Break Through!

The **Bible** for Young Catholics

Do not let anyone look down on you because you are young,
but be an example for the believers in your speech,
your conduct, your love, faith, and purity.

1 Timothy 4:12

This Bible belongs to:

_____

Given by: _____

Date: _____

Occasion: _____

saint mary's press

CONTENTS

OLD TESTAMENT

NEW TESTAMENT

GOD BREAKS THROUGH:
SALVATION HISTORY TIME LINE

BIBLE BOOK
Genesis, chapters 1–11

BIBLE BOOK
Genesis, chapters 12–50

BIBLE PEOPLE
• Adam & Eve • Cain & Abel • Noah

BIBLE PEOPLE
• Abraham • Sarah • Isaac & Rebecca
• Jacob, Leah, & Rachel • Esau • Joseph

PRIMEVAL HISTORY

PATRIARCHS

CREATION   2000 BC   2000 BC   1700 BC

The Bible begins with imaginative stories about how God created everything that exists. These are sometimes called "primeval" stories, meaning they are stories of things that happened before recorded history. The stories of Adam and Eve, Cain and Abel, Noah and the flood, and the tower of Babylon teach us that God created everything and that human beings have a special place in creation. They teach us that sin destroys our relationships with God and each other. They teach us that sin spreads and that without God's help, sin leads to death and destruction.

In this period of salvation history, God begins to form a special relationship with a chosen race of people. He makes a special promise, called a Covenant, with a man named Abraham and his wife, Sarah. God promises that their descendants will be numerous and that they will inherit a Promised Land. This is followed by the stories of Abraham and Sarah's son, Isaac; their grandsons, Jacob and Esau; and their great-grandchildren, Joseph and his brothers and sister. These stories show us that even though Abraham and Sarah's descendants had many problems, God was faithful to his Covenant with them. Jacob's sons become the patriarchs— that is, founding fathers—of the Twelve Tribes of Israel.

The Bible tells the story of how God breaks through to save human beings from sin and bring us to eternal life. History told from the perspective of God's breaking through is called salvation history. This time line shows the major periods of salvation history as told in the Bible's stories. Each period lists some Bible books that tell the stories from that period, lists some important people of that period, and briefly describes what God is doing.

BIBLE BOOK
Exodus

BIBLE BOOKS
Joshua, Judges, Ruth

BIBLE PEOPLE
• Moses • Aaron & Miriam • Pharaoh

BIBLE PEOPLE
• Joshua • Deborah • Gideon
• Samson • Ruth

EGYPT AND THE EXODUS

1700 BC — 1250 BC

SETTLING THE PROMISED LAND

1250 BC — 1050 BC

At the beginning of the Book of Exodus, we discover that the descendants of Jacob's children—now called Israelites—are in slavery in Egypt. God hears their cries and calls Moses to lead the people out of slavery. But Pharaoh, the Egyptian leader, has a hard heart. God has to send terrible plagues to make him let the Israelites go. The Israelites' escape from Egypt and journey to the Holy Land is called the Exodus.

On the way to the Promised Land, the Israelites stop at Mount Sinai. There God extends the Covenant he made with Abraham to all the Israelites. He gives Moses the Ten Commandments, which the people must obey as part of the Covenant.

Moses dies before the Israelites enter the Promised Land. God calls a new leader, Joshua, to lead the people into the land. Much of the land is inhabited by other people. The Israelites must fight to gain control of the land. When they trust God, they are successful in their battles; when they do not trust God, they fail. Eventually they gain control of the land, and each of the twelve tribes is given their own section of the land.

New invaders, the Philistines, try to capture the land. At this time the Israelites have no king, because God is their ruler. But God calls special prophets and warriors, called judges, to help deliver justice and defend the land against the Philistine invasion.

Time Line (continued)

BIBLE BOOKS
1 Samuel, 2 Samuel, 1 Kings,
2 Kings, Micah, Isaiah, Jeremiah

BIBLE BOOKS
Ezra, Nehemiah, Esther, Isaiah,
2 Maccabees, Ezekiel, Daniel, Jonah

BIBLE PEOPLE
• Samuel • King Solomon
• Elijah & Elisha • King Saul
• King David • King Hezekiah
• King Josiah • Amos • Hosea
• Isaiah • Jeremiah

BIBLE PEOPLE
• Ezekiel • Ezra & Nehemiah
• the Maccabees • Judith • Esther

KINGDOMS OF JUDAH & ISRAEL

1050 BC   587 BC

EXILE AND RETURN

587 BC   AD 1

At the end of the period of the judges, the Israelites want their own king. God has Samuel—the last of the judges— anoint Saul as the first king of Israel. David follows Saul as the next king. David is a mighty warrior and unites all the Twelve Tribes into one kingdom. David's son, Solomon, builds a Temple at Jerusalem, the capital city.

After Solomon's death there is disagreement between the tribes, and the kingdom splits in two. Israel is the name of the northern kingdom and Judah is the name of the southern kingdom. Many of the kings of Israel and Judah worshiped foreign gods and allowed injustice in the kingdom. Prophets like Amos, Hosea, and Isaiah called the people to stop worshiping idols, to practice justice, and to care for people in need.

Despite the prophets' warnings, the people of Israel and Judah continued to turn away from God's Covenant with them. So God let their kingdoms be conquered. Israel was conquered by the Assyrians in 721 BC. Judah was conquered by the Babylonians in 587 BC. Many of the people were taken into captivity, so this time was called the Exile. Prophets like Ezekiel comforted the Israelites with the promise that God was still with them. Fifty years passed in exile. Then a new king allowed the people—now called Judeans or Jews—to return to rebuild Jerusalem and the Temple. The people saw God's hand at work. During this troubled time, the people were hoping for a messiah, or savior, to make them great again.

BIBLE BOOKS
Matthew, Mark, Luke, John

BIBLE BOOKS
Acts of the Apostles, Romans,
1 Corinthians, Galatians, James, Philippians,
1 Timothy, Hebrews, 1 Peter,
1,2,3 John, Revelation

BIBLE PEOPLE
- Mary of Nazareth • John the Baptist
- Jesus Christ
- Peter • Mary Magdalene
- The Twelve Apostles
- Mary & Martha of Bethany

BIBLE PEOPLE
- Peter • Paul • Barnabas • Timothy
- Priscilla & Aquila

LIFE OF JESUS CHRIST

AD 1   AD 33

EARLY CHRISTIAN CHURCH

AD 33   AD 100

When the time was right, God sent his only Son, Jesus Christ, into the world. When Jesus was born, the Romans ruled Israel. Some of the Jews were hoping for a mighty warrior and king like David, who would drive the Romans out. Instead, Jesus showed a different way. He preached love, justice, and forgiveness. He healed and worked miracles as signs of God's power.

Jesus' followers, called disciples, came to see that he was the Messiah, the Savior. Jesus showed that salvation comes through faith and a change of heart, not through violence and political power. When Jesus was killed by the Romans—with the approval of the Jewish leaders—his followers thought that all was lost. Instead, after three days God raised Jesus from the dead!

After his Resurrection, Jesus instructed his closest followers, the Apostles, to go and spread the Good News of salvation to all people. The Holy Spirit gave them the courage to tell others about Jesus Christ. They started by first preaching to other Jews. Sometimes they were persecuted by Jewish leaders who did not believe in Jesus.

One of those persecutors—whose name was Paul—had a vision of Jesus and became a Christian. God revealed to Paul that Christ came for all people. Paul began preaching to non-Jews, who were called Gentiles. Wherever he traveled he started new Christian communities. He was helped by many other believers, women and men. Soon Christianity spread throughout the whole Roman Empire—even to Rome.

BIBLE
PEOPLE INTERVIEWS

ABOUT THIS BIBLE

Welcome to *Breakthrough! The Bible for Young Catholics.* Growing out of childhood and into your teens is an exciting time of life. It can also be difficult at times. The good news is that no matter what you are feeling or what situation you are in, God never stops trying to **break through** and let you know that he loves you. That is why the title of this special Bible for young people is *Breakthrough!*

Through the words of the Bible, God speaks to all people. The Bible is the story of God's love relationship with the human race. This story is told through many different kinds of writing because the Bible is not one book—it is a collection of books. There are seventy-three books in Catholic Bibles: forty-six books in the Old Testament and twenty-seven books in the New Testament.

Catholic Connections

Scripture and Tradition

God wants us to know him. So throughout history God has revealed himself to human beings. We call this "revelation." God's most complete revelation was through the person of his son, Jesus Christ. Through the power of the Holy Spirit, the Apostles handed on to others what they had learned from their experience of Jesus. They passed on everything that our loving God revealed to save us from sin and death. Through the power of the Holy Spirit, the bishops of the Church continue to pass on this revelation without error for all ages.

This revelation is handed on in a special way through the Bible—in both the Old and New Testaments. It is also handed on through something called Tradition, a word which actually means "handing on." Tradition includes some teachings and practices that may not be found explicitly in the Scriptures (another word for the Bible). In fact, some of God's revelation is known chiefly through Tradition rather than through the Bible. That is why the Bible alone is not enough to learn about all of God's revelation. Both the Bible and Tradition are needed to learn the fullness of God's revelation.

Catholic Connections articles explain how Catholic beliefs are part of God's revelation and are taught through the Bible. They discuss things like our belief in the sacraments, our devotion to Mary, and the special role of the Pope and bishops. If you read all the Catholic Connections articles, it will be like getting a mini introduction to the main beliefs of the Catholic Church!

Breakthrough! was created to help young people read and understand the books of the Bible. We started by using the Good News Translation, a version of the Bible that is easier for young people to read. Then we added short articles to help you understand what you read. There are four different types of articles in this Bible: Study It!, Pray It!, Live It!, and Catholic Connections. Samples of these four types of articles are on these pages so you can see what they look like.

Reading Helps in *Breakthrough!*

Everyone needs help reading the Bible. It is not an easy book for beginners to pick up and understand. Along with the articles that we added to the Bible books, *Breakthrough!* has the following additional reading helps to assist you in understanding what God reveals through the words of the Bible.

Salvation History Time Line

God has had a plan for saving human beings from sin and death since the sin of our original parents, Adam and Eve. We call the story of God's saving plan "salvation history." The books of the Bible teach us about the people and

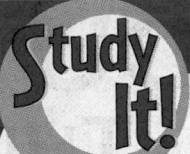

Background for Understanding

The Bible was written a long time ago. So it is not surprising that we might need some help understanding the full meaning of the stories and teachings. This is true for adults as well as youth!

The Study It! articles give you information to help you better understand the Bible story you are reading. Some of the Study It! articles focus on the symbols the author used in the stories. Some help you understand the history behind the story. Some help you understand the story by explaining how people lived back then. The main purpose of the Study It! articles is to help you understand what the original author of the story was trying to get across.

Pray It!

Talking with God

Think of reading the Bible as sort of like having a conversation with God. Whenever you read the Bible, start by asking God for help in understanding what you read. After you read a section, listen for what God is telling you in the story. Then you will want to respond to God. This is one way of praying—by talking to God and listening for God's voice in what you read.

The Pray It! articles will help you do that. They contain prayers or ideas for how you might pray. Sometimes they make connections with the way we pray together at church. You may want to keep a journal to write down your thoughts—and to make up your own prayers—as you read the Bible.

events that are part of salvation history. In order to fully understand the meaning of these stories, it is helpful to know how they fit into the big picture of God's saving plan. To help you with this, a Bible time line, called "God Breaks Through: Salvation History Time Line," is provided in the next section. Read this section before you start reading the rest of *Breakthrough!*

Bible People Interviews

The stories in the Bible tell us how God broke through to certain people as part of salvation history. You will meet some of those people through imaginative interviews contained in the color sections inserted throughout *Breakthrough!* The interviews will help you understand the role these people had in God's great plan of salvation. Let them inspire you to answer God's call in your life!

Reading Plan

It is good to have a plan for reading the Bible. But don't start by trying to read through the whole Bible from beginning to end! In fact, for young Christians we don't even suggest you try to read all seventy-three books. We have picked forty books for you to focus on. Reading these books will give you a very good overview of salvation history. The section "Reading Plan" gives you a chart for keeping track of your progress in reading these books.

Study and Prayer Helps

You will find some important study and prayer helps in the back of *Breakthrough!* Included is an index to help you find the stories of important Bible events and Jesus' miracles, parables, and teachings. Another index contains all of the subjects covered in the Pray It!, Study It!, Live It!, and Catholic Connections articles. A glossary will help you understand unfamiliar Bible words, and other sections will help you find important Catholic prayers and teachings. "Bible Passages for Special Occasions" suggests

Bible passages for you to read at important moments in your life. Finally, nine maps show the location of important events in the Bible. The more you use these helps, the better you will be able to understand the Bible and to pray with it.

Some Important Questions

Who wrote the Bible?

Many of the Bible's stories were first told by storytellers around campfires and in religious gatherings. Or they were messages given in public places by prophets and evangelists. Eventually these stories and messages were written down. Other people added to them, combined them, and rewrote them. The Bible was written so long ago that we have no idea who most of the original writers and editors were. What we do know is that

Live It!

Following God in Everyday Life

Reading the Bible will change your life, especially if you are open to hearing God's call in the Bible. Even though the stories and teachings of the Bible were written long ago, they still apply today. God's Word is eternal— which is a way of saying that it applies to everyone, all through history.

The Live It! articles will help you understand how these ancient stories apply to your life today. They show how the Bible is a guide to building good relationships—with your friends, your family, and other people in your school and community. Live It! articles also show how God wants us to serve others who are in need and bring justice and peace to the world.

the Holy Spirit was at work through the whole process, inspiring these authors to communicate God's truth.

Why do we say the Bible is the Word of God?

We know that the Bible is the Word of God because the Holy Spirit inspired the human authors who wrote it. This means that God helped the human authors communicate what he wanted us to know and that he is the ultimate author of the Bible. It means that the Bible is God's Word. He wants to communicate his truth and love to us. By inspiring the human authors, God made sure they communicated the things we need to know about him and how he saves us without any errors.

Inspiration does not mean that the Holy Spirit took over the minds of the human authors who wrote the books of the Bible. The human authors wrote as human beings, using the knowledge and language they had available. Being inspired did not change their human limitations. Despite these limitations, under the Holy Spirit's guidance, they communicated the truth we need to know about God and his plan for us.

How do I find Bible passages?

The Bible is organized in a way that helps you locate specific Bible passages. Each book in the Bible is divided into chapters (except for some very short books). The chapter numbers are the larger ones on the page. Each chapter is divided into verses. A verse is usually about a sentence long. The verse numbers are the smaller numbers in each chapter and start with verse 1 in each new chapter.

A Bible citation has a book name, a chapter number, and verse numbers. Here is an example: John 3:16–21. In this example, the book is John, meaning the Gospel of John. The chapter number is 3, and the verse numbers are 16 through 21. Go ahead, try and find John 3:16–21. If you need help finding where the book is in the Bible, use the handy chart in the back of *Breakthrough!*

Name of Book   Verse(s)

Jn 3:16–17

Chapter

What is a good way to study the Bible?

It is not a good idea to start at the beginning of the Bible and try to read it all the way through to the end, like you would a novel. Instead, start with a book you find interesting and read a chapter or two every day until you finish it. Then pick another book and read through it.

It is also a good idea to have a little ritual each time you read. This will help you to be more focused on what God wants to say to you as you read the Bible. Here are some simple steps you might try:

1. Start with a short prayer asking for God's help in understanding what you read. There is a prayer in the front of *Breakthrough!* that you can use.

2. Read carefully through the chapter or passage. Don't rush. Try to hear every word and let its meaning sink in.

3. Think about what you just read. Try to imagine yourself in the story. How would you feel? What do you think God is saying to you through the words you read?

4. Read the Study It!, Pray It!, Live It!, or Catholic Connections article if there is one connected to the passage you read.

5. Finish by thinking about how the reading might apply to your life. Is God comforting you about a hard situation? Is God calling you to make a change or try something new? Talk with God about whatever you are thinking or feeling.

READING PLAN

As a young person, you will want to get familiar with the people and stories in the Bible. A good way to do this is by reading complete books of the Bible. However, we do not recommend that you start at the beginning of the Bible and try to read it straight through. Because the Bible is a collection of many different kinds of books, it was not meant to be read like that. A better approach is to go back and forth between books in the Old and New Testaments. That way you can see the connections between both testaments.

The following chart lists the forty books that we have filled with extra articles. We chose these books because reading them will help you see the big picture of God's revelation. You don't have to read the books in this order though; read them in whatever order you wish. We have listed all the chapters in each book so you can check them off as you read them. There are 943 chapters all together. To read them all in one year, you would have to read about two or three chapters a day; to read them over three years, you would have to read about one chapter a day. There is no need to rush, the important thing is to open yourself up to what God wishes to say to you.

MARK
❏1 ❏2 ❏3 ❏4 ❏5 ❏6 ❏7 ❏8 ❏9 ❏10 ❏11
❏12 ❏13 ❏14 ❏15 ❏16

GENESIS
❏1 ❏2 ❏3 ❏4 ❏5 ❏6 ❏7 ❏8 ❏9 ❏10 ❏11
❏12 ❏13 ❏14 ❏15 ❏16 ❏17 ❏18 ❏19 ❏20
❏21 ❏22 ❏23 ❏24 ❏25 ❏26 ❏27 ❏28 ❏29
❏30 ❏31 ❏32 ❏33 ❏34 ❏35 ❏36 ❏37 ❏38
❏39 ❏40 ❏41 ❏42 ❏43 ❏44 ❏45 ❏46 ❏47
❏48 ❏49 ❏50

EXODUS
❏1 ❏2 ❏3 ❏4 ❏5 ❏6 ❏7 ❏8 ❏9 ❏10 ❏11
❏12 ❏13 ❏14 ❏15 ❏16 ❏17 ❏18 ❏19 ❏20
❏21 ❏22 ❏23 ❏24 ❏25 ❏26 ❏27 ❏28 ❏29
❏30 ❏31 ❏32 ❏33 ❏34 ❏35 ❏36 ❏37 ❏38
❏39 ❏40

JOSHUA
❏1 ❏2 ❏3 ❏4 ❏5 ❏6 ❏7 ❏8 ❏9 ❏10 ❏11
❏12 ❏13 ❏14 ❏15 ❏16 ❏17 ❏18 ❏19 ❏20
❏21 ❏22 ❏23 ❏24

LUKE
❏1 ❏2 ❏3 ❏4 ❏5 ❏6 ❏7 ❏8 ❏9 ❏10 ❏11
❏12 ❏13 ❏14 ❏15 ❏16 ❏17 ❏18 ❏19 ❏20
❏21 ❏22 ❏23 ❏24

ACTS
❏1 ❏2 ❏3 ❏4 ❏5 ❏6 ❏7 ❏8 ❏9 ❏10 ❏11
❏12 ❏13 ❏14 ❏15 ❏16 ❏17 ❏18 ❏19 ❏20
❏21 ❏22 ❏23 ❏24 ❏25 ❏26 ❏27 ❏28

JUDGES
❏1 ❏2 ❏3 ❏4 ❏5 ❏6 ❏7 ❏8 ❏9 ❏10 ❏11
❏12 ❏13 ❏14 ❏15 ❏16 ❏17 ❏18 ❏19 ❏20
❏21

RUTH
❏1 ❏2 ❏3 ❏4

I SAMUEL
❏1 ❏2 ❏3 ❏4 ❏5 ❏6 ❏7 ❏8 ❏9 ❏10 ❏11
❏12 ❏13 ❏14 ❏15 ❏16 ❏17 ❏18 ❏19 ❏20
❏21 ❏22 ❏23 ❏24 ❏25 ❏26 ❏27 ❏28 ❏29
❏30 ❏31

I TIMOTHY
❏1 ❏2 ❏3 ❏4 ❏5 ❏6

2 TIMOTHY
❏1 ❏2 ❏3 ❏4

I CORINTHIANS
❏1 ❏2 ❏3 ❏4 ❏5 ❏6 ❏7 ❏8 ❏9 ❏10 ❏11
❏12 ❏13 ❏14 ❏15 ❏16

2 SAMUEL
❏1 ❏2 ❏3 ❏4 ❏5 ❏6 ❏7 ❏8 ❏9 ❏10 ❏11
❏12 ❏13 ❏14 ❏15 ❏16 ❏17 ❏18 ❏19 ❏20
❏21 ❏22 ❏23 ❏24

I KINGS
❏1 ❏2 ❏3 ❏4 ❏5 ❏6 ❏7 ❏8 ❏9 ❏10 ❏11
❏12 ❏13 ❏14 ❏15 ❏16 ❏17 ❏18 ❏19 ❏20
❏21 ❏22

2 KINGS
❏1 ❏2 ❏3 ❏4 ❏5 ❏6 ❏7 ❏8 ❏9 ❏10 ❏11
❏12 ❏13 ❏14 ❏15 ❏16 ❏17 ❏18 ❏19 ❏20
❏21 ❏22 ❏23 ❏24 ❏25

ISAIAH
❑ 1 ❑ 2 ❑ 3 ❑ 4 ❑ 5 ❑ 6 ❑ 7 ❑ 8 ❑ 9 ❑ 10 ❑ 11
❑ 12 ❑ 13 ❑ 14 ❑ 15 ❑ 16 ❑ 17 ❑ 18 ❑ 19 ❑ 20
❑ 21 ❑ 22 ❑ 23 ❑ 24 ❑ 25 ❑ 26 ❑ 27 ❑ 28 ❑ 29
❑ 30 ❑ 31 ❑ 32 ❑ 33 ❑ 34 ❑ 35 ❑ 36 ❑ 37 ❑ 38
❑ 39 ❑ 40 ❑ 41 ❑ 42 ❑ 43 ❑ 44 ❑ 45 ❑ 46 ❑ 47
❑ 48 ❑ 49 ❑ 50 ❑ 51 ❑ 52 ❑ 53 ❑ 54 ❑ 55 ❑ 56
❑ 57 ❑ 58 ❑ 59 ❑ 60 ❑ 61 ❑ 62 ❑ 63 ❑ 64 ❑ 65
❑ 66

MATTHEW
❑ 1 ❑ 2 ❑ 3 ❑ 4 ❑ 5 ❑ 6 ❑ 7 ❑ 8 ❑ 9 ❑ 10 ❑ 11
❑ 12 ❑ 13 ❑ 14 ❑ 15 ❑ 16 ❑ 17 ❑ 18 ❑ 19 ❑ 20
❑ 21 ❑ 22 ❑ 23 ❑ 24 ❑ 25 ❑ 26 ❑ 27 ❑ 28

PSALMS
❑ 1 ❑ 2 ❑ 3 ❑ 4 ❑ 5 ❑ 6 ❑ 7 ❑ 8 ❑ 9 ❑ 10 ❑ 11
❑ 12 ❑ 13 ❑ 14 ❑ 15 ❑ 16 ❑ 17 ❑ 18 ❑ 19 ❑ 20
❑ 21 ❑ 22 ❑ 23 ❑ 24 ❑ 25 ❑ 26 ❑ 27 ❑ 28 ❑ 29
❑ 30 ❑ 31 ❑ 32 ❑ 33 ❑ 34 ❑ 35 ❑ 36 ❑ 37 ❑ 38
❑ 39 ❑ 40 ❑ 41 ❑ 42 ❑ 43 ❑ 44 ❑ 45 ❑ 46 ❑ 47
❑ 48 ❑ 49 ❑ 50 ❑ 51 ❑ 52 ❑ 53 ❑ 54 ❑ 55 ❑ 56
❑ 57 ❑ 58 ❑ 59 ❑ 60 ❑ 61 ❑ 62 ❑ 63 ❑ 64 ❑ 65
❑ 66 ❑ 67 ❑ 68 ❑ 69 ❑ 70 ❑ 71 ❑ 72 ❑ 73 ❑ 74
❑ 75 ❑ 76 ❑ 77 ❑ 78 ❑ 79 ❑ 80 ❑ 81 ❑ 82 ❑ 83
❑ 84 ❑ 85 ❑ 86 ❑ 87 ❑ 88 ❑ 89 ❑ 90 ❑ 91 ❑ 92
❑ 93 ❑ 94 ❑ 95 ❑ 96 ❑ 97 ❑ 98 ❑ 99 ❑ 100 ❑ 101
❑ 102 ❑ 103 ❑ 104 ❑ 105 ❑ 106 ❑ 107 ❑ 108
❑ 109 ❑ 110 ❑ 111 ❑ 112 ❑ 113 ❑ 114 ❑ 115
❑ 116 ❑ 117 ❑ 118 ❑ 119 ❑ 120 ❑ 121 ❑ 122
❑ 123 ❑ 124 ❑ 125 ❑ 126 ❑ 127 ❑ 128 ❑ 129
❑ 130 ❑ 131 ❑ 132 ❑ 133 ❑ 134 ❑ 135 ❑ 136
❑ 137 ❑ 138 ❑ 139 ❑ 140 ❑ 141 ❑ 142 ❑ 143
❑ 144 ❑ 145 ❑ 146 ❑ 147 ❑ 148 ❑ 149 ❑ 150

PHILIPPIANS
❑ 1 ❑ 2 ❑ 3 ❑ 4

AMOS
❑ 1 ❑ 2 ❑ 3 ❑ 4 ❑ 5 ❑ 6 ❑ 7 ❑ 8 ❑ 9

MICAH
❑ 1 ❑ 2 ❑ 3 ❑ 4 ❑ 5 ❑ 6 ❑ 7

JEREMIAH
❑ 1 ❑ 2 ❑ 3 ❑ 4 ❑ 5 ❑ 6 ❑ 7 ❑ 8 ❑ 9 ❑ 10 ❑ 11
❑ 12 ❑ 13 ❑ 14 ❑ 15 ❑ 16 ❑ 17 ❑ 18 ❑ 19 ❑ 20
❑ 21 ❑ 22 ❑ 23 ❑ 24 ❑ 25 ❑ 26 ❑ 27 ❑ 28 ❑ 29
❑ 30 ❑ 31 ❑ 32 ❑ 33 ❑ 34 ❑ 35 ❑ 36 ❑ 37 ❑ 38
❑ 39 ❑ 40 ❑ 41 ❑ 42 ❑ 43 ❑ 44 ❑ 45 ❑ 46 ❑ 47
❑ 48 ❑ 49 ❑ 50 ❑ 51 ❑ 52

JAMES
❑ 1 ❑ 2 ❑ 3 ❑ 4 ❑ 5

GALATIANS
❑ 1 ❑ 2 ❑ 3 ❑ 4 ❑ 5 ❑ 6

ESTHER
❑ A ❑ 1 ❑ 2 ❑ 3 ❑ B ❑ 4 ❑ C ❑ D ❑ 5 ❑ 6 ❑ 7
❑ 8 ❑ E ❑ 9 ❑ 10 ❑ F

DANIEL
❑ 1 ❑ 2 ❑ 3 ❑ 4 ❑ 5 ❑ 6 ❑ 7 ❑ 8 ❑ 9 ❑ 10 ❑ 11
❑ 12 ❑ 13 ❑ 14

JOB
❑ 1 ❑ 2 ❑ 3 ❑ 4 ❑ 5 ❑ 6 ❑ 7 ❑ 8 ❑ 9 ❑ 10 ❑ 11
❑ 12 ❑ 13 ❑ 14 ❑ 15 ❑ 16 ❑ 17 ❑ 18 ❑ 19 ❑ 20
❑ 21 ❑ 22 ❑ 23 ❑ 24 ❑ 25 ❑ 26 ❑ 27 ❑ 28 ❑ 29
❑ 30 ❑ 31 ❑ 32 ❑ 33 ❑ 34 ❑ 35 ❑ 36 ❑ 37 ❑ 38
❑ 39 ❑ 40 ❑ 41 ❑ 42

I PETER
❑ 1 ❑ 2 ❑ 3 ❑ 4 ❑ 5

EZEKIEL
❑ 1 ❑ 2 ❑ 3 ❑ 4 ❑ 5 ❑ 6 ❑ 7 ❑ 8 ❑ 9 ❑ 10 ❑ 11
❑ 12 ❑ 13 ❑ 14 ❑ 15 ❑ 16 ❑ 17 ❑ 18 ❑ 19 ❑ 20
❑ 21 ❑ 22 ❑ 23 ❑ 24 ❑ 25 ❑ 26 ❑ 27 ❑ 28 ❑ 29
❑ 30 ❑ 31 ❑ 32 ❑ 33 ❑ 34 ❑ 35 ❑ 36 ❑ 37 ❑ 38
❑ 39 ❑ 40 ❑ 41 ❑ 42 ❑ 43 ❑ 44 ❑ 45 ❑ 46 ❑ 47
❑ 48

JONAH
❑ 1 ❑ 2 ❑ 3 ❑ 4

EZRA
❑ 1 ❑ 2 ❑ 3 ❑ 4 ❑ 5 ❑ 6 ❑ 7 ❑ 8 ❑ 9 ❑ 10

NEHEMIAH
❑ 1 ❑ 2 ❑ 3 ❑ 4 ❑ 5 ❑ 6 ❑ 7 ❑ 8 ❑ 9 ❑ 10 ❑ 11
❑ 12 ❑ 13

HEBREWS
❑ 1 ❑ 2 ❑ 3 ❑ 4 ❑ 5 ❑ 6 ❑ 7 ❑ 8 ❑ 9 ❑ 10 ❑ 11
❑ 12 ❑ 13

ROMANS
❑ 1 ❑ 2 ❑ 3 ❑ 4 ❑ 5 ❑ 6 ❑ 7 ❑ 8 ❑ 9 ❑ 10 ❑ 11
❑ 12 ❑ 13 ❑ 14 ❑ 15 ❑ 16

PROVERBS
❑ 1 ❑ 2 ❑ 3 ❑ 4 ❑ 5 ❑ 6 ❑ 7 ❑ 8 ❑ 9 ❑ 10 ❑ 11
❑ 12 ❑ 13 ❑ 14 ❑ 15 ❑ 16 ❑ 17 ❑ 18 ❑ 19 ❑ 20
❑ 21 ❑ 22 ❑ 23 ❑ 24 ❑ 25 ❑ 26 ❑ 27 ❑ 28 ❑ 29
❑ 30 ❑ 31

SONG OF SONGS
❑ 1 ❑ 2 ❑ 3 ❑ 4 ❑ 5 ❑ 6 ❑ 7 ❑ 8

2 MACCABEES
❑ 1 ❑ 2 ❑ 3 ❑ 4 ❑ 5 ❑ 6 ❑ 7 ❑ 8 ❑ 9 ❑ 10 ❑ 11
❑ 12 ❑ 13 ❑ 14 ❑ 15

JOHN
❑ 1 ❑ 2 ❑ 3 ❑ 4 ❑ 5 ❑ 6 ❑ 7 ❑ 8 ❑ 9 ❑ 10 ❑ 11
❑ 12 ❑ 13 ❑ 14 ❑ 15 ❑ 16 ❑ 17 ❑ 18 ❑ 19 ❑ 20
❑ 21

I JOHN
❑ 1 ❑ 2 ❑ 3 ❑ 4 ❑ 5

REVELATION
❑ 1 ❑ 2 ❑ 3 ❑ 4 ❑ 5 ❑ 6 ❑ 7 ❑ 8 ❑ 9 ❑ 10 ❑ 11
❑ 12 ❑ 13 ❑ 14 ❑ 15 ❑ 16 ❑ 17 ❑ 18 ❑ 19 ❑ 20
❑ 21 ❑ 22

Imprimatur information for the text of the articles and the introductions:
Nihil Obstat: Rev. Robert S. Horihan, STL
                      Censor Librorum
                      October 28, 2005
Imprimatur: †Most Reverend Bernard J. Harrington, DD
                      Bishop of Winona
                      October 28, 2005

The nihil obstat and imprimatur are official declarations that a book or pamphlet is free of doctrinal or moral error. No implication is contained therein that those who have granted the nihil obstat or imprimatur agree with the contents, opinions, or statements expressed, nor do they assume any legal responsibility associated with publication.

Imprimatur information for the text of the Good News Translation, Catholic Edition:
Imprimatur: †Most Reverend William H. Keeler, DD
                      President, National Conference of Catholic Bishops
                      March 10, 1993

Writers:
Nora Bradbury-Haehl, Lisa-Marie Calderone-Stewart, Virginia Halbur, Shirley Kelter, Marilyn Kielbasa, Larry Schatz, Victoria Shepp, Brian Singer-Towns

Publishing team:
The publishing team included Gloria Shahin, editorial director; Brian Singer-Towns, general editor; Virginia Halbur, coeditor. Prepress and manufacturing coordinated by the production departments of Saint Mary's Press.

Acknowledgments continued on page 1858.

Printed in the United States of America

4141 (PO3922)

ISBN 978-1-59982-339-3, paper
ISBN 978-1-59982-342-3, hardcover
ISBN 978-1-59982-340-9, ebook

Library of Congress Cataloging-in-Publication Data

Bible. English. Good News Translation. 2013.
   Breakthrough! : the Bible for young Catholics.
      p. cm.
Includes index.
ISBN 978-1-59982-339-3 (pbk.)—ISBN 978-1-59982-342-3 (hardcover)—ISBN 978-1-59982-340-9 (ebook)
I. Title.
BS195.T63 2013b
220.5'2082—dc23
                                    2012042652

FOREWORD TO THE
CATHOLIC EDITION OF THE
GOOD NEWS TRANSLATION

In the *Dogmatic Constitution on Divine Revelation* (*Dei Verbum*), promulgated in 1965, the Second Vatican Council urged that "easy access to Sacred Scripture should be provided for all the Christian faithful," and encouraged the preparation of new translations of the Scriptures "since the word of God should be accessible at all times" (*Dei Verbum* 22). Just one year later, the American Bible Society published *Good News for Modern Man: The New Testament in Today's English Version*, and it immediately became an international best-seller. This success encouraged the American Bible Society to undertake the translation of the Old Testament and to publish the first edition of the *Good News Bible* in 1976. Even as the Old Testament was being translated from Hebrew, discussions between the ABS and Roman Catholic officials began concerning the possibility of translating the Old Testament books that Roman Catholic Bibles always include but which are not based on Hebrew texts. These books are sometimes called "deuterocanonical" to suggest that they were added to the list (canon) of books that Catholics consider to be sacred Scripture and a worthy basis for doctrine at a somewhat later date than those books that were translated from Hebrew. The deuterocanonical books exist in Greek and Latin sources and have always been included in English Bibles translated from the Latin Vulgate.

Consequently, the American Bible Society published the *Good News Bible with Deuterocanonicals/Apocrypha* in 1979. This "interconfessional" text included all the deuterocanonical books plus a number of additional books not usually found in Catholic Bibles, but which other Christian traditions revere and employ in worship. This was the first edition of the *Good News Bible* to receive an *Imprimatur* (which means "let it be printed") from a Roman Catholic bishop, the Archbishop John Francis Whealon, the late archbishop of Hartford, Connecticut. While the *Imprimatur* does not constitute an endorsement, it assures the reader that the book does not contain anything contrary to the Catholic faith. When the *Good News Translation* was revised in 1992, it too received the *Imprimatur*, this time from the National Conference of Catholic Bishops under the signature of the then-Archbishop (now Cardinal) William H. Keeler, Archbishop of Baltimore.

The Catholic edition of the *Good News Bible* you hold in your hands contains the 1992 revised text in the order and format most preferred by Roman Catholics. It contains only those books considered sacred Scripture by Catholics and presents them in the sequence that follows the one used in all Catholic Bibles in the Latin Vulgate tradition. If you are unfamiliar with the *Good News Translation*, or if you are looking for a translation that will help you better understand the Good News of Jesus Christ for you and the world today, I encourage you to read on.

Jean-Pierre Ruiz, STD
St. John's University, New York
Epiphany 2003

OLD TESTAMENT

The Bible is divided into two major sections, the Old Testament and the New Testament. The Old Testament in Catholic Bibles contains forty-six books. The Bibles that most Protestants use has thirty-nine books in the Old Testament. They do not include the books of Tobit, Judith, 1 and 2 Maccabees, Wisdom, Sirach, Baruch, and some parts of Esther and Daniel. That is the main difference between Catholic and Protestant Bibles.

The Old Testament books include many different kinds of writings. You will find history, poetry, legends, laws, wise sayings, short stories, and the words of prophets. The Old Testament books are primarily about God's special relationship with his Chosen People. At different times these people are called Hebrews, Israelites, Judeans, and Jews. During their history God breaks through and calls the Chosen People to recognize him as their one and only God. God promises to bless them in a special way, and he asks the Chosen People to be faithful in following his commands.

This holy promise between God and the Chosen People is called a covenant. *Testament* is another word for *covenant*, so the Old Testament is the story of the Covenant between God and his special people—the Jews. Because of this, most of the books of the Old Testament are also the sacred Scriptures of the Jewish people. Since the books were written in Hebrew, they are sometimes called the Hebrew Scriptures. So the Old Testament isn't "old" because it is out of date. It is "old" because it is the story of how God first made his Covenant with his Chosen People.

The Old Testament in Christian Bibles is divided into four different sections. The table of contents shows the books that are in each section. Here is some information on each section:

The Pentateuch or Torah. These five books are the heart of the Old Testament. They contain the stories of Creation and stories about how sin entered the world. They tell how God broke through to first make his Covenant with Noah and Abraham. The Book of Exodus tells how God led his people out of slavery through the leadership of Moses. At Mount Sinai, God extended the Covenant to all his Chosen People and gave them the Ten Commandments.

The Historical Books. These sixteen books are mostly religious history and some short novels. They tell how the Chosen People settled in the Promised Land. Eventually they became a kingdom led by kings like Saul, David, and Solomon. But the rulers and the people often worshiped false gods and ignored the poor. So God sent prophets like Elijah and Elisha to call the people to be faithful to the Covenant. The historical books have imaginative stories about heroes like Ruth, Tobit, Judith, and Esther.

The Wisdom Books. These seven books contain the collected wisdom of the Chosen People. They contain the songs they used in worship and prayer. They contain advice for living a good and holy life. The Song of Songs has poetry about the goodness of sexuality. The Book of Job is a debate about why good people suffer bad things.

The Books of the Prophets. These eighteen books contain the messages of important prophets. The prophets delivered God's message to the Chosen People. They warned the Chosen People against worshiping false gods. They challenged the Chosen People to act fairly and to care for the poor. The prophets also offered comfort and hope when the people thought God had abandoned them. And some of the prophets promised a future savior, the Messiah, who would bring God's love, justice, and peace to the world.

To fully understand God's plan for the human race, we need both the Old and the New Testament. In the Old Testament, God reveals the love he has for us. The stories teach us how sin keeps us from being in a completely loving relationship with God. The Old Testament shows how, through various people, God broke through to put his Chosen People on the right path. The stories prepare us to understand how Jesus Christ fulfills God's promise to save us from sin and death.

Jake's mom keeps photo albums and scrapbooks. Chantal's dad videotapes the major moments in her life—and the not-so-major ones. Frederick's grandparents tell stories about what life was like when they were young. Human beings need to keep track of their memories. They also need to understand where they came from and where they are going.

The Book of Genesis does these things for the family of God. It starts out with stories about how God created the world, how evil came to be, and what God did about it. Then it tells the history of God's people—people who are holy (sometimes), good (except when they're bad), and faithful to God (eventually). Most of all, the Book of Genesis is the beginning of a love story between God and us.

Chap. 22

Headlines

- God Creates Stars, Seas, and Slimy Things (chapters 1–2)
- First Sin Leads to First Punishment (3:1–24)
- Flood Warning! Noah Evacuates (chapters 7–8)
- God Calls, Abram Listens (12:1–9)
- Treachery and Trickery: Twin Steals Inheritance (27:1–45)
- Jacob Tricked, Marries Wrong Sister! (29:15–30)
- Pharaoh Appoints Israelite Governor (41:37–57)

FACTOIDS

Who wrote this book? A tradition says Moses wrote Genesis, but that is unlikely. It was probably written by one or more authors who collected stories that were passed from generation to generation by word of mouth.

Why was it written? Genesis was written to explain how God created the world, how sin became part of life, and how the Israelites came to be God's Chosen People.

How does it fit into the Bible? Genesis is the first book of the Bible. It is part of the Pentateuch, the five books of the Bible that Jews call the Torah.

How is it organized? The first eleven chapters tell the story of Creation, the Fall, and God's Covenant with Noah. The rest of the book starts the history of God's Chosen People, beginning with Abraham and Sarah.

Important themes
- Everything God created is good and holy.
- Sin and evil are real.
- God promises to care for those who are faithful.

GENESIS

The Story of Creation

1 ¹In the beginning, when God created the universe,ᵃ ²the earth was formless and desolate. The raging ocean that covered everything was engulfed in total darkness, and the Spirit of Godᵇ was moving over the water. ³Then God commanded, "Let there be light"—and light appeared. ⁴God was pleased with what he saw. Then he separated the light from the darkness, ⁵and he named the light "Day" and the darkness "Night." Evening passed and morning came—that was the first day.

⁶⁻⁷Then God commanded, "Let there be a dome to divide the water and to keep it in two separate places"—and it was done. So God made a dome, and it separated the water under it from the water above it. ⁸He named the dome "Sky." Evening passed and morning came—that was the second day.

⁹Then God commanded, "Let the water below the sky come together in one place, so that the land will appear"—and it was done. ¹⁰He named the land "Earth," and the water which had come together he named "Sea." And God was pleased with what he saw. ¹¹Then he commanded, "Let the earth produce all kinds of plants, those that bear grain and those that bear fruit"—and it was done. ¹²So the earth produced all kinds of plants, and God was pleased with what he saw. ¹³Evening passed and morning came—that was the third day.

¹⁴Then God commanded, "Let lights appear in the sky to separate day from night and to show the time when days, years, and religious festivalsᶜ begin; ¹⁵they will shine in the sky to give light to the earth"—and it was done. ¹⁶So God made the two larger lights, the sun to rule over the day and the moon to rule over the night; he also made the stars. ¹⁷He placed the lights in the sky to shine on the earth, ¹⁸to rule over the day

And God Was Pleased

The Bible says that every time God created something, God was pleased. God never made a mistake in creation, never started over, never even said "oops!" Poison ivy, grizzly bears, hurricanes, spiders, bacteria, vultures, and aardvarks were all worthy of God's pride.

God was especially proud of the human beings he made on the sixth day (Genesis 1:31). No human being who lives on this planet was a mistake. You are here because God wanted YOU at this time in this place for a special reason. The same goes for the person at school whom you really don't like and the person halfway across the world who lives in an "enemy" country.

The next time you're down on yourself or someone else, remember that everyone has a bad day once in a while and try to imagine God saying, "I am *very* pleased! I do great work!"

— Genesis 1:1—2:4

and the night, and to separate light from darkness. And God was pleased with what he saw. ¹⁹Evening passed and morning came—that was the fourth day.

²⁰Then God commanded, "Let the water be filled with many kinds of living beings,

---

ᵃ **1:1** In the beginning . . . the universe; *or* In the beginning God created the universe; *or* When God began to create the universe.   ᵇ **1:2** the Spirit of God; *or* the power of God; *or* a wind from God; *or* an awesome wind.
ᶜ **1:14** religious festivals; *or* seasons.
1:3 2 Macc 7:28; 2 Cor 4:6   **1:6–8** 2 Pet 3:5

So God made them all, and was pleased with what he saw. (1:25)

and let the air be filled with birds." ²¹So God created the great sea monsters, all kinds of creatures that live in the water, and all kinds of birds. And God was pleased with what he saw. ²²He blessed them all and told the creatures that live in the water to reproduce and to fill the sea, and he told the birds to increase in number. ²³Evening passed and morning came—that was the fifth day.

²⁴Then God commanded, "Let the earth produce all kinds of animal life: domestic and wild, large and small"—and it was done. ²⁵So God made them all, and he was pleased with what he saw.

²⁶Then God said, "And now we will make human beings; they will be like us and resemble us. They will have power over the fish, the birds, and all animals, domestic and wild,ᵈ large and small." ²⁷So God created human beings, making them to be like himself. He created them male and female, ²⁸blessed them, and said, "Have many children, so that your descendants will live all over the earth and bring it under their control. I am putting you in charge of the fish, the birds, and all the wild animals. ²⁹I have provided all kinds of grain and all kinds of fruit for you to eat; ³⁰but for all the wild animals and for all the birds I have provided

grass and leafy plants for food"—and it was done. ³¹God looked at everything he had made, and he was very pleased. Evening passed and morning came—that was the sixth day.

2 ¹And so the whole universe was completed. ²By the seventh day God finished what he had been doing and stopped working. ³He blessed the seventh day and set it apart as a special day, because by that day he had completed his creationᵉ and stopped working. ⁴And that is how the universe was created.

So God created human beings . . . and he was very pleased. (1:27–31)

ᵈ **1:26** *One ancient translation* animals, domestic and wild; *Hebrew* domestic animals and all the earth.   ᵉ **2:3** by that day he had completed his creation; *or* on that day he completed his creation.
1:26 Wis 2:23; Sir 17:3, 4; 1 Cor 11:7   **1:27, 28** Gen 5:1, 2   **1:27** Mt 19:4; Mk 10:6   **2:2, 3** Ex 20:11
2:2 Heb 4:4, 10

Count the number of times the phrase "God was pleased" appears in Genesis, chapter 1.

Genesis

The Garden of Eden

When the LORD[f] God made the universe, [5]there were no plants on the earth and no seeds had sprouted, because he had not sent any rain, and there was no one to cultivate the land; [6]but water would come up from beneath the surface and water the ground.

[7]Then the LORD God took some soil from the ground[g] and formed a man[g] out of it; he breathed life-giving breath into his nostrils and the man began to live.

[8]Then the LORD God planted a garden in Eden, in the East, and there he put the man he had formed. [9]He made all kinds of beautiful trees grow there and produce good fruit. In the middle of the garden stood the tree that gives life and the tree that gives knowledge of what is good and what is bad.[h]

[10]A stream flowed in Eden and watered the garden; beyond Eden it divided into four rivers. [11]The first river is the Pishon; it flows around the country of Havilah. ([12]Pure gold is found there and also rare perfume and precious stones.) [13]The second river is the Gihon; it flows around the country of Cush.[i] [14]The third river is the Tigris, which flows east of Assyria, and the fourth river is the Euphrates.

[15]Then the LORD God placed the man in the Garden of Eden to cultivate it and guard it. [16]He told him, "You may eat the fruit of any tree in the garden, [17]except the tree that gives knowledge of what is good and what is bad.[j] You must not eat the fruit of that tree; if you do, you will die the same day."

[18]Then the LORD God said, "It is not good for the man to live alone. I will make a suitable companion to help him." [19]So he took some soil from the ground and formed all the animals and all the birds. Then he brought them to the man to see what he would name them; and that is how they all

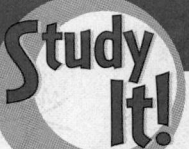

Uncovering the Truth

The first two chapters of Genesis tell two different stories of Creation. Some people believe that everything happened just as the Bible says it did. But Bible scholars tell us that neither of these stories gives us the scientific or historical *facts* about Creation. For example, God did not really create the world in six twenty-four-hour days. Neither God nor Adam named anything. And God did not take a rib from Adam to create Eve.

The stories in Genesis are symbolic stories. They may not contain scientific facts, but they tell us some important truths about God:

- God always was, even before the universe was created.
- God created everything.
- God loves all of Creation.
- God created humans in the image of God.
- God created us to be happy and live in perfect harmony with him, each other, and all creation.

There are many ways to communicate religious truth, and the Bible uses most of them. Believing the religious truth that the Bible teaches is the thing that really matters.

— Genesis 2:5–25

---

[f] **2:4** THE LORD: *Where the Hebrew text has Yahweh, traditionally transliterated as Jehovah, this translation employs* LORD *with capital letters, following a usage which is widespread in English versions.* [g] **2:7** GROUND . . . MAN: *The Hebrew words for "man" and "ground" have similar sounds.* [h] **2:9** knowledge of what is good and what is bad; *or* knowledge of everything. [i] **2:13** CUSH: *usually means Ethiopia, but here may refer to a place in Mesopotamia.* [j] **2:17** knowledge of what is good and what is bad; *or* knowledge of everything.
2:7 Wis 15:8, 11; 1 Cor 15:45   **2:9** Rev 2:7; 22:2, 14

Genesis means "source" or "beginning." It means that this book is about the beginning of things: the world, human beings, sin, the Covenant with God.

got their names. 20So the man named all the birds and all the animals; but not one of them was a suitable companion to help him.

21Then the LORD God made the man fall into a deep sleep, and while he was sleeping, he took out one of the man's ribs and closed up the flesh. 22He formed a woman out of the rib and brought her to him. 23Then the man said,

"At last, here is one of my own kind—
Bone taken from my bone, and flesh from
  my flesh.
'Woman' is her name because she was
  taken out of man."[k]

24That is why a man leaves his father and mother and is united with his wife, and they become one.

25The man and the woman were both naked, but they were not embarrassed.

Human Disobedience

3 1Now the snake was the most cunning animal that the LORD God had made. The snake asked the woman, "Did God really tell you not to eat fruit from any tree in the garden?"

2"We may eat the fruit of any tree in the garden," the woman answered, 3"except the tree in the middle of it. God told us not to eat the fruit of that tree or even touch it; if we do, we will die."

4The snake replied, "That's not true; you will not die. 5God said that because he knows that when you eat it, you will be like God[l] and know what is good and what is bad."[m]

6The woman saw how beautiful the tree was and how good its fruit would be to eat, and she thought how wonderful it would be to become

How wonderful it would be to become wise! (3:6)

wise. So she took some of the fruit and ate it. Then she gave some to her husband, and he also ate it. 7As soon as they had eaten it, they were given understanding and realized that they were naked; so they sewed fig leaves together and covered themselves.

8That evening they heard the LORD God walking in the garden, and they hid from him among the trees. 9But the LORD God called out to the man, "Where are you?"

10He answered, "I heard you in the garden; I was afraid and hid from you, because I was naked."

11"Who told you that you were naked?" God asked. "Did you eat the fruit that I told you not to eat?"

12The man answered, "The woman you put here with me gave me the fruit, and I ate it."

13The LORD God asked the woman, "Why did you do this?"

She replied, "The snake tricked me into eating it."

God Pronounces Judgment

14Then the LORD God said to the snake, "You will be punished for this; you alone of all the animals must bear this curse: From now on you will crawl on your belly, and you will have to eat dust as long as you live. 15I will make you and the woman hate each other; her offspring and yours will always be enemies. Her offspring will crush your head, and you will bite her offspring's[n] heel."

16And he said to the woman, "I will increase your trouble in pregnancy and your pain in giving birth. In spite of this, you will still have desire for your husband, yet you will be subject to him."

17And he said to the man, "You listened to your wife and ate the fruit which I told you not to eat. Because of what you have done, the ground will be under a curse. You will have to work hard all your life to make it produce enough food for you. 18It will produce weeds and thorns, and you will have to eat wild plants. 19You will have to work

_k_ **2:23** WOMAN . . . MAN: _The Hebrew words for "woman" and "man" have rather similar sounds._   _l_ **3:5** God; _or the_ gods.   _m_ **3:5** know what is good and what is bad; _or_ know everything.   _n_ **3:15** her offspring's; _or_ their.
2:24 Mt 19:5; Mk 10:7, 8; 1 Cor 6:16; Eph 5:31   **3:1** Wis 2:24; Rev 12:9; 20:2   **3:13** 2 Cor 11:3; 1 Tim 2:14   **3:15** Rev 12:17   **3:17, 18** Heb 6:8

Original Sin

Catholic Connections

In Genesis, chapter 3, a serpent told Adam and Eve that they could be just like God if they ate fruit from a certain tree. The trouble was that God told them not to. They knew it was wrong, but they ate it anyway. As a consequence God told them to leave the garden and promised that they would now have a hard life. Their problems were passed to all future generations—including ours.

Just like the Creation stories, the story about the serpent is a symbolic story that teaches a great truth: human beings turned away from God. The Church calls this turning away from God original sin. Just as you got your brown eyes from your mom or your gift for music from your grandfather, you were born with original sin because of the sin of the first human beings—Adam and Eve.

Because of original sin, human beings are more likely to disobey God; there is evil in the world; our relationships are sometimes difficult. But through our Baptism, original sin is forgiven and we are born to a new life as sons and daughters of God.

— Genesis 3:1–24

hard and sweat to make the soil produce anything, until you go back to the soil from which you were formed. You were made from soil, and you will become soil again."

20 Adam[o] named his wife Eve,[p] because she was the mother of all human beings. 21 And the LORD God made clothes out of animal skins for Adam and his wife, and he clothed them.

Adam and Eve Are Sent Out of the Garden

22 Then the LORD God said, "Now these human beings have become like one of us and have knowledge of what is good and what is bad.[q] They must not be allowed to take fruit from the tree that gives life, eat it, and live forever." 23 So the LORD God sent them out of the Garden of Eden and made them cultivate the soil from which they had been formed. 24 Then at the east side of the

garden he put living creatures[r] and a flaming sword which turned in all directions. This was to keep anyone from coming near the tree that gives life.

Cain and Abel

4 1 Then Adam had intercourse with his wife, and she became pregnant. She bore a son and said, "By the LORD's help I have gotten a son." So she named him Cain.[s] 2 Later she gave birth to another son, Abel. Abel became a shepherd, but Cain was a farmer. 3 After some time Cain brought some of his harvest and gave it as an offering to the LORD. 4 Then Abel brought the first lamb born to one of his sheep, killed it, and gave the best parts of it as an offering. The LORD was pleased with Abel and his offering, 5 but he rejected Cain and his offering. Cain became furious, and he scowled in anger. 6 Then the LORD said to Cain, "Why

o **3:20** ADAM: *This name in Hebrew means "all human beings."* p **3:20** EVE: *This name sounds similar to the Hebrew word for "living," which is rendered in this context as "human beings."* q **3:22** knowledge of what is good and what is bad; *or* knowledge of everything. r **3:24** LIVING CREATURES: *See Word List.* s **4:1** CAIN: *This name sounds like the Hebrew for "gotten."*

3:22 Rev 22:14   **4:4** Heb 11:4

Pray It!

Am I Like Cain?

Am I like Cain, God?
I know I sometimes don't do my best. I do just enough to barely get by. Then when someone tells me it's not good enough, I get angry.
Am I like Cain, God?
Sometimes I hurt those who do well at the things I'd like to be good at. I hurt them with my words, my attitudes, and my actions.
Am I like Cain, God?
When I'm punished for something I did wrong, I complain about the unfairness of it all. I don't take responsibility for what I did.
Am I like Cain, God?
If I am, I'm sorry. Please help me let go of the anger and jealousy that's in my heart. Replace it with kindness, fairness, and the ability to see myself as you see me.
Amen.

— Genesis 4:1–16

are you angry? Why that scowl on your face? ⁷If you had done the right thing, you would be smiling;ᵗ but because you have done evil, sin is crouching at your door. It wants to rule you, but you must overcome it."

⁸Then Cain said to his brother Abel, "Let's go out in the fields."ᵘ When they were out in the fields, Cain turned on his brother and killed him.

⁹The LORD asked Cain, "Where is your brother Abel?"

He answered, "I don't know. Am I supposed to take care of my brother?"

¹⁰Then the LORD said, "Why have you done this terrible thing? Your brother's blood is crying out to me from the ground, like a voice calling for revenge. ¹¹You are placed under a curse and can no longer farm the soil. It has soaked up your brother's blood as if it had opened its mouth to receive it when

"Why that scowl on your face?" (4:6)

ᵗ **4:7** you would be smiling; *or* I would have accepted your offering.   ᵘ **4:8** *Some ancient translations* Let's go out in the fields; *Hebrew does not have these words.*
4:8 Wis 10:3; Mt 23:35; Lk 11:51; 1 Jn 3:12   **4:10** Heb 12:24

The Fall is the name given to the events that led to Adam and Eve's being thrown out of the Garden of Eden.

Respecting Life

Ca†holic
Connec†ions

Cain tried to hide it at first. When God asked about Abel, he said, "I don't know. Am I supposed to take care of my brother?" (Genesis 4:9) But God knew the truth: Cain killed his brother.

In many parts of the world (including the United States), if someone kills another person, he or she can be put to death for the crime. But God spared Cain from that fate. He even put a mark on Cain to warn others not to kill him. The rest of his life was miserable, but he lived.

The Catholic Church teaches that all of life is sacred—even the life of a person who takes someone else's life. For that reason the death penalty must not be used if there are other ways to keep the murderer from hurting someone else. God calls us to have respect for all life.

— Genesis 4:8–16

you killed him. 12 If you try to grow crops, the soil will not produce anything; you will be a homeless wanderer on the earth."

13 And Cain said to the LORD, "This punishment is too hard for me to bear. 14 You are driving me off the land and away from your presence. I will be a homeless wanderer on the earth, and anyone who finds me will kill me."

15 But the LORD answered, "No. If anyone kills you, seven lives will be taken in revenge." So the LORD put a mark on Cain to warn anyone who met him not to kill him. 16 And Cain went away from the LORD's presence and lived in a land called "Wandering," which is east of Eden.

The Descendants of Cain

17 Cain and his wife had a son and named him Enoch. Then Cain built a city and named it after his son. 18 Enoch had a son named Irad, who was the father of Mehujael, and Mehujael had a son named

Methushael, who was the father of Lamech. 19 Lamech had two wives, Adah and Zillah. 20 Adah gave birth to Jabal, who was the ancestor of those who raise livestock and live in tents. 21 His brother was Jubal, the ancestor of all musicians who play the harp and the flute. 22 Zillah gave birth to Tubal Cain, who made all kinds of tools out of bronze and iron.ᵛ The sister of Tubal Cain was Naamah.

23 Lamech said to his wives,
"Adah and Zillah, listen to me:
I have killed a young man because he
    struck me.
24 If seven lives are taken to pay for killing
    Cain,
Seventy-seven will be taken if anyone kills
    me."

Seth and Enosh

25 Adam and his wife had another son. She said, "God has given me a son to replace Abel, whom Cain killed." So she named him Seth.ʷ 26 Seth had a son whom he named

ᵛ **4:22** who made all kinds of tools out of bronze and iron; *one ancient translation* who was the ancestor of all metalworkers.   ʷ **4:25** SETH: *This name sounds like the Hebrew for "has given."*

Cain committed the sin of murder, but his story also contains other sins, such as jealous behavior and lying. Can you find more?

Enosh. It was then that people began using the LORD's holy name in worship.

The Descendants of Adam
(1 Chronicles 1:1–4)

5 ¹This is the list of the descendants of Adam. (When God created human beings, he made them like himself. ²He created them male and female, blessed them, and named them "Human Beings.") ³When Adam was 130 years old, he had a son who was like him, and he named him Seth. ⁴After that, Adam lived another 800 years. He had other children ⁵and died at the age of 930.

⁶When Seth was 105, he had a son, Enosh, ⁷and then lived another 807 years. He had other children ⁸and died at the age of 912.

⁹When Enosh was 90, he had a son, Kenan, ¹⁰and then lived another 815 years. He had other children ¹¹and died at the age of 905.

¹²When Kenan was 70, he had a son, Mahalalel, ¹³and then lived another 840 years. He had other children ¹⁴and died at the age of 910.

¹⁵When Mahalalel was 65, he had a son, Jared, ¹⁶and then lived another 830 years. He had other children ¹⁷and died at the age of 895.

¹⁸When Jared was 162, he had a son, Enoch, ¹⁹and then lived another 800 years. He had other children ²⁰and died at the age of 962.

²¹When Enoch was 65, he had a son, Methuselah. ²²After that, Enoch lived in fellowship with God for 300 years and had other children. ²³He lived to be 365 years old. ²⁴He spent his life in fellowship with God, and then he disappeared, because God took him away.

²⁵When Methuselah was 187, he had a son, Lamech, ²⁶and then lived another 782 years. He had other children ²⁷and died at the age of 969.

²⁸When Lamech was 182, he had a son ²⁹and said, "From the very ground on which the LORD put a curse, this child will bring us relief from all our hard work"; so he named him Noah.^x ³⁰Lamech lived another 595 years. He had other children ³¹and died at the age of 777.

³²After Noah was 500 years old, he had three sons, Shem, Ham, and Japheth.

Human Wickedness

6 ¹When people had spread all over the world, and daughters were being born, ²some of the heavenly beings^y saw that these young women were beautiful, so they took the ones they liked. ³Then the LORD said, "I will not allow people to live forever; they are mortal. From now on they will live no

Live It!

God's Bright Spot

God was fed up with human beings. Even though they were created in God's image, they insisted on disobeying God—*big* time! So God decided to destroy everyone and start from scratch. "I will wipe out these people I have created, and also the animals and the birds, because I am sorry that I made any of them" (Genesis 6:7).

But there was one bright spot: Noah and his family. They were good people who always made God number one in their life. They were the only ones in the world who lived as God wanted them to live. Because of them, God decided that the world was worth saving after all.

Does God always come first in your life? Are you God's bright spot?

— Genesis 6:1–12

---

^x **5:29** NOAH: *This name sounds like the Hebrew for "relief."*   ^y **6:2** heavenly beings; *or* sons of the gods; *or* sons of God.

5:1, 2 Gen 1:27, 28   **5:2** Mt 19:4; Mk 10:6   **5:24** Sir 44:16; 49:14; Heb 11:5; Jude 14   **6:1–4** Job 1:6; 2:1

Genesis

longer than 120 years." ⁴In those days, and even later, there were giants on the earth who were descendants of human women and the heavenly beings. They were the great heroes and famous men of long ago.

⁵When the LORD saw how wicked everyone on earth was and how evil their thoughts were all the time, ⁶he was sorry that he had ever made them and put them on the earth. He was so filled with regret ⁷that he said, "I will wipe out these people I have created, and also the animals and the birds, because I am sorry that I made any of them." ⁸But the LORD was pleased with Noah.

Noah

⁹⁻¹⁰This is the story of Noah. He had three sons, Shem, Ham, and Japheth. Noah had no faults and was the only good man of his time. He lived in fellowship with God, ¹¹but everyone else was evil in God's sight, and violence had spread everywhere. ¹²God looked at the world and saw that it was evil, for the people were all living evil lives.

¹³God said to Noah, "I have decided to put an end to all people. I will destroy them completely, because the world is full of their violent deeds. ¹⁴Build a boat for yourself out of good timber; make rooms in it and cover it with tar inside and out. ¹⁵Make it 450 feet long, 75 feet wide, and 45 feet high. ¹⁶Make a roofᶻ for the boat and leave a space of 18 inches between the roofᶻ and the sides. Build it with three decks and put a door in the side. ¹⁷I am going to send a flood on the earth to destroy every living being. Everything on the earth will die, ¹⁸but I will make a covenant with you. Go into the boat with your wife, your sons, and their wives. ¹⁹⁻²⁰Take into the boat with you a male and a female of every kind of animal and of every kind of bird, in order to keep them alive. ²¹Take along all kinds of food for you and for them." ²²Noah did everything that God commanded.

The Flood

7 ¹The LORD said to Noah, "Go into the boat with your whole family; I have found that you are the only one in all the world who does what is right. ²Take with you seven pairs of each kind of ritually clean animal, but only one pair of each kind of unclean animal. ³Take also seven pairs of each kind of bird. Do this so that every kind of animal and bird will be kept alive to reproduce again on the earth. ⁴Seven days from now I am going to send rain that will fall for forty days and nights, in order to destroy all the living beings that I have made." ⁵And Noah did everything that the LORD commanded.

⁶Noah was six hundred years old when the flood came on the earth. ⁷He and his wife, and his sons and their wives, went into the boat to escape the flood. ⁸A male and a female of every kind of animal and bird, whether ritually clean or unclean, ⁹went into the boat with Noah, as God had commanded. ¹⁰Seven days later the flood came.

Every kind of animal and bird . . . went into the boat. (7:8, 9)

¹¹When Noah was six hundred years old, on the seventeenth day of the second month all the outlets of the vast body of water beneath the earth burst open, all the floodgates of the sky were opened, ¹²and rain fell on the earth for forty days and nights. ¹³On that same day Noah and his wife went into the boat with their three sons, Shem, Ham, and Japheth, and their wives. ¹⁴With them went every kind of animal, domestic and wild, large and small, and every kind of bird. ¹⁵A male and a female of each kind of living

---

ᶻ **6:16** roof; *or* window.
6:4 Num 13:33; Sir 16:7; Bar 3:26   **6:5–8** Mt 24:37; Lk 17:26; 1 Pet 3:20   **6:9** Sir 44:17, 18; 2 Pet 2:5
6:22 Heb 11:7   **7:7** Mt 24:38, 39; Lk 17:27   **7:11** 2 Pet 3:6

being went into the boat with Noah, ¹⁶as God had commanded. Then the LORD shut the door behind Noah.

¹⁷The flood continued for forty days, and the water became deep enough for the boat to float. ¹⁸The water became deeper, and the boat drifted on the surface. ¹⁹It became so deep that it covered the highest mountains; ²⁰it went on rising until it was about twenty-five feet above the tops of the mountains. ²¹Every living being on the earth died— every bird, every animal, and every person. ²²Everything on earth that breathed died. ²³The LORD destroyed all living beings on the earth—human beings, animals, and birds. The only ones left were Noah and those who were with him in the boat. ²⁴The water did not start going down for a hundred and fifty days.

Everything on earth that breathed died. (7:22)

The End of the Flood

8 ¹God had not forgotten Noah and all the animals with him in the boat; he caused a wind to blow, and the water started going down. ²The outlets of the water beneath the earth and the floodgates of the sky were closed. The rain stopped, ³and the water gradually went down for 150 days. ⁴On the seventeenth day of the seventh month the boat came to rest on a mountain in the Ararat range. ⁵The water kept going down, and on the first day of the tenth month the tops of the mountains appeared.

⁶After forty days Noah opened a window ⁷and sent out a raven. It did not come back, but kept flying around until the water was

completely gone. ⁸Meanwhile, Noah sent out a dove to see if the water had gone down, ⁹but since the water still covered all the land, the dove did not find a place to light. It flew back to the boat, and Noah reached out and took it in. ¹⁰He waited another seven days and sent out the dove again. ¹¹It returned to him in the evening with a fresh olive leaf in its beak. So Noah knew that the water had gone down. ¹²Then he waited another seven days and sent out the dove once more; this time it did not come back.

The water had gone down. (8:11)

¹³When Noah was 601 years old, on the first day of the first month, the water was gone. Noah removed the covering of the boat, looked around, and saw that the ground was getting dry. ¹⁴By the twenty-seventh day of the second month the earth was completely dry.

¹⁵God said to Noah, ¹⁶"Go out of the boat with your wife, your sons, and their wives. ¹⁷Take all the birds and animals out with you, so that they may reproduce and spread over all the earth." ¹⁸So Noah went out of the boat with his wife, his sons, and their wives. ¹⁹All the animals and birds went out of the boat in groups of their own kind.

Noah Offers a Sacrifice

²⁰Noah built an altar to the LORD; he took one of each kind of ritually clean animal and bird, and burned them whole as a sacrifice on the altar. ²¹The odor of the sacrifice pleased the LORD, and he said to himself,

The name *Noah* means "to comfort" or "to give rest" in Hebrew.

Got Gratitude?

When Noah and his family left the boat, the first thing Noah did was build an altar and offer prayers of thanksgiving to God. He was grateful to God for saving them and giving them a chance to start all over again. After receiving Noah's act of gratitude God decided never to destroy the world again.

If you never say thank you to the people in your life, they might feel like you take them for granted or don't appreciate them. Gratitude is also an important part of your relationship with God. Have you thanked God lately? For what are you grateful?

— Genesis 8:20–22

"Never again will I put the earth under a curse because of what people do; I know that from the time they are young their thoughts are evil. Never again will I destroy all living beings, as I have done this time. 22 As long as the world exists, there will be a time for planting and a time for harvest. There will always be cold and heat, summer and winter, day and night."

God's Covenant with Noah

9 1God blessed Noah and his sons and said, "Have many children, so that your descendants will live all over the earth. 2 All the animals, birds, and fish will live in fear of you. They are all placed under your power. 3 Now you can eat them, as well as green plants; I give them all to you for food. 4 The one thing you must not eat is meat with blood still in it; I forbid this because the life is in the blood. 5 If anyone takes human life, he will be punished. I will punish with death any animal that takes a human life. 6 Human beings were made like God, so whoever murders one of them will be killed by someone else.

7 "You must have many children, so that your descendants will live all over the earth."

8 God said to Noah and his sons, 9 "I am now making my covenant with you and with your descendants, 10 and with all living beings—all birds and all animals—everything that came out of the boat with you. 11 With these words I make my covenant with you: I promise that never again will all living beings be destroyed by a flood; never again will a flood destroy the earth. 12 As a sign of this everlasting covenant which I am making with you and with all living beings, 13 I am putting my bow in the clouds. It will be the sign of my covenant with the world. 14 Whenever I

The sign of my covenant with the world (9:13)

cover the sky with clouds and the rainbow appears, 15 I will remember my promise to you and to all the animals that a flood will never again destroy all living beings. 16 When the rainbow appears in the clouds, I will see it and remember the everlasting covenant between me and all living beings on earth.

9:1 Gen 1:28   **9:4** Lev 7:26, 27; 17:10–14; 19:26; Deut 12:16, 23; 15:23   **9:6** Ex 20:13; Gen 1:26   **9:7** Gen 1:28

Compare Genesis 1:29 and 9:2–3. What did God add to the human diet?

Pray It!   A Promising Sign

"I am putting my bow in the clouds. It will be the sign of my covenant with the world" (Genesis 9:13). After it was all over, God sent a rainbow as a sign to Noah, his family, and all living beings that God would never leave them and would never use a flood to destroy the world again. The rainbow was a symbol of God's *covenant,* a solemn promise made to Noah and to everyone who lived after him—including *you.*

Dear God,
When I am overwhelmed by the destruction and evil that exists in the world today,
help me to remember the promise you made to Noah and his family. When I am fear-
ful, fill me with your peace. Each time I see a rainbow, may it remind me that you are
always with me and will never leave me. Amen.

— Genesis 9:8–17

17That is the sign of the promise which I am making to all living beings."

Noah and His Sons

18The sons of Noah who went out of the boat were Shem, Ham, and Japheth. (Ham was the father of Canaan.) 19These three sons of Noah were the ancestors of all the people on earth.

20Noah, who was a farmer, was the first man to plant a vineyard. 21After he drank some of the wine, he became drunk, took off his clothes, and lay naked in his tent. 22When Ham, the father of Canaan, saw that his father was naked, he went out and told his two brothers. 23Then Shem and Japheth took a robe and held it behind them on their shoulders. They walked backward into the tent and covered their father, keeping their faces turned away so as not to see him naked. 24When Noah sobered up and learned what his youngest son had done to him, 25he said,

"A curse on Canaan!
He will be a slave to his brothers.
26Give praise to the LORD, the God of
Shem!
Canaan will be the slave of Shem.
27May God cause Japheth*a* to increase!

May his descendants live with the people of Shem!
Canaan will be the slave of Japheth."
28After the flood Noah lived 350 years 29and died at the age of 950.

The Descendants of Noah's Sons
(1 Chronicles 1:5–23)

10 1These are the descendants of Noah's sons, Shem, Ham, and Japheth. These three had sons after the flood.

2The sons of Japheth—Gomer, Magog, Madai, Javan, Tubal, Meshech, and Tiras—were the ancestors of the peoples who bear their names. 3The descendants of Gomer were the people of Ashkenaz, Riphath, and Togarmah. 4The descendants of Javan were the people of Elishah, Spain, Cyprus, and Rhodes; 5they were the ancestors of the people who live along the coast and on the islands. These are the descendants of Japheth, living in their different tribes and countries, each group speaking its own language.

6The sons of Ham—Cush, Egypt, Libya, and Canaan—were the ancestors of the peoples who bear their names. 7The descendants of Cush were the people of Seba, Havilah, Sabtah, Raamah, and Sabteca. The descendants

a **9:27** JAPHETH: *This name sounds like the Hebrew for "increase."*

of Raamah were the people of Sheba and Dedan. 8Cush had a son named Nimrod, who became the world's first great conqueror. 9By the LORD's help he was a great hunter, and that is why people say, "May the LORD make you as great a hunter as Nimrod!" 10At first his kingdom included Babylon, Erech, and Accad, all three of them in Babylonia. 11From that land he went to Assyria and built the cities of Nineveh, Rehoboth Ir, Calah, 12and Resen, which is between Nineveh and the great city of Calah.

13The descendants of Egypt were the people of Lydia, Anam, Lehab, Naphtuh, 14Pathrus, Casluh, and of Crete, from whom the Philistines are descended.[b]

15Canaan's sons—Sidon, the oldest, and Heth—were the ancestors of the peoples who bear their names. 16Canaan was also the ancestor of the Jebusites, the Amorites, the Girgashites, 17the Hivites, the Arkites, the Sinites, 18the Arvadites, the Zemarites, and the Hamathites. The different tribes of the Canaanites spread out, 19until the Canaanite borders reached from Sidon southward to Gerar near Gaza, and eastward to Sodom, Gomorrah, Admah, and Zeboiim near Lasha. 20These are the descendants of Ham, living in their different tribes and countries, each group speaking its own language.

21Shem, the older brother of Japheth, was the ancestor of all the Hebrews. 22Shem's sons—Elam, Asshur, Arpachshad, Lud, and Aram—were the ancestors of the peoples who bear their names. 23The descendants of Aram were the people of Uz, Hul, Gether, and Meshek. 24Arpachshad was the father of Shelah, who was the father of Eber. 25Eber had two sons: one was named Peleg,[c] because during his time the people of the world were divided; and the other was named Joktan. 26The descendants of Joktan were the people of Almodad, Sheleph, Hazarmaveth, Jerah, 27Hadoram, Uzal, Diklah, 28Obal, Abimael, Sheba, 29Ophir, Havilah, and Jobab. All of them were descended from Joktan. 30The land in which they lived extended from Mesha to Sephar in the east-

ern hill country. 31These are the descendants of Shem, living in their different tribes and countries, each group speaking its own language.

32All these peoples are the descendants of Noah, nation by nation, according to their different lines of descent. After the flood all the nations of the earth were descended from the sons of Noah.

The Tower of Babylon

11 1At first, the people of the whole world had only one language and used the same words. 2As they wandered about in the East, they came to a plain in Babylonia and settled there. 3They said to one another, "Come on! Let's make bricks and bake them hard." So they had bricks to build with and tar to hold them together. 4They said, "Now let's build a city with a tower that reaches the sky, so that we can make a name for ourselves and not be scattered all over the earth."

5Then the LORD came down to see the city and the tower which they had built, 6and he said, "Now then, these are all one people and they speak one language; this is just the beginning of what they are going to do. Soon they will be able to do anything they want! 7Let us go down and mix up their language so that they will not understand each other." 8So the LORD scattered them all over the earth, and they stopped building the city. 9The city was called Babylon,[d] because there the LORD mixed up the language of all the people, and from there he scattered them all over the earth.

The Descendants of Shem
(1 Chronicles 1:24–27)

10These are the descendants of Shem. Two years after the flood, when Shem was 100 years old, he had a son, Arpachshad. 11After that, he lived another 500 years and had other children.

12When Arpachshad was 35 years old, he

---

[b] **10:14** *Probable text* and of Crete . . . descended; *Hebrew* from whom the Philistines are descended, and Crete.   [c] **10:25** PELEG: *This name sounds like the Hebrew for "divide."*   [d] **11:9** BABYLON: *This name sounds like the Hebrew for "mixed up."*

son, Peleg; [17]after that, he lived another 430 years and had other children.

[18]When Peleg was 30 years old, he had a son, Reu; [19]after that, he lived another 209 years and had other children.

[20]When Reu was 32 years old, he had a son, Serug; [21]after that, he lived another 207 years and had other children.

[22]When Serug was 30 years old, he had a son, Nahor; [23]after that, he lived another 200 years and had other children.

[24]When Nahor was 29 years old, he had a son, Terah; [25]after that, he lived another 119 years and had other children.

[26]After Terah was 70 years old, he became the father of Abram, Nahor, and Haran.

The Descendants of Terah

[27]These are the descendants of Terah, who was the father of Abram, Nahor, and Haran. Haran was the father of Lot, [28]and Haran died in his hometown of Ur in Babylonia, while his father was still living. [29]Abram married Sarai, and Nahor married Milcah, the daughter of Haran, who was also the father of Iscah. [30]Sarai was not able to have children.

[31]Terah took his son Abram, his grandson Lot, who was the son of Haran, and his daughter-in-law Sarai, Abram's wife, and with them he left the city of Ur in Babylonia to go to the land of Canaan. They went as far as Haran and settled there. [32]Terah died there at the age of 205.

God's Call to Abram

12 [1]The LORD said to Abram, "Leave your country, your relatives, and your father's home, and go to a land that I am going to show you. [2]I will give you many descendants, and they will become a great nation. I will bless you and make your name famous, so that you will be a blessing. [3]I will bless those who bless you,

But I will curse those who curse you.

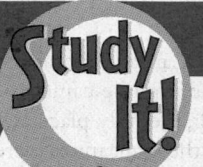

Watch Your Language!

As the Bible story goes, people used to speak the same language—until the people of Babylon tried to build a tower to the sky, that is. They wanted to show off their greatness; they wanted to be like God. God wanted to put a stop to their work, so God "mixed up the language of all the people, and from there he scattered them all over the earth" (Genesis 11:9).

The writers of Genesis were trying to explain the fact that people around the world spoke different languages, so they used a story about a tower. Like the other stories in the first eleven chapters of Genesis, it may not contain many historical facts, but it is true. Language can be used in ways that are hurtful or helpful. It can be used to build up relationships or to tear them down. It can be a source of prejudice, or it can be a source of pride.

God gave human beings the gift of language for a reason: to build a world that pleases and honors God.

— Genesis 11:1–9

---

had a son, Shelah; [13]after that, he lived another 403 years and had other children.

[14]When Shelah was 30 years old, he had a son, Eber; [15]after that, he lived another 403 years and had other children.

[16]When Eber was 34 years old, he had a

12:1 Wis 10:5; Acts 7:2, 3; Heb 11:8   **12:3** Gal 3:8

For the next month or so, try to learn at least one new word or phrase a day in another langusge.

Genesis

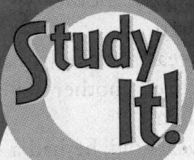

From Story to History

In the first part of the Book of Genesis (chapters 1–11), God speaks to us through stories about symbolic people in a time before recorded history. Though these chapters do not contain many historical facts, they are full of truth about God. The genealogy, or family tree, in Genesis 11:10–32 makes a transition to the second part of Book of Genesis.

Starting with the story of Abram and Sarai (who are later renamed Abraham and Sarah) in chapter 12, Genesis becomes more like a history book. The names of people and places are real. The events described in the second part of the book are not unusual; they are events that happen to real people. The characters struggle with some of the same things that we struggle with.

Both parts of Genesis are important. They are the foundation of all that we believe about God and God's relationship with us since the beginning of time.

— Genesis 11:10–32

And through you I will bless all the nations."[e]

[4] When Abram was seventy-five years old, he started out from Haran, as the LORD had told him to do; and Lot went with him. [5] Abram took his wife Sarai, his nephew Lot, and all the wealth and all the slaves they had acquired in Haran, and they started out for the land of Canaan.

When they arrived in Canaan, [6] Abram traveled through the land until he came to the sacred tree of Moreh, the holy place at Shechem. (At that time the Canaanites were still living in the land.) [7] The LORD appeared to Abram and said to him, "This is the country that I am going to give to your descendants." Then Abram built an altar there to the LORD, who had appeared to him. [8] After that, he moved on south to the hill country east of the city of Bethel and set up his camp between Bethel on the west and Ai on the east. There also he built an altar and worshiped the LORD. [9] Then he moved on from place to place, going toward the southern part of Canaan.

Abram in Egypt

[10] But there was a famine in Canaan, and it was so bad that Abram went farther south to Egypt, to live there for a while. [11] When he was about to cross the border into Egypt, he said to his wife Sarai, "You are a beautiful woman. [12] When the Egyptians see you, they will assume that you are my wife, and so they will kill me and let you live. [13] Tell them that you are my sister; then because of you they will let me live and treat me well." [14] When he crossed the border into Egypt, the Egyptians did see that his wife was beautiful. [15] Some of the court officials saw her and told the king how beautiful she was; so she was taken to his palace. [16] Because of her the king treated Abram well and gave him flocks of sheep and goats, cattle, donkeys, slaves, and camels.

[17] But because the king had taken Sarai, the LORD sent terrible diseases on him and on the people of his palace. [18] Then the king sent for Abram and asked him, "What have you done to me? Why didn't you tell me that she was your wife? [19] Why did you say

[e] **12:3** And through . . . nations; *or* All the nations will ask me to bless them as I have blessed you.
12:7 Acts 7:5; Gal 3:16   **12:13** Gen 20:2; 26:7

Chapters 12–50 of the Book of Genesis are mainly about Abraham, his son Isaac, Abraham's grandson Jacob, and Abraham's great-grandson Joseph.

An Act of Faith

**What would you do if someone
told you to leave your home, your
family, and your friends and move
to a new country? This person
says that if you do as asked, you
will be famous. Would you trust
him or her? Would you do it?**

That's exactly what happened
to Abram. He and his wife Sarai
were living a comfortable life in
Haran. God told them to pick up
everything and move—not just to
the next town, but to a new country. And they listened.

Why did Abram do it? Because
he had faith. Through his faith, he
came to know that God had great
plans for him. He knew that his
faith was a gift; he worked hard
to understand what God wanted
of him and took the steps to make
it happen. It wasn't always easy,
but every time Abram acted out
of faith, his relationship with God
got deeper.

God also gave you the gift of
faith. Though God may not be
telling you to leave home, he is
inviting you to live out your faith
every day. Are you listening carefully? What do you think God is
asking of you?

— Genesis 12:1–9

Abram and Lot Separate

13 ¹Abram went north out of Egypt to
the southern part of Canaan with
his wife and everything he owned, and Lot
went with him. ²Abram was a very rich
man, with sheep, goats, and cattle, as well as
silver and gold. ³Then he left there and
moved from place to place, going toward
Bethel. He reached the place between Bethel
and Ai where he had camped before ⁴and
had built an altar. There he worshiped the
Lord.

⁵Lot also had sheep, goats, and cattle, as
well as his own family and servants. ⁶And so
there was not enough pasture land for the
two of them to stay together, because they
had too many animals. ⁷So quarrels broke
out between the men who took care of
Abram's animals and those who took care of
Lot's animals. (At that time the Canaanites
and the Perizzites were still living in the
land.)

⁸Then Abram said to Lot, "We are relatives, and your men and my men shouldn't
be quarreling. ⁹So let's separate. Choose any
part of the land you want. You go one way,
and I'll go the other."

¹⁰Lot looked around and saw that the
whole Jordan Valley, all the way to Zoar, had
plenty of water, like the Garden of the
Lord*ᶠ* or like the land of Egypt. (This was
before the Lord had destroyed the cities of
Sodom and Gomorrah.) ¹¹So Lot chose the
whole Jordan Valley for himself and moved
away toward the east. That is how the two
men parted. ¹²Abram stayed in the land of
Canaan, and Lot settled among the cities in
the valley and camped near Sodom, ¹³whose
people were wicked and sinned against the
Lord.

Abram Moves to Hebron

¹⁴After Lot had left, the Lord said to
Abram, "From where you are, look carefully
in all directions. ¹⁵I am going to give you
and your descendants all the land that you
see, and it will be yours forever. ¹⁶I am going
to give you so many descendants that no one

that she was your sister, and let me take her
as my wife? Here is your wife; take her and
get out!" ²⁰The king gave orders to his men,
so they took Abram and put him out of the
country, together with his wife and everything he owned.

ᶠ **13:10** GARDEN OF THE LORD: *a reference to the Garden of Eden.*
13:10 Gen 2:10   **13:15** Acts 7:5

will be able to count them all; it would be as easy to count all the specks of dust on earth! [17]Now, go and look over the whole land, because I am going to give it all to you." [18]So Abram moved his camp and settled near the sacred trees of Mamre at Hebron, and there he built an altar to the LORD.

Abram Rescues Lot

14 [1]Four kings, Amraphel of Babylonia, Arioch of Ellasar, Chedorlaomer of Elam, and Tidal of Goiim, [2]went to war against five other kings: Bera of Sodom, Birsha of Gomorrah, Shinab of Admah, Shemeber of Zeboiim, and the king of Bela (or Zoar). [3]These five kings had formed an alliance and joined forces in Siddim Valley, which is now the Dead Sea. [4]They had been under the control of Chedorlaomer for twelve years, but in the thirteenth year they rebelled against him. [5]In the fourteenth year Chedorlaomer and his allies came with their armies and defeated the Rephaim in Ashteroth Karnaim, the Zuzim in Ham, the Emim in the plain of Kiriathaim, [6]and the Horites in the mountains of Edom, pursuing them as far as Elparan on the edge of the desert. [7]Then they turned around and came back to Kadesh (then known as Enmishpat). They conquered all the land of

the Amalekites and defeated the Amorites who lived in Hazazon Tamar.

[8]Then the kings of Sodom, Gomorrah, Admah, Zeboiim, and Bela drew up their armies for battle in Siddim Valley and fought [9]against the kings of Elam, Goiim, Babylonia, and Ellasar, five kings against four. [10]The valley was full of tar pits, and when the kings of Sodom and Gomorrah tried to run away from the battle, they fell into the pits; but the other three kings escaped to the mountains. [11]The four kings took everything in Sodom and Gomorrah, including the food, and went away. [12]Lot, Abram's nephew, was living in Sodom, so they took him and all his possessions.

[13]But a man escaped and reported all this to Abram, the Hebrew, who was living near the sacred trees belonging to Mamre the Amorite. Mamre and his brothers Eshcol and Aner were Abram's allies. [14]When Abram heard that his nephew had been captured, he called together all the fighting men in his camp, 318 in all, and pursued the four kings all the way to Dan. [15]There he divided his men into groups, attacked the enemy by night, and defeated them. He chased them as far as Hobah, north of Damascus, [16]and got back all the loot that had been taken. He also brought back his nephew Lot and his possessions, together with the women and the other prisoners.

Priest of the Most High God

Catholic Connections

When Abram won a battle, Melchizedek—a king and a "priest of the Most High God" (Genesis 14:18)—blessed him. But it was an unusual blessing. Melchizedek offered Abram bread and wine, just as Jesus did at the Last Supper. It was different for Jesus, though. When he blessed the bread and shared it with his Apostles, it was no longer bread and wine. It was his body and blood.

Melchizedek is a priest of the Covenant between God and Abram. Jesus Christ is the High Priest of the New Covenant that God made with the whole human race—the Most High Priest of the Most High God. Every priest ordained in the Catholic Church carries on the work of Melchizedek and above all of Jesus in serving God's people.

— Genesis 14:17–20

Pray It!

Fear and Faith

Dear God,

Abram trusted you all the time. He did what you asked him to do and went where you asked him to go. Abraham had great faith and knew that you were leading him. But even he was afraid. He worried a lot. He was so afraid that he had nightmares.

Sometimes I'm afraid, too, God. I'm afraid of what the future will bring, what to do when I grow up, and what will happen to the people I love. I'm afraid of the tests I have in school and the tests I have in life.

I believe in you, God. I know that you are with me all the time—especially when I'm afraid. Please take care of me. Amen.

— *Genesis 15:1–15*

Melchizedek Blesses Abram

17 When Abram came back from his victory over Chedorlaomer and the other kings, the king of Sodom went out to meet him in Shaveh Valley (also called King's Valley). 18 And Melchizedek, who was king of Salem and also a priest of the Most High God, brought bread and wine to Abram, 19 blessed him, and said, "May the Most High God, who made heaven and earth, bless Abram! 20 May the Most High God, who gave you victory over your enemies, be praised!" And Abram gave Melchizedek a tenth of all the loot he had recovered.

21 The king of Sodom said to Abram, "Keep the loot, but give me back all my people."

22 Abram answered, "I solemnly swear before the LORD, the Most High God, Maker of heaven and earth, 23 that I will not keep anything of yours, not even a thread or a sandal strap. Then you can never say, 'I am the one who made Abram rich.' 24 I will take nothing for myself. I will accept only what my men have used. But let my allies, Aner, Eshcol, and Mamre, take their share."

God's Covenant with Abram

15 1 After this, Abram had a vision and heard the LORD say to him, "Do not be afraid, Abram. I will shield you from danger and give you a great reward."

2 But Abram answered, "Sovereign LORD, what good will your reward do me, since I have no children? My only heir is Eliezer of Damascus.*g* 3 You have given me no children, and one of my slaves will inherit my property."

4 Then he heard the LORD speaking to him again: "This slave Eliezer will not inherit your property; your own son will be your heir." 5 The LORD took him outside and said, "Look at the sky and try to count the stars; you will have as many descendants as that."

6 Abram put his trust in the LORD, and because of this the LORD was pleased with him and accepted him.

7 Then the LORD said to him, "I am the LORD, who led you out of Ur in Babylonia, to give you this land as your own."

8 But Abram asked, "Sovereign LORD, how can I know that it will be mine?"

9 He answered, "Bring me a cow, a goat,

g **15:2** My . . . Damascus; *Hebrew unclear; literally,* The heir of my house, he of Damascus, Eliezer.
14:18–20 Heb 7:1–10   **15:5** Rom 4:18; Heb 11:12   **15:6** 1 Macc 2:52; Rom 4:3; Gal 3:6; Jas 2:23

Check out Hebrews 7:1–10 for more about Melchizedek. You may also hear his name at Mass in the Eucharistic prayer.

and a ram, each of them three years old, and a dove and a pigeon." 10Abram brought the animals to God, cut them in half, and placed the halves opposite each other in two rows; but he did not cut up the birds. 11Vultures came down on the bodies, but Abram drove them off.

12When the sun was going down, Abram fell into a deep sleep, and fear and terror came over him. 13The LORD said to him, "Your descendants will be strangers in a foreign land; they will be slaves there and will be treated cruelly for four hundred years. 14But I will punish the nation that enslaves them, and when they leave that foreign land, they will take great wealth with them. 15You yourself will live to a ripe old age, die in peace, and be buried. 16It will be four generations before your descendants come back here, because I will not drive out the Amorites until they become so wicked that they must be punished."

17When the sun had set and it was dark, a smoking fire pot and a flaming torch suddenly appeared and passed between the pieces of the animals. 18Then and there the LORD made a covenant with Abram. He said, "I promise to give your descendants all this land from the border of Egypt to the Euphrates River, 19including the lands of the Kenites, the Kenizzites, the Kadmonites, 20the Hittites, the Perizzites, the Rephaim, 21the Amorites, the Canaanites, the Girgashites, and the Jebusites."

Hagar and Ishmael

16 1Abram's wife Sarai had not borne him any children. But she had an Egyptian slave woman named Hagar, 2and so she said to Abram, "The LORD has kept me from having children. Why don't you sleep with my slave? Perhaps she can have a child for me." Abram agreed with what Sarai

said. 3So she gave Hagar to him to be his concubine. (This happened after Abram had lived in Canaan for ten years.) 4Abram had intercourse with Hagar, and she became pregnant. When she found out that she was pregnant, she became proud and despised Sarai.

5Then Sarai said to Abram, "It's your fault that Hagar despises me.h I myself gave her to you, and ever since she found out that she was pregnant, she has despised me. May the LORD judge which of us is right, you or me!"

6Abram answered, "Very well, she is your slave and under your control; do whatever you want with her." Then Sarai treated Hagar so cruelly that she ran away.

7The angel of the LORD met Hagar at a spring in the desert on the road to Shur 8and said, "Hagar, slave of Sarai, where have you come from and where are you going?"

She answered, "I am running away from my mistress."

9He said, "Go back to her and be her slave." 10Then he said, "I will give you so many descendants that no one will be able to count them. 11You are going to have a son, and you will name him Ishmael,i because the LORD has heard your cry of distress. 12But your son will live like a wild donkey; he will be against everyone, and everyone will be against him. He will live apart from all his relatives."

13Hagar asked herself, "Have I really seen God and lived to tell about it?"j So she called the LORD, who had spoken to her, "A God Who Sees." 14That is why people call the well between Kadesh and Bered "The Well of the Living One Who Sees Me."

15Hagar bore Abram a son, and he named him Ishmael. 16Abram was eighty-six years old at the time.

h **16:5** It's your fault...me; or May you suffer for this wrong done against me.   i **16:11** ISHMAEL: *This name in Hebrew means "God hears."*   j **16:13** *Probable text* lived to tell about it?; *Hebrew unclear.*
15:12 Job 4:13, 14   **15:13** Ex 1:1–14; Acts 7:6   **15:14** Ex 12:40, 41; Acts 7:7   **15:18** Acts 7:5   **16:15** Gal 4:22

Circumcision, the Sign of the Covenant

17 ¹When Abram was ninety-nine years old, the LORD appeared to him and said, "I am the Almighty God. Obey me and always do what is right. ²I will make my covenant with you and give you many descendants." ³Abram bowed down with his face touching the ground, and God said, ⁴"I make this covenant with you: I promise that you will be the ancestor of many nations. ⁵Your name will no longer be Abram, but Abraham,ᵏ because I am making you the ancestor of many nations. ⁶I will give you many descendants, and some of them will be kings. You will have so many descendants that they will become nations.

⁷"I will keep my promise to you and to your descendants in future generations as an everlasting covenant. I will be your God and the God of your descendants. ⁸I will give to you and to your descendants this land in which you are now a foreigner. The whole land of Canaan will belong to your descendants forever, and I will be their God."

⁹God said to Abraham, "You also must agree to keep the covenant with me, both you and your descendants in future generations. ¹⁰You and your descendants must all agree to circumcise every male among you. ¹¹⁻¹²From now on you must circumcise every baby boy when he is eight days old, including slaves born in your homes and slaves bought from foreigners. This will show that there is a covenant between you and me. ¹³Each one must be circumcised, and this will be a physical sign to show that my covenant with you is everlasting. ¹⁴Any male who has not been circumcised will no longer be considered one of my people, because he has not kept the covenant with me."

¹⁵God said to Abraham, "You must no longer call your wife Sarai; from now on her name is Sarah.ˡ ¹⁶I will bless her, and I will give you a son by her. I will bless her, and she will become the mother of nations, and there will be kings among her descendants."

¹⁷Abraham bowed down with his face

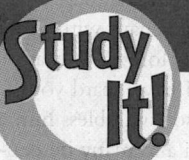

What's in a Name?

Abram was faithful to God, and God was faithful to Abram. As a sign of that faithfulness, God made a covenant with him—a solemn promise to bless Abram with many descendants. Abram did not understand how this could happen—he had only one son at the time, Ishmael, whose mother was a slave. Abram's real wife, Sarai, was old—too old to have children. But Abram trusted God, just like he always did.

As a sign of the covenant between them, God changed Abram's name from Abram (which means "father") to Abraham (which means "father of many"). His wife's name was changed from Sarai to Sarah (meaning "princess"). As a physical sign of the covenant, God told Abram to be circumcised and to have his son and all the males in his house circumcised.

It happened just as God said it would. Sarah had a son named Isaac (meaning "God laughs"). Ishmael (meaning "God hears") also took his place among Abraham's descendants.

— **Genesis 17:1–22**

touching the ground, but he began to laugh when he thought, "Can a man have a child when he is a hundred years old? Can Sarah have a child at ninety?" ¹⁸He asked God, "Why not let Ishmael be my heir?"

¹⁹But God said, "No. Your wife Sarah will

ᵏ **17:5** ABRAHAM: *This name sounds like the Hebrew for "ancestor of many nations."* ˡ **17:15** SARAH: *This name in Hebrew means "princess."*
17:5 Rom 4:17   **17:7** Lk 1:55   **17:8** Acts 7:5   **17:10** Acts 7:8; Rom 4:11

Genesis

bear you a son and you will name him Isaac.[m] I will keep my covenant with him and with his descendants forever. It is an everlasting covenant. 20I have heard your request about Ishmael, so I will bless him and give him many children and many descendants. He will be the father of twelve princes, and I will make a great nation of his descendants. 21But I will keep my covenant with your son Isaac, who will be born to Sarah about this time next year." 22When God finished speaking to Abraham, he left him.

23On that same day Abraham obeyed God and circumcised his son Ishmael and all the other males in his household, including the slaves born in his home and those he had bought. 24Abraham was ninety-nine years old when he was circumcised, 25and his son Ishmael was thirteen. 26They were both circumcised on the same day, 27together with all of Abraham's slaves.

A Son Is Promised to Abraham

18 1The LORD appeared to Abraham at the sacred trees of Mamre. As Abraham was sitting at the entrance of his tent during the hottest part of the day, 2he looked up and saw three men standing there. As soon as he saw them, he ran out to meet them. Bowing down with his face touching the ground, 3he said, "Sirs, please do not pass by my home without stopping; I am here to serve you. 4Let me bring some water for you to wash your feet; you can rest here beneath this tree. 5I will also bring a bit of food; it will give you strength to continue your journey. You have honored me by coming to my home, so let me serve you."

They replied, "Thank you; we accept."

6Abraham hurried into the tent and said to Sarah, "Quick, take a sack of your best flour, and bake some bread." 7Then he ran to the herd and picked out a calf that was tender and fat, and gave it to a servant, who hurried to get it ready. 8He took some cream, some milk, and the meat, and set the food before the men. There under the tree he served them himself, and they ate.

Surprises from God

One day Abraham and Sarah had visitors—one of whom was actually God. God promised Abraham that Sarah would have a baby. When Sarah heard the visitors' comments, she laughed. She couldn't *possibly* have a baby at this point in her life. She was too old. But Sarah didn't understand that it was God talking. And God can do surprising things.

Did God ever surprise you? Did something wonderful but unexpected ever happen to you? It might be something small, like a phone call from a friend or a piece of music that brings back good memories. Maybe it's something bigger, like a new job for a parent who is unemployed or finding out that you really like being a teacher's aide for younger kids. Those are gifts from God.

God is full of surprises. All you have to do is keep your eyes, your ears, and your heart open.

— Genesis 18:1–15

9Then they asked him, "Where is your wife Sarah?"

"She is there in the tent," he answered.

10One of them said, "Nine months from now[n] I will come back, and your wife Sarah will have a son."

Sarah was behind him, at the door of the tent, listening. 11Abraham and Sarah were very old, and Sarah had stopped having her monthly periods. 12So Sarah laughed to herself and said, "Now that I am old and worn out, can I still enjoy sex? And besides, my husband is old too."

13Then the LORD asked Abraham, "Why

---

[m] **17:19** ISAAC: *This name in Hebrew means "he laughs."*   [n] **18:10** Nine months from now; *or* This time next year.
18:2a Heb 13:2   **18:10** Rom 9:9   **18:12** 1 Pet 3:6

did Sarah laugh and say, 'Can I really have a child when I am so old?' [14]Is anything too hard for the LORD? As I said, nine months from now I will return, and Sarah will have a son."

[15]Because Sarah was afraid, she denied it. "I didn't laugh," she said.

"Yes, you did," he replied. "You laughed."

Abraham Pleads for Sodom

[16]Then the men left and went to a place where they could look down at Sodom, and Abraham went with them to send them on their way. [17]And the LORD said to himself, "I will not hide from Abraham what I am going to do. [18]His descendants will become a great and mighty nation, and through him I will bless all the nations.[o] [19]I have chosen him in order that he may command his sons and his descendants to obey me and to do what is right and just. If they do, I will do everything for him that I have promised."

[20]Then the LORD said to Abraham, "There are terrible accusations against Sodom and Gomorrah, and their sin is very great. [21]I must go down to find out whether or not the accusations which I have heard are true."

[22]Then the two men left and went on toward Sodom, but the LORD remained with Abraham. [23]Abraham approached the LORD and asked, "Are you really going to destroy the innocent with the guilty? [24]If there are fifty innocent people in the city, will you destroy the whole city? Won't you spare it in order to save the fifty? [25]Surely you won't kill the innocent with the guilty. That's impossible! You can't do that. If you did, the innocent would be punished along with the guilty. That is impossible. The judge of all the earth has to act justly."

[26]The LORD answered, "If I find fifty innocent people in Sodom, I will spare the whole city for their sake."

[27]Abraham spoke again: "Please forgive my boldness in continuing to speak to you, Lord. I am only a man and have no right to say anything. [28]But perhaps there will be only forty-five innocent people instead of fifty. Will you destroy the whole city because there are five too few?"

The LORD answered, "I will not destroy the city if I find forty-five innocent people."

[29]Abraham spoke again: "Perhaps there will be only forty."

He replied, "I will not destroy it if there are forty."

[30]Abraham said, "Please don't be angry, Lord, but I must speak again. What if there are only thirty?"

He said, "I will not do it if I find thirty."

[31]Abraham said, "Please forgive my boldness in continuing to speak to you, Lord. Suppose that only twenty are found?"

He said, "I will not destroy the city if I find twenty."

[32]Abraham said, "Please don't be angry, Lord, and I will speak only once more. What if only ten are found?"

He said, "I will not destroy it if there are ten." [33]After he had finished speaking with Abraham, the LORD went away, and Abraham returned home.

The Sinfulness of Sodom

19 [1]When the two angels came to Sodom that evening, Lot was sitting at the city gate. As soon as he saw them, he got up and went to meet them. He bowed down before them [2]and said, "Sirs, I am here to serve you. Please come to my house. You can wash your feet and spend the night. In the morning you can get up early and go on your way."

But they answered, "No, we will spend the night here in the city square."

[3]He kept on urging them, and finally they went with him to his house. Lot ordered his servants to bake some bread and prepare a fine meal for the guests. When it was ready, they ate it.

---

[o] **18.18** through . . . nations; *or* all the nations will ask me to bless them as I have blessed him.
18.14 Lk 1:37

In Genesis 18:16–33 Abraham takes the daring step of questioning God. Are you willing to share with God everything you are thinking and feeling?

4Before the guests went to bed, the men of Sodom surrounded the house. All the men of the city, both young and old, were there. **5**They called out to Lot and asked, "Where are the men who came to stay with you tonight? Bring them out to us!" The men of Sodom wanted to have sex with them.

6Lot went outside and closed the door behind him. **7**He said to them, "Friends, I beg you, don't do such a wicked thing! **8**Look, I have two daughters who are still virgins. Let me bring them out to you, and you can do whatever you want with them. But don't do anything to these men; they are guests in my house, and I must protect them."

9But they said, "Get out of our way, you foreigner! Who are you to tell us what to do? Out of our way, or we will treat you worse than them." They pushed Lot back and moved up to break down the door. **10**But the two men inside reached out, pulled Lot back into the house, and shut the door. **11**Then they struck all the men outside with blindness, so that they couldn't find the door.

Lot Leaves Sodom

12The two men said to Lot, "If you have anyone else here—sons, daughters, sons-in-law, or any other relatives living in the city—get them out of here, **13**because we are going to destroy this place. The LORD has heard the terrible accusations against these people and has sent us to destroy Sodom."

14Then Lot went to the men that his daughters were going to marry, and said, "Hurry up and get out of here; the LORD is going to destroy this place." But they thought he was joking.

15At dawn the angels tried to make Lot hurry. "Quick!" they said. "Take your wife and your two daughters and get out, so that you will not lose your lives when the city is

destroyed." **16**Lot hesitated. The LORD, however, had pity on him; so the men took him, his wife, and his two daughters by the hand and led them out of the city. **17**Then one of the angels said, "Run for your lives! Don't look back and don't stop in the valley. Run to the hills, so that you won't be killed."

Live It!

Don't Look Back

Evil surrounded Lot and his family. They lived in Sodom, a town where people did awful things. Finally, God had enough. He decided to destroy Sodom and Gomorrah, a neighboring town. But Lot and his family were good people. God wanted to spare them, so he told them to "Run for your lives! Don't look back . . . (Genesis 19:17)."

As you grow up you, too, will come face to face with evil. You may face pressure to drink or do drugs. You may be tempted to watch sexually suggestive images or pornography. You may get caught up with games that portray acts of violence or destruction as fun. These activities may not seem dangerous at first, but if you get deeper into them they will eventually lead to death and destruction.

When you are faced with a situation you know is wrong, do the right thing and take God's advice: "Run for your lives! Don't look back."

— Genesis 19:1–29

19:5–8 Judg 19:22–24   **19:11** 2 Kings 6:18   **19:16** 2 Pet 2:7

What is the connection between the story of Lot and his family (Genesis, chapter 19) and the story of Noah (Genesis, chapter 7)?

18But Lot answered, "No, please don't make us do that, sir. 19You have done me a great favor and saved my life. But the hills are too far away; the disaster will overtake me, and I will die before I get there. 20Do you see that little town? It is near enough. Let me go over there—you can see it is just a small place—and I will be safe."

21He answered, "All right, I agree. I won't destroy that town. 22Hurry! Run! I can't do anything until you get there."

Because Lot called it small, the town was named Zoar.p

The Destruction of Sodom and Gomorrah

23The sun was rising when Lot reached Zoar. 24Suddenly the LORD rained burning sulfur on the cities of Sodom and Gomorrah 25and destroyed them and the whole valley, along with all the people there and everything that grew on the land. 26But Lot's wife looked back and was turned into a pillar of salt.

Lot's wife looked back. (19:26)

27Early the next morning Abraham hurried to the place where he had stood in the presence of the LORD. 28He looked down at Sodom and Gomorrah and the whole valley and saw smoke rising from the land, like smoke from a huge furnace. 29But when God destroyed the cities of the valley where

Lot was living, he kept Abraham in mind and allowed Lot to escape to safety.

The Origin of the Moabites and Ammonites

30Because Lot was afraid to stay in Zoar, he and his two daughters moved up into the hills and lived in a cave. 31The older daughter said to her sister, "Our father is getting old, and there are no men in the whole worldq to marry us so that we can have children. 32Come on, let's get our father drunk, so that we can sleep with him and have children by him." 33That night they gave him wine to drink, and the older daughter had intercourse with him. But he was so drunk that he didn't know it.

34The next day the older daughter said to her sister, "I slept with him last night; now let's get him drunk again tonight, and you sleep with him. Then each of us will have a child by our father." 35So that night they got him drunk, and the younger daughter had intercourse with him. Again he was so drunk that he didn't know it. 36In this way both of Lot's daughters became pregnant by their own father. 37The older daughter had a son, whom she named Moab.r He was the ancestor of the present-day Moabites. 38The younger daughter also had a son, whom she named Benammi.s He was the ancestor of the present-day Ammonites.

Abraham and Abimelech

20 1Abraham moved from Mamre to the southern part of Canaan and lived between Kadesh and Shur. Later, while he was living in Gerar, 2he said that his wife Sarah was his sister. So King Abimelech of Gerar had Sarah brought to him. 3One night God appeared to him in a dream and said, "You are going to die, because you have taken this woman; she is already married."

4But Abimelech had not come near her, and he said, "Lord, I am innocent! Would

p **19:22** ZOAR: *This name sounds like the Hebrew for "small."* q **19:31** the whole world; or this land. r **19:37** MOAB: *This name sounds like the Hebrew for "from my father."* s **19:38** BENAMMI: *This name in Hebrew means "son of my relative" and sounds like the Hebrew for "Ammonite."*
19:24, 25 Mt 10:15; 11:23, 24; Lk 10:12; 17:29; 2 Pet 2:6; Jude 7 **19:26** Wis 10:7; Lk 17:32 **20:2** Gen 12:13; 26:7

you destroy me and my people? 5 Abraham himself said that she was his sister, and she said the same thing. I did this with a clear conscience, and I have done no wrong."

6 God replied in the dream, "Yes, I know that you did it with a clear conscience; so I kept you from sinning against me and did not let you touch her. 7 But now, give the woman back to her husband. He is a prophet, and he will pray for you, so that you will not die. But if you do not give her back, I warn you that you are going to die, you and all your people."

8 Early the next morning Abimelech called all his officials and told them what had happened, and they were terrified. 9 Then Abimelech called Abraham and asked, "What have you done to us? What wrong have I done to you to make you bring this disaster on me and my kingdom? No one should ever do what you have done to me. 10 Why did you do it?"

11 Abraham answered, "I thought that there would be no one here who has reverence for God and that they would kill me to get my wife. 12 She really is my sister. She is the daughter of my father, but not of my mother, and I married her. 13 So when God sent me from my father's house into foreign lands, I said to her, 'You can show how loyal you are to me by telling everyone that I am your brother.' "

14 Then Abimelech gave Sarah back to Abraham, and at the same time he gave him sheep, cattle, and slaves. 15 He said to Abraham, "Here is my whole land; live anywhere you like." 16 He said to Sarah, "I am giving your brother a thousand pieces of silver as proof to all who are with you that you are innocent; everyone will know that you have done no wrong."

17-18 Because of what had happened to Sarah, Abraham's wife, the LORD had made it impossible for any woman in Abimelech's palace to have children. So Abraham prayed for Abimelech, and God healed him. He also healed his wife and his slave women, so that they could have children.

The Birth of Isaac

21 1 The LORD blessed Sarah, as he had promised, 2 and she became pregnant and bore a son to Abraham when he was old. The boy was born at the time God had said he would be born. 3 Abraham named him Isaac, 4 and when Isaac was eight days old, Abraham circumcised him, as God had commanded. 5 Abraham was a hundred years old when Isaac was born. 6 Sarah said, "God has brought me joy and laughter.*t* Everyone who hears about it will laugh with me." 7 Then she added, "Who would have said to Abraham that Sarah would nurse children? Yet I have borne him a son in his old age."

8 The child grew, and on the day that he was weaned, Abraham gave a great feast.

Hagar and Ishmael Are Sent Away

9 One day Ishmael, whom Hagar the Egyptian had borne to Abraham, was playing with*u* Sarah's son Isaac.*v* 10 Sarah saw them and said to Abraham, "Send this slave and her son away. The son of this woman must not get any part of your wealth, which my son Isaac should inherit." 11 This troubled Abraham very much, because Ishmael also was his son. 12 But God said to Abraham, "Don't be worried about the boy and your slave Hagar. Do whatever Sarah tells you, because it is through Isaac that you will have the descendants I have promised. 13 I will also give many children to the son of the slave woman, so that they will become a nation. He too is your son."

14 Early the next morning Abraham gave Hagar some food and a leather bag full of water. He put the child on her back and sent her away. She left and wandered about in the wilderness of Beersheba. 15 When the water was all gone, she left the child under a bush 16 and sat down about a hundred yards away. She said to herself, "I can't bear to see my child die." While she was sitting there, she*w* began to cry.

17 God heard the boy crying, and from

---

t **21:6** LAUGHTER: *The name Isaac in Hebrew means "he laughs" (see also 17:17–19).*   *u* **21:9** playing with; *or making fun of.*   *v* **21:9** *Some ancient translations* with Sarah's son Isaac; *Hebrew does not have these words.*
w **21:16** she; *one ancient translation* the child.
21:2 Heb 11:11   **21:4** Gen 17:12; Acts 7:8   **21:10** Gal 4:29, 30   **21:12** Rom 9:7; Heb 11:18

Jealousy

Tina was beautiful, smart, and athletic. Her closets were bursting with the latest fashions. If Tina wanted something, she got it. Rene had the things she needed, but seldom got anything just because she wanted it. Both girls were on the softball team.

Everyone liked Rene. She was a great softball player and captain of the team. Just like Sarah was jealous of Hagar, Tina was jealous of Rene's success and happiness. Tina tried hard to get everyone on the team to turn on Rene. Some people did. Most did not.

It was a good year for Rene. She loved softball and loved being captain of the team. For Tina it wasn't a great season. Her jealousy got the best of her. She hurt a lot of people. Finally, she quit the team.

Jealousy is a feeling that keeps on growing like mold on a peach. It destroys the goodness of a person and hurts everyone around him or her. Are you jealous of someone? How does your jealousy affect your relationship with that person? Ask God to help you to let go of your jealousy.

— Genesis 21:9–21

him. I will make a great nation out of his descendants." [19] Then God opened her eyes, and she saw a well. She went and filled the leather bag with water and gave some to the boy. [20] God was with the boy as he grew up; he lived in the wilderness of Paran and became a skillful hunter. [21] His mother got an Egyptian wife for him.

The Agreement between Abraham and Abimelech

[22] At that time Abimelech went with Phicol, the commander of his army, and said to Abraham, "God is with you in everything you do. [23] So make a vow here in the presence of God that you will not deceive me, my children, or my descendants. I have been loyal to you, so promise that you will also be loyal to me and to this country in which you are living."

[24] Abraham said, "I promise."

[25] Abraham complained to Abimelech about a well which the servants of Abimelech had seized. [26] Abimelech said, "I don't know who did this. You didn't tell me about it, and this is the first I have heard of it."

[27] Then Abraham gave some sheep and cattle to Abimelech, and the two of them made an agreement. [28] Abraham separated seven lambs from his flock, [29] and Abimelech asked him, "Why did you do that?"

[30] Abraham answered, "Accept these seven lambs. By doing this, you admit that I am the one who dug this well." [31] And so the place was called Beersheba,^{x} because it was there that the two of them made a vow.

[32] After they had made this agreement at Beersheba, Abimelech and Phicol went back to Philistia. [33] Then Abraham planted a tamarisk tree in Beersheba and worshiped the LORD, the Everlasting God. [34] Abraham lived in Philistia for a long time.

heaven the angel of God spoke to Hagar, "What are you troubled about, Hagar? Don't be afraid. God has heard the boy crying. [18] Get up, go and pick him up, and comfort

---

^{x} **21:31** BEERSHEBA: *This name in Hebrew means "Well of the Vow" or "Well of Seven" (see also 26.33).*
21:22 Gen 26.26

The story of Hagar and Ishmael in Genesis, chapter 21, shows that God takes care of poor and powerless people.

The Ultimate Sacrifice

Catholic Connections

God asked Abraham to do the unthinkable: kill his son Isaac. Abraham must have been horrified! After all, God promised him that he would have many descendants. But Abraham trusted God, so he loaded his donkey with wood and took Isaac up the mountain. Just as Abraham raised the knife, an angel stopped him. This story teaches us two things. First, that Abraham had complete faith in God. Second, that human sacrifice is against God's will.

In the New Testament, God again asks the unthinkable: he asks Jesus to be willing to sacrifice his life. Like Abraham, Jesus totally trusts his Father and obeys. Those who wish to kill Jesus do not listen to God as Abraham did. Jesus suffers a horrible death. But that is not the end, for God raised Jesus from the dead, thus sealing once and for all the New Covenant through which all people can have eternal life.

Because Abraham trusted God, his descendants would become God's special people. Because Jesus trusted God, all people can become part of God's family.

— Genesis 22:1–19

God Commands Abraham to Offer Isaac

22 ¹Some time later God tested Abraham; he called to him, "Abraham!" And Abraham answered, "Yes, here I am!"

²"Take your son," God said, "your only son, Isaac, whom you love so much, and go to the land of Moriah. There on a mountain that I will show you, offer him as a sacrifice to me."

³Early the next morning Abraham cut some wood for the sacrifice, loaded his donkey, and took Isaac and two servants with him. They started out for the place that God had told him about. ⁴On the third day Abraham saw the place in the distance. ⁵Then he said to the servants, "Stay here with the donkey. The boy and I will go over there and worship, and then we will come back to you."

⁶Abraham made Isaac carry the wood for the sacrifice, and he himself carried a knife and live coals for starting the fire. As they walked along together, ⁷Isaac spoke up, "Father!"

He answered, "Yes, my son?"

Isaac asked, "I see that you have the coals and the wood, but where is the lamb for the sacrifice?"

⁸Abraham answered, "God himself will provide one." And the two of them walked on together.

⁹When they came to the place which God had told him about, Abraham built an altar and arranged the wood on it. He tied up his son and placed him on the altar, on top of the wood. ¹⁰Then he picked up the knife to kill him. ¹¹But the angel of the LORD called to him from heaven, "Abraham, Abraham!"

22:1–13 Wis 10:5; Sir 44:20; Heb 11:17–19   **22:2** 2 Chr 3:1   **22:9** Jas 2:21

"All the nations will ask me to bless them as I have blessed your descendants—all because you obeyed my command" (Genesis 22:18).

He answered, "Yes, here I am."

12"Don't hurt the boy or do anything to him," he said. "Now I know that you honor and obey God, because you have not kept back your only son from him."

"Now I know that you honor and obey God." (22:12)

13Abraham looked around and saw a ram caught in a bush by its horns. He went and got it and offered it as a burnt offering instead of his son. 14Abraham named that place "The LORD Provides."y And even today people say, "On the LORD's mountain he provides."z

15The angel of the LORD called to Abraham from heaven a second time, 16"I make a vow by my own name—the LORD is speaking—that I will richly bless you. Because you did this and did not keep back your only son from me, 17I promise that I will give you as many descendants as there are stars in the sky or grains of sand along the seashore. Your descendants will conquer their enemies. 18All the nations will ask me to bless them as I have blessed your descendants—all because you obeyed my command." 19Abraham went back to his servants, and they went together to Beersheba, where Abraham settled.

The Descendants of Nahor

20Some time later Abraham learned that Milcah had borne eight children to his brother Nahor: 21Uz the first-born, Buz his brother, Kemuel the father of Aram, 22Chesed, Hazo, Pildash, Jidlaph, and Bethuel, 23Rebecca's father. Milcah bore these eight sons to Nahor, Abraham's brother. 24Reumah, Nahor's concubine, bore Tebah, Gaham, Tahash, and Maacah.

Sarah Dies and Abraham Buys a Burial Ground

23 1Sarah lived to be 127 years old. 2She died in Hebron in the land of Canaan, and Abraham mourned her death.

3He left the place where his wife's body was lying, went to the Hittites, and said, 4"I am a foreigner living here among you; sell me some land, so that I can bury my wife."

5They answered, 6"Listen to us, sir. We look upon you as a mighty leader; bury your wife in the best grave that we have. Any of us would be glad to give you a grave, so that you can bury her."

7Then Abraham bowed before them 8and said, "If you are willing to let me bury my wife here, please ask Ephron son of Zohar 9to sell me Machpelah Cave, which is near the edge of his field. Ask him to sell it to me for its full price, here in your presence, so that I can own it as a burial ground."

10Ephron himself was sitting with the other Hittites at the meeting place at the city gate; he answered in the hearing of everyone there, 11"Listen, sir; I will give you the whole field and the cave that is in it. Here in the presence of my own people, I will give it to you, so that you can bury your wife."

12But Abraham bowed before the Hittites 13and said to Ephron, so that everyone could hear, "May I ask you, please, to listen. I will buy the whole field. Accept my payment, and I will bury my wife there."

14Ephron answered, 15"Sir, land worth only four hundred pieces of silver—what is that between us? Bury your wife in it."

---

y **22:14** Provides; *or* Sees.   z **22:14** provides; *or* is seen.
22:16, 17 Heb 6:13, 14   **22:17** Heb 11:12   **22:18** Acts 3:25   **23:4** Heb 11:9, 13; Acts 7:16

Genesis

[16] Abraham agreed and weighed out the amount that Ephron had mentioned in the hearing of the people—four hundred pieces of silver, according to the standard weights used by the merchants.

[17] That is how the property which had belonged to Ephron at Machpelah east of Mamre, became Abraham's. It included the field, the cave which was in it, and all the trees in the field up to the edge of the property. [18] It was recognized as Abraham's property by all the Hittites who were there at the meeting.

[19] Then Abraham buried his wife Sarah in that cave in the land of Canaan. [20] So the field which had belonged to the Hittites, and the cave in it, became the property of Abraham for a burial ground.

A Wife for Isaac

24 [1] Abraham was now very old, and the LORD had blessed him in everything he did. [2] He said to his oldest servant, who was in charge of all that he had, "Place your hand between my thighs[a] and make a vow. [3] I want you to make a vow in the name of the LORD, the God of heaven and earth, that you will not choose a wife for my son from the people here in Canaan. [4] You must go back to the country where I was born and get a wife for my son Isaac from among my relatives."

[5] But the servant asked, "What if the young woman will not leave home to come with me to this land? Shall I send your son back to the land you came from?"

[6] Abraham answered, "Make sure that you don't send my son back there! [7] The LORD, the God of heaven, brought me from the home of my father and from the land of my relatives, and he solemnly promised me that he would give this land to my descendants. He will send his angel before you, so that you can get a wife there for my son. [8] If the young woman is not willing to come with you, you will be free from this promise. But you must not under any circumstances take my son back there." [9] So the servant put his hand between the thighs of Abraham, his master, and made a vow to do what Abraham had asked.

[10] The servant, who was in charge of Abraham's property, took ten of his master's camels and went to the city where Nahor had lived in northern Mesopotamia. [11] When he arrived, he made the camels kneel down at the well outside the city. It was late afternoon, the time when women came out to get water. [12] He prayed, " LORD, God of my master Abraham, give me success today and keep your promise to my master. [13] Here I am at the well where the young women of the city will be coming to get water. [14] I will say to one of them, 'Please, lower your jar and let me have a drink.' If she says, 'Drink, and I will also bring water for your camels,' may she be the one that you have chosen for your servant Isaac. If this happens, I will know that you have kept your promise to my master."

[15] Before he had finished praying, Rebecca arrived with a water jar on her shoulder. She was the daughter of Bethuel, who was the son of Abraham's brother Nahor and his wife Milcah. [16] She was a very beautiful young woman and still a virgin. She went down to the well, filled her jar, and came back. [17] The servant ran to meet her and said, "Please give me a drink of water from your jar."

[18] She said, "Drink, sir," and quickly lowered her jar from her shoulder and held it while he drank. [19] When he had finished, she said, "I will also bring water for your camels

Rebecca arrived. (24:15)

---

[a] **24:2** PLACE . . . THIGHS: *This was the way in which a vow was made absolutely unchangeable.*

and let them have all they want." 20She quickly emptied her jar into the animals' drinking trough and ran to the well to get more water, until she had watered all his camels. 21The man kept watching her in silence, to see if the LORD had given him success.

22When she had finished, the man took an expensive gold ring and put it in her nose and put two large gold bracelets on her arms. 23He said, "Please tell me who your father is. Is there room in his house for my men and me to spend the night?"

24"My father is Bethuel son of Nahor and Milcah," she answered. 25"There is plenty of straw and fodder at our house, and there is a place for you to stay."

26Then the man knelt down and worshiped the LORD. 27He said, "Praise the LORD, the God of my master Abraham, who has faithfully kept his promise to my master. The LORD has led me straight to my master's relatives."

28The young woman ran to her mother's house and told the whole story. 29Now Rebecca had a brother named Laban, and he ran outside to go to the well where Abraham's servant was. 30Laban had seen the nose ring and the bracelets on his sister's arms and had heard her say what the man had told her. He went to Abraham's servant, who was standing by his camels at the well, 31and said, "Come home with me. You are a man whom the LORD has blessed. Why are you standing out here? I have a room ready for you in my house, and there is a place for your camels."

32So the man went into the house, and Laban unloaded the camels and gave them straw and fodder. Then he brought water for Abraham's servant and his men to wash their feet. 33When food was brought, the man said, "I will not eat until I have said what I have to say."

Laban said, "Go on and speak."

34"I am the servant of Abraham," he began. 35"The LORD has greatly blessed my master and made him a rich man. He has given him flocks of sheep and goats, cattle, silver, gold, male and female slaves, camels, and donkeys. 36Sarah, my master's wife, bore him a son when she was old, and my master has given everything he owns to him. 37My master made me promise with a vow to obey his command. He said, 'Do not choose a wife for my son from the young women in the land of Canaan. 38Instead, go to my father's people, to my relatives, and choose a wife for him.' 39And I asked my master, 'What if she will not come with me?' 40He answered, 'The LORD, whom I have always obeyed, will send his angel with you and give you success. You will get for my son a wife from my own people, from my father's family. 41There is only one way for you to be free from your vow: if you go to my relatives and they refuse you, then you will be free.'

42"When I came to the well today, I prayed, ' LORD, God of my master Abraham, please give me success in what I am doing. 43Here I am at the well. When a young woman comes out to get water, I will ask her to give me a drink of water from her jar. 44If she agrees and also offers to bring water for my camels, may she be the one that you have chosen as the wife for my master's son.' 45Before I had finished my silent prayer, Rebecca came with a water jar on her shoulder and went down to the well to get water. I said to her, 'Please give me a drink.' 46She quickly lowered her jar from her shoulder and said, 'Drink, and I will also water your camels.' So I drank, and she watered the camels. 47I asked her, 'Who is your father?' And she answered, 'My father is Bethuel son of Nahor and Milcah.' Then I put the ring in her nose and the bracelets on her arms. 48I knelt down and worshiped the LORD. I praised the LORD, the God of my master Abraham, who had led me straight to my master's relative, where I found his daughter for my master's son. 49Now, if you intend to fulfill your responsibility toward my master and treat him fairly, please tell me; if not, say so, and I will decide what to do."

50Laban and Bethuel answered, "Since this

Rebecca had a gift for hospitality. She welcomed strangers and took care of them (Genesis 24:15–20). Who do you know who has the gift of hospitality?

matter comes from the LORD, it is not for us to make a decision. 51Here is Rebecca; take her and go. Let her become the wife of your master's son, as the LORD himself has said."

52When the servant of Abraham heard this, he bowed down and worshiped the LORD. 53Then he brought out clothing and silver and gold jewelry, and gave them to Rebecca. He also gave expensive gifts to her brother and to her mother.

54Then Abraham's servant and the men with him ate and drank, and spent the night there. When they got up in the morning, he said, "Let me go back to my master."

55But Rebecca's brother and her mother said, "Let her stay with us a week or ten days, and then she may go."

56But he said, "Don't make us stay. The LORD has made my journey a success; let me go back to my master."

57They answered, "Let's call her and find out what she has to say." 58So they called Rebecca and asked, "Do you want to go with this man?"

"Yes," she answered.

59So they let Rebecca and her old family servant go with Abraham's servant and his men. 60And they gave Rebecca their blessing in these words:

"May you, sister, become the mother of
    millions!
May your descendants conquer the cities
    of their enemies!"

61Then Rebecca and her young women got ready and mounted the camels to go with Abraham's servant, and they all started out.

62Isaac had come into the wilderness of[b] "The Well of the Living One Who Sees Me" and was staying in the southern part of Canaan. 63He went out in the early evening to take a walk in the fields and saw camels coming. 64When Rebecca saw Isaac, she got down from her camel 65and asked Abraham's servant, "Who is that man walking toward us in the field?"

"He is my master," the servant answered. So she took her scarf and covered her face.

A Match Made in Heaven

Isaac and Rebecca were meant for each other. God guided Abraham's servant and Rebecca's family to bring these two young people together so that they could be married. They raised a family and had a long life. "Isaac loved Rebecca . . ." (Genesis 24:67). And we presume that Rebecca loved Isaac, too.

What do you think you will be doing twenty years from now? Will you be married? Will you have children? Would you consider being a priest or a brother or a sister? Will you stay single? These lifestyles are known as *vocations,* and each one is a unique way to live the life God intends for you.

As you grow up, choosing a vocation will be one of your main responsibilities. Just as God brought Isaac and Rebecca together, God will guide you in lots of different ways. Keep your eyes, ears, and heart open to all possibilities. If you do, twenty years from now you and your life will be a match made in heaven!

— Genesis 24:57–67

66The servant told Isaac everything he had done. 67Then Isaac brought Rebecca into the tent that his mother Sarah had lived in, and she became his wife. Isaac loved Rebecca, and so he was comforted for the loss of his mother.

[b] 24:62 *Some ancient translations* into the wilderness of; *Hebrew* from coming.

After Sarah died Abraham married again and had more children. He died at a very old age. God's promises were fulfilled.

Pray It!

Thanks for Siblings

Jacob and Esau were brothers, twin sons of Isaac and Rebecca. They were very different from each other. Sometimes they got along, sometimes they didn't. Their conflicts continued throughout their life.

How do you get along with your brothers and sisters, your siblings? Do you help one another or hurt one another? Have you ever said thank you to God for them? Here's a prayer to help you do that.

Dear God,
I don't often say thanks for my siblings.
Usually, I complain to you about them.
We argue, we fight, and we get in one another's way.
We also laugh a lot and have fun together.
Deep down, I love them, and I know they love me.
My life would be a lot more boring without them.
So thank you, God, for sisters and brothers.
Please keep them safe and happy. Amen.

— Genesis 25:19–34

Other Descendants of Abraham
(1 Chronicles 1:32, 33)

25 [1]Abraham married another woman, whose name was Keturah. [2]She bore him Zimran, Jokshan, Medan, Midian, Ishbak, and Shuah. [3]Jokshan was the father of Sheba and Dedan, and the descendants of Dedan were the Asshurim, the Letushim, and the Leummim. [4]The sons of Midian were Ephah, Epher, Hanoch, Abida, and Eldaah. All these were Keturah's descendants.

[5]Abraham left everything he owned to Isaac; [6]but while he was still alive, he gave presents to the sons his other wives had borne him. Then he sent these sons to the land of the East, away from his son Isaac.

The Death and Burial of Abraham

[7-8]Abraham died at the ripe old age of 175. [9]His sons Isaac and Ishmael buried him in Machpelah Cave, in the field east of Mamre that had belonged to Ephron son of Zohar the Hittite. [10]It was the field that Abraham had bought from the Hittites; both Abraham and his wife Sarah were buried there. [11]After the death of Abraham, God blessed his son Isaac, who lived near "The Well of the Living One Who Sees Me."

The Descendants of Ishmael
(1 Chronicles 1:28–31)

[12]Ishmael, whom Hagar, the Egyptian slave of Sarah, bore to Abraham, [13]had the following sons, listed in the order of their birth: Nebaioth, Kedar, Adbeel, Mibsam, [14]Mishma, Dumah, Massa, [15]Hadad, Tema, Jetur, Naphish, and Kedemah. [16]They were the ancestors of twelve tribes, and their names were given to their villages and camping places. [17]Ishmael was 137 years old when he died. [18]The descendants of Ishmael lived in the territory between Havilah and Shur, to the east of Egypt on the way to Assyria. They lived apart from the other descendants of Abraham.

The Birth of Esau and Jacob

19 This is the story of Abraham's son Isaac. 20 Isaac was forty years old when he married Rebecca, the daughter of Bethuel (an Aramean from Mesopotamia) and sister of Laban. 21 Because Rebecca had no children, Isaac prayed to the LORD for her. The LORD answered his prayer, and Rebecca became pregnant. 22 She was going to have twins, and before they were born, they struggled against each other in her womb. She said, "Why should something like this happen to me?" So she went to ask the LORD for an answer. 23 The LORD said to her,

"Two nations are within you;
You will give birth to two rival peoples.
One will be stronger than the other;
The older will serve the younger."

24 The time came for her to give birth, and she had twin sons. 25 The first one was reddish, and his skin was like a hairy robe, so he was named Esau.c 26 The second one was born holding on tightly to the heel of Esau, so he was named Jacob.d Isaac was sixty years old when they were born.

Esau Sells His Rights as the First-Born Son

27 The boys grew up, and Esau became a skilled hunter, a man who loved the outdoors, but Jacob was a quiet man who stayed at home. 28 Isaac preferred Esau, because he enjoyed eating the animals Esau killed, but Rebecca preferred Jacob.

29 One day while Jacob was cooking some bean soup, Esau came in from hunting. He was hungry 30 and said to Jacob, "I'm starving; give me some of that red stuff." (That is why he was named Edom.e)

31 Jacob answered, "I will give it to you if you give me your rights as the first-born son."

32 Esau said, "All right! I am about to die; what good will my rights do me?"

33 Jacob answered, "First make a vow that you will give me your rights."

Esau made the vow and gave his rights to Jacob. 34 Then Jacob gave him some bread and some of the soup. He ate and drank and then got up and left. That was all Esau cared about his rights as the first-born son.

Then Jacob gave him . . . some of the soup. (25:34)

Isaac Lives at Gerar

26 1 There was another famine in the land besides the earlier one during the time of Abraham. Isaac went to Abimelech, king of the Philistines, at Gerar. 2 The LORD had appeared to Isaac and had said, "Do not go to Egypt; stay in this land, where I tell you to stay. 3 Live here, and I will be with you and bless you. I am going to give all this territory to you and to your descendants. I will keep the promise I made to your father Abraham. 4 I will give you as many descendants as there are stars in the sky, and I will give them all this territory. All the nations will ask me to bless them as I have blessed your descendants. 5 I will bless you, because Abraham obeyed me and kept all my laws and commands."

6 So Isaac lived at Gerar. 7 When the men there asked about his wife, he said that she was his sister. He would not admit that she was his wife, because he was afraid that the men there would kill him to get Rebecca, who was very beautiful. 8 When Isaac had

---

c **25:25** ESAU: *This name is taken to refer to Seir, the territory later inhabited by Esau's descendants; Seir sounds like the Hebrew for "hairy."* d **25:25** JACOB: *This name sounds like the Hebrew for "heel."* e **25:30** EDOM: *This name sounds like the Hebrew for "red."*
25:23 Rom 9:12   **25:33** Heb 12:16   **26:3, 4** Gen 22:16–18   **26:7** Gen 12:13; 20:2

been there for some time, King Abimelech looked down from his window and saw Isaac and Rebecca making love. 9 Abimelech sent for Isaac and said, "So she is your wife! Why did you say she was your sister?"

He answered, "I thought I would be killed if I said she was my wife."

10 "What have you done to us?" Abimelech said. "One of my men might easily have slept with your wife, and you would have been responsible for our guilt." 11 Abimelech warned all the people: "Anyone who mistreats this man or his wife will be put to death."

12 Isaac sowed crops in that land, and that year he harvested a hundred times as much as he had sown, because the LORD blessed him. 13 He continued to prosper and became a very rich man. 14 Because he had many herds of sheep and cattle and many servants, the Philistines were jealous of him. 15 So they filled in all the wells which the servants of his father Abraham had dug while Abraham was alive.

16 Then Abimelech said to Isaac, "Leave our country. You have become more powerful than we are." 17 So Isaac left and set up his camp in Gerar Valley, where he stayed for some time. 18 He dug once again the wells which had been dug during the time of Abraham and which the Philistines had stopped up after Abraham's death. Isaac gave the wells the same names that his father had given them.

19 Isaac's servants dug a well in the valley and found water. 20 The shepherds of Gerar quarreled with Isaac's shepherds and said, "This water belongs to us." So Isaac named the well "Quarrel."

21 Isaac's servants dug another well, and there was a quarrel about that one also, so he named it "Enmity." 22 He moved away from there and dug another well. There was no dispute about this one, so he named it "Freedom." He said, "Now the LORD has given us freedom to live in the land, and we will be prosperous here."

23 Isaac left and went to Beersheba. 24 That night the LORD appeared to him and said, "I am the God of your father Abraham. Do not be afraid; I am with you. I will bless you and give you many descendants because of my promise to my servant Abraham." 25 Isaac built an altar there and worshiped the LORD. Then he set up his camp there, and his servants dug another well.

The Agreement between Isaac and Abimelech

26 Abimelech came from Gerar with Ahuzzath his adviser and Phicol the commander of his army to see Isaac. 27 So Isaac asked, "Why have you now come to see me, when you were so unfriendly to me before and made me leave your country?"

28 They answered, "Now we know that the LORD is with you, and we think that there should be a solemn agreement between us. We want you to promise 29 that you will not harm us, just as we did not harm you. We were kind to you and let you go peacefully. Now it is clear that the LORD has blessed you." 30 Isaac prepared a feast for them, and they ate and drank. 31 Early next morning each man made his promise and sealed it with a vow. Isaac said good-bye to them, and they parted as friends.

32 On that day Isaac's servants came and told him about the well which they had dug. They said, "We have found water." 33 He named the well "Vow." That is how the city of Beersheba[f] got its name.

Esau's Foreign Wives

34 When Esau was forty years old, he married two Hittites, Judith the daughter of Beeri, and Basemath the daughter of Elon. 35 They made life miserable for Isaac and Rebecca.

---

f **26:33** BEERSHEBA: *This name in Hebrew means "Well of the Vow" or "Well of Seven" (see also 21.31).*
26:26 Gen 21:22

How were Jacob and Esau different? Read Genesis 25:19–34 to find out. How are you different from your siblings?

Isaac Blesses Jacob

27 [1]Isaac was now old and had become blind. He sent for his older son Esau and said to him, "Son!"

"Yes," he answered.

[2]Isaac said, "You see that I am old and may die soon. [3]Take your bow and arrows, go out into the country, and kill an animal for me. [4]Cook me some of that tasty food that I like, and bring it to me. After I have eaten it, I will give you my final blessing before I die."

[5]While Isaac was talking to Esau, Rebecca was listening. So when Esau went out to hunt, [6]she said to Jacob, "I have just heard your father say to Esau, [7]'Bring me an animal and cook it for me. After I have eaten it, I will give you my blessing in the presence of the LORD before I die.' [8]Now, son," Rebecca continued, "listen to me and do what I say. [9]Go to the flock and pick out two fat young goats, so that I can cook them and make some of that food your father likes so much. [10]You can take it to him to eat, and he will give you his blessing before he dies."

[11]But Jacob said to his mother, "You know that Esau is a hairy man, but I have smooth skin. [12]Perhaps my father will touch me and find out that I am deceiving him; in this way, I will bring a curse on myself instead of a blessing."

[13]His mother answered, "Let any curse against you fall on me, my son; just do as I say, and go and get the goats for me." [14]So he went to get them and brought them to her, and she cooked the kind of food that his father liked. [15]Then she took Esau's best clothes, which she kept in the house, and put them on Jacob. [16]She put the skins of the goats on his arms and on the hairless part of his neck. [17]She handed him the tasty food, along with the bread she had baked.

[18]Then Jacob went to his father and said, "Father!"

"Yes," he answered. "Which of my sons are you?"

[19]Jacob answered, "I am your older son Esau; I have done as you told me. Please sit

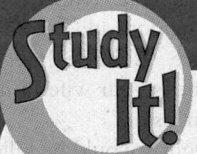

Esau's Dilemma

My brother Jacob did it to me again. First he tricked me into giving him my rights as the oldest son (Genesis 25:27–34). Then he tricked my father into giving him his blessing—the blessing of a dying father for his firstborn son (Genesis 27:1–29). My mother was behind it all, I know. She always liked Jacob best. My father is upset. He only had one blessing to give, and Jacob stole it from me.

Mom said God wanted it this way. God had plans for Jacob. But what about me? What about my life and my plans? With our father's blessing, Jacob will have a good life. The rest of my life will probably be miserable—all because Jacob is a thief and a liar. My father says what's done is done, and we all have to move on with our life. I'm not so sure I can let it go. Jacob ruined my life, and I'd like to kill him for it.

What would you do? Do you think what my mother and brother did to me and my father was fair? Okay, maybe I have some responsibility—I did make a stupid decision because of my hunger. But does doing wrong in the name of God make it right? Can God make good come out of deceit and trickery?

— Genesis 27:1–29

up and eat some of the meat that I have brought you, so that you can give me your blessing."

20 Isaac said, "How did you find it so quickly, son?"

Jacob answered, "The LORD your God helped me find it."

21 Isaac said to Jacob, "Please come closer so that I can touch you. Are you really Esau?" 22 Jacob moved closer to his father, who felt him and said, "Your voice sounds like Jacob's voice, but your arms feel like Esau's arms." 23 He did not recognize Jacob, because his arms were hairy like Esau's. He was about to give him his blessing, 24 but asked again, "Are you really Esau?"

"I am," he answered.

25 Isaac said, "Bring me some of the meat. After I eat it, I will give you my blessing." Jacob brought it to him, and he also brought him some wine to drink. 26 Then his father said to him, "Come closer and kiss me, son." 27 As he came up to kiss him, Isaac smelled his clothes—so he gave him his blessing. He said, "The pleasant smell of my son is like the smell of a field which the LORD has blessed. 28 May God give you dew from heaven and make your fields fertile! May he give you plenty of grain and wine! 29 May nations be your servants, and may peoples bow down before you. May you rule over all your relatives, and may your mother's descendants bow down before you. May those who curse you be cursed, and may those who bless you be blessed."

He gave him his blessing. (27:27)

Esau Begs for Isaac's Blessing

30 Isaac finished giving his blessing, and as soon as Jacob left, his brother Esau came in from hunting. 31 He also cooked some tasty food and took it to his father. He said, "Please, father, sit up and eat some of the meat that I have brought you, so that you can give me your blessing."

32 "Who are you?" Isaac asked.

"Your older son Esau," he answered.

33 Isaac began to tremble and shake all over, and he asked, "Who was it, then, who killed an animal and brought it to me? I ate it just before you came. I gave him my final blessing, and so it is his forever."

34 When Esau heard this, he cried out loudly and bitterly and said, "Give me your blessing also, father!"

35 Isaac answered, "Your brother came and deceived me. He has taken away your blessing."

36 Esau said, "This is the second time that he has cheated me. No wonder his name is Jacob.[g] He took my rights as the first-born son, and now he has taken away my blessing. Haven't you saved a blessing for me?"

37 Isaac answered, "I have already made him master over you, and I have made all his relatives his slaves. I have given him grain and wine. Now there is nothing that I can do for you, son!"

38 Esau continued to plead with his father: "Do you have only one blessing, father? Bless me too, father!" He began to cry.

39 Then Isaac said to him,

"No dew from heaven for you,
No fertile fields for you.
40 You will live by your sword,
But be your brother's slave.
Yet when you rebel,[h]
You will break away from his control."

41 Esau hated Jacob, because his father had given Jacob the blessing. He thought, "The time to mourn my father's death is near; then I will kill Jacob."

42 But when Rebecca heard about Esau's plan, she sent for Jacob and said, "Listen, your brother Esau is planning to get even with

g **27:36** JACOB: *This name sounds like the Hebrew for "cheat."*   h **27:40** rebel; *or* grow restless.
27:27–29 Heb 11:20   **27:29** Gen 12:3   **27:36** Gen 25:29–34   **27:38** Heb 12:17   **27:39, 40** Heb 11:20
27:40 Gen 36:8; 2 Kings 8:20   **27:42** Wis 10:10

you and kill you. ⁴³Now, son, do what I say.
Go at once to my brother Laban in Haran,
⁴⁴and stay with him for a while, until your
brother's anger cools down ⁴⁵and he forgets
what you have done to him. Then I will send
someone to bring you back. Why should I
lose both of my sons on the same day?"

Isaac Sends Jacob to Laban

⁴⁶Rebecca said to Isaac, "I am sick and
tired of Esau's foreign wives. If Jacob also
marries one of these Hittites, I might as well
die."

28 ¹Isaac called Jacob, greeted him, and
told him, "Don't marry a Canaanite.
²Go instead to Mesopotamia, to the home of
your grandfather Bethuel, and marry one of
the young women there, one of your uncle
Laban's daughters. ³May Almighty God bless
your marriage and give you many children,
so that you will become the father of many
nations! ⁴May he bless you and your descendants as he blessed Abraham, and may you
take possession of this land, in which you
have lived and which God gave to Abraham!" ⁵Isaac sent Jacob away to
Mesopotamia, to Laban, who was the son of
Bethuel the Aramean and the brother of
Rebecca, the mother of Jacob and Esau.

Esau Takes Another Wife

⁶Esau learned that Isaac had blessed Jacob
and sent him away to Mesopotamia to find a
wife. He also learned that when Isaac blessed
him, he commanded him not to marry a
Canaanite woman. ⁷He found out that Jacob
had obeyed his father and mother and had
gone to Mesopotamia. ⁸Esau then understood that his father Isaac did not approve of
Canaanite women. ⁹So he went to Ishmael
son of Abraham and married his daughter
Mahalath, who was the sister of Nebaioth.

Jacob's Dream at Bethel

¹⁰Jacob left Beersheba and started toward
Haran. ¹¹At sunset he came to a holy place[i]

A stairway reaching from earth to heaven (28:12)

and camped there. He lay down to sleep,
resting his head on a stone. ¹²He dreamed
that he saw a stairway reaching from earth to
heaven, with angels going up and coming
down on it. ¹³And there was the LORD
standing beside him.[j] "I am the LORD, the
God of Abraham and Isaac," he said. "I will
give to you and to your descendants this
land on which you are lying. ¹⁴They will be
as numerous as the specks of dust on the
earth. They will extend their territory in all
directions, and through you and your
descendants I will bless all the nations.[k]
¹⁵Remember, I will be with you and protect
you wherever you go, and I will bring you

---

[i] **28:11** a holy place; *or* a place.   [j] **28:13** beside him; *or* on it.   [k] **28:14** through you . . . nations; *or* all the
nations will ask me to bless them as I have blessed you and your descendants.
28:4 Gen 17:4–8   **28:10** Wis 10:10   **28:12** Jn 1:51   **28:13** Gen 13:14, 15   **28:14** Gen 12:3; 22:18

back to this land. I will not leave you until I have done all that I have promised you."

¹⁶Jacob woke up and said, "The LORD is here! He is in this place, and I didn't know it!" ¹⁷He was afraid and said, "What a terrifying place this is! It must be the house of God; it must be the gate that opens into heaven."

¹⁸Jacob got up early next morning, took the stone that was under his head, and set it up as a memorial. Then he poured olive oil on it to dedicate it to God. ¹⁹He named the place Bethel.¹ (The town there was once known as Luz.) ²⁰Then Jacob made a vow to the LORD: "If you will be with me and protect me on the journey I am making and give me food and clothing, ²¹and if I return safely to my father's home, then you will be my God. ²²This memorial stone which I have set up will be the place where you are worshiped, and I will give you a tenth of everything you give me."

Jacob Arrives at Laban's Home

29 ¹Jacob continued on his way and went toward the land of the East. ²Suddenly he came upon a well out in the fields with three flocks of sheep lying around it. The flocks were watered from this well, which had a large stone over the opening. ³Whenever all the flocks came together there, the shepherds would roll the stone back and water them. Then they would put the stone back in place.

⁴Jacob asked the shepherds, "My friends, where are you from?"

"From Haran," they answered.

⁵He asked, "Do you know Laban, grandson of Nahor?"

"Yes, we do," they answered.

⁶"Is he well?" he asked.

"He is well," they answered. "Look, here comes his daughter Rachel with his flock."

⁷Jacob said, "Since it is still broad daylight and not yet time to bring the flocks in, why don't you water them and take them back to pasture?"

⁸They answered, "We can't do that until all the flocks are here and the stone has been rolled back; then we will water the flocks."

⁹While Jacob was still talking with them, Rachel arrived with the flock. ¹⁰When Jacob saw Rachel with his uncle Laban's flock, he went to the well, rolled the stone back, and watered the sheep. ¹¹Then he kissed her and began to cry for joy. ¹²He told her, "I am your father's relative, the son of Rebecca."

She ran to tell her father; ¹³and when he heard the news about his nephew Jacob, he ran to meet him, hugged him and kissed him, and brought him into the house. When Jacob told Laban everything that had happened, ¹⁴Laban said, "Yes, indeed, you are my own flesh and blood." Jacob stayed there a whole month.

Jacob Serves Laban for Rachel and Leah

¹⁵Laban said to Jacob, "You shouldn't work for me for nothing just because you are my relative. How much pay do you want?" ¹⁶Laban had two daughters; the older was named Leah, and the younger Rachel. ¹⁷Leah had lovely*m* eyes, but Rachel was shapely and beautiful.

¹⁸Jacob was in love with Rachel, so he said, "I will work seven years for you, if you will let me marry Rachel."

¹⁹Laban answered, "I would rather give her to you than to anyone else; stay here with me." ²⁰Jacob worked seven years so that he could have Rachel, and the time seemed like only a few days to him, because he loved her.

²¹Then Jacob said to Laban, "The time is up; let me marry your daughter." ²²So Laban gave a wedding feast and invited everyone. ²³But that night, instead of Rachel, he took Leah to Jacob, and Jacob had intercourse with her. (²⁴Laban gave his slave woman Zilpah to his daughter Leah as her maid.) ²⁵Not until the next morning did Jacob discover that it was Leah. He went to Laban and said,

¹ **28:19** BETHEL: *This name in Hebrew means "house of God."*   *m* **29:17** lovely; *or* weak.

Jacob asked three things from God. Read Genesis 28:20–22 to find out what they are. What do you need from God?

"Why did you do this to me? I worked to get Rachel. Why have you tricked me?"

26Laban answered, "It is not the custom here to give the younger daughter in marriage before the older. 27Wait until the week's marriage celebrations are over, and I will give you Rachel, if you will work for me another seven years."

28Jacob agreed, and when the week of marriage celebrations was over, Laban gave him his daughter Rachel as his wife. (29Laban gave his slave woman Bilhah to his daughter Rachel as her maid.) 30Jacob had intercourse with Rachel also, and he loved her more than Leah. Then he worked for Laban another seven years.

The Children Born to Jacob

31When the LORD saw that Leah was loved less than Rachel, he made it possible for her to have children, but Rachel remained childless. 32Leah became pregnant and gave birth to a son. She said, "The LORD has seen my trouble, and now my husband will love me"; so she named him Reuben.*n* 33She became pregnant again and gave birth to another son. She said, "The LORD has given me this son also, because he heard that I was not loved"; so she named him Simeon.*o* 34Once again she became pregnant and gave birth to another son. She said, "Now my husband will be bound more tightly to me, because I have borne him three sons"; so she named him Levi.*p* 35Then she became pregnant again and gave birth to another son. She said, "This time I will praise the LORD"; so she named him Judah.*q* Then she stopped having children.

30 1But Rachel had not borne Jacob any children, and so she became jealous of her sister and said to Jacob, "Give me children, or I will die."

2Jacob became angry with Rachel and said, "I can't take the place of God. He is the one who keeps you from having children."

3She said, "Here is my slave Bilhah; sleep with her, so that she can have a child for me. In this way I can become a mother through her." 4So she gave Bilhah to her husband, and he had intercourse with her. 5Bilhah became pregnant and bore Jacob a son. 6Rachel said, "God has judged in my favor. He has heard my prayer and has given me a son"; so she named him Dan.*r* 7Bilhah became pregnant again and bore Jacob a second son. 8Rachel said, "I have fought a hard fight with my sister, but I have won"; so she named him Naphtali.*s*

9When Leah realized that she had stopped having children, she gave her slave Zilpah to Jacob as his wife. 10Then Zilpah bore Jacob a son. 11Leah said, "I have been lucky"; so she named him Gad.*t* 12Zilpah bore Jacob another son, 13and Leah said, "How happy I am! Now women will call me happy"; so she named him Asher.*u*

14During the wheat harvest Reuben went into the fields and found mandrakes,*v* which he brought to his mother Leah. Rachel said to Leah, "Please give me some of your son's mandrakes."

15Leah answered, "Isn't it enough that you have taken away my husband? Now you are even trying to take away my son's mandrakes."

Rachel said, "If you will give me your son's mandrakes, you can sleep with Jacob tonight."

16When Jacob came in from the fields in the evening, Leah went out to meet him and said, "You are going to sleep with me tonight, because I have paid for you with my son's mandrakes." So he had intercourse with her that night.

17God answered Leah's prayer, and she

n **29:32** REUBEN: *This name sounds like the Hebrew for "see, a son" and "has seen my trouble."*   *o* **29:32** SIMEON: *This name sounds like the Hebrew for "hear."*   *p* **29:32** LEVI: *This name sounds like the Hebrew for "bound."*   *q* **29:32** JUDAH: *This name sounds like the Hebrew for "praise."*   *r* **30:6** DAN: *This name sounds like the Hebrew for "judge in favor."*   *s* **30:8** NAPHTALI: *This name sounds like the Hebrew for "fight."*   *t* **30:11** GAD: *This name in Hebrew means "luck."*   *u* **30:13** ASHER: *This name in Hebrew means "happy."*   *v* **30:14** MANDRAKES: *Plants which were believed to produce fertility and were used as love charms.*

Rachel had a difficult time getting pregnant. Who was another woman in Genesis with the same difficulty? (Hint: It was Jacob's grandmother.)

An Imperfect Believer

Jacob was not the most honest guy in the world. Most of what he had he got from tricking or cheating other people:

- He took advantage of Esau's hunger to get Esau's rights as a firstborn son (Genesis 25:27–34).
- He tricked Isaac into giving him the blessing that was rightfully Esau's (27:1–29).
- He cleverly arranged to receive Laban's strongest sheep as payment for his service to his father-in-law. After twenty years of working for Laban, Jacob was a rich man (30:25–43).

Jacob's trickery had consequences. His brother, Esau, hated him and wanted to kill him. His father-in-law tricked him into working for him for fourteen years. Yet with all his shortcomings, Jacob loved God deeply, and God had big plans for him. The twelve tribes that made up the great nation of Israel were descendants of Jacob's sons. Jacob's story teaches us something important: God can work through everyone—not just those who appear to be saintly or perfect. As long as you keep working on your relationship with God, God will work through you. You don't need to be perfect, just willing to trust God and do your best!

— Genesis 30:25–43

became pregnant and bore Jacob a fifth son. [18] Leah said, "God has given me my reward, because I gave my slave to my husband"; so she named her son Issachar. [w] [19] Leah became pregnant again and bore Jacob a sixth son. [20] She said, "God has given me a fine gift. Now my husband will accept me, because I have borne him six sons"; so she named him Zebulun. [x] [21] Later she bore a daughter, whom she named Dinah.

[22] Then God remembered Rachel; he answered her prayer and made it possible for her to have children. [23] She became pregnant and gave birth to a son. She said, "God has taken away my disgrace by giving me a son. [24] May the LORD give me another son"; so she named him Joseph. [y]

Jacob's Bargain with Laban

[25] After the birth of Joseph, Jacob said to Laban, "Let me go, so that I can return home. [26] Give me my wives and children that I have earned by working for you, and I will leave. You know how well I have served you."

[27] Laban said to him, "Let me say this: I have learned by divination that the LORD has blessed me because of you. [28] Name your wages, and I will pay them."

[29] Jacob answered, "You know how I have worked for you and how your flocks have prospered under my care. [30] The little you had before I came has grown enormously, and the LORD has blessed you wherever I went. [z] Now it is time for me to look out for my own interests."

[31] "What shall I pay you?" Laban asked.

Jacob answered, "I don't want any wages. I will continue to take care of your flocks if you agree to this suggestion: [32] Let me go through all your flocks today and take every black lamb [a] and every spotted or speckled young goat. That is all the wages I want. [33] In the future you can easily find out if I have been honest. When you come to check up on my wages, if I have any goat that isn't

---

[w] **30:18** ISSACHAR: *This name sounds like the Hebrew for "a man is hired" and "there is reward."* [x] **30:20** ZEBULUN: *This name sounds like the Hebrew for "accept" and "gift."* [y] **30:24** JOSEPH: *This name sounds like the Hebrew for "may he give another" and "he has taken away."* [z] **30:30** wherever I went; *or* because of me. [a] **30:32** *One ancient translation* every black lamb; *Hebrew* every spotted and speckled lamb, and every black lamb.

speckled or spotted or any sheep that isn't black, you will know that it has been stolen."

³⁴Laban answered, "Agreed. We will do as you suggest." ³⁵But that day Laban removed the male goats that had stripes or spots and all the females that were speckled and spotted or which had white on them; he also removed all the black sheep. He put his sons in charge of them, ³⁶and then went away from Jacob with this flock as far as he could travel in three days. Jacob took care of the rest of Laban's flocks.

³⁷Jacob got green branches of poplar, almond, and plane trees and stripped off some of the bark so that the branches had white stripes on them. ³⁸He placed these branches in front of the flocks at their drinking troughs. He put them there, because the animals mated when they came to drink. ³⁹So when the goats bred in front of the branches, they produced young that were streaked, speckled, and spotted.

⁴⁰Jacob kept the sheep separate from the goats and made them face in the direction of the streaked and black animals of Laban's flock. In this way he built up his own flock and kept it apart from Laban's.

⁴¹When the healthy animals were mating, Jacob put the branches in front of them at the drinking troughs, so that they would breed among the branches. ⁴²But he did not put the branches in front of the weak animals. Soon Laban had all the weak animals, and Jacob all the healthy ones. ⁴³In this way Jacob became very wealthy. He had many flocks, slaves, camels, and donkeys.

Jacob Flees from Laban

31 ¹Jacob heard that Laban's sons were saying, "Jacob has taken everything that belonged to our father. He got all his wealth from what our father owned." ²He also saw that Laban was no longer as friendly as he had been earlier. ³Then the LORD said to him, "Go back to the land of your fathers and to your relatives. I will be with you."

⁴So Jacob sent word to Rachel and Leah to meet him in the field where his flocks were. ⁵He said to them, "I have noticed that

your father is not as friendly toward me as he used to be; but my father's God has been with me. ⁶You both know that I have worked for your father with all my strength. ⁷Yet he has cheated me and changed my wages ten times. But God did not let him harm me. ⁸Whenever Laban said, 'The speckled goats shall be your wages,' all the flocks produced speckled young. When he said, 'The striped goats shall be your wages,' all the flocks produced striped young. ⁹God has taken flocks away from your father and given them to me.

¹⁰"During the breeding season I had a dream, and I saw that the male goats that were mating were striped, spotted, and speckled. ¹¹The angel of God spoke to me in the dream and said, 'Jacob!' 'Yes,' I answered. ¹²'Look,' he continued, 'all the male goats that are mating are striped, spotted, and speckled. I am making this happen because I have seen all that Laban is doing to you. ¹³I am the God who appeared to you at Bethel, where you dedicated a stone as a memorial by pouring olive oil on it and where you made a vow to me. Now get ready and go back to the land where you were born.' "

¹⁴Rachel and Leah answered Jacob, "There is nothing left for us to inherit from our father. ¹⁵He treats us like foreigners. He sold us, and now he has spent all the money he was paid for us. ¹⁶All this wealth which God has taken from our father belongs to us and to our children. Do whatever God has told you."

¹⁷⁻¹⁸So Jacob got ready to go back to his father in the land of Canaan. He put his children and his wives on the camels, and drove all his flocks ahead of him, with everything that he had gotten in Mesopotamia. ¹⁹Laban had gone to shear his sheep, and during his absence Rachel stole the household gods that belonged to her father. ²⁰Jacob deceived Laban by not letting him know that he was leaving. ²¹He took everything he owned and left in a hurry. He crossed the Euphrates River and started for the hill country of Gilead.

Jacob drove all his flocks ahead of him. (31:18)

Laban Pursues Jacob

22 Three days later Laban was told that Jacob had fled. 23 He took his men with him and pursued Jacob for seven days until he caught up with him in the hill country of Gilead. 24 In a dream that night God came to Laban and said to him, "Be careful not to threaten Jacob in any way." 25 Jacob had set up his camp on a mountain, and Laban set up his camp with his relatives in the hill country of Gilead.

26 Laban said to Jacob, "Why did you deceive me and carry off my daughters like women captured in war? 27 Why did you deceive me and slip away without telling me? If you had told me, I would have sent you on your way with rejoicing and singing to the music of tambourines and harps. 28 You did not even let me kiss my grandchildren and my daughters good-bye. That was a foolish thing to do! 29 I have the power to do you harm, but last night the God of your father warned me not to threaten you in any way. 30 I know that you left because you were so anxious to get back home, but why did you steal my household gods?"

31 Jacob answered, "I was afraid, because I thought that you might take your daughters away from me. 32 But if you find that anyone here has your gods, he will be put to death. Here, with our men as witnesses, look for anything that belongs to you and take what is yours." Jacob did not know that Rachel had stolen Laban's gods.

33 Laban went and searched Jacob's tent; then he went into Leah's tent, and the tent of the two slave women, but he did not find his gods. Then he went into Rachel's tent. 34 Rachel had taken the household gods and put them in a camel's saddlebag and was sitting on them. Laban searched through the whole tent, but did not find them. 35 Rachel said to her father, "Do not be angry with me, sir, but I am not able to stand up in your presence; I am having my monthly period." Laban searched but did not find his household gods.

36 Then Jacob lost his temper. "What crime have I committed?" he asked angrily. "What law have I broken that gives you the right to hunt me down? 37 Now that you have searched through all my belongings, what household article have you found that belongs to you? Put it out here where your men and mine can see it, and let them decide which one of us is right. 38 I have been with you now for twenty years; your sheep and your goats have not failed to

reproduce, and I have not eaten any rams from your flocks. [39]Whenever a sheep was killed by wild animals, I always bore the loss myself. I didn't take it to you to show that it was not my fault. You demanded that I make good anything that was stolen during the day or during the night. [40]Many times I suffered from the heat during the day and from the cold at night. I was not able to sleep. [41]It was like that for the whole twenty years I was with you. For fourteen years I worked to win your two daughters—and six years for your flocks. And even then, you changed my wages ten times. [42]If the God of my fathers, the God of Abraham and Isaac, had not been with me, you would have already sent me away empty-handed. But God has seen my trouble and the work I have done, and last night he gave his judgment."

The Agreement between Jacob and Laban

[43]Laban answered Jacob, "These young women are my daughters; their children belong to me, and these flocks are mine. In fact, everything you see here belongs to me. But since I can do nothing to keep my daughters and their children, [44]I am ready to make an agreement with you. Let us make a pile of stones to remind us of our agreement."

[45]So Jacob got a stone and set it up as a memorial. [46]He told his men to gather some rocks and pile them up. Then they ate a meal beside the pile of rocks. [47]Laban named it Jegar Sahadutha,[b] while Jacob named it Galeed.[c] [48]Laban said to Jacob, "This pile of rocks will be a reminder for both of us." That is why that place was named Galeed. [49]Laban also said, "May the LORD keep an eye on us while we are separated from each other." So the place was also named Mizpah.[d] [50]Laban went on, "If you mistreat my daughters or if you marry other women, even though I don't

know about it, remember that God is watching us. [51]Here are the rocks that I have piled up between us, and here is the memorial stone. [52]Both this pile and this memorial stone are reminders. I will never go beyond this pile to attack you, and you must never go beyond it or beyond this memorial stone to attack me. [53]The God of Abraham and the God of Nahor[e] will judge between us." Then, in the name of the God whom his father Isaac worshiped, Jacob solemnly vowed to keep this promise. [54]He killed an animal, which he offered as a sacrifice on the mountain, and he invited his men to the meal. After they had eaten, they spent the night on the mountain. [55]Early the next morning Laban kissed his grandchildren and his daughters good-bye, and left to go back home.

Jacob Prepares to Meet Esau

32 [1]As Jacob went on his way, some angels met him. [2]When he saw them, he said, "This is God's camp"; so he named the place Mahanaim.[f]

[3]Jacob sent messengers ahead of him to his brother Esau in the country of Edom. [4]He instructed them to say: "I, Jacob, your obedient servant, report to my master Esau that I have been staying with Laban and that I have delayed my return until now. [5]I own cattle, donkeys, sheep, goats, and slaves. I am sending you word, sir, in the hope of gaining your favor."

[6]When the messengers came back to Jacob, they said, "We went to your brother Esau, and he is already on his way to meet you. He has four hundred men with him." [7]Jacob was frightened and worried. He divided into two groups the people who were with him, and also his sheep, goats, cattle, and camels. [8]He thought, "If Esau comes and attacks the first group, the other may be able to escape."

---

[b] **31:47** JEGAR SAHADUTHA: *This name in Aramaic means "a pile to remind us."* [c] **31:47** GALEED: *This name in Hebrew means "a pile to remind us."* [d] **31:49** MIZPAH: *This name sounds like the Hebrew for "place from which to watch."* [e] **31:53** ABRAHAM . . . NAHOR: *Abraham was Jacob's grandfather and Nahor was Laban's grandfather.* [f] **32:2** MAHANAIM: *This name in Hebrew means "two camps."*

Have you ever felt like God wanted you to do something you didn't want to do? If so, you've wrestled with God.

⁹Then Jacob prayed, "God of my grand-father Abraham and God of my father Isaac, hear me! You told me, LORD, to go back to my land and to my relatives, and you would make everything go well for me. ¹⁰I am not worth all the kindness and faithfulness that you have shown me, your servant. I crossed the Jordan with nothing but a walking stick, and now I have come back with these two groups. ¹¹Save me, I pray, from my brother Esau. I am afraid—afraid that he is coming to attack us and destroy us all, even the women and children. ¹²Remember that you promised to make everything go well for me and to give me more descendants than any-one could count, as many as the grains of sand along the seashore."

¹³⁻¹⁵After spending the night there, Jacob chose from his livestock as a present for his brother Esau: 200 female goats and 20 males, 200 female sheep and 20 males, 30 milk camels with their young, 40 cows and 10 bulls, 20 female donkeys and 10 males. ¹⁶He divided them into herds and put one of his servants in charge of each herd. He said to them, "Go ahead of me, and leave a space between each herd and the one behind it." ¹⁷He ordered the first servant, "When my brother Esau meets you and asks, 'Who is your master? Where are you going? Who owns these animals in front of you?' ¹⁸you must answer, 'They belong to your servant Jacob. He sends them as a present to his mas-ter Esau. Jacob himself is right behind us.' " ¹⁹He gave the same order to the second, the third, and to all the others who were in charge of the herds: "This is what you must say to Esau when you meet him. ²⁰You must say, 'Yes, your servant Jacob is right behind us.' " Jacob was thinking, "I will win him over with the gifts, and when I meet him, perhaps he will forgive me." ²¹He sent the gifts on ahead of him and spent that night in camp.

Jacob Wrestles at Peniel

²²That same night Jacob got up, took his two wives, his two concubines, and his eleven children, and crossed the Jabbok River. ²³After he had sent them across, he

Jacob's Wrestling Match

Did you ever have your favorite television show interrupted by an important announcement? That's what happens in the story about Jacob and Esau. They are just about to meet after twenty years when the writer stops the action and switches to another story: Jacob's wrestling match.

Jacob must have planned to get a good night's sleep before the meeting with Esau, which he was dreading. He sent everyone ahead while he stayed behind. That night a man came to him and started wrestling with him. They wrestled all night long. The man would not tell Jacob his name, but Jacob knew it was God. When they finished God blessed him and changed his name: Jacob's new name was Israel, which means "he struggles with God."

Jacob's life changed that day. He knew he was destined for great things. He worked hard to be the person God wanted him to be. He knew he had to make things right with Esau. After all, he had God's promise that he would be the founder and the father of the great nation of Israel.

— Genesis 32:22–32

also sent across all that he owned, ²⁴but he stayed behind, alone.

Then a man came and wrestled with him until just before daybreak. ²⁵When the man saw that he was not winning the struggle, he hit Jacob on the hip, and it was thrown out

32:12 Gen 22:17   **32:23** Wis 10:12   **32:24–26** Hos 12:3, 4

A man came and wrestled with him. (32:24)

Esau . . . threw his arms around him. (33:4)

of joint. 26 The man said, "Let me go; daylight is coming."

"I won't, unless you bless me," Jacob answered.

27 "What is your name?" the man asked.

"Jacob," he answered.

28 The man said, "Your name will no longer be Jacob. You have struggled with God and with men, and you have won; so your name will be Israel." *g*

29 Jacob said, "Now tell me your name."

But he answered, "Why do you want to know my name?" Then he blessed Jacob.

30 Jacob said, "I have seen God face to face, and I am still alive"; so he named the place Peniel. *h* 31 The sun rose as Jacob was leaving Peniel, and he was limping because of his hip. 32 Even today the descendants of Israel do not eat the muscle which is on the hip joint, because it was on this muscle that Jacob was hit.

Jacob Meets Esau

33 1 Jacob saw Esau coming with his four hundred men, so he divided the children among Leah, Rachel, and the two concubines. 2 He put the concubines and their children first, then Leah and her children, and finally Rachel and Joseph at the rear. 3 Jacob went ahead of them and bowed down to the ground seven times as

he approached his brother. 4 But Esau ran to meet him, threw his arms around him, and kissed him. They were both crying. 5 When Esau looked around and saw the women and the children, he asked, "Who are these people with you?"

"These, sir, are the children whom God has been good enough to give me," Jacob answered. 6 Then the concubines came up with their children and bowed down; 7 then Leah and her children came, and last of all Joseph and Rachel came and bowed down.

8 Esau asked, "What about that other group I met? What did that mean?"

Jacob answered, "It was to gain your favor."

9 But Esau said, "I have enough, my brother; keep what you have."

10 Jacob said, "No, please, if I have gained your favor, accept my gift. To see your face is

"If I have gained your favor" (33:10)

g **32:28** ISRAEL: *This name sounds like the Hebrew for "he struggles with God" or "God struggles."* h **32:30** PENIEL: *This name sounds like the Hebrew for "the face of God."*
32:28 Gen 35:10   **32:29** Judg 13:17, 18

Pray It!

A Moment of Great Power

The story of Jacob and Esau ends with a powerful moment: a moment of reconciliation. Jacob begs for Esau's forgiveness, and Esau forgives him. Esau did not hold a grudge against his brother. Jacob must have felt tremendous relief after so many years of worrying. In fact, meeting for the first time was such an intense experience that both brothers cried as they hugged each other. Their relationship was healed.

Are you more like Jacob who needed forgiveness? Or are you more like Esau who needed to forgive? Is there a relationship in your life that needs healing? Pray for the courage to let go of your grudges. Pray for the virtue of humility. Ask God to make your heart ready for a moment of great power.

— Genesis 33:1–11

for me like seeing the face of God, now that you have been so friendly to me. ¹¹Please accept this gift which I have brought for you; God has been kind to me and given me everything I need." Jacob kept on urging him until he accepted.

¹²Esau said, "Let's get ready and leave. I will go ahead of you."

¹³Jacob answered, "You know that the children are weak, and I must think of the sheep and livestock with their young. If they are driven hard for even one day, the whole herd will die. ¹⁴Please go on ahead of me, and I will follow slowly, going as fast as I can with the livestock and the children until I catch up with you in Edom."

¹⁵Esau said, "Then let me leave some of my men with you."

But Jacob answered, "There is no need for that for I only want to gain your favor."*ⁱ*
¹⁶So that day Esau started on his way back to Edom. ¹⁷But Jacob went to Sukkoth, where he built a house for himself and shelters for his livestock. That is why the place was named Sukkoth.*ʲ*

¹⁸On his return from Mesopotamia Jacob arrived safely at the city of Shechem in the land of Canaan and set up his camp in a field near the city. ¹⁹He bought that part of the field from the descendants of Hamor father of Shechem for a hundred pieces of silver. ²⁰He put up an altar there and named it for El, the God of Israel.

The Rape of Dinah

34 ¹One day Dinah, the daughter of Jacob and Leah, went to visit some of the Canaanite women. ²When Shechem son of Hamor the Hivite, who was chief of that region, saw her, he took her and raped her. ³But he found the young woman so attractive that he fell in love with her and tried to win her affection.*ᵏ* ⁴He told his father, "I want you to get Dinah for me as my wife."

⁵Jacob learned that his daughter had been disgraced, but because his sons were out in the fields with his livestock, he did nothing until they came back. ⁶Shechem's father

ⁱ **33:15** for I only want to gain your favor; *or* if it's all right with you.   *ʲ* **33:17** SUKKOTH: *This name in Hebrew means "shelters."*   *ᵏ* **34:3** tried to win her affection; *or* comforted her.
33:19 Josh 24:32; Jn 4:5

Jacob was *really* nervous about meeting Esau. Read 32:13–21 and 33:1–17. How would you have handled it?

Hamor went out to talk with Jacob, 7just as Jacob's sons were coming in from the fields. When they heard about it, they were shocked and furious that Shechem had done such a thing and had insulted the people of Israel by raping Jacob's daughter. 8Hamor said to him, "My son Shechem has fallen in love with your daughter; please let him marry her. 9Let us make an agreement that there will be intermarriage between our people and yours. 10Then you may stay here in our country with us; you may live anywhere you wish, trade freely, and own property."

11Then Shechem said to Dinah's father and brothers, "Do me this favor, and I will give you whatever you want. 12Tell me what presents you want, and set the payment for the bride as high as you wish; I will give you whatever you ask, if you will only let me marry her."

13Because Shechem had disgraced their sister Dinah, Jacob's sons answered Shechem and his father Hamor in a deceitful way. 14They said to him, "We cannot let our sister marry a man who is not circumcised; that would be a disgrace for us. 15We can agree only on the condition that you become like us by circumcising all your males. 16Then we will agree to intermarriage. We will settle among you and become one people with you. 17But if you will not accept our terms and be circumcised, we will take her and leave."

18These terms seemed fair to Hamor and his son Shechem, 19and the young man lost no time in doing what was suggested, because he was in love with Jacob's daughter. He was the most important member of his family.

20Hamor and his son Shechem went to the meeting place at the city gate and spoke to the people of the town: 21"These men are friendly; let them live in the land with us and travel freely. The land is large enough for them also. Let us marry their daughters and give them ours in marriage. 22But these men will agree to live among us and be one peo-

ple with us only on the condition that we circumcise all our males, as they are circumcised. 23Won't all their livestock and everything else they own be ours? So let us agree that they can live among us." 24All the citizens of the city agreed with what Hamor and Shechem proposed, and all the males were circumcised.

25Three days later, when the men were still sore from their circumcision, two of Jacob's sons, Simeon and Levi, the brothers of Dinah, took their swords, went into the city without arousing suspicion, and killed all the men, 26including Hamor and his son Shechem. Then they took Dinah from Shechem's house and left. 27After the slaughter Jacob's other sons looted the town to take revenge for their sister's disgrace. 28They took the flocks, the cattle, the donkeys, and everything else in the city and in the fields. 29They took everything of value, captured all the women and children, and carried off everything in the houses.

30Jacob said to Simeon and Levi, "You have gotten me into trouble; now the Canaanites, the Perizzites, and everybody else in the land will hate me. I do not have many men; if they all band together against me and attack me, our whole family will be destroyed."

31But they answered, "We cannot let our sister be treated like a common whore."

God Blesses Jacob at Bethel

35 1God said to Jacob, "Go to Bethel at once, and live there. Build an altar there to me, the God who appeared to you when you were running away from your brother Esau."

2So Jacob said to his family and to all who were with him, "Get rid of the foreign gods that you have; purify yourselves and put on clean clothes. 3We are going to leave here and go to Bethel, where I will build an altar to the God who helped me in the time of my trouble and who has been with me

35:1 Gen 28:11–17

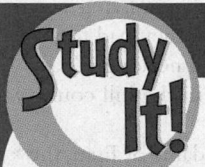

A Crime Then and Now

The story of Dinah in Genesis, chapter 34, is shocking. Dinah was raped. Even though life was different then, rape was still considered a crime. But we don't hear how Dinah felt about it, just how her brothers felt. Back then people were more concerned about bringing dishonor to the family rather than the hurt caused to a living, breathing human being.

The man who raped Dinah, Shechem, wants to marry her. So Shechem's father and Dinah's father, Jacob, arrange the marriage of Shechem and Dinah. Dinah was never even asked how she felt about this! In biblical times, girls and women were the property of men—like land, animals, and tools. They could not own anything. They had little say in whom they married. They were expected to have many children—especially male children. They had no rights.

Today we see men and women as persons with equal rights. And our definition of sexual abuse includes not only rape but also unwanted sexual touching and unwanted sexual language and suggestions. You have probably heard about sexual abuse at school. If you or someone you know is being abused, tell an adult whom you trust. The adult should help bring an end to the abuse; if not, tell another adult. Rape and sexual abuse were horrible crimes in biblical times. They are still horrible crimes today.

— Genesis, chapter 34

everywhere I have gone." [4]So they gave Jacob all the foreign gods that they had and also the earrings that they were wearing. He buried them beneath the oak tree near Shechem.

[5]When Jacob and his sons started to leave, great fear fell on the people of the nearby towns, and they did not pursue them. [6]Jacob came with all his people to Luz, which is now known as Bethel, in the land of Canaan. [7]He built an altar there and named the place for the God of Bethel, because God had revealed himself to him there when he was running away from his brother. [8]Rebecca's nurse Deborah died and was buried beneath the oak south of Bethel. So it was named "Oak of Weeping."

[9]When Jacob returned from Mesopotamia, God appeared to him again and blessed him. [10]God said to him, "Your name is Jacob, but from now on it will be Israel." So God named him Israel. [11]And God said to him, "I am Almighty God. Have many children. Nations will be descended from you, and you will be the ancestor of kings. [12]I will give you the land which I gave to Abraham and to Isaac, and I will also give it to your descendants after you." [13]Then God left him. [14]There, where God had spoken to him, Jacob set up a memorial stone and consecrated it by pouring wine and olive oil on it. [15]He named the place Bethel.

The Death of Rachel

[16]Jacob and his family left Bethel, and when they were still some distance from Ephrath, the time came for Rachel to have her baby, and she was having difficult labor. [17]When her labor pains were at their worst, the midwife said to her, "Don't be afraid, Rachel; it's another boy." [18]But she was dying, and as she breathed her last, she named her son Benoni,[l] but his father named him Benjamin.[m]

[19]When Rachel died, she was buried

[l] **35.18** BENONI: *This name in Hebrew means "son of my sorrow."* [m] **35:18** BENJAMIN: *This name in Hebrew means "son who will be fortunate."*
35:10 Gen 32:28 **35:11, 12** Gen 17:4–8
35:14, 15 Gen 28:18, 19

beside the road to Ephrath, now known as Bethlehem. 20Jacob set up a memorial stone there, and it still marks Rachel's grave to this day. 21Jacob moved on and set up his camp on the other side of the tower of Eder.

The Sons of Jacob
(1 Chronicles 2:1, 2)

22While Jacob was living in that land, Reuben had sexual intercourse with Bilhah, one of his father's concubines; Jacob heard about it and was furious.*n*

Jacob had twelve sons. 23The sons of Leah were Reuben (Jacob's oldest son), Simeon, Levi, Judah, Issachar, and Zebulun. 24The sons of Rachel were Joseph and Benjamin. 25The sons of Rachel's slave Bilhah were Dan and Naphtali. 26The sons of Leah's slave Zilpah were Gad and Asher. These sons were born in Mesopotamia.

The Death of Isaac

27Jacob went to his father Isaac at Mamre, near Hebron, where Abraham and Isaac had lived. 28Isaac lived to be a hundred and eighty years old 29and died at a ripe old age; and his sons Esau and Jacob buried him.

The Descendants of Esau
(1 Chronicles 1:34–37)

36 1These are the descendants of Esau, also called Edom. 2Esau married Canaanite women: Adah, the daughter of Elon the Hittite; Oholibamah, the daughter of Anah son*o* of Zibeon the Hivite; 3and Basemath, the daughter of Ishmael and sister of Nebaioth. 4Adah bore Eliphaz; Basemath bore Reuel; 5and Oholibamah bore Jeush, Jalam, and Korah. All these sons were born to Esau in the land of Canaan.

6Then Esau took his wives, his sons, his daughters, and all the people of his house, along with all his livestock and all the possessions he had gotten in the land of Canaan, and went away from his brother Jacob to another land. 7He left because the

land where he and Jacob were living was not able to support them; they had too much livestock and could no longer stay together. 8So Esau lived in the hill country of Edom.

9These are the descendants of Esau, the ancestor of the Edomites. 10-13Esau's wife Adah bore him one son, Eliphaz, and Eliphaz had five sons: Teman, Omar, Zepho, Gatam, and Kenaz. And by another wife, Timna, he had one more son, Amalek.

Esau's wife Basemath bore him one son, Reuel, and Reuel had four sons: Nahath, Zerah, Shammah, and Mizzah.

14Esau's wife Oholibamah, the daughter of Anah son*o* of Zibeon, bore him three sons: Jeush, Jalam, and Korah.

15These are the tribes descended from Esau. Esau's first son Eliphaz was the ancestor of the following tribes: Teman, Omar, Zepho, Kenaz, 16Korah, Gatam, and Amalek. These were all descendants of Esau's wife Adah.

17Esau's son Reuel was the ancestor of the following tribes: Nahath, Zerah, Shammah, and Mizzah. These were all descendants of Esau's wife Basemath.

18The following tribes were descended from Esau by his wife Oholibamah, the daughter of Anah: Jeush, Jalam, and Korah. 19All these tribes were descended from Esau.

The Descendants of Seir
(1 Chronicles 1:38–42)

20-21The original inhabitants of the land of Edom were divided into tribes which traced their ancestry to the following descendants of Seir, a Horite: Lotan, Shobal, Zibeon, Anah, Dishon, Ezer, and Dishan.

22Lotan was the ancestor of the clans of Hori and Heman. (Lotan had a sister named Timna.)

23Shobal was the ancestor of the clans of Alvan, Manahath, Ebal, Shepho, and Onam. 24Zibeon had two sons, Aiah and Anah. (This is the Anah who found the hot springs in the wilderness when he was taking care of

---

n **35:22** *One ancient translation* and was furious; *Hebrew does not have these words.*   *o* **36:2,14** *Some ancient translations* son; *Hebrew* daughter; *or* granddaughter.
35:22 Gen 49:4   **35:27** Gen 13:18   **36:2** Gen 26:34   **36:3** Gen 28:9

his father's donkeys.) 25-26Anah was the father of Dishon, who was the ancestor of the clans of Hemdan, Eshban, Ithran, and Cheran. Anah also had a daughter named Oholibamah.

27Ezer was the ancestor of the clans of Bilhan, Zaavan, and Akan.

28Dishan was the ancestor of the clans of Uz and Aran.

29-30These are the Horite tribes in the land of Edom: Lotan, Shobal, Zibeon, Anah, Dishon, Ezer, and Dishan.

The Kings of Edom
(1 Chronicles 1:43–54)

31-39Before there were any kings in Israel, the following kings ruled the land of Edom in succession:

Bela son of Beor from Dinhabah
Jobab son of Zerah from Bozrah
Husham from the region of Teman
Hadad son of Bedad from Avith (he
    defeated the Midianites in a battle in
    the country of Moab)
Samlah from Masrekah
Shaul from Rehoboth-on-the-River
Baal Hanan son of Achbor
Hadad from Pau (his wife was Mehetabel,
    the daughter of Matred and
    granddaughter of Mezahab)

40-43Esau was the ancestor of the following Edomite tribes: Timna, Alvah, Jetheth, Oholibamah, Elah, Pinon, Kenaz, Teman, Mibzar, Magdiel, and Iram. The area where each of these tribes lived was known by the name of the tribe.

Joseph and His Brothers

37 ¹Jacob continued to live in the land of Canaan, where his father had lived, ²and this is the story of Jacob's family.

Joseph, a young man of seventeen, took care of the sheep and goats with his brothers, the sons of Bilhah and Zilpah, his father's concubines. He brought bad reports to his father about what his brothers were doing.

Live It!

Favored Sibling

Richard and William were goofing around in the living room. The lamp fell and smashed into many pieces. William told his dad that it was Richard's fault. His dad believed him. Richard was older and stronger, he said. He should have known better.

Maya was the baby in the family. Even though she was eleven, she acted like a baby—when it suited her. She got everything she wanted. LeBron had to save his own money to buy a CD player. Maya got one for her birthday.

Do you ever feel like your parents favor your brother or sister over you? It may be true sometimes, as in the case with Joseph and his brothers (Genesis 37:3), but most parents love their children equally. They try to be fair, and that means occasionally giving someone special treatment. The next time you feel like your parents are unjust, try to remember a time when you were on the receiving end of their favoritism. If you can't remember, ask your siblings. They are sure to come up with a time when it seemed that your mom or dad liked you best.

— Genesis, chapter 37

---

³Jacob loved Joseph more than all his other sons, because he had been born to him when he was old. He made a long robe with full sleeves*p* for him. ⁴When his brothers saw that their father loved Joseph more than he

p **37:3** robe with full sleeves; *or* decorated robe.

Starting with Genesis, chapter 37, through the end of the book, Joseph takes over as the main character.

loved them, they hated their brother so much that they would not speak to him in a friendly manner.

5 One time Joseph had a dream, and when he told his brothers about it, they hated him even more. 6 He said, "Listen to the dream I had. 7 We were all in the field tying up sheaves of wheat, when my sheaf got up and stood up straight. Yours formed a circle around mine and bowed down to it."

8 "Do you think you are going to be a king and rule over us?" his brothers asked. So they hated him even more because of his dreams and because of what he said about them.

9 Then Joseph had another dream and told his brothers, "I had another dream, in which I saw the sun, the moon, and eleven stars bowing down to me."

10 He also told the dream to his father, and his father scolded him: "What kind of a dream is that? Do you think that your mother, your brothers, and I are going to come and bow down to you?" 11 Joseph's brothers were jealous of him, but his father kept thinking about the whole matter.

Joseph Is Sold and Taken to Egypt

12 One day when Joseph's brothers had gone to Shechem to take care of their father's flock, 13 Jacob said to Joseph, "I want you to go to Shechem, where your brothers are taking care of the flock."

Joseph answered, "I am ready."

14 His father told him, "Go and see if your brothers are safe and if the flock is all right; then come back and tell me." So his father sent him on his way from Hebron Valley.

Joseph arrived at Shechem 15 and was wandering around in the country when a man saw him and asked him, "What are you looking for?"

16 "I am looking for my brothers, who are taking care of their flock," he answered. "Can you tell me where they are?"

17 The man said, "They have already left. I heard them say that they were going to Dothan." So Joseph went after his brothers and found them at Dothan.

18 They saw him in the distance, and before he reached them, they plotted against him and decided to kill him. 19 They said to one another, "Here comes that dreamer. 20 Come on now, let's kill him and throw his body into one of the dry wells. We can say that a wild animal killed him. Then we will see what becomes of his dreams."

21 Reuben heard them and tried to save Joseph. "Let's not kill him," he said. 22 "Just throw him into this well in the wilderness, but don't hurt him." He said this, planning to save him from them and send him back to his father. 23 When Joseph came up to his brothers, they ripped off his long robe with full sleeves.p 24 Then they took him and threw him into the well, which was dry.

25 While they were eating, they suddenly saw a group of Ishmaelites traveling from Gilead to Egypt. Their camels were loaded with spices and resins. 26 Judah said to his brothers, "What will we gain by killing our brother and covering up the murder? 27 Let's sell him to these Ishmaelites. Then we won't have to hurt him; after all, he is our brother, our own flesh and blood." His brothers agreed, 28 and when some Midianite traders came by, the brothersq pulled Joseph out of the well and sold him for twenty pieces of silver to the Ishmaelites, who took him to Egypt.

29 When Reuben came back to the well and found that Joseph was not there, he tore his clothes in sorrow. 30 He returned to his brothers and said, "The boy is not there! What am I going to do?"

31 Then they killed a goat and dipped Joseph's robe in its blood. 32 They took the robe to their father and said, "We found this. Does it belong to your son?"

33 He recognized it and said, "Yes, it is his! Some wild animal has killed him. My son

---

p **37:23** robe with full sleeves; or decorated robe.   q **37:28** the brothers; Hebrew they.
37:11 Acts 7:9   **37:28** Wis 10:13; Acts 7:9

The story of Joseph was made into a popular musical called *Joseph and the Amazing Technicolor Dreamcoat.*

The Ishmaelites . . . took him to Egypt. (37:28)

Joseph has been torn to pieces!" [34]Jacob tore his clothes in sorrow and put on sackcloth. He mourned for his son a long time. [35]All his sons and daughters came to comfort him, but he refused to be comforted and said, "I will go down to the world of the dead still mourning for my son." So he continued to mourn for his son Joseph.

[36]Meanwhile, in Egypt the Midianites had sold Joseph to Potiphar, one of the king's officers, who was the captain of the palace guard.

Judah and Tamar

38 [1]About that time Judah left his brothers and went to stay with a man named Hirah, who was from the town of Adullam. [2]There Judah met a young Canaanite woman whose father was named Shua. He married her, [3]and she bore him a son, whom he named Er. [4]She became pregnant again and bore another son and named him Onan. [5]Again she had a son and named him Shelah. Judah was at Achzib when the boy was born.

[6]For his first son Er, Judah got a wife whose name was Tamar. [7]Er's conduct was evil, and it displeased the LORD, so the LORD killed him. [8]Then Judah said to Er's brother Onan, "Go and sleep with your brother's widow. Fulfill your obligation to her as her husband's brother, so that your brother may have descendants." [9]But Onan knew that the children would not belong to him, so when he had intercourse with his brother's widow, he let the semen spill on the ground, so that there would be no chil-

dren for his brother. [10]What he did displeased the LORD, and the LORD killed him also. [11]Then Judah said to his daughter-in-law Tamar, "Return to your father's house and remain a widow until my son Shelah grows up." He said this because he was afraid that Shelah would be killed, as his brothers had been. So Tamar went back home.

[12]After some time Judah's wife died. When he had finished the time of mourning, he and his friend Hirah of Adullam went to Timnah, where his sheep were being sheared. [13]Someone told Tamar that her father-in-law was going to Timnah to shear his sheep. [14]So she changed from the widow's clothes she had been wearing, covered her face with a veil, and sat down at the entrance to Enaim, a town on the road to Timnah. As she well knew, Judah's youngest son Shelah was now grown up, and yet she had not been given to him in marriage.

[15]When Judah saw her, he thought that she was a prostitute, because she had her face covered. [16]He went over to her at the side of the road and said, "All right, how much do you charge?" (He did not know that she was his daughter-in-law.)

She said, "What will you give me?"

[17]He answered, "I will send you a young goat from my flock."

She said, "All right, if you will give me something to keep as a pledge until you send the goat."

[18]"What shall I give you as a pledge?" he asked.

She answered, "Your seal with its cord and the walking stick you are carrying." He gave them to her. Then they had intercourse, and she became pregnant. [19]Tamar went home, took off her veil, and put her widow's clothes back on.

[20]Judah sent his friend Hirah to take the goat and get back from the woman the articles he had pledged, but Hirah could not find her. [21]He asked some men at Enaim, "Where is the prostitute who was here by the road?"

"There has never been a prostitute here," they answered.

[22]He returned to Judah and said, "I couldn't find her. The men of the place said that there had never been a prostitute there."

23 Judah said, "Let her keep the things. We don't want people to laugh at us. I did try to pay her, but you couldn't find her."

24 About three months later someone told Judah, "Your daughter-in-law Tamar has been acting like a whore, and now she is pregnant."

Judah ordered, "Take her out and burn her to death."

25 As she was being taken out, she sent word to her father-in-law: "I am pregnant by the man who owns these things. Look at them and see whose they are—this seal with its cord and this walking stick."

26 Judah recognized them and said, "She is in the right. I have failed in my obligation to her—I should have given her to my son Shelah in marriage." And Judah never had intercourse with her again.

27 When the time came for her to give birth, it was discovered that she was going to have twins. 28 While she was in labor, one of them put out an arm; the midwife caught it, tied a red thread around it, and said, "This one was born first." 29 But he pulled his arm back, and his brother was born first. Then the midwife said, "So this is how you break your way out!" So he was named Perez.[r]
30 Then his brother was born with the red thread on his arm, and he was named Zerah.[s]

Joseph and Potiphar's Wife

39 ¹Now the Ishmaelites had taken Joseph to Egypt and sold him to Potiphar, one of the king's officers, who was the captain of the palace guard. ²The LORD was with Joseph and made him successful. He lived in the house of his Egyptian master, ³who saw that the LORD was with Joseph and had made him successful in everything he did. ⁴Potiphar was pleased with him and made him his personal servant; so he put him in charge of his house and everything he owned. ⁵From then on, because of Joseph the LORD blessed the household of the Egyptian and everything that he had in his house and in his fields.

⁶Potiphar turned over everything he had to the care of Joseph and did not concern himself with anything except the food he ate.

Joseph was well-built and good-looking, ⁷and after a while his master's wife began to desire Joseph and asked him to go to bed with her. ⁸He refused and said to her, "Look, my master does not have to concern himself with anything in the house, because I am here. He has put me in charge of everything he has. ⁹I have as much authority in this house as he has, and he has not kept back anything from me except you. How then could I do such an immoral thing and sin against God?" ¹⁰Although she asked Joseph day after day, he would not go to bed with her.

¹¹But one day when Joseph went into the house to do his work, none of the house servants was there. ¹²She caught him by his robe and said, "Come to bed with me." But he escaped and ran outside, leaving his robe in her hand. ¹³When she saw that he had left his robe and had run out of the house, ¹⁴she called to her house servants and said, "Look at this! This Hebrew that my husband brought to the house is insulting us. He came into my room and tried to rape me, but I screamed as loud as I could. ¹⁵When he heard me scream, he ran outside, leaving his robe beside me."

¹⁶She kept his robe with her until Joseph's master came home. ¹⁷Then she told him the same story: "That Hebrew slave that you brought here came into my room and insulted me. ¹⁸But when I screamed, he ran outside, leaving his robe beside me."

¹⁹Joseph's master was furious ²⁰and had Joseph arrested and put in the prison where the king's prisoners were kept, and there he stayed. ²¹But the LORD was with Joseph and blessed him, so that the jailer was pleased with him. ²²He put Joseph in charge of all the other prisoners and made him responsible for everything that was done in the prison. ²³The jailer did not have to look after anything for which Joseph was responsible, because the LORD was with Joseph and made him succeed in everything he did.

---

r **38:29** PEREZ: *This name in Hebrew means "breaking out."*   *s* **38:29** ZERAH: *This name sounds like a Hebrew word for the red brightness of dawn.*
39:2 Acts 7:9   **39:21** Acts 7:9

Joseph's Tough Times

Joseph was in a tough spot. He was a slave in Egypt, having been sold by his brothers. But he made the best of it. He kept at it and worked hard. His master was pleased, so he made him his personal servant. Later, when Joseph was falsely accused of a crime and thrown into jail, the jailer recognized that Joseph had a special gift for understanding dreams. Eventually, he became governor of Egypt with power over many people—including his brothers.

Joseph could not have done it without God. He knew that God was everywhere, and he called on God for help. "The LORD was with Joseph and made him successful" (Genesis 39:2).

Do you ever feel like nothing is right? Does it seem like you'll never get ahead sometimes? Are you stressed and worried? Do what Joseph did:
• Persevere. That means keep on doing what you have to do.
• Do your very best.
• Ask God for help.
Someday you will look back at your tough times and say, "The Lord was with me and made me successful."

— Genesis 39:1–6

Joseph Interprets the Prisoners' Dreams

40 ¹Some time later the king of Egypt's wine steward and his chief baker offended the king. ²He was angry with these two officials ³and put them in prison in the house of the captain of the guard, in the same place where Joseph was being kept. ⁴They spent a long time in prison, and the captain assigned Joseph as their servant.

⁵One night there in prison the wine steward and the chief baker each had a dream, and the dreams had different meanings. ⁶When Joseph came to them in the morning, he saw that they were upset. ⁷He asked them, "Why do you look so worried today?"

⁸They answered, "Each of us had a dream, and there is no one here to explain what the dreams mean."

"It is God who gives the ability to interpret dreams," Joseph said. "Tell me your dreams."

⁹So the wine steward said, "In my dream there was a grapevine in front of me ¹⁰with three branches on it. As soon as the leaves came out, the blossoms appeared, and the grapes ripened. ¹¹I was holding the king's cup; so I took the grapes and squeezed them into the cup and gave it to him."

¹²Joseph said, "This is what it means: the three branches are three days. ¹³In three days the king will release you, pardon you, and restore you to your position. You will give him his cup as you did before when you were his wine steward. ¹⁴But please remember me when everything is going well for you, and please be kind enough to mention me to the king and help me get out of this prison. ¹⁵After all, I was kidnapped from the land of the Hebrews, and even here in Egypt I didn't do anything to deserve being put in prison."

¹⁶When the chief baker saw that the interpretation of the wine steward's dream was favorable, he said to Joseph, "I had a dream too; I was carrying three breadbaskets on my head. ¹⁷In the top basket there were all kinds of baked goods for the king, and the birds were eating them."

¹⁸Joseph answered, "This is what it means: the three baskets are three days. ¹⁹In three days the king will release you—and have your

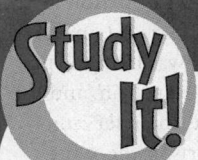

Catching Dreams

Long ago, a spiritual leader of the Lakota people, a Native American nation, had a vision of a spider named Iktomi who spoke in a sacred language. Iktomi took a willow hoop with beads, feathers, and horsehair on it. He began to spin a web as he spoke to the leader about the cycle of life and good and bad dreams. He said that the good dreams will lead a person in the right direction. Bad dreams will lead a person astray.

Iktomi gave the leader the hoop, which was a perfect circle with a hole in the center of the web. He told the leader that if he believed in the Great Spirit, the web would catch his good dreams, and he would lead his people well. The bad ones would pass through the hole in the center and disappear with the morning sun.

Even today, Lakota people—as well as many other people—hang dream catchers in their homes to sift their dreams and visions. They believe that dreams are messages from the Great Spirit, whom we call God. Their belief reflects the Bible stories of people like Joseph who had the gift of interpreting dreams as messages from God.

— Genesis 41:1–36

gave a banquet for all his officials; he released his wine steward and his chief baker and brought them before his officials. 21He restored the wine steward to his former position, 22but he executed the chief baker. It all happened just as Joseph had said. 23But the wine steward never gave Joseph another thought—he forgot all about him.

Joseph Interprets the King's Dreams

41 1After two years had passed, the king of Egypt dreamed that he was standing by the Nile River, 2when seven cows, fat and sleek, came up out of the river and began to feed on the grass. 3Then seven other cows came up; they were thin and bony. They came and stood by the other cows on the riverbank, 4and the thin cows ate up the fat cows. Then the king woke up. 5He fell asleep again and had another dream. Seven heads of grain, full and ripe, were growing on one stalk. 6Then seven other heads of grain sprouted, thin and scorched by the desert wind, 7and the thin heads of grain swallowed the full ones. The king woke up and realized that he had been dreaming. 8In the morning he was worried, so he sent for all the magicians and wise men of Egypt. He told them his dreams, but no one could explain them to him.

9Then the wine steward said to the king, "I must confess today that I have done wrong. 10You were angry with the chief baker and me, and you put us in prison in the house of the captain of the guard. 11One night each of us had a dream, and the dreams had different meanings. 12A young Hebrew was there with us, a slave of the captain of the guard. We told him our dreams, and he interpreted them for us. 13Things turned out just as he said: you restored me to my position, but you executed the baker."

14The king sent for Joseph, and he was immediately brought from the prison. After he had shaved and changed his clothes, he

head cut off! Then he will hang your body on a pole, and the birds will eat your flesh."

20On his birthday three days later the king

41:8 Dan 2:2

HIGHLIGHTS IN JOSEPH'S LIFE (37—46)
(Numbers refer to chapter and verse in Genesis)

came into the king's presence. ¹⁵The king said to him, "I have had a dream, and no one can explain it. I have been told that you can interpret dreams."

¹⁶Joseph answered, "I cannot, Your Majesty, but God will give a favorable interpretation."

¹⁷The king said, "I dreamed that I was standing on the bank of the Nile, ¹⁸when

seven cows, fat and sleek, came up out of the river and began feeding on the grass. ¹⁹Then seven other cows came up which were thin and bony. They were the poorest cows I have ever seen anywhere in Egypt. ²⁰The thin cows ate up the fat ones, ²¹but no one would have known it, because they looked just as bad as before. Then I woke up. ²²I also dreamed that I saw seven heads of grain which were full and ripe, growing on one stalk. 23 Then seven heads of grain sprouted, thin and scorched by the desert wind, 24 and the thin heads of grain swallowed the full ones. I told the dreams to the magicians, but none of them could explain them to me."

25 Joseph said to the king, "The two dreams mean the same thing; God has told you what he is going to do. 26 The seven fat cows are seven years, and the seven full heads of grain are also seven years; they have the same meaning. 27 The seven thin cows which came up later and the seven thin heads of grain scorched by the desert wind are seven years of famine. 28 It is just as I told you— God has shown you what he is going to do. 29 There will be seven years of great plenty in all the land of Egypt. 30 After that, there will be seven years of famine, and all the good years will be forgotten, because the famine will ruin the country. 31 The time of plenty will be entirely forgotten, because the famine which follows will be so terrible. 32 The repetition of your dream means that the matter is fixed by God and that he will make it happen in the near future.

33 "Now you should choose some man with wisdom and insight and put him in charge of the country. 34 You must also appoint other officials and take a fifth of the crops during the seven years of plenty. 35 Order them to collect all the food during the good years that are coming, and give them authority to store up grain in the cities and guard it. 36 The food will be a reserve supply for the country during the seven years of famine which are going to come on Egypt. In this way the people will not starve."

Joseph Is Made Governor over Egypt

37 The king and his officials approved this plan, 38 and he said to them, "We will never find a better man than Joseph, a man who has God's spirit in him." 39 The king said to Joseph, "God has shown you all this, so it is obvious that you have greater wisdom and insight than anyone else. 40 I will put you in charge of my country, and all my people will

obey your orders. Your authority will be second only to mine. 41 I now appoint you governor over all Egypt." 42 The king removed from his finger the ring engraved with the royal seal and put it on Joseph's finger. He put a fine linen robe on him, and placed a gold chain around his neck. 43 He gave him the second royal chariot to ride in, and his guard of honor went ahead of him and cried out, "Make way! Make way!" And so Joseph was appointed governor over all Egypt. 44 The king said to him, "I am the king—and no one in all Egypt shall so much as lift a hand or a foot without your permission." 45-46 He gave Joseph the Egyptian name Zaphenath Paneah, and he gave him a wife, Asenath, the daughter of Potiphera, a priest in the city of Heliopolis.

Joseph was thirty years old when he began to serve the king of Egypt. He left the king's court and traveled all over the land. 47 During the seven years of plenty the land produced abundant crops, 48 all of which Joseph collected and stored in the cities. In each city he stored the food from the fields around it. 49 There was so much grain that Joseph stopped measuring it—it was like the sand of the sea.

50 Before the years of famine came, Joseph had two sons by Asenath. 51 He said, "God has made me forget all my sufferings and all my father's family"; so he named his first son Manasseh.[t] 52 He also said, "God has given me children in the land of my trouble"; so he named his second son Ephraim.[u]

53 The seven years of plenty that the land of Egypt had enjoyed came to an end, 54 and the seven years of famine began, just as Joseph had said. There was famine in every other country, but there was food throughout Egypt. 55 When the Egyptians began to be hungry, they cried out to the king for food. So he ordered them to go to Joseph and do what he told them. 56 The famine grew worse and spread over the whole country, so Joseph opened all the storehouses and sold grain to the Egyptians. 57 People came to Egypt from all over the world to buy grain from Joseph, because the famine was severe everywhere.

---

[t] **41:51** MANASSEH: *This name sounds like the Hebrew for "cause to forget."* [u] **41:51** EPHRAIM: *This name sounds like the Hebrew for "give children."*
41:40 Acts 7:10   **41:42** Dan 5:29   **41:54** Acts 7:11

Joseph's Brothers Go to Egypt to Buy Grain

42 ¹When Jacob learned that there was grain in Egypt, he said to his sons, "Why don't you do something? ²I hear that there is grain in Egypt; go there and buy some to keep us from starving to death." ³So Joseph's ten half brothers went to buy grain in Egypt, ⁴but Jacob did not send Joseph's full brother Benjamin with them, because he was afraid that something might happen to him.

⁵The sons of Jacob came with others to buy grain, because there was famine in the land of Canaan. ⁶Joseph, as governor of the land of Egypt, was selling grain to people from all over the world. So Joseph's brothers came and bowed down before him with their faces to the ground. ⁷When Joseph saw his brothers, he recognized them, but he acted as if he did not know them. He asked them harshly, "Where do you come from?"

"We have come from Canaan to buy food," they answered.

⁸Although Joseph recognized his brothers, they did not recognize him. ⁹He remembered the dreams he had dreamed about them and said, "You are spies; you have come to find out where our country is weak."

¹⁰"No, sir," they answered. "We have come as your slaves, to buy food. ¹¹We are all brothers. We are not spies, sir, we are honest men."

¹²Joseph said to them, "No! You have come to find out where our country is weak."

¹³They said, "We were twelve brothers in all, sir, sons of the same man in the land of Canaan. One brother is dead, and the youngest is now with our father."

¹⁴"It is just as I said," Joseph answered. "You are spies. ¹⁵This is how you will be tested: I swear by the name of the king that you will never leave unless your youngest brother comes here. ¹⁶One of you must go and get him. The rest of you will be kept under guard until the truth of what you say can be tested. Otherwise, as sure as the king

The Great River of Blessings

People were starving. There just was not enough food to feed everyone. A drought made growing crops difficult. Many people outside of Egypt went there to see if they could buy grain. Thanks to Joseph the Egyptians had storehouses of grain. He shared it with both Egyptians and non-Egyptians.

The Egyptians had the Nile River to thank for their good fortune. The Nile is the longest river in the world, and the land along the river is rich and fertile. So even when a drought hit the land, the river provided water for the crops.

God's creation provides plenty of food for the people of the world. Unfortunately, those countries that are blessed with riches often do not share with struggling countries. Even in our own country, every day people go hungry while others eat too much, waste food, or throw it away.

What can you do to make a difference in the world's hunger problem? What can you do to help with hunger in your own city or community?

— Genesis 42:1–11

lives, you are spies." ¹⁷With that, he put them in prison for three days.

¹⁸On the third day Joseph said to them, "I am a God-fearing man, and I will spare your lives on one condition. ¹⁹To prove that you

42:2 Acts 7:12   **42:9** Gen 37:5–10

Remember Joseph's dream in Genesis 37:5–11? It comes true in Egypt (see Genesis 42:6). But this time, Joseph doesn't brag about it.

are honest, one of you will stay in the prison where you have been kept; the rest of you may go and take back to your starving families the grain that you have bought. [20] Then you must bring your youngest brother to me. This will prove that you have been telling the truth, and I will not put you to death."

They agreed to this [21] and said to one another, "Yes, now we are suffering the consequences of what we did to our brother; we saw the great trouble he was in when he begged for help, but we would not listen. That is why we are in this trouble now."

[22] Reuben said, "I told you not to harm the boy, but you wouldn't listen. And now we are being paid back for his death." [23] Joseph understood what they said, but they did not know it, because they had been speaking to him through an interpreter. [24] Joseph left them and began to cry. When he was able to speak again, he came back, picked out Simeon, and had him tied up in front of them.

Joseph's Brothers Return to Canaan

[25] Joseph gave orders to fill his brothers' packs with grain, to put each man's money back in his sack, and to give them food for the trip. This was done. [26] The brothers loaded their donkeys with the grain they had bought, and then they left. [27] At the place where they spent the night, one of them opened his sack to feed his donkey and found his money at the top of the sack. [28] "My money has been returned to me," he called to his brothers. "Here it is in my sack!" Their hearts sank, and in fear they asked one another, "What has God done to us?"

[29] When they came to their father Jacob in Canaan, they told him all that had happened to them: [30] "The governor of Egypt spoke harshly to us and accused us of spying against his country. [31] 'We are not spies,' we answered, 'we are honest men. [32] We were twelve brothers in all, sons of the same

father. One brother is dead, and the youngest is still in Canaan with our father.' [33] The man answered, 'This is how I will find out if you are honest men: One of you will stay with me; the rest will take grain for your starving families and leave. [34] Bring your youngest brother to me. Then I will know that you are not spies, but honest men; I will give your brother back to you, and you can stay here and trade.' "

[35] Then when they emptied out their sacks, every one of them found his bag of money; and when they saw the money, they and their father Jacob were afraid. [36] Their father said to them, "Do you want to make me lose all my children? Joseph is gone; Simeon is gone; and now you want to take away Benjamin. I am the one who suffers!"

[37] Reuben said to his father, "If I do not bring Benjamin back to you, you can kill my two sons. Put him in my care, and I will bring him back."

[38] But Jacob said, "My son cannot go with you; his brother is dead, and he is the only one left. Something might happen to him on the way. I am an old man, and the sorrow you would cause me would kill me."

Joseph's Brothers Return to Egypt with Benjamin

43 [1] The famine in Canaan got worse, [2] and when the family of Jacob had eaten all the grain which had been brought from Egypt, Jacob said to his sons, "Go back and buy a little food for us."

[3] Judah said to him, "The man sternly warned us that we would not be admitted to his presence unless we had our brother with us. [4] If you are willing to send our brother with us, we will go and buy food for you. [5] If you are not willing, we will not go, because the man told us we would not be admitted to his presence unless our brother was with us."

[6] Jacob said, "Why did you cause me so much trouble by telling the man that you had another brother?"

42:22 Gen 37:21, 22

Genesis 43:34 says Benjamin was served five times as much food as the others. It was just a way of saying "much more."

7They answered, "The man kept asking about us and our family, 'Is your father still living? Do you have another brother?' We had to answer his questions. How could we know that he would tell us to bring our brother with us?"

8Judah said to his father, "Send the boy with me, and we will leave at once. Then none of us will starve to death. **9**I will pledge my own life, and you can hold me responsible for him. If I do not bring him back to you safe and sound, I will always bear the blame. **10**If we had not waited so long, we could have been there and back twice by now."

11Their father said to them, "If that is how it has to be, then take the best products of the land in your packs as a present for the governor: a little resin, a little honey, spices, pistachio nuts, and almonds. **12**Take with you also twice as much money, because you must take back the money that was returned in the top of your sacks. Maybe it was a mistake. **13**Take your brother and return at once. **14**May Almighty God cause the man to have pity on you, so that he will give Benjamin and your other brother back to you. As for me, if I must lose my children, I must lose them."

15So the brothers took the gifts and twice as much money, and set out for Egypt with Benjamin. There they presented themselves to Joseph. **16**When Joseph saw Benjamin with them, he said to the servant in charge of his house, "Take these men to my house. They are going to eat with me at noon, so kill an animal and prepare it." **17**The servant did as he was commanded and took the brothers to Joseph's house.

18As they were being brought to the house, they were afraid and thought, "We are being brought here because of the money that was returned in our sacks the first time. They will suddenly attack us, take our donkeys, and make us his slaves." **19**So at the door of the house, they said to the servant in charge, **20**"If you please, sir, we came here once before to buy food. **21**When we set up camp on the way home, we opened our sacks, and each man found his money in the top of his sack—every bit of it. We have brought it back to you. **22**We have also brought some more money with us to buy

more food. We do not know who put our money back in our sacks."

23The servant said, "Don't worry. Don't be afraid. Your God, the God of your father, must have put the money in your sacks for you. I received your payment." Then he brought Simeon to them.

24The servant took the brothers into the house. He gave them water so that they could wash their feet, and he fed their donkeys. **25**They got their gifts ready to present to Joseph when he arrived at noon, because they had been told that they were to eat with him. **26**When Joseph got home, they took the gifts into the house to him and bowed down to the ground before him. **27**He asked about their health and then said, "You told me about your old father—how is he? Is he still alive and well?"

28They answered, "Your humble servant, our father, is still alive and well." And they knelt and bowed down before him.

29When Joseph saw his brother Benjamin, he said, "So this is your youngest brother, the one you told me about. God bless you, my son." **30**Then Joseph left suddenly, because his heart was full of tender feelings for his brother. He was about to break down, so he went to his room and cried. **31**After he had washed his face, he came out, and controlling himself, he ordered the meal to be served. **32**Joseph was served at one table and his brothers at another. The Egyptians who were eating there were served separately, because they considered it beneath their dignity to eat with Hebrews. **33**The brothers had been seated at the table, facing Joseph, in the order of their age from the oldest to the youngest. When they saw how they had been seated, they looked at one another in amazement. **34**Food was served to them from Joseph's table, and Benjamin was served five times as much as the rest of them. So they ate and drank with Joseph until they were drunk.

The Missing Cup

44 **1**Joseph commanded the servant in charge of his house, "Fill the men's sacks with as much food as they can carry, and put each man's money in the top of his

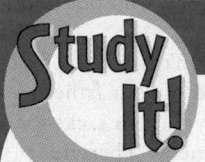

Another Name for the Israelites

You may have noticed that the word *Hebrew* is used several times in Genesis to refer to Abraham, Jacob, and Jacob's sons. It is a name that foreigners used to refer to Abraham and his descendants. They were called Hebrews before they were called Israelites. It described the Chosen People as an ethnic group, just as we would use terms like Hmong or Hispanic to describe a person's ethnicity.

Hebrew is also the name of the language of the Jewish people and is still used in Jewish worship around the world.

— Genesis 43:32

sack. 2Put my silver cup in the top of the youngest brother's sack, together with the money for his grain." He did as he was told. 3Early in the morning the brothers were sent on their way with their donkeys. 4When they had gone only a short distance from the city, Joseph said to the servant in charge of his house, "Hurry after those men. When you catch up with them, ask them, 'Why have you paid back evil for good? 5Why did you steal my master's silver cup?*v* It is the one he drinks from, the one he uses for divination. You have committed a serious crime!' "

6When the servant caught up with them, he repeated these words. 7They answered him, "What do you mean, sir, by talking like this? We swear that we have done no such thing. 8You know that we brought back to you from the land of Canaan the money we found in the top of our sacks. Why then should we steal silver or gold from your master's house? 9Sir, if any one of us is found to have it, he will be put to death, and the rest of us will become your slaves."

10He said, "I agree; but only the one who has taken the cup will become my slave, and the rest of you can go free." 11So they quickly lowered their sacks to the ground, and each man opened his sack. 12Joseph's servant searched carefully, beginning with the oldest and ending with the youngest, and the cup was found in Benjamin's sack. 13The brothers tore their clothes in sorrow, loaded their donkeys, and returned to the city.

14When Judah and his brothers came to Joseph's house, he was still there. They bowed down before him, 15and Joseph said, "What have you done? Didn't you know that a man in my position could find you out by practicing divination?"

16"What can we say to you, sir?" Judah answered. "How can we argue? How can we clear ourselves? God has uncovered our guilt. All of us are now your slaves and not just the one with whom the cup was found."

17Joseph said, "Oh, no! I would never do that! Only the one who had the cup will be my slave. The rest of you may go back safe and sound to your father."

Judah Pleads for Benjamin

18Judah went up to Joseph and said, "Please, sir, allow me to speak with you freely. Don't be angry with me; you are like the king himself. 19Sir, you asked us, 'Do you have a father or another brother?' 20We answered, 'We have a father who is old and a younger brother, born to him in his old age. The boy's brother is dead, and he is the only one of his mother's children still alive; his father loves him very much.' 21Sir, you told us to bring him here, so that you could see him, 22and we answered that the boy could not leave his father; if he did, his father would die. 23Then you said, 'You will not be admitted to my presence again unless your youngest brother comes with you.'

24"When we went back to our father, we told him what you had said. 25Then he told us to return and buy a little food. 26We

---

v **44:5** *One ancient translation* Why did you steal my master's silver cup?; *Hebrew does not have these words.*

answered, 'We cannot go; we will not be admitted to the man's presence unless our youngest brother is with us. We can go only if our youngest brother goes also.' 27 Our father said to us, 'You know that my wife Rachel bore me only two sons. 28 One of them has already left me. He must have been torn to pieces by wild animals, because I have not seen him since he left. 29 If you take this one from me now and something happens to him, the sorrow you would cause me would kill me, as old as I am.'

30-31 "And now, sir," Judah continued, "if I go back to my father without the boy, as soon as he sees that the boy is not with me, he will die. His life is wrapped up in the life of the boy, and he is so old that the sorrow we would cause him would kill him. 32 What is more, I pledged my life to my father for the boy. I told him that if I did not bring the boy back to him, I would bear the blame all my life. 33 And now, sir, I will stay here as your slave in place of the boy; let him go back with his brothers. 34 How can I go back to my father if the boy is not with me? I cannot bear to see this disaster come upon my father."

Joseph Tells His Brothers Who He Is

45 1 Joseph was no longer able to control his feelings in front of his servants, so he ordered them all to leave the room. No one else was with him when Joseph told his brothers who he was. 2 He cried with such loud sobs that the Egyptians heard it, and the news was taken to the king's palace. 3 Joseph said to his brothers, "I am Joseph. Is my father still alive?" But when his brothers heard this, they were so terrified that they could not answer. 4 Then Joseph said to them, "Please come closer." They did, and he said, "I am your brother Joseph, whom you sold into Egypt. 5 Now do not be upset or blame yourselves because you sold me here. It was really God who sent me ahead of you to save people's lives. 6 This is

only the second year of famine in the land; there will be five more years in which there will be neither plowing nor reaping. 7 God sent me ahead of you to rescue you in this amazing way and to make sure that you and your descendants survive. 8 So it was not really you who sent me here, but God. He has made me the king's highest official. I am in charge of his whole country; I am the ruler of all Egypt.

9 "Now hurry back to my father and tell him that this is what his son Joseph says: 'God has made me ruler of all Egypt; come to me without delay. 10 You can live in the region of Goshen, where you can be near me—you, your children, your grandchildren, your sheep, your goats, your cattle, and everything else that you have. 11 If you are in Goshen, I can take care of you. There will still be five years of famine; and I do not want you, your family, and your livestock to starve.' "

12 Joseph continued, "Now all of you, and you too, Benjamin, can see that I am really Joseph. 13 Tell my father how powerful I am here in Egypt and tell him about everything that you have seen. Then hurry and bring him here."

14 He threw his arms around his brother Benjamin and began to cry; Benjamin also cried as he hugged him. 15 Then, still weeping, he embraced each of his brothers and kissed them. After that, his brothers began to talk with him.

16 When the news reached the palace that Joseph's brothers had come, the king and his officials were pleased. 17 He said to Joseph, "Tell your brothers to load their animals and to return to the land of Canaan. 18 Let them get their father and their families and come back here. I will give them the best land in Egypt, and they will have more than enough to live on. 19 Tell them also to take wagons with them from Egypt for their wives and small children and to bring their father with them. 20 They are not to worry about leaving

45:1 Acts 7:13   45:9–11 Acts 7:14

Pray It!

The Way to Peace

Joseph had every reason to get even with his brothers, and he had the power to do it. But instead Joseph used his power to reunite his family. He made his father, Jacob, a very happy man in his old age. Joseph knew that revenge does not bring peace. Only forgiveness does.

The next time you want to get even with someone, think about Joseph and his brothers. Then say this famous prayer for peace, which is attributed to Saint Francis of Assisi:

> Lord, make me an instrument of your peace:
> where there is hatred, let me sow love;
> where there is injury, pardon;
> where there is doubt, faith;
> where there is despair, hope;
> where there is darkness, light;
> and where there is sadness, joy.
> O Divine Master,
> grant that I may not so much seek
> to be consoled as to console,
> to be understood as to understand,
> to be loved as to love.
> For it is in giving that we receive,
> it is in pardoning that we are pardoned,
> and it is in dying that we are born to eternal life.

— Genesis, chapter 45

their possessions behind; the best in the whole land of Egypt will be theirs."

21 Jacob's sons did as they were told. Joseph gave them wagons, as the king had ordered, and food for the trip. 22 He also gave each of them a change of clothes, but he gave Benjamin three hundred pieces of silver and five changes of clothes. 23 He sent his father ten donkeys loaded with the best Egyptian goods and ten donkeys loaded with grain, bread, and other food for the trip. 24 He sent his brothers off and as they left, he said to them, "Don't quarrel on the way."

25 They left Egypt and went back home to their father Jacob in Canaan. 26 "Joseph is still alive!" they told him. "He is the ruler of all

Egypt!" Jacob was stunned and could not believe them.

27 But when they told him all that Joseph had said to them, and when he saw the wagons which Joseph had sent to take him to Egypt, he recovered from the shock. 28 "My son Joseph is still alive!" he said. "This is all I could ask for! I must go and see him before I die."

Jacob and His Family Go to Egypt

46 ¹Jacob packed up all he had and went to Beersheba, where he offered sacrifices to the God of his father

Journeys to buy grain from Egypt in times of famine were so common that they are illustrated in Egyptian art.

Isaac. 2God spoke to him in a vision at night and called, "Jacob, Jacob!"

"Yes, here I am," he answered.

3"I am God, the God of your father," he said. "Do not be afraid to go to Egypt; I will make your descendants a great nation there. 4I will go with you to Egypt, and I will bring your descendants back to this land. Joseph will be with you when you die."

5Jacob set out from Beersheba. His sons put him, their small children, and their wives in the wagons which the king of Egypt had sent. 6They took their livestock and the possessions they had acquired in Canaan and went to Egypt. Jacob took all his descendants with him: 7his sons, his grandsons, his daughters, and his granddaughters.

8The members of Jacob's family who went to Egypt with him were his oldest son Reuben 9and Reuben's sons: Hanoch, Pallu, Hezron, and Carmi. 10Simeon and his sons: Jemuel, Jamin, Ohad, Jachin, Zohar, and Shaul, the son of a Canaanite woman. 11Levi and his sons: Gershon, Kohath, and Merari. 12Judah and his sons: Shelah, Perez, and Zerah. (Judah's other sons, Er and Onan, had died in Canaan.) Perez' sons were Hezron and Hamul. 13Issachar and his sons: Tola, Puah, Jashub, and Shimron. 14Zebulun and his sons: Sered, Elon, and Jahleel. 15These are the sons that Leah had borne to Jacob in Mesopotamia, besides his daughter Dinah. In all, his descendants by Leah numbered thirty-three.

16Gad and his sons: Zephon, Haggi, Shuni, Ezbon, Eri, Arod, and Areli. 17Asher and his sons: Imnah, Ishvah, Ishvi, Beriah, and their sister Serah. Beriah's sons were Heber and Malchiel. 18These sixteen are the descendants of Jacob by Zilpah, the slave woman whom Laban gave to his daughter Leah.

19Jacob's wife Rachel bore him two sons: Joseph and Benjamin. 20In Egypt Joseph had two sons, Manasseh and Ephraim, by Asenath, the daughter of Potiphera, a priest in Heliopolis. 21Benjamin's sons were Bela, Becher, Ashbel, Gera, Naaman, Ehi, Rosh, Muppim, Huppim, and Ard. 22These fourteen are the descendants of Jacob by Rachel.

23Dan and his son Hushim. 24Naphtali and his sons: Jahzeel, Guni, Jezer, and Shillem. 25These seven are the descendants of Jacob by Bilhah, the slave woman whom Laban gave to his daughter Rachel.

26The total number of the direct descendants of Jacob who went to Egypt was sixty-six, not including his sons' wives. 27Two sons were born to Joseph in Egypt, bringing to seventy the total number of Jacob's family who went there.

Jacob and His Family in Egypt

28Jacob sent Judah ahead to ask Joseph to meet them in Goshen. When they arrived, 29Joseph got in his chariot and went to Goshen to meet his father. When they met, Joseph threw his arms around his father's neck and cried for a long time. 30Jacob said to Joseph, "I am ready to die, now that I have seen you and know that you are still alive."

31Then Joseph said to his brothers and the rest of his father's family, "I must go and tell the king that my brothers and all my father's family, who were living in Canaan, have come to me. 32I will tell him that you are shepherds and take care of livestock and that you have brought your flocks and herds and everything else that belongs to you. 33When the king calls for you and asks what your occupation is, 34be sure to tell him that you have taken care of livestock all your lives, just as your ancestors did. In this way he will let you live in the region of Goshen." Joseph said this because Egyptians will have nothing to do with shepherds.

47 1So Joseph took five of his brothers and went to the king. He told him, "My father and my brothers have come from Canaan with their flocks, their herds, and all that they own. They are now in the region of Goshen." 2He then presented his brothers to the king. 3The king asked them, "What is your occupation?"

"We are shepherds, sir, just as our ancestors were," they answered. 4"We have come to live in this country, because in the land of Canaan the famine is so severe that there is no pasture for our flocks. Please give us permission to live in the region of Goshen." ⁵The king said to Joseph, "Now that your father and your brothers have arrived, ⁶the land of Egypt is theirs. Let them settle in the region of Goshen, the best part of the land. And if there are any capable men among them, put them in charge of my own livestock."

⁷Then Joseph brought his father Jacob and presented him to the king. Jacob gave the king his blessing, ⁸and the king asked him, "How old are you?"

⁹Jacob answered, "My life of wandering has lasted a hundred and thirty years. Those years have been few and difficult, unlike the long years of my ancestors in their wanderings." ¹⁰Jacob gave the king a farewell blessing and left. ¹¹Then Joseph settled his father and his brothers in Egypt, giving them property in the best of the land near the city of Rameses, as the king had commanded. ¹²Joseph provided food for his father, his brothers, and all the rest of his father's family, including the very youngest.

The Famine

¹³The famine was so severe that there was no food anywhere, and the people of Egypt and Canaan became weak with hunger. ¹⁴As they bought grain, Joseph collected all the money and took it to the palace. ¹⁵When all the money in Egypt and Canaan was spent, the Egyptians came to Joseph and said, "Give us food! Don't let us die. Do something! Our money is all gone."

¹⁶Joseph answered, "Bring your livestock; I will give you food in exchange for it if your money is all gone." ¹⁷So they brought their livestock to Joseph, and he gave them food in exchange for their horses, sheep, goats, cattle, and donkeys. That year he supplied them with food in exchange for all their livestock.

¹⁸The following year they came to him and said, "We will not hide the fact from you, sir, that our money is all gone and our livestock belongs to you. There is nothing left to give you except our bodies and our lands. ¹⁹Don't let us die. Do something!

Don't let our fields be deserted. Buy us and our land in exchange for food. We will be the king's slaves, and he will own our land. Give us grain to keep us alive and seed so that we can plant our fields."

²⁰Joseph bought all the land in Egypt for the king. Every Egyptian was forced to sell his land, because the famine was so severe; and all the land became the king's property. ²¹Joseph made slaves of the people from one end of Egypt to the other. ²²The only land he did not buy was the land that belonged to the priests. They did not have to sell their lands, because the king gave them an allowance to live on. ²³Joseph said to the people, "You see, I have now bought you and your lands for the king. Here is seed for you to sow in your fields. ²⁴At the time of harvest you must give one-fifth to the king. You can use the rest for seed and for food for yourselves and your families."

²⁵They answered, "You have saved our lives; you have been good to us, sir, and we will be the king's slaves." ²⁶So Joseph made it a law for the land of Egypt that one-fifth of the harvest should belong to the king. This law still remains in force today. Only the lands of the priests did not become the king's property.

Jacob's Last Request

²⁷The Israelites lived in Egypt in the region of Goshen, where they became rich and had many children. ²⁸Jacob lived in Egypt seventeen years, until he was a hundred and forty-seven years old. ²⁹When the time drew near for him to die, he called for his son Joseph and said to him, "Place your hand between my thighsʷ and make a solemn vow that you will not bury me in Egypt. ³⁰I want to be buried where my fathers are; carry me out of Egypt and bury me where they are buried."

Joseph answered, "I will do as you say."

³¹Jacob said, "Make a vow that you will." Joseph made the vow, and Jacob gave thanks there on his bed.

ʷ **47:29** PLACE ... THIGHS: *See 24:2.*
47:29, 30 Gen 49:29–32; 50:6

Jacob Blesses Ephraim and Manasseh

48 ¹Some time later Joseph was told that his father was ill. So he took his two sons, Manasseh and Ephraim, and went to see Jacob. ²When Jacob was told that his son Joseph had come to see him, he gathered his strength and sat up in bed. ³Jacob said to Joseph, "Almighty God appeared to me at Luz in the land of Canaan and blessed me. ⁴He said to me, 'I will give you many children, so that your descendants will become many nations; I will give this land to your descendants as their possession forever.' "

⁵Jacob continued, "Joseph, your two sons, who were born to you in Egypt before I came here, belong to me; Ephraim and Manasseh are just as much my sons as Reuben and Simeon. ⁶If you have any more sons, they will not be considered mine; the inheritance they get will come through Ephraim and Manasseh. ⁷I am doing this because of your mother Rachel. To my great sorrow she died in the land of Canaan, not far from Ephrath, as I was returning from Mesopotamia. I buried her there beside the road to Ephrath." (Ephrath is now known as Bethlehem.)

⁸When Jacob saw Joseph's sons, he asked, "Who are these boys?"

⁹Joseph answered, "These are my sons, whom God has given me here in Egypt."

Jacob said, "Bring them to me so that I may bless them." ¹⁰Jacob's eyesight was failing because of his age, and he could not see very well. Joseph brought the boys to him, and he hugged them and kissed them. ¹¹Jacob said to Joseph, "I never expected to see you again, and now God has even let me see your children." ¹²Then Joseph took them from Jacob's lap and bowed down before him with his face to the ground.

¹³Joseph put Ephraim at Jacob's left and Manasseh at his right. ¹⁴But Jacob crossed his hands, and put his right hand on the head of Ephraim, even though he was the younger, and his left hand on the head of Manasseh, who was the older. ¹⁵Then he blessed Joseph:ˣ

"May God . . . bless these boys!" (48:15)

"May God, whom my fathers Abraham
    and Isaac served, bless these boys!
May God, who has led me to this very
    day, bless them!
¹⁶May the angel, who has rescued me from
    all harm, bless them!
May my name and the name of my
    fathers Abraham and Isaac live on
    through these boys!
May they have many children, many
    descendants!"

¹⁷Joseph was upset when he saw that his father had put his right hand on Ephraim's head; so he took his father's hand to move it from Ephraim's head to the head of Manasseh. ¹⁸He said to his father, "Not that way, father. This is the older boy; put your right hand on his head."

¹⁹His father refused, saying, "I know, son, I know. Manasseh's descendants will also become a great people. But his younger brother will be greater than he, and his descendants will become great nations."

²⁰So he blessed them that day, saying, "The

ˣ **48:15** JOSEPH: *In blessing Ephraim and Manasseh, Jacob was in fact blessing Joseph.*
48:3, 4 Gen 28:13, 14   **48:7** Gen 35:16–19   **48:20** Heb 11:21

Jacob adopted Joseph's sons as his own. Read about it in Genesis 48:5–7.

Israelites will use your names when they pronounce blessings. They will say, 'May God make you like Ephraim and Manasseh.' " In this way Jacob put Ephraim before Manasseh.

21 Then Jacob said to Joseph, "As you see, I am about to die, but God will be with you and will take you back to the land of your ancestors. 22 It is to you and not to your brothers that I am giving Shechem, that fertile region which I took from the Amorites with my sword and my bow."

The Last Words of Jacob

49 1 Jacob called for his sons and said, "Gather around, and I will tell you what will happen to you in the future:

2 "Come together and listen, sons of Jacob.
Listen to your father Israel.

3 "Reuben, my first-born, you are my
strength
And the first child of my manhood,
The proudest and strongest of all my sons.
4 You are like a raging flood,
But you will not be the most important,
For you slept with my concubine
And dishonored your father's bed.

5 "Simeon and Levi are brothers.
They use their weapons to commit
violence.
6 I will not join in their secret talks,
Nor will I take part in their meetings,
For they killed people in anger
And they crippled bulls for sport.
7 A curse be on their anger, because it is so
fierce,
And on their fury, because it is so cruel.
I will scatter them throughout the land of
Israel.
I will disperse them among its people.

8 "Judah, your brothers will praise you.
You hold your enemies by the neck.

Your brothers will bow down before you.
9 Judah is like a lion,
Killing his victim and returning to his den,
Stretching out and lying down.
No one dares disturb him.
10 Judah will hold the royal scepter,
And his descendants will always rule.
Nations will bring him tribute*y*
And bow in obedience before him.
11 He ties his young donkey to a grapevine,
To the very best of the vines.
He washes his clothes in blood-red wine.
12 His eyes are bloodshot from drinking
wine,
His teeth white from drinking milk. *z*

13 "Zebulun will live beside the sea.
His shore will be a haven for ships.
His territory will reach as far as Sidon.

14 "Issachar is no better than a donkey
That lies stretched out between its
saddlebags.
15 But he sees that the resting place is good
And that the land is delightful.
So he bends his back to carry the load
And is forced to work as a slave.

16 "Dan will be a ruler for his people.
They will be like the other tribes of Israel.
17 Dan will be a snake at the side of the road,
A poisonous snake beside the path,
That strikes at the horse's heel,
So that the rider is thrown off backward.

18 "I wait for your deliverance, LORD.

19 "Gad will be attacked by a band of
robbers,
But he will turn and pursue them.

20 "Asher's land will produce rich food.
He will provide food fit for a king.

21 "Naphtali is a deer that runs free,
Who bears lovely fawns. *a*

22 "Joseph is like a wild donkey by a spring,

---

y **49:10** *Probable text* Nations . . . tribute; *Hebrew unclear.*   *z* **49:12** His eyes . . . milk; *or* His eyes are darker than wine, his teeth are whiter than milk.   *a* **49:21** Naphtali . . . fawns *or* Naphtali is a spreading tree that puts out lovely branches.
49:9 Num 24:9; Rev 5:5

Jacob's sons are the patriarchs, or fathers, of families that will become the Twelve Tribes of Israel.

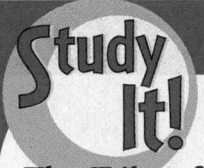

The Tribe of Judah

In his final words, Jacob blesses or curses each of his sons. Some of the blessings also include predictions of what will happen to each of the twelve tribes that descend from his sons. For example, Jacob predicted that people will bring Judah tribute and bow down before him. It was his way of saying that the tribe of Judah would become the strongest of the Twelve Tribes of Israel. He also predicted that Judah "will hold the royal scepter" (Genesis 49:10). This was another way of saying that a descendant of Judah would be king. Sure enough, King David was a descendant of Judah. You can read about him in the Second Book of Samuel.

Jesus was a descendant of David. He is often referred to as the Son of David. Jesus is the one who Jacob predicts "will always rule" (49:10). Jesus is the fulfillment of God's Covenant, or promise, with Abraham and Jacob.

— Genesis 49:8–12

The Almighty God who blesses you
With blessings of rain from above
And of deep waters from beneath the
    ground,
Blessings of many cattle and children,
26 Blessings of grain and flowers, *d*
Blessings of ancient mountains, *e*
Delightful things from everlasting hills.
May these blessings rest on the head of
    Joseph,
On the brow of the one set apart from his
    brothers.

27 "Benjamin is like a vicious wolf.
Morning and evening he kills and
    devours."

28 These are the twelve tribes of Israel, and this is what their father said as he spoke a suitable word of farewell to each son.

The Death and Burial of Jacob

29 Then Jacob commanded his sons, "Now that I am going to join my people in death, bury me with my fathers in the cave that is in the field of Ephron the Hittite, 30 at Machpelah east of Mamre in the land of Canaan. Abraham bought this cave and field from Ephron for a burial ground. 31 That is where they buried Abraham and his wife Sarah; that is where they buried Isaac and his wife Rebecca; and that is where I buried Leah. 32 The field and the cave in it were bought from the Hittites. Bury me there." 33 When Jacob had finished giving instructions to his sons, he lay back down and died.

50 1 Joseph threw himself on his father, crying and kissing his face. 2 Then Joseph gave orders to embalm his father's body. 3 It took forty days, the normal time for embalming. The Egyptians mourned for him seventy days.

4 When the time of mourning was over, Joseph said to the king's officials, "Please take this message to the king: 5 'When my father was about to die, he made me promise him that I would bury him in the tomb which

A wild colt on a hillside. *b*
23 His enemies attack him fiercely
And pursue him with their bows and
    arrows.
24 But his bow remains steady,
And his arms are made strong *c*
By the power of the Mighty God of Jacob,
By the Shepherd, the Protector of Israel.
25 It is your father's God who helps you,

b **49:22** Joseph . . . hillside; *or* Joseph is like a tree by a spring, a fruitful tree that spreads over a wall.
c **49:24** But . . . strong; *or* But their bows were broken and splintered, the muscles of their arms torn apart.
d **49:26** *Probable text* grain and flowers; *Hebrew* your fathers are mightier than.   *e* **49:26** *One ancient translation* ancient mountains; *Hebrew* my ancestors to.
49:30 Gen 23:3–20   **49:31** a Gen 25:9, 10; b Gen 35:29   **49:33** Acts 7:15   **50:5** Gen 47:29–31

he had prepared in the land of Canaan. So please let me go and bury my father, and then I will come back.' "

⁶The king answered, "Go and bury your father, as you promised you would."

⁷So Joseph went to bury his father. All the king's officials, the senior men of his court, and all the leading men of Egypt went with Joseph. ⁸His family, his brothers, and the rest of his father's family all went with him. Only their small children and their sheep, goats, and cattle stayed in the region of Goshen. ⁹Men in chariots and men on horseback also went with him; it was a huge group.

¹⁰When they came to the threshing place at Atad east of the Jordan, they mourned loudly for a long time, and Joseph performed mourning ceremonies for seven days. ¹¹When the citizens of Canaan saw those people mourning at Atad, they said, "What a solemn ceremony of mourning the Egyptians are holding!" That is why the place was named Abel Mizraim.ᶠ

¹²So Jacob's sons did as he had commanded them; ¹³they carried his body to Canaan and buried it in the cave at Machpelah east of Mamre in the field which Abraham had bought from Ephron the Hittite for a burial ground. ¹⁴After Joseph had buried his father, he returned to Egypt with his brothers and all who had gone with him for the funeral.

Joseph Reassures His Brothers

¹⁵After the death of their father, Joseph's brothers said, "What if Joseph still hates us and plans to pay us back for all the harm we did to him?" ¹⁶So they sent a message to Joseph: "Before our father died, ¹⁷he told us to ask you, 'Please forgive the crime your brothers committed when they wronged you.' Now please forgive us the wrong that we, the servants of your father's God, have done." Joseph cried when he received this message.

¹⁸Then his brothers themselves came and

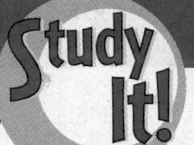

To Be Continued

The Book of Genesis ends on a positive note. Jacob and his family are reunited. He blesses his sons and their children and tells them what they can expect in the future. Then he dies a happy man at a very old age. Joseph's brothers were afraid that Joseph would get even with them after the death of Jacob, but Joseph told them not to be afraid.

Joseph and his brothers and their families continued to live in Egypt, far away from home and far from the land that God promised to Abraham and his descendants. The next book of the Bible, Exodus, is a continuation of the story, long after the death of Joseph and his brothers.

Life will get very difficult for the descendants of Abraham, Isaac, and Jacob. But as always, God will be with them. The main message of Genesis is that God will not abandon his Creation, his promises, or his people.

— Genesis; chapter 50

bowed down before him. "Here we are before you as your slaves," they said.

¹⁹But Joseph said to them, "Don't be afraid; I can't put myself in the place of God. ²⁰You plotted evil against me, but God turned it into good, in order to preserve the lives of many people who are alive today because of what happened. ²¹You have nothing to fear. I will take care of you and your children." So he reassured them with kind words that touched their hearts.

ᶠ**50:11** ABEL MIZRAIM: *This name sounds like the Hebrew for "mourning of the Egyptians."*
50:13 Acts 7:16

The Death of Joseph

22Joseph continued to live in Egypt with his father's family; he was a hundred and ten years old when he died. 23He lived to see Ephraim's children and grandchildren. He also lived to receive the children of Machir son of Manasseh into the family. 24He said to his brothers, "I am about to die, but God will certainly take care of you and lead you out of this land to the land he solemnly promised to Abraham, Isaac, and Jacob." 25Then Joseph asked his people to make a vow. "Promise me," he said, "that when God leads you to that land, you will take my body with you." 26So Joseph died in Egypt at the age of a hundred and ten. They embalmed his body and put it in a coffin.

50:25 Ex 13:19; Josh 24:32; Heb 11:22

Your Next Step Congratulations on finishing the Book of Genesis! Use this space to write your thoughts and questions about this book. If you are following the suggested reading plan, go on to the Book of Exodus to find out how God delivered the people from slavery in Egypt.

A bold escape! A reluctant hero! Spectacular effects! Plagues of insects! Outbursts of rage! Passion and tenderness! Sounds like a blockbuster film, doesn't it? Hollywood film producers thought so too. In fact, only the story of Jesus has probably been the subject of more Bible-based movies than the Book of Exodus.

Aside from some great movie moments, Exodus is the story of how the Israelites came to be God's people. It is a story of slavery and freedom from slavery, promises and broken promises, anger and compassion, disappointment and hope. Led by Moses and his siblings, the Israelites came to know that God loves them, watches over them, and is *always* faithful.

Chap. 14

Head lines

- Midwives Trick Pharaoh, Boy Lives (1:15—2:10)
- God's Voice Heard in Burning Bush! (3:1—4:17)
- Forecast: Hail with a Chance of Locusts (7:14—10:29)
- Angel of Death Passes Over (12:21–42)
- Red Sea Parts for Israelites (14:1–31)
- God Lays Down the Laws (20:1–17)
- Doubting Israelites Worship Gold Calf (32:1–24)

FACTOIDS

Who wrote this book? Exodus was written by an unknown author, possibly a group. The author collected stories that had been passed down for hundreds of years and put them together to make this book.

How does it fit into the Bible? It is the second book of the Bible. It is also the second book of the Pentateuch, that is, the Jewish Torah.

Who are the main characters? Moses, the Israelites, and Yahweh (God)

How is it organized? It has two main sections. The first section is about the freeing of the Israelites from slavery and their journey out of Egypt. The second section begins in chapter 19, when the Israelites reach Mount Sinai.

Important themes
- God frees people from slavery.
- God is always with the Chosen People, taking care of them.
- The Covenant between God and his people is rooted in love.

EXODUS

The Israelites Are Treated Cruelly in Egypt

1 ¹ The sons of Jacob who went to Egypt with him, each with his family, were ²Reuben, Simeon, Levi, Judah, ³Issachar, Zebulun, Benjamin, ⁴Dan, Naphtali, Gad, and Asher. ⁵The total number of these people directly descended from Jacob was seventy.ᵃ His son Joseph was already in Egypt. ⁶In the course of time Joseph, his brothers, and all the rest of that generation died, ⁷but their descendants, the Israelites, had many children and became so numerous and strong that Egypt was filled with them.

⁸Then, a new king, who knew nothing about Joseph, came to power in Egypt. ⁹He said to his people, "These Israelites are so numerous and strong that they are a threat to us. ¹⁰In case of war they might join our enemies in order to fight against us, and might escape fromᵇ the country. We must find some way to keep them from becomming even more numerous." ¹¹So the Egyptians put slave drivers over them to crush their spirits with hard labor. The Israelites built the cities of Pithom and Rameses to serve as supply centers for the king. ¹²But the more the Egyptians oppressed the Israelites, the more they increased in number and the farther they spread through the land. The Egyptians came to fear the Israelites ¹³⁻¹⁴and made their lives miserable by forcing them into cruel slavery. They made them work on their building projects and in their fields, and they had no pity on them.

¹⁵Then the king of Egypt spoke to Shiphrah and Puah, the two midwives who helped the Hebrew women. ¹⁶"When you help the Hebrew women give birth," he said to them, "kill the baby if it is a boy; but if it is a girl, let it live." ¹⁷But the midwives were God-fearing and so did not obey the king; instead, they let the boys live. ¹⁸So the king sent for the midwives and asked them, "Why

Live It!

Doing the Right Thing

At the end of the Book of Genesis, life was good for the Israelites. But a few hundred years passed, and life was terrible. They were slaves and were treated cruelly by the Egyptians.

The family of Jacob's descendants—which was big to begin with—grew even bigger. His descendants numbered in the thousands. The Egyptians were afraid that the Israelites would gain power and take over. As a way of controlling the population, Pharaoh told the midwives— women skilled in helping with births—to kill all baby boys born to Hebrew women. Two midwives—Puah and Shiphrah— decided that it was the wrong thing to do. They knew they would be in trouble if Pharaoh found out, so they made up a story about why they did not kill the babies. Because of their decision to do the right thing, a baby boy named Moses grew up to free the Israelites from slavery and lead them out of Egypt.

Doing the right thing is not always easy, but it is always the best choice for those who want to be right with God.

— Exodus 1:15–22

ᵃ **1:5** *One ancient translation* seventy-five *(see Acts 7:14).*   ᵇ **1:10** escape from; *or* take control of.
1:1–4 Gen 46:8–27   **1:7** Acts 7:17   **1:8** Acts 7:18   **1:10** Acts 7:19

are you doing this? Why are you letting the boys live?"

[19]They answered, "The Hebrew women are not like Egyptian women; they give birth easily, and their babies are born before either of us gets there." [20-21]Because the midwives were God-fearing, God was good to them and gave them families of their own. And the Israelites continued to increase and become strong. [22]Finally the king issued a command to all his people: "Take every newborn Hebrew boy and throw him into the Nile, but let all the girls live."

The Birth of Moses

2 [1]During this time a man from the tribe of Levi married a woman of his own tribe, [2]and she bore him a son. When she saw what a fine baby he was, she hid him for three months. [3]But when she could not hide him any longer, she took a basket made of reeds and covered it with tar to make it watertight. She put the baby in it and then placed it in the tall grass at the edge of the river. [4]The baby's sister stood some distance away to see what would happen to him.

[5]The king's daughter came down to the river to bathe, while her servants walked along the bank. Suddenly she noticed the basket in the tall grass and sent a slave

The king's daughter . . . noticed the basket. (2:5)

woman to get it. [6]The princess opened it and saw a baby boy. He was crying, and she felt sorry for him. "This is one of the Hebrew babies," she said.

[7]Then his sister asked her, "Shall I go and call a Hebrew woman to nurse the baby for you?"

[8]"Please do," she answered. So the girl went and brought the baby's own mother. [9]The princess told the woman, "Take this baby and nurse him for me, and I will pay you." So she took the baby and nursed him. [10]Later, when the child was old enough, she took him to the king's daughter, who adopted him as her own son. She said to herself, "I pulled him out of the water, and so I name him Moses."[c]

Moses Escapes to Midian

[11]When Moses had grown up, he went out to visit his people, the Hebrews, and he saw how they were forced to do hard labor. He even saw an Egyptian kill a Hebrew, one of Moses' own people. [12]Moses looked all around, and when he saw that no one was watching, he killed the Egyptian and hid his body in the sand. [13]The next day he went back and saw two Hebrew men fighting. He said to the one who was in the wrong, "Why are you beating up a fellow Hebrew?"

[14]The man answered, "Who made you our ruler and judge? Are you going to kill me just as you killed that Egyptian?" Then Moses was afraid and said to himself, "People have found out what I have done." [15-16]When the king heard about what had happened, he tried to have Moses killed, but Moses fled and went to live in the land of Midian.

One day, when Moses was sitting by a well, seven daughters of Jethro, the priest of Midian, came to draw water and fill the troughs for their father's sheep and goats. [17]But some shepherds drove Jethro's daughters away. Then Moses went to their rescue

[c] **2:10** MOSES: *This name sounds like the Hebrew for "pull out."*
1:22 Acts 7:19   **2:2** Acts 7:20; Heb 11:23   **2:10** Acts 7:21   **2:11–14** Acts 7:23–28   **2:11** Heb 11:24
2:15 Acts 7:29; Heb 11:27

The king wanted all Jewish boys killed because they could be future leaders. Only men were expected to be leaders at that time.

Exodus

Standing Up for Right

Moses had a good life as the adopted son of Pharaoh's daughter. While his fellow Hebrews were working as slaves, Moses had the best of everything. Still, it bothered him when he saw people hurting others.

- When he saw an Egyptian slave master beating a Hebrew slave, he was so angry that he killed the Egyptian (Exodus 2:11–12).
- He stepped in and tried to stop two Hebrews from fighting (2:13).
- He defended seven sisters against some shepherds and helped them get water (2:16–17).

Moses should not have killed the slave master, and he ran away to save his life. God knew that his heart was in the right place, though, and used Moses to lead the people out of Egypt.

When you see someone being hurt by the actions or words of others, how do you react? Do you always stand up for what is right? How is God using you to right the wrongs of the world?

— Exodus 2:11–17

and watered their animals for them. [18]When they returned to their father, he asked, "Why have you come back so early today?"

[19]"An Egyptian rescued us from the shepherds," they answered, "and he even drew water for us and watered our animals."

[20]"Where is he?" he asked his daughters. "Why did you leave the man out there? Go and invite him to eat with us."

[21]So Moses decided to live there, and Jethro gave him his daughter Zipporah in marriage, [22]who bore him a son. Moses said to himself, "I am a foreigner in this land, and so I name him Gershom."[d]

[23]Years later the king of Egypt died, but the Israelites were still groaning under their slavery and cried out for help. Their cry went up to God, [24]who heard their groaning and remembered his covenant with Abraham, Isaac, and Jacob. [25]He saw the slavery of the Israelites and was concerned for them.[e]

God Calls Moses

3 [1]One day while Moses was taking care of the sheep and goats of his father-in-law Jethro, the priest of Midian, he led the flock across the desert and came to Sinai, the holy mountain. [2]There the angel of the LORD appeared to him as a flame coming from the middle of a bush. Moses saw that the bush was on fire but that it was not burning up. [3]"This is strange," he thought. "Why isn't the bush burning up? I will go closer and see."

[4]When the LORD saw that Moses was coming closer, he called to him from the middle of the bush and said, "Moses! Moses!"

He answered, "Yes, here I am."

[5]God said, "Do not come any closer. Take off your sandals, because you are standing on holy ground. [6]I am the God of your ancestors, the God of Abraham, Isaac, and Jacob." So Moses covered his face, because he was afraid to look at God.

[7]Then the LORD said, "I have seen how cruelly my people are being treated in Egypt; I have heard them cry out to be rescued from their slave drivers. I know all about their sufferings, [8]and so I have come down to rescue them from the Egyptians and to bring them out of Egypt to a spacious land, one which is rich and fertile and in which the Canaanites, the Hittites, the Amorites, the Perizzites, the Hivites, and the Jebusites now live. [9]I have indeed heard the cry of my people, and I see how the Egyptians are oppressing them. [10]Now I am

[d] **2:22** GERSHOM: *This name sounds like the Hebrew for "foreigner."* [e] **2:25** was concerned for them; *one ancient translation* revealed himself to them.
2:24 Gen 15:13, 14　**3:2–10** Acts 7:30–34

Exodus

Pray It!

A God of Many Names

When Moses asks for God's name, God tells him it is "I am who I am." Jews consider this name of God to be too sacred to say or even to write. To make sure no one reading the Hebrew Bible accidentally pronounced the name of God, Jewish scholars used the vowel symbols for the word "Lord" when writing the consonants for God's name (YHWH). Readers encountered this unusual spelling in the text would then either say "Lord" or "the Name." In a similar way, many English Bibles signal the specialness of God's name by representing it as "LORD".

God is a God of many names. We call God healer, creator, and comforter. We say God is a God of hope, a wonder worker, and our eternal friend. We talk about God the Father and sometimes also God as Mother.

What names for God do you hear in the words and music during Mass? Which names are most meaningful to you? Make a list of your favorite names for God. Each day, say one name over and over and think about what it means.

— Exodus 3:14

sending you to the king of Egypt so that you can lead my people out of his country."

11 But Moses said to God, "I am nobody. How can I go to the king and bring the Israelites out of Egypt?"

12 God answered, "I will be with you, and when you bring the people out of Egypt, you will worship me on this mountain. That will be the proof that I have sent you."

13 But Moses replied, "When I go to the Israelites and say to them, 'The God of your ancestors sent me to you,' they will ask me, 'What is his name?' So what can I tell them?"

14 God said, "I am who I am. You must tell them: 'The one who is called I AM*f* has sent me to you.' **15** Tell the Israelites that I, the LORD, the God of their ancestors, the God of Abraham, Isaac, and Jacob, have sent you to them. This is my name forever; this is what all future generations are to call me. **16** Go and gather the leaders of Israel together and tell them that I, the LORD, the God of their ancestors, the God of Abraham, Isaac, and Jacob, appeared to you. Tell them that I have come to them and have seen what the Egyptians are doing to them. **17** I

have decided that I will bring them out of Egypt, where they are being treated cruelly, and will take them to a rich and fertile land—the land of the Canaanites, the Hittites, the Amorites, the Perizzites, the Hivites, and the Jebusites.

18 "My people will listen to what you say to them. Then you must go with the leaders

"I am who I am. . . . This is my name forever."
(3:14-15)

f **3:14** I am who I am . . . I AM; *or* I will be who I will be . . . I WILL BE. *"I am" sounds like the Hebrew name Yahweh traditionally transliterated as Jehovah. This name is represented in this translation by "the LORD" in capital letters, following a usage which is widespread in English versions.*
3:13 Ex 6:2, 3   **3:14** Rev 1:4, 8

of Israel to the king of Egypt and say to him, 'The LORD, the God of the Hebrews, has revealed himself to us. Now allow us to travel three days into the desert to offer sacrifices to the LORD, our God.' ¹⁹I know that the king of Egypt will not let you go unless he is forced to do so. ²⁰But I will use my power and will punish Egypt by doing terrifying things there. After that he will let you go.

²¹"I will make the Egyptians respect you so that when my people leave, they will not go empty-handed. ²²Every Israelite woman will go to her Egyptian neighbors and to any Egyptian woman living in her house and will ask for clothing and for gold and silver jewelry. The Israelites will put these things on their sons and daughters and carry away the wealth of the Egyptians."

God Gives Moses Miraculous Power

4 ¹Then Moses answered the LORD, "But suppose the Israelites do not believe me and will not listen to what I say. What shall I do if they say that you did not appear to me?"

²So the LORD asked him, "What are you holding?"

"A walking stick," he answered.

³The LORD said, "Throw it on the ground." When Moses threw it down, it turned into a snake, and he ran away from it. ⁴Then the LORD said to Moses, "Reach down and pick it up by the tail." So Moses reached down and caught it, and it became a walking stick again. ⁵The LORD said, "Do this to prove to the Israelites that the LORD, the God of their ancestors, the God of Abraham, Isaac, and Jacob, has appeared to you."

⁶The LORD spoke to Moses again, "Put your hand inside your robe." Moses obeyed; and when he took his hand out, it was diseased, covered with white spots, like snow. ⁷Then the LORD said, "Put your hand inside your robe again." He did so, and when he took it out this time, it was healthy, just like the rest of his body. ⁸The LORD said, "If they will not believe you or be convinced by the

Moses' Problem

Are you self-conscious about your height or your weight? Do you have a funny scar or wild hair? Do you believe that you're not very smart? Are you afraid of being made fun of? So was Moses.

Moses kept trying to tell God that he was the wrong guy for the job of leading the Israelites out of Egypt. He kept coming up with excuses. In Exodus, chapter 4, we find out that Moses had a speech problem and he was self-conscious about it. "I am a poor speaker, slow and hesitant" (Exodus 4:10). God did not back down though. God knew that Moses could do the job and promised to help him. Aaron would be his assistant, God said. Aaron would do the speaking. Moses would do the leading.

God created Moses—and you—for a purpose. God loves you just the way you are and plans to use every bit of who you are to build a better world. You are a perfect creation in God's eyes—flaws and all.

— Exodus 4:1–17

"To prove . . . that the LORD has appeared to you" (4:5)

Read chapter 1 in the Book of Jeremiah. How does Jeremiah's story compare with Moses' story in Exodus, chapter 3?

Exodus

first miracle, then this one will convince them. 9If in spite of these two miracles they still will not believe you, and if they refuse to listen to what you say, take some water from the Nile and pour it on the ground. The water will turn into blood."

10But Moses said, "No, LORD, don't send me. I have never been a good speaker, and I haven't become one since you began to speak to me. I am a poor speaker, slow and hesitant."

11The LORD said to him, "Who gives man his mouth? Who makes him deaf or dumb? Who gives him sight or makes him blind? It is I, the LORD. 12Now, go! I will help you to speak, and I will tell you what to say."

13But Moses answered, "No, Lord, please send someone else."

14At this the LORD became angry with Moses and said, "What about your brother Aaron, the Levite? I know that he can speak well. In fact, he is now coming to meet you and will be glad to see you. 15You can speak to him and tell him what to say. I will help both of you to speak, and I will tell you both what to do. 16He will be your spokesman and speak to the people for you. Then you will be like God, telling him what to say. 17Take this walking stick with you; for with it you will perform miracles."

Moses Returns to Egypt

18Then Moses went back to Jethro, his father-in-law, and said to him, "Please let me go back to my relatives in Egypt to see if they are still alive." Jethro agreed and told him good-bye.

19While Moses was still in Midian, the LORD said to him, "Go back to Egypt, for all those who wanted to kill you are dead." 20So Moses took his wife and his sons, put them on a donkey, and set out with them for Egypt, carrying the walking stick that God had told him to take.

21Again the LORD said to Moses, "Now

that you are going back to Egypt, be sure to perform before the king all the miracles which I have given you the power to do. But I will make the king stubborn, and he will not let the people go. 22Then you must tell him that I, the LORD, say, 'Israel is my first-born son. 23I told you to let my son go, so that he might worship me, but you refused. Now I am going to kill your first-born son.'"

24At a camping place on the way to Egypt, the LORD met Moses and tried to kill him. 25-26Then Zipporah, his wife, took a sharp stone, cut off the foreskin of her son, and touched Moses' feet*g* with it. Because of the rite of circumcision she said to Moses, "You are a husband of blood to me." And so the LORD spared Moses' life.

27Meanwhile the LORD had said to Aaron, "Go into the desert to meet Moses." So he went to meet him at the holy mountain; and when he met him, he kissed him. 28Then Moses told Aaron everything that the LORD had said when he told him to return to Egypt; he also told him about the miracles which the LORD had ordered him to perform. 29So Moses and Aaron went to Egypt and gathered all the Israelite leaders together. 30Aaron told them everything that the LORD had said to Moses, and then Moses performed all the miracles in front of the people. 31They believed, and when they heard that the LORD had come to them and had seen how they were being treated cruelly, they bowed down and worshiped.

Moses and Aaron before the King of Egypt

5 1Then Moses and Aaron went to the king of Egypt and said, "The LORD, the God of Israel, says, 'Let my people go, so that they can hold a festival in the desert to honor me.'"

2"Who is the LORD?" the king demanded. "Why should I listen to him and let Israel

---

g 4:25–26 FEET: *This reference to "feet" is thought by some to be a euphemism for the genitals.*
4:23 Ex 12:29

"Now, go! I will help you to speak, and I will tell you what to say"
(Exodus 4:12).

go? I do not know the LORD; and I will not let Israel go."

³Moses and Aaron replied, "The God of the Hebrews has revealed himself to us. Allow us to travel three days into the desert to offer sacrifices to the LORD our God. If we don't do so, he will kill us with disease or by war."

⁴The king said to Moses and Aaron, "What do you mean by making the people neglect their work? Get those slaves back to work! ⁵You people have become more numerous than the Egyptians. And now you want to stop working!"

⁶That same day the king commanded the Egyptian slave drivers and the Israelite foremen: ⁷"Stop giving the people straw for making bricks. Make them go and find it for themselves. ⁸But still require them to make the same number of bricks as before, not one brick less. They don't have enough work to do, and that is why they keep asking me to let them go and offer sacrifices to their God! ⁹Make them work harder and keep them busy, so that they won't have time to listen to a pack of lies."

¹⁰The slave drivers and the Israelite foremen went out and said to the Israelites, "The king has said that he will not supply you with any more straw. ¹¹He says that you must go and get it for yourselves wherever you can find it, but you must still make the same number of bricks." ¹²So the people went all over Egypt looking for straw. ¹³The slave drivers kept trying to force them to make the same number of bricks every day as they had made when they were given straw. ¹⁴The Egyptian slave drivers beat the Israelite foremen, whom they had put in charge of the work. They demanded, "Why aren't you people making the same number of bricks that you made before?"

¹⁵Then the foremen went to the king and complained, "Why do you do this to us, Your Majesty? ¹⁶We are given no straw, but we are still ordered to make bricks! And now we are being beaten. It is your people that are at fault."

¹⁷The king answered, "You are lazy and don't want to work, and that is why you ask me to let you go and offer sacrifices to the LORD. ¹⁸Now get back to work! You will not be given any straw, but you must still

Now What?

Moses and Aaron did just as God wanted them to do. They returned to Egypt to tell the king to free the Israelites. Everything went according to the plan except for one thing: the king refused. In fact, he treated the Israelites even more cruelly than before. Moses and Aaron weren't sure what to do next.

Did you ever try to fix something that was wrong, only to have it turn out worse than before? For example, you might have decided to stop cheating, only to be accused by a teacher of copying someone's answers on a big test. Maybe you tried to patch up a relationship with someone, but had a huge fight instead.

When that happens to you, follow Moses' example and do two things:

- Talk to God. Of course God knew what happened, but Moses made his feelings known anyway.
- Be patient. God had a plan to change Pharaoh's mind, but it would take time. Moses had to let God do his work.

Bad things happen to everyone, but if you are right with God, everything will work out. Believe it!

— Exodus 5:1–22

make the same number of bricks." ¹⁹The foremen realized that they were in trouble when they were told that they had to make the same number of bricks every day as they had made before.

²⁰As they were leaving, they met Moses and Aaron, who were waiting for them. ²¹They said to Moses and Aaron, "The

Exodus

LORD has seen what you have done and will punish you for making the king and his officers hate us. You have given them an excuse to kill us."

Moses Complains to the LORD

²²Then Moses turned to the LORD again and said, "Lord, why do you mistreat your people? Why did you send me here? ²³Ever since I went to the king to speak for you, he has treated them cruelly. And you have done nothing to help them!"

6 ¹Then the LORD said to Moses, "Now you are going to see what I will do to the king. I will force him to let my people go. In fact, I will force him to drive them out of his land."

God Calls Moses

²God spoke to Moses and said, "I am the LORD. ³I appeared to Abraham, to Isaac, and to Jacob as Almighty God, but I did not make myself known to them by my holy name, the LORD.ʰ ⁴I also made my covenant with them, promising to give them the land of Canaan, the land in which they had lived as foreigners. ⁵Now I have heard the groaning of the Israelites, whom the Egyptians have enslaved, and I have remembered my covenant. ⁶So tell the Israelites that I say to them, 'I am the LORD; I will rescue you and set you free from your slavery to the Egyptians. I will raise my mighty arm to bring terrible punishment upon them, and I will save you. ⁷I will make you my own people, and I will be your God. You will know that I am the LORD your God when I set you free from slavery in Egypt. ⁸I will bring you to the land that I solemnly promised to give to Abraham, Isaac, and Jacob; and I will give it to you as your own possession. I am the LORD.' " ⁹Moses told this to the Israelites, but they would not listen to him, because their spirit had been broken by their cruel slavery.

¹⁰Then the LORD said to Moses, ¹¹"Go and tell the king of Egypt that he must let the Israelites leave his land."

¹²But Moses replied, "Even the Israelites

Not Me, Lord!

Logan was fed up. "I can't do anything about stuff that happens in places I don't know anything about!" he said. He kept hearing about how young people could make a difference, how they could change the world. He was tired of hearing that it was all up to him. His parents wouldn't let him stay up past 9 o'clock on school nights. Like Moses, Logan was thinking, "How could I change the world?"

One day Logan saw a poster: "We must be the change we wish to see in the world." At first, he was confused, but when he thought about it, it started to make sense. He could make things better in *his* world. If he was kind to people, those people might start doing nice things for others. And on it would go.

Logan secretly started doing things for others every day. His kindness changed his attitude. It made people smile. It changed his world—one kind act at a time.

— Exodus 6:12–13

will not listen to me, so why should the king? I am such a poor speaker."

¹³The LORD commanded Moses and Aaron: "Tell the Israelites and the king of Egypt that I have ordered you to lead the Israelites out of Egypt."

The Family Record of Moses and Aaron

¹⁴Reuben, Jacob's first-born, had four sons: Hanoch, Pallu, Hezron, and Carmi; they were the ancestors of the clans that bear

ʰ **6:3** THE LORD: See *3:14*.
6:2, 3 Gen 17:1; 28:3; 35:11; Ex 3:13–15

their names. 15Simeon had six sons: Jemuel, Jamin, Ohad, Jachin, Zohar, and Shaul, the son of a Canaanite woman; they were the ancestors of the clans that bear their names. 16Levi had three sons: Gershon, Kohath, and Merari; they were the ancestors of the clans that bear their names. Levi lived 137 years. 17Gershon had two sons: Libni and Shimei, and they had many descendants. 18Kohath had four sons: Amram, Izhar, Hebron, and Uzziel. Kohath lived 133 years. 19Merari had two sons: Mahli and Mushi. These are the clans of Levi with their descendants.

20Amram married his father's sister Jochebed, who bore him Aaron and Moses. Amram lived 137 years. 21Izhar had three sons: Korah, Nepheg, and Zichri. 22Uzziel also had three sons: Mishael, Elzaphan, and Sithri.

23Aaron married Elisheba, the daughter of Amminadab and sister of Nahshon; she bore him Nadab, Abihu, Eleazar, and Ithamar. 24Korah had three sons: Assir, Elkanah, and Abiasaph; they were the ancestors of the divisions of the clan of Korah. 25Eleazar, Aaron's son, married one of Putiel's daughters, who bore him Phinehas. These were the heads of the families and the clans of the tribe of Levi.

26Aaron and Moses were the ones to whom the LORD said, "Lead the tribes of Israel out of Egypt." 27They were the men who told the king of Egypt to free the Israelites.

The LORD's Command to Moses and Aaron

28When the LORD spoke to Moses in the land of Egypt, 29he said, "I am the LORD. Tell the king of Egypt everything I tell you."

30But Moses answered, "You know that I am such a poor speaker; why should the king listen to me?"

7 1The LORD said, "I am going to make you like God to the king, and your brother Aaron will speak to him as your prophet. 2Tell Aaron everything I command you, and he will tell the king to let the Israelites leave his country. 3-4But I will make the king stubborn, and he will not listen to you, no matter how many terrifying things I do in Egypt. Then I will bring severe punishment on Egypt and lead the tribes of my people out of the land. 5The Egyptians will then know that I am the LORD, when I raise my hand against them and bring the Israelites out of their country." 6Moses and Aaron did what the LORD commanded. 7At the time when they spoke to the king, Moses was eighty years old, and Aaron was eighty-three.

Aaron's Walking Stick

8The LORD said to Moses and Aaron, 9"If the king demands that you prove yourselves by performing a miracle, tell Aaron to take his walking stick and throw it down in front of the king, and it will turn into a snake." 10So Moses and Aaron went to the king and did as the LORD had commanded. Aaron threw his walking stick down in front of the king and his officers, and it turned into a snake. 11Then the king called for his wise men and magicians, and by their magic they did the same thing. 12They threw down their walking sticks, and the sticks turned into snakes. But Aaron's stick swallowed theirs. 13The king, however, remained stubborn and, just as the LORD had said, the king would not listen to Moses and Aaron.

Disasters Strike Egypt
Blood

14Then the LORD said to Moses, "The king is very stubborn and refuses to let the people go. 15So go and meet him in the morning when he goes down to the Nile. Take with you the walking stick that was turned into a snake, and wait for him on the riverbank. 16Then say to the king, 'The LORD, the God of the Hebrews, sent me to

6:16–19 Num 3.17–20; 26:57, 58; 1 Chr 6:16–19   7:3 Acts 7:36   7:14–24 Wis 11:6–8

Moses tried *again* to get out of leading the Israelites. Read Exodus 6:10–13 and Exodus 6:28—7:7 to see what he said and how God replied.

Exodus

tell you to let his people go, so that they can worship him in the desert. But until now you have not listened. [17]Now, Your Majesty, the LORD says that you will find out who he is by what he is going to do. Look, I am going to strike the surface of the river with this stick, and the water will be turned into blood. [18]The fish will die, and the river will stink so much that the Egyptians will not be able to drink from it.' "

[19]The LORD said to Moses, "Tell Aaron to take his stick and hold it out over all the rivers, canals, and pools in Egypt. The water will become blood, and all over the land there will be blood, even in the wooden tubs and stone jars."

[20]Then Moses and Aaron did as the LORD commanded. In the presence of the king and his officers, Aaron raised his stick and struck the surface of the river, and all the water in it was turned into blood. [21]The fish in the river died, and it smelled so bad that the Egyptians could not drink from it. There was blood everywhere in Egypt. [22]Then the king's magicians did the same thing by means of their magic, and the king was as stubborn as ever. Just as the LORD had said, the king refused to listen to Moses and Aaron. [23]Instead, he turned and went back to his palace without paying any attention even to this. [24]All the Egyptians dug along the bank of the river for drinking water, because they were not able to drink water from the river.

[25]Seven days passed after the LORD struck the river.

Frogs

8 [1]Then the LORD said to Moses, "Go to the king and tell him that the LORD says, 'Let my people go, so that they can worship me. [2]If you refuse, I will punish your country by covering it with frogs. [3]The Nile will be so full of frogs that they will leave it and go into your palace, your bedroom, your bed, the houses of your officials

Ten Terrible Troubles

The king would not listen to God's message through Moses and Aaron, so God did ten terrible things to Egypt to change the king's mind. Each one was worse than the others. Because of these ten plagues, God said, "The Egyptians will then know that I am the LORD" (Exodus 7:5).

Biblical scholars think that most of the plagues were like natural disasters that occasionally happened in Egypt anyway. What made them different in this story is that each plague started and stopped when Moses commanded it to.

Highlight or make a list of the ten plagues that God sent to the Egyptians. Which was the one that finally changed the king's mind and heart?

— Exodus 7:14–18

and your people, and even into your ovens and baking pans. [4]They will jump up on you, your people, and all your officials.' "

[5]The LORD said to Moses, "Tell Aaron to hold out his walking stick over the rivers, the canals, and the pools, and make frogs come up and cover the land of Egypt." [6]So Aaron held it out over all the water, and the frogs came out and covered the land. [7]But the magicians used magic, and they also made frogs come up on the land.

[8]The king called for Moses and Aaron and said, "Pray to the LORD to take away these

How old were Moses and Aaron when they started the journey out of Egypt? Check the first few verses of Exodus, chapter 7.

Pray It!

On Being Stubborn

The king of Egypt was stubborn, God. He refused to listen to you. His heart was hard.
He was too proud to pay attention to your messengers.
I'm afraid that I'm like the king sometimes, God.
> *I laugh at people who are hurting.*
> *I don't treat people fairly.*
> *I ignore people who talk about you.*
> *I refuse to change my ways.*
Soften my heart, God, so that it is a more welcoming place for you. When I feel like
being stubborn, fill my mind with thoughts of your love. When I act proudly, help me
remember that you are a God of justice. When I refuse to listen to those who share
your words, speak to me of the comfort that your Word brings. Amen.

— Exodus 8:5–19

---

frogs, and I will let your people go, so that they can offer sacrifices to the LORD."

⁹Moses replied, "I will be glad to pray for you. Just set the time when I am to pray for you, your officers, and your people. Then you will be rid of the frogs, and there will be none left except in the Nile."

¹⁰The king answered, "Pray for me tomorrow."

Moses said, "I will do as you ask, and then you will know that there is no other god like the LORD, our God. ¹¹You, your officials, and your people will be rid of the frogs, and there will be none left except in

They will jump up on you. (8:4)

the Nile." ¹²Then Moses and Aaron left the king, and Moses prayed to the LORD to take away the frogs which he had brought on the king. ¹³The LORD did as Moses asked, and the frogs in the houses, the courtyards, and the fields died. ¹⁴The Egyptians piled them up in great heaps, until the land stank with them. ¹⁵When the king saw that the frogs were dead, he became stubborn again and, just as the LORD had said, the king would not listen to Moses and Aaron.

Gnats

¹⁶The LORD said to Moses, "Tell Aaron to strike the ground with his stick, and all over the land of Egypt the dust will change into gnats." ¹⁷So Aaron struck the ground with his stick, and all the dust in Egypt was turned into gnats, which covered the people and the animals. ¹⁸The magicians tried to use their magic to make gnats appear, but they failed. There were gnats everywhere, ¹⁹and the magicians said to the king, "God has done this!" But the king was stubborn and, just as the LORD had said, the king would not listen to Moses and Aaron.

Flies

20The LORD said to Moses, "Early tomorrow morning go and meet the king as he goes to the river, and tell him that the LORD says, 'Let my people go, so that they can worship me. **21**I warn you that if you refuse, I will punish you by sending flies on you, your officials, and your people. The houses of the Egyptians will be full of flies, and the ground will be covered with them. **22**But I will spare the region of Goshen, where my people live, so that there will be no flies there. I will do this so that you will know that I, the LORD, am at work in this land. **23**I will make a distinction[i] between my people and your people. This miracle will take place tomorrow.' " **24**The LORD sent great swarms of flies into the king's palace and the houses of his officials. The whole land of Egypt was brought to ruin by the flies.

25Then the king called for Moses and Aaron and said, "Go and offer sacrifices to your God here in this country."

26"It would not be right to do that," Moses answered, "because the Egyptians would be offended by our sacrificing the animals that we offer to the LORD our God. If we use these animals and offend the Egyptians by sacrificing them where they can see us, they will stone us to death. **27**We must travel three days into the desert to offer sacrifices to the LORD our God, just as he commanded us."

28The king said, "I will let you go to sacrifice to the LORD, your God, in the desert, if you do not go very far. Pray for me."

29Moses answered, "As soon as I leave, I will pray to the LORD that tomorrow the flies will leave you, your officials, and your people. But you must not deceive us again and prevent the people from going to sacrifice to the LORD."

30Moses left the king and prayed to the LORD, **31**and the LORD did as Moses asked. The flies left the king, his officials, and his people; not one fly remained. **32**But even this time the king became stubborn, and again he would not let the people go.

Death of the Animals

9 **1**The LORD said to Moses, "Go to the king and tell him that the LORD, the God of the Hebrews, says, 'Let my people go, so that they may worship me. **2**If you again refuse to let them go, **3**I will punish you by sending a terrible disease on all your animals—your horses, donkeys, camels, cattle, sheep, and goats. **4**I will make a distinction between the animals of the Israelites and those of the Egyptians, and no animal that belongs to the Israelites will die. **5**I, the LORD, have set tomorrow as the time when I will do this.' "

6The next day the LORD did as he had said, and all the animals of the Egyptians died, but not one of the animals of the Israelites died. **7**The king asked what had happened and was told that none of the animals of the Israelites had died. But he was stubborn and would not let the people go.

Boils

8Then the LORD said to Moses and Aaron, "Take a few handfuls of ashes from a furnace; Moses is to throw them into the air in front of the king. **9**They will spread out like fine dust over all the land of Egypt, and everywhere they will produce boils that become open sores on the people and the animals." **10**So they got some ashes and stood before the king; Moses threw them into the air, and they produced boils that became open sores on the people and the animals. **11**The magicians were not able to appear before Moses, because they were covered with boils, like all the other Egyptians. **12**But the LORD made the king stubborn and, just as the LORD had said, the king would not listen to Moses and Aaron.

Hail

13The LORD then said to Moses, "Early tomorrow morning meet with the king and tell him that the LORD, the God of the Hebrews, says, 'Let my people go, so that they may worship me. **14**This time I will punish not only your officials and your people, but I

---

[i] **8:23** *Some ancient translations* a distinction; *Hebrew* redemption.
9:10 Rev 16:2

Promise Breakers and Promise Keepers?

It was a huge hailstorm—the worst the king had ever seen. Finally he had enough. He called Moses and Aaron and told them to take the Israelites away. In return, Moses promised to stop the storm. As soon as he got outside the city, he raised his hands to God, and the rain, thunder, and hail stopped. But when things were back to normal, the king refused to let the people go. Just because life got better, he broke the promise he had made to Moses and Aaron—and to God.

Many people turn to God when life gets hard. They promise that if God will help them, they will pray more, help poor people, and resist temptation. But when life gets back to normal, they forget about their promises—and about God. But God promised to be with us always, no matter what happens.

Have you made any promises to God lately? How about to other people? Are you a promise breaker, like Pharaoh? Or are you a promise keeper, like God?

— Exodus 9:13–35

that my fame might spread over the whole world. ¹⁷Yet you are still arrogant and refuse to let my people go. ¹⁸This time tomorrow I will cause a heavy hailstorm, such as Egypt has never known in all its history. ¹⁹Now give orders for your livestock and everything else you have in the open to be put under shelter. Hail will fall on the people and animals left outside unprotected, and they will all die.' " ²⁰Some of the king's officials were afraid because of what the LORD had said, and they brought their slaves and animals indoors for shelter. ²¹Others, however, paid no attention to the LORD's warning and left their slaves and animals out in the open.

²²Then the LORD said to Moses, "Raise your hand toward the sky, and hail will fall over the whole land of Egypt—on the people, the animals, and all the plants in the fields." ²³So Moses raised his stick toward the sky, and the LORD sent thunder and hail, and lightning struck the ground. The LORD sent ²⁴a heavy hailstorm, with lightning flashing back and forth. It was the worst storm that Egypt had ever known in all its history. ²⁵All over Egypt the hail struck down everything in the open, including all the people and all the animals. It beat down all the plants in the fields and broke all the trees. ²⁶The region of Goshen, where the Israelites lived, was the only place where there was no hail.

²⁷The king sent for Moses and Aaron and said, "This time I have sinned; the LORD is in the right, and my people and I are in the wrong. ²⁸Pray to the LORD! We have had enough of this thunder and hail! I promise to let you go; you don't have to stay here any longer."

²⁹Moses said to him, "As soon as I go out of the city, I will lift up my hands in prayer to the LORD. The thunder will stop, and there will be no more hail, so that you may know that the earth belongs to the LORD. ³⁰But I know that you and your officials do not yet fear the LORD God."

³¹The flax and the barley were ruined, because the barley was ripe, and the flax was

will punish you as well, so that you may know that there is no one like me in all the world. ¹⁵If I had raised my hand to strike you and your people with disease, you would have been completely destroyed. ¹⁶But to show you my power I have let you live so

9:16 Rom 9:17   9:24 Rev 8:7; 16:21

The king refused to give in, even though he was only hurting himself. Have you ever been that stubborn?

budding. [32]But none of the wheat was ruined, because it ripens later.

[33]Moses left the king, went out of the city, and lifted up his hands in prayer to the LORD. The thunder, the hail, and the rain all stopped. [34]When the king saw what had happened, he sinned again. He and his officials remained as stubborn as ever [35]and, just as the LORD had foretold through Moses, the king would not let the Israelites go.

Locusts

10 [1]Then the LORD said to Moses, "Go and see the king. I have made him and his officials stubborn, in order that I may perform these miracles among them [2]and in order that you may be able to tell your children and grandchildren how I made fools of the Egyptians when I performed the miracles. All of you will know that I am the LORD."

[3]So Moses and Aaron went to the king and said to him, "The LORD, the God of the Hebrews, says, 'How much longer will you refuse to submit to me? Let my people go, so that they may worship me. [4]If you keep on refusing, then I will bring locusts into your country tomorrow. [5]There will be so many that they will completely cover the ground. They will eat everything that the hail did not destroy, even the trees that are left. [6]They will fill your palaces and the houses of all your officials and all your people. They will be worse than anything your ancestors ever saw.'" Then Moses turned and left.

[7]The king's officials said to him, "How long is this man going to give us trouble? Let the Israelite men go, so that they can worship the LORD their God. Don't you realize that Egypt is ruined?"

[8]So Moses and Aaron were brought back to the king, and he said to them, "You may go and worship the LORD your God. But exactly who will go?"

[9]Moses answered, "We will all go, including our children and our old people. We will take our sons and daughters, our sheep and goats, and our cattle, because we must hold a festival to honor the LORD."

[10]The king said, "I swear by the LORD that I will never let you take your women and children! It is clear that you are plotting to revolt. [11]No! Only the men may go and worship the LORD if that is what you want." With that, Moses and Aaron were driven out of the king's presence.

[12]Then the LORD said to Moses, "Raise your hand over the land of Egypt to bring the locusts. They will come and eat everything that grows, everything that has survived the hail." [13]So Moses raised his stick, and the LORD caused a wind from the east to blow on the land all that day and all that night. By morning it had brought the locusts. [14]They came in swarms and settled over the whole country. It was the largest swarm of locusts that had ever been seen or that ever would be seen again. [15]They covered the ground until it was black with them; they ate everything that the hail had left, including all the fruit on the trees. Not a green thing was left on any tree or plant in all the land of Egypt.

[16]Then the king hurriedly called Moses and Aaron and said, "I have sinned against the LORD your God and against you. [17]Now forgive my sin this one time and pray to the LORD your God to take away this fatal punishment from me." [18]Moses left the king and prayed to the LORD. [19]And the LORD changed the east wind into a very strong west wind, which picked up the locusts and blew them into the Gulf of Suez.[j] Not one locust was left in all of Egypt. [20]But the LORD made the king stubborn, and he did not let the Israelites go.

Darkness

[21]The LORD then said to Moses, "Raise your hand toward the sky, and a darkness thick enough to be felt will cover the land

[j] **10:19** GULF OF SUEZ: *See Red Sea in 13:18.*
10:14, 15 Rev 9:2, 3   **10:21–23** Wis 17:1–21

"I have sinned against the LORD your God and against you" *(Exodus 10:16).*
The king said it, but he didn't mean it.

Breaking Families Apart

The king of Egypt was getting tired of Moses and Aaron pestering him to let the Israelites go to worship their God. Finally, he told Moses to take just the men. But Moses wanted everyone to go. He wanted to keep families together. The king refused.

Today, no evil leader is probably forcing your family members to separate from one another. But we face other challenges that make it hard for us to build strong relationships. Work schedules and extreme busyness are some reasons families cannot find time to do things together. Separation and divorce pose other barriers that keep families apart.

Do you think your family spends enough time together? If not, what are some of the reasons? What can you do to build stronger relationships with the people you live with? Say a prayer asking God to bless all the people you consider to be "family."

— Exodus 10:7–11

not one will be left behind. We ourselves must select the animals with which to worship the LORD our God. And until we get there, we will not know what animals to sacrifice to him."

27 The LORD made the king stubborn, and he would not let them go. 28 He said to Moses, "Get out of my sight! Don't let me ever see you again! On the day I do, you will die!"

29 "You are right," Moses answered. "You will never see me again."

Moses Announces the Death of the First-Born

11 1 Then the LORD said to Moses, "I will send only one more punishment on the king of Egypt and his people. After that he will let you leave. In fact, he will drive all of you out of here. 2 Now speak to the people of Israel and tell all of them to ask their neighbors for gold and silver jewelry." 3 The LORD made the Egyptians respect the Israelites. Indeed, the officials and all the people considered Moses to be a very great man.

4 Moses then said to the king, "The LORD says, 'At about midnight I will go through Egypt, 5 and every first-born son in Egypt will die, from the king's son, who is heir to the throne, to the son of the slave woman who grinds grain. The first-born of all the cattle will die also. 6 There will be loud crying all over Egypt, such as there has never been before or ever will be again. 7 But not even a dog will bark at the Israelites or their animals. Then you will know that I, the LORD, make a distinction between the Egyptians and the Israelites.' " 8 Moses concluded by saying, "All your officials will come to me and bow down before me, and they will beg me to take all my people and go away. After that, I will leave." Then in great anger Moses left the king.

9 The LORD said to Moses, "The king will continue to refuse to listen to you, in order that I may do more of my miracles in Egypt." 10 Moses and Aaron performed all these miracles before the king, but the LORD made him stubborn, and he would not let the Israelites leave his country.

of Egypt." 22 Moses raised his hand toward the sky, and there was total darkness throughout Egypt for three days. 23 The Egyptians could not see each other, and no one left his house during that time. But the Israelites had light where they were living.

24 The king called Moses and said, "You may go and worship the LORD; even your women and children may go with you. But your sheep, goats, and cattle must stay here."

25 Moses answered, "Then you would have to provide us with animals for sacrifices and burnt offerings to offer to the LORD our God. 26 No, we will take our animals with us;

Exodus

The Passover

12 [1] The LORD spoke to Moses and Aaron in Egypt: [2] "This month is to be the first month of the year for you. [3] Give these instructions to the whole community of Israel: On the tenth day of this month each man must choose either a lamb or a young goat for his household. [4] If his family is too small to eat a whole animal, he and his next-door neighbor may share an animal, in proportion to the number of people and the amount that each person can eat. [5] You may choose either a sheep or a goat, but it must be a one-year-old male without any defects. [6] Then, on the evening of the fourteenth day of the month, the whole community of Israel will kill the animals. [7] The people are to take some of the blood and put it on the door-posts and above the doors of the houses in which the animals are to be eaten. [8] That night the meat is to be roasted, and eaten with bitter herbs and with bread made without yeast. [9] Do not eat any of it raw or boiled, but eat it roasted whole, including the head, the legs, and the internal organs. [10] You must not leave any of it until morning; if any is left over, it must be burned. [11] You are to eat it quickly, for you are to be dressed for travel, with your sandals on your feet and your walking stick in your hand. It is the Passover Festival to honor me, the LORD.

[12] "On that night I will go through the land of Egypt, killing every first-born male, both human and animal, and punishing all the gods of Egypt. I am the LORD. [13] The blood on the doorposts will be a sign to mark the houses in which you live. When I see the blood, I will pass over you and will not harm you when I punish the Egyptians. [14] You must celebrate this day as a religious festival to remind you of what I, the LORD, have done. Celebrate it for all time to come."

The Festival of Unleavened Bread

[15] The LORD said, "For seven days you must not eat any bread made with yeast—eat only unleavened bread. On the first day you are to get rid of all the yeast in your houses, for if anyone during those seven days eats bread made with yeast, he shall no longer be considered one of my people. [16] On the first day and again on the seventh day you are to meet for worship. No work is to be done on those days, but you may prepare food. [17] Keep this festival, because it was on this day that I brought your tribes out of Egypt. For all time to come you must celebrate this day as a festival. [18] From the evening of the fourteenth day of the first month to the evening of the twenty-first day, you must not eat any bread made with yeast. [19-20] For seven days no yeast must be found in your houses, for if anyone, native-born or foreign, eats bread made with yeast, he shall no longer be considered one of my people."

The First Passover

[21] Moses called for all the leaders of Israel and said to them, "Each of you is to choose a lamb or a young goat and kill it, so that your families can celebrate Passover. [22] Take a sprig of hyssop, dip it in the bowl containing[k] the animal's blood, and wipe the blood on the doorposts and the beam above the door of your house. Not one of you is to leave the house until morning. [23] When the LORD goes through Egypt to kill the Egyptians, he will see the blood on the beams and the doorposts and will not let the Angel of Death enter your houses and kill you. [24] You and your children must obey these rules forever. [25] When you enter the land that the LORD has promised to give you, you must perform this ritual. [26] When your children ask you, 'What does this ritual mean?' [27] you will answer, 'It is the sacrifice of Passover to honor the LORD, because he passed over the houses of the Israelites in Egypt. He killed the Egyptians, but spared us.' "

The Israelites knelt down and worshiped. [28] Then they went and did what the LORD had commanded Moses and Aaron.

k **12:22** dip it in the bowl containing; *or* put it on the threshold covered with.
12:1–13 Lev 23:5; Num 9:1–5; 28:16; Deut 16:1, 2 **12:14–20** Ex 23:15; 34:18; Lev 23:6–8; Num 28:17–25; Deut 16:3–8 **12:23** Heb 11:28

Saved by the Blood of the Lamb

Ca✝**holic Connec**✝**ions**

Every spring Jewish families celebrate
Passover to remember the story described in
Exodus, chapter 12. God gave the Israelites
specific instructions for preparing the last meal they would eat as slaves of
the Egyptians. God also told them to sacrifice a lamb and spread its blood
on their doorposts. Their families would then be saved from the Angel of
Death that God would send to kill the Egyptian first-born males.

Jesus and his disciples were probably sharing a Passover meal (also
known as a Paschal feast or a seder meal) on the night before he died.
Through this meal, which we know as the Last Supper, Jesus helped his followers understand his own death. The sacrifice of his body and blood would
save the world. Just as the blood of the lamb freed the Israelites from the
slavery of the Egyptians, Jesus freed the world from the slavery of sin. That
is why the New Testament calls Jesus the Lamb of God.

We commemorate the life, death, and Resurrection of Jesus—the Paschal
sacrifice—every time we celebrate the Eucharist.

— Exodus 12:21–28

The Death of the First-Born

²⁹At midnight the LORD killed all the
first-born sons in Egypt, from the king's son,
who was heir to the throne, to the son of
the prisoner in the dungeon; all the first-
born of the animals were also killed. ³⁰That
night, the king, his officials, and all the other
Egyptians were awakened. There was loud
crying throughout Egypt, because there was
not one home in which there was not a
dead son. ³¹That same night the king sent
for Moses and Aaron and said, "Get out, you
and your Israelites! Leave my country; go
and worship the LORD, as you asked. ³²Take
your sheep, goats, and cattle, and leave. Also
pray for a blessing on me."

³³The Egyptians urged the people to
hurry and leave the country; they said, "We
will all be dead if you don't leave." ³⁴So the
people filled their baking pans with unleavened dough, wrapped them in clothing, and

carried them on their shoulders. ³⁵The
Israelites had done as Moses had said, and had
asked the Egyptians for gold and silver jewelry and for clothes. ³⁶The LORD made the
Egyptians respect the people and give them
what they asked for. In this way the Israelites
carried away the wealth of the Egyptians.

The Israelites Leave Egypt

³⁷The Israelites set out on foot from Rameses for Sukkoth. There were about 600,000
men, not counting women and children. ³⁸A

*The people filled their baking pans with
unleavened dough. (12:34)*

12:29 Ex 4:22–32   **12:35, 36** Ex 3:21, 22

Exodus

large number of other people and many sheep, goats, and cattle also went with them. ³⁹They baked unleavened bread from the dough that they had brought out of Egypt, for they had been driven out of Egypt so suddenly that they did not have time to get their food ready or to prepare leavened dough.

⁴⁰The Israelites had lived in Egypt for 430 years. ⁴¹On the day the 430 years ended, all the tribes of the LORD's people left Egypt. ⁴²It was a night when the LORD kept watch to bring them out of Egypt; this same night is dedicated to the LORD for all time to come as a night when the Israelites must keep watch.

Regulations about Passover

⁴³The LORD said to Moses and Aaron, "These are the Passover regulations: No foreigner shall eat the Passover meal, ⁴⁴but any slave that you have bought may eat it if you circumcise him first. ⁴⁵No temporary resident or hired worker may eat it. ⁴⁶The whole meal must be eaten in the house in which it was prepared; it must not be taken outside. And do not break any of the animal's bones. ⁴⁷The whole community of Israel must celebrate this festival, ⁴⁸but no uncircumcised man may eat it. If a foreigner has settled among you and wants to celebrate Passover to honor the LORD, you must first circumcise all the males of his household. He is then to be treated like a native-born Israelite and may join in the festival. ⁴⁹The same regulations apply to native-born Israelites and to foreigners who settle among you." ⁵⁰All the Israelites obeyed and did what the LORD had commanded Moses and Aaron. ⁵¹On that day the LORD brought the Israelite tribes out of Egypt.

Dedication of the First-Born

13 ¹The LORD said to Moses, ²"Dedicate all the first-born males to me, for every first-born male Israelite and every first-born male animal belongs to me."

The Festival of Unleavened Bread

³Moses said to the people, "Remember this day—the day on which you left Egypt, the place where you were slaves. This is the day the LORD brought you out by his great power. No leavened bread is to be eaten. ⁴You are leaving Egypt on this day in the first month, the month of Abib. ⁵The LORD solemnly promised your ancestors to give you the land of the Canaanites, the Hittites, the Amorites, the Hivites, and the Jebusites. When he brings you into that rich and fertile land, you must celebrate this festival in the first month of every year. ⁶For seven days you must eat unleavened bread and on the seventh day there is to be a festival to honor the LORD. ⁷For seven days you must not eat any bread made with yeast; there must be no yeast or leavened bread anywhere in your land. ⁸When the festival begins, explain to your sons that you do all this because of what the LORD did for you when you left Egypt. ⁹This observance will be a reminder, like something tied on your hand or on your forehead; it will remind you to continue to recite and study the Law of the LORD, because the LORD brought you out of Egypt by his great power. ¹⁰Celebrate this festival at the appointed time each year.

The First-Born

¹¹"The LORD will bring you into the land of the Canaanites, which he solemnly promised to you and your ancestors. When he gives it to you, ¹²you must offer every first-born male to the LORD. Every first-born male of your animals belongs to the LORD, ¹³but you must buy back from him every first-born male donkey by offering a lamb in its place. If you do not want to buy back the donkey, break its neck. You must buy back every first-born male child of yours. ¹⁴In the future, when your son asks what this observance means, you will answer him, 'By using

12:40 Gen 15:13; Gal 3:17   **12:46** Num 9:12; Jn 19:36   **13:2** Num 3:13; Lk 2:23   **13:12** Ex 34:19, 20; Lk 2:23

Why didn't the Israelites take the shortest way out of Egypt? The answer is somewhere in the last part of Exodus, chapter 13.

Pray It!

God, Be My Pillar

God of light and God of darkness, the Israelites knew you were with them as they made their way out of Egypt. They saw you as a pillar (column) of cloud in front of them during the day and a pillar of fire at night, guiding and lighting their way.

I wish I could see you sometimes. It would make life a lot easier. At least I would know that I'm heading in the right direction. I know that you're always with me, too, but sometimes I don't feel it.

I think that you put "pillars" in my life to guide me, just as you guided the Israelites. After all, I have parents, teachers, relatives, and friends who look out for me. They teach me, give me directions, and light my way when I'm lost or confused. They are gifts from you—your way of being my very own pillar of cloud and fire. Thank you, God, for them. Amen.

— Exodus 13:20–22

great power the LORD brought us out of Egypt, the place where we were slaves. ¹⁵When the king of Egypt was stubborn and refused to let us go, the LORD killed every first-born male in the land of Egypt, both human and animal. That is why we sacrifice every first-born male animal to the LORD, but buy back our first-born sons. ¹⁶This observance will be a reminder, like something tied on our hands or on our foreheads; it will remind us that the LORD brought us out of Egypt by his great power.' "

The Pillar of Cloud and the Pillar of Fire

¹⁷When the king of Egypt let the people go, God did not take them by the road that goes up the coast to Philistia, although it was the shortest way. God thought, "I do not want the people to change their minds and return to Egypt when they see that they are going to have to fight." ¹⁸Instead, he led them in a roundabout way through the desert toward the Red Sea.*¹* The Israelites were armed for battle.

¹⁹Moses took the body of Joseph with

him, as Joseph had made the Israelites solemnly promise to do. Joseph had said, "When God rescues you, you must carry my body with you from this place."

²⁰The Israelites left Sukkoth and camped at Etham on the edge of the desert. ²¹During the day the LORD went in front of them in a pillar of cloud to show them the way, and during the night he went in front of them in a pillar of fire to give them light, so that they could travel night and day. ²²The pillar of cloud was always in front of the people during the day, and the pillar of fire at night.

Crossing the Red Sea

14 ¹Then the LORD said to Moses, ²"Tell the Israelites to turn back and camp in front of Pi Hahiroth, between Migdol and the Red Sea, near Baal Zephon. ³The king will think that the Israelites are wandering around in the country and are closed in by the desert. ⁴I will make him stubborn, and he will pursue you, and my victory over the king and his army will bring me honor. Then the Egyptians will

*¹ **13:18** RED SEA: (in Hebrew literally "Sea of Reeds") evidently referred to (1) a series of lakes and marshes between the head of the Gulf of Suez and the Mediterranean, the region generally regarded as the site of the events described in Exodus 13, and was also used to designate (2) the Gulf of Suez, and (3) the Gulf of Aqaba.*
13:19 Gen 50:25; Josh 24:32   **13:22** Wis 10:17, 18; 18:3

The LORD went in front of them. (13:21)

know that I am the LORD." The Israelites did as they were told.

⁵When the king of Egypt was told that the people had escaped, he and his officials changed their minds and said, "What have we done? We have let the Israelites escape, and we have lost them as our slaves!" ⁶The king got his war chariot and his army ready. ⁷He set out with all his chariots, including the six hundred finest, commanded by their officers. ⁸The LORD made the king stubborn, and he pursued the Israelites, who were leaving triumphantly.ᵐ ⁹The Egyptian army, with all the horses, chariots, and drivers, pursued them and caught up with them where they were camped by the Red Sea near Pi Hahiroth and Baal Zephon.

¹⁰When the Israelites saw the king and his army marching against them, they were terrified and cried out to the LORD for help. ¹¹They said to Moses, "Weren't there any graves in Egypt? Did you have to bring us out here in the desert to die? Look what you have done by bringing us out of Egypt! ¹²Didn't we tell you before we left that this would happen? We told you to leave us alone and let us go on being slaves of the Egyptians. It would be better to be slaves there than to die here in the desert."

¹³Moses answered, "Don't be afraid! Stand your ground, and you will see what the LORD will do to save you today; you will never see these Egyptians again. ¹⁴The LORD will fight for you, and all you have to do is keep still."

¹⁵The LORD said to Moses, "Why are you crying out for help? Tell the people to move forward. ¹⁶Lift up your walking stick and hold it out over the sea. The water will divide, and the Israelites will be able to walk through the sea on dry ground. ¹⁷I will make the Egyptians so stubborn that they will go in after them, and I will gain honor by my victory over the king, his army, his chariots,

ᵐ **14:8** triumphantly; *or* under the protection of the LORD.

and his drivers. [18]When I defeat them, the Egyptians will know that I am the LORD."

[19]The angel of God, who had been in front of the army of Israel, moved and went to the rear. The pillar of cloud also moved until it was [20]between the Egyptians and the Israelites. The cloud made it dark for the Egyptians, but gave light to the people of Israel,[n] and so the armies could not come near each other all night.

[21]Moses held out his hand over the sea, and the LORD drove the sea back with a strong east wind. It blew all night and turned the sea into dry land. The water was divided, [22]and the Israelites went through the sea on dry ground, with walls of water on both sides. [23]The Egyptians pursued them and went after them into the sea with all their horses, chariots, and drivers. [24]Just before dawn the LORD looked down from the pillar of fire and cloud at the Egyptian army and threw them into a panic. [25]He made the wheels of their chariots get stuck, so that they moved with great difficulty. The Egyptians said, "The LORD is fighting for the Israelites against us. Let's get out of here!"

The Egyptians will know that I am the LORD.
(14:18)

[26]The LORD said to Moses, "Hold out your hand over the sea, and the water will come back over the Egyptians and their chariots and drivers." [27]So Moses held out his hand over the sea, and at daybreak the water returned to its normal level. The Egyptians tried to escape from the water, but the LORD threw them into the sea. [28]The water returned and covered the chariots, the drivers, and all the Egyptian army that had followed the Israelites into the sea; not one of them was left. [29]But the Israelites walked through the sea on dry ground, with walls of water on both sides.

[30]On that day the LORD saved the people of Israel from the Egyptians, and the Israelites saw them lying dead on the seashore. [31]When the Israelites saw the great power with which the LORD had defeated the Egyptians, they stood in awe of the LORD; and they had faith in the LORD and in his servant Moses.

The Song of Moses

15 [1]Then Moses and the Israelites sang this song to the LORD:

"I will sing to the LORD, because he has
      won a glorious victory;
  he has thrown the horses and their
      riders into the sea.
[2]The LORD is my strong defender;
  he is the one who has saved me.
He is my God, and I will praise him,
  my father's God, and I will sing about
      his greatness.
[3]The LORD is a warrior;
  the LORD is his name.

[4]"He threw Egypt's army and its chariots
      into the sea;
  the best of its officers were drowned in
      the Red Sea.
[5]The deep sea covered them;
  they sank to the bottom like a stone.

[n] **14:20** *Probable text* The cloud . . . Israel; *Hebrew unclear.*
14:22 1 Cor 10:1, 2; Heb 11:29   **15:1** Rev 15:3   **15:2** Ps 118:14; Isa 12:2

Why couldn't Pharaoh's army see the Israelites crossing the Red Sea? Read Exodus 14:19–20 to find out.

Exodus

Pray It!

We Did It, God!

After the Israelites make it across the Red Sea, they stopped to thank God and sing a song of praise. After all, they could not have done it without God's help.

What has God done for you lately? How has God gotten you through your own "Red Sea"?

• Has God gotten you through a hard time? Maybe God gave you the right words to say to someone you needed to apologize to after a huge fight.

• Has God blessed you with a special gift? Maybe God sent a new friend or a great tutor that has given you a better handle on math.

• Has God taken care of someone in your family? Maybe God led your mom to a better job or gave a relative the strength to get through an illness.

Read through Moses' prayer of praise and thanksgiving, then write your own. In it, tell the story of God's goodness in your life. Praise God with all the enthusiasm you can muster in your heart.

— Exodus, chapter 15

6 "Your right hand, LORD, is awesome in
    power;
  it breaks the enemy in pieces.
7 In majestic triumph you overthrow your
    foes;
  your anger blazes out and burns them
    up like straw.
8 You blew on the sea and the water piled
    up high;
  it stood up straight like a wall;
  the deepest part of the sea became
    solid.
9 The enemy said, 'I will pursue them and
    catch them;
  I will divide their wealth and take all I
    want;
  I will draw my sword and take all they
    have.'
10 But one breath from you, LORD, and the
    Egyptians were drowned;
  they sank like lead in the terrible water.
11 "LORD, who among the gods is like you?
  Who is like you, wonderful in holiness?
  Who can work miracles and mighty
    acts like yours?

12 You stretched out your right hand,
  and the earth swallowed our enemies.
13 Faithful to your promise, you led the
    people you had rescued;
  by your strength you guided them to
    your sacred land.
14 The nations have heard, and they tremble
    with fear;
  the Philistines are seized with terror.
15 The leaders of Edom are terrified;
  Moab's mighty men are trembling;
  the people of Canaan lose their
    courage.
16 Terror and dread fall upon them.
  They see your strength, O LORD,
    and stand helpless with fear
  until your people have marched past—
    the people you set free from slavery.
17 You bring them in and plant them on
    your mountain,
  the place that you, LORD, have chosen
    for your home,
  the Temple that you yourself have built.
18 You, LORD, will be king forever and
    ever."

Moses' sister led the women in singing praises to God and dancing. What was her name? You'll find it in Exodus, chapter 15.

The Song of Miriam

19 The Israelites walked through the sea on dry ground. But when the Egyptian chariots with their horses and drivers went into the sea, the LORD brought the water back, and it covered them.

20 The prophet Miriam, Aaron's sister, took her tambourine, and all the women followed her, playing tambourines and dancing. **21** Miriam sang for them:

> "Sing to the LORD, because he has won a
>   glorious victory;
>   he has thrown the horses and their
>   riders into the sea."

Bitter Water

22 Then Moses led the people of Israel away from the Red Sea into the desert of Shur. For three days they walked through the desert, but found no water. **23** Then they came to a place called Marah, but the water there was so bitter that they could not drink it. That is why it was named Marah.* **24** The people complained to Moses and asked, "What are we going to drink?" **25** Moses prayed earnestly to the LORD, and the LORD showed him a piece of wood, which he threw into the water; and the water became fit to drink.

There the LORD gave them laws to live by, and there he also tested them. **26** He said, "If you will obey me completely by doing what I consider right and by keeping my commands, I will not punish you with any of the diseases that I brought on the Egyptians. I am the LORD, the one who heals you."

27 Next they came to Elim, where there were twelve springs and seventy palm trees; there they camped by the water.

The Manna and the Quails

16 **1** The whole Israelite community set out from Elim, and on the fifteenth day of the second month after they had left Egypt, they came to the desert of Sin, which is between Elim and Sinai. **2** There in the desert they all complained to Moses and Aaron **3** and said to them, "We wish that the LORD had killed us in Egypt. There we could at least sit down and eat meat and as much other food as we wanted. But you have brought us out into this desert to starve us all to death."

4 The LORD said to Moses, "Now I am going to cause food to rain down from the sky for all of you. The people must go out every day and gather enough for that day. In this way I can test them to find out if they will follow my instructions. **5** On the sixth day they are to bring in twice as much as usual and prepare it."

6 So Moses and Aaron said to all the Israelites, "This evening you will know that it was the LORD who brought you out of Egypt. **7** In the morning you will see the dazzling light of the LORD's presence. He has heard your complaints against him—yes, against him, because we are only carrying out his instructions." **8** Then Moses said, "It is the LORD who will give you meat to eat in the evening and as much bread as you want in the morning, because he has heard how much you have complained against him. When you complain against us, you are really complaining against the LORD."

9 Moses said to Aaron, "Tell the whole community to come and stand before the LORD, because he has heard their complaints." **10** As Aaron spoke to the whole community, they turned toward the desert, and suddenly the dazzling light of the LORD appeared in a cloud. **11** The LORD said to Moses, **12** "I have heard the complaints of the Israelites. Tell them that at twilight they will have meat to eat, and in the morning they will have all the bread they want. Then they will know that I, the LORD, am their God."

13 In the evening a large flock of quails flew in, enough to cover the camp, and in the morning there was dew all around the camp. **14** When the dew evaporated, there was something thin and flaky on the surface of the desert. It was as delicate as frost. **15** When the Israelites saw it, they didn't

---

o **15:23** MARAH: *This name in Hebrew means "bitter."*
15:25 Sir 38:5   **16:4** Wis 16:20–29; Jn 6:31   **16:15** 1 Cor 10:3

Exodus

The food that the LORD has given you to eat (16:15)

know what it was and asked each other, "What is it?"

Moses said to them, "This is the food that the LORD has given you to eat. ¹⁶The LORD has commanded that each of you is to gather as much of it as he needs, two quarts for each member of his household."

¹⁷The Israelites did this, some gathering more, others less. ¹⁸When they measured it, those who gathered much did not have too much, and those who gathered less did not have too little. Each had gathered just what he needed. ¹⁹Moses said to them, "No one is to keep any of it for tomorrow." ²⁰But some of them did not listen to Moses and saved part of it. The next morning it was full of worms and smelled rotten, and Moses was angry with them. ²¹Every morning each one gathered as much as he needed; and when the sun grew hot, what was left on the ground melted.

²²On the sixth day they gathered twice as much food, four quarts for each person. All the leaders of the community came and told Moses about it, ²³and he said to them, "The LORD has commanded that tomorrow is a holy day of rest, dedicated to him. Bake today what you want to bake and boil what you want to boil. Whatever is left should be put aside and kept for tomorrow." ²⁴As Moses had commanded, they kept what was left until the next day; it did not spoil or get worms in it. ²⁵Moses said, "Eat this today, because today is the Sabbath, a day of rest

Come and Get It!

The Israelites hadn't had much to eat since they left Egypt. They were hungry, so they complained to Moses. Moses did his usual thing—talked to God about it. God sent manna, a kind of sweet, flaky breadlike substance. It was the first time the Israelites had seen this. In fact, manna means "what is it?" in Hebrew. God also sent small birds called quails so the travelers would have some meat.

Small quantities of manna and quails still appear in that part of the world today. The miracle was that God sent enough to feed everyone for a long time. Manna in the morning. Quails at night. Quite a feast!

When we celebrate Eucharist, the priest consecrates bread and wine, and it becomes the body and blood of Jesus. This is God's way of giving us food for our spiritual journey, just like he did for the Israelites.

— Exodus, chapter 16

dedicated to the LORD, and you will not find any food outside the camp. ²⁶You must gather food for six days, but on the seventh day, the day of rest, there will be none."

²⁷On the seventh day some of the people went out to gather food, but they did not find any. ²⁸Then the LORD said to Moses, "How much longer will you people refuse to obey my commands? ²⁹Remember that I, the LORD, have given you a day of rest, and that is why on the sixth day I will always give you enough food for two days. Everyone is to stay where he is on the seventh day

and not leave his home." ³⁰So the people did no work on the seventh day.

³¹The people of Israel called the food manna.*p* It was like a small white seed, and tasted like thin cakes made with honey. ³²Moses said, "The LORD has commanded us to save some manna, to be kept for our descendants, so that they can see the food which he gave us to eat in the desert when he brought us out of Egypt." ³³Moses said to Aaron, "Take a jar, put two quarts of manna in it, and place it in the LORD's presence to be kept for our descendants." ³⁴As the LORD had commanded Moses, Aaron put it in front of the Covenant Box, so that it could be kept. ³⁵The Israelites ate manna for the next forty years, until they reached the land of Canaan, where they settled. (³⁶The standard dry measure then in use equaled twenty quarts.)

Water from the Rock
(Numbers 20:1–13)

17 ¹The whole Israelite community left the desert of Sin, moving from one place to another at the command of the LORD. They camped at Rephidim, but there was no water there to drink. ²They complained to Moses and said, "Give us water to drink."

Moses answered, "Why are you complaining? Why are you putting the LORD to the test?"

³But the people were very thirsty and continued to complain to Moses. They said, "Why did you bring us out of Egypt? To kill us and our children and our livestock with thirst?"

⁴Moses prayed earnestly to the LORD and said, "What can I do with these people? They are almost ready to stone me."

⁵The LORD said to Moses, "Take some of the leaders of Israel with you, and go on ahead of the people. Take along the stick with which you struck the Nile. ⁶I will stand before you on a rock at Mount Sinai. Strike the rock, and water will come out of it for the people to drink." Moses did so in the presence of the leaders of Israel.

No More Whining!

Moses was trying his best to lead the Israelites out of Egypt. But life was hard, and the Israelites complained a lot. They were hungry. They were thirsty. They were lost. Let's face it: These Israelites were whiners.

Parents, teachers, and others in authority do their best to lead the way God wants them to, but some people do not appreciate their efforts. They whine because they are only concerned about themselves. When the Israelites complained, Moses went to God and said, "What can I do with these people?" (Exodus 17:4). Could your parents, teachers, and friends be asking God the same question about you?

The next time you feel like complaining, check your attitude and ask yourself two questions:
• Is complaining going to make things better or worse for everyone?
• What can I do *myself* to make the situation better?

Then say a prayer for the people in your life who do their best to listen to God and guide you in the right direction.

— Exodus 17:1–7

p **16:31** MANNA: *This word sounds like the Hebrew for "what is it?" (see verse 15).*
16:31 Num 11:7, 8   **16:33** Heb 9:4   **16:35** Josh 5:12   **17:1–7** Num 20:2–13

Compare the story in Exodus, chapter 16, with the story in Matthew 14:13–21. How are they similar?

7 The place was named Massah and Meribah,*q* because the Israelites complained and put the LORD to the test when they asked, "Is the LORD with us or not?"

War with the Amalekites

8 The Amalekites came and attacked the Israelites at Rephidim. 9 Moses said to Joshua, "Pick out some men to go and fight the Amalekites tomorrow. I will stand on top of the hill holding the stick that God told me to carry." 10 Joshua did as Moses commanded him and went out to fight the Amalekites, while Moses, Aaron, and Hur went up to the top of the hill. 11 As long as Moses held up his arms, the Israelites won, but when he put his arms down, the Amalekites started winning. 12 When Moses' arms grew tired, Aaron and Hur brought a stone for him to sit on, while they stood beside him and held up his arms, holding them steady until the sun went down. 13 In this way Joshua totally defeated the Amalekites.

They held his arms steady until the sun went down.
(17:12)

14 Then the LORD said to Moses, "Write an account of this victory, so that it will be remembered. Tell Joshua that I will completely destroy the Amalekites." 15 Moses built an altar and named it "The LORD is my Banner." 16 He said, "Hold high the banner of the LORD!*r* The LORD will continue to fight against the Amalekites forever!"

Jethro Visits Moses

18 1 Moses' father-in-law Jethro, the priest of Midian, heard about everything that God had done for Moses and the people of Israel when he led them out of Egypt. 2 So he came to Moses, bringing with him Moses' wife Zipporah, who had been left behind, 3 and Gershom and Eliezer, her two sons. (Moses had said, "I have been a foreigner in a strange land"; so he had named one son Gershom.*s* 4 He had also said, "The God of my father helped me and saved me from being killed by the king of Egypt"; so he had named the other son Eliezer.*t*) 5 Jethro came with Moses' wife and her two sons into the desert where Moses was camped at the holy mountain. 6 He had sent word to Moses that they were coming, 7 so Moses went out to meet him, bowed before him, and kissed him. They asked about each other's health and then went into Moses' tent. 8 Moses told Jethro everything that the LORD had done to the king and the people of Egypt in order to rescue the Israelites. He also told him about the hardships the people had faced on the way and how the LORD had saved them. 9 When Jethro heard all this, he was happy 10 and said, "Praise the LORD, who saved you from the king and the people of Egypt! Praise the LORD, who saved his people from slavery! 11 Now I know that the LORD is greater than all the gods, because he did this when the Egyptians treated the Israelites with such contempt." 12 Then Jethro brought an offering to be burned whole and other sacrifices to be offered to God; and Aaron and all the leaders of Israel went with him to eat the sacred meal as an act of worship.

---

q **17:7** MASSAH . . . MERIBAH: *These names in Hebrew mean "testing" and "complaining."*   *r* **17:16** *Probable text* Hold . . . LORD; *Hebrew unclear.*   *s* **18:3** GERSHOM: *This name sounds like the Hebrew for "foreigner."*   *t* **18:4** ELIEZER: *This name sounds like the Hebrew for "God helps me."*
17:14 Deut 25:17–19; 1 Sam 15:2–9   **18:2, 3** Ex 2:21, 22   **18:3** Acts 7:29

Pray It!

A Friend in Need

Jethro must have known that Moses needed someone to talk to. When he heard about everything that had happened, he went to find his son-in-law. Moses was glad to see him. He told him about what God had done for them and how hard the journey had been. Jethro was thrilled at everything Moses had accomplished and praised God. He also gave Moses some good advice to help ease Moses' burden. Maybe he helped Moses see all his struggles in a new light.

Does someone in your life seem to know when you need a friend? This person is probably a good listener and helps you see things in a way you never thought about before. Say the following prayer for the Jethro in your life:

Thank you, God, for my friend (name of person).
She (or he) . . .
  Knows when I need someone to listen.
  Lets me talk about my worries and struggles.
  Shows me the good side when I can only see the bad.
  Laughs with me, not at me.
  Gives me good advice.
  Lets me talk about you.
Thank you, God, for (name). Please let me be a friend like that for someone else. Amen.

— Exodus 18:1–27

The Appointment of Judges
(Deuteronomy 1:9–18)

13 The next day Moses was settling disputes among the people, and he was kept busy from morning till night. **14** When Jethro saw everything that Moses had to do, he asked, "What is all this that you are doing for the people? Why are you doing this all alone, with people standing here from morning till night to consult you?"

15 Moses answered, "I must do this because the people come to me to learn God's will. **16** When two people have a dispute, they come to me, and I decide which one of them is right, and I tell them God's commands and laws."

17 Then Jethro said, "You are not doing this right. **18** You will wear yourself out and these people as well. This is too much for you to do alone. **19** Now let me give you some good advice, and God will be with you. It is right for you to represent the people before God and bring their disputes to him. **20** You should

teach them God's commands and explain to them how they should live and what they should do. **21** But in addition, you should choose some capable men and appoint them as leaders of the people: leaders of thousands, hundreds, fifties, and tens. They must be God-fearing men who can be trusted and who cannot be bribed. **22** Let them serve as judges for the people on a permanent basis. They can bring all the difficult cases to you, but they themselves can decide all the smaller disputes. That will make it easier for you, as they share your burden. **23** If you do this, as God commands, you will not wear yourself out, and all these people can go home with their disputes settled."

24 Moses took Jethro's advice **25** and chose capable men from among all the Israelites. He appointed them as leaders of thousands, hundreds, fifties, and tens. **26** They served as judges for the people on a permanent basis, bringing the difficult cases to Moses but deciding the smaller disputes themselves.

27 Then Moses said good-bye to Jethro, and Jethro went back home.

The Israelites at Mount Sinai

19

1-2 The people of Israel left Rephidim, and on the first day of the third month after they had left Egypt they came to the desert of Sinai. There they set up camp at the foot of Mount Sinai, 3 and Moses went up the mountain to meet with God.

The LORD called to him from the mountain and told him to say to the Israelites, Jacob's descendants: 4 "You saw what I, the LORD, did to the Egyptians and how I carried you as an eagle carries her young on her wings, and brought you here to me. 5 Now, if you will obey me and keep my covenant, you will be my own people. The whole earth is mine, but you will be my chosen people, 6 a people dedicated to me alone, and you will serve me as priests." 7 So Moses went down and called the leaders of the people together and told them everything that the LORD had commanded him. 8 Then all the people answered together, "We will do everything that the LORD has said," and Moses reported this to the LORD.

9 The LORD said to Moses, "I will come to you in a thick cloud, so that the people will hear me speaking with you and will believe you from now on."

Moses told the LORD what the people had answered, 10 and the LORD said to him, "Go to the people and tell them to spend today and tomorrow purifying themselves for worship. They must wash their clothes 11 and be ready the day after tomorrow. On that day I will come down on Mount Sinai, where all the people can see me. 12 Mark a boundary around the mountain that the people must not cross, and tell them not to go up the mountain or even get near it. If any of you set foot on it, you are to be put to death; 13 you must either be stoned or shot with arrows, without anyone touching you. This applies to both people and animals; they must be put to death. But when the trumpet is blown, then the people are to go up to the mountain."

14 Then Moses came down the mountain and told the people to get ready for worship. So they washed their clothes, 15 and Moses told them, "Be ready by the day after tomorrow and don't have sexual intercourse in the meantime."

16 On the morning of the third day there was thunder and lightning, a thick cloud appeared on the mountain, and a very loud trumpet blast was heard. All the people in the camp trembled with fear. 17 Moses led them out of the camp to meet God, and they stood at the foot of the mountain. 18 All of Mount Sinai was covered with smoke, because the LORD had come down on it in fire. The smoke went up like the smoke of a furnace, and the whole mountain[u] trembled violently. 19 The sound of the trumpet became louder and louder. Moses spoke, and God answered him with thunder. 20 The LORD came down on the top of Mount Sinai and called Moses to the top of the mountain. Moses went up 21 and the LORD said to him, "Go down and warn the people not to cross the boundary to come and look at me; if they do, many of them will die. 22 Even the priests who come near me must purify themselves, or I will punish them."

God answered him with thunder. (19:19)

23 Moses said to the LORD, "The people cannot come up, because you commanded us to consider the mountain sacred and to mark a boundary around it."

24 The LORD replied, "Go down and bring Aaron back with you. But the priests and the

u **19:18** the whole mountain; *one ancient translation and some Hebrew manuscripts* all the people.
19:5, 6 1 Pet 2:9   **19:5** Deut 4:20; 7:6; 14:2; 26:18; Titus 2:14   **19:6** Rev 1:6; 5:10   **19:12, 13** Heb 12:18–20   **19:16** Rev 4:5   **19:16–18** Deut 4:11, 12

Pray It!

Sensing God's Power

It's no wonder the Israelites were petrified. Wouldn't you be? Mount Sinai was in flames and shaking violently. There was thunder, lightning, and trumpets. Let's just say it was a powerful day—one that the Israelites would not forget.

We usually think of God's power as flashy and showy, like a disaster film at the theater. But God's power can be quiet, too. Every one of your senses experiences God's power. All you have to do is pay attention and not take God's power for granted.

Try these "power prayers":

- Look at the sunset, the ocean, or the stars and see God's power.
- Listen to a gentle rain, people laughing, or your heartbeat to hear God's power.
- Touch a rock, the trunk of a tree, or your own skin to feel God's power.
- Breathe in the scent of fire, a flower, or fresh-baked bread to smell God's power.
- Enjoy an orange, a slice of pizza, or a bowl of soup to taste God's power.

When you are aware of God's power all around you, repeat the words of the Israelites: "We will do everything that the LORD has said" (Exodus 19:8).

— Exodus 19:16–25

people must not cross the boundary to come up to me, or I will punish them." 25Moses then went down to the people and told them what the LORD had said.

The Ten Commandments
(Deuteronomy 5:1–21)

20 1God spoke, and these were his words: 2"I am the LORD your God who brought you out of Egypt, where you were slaves.

3 "Worship no god but me.

4 "Do not make for yourselves images of anything in heaven or on earth or in the water under the earth. 5Do not bow down to any idol or worship it, because I am the LORD your God and I tolerate no rivals. I

bring punishment on those who hate me and on their descendants down to the third and fourth generation. 6But I show my love to thousands of generations*v* of those who love me and obey my laws.

7 "Do not use my name for evil purposes, for I, the LORD your God, will punish anyone who misuses my name.

8 "Observe the Sabbath and keep it holy. 9You have six days in which to do your work, 10but the seventh day is a day of rest dedicated to me. On that day no one is to work—neither you, your children, your slaves, your animals, nor the foreigners who live in your country. 11In six days I, the LORD, made the earth, the sky, the seas, and everything in them, but on the seventh day I

v **20:6** thousands of generations; *or* thousands.
20:4, 5 Ex 34:17; Lev 19:4; 26:1; Deut 4:15–18; 27:15   **20:5, 6** Ex 34:6, 7; Num 14:18; Deut 7:9, 10
20:7 Lev 19:12   **20:8** Ex 16:23–30; 31:12–14   **20:9, 10** Ex 23:12; 31:15; 34:21; 35:2; Lev 23:3   **20:11** Gen 2:1–3; Ex 31:17

God makes a covenant with the Israelites in Exodus 19:3–8. With whom did God make other covenants? Hint: Check out Genesis.

The Ten Commandments

Catholic Connections

The Ten Commandments are one of the most famous parts of the Bible. They are a summary of the entire Law God gave to Moses on Mount Sinai. For Christians and Jews, these Commandments play a key role in how we make decisions, how we treat each other, and how we go about being right with God.

As Catholics, we believe that the Ten Commandments and the teachings of Jesus (especially the Beatitudes in Matthew 5:3–11) are the core of what God reveals about morality. (Morality is knowing what is good and evil, right and wrong.) The *Catechism of the Catholic Church*—which is the official summary of Church teachings—uses the Ten Commandments as the outline for Christian morality.

Can you name all Ten Commandments? If not, try to memorize them. More important, try to live by them at all times.

— Exodus 20:1–17

rested. That is why I, the LORD, blessed the Sabbath and made it holy.

12 "Respect your father and your mother, so that you may live a long time in the land that I am giving you.

13 "Do not commit murder.

14 "Do not commit adultery.

15 "Do not steal.

16 "Do not accuse anyone falsely.

17 "Do not desire another man's house; do not desire his wife, his slaves, his cattle, his donkeys, or anything else that he owns."

The People's Fear
(Deuteronomy 5:22–33)

18 When the people heard the thunder and the trumpet blast and saw the lightning and the smoking mountain, they trembled with fear and stood a long way off. 19 They said to Moses, "If you speak to us, we will listen; but

we are afraid that if God speaks to us, we will die."

20 Moses replied, "Don't be afraid; God has only come to test you and make you keep on obeying him, so that you will not sin." 21 But the people continued to stand a long way off, and only Moses went near the dark cloud where God was.

Laws about Altars

22 The LORD commanded Moses to tell the Israelites: "You have seen how I, the LORD, have spoken to you from heaven. 23 Do not make for yourselves gods of silver or gold to be worshiped in addition to me. 24 Make an altar of earth for me, and on it sacrifice your sheep and your cattle as offerings to be completely burned and as fellowship offerings. In every place that I set aside for you to worship me, I will come to you

20:12 a Deut 27:16; Mt 15:4; 19:19; Mk 7:10; 10:19; Lk 18:20; Eph 6:2; b Eph 6:3 20:13 Gen 9:6; Lev 24:17; Mt 5:21; 19:18; Mk 10:19; Lk 18:20; Rom 13:9; Jas 2:11 20:14 Lev 20:10; Mt 5:27; 19:18; Mk 10:19; Lk 18:20; Rom 13:9; Jas 2:11 20:15 Lev 19:11; Mt 19:18; Mk 10:19; Lk 18:20; Rom 13:9 20:16 Ex 23:1; Mt 19:18; Mk 10:19; Lk 18:20 20:17 Rom 7:7; 13:9 20:18, 19 Heb 12:18, 19

Jesus summed up the Ten Commandments in two statements. Read Mark 12:28–31 to find out what they are.

and bless you. 25If you make an altar of stone for me, do not build it out of cut stones, because when you use a chisel on stones, you make them unfit for my use. 26Do not build an altar for me with steps leading up to it; if you do, you will expose yourselves as you go up the steps.

The Treatment of Slaves
(Deuteronomy 15:12–18)

21 1"Give the Israelites the following laws: 2If you buy a Hebrew slave, he shall serve you for six years. In the seventh year he is to be set free without having to pay anything. 3If he was unmarried when he became your slave, he is not to take a wife with him when he leaves; but if he was married when he became your slave, he may take his wife with him. 4If his master gave him a wife and she bore him sons or daughters, the woman and her children belong to the master, and the man is to leave by himself. 5But if the slave declares that he loves his master, his wife, and his children and does not want to be set free, 6then his master shall take him to the place of worship. There he is to make him stand against the door or the doorpost and put a hole through his ear. Then he will be his slave for life.

7"If a man sells his daughter as a slave, she is not to be set free, as male slaves are. 8If she is sold to someone who intends to make her his wife, but he doesn't like her, then she is to be sold back to her father; her master cannot sell her to foreigners, because he has treated her unfairly. 9If a man buys a female slave to give to his son, he is to treat her like a daughter. 10If a man takes a second wife, he must continue to give his first wife the same amount of food and clothing and the same rights that she had before. 11If he does not fulfill these duties to her, he must set her free and not receive any payment.

Laws about Violent Acts

12"Whoever hits someone and kills him is to be put to death. 13But if it was an acci-dent and he did not mean to kill him, he can escape to a place which I will choose for you, and there he will be safe. 14But when someone gets angry and deliberately kills someone else, he is to be put to death, even if he has run to my altar for safety.

15"Whoever hits his father or his mother is to be put to death.

16"Whoever kidnaps someone, either to sell him or to keep him as a slave, is to be put to death.

17"Whoever curses his father or his mother is to be put to death.

18-19"If there is a fight and someone hits someone else with a stone or with his fist, but does not kill him, he is not to be punished. If the one who was hit has to stay in bed, but later is able to get up and walk outside with the help of a cane, the one who hit him is to pay for his lost time and take care of him until he gets well.

20"If a slave owner takes a stick and beats his slave, whether male or female, and the slave dies on the spot, the owner is to be punished. 21But if the slave does not die for a day or two, the master is not to be punished. The loss of his property is punishment enough.

22"If some men are fighting and hurt a pregnant woman so that she loses her child, but she is not injured in any other way, the one who hurt her is to be fined whatever amount the woman's husband demands, subject to the approval of the judges. 23But if the woman herself is injured, the punishment shall be life for life, 24eye for eye, tooth for tooth, hand for hand, foot for foot, 25burn for burn, wound for wound, bruise for bruise.

26"If someone hits his male or female slave in the eye and puts it out, he is to free the slave as payment for the eye. 27If he knocks out a tooth, he is to free the slave as payment for the tooth.

The Responsibility of Owners

28"If a bull gores someone to death, it is to be stoned, and its flesh shall not be eaten; but its owner is not to be punished. 29But if

20:25 Deut 27:5–7; Josh 8:31   **21:2–6** Lev 25:39–46   **21:12** Lev 24:17   **21:13** Num 35:10–34; Deut 19:1–13; Josh 20:1–9   **21:16** Deut 24:7   **21:17** Lev 20:9; Mt 15:4; Mk 7:10   **21:24** Lev 24:19, 20; Deut 19:21; Mt 5:38

Getting Even

Riley just wanted to punch something, he was so mad. Zach made fun of him in gym class, and all the other guys laughed. That wasn't the worst of it though. It carried over to the cafeteria. It was the longest lunch period of his life. Now he was trying to figure out a way to get back at Zach. He wanted revenge.

Many people use Exodus 21:23–25 to justify getting even with someone. Even some laws are based on it, like the death penalty for a person who commits murder. But Jesus had a different idea. He said, "If anyone slaps you on the right cheek, let him slap your left cheek too" (Matthew 5:39).

An eye for an eye only leaves two people who can't see very well. A wound for a wound only leaves two people who are hurting. Instead of getting back at Zach, Riley should use his energy to do something kind for someone else who might be hurting.

Is there someone you want to get even with? What can you do instead that will make you feel better and help someone else? What would Jesus do?

— Exodus 21:23–25

same rule applies. ³²If the bull kills a male or female slave, its owner shall pay the owner of the slave thirty pieces of silver, and the bull shall be stoned to death.

³³"If someone takes the cover off a pit or if he digs one and does not cover it, and a bull or a donkey falls into it, ³⁴he must pay for the animal. He is to pay the money to the owner and may keep the dead animal. ³⁵If someone's bull kills someone else's bull, the two of them shall sell the live bull and divide the money; they shall also divide up the meat from the dead animal. ³⁶But if it was known that the bull had been in the habit of attacking and its owner did not keep it penned up, he must make good the loss by giving the other man a live bull, but he may keep the dead animal.

Laws about Repayment

22 ¹"If someone steals a cow or a sheep and kills it or sells it, he must pay five cows for one cow and four sheep for one sheep. ²⁻⁴He must pay for what he stole. If he owns nothing, he shall be sold as a slave to pay for what he has stolen. If the stolen animal, whether a cow, a donkey, or a sheep, is found alive in his possession, he shall pay two for one.

"If a thief is caught breaking into a house at night and is killed, the one who killed him is not guilty of murder. But if it happens during the day, he is guilty of murder.

⁵"If someone lets his animals graze in a field or a vineyard and they stray away and eat up the crops*ʷ* growing in someone else's field, he must make good the loss with the crops from his own fields or vineyards.

They . . . eat up the crops growing in someone else's field. (22:5)

the bull had been in the habit of attacking people and its owner had been warned, but did not keep it penned up—then if it gores someone to death, it is to be stoned, and its owner is to be put to death also. ³⁰However, if the owner is allowed to pay a fine to save his life, he must pay the full amount required. ³¹If the bull kills a boy or a girl, the

---

ʷ **22:5** If . . . crops; *or* If someone burns off a field or a vineyard, and lets the fire get out of control and burn up the crops.

6"If someone starts a fire in his own field and it spreads through the weeds to someone else's field and burns up grain that is growing or that has been cut and stacked, the one who started the fire is to pay for the damage.

7"If anyone agrees to keep someone else's money or other valuables for him and they are stolen from his house, the thief, if found, shall repay double. **8**But if the thief is not found, the one who was keeping the valuables is to be brought to the place of worship and there he must take an oath that he has not stolen the other one's property.

9"In every case of a dispute about property, whether it involves cattle, donkeys, sheep, clothing, or any other lost object, the two people claiming the property shall be taken to the place of worship. The one whom God declares to be guilty shall pay double to the other one.

10"If anyone agrees to keep someone else's donkey, cow, sheep, or other animal for him, and the animal dies or is injured or is carried off in a raid, and if there was no witness, **11**the man must go to the place of worship and take an oath that he has not stolen the other man's animal. If the animal was not stolen, the owner shall accept the loss, and the other man need not repay him; **12**but if the animal was stolen, the man must repay the owner. **13**If it was killed by wild animals, the man is to bring the remains as evidence; he need not pay for what has been killed by wild animals.

14"If anyone borrows an animal from someone else and it is injured or dies when its owner is not present, he must pay for it. **15**But if that happens when the owner is present, he need not repay. If it is a rented animal, the loss is covered by the rental price.

Moral and Religious Laws

16"If a man seduces a virgin who is not engaged, he must pay the bride price for her and marry her. **17**But if her father refuses to

Rules and More Rules

"This place has too many rules!" Erika cried. "I'm afraid to say anything, do anything, or be different anymore. I might break a rule." Too many rules can be frustrating, but without them life would be a mess. Think of what the school day would be like without rules. What would it be like to ride in a car if there were no traffic laws? What would life be like at home without rules?

Many laws are listed in the Book of Exodus, after the Ten Commandments. These new laws helped the Israelites to build a fair society rather than one that was based on greed and violence. Some of the laws still hold true for us. Others no longer apply because of changes in culture, and the teaching of Jesus.

Rules are made for good reasons, and it is best to try to follow them. If you think a rule is unfair, talk respectfully to the people who made it. Try to understand why they felt the rule was necessary. Maybe you can work together to change it in a way that is fair to everyone.

— Exodus 22:1–8

let him marry her, he must pay the father a sum of money equal to the bride price for a virgin.

18"Put to death any woman who practices magic.

19"Put to death anyone who has sexual relations with an animal.

22:16, 17 Deut 22:28, 29   **22:18** Deut 18:10, 11   **22:19** Lev 18:23; 20:15, 16; Deut 27:21

Which laws in Exodus, chapters 21–23, seem fair to you? Find some that no longer make sense in our culture or because of the teaching of Jesus.

20"Condemn to death anyone who offers sacrifices to any god except to me, the LORD.

21"Do not mistreat or oppress a foreigner; remember that you were foreigners in Egypt. 22Do not mistreat any widow or orphan. 23If you do, I, the LORD, will answer them when they cry out to me for help, 24and I will become angry and kill you in war. Your wives will become widows, and your children will be fatherless.

25"If you lend money to any of my people who are poor, do not act like a moneylender and require him to pay interest. 26If you take someone's cloak as a pledge that he will pay you, you must give it back to him before the sun sets, 27because it is the only covering he has to keep him warm. What else can he sleep in? When he cries out to me for help, I will answer him because I am merciful.

28"Do not speak evil of God,ˣ and do not curse a leader of your people.

29"Give me the offerings from your grain, your wine, and your olive oil when they are due.

"Give me your first-born sons. 30Give me the first-born of your cattle and your sheep. Let the first-born male stay with its mother for seven days, and on the eighth day offer it to me.

31"You are my people, so you must not eat the meat of any animal that has been killed by wild animals; instead, give it to the dogs.

Justice and Fairness

23 1"Do not spread false rumors, and do not help a guilty person by giving false testimony. 2Do not follow the majority when they do wrong or when they give testimony that perverts justice. 3Do not show partiality to a poor person at his trial.

4"If you happen to see your enemy's cow or donkey running loose, take it back to him. 5If his donkey has fallen under its load, help him get the donkey to its feet again; don't just walk off.

6"Do not deny justice to a poor person when he appears in court. 7Do not make false accusations, and do not put an innocent person to death, for I will condemn anyone who does such an evil thing. 8Do not accept a bribe, for a bribe makes people blind to what is right and ruins the cause of those who are innocent.

9"Do not mistreat a foreigner; you know how it feels to be a foreigner, because you were foreigners in Egypt.

The Seventh Year and the Seventh Day

10"For six years plant your land and gather in what it produces. 11But in the seventh year let it rest, and do not harvest anything that grows on it. The poor may eat what grows there, and the wild animals can have what is left. Do the same with your vineyards and your olive trees.

12"Work six days a week, but do no work on the seventh day, so that your slaves and the foreigners who work for you and even your animals can rest.

13"Listen to everything that I, the LORD, have said to you. Do not pray to other gods; do not even mention their names.

The Three Great Festivals
(Exodus 34:18–26; Deuteronomy 16:1–17)

14"Celebrate three festivals a year to honor me. 15In the month of Abib, the month in which you left Egypt, celebrate the Festival of Unleavened Bread in the way that I commanded you. Do not eat any bread made with yeast during the seven days of

---

ˣ **22:28** God; *or* the judges.
22:20 Deut 17:2–7 **22:21, 22** Ex 23:9; Lev 19:33, 34; Deut 24:17, 18; 27:19 **22:25** Lev 25:35–38; Deut 15:7–11; 23:19, 20 **22:26, 27** Deut 24:10–13 **22:28** Acts 23:5 **22:31** Lev 17:15 **23:1** Ex 20:16; Lev 19:11, 12; Deut 5:20 **23:3** Lev 19:15 **23:4, 5** Deut 22:1–4 **23:6–8** Lev 19:15; Deut 16:19 **23:9** Ex 22:21; Lev 19:33, 34; Deut 24:17, 18; 27:19 **23:10, 11** Lev 25:1–7 **23:12** Ex 20:9–11; 31:15; 34:21; 35:2; Lev 23:3; Deut 5:13, 14 **23:15** Ex 12:14–20; Lev 23:6–8; Num 28:17–25

Which verse in Exodus 23:1–9 deals with peer pressure? What does it say about following the crowd?

Everyday Justice

If a teacher asked you and your friends to come up with guidelines for being a person who is well liked and respected, your list would probably include some of the following rules:

• Don't spread rumors.

• Don't cover for someone who has done something wrong.

• Don't give in to peer pressure, especially when peers lie or cheat.

• If you find something that belongs to someone else, return it to that person.

• Be fair to everyone, even those who are different or don't seem to fit in.

The words may be different, but these rules come straight from the Bible (Exodus 23:1–9). They were written hundreds of years ago, but they make as much sense today as they did then. If you want to be well liked and respected as you grow up, you will want to live by these rules.

The Bible is not just a book for and about people who lived many centuries ago. It is a book that was written for and about you, too. Read it often and use it as a guide to becoming the person God wants you to be.

— Exodus 23:1–9

this festival. Never come to worship me without bringing an offering.

¹⁶"Celebrate the Harvest Festival when you begin to harvest your crops.

"Celebrate the Festival of Shelters in the autumn, when you gather the fruit from your vineyards and orchards. ¹⁷Every year at these three festivals all your men must come to worship me, the Lord your God.

¹⁸"Do not offer bread made with yeast when you sacrifice an animal to me. The fat of animals sacrificed to me during these festivals is not to be left until the following morning.

¹⁹"Each year bring to the house of the LORD your God the first grain that you harvest.

"Do not cook a young sheep or goat in its mother's milk.

Promises and Instructions

²⁰"I will send an angel ahead of you to protect you as you travel and to bring you to the place which I have prepared. ²¹Pay attention to him and obey him. Do not rebel against him, for I have sent him, and he will not pardon such rebellion. ²²But if you obey him and do everything I command, I will fight against all your enemies. ²³My angel will go ahead of you and take you into the land of the Amorites, the Hittites, the Perizzites, the Canaanites, the Hivites, and the Jebusites, and I will destroy them. ²⁴Do not bow down to their gods or worship them, and do not adopt their religious practices. Destroy their gods and break down their sacred stone pillars. ²⁵If you worship me, the LORD your God, I will bless you with food and water and take away all your sicknesses. ²⁶In your land no woman will have a miscarriage or be without children. I will give you long lives.

²⁷"I will make the people who oppose you afraid of me; I will bring confusion among the people against whom you fight, and I will make all your enemies turn and run from you. ²⁸I will throw your enemies into panic;ʸ I will drive out the Hivites, the Canaanites, and the Hittites as you advance. ²⁹I will not drive them out within a year's time; if I did, the land would become deserted, and the wild animals would be too many for you. ³⁰Instead, I will drive them out little by little, until there are enough of you to take possession of the land. ³¹I will make the borders of your land extend from

ʸ 23:28 I will . . . panic; *or* I will send hornets among your enemies.
23:16 a Lev 23:15–21; Num 28:26–31; b Lev 23:39–43   23:19 Deut 26:2; Ex 34:26; Deut 14:21

the Gulf of Aqaba to the Mediterranean Sea and from the desert to the Euphrates River. I will give you power over the inhabitants of the land, and you will drive them out as you advance. ³²Do not make any agreement with them or with their gods. ³³Do not let those people live in your country; if you do, they will make you sin against me. If you worship their gods, it will be a fatal trap for you."

The Covenant Is Sealed

24 ¹The LORD said to Moses, "Come up the mountain to me, you and Aaron, Nadab, Abihu, and seventy of the leaders of Israel; and while you are still some distance away, bow down in worship. ²You alone, and none of the others, are to come near me. The people are not even to come up the mountain."

³Moses went and told the people all the LORD's commands and all the ordinances, and all the people answered together, "We will do everything that the LORD has said." ⁴Moses wrote down all the LORD's commands. Early the next morning he built an altar at the foot of the mountain and set up twelve stones, one for each of the twelve tribes of Israel. ⁵Then he sent young men, and they burned sacrifices to the LORD and sacrificed some cattle as fellowship offerings. ⁶Moses took half of the blood of the animals and put it in bowls; and the other half he threw against the altar. ⁷Then he took the book of the covenant, in which the LORD's commands were written, and read it aloud to the people. They said, "We will obey the LORD and do everything that he has commanded."

⁸Then Moses took the blood in the bowls and threw it on the people. He said, "This is the blood that seals the covenant which the LORD made with you when he gave all these commands."

⁹Moses, Aaron, Nadab, Abihu, and seventy of the leaders of Israel went up the mountain ¹⁰and they saw the God of Israel. Beneath his feet was what looked like a pavement of sapphire, as blue as the sky.

The Covenant of Covenants

God made important covenants before this one. In the Bible a covenant is a set of promises made between God and a person or a group. The Book of Genesis tells about covenants God made with Noah, Abraham, and Jacob. But the Sinai Covenant is the Covenant of Covenants. At Sinai God made clear what his covenant with Abraham would now mean for all of Abraham's descendants. When Moses read the Law—the Ten Commandments—from the book of the Covenant, the Israelites replied, "We will obey the LORD and do everything that he has commanded" (Exodus 24:7). To seal the deal, Moses went up Mount Sinai, where God gave him stone tablets on which the Law was written. The Sinai Covenant and the Law that was part of that Covenant continue to guide Jewish and Christian believers today.

God's Covenant with the Israelites meant that they were now and forever the People of God. Nothing would ever change that, even though the Israelites would make some huge mistakes. As sons and daughters of Abraham through our faith, we are also the People of God—now and forever.

— Exodus 24:1–18

¹¹God did not harm these leading men of Israel; they saw God, and then they ate and drank together.

24:8 a Mt 26:28; Mk 14:24; Lk 22:20; 1 Cor 11:25; Heb 10:29; **b** Heb 9:19, 20

Exodus

Moses on Mount Sinai

12 The LORD said to Moses, "Come up the mountain to me, and while you are here, I will give you two stone tablets which contain all the laws that I have written for the instruction of the people." 13 Moses and his helper Joshua got ready, and Moses beganᶻ to go up the holy mountain. 14 Moses said to the leaders, "Wait here in the camp for us until we come back. Aaron and Hur are here with you; and so whoever has a dispute to settle can go to them."

15 Moses went up Mount Sinai, and a cloud covered it. 16-17 The dazzling light of the LORD's presence came down on the mountain. To the Israelites the light looked like a fire burning on top of the mountain. The cloud covered the mountain for six days, and on the seventh day the LORD called to Moses from the cloud. 18 Moses went on up the mountain into the cloud. There he stayed for forty days and nights.

Offerings for the Sacred Tent
(Exodus 35:4–9)

25 1 The LORD said to Moses, 2 "Tell the Israelites to make an offering to me. Receive whatever offerings anyone wishes to give. 3 These offerings are to be: gold, silver, and bronze; 4 fine linen; blue, purple, and red wool; cloth made of goats' hair; 5 rams' skin dyed red; fine leather; acacia wood; 6 oil for the lamps; spices for the anointing oil and for the sweet-smelling incense; 7 carnelians and other jewels to be set in the ephodᵃ of the High Priest and in his breastpiece. 8 The people must make a sacred Tent for me, so that I may live among them. 9 Make it and all its furnishings according to the plan that I will show you.

The Covenant Box
(Exodus 37:1–9)

10 "Make a Box out of acacia wood, 45 inches long, 27 inches wide, and 27 inches high. 11 Cover it with pure gold inside and out and put a gold border all around it. 12 Make four carrying rings of gold for it and attach them to its four legs, with two rings on each side. 13 Make carrying poles of acacia wood and cover them with gold 14 and put them through the rings on each side of the Box. 15 The poles are to be left in the rings and must not be taken out. 16 Then put in the Box the two stone tablets that I will give you, on which the commandments are written.

17 "Make a lid of pure gold, 45 inches long and 27 inches wide. 18 Make two winged creaturesᵇ of hammered gold, 19 one for each end of the lid. Make them so that they form one piece with the lid. 20 The winged creatures are to face each other across the lid, and their outspread wings are to cover it. 21 Put the two stone tablets inside the Box and put the lid on top of it. 22 I will meet you there, and from above the lid between the two winged creatures I will give you all my laws for the people of Israel.

The Table for the Bread Offered to God
(Exodus 37:10–16)

23 "Make a table out of acacia wood, 36 inches long, 18 inches wide, and 27 inches high. 24 Cover it with pure gold and put a gold border around it. 25 Make a rim 3 inches wide around it and a gold border around the rim. 26 Make four carrying rings of gold for it and put them at the four corners, where the legs are. 27 The rings to hold the poles for carrying the table are to be placed near the rim. 28 Make the poles of acacia wood and cover them with gold. 29 Make

---

ᶻ **24:13** *Moses began; one ancient translation* they began.   ᵃ **25:7** EPHOD: *In most contexts the term ephod refers to a type of shoulder garment, in certain respects resembling a vest. It was made of costly and colorful cloth and to it was attached a kind of pouch containing the Urim and Thummim, two objects used in determining God's will.*   ᵇ **25:18** WINGED CREATURES. *See Word List.*
24:18 Deut 9:9   **25:17** Heb 9:5

The stone tablets were to be kept in the Covenant Box described in Exodus 25:10–22. The Covenant Box is also called the Ark of the Covenant in other Bibles.

plates, cups, jars, and bowls to be used for the wine offerings. All of these are to be made of pure gold. ³⁰The table is to be placed in front of the Covenant Box, and on the table there is always to be the sacred bread offered to me.

The Lampstand
(Exodus 37:17–24)

³¹"Make a lampstand of pure gold. Make its base and its shaft of hammered gold; its decorative flowers, including buds and petals, are to form one piece with it. ³²Six branches shall extend from its sides, three from each side. ³³Each of the six branches is to have three decorative flowers shaped like almond blossoms with buds and petals. ³⁴The shaft of the lampstand is to have four decorative flowers shaped like almond blossoms with buds and petals. ³⁵There is to be one bud below each of the three pairs of branches. ³⁶The buds, the branches, and the lampstand are to be a single piece of pure hammered gold. ³⁷Make seven lamps for the lampstand and set them up so that they shine toward the front. ³⁸Make its tongs and trays of pure gold. ³⁹Use seventy-five pounds of pure gold to make the lampstand and all this equipment. ⁴⁰Take care to make them according to the plan that I showed you on the mountain.

The Tent of the LORD's Presence
(Exodus 36:8–38)

26 ¹"Make the interior of the sacred Tent, the Tent of my presence, out of ten pieces of fine linen woven with blue, purple, and red wool. Embroider them with figures of winged creatures. ²Make each piece the same size, 14 yards long and 2 yards wide. ³Sew five of them together in one set, and do the same with the other five. ⁴Make loops of blue cloth on the edge of the outside piece in each set. ⁵Put fifty loops on the first piece of the first set and fifty

loops matching them on the last piece of the second set. ⁶Make fifty gold hooks with which to join the two sets into one piece.

⁷"Make a cover for the Tent out of eleven pieces of cloth made of goats' hair. ⁸Make them all the same size, 15 yards long and 2 yards wide. ⁹Sew five of them together in one set, and the other six in another set. Fold the sixth piece double over the front of the Tent. ¹⁰Put fifty loops on the edge of the last piece of one set, and fifty loops on the edge of the other set. ¹¹Make fifty bronze hooks and put them in the loops to join the two sets so as to form one cover. ¹²Hang the extra half piece over the back of the Tent. ¹³The extra half yard on each side of the length is to hang over the sides of the Tent to cover it.

¹⁴"Make two more coverings, one of rams' skin dyed red and the other of fine leather, to serve as the outer cover.

¹⁵"Make upright frames for the Tent out of acacia wood. ¹⁶Each frame is to be 15 feet long and 27 inches wide, ¹⁷with two matching projections, so that the frames can be joined together. All the frames are to have these projections. ¹⁸Make twenty frames for the south side ¹⁹and forty silver bases to go under them, two bases under each frame to hold its two projections. ²⁰Make twenty frames for the north side of the Tent ²¹and forty silver bases, two under each frame. ²²For the back of the Tent on the west, make six frames, ²³and two frames for the corners. ²⁴These corner frames are to be joined at the bottom and connected all the way to the top. The two frames that form the two corners are to be made in this way. ²⁵So there will be eight frames with their sixteen silver bases, two under each frame.

²⁶"Make fifteen crossbars of acacia wood, five for the frames on one side of the Tent, ²⁷five for the frames on the other side, and five for the frames on the west end, at the back. ²⁸The middle crossbar, set halfway up the frames, is to extend from one end of the

---

c **26:1** TENT OF THE LORD'S PRESENCE: *See Word List.*
25:30 Lev 24:5-8   **25:40** Acts 7:44; Heb 8:5

The Tent of the LORD's Presence is also called a tabernacle in other Bible translations.

Portable God

Martina was going away with her friend's family for a few days. Her mom went shopping and bought several travel-sized items for Martina to take along—shampoo, toothpaste, and other things she needed for the trip. They were small and a lot easier to pack than the stuff she had at home.

Exodus, chapters 25–31, contain instructions for building a travel-sized worship space. As the Israelites continued their journey from Sinai, God wanted them to know that he was always with them, always blessing them. They needed a place to worship God and listen to him. The Tent of the LORD's presence and its furnishings weren't exactly small and light, but they could be packed up and carried from place to place.

God is always with us, but sometimes we need to be reminded of his presence. Some people wear a cross or medal. Others pray when they hear church bells. Others post pictures and poems that remind them of God in places where they will see them every day.

As you travel on your journey through life, what reminds you that God is with you?

— Exodus, chapter 26

with blue, purple, and red wool. Embroider it with figures of winged creatures. 32 Hang it on four posts of acacia wood covered with gold, fitted with hooks, and set in four silver bases. 33 Place the curtain under the row of hooks in the roof of the Tent, and put behind the curtain the Covenant Box containing the two stone tablets. The curtain will separate the Holy Place from the Most Holy Place. 34 Put the lid on the Covenant Box. 35 Outside the Most Holy Place put the table against the north side of the Tent and the lampstand against the south side.

36 "For the entrance of the Tent make a curtain of fine linen woven with blue, purple, and red wool and decorated with embroidery. 37 For this curtain make five posts of acacia wood covered with gold and fitted with gold hooks; make five bronze bases for these posts.

The Altar
(Exodus 38:1–7)

27 1 "Make an altar out of acacia wood. It is to be square, 7½ feet long and 7½ feet wide, and it is to be 4½ feet high. 2 Make projections at the top of the four corners. They are to form one piece with the altar, and the whole is to be covered with bronze. 3 Make pans for the greasy ashes, and make shovels, bowls, hooks, and fire pans. All this equipment is to be made of bronze. 4 Make a bronze grating and put four bronze carrying rings on its corners. 5 Put the grating under the rim of the altar, so that it reaches halfway up the altar. 6 Make carrying poles of acacia wood, cover them with bronze, 7 and put them in the rings on each side of the altar when it is carried. 8 Make the altar out of boards and leave it hollow, according to the plan that I showed you on the mountain.

The Enclosure for the Tent of the LORD's Presence
(Exodus 38:9–20)

9 "For the Tent of my presence make an enclosure out of fine linen curtains. On the south side the curtains are to be 50 yards

Tent to the other. 29 Cover the frames with gold and fit them with gold rings to hold the crossbars, which are also to be covered with gold. 30 Set up the Tent according to the plan that I showed you on the mountain.

31 "Make a curtain of fine linen woven

Exodus

Pray It!

A Traveler's Prayer

Saint Patrick was a missionary who brought Christ to the people of Ireland. Because of his efforts to spread the Gospel, Patrick is known as the Apostle of Ireland and its patron saint.

Inside the Tent of the LORD's presence, in front of the Covenant Box, a lamp was to be kept burning all night as a sign of God's presence. Like that lamp, this prayer of Saint Patrick will remind you that God is always with you and around you on the journey of life.

Christ, be with me, Christ before me, Christ behind me.
Christ in me, Christ beneath me, Christ above me,
Christ on my right, Christ on my left.
Christ where I lie, Christ where I sit, Christ where I arise.
Christ in the heart of every one who thinks of me,
Christ in the mouth of every one who speaks of me.
Christ in every eye that sees me.
Christ in every ear that hears me.

— Exodus 27:20–21

long, 10supported by twenty bronze posts in twenty bronze bases, with hooks and rods made of silver. 11Do the same on the north side of the enclosure. 12On the west side there are to be curtains 25 yards long, with ten posts and ten bases. 13On the east side, where the entrance is, the enclosure is also to be 25 yards wide. 14-15On each side of the entrance there are to be 7½ yards of curtains, with three posts and three bases. 16For the entrance itself there is to be a curtain 10 yards long made of fine linen woven with blue, purple, and red wool, and decorated with embroidery. It is to be supported by four posts in four bases. 17All the posts around the enclosure are to be connected with silver rods, and their hooks are to be made of silver and their bases of bronze. 18The enclosure is to be 50 yards long, 25 yards wide, and 2½ yards high. The curtains are to be made of fine linen and the bases of bronze. 19All the equipment that is used in the Tent and all the pegs for the Tent and for the enclosure are to be made of bronze.

Taking Care of the Lamp
(Leviticus 24:1–4)

20"Command the people of Israel to bring you the best olive oil for the lamp, so that it can be lit each evening. 21Aaron and his sons are to set up the lamp in the Tent of my presence outside the curtain which is in front of the Covenant Box. There in my presence it is to burn from evening until morning. This command is to be kept forever by the Israelites and their descendants.

Garments for the Priests
(Exodus 39:1–7)

28 1"Summon your brother Aaron and his sons, Nadab, Abihu, Eleazar, and Ithamar. Separate them from the people of Israel, so that they may serve me as priests. 2Make priestly garments for your brother Aaron, to provide him with dignity and beauty. 3Call all the skilled workers to whom I have given ability, and tell them to make Aaron's clothes, so that he may be dedicated as a priest in my service. 4Tell them to make a breastpiece, an ephod, a robe, an embroi-

Catholic Connections

Vestments

In Exodus, chapter 28, God gave Moses directions for the clothing—called *vestments*—that the priests of the temple were to wear to honor God. It was to be brightly colored and made of the finest materials.

Catholic priests and deacons also wear vestments when they celebrate the sacraments. The next time you are at Mass, see if you can identify the following vestments:

- Alb: a long, white tunic. It may be tied around the waist with a rope, known as a *cincture.*
- Stole: a long, narrow strip of fabric. Priests wear a stole over both shoulders. Deacons wear a stole over one shoulder.
- Chasuble: the outer garment worn by a priest. The color of the chasuble is determined by the liturgical season or type of Mass being celebrated.

— Exodus, chapter 28

dered shirt, a turban, and a sash. They are to make these priestly garments for your brother Aaron and his sons, so that they can serve me as priests. 5 The skilled workers are to use blue, purple, and red wool, gold thread, and fine linen.

6 "They are to make the ephod of blue, purple, and red wool, gold thread, and fine linen, decorated with embroidery. 7 Two shoulder straps, by which it can be fastened, are to be attached to the sides. 8 A finely woven belt made of the same materials is to be attached to the ephod so as to form one piece with it. 9 Take two carnelian stones and engrave on them the names of the twelve sons of Jacob, 10 in the order of their birth, with six on one stone and six on the other. 11 Have a skillful jeweler engrave on the two stones the names of the sons of Jacob, and mount the stones in gold settings. 12 Put them on the shoulder straps of the ephod to represent the twelve tribes of Israel. In this way Aaron will carry their names on his shoulders, so that I, the LORD, will always

remember my people. 13 Make two gold settings 14 and two chains of pure gold twisted like cords, and attach them to the settings.

The Breastpiece
(Exodus 39:8–21)

15 "Make a breastpiece for the High Priest to use in determining God's will. It is to be made of the same materials as the ephod and with similar embroidery. 16 It is to be square and folded double, 9 inches long and 9 inches wide. 17 Mount four rows of precious stones on it; in the first row mount a ruby, a topaz, and a garnet; 18 in the second row, an emerald, a sapphire, and a diamond; 19 in the third row, a turquoise, an agate, and an amethyst; 20 and in the fourth row, a beryl, a carnelian, and a jasper. These are to be mounted in gold settings. 21 Each of these twelve stones is to have engraved on it the name of one of the sons of Jacob, to represent the tribes of Israel. 22 For the breastpiece make chains of pure gold, twisted like cords.

Breastpiece: A linen pocket that was attached to another garment and worn like an apron. It held special items.

23 Make two gold rings and attach them to the upper corners of the breastpiece, 24 and fasten the two gold cords to the two rings. 25 Fasten the other two ends of the cords to the two settings, and in this way attach them in front to the shoulder straps of the ephod. 26 Then make two rings of gold and attach them to the lower corners of the breastpiece on the inside edge next to the ephod. 27 Make two more gold rings and attach them to the lower part of the front of the two shoulder straps of the ephod, near the seam and above the finely woven belt. 28 Tie the rings of the breastpiece to the rings of the ephod with a blue cord, so that the breastpiece rests above the belt and does not come loose.

29 "When Aaron enters the Holy Place, he will wear this breastpiece engraved with the names of the tribes of Israel, so that I, the LORD, will always remember my people. 30 Put the Urim and Thummim*d* in the breastpiece, so that Aaron will carry them when he comes into my holy presence. At such times he must always wear this breast-piece, so that he can determine my will for the people of Israel.

The Other Priestly Garments
(Exodus 39:22–31)

31 "The robe that goes under the ephod is to be made entirely of blue wool. 32 It is to have a hole for the head, and this hole is to be reinforced with a woven binding to keep it from tearing. 33-34 All around its lower hem put pomegranates of blue, purple, and red wool, alternating with gold bells. 35 Aaron is to wear this robe when he serves as priest. When he comes into my presence in the Holy Place or when he leaves it, the sound of the bells will be heard, and he will not be killed.

36 "Make an ornament of pure gold and engrave on it 'Dedicated to the LORD.' 37 Tie it to the front of the turban with a blue cord.

38 Aaron is to wear it on his forehead, so that I, the LORD, will accept all the offerings that the Israelites dedicate to me, even if the people commit some error in offering them.

39 "Weave Aaron's shirt of fine linen and make a turban of fine linen and also a sash decorated with embroidery.

40 "Make shirts, sashes, and caps for Aaron's sons, to provide them with dignity and beauty. 41 Put these clothes on your brother Aaron and his sons. Then ordain them and dedicate them by anointing them with olive oil, so that they may serve me as priests. 42 Make linen shorts for them, reaching from the waist to the thighs, so that they will not expose themselves. 43 Aaron and his sons must always wear them when they go into the Tent of my presence or approach the altar to serve as priests in the Holy Place, so that they will not be killed for exposing themselves. This is a permanent rule for Aaron and his descendants.

Instructions for Ordaining Aaron and His Sons as Priests
(Leviticus 8:1–36)

29 1 "This is what you are to do to Aaron and his sons to dedicate them as priests in my service. Take one young bull and two rams without any defects. 2 Use the best wheat flour, but no yeast, and make some bread with olive oil, some without it, and some in the form of thin cakes brushed with oil. 3 Put them in a basket and offer them to me when you sacrifice the bull and the two rams.

4 "Bring Aaron and his sons to the entrance of the Tent of my presence, and have them take a ritual bath. 5 Then dress Aaron in the priestly garments—the shirt, the robe that goes under the ephod, the ephod, the breastpiece, and the belt. 6 Put the turban on him and tie on it the sacred sign of dedication engraved 'Dedicated to the

---

d **28:30** URIM AND THUMMIM: *Two objects used by the priest to determine God's will; it is not known precisely how they were used.*
28:30 Num 27:21; Deut 33:8; Ezra 2:63; Neh 7:65   **28:33, 34** Sir 45:9

Ordination is the religious ritual in which someone becomes a priest by being given priestly powers and responsibilities.

LORD.' 7 Then take the anointing oil, pour it on his head, and anoint him.

8 "Bring his sons and put shirts on them; 9 put sashes around their waists and tie caps on their heads. That is how you are to ordain Aaron and his sons. They and their descendants are to serve me as priests forever.

10 "Bring the bull to the front of the Tent of my presence and tell Aaron and his sons to put their hands on its head. 11 Kill the bull there in my holy presence at the entrance of the Tent. 12 Take some of the bull's blood and with your finger put it on the projections of the altar. Then pour out the rest of the blood at the base of the altar. 13 Next, take all the fat which covers the internal organs, the best part of the liver, and the two kidneys with the fat on them, and burn them on the altar as an offering to me. 14 But burn the bull's flesh, its skin, and its intestines outside the camp. This is an offering to take away the sins of the priests.

15 "Take one of the rams and tell Aaron and his sons to put their hands on its head. 16 Kill it, and take its blood and throw it against all four sides of the altar. 17 Cut the ram in pieces; wash its internal organs and its hind legs, and put them on top of the head and the other pieces. 18 Burn the whole ram on the altar as a food offering. The odor of this offering pleases me.

19 "Take the other ram—the ram used for dedication—and tell Aaron and his sons to put their hands on its head. 20 Kill it, and take some of its blood and put it on the lobes of the right ears of Aaron and his sons, on the thumbs of their right hands and on the big toes of their right feet. Throw the rest of the blood against all four sides of the altar. 21 Take some of the blood that is on the altar and some of the anointing oil, and sprinkle it on Aaron and his clothes and on his sons and their clothes. He, his sons, and their clothes will then be dedicated to me.

22 "Cut away the ram's fat, the fat tail, the fat covering the internal organs, the best part of the liver, the two kidneys with the fat on them, and the right thigh. 23 From the basket of bread which has been offered to me, take

one loaf of each kind: one loaf made with olive oil and one made without it and one thin cake. 24 Put all this food in the hands of Aaron and his sons and have them dedicate it to me as a special gift. 25 Then take it from them and burn it on the altar, on top of the burnt offering, as a food offering to me. The odor of this offering pleases me.

26 "Take the breast of this ram and dedicate it to me as a special gift. This part of the animal will be yours.

27 "When a priest is ordained, the breast and the thigh of the ram being used for the ordination are to be dedicated to me as a special gift and set aside for the priests. 28 It is my unchanging decision that when my people make their fellowship offerings, the breast and the thigh of the animal belong to the priests. This is the people's gift to me, the LORD.

29 "Aaron's priestly garments are to be handed on to his sons after his death, for them to wear when they are ordained. 30 The son of Aaron who succeeds him as priest and who goes into the Tent of my presence to serve in the Holy Place is to wear these garments for seven days.

31 "Take the meat of the ram used for the ordination of Aaron and his sons and boil it in a holy place. 32 At the entrance of the Tent of my presence they are to eat it along with the bread left in the basket. 33 They shall eat what was used in the ritual of forgiveness at their ordination. Only priests may eat this food, because it is sacred. 34 If some of the meat or some of the bread is not eaten by morning, it is to be burned; it is not to be eaten, for it is sacred.

35 "Perform the rites of ordination for Aaron and his sons for seven days exactly as I have commanded you. 36 Each day you must offer a bull as a sacrifice, so that sin may be forgiven. This will purify the altar. Then anoint it with olive oil to make it holy. 37 Do this every day for seven days. Then the altar will be completely holy, and anyone or anything that touches it will be harmed by the power of its holiness.*e*

---

e **29:37** BE HARMED BY THE POWER OF ITS HOLINESS: *It was believed that ordinary people or things would be harmed by touching something holy.*
29:18 Eph 5:2; Phil 4:18

The Daily Offerings
(Numbers 28:1–8)

38 "Every day for all time to come, sacrifice on the altar two one-year-old lambs. 39 Sacrifice one of the lambs in the morning and the other in the evening. 40 With the first lamb offer two pounds of fine wheat flour mixed with one quart of pure olive oil. Pour out one quart of wine as an offering. 41 Sacrifice the second lamb in the evening, and offer with it the same amounts of flour, olive oil, and wine as in the morning. This is a food offering to me, the LORD, and its odor pleases me. 42 For all time to come, this burnt offering is to be offered in my presence at the entrance of the Tent of my presence. That is where I will meet my people and speak to you. 43 There I will meet the people of Israel, and the dazzling light of my presence will make the place holy. 44 I will make the Tent and the altar holy, and I will set Aaron and his sons apart to serve me as priests. 45 I will live among the people of Israel, and I will be their God. 46 They will know that I am the LORD their God who brought them out of Egypt so that I could live among them. I am the LORD their God.

The Altar for Burning Incense
(Exodus 37:25–28)

30 1 "Make an altar out of acacia wood, for burning incense. 2 It is to be square, 18 inches long and 18 inches wide, and it is to be 36 inches high. Its projections at the four corners are to form one piece with it. 3 Cover its top, all four sides, and its projections with pure gold, and put a gold border around it. 4 Make two gold carrying rings for it and attach them below the border on two sides to hold the poles with which it is to be carried. 5 Make these poles of acacia wood and cover them with gold. 6 Put this altar outside the curtain which hangs in front of the Covenant Box. That is the place where I will meet you. 7 Every morning when Aaron comes to take care of the lamps, he is to burn sweet-smelling incense on it. 8 He must do the same when he lights the lamps in the evening. This offering of incense is to continue without interruption for all time to come. 9 Do not offer on this altar any forbidden incense, any animal offering, or any grain offering, and do not pour out any wine offering on it. 10 Once a year Aaron is to perform the ritual for purifying the altar by putting on its four projections the blood of the animal sacrificed for sin. This is to be done every year for all time to come. This altar is to be completely holy, dedicated to me, the LORD."

The Tax for the Tent of the LORD's Presence

11 The LORD said to Moses, 12 "When you take a census of the people of Israel, each man is to pay me a price for his life, so that no disaster will come on him while the census is being taken. 13 Everyone included in the census must pay the required amount of money, weighed according to the official standard. Everyone must pay this as an offering to me. 14 Everyone being counted in the census, that is, every man twenty years old or older, is to pay me this amount. 15 The rich man is not to pay more, nor the poor man less, when they pay this amount for their lives. 16 Collect this money from the people of Israel and spend it for the upkeep of the Tent of my presence. This tax will be the payment for their lives, and I will remember to protect them."

The Bronze Basin

17 The LORD said to Moses, 18 "Make a bronze basin with a bronze base. Place it between the Tent and the altar, and put water in it. 19 Aaron and his sons are to use the water to wash their hands and feet 20 before they go into the Tent or approach the altar to offer the food offering. Then they will not be killed. 21 They must wash their hands and feet, so that they will not die. This is a rule which they and their descendants are to observe forever."

30:13 Ex 38:25, 26; Mt 17:24   **30:18** Ex 38:8

The Anointing Oil

22 The LORD said to Moses, 23 "Take the finest spices—12 pounds of liquid myrrh, 6 pounds of sweet-smelling cinnamon, 6 pounds of sweet-smelling cane, 24 and 12 pounds of cassia (all weighed according to the official standard). Add one gallon of olive oil, 25 and make a sacred anointing oil, mixed like perfume. 26 Use it to anoint the Tent of my presence, the Covenant Box, 27 the table and all its equipment, the lampstand and its equipment, the altar for burning incense, 28 the altar for burning offerings, together with all its equipment, and the washbasin with its base. 29 Dedicate these things in this way, and they will be completely holy, and anyone or anything that touches them will be harmed by the power of its holiness.ᶠ 30 Then anoint Aaron and his sons, and ordain them as priests in my service. 31 Say to the people of Israel, 'This holy anointing oil is to be used in my service for all time to come. 32 It must not be poured on ordinary men, and you must not use the same formula to make any mixture like it. It is holy, and you must treat it as holy. 33 Whoever makes any like it or uses any of it on anyone who is not a priest will no longer be considered one of my people.' "

The Incense

34 The LORD said to Moses, "Take an equal part of each of the following sweet spices—stacte, onycha, galbanum, and pure frankincense. 35 Use them to make incense, mixed like perfume. Add salt to keep it pure and holy. 36 Beat part of it into a fine powder, take it into the Tent of my presence, and sprinkle it in front of the Covenant Box. Treat this incense as completely holy. 37 Do not use the same formula to make any incense like it for yourselves. Treat it as a holy thing dedicated to me. 38 If anyone makes any like it for use as perfume, he will no longer be considered one of my people."

God-Given Gifts

Bezalel could do just about anything. He was skilled at working with wood, precious metals, and cloth. He was famous for his wonderful designs. Where did he get such talent? From God. "I have filled him with my power. I have given him understanding, skill, and ability for every kind of artistic work" (Exodus 31:3).

God gave you a special gift, too, and is counting on you to use it to honor him. You may have a gift of working with your hands or for working with people. Maybe you are good at decorating or writing. Perhaps you are a good leader or a good follower. We use our gifts from God in ways that honor him.

• What special gift or gifts has God given you?
• What do you think God is asking you to do with your gift right now?
• How will you honor God with your gift?

~ Exodus 31:1–11

Craftsmen for the Tent of the LORD's Presence
(Exodus 35:30—36:1)

31 1 The LORD said to Moses, 2 "I have chosen Bezalel, the son of Uri and grandson of Hur, from the tribe of Judah, 3 and I have filled him with my power.ᵍ I have given him understanding, skill, and ability for

---

ᶠ **30:29** HARMED BY THE POWER OF ITS HOLINESS: *See* 29:37.   ᵍ **31:3** power; *or* spirit.
30:22–38 Ex 37:29

The Jewish Sabbath (like Sunday in the Christian Church) is supposed to be a day of rest. Why? Check out Exodus, chapter 31.

Exodus

every kind of artistic work— 4for planning skillful designs and working them in gold, silver, and bronze; 5for cutting jewels to be set; for carving wood; and for every other kind of artistic work. 6I have also selected Oholiab son of Ahisamach, from the tribe of Dan, to work with him. I have also given great ability to all the other skilled workers, so that they can make everything I have commanded to be made: 7the Tent of my presence, the Covenant Box and its lid, all the furnishings of the Tent, 8the table and its equipment, the lampstand of pure gold and all its equipment, the altar for burning incense, 9the altar for burnt offerings and all its equipment, the washbasin and its base, 10the magnificent priestly garments for Aaron and his sons to use when they serve as priests, 11the anointing oil, and the sweet-smelling incense for the Holy Place. In making all these things, they are to do exactly as I have commanded you."

Sabbath, the Day of Rest

12The LORD commanded Moses 13to tell the people of Israel, "Keep the Sabbath, my day of rest, because it is a sign between you and me for all time to come, to show that I, the LORD, have made you my own people. 14You must keep the day of rest, because it is sacred. Whoever does not keep it, but works on that day, is to be put to death. 15You have six days in which to do your work, but the seventh day is a solemn day of rest dedicated to me. Whoever does any work on that day is to be put to death. 16The people of Israel are to keep this day as a sign of the covenant. 17It is a permanent sign between the people of Israel and me, because I, the LORD, made heaven and earth in six days, and on the seventh day I stopped working and rested."

18When God had finished speaking to Moses on Mount Sinai, he gave him the two stone tablets on which God himself had written the commandments.

The Gold Bull-Calf
(Deuteronomy 9:6–29)

32 1When the people saw that Moses had not come down from the mountain but was staying there a long time, they gathered around Aaron and said to him, "We do not know what has happened to this man Moses, who led us out of Egypt; so make us a god[h] to lead us."

2Aaron said to them, "Take off the gold earrings which your wives, your sons, and your daughters are wearing, and bring them to me." 3So all the people took off their gold earrings and brought them to Aaron. 4He took the earrings, melted them, poured the gold into a mold, and made a gold bull-calf.

The people said, "Israel, this is our god, who led us out of Egypt!"

5Then Aaron built an altar in front of the gold bull-calf and announced, "Tomorrow there will be a festival to honor the LORD." 6Early the next morning they brought some animals to burn as sacrifices and others to eat as fellowship offerings. The people sat down to a feast, which turned into an orgy of drinking and sex.

7The LORD said to Moses, "Hurry and go back down, because your people, whom you led out of Egypt, have sinned and rejected me. 8They have already left the way that I commanded them to follow; they have made a bull-calf out of melted gold and have worshiped it and offered sacrifices to it. They are saying that this is their god, who led them out of Egypt. 9I know how stubborn these people are. 10Now, don't try to stop me. I am angry with them, and I am going to destroy them. Then I will make you and your descendants into a great nation."

11But Moses pleaded with the LORD his God and said, " LORD, why should you be so angry with your people, whom you rescued from Egypt with great might and power? 12Why should the Egyptians be able to say

h **32:1** a god; *or* some gods.
31:15 Ex 20:8–11; 23:12; 34:21; 35:2; Lev 23:3; Deut 5:12–14　**31:17** Ex 20:11　**32:1** Acts 7:40
32:4 1 Kings 12:28; Acts 7:41　**32:6** 1 Cor 10:7　**32:11–14** Num 14:13–19

How did God punish the Israelites? You'll find the answer near the end of Exodus, chapter 32.

that you led your people out of Egypt, planning to kill them in the mountains and destroy them completely? Stop being angry; change your mind and do not bring this disaster on your people. ¹³Remember your servants Abraham, Isaac, and Jacob. Remember the solemn promise you made to them to give them as many descendants as there are stars in the sky and to give their descendants all that land you promised would be their possession forever." ¹⁴So the LORD changed his mind and did not bring on his people the disaster he had threatened.

¹⁵Moses went back down the mountain, carrying the two stone tablets with the commandments written on both sides. ¹⁶God himself had made the tablets and had engraved the commandments on them.

¹⁷Joshua heard the people shouting and said to Moses, "I hear the sound of battle in the camp."

¹⁸Moses said, "That doesn't sound like a shout of victory or a cry of defeat; it's the sound of singing."

¹⁹When Moses came close enough to the camp to see the bull-calf and to see the people dancing, he became furious. There at the foot of the mountain, he threw down the tablets he was carrying and broke them. ²⁰He took the bull-calf which they had made, melted it, ground it into fine powder, and mixed it with water. Then he made the people of Israel drink it. ²¹He said to Aaron, "What did these people do to you, that you have made them commit such a terrible sin?"

²²Aaron answered, "Don't be angry with me; you know how determined these people are to do evil. ²³They said to me, 'We don't know what has happened to this man Moses, who brought us out of Egypt; so make us a god to lead us.' ²⁴I asked them to bring me their gold ornaments, and those who had any took them off and gave them to me. I threw the ornaments into the fire and out came this bull-calf!"

²⁵Moses saw that Aaron had let the people get out of control and make fools of themselves in front of their enemies. ²⁶So he stood at the gate of the camp and shouted, "Everyone who is on the LORD's side come over here!" So all the Levites gathered

Live It!

Sinful but Forgiven

How could the Israelites do something like this! Forty days earlier they promised God that they would obey his commandments. Then, while Moses was on Mount Sinai, they asked Aaron to make a bull-calf out of gold so that they could worship it. They broke the very first commandment, "Do not bow down to any idol or worship it" (Exodus 20:5).

Moses was so angry that he threw the stone tablets, and they cracked into pieces. God wanted to destroy the Israelites, but Moses knew that God loved them. Even though the people sinned, Moses asked God to forgive them. God did just that—over and over again.

We shouldn't be too hard on the Israelites. Most of us do something to betray God on a pretty regular basis. But as soon as we say we're sorry and promise to do better, God forgives us. And he keeps on forgiving us, simply because we are God's people, God is our God, and God loves us. No sin is big enough to change that.

It is important to be aware of your sins—even though you might not have angry people breaking stone tablets nearby. When you are aware of a sin, say a prayer asking God's forgiveness and try to go to the sacrament of Penance and Reconciliation, especially if it is a serious sin. Then let yourself feel God's love surround you.

— Exodus, chapter 32

32:13 Gen 22:16, 17; Gen 17:8

around him, ²⁷and he said to them, "The
LORD God of Israel commands every one of
you to put on your sword and go through
the camp from this gate to the other and kill
your brothers, your friends, and your neighbors." ²⁸The Levites obeyed, and killed about
three thousand men that day. ²⁹Moses said to
the Levites, "Today you have consecrated
yourselvesⁱ as priests in the service of the
LORD by killing your sons and brothers, so
the LORD has given you his blessing."

³⁰The next day Moses said to the people,
"You have committed a terrible sin. But
now I will again go up the mountain to the
LORD; perhaps I can obtain forgiveness for
your sin." ³¹Moses then returned to the
LORD and said, "These people have committed a terrible sin. They have made a god out
of gold and worshiped it. ³²Please forgive
their sin; but if you won't, then remove my
name from the book in which you have
written the names of your people."

³³The LORD answered, "It is those who
have sinned against me whose names I will
remove from my book. ³⁴Now go, lead the
people to the place I told you about.
Remember that my angel will guide you,
but the time is coming when I will punish
these people for their sin."

³⁵So the LORD sent a disease on the people, because they had caused Aaron to make
the gold bull-calf.

The LORD Orders Israel to Leave Mount Sinai

33 ¹ The LORD said to Moses, "Leave
this place, you and the people you
brought out of Egypt, and go to the land
that I promised to give to Abraham, Isaac,
and Jacob and to their descendants. ²I will
send an angel to guide you, and I will drive
out the Canaanites, the Amorites, the Hittites, the Perizzites, the Hivites, and the
Jebusites. ³You are going to a rich and fertile
land. But I will not go with you myself,
because you are a stubborn people, and I
might destroy you on the way."

⁴When the people heard this, they began
to mourn and did not wear jewelry any more.
⁵For the LORD had commanded Moses to tell
them, "You are a stubborn people. If I were to
go with you even for a moment, I would
completely destroy you. Now take off your
jewelry, and I will decide what to do with
you." ⁶So after they left Mount Sinai, the
people of Israel no longer wore jewelry.

The Tent of the LORD's Presence

⁷Whenever the people of Israel set up camp,
Moses would take the sacred Tent and put it up
some distance outside the camp. It was called
the Tent of the LORD's presence, and anyone
who wanted to consult the LORD would go
out to it. ⁸Whenever Moses went out there,
the people would stand at the door of their
tents and watch Moses until he entered it.
⁹After Moses had gone in, the pillar of cloud
would come down and stay at the door of the
Tent, and the LORD would speak to Moses
from the cloud. ¹⁰As soon as the people saw
the pillar of cloud at the door of the Tent, they
would bow down. ¹¹The LORD would speak
with Moses face to face, just as someone speaks
with a friend. Then Moses would return to the
camp. But the young man who was his helper,
Joshua son of Nun, stayed in the Tent.

The LORD Promises to Be with His People

¹²Moses said to the LORD, "It is true that
you have told me to lead these people to
that land, but you did not tell me whom you
would send with me. You have said that you
know me well and are pleased with me.
¹³Now if you are, tell me your plans, so that
I may serve you and continue to please you.

They would bow down. (33:10)

ⁱ **32:29** *Some ancient translations* Today you have consecrated yourselves; *Hebrew* Consecrate yourselves today; *or*
You have been consecrated today.
32:32 Ps 69:28; Rev 3:5　**33:1 a** Gen 12:7; **b** Gen 26:3; **c** Gen 28:13

Pray It!

How Will I Know, God?

Moses had a lot of questions for God. He wanted to be sure he was headed in the right direction and that God was pleased with him. In Exodus 33:12–23, Moses and God have a conversation that shows the love they have for each other. Moses' prayer might have sounded something like this:

God, I try to do what I think you want me to do, but am I doing it right?
How will I know?
Are you pleased with me, God? When you look at me, do you feel proud?
How will I know?
I want to believe that you're on the journey with me—even when I mess
things up, but how will I know?
I wish I could see you, God. Maybe I do—but I just don't know it's you.
How will I know?
I'd like some answers soon, God. But I have to trust that you will show me
what I need to know even if it isn't everything that I would want to know.

— Exodus 33:12–23

Remember also that you have chosen this nation to be your own."

14 The LORD said, "I will go with you, and I will give you victory."

15 Moses replied, "If you do not go with us, don't make us leave this place. 16 How will anyone know that you are pleased with your people and with me if you do not go with us? Your presence with us will distinguish us from any other people on earth."

17 The LORD said to Moses, "I will do just as you have asked, because I know you very well and I am pleased with you."

18 Then Moses requested, "Please, let me see the dazzling light of your presence."

19 The LORD answered, "I will make all my splendor pass before you and in your presence I will pronounce my sacred name. I am the LORD, and I show compassion and pity on those I choose. 20 I will not let you see my face, because no one can see me and stay alive, 21 but here is a place beside me where you can stand on a rock. 22 When the

dazzling light of my presence passes by, I will put you in an opening in the rock and cover you with my hand until I have passed by. 23 Then I will take my hand away, and you will see my back but not my face."

The Second Set of Stone Tablets
(Deuteronomy 10:1–5)

34 1 The LORD said to Moses, "Cut two stone tablets like the first ones, and I will write on them the words that were on the first tablets, which you broke. 2 Get ready tomorrow morning, and come up Mount Sinai to meet me there at the top. 3 No one is to come up with you; no one is to be seen on any part of the mountain; and no sheep or cattle are to graze at the foot of the mountain." 4 So Moses cut two more stone tablets, and early the next morning he carried them up Mount Sinai, just as the LORD had commanded.

5 The LORD came down in a cloud, stood

33:19 Rom 9:15

Why did God think about sending an angel to go with the Israelites instead of going himself? Read Exodus 33:1–6.

Exodus

Party Time!

Catholic Connections

The Harvest Festival mentioned in Exodus 34:22 was a celebration of the wheat harvest. It was also known as Pentecost. Some Bibles also call it the Feast of Weeks. The Israelites received the Covenant Law from God on Mount Sinai during harvest time, so the feast of Pentecost came to be a celebration of the Covenant between God and his Chosen People.

When Jesus' followers were celebrating Pentecost after Jesus ascended into heaven, an important event happened. The Holy Spirit came to be with them, just as Jesus promised before he died. Check out Acts, chapter 2, to read all about it. In the New Testament, Pentecost marks the time when Jesus' followers began going out to preach and baptize new believers. So Pentecost is sometimes called the birthday of the Church. Catholics celebrate the feast of Pentecost fifty days after Easter.

— Exodus 34:22

with him there, and pronounced his holy name, the LORD.*j* 6 The LORD then passed in front of him and called out, "I, the LORD, am a God who is full of compassion and pity, who is not easily angered and who shows great love and faithfulness. 7 I keep my promise for thousands of generations*k* and forgive evil and sin; but I will not fail to punish children and grandchildren to the third and fourth generation for the sins of their parents."

8 Moses quickly bowed down to the ground and worshiped. 9 He said, "Lord, if you really are pleased with me, I ask you to go with us. These people are stubborn, but forgive our evil and our sin, and accept us as your own people."

The Covenant Is Renewed
(Exodus 23:14–19; Deuteronomy 7:1–5; 16:1–17)

10 The LORD said to Moses, "I now make a covenant with the people of Israel. In their presence I will do great things such as have

never been done anywhere on earth among any of the nations. All the people will see what great things I, the LORD, can do, because I am going to do an awesome thing for you. 11 Obey the laws that I am giving you today. I will drive out the Amorites, the Canaanites, the Hittites, the Perizzites, the Hivites, and the Jebusites, as you advance. 12 Do not make any treaties with the people of the country into which you are going, because this could be a fatal trap for you. 13 Instead, tear down their altars, destroy their sacred pillars, and cut down their symbols of the goddess Asherah.

14 "Do not worship any other god, because I, the LORD, tolerate no rivals. 15 Do not make any treaties with the people of the country, because when they worship their pagan gods and sacrifice to them, they will invite you to join them, and you will be tempted to eat the food they offer to their gods. 16 Your sons might marry those foreign women, who would lead them to be unfaithful to me and to worship their pagan gods.

j **34:5** THE LORD: *See 3:14, and Word List.*   *k* **34:7** thousands of generations; *or* thousands.
34:6, 7 Ex 20:5, 6; Num 14:18; Deut 5:9, 10; 7:9, 10   **34:13** Deut 16:21

"I, the LORD, am a God who is full of compassion and pity, who is not easily angered and who shows great love and faithfulness" (Exodus 34:6).

Exodus

Pray It!

A Moment with God

Moses' face was beaming! He had just come down from Mount Sinai, where he spent some time talking to God. His time on Mount Sinai was just what he needed to continue living the life God wanted him to live.

You can be with God whenever you want to. You do not need to do anything special—except be mindful that God is with you. To help you find that place of mindfulness, you might say a short prayer over and over, like "Be with me, God" or "God, you are my God, and I am yours." When you are focused, you can talk to God, read a prayer, say one that you know, or just be quiet and feel God's love for you.

Don't be too concerned about *how* you pray. It's more important *that* you pray. God is waiting for you to climb Mount Sinai in your heart.

— Exodus 34:29–35

17 "Do not make gods of metal and worship them.

18 "Keep the Festival of Unleavened Bread. As I have commanded you, eat unleavened bread for seven days in the month of Abib, because it was in that month that you left Egypt.

19 "Every first-born son and first-born male domestic animal belongs to me, 20 but you are to buy back every first-born donkey by offering a lamb in its place. If you do not buy it back, break its neck. Buy back every first-born son.

"No one is to appear before me without an offering.

21 "You have six days in which to do your work, but do not work on the seventh day, not even during plowing time or harvest.

22 "Keep the Harvest Festival when you begin to harvest the first crop of your wheat, and keep the Festival of Shelters in the autumn when you gather your fruit.

23 "Three times a year all of your men must come to worship me, the LORD, the God of Israel. 24 After I have driven out the nations before you and extended your territory, no one will try to conquer your country during the three festivals.

25 "Do not offer bread made with yeast when you sacrifice an animal to me. Do not keep until the following morning any part of the animal killed at the Passover Festival.

26 "Each year bring to the house of the LORD the first grain that you harvest.

"Do not cook a young sheep or goat in its mother's milk."

27 The LORD said to Moses, "Write these words down, because it is on the basis of these words that I am making a covenant with you and with Israel." 28 Moses stayed there with the LORD forty days and nights, eating and drinking nothing. He wrote on the tablets the words of the covenant—the Ten Commandments.

Moses Goes Down from Mount Sinai

29 When Moses went down from Mount Sinai carrying the Ten Commandments, his face was shining because he had been speaking with the LORD; but he did not know it. 30 Aaron and all the people looked at Moses and saw that his face was shining, and they were afraid to go near him. 31 But Moses called them, and Aaron and all the leaders of the community went to him, and Moses

34:17 Ex 20:4; Lev 19:4; Deut 5:8; 27:15 **34:18** Ex 12:14–20; Lev 23:6–8; Num 28:16–25 **34:19** Ex 13:2 **34:20** Ex 13:13 **34:21** Ex 20:9, 10; 23:12; 31:15; 35:2; Lev 23:3; Deut 5:13, 14 **34:22 a** Lev 23:15–21; Num 28:26–31; **b** Lev 23:39–43 **34:25** Ex 12:10 **34:26 a** Deut 26:2; **b** Deut 14:21 **34:29–35** 2 Cor 3:7–16 spoke with them. [32] After that, all the people of Israel gathered around him, and Moses gave them all the laws that the LORD had given him on Mount Sinai. [33] When Moses had finished speaking with them, he covered his face with a veil. [34] Whenever Moses went into the Tent of the LORD's presence to speak to the LORD, he would take the veil off. When he came out, he would tell the people of Israel everything that he had been commanded to say, [35] and they would see that his face was shining. Then he would put the veil back on until the next time he went to speak with the LORD.

Regulations for the Sabbath

35 [1] Moses called together the whole community of the people of Israel and said to them, "This is what the LORD has commanded you to do: [2] You have six days in which to do your work, but the seventh day is to be sacred, a solemn day of rest dedicated to me, the LORD. Anyone who does any work on that day is to be put to death. [3] Do not even light a fire in your homes on the Sabbath."

Offerings for the Sacred Tent
(Exodus 25:1–9)

[4] Moses said to all the people of Israel, "This is what the LORD has commanded: [5] Make an offering to the LORD. Everyone who wishes to do so is to bring an offering of gold, silver, or bronze; [6] fine linen; blue, purple, and red wool; cloth made of goats' hair; [7] rams' skin dyed red; fine leather; acacia wood; [8] oil for the lamps; spices for the anointing oil and for the sweet-smelling incense; [9] carnelians and other jewels to be set in the High Priest's ephod and in his breastpiece.

Articles for the Tent of the LORD's Presence
(Exodus 39:32–43)

[10] "All the skilled workers among you are to come and make everything that the LORD commanded: [11] the Tent, its covering and its outer covering, its hooks and its frames, its crossbars, its posts, and its bases; [12] the Covenant Box, its poles, its lid, and the curtain to screen it off; [13] the table, its poles, and all its equipment; the bread offered to God; [14] the lampstand for the light and its equipment; the lamps with their oil; [15] the altar for burning incense and its poles; the anointing oil; the sweet-smelling incense; the curtain for the entrance of the Tent; [16] the altar on which to burn offerings, with its bronze grating attached, its poles, and all its equipment; the washbasin and its base; [17] the curtains for the enclosure, its posts and bases; the curtain for the entrance of the enclosure; [18] the Tent pegs and ropes for the Tent and the enclosure; [19] and the magnificent garments the priests are to wear when they serve in the Holy Place—the sacred clothes for Aaron the priest and for his sons."

The People Bring Their Offerings

[20] All the people of Israel left, [21] and everyone who wished to do so brought an offering to the LORD for making the Tent of the LORD's presence. They brought everything needed for use in worship and for making the priestly garments. [22] All who wanted to, both men and women, brought decorative pins, earrings, rings, necklaces, and all kinds of gold jewelry and dedicated them to the LORD. [23] Everyone who had fine linen; blue, purple, or red wool; cloth of goats' hair; rams' skin dyed red; or fine leather, brought it. [24] All who were able to contribute silver or bronze brought their offering for the LORD, and all who had acacia wood which could be used for any of the work brought it. [25] All the skilled women brought fine linen thread and thread of blue, purple, and red wool, which they had made. [26] They also made thread of goats' hair. [27] The leaders brought carnelians and other jewels to be set in the ephod and the breastpiece [28] and spices and oil for the lamps, for the anointing oil, and for the sweet-smelling incense. [29] All the people of Israel who wanted to brought their offering to the LORD for the work which he had commanded Moses to do.

35:2 Ex 20:8–11; 23:12; 31:15; 34:21; Lev 23:3; Deut 5:12–14

Workers to Make the Tent of the Lord's Presence
(Exodus 31:1–11)

[30] Moses said to the Israelites, "The Lord has chosen Bezalel, the son of Uri and grandson of Hur from the tribe of Judah. [31] God has filled him with his power[l] and given him skill, ability, and understanding for every kind of artistic work, [32] for planning skillful designs and working them in gold, silver, and bronze; [33] for cutting jewels to be set; for carving wood; and for every other kind of artistic work. [34] The Lord has given to him and to Oholiab son of Ahisamach, from the tribe of Dan, the ability to teach their crafts to others. [35] He has given them skill in all kinds of work done by engravers, designers, and weavers of fine linen; blue, purple, and red wool; and other cloth. They are able to do all kinds of work and are skillful designers.

36 [1] "Bezalel, Oholiab, and all the other workers to whom the Lord has given skill and understanding, who know how to make everything needed to build the sacred Tent, are to make everything just as the Lord has commanded."

The People Bring Many Gifts

[2] Moses called Bezalel, Oholiab, and all the other skilled men to whom the Lord had given ability and who were willing to help, and Moses told them to start working. [3] They received from him all the offerings which the Israelites had brought for constructing the sacred Tent. But the people of Israel continued to bring Moses their offerings every morning. [4] Then the skilled men who were doing the work went [5] and told Moses, "The people are bringing more than is needed for the work which the Lord commanded to be done."

[6] So Moses sent a command throughout the camp that no one was to make any further contribution for the sacred Tent; so the people did not bring any more. [7] What had already been brought was more than enough to finish all the work.

Making the Tent of the Lord's Presence
(Exodus 26:1–37)

[8] The most skilled men among those doing the work made the Tent of the Lord's

Every Little Something Counts

When work finally started on the portable worship space, everyone wanted to contribute something. People brought jewels, colorful cloths, animal skins, oil, and whatever else they could think of to create a proper place to worship God together. In the end, the craftsmen had "more than enough to finish all the work" (Exodus 36:7).

How do you contribute to the life of your parish community? Do you help with parish programs and events? Do you contribute money to support the work of the Church and help those who are needy? Do you use the gifts God gave you to make your parish a better place? Do you share your ideas with parish leaders? You may be young, but you have a lot to give. Being young is no excuse for not doing your part.

Everyone can do something, and every little something counts. What *can* you do? What *will* you do?

— Exodus 36:2–7

---

[l] **35:31** power; *or* spirit.

presence. They made it out of ten pieces of fine linen woven with blue, purple, and red wool and embroidered with figures of winged creatures. ⁹Each piece was the same size, 14 yards long and 2 yards wide. ¹⁰They sewed five of them together in one set and did the same with the other five. ¹¹They made loops of blue cloth on the edge of the outside piece in each set. ¹²They put fifty loops on the first piece of the first set and fifty loops matching them on the last piece of the second set. ¹³They made fifty gold hooks, with which to join the two sets into one piece.

¹⁴Then they made a cover for the Tent out of eleven pieces of cloth made of goats' hair. ¹⁵They made them all the same size, 15 yards long and 2 yards wide. ¹⁶They sewed five of them together in one set and the other six in another set. ¹⁷They put fifty loops on the edge of the last piece of one set and fifty loops on the edge of the other set. ¹⁸They made fifty bronze hooks to join the two sets, so as to form one cover. ¹⁹They made two more coverings, one of rams' skin dyed red and the other of fine leather, to serve as an outer cover.

²⁰They made upright frames of acacia wood for the Tent. ²¹Each frame was 15 feet tall and 27 inches wide, ²²with two matching projections, so that the frames could be joined together. All the frames had these projections. ²³They made twenty frames for the south side ²⁴and forty silver bases to go under them, two bases under each frame to hold its two projections. ²⁵They made twenty frames for the north side of the Tent ²⁶and forty silver bases, two under each frame. ²⁷For the back of the Tent, on the west, they made six frames ²⁸and two frames for the corners. ²⁹These corner frames were joined at the bottom and connected all the way to the top. The two frames that formed the two corners were made in this way. ³⁰So there were eight frames and sixteen silver bases, two under each frame.

³¹They made fifteen crossbars of acacia wood, five for the frames on one side of the Tent, ³²five for the frames on the other side,

and five for the frames on the west end, at the back. ³³The middle crossbar, set halfway up the frames, extended from one end of the Tent to the other. ³⁴They covered the frames with gold and fitted them with gold rings to hold the crossbars, which were also covered with gold.

³⁵They made a curtain of fine linen, woven with blue, purple, and red wool and embroidered it with figures of winged creatures. ³⁶They made four posts of acacia wood to hold the curtain, covered them with gold, and fitted them with gold hooks. Then they made four silver bases to hold the posts. ³⁷For the entrance of the Tent they made a curtain of fine linen woven with blue, purple, and red wool and decorated with embroidery. ³⁸For this curtain they made five posts fitted with hooks, covered their tops and their rods with gold, and made five bronze bases for the posts.

Making the Covenant Box
(Exodus 25:10–22)

37 ¹Bezalel made the Covenant Box out of acacia wood, 45 inches long, 27 inches wide, and 27 inches high. ²He covered it with pure gold inside and out and put a gold border all around it. ³He made four carrying rings of gold for it and attached them to its four feet, with two rings on each side. ⁴He made carrying poles of acacia wood, covered them with gold, ⁵and put them through the rings on each side of the Box. ⁶He made a lid of pure gold, 45 inches long and 27 inches wide. ⁷He made two winged creatures of hammered gold, ⁸one for each end of the lid. He made them so that they formed one piece with the lid. ⁹The winged creatures faced each other across the lid, and their outspread wings covered it.

Can you think of a movie about finding the Covenant Box (the Ark of the Covenant)? If not, ask a relative or a teacher.

Making the Table for the Bread Offered to God
(Exodus 25:23–30)

10He made the table out of acacia wood, 36 inches long, 18 inches wide, and 27 inches high. 11He covered it with pure gold and put a gold border around it. 12He made a rim 3 inches wide around it and put a gold border around the rim. 13He made four carrying rings of gold for it and put them at the four corners, where the legs were. 14The rings to hold the poles for carrying the table were placed near the rim. 15He made the poles of acacia wood and covered them with gold. 16He made the dishes of pure gold for the table: the plates, the cups, the jars, and the bowls to be used for the wine offering.

Making the Lampstand
(Exodus 25:31–40)

17He made the lampstand of pure gold. He made its base and its shaft of hammered gold; its decorative flowers, including buds and petals, formed one piece with it. 18Six branches extended from its sides, three from each side. 19Each of the six branches had three decorative flowers shaped like almond blossoms with buds and petals. 20The shaft of the lampstand had four decorative flowers shaped like almond blossoms with buds and petals. 21There was one bud below each of the three pairs of branches. 22The buds, the branches, and the lampstand were a single piece of pure hammered gold. 23He made seven lamps for the lampstand, and he made its tongs and trays of pure gold. 24He used seventy-five pounds of pure gold to make the lampstand and all its equipment.

Making the Altar for Burning Incense
(Exodus 30:1–5)

25He made an altar out of acacia wood, for burning incense. It was square, 18 inches long and 18 inches wide, and it was 36 inches high. Its projections at the four corners formed one piece with it. 26He covered its top, all four sides, and its projections with pure gold and put a gold border around it.

27He made two gold carrying rings for it and attached them below the border on the two sides, to hold the poles with which it was to be carried. 28He made the poles of acacia wood and covered them with gold.

Making the Anointing Oil and the Incense
(Exodus 30:22–38)

29He also made the sacred anointing oil and the pure sweet-smelling incense, mixed like perfume.

Making the Altar for Burning Offerings
(Exodus 27:1–8)

38 1For burning offerings, he made an altar out of acacia wood. It was square, 7½ feet long and 7½ feet wide, and it was 4½ feet high. 2He made the projections at the top of the four corners, so that they formed one piece with the altar. He covered it all with bronze. 3He also made all the equipment for the altar: the pans, the shovels, the bowls, the hooks, and the fire pans. All this equipment was made of bronze. 4He made a bronze grating and put it under the rim of the altar, so that it reached halfway up the altar. 5He made four carrying rings and put them on the four corners. 6He made carrying poles of acacia wood, covered them with bronze, 7and put them in the rings on each side of the altar. The altar was made of boards and was hollow.

Making the Bronze Basin
(Exodus 30:18)

8He made the bronze basin and its bronze base out of the mirrors belonging to the women who served at the entrance of the Tent of the LORD's presence.

The Enclosure for the Tent of the LORD's Presence
(Exodus 27:9–19)

9For the Tent of the LORD's presence he

made the enclosure out of fine linen curtains. On the south side the curtains were 50 yards long, [10]supported by twenty bronze posts in twenty bronze bases, with hooks and rods made of silver. [11]The enclosure was the same on the north side. [12]On the west side there were curtains 25 yards long, with ten posts and ten bases and with hooks and rods made of silver. [13]On the east side, where the entrance was, the enclosure was also 25 yards wide. [14-15]On each side of the entrance there were 7½ yards of curtains, with three posts and three bases. [16]All the curtains around the enclosure were made of fine linen. [17]The bases for the posts were made of bronze, and the hooks, the rods, and the covering of the tops of the posts were made of silver. All the posts around the enclosure were connected with silver rods. [18]The curtain for the entrance of the enclosure was made of fine linen woven with blue, purple, and red wool and decorated with embroidery. It was 10 yards long and 2½ yards high, like the curtains of the enclosure. [19]It was supported by four posts in four bronze bases. Their hooks, the covering of their tops, and their rods were made of silver. [20]All the pegs for the Tent and for the surrounding enclosure were made of bronze.

Metals Used in the Tent of the LORD's Presence

[21]Here is a list of the amounts of the metals used in the Tent of the LORD's presence, where the two stone tablets were kept on which the Ten Commandments were written. The list was ordered by Moses and made by the Levites who worked under the direction of Ithamar son of Aaron the priest. [22]Bezalel, the son of Uri and grandson of Hur from the tribe of Judah, made everything that the LORD had commanded. [23]His helper, Oholiab son of Ahisamach, from the tribe of Dan, was an engraver, a designer, and a weaver of fine linen and of blue, purple, and red wool. [24]All the gold that had been dedicated to the LORD for the sacred Tent weighed 2,195 pounds, weighed according to the official standard. [25]The silver from the census of the community weighed 7,550 pounds, weighed

according to the official standard. [26]This amount equaled the total paid by all persons enrolled in the census, each one paying the required amount, weighed according to the official standard. There were 603,550 men twenty years old or older enrolled in the census. [27]Of the silver, 7,500 pounds were used to make the hundred bases for the sacred Tent and for the curtain, 75 pounds for each base. [28]With the remaining 50 pounds of silver Bezalel made the rods, the hooks for the posts, and the covering for their tops. [29]The bronze which was dedicated to the LORD amounted to 5,310 pounds. [30]With it he made the bases for the entrance of the Tent of the LORD's presence, the bronze altar with its bronze grating, all the equipment for the altar, [31]the bases for the surrounding enclosure and for the entrance of the enclosure, and all the pegs for the Tent and the surrounding enclosure.

Making the Garments for the Priests
(Exodus 28:1–14)

39 [1]With the blue, purple, and red wool they made the magnificent garments which the priests were to wear when they served in the Holy Place. They made the priestly garments for Aaron, as the LORD had commanded Moses.

[2]They made the ephod of fine linen; blue, purple, and red wool; and gold thread. [3]They hammered out sheets of gold and cut them into thin strips to be worked into the fine linen and into the blue, purple, and red wool. [4]They made two shoulder straps for the ephod and attached them to its sides, so that it could be fastened. [5]The finely woven belt, made of the same materials, was attached to the ephod so as to form one piece with it, as the LORD had commanded Moses. [6]They prepared the carnelians and mounted them in gold settings; they were skillfully engraved with the names of the twelve sons of Jacob. [7]They put them on the shoulder straps of the ephod to represent the twelve tribes of Israel, just as the LORD had commanded Moses.

38:25, 26 Ex 30:11–16   **38:26** Mt 17:24

Making the Breastpiece
(Exodus 28:15–30)

8 They made the breastpiece of the same materials as the ephod and with similar embroidery. 9 It was square and folded double, 9 inches long and 9 inches wide. 10 They mounted four rows of precious stones on it: in the first row they mounted a ruby, a topaz, and a garnet; 11 in the second row, an emerald, a sapphire, and a diamond; 12 in the third row, a turquoise, an agate, and an amethyst; 13 and in the fourth row, a beryl, a carnelian, and a jasper. These were mounted in gold settings. 14 Each of the twelve stones had engraved on it the name of one of the sons of Jacob, in order to represent the twelve tribes of Israel. 15 For the breastpiece they made chains of pure gold, twisted like cords. 16 They made two gold settings and two gold rings and attached the two rings to the upper corners of the breastpiece. 17 They fastened the two gold cords to the two rings 18 and fastened the other two ends of the cords to the two settings and in this way attached them in front to the shoulder straps of the ephod. 19 They made two rings of gold and attached them to the lower corners of the breastpiece, on the inside edge next to the ephod. 20 They made two more gold rings and attached them to the lower part of the front of the two shoulder straps of the ephod, near the seam and above the finely woven belt. 21 Just as the LORD had commanded Moses, they tied the rings of the breastpiece to the rings of the ephod with a blue cord, so that the breastpiece rested above the belt and did not come loose.

Making the Other Priestly Garments
(Exodus 28:31–43)

22 The robe that goes under the ephod was made entirely of blue wool. 23 The hole for the head was reinforced with a woven binding to keep it from tearing. 24-26 All around its lower hem they put pomegranates of fine linen and of blue, purple, and red wool, alternating with bells of pure gold, just as the LORD had commanded Moses.

27 They made the shirts for Aaron and his sons, 28 and the turban, the caps, the linen shorts, 29 and the sash of fine linen and of blue, purple, and red wool, decorated with embroidery, as the LORD had commanded Moses. 30 They made the ornament, the sacred sign of dedication, out of pure gold, and they engraved on it "Dedicated to the LORD." 31 They tied it to the front of the turban with a blue cord, just as the LORD had commanded Moses.

The Completion of the Work
(Exodus 35:10–19)

32 All the work on the Tent of the LORD's presence was finally completed. The Israelites made everything just as the LORD had commanded Moses. 33 They brought to Moses the Tent and all its equipment, its hooks, its frames, its crossbars, its posts, and its bases; 34 the covering of rams' skin dyed red; the covering of fine leather; the curtain; 35 the Covenant Box containing the stone tablets, its poles, and its lid; 36 the table and all its equipment, and the bread offered to God; 37 the lampstand of pure gold, its lamps, all its equipment, and the oil for the lamps; 38 the gold altar; the anointing oil; the sweet-smelling incense; the curtain for the entrance of the Tent; 39 the bronze altar with its bronze grating, its poles, and all its equipment; the washbasin and its base; 40 the curtains for the enclosure and its posts and bases; the curtain for the entrance of the enclosure and its ropes; the Tent pegs; all the equipment to be used in the Tent; 41 and the magnificent garments the priests were to wear in the Holy Place—the sacred clothes for Aaron the priest and for his sons. 42 The Israelites had done all the work just as the LORD had commanded Moses. 43 Moses examined everything and saw that they had made it all just as the LORD had commanded. So Moses blessed them.

How many stones were in the breastpiece? Why that number? What was engraved on each? Check out Exodus, chapter 39.

Exodus

Way to Go!

When the Israelites finished their work, Moses looked it over, and because they had done what God asked, he blessed them. They had every reason to be proud of themselves, just like these three people who are about your age:

- Mitchell's scout leader told his mom that he could always count on Mitch to get things done. Mitch and his mom were very proud.
- Desiree was proud of her family. They all worked together, supported one another, and cared for one another.
- Amanda was proud of her ability to play the clarinet. She was thrilled when the music director at church asked her to be part of the music group for the first Communion liturgy.

What are you proud of? Is it a special talent? a personality trait? something you work hard at? something you are part of? You can have pride in anything you do or are that is pleasing to God. When you are proud of yourself for the right reasons, God blesses you.

— Exodus 39:32–43

Setting Up and Dedicating the Tent of the LORD's Presence

40 ¹The LORD said to Moses, ²"On the first day of the first month set up the Tent of the LORD's presence. ³Place in it the Covenant Box containing the Ten Commandments and put the curtain in front of it. ⁴Bring in the table and place the equip-ment on it. Also bring in the lampstand and set up the lamps on it. ⁵Put the gold altar for burning incense in front of the Covenant Box and hang the curtain at the entrance of the Tent. ⁶Put in front of the Tent the altar for burning offerings. ⁷Put the washbasin between the Tent and the altar and fill it with water. ⁸Put up the surrounding enclosure and hang the curtain at its entrance.

⁹"Then dedicate the Tent and all its equipment by anointing it with the sacred oil, and it will be holy. ¹⁰Next, dedicate the altar and all its equipment by anointing it, and it will be completely holy. ¹¹Also dedicate the washbasin and its base in the same way.

¹²"Bring Aaron and his sons to the entrance of the Tent, and have them take a ritual bath. ¹³Dress Aaron in the priestly garments, anoint him, and in this way consecrate him, so that he can serve me as priest. ¹⁴Bring his sons and put the shirts on them. ¹⁵Then anoint them, just as you anointed their father, so that they can serve me as priests. This anointing will make them priests for all time to come."

¹⁶Moses did everything just as the LORD had commanded. ¹⁷So on the first day of the first month of the second year after they left Egypt, the Tent of the LORD's presence was set up. ¹⁸Moses put down its bases, set up its frames, attached its crossbars, and put up its posts. ¹⁹He spread out the covering over the Tent and put the outer covering over it, just as the LORD had commanded. ²⁰Then he took the two stone tablets and put them in the Covenant Box. He put the poles in the rings of the Box and put the lid on it. ²¹Then he put the Box in the Tent and hung up the curtain. In this way he screened off the Covenant Box, just as the LORD had commanded.

²²He put the table in the Tent, on the north side outside the curtain, ²³and placed on it the bread offered to the LORD, just as the LORD had commanded. ²⁴He put the lampstand in the Tent, on the south side, opposite the table, ²⁵and there in the LORD's presence he lit the lamps, just as the LORD had commanded. ²⁶He put the gold altar in the Tent, in front of

How many times does the phrase "LORD had commanded" appear in chapter 40? Why does it appear so many times?

the curtain, 27and burned the sweet-smelling incense, just as the LORD had commanded. 28He hung the curtain at the entrance of the Tent, 29and there in front of the curtain he placed the altar for burning offerings. On it he sacrificed the burnt offering and the grain offering, just as the LORD had commanded. 30He put the washbasin between the Tent and the altar and filled it with water. 31Moses, Aaron, and his sons washed their hands and their feet there 32whenever they went into the Tent or to the altar, just as the LORD had commanded. 33Moses set up the enclosure around the Tent and the altar and hung the curtain at the entrance of the enclosure. So he finished all the work.

The Cloud over the Tent of the LORD's Presence
(Numbers 9:15–23)

34Then the cloud covered the Tent and the dazzling light of the LORD's presence filled it. 35Because of this, Moses could not go into the Tent. 36The Israelites moved their camp to another place only when the cloud lifted from the Tent. 37As long as the cloud stayed there, they did not move their camp. 38During all their wanderings they could see the cloud of the LORD's presence over the Tent during the day and a fire burning above it during the night.

40:34 1 Kings 8:10, 11; Isa 6:4; Ezek 43:4, 5; Rev 15:8

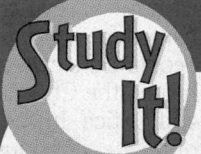

To Be Continued

At the end of the Book of Exodus, the Israelites leave Mount Sinai. They would not reach Canaan—the land that God promised to Abraham—for many years. The story of the journey to the Promised Land is continued in the Book of Numbers, then in Deuteronomy, and finally in the Book of Joshua.

During their years of wandering through the desert, the Israelites experienced many encounters with God and made many mistakes. They celebrated together and they fought. People died and babies were born. In other words, in their journey to the Promised Land, life happened.

The same is true for us. Each day, we move toward our own promised land: heaven. Like the Israelites, we walk with other people who are headed in the same direction, guided by God.

— Exodus, chapter 40

Your Next Step

Congratulations on finishing the Book of Exodus! Use this space to write your thoughts and questions about this book. If you are following the suggested reading plan, move ahead to the Book of Joshua, which tells how the Israelites moved into the Promised Land.

Leviticus

"Leviticus Rules!" That's what you might say if you really liked rules. Leviticus is a law book for God's people. The book is named for a group of priests from the tribe of Levi. God's Chosen People were expected to live by these laws. The laws in Leviticus helped the Chosen People put God first and live lives of holiness and justice. In the same way, Christians are called to live lives of holiness and justice—even when it doesn't seem to be very popular.

Most of these laws are no longer followed by Christians. The Holy Spirit led the early Christians to understand that many of these laws were no longer necessary for Christians. But we can appreciate the intent of these laws, to live lives that are holy and pleasing to God!

Chap. 8

Head lines

- Moses's Brother Is Ordained a Priest (8:1–36)
- Be Careful What You Eat (chapter 11)
- Scapegoat Takes Rap for Sinners! (16:20–22)
- God's People Told to Love Neighbors (19:1–18)
- Fifty Year Celebration: Time to Party! (25:8–17)
- Blessings Promised for Obeying Laws! (26:1–13)

FACTOIDS

Who wrote this book? This collection of laws and regulations, which were handed down orally, was probably compiled by several priestly writers and editors over a long period of time.

When was it written? The laws were established in the desert wilderness, after the Israelites escaped from Egypt. However, the writing and editing was probably done hundreds of years later.

Why was it written? Leviticus was written to bring about holiness and to unify the Israelite people.

What literary style is used? This book is written in the "priestly style," which is formal and portrays God as distant. Rules are rules, and it is the job of God's People to follow them.

Important themes

- Actions have consequences. If we follow the laws, we will be holy.
- Don't let the negative influence of others persuade you to sin.
- The blessings that God gives us are meant to be shared.

Sacrifices Burned Whole

1 ¹The LORD called to Moses from the Tent of the LORD's presence and gave him the following rules ²for the Israelites to observe when they offer their sacrifices.

When you offer an animal sacrifice, it may be one of your cattle or one of your sheep or goats. ³If you are offering one of your cattle as a burnt offering, you must bring a bull without any defects. You must present it at the entrance of the Tent of the LORD's presence so that the LORD will accept you. ⁴You shall put your hand on its head, and it will be accepted as a sacrifice to take away your sins. ⁵You shall kill the bull there, and the Aaronite priests shall present the blood to the LORD and then throw it against all four sides of the altar located at the entrance of the Tent. ⁶Then you shall skin the animal and cut it up, ⁷and the priests shall arrange firewood on the altar and light it. ⁸They shall put on the fire the pieces of the animal, including the head and the fat. ⁹You must wash the internal organs and the hind legs, and the officiating priest will burn the whole sacrifice on the altar. The odor of this food offering is pleasing to the LORD.

¹⁰If you are offering one of your sheep or goats, it must be a male without any defects. ¹¹You shall kill it on the north side of the altar, and the priests shall throw its blood on all four sides of the altar. ¹²After you cut it up, the officiating priest shall put on the fire all the parts, including the head and the fat. ¹³You must wash the internal organs and the hind legs, and the priest will present the sacrifice to the LORD and burn all of it on the altar. The odor of this food offering is pleasing to the LORD.

¹⁴If you are offering a bird as a burnt offering, it must be a dove or a pigeon. ¹⁵The priest shall present it at the altar, wring its neck, and burn its head on the altar. Its blood shall be drained out against the side of the altar. ¹⁶He shall remove the crop and its contents and throw them away on the east side of the altar where the ashes are put. ¹⁷He shall take hold of its wings and tear its body open, without tearing the wings off, and then burn it whole on the altar. The odor of this food offering is pleasing to the LORD.

Grain Offerings

2 ¹When any of you present an offering of grain to the LORD, you must first grind it into flour. You must put olive oil and incense on it ²and bring it to the Aaronite priests. The officiating priest shall take a handful of the flour and oil and all of the incense and burn it on the altar as a token that it has all been offered to the LORD. The odor of this food offering is pleasing to the LORD. ³The rest of the grain offering belongs to the priests; it is very holy, since it is taken from the food offered to the LORD.

⁴If the offering is bread baked in an oven, it must be made without yeast. It may be thick loaves made of flour mixed with olive oil or thin cakes brushed with olive oil.

⁵If the offering is bread cooked on a griddle, it is to be made of flour mixed with olive oil but without yeast. ⁶Crumble it up and pour the oil on it when you present it as an offering.

⁷If the offering is bread cooked in a pan, it is to be made of flour and olive oil. ⁸Bring it as an offering to the LORD and present it to the priest, who will take it to the altar. ⁹The priest will take part of it as a token that it has all been offered to the LORD, and he will burn it on the altar. The odor of this food offering is pleasing to the LORD. ¹⁰The rest of the offering belongs to the priests; it is very holy, since it is taken from the food offered to the LORD.

¹¹None of the grain offerings which you present to the LORD may be made with yeast; you must never use yeast or honey in food offered to the LORD. ¹²An offering of the first grain that you harvest each year shall be brought to the LORD, but it is not to be burned on the altar. ¹³Put salt on every grain offering, because salt represents the covenant

between you and God. (You must put salt on all your offerings.) ¹⁴When you bring to the LORD an offering of the first grain harvested, offer roasted grain or ground meal. ¹⁵Add olive oil and put incense on it. ¹⁶The priest will burn that part of the meal and oil that is to serve as a token, and also all the incense, as a food offering to the LORD.

Fellowship Offerings

3 ¹When any of you offer one of your cattle as a fellowship offering, it is to be a bull or a cow without any defects. ²You shall put your hand on the head of the animal and kill it at the entrance of the Tent of the LORD's presence. The Aaronite priests shall throw the blood against all four sides of the altar ³and present the following parts of the animal as a food offering to the LORD: all the fat on the internal organs, ⁴the kidneys and the fat on them, and the best part of the liver. ⁵The priests shall burn all this on the altar along with the burnt offerings. The odor of this food offering is pleasing to the LORD.

⁶If a sheep or goat is used as a fellowship offering, it may be male or female, but it must be without any defects. ⁷If you offer a sheep, ⁸you shall put your hand on its head and kill it in front of the Tent. The priests shall throw its blood against all four sides of the altar ⁹and present the following parts of the animal as a food offering to the LORD: the fat, the entire fat tail cut off near the backbone, all the fat covering the internal organs, ¹⁰the kidneys and the fat on them, and the best part of the liver. ¹¹The officiating priest shall burn all this on the altar as a food offering to the LORD.

¹²If you offer a goat, ¹³you shall put your hand on its head and kill it in front of the Tent. The priests shall throw its blood against all four sides of the altar ¹⁴and present the following parts as a food offering to the LORD: all the fat on the internal organs, ¹⁵the kidneys and the fat on them, and the best part of the liver. ¹⁶The priest shall burn all this on the altar as a food offering pleasing to the LORD. All the fat belongs to the LORD. ¹⁷No Israelite may eat any fat or any blood; this is a rule to be kept forever by all Israelites wherever they live.

Offerings for Unintentional Sins

4 ¹The LORD commanded Moses ²to tell the people of Israel that anyone who sinned and broke any of the LORD's commands without intending to, would have to observe the following rules.

³If it is the High Priest who sins and so brings guilt on the people, he shall present a young bull without any defects and sacrifice it to the LORD for his sin. ⁴He shall bring the bull to the entrance of the Tent, put his hand on its head, and kill it there in the LORD's presence. ⁵Then the High Priest shall take some of the bull's blood and carry it into the Tent. ⁶He shall dip his finger in the blood and sprinkle it in front of the sacred curtain seven times. ⁷Then he shall put some of the blood on the projections at the corners of the incense altar in the Tent. He shall pour out the rest of the blood at the base of the altar used for burning sacrifices, which is at the entrance of the Tent. ⁸From this bull he shall take all the fat, the fat on the internal organs, ⁹the kidneys and the fat on them, and the best part of the liver. ¹⁰The priest shall take this fat and burn it on the altar used for the burnt offerings, just as he does with the fat from the animal killed for the fellowship offering. ¹¹But he shall take its skin, all its flesh, its head, its legs, and its internal organs, including the intestines, ¹²carry it all outside the camp to the ritually clean place where the ashes are poured out, and there he shall burn it on a wood fire.

¹³If it is the whole community of Israel

He shall bring the bull. (4:4)

that sins and becomes guilty of breaking one of the LORD's commands without intending to, [14]then as soon as the sin becomes known, the community shall bring a young bull as a sin offering. They shall bring it to the Tent of the LORD's presence; [15]the leaders of the community shall put their hands on its head, and it shall be killed there. [16]The High Priest shall take some of the bull's blood into the Tent, [17]dip his finger in it, and sprinkle it in front of the curtain seven times. [18]He shall put some of the blood on the projections at the corners of the incense altar inside the Tent and pour out the rest of it at the base of the altar used for burning sacrifices, which is at the entrance of the Tent. [19]Then he shall take all its fat and burn it on the altar. [20]He shall do the same thing with this bull as he does with the bull for the sin offering, and in this way he shall make the sacrifice for the people's sin, and they will be forgiven. [21]Then he shall take the bull outside the camp and burn it, just as he burns the bull offered for his own sin. This is an offering to take away the sin of the community.

[22]If it is a ruler who sins and becomes guilty of breaking one of the LORD's commands without intending to, [23]then as soon as the sin is called to his attention, he shall bring as his offering a male goat without any defects. [24]He shall put his hand on its head and kill it on the north side of the altar, where the animals for the burnt offerings are killed. This is an offering to take away sin. [25]The priest shall dip his finger in the blood of the animal, put it on the projections at the corners of the altar, and pour out the rest of it at the base of the altar. [26]Then he shall burn all of its fat on the altar, just as he burns the fat of the animals killed for the fellowship offerings. In this way the priest shall offer the sacrifice for the sin of the ruler, and he will be forgiven.

[27]If any of you people sin and become guilty of breaking one of the LORD's commands without intending to, [28]then as soon as the sin is called to your attention, you shall bring as your offering a female goat without any defects. [29]You shall put your hand on its head and kill it on the north side of the altar, where the animals for the burnt offerings are killed. [30]The priest shall dip his finger in the blood of the animal, put it on the projections at the corners of the altar, and pour out the rest of it at the base of the altar. [31]Then he shall remove all its fat, just as the fat is removed from the animals killed for the fellowship offerings, and he shall burn it on the altar as an odor pleasing to the LORD. In this way the priest shall offer the sacrifice for the man's sin, and he will be forgiven.

[32]If you bring a sheep as a sin offering, it must be a female without any defects. [33]You shall put your hand on its head and kill it on the north side of the altar, where the animals for the burnt offerings are killed. [34]The priest shall dip his finger in the blood of the animal, put it on the projections at the corners of the altar, and pour out the rest of it at the base of the altar. [35]Then he shall remove all its fat, just as the fat is removed from the sheep killed for the fellowship offerings, and he shall burn it on the altar along with the food offerings given to the LORD. In this way the priest shall offer the sacrifice for your sin, and you will be forgiven.

Cases Requiring Sin Offerings

5 [1]Sin offerings are required in the following cases.

If you are officially summoned to give evidence in court and do not give information about something you have seen or heard, you must suffer the consequences.

[2]If you unintentionally touch anything ritually unclean, such as a dead animal, you are unclean and guilty as soon as you realize what you have done.

[3]If you unintentionally touch anything of human origin that is unclean, whatever it may be, you are guilty as soon as you realize what you have done.

[4]If you make a careless vow, no matter what it is about, you are guilty as soon as you realize what you have done.

[5]When you are guilty, you must confess the sin, [6]and as the penalty for your sin you must bring to the LORD a female sheep or

Leviticus

goat as an offering. The priest shall offer the sacrifice for your sin.

7 If you cannot afford a sheep or a goat, you shall bring to the LORD as the payment for your sin two doves or two pigeons, one for a sin offering and the other for a burnt offering. 8 You shall bring them to the priest, who will first offer the bird for the sin offering. He will break its neck without pulling off its head 9 and sprinkle some of its blood against the side of the altar. The rest of the blood will be drained out at the base of the altar. This is an offering to take away sin. 10 Then he shall offer the second bird as a burnt offering, according to the regulations. In this way the priest shall offer the sacrifice for your sin, and you will be forgiven.

11 If you cannot afford two doves or two pigeons, you shall bring two pounds of flour as a sin offering. You shall not put any olive oil or any incense on it, because it is a sin offering, not a grain offering. 12 You shall bring it to the priest, who will take a handful of it as a token that it has all been offered to the LORD, and he will burn it on the altar as a food offering. It is an offering to take away sin. 13 In this way the priest shall offer the sacrifice for your sin, and you will be forgiven. The rest of the flour belongs to the priest, just as in the case of a grain offering.

Repayment Offerings

14 The LORD gave the following regulations to Moses. 15 If any of you sin unintentionally by failing to hand over the payments that are sacred to the LORD, you shall bring as your repayment offering to the LORD a male sheep or goat without any defects. Its value is to be determined according to the official standard. 16 You must make the payments you have failed to hand over and must pay an additional 20 percent. You shall give it to the priest, and the priest shall offer the animal as a sacrifice for your sin, and you will be forgiven.

17 If any of you sin unintentionally by breaking any of the LORD's commands, you are guilty and must pay the penalty. 18 You must bring to the priest as a repayment offering a male sheep or goat without any

defects. Its value is to be determined according to the official standard. The priest shall offer the sacrifice for the sin which you committed unintentionally, and you will be forgiven. 19 It is a repayment offering for the sin you committed against the LORD.

6 1 The LORD gave the following regulations to Moses. 2 An offering is to be made if any of you sin against the LORD by refusing to return what another Israelite has left as a deposit or by stealing something from him or by cheating him 3 or by lying about something that has been lost and swearing that you did not find it. 4-5 When you sin in any of these ways, you must repay whatever you got by dishonest means. On the day you are found guilty, you must repay the owner in full, plus an additional 20 percent. 6 You shall bring to the priest as your repayment offering to the LORD a male sheep or goat without any defects. Its value is to be determined according to the official standard. 7 The priest shall offer the sacrifice for your sin, and you will be forgiven.

Sacrifices Burned Whole

8 The LORD commanded Moses 9 to give Aaron and his sons the following regulations for burnt offerings. A burnt offering is to be left on the altar all night long, and the fire is to be kept burning. 10 Then the priest, wearing his linen robe and linen shorts, shall remove the greasy ashes left on the altar and put them at the side of the altar. 11 Then he shall change his clothes and take the ashes outside the camp to a ritually clean place. 12 The fire on the altar must be kept burning and never allowed to go out. Every morning the priest shall put firewood on it, arrange the burnt offering on it, and burn the fat of the fellowship offering. 13 The fire must always be kept burning on the altar and never allowed to go out.

Grain Offerings

14 The following are the regulations for grain offerings. An Aaronite priest shall present the grain offering to the LORD in front

of the altar. 15Then he shall take a handful of the flour and oil, and the incense on it, and burn it on the altar as a token that all of it has been offered to the LORD. The odor of this offering is pleasing to the LORD. 16-17The priests shall eat the rest of it. It shall be made into bread baked without yeast and eaten in a holy place, the courtyard of the Tent of the LORD's presence. The LORD has given it to the priests as their part of the food offerings. It is very holy, like the sin offerings and the repayment offerings. 18For all time to come any of the male descendants of Aaron may eat it as their continuing share of the food offered to the LORD. Anyone else who touches a food offering will be harmed by the power of its holiness.

19The LORD gave Moses the following regulations 20for the ordination of an Aaronite priest. On the day he is ordained, he shall present as an offering to the LORD two pounds of flour (the same amount as the daily grain offering), half in the morning and half in the evening. 21It is to be mixed with oil and cooked on a griddle and then crumbled and presented as a grain offering, an odor pleasing to the LORD. 22For all time to come this offering is to be made by every descendant of Aaron who is serving as High Priest. It shall be completely burned as a sacrifice to the LORD. 23No part of a grain offering that a priest makes may be eaten; all of it must be burned.

Sin Offerings

24The LORD commanded Moses 25to give Aaron and his sons the following regulations for sin offerings. The animal for a sin offering shall be killed on the north side of the altar, where the animals for the burnt offerings are killed. This is a very holy offering. 26The priest who sacrifices the animal shall eat it in a holy place, the courtyard of the Tent of the LORD's presence. 27Anyone or anything that touches the flesh of the animal will be harmed by the power of its holiness. If any article of clothing is spattered with the animal's blood, it must be washed in a holy place. 28Any clay pot in which the meat is boiled must be broken, and if a metal pot is used, it must be scrubbed and rinsed with

water. 29Any male of the priestly families may eat this offering; it is very holy. 30But if any of the blood is brought into the Tent and used in the ritual to take away sin, the animal must not be eaten; it must be burned.

Repayment Offerings

7 1The following are the regulations for repayment offerings, which are very holy. 2The animal for this offering is to be killed on the north side of the altar, where the animals for the burnt offerings are killed, and its blood is to be thrown against all four sides of the altar. 3All of its fat shall be removed and offered on the altar: the fat tail, the fat covering the internal organs, 4the kidneys and the fat on them, and the best part of the liver. 5The priest shall burn all the fat on the altar as a food offering to the LORD. It is a repayment offering. 6Any male of the priestly families may eat it, but it must be eaten in a holy place, because it is very holy.

7There is one regulation that applies to both the sin offering and the repayment offering: the meat belongs to the priest who offers the sacrifice. 8The skin of an animal offered as a burnt offering belongs to the priest who offers the sacrifice. 9Every grain offering that has been baked in an oven or prepared in a pan or on a griddle belongs to the priest who has offered it to God. 10But all uncooked grain offerings, whether mixed with oil or dry, belong to all the Aaronite priests and must be shared equally among them.

Fellowship Offerings

11The following are the regulations for the fellowship offerings presented to the LORD. 12If you make this offering as a thanksgiving offering to God, you shall present, together with the animal to be sacrificed, an offering of bread made without yeast: either thick loaves made of flour mixed with olive oil or thin cakes brushed with olive oil or cakes made of flour mixed with olive oil. 13In addition, you shall offer loaves of bread baked with yeast. 14You shall present one part of each kind of bread as a special contribution to the LORD; it belongs to the priest who takes the blood of the animal and throws it against the altar. 15The flesh of the animal must be eaten on the day it is sacrificed; none of it may be left until the next morning.

16If you bring a fellowship offering as fulfillment of a vow or as your own freewill offering, not all of it has to be eaten on the day it is offered, but any that is left over may be eaten on the following day. 17Any meat that still remains on the third day must be burned. 18If any of it is eaten on the third day, God will not accept your offering. The offering will not be counted to your credit but will be considered unclean, and whoever eats it will suffer the consequences. 19If the meat comes into contact with anything ritually unclean, it must not be eaten, but must be burned.

Any of you that are ritually clean may eat the meat, 20but if any of you who are not clean eat it, you shall no longer be considered one of God's people. 21Also, if you eat the meat of this offering after you have touched anything ritually unclean, whether from a person or an animal, you shall no longer be considered one of God's people.

22The LORD gave Moses the following regulations 23for the people of Israel. No fat of cattle, sheep, or goats shall be eaten. 24The fat of an animal that has died a natural death or has been killed by a wild animal must not be eaten, but it may be used for any other purpose. 25Anyone who eats the fat of an animal that may be offered as a food offering to the LORD will no longer be considered one of God's people. 26No matter where the Israelites live, they must never use the blood of birds or animals for food. 27Anyone who breaks this law will no longer be considered one of God's people.

28The LORD gave Moses the following regulations 29for the people of Israel. When any of you offer a fellowship offering you must bring part of it as a special gift to the LORD, 30bringing it with your own hands as a food offering. You shall bring the fat of the animal with its breast and present it as a special gift to the LORD. 31The priest shall burn the fat on the altar, but the breast shall belong to the priests. 32The right hind leg of the animal shall be given as a special contribution 33to the priest who offers the blood and the fat of the fellowship offering. 34The breast of the animal is a special gift, and the right hind leg is a special contribution that the LORD has taken from the people of Israel and given to the priests. This is what the people of Israel must give to the priests for all time to come. 35This is the part of the food offered to the LORD that was given to Aaron and his sons on the day they were ordained as priests. 36On that day the LORD commanded the people of Israel to give them this part of the offering. It is a regulation that the people of Israel must obey for all time to come.

37These, then, are the regulations for the burnt offerings, the grain offerings, the sin offerings, the repayment offerings, the ordination offerings, and the fellowship offerings. 38There on Mount Sinai in the desert, the LORD gave these commands to Moses on the day he told the people of Israel to make their offerings.

The Ordination of Aaron and His Sons
(Exodus 29:1–37)

8 1The LORD said to Moses, 2"Take Aaron and his sons to the entrance of the Tent of my presence and bring the priestly garments, the anointing oil, the young bull for the sin offering, the two rams, and the basket of unleavened bread. 3Then call the whole community together there."

4Moses did as the LORD had commanded, and when the community had assembled, 5he said to them, "What I am now about to do is what the LORD has commanded."

6Moses brought Aaron and his sons forward and had them take a ritual bath. 7He put the shirt and the robe on Aaron and the sash around his waist. He put the ephod*a* on him and fastened it by putting its finely woven belt around his waist. 8He put the breastpiece on him and put the Urim and Thummim*b* in it. 9He placed the turban on his head, and on the front of it he put the

---

a **8:7** EPHOD: *See Word List.*　　*b* **8:8** URIM AND THUMMIM: *Two objects used by the priest to determine God's will; it is not known precisely how they were used.*
7:26, 27 Gen 9:4; Lev 17:10–14; 19:26; Deut 12:16, 23; 15:23

gold ornament, the sacred sign of dedication, just as the LORD had commanded him.

10 Then Moses took the anointing oil and put it on the Tent of the LORD's presence and everything that was in it, and in this way he dedicated it all to the LORD. 11 He took some of the oil and sprinkled it seven times on the altar and its equipment and on the basin and its base, in order to dedicate them to the LORD. 12 He ordained Aaron by pouring some of the anointing oil on his head. 13 Next, Moses brought the sons of Aaron forward and put shirts on them, put sashes around their waists, and tied caps on their heads, just as the LORD had commanded.

14 Then Moses brought the young bull for the sin offering, and Aaron and his sons put their hands on its head. 15 Moses killed it and took some of the blood, and with his finger put it on the projections at the corners of the altar, in order to dedicate it. He then poured out the rest of the blood at the base of the altar. In this way he dedicated it and purified it. 16 Moses took all the fat on the internal organs, the best part of the liver, and the kidneys with the fat on them, and burned it all on the altar. 17 He took the rest of the bull, including its skin, flesh, and intestines, and burned it outside the camp, just as the LORD had commanded.

18 Next, Moses brought the ram for the burnt offering, and Aaron and his sons put their hands on its head. 19 Moses killed it and threw the blood on all four sides of the altar. 20-21 He cut the ram in pieces, washed the internal organs and the hind legs with water, and burned the head, the fat, and all the rest of the ram on the altar, just as the LORD had commanded. This burnt offering was a food offering, and its odor was pleasing to the LORD.

22 Then Moses brought the second ram, which was for the ordination of priests, and Aaron and his sons put their hands on its head. 23 Moses killed it and took some of the blood and put it on the lobe of Aaron's right ear, on the thumb of his right hand, and on the big toe of his right foot. 24 Then he brought Aaron's sons forward and put some of the blood on the lobes of their right ears,

on the thumbs of their right hands, and on the big toes of their right feet. Moses then threw the rest of the blood on all four sides of the altar. 25 He took the fat, the fat tail, all the fat covering the internal organs, the best part of the liver, the kidneys with the fat on them, and the right hind leg. 26 Then he took one loaf of bread from the basket of unleavened bread dedicated to the LORD, one loaf made with oil, and one thin cake, and he put them on top of the fat and the right hind leg. 27 He put all of this food in the hands of Aaron and his sons, and they presented it as a special gift to the LORD. 28 Then Moses took the food from them and burned it on the altar, on top of the burnt offering, as an ordination offering. This was a food offering, and its odor was pleasing to the LORD. 29 Then Moses took the breast and presented it as a special gift to the LORD. It was Moses' part of the ordination ram. Moses did everything just as the LORD had commanded.^c

30 Moses took some of the anointing oil and some of the blood that was on the altar and sprinkled them on Aaron and his sons and on their clothes. In this way he consecrated them and their clothes to the LORD.

31 Moses said to Aaron and his sons, "Take the meat to the entrance of the Tent of the LORD's presence, boil it, and eat it there with the bread that is in the basket of ordination offerings, just as the LORD commanded.^c 32 Burn up any meat or bread that is left over. 33 You shall not leave the entrance of the Tent for seven days, until your ordination rites are completed. 34 The LORD commanded us to do what we have done today, in order to take away your sin. 35 You must stay at the entrance of the Tent day and night for

In this way he consecrated them. (8:30)

seven days, doing what the LORD has commanded. If you don't, you will die. This is
what the LORD has commanded me." 36So
Aaron and his sons did everything that the
LORD had commanded through Moses.

Aaron Offers Sacrifices

9 1The day after the ordination rites were
completed, Moses called Aaron and his
sons and the leaders of Israel. 2He said to
Aaron, "Take a young bull and a ram without any defects and offer them to the LORD,
the bull for a sin offering and the ram for a
burnt offering. 3Then tell the people of
Israel to take a male goat for a sin offering, a
one-year-old calf, and a one-year-old lamb
without any defects for a burnt offering,
4and a bull and a ram for a fellowship offering. They are to sacrifice them to the LORD
with the grain offering mixed with oil. They
must do this because the LORD will appear
to them today."

5They brought to the front of the Tent
everything that Moses had commanded, and
the whole community assembled there to
worship the LORD. 6Moses said, "The LORD
has commanded you to do all this, so that
the dazzling light of his presence can appear
to you." 7Then he said to Aaron, "Go to the
altar and offer the sin offering and the burnt
offering to take away your sins and the sins
of the people. Present this offering to take
away the sins of the people, just as the LORD
commanded."

8Aaron went to the altar and killed the
young bull which was for his own sin offering. 9His sons brought him the blood, and
he dipped his finger in it, put some of it on
the projections at the corners of the altar,
and poured out the rest of it at the base of
the altar. 10Then he burned on the altar the
fat, the kidneys, and the best part of the liver,
just as the LORD had commanded Moses.
11But he burned the meat and the skin outside the camp.

12He killed the animal which was for his
own burnt offering. His sons brought him
the blood, and he threw it on all four sides
of the altar. 13They handed him the head

and the other pieces of the animal, and he
burned them on the altar. 14Then he washed
the internal organs and the hind legs and
burned them on the altar on top of the rest
of the burnt offering.

15After that, he presented the people's
offerings. He took the goat that was to be
offered for the people's sins, killed it, and offered it, as he had done with his own sin
offering. 16He also brought the animal for
the burnt offering and offered it according
to the regulations. 17He presented the grain
offering and took a handful of flour and
burned it on the altar. (This was in addition
to the daily burnt offering.) 18He killed the
bull and the ram as a fellowship offering for
the people. His sons brought him the blood,
and he threw it on all four sides of the altar.
19Aaron put the fat parts of the bull and the
ram 20on top of the breasts of the animals
and carried it all to the altar. He burned the
fat on the altar 21and presented the breasts
and the right hind legs as the special gift to
the LORD for the priests, as Moses had commanded.

22When Aaron had finished all the sacrifices, he raised his hands over the people and
blessed them, and then stepped down.
23Moses and Aaron went into the Tent of the
LORD's presence, and when they came out,
they blessed the people, and the dazzling
light of the LORD's presence appeared to all
the people. 24Suddenly the LORD sent a fire,
and it consumed the burnt offering and the
fat parts on the altar. When the people saw
it, they all shouted and bowed down with
their faces to the ground.

The Sin of Nadab and Abihu

10 1Aaron's sons, Nadab and Abihu,
each took his fire pan, put live coals
in it, added incense, and presented it to the
LORD. But this fire was not holy, because the
LORD had not commanded them to present
it. 2Suddenly the LORD sent fire, and it
burned them to death there in the presence
of the LORD. 3Then Moses said to Aaron,
"This is what the LORD was speaking about
when he said, 'All who serve me must

respect my holiness; I will reveal my glory to my people.' "[d] But Aaron remained silent.

[4] Moses called Mishael and Elzaphan, the sons of Uzziel, Aaron's uncle, and said to them, "Come here and carry your cousins' bodies away from the sacred Tent and put them outside the camp." [5] So they came and took hold of the clothing on the corpses and carried them outside the camp, just as Moses had commanded.

[6] Then Moses said to Aaron and to his sons Eleazar and Ithamar, "Do not leave your hair uncombed or tear your clothes to show that you are in mourning. If you do, you will die, and the LORD will be angry with the whole community. But all other Israelites are allowed to mourn this death caused by the fire which the LORD sent. [7] Do not leave the entrance of the Tent or you will die, because you have been consecrated by the anointing oil of the LORD." So they did as Moses said.

Rules for Priests

[8] The LORD said to Aaron, [9] "You and your sons are not to enter the Tent of my presence after drinking wine or beer; if you do, you will die. This is a law to be kept by all your descendants. [10] You must distinguish between what belongs to God and what is for general use, between what is ritually clean and what is unclean. [11] You must teach the people of Israel all the laws which I have given to you through Moses."

[12] Moses said to Aaron and his two remaining sons, Eleazar and Ithamar, "Take the grain offering that is left over from the food offered to the LORD, make unleavened bread with it and eat it beside the altar, because this offering is very holy. [13] Eat it in a holy place; it is the part that belongs to you and your sons from the food offered to the LORD. That is what the LORD commanded me. [14] But you and your families may eat the breast and the hind leg that are presented as the special gift and the special contribution to the LORD for the priests. You may eat them in any ritually clean place. These offerings have been given to you and your children as the part that belongs to you from the fellowship offerings of the people of Israel. [15] They shall bring the hind leg and the breast at the time the fat is presented as a food offering to the LORD. These parts belong to you and your children forever, just as the LORD commanded."

[16] Moses asked about the goat for the sin offering and learned that it had already been burned. This made him angry at Eleazar and Ithamar, and he demanded, [17] "Why didn't you eat the sin offering in a sacred place? It is very holy, and the LORD has given it to you in order to take away the sin of the community. [18] Since its blood was not brought into the sacred Tent, you should have eaten the sacrifice there, as I commanded."

[19] Aaron answered, "If I had eaten the sin offering today, would the LORD have approved? The people presented their sin offering to the LORD today, and they brought their burnt offering, but still these terrible things have happened to me." [20] When Moses heard this, he was satisfied.

Animals That May Be Eaten
(Deuteronomy 14:3–21)

11 [1] The LORD gave Moses and Aaron the following regulations [2] for the people of Israel. You may eat any land animal [3] that has divided hoofs and that also chews the cud, [4-6] but you must not eat camels, rock badgers, or rabbits. These must be considered unclean; they chew the cud, but do not have divided hoofs. [7] Do not eat pigs. They must be considered unclean; they have divided hoofs, but do not chew the cud. [8] Do not eat these animals or even touch their dead bodies; they are unclean.

[9] You may eat any kind of fish that has fins and scales, [10] but anything living in the water that does not have fins and scales must not be eaten. [11] Such creatures must be considered unclean. You must not eat them or even touch their dead bodies. [12] You must not eat anything that lives in the water and does not have fins and scales.

[13-19] You must not eat any of the following

---

[d] **10:3** I will reveal my glory to my people; *or* my people must honor me.
10:12, 13 Lev 6:14–18   **10:14, 15** Lev 7:30–34   **10:17** Lev 6:24–26

Leviticus

The unclean animals (11)

birds: eagles, owls, hawks, falcons; buzzards, vultures, crows; ostriches; seagulls, storks, herons, pelicans, cormorants;*e* hoopoes; or bats.

20 All winged insects are unclean, **21** except those that hop. **22** You may eat locusts, crickets, or grasshoppers. **23** But all other small things that have wings and also crawl must be considered unclean.

24-28 If you touch the dead bodies of the following animals, you will be unclean until evening: all animals with hoofs, unless their hoofs are divided and they chew the cud, and all four-footed animals with paws. If you carry their dead bodies, you must wash your clothes, but you will still be unclean until evening.

29-30 Moles, rats, mice, and lizards must be considered unclean. **31** Whoever touches them or their dead bodies will be unclean until evening. **32** And if their dead bodies fall on anything, it will be unclean. This applies to any article of wood, cloth, leather, or sacking, no matter what it is used for. It shall be dipped in water, but it will remain unclean until evening. **33** And if their bodies fall into a clay pot, everything that is in it shall be unclean, and you must break the pot. **34** Any food which could normally be eaten, but on which water from such a pot has been poured, will be unclean, and any-

thing drinkable in such a pot is unclean. **35** Anything on which the dead bodies fall is unclean; a clay stove or oven shall be broken, **36** but a spring or a cistern remains clean, although anything else that touches their dead bodies is unclean. **37** If one of them falls on seed that is going to be planted, the seed remains clean. **38** But if the seed is soaking in water and one of them falls on it, the seed is unclean.

39 If any animal that may be eaten dies, anyone who touches it will be unclean until evening. **40** And if any of you eat any part of the animal, you must wash your clothes, but you will still be unclean until evening; any of you who carry the dead body must wash your clothes, but you will still be unclean until evening.

41 You must not eat any of the small animals that move on the ground, **42** whether they crawl, or walk on four legs, or have many legs. **43** Do not make yourselves unclean by eating any of these. **44** I am the LORD your God, and you must keep yourselves holy, because I am holy. **45** I am the LORD who brought you out of Egypt so that I could be your God. You must be holy, because I am holy.

46 This, then, is the law about animals and birds, about everything that lives in the water, and everything that moves on the

e **11:13–19** *The identification of some of the birds in verses 13–19 is uncertain.*
11:44 Lev 19:2; 1 Pet 1:16

ground. [47]You must be careful to distinguish between what is ritually clean and unclean, between animals that may be eaten and those that may not.

The Purification of Women after Childbirth

12 [1]The LORD gave Moses the following regulations [2]for the people of Israel. For seven days after a woman gives birth to a son, she is ritually unclean, as she is during her monthly period. [3]On the eighth day, the child shall be circumcised. [4]Then it will be thirty-three more days until she is ritually clean from her loss of blood; she must not touch anything that is holy or enter the sacred Tent until the time of her purification is completed.

[5]For fourteen days after a woman gives birth to a daughter, she is ritually unclean, as she is during her monthly period. Then it will be sixty-six more days until she is ritually clean from her loss of blood.

[6]When the time of her purification is completed, whether for a son or daughter, she shall bring to the priest at the entrance of the Tent of the LORD's presence a one-year-old lamb for a burnt offering and a pigeon or a dove for a sin offering. [7]The priest shall present her offering to the LORD and perform the ritual to take away her impurity, and she will be ritually clean. This, then, is what a woman must do after giving birth.

[8]If the woman cannot afford a lamb, she shall bring two doves or two pigeons, one for a burnt offering and the other for a sin offering, and the priest shall perform the ritual to take away her impurity, and she will be ritually clean.

Laws concerning Skin Diseases

13 [1]The LORD gave Moses and Aaron these regulations. [2]If any of you have a sore on your skin or a boil or an inflammation which could develop into a dreaded skin disease, you shall be brought to the Aaronite priest. [3]The priest shall examine the sore, and if the hairs in it have turned

white and the sore appears to be deeper than the surrounding skin, it is a dreaded skin disease, and the priest shall pronounce you unclean. [4]But if the sore is white and does not appear to be deeper than the skin around it and the hairs have not turned white, the priest shall isolate you for seven days. [5]The priest shall examine you again on the seventh day, and if in his opinion the sore looks the same and has not spread, he shall isolate you for another seven days. [6]The priest shall examine you again on the seventh day, and if the sore has faded and has not spread, he shall pronounce you ritually clean; it is only a sore. You shall wash your clothes and be ritually clean. [7]But if the sore spreads after the priest has examined you and pronounced you clean, you must appear before the priest again. [8]The priest will examine you again, and if it has spread, he shall pronounce you unclean; it is a dreaded skin disease.

[9]If any of you have a dreaded skin disease, you shall be brought to the priest, [10]who will examine you. If there is a white sore on your skin which turns the hairs white and is full of pus, [11]it is a chronic skin disease. The priest shall pronounce you unclean; there is no need to isolate you, because you are obviously unclean. [12]If the skin disease spreads and covers you from head to foot, [13]the priest shall examine you again. If he finds that it actually has covered the whole body, he shall pronounce you ritually clean. If your whole skin has turned white, you are ritually clean. [14]But from the moment an open sore appears, you are unclean. [15]The priest shall examine you again, and if he sees an open sore, he shall pronounce you unclean. An open sore means a dreaded skin disease, and you are unclean. [16]But when the sore heals and becomes white again, you shall go to the priest, [17]who will examine you again. If the sore has turned white, you are ritually clean, and the priest shall pronounce you clean.

[18]If any of you have a boil that has healed [19]and if afterward a white swelling or a reddish-white spot appears where the boil was, you shall go to the priest. [20]The priest shall

examine you, and if the spot seems to be deeper than the surrounding skin and the hairs in it have turned white, he shall pronounce you unclean. It is a dreaded skin disease that has started in the boil. 21But if the priest examines it and finds that the hairs in it have not turned white and that it is not deeper than the surrounding skin, but is light in color, the priest shall isolate you for seven days. 22If the spot spreads, the priest shall pronounce you unclean; you are diseased. 23But if it remains unchanged and does not spread, it is only the scar left from the boil, and the priest shall pronounce you ritually clean.

The priest shall examine you. (13:20)

24In case any of you have been burned, if the raw flesh becomes white or reddish-white, 25the priest shall examine you. If the hairs in the spot have turned white and it appears deeper than the surrounding skin, it is a dreaded skin disease that has started in the burn, and the priest shall pronounce you unclean. 26But if the hairs in it have not turned white and it is not deeper than the surrounding skin, but is light in color, the priest shall isolate you for seven days. 27The priest shall examine you again on the seventh day, and if it is spreading, it is a dreaded skin disease, and the priest shall pronounce you unclean. 28But if the spot remains unchanged and does not spread and is light in color, it is not a dreaded skin disease. The priest shall pronounce you ritually clean, because it is only a scar from the burn.

29When any of you, male or female, have a sore on your head or chin, 30the priest shall examine it. If it seems to be deeper than the surrounding skin and the hairs in it are yellowish and thin, it is a dreaded skin disease, and he shall pronounce you unclean. 31If, when the priest examines you, the sore does not appear to be deeper than the surrounding skin, but there are still no healthy hairs in it, he shall isolate you for seven days. 32The priest shall examine the sore again on the seventh day, and if it has not spread and there are no yellowish hairs in it and it does not seem to be deeper than the surrounding skin, 33you shall shave the head except the area around the sore. The priest shall then isolate you for another seven days. 34On the seventh day the priest shall again examine the sore, and if it has not spread and does not seem to be deeper than the surrounding skin, he shall pronounce you ritually clean. You shall wash your clothes, and you will be clean. 35But if the sore spreads after you have been pronounced clean, 36the priest shall examine you again. If the sore has spread, he need not look for yellowish hairs; you are obviously unclean. 37But if in the priest's opinion the sore has not spread and healthy hairs are growing in it, the sore has healed, and the priest shall pronounce you ritually clean.

38When any of you, male or female, have white spots on the skin, 39the priest shall examine you. If the spots are dull white, it is only a blemish that has broken out on the skin; you are ritually clean.

40-41If you lose your hair at the back or the front of your head, this does not make you unclean. 42But if a reddish-white sore appears on the bald spot, it is a dreaded skin disease. 43The priest shall examine you, and if there is a reddish-white sore, 44the priest shall pronounce you unclean, because of the dreaded skin disease on your head.

45If you have a dreaded skin disease, you must wear torn clothes, leave your hair uncombed, cover the lower part of your face, and call out, "Unclean, unclean!" 46You remain unclean as long as you have the disease, and you must live outside the camp, away from others.

Laws concerning Mildew

47When there is mildew^f on clothing, whether wool or linen, **48**or on any piece of linen or wool cloth or on leather or anything made of leather, **49**if it is greenish or reddish, it is a spreading mildew and must be shown to the priest. **50**The priest shall examine it and put the object away for seven days. **51**He shall examine it again on the seventh day, and if the mildew has spread, the object is unclean. **52**The priest shall burn it, because it is a spreading mildew which must be destroyed by fire.

53But if, when he examines it, the priest finds that the mildew has not spread on the object, **54**he shall order that it be washed and put away for another seven days. **55**Then he shall examine it, and if the mildew has not changed color, even though it has not spread, it is still unclean; you must burn the object, whether the rot is on the front or the back. **56**But if, when the priest examines it again, the mildew has faded, he shall tear it out of the clothing or leather. **57**Then, if the mildew reappears, it is spreading again, and the owner shall burn the object. **58**If he washes the object and the spot disappears, he shall wash it again, and it will be ritually clean.

59This, then, is the law about mildew on clothing, whether it is wool or linen, or on linen or wool cloth or on anything made of leather; this is how the decision is made as to whether it is ritually clean or unclean.

Purification after Having Skin Diseases

14 **1**The LORD gave Moses **2**the following regulations about the ritual purification of those of you cured of a dreaded skin disease. On the day you are to be pronounced clean, you shall be brought to the priest, **3**and the priest shall take you outside the camp and examine you. If the disease is healed, **4**the priest shall order that two ritually clean birds be brought, along with a piece of cedar wood, a red cord, and a sprig of hyssop. **5**Then the priest shall order

that one of the birds be killed over a clay bowl containing fresh spring water. **6**He shall take the other bird and dip it, together with the cedar wood, the red cord, and the hyssop, in the blood of the bird that was killed. **7**He shall sprinkle the blood seven times on the one of you who is to be purified from your skin disease, and then he shall pronounce you clean. He shall let the live bird fly away over the open fields. **8**You shall wash your clothes, shave off all your hair, and take a bath; you will then be ritually clean. You may enter the camp, but you must live outside your tent for seven days. **9**On the seventh day you shall again shave your head, your beard, your eyebrows, and all the rest of the hair on your body; you shall wash your clothes and take a bath, and then you will be ritually clean.

10On the eighth day you shall bring two male lambs and one female lamb a year old that are without any defects, five pounds of flour mixed with olive oil, and half a pint of olive oil. **11**The priest shall take you and these offerings to the entrance of the Tent of the LORD's presence. **12**Then the priest shall take one of the male lambs and together with the half pint of oil he shall offer it as a repayment offering. He shall present them as a special gift to the LORD for the priest. **13**He shall kill the lamb in the holy place where the animals for the sin offerings and the burnt offerings are killed. He must do this because the repayment offering, like the sin offering, belongs to the priest and is very holy. **14**The priest shall take some of the blood of the lamb and put it on the lobe of the right ear, on the thumb of the right hand, and on the big toe of the right foot of the one of you to be declared ritually clean. **15**The priest shall take some of the olive oil and pour it in the palm of his own left hand, **16**dip a finger of his right hand in it, and sprinkle some of it seven times there in the LORD's presence. **17**He shall take some of the oil that is in the palm of his hand and some of the blood of the lamb and put them on the lobe of the right ear, on the thumb of the right hand, and on the big toe of the right foot of the one of you to be declared

Leviticus

---

^{f} **13:47** MILDEW: *The Hebrew word for "dreaded skin disease" and "mildew" is the same.*
14:2 Mt 8:4; Mk 1:44; Lk 5:14; 17:14

ritually clean. 18He shall put the rest of the oil that is in the palm of his hand on your head. In this way he shall perform the ritual of purification.

19Then the priest shall offer the sin offering and perform the ritual of purification. After that, he shall kill the animal for the burnt offering 20and offer it with the grain offering on the altar. In this way the priest shall perform the ritual of purification, and you will be ritually clean.

21If you are poor and cannot afford any more, you shall bring for your purification only one male lamb as your repayment offering, a special gift to the LORD for the priest. You shall bring only two pounds of flour mixed with olive oil for a grain offering and half a pint of olive oil. 22You shall also bring two doves or two pigeons, one for the sin offering and one for the burnt offering. 23On the eighth day of your purification you shall bring them to the priest at the entrance of the Tent. 24The priest shall take the lamb and the olive oil and present them as a special gift to the LORD for the priest. 25He shall kill the lamb and take some of the blood and put it on the lobe of your right ear, on the thumb of your right hand, and on the big toe of your right foot. 26The priest shall pour some of the oil into the palm of his own left hand 27and with a finger of his right hand sprinkle some of it seven times there in the LORD's presence. 28He shall put some of the oil on the same places he put the blood: on the lobe of your right ear, on the thumb of your right hand, and on the big toe of your right foot. 29The rest of the oil that is in his palm he shall put on your head and in this way perform the ritual of purification. 30Then he shall offer one of the doves or pigeons 31as the sin offering and the other as the burnt offering with the grain offering. In this way the priest shall perform the ritual of purification. 32This is the law for those who have a dreaded skin disease but who cannot afford the normal offerings required for his purification.

Mildew in Houses

33The LORD gave Moses and Aaron 34-35the following regulations about houses affected by spreading mildew. (These were to apply after the people of Israel entered the land of Canaan, which the LORD was going to give them as their possession.) If any of you find that the LORD has sent mildew on your house, then you must go and tell the priest about it. 36The priest shall order everything to be moved out of the house before he goes to examine the mildew; otherwise everything in the house will be declared unclean. Then he shall go to the house 37and examine the mildew. If there are greenish or reddish spots that appear to be eating into the wall, 38he shall leave the house and lock it up for seven days. 39On the seventh day he shall return and examine it again. If the mildew has spread, 40he shall order that the stones on which the mildew is found be removed and thrown into some unclean place outside the city. 41After that he must have all the interior walls scraped and the plaster dumped in an unclean place outside the city. 42Then other stones are to be used to replace the stones that were removed, and new plaster will be used to cover the walls.

The stones shall be removed. (14:40)

43If the mildew breaks out again in the house after the stones have been removed and the house has been scraped and plastered, 44the priest shall go and look. If it has spread, the house is unclean. 45It must be torn down, and its stones, its wood, and all its plaster must be carried out of the city to an unclean place. 46Any who enter the house while it is locked up will be unclean until evening. 47Any who lie down or eat in the house must wash their clothes.

⁴⁸If, when the priest comes to look, the mildew has not reappeared after the house has been replastered, he shall pronounce the house ritually clean, because the mildew has been completely removed. ⁴⁹To purify the house, he shall take two birds, some cedar wood, a red cord, and a sprig of hyssop. ⁵⁰He shall kill one of the birds over a clay bowl containing fresh spring water. ⁵¹Then he shall take the cedar wood, the hyssop, the red cord, and the live bird and shall dip them in the blood of the bird that was killed and in the fresh water. And he shall sprinkle the house seven times. ⁵²In this way he shall purify the house with the bird's blood, the fresh water, the live bird, the cedar wood, the hyssop, and the red cord. ⁵³Then he shall let the live bird fly away outside the city over the open fields. In this way he shall perform the ritual of purification for the house, and it will be ritually clean.

⁵⁴These are the laws about dreaded skin diseases; ⁵⁵⁻⁵⁶sores, boils, or inflammations; and about mildew in clothes or houses. ⁵⁷These laws determine when something is unclean and when it is clean.

Unclean Bodily Discharges

15 ¹The LORD gave Moses and Aaron the following regulations ²for the people of Israel. When any man has a discharge from his penis, the discharge is unclean, ³whether the penis runs with it or is stopped up by it. ⁴Any bed on which he sits or lies is unclean. ⁵Anyone who touches his bed ⁶or sits on anything the man has sat on must wash his clothes and take a bath, and he remains unclean until evening. ⁷Anyone who touches the man with the discharge must wash his clothes and take a bath, and he remains unclean until evening. ⁸If the man with the discharge spits on anyone who is ritually clean, that person must wash his clothes and take a bath, and he remains unclean until evening. ⁹Any saddle or seat on which the man with the discharge sits is unclean. ¹⁰Anyone who touches anything on which the man sat is unclean until evening. Anyone who carries anything on which the man sat must wash his clothes and take a bath, and he remains unclean until evening.

¹¹If a man who has a discharge touches one of you without first having washed his hands, you must wash your clothes and take a bath, and you remain unclean until evening. ¹²Any clay pot that the man touches must be broken, and any wooden bowl that he touches must be washed.

¹³After the man is cured of his discharge, he must wait seven days and then wash his clothes and take a bath in fresh spring water, and he will be ritually clean. ¹⁴On the eighth day he shall take two doves or two pigeons to the entrance of the Tent of the LORD's presence and give them to the priest. ¹⁵The priest shall offer one of them as a sin offering and the other as a burnt offering. In this way he will perform the ritual of purification for the man.

¹⁶When a man has an emission of semen, he must bathe his whole body, and he remains unclean until evening. ¹⁷Anything made of cloth or leather on which the semen falls must be washed, and it remains unclean until evening. ¹⁸After sexual intercourse both the man and the woman must take a bath, and they remain unclean until evening.

¹⁹When a woman has her monthly period, she remains unclean for seven days. Anyone who touches her is unclean until evening. ²⁰Anything on which she sits or lies during her monthly period is unclean. ²¹⁻²³Any who touch her bed or anything on which she has sat must wash their clothes and take a bath, and they remain unclean until evening. ²⁴If a man has sexual intercourse with her during her period, he is contaminated by her impurity and remains unclean for seven days, and any bed on which he lies is unclean.

²⁵If a woman has a flow of blood for several days outside her monthly period or if her flow continues beyond her regular period, she remains unclean as long as the flow continues, just as she is during her monthly period. ²⁶Any bed on which she lies and anything on which she sits during this time is unclean. ²⁷Any who touch them are unclean and must wash their clothes and take a bath; they remain unclean until evening. ²⁸After her flow stops, she must wait seven days, and then she will be ritually clean. ²⁹On the eighth day she shall take two

doves or two pigeons to the priest at the entrance of the Tent of the LORD's presence. [30] The priest shall offer one of them as a sin offering and the other as a burnt offering, and in this way he will perform the ritual of purification for her.

[31] The LORD told Moses to warn the people of Israel about their uncleanness, so that they would not defile the Tent of his presence, which was in the middle of the camp. If they did, they would be killed.

[32] These are the regulations about a man who has a discharge or an emission of semen, [33] a woman during her monthly period, or a man who has sexual intercourse with a woman who is ritually unclean.

The Day of Atonement

16 [1] The LORD spoke to Moses after the death of the two sons of Aaron who were killed when they offered unholy fire to the LORD. [2] He said, "Tell your brother Aaron that only at the proper time is he to go behind the curtain into the Most Holy Place, because that is where I appear in a cloud above the lid on the Covenant Box. If he disobeys, he will be killed. [3] He may enter the Most Holy Place only after he has brought a young bull for a sin offering and a ram for a burnt offering."

[4] Then the LORD gave the following instructions. Before Aaron goes into the Most Holy Place, he must take a bath and put on the priestly garments: the linen robe and shorts, the belt, and the turban.

[5] The community of Israel shall give Aaron two male goats for a sin offering and a ram for a burnt offering. [6] He shall offer a bull as a sacrifice to take away his own sins and those of his family. [7] Then he shall take the two goats to the entrance of the Tent of the LORD's presence. [8] There he shall draw lots, using two stones, one marked "for the LORD" and the other "for Azazel." [g] [9] Aaron shall sacrifice the goat chosen by lot for the LORD and offer it as a sin offering. [10] The goat chosen for Azazel shall be presented alive to the LORD and sent off into the

desert to Azazel, in order to take away the sins of the people.

[11] When Aaron sacrifices the bull as the sin offering for himself and his family, [12] he shall take a fire pan full of burning coals from the altar and two handfuls of fine incense and bring them into the Most Holy Place. [13] There in the LORD's presence he shall put the incense on the fire, and the smoke of the incense will hide the lid of the Covenant Box so that he will not see it and die. [14] He shall take some of the bull's blood and with his finger sprinkle it on the front of the lid and then sprinkle some of it seven times in front of the Covenant Box.

[15] After that, he shall kill the goat for the sin offering for the people, bring its blood into the Most Holy Place, and sprinkle it on the lid and then in front of the Covenant Box, as he did with the bull's blood. [16] In this way he will perform the ritual to purify the Most Holy Place from the uncleanness of the people of Israel and from all their sins. He must do this to the Tent, because it stands in the middle of the camp, which is ritually unclean. [17] From the time Aaron enters the Most Holy Place to perform the ritual of purification until he comes out, there must be no one in the Tent. When he has performed the ritual for himself, his family, and the whole community, [18] he must then go out to the altar for burnt offerings and purify it. He must take some of the bull's blood and some of the goat's blood and put it all over the projections at the corners of the altar. [19] With his finger he must sprinkle some of the blood on the altar seven times. In this way he is to purify it from the sins of the people of Israel and make it holy.

The Scapegoat

[20] When Aaron has finished performing the ritual to purify the Most Holy Place, the rest of the Tent of the LORD's presence, and the altar, he shall present to the LORD the live goat chosen for Azazel. [g] [21] He shall put both of his hands on the goat's head and confess over it all the evils, sins, and rebellions of the people of Israel, and so transfer them to the

g **16:8,20** AZAZEL: *The meaning of this Hebrew word is unknown; it may be the name of a desert demon.*
16:2 Heb 6:19   **16:3** Heb 9:7   **16:15** Heb 9:12   **16:21, 22** Tob 8:3

goat's head. Then the goat is to be driven off into the desert by someone appointed to do it. 22 The goat will carry all their sins away with him into some uninhabited land.

The goat will carry all their sins away. (16:22)

23 Then Aaron shall go into the Tent, take off the priestly garments that he had put on before entering the Most Holy Place, and leave them there. 24 He must take a bath in a holy place and put on his own clothes. After that, he shall go out and offer the burnt offering to remove his own sins and those of the people. 25 He shall burn on the altar the fat of the animal for the sin offering. 26 The man who drove the goat into the desert to Azazel must wash his clothes and take a bath before he comes back into camp. 27 The bull and the goat used for the sin offering, whose blood was brought into the Most Holy Place to take away sin, shall be carried outside the camp and burned. Skin, meat, and intestines shall all be burned. 28 The one who burns them must wash his clothes and take a bath before he returns to camp.

Observing the Day of Atonement

29 The following regulations are to be observed for all time to come. On the tenth day of the seventh month the Israelites and the foreigners living among them must fast and must not do any work. 30 On that day the ritual is to be performed to purify them from all their sins, so that they will be ritually clean. 31 That day is to be a very holy day, one on which they fast and do no work at all. These regulations are to be observed for all time to come. 32 The High Priest, properly ordained and consecrated to succeed his father, is to perform the ritual of purification. He shall put on the priestly garments 33 and perform the ritual to purify the Most Holy Place, the rest of the Tent of the LORD's presence, the altar, the priests, and all the people of the community. 34 These regulations are to be observed for all time to come. This ritual must be performed once a year to purify the people of Israel from all their sins.

So Moses*h* did as the LORD had commanded.

The Sacredness of Blood

17 1 The LORD commanded Moses 2 to give Aaron and his sons and all the people of Israel the following regulations. 3-4 Any Israelites who kill a cow or a sheep or a goat as an offering to the LORD anywhere except at the entrance of the Tent of the LORD's presence have broken the Law. They have shed blood and shall no longer be considered God's people. 5 The meaning of this command is that the people of Israel shall now bring to the LORD the animals which they used to kill in the open country. They shall now bring them to the priest at the entrance of the Tent and kill them as fellowship offerings. 6 The priest shall throw the blood against the sides of the altar at the entrance of the Tent and burn the fat to produce an odor that is pleasing to the LORD. 7 The people of Israel must no longer be unfaithful to the LORD by killing their animals in the fields as sacrifices to the goat demons. The people of Israel must keep this regulation for all time to come.

8 Any Israelites or any foreigners living in the community who offer a burnt offering or any other sacrifice 9 as an offering to the LORD anywhere except at the entrance of the Tent shall no longer be considered God's people.

10 If any Israelites or any foreigners living

h **16:34** Moses; *or* Aaron.
16:23 Ezek 44:19   **16:27** Heb 13:11   **16:29–34** Lev 23:26–32; Num 29:7–11   **17:10** Gen 9:4; Lev 7:26, 27; 19:26; Deut 12:16, 23; 15:23

in the community eat meat with blood still in it, the LORD will turn against them and no longer consider them his people. [11]The life of every living thing is in the blood, and that is why the LORD has commanded that all blood be poured out on the altar to take away the people's sins. Blood, which is life, takes away sins. [12]That is why the LORD has told the people of Israel that neither they nor any foreigner living among them shall eat any meat with blood still in it.

[13]If any Israelites or any foreigners living in the community catch an animal or a bird which is ritually clean, they must pour its blood out on the ground and cover it with dirt. [14]The life of every living thing is in the blood, and that is why the LORD has told the people of Israel that they shall not eat any meat with blood still in it and that anyone who does so will no longer be considered one of his people.

[15]Any people, Israelites or foreigners, who eat meat from an animal that has died a natural death or has been killed by wild animals must wash their clothes, take a bath, and wait until evening before they are ritually clean. [16]If they do not, they must suffer the consequences.

Forbidden Sexual Practices

18 [1]The LORD told Moses [2]to say to the people of Israel, "I am the LORD your God. [3]Do not follow the practices of the people of Egypt, where you once lived, or of the people in the land of Canaan, where I am now taking you. [4]Obey my laws and do what I command. I am the LORD your God. [5]Follow the practices and the laws that I give you; you will save your life by doing so. I am the LORD."

[6]The LORD gave the following regulations. Do not have sexual intercourse with any of your relatives. [7]Do not disgrace your father by having intercourse with your mother. You must not disgrace your own mother. [8]Do not disgrace your father by having intercourse with any of his other wives. [9]Do not have

intercourse with your sister or your half sister, whether or not she was brought up in the same house with you. [10]Do not have intercourse with your granddaughter; that would be a disgrace to you. [11]Do not have intercourse with a stepsister; she, too, is your sister. [12-13]Do not have intercourse with an aunt, whether she is your father's sister or your mother's sister. [14]Do not have intercourse with your uncle's wife; she, too, is your aunt. [15]Do not have intercourse with your daughter-in-law [16]or with your brother's wife. [17]Do not have intercourse with the daughter or granddaughter of a woman with whom you have had intercourse; they may be related to you, and that would be incest. [18]Do not take your wife's sister as one of your wives, as long as your wife is living.

[19]Do not have intercourse with a woman during her monthly period, because she is ritually unclean. [20]Do not have intercourse with another man's wife; that would make you ritually unclean. [21]Do not hand over any of your children to be used in the worship of the god Molech, because that would bring disgrace on the name of God, the LORD. [22]No man is to have sexual relations with another man; God hates that. [23]No man or woman is to have sexual relations with an animal; that perversion makes you ritually unclean.

[24]Do not make yourselves unclean by any of these acts, for that is how the pagans made themselves unclean, those pagans who lived in the land before you and whom the LORD is driving out so that you can go in. [25]Their actions made the land unclean, and so the LORD is punishing the land and making it reject the people who lived there. [26-27]They did all these disgusting things and made the land unclean, but you must not do them. All of you, whether Israelites or foreigners living with you, must keep the LORD's laws and commands, [28]and then the land will not reject you, as it rejected the pagans who lived there before you. [29]You know that whoever does any of these disgusting things will no longer be considered one of God's people.

[30]And the LORD said, "Obey the com-

17:11 Heb 9:22   **18:5** Neh 9:29; Ezek 18:9; 20:11–13; Lk 10:28; Rom 10:5; Gal 3:12   **18:8** Lev 20:11; Deut 22:30; 27:20   **18:9** Lev 20:17; Deut 27:22   **18:12–14** Lev 20:19, 20   **18:15** Lev 20:12   **18:16** Lev 20:21 **18:17** Lev 20:14; Deut 27:23   **18:19** Lev 20:18   **18:20** Lev 20:10   **18:21** Lev 20:1–5   **18:22** Lev 20:13 **18:23** Ex 22:19; Lev 20:15, 16; Deut 27:21

mands I give and do not follow the practices of the people who lived in the land before you, and do not make yourselves unclean by doing any of these things. I am the LORD your God."

Laws of Holiness and Justice

19 ¹The LORD told Moses ²to say to the community of Israel, "Be holy, because I, the LORD your God, am holy. ³Each of you must respect your mother and your father, and must keep the Sabbath, as I have commanded. I am the LORD your God.

⁴"Do not abandon me and worship idols; do not make gods of metal and worship them. I am the LORD your God.

⁵"When you kill an animal for a fellowship offering, keep the regulations that I have given you, and I will accept the offering. ⁶The meat must be eaten on the day the animal is killed or on the next day. Any meat left on the third day must be burned, ⁷because it is ritually unclean, and if anyone eats it, I will not accept the offering. ⁸Any who eat it will be guilty of treating as ordinary what is dedicated to me, and they will no longer be considered my people.

⁹"When you harvest your fields, do not cut the grain at the edges of the fields, and do not go back to cut the heads of grain that were left. ¹⁰Do not go back through your vineyard to gather the grapes that were missed or to pick up the grapes that have fallen; leave them for poor people and foreigners. I am the LORD your God.

¹¹"Do not steal or cheat or lie. ¹²Do not make a promise in my name if you do not intend to keep it; that brings disgrace on my name. I am the LORD your God.

¹³"Do not rob or take advantage of anyone. Do not hold back the wages of someone you have hired, not even for one night. ¹⁴Do not curse the deaf or put something in front of the blind so as to make them stumble over it. Obey me; I am the LORD your God.

¹⁵"Be honest and just when you make decisions in legal cases; do not show

You Can Be Holy!

Chapters 17–26 of Leviticus are called the holiness code, or holiness laws. In these chapters God says, "Be holy, because I, the LORD your God, am holy" (19:2), and, "Obey my laws, because I am the LORD and I make you holy" (20:8). The message is clear: God wants us to be holy as he is holy. To be holy is to be like God, and holiness is basically imitating God.

All of these laws in the holiness code were ways of living God's values. The laws had to do with avoiding sinful behavior, how to avoid sickness and disease, how to worship God properly, and how to live fairly with other people. Some of these laws don't apply to us today because Christians have a different understanding today of how to live out these same values. But the values are still there for us to live out in every part of our lives.

The call to holiness takes a new twist in the New Testament. Because Jesus is God we are now called to imitate Jesus. Imitating Jesus means being peacemakers, being forgiving even to those who hate us, caring for everyone, especially people with special needs, and accepting suffering with grace. Try this. Make a list of all the things you can do to be like Jesus. Then ask Jesus to help you do them!

— Leviticus 19:1–3

Leviticus

19:2 Lev 11:44, 45; 1 Pet 1:16　**19:3** a Ex 20:12; Deut 5:16; b Ex 20:8; Deut 5:12　**19:4** a Lev 26:1; b Ex 20:23; 34:17; Deut 17:25　**19:9, 10** Lev 27:15; Deut 24:19–22　**19:11** a Ex 20:15; Deut 5:19; b Ex 20:16; Deut 5:20　**19:12** Ex 20:7; Deut 5:11; Mt 5:33　**19:13** Deut 24:14, 15　**19:14** Deut 27:18　**19:15** Ex 23:6–8; Deut 16:19

Leviticus

favoritism to the poor or fear the rich. 16Do not spread lies about anyone, and when someone is on trial for his life, speak out if your testimony can help him. I am the LORD.

17"Do not bear a grudge against others, but settle your differences with them, so that you will not commit a sin because of them.*i* 18Do not take revenge on others or continue to hate them, but love your neighbors as you love yourself. I am the LORD.

"Do not bear a grudge." (19:17)

19"Obey my commands. Do not cross-breed domestic animals. Do not plant two kinds of seed in the same field. Do not wear clothes made of two kinds of material.

20"If a slave woman is the recognized concubine of a man and she has not been paid for and freed, then if another man has sexual relations with her, they will be punished, but not*j* put to death, since she is a slave. 21The man shall bring a ram to the entrance of the Tent of my presence as his repayment offering, 22and with it the priest shall perform the ritual of purification to remove the man's sin, and God will forgive him.

23"When you come into the land of Canaan and plant any kind of fruit tree, consider the fruit ritually unclean for the first three years. During that time you must not eat it. 24In the fourth year all the fruit shall be dedicated as an offering to show your gratitude to me,*k* the LORD. 25But in the fifth year you may eat the fruit. If you do all this, your trees will bear more fruit. I am the LORD your God.

Show respect for old people. (19:32)

26"Do not eat any meat with blood still in it. Do not practice any kind of magic. 27Do not cut the hair on the sides of your head or trim your beard 28or tattoo yourselves or cut gashes in your body to mourn for the dead. I am the LORD.

29"Do not disgrace your daughters by making them temple prostitutes;*l* if you do, you will turn to other gods and the land will be full of immorality. 30Keep the Sabbath, and honor the place where I am worshiped. I am the LORD.

31"Do not go for advice to people who consult the spirits of the dead. If you do, you will be ritually unclean. I am the LORD your God.

32"Show respect for old people and honor them. Reverently obey me; I am the LORD.

33"Do not mistreat foreigners who are living in your land. 34Treat them as you would an Israelite, and love them as you love yourselves. Remember that you were once foreigners in the land of Egypt. I am the LORD your God.

35"Do not cheat anyone by using false measures of length, weight, or quantity. 36Use honest scales, honest weights, and honest measures. I am the LORD your God,

---

i **19:17** so . . . them; *or* so that you do not commit this sin against them.　*j* **19:20** they . . . not; *or* an investigation will be made but they will not be.　*k* **19:24** to show your gratitude to me; *or* in praise of me.
l **19:29** TEMPLE PROSTITUTES: *These women were found in Canaanite temples, where fertility gods were worshiped. It was believed that intercourse with these prostitutes assured fertile fields and herds.*

19:17 Mt 18:15　**19:18** Mt 5:43; 19:19; 22:39; Mk 12:31; Lk 10:27; Rom 13:9; Gal 5:14; Jas 2:8　**19:19** Deut 22:9–11　**19:26 a** Gen 9:4; Lev 7:26, 27; 17:10–14; Deut 12:16, 23; 15:23; **b** Deut 18:10　**19:27, 28** Lev 21:5; Deut 14:1　**19:29** Deut 23:17　**19:30** Lev 26:2　**19:31** Deut 18:11; 1 Sam 28:3; 2 Kings 23:4; Isa 8:19　**19:33, 34** Ex 22:21; Deut 24:17, 18; 27:19　**19:35, 36** Deut 25:13–16; Prov 20:10; Ezek 45:10

Love them as you love yourselves. (19:34)

and I brought you out of Egypt. 37Obey all my laws and commands. I am the LORD."

Penalties for Disobedience

20 1The LORD told Moses 2to say to the people of Israel, "Any of you or any foreigner living among you who gives any children to be used in the worship of the god Molech shall be stoned to death by the whole community. 3If any of you give one of your children to Molech and make my sacred Tent unclean and disgrace my holy name, I will turn against you and will no longer consider you my people. 4But if the community ignores what you have done and does not put you to death, 5I myself will turn against you and your whole family and against all who join you in being unfaithful to me and worshiping Molech. I will no longer consider any of you my people.

6"If any of you go for advice to people who consult the spirits of the dead, I will turn against you and will no longer consider you one of my people. 7Keep yourselves holy, because I am the LORD your God. 8Obey my laws, because I am the LORD and I make you holy."

9The LORD gave the following regulations. Any of you that curse your father or mother shall be put to death; you are responsible for your own death.

10If a man commits adultery with the wife of an Israelite, both he and the woman shall be put to death. 11A man who has inter-course with one of his father's wives disgraces his father, and both he and the woman shall be put to death. They are responsible for their own death. 12If a man has intercourse with his daughter-in-law, they shall both be put to death. They have committed incest and are responsible for their own death. 13If a man has sexual relations with another man, they have done a disgusting thing, and both shall be put to death. They are responsible for their own death. 14If a man marries a woman and her mother, all three shall be burned to death because of the disgraceful thing they have done; such a thing must not be permitted among you. 15If a man has sexual relations with an animal, he and the animal shall be put to death. 16If a woman tries to have sexual relations with an animal, she and the animal shall be put to death. They are responsible for their own death.

17If a man marries his sister or half sister, they shall be publicly disgraced and driven out of the community. He has had intercourse with his sister and must suffer the consequences. 18If a man has intercourse with a woman during her monthly period, both of them are to be driven out of the community, because they have broken the regulations about ritual uncleanness.

19If a man has intercourse with his aunt, both of them must suffer the consequences for incest. 20If a man has intercourse with his uncle's wife, he disgraces his uncle, and he and the woman will pay the penalty; neither one will have children. 21If a man takes his brother's wife, they will die childless. He has done a ritually unclean thing and has disgraced his brother.

22The LORD said, "Keep all my laws and commands, so that you will not be rejected by the land of Canaan, into which I am bringing you. 23Do not adopt the customs of the people who live there; I am driving out those pagans so that you can enter the land. They have disgusted me with all their evil practices. 24But I have promised you this rich and fertile land as your possession, and I will give it to you. I am the LORD your

20:9 Ex 21:17; Mt 15:4; Mk 7:10   20:10 Ex 20:14; Lev 18:20; Deut 5:18   20:11 Lev 18:8; Deut 22:30; 27:20   20:12 Lev 18:15   20:13 Lev 18:22   20:14 Lev 18:17; Deut 27:23   20:15, 16 Ex 22:19; Lev 18:23; Deut 27:21   20:17 Lev 18:9; Deut 27:22   20:18 Lev 18:19   20:19, 20 Lev 18:12–14   20:21 Lev 18:16

Leviticus

God, and I have set you apart from the other nations. 25 So then, you must make a clear distinction between animals and birds that are ritually clean and those that are not. Do not eat unclean animals or birds. I have declared them unclean, and eating them would make you unclean. 26 You shall be holy and belong only to me, because I am the LORD and I am holy. I have set you apart from the other nations so that you would belong to me alone.

27 "Any man or woman who consults the spirits of the dead shall be stoned to death; any of you that do this are responsible for your own death."

The Holiness of the Priests

21 1 The LORD commanded Moses to tell the Aaronite priests, "No priest is to make himself ritually unclean by taking part in the funeral ceremonies when a relative dies, 2 unless it is his mother, father, son, daughter, brother, 3 or unmarried sister living in his house. 4 He shall not make himself unclean at the death of those related to him by marriage.*m*

5 "No priest shall shave any part of his head or trim his beard or cut gashes on his body to show that he is in mourning. 6 He must be holy and must not disgrace my name. He offers food offerings to me, and he must be holy. 7 A priest shall not marry a woman who has been a prostitute or a woman who is not a virgin or who is divorced; he is holy. 8 The people must consider the priest holy, because he presents the food offerings to me. I am the LORD; I am holy and I make my people holy. 9 If a priest's daughter becomes a prostitute, she disgraces her father; she shall be burned to death.

10 "The High Priest has had the anointing oil poured on his head and has been consecrated to wear the priestly garments, so he must not leave his hair uncombed or tear his clothes to show that he is in mourning. 11-12 He has been dedicated to me and is not to make himself ritually unclean nor is he to defile my sacred Tent by leaving it and entering a house where there is a dead person,

even if it is his own father or mother. 13 He shall marry a virgin, 14 not a widow or a divorced woman or a woman who has been a prostitute. He shall marry only a virgin from his own clan. 15 Otherwise, his children, who ought to be holy, will be ritually unclean. I am the LORD and I have set him apart as the High Priest."

16 The LORD commanded Moses 17 to tell Aaron, "None of your descendants who has any physical defects may present the food offering to me. This applies for all time to come. 18 No man with any physical defects may make the offering: no one who is blind, lame, disfigured, or deformed; 19 no one with a crippled hand or foot; 20 no one who is a hunchback or a dwarf; no one with any eye or skin disease; and no eunuch. 21 No descendant of Aaron the priest who has any physical defects may present the food offering to me. 22 Such a man may eat the food offered to me, both the holy food offering and the very holy food offering, 23 but because he has a physical defect, he shall not come near the sacred curtain or approach the altar. He must not profane these holy things, because I am the LORD and I make them holy."

24 This, then, is what Moses said to Aaron, the sons of Aaron, and to all the people of Israel.

The Holiness of the Offerings

22 1 The LORD commanded Moses 2 to tell Aaron and his sons, "You must not bring disgrace on my holy name, so treat with respect the sacred offerings that the people of Israel dedicate to me. I am the LORD. 3 If any of your descendants, while he is ritually unclean, comes near the sacred offerings which the people of Israel have dedicated to me, he can never again serve at the altar. This applies for all time to come. I am the LORD.

4 "None of the descendants of Aaron who has a dreaded skin disease or a discharge may eat any of the sacred offerings until he is ritually clean. Any priest is unclean if he touches anything which is unclean through contact with a corpse or if he has an emis-

m 21:4 *Verse 4 in Hebrew is unclear.*
21:5 Lev 19:27, 28; Deut 14:1

sion of semen [5]or if he has touched an unclean animal or person. [6]Any priest who becomes unclean remains unclean until evening, and even then he may not eat any of the sacred offerings until he has taken a bath. [7]After the sun sets he is clean, and then he may eat the sacred offerings, which are his food. [8]He shall not eat the meat of any animal that has died a natural death or has been killed by wild animals; it will make him unclean. I am the LORD.

[9]"All priests shall observe the regulations that I have given. Otherwise, they will become guilty and die, because they have disobeyed the sacred regulations. I am the LORD and I make them holy.

[10]"Only a member of a priestly family may eat any of the sacred offerings; no one else may eat them—not even someone staying with a priest or hired by him. [11]But a priest's slaves, bought with his own money or born in his home, may eat the food the priest receives. [12]A priest's daughter who marries someone who is not a priest may not eat any of the sacred offerings. [13]But a widowed or divorced daughter who has no children and who has returned to live in her father's house as a dependent may eat the food her father receives as a priest. Only a member of a priestly family may eat any of it.

[14]"If any people who are not members of a priestly family eat any of the sacred offerings without intending to, they must repay the priest its full value plus an additional 20 percent. [15]The priests shall not profane the sacred offerings [16]by letting any unauthorized people eat them; this would bring guilt and punishment on such people. I am the LORD and I make the offerings holy."

[17]The LORD commanded Moses [18]to give Aaron and his sons and all the people of Israel the following regulations. When any Israelite or any foreigner living in Israel presents a burnt offering, whether as fulfillment of a vow or as a freewill offering, the animal must not have any defects. [19]To be accepted, it must be a male without any defects. [20]If you offer any animal that has any defects, the LORD will not accept it. [21]When anyone

presents a fellowship offering to the LORD, whether as fulfillment of a vow or as a freewill offering, the animal must be without any defects if it is to be accepted. [22]Do not offer to the LORD any animal that is blind or crippled or mutilated, or that has a running sore or a skin eruption or scabs. Do not offer any such animals on the altar as a food offering. [23]As a freewill offering you may offer an animal that is stunted or not perfectly formed, but it is not acceptable in fulfillment of a vow. [24]Do not offer to the LORD any animal whose testicles have been crushed, cut, bruised, or torn off. This is not permitted in your land.

[25]Do not offer as a food offering any animal obtained from a foreigner. Such animals are considered defective and are not acceptable.

[26-27]When a calf or a lamb or a kid is born, it must not be taken from its mother for seven days, but after that it is acceptable as a food offering. [28]Do not sacrifice a cow and its calf or a sheep and its lamb or a goat and its kid on the same day. [29]When you offer a sacrifice of thanksgiving to the LORD, follow the rules so that you will be accepted; [30]eat it the same day and leave none of it until the next morning.

[31]The LORD said, "Obey my commands; I am the LORD. [32]Do not bring disgrace on my holy name; all the people of Israel must acknowledge me to be holy. I am the LORD and I make you holy; [33]and I brought you out of Egypt to become your God. I am the LORD."

The Religious Festivals

23 [1]The LORD gave Moses [2]the following regulations for the religious festivals, when the people of Israel are to gather for worship. [3]You have six days in which to do your work, but remember that the seventh day, the Sabbath, is a day of rest. On that day do not work, but gather for worship. The Sabbath belongs to the LORD, no matter where you live. [4]Proclaim the following festivals at the appointed times.

Passover and Unleavened Bread
(Numbers 28:16–25)

5 The Passover, celebrated to honor the LORD, begins at sunset on the fourteenth day of the first month. 6 On the fifteenth day the Festival of Unleavened Bread begins, and for seven days you must not eat any bread made with yeast. 7 On the first of these days you shall gather for worship and do none of your daily work. 8 Offer your food offerings to the LORD for seven days. On the seventh day you shall again gather for worship, but you shall do none of your daily work.

9-10 When you come into the land that the LORD is giving you and you harvest your grain, take the first sheaf to the priest. 11 He shall present it as a special offering to the LORD, so that you may be accepted. The priest shall present it the day after the Sabbath. 12 On the day you present the offering of grain, also sacrifice as a burnt offering a one-year-old male lamb that has no defects. 13 With it you shall present four pounds of flour mixed with olive oil as a food offering. The odor of this offering is pleasing to the LORD. You shall also present with it an offering of one quart of wine. 14 Do not eat any of the new grain, whether raw, roasted, or baked into bread, until you have brought this offering to God. This regulation is to be observed by all your descendants for all time to come.

The Harvest Festival
(Numbers 28:26–31)

15 Count seven full weeks from the day after the Sabbath on which you bring your sheaf of grain to present to the LORD. 16 On the fiftieth day, the day after the seventh Sabbath, present to the LORD another new offering of grain. 17 Each family is to bring two loaves of bread and present them to the LORD as a special gift. Each loaf shall be made of four pounds of flour baked with yeast and shall be presented to the LORD as an offering of the first grain to be harvested. 18 And with the bread the community is to present seven one-year-old lambs, one bull,

and two rams, none of which may have any defects. They shall be offered as a burnt offering to the LORD, along with a grain offering and a wine offering. The odor of this offering is pleasing to the LORD. 19 Also offer one male goat as a sin offering and two one-year-old male lambs as a fellowship offering. 20 The priest shall present the bread with the two lambs as a special gift to the LORD for the priests. These offerings are holy. 21 On that day do none of your daily work, but gather for worship. Your descendants are to observe this regulation for all time to come, no matter where they live.

22 When you harvest your fields, do not cut the grain at the edges of the fields, and do not go back to cut the heads of grain that were left; leave them for poor people and foreigners. The LORD is your God.

Leave them for poor people. (23:22)

The New Year Festival
(Numbers 29:1–6)

23-24 On the first day of the seventh month observe a special day of rest, and come together for worship when the trumpets sound. 25 Present a food offering to the LORD and do none of your daily work.

The Day of Atonement
(Numbers 29:7–11)

26-27 The tenth day of the seventh month is the day when the annual ritual is to be performed to take away the sins of the people. On that day do not eat anything at all; come together for worship, and present a food offering to the LORD. 28 Do no work on that day, because it is the day for performing the ritual to take away sin. 29 Any

23:5 Ex 12:1–13; Deut 16:1, 2 **23:6–8** Ex 12:14–20; 23:15; 34:18; Deut 16:3–8 **23:15–21** Ex 23:16; 34:22; Deut 16:9–12 **23:22** Lev 19:9, 10; Deut 24:19–22 **23:26–32** Lev 16:29–34

who eat anything on that day will no longer be considered God's people. ³⁰And if any do any work on that day, the LORD himself will put them to death. ³¹This regulation applies to all your descendants, no matter where they live. ³²From sunset on the ninth day of the month to sunset on the tenth observe this day as a special day of rest, during which nothing may be eaten.

The Festival of Shelters
(Numbers 29:12–40)

³³⁻³⁴The Festival of Shelters begins on the fifteenth day of the seventh month and continues for seven days. ³⁵On the first of these days come together for worship and do none of your daily work. ³⁶Each day for seven days you shall present a food offering. On the eighth day come together again for worship and present a food offering. It is a day for worship, and you shall do no work.

(³⁷These are the religious festivals on which you honor the LORD by gathering together for worship and presenting food offerings, burnt offerings, grain offerings, sacrifices, and wine offerings, as required day by day. ³⁸These festivals are in addition to the regular Sabbaths, and these offerings are in addition to your regular gifts, your offerings as fulfillment of vows, and your freewill offerings that you give to the LORD.)

³⁹When you have harvested your fields, celebrate this festival for seven days, beginning on the fifteenth day of the seventh month. The first day shall be a special day of rest. ⁴⁰On that day take some of the best fruit from your trees, take palm branches and limbs from leafy trees, and begin a religious festival to honor the LORD your God. ⁴¹Celebrate it for seven days. This regulation is to be kept by your descendants for all time to come. ⁴²All the people of Israel shall live in shelters for seven days, ⁴³so that your descendants may know that the LORD made the people of Israel live in simple shelters when he led them out of Egypt. He is the LORD your God.

⁴⁴So in this way Moses gave the people of Israel the regulations for observing the religious festivals to honor the LORD.

Taking Care of the Lamps
(Exodus 27:20, 21)

24 ¹The LORD told Moses ²to give the following orders to the people of Israel: Bring pure olive oil of the finest quality for the lamps in the Tent, so that a light might be kept burning regularly. ³Each evening Aaron shall light them and keep them burning until morning, there in the LORD's presence outside the curtain in front of the Covenant Box, which is in the Most Holy Place. This regulation is to be observed for all time to come. ⁴Aaron shall take care of the lamps on the lampstand of pure gold and must see that they burn regularly in the LORD's presence.

The Bread Offered to God

⁵Take twenty-four pounds of flour and bake twelve loaves of bread. ⁶Put the loaves in two rows, six in each row, on the table covered with pure gold, which is in the LORD's presence. ⁷Put some pure incense on each row, as a token food offering to the LORD to take the place of the bread. ⁸Every Sabbath, for all time to come, the bread must be placed in the presence of the LORD. This is Israel's duty forever. ⁹The bread belongs to Aaron and his descendants, and they shall eat it in a holy place, because this is a very holy part of the food offered to the LORD for the priests.

An Example of Just and Fair Punishment

¹⁰⁻¹¹There was a man whose father was an Egyptian and whose mother was an Israelite named Shelomith, the daughter of Dibri from the tribe of Dan. There in the camp this man quarreled with an Israelite. During the quarrel he cursed the LORD, so they took him to Moses, ¹²put him under guard, and waited for the LORD to tell them what to do with him.

¹³The LORD said to Moses, ¹⁴"Take that man out of the camp. Everyone who heard him curse shall put his hands on the man's head to testify that he is guilty, and then the

whole community shall stone him to death. [15]Then tell the people of Israel that anyone who curses God must suffer the consequences [16]and be put to death. Any Israelite or any foreigner living in Israel who curses the LORD shall be stoned to death by the whole community.

[17]"Any who commit murder shall be put to death, [18]and any who kill an animal belonging to someone else must replace it. The principle is a life for a life.

[19]"If any of you injure another person, whatever you have done shall be done to you. [20]If you break a bone, one of your bones shall be broken; if you put out an eye, one of your eyes shall be put out; if you knock out a tooth, one of your teeth shall be knocked out. Whatever injury you cause another person shall be done to you in return. [21]Whoever kills an animal shall replace it, but whoever kills a human being shall be put to death. [22]This law applies to all of you, to Israelites and to foreigners living among you, because I am the LORD your God."

[23]When Moses had said this to the people of Israel, they took the man outside the camp and stoned him to death. In this way the people of Israel did what the LORD had commanded Moses.

The Seventh Year
(Deuteronomy 15:1–11)

25 [1]The LORD spoke to Moses on Mount Sinai and commanded him [2]to give the following regulations to the people of Israel. When you enter the land that the LORD is giving you, you shall honor the LORD by not cultivating the land every seventh year. [3]You shall plant your fields, prune your vineyards, and gather your crops for six years. [4]But the seventh year is to be a year of complete rest for the land, a year dedicated to the LORD. Do not plant your fields or prune your vineyards. [5]Do not even harvest the grain that grows by itself without being planted, and do not gather the grapes from your unpruned vines; it is a year of complete rest for the land. [6]Although the land has not been cultivated during that

year, it will provide food for you, your slaves, your hired men, the foreigners living with you, [7]your domestic animals, and the wild animals in your fields. Everything that it produces may be eaten.

The Year of Restoration

[8]Count seven times seven years, a total of forty-nine years. [9]Then, on the tenth day of the seventh month, the Day of Atonement, send someone to blow a trumpet throughout the whole land. [10]In this way you shall set the fiftieth year apart and proclaim freedom to all the inhabitants of the land. During this year all property that has been sold shall be restored to the original owner or the descendants, and any who have been sold as slaves shall return to their families. [11]You shall not plant your fields or harvest the grain that grows by itself or gather the grapes in your unpruned vineyards. [12]The whole year shall be sacred for you; you shall eat only what the fields produce of themselves.

[13]In this year all property that has been sold shall be restored to its original owner. [14]So when you sell land to an Israelite or buy land, do not deal unfairly. [15]The price is to be set according to the number of years the land can produce crops before the next Year of Restoration. [16]If there are many years, the price shall be higher, but if there are only a few years, the price shall be lower, because what is being sold is the number of crops the land can produce. [17]Do not cheat an Israelite, but obey the LORD your God.

The Problem of the Seventh Year

[18]Obey all the LORD's laws and commands, so that you may live in safety in the land. [19]The land will produce its crops, and you will have all you want to eat and will live in safety.

[20]But someone may ask what there will be to eat during the seventh year, when no fields are planted and no crops gathered. [21]The LORD will bless the land in the sixth year so that it will produce enough food for two years. [22]When you plant your fields in

---

24:17 Ex 21:12   **24:20** Ex 21:23–25; Deut 19:21; Mt 5:38   **24:22** Num 15:16   **25:1–7** Ex 23:10, 11

the eighth year, you will still be eating what you harvested during the sixth year, and you will have enough to eat until the crops you plant that year are harvested.

Restoration of Property

23 Your land must not be sold on a permanent basis, because you do not own it; it belongs to God, and you are like foreigners who are allowed to make use of it.
24 When land is sold, the right of the original owner to buy it back must be recognized. 25 If any of you Israelites become poor and are forced to sell your land, your closest relative is to buy it back. 26 If you have no relative to buy it back, you may later become prosperous and have enough to buy it back yourself. 27 In that case you must pay to the one who bought it a sum that will make up for the years remaining until the next Year of Restoration, when you would in any event recover your land. 28 But if you do not have enough money to buy the land back, it remains under the control of the one who bought it until the next Year of Restoration. In that year it will be returned to its original owner.
29 If you sell a house in a walled city, you have the right to buy it back during the first full year from the date of sale. 30 But if you do not buy it back within the year, you lose the right of repurchase, and the house becomes the permanent property of the purchasers and their descendants; it will not be returned in the Year of Restoration. 31 But houses in unwalled villages are to be treated like fields; the original owner has the right to buy them back, and they are to be returned in the Year of Restoration. 32 However, Levites have the right to buy back at any time their property in the cities assigned to them. 33 If a house in one of these cities is sold by a Levite and is not bought back, it must be returned in the Year of Restoration,*n* because the houses which the Levites own in their cities are their permanent property among the people of Israel. 34 But the pasture land around the Levite cities shall never be sold; it is their property forever.

Loans to the Poor

35 If any Israelites living near you become poor and cannot support themselves, you must provide for them as you would for a hired worker, so that they can continue to live near you. 36 Do not charge Israelites any interest, but obey God and let them live near you. 37 Do not make them pay interest on the money you lend them, and do not make a profit on the food you sell them. 38 This is the command of the LORD your God, who brought you out of Egypt in order to give you the land of Canaan and to be your God.

You must provide for them. (25:35)

Release of Slaves

39 If any Israelites living near you become so poor that they sell themselves to you as a slave, you shall not make them do the work of a slave. 40 They shall stay with you as hired workers and serve you until the next Year of Restoration. 41 At that time they and their children shall leave you and return to their family and to the property of their ancestors. 42 The people of Israel are the LORD's slaves, and he brought them out of Egypt; they must not be sold into slavery. 43 Do not treat them harshly, but obey your God. 44 If you need slaves, you may buy them from the nations around you. 45 You may also buy the children of the foreigners who are living among you. Such children born in your land may become your property, 46 and you may leave them as an inheritance to your children,

---

n **25:33** *Probable text* If a house . . . Restoration; *Hebrew unclear.*
25:35 Deut 15:7, 8   **25:37** Ex 22:25; Deut 23:19, 20   **25:39–46** Ex 21:2–6; Deut 15:12–18

whom they must serve as long as they live. But you must not treat any Israelites harshly.

47Suppose a foreigner living with you becomes rich, while some Israelites become poor and sell themselves as slaves to that foreigner or to a member of that foreigner's family. 48After they are sold, they still have the right to be bought back. A brother 49or an uncle or a cousin or another close relative may buy them back; or if they themselves earn enough, they may buy their own freedom. 50They must consult the one who bought them, and they must count the years from the time they sold themselves until the next Year of Restoration and must set the price for their release on the basis of the wages paid hired workers. 51-52They must refund a part of the purchase price according to the number of years left, 53as if they had been hired on an annual basis. Their master must not treat them harshly. 54If they are not set free in any of these ways, they and their children must be set free in the next Year of Restoration. 55Israelites cannot be permanent slaves, because the people of Israel are the LORD's slaves. He brought them out of Egypt; he is the LORD their God.

Blessings for Obedience
(Deuteronomy 7:12–24; 28:1–14)

26 1The LORD said, "Do not make idols or set up statues, stone pillars, or carved stones to worship. I am the LORD your God. 2Keep the religious festivals and honor the place where I am worshiped. I am the LORD.

3"If you live according to my laws and obey my commands, 4I will send you rain at the right time, so that the land will produce crops and the trees will bear fruit. 5Your crops will be so plentiful that you will still be harvesting grain when it is time to pick grapes, and you will still be picking grapes when it is time to plant grain. You will have all that you want to eat, and you can live in safety in your land.

6"I will give you peace in your land, and you can sleep without being afraid of anyone. I will get rid of the dangerous animals

in the land, and there will be no more war there. 7You will be victorious over your enemies; 8five of you will be able to defeat a hundred, and a hundred will be able to defeat ten thousand. 9I will bless you and give you many children; I will keep my part of the covenant that I made with you. 10Your harvests will be so plentiful that they will last for a year, and even then you will have to throw away what is left of the old harvest to make room for the new. 11I will live among you in my sacred Tent, and I will never turn away from you. 12I will be with you; I will be your God, and you will be my people. 13I, the LORD your God, brought you out of Egypt so that you would no longer be slaves. I broke the power that held you down and I let you walk with your head held high."

Punishment for Disobedience
(Deuteronomy 28:15–68)

14The LORD said, "If you will not obey my commands, you will be punished. 15If you refuse to obey my laws and commands and break the covenant I have made with you, 16I will punish you. I will bring disaster on you—incurable diseases and fevers that will make you blind and cause your life to waste away. You will plant your crops, but it will do you no good, because your enemies will conquer you and eat what you have grown. 17I will turn against you, so that you will be defeated, and those who hate you will rule over you; you will be so terrified that you will run when no one is chasing you.

18"If even after all of this you still do not obey me, I will increase your punishment seven times. 19I will break your stubborn pride; there will be no rain, and your land will be dry and as hard as iron. 20All your hard work will do you no good, because your land will not produce crops and the trees will not bear fruit.

21"If you still continue to resist me and refuse to obey me, I will again increase your punishment seven times. 22I will send dangerous animals among you, and they will kill your children, destroy your livestock, and leave so few of you that your roads will be deserted.

23 "If after all of this punishment you still do not listen to me, but continue to defy me, **24** then I will turn on you and punish you seven times harder than before. **25** I will bring war on you to punish you for breaking our covenant, and if you gather in your cities for safety, I will send incurable diseases among you, and you will be forced to surrender to your enemies. **26** I will cut off your food supply, so that ten women will need only one oven to bake all the bread they have. They will ration it out, and when you have eaten it all, you will still be hungry.

27 "If after all of this you still continue to defy me and refuse to obey me, **28** then in my anger I will turn on you and again make your punishment seven times worse than before. **29** Your hunger will be so great that you will eat your own children. **30** I will destroy your places of worship on the hills, tear down your incense altars, and throw your dead bodies on your fallen idols. In utter disgust **31** I will turn your cities into ruins, destroy your places of worship, and refuse to accept your sacrifices. **32** I will destroy your land so completely that the enemies who occupy it will be shocked at the destruction. **33** I will bring war on you and scatter you in foreign lands. Your land will be deserted, and your cities left in ruins. **34-35** Then the land will enjoy the years of complete rest that you would not give it; it will lie abandoned and get its rest while you are in exile in the land of your enemies.

36 "I will make those of you who are in exile so terrified that the sound of a leaf blowing in the wind will make you run. You will run as if you were being pursued in battle, and you will fall when there is no enemy near you. **37** You will stumble over one another when no one is chasing you, and you will be unable to fight against any enemy. **38** You will die in exile, swallowed up by the land of your enemies. **39** The few of you who survive in the land of your enemies will waste away because of your own sin and the sin of your ancestors.

40 "But your descendants will confess their sins and the sins of their ancestors, who resisted me and rebelled against me, **41** and caused me to turn against them and send them into exile in the land of their enemies. At last, when your descendants are humbled and they have paid the penalty for their sin and rebellion, **42** I will remember my covenant with Jacob and with Isaac and with Abraham, and I will renew my promise to give my people the land. **43** First, however, the land must be rid of its people, so that it can enjoy its complete rest, and they must pay the full penalty for having rejected my laws and my commands. **44** But even then, when they are still in the land of their enemies, I will not completely abandon them or destroy them. That would put an end to my covenant with them, and I am the LORD their God. **45** I will renew the covenant that I made with their ancestors when I showed all the nations my power by bringing my people out of Egypt, in order that I, the LORD, might be their God."

46 All these are the laws and commands that the LORD gave to Moses on Mount Sinai for the people of Israel.

Laws concerning Gifts to the LORD

27 **1** The LORD gave Moses **2** the following regulations for the people of Israel. When any of you have been given to the LORD in fulfillment of a special vow, you may be set free by the payment of the following sums of money, **3-7** according to the official standard:

—adult male, twenty to sixty years old: 50 pieces of silver
—adult female: 30 pieces of silver
—young male, five to twenty years old: 20 pieces of silver
—young female: 10 pieces of silver
—infant male under five: 5 pieces of silver
—infant female: 3 pieces of silver
—male above sixty years of age: 15 pieces of silver
—female above sixty: 10 pieces of silver

8 If any of you make a vow and are too poor to pay the standard price, you shall bring the person to the priest, and the priest

26:42 **a** Gen 28:13, 14; **b** Gen 26:3, 4; **c** Gen 17:7, 8

will set a lower price, according to your ability to pay.

9 If your vow concerns an animal that is acceptable as an offering to the LORD, then every gift made to the LORD is sacred, 10 and you may not substitute another animal for it. If you do, both animals belong to the LORD. 11 But if your vow concerns a ritually unclean animal, which is not acceptable as an offering to the LORD, you shall take the animal to the priest. 12 The priest shall set a price for it, according to its good or bad qualities, and the price will be final. 13 If you wish to buy it back, you must pay the price plus an additional 20 percent.

14 When any of you dedicate your house to the LORD, the priest shall set the price according to its good or bad points, and the price will be final. 15 If you wish to buy your house back, you must pay the price plus an additional 20 percent.

16 If any of you dedicate part of your land to the LORD, the price shall be set according to the amount of seed it takes to sow it, at the rate of ten pieces of silver per bushel of barley. 17 If you dedicate the land immediately after a Year of Restoration, the full price applies. 18 If you dedicate it any time later, the priest shall estimate the cash value according to the number of years left until the next Year of Restoration, and set a reduced price. 19 If you wish to buy your field back, you must pay the price plus an additional 20 percent. 20 If you sell the field to someone else without first buying it back from the LORD, you lose the right to buy it back. 21 At the next Year of Restoration the field will become the LORD's permanent property; it shall belong to the priests.

22 If you dedicate to the LORD a field that you have bought, 23 the priest shall estimate its value according to the number of years until the next Year of Restoration, and you must pay the price that very day; the money belongs to the LORD. 24 At the Year of Restoration the field shall be returned to the original owner or to the descendants.

25 All prices shall be set according to the official standard.

26 The first-born of an animal already belongs to the LORD, so no one may dedicate it to him as a freewill offering. A calf, a lamb, or a kid belongs to the LORD, 27 but the first-born of an unclean animal may be bought back at the standard price plus an additional 20 percent. If it is not bought back, it may be sold to someone else at the standard price.

28 None of you may sell or buy back what you have unconditionally dedicated° to the LORD, whether it is a human being, an animal, or land. It belongs permanently to the LORD. 29 Not even human beings who have been unconditionally dedicated may be bought back; they must be put to death.

30 One tenth of all the produce of the land, whether grain or fruit, belongs to the LORD. 31 If you wish to buy any of it back, you must pay the standard price plus an additional 20 percent. 32 One of every ten domestic animals belongs to the LORD. When the animals are counted, every tenth one belongs to the LORD. 33 You may not arrange the animals so that the poor animals are chosen, and you may not make any substitutions. If you do substitute one animal for another, then both animals will belong to the LORD and may not be bought back.

34 These are the commands that the LORD gave Moses on Mount Sinai for the people of Israel.

° 27:28 UNCONDITIONALLY DEDICATED: *Anything dedicated in this way belonged completely to the LORD and could not be used; it had to be destroyed.*
27:28 Num 18:14   **27:30–33** Num 18:21; Deut 14:22–29

Are we there yet? I'm hungry! He's bugging me! Why do you get the front seat? Traveling together can have its joys, and its struggles. The Book of Numbers tells the story of the Israelites' journey from Sinai to Moab as they prepare to enter the Promised Land.

As with most trips, the Israelites' journey began by making sure everyone was counted and knew the rules for the journey. The trip had its memorable moments—a fiery cloud, spies, and even a talking donkey. And then there were those who complained about everything. Their rebellion stood in contrast to God's faithfulness, patience, and love. As time passed, a new generation emerged that was more faithful and obedient to God. They were the ones to finally settle the Promised Land.

Chap. 21

Headlines

- Moses Takes Census and Divides Camps (1:1—2:34)
- Fiery Cloud Hovers Over Tent (9:15–23)
- Road Trip: Israelites Head to Moab (10:33–36)
- Moses Sends Spies to Scout Canaan (13:1–25)
- Walking Stick Blossoms Overnight! (17:1–12)
- Donkey Talks, Owner Confesses! (22:22–33)
- Joshua Chosen as Moses' Successor (27:15–23)

FACTOIDS

Who wrote this book? Priestly scribes most likely wrote this book hundreds of years after the events took place.

When was it written? The final version of the book was probably composed sometime during the Babylonian exile (587–538 BC).

Why was it written? This book records the story of the Israelites where Exodus leaves off. It makes clear for God's people the importance of being holy, faithful, and grateful for God's blessings.

How does it fit into the Bible? It is the fourth book in the Pentateuch (the first five books of the Bible) and tells the early experiences of God's people.

Important themes
- Faithfulness and gratefulness to God is rewarded.
- Don't lose faith in God when things get hard.
- God is always patient, present, and caring despite the faults and failings of his people.

NUMBERS

The First Census of Israel

1 ¹On the first day of the second month in the second year after the people of Israel left Egypt, the LORD spoke to Moses there in the Tent of his presence in the Sinai Desert. He said, ²"You and Aaron are to take a census of the people of Israel by clans and families. List the names of all the men ³twenty years old or older who are fit for military service. ⁴Ask one clan chief from each tribe to help you." ⁵⁻¹⁶These are the men, leaders within their tribes, who were chosen from the community for this work:

Tribe	Clan chief
Reuben	Elizur son of Shedeur
Simeon	Shelumiel son of Zurishaddai
Judah	Nahshon son of Amminadab
Issachar	Nethanel son of Zuar
Zebulun	Eliab son of Helon
Ephraim	Elishama son of Ammihud
Manasseh	Gamaliel son of Pedahzur
Benjamin	Abidan son of Gideoni
Dan	Ahiezer son of Ammishaddai
Asher	Pagiel son of Ochran
Gad	Eliasaph son of Deuel
Naphtali	Ahira son of Enan

¹⁷With the help of these twelve men Moses and Aaron ¹⁸called together the whole community on the first day of the second month and registered all the people by clans and families. The names of all the men twenty years old or older were recorded and counted, ¹⁹as the LORD had commanded. In the Sinai Desert, Moses registered the people. ²⁰⁻⁴⁶The men twenty years old or older who were fit for military service were registered by name according to clan and family, beginning with the tribe of Reuben, Jacob's oldest son. The totals were as follows:

Tribe	Number
Reuben	46,500
Simeon	59,300
Gad	45,650
Judah	74,600
Issachar	54,400
Zebulun	57,400
Ephraim	40,500
Manasseh	32,200
Benjamin	35,400
Dan	62,700
Asher	41,500
Naphtali	53,400
Total:	603,550

⁴⁷The Levites were not registered with the other tribes, ⁴⁸because the LORD had said to Moses, ⁴⁹"When you take a census of the men fit for military service, do not include the tribe of Levi. ⁵⁰Instead, put the Levites in charge of the Tent of my presence and all its equipment. They shall carry it and its equipment, serve in it, and set up their camp around it. ⁵¹Whenever you move your camp, the Levites shall take the Tent down and set it up again at each new campsite. Anyone else who comes near the Tent shall be put to death. ⁵²The rest of the Israelites shall set up camp, company by company, each man with his own group and under his own banner. ⁵³But the Levites shall camp around the Tent to guard it, so that no one may come near and cause my anger to strike the community of Israel." ⁵⁴So the people of Israel did everything that the LORD had commanded Moses.

The Arrangement of the Tribes in Camp

2 ¹The LORD gave Moses and Aaron the following instructions. ²When the Israelites set up camp, each man will camp under the banner of his division and the flag of his own clan. The camp is to be set up all around the Tent.

³⁻⁹On the east side, those under the banner of the division of Judah shall camp in their groups, under their leaders, as follows:

Tribe	Leader	Number
Judah	Nahshon son of Amminadab	74,600
Issachar	Nethanel son of Zuar	54,400
Zebulun	Eliab son of Helon	57,400
	Total:	186,400

The division of Judah shall march first.

10-16 On the south, those under the banner of the division of Reuben shall camp in their groups, under their leaders, as follows:

Tribe	Leader	Number
Reuben	Elizur son of Shedeur	46,500
Simeon	Shelumiel son of Zurishaddai	59,300
Gad	Eliasaph son of Deuel	45,650
	Total:	151,450

The division of Reuben shall march second.

17 Then, between the first two divisions and the last two the Levites are to march carrying the Tent. Each division shall march in the same order as they camp, each in position under its banner.

18-24 On the west, those under the banner of the division of Ephraim shall camp in their groups, under their leaders, as follows:

Tribe	Leader	Number
Ephraim	Elishama son of Ammihud	40,500
Manasseh	Gamaliel son of Pedahzur	32,200
Benjamin	Abidan son of Gideoni	35,400
	Total:	108,100

The division of Ephraim shall march third.

25-31 On the north, those under the banner of the division of Dan shall camp in their groups, under their leaders, as follows:

Tribe	Leader	Number
Dan	Ahiezer son of Ammishaddai	62,700

Asher	Pagiel son of Ochran	41,500
Naphtali	Ahira son of Enan	53,400
	Total:	157,600

The division of Dan shall march last.

32 The total number of the people of Israel enrolled in the divisions, group by group, was 603,550. **33** As the LORD had commanded Moses, the Levites were not registered with the rest of the Israelites.

34 So the people of Israel did everything the LORD had commanded Moses. They camped, each under his own banner, and they marched, each with his own clan.

Aaron's Sons

3 **1** This is the family of Aaron and Moses at the time the LORD spoke to Moses on Mount Sinai. **2** Aaron had four sons: Nadab, the oldest, Abihu, Eleazar, and Ithamar. **3** They were anointed and ordained as priests, **4** but Nadab and Abihu were killed when they offered unholy fire to the LORD in the Sinai Desert. They had no children, so Eleazar and Ithamar served as priests during Aaron's lifetime.

The Levites Are Appointed to Serve the Priests

5 The LORD said to Moses, **6** "Bring forward the tribe of Levi and appoint them as servants of Aaron the priest. **7** They shall do the work required for the Tent of my presence and perform duties for the priests and for the whole community. **8** They shall take charge of all the equipment of the Tent and perform the duties for the rest of the Israelites. **9** The only responsibility the Levites have is to serve Aaron and his sons. **10** You shall appoint Aaron and his sons to carry out the duties of the priesthood; anyone else who tries to do so shall be put to death."

11 The LORD said to Moses, **12-13** "The Levites are now to be mine. When I killed all the first-born of the Egyptians, I consecrated as my own the oldest son of each Israelite family and the first-born of every animal. Now, instead of having the first-born sons of

Numbers

Israel as my own, I have the Levites; they will belong to me. I am the LORD."

The Census of the Levites

14In the Sinai Desert the LORD commanded Moses 15to register the Levites by clans and families, enrolling every male a month old or older, 16and Moses did so. 17-20Levi had three sons: Gershon, Kohath, and Merari, who were the ancestors of the clans that bear their names. Gershon had two sons: Libni and Shimei; Kohath had four sons: Amram, Izhar, Hebron, and Uzziel; and Merari had two sons: Mahli and Mushi. They were the ancestors of the families that bear their names.

21The clan of Gershon was composed of the families of Libni and Shimei. 22The total number of males one month old or older that were enrolled was 7,500. 23This clan was to camp on the west behind the Tent, 24with Eliasaph son of Lael as chief of the clan. 25They were responsible for the Tent, its inner cover, its outer cover, the curtain for the entrance, 26the curtains for the court which is around the Tent and the altar, and the curtain for the entrance of the court. They were responsible for all the service connected with these items.

27The clan of Kohath was composed of the families of Amram, Izhar, Hebron, and Uzziel. 28The total number of males one month old or older that were enrolled was 8,600. 29This clan was to camp on the south side of the Tent, 30with Elizaphan son of Uzziel as chief of the clan. 31They were responsible for the Covenant Box, the table, the lampstand, the altars, the utensils the priests use in the Holy Place, and the curtain at the entrance to the Most Holy Place. They were responsible for all the service connected with these items.

32The chief of the Levites was Eleazar son of Aaron the priest. He was in charge of those who carried out the duties in the Holy Place.

33The clan of Merari was composed of the families of Mahli and Mushi. 34The total number of males one month old or older that were enrolled was 6,200. 35This clan was to camp on the north side of the Tent,

with Zuriel son of Abihail as chief of the clan. 36They were assigned responsibility for the frames for the Tent, its bars, posts, bases, and all its fittings. They were responsible for all the service connected with these items. 37They were also responsible for the posts, bases, pegs, and ropes for the outer court.

38Moses and Aaron and his sons were to camp in front of the Tent on the east. They were responsible for carrying out the services performed in the Holy Place for the people of Israel. Anyone else who tried to do so was to be put to death. 39The total number of all the Levite males one month old or older that Moses enrolled by clans at the command of the LORD, was 22,000.

The Levites Take the Place of the First-Born Sons

40-41The LORD said to Moses, "All of Israel's first-born sons belong to me. So register by name every first-born male Israelite, one month old or older. But in place of them I claim all the Levites as mine! I am the LORD! I also claim the livestock of the Levites in place of all the first-born of the livestock." 42Moses obeyed, and registered all the first-born males 43one month old or older; the total was 22,273.

44The LORD said to Moses, 45"Now dedicate the Levites as mine in place of all the first-born Israelite sons, and dedicate the livestock of the Levites in place of the first-born of the Israelites' livestock. 46Since the first-born Israelite sons outnumber the Levites by 273, you must buy back the extra sons. 47For each one pay five pieces of silver, according to the official standard, 48and give this money to Aaron and his sons." 49Moses obeyed and took 50the 1,365 pieces of silver 51and gave them to Aaron and his sons.

The Duties of the Levite Clan of Kohath

4 1The LORD told Moses 2to take a census of the Levite clan of Kohath by sub-clans and families, 3and to register all the men between the ages of thirty and fifty who were qualified to work in the Tent of

the LORD's presence. ⁴Their service involves the most holy things.

⁵The LORD gave Moses the following instructions. When it is time to break camp, Aaron and his sons shall enter the Tent, take down the curtain in front of the Covenant Box, and cover the Box with it. ⁶They shall put a fine leather cover over it, spread a cloth of solid blue on top, and then insert the carrying poles.

⁷They shall spread a blue cloth over the table for the bread offered to the LORD and put on it the dishes, the incense bowls, the offering bowls, and the jars for the wine offering. There shall always be bread on the table. ⁸They shall spread a red cloth over all of this, put a fine leather cover over it, and then insert the carrying poles.

⁹They shall take a blue cloth and cover the lampstand, with its lamps, tongs, trays, and all the olive oil containers. ¹⁰They shall wrap it and all its equipment in a fine leather cover and place it on a carrying frame.

¹¹Next they shall spread a blue cloth over the gold altar, put a fine leather cover over it, and then insert the carrying poles. ¹²They shall take all the utensils used in the Holy Place, wrap them in a blue cloth, put a fine leather cover over them, and place them on a carrying frame. ¹³They shall remove the greasy ashes from the altar and spread a purple cloth over it. ¹⁴They shall put on it all the equipment used in the service at the altar: fire pans, hooks, shovels, and basins. Then they shall put a fine leather cover over it and insert the carrying poles. ¹⁵When it is time to break camp, the clan of Kohath shall

come to carry the sacred objects only after Aaron and his sons have finished covering them and all their equipment. The Kohath clan must not touch the sacred objects, or they will die.

These are the responsibilities of the Kohath clan whenever the Tent is moved.

¹⁶Eleazar son of Aaron the priest shall be responsible for the whole Tent and for the oil for the lamps, the incense, the grain offerings, the anointing oil, and everything else in the Tent that has been consecrated to the LORD.

¹⁷The LORD said to Moses and Aaron, ¹⁸"Do not let the clan of Kohath ¹⁹be killed by coming near these most sacred objects. To prevent this from happening, Aaron and his sons shall go in and assign each man his task and tell him what to carry. ²⁰But if the Kohathites enter the Tent and see the priests preparing the sacred objects for moving,ᵃ they will die."

The Duties of the Levite Clan of Gershon

²¹The LORD told Moses ²²to take a census of the Levite clan of Gershon by subclans and families, ²³and to register all the men between the ages of thirty and fifty who were qualified to work in the Tent of the LORD's presence. ²⁴They shall be responsible for carrying the following objects: ²⁵the Tent, its inner cover, its outer cover, the fine leather cover on top of it, the curtain for the entrance, ²⁶the curtains and ropes for the court that is around the Tent and the altar,

---

ᵃ **4:20** see . . . moving; *or* see the sacred objects even for a moment.

Qualified to work in the Tent (4:23)

the curtains for the entrance of the court, and all the fittings used in setting up these objects. They shall perform all the tasks required for these things. 27 Moses and Aaron shall see to it that the Gershonites perform all the duties and carry everything that Aaron and his sons assign to them. 28 These are the responsibilities of the Gershon clan in the Tent; they shall carry them out under the direction of Ithamar son of Aaron the priest.

The Duties of the Levite Clan of Merari

29 The LORD told Moses to take a census of the Levite clan of Merari by subclans and families, 30 and to register all the men between the ages of thirty and fifty who were qualified to work in the Tent of the LORD's presence. 31 They shall be responsible for carrying the frames, bars, posts, and bases of the Tent, 32 and the posts, bases, pegs, and ropes of the court around the Tent, with all the fittings used in setting them up. Each man will be responsible for carrying specific items. 33 These are the responsibilities of the Merari clan in their service in the Tent; they shall carry them out under the direction of Ithamar son of Aaron the priest.

The Census of the Levites

34-48 Following the LORD's command, Moses, Aaron, and the leaders of the community took a census of the three Levite clans, Kohath, Gershon, and Merari. They did this by subclans and families and registered all the men between the ages of thirty and fifty who were qualified to work in the Tent of the LORD's presence, as follows:

Clan	Number
Kohath	2,750
Gershon	2,630
Merari	3,200
	Total: 8,580

49 Each man was registered as the LORD had commanded Moses; and at the command of the LORD given through Moses, each man was assigned responsibility for his task of serving or carrying.

Unclean People

5 ¹The LORD said to Moses, ² "Command the people of Israel to expel from the camp everyone with a dreaded skin disease or a bodily discharge and everyone who is unclean by contact with a corpse. ³ Send all these ritually unclean people out, so that they will not defile the camp, where I live among my people." ⁴ The Israelites obeyed and expelled them all from the camp.

Repayment for Wrongs Done

⁵ The LORD gave Moses ⁶ the following instructions for the people of Israel. When any of you are unfaithful to the LORD and commit a wrong against someone, ⁷ you must confess your sin and make full repayment, plus an additional 20 percent, to the person you have wronged. ⁸ But if that person has died and has no near relative to whom payment can be made, it shall be given to the LORD for the priest. This payment is in addition to the ram used to perform the ritual of purification for the guilty person. ⁹ Also every special contribution which the Israelites offer to the LORD belongs to the priest to whom they present it. ¹⁰ Each priest shall keep the offerings presented to him.

Cases of Wives with Suspicious Husbands

¹¹ The LORD commanded Moses ¹²⁻¹⁴ to give the Israelites the following instructions. It may happen that a man becomes suspicious that his wife is unfaithful to him and has defiled herself by having intercourse with another man. But the husband may not be certain, for his wife may have kept it secret—there was no witness, and she was not caught in the act. Or it may happen that a husband becomes suspicious of his wife, even though she has not been unfaithful. ¹⁵ In either case the man shall take his wife to the priest. He shall also take the required offering of two pounds of barley flour, but he shall not pour any olive oil on it or put any incense on it, because it is an offering

from a suspicious husband, made to bring the truth to light.

¹⁶The priest shall bring the woman forward and have her stand in front of the altar. ¹⁷He shall pour some holy water into a clay bowl and take some of the earth that is on the floor of the Tent of the LORD's presence and put it in the water to make it bitter. ¹⁸Then he shall loosen the woman's hair and put the offering of flour in her hands. In his hands the priest shall hold the bowl containing the bitter water that brings a curse. ¹⁹Then the priest shall make the woman agree to this oath spoken by the priest: "If you have not committed adultery, you will not be harmed by the curse that this water brings. ²⁰But if you have committed adultery, ²¹may the LORD make your name a curse among your people. May he cause your genital organs to shrink and your stomach to swell up. ²²May this water enter your stomach and cause it to swell up and your genital organs to shrink."

The woman shall respond, "I agree; may the LORD do so."

²³Then the priest shall write this curse down and wash the writing off into the bowl of bitter water. ²⁴Before he makes the woman drink the water, which may then cause her bitter pain, ²⁵the priest shall take the offering of flour out of the woman's hands, hold it out in dedication to the LORD, and present it on the altar. ²⁶Then he shall take a handful of it as a token offering and burn it on the altar. Finally, he shall make the woman drink the water. ²⁷If she has committed adultery, the water will cause bitter pain; her stomach will swell up and her genital organs will shrink. Her name will become a curse among her people. ²⁸But if she is innocent, she will not be harmed and will be able to bear children.

²⁹⁻³⁰This is the law in cases where a man is jealous and becomes suspicious that his wife has committed adultery. The woman shall be made to stand in front of the altar, and the priest shall perform this ritual. ³¹The husband shall be free of guilt, but the woman, if guilty, must suffer the consequences.

Rules for Nazirites

6 ¹The LORD commanded Moses ²to give the following instructions to the people of Israel. Any of you, male or female, who make a special vow to become a nazirite and dedicate yourself to the LORD ³shall abstain from wine and beer. You shall not drink any kind of drink made from grapes or eat any grapes or raisins. ⁴As long as you are a nazirite, you shall not eat anything that comes from a grapevine, not even the seeds or skins of grapes.

⁵As long as you are under the nazirite vow, you must not cut your hair or shave. You are bound by the vow for the full time that you are dedicated to the LORD, and you shall let your hair grow. ⁶⁻⁷Your hair is the sign of your dedication to God, and so you must not defile yourself by going near a corpse, not even that of your father, mother, brother, or sister. ⁸As long as you are a nazirite, you are consecrated to the LORD.

⁹If your consecrated hair is defiled because you are right beside someone who suddenly dies, you must wait seven days and then shave your head; and so you become ritually clean. ¹⁰On the eighth day you shall bring two doves or two pigeons to the priest at the entrance of the Tent of the LORD's presence. ¹¹The priest shall offer one as a sin offering and the other as a burnt offering, to perform the ritual of purification for you because of your contact with a corpse. On the same day you shall reconsecrate your hair ¹²and rededicate to the LORD your time as a nazirite. The previous period of time doesn't count, because your consecrated hair was defiled. As a repayment offering you shall bring a one-year-old lamb.

¹³When you complete your nazirite vow, you shall perform this ritual. You shall go to the entrance of the Tent ¹⁴and present to the LORD three animals without any defects: a one-year-old male lamb for a burnt offering, a one-year-old ewe lamb for a sin offering, and a ram for a fellowship offering. ¹⁵You shall also offer a basket of bread made without yeast: thick loaves made of flour mixed with olive oil and thin cakes brushed with

6:3 Lk 1:15   **6:13–21** Acts 21:23, 24

olive oil, and in addition the required offerings of grain and wine.

¹⁶The priest shall present all these to the LORD and offer the sin offering and the burnt offering. ¹⁷He shall sacrifice the ram to the LORD as a fellowship offering, and offer it with the basket of bread; he shall also present the offerings of grain and wine. ¹⁸At the entrance of the Tent you nazirites shall shave off your hair and put it on the fire on which the fellowship offering is being burned.

¹⁹Then, when the shoulder of the ram is boiled, the priest shall take it and put it, together with one thick loaf of bread and one thin cake from the basket, into the hands of the nazirite. ²⁰Next, the priest shall present them as a special gift to the LORD; they are a sacred offering for the priest, in addition to the breast and the leg of the ram which by law belong to the priest. After that, the nazirite may drink wine.

²¹These are the regulations for you nazirites; but if you promise an offering beyond what your vow requires you to give, you must fulfill exactly the promise you made.

The Priestly Blessing

²²The LORD commanded Moses ²³to tell Aaron and his sons to use the following words in blessing the people of Israel:
²⁴May the LORD bless you and take care of you;
²⁵May the LORD be kind and gracious to you;
²⁶May the LORD look on you with favor and give you peace.

²⁷And the LORD said, "If they pronounce my name as a blessing upon the people of Israel, I will bless them."

The Offerings of the Leaders

7 ¹On the day Moses finished setting up the Tent of the LORD's presence, he anointed and dedicated the Tent and all its equipment, and the altar and all its equipment. ²Then the clan chiefs who were leaders in the tribes of Israel, the same men who were in charge of the census, ³brought their offerings to the LORD: six wagons and twelve oxen, a wagon for every two leaders and an ox for each leader. After they had presented them, ⁴the LORD said to Moses, ⁵"Accept these gifts for use in the work to be done for the Tent; give them to the Levites according to the work they have to do." ⁶So Moses gave the wagons and the oxen to the Levites. ⁷He gave two wagons and four oxen to the Gershonites, ⁸and four wagons and eight oxen to the Merarites. All their work was to be done under the direction of Ithamar son of Aaron. ⁹But Moses gave no wagons or oxen to the Kohathites, because the sacred objects they took care of had to be carried on their shoulders.

¹⁰The leaders also brought offerings to celebrate the dedication of the altar. When they were ready to present their gifts at the altar, ¹¹the LORD said to Moses, "Tell them that each day for a period of twelve days one of the leaders is to present his gifts for the dedication of the altar."

¹²⁻⁸³They presented their offerings in the following order:

Day	Tribe	Leader
1st	Judah	Nahshon son of Amminadab
2nd	Issachar	Nethanel son of Zuar
3rd	Zebulun	Eliab son of Helon
4th	Reuben	Elizur son of Shedeur
5th	Simeon	Shelumiel son of Zurishaddai
6th	Gad	Eliasaph son of Deuel
7th	Ephraim	Elishama son of Ammihud
8th	Manasseh	Gamaliel son of Pedahzur
9th	Benjamin	Abidan son of Gideoni
10th	Dan	Ahiezer son of Ammishaddai
11th	Asher	Pagiel son of Ochran
12th	Naphtali	Ahira son of Enan

The offerings each one brought were identical: one silver bowl weighing 50 ounces and one silver basin weighing 30 ounces, by the official standard, both of them full of flour mixed with oil for the grain offering; one gold dish weighing 4 ounces, full of incense; one young bull, one ram, and a one-year-old lamb, for the burnt offering; one goat for the sin offering; and two bulls, five rams, five goats, and five one-year-old lambs, for the fellowship offering.

84-88 The totals of the offerings brought by the twelve leaders for the dedication of the altar were as follows:

- –twelve silver bowls and twelve silver basins weighing a total of 60 pounds
- –twelve gold dishes weighing a total of 48 ounces, filled with incense
- –twelve bulls, twelve rams, and twelve one-year-old lambs, plus the grain offerings that go with them, for the burnt offerings
- –twelve goats for the sin offerings
- –twenty-four bulls, sixty rams, sixty goats, sixty one-year-old lambs, for the fellowship offerings

89 When Moses went into the Tent to talk with the LORD, he heard the LORD speaking to him from above the lid on the Covenant Box, between the two winged creatures.*b*

Placing the Lamps

8 **1** The LORD said to Moses, **2** "Tell Aaron that when he puts the seven lamps on the lampstand, he should place them so that the light shines toward the front." **3** Aaron obeyed and placed the lamps facing the front of the lampstand. **4** From top to bottom the lampstand was made of hammered gold, according to the pattern that the LORD had shown Moses.

The Purification and Dedication of the Levites

5 The LORD said to Moses, **6** "Separate the Levites from the rest of the people of Israel and purify them **7** in the following way: sprinkle them with the water of purification and have them shave their whole bodies and have them wash their clothes. Then they will be ritually clean. **8** Then they are to take a young bull and the required grain offering of flour mixed with olive oil; and you are to take another bull for the sin offering. **9** Then

assemble the whole community of Israel and have the Levites stand in front of the Tent of my presence. **10** The people of Israel are to place their hands on the heads of the Levites, **11** and then Aaron shall dedicate the Levites to me as a special gift from the Israelites, so that they may do my work. **12** The Levites shall then put their hands on the heads of the two bulls; one is to be offered as a sin offering and the other as a burnt offering, in order to perform the ritual of purification for the Levites.

13 "Dedicate the Levites as a special gift to me, and put Aaron and his sons in charge of them. **14** Separate the Levites in this way from the rest of the Israelites, so that they will belong to me. **15** After you have purified and dedicated the Levites, they will be qualified to work in the Tent. **16** I have claimed them in the place of all the first-born sons of the Israelites, and they belong to me alone. **17** When I killed all the first-born in Egypt, I consecrated as my own the oldest son of each Israelite family and the first-born of every animal. **18** I am now taking the Levites instead of all the first-born of the Israelites, **19** and I assign the Levites to Aaron and his sons, as a gift from the Israelites, to work in the Tent for the people of Israel and to protect the Israelites from the disaster that would strike them if they came too near the Holy Place."

20 So Moses, Aaron, and all the people of Israel dedicated the Levites, as the LORD commanded Moses. **21** The Levites purified themselves and washed their clothes, and Aaron dedicated them as a special gift to the LORD. He also performed the ritual of purification for them. **22** The people did everything the LORD had commanded Moses concerning the Levites. And so the Levites were qualified to work in the Tent under Aaron and his sons.

23 The LORD said to Moses, **24** "From the age of twenty-five each Levite shall perform his duties in the Tent of my presence, **25** and at the age of fifty he shall retire. **26** After that, he may help his fellow Levites in performing their duties in the Tent, but he must not perform any service by himself. This is how you are to regulate the duties of the Levites."

b **7:89** WINGED CREATURES: *See Word List.*
8:1–4 Ex 25:31–40; 37:17–24   **8:17** Ex 13:2

The Second Passover

9 ¹ The LORD spoke to Moses in the Sinai Desert in the first month of the second year after the people of Israel had left Egypt. He said, ²-³ "On the fourteenth day of this month, beginning at sunset, the people of Israel are to observe the Passover according to all the rules and regulations for it." ⁴So Moses told the people to observe the Passover, ⁵and on the evening of the fourteenth day of the first month they did so in the Sinai Desert. The people did everything just as the LORD had commanded Moses.

⁶But there were some people who were ritually unclean because they had touched a corpse, and they were not able to keep the Passover on that day. They went to Moses and Aaron ⁷and said, "We are unclean because we have touched a corpse, but why should we be excluded from presenting the LORD's offering with the rest of the Israelites?"

⁸Moses answered, "Wait until I receive instructions from the LORD."

⁹The LORD told Moses ¹⁰to say to the people of Israel, "When any of you or your descendants are unclean from touching a corpse or are far away on a journey, but still want to keep the Passover, ¹¹you are permitted to observe it one month later instead, on the evening of the fourteenth day of the second month. Celebrate it with unleavened bread and bitter herbs. ¹²Do not leave any of the food until the following morning and do not break any of the animal's bones. Observe the Passover according to all the regulations. ¹³But if any of you are ritually clean and not away on a journey and do not observe the Passover, you shall no longer be considered my people, because you did not present the offering to me at the appointed time. You must suffer the consequences of your sin.

¹⁴ "If foreigners living among you want to keep the Passover, they must observe it according to all the rules and regulations. The same law applies to everyone, whether native or foreigner."

The Fiery Cloud
(Exodus 40:34–38)

¹⁵-¹⁶On the day the Tent of the LORD's presence was set up, a cloud came and covered it. At night the cloud looked like fire. ¹⁷Whenever the cloud lifted, the people of Israel broke camp, and they set up camp again in the place where the cloud came down. ¹⁸The people broke camp at the command of the LORD, and at his command they set up camp. As long as the cloud stayed over the Tent, they stayed in the same camp. ¹⁹When the cloud stayed over the Tent for a long time, they obeyed the LORD and did not move on. ²⁰Sometimes the cloud remained over the Tent for only a few days; in any case, they remained in camp or moved, according to the command of the LORD. ²¹Sometimes the cloud remained only from evening until morning, and they moved on as soon as the cloud lifted. Whenever the cloud lifted, they moved on. ²²Whether it was two days, a month, a year, or longer, as long as the cloud remained over the Tent, they did not move on; but when it lifted, they moved. ²³They set up camp and broke camp in obedience to the commands which the LORD gave through Moses.

The Silver Trumpets

10 ¹The LORD said to Moses, ² "Make two trumpets of hammered silver to use for calling the people together and for breaking camp. ³When long blasts are sounded on both trumpets, the whole community is to gather around you at the entrance to the Tent of my presence. ⁴But when only one trumpet is sounded, then only the leaders of the clans are to gather around you. ⁵When short blasts are sounded, the tribes camped on the east will move out. ⁶When short blasts are sounded a second time, the tribes on the south will move out. So short blasts are to be sounded to break camp, ⁷but in order to call the community together, long blasts are to be sounded. ⁸The trumpets are to be blown by Aaron's sons, the priests.

"The following rule is to be observed for

all time to come. 9 When you are at war in your land, defending yourselves against an enemy who has attacked you, sound the signal for battle on these trumpets. I, the LORD your God, will help you and save you from your enemies. 10 Also on joyful occasions—at your New Moon Festivals and your other religious festivals—you are to blow the trumpets when you present your burnt offerings and your fellowship offerings. Then I will help you. I am the LORD your God."

The Israelites Break Camp

11 On the twentieth day of the second month in the second year after the people left Egypt, the cloud over the Tent of the LORD's presence lifted, 12 and the Israelites started on their journey out of the Sinai Desert. The cloud came to rest in the wilderness of Paran.

13 They began to march at the command of the LORD through Moses, 14 and each time they moved, they were in the same order. Those under the banner of the division led by the tribe of Judah started out first, company by company, with Nahshon son of Amminadab in command. 15 Nethanel son of Zuar was in command of the tribe of Issachar, 16 and Eliab son of Helon was in command of the tribe of Zebulun.

17 Then the Tent would be taken down, and the clans of Gershon and Merari, who carried it, would start out.

When only one trumpet is sounded (10:4)

18 Next, those under the banner of the division led by the tribe of Reuben would start out, company by company, with Elizur son of Shedeur in command. 19 Shelumiel son of Zurishaddai was in command of the tribe of Simeon, 20 and Eliasaph son of Deuel was in command of the tribe of Gad.

21 Then the Levite clan of Kohath would start out, carrying the sacred objects. By the time they arrived at the next camp, the Tent had been set up again.

22 Next, those under the banner of the division led by the tribe of Ephraim would start out, company by company, with Elishama son of Ammihud in command. 23 Gamaliel son of Pedahzur was in command of the tribe of Manasseh, 24 and Abidan son of Gideoni was in command of the tribe of Benjamin.

25 Finally, those under the banner of the division led by the tribe of Dan, serving as the rear guard of all the divisions, would start out, company by company, with Ahiezer son of Ammishaddai in command. 26 Pagiel son of Ochran was in command of the tribe of Asher, 27 and Ahira son of Enan was in command of the tribe of Naphtali. 28 This, then, was the order of march, company by company, whenever the Israelites broke camp and set out.

29 Moses said to his brother-in-law Hobab son of Jethro the Midianite, "We are about to start out for the place which the LORD said he would give us. He has promised to make Israel prosperous, so come with us, and we will share our prosperity with you."

30 Hobab answered, "No, I am going back to my native land."

31 "Please don't leave us," Moses said. "You know where we can camp in the wilderness, and you can be our guide. 32 If you come with us, we will share with you all the blessings that the LORD gives us."

The People Set Out

33 When the people left Sinai, the holy mountain, they traveled three days. The LORD's Covenant Box always went ahead of them to find a place for them to camp. 34 As they moved on from each camp, the cloud of the LORD was over them by day.

35 Whenever the Covenant Box started out, Moses would say, "Arise, LORD; scatter your enemies and put to flight those who hate you!" 36 And whenever it stopped, he would say, "Return, LORD, to the thousands of families of Israel."c

The Place Named Taberah

11 1 The people began to complain to the LORD about their troubles. When the LORD heard them, he became angry and sent fire on the people. It burned among them and destroyed one end of the camp. 2 The people cried out to Moses for help; he prayed to the LORD, and the fire died down. 3 So the place was named Taberah,d because there the fire of the LORD burned among them.

Moses Chooses Seventy Leaders

4 There were foreigners traveling with the Israelites. They had a strong craving for meat, and even the Israelites themselves began to complain: "If only we could have some meat! 5 In Egypt we used to eat all the fish we wanted, and it cost us nothing. Remember the cucumbers, the watermelons, the leeks, the onions, and the garlic we had? 6 But now our strength is gone. There is nothing at all to eat—nothing but this manna day after day!"

(7 Manna was like small seeds, whitish yellow in color. 8-9 It fell on the camp at night along with the dew. The next morning the people would go around and gather it, grind it or pound it into flour, and then boil it and make it into flat cakes. It tasted like bread baked with olive oil.)

10 Moses heard all the people complaining as they stood around in groups at the entrances of their tents. He was distressed because the LORD had become angry with them, 11 and he said to the LORD, "Why have you treated me so badly? Why are you displeased with me? Why have you given me the responsibility for all these people? 12 I didn't create them or bring them to birth!

Quit Your Griping

Throughout the Book of Numbers, there were many times when the Israelites complained to Moses. They complained about a lot of things, including a lack of food and water and Moses' leadership. When they got to the Promised Land, they complained because strong people were already living there. They complained so much that Moses asked God to kill him so he wouldn't have to listen to their complaints anymore!

The Israelites complained so much because they were discouraged and afraid. What the author of Numbers wants us to know is that when things get hard, we need to trust in God even more. Our grumbling, griping, and complaining may sound like we don't appreciate what God does for us. It might be a symptom that we don't trust that God is there for us.

Think about how you act at home. Do you grumble and gripe about what your parents feed you? Do you complain about your chores or your sisters and brothers? Does your griping make you sound ungrateful? If so, you may want to try to replace griping with either silence or praise. What if you praise the brussels sprouts at your table because God did create them? What if you praise your siblings for keeping you from being bored? The next time you're ready to complain, grumble, or gripe, remember these stories.

— Numbers 11:1–15

---

c **10:36** Return . . . Israel; or Return, LORD, you who are like an army of millions for Israel.   d **11:3** TABERAH: This name sounds like the Hebrew for "burning."
10:35 Ps 68:1   **11:7, 8** Ex 16:31   **11:9** Ex 16:13–15

Why should you ask me to act like a nurse and carry them in my arms like babies all the way to the land you promised to their ancestors? 13 Where could I get enough meat for all these people? They keep whining and asking for meat. 14 I can't be responsible for all these people by myself; it's too much for me! 15 If you are going to treat me like this, have pity on me and kill me, so that I won't have to endure your cruelty any longer."

"I can't be responsible for all these people!" (11:14)

16 The LORD said to Moses, "Assemble seventy respected men who are recognized as leaders of the people, bring them to me at the Tent of my presence, and tell them to stand there beside you. 17 I will come down and speak with you there, and I will take some of the spirit I have given you and give it to them. Then they can help you bear the responsibility for these people, and you will not have to bear it alone. 18 Now tell the people, 'Purify yourselves for tomorrow; you will have meat to eat. The LORD has heard you whining and saying that you wished you had some meat and that you were better off in Egypt. Now the LORD will give you meat, and you will have to eat it. 19 You will have to eat it not just for one or two days, or five, or ten, or even twenty days, 20 but for a whole month, until it comes out of your ears, until you are sick of it. This will happen because you have rejected the LORD who is here among you and have complained to him that you should never have left Egypt.' "

21 Moses said to the LORD, "Here I am leading 600,000 people, and you say that you will give them enough meat for a month? 22 Could enough cattle and sheep be killed to satisfy them? Are all the fish in the sea enough for them?"

23 "Is there a limit to my power?" the LORD answered. "You will soon see whether what I have said will happen or not!"

24 So Moses went out and told the people what the LORD had said. He assembled seventy of the leaders and placed them around the Tent. 25 Then the LORD came down in the cloud and spoke to him. He took some of the spirit he had given to Moses and gave it to the seventy leaders. When the spirit came on them, they began to shout like prophets, but not for long.

26 Two of the seventy leaders, Eldad and Medad, had stayed in the camp and had not gone out to the Tent. There in the camp the spirit came on them, and they too began to shout like prophets. 27 A young man ran out to tell Moses what Eldad and Medad were doing.

28 Then Joshua son of Nun, who had been Moses' helper since he was a young man, spoke up and said to Moses, "Stop them, sir!"

29 Moses answered, "Are you concerned about my interests? I wish that the LORD would give his spirit to all his people and make all of them shout like prophets!" 30 Then Moses and the seventy leaders of Israel went back to camp.

The LORD Sends Quails

31 Suddenly the LORD sent a wind that brought quails from the sea, flying three feet above the ground. They settled on the camp and all around it for miles and miles in every direction.e 32 So all that day, all night, and all the next day, the people worked catching quails; no one gathered less than fifty bushels. They spread them out to dry all around the camp. 33 While there was still plenty of meat for them to eat, the LORD became angry with the people and caused an epidemic to break out among them. 34 That place was named Kibroth Hattaavah (which means "Graves of Craving"), because there they buried the people who had craved meat.

e **11:31** sea, flying . . . direction; *or* sea. They settled in the camp and all around it for miles and miles in every direction, until they were piled up three feet deep on the ground.

Catching quails (11:32)

35From there the people moved to Hazeroth, where they made camp.

Miriam Is Punished

12 1Moses had married a Cushite*f*
woman, and Miriam and Aaron criticized him for it. 2They said, "Has the LORD
spoken only through*g* Moses? Hasn't he also
spoken through*g* us?" The LORD heard what
they said. (3Moses was a humble man, more
humble than anyone else on earth.)

4Suddenly the LORD said to Moses,
Aaron, and Miriam, "I want the three of
you to come out to the Tent of my presence." They went, 5and the LORD came
down in a pillar of cloud, stood at the
entrance of the Tent, and called out,
"Aaron! Miriam!" The two of them stepped
forward, 6and the LORD said, "Now hear
what I have to say! When there are prophets
among you,*h* I reveal myself to them in
visions and speak to them in dreams. 7It is
different when I speak with my servant
Moses; I have put him in charge of all my
people Israel.*i* 8So I speak to him face to
face, clearly and not in riddles; he has even
seen my form! How dare you speak against
my servant Moses?"

9The LORD was angry with them; and so
as he departed 10and the cloud left the Tent,
Miriam's skin was suddenly covered with a
dreaded disease and turned as white as snow.

When Aaron looked at her and saw that she
was covered with the disease, 11he said to
Moses, "Please, sir, do not make us suffer this
punishment for our foolish sin. 12Don't let
her become like something born dead with
half its flesh eaten away."

13So Moses cried out to the LORD, "O
God, heal her!"

"O God, heal her!" (12:13)

14The LORD answered, "If her father had
spit in her face, she would have to bear her
disgrace for seven days. So let her be shut
out of the camp for a week, and after that
she can be brought back in." 15Miriam was
shut out of the camp for seven days, and
the people did not move on until she was
brought back in. 16Then they left Hazeroth
and set up camp in the wilderness of Paran.

---

f **12:1** Cushite *(compare Heb 3:7); or* Midianite; *or* Ethiopian.   *g* **12:2** through; *or to.*   *h* **12:6** *Some ancient
translations* When . . . you; *Hebrew unclear.*   *i* **12:7** I have put . . . Israel; *or* he can be trusted with all my affairs.
12:3 Sir 45:4   **12:7** Heb 3:2   **12:14** Num 5:2, 3

The Spies
(Deuteronomy 1:19–33)

13 [1] The LORD said to Moses, [2] "Choose one of the leaders from each of the twelve tribes and send them as spies to explore the land of Canaan, which I am giving to the Israelites." [3-15] Moses obeyed and from the wilderness of Paran he sent out leaders, as follows:

Tribe	Leader
Reuben	Shammua son of Zaccur
Simeon	Shaphat son of Hori
Judah	Caleb son of Jephunneh
Issachar	Igal son of Joseph
Ephraim	Hoshea son of Nun
Benjamin	Palti son of Raphu
Zebulun	Gaddiel son of Sodi
Manasseh	Gaddi son of Susi
Dan	Ammiel son of Gemalli
Asher	Sethur son of Michael
Naphtali	Nahbi son of Vophsi
Gad	Geuel son of Machi

[16] These are the spies Moses sent to explore the land. He changed the name of Hoshea son of Nun to Joshua.

[17] When Moses sent them out, he said to them, "Go north from here into the southern part of the land of Canaan and then on into the hill country. [18] Find out what kind of country it is, how many people live there, and how strong they are. [19] Find out whether the land is good or bad and whether the people live in open towns or in fortified cities. [20] Find out whether the soil is fertile and whether the land is wooded. And be sure to bring back some of the fruit that grows there." (It was the season when grapes were beginning to ripen.)

[21] So the men went north and explored the land from the wilderness of Zin in the south all the way to Rehob, near Hamath Pass in the north. [22] They went first into the southern part of the land and came to Hebron, where the clans of Ahiman, Sheshai, and Talmai, the descendants of a race of giants called the Anakim, lived. (Hebron was founded seven years before Zoan in Egypt.)

[23] They came to Eshcol Valley, and there they cut off a branch which had one bunch of grapes on it so heavy that it took two men to carry it on a pole between them. They also brought back some pomegranates and figs. ([24] That place was named Eshcol[j] Valley because of the bunch of grapes the Israelites cut off there.)

It took two men to carry it. (13:23)

[25] After exploring the land for forty days, the spies returned [26] to Moses, Aaron, and the whole community of Israel at Kadesh in the wilderness of Paran. They reported what they had seen and showed them the fruit they had brought. [27] They told Moses, "We explored the land and found it to be rich and fertile; and here is some of its fruit. [28] But the people who live there are powerful, and their cities are very large and well fortified. Even worse, we saw the descendants of the giants there. [29] Amalekites live in the southern part of the land; Hittites, Jebusites, and Amorites live in the hill country; and Canaanites live by the Mediterranean Sea and along the Jordan River."

[30] Caleb silenced the people who were complaining against[k] Moses, and said, "We should attack now and take the land; we are strong enough to conquer it."

[31] But the men who had gone with Caleb said, "No, we are not strong enough to attack them; the people there are more powerful than we are." [32] So they spread a false report among the Israelites about the land they had explored. They said, "That land doesn't even produce enough to feed the people who live there. Everyone we saw was very tall, [33] and we even saw giants there, the

---

j **13:24** ESHCOL: *This name in Hebrew means "bunch of grapes."*   *k* **13:30** complaining against; *or* gathered around.
13:33 Gen 6:4

descendants of Anak. We felt as small as grasshoppers, and that is how we must have looked to them."

The People Complain

14 ¹All night long the people cried out in distress. ²They complained against Moses and Aaron, and said, "It would have been better to die in Egypt or even here in the wilderness! ³Why is the LORD taking us into that land? We will be killed in battle, and our wives and children will be captured. Wouldn't it be better to go back to Egypt?" ⁴So they said to one another, "Let's choose a leader and go back to Egypt!"

⁵Then Moses and Aaron bowed to the ground in front of all the people. ⁶And Joshua son of Nun and Caleb son of Jephunneh, two of the spies, tore their clothes in sorrow ⁷and said to the people, "The land we explored is an excellent land. ⁸If the LORD is pleased with us, he will take us there and give us that rich and fertile land. ⁹Do not rebel against the LORD and don't be afraid of the people who live there. We will conquer them easily. The LORD is with us and has defeated the gods who protected them; so don't be afraid." ¹⁰The whole community was threatening to stone them to death, but suddenly the people saw the dazzling light of the LORD's presence appear over the Tent.

Moses Prays for the People

¹¹The LORD said to Moses, "How much longer will these people reject me? How much longer will they refuse to trust in me, even though I have performed so many miracles among them? ¹²I will send an epidemic and destroy them, but I will make you the father of a nation that is larger and more powerful than they are!"

¹³But Moses said to the LORD, "You brought these people out of Egypt by your power. When the Egyptians hear what you have done to your people, ¹⁴they will tell it to the people who live in this land. These people have already heard that you, LORD, are with us, that you appear in plain sight when your cloud stops over us, and that you go before us in a pillar of cloud by day and a pillar of fire by night. ¹⁵Now if you kill all your people, the nations who have heard of your fame will say ¹⁶that you killed your people in the wilderness because you were not able to bring them into the land you promised to give them. ¹⁷So now, LORD, I pray, show us your power and do what you promised when you said, ¹⁸'I, the LORD, am not easily angered, and I show great love and faithfulness and forgive sin and rebellion. Yet I will not fail to punish children and grandchildren to the third and fourth generation for the sins of their parents.' ¹⁹And now, LORD, according to the greatness of your unchanging love, forgive, I pray, the sin of these people, just as you have forgiven them ever since they left Egypt."

²⁰The LORD answered, "I will forgive them, as you have asked. ²¹But I promise that as surely as I live and as surely as my presence fills the earth, ²²none of these people will live to enter that land. They have seen the dazzling light of my presence and the miracles that I performed in Egypt and in the wilderness, but they have tried my patience over and over again and have refused to obey me. ²³They will never enter the land which I promised to their ancestors. None of those who have rejected me will ever enter it. ²⁴But because my servant Caleb has a different attitude and has remained loyal to me, I will bring him into the land which he explored, and his descendants will possess the land ²⁵in whose valleys the Amalekites and the Canaanites now live. Turn back tomorrow and go into the wilderness in the direction of the Gulf of Aqaba."

The LORD Punishes the People for Complaining

²⁶The LORD said to Moses and Aaron, ²⁷"How much longer are these wicked people going to complain against me? I have heard enough of these complaints! ²⁸Now give them this answer: 'I swear that as surely as I live, I will do to you just what you have

14:9 Heb 3:16   **14:13–19** Ex 32:11–14   **14:18** Ex 20:5, 6; 34:6, 7; Deut 5:9, 10; 7:9, 10   **14:21–23** Heb 3:18   **14:24** Josh 14:9–12

asked. I, the LORD, have spoken. ²⁹You will die and your corpses will be scattered across this wilderness. Because you have complained against me, none of you over twenty years of age will enter that land. ³⁰I promised to let you live there, but not one of you will, except Caleb and Joshua. ³¹You said that your children would be captured, but I will bring them into the land that you rejected, and it will be their home. ³²You will die here in this wilderness. ³³Your children will wander in the wilderness for forty years, suffering for your unfaithfulness, until the last one of you dies. ³⁴You will suffer the consequences of your sin for forty years, one year for each of the forty days you spent exploring the land. You will know what it means to have me against you! ³⁵I swear that I will do this to you wicked people who have gathered together against me. Here in the wilderness every one of you will die. I, the LORD, have spoken.' "

³⁶⁻³⁷The men Moses had sent to explore the land brought back a false report which caused the people to complain against the LORD. And so the LORD struck them with a disease, and they died. ³⁸Of the twelve spies only Joshua and Caleb survived.

The First Attempt to Invade the Land
(Deuteronomy 1:41–46)

³⁹When Moses told the Israelites what the LORD had said, they mourned bitterly. ⁴⁰Early the next morning they started out to invade the hill country, saying, "Now we are ready to go to the place which the LORD told us about. We admit that we have sinned."

⁴¹But Moses said, "Then why are you disobeying the LORD now? You will not succeed! ⁴²Don't go. The LORD is not with you, and your enemies will defeat you. ⁴³When you face the Amalekites and the Canaanites, you will die in battle; the LORD will not be with you, because you have refused to follow him."

⁴⁴Yet they still dared to go up into the hill country, even though neither the LORD's

Covenant Box nor Moses left the camp. ⁴⁵Then the Amalekites and the Canaanites who lived there attacked and defeated them, and pursued them as far as Hormah.*ˡ*

Laws about Sacrifice

15 ¹The LORD gave Moses ²the following regulations for the people of Israel to observe in the land that he was going to give them. ³A bull, a ram, a sheep, or a goat may be presented to the LORD as a burnt offering or as a sacrifice in fulfillment of a vow or as a freewill offering or as an offering at your regular religious festivals; the odor of these food offerings is pleasing to the LORD. ⁴⁻⁵Whoever presents a sheep or a goat as a burnt offering to the LORD is to bring with each animal 2 pounds of flour mixed with 2 pints of olive oil as a grain offering, together with 2 pints of wine. ⁶When a ram is offered, 4 pounds of flour mixed with 3 pints of olive oil are to be presented as a grain offering, ⁷together with 3 pints of wine. The odor of these sacrifices is pleasing to the LORD. ⁸When a bull is offered to the LORD as a burnt offering or as a sacrifice in fulfillment of a vow or as a fellowship offering, ⁹a grain offering of 6 pounds of flour mixed with 4 pints of olive oil is to be presented, ¹⁰together with 4 pints of wine. The odor of this sacrifice is pleasing to the LORD.

¹¹That is what shall be offered with each bull, ram, sheep, or goat. ¹²When more than one animal is offered, the accompanying offering is to be increased proportionately. ¹³All native Israelites are to do this when they present a food offering, an odor pleasing to the LORD. ¹⁴And if at any time foreigners living among you, whether on a temporary or a permanent basis, make a food offering, an odor that pleases the LORD, they are to observe the same regulations. ¹⁵For all time to come, the same*ᵐ* rules are binding on you and on the foreigners who live among you. You and they are alike in the LORD's sight; ¹⁶the same laws and regulations apply to you and to them.

Numbers

ˡ **14:45** HORMAH: *This name in Hebrew means "destruction."*   *ᵐ* **15:15** *Some ancient translations* the same; *Hebrew* the congregation the same.
14:29 Heb 3:17   **14:33** Acts 7:36   **15:16** Lev 24:22

17The LORD gave Moses 18the following regulations for the people of Israel to observe in the land that he was going to give them. 19When any food produced there is eaten, some of it is to be set aside as a special contribution to the LORD. 20When you bake bread, the first loaf of the first bread made from the new grain is to be presented as a special contribution to the LORD. This is to be presented in the same way as the special contribution you make from the grain you thresh. 21For all time to come, this special gift is to be given to the LORD from the bread you bake.

22But suppose someone unintentionally fails to keep some of these regulations which the LORD has given Moses. 23And suppose that in the future the community fails to do everything that the LORD commanded through Moses. 24If the mistake was made because of the ignorance of the community, they are to offer a bull as a burnt offering, an odor that pleases the LORD, with the proper grain offering and wine offering. In addition, they are to offer a male goat as a sin offering. 25The priest shall perform the ritual of purification for the community, and they will be forgiven, because the mistake was unintentional and they brought their sin offering as a food offering to the LORD. 26The whole community of Israel and the foreigners living among them will be forgiven, because everyone was involved in the mistake.

27If any of you sin unintentionally, you are to offer a one-year-old female goat as a sin offering. 28At the altar the priest shall perform the ritual of purification to purify you from your sin, and you will be forgiven. 29The same regulation applies to all who unintentionally commit a sin, whether they are native Israelites or resident foreigners.

30But any who sin deliberately, whether they are natives or foreigners, are guilty of treating the LORD with contempt, and they shall be put to death, 31because they have rejected what the LORD said and have deliberately broken one of his commands. They are responsible for their own death.

The Man Who Broke the Sabbath

32Once, while the Israelites were still in the wilderness, a man was found gathering firewood on the Sabbath. 33He was taken to Moses, Aaron, and the whole community, 34and was put under guard, because it was not clear what should be done with him. 35Then the LORD said to Moses, "The man must be put to death; the whole community is to stone him to death outside the camp." 36So the whole community took him outside the camp and stoned him to death, as the LORD had commanded.

Rules about Tassels

37The LORD commanded Moses 38to say to the people of Israel: "Make tassels on the corners of your garments and put a blue cord on each tassel. You are to do this for all time to come. 39The tassels will serve as reminders, and each time you see them you will remember all my commands and obey them; then you will not turn away from me and follow your own wishes and desires. 40The tassels will remind you to keep all my commands, and you will belong completely to me. 41I am the LORD your God; I brought you out of Egypt to be your God. I am the LORD."

The Rebellion of Korah, Dathan, and Abiram

16 1-2Korah son of Izhar, from the Levite clan of Kohath, rebelled against the leadership of Moses. He was joined by three members of the tribe of Reuben—Dathan and Abiram, the sons of Eliab, and On son of Peleth—and by 250 other Israelites, well-known leaders chosen by the community. 3They assembled before Moses and Aaron and said to them, "You have gone too far! All the members of the community belong to the LORD, and the LORD is with all of us. Why, then, Moses, do you set yourself above the LORD's community?"

4When Moses heard this, he threw himself on the ground and prayed. 5Then he said to Korah and his followers, "Tomorrow morning the LORD will show us who belongs to him; he will let the one who belongs to him, that is, the one he has chosen, approach him at the altar. 6-7Tomorrow morning you and your followers take fire pans, put live coals and incense on them, and take them to the altar. Then we will see which of us the LORD has chosen. You Levites are the ones who have gone too far!"

8Moses continued to speak to Korah. "Listen, you Levites! 9Do you consider it a small matter that the God of Israel has set you apart from the rest of the community, so that you can approach him, perform your service in the LORD's Tent, and minister to the community and serve them? 10He has let you and all the other Levites have this honor—and now you are trying to get the priesthood too! 11When you complain against Aaron, it is really against the LORD that you and your followers are rebelling."

12Then Moses sent for Dathan and Abiram, but they said, "We will not come! 13Isn't it enough that you have brought us out of the fertile land of Egypt to kill us here in the wilderness? Do you also have to lord it over us? 14You certainly have not brought us into a fertile land or given us fields and vineyards as our possession, and now you are trying to deceive us. We will not come!"

15Moses became angry and said to the LORD, "Do not accept any offerings these men bring. I have not wronged any of them; I have not even taken one of their donkeys."

16Moses said to Korah, "Tomorrow you and your 250 followers must come to the Tent of the LORD's presence; Aaron will also be there. 17Each of you will take his fire pan, put incense on it, and then present it at the altar." 18So they each took their fire pans, put live coals and incense on them, and stood at the entrance of the Tent with Moses and Aaron. 19Then Korah gathered the whole community, and they stood facing Moses and Aaron at the entrance of the Tent. Suddenly the dazzling light of the LORD's presence appeared to the whole community, 20and the LORD said to Moses and Aaron, 21"Move back from these people, and I will destroy them immediately."

22But Moses and Aaron bowed down with their faces to the ground and said, "O God, you are the source of all life. When one of us sins, do you become angry with the whole community?"

23The LORD said to Moses, 24"Tell the people to move away from the tents of Korah, Dathan, and Abiram."

25Then Moses, accompanied by the leaders of Israel, went to Dathan and Abiram. 26He said to the people, "Get away from the tents of these wicked men and don't touch anything that belongs to them. Otherwise, you will be wiped out with them for all their sins." 27So they moved away from the tents of Korah, Dathan, and Abiram.

Dathan and Abiram had come out and were standing at the entrance of their tents, with their wives and children. 28Moses said to the people, "This is how you will know that the LORD has sent me to do all these things and that it is not by my own choice that I have done them. 29If these men die a natural death without some punishment from God, then the LORD did not send me. 30But if the LORD does something unheard of, and the earth opens up and swallows them with all they own, so that they go down alive to the world of the dead, you will know that these men have rejected the LORD."

The earth opens up and swallows them. (16:30)

31As soon as he had finished speaking, the ground under Dathan and Abiram split open 32and swallowed them and their families, together with all of Korah's followers and their possessions. 33So they went down alive to the world of the dead, with their possessions. The earth closed over them, and they vanished. 34All the people of Israel who were

Between the living and the dead (16:48)

there fled when they heard their cry. They shouted, "Run! The earth might swallow us too!"

³⁵ Then the LORD sent a fire that blazed out and burned up the 250 men who had presented the incense.

The Fire Pans

³⁶ Then the LORD said to Moses, ³⁷ "Tell Eleazar son of Aaron the priest to remove the bronze fire pans from the remains of those who have been burned, and scatter the coals from the fire pans somewhere else, because the fire pans are holy. ³⁸ They became holy when they were presented at the LORD's altar. So take the fire pans of these who were put to death for their sin, beat them into thin plates, and make a covering for the altar. It will be a warning to the people of Israel." ³⁹ So Eleazar the priest took the fire pans and had them beaten into thin plates to make a covering for the altar. ⁴⁰ This was a warning to the Israelites that no one who was not a descendant of Aaron should come to the altar to burn incense for the LORD. Otherwise he would be destroyed like Korah and his men. All this was done as the LORD had commanded Eleazar through Moses.

Aaron Saves the People

⁴¹ The next day the whole community complained against Moses and Aaron and said, "You have killed some of the LORD's people." ⁴² After they had all gathered to protest to Moses and Aaron, they turned toward the Tent and saw that the cloud was covering it and that the dazzling light of the LORD's presence had appeared. ⁴³ Moses and Aaron went and stood in front of the Tent, ⁴⁴ and the LORD said to Moses, ⁴⁵ "Move back from these people, and I will destroy them on the spot!"

The two of them bowed down with their faces to the ground, ⁴⁶ and Moses said to Aaron, "Take your fire pan, put live coals from the altar in it, and put some incense on the coals. Then hurry with it to the people and perform the ritual of purification for them. Hurry! The LORD's anger has already broken out and an epidemic has already begun." ⁴⁷ Aaron obeyed, took his fire pan and ran into the middle of the assembled people. When he saw that the plague had already begun, he put the incense on the coals and performed the ritual of purification for the people. ⁴⁸ This stopped the plague, and he was left standing between the living and the dead. ⁴⁹ The number of people who died was 14,700, not counting those who died in Korah's rebellion. ⁵⁰ When the

16:44–48 Wis 18:20–25

plague had stopped, Aaron returned to Moses at the entrance of the Tent.

Aaron's Walking Stick

17 [1]The LORD said to Moses, [2]"Tell the people of Israel to give you twelve walking sticks, one from the leader of each tribe. Write each man's name on his stick [3]and then write Aaron's name on the stick representing Levi. There will be one stick for each tribal leader. [4]Take them to the Tent of my presence and put them in front of the Covenant Box, where I meet you. [5]Then the stick of the man I have chosen will sprout. In this way I will put a stop to the constant complaining of these Israelites against you."

[6]So Moses spoke to the Israelites, and each of their leaders gave him a stick, one for each tribe, twelve in all, and Aaron's stick was put with them. [7]Moses then put all the sticks in the Tent in front of the LORD's Covenant Box.

[8]The next day, when Moses went into the Tent, he saw that Aaron's stick, representing the tribe of Levi, had sprouted. It had budded, blossomed, and produced ripe almonds! [9]Moses took all the sticks and showed them to the Israelites. They saw what had happened, and each leader took his own stick back. [10]The LORD said to Moses, "Put Aaron's stick back in front of the Covenant Box. It is to be kept as a warning to the rebel Israelites

Aaron's stick . . . produced ripe almonds. (17:8)

that they will die unless their complaining stops." [11]Moses did as the LORD commanded.

[12]The people of Israel said to Moses, "Then that's the end of us! [13]If anyone who even comes near the Tent must die, then we are all as good as dead!"

17:8–10 Heb 9:4

Duties of Priests and Levites

18 [1]The LORD said to Aaron, "You, your sons, and the Levites must suffer the consequences of any guilt connected with serving in the Tent of my presence; but only you and your sons will suffer the consequences of service in the priesthood. [2]Bring in your relatives, the tribe of Levi, to work with you and help you while you and your sons are serving at the Tent. [3]They are to fulfill their duties to you and their responsibilities for the Tent, but they must not have any contact with sacred objects in the Holy Place or with the altar. If they do, both they and you will be put to death. [4]They are to work with you and fulfill their responsibilities for all the service in the Tent, but no unqualified person may work with you. [5]You and your sons alone must fulfill the responsibilities for the Holy Place and the altar, so that my anger will not again break out against the people of Israel. [6]I am the one who has chosen your relatives the Levites from among the Israelites as a gift to you. They are dedicated to me, so that they can carry out their duties in the Tent. [7]But you and your sons alone shall fulfill all the responsibilities of the priesthood that concern the altar and what is in the Most Holy Place. These things are your responsibility, because I have given you the gift of the priesthood. Any unqualified person who comes near the sacred objects shall be put to death."

The Share of the Priests

[8]The LORD said to Aaron, "Remember that I am giving you all the special contributions made to me that are not burned as sacrifices. I am giving them to you and to your descendants as the part assigned to you forever. [9]Of the most sacred offerings not burned on the altar, the following belong to you: the grain offerings, the sin offerings, and the repayment offerings. Everything that is presented to me as a sacred offering belongs to you and your sons. [10]You must eat these things in a holy place, and only males may eat them; consider them holy.

Numbers

11 "In addition, any other special contributions that the Israelites present to me shall be yours. I am giving them to you, your sons, and your daughters for all time to come. Every member of your family who is ritually clean may eat them.

12 "I am giving you all the best of the first produce which the Israelites give me each year: olive oil, wine, and grain. 13 It all belongs to you. Every member of your family who is ritually clean may eat it.

14 "Everything in Israel that has been unconditionally dedicated to me belongs to you.

15 "Every first-born child or animal that the Israelites present to me belongs to you. But you must accept payment to buy back every first-born child, and must also accept payment for every first-born animal that is ritually unclean. 16 Children shall be bought back at the age of one month for the fixed price of five pieces of silver, according to the official standard. 17 But the first-born of cows, sheep, and goats are not to be bought back; they belong completely to me and are to be sacrificed. Throw their blood against the altar and burn their fat as a food offering, an odor pleasing to me. 18 The meat from them belongs to you, like the breast and the right hind leg of the special offering.

19 "I am giving to you, to your sons, and to your daughters, for all time to come, all the special contributions which the Israelites present to me. This is an unbreakable covenant that I have made with you and your descendants."

20 The LORD said to Aaron, "You will not receive any property that can be inherited, and no part of the land of Israel will be assigned to you. I, the LORD, am all you need."

The Share of the Levites

21 The LORD said, "I have given to the Levites every tithe that the people of Israel present to me. This is in payment for their service in taking care of the Tent of my presence. 22 The other Israelites must no longer approach the Tent and in this way bring on

themselves the penalty of death. 23 From now on only the Levites will take care of the Tent and bear the full responsibility for it. This is a permanent rule that applies also to your descendants. The Levites shall have no permanent property in Israel, 24 because I have given to them as their possession the tithe which the Israelites present to me as a special contribution. That is why I told them that they would have no permanent property in Israel."

The Levites' Tithe

25 The LORD commanded Moses 26 to say to the Levites: "When you receive from the Israelites the tithe that the LORD gives you as your possession, you must present a tenth of it as a special contribution to the LORD. 27 This special contribution will be considered as the equivalent of the offering which the farmer makes of new grain and new wine. 28 In this way you also will present the special contribution that belongs to the LORD from all the tithes which you receive from the Israelites. You are to give this special contribution for the LORD to Aaron the priest. 29 Give it from the best that you receive. 30 When you have presented the best part, you may keep the rest, just as the farmer keeps what is left after he makes his offering. 31 You and your families may eat the rest anywhere, because it is your wages for your service in the Tent. 32 You will not become guilty when you eat it, as long as you have presented the best of it to the LORD. But be sure not to profane the sacred gifts of the Israelites by eating any of the gifts before the best part is offered; if you do, you will be put to death."

Ashes of the Red Cow

19 1 The LORD commanded Moses and Aaron 2 to give the Israelites the following regulations. Bring to Moses and Aaron a red cow which has no defects and which has never been worked, 3 and they will give it to Eleazar the priest. It is to be taken outside the camp and killed in his presence.ⁿ 4 Then Eleazar is to take some of

its blood and with his finger sprinkle it seven times in the direction of the Tent. ⁵The whole animal, including skin, meat, blood, and intestines, is to be burned in the presence of the priest. ⁶Then he is to take some cedar wood, a sprig of hyssop, and a red cord and throw them into the fire. ⁷After that, he is to wash his clothes and pour water over himself, and then he may enter the camp; but he remains ritually unclean until evening. ⁸The one who burned the cow must also wash his clothes and pour water over himself, but he also remains unclean until evening. ⁹Then someone who is ritually clean is to collect the ashes of the cow and put them in a ritually clean place outside the camp, where they are to be kept for the Israelite community to use in preparing the water for removing ritual uncleanness. This ritual is performed to remove sin. ¹⁰The one who collected the ashes must wash his clothes, but he remains unclean until evening. This regulation is valid for all time to come, both for the Israelites and for the foreigners living among them.

Contact with a Corpse

¹¹Those who touch a corpse are ritually unclean for seven days. ¹²They must purify themselves with the water for purification on the third day and on the seventh day, and then they will be clean. But if they do not purify themselves on both the third and the seventh day, they will not be clean. ¹³Those who touch a corpse and do not purify themselves remain unclean, because the water for purification has not been thrown over them. They defile the LORD's Tent, and they will no longer be considered God's people.

¹⁴In the case of a person who dies in a tent, anyone who is in the tent at the time of death or who enters it becomes ritually unclean for seven days. ¹⁵Every jar and pot in the tent that has no lid° on it also becomes unclean. ¹⁶If any touch a person who has been killed or has died a natural death outdoors or if any touch a human bone or a grave, they become unclean for seven days.

¹⁷To remove the uncleanness, some ashes from the red cow which was burned to remove sin shall be taken and put in a pot, and fresh water added. ¹⁸In the first case, someone who is ritually clean is to take a sprig of hyssop, dip it in the water, and sprinkle the tent, everything in it, and the people who were there. In the second case, someone who is ritually clean is to sprinkle the water on those who had touched the human bone or the dead body or the grave. ¹⁹On the third day and on the seventh the person who is ritually clean is to sprinkle the water on the unclean persons. On the seventh day he is to purify those, who, after washing their clothes and pouring water over themselves, become ritually clean at sunset.

²⁰Those who have become ritually unclean and do not purify themselves remain unclean, because the water for purification has not been thrown over them. They defile the LORD's Tent and will no longer be considered God's people. ²¹You are to observe this rule for all time to come. The person who sprinkles the water for purification must also wash his clothes; anyone who touches the water remains ritually unclean until evening. ²²Whatever an unclean person touches is unclean, and anyone else who touches it remains unclean until evening.

Events at Kadesh
(Exodus 17:1–7)

20 ¹In the first month the whole community of Israel came to the wilderness of Zin and camped at Kadesh. There Miriam died and was buried.

²There was no water where they camped, so the people gathered around Moses and Aaron ³and complained: "It would have been better if we had died in front of the LORD's Tent along with the other Israelites. ⁴Why have you brought us out into this wilderness? Just so that we can die here with our animals? ⁵Why did you bring us out of Egypt into this miserable place where nothing will grow? There's no grain, no figs, no grapes, no

pomegranates. There is not even any water to drink!" 6Moses and Aaron moved away from the people and stood at the entrance of the Tent. They bowed down with their faces to the ground, and the dazzling light of the LORD's presence appeared to them.

7The LORD said to Moses, 8"Take the stick that is in front of the Covenant Box, and then you and Aaron assemble the whole community. There in front of them all speak to that rock over there, and water will gush out of it. In this way you will bring water out of the rock for the people, for them and their animals to drink." 9Moses went and got the stick, as the LORD had commanded.

10He and Aaron assembled the whole community in front of the rock, and Moses said, "Listen, you rebels! Do we have to get water out of this rock for you?" 11Then Moses raised the stick and struck the rock twice with it, and a great stream of water gushed out, and all the people and animals drank.

12But the LORD reprimanded Moses and Aaron. He said, "Because you did not have

A great stream of water gushed out. (20:11)

enough faith to acknowledge my holy power before the people of Israel, you will not lead them into the land that I promised to give them."

13This happened at Meribah,*p* where the people of Israel complained against the LORD and where he showed them that he is holy.

The King of Edom Refuses to Let Israel Pass

14Moses sent messengers from Kadesh to the king of Edom. They said, "This message is from your kinsmen, the tribes of Israel. You know the hardships we have suffered, 15how our ancestors went to Egypt, where we lived many years. The Egyptians mistreated our ancestors and us, 16and we cried to the LORD for help. He heard our cry and sent an angel, who led us out of Egypt. Now we are at Kadesh, a town at the border of your territory. 17Please permit us to pass through your land. We and our cattle will not leave the road or go into your fields or vineyards, and we will not drink from your wells. We will stay on the main road*q* until we are out of your territory."

18But the Edomites answered, "We refuse to let you pass through our country! If you try, we will march out and attack you."

19The people of Israel said, "We will stay on the main road, and if we or our animals drink any of your water, we will pay for it— all we want is to pass through."

20The Edomites repeated, "We refuse!" and they marched out with a powerful army to attack the people of Israel. 21Because the Edomites would not let the Israelites pass through their territory, the Israelites turned and went another way.

The Death of Aaron

22The whole community of Israel left Kadesh and arrived at Mount Hor, 23on the border of Edom. There the LORD said to Moses and Aaron, 24"Aaron is not going to enter the land which I promised to give to Israel; he is going to die, because the two of you rebelled against my command at Meribah. 25Take Aaron and his son Eleazar up Mount Hor, 26and there remove Aaron's priestly robes and put them on Eleazar. Aaron is going to die there." 27Moses did

p **20:13** MERIBAH: *This name in Hebrew means "complaining."*   *q* **20:17** main road; *or* King's Highway.
20:11 Wis 11:4

what the LORD had commanded. They went up Mount Hor in the sight of the whole community, 28and Moses removed Aaron's priestly robes and put them on Eleazar. There on the top of the mountain Aaron died, and Moses and Eleazar came back down. 29The whole community learned that Aaron had died, and they all mourned for him for thirty days.

Victory over the Canaanites

21 1When the Canaanite king of Arad in the southern part of Canaan heard that the Israelites were coming by way of Atharim, he attacked them and captured some of them. 2Then the Israelites made a vow to the LORD: "If you will let us conquer these people, we will unconditionally dedicate[r] them and their cities to you and will destroy them." 3The LORD heard them and helped them conquer the Canaanites. So the Israelites completely destroyed them and their cities, and named the place Hormah.[s]

The Snake Made of Bronze

4The Israelites left Mount Hor by the road that leads to the Gulf of Aqaba, in order to go around the territory of Edom. But on the way the people lost their patience 5and spoke against God and Moses. They complained, "Why did you bring us out of Egypt to die in this desert, where there is no food or water? We can't stand any more of this miserable food!" 6Then the LORD sent poisonous snakes among the people, and many Israelites were bitten and died. 7The people came to Moses and said, "We sinned when we spoke against the LORD and against you. Now pray to the LORD to take these snakes away." So Moses prayed for the people. 8Then the LORD told Moses to make a metal snake and put it on a pole, so that anyone who was bitten could look at it and be healed. 9So Moses made a bronze snake and put it on a pole. Anyone who had been bitten would look at the bronze snake and be healed.

From Mount Hor to the Valley of the Moabites

10The Israelites moved on and camped at Oboth. 11After leaving that place, they camped at the ruins of Abarim in the wilderness east of Moabite territory. 12Then they camped in Zered Valley. 13From there they moved again and camped on the north side of the Arnon River, in the wilderness which extends into Amorite territory. (The Arnon was the border between the Moabites and the Amorites.) 14That is why *The Book of the LORD's Battles* speaks of " . . . the town of Waheb in the area of Suphah, and the valleys; the Arnon River, 15and the slope of the valleys that extend to the town of Ar and toward the border of Moab."

16From there they went on to a place called Wells, where the LORD said to Moses, "Bring the people together, and I will give them water." 17At that time the people of Israel sang this song:

"Wells, produce your water;
And we will greet it with a song—
18The well dug by princes
And by leaders of the people,
Dug with a royal scepter
And with their walking sticks."

They moved from the wilderness to Mattanah, 19and from there they went on to Nahaliel, and from Nahaliel to Bamoth, 20and from Bamoth to the valley in the

Anyone who was bitten could look at it and be healed. (21:8)

---

[r] **21:2** UNCONDITIONALLY DEDICATE: *Anything dedicated in this way belonged completely to the LORD and could not be used; it had to be destroyed.*   [s] **21:3** HORMAH: *This name in Hebrew means "destruction."*
20:28 Ex 29:29; Num 33:38; Deut 10:6   **21:1** Num 33:40   **21:4** Deut 2:1   **21:5, 6** 1 Cor 10:9
21:9 2 Kings 18:4; Jn 3:14

territory of the Moabites, below the top of Mount Pisgah, looking out over the desert.

Victory over King Sihon and King Og
(Deuteronomy 2:26—3:11)

21 Then the people of Israel sent messengers to the Amorite king Sihon to say: 22 "Let us pass through your land. We and our cattle will not leave the road and go into your fields or vineyards, and we will not drink water from your wells; we will stay on the main road*t* until we are out of your territory." 23 But Sihon would not permit the people of Israel to pass through his territory. He gathered his army and went out to Jahaz in the wilderness and attacked the Israelites. 24 But the Israelites killed many of the enemy in battle and occupied their land from the Arnon River north to the Jabbok, that is, to the Ammonites, because the Ammonite border was strongly defended.*u* 25 So the people of Israel captured all the Amorite cities, including Heshbon and all the surrounding towns, and settled in them. 26 Heshbon was the capital city of the Amorite king Sihon, who had fought against the former king of Moab and had captured all his land as far as the Arnon River. 27 That is why the poets sing,

"Come to Heshbon, to King Sihon's city!
We want to see it rebuilt and restored.
28 Once from this city of Heshbon
Sihon's army went forth like a fire;
It destroyed the city of Ar in Moab
And devoured*v* the hills of the upper
   Arnon.
29 How terrible for you, people of Moab!
You worshipers of Chemosh are brought
   to ruin!
Your god let the men become refugees,
And the women became captives of the
   Amorite king.
30 But now their descendants are destroyed,
All the way from Heshbon to Dibon,
From Nashim to Nophah, near
   Medeba."*w*

31 So the people of Israel settled in the territory of the Amorites, 32 and Moses sent men to find the best way to attack the city of Jazer. The Israelites captured it and its surrounding towns and drove out the Amorites living there.

33 Then the Israelites turned and took the road to Bashan, and King Og of Bashan marched out with his army to attack them at Edrei. 34 The LORD said to Moses, "Do not be afraid of him. I will give you victory over him, all his people, and his land. Do to him what you did to Sihon, the Amorite king who ruled at Heshbon." 35 So the Israelites killed Og, his sons, and all his people, leaving no survivors, and then they occupied his land.

The King of Moab Sends for Balaam

22 1 The Israelites moved on and set up camp in the plains of Moab east of the Jordan and opposite Jericho.

2 When the king of Moab, Balak son of Zippor, heard what the Israelites had done to the Amorites and how many Israelites there were, 3 he and all his people became terrified. 4 The Moabites said to the leaders of the Midianites, "This horde will soon destroy everything around us, like a bull eating the grass in a pasture." So King Balak 5 sent messengers to summon Balaam son of Beor, who was at Pethor near the Euphrates River in the land of Amaw. They brought him this message from Balak: "I want you to know that a whole nation has come from Egypt; its people are spreading out everywhere and threatening to take over our land. 6 They outnumber us, so please come and put a curse on them for me. Then perhaps we will be able to defeat them and drive them out of the land. I know that when you pronounce a blessing, people are blessed, and when you pronounce a curse, they are placed under a curse."

7 So the Moabite and Midianite leaders took with them the payment for the curse, went to Balaam, and gave him Balak's message. 8 Balaam said to them, "Spend the night

---

t 21:22 main road; *or* King's Highway.   *u* 21:24 because . . . strongly defended; *some ancient translations* as far as Jazer on the Ammonite border.   *v* 21:28 *One ancient translation* devoured; *Hebrew* the lords of.   *w* 21:30 *Verse 30 in Hebrew is unclear.*

21:28, 29 Jer 48:45, 46   22:5 Num 31:8; 2 Pet 2:15, 16; Jude 11 here, and tomorrow I will report to you whatever the LORD tells me." So the Moabite leaders stayed with Balaam.

⁹God came to Balaam and asked, "Who are these people that are staying with you?"

¹⁰He answered, "King Balak of Moab has sent them to tell me ¹¹that a people who came from Egypt has spread out over the whole land. He wants me to curse them for him, so that he can fight them and drive them out."

¹²God said to Balaam, "Do not go with them, and do not put a curse on the people of Israel, because they have my blessing."

¹³The next morning Balaam went to Balak's messengers and said, "Go back home;

HIGHLIGHTS FROM THE STORY OF BALAAM
(Numbers refer to chapter and verse in Numbers)

the LORD has refused to let me go with you." [14]So they returned to Balak and told him that Balaam had refused to come with them.

[15]Then Balak sent a larger number of leaders, who were more important than the first. [16]They went to Balaam and gave him this message from Balak: "Please don't let anything prevent you from coming to me! [17]I will reward you richly and do anything you say. Please come and curse these people for me."

[18]But Balaam answered, "Even if Balak gave me all the silver and gold in his palace, I could not disobey the command of the LORD my God in even the smallest matter. [19]But please spend the night, as the others did, so that I may learn whether or not the LORD has something else to tell me."

[20]That night God came to Balaam and said, "If these men have come to ask you to go with them, get ready and go, but do only what I tell you." [21]So the next morning Balaam saddled his donkey and went with the Moabite leaders.

Balaam and His Donkey

[22]God was angry that Balaam was going, and as Balaam was riding along on his donkey, accompanied by his two servants, the angel of the LORD stood in the road to bar his way. [23]When the donkey saw the angel standing there holding a sword, it left the road and turned into the fields. Balaam beat the donkey and brought it back onto the road. [24]Then the angel stood where the road narrowed between two vineyards and had a stone wall on each side. [25]When the donkey saw the angel, it moved over against the wall and crushed Balaam's foot against it. Again Balaam beat the donkey. [26]Once more the angel moved ahead; he stood in a narrow place where there was no room at all to pass on either side. [27]This time, when the donkey saw the angel, it lay down. Balaam lost his temper and began to beat the donkey with his stick. [28]Then the LORD gave the donkey the power of speech, and it said to Balaam, "What have I done to you?

Why have you beaten me these three times?"

[29]Balaam answered, "Because you have made a fool of me! If I had a sword, I would kill you."

[30]The donkey replied, "Am I not the same donkey on which you have ridden all your life? Have I ever treated you like this before?"

"No," he answered.

[31]Then the LORD let Balaam see the angel standing there with his sword; and Balaam threw himself face downward on the ground. [32]The angel demanded, "Why have you beaten your donkey three times like this? I have come to bar your way, because you should not be making this journey.[x] [33]But your donkey saw me and turned aside three times. If it hadn't, I would have killed you and spared the donkey."

[34]Balaam replied, "I have sinned. I did not know that you were standing in the road to oppose me; but now if you think it is wrong for me to go on, I will return home."

[35]But the angel said, "Go on with these men, but say only what I tell you to say." So Balaam went on with them.

Balak Welcomes Balaam

[36]When Balak heard that Balaam was coming, he went to meet him at Ar, a city on the Arnon River at the border of Moab. [37]Balak said to him, "Why didn't you come when I sent for you the first time? Did you think I wasn't able to reward you enough?"

[38]Balaam answered, "I came, didn't I? But now, what power do I have? I can say only what God tells me to say." [39]So Balaam went with Balak to the town of Huzoth, [40]where Balak slaughtered cattle and sheep and gave some of the meat to Balaam and the leaders who were with him.

Balaam's First Prophecy

[41]The next morning Balak took Balaam up to Bamoth Baal, from where Balaam could see a part of the people of Israel.

---

x **22:32** *Probable text* you should . . . journey; *Hebrew unclear.*

23

¹He said to Balak, "Build seven altars here for me, and bring me seven bulls and seven rams."

²Balak did as he was told, and he and Balaam offered a bull and a ram on each altar. ³Then Balaam said to Balak, "Stand here by your burnt offering, while I go to see whether or not the LORD will meet me. I will tell you whatever he reveals to me." So he went alone to the top of a hill, ⁴and God met him. Balaam said to him, "I have built the seven altars and offered a bull and a ram on each."

⁵The LORD told Balaam what to say and sent him back to Balak to give him his message. ⁶So he went back and found Balak still standing by his burnt offering with all the leaders of Moab.

⁷Balaam uttered this prophecy:

"Balak king of Moab has brought me
From Syria, from the eastern mountains.
'Come speak for me,' he said.
'Put a curse on the people of Israel.'
⁸How can I curse what God has not cursed,
Or speak of doom when the LORD has not?
⁹From the high rocks I can see them;
I can watch them from the hills.
They are a nation that lives alone;
They know they are blessed more than other nations.
¹⁰The descendants of Israel are like the dust—
There are too many of them to be counted.
Let me end my days like one of God's people;
Let me die in peace like the righteous."

¹¹Then Balak said to Balaam, "What have you done to me? I brought you here to curse my enemies, but all you have done is bless them."

¹²He answered, "I can say only what the LORD tells me to say."

Balaam's Second Prophecy

¹³Then Balak said to Balaam, "Come with me to another place from which you can see only some of the Israelites. Curse them for me from there." ¹⁴He took him to the field of Zophim on the top of Mount Pisgah. There also he built seven altars and offered a bull and a ram on each of them.

¹⁵Balaam said to Balak, "Stand here by your burnt offering, and I will meet God over there."

¹⁶The LORD met Balaam, told him what to say, and sent him back to Balak to give him his message. ¹⁷So he went back and found Balak still standing by his burnt offering, with the leaders of Moab. Balak asked what the LORD had said, ¹⁸and Balaam uttered this prophecy:

"Come, Balak son of Zippor,
And listen to what I have to say.
¹⁹God is not like people, who lie;
He is not a human who changes his mind.
Whatever he promises, he does;
He speaks, and it is done.
²⁰I have been instructed to bless,
And when God blesses, I cannot call it back.
²¹I foresee that Israel's future
Will bring her no misfortune or trouble.
The LORD their God is with them;
They proclaim that he is their king.
²²God has brought them out of Egypt;
He fights for them like a wild ox.
²³There is no magic charm, no witchcraft,
That can be used against the nation of Israel.ʸ
Now people will say about Israel,
'Look what God has done!'
²⁴The nation of Israel is like a mighty lion:
It doesn't rest until it has torn and devoured,
Until it has drunk the blood of those it has killed."

²⁵Then Balak said to Balaam, "You refuse to curse the people of Israel, but at least don't bless them!"

²⁶Balaam answered, "Didn't I tell you that I had to do everything that the LORD told me?"

ʸ 23:23 There . . . Israel; *or* No magic charms are used in Israel, no witchcraft is practiced there.

Balaam's Third Prophecy

27Balak said, "Come with me, and I will take you to another place. Perhaps God will be willing to let you curse them for me from there." 28So he took Balaam to the top of Mount Peor overlooking the desert. 29Balaam said to him, "Build seven altars for me here and bring me seven bulls and seven rams." 30Balak did as he was told, and offered a bull and a ram on each altar.

24 1By now Balaam knew that the LORD wanted him to bless the people of Israel, so he did not go to look for omens, as he had done before. He turned toward the desert 2and saw the people of Israel camped tribe by tribe. The spirit of God took control of him, 3and he uttered this prophecy:

"The message of Balaam son of Beor,
The words of the man who can see
    clearly,*z*
4Who can hear what God is saying.
With staring eyes I see in a trance
A vision from Almighty God.
5The tents of Israel are beautiful,
6Like long rows of palms
Or gardens beside a river,
Like aloes planted by the LORD
Or cedars beside the water.
7They will have abundant rainfall
And plant their seed in well-watered
    fields.*a*
Their king shall be greater than Agag,
And his rule shall be extended far and
    wide.
8God brought them out of Egypt;
He fights for them like a wild ox.
They devour their enemies,
Crush their bones, smash their arrows.
9The nation is like a mighty lion;
When it is sleeping, no one dares wake it.
Whoever blesses Israel will be blessed,
And whoever curses Israel will be cursed."

10Balak clenched his fists in anger and said to Balaam, "I called you to curse my enemies, but three times now you have blessed

them instead. 11Now get on home! I promised to reward you, but the LORD has kept you from getting the reward."

12Balaam answered, "I told the messengers you sent to me that 13even if you gave me all the silver and gold in your palace, I could not disobey the command of the LORD by doing anything of myself. I will say only what the LORD tells me to say."

Balaam's Final Prophecies

14Balaam said to Balak, "Now I am going back to my own people, but before I go, I am warning you what the people of Israel will do to your people in the future." 15Then he uttered this prophecy:

"The message of Balaam son of Beor,
The words of the man who can see
    clearly,*b*
16Who can hear what God is saying
And receive the knowledge that comes
    from the Most High.
With staring eyes I see in a trance
A vision from Almighty God.
17I look into the future,
And I see the nation of Israel.
A king, like a bright star, will arise in that
    nation.
Like a comet he will come from Israel.
He will strike the leaders of Moab
And beat down all the people of Seth.*c*
18He will conquer his enemies in Edom
And make their land his property,
While Israel continues victorious.
19The nation of Israel will trample them
    down
And wipe out the last survivors."

20Then in his vision Balaam saw the Amalekites and uttered this prophecy:
"Amalek was the most powerful nation of
    all,
But at the end it will perish forever."
21In his vision he saw the Kenites, and uttered this prophecy:
"The place where you live is secure,
Safe as a nest set high on a cliff,

---

z **24:3** who can see clearly; *or* whose eyes are closed.   *a* **24:7** *One ancient translation* They . . . fields; *Hebrew unclear.*   *b* **24:15** who can see clearly; *or* whose eyes are closed.   *c* **24:17** the people of Seth; *or* who are proud and violent.
24:9 *a* Gen 49:9; *b* Gen 12:3

22 But you Kenites will be destroyed
When Assyria takes you captive." *d*
23 Balaam uttered this prophecy:
"Who are these people gathering in the
north?*e*
24 Invaders will sail from Cyprus;
They will conquer Assyria and Eber,
But they, in turn, will perish forever."
25 Then Balaam got ready and went back
home, and Balak went on his way.

The People of Israel at Peor

25 ¹When the Israelites were camped at
Acacia Valley, the men began to have
sexual intercourse with the Moabite women
who were there. ²These women invited
them to sacrificial feasts, where the god of
Moab was worshiped. The Israelites ate the
food and worshiped the god ³Baal of Peor.
So the LORD was angry with them ⁴and said
to Moses, "Take all the leaders of Israel and,
in obedience to me, execute them in broad
daylight,*f* and then I will no longer be angry
with the people." ⁵Moses said to the officials,
"Each of you is to kill every man in your
tribe who has become a worshiper of Baal
of Peor."

⁶One of the Israelites took a Midianite
woman into his tent in the sight of Moses
and the whole community, while they were
mourning at the entrance of the Tent of the
LORD's presence. ⁷When Phinehas, the son
of Eleazar and grandson of Aaron the priest,
saw this, he got up and left the assembly. He
took a spear, ⁸followed the man and the
woman into the tent, and drove the spear
through both of them. In this way the epidemic that was destroying Israel was stopped,
⁹but it had already killed twenty-four thousand people.

¹⁰The LORD said to Moses, ¹¹"Because of
what Phinehas has done, I am no longer
angry with the people of Israel. He refused
to tolerate the worship of any god but me,
and that is why I did not destroy them in my
anger. ¹²So tell him that I am making a
covenant with him that is valid for all time
to come. ¹³He and his descendants are per-

manently established as priests, because he
did not tolerate any rivals to me and brought
about forgiveness for the people's sin."

¹⁴The name of the Israelite who was
killed with the Midianite woman was Zimri
son of Salu, the head of a family in the tribe
of Simeon. ¹⁵The woman's name was Cozbi.
Zur, her father, was chief of a group of Midianite clans.

¹⁶The LORD commanded Moses,
¹⁷"Attack the Midianites and destroy them,
¹⁸because of the evil they did to you when
they deceived you at Peor, and because of
Cozbi, who was killed at the time of the
epidemic at Peor."

The Second Census

26 ¹After the epidemic the LORD said
to Moses and Eleazar son of Aaron,
²"Take a census by families of the whole
community of Israel, of all men twenty years
old or older who are fit for military service."
³⁻⁴Moses and Eleazar obeyed and called
together all the men of that age group. They
assembled in the plains of Moab across the
Jordan River from Jericho.

These were the Israelites who came out of
Egypt:

⁵The tribe of Reuben (Reuben was the
oldest son of Jacob): the clans of Hanoch,
Pallu, ⁶Hezron, and Carmi. ⁷These clans
numbered 43,730 men. ⁸The descendants of
Pallu were Eliab ⁹and his sons Nemuel,
Dathan, and Abiram. (These are the Dathan
and Abiram who were chosen by the community. They defied Moses and Aaron and
joined the followers of Korah when they
rebelled against the LORD. ¹⁰The ground
opened and swallowed them, and they died
with Korah and his followers when fire
destroyed 250 men; they became a warning
to the people. ¹¹But the sons of Korah were
not killed.)

¹²The tribe of Simeon: the clans of
Nemuel, Jamin, Jachin, ¹³Zerah, and Shaul.
¹⁴These clans numbered 22,200 men.
¹⁵The tribe of Gad: the clans of Zephon,

d **24:22** *Verse 22 in Hebrew is unclear.*   *e* **24:23** *Probable text* Who . . . north; *Hebrew unclear.*   *f* **25:4** in broad
daylight; *or* publicly.
26:1–51 Num 1:1–46

Haggi, Shuni, [16]Ozni, Eri, [17]Arod, and Areli. [18]These clans numbered 40,500 men.

[19-21]The tribe of Judah: the clans of Shelah, Perez, Zerah, Hezron, and Hamul. (Two of Judah's sons, Er and Onan, had died in the land of Canaan.) [22]These clans numbered 76,500 men.

[23]The tribe of Issachar: the clans of Tola, Puah, [24]Jashub, and Shimron. [25]These clans numbered 64,300 men.

[26]The tribe of Zebulun: the clans of Sered, Elon, and Jahleel. [27]These clans numbered 60,500 men.

[28]The tribes of Joseph, who was the father of two sons, Manasseh and Ephraim.

[29]The tribe of Manasseh. Machir son of Manasseh was the father of Gilead, and the following clans traced their ancestry to Gilead: [30]the clans of Iezer, Helek, [31]Asriel, Shechem, [32]Shemida, and Hepher. [33]Zelophehad son of Hepher had no sons, but only daughters; their names were Mahlah, Noah, Hoglah, Milcah, and Tirzah. [34]These clans numbered 52,700 men.

[35]The tribe of Ephraim: the clans of Shuthelah, Becher, and Tahan. [36]The clan of Eran traced its descent from Shuthelah. [37]These clans numbered 32,500 men.

These are the clans descended from Joseph.

[38]The tribe of Benjamin: the clans of Bela, Ashbel, Ahiram, [39]Shephupham, and Hupham. [40]The clans of Ard and Naaman traced their descent from Bela. [41]These clans numbered 45,600 men.

[42]The tribe of Dan: the clan of Shuham, [43]which numbered 64,400 men.

[44]The tribe of Asher: the clans of Imnah, Ishvi, and Beriah. [45]The clans of Heber and Malchiel traced their descent from Beriah. [46]Asher had a daughter named Serah. [47]These clans numbered 53,400 men.

[48]The tribe of Naphtali: the clans of Jahzeel, Guni, [49]Jezer, and Shillem. [50]These clans numbered 45,400 men.

[51]The total number of the Israelite men was 601,730.

[52]The LORD said to Moses, [53]"Divide the land among the tribes, according to their size. [54-56]Divide the land by drawing lots,

and give a large share to a large tribe and a small one to a small tribe."

[57]The tribe of Levi consisted of the clans of Gershon, Kohath, and Merari. [58]Their descendants included the subclans of Libni, Hebron, Mahli, Mushi, and Korah. Kohath was the father of Amram, [59]who was married to Levi's daughter Jochebed, who was born in Egypt. She bore Amram two sons, Aaron and Moses, and a daughter, Miriam. [60]Aaron had four sons, Nadab, Abihu, Eleazar, and Ithamar. [61]Nadab and Abihu died when they offered unholy fire to the LORD. [62]The male Levites who were one month old or older numbered 23,000. They were listed separately from the rest of the Israelites, because they were not given any property in Israel.

[63]All these clans were listed by Moses and Eleazar when they took a census of the Israelites in the plains of Moab across the Jordan River from Jericho. [64]There was not even one man left among those whom Moses and Aaron had listed in the first census in the Sinai Desert. [65]The LORD had said that all of them would die in the wilderness, and except for Caleb son of Jephunneh and Joshua son of Nun they all did.

The Daughters of Zelophehad

27 [1]Mahlah, Noah, Hoglah, Milcah, and Tirzah were the daughters of Zelophehad son of Hepher, son of Gilead, son of Machir, son of Manasseh, son of Joseph. [2]They went and stood before Moses, Eleazar the priest, the leaders, and the whole community at the entrance of the Tent of the LORD's presence and said, [3]"Our father died in the wilderness without leaving any sons. He was not among the followers of Korah, who rebelled against the LORD; he died because of his own sin. [4]Just because he had no sons, why should our father's name disappear from Israel? Give us property among our father's relatives."

[5]Moses presented their case to the LORD, [6]and the LORD said to him, [7]"What the daughters of Zelophehad request is right; give them property among their father's rela-

Take Joshua . . . a capable man. (27:18)

tives. Let his inheritance pass on to them. ⁸Tell the people of Israel that whenever a man dies without leaving a son, his daughter is to inherit his property. ⁹If he has no daughter, his brothers are to inherit it. ¹⁰If he has no brothers, his father's brothers are to inherit it. ¹¹If he has no brothers or uncles, then his nearest relative is to inherit it and hold it as his own property. The people of Israel are to observe this as a legal requirement, just as I, the LORD, have commanded you."

Joshua Is Chosen as Successor to Moses
(Deuteronomy 31:1–8)

¹²The LORD said to Moses, "Go up the Abarim Mountains and look out over the land that I am giving to the Israelites. ¹³After you have seen it, you will die, as your brother Aaron did, ¹⁴because both of you rebelled against my command in the wilderness of Zin. When the whole community complained against me at Meribah, you refused to acknowledge my holy power before

them." (Meribah is the spring at Kadesh in the wilderness of Zin.)

¹⁵Moses prayed, ¹⁶" LORD God, source of all life, appoint, I pray, a man who can lead the people ¹⁷and can command them in battle, so that your community will not be like sheep without a shepherd."

¹⁸The LORD said to Moses, "Take Joshua son of Nun, a capable man, and place your hands on his head. ¹⁹Have him stand in front of Eleazar the priest and the whole community, and there before them all proclaim him as your successor. ²⁰Give him some of your own authority, so that the whole community of Israel will obey him. ²¹He will depend on Eleazar the priest, who will learn my will by using the Urim and Thummim.ᵍ In this way Eleazar will direct Joshua and the whole community of Israel in all their affairs." ²²Moses did as the LORD had commanded him. He had Joshua stand before Eleazar the priest and the whole community. ²³As the LORD had commanded, Moses put his hands on Joshua's head and proclaimed him as his successor.

ᵍ **27:21** URIM AND THUMMIM: *Two objects used by the priest to determine God's will; it is not known precisely how they were used.*
27:12–14 Deut 3:23–27; 32:48–52   **27:17** 1 Kings 22:17; Ezek 34:5; Mt 9:36; Mk 6:34   **27:18** Ex 24:13
27:21 Ex 28:30; 1 Sam 14:41; 28:6   **27:23** Deut 31:23

The Regular Offerings
(Exodus 29:38–46)

28 ¹The LORD commanded Moses ²to instruct the Israelites to present to God at the appointed times the required food offerings that are pleasing to him.

³These are the food offerings that are to be presented to the LORD: for the daily burnt offering, two one-year-old male lambs without any defects. ⁴Offer the first lamb in the morning, and the second in the evening, ⁵each with a grain offering of 2 pounds of flour, mixed with 2 pints of the best olive oil. ⁶This is the daily offering that is completely burned, which was first offered at Mount Sinai as a food offering, an odor pleasing to the LORD. ⁷As the wine offering with the first lamb, pour out at the altar 2 pints of wine. ⁸In the evening offer the second lamb in the same way as the morning offering, together with its wine offering. It also is a food offering, an odor pleasing to the LORD.

The Sabbath Offering

⁹On the Sabbath day offer two one-year-old male lambs without any defects, 4 pounds of flour mixed with olive oil as a grain offering, and the wine offering. ¹⁰This burnt offering is to be offered every Sabbath in addition to the daily offering with its wine offering.

The Offering on the First Day of the Month

¹¹Present a burnt offering to the LORD at the beginning of each month: two young bulls, one ram, seven one-year-old male lambs, all without any defects. ¹²As a grain offering, offer flour mixed with olive oil: with each bull, 6 pounds of flour; with the ram, 4 pounds; ¹³and with each lamb, 2 pounds. These burnt offerings are food offerings, an odor pleasing to the LORD. ¹⁴The proper wine offering is 4 pints of wine with each bull, 3 pints with the ram, and 2 pints with each lamb. This is the regulation for the burnt offering for the first day of each month throughout the year. ¹⁵And in addition to the daily burnt offering with its wine offering, offer one male goat as a sin offering.

The Offerings at the Festival of Unleavened Bread
(Leviticus 23:5–14)

¹⁶The Passover Festival in honor of the LORD is to be held on the fourteenth day of the first month. ¹⁷On the fifteenth day a religious festival begins which lasts seven days, during which only bread prepared without yeast is to be eaten. ¹⁸On the first day of the festival you are to gather for worship, and no work is to be done. ¹⁹Offer a burnt offering as a food offering to the LORD: two young bulls, one ram, and seven one-year-old male lambs, all without any defects. ²⁰Offer the proper grain offering of flour mixed with olive oil: 6 pounds with each bull, 4 pounds with the ram, ²¹and 2 pounds with each lamb. ²²Also offer one male goat as a sin offering, and in this way perform the ritual of purification for the people. ²³Offer these in addition to the regular morning burnt offering. ²⁴In the same way, for seven days offer to the LORD a food offering, an odor pleasing to him. Offer this in addition to the daily burnt offering and wine offering. ²⁵Meet for worship on the seventh day and do no work.

The Offerings at the Harvest Festival
(Leviticus 23:15–22)

²⁶On the first day of the Harvest Festival, when you present the offering of new grain to the LORD, you are to gather for worship, and no work is to be done. ²⁷Offer a burnt offering as an odor pleasing to the LORD: two young bulls, one ram, and seven one-year-old male lambs, all without any defects. ²⁸Offer the proper grain offering of flour mixed with olive oil: 6 pounds with each bull, 4 pounds with the ram, ²⁹and 2 pounds with each lamb. ³⁰Also offer one male goat as a sin offering, and in this way perform the ritual of purification for the people.

28:16 Ex 12:1–13; Deut 16:1, 2   **28:17–25** Ex 12:14–20; 23:15; 34:18; Deut 16:3–8   **28:26–31** Ex 23:16; 34:22; Deut 16:9–12

31 Offer these and the wine offering in addition to the daily burnt offering and grain offering.

The Offerings at the New Year Festival
(Leviticus 23:23–25)

29 ¹On the first day of the seventh month you are to gather for worship, and no work is to be done. On that day trumpets are to be blown. ²Present a burnt offering to the LORD, an odor pleasing to him: one young bull, one ram, and seven one-year-old male lambs, all without any defects. ³Offer the proper grain offering of flour mixed with olive oil: 6 pounds of flour with the bull, 4 pounds with the ram, ⁴and 2 pounds with each lamb. ⁵Also offer one male goat as a sin offering, and in this way perform the ritual of purification for the people. ⁶Offer these in addition to the regular burnt offering for the first day of the month with its grain offering, and the daily burnt offering with its grain offering and wine offering. These food offerings are an odor pleasing to the LORD.

The Offerings at the Day of Atonement
(Leviticus 23:26–32)

⁷Gather for worship on the tenth day of the seventh month; eat no food and do no work. ⁸Offer a burnt offering to the LORD, an odor pleasing to him: one young bull, one ram, and seven one-year-old male lambs, all without any defects. ⁹Offer the proper grain offering of flour mixed with olive oil: 6 pounds of flour with the bull, 4 pounds with the ram, ¹⁰and 2 pounds with each lamb. ¹¹Also offer one male goat as a sin offering, in addition to the goat offered in the ritual of purification for the people, and the daily burnt offering with its grain offering and wine offering.

The Offerings at the Festival of Shelters
(Leviticus 23:33–44)

¹²Gather for worship on the fifteenth day of the seventh month. Celebrate this festival in honor of the LORD for seven days and do no work. ¹³On this first day offer a food offering to the LORD, an odor pleasing to him: thirteen young bulls, two rams, and fourteen one-year-old male lambs, all without any defects. ¹⁴Offer the proper grain offering of flour mixed with olive oil: 6 pounds of flour with each bull, 4 pounds with each ram, ¹⁵and 2 pounds with each lamb, with the required wine offerings. ¹⁶Also offer one male goat as a sin offering. Offer these in addition to the daily burnt offering with its grain offering and wine offering.

¹⁷On the second day offer twelve young bulls, two rams, and fourteen one-year-old male lambs, all without any defects. ¹⁸⁻¹⁹Offer with them all the other offerings required for the first day.

²⁰On the third day offer eleven young bulls, two rams, and fourteen one-year-old male lambs, all without any defects. ²¹⁻²²Offer with them all the other offerings required for the first day.

²³On the fourth day offer ten young bulls, two rams, and fourteen one-year-old male lambs, all without any defects. ²⁴⁻²⁵Offer with them all the other offerings required for the first day.

²⁶On the fifth day offer nine young bulls, two rams, and fourteen one-year-old male lambs, all without any defects. ²⁷⁻²⁸Offer with them all the other offerings required for the first day.

²⁹On the sixth day offer eight young bulls, two rams, and fourteen one-year-old male lambs, all without any defects. ³⁰⁻³¹Offer with them all the other offerings required for the first day.

³²On the seventh day offer seven young bulls, two rams, and fourteen one-year-old male lambs, all without any defects. ³³⁻³⁴Offer with them all the other offerings required for the first day.

³⁵On the eighth day gather for worship

29:7–11 Lev 16:29–34   **29:12–38** Lev 23:34; Deut 16:13–15

Numbers

and do no work. 36Offer a burnt offering as a food offering to the LORD, an odor pleasing to him: one young bull, one ram, and seven one-year-old male lambs, all without any defects. 37-38Offer with them all the other offerings required for the first day.

39These are the regulations concerning the burnt offerings, grain offerings, wine offerings, and fellowship offerings that you are to make to the LORD at your appointed festivals. These are in addition to the offerings you give in fulfillment of a vow or as freewill offerings.

40So Moses told the people of Israel everything that the LORD had commanded him.

Rules about Vows

30 1Moses gave the following instructions to the leaders of the tribes of Israel. 2When a man makes a vow to give something to the LORD or takes an oath to abstain from something, he must not break his promise, but must do everything that he said he would.

3When a young woman still living in her father's house makes a vow to give something to the LORD or promises to abstain from something, 4she must do everything that she vowed or promised unless her father raises an objection when he hears about it. 5But if her father forbids her to fulfill the vow when he hears about it, she is not required to keep it. The LORD will forgive her, because her father refused to let her keep it.

6If an unmarried woman makes a vow, whether deliberately or carelessly, or promises to abstain from something, and then marries, 7she must do everything that she vowed or promised unless her husband raises an objection when he hears about it. 8But if her husband forbids her to fulfill the vow when he hears about it, she is not required to keep it. The LORD will forgive her.

9A widow or a divorced woman must keep every vow she makes and every promise to abstain from something.

10If a married woman makes a vow or promises to abstain from something, 11she must do everything that she vowed or promised unless her husband raises an objection when he hears about it. 12But if her husband forbids her to fulfill the vow when he hears about it, she is not required to keep it. The LORD will forgive her, because her husband prevented her from keeping her vow. 13Her husband has the right to affirm or to annul any vow or promise that she has made. 14But if, by the day after he hears of the vow, he has raised no objection, she must do everything that she has vowed or promised. He has affirmed the vow by not objecting on the day he heard of it. 15But if he later annuls the vow, he must suffer the consequences for the failure to fulfill the vow.

16These are the rules that the LORD gave Moses concerning vows made by an unmarried woman living in her father's house or by a married woman.

The Holy War against Midian

31 1The LORD said to Moses, 2"Punish the Midianites for what they did to the people of Israel. After you have done that, you will die."

3So Moses said to the people, "Get ready for war, so that you can attack Midian and punish them for what they did to the LORD. 4From each tribe of Israel send a thousand men to war."

5So a thousand men were chosen from each tribe, a total of twelve thousand men ready for battle. 6Moses sent them to war under the command of Phinehas son of Eleazar the priest, who took charge of the sacred objects and the trumpets for giving signals. 7They attacked Midian, as the LORD had commanded Moses, and killed all the men, 8including the five kings of Midian: Evi, Rekem, Zur, Hur, and Reba. They also killed Balaam son of Beor.

9The people of Israel captured the Midianite women and children, took their cattle and their flocks, plundered all their wealth, 10and burned all their cities and camps. 11They took all the loot that they had captured, including the prisoners and the animals, 12and brought them to Moses and

30:2 Deut 23:21–23; Mt 5:33

Eleazar and to the community of the people of Israel, who were at the camp on the plains of Moab across the Jordan from Jericho.

The Army Returns

13 Moses, Eleazar, and all the other leaders of the community went out of the camp to meet the army. 14 Moses became angry with the officers, the commanders of battalions and companies, who had returned from the war. 15 He asked them, "Why have you kept all the women alive? 16 Remember that it was the women who followed Balaam's instructions and at Peor led the people to be unfaithful to the LORD. That was what brought the epidemic on the LORD's people. 17 So now kill every boy and kill every woman who has had sexual intercourse, 18 but keep alive for yourselves all the girls and all the women who are virgins. 19 Now all of you who have killed anyone or have touched a corpse must stay outside the camp for seven days. On the third day and on the seventh day purify yourselves and the women you have captured. 20 You must also purify every piece of clothing and everything made of leather, goats' hair, or wood."

21 Eleazar the priest said to the men who had returned from battle, "These are the regulations that the LORD has given to Moses. 22-23 Everything that will not burn, such as gold, silver, bronze, iron, tin, or lead, is to be purified by passing it through fire. Everything else is to be purified by the water for purification. 24 On the seventh day you must wash your clothes; then you will be ritually clean and will be permitted to enter the camp."

Division of the Loot

25 The LORD said to Moses, 26 "You and Eleazar, together with the other leaders of the community, are to count everything that has been captured, including the prisoners and the animals. 27 Divide what was taken into two equal parts, one part for the soldiers and the other part for the rest of the community. 28 From the part that belongs to the

soldiers, withhold as a tax for the LORD one out of every five hundred prisoners and the same proportion of the cattle, donkeys, sheep, and goats. 29 Give them to Eleazar the priest as a special contribution to the LORD. 30 From the part given to the rest of the people, take one out of every fifty prisoners and the same proportion of the cattle, donkeys, sheep, and goats. Give them to the Levites who are in charge of the LORD's Tent." 31 Moses and Eleazar did what the LORD commanded.

32-35 The following is a list of what was captured by the soldiers, in addition to what they kept for themselves: 675,000 sheep and goats, 72,000 cattle, 61,000 donkeys, and 32,000 virgins. 36-40 The half share of the soldiers was 337,500 sheep and goats, of which 675 were the tax for the LORD; 36,000 cattle for the soldiers, of which 72 were the tax for the LORD; 30,500 donkeys for the soldiers, of which 61 were the tax for the LORD; and 16,000 virgins for the soldiers, of which 32 were the tax for the LORD. 41 So Moses gave Eleazar the tax as a special contribution to the LORD, as the LORD had commanded.

42-46 The share of the community was the same as that for the soldiers: 337,500 sheep and goats, 36,000 cattle, 30,500 donkeys, and 16,000 virgins. 47 From this share Moses took one out of every fifty prisoners and animals, and as the LORD had commanded, gave them to the Levites who were in charge of the LORD's Tent.

48 Then the officers who had commanded the army went to Moses 49 and reported, "Sir, we have counted the soldiers under our command and not one of them is missing. 50 So we are bringing the gold ornaments, armlets, bracelets, rings, earrings, and necklaces that each of us has taken. We offer them to the LORD as a payment for our lives, so that he will protect us." 51 Moses and Eleazar received the gold, all of which was in the form of ornaments. 52 The total contribution of the officers weighed over four hundred pounds. 53 Those who were not officers kept the loot they had taken. 54 So Moses and Eleazar took the gold to the Tent, so that the LORD would protect the people of Israel.

The gold ornaments. (31:50)

The Tribes East of the Jordan
(Deuteronomy 3:12–22)

32 ¹The tribes of Reuben and Gad had a lot of livestock. When they saw how suitable the land of Jazer and Gilead was for cattle, ²they went to Moses, Eleazar, and the other leaders of the community and said, ³⁻⁴"This region which the LORD has helped the Israelites occupy—the towns of Ataroth, Dibon, Jazer, Nimrah, Heshbon, Elealeh, Sibmah, Nebo, and Beon—is good land for livestock, and we have so much livestock. ⁵Please give us this land as our property, and do not make us cross the Jordan River and settle there."

⁶Moses replied, "Do you want to stay here while the other Israelites go to war? ⁷How dare you try to discourage the people of Israel from crossing the Jordan into the land which the LORD has given them? ⁸That is what your fathers did when I sent them from Kadesh Barnea to explore the land. ⁹They went as far as Eshcol Valley and saw the land, but when they returned, they discouraged the people from entering the land which the LORD had given them. ¹⁰The LORD became angry that day and made a promise: ¹¹'I swear that because they did not remain loyal to me, none of the men twenty years old or older who came out of Egypt will enter the land that I promised to Abraham, Isaac, and Jacob.' ¹²This included everyone, except Caleb son of Jephunneh the Kenizzite and Joshua son of Nun; they remained loyal to the LORD. ¹³The LORD became angry with the people and made them wander in the wilderness forty years until that whole generation that had dis-

pleased him was dead. ¹⁴And now you have taken your ancestors' place, a new generation of sinful people ready to bring down the fierce anger of the LORD on Israel again. ¹⁵If you people of Reuben and Gad refuse to follow him now, he will once again abandon all these people in the wilderness, and you will be responsible for their destruction."

¹⁶They approached Moses and said, "First, allow us to build stone enclosures here for our sheep and fortified towns for our dependents. ¹⁷Then we will be ready to go with the other Israelites into battle and lead the attack until we have settled them in the land that will be theirs. In the meantime, our dependents can live here in the fortified towns, safe from the people of this land. ¹⁸We will not return to our homes until all the other Israelites have taken possession of the land assigned to them. ¹⁹We will not take possession of any property among them on the other side of the Jordan, because we have received our share here east of the Jordan."

²⁰Moses answered, "If you really mean what you say, then here in the presence of the LORD get ready to go into battle. ²¹All your fighting men are to cross the Jordan and under the command of the LORD they are to attack our enemies until the LORD defeats them ²²and takes possession of the land. After that, you may return, because you will have fulfilled your obligation to the LORD and to the other Israelites. Then the LORD will acknowledge that this land east of the Jordan is yours. ²³But if you do not keep your promise, I warn you that you will be sinning against the LORD. Make no mistake about it; you will be punished for your sin. ²⁴So build your towns and the enclosures for your sheep, but do what you have promised!"

²⁵The men of Gad and Reuben said, "Sir, we will do as you command. ²⁶Our wives and children and our cattle and sheep will remain here in the towns of Gilead. ²⁷But all of us are ready to go into battle under the LORD's command. We will cross the Jordan and fight, just as you have said."

²⁸So Moses gave these commands to Eleazar, Joshua, and the other leaders of Israel: ²⁹"If the men of Gad and Reuben

cross the Jordan ready for battle at the LORD's command and if with their help you are able to conquer the land, then give them the land of Gilead as their property. ³⁰But if they do not cross the Jordan and go into battle with you, they are to receive their share of the property in the land of Canaan, as you do."

³¹The men of Gad and Reuben answered, "Sir, we will do as the LORD has commanded. ³²Under his command we will cross into the land of Canaan and go into battle, so that we can retain our property here east of the Jordan."

³³So Moses assigned to the tribes of Gad and Reuben and to half the tribe of Manasseh all the territory of King Sihon of the Amorites and King Og of Bashan, including the towns and the country around them. ³⁴The tribe of Gad rebuilt the fortified towns of Dibon, Ataroth, Aroer, ³⁵Atroth Shophan, Jazer, Jogbehah, ³⁶Beth Nimrah, and Beth Haran. ³⁷The tribe of Reuben rebuilt Heshbon, Elealeh, Kiriathaim, ³⁸Nebo, Baal Meon (this name was changed), and Sibmah. They gave new names to the towns they rebuilt.

³⁹The clan of Machir son of Manasseh invaded the land of Gilead, occupied it, and drove out the Amorites who were there. ⁴⁰So Moses gave Gilead to the clan of Machir, and they lived there. ⁴¹Jair, of the tribe of Manasseh, attacked and captured some villages and named them "Villages of Jair." ⁴²Nobah attacked and captured Kenath and its villages, and he renamed it Nobah, after himself.

The Journey from Egypt to Moab

33 ¹The following account gives the names of the places where the Israelites set up camp after they left Egypt in their tribes under the leadership of Moses and Aaron. ²At the command of the LORD, Moses wrote down the name of the place each time they set up camp.

³The people of Israel left Egypt on the fifteenth day of the first month of the year, the day after the first Passover. Under the LORD's protection they left the city of Rameses in full view of the Egyptians, ⁴who were burying the first-born sons that the LORD had killed. By doing this, the LORD showed that he was more powerful than the gods of Egypt.

⁵The people of Israel left Rameses and set up camp at Sukkoth. ⁶Their next camp was at Etham on the edge of the desert. ⁷From there they turned back to Pi Hahiroth, east of Baal Zephon, and camped near Migdol. ⁸They left Pi Hahiroth and passed through the Red Sea*ʰ* into the desert of Shur; after a three days' march they camped at Marah. ⁹From there they went to Elim, where they camped, because there were twelve springs of water and seventy palm trees there.

¹⁰They left Elim and camped near the Gulf of Suez. ¹¹Their next camp was in the desert of Sin. ¹²Then they camped at Dophkah, ¹³and after that at Alush. ¹⁴Next was Rephidim, where there was no water for them to drink.

¹⁵⁻³⁷From Rephidim to Mount Hor they set up camp at the following places: the Sinai Desert, Kibroth Hattaavah (or "Graves of Craving"), Hazeroth, Rithmah, Rimmon Perez, Libnah, Rissah, Kehelathah, Mount Shepher, Haradah, Makheloth, Tahath, Terah, Mithkah, Hashmonah, Moseroth, Bene Jaakan, Hor Haggidgad, Jotbathah, Abronah, Eziongeber, the wilderness of Zin (that is, Kadesh), and Mount Hor, at the edge of the land of Edom.

³⁸⁻³⁹At the command of the LORD, Aaron the priest climbed Mount Hor. At the age of 123 he died there on the first day of the fifth month of the fortieth year after the Israelites had left Egypt.

⁴⁰The king of Arad in southern Canaan heard that the Israelites were coming.

⁴¹⁻⁴⁹From Mount Hor to the plains of Moab the Israelites set up camp at the following places: Zalmonah, Punon, Oboth, the ruins of Abarim in the territory of Moab, Dibon Gad, Almon Diblathaim, the Abarim Mountains near Mount Nebo, and in the plains of Moab across the Jordan River from Jericho, between Beth Jeshimoth and Acacia Valley.

ʰ **33:8** RED SEA: *See Word List.*
33:38 Num 20:22–28; Deut 10:6; 32:50   **33:40** Num 21:1

Instructions before Crossing the Jordan

50There in the plains of Moab across the Jordan from Jericho the LORD gave Moses 51the following instructions for Israel: "When you cross the Jordan into the land of Canaan, 52you must drive out all the inhabitants of the land. Destroy all their stone and metal idols and all their places of worship. 53Occupy the land and settle in it, because I am giving it to you. 54Divide the land among the various tribes and clans by drawing lots, giving a large piece of property to a large clan and a small one to a small clan. 55But if you do not drive out the inhabitants of the land, those that are left will be as troublesome as splinters in your eyes and thorns in your sides, and they will fight against you. 56If you do not drive them out, I will destroy you, as I planned to destroy them."

The Boundaries of the Land

34 1The LORD gave Moses 2the following instructions for the people of Israel: "When you enter Canaan, the land which I am giving you, the borders of your territory will be as follows. 3The southern border will extend from the wilderness of Zin along the border of Edom. It will begin on the east at the southern end of the Dead Sea. 4Then it will turn southward toward Akrabbim Pass and continue on through Zin as far south as Kadesh Barnea. Then it will turn northwest to Hazar Addar and on to Azmon, 5where it will turn toward the valley at the border of Egypt and end at the Mediterranean.

6"The western border will be the Mediterranean Sea.

7"The northern border will follow a line from the Mediterranean to Mount Hor 8and from there to Hamath Pass. It will continue to Zedad 9and to Ziphron, and will end at Hazar Enan.

10"The eastern border will follow a line from Hazar Enan to Shepham. 11It will then go south to Harbel, east of Ain, and on to the hills on the eastern shore of Lake Galilee, 12then south along the Jordan River to the Dead Sea.

"These will be the four borders of your land."

13So Moses said to the Israelites, "This is the land that you will receive by drawing lots, the land that the LORD has assigned to the nine and one-half tribes. 14The tribes of Reuben and Gad and the eastern half of Manasseh have received their property, divided according to their families, 15on the eastern side of the Jordan, opposite Jericho."

The Leaders Responsible for Dividing the Land

16The LORD said to Moses, 17"Eleazar the priest and Joshua son of Nun will divide the land for the people. 18Take also one leader from each tribe to help them divide it." 19-28These are the men the LORD chose:

Tribe	Leader
Judah	Caleb son of Jephunneh
Simeon	Shelumiel son of Ammihud
Benjamin	Elidad son of Chislon
Dan	Bukki son of Jogli
Manasseh	Hanniel son of Ephod
Ephraim	Kemuel son of Shiphtan
Zebulun	Elizaphan son of Parnach
Issachar	Paltiel son of Azzan
Asher	Ahihud son of Shelomi
Naphtali	Pedahel son of Ammihud

29These are the men that the LORD assigned to divide the property for the people of Israel in the land of Canaan.

The Cities Assigned to the Levites

35 1In the plains of Moab across the Jordan from Jericho the LORD said to Moses, 2"Tell the Israelites that from the property they receive they must give the Levites some cities to live in and pasture land around the cities. 3These cities will belong to the Levites, and they will live there. The pasture land will be for their cattle and all their other animals. 4The pasture land is to extend outward from the city walls five hundred yards in each direction, 5so that

33:54 Num 26:54–56   34:13 Num 26:52–56   34:13–15 Josh 14:1–5   35:1–8 Josh 21:1–42 there is a square area measuring one thousand yards on each side, with the city in the middle. 6 You are to give the Levites six cities of refuge to which any of you can escape if you kill someone accidentally. In addition, give them forty-two other cities 7 with their pasture land, making a total of forty-eight. 8 The number of Levite cities in each tribe is to be determined according to the size of its territory."

The Cities of Refuge
(Deuteronomy 19:1–13; Joshua 20:1–9)

9 The LORD told Moses 10 to say to the people of Israel: "When you cross the Jordan River and enter the land of Canaan, 11 you are to choose cities of refuge to which any of you can escape if you kill someone accidentally. 12 There you will be safe from the dead person's relative who seeks revenge. No one accused of manslaughter is to be put to death without a public trial. 13 Choose six cities, 14 three east of the Jordan and three in the land of Canaan. 15 These will serve as cities of refuge for Israelites and for foreigners who are temporary or permanent residents. Anyone who kills someone accidentally can escape to one of them.

16-18 "If, however, any of you use a weapon of iron or stone or wood to kill someone, you are guilty of murder and are to be put to death. 19 The dead person's nearest relative has the responsibility for putting the murderer to death. When he finds you, he is to kill you.

20 "If you hate someone and kill him by pushing him down or by throwing something at him 21 or by striking him with your fist, you are guilty of murder and are to be put to death. The dead person's nearest relative has the responsibility for putting the murderer to death. When he finds you, he is to kill you.

22 "But suppose you accidentally kill someone you do not hate, whether by pushing him down or by throwing something at him. 23 Or suppose that, without looking, you throw a stone that kills someone whom you did not intend to hurt and who was not your enemy. 24 In such cases the community shall judge in your favor and not in favor of the dead person's relative who is seeking revenge. 25 You are guilty only of manslaughter, and the community is to rescue you from the dead person's relative, and they are to return you to the city of refuge to which you had escaped. You must live there until the death of the man who is then High Priest. 26 If you leave the city of refuge to which you have escaped 27 and if the dead person's relative finds you and kills you, this act of revenge is not murder. 28 Any of you guilty of manslaughter must remain in the city of refuge until the death of the High Priest, but after that you may return home. 29 These rules apply to you and your descendants wherever you may live.

30 "Those accused of murder may be found guilty and put to death only on the evidence of two or more witnesses; the evidence of one witness is not sufficient to support an accusation of murder. 31 Murderers must be put to death. They cannot escape this penalty by the payment of money. 32 If they have fled to a city of refuge, do not allow them to make a payment in order to return home before the death of the High Priest. 33 If you did this, you would defile the land where you are living. Murder defiles the land, and except by the death of the murderer there is no way to perform the ritual of purification for the land where someone has been murdered. 34 Do not defile the land where you are living, because I am the LORD and I live among the people of Israel."

The Inheritance of Married Women

36 1 The heads of the families in the clan of Gilead, the son of Machir and grandson of Manasseh son of Joseph, went to Moses and the other leaders. 2 They said, "The LORD commanded you to distribute the land to the people of Israel by drawing lots. He also commanded you to give the property of our relative Zelophehad to his daughters. 3 But remember, if they marry men of another tribe, their property will then belong to that tribe, and the total

35:9–28 Deut 19:2–4; Jas 20:1–9   **35:30** Deut 17:6; 19:15   **36:2** Num 27:7

allotted to us will be reduced. ⁴In the Year of Restoration, when all property that has been sold is restored to its original owners, the property of Zelophehad's daughters will be permanently added to the tribe into which they marry and will be lost to our tribe."

⁵So Moses gave the people of Israel the following command from the LORD. He said, "What the tribe of Manasseh says is right, ⁶and so the LORD says that the daughters of Zelophehad are free to marry anyone they wish but only within their own tribe. ⁷The property of every Israelite will remain attached to his tribe. ⁸Every woman who inherits property in an Israelite tribe must marry a man belonging to that tribe. In this way all Israelites will inherit the property of their ancestors, ⁹and the property will not pass from one tribe to another. Each tribe will continue to possess its own property."

¹⁰⁻¹¹So Mahlah, Tirzah, Hoglah, Milcah, and Noah, the daughters of Zelophehad, did as the LORD had commanded Moses, and they married their cousins. ¹²They married within the clans of the tribe of Manasseh son of Joseph, and their property remained in their father's tribe.

¹³These are the rules and regulations that the LORD gave the Israelites through Moses in the plains of Moab across the Jordan River from Jericho.

Has your family ever had to move to a brand new city where you didn't know anyone? If you have, you know that you can feel both scared and excited at the same time. So picture a whole nation of people about to enter a foreign country, and not sure what kind of welcome they are going to receive. This was the situation of the Israelites after their years of wandering in the desert. They were feeling both excited and afraid and needed a morale boost. Deuteronomy is made up of Moses' last words of encouragement to the Israelites before he dies and turns over the leadership to Joshua.

Before Moses gives his final blessing, he tells the people that they have to choose—life or death, blessings or curses, faithfulness to God or disobedience. Moses encourages them to choose life by loving and holding fast to God so that they and their children may live and prosper in the land that God promised.

Chap. 34

Headlines

- Obedience Has Its Rewards (4:1–14)
- Remember This One Thing (6:4–9)
- Don't Make God Angry Again! (chapter 9)
- Seven Is the Magic Number (15:1–11)
- Remember to Celebrate! (16:1–17)
- Be Sexually Pure (22:13–30)
- Moses' Final Farewell (32:45–52)

FACTOIDS

Who wrote this book? It was written by elders or scribes who summarized the first Law given to the Israelites in the desert to meet the Israelites' changing needs. *Deuteronomy* means a "second Law."

When was it written? During the Babylonian exile, while the Israelites were figuring out how to preserve their laws and beliefs.

Why was it written? Deuteronomy was written to encourage the people to have hope and to trust in their Covenant relationship with God.

What is the Jesus connection? Jesus quotes Deuteronomy 6:4–9 when asked about the greatest commandment. See Matthew 22:37–39.

Important themes

- God promises to bless those who are faithful.
- God's people are called to protect the weak, feed and clothe poor people, bring justice for widows and orphans, and welcome the stranger.

DEUTERONOMY

Introduction

1 ¹In this book are the words that Moses spoke to the people of Israel when they were in the wilderness east of the Jordan River. They were in the Jordan Valley near Suph, between the town of Paran on one side and the towns of Tophel, Laban, Hazeroth, and Dizahab on the other. (²It takes eleven days to travel from Mount Sinai to Kadesh Barnea by way of the hill country of Edom.) ³On the first day of the eleventh month of the fortieth year after they had left Egypt, Moses told the people everything the LORD had commanded him to tell them. ⁴This was after the LORD*a* had defeated King Sihon of the Amorites, who ruled in the town of Heshbon, and King Og of Bashan, who ruled in the towns of Ashtaroth and Edrei. ⁵It was while the people were east of the Jordan in the territory of Moab that Moses began to explain God's laws and teachings.

He said, ⁶"When we were at Mount Sinai, the LORD our God said to us, 'You have stayed long enough at this mountain. ⁷Break camp and move on. Go to the hill country of the Amorites and to all the surrounding regions—to the Jordan Valley, to the hill country and the lowlands, to the southern region, and to the Mediterranean coast. Go to the land of Canaan and on beyond the Lebanon Mountains as far as the great Euphrates River. ⁸All of this is the land which I, the LORD, promised to give to your ancestors, Abraham, Isaac, and Jacob, and to their descendants. Go and occupy it.' "

Moses Appoints Judges
(Exodus 18:13–27)

⁹Moses said to the people, "While we were still at Mount Sinai, I told you, 'The responsibility for leading you is too much for me. I can't do it alone. ¹⁰The LORD your God has made you as numerous as the stars in the sky. ¹¹May the LORD, the God of your ancestors, make you increase a thousand times more and make you prosperous, as he promised! ¹²But how can I alone bear the heavy responsibility for settling your disputes? ¹³Choose some wise, understanding, and experienced men from each tribe, and I will put them in charge of you.' ¹⁴And you agreed that this was a good thing to do. ¹⁵So I took the wise and experienced leaders you chose from your tribes, and I placed them in charge of you. Some were responsible for a thousand people, some for a hundred, some for fifty, and some for ten. I also appointed other officials throughout the tribes.

¹⁶"At that time I instructed them, 'Listen to the disputes that come up among your people. Judge every dispute fairly, whether it concerns only your own people or involves foreigners who live among you. ¹⁷Show no partiality in your decisions; judge everyone on the same basis, no matter who they are. Do not be afraid of anyone, for the decisions you make come from God. If any case is too difficult for you, bring it to me, and I will decide it.' ¹⁸At the same time I gave you instructions for everything else you were to do.

The Spies Are Sent Out from Kadesh Barnea
(Numbers 13:1–33)

¹⁹"We did what the LORD our God commanded us. We left Mount Sinai and went through that vast and fearful desert on the way to the hill country of the Amorites. When we reached Kadesh Barnea, ²⁰⁻²¹I told you, 'You have now come to the hill country of the Amorites, which the LORD our God, the God of our ancestors, is giving us. Look, there it is. Go and occupy it as he commanded. Do not hesitate or be afraid.'

²²"But you came to me and said, 'Let's send men ahead of us to spy out the land, so

---

a **1:4** the LORD; *or* Moses.
1:4 Num 21:21–35

that they can tell us the best route to take and what kind of cities are there.'

23 "That seemed like a good thing to do, so I selected twelve men, one from each tribe. **24** They went into the hill country as far as Eshcol Valley and explored it. **25** They brought us back some fruit they found there, and reported that the land which the LORD our God was giving us was very fertile.

26 "But you rebelled against the command of the LORD your God, and you would not enter the land. **27** You grumbled to one another: 'The LORD hates us. He brought us out of Egypt just to hand us over to these Amorites, so that they could kill us. **28** Why should we go there? We are afraid. The men we sent tell us that the people there are stronger and taller than we are, and that they live in cities with walls that reach the sky. They saw giants there!'

29 "But I told you, 'Don't be afraid of those people. **30** The LORD your God will lead you, and he will fight for you, just as you saw him do in Egypt **31** and in the desert. You saw how he brought you safely all the way to this place, just as a father would carry his son.' **32** But in spite of what I said, you still would not trust the LORD, **33** even though he always went ahead of you to find a place for you to camp. To show you the way, he went in front of you in a pillar of fire by night and in a pillar of cloud by day.

The LORD Punishes Israel
(Numbers 14:20–45)

34 "The LORD heard your complaints and became angry, and so he solemnly declared, **35** 'Not one of you from this evil generation will enter the fertile land that I promised to give your ancestors. **36** Only Caleb son of Jephunneh will enter it. He has remained faithful to me, and I will give him and his descendants the land that he has explored.' **37** Because of you the LORD also became angry with me and said, 'Not even you, Moses, will enter the land. **38** But strengthen the determination of your helper, Joshua son of Nun. He will lead Israel to occupy the land.'

39 "Then the LORD said to all of us, 'Your children, who are still too young to know right from wrong, will enter the land– the children you said would be seized by your enemies. I will give the land to them, and they will occupy it. **40** But as for you people, turn around and go back into the desert on the road to the Gulf of Aqaba.'

41 "You replied, 'Moses, we have sinned against the LORD. But now we will attack, just as the LORD our God commanded us.' Then each one of you got ready to fight, thinking it would be easy to invade the hill country.

42 "But the LORD said to me, 'Warn them not to attack, for I will not be with them, and their enemies will defeat them.' **43** I told you what the LORD had said, but you paid no attention. You rebelled against him, and in your pride you marched into the hill country. **44** Then the Amorites who lived in those hills came out against you like a swarm of bees. They chased you as far as Hormah and defeated you there in the hill country of Edom. **45** So you cried out to the LORD for help, but he would not listen to you or pay any attention to you.

The Years in the Desert

46 "So then, after we had stayed at Kadesh for a long time, **1** we finally turned and went into the desert, on the road to the Gulf of Aqaba, as the LORD had commanded, and we spent a long time wandering about in the hill country of Edom.

2 "Then the LORD told me **3** that we had spent enough time wandering about in those hills and that we should go north. **4** He told me to give you the following instructions 'You are about to go through the hill country of Edom, the territory of your distant relatives, the descendants of Esau. They will be afraid of you, **5** but you must not start a war with them, because I am not going to give you so much as a square foot of their land. I have given Edom to Esau's descendants. **6** You may buy food and water from them.'

7 "Remember how the LORD your God has blessed you in everything that you have done. He has taken care of you as you wandered through this vast desert. He has been with you these forty years, and you have had everything you needed.

8 "So we moved on and left the road that goes from the towns of Elath and Eziongeber to the Dead Sea, and we turned northeast toward Moab. 9 The LORD said to me, 'Don't trouble the people of Moab, the descendants of Lot, or start a war against them. I have given them the city of Ar, and I am not going to give you any of their land.' "

(10 A mighty race of giants called the Emim used to live in Ar. They were as tall as the Anakim, another race of giants. 11 Like the Anakim they were also known as Rephaim; but the Moabites called them Emim. 12 The Horites used to live in Edom, but the descendants of Esau chased them out, destroyed their nation, and settled there themselves, just as the Israelites later chased their enemies out of the land that the LORD gave them.)

13 "Then we crossed the Zered River as the LORD told us to do. 14 This was thirty-eight years after we had left Kadesh Barnea. All the fighting men of that generation had died, as the LORD had said they would. 15 The LORD kept on opposing them until he had destroyed them all.

16 "After they had all died, 17 the LORD said to us, 18 'Today you are to pass through the territory of Moab by way of Ar. 19 You will then be near the land of the Ammonites, the descendants of Lot. Don't trouble them or start a war against them, because I am not going to give you any of the land that I have given them.' "

(20 This territory is also known as the land of the Rephaim, the name of the people who used to live there; the Ammonites called them Zamzummim. 21 They were as tall as the Anakim. There were many of them, and they were a mighty race. But the LORD destroyed them, so that the Ammonites took over their land and settled there. 22 The LORD had done the same thing for the Edomites, the descendants of Esau, who live in the hill country of Edom. He destroyed the Horites, so that the Edomites took over their land and settled there, where they still live. 23 The land along the Mediterranean coast had been settled by people from the island of Crete. They had destroyed the Avvim, the original inhabitants, and had taken over all their land as far south as the city of Gaza.)

24 "After we had passed through Moab, the LORD told us, 'Now, start out and cross the Arnon River. I am placing in your power Sihon, the Amorite king of Heshbon, along with his land. Attack him, and begin occupying his land. 25 From today on I will make people everywhere afraid of you. Everyone will tremble with fear at the mention of your name.'

Israel Defeats King Sihon
(Numbers 21:21–30)

26 "Then I sent messengers from the desert of Kedemoth to King Sihon of Heshbon with the following offer of peace: 27 'Let us pass through your country. We will go straight through and not leave the road. 28 We will pay for the food we eat and the water we drink. All we want to do is to pass through your country, 29 until we cross the Jordan River into the land that the LORD our God is giving us. The descendants of Esau, who live in Edom, and the Moabites, who live in Ar, allowed us to pass through their territory.'

30 "But King Sihon would not let us pass through his country. The LORD your God had made him stubborn and rebellious, so that we could defeat him and take his territory, which we still occupy.

31 "Then the LORD said to me, 'Look, I have made King Sihon and his land helpless before you; take his land and occupy it.' 32 Sihon came out with all his men to fight us near the town of Jahaz, 33 but the LORD our God put him in our power, and we killed him, his sons, and all his men. 34 At the same time we captured and destroyed every town, and put everyone to death, men, women, and children. We left no survivors. 35 We took the livestock and plundered the towns. 36 The LORD our God let us capture

all the towns from Aroer, on the edge of the Arnon Valley, and the city in the middle of that valley, all the way to Gilead. No town had walls too strong for us. [37]But we did not go near the territory of the Ammonites or to the banks of the Jabbok River or to the towns of the hill country or to any other place where the LORD our God had commanded us not to go.

Israel Conquers King Og
(Numbers 21:31–35)

3 [1]"Next, we moved north toward the region of Bashan, and King Og came out with all his men to fight us near the town of Edrei. [2]But the LORD said to me, 'Don't be afraid of him. I am going to give him, his men, and all his territory to you. Do the same thing to him that you did to Sihon the Amorite king who ruled in Heshbon.'

[3]"So the LORD also placed King Og and his people in our power, and we slaughtered them all. [4]At the same time we captured all his towns—there was not one that we did not take. In all we captured sixty towns—the whole region of Argob, where King Og of Bashan ruled. [5]All these towns were fortified with high walls, gates, and bars to lock the gates, and there were also many villages without walls. [6]We destroyed all the towns and put to death all the men, women, and children, just as we did in the towns that belonged to King Sihon of Heshbon. [7]We took the livestock and plundered the towns.

[8]"At that time we took from those two Amorite kings the land east of the Jordan River, from the Arnon River to Mount Hermon. ([9]Mount Hermon is called Sirion by the Sidonians, and Senir by the Amorites.) [10]We took all the territory of King Og of Bashan: the cities on the plateau, the regions of Gilead and of Bashan, as far east as the towns of Salecah and Edrei."

([11]King Og was the last of the Rephaim. His coffin,[b] made of stone,[c] was six feet wide and almost fourteen feet long, according to standard measurements. It can still be seen in the Ammonite city of Rabbah.)

The Tribes That Settled East of the Jordan
(Numbers 32:1–42)

[12]"When we took possession of the land, I assigned to the tribes of Reuben and Gad the territory north of the town of Aroer near the Arnon River and part of the hill country of Gilead, along with its towns. [13]To half the tribe of Manasseh I assigned the rest of Gilead and also all of Bashan, where Og had ruled, that is, the entire Argob region."

(Bashan was known as the land of the Rephaim. [14]Jair, from the tribe of Manasseh, took the entire region of Argob, that is, Bashan, as far as the border of Geshur and Maacah. He named the villages after himself, and they are still known as the villages of Jair.)

[15]"I assigned Gilead to the clan of Machir of the tribe of Manasseh. [16]And to the tribes of Reuben and Gad I assigned the territory from Gilead to the Arnon River. The middle of the river was their southern boundary, and their northern boundary was the Jabbok River, part of which formed the Ammonite border. [17]On the west their territory extended to the Jordan River, from Lake Galilee in the north down to the Dead Sea in the south and to the foot of Mount Pisgah on the east.

[18]"At the same time, I gave them the following instructions: 'The LORD our God has given you this land east of the Jordan to occupy. Now arm your fighting men and send them across the Jordan ahead of the other tribes of Israel, to help them occupy their land. [19]Only your wives, children, and livestock—I know you have a lot of livestock—will remain behind in the towns that I have assigned to you. [20]Help the other Israelites until they occupy the land that the LORD is giving them west of the Jordan and until the LORD lets them live there in peace, as he has already done here for you. After that, you may return to this land that I have assigned to you.'

[21]"Then I instructed Joshua: 'You have seen all that the LORD your God did to those two kings, Sihon and Og; and he will do the same thing to everyone else whose land you invade. [22]Don't be afraid of them, for the LORD your God will fight for you.'

---

[b] **3:11** coffin; *or* bed.   [c] **3:11** stone; *or* iron.
3:18–20 Josh 1:12–15

Moses Is Not Permitted to Enter Canaan

23"At that time I earnestly prayed, 24"Sovereign LORD, I know that you have shown me only the beginning of the great and wonderful things you are going to do. There is no god in heaven or on earth who can do the mighty things that you have done! 25Let me cross the Jordan River, LORD, and see the fertile land on the other side, the beautiful hill country and the Lebanon Mountains.'

26"But because of you people the LORD was angry with me and would not listen. Instead, he said, 'That's enough! Don't mention this again! 27Go to the peak of Mount Pisgah and look to the north and to the south, to the east and to the west. Look carefully at what you see, because you will never go across the Jordan. 28Give Joshua his instructions. Strengthen his determination, because he will lead the people across to occupy the land that you see.'

29"So we remained in the valley opposite the town of Bethpeor."

Moses Urges Israel to Be Obedient

4 1Then Moses said to the people, "Obey all the laws that I am teaching you, and you will live and occupy the land which the LORD, the God of your ancestors, is giving you. 2Do not add anything to what I command you, and do not take anything away. Obey the commands of the LORD your God that I have given you. 3You yourselves saw what the LORD did at Mount Peor. He destroyed everyone who worshiped Baal there, 4but those of you who were faithful to the LORD your God are still alive today.

5"I have taught you all the laws, as the LORD my God told me to do. Obey them in the land that you are about to invade and occupy. 6Obey them faithfully, and this will show the people of other nations how wise you are. When they hear of all these laws, they will say, 'What wisdom and understanding this great nation has!'

7"No other nation, no matter how great, has a god who is so near when they need him as the LORD our God is to us. He answers us whenever we call for help. 8No other nation, no matter how great, has laws so just as those that I have taught you today. 9Be on your guard! Make certain that you do not forget, as long as you live, what you have seen with your own eyes. Tell your children and your grandchildren 10about the day you stood in the presence of the LORD your God at Mount Sinai, when he said to me, 'Assemble the people. I want them to hear what I have to say, so that they will learn to obey me as long as they live and so that they will teach their children to do the same.'

11"Tell your children how you went and stood at the foot of the mountain which was covered with thick clouds of dark smoke and fire blazing up to the sky. 12Tell them how the LORD spoke to you from the fire, how you heard him speaking but did not see him in any form at all. 13He told you what you must do to keep the covenant he made with you—you must obey the Ten Commandments, which he wrote on two stone tablets. 14The LORD told me to teach you all the laws that you are to obey in the land that you are about to invade and occupy.

Warning against Idolatry

15"When the LORD spoke to you from the fire on Mount Sinai, you did not see any form. For your own good, then, make certain 16that you do not sin by making for yourselves an idol in any form at all—whether man or woman, 17animal or bird, 18reptile or fish. 19Do not be tempted to worship and serve what you see in the sky—the sun, the moon, and the stars. The LORD your God has given these to all other peoples for them to worship. 20But you are the people he rescued from Egypt, that blazing furnace. He brought you out to make you his own people, as you are today. 21Because of you the LORD your God was angry with me and solemnly declared that I would not

3:23–27 Num 27:12–14; Deut 32:48–52 **4:2** Rev 22:18, 19 **4:3** Num 25:1–9 **4:11, 12** Ex 19:16–18; Heb 12:18, 19 **4:13** Ex 31:18; 34:28; Deut 9:10 **4:14** Ex 21:1 **4:16** Ex 20:4; Lev 26:1; Deut 5:8; 27:15 **4:17, 18a** Rom 1:23 **4:20** Ex 19:5; Deut 7:6; 14:2; 26:18; Titus 2:14; 1 Pet 2:9 **4:21** Num 20:12

cross the Jordan River to enter the fertile land which he is giving you. 22I will die in this land and never cross the river, but you are about to go across and occupy that fertile land. 23Be certain that you do not forget the covenant that the LORD your God made with you. Obey his command not to make yourselves any kind of idol, 24because the LORD your God is like a flaming fire; he tolerates no rivals.

25"Even when you have been in the land a long time and have children and grandchildren, do not sin by making for yourselves an idol in any form at all. This is evil in the LORD's sight, and it will make him angry. 26I call heaven and earth as witnesses against you today that, if you disobey me, you will soon disappear from the land. You will not live very long in the land across the Jordan that you are about to occupy. You will be completely destroyed. 27The LORD will scatter you among other nations, where only a few of you will survive. 28There you will serve gods made by human hands, gods of wood and stone, gods that cannot see or hear, eat or smell. 29There you will look for the LORD your God, and if you search for him with all your heart, you will find him. 30When you are in trouble and all those things happen to you, then you will finally turn to the LORD and obey him. 31He is a merciful God. He will not abandon you or destroy you, and he will not forget the covenant that he himself made with your ancestors.

32"Search the past, the time before you were born, all the way back to the time when God created human beings on the earth. Search the entire earth. Has anything as great as this ever happened before? Has anyone ever heard of anything like this? 33Have any people ever lived after hearing a god speak to them from a fire, as you have? 34Has any god ever dared to go and take a people from another nation and make them his own, as the LORD your God did for you in Egypt? Before your very eyes he used his great power and strength; he brought plagues and war, worked miracles and wonders, and caused terrifying things to happen. 35The

LORD has shown you this, to prove to you that he alone is God and that there is no other. 36He let you hear his voice from heaven so that he could instruct you; and here on earth he let you see his holy fire, and he spoke to you from it. 37Because he loved your ancestors, he chose you, and by his great power he himself brought you out of Egypt. 38As you advanced, he drove out nations greater and more powerful than you, so that he might bring you in and give you their land, the land which still belongs to you. 39So remember today and never forget: the LORD is God in heaven and on earth. There is no other god. 40Obey all his laws that I have given you today, and all will go well with you and your descendants. You will continue to live in the land that the LORD your God is giving you to be yours forever."

The Cities of Refuge East of the Jordan

41Then Moses set aside three cities east of the Jordan River 42to which a man could escape and be safe if he had accidentally killed someone who had not been his enemy. He could escape to one of these cities and not be put to death. 43For the tribe of Reuben there was the city of Bezer, on the desert plateau; for the tribe of Gad there was Ramoth, in the territory of Gilead; and for the tribe of Manasseh there was Golan, in the territory of Bashan.

Introduction to the Giving of God's Law

44Moses gave God's laws and teachings to the people of Israel. 45-46It was after they had come out of Egypt and were in the valley east of the Jordan River, opposite the town of Bethpeor, that he gave them these laws. This was in the territory that had belonged to King Sihon of the Amorites, who had ruled in the town of Heshbon. Moses and the people of Israel defeated him when they came out of Egypt. 47They occupied his land and the land of King Og of Bashan, the other Amorite king who lived east of the

4:24 Heb 12:29   **4:27, 28** Deut 28:36   **4:29** Jer 29:13   **4:35** Mk 12:32   **4:41–43** Josh 20:8, 9

Jordan. ⁴⁸This land extended from the town of Aroer, on the edge of the Arnon River, all the way north to Mount Sirion,ᵈ that is, Mount Hermon. ⁴⁹It also included all the region east of the Jordan River as far south as the Dead Sea and east to the foot of Mount Pisgah.

The Ten Commandments
(Exodus 20:1–17)

5 ¹Moses called together all the people of Israel and said to them, "People of Israel, listen to all the laws that I am giving you today. Learn them and be sure that you obey them. ²At Mount Sinai the LORD our God made a covenant, ³not only with our fathers, but with all of us who are living today. ⁴There on the mountain the LORD spoke to you face to face from the fire. ⁵I stood between you and the LORD at that time to tell you what he said, because you were afraid of the fire and would not go up the mountain.

"The LORD said, ⁶'I am the LORD your God, who rescued you from Egypt, where you were slaves.

The LORD our God made a covenant. (5:2)

⁷" 'Worship no god but me.

⁸" 'Do not make for yourselves images of anything in heaven or on earth or in the water under the earth. ⁹Do not bow down to any idol or worship it, for I am the LORD your God and I tolerate no rivals. I bring punishment on those who hate me and on their descendants down to the third and fourth generation. ¹⁰But I show my love to thousands of generationsᵉ of those who love me and obey my laws.

¹¹" 'Do not use my name for evil purposes, for I, the LORD your God, will punish anyone who misuses my name.

¹²" 'Observe the Sabbath and keep it holy, as I, the LORD your God, have commanded you. ¹³You have six days in which to do your work, ¹⁴but the seventh day is a day of rest dedicated to me. On that day no one is to work—neither you, your children, your slaves, your animals, nor the foreigners who live in your country. Your slaves must rest just as you do. ¹⁵Remember that you were slaves in Egypt, and that I, the LORD your God, rescued you by my great power and strength. That is why I command you to observe the Sabbath.

¹⁶" 'Respect your father and your mother, as I, the LORD your God, command you, so that all may go well with you and so that you may live a long time in the land that I am giving you.

¹⁷" 'Do not commit murder.

¹⁸" 'Do not commit adultery.

¹⁹" 'Do not steal.

²⁰" 'Do not accuse anyone falsely.

²¹" 'Do not desire another man's wife; do not desire his house, his land, his slaves, his cattle, his donkeys, or anything else that he owns.'

²²"These are the commandments the LORD gave to all of you when you were gathered at the mountain. When he spoke with a mighty voice from the fire and from the thick clouds, he gave these commandments and no others. Then he wrote them on two stone tablets and gave them to me.

ᵈ **4:48** *One ancient translation* Sirion; *Hebrew* Sion.   ᵉ **5:10** thousands of generations; *or* thousands.
5:8, 9 Lev 26:1; Deut 4:15–18; 27:15   **5:9, 10** Ex 34:6, 7; Num 14:18; Deut 7:9, 10   **5:11** Lev 19:12
5:12 Ex 16:23–30; 31:12–14   **5:13, 14** Ex 23:12; 31:15; 34:21; 35:2; Lev 23:3   **5:16 a** Deut 27:16; Sir 3:1–16; Mt 15:4; 19:19; Mk 7:10; 10:19; Lk 18:20; Eph 6:2; **b** Eph 6:3   **5:17** Gen 9:6; Lev 24:17; Mt 5:21; 19:18; Mt 19:18; Lk 18:20; Rom 13:9; Jas 2:11   **5:18** Lev 20:10; Mt 5:27; 19:18; Mk 10:19; Lk 18:20; Rom 13:9; Jas 2:11   **5:19** Lev 19:11; Mt 19:18; Mk 10:19; Lk 18:20; Rom 13:9   **5:20** Ex 23:1; Mt 19:18; Mk 10:19; Lk 18:20   **5:21** Rom 7:7; 13:9   **5:22–27** Heb 12:18, 19

The People's Fear

(Exodus 20:18-21)

23 "When the whole mountain was on fire and you heard the voice from the darkness, your leaders and the chiefs of your tribes came to me 24 and said, 'The LORD our God showed us his greatness and his glory when we heard him speak from the fire! Today we have seen that it is possible for people to continue to live, even though God has spoken to them. 25 But why should we risk death again? That terrible fire will destroy us. We are sure to die if we hear the LORD our God speak again. 26 Has any human being ever lived after hearing the living God speak from a fire? 27 Go back, Moses, and listen to everything that the LORD our God says. Then return and tell us what he said to you. We will listen and obey.'

28 "When the LORD heard this, he said to me, 'I have heard what these people said, and they are right. 29 If only they would always feel this way! If only they would always honor me and obey all my commands, so that everything would go well with them and their descendants forever. 30 Go and tell them to return to their tents. 31 But you, Moses, stay here with me, and I will give you all my laws and commands. Teach them to the people, so that they will obey them in the land that I am giving them.'

32 "People of Israel, be sure that you do everything that the LORD your God has commanded you. Do not disobey any of his laws. 33 Obey them all, so that everything will go well with you and so that you will continue to live in the land that you are going to occupy.

The Great Commandment

6 1 "These are all the laws that the LORD your God commanded me to teach you. Obey them in the land that you are about to enter and occupy. 2 As long as you live, you and your descendants are to honor the LORD your God and obey all his laws that I am giving you, so that you may live in

that land a long time. 3 Listen to them, people of Israel, and obey them! Then all will go well with you, and you will become a mighty nation and live in that rich and fertile land, just as the LORD, the God of our ancestors, has promised.

4 "Israel, remember this! The LORD—and the LORD alone—is our God.*f* 5 Love the LORD your God with all your heart, with all your soul, and with all your strength. 6 Never forget these commands that I am giving you today. 7 Teach them to your children. Repeat them when you are at home and when you are away, when you are resting and when you are working. 8 Tie them on your arms and wear them on your foreheads as a reminder. 9 Write them on the doorposts of your houses and on your gates.

Write them on the doorposts. (6:9)

Warning against Disobedience

10 "Just as the LORD your God promised your ancestors, Abraham, Isaac, and Jacob, he will give you a land with large and prosperous cities which you did not build. 11 The houses will be full of good things which you did not put in them, and there will be wells that you did not dig, and vineyards and olive orchards that you did not plant. When the LORD brings you into this land and you have all you want to eat, 12 make certain that you do not forget the LORD who rescued

f **6:4** The LORD . . . is our God; *or* The LORD, our God, is the only God; *or* The LORD our God is one.
6:4 Mk 12:29   **6:5** Mt 22:37; Mk 12:30; Lk 10:27   **6:6-9** Deut 11:18-20   **6:10** a Gen 12:7; b Gen 26:3;
c Gen 28:13

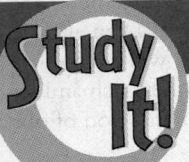

How Shall You Love God?

Deuteronomy 6:4–9 is part of a prayer called the Shema. Chapter 6, verse 4 may even be the most famous verse of the Old Testament, "Israel, remember this! The LORD—and the LORD alone—is our God." The next verse also tells you how to love God: "Love the LORD your God with all your heart, with all your soul, and with all your strength." Being surrounded by people who do not believe in their God was a temptation for the Israelites. They could and often did start following the false gods of other nations. The Shema was a constant reminder to be faithful to God—heart, soul, and strength.

The passage goes on to say don't just believe this, but talk about it with your family, wear the words on your clothing, and display the words on your doorposts (6:7–9)! Even today, this happens. When they pray, Orthodox Jews wear phylacteries, which are tiny leather pouches that hold small scrolls. The scrolls have the words of Deuteronomy 6:4–9 written on them. Their homes also have a mezuzah, a small container holding such a scroll, on their doorpost.

In the Gospel of Matthew (22:34–39) Jesus was asked what the greatest commandment was. He quoted this passage from Deuteronomy as his answer.

— Deuteronomy 6:4–9

you from Egypt, where you were slaves. ¹³Honor the LORD your God, worship only him, and make your promises in his name alone. ¹⁴Do not worship other gods, any of the gods of the peoples around you. ¹⁵If you do worship other gods, the LORD's anger will come against you like fire and will destroy you completely, because the LORD your God, who is present with you, tolerates no rivals.

¹⁶"Do not put the LORD your God to the test, as you did at Massah. ¹⁷Be sure that you obey all the laws that he has given you. ¹⁸Do what the LORD says is right and good, and all will go well with you. You will be able to take possession of the fertile land that the LORD promised your ancestors, ¹⁹and you will drive out your enemies, as he promised.

²⁰"In times to come your children will ask you, 'Why did the LORD our God command us to obey all these laws?' ²¹Then tell them, 'We were slaves of the king of Egypt, and the LORD rescued us by his great power. ²²With our own eyes we saw him work miracles and do terrifying things to the Egyptians and to their king and to all his officials. ²³He freed us from Egypt to bring us here and give us this land, as he had promised our ancestors he would. ²⁴Then the LORD our God commanded us to obey all these laws and to honor him. If we do, he will always watch over our nation and keep it prosperous. ²⁵If we faithfully obey everything that God has commanded us, he will be pleased with us.'ᵍ

The LORD's Own People
(Exodus 34:11–16)

7 ¹ "The LORD your God will bring you into the land that you are going to occupy, and he will drive many nations out of it. As you advance, he will drive out seven nations larger and more powerful than you: the Hittites, the Girgashites, the Amorites, the Canaanites, the Perizzites, the Hivites, and the Jebusites. ²When the LORD your God places these people in your power and you defeat them, you must put them all to death. Do not make an alliance with them

ᵍ **6:25** If we faithfully . . . with us; *or* The right thing for us to do is to obey faithfully everything that God has commanded us.
6:13 Mt 4:10; Lk 4:8   **6:16 a** Mt 4:7; Lk 4:12; **b** Ex 17:1–7   **7:1** Acts 13:19

or show them any mercy. [3]Do not marry any of them, and do not let your children marry any of them, [4]because then they would lead your children away from the LORD to worship other gods. If that happens, the LORD will be angry with you and destroy you at once. [5]So then, tear down their altars, break their sacred stone pillars in pieces, cut down their symbols of the goddess Asherah, and burn their idols. [6]Do this because you belong to the LORD your God. From all the peoples on earth he chose you to be his own special people.

[7]"The LORD did not love you and choose you because you outnumbered other peoples; you were the smallest nation on earth. [8]But the LORD loved you and wanted to keep the promise that he made to your ancestors. That is why he saved you by his great might and set you free from slavery to the king of Egypt. [9]Remember that the LORD your God is the only God and that he is faithful. He will keep his covenant and show his constant love to a thousand generations of those who love him and obey his commands, [10]but he will not hesitate to punish those who hate him. [11]Now then, obey what you have been taught; obey all the laws that I have given you today.

The Blessings of Obedience
(Deuteronomy 28:1–14)

[12]"If you listen to these commands and obey them faithfully, then the LORD your God will continue to keep his covenant with you and will show you his constant love, as he promised your ancestors. [13]He will love you and bless you, so that you will increase in number and have many children; he will bless your fields, so that you will have grain, wine, and olive oil; and he will bless you by giving you many cattle and sheep. He will give you all these blessings in the land that he promised your ancestors he would give to you. [14]No people in the world will be as richly blessed as you. None of you nor any of your livestock will be sterile. [15]The LORD will protect you from all sickness, and he will

not bring on you any of the dreadful diseases that you experienced in Egypt, but he will bring them on all your enemies. [16]Destroy every nation that the LORD your God places in your power, and do not show them any mercy. Do not worship their gods, for that would be fatal.

[17]"Do not tell yourselves that these peoples outnumber you and that you cannot drive them out. [18]Do not be afraid of them; remember what the LORD your God did to the king of Egypt and to all his people. [19]Remember the terrible plagues that you saw with your own eyes, the miracles and wonders, and the great power and strength by which the LORD your God set you free. In the same way that he destroyed the Egyptians, he will destroy all these people that you now fear. [20]He will even cause panic[h] among them and will destroy those who escape and go into hiding. [21]So do not be afraid of these people. The LORD your God is with you; he is a great God and one to be feared. [22]Little by little he will drive out these nations as you advance. You will not be able to destroy them all at once, for, if you did, the number of wild animals would increase and be a threat to you. [23]The LORD will put your enemies in your power and make them panic until they are destroyed. [24]He will put their kings in your power. You will kill them, and they will be forgotten. No one will be able to stop you; you will destroy everyone. [25]Burn their idols. Do not desire the silver or gold that is on them, and do not take it for yourselves. If you do, that will be fatal, because the LORD hates idolatry. [26]Do not bring any of these idols into your homes, or the same curse will be on you that is on them. You must hate and despise these idols, because they are under the LORD's curse.

A Good Land to Be Possessed

8 [1]"Obey faithfully all the laws that I have given you today, so that you may live, increase in number, and occupy the land that the LORD promised to your ancestors.

---

[h] **7:20** cause panic; *or* send hornets, *or* send plagues.
7:5 Deut 12:3   **7:6** Ex 19:5; Deut 4:20; 14:2; 26:18; Titus 2:14; 1 Pet 2:9   **7:9, 10** Ex 20:5, 6; 34:6, 7; Num 14:18; Deut 5:9, 10   **7:12–16** Deut 11:13–17

²Remember how the LORD your God led you on this long journey through the desert these past forty years, sending hardships to test you, so that he might know what you intended to do and whether you would obey his commands. ³He made you go hungry, and then he gave you manna to eat, food that you and your ancestors had never eaten before. He did this to teach you that you must not depend on bread alone to sustain you, but on everything that the LORD says. ⁴During these forty years your clothes have not worn out, nor have your feet swollen up. ⁵Remember that the LORD your God corrects and punishes you just as parents discipline their children. ⁶So then, do as the LORD has commanded you: live according to his laws and obey him. ⁷The LORD your God is bringing you into a fertile land—a land that has rivers and springs, and underground streams gushing out into the valleys and hills; ⁸a land that produces wheat and barley, grapes, figs, pomegranates, olives, and honey. ⁹There you will never go hungry or ever be in need. Its rocks have iron in them, and from its hills you can mine copper. ¹⁰You will have all you want to eat, and you will give thanks to the LORD your God for the fertile land that he has given you.

Warnings against Forgetting the LORD

¹¹"Make certain that you do not forget the LORD your God; do not fail to obey any of his laws that I am giving you today. ¹²When you have all you want to eat and have built good houses to live in ¹³and when your cattle and sheep, your silver and gold, and all your other possessions have increased, ¹⁴be sure that you do not become proud and forget the LORD your God who rescued you from Egypt, where you were slaves. ¹⁵He led you through that vast and terrifying desert where there were poisonous snakes and scorpions. In that dry and waterless land he made water flow out of solid rock for you. ¹⁶In the desert he gave you manna to eat, food that your ancestors had never eaten. He sent hardships on you to test you, so that in the end he could bless you with good things. ¹⁷So then, you must never think that you have made yourselves wealthy by your own power and strength. ¹⁸Remember that it is the LORD your God who gives you the power to become rich. He does this because he is still faithful today to the covenant that he made with your ancestors. ¹⁹Never forget the LORD your God or turn to other gods to worship and serve them. If you do, then I warn you today that you will certainly be destroyed. ²⁰If you do not obey the LORD, then you will be destroyed just like those nations that he is going to destroy as you advance.

The People's Disobedience

9 ¹"Listen, people of Israel! Today you are about to cross the Jordan River and occupy the land belonging to nations greater and more powerful than you. Their cities are large, with walls that reach the sky. ²The people themselves are tall and strong; they are giants, and you have heard it said that no one can stand against them. ³But now you will see for yourselves that the LORD your God will go ahead of you like a raging fire. He will defeat them as you advance, so that you will drive them out and destroy them quickly, as he promised.

⁴"After the LORD your God has driven them out for you, do not say to yourselves that he brought you in to possess this land because you deserved it. No, the LORD is going to drive these people out for you because they are wicked. ⁵It is not because you are good and do what is right that the LORD is letting you take their land. He will drive them out because they are wicked and because he intends to keep the promise that he made to your ancestors, Abraham, Isaac, and Jacob. ⁶You can be sure that the LORD is not giving you this fertile land because you deserve it. No, you are a stubborn people.

⁷"Never forget how you made the LORD your God angry in the desert. From the day that you left Egypt until the day you arrived here, you have rebelled against him. ⁸Even at Mount Sinai you made the LORD angry— angry enough to destroy you. ⁹I went up the

mountain to receive the stone tablets on which was written the covenant that the LORD had made with you. I stayed there forty days and nights and did not eat or drink anything. [10] Then the LORD gave me the two stone tablets on which he had written with his own hand what he had said to you from the fire on the day that you were gathered there at the mountain. [11] Yes, after those forty days and nights the LORD gave me the two stone tablets on which he had written the covenant.

[12] "Then the LORD said to me, 'Go down the mountain at once, because your people, whom you led out of Egypt, have become corrupt and have done evil. They have already turned away from what I commanded them to do, and they have made an idol for themselves.'

[13] "The LORD also said to me, 'I know how stubborn these people are. [14] Don't try to stop me. I intend to destroy them so that no one will remember them any longer. Then I will make you the father of a nation larger and more powerful than they are.'

[15] "So I turned and went down the mountain, carrying the two stone tablets on which the covenant was written. Flames of fire were coming from the mountain. [16] I saw that you had already disobeyed the command that the LORD your God had given you, and that you had sinned against him by making yourselves a metal idol in the form of a bull-calf. [17] So there in front of you I threw the stone tablets down and broke them to pieces. [18] Then once again I lay face downward in the LORD's presence for forty days and nights and did not eat or drink anything. I did this because you had sinned against the LORD and had made him angry. [19] I was afraid of the LORD's fierce anger, because he was furious enough to destroy you; but once again the LORD listened to me. [20] The LORD was also angry enough with Aaron to kill him, so I prayed for Aaron at the same time. [21] I took that sinful thing that you had made—that metal bull-calf—and threw it into the fire. Then I broke it in pieces, ground it to dust, and threw the dust into the stream that flowed down the mountain.

[22] "You also made the LORD your God angry when you were at Taberah, Massah, and Kibroth Hattaavah. [23] And when he sent you from Kadesh Barnea with orders to go and take possession of the land that he was giving you, you rebelled against him; you did not trust him or obey him. [24] Ever since I have known you, you have rebelled against the LORD.

[25] "So I lay face downward in the LORD's

I threw the stone tablets down and broke them to pieces. (9:17)

presence those forty days and nights, because I knew that he was determined to destroy you. 26 And I prayed, 'Sovereign LORD, don't destroy your own people, the people you rescued and brought out of Egypt by your great strength and power. 27 Remember your servants, Abraham, Isaac, and Jacob, and do not pay any attention to the stubbornness, wickedness, and sin of this people. 28 Otherwise, the Egyptians will say that you were unable to take your people into the land that you had promised them. They will say that you took your people out into the desert to kill them, because you hated them. 29 After all, these are the people whom you chose to be your own and whom you brought out of Egypt by your great power and might.'

Moses Receives the Commandments Again
(Exodus 34:1–10)

10 1 "Then the LORD said to me, 'Cut two stone tablets like the first ones and make a wooden Box to put them in. Come up to me on the mountain, 2 and I will write on those tablets what I wrote on the tablets that you broke, and then you are to put them in the Box.'

3 "So I made a Box of acacia wood and cut two stone tablets like the first ones and took them up the mountain. 4 Then the LORD wrote on those tablets the same words that he had written the first time, the Ten Commandments that he gave you when he spoke from the fire on the day you were gathered at the mountain. The LORD gave me the tablets, 5 and I turned and went down the mountain. Then, just as the LORD had commanded, I put them in the Box that I had made—and they have been there ever since."

(6 The Israelites set out from the wells that belonged to the people of Jaakan, and went to Moserah. There Aaron died and was buried, and his son Eleazar succeeded him as priest. 7 From there they went to Gudgodah and then on to Jotbathah, a well-watered place. 8 At that time the LORD appointed the men of the tribe of Levi to be in charge of the Covenant Box, to serve him as priests, and to pronounce blessings in his name. And these are still their duties. 9 That is why the tribe of Levi received no land as the other tribes did; what they received was the privilege of being the LORD's priests, as the LORD your God promised.)

10 "I stayed on the mountain forty days and nights, as I did the first time. The LORD listened to me once more and agreed not to destroy you. 11 Then he told me to go and lead you, so that you could take possession of the land that he had promised to give to your ancestors.

What God Demands

12 "Now, people of Israel, listen to what the LORD your God demands of you: Worship the LORD and do all that he commands. Love him, serve him with all your heart, 13 and obey all his laws. I am giving them to you today for your benefit. 14 To the LORD belong even the highest heavens; the earth is his also, and everything on it. 15 But the LORD's love for your ancestors was so strong that he chose you instead of any other people, and you are still his chosen people. 16 So then, from now on be obedient to the LORD and stop being stubborn. 17 The LORD your God is supreme over all gods and over all powers. He is great and mighty, and he is to be obeyed. He does not show partiality, and he does not accept bribes. 18 He makes sure that orphans and widows are treated fairly; he loves the foreigners who live with our people, and gives them food and clothes. 19 So then, show love for those foreigners, because you were once foreigners in Egypt. 20 Have reverence for the LORD your God and worship only him. Be faithful to him and make your promises in his name alone. 21 Praise him—he is your God, and you have seen with your own eyes the great and astounding things that he has done for you. 22 When your ancestors went to Egypt, there were only seventy of them. But now the LORD your God has made you as numerous as the stars in the sky.

10:6 Num 20:28; 33:38   10:8 Num 3:5–8   10:10 Ex 34:28   10:17 1 Tim 6:15; Rev 17:14; 19:16; Acts 10:34; Rom 2:11; Gal 2:6; Eph 6:9   10:18 Sir 35:12–15   10:22 a Gen 46:27; b Gen 15:5; 22:17

The Lord's Greatness

11 ¹"Love the Lord your God and always obey all his laws. ²Remember today what you have learned about the Lord through your experiences with him. It was you, not your children, who had these experiences. You saw the Lord's greatness, his power, his might, ³and his miracles. You saw what he did to the king of Egypt and to his entire country. ⁴You saw how the Lord completely wiped out the Egyptian army, along with their horses and chariots, by drowning them in the Red Sea*ⁱ* when they were pursuing you. ⁵You know what the Lord did for you in the desert before you arrived here. ⁶You recall what he did to Dathan and Abiram, the sons of Eliab of the tribe of Reuben. In the sight of everyone the earth opened up and swallowed them, along with their families, their tents, and all their servants and animals. ⁷Yes, you are the ones who have seen all these great things that the Lord has done.

The Blessings of the Promised Land

⁸"Obey everything that I have commanded you today. Then you will be able to cross the river and occupy the land that you are about to enter. ⁹And you will live a long time in the rich and fertile land that the Lord promised to give your ancestors and their descendants. ¹⁰The land that you are about to occupy is not like the land of Egypt, where you lived before. There, when you planted grain, you had to work hard to irrigate the fields; ¹¹but the land that you are about to enter is a land of mountains and valleys, a land watered by rain. ¹²The Lord your God takes care of this land and watches over it throughout the year.

¹³"So then, obey the commands that I have given you today; love the Lord your God and serve him with all your heart. ¹⁴If you do, he will send rain on your land when it is needed, in the autumn and in the spring, so that there will be grain, wine, and olive oil for you, ¹⁵and grass for your livestock. You will have all the food you want. ¹⁶Do not let yourselves be led away from the Lord to worship and serve other gods. ¹⁷If you do, the Lord will become angry with you. He will hold back the rain, and your ground will become too dry for crops to grow. Then you will soon die there, even though it is a good land that he is giving you.

¹⁸"Remember these commands and cherish them. Tie them on your arms and wear them on your foreheads as a reminder. ¹⁹Teach them to your children. Talk about them when you are at home and when you are away, when you are resting and when you are working. ²⁰Write them on the doorposts of your houses and on your gates. ²¹Then you and your children will live a long time in the land that the Lord your God promised to give to your ancestors. You will live there as long as there is a sky above the earth.

Teach them to your children. (11:19)

²²"Obey faithfully everything that I have commanded you: Love the Lord your God, do everything he commands, and be faithful to him. ²³Then he will drive out all those nations as you advance, and you will occupy

---

ⁱ **11:4:** RED SEA: *See Word List.*
11:3 Ex 7:8—12:13   **11:4** Ex 14:28   **11:6** Num 16:31, 32   **11:13–17** Lev 26:3–5; Deut 7:12–16; 28:1–14
11:18–20 Deut 6:6–9

Deuteronomy

the land belonging to nations greater and more powerful than you. 24All the ground that you march over will be yours. Your territory will extend from the desert in the south to the Lebanon Mountains in the north, and from the Euphrates River in the east to the Mediterranean Sea in the west. 25Wherever you go in that land, the LORD your God will make the people fear you, as he has promised, and no one will be able to stop you.

26"Today I am giving you the choice between a blessing and a curse— 27a blessing, if you obey the commands of the LORD your God that I am giving you today; 28but a curse, if you disobey these commands and turn away to worship other gods that you have never worshiped before. 29When the LORD brings you into the land that you are going to occupy, you are to proclaim the blessing from Mount Gerizim and the curse from Mount Ebal. (30These two mountains are west of the Jordan River in the territory of the Canaanites who live in the Jordan Valley. They are toward the west, not far from the sacred trees of Moreh near the town of Gilgal.) 31You are about to cross the Jordan River and occupy the land that the LORD your God is giving you. When you take it and settle there, 32be sure to obey all the laws that I am giving you today.

The One Place for Worship

12 1"Here are the laws that you are to obey as long as you live in the land that the LORD, the God of your ancestors, is giving you. Listen to them! 2In the land that you are taking, destroy all the places where the people worship their gods on high mountains, on hills, and under green trees. 3Tear down their altars and smash their sacred stone pillars to pieces. Burn their symbols of the goddess Asherah and chop down their idols, so that they will never again be worshiped at those places.

4"Do not worship the LORD your God in the way that these people worship their gods. 5Out of the territory of all your tribes the LORD will choose the one place where the people are to come into his presence and

worship him. 6There you are to offer your sacrifices that are to be burned and your other sacrifices, your tithes and your offerings, the gifts that you promise to the LORD, your freewill offerings, and the first-born of your cattle and sheep. 7There, in the presence of the LORD your God, who has blessed you, you and your families will eat and enjoy the good things that you have worked for.

8"When that time comes, you must not do as you have been doing. Until now you have all been worshiping as you please, 9because you have not yet entered the land that the LORD your God is giving you, where you can live in peace. 10When you cross the Jordan River, the LORD will let you occupy the land and live there. He will keep you safe from all your enemies, and you will live in peace. 11The LORD will choose a single place where he is to be worshiped, and there you must bring to him everything that I have commanded: your sacrifices that are to be burned and your other sacrifices, your tithes and your offerings, and those special gifts that you have promised to the LORD. 12Be joyful there in his presence, together with your children, your servants, and the Levites who live in your towns; remember that the Levites will have no land of their own. 13You are not to offer your sacrifices wherever you choose; 14you must offer them only in the one place that the LORD will choose in the territory of one of your tribes. Only there are you to offer your sacrifices that are to be burned and do all the other things that I have commanded you.

Tear down their altars. (12:3)

11:24, 25 Josh 1:3–5   **11:29** Deut 27:11–14; Josh 8:33–35   **12:3** Deut 7:5

15"But you are free to kill and eat your animals wherever you live. You may eat as many as the LORD gives you. All of you, whether ritually clean or unclean, may eat them, just as you would eat the meat of deer or antelope. 16But you must not eat their blood; you must pour it out on the ground like water. 17Nothing that you offer to the LORD is to be eaten in the places where you live: neither the tithes of your grain, your wine, or your olive oil, nor the first-born of your cattle and sheep, the gifts that you promise to the LORD, your freewill offerings, or any other offerings. 18You and your children, together with your servants and the Levites who live in your towns, are to eat these offerings only in the presence of the LORD your God, in the one place of worship chosen by the LORD your God. And you are to be happy there over everything that you have done. 19Be sure, also, not to neglect the Levites, as long as you live in your land.

20"When the LORD your God enlarges your territory, as he has promised, you may eat meat whenever you want to. 21If the one place of worship is too far away, then, whenever you wish, you may kill any of the cattle or sheep that the LORD has given you, and you may eat the meat at home, as I have told you. 22Anyone, ritually clean or unclean, may eat that meat, just as he would eat the meat of deer or antelope. 23Only do not eat meat with blood still in it, for the life is in the blood, and you must not eat the life with the meat. 24Do not use the blood for food; instead, pour it out on the ground like water. 25If you obey this command, the LORD will be pleased, and all will go well for you and your descendants. 26Take to the one place of worship your offerings and the gifts that you have promised the LORD. 27Offer there the sacrifices which are to be completely burned on the LORD's altar. Also offer those sacrifices in which you eat the meat and pour the blood out on the altar. 28Obey faithfully everything that I have commanded you, and all will go well for you and your descendants forever, because you will be doing what is right and what pleases the LORD your God.

Warning against Idolatry

29"The LORD your God will destroy the nations as you invade their land, and you will occupy it and settle there. 30After the LORD destroys those nations, make sure that you don't follow their religious practices, because that would be fatal. Don't try to find out how they worship their gods, so that you can worship in the same way. 31Do not worship the LORD your God in the way they worship their gods, for in the worship of their gods they do all the disgusting things that the LORD hates. They even sacrifice their children in the fires on their altars.

32"Do everything that I have commanded you; do not add anything to it or take anything from it.

13 1"Prophets or interpreters of dreams may promise a miracle or a wonder, 2in order to lead you to worship and serve gods that you have not worshiped before. Even if what they promise comes true, 3do not pay any attention to them. The LORD your God is using them to test you, to see if you love the LORD with all your heart. 4Follow the LORD and honor him; obey him and keep his commands; worship him and be faithful to him. 5But put to death any interpreters of dreams or prophets that tell you to rebel against the LORD, who rescued you from Egypt, where you were slaves. Such people are evil and are trying to lead you away from the life that the LORD has commanded you to live. They must be put to death, in order to rid yourselves of this evil.

6"Even your brother or your son or your daughter or the wife you love or your closest friend may secretly encourage you to worship other gods, gods that you and your ancestors have never worshiped. 7Some of them may encourage you to worship the gods of the people who live near you or the gods of those who live far away. 8But do not let any of them persuade you; do not even listen to them. Show them no mercy or pity, and do not protect them. 9Kill them! Be the first to stone them, and then let everyone else stone them too. 10Stone them to death! They tried to lead you away from the LORD your God, who

Do not even listen to them. (13:8)

rescued you from Egypt, where you were slaves. ¹¹Then all the people of Israel will hear what happened; they will be afraid, and no one will ever again do such an evil thing.

¹²"When you are living in the towns that the LORD your God gives you, you may hear ¹³that some worthless people of your nation have misled the people of their town to worship gods that you have never worshiped before. ¹⁴If you hear such a rumor, investigate it thoroughly; and if it is true that this evil thing did happen, ¹⁵then kill all the people in that town and all their livestock too. Destroy that town completely. ¹⁶Bring together all the possessions of the people who live there and pile them up in the town square. Then burn the town and everything in it as an offering to the LORD your God. It must be left in ruins forever and never again be rebuilt. ¹⁷Do not keep for yourselves anything that was condemned to destruction, and then the LORD will turn from his fierce anger and show you mercy. He will be merciful to you and make you a numerous people, as he promised your ancestors, ¹⁸if you obey all his commands that I have given you today, and do what he requires.

A Forbidden Mourning Practice

14 ¹"You are the people of the LORD your God. So when you mourn for the dead, don't gash yourselves or shave the front of your head, as other people do. ²You belong to the LORD your God; he has chosen you to be his own people from among all the peoples who live on earth.

Clean and Unclean Animals
(Leviticus 11:1–47)

³"Do not eat anything that the LORD has declared unclean. ⁴You may eat these animals: cattle, sheep, goats, ⁵deer, wild sheep, wild goats, or antelopes— ⁶any animals that have divided hoofs and that also chew the cud. ⁷But no animals may be eaten unless they have divided hoofs and also chew the cud. You may not eat camels, rabbits, or rock badgers. They must be considered unclean; they chew the cud but do not have divided hoofs. ⁸Do not eat pigs. They must be considered unclean; they have divided hoofs but do not chew the cud. Do not eat any of these animals or even touch their dead bodies.

⁹"You may eat any kind of fish that has fins and scales, ¹⁰but anything living in the water that does not have fins and scales may not be eaten; it must be considered unclean.

¹¹"You may eat any clean bird. ¹²⁻¹⁸But these are the kinds of birds you are not to eat: eagles, owls, hawks, falcons; buzzards, vultures, crows; ostriches; seagulls, storks, herons, pelicans, cormorants;ʲ hoopoes; and bats.

¹⁹"All winged insects are unclean; do not eat them. ²⁰You may eat any clean insect.

²¹"Do not eat any animal that dies a natural death. You may let the foreigners who live among you eat it, or you may sell it to other foreigners. But you belong to the LORD your God; you are his people.

"Do not cook a young sheep or goat in its mother's milk.

The Law of the Tithe

²²"Set aside a tithe—a tenth of all that your fields produce each year. ²³Then go to the one place where the LORD your God has chosen to be worshiped; and there in his presence eat the tithes of your grain, wine, and olive oil, and the first-born of your cat-

ʲ **14:12–18** *The identification of some of these birds is uncertain.*
14:1 Lev 19:28; 21:5   **14:2** Ex 19:5, 6; Deut 4:20; 7:6; 26:18; Titus 2:14; 1 Pet 2:9   **14:21** Ex 23:19; 34:26
14:22–29 Lev 27:30–33; Num 18:21

tle and sheep. Do this so that you may learn to honor the LORD your God always. 24 If the place of worship is too far from your home for you to carry there the tithe of the produce that the LORD has blessed you with, then do this: 25 Sell your produce and take the money with you to the one place of worship. 26 Spend it on whatever you want—beef, lamb, wine, beer—and there, in the presence of the LORD your God, you and your families are to eat and enjoy yourselves.

27 "Do not neglect the Levites who live in your towns; they have no property of their own. 28 At the end of every third year bring the tithe of all your crops and store it in your towns. 29 This food is for the Levites, since they own no property, and for the foreigners, orphans, and widows who live in your towns. They are to come and get all they need. Do this, and the LORD your God will bless you in everything you do.

The Seventh Year
(Leviticus 25:1–7)

15 1 "At the end of every seventh year you are to cancel the debts of those who owe you money. 2 This is how it is to be done. Each of you who has lent money to any Israelite is to cancel the debt; you must not try to collect the money; the LORD himself has declared the debt canceled. 3 You may collect what a foreigner owes you, but you must not collect what any of your own people owe you.

4 "The LORD your God will bless you in the land that he is giving you. Not one of your people will be poor 5 if you obey him and carefully observe everything that I command you today. 6 The LORD will bless you, as he has promised. You will lend money to many nations, but you will not have to borrow from any; you will have control over many nations, but no nation will have control over you.

7 "If in any of the towns in the land that the LORD your God is giving you there are Israelites in need, then do not be selfish and refuse to help them. 8 Instead, be generous and lend them as much as they need. 9 Do

not refuse to lend them something, just because the year when debts are canceled is near. Do not let such an evil thought enter your mind. If you refuse to make the loan, they will cry out to the LORD against you, and you will be held guilty. 10 Give to them freely and unselfishly, and the LORD will bless you in everything you do. 11 There will always be some Israelites who are poor and in need, and so I command you to be generous to them.

The Treatment of Slaves
(Exodus 21:1–11)

12 "If any Israelites, male or female, sell themselves[k] to you as slaves, you are to release them after they have served you for six years. When the seventh year comes, you must let them go free. 13 When you set them free, do not send them away empty-handed. 14 Give to them generously from what the LORD has blessed you with—sheep, grain, and wine. 15 Remember that you were slaves in Egypt and the LORD your God set you free; that is why I am now giving you this command.

Do not send them away empty-handed. (15:13)

16 "But your slave may not want to leave; he may love you and your family and be content to stay. 17 Then take him to the door of your house and there pierce his ear; he will

k **15:12** sell themselves, *or* are sold.
15:7, 8 Lev 25:35   **15:11** Mt 26:11; Mk 14:7; Jn 12:8   **15:12–18** Lev 25:39–46

then be your slave for life. Treat your female slave in the same way. [18]Do not be resentful when you set slaves free; after all, they have served you for six years at half the cost of hired servants.[l] Do this, and the LORD your God will bless you in all that you do.

The First-Born Cattle and Sheep

[19]"Set aside for the LORD your God all the first-born males of your cattle and sheep; don't use any of these cattle for work and don't shear any of these sheep. [20]Each year you and your family are to eat them in the LORD's presence at the one place of worship. [21]But if there is anything wrong with the animals, if they are crippled or blind or have any other serious defect, you must not sacrifice them to the LORD your God. [22]You may eat such animals at home. All of you, whether ritually clean or unclean, may eat them, just as you eat deer or antelope. [23]But do not use their blood for food; instead, you must pour it out on the ground like water.

The Passover
(Exodus 12:1–20)

16 [1]"Honor the LORD your God by celebrating Passover in the month of Abib; it was on a night in that month that he rescued you from Egypt. [2]Go to the one place of worship and slaughter there one of your sheep or cattle for the Passover meal to honor the LORD your God. [3]When you eat this meal, do not eat bread prepared with yeast. For seven days you are to eat bread prepared without yeast, as you did when you had to leave Egypt in such a hurry. Eat this bread—it will be called the bread of suffering—so that as long as you live you will remember the day you came out of Egypt, that place of suffering. [4]For seven days no one in your land is to have any yeast in the house; and the meat of the animal killed on the evening of the first day must be eaten that same night.

[5-6]"Slaughter the Passover animals at the one place of worship—and nowhere else in the land that the LORD your God will give you. Do it at sunset, the time of day when you left Egypt. [7]Boil the meat and eat it at the one place of worship; and the next morning return home. [8]For the next six days you are to eat bread prepared without yeast, and on the seventh day assemble to worship the LORD your God, and do no work on that day.

The Harvest Festival
(Exodus 34:22; Leviticus 23:15–21)

[9]"Count seven weeks from the time that you begin to harvest the grain, [10]and then celebrate the Harvest Festival, to honor the LORD your God, by bringing him a freewill offering in proportion to the blessing he has given you. [11]Be joyful in the LORD's presence, together with your children, your servants, and the Levites, foreigners, orphans, and widows who live in your towns. Do this at the one place of worship. [12]Be sure that you obey these commands; do not forget that you were slaves in Egypt.

The Festival of Shelters
(Leviticus 23:33–43)

[13]"After you have threshed all your grain and pressed all your grapes, celebrate the Festival of Shelters for seven days. [14]Enjoy it with your children, your servants, and the Levites, foreigners, orphans, and widows who live in your towns. [15]Honor the LORD your God by celebrating this festival for seven days at the one place of worship. Be joyful, because the LORD has blessed your harvest and your work.

[16]"All the men of your nation are to come to worship the LORD three times a year at the one place of worship: at Passover, Harvest Festival, and the Festival of Shelters. Each man is to bring a gift [17]as he is able, in proportion to the blessings that the LORD your God has given him.

---

l **15:18** at half . . . servants; *or* and have worked twice as hard as hired servants.
15:19 Ex 13:12   **15:23** Gen 9:4; Lev 7:26, 27; 17:10–14; 19:26; Deut 12:16, 23   **16:1–8** Ex 12:1–20; Lev 23:5–8; Num 28:16–25   **16:9–12** Lev 23:15–21; Num 28:26–31   **16:13–15** Lev 23:33–36, 39–43; Num 29:12–38

Each man is to bring a gift. (16:16)

The Administration of Justice

18"Appoint judges and other officials in every town that the LORD your God gives you. These men are to judge the people impartially. 19They are not to be unjust or show partiality in their judgments; and they are not to accept bribes, for gifts blind the eyes even of wise and honest men, and cause them to give wrong decisions. 20Always be fair and just, so that you will occupy the land that the LORD your God is giving you and so that you will continue to live there.

21"When you make an altar for the LORD your God, do not put beside it a wooden symbol of the goddess Asherah. 22And do not set up any stone pillar for idol worship; the LORD hates them.

17 1"Do not sacrifice to the LORD your God cattle or sheep that have any defects; the LORD hates this.

2"Suppose you hear that in one of your towns some men or women have sinned against the LORD and broken his covenant 3by worshiping and serving other gods or the sun or the moon or the stars, contrary to the LORD's command. 4If you hear such a report, then investigate it thoroughly. If it is true that this evil thing has happened in Israel, 5then take them outside the town and stone them to death. 6However, they may be put to death only if two or more witnesses testify against them; they are not to be put to death if there is only one witness. 7The

witnesses are to throw the first stones, and then the rest of the people are to stone them; in this way you will get rid of this evil.

8"It may be that some cases will be too difficult for the local judges to decide, such as certain cases of property rights or of bodily injury or those cases that involve a distinction between murder and manslaughter. When this happens, go to the one place of worship chosen by the LORD your God, 9and present your case to the levitical priests and to the judge who is in office at that time, and let them decide the case. 10They will give their decision, and you are to do exactly as they tell you. 11Accept their verdict and follow their instructions in every detail. 12Anyone who dares to disobey either the judge or the priest on duty is to be put to death; in this way you will remove this evil from Israel. 13Then everyone will hear of it and be afraid, and no one else will dare to act in such a way.

Instructions concerning a King

14"After you have taken possession of the land that the LORD your God is going to give you and have settled there, then you will decide you need a king like all the nations around you. 15Be sure that the man you choose to be king is the one whom the LORD has chosen. He must be one of your own people; do not make a foreigner your

16:19 Ex 23:6–8; Lev 19:15   **16:21** Ex 34:13   **16:22** Lev 26:1   **17:3** Ex 22:20   **17:6** Num 35:30; Deut 19:15; Mt 18:16; 2 Cor 13:1; 1 Tim 5:19; Heb 10:28   **17:7** 1 Cor 5:13   **17:14** 1 Sam 8:5

king. 16The king is not to have a large number of horses for his army, and he is not to send people to Egypt to buy horses,[m] because the LORD has said that his people are never to return there. 17The king is not to have many wives, because this would make him turn away from the LORD; and he is not to make himself rich with silver and gold. 18When he becomes king, he is to have a copy of the book of God's laws and teachings made from the original copy kept by the levitical priests. 19He is to keep this book near him and read from it all his life, so that he will learn to honor the LORD and to obey faithfully everything that is commanded in it. 20This will keep him from thinking that he is better than other Israelites and from disobeying the LORD's commands in any way. Then he will reign for many years, and his descendants will rule Israel for many generations.

The Share of the Priests

18 1"The priestly tribe of Levi is not to receive any share of land in Israel; instead, they are to live on the offerings and other sacrifices given to the LORD. 2They are to own no land, as the other tribes do; their share is the privilege of being the LORD's priests, as the LORD has promised.

3"Whenever cattle or sheep are sacrificed, the priests are to be given the shoulder, the jaw, and the stomach. 4They are to receive the first share of the grain, wine, olive oil, and wool. 5The LORD chose from all your tribes the tribe of Levi to serve him as priests forever.

6"Any Levite who wants to may come from any town in Israel to the one place of worship 7and may serve there as a priest of the LORD his God, like the other Levites who are serving there. 8He is to receive the same amount of food as the other priests, and he may keep whatever his family sends him.[n]

Warning against Pagan Practices

9"When you come into the land that the LORD your God is giving you, don't follow the disgusting practices of the nations that are there. 10Don't sacrifice your children in the fires on your altars; and don't let your people practice divination or look for omens or use spells 11or charms, and don't let them consult the spirits of the dead. 12The LORD your God hates people who do these disgusting things, and that is why he is driving those nations out of the land as you advance. 13Be completely faithful to the LORD."

The Promise to Send a Prophet

14Then Moses said, "In the land you are about to occupy, people follow the advice of those who practice divination and look for omens, but the LORD your God does not allow you to do this. 15Instead, he will send you a prophet like me from among your own people, and you are to obey him.[o]

16"On the day that you were gathered at Mount Sinai, you begged not to hear the LORD speak again or to see his fiery presence any more, because you were afraid you would die. 17So the LORD said to me, 'They have made a wise request. 18I will send them a prophet like you from among their own people; I will tell him what to say, and he[p] will tell the people everything I command. 19He will speak in my name, and I[q] will punish anyone who refuses to obey him. 20But if any prophet dares to speak a message in my name when I did not command him to do so, he must die for it, and so must any prophet who speaks in the name of other gods.'

21"You may wonder how you can tell when a prophet's message does not come from the LORD. 22If a prophet speaks in the name of the LORD and what he says does not come true, then it is not the LORD's message. That prophet has spoken on his own authority, and you are not to fear him.

m **17:16** to buy horses; *or* in exchange for horses.   *n* **18:8** *Probable text* and he may keep . . . sends him; *Hebrew unclear.*   *o* **18:15** a prophet . . . him; *or* prophets . . . them.   *p* **18:18** a prophet . . . him . . . he; *or* prophets . . . them . . . they.   *q* **18:19** He will speak . . . and I; *or* When a prophet speaks in my name, I.
17:16 1 Kings 10:28; 2 Chr 1:16; 9:28   **17:17 a** 1 Kings 11:1–8; **b** 1 Kings 10:14–22, 27; 2 Chr 1:15; 9:27   **18:2** Num 18:20   **18:10 a** Lev 19:26; **b** Ex 22:18   **18:11** Lev 19:31   **18:13** Mt 5:48   **18:15** Acts 3:22; 7:37   **18:19** Acts 3:23

The Cities of Refuge
(Numbers 35:9–34; Joshua 20:1–9)

19 ¹ "After the LORD your God has destroyed the people whose land he is giving you and after you have taken their cities and houses and settled there, ²⁻³ divide the territory into three parts, each with a city that can be easily reached. Then any of you that kill will be able to escape to one of them for protection. ⁴ If you accidentally kill someone who is not your enemy, you may escape to any of these cities and be safe. ⁵ For example, if two of you go into the forest together to cut wood and if, as one of you is chopping down a tree, the ax head comes off the handle and kills the other, you can run to one of those three cities and be safe. ⁶ If there were only one city, the distance to it might be too great, and the relative who is responsible for taking revenge for the killing might catch you and angrily kill an innocent person. After all, it was by accident that you killed someone who was not your enemy. ⁷ This is why I order you to set aside three cities.

⁸ "When the LORD your God enlarges your territory, as he told your ancestors he would, and gives you all the land he has promised, ⁹ then you are to select three more cities. (He will give you this land if you do everything that I command you today and if you love the LORD your God and live according to his teachings.) ¹⁰ Do this, so that innocent people will not die and so that you will not be guilty of putting them to death in the land that the LORD is giving you.

¹¹ "But suppose you deliberately murder your enemy in cold blood and then escape to one of those cities for protection. ¹² In that case, the leaders of your own town are to send for you and hand you over to the relative responsible for taking revenge for the murder, so that you may be put to death. ¹³ No mercy will be shown to you. Israel must rid itself of murderers, so that all will go well.

Ancient Property Lines

¹⁴ "Do not move your neighbor's property line, established long ago in the land that the LORD your God is giving you.

Concerning Witnesses

¹⁵ "One witness is not enough to convict someone of a crime; at least two witnesses are necessary to prove that someone is guilty. ¹⁶ If any of you try to harm another by false accusations, ¹⁷ both of you are to go to the one place of worship and be judged by the priests and judges who are then in office. ¹⁸ The judges will investigate the case thoroughly; and if you have made a false accusation, ¹⁹ you are to receive the punishment the accused would have received. In this way your nation will get rid of this evil. ²⁰ Then everyone else will hear what happened; they will be afraid, and no one will ever again do such an evil thing. ²¹ In such cases show no

It was by accident that you killed someone. (19:6)

19:1–13 Josh 20:1–9   **19:14** Deut 27:17   **19:15** Num 35:30; Deut 17:6; Mt 18:16; Jn 8:17; 2 Cor 13:1; 1 Tim 5:19; Heb 10:28   **19:21** Ex 21:23–25; Lev 24:19, 20; Mt 5:38

mercy; the punishment is to be a life for a life, an eye for an eye, a tooth for a tooth, a hand for a hand, and a foot for a foot.

Concerning War

20 ¹"When you go out to fight against your enemies and you see chariots and horses and an army that outnumbers yours, do not be afraid of them. The LORD your God, who rescued you from Egypt, will be with you. ²Before you start fighting, a priest is to come forward and say to the army, ³'Men of Israel, listen! Today you are going into battle. Do not be afraid of your enemies or lose courage or panic. ⁴The LORD your God is going with you, and he will give you victory.'

⁵"Then the officers will address the men and say, 'Is there any man here who has just built a house, but has not yet dedicated it? If so, he is to go home. Otherwise, if he is killed in battle, someone else will dedicate his house. ⁶Is there any man here who has just planted a vineyard, but has not yet had the chance to harvest its grapes? If so, he is to go home. Otherwise, if he is killed in battle, someone else will enjoy the wine. ⁷Is there anyone here who is engaged to be married? If so, he is to go home. Otherwise, if he is killed in battle, someone else will marry the woman he is engaged to.'

⁸"The officers will also say to the men, 'Is there any man here who has lost his nerve and is afraid? If so, he is to go home. Otherwise, he will destroy the morale of the others.' ⁹When the officers have finished speaking to the army, leaders are to be chosen for each unit.

¹⁰"When you go to attack a city, first give its people a chance to surrender. ¹¹If they open the gates and surrender, they are all to become your slaves and do forced labor for you. ¹²But if the people of that city will not surrender, but choose to fight, surround it with your army. ¹³Then, when the LORD your God lets you capture the city, kill every man in it. ¹⁴You may, however, take for yourselves the women, the children, the livestock, and everything else in the city. You may use everything that belongs to your enemies. The LORD has given it to you.

¹⁵That is how you are to deal with those cities that are far away from the land you will settle in.

¹⁶"But when you capture cities in the land that the LORD your God is giving you, kill everyone. ¹⁷Completely destroy all the people: the Hittites, the Amorites, the Canaanites, the Perizzites, the Hivites, and the Jebusites, as the LORD ordered you to do. ¹⁸Kill them, so that they will not make you sin against the LORD by teaching you to do all the disgusting things that they do in the worship of their gods.

¹⁹"When you are trying to capture a city, do not cut down its fruit trees, even though the siege lasts a long time. Eat the fruit, but do not destroy the trees; the trees are not your enemies. ²⁰You may cut down the other trees and use them in the siege mounds until the city is captured.

Concerning Unsolved Murders

21 ¹"Suppose someone is found murdered in a field in the land that the LORD your God is going to give you, and you do not know who killed him. ²Your leaders and judges are to go out and measure the distance from the place where the body was found to each of the nearby towns. ³Then the leaders of the town nearest to where the body was found are to select a young cow that has never been used for work. ⁴They are to take it down to a spot near a stream that never runs dry and where the ground has never been plowed or planted, and there they are to break its neck. ⁵The levitical priests are to go there also, because they are to decide every legal case involving violence. The LORD your God has chosen them to serve him and to pronounce blessings in his name. ⁶Then all the leaders from the town nearest the place where the murdered person was found are to wash their hands over the cow ⁷and say, 'We did not murder this one, and we do not know who did it. ⁸LORD, forgive your people Israel, whom you rescued from Egypt. Forgive us and do not hold us responsible for the murder of an innocent person.' ⁹And so, by doing what the LORD requires, you will not be held responsible for the murder.

Concerning Women Prisoners of War

10 "When the LORD your God gives you victory in battle and you take prisoners, 11 you may see among them a beautiful woman that you like and want to marry. 12 Take her to your home, where she will shave her head,[r] cut her fingernails, 13 and change her clothes. She is to stay in your home and mourn for her parents for a month; after that, you may marry her. 14 Later, if you no longer want her, you are to let her go free. Since you forced her to have intercourse with you, you cannot treat her as a slave and sell her.

Concerning the First Son's Inheritance

15 "Suppose a man has two wives and they both bear him sons, but the first son is not the child of his favorite wife. 16 When the man decides how he is going to divide his property among his children, he is not to show partiality to the son of his favorite wife by giving him the share that belongs to the first-born son. 17 He is to give a double share of his possessions to his first son, even though he is not the son of his favorite wife. A man must acknowledge his first son and give him the share he is legally entitled to.

Concerning a Disobedient Son

18 "Suppose someone has a son who is stubborn and rebellious, a son who will not obey his parents, even though they punish him. 19 His parents are to take him before the leaders of the town where he lives and make him stand trial. 20 They are to say to them, 'Our son is stubborn and rebellious and refuses to obey us; he wastes money and is a drunkard.' 21 Then the men of the city are to stone him to death, and so you will get rid of this evil. Everyone in Israel will hear what has happened and be afraid.

Various Laws

22 "If someone has been put to death for a crime and the body is hung on a post, 23 it is not to remain there overnight. It must be buried the same day, because a dead body hanging on a post brings God's curse on the land. Bury the body, so that you will not defile the land that the LORD your God is giving you.

22 1 "If you see an Israelite's cow or sheep running loose, do not ignore it; take it back. 2 But if its owner lives a long way off or if you don't know who owns it, then take it home with you. When its owner comes looking for it, give it to him. 3 Do the same thing if you find a donkey, a piece of clothing, or anything else that an Israelite may have lost.

When its owner comes . . . . give it to him. (22:2)

4 "If an Israelite's donkey or cow has fallen down, don't ignore it; help him get the animal to its feet again.

If an Israelite's donkey . . . has fallen down (22:4)

Deuteronomy

5"Women are not to wear men's clothing, and men are not to wear women's clothing; the LORD your God hates people who do such things.

6"If you happen to find a bird's nest in a tree or on the ground with the mother bird sitting either on the eggs or with her young, you are not to take the mother bird. 7You may take the young birds, but you must let the mother bird go, so that you will live a long and prosperous life.

8"When you build a new house, be sure to put a railing around the edge of the roof. Then you will not be responsible if someone falls off and is killed.

9"Do not plant any crop in the same field with your grapevines; if you do, you are forbidden to use either the grapes or the produce of the other crop.

10"Do not hitch an ox and a donkey together for plowing.

11"Do not wear cloth made by weaving wool and linen together.

12"Sew tassels on the four corners of your clothes.

Laws concerning Sexual Purity

13"Suppose a man marries a young woman and later he decides he doesn't want her. 14So he makes up false charges against her, accusing her of not being a virgin when they got married.

15"If this happens, the young woman's parents are to take the blood-stained wedding sheet that proves she was a virgin, and they are to show it in court to the town leaders. 16Her father will say to them, 'I gave my daughter to this man in marriage, and now he doesn't want her. 17He has made false charges against her, saying that she was not a virgin when he married her. But here is the proof that my daughter was a virgin; look at the bloodstains on the wedding sheet!' 18Then the town leaders are to take the husband and beat him. 19They are also to fine him a hundred pieces of silver and give the money to the young woman's father, because the man has brought disgrace on an Israelite woman. Moreover, she will continue to be his wife, and he can never divorce her as long as he lives.

20"But if the charge is true and there is no proof that she was a virgin, 21then they are to take her out to the entrance of her father's house, where the men of her city are to stone her to death. She has done a shameful thing among our people by having intercourse before she was married, while she was still living in her father's house. In this way you will get rid of this evil.

22"If a man is caught having intercourse with another man's wife, both of them are to be put to death. In this way you will get rid of this evil.

23"Suppose a man is caught in a town having intercourse with a young woman who is engaged to someone else. 24You are to take them outside the town and stone them to death. She is to die because she did not cry out for help, although she was in a town, where she could have been heard. And the man is to die because he had intercourse with someone who was engaged. In this way you will get rid of this evil.

25"Suppose a man out in the countryside rapes a young woman who is engaged to someone else. Then only the man is to be put to death; 26nothing is to be done to the woman, because she has not committed a sin worthy of death. This case is the same as when one man attacks another man and murders him. 27The man raped the engaged woman in the countryside, and although she cried for help, there was no one to help her.

28"Suppose a man is caught raping a young woman who is not engaged. 29He is to pay her father the bride price of fifty pieces of silver, and she is to become his wife, because he forced her to have intercourse with him. He can never divorce her as long as he lives.

30"No man is to disgrace his father by having intercourse with any of his father's wives.

Exclusion from the LORD's People

23 1"No man who has been castrated or whose penis has been cut off may be included among the LORD's people.

2"No one born out of wedlock or any

descendant of such a person, even in the tenth generation, may be included among the LORD's people.

3 "No Ammonite or Moabite—or any of their descendants, even in the tenth generation—may be included among the LORD's people. 4 They refused to provide you with food and water when you were on your way out of Egypt, and they hired Balaam son of Beor, from the city of Pethor in Mesopotamia, to curse you. 5 But the LORD your God would not listen to Balaam; instead he turned the curse into a blessing, because he loved you. 6 As long as you are a nation, never do anything to help these nations or to make them prosperous.

7 "Do not despise the Edomites; they are your relatives. And do not despise the Egyptians; you once lived in their land. 8 From the third generation onward their descendants may be included among the LORD's people.

Keeping the Military Camp Clean

9 "When you are in camp in time of war, you are to avoid anything that would make you ritually unclean. 10 If a man becomes unclean because he has had a wet dream during the night, he is to go outside the camp and stay there. 11 Toward evening he is to wash himself, and at sunset he may come back into camp.

12 "You are to have a place outside the camp where you can go when you need to relieve yourselves. 13 Carry a stick as part of your equipment, so that when you have a bowel movement you can dig a hole and cover it up. 14 Keep your camp ritually clean, because the LORD your God is with you in your camp to protect you and to give you victory over your enemies. Do not do anything indecent that would cause the LORD to turn his back on you.

Various Laws

15 "If slaves run away from their owners and come to you for protection, do not send them back. 16 They may live in any of your towns that they choose, and you are not to treat them harshly.

17 "No Israelite, man or woman, is to become a temple prostitute. 18 Also, no money earned in this way may be brought into the house of the LORD your God in fulfillment of a vow. The LORD hates temple prostitutes.

19 "When you lend money or food or anything else to Israelites, do not charge them interest. 20 You may charge interest on what you lend to foreigners, but not on what you lend to Israelites. Obey this rule, and the LORD your God will bless everything you do in the land that you are going to occupy.

21 "When you make a vow to the LORD your God, do not put off doing what you promised; the LORD will hold you to your vow, and it is a sin not to keep it. 22 It is no sin not to make a vow to the LORD, 23 but if you make one voluntarily, be sure that you keep it.

24 "When you walk along a path in someone else's vineyard, you may eat all the grapes you want, but you must not carry any away in a container. 25 When you walk along a path in someone else's grainfield, you may eat all the

You may eat all the grapes you want. (23:24)

But you must not carry any away in a container. (23:24)

23:3–5 Neh 13:1, 2   23:4 Num 22:1–6   23:5 Num 23:7—24:9   23:17 Lev 19:29   23:19, 20 Ex 22:25; Lev 25:36, 37; Deut 15:7–11   23:21 Num 30:1–16; Mt 5:33

grain you can pull off with your hands, but you must not cut any grain with a sickle.

Divorce and Remarriage

24 [1] "Suppose a man marries a woman and later decides that he doesn't want her, because he finds something about her that he doesn't like.[s] So he writes out divorce papers, gives them to her, and sends her away from his home. [2] Then suppose she marries another man, [3] and he also decides that he doesn't want her, so he also writes out divorce papers, gives them to her, and sends her away from his home. Or suppose her second husband dies. [4] In either case, her first husband is not to marry her again; he is to consider her defiled. If he married her again, it would be offensive to the LORD. You are not to commit such a terrible sin in the land that the LORD your God is giving you.

Various Laws

[5] "When a man is newly married, he is not to be drafted into military service or any other public duty; he is to be excused from duty for one year, so that he can stay at home and make his wife happy.[t]

[6] "When you lend someone something, you are not to take as security his millstones used for grinding his grain. This would take away the family's means of preparing food to stay alive.

[7] "If any of you kidnap Israelites and make them your slaves or sell them into slavery, you are to be put to death. In this way your nation will get rid of this evil.

[8] "When you are suffering from a dreaded skin disease, be sure to do exactly what the levitical priests tell you; follow the instructions that I have given them. [9] Remember what the LORD your God did to Miriam as you were coming from Egypt.

[10] "When you lend someone something, do not go into his house to get the garment he is going to give you as security; [11] wait

outside and let him bring it to you himself. [12] If he is poor, do not keep it overnight; [13] return it to him each evening, so that he can have it to sleep in. Then he will be grateful, and the LORD your God will be pleased with you.

[14] "Do not cheat poor and needy hired servants, whether they are Israelites or foreigners living in one of your towns. [15] Each day before sunset pay them for that day's work; they need the money and have counted on getting it. If you do not pay them, they will cry out against you to the LORD, and you will be guilty of sin.

[16] "Parents are not to be put to death for crimes committed by their children, and children are not to be put to death for crimes committed by their parents; people are to be put to death only for a crime they themselves have committed.

[17] "Do not deprive foreigners and orphans of their rights; and do not take a widow's garment as security for a loan. [18] Remember that you were slaves in Egypt and that the LORD your God set you free; that is why I have given you this command.

[19] "When you gather your crops and fail to bring in some of the grain that you have cut, do not go back for it; it is to be left for the foreigners, orphans, and widows, so that the LORD your God will bless you in everything you do. [20] When you have picked your olives once, do not go back and get those that are left; they are for the foreigners, orphans, and widows. [21] When you have gathered your grapes once, do not go back over the vines a second time; the grapes that are left are for the foreigners, orphans, and widows. [22] Never forget that you were slaves in Egypt; that is why I have given you this command.

25 [1] "Suppose two Israelites go to court to settle a dispute, and one is declared innocent and the other guilty. [2] If the guilty one is sentenced to be beaten, the judge is to make him lie face downward and have him whipped. The number of lashes will depend on the crime he has committed.

[s] **24:1** something . . . like; *or* that she is guilty of some shameful conduct.   [t] **24:5** make his wife happy; *or* be happy with his wife.
24:1 Mt 5:31; 19:7; Mk 10:4   **24:7** Ex 21:16   **24:8** Lev 13:1—14:54   **24:9** Num 12:10   **24:10–13** Ex 22:26, 27   **24:14, 15** Lev 19:13   **24:16** 2 Kings 14:6; 2 Chr 25:4; Ezek 18:20   **24:17, 18** Ex 23:9; Lev 19:33, 34; Deut 27:19   **24:19–21** Lev 19:9, 10; 23:22

3He may be given as many as forty lashes, but no more; more than that would humiliate him publicly.

4"Do not muzzle an ox when you are using it to thresh grain.

Duty to a Dead Brother

5"If two brothers live on the same property and one of them dies, leaving no son, then his widow is not to be married to someone outside the family; it is the duty of the dead man's brother to marry her. 6The first son that they have will be considered the son of the dead man, so that his family line will continue in Israel. 7But if the dead man's brother does not want to marry her, she is to go before the town leaders and say, 'My husband's brother will not do his duty; he refuses to give his brother a descendant among the people of Israel.' 8Then the town leaders are to summon him and speak to him. If he still refuses to marry her, 9his brother's widow is to go up to him in the presence of the town leaders, take off one of his sandals, spit in his face, and say, 'This is what happens to the man who refuses to give his brother a descendant.' 10His family will be known in Israel as 'the family of the man who had his sandal pulled off.'

Other Laws

11"If two men are having a fight and the wife of one tries to help her husband by grabbing hold of the other man's genitals, 12show her no mercy; cut off her hand.

13-14"Do not cheat when you use weights and measures. 15Use true and honest weights and measures, so that you may live a long time in the land that the LORD your God is giving you. 16The LORD hates people who cheat.

The Command to Kill the Amalekites

17"Remember what the Amalekites did to you as you were coming from Egypt. 18They had no fear of God, and so they attacked you

from the rear when you were tired and exhausted, and killed all who were straggling behind. 19So then, when the LORD your God has given you the land and made you safe from all your enemies who live around you, be sure to kill all the Amalekites, so that no one will remember them any longer. Do not forget!

Harvest Offerings

26 1"After you have occupied the land that the LORD your God is giving you and have settled there, 2each of you must place in a basket the first part of each crop that you harvest and you must take it with you to the one place of worship. 3Go to the priest in charge at that time and say to him, 'I now acknowledge to the LORD my God that I have entered the land that he promised our ancestors to give us.'

4"The priest will take the basket from you and place it before the altar of the LORD your God. 5Then, in the LORD's presence you will recite these words: 'My ancestor was a wandering Aramean, who took his family to Egypt to live. They were few in number when they went there, but they became a large and powerful nation. 6The Egyptians treated us harshly and forced us to work as slaves. 7Then we cried out for help to the LORD, the God of our ancestors. He heard us and saw our suffering, hardship, and misery. 8By his great power and strength he rescued us from Egypt. He worked miracles and wonders, and caused terrifying things to happen. 9He brought us here and gave us this rich and fertile land. 10So now I bring to the LORD the first part of the harvest that he has given me.'

"Then set the basket down in the LORD's presence and worship there. 11Be grateful for the good things that the LORD your God has given you and your family; and let the Levites and the foreigners who live among you join in the celebration.

12"Every third year give the tithe—a tenth of your crops—to the Levites, the foreigners, the orphans, and the widows, so

25:3 2 Cor 11:24 **25:4** 1 Cor 9:9; 1 Tim 5:18 **25:5, 6** Mt 22:24; Mk 12:19; Lk 20:28 **25:7–10** Ruth 4:7, 8 **25:13–16** Lev 19:35, 36 **25:17–19** Ex 17:8–14; 1 Sam 15:2–9 **26:2** Ex 23:19 **26:12** Deut 14:28, 29

that in every community they will have all they need to eat. When you have done this, [13]say to the LORD, 'None of the sacred tithe is left in my house; I have given it to the Levites, the foreigners, the orphans, and the widows, as you commanded me to do. I have not disobeyed or forgotten any of your commands concerning the tithe. [14]I have not eaten any of it when I was mourning; I have not taken any of it out of my house when I was ritually unclean; and I have not given any of it as an offering for the dead.[u] I have obeyed you, O LORD; I have done everything you commanded concerning the tithe. [15]Look down from your holy place in heaven and bless your people Israel; bless also the rich and fertile land that you have given us, as you promised our ancestors.'

The LORD's Own People

[16]"Today the LORD your God commands you to obey all his laws; so obey them faithfully with all your heart. [17]Today you have acknowledged the LORD as your God; you have promised to obey him, to keep all his laws, and to do all that he commands. [18]Today the LORD has accepted you as his own people, as he promised you; and he commands you to obey all his laws. [19]He will make you greater than any other nation that he has created, and you will bring praise and honor to his name.[v] You will be his own people, as he promised."

God's Laws Written on Stones

27 [1]Then Moses, together with the leaders of Israel, said to the people, "Obey all the instructions that I am giving you today. [2]On the day you cross the Jordan River and enter the land that the LORD your God is giving you, you are to set up some large stones, cover them with plaster, [3]and write on them all these laws and teachings. When you have entered the rich and fertile land that the LORD, the God of your ancestors, promised you, [4]and you are on the

other side of the Jordan, set up these stones on Mount Ebal, as I am instructing you today, and cover them with plaster. [5]Build an altar there made of stones that have had no iron tools used on them, [6]because any altar you build for the LORD your God must be made of uncut stones. There you are to offer the sacrifices that are to be burned, [7]and there you are to sacrifice and eat your fellowship offerings and be grateful in the presence of the LORD your God. [8]On the stones covered with plaster write clearly every word of God's laws."

[9]Then Moses, together with the levitical priests, said to all the people of Israel, "Give me your attention, people of Israel, and listen to me. Today you have become the people of the LORD your God; [10]so obey him and keep all his laws that I am giving you today."

"People of Israel . . . listen to me." (27:9)

The Curses on Disobedience

[11]Then Moses said to the people of Israel, [12]"After you have crossed the Jordan, the following tribes are to stand on Mount Gerizim when the blessings are pronounced on the people: Simeon, Levi, Judah, Issachar, Joseph, and Benjamin. [13]And the following tribes will stand on Mount Ebal when the curses are pronounced: Reuben, Gad, Asher, Zebulun, Dan, and Naphtali. [14]The Levites will speak these words in a loud voice:

[15]" 'God's curse on anyone who makes an idol of stone, wood, or metal and secretly worships it; the LORD hates idolatry.'

"And all the people will answer, 'Amen!'

[16]" 'God's curse on anyone who dishonors his father or mother.'

"And all the people will answer, 'Amen!'"

17" 'God's curse on anyone who moves a neighbor's property line.'

"And all the people will answer, 'Amen!'"

18" 'God's curse on anyone who leads a blind person in the wrong direction.'

"And all the people will answer, 'Amen!'"

19" 'God's curse on anyone who deprives foreigners, orphans, and widows of their rights.'

"And all the people will answer, 'Amen!'"

20" 'God's curse on anyone who disgraces his father by having intercourse with any of his father's wives.'

"And all the people will answer, 'Amen!'"

21" 'God's curse on anyone who has sexual relations with an animal.'

"And all the people will answer, 'Amen!'"

22" 'God's curse on anyone who has intercourse with his sister or half sister.'

"And all the people will answer, 'Amen!'"

23" 'God's curse on anyone who has intercourse with his mother-in-law.'

"And all the people will answer, 'Amen!'"

24" 'God's curse on anyone who secretly commits murder.'

"And all the people will answer, 'Amen!'"

25" 'God's curse on anyone who accepts money to murder an innocent person.'

"And all the people will answer, 'Amen!'"

26" 'God's curse on anyone who does not obey all of God's laws and teachings.'

"And all the people will answer, 'Amen!'"

The Blessings of Obedience
(Leviticus 26:3–13; Deuteronomy 7:12–24)

28 1 "If you obey the LORD your God and faithfully keep all his commands that I am giving you today, he will make you greater than any other nation on earth. 2Obey the LORD your God and all these blessings will be yours:

3 "The LORD will bless your towns and your fields.

4 "The LORD will bless you with many children, with abundant crops, and with many cattle and sheep.

5 "The LORD will bless your grain crops and the food you prepare from them.

6 "The LORD will bless everything you do.

7 "The LORD will defeat your enemies when they attack you. They will attack from one direction, but they will run from you in all directions.

8 "The LORD your God will bless your work and fill your barns with grain. He will bless you in the land that he is giving you.

9 "If you obey the LORD your God and do everything he commands, he will make you his own people, as he has promised. 10Then all the peoples on earth will see that the LORD has chosen you to be his own people, and they will be afraid of you. 11The LORD will give you many children, many cattle, and abundant crops in the land that he promised your ancestors to give you. 12He will send rain in season from his rich storehouse in the sky and bless all your work, so that you will lend to many nations, but you will not have to borrow from any. 13The LORD your God will make you the leader among the nations and not a follower; you will always prosper and never fail if you obey faithfully all his commands that I am giving you today. 14But you must never disobey them in any way, or worship and serve other gods.

The Consequences of Disobedience
(Leviticus 26:14–46)

15 "But if you disobey the LORD your God and do not faithfully keep all his commands and laws that I am giving you today, all these evil things will happen to you:

16 "The LORD will curse your towns and your fields.

17 "The LORD will curse your grain crops and the food you prepare from them.

18 "The LORD will curse you by giving you only a few children, poor crops, and few cattle and sheep.

19 "The LORD will curse everything you do.

20 "If you do evil and reject the LORD, he will bring on you disaster, confusion, and

27:17 Deut 19:14   **27:18** Lev 19:14   **27:19** Ex 22:21; 23:9; Lev 19:33, 34; Deut 24:17, 18   **27:20** Lev 18:8; 20:11; Deut 22:30   **27:21** Ex 22:19; Lev 18:23; 20:15   **27:22** Lev 18:9; 20:17   **27:23** Lev 18:17; 20:14   **27:26** Gal 3:10   **28:1–14** Deut 11:13–17

But if you disobey the LORD (28:15)

trouble in everything you do, until you are quickly and completely destroyed. 21He will send disease after disease on you until there is not one of you left in the land that you are about to occupy. 22The LORD will strike you with infectious diseases, with swelling and fever; he will send drought and scorching winds to destroy your crops. These disasters will be with you until you die. 23No rain will fall, and your ground will become as hard as iron. 24Instead of rain, the LORD will send down duststorms and sandstorms until you are destroyed.

25"The LORD will give your enemies victory over you. You will attack them from one direction, but you will run from them in all directions, and all the people on earth will be terrified when they see what happens to you. 26When you die, birds and wild animals will come and eat your bodies, and there will be no one to scare them off. 27The LORD will send boils on you, as he did on the Egyptians. He will make your bodies break out with sores. You will be covered with scabs, and you will itch, but there will be no cure. 28The LORD will make you lose your mind; he will strike you with

blindness and confusion. 29You will grope about in broad daylight like someone blind, and you will not be able to find your way. You will not prosper in anything you do. You will be constantly oppressed and robbed, and there will be no one to help you.

30"You will be engaged to a young woman—but someone else will marry her. You will build a house—but never live in it. You will plant a vineyard—but never eat its grapes. 31Your cattle will be butchered before your very eyes, but you will not eat any of the meat. Your donkeys will be dragged away while you look on, and they will not be given back to you. Your sheep will be given to your enemies, and there will be no one to help you. 32Your sons and daughters will be given as slaves to foreigners while you look on. Every day you will strain your eyes, looking in vain for your children to return. 33A foreign nation will take all the crops that you have worked so hard to grow, while you receive nothing but constant oppression and harsh treatment. 34Your sufferings will make you lose your mind. 35The LORD will cover your legs with incurable, painful sores; boils will cover you from head to foot.

36"The LORD will take you and your king away to a foreign land, where neither you nor your ancestors ever lived before; there you will serve gods made of wood and stone. 37In the countries to which the LORD will scatter you, the people will be shocked at what has happened to you; they will make fun of you and ridicule you.

38"You will plant plenty of seed, but reap only a small harvest, because the locusts will eat your crops. 39You will plant vineyards and take care of them, but you will not gather their grapes or drink wine from them, because worms will eat the vines. 40Olive trees will grow everywhere in your land, but you will not have any olive oil, because the olives will drop off. 41You will have sons and daughters, but you will lose them, because they will be taken away as prisoners of war. 42All your trees and crops will be devoured by insects.

43"Foreigners who live in your land will gain more and more power, while you gradually lose yours. 44They will have money to lend you, but you will have none to lend them. In the end they will be your rulers.

45 "All these disasters will come on you, and they will be with you until you are destroyed, because you did not obey the LORD your God and keep all the laws that he gave you. 46 They will be the evidence of God's judgment on you and your descendants forever. 47 The LORD blessed you in every way, but you would not serve him with glad and joyful hearts. 48 So then, you will serve the enemies that the LORD is going to send against you. You will be hungry, thirsty, and naked—in need of everything. The LORD[w] will oppress you harshly until you are destroyed. 49 The LORD will bring against you a nation from the ends of the earth, a nation whose language you do not know. They will swoop down on you like an eagle. 50 They will be ruthless and show no mercy to anyone, young or old. 51 They will eat your livestock and your crops, and you will starve to death. They will not leave you any grain, wine, olive oil, cattle, or sheep; and you will die. 52 They will attack every town in the land that the LORD your God is giving you, and the high, fortified walls in which you trust will fall.

53 "When your enemies are besieging your towns, you will become so desperate for food that you will even eat the children that the LORD your God has given you. 54-55 Even the most refined man of noble birth will become so desperate during the siege that he will eat some of his own children because he has no other food. He will not even give any to his brother or to the wife he loves or to any of his children who are left. 56-57 Even the most refined woman of noble birth, so rich that she has never had to walk anywhere, will behave in the same way. When the enemy besieges her town, she will become so desperate for food that she will secretly eat her newborn child and the afterbirth as well. She will not share them with the husband she loves or with any of her children.

58 "If you do not obey faithfully all of God's teachings that are written in this book

and if you do not honor the wonderful and awesome name of the LORD your God, 59 he will send on you and on your descendants incurable diseases and horrible epidemics that can never be stopped. 60 He will bring on you once again all the dreadful diseases you experienced in Egypt, and you will never recover. 61 He will also send all kinds of diseases and epidemics that are not mentioned in this book of God's laws and teachings, and you will be destroyed. 62 Although you become as numerous as the stars in the sky, only a few of you will survive, because you did not obey the LORD your God. 63 Just as the LORD took delight in making you prosper and in making you increase in number, so he will take delight in destroying you and in bringing ruin on you. You will be uprooted from the land that you are about to occupy.

64 "The LORD will scatter you among all the nations, from one end of the earth to the other, and there you will serve gods made of wood and stone, gods that neither you nor your ancestors have ever worshiped before. 65 You will find no peace anywhere, no place to call your own; the LORD will overwhelm you with anxiety, hopelessness, and despair. 66 Your life will always be in danger. Day and night you will be filled with terror, and you will live in constant fear of death. 67 Your hearts will pound with fear at everything you see. Every morning you will wish for evening; every evening you will wish for morning. 68 The LORD will send you back to Egypt in ships, even though he[x] said that you would never have to go there again. There you will try to sell yourselves to your enemies as slaves, but no one will want to buy you."

The LORD's Covenant with Israel in the Land of Moab

29 1 These are the terms of the covenant that the LORD commanded Moses to make with the people of Israel in the land of Moab; all this was in addition to the covenant which the LORD had made with them at Mount Sinai.

---

w **28:48** The LORD; or Your enemies.   x **28:68** he; or I.
28:57 2 Kings 6:28, 29; Lam 4:10

²Moses called together all the people of Israel and said to them, "You saw for yourselves what the LORD did to the king of Egypt, to his officials, and to his entire country. ³You saw the terrible plagues, the miracles, and the great wonders that the LORD performed. ⁴But to this very day he has not let you understand what you have experienced. ⁵For forty years the LORD led you through the desert, and your clothes and sandals never wore out. ⁶You did not have bread to eat or wine or beer to drink, but the LORD provided for your needs in order to teach you that he is your God. ⁷And when we came to this place, King Sihon of Heshbon and King Og of Bashan came out to fight against us. But we defeated them, ⁸took their land, and divided it among the tribes of Reuben and Gad, and half the tribe of Manasseh. ⁹Obey faithfully all the terms of this covenant, so that you will be successful in everything you do.

¹⁰"Today you are standing in the presence of the LORD your God, all of you—your leaders and officials, your men, ¹¹women, and children, and the foreigners who live among you and cut wood and carry water for you. ¹²You are here today to enter into this covenant that the LORD your God is making with you and to accept its obligations, ¹³so that the LORD may now confirm you as his people and be your God, as he promised you and your ancestors, Abraham, Isaac, and Jacob. ¹⁴You are not the only ones with whom the LORD is making this covenant with its obligations. ¹⁵He is making it with all of us who stand here in his presence today and also with our descendants who are not yet born.

¹⁶"You remember what life was like in Egypt and what it was like to travel through the territory of other nations. ¹⁷You saw their disgusting idols made of wood, stone, silver, and gold. ¹⁸Make sure that no man, woman, family, or tribe standing here today turns from the LORD our God to worship the gods of other nations. This would be like a root that grows to be a bitter and poisonous plant. ¹⁹Make sure that there is no one here today who hears these solemn demands

and yet convinces himself that all will be well with him, even if he stubbornly goes his own way. That would destroy all of you, good and evil alike. ²⁰The LORD will not forgive such a man. Instead, the LORD's burning anger will flame up against him, and all the disasters written in this book will fall on him until the LORD has destroyed him completely. ²¹The LORD will make an example of him before all the tribes of Israel and will bring disaster on him in accordance with all the curses listed in the covenant that is written in this book of the LORD's teachings.

²²"In future generations your descendants and foreigners from distant lands will see the disasters and sufferings that the LORD has brought on your land. ²³The fields will be a barren waste, covered with sulfur and salt; nothing will be planted, and not even weeds will grow there. Your land will be like the cities of Sodom and Gomorrah, of Admah and Zeboiim, which the LORD destroyed when he was furiously angry. ²⁴Then the whole world will ask, 'Why did the LORD do this to their land? What was the reason for his fierce anger?' ²⁵And the answer will be, 'It is because the LORD's people broke the covenant they had made with him, the God of their ancestors, when he brought them out of Egypt. ²⁶They served other gods that they had never worshiped before, gods that the LORD had forbidden them to worship. ²⁷And so the LORD became angry with his people and brought on their land all the disasters written in this book. ²⁸The LORD became furiously angry, and in his great anger he uprooted them from their land and threw them into a foreign land, and there they are today.'

²⁹"There are some things that the LORD our God has kept secret; but he has revealed his Law, and we and our descendants are to obey it forever.

Conditions for Restoration and Blessing

30 ¹"I have now given you a choice between a blessing and a curse. When all these things have happened to you,

29:7 a Num 21:21–30; b Num 21:31–35   **29:8** Num 32:33   **29:18** Heb 12:15   **29:23** Gen 19:24, 25

and you are living among the nations where the LORD your God has scattered you, you will remember the choice I gave you. ²If you and your descendants will turn back to the LORD and with all your heart obey his commands that I am giving you today, ³then the LORD your God will have mercy on you. He will bring you back from the nations where he has scattered you, and he will make you prosperous again. ⁴Even if you are scattered to the farthest corners of the earth, the LORD your God will gather you together and bring you back, ⁵so that you may again take possession of the land where your ancestors once lived. And he will make you more prosperous and more numerous than your ancestors ever were. ⁶The LORD your God will give you and your descendants obedient hearts, so that you will love him with all your heart, and you will continue to live in that land. ⁷He will turn all these curses against your enemies, who hated you and oppressed you, ⁸and you will again obey him and keep all his commands that I am giving you today. ⁹The LORD will make you prosperous in all that you do; you will have many children and a lot of livestock, and your fields will produce abundant crops. He will be as glad to make you prosperous as he was to make your ancestors prosperous, ¹⁰but you will have to obey him and keep all his laws that are written in this book of his teachings. You will have to turn to him with all your heart.

¹¹"The command that I am giving you today is not too difficult or beyond your reach. ¹²It is not up in the sky. You do not have to ask, 'Who will go up and bring it down for us, so that we can hear it and obey it?' ¹³Nor is it on the other side of the ocean. You do not have to ask, 'Who will go across the ocean and bring it to us, so that we may hear it and obey it?' ¹⁴No, it is here with you. You know it and can quote it, so now obey it.

¹⁵"Today I am giving you a choice between good and evil, between life and death. ¹⁶If you obey the commands of the LORD your God,ʸ which I give you today, if you love him, obey him, and keep all his

laws, then you will prosper and become a nation of many people. The LORD your God will bless you in the land that you are about to occupy. ¹⁷But if you disobey and refuse to listen, and are led away to worship other gods, ¹⁸you will be destroyed—I warn you here and now. You will not live long in that land across the Jordan that you are about to occupy. ¹⁹I am now giving you the choice between life and death, between God's blessing and God's curse, and I call heaven and earth to witness the choice you make. Choose life. ²⁰Love the LORD your God, obey him and be faithful to him, and then you and your descendants will live long in the land that he promised to give your ancestors, Abraham, Isaac, and Jacob."

Choose life. (30:19)

Joshua Becomes Moses' Successor

31 ¹Moses continued speaking to the people of Israel, ²and said, "I am now a hundred and twenty years old and am

---

ʸ **30:16** *One ancient translation* If you obey the commands of the LORD your God; *Hebrew does not have these words.*

30:12–14 Rom 10:6–8   **30:15** Sir 15:16, 17   **30:20 a** Gen 12:7; **b** Gen 26:3; **c** Gen 28:13   **31:2** Num 20:12

Deuteronomy

no longer able to be your leader. And besides this, the LORD has told me that I will not cross the Jordan. ³The LORD your God himself will go before you and destroy the nations living there, so that you can occupy their land; and Joshua will be your leader, as the LORD has said. ⁴The LORD will destroy those people, just as he defeated Sihon and Og, kings of the Amorites, and destroyed their country. ⁵The LORD will give you victory over them, and you are to treat them exactly as I have told you. ⁶Be determined and confident. Do not be afraid of them. Your God, the LORD himself, will be with you. He will not fail you or abandon you."

⁷Then Moses called Joshua and said to him in the presence of all the people of Israel, "Be determined and confident; you are the one who will lead these people to occupy the land that the LORD promised to their ancestors. ⁸The LORD himself will lead you and be with you. He will not fail you or abandon you, so do not lose courage or be afraid."

The Law Is to Be Read Every Seven Years

⁹So Moses wrote down God's Law and gave it to the levitical priests, who were in charge of the LORD's Covenant Box, and to the leaders of Israel. ¹⁰He commanded them, "At the end of every seven years, when the year that debts are canceled comes around, read this aloud at the Festival of Shelters. ¹¹Read it to the people of Israel when they come to worship the LORD your God at the one place of worship. ¹²Call together all the men, women, and children, and the foreigners who live in your towns, so that everyone may hear it and learn to honor the LORD your God and to obey his teachings faithfully. ¹³In this way your descendants who have never heard the Law of the LORD your God will hear it. And so they will learn to obey him as long as they live in the land that you are about to occupy across the Jordan."

The LORD's Last Instructions to Moses

¹⁴Then the LORD said to Moses, "You do not have much longer to live. Call Joshua and bring him to the Tent, so that I may give him his instructions." Moses and Joshua went to the Tent, ¹⁵and the LORD appeared to them there in a pillar of cloud that stood by the door of the Tent.

¹⁶The LORD said to Moses, "You will soon die, and after your death the people will become unfaithful to me and break the covenant that I made with them. They will abandon me and worship the pagan gods of the land they are about to enter. ¹⁷When that happens, I will become angry with them; I will abandon them, and they will be destroyed. Many terrible disasters will come upon them, and then they will realize that these things are happening to them because I, their God, am no longer with them. ¹⁸And I will refuse to help them then, because they have done evil and worshiped other gods.

¹⁹"Now, write down this song. Teach it to the people of Israel, so that it will stand as evidence against them. ²⁰I will take them into this rich and fertile land, as I promised their ancestors. There they will have all the food they want, and they will live comfortably. But they will turn away and worship other gods. They will reject me and break my covenant, ²¹and many terrible disasters will come on them. But this song will still be sung, and it will stand as evidence against them. Even now, before I take them into the land that I promised to give them, I know what they are thinking."

²²That same day Moses wrote down the song and taught it to the people of Israel.

²³Then the LORD spoke to Joshua son of Nun and told him, "Be confident and determined. You will lead the people of Israel into the land that I promised them, and I will be with you."

²⁴Moses wrote God's Law in a book, taking care not to leave out anything. ²⁵When he finished, he said to the levitical priests, who were in charge of the LORD's Covenant Box, ²⁶"Take this book of God's Law and place it beside the Covenant Box of the LORD your

God, so that it will remain there as a witness against his people. ²⁷I know how stubborn and rebellious they are. They have rebelled against the LORD during my lifetime, and they will rebel even more after I am dead. ²⁸Assemble all your tribal leaders and officials before me, so that I can tell them these things; I will call heaven and earth to be my witnesses against them. ²⁹I know that after my death the people will become wicked and reject what I have taught them. And in time to come they will meet with disaster, because they will have made the LORD angry by doing what he has forbidden."

The Song of Moses

³⁰Then Moses recited the entire song while all the people of Israel listened.

32 ¹"Earth and sky, hear my words,
listen closely to what I say.
²My teaching will fall like drops of rain
and form on the earth like dew.
My words will fall like showers on young plants,
like gentle rain on tender grass.
³I will praise the name of the LORD,
and his people will tell of his greatness.

⁴"The LORD is your mighty defender,
perfect and just in all his ways;
Your God is faithful and true;
he does what is right and fair.
⁵But you are unfaithful, unworthy to be his people,ᶻ
a sinful and deceitful nation.
⁶Is this the way you should treat the LORD,
you foolish, senseless people?
He is your father, your Creator,
he made you into a nation.

⁷"Think of the past, of the time long ago;
ask your parents to tell you what happened,
ask the old people to tell of the past.
⁸The Most High assigned nations their lands;
he determined where peoples should live.

He assigned to each nation a heavenly being,
⁹ but Jacob's descendants he chose for himself.

¹⁰"He found them wandering through the desert,
a desolate, wind-swept wilderness.
He protected them and cared for them,
as he would protect himself.
¹¹Like an eagle teaching its young to fly,ᵃ
catching them safely on its spreading wings,
the LORD kept Israel from falling.
¹²The LORD alone led his people
without the help of a foreign god.

¹³"He let them rule the highlands,
and they ate what grew in the fields.
They found wild honey among the rocks;
their olive trees flourished in stony ground.
¹⁴Their cows and goats gave plenty of milk;
they had the best sheep, goats, and cattle,
the finest wheat, and the choicest wine.

¹⁵"The LORD's people grew rich, but rebellious;
they were fat and stuffed with food.
They abandoned God their Creator
and rejected their mighty savior.
¹⁶Their idolatry made the LORD jealous;
the evil they did made him angry.
¹⁷They sacrificed to gods that are not real,
new gods their ancestors had never known,
gods that Israel had never obeyed.
¹⁸They forgot their God, their mighty savior,
the one who had given them life.

¹⁹"When the LORD saw this, he was angry
and rejected his sons and daughters.
²⁰'I will no longer help them,' he said;
'then I will see what happens to them,
those stubborn, unfaithful people.
²¹With their idols they have made me angry,
jealous with their so-called gods,
gods that are really not gods.

ᶻ **32:5** *Probable text* But you . . . people; *Hebrew unclear.*   ᵃ **32:11** teaching its young to fly; *or* watching over its young.
32:8 Acts 17:26   **32:17** 1 Cor 10:20   **32:21 a** 1 Cor 10:22; **b** Rom 10:19

So I will use a so-called nation to make
  them angry;
  I will make them jealous with a nation
    of fools.
22 My anger will flame up like fire
  and burn everything on earth.
It will reach to the world below[b]
  and consume the roots of the
    mountains.

23 " 'I will bring on them endless disasters
  and use all my arrows against them.
24 They will die from hunger and fever;
  they will die from terrible diseases.
I will send wild animals to attack them,
  and poisonous snakes to bite them.
25 War will bring death in the streets;
  terrors will strike in the homes.
Young men and young women will die;
  neither babies nor old people will be
    spared.
26 I would have destroyed them completely,
  so that no one would remember them.
27 But I could not let their enemies boast
  that they had defeated my people,
  when it was I myself who had crushed
    them.'

28 "Israel is a nation without sense;
  they have no wisdom at all.
29 They fail to see why they were defeated;
  they cannot understand what happened.
30 Why were a thousand defeated by one,
  and ten thousand by only two?
The LORD, their God, had abandoned
    them;
  their mighty God had given them up.
31 Their enemies know that their own gods
    are weak,
  not mighty like Israel's God.
32 Their enemies, corrupt as Sodom and
    Gomorrah,
  are like vines that bear bitter and
    poisonous grapes,
33 like wine made from the venom of
    snakes.
34 "The LORD remembers what their
    enemies have done;
  he waits for the right time to punish
    them.

35 The LORD will take revenge and punish
    them;
  the time will come when they will fall;
  the day of their doom is near.
36 The LORD will rescue his people
  when he sees that their strength is
    gone.
He will have mercy on those who serve
    him,
  when he sees how helpless they are.
37 Then the LORD will ask his people,
  'Where are those mighty gods you
    trusted?
38 You fed them the fat of your sacrifices
  and offered them wine to drink.
Let them come and help you now;
  let them run to your rescue.

39 " 'I, and I alone, am God;
  no other god is real.
I kill and I give life, I wound and I heal,
  and no one can oppose what I do.
40 As surely as I am the living God,
  I raise my hand and I vow
41 that I will sharpen my flashing sword
  and see that justice is done.
I will take revenge on my enemies
  and punish those who hate me.
42 My arrows will drip with their blood,
  and my sword will kill all who oppose
    me.
I will spare no one who fights against me;
  even the wounded and prisoners will
    die.'

43 "Nations, you must praise the LORD's
    people—
  he punishes all who kill them.
He takes revenge on his enemies
  and forgives the sins of his people."

44 Moses and Joshua son of Nun recited this
song, so that the people of Israel could hear it.

Moses' Final Instructions

45 When Moses had finished giving God's
teachings to the people, 46 he said, "Be sure to
obey all these commands that I have given
you today. Repeat them to your children, so
that they may faithfully obey all of God's

---

b 32:22 THE WORLD BELOW: *This refers to the world of the dead.*
32:35 Rom 12:19; Heb 10:30   32:36a Ps 135:14   32:43 Rom 15:10; Rev 19:2

teachings. ⁴⁷These teachings are not empty words; they are your very life. Obey them and you will live long in that land across the Jordan that you are about to occupy."

⁴⁸That same day the LORD said to Moses, ⁴⁹"Go to the Abarim Mountains in the land of Moab opposite the city of Jericho; climb Mount Nebo and look at the land of Canaan that I am about to give the people of Israel. ⁵⁰You will die on that mountain as your brother Aaron died on Mount Hor, ⁵¹because both of you were unfaithful to me in the presence of the people of Israel. When you were at the waters of Meribah, near the town of Kadesh in the wilderness of Zin, you dishonored me in the presence of the people. ⁵²You will look at the land from a distance, but you will not enter the land that I am giving the people of Israel."

Moses Blesses the Tribes of Israel

33 ¹These are the blessings that Moses, the man of God, pronounced on the people of Israel before he died.

² The LORD came from Mount Sinai;
   he rose like the sun over Edom
   and shone on his people from Mount
     Paran.
   Ten thousand angels were with him,
   a flaming fire at his right hand.^c
³ The LORD loves his people^d
   and protects those who belong to him.
   So we bow at^e his feet
   and obey his commands.
⁴ We obey the Law that Moses gave us,
   our nation's most treasured possession.
⁵ The LORD became king of his people Israel
   when their tribes and leaders were
     gathered together.

⁶Moses said about the tribe of Reuben:
   "May Reuben never die out,
   Although their people are few."

⁷About the tribe of Judah he said:
   "LORD, listen to their cry for help;

Unite them again with the other tribes.
Fight for them, LORD,
And help them against their enemies."^f

⁸About the tribe of Levi he said:
   "You, LORD, reveal your will by the Urim
     and Thummim^g
   Through your faithful servants, the
     Levites;
   You put them to the test at Massah
   And proved them true at the waters of
     Meribah.
⁹ They showed greater loyalty to you
   Than to parents, brothers, or children.
   They obeyed your commands
   And were faithful to your covenant.
¹⁰ They will teach your people to obey your
     Law;
   They will offer sacrifices on your altar.
¹¹ LORD, help their tribe to grow strong;
   Be pleased with what they do.
   Crush all their enemies;
   Let them never rise again."

¹²About the tribe of Benjamin he said:
   "This is the tribe the LORD loves and
     protects;
   He guards them all the day long,
   And he dwells in their midst."^h

¹³About the tribe of Joseph he said:
   "May the LORD bless their land with rain
   And with water from under the earth.
¹⁴ May their land be blessed with sun-
     ripened fruit,
   Rich with the best fruits of each season.
¹⁵ May their ancient hills be covered with
     choice fruit.
¹⁶ May their land be filled with all that is
     good,
   Blessed by the goodness of the LORD,
   Who spoke from the burning bush.
   May these blessings come to the tribe of
     Joseph,
   Because he was the leader among his
     brothers.
¹⁷ Joseph has the strength of a bull,
   The horns of a wild ox.

---

^c **33:2** *Probable text* Ten thousand . . . right hand; *Hebrew unclear.*   ^d **33:3** *One ancient translation* his people; *Hebrew* the peoples.   ^e **33:3** *Probable text* bow at; *Hebrew unclear.*   ^f **33:7** *Probable text* Fight for . . . enemies; *Hebrew* The tribe of Judah will fight for itself, and the LORD will help it against its enemies.   ^g **33:8** URIM AND THUMMIM: *Two objects used by the priest to determine God's will; it is not known precisely how they were used.*   ^h **33:12** And he . . . midst; *or* They live under his protection.

32:48–52 Num 27:12–14; Deut 3:23–27   **33:8 a** Ex 28:30; **b** Ex 17:7; **c** Ex 17:7; Num 20:13

His horns are Manasseh's thousands
And Ephraim's ten thousands.
With them he gores the nations
And pushes them to the ends of the
    earth."

18 About the tribes of Zebulun and
Issachar he said:
"May Zebulun be prosperous in their
    trade on the sea,
And may Issachar's wealth increase at
    home.
19 They invite foreigners to their mountain
And offer the right sacrifices there.
They get their wealth from the sea
And from the sand along the shore."

20 About the tribe of Gad he said:
"Praise God, who made their territory
    large.
Gad waits like a lion
To tear off an arm or a scalp.
21 They took the best of the land for
    themselves;
A leader's share was assigned to them.
They obeyed the LORD's commands and
    laws
When the leaders of Israel were gathered
    together."[i]

22 About the tribe of Dan he said:
"Dan is a young lion;
He leaps out from Bashan."

23 About the tribe of Naphtali he said:
"Naphtali is richly blessed by the LORD's
    good favor;

Their land reaches to the south from Lake
    Galilee."

24 About the tribe of Asher he said:
"Asher is blessed more than the other
    tribes.
May he be the favorite of his brothers,
And may his land be rich with olive trees.
25 May his towns be protected with iron
    gates,
And may he always live secure."

26 People of Israel, no god is like your God,
    riding in splendor across the sky,
    riding through the clouds to come to
        your aid.
27 God has always been your defense;
    his eternal arms are your support.
He drove out your enemies as you
        advanced,
    and told you to destroy them all.
28 So Jacob's descendants live in peace,
    secure in a land full of grain and wine,
    where dew from the sky waters the
        ground.
29 Israel, how happy you are!
    There is no one like you,
    a nation saved by the LORD.
The LORD himself is your shield and your
        sword,
    to defend you and give you victory.
Your enemies will come begging for
        mercy,
    and you will trample them down.

---

[i] *33:21* One ancient translation When the leaders . . . together; Hebrew unclear.

The LORD showed him the whole land. (34:1)

The Death of Moses

34 ¹Moses went up from the plains of Moab to Mount Nebo, to the top of Mount Pisgah east of Jericho, and there the LORD showed him the whole land: the territory of Gilead as far north as the town of Dan; ²the entire territory of Naphtali; the territories of Ephraim and Manasseh; the territory of Judah as far west as the Mediterranean Sea; ³the southern part of Judah; and the plain that reaches from Zoar to Jericho, the city of palm trees. ⁴Then the LORD said to Moses, "This is the land that I promised Abraham, Isaac, and Jacob I would give to their descendants. I have let you see it, but I will not let you go there."

⁵So Moses, the LORD's servant, died there in the land of Moab, as the LORD had said he would. ⁶The LORD buried him in a valley in Moab, opposite the town of Bethpeor, but to this day no one knows the exact place of his burial. ⁷Moses was a hundred and twenty years old when he died; he was as strong as ever, and his eyesight was still good. ⁸The people of Israel mourned for him for thirty days in the plains of Moab.

⁹Joshua son of Nun was filled with wisdom, because Moses had appointed him to be his successor. The people of Israel obeyed Joshua and kept the commands that the LORD had given them through Moses.

¹⁰There has never been a prophet in Israel like Moses; the LORD spoke with him face to face. ¹¹No other prophet has ever done miracles and wonders like those that the LORD sent Moses to perform against the king of Egypt, his officials, and the entire country. ¹²No other prophet has been able to do the great and terrifying things that Moses did in the sight of all Israel.

34:4 a Gen 12:7; b Gen 26:3; c Gen 28:13   34:10 Ex 33:11; Sir 45:1–5

Deuteronomy

THE BOOK OF Joshua

Action, adventure, spies, sieges, battles—the Book of Joshua is full of great stories. It is also part of a larger story, the story of the People of God. Moses led them out of slavery and through the wilderness. Now Joshua is their leader. They are about to enter the Promised Land. The people see their military victories as God's reward for their obedience. The Book of Joshua shows God's faithfulness in fulfilling his promise to his people.

Chap. 6

Head_{lines}

- Rahab Rescues Spies on the Roof! (2:1–24)
- The Walls Come Tumbling Down (5:13—6:27)
- Disguise Fools Joshua (9:3–15)
- Women Request Right to Land! (17:3–6)
- Argument Erupts Over Monument (22:13–20)
- People Vow to Serve the Lord (24:14–18)

FACTOIDS

Who wrote this book? The author is not known. Some scholars think it was the same person or group who wrote Deuteronomy.

When was it written? The book probably went through several stages as various stories were collected and written down. The final version was probably written during the Babylonian Exile.

Why was it written? The Book of Joshua was written to reinforce the idea that obedience to God will be rewarded and disobedience will be punished

What is the Jesus connection? The name Jesus is the Greek form of the Hebrew name Joshua.

Important themes

- God is always with his people, no matter where they are.
- God gives those who are faithful and obedient the Promised Land.
- Do not worship false gods but serve only the God of Israel.

JOSHUA

Big Shoes to Fill

Moses had led the Israelites out of Egypt and through the wilderness. He had been with them as their leader for forty years! Now Joshua is chosen as the one to lead the people after Moses died. That must have been scary for Joshua. But God promises Joshua, "I will always be with you; I will never abandon you" (1:5). Read chapter 34 of Deuteronomy to see how Joshua's story is a continuation of the story of Moses and God's Chosen People, the Israelites.

It can be hard to follow others who were really good at something. Maybe you are on the basketball team the year after the previous team won the regional title. Maybe you're following an older brother or sister who got all A's in school. If you sometimes feel like you have big shoes to fill, remember Joshua and fear not! God will be with you and never abandon you. God doesn't ask you to be successful, just to be faithful to him.

— Joshua 1:1–9

God Commands Joshua to Conquer Canaan

1 ¹After the death of the LORD's servant Moses, the LORD spoke to Moses' helper, Joshua son of Nun. ²He said, "My servant Moses is dead. Get ready now, you and all the people of Israel, and cross the Jordan River into the land that I am giving them. ³As I told Moses, I have given you and all my people the entire land that you will be marching over. ⁴Your borders will reach from the desert in the south to the Lebanon Mountains in the north; from the great Euphrates River in the east, through the Hittite country, to the Mediterranean Sea in the west. ⁵Joshua, no one will be able to defeat you as long as you live. I will be with you as I was with Moses. I will always be with you; I will never abandon you. ⁶Be determined and confident, for you will be the leader of these people as they occupy this land which I promised their ancestors. ⁷Just be determined, be confident; and make sure that you obey the whole Law that my servant Moses gave you. Do not neglect any part of it and you will succeed wherever you go. ⁸Be sure that the book of the Law is always read in your worship. Study it day and night, and make sure that you obey everything written in it. Then you will be prosperous and successful. ⁹Remember that I have commanded you to be determined and confident! Do not be afraid or discouraged, for I, the LORD your God, am with you wherever you go."

Joshua Gives Orders to the People

¹⁰Then Joshua ordered the leaders to ¹¹go through the camp and say to the people, "Get some food ready, because in three days you are going to cross the Jordan River to occupy the land that the LORD your God is giving you."

¹²Joshua said to the tribes of Reuben and Gad and to half the tribe of Manasseh, ¹³"Remember how the LORD's servant Moses told you that the LORD your God would give you this land on the east side of the Jordan as your home. ¹⁴Your wives, your children, and your livestock will stay here, but your soldiers, armed for battle, will cross over ahead of the other Israelites in order to help them ¹⁵until

---

1:3–5 Deut 11:24, 25   **1:5** Deut 31:6, 8; Heb 13:5   **1:6** Deut 31:6, 7, 23   **1:12–15** Num 32:28–32; Deut 3:18–20; Josh 22:1–6

they have occupied the land west of the Jordan that the LORD your God has given them. When he has given safety to all the tribes of Israel, then you may come back and settle here in your own land east of the Jordan, which Moses, the LORD's servant, gave to you."

16They answered Joshua, "We will do everything you have told us and will go anywhere you send us. 17We will obey you, just as we always obeyed Moses, and may the LORD your God be with you as he was with Moses! 18Whoever questions your authority or disobeys any of your orders will be put to death. Be determined and confident!"

Joshua Sends Spies into Jericho

2 1Then Joshua sent two spies from the camp at Acacia with orders to go and secretly explore the land of Canaan, especially the city of Jericho. When they came to the city, they went to spend the night in the house of a prostitute named Rahab. 2The king of Jericho heard that some Israelites had come that night to spy out the country, 3so he sent word to Rahab: "The men in your house have come to spy out the whole country! Bring them out!"

4-6"Some men did come to my house," she answered, "but I don't know where they were from. They left at sundown before the city gate was closed. I didn't find out where they were going, but if you start after them quickly, you can catch them." (Now Rahab had taken the two spies up on the roof and hidden them under some stalks of flax that she had put there.) 7The king's men left the city, and then the gate was shut. They went looking for the Israelite spies as far as the place where the road crosses the Jordan.

8Before the spies settled down for the night, Rahab went up on the roof 9and said to them, "I know that the LORD has given you this land. Everyone in the country is terrified of you. 10We have heard how the LORD dried up the Red Sea in front of you when you were leaving Egypt. We have also heard how you killed Sihon and Og, the two Amorite kings east of the Jordan. 11We were afraid as soon as we heard about it; we have all lost our courage because of you. The LORD your God is God in heaven above and here on earth. 12Now swear by him that you will treat my family as kindly as I have treated you, and give me some sign that I can trust you. 13Promise me that you will save my father and mother, my brothers and sisters, and all their families! Don't let us be killed!"

14The men said to her, "May God take our lives if we don't do as we say!a If you do not tell anyone what we have been doing, we promise you that when the LORD gives us this land, we will treat you well."

15Rahab lived in a house built into the city

Explore the land . . . especially the city of Jericho. (2:1)

a 2:14 May God . . . say; or We will protect you if you protect us.
2:1 Heb 11:31; Jas 2:25   **2:10 a** Ex 14:21; **b** Num 21:21–35

Remember the Parable of the Good Samaritan (*Luke 10:30–37*)? What similarities are there between Rahab and the Good Samaritan?

Pray It!

The Lord Your God Is God

God is all around us, all the time, every minute of every day. And yet we fail to recognize God's power and presence. Rahab, the woman who hides the Israelite spies, tells them that she believes their God is the true God of heaven and earth. This story has a little irony in it. Rahab is a Canaanite. She is the enemy of the Israelites. But her belief in the power of their God is what saves the Israelite spies.

Take a few minutes to write down the evidence of God you have seen in your own life. What are the signs, big and small, that come your way and remind you of God's power and presence? Some people like to keep a journal of the times they notice God's action in their lives and look back on it from time to time. It can help us recognize God's power and presence the way Rahab did.

— Joshua 2:1–13

wall, so she let the men down from the window by a rope. 16"Go into the hill country," she said, "or the king's men will find you. Hide there for three days until they come back. After that, you can go on your way."

17The men said to her, "We will keep the promise that you have made us give. 18This is what you must do. When we invade your land, tie this red cord to the window you let us down from. Get your father and mother, your brothers, and all your father's family together in your house. 19If anyone goes out of the house, his death will be his own fault, and we will not be responsible; but if anyone in the house with you is harmed, then we will be responsible. 20However, if you tell anyone what we have been doing, then we will not have to keep our promise which you have made us give you." 21She agreed and sent them away. When they had gone, she tied the red cord to the window.

22The spies went into the hills and hid. The king's men looked for them all over the countryside for three days, but they did not find them, so they returned to Jericho. 23Then the two spies came down from the hills, crossed the river, and went back to Joshua. They told him everything that had happened, 24and then said, "We are sure that the LORD has given us the whole country. All the people there are terrified of us."

The People of Israel Cross the Jordan

3 1The next morning Joshua and all the people of Israel got up early, left the camp at Acacia, and went to the Jordan, where they camped while waiting to cross it. 2Three days later the leaders went through the camp 3and told the people, "When you see the priests carrying the Covenant Box of the LORD your God, break camp and follow them. 4You have never been here before, so they will show you the way to go. But do not get near the Covenant Box; stay about half a mile behind it."

5Joshua told the people, "Purify yourselves, because tomorrow the LORD will perform miracles among you." 6Then he told the priests to take the Covenant Box and go with it ahead of the people. They did as he said.

7The LORD said to Joshua, "What I do today will make all the people of Israel begin to honor you as a great man, and they will realize that I am with you as I was with Moses. 8Tell the priests carrying the Covenant Box that when they reach the river, they must wade in and stand near the bank."

9Then Joshua said to the people, "Come here and listen to what the LORD your God has to say. 10As you advance, he will surely drive out the Canaanites, the Hittites, the Hivites, the Perizzites, the Girgashites, the

Joshua

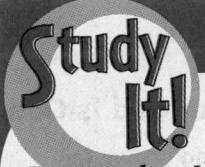

Remember When . . .

Remember when Moses brought the people of Israel across the Red Sea (Exodus 14:21–31)? The story of Joshua leading the people across the Jordan is meant to remind people of Moses. A miracle happens. The waters are parted. All the people are able to cross over safely. Why might the author want people to compare Joshua to Moses?

— Joshua 3:14–17

Amorites, and the Jebusites. You will know that the living God is among you ¹¹when the Covenant Box of the Lord of all the earth crosses the Jordan ahead of you. ¹²Now choose twelve men, one from each of the tribes of Israel. ¹³When the priests who carry the Covenant Box of the LORD of all the earth put their feet in the water, the Jordan will stop flowing, and the water coming downstream will pile up in one place."

¹⁴⁻¹⁵It was harvest time, and the river was in flood.

When the people left the camp to cross the Jordan, the priests went ahead of them, carrying the Covenant Box. As soon as the priests stepped into the river, ¹⁶the water stopped flowing and piled up, far upstream at Adam, the city beside Zarethan. The flow downstream to the Dead Sea was completely cut off, and the people were able to cross over near Jericho. ¹⁷While the people walked across on dry ground, the priests carrying the LORD's Covenant Box stood on dry ground in the middle of the Jordan until all the people had crossed over.

Memorial Stones Are Set Up

4 ¹When the whole nation had crossed the Jordan, the LORD said to Joshua, ²"Choose twelve men, one from each tribe, ³and command them to take twelve stones out of the middle of the Jordan, from the very place where the priests were standing. Tell them to carry these stones with them and to put them down where you camp tonight."

⁴Then Joshua called the twelve men he had chosen, ⁵and he told them, "Go into the Jordan ahead of the Covenant Box of the LORD your God. Each one of you take a stone on your shoulder, one for each of the

The people hurried across the river. (4:10)

tribes of Israel. 6These stones will remind the people of what the LORD has done. In the future, when your children ask what these stones mean to you, 7you will tell them that the water of the Jordan stopped flowing when the LORD's Covenant Box crossed the river. These stones will always remind the people of Israel of what happened here."

8The men followed Joshua's orders. As the LORD had commanded Joshua, they took twelve stones from the middle of the Jordan, one for each of the tribes of Israel, carried them to the camping place, and put them down there. 9Joshua also set up twelve stones in the middle of the Jordan, where the priests carrying the Covenant Box had stood. (Those stones are still there.) 10The priests stood in the middle of the Jordan until everything had been done that the LORD ordered Joshua to tell the people to do. This is what Moses had commanded.

Twelve stones in the middle of the Jordan (4:9)

The people hurried across the river. 11When they were all on the other side, the priests with the LORD's Covenant Box went on ahead of the people. 12The men of the tribes of Reuben and Gad and of half the tribe of Manasseh, ready for battle, crossed ahead of the rest of the people, as Moses had told them to do. 13In the presence of the LORD about forty thousand men ready for war crossed over to the plain near Jericho. 14What the LORD did that day made the people of Israel consider Joshua a great man. They honored him all his life, just as they had honored Moses.

15Then the LORD told Joshua 16to command the priests carrying the Covenant Box

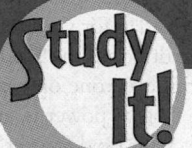

An Important Dozen

There are twelve tribes of Israel, descended from the twelve sons of Jacob (Genesis 35:23–26). After the Israelites had passed through the Jordan, the Lord had each tribe take a large stone from the riverbed. They carried the stones to dry land and made an altar in honor of God's power. It was a custom to make an altar to honor God as a memorial wherever a special event occurred.

Throughout the Old Testament, God guides the twelve tribes that make up the whole nation. Sometimes they fight among themselves, but often, especially in the Book of Joshua, they work together and try hard to be unified. Jesus chose twelve Apostles to be his closest followers. The number is meant to remind everyone that Jesus' mission is a continuation of the salvation begun in the Hebrew Scriptures.

— Joshua 4:19–24

Joshua

to come up out of the Jordan. 17Joshua did so, 18and when the priests reached the riverbank, the river began flowing once more and flooded its banks again.

19The people crossed the Jordan on the tenth day of the first month and camped at Gilgal, east of Jericho. 20There Joshua set up the twelve stones taken from the Jordan. 21And he said to the people of Israel, "In the future, when your children ask you what these stones mean, 22you will tell them about the time when Israel crossed the Jordan on dry

The Covenant Box is also called the Ark of the Covenant. It was a sign of God's presence and leadership.

ground. 23 Tell them that the LORD your God dried up the water of the Jordan for you until you had crossed, just as he dried up the Red Sea for us. 24 Because of this everyone on earth will know how great the LORD's power is, and you will honor the LORD your God forever."

5 ¹All the Amorite kings west of the Jordan and all the Canaanite kings along the Mediterranean Sea heard that the LORD had dried up the Jordan until the people of Israel had crossed it. They became afraid and lost their courage because of the Israelites.

The Circumcision at Gilgal

2 Then the LORD told Joshua, "Make some knives out of flint and circumcise the Israelites." 3 So Joshua did as the LORD had commanded, and he circumcised the Israelites at a place called Circumcision Hill. 4-6 When the people of Israel left Egypt, all the males were already circumcised. However, during the forty years the people spent crossing the desert, none of the baby boys had been circumcised. Also, by the end of that time all the men who were of fighting age when they left Egypt had died because they had disobeyed the LORD. Just as he had sworn, they were not allowed to see the rich and fertile land that he had promised their ancestors. 7 The sons of these men had never been circumcised, and it was this new generation that Joshua circumcised.

8 After the circumcision was completed, the whole nation stayed in the camp until the wounds had healed. 9 The LORD said to Joshua, "Today I have removed from you the disgrace of being slaves in Egypt." That is why the place was named Gilgal,ᵇ the name it still has.

10 While the Israelites were camping at Gilgal on the plain near Jericho, they observed Passover on the evening of the fourteenth day of the month. 11 The next day was the first time they ate food grown in Canaan: roasted grain and bread made with-out yeast. 12 The manna stopped falling then, and the Israelites no longer had any. From that time on they ate food grown in Canaan.

Following God's Will

The Israelites have done what God has asked them to do. God rewards them by bringing them into the Promised Land. But even though they had Moses and Aaron to lead them, they have not always followed God's will. They had to wander in the desert for forty years because they had been disobedient. All the adult men and women who had been adults when they left their life of slavery in Egypt had died during those years. Now a new generation would pick up where the older generation left off.

How do we know what God's will is for us? We have a number of guides along our path: the Bible, the teachings of the Church, the people of faith who are around us, and our own con-science. All these things help us understand what God wants for us. And the sacraments of the Church are a physical sign of God's power in our life and our promise to follow God's will. You have a responsibility for keeping the mis-sion of Jesus, to bring God's heal-ing love and forgiveness to others, alive in the world!

— Joshua 5:2-9

ᵇ 5:9 GILGAL: *This name sounds like the Hebrew for "removed."*
5:6 Num 14:28–35   5:10 Ex 12:1–13   5:12 Ex 16:35

"Everyone on earth will know how great the LORD's power is, and you will honor the LORD your God forever" (Joshua 4:24).

The Angel's Promise

In the Bible, angels have a number of different roles. They bring messages, they give advice, they guide, and they encourage. After the Israelites enter the Promised Land, an angel with a sword appears to Joshua as a sign that God will be with them in the battles to come. The angel is a reminder that God is with Joshua in the same way God was with Moses. The angel in this story even uses the same words as the angel who spoke to Moses (Exodus 3:5): "Take your sandals off; you are standing on holy ground" (Joshua 5:15).

What are some times when you feel a special need for God's reassurance? During those times look for little signs that God is with you. Joshua had to notice the angel and even go ask him why he was there. The signs of God's love and presence are often just little things: the smile of a stranger or a song on the radio with a special message for you. And don't be afraid to ask a parent, a friend, or another adult you trust for a little extra support. They are also God's messengers in your life.

— Joshua 5:13–15

Joshua and the Man with a Sword

¹³While Joshua was near Jericho, he suddenly saw a man standing in front of him, holding a sword. Joshua went up to him and asked, "Are you one of our soldiers, or an enemy?"

¹⁴"Neither," the man answered. "I am here as the commander of the LORD's army."

Joshua threw himself on the ground in worship and said, "I am your servant, sir. What do you want me to do?"

¹⁵And the commander of the LORD's army told him, "Take your sandals off; you are standing on holy ground." And Joshua did as he was told.

The Fall of Jericho

6 ¹The gates of Jericho were kept shut and guarded to keep the Israelites out. No one could enter or leave the city. ²The LORD said to Joshua, "I am putting into your hands Jericho, with its king and all its brave soldiers. ³You and your soldiers are to march around the city once a day for six days. ⁴Seven priests, each carrying a trumpet, are to go in front of the Covenant Box. On the seventh day you and your soldiers are to march around the city seven times while the priests blow the trumpets. ⁵Then they are to sound one long note. As soon as you hear it, all the people are to give a loud shout, and the city walls will collapse. Then the whole army will go straight into the city."

⁶Joshua called the priests and told them, "Take the Covenant Box, and seven of you go in front of it, carrying trumpets." ⁷Then he ordered the people to start marching around the city, with an advance guard going on ahead of the LORD's Covenant Box.

⁸⁻⁹So, just as Joshua had ordered, an advance guard started out ahead of the priests who were blowing trumpets; behind these came the priests who were carrying the Covenant Box, followed by a rear guard. All this time the trumpets were sounding. ¹⁰But Joshua had ordered the people not to shout, not to say a word until he gave the order. ¹¹So he had this group of men take the LORD's Covenant Box around the city one time. Then they came back to camp and spent the night there.

¹²⁻¹³Joshua got up early the next morning, and for the second time the priests and soldiers marched around the city in the same order as the day before: first, the advance guard; next, the seven priests blowing the seven trumpets; then, the priests carrying the LORD's Covenant Box; and finally, the rear guard. All this time the trumpets were sounding. ¹⁴On this second day they again marched around the city one time and then returned to camp. They did this for six days.

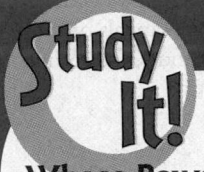

Whose Power Won?

The fall of Jericho is important because it is the first military victory of the Israelites. But when you read the story, notice the strange way they win. God has Joshua's army march around the city once a day for seven days. They are led by the priests who carry the Covenant Box. On the seventh day the priests blow their trumpets, and the army shouts, and the walls that protect the city collapse, leaving it defenseless! What does this mean?

In the Bible, numbers have symbolic meanings. Seven is a number that symbolizes completeness and God's power—remember the seven days of creation in the opening chapters of the Book of Genesis? The seven marches on seven days show that the victory belongs not to a leader or an army but to God.

— Joshua 6:1–20

15On the seventh day they got up at daybreak and marched seven times around the city in the same way—this was the only day that they marched around it seven times. 16The seventh time around, when the priests were about to sound the trumpets, Joshua ordered the people to shout, and he said, "The LORD has given you the city! 17The city and everything in it must be totally destroyed as an offering to the LORD. Only the prostitute Rahab and her household will be spared, because she hid our spies. 18But you are not to take anything that is to be destroyed; if you do, you will bring trouble and destruction on the Israelite camp. 19Everything made of silver, gold, bronze, or iron is set apart for the LORD. It is to be put in the LORD's treasury."

20So the priests blew the trumpets. As soon as the people heard it, they gave a loud shout, and the walls collapsed. Then all the army went straight up the hill into the city and captured it. 21With their swords they killed everyone in the city, men and women, young and old. They also killed the cattle, sheep, and donkeys.

22Joshua then told the two men who had served as spies, "Go into the prostitute's house, and bring her and her family out, as you promised her." 23So they went and

6:20 Heb 11:30

They gave a loud shout, and the walls collapsed. (6:20)

Joshua

Can There Be Holy War?

In the Old Testament there are many stories of war victories that are portrayed as the fulfillment of God's wishes. Joshua and the Israelites saw the Canaanites as a threat to their beliefs and felt that it was God's will that they should kill them all. They even felt that wars against unbelievers were holy and commanded by God. When their army was victorious in battle, the Israelites understood it to mean that God was on their side.

For Christians this view of war is a problem. Because of Jesus' teachings, the terms *holy* and *war* seem to contradict each other. Jesus taught us to love our enemies and to do good to those who persecute us. We interpret the Old Testament in the light of Jesus' teachings. Because of this, the Church teaches that war is only to be used as a last resort under very specific circumstances. War is not holy and marks a failure by somebody to live by God's will. Every effort should be made to find nonviolent solutions before resorting to war.

— Joshua 6:21

brought Rahab out, along with her father and mother, her brothers, and the rest of her family. They took them all, family and slaves, to safety near the Israelite camp. ²⁴Then they set fire to the city and burned it to the ground, along with everything in it, except

6:25 Heb 11:31 6:26 1 Kings 16:34

the things made of gold, silver, bronze, and iron, which they took and put in the LORD's treasury. ²⁵But Joshua spared the lives of the prostitute Rahab and all her relatives, because she had hidden the two spies that he had sent to Jericho. (Her descendants have lived in Israel to this day.)

²⁶At this time Joshua issued a solemn warning: "Anyone who tries to rebuild the city of Jericho will be under the LORD's curse.

Whoever lays the foundation will lose his oldest son;
Whoever builds the gates will lose his youngest."

²⁷So the LORD was with Joshua, and his fame spread through the whole country.

Achan's Sin

7 ¹The LORD's command to Israel not to take from Jericho anything that was to be destroyed was not obeyed. A man named Achan disobeyed that order, and so the LORD was furious with the Israelites. (Achan was the son of Carmi and grandson of Zabdi, and belonged to the clan of Zerah, a part of the tribe of Judah.)

²Joshua sent some men from Jericho to Ai, a city east of Bethel, near Bethaven, with orders to go and explore the land. When they had done so, ³they reported back to Joshua: "There is no need for everyone to attack Ai. Send only about two or three thousand men. Don't send the whole army up there to fight; it is not a large city." ⁴So about three thousand Israelites made the attack, but they were forced to retreat. ⁵The men of Ai chased them from the city gate as far as some quarries and killed about thirty-six of them on the way down the hill. Then the Israelites lost their courage and were afraid.

⁶Joshua and the leaders of Israel tore their clothes in grief, threw themselves to the ground before the LORD's Covenant Box, and lay there till evening, with dust on their

Joshua

heads to show their sorrow. 7 And Joshua said, "Sovereign LORD! Why did you bring us across the Jordan at all? To turn us over to the Amorites? To destroy us? Why didn't we just stay on the other side of the Jordan? 8 What can I say, O Lord, now that Israel has retreated from the enemy? 9 The Canaanites and everyone else in the country will hear about it. They will surround us and kill every one of us! And then what will you do to protect your honor?"

10 The LORD said to Joshua, "Get up! Why are you lying on the ground like this? 11 Israel has sinned! They have broken the agreement with me that I ordered them to keep. They have taken some of the things condemned to destruction. They stole them, lied about it, and put them with their own things. 12 This is why the Israelites cannot stand against their enemies. They retreat from them because they themselves have now been condemned to destruction! I will not stay with you any longer unless you destroy the things you were ordered not to take! 13 Get up! Purify the people and get them ready to come before me. Tell them to be ready tomorrow, because I, the LORD God of Israel, have this to say: 'Israel, you have in your possession some things that I ordered you to destroy! You cannot stand against your enemies until you get rid of these things!' 14 So tell them that in the morning they will be brought forward, tribe by tribe. The tribe that I pick out will then come forward, clan by clan. The clan that I pick out will come forward, family by family. The family that I pick out will come forward, one by one. 15 The one who is then picked out and found with the condemned goods will be burned, along with his family and everything he owns, for he has brought terrible shame on Israel and has broken my covenant."

16 Early the next morning Joshua brought Israel forward, tribe by tribe, and the tribe of Judah was picked out. 17 He brought the tribe of Judah forward, clan by clan, and the clan of Zerah was picked out. Then he

Consequences

Actions have consequences. Have you ever gotten grounded by your parents for breaking the rules? Ever had a friend stop trusting you because of something you did or said? Usually the people who love us and care about us will forgive us when we make mistakes or even when we do something wrong on purpose. Sometimes, though, the consequences are bigger than we can handle or fix. We might spread a rumor that ruins a person's reputation. When someone drives drunk and kills another person in an accident, the consequences affect many people for years to come.

This is what happened to the Israelites with Achan. God commanded the people not to take anything from the city of Jericho. It seemed God wanted this first battle to not be about gaining wealth or possessions. But Achan took gold, silver, and clothing. His disobedience had consequences not only for him but also for all the Israelites. They lost the very next battle they fought.

The next time you're tempted to do something wrong, consider the consequences. How will this action hurt you and possibly other people?

— Joshua, chapter 7

brought the clan of Zerah forward, family by family, and the family of Zabdi was picked out. 18 He then brought Zabdi's family for-

The valley of trouble is called Achor, which means "misery" or "affliction" in the Hebrew language.

Pray It!

Courage

"Don't be afraid or discouraged. I will give you victory" (Joshua 8:1). Joshua and the people of Israel trusted their lives to God. Do you rely on God? Trusting in God can be a hard thing to do. We want to do it ourselves, our own way. God sometimes asks us to take chances and step beyond where we are comfortable.

> God help me to rely on you.
> Give me the courage to follow your will
>   as I reach out to others and as I learn new things.
> Help me to have the confidence that you
>   will always be there to guide me and protect me. Amen.

— Joshua 8:1–2

ward, one by one, and Achan, the son of Carmi and grandson of Zabdi, was picked out. ¹⁹Joshua said to him, "My son, tell the truth here before the LORD, the God of Israel, and confess. Tell me now what you have done. Don't try to hide it from me."

²⁰"It's true," Achan answered. "I have sinned against the LORD, Israel's God, and this is what I did. ²¹Among the things we seized I saw a beautiful Babylonian cloak, about five pounds of silver, and a bar of gold weighing over one pound. I wanted them so much that I took them. You will find them buried inside my tent, with the silver at the bottom."

²²So Joshua sent some men, who ran to the tent and found that the condemned things really were buried there, with the silver at the bottom. ²³They brought them out of the tent, took them to Joshua and all the Israelites, and laid them down in the presence of the LORD. ²⁴Joshua, along with all the people of Israel, seized Achan, the silver, the cloak, the bar of gold, together with Achan's sons and daughters, his cattle, donkeys, and sheep, his tent, and everything else he owned; and they took them to Trouble Valley. ²⁵And Joshua said, "Why have you brought such trouble on us? The LORD will now bring trouble on you!" All the people then stoned Achan to death; they also stoned and burned his family and possessions.

²⁶They put a huge pile of stones over him, which is there to this day. That is why that place is still called Trouble Valley.

Then the LORD was no longer furious.

The Capture and Destruction of Ai

8 ¹The LORD said to Joshua, "Take all the soldiers with you and go on up to Ai. Don't be afraid or discouraged. I will give you victory over the king of Ai; his people, city, and land will be yours. ²You are to do to Ai and its king what you did to Jericho and its king, but this time you may keep its goods and livestock for yourselves. Prepare to attack the city by surprise from the rear."

³So Joshua got ready to go to Ai with all his soldiers. He picked out thirty thousand of his best troops and sent them out at night ⁴with these orders: "Hide on the other side of the city, but not too far away from it; be ready to attack. ⁵My men and I will approach the city. When the men of Ai come out against us, we will turn and run, just as we did the first time. ⁶They will pursue us until we have led them away from the city. They will think that we are running from them, as we did before. ⁷Then you will come out of hiding and capture the city. The LORD your God will give it to you. ⁸After you have taken the city, set it on fire, just as the LORD has commanded.

Joshua

These are your orders." 9So Joshua sent them out, and they went to their hiding place and waited there, west of Ai, between Ai and Bethel. Joshua spent the night in camp.

10Early in the morning Joshua got up and called the soldiers together. Then he and the leaders of Israel led them to Ai. 11The soldiers with him went toward the main entrance to the city and set up camp on the north side, with a valley between themselves and Ai. 12He took about five thousand men and put them in hiding west of the city, between Ai and Bethel. 13The soldiers were arranged for battle with the main camp north of the city and the rest of the men to the west. Joshua spent the night in the valley. 14When the king of Ai saw Joshua's men, he acted quickly. He and all his men went out toward the Jordan Valley to fight the Israelites at the same place as before, not knowing that he was about to be attacked from the rear. 15Joshua and his men pretended that they were retreating, and ran away toward the barren country. 16All the men in the city had been called together to go after them, and as they pursued Joshua, they kept getting farther away from the city. 17Every man in Ai*c* went after the Israelites, and the city was left wide open, with no one to defend it.

18Then the LORD said to Joshua, "Point your spear at Ai; I am giving it to you." Joshua did as he was told, 19and as soon as he lifted his hand, the men who had been hiding got up quickly, ran into the city and captured it. They immediately set the city on fire. 20When the men of Ai looked back, they saw the smoke rising to the sky. There was no way for them to escape, because the Israelites who had run toward the barren country now turned around to attack them. 21When Joshua and his men saw that the others had taken the city and that it was on fire, they turned around and began killing the men of Ai. 22The Israelites in the city now came down to join the battle. So the men of Ai found themselves completely surrounded by Israelites, and they were all

killed. No one got away, and no one lived through it 23except the king of Ai. He was captured and taken to Joshua.

24The Israelites killed every one of the enemy in the barren country where they had chased them. Then they went back to Ai and killed everyone there. 25-26Joshua kept his spear pointed at Ai and did not put it down until every person there had been killed. The whole population of Ai was killed that day—twelve thousand men and women. 27The Israelites kept for themselves the livestock and goods captured in the city, as the LORD had told Joshua. 28Joshua burned Ai and left it in ruins. It is still like that today. 29He hanged the king of Ai from a tree and left his body there until evening. At sundown Joshua gave orders for the body to be removed, and it was thrown down at the entrance to the city gate. They covered it with a huge pile of stones, which is still there today.

The Law Is Read at Mount Ebal

30Then Joshua built on Mount Ebal an altar to the LORD, the God of Israel. 31He made it according to the instructions that Moses, the LORD's servant, had given the Israelites, as it says in the Law of Moses: "an altar made of stones which have not been cut with iron tools." On it they offered burnt sacrifices to the LORD, and they also presented their fellowship offerings. 32There, with the Israelites looking on, Joshua made on the stones*d* a copy of the Law which Moses had written. 33The Israelites, with their leaders, officers, and judges, as well as the foreigners among them, stood on two sides of the LORD's Covenant Box, facing the levitical priests who carried it. Half of the people stood with their backs to Mount Gerizim and the other half with their backs to Mount Ebal. The LORD's servant Moses had commanded them to do this when the time came for them to receive the blessing. 34Joshua then read aloud the whole Law, including the blessings and the curses, just as they are

c 8:17 *One ancient translation* Ai; *Hebrew* Ai and Bethel. *d* 8:32 the stones; *or* stones.
8:30–32 Deut 27:2–8 **8:31** Ex 20:25 **8:33–35** Deut 11:29; 27:11–14

Altars

Catholic Connections

The Israelites built an altar at Mount Ebal to offer sacrifice in praise and thanksgiving to God. This altar was a renewal of their promise to be obedient to God. Altars were a way to offer thanksgiving and praise to God. The altar at Mount Ebal reminded them that even though they were in a new place, their identity was the same. They were still the People of God. Joshua emphasized this by reading aloud the whole Law to the people.

Every Catholic church has an altar. We also offer thanks and praise to God. It's where we celebrate who we are. At the alter we celebrate and renew Jesus' sacrifice and gather as one family around the table of the Lord. The altar helps us remember our identity as followers of Jesus, the family of God.

— Joshua 8:30–35

written in the book of the Law. ³⁵Every one of the commandments of Moses was read by Joshua to the whole gathering, which included women and children, as well as the foreigners living among them.

The Gibeonites Deceive Joshua

9 ¹The victories of Israel became known to all the kings west of the Jordan—in the hills, in the foothills, and all along the coastal plain of the Mediterranean Sea as far north as Lebanon; these were the kings of the Hittites, the Amorites, the Canaanites, the Perizzites, the Hivites, and the Jebusites. ²They all came together and joined forces to fight against Joshua and the Israelites.

³But the people of Gibeon, who were Hivites, heard what Joshua had done to Jericho and Ai, ⁴and they decided to deceive him. They went and got some food and loaded their donkeys with worn-out sacks and patched-up wineskins. ⁵They put on ragged clothes and worn-out sandals that had been mended. The bread they took with them was dry and moldy. ⁶Then they

went to the camp at Gilgal and said to Joshua and the Israelites, "We have come from a distant land. We want you to make a treaty with us."

⁷But the Israelites said, "Why should we make a treaty with you? Maybe you live nearby."

⁸They said to Joshua, "We are at your service."

Joshua asked them, "Who are you? Where do you come from?"

⁹Then they told him this story: "We have come from a very distant land, sir, because we have heard of the LORD your God. We have heard about everything that he did in Egypt ¹⁰and what he did to the two Amorite kings east of the Jordan: King Sihon of Heshbon and King Og of Bashan, who lived in Ashtaroth. ¹¹Our leaders and all the people that live in our land told us to get some food ready for a trip and to go and meet you. We were told to put ourselves at your service and ask you to make a treaty with us. ¹²Look at our bread. When we left home with it and started out to meet you, it was still warm. But look! Now it is dry and

Joshua

9:7 Ex 23:32; 34:12; Deut 7:2   **9:10** Num 21:21–35

Sometimes in the Bible it's the crafty or clever people who succeed. The people of Gibeon trick Joshua into an alliance, and so they survive.

moldy. 13When we filled these wineskins, they were new, but look! They are torn. Our clothes and sandals are worn out from the long trip."

"But look! They are torn." (9:13)

14The Israelites accepted some food from them, but did not consult the LORD about it. 15Joshua made a treaty of friendship with the people of Gibeon and allowed them to live. The leaders of the community of Israel gave their solemn promise to keep the treaty.

16Three days after the treaty had been made, the Israelites learned that these people did indeed live nearby. 17So the people of Israel started out and three days later arrived at the cities where these people lived: Gibeon, Chephirah, Beeroth, and Kiriath Jearim. 18But the Israelites could not kill them, because their leaders had made a solemn promise to them in the name of the LORD, Israel's God. All the people complained to the leaders about this, 19but they answered, "We have made our solemn promise to them in the name of the LORD God of Israel. Now we cannot harm them. 20We must let them live because of our promise; if we don't, God will punish us. 21Let them live, but they will have to cut wood and carry water for us." This was what the leaders suggested.

22Joshua ordered the people of Gibeon to be brought to him, and he asked them, "Why did you deceive us and tell us that you were from far away, when you live right here? 23Because you did this, God has condemned you. Your people will always be slaves, cutting wood and carrying water for the sanctuary of my God."

24They answered, "We did it, sir, because we learned that it was really true that the LORD your God had commanded his servant Moses to give you the whole land and to kill the people living in it as you advanced. We did it because we were terrified of you; we were in fear of our lives. 25Now we are in your power; do with us what you think is right." 26So this is what Joshua did: he protected them and did not allow the people of Israel to kill them. 27But at the same time he made them slaves, to cut wood and carry water for the people of Israel and for the LORD's altar. To this day they have continued to do this work in the place where the LORD has chosen to be worshiped.

The Amorites Are Defeated

10 1Adonizedek, the king of Jerusalem,*e* heard that Joshua had captured and totally destroyed Ai and had killed its king, just as he had done to Jericho and its king. He also heard that the people of Gibeon had made peace with the Israelites and were living among them. 2The people of Jerusalem were greatly alarmed at this because Gibeon was as large as any of the cities that had a king; it was larger than Ai, and its men were good fighters. 3So Adonizedek sent the following message to King Hoham of Hebron, King Piram of Jarmuth, King Japhia of Lachish, and to King Debir of Eglon: 4"Come and help me attack Gibeon, because its people have made peace with Joshua and the Israelites." 5These five Amorite kings, the kings of Jerusalem, Hebron, Jarmuth, Lachish, and Eglon, joined forces, surrounded Gibeon, and attacked it.

6The men of Gibeon sent word to Joshua at the camp in Gilgal: "Do not abandon us, sir! Come at once and help us! Save us! All

e 10:1 JERUSALEM: *At that time it was a Jebusite city.*

Joshua

Pray It!

Helpful Hail

Have you ever witnessed a powerful storm? It can be scary, but it can be beautiful. It can also remind us of the tremendous power of nature. As Joshua's army chased down its enemies, strange things were going on in the sky that helped their battle. In biblical times, natural phenomena like earthquakes, solar and lunar eclipses, volcanic eruptions, and powerful storms were often seen as signs of God's punishment or power. Because we understand how weather develops and what causes earthquakes, we can sometimes take the forces of nature for granted.

> *God of all creation,*
> *you made everything*
> *from the depths of the earth to the farthest star.*
> *Wind and water, sun and sky,*
> *you made everything.*
> *Help me to remember*
> *when I see a beautiful sunset or a powerful storm,*
> *when nature amazes me,*
> *that you made everything. Amen.*

— Joshua 10:11–14

Joshua

the Amorite kings in the hill country have joined forces and have attacked us!"

7So Joshua and his whole army, including the best troops, started out from Gilgal. 8The LORD said to Joshua, "Do not be afraid of them. I have already given you the victory. Not one of them will be able to stand against you." 9All night Joshua and his army marched from Gilgal to Gibeon, and they made a surprise attack on the Amorites. 10The LORD made the Amorites panic at the sight of Israel's army. The Israelites slaughtered them at Gibeon and pursued them down the mountain pass at Beth Horon, keeping up the attack as far south as Azekah and Makkedah. 11While the Amorites were running down the pass from the Israelite army, the LORD made large hailstones fall down on them all the way to Azekah. More were killed by the hailstones than by the Israelites.

12On the day that the LORD gave the men of Israel victory over the Amorites, Joshua

spoke to the LORD. In the presence of the Israelites he said,

"Sun, stand still over Gibeon;
Moon, stop over Aijalon Valley."

13The sun stood still and the moon did not move until the nation had conquered its enemies. This is written in the Book of Jashar. The sun stood still in the middle of the sky and did not go down for a whole day. 14Never before, and never since, has there been a day like it, when the LORD obeyed a human being. The LORD fought on Israel's side!

15After this, Joshua and his army went back to the camp at Gilgal.

Joshua Captures the Five Amorite Kings

16The five Amorite kings, however, had escaped and were hiding in the cave at Makkedah. 17Someone found them, and Joshua was told where they were hiding. 18He said, "Roll some big stones in front of the entrance to the cave. Place some guards there, ¹⁹but don't stay there yourselves. Keep on after the enemy and attack them from the rear; don't let them get to their cities! The LORD your God has given you victory over them." ²⁰Joshua and the men of Israel slaughtered them, although some managed to find safety inside their city walls and were not killed. ²¹Then all of Joshua's men came back safe to him at the camp at Makkedah.

No one in the land dared even to speak against the Israelites.

Bring those five kings out to me. (10:22)

²²Then Joshua said, "Open the entrance to the cave and bring those five kings out to me." ²³So the cave was opened, and the kings of Jerusalem, Hebron, Jarmuth, Lachish, and Eglon were brought out ²⁴and taken to Joshua. Joshua then called all the men of Israel to him and ordered the officers who had gone with him to come and put their feet on the necks of the kings. They did so. ²⁵Then Joshua said to his officers, "Don't be afraid or discouraged. Be determined and confident because this is what the LORD is going to do to all your enemies." ²⁶Then Joshua killed the kings and hanged them on five trees, where their bodies stayed until evening. ²⁷At sundown Joshua gave orders, and their bodies were taken down and thrown into the same cave where they had hidden earlier. Large stones were placed at the entrance to the cave, and they are still there.

Joshua Captures More Amorite Territory

²⁸Joshua attacked and captured Makkedah and its king that day. He put everyone in the city to death; no one was left alive. He did to the king of Makkedah what he had done to the king of Jericho.

²⁹After this, Joshua and his army went on from Makkedah to Libnah and attacked it. ³⁰The LORD also gave the Israelites victory over this city and its king. They spared no one, but killed every person in it. They did to the king what they had done to the king of Jericho.

³¹After this, Joshua and his army went on from Libnah to Lachish, surrounded it and attacked it. ³²The LORD gave the Israelites victory over Lachish on the second day of the battle. Just as they had done at Libnah, they spared no one, but killed every person in the city. ³³King Horam of Gezer came to the aid of Lachish, but Joshua defeated him and his army and left none of them alive.

³⁴Next, Joshua and his army went on from Lachish to Eglon, surrounded it and attacked it. ³⁵They captured it the same day and put everyone there to death, just as they had done at Lachish.

³⁶After this, Joshua and his army went from Eglon up into the hills to Hebron, attacked it ³⁷and captured it. They killed the king and everyone else in the city as well as in the nearby towns. Joshua condemned the city to total destruction, just as he had done to Eglon. No one in it was left alive.

³⁸Then Joshua and his army turned back to Debir and attacked it. ³⁹He captured it, with its king and all the nearby towns. They put everyone there to death. Joshua did to Debir and its king what he had done to Hebron and to Libnah and its king.

⁴⁰Joshua conquered the whole land. He defeated the kings of the hill country, the eastern slopes, and the western foothills, as well as those of the dry country in the south. He spared no one; everyone was put to death. This was what the LORD God of Israel had commanded. ⁴¹Joshua's campaign took him from Kadesh Barnea in the south to Gaza near the coast, including all the area of Goshen, and as far north as Gibeon. ⁴²Joshua conquered all these kings and their territory in one campaign because the LORD, Israel's God, was fighting for Israel.

[43] After this, Joshua and his army went back to the camp at Gilgal.

Joshua Defeats Jabin and His Allies

11 [1] When the news of Israel's victories reached King Jabin of Hazor, he sent word to King Jobab of Madon, to the kings of Shimron and Achshaph, [2] and to the kings in the hill country in the north, in the Jordan Valley south of Lake Galilee, in the foothills, and on the coast near Dor. [3] He also sent word to the Canaanites on both sides of the Jordan, to the Amorites, the Hittites, the Perizzites, and the Jebusites in the hill country, as well as to the Hivites who lived at the foot of Mount Hermon in the land of Mizpah. [4] They came with all their soldiers—an army with as many men as there are grains of sand on the seashore. They also had many horses and chariots. [5] All of these kings joined forces and came together and set up camp at Merom Brook to fight against Israel.

[6] The LORD said to Joshua, "Do not be afraid of them. By this time tomorrow I will have killed all of them for Israel. You are to cripple their horses and burn their chariots." [7] So Joshua and all his men attacked them by surprise at Merom Brook. [8] The LORD gave the Israelites victory over them; the Israelites attacked and pursued them as far north as Misrephoth Maim and Sidon, and as far east as the valley of Mizpah. The fight continued until none of the enemy was left alive. [9] Joshua did to them what the LORD had commanded: he crippled their horses and burned their chariots.

[10] Joshua then turned back, captured Hazor and killed its king. (At that time Hazor was the most powerful of all those kingdoms.) [11] They put everyone there to death; no one was left alive, and the city was burned.

[12] Joshua captured all these cities and their kings, putting everyone to death, just as Moses, the LORD's servant, had commanded. [13] However, the Israelites did not burn any of the cities built on mounds, except Hazor, which Joshua did burn. [14] The people of Israel took all the valuables and livestock from these cities and kept them for themselves. But they put every person to death; no one was left alive. [15] The LORD had given his commands to his servant Moses, Moses had given them to Joshua, and Joshua obeyed them. He did everything that the LORD had commanded Moses.

The Territory Taken by Joshua

[16] Joshua captured all the land—the hill country and foothills, both north and south, all the area of Goshen and the dry country south of it, as well as the Jordan Valley. [17-18] The territory extended from Mount Halak in the south near Edom, as far as Baal-gad in the north, in the valley of Lebanon south of Mount Hermon. Joshua was at war with the kings of this territory for a long time, but he captured them all and put them to death. [19] The only city that made peace with the people of Israel was Gibeon, where some of the Hivites lived. All the others were conquered in battle. [20] The LORD had made them determined to fight the Israelites, so that they would be condemned to total destruction and all be killed without mercy. This was what the LORD had commanded Moses.

[21] At this time Joshua went and destroyed the race of giants called the Anakim who lived in the hill country—in Hebron, Debir, Anab, and in all the hill country of Judah and Israel. Joshua completely destroyed them and their cities. [22] None of the Anakim were left in the land of Israel; a few, however, were left in Gaza, Gath, and Ashdod.

[23] Joshua captured the whole land, as the LORD had commanded Moses. Joshua gave it to the Israelites as their own and divided it into portions, one for each tribe.

So the people rested from war.

Joshua

11:20 Deut 7:16

The city of Hazor (Joshua 11:10) was the largest city of Joshua's time. With 40,000 inhabitants, it was almost ten times the size of Jerusalem.

The Kings Defeated by Moses

12 ¹ The people of Israel had already conquered and occupied the land east of the Jordan, from the Arnon Valley up the Jordan Valley and as far north as Mount Hermon. They defeated two kings. ²One was Sihon, the Amorite king who ruled at Heshbon. His kingdom included half of Gilead: from Aroer (on the edge of the Arnon Valley) and from the city inᶠ the middle of that valley, as far as the Jabbok River, the border of Ammon; ³it included the Jordan Valley from Lake Galilee south to Beth Jeshimoth (east of the Dead Sea) and on toward the foot of Mount Pisgah.

⁴They also defeated King Og of Bashan, who was one of the last of the Rephaim; he ruled at Ashtaroth and Edrei. ⁵His kingdom included Mount Hermon, Salecah, and all of Bashan as far as the boundaries of Geshur and Maacah, as well as half of Gilead, as far as the territory of King Sihon of Heshbon.

⁶These two kings were defeated by Moses and the people of Israel. Moses, the LORD's servant, gave their land to the tribes of Reuben and Gad and to half the tribe of Manasseh, to be their possession.

The Kings Defeated by Joshua

⁷Joshua and the people of Israel defeated all the kings in the territory west of the Jordan, from Baalgad in the valley of Lebanon to Mount Halak in the south near Edom. Joshua divided this land among the tribes and gave it to them as a permanent possession. ⁸This portion included the hill country, the western foothills, the Jordan Valley and its foothills, the eastern slopes, and the dry country in the south. This land had been the home of the Hittites, the Amorites, the Canaanites, the Perizzites, the Hivites, and the Jebusites. ⁹The people of Israel defeated the kings of the following cities: Jericho, Ai

Conquering Canaan

In a time when winning a battle was seen as a sign of God's blessing, Joshua was very blessed. Chapter 12 of Joshua lists all the kings defeated by Moses and Joshua. Even though Joshua was not a king himself, God had given him victory over kings. This list shows that the Israelites had won everything that God had promised them so far. The list includes all the different types of land in Palestine: hill country, the Jordan river valley, foothills, and plains. The Israelites were well on their way to gaining control over the Promised Land.

— Joshua, chapter 12

(near Bethel), ¹⁰Jerusalem, Hebron, ¹¹Jarmuth, Lachish, ¹²Eglon, Gezer, ¹³Debir, Geder, ¹⁴Hormah, Arad, ¹⁵Libnah, Adullam, ¹⁶Makkedah, Bethel, ¹⁷Tappuah, Hepher, ¹⁸Aphek, Lasharon, ¹⁹Madon, Hazor, ²⁰Shimron Meron, Achshaph, ²¹Taanach, Megiddo, ²²Kedesh, Jokneam (in Carmel), ²³Dor (on the coast), Goiim (in Galileeᵍ), ²⁴and Tirzah—thirty-one kings in all.

The Land Still to Be Taken

13 ¹Joshua was now very old. The LORD said to him, "You are very old, but there is still much land to be taken: ²all the territory of Philistia and Geshur, ³as well as all the territory of the Avvim to the

ᶠ **12:2** *Probable text (see 13:16; Deut 2:36)* the city in; *Hebrew does not have these words.* ᵍ **12:23** *One ancient translation* Galilee; *Hebrew* Gilgal.
12:1–5 Num 21:21–35; Deut 2:26—3:11   **12:6** Num 32:33; Deut 3:12

The tribes mentioned in Joshua 12:6 will have a big argument over an altar with the rest of the tribes of Israel in Joshua, chapter 22.

south. (The land from the stream Shihor, at the Egyptian border, as far north as the border of Ekron was considered Canaanite; the kings of the Philistines lived at Gaza, Ashdod, Ashkelon, Gath, and Ekron.) 4There is still all the Canaanite country, and Mearah (which belonged to the Sidonians), as far as Aphek, at the Amorite border; 5the land of the Gebalites; all of Lebanon to the east, from Baalgad, which is south of Mount Hermon, to Hamath Pass. 6This includes all the territory of the Sidonians, who live in the hill country between the Lebanon Mountains and Misrephoth Maim. I will drive all these peoples out as the people of Israel advance. You must divide the land among the Israelites, just as I have commanded you to do. 7Now then, divide this land among the other nine tribes and half of the tribe of Manasseh, for them to possess as their own."

The Division of the Territory East of the Jordan

8The tribes of Reuben and Gad and the other half of the tribe of Manasseh had already received the land that Moses, the LORD's servant, had given them; it was on the east side of the Jordan River. 9Their territory extended to Aroer (on the edge of the Arnon Valley) and the city in the middle of that valley and included all of the plateau from Medeba to Dibon. 10It went as far as the border of Ammon and included all the cities that had been ruled by the Amorite king Sihon, who had ruled at Heshbon. 11It included Gilead, the regions of Geshur and Maacah, all of Mount Hermon, and all of Bashan as far as Salecah. 12It included the kingdom of Og, the last of the Rephaim, who had ruled at Ashtaroth and Edrei. Moses had defeated these people and driven them out. 13However, the Israelites did not drive out the people of Geshur and Maacah; they still live in Israel.

14Moses had given no land to the tribe of Levi. As the LORD had told Moses, they were to receive as their possession a share of the sacrifices burned on the altar to the LORD God of Israel.

Older and Wiser

Do you know an older person who has a strong faith in God? What do you think made their faith so strong? Often it's not because they've had an easy life but because they've learned that they needed to count on God. They've learned that when life got hard, they couldn't get by when they tried to do it on their own power.

When God commands Joshua to divide the land, Joshua is an old man. Joshua has followed God faithfully all his life. He has learned by experience that if you rely on God, God will always be there for you. During the rest of the book, Joshua doesn't fight any more battles. But he is still the wise leader the people come to for advice and inspiration.

What older person can you go to for advice and inspiration? Many young people have grandparents who fill that role. Ask that older person what he or she has learned about getting through life's hard times. Let that person's experiences inspire you.

— Joshua 13:1–7

The Territory Assigned to Reuben

15Moses had given a part of the land to the families of the tribe of Reuben as their possession. 16Their territory extended to Aroer (on the edge of the Arnon Valley) and the city in the middle of that valley and included all the plateau around Medeba. 17It included Heshbon and all the cities on the plateau: Dibon, Bamoth Baal, Beth Baalmeon, 18Jahaz, Kedemoth, Mephaath, 19Kiriathaim, Sibmah, Zereth Shahar on the hill in the valley,

13:6 Num 33:54   **13:8** Num 32:33; Deut 3:12   **13:14** Deut 18:1

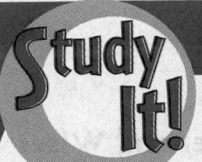

Dividing the Land

Chapter 13 of Joshua begins the second major part of this book. In this section the Promised Land is divided among the Twelve Tribes of Israel. Even though the major battles have been fought and most of the land has been won, there is still work to be done. In these chapters you will read about promises made and kept. Even though the division of the land all sounds pretty peaceful and orderly, the reality was probably a lot messier. Keep in mind that the guiding theme is that the promises God made to Moses and the Israelites at Mount Sinai are now being fulfilled.

— Joshua, chapter 13

20 Bethpeor, the slopes of Mount Pisgah, and Beth Jeshimoth. 21 It included all the cities of the plateau and the whole kingdom of the Amorite king Sihon, who had ruled at Heshbon. Moses defeated him, as well as the rulers of Midian: Evi, Rekem, Zur, Hur, and Reba. All of them had ruled the land for King Sihon. 22 Among those whom the people of Israel killed was the fortune teller Balaam son of Beor. 23 The Jordan was the western border of the tribe of Reuben. These were the cities and towns given to the families of the tribe of Reuben as their possession.

The Territory Assigned to Gad

24 Moses had also given a part of the land to the families of the tribe of Gad as their possession. 25 Their territory included Jazer and all the cities of Gilead, half the land of

Ammon as far as Aroer, which is east of Rabbah; 26 their land extended from Heshbon to Ramath Mizpeh and Betonim, from Mahanaim to the border of Lodebar. 27 In the Jordan Valley it included Beth Haram, Bethnimrah, Sukkoth, and Zaphon, the rest of the kingdom of King Sihon of Heshbon. Their western border was the Jordan River as far north as Lake Galilee. 28 These were the cities and towns given to the families of the tribe of Gad as their possession.

The Territory Assigned to East Manasseh

29 Moses had given a part of the land to the families of half the tribe of Manasseh as their possession. 30 Their territory extended to Mahanaim and included all of Bashan— the whole kingdom of Og, the king of Bashan, as well as all sixty of the villages of Jair in Bashan. 31 It included half of Gilead, as well as Ashtaroth and Edrei, the capital cities of Og's kingdom in Bashan. All this was given to half the families descended from Machir son of Manasseh.

32 This is how Moses divided the land east of Jericho and the Jordan when he was in the plains of Moab. 33 But Moses did not assign any land to the tribe of Levi. He told them that their possession was to be a share of the offerings to the LORD God of Israel.

The Division of the Territory West of the Jordan

14 1 What follows is an account of how the land of Canaan west of the Jordan was divided among the people of Israel. Eleazar the priest, Joshua son of Nun, and the leaders of the families of the Israelite tribes divided it among the population. 2 As the LORD had commanded Moses, the territories of the nine and one-half tribes west of the Jordan were determined by drawing lots.[h] 3-4 Moses had already assigned the land east of the Jordan to the other two and one-half tribes. (The descendants of Joseph were divided into two tribes: Manasseh and Ephraim.) However, Moses gave the Levites

[h] **14:2** DRAWING LOTS: *This was usually done by using specially marked stones to determine God's will.*
13:33 Num 18:20; Deut 18:2   **14:2** Num 26:52–56; 34:13   **14:3, 4** Num 32:33; 34:14, 15; Deut 3:12–17

no portion of the territory. Instead, they received cities to live in, with fields for their cattle and flocks. ⁵The people of Israel divided the land as the LORD had commanded Moses.

Hebron Is Given to Caleb

⁶One day some people from the tribe of Judah came to Joshua at Gilgal. One of them, Caleb son of Jephunneh the Kenizzite, said to him, "You know what the LORD said in Kadesh Barnea about you and me to Moses, the man of God. ⁷I was forty years old when the LORD's servant Moses sent me from Kadesh Barnea to spy out this land. I brought an honest report back to him. ⁸The men who went with me, however, made our people afraid. But I faithfully obeyed the LORD my God. ⁹Because I did, Moses promised me that my children and I would certainly receive as our possession the land which I walked over. ¹⁰But now, look. It has been forty-five years since the LORD said that to Moses. That was when Israel was going through the desert, and the LORD, as he promised, has kept me alive ever since. Look at me! I am eighty-five years old ¹¹and am just as strong today as I was when Moses sent me out. I am still strong enough for war or for anything else. ¹²Now then, give me the hill country that the LORD promised me on that day when my men and I reported. We told you then that the race of giants called the Anakim were there in large walled cities. Maybe the LORD will be with me, and I will drive them out, just as the LORD said."

¹³Joshua blessed Caleb son of Jephunneh and gave him the city of Hebron as his possession. ¹⁴Hebron still belongs to the descendants of Caleb son of Jephunneh the Kenizzite, because he faithfully obeyed the LORD, the God of Israel. ¹⁵Before this, Hebron was called the city of Arba. (Arba had been the greatest of the Anakim.)

There was now peace in the land.

Caleb's Reward

Caleb is given a special reward when the land is divided because of his faithfulness to God. We are also rewarded when we are faithful to God. Have you ever experienced any of the following rewards?
- Feeling good about yourself because you've been kind to others.
- Becoming more happy and joyful because you made a decision based upon what God wants rather than on what other people think or do.
- Becoming less stressed because you know that God is with you.

What other rewards have you received for trying to follow God's way?

— Joshua 14:6–15

The Territory Assigned to Judah

15 ¹The families of the tribe of Judah received a part of the land described as follows:

The land reached south to the southernmost point of the wilderness of Zin, at the border of Edom. ²This southern border ran from the south end of the Dead Sea, ³went southward from the Akrabbim Pass and on to Zin. It ran south of Kadesh Barnea, past Hezron and up to Addar, turned toward Karka, ⁴went on to Azmon, and followed the stream on the border of Egypt to the Mediterranean Sea, where the border ended. That was the southern border of Judah.

⁵The eastern border was the Dead Sea, all

Joshua

14:6 Num 14:30   14:7 Num 13:1–30   14:9 Num 14:24

What was special about the tribe of Levi, and why don't they receive land like the rest of the tribes? (See Deuteronomy 18:1–8.)

the way up to the inlet where the Jordan empties into it.

The northern border began there, [6] extended up to Beth Hoglah, and went north of the ridge overlooking the Jordan Valley. Then it went up to the Stone of Bohan (Bohan was a son of Reuben), [7] from Trouble Valley up to Debir, and then turned north toward Gilgal, which faces Adummim Pass on the south side of the valley. It then went on to the springs of Enshemesh, out to Enrogel, [8] and up through Hinnom Valley on the south side of the hill where the Jebusite city of Jerusalem was located. The border then proceeded up to the top of the hill on the west side of Hinnom Valley, at the northern end of Rephaim Valley. [9] From there it went to the Springs of Nephtoah and out to the cities near Mount Ephron. There it turned toward Baalah (or Kiriath Jearim), [10] where it circled west of Baalah toward the hill country of Edom, went on the north side of Mount Jearim (or Chesalon), down to Beth Shemesh, and on past Timnah. [11] The border then went out to the hill north of Ekron, turned toward Shikkeron, past Mount Baalah, and on to Jamnia. It ended at the Mediterranean Sea, [12] which formed the western border.

Within these borders lived the people of the families of Judah.

Caleb Conquers Hebron and Debir
(Judges 1:11–15)

[13] As the LORD commanded Joshua, part of the territory of Judah was given to Caleb son of Jephunneh, from the tribe of Judah. He received Hebron, the city belonging to Arba, father of Anak. [14] Caleb drove the descendants of Anak out of the city—the clans of Sheshai, Ahiman, and Talmai. [15] From there he went to attack the people living in Debir. (This city used to be called Kiriath Sepher.) [16] Caleb said, "I will give my daughter Achsah in marriage to the man who suc-

ceeds in capturing Kiriath Sepher." [17] Othniel, the son of Caleb's brother Kenaz, captured the city, so Caleb gave him his daughter Achsah in marriage. [18] On the wedding day Othniel urged her[i] to ask her father for a field. She got down from her donkey, and Caleb asked her what she wanted. [19] She answered, "I want some water holes. The land you have given me is in the dry country." So Caleb gave her the upper and lower springs.

The Cities of Judah

[20] This is the land that the families of the tribe of Judah received as their possession. [21] The cities farthest south that belonged to them, those that were near the border of Edom, were Kabzeel, Eder, Jagur, [22] Kinah, Dimonah, Adadah, [23] Kedesh, Hazor, Ithnan, [24] Ziph, Telem, Bealoth, [25] Hazor Hadattah, Kerioth Hezron (or Hazor), [26] Amam, Shema, Moladah, [27] Hazar Gaddah, Heshmon, Bethpelet, [28] Hazar Shual, Beersheba, Biziothiah, [29] Baalah, Iim, Ezem, [30] Eltolad, Chesil, Hormah, [31] Ziklag, Madmannah, Sansannah, [32] Lebaoth, Shilhim, Ain, and Rimmon: twenty-nine cities in all, along with the towns around them.

[33] The cities in the foothills were Eshtaol, Zorah, Ashnah, [34] Zanoah, Engannim, Tappuah, Enam, [35] Jarmuth, Adullam, Socoh, Azekah, [36] Shaaraim, Adithaim, Gederah, and Gederothaim: fourteen cities, along with the towns around them.

[37] There were also Zenan, Hadashah, Migdalgad, [38] Dilean, Mizpah, Joktheel, [39] Lachish, Bozkath, Eglon, [40] Cabbon, Lahmam, Chitlish, [41] Gederoth, Bethdagon, Naamah, and Makkedah: sixteen cities, along with the towns around them.

[42] There were also Libnah, Ether, Ashan, [43] Iphtah, Ashnah, Nezib, [44] Keilah, Achzib, and Mareshah: nine cities, along with the towns around them.

[45] There was Ekron with its towns and vil-

---

[i] **15:18** Probable text (see Judg 1:14) Othniel urged her; Hebrew she urged Othniel.
15:13, 14 Judg 1:20

Othniel (Joshua 15:17) **will become the first judge of Israel. More of his story appears in Judges 3:7–11.**

lages, 46and all the cities and towns near Ashdod, from Ekron to the Mediterranean Sea.

47There were Ashdod and Gaza, with their towns and villages, reaching to the stream on the border of Egypt and the coast of the Mediterranean Sea.

48In the hill country there were Shamir, Jattir, Socoh, 49Dannah, Kiriath Sepher (or Debir), 50Anab, Eshtemoa, Anim, 51Goshen, Holon, and Giloh: eleven cities, along with the towns around them.

52There were Arab, Dumah, Eshan, 53Janim, Beth Tappuah, Aphekah, 54Humtah, Hebron, and Zior: nine cities, along with the towns around them.

55There were Maon, Carmel, Ziph, Juttah, 56Jezreel, Jokdeam, Zanoah, 57Kain, Gibeah, and Timnah: ten cities, along with the towns around them.

58There were Halhul, Bethzur, Gedor, 59Maarath, Bethanoth, and Eltekon: six cities, along with the towns around them.

60There were Kiriath Baal (or Kiriath Jearim) and Rabbah: two cities, along with the towns around them.

61In the desert there were Beth Arabah, Middin, Secacah, 62Nibshan, Salt City, and Engedi: six cities, along with the towns around them.

63But the people of Judah were not able to drive out the Jebusites, who lived in Jerusalem. The Jebusites still live there with the people of Judah.

The Territory Assigned to Ephraim and West Manasseh

16 1The southern boundary of the land assigned to the descendants of Joseph started from the Jordan near Jericho, at a point east of the springs of Jericho, and went into the desert. It went from Jericho up into the hill country as far as Bethel. 2From Bethel it went to Luz, passing on to Ataroth Addar, where the Archites lived. 3It then went west to the area of the Japhletites, as far as the area of Lower Beth Horon. It went on from there to Gezer and ended at the Mediterranean Sea.

4The descendants of Joseph, the tribes of Ephraim and West Manasseh, received this land as their possession.

Ephraim

5This was the territory of the Ephraimite families: their border ran from Ataroth Addar eastward to Upper Beth Horon, 6and from there to the Mediterranean Sea. Michmethath was on their north. East of there the border bent toward Taanath Shiloh and went past it on the east to Janoah. 7Then it went down from Janoah to Ataroth and Naarah, reaching Jericho and ending at the Jordan. 8The border went west from Tappuah to the stream Kanah and ended at the Mediterranean Sea. This was the land given to the families of the tribe of Ephraim as their possession, 9along with some towns and villages that were within the borders of Manasseh, but given to the Ephraimites. 10But they did not drive out the Canaanites who lived in Gezer, so the Canaanites have lived among the Ephraimites to this day, but they have been forced to work as slaves.

West Manasseh

17 1A part of the land west of the Jordan was assigned to some of the families descended from Joseph's older son Manasseh. Machir, the father of Gilead, was Manasseh's oldest son and a military hero, so Gilead and Bashan, east of the Jordan, were assigned to him. 2Land west of the Jordan was assigned to the rest of the families of Manasseh: Abiezer, Helek, Asriel, Shechem, Hepher, and Shemida. These were male descendants of Manasseh son of Joseph, and they were heads of families. 3Zelophehad, son of Hepher, son of Gilead, son of Machir, son of Manasseh, did not have any sons, but only daughters. Their names were Mahlah, Noah, Hoglah, Milcah, and Tirzah. 4They went to Eleazar the priest and to Joshua son of Nun and to the leaders, and said, "The LORD commanded Moses to give us, as well as our male relatives, a part of the land to possess." So, as the LORD had commanded, they were given land along with their male

Joshua

15:63 Judg 1:21; 2 Sam 5:6; 1 Chr 11:4   16:10 Judg 1:29   17:4 Num 27:1–7 relatives. 5 This is why Manasseh received ten shares in addition to Gilead and Bashan on the east side of the Jordan, 6 since his female descendants as well as his male descendants were assigned land. The land of Gilead was assigned to the rest of the descendants of Manasseh.

7 The territory of Manasseh reached from Asher to Michmethath, east of Shechem. The border then went south to include the people of Entappuah. 8 The land around Tappuah belonged to Manasseh, but the town of Tappuah, on the border, belonged to the descendants of Ephraim. 9 The border then went down to the stream Kanah. The cities south of the stream belonged to Ephraim, even though they were in the territory of Manasseh. The border of Manasseh proceeded along the north side of the stream and ended at the Mediterranean Sea. 10 Ephraim was to the south, and Manasseh was to the north, with the Mediterranean Sea as their western border. Asher was to the northwest, and Issachar to the northeast. 11 Within the territories of Issachar and Asher, Manasseh possessed Beth Shan and Ibleam, along with their surrounding towns, as well as Dor (the one on the coast),ʲ Endor, Taanach, Megiddo, and their surrounding towns. 12 The people of Manasseh, however, were not able to drive out the people living in those cities, so the Canaanites continued to live there. 13 Even when the Israelites became stronger, they did not drive out all the Canaanites, but they did force them to work for them.

Ephraim and West Manasseh Request More Land

14 The descendants of Joseph said to Joshua, "Why have you given us only one part of the land to possess as our own? There are very many of us because the LORD has blessed us."

15 Joshua answered, "If there are so many of you and the hill country of Ephraim is too small for you, then go into the forests and clear ground for yourselves in the land of the Perizzites and the Rephaim."

Women Have Rights, Too!

In Numbers, chapter 27, the daughters of Zelophehad have a serious talk with Moses. Keep in mind that at this time, women cannot inherit land. Their father is dead, and they don't have any brothers. They ask Moses for the right to inherit land so that their father will be remembered. These remarkable women are mentioned four times in the Scriptures: twice in Numbers, once in Joshua, and again in Chronicles. Joshua keeps the promise that Moses made to these women. Because they speak up and ask that their rights be protected, they are given land to preserve their family name.

Many people find the story of these outspoken women an important one today. It is a story that shows that women are entitled to human rights and human dignity. Are boys and girls treated the same in your school and community? Does either group get more attention or more privileges? Can you think of any ways that the dignity and rights of women still need protection today?

— Joshua 17:3–6

16 They replied, "The hill country is not big enough for us, but the Canaanites in the plains have iron chariots, both those who live in Beth Shan and its surrounding towns and those who live in Jezreel Valley."

17 Joshua said to the tribes of Ephraim and West Manasseh, "There are indeed many of

ʲ 17:11 *Probable text* Dor (the one on the coast); *Hebrew unclear.*
17:12, 13 Judg 1:27, 28

you, and you are very powerful. You shall have more than one share. 18 The hill country will be yours. Even though it is a forest, you will clear it and take possession of it from one end to the other. As for the Canaanites, you will drive them out, even though they do have iron chariots and are a strong people."

The Division of the Rest of the Land

18 1 After they had conquered the land, the entire community of Israel assembled at Shiloh and set up the Tent of the LORD's presence. 2 There were still seven tribes of the people of Israel who had not yet been assigned their share of the land. 3 So Joshua said to the people of Israel, "How long are you going to wait before you go in and take the land that the LORD, the God of your ancestors, has given you? 4 Let me have three men from each tribe. I will send them out over the whole country to map out the territory that they would like to have as their possession. Then they are to come back to me. 5 The land will be divided among them in seven parts; Judah will stay in its territory in the south, and Joseph in its territory in the north. 6 Write down a description of these seven divisions and bring it to me.

k **18:6** DRAW LOTS: *See 14:2.*

Then I will draw lots *k* to consult the LORD our God for you. 7 The Levites, however, will not receive a share of the land with the rest of you, because their share is to serve as the LORD's priests. And of course, the tribes of Gad, Reuben, and East Manasseh have already received their land east of the Jordan, which Moses, the LORD's servant, gave to them."

8 The men went on their way to map out the land after Joshua had given them these instructions: "Go all over the land and map it out, and come back to me. And then here in Shiloh I will consult the LORD for you by drawing lots." 9 So the men went all over the land and set down in writing how they divided it into seven parts, making a list of the towns. Then they went back to Joshua in the camp at Shiloh. 10 Joshua drew lots to consult the LORD for them, and assigned each of the remaining tribes of Israel a certain part of the land.

The Territory Assigned to Benjamin

11 The territory belonging to the families of the tribe of Benjamin was the first to be assigned. Their land lay between the tribes of Judah and Joseph. 12 On the north their border began at the Jordan and then went up

Go all over the land and map it out. (18:8)

Many of the names of people became the names of places as the tribes settled into the territories that were given to them.

the slope north of Jericho and westward through the hill country as far as the desert of Bethaven. ¹³The border then went to the slope on the south side of Luz (also called Bethel), then down to Ataroth Addar, on the mountain south of Lower Beth Horon. ¹⁴The border then went in another direction, turning south from the western side of this mountain and going to Kiriath Baal (or Kiriath Jearim), which belongs to the tribe of Judah. This was the western border. ¹⁵The southern border started on the edge of Kiriath Jearim and went[l] to the Springs of Nephtoah. ¹⁶It then went down to the foot of the mountain that overlooks Hinnom Valley, at the north end of Rephaim Valley. It then went south through Hinnom Valley, south of the Jebusite ridge, toward Enrogel. ¹⁷It then turned north to Enshemesh and then on to Geliloth, opposite Adummim Pass. The border then went down to the Stone of Bohan (Bohan was a son of Reuben) ¹⁸and passed north of the ridge overlooking the Jordan Valley. It then went down into the valley, ¹⁹passing north of the ridge of Beth Hoglah, and ended at the northern inlet on the Dead Sea, where the Jordan River empties into it. This was the southern border. ²⁰The Jordan was the eastern border. These were the borders of the land which the families of the tribe of Benjamin received as their possession.

²¹The cities belonging to the families of the tribe of Benjamin were Jericho, Beth Hoglah, Emek Keziz, ²²Beth Arabah, Zemaraim, Bethel, ²³Avvim, Parah, Ophrah, ²⁴Chepharammoni, Ophni, and Geba: twelve cities, along with the towns around them. ²⁵There were also Gibeon, Ramah, Beeroth, ²⁶Mizpah, Chephirah, Mozah, ²⁷Rekem, Irpeel, Taralah, ²⁸Zela, Haeleph, Jebus (or Jerusalem), Gibeah, and Kiriath Jearim: fourteen cities, along with the towns around them. This is the land which the families of the tribe of Benjamin received as their possession.

The Territory Assigned to Simeon

19

¹The second assignment made was for the families of the tribe of Simeon. Its territory extended into the land assigned to the tribe of Judah. ²It included Beersheba, Sheba, Moladah, ³Hazar Shual, Balah, Ezem, ⁴Eltolad, Bethul, Hormah, ⁵Ziklag, Beth Marcaboth, Hazar Susah, ⁶Beth Lebaoth, and Sharuhen: thirteen cities, along with the towns around them.

⁷There were also Ain, Rimmon, Ether, and Ashan: four cities, along with the towns around them. ⁸This included all the towns around these cities as far as Baalath Beer (or Ramah), in the south. This was the land which the families of the tribe of Simeon received as their possession. ⁹Since Judah's assignment was larger than was needed, part of its territory was given to the tribe of Simeon.

The Territory Assigned to Zebulun

¹⁰The third assignment made was for the families of the tribe of Zebulun. The land which they received reached as far as Sarid. ¹¹From there the border went west to Mareal, touching Dabbesheth and the stream east of Jokneam. ¹²On the other side of Sarid it went east to the border of Chisloth Tabor, then to Daberath and up to Japhia. ¹³It continued east from there to Gath Hepher and Ethkazin, turning in the direction of Neah on the way to Rimmon. ¹⁴On the north the border turned toward Hannathon, ending at Iphtahel Valley. ¹⁵It included Kattath, Nahalal, Shimron, Idalah, and Bethlehem: twelve cities, along with the towns around them. ¹⁶These cities and their towns were in the land which the families of the tribe of Zebulun received as their possession.

The Territory Assigned to Issachar

¹⁷The fourth assignment made was for the families of the tribe of Issachar. ¹⁸Its area

---

[l] **18:15** *Probable text* and went; *Hebrew* and went westward.
19:2–8 1 Chr 4:28–33

Shiloh (Joshua 19:51) **was an important place. The Tent of the Lord's Presence, which is also called the Tent of meeting, is set up there. It was a holy place.**

included Jezreel, Chesulloth, Shunem, [19]Hapharaim, Shion, Anaharath, [20]Rabbith, Kishion, Ebez, [21]Remeth, Engannim, Enhaddah, and Bethpazzez. [22]The border also touched Tabor, Shahazumah, and Beth Shemesh, ending at the Jordan. It included sixteen cities along with the towns around them. [23]These cities and their towns were in the land which the families of the tribe of Issachar received as their possession.

The Territory Assigned to Asher

[24]The fifth assignment made was for the families of the tribe of Asher. [25]Its area included Helkath, Hali, Beten, Achshaph, [26]Allam Melech, Amad, and Mishal. On the west it touched Carmel and Shihor Libnath. [27]As it turned east, the border went to Bethdagon, touching Zebulun and Iphtahel Valley on the way north to Bethemek and Neiel. It continued north to Cabul, [28]Ebron, Rehob, Hammon, and Kanah, as far as Sidon. [29]The border then turned to Ramah, reaching the fortified city of Tyre; then it turned to Hosah and ended at the Mediterranean Sea. It included Mahalab, Achzib, [30]Ummah, Aphek, and Rehob: twenty-two cities, along with the towns around them. [31]These cities and their towns were in the land which the families of the tribe of Asher received as their possession.

The Territory Assigned to Naphtali

[32]The sixth assignment made was for the families of the tribe of Naphtali. [33]Its border went from Heleph to the oak in Zaanannim, on to Adaminekeb and to Jamnia, as far as Lakkum, and ended at the Jordan. [34]There the border turned west to Aznoth Tabor, from there to Hukkok, touching Zebulun on the south, Asher on the west, and the Jordan[m] on the east. [35]The fortified cities were Ziddim, Zer, Hammath, Rakkath, Chinnereth, [36]Adamah, Ramah, Hazor, [37]Kedesh, Edrei, Enhazor, [38]Yiron, Migdalel, Horem, Bethanath, and Beth Shemesh: nineteen cities, along with the towns around them. [39]These cities and their towns were in the

land which the families of the tribe of Naphtali received as their possession.

The Territory Assigned to Dan

[40]The seventh assignment made was for the families of the tribe of Dan. [41]Its area included Zorah, Eshtaol, Irshemesh, [42]Shaalbim, Aijalon, Ithlah, [43]Elon, Timnah, Ekron, [44]Eltekeh, Gibbethon, Baalath, [45]Jehud, Beneberak, Gathrimmon, [46]Mejarkon, and Rakkon, as well as the territory around Joppa. [47]When the people of Dan lost their land, they went to Laish and attacked it. They captured it, killed its people, and claimed it for themselves. They settled there and changed the name of the city from Laish to Dan, naming it after their ancestor Dan. [48]These cities and their towns were in the land which the families of the tribe of Dan received as their possession.

The Final Assignment of the Land

[49]When the people of Israel finished dividing up the land, they gave Joshua son of Nun a part of the land as his own. [50]As the LORD had commanded, they gave him the city he asked for: Timnath Serah, in the hill country of Ephraim. He rebuilt the city and settled there.

[51]Eleazar the priest, Joshua son of Nun, and the leaders of the families of the tribes of Israel assigned these parts of the land by drawing lots[n] to consult the LORD at Shiloh, at the entrance of the Tent of the LORD's presence. In this way they finished dividing the land.

The Cities of Refuge

20 [1]Then the LORD told Joshua [2]to say to the people of Israel, "Choose the cities of refuge that I had Moses tell you about. [3]If any of you accidentally kills someone, you can go there and escape the one who is looking for revenge. [4]You can run away to one of these cities, go to the place of judgment at the entrance to the city, and explain to the leaders what happened. Then

---

[m] **19:34** *One ancient translation* the Jordan; *Hebrew* Judah at the Jordan.   [n] **19:51** DRAWING LOTS: *See 14:2.*
19:47 Judg 18:27–29   **20:1–9** Num 35:9–34; Deut 4:41–43; 19:1–13

Pray It!

A Second Chance

If someone killed another person in ancient Israel, the dead person's family was expected to take revenge. They could, by law, kill the killer. That was the justice of the time, even if the death was accidental. This passage from Joshua establishes safe places for anyone in danger of being killed for the sake of revenge. The cities of refuge were places where someone could start a new life and be assured of protection. They were places where the hopeless could get a second chance.

Have you ever needed a second chance? Maybe you made a big mistake, or maybe you started hanging around the wrong people. Maybe you just forgot the kind of person you wanted to be and started doing things you knew you shouldn't do. Well, fortunately, God is a God of second chances. In the same way the cities of refuge were established to protect and give new life, Jesus gives us new life—forgiveness, safety, a second chance.

> *God of new life,*
> *be my city of refuge*
> *When I have done wrong,*
> *I will come to you.*
> *You will be my safe place in this world*
> *until I can set things right again. Amen.*

— Joshua, chapter 20

they will let you into the city and give you a place to live in, so that you can stay there. ⁵If the one looking for revenge follows you there, the people of the city must not hand you over to that one. They must protect you because you killed the person accidentally and not out of anger. ⁶You may stay in the city until you have received a public trial and until the death of the man who is then the High Priest. Then you may go back home to your own town, from which you had run away."

⁷So, on the west side of the Jordan they set aside Kedesh in Galilee, in the hill country of Naphtali; Shechem, in the hill country of Ephraim; and Hebron, in the hill country of Judah. ⁸East of the Jordan, on the desert plateau east of Jericho, they chose Bezer in the territory of Reuben; Ramoth in Gilead, in the territory of Gad; and Golan in Bashan, in the territory of Manasseh. ⁹These were the cities of refuge chosen for all the

people of Israel and for any foreigner living among them. Any who killed a person accidentally could find protection there from the one looking for revenge; they could not be killed unless they had first received a public trial.

The Cities of the Levites

21 ¹The leaders of the Levite families went to Eleazar the priest, Joshua son of Nun, and to the heads of the families of all the tribes of Israel. ²There at Shiloh in the land of Canaan they said to them, "The LORD commanded through Moses that we were to be given cities to live in, as well as pasture land around them for our livestock." ³So in accordance with the LORD's command the people of Israel gave the Levites certain cities and pasture lands out of their own territories.

⁴The families of the Levite clan of Kohath

were the first to be assigned cities. The families who were descended from Aaron the priest were assigned thirteen cities from the territories of Judah, Simeon, and Benjamin. [5] The rest of the clan of Kohath was assigned ten cities from the territories of Ephraim, Dan, and West Manasseh.

[6] The clan of Gershon was assigned thirteen cities from the territories of Issachar, Asher, Naphtali, and East Manasseh.

[7] The families of the clan of Merari were assigned twelve cities from the territories of Reuben, Gad, and Zebulun.

[8] By drawing lots,[n] the people of Israel assigned these cities and their pasture lands to the Levites, as the LORD had commanded through Moses.

[9] These are the names of the cities from the territories of Judah and Simeon which were given [10] to the descendants of Aaron who were of the clan of Kohath, which was descended from Levi. Their assignment was the first to be made. [11] They were given the city of Arba (Arba was Anak's father), now called Hebron, in the hill country of Judah, along with the pasture land surrounding it. [12] However, the fields of the city, as well as its towns, had already been given to Caleb son of Jephunneh as his possession.

[13] In addition to Hebron (one of the cities of refuge), the following cities were assigned to the descendants of Aaron the priest: Libnah, [14] Jattir, Eshtemoa, [15] Holon, Debir, [16] Ain, Juttah, and Beth Shemesh, with their pasture lands: nine cities from the tribes of Judah and Simeon. [17] From the territory of Benjamin they were given four cities: Gibeon, Geba, [18] Anathoth, and Almon, with their pasture lands. [19] Thirteen cities in all, with their pasture lands, were given to the priests, the descendants of Aaron.

[20] The other families of the Levite clan of Kohath were assigned some cities from the territory of Ephraim. [21] They were given four cities: Shechem and its pasture lands in the hill country of Ephraim (one of the cities of refuge), Gezer, [22] Kibzaim, and Beth Horon, with their pasture lands. [23] From the territory of Dan they were given four cities: Eltekeh, Gibbethon, [24] Aijalon, and Gathrimmon, with their pasture lands. [25] From the territory of West Manasseh they were given two cities: Taanach and Gathrimmon, with their pasture lands. [26] These families of the clan of Kohath received ten cities in all, with their pasture lands.

[27] Another group of Levites, the clan of Gershon, received from the territory of East Manasseh two cities: Golan in Bashan (one of the cities of refuge) and Beeshterah, with their pasture lands. [28] From the territory of Issachar they received four cities: Kishion, Daberath, [29] Jarmuth, and Engannim, with their pasture lands. [30] From the territory of Asher they received four cities: Mishal, Abdon, [31] Helkath, and Rehob, with their pasture lands. [32] From the territory of Naphtali they received three cities: Kedesh in Galilee, with its pasture lands (one of the cities of refuge), Hammoth Dor, and Kartan, with their pasture lands. [33] The various families of the clan of Gershon received a total of thirteen cities with their pasture lands.

[34] The rest of the Levites, the clan of Merari, received from the territory of Zebulun four cities: Jokneam, Kartah, [35] Dimnah, and Nahalal, with their pasture lands. [36] From the territory of Reuben they received four cities: Bezer, Jahaz, [37] Kedemoth, and Mephaath, with their pasture lands. [38] From the tribe of Gad they received four cities: Ramoth in Gilead, with its pasture lands (one of the cities of refuge), Mahanaim, [39] Heshbon, and Jazer, with their pasture lands. [40] So the clan of Merari was assigned a total of twelve cities.

[41-42] From the land that the people of Israel possessed, a total of forty-eight cities, with the pasture lands around them, was given to the Levites.

Joshua

[n] 21:8 DRAWING LOTS: *See 14:2.*

There are six cities of refuge: Kedesh, Shechem, Hebron, Bezer, Ramoth, and Golan. Can you find all six on Map 3 in the back of this Bible?

Israel Takes Possession of the Land

⁴³So the LORD gave to Israel all the land that he had solemnly promised their ancestors he would give them. When they had taken possession of it, they settled down there. ⁴⁴The LORD gave them peace throughout the land, just as he had promised their ancestors. Not one of all their enemies had been able to stand against them, because the LORD gave the Israelites the victory over all their enemies. ⁴⁵The LORD kept every one of the promises that he had made to the people of Israel.

Joshua Sends the Eastern Tribes Home

22 ¹Then Joshua called together the people of the tribes of Reuben, Gad, and East Manasseh. ²He said to them, "You have done everything that Moses the LORD's servant ordered you to do, and you have obeyed all my commands. ³All this time you have never once deserted the other Israelites. You have been careful to obey the commands of the LORD your God. ⁴Now, as he promised, the LORD your God has given the other Israelites peace. So go back home to the land which you claimed for your own, the land on the east side of the Jordan, that Moses, the LORD's servant, gave you. ⁵Make sure you obey the law that Moses commanded you: love the LORD your God, do his will, obey his commandments, be faithful to him, and serve him with all your heart and soul."

⁶⁻⁸Joshua sent them home with his blessing and with these words: "You are going back home very rich, with a lot of livestock, silver, gold, bronze, iron, and many clothes. Share with your fellow tribesmen what you took from your enemies." Then they left for home.

Moses had given land east of the Jordan to one half of the tribe of Manasseh, but to the other half Joshua had given land west of the Jordan, along with the other tribes.

⁹So the people of the tribes of Reuben, Gad, and East Manasseh went back home. They left the rest of the people of Israel at

Who Do They Think They Are?

"Look at the way he's dressed!" "She thinks she's so great." Sometimes we judge people without really understanding them. That's what happens in Joshua, chapter 22. The tribes that settled on the eastern side of the Jordan wanted to make sure that the rest of Israel knew that they also served God, so they built an altar that was big enough to be seen all the way across the river. They even named it Witness.

But the tribes on the western side of the Jordan saw the altar as a threat. They thought it meant the tribes on the eastern side were worshiping foreign gods. They talked about going to war against their fellow Israelites! Phinehas is sent to talk to the eastern tribes and quickly sees that the eastern tribes have been misjudged.

When we quickly judge somebody's actions, we might be in danger of misjudgment. We can end up angry or hateful, and the other person can feel attacked or left out. When you see something happening you don't understand, be sure to do what the Israelites did. Take time to find out what the other person really meant by what he or she did.

— Joshua, chapter 22

Chapter 22 begins the third major section of the Book of Joshua. This section describes what happens after all the tribes were settled in their given lands.

Shiloh in the land of Canaan and started out for their own land, the land of Gilead, which they had taken as the LORD had commanded them through Moses.

The Altar by the Jordan

10 When the tribes of Reuben, Gad, and East Manasseh arrived at Geliloth, still on the west side*o* of the Jordan, they built a large, impressive altar there by the river. 11 The rest of the people of Israel were told, "Listen! The people of the tribes of Reuben, Gad, and East Manasseh have built an altar at Geliloth, on our side of the Jordan!" 12 When the people of Israel heard this, the whole community came together at Shiloh to go to war against the eastern tribes.

13 Then the people of Israel sent Phinehas, the son of Eleazar the priest, to the people of the tribes of Reuben, Gad, and East Manasseh in the land of Gilead. 14 Ten leading men went with Phinehas, one from each of the western tribes and each one the head of a family among the clans. 15 They came to the land of Gilead, to the people of Reuben, Gad, and East Manasseh, 16 and speaking for the whole community of the LORD, they said to them, "Why have you done this evil thing against the God of Israel? You have rebelled against the LORD by building this altar for yourselves! You are no longer following him! 17 Remember our sin at Peor, when the LORD punished his own people with an epidemic? We are still suffering because of that. Wasn't that sin enough? 18 Are you going to refuse to follow him now? If you rebel against the LORD today, he will be angry with everyone in Israel tomorrow. 19 Now then, if your land is not fit to worship in, come over into the LORD's land, where his Tent is. Claim some land among us. But don't rebel against the LORD or make rebels out of us by building an altar in addition to the altar of the LORD our God. 20 Remember how Achan son of Zerah refused to obey the command about the things condemned to destruction; the whole community of Israel was punished for that.

Achan was not the only one who died because of his sin."

21 The people of the tribes of Reuben, Gad, and East Manasseh answered the heads of the families of the western tribes: 22 "The Mighty One is God! He is the LORD! The Mighty One is God! He is the LORD! He knows why we did this, and we want you to know too! If we rebelled and did not keep faith with the LORD, do not let us live any longer! 23 If we disobeyed the LORD and built our own altar to burn sacrifices on or to use for grain offerings or fellowship offerings, let the LORD himself punish us. 24 No! We did it because we were afraid that in the future your descendants would say to ours, 'What do you have to do with the LORD, the God of Israel? 25 He made the Jordan a boundary between us and you people of Reuben and Gad. You have nothing to do with the LORD.' Then your descendants might make our descendants stop worshiping the LORD. 26 So we built an altar, not to burn sacrifices or make offerings, 27 but instead, as a sign for our people and yours, and for the generations after us, that we do indeed worship the LORD before his sacred Tent with our offerings to be burned and with sacrifices and fellowship offerings. This was to keep your descendants from saying that ours have nothing to do with the LORD. 28 It was our idea that, if this should ever happen, our descendants could say, 'Look! Our ancestors made an altar just like the LORD's altar. It was not for burning offerings or for sacrifice, but as a sign for our people and yours.' 29 We would certainly not rebel against the LORD or stop following him now by building an altar to burn offerings on or for grain offerings or sacrifices. We would not build any other altar than the altar of the LORD our God that stands in front of the Tent of his presence."

30 Phinehas the priest and the ten leading men of the community who were with him, the heads of families of the western tribes, heard what the people of the tribes of Reuben, Gad, and East Manasseh had to say, and they were satisfied. 31 Phinehas, the son of Eleazar the priest, said to them, "Now we

o **22:10** still on the west side; *or* on the east side.
22:16 Deut 12:13, 14   **22:17** Num 25:1–9   **22:20** Josh 7:1–26

know that the LORD is with us. You have not rebelled against him, and so you have saved the people of Israel from the LORD's punishment."

32 Then Phinehas and the leaders left the people of Reuben and Gad in the land of Gilead and went back to Canaan, to the people of Israel, and reported to them. 33 The Israelites were satisfied and praised God. They no longer talked about going to war to devastate the land where the people of Reuben and Gad had settled.

34 The people of Reuben and Gad said, "This altar is a witness to all of us that the LORD is God." And so they named it "Witness."

Joshua's Farewell Address

23 ¹Much later the LORD gave Israel security from their enemies around them. By that time Joshua was very old, ²so he called all Israel, the elders, leaders, judges, and officers of the people, and said, "I am very old now. ³You have seen everything that the LORD your God has done to all these nations because of you. The LORD your God has been fighting for you. ⁴I have assigned as the possession of your tribes the land of the nations that are still left, as well as of all the nations that I have already conquered, from the Jordan River in the east to the Mediterranean Sea in the west. ⁵The LORD your God will make them retreat from you, and he will drive them away as you advance. You shall have their land, as the LORD your God has promised you. ⁶So be careful to obey and do everything that is written in the book of the Law of Moses. Do not neglect any part of it, ⁷and then you will not associate with these peoples left among you or speak the names of their gods or use those names in taking vows or worship those gods or bow down to them. ⁸Instead, be faithful to the LORD, as you have been till now. ⁹The LORD has driven great and powerful nations out as you advanced, and no one has ever been able to stand against you. ¹⁰Any one of you can make a thousand men run away, because the LORD your God is fighting for you, just as he promised. ¹¹Be careful, then, to love the

LORD your God. ¹²If you are disloyal and join with the nations that are still left among you and intermarry with them, ¹³you may be sure that the LORD your God will no longer drive these nations out as you advance. Rather, they will be as dangerous for you as a trap or a pit and as painful as a whip on your back or thorns in your eyes. And this will last until none of you are left in this good land which the LORD your God has given you.

¹⁴"Now my time has come to die. Every one of you knows in his heart and soul that the LORD your God has given you all the good things that he promised. Every promise he made has been kept; not one has failed. ¹⁵But just as he kept every promise that he made to you, so he will carry out every threat. ¹⁶If you do not keep the covenant which the LORD your God commanded you to keep and if you serve and worship other gods, then in his anger he will punish you, and soon none of you will be left in this good land that he has given you."

Joshua Speaks to the People at Shechem

24 ¹Joshua gathered all the tribes of Israel together at Shechem. He called the elders, the leaders, the judges, and the officers of Israel, and they came into the presence of God. ²Joshua said to all the people, "This is what the LORD, the God of Israel, has to say: 'Long ago your ancestors lived on the other side of the Euphrates River and worshiped other gods. One of those ancestors was Terah, the father of Abraham and Nahor. ³Then I took Abraham, your ancestor, from the land across the Euphrates and led him through the whole land of Canaan. I gave him many descendants. I gave him Isaac, ⁴and to Isaac I gave Jacob and Esau. I gave Esau the hill country of Edom as his possession, but your ancestor Jacob and his children went down to Egypt. ⁵Later I sent Moses and Aaron, and I brought great trouble on Egypt. But I led you out; ⁶I brought your ancestors out of Egypt, and the Egyptians pursued them with chariots and cavalry. But when your ances-

23:10 a Deut 32:30; b Deut 3:22 **24:2** Gen 11:27 **24:3** a Gen 12:1–9; b Gen 21:1–3 **24:4** a Gen 25:24–26; b Gen 36:8; Deut 2:5; c Gen 46:1–7 **24:5** Ex 3:1—12:42

Pray It!

Remembering God's Goodness

Joshua recounts to the people all the things God has done for them. He reminds them of God's goodness and guidance to them throughout the years. Just like these ancient Israelites, every good thing we have comes from God. Take some time to remember all the times God has been good to you. Remember all your friendships, the love of your family, and the important lessons that you've learned.

As part of their prayer, some people like to keep a gratitude list or gratitude journal. At the end of every day, they write down all the good things that happened to them that day. No matter how bad the day was, they try to write down at least one good thing. It is surprising how something this simple can help you see God at work in your life! Is this something you might try?

— Joshua 24:1–15

tors got to the Red Sea [7]they cried out to me for help, and I put darkness between them and the Egyptians. I made the sea come rolling over the Egyptians and drown them. You know what I did to Egypt.

"'You lived in the desert a long time. [8]Then I brought you to the land of the Amorites, who lived on the east side of the Jordan. They fought you, but I gave you victory over them. You took their land, and I destroyed them as you advanced. [9]Then the king of Moab, Balak son of Zippor, fought against you. He sent word to Balaam son of Beor and asked him to put a curse on you. [10]But I would not listen to Balaam, so he blessed you, and in this way I rescued you from Balak. [11]You crossed the Jordan and came to Jericho. The men of Jericho fought you, as did the Amorites, the Perizzites, the Canaanites, the Hittites, the Girgashites, the Hivites, and the Jebusites. But I gave you victory over them all. [12]As you advanced, I threw them into panic in order to drive out the two Amorite kings. Your swords and bows had nothing to do with it. [13]I gave you a land that you had never

worked and cities that you had not built. Now you are living there and eating grapes from vines that you did not plant, and olives from trees that you did not plant.'

[14]"Now then," Joshua continued, "honor the LORD and serve him sincerely and faithfully. Get rid of the gods which your ancestors used to worship in Mesopotamia and in Egypt, and serve only the LORD. [15]If you are not willing to serve him, decide today whom you will serve, the gods your ancestors worshiped in Mesopotamia or the gods of the Amorites, in whose land you are now living. As for my family and me, we will serve the LORD."

[16]The people replied, "We would never leave the LORD to serve other gods! [17]The LORD our God brought our fathers and us out of slavery in Egypt, and we saw the miracles that he performed. He kept us safe wherever we went among all the nations through which we passed. [18]As we advanced into this land, the LORD drove out all the Amorites who lived here. So we also will serve the LORD; he is our God."

24:6, 7 Ex 14:1–31   **24:8** Num 21:21–35   **24:9, 10** Num 22:1—24:25   **24:11 a** Josh 3:14–17; **b** Josh 6:1–21   **24:12** Ex 23:28; Deut 7:20   **24:13** Deut 6:10, 11

Joshua

"As for my family and me, we will serve the LORD" *(Joshua 24:15).*

"As for my family and me, we will serve the Lord." (24:15)

¹⁹Joshua said to the people, "But you may not be able to serve the LORD. He is a holy God and will not forgive your sins. He will tolerate no rivals, ²⁰and if you leave him to serve foreign gods, he will turn against you and punish you. He will destroy you, even though he was good to you before."

²¹The people said to Joshua, "No! We will serve the LORD."

²²Joshua told them, "You are your own witnesses to the fact that you have chosen to serve the LORD."

"Yes," they said, "we are witnesses."

²³"Then get rid of those foreign gods that you have," he demanded, "and pledge your loyalty to the LORD, the God of Israel."

²⁴The people then said to Joshua, "We will serve the LORD our God. We will obey his commands."

²⁵So Joshua made a covenant for*ᵖ* the people that day, and there at Shechem he gave them laws and rules to follow. ²⁶Joshua wrote these commands in the book of the Law of God. Then he took a large stone and set it up under the oak tree in the LORD's sanctuary. ²⁷He said to all the people, "This stone will be our witness. It has heard all the words that the LORD has spoken to us. So it will be a witness against you, to keep you from rebelling against your God." ²⁸Then Joshua sent the people away, and everyone returned to their own part of the land.

Joshua and Eleazar Die

²⁹After that, the LORD's servant Joshua son of Nun died at the age of a hundred and ten. ³⁰They buried him on his own land at Timnath Serah in the hill country of Ephraim north of Mount Gaash.

³¹As long as Joshua lived, the people of Israel served the LORD, and after his death they continued to do so as long as those leaders were alive who had seen for themselves everything that the LORD had done for Israel.

³²The body of Joseph, which the people of Israel had brought from Egypt, was buried at Shechem, in the piece of land that Jacob had bought from the sons of Hamor, the father of Shechem, for a hundred pieces of silver. This land was inherited by Joseph's descendants.

³³Eleazar son of Aaron died and was buried at Gibeah, the town in the hill country of Ephraim which had been given to his son Phinehas.

ᵖ 24:25 for; *or* with.
24:30 Josh 19:49, 50   24:32 Gen 33:19; 50:24, 25; Ex 13:19; Jn 4:5; Acts 7:16

Your Next Step

Congratulations on finishing the Book of Joshua! Use this space to write your thoughts and questions about this book. If you are following the suggested reading plan, go ahead to the New Testament and the Gospel according to Luke. Look for ways the Gospel makes connections with the Old Testament people you have read about so far.

Joshua

Have you ever met someone who just seems born to lead? Maybe that person is good at talking to people, or they are very athletic. After the strong leadership of Moses and Joshua and before the great kings, the leaders of the Israelites were called judges. They were not like the judges you see in a courtroom. Some were military leaders or local heroes. Others were simply respected members of the community. They were natural leaders.

The Book of Judges tells the story of Israel in an in-between time. Even though the Israelites had entered the Promised Land, they needed to remain faithful to their covenant with God. Yet even the judges failed to always be faithful to God. Still, no matter how many times the people of Israel turned away from God, God was always ready to rescue them.

Chap. 16

Headlines

- Israelites Abandon God, Had a Baal! (2:11–15)
- Woman Murders Sleeping General (4:12–24)
- Deborah's Song: A New Top 40 Hit! (chapter 5)
- Gideon Looks for a Sign (6:36–40)
- Judge Makes Foolish Promise (11:29–39)
- Angel Announces Child's Birth (chapter 13)
- Bad Haircut Leads to Blindness (16:1–22)

FACTOIDS

Who wrote this book? The author is unknown, but someone during the Exile gathered these stories into this one collection. Some think it was the same person or group who wrote Deuteronomy.

When did these events take place? After the conquest of Canaan and before the time of the Israelite kings.

Why was it written? The Book of Judges was written to record the stories of the judges and show that whenever Israel turned away from God, it fell into ruin. Faithfulness to God was the key to the Israelites' survival.

Important themes

- When the people turn to God, God raises up heroes to lead them.
- Faithfulness leads to blessings, and unfaithfulness is punished.
- God is always merciful when the people repent.

JUDGES

The Tribes of Judah and Simeon Capture Adonibezek

1 ¹After Joshua's death the people of Israel asked the LORD, "Which of our tribes should be the first to go and attack the Canaanites?"

²The LORD answered, "The tribe of Judah will go first. I am giving them control of the land."

³The people of Judah said to the people of Simeon, "Go with us into the territory assigned to us, and we will fight the Canaanites together. Then we will go with you into the territory assigned to you." So the tribes of Simeon ⁴and Judah went into battle together. The LORD gave them victory over the Canaanites and the Perizzites, and they defeated ten thousand men at Bezek. ⁵They found Adonibezek there and fought him. ⁶He ran away, but they chased him, caught him, and cut off his thumbs and big toes. ⁷Adonibezek said, "Seventy kings with their thumbs and big toes cut off have picked up scraps under my table. God has now done to me what I did to them." He was taken to Jerusalem, where he died.

The Tribe of Judah Conquers Jerusalem and Hebron

⁸The people of Judah attacked Jerusalem and captured it. They killed its people and set fire to the city. ⁹After this they went on to fight the Canaanites who lived in the hill country, in the foothills, and in the dry country to the south. ¹⁰They marched against the Canaanites living in the city of Hebron, which used to be called Kiriath Arba. There they defeated the clans of Sheshai, Ahiman, and Talmai.

Othniel Conquers the City of Debir
(Joshua 15:13–19)

¹¹From there the men of Judah marched against the city of Debir, at that time called Kiriath Sepher. ¹²One of them, called Caleb, said, "I will give my daughter Achsah in marriage to the man who succeeds in capturing Kiriath Sepher." ¹³Othniel, the son of Caleb's younger brother Kenaz, captured the city, so Caleb gave him his daughter Achsah in marriage. ¹⁴On the wedding day Othniel urged her*a* to ask her father for a field. She got down from her donkey, and Caleb asked her what she wanted. ¹⁵She answered, "I want some water holes. The land you have given me is in the dry country." So Caleb gave her the upper and lower springs.

The Victories of the Tribes of Judah and Benjamin

¹⁶The descendants of Moses' father-in-law, the Kenite, went on with the people of Judah from Jericho, the city of palm trees, into the barren country south of Arad in Judah. There they settled among the Amalekites.*b* ¹⁷The people of Judah went with the people of Simeon, and together they defeated the Canaanites who lived in the city of Zephath. They put a curse on the city, destroyed it, and named it Hormah.*c* ¹⁸⁻¹⁹The LORD helped the people of Judah, and they took possession of the hill country. But they did not capture*d* Gaza, Ashkelon, or Ekron, with their surrounding territories. These people living along the coast had iron chariots, and so the people of Judah were not able to drive them out. ²⁰As Moses had commanded, Hebron was given to Caleb, who drove out of the city the three clans descended from Anak. ²¹But the people of the tribe of Ben-

---

a **1:14** *Some ancient translations* Othniel urged her; *Hebrew* she urged Othniel.   *b* **1:16** *Some ancient translations* Amalekites; *Hebrew* people.   *c* **1:17** HORMAH: *This name in Hebrew means "destruction."*   *d* **1:18–19** *One ancient translation* But they did not capture; *Hebrew* And they captured.
1:20 Josh 15:13, 14   **1:21** Josh 15:63; 2 Sam 5:6; 1 Chr 11:4

Speak Up

Caleb's daughter Achsah knows that her people will need water. The land they are given is in the desert. She asks her father, and he gives her two springs, or watering holes. Do you suffer in silence when you need something? Be bold like Achsah and ask for what you need. You can ask God for help with any problem. But sometimes you need to ask a parent or a friend for help, too. People can't help you if they don't know what you need!

— Judges 1:12–15

jamin did not drive out the Jebusites living in Jerusalem, and the Jebusites have continued to live there with the people of Benjamin ever since.

The Tribes of Ephraim and Manasseh Conquer Bethel

22-23 The tribes of Ephraim and Manasseh went to attack the city of Bethel, at that time called Luz. The LORD helped them. They sent spies to the city, 24 who saw a man leaving and said to him, "Show us how to get into the city, and we won't hurt you." 25 So he showed them, and the people of Ephraim and Manasseh killed everyone in the city, except this man and his family. 26 He later went to the land of the Hittites, built a city there, and named it Luz, which is still its name.

ᵉ 1:36 *One ancient translation* Edomite; *Hebrew* Amorite.
1:27, 28 Josh 17:11–13   **1:29** Josh 16:10

People Who Were Not Driven Out by the Israelites

27 The tribe of Manasseh did not drive out the people living in the cities of Beth Shan, Taanach, Dor, Ibleam, Megiddo, and the nearby towns; the Canaanites continued to live there. 28 When the Israelites became stronger, they forced the Canaanites to work for them, but still they did not drive them all out.

29 The tribe of Ephraim did not drive out the Canaanites living in the city of Gezer, and so the Canaanites continued to live there with them.

30 The tribe of Zebulun did not drive out the people living in the cities of Kitron and Nahalal, and so the Canaanites continued to live there with them and were forced to work for them.

31 The tribe of Asher did not drive out the people living in the cities of Acco, Sidon, Ahlab, Achzib, Helbah, Aphek, and Rehob. 32 The people of Asher lived with the local Canaanites, since they had not been driven out.

33 The tribe of Naphtali did not drive out the people living in the cities of Beth Shemesh and Bethanath. The people of Naphtali lived with the local Canaanites, but forced them to work for them.

34 The Amorites forced the people of the tribe of Dan into the hill country and did not let them come down to the plain. 35 The Amorites continued to live at Aijalon, Shaalbim, and Mount Heres, but the tribes of Ephraim and Manasseh kept them under their rule and forced them to work for them.

36 North of Sela, the Edomiteᵉ border ran through Akrabbim Pass.

The Angel of the LORD at Bochim

2 ¹ The angel of the LORD went from Gilgal to Bochim and said to the Israelites, "I took you out of Egypt and

Pray It!

Turning Your Back on God

The Israelites turned their back on God by worshiping the Baals and Astartes, the gods and goddesses of other peoples. They had promised to have no other God but Yahweh. It is hard to imagine why they would do this after all that God had done for them.

We should be careful, though, before judging the Israelites too harshly. There is more than one way to turn your back on God. We can put other things before God. We're too busy to pray or go to church. We don't notice other people in need because we're too distracted by things we want. It's all too easy to do.

God, help me never to turn my back on you,
*   because you never turn your back on me.*
Remind me when I forget you,
*   that I am yours and you are mine.*
Help me commit to putting you first,
*   by praying,*
*   by doing something for someone in need,*
*   by being an active member of my church. Amen.*

— Judges 2:10–13

brought you to the land that I promised to your ancestors. I said, 'I will never break my covenant with you. ²You must not make any covenant with the people who live in this land. You must tear down their altars.' But you have not done what I told you. You have done just the opposite! ³So I tell you now that I will not drive these people out as you advance. They will be your enemies,ᶠ and you will be trapped by the worship of their gods." ⁴When the angel had said this, all the people of Israel began to cry, ⁵and that is why the place is called Bochim.ᵍ There they offered sacrifices to the LORD.

The Death of Joshua

⁶Joshua sent the people of Israel on their way, and each man went to take possession of his own share of the land. ⁷As long as Joshua lived, the people of Israel served the LORD, and even after his death they continued to do so as long as the leaders were alive who had seen for themselves all the great things that the LORD had done for Israel. ⁸The LORD's servant Joshua son of Nun died at the age of a hundred and ten. ⁹He was buried in his own part of the land at Timnath Serah in the hill country of Ephraim north of Mount Gaash. ¹⁰That whole generation also died, and the next generation forgot the LORD and what he had done for Israel.

Israel Stops Worshiping the LORD

¹¹Then the people of Israel sinned against the LORD and began to serve the Baals. ¹²They stopped worshiping the LORD, the

ᶠ **2:3** *Some ancient translations* enemies; *Hebrew* sides.   ᵍ **2:5** BOCHIM: *This name in Hebrew means "those who cry."*
2:2 Ex 34:12, 13; Deut 7:2–5   **2:9** Josh 19:49, 50

Baals were the gods of the Canaanites, and the Astartes their goddesses.

God of their ancestors, the God who had brought them out of Egypt, and they began to worship other gods, the gods of the peoples around them. They bowed down to them and made the LORD angry. 13 They stopped worshiping the LORD and served the Baals and the Astartes. 14 And so the LORD became furious with Israel and let raiders attack and rob them. He let the enemies all around overpower them, and the Israelites could no longer protect themselves. 15 Every time they would go into battle, the LORD was against them, just as he had said he would be. They were in great distress.

16 Then the LORD gave the Israelites leaders who saved them from the raiders. 17 But the Israelites paid no attention to their leaders. Israel was unfaithful to the LORD and worshiped other gods. Their fathers had obeyed the LORD's commands, but this new generation soon stopped doing so. 18 Whenever the LORD gave Israel a leader, the LORD would help that leader and would save the people from their enemies as long as that leader lived. The LORD would have mercy on them because they groaned under their suffering and oppression. 19 But when the leader died, the people would return to the old ways and behave worse than the previous generation. They would serve and worship other gods, and stubbornly continue their own evil ways. 20 Then the LORD would become furious with Israel and say, "This

nation has broken the covenant that I commanded their ancestors to keep. Because they have not obeyed me, 21 I will no longer drive out any of the nations that were still in the land when Joshua died. 22 I will use them to find out whether or not these Israelites will follow my ways, as their ancestors did." 23 So the LORD allowed these nations to remain in the land; he did not give Joshua victory over them, nor did he drive them out soon after Joshua's death.

The Nations Remaining in the Land

3 1 So then, the LORD left some nations in the land to test the Israelites who had not been through the wars in Canaan. 2 He did this only in order to teach each generation of Israelites about war, especially those who had never been in battle before. 3 Those left in the land were the five Philistine cities, all the Canaanites, the Sidonians, and the Hivites who lived in the Lebanon Mountains from Mount Baal Hermon as far as Hamath Pass. 4 They were to be a test for Israel, to find out whether or not the Israelites would obey the commands that the LORD had given their ancestors through Moses. 5 And so the people of Israel settled down among the Canaanites, the Hittites, the Amorites, the Perizzites, the Hivites, and the Jebusites. 6 They intermarried with them and worshiped their gods.

Othniel

7 The people of Israel forgot the LORD their God; they sinned against him and worshiped the idols of Baal and Asherah. 8 So the LORD became angry with Israel and let King Cushan Rishathaim of Mesopotamia conquer them. They were subject to him for eight years. 9 Then the Israelites cried out to the LORD, and he sent someone to free them. This was Othniel, the son of Caleb's younger brother Kenaz. 10 The spirit of the LORD came upon him, and he became Israel's leader. Othniel went to war, and the LORD gave him the victory over the king of Mesopotamia. 11 There was peace in the land for forty years, and then Othniel died.

Israel . . . worshiped other gods. (2:17)

Judges

Ehud

12 The people of Israel sinned against the LORD again. Because of this the LORD made King Eglon of Moab stronger than Israel. **13** Eglon joined the Ammonites and the Amalekites; they defeated Israel and captured Jericho, the city of palm trees. **14** The Israelites were subject to Eglon for eighteen years.

15 Then the Israelites cried out to the LORD, and he sent someone to free them. This was Ehud, a left-handed man, who was the son of Gera, from the tribe of Benjamin. The people of Israel sent Ehud to King Eglon of Moab with gifts for him. **16** Ehud had made himself a double-edged sword about a foot and a half long. He had it fastened on his right side under his clothes. **17** Then he took the gifts to Eglon, who was a very fat man. **18** When Ehud had given him the gifts, he told the men who had carried them to go back home. **19** But Ehud himself turned back at the carved stones near Gilgal, went back to Eglon, and said, "Your Majesty, I have a secret message for you."

So the king ordered his servants, "Leave us alone!" And they all went out.

20 Then, as the king was sitting there alone in his cool room on the roof, Ehud went over to him and said, "I have a message from God for you." The king stood up. **21** With his left hand Ehud took the sword from his right side and plunged it into the king's belly. **22** The whole sword went in, handle and all, and the fat covered it up. Ehud did not pull it out of the king's belly, and it stuck out behind, between his legs.[h] **23** Then Ehud went outside, closed the doors behind him, locked them, **24** and left. The servants came and saw that the doors were locked, but they only thought that the king was inside, relieving himself. **25** They waited as long as they thought they should, but when he still did not open the door, they took the key and opened it. And there was their master, lying dead on the floor.

26 Ehud got away while they were waiting. He went past the carved stones and escaped to Seirah. **27** When he arrived there in the hill country of Ephraim, he blew a trumpet to call the people of Israel to battle; then he led

them down from the hills. **28** He told them, "Follow me! The LORD has given you victory over your enemies, the Moabites." So they followed Ehud down and captured the place where the Moabites were to cross the Jordan; they did not allow anyone to cross. **29** That day they killed about ten thousand of the best Moabite soldiers; none of them escaped. **30** That day the Israelites defeated Moab, and there was peace in the land for eighty years.

Shamgar

31 The next leader was Shamgar son of Anath. He too rescued Israel, and did so by killing six hundred Philistines with an oxgoad.

Deborah and Barak

4 **1** After Ehud died, the people of Israel sinned against the LORD again. **2** So the LORD let them be conquered by Jabin, a Canaanite king who ruled in the city of Hazor. The commander of his army was Sisera, who lived at Harosheth-of-the-Gentiles. **3** Jabin had nine hundred iron chariots, and he ruled the people of Israel with cruelty and violence for twenty years. Then the people of Israel cried out to the LORD for help.

4 Now Deborah, the wife of Lappidoth, was a prophet, and she was serving as a judge for the Israelites at that time. **5** She would sit under a certain palm tree between Ramah and Bethel in the hill country of Ephraim, and the people of Israel would go there for her decisions. **6** One day she sent for Barak son of Abinoam from the city of Kedesh in Naphtali and said to him, "The LORD, the God of Israel, has given you this command: 'Take ten thousand men from the tribes of Naphtali and Zebulun and lead them to Mount Tabor. **7** I will bring Sisera, the commander of Jabin's army, to fight you at the Kishon River. He will have his chariots and soldiers, but I will give you victory over him.'"

8 Then Barak replied, "I will go if you go with me, but if you don't go with me, I won't go either."

---

h **3:22** *Probable text* it stuck . . . legs; *Hebrew unclear.*

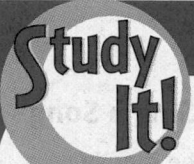

A Brave and Wise Woman

Deborah is very unusual for her time. She is the fourth judge of Israel, and the only woman known to be a judge. She sits under her palm tree and gives wise advice to all the people who come to her. Then she receives a message from God and commands Barak to go to war. Barak refuses unless Deborah agrees to go with him. Barak must have felt the army would only follow him if they saw that Deborah was with him. Barak and the people who came to Deborah for judgment and advice must have trusted her a lot.

What woman do you know who is wise and courageous?

— Judges 4:1–8

9She answered, "All right, I will go with you, but you won't get any credit for the victory, because the LORD will hand Sisera over to a woman." So Deborah set off for Kedesh with Barak. **10**Barak called the tribes of Zebulun and Naphtali to Kedesh, and ten thousand men followed him. Deborah went with him.

11In the meantime Heber the Kenite had set up his tent close to Kedesh near the oak tree at Zaanannim. He had moved away from the other Kenites, the descendants of Hobab, the brother-in-law of Moses.

12When Sisera learned that Barak had gone up to Mount Tabor, **13**he called out his nine hundred iron chariots and all his men, and sent them from Harosheth-of-the-Gentiles to the Kishon River.

14Then Deborah said to Barak, "Go! The LORD is leading you! Today he has given you victory over Sisera." So Barak went down from Mount Tabor with his ten thousand men. **15**When Barak attacked with his army, the LORD threw Sisera into confusion together with all his chariots and men. Sisera got down from his chariot and fled on foot. **16**Barak pursued the chariots and the army to Harosheth-of-the-Gentiles, and Sisera's whole army was killed. Not a man was left.

The LORD threw . . . into confusion . . . all his chariots and men. (4:15)

17Sisera ran away to the tent of Jael, the wife of Heber the Kenite, because King Jabin of Hazor was at peace with Heber's family. **18**Jael went out to meet Sisera and said to him, "Come in, sir; come into my tent. Don't be afraid." So he went in, and she hid him behind a curtain.[i] **19**He said to her, "Please give me a drink of water; I'm thirsty." She opened a leather bag of milk, gave him a drink, and hid him again. **20**Then he told her, "Stand at the door of the tent, and if anyone comes and asks you if anyone is here, say no."

21Sisera was so tired that he fell sound asleep. Then Jael took a hammer and a tent peg, quietly went up to him, and killed him by driving the peg right through the side of his head and into the ground. **22**When Barak came looking for Sisera, Jael went out to meet him and said to him, "Come here! I'll show you the man you're looking for." So he went in with her, and there was Sisera on the ground, dead, with the tent peg through his head.

23That day God gave the Israelites victory

Judges

---

i **4:18** hid him behind a curtain; *or* covered him with a rug.

Pray It!

Sing a Song

After their victory over the Canaanites, Deborah and Barak sing the song in Judges, chapter 5. The song recounts the victory over Sisera's army and the brave acts of those who helped. If you wrote a song that praised God for the good he has done in your life, what would you say? If you could choose a song that celebrates what God has done for you, what song would you choose?

Some people find that music helps them pray. They may listen to popular music on the radio or music by Christian singers or bands. If you want to pray with music, you might ask a youth leader at your church for some suggestions.

— Judges, chapter 5

over Jabin, the Canaanite king. ²⁴ They pressed harder and harder against him until they destroyed him.

The Song of Deborah and Barak

5 ¹On that day Deborah and Barak son of Abinoam sang this song:

² Praise the LORD!
  The Israelites were determined to fight;
  the people gladly volunteered.
³ Listen, you kings!
  Pay attention, you rulers!
  I will sing and play music
  to Israel's God, the LORD.
⁴ LORD, when you left the mountains of Seir,
  when you came out of the region of Edom,
  the earth shook, and rain fell from the sky.
  Yes, water poured down from the clouds.
⁵ The mountains quaked before the LORD of Sinai,
  before the LORD, the God of Israel.

⁶ In the days of Shamgar son of Anath,
  in the days of Jael,
caravans no longer went through the land,
  and travelers used the back roads.
⁷ The towns of Israel stood abandoned, Deborah;
  they stood empty until you came,ʲ
  came like a mother for Israel.
⁸ Then there was war in the land
  when the Israelites chose new gods.
  Of the forty thousand men in Israel,
  did anyone carry shield or spear?
⁹ My heart is with the commanders of Israel,
  with the people who gladly volunteered.
  Praise the LORD!
¹⁰ Tell ofᵏ it, you that ride on white donkeys,
  sitting on saddles,
  and you that must walk wherever you go.
¹¹ Listen! The noisy crowds around the wells
  are telling of the LORD's victories,
  the victories of Israel's people!

Then the LORD's people marched down
  from their cities.ˡ

ʲ **5:7** abandoned, Deborah . . . you came; *or* abandoned; they stood empty until I, Deborah, came.
ᵏ **5:10** Tell of; *or* Think about.   ˡ **5:11** from their cities; *or* to their gates.
5:5 Ex 19:18

12 Lead on, Deborah, lead on!
   Lead on! Sing a song! Lead on!
   Forward, Barak son of Abinoam,
   lead your captives away!
13 Then the faithful ones came down to
   their leaders;
   the LORD's people came to him[m] ready
   to fight.
14 They came[n] from Ephraim into the
   valley,[o]
   behind the tribe of Benjamin and its
   people.
   The commanders came down from
   Machir,
   the officers down from Zebulun.
15 The leaders of Issachar came with
   Deborah;
   yes, Issachar came and Barak too,
   and they followed him into the valley.
   But the tribe of Reuben was divided;
   they could not decide to come.
16 Why did they stay behind with the sheep?
   To listen to shepherds calling the
   flocks?
   Yes, the tribe of Reuben was divided;
   they could not decide to come.
17 The tribe of Gad stayed east of the
   Jordan,
   and the tribe of Dan remained by the
   ships.
   The tribe of Asher stayed by the seacoast;
   they remained along the shore.
18 But the people of Zebulun and Naphtali
   risked their lives on the battlefield.

19 At Taanach, by the stream of Megiddo,
   the kings came and fought;
   the kings of Canaan fought,
   but they took no silver away.
20 The stars fought from the sky;
   as they moved across the sky,
   they fought against Sisera.
21 A flood in the Kishon swept them
   away—
   the onrushing Kishon River.
   I shall march, march on, with strength!
22 Then the horses came galloping on,
   stamping the ground with their hoofs.

23 "Put a curse on Meroz," says the angel of
   the LORD,
   "a curse, a curse on those who live
   there.
   They did not come to help the LORD,
   come as soldiers to fight for him."

24 The most fortunate of women is Jael,
   the wife of Heber the Kenite—
   the most fortunate of women who live
   in tents.
25 Sisera asked for water, but she gave him
   milk;
   she brought him cream in a beautiful
   bowl.
26 She took a tent peg in one hand,
   a worker's hammer in the other;
   she struck Sisera and crushed his skull;
   she pierced him through the head.
27 He sank to his knees,
   fell down and lay still at her feet.
   At her feet he sank to his knees and fell;
   he fell to the ground, dead.

28 Sisera's mother looked out of the
   window;
   she gazed[p] from behind the lattice.
   "Why is his chariot so late in coming?"
   she asked.
   "Why are his horses so slow to
   return?"
29 Her wisest friends answered her,
   and she told herself over and over,
30 "They are only finding things to capture
   and divide,
   a woman or two for every soldier,
   rich cloth for Sisera,
   embroidered pieces for the neck of the
   queen."[q]

31 So may all your enemies die like that,
   O LORD,
   but may your friends shine like the
   rising sun!

And there was peace in the land for forty
years.

---

[m] **5:13** One ancient translation him; Hebrew me.   [n] **5:14** Probable text They came; Hebrew Their root.
[o] **5:14** One ancient translation into the valley; Hebrew in Amalek.   [p] **5:28** Some ancient translations gazed; Hebrew
cried out.   [q] **5:30** Probable text queen; Hebrew plunder.

Gideon

6 ¹Once again the people of Israel sinned against the LORD, so he let the people of Midian rule them for seven years. ²The Midianites were stronger than Israel, and the people of Israel hid from them in caves and other safe places in the hills. ³Whenever the Israelites would plant their crops, the Midianites would come with the Amalekites and the desert tribes and attack them. ⁴They would camp on the land and destroy the crops as far south as the area around Gaza. They would take all the sheep, cattle, and donkeys, and leave nothing for the Israelites to live on. ⁵They would come with their livestock and tents, as thick as locusts. They and their camels were too many to count. They came and devastated the land, ⁶and Israel was helpless against them.

⁷Then the people of Israel cried out to the LORD for help against the Midianites, ⁸and he sent them a prophet who brought them this message from the LORD, the God of Israel: "I brought you out of slavery in Egypt. ⁹I rescued you from the Egyptians and from the people who fought you here in this land. I drove them out as you advanced, and I gave you their land. ¹⁰I told you that I am the LORD your God and that you should not worship the gods of the Amorites, whose land you are now living in. But you have not listened to me."

¹¹Then the LORD's angel came to the village of Ophrah and sat under the oak tree that belonged to Joash, a man of the clan of Abiezer. His son Gideon was threshing some wheat secretly in a wine press, so that the Midianites would not see him. ¹²The LORD's angel appeared to him there and said, "The LORD is with you, brave and mighty man!"

¹³Gideon said to him, "If I may ask, sir, why has all this happened to us if the LORD is with us? What happened to all the wonderful things that our fathers told us the LORD used to do—how he brought them out of Egypt? The LORD has abandoned us and left us to the mercy of the Midianites."

¹⁴Then the LORD ordered him, "Go with all your great strength and rescue Israel from the Midianites. I myself am sending you."

¹⁵Gideon replied, "But Lord, how can I rescue Israel? My clan is the weakest in the tribe of Manasseh, and I am the least important member of my family."

¹⁶The LORD answered, "You can do it because I will help you. You will crush the Midianites as easily as if they were only one man."

¹⁷Gideon replied, "If you are pleased with me, give me some proof that you are really the LORD. ¹⁸Please do not leave until I bring you an offering of food."

He said, "I will stay until you come back."

¹⁹So Gideon went into his house and cooked a young goat and used a bushel of flour to make bread without any yeast. He put the meat in a basket and the broth in a pot, brought them to the LORD's angel under the oak tree, and gave them to him. ²⁰The angel told him, "Put the meat and the bread on this rock, and pour the broth over them." Gideon did so. ²¹Then the LORD's angel reached out and touched the meat and the bread with the end of the stick he was holding. Fire came out of the rock and burned up the meat and the bread. Then the angel disappeared.

²²Gideon then realized that it was the LORD's angel he had seen, and he said in terror, "Sovereign LORD! I have seen your angel face to face!"

²³But the LORD told him, "Peace. Don't be afraid. You will not die." ²⁴Gideon built an altar to the LORD there and named it "The LORD is Peace." (It is still standing at Ophrah, which belongs to the clan of Abiezer.)

"The LORD is with you, brave and mighty man!"
(6:12)

But Lord . . .

It's a familiar pattern in the Bible. God calls someone, and they have a long list of reasons why they can't respond. Gideon tells the Lord that he can't lead because he's too unimportant. God tells Gideon though, "You can do it because I will help you" (Judges 6:16).

Have you ever thought that you would like to make a difference in the world, but felt as though you were too young or too shy or not smart enough or not popular enough? God says, "You can do it because I will be there to help you!"

That's one of the great things about God. Things that may not have seemed possible before *are* possible. God calls all sorts of people (usually not the richest or the prettiest) to do good in the world. God's calling you too! Gideon said yes. What will your answer be?

— Judges 6:11–16

25 That night the LORD told Gideon, "Take your father's bull and another bull seven years old, *r* tear down your father's altar to Baal, and cut down the symbol of the goddess Asherah, which is beside it. 26 Build a well-constructed altar to the LORD your God on top of this mound. Then take the second bull *s* and burn it whole as an offering, using for firewood the symbol of Asherah you have cut down." 27 So Gideon took

ten of his servants and did what the LORD had told him. He was too afraid of his family and the people in town to do it by day, so he did it at night.

28 When the people in town got up early the next morning, they found that the altar to Baal and the symbol of Asherah had been cut down, and that the second bull had been burned on the altar that had been built there. 29 They asked each other, "Who did this?" They investigated and found out that Gideon son of Joash had done it. 30 Then they said to Joash, "Bring your son out here, so that we can kill him! He tore down the altar to Baal and cut down the symbol of Asherah beside it."

31 But Joash said to all those who confronted him, "Are you arguing for Baal? Are you defending him? Anyone who argues for him will be killed before morning. If Baal is a god, let him defend himself. It is his altar that was torn down." 32 From then on Gideon was known as Jerubbaal, *t* because Joash said, "Let Baal defend himself; it is his altar that was torn down."

33 Then all the Midianites, the Amalekites, and the desert tribes assembled, crossed the Jordan River, and camped in Jezreel Valley. 34 The spirit of the LORD took control of Gideon, and he blew a trumpet to call the men of the clan of Abiezer to follow him. 35 He sent messengers throughout the territory of both parts of Manasseh to call them to follow him. He sent messengers to the tribes of Asher, Zebulun, and Naphtali, and they also came to join him.

36 Then Gideon said to God, "You say that you have decided to use me to rescue Israel. 37 Well, I am putting some wool on the ground where we thresh the wheat. If in the morning there is dew only on the wool but not on the ground, then I will know that you are going to use me to rescue Israel." 38 That is exactly what happened. When Gideon got up early the next morning, he squeezed the wool and wrung enough dew

Judges

r **6:25** bull and another bull seven years old; *or* bull, the seven-year-old one.   *s* **6:26** the second bull; *or* the bull.
t **6:32** JERUBBAAL: *This name in Hebrew means "Let Baal defend himself."*

The Midianites were descendants of Abraham! Midian was Abraham's son by Keturah (*Genesis 25:1–2*).

Miracles

Gideon asks for a sign from God. He wants to be sure that this is what God really wants him to do. God's response to Gideon is to show him not just one but two miracles. In one miracle God caused fire to come from a rock and burn up bread and meat. In the second miracle God caused the morning dew to be only on some wool Gideon put out, while leaving no dew on the ground. The next day the morning dew was only on ground, and the wool was completely dry.

   The Catholic Church teaches that miracles still happen today. Many miracles are healings of people who are sick or diseased. These healings happen without any medical explanation. We cannot force God to perform a miracle, especially as a test, like Gideon. But we can ask God for what we need and trust he will give us what is best for us.

— Judges 6:17–22,36–40

out of it to fill a bowl with water. 39 Then Gideon said to God, "Don't be angry with me; let me speak just once more. Please let me make one more test with the wool. This time let the wool be dry, and the ground be wet." 40 That night God did that very thing. The next morning the wool was dry, but the ground was wet with dew.

Gideon Defeats the Midianites

7 ¹One day Gideon and all his men got up early and camped beside Harod Spring. The Midianite camp was in the valley to the north of them by Moreh Hill.

   ²The LORD said to Gideon, "The men you have are too many for me to give them victory over the Midianites. They might think that they had won by themselves, and so give me no credit. ³Announce to the people, 'Anyone who is afraid should go back home, and we will stay here at Mount Gilead.'" So twenty-two thousand went back, but ten thousand stayed.

   ⁴Then the LORD said to Gideon, "You still have too many men. Take them down to the water, and I will separate them for you there. If I tell you a man should go with you, he will go. If I tell you a man should not go with you, he will not go." ⁵Gideon took the men down to the water, and the LORD told him, "Separate everyone who laps up the water with his tongue like a dog, from everyone who gets down on his knees to drink." ⁶There were three hundred men who scooped up water in their hands and lapped it; all the others got down on their knees to drink. ⁷The LORD said to Gideon, "I will rescue you and give you victory over the Midianites with the three hundred men who lapped the water. Tell everyone else to

"Separate everyone who laps up the water." (7:5)

7:3 Deut 20:8

Gideon's strategy is surprise! Check out the strategy he used to defeat the Midianites with only a handful of soldiers!

go home." [8] So Gideon sent all the Israelites home, except the three hundred, who kept all the supplies and trumpets. The Midianite camp was below them in the valley.

[9] That night the Lord commanded Gideon, "Get up and attack the camp; I am giving you victory over it. [10] But if you are afraid to attack, go down to the camp with your servant Purah. [11] You will hear what they are saying, and then you will have the courage to attack." So Gideon and his servant Purah went down to the edge of the enemy camp. [12] The Midianites, the Amalekites, and the desert tribesmen were spread out in the valley like a swarm of locusts, and they had as many camels as there are grains of sand on the seashore.

[13] When Gideon arrived, he heard a man telling a friend about a dream. He was saying, "I dreamed that a loaf of barley bread rolled into our camp and hit a tent. The tent collapsed and lay flat on the ground."

[14] His friend replied, "It's the sword of the Israelite, Gideon son of Joash! It can't mean anything else! God has given him victory over Midian and our whole army!"

[15] When Gideon heard about the man's dream and what it meant, he fell to his knees and worshiped the Lord. Then he went back to the Israelite camp and said, "Get up! The Lord is giving you victory over the Midianite army!" [16] He divided his three hundred men into three groups and gave each man a trumpet and a jar with a torch inside it. [17] He told them, "When I get to the edge of the camp, watch me, and do what I do. [18] When my group and I blow our trumpets, then you blow yours all around the camp and shout, 'For the Lord and for Gideon!' "

[19] Gideon and his one hundred men came to the edge of the camp a while before midnight, just after the guard had been changed. Then they blew the trumpets and broke the jars they were holding, [20] and the other two groups did the same. They all held the torches in their left hands, the trumpets in their right, and shouted, "A sword for the Lord and for Gideon!" [21] Every man stood in his place around the camp, and the whole enemy army ran away yelling. [22] While

Gideon's men were blowing their trumpets, the Lord made the enemy troops attack each other with their swords. They ran toward Zarethan as far as Beth Shittah, as far as the town of Abel Meholah near Tabbath.

[23] Then men from the tribes of Naphtali, Asher, and both parts of Manasseh were called out, and they pursued the Midianites. [24] Gideon sent messengers through all the hill country of Ephraim to say, "Come down and fight the Midianites. Hold the Jordan River and the streams as far as Bethbarah, to keep the Midianites from crossing them." The men of Ephraim were called together, and they held the Jordan River and the streams as far as Bethbarah. [25] They captured the two Midianite chiefs, Oreb and Zeeb; they killed Oreb at Oreb Rock, and Zeeb at the Winepress of Zeeb. They continued to pursue the Midianites and brought the heads of Oreb and Zeeb to Gideon, who was now east of the Jordan.

The Final Defeat of the Midianites

8 [1] Then the people of Ephraim said to Gideon, "Why didn't you call us when you went to fight the Midianites? Why did you treat us like this?" They complained bitterly about it.

[2] But he told them, "What I was able to do is nothing compared with what you have done. Even the little that you people of Ephraim did is worth more than what my whole clan has done. [3] After all, through the power of God you killed the two Midianite chiefs, Oreb and Zeeb. What have I done to compare with that?" When he said this, they were no longer so angry.

[4] By this time Gideon and his three hundred men had come to the Jordan River and had crossed it. They were exhausted, but were still pursuing the enemy. [5] When they arrived at Sukkoth, he said to the men of the town, "Please give my men some loaves of bread. They are exhausted, and I am chasing Zebah and Zalmunna, the Midianite kings."

[6] But the leaders of Sukkoth said, "Why should we give your army any food? You haven't captured Zebah and Zalmunna yet."

8:3–5 Ps 83:11

While Gideon's men were blowing their trumpets, the LORD made the enemy troops attack each other. (7:22)

7So Gideon said, "All right! When the LORD has handed Zebah and Zalmunna over to me, I will beat you with thorns and briers from the desert!" 8Gideon went on to Penuel and made the same request of the people there, but the men of Penuel gave the same answer as the men of Sukkoth. 9So he said to them, "I am going to come back safe and sound, and when I do, I will tear this tower down!"

10Zebah and Zalmunna were at Karkor with their army. Of the whole army of desert tribesmen, only about 15,000 were left; 120,000 soldiers had been killed. 11Gideon went on the road along the edge of the desert, east of Nobah and Jogbehah, and attacked the army by surprise. 12The two Midianite kings, Zebah and Zalmunna, ran away, but he pursued them and captured them, and caused their whole army to panic.

13When Gideon was returning from the battle by way of Heres Pass, 14he captured a young man from Sukkoth and questioned him. The young man wrote down for Gideon the names of the seventy-seven leading men of Sukkoth. 15Then Gideon went to the men of Sukkoth and said, "Remember when you refused to help me? You said that you couldn't give any food to my exhausted army because I hadn't captured Zebah and Zalmunna yet. Well, here they are!" 16He then took thorns and briers from the desert and used them to punish the leaders of Sukkoth. 17He also tore down the tower at Penuel and killed the men of that city.

18Then Gideon asked Zebah and Zalmunna, "What about the men you killed at Tabor?"

They answered, "They looked like you—every one of them like the son of a king."

19Gideon said, "They were my brothers, my own mother's sons. I solemnly swear that if you had not killed them, I would not kill you." 20Then he said to Jether, his oldest son, "Go ahead, kill them!" But the boy did not draw his sword. He hesitated, because he was still only a boy.

²¹Then Zebah and Zalmunna said to Gideon, "Come on, kill us yourself. It takes a man to do a man's job." So Gideon killed them and took the ornaments that were on the necks of their camels.

²²After that, the Israelites said to Gideon, "Be our ruler—you and your descendants after you. You have saved us from the Midianites."

²³Gideon answered, "I will not be your ruler, nor will my son. The LORD will be your ruler." ²⁴But he went on to say, "Let me ask one thing of you. Every one of you give me the earrings you took." (The Midianites, like other desert people, wore gold earrings.)

²⁵The people answered, "We'll be glad to give them to you." They spread out a cloth, and everyone put on it the earrings that he had taken. ²⁶The gold earrings that Gideon got weighed over forty pounds, and this did not include the ornaments, necklaces, and purple clothes that the kings of Midian wore, nor the collars that were around the necks of their camels. ²⁷Gideon made an idol from the gold and put it in his hometown, Ophrah. All the Israelites abandoned God and went there to worship the idol. It was a trap for Gideon and his family.

²⁸So Midian was defeated by the Israelites and was no longer a threat. The land was at peace for forty years, until Gideon died.

The Death of Gideon

²⁹Gideon went back to his own home and lived there. ³⁰He had seventy sons, because he had many wives. ³¹He also had a concubine in Shechem; she bore him a son, and he named him Abimelech. ³²Gideon son of Joash died at a ripe old age and was buried in the tomb of his father Joash, at Ophrah, the town of the clan of Abiezer.

³³After Gideon's death the people of Israel were unfaithful to God again and worshiped the Baals. They made Baal-of-the-Covenant their god, ³⁴and no longer served the LORD

I Will Not Rule Over You

The Israelites had many powerful leaders through the years: Abraham, Moses, Joshua, and now the judges. But they had never had a king. They want to make Gideon a king, but he refuses the honor. He feels that the Israelites should only honor God as their king.

After the time of the judges, the Israelites will have their own kings. During this time you will see that Gideon's opinion about kings is justified. Many of the kings are not faithful to God and the Covenant God made with the Israelites.

— Judges 8:22–23

their God, who had saved them from all their enemies around them. ³⁵They were not grateful to the family of Gideon for all the good that he had done for Israel.

Abimelech

9 ¹Gideon's son Abimelech went to the town of Shechem, where all his mother's relatives lived, and told them ²to ask the men of Shechem, "Which would you prefer? To have all seventy of Gideon's sons govern you or to have just one man? Remember that Abimelech is your own flesh and blood." ³His mother's relatives talked to the men of Shechem about this for him, and the men of Shechem decided to follow Abimelech because he was their relative. ⁴They gave him seventy pieces of silver from the temple of Baal-of-the-Covenant, and with this money he hired a bunch of worthless

Judges

"I will not be your ruler, nor will my son. The LORD will be your ruler" (*Judges 8:23*).

Pray It!

Prayer of a Humble Leader

Abimelech's father, Gideon, was a humble hero. Abimelech was not like his father at all. God chose Gideon. Abimelech chose himself. He decided that he wanted to lead, so he killed all seventy of his brothers except one. The surviving brother curses Abimelech and the people of Shechem who supported him. Even though Abimelech experiences some military successes, he dies without honor. His own people turn on him.

God make me a humble leader.
Help me to lead not because I want to
*   but when you call me to lead.*
Help me to lead not for my personal glory
*   but to bring glory to you.*
Help me not to think of what I want
*   but to put the needs of others before my own needs. Amen.*

— Judges, chapter 9

scoundrels to join him. ⁵He went to his father's house at Ophrah, and there on top of a single stone he killed his seventy brothers, Gideon's sons. But Jotham, Gideon's youngest son, hid and was not killed. ⁶Then all the men of Shechem and Bethmillo got together and went to the sacred oak tree at Shechem, where they made Abimelech king.

⁷When Jotham heard about this, he went and stood on top of Mount Gerizim and shouted out to them, "Listen to me, you men of Shechem, and God may listen to you! ⁸Once upon a time the trees went out to choose a king for themselves. They said to the olive tree, 'Be our king.' ⁹The olive tree answered, 'In order to govern you, I would have to stop producing my oil, which is used to honor gods and human beings.' ¹⁰Then the trees said to the fig tree, 'You come and be our king.' ¹¹But the fig tree answered, 'In order to govern you, I would have to stop producing my good sweet fruit.' ¹²So the trees then said to the grapevine, 'You come and be our king.' ¹³But the vine answered, 'In order to govern you, I would have to

stop producing my wine, that makes gods and human beings happy.' ¹⁴So then all the trees said to the thorn bush, 'You come and be our king.' ¹⁵The thorn bush answered, 'If you really want to make me your king, then come and take shelter in my shade. If you don't, fire will blaze out of my thorny branches and burn up the cedars of Lebanon.'

¹⁶"Now then," Jotham continued, "were you really honest and sincere when you made Abimelech king? Did you respect Gideon's memory and treat his family properly, as his actions deserved? ¹⁷Remember that my father fought for you. He risked his life to save you from the Midianites. ¹⁸But today you turned against my father's family. You killed his sons—seventy men on a single stone—and just because Abimelech, his son by his servant woman, is your relative, you have made him king of Shechem. ¹⁹Now then, if what you did today to Gideon and his family was sincere and honest, then be happy with Abimelech and let him be happy with you. ²⁰But if not, may fire blaze out

Part of Abimelech's problem is that he is pretty stuck on himself. Who else in the Bible has a similar problem?

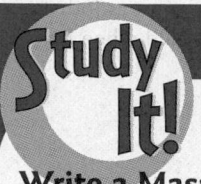

Write a Masal

Abimelech's brother Jotham uses a story about trees to describe what Abimelech's leadership will be like and to predict Abimelech's doom. In ancient Israel this kind of story is called a *masal*. A *masal* uses a saying or story to make a comparison with a situation the listeners are familiar with. In Jotham's story, he says Abimelech is like the thorn bush that is good only for burning. Sooner or later those who follow him will be destroyed by him.

Think of some situation of wrongdoing or injustice in the world today. What kind of story could you tell to describe to people what will happen if they don't set things right? Write your own masal that tells about this problem.

— Judges 9:7–15

from Abimelech and burn up the men of Shechem and Bethmillo. May fire blaze out from the men of Shechem and Bethmillo and burn Abimelech up." 21 Then because he was afraid of his brother Abimelech, Jotham ran away and went to live at Beer.

22 Abimelech ruled Israel for three years. 23 Then God made Abimelech and the men of Shechem hostile to each other, and they rebelled against Abimelech. 24 This happened so that Abimelech and the men of Shechem, who encouraged him to murder Gideon's seventy sons, would pay for their crime. 25 The men of Shechem put men in ambush against Abimelech on the mountaintops, and they robbed everyone who passed their way. Abimelech was told about this.

26 Then Gaal son of Ebed came to Shechem with his brothers, and the men of Shechem put their confidence in him. 27 They all went out into their vineyards and picked the grapes, made wine from them, and held a festival. They went into the temple of their god, where they ate and drank and made fun of Abimelech. 28 Gaal said, "What kind of men are we in Shechem? Why are we serving Abimelech? Who is he, anyway? The son of Gideon! And Zebul takes orders from him, but why should we serve him? Be loyal to your ancestor Hamor, who founded your clan! 29 I wish I were leading this people! I would get rid of Abimelech! I would tell^u him, 'Reinforce your army, come on out and fight!' "

30 Zebul, the ruler of the city, became angry when he heard what Gaal had said. 31 He sent messengers to Abimelech at Arumah^v to say, "Gaal son of Ebed and his brothers have come to Shechem, and they are not going to let you into the city. 32 Now then, you and your men should move by night and hide in the fields. 33 Get up tomorrow morning at sunrise and make a sudden attack on the city. Then when Gaal and his men come out against you, hit them with all you've got!"

34 So Abimelech and all his men made their move at night and hid outside Shechem in four groups. 35 When Abimelech and his men saw Gaal come out and stand at the city gate, they got up from their hiding places. 36 Gaal saw them and said to Zebul, "Look! There are men coming down from the mountaintops!"

"Those are not men," Zebul answered. "They are just shadows on the mountains."

37 Gaal said again, "Look! There are men coming down the crest of the mountain and one group is coming along the road from the oak tree of the fortunetellers!"

38 Then Zebul said to him, "Where is all your big talk now? You were the one who asked why we should serve this man Abimelech. These are the men you were making fun of. Go on out now and fight them."

39 Gaal led the men of Shechem out and fought Abimelech. 40 Abimelech started after Gaal, and Gaal ran. Many were wounded, even at the city gate. 41 Abimelech lived in

Arumah, and Zebul drove Gaal and his brothers out of Shechem, so that they could no longer live there.

⁴²The next day Abimelech found out that the people of Shechem were planning to go out into the fields, ⁴³so he took his men, divided them into three groups, and hid in the fields, waiting. When he saw the people coming out of the city, he came out of hiding to kill them. ⁴⁴While Abimelech and his group hurried forward to guard the city gate, the other two companies attacked the people in the fields and killed them all. ⁴⁵The fighting continued all day long. Abimelech captured the city, killed its people, tore it down, and covered the ground with salt.

⁴⁶When all the leading men in the fort at Shechem heard about this, they sought safety in the stronghold of the temple of Baal-of-the-Covenant. ⁴⁷Abimelech was told that they had gathered there, ⁴⁸so he went up to Mount Zalmon with his men. There he took an ax, cut a limb off a tree, and put it on his shoulder. He told his men to hurry and do the same thing. ⁴⁹So everyone cut off a tree limb; then they followed Abimelech and piled the wood up against the stronghold. They set it on fire, with the people inside, and all the people of the fort died—about a thousand men and women.

⁵⁰Then Abimelech went to Thebez, surrounded that city, and captured it. ⁵¹There was a strong tower there, and every man and woman in the city, including the leaders, ran to it. They locked themselves in and went up to the roof. ⁵²When Abimelech came to attack the tower, he went up to the door to set the tower on fire. ⁵³But a woman threw a millstone down on his head and fractured his skull. ⁵⁴Then he quickly called the young man who was carrying his weapons and told him, "Draw your sword and kill me. I don't want it said that a woman killed me." So the young man ran him through, and he died. ⁵⁵When the Israelites saw that Abimelech was dead, they all went home.

⁵⁶And so it was that God paid Abimelech back for the crime that he committed against his father in killing his seventy brothers. ⁵⁷God also made the men of Shechem

suffer for their wickedness, just as Jotham, Gideon's son, said they would when he cursed them.

Tola

10 ¹After Abimelech's death Tola, the son of Puah and grandson of Dodo, came to free Israel. He was from the tribe of Issachar and lived at Shamir in the hill country of Ephraim. ²He was Israel's leader for twenty-three years. Then he died and was buried at Shamir.

Jair

³After Tola came Jair from Gilead. He led Israel for twenty-two years. ⁴He had thirty sons who rode thirty donkeys. They had thirty cities in the land of Gilead, which are still called the villages of Jair. ⁵Jair died and was buried at Kamon.

Jephthah

⁶Once again the Israelites sinned against the LORD by worshiping the Baals and the Astartes, as well as the gods of Syria, of Sidon, of Moab, of Ammon, and of Philistia. They abandoned the LORD and stopped worshiping him. ⁷So the LORD became angry with the Israelites, and let the Philistines and the Ammonites conquer them. ⁸For eighteen years they oppressed and persecuted all the Israelites who lived in Amorite country east of the Jordan River in Gilead. ⁹The Ammonites even crossed the Jordan to fight the tribes of Judah, Benjamin, and Ephraim. Israel was in great distress.

¹⁰Then the Israelites cried out to the LORD and said, "We have sinned against you, for we left you, our God, and worshiped the Baals."

¹¹The LORD gave them this answer: "The Egyptians, the Amorites, the Ammonites, the Philistines, ¹²the Sidonians, the Amalekites, and the Maonites oppressed you in the past, and you cried out to me. Did I not save you from them? ¹³But you still left me and worshiped other gods, so I am not going to rescue you again. ¹⁴Go and cry out to the gods

you have chosen. Let them rescue you when you get in trouble."

15 But the people of Israel said to the LORD, "We have sinned. Do whatever you like, but please, save us today." **16** So they got rid of their foreign gods and worshiped the LORD; and he became troubled over Israel's distress.

17 Then the Ammonite army prepared for battle and camped in Gilead. The people of Israel came together and camped at Mizpah in Gilead. **18** There the people and the leaders of the Israelite tribes asked one another, "Who will lead the fight against the Ammonites? Whoever does will be the leader of everyone in Gilead."

11 **1** Jephthah, a brave soldier from Gilead, was the son of a prostitute. His father Gilead **2** had other sons by his wife, and when they grew up, they forced Jephthah to leave home. They told him, "You will not inherit anything from our father; you are the son of another woman." **3** Jephthah fled from his brothers and lived in the land of Tob. There he attracted a group of worthless men, and they went around with him.

4 It was some time later that the Ammonites went to war against Israel. **5** When this happened, the leaders of Gilead went to bring Jephthah back from the land of Tob. **6** They told him, "Come and lead us, so that we can fight the Ammonites."

7 But Jephthah answered, "You hated me so much that you forced me to leave my father's house. Why come to me now that you're in trouble?"

8 They said to Jephthah, "We are turning to you now because we want you to go with us and fight the Ammonites and lead all the people of Gilead."

9 Jephthah said to them, "If you take me back home to fight the Ammonites and the LORD gives me victory, I will be your ruler."

10 They replied, "We agree. The LORD is our witness." **11** So Jephthah went with the leaders of Gilead, and the people made him

An Unexpected Leader

Sometimes prejudice and jealousy can get in the way of someone using his or her gifts. Jephthah was driven away from his home by his half-brothers. His mother and father weren't married, and his brothers did not want to share their inheritance with him.

Have you ever been discriminated against because you dress or talk differently? Have you ever kept someone else from being a part of the group because they like to do different things than you? Fortunately for the Israelites, Jephthah helped them anyway, even though they had rejected him. He was a brave soldier and a good leader. God works through all kinds of people! We risk missing out on some really great people when we only stick with the ones who are just like us! Branch out and see what God has in store for you!

— Judges 11:1–11

Judges

their ruler and leader. Jephthah stated his terms at Mizpah in the presence of the LORD.

12 Then Jephthah sent messengers to the king of Ammon to say, "What is your quarrel with us? Why have you invaded our country?"

13 The king of Ammon answered Jephthah's messengers, "When the Israelites came out of Egypt, they took away my land from the Arnon River to the Jabbok River and the Jordan River. Now you must give it back peacefully."

14 Jephthah sent messengers back to the king of Ammon **15** with this answer: "It is not true that Israel took away the land of Moab or the land of Ammon. 16 This is what happened: when the Israelites left Egypt, they went through the desert to the Gulf of Aqaba and came to Kadesh. 17 Then they sent messengers to the king of Edom to ask permission to go through his land. But the king of Edom would not let them. They also asked the king of Moab, but neither would he let them go through his land. So the Israelites stayed at Kadesh. 18 Then they went on through the desert, going around the land of Edom and the land of Moab until they came to the east side of Moab, on the other side of the Arnon River. They camped there, but they did not cross the Arnon because it was the boundary of Moab. 19 Then the Israelites sent messengers to Sihon, the Amorite king of Heshbon, and asked him for permission to go through his country to their own land. 20 But Sihon would not let Israel do it. He brought his whole army together, camped at Jahaz, and attacked Israel. 21 But the LORD, the God of Israel, gave the Israelites victory over Sihon and his army. So the Israelites took possession of all the territory of the Amorites who lived in that country. 22 They occupied all the Amorite territory from the Arnon in the south to the Jabbok in the north and from the desert on the east to the Jordan on the west. 23 So it was the LORD, the God of Israel, who drove out the Amorites for his people, the Israelites. 24 Are you going to try to take it back? You can keep whatever your god Chemosh has given you. But we are going to keep everything that the LORD, our God, has taken for us. 25 Do you think you are any better than Balak son of Zippor, king of Moab? He never challenged Israel, did he? Did he ever go to war against us? 26 For three hundred years Israel has occupied Heshbon and Aroer, and the towns around them, and all the cities on the banks of the Arnon River. Why haven't you taken them back in all

this time? 27 No, I have not done you any wrong. You are doing wrong by making war on me. The LORD is the judge. He will decide today between the Israelites and the Ammonites." 28 But the king of Ammon paid no attention to this message from Jephthah.

29 Then the spirit of the LORD came upon Jephthah. He went through Gilead and Manasseh and returned to Mizpah in Gilead and went on to Ammon. 30 Jephthah promised the LORD: "If you will give me victory over the Ammonites, 31 I will burn as an offering the first person that comes out of my house to meet me, when I come back from the victory. I will offer that person to you as a sacrifice."

32 So Jephthah crossed the river to fight the Ammonites, and the LORD gave him victory. 33 He struck at them from Aroer to the area around Minnith, twenty cities in all, and as far as Abel Keramim. There was a great slaughter, and the Ammonites were defeated by Israel.

Jephthah's Daughter

34 When Jephthah went back home to Mizpah, there was his daughter coming out

Dancing and playing the tambourine (11:34)

11:17 Num 20:14–21   11:18 Num 21:4   11:19–22 Num 21:21–24   11:25 Num 22:1–6

Jephthah makes a vow to sacrifice a human being even though the Abraham and Isaac story teaches that God doesn't want that.

Pray It!

Friends to Count On

Jephthah made a terrible promise, and his daughter is sacrificed. She will die without getting married or having children. Her friends go with her into the mountains to help her mourn. It couldn't have been easy being with her when they knew she was going to be killed. Have you ever known someone who knew they were dying? A lot of people pull away when someone is dying or even just very sick. They just don't want to have to deal with pain or struggle.

> *God of love, give me friends I can count on*
> *when I have something difficult to face*
> *or if I just need a shoulder to cry on.*
> *Help me in turn to be a good friend*
> *and offer comfort to the people who count on me. Amen.*

> — **Judges 11:34–40**

to meet him, dancing and playing the tambourine. She was his only child. ³⁵When he saw her, he tore his clothes in sorrow and said, "Oh, my daughter! You are breaking my heart! Why must it be you that causes me pain? I have made a solemn promise to the LORD, and I cannot take it back!"

³⁶She told him, "If you have made a promise to the LORD, do what you said you would do to me, since the LORD has given you revenge on your enemies, the Ammonites." ³⁷But she asked her father, "Do this one thing for me. Leave me alone for two months, so that I can go with my friends to wander in the mountains and grieve that I must die a virgin." ³⁸He told her to go and sent her away for two months. She and her friends went up into the mountains and grieved because she was going to die unmarried and childless. ³⁹After two months she came back to her father. He did what he had promised the LORD, and she died still a virgin.

This was the origin of the custom in Israel ⁴⁰that the Israelite women would go out for four days every year to grieve for the daughter of Jephthah of Gilead.

Jephthah and the Ephraimites

12 ¹The men of Ephraim prepared for battle; they crossed the Jordan River to Zaphon and said to Jephthah, "Why did you cross the border to fight the Ammonites without calling us to go with you? We'll burn the house down over your head!"

²But Jephthah told them, "My people and I had a serious quarrel with the Ammonites. I did call you, but you would not rescue me from them. ³When I saw that you were not going to, I risked my life and crossed the border to fight them, and the LORD gave me victory over them. So why are you coming up to fight me now?" ⁴Then Jephthah brought all the men of Gilead together, fought the men of Ephraim and defeated them. (The Ephraimites had said, "You Gileadites in Ephraim and Manasseh, you are deserters from Ephraim!") ⁵In order to keep the Ephraimites from escaping, the Gileadites captured the places where the Jordan could be crossed. When any Ephraimite who was trying to escape would ask permission to cross, the men of Gilead would ask, "Are you an Ephraimite?" If he said, "No," ⁶they would tell him to say "Shibboleth." But he would say "Sibboleth," because he could not

Judges

pronounce it correctly. Then they would grab him and kill him there at one of the Jordan River crossings. At that time forty-two thousand of the Ephraimites were killed.

7 Jephthah led Israel for six years. Then he died and was buried in his hometown[w] in Gilead.

Ibzan, Elon, and Abdon

8 After Jephthah, Ibzan from Bethlehem led Israel. 9 He had thirty sons and thirty daughters. He gave his daughters in marriage outside the clan and brought thirty young women from outside the clan for his sons to marry. Ibzan led Israel for seven years, 10 then he died and was buried at Bethlehem.

11 After Ibzan, Elon from Zebulun led Israel for ten years. 12 Then he died and was buried at Aijalon in the territory of Zebulun.

13 After Elon, Abdon son of Hillel from Pirathon led Israel. 14 He had forty sons and thirty grandsons, who rode on seventy donkeys. Abdon led Israel for eight years, 15 then he died and was buried at Pirathon in the territory of Ephraim in the hill country of the Amalekites.

The Birth of Samson

13 1 The Israelites sinned against the LORD again, and he let the Philistines rule them for forty years.

2 At that time there was a man named Manoah from the town of Zorah. He was a member of the tribe of Dan. His wife had never been able to have children. 3 The LORD's angel appeared to her and said, "You have never been able to have children, but you will soon be pregnant and have a son. 4 Be sure not to drink any wine or beer, or eat any forbidden food; 5 and after your son is born, you must never cut his hair, because from the day of his birth he will be dedicated to God as a nazirite.[x] He will begin the work of rescuing Israel from the Philistines."

6 Then the woman went and told her hus-

A Sneak Preview

Pay attention when an angel visits! You can usually bet something big is about to happen. It's a sneak preview, a way to let the audience know that something important is coming soon. Manoah and his wife each see an angel who promises them they will have a son. They have not been able to have a child, so this is wonderful news. However, they must raise him as a nazirite—someone who is especially dedicated to God.

Can you think of other childless couples in the Bible who receive special visits from angels? One couple is in the Book of Genesis, and two others are in the beginning of the Gospel of Luke.

— Judges 13:2–24

band, "A man of God has come to me, and he looked as frightening as the angel[y] of God. I didn't ask him where he came from, and he didn't tell me his name. 7 But he did tell me that I would become pregnant and have a son. He told me not to drink any wine or beer, or eat any forbidden food, because the boy is to be dedicated to God as a nazirite as long as he lives."

8 Then Manoah prayed to the LORD, "Please, LORD, let the man of God that you sent come back to us and tell us what we must do with the boy when he is born."

9 God did what Manoah asked, and his angel came back to the woman while she was sitting in the field. Her husband Manoah was not with her, 10 so she ran at once and

---

w **12:7** *One ancient translation* his hometown; *Hebrew* the towns.   x **13:5** NAZIRITE: *A person who showed devotion to God by taking vows not to drink wine or beer or allow any hair to be cut or touch corpses (see Num 6:1–8).* y **13:6** the angel; *or* an angel.
13:5 Num 6:1–5

told him, "Look! The man who came to me the other day has appeared to me again."

[11] Manoah got up and followed his wife. He went to the man and asked, "Are you the man who talked to my wife?"

"Yes," he answered.

[12] Then Manoah said, "Now then, when your words come true, what must the boy do? What kind of a life must he lead?"

[13] The LORD's angel answered, "Your wife must be sure to do everything that I have told her. [14] She must not eat anything that comes from the grapevine; she must not drink any wine or beer, or eat any forbidden food. She must do everything that I have told her."

[15-16] Not knowing that it was the LORD's angel, Manoah said to him, "Please do not go yet. Let us cook a young goat for you."

But the angel said, "If I do stay, I will not eat your food. But if you want to prepare it, burn it as an offering to the LORD."

[17] Manoah replied, "Tell us your name, so that we can honor you when your words come true."

[18] The angel asked, "Why do you want to know my name? It is a name of wonder." [z]

[19] So Manoah took a young goat and some grain, and offered them on the rock altar to the LORD who works wonders. [a]

[20-21] While the flames were going up from the altar, Manoah and his wife saw the LORD's angel go up toward heaven in the flames. Manoah realized then that the man had been the LORD's angel, and he and his wife threw themselves face downward on the ground. They never saw the angel again.

[22] Manoah said to his wife, "We are sure to die, because we have seen God!"

[23] But his wife answered, "If the LORD had wanted to kill us, he would not have accepted our offerings; he would not have shown us all this or told us such things at this time."

[24] The woman gave birth to a son and named him Samson. The child grew and the LORD blessed him. [25] And the LORD's power

Manoah and his wife saw the LORD's angel. (13:21)

began to strengthen him while he was between Zorah and Eshtaol in the Camp of Dan.

Samson and the Woman from Timnah

14 [1] One day Samson went down to Timnah, where he noticed a certain young Philistine woman. [2] He went back home and told his father and mother, "There is a Philistine woman down at Timnah who caught my attention. Get her for me; I want to marry her."

[3] But his father and mother asked him, "Why do you have to go to those heathen Philistines to get a wife? Can't you find someone in our own clan, among all our people?"

But Samson told his father, "She is the one I want you to get for me. I like her."

---

[z] **13:18** *name of wonder; or* mysterious name.   [a] **13:19** *Some ancient translations* who works wonders; *Hebrew* and working wonders while Manoah and his wife watched.

Samson eats wild honey and is known as something of a wild man. Can you think of a wild man from the Gospels that eats wild honey?

⁴His parents did not know that it was the LORD who was leading Samson to do this, for the LORD was looking for a chance to fight the Philistines. At this time the Philistines were ruling Israel.

⁵So Samson went down to Timnah with his father and mother. As they were going through the vineyards there, he heard a young lion roaring. ⁶Suddenly the power of the LORD made Samson strong, and he tore the lion apart with his bare hands, as if it were a young goat. But he did not tell his parents what he had done.

⁷Then he went and talked to the young woman, and he liked her. ⁸A few days later Samson went back to marry her. On the way he left the road to look at the lion he had killed, and he was surprised to find a swarm of bees and some honey inside the dead body. ⁹He scraped the honey out into his hands and ate it as he walked along. Then he went to his father and mother and gave them some. They ate it, but Samson did not tell them that he had taken the honey from the dead body of a lion.

¹⁰His father went to the woman's house, and Samson gave a banquet there. This was a custom among the young men. ¹¹When the Philistines saw him, they sent thirty young men to stay with him. ¹²⁻¹³Samson said to them, "Let me tell you a riddle. I'll bet each one of you a piece of fine linen and a change of fine clothes that you can't tell me its meaning before the seven days of the wedding feast are over."

"Tell us your riddle," they said. "Let's hear it."

¹⁴He said,

"Out of the eater came something to eat;
Out of the strong came something sweet."

Three days later they had still not figured out what the riddle meant.

¹⁵On the fourth[b] day they said to Samson's wife, "Trick your husband into telling us what the riddle means. If you don't, we'll set fire to your father's house and burn you

Samson in Trouble

Samson, for all his feats of strength, seems to keep getting himself in trouble. If he would only think first, he might not get into trouble so much. His anger also gets him into trouble. First, he told a riddle at his wedding feast that he thought no one could guess. But the guests found out the answer from his new wife, which made Samson furious. Besides killing thirty Philistine men, he stormed away from his new wife. When her father then married her to the best man, Samson was even more furious. He tied burning torches to foxes' tails, and they set fire to the Philistine crops and orchards. In revenge the Philistines killed his wife and her family. It just kept getting worse and worse.

When you get upset, do you stop and think, or do you just react? In the end Samson forgets that God is where his real strength lies. Can you remember and keep cool when things around you heat up? Try remembering that God is your strength next time you get angry or upset!

— Judges 14:15—15:8

with it.[c] You two invited us so that you could rob us, didn't you?"

¹⁶So Samson's wife went to him in tears and said, "You don't love me! You just hate

[b] **14:15** *Some ancient translations* fourth; *Hebrew* seventh.   [c] **14:15** set fire . . . you with it; *or* burn you and your family.

Three thousand men came to capture one man! Silly? Well, not if he can kill a thousand men with a jawbone of a donkey!

me! You told my friends a riddle and didn't tell me what it means!"

He said, "Look, I haven't even told my father and mother. Why should I tell you?" ¹⁷She cried about it for the whole seven days of the feast. But on the seventh day he told her what the riddle meant, for she nagged him so about it. Then she told the Philistines. ¹⁸So on the seventh day, before Samson went into the bedroom,ᵈ the men of the city said to him,

"What could be sweeter than honey?
What could be stronger than a lion?"
Samson replied,

"If you hadn't been plowing with my
    cow,
You wouldn't know the answer now."

¹⁹Suddenly the power of the LORD made him strong, and he went down to Ashkelon, where he killed thirty men, stripped them, and gave their fine clothes to the men who had solved the riddle. After that, he went back home, furious about what had happened, ²⁰and his wife was given to the man that had been his best man at the wedding.

15 ¹Some time later Samson went to visit his wife during the wheat harvest and took her a young goat. He told her father, "I want to go to my wife's room."

But he wouldn't let him in. ²He told Samson, "I really thought that you hated her, so I gave her to your friend. But her younger sister is prettier, anyway. You can have her, instead."

³Samson said, "This time I'm not going to be responsible for what I do to the Philistines!" ⁴So he went and caught three hundred foxes. Two at a time, he tied their tails together and put torches in the knots. ⁵Then he set fire to the torches and turned the foxes loose in the Philistine wheat fields. In this way he burned up not only the wheat that had been harvested but also the wheat that was still in the fields. The olive orchards were also burned. ⁶When the Philistines asked who had done this, they learned that Samson had done it because his father-in-law, a man from Timnah, had given Samson's wife to a friend of Samson's.

So the Philistines went and burned the woman to death and burned down her father's house.ᵉ

⁷Samson told them, "So this is how you act! I swear that I won't stop until I pay you back!" ⁸He attacked them fiercely and killed many of them. Then he went and stayed in the cave in the cliff at Etam.

Samson Defeats the Philistines

⁹The Philistines came and camped in Judah, and attacked the town of Lehi. ¹⁰The men of Judah asked them, "Why are you attacking us?"

They answered, "We came to take Samson prisoner and to treat him as he treated us." ¹¹So these three thousand men of Judah went to the cave in the cliff at Etam and said to Samson, "Don't you know that the Philistines are our rulers? What have you done to us?"

He answered, "I did to them just what they did to me."

¹²They told him, "We have come here to tie you up, so we can hand you over to them."

Samson said, "Give me your word that you won't kill me yourselves."

¹³"All right," they said, "we are only going to tie you up and hand you over to them. We won't kill you." So they tied him up with two new ropes and brought him back from the cliff.

¹⁴When he got to Lehi, the Philistines came running toward him, shouting at him.

*He tied their tails together and put torches in
the knots. (15:4)*

ᵈ **14:18** *Probable text* bedroom; *Hebrew* sun.   ᵉ **15:6** burned the woman . . . house; *or* burned the woman and her family to death.

He broke the ropes around his arms. (15:14)

Suddenly the power of the LORD made him strong, and he broke the ropes around his arms and hands as if they were burnt thread. ¹⁵Then he found a jawbone of a donkey that had recently died. He reached down and picked it up, and killed a thousand men with it. ¹⁶So Samson sang,

"With the jawbone of a donkey I killed a
    thousand men;
With the jawbone of a donkey I piled
    them up in piles."*f*

¹⁷After that, he threw the jawbone away. The place where this happened was named Ramath Lehi.*g*

¹⁸Then Samson became very thirsty, so he called to the LORD and said, "You gave me this great victory; am I now going to die of thirst and be captured by these heathen Philistines?" ¹⁹Then God opened a hollow place in the ground there at Lehi, and water came out of it. Samson drank it and began to feel much better. So the spring was named Hakkore;*h* it is still there at Lehi.

²⁰Samson led Israel for twenty years while the Philistines ruled the land.

Samson at Gaza

16 ¹One day Samson went to the Philistine city of Gaza, where he met a prostitute and went to bed with her. ²The people of Gaza found out that Samson was there, so they surrounded the place and waited for him all night long at the city gate. They were quiet all night, thinking to themselves, "We'll wait until daybreak, and then we'll kill him." ³But Samson stayed in bed only until midnight. Then he got up and took hold of the city gate and pulled it up—doors, posts, lock, and all. He put them on his shoulders and carried them far off to the top of the hill overlooking Hebron.

Samson and Delilah

⁴After this, Samson fell in love with a woman named Delilah, who lived in Sorek Valley. ⁵The five Philistine kings went to her and said, "Trick Samson into telling you why he is so strong and how we can overpower him, tie him up, and make him helpless. Each one of us will give you eleven hundred pieces of silver."

⁶So Delilah said to Samson, "Please tell me what makes you so strong. If someone wanted to tie you up and make you helpless, how could he do it?"

⁷Samson answered, "If they tie me up with seven new bowstrings that are not dried out, I'll be as weak as anybody else."

⁸So the Philistine kings brought Delilah seven new bowstrings that were not dried out, and she tied Samson up. ⁹She had some men waiting in another room, so she shouted, "Samson! The Philistines are coming!" But he snapped the bowstrings just as thread breaks when fire touches it. So they still did not know the secret of his strength.

¹⁰Delilah told Samson, "Look, you've been making a fool of me and not telling me the truth. Please tell me how someone could tie you up."

¹¹He told her, "If they tie me with new ropes that have never been used, I'll be as weak as anybody else."

¹²So Delilah got some new ropes and tied

---

f **15:16** PILES: *This word sounds like the Hebrew for "donkey."*   *g* **15:17** RAMATH LEHI: *This name in Hebrew means "Jawbone Hill."*   *h* **15:19** HAKKORE: *This name in Hebrew means "caller."*

Be Careful Whom You Trust

Lisa didn't like her middle name. It was old fashioned, and it embarrassed her. She never told anyone what it was, especially at school. Then one day Marci invited Lisa over after school. Lisa didn't know Marci very well, but Marci was popular. They did their homework and had a nice time. Then Marci wanted to play Truth or Dare. She asked Lisa what her middle name was. Lisa wasn't sure if Marci would keep her secret, but she wanted Marci to like her. Lisa told Marci her middle name and asked her not to tell anyone else. The next day at school Lisa walked into the classroom and someone had written her whole name in big letters on the board at the front of the classroom. Lisa had never been so embarrassed or felt such betrayal in her whole life.

Samson, like Lisa, shared his secret with someone who wasn't trustworthy. What was wrong with Samson? Why couldn't he see that Delilah was trying to trick him? Why did he trust her with his most important secret? What about Lisa? Why would she tell someone she hardly knew one of her biggest secrets? Read Sirach 6:5–17 and write down your own advice about being taken advantage of.

— Judges 16:4–22

him up. Then she shouted, "Samson! The Philistines are coming!" The men were waiting in another room. But he snapped the ropes off his arms like thread.

13 Delilah said to Samson, "You're still making a fool of me and not telling me the truth. Tell me how someone could tie you up."

He told her, "If you weave my seven locks of hair into a loom, and make it tight with a peg, I'll be as weak as anybody else."

14 Delilah then lulled him to sleep, took his seven locks of hair, and wove them into the loom.*i* She made it tight with a peg and shouted, "Samson! The Philistines are coming!" But he woke up and pulled his hair loose from the loom.

15 So she said to him, "How can you say you love me, when you don't mean it? You've made a fool of me three times, and you still haven't told me what makes you so strong." 16 She kept on asking him, day after day. He got so sick and tired of her bothering him about it 17 that he finally told her the truth. "My hair has never been cut," he said. "I have been dedicated to God as a nazirite*j* from the time I was born. If my hair were cut, I would lose my strength and be as weak as anybody else."

18 When Delilah realized that he had told her the truth, she sent a message to the Philistine kings and said, "Come back one more time. He has told me the truth." Then they came and brought the money with them. 19 Delilah lulled Samson to sleep in her lap and then called a man, who cut off*k* Samson's seven locks of hair. Then she began to torment him, for he had lost his strength. 20 Then she shouted, "Samson! The Philistines are coming!" He woke up and thought, "I'll get loose and go free, as always." He did not know that the LORD had left him. 21 The Philistines captured him and put his eyes out. They took him to Gaza, chained him with bronze chains, and put him to work grinding at the mill in the prison. 22 But his hair started growing back.

Judges

---

i **16:14** *One ancient translation* and make it tight *(in verse 13)* . . . *into the loom (in verse 14); Hebrew does not have these words.* *j* **16:17** NAZIRITE: *See 13:5.* *k* **16:19** *Probable text* who cut off; *Hebrew* and she cut off.

Samson gave in to Delilah because she kept bothering him. What should Samson have done instead?

Pray It!

Prayer in Despair

Samson had once been strong and in control of every situation. He lost his strength because he forgot that it came from the Lord. But even though he has nothing left, he turns to God and asks for help. The next time you are in despair, lose hope and want to give up, try Samson's prayer:

"*Sovereign Lord, please remember me; please, God, give me my strength*" (Judges 16:28).

— Judges 16:23–31

The Death of Samson

23 The Philistine kings met together to celebrate and offer a great sacrifice to their god Dagon. They sang, "Our god has given us victory over our enemy Samson!" 24-25 They were enjoying themselves, and so they said, "Call Samson, and let's make him entertain us!"[l] When they brought Samson out of the prison, they made him entertain them[m] and made him stand between the columns. When the people saw him, they sang praise to their god: "Our god has given us victory over our enemy, who devastated our land and killed so many of us!" 26 Samson said to the boy who was leading him by the hand, "Let me touch the columns that hold up the building. I want to lean on them." 27 The building was crowded with men and women. All five Philistine kings were there, and there were about three thousand men and women on the roof, watching Samson entertain them.[n] 28 Then Samson prayed, "Sovereign Lord, please remember me; please, God, give me my strength just this one time more, so that with this one blow I can get even with the Philistines for putting out my two eyes." 29 So Samson took hold of the two middle columns holding up the building. Putting one hand on each column, he pushed against them 30 and shouted, "Let me die with the Philistines!" He pushed with all his might, and the building fell down on the five kings and everyone else. Samson killed more people at his death than he had killed during his life.

31 His brothers and the rest of his family came down to get his body. They took him back and buried him between Zorah and Eshtaol in the tomb of his father Manoah. He had been Israel's leader for twenty years.

He pushed with all his might. (16:30)

l 16:24–25 make him entertain us; *or* make fun of him.   m 16:24–25 made him entertain them; *or* made fun of him.   n 16:27 entertain them; *or* and making fun of him.

In the Book of Judges, the people worship God at Shiloh in a tent. Do you know which king builds a Temple to worship God? What city is it built in?

Micah's Idols

17 ¹There was once a man named Micah, who lived in the hill country of Ephraim. ²He told his mother, "When someone stole those eleven hundred pieces of silver from you, you put a curse on the robber. I heard you do it. Look, I have the money. I am the one who took it."

His mother said, "May the LORD bless you, my son!" ³He gave the money back to his mother, and she said, "To keep the curse from falling on my son, I myself am solemnly dedicating the silver to the LORD. It will be used to make a wooden idol covered with silver. So now I will give the pieces of silver back to you." ⁴Then he gave them back to his mother. She took two hundred of the pieces of silver and gave them to a metalworker, who made an idol, carving it from wood and covering it with the silver. It was placed in Micah's house.

⁵This man Micah had his own place of worship. He made some idols and an ephod,ᵒ and appointed one of his sons as his priest. ⁶There was no king in Israel at that time; everyone did whatever they wanted.

⁷At that same time there was a young Levite who had been living in the town of Bethlehem in Judah. ⁸He left Bethlehem to find another place to live. While he was traveling, he came to Micah's house in the hill country of Ephraim. ⁹Micah asked him, "Where do you come from?"

He answered, "I am a Levite from Bethlehem in Judah. I am looking for a place to live."

¹⁰Micah said, "Stay with me. Be my adviser and priest, and I will give you ten pieces of silver a year, some clothes, and your food."ᵖ ¹¹The young Levite agreed to stay with Micah and became like a son to him. ¹²Micah appointed him as his priest, and he lived in Micah's home. ¹³Micah said, "Now that I have a Levite as my priest, I know that the LORD will make things go well for me."

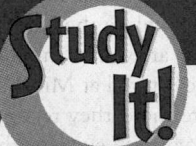

What's Wrong with This Picture?

Read Judges, chapters 17–18, carefully. Does anything strike you as terribly wrong with the actions of the people in this story? Did you notice the following?

- Micah steals from his mother (17:2).
- Micah has the stolen silver made into an idol. In addition he has several other idols (17:4–5).
- The spies steal from Micah. The priest doesn't stop the spies from stealing (18:18).
- When Micah and his neighbors try to stop the Danite army, they act like nothing is wrong (18:23).
- The Danites kill a whole town of peaceful people and burn it to the ground (18:27).

These actions are against several of the Ten Commandments. Twice the author mentions, "There was no king in Israel at that time" (17:6; 18:1). The Book of Judges was written later, at a time when there was a king. It seems like the author may be suggesting that things are better with kings.

— Judges, chapters 17–18

Micah and the Tribe of Dan

18 ¹There was no king in Israel at that time. In those days the tribe of Dan was looking for territory to claim and settle in because they had not yet received any land of their own among the tribes of Israel. ²So the people of Dan chose five qualifiedᵠ men out of all the families in the tribe and

---

ᵒ **17:5** EPHOD: *See Word List.*   ᵖ **17:10** *Probable text* your food; *Hebrew* your food. So the Levite went.
ᵠ **18:2** qualified; *or* brave.
17:6 Judg 21:25

sent them from the towns of Zorah and Eshtaol with instructions to explore the land and spy on it. When they arrived in the hill country of Ephraim, they stayed at Micah's house. ³While they were there, they recognized the accent of the young Levite, so they went up to him and asked, "What are you doing here? Who brought you here?"

⁴He answered, "I have an arrangement with Micah, who pays me to serve as his priest."

⁵They said to him, "Please ask God if we are going to be successful on our trip."

⁶The priest answered, "You have nothing to worry about. The LORD is taking care of you on this trip."

⁷So the five men left and went to the town of Laish. They saw how the people there lived in security like the Sidonians. They were a peaceful, quiet people, with no argument with anyone; they had all they needed.ʳ They lived far away from the Sidonians and had no dealings with any other people. ⁸When the five men returned to Zorah and Eshtaol, the people asked them what they had found out. ⁹"Come on," they replied. "Let's attack Laish. We saw the land, and it's very good. Don't stay here doing nothing; hurry! Go on in and take it over! ¹⁰When you get there, you will find that the people don't suspect a thing. It is a big country; it has everything a person could want, and God has given it to you."

¹¹So six hundred men from the tribe of Dan left Zorah and Eshtaol, ready for battle. ¹²They went up and camped west of Kiriath Jearim in Judah. That is why the place is still called Camp of Dan. ¹³They went on from there and came to Micah's house in the hill country of Ephraim.

¹⁴Then the five men who had gone to spy on the country around Laish said to their companions, "Did you know that here in one of these houses there is a wooden idol covered with silver? There are also other idols and an ephod. What do you think we should do?" ¹⁵So they went into Micah's house, where the young Levite lived, and asked the Levite how he was getting along. ¹⁶Meanwhile the six hundred Danite soldiers, ready for battle, were standing at the gate. ¹⁷The five spies went straight on into the house and took the wooden idol covered with silver, the other idols, and the ephod, while the priest stayed at the gate with the six hundred armed men.

¹⁸When the men went into Micah's house and took the sacred objects, the priest asked them, "What are you doing?"

¹⁹They told him, "Keep quiet. Don't say a word. Come with us and be our priest and adviser. Wouldn't you rather be a priest for a whole Israelite tribe than for the family of one man?" ²⁰This made the priest very happy, so he took the sacred objects and went along with them.

²¹They turned around and started off, with their children, their livestock, and their belongings going ahead. ²²They had traveled a good distance from the house when Micah called his neighbors out for battle. They caught up with the Danites ²³and shouted at them. The Danites turned around and asked Micah, "What's the matter? Why all this mob?"

²⁴Micah answered, "What do you mean, 'What's the matter?' You take my priest and the gods that I made, and walk off! What have I got left?"

²⁵The Danites told him, "You had better not say anything else unless you want these men to get angry and attack you. You and your whole family would die." ²⁶Then the Danites went on. Micah saw that they were too strong for him, so he turned and went back home.

²⁷⁻²⁸After the Danites had taken the priest and the things that Micah had made, they went and attacked Laish, that town of peaceful, quiet people which was in the same valley as Bethrehob. They killed the inhabitants and burned the town. There was no one to save them, because Laish was a long way from Sidon, and they had no dealings with any other people. The Danites rebuilt the town and settled down there. ²⁹They changed its name from Laish to Dan, after their ancestor Dan, the son of Jacob. ³⁰The Danites set up the idol to be worshiped, and Jonathan, the son of Gershom and grandson

---

ʳ **18:7** *Probable text* They were . . . needed; *Hebrew unclear.*

Adam & Eve

Breakthrough!: So glad to finally meet you! You two are the original originals!

Adam: We may be the original originals, but we're stand-ins for the real thing.

B: Huh?

Eve: What Adam is trying to say is that we're characters in a story that isn't really history.

B: But you've got real names! And you're in the Bible!

Adam: Actually, my name simply means "human being."

Eve: And my name means "living."

B: You mean, you never existed?

Adam: I wouldn't say that. God created human beings and there was a first set of human parents, right? But the first human beings lived long before recorded history. So in the opening stories of the Bible, we are the symbols for the first man and woman.

B: Then what about the part about the Garden of Eden?

Eve: The Garden is another symbolic part of the story. It explains the way things should be between God and human beings. God created us with a free will and meant us to live in perfect harmony with him, each other, and all creation. But we chose to give in to temptation and disobeyed God.

Adam: Our sin has been passed on to everyone who lived after us—except Jesus and his mother, Mary.

Eve: Have you ever heard of Original Sin? That's what Adam is talking about. It means that every person is born somewhat separated from God and has a tendency to choose sin.

B: Does that mean we're all bad?

Adam: Absolutely not. Everything God created is good and holy. Sometimes we make bad choices, but God's love is much greater than our weaknesses.

Eve: Right. Even though we sometimes turn away from God, God never turns away from us. And that's the truth!

c1

Abraham

Breakthrough!: Abraham. That wasn't always your name, was it?

Abraham: No, it was Abram at first. God changed it as a sign of the Covenant he made with me. My wife's name was changed to Sarah.

B: Covenant?

Abraham: That's a special agreement between God and me. I promised to do what God asked. God promised to give me many descendants and a land to call our own. That took some faith because Sarah and I were both pretty old, but I didn't ask too many questions—God being God and all.

B: Speaking of being old, you were not a young man when God asked you to pack up and leave your family. What was that all about?

Abraham: Like I said, I didn't ask too many questions. God promised to bless me and make me famous. Did you expect me to say no?

B: Wasn't it hard though?

Abraham: Sure it was. We had a comfortable life in Haran [HAIR-uhn]. It was not an easy trip. It was downright terrifying sometimes.

B: What are some of the amazing things God did during your lifetime?

Abraham: Well, of course, there was the wonderful day Isaac was born. The destruction of Sodom and Gomorrah showed me how God treats those who do not live a good life. Then there was the day God told me to sacrifice Isaac. It was the worst day of my life. I had to make a choice: my son or my God. I didn't know it at the time, but God was testing me. You can read about my and Sarah's adventures in the Book of Genesis.

B: What's the most important thing you learned from God?

Abraham: Listen, and have faith. God may surprise you. Look what happened to me. I became the father of the Jewish, Christian, and Muslim peoples.

Sarah

Breakthrough!: Should we call you Sarah or Sarai?

Sarah: Sarah, please. Sarai was my name before God made the Covenant with my husband, Abraham.

B: What was life like for you and Abraham?

Sarah: Abraham was a good man. We lived a comfortable life in Haran [HAIR-uhn]. The other women and I were good friends. Then one day God told Abraham to pick up everything and leave. I had nothing to say about it. Women did not have much say back then. So we went—Abraham, his nephew Lot, all our belongings, our servants, and me.

B: How was the trip?

Sarah: Long. We ended up in Egypt because of a famine. The Pharaoh [FAIR-oh] took me to live with him, but he let me go when God gave him a terrible disease.

B: Any children?

Sarah: That's a sore spot—and the high point of my life. Abraham and I wanted a son in the worst way, but God never gave us any children. Then one day I overheard some visitors telling Abraham that I would have a son. I laughed to myself; I was much too old to have children. We found out later that these visitors were from God.

B: Then what happened?

Sarah: Nine months later I had a bouncing baby boy. We named him Isaac.

B: Isaac is an unusual name. What does it mean?

Sarah: It means, "He laughs."

B: What lessons did you try to pass on to Isaac?

Sarah: Nothing is impossible with God. Put your trust in the God who is always with you. And keep on laughing.

Isaac

Breakthrough!: Isaac, how would you describe yourself?

Isaac: I'm a peaceful guy. I may get upset, but I'm not one to get even. I trust that God will take care of things. I guess I learned that from my dad, Abraham.

B: Tell me about your wife.

Isaac: Oh, how I loved Rebecca! I didn't exactly choose her. Like all weddings at that time, our families arranged for us to marry. God had a hand in it, I'm sure.

B: Did you have children?

Isaac: We had twin boys, Esau [EE-saw] and Jacob. Esau was my favorite, partly because he always brought me meat from his hunting trips. Jacob was quiet but feisty—just like his mother. Rebecca liked him better.

B: Didn't Esau give away his special rights as your firstborn son?

Isaac: Yes, he gave away his birthright. For what? Food! I swear, that guy would eat anything that didn't eat him first!

B: Tell us about "the switch."

Isaac: I couldn't believe I was tricked like that! I was supposed to give Esau a special blessing, but Rebecca decided that Jacob should have it. She put an animal skin on Jacob's arm. I was blind, so I had to go by what I felt. I knew Esau was a lot hairier than his brother, so when I touched Jacob's hairy arm, I thought he was Esau. So I blessed the wrong son—or was it the right one?

B: How did Esau react?

Isaac: He was upset, and so was I. He begged me for a blessing, but I only had one special blessing to give. Esau wanted to get even with Jacob, but we sent Jacob away for his own protection.

B: What did you try to teach your sons about God?

Isaac: Trust in God. God has a way of making things work out.

Jacob

Breakthrough!: You had a major role in the history of the Chosen People, didn't you?

Jacob: I'd like to think so.

B: How do you explain the dishonest start to your career?

Jacob: You must be talking about the birthright and blessing that I tricked my brother, Esau [EE-saw], out of. I'm not proud of it, but let's just say that God intended things to be different. Don't forget that I was on the receiving end of one of those switches, too.

B: Do you mean your father-in-law, Laban [LAY-buhn]?

Jacob: Yes. When I met Rachel, I fell in love with her immediately. I told her father that I would work for him for seven years if he would let me marry her. He agreed, but when the time came, he secretly gave me his older daughter, Leah [LEE-uh], instead. So I hung around and worked another seven years so I could marry Rachel, too.

B: Did you father any children?

Jacob: Twelve sons and one daughter. The Twelve Tribes of Israel [IZ-ry-el] are named for my sons and two grandsons. That must have been what God meant when he promised my grandfather, Abraham, that he would have many descendants.

B: Did you have a favorite?

Jacob: Yes; Joseph and Benjamin, the sons of Rachel. That caused a few problems.

B: Tell us more.

Jacob: My older sons were jealous, especially of Joseph. They sold Joseph as a slave and told me he was dead. I was heartbroken. But our amazing God made it all come out okay in the end.

B: Do you have a message for our readers?

Jacob: Never lose hope. God came through for us and made me the father of the Twelve Tribes of Israel!

Leah & Rachel

Breakthrough!: You two are sisters, right?

Leah [LEE-uh]: Yes. We are the daughters of Laban [LAY-buhn]. I am the oldest.

B: You were both married to Jacob. How did that happen?

Rachel: Jacob was in love with me. He promised to work for my father for seven years if he would let us get married. My father agreed, but at the last minute, he tricked Jacob into marrying Leah.

Leah: My face was covered with a veil, so Jacob couldn't see me. I didn't know what was going on. I just did as my father told me. Besides, it was our custom that the oldest daughter married first. If Rachel married before me, people would have thought there was something terribly wrong with me.

B: How did Jacob react?

Rachel: He was angry, but I think he understood why my father tricked him. We got married a week later, but he had to work for my father for another seven years. I knew that he must have loved me very much to do that.

Leah: It was very obvious that Jacob loved Rachel more than me. She was prettier. Sometimes it hurt.

B: So you both had children?

Leah: I gave Jacob many children—six sons and a daughter. That pleased him.

Rachel: I was jealous of Leah. It seemed like I would never have children. Finally, I had Joseph. Such a joy! A few years later, I got pregnant again. It was a difficult birth. I died after Benjamin was born.

B: What do you think your greatest contribution to God's plan is?

Leah: Rachel and I, along with Sarah and Rebecca, were the founding mothers of Israel [IZ-ry-el].

Rachel: That's right. The men could not have done it without our faith and wisdom!

Joseph

Breakthrough!: Nice coat!

Joseph: Thanks. It was a gift from my father.

B: Colorful! Is that how you would describe your life?

Joseph: Yes. I was the son of Jacob and Rachel. I didn't know my mother well. She died when my brother, Benjamin, was born. My father talked about her all the time. He really loved her.

B: You had eleven brothers and a sister. Was there any sibling rivalry?

Joseph: Big time. My brothers were so jealous of me that they sold me. I ended up as a slave in Egypt.

B: It must have been a hard life.

Joseph: It was, but God was with me. I did well, and became the slave of an important official. But then I was accused of something I didn't do and got thrown into prison. Luckily, God gave me the gift of understanding dreams. That's how I got out of prison.

B: Whose dreams did you interpret?

Joseph: First it was the baker and the wine steward. Eventually Pharaoh [FAIR-oh] called me in to interpret his dreams. He was so pleased that he made me governor of Egypt.

B: Did you ever see your family again?

Joseph: Yes. Because of a drought in Canaan [KAY-nuhn], there was no food. My brothers came to Egypt to buy grain. They didn't recognize me, but I knew who they were. I made them sweat a little before I gave them food. It was payback time, if you know what I mean. You can read the story in Genesis, chapters 42–47. Eventually the entire family came to Egypt.

B: Any advice for our readers?

Joseph: Three things: Do your best wherever you are, take care of the needy, and don't try to get even.

Moses

Breakthrough!: So, Moses, it's great to finally meet you! You have many fans. Many people even call you a hero!

Moses: Well, I don't know about that. Early in my life, I didn't even know who I was.

B: Really?

Moses: Yes, I was actually born a slave, but my mother and sister saved my life. The pharaoh's daughter adopted me, and I lived like an Egyptian prince. When I finally realized how badly my blood relatives were treated, I kind of flew off the handle. But God has always come through for me.

B: Could you tell us a little about a time God came through for you?

Moses: Well, the most amazing time was when I led my people to freedom. Pharaoh and his whole army were after us! We were pretty scared, but God told me to stretch my staff out over the water, and we crossed over on dry land. But the water closed over Pharaoh's army and drowned them, and we were able to escape.

B: Why do you think God chose you to lead the people out of Egypt?

Moses: You know, that's something I never could figure out. I'm not a good public speaker. I'm not very brave. I killed a man, a soldier who was beating a slave, and had to run away and hide. I was really afraid. I certainly didn't want to go back to Egypt. I pleaded with God to send someone else. I guess God must have seen something in me that I couldn't.

B: What advice would you like to give our readers?

Moses: I have to say that the Ten Commandments God gave me on Mount Sinai [SY-ny] are the best advice I could give anyone.

of Moses, served as a priest for the Danites, and his descendants served as their priests until the people were taken away into exile. [31] Micah's idol remained there as long as the Tent where God was worshiped remained at Shiloh.

The Levite and His Concubine

19 [1] In those days before Israel had a king, there was a Levite living far back in the hill country of Ephraim. He took a young woman from Bethlehem in Judah to be his concubine. [2] But she became angry with him,⁵ went back to her father's house in Bethlehem, and stayed there four months. [3] Then the man decided to go after her and try to persuade her to return to him. He took his servant and two donkeys with him. The woman showed the Levite into the house, and when her father saw him, he gave him a hearty greeting. [4] The father insisted that he stay, and so he stayed for three days. The couple had their meals and spent the nights there. [5] On the morning of the fourth day they woke up early and got ready to go. But the woman's father said to the Levite, "Have something to eat first. You'll feel better. You can go later."

[6] So the two men sat down and ate and drank together. Then the woman's father told him, "Please spend the night and enjoy yourself."

[7] The Levite got up to go, but the father urged him to stay, so he spent another night there. [8] Early in the morning of the fifth day he started to leave, but the woman's father said, "Eat something, please. Wait until later in the day." So the two men ate together.

[9] When the man, his concubine, and the servant once more started to leave, the father said, "Look, it's almost evening now; you might as well stay all night. It will be dark soon; stay here and have a good time. Tomorrow you can get up early for the trip and go home."

⁵ **19:2** *One ancient translation* became angry with him; *another translation* left him; *Hebrew* was faithful to him.

No More Violence Against Women

In the last few chapters of the Book of Judges, things go terribly wrong. The story starts with a man—a Levite or a priest—who has reclaimed his concubine. Ironically he passes by a non-Israelite town to stay overnight in a city of Israelites. Only an old man shows them any hospitality. Then a gang shows up and wants to rape the visiting Levite. To save himself he hands over his concubine, and overnight the gang rapes and abuses her to death.

The story doesn't get any better. The Levite takes the dead woman and cuts her into twelve pieces, and sends them to all twelve tribes of Israel. Of course everyone is shocked, and they agree to go to war against the tribe of Benjamin. The whole nation of Israel ends up in civil war.

In this disturbing story, women were treated as objects used by men. Not just the gang but even by the Levite who fails to defend his concubine. Unfortunately, this horrible behavior still happens today. Women are treated as objects for display in advertising and pornography. Men abuse women violently every day. Violence against women is wrong. Men and women (including young men and young women) need to stand up and speak out against this kind of violence.

— Judges, chapter 19

Judges

Do you know where to find help if someone you know has been physically or sexually abused?

10-11But the man did not want to spend another night there, so he and his concubine started on their way, with their servant and two donkeys with pack saddles. It was late in the day when they came near Jebus (that is, Jerusalem), so the servant said to his master, "Why don't we stop and spend the night here in this Jebusite city?"

12-13But his master said, "We're not going to stop in a city where the people are not Israelites. We'll pass on by and go a little farther and spend the night at Gibeah or Ramah." 14So they passed by Jebus and continued on their way. It was sunset when they came to Gibeah in the territory of the tribe of Benjamin. 15They turned off the road to go and spend the night there. They went into town and sat down in the city square, but no one offered to take them home for the night.

16While they were there, an old man came by at the end of a day's work on the farm. He was originally from the hill country of Ephraim, but he was now living in Gibeah. (The other people there were from the tribe of Benjamin.) 17The old man noticed the traveler in the city square and asked him, "Where do you come from? Where are you going?"

18The Levite answered, "We have been in Bethlehem in Judah, and now we are on our way home*f* deep in the hill country of Ephraim. No one will put us up for the night, 19even though we have fodder and straw for our donkeys, as well as bread and wine for my concubine and me and for my servant. We have everything we need."

20The old man said, "You are welcome in my home! I'll take care of you; you don't have to spend the night in the square." 21So he took them home with him and fed their donkeys. His guests washed their feet and had a meal.

22They were enjoying themselves when all of a sudden some sexual perverts from the town surrounded the house and started beating on the door. They said to the old man, "Bring out that man that came home with you! We want to have sex with him!"

23But the old man went outside and said to them, "No, my friends! Please! Don't do such an evil, immoral thing! This man is my guest. 24Look! Here is his concubine and my own virgin daughter. I'll bring them out now, and you can have them. Do whatever you want to with them. But don't do such an awful thing to this man!" 25But the men would not listen to him. So the Levite took his concubine and put her outside with them. They raped her and abused her all night long and didn't stop until morning.

26At dawn the woman came and fell down at the door of the old man's house, where her husband was. She was still there when daylight came. 27Her husband got up that morning, and when he opened the door to go on his way, he found his concubine lying in front of the house with her hands reaching for the door. 28He said, "Get up. Let's go." But there was no answer. So he put her body across the donkey and started on his way home. 29When he arrived, he went in the house and got a knife. He took his concubine's body, cut it into twelve pieces, and sent one piece to each of the twelve tribes of Israel. 30Everyone who saw it said, "We have never heard of such a thing! Nothing like this has ever happened since the Israelites left Egypt! We have to do something about this! What will it be?"

Israel Prepares for War

20 1All the people of Israel from Dan in the north to Beersheba in the south, as well as from the land of Gilead in the east, answered the call. They gathered in one body in the LORD's presence at Mizpah. 2The leaders of all the tribes of Israel were present at this gathering of God's people,

f **19:18** *One ancient translation* home; *Hebrew* to the house of the LORD.
19:22–24 Gen 19:5–8   **19:29** 1 Sam 11:7

Concubine: A servant woman who, although not a wife, has sexual relations with her master. She was often treated like a second wife.

and there were 400,000 foot soldiers.
³Meanwhile the people of Benjamin heard
that all the other Israelites had gathered at
Mizpah.

The Israelites asked, "Tell us, how was this
crime committed?" ⁴The Levite whose concubine had been murdered answered, "My
concubine and I went to Gibeah in the territory of Benjamin to spend the night. ⁵The
men of Gibeah came to get me and surrounded the house at night. They intended
to kill me; instead they raped my concubine,
and she died. ⁶I took her body, cut it in
pieces, and sent one piece to each of the
twelve tribes of Israel. These people have
committed an evil and immoral act among
us. ⁷All of you here are Israelites. What are
we going to do about this?"

⁸All the people stood up together and
said, "None of us, whether he lives in a tent
or in a house, will go home. ⁹This is what
we will do: we will draw lots and choose
some men to attack Gibeah.ᵘ ¹⁰One tenth of
the men in Israel will provide food for the
army, and the others will go and punish
Gibeahᵛ for this immoral act that they have
committed in Israel." ¹¹So all the men in
Israel assembled with one purpose—to
attack the town.

¹²The Israelite tribes sent messengers all
through the territory of the tribe of Benjamin to say, "What is this crime that you
have committed? ¹³Now hand over those
perverts in Gibeah, so that we can kill them
and remove this evil from Israel." But the
people of Benjamin paid no attention to the
other Israelites. ¹⁴From all the cities of Benjamin they came to Gibeah to fight the
other people of Israel. ¹⁵⁻¹⁶They called out
twenty-six thousand soldiers from their cities
that day. Besides these, the citizens of Gibeah
gathered seven hundred specially chosen
menʷ who were left-handed. Every one of
them could sling a stone at a strand of hair
and never miss. ¹⁷Not counting the tribe of
Benjamin, the Israelites gathered 400,000
trained soldiers.

The War against the Benjaminites

¹⁸The Israelites went to the place of worship at Bethel, and there they asked God,
"Which tribe should attack the Benjaminites
first?"

The LORD answered, "The tribe of Judah."

¹⁹So the Israelites started out the next
morning and camped near the city of
Gibeah. ²⁰They went to attack the army of
Benjamin, and placed the soldiers in position
facing the city. ²¹The army of Benjamin
came out of the city, and before the day was
over they had killed twenty-two thousand
Israelite soldiers. ²²⁻²³Then the Israelites went
to the place of worship and mourned in the
presence of the LORD until evening. They
asked him, "Should we go again into battle
against our brothers the Benjaminites?"

The LORD answered, "Yes."

So the Israelite army was encouraged,
and they placed their soldiers in position
again, where they had been the day before.
²⁴They marched against the army of Benjamin a second time. ²⁵And for the second
time the Benjaminites came out of Gibeah,
and this time they killed eighteen thousand
trained Israelite soldiers. ²⁶Then all the
people of Israel went up to Bethel and
mourned. They sat there in the LORD's
presence and did not eat until evening.
They offered fellowship sacrifices and
burned some sacrifices whole—all in the
presence of the LORD. ²⁷⁻²⁸God's Covenant
Box was there at Bethel in those days, and
Phinehas, the son of Eleazar and grandson
of Aaron, was in charge of it. The people
asked the LORD, "Should we go out to fight
our brothers the Benjaminites again, or
should we give up?"

The LORD answered, "Fight. Tomorrow I
will give you victory over them."

²⁹So the Israelites put some soldiers in
hiding around Gibeah. ³⁰Then for the third
straight day they marched against the army
of Benjamin and placed their soldiers in
battle position facing Gibeah, as they had
done before. ³¹The Benjaminites came out
to fight and were led away from the city. As

ᵘ **20:9** *One ancient translation* to attack Gibeah; *Hebrew* to Gibeah. ᵛ **20:10** *One ancient translation* Gibeah;
Hebrew Geba. ʷ **20:15–16** *Some ancient translations* men; *Hebrew* men. In all this number there were seven
hundred specially chosen men.

they had before, they began killing some Israelites in the open country, on the road to Bethel and on the road to Gibeah. They killed about thirty Israelites. 32 The Benjaminites said, "We've beaten them just as before."

But the Israelites had planned to retreat and lead them away from the city onto the roads. 33 So when the main army of the Israelites pulled back and regrouped at Baaltamar, the men surrounding Gibeah suddenly rushed out of their hiding places in the rocky country around the city.ˣ 34 Ten thousand men, specially chosen out of all Israel, attacked Gibeah, and the fighting was hard. The Benjaminites had not realized that they were about to be destroyed. 35 The LORD gave Israel victory over the army of Benjamin. The Israelites killed 25,100 of the enemy that day, 36 and the Benjaminites realized they were defeated.

How the Israelites Won

The main body of the Israelite army had retreated from the Benjaminites because they were relying on the men that they had put in hiding around Gibeah. 37 These men ran quickly toward Gibeah; they spread out in the city and killed everyone there. 38 The main Israelite army and the men in hiding had arranged a signal. When they saw a big cloud of smoke going up from the town, 39 the Israelites out on the battlefield were to turn around. By this time the Benjaminites had already killed the thirty Israelites. They told themselves, "Yes, we've beaten them just as before." 40 Then the signal appeared; a cloud of smoke began to go up from the town. The Benjaminites looked behind them and were amazed to see the whole city going up in flames. 41 Then the Israelites turned around, and the Benjaminites were thrown into panic because they realized that they were about to be destroyed. 42 They retreated from the Israelites and ran toward the open country, but they could not escape. They were caught between the main army and the men who were now coming out of

Civil War

The rape of the Levite's concubine has resulted in a horrible civil war. This is not the first time, and it won't be the last, that Israel has gone to war against itself. The Israelites realize just before it's too late that they must stop the fighting or the tribe of Benjamin will come to an end. Since the other tribes have killed all the Benjaminite women, the remaining men have no one left to marry. So they commit even more violence so the men of Benjamin will have wives. Yikes! This is a frightening story of violence and revenge gone out of control.

Have you ever been in an argument with a group of friends? Has it ever happened that people take sides with each side acting worse and worse to each other? The only way this can end is with everyone hating each other—or if someone says *stop* and reaches out a hand asking for forgiveness. Can you be that person?

— Judges, chapters 20–21

the city,ʸ and they were destroyed. 43 The Israelites had the enemy trapped, and without stopping they pursued them as far as a point east of Gibeah, killing them as they went.ᶻ 44 Eighteen thousand of the best Benjaminite soldiers were killed. 45 The others turned and ran toward the open country to Rimmon Rock. Five thousand of them were killed on the roads. The Israelites continued to pursue the rest to Gidom, killing two thousand. 46 In all, twenty-five thousand Ben-

ˣ **20:33** *One ancient translation* the city (that is, Gibeah); *Hebrew* Geba. ʸ **20:42** *Probable text* city; *Hebrew* cities.
ᶻ **20:43** *Verse 43 in Hebrew is unclear.*

jaminites were killed that day—all of them brave soldiers.

47But six hundred men were able to escape to the open country to Rimmon Rock, and they stayed there four months. **48**The Israelites turned back against the rest of the Benjaminites and killed them all— men, women, and children, and animals as well. They burned every town in the area.

Wives for the Tribe of Benjamin

21 **1**When the Israelites had gathered at Mizpah, they had made a solemn promise to the LORD: "None of us will allow a Benjaminite to marry a daughter of ours." **2**So now the people of Israel went to Bethel and sat there in the presence of God until evening. Loudly and bitterly they mourned: **3**"LORD God of Israel, why has this happened? Why is the tribe of Benjamin about to disappear from Israel?"

4Early the next morning the people got up and built an altar there. They offered fellowship sacrifices and burned some sacrifices whole. **5**They asked, "Is there any group out of all the tribes of Israel that did not go to the gathering in the LORD's presence at Mizpah?" (They had taken a solemn oath that anyone who had not gone to Mizpah would be put to death.) **6**The people of Israel felt sorry for their brothers the Benjaminites and said, "Today Israel has lost one of its tribes. **7**What shall we do to provide wives for the men of Benjamin who are left? We have made a solemn promise to the LORD that we will not give them any of our daughters."

8When they asked if there was some group out of the tribes of Israel that had not gone to the gathering at Mizpah, they found out that no one from Jabesh in Gilead had been there; **9**at the roll call of the army no one from Jabesh had responded. **10**So the assembly sent twelve thousand of their bravest men with the orders, "Go and kill everyone in Jabesh, including women and children. **11**Kill all the males, and also every woman who is not a virgin." **12**They found four hundred young virgins among the people in Jabesh, so they brought them to the camp at Shiloh, which is in the land of Canaan.

13Then the whole assembly sent word to the Benjaminites who were at Rimmon Rock and offered to end the war. **14**The Benjaminites came back, and the other Israelites gave them the young women from Jabesh whom they had not killed. But there were not enough of them.

15The people felt sorry for the Benjaminites because the LORD had broken the unity of the tribes of Israel. **16**So the leaders of the gathering said, "There are no more women in the tribe of Benjamin. What shall we do to provide wives for the men who are left? **17**Israel must not lose one of its twelve tribes. We must find a way for the tribe of Benjamin to survive, **18**but we cannot allow them to marry our daughters, because we have put a curse on anyone who allows a Benjaminite to marry one of our daughters."

19Then they thought, "The yearly festival of the LORD at Shiloh is coming soon." (Shiloh is north of Bethel, south of Lebonah, and east of the road between Bethel and Shechem.) **20**They told the Benjaminites, "Go and hide in the vineyards **21**and watch. When the young women of Shiloh come out to dance during the festival, you come out of the vineyards. Each of you take a wife by force from among them and take her back to the territory of Benjamin with you. **22**If their fathers or brothers come to you*a* and protest, you*b* can tell them, 'Please let us keep them, because we did not take them from you in battle to be our wives. And since you did not give them to us, you are not guilty of breaking your promise.' "

23The Benjaminites did this; each of them chose a wife from the young women who

---

a **21:22** *One ancient translation* you; *Hebrew* us.　　*b* **21:22** *Probable text* you; *Hebrew* we.

The city of Gibeah had 700 left-handed warriors who were excellent with slings. Do you recall an earlier judge who was also left-handed?

were dancing at Shiloh and carried her away. Then they went back to their own territory, rebuilt their towns, and lived there. 24 At the same time the rest of the Israelites left, and

every man went back to his own tribe and family and to his own property.

25 There was no king in Israel at that time. Everyone did whatever they pleased.

21:25 Judg 17:6

Your Next Step

Congratulations on finishing the Book of Judges! Use this space to write your thoughts and questions about this book. If you are following the suggested reading plan, go on to the Book of Ruth. This little short story about faithful love happens during the time of the judges.

THE BOOK OF *Ruth*

Ruth is a love story, but not the kind that we're used to hearing. It is the story of the love and devotion of a daughter-in-law for her mother-in-law. The story begins with Ruth as a poor widow. She has nothing but her faith in God and her love for Naomi, her widowed mother-in-law. Ruth refuses to leave Naomi. Ruth's faithfulness is rewarded with marriage to a wealthy man. Even more, the Bible tells us that Ruth will become the great-grandmother of the famous King David. So Ruth is also an ancestor of Jesus. You will enjoy this dramatic story of tragedy, hope for the future, and faith in God.

Chap. 3

Head lines

- Desperate Widow Sends Sons' Wives Away! (1:1–14)
- Faithful Daughter-in-law Refuses to Leave (1:16–22)
- Rich Relative Helps Ruth (2:1–16)
- Boaz Takes Off Sandal, Seals Deal! (4:1–12)
- Boy Destined for Fame! (4:13–22)

FACTOIDS

Who wrote this book? The author is not known.

When was it written? The story of Ruth is set during the time of the judges, but the book was written much later than that.

Why was it written? Ruth was written to remind people of the values of faithfulness, obedience, and love. Ruth is offered as the model of all these things even though she is a foreigner.

What is the Jesus connection? Ruth is the great-grandmother of King David. David was a shepherd as a young man. He was the ancestor of Jesus who would also be called shepherd and king.

Important themes

- Faithfulness and generosity will be rewarded.
- God works through ordinary people.
- God's love and favor extends to people of different faiths and cultures.

RUTH

Elimelech and His Family Move to Moab

1 ¹⁻²Long ago, in the days before Israel had a king, there was a famine in the land. So a man named Elimelech, who belonged to the clan of Ephrath and who lived in Bethlehem in Judah, went with his wife Naomi and their two sons Mahlon and Chilion to live for a while in the country of Moab. While they were living there, ³Elimelech died, and Naomi was left alone with her two sons, ⁴who married Moabite women, Orpah and Ruth. About ten years later ⁵Mahlon and Chilion also died, and Naomi was left all alone, without husband or sons.

Naomi and Ruth Return to Bethlehem

⁶Some time later Naomi heard that the LORD had blessed his people by giving them good crops; so she got ready to leave Moab with her daughters-in-law. ⁷They started out together to go back to Judah, but on the way ⁸she said to them, "Go back home and stay with your mothers. May the LORD be as good to you as you have been to me and to those who have died. ⁹And may the LORD make it possible for each of you to marry again and have a home."

So Naomi kissed them good-bye. But they started crying ¹⁰and said to her, "No! We will go with you to your people."

¹¹"You must go back, my daughters," Naomi answered. "Why do you want to come with me? Do you think I could have sons again for you to marry? ¹²Go back home, for I am too old to get married again. Even if I thought there was still hope, and so got married tonight and had sons, ¹³would you wait until they had grown up? Would this keep you from marrying someone else? No, my daughters, you know that's impossible. The LORD has turned against me, and I feel very sorry for you."[a]

When Bad Things Happen

The events in the Book of Ruth happened a long time ago, but the lessons it teaches can still help us today. Ruth was a widow. Her husband died at a young age before they had any children. In Ruth's time a widow faced poverty and even starvation unless she remarried. Her mother-in-law, Naomi, wants Ruth to go back to her birth family. But Ruth holds tight to her new faith in God and to Naomi, whom she loves and who probably taught Ruth about God. Ruth knows that staying with her new family and counting on God's help is better than each facing hard times alone.

When things get hard, prayer, family, and friendship are sometimes the only things that can get us through. Think of the last time you faced something really sad or difficult. How did you handle it? Whom did you rely on? The next time something bad happens, remember the people you can count on and remember to turn to God.

— Ruth, chapter 1

¹⁴Again they started crying. Then Orpah kissed her mother-in-law good-bye and went back home,[b] but Ruth held on to her. ¹⁵So Naomi said to her, "Ruth, your sister-in-law has gone back to her people and to her god.[c] Go back home with her."

---

[a] **1:13** sorry for you; *or* bitter about what has happened to you.   [b] **1:14** *One ancient translation* and went back home; *Hebrew does not have these words.*   [c] **1:15** god; *or* gods.

16But Ruth answered, "Don't ask me to leave you! Let me go with you. Wherever you go, I will go; wherever you live, I will live. Your people will be my people, and your God will be my God. 17Wherever you die, I will die, and that is where I will be buried. May the LORD's worst punishment come upon me if I let anything but death*d* separate me from you!"

18When Naomi saw that Ruth was determined to go with her, she said nothing more.

19They went on until they came to Bethlehem. When they arrived, the whole town became excited, and the women there exclaimed, "Is this really Naomi?"

They went on until they came to Bethlehem. (1:19)

20"Don't call me Naomi," she answered; "call me Marah,*e* because Almighty God has made my life bitter. 21When I left here, I had plenty, but the LORD has brought me back without a thing. Why call me Naomi when the LORD Almighty has condemned me and sent me trouble?"

22This, then, was how Naomi came back from Moab with Ruth, her Moabite daughter-in-law. When they arrived in Bethlehem, the barley harvest was just beginning.

Ruth Works in the Field of Boaz

2 1Naomi had a relative named Boaz, a rich and influential man who belonged to the family of her husband Elimelech.

2One day Ruth said to Naomi, "Let me go to the fields to gather the grain that the harvest workers leave. I am sure to find someone who will let me work with him."

Naomi answered, "Go ahead, daughter."

3So Ruth went out to the fields and walked behind the workers, picking up the heads of grain which they left. It so happened that she was in a field that belonged to Boaz.

Ruth went out . . . picking up the heads of grain. (2:3)

4Some time later Boaz himself arrived from Bethlehem and greeted the workers. "The LORD be with you!" he said.

"The LORD bless you!" they answered.

5Boaz asked the man in charge, "Who is that young woman?"

6The man answered, "She is the foreigner who came back from Moab with Naomi. 7She asked me to let her follow the workers and gather grain. She has been working since early morning and has just now stopped to rest for a while under the shelter."

8Then Boaz said to Ruth, "Let me give you some advice. Don't gather grain anywhere except in this field. Work with the women here; 9watch them to see where they are reaping and stay with them. I have

d **1:17** *anything but death; or even death.* *e* **1:20** NAOMI . . . MARAH: *In Hebrew Naomi means "pleasant" and Marah means "bitter."*
2:2 Lev 19:9, 10; Deut 24:19

Caring for Poor People

The Law of Moses had strict laws regarding how poor people were to be cared for. They recognized that orphans and widows relied on the kindness of other people. For example, Ruth gleaned in the fields of Boaz, which means she followed the harvesters and picked the grain they left behind. The Law of Moses required that this be allowed to provide for poor people and foreigners (Leviticus 19:9–10).

In a similar way, the Catholic Church teaches that we must love poor people and help provide for their needs. This is sometimes called the preferential love for the poor. There are a number of organizations that put this teaching into action on a national and global scale. The Catholic Campaign for Human Development helps people in the United States. Catholic Relief Services helps people in need all over the world. Both organizations are sponsored by the Catholic Church in the United States and have special opportunities for youth to help. Find their Web sites online and learn more about what you can do.

— Ruth 2:1–3

Catholic Connections

ordered my men not to molest you. And whenever you are thirsty, go and drink from the water jars that they have filled."

¹⁰Ruth bowed down with her face touching the ground, and said to Boaz, "Why should you be so concerned about me? Why should you be so kind to a foreigner?"

¹¹Boaz answered, "I have heard about everything that you have done for your mother-in-law since your husband died. I know how you left your father and mother and your own country and how you came to live among a people you had never known before. ¹²May the LORD reward you for what you have done. May you have a full reward from the LORD God of Israel, to whom you have come for protection!"

¹³Ruth answered, "You are very kindᶠ to me, sir. You have made me feel better by speaking gently to me, even though I am not the equal of one of your servants."

¹⁴At mealtime Boaz said to Ruth, "Come and have a piece of bread, and dip it in the sauce." So she sat with the workers, and Boaz passed some roasted grain to her. She ate until she was satisfied, and she still had some food left over. ¹⁵-¹⁶After she had left to go and gather grain, Boaz ordered the workers, "Let her gather grain even where the bundles are lying, and don't say anything to stop her. Besides that, pull out some heads of grain from the bundles and leave them for her to pick up."

¹⁷So Ruth gathered grain in the field until evening, and when she had beaten it out, she found she had nearly twenty-five pounds. ¹⁸She took the grain back into town and showed her mother-in-law how much she had gathered. She also gave her the food left over from the meal. ¹⁹Naomi asked her, "Where did you gather all this grain today? Whose field have you been working in? May God bless the man who took an interest in you!"

So Ruth told Naomi that she had been

ᶠ **2:13** You are very kind; or Please be kind.

Ruth

Ruth is also a love story. What signs do you see in chapter 2 that Boaz is falling in love with Ruth?

A Good Reputation

What kind of reputation do you have? Do people know you as a kind person? a hard worker? a person with good morals?

Ruth's faithfulness to her mother-in-law is already the talk of the town when Boaz meets her. Often we hear about ugly rumors and negative gossip, but word can also spread when people do good things. Normally, someone like Boaz would be suspicious of Ruth because she is a foreigner. But Ruth's good reputation has made her path smoother. Because Ruth has been kind to Naomi, Boaz is generous to her.

A good reputation generally takes time to build. It comes from consistently being generous, positive, and faithful over time. A good reputation doesn't guarantee success, but it can be a valuable asset. Think about what you want your reputation to be and what you have to do to build it.

— Ruth 2:11–12

working in a field belonging to a man named Boaz.

20"May the LORD bless Boaz!" Naomi exclaimed. "The LORD always keeps his promises to the living and the dead." And she went on, "That man is a close relative of ours, one of those responsible for taking care of us."

21Then Ruth said, "Best of all, he told me to keep gathering grain with his workers until they finish the harvest."

22Naomi said to Ruth, "Yes, daughter, it will be better for you to work with the women in Boaz' field. You might be molested if you went to someone else's field." 23So

Ruth worked with them and gathered grain until all the barley and wheat had been harvested. And she continued to live with her mother-in-law.

Ruth Finds a Husband

3 ¹Some time later Naomi said to Ruth, "I must find a husband for you, so that you will have a home of your own. ²Remember that this man Boaz, whose women you have been working with, is our relative. Now listen. This evening he will be threshing the barley. ³So wash yourself, put on some perfume, and get dressed in your best clothes. Then go where he is threshing, but don't let him know you are there until he has finished eating and drinking. ⁴Be sure to notice where he lies down, and after he falls asleep, go and lift the covers and lie down at his feet. He will tell you what to do."

⁵Ruth answered, "I will do everything you say."

⁶So Ruth went to the threshing place and did just what her mother-in-law had told her. ⁷When Boaz had finished eating and drinking, he was in a good mood. He went to the pile of barley and lay down to sleep. Ruth slipped over quietly, lifted the covers and lay down at his feet. ⁸During the night he woke up suddenly, turned over, and was surprised to find a woman lying at his feet. ⁹"Who are you?" he asked.

"It's Ruth, sir," she answered. "Because you are a close relative, you are responsible for taking care of me. So please marry me."

¹⁰"The LORD bless you," he said. "You are showing even greater family loyalty in what you are doing now than in what you did for your mother-in-law. You might have gone looking for a young man, either rich or poor, but you haven't. ¹¹Now don't worry, Ruth. I will do everything you ask; as everyone in town knows, you are a fine woman. ¹²It is true that I am a close relative and am responsible for you, but there is a man who is a closer relative than I am. ¹³Stay here the rest of the night, and in the morning we will find out whether or not he will take responsibility for you. If so, well and good; if not,

Ruth

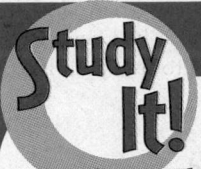

Marriage Then and Now

It probably seems strange that Boaz feels he has to clear it with another relative to marry Ruth. Marriage in Ruth's time was rarely about love. Usually it was an arrangement made by fathers of different families. If the father was dead or far away, then the next closest male relative could make arrangements. The male relative may even have married a widowed woman himself. Ruth's actions are surprising because she appeals on her own behalf to Boaz for his protection.

Boaz does indeed love Ruth and wants to marry her, but he has to clear it with the other male relative. So he makes the arrangements with the city elders and her closest male relative for the marriage. Christian marriage is different because we see marriage as a sacrament that requires the consent of both the man and the woman. This is another sign that our understanding of the rights of women has come quite a way since biblical times.

— Ruth 4:1–12

then I swear by the living LORD that I will take the responsibility. Now lie down and stay here till morning."

¹⁴So she lay there at his feet, but she got up before it was light enough for her to be seen, because Boaz did not want anyone to know that she had been there. ¹⁵Boaz said to her, "Take off your cloak and spread it out here." She did, and he poured out almost fifty pounds of barley and helped her lift it

to her shoulder. Then she returned to town with it. ¹⁶When she arrived home, her mother-in-law asked her, "How did you get along, daughter?"

Ruth told her everything that Boaz had done for her. ¹⁷She added, "He told me I must not come back to you empty-handed, so he gave me all this barley."

¹⁸Naomi said to her, "Now be patient, Ruth, until you see how this all turns out. Boaz will not rest today until he settles the matter."

Boaz Marries Ruth

4 ¹Boaz went to the meeting place at the town gate and sat down there. Then Elimelech's nearest relative, the man whom Boaz had mentioned, came by, and Boaz called to him, "Come over here, my friend, and sit down." So he went over and sat down. ²Then Boaz got ten of the leaders of the town and asked them to sit down there too. When they were seated, ³he said to his relative, "Now that Naomi has come back from Moab, she wants to sell the field that belonged to our relative Elimelech, ⁴and I think you ought to know about it. Now then, if you want it, buy it in the presence of these men sitting here. But if you don't want it, say so, because the right to buy it belongs first to you and then to me."

The man said, "I will buy it."

⁵Boaz said, "Very well, if you buy the field from Naomi, then you are also buying Ruth,ᵍ the Moabite widow, so that the field will stay in the dead man's family."

⁶The man answered, "In that case I will give up my right to buy the field, because it would mean that my own children would not inherit it. You buy it; I would rather not."

⁷Now in those days, to settle a sale or an exchange of property, it was the custom for the seller to take off his sandal and give it to the buyer. In this way the Israelites showed that the matter was settled.

⁸So when the man said to Boaz, "You buy it," he took off his sandal and gave it to Boaz.ʰ ⁹Then Boaz said to the leaders and all

---

ᵍ **4:5** *Some ancient translations* Naomi . . . Ruth; *Hebrew* Naomi and from Ruth.   ʰ **4:8** *One ancient translation* and gave it to Boaz; *Hebrew does not have these words.*
4:7, 8 Deut 25:9   **4:10** Deut 25:5, 6

It was the custom for the seller to take off his sandal.
(4:7)

the others there, "You are all witnesses today
that I have bought from Naomi everything
that belonged to Elimelech and to his sons
Chilion and Mahlon. [10]In addition, Ruth the
Moabite, Mahlon's widow, becomes my wife.
This will keep the property in the dead man's
family, and his family line will continue
among his people and in his hometown. You
are witnesses to this today."

[11]The leaders and the others said, "Yes, we

are witnesses. May the LORD make your
wife become like Rachel and Leah, who
bore many children to Jacob. May you
become rich in the clan of Ephrath and
famous in Bethlehem. [12]May the children
that the LORD will give you by this young
woman make your family like the family of
Perez, the son of Judah and Tamar."

Boaz and His Descendants

[13]So Boaz took Ruth home as his wife.
The LORD blessed her, and she became
pregnant and had a son. [14]The women said
to Naomi, "Praise the LORD! He has given
you a grandson today to take care of you.
May the boy become famous in Israel!
[15]Your daughter-in-law loves you, and has
done more for you than seven sons. And
now she has given you a grandson, who will
bring new life to you and give you security
in your old age." [16]Naomi took the child,
held him close,[i] and took care of him.

[17]The women of the neighborhood
named the boy Obed. They told everyone,
"A son has been born to Naomi!"

Obed became the father of Jesse, who was
the father of David.

[18-22]This is the family line from Perez to
David: Perez, Hezron, Ram, Amminadab,
Nahshon, Salmon, Boaz, Obed, Jesse, David.

[i] **4:16** held him close; *or* adopted him.
4:11 Gen 29:31   **4:12** Gen 38:27–30

Ruth

Your Next Step

Congratulations on finishing the Book of Ruth! Use
this space to write your thoughts and questions
about this book. If you are following the suggested
reading plan, go on to the First Book of Samuel.
This book tells about Samuel, the last judge of
Israel, and about Saul, the first king of Israel.

"Okay, okay—have it your way. But don't say I didn't warn you!"

Perhaps you have heard these words somewhere along the line. This is the message God gives the people through Samuel, the last of the judges. The people want a king. It seems as if that's all they care about. They want to be just like every other nation. So God agrees. That sets into motion a new era in Israel's history. The two books of Samuel, which were originally one long book, tell the stories of the time of change in leadership—from the judges, the military rulers of Israel, to the kings. This will pose a whole new set of challenges for the people. The Israelites and their kings will have to remember that the true king of Israel is God.

Chap. 17

Headlines

- Sleeping Boy Is Awakened by Voice (3:1–19)
- Saul Is Chosen as First King (10:17–27)
- Disobedient King Rejected by God (15:10–23)
- Shepherd Boy Is Anointed Next King (16:1–13)
- Giant Slain with a Slingshot (17:41–54)
- Loyal Prince Risks Life for David (20:9–17)
- Wise Wife Saves Foolish Husband (25:2–35)

FACTOIDS

Why was it written? This book was probably compiled using ancient court records and stories of heroes. It was written to tell the story of the beginning of the monarchy (kings) in Israel.

What time period does it cover? About 1040 to 1000 BC.

How does it fit into the Bible? First and Second Samuel are very important books because they tell the story of Israel's greatest king, David.

Jesus connection: Jesus is from the line of David and is often compared to David.

Important themes

- Faithfulness to God leads to success; disobedience leads to disaster.
- Israel's kings are chosen by God and are responsible for God's interests.
- The person God chooses is often not the person we might choose.

1 SAMUEL

Elkanah and His Family at Shiloh

1 ¹There was a man named Elkanah, from the tribe of Ephraim, who lived in the town of Ramah in the hill country of Ephraim. He was the son of Jeroham and grandson of Elihu, and belonged to the family of Tohu, a part of the clan of Zuph. ²Elkanah had two wives, Hannah and Peninnah. Peninnah had children, but Hannah did not. ³Every year Elkanah went from Ramah to worship and offer sacrifices to the LORD Almighty at Shiloh, where Hophni and Phinehas, the two sons of Eli, were priests of the LORD. ⁴Each time Elkanah offered his sacrifice, he would give one share of the meat to Peninnah and one share to each of her children. ⁵And even though he loved Hannah very much he would give her only one share, because*a* the LORD had kept her from having children. ⁶Peninnah, her rival, would torment and humiliate her, because the LORD had kept her childless. ⁷This went on year after year; whenever they went to the house of the LORD, Peninnah would upset Hannah so much that she would cry and refuse to eat anything. ⁸Her husband Elkanah would ask her, "Hannah, why are you crying? Why won't you eat? Why are you always so sad? Don't I mean more to you than ten sons?"

Hannah and Eli

⁹⁻¹⁰One time, after they had finished their meal in the house of the LORD at Shiloh, Hannah got up. She was deeply distressed, and she cried bitterly as she prayed to the LORD. Meanwhile, Eli the priest was sitting in his place by the door. ¹¹Hannah made a solemn promise: "LORD Almighty, look at me, your servant! See my trouble and remember me! Don't forget me! If you give me a son, I promise that I will dedicate him to you for his whole life and that he will never have his hair cut."*b*

¹²Hannah continued to pray to the LORD for a long time, and Eli watched her lips. ¹³She was praying silently; her lips were

a **1:5** And even . . . because; *or* To Hannah, however, he would give a special share, because he loved her very much, even though. *b* **1:11** NEVER HAVE HIS HAIR CUT: *A sign of dedication to the LORD (see Num 6:5).*
1:11 Num 6:5

Pray It!

I'm Praying, Really!

Hannah is praying silently to the Lord, but her lips are moving. She is begging the Lord to give her a son. Eli, the priest, is watching her and thinks that she must be drunk and tells her to sober up. Have you ever judged someone else's behavior only to find out you were wrong? Try this prayer when you are tempted to judge someone else without knowing what is really going on.

Lord, help me not to be too quick to judge others, especially during a prayer service or Mass. Even though it may look like they are sleeping or daydreaming, they may also be deep in prayer, as I should be at those times. Give me the deep faith of Hannah and let me focus on you during prayer, not the actions of those around me. Amen.

— 1 Samuel 1:12–18

moving, but she made no sound. So Eli thought that she was drunk, ¹⁴and he said to her, "Stop making a drunken show of yourself! Stop your drinking and sober up!"

"Stop making a drunken show of yourself!" (1:14)

¹⁵"No, I'm not drunk, sir," she answered. "I haven't been drinking! I am desperate, and I have been praying, pouring out my troubles to the LORD. ¹⁶Don't think I am a worthless woman. I have been praying like this because I'm so miserable."

¹⁷"Go in peace," Eli said, "and may the God of Israel give you what you have asked him for."

¹⁸"May you always think kindly of me," she replied. Then she went away, ate some food, and was no longer sad.

Samuel's Birth and Dedication

¹⁹The next morning Elkanah and his family got up early, and after worshiping the LORD, they went back home to Ramah. Elkanah had intercourse with his wife Hannah, and the LORD answered her prayer. ²⁰So it was that she became pregnant and gave birth to a son. She named him Samuel,ᶜ and explained, "I asked the LORD for him."

²¹The time came again for Elkanah and his family to go to Shiloh and offer to the LORD the yearly sacrifice and the special sacrifice he had promised. ²²But this time Hannah did not go. She told her husband, "As soon as the child is weaned, I will take him to the house of the LORD, where he will stay all his life."

²³Elkanah answered, "All right, do whatever you think best; stay at home until you have weaned him. And may the LORD make yourᵈ promise come true." So Hannah stayed at home and nursed her child.

²⁴After she had weaned him, she took him to Shiloh, taking along a three-year-old bull,ᵉ a bushel of flour, and a leather bag full of wine. She took Samuel, young as he was, to the house of the LORD at Shiloh. ²⁵After they had killed the bull, they took the child to Eli. ²⁶Hannah said to him, "Excuse me, sir. Do you remember me? I am the woman you saw standing here, praying to the LORD. ²⁷I asked him for this child, and he gave me what I asked for. ²⁸So I am dedicating him to the LORD. As long as he lives, he will belong to the LORD."

Then theyᶠ worshiped the LORD there.

Hannah's Prayer

2 ¹ Hannah prayed:

"The LORD has filled my heart with joy;
   how happy I am because of what he
     has done!
I laugh at my enemies;
   how joyful I am because God has
     helped me!

²"No one is holy like the LORD;
   there is none like him,
   no protector like our God.

ᶜ **1:20** SAMUEL: *This name, which in Hebrew means "name of God," is here related to the Hebrew verb for "ask."*
ᵈ **1:23** *Some ancient translations* your; *Hebrew* his.   ᵉ **1:24** *Some ancient translations* a three-year-old bull; *Hebrew* three bulls.   ᶠ **1:28** *Some ancient translations* they; *Hebrew* he.
2:1–10 Lk 1:46–55

3 Stop your loud boasting;
  silence your proud words.
For the LORD is a God who knows,
  and he judges all that people do.
4 The bows of strong soldiers are broken,
  but the weak grow strong.
5 The people who once were well fed
  now hire themselves out to get food,
  but the hungry are hungry no more.
The childless wife has borne seven
  children,
  but the mother of many is left with
  none.
6 The LORD kills and restores to life;
  he sends people to the world of the
  dead
  and brings them back again.
7 He makes some people poor and others
  rich;
  he humbles some and makes others
  great.
8 He lifts the poor from the dust
  and raises the needy from their misery.
He makes them companions of princes
  and puts them in places of honor.
The foundations of the earth belong to
  the LORD;
  on them he has built the world.

9 "He protects the lives of his faithful
  people,
  but the wicked disappear in darkness;
  a man does not triumph by his own
  strength.
10 The LORD's enemies will be destroyed;
  he will thunder against them from
  heaven.
The LORD will judge the whole world;
  he will give power to his king,
  he will make his chosen king
  victorious."

11 Then Elkanah went back home to
Ramah, but the boy Samuel stayed in Shiloh
and served the LORD under the priest Eli.

The Sons of Eli

12 The sons of Eli were scoundrels. They
paid no attention to the LORD 13 or to the
regulations concerning what the priests

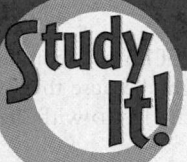

Two Women at Prayer

Read Hannah's prayer at the beginning of 1 Samuel, chapter 2. Hannah is filled with joy because God heard her prayer for a son. Now turn to the Gospel of Luke and read Luke 1:46–55. This is Mary's prayer when she visits her cousin Elizabeth. Notice all the similarities between the two prayers. Both women gave birth to sons who were destined for greatness.

Hannah and Elizabeth, although separated by one thousand years, also have a lot in common. Neither woman could have children, but finally both were given a son. Their sons, Samuel and John the Baptist, play key roles in preparing the way for great kings. Samuel anointed King David, and John baptized Jesus.

— 1 Samuel 2:1–10

could demand from the people. Instead, when someone was offering a sacrifice, the priest's servant would come with a three-pronged fork. While the meat was still cooking, 14 he would stick the fork into the cooking pot, and whatever the fork brought out belonged to the priest. All the Israelites who came to Shiloh to offer sacrifices were treated like this. 15 In addition, even before the fat was taken off and burned, the priest's servant would come and say to the one offering the sacrifice, "Give me some meat for the priest to roast; he won't accept boiled meat from you, only raw meat."

16 If the person answered, "Let us do what is right and burn the fat first; then take what you want," the priest's servant would say,

I Samuel

"No! Give it to me now! If you don't, I will have to take it by force!"

17 This sin of the sons of Eli was extremely serious in the LORD's sight, because they treated the offerings to the LORD with such disrespect.

Samuel at Shiloh

18 In the meantime the boy Samuel continued to serve the LORD, wearing a sacred linen apron. 19 Each year his mother would make a little robe and take it to him when she accompanied her husband to offer the yearly sacrifice. 20 Then Eli would bless Elkanah and his wife, and say to Elkanah, "May the LORD give you other children by this woman to take the place of the one you dedicated to him."

Each year his mother would make a little robe. (2:19)

After that they would go back home. 21 The LORD did bless Hannah, and she had three more sons and two daughters. The boy Samuel grew up in the service of the LORD.

Eli and His Sons

22 Eli was now very old. He kept hearing about everything his sons were doing to the Israelites and that they were even sleeping with the women who worked at the entrance to the Tent of the LORD's presence. 23 So he said to them, "Why are you doing these things? Everybody tells me about the evil you are doing. 24 Stop it, my sons! This is an awful thing the people of the LORD are talking about! 25 If anyone sins against someone else, God can defend the one who is wrong; but who can defend someone who sins against the LORD?"

But they would not listen to their father, for the LORD had decided to kill them.

26 The boy Samuel continued to grow and to gain favor both with the LORD and with people.

The Prophecy against Eli's Family

27 A prophet came to Eli with this message from the LORD: "When your ancestor Aaron and his family were slaves of the king of Egypt, I revealed myself to Aaron. 28 From all the tribes of Israel I chose his family to be my priests, to serve at the altar, to burn the incense, and to wear the ephod*g* to consult me. And I gave them the right to keep a share of the sacrifices burned on the altar. 29 Why, then, do you look with greed*h* at the sacrifices and offerings which I require from my people? Why, Eli, do you honor your sons more than me by letting them fatten themselves on the best parts of all the sacrifices my people offer to me? 30 I, the LORD God of Israel, promised in the past that your family and your clan would serve me as priests for all time. But now I say that I won't have it any longer! Instead, I will honor those who honor me, and I will treat with contempt those who despise me. 31 Listen, the time is coming when I will kill all the young men in your family and your clan, so that no man in your family will live to be old. 32 You will be troubled and look with envy*i* on all the blessings I will give to the other people of Israel, but no one in your family will ever again live to old age. 33 Yet I will keep one of your descendants alive, and he will serve me as priest. But he*j* will become blind and lose all

g 2:28 EPHOD: *See Word List.*   *h* 2:29 *One ancient translation* look with greed; *Hebrew unclear.*   *i* 2:32 *Probable text* look with envy; *Hebrew unclear.*   *j* 2:33 *One ancient translation* he; *Hebrew* you.
2:26 Sir 46:13; Lk 2:52   2:28 a Ex 28:1–4; b Lev 7:35, 36

Pray It!

Speak, Lord

Read the wonderful story of God calling young Samuel (1 Samuel 3:1–14). At first Samuel thinks it is Eli calling him, and so he asks Eli what he wants. Then Eli catches on. He knows that God is calling Samuel, and suggests a great response to Samuel: "Speak, LORD, your servant is listening." This is a great way for us to hear God as well. Here are a few prayer ideas you can try using.

- Read a Bible passage and then say, "Speak, Lord, your servant is listening."
- Tell God about a problem you are dealing with. Then say, "Speak, Lord, your servant is listening."
- Place yourself in a quiet space and say, "Speak, Lord, your servant is listening." To make it even more personal, add your own name after the phrase "your servant." Repeat the phrase a few times, and then sit quietly and listen.

— 1 Samuel 3:1–10

hope, and all your other descendants will die a violent death. ³⁴When your two sons Hophni and Phinehas both die on the same day, this will show you that everything I have said will come true. ³⁵I will choose a priest who will be faithful to me and do everything I want him to. I will give him descendants, who will always serve in the presence of my chosen king. ³⁶Any of your descendants who survive will have to go to that priest and ask him for money and food, and beg to be allowed to help the priests, in order to have something to eat."

The LORD Appears to Samuel

3 ¹In those days, when the boy Samuel was serving the LORD under the direction of Eli, there were very few messages from the LORD, and visions from him were quite rare. ²One night Eli, who was now almost blind, was sleeping in his own room; ³Samuel was sleeping in the sanctuary, where the sacred Covenant Box was. Before dawn, while the lamp was still burning, ⁴the LORD called Samuel. He answered, "Yes, sir!" ⁵and

ran to Eli and said, "You called me, and here I am."

But Eli answered, "I didn't call you; go back to bed." So Samuel went back to bed.

⁶⁻⁷The LORD called Samuel again. The boy did not know that it was the LORD, because the LORD had never spoken to him before. So he got up, went to Eli, and said, "You called me, and here I am."

But Eli answered, "My son, I didn't call you; go back to bed."

⁸The LORD called Samuel a third time; he got up, went to Eli, and said, "You called me, and here I am."

Then Eli realized that it was the LORD who was calling the boy, ⁹so he said to him, "Go back to bed; and if he calls you again, say, 'Speak, LORD, your servant is listening.'" So Samuel went back to bed.

¹⁰The LORD came and stood there, and called as he had before, "Samuel! Samuel!"

Samuel answered, "Speak; your servant is listening."

¹¹The LORD said to him, "Some day I am going to do something to the people of Israel

1 Samuel

2:34 1 Sam 4:11

Eli's ancestor is Aaron, the first high priest of the Israelites.
Who were Aaron's brother and sister (see Exodus, chapters 4 and 15)?

"Speak; your servant is listening." (3:10)

that is so terrible that everyone who hears about it will be stunned. 12On that day I will carry out all my threats against Eli's family, from beginning to end. 13I have already told him[k] that I am going to punish his family forever because his sons have spoken evil things against me. Eli knew they were doing this, but he did not stop them. 14So I solemnly declare to the family of Eli that no sacrifice or offering will ever be able to remove the consequences of this terrible sin."

15Samuel stayed in bed until morning; then he got up and opened the doors of the house of the LORD. He was afraid to tell Eli about the vision. 16Eli called him, "Samuel, my boy!"

"Yes, sir," answered Samuel.

17"What did the LORD tell you?" Eli asked. "Don't keep anything from me. God will punish you severely if you don't tell me everything he said." 18So Samuel told him everything; he did not keep anything back. Eli said, "He is the LORD; he will do whatever seems best to him."

19As Samuel grew up, the LORD was with him and made come true everything that Samuel said. 20So all the people of Israel, from one end of the country to the other, knew that Samuel was indeed a prophet of the LORD. 21The LORD continued to reveal himself at Shiloh, where he had appeared to Samuel and had spoken to him. And when Samuel spoke, all Israel listened.

The Capture of the Covenant Box

4 1At that time the Philistines gathered to go to war against Israel, so[l] the Israelites set out to fight them. The Israelites set up their camp at Ebenezer and the Philistines at Aphek. 2The Philistines attacked, and after fierce fighting they defeated the Israelites and killed about four thousand men on the battlefield. 3When the survivors came back to camp, the leaders of Israel said, "Why did the LORD let the Philistines defeat us today? Let's go and bring the LORD's Covenant Box from Shiloh, so that he[m] will go with us and save us from our enemies." 4So they sent messengers to Shiloh and got the Covenant Box of the LORD Almighty, who is enthroned above the winged creatures.[n] And Eli's two sons, Hophni and Phinehas, came along with the Covenant Box.

5When the Covenant Box arrived, the Israelites gave such a loud shout of joy that the earth shook. 6The Philistines heard the shouting and said, "Listen to all that shouting in the Hebrew camp! What does it mean?" When they found out that the LORD's Covenant Box had arrived in the Hebrew camp, 7they were afraid, and said, "A god has come into their camp! We're lost! Nothing like this has ever happened to us before! 8Who can save us from those powerful gods? They are the gods who slaughtered the Egyptians in the desert! 9Be brave, Philistines! Fight like men, or we will become slaves to the Hebrews, just as they were our slaves. So fight like men!"

10The Philistines fought hard and defeated the Israelites, who went running to their homes. There was a great slaughter: thirty thousand Israelite soldiers were killed. 11God's Covenant Box was captured, and Eli's sons, Hophni and Phinehas, were both killed.

k **3:13** *One ancient translation* I have already told him; *Hebrew* I will tell him.   l **4:1** *One ancient translation* the Philistines . . . so; *Hebrew does not have these words.*   m **4:3** he; *or it.*   n **4:4** WINGED CREATURES: *See Word List.* **4:4** Ex 25:22

Thousands! Add up the number of Israelites the Philistines killed in I Samuel, chapter 4. Keep in mind that sometimes numbers are exaggerated in the Bible.

The Death of Eli

12 A man from the tribe of Benjamin ran all the way from the battlefield to Shiloh and arrived there the same day. To show his grief, he had torn his clothes and put dirt on his head. 13 Eli, who was very worried about the Covenant Box, was sitting in his seat beside the road, staring. The man spread the news throughout the town, and everyone cried out in fear. 14 Eli heard the noise and asked, "What is all this noise about?" The man hurried to Eli to tell him the news. (15 Eli was now ninety-eight years old and almost completely blind.) 16 The man said, "I have escaped from the battle and have run all the way here today."

Eli asked him, "What happened, my son?"

17 The messenger answered, "Israel ran away from the Philistines; it was a terrible defeat for us! Besides that, your sons Hophni and Phinehas were killed, and God's Covenant Box was captured!"

18 When the man mentioned the Covenant Box, Eli fell backward from his seat beside the gate. He was so old and fat that the fall broke his neck, and he died. He had been a leader in Israel for forty years.

The Death of the Widow of Phinehas

19 Eli's daughter-in-law, the wife of Phinehas, was pregnant, and it was almost time for her baby to be born. When she heard that God's Covenant Box had been captured and that her father-in-law and her husband were dead, she suddenly went into labor and gave birth. 20 As she was dying, the women helping her said to her, "Be brave! You have a son!" But she paid no attention and did not answer. 21 She named the boy Ichabod,[o] explaining, "God's glory has left Israel"— referring to the capture of the Covenant Box and the death of her father-in-law and her husband. 22 "God's glory has left Israel," she said, "because God's Covenant Box has been captured."

The Covenant Box among the Philistines

5 1 After the Philistines captured the Covenant Box, they carried it from Ebenezer to their city of Ashdod, 2 took it into the temple of their god Dagon, and set it up beside his statue. 3 Early the next morning the people of Ashdod saw that the statue of Dagon had fallen face downward on the ground in front of the LORD's Covenant Box. So they lifted it up and put it back in its place. 4 Early the following morning they saw that the statue had again fallen down in front of the Covenant Box. This time its head and both its arms were broken off and were lying in the doorway; only the body was left. (5 That is why even today the priests of Dagon and all his worshipers in Ashdod step over that place and do not walk on it.)

6 The LORD punished the people of Ashdod severely and terrified them. He punished them and the people in the surrounding territory by causing them to have tumors.[p] 7 When they saw what was happening, they said, "The God of Israel is punishing us and our god Dagon. We can't let the Covenant Box stay here any longer." 8 So they sent messengers and called together all five of the Philistine kings and asked them, "What shall we do with the Covenant Box of the God of Israel?"

"Take it over to Gath," they answered; so they took it to Gath, another Philistine city. 9 But after it arrived there, the LORD punished that city too and caused a great panic. He punished them with tumors which developed in all the people of the city, young and old alike. 10 So they sent the Covenant Box to Ekron, another Philistine city; but when it arrived there, the people cried out, "They have brought the Covenant Box of the God of Israel here, in order to kill us all!" 11 So again they sent for all the Philistine kings and said, "Send the Covenant Box of Israel back to its own place, so that it won't kill us and our families." There was panic throughout the city because God was punishing them so severely. 12 Even those who did not die developed tumors and the people cried out to their gods for help.

o 4:21 ICHABOD: *This name in Hebrew means "no glory."* p 5:6 TUMORS: *The association of tumors with an abundance of mice suggests that this was a case of bubonic plague (see 6:5).*

Stealing Has Consequences

The Covenant Box—also know as the Ark of the Covenant—was the holiest object in all of Israel. That it had been stolen was so shocking that it caused old Eli to fall out of his chair and break his neck (1 Samuel 4:18). Note what happened to the Philistines after they had stolen the Covenant Box. Many people developed tumors, and some even died. Soon, they couldn't wait to get rid of it. So, what's the point of this story?

One point is that there are consequences for stealing. When we take something that is of value to someone else, we rarely get away with it. We may not get tumors like the Philistines, but we may get caught and have to face legal consequences or the loss of a friendship. Even if we don't get caught, we have taken what does not belong to us, and that is a violation of God's Law, a sin. If we don't seek forgiveness, our hearts begin to harden. We no longer care about the effects of our actions on others. We drift away from God.

Have you ever had to return something you stole and ask for forgiveness? That can serve as a powerful lesson and helps to make things right—with others and with God.

— 1 Samuel, chapter 5

The Return of the Covenant Box

6 ¹After the LORD's Covenant Box had been in Philistia for seven months, ²the people called the priests and the magicians and asked, "What shall we do with the Covenant Box of the LORD? If we send it back where it belongs, what shall we send with it?"

³They answered, "If you return the Covenant Box of the God of Israel, you must, of course, send with it a gift to him to pay for your sin. The Covenant Box must not go back without a gift. In this way you will be healed, and you will find out why he has kept on punishing you."

⁴"What gift shall we send him?" the people asked.

They answered, "Five gold models of tumors and five gold mice, one of each for each Philistine king. The same plague was sent on all of you and on the five kings. ⁵You must make these models of the tumors and of the mice that are ravaging your country, and you must give honor to the God of Israel. Perhaps he will stop punishing you, your gods, and your land. ⁶Why should you be stubborn, as the king of Egypt and the Egyptians were? Don't forget how God made fools of them until they let the Israelites leave Egypt. ⁷So prepare a new wagon and two cows that have never been yoked; hitch them to the wagon and drive their calves back to the barn. ⁸Take the LORD's Covenant Box, put it on the wagon, and place in a box beside it the gold models that you are sending to him as a gift to pay for your sins. Start the wagon on its way and let it go by itself. ⁹Then watch it go; if it goes toward the town of Beth Shemesh, this means that it is the God of the Israelites who has sent this terrible disaster on us. But if it doesn't, then we will know that he did not send the plague; it was only a matter of chance."

¹⁰They did what they were told: they took two cows and hitched them to the wagon, and shut the calves in the barn. ¹¹They put the Covenant Box in the wagon, together with the box containing the gold models of the mice and of the tumors. ¹²The cows started off on the road to Beth Shemesh and headed straight toward it, without turning off the road. They were mooing as they went. The five Philistine kings followed them as far as the border of Beth Shemesh.

¹³The people of Beth Shemesh were reaping wheat in the valley, when suddenly

they looked up and saw the Covenant Box. They were overjoyed at the sight. ¹⁴The wagon came to a field belonging to a man named Joshua, who lived in Beth Shemesh, and it stopped there near a large rock. The people chopped up the wooden wagon and killed the cows and burned them as a burnt sacrifice to the LORD. ¹⁵The Levites lifted off the Covenant Box of the LORD and the box with the gold models in it, and placed them on the large rock. Then the people of Beth Shemesh offered burnt sacrifices and other sacrifices to the LORD. ¹⁶The five Philistine kings watched them do this and then went back to Ekron that same day.

The wagon came to a field belonging to a man named Joshua. (6:14)

¹⁷The Philistines sent the five gold tumors to the LORD as a gift to pay for their sins, one each for the cities of Ashdod, Gaza, Ashkelon, Gath, and Ekron. ¹⁸They also sent gold mice, one for each of the cities ruled by the five Philistine kings, both the fortified towns and the villages without walls. The large rock in the field of Joshua of Beth Shemesh, on which they placed the LORD's Covenant Box, is still there as a witness to what happened.

¹⁹The LORD killed seventy of the men of Beth Shemesh because they looked inside the Covenant Box. And the people mourned

because the LORD had caused such a great slaughter among them.

The Covenant Box at Kiriath Jearim

²⁰So the men of Beth Shemesh said, "Who can stand before the LORD, this holy God? Where can we send him to get him away from us?" ²¹They sent messengers to the people of Kiriath Jearim to say, "The Philistines have returned the LORD's Covenant Box. Come down and get it."

7 ¹ So the people of Kiriath Jearim got the LORD's Covenant Box and took it to the house of a man named Abinadab, who lived on a hill. They consecrated his son Eleazar to be in charge of it.

Samuel Rules Israel

²The Covenant Box of the LORD stayed in Kiriath Jearim a long time, some twenty years. During this time all the Israelites cried to the LORD for help.

³Samuel said to the people of Israel, "If you are going to turn to the LORD with all your hearts, you must get rid of all the foreign gods and the images of the goddess Astarte. Dedicate yourselves completely to the LORD and worship only him, and he will rescue you from the power of the Philistines." ⁴So the Israelites got rid of their idols of Baal and Astarte, and worshiped only the LORD.

⁵Then Samuel called for all the Israelites to meet at Mizpah, telling them, "I will pray to the LORD for you there." ⁶So they all gathered at Mizpah. They drew some water and poured it out as an offering to the LORD and fasted that whole day. They said, "We have sinned against the LORD." (It was at Mizpah where Samuel settled disputes among the Israelites.)

⁷When the Philistines heard that the Israelites had gathered at Mizpah, the five Philistine kings started out with their men to attack them. The Israelites heard about it and

7:1 2 Sam 6:2–4; 1 Chr 13:5–7

I Samuel

were afraid, ⁸and said to Samuel, "Keep praying to the LORD our God to save us from the Philistines." ⁹Samuel killed a young lamb and burned it whole as a sacrifice to the LORD. Then he prayed to the LORD to help Israel, and the LORD answered his prayer. ¹⁰While Samuel was offering the sacrifice, the Philistines moved forward to attack; but just then the LORD thundered from heaven against them. They became completely confused and fled in panic. ¹¹The Israelites marched out from Mizpah and pursued the Philistines almost as far as Bethcar, killing them along the way.

¹²Then Samuel took a stone, set it up between Mizpah and Shen, and said, "The LORD has helped us all the way"—and he named it "Stone of Help." ¹³So the Philistines were defeated, and the LORD prevented them from invading Israel's territory as long as Samuel lived. ¹⁴All the cities which the Philistines had captured between Ekron and Gath were returned to Israel, and so Israel got back all its territory. And there was peace also between the Israelites and the Canaanites.

¹⁵Samuel ruled Israel as long as he lived. ¹⁶Every year he would go around to Bethel, Gilgal, and Mizpah, and in these places he would settle disputes. ¹⁷Then he would go back to his home in Ramah, where also he would serve as judge. In Ramah he built an altar to the LORD.

The People Ask for a King

8 ¹When Samuel grew old, he made his sons judges in Israel. ²The older son was named Joel and the younger one Abijah; they were judges in Beersheba. ³But they did not follow their father's example; they were interested only in making money, so they accepted bribes and did not decide cases honestly.

⁴Then all the leaders of Israel met together, went to Samuel in Ramah, ⁵and said to him, "Look, you are getting old and your sons

don't follow your example. So then, appoint a king to rule over us, so that we will have a king, as other countries have." ⁶Samuel was displeased with their request for a king; so he prayed to the LORD, ⁷and the LORD said, "Listen to everything the people say to you.

Live It!

Who's the King?

So, who is in charge around here?

That is a question that could have been asked by almost any of Israel's neighbors because the Israelites had no clear ruler. The question is one of authority. A lot of times, we don't really like to be told what to do. You probably feel this way a lot at home or in school. It almost seems as if adults have it in for you. Why can't they just leave you alone?

That's a good question. Here's an answer. We need to realize that in order for the world to work right, we need leaders. Good leaders challenge us to work together and inspire us to be the best people we can be. Ultimately, our leader is God. God is The Authority. The best leaders are those who carry out the will of God in all that they do.

Like all their neighbors, the Israelites wanted to have a king, a definite person in charge. Samuel is worried that they will forget who is really in charge. We may forget, too. If God is not number 1 in our lives, we need to look at what is.

— 1 Samuel, chapter 8

7:9 Sir 46:16–18   **8:5** Deut 17:14

I Samuel

Samuel tells the people that having a king will change their lives. Name at least five changes that Samuel lists.

You are not the one they have rejected; I am the one they have rejected as their king. 8 Ever since I brought them out of Egypt, they have turned away from me and worshiped other gods; and now they are doing to you what they have always done to me. 9 So then, listen to them, but give them strict warnings and explain how their kings will treat them."

10 Samuel told the people who were asking him for a king everything that the LORD had said to him. 11 "This is how your king will treat you," Samuel explained. "He will make soldiers of your sons; some of them will serve in his war chariots, others in his cavalry, and others will run before his chariots. 12 He will make some of them officers in charge of a thousand men, and others in charge of fifty men. Your sons will have to plow his fields, harvest his crops, and make his weapons and the equipment for his chariots. 13 Your daughters will have to make perfumes for him and work as his cooks and his bakers. 14 He will take your best fields, vineyards, and olive groves, and give them to his officials. 15 He will take a tenth of your grain and of your grapes for his court officers and other officials. 16 He will take your servants and your best cattle q and donkeys, and make them work for him. 17 He will take a tenth of your flocks. And you yourselves will become his slaves. 18 When that time comes, you will complain bitterly because of your king, whom you yourselves chose, but the LORD will not listen to your complaints."

19 The people paid no attention to Samuel, but said, "No! We want a king, 20 so that we will be like other nations, with our own king to rule us and to lead us out to war and to fight our battles." 21 Samuel listened to everything they said and then went and told it to the LORD. 22 The LORD answered, "Do what they want and give them a king." Then Samuel told all the men of Israel to go back home.

Saul Meets Samuel

9 1 There was a wealthy and influential man named Kish, from the tribe of Benjamin; he was the son of Abiel and grandson of Zeror, and belonged to the family of Becorath, a part of the clan of Aphiah. 2 He had a son named Saul, a handsome man in the prime of life. Saul was a foot taller than anyone else in Israel and more handsome as well.

3 Some donkeys belonging to Kish had wandered off, so he said to Saul, "Take one of the servants with you and go and look for the donkeys." 4 They went through the hill country of Ephraim and the region of Shalishah, but did not find them; so they went on through the region of Shaalim, but the donkeys were not there. Then they went through the territory of Benjamin, but still did not find them. 5 When they came into the region of Zuph, Saul said to his servant, "Let's go back home, or my father might stop thinking about the donkeys and start worrying about us."

6 The servant answered, "Wait! In this town there is a holy man who is highly respected because everything he says comes true. Let's go to him, and maybe he can tell us where we can find the donkeys."

7 "If we go to him, what can we give him?" Saul asked. "There is no food left in our packs, and we don't have a thing to give him, do we?"

8 The servant answered, "I have a small silver coin. I can give him that, and then he will tell us where we can find them."

9-11 Saul replied, "A good idea! Let's go." So they went to the town where the holy man lived. As they were going up the hill to the town, they met some young women who were coming out to draw water. They asked these women, "Is the seer in town?"

(At that time a prophet was called a seer, and so whenever someone wanted to ask God a question, he would say, "Let's go to the seer.")

12-13 "Yes, he is," the young women answered. "In fact, he is just ahead of you. If you hurry, you will catch up with him. As soon as you go into town, you will find him. He arrived in town today because the people are going to offer a sacrifice on the altar on the hill. The people who are invited won't start eating until he gets there, because

I Samuel

Tall Saul

Saul, the first king, is described as the most handsome man in Israel. He was also a foot taller than anyone else in Israel. No doubt that in our society he would be on the cover of almost every magazine.

Next time you are at a magazine rack, look at all the covers that feature people. Do you see any without someone beautiful or handsome on them? It is very clear that looks and appearance matter a lot in our society. So, where does that leave us? Most of us can never hope to measure up to the standards set by Hollywood. Almost everyone wishes they were better looking or taller or thinner or . . . you fill in the blank!

To the biblical writers, it was important that the first king of Israel stand apart, so Saul is described as being tall and very handsome. However, as we will find out in the stories about Saul, there are other things that are much more important than looks. We cannot all be models or movie stars, but we can be people whom others admire in the things that really matter. And we can all be models of faith, if we work at it.

What one thing can you do today to deepen your relationship with God and strengthen your faith?

— 1 Samuel 9:2

in, they saw Samuel coming out toward them on his way to the place of worship.

15 Now on the previous day the LORD had told Samuel, 16 "Tomorrow about this time I will send you a man from the tribe of Benjamin; anoint him as ruler of my people Israel, and he will rescue them from the Philistines. I have seen the suffering of my people and have heard their cries for help."

17 When Samuel caught sight of Saul, the LORD said to him, "This is the man I told you about. He will rule my people." 18 Then Saul went over to Samuel, who was near the gate, and asked, "Tell me, where does the seer live?"

19 Samuel answered, "I am the seer. Go on ahead of me to the place of worship. Both of you are to eat with me today. Tomorrow morning I will answer all your questions and send you on your way. 20 As for the donkeys that were lost three days ago, don't worry about them; they have already been found. But who is it that the people of Israel want so much?ʳ It is you—you and your father's family."

21 Saul answered, "I belong to the tribe of Benjamin, the smallest tribe in Israel, and my

"I am the seer." (9:19)

he has to bless the sacrifice first. If you go now, you will find him before he goes up the hill to eat." 14 So Saul and his servant went on to the town, and as they were going family is the least important one in the tribe. Why, then, do you talk like this to me?"

22 Then Samuel led Saul and his servant into the large room and gave them a place at the head of the table where the guests, about thirty in all, were seated. 23 Samuel said to the cook, "Bring the piece of meat I gave you, which I told you to set aside." 24 So the cook brought the choice piece of the leg and placed it before Saul. Samuel[s] said, "Look, here is the piece that was kept for you. Eat it. I saved it for you to eat at this time with the people I invited."[t]

So Saul ate with Samuel that day. 25 When they went down from the place of worship to the town, they fixed up a bed for Saul[u] on the roof,[v] 26 and he slept there.[w]

Samuel Anoints Saul as Ruler

At dawn Samuel called to Saul on the roof, "Get up, and I will send you on your way." Saul got up, and he and Samuel went out to the street together. 27 When they arrived at the edge of town, Samuel said to Saul, "Tell the servant to go on ahead of us." The servant left, and Samuel continued, "Stay here a minute, and I will tell you what God has said."

10 1 Then Samuel took a jar of olive oil and poured it on Saul's head, kissed him, and said, "The LORD anoints you as ruler of his people Israel. You will rule his people and protect them from all their enemies. And this is the proof to you that the LORD has chosen you[x] to be the ruler of his people: 2 When you leave me today, you will meet two men near Rachel's tomb at Zelzah in the territory of Benjamin. They will tell you that the donkeys you were looking for have been found, so that your father isn't worried any more about them but about you, and he keeps asking, 'What shall I do

about my son?' 3 You will go on from there until you come to the sacred tree at Tabor, where you will meet three men on their way to offer a sacrifice to God at Bethel. One of them will be leading three young goats, another one will be carrying three loaves of bread, and the third one will have a leather bag full of wine. 4 They will greet you and offer you two of the loaves, which you are to accept. 5 Then you will go to the Hill of God in Gibeah, where there is a Philistine camp. At the entrance to the town you will meet a group of prophets coming down from the altar on the hill, playing harps, drums, flutes, and lyres. They will be dancing and shouting. 6 Suddenly the spirit of the LORD will take control of you, and you will join in their religious dancing and shouting and will become a different person. 7 When these things happen, do whatever God leads you to do. 8 You will go ahead of me to Gilgal, where I will meet you and offer burnt sacrifices and

"The LORD anoints you as ruler of his people." (10:1)

---

[s] 9:24 *Some ancient translations* Samuel; *Hebrew* He (that is, the cook).   [t] 9:24 *Probable text* I saved it . . . invited; *Hebrew unclear.*   [u] 9:25 *One ancient translation* they fixed up a bed for Saul; *Hebrew* he spoke with Saul.   [v] 9:25 ON THE ROOF: *At that time houses had flat roofs, and it was common for people to sleep on them.*   [w] 9:26 *Some ancient translations* and he slept there; *Hebrew* and they got up early.   [x] 10:1 *Some ancient translations* as ruler of his people . . . the LORD has chosen you; *Hebrew does not have these words.*

Can you find three things that looked like accidents that led to Saul's meeting Samuel? What does this say about how God works?

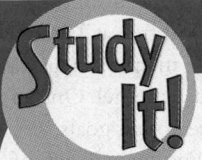

Study It!

Being Anointed

It may seem rather odd that the kings of Israel are anointed rather than crowned, especially when we realize that to be anointed means having olive oil poured over your head. Yet this action is indeed a very important sign. When Samuel pours oil over Saul's head and blesses him, Samuel tells him that he has been chosen and anointed by God. Every king from then on will be anointed in the same way. Anointing with oil is an ancient symbol of holiness. The word *Messiah* in Hebrew and *Christ* in Greek translate as "the Anointed One."

In the Catholic Church, we continue that tradition in the sacraments of Baptism, Confirmation, and Anointing of the Sick. In each of these sacraments, oil is used in the blessing and is a sign that the power of the Holy Spirit is being poured out on the person.

— 1 Samuel 10:1

fellowship sacrifices. Wait there seven days until I come and tell you what to do."

9 When Saul turned to leave Samuel, God gave Saul a new nature. And everything Samuel had told him happened that day. 10 When Saul and his servant arrived at Gibeah, a group of prophets met him. Suddenly the spirit of God took control of him, and he joined in their ecstatic dancing and shouting. 11 People who had known him

before saw him doing this and asked one another, "What has happened to the son of Kish? Has Saul become a prophet?" 12 A man who lived there asked, "How about these other prophets—who do you think their fathers are?" This is how the saying originated, "Has even Saul become a prophet?" 13 When Saul finished his ecstatic dancing and shouting, he went to the altar on the hill.

14 Saul's uncle saw him and the servant, and he asked them, "Where have you been?"

"Looking for the donkeys," Saul answered. "When we couldn't find them, we went to see Samuel."

15 "And what did he tell you?" Saul's uncle asked.

16 "He told us that the animals had been found," Saul answered—but he did not tell his uncle what Samuel had said about his becoming king.

Saul Is Acclaimed as King

17 Samuel called the people together for a religious gathering at Mizpah 18 and said to them, "The LORD, the God of Israel, says, 'I brought you out of Egypt and rescued you from the Egyptians and all the other peoples who were oppressing you. 19 I am your God, the one who rescues you from all your troubles and difficulties, but today you have rejected me and have asked me to give you a king. Very well, then, gather yourselves before the LORD by tribes and by clans.'"

20 Then Samuel had each tribe come forward, and the LORD picked the tribe of Benjamin. 21 Then Samuel had the families of the tribe of Benjamin come forward, and the family of Matri was picked out. Then the men of the family of Matri came forward,*y* and Saul son of Kish was picked out. They looked for him, but when they could not find him, 22 they asked the LORD, "Is there still someone else?"

y **10:21** *One ancient translation* Then the men of the family of Matri came forward; *Hebrew does not have these words.*
10:12 1 Sam 19:23, 24

Saul is acclaimed as king at Mizpah. Locate Mizpah on Map 3 in the back of this Bible. What other important city is it close to?

The LORD answered, "Saul is over there, hiding behind the supplies."

23 So they ran and brought Saul out to the people, and they could see that he was a foot taller than anyone else. 24 Samuel said to the people, "Here is the man the LORD has chosen! There is no one else among us like him."

All the people shouted, "Long live the king!"

25 Samuel explained to the people the rights and duties of a king, and then wrote them in a book, which he deposited in a holy place. Then he sent everyone home. 26 Saul also went back home to Gibeah. Some powerful men,z whose hearts God had touched, went with him. 27 But some worthless people said, "How can this fellow do us any good?" They despised Saul and did not bring him any gifts.

Saul Defeats the Ammonites

11 1 About a month later King Nahash of Ammon led his army against the town of Jabesh in the territory of Gilead and besieged it. The men of Jabesh said to Nahash, "Make a treaty with us, and we will accept you as our ruler."

2 Nahash answered, "I will make a treaty with you on one condition: I will put out everyone's right eye and so bring disgrace on all Israel."

3 The leaders of Jabesh said, "Give us seven days to send messengers throughout the land of Israel. If no one will help us, then we will surrender to you."

4 The messengers arrived at Gibeah, where Saul lived, and when they told the news, the people started crying in despair. 5 Saul was just then coming in from the field with his oxen, and he asked, "What's wrong? Why is everyone crying?" They told him what the messengers from Jabesh had reported. 6 When Saul heard this, the spirit of God took control of him, and he became furious. 7 He took two oxen, cut them in pieces, and had messengers carry the pieces throughout the land of Israel with this warning: "Who-

ever does not follow Saul and Samuel into battle will have this done to his oxen!"

The people of Israel were afraid of what the LORD might do, and all of them, without exception, came out together. 8 Saul gathered them at Bezek: there were 300,000 from Israel and 30,000 from Judah. 9 They said to the messengers from Jabesh, "Tell your people that before noon tomorrow they will be rescued." When the people of Jabesh received the message, they were overjoyed 10 and said to Nahash, "Tomorrow we will surrender to you, and you can do with us whatever you wish."

11 That night Saul divided his men into three groups, and at dawn the next day they rushed into the enemy camp and attacked the Ammonites. By noon they had slaughtered them. The survivors scattered, each man running off by himself.

12 Then the people of Israel said to Samuel, "Where are the people who said that Saul should not be our king? Hand them over to us, and we will kill them!"

13 But Saul said, "No one will be put to death today, for this is the day the LORD rescued Israel." 14 And Samuel said to them, "Let us all go to Gilgal and once more proclaim Saul as our king." 15 So they all went to Gilgal, and there at the holy place they proclaimed Saul king. They offered fellowship sacrifices, and Saul and all the people of Israel celebrated the event.

Samuel Addresses the People

12 1 Then Samuel said to the people of Israel, "I have done what you asked me to do. I have given you a king to rule you, 2 and now you have him to lead you. As for me, I am old and gray, and my sons are with you. I have been your leader from my youth until now. 3 Here I am. If I have done anything wrong, accuse me now in the presence of the LORD and the king he has chosen. Have I taken anybody's cow or anybody's donkey? Have I cheated or oppressed anyone? Have I accepted a bribe from

z **10:26** *One ancient translation* Some powerful men; *Hebrew* The army.
12:3 Sir 46:19

anyone? If I have done any of these things, I will pay back what I have taken."

⁴The people answered, "No, you have not cheated us or oppressed us; you have not taken anything from anyone."

⁵Samuel replied, "The LORD and the king he has chosen are witnesses today that you have found me to be completely innocent."

"Yes, the LORD is our witness," they answered.

⁶Samuel continued, "The LORD is the one who chose Moses and Aaron and who brought your ancestors out of Egypt. ⁷Now stand where you are, and I will accuse you before the LORD by reminding you*ᵃ* of all the mighty actions the LORD did to save you and your ancestors. ⁸When Jacob and his family went to Egypt and the Egyptians oppressed them,*ᵇ* your ancestors cried to the LORD for help, and he sent Moses and Aaron, who brought them out of Egypt and settled them in this land. ⁹But the people forgot the LORD their God, and so he let the Philistines and the king of Moab and Sisera, commander of the army of the city of Hazor, fight against your ancestors and conquer them. ¹⁰Then they cried to the LORD for help and said, 'We have sinned, because we turned away from you, LORD, and worshiped the idols of Baal and Astarte. Rescue us from our enemies, and we will worship you!' ¹¹And the LORD sent Gideon, Barak,*ᶜ* Jephthah, and finally me. Each of us rescued you from your enemies, and you lived in safety. ¹²But when you saw that King Nahash of Ammon was about to attack you, you rejected the LORD as your king and said to me, 'We want a king to rule us.'

¹³"Now here is the king you chose; you asked for him, and now the LORD has given him to you. ¹⁴All will go well with you if you honor the LORD your God, serve him, listen to him, and obey his commands, and if you and your king follow him. ¹⁵But if you do not listen to the LORD but disobey his commands, he will be against you and your king.*ᵈ* ¹⁶So then, stand where you are, and

A Simple Choice

Okay, the Israelites got what they wanted: a king. So now, Samuel lays out for them in simple terms what they need to do: honor, serve, listen, and obey God, and all will go well. If you don't listen to God and disobey, things will not go well.

Isn't this also our choice in life? It seems that when our faith is strong and we try our best to follow God's will, things have a way of working out. Even terrible things—like losing someone we love or dealing with addictions—will gradually get better when we keep trying to put God first. But when we follow another path and shut God out, it doesn't take long for our lives to get pretty messed up.

Think of the bad choices so many young people make: drugs, alcohol, gangs, violence. None of these will bring us closer to God and true happiness. Oh, it may seem so at the time, but it doesn't take long and soon we find ourselves very far from the person God wants us to be. We have not honored, served, listened, or obeyed God. However, it is never too late to turn to God and start over. The Israelites learned this lesson time and time again through their history. What about us?

— 1 Samuel 12:13–15

ᵃ **12:7** *One ancient translation* by reminding you; *Hebrew does not have these words.*   *ᵇ* **12:8** *One ancient translation* and the Egyptians oppressed them; *Hebrew does not have these words.*   *ᶜ* **12:11** *Some ancient translations* Barak; *Hebrew* Bedan.   *ᵈ* **12:15** *One ancient translation* your king; *Hebrew* your ancestors.
12:6 Ex 6:26   **12:8** Ex 2:23   **12:9** a Judg 4:2; b Judg 13:1; c Judg 3:12   **12:10** Judg 10:10–15
12:11 a Judg 7:1; b Judg 4:6; c Judg 11:29; d 1 Sam 3:20   **12:12** 1 Sam 8:19

you will see the great thing which the LORD is going to do. ¹⁷It's the dry season, isn't it? But I will pray, and the LORD will send thunder and rain. When this happens, you will realize that you committed a great sin against the LORD when you asked him for a king."

¹⁸So Samuel prayed, and on that same day the LORD sent thunder and rain. Then all the people became afraid of the LORD and of Samuel, ¹⁹and they said to Samuel, "Please, sir, pray to the LORD your God for us, so that we won't die. We now realize that, besides all our other sins, we have sinned by asking for a king."

²⁰"Don't be afraid," Samuel answered. "Even though you have done such an evil thing, do not turn away from the LORD, but serve him with all your heart. ²¹Don't go after^e false gods; they cannot help you or save you, for they are not real. ²²The LORD has made a solemn promise, and he will not abandon you, for he has decided to make you his own people. ²³As for me, the LORD forbid that I should sin against him by no longer praying for you. Instead, I will teach you what is good and right for you to do. ²⁴Obey the LORD and serve him faithfully with all your heart. Remember the great things he has done for you. ²⁵But if you continue to sin, you and your king will be destroyed."

War against the Philistines

13 ^{f 2}Saul picked three thousand men, keeping two thousand of them with him in Michmash and in the hill country of Bethel and sending one thousand with his son Jonathan to Gibeah, in the territory of the tribe of Benjamin. The rest of the men Saul sent home.

³Jonathan killed the Philistine commander^g in Geba, and all the Philistines

heard about it. Then Saul sent messengers to call the Hebrews to war by blowing a trumpet throughout the whole country. ⁴All the Israelites were told that Saul had killed the Philistine commander and that the Philistines hated them. So the people answered the call to join Saul at Gilgal.

⁵The Philistines assembled to fight the Israelites; they had thirty thousand war chariots, six thousand cavalry troops, and as many soldiers as there are grains of sand on the seashore. They went to Michmash, east of Bethaven, and camped there. ⁶Then they launched a strong attack against the Israelites, putting them in a desperate situation. Some of the Israelites hid in caves and holes or among the rocks or in pits and wells; ⁷others crossed the Jordan River into the territories of Gad and Gilead.

Saul was still at Gilgal, and the people with him were trembling with fear. ⁸He waited seven days for Samuel, as Samuel had instructed him to do, but Samuel still had not come to Gilgal. The people began to desert Saul, ⁹so he said to them, "Bring me the burnt sacrifices and the fellowship sacrifices." He offered a burnt sacrifice, ¹⁰and just as he was finishing, Samuel arrived. Saul went out to meet him and welcome him, ¹¹but Samuel said, "What have you done?"

Saul answered, "The people were deserting me, and you had not come when you said you would; besides that, the Philistines are gathering at Michmash. ¹²So I thought, 'The Philistines are going to attack me here in Gilgal, and I have not tried to win the LORD's favor.' So I felt I had to offer a sacrifice."

¹³"That was a foolish thing to do," Samuel answered. "You have not obeyed the command the LORD your God gave you. If you had obeyed, he would have let you and your descendants rule over Israel forever. ¹⁴But now your rule will not continue. Because

---

^e **12:21** *Some ancient translations* after; *Hebrew* because after.   ^f **13:1** *One ancient translation does not have verse 1; Hebrew has as verse 1* Saul was . . . years old when he became king, and he was king of Israel for two years. *The Hebrew text is defective at two points in this verse.*   ^g **13:3** killed the Philistine commander; *or* defeated the Philistines camping.

13:8 1 Sam 10:8

"Obey the LORD and serve him faithfully with all your heart. Remember the great things he has done for you" (*1 Samuel 12:24*).

you have disobeyed him, the LORD will find the kind of man he wants and make him ruler of his people."

15 Samuel left Gilgal and went on his way. The rest of the people followed Saul as he went to join his soldiers. They went from Gilgal[h] to Gibeah in the territory of Benjamin. Saul inspected his troops, about six hundred men. 16 Saul, his son Jonathan, and their men camped in Geba in the territory of Benjamin; the Philistine camp was at Michmash. 17 The Philistine soldiers went out on raids from their camp in three groups: one group went toward Ophrah in the territory of Shual, 18 another went toward Beth Horon, and the other one went to the border overlooking Zeboim Valley and the wilderness.

19 There were no blacksmiths in Israel because the Philistines were determined to keep the Hebrews from making swords and spears. (20 The Israelites had to go to the Philistines to get their plows, hoes, axes, and sickles[i] sharpened; 21 the charge was one small coin for sharpening axes and for fixing goads,[j] and two coins for sharpening plows or hoes.) 22 And so on the day of battle none of the Israelite soldiers except Saul and his son Jonathan had swords or spears.

23 The Philistines sent a group of soldiers to defend Michmash Pass.

Jonathan's Daring Deed

14 1 One day Jonathan said to the young man who carried his weapons, "Let's go across to the Philistine camp." But Jonathan did not tell his father Saul, 2 who was camping under a pomegranate tree in Migron, not far from Gibeah; he had about six hundred men with him. 3 (The priest carrying the ephod was Ahijah, the son of Ichabod's brother Ahitub, who was

the son of Phinehas and grandson of Eli, the priest of the LORD in Shiloh.) The men did not know that Jonathan had left.

4 In Michmash Pass, which Jonathan had to go through to get over to the Philistine camp, there were two large jagged rocks, one on each side of the pass: one was called Bozez and the other Seneh. 5 One was on the north side of the pass, facing Michmash, and the other was on the south side, facing Geba.

6 Jonathan said to the young man, "Let's cross over to the camp of those heathen Philistines. Maybe the LORD will help us; if he does, nothing can keep him from giving us the victory, no matter how few of us there are."

7 The young man answered, "Whatever you want to do,[k] I'm with you."

8 "All right," Jonathan said. "We will go across and let the Philistines see us. 9 If they tell us to wait for them to come to us, then we will stay where we are. 10 But if they tell us to go to them, then we will, because that will be the sign that the LORD has given us victory over them."

11 So they let the Philistines see them, and the Philistines said, "Look! Some Hebrews are coming out of the holes they have been hiding in!" 12 Then they called out to Jonathan and the young man, "Come on up here! We have something to tell[l] you!"

Jonathan said to the young man, "Follow me. The LORD has given Israel victory over them." 13 Jonathan climbed up out of the pass on his hands and knees, and the young man followed him. Jonathan attacked the Philistines and knocked them down, and the young man killed them. 14 In that first slaughter Jonathan and the young man killed about twenty men in an area of about half an acre.[m] 15 All the Philistines in the countryside were terrified; the raiders and the sol-

---

[h] **13:15** *Some ancient translations* on his way . . . went from Gilgal; *Hebrew does not have these words.*   [i] **13:20** *One ancient translation* sickles; *Hebrew* plows.   [j] **13:21** *Probable text* the charge . . . fixing goads; *Hebrew unclear.*
[k] **14:7** *One ancient translation* you want to do; *Hebrew* you want to do. Turn.   [l] **14:12** tell; *or show.*   [m] **14:14** *Probable text* in an area of about half an acre; *Hebrew unclear.*
13:14 Acts 13:22

Saul's son Jonathan (*1 Samuel 13:2*) **will play a very important role in David's life. Stay tuned.**

diers in the camp trembled with fear; the earth shook, and there was great panic.

The Defeat of the Philistines

[16]Saul's men on watch at Gibeah in the territory of Benjamin saw the Philistines running in confusion. [17]So Saul said to his men, "Count the soldiers and find out who is missing." They did so and found that Jonathan and the young man who carried his weapons were missing. [18]"Bring the ephod[n] here," Saul said to Ahijah the priest. (On that day Ahijah was carrying it in front of the people of Israel.)[o] [19]As Saul was speaking to the priest, the confusion in the Philistine camp kept getting worse, so Saul said to him, "There's no time to consult the LORD!" [20]Then he and his men marched into battle against the Philistines, who were fighting each other in complete confusion. [21]Some Hebrews, who had been on the Philistine side and had gone with them to the camp, changed sides again[p] and joined Saul and Jonathan. [22]Others, who had been hiding in the hills of Ephraim, heard that the Philistines were running away, so they also joined in and attacked the Philistines, [23]fighting all the way beyond Bethaven. The LORD saved Israel that day.

Events after the Battle

[24]The Israelites were weak with hunger that day, because Saul, with a solemn oath, had given the order: "A curse be on anyone who eats any food today before I take revenge on my enemies." So nobody had eaten anything all day. [25]They all[q] came into a wooded area and found honey everywhere. [26]The woods were full of honey, but no one ate any of it because they were all afraid of Saul's curse. [27]But Jonathan had not heard his father threaten the people with a curse; so he reached out with the stick he was carrying, dipped it in a honeycomb, and ate some honey. At once he felt much better.

[28]But one of the men told him, "We are all weak from hunger, but your father threatened us and said, 'A curse be on anyone who eats any food today.' "

[29]Jonathan answered, "What a terrible thing my father has done to our people! See how much better I feel because I ate some honey! [30]How much better it would have been today if our people had eaten the food they took when they defeated the enemy. Just think how many more Philistines they would have killed!"

[31]That day the Israelites defeated the Philistines, fighting all the way from Michmash to Aijalon. By this time the Israelites were very weak from hunger, [32]and so they rushed over to what they had captured from the enemy, took sheep and cattle, slaughtered them on the spot, and ate the meat with the blood still in it. [33]Saul was told, "Look, the people are sinning against the LORD by eating meat with the blood in it."

"You are traitors!" Saul cried out. "Roll a big stone over here[r] to me." [34]Then he gave another order: "Go among the people and tell them all to bring their cattle and sheep here. They are to slaughter them and eat them here; they must not sin against the LORD by eating meat with blood in it." So that night they all brought their cattle and slaughtered them there. [35]Saul built an altar to the LORD, the first one that he built.

[36]Saul said to his men, "Let's go down and attack the Philistines in the night, plunder them until dawn, and kill them all."

"Do whatever you think best," they answered.

But the priest said, "Let's consult God first."

[37]So Saul asked God, "Shall I attack the Philistines? Will you give us victory?" But God did not answer that day. [38]Then Saul said to the leaders of the people, "Come here and find out what sin was committed today. [39]I promise by the living LORD, who gives Israel victory, that the guilty one will be put to death, even if he is my son

---

[n] **14:18** *One ancient translation* ephod (see 2:28); *Hebrew* Covenant Box.   [o] **14:18** *One ancient translation* On that day . . . Israel; *Hebrew* Because on that day God's Covenant Box and the people of Israel.   [p] **14:21** *Some ancient translations* changed sides again; *Hebrew* around also.   [q] **14:25** *Probable text* They all; *Hebrew* All the land.
[r] **14:33** *One ancient translation* here; *Hebrew* today.
14:33 Gen 9:4; Lev 7:26, 27; 17:10–14; 19:26; Deut 12:16, 23; 15:23

Pray It!

"Do Whatever You Think Best"

"Do whatever you think best" is repeated twice by Saul's troops (1 Samuel 14:36,40). It shows that they have confidence in Saul's decisions and will do what he tells them.

This sentence also serves as a deep statement of faith in another person. To know that others are counting on you to do whatever you think best means that they have a lot of confidence in you. This responsibility can be almost scary when you are babysitting or watching over younger brothers or sisters. If there's any danger—a bad storm, someone gets sick, or there is an accident—people are counting on you to do whatever you think is best. If you are in a difficult situation and are unsure what to do, say a prayer to God for guidance. You'd be amazed at how God can calm your fears and show you a way. Even if it doesn't work out perfectly, you will remember that God is with you.

— 1 Samuel 14:36,40

Jonathan." But no one said anything. 40 Then Saul said to them, "All of you stand over there, and Jonathan and I will stand over here."

"Do whatever you think best," they answered.

41 Saul said to the LORD, the God of Israel, "LORD, why have you not answered me today? LORD, God of Israel, answer me by the sacred stones. If the guilt is Jonathan's or mine, answer by the Urim; but if it belongs to your people Israel,*s* answer by the Thummim."*t* The answer indicated Jonathan and Saul; and the people were cleared. 42 Then Saul said, "Decide between my son Jonathan and me." And Jonathan was indicated. 43 Then Saul asked Jonathan, "What have you done?"

Jonathan answered, "I ate a little honey with the stick I was holding. Here I am—I am ready to die."

44 Saul said to him, "May God strike me dead if you are not put to death!"

45 But the people said to Saul, "Will Jonathan, who won this great victory for Israel, be put to death? No! We promise by the living LORD that he will not lose even a hair from his head. What he did today was done with God's help." So the people saved Jonathan from being put to death.

46 After that, Saul stopped pursuing the Philistines, and they went back to their own territory.

Saul's Reign and Family

47 After Saul became king of Israel, he fought all his enemies everywhere: the people of Moab, of Ammon, and of Edom, the kings of Zobah, and the Philistines. Wherever he fought he was victorious.*u* 48 He fought heroically and defeated even the people of Amalek. He saved the Israelites from all attacks.

49 Saul's sons were Jonathan, Ishvi, and Malchishua. His older daughter was named Merab, and the younger one Michal. 50 His wife was Ahinoam, the daughter of Ahimaaz; his army commander was his cousin Abner, the son of his uncle Ner. 51 Saul's father Kish and Abner's father Ner were sons of Abiel.

52 As long as he lived, Saul had to fight

---

s **14:41** *Some ancient translations* answer me by the sacred stones . . . your people Israel; *Hebrew does not have these words.* *t* **14:41** URIM . . . THUMMIM: *Two stones used by the priest to determine God's will; it is not known precisely how they were used.* *u* **14:47** *One ancient translation* was victorious; *Hebrew* acted wickedly.

14:41 Num 27:21; 1 Sam 28:6

fiercely against the Philistines. So whenever he found a man who was strong or brave, he would enlist him in his army.

War against the Amalekites

15 [1] Samuel said to Saul, "I am the one whom the LORD sent to anoint you king of his people Israel. Now listen to what the LORD Almighty says. [2] He is going to punish the people of Amalek because their ancestors opposed the Israelites when they were coming from Egypt. [3] Go and attack the Amalekites and completely destroy everything they have. Don't leave a thing; kill all the men, women, children, and babies; the cattle, sheep, camels, and donkeys."

[4] Saul called his forces together and inspected them at Telem: there were 200,000 soldiers from Israel and 10,000 from Judah. [5] Then he and his men went to the city of Amalek and waited in ambush in a dry riverbed. [6] He sent a warning to the Kenites, a people whose ancestors had been kind to the Israelites when they came from Egypt: "Go away and leave the Amalekites, so that I won't kill you along with them." So the Kenites left.

[7] Saul defeated the Amalekites, fighting all the way from Havilah to Shur, east of Egypt; [8] he captured King Agag of Amalek alive and killed all the people. [9] But Saul and his men spared Agag's life and did not kill the best sheep and cattle, the best calves and lambs,[v] or anything else that was good; they destroyed only what was useless or worthless.[w]

Saul Is Rejected as King

[10] The LORD said to Samuel, [11] "I am sorry that I made Saul king; he has turned away from me and disobeyed my commands." Samuel was angry, and all night long he pleaded with the LORD. [12] Early the following morning he went off to find Saul. He heard that Saul had gone to the town of Carmel, where he had built a monument to himself, and then had gone on to Gilgal. [13] Samuel went up to Saul, who greeted him, saying, "The LORD bless you, Samuel! I have obeyed the LORD's command."

[14] Samuel asked, "Why, then, do I hear cattle mooing and sheep bleating?"

[15] Saul answered, "My men took them from the Amalekites. They kept the best sheep and cattle to offer as a sacrifice to the LORD your God, and the rest we have destroyed completely."[x]

[16] "Stop," Samuel ordered, "and I will tell you what the LORD said to me last night."

"Tell me," Saul said.

[17] Samuel answered, "Even though you consider yourself of no importance, you are the leader of the tribes of Israel. The LORD anointed you king of Israel, [18] and he sent you out with orders to destroy those wicked people of Amalek. He told you to fight until you had killed them all. [19] Why, then, did you not obey him? Why did you rush to grab the loot, and so do what displeases the LORD?"

[20] "I did obey the LORD," Saul replied. "I went out as he told me to, brought back King Agag, and killed all the Amalekites. [21] But my men did not kill the best sheep and cattle that they captured; instead, they brought them here to Gilgal to offer as a sacrifice to the LORD your God."

[22] Samuel said, "Which does the LORD prefer: obedience or offerings and sacrifices? It is better to obey him than to sacrifice the best sheep to him. [23] Rebellion against him is as bad as witchcraft, and arrogance is as sinful as idolatry. Because you rejected the LORD's command, he has rejected you as king."

[24] "Yes, I have sinned," Saul replied. "I disobeyed the LORD's command and your instructions. I was afraid of my men and did

[v] **15:9** *One ancient translation* the best calves and lambs; *Hebrew unclear.*   [w] **15:9** *Some ancient translations* useless or worthless; *Hebrew unclear.*   [x] **15:15** DESTROYED COMPLETELY: *These animals had been unconditionally dedicated to the LORD and had to be destroyed (see Lev 27:28).*
15:1 1 Sam 10:1   **15:2** Ex 17:8–14; Deut 25:17–19

I Samuel

Urim and Thummim were two stones or sticks used by Israelite priests to try to determine God's will. They were probably thrown like dice.

Who Do You Think You Are?

Samuel tells the disobedient Saul that arrogance is as sinful as idolatry. Idolatry means worshiping false gods. What does arrogance mean, and why is it so bad?

To be arrogant is to think that you are better than other people and to act like it. We might also call such a person a snob. While it is not right for us to judge others, we can usually tell when we are in the presence of someone who is arrogant. They have a way of making us feel unimportant or of even ignoring us. It is almost as if they assume that somehow God has made them superior to others. We all know that some of us are richer than others and some of us are better looking or better athletes, but we also know that all of us are created in God's image. God does not approve when we act as if we're better than other people—because then we are not only arrogant toward other people, but we are also arrogant toward God!

Arrogance is often easy to spot in others, but not always easy to see in ourselves. Ask Jesus to help you see if any of your actions or behavior could be seen as arrogant by someone else.

— 1 Samuel 15:17–25

what they wanted. 25 But now I beg you, forgive my sin and go back with me, so that I can worship the LORD."

26 "I will not go back with you," Samuel answered. "You rejected the LORD's command, and he has rejected you as king of Israel."

27 Then Samuel turned to leave, but Saul caught hold of his cloak, and it tore. 28 Samuel said to him, "The LORD has torn the kingdom of Israel away from you today and given it to someone who is a better man than you. 29 Israel's majestic God does not lie or change his mind. He is not a human being—he does not change his mind."

"The LORD has torn the kingdom . . . away from you." (15:28)

30 "I have sinned," Saul replied. "But at least show me respect in front of the leaders of my people and all of Israel. Go back with me so that I can worship the LORD your God." 31 So Samuel went back with him, and Saul worshiped the LORD.

32 "Bring King Agag here to me," Samuel ordered. Agag came to him, trembling with fear, thinking to himself, "What a bitter thing it is to die!" *y* 33 Samuel said, "As your sword has made many mothers childless, so now your mother will become childless." And he cut Agag to pieces in front of the altar in Gilgal.

34 Then Samuel went to Ramah, and King Saul went home to Gibeah. 35 As long as Samuel lived, he never again saw the king; but he grieved over him. The LORD was sorry that he had made Saul king of Israel.

y **15:32** trembling with fear . . . die; *or* confidently, thinking to himself, "Surely the bitter danger of death is past!"
15:27, 28 1 Sam 28:17; 1 Kings 11:30, 31

Jesse is the son of Obed, and Obed is Ruth and Boaz's son. That makes Ruth—who was not an Israelite by birth—King David's great-grandmother.

David Is Anointed King

16 ¹The LORD said to Samuel, "How long will you go on grieving over Saul? I have rejected him as king of Israel. But now get some olive oil and go to Bethlehem, to a man named Jesse, because I have chosen one of his sons to be king."

²"How can I do that?" Samuel asked. "If Saul hears about it, he will kill me!"

The LORD answered, "Take a calf with you and say that you are there to offer a sacrifice to the LORD. ³Invite Jesse to the sacrifice, and I will tell you what to do. You will anoint as king the man I tell you to."

⁴Samuel did what the LORD told him to do and went to Bethlehem, where the city leaders came trembling to meet him and asked, "Is this a peaceful visit, seer?"

⁵"Yes," he answered. "I have come to offer a sacrifice to the LORD. Purify yourselves and come with me." He also told Jesse and his sons to purify themselves, and he invited them to the sacrifice.

⁶When they arrived, Samuel saw Jesse's son Eliab and said to himself, "This man standing here in the LORD's presence is surely the one he has chosen." ⁷But the LORD said to him, "Pay no attention to how tall and handsome he is. I have rejected him, because I do not judge as people judge. They look at the outward appearance, but I look at the heart."

⁸Then Jesse called his son Abinadab and brought him to Samuel. But Samuel said, "No, the LORD hasn't chosen him either." ⁹Jesse then brought Shammah. "No, the LORD hasn't chosen him either," Samuel said. ¹⁰In this way Jesse brought seven of his sons to Samuel. And Samuel said to him, "No, the LORD hasn't chosen any of these." ¹¹Then he asked him, "Do you have any more sons?"

Jesse answered, "There is still the youngest, but he is out taking care of the sheep."

"Tell him to come here," Samuel said. "We won't offer the sacrifice until he comes." ¹²So Jesse sent for him. He was a handsome, healthy young man, and his eyes sparkled. The LORD said to Samuel, "This is the one—anoint him!" ¹³Samuel took the olive oil and anointed David in front of his brothers. Immediately the spirit of the LORD took

Study It!

The Heart of the Matter

God gives Samuel a very important message when he visits Jesse. Samuel has to determine which one of Jesse's eight sons will become the next king. It would make perfect sense that Eliab, the oldest son, would become the king. In biblical times, that's the way it worked: the first-born son would inherit the most. Eliab was also tall and handsome. He seemed like the natural choice. But God tells Samuel: "Pay no attention to how tall and handsome he is. . . . I do not judge as people judge. They look at the outward appearance, but I look at the heart" (1 Samuel 16:7).

So much for being the best looking or the richest or the smartest or the best athlete. That matters little in God's eyes. God cuts right through all of what the world considers important and sees the heart of each person. It is there that the true greatness of a person lies. David is the youngest of his family. In fact, he is not even present when Samuel comes to visit. He is tending the sheep. But God saw in young David what no one else did—a person after his own heart. Sometimes on a team, the coach may choose a player who clearly isn't as gifted an athlete as someone else, but that coach knows that this young person will put his or her heart in it. That often counts for more than ability. Don't ever underestimate yourself. God knows what is in your heart. It doesn't matter what the world thinks.

— 1 Samuel 16:1–13

1 Samuel

control of David and was with him from that day on. Then Samuel returned to Ramah.

David in Saul's Court

14 The LORD's spirit left Saul, and an evil spirit sent by the LORD tormented him. 15 His servants said to him, "We know that an evil spirit sent by God is tormenting you. 16 So give us the order, sir, and we will look for a man who knows how to play the harp. Then when the evil spirit comes on you, the man can play his harp, and you will be all right again."

17 Saul ordered them, "Find me a man who plays well and bring him to me."

18 One of his attendants said, "Jesse of the town of Bethlehem has a son who is a good musician. He is also a brave and handsome man, a good soldier, and an able speaker. The LORD is with him."

19 So Saul sent messengers to Jesse to say, "Send me your son David, the one who takes care of the sheep." 20 Jesse sent David to Saul with a young goat, a donkey loaded with bread, and a leather bag full of wine. 21 David came to Saul and entered his service. Saul liked him very much and chose him as the man to carry his weapons. 22 Then Saul sent a message to Jesse: "I like David. Let him stay here in my service." 23 From then on, whenever the evil spirit sent by God came on Saul, David would get his harp and play it. The evil spirit would leave, and Saul would feel better and be all right again.

David would get his harp and play it. (16:23)

Goliath Challenges the Israelites

17 ¹The Philistines gathered for battle in Socoh, a town in Judah; they camped at a place called Ephes Dammim, between Socoh and Azekah. ²Saul and the

The Power of Music

David had many talents. One was that he could write songs and play the harp. In fact, whenever Saul was tormented by an evil spirit causing Saul to feel bad, David would play his harp. Saul's advisers knew what all of us know today: music can have a powerful effect on our moods. If we've had a bad day, often we turn to our favorite music to help us feel better. Or if we're feeling great, we often turn to music to celebrate as well. Everyone has their favorite songs, their favorite performers, and their favorite types of music. Music is a great gift, and there is an amazing variety of it.

Music should raise us to a higher level. Every major religion includes music in its worship, because music has power to lift us up. It is also true that there are songs and artists whose music often sends negative messages about life and relationships. Music that accepts violence, drug use, and immoral sex does not lift us up but can tear us down. Look at the lyrics (words) of the music you listen to most often. What messages are coming through? What choices can you make to limit your exposure to negative messages in music?

~ 1 Samuel 16:14–23

Israelites assembled and camped in Elah Valley, where they got ready to fight the Philistines. ³The Philistines lined up on one hill and the Israelites on another, with a valley between them.

⁴A man named Goliath, from the city of Gath, came out from the Philistine camp to

"I dare you to pick someone to fight me!" (17:10)

challenge the Israelites. He was over nine feet[z] tall [5]and wore bronze armor that weighed about 125 pounds and a bronze helmet. [6]His legs were also protected by bronze armor, and he carried a bronze javelin slung over his shoulder. [7]His spear was as thick as the bar on a weaver's loom, and its iron head weighed about fifteen pounds. A soldier walked in front of him carrying his shield. [8]Goliath stood and shouted at the Israelites, "What are you doing there, lined up for battle? I am a Philistine, you slaves of Saul! Choose one of your men to fight me. [9]If he wins and kills me, we will be your slaves; but if I win and kill him, you will be our slaves. [10]Here and now I challenge the Israelite army. I dare you to pick someone to fight me!" [11]When Saul and his men heard this, they were terrified.

David in Saul's Camp

[12]David was the son of Jesse, who was an Ephrathite from Bethlehem in Judah. Jesse had eight sons, and at the time Saul was king, he was already a very old man.[a] [13]His three oldest sons had gone with Saul to war. The oldest was Eliab, the next was Abinadab, and the third was Shammah. [14]David was the youngest son, and while the three oldest brothers stayed with Saul, [15]David would go back to Bethlehem from time to time, to take care of his father's sheep.

[16]Goliath challenged the Israelites every morning and evening for forty days.

[17]One day Jesse said to David, "Take a half-bushel of this roasted grain and these ten loaves of bread, and hurry with them to your brothers in the camp. [18]And take these ten cheeses to the commanding officer. Find out how your brothers are getting along and bring back something to show that you saw them and that they are well. [19]King Saul, your brothers, and all the other Israelites are in Elah Valley fighting the Philistines."

[20]David got up early the next morning, left someone else in charge of the sheep, took the food, and went as Jesse had told him to. He arrived at the camp just as the Israelites were going out to their battle line, shouting the war cry. [21]The Philistine and the Israelite armies took positions for battle, facing each other. [22]David left the food with the officer in charge of the supplies, ran to

[z] **17:4** *Hebrew* nine feet; *one ancient Hebrew manuscript and one ancient translation* seven feet.
[a] **17:12** *Some ancient translations* a very old man; *Hebrew unclear.*

Philistia is the land of the Philistines. Locate Goliath's homeland on Map 3 in the back of this Bible.

the battle line, went to his brothers, and asked how they were getting along. 23As he was talking with them, Goliath came forward and challenged the Israelites as he had done before. And David heard him. 24When the Israelites saw Goliath, they ran away in terror. 25"Look at him!" they said to each other. "Listen to his challenge! King Saul has promised to give a big reward to the man who kills him; the king will also give him his daughter to marry and will not require his father's family to pay taxes."b

26David asked the men who were near him, "What will the man get who kills this Philistine and frees Israel from this disgrace? After all, who is this heathen Philistine to defy the army of the living God?" 27They told him what would be done for the man who killed Goliath.

28Eliab, David's oldest brother, heard David talking to the men. He became angry with David and said, "What are you doing here? Who is taking care of those sheep of yours out there in the wilderness? You smart aleck, you! You just came to watch the fighting!"

29"Now what have I done?" David asked. "Can't I even ask a question?" 30He turned to another man and asked him the same question, and every time he asked, he got the same answer.

31Some men heard what David had said, and they told Saul, who sent for him. 32David said to Saul, "Your Majesty, no one should be afraid of this Philistine! I will go and fight him."

33"No," answered Saul. "How could you fight him? You're just a boy, and he has been a soldier all his life!"

34"Your Majesty," David said, "I take care of my father's sheep. Any time a lion or a bear carries off a lamb, 35I go after it, attack it, and rescue the lamb. And if the lion or bear turns on me, I grab it by the throat and beat it to death. 36I have killed lions and bears, and I will do the same to this heathen Philistine, who has defied the army of the living God. 37The LORD has saved me from

b **17:25** to pay taxes; *or* either to pay taxes or serve him.

Taking a Big Risk

The story of David defeating Goliath is one of the best known in the Bible. Think about what a risk David was taking. With only a slingshot, he took on a giant warrior dressed in full armor. We can be sure that what drove David to take on Goliath was his deep faith and trust that God was with him.

Taking risks is an important part of life, but we always have to weigh those risks. At times, some of the risks we face may seem like Goliaths. Sometimes our fears make the risk seem even bigger than it is. Sometimes we decide that the risk is not worth it or will not be a healthy choice for us. We know that abusing drugs or other substances and having any kind of sex before marriage are very dangerous and harmful behaviors. These are bad risks to take! However, challenging ourselves to try a new activity and to reach out to a new person in friendship are risks worth taking. If our faith and trust in God guide us in our decision making, we will most likely take risks that will help us grow, no matter how challenging they seem.

The next time you are thinking of trying something that involves risk, picture David approaching giant Goliath armed with only his slingshot and his deep faith in God.

— 1 Samuel, chapter 17

When David fought Goliath he put his complete trust in God—a good reminder that we also need to put our trust in God every day.

lions and bears; he will save me from this Philistine."

"All right," Saul answered. "Go, and the LORD be with you." 38 He gave his own armor to David for him to wear: a bronze helmet, which he put on David's head, and a coat of armor. 39 David strapped Saul's sword over the armor and tried to walk, but he couldn't, because he wasn't used to wearing them. "I can't fight with all this," he said to Saul. "I'm not used to it." So he took it all off. 40 He took his shepherd's stick and then picked up five smooth stones from the stream and put them in his bag. With his sling ready, he went out to meet Goliath.

"Do you think I'm a dog?" (17:43)

He . . . picked up five smooth stones. (17:40)

David Defeats Goliath

41 The Philistine started walking toward David, with his shield bearer walking in front of him. He kept coming closer, 42 and when he got a good look at David, he was filled with scorn for him because he was just a nice, good-looking boy. 43 He said to David, "What's that stick for? Do you think I'm a dog?" And he called down curses from his god on David. 44 "Come on," he challenged David, "and I will give your body to the birds and animals to eat."

45 David answered, "You are coming against me with sword, spear, and javelin, but I come against you in the name of the LORD Almighty, the God of the Israelite armies, which you have defied. 46 This very day the LORD will put you in my power; I will defeat you and cut off your head. And I will give the bodies of the Philistine soldiers to the birds and animals to eat. Then the whole

world will know that Israel has a God, 47 and everyone here will see that the LORD does not need swords or spears to save his people. He is victorious in battle, and he will put all of you in our power."

48 Goliath started walking toward David again, and David ran quickly toward the Philistine battle line to fight him. 49 He reached into his bag and took out a stone, which he slung at Goliath. It hit him on the forehead and broke his skull, and Goliath fell face downward on the ground. 50 And so, without a sword, David defeated and killed Goliath with a sling and a stone! 51 He ran to him, stood over him, took Goliath's sword out of its sheath, and cut off his head and killed him.

When the Philistines saw that their hero was dead, they ran away. 52 The men of Israel and Judah shouted and ran after them,

David defeated and killed Goliath. (17:50)

I Samuel

pursuing them all the way to Gath[c] and to the gates of Ekron. The Philistines fell wounded all along the road that leads to Shaaraim, as far as Gath and Ekron. [53] When the Israelites came back from pursuing the Philistines, they looted their camp. [54] David got Goliath's head and took it to Jerusalem, but he kept Goliath's weapons in his own tent.

David Is Presented to Saul

[55] When Saul saw David going out to fight Goliath, he asked Abner, the commander of his army, "Abner, whose son is he?"

"I have no idea, Your Majesty," Abner answered.

[56] "Then go and find out," Saul ordered.

[57] So when David returned to camp after killing Goliath, Abner took him to Saul. David was still carrying Goliath's head. [58] Saul asked him, "Young man, whose son are you?"

"I am the son of your servant Jesse from Bethlehem," David answered.

18 [1] Saul and David finished their conversation. After that, Saul's son Jonathan was deeply attracted to David and came to love him as much as he loved himself. [2] Saul kept David with him from that day on and did not let him go back home. [3] Jonathan swore eternal friendship with David because of his deep affection for him. [4] He took off the robe he was wearing and gave it to David, together with his armor and also his sword, bow, and belt. [5] David was successful in all the missions on which Saul sent

Jonathan swore eternal friendship with David. (18:3)

Friends for Life

Throughout the rest of First Samuel, it is clear that David and Jonathan have become very close friends. Jonathan even shares his clothes with David. It is not easy to be a good and loyal friend. It takes a lot of work, and in Jonathan's case, he has to deal with the growing jealousy of his father, King Saul, toward David. Several times, Jonathan takes great risks to help David because of their deep friendship. There are things you trust your best friend with that you tell no one else. It is all about trust and staying loyal to each other through thick and thin. Most of us can count on one hand those individuals we call true friends.

Think about how good and loyal a friend you are. Think about how you can make friends and also deepen a friendship you already have. Ask God to help you. Pray for your friends every day. Pray that you will be a loyal friend.

— 1 Samuel 18:1–5

him, and so Saul made him an officer in his army. This pleased all of Saul's officers and men.

Saul Becomes Jealous of David

[6] As David was returning after killing Goliath and as the soldiers were coming back home, women from every town in Israel came out to meet King Saul. They were singing joyful songs, dancing, and playing

[c] **17:52** One ancient translation Gath; *Hebrew* a valley.
18:7 1 Sam 21:11; 29:5

I Samuel

tambourines and lyres. [7]In their celebration the women sang, "Saul has killed thousands, but David tens of thousands." [8]Saul did not like this, and he became very angry. He said, "For David they claim tens of thousands, but only thousands for me. They will be making him king next!" [9]And so he was jealous and suspicious of David from that day on.

[10]The next day an evil spirit from God suddenly took control of Saul, and he raved in his house like a madman. David was playing the harp, as he did every day, and Saul was holding a spear. [11]"I'll pin him to the wall," Saul said to himself, and he threw the spear at him twice; but David dodged each time.

"I'll pin him to the wall." (18:11)

[12]Saul was afraid of David because the LORD was with David but had abandoned him. [13]So Saul sent him away and put him in command of a thousand men. David led his men in battle [14]and was successful in all he did, because the LORD was with him. [15]Saul noticed David's success and became even more afraid of him. [16]But everyone in Israel and Judah loved David because he was such a successful leader.

David Marries Saul's Daughter

[17]Then Saul said to David, "Here is my older daughter Merab. I will give her to you as your wife on condition that you serve me as a brave and loyal soldier, and fight the LORD's battles." (Saul was thinking that in this way the Philistines would kill David, and he would not have to do it himself.)

[18]David answered, "Who am I and what is my family that I should become the king's

son-in-law?" [19]But when the time came for Merab to be given to David, she was given instead to a man named Adriel from Meholah.

[20]Saul's daughter Michal, however, fell in love with David, and when Saul heard of this, he was pleased. [21]He said to himself, "I'll give Michal to David; I will use her to trap him, and he will be killed by the Philistines." So for the second time Saul said to David, "You will be my son-in-law." [22]He ordered his officials to speak privately with David and tell him, "The king is pleased with you and all his officials like you; now is a good time for you to marry his daughter."

[23]So they told this to David, and he answered, "It's a great honor to become the king's son-in-law, too great for someone poor and insignificant like me."

[24]The officials told Saul what David had said, [25]and Saul ordered them to tell David: "All the king wants from you as payment for the bride are the foreskins of a hundred dead Philistines, as revenge on his enemies." (This was how Saul planned to have David killed by the Philistines.) [26]Saul's officials reported to David what Saul had said, and David was delighted with the thought of becoming the king's son-in-law. Before the day set for the wedding, [27]David and his men went and killed two hundred Philistines. He took their foreskins to the king and counted them all out to him, so that he might become his son-in-law. So Saul had to give his daughter Michal in marriage to David.

[28]Saul realized clearly that the LORD was with David and also that his daughter Michal loved him. [29]So he became even more afraid of David and was his enemy as long as he lived.

[30]The Philistine armies would come and fight, but in every battle David was more successful than any of Saul's other officers. As a result David became very famous.

I Samuel

Saul's oldest daughter, Merab, was first promised in marriage to David, but David ended up marrying a different daughter. What was her name?

Pray It!

The Jealousy Monster

Jealousy can really eat away at our relationships and destroy friendships. Jealousy turns Saul into a crazed man who publicly tries to kill David! Eventually it destroys this once great man. When you feel jealousy for another, try this prayer:

Dear God, I need your help in dealing with my jealousy toward _____.
Help me to step back and not judge this person.
Help me to realize how quickly my feelings of jealousy can take over and can lead me
    to say and do things that go against your command to love one another.
I want to pray that you bless _____
    and that I can accept whatever differences there are between us.
Help me to move on and not let jealousy get the best of me.
Amen.

— 1 Samuel, chapter 19

David Is Persecuted by Saul

19 ¹Saul told his son Jonathan and all his officials that he planned to kill[d] David. But Jonathan was very fond of David, ²and so he told him, "My father is trying to kill you. Please be careful tomorrow morning; hide in some secret place and stay there. ³I will go and stand by my father in the field where you are hiding, and I will speak to him about you. If I find out anything, I will let you know."

⁴Jonathan praised David to Saul and said, "Sir, don't do wrong to your servant David. He has never done you any wrong; on the contrary, everything he has done has been a great help to you. ⁵He risked his life when he killed Goliath, and the LORD won a great victory for Israel. When you saw it, you were glad. Why, then, do you now want to do wrong to an innocent man and kill David for no reason at all?"

⁶Saul was convinced by what Jonathan said and made a vow in the LORD's name that he would not kill David. ⁷So Jonathan called David and told him everything; then he took him to Saul, and David served the king as he had before.

⁸War with the Philistines broke out again. David attacked them and defeated them so thoroughly that they fled.

⁹One day an evil spirit from the LORD took control of Saul. He was sitting in his house with his spear in his hand, and David was there, playing his harp. ¹⁰Saul tried to pin David to the wall with his spear, but David dodged, and the spear stuck in the wall. David ran away and escaped.

¹¹That same night Saul sent some men to watch David's house and kill him the next morning. Michal, David's wife, warned him, "If you don't get away tonight, tomorrow you will be dead." ¹²She let him down from a window, and he ran away and escaped. ¹³Then she took the household idol, laid it on the bed, put a pillow made of goats' hair

---

[d] **19:1** that he planned to kill; *or* to kill.
19:11 Ps 59 Title

I Samuel

How does David's wife fool Saul's soldiers into thinking he is sick? It's a trick you sometimes see in movies.

at its head, and put a cover over it. ¹⁴When Saul's men came to get David, Michal told them that he was sick. ¹⁵But Saul sent them back to see David for themselves. He ordered them, "Carry him here in his bed, and I will kill him." ¹⁶They went inside and found the household idol in the bed and the goats' hair pillow at its head. ¹⁷Saul asked Michal, "Why have you tricked me like this and let my enemy escape?"

She answered, "He said he would kill me if I didn't help him escape."

¹⁸David escaped and went to Samuel in Ramah and told him everything that Saul had done to him. Then he and Samuel went to Naioth and stayed there. ¹⁹Saul was told that David was in Naioth in Ramah, ²⁰so he sent some men to arrest him. They saw⸋ the group of prophets dancing and shouting, with Samuel as their leader. Then the spirit of God took control of Saul's men, and they also began to dance and shout. ²¹When Saul heard of this, he sent more messengers, and they also began to dance and shout. He sent messengers the third time, and the same thing happened to them. ²²Then he himself started out to Ramah. When he came to the large well in Secu, he asked where Samuel and David were and was told that they were at Naioth. ²³As he was going there, the spirit of God took control of him also, and he danced and shouted all the way to Naioth. ²⁴He took off his clothes and danced and shouted in Samuel's presence, and lay naked all that day and all that night. (This is how the saying originated, "Has even Saul become a prophet?")

Jonathan Helps David

20 ¹Then David fled from Naioth in Ramah and went to Jonathan. "What have I done?" he asked. "What crime have I committed? What wrong have I done to your father to make him want to kill me?"

²Jonathan answered, "God forbid that you should die! My father tells me everything he does, important or not, and he would not hide this from me. It just isn't so!"

³But David answered,ᶠ "Your father knows very well how much you like me, and he has decided not to let you know what he plans to do, because you would be deeply hurt. I swear to you by the living LORD that I am only a step away from death!"

⁴Jonathan said, "I'll do anything you want."

⁵"Tomorrow is the New Moon Festival," David replied, "and I am supposed to eat with the king. But if it's all right with you, I will go and hide in the fields until the evening of the day after tomorrow. ⁶If your father notices that I am not at the table, tell him that I begged your permission to hurry home to Bethlehem, since it's the time for the annual sacrifice there for my whole family. ⁷If he says, 'All right,' I will be safe; but if he becomes angry, you will know that he is determined to harm me. ⁸Please do me this favor, and keep the sacred promise you made to me. But if I'm guilty, kill me yourself! Why take me to your father to be killed?"

⁹"Don't even think such a thing!" Jonathan answered. "If I knew for sure that my father was determined to harm you, wouldn't I tell you?"

¹⁰David then asked, "Who will let me know if your father answers you angrily?"

¹¹"Let's go out to the fields," Jonathan answered. So they went, ¹²and Jonathan said to David, "May the LORD God of Israel be our witness!ᵍ At this time tomorrow and on the following day I will question my father. If his attitude toward you is good, I will send you word. ¹³If he intends to harm you, may the LORD strike me dead if I don't let you know about it and get you safely away. May the LORD be with you as he was with my father! ¹⁴And if I remain alive, please keep your sacred promise and be loyal to me; but if I die,ʰ ¹⁵show the same kind of loyalty to my family forever. And when the LORD has completely destroyed all your enemies, ¹⁶may our promise to each other still be unbroken. If it is broken, the LORD will punish you."ⁱ

I Samuel

ᵉ **19:20** *Some ancient translations* They saw; *Hebrew* He saw. ᶠ **20:3** *One ancient translation* answered; *Hebrew* made a vow again. ᵍ **20:12** *One ancient translation* be our witness; *Hebrew does not have these words.* ʰ **20:14** *Some ancient translations* if I die; *Hebrew* that I may not die. ⁱ **20:16** *Verses 15–16 in Hebrew are unclear.*

19:24 1 Sam 10:11, 12 **20:5** Num 28:11 **20:15** 2 Sam 9:1

¹⁷Once again Jonathan made David promise to love him, for Jonathan loved David as much as he loved himself. ¹⁸Then Jonathan said to him, "Since tomorrow is the New Moon Festival, your absence will be noticed if you aren't at the meal. ¹⁹The day after tomorrow your absence will be noticed[j] even more; so go to the place where you hid yourself the other time, and hide behind the pile of stones there.[k] ²⁰I will then shoot three arrows at it, as though it were a target. ²¹Then I will tell my servant to go and find them. And if I tell him, 'Look, the arrows are on this side of you; get them,' that means that you are safe and can come out. I swear by the living LORD that you will be in no danger. ²²But if I tell him, 'The arrows are on the other side of you,' then leave, because the LORD is sending you away. ²³As for the promise we have made to each other, the LORD will make sure that we will keep it forever."

²⁴So David hid in the fields. At the New Moon Festival, King Saul came to the meal ²⁵and sat in his usual place by the wall. Abner sat next to him, and Jonathan sat across the table from him.[l] David's place was empty, ²⁶but Saul said nothing that day, because he thought, "Something has happened to him, and he is not ritually pure." ²⁷On the following day, the day after the New Moon Festival, David's place was still empty, and Saul asked Jonathan, "Why didn't David come to the meal either yesterday or today?"

²⁸Jonathan answered, "He begged me to let him go to Bethlehem. ²⁹'Please let me go,' he said, 'because our family is celebrating the sacrificial feast in town, and my brother ordered me to be there. So then, if you are my friend, let me go and see my relatives.' That is why he isn't in his place at your table."

³⁰Saul became furious with Jonathan and said to him, "How rebellious and faithless your mother was! Now I know you are taking sides with David and are disgracing yourself and that mother of yours! ³¹Don't

you realize that as long as David is alive, you will never be king of this country? Now go and bring him here—he must die!"

³²"Why should he die?" Jonathan replied. "What has he done?"

³³At that, Saul threw his spear at Jonathan to kill him, and Jonathan realized that his father was really determined to kill David. ³⁴Jonathan got up from the table in a rage and ate nothing that day—the second day of the New Moon Festival. He was deeply distressed about David, because Saul had insulted him. ³⁵The following morning Jonathan went to the fields to meet David, as they had agreed. He took a young boy with him ³⁶and said to him, "Run and find the arrows I'm going to shoot." The boy ran, and Jonathan shot an arrow beyond him. ³⁷When the boy reached the place where the arrow had fallen, Jonathan shouted to him, "The arrow is farther on! ³⁸Don't just stand there! Hurry up!" The boy picked up the arrow and returned to his master, ³⁹not knowing what it all meant; only Jonathan and David knew. ⁴⁰Jonathan gave his weapons to the boy and told him to take them back to town.

⁴¹After the boy had left, David got up from behind the pile of stones,[m] fell on his knees and bowed with his face to the ground three times. Both he and Jonathan were crying as they kissed each other; David's grief was even greater than Jonathan's.[n] ⁴²Then Jonathan said to David, "God be with you. The LORD will make sure that you and I, and your descendants and mine, will forever keep

"God be with you!" (20:42)

---

the sacred promise we have made to each other." Then David left, and Jonathan went back to the town.

David Flees from Saul

21 ¹ David went to the priest Ahimelech in Nob. Ahimelech came out trembling to meet him and asked, "Why did you come here all by yourself?"

² "I am here on the king's business," David answered. "He told me not to let anyone know what he sent me to do. As for my men, I have told them to meet me at a certain place. ³ Now, then, what supplies do you have? Give me five loaves of bread or anything else you have."

⁴ The priest said, "I don't have any ordinary bread, only sacred bread; you can have it if your men haven't had sexual relations recently."

⁵ "Of course they haven't," answered David. "My men always keep themselves ritually pure even when we go out on an ordinary mission; how much more this time when we are on a special mission!"

⁶ So the priest gave David the sacred bread, because the only bread he had was the loaves offered to God, which had been removed from the sacred table and replaced by fresh bread.

(⁷ Saul's chief herdsman, Doeg, who was from Edom, happened to be there that day, because he had to fulfill a religious obligation.)

⁸ David said to Ahimelech, "Do you have a spear or a sword you can give me? The king's orders made me leave in such a hurry that I didn't have time to get my sword or any other weapon."

⁹ Ahimelech answered, "I have the sword of Goliath the Philistine, whom you killed in Elah Valley; it is behind the ephod, wrapped in a cloth. If you want it, take it—it's the only weapon here."

"Give it to me," David said. "There is not a better sword anywhere!"

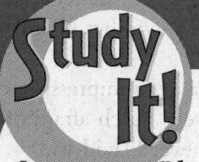

Innocent Blood

Saul has clearly let his anger and jealousy overtake him. Because the priest Ahimelech has helped David feed his men, Saul decides to take revenge and orders eighty-five priests killed. Then he has everyone else in the city of Nob killed as well, including children and even babies. This slaughter of innocent blood is a terrible sin. Throughout history we have examples of innocent people being killed. Every continent and every century has its own horror stories about innocent people being put to death.

To some people in power, life is cheap. They have no regard for the sanctity of human life. They are like bullies on the playground who pick on people or beat them up simply to show that they are tougher, but they do it on a larger and much deadlier scale. Bullies—large and small—often come to a violent end themselves.

If you are being bullied, let a trusted adult know. If you are involved in being a bully, take a good, hard look at who you are bullying and why. Decide not to add to the violence in the world.

— 1 Samuel 21:1–6; 22:9–19

¹⁰ So David left, fleeing from Saul, and went to King Achish of Gath. ¹¹ The king's officials said to Achish, "Isn't this David, the king of his country? This is the man about

21:1–6 Mt 12:3, 4; Mk 2:25, 26; Lk 6:3   21:6 Lev 24:5–9   21:9 1 Sam 17:51   21:11 1 Sam 18:7; 29:5

I Samuel

This story of the sacred bread in 1 Samuel, chapter 21, is used by Jesus to make a point about the Sabbath. Check it out in Matthew 12:1–4.

whom the women sang, as they danced, 'Saul has killed thousands, but David has killed tens of thousands.' "

12 Their words made a deep impression on David, and he became very much afraid of King Achish. 13 So whenever David was around them, he pretended to be insane and acted like a madman when they tried to restrain him; he would scribble on the city[o] gates and let spit drool down his beard. 14 So Achish said to his officials, "Look! The man is crazy! Why did you bring him to me? 15 Don't I have enough madmen already? Why bring another one to bother me with his crazy actions right here in my own house?"

The Slaughter of the Priests

22 ¹ David fled from the city of Gath and went to a cave near the town of Adullam. When his brothers and the rest of the family heard that he was there, they joined him. ²People who were oppressed or in debt or dissatisfied went to him, about four hundred men in all, and he became their leader.

³David went on from there to Mizpah in Moab and said to the king of Moab, "Please let my father and mother come and stay with you until I find out what God is going to do for me." ⁴So David left his parents with the king of Moab, and they stayed there as long as David was hiding out in the cave.

⁵Then the prophet Gad came to David and said, "Don't stay here; go at once to the land of Judah." So David left and went to the forest of Hereth.

⁶One day Saul was in Gibeah, sitting under a tamarisk tree on a hill, with his spear in his hand, and all his officers were standing around him. He was told that David and his men had been located, ⁷and he said to his officers, "Listen, men of Benjamin! Do you

think that David will give fields and vineyards to all of you, and make you officers in his army? ⁸Is that why you are plotting against me? Not one of you told me that my own son had made an alliance with David. No one is concerned about me or tells me that David, one of my own men, is right now looking for a chance to kill me, and that my son has encouraged him!"

⁹Doeg was standing there with Saul's officers, and he said, "I saw David when he went to Ahimelech son of Ahitub in Nob. ¹⁰Ahimelech asked the LORD what David should do, and then he gave David some food and the sword of Goliath the Philistine."

¹¹So King Saul sent for the priest Ahimelech and all his relatives, who were also priests in Nob, and they came to him. ¹²Saul said to Ahimelech, "Listen, Ahimelech!"

"At your service, sir," he answered.

¹³Saul asked him, "Why are you and David plotting against me? Why did you give him some food and a sword, and consult God for him? Now he has turned against me and is waiting for a chance to kill me!"

¹⁴Ahimelech answered, "David is the most faithful officer you have! He is your own son-in-law, captain of[p] your bodyguard, and highly respected by everyone in the royal court. ¹⁵Yes, I consulted God for him, and it wasn't the first time.[q] As for plotting against you, Your Majesty must not accuse me or anyone else in my family. I don't know anything about this matter!"

¹⁶The king said, "Ahimelech, you and all your relatives must die." ¹⁷Then he said to the guards standing near him, "Kill the LORD's priests! They conspired with David and did not tell me that he had run away, even though they knew it all along." But the guards refused to lift a hand to kill the LORD's priests. ¹⁸So Saul said to Doeg, "You

o 21:13 city; or palace.   p 22:14 Some ancient translations captain of; Hebrew he turned to   q 22:15 Yes, I consulted . . . time; or Now, have I done something wrong today by consulting God for him? Not at all!   21:12 Ps 56 Title   21:13 Ps 34 Title   22:1 Ps 57 Title; Ps 142 Title   22:9, 10 1 Sam 21:7–9; Ps 52 Title

The wilderness near Ziph where David hid from Saul was most likely a very rocky and difficult area in which to travel, so no one lived there.

I Samuel

kill them!"—and Doeg killed them all. On that day he killed eighty-five priests who were qualified to carry the ephod. ¹⁹Saul also had all the other inhabitants of Nob, the city of priests, put to death: men and women, children and babies, cattle, donkeys, and sheep—they were all killed.

²⁰But Abiathar, one of Ahimelech's sons, escaped, and went and joined David. ²¹He told him how Saul had slaughtered the priests of the LORD. ²²David said to him, "When I saw Doeg there that day, I knew that he would be sure to tell Saul. So I am responsible ʳ for the death of all your relatives. ²³Stay with me and don't be afraid. Saul wants to kill both you and me, but you will be safe with me."

David Saves the Town of Keilah

23 ¹David heard that the Philistines were attacking the town of Keilah and were stealing the newly harvested grain. ²So he asked the LORD, "Shall I go and attack the Philistines?"

"Yes," the LORD answered. "Attack them and save Keilah."

³But David's men said to him, "We have enough to be afraid of here in Judah; it will be much worse if we go to Keilah and attack the Philistine forces!" ⁴So David consulted the LORD again, and the LORD said to him, "Go and attack Keilah, because I will give you victory over the Philistines." ⁵So David and his men went to Keilah and attacked the Philistines; they killed many of them and took their livestock. And so it was that David saved the town.

⁶When Abiathar son of Ahimelech escaped and joined David in Keilah, he took the ephod with him.

⁷Saul was told that David had gone to Keilah, and he said, "God has put him in my power. David has trapped himself by going into a walled town with fortified gates." ⁸So Saul called his troops to war, to march against Keilah and besiege David and his men.

⁹When David heard that Saul was planning to attack him, he said to the priest Abi-

athar, "Bring the ephod here." ¹⁰Then David said, " LORD, God of Israel, I have heard that Saul is planning to come to Keilah and destroy it on account of me, your servant. ¹¹Will the citizens of Keilah hand me over to Saul? Will Saul really come, as I have heard? LORD, God of Israel, I beg you to answer me!"

The LORD answered, "Saul will come."

¹²"And will the citizens of Keilah hand my men and me over to Saul?" David asked again.

"They will," the LORD answered.

¹³So David and his men—about six hundred in all—left Keilah at once and kept on the move. When Saul heard that David had escaped from Keilah, he gave up his plan.

David in the Hill Country

¹⁴David stayed in hiding in the hill country, in the wilderness near Ziph. Saul was always trying to find him, but God did not turn David over to him. ¹⁵David saw that Saul was out to kill him.

David was at Horesh, in the wilderness near Ziph. ¹⁶Jonathan went to him there and encouraged him with assurances of God's protection, ¹⁷saying to him, "Don't be afraid. My father Saul won't be able to harm you. He knows very well that you are the one who will be the king of Israel and that I will be next in rank to you." ¹⁸The two of them made a sacred promise of friendship to each other. David stayed at Horesh, and Jonathan went home.

¹⁹Some people from Ziph went to Saul at Gibeah and said, "David is hiding out in our territory at Horesh on Mount Hachilah, in the southern part of the Judean wilderness. ²⁰We know, Your Majesty, how much you want to capture him; so come to our territory, and we will make sure that you catch him."

²¹Saul answered, "May the LORD bless you for being so kind to me! ²²Go and make sure once more; find out for certain where he is and who has seen him there. I hear that he is very cunning. ²³Find out exactly the

ʳ 22:22 *Some ancient translations* I am responsible; *Hebrew* I have turned.
23:18 1 Sam 18:3   23:19 Ps 54 Title

I Samuel

places where he hides, and be sure to bring back a report to me right away. Then I will go with you, and if he is still in the region, I will hunt him down, even if I have to search the whole land of Judah."

24 So they left and returned to Ziph ahead of Saul. David and his men were in the wilderness of Maon, in a desolate valley in the southern part of the Judean wilderness. 25 Saul and his men set out to look for David, but he heard about it and went to a rocky hill in the wilderness of Maon and stayed there. When Saul heard about this, he went after David. 26 Saul and his men were on one side of the hill, separated from David and his men, who were on the other side. They were hurrying to get away from Saul and his men, who were closing in on them and were about to capture them. 27 Just then a messenger arrived and said to Saul, "Come back at once! The Philistines are invading the country!" 28 So Saul stopped pursuing David and went to fight the Philistines. That is why that place is called Separation Hill. 29 David left and went to the region of En-gedi, where he stayed in hiding.

David Spares Saul's Life

24 ¹When Saul came back from fighting the Philistines, he was told that David was in the wilderness near Engedi. ²Saul took three thousand of the best soldiers in Israel and went looking for David and his men east of Wild Goat Rocks. ³He came to a cave close to some sheep pens by the road and went in to relieve himself. It happened to be the very cave in which David and his men were hiding far back in the cave. ⁴They said to him, "This is your chance! The LORD has told you that he would put your enemy in your power and you could do to him whatever you wanted to." David crept over and cut off a piece of Saul's robe without Saul's knowing it. ⁵But then David's conscience began to hurt, ⁶and he said to his men, "May the LORD keep me from doing any harm to my master, whom the LORD chose as king! I must not harm him in the least, because he is the king cho-

David . . . cut off a piece of Saul's robe. (24:4)

sen by the LORD!" ⁷So David convinced his men that they should not attack Saul.

Saul got up, left the cave, and started away. ⁸Then David went out after him and called to him, "Your Majesty!" Saul turned around, and David bowed down to the ground in respect ⁹and said, "Why do you listen to people who say that I am trying to harm you? ¹⁰You can see for yourself that just now in the cave the LORD put you in my power. Some of my men told me to kill you, but I felt sorry for you and said that I would not harm you in the least, because you are the one whom the LORD chose to be king. ¹¹Look, my father, look at the piece of your robe I am holding! I could have killed you, but instead I only cut this off. This should convince you that I have no thought of rebelling against you or of harming you. You are hunting me down to kill me, even though I have not done you any wrong. ¹²May the LORD judge which one of us is wrong! May he punish you for your action against me, for I will not harm you in the least. ¹³You know the old saying, 'Evil is done only by evil people.' And

"I could have killed you!" (24:11)

Pray It!

Respect

Try to imagine David's situation in 1 Samuel, chapter 24. He could very easily have killed Saul. He knew that Saul would kill him, if given the chance. So why did he spare Saul's life?

It's simple: respect. David knew that even though Saul had fallen out of favor with God, Saul was still God's chosen king, and he had great respect for both God and for his king. This says a lot about David's character.

Respect is a very important virtue and is a sign of maturity. We need to respect those in authority. We may not always agree with them, but we still respect their position. One way you can show your respect for people in authority is to pray for them. Here is a checklist of people you could pray for:

- your parents or guardians
- your principal and teachers
- your mayor and city council or county board
- your state's governor and representatives
- state and federal judges
- the president and Congress
- leaders of all the nations of the world

— 1 Samuel, chapter 24

so I will not harm you. ¹⁴Look at what the king of Israel is trying to kill! Look at what he is chasing! A dead dog, a flea! ¹⁵The LORD will judge, and he will decide which one of us is wrong. May he look into the matter, defend me, and save me from you."

¹⁶When David had finished speaking, Saul said, "Is that really you, David my son?" And he started crying. ¹⁷Then he said to David, "You are right, and I am wrong. You have been so good to me, while I have done such wrong to you! ¹⁸Today you have shown how good you are to me, because you did not kill me, even though the LORD put me in your power. ¹⁹How often does someone catch an enemy and then let him get away unharmed? The LORD bless you for what you have done to me today! ²⁰Now I am sure that you will be king of Israel and that the kingdom will continue under your rule. ²¹But promise me

in the LORD's name that you will spare my descendants, so that my name and my family's name will not be completely forgotten." ²²David promised that he would.

Then Saul went back home, and David and his men went back to their hiding place.

The Death of Samuel

25 ¹Samuel died, and all the Israelites came together and mourned for him. Then they buried him at his home in Ramah.

David and Abigail

After this, David went to the wilderness of Paran. ²⁻³There was a man of the clan of Caleb named Nabal, who was from the town of Maon, and who owned land near the

"Then he (Saul) said to David, 'You are right and I am wrong. You have been so good to me, while I have done such wrong to you!'" (1 Samuel 24:17).

town of Carmel. He was a very rich man, the owner of three thousand sheep and one thousand goats. His wife Abigail was beautiful and intelligent, but he was a mean, bad-tempered man.

Nabal was shearing his sheep in Carmel, ⁴and David, who was in the wilderness, heard about it, ⁵so he sent ten young men with orders to go to Carmel, find Nabal, and give him his greetings. ⁶He instructed them to say to Nabal: "David sends you greetings, my friend, with his best wishes for you, your family, and all that is yours. ⁷He heard that you were shearing your sheep, and he wants you to know that your shepherds have been with us and we did not harm them. Nothing that belonged to them was stolen all the time they were at Carmel. ⁸Just ask them, and they will tell you. We have come on a feast day, and David asks you to receive us kindly. Please give what you can to us your servants and to your dear friend David."

⁹David's men delivered this message to Nabal in David's name. Then they waited there, ¹⁰and Nabal finally answered, "David? Who is he? I've never heard of him! The country is full of runaway slaves nowadays! ¹¹I'm not going to take my bread and water, and the animals I have butchered for my sheepshearers, and give them to people who come from I don't know where!"

¹²David's men went back to him and told him what Nabal had said. ¹³"Buckle on your swords!" he ordered, and they all did. David also buckled on his sword and left with about four hundred of his men, leaving two hundred behind with the supplies.

¹⁴One of Nabal's servants said to Nabal's wife Abigail, "Have you heard? David sent some messengers from the wilderness with greetings for our master, but he insulted them. ¹⁵Yet they were very good to us; they never bothered us, and all the time we were with them in the fields, nothing that belonged to us was stolen. ¹⁶They protected us day and night the whole time we were

with them looking after our flocks. ¹⁷Please think this over and decide what to do. This could be disastrous for our master and all his family. He is so mean that he won't listen to anybody!"

¹⁸Abigail quickly gathered two hundred loaves of bread, two leather bags full of wine, five roasted sheep, two bushels of roasted grain, a hundred bunches of raisins, and two hundred cakes of dried figs, and loaded them on donkeys. ¹⁹Then she said to the servants, "You go on ahead and I will follow you." But she said nothing to her husband.

²⁰She was riding her donkey around a bend on a hillside when suddenly she met David and his men coming toward her. ²¹David had been thinking, "Why did I ever protect that fellow's property out here in the wilderness? Not a thing that belonged to him was stolen, and this is how he pays me back for the help I gave him! ²²May God strike me*s* dead if I don't kill every last one of those men before morning!"

²³When Abigail saw David, she quickly dismounted and threw herself on the ground ²⁴at David's feet, and said to him, "Please, sir, listen to me! Let me take the blame. ²⁵Please, don't pay any attention to Nabal, that good-for-nothing! He is exactly what his name means—a fool!*t* I wasn't there when your

When Abigail saw David . . . (25:23)

---

s **25:22** *One ancient translation* me; *Hebrew* my enemies. Nabal.   *t* **25:25** A FOOL: *This is the meaning of the Hebrew name Nabal.*

Did you ever wonder what kind of food the ancient Israelites ate? Check the list in I Samuel 25:18.

servants arrived, sir. 26It is the LORD who has kept you from taking revenge and killing your enemies. And now I swear to you by the living LORD that your enemies and all who want to harm you will be punished like Nabal. 27Please, sir, accept this present I have brought you, and give it to your men. 28Please forgive me, sir, for any wrong I have done. The LORD will make you king, and your descendants also, because you are fighting his battles; and you will not do anything evil*u* as long as you live. 29If anyone should attack you and try to kill you, the LORD your God will keep you safe, as someone guards a precious treasure. As for your enemies, however, he will throw them away, as someone hurls stones with a sling. 30And when the LORD has done all the good things he has promised you and has made you king of Israel, 31then you will not have to feel regret or remorse, sir, for having killed without cause or for having taken your own revenge. And when the LORD has blessed you, sir, please do not forget me."

32David said to her, "Praise the LORD, the God of Israel, who sent you today to meet me! 33Thank God for your good sense and for what you have done today in keeping me from the crime of murder and from taking my own revenge. 34The LORD has kept me from harming you. But I swear by the living God of Israel that if you had not hurried to meet me, all of Nabal's men would have been dead by morning!" 35Then David accepted what she had brought him and said to her, "Go back home and don't worry. I will do what you want."

36Abigail went back to Nabal, who was at home having a feast fit for a king. He was drunk and in a good mood, so she did not tell him anything until the next morning. 37Then, after he had sobered up, she told him everything. He suffered a stroke and was completely paralyzed. 38Some ten days later the LORD struck Nabal and he died.

39When David heard that Nabal had died, he said, "Praise the LORD! He has taken revenge on Nabal for insulting me and has

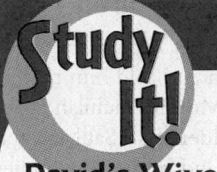

David's Wives

The final verses of 1 Samuel, chapter 25, list a few of David's wives. The religious and civil laws in our country forbid polygamy, which means having more than one spouse. However, during the time of David, it was very common for men to have more than one wife. It was especially common for a ruler or military leader to have several wives. One of the reasons was to protect women. In biblical times, women had no rights and were generally considered property. An adult woman who wasn't married didn't "belong" to anyone and had no protector. We have a very different attitude toward women and marriage today.

— 1 Samuel 25:43–44

kept me his servant from doing wrong. The LORD has punished Nabal for his evil."

Then David sent a proposal of marriage to Abigail. 40His servants went to her at Carmel and said to her, "David sent us to take you to him to be his wife."

41Abigail bowed down to the ground and said, "I am his servant, ready to wash the feet of his servants." 42She rose quickly and mounted her donkey. Accompanied by her five maids, she went with David's servants and became his wife.

43David had married Ahinoam from Jezreel, and now Abigail also became his wife. 44Meanwhile, Saul had given his daughter Michal, who had been David's wife, to Palti son of Laish, who was from the town of Gallim.

u 25:28 you will not do anything evil; *or* no evil will happen to you.
25:44 2 Sam 3:14–16

I Samuel

David Spares Saul's Life Again

26 ¹ Some men from Ziph came to Saul at Gibeah and told him that David was hiding on Mount Hachilah at the edge of the Judean wilderness. ²Saul went at once with three thousand of the best soldiers in Israel to the wilderness of Ziph to look for David, ³and camped by the road on Mount Hachilah. David was still in the wilderness, and when he learned that Saul had come to look for him, ⁴he sent spies and found out that Saul was indeed there. ⁵He went at once and located the exact place where Saul and Abner son of Ner, commander of Saul's army, slept. Saul slept inside the camp, and his men camped around him.

⁶Then David asked Ahimelech the Hittite, and Abishai the brother of Joab (their mother was Zeruiah), "Which of you two will go to Saul's camp with me?"

"I will," Abishai answered.

⁷So that night David and Abishai entered Saul's camp and found Saul sleeping in the center of the camp with his spear stuck in the ground near his head. Abner and the troops were sleeping around him. ⁸Abishai said to David, "God has put your enemy in your power tonight. Now let me plunge his own spear through him and pin him to the ground with just one blow—I won't have to strike twice!"

⁹But David said, "You must not harm him! The LORD will certainly punish whoever harms his chosen king. ¹⁰By the living LORD," David continued, "I know that the LORD himself will kill Saul, either when his time comes to die a natural death or when he dies in battle. ¹¹The LORD forbid that I should try to harm the one whom the LORD has made king! Let's take his spear and his water jar, and go." ¹²So David took the spear and the water jar from right beside Saul's head, and he and Abishai left. No one saw it or knew what had happened or even woke up—they were all sound asleep, because the LORD had sent a heavy sleep on them all.

¹³Then David crossed over to the other side of the valley to the top of the hill, a safe distance away, ¹⁴and shouted to Saul's troops and to Abner, "Abner! Can you hear me?"

"Who is that shouting and waking up the king?" Abner asked.

¹⁵David answered, "Abner, aren't you the greatest man in Israel? So why aren't you protecting your master, the king? Just now someone entered the camp to kill your master. ¹⁶You failed in your duty, Abner! I swear by the living LORD that all of you deserve to die, because you have not protected your master, whom the LORD made king. Look! Where is the king's spear? Where is the water jar that was right by his head?"

¹⁷Saul recognized David's voice and asked, "David, is that you, my son?"

"Yes, Your Majesty," David answered. ¹⁸And he added, "Why, sir, are you still pursuing me, your servant? What have I done? What crime have I committed? ¹⁹Your Majesty, listen to what I have to say. If it is the LORD who has turned you against me, an offering to him will make him change his mind; but if some people have done it, may the LORD's curse fall on them. For they have driven me out from the LORD's land to a country where I can only worship foreign gods. ²⁰Don't let me be killed on foreign soil, away from the LORD. Why should the king of Israel come to kill a flea like me? Why should he hunt me down like a wild bird?"

²¹Saul answered, "I have done wrong. Come back, David, my son! I will never harm you again, because you have spared my life tonight. I have been a fool! I have done a terrible thing!"

²²David replied, "Here is your spear, Your Majesty. Let one of your men come over and get it. ²³The LORD rewards those who are faithful and righteous. Today he put you in my power, but I did not harm you, whom the LORD made king. ²⁴Just as I have spared your life today, may the LORD do the same to me and free me from all troubles!"

²⁵Saul said to David, "God bless you, my son! You will succeed in everything you do!"

So David went on his way, and Saul returned home.

26:1 Ps 54 Title   26:11 1 Sam 24:6

David among the Philistines

27 ¹David said to himself, "One of these days Saul will kill me. The best thing for me to do is to escape to Philistia. Then Saul will give up looking for me in Israel, and I will be safe." ²So David and his six hundred men went over at once to Achish son of Maoch, king of Gath. ³David and his men settled there in Gath with their families. David had his two wives with him, Ahinoam from Jezreel, and Abigail, Nabal's widow, from Carmel. ⁴When Saul heard that David had fled to Gath, he gave up trying to find him.

⁵David said to Achish, "If you are my friend, let me have a small town to live in. There is no need, sir, for me to live with you in the capital city." ⁶So Achish gave him the town of Ziklag, and for this reason Ziklag has belonged to the kings of Judah ever since. ⁷David lived in Philistia for sixteen months.

⁸During that time David and his men would attack the people of Geshur, Girzi, and Amalek, who had been living in the region a very long time. He would raid their land as far as Shur, all the way down to Egypt, ⁹killing all the men and women and taking the sheep, cattle, donkeys, camels, and even the clothes. Then he would come back to Achish, ¹⁰who would ask him, "Where did you go on a raid this time?" and David would tell him that he had gone to the southern part of Judah or to the territory of the clan of Jerahmeel or to the territory where the Kenites lived. ¹¹David would kill everyone, men and women, so that no one could go back to Gath and report what he and his men had really done. This is what David did the whole time he lived in Philistia. ¹²But Achish trusted David and said to himself, "He is hated so much by his own people the Israelites that he will have to serve me all his life."

28 ¹Some time later the Philistines gathered their troops to fight Israel, and Achish said to David, "Of course you understand that you and your men are to fight on my side."

²"Of course," David answered. "I am your servant, and you will see for yourself what I can do."

Achish said, "Good! I will make you my permanent bodyguard."

Saul Consults a Medium

³Now Samuel had died, and all the Israelites had mourned for him and had buried him in his hometown of Ramah. Saul had forced all the fortunetellers and mediums to leave Israel.

⁴The Philistine troops assembled and camped near the town of Shunem; Saul gathered the Israelites and camped at Mount Gilboa. ⁵When Saul saw the Philistine army, he was terrified, ⁶and so he asked the LORD what to do. But the LORD did not answer him at all, either by dreams or by the use of Urim and Thummim or by prophets. ⁷Then Saul ordered his officials, "Find me a woman who is a medium, and I will go and consult her."

"There is one in Endor," they answered.

⁸So Saul disguised himself; he put on different clothes, and after dark he went with two of his men to see the woman. "Consult the spirits for me and tell me what is going to happen," he said to her. "Call up the spirit of the man I name."

⁹The woman answered, "Surely you know what King Saul has done, how he forced the fortunetellers and mediums to leave Israel.ᵛ Why, then, are you trying to trap me and get me killed?"

¹⁰Then Saul made a sacred vow. "By the living LORD I promise that you will not be punished for doing this," he told her.

¹¹"Whom shall I call up for you?" the woman asked.

ᵛ **28:9** he forced . . . Israel; *or* he put to death the fortunetellers and mediums in Israel.
28:3 1 Sam 25:1   **28:3** Lev 20:27; Deut 18:10, 11   **28:6** Num 27:21   **28:11** Sir 46:20

I Samuel

Twice David has a chance to kill Saul; twice he takes something of Saul's to prove he was close to him. What are the two objects?

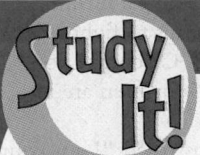

Calling Up the Dead

In a rather frightening episode, Saul contacts a medium, that is, someone who calls people back from the dead. Saul, who is terrified of the Philistines, grows more and more desperate. He has the medium conjure up the spirit of the dead judge and prophet Samuel. This is a very serious violation of God's Law. The Israelites were supposed to trust in God, not in magic and the rituals used by people who worshiped false gods. In the end, Saul is given a message by Samuel's spirit that he and his sons would die in battle. This message hurt more than it helped because it terrified Saul.

We must avoid things like séances and Ouija boards, which supposedly allow communication with the spirits of dead people. People who get deeply involved in this get taken advantage of by con artists. They get fooled into thinking there are powers other than God. It is all a lack of trust in God's power. Our faith tells us that if we follow God's path of life, we have little to worry about when our own life ends.

— 1 Samuel 28:3–19

"Samuel," he answered.

12 When the woman saw Samuel, she screamed and said to Saul, "Why have you tricked me? You are King Saul!"

13 "Don't be afraid!" the king said to her. "What do you see?"

"I see a spirit coming up from the earth," she answered.

14 "What does it look like?" he asked.

"It's an old man coming up," she answered. "He is wearing a cloak."

Then Saul knew that it was Samuel, and he bowed to the ground in respect.

15 Samuel said to Saul, "Why have you disturbed me? Why did you make me come back?"

Saul answered, "I am in great trouble! The Philistines are at war with me, and God has abandoned me. He doesn't answer me any more, either by prophets or by dreams. And so I have called you, for you to tell me what I must do."

16 Samuel said, "Why do you call me when the LORD has abandoned you and become your enemy? 17 The LORD has done to you what he told you through me: he has taken the kingdom away from you and given it to David instead. 18 You disobeyed the LORD's command and did not completely destroy the Amalekites and all they had. That is why the LORD is doing this to you now. 19 He will give you and Israel over to the Philistines. Tomorrow you and your sons will join me, and the LORD will also give the army of Israel over to the Philistines."

20 At once Saul fell down and lay stretched out on the ground, terrified by what Samuel had said. He was weak, because he had not eaten anything all day and all night. 21 The woman went over to him and saw that he was terrified, so she said to him, "Please, sir, I risked my life by doing what you asked. 22 Now please do what I ask. Let me fix you some food. You must eat so that you will be strong enough to travel."

23 Saul refused and said he would not eat anything. But his officers also urged him to eat. He finally gave in, got up from the ground, and sat on the bed. 24 The woman quickly killed a calf which she had been fattening. Then she took some flour, prepared it,

28:17 1 Sam 15:28   **28:18** 1 Sam 15:3–9

Why don't the Philistine commanders want David to fight with them against Saul?

and baked some bread without yeast. 25She set the food before Saul and his officers, and they ate it. And they left that same night.

David Is Rejected by the Philistines

29 1The Philistines brought all their troops together at Aphek, while the Israelites camped at the spring in Jezreel Valley. 2The five Philistine kings marched out with their units of a hundred and of a thousand men; David and his men marched in the rear with King Achish. 3The Philistine commanders saw them and asked, "What are these Hebrews doing here?"

Achish answered, "This is David, an official of King Saul of Israel. He has been with me for quite some time now. He has done nothing I can find fault with since the day he came over to me."

4But the Philistine commanders were angry with Achish and said to him, "Send that fellow back to the town you gave him. Don't let him go into battle with us; he might turn against us during the fighting. What better way is there for him to win back his master's favor than by the death of our men? 5After all, this is David, the one about whom the women sang, as they danced, 'Saul has killed thousands, but David has killed tens of thousands.' "

6Achish called David and said to him, "I swear by the living God of Israel that you have been loyal to me; and I would be pleased to have you go with me and fight in this battle. I have not found any fault in you from the day you came over to me. But the other kings don't approve of you. 7So go back home in peace, and don't do anything that would displease them."

8David answered, "What have I done wrong, sir? If, as you say, you haven't found any fault in me since the day I started serving you, why shouldn't I go with you, my master and king, and fight your enemies?"

9"I agree," Achish replied. "I consider you as loyal as an angel of God. But the other kings have said that you can't go with us into battle. 10So then, David, tomorrow morning all of you who left Saul and came over to me will have to get up early and leave as soon as it's light."

11So David and his men started out early the following morning to go back to Philistia, and the Philistines went on to Jezreel.

The War against the Amalekites

30 1Two days later David and his men arrived back at Ziklag. The Amalekites had raided southern Judah and attacked Ziklag. They had burned down the town 2and captured all the women; they had not killed anyone, but had taken everyone with them when they left. 3When David and his men arrived, they found that the town had been burned down and that their wives, sons, and daughters had been carried away. 4David and his men started crying and did not stop until they were completely exhausted. 5Even David's two wives, Ahinoam and Abigail, had been taken away.

6David was now in great trouble, because his men were all very bitter about losing their children, and they were threatening to stone him; but the LORD his God gave him courage. 7David said to the priest Abiathar son of Ahimelech, "Bring me the ephod," and Abiathar brought it to him. 8David asked the LORD, "Shall I go after those raiders? And will I catch them?"

He answered, "Go after them; you will catch them and rescue the captives."

9So David and his six hundred men started out, and when they arrived at Besor Brook, some of them stayed there. 10David continued on his way with four hundred men; the other two hundred men were too tired to cross the brook and so stayed behind. 11The men with David found a young Egyptian out in the country and brought him to David. They gave him some food and water, 12some dried figs, and two bunches of raisins. After he had eaten, his strength returned; he had not had anything to eat or drink for three full days. 13David asked him, "Who is your master, and where are you from?"

"I am an Egyptian, the slave of an Amalekite," he answered. "My master left me behind three days ago because I got sick.

29:5 1 Sam 18:7; 21:11   **30:5** 1 Sam 25:42, 43   **30:7** 1 Sam 22:20–23

14 We had raided the territory of the Cherethites in the southern part of Judah and the territory of the clan of Caleb, and we burned down Ziklag."

15 "Will you lead me to those raiders?" David asked him.

He answered, "I will if you promise me in God's name that you will not kill me or hand me over to my master." 16 And he led David to them.

The raiders were scattered all over the place, eating, drinking, and celebrating because of the enormous amount of loot they had captured from Philistia and Judah. 17 At dawn the next day David attacked them and fought until evening. Except for four hundred young men who mounted camels and got away, none of them escaped. 18 David rescued everyone and everything the Amalekites had taken, including his two wives; 19 nothing at all was missing. David got back all his men's sons and daughters, and all the loot the Amalekites had taken. 20 He also recovered all the flocks and herds; his men drove all the livestock in front of them*w* and said, "This belongs to David!"

21 Then David went back to the two hundred men who had been too weak to go with him and had stayed behind at Besor Brook. They came forward to meet David and his men, and David went up to them and greeted them warmly. 22 But some mean and worthless men who had gone with David said, "They didn't go with us, and so we won't give them any of the loot. They can take their wives and children and go away."

23 But David answered, "My brothers, you can't do this with what the LORD has given us! He kept us safe and gave us victory over the raiders. 24 No one can agree with what you say! All must share alike: whoever stays behind with the supplies gets the same share as the one who goes into battle." 25 David made this a rule, and it has been followed in Israel ever since.

26 When David returned to Ziklag, he sent part of the loot to his friends, the leaders of Judah, with the message, "Here is a present for you from the loot we took from the LORD's enemies." 27 He sent it to the people

Share and Share Alike

Sharing. David makes it a rule for his troops to follow. It is something we are taught and reminded of often as little children. Why is sharing so difficult? Probably because sharing goes against our culture which says to get as much as you can. God always calls us not to think of just ourselves. We have a duty to share what we have with others. If we make a practice of sharing when we are younger, as we grow older sharing becomes a habit. From something as simple as offering others a piece of gum to putting money into the collection basket each week, we are better people when we share what we have. Sharing reminds us that everything we have is really a gift from God.

- Who has shared something with you recently?
- What have you shared with others?

— 1 Samuel 30:17–25

in Bethel, to the people in Ramah in the southern part of Judah, and to the people in the towns of Jattir, 28 Aroer, Siphmoth, Eshtemoa, 29 and Racal; to the clan of Jerahmeel, to the Kenites, 30 and to the people in the towns of Hormah, Borashan, Athach, 31 and Hebron. He sent it to all the places where he and his men had roamed.

The Death of Saul and His Sons
(1 Chronicles 10:1–12)

31 ¹ The Philistines fought a battle against the Israelites on Mount Gilboa. Many Israelites were killed there, and the rest of them, including King Saul and his

---

w **30:20** *Probable text his men . . . front of them; Hebrew unclear.*

sons, fled. ²But the Philistines caught up with them and killed three of Saul's sons, Jonathan, Abinadab, and Malchishua. ³The fighting was heavy around Saul, and he himself was hit by enemy arrows and badly wounded. ⁴He said to the young man carrying his weapons, "Draw your sword and kill me, so that these godless Philistines won't gloat over me and kill me." But the young man was too terrified to do it. So Saul took his own sword and threw himself on it. ⁵The young man saw that Saul was dead, so he too threw himself on his own sword and died with Saul. ⁶And that is how Saul, his three sons, and the young man died; all of Saul's men died that day. ⁷When the Israelites on the other side of Jezreel Valley and east of the Jordan River heard that the Israelite army had fled and that Saul and his sons had been killed, they abandoned their towns and fled. Then the Philistines came and occupied the towns.

⁸The day after the battle the Philistines went to plunder the corpses, and they found the bodies of Saul and his three sons lying on Mount Gilboa. ⁹They cut off Saul's head, stripped off his armor, and sent messengers with them throughout Philistia to tell the good news to their idols and to their people. ¹⁰Then they put his weapons in the temple of the goddess Astarte, and they nailed his body to the wall of the city of Beth Shan.

¹¹When the people of Jabesh in Gilead heard what the Philistines had done to Saul, ¹²the bravest men started out and marched all night to Beth Shan. They took down the bodies of Saul and his sons from the wall, brought them back to Jabesh, and burned them there. ¹³Then they took the bones and buried them under the tamarisk tree in town, and fasted for seven days.

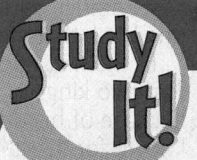

A Tragic End

Saul's story is a very sad one. He and his sons meet a brutal and bloody end. What happened to this once-promising king of Israel? There are lots of answers, but the simplest is ego. Saul let his ego take over, and he forgot about God; he disobeyed, and he did not follow God's will. He spent his last days chasing after David, slaughtering priests, calling up Samuel's spirit, and finally committing suicide. His sons, including David's best friend Jonathan, are also dead.

Saul failed as king. He failed and met such a tragic end because he turned away from God. And he was too stubborn or too proud to change his ways and get off the path of destruction he was on. Let us remember that it is never too late to turn away from sin and return to God.

— 1 Samuel, chapter 31

Your Next Step

Congratulations on finishing the First Book of Samuel! Use this space to write your thoughts and questions about this book. If you are following the suggested reading plan, move ahead to the First Letter of Timothy in the New Testament. This letter is filled with advice to a Christian leader in the early Church about how to lead wisely.

I Samuel

If you are thinking that there might be a sequel to First Samuel, you're right! First and Second Samuel were originally one book that was split into two separate books.

In the first book, Samuel, a prophet of the Lord, anoints the first two kings of Israel—Saul, who is later rejected by God because of his disobedience, and David, a shepherd boy well-known for defeating a giant with a slingshot.

In the second book, David reigns as king. Even though David is a good warrior and a successful king, he's not perfect. David commits some very serious sins and has to pay the consequences. He also has to deal with the violent death of two of his sons. David is a good example for us because he admitted his sins and remained faithful to God, no matter what.

Chap. 11

Head lines

- David Grieves for Dead Friend and King (1:1–12)
- David Named King of Israel and Judah (5:1–12)
- Sex Scandal in the Palace (chapter 11)
- Prophet Uncovers Crime, King Repents (chapter 12)
- King's Son Plans Rebellion! (15:1–12)
- King's Son Dies in Tree (18:4–18)
- David's Song Praises God's Victory (chapter 22)

FACTOIDS

Why was this book written? This book was written to tell the story of David's rise to power as the second king of Israel, his fall into sin, and his reliance on God.

What time period does it cover? About 1000 to 960 BC.

How does it fit into the Bible? This book continues the saga begun in First Samuel and covers the reign of Israel's greatest king, David.

Jesus connection: David is promised an eternal dynasty, from which Jesus will come one thousand years later (7:1–17).

Important themes

- When David sins, he admits it and asks God for forgiveness.
- Violence, jealousy, and power easily lead to a multitude of sins.
- God keeps the Covenant with his people through all of history.

2 SAMUEL

David Learns of Saul's Death

1 ¹After Saul's death David came back from his victory over the Amalekites and stayed in Ziklag for two days. ²The next day a young man arrived from Saul's camp. To show his grief, he had torn his clothes and put dirt on his head. He went to David and bowed to the ground in respect. ³David asked him, "Where have you come from?"

"I have escaped from the Israelite camp," he answered.

⁴"Tell me what happened," David said.

"Our army ran away from the battle," he replied, "and many of our men were killed. Saul and his son Jonathan were also killed."

⁵"How do you know that Saul and Jonathan are dead?" David asked him.

⁶He answered, "I happened to be on Mount Gilboa, and I saw that Saul was leaning on his spear and that the chariots and cavalry of the enemy were closing in on him. ⁷Then he turned around, saw me, and called to me. I answered, 'Yes, sir!' ⁸He asked who I was, and I told him that I was an Amalekite. ⁹Then he said, 'Come here and kill me! I have been badly wounded, and I'm about to die.' ¹⁰So I went up to him and killed him, because I knew that he would die anyway as soon as he fell. Then I took the crown from his head and the bracelet from his arm, and I have brought them to you, sir."

¹¹David tore his clothes in sorrow, and all his men did the same. ¹²They grieved and mourned and fasted until evening for Saul and Jonathan and for Israel, the people of the LORD, because so many had been killed in battle.

¹³David asked the young man who had brought him the news, "Where are you from?"

He answered, "I'm an Amalekite, but I live in your country."

¹⁴David asked him, "How is it that you

David tore his clothes in sorrow. (1:11)

dared kill the LORD's chosen king?" ¹⁵Then David called one of his men and said, "Kill him!" The man struck the Amalekite and mortally wounded him, ¹⁶and David said to the Amalekite, "You brought this on yourself. You condemned yourself when you confessed that you killed the one whom the LORD chose to be king."

David's Lament for Saul and Jonathan

¹⁷David sang this lament for Saul and his son Jonathan, ¹⁸and ordered it[a] to be taught to the people of Judah. (It is recorded in *The Book of Jashar.*)

¹⁹"On the hills of Israel our leaders are dead!
The bravest of our soldiers have fallen!
²⁰Do not announce it in Gath
or in the streets of Ashkelon.
Do not make the women of Philistia glad;
do not let the daughters of pagans
rejoice.

²¹"May no rain or dew fall on Gilboa's hills;
may its fields be always barren!

---

[a] **1:18** *One ancient translation* it; *Hebrew* the bow.
1:6–10 1 Sam 31:1–6; 1 Chr 10:1–6   **1:18** Josh 10:13

Torn Apart

When David learned that both Saul and Jonathan were dead, he "tore his clothes in sorrow, and all his men did the same" (2 Samuel 1:11). This may strike us as a bit strange, and definitely a waste of clothing! But think for a moment about this action and what it might stand for. Many of us have experienced the loss of someone we are close to, either a family member or a close friend. Doesn't it often feel as if he or she were suddenly torn from our lives?

No matter how good someone is at sewing or patching, once a piece of clothing is ripped, it is never the same. So it is with us: when people we love die, they leave their mark on our lives, and we will never be the same. When we trust in God's goodness, the pain and grief we experience will be replaced by good memories over time. Think about someone in your life who died and how it felt when he or she was gone.

— 2 Samuel 1:1–12

For the shields of the brave lie there in disgrace;
the shield of Saul is no longer polished with oil.
²²Jonathan's bow was deadly,
the sword of Saul was merciless,
striking down the mighty, killing the enemy.

²³ "Saul and Jonathan, so wonderful and dear;
together in life, together in death;
swifter than eagles, stronger than lions.

²⁴ "Women of Israel, mourn for Saul!
He clothed you in rich scarlet dresses
and adorned you with jewels and gold.

²⁵ "The brave soldiers have fallen,
they were killed in battle.
Jonathan lies dead in the hills.

²⁶ "I grieve for you, my brother Jonathan;
how dear you were to me!
How wonderful was your love for me,
better even than the love of women.

²⁷ "The brave soldiers have fallen,
their weapons abandoned and useless."

David Is Made King of Judah

2 ¹After this, David asked the LORD, "Shall I go and take control of one of the towns of Judah?"

"Yes," the LORD answered.

"Which one?" David asked.

"Hebron," the LORD said. ²So David went to Hebron, taking with him his two wives: Ahinoam, who was from Jezreel, and Abigail, Nabal's widow, who was from Carmel. ³He also took his men and their families, and they settled in the towns around Hebron. ⁴Then the men of Judah came to Hebron and anointed David as king of Judah.

When David heard that the people of Jabesh in Gilead had buried Saul, ⁵he sent some men there with the message: "May the LORD bless you for showing your loyalty to your king by burying him. ⁶And now may the LORD be kind and faithful to you. I too will treat you well because of what you have done. ⁷Be strong and brave! Saul your king is dead, and the people of Judah have anointed me as their king."

2:2 1 Sam 25:42, 43   **2:4** 1 Sam 31:11–13

Find out how long David ruled over Judah (*2 Samuel 2:11*), **and locate Judah on Map 3 in the back of this Bible.**

2 Samuel

Ishbosheth Is Made King of Israel

8 The commander of Saul's army, Abner son of Ner, had fled with Saul's son Ishbosheth across the Jordan to Mahanaim. **9** There Abner made Ishbosheth king of the territories of Gilead, Asher,*b* Jezreel, Ephraim, and Benjamin, and indeed over all Israel. **10** He was forty years old when he was made king of Israel, and he ruled for two years.

But the tribe of Judah was loyal to David, **11** and he ruled in Hebron over Judah for seven and a half years.

War between Israel and Judah

12 Abner and the officials of Ishbosheth went from Mahanaim to the city of Gibeon. **13** Joab, whose mother was Zeruiah, and David's other officials met them at the pool, where they all sat down, one group on one side of the pool and the other group on the opposite side. **14** Abner said to Joab, "Let's have some of the young men from each side fight an armed contest."

"All right," Joab answered.

15 So twelve men, representing Ishbosheth and the tribe of Benjamin, fought twelve of David's men. **16** Each man caught his opponent by the head and plunged his sword into his opponent's side, so that all twenty-four of them fell down dead together. And so that place in Gibeon is called "Field of Swords."

17 Then a furious battle broke out, and Abner and the Israelites were defeated by David's men. **18** The three sons of Zeruiah were there: Joab, Abishai, and Asahel. Asahel, who could run as fast as a wild deer, **19** started chasing Abner, running straight for him. **20** Abner looked back and said, "Is that you, Asahel?"

"Yes," he answered.

21 "Stop chasing me!" Abner said. "Run after one of the soldiers and take what he has." But Asahel kept on chasing him. **22** Once more Abner said to him, "Stop chasing me! Why force me to kill you? How could I face your brother Joab?" **23** But Asahel would not quit; so Abner, with a backward thrust*c* of his spear, struck him through the stomach so that the spear came out at his back. Asahel dropped to the ground dead, and everyone who came to the place where he was lying stopped and stood there.

24 But Joab and Abishai started out after Abner, and at sunset they came to the hill of Ammah, which is to the east of Giah on the road to the wilderness of Gibeon. **25** The men from the tribe of Benjamin gathered around Abner again and took their stand on the top of a hill. **26** Abner called out to Joab, "Do we have to go on fighting forever? Can't you see that in the end there will be nothing but bitterness? We are your relatives. How long will it be before you order your men to stop chasing us?"

27 "I swear by the living God," Joab answered, "that if you had not spoken, my men would have kept on chasing you until tomorrow morning." **28** Then Joab blew the trumpet as a signal for his men to stop pursuing the Israelites; and so the fighting stopped.

29 Abner and his men marched through the Jordan Valley all that night; they crossed the Jordan River, and after marching all the next morning, they arrived back at Mahanaim.

30 When Joab gave up the chase, he gathered all his men and found that nineteen of them were missing, in addition to Asahel. **31** David's men had killed 360 of Abner's men from the tribe of Benjamin. **32** Joab and his men took Asahel's body and buried it in the family tomb at Bethlehem. Then they marched all night and at dawn arrived back at Hebron.

3 **1** The fighting between the forces supporting Saul's family and those supporting David went on for a long time. As David became stronger and stronger, his opponents became weaker and weaker.

David's Sons

2 The following six sons, in order of their birth, were born to David at Hebron: Amnon, whose mother was Ahinoam, from Jezreel; **3** Chileab, whose mother was Abigail, Nabal's widow, from Carmel; Absalom, whose mother was Maacah, the daughter of King

---

b **2:9** *One ancient translation* Asher; *Hebrew* Assyria.   *c* **2:23** *Probable text* with a backward thrust; *Hebrew unclear.*

Talmai of Geshur; 4Adonijah, whose mother was Haggith; Shephatiah, whose mother was Abital; 5Ithream, whose mother was Eglah. All of these sons were born in Hebron.

Abner Joins David

6As the fighting continued between David's forces and the forces loyal to Saul's family, Abner became more and more powerful among Saul's followers.

7One day Ishbosheth son of Saul accused Abner of sleeping with Saul's concubine Rizpah, the daughter of Aiah. 8This made Abner furious. "Do you think that I would betray Saul? Do you really think I'm serving Judah?" he exclaimed. "From the very first I have been loyal to the cause of your father Saul, his brothers, and his friends, and I have kept you from being defeated by David; yet today you find fault with me about a woman! 9-10The LORD promised David that he would take the kingdom away from Saul and his descendants and would make David king of both Israel and Judah, from one end of the country to the other. Now may God strike me dead if I don't make this come true!" 11Ishbosheth was so afraid of Abner that he could not say a word.

12Abner sent messengers to David, who at that time was at Hebron,d to say, "Who is going to rule this land? Make an agreement with me, and I will help you win all Israel over to your side."

13"Good!" David answered. "I will make an agreement with you on one condition: you must bring Saul's daughter Michal to me when you come to see me." 14And David also sent messengers to Ishbosheth to say, "Give me back my wife Michal. I paid a hundred Philistine foreskins in order to marry her." 15So Ishbosheth had her taken from her husband Paltiel son of Laish. 16Paltiel followed her all the way to the town of Bahurim, crying as he went. But when Abner said, "Go back home," he did.

17Abner went to the leaders of Israel and said to them, "For a long time you have wanted David to be your king. 18Now here is your chance. Remember that the LORD has said, 'I will use my servant David to rescue my people Israel from the Philistines and from all their other enemies.' " 19Abner spoke also to the people of the tribe of Benjamin and then went to Hebron to tell David what the people of Benjamin and of Israel had agreed to do.

20When Abner came to David at Hebron with twenty men, David gave a feast for them. 21Abner told David, "I will go now and win all Israel over to Your Majesty. They will accept you as king, and then you will get what you have wanted and will rule over the whole land." David gave Abner a guarantee of safety and sent him on his way.

Abner Is Murdered

22Later on Joab and David's other officials returned from a raid, bringing a large amount of loot with them. Abner, however, was no longer there at Hebron with David, because David had sent him away with a guarantee of safety. 23When Joab and his men arrived, he was told that Abner had come to King David and had been sent away with a guarantee of safety. 24So Joab went to the king and said to him, "What have you done? Abner came to you—why did you let him go like that? 25He came here to deceive you and to find out everything you do and everywhere you go. Surely you know that!"

26After leaving David, Joab sent messengers to get Abner, and they brought him back from Sirah Well; but David knew nothing about it. 27When Abner arrived in Hebron, Joab took him aside at the gate, as though he wanted to speak privately with him, and there he stabbed him in the stomach. And so Abner was murdered because he had killed Joab's brother Asahel. 28When David heard the news, he said, "The LORD knows that my subjects and I are completely innocent of the murder of Abner. 29May the punishment for it fall on Joab and all his family! In every generation may there be some man in his family who has gonorrhea or a dreaded skin disease or is fit only to do a woman's work or is killed in battle or doesn't have enough to

---

d 3:12 One ancient translation at Hebron; Hebrew where he (Abner) was.
3:10 1 Sam 15:28   3:14 1 Sam 18:27

Afflictions

David curses the descendants of Joab, asking that in every generation someone be afflicted with gonorrhea, a skin disease, weakness, death in battle, or hunger. It doesn't sound very nice but neither was Joab's sneaky killing of Abner. Jesus taught us that God doesn't punish children for their parents' sins, but it was a popular belief in Old Testament times.

You probably know that gonorrhea is a sexually transmitted disease (STD). It has been around a very long time. Keep in mind that it is transmitted almost only though sexual intercourse. Also keep in mind that if you and your future spouse follow the Church's teaching on sexuality, you should not need to worry unduly about gonorrhea or any other STD.

Make a pledge now to avoid intimate sexual activity until you get married. You might want to visit the True Love Waits Web site for more information.

— 2 Samuel 3:26–30

eat!" 30 So Joab and his brother Abishai took revenge on Abner for killing their brother Asahel in the battle at Gibeon.

Abner Is Buried

31 Then David ordered Joab and his men to tear their clothes, wear sackcloth, and mourn for Abner. And at the funeral King David himself walked behind the coffin. 32 Abner was buried at Hebron, and the king wept aloud at the grave, and so did all the people. 33 David sang this lament for Abner:

"Why did Abner have to die like a fool?
34 His hands were not tied,
    And his feet were not bound;
    He died like someone killed by criminals!"

And the people wept for him again.

35 All day long the people tried to get David to eat something, but he made a solemn promise, "May God strike me dead if I eat anything before the day is over!" 36 They took note of this and were pleased. Indeed, everything the king did pleased the people. 37 All of David's people and all the people in Israel understood that the king had no part in the murder of Abner. 38 The king said to his officials, "Don't you realize that this day a great leader in Israel has died? 39 Even though I am the king chosen by God, I feel weak today. These sons of Zeruiah are too violent for me. May the LORD punish these criminals as they deserve!"

Ishbosheth Is Murdered

4 1 When Saul's son Ishbosheth heard that Abner had been killed in Hebron, he was afraid, and all the people of Israel were alarmed. 2 Ishbosheth had two officers who were leaders of raiding parties, Baanah and Rechab, sons of Rimmon, from Beeroth in the tribe of Benjamin. (Beeroth is counted as part of Benjamin. 3 Its original inhabitants had fled to Gittaim, where they have lived ever since.)

4 Another descendant of Saul was Jonathan's son Mephibosheth, who was five years old when Saul and Jonathan were killed. When the news about their death came from the city of Jezreel, his nurse picked him up and fled; but she was in such a hurry that she dropped him, and he became crippled.

4:4 2 Sam 9:3

2 Samuel

Mephibosheth is Jonathan's son. How did he become crippled?

5Rechab and Baanah set out for Ish-bosheth's house and arrived there about noon, while he was taking his midday rest. 6The woman at the door had become drowsy while she was sifting wheat and had fallen asleep, so Rechab and Baanah slipped in.*e* 7Once inside, they went to Ishbosheth's bedroom, where he was sound asleep, and killed him. Then they cut off his head, took it with them, and walked all night through the Jordan Valley. 8They presented the head to King David at Hebron and said to him, "Here is the head of Ishbosheth, the son of your enemy Saul, who tried to kill you. Today the LORD has allowed Your Majesty to take revenge on Saul and his descendants."

9David answered them, "I take a vow by the living LORD, who has saved me from all dangers! 10The messenger who came to me at Ziklag and told me of Saul's death thought he was bringing good news. I seized him and had him put to death. That was the reward I gave him for his good news! 11How much worse it will be for evil men who murder an innocent man asleep in his own house! I will now take revenge on you for murdering him and will wipe you off the face of the earth!" 12David gave the order, and his soldiers killed Rechab and Baanah and cut off their hands and feet, which they hung up near the pool in Hebron. They took Ishbosheth's head and buried it in Abner's tomb there at Hebron.

David Becomes King of Israel and Judah
(1 Chronicles 11:1–9; 14:1–7)

5 1Then all the tribes of Israel went to David at Hebron and said to him, "We are your own flesh and blood. 2In the past, even when Saul was still our king, you led the people of Israel in battle, and the LORD promised you that you would lead his people and be their ruler." 3So all the leaders of Israel came to King David at Hebron. He made a sacred alliance with them, they anointed him, and he became king of Israel. 4David was thirty years old when he became king, and he ruled for forty years. 5He ruled in Hebron over Judah for seven and a half years, and in Jerusalem over all Israel and Judah for thirty-three years.

6The time came when King David and his men set out to attack Jerusalem. The Jebusites, who lived there, thought that David would not be able to conquer the city, and so they said to him, "You will never get in here; even the blind and the crippled could keep you out." (7But David did capture their fortress of Zion, and it became known as "David's City.")

8That day David said to his men, "Does anybody here hate the Jebusites as much as I do? Enough to kill them? Then go up through the water tunnel and attack those poor blind cripples." (That is why it is said, "The blind and the crippled cannot enter the LORD's house.")*f*

9After capturing the fortress, David lived in it and named it "David's City." He built the city around it, starting at the place where land was filled in on the east side of the hill. 10He grew stronger all the time, because the LORD God Almighty was with him.

11King Hiram of Tyre sent a trade mission to David; he provided him with cedar logs and with carpenters and stone masons to build a palace. 12And so David realized that the LORD had established him as king of Israel and was making his kingdom prosperous for the sake of his people.

13After moving from Hebron to Jerusalem, David took more concubines and wives, and had more sons and daughters. 14The following children were born to him in Jerusalem: Shammua, Shobab, Nathan, Solomon, 15Ibhar, Elishua, Nepheg, Japhia, 16Elishama, Eliada, and Eliphelet.

---

e **4:6** *Verse 6 follows one ancient translation; Hebrew* They went on into the house carrying wheat, and struck him in the belly. Then Rechab and his brother Baanah escaped. *f* **5:8** *Verse 8 in Hebrew is unclear.*
4:10 2 Sam 1:1–16   **5:4, 5** 1 Kings 2:11; 1 Chr 3:4; 29:27   **5:6** Josh 15:63; Judg 1:21

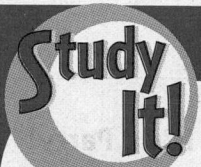

Jerusalem, the Holy City

When David captured the city of Jerusalem from the Jebusites, it became known as David's City. When David captured it, it wasn't all that big or famous. But under David and Solomon's rule, it became the largest and most important city in Israel.

Jerusalem today continues to be a very important city. It has become a holy city for three of the world's major religions: Judaism, Christianity, and Islam. For Jews, Jerusalem contains a wall from the Great Temple built by King Herod and destroyed by the Romans in AD 70. For Christians, Jerusalem is the city where Jesus was crucified, buried, and raised from the dead. For Islam, Jerusalem is one of the three holy cities. It contains the Dome of the Rock, a mosque built over the site where all three faiths believe Abraham took his son to be sacrificed.

— 2 Samuel 5:6–9

Victory over the Philistines
(1 Chronicles 14:8–17)

17 The Philistines were told that David had been made king of Israel, so their army set out to capture him. When David heard of it, he went down to a fortified place. 18 The Philistines arrived at Rephaim Valley and occupied it. 19 David asked the LORD, "Shall I attack the Philistines? Will you give me the victory?"

"Yes, attack!" the LORD answered. "I will give you the victory!"

20 So David went to Baal Perazim and there he defeated the Philistines. He said, "The LORD has broken through my enemies like a flood." And so that place is called Baal Perazim.*g* 21 When the Philistines fled, they left their idols behind, and David and his men carried them away.

22 Then the Philistines went back to Rephaim Valley and occupied it again. 23 Once more David consulted the LORD, who answered, "Don't attack them from here, but go around and get ready to attack them from the other side, near the balsam trees. 24 When you hear the sound of marching in the treetops, then attack because I will be marching ahead of you to defeat the Philistine army." 25 David did what the LORD had commanded, and was able to drive the Philistines back from Geba all the way to Gezer.

The Covenant Box Is Brought to Jerusalem
(1 Chronicles 13:1–14; 15:25 —16:6, 43)

6 1 Once more David called together the best soldiers in Israel, a total of thirty thousand men, 2 and led them to Baalah*h* in Judah, in order to bring from there God's Covenant Box, bearing the name of the LORD Almighty, whose throne is above the winged creatures.*i* 3 They took it from Abinadab's home on the hill and placed it on a new cart. Uzzah and Ahio, sons of Abinadab, were guiding the cart, 4 with Ahio walking in front. 5 David and all the Israelites were dancing and singing with all their might*j* to honor the LORD. They were playing harps, lyres, drums, rattles, and cymbals.

The Israelites were dancing and singing. (6:5)

2 Samuel

---

g **5:20** BAAL PERAZIM: *This name in Hebrew means "Lord of the Breakthrough."*   *h* **6:2** *Probable text (see 1 Chr 13:6)* to Baalah; *Hebrew* from Baaley, or from the leaders.   *i* **6:2** WINGED CREATURES: *See Word List.*   *j* **6:5** *One ancient translation (and see 1 Chr 13:8) and singing with all their might; Hebrew with all the fir trees.*
6:2 Ex 25:22   **6:3** 1 Sam 7:1, 2

⁶As they came to the threshing place of Nacon, the oxen stumbled, and Uzzah reached out and took hold of the Covenant Box. ⁷At once the LORD God became angry with Uzzah and killed him because of his irreverence.ᵏ Uzzah died there beside the Covenant Box, ⁸and so that place has been called Perez Uzzahˡ ever since. David was furious because the LORD had punished Uzzah in anger.

⁹Then David was afraid of the LORD and said, "How can I take the Covenant Box with me now?" ¹⁰So he decided not to take it with him to Jerusalem; instead, he turned off the road and took it to the house of Obed Edom, a native of the city of Gath. ¹¹It stayed there three months, and the LORD blessed Obed Edom and his family.

¹²King David heard that because of the Covenant Box the LORD had blessed Obed Edom's family and all that he had; so he got the Covenant Box from Obed's house to take it to Jerusalem with a great celebration. ¹³After the men carrying the Covenant Box had gone six steps, David had them stop while he offered the LORD a sacrifice of a bull and a fattened calf. ¹⁴David, wearing only a linen cloth around his waist, danced with all his might to honor the LORD. ¹⁵And so he and all the Israelites took the Covenant Box up to Jerusalem with shouts of joy and the sound of trumpets.

¹⁶As the Box was being brought into the city, Michal, Saul's daughter, looked out of the window and saw King David dancing and jumping around in the sacred dance, and she was disgusted with him. ¹⁷They brought the Box and put it in its place in the Tent that David had set up for it. Then he offered sacrifices and fellowship offerings to the LORD. ¹⁸When he had finished offering the sacrifices, he blessed the people in the name of the LORD Almighty ¹⁹and distributed food to them all. He gave each man and woman in Israel a loaf of bread, a piece of roasted meat,ᵐ and some raisins. Then everyone went home.

²⁰Afterward, when David went home to greet his family, Michal came out to meet him. "The king of Israel made a big name

It's a Party!

Try to imagine the president of the United States leading a parade to the Capitol building in Washington, D.C., by publicly dancing! When King David did something similar in the capital city of Jerusalem, he certainly got people's attention. He was leading the holiest object of the Jewish faith, the Covenant Box or Ark of the Covenant. It was going to its new home in the center of the city. To fully praise God, King David decided to throw a party, or festival, which he would lead. He also served everyone a meal.

One of David's wives, Michal, thought he was being a show-off, but he told her that this was the least he could do to honor God. What David did may not have seemed very kingly, but he did it out of a deep desire to show his love for God. And he wasn't the least bit embarrassed. Sometimes because religion isn't "cool," we get embarrassed when others find out that we pray or read the Bible or go to Church every Sunday.

Think of a time when you became embarrassed about publicly expressing your faith. What caused you to react in such a way, and how would you do it differently now? Next time you feel yourself becoming embarrassed about expressing your faith, picture David dancing before the Lord.

— 2 Samuel 6:12–23

ᵏ **6:7** *Probable text* his irreverence; *Hebrew unclear.* ˡ **6:8** PEREZ UZZAH: *This name in Hebrew means "Punishment of Uzzah."* ᵐ **6:19** a piece of roasted meat; *or* a cake of dates.
6:11 1 Chr 26:4, 5   **6:19, 20** 1 Chr 16:43

for himself today!" she said. "He exposed himself like a fool in the sight of the servant women of his officials!"

[21]David answered, "I was dancing to honor the LORD, who chose me instead of your father and his family to make me the leader of his people Israel. And I will go on dancing to honor the LORD, [22]and will disgrace myself even more. You[n] may think I am nothing, but those women will think highly of me!"

[23]Michal, Saul's daughter, never had any children.

Nathan's Message to David
(1 Chronicles 17:1–15)

7 [1]King David was settled in his palace, and the LORD kept him safe from all his enemies. [2]Then the king said to the prophet Nathan, "Here I am living in a house built of cedar, but God's Covenant Box is kept in a tent!"

[3]Nathan answered, "Do whatever you have in mind, because the LORD is with you." [4]But that night the LORD said to Nathan, [5]"Go and tell my servant David that I say to him, 'You are not the one to build a temple for me to live in. [6]From the time I rescued the people of Israel from Egypt until now, I have never lived in a temple; I have traveled around living in a tent. [7]In all my traveling with the people of Israel I never asked any of the leaders[o] that I appointed why they had not built me a temple made of cedar.'

[8]"So tell my servant David that I, the LORD Almighty, say to him, 'I took you from looking after sheep in the fields and made you the ruler of my people Israel. [9]I have been with you wherever you have gone, and I have defeated all your enemies as you advanced. I will make you as famous as the greatest leaders in the world. [10-11]I have chosen a place for my people Israel and have settled them there, where they will live

without being oppressed any more. Ever since they entered this land, they have been attacked by violent people, but this will not happen again. I promise to keep you safe from all your enemies and to give you descendants. [12]When you die and are buried with your ancestors, I will make one of your sons king and will keep his kingdom strong. [13]He will be the one to build a temple for me, and I will make sure that his dynasty continues forever. [14]I will be his father, and he will be my son. When he does wrong, I will punish him as a father punishes his son. [15]But I will not withdraw my support from him as I did from Saul, whom I removed so that you could be king. [16]You will always have descendants, and I will make your kingdom last forever. Your dynasty will never end.' "

[17]Nathan told David everything that God had revealed to him.

David's Prayer of Thanksgiving
(1 Chronicles 17:16–27)

[18]Then King David went into the Tent of the LORD's presence, sat down and prayed, "Sovereign LORD, I am not worthy of what you have already done for me, nor is my family. [19]Yet now you are doing even more, Sovereign LORD; you have made promises about my descendants in the years to come. And you let a man see this,[p] Sovereign LORD! [20]What more can I say to you! You know me, your servant. [21]It was your will and purpose to do this; you have done all these great things in order to instruct me. [22]How great you are, Sovereign LORD! There is none like you; we have always known that you alone are God. [23]There is no other nation on earth like Israel, whom you rescued from slavery to make them your own people. The great and wonderful things you did for them[q] have spread your fame throughout the world. You drove out[r] other

Notice the musical instruments used in David's time *(2 Samuel 6:5)*. **Which ones do we still use today?**

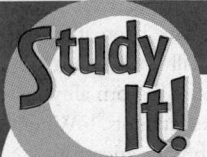

An Eternal Kingdom

In 2 Samuel, chapter 7, Nathan gives David a very important message from God. David is promised by God that his kingdom will last forever, that David's dynasty will never end. A dynasty is the line of rulers or powerful people who are descendants of one person. What this promise, or covenant, seemed to mean was that a descendant of David would always sit on the throne of Israel.

But as we will see, there comes a time when David's descendants no longer sit on the throne. It's not that the covenant was wrong, it was just going to be fulfilled in an unexpected way. This covenant God makes with David is fulfilled in Jesus Christ. Jesus was a descendant of David. Jesus established God's kingdom on earth, a kingdom that has no end.

During Advent we hear the phrase "the root of Jesse." That refers to Jesus, who traces his ancestry back to David, the son of Jesse. David responds to this covenant with a beautiful prayer in 2 Samuel 7:18–29.

— 2 Samuel 7:12–29

25 "And now, LORD God, fulfill for all time the promise you made about me and my descendants, and do what you said you would. 26 Your fame will be great, and people will forever say, 'The LORD Almighty is God over Israel.' And you will preserve my dynasty for all time. 27 LORD Almighty, God of Israel! I have the courage to pray this prayer to you, because you have revealed all this to me, your servant, and have told me that you will make my descendants kings.

28 "And now, Sovereign LORD, you are God; you always keep your promises, and you have made this wonderful promise to me. 29 I ask you to bless my descendants so that they will continue to enjoy your favor. You, Sovereign LORD, have promised this, and your blessing will rest on my descendants forever."

David's Military Victories
(1 Chronicles 18:1–17)

8 ¹Some time later King David attacked the Philistines again, defeated them, and ended their control over the land.*s*

² Then he defeated the Moabites. He made the prisoners lie down on the ground and put two out of every three of them to death. So the Moabites became his subjects and paid taxes to him.

³ Then he defeated the king of the Syrian state of Zobah, Hadadezer son of Rehob, as Hadadezer was on his way to restore his control over the territory by the upper Euphrates River. ⁴ David captured seventeen hundred of his cavalry and twenty thousand of his foot soldiers. He kept enough horses for a hundred chariots and crippled all the rest.

⁵ When the Syrians of Damascus sent an army to help King Hadadezer, David attacked it and killed twenty-two thousand men. ⁶ Then he set up military camps in*t* their territory, and they became his subjects and paid taxes to him. The LORD made David victorious everywhere. ⁷ David captured the gold shields carried by Hadadezer's

nations and their gods as your people advanced, the people whom you set free from Egypt to be your own. 24 You have made Israel your own people forever, and you, LORD, have become their God.

s **8:1** *Probable text* over the land; *Hebrew unclear.*   *t* **8:6** set up military camps in; *or* placed military commanders over.

Joram gives David presents made of what three metals? How are they connected to the Olympics today?

officials and took them to Jerusalem. ⁸He also took a great quantity of bronze from Betah and Berothai, cities ruled by Hadadezer.

⁹King Toi of Hamath heard that David had defeated all of Hadadezer's army. ¹⁰So he sent his son Joram to greet King David and congratulate him for his victory over Hadadezer, against whom Toi had fought many times. Joram took David presents made of gold, silver, and bronze. ¹¹King David dedicated them for use in worship, along with the silver and gold he took from the nations he had conquered—¹²Edom, Moab, Ammon, Philistia, and Amalek—as well as part of the loot he had taken from Hadadezer.

¹³David became even more famous when he returned from killing eighteen thousand Edomites in Salt Valley. ¹⁴He set up military camps*ᵘ* throughout Edom, and the people there became his subjects. The LORD made David victorious everywhere.

¹⁵David ruled over all of Israel and made sure that his people were always treated fairly and justly. ¹⁶Joab, whose mother was Zeruiah, was the commander of the army; Jehoshaphat son of Ahilud was in charge of the records; ¹⁷Zadok son of Ahitub and Ahimelech son of Abiathar were priests; Seraiah was the court secretary; ¹⁸Benaiah son of Jehoiada was in charge of*ᵛ* David's bodyguards; and David's sons were priests.

David and Mephibosheth

9 ¹One day David asked, "Is there anyone left of Saul's family? If there is, I would like to show him kindness for Jonathan's sake."

²There was a servant of Saul's family named Ziba, and he was told to go to David. "Are you Ziba?" the king asked.

"At your service, sir," he answered.

³The king asked him, "Is there anyone left of Saul's family to whom I can show loyalty and kindness, as I promised God I would?"

Ziba answered, "There is still one of Jonathan's sons. He is crippled."

⁴"Where is he?" the king asked.

"At the home of Machir son of Ammiel

He is crippled. (9:3)

in Lodebar," Ziba answered. ⁵So King David sent for him.

⁶When Mephibosheth, the son of Jonathan and grandson of Saul, arrived, he bowed down before David in respect. David said, "Mephibosheth," and he answered, "At your service, sir."

⁷"Don't be afraid," David replied. "I will be kind to you for the sake of your father Jonathan. I will give you back all the land that belonged to your grandfather Saul, and you will always be welcome at my table."

⁸Mephibosheth bowed again and said, "I am no better than a dead dog, sir! Why should you be so good to me?"

⁹Then the king called Ziba, Saul's servant, and said, "I am giving Mephibosheth, your master's grandson, everything that belonged

"Don't be afraid . . . I will be kind to you." (9:7)

ᵘ **8:14** set up military camps; *or* placed military commanders.   *ᵛ* **8:18** *Some ancient translations* was in charge of; *Hebrew does not have these words.*

8:13 Ps 60 Title   **9:1** 1 Sam 20:15–17   **9:3** 2 Sam 4:4

Live Your Potential

In 2 Samuel, chapter 9, King David met the only surviving son of his best friend, Jonathan. He saw that Mephibosheth was injured in both legs. David treated him like his own son and made sure all the land taken from his family was returned. Just because Mephibosheth was injured was not a reason for him not to be treated fairly.

Today we have a variety of terms for people who have physical disabilities. The term often used to describe such persons is "differently abled." We want to emphasize the positive, that people can live full and satisfying lives even with a disability. Often in biblical times such persons were avoided because people believed that God was punishing them for their sins. Today, we know better. We understand that there are a variety of people, that everyone has different abilities, and that all people are to be treated with fairness and respect because they are created in the image of God.

Think about a time when you saw a person with different physical or mental abilities treated with a lack of respect. What can you do if that happens again?

— 2 Samuel, chapter 9

So Mephibosheth ate at the king's[w] table, just like one of the king's sons. 12Mephibosheth had a young son named Mica. All the members of Ziba's family became servants of Mephibosheth. 13So Mephibosheth, who was crippled in both feet, lived in Jerusalem, eating all his meals at the king's table.

David Defeats the Ammonites and the Syrians
(1 Chronicles 19:1–19)

10 1Some time later King Nahash of Ammon died, and his son Hanun became king. 2King David said, "I must show loyal friendship to Hanun, as his father Nahash did to me." So David sent messengers to express his sympathy.

When they arrived in Ammon, 3the Ammonite leaders said to the king, "Do you think that it is in your father's honor that David has sent these men to express sympathy to you? Of course not! He has sent them here as spies to explore the city, so that he can conquer us!"

4Hanun seized David's messengers, shaved off one side of their beards, cut off their clothes at the hips, and sent them away. 5They were too ashamed to return home. When David heard about what had happened, he sent word for them to stay in Jericho and not return until their beards had grown again.

6The Ammonites realized that they had made David their enemy, so they hired twenty thousand Syrian soldiers from Bethrehob and Zobah, twelve thousand men from Tob, and the king of Maacah with a thousand men. 7David heard of it and sent Joab against them with the whole army. 8The Ammonites marched out and took up their position at the entrance to Rabbah, their capital city, while the others, both the Syrians and the men from Tob and Maacah, took up their position in the open countryside.

9Joab saw that the enemy troops would attack him in front and from the rear, so he chose the best of Israel's soldiers and put them in position facing the Syrians. 10He placed the rest of his troops under the com-

to Saul and his family. 10You, your sons, and your servants will farm the land for your master Saul's family and bring in the harvest, to provide food for them. But Mephibosheth himself will always be a guest at my table." (Ziba had fifteen sons and twenty servants.)

11Ziba answered, "I will do everything Your Majesty commands."

---

w 9:11 One ancient translation the king's; *Hebrew* my.

Cruelty

In 2 Samuel 10:3–4, we read
about how Hanun, the king of
Ammon, treats David's messengers. He cuts off one side of their
beards and cuts off their clothes
at the hips. They are too ashamed
and embarrassed to return home
until their beards have grown
back. This is a grave insult to King
David, who sent them to express
his sympathy for Hanun's father,
who had died.

Perhaps the actions done to
David's men seem strange to us,
but they were done to make fun
of these men and to embarrass
them and their king, David. It
seems like a childish thing to do,
until we think about the ways that
we make fun of others, especially
those we don't like. We can do it
through actions that belittle others, or we can do it through
words. Either way, the result is the
same: we have tried to make ourselves better than someone else,
while in reality we have only
shown our immaturity.

Think about a time when you
made fun of someone else or did
something cruel to them. How do
you feel about it now? How do
you think it made them feel? Is it
possible to make it up to them?

— 2 Samuel 10:4–5

mand of his brother Abishai, who put them
in position facing the Ammonites. ¹¹Joab said
to him, "If you see that the Syrians are

defeating me, come and help me, and if the
Ammonites are defeating you, I will go and
help you. ¹²Be strong and courageous! Let's
fight hard for our people and for the cities of
our God. And may the LORD's will be done!"

¹³Joab and his men advanced to attack,
and the Syrians fled. ¹⁴When the Ammonites
saw the Syrians running away, they fled from
Abishai and retreated into the city. Then Joab
turned back from fighting the Ammonites
and went back to Jerusalem.

¹⁵The Syrians realized that they had been
defeated by the Israelites, and so they called
all their troops together. ¹⁶King Hadadezer
sent for the Syrians who were on the east
side of the Euphrates River, and they came
to Helam under the command of Shobach,
commander of the army of King Hadadezer
of Zobah. ¹⁷When David heard of it, he
gathered the Israelite troops, crossed the Jordan River, and marched to Helam, where
the Syrians took up their position facing
him. The fighting began, ¹⁸and the Israelites
drove the Syrian army back. David and his
men killed seven hundred Syrian chariot
drivers and forty thousand cavalry, and they
wounded Shobach, the enemy commander,
who died on the battlefield. ¹⁹When the
kings who were subject to Hadadezer realized that they had been defeated by the
Israelites, they made peace with them and
became their subjects. And the Syrians were
afraid to help the Ammonites any more.

David and Bathsheba

11 ¹The following spring, at the time
of the year when kings usually go to
war, David sent out Joab with his officers
and the Israelite army; they defeated the
Ammonites and besieged the city of Rabbah. But David himself stayed in Jerusalem.

²One day, late in the afternoon, David got
up from his nap and went to the palace roof.
As he walked around up there, he saw a
woman taking a bath in her house. She was
very beautiful. ³So he sent a messenger to

2 Samuel

11:1 1 Chr 20:1

**"Be strong and courageous! Let's fight hard for our people and for the cities of
our God. And may the LORD's will be done!"** *(2 Samuel 10:12)*.

Pray It!

Facing the Truth

King David seemed to have it all. So much was going his way. But one day, he seemed to forget who he was and what God had called him to be. He saw a beautiful woman and decided he wanted her for himself. The only problem was that she happened to be married to a man named Uriah. Because the woman—named Bathsheba—became pregnant with David's child, he had her husband, Uriah, killed. Clearly, he abused his power. Nathan the prophet served as God's voice here. Through a clever story, he got David to admit his own sin. It was a powerful moment for both men. David could not undo what had been done, but he did repent and admitted that he had sinned. He didn't try to make excuses or have Nathan silenced.

David may have written Psalm 51 as a way of asking for forgiveness. You can read Psalm 51 as a prayer asking for forgiveness, too.

> *Be merciful to me, O God,*
> *because of your constant love.*
> *Because of your great mercy*
> *wipe away my sins!*
> *Wash away all my evil*
> *and make me clean from my sin!* (Psalm 51:1–2)

— 2 Samuel, chapters 11–12

find out who she was, and learned that she was Bathsheba, the daughter of Eliam and the wife of Uriah the Hittite. [4]David sent messengers to get her; they brought her to him and he made love to her. (She had just finished her monthly ritual of purification.) Then she went back home. [5]Afterward she discovered that she was pregnant and sent a message to David to tell him.

[6]David then sent a message to Joab: "Send me Uriah the Hittite." So Joab sent him to David. [7]When Uriah arrived, David asked him if Joab and the troops were well, and how the fighting was going. [8]Then he said to Uriah, "Go on home and rest a while." Uriah left, and David had a present sent to his home. [9]But Uriah did not go home; instead he slept at the palace gate with the king's guards. [10]When David heard that Uriah had not gone home, he asked him, "You have just returned after a long absence; why didn't you go home?"

[11]Uriah answered, "The men of Israel and Judah are away in battle, and the Covenant Box is with them; my commander Joab and his officers are camping out in the open. How could I go home, eat and drink, and sleep with my wife? By all that's sacred, I swear that I could never do such a thing!"

[12]So David said, "Then stay here the rest of the day, and tomorrow I'll send you back." So Uriah stayed in Jerusalem that day and the next. [13]David invited him to supper and got him drunk. But again that night Uriah did not go home; instead he slept on his blanket[x] in the palace guardroom.

[x] **11:13** blanket; *or* cot.

2 Samuel

David wants Uriah to go home and sleep with his wife, Bathsheba. Why does David want this?

14The next morning David wrote a letter to Joab and sent it by Uriah. 15He wrote: "Put Uriah in the front line, where the fighting is heaviest, then retreat and let him be killed." 16So while Joab was besieging the city, he sent Uriah to a place where he knew the enemy was strong. 17The enemy troops came out of the city and fought Joab's forces; some of David's officers were killed, and so was Uriah.

18Then Joab sent a report to David telling him about the battle, 19and he instructed the messenger, "After you have told the king all about the battle, 20he may get angry and ask you, 'Why did you go so near the city to fight them? Didn't you realize that they would shoot arrows from the walls? 21Don't you remember how Abimelech son of Gideon was killed? It was at Thebez, where a woman threw a millstone down from the wall and killed him. Why, then, did you go so near the wall?' If the king asks you this, tell him, 'Your officer Uriah was also killed.' "

22So the messenger went to David and told him what Joab had commanded him to say. 23He said, "Our enemies were stronger than we were and came out of the city to fight us in the open, but we drove them back to the city gate. 24Then they shot arrows at us from the wall, and some of Your Majesty's officers were killed; your officer Uriah was also killed."

25David said to the messenger, "Encourage Joab and tell him not to be upset, since you never can tell who will die in battle. Tell him to launch a stronger attack on the city and capture it."

26When Bathsheba heard that her husband had been killed, she mourned for him. 27When the time of mourning was over, David had her brought to the palace; she became his wife and bore him a son. But the LORD was not pleased with what David had done.

Nathan's Message and David's Repentance

12 ¹The LORD sent the prophet Nathan to David. Nathan went to him and said, "There were two men who lived in the same town; one was rich and the other poor. ²The rich man had many cattle and sheep, ³while the poor man had only one lamb, which he had bought. He took care of it, and it grew up in his home with his children. He would feed it some of his own food, let it drink from his cup, and hold it in his lap. The lamb was like a daughter to him. ⁴One day a visitor arrived at the rich man's home. The rich man didn't want to kill one of his own animals to fix a meal for him; instead, he took the poor man's lamb and prepared a meal for his guest."

⁵David became very angry at the rich man and said, "I swear by the living LORD that the man who did this ought to die! ⁶For having done such a cruel thing, he must pay back four times as much as he took."

⁷"You are that man," Nathan said to David. "And this is what the LORD God of Israel says: 'I made you king of Israel and rescued you from Saul. ⁸I gave you his kingdom and his wives; I made you king over Israel and Judah. If this had not been enough, I would have given you twice as much. ⁹Why, then, have you disobeyed my commands? Why did

The rich man had many cattle and sheep. (12:2) • *The poor man had only one lamb. (12:3)*

He took the poor man's lamb. (12:4)

you do this evil thing? You had Uriah killed in battle; you let the Ammonites kill him, and then you took his wife! ¹⁰Now, in every generation some of your descendants will die a violent death because you have disobeyed me and have taken Uriah's wife. ¹¹I swear to you that I will cause someone from your own family to bring trouble on you. You will see it when I take your wives from you and give them to another man; and he will have intercourse with them in broad daylight. ¹²You sinned in secret, but I will make this happen in broad daylight for all Israel to see.' "

¹³"I have sinned against the LORD," David said.

Nathan replied, "The LORD forgives you; you will not die. ¹⁴But because you have shown such contempt for the LORD in doing this, your child will die." ¹⁵Then Nathan went home.

David's Son Dies

The LORD caused the child that Uriah's wife had borne to David to become very sick. ¹⁶David prayed to God that the child would get well. He refused to eat anything, and every night he went into his room and spent the night lying on the floor. ¹⁷His court officials went to him and tried to make him get up, but he refused and would not eat anything with them. ¹⁸A week later the child died, and David's officials were afraid to tell him the news. They said, "While the child was living, David wouldn't answer us when we spoke to him. How can we tell him that his child is dead? He might do himself some harm!"

¹⁹When David noticed them whispering to each other, he realized that the child had died. So he asked them, "Is the child dead?"

"Yes, he is," they answered.

²⁰David got up from the floor, took a bath, combed his hair, and changed his clothes. Then he went and worshiped in the house of the LORD. When he returned to the palace, he asked for food and ate it as soon as it was served. ²¹"We don't understand this," his officials said to him. "While the child was alive, you wept for him and would not eat; but as soon as he died, you got up and ate!"

²²"Yes," David answered, "I did fast and weep while he was still alive. I thought that the LORD might be merciful to me and not let the child die. ²³But now that he is dead, why should I fast? Could I bring the child back to life? I will some day go to where he is, but he can never come back to me."

Solomon Is Born

²⁴Then David comforted his wife Bathsheba. He had intercourse with her, and she bore a son, whom David named Solomon. The LORD loved the boy ²⁵and commanded the prophet Nathan to name the boy Jedidiah,ʸ because the LORD loved him.

David Captures Rabbah
(1 Chronicles 20:1–3)

²⁶Meanwhile Joab continued his campaign against Rabbah, the capital city of Ammon, and was about to capture it. ²⁷He sent messengers to David to report: "I have attacked Rabbah and have captured its water

---

ʸ **12:25** JEDIDIAH: *This name in Hebrew means "Beloved of the LORD."*
12:11, 12 2 Sam 16:22

supply. ²⁸Now gather the rest of your forces, attack the city and take it yourself. I don't want to get the credit for capturing it." ²⁹So David gathered his forces, went to Rabbah, attacked it, and conquered it. ³⁰From the head of the idol of the Ammonite god Molech ᶻ David took a gold crown which weighed about seventy-five pounds and had a jewel in it. David took the jewel and put it in his own crown.ᵃ He also took a large amount of loot from the city ³¹and put its people to work with saws, iron hoes, and iron axes, and forced them to work atᵇ making bricks. He did the same to the people of all the other towns of Ammon. Then he and his men returned to Jerusalem.

Amnon and Tamar

13 ¹David's son Absalom had a beautiful unmarried sister named Tamar. Amnon, another of David's sons, fell in love with her. ²He was so much in love with her that he became sick, because it seemed impossible for him to have her; as a virgin, she was kept from meeting men. ³But he had a friend, a very shrewd man named Jonadab, the son of David's brother Shammah. ⁴Jonadab said to Amnon, "You are the king's son, yet day after day I see you looking sad. What's the matter?"

"I'm in love with Tamar, the sister of my half brother Absalom," he answered.

⁵Jonadab said to him, "Pretend that you are sick and go to bed. When your father comes to see you, say to him, 'Please ask my sister Tamar to come and feed me. I want her to fix the food here where I can see her, and then serve it to me herself.' " ⁶So Amnon pretended that he was sick and went to bed.

King David went to see him, and Amnon said to him, "Please let Tamar come and make a few cakes here where I can see her, and then serve them to me herself."

⁷So David sent word to Tamar in the palace: "Go to Amnon's house and fix him

Tell Someone!

In the beginning of 2 Samuel, chapter 13, we read about a horrible event: David's oldest son, Amnon, rapes his half sister, Tamar. It may surprise us to read that people in the Bible do such things, but it reminds us that biblical people are human beings like us. And often human beings do cruel things to one another. When bad things happen within families, it is especially difficult because family members are supposed to look out for one another. What Amnon did to Tamar is a sin and a crime. His actions also tore David's family apart.

Today we would counsel Tamar to tell someone about what happened and to make sure that she receives the care she needs. Amnon would be arrested for his crime to his sister.

If you or someone you know is ever the victim of sexual abuse, whether the perpetrator is a family member or someone else, make sure to let someone know about it. Tell a trusted adult outside the family—a teacher or a counselor perhaps. The abused person's welfare is more important than someone's reputation.

— 2 Samuel 13:1–21

some food." ⁸She went there and found him in bed. She took some dough, prepared it, and made some cakes there where he could see her. Then she baked the cakes ⁹and

---

ᶻ **12:30** idol of the Ammonite god Molech; *or* Ammonite king.   ᵃ **12:30** jewel . . . crown; *or* crown and put it on his own head.   ᵇ **12:31** *Probable text (see 1 Chr 20:3)* work at; *Hebrew* pass through.

2 Samuel

Look back at Nathan's prophecy to David in 2 Samuel 12:10. How is it fulfilled in chapter 13?

emptied them out of the pan for him to eat, but he wouldn't. He said, "Send everyone away"—and they all left. [10]Then he said to her, "Bring the cakes here to my bed and serve them to me yourself." She took the cakes and went over to him. [11]As she offered them to him, he grabbed her and said, "Come to bed with me!"

[12]"No," she said. "Don't force me to do such a degrading thing! That's awful! [13]How could I ever hold up my head in public again? And you—you would be completely disgraced in Israel. Please, speak to the king, and I'm sure that he will give me to you."

[14]But he would not listen to her; and since he was stronger than she was, he overpowered her and raped her.

[15]Then Amnon was filled with a deep hatred for her; he hated her now even more than he had loved her before. He said to her, "Get out!"

[16]"No," she answered. "To send me away like this is a greater crime[c] than what you just did!"

But Amnon would not listen to her; [17]he called in his personal servant and said, "Get this woman out of my sight! Throw her out and lock the door!" [18]The servant put her out and locked the door.

Tamar was wearing a long robe with full sleeves,[d] the usual clothing for an unmarried princess in those days.[e] [19]She sprinkled ashes on her head, tore her robe, and with her face buried in her hands went away crying. [20]When her brother Absalom saw her, he asked, "Has Amnon molested you? Please, sister, don't let it upset you so much. He is your half brother, so don't tell anyone about it." So Tamar lived in Absalom's house, sad and lonely.

[21]When King David heard what had happened, he was furious. [22]And Absalom hated Amnon so much for having raped his sister Tamar that he would no longer even speak to him.

Absalom's Revenge

[23]Two years later Absalom was having his sheep sheared at Baal Hazor, near the town of Ephraim, and he invited all the king's sons to be there. [24]He went to King David and said, "Your Majesty, I am having my sheep sheared. Will you and your officials come and take part in the festivities?"

[25]"No, my son," the king answered. "It would be too much trouble for you if we all went." Absalom insisted, but the king would not give in, and he asked Absalom to leave.

[26]But Absalom said, "Well, then, will you at least let my brother Amnon come?"

"Why should he?" the king asked. [27]But Absalom kept on insisting until David finally let Amnon and all his other sons go with Absalom.

Absalom prepared a banquet fit for a king[f] [28]and instructed his servants: "Notice when Amnon has had too much to drink, and then when I give the order, kill him. Don't be afraid. I will take the responsibility myself. Be brave and don't hesitate!" [29]So the servants followed Absalom's instructions and killed Amnon. All the rest of David's sons mounted their mules and fled.

[30]While they were on their way home, David was told: "Absalom has killed all your sons—not one of them is left!" [31]The king stood up, tore his clothes in sorrow, and threw himself to the ground. The servants who were there with him tore their clothes also. [32]But Jonadab, the son of David's brother Shammah, said, "Your Majesty, they haven't killed all your sons. Only Amnon is dead. You could tell by looking at Absalom that he had made up his mind to do this from the time that Amnon raped his sister Tamar. [33]So don't believe the news that all your sons are dead; only Amnon was killed."

[34]In the meantime Absalom had fled.

Just then the soldier on sentry duty saw a large crowd coming down the hill on the

---

[c] **13:16** *Probable text* To send me . . . crime; *Hebrew unclear.* [d] **13:18** long robe with full sleeves; *or* decorated robe *(see Gen 37:3).* [e] **13:18** *Probable text* in those days; *Hebrew* garments. [f] **13:27** *Some ancient translations* Absalom prepared a banquet fit for a king; *Hebrew does not have these words.*

The sexual abuse and family violence in the story of Amnon, Tamar, and Absalom still happens today. Say a prayer for the victims of abuse.

"Those are your sons coming." (13:35)

road from Horonaim.*g* He went to the king and reported what he had seen.*h* 35Jonadab said to David, "Those are your sons coming, just as I said they would." 36As soon as he finished saying this, David's sons came in; they started crying, and David and his officials also cried bitterly.

37-38Absalom fled and went to the king of Geshur, Talmai son of Ammihud, and stayed there three years. David mourned a long time for his son Amnon; 39but when he got over Amnon's death, he was filled with longing for his son Absalom.

Joab Arranges for Absalom's Return

14 1Joab knew that King David missed Absalom very much, 2so he sent for a clever woman who lived in Tekoa. When she arrived, he said to her, "Pretend that you are in mourning; put on your mourning clothes, and don't comb your hair. Act like a woman who has been in mourning for a long time. 3Then go to the king and say to him what I tell you to say." Then Joab told her what to say.

4The woman went to the king, bowed down to the ground in respect, and said, "Help me, Your Majesty!"

5"What do you want?" he asked her.

"I am a poor widow, sir," she answered.

Fathers and Sons

No matter how much parents and children love one another, there will come times when they won't get along. It happens in every family. Even the great King David had difficulties with his son Absalom, big ones. Absalom had killed his half brother, Amnon, because Amnon had raped Absalom's sister Tamar. Talk about your family troubles! Eventually David and Absalom were reconciled, but the struggles continued.

In some families, certain family members or relatives do not talk to one another. This may have gone on for years. As hard as it is sometimes, we have to be willing to do two things with our parents or guardians and siblings: show them the respect and love they deserve and always try to make things right. We shouldn't leave the house or go to our room at the end of the day angry with a family member. Try to reconcile. Take the first step if you need to. Family is just too important a part of our lives for us to stay mad at one another.

Is there someone in your family you need to be reconciled with? What's keeping you from doing it? Ask God for help.

— 2 Samuel, chapter 14

"My husband is dead. 6Sir, I had two sons, and one day they got into a quarrel out in the fields, where there was no one to separate them, and one of them killed the other. 7And now, sir, all my relatives have turned

---

g **13:34** *Probable text* from Horonaim; *Hebrew* behind him. *h* **13:34** *One ancient translation* He went . . . had seen; *Hebrew does not have these words.*
13:37 2 Sam 3:3

2 Samuel

against me and are demanding that I hand my son over to them, so that they can kill him for murdering his brother. If they do this, I will be left without a son. They will destroy my last hope and leave my husband without a son to keep his name alive."

8 "Go back home," the king answered, "and I will take care of the matter."

9 "Your Majesty," she said, "whatever you do, my family and I will take the blame; you and the royal family are innocent."

10 The king replied, "If anyone threatens you, bring him to me, and he will never bother you again."

11 She said, "Your Majesty, please pray to the LORD your God, so that my relative who is responsible for avenging the death of my son will not commit a greater crime by killing my other son."

"I promise by the living LORD," David replied, "that your son will not be harmed in the least."

12 "Please, Your Majesty, let me say just one more thing," the woman said.

"All right," he answered.

13 She said to him, "Why have you done such a wrong to God's people? You have not allowed your own son to return from exile, and so you have condemned yourself by what you have just said. 14 We will all die; we are like water spilled on the ground, which can't be gathered again. Even God does not bring the dead back to life, but the king can at least find a way to bring a man back from exile.[i] 15 Now, Your Majesty, the reason I have come to speak to you is that the people threatened me, and so I said to myself that I would speak to you in the hope that you would do what I ask. 16 I thought you would listen to me and save me from the one who is trying to kill my son and me and so remove us from the land God gave his people. 17 I said to myself that your promise, sir, would make me safe, because the king is like God's angel and can distinguish good from evil.[j] May the LORD your God be with you!"

18 The king answered, "I'm going to ask you a question, and you must tell me the whole truth."

"Ask me anything, Your Majesty," she answered.

19 "Did Joab put you up to this?" he asked her.

She answered, "I swear by all that is sacred, Your Majesty, that there is no way to avoid answering your question.[k] It was indeed your officer Joab who told me what to do and what to say. 20 But he did it in order to straighten out this whole matter. Your Majesty is as wise as the angel of God and knows everything that happens."

21 Later on the king said to Joab, "I have decided to do what you want. Go and get the young man Absalom and bring him back here."

22 Joab threw himself to the ground in front of David in respect, and said, "God bless you, Your Majesty! Now I know that you are pleased with me, because you have granted my request." 23 Then he got up and went to Geshur and brought Absalom back to Jerusalem. 24 The king, however, gave orders that Absalom should not live in the palace. "I don't want to see him," the king said. So Absalom lived in his own house and did not appear before the king.

Absalom Is Reconciled to David

25 There was no one in Israel as famous for his good looks as Absalom; he had no defect from head to toe. 26 His hair was very thick, and he had to cut it once a year, when it grew too long and heavy. It would weigh about five pounds according to the royal standard of weights. 27 Absalom had three sons and one daughter named Tamar, a very beautiful woman.

28 Absalom lived two years in Jerusalem without seeing the king. 29 Then he sent for Joab, to ask him to go to the king for him; but Joab would not come. Again Absalom sent for him, and again Joab refused to come. 30 So Absalom said to his servants, "Look, Joab's field is next to mine, and it has barley growing in it. Go and set fire to it." So they went and set the field on fire.

31 Joab went to Absalom's house and

demanded, "Why did your servants set fire to my field?"

32 Absalom answered, "Because you wouldn't come when I sent for you. I wanted you to go to the king and ask for me: 'Why did I leave Geshur and come here? It would have been better for me to have stayed there.'" And Absalom went on, "I want you to arrange for me to see the king, and if I'm guilty, then let him put me to death."

33 So Joab went to King David and told him what Absalom had said. The king sent for Absalom, who went to him and bowed down to the ground in front of him. The king welcomed him with a kiss.

Absalom would . . . take hold of him . . . and kiss him. (15:5)

Absalom Plans Rebellion

15 ¹After this, Absalom provided a chariot and horses for himself, and an escort of fifty men. ²He would get up early and go and stand by the road at the city gate. Whenever someone came there with a dispute that he wanted the king to settle, Absalom would call him over and ask him where he was from. And after the man had told him what tribe he was from, ³Absalom would say, "Look, the law is on your side, but there is no representative of the king to hear your case." ⁴And he would add, "How I wish I were a judge! Then anyone who had a dispute or a claim could come to me, and I would give him justice." ⁵When the man would approach Absalom to bow down before him, Absalom would reach out, take hold of him, and kiss him. ⁶Absalom did this with every Israelite who came to the king for judgment, and so he won their loyalty.

⁷After four¹ years Absalom said to King David, "Sir, let me go to Hebron and keep a promise I made to the LORD. ⁸While I was living in Geshur in Syria, I promised the LORD that if he would take me back to Jerusalem, I would worship him in Hebron."ᵐ

⁹"Go in peace," the king said. So Absalom went to Hebron. ¹⁰But he sent messengers to all the tribes of Israel to say, "When you hear the sound of trumpets, shout, 'Absalom has become king at Hebron!'" ¹¹There were two hundred men who at Absalom's invitation had gone from Jerusalem with him; they knew nothing of the plot and went in all good faith. ¹²And while he was offering sacrifices, Absalom also sent to the town of Gilo for Ahithophel, who was one of King David's advisers. The plot against the king gained strength, and Absalom's followers grew in number.

David Flees from Jerusalem

¹³A messenger reported to David, "The Israelites are pledging their loyalty to Absalom."

¹⁴So David said to all his officials who were with him in Jerusalem, "We must get away at once if we want to escape from Absalom! Hurry! Or else he will soon be here and defeat us and kill everyone in the city!"

¹⁵"Yes, Your Majesty," they answered. "We are ready to do whatever you say." ¹⁶So the king left, accompanied by all his family and officials, except for ten concubines, whom he left behind to take care of the palace.

¹⁷As the king and all his men were leaving the city, they stopped at the last house. ¹⁸All

---

¹ **15:7** *Some ancient translations* four; *Hebrew* forty.   ᵐ **15:8** *One ancient translation* in Hebron; *Hebrew does not have these words.*

2 Samuel

How did Absalom get Joab's attention when Joab was ignoring him?

So the king left, accompanied by all his family. (15:16)

his officials stood[n] next to him as the royal bodyguards passed by in front of him. The six hundred soldiers who had followed him from Gath also passed by, 19and the king said to Ittai, their leader, "Why are you going with us? Go back and stay with the new king. You are a foreigner, a refugee away from your own country. 20You have lived here only a short time, so why should I make you wander around with me? I don't even know where I'm going. Go back and take all your people with you—and may the LORD be kind and faithful to you."[o]

21But Ittai answered, "Your Majesty, I swear to you in the LORD's name that I will always go with you wherever you go, even if it means death."

22"Fine!" David answered. "March on!" So Ittai went on with all his men and their dependents. 23The people cried loudly as David's followers left. The king crossed Kidron Brook, followed by his men, and together they went out toward the wilderness.

24Zadok the priest was there, and with him were the Levites, carrying the sacred Covenant Box. They set it down[p] and didn't pick it up again until all the people had left the city. The priest Abiathar was there too.[q] 25Then the king said to Zadok, "Take the Covenant Box back to the city. If the LORD is pleased with me, some day he will let me come back to see it and the place where it stays. 26But if he isn't pleased with me—well, then, let him do to me what he wishes." 27And he went on to say to Zadok, "Look,[r] take your son Ahimaaz and Abiathar's son Jonathan and go back to the city in peace. 28Meanwhile, I will wait at the river crossings in the wilderness until I receive news from you." 29So Zadok and Abiathar took the Covenant Box back into Jerusalem and stayed there.

30David went on up the Mount of Olives crying; he was barefoot and had his head covered as a sign of grief. All who followed him covered their heads and cried also. 31When David was told[s] that Ahithophel had joined Absalom's rebellion, he prayed, "Please, LORD, turn Ahithophel's advice into nonsense!"

32When David reached the top of the hill, where there was a place of worship, his trusted friend Hushai the Archite met him with his clothes torn and with dirt on his head. 33David said to him, "You will be of no help to me if you come with me, 34but you can help me by returning to the city and telling Absalom that you will now serve him as faithfully as you served his father. And do all you can to oppose any advice that Ahithophel gives. 35The priests Zadok and Abiathar will be there; tell them everything you

David went on up the Mount of Olives crying. (15:30)

---

[n] **15:18** *Probable text* stood; *Hebrew* passed.   [o] **15:20** *One ancient translation* and may the LORD be kind and faithful to you; *Hebrew* kindness and faithfulness.   [p] **15:24** *Probable text* set it down; *Hebrew* poured it out.   [q] **15:24** *Probable text* was there too; *Hebrew* went up.   [r] **15:27** *Some ancient translations* Look; *Hebrew* Are you the seer?   [s] **15:31** *One ancient translation* was told; *Hebrew* told.

Did Mephibosheth really betray David as his servant Ziba says he did? Check out 2 Samuel 19:24–30 for Mephibosheth's side of the story.

hear in the king's palace. 36 They have their sons Ahimaaz and Jonathan with them, and you can send them to me with all the information you gather."

37 So Hushai, David's friend, returned to the city just as Absalom was arriving.

David and Ziba

16 1 When David had gone a little beyond the top of the hill, he was suddenly met by Ziba, the servant of Mephibosheth, who had with him a couple of donkeys loaded with two hundred loaves of bread, a hundred bunches of raisins, a hundred bunches of fresh fruit, and a leather bag full of wine. 2 King David asked him, "What are you going to do with all that?"

Ziba answered, "The donkeys are for Your Majesty's family to ride, the bread and the fruit are for the men to eat, and the wine is for them to drink when they get tired in the wilderness."

3 "Where is Mephibosheth, the grandson of your master Saul?" the king asked him.

"He is staying in Jerusalem," Ziba answered, "because he is convinced that the Israelites will now restore to him the kingdom of his grandfather Saul."

4 The king said to Ziba, "Everything that belonged to Mephibosheth is yours."

"I am your servant," Ziba replied. "May I always please Your Majesty!"

David and Shimei

5 When King David arrived at Bahurim, one of Saul's relatives, Shimei son of Gera, came out to meet him, cursing him as he came. 6 Shimei started throwing stones at David and his officials, even though David was surrounded by his men and his bodyguards. 7 Shimei cursed him and said, "Get out! Get out! Murderer! Criminal! 8 You took Saul's kingdom, and now the LORD is punishing you for murdering so many of Saul's family. The LORD has given the kingdom to your son Absalom, and you are ruined, you murderer!"

9 Abishai, whose mother was Zeruiah, said to the king, "Your Majesty, why do you let this dog curse you? Let me go over there and cut off his head!"

10 "This is none of your business," the king said to Abishai and his brother Joab. "If he curses me because the LORD told him to, who has the right to ask why he does it?" 11 And David said to Abishai and to all his officials, "My own son is trying to kill me; so why should you be surprised at this Benjaminite? The LORD told him to curse; so leave him alone and let him do it. 12 Perhaps the LORD will notice my misery[t] and give me some blessings to take the place of his curse." 13 So David and his men continued along the road. Shimei kept up with them, walking on the hillside; he was cursing and throwing stones and dirt at them as he went. 14 The king and all his men were worn out when they reached the Jordan,[u] and there they rested.

Shimei kept up with them, . . . cursing and throwing stones. (16:13)

Absalom in Jerusalem

15 Absalom and all the Israelites with him entered Jerusalem, and Ahithophel was with them. 16 When Hushai, David's trusted friend, met Absalom, he shouted, "Long live the king! Long live the king!"

17 "What has happened to your loyalty to your friend David?" Absalom asked him. "Why didn't you go with him?"

18 Hushai answered, "How could I? I am for the one chosen by the LORD, by these people, and by all the Israelites. I will stay with you. 19 After all, whom should I serve, if

---

[t] **16:12** *Some ancient translations* misery; *Hebrew* wickedness.   [u] **16:14** *One ancient translation* the Jordan; *Hebrew does not have these words.*

16:1 2 Sam 9:9, 10   **16:3** 2 Sam 19:25–27

not my master's son? As I served your father, so now I will serve you."

20 Then Absalom turned to Ahithophel and said, "Now that we are here, what do you advise us to do?"

21 Ahithophel answered, "Go and have intercourse with your father's concubines whom he left behind to take care of the palace. Then everyone in Israel will know that your father regards you as his enemy, and your followers will be greatly encouraged." 22 So they set up a tent for Absalom on the palace roof, and in the sight of everyone Absalom went in and had intercourse with his father's concubines.

23 Any advice that Ahithophel gave in those days was accepted as though it were the very word of God; both David and Absalom followed it.

Hushai Misleads Absalom

17 1 Not long after that, Ahithophel said to Absalom, "Let me choose twelve thousand men, and tonight I will set out after David. 2 I will attack him while he is tired and discouraged. He will be frightened, and all his men will run away. I will kill only the king 3 and then bring back all his men to you, like a bride returning to her husband. You want to kill only one man;*v* the rest of the people will be safe." 4 This seemed like good advice to Absalom and all the Israelite leaders.

5 Absalom said, "Now call Hushai, and let us hear what he has to say." 6 When Hushai arrived, Absalom said to him, "This is the advice that Ahithophel has given us; shall we follow it? If not, you tell us what to do."

7 Hushai answered, "The advice Ahithophel gave you this time is no good. 8 You know that your father David and his men are hard fighters and that they are as fierce as a mother bear robbed of her cubs. Your father is an experienced soldier and does not stay with his men at night. 9 Right now he is probably hiding in a cave or some other place. As soon as David attacks your men, whoever hears about it will say that your men have been defeated. 10 Then even the bravest men, as fearless as lions, will be

afraid because everyone in Israel knows that your father is a great soldier and that his men are hard fighters. 11 My advice is that you bring all the Israelites together from one end of the country to the other, as many as the grains of sand on the seashore, and that you lead them personally in battle. 12 We will find David wherever he is, and attack him before he knows what's happening. Neither he nor any of his men will survive. 13 If he retreats into a city, our people will all bring ropes and just pull the city*w* into the valley below. Not a single stone will be left there on top of the hill."

14 Absalom and all the Israelites said, "Hushai's advice is better than Ahithophel's." The LORD had decided that Ahithophel's good advice would not be followed, so that disaster would come on Absalom.

David Is Warned and Escapes

15 Then Hushai told the priests Zadok and Abiathar what advice he had given to Absalom and the Israelite leaders and what advice Ahithophel had given. 16 Hushai added, "Quick, now! Send a message to David not to spend the night at the river crossings in the wilderness, but to cross the Jordan at once, so that he and his men won't all be caught and killed."

17 Abiathar's son Jonathan and Zadok's son Ahimaaz were waiting at the spring of Enrogel, on the outskirts of Jerusalem, because they did not dare be seen entering the city. A servant woman would regularly go and tell them what was happening, and then they would go and tell King David. 18 But one day a boy happened to see them, and he told Absalom; so they hurried off to hide in the house of a certain man in Bahurim. He had a well near his house, and they got down in it. 19 The man's wife took a covering, spread it over the opening of the well and scattered grain over it, so that no one would notice anything. 20 Absalom's officials came to the house and asked the woman, "Where are Ahimaaz and Jonathan?"

"They crossed the river," she answered.

The men looked for them but could not find them, and so they returned to Jerusalem.

---

v **17:3** *One ancient translation* like a bride . . . only one man; *Hebrew* like the return of the whole, so is the man you seek.   *w* **17:13** *Some ancient translations* the city; *Hebrew* him.
16:22 2 Sam 12:11, 12

21 After they left, Ahimaaz and Jonathan came up out of the well and went and reported to King David. They told him what Ahithophel had planned against him and said, "Hurry up and cross the river." 22 So David and his men started crossing the Jordan, and by daybreak they had all gone across.

23 When Ahithophel saw that his advice had not been followed, he saddled his donkey and went back to his hometown. After putting his affairs in order, he hanged himself. He was buried in the family grave.

24 David had reached the town of Mahanaim by the time Absalom and the Israelites had crossed the Jordan. (25 Absalom had put Amasa in command of the army in the place of Joab. Amasa was the son of Jether the Ishmaelite;x his mother was Abigail, the daughter of Nahash and the sister of Joab's mother Zeruiah.) 26 Absalom and his men camped in the land of Gilead.

27 When David arrived at Mahanaim, he was met by Shobi son of Nahash, from the city of Rabbah in Ammon, and by Machir son of Ammiel, from Lodebar, and by Barzillai, from Rogelim in Gilead. 28-29 They brought bowls, clay pots, and bedding, and also food for David and his men: wheat, barley, meal, roasted grain, beans, peas,y honey, cheese, cream, and some sheep. They knew that David and his men would get hungry, thirsty, and tired in the wilderness.

For David and his men (17:28)

Absalom Is Defeated and Killed

18 1 King David brought all his men together, divided them into units of a thousand and of a hundred, and placed

officers in command of them. 2 Then he sent them out in three groups, with Joab and Joab's brother Abishai and Ittai from Gath, each in command of a group. And the king said to his men, "I will go with you myself."

3 "You mustn't go with us," they answered. "It won't make any difference to the enemy if the rest of us turn and run, or even if half of us are killed; but you are worth ten thousand of us. It will be better if you stay here in the city and send us help."

4 "I will do whatever you think best," the king answered. Then he stood by the side of the gate as his men marched out in units of a thousand and of a hundred. 5 He gave orders to Joab, Abishai, and Ittai: "For my sake don't harm the young man Absalom." And all the troops heard David give this command to his officers.

"Don't harm the young man Absalom." (18:5)

6 David's army went out into the countryside and fought the Israelites in Ephraim Forest. 7 The Israelites were defeated by David's men; it was a terrible defeat, with twenty thousand men killed that day. 8 The fighting spread over the countryside, and more men died in the forest than were killed in battle.

9 Suddenly Absalom met some of David's men. Absalom was riding a mule, and as it went under a large oak tree, Absalom's head

2 Samuel

x **17:25** *One ancient translation (and see 1 Chr 2:17)* Ishmaelite; *Hebrew* Israelite.　y **17:28-29** *Some ancient translations* peas; *Hebrew* peas and roasted grain.

Absalom's head got caught in the branches. (18:9)

got caught in the branches. The mule ran on and Absalom was left hanging in midair. 10One of David's men saw him and reported to Joab, "Sir, I saw Absalom hanging in an oak tree!"

11Joab answered, "If you saw him, why didn't you kill him on the spot? I myself would have given you ten pieces of silver and a belt."

12But the man answered, "Even if you gave me a thousand pieces of silver, I wouldn't lift a finger against the king's son. We all heard the king command you and Abishai and Ittai, 'For my sake don't harm the young man Absalom.' 13But if I had disobeyed the king and killed Absalom, the king would have heard about it—he hears about everything—and you would not have defended me."

14"I'm not going to waste any more time with you," Joab said. He took three spears and plunged them into Absalom's chest while he was still alive, hanging in the oak tree. 15Then ten of Joab's soldiers closed in on Absalom and finished killing him.

16Joab had the trumpet blown to stop the fighting, and his troops came back from pursuing the Israelites. 17They took Absalom's body, threw it into a deep pit in the forest, and covered it with a huge pile of stones. All the Israelites fled to their own hometowns.

18During his lifetime Absalom had built a monument for himself in King's Valley, because he had no son to keep his name alive. So he named it after himself, and to this day it is known as Absalom's Monument.

David Is Told of Absalom's Death

19Then Ahimaaz son of Zadok said to Joab, "Let me run to the king with the good news that the LORD has saved him from his enemies."

20"No," Joab said, "today you will not take any good news. Some other day you may do so, but not today, for the king's son is dead." 21Then he said to his Ethiopian z slave, "Go and tell the king what you have seen." The slave bowed and ran off.

22Ahimaaz insisted, "I don't care what happens; please let me take the news also."

"Why do you want to do it, my son?" Joab asked. "You will get no reward for it."

23"Whatever happens," Ahimaaz said again, "I want to go."

"Then go," Joab said. So Ahimaaz ran off down the road through the Jordan Valley, and soon he passed the slave.

24David was sitting in the space between the inner and outer gates of the city. The lookout went up to the top of the wall and stood on the roof of the gateway; he looked out and saw a man running alone. 25He called down and told the king, and the king said, "If he is alone, he is bringing good news." The runner kept coming closer.

26Then the lookout saw another man running alone, and he called down to the gatekeeper, "Look! There's another man running!"

The king answered, "This one also is bringing good news."

27The lookout said, "I can see that the first man runs like Ahimaaz."

"He's a good man," the king said, "and he is bringing good news."

28Ahimaaz called out a greeting to the king, threw himself down to the ground

z **18:21** *Hebrew* Cushite: *Cush is the ancient name of the extensive territory south of the First Cataract of the Nile River. This region was called Ethiopia in Graeco-Roman times, and included within its borders most of modern Sudan and some of present-day Ethiopia (Abyssinia).*

Check out 2 Samuel 14:25–26 to understand what caused Absalom to get caught in the tree.

Pray It!

If Only

David grieves over the death of his son Absalom, and says: "If only I had died in your place" (2 Samuel 18:33). We understand David's mourning for his dead son, but we have to be careful of getting too caught up in "if onlys." David becomes so trapped wishing things were different that he fails to be the strong leader his people need him to be. We can always find something about ourselves or our lives that we would like to change. Sometimes we can change things, but not always. We need to ask God for the ability to determine what we can and cannot change. Next time you find yourself saying, "If only . . . ," try this prayer.

Dear God, things haven't turned out like I hoped.
Sometimes I find myself wishing things had gone differently.
When I am tempted to say, "If only . . . ," open my eyes to all the blessings around me.
Let me make the most of what you have given me.
Help me to know when to work at changing things,
*   and when to accept things as they are and make the best of them.*
I need your help God, please. Amen.

— 2 Samuel 18:33

---

before him, and said, "Praise the LORD your God, who has given you victory over the men who rebelled against Your Majesty!"

29 "Is the young man Absalom all right?" the king asked.

Ahimaaz answered, "Sir, when your officer Joab sent me, I saw a great commotion, but I couldn't tell what it was."

30 "Stand over there," the king told him; and he went over and stood there.

31 Then the Ethiopian[z] slave arrived and said to the king, "I have good news for Your Majesty! Today the LORD has given you victory over all who rebelled against you!"

32 "Is the young man Absalom all right?" the king asked.

The slave answered, "I wish that what has happened to him would happen to all your enemies, sir, and to all who rebel against you."

33 The king was overcome with grief. He went up to the room over the gateway and wept. As he went, he cried, "O my son! My son Absalom! Absalom, my son! If only I had

died in your place, my son! Absalom, my son!"

Joab Reprimands David

19 ¹Joab was told that King David was weeping and mourning for Absalom. ²And so the joy of victory was turned into sadness for all of David's troops that day, because they heard that the king was mourning for his son. ³They went back into the city quietly, like soldiers who are ashamed because they are running away from battle. ⁴The king covered his face and cried loudly, "O my son! My son Absalom! Absalom, my son!"

⁵Joab went to the king's house and said to him, "Today you have humiliated your men—the men who saved your life and the lives of your sons and daughters and of your wives and concubines. ⁶You oppose those who love you and support those who hate you! You have made it clear that your

---

z **18:31** *Hebrew Cushite: Cush is the ancient name of the extensive territory south of the First Cataract of the Nile River. This region was called Ethiopia in Graeco-Roman times, and included within its borders most of modern Sudan and some of present-day Ethiopia (Abyssinia).*

2 Samuel

"O my son! My son Absalom!" (19:4)

officers and men mean nothing to you. I can see that you would be quite happy if Absalom were alive today and all of us were dead. [7]Now go and reassure your men. I swear by the LORD's name that if you don't, not one of them will be with you by tomorrow morning. That would be the worst disaster you have suffered in all your life." [8]Then the king got up, and went and sat near the city gate. His men heard that he was there, and they all gathered around him.

David Starts Back to Jerusalem

Meanwhile all the Israelites had fled to their own hometowns. [9]All over the country they started quarreling among themselves. "King David saved us from our enemies," they said to one another. "He rescued us from the Philistines, but now he has fled from Absalom and left the country. [10]We anointed Absalom as our king, but he has been killed in battle. So why doesn't somebody try to bring King David back?"

[11]The news of what the Israelites were saying reached King David.[a] So he sent the priests Zadok and Abiathar to ask the leaders of Judah, "Why should you be the last to help bring the king back to his palace? [12]You are my relatives, my own flesh and blood; why should you be the last to bring

me back?" [13]David also told them to say to Amasa, "You are my relative. From now on I am putting you in charge of the army in place of Joab. May God strike me dead if I don't!" [14]David's words won the complete loyalty of all the men of Judah, and they sent him word to return with all his officials.

[15]On his way back the king was met at the Jordan River by the men of Judah, who had come to Gilgal to escort him across the river. [16]At the same time the Benjaminite Shimei son of Gera from Bahurim hurried to the Jordan to meet King David. [17]He had with him a thousand men from the tribe of Benjamin. And Ziba, the servant of Saul's family, also came with his fifteen sons and twenty servants, and they arrived at the Jordan before the king. [18]They crossed[b] the river to escort the royal party across and to do whatever the king wanted.

David Shows Kindness to Shimei

As the king was getting ready to cross, Shimei threw himself down in front of him [19]and said, "Your Majesty, please forget the wrong I did that day you left Jerusalem. Don't hold it against me or think about it any more. [20]I know, sir, that I have sinned, and this is why I am the first one from the northern tribes to come and meet Your Majesty today."

[21]Abishai son of Zeruiah spoke up: "Shimei should be put to death because he cursed the one whom the LORD chose as king."

[22]But David said to Abishai and his brother Joab, "Who asked your opinion? Are you going to give me trouble? I am the one who is king of Israel now, and no Israelite will be put to death today." [23]And he said to Shimei, "I give you my word that you will not be put to death."

David Shows Kindness to Mephibosheth

[24]Then Mephibosheth, Saul's grandson, came down to meet the king. He had not washed his feet, trimmed his beard, or washed his clothes from the time the king left

---

[a] **19:11** *Some ancient translations* The news . . . David; *Hebrew* The news . . . David, to his palace, *and places this sentence at the end of the verse.* [b] **19:18** *Probable text* They crossed; *Hebrew* The crossing crossed.
19:16 2 Sam 16:5–13   **19:24** 2 Sam 9:1–13; 16:1–4

Old Friends

Some young people don't like going into care facilities where lots of older adults live. They don't like being around old people. They often say, "It's too depressing." One of King David's supporters, Barzillai, is eighty years old. He tells David some of the things he struggles with, which are the same things old people deal with today.

    Think about what a difference you can make in the lives of older adults when you go to visit them. It is rare that they see any young people. See if you can volunteer at a nearby residence for older adults. Often residents like to play cards or checkers or just to visit. They each have a lifetime of stories to tell. Look around their rooms and ask them about photos and objects that you see. All you need to bring with you is a smile and the willingness to be patient. You can really be a gift in an older person's life!

— 2 Samuel 19:31–39

angel, so do what seems right to you. 28All of my father's family deserved to be put to death by Your Majesty, but you gave me the right to eat at your table. I have no right to ask for any more favors from Your Majesty."

29The king answered, "You don't have to say anything more. I have decided that you and Ziba will share Saul's property."

30"Let Ziba have it all," Mephibosheth answered. "It's enough for me that Your Majesty has come home safely."

David Shows Kindness to Barzillai

31Barzillai, from Gilead, had also come down from Rogelim to escort the king across the Jordan. 32Barzillai was a very old man, eighty years old. He was very rich and had supplied the king with food while he was staying at Mahanaim. 33The king said to him, "Come with me to Jerusalem, and I will take care of you."

34But Barzillai answered, "I don't have long to live; why should I go with Your Majesty to Jerusalem? 35I am already eighty years old, and nothing gives me pleasure any more. I can't taste what I eat and drink, and I can't hear the voices of singers. I would only be a burden to Your Majesty. 36I don't deserve such a great reward. So I will go just a little way with you beyond the Jordan. 37Then let me go back home and die near my parents' grave. Here is my son Chimham, who will serve you; take him with you, Your Majesty, and do for him as you think best."

38The king answered, "I will take him with me and do for him whatever you want. And I will do for you anything you ask." 39Then David and all of his men crossed the Jordan. He kissed Barzillai and gave him his blessing, and Barzillai went back home.

Judah and Israel Argue over the King

40When the king had crossed, escorted by all the people of Judah and half the people

Jerusalem until he returned victorious. 25When Mephibosheth arrived from*c* Jerusalem to meet the king, the king said to him, "Mephibosheth, you didn't go with me. Why not?"

26He answered, "As you know, Your Majesty, I am crippled. I told my servant to saddle my donkey so that I could ride along with you, but he betrayed me. 27He lied about me to Your Majesty, but you are like God's

c **19:25** *One ancient translation* from; *Hebrew* at.
19:31 2 Sam 17:27–29

After his son Absalom's death, David could be angry and revengeful or kind and forgiving. Which does he choose?

of Israel, he went on to Gilgal, and Chimham went with him. 41 Then all the Israelites went to the king and said to him, "Your Majesty, why did our brothers, the men of Judah, think they had the right to take you away and escort you, your family, and your men across the Jordan?"

42 The men of Judah answered, "We did it because the king is one of us. So why should this make you angry? He hasn't paid for our food nor has he given us anything."

43 The Israelites replied, "We have ten times as many claims on King David as you have, even if he is one of you. Why do you look down on us? Don't forget that we were the first to talk about bringing the king back!"

But the men of Judah were more violent in making their claims than the men of Israel.

Sheba's Rebellion

20 ¹ There happened to be in Gilgal a worthless character named Sheba son of Bikri, of the tribe of Benjamin. He blew the trumpet and called out, "Down with David! We won't follow him! Men of Israel, let's go home!" 2 So the Israelites deserted David and went with Sheba, but the men of Judah remained loyal and followed David from the Jordan to Jerusalem.

3 When David arrived at his palace in Jerusalem, he took the ten concubines he had left to take care of the palace, and put them under guard. He provided for their needs, but did not have intercourse with them. They were kept confined for the rest of their lives, living like widows.

4 The king said to Amasa, "Call the men of Judah together and be back here with them by the day after tomorrow." 5 Amasa went to call them, but he did not get back by the time the king had told him to. 6 So the king said to Abishai, "Sheba will give us more trouble than Absalom. Take my men and go after him, or else he may occupy some forti-

fied towns and escape from us." 7 So Joab's men, the royal bodyguards, and all the other soldiers left Jerusalem with Abishai to go after Sheba. 8 When they reached the large rock at Gibeon, Amasa met them. Joab was dressed for battle, with a sword in its sheath fastened to his belt. As he came forward, the sword fell out. 9 Joab said to Amasa, "How are you, my friend?" and took hold of his beard with his right hand in order to kiss him. 10 Amasa was not on guard against the sword that Joab was holding in his other hand, and Joab stabbed him in the belly, and his insides spilled out on the ground. He died immediately, and Joab did not have to strike again.

Then Joab and his brother Abishai went on after Sheba. 11 One of Joab's men stood by Amasa's body and called out, "Everyone who is for Joab and David follow Joab!" 12 Amasa's body, covered with blood, was lying in the middle of the road. Joab's man saw that everybody was stopping, so he dragged the body from the road out into the field and threw a blanket over it. 13 After the body had been removed from the road, everyone followed Joab in pursuit of Sheba.

14 Sheba passed through the territory of all the tribes of Israel and came to the city of Abel Beth Maacah, and all the members of the clan of Bikri ᵈ assembled and followed him into the city. 15 Joab's men heard that Sheba was there, and so they went and besieged the city. They built ramps of earth against the outer wall and also began to dig under the wall to make it fall down. 16 There was a wise woman in the city who shouted from the wall, "Listen! Listen! Tell Joab to come here; I want to speak with him." 17 Joab went, and she asked, "Are you Joab?"

"Yes, I am," he answered.

"Listen to me, sir," she said.

"I'm listening," he answered.

18 She said, "Long ago they used to say, 'Go and get your answer in the city of Abel'—and that's just what they did. 19 Ours is a great city, one of the most peaceful and loyal in Israel.

ᵈ 20:14 *Probable text* Bikri; *Hebrew* Beri.
20:1 1 Kings 12:16; 2 Chr 10:16   20:3 2 Sam 16:22

The cabinet of the president is made up of the officials who help the president run the country. Who is in David's cabinet, and what are their duties?

Why are you trying to destroy it? Do you want to ruin what belongs to the LORD?"

20 "Never!" Joab answered. "I will never ruin or destroy your city! 21 That is not our plan. A man named Sheba son of Bikri, who is from the hill country of Ephraim, started a rebellion against King David. Hand over this one man, and I will withdraw from the city."

"We will throw his head over the wall to you," she said. 22 Then she went to the people of the city with her plan, and they cut off Sheba's head and threw it over the wall to Joab. He blew the trumpet as a signal for his men to leave the city, and they went back home. And Joab returned to Jerusalem to the king.

David's Officials

23 Joab was in command of the army of Israel; Benaiah son of Jehoiada was in charge of David's bodyguards; 24 Adoniram was in charge of the forced labor; Jehoshaphat son of Ahilud was in charge of the records; 25 Sheva was the court secretary; Zadok and Abiathar were the priests, 26 and Ira from the town of Jair was also one of David's priests.

Saul's Descendants Are Put to Death

21 ¹During David's reign there was a severe famine which lasted for three full years. So David consulted the LORD about it, and the LORD said, "Saul and his family are guilty of murder; he put the people of Gibeon to death." (²The people of Gibeon were not Israelites; they were a small group of Amorites whom the Israelites had promised to protect, but Saul had tried to destroy them because of his zeal for the people of Israel and Judah.) ³So David summoned the people of Gibeon and said to them, "What can I do for you? I want to make up for the wrong that was done to you, so that you will bless the LORD's people."

⁴They answered, "Our quarrel with Saul and his family can't be settled with silver or gold, nor do we want to kill any Israelite."

"What, then, do you think I should do for you?" David asked.

⁵They answered, "Saul wanted to destroy us and leave none of us alive anywhere in Israel. ⁶So hand over seven of his male descendants, and we will hang them before the LORD at Gibeah, the hometown of Saul, the LORD's chosen king."

"I will hand them over," the king answered.

⁷But because of the sacred promise that he and Jonathan had made to each other, David spared Jonathan's son Mephibosheth, the grandson of Saul. ⁸However, he took Armoni and Mephibosheth, the two sons that Rizpah the daughter of Aiah had borne to Saul; he also took the five sons of Saul's daughter Merab, whom she had borne to Adriel son of Barzillai, who was from Meholah. ⁹David handed them over to the people of Gibeon, who hanged them on the mountain before the LORD—and all seven of them died together. It was late in the spring, at the beginning of the barley harvest, when they were put to death.

¹⁰Then Saul's concubine Rizpah, the daughter of Aiah, used sackcloth to make a shelter for herself on the rock where the corpses were, and she stayed there from the beginning of harvest until the autumn rains came. During the day she would keep the birds away from the corpses, and at night she would protect them from wild animals.

¹¹When David heard what Rizpah had done, ¹²he went and got the bones of Saul and of his son Jonathan from the people of Jabesh in Gilead. (They had stolen them from the public square in Beth Shan, where the Philistines had hanged the bodies on the day they killed Saul on Mount Gilboa.) ¹³David took the bones of Saul and Jonathan and also gathered up the bones of the seven men who had been hanged. ¹⁴Then they buried the bones of Saul and Jonathan in the grave of Saul's father Kish, in Zela in the territory of Benjamin, doing all that the king had commanded. And after that, God answered their prayers for the country.

Battles against Philistine Giants
(1 Chronicles 20:4–8)

¹⁵There was another war between the Philistines and Israel, and David and his men

21:2 Josh 9:3–15   21:7 1 Sam 20:15–17; 2 Sam 9:1–7   21:8 1 Sam 18:19   21:12 1 Sam 31:8–13

Respect for the Dead

Notice how David pays respect to the remains of Saul and Jonathan. Honoring the dead is a strong tradition in the Catholic Church. A special day has been set aside in the year to do that. It is November 2 and is often called All Souls' Day. Mexicans have a tradition called Day of the Dead, in which they celebrate with those who have died by having picnics at the graves of departed family members. The Church also has a tradition of honoring relics, which sometimes are bones or bone fragments of saints and holy people. Because these relics were once part of the living body of a saint, they too are considered holy.

All this comes from the belief that we are to honor and revere the memory and resting places of the dead. We know that the souls of those who die in God's friendship will one day be united with God and with all the saints in heaven after death. At the end of the world, their bodies will rise again to be united with their souls. So even though our dead loved ones are no longer physically here on earth, we can be connected to them spiritually. We call this spiritual family of living and dead believers the Communion of Saints. If we remain faithful to God, we too will be part of the Communion of Saints in this life and after our death.

— 2 Samuel 21:11–14

went and fought the Philistines. During one of the battles David grew tired. ¹⁶A giant named Ishbibenob, who was carrying a bronze spear that weighed about seven and a half pounds and who was wearing a new sword, thought he could kill David. ¹⁷But Abishai son of Zeruiah came to David's help, attacked the giant, and killed him. Then David's men made David promise that he would never again go out with them to battle. "You are the hope of Israel, and we don't want to lose you," they said.

¹⁸After this there was a battle with the Philistines at Gob, during which Sibbecai from Hushah killed a giant named Saph.

¹⁹There was another battle with the Philistines at Gob, and Elhanan son of Jair[e] from Bethlehem killed Goliath from Gath, whose spear had a shaft as thick as the bar on a weaver's loom.

²⁰Then there was another battle at Gath, where there was a giant who loved to fight. He had six fingers on each hand and six toes on each foot. ²¹He defied the Israelites, and

Jonathan, the son of David's brother Shammah, killed him.

²²These four were descendants of the giants of Gath, and they were killed by David and his men.

David's Song of Victory
(Psalm 18)

22 ¹When the LORD saved David from Saul and his other enemies, David sang this song to the LORD:

² The LORD is my protector;
   he is my strong fortress.
³ My God is my protection,
   and with him I am safe.
 He protects me like a shield;
   he defends me and keeps me safe.
 He is my savior;
   he protects me and saves me from
      violence.
⁴ I call to the LORD,
   and he saves me from my enemies.
 Praise the LORD!

ᵉ **21:19** *Probable text (see 1 Chr 20:5)* Jair; *Hebrew* Jaareoregim.
21:17 1 Kings 11:36; Ps 132:17

5 The waves of death were all around
 me;
  the waves of destruction rolled over
   me.
6 The danger of death was around me,
  and the grave set its trap for me.
7 In my trouble I called to the LORD;
  I called to my God for help.
 In his temple he heard my voice;
  he listened to my cry for help.

8 Then the earth trembled and shook;
  the foundations of the sky rocked and
   quivered
  because God was angry!
9 Smoke poured out of his nostrils,
  a consuming flame and burning coals
   from his mouth.
10 He tore the sky open and came down,
  with a dark cloud under his feet.
11 He flew swiftly on his winged creature;*f*
  he traveled on the wings of the wind.

The LORD is my protector! (22:2)

12 He covered himself with darkness;
  thick clouds, full of*g* water, surrounded
   him;
13 burning coals flamed up from the
   lightning before him.
14 Then the LORD thundered from the sky,
  and the voice of Almighty God was
   heard.
15 He shot his arrows and scattered his
   enemies;
  with flashes of lightning he sent them
   running.
16 The floor of the ocean was laid bare,
  and the foundations of the earth were
   uncovered
  when the LORD rebuked his enemies
  and roared at them in anger.

17 The LORD reached down from above and
   took hold of me;
  he pulled me out of the deep waters.
18 He rescued me from my powerful enemies
  and from all those who hate me—
  they were too strong for me.
19 When I was in trouble, they attacked
   me,
  but the LORD protected me.
20 He helped me out of danger;
  he saved me because he was pleased
   with me.

21 The LORD rewards me because I do what
   is right;
  he blesses me because I am innocent.
22 I have obeyed the law of the LORD;
  I have not turned away from my God.
23 I have observed all his laws;
  I have not disobeyed his commands.
24 He knows that I am faultless,
  that I have kept myself from doing
   wrong.
25 And so he rewards me because I do what
   is right,
  because he knows that I am
   innocent.

f **22:11** WINGED CREATURE: *See Word List.* *g* **22:12** *Some ancient translations (and see Ps 18:11) full of; Hebrew unclear.*

26 O LORD, you are faithful to those who
        are faithful to you,
    and completely good to those[h] who are
        perfect.
27 You are pure to those who are pure,
    but hostile to those who are wicked.
28 You save those who are humble,
    but you humble those who are proud.

29 You, LORD, are my light;
    you dispel my darkness.
30 You give me strength to attack my enemies
    and power to overcome their defenses.

31 This God—how perfect are his deeds,
    how dependable his words!
  He is like a shield
    for all who seek his protection.
32 The LORD alone is God;
    God alone is our defense.
33 This God is my strong refuge;
    he makes[i] my pathway safe.
34 He makes me sure-footed as a deer;
    he keeps me safe on the mountains.
35 He trains me for battle,
    so that I can use the strongest bow.

36 O LORD, you protect me and save me;
    your help has made me great.
37 You have kept me from being captured,
    and I have never fallen.
38 I pursue my enemies and defeat them;
    I do not stop until I destroy them.
39 I strike them down, and they cannot
        rise;
    they lie defeated before me.
40 You give me strength for the battle
    and victory over my enemies.
41 You make my enemies run from me;
    I destroy those who hate me.
42 They look for help, but no one saves
        them;
    they call to the LORD, but he does not
        answer.
43 I crush them, and they become like
        dust;

I trample on them like mud in the
        streets.
44 You saved me from my rebellious people
    and maintained my rule over the
        nations;
    people I did not know have now
        become my subjects.
45 Foreigners bow before me;
    when they hear me, they obey.
46 They lose their courage
    and come trembling[j] from their
        fortresses.

47 The LORD lives! Praise my defender!
    Proclaim the greatness of the strong
        God who saves me!
48 He gives me victory over my enemies;
    he subdues the nations under me
49   and saves me from my foes.

  O LORD, you give me victory over my
        enemies
    and protect me from violent men.
50 And so I praise you among the nations;
    I sing praises to you.
51 God gives great victories to his king;
    he shows constant love to the one he
        has chosen,
    to David and his descendants
        forever.

David's Last Words

23 ¹David son of Jesse was the man
    whom God made great, whom the
God of Jacob chose to be king, and who was
the composer of beautiful songs for Israel.
These are David's last words:

2 The spirit of the LORD speaks through
        me;
    his message is on my lips.
3 The God of Israel has spoken;
    the protector of Israel said to me:
  "The king who rules with justice,
    who rules in obedience to God,

---

h **22:26** *Probable text (see Ps 18:25)* those; *Hebrew* the strong.   i **22:33** *Probable text (see Ps 18:32)* he makes;
Hebrew unclear.   j **22:46** *Probable text (see Ps 18:45)* come trembling; *Hebrew* come ready to fight.
22:34 Hab 3:19   **22:50** Rom 15:9

Who were "The Three," and what did each of them do to become famous?

The Man Whom God Made Great

David is described well in the first sentence of 2 Samuel, chapter 23. Think about how far David has come. When we first met him back in 1 Samuel, chapter 16, he was a lowly shepherd, the youngest of eight sons. And yet God knew what was in David's heart and could see what kind of man David would become. He certainly wasn't perfect, but through all his life David remained faithful to God.

There is so much potential in each one of us. We too have greatness within us. We only have to believe in ourselves and trust that God can and will call forth marvelous things from us. After all, we are created in God's image. Let God's grace flow through you. Ask God to help you become the person you were created to be. David composed beautiful songs for Israel. Let your life be a song of God's grace.

— 2 Samuel 23:1

4 is like the sun shining on a cloudless dawn,
    the sun that makes the grass sparkle
        after rain."

5 And that is how God will bless my
    descendants,
    because he has made an eternal
        covenant with me,
    an agreement that will not be broken,
    a promise that will not be changed.
That is all I desire;
    that will be my victory,
    and God will surely bring it about.

6 But godless people are like thorns that are
        thrown away;
    no one can touch them barehanded.
7 You must use an iron tool or a spear;
    they will be burned completely. [k]

David's Famous Soldiers
(1 Chronicles 11:10–41)

8 These are the names of David's famous soldiers: the first was Josheb Basshebeth from Tachemon, who was the leader of "The Three"; [l] he fought with his spear [m] against eight hundred men and killed them all in one battle.

9 The second of the famous three was Eleazar son of Dodo, of the clan of Ahoh. One day he and David challenged the Philistines who had gathered for battle. The Israelites fell back, 10 but he stood his ground and fought the Philistines until his hand was so cramped that he could not let go of his sword. The LORD won a great victory that day. After it was over, the Israelites returned to where Eleazar was and stripped the armor from the dead.

11 The third of the famous three was Shammah son of Agee from Harar. The Philistines had gathered at Lehi, where there was a field of peas. The Israelites fled from the Philistines, 12 but Shammah stood his ground in the field, defended it, and killed the Philistines. The LORD won a great victory that day.

13 Near the beginning of harvest time [n] three of "The Thirty" went down to Adullam Cave, where David was, while a band of Philistines was camping in Rephaim Valley. 14 At that time David was on a fortified hill, and a group of Philistines had occupied Bethlehem. 15 David grew homesick and said, "How I wish someone would bring me a drink of water from the well by the gate at Bethlehem!" 16 The three famous soldiers forced their way through the Philistine camp, drew some water from the well, and brought it back to David. But he would not drink it; instead he poured it out as an offering to the LORD 17 and said, "LORD, I could

---

[k] 23:7 Verses 6-7 in Hebrew are unclear.   [l] 23:8 One ancient translation "The Three"; Hebrew the third.

[m] 23:8 Probable text (see 1 Chr 11:11) he fought with his spear; Hebrew unclear.   [n] 23:13 Probable text Near the beginning of harvest time; Hebrew unclear.

2 Samuel

never drink this! It would be like drinking the blood of these men who risked their lives!" So he refused to drink it.

Those were the brave deeds of the three famous soldiers.

18 Joab's brother Abishai (their mother was Zeruiah) was the leader of "The Famous Thirty." He fought with his spear against three hundred men and killed them, and became famous among "The Thirty."*o* 19 He was the most famous of "The Thirty"*p* and became their leader, but he was not as famous as "The Three."

20 Benaiah son of Jehoiada from Kabzeel was another famous soldier; he did many brave deeds, including killing two great Moabite warriors. He once went down into a pit on a snowy day and killed a lion. 21 He also killed an Egyptian, a huge man who was armed with a spear. Benaiah attacked him with his club, snatched the spear from the Egyptian's hand, and killed him with it. 22 Those were the brave deeds of Benaiah, who was one of "The Thirty."*p* 23 He was outstanding among them, but was not as famous as "The Three." David put him in charge of his bodyguard.

24-39 Other members of "The Thirty" included:

Asahel, Joab's brother
Elhanan son of Dodo from Bethlehem
Shammah and Elika from Harod
Helez from Pelet
Ira son of Ikkesh from Tekoa
Abiezer from Anathoth
Mebunnai from Hushah
Zalmon from Ahoh
Maharai from Netophah
Heleb son of Baanah from Netophah
Ittai son of Ribai from Gibeah in Benjamin
Benaiah from Pirathon
Hiddai from the valleys near Gaash
Abialbon from Arabah
Azmaveth from Bahurim
Eliahba from Shaalbon
The sons of Jashen
Jonathan

Shammah from Harar
Ahiam son of Sharar from Harar
Eliphelet son of Ahasbai from Maacah
Eliam son of Ahithophel from Gilo
Hezro from Carmel
Paarai from Arab
Igal son of Nathan from Zobah
Bani from Gad
Zelek from Ammon
Naharai from Beeroth, Joab's armorbearer
Ira and Gareb from Jattir
Uriah the Hittite.

There were thirty-seven famous soldiers in all.

David Takes a Census
(1 Chronicles 21:1–27)

24 1 On another occasion the LORD was angry with Israel, and he made David bring trouble on them. The LORD said to him, "Go and count the people of Israel and Judah." 2 So David gave orders to Joab, the commander of his army: "Go with your officers through all the tribes of Israel from one end of the country to the other, and count the people. I want to know how many there are."

3 But Joab answered the king, "Your Majesty, may the LORD your God make the people of Israel a hundred times more numerous than they are now, and may you live to see him do it. But why does Your Majesty want to do this?" 4 But the king made Joab and his officers obey his order; they left his presence and went out to count the people of Israel.

5 They crossed the Jordan and camped south of Aroer, the city in the middle of the valley, in the territory of Gad.*q* From there they went north to Jazer, 6 and on to Gilead and to Kadesh, in Hittite territory.*r* Then they went to Dan, and from Dan they went*s* west to Sidon. 7 Then they went south to the fortified city of Tyre, on to all the cities of the Hivites and the Canaanites, and finally to Beersheba, in the southern part of Judah. 8 So

---

o **23:18** One ancient translation "The Thirty"; Hebrew "The Three."   *p* **23:19,22** Probable text "The Thirty"; Hebrew "The Three."   *q* **24:5** Probable text Aroer . . . Gad; Hebrew unclear.   *r* **24:6** One ancient translation Kadesh, in Hittite territory; Hebrew to the land of Tahtim, Hodshi.   *s* **24:6** Probable text and from Dan they went; Hebrew unclear.

2 Samuel

Pray It!

Guilty Conscience

What do we do when, like David, our conscience begins to hurt? Try this prayer.

O God, sometimes I can coast along in life, and everything seems to be going great. At other times, I know something is wrong. I don't feel right inside. Help me to pay attention to my conscience. If I am feeling guilty, help me to be honest with myself and with you. Help me to ask forgiveness if I've done something wrong. Help me to do the right thing, and when I fail, help me to learn from my failure and make up my mind to do better. You are with me through it all. Don't let me forget that! Amen.

— 2 Samuel 24:10

after nine months and twenty days they returned to Jerusalem, having traveled through the whole country. 9They reported to the king the total number of men capable of military service: 800,000 in Israel and 500,000 in Judah.

10But after David had taken the census, his conscience began to hurt, and he said to the LORD, "I have committed a terrible sin in doing this! Please forgive me. I have acted foolishly."

11-12The LORD said to Gad, David's prophet, "Go and tell David that I am giving him three choices. I will do whichever he chooses." The next morning, after David had gotten up, 13Gad went to him, told him what the LORD had said, and asked, "Which is it to be? Three*t* years of famine in your land or three months of running away from your enemies or three days of an epidemic in your land? Now think it over, and tell me what answer to take back to the LORD."

14David answered, "I am in a desperate situation! But I don't want to be punished by people. Let the LORD himself be the one to punish us, for he is merciful." 15So the LORD sent an epidemic on Israel, which lasted from that morning until the time that he had chosen. From one end of the coun-

try to the other seventy thousand Israelites died. 16When the LORD's angel was about to destroy Jerusalem, the LORD changed his mind about punishing the people and said to the angel who was killing them, "Stop! That's enough!" The angel was by the threshing place of Araunah, a Jebusite.

17David saw the angel who was killing the people, and said to the LORD, "I am the guilty one. I am the one who did wrong. What have these poor people done? You should punish me and my family."

18That same day Gad went to David and said to him, "Go up to Araunah's threshing place and build an altar to the LORD." 19David obeyed the LORD's command and went as Gad had told him to. 20Araunah looked down and saw the king and his officials coming up to him. He threw himself on the ground in front of David 21and asked, "Your Majesty, why are you here?"

David answered, "To buy your threshing place and build an altar for the LORD, in order to stop the epidemic."

22"Take it, Your Majesty," Araunah said, "and offer to the LORD whatever you wish. Here are these oxen to burn as an offering on the altar; here are their yokes and the threshing boards to use as fuel." 23Araunah

t 24:13 Some ancient translations (and see 1 Chr 21:12) Three; Hebrew Seven.

2 Samuel

What is the total number of men capable of military service in David's kingdom? You will have to add those in Israel and those in Judah.

gave it all to the king^u and said to him, "May the LORD your God accept your offering."

24 But the king answered, "No, I will pay you for it. I will not offer to the LORD my God sacrifices that have cost me nothing."

And he bought the threshing place and the oxen for fifty pieces of silver. 25 Then he built an altar to the LORD and offered burnt offerings and fellowship offerings. The LORD answered his prayer, and the epidemic in Israel was stopped.

^u 24:23 *Probable text* to the king; *Hebrew* to the king the king.

Your Next Step

Congratulations on finishing the Second Book of Samuel! Use this space to write your thoughts and questions about this book. If you are following the suggested reading plan, go ahead to the First Book of Kings. It continues with the story of King Solomon and the kings who followed him.

Just as the great pyramids record the golden years of Egypt, Israel's golden years are recorded in the First Book of Kings. The story of Israel's kings began in First and Second Samuel with Saul and David. The story continues in First Kings when David's son Solomon becomes the next king. He is a powerful and wise king who accumulates great wealth and builds Jerusalem into a great city.

Solomon is famous for building the Temple in Jerusalem. However, Solomon does not remain obedient to God, and his kingdom is eventually split in two—the kingdom of Judah in the south and the kingdom of Israel in the north. Prophets, who speak for God and are often critical of the kings, begin to play an important role in both First and Second Kings.

Chap. 18

Headlines

- Young Solomon Prays for Wisdom (3:4–15)
- King Orders Baby Cut in Two! (3:16–28)
- Temple Construction Begins (6:1–14)
- Northern Tribes Revolt, Kingdom Splits (12:1–20)
- Prophet's Prayers Restore Child's Life (17:8–24)
- Elijah Proves Yahweh Supreme (18:16–40)
- Evil Deeds by King and Queen (chapter 21)

FACTOIDS

Who wrote this book? First and Second Kings were originally one book, but the author is unknown.

When was it written? It was probably written sometime after the fall of Jerusalem (587 BC). The author or authors used court records and other written histories as sources.

What time period does it cover? From 960 to 850 BC.

Why was it written? It was written to show that Israel's history was guided by God.

Important themes

- The success of the king's reign relies on his obedience to God.
- Disobeying God's Law and worshipping false gods result in the loss of the kingdom.
- God offers hope and continues to speak to his people through the prophets.

1 KINGS

King David in His Old Age

1 ¹King David was now a very old man, and although his servants covered him with blankets, he could not keep warm. ²So his officials said to him, "Your Majesty, let us find a young woman to stay with you and take care of you. She will lie close to you and keep you warm." ³A search was made all over Israel for a beautiful young woman, and in Shunem they found such a woman named Abishag, and brought her to the king. ⁴She was very beautiful, and waited on the king and took care of him, but he did not have intercourse with her.

Adonijah Claims the Throne

⁵⁻⁶Now that Absalom was dead, Adonijah, the son of David and Haggith, was the oldest surviving son. He was a very handsome man. David had never reprimanded him about anything, and he was ambitious to be king. He provided for himself chariots, horses, and an escort of fifty men. ⁷He talked with Joab (whose mother was Zeruiah) and with Abiathar the priest, and they agreed to support his cause. ⁸But Zadok the priest, Benaiah son of Jehoiada, Nathan the prophet, Shimei, Rei, and David's bodyguards were not on Adonijah's side.

⁹One day Adonijah offered a sacrifice of sheep, bulls, and fattened calves at Snake Rock, near the spring of Enrogel. He invited the other sons of King David and the king's officials who were from Judah to come to this sacrificial feast, ¹⁰but he did not invite his half brother Solomon or Nathan the prophet or Benaiah or the king's bodyguards.

Solomon Is Made King

¹¹Then Nathan went to Bathsheba, Solomon's mother, and asked her, "Haven't you heard that Haggith's son Adonijah has made himself king? And King David doesn't know anything about it! ¹²If you want to save your life and the life of your son Solomon, I would advise you to ¹³go at once to King David and ask him, 'Your Majesty, didn't you solemnly promise me that my son Solomon would succeed you as king? How is it, then, that Adonijah has become king?' " ¹⁴And Nathan added, "Then, while you are still talking with King David, I will come in and confirm your story."

¹⁵So Bathsheba went to see the king in his bedroom. He was very old, and Abishag, the young woman from Shunem, was taking care of him. ¹⁶Bathsheba bowed low before the king, and he asked, "What do you want?"

¹⁷She answered, "Your Majesty, you made me a solemn promise in the name of the LORD your God that my son Solomon would be king after you. ¹⁸But Adonijah has already become king, and you don't know anything about it. ¹⁹He has offered a sacrifice of many bulls, sheep, and fattened calves, and he invited your sons, and Abiathar the priest, and Joab the commander of your army to the feast, but he did not invite your son Solomon. ²⁰Your Majesty, all the people of Israel are looking to you to tell them who is to succeed you as king. ²¹If you don't, as soon as you are dead, my son Solomon and I will be treated as traitors."

²²She was still speaking, when Nathan arrived at the palace. ²³The king was told that the prophet was there, and Nathan went in and bowed low before the king. ²⁴Then he said, "Your Majesty, have you announced that Adonijah would succeed you as king? ²⁵This very day he has gone and offered a sacrifice of many bulls, sheep, and fattened calves. He invited all your sons, Joab the commander of your army,ᵃ and Abiathar the priest, and right now they are feasting with him and shouting, 'Long live King Adonijah!' ²⁶But he did not invite me, sir, or Zadok the priest or Benaiah or Solomon. ²⁷Did Your Majesty approve all this and not

---

ᵃ **1:25** *One ancient translation* Joab the commander of your army; *Hebrew* your army commanders.
1:5 2 Sam 3:4 **1:11** 2 Sam 12:24

even tell your officials who is to succeed you as king?"

28 King David said, "Ask Bathsheba to come back in"—and she came and stood before him. 29 Then he said to her, "I promise you by the living LORD, who has rescued me from all my troubles, 30 that today I will keep the promise I made to you in the name of the LORD, the God of Israel, that your son Solomon would succeed me as king."

31 Bathsheba bowed low and said, "May my lord the king live forever!"

32 Then King David sent for Zadok, Nathan, and Benaiah. When they came in, 33 he said to them, "Take my court officials with you; have my son Solomon ride my own mule, and escort him down to Gihon Spring, 34 where Zadok and Nathan are to anoint him as king of Israel. Then blow the trumpet and shout, 'Long live King Solomon!' 35 Follow him back here when he comes to sit on my throne. He will succeed me as king, because he is the one I have chosen to be the ruler of Israel and Judah."

36 "It shall be done," answered Benaiah, "and may the LORD your God confirm it! 37 As the LORD has been with Your Majesty, may he also be with Solomon and make his reign even more prosperous than yours."

38 So Zadok, Nathan, Benaiah, and the royal bodyguards put Solomon on King David's mule and escorted him to Gihon Spring. 39 Zadok took the container of olive oil which he had brought from the Tent of the LORD's presence, and anointed Solomon. They blew the trumpet, and all the people shouted, "Long live King Solomon!" 40 Then they all followed him back, shouting for joy and playing flutes, making enough noise to shake the ground.

41 As Adonijah and all his guests were finishing the feast, they heard the noise. And when Joab heard the trumpet, he asked, "What's the meaning of all that noise in the city?" 42 Before he finished speaking, Jonathan, the son of the priest Abiathar,

arrived. "Come on in," Adonijah said. "You're a good man—you must be bringing good news."

43 "I'm afraid not," Jonathan answered. "His Majesty King David has made Solomon king. 44 He sent Zadok, Nathan, Benaiah, and the royal bodyguards to escort him. They had him ride on the king's mule, 45 and Zadok and Nathan anointed him as king at Gihon Spring. Then they went into the city, shouting for joy, and the people are now in an uproar. That's the noise you just heard. 46 Solomon is now the king. 47 What is more, the court officials went in to pay their respects to His Majesty King David and said, 'May your God make Solomon even more famous than you, and may Solomon's reign be even more prosperous than yours.' Then King David bowed in worship on his bed 48 and prayed, 'Let us praise the LORD, the God of Israel, who has today made one of my descendants succeed me as king, and has let me live to see it!' "

49 Then Adonijah's guests were afraid, and they all got up and left, each going his own way. 50 Adonijah, in great fear of Solomon, went to the Tent of the LORD's presence and took hold of the corners of the altar.[b] 51 King Solomon was told that Adonijah was afraid of him and that he was holding on to the corners of the altar and had said, "First, I want King Solomon to swear to me that he will not have me put to death."

52 Solomon replied, "If he is loyal, not even a hair on his head will be touched; but if he is not, he will die." 53 King Solomon then sent for Adonijah and had him brought down from the altar. Adonijah went to the king and bowed low before him, and the king said to him, "You may go home."

David's Last Instructions to Solomon

2 ¹ When David was about to die, he called his son Solomon and gave him his last instructions: 2 "My time to die has

---

b 1:50 CORNERS OF THE ALTAR: Small projections at the four corners of the altar that looked like horns. Anyone holding on to them was safe from being killed.

Read about King David as a young hero in I Samuel, chapters 16–18. This shivering old man was once a handsome shepherd boy.

I Kings

Good Advice

Solomon has just become king. David's advice to his son Solomon is to follow the Law of Moses and to obey God in everything. Even though David made some pretty big mistakes, he always tried to obey God. When he was wrong, he admitted it and tried to set things right.

Think of someone you know who seems to have a good relationship with God—someone whose actions match his or her words, someone who puts his or her complete faith and trust in God. What advice do you think that person would give you about following God? Why not ask him or her?

— 1 Kings 2:1–4

come. Be confident and determined, ³and do what the LORD your God orders you to do. Obey all his laws and commands, as written in the Law of Moses, so that wherever you go you may prosper in everything you do. ⁴If you obey him, the LORD will keep the promise he made when he told me that my descendants would rule Israel as long as they were careful to obey his commands faithfully with all their heart and soul.

⁵"There is something else. You remember what Joab did to me by killing the two commanders of Israel's armies, Abner son of Ner and Amasa son of Jether. You remember how he murdered them in time of peace as revenge for deaths they had caused in time

of war. He killed innocent men,ᶜ and now I bear the responsibility for what he did, and I sufferᵈ the consequences. ⁶You know what to do; you must not let him die a natural death.

⁷"But show kindness to the sons of Barzillai from Gilead and take care of them, because they were kind to me when I was fleeing from your brother Absalom.

⁸"There is also Shimei son of Gera, from the town of Bahurim in Benjamin. He cursed me bitterly the day I went to Mahanaim, but when he met me at the Jordan River, I gave him my solemn promise in the name of the LORD that I would not have him killed. ⁹But you must not let him go unpunished. You know what to do, and you must see to it that he is put to death."

The Death of David

¹⁰David died and was buried in David's City. ¹¹He had been king of Israel for forty years, ruling seven years in Hebron and thirty-three years in Jerusalem. ¹²Solomon succeeded his father David as king, and his royal power was firmly established.

The Death of Adonijah

¹³Then Adonijah, whose mother was Haggith, went to Bathsheba, who was Solomon's mother. "Is this a friendly visit?" she asked.

"It is," he answered, ¹⁴and then he added, "I have something to ask of you."

"What is it?" she asked.

¹⁵He answered, "You know that I should have become king and that everyone in Israel expected it. But it happened differently, and my brother became king because it was the LORD's will. ¹⁶And now I have one request to make; please do not refuse me."

"What is it?" Bathsheba asked.

ᶜ **2:5** *Some ancient translations* innocent men; *Hebrew* men in battle.   ᵈ **2:5** *Some ancient translations* I bear . . . and I suffer; *Hebrew* he bears . . . and he suffers.

2:5 a 2 Sam 3:27; **b** 2 Sam 20:10   **2:7** 2 Sam 17:27–29   **2:8** 2 Sam 16:5–13; 19:16–23   **2:11** 2 Sam 5:4, 5; 1 Chr 3:4   **2:12** 1 Chr 29:23

Solomon is anointed with oil when he becomes king. Catholics use oil for anointing in four of the Seven Sacraments. Can you name them?

17He answered, "Please ask King Solomon—I know he won't refuse you—to let me have Abishag, the young woman from Shunem, as my wife."

18"Very well," she answered. "I will speak to the king for you."

19So Bathsheba went to the king to speak to him on behalf of Adonijah. The king stood up to greet his mother and bowed to her. Then he sat on his throne and had another one brought in on which she sat at his right. 20She said, "I have a small favor to ask of you; please do not refuse me."

"What is it, mother?" he asked. "I will not refuse you."

21She answered, "Let your brother Adonijah have Abishag as his wife."

22"Why do you ask me to give Abishag to him?" the king asked. "You might as well ask me to give him the throne too. After all, he is my older brother, and Abiathar the priest and Joab are on his side!"e 23Then Solomon made a solemn promise in the LORD's name, "May God strike me dead if I don't make Adonijah pay with his life for asking this! 24The LORD has firmly established me on the throne of my father David; he has kept his promise and given the kingdom to me and my descendants. I swear by the living LORD that Adonijah will die this very day!"

25So King Solomon gave orders to Benaiah, who went out and killed Adonijah.

Abiathar's Banishment and Joab's Death

26Then King Solomon said to Abiathar the priest, "Go to your country home in Anathoth. You deserve to die, but I will not have you put to death now, for you were in charge of the LORD's Covenant Box while you were with my father David, and you shared in all his troubles." 27Then Solomon dismissed Abiathar from serving as a priest of the LORD, and so made come true what the LORD had said in Shiloh about the priest Eli and his descendants.

28Joab heard what had happened. (He had supported Adonijah, but not Absalom.) So he fled to the Tent of the LORD's presence and took hold of the corners of the altar.f 29When the news reached King Solomon that Joab had fled to the Tent and was by the altar, Solomon sent a messenger to Joab to ask him why he had fled to the altar. Joab answered that he had fled to the LORD because he was afraid of Solomon. So King Solomon sent Benaiahg to kill Joab. 30He went to the Tent of the LORD's presence and said to Joab, "The king orders you to come out."

"No," Joab answered. "I will die here."

Benaiah went back to the king and told him what Joab had said.

31"Do what Joab says," Solomon answered. "Kill him and bury him. Then neither I nor any other of David's descendants will any longer be held responsible for what Joab did when he killed innocent men. 32The LORD will punish Joab for those murders, which he committedh without my father David's knowledge. Joab killed two innocent men who were better men than he: Abner, commander of the army of Israel, and Amasa, commander of the army of Judah. 33The punishment for their murders will fall on Joab and on his descendants forever. But the LORD will always give success to David's descendants who sit on his throne."

34So Benaiah went to the Tent of the LORD's presence and killed Joab, and he was buried at his home in the open country. 35The king made Benaiah commander of the army in Joab's place and put Zadok the priest in Abiathar's place.

The Death of Shimei

36Then the king sent for Shimei and said to him, "Build a house for yourself here in Jerusalem. Live in it and don't leave the city. 37If you ever leave and go beyond Kidron Brook, you will certainly die—and you yourself will be to blame."

38"Very well, Your Majesty," Shimei answered. "I will do what you say." So he lived in Jerusalem a long time.

---

e 2:22 Some ancient translations and Abiathar the priest . . . on his side; Hebrew unclear. f 2:28 CORNERS OF THE ALTAR: See 1:50. g 2:29 One ancient translation Solomon sent a messenger . . . sent Benaiah; Hebrew Solomon sent Benaiah. h 2:32 will punish . . . committed; or will kill Joab, because he committed those murders.
2:17 1 Kings 1:3, 4   2:26 a 2 Sam 15:24; b 1 Sam 22:20–23   2:27 1 Sam 2:27–36

[39]Three years later, however, two of Shimei's slaves ran away to the king of Gath, Achish son of Maacah. When Shimei heard that they were in Gath, [40]he saddled his donkey and went to King Achish in Gath, to find his slaves. He found them and brought them back home. [41]When Solomon heard what Shimei had done, [42]he sent for him and said, "I made you promise in the LORD's name not to leave Jerusalem. And I warned you that if you ever did, you would certainly die. Did you not agree to it and say that you would obey me? [43]Why, then, have you broken your promise and disobeyed my command? [44]You know very well all the wrong that you did to my father David. The LORD will punish you for it. [45]But he will bless me, and he will make David's kingdom secure forever."

[46]Then the king gave orders to Benaiah, who went out and killed Shimei. Solomon was now in complete control.

Solomon Prays for Wisdom
(2 Chronicles 1:3–12)

3 [1]Solomon made an alliance with the king of Egypt by marrying his daughter. He brought her to live in David's City until he had finished building his palace, the Temple, and the wall around Jerusalem. [2]A temple had not yet been built for the LORD, and so the people were still offering sacrifices at many different altars. [3]Solomon loved the LORD and followed the instructions of his father David, but he also slaughtered animals and offered them as sacrifices on various altars.

[4]On one occasion he went to Gibeon to offer sacrifices because that was where the most famous altar was. He had offered hundreds of burnt offerings there in the past. [5]That night the LORD appeared to him in a dream and asked him, "What would you like me to give you?"

[6]Solomon answered, "You always showed great love for my father David, your servant, and he was good, loyal, and honest in his relation with you. And you have continued to show him your great and constant love by giving him a son who today rules in his place. [7]O LORD God, you have let me succeed my father as king, even though I am very young and don't know how to rule. [8]Here I am among the people you have chosen to be your own, a people who are so many that they cannot be counted. [9]So give me the wisdom I need to rule your people with justice and to know the difference between good and evil. Otherwise, how would I ever be able to rule this great people of yours?"

"Give me the wisdom I need." (3:9)

[10]The Lord was pleased that Solomon had asked for this, [11]and so he said to him, "Because you have asked for the wisdom to rule justly, instead of long life for yourself or riches or the death of your enemies, [12]I will do what you have asked. I will give you more wisdom and understanding than anyone has ever had before or will ever have again. [13]I will also give you what you have not asked for: all your life you will have wealth and honor, more than that of any other king. [14]And if you obey me and keep my laws and commands, as your father David did, I will give you a long life."

[15]Solomon woke up and realized that God had spoken to him in the dream. Then he went to Jerusalem and stood in front of the LORD's Covenant Box and offered burnt offerings and fellowship offerings to the LORD. After that he gave a feast for all his officials.

Pray It!

Not a Perfect Person

Solomon has gained the throne and scarcely begun to rule. Already we see he is jealous and fearful of his half brother Adonijah. Solomon even has him killed. So why is it that long after Solomon's death, people will refer to Solomon's wisdom and his riches? Probably because even though Solomon is far from perfect, he struggles to follow God's laws.

Every person has strengths and weaknesses. Solomon realizes this. So he turns to God and asks for the gift of wisdom. You can do this, too. When you're feeling less than perfect, pray this prayer patterned after Solomon's prayer.

Loving God,
You have showed great love to your people.
You have given me many gifts
  even though I am very young
  and don't yet know everything I will need to know.
Here I am
  among your people.
Give me the wisdom I need to follow you.
Help me to see what is right and what is wrong.
Help me to be a sign of your love in the world. Amen.

— 1 Kings 3:6–9

Solomon Judges a Difficult Case

16One day two prostitutes came and presented themselves before King Solomon. 17One of them said, "Your Majesty, this woman and I live in the same house, and I gave birth to a baby boy at home while she was there. 18Two days after my child was born, she also gave birth to a baby boy. Only the two of us were there in the house—no one else was present. 19Then one night she accidentally rolled over on her baby and smothered it. 20She got up during the night, took my son from my side while I was asleep, and carried him to her bed; then she put the dead child in my bed. 21The next morning, when I woke up and was going to nurse my baby, I saw that it was dead. I looked at it more closely and saw that it was not my child."

22But the other woman said, "No! The living child is mine, and the dead one is yours!"

The first woman answered back, "No! The dead child is yours, and the living one is mine!"

And so they argued before the king.

23Then King Solomon said, "Each of you claims that the living child is hers and that the dead child belongs to the other one." 24He sent for a sword, and when it was brought, 25he said, "Cut the living child in two and give each woman half of it."

26The real mother, her heart full of love for her son, said to the king, "Please, Your Majesty, don't kill the child! Give it to her!"

But the other woman said, "Don't give it to either of us; go on and cut it in two."

27Then Solomon said, "Don't kill the

Solomon makes a wise political move by marrying the King of Egypt's daughter, but it may not be the best choice as far as God is concerned. Why?

I Kings

"Don't kill the child!" (3:27)

child! Give it to the first woman—she is its real mother."

28 When the people of Israel heard of Solomon's decision, they were all filled with deep respect for him, because they knew then that God had given him the wisdom to settle disputes fairly.

Solomon's Officials

4 1 Solomon was king of all Israel, 2 and these were his high officials:

The priest: Azariah son of Zadok

3 The court secretaries: Elihoreph and Ahijah, sons of Shisha

In charge of the records: Jehoshaphat son of Ahilud

4 Commander of the army: Benaiah son of Jehoiada

Priests: Zadok and Abiathar

5 Chief of the district governors: Azariah son of Nathan

Royal Adviser: the priest Zabud son of Nathan

6 In charge of the palace servants: Ahishar

In charge of the forced labor: Adoniram son of Abda

7 Solomon appointed twelve men as district governors in Israel. They were to provide food from their districts for the king and his household, each man being responsible for one month out of the year. 8 The fol-

lowing are the names of these twelve officers and the districts they were in charge of:

Benhur: the hill country of Ephraim

9 Bendeker: the cities of Makaz, Shaalbim, Beth Shemesh, Elon, and Beth Hanan

10 Benhesed: the cities of Arubboth and Socoh and all the territory of Hepher

11 Benabinadab, who was married to Solomon's daughter Taphath: the whole region of Dor

12 Baana son of Ahilud: the cities of Taanach, Megiddo, and all the region near Beth Shan, near the town of Zarethan, south of the town of Jezreel, as far as the city of Abel Meholah and the city of Jokmeam

13 Bengeber: the city of Ramoth in Gilead, and the villages in Gilead belonging to the clan of Jair, a descendant of Manasseh, and the region of Argob in Bashan, sixty large towns in all, fortified with walls and with bronze bars on the gates

14 Ahinadab son of Iddo: the district of Mahanaim

15 Ahimaaz, who was married to Basemath, another of Solomon's daughters: the territory of Naphtali

16 Baana son of Hushai: the region of Asher and the town of Bealoth

17 Jehoshaphat son of Paruah: the territory of Issachar

18 Shimei son of Ela: the territory of Benjamin

19 Geber son of Uri: the region of Gilead, which had been ruled by King Sihon of the Amorites and King Og of Bashan

Besides these twelve, there was one governor over the whole land.

Solomon's Prosperous Reign

20 The people of Judah and Israel were as numerous as the grains of sand on the seashore; they ate and drank, and were happy.

Do you remember hearing the phrase "grains of sand on the seashore" before? Check out Genesis 22:17.

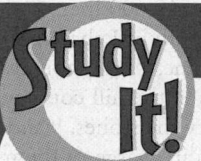

Three Thousand Proverbs!

Solomon's fame spread. His rule was a time of peace and riches. Even though some of the numbers might be exaggerated to make a point, clearly there was something special about Solomon. He was not only wise about leadership and human nature, but he knew about science, the natural world, plants, and animals. He was a writer and a composer, making over three thousand proverbs and one thousand songs! No wonder people thought that he might have been the author of other Old Testament books, such as the Song of Songs, Ecclesiastes, Proverbs, and the Book of Wisdom.

— 1 Kings 4:20–34

²¹Solomon's kingdom included all the nations from the Euphrates River to Philistia and the Egyptian border. They paid him taxes and were subject to him all his life.

²²The supplies Solomon needed each day were 150 bushels of fine flour and 300 bushels of meal; ²³10 stall-fed cattle, 20 pasture-fed cattle, and 100 sheep, besides deer, gazelles, roebucks, and poultry.

²⁴Solomon ruled over all the land west of the Euphrates River, from Tiphsah on the Euphrates as far west as the city of Gaza. All the kings west of the Euphrates were subject to him, and he was at peace with all the neighboring countries. ²⁵As long as he lived, the people throughout Judah and Israel lived in safety, each family with its own grapevines and fig trees.

²⁶Solomon had forty thousand stalls for his chariot horses and twelve thousand caval-ry horses. ²⁷His twelve governors, each one in the month assigned to him, supplied the food King Solomon needed for himself and for all who ate in the palace; they always supplied everything needed. ²⁸Each governor also supplied his share of barley and straw, where it was needed,ⁱ for the chariot horses and the work animals.

²⁹God gave Solomon unusual wisdom and insight, and knowledge too great to be measured. ³⁰Solomon was wiser than the wise men of the East or the wise men of Egypt. ³¹He was the wisest of all men: wiser than Ethan the Ezrahite, and Heman, Calcol, and Darda, the sons of Mahol, and his fame spread throughout all the neighboring countries. ³²He composed three thousand proverbs and more than a thousand songs. ³³He spoke of trees and plants, from the Lebanon cedars to the hyssop that grows on walls; he talked about animals, birds, reptiles, and fish. ³⁴Kings all over the world heard of his wisdom and sent people to listen to him.

Solomon Prepares to Build the Temple
(2 Chronicles 2:1–18)

5 ¹King Hiram of Tyre had always been a friend of David's, and when he heard that Solomon had succeeded his father David as king, he sent ambassadors to him. ²Solomon sent back this message to Hiram: ³"You know that because of the constant wars my father David had to fight against the enemy countries all around him, he could not build a temple for the worship of the LORD his God until the LORD had given him victory over all his enemies. ⁴But now the LORD my God has given me peace on all my borders. I have no enemies, and there is no danger of attack. ⁵The LORD promised my father David, 'Your son, whom I will make king after you, will build a temple for me.' And I have now decided to build that temple for the worship of the LORD my God. ⁶So send your men to Lebanon to cut down cedars for me. My men will work with them, and I will pay your men whatever you decide. As you well know, my men don't know how to cut down trees as well as yours do."

7Hiram was extremely pleased when he received Solomon's message, and he said, "Praise the LORD today for giving David such a wise son to succeed him as king of that great nation!" 8Then Hiram sent Solomon the following message: "I have received your message, and I am ready to do what you ask. I will provide the cedars and the pine trees. 9My men will bring the logs down from Lebanon to the sea and will tie them together in rafts to float them down the coast to the place you choose. There my men will untie them, and your men will take charge of them. On your part, I would like you to supply the food for my men."

10So Hiram supplied Solomon with all the cedar and pine logs that he wanted, 11and Solomon provided Hiram with 100,000 bushels of wheat and 110,000 gallons*j* of pure olive oil every year to feed his men.

12The LORD kept his promise and gave

Hiram supplied Solomon with . . . cedar and pine logs. (5:10)

Solomon wisdom. There was peace between Hiram and Solomon, and they made a treaty with each other.

13King Solomon drafted 30,000 men as forced labor from all over Israel, 14and put Adoniram in charge of them. He divided

them into three groups of 10,000 men, and each group spent one month in Lebanon and two months back home. 15Solomon also had 80,000 stone cutters in the hill country, with 70,000 men to carry the stones, 16and he placed 3,300 foremen in charge of them to supervise their work. 17At King Solomon's command they cut fine large stones for the foundation of the Temple. 18Solomon's and Hiram's workers and men from the city of Byblos prepared the stones and the timber to build the Temple.

Solomon Builds the Temple

6 1Four hundred and eighty years after the people of Israel left Egypt, during the fourth year of Solomon's reign over Israel, in the second month, the month of Ziv, Solomon began work on the Temple. 2Inside it was 90 feet long, 30 feet wide, and 45 feet high. 3The entrance room was 15 feet deep and 30 feet wide, as wide as the sanctuary itself. 4The walls of the Temple had openings in them, narrower on the outside than on the inside. 5Against the outside walls, on the sides and the back of the Temple, a three-storied annex was built, each story 7½ feet high. 6Each room in the lowest story was 7½ feet wide, in the middle story 9 feet wide, and in the top story 10½ feet wide. The Temple wall on each floor was thinner than on the floor below, so that the rooms could rest on the wall without having their beams built into it.

7The stones with which the Temple was built had been prepared at the quarry, so that there was no noise made by hammers, axes, or any other iron tools as the Temple was being built.

8The entrance to the lowest*k* story of the annex was on the south side of the Temple, with stairs leading up to the second and third stories. 9So King Solomon finished building the Temple. He put in a ceiling made of beams and boards of cedar. 10The three-storied annex, each story*l* 7½ feet high, was built against the outside walls of the Temple, and was joined to them by cedar beams.

11The LORD said to Solomon, 12"If you

A Place to Worship

Catholic Connections

The Temple building is described here in great detail. Solomon spared no expense and built an impressive resting place for the Covenant Box, also called the Ark of the Covenant. Christians have done the same thing. In many of the great cities of the world are beautiful cathedrals and churches where people go to worship God. Some people make it a practice to visit famous churches when they visit a new city. They may try to attend Mass at well-known Catholic churches. If your family travels a lot, you might want to try this. It is inspiring to see the beautiful buildings and art created to honor God. Though the Temple and our churches today were built centuries apart, they were built for the same purpose: "for the worship of the LORD my God" (1 Kings 5:5).

— 1 Kings, chapters 5–6

obey all my laws and commands, I will do for you what I promised your father David. **13** I will live among my people Israel in this Temple that you are building, and I will never abandon them."

14 So Solomon finished building the Temple.

The Interior Furnishings of the Temple
(2 Chronicles 3:8–14)

15 The inside walls were covered with cedar panels from the floor to the ceiling, and the floor was made of pine. **16** An inner room, called the Most Holy Place, was built in the rear of the Temple. It was 30 feet long and was partitioned off by cedar boards reaching from the floor to the ceiling.[m] **17** The room in front of the Most Holy Place was 60 feet long. **18** The cedar panels were decorated with carvings of gourds and flowers; the whole interior was covered with

cedar, so that the stones of the walls could not be seen.

19 In the rear of the Temple an inner room was built, where the LORD's Covenant Box was to be placed. **20** This inner room was 30 feet long, 30 feet wide, and 30 feet high, all covered with pure gold. The altar was covered with cedar panels.[n] **21** The inside of the Temple was covered with gold, and gold chains were placed across the entrance of the inner room, which was also covered with gold. **22** The whole interior of the Temple was covered with gold, as well as the altar in the Most Holy Place.

23 Two winged creatures were made of olive wood and placed in the Most Holy Place, each one 15 feet tall. **24-26** Both were of the same size and shape. Each had two wings, each wing 7½ feet long, so that the distance from one wing tip to the other was 15 feet. **27** They were placed side by side in the Most Holy Place, so that two of their outstretched wings touched each other in the middle of the room, and the other two

[m] **6:16** *One ancient translation* ceiling; *Hebrew* walls.　[n] **6:20** *Verse 20 in Hebrew is unclear.*
6:16 Ex 26:33, 34　**6:22** Ex 30:1–3　**6:23–28** Ex 25:18–20

The plants and animals carved and gilded in the Temple had symbolic meaning. They represented power, happiness, and blessing.

wings touched the walls. 28The two winged creatures were covered with gold.

29The walls of the main room and of the inner room were all decorated with carved figures of winged creatures, palm trees, and flowers. 30Even the floor was covered with gold.

31A double door made of olive wood was set in place at the entrance of the Most Holy Place; the top of the doorway was a pointed arch. 32The doors were decorated with carved figures of winged creatures, palm trees, and flowers. The doors, the winged creatures, and the palm trees were covered with gold. 33For the entrance to the main room a rectangular doorframe of olive wood was made. 34There were two folding doors made of pine 35and decorated with carved figures of winged creatures, palm trees, and flowers, which were evenly covered with gold.

36An inner court was built in front of the Temple, enclosed with walls which had one layer of cedar beams for every three layers of stone.

37The foundation of the Temple was laid in the second month, the month of Ziv, in the fourth year of Solomon's reign. 38In the eighth month, the month of Bul, in the eleventh year of Solomon's reign, the Temple was completely finished exactly as it had been planned. It had taken Solomon seven years to build it.

Solomon's Palace

7 1Solomon also built a palace for himself, and it took him thirteen years. 2-3The Hall of the Forest of Lebanon⁰ was 150 feet long, 75 feet wide, and 45 feet high. It had threeᵖ rows of cedar pillars, 15 in each row, with cedar beams resting on them. The ceiling was of cedar, extending over storerooms, which were supported by the pillars. 4On each of the two side walls there were

three rows of windows. 5The doorways and the windowsᑫ had rectangular frames, and the three rows of windows in each wall faced the opposite rows.

6The Hall of Columns was 75 feet long and 45 feet wide. It had a covered porch, supported by columns.

7The Throne Room, also called the Hall of Judgment, where Solomon decided cases, had cedar panels from the floor to the rafters.ʳ

8Solomon's own quarters, in another court behind the Hall of Judgment, were made like the other buildings. He also built the same kind of house for his wife, the daughter of the king of Egypt.

9All these buildings and the great court were made of fine stones from the foundations to the eaves. The stones were prepared at the quarry and cut to measure, with their inner and outer sides trimmed with saws. 10The foundations were made of large stones prepared at the quarry, some of them twelve feet long and others fifteen feet long. 11On top of them were other stones, cut to measure, and cedar beams. 12The palace court, the inner court of the Temple, and the entrance room of the Temple had walls with one layer of cedar beams for every three layers of cut stones.

Huram's Task
(2 Chronicles 2:13,14)

13King Solomon sent for a man named Huram, a craftsman living in the city of Tyre, who was skilled in bronze work. 14His father, who was no longer living, was from Tyre, and had also been a skilled bronze craftsman; his mother was from the tribe of Naphtali. Huram was an intelligent and experienced craftsman. He accepted King Solomon's invitation to be in charge of all the bronze work.

⁰ **7:2–3** HALL OF THE FOREST OF LEBANON: *A large ceremonial hall in the palace, probably so called because it was paneled in cedar.*   ᵖ **7:2–3** *One ancient translation* three; *Hebrew* four.   ᑫ **7:5** *One ancient translation* windows; *Hebrew* doorposts.   ʳ **7:7** *Some ancient translations* rafters; *Hebrew* floor.
7:8 1 Kings 3:1

Huram was a busy guy! Read the list of everything he made for the Temple in I Kings 7:40–45.

The Two Bronze Columns
(2 Chronicles 3:15–17)

15 Huram cast two bronze columns, each one 27 feet tall and 18 feet in circumference,ˢ and placed them at the entrance of the Temple. **16** He also made two bronze capitals, each one 7½ feet tall, to be placed on top of the columns. **17** The top of each column was decorated with a design of interwoven chainsᵗ **18** and two rows of bronze pomegranates.

19 The capitals were shaped like lilies, 6 feet tall, **20** and were placed on a rounded section which was above the chain design. There were 200 pomegranates in two rows around eachᵘ capital.

21 Huram placed these two bronze columns in front of the entrance of the Temple: the one on the south side was named Jachinᵛ and the one on the north was named Boaz.ʷ **22** The lily-shaped bronze capitals were on top of the columns.

And so the work on the columns was completed.

The Bronze Tank
(2 Chronicles 4:2–5)

23 Huram made a round tank of bronze, 7½ feet deep, 15 feet in diameter, and 45 feet in circumference. **24** All around the outer edge of the rim of the tankˣ were two rows of bronze gourds, which had been cast all in one piece with the rest of the tank. **25** The tank rested on the backs of twelve bronze bulls that faced outward, three facing in each direction. **26** The sides of the tank were 3 inches thick. Its rim was like the rim of a cup, curving outward like the petals of a lily. The tank held about 10,000 gallons.

The Bronze Carts

27 Huram also made ten bronze carts; each was 6 feet long, 6 feet wide, and 4½ feet high. **28** They were made of square panels which were set in frames, **29** with the figures of lions, bulls, and winged creatures on the panels; and on the frames, above and underneath the lions and bulls, there were spiral figures in relief. **30** Each cart had four bronze wheels with bronze axles. At the four corners were bronze supports for a basin; the supports were decorated with spiral figures in relief. **31** There was a circular frame on top for the basin. It projected upward 18 inches from the top of the cart and 7 inches down into it. It had carvings around it. **32** The wheels were 25 inches high; they were under the panels, and the axles were of one piece with the carts. **33** The wheels were like chariot wheels; their axles, rims, spokes, and hubs were all of bronze. **34** There were four supports at the bottom corners of each cart, which were of one piece with the cart. **35** There was a 9-inch band around the top of each cart; its supports and the panels were of one piece with the cart. **36** The supports and panels were decorated with figures of winged creatures, lions, and palm trees, wherever there was space for them, with spiral figures all around. **37** This, then, is how the carts were made; they were all alike, having the same size and shape.

38 Huram also made ten basins, one for each cart. Each basin was 6 feet in diameter and held 200 gallons. **39** He placed five of the carts on the south side of the Temple, and the other five on the north side; the tank he placed at the southeast corner.

Summary List of Temple Furnishings
(2 Chronicles 4:11—5:1)

40-45 Huram also made pots, shovels, and bowls. He completed all his work for King Solomon for the LORD's Temple. This is what he made:

> The two columns
> The two bowl-shaped capitals on top of the columns

ˢ **7:15** *Some ancient translations* each one . . . circumference; *Hebrew* the first column was 27 feet tall and the second column was 18 feet in circumference.   ᵗ **7:17** *Verse 17 in Hebrew is unclear.*   ᵘ **7:20** *One ancient translation* each; *Hebrew* the second.   ᵛ **7:21** JACHIN: *This name sounds like the Hebrew for "he (God) establishes."*   ʷ **7:21** BOAZ: *This name sounds like the Hebrew for "by his (God's) strength."*   ˣ **7:24** *Probable text* All around . . . tank; *Hebrew unclear.*

7:38 Ex 30:17–21

The design of interwoven chains on each
capital
The 400 bronze pomegranates, in two
rows of 100 each around the design
on each capital
The ten carts
The ten basins
The tank
The twelve bulls supporting the tank
The pots, shovels, and bowls

All this equipment for the Temple, which
Huram made for King Solomon, was of polished bronze. [46]The king had it all made in
the foundry between Sukkoth and Zarethan,
in the Jordan Valley. [47]Solomon did not have
these bronze objects weighed, because there
were too many of them, and so their weight
was never determined.

[48]Solomon also had gold furnishings made
for the Temple: the altar, the table for the
bread offered to God, [49]the ten lampstands
that stood in front of the Most Holy Place,
five on the south side and five on the north;
the flowers, lamps, and tongs; [50]the cups,
lamp snuffers, bowls, dishes for incense, and
the pans used for carrying live coals; and the
hinges for the doors of the Most Holy Place
and of the outer doors of the Temple. All
these furnishings were made of gold.

[51]When King Solomon finished all the
work on the Temple, he placed in the Temple storerooms all the things that his father
David had dedicated to the LORD—the silver, gold, and other articles.

The Covenant Box Is Brought to the Temple
(2 Chronicles 5:2— 6:2)

8 [1] Then King Solomon summoned all
the leaders of the tribes and clans of
Israel to come to him in Jerusalem in order
to take the LORD's Covenant Box from
Zion, David's City, to the Temple. [2]They all
assembled during the Festival of Shelters in
the seventh month, in the month of
Ethanim. [3]When all the leaders had gathered, the priests lifted the Covenant Box
[4]and carried it to the Temple. The Levites
and the priests also moved the Tent of the

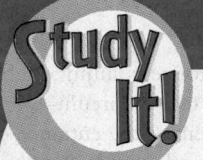

Old and New

After the Temple is built, the peo-
ple come together to place the
Covenant Box in the Most Holy
Place. The Most Holy Place was a
special room in the back of the
Temple. Only the high priest could
enter the Most Holy Place after the
Covenant Box was placed there.

The Covenant Box contained
the stone tablets with the laws
that Moses brought down from
Mount Sinai. It connected the
Israelite people with their history.
It was a coming together of their
old way of life, when they were
wandering tribes, with their new
way of life, as a nation with a king.
Even though they had changed
their way of life, they were still the
Chosen People, blessed by God
and made holy by God's presence.

— 1 Kings 8:1–9

LORD's presence and all its equipment to the
Temple. [5]King Solomon and all the people
of Israel assembled in front of the Covenant
Box and sacrificed a large number of sheep
and cattle—too many to count. [6]Then the
priests carried the Covenant Box into the
Temple and put it in the Most Holy Place,
beneath the winged creatures. [7]Their outstretched wings covered the box and the
poles it was carried by. [8]The ends of the
poles could be seen by anyone standing
directly in front of the Most Holy Place, but
from nowhere else. (The poles are still there
today.) [9]There was nothing inside the
Covenant Box except the two stone tablets
which Moses had placed there at Mount

7:48 a Ex 30:1–3; b Ex 25:23–30   **7:49** Ex 25:31–40   **7:51** 2 Sam 8:11; 1 Chr 18:11   **8:1** 2 Sam 6:12–16;
1 Chr 15:25–29   **8:2** Lev 23:34   **8:9** Deut 10:5

Sinai, when the LORD made a covenant with the people of Israel as they were coming from Egypt.

10 As the priests were leaving the Temple, it was suddenly filled with a cloud 11 shining with the dazzling light of the LORD's presence, and they could not go back in to perform their duties. 12 Then Solomon prayed:

"You, LORD, have placed the sun in the
   sky,y

   yet you have chosen to live in clouds
   and darkness.

13 Now I have built a majestic temple for
   you,

   a place for you to live in forever."

Solomon's Address to the People
(2 Chronicles 6:3–11)

14 As the people stood there, King Solomon turned to face them, and he asked God's blessing on them. 15 He said, "Praise the LORD God of Israel! He has kept the promise he made to my father David, when he told him, 16 'From the time I brought my people out of Egypt, I have not chosen any city in all the land of Israel in which a temple should be built where I would be worshiped. But I chose you, David, to rule my people.' "

17 And Solomon continued, "My father David planned to build a temple for the worship of the LORD God of Israel, 18 but the LORD said to him, 'You were right in wanting to build a temple for me, 19 but you will never build it. It is your son, your own son, who will build my temple.'

20 "And now the LORD has kept his promise. I have succeeded my father as king of Israel, and I have built the Temple for the worship of the LORD God of Israel. 21 I have also provided a place in the Temple for the Covenant Box containing the stone tablets of the covenant which the LORD made with our ancestors when he brought them out of Egypt."

Solomon's Prayer
(2 Chronicles 6:12–42)

22 Then in the presence of the people Solomon went and stood in front of the altar, where he raised his arms 23 and prayed, "LORD God of Israel, there is no god like you in heaven above or on earth below! You keep your covenant with your people and show them your love when they live in wholehearted obedience to you. 24 You have kept the promise you made to my father David; today every word has been fulfilled. 25 And now, LORD God of Israel, I pray that you will also keep the other promise you made to my father when you told him that there would always be one of his descendants ruling as king of Israel, provided they obeyed you as carefully as he did. 26 So now, O God of Israel, let everything come true that you promised to my father David, your servant.

27 "But can you, O God, really live on earth? Not even all of heaven is large enough to hold you, so how can this Temple that I have built be large enough? 28 LORD my God, I am your servant. Listen to my prayer, and grant the requests I make to you today. 29 Watch over this Temple day and night, this place where you have chosen to be worshiped. Hear me when I face this Temple and pray. 30 Hear my prayers and the prayers of your people when they face this place and pray. In your home in heaven hear us and forgive us.

31 "When a person is accused of wronging another and is brought to your altar in this Temple to take an oath that he is innocent, 32 O LORD, listen in heaven and judge your servants. Punish the guilty one as he deserves, and acquit the one who is innocent.

33 "When your people Israel are defeated by their enemies because they have sinned against you, and then when they turn to you and come to this Temple, humbly praying to

---

y 8:12 One ancient translation You . . . sky; Hebrew does not have these words.

8:10, 11 Ex 40:34, 35   8:12 Ps 18:11; 97:2   8:16 2 Sam 7:4–11; 1 Chr 17:3–10   8:17, 18 2 Sam 7:1–3;
1 Chr 17:1, 2   8:19 2 Sam 7:12, 13; 1 Chr 17:11, 12   8:25 1 Kings 2:4   8:27 2 Chr 2:6   8:29 Deut 12:11

"LORD God of Israel, there is no god like you in heaven above or on earth below!" (I Kings 8:23).

God in a Box?

Solomon recognizes that even though he has built a magnificent temple, God cannot be held inside a building. He wisely prays, "Not even all of heaven is large enough to hold you" (1 Kings 8:27). Sometimes we make the mistake of thinking that God is only in a building, our church. We think that somehow God is only with us when we go to church. The amazing thing we must remember is that God is present to us every minute of every day. All we have to do is open our eyes!

Jesse Manibusan, a popular Catholic singer and speaker, wrote a great song called "Open My Eyes." It makes a great prayer. Try using it throughout the day to remember God is with you.

Open my eyes, Lord, help me to see
your face.
Open my eyes, Lord, help me to see.
Open my ears, Lord, help me to hear
your voice.
Open my ears, Lord, help me to hear.

— 1 Kings 8:27

© 1988 Jesse Manibusan

you for forgiveness, 34listen to them in heaven. Forgive the sins of your people and bring them back to the land which you gave to their ancestors.

35 "When you hold back the rain because your people have sinned against you, and then when they repent and face this Temple, humbly praying to you, 36listen to them in heaven. Forgive the sins of the king and of the people of Israel, and teach them to do

what is right. Then, O LORD, send rain on this land of yours, which you gave to your people as a permanent possession.

37 "When there is famine in the land or an epidemic or the crops are destroyed by scorching winds or swarms of locusts, or when your people are attacked by their enemies, or when there is disease or sickness among them, 38listen to their prayers. If any of your people Israel, out of heartfelt sorrow, stretch out their hands in prayer toward this Temple, 39hear their prayer. Listen to them in your home in heaven, forgive them, and help them. You alone know the thoughts of the human heart. Deal with each person as he deserves, 40so that your people may obey you all the time they live in the land which you gave to our ancestors.

41-42 "When a foreigner who lives in a distant land hears of your fame and of the great things you have done for your people and comes to worship you and to pray at this Temple, 43listen to his prayer. In heaven, where you live, hear him and do what he asks you to do, so that all the peoples of the world may know you and obey you, as your people Israel do. Then they will know that this Temple I have built is the place where you are to be worshiped.

44 "When you command your people to go into battle against their enemies and they pray to you, wherever they are, facing this city which you have chosen and this Temple which I have built for you, 45listen to their prayers. Hear them in heaven and give them victory.

46 "When your people sin against you— and there is no one who does not sin—and in your anger you let their enemies defeat them and take them as prisoners to some other land, even if that land is far away, 47listen to your people's prayers. If there in that land they repent and pray to you, confessing how sinful and wicked they have been, hear their prayers, O LORD. 48If in that land they truly and sincerely repent and pray to you as they face toward this land which you gave to our ancestors, this city which you have cho-

King Solomon had many important allies. King Hiram of Tyre was one of them. Can you name one of the favors that King Hiram did for Solomon?

sen, and this Temple which I have built for you, [49]then listen to their prayers. In your home in heaven hear them and be merciful to them. [50]Forgive all their sins and their rebellion against you, and make their enemies treat them with kindness. [51]They are your own people, whom you brought out of Egypt, that blazing furnace.

[52]"Sovereign LORD, may you always look with favor on your people Israel and their king, and hear their prayer whenever they call to you for help. [53]You chose them from all the peoples to be your own people, as you told them through your servant Moses when you brought our ancestors out of Egypt."

The Final Prayer

[54]After Solomon had finished praying to the LORD, he stood up in front of the altar, where he had been kneeling with uplifted hands. [55]In a loud voice he asked God's blessings on all the people assembled there. He said, [56]"Praise the LORD who has given his people peace, as he promised he would. He has kept all the generous promises he made through his servant Moses. [57]May the LORD our God be with us as he was with our ancestors; may he never leave us or abandon us; [58]may he make us obedient to him, so that we will always live as he wants us to live, keeping all the laws and commands he gave our ancestors. [59]May the LORD our God remember at all times this prayer and these petitions I have made to him. May he always be merciful to the people of Israel and to their king, according to their daily needs. [60]And so all the nations of the world will know that the LORD alone is God—there is no other. [61]May you, his people, always be faithful to the LORD our God, obeying all his laws and commands as you do today."

The Dedication of the Temple
(2 Chronicles 7:4–10)

[62]Then King Solomon and all the people there offered sacrifices to the LORD. [63]He sacrificed 22,000 head of cattle and 120,000 sheep as fellowship offerings. And so the king and all the people dedicated the Temple. [64]That same day he also consecrated the central part of the courtyard, the area in front of the Temple, and then he offered there the sacrifices burned whole, the grain offerings, and the fat of the animals for the fellowship offerings. He did this because the bronze altar was too small for all these offerings.

[65]There at the Temple, Solomon and all the people of Israel celebrated the Festival of Shelters for seven[z] days. There was a huge crowd of people from as far away as Hamath Pass in the north and the Egyptian border in the south. [66]On the eighth day Solomon sent the people home. They all praised him and went home happy because of all the blessings that the LORD had given his servant David and his people Israel.

God Appears to Solomon Again
(2 Chronicles 7:11–22)

9 [1]After King Solomon had finished building the Temple and the palace and everything else he wanted to build, [2]the LORD appeared to him again, as he had in Gibeon. [3]The LORD said to him, "I have heard your prayer. I consecrate this Temple which you have built as the place where I shall be worshiped forever. I will watch over it and protect it for all time. [4]If you will serve me in honesty and integrity, as your father David did, and if you obey my laws and do everything I have commanded you, [5]I will keep the promise I made to your father David when I told him that Israel would always be ruled by his descendants. [6]But if you or your descendants stop following me, disobey the laws and commands I have given you, and worship other gods, [7]then I will remove my people Israel from the land that I have given them. I will also abandon this Temple which I have consecrated as the place where I am to be worshiped. People everywhere will ridicule Israel and treat her with contempt. [8]This Temple will become a pile of ruins,[a] and

---

[z] *8:65* One ancient translation seven; *Hebrew* fourteen.   [a] *9:8* Some ancient translations a pile of ruins; *Hebrew* high.
8:56 Deut 12:10; Josh 21:44, 45   **9:2** 1 Kings 3:5; 2 Chr 1:7   **9:5** 1 Kings 2:4   **9:8** 2 Kings 25:9; 2 Chr 36:19

everyone who passes by will be shocked and amazed. 'Why did the LORD do this to this land and this Temple?' they will ask. [9]People will answer, 'It is because they abandoned the LORD their God, who brought their ancestors out of Egypt. They gave their allegiance to other gods and worshiped them. That is why the LORD has brought this disaster on them.' "

Solomon's Agreement with Hiram
(2 Chronicles 8:1, 2)

[10]It took Solomon twenty years to build the Temple and his palace. [11]King Hiram of Tyre had provided him with all the cedar and pine and with all the gold he wanted for this work. After it was finished, King Solomon gave Hiram twenty towns in the region of Galilee. [12]Hiram went to see them, and he did not like them. [13]So he said to Solomon, "So these, my brother, are the towns you have given me!" For this reason the area is still called Cabul.[b] [14]Hiram had sent Solomon almost five tons of gold.

Further Achievements of Solomon
(2 Chronicles 8:3–18)

[15]King Solomon used forced labor to build the Temple and the palace, to fill in land on the east side of the city, and to build the city wall. He also used it to rebuild the cities of Hazor, Megiddo, and Gezer. ([16]The king of Egypt had attacked Gezer and captured it, killing its inhabitants and setting fire to the city. Then he gave it as a wedding present to his daughter when she married Solomon, [17]and Solomon rebuilt it.) Using his forced labor, Solomon also rebuilt Lower Beth Horon, [18]Baalath, Tamar in the wilderness of Judah, [19]the cities where his supplies were kept, the cities for his horses and chariots, and everything else he wanted to build in Jerusalem, in Lebanon, and elsewhere in his kingdom. [20-21]For his forced labor Solomon used the descendants of the people of Canaan whom the Israelites had not killed

when they took possession of their land. These included Amorites, Hittites, Perizzites, Hivites, and Jebusites, whose descendants continue to be slaves down to the present time. [22]Solomon did not make slaves of Israelites; they served as his soldiers, officers, commanders, chariot captains, and cavalry.

[23]There were 550 officials in charge of the forced labor working on Solomon's various building projects.

[24]Solomon filled in the land on the east side of the city, after his wife, the daughter of the king of Egypt, had moved from David's City to the palace Solomon built for her.

[25]Three times a year Solomon offered burnt offerings and fellowship offerings on the altar he had built to the LORD. He also burned incense[c] to the LORD. And so he finished building the Temple.

[26]King Solomon also built a fleet of ships at Eziongeber, which is near Elath on the shore of the Gulf of Aqaba, in the land of Edom. [27]King Hiram sent some experienced sailors from his fleet to serve with Solomon's men. [28]They sailed to the land of Ophir and brought back to Solomon about sixteen tons of gold.

The Visit of the Queen of Sheba
(2 Chronicles 9:1–12)

10 [1]The queen of Sheba heard of Solomon's fame,[d] and she traveled to Jerusalem to test him with difficult questions. [2]She brought with her a large group of attendants, as well as camels loaded with spices, jewels, and a large amount of gold. When she and Solomon met, she asked him all the questions that she could think of. [3]He answered them all; there was nothing too difficult for him to explain. [4]The queen of Sheba heard Solomon's wisdom and saw the palace he had built. [5]She saw the food that was served at his table, the living quarters for his officials, the organization of his palace staff and the uniforms they wore, the servants who waited on him at feasts, and the sacrifices he offered in the Temple. It left her

---

[b] *9:13* CABUL: *This name sounds like "ke-bal," the Hebrew for "worthless."*   [c] *9:25 Hebrew has two additional words, the meaning of which is unclear.*   [d] *10:1 Probable text (see 2 Chr 9:1)* Solomon's fame; *Hebrew* Solomon's fame concerning the name of the LORD.
9:25 Ex 23:17; 34:23; Deut 16:16   **10:1–10** Mt 12:42; Lk 11:31

The queen of Sheba heard of Solomon's fame. (10:1)

breathless and amazed. [6]She said to King Solomon, "What I heard in my own country about you[e] and your wisdom is true! [7]But I couldn't believe it until I had come and seen it all for myself. But I didn't hear even half of it; your wisdom and wealth are much greater than what I was told. [8]How fortunate are your wives![f] And how fortunate your servants, who are always in your presence and are privileged to hear your wise sayings! [9]Praise the LORD your God! He has shown how pleased he is with you by making you king of Israel. Because his love for Israel is eternal, he has made you their king so that you can maintain law and justice."

[10]She presented to King Solomon the gifts she had brought: almost five tons of gold and a very large amount of spices and jewels. The amount of spices she gave him was by far the greatest that he ever received at any time.

([11]Hiram's fleet, which had brought gold from Ophir, also brought from there a large amount of juniper wood and jewels. [12]Solomon used the wood to build railings in the Temple and the palace, and also to make harps and lyres for the musicians. It

was the finest juniper wood ever imported into Israel; none like it has ever been seen again.)

[13]King Solomon gave the queen of Sheba everything she asked for, besides all the other customary gifts that he had generously given her. Then she and her attendants returned to the land of Sheba.

King Solomon's Wealth
(2 Chronicles 9:13–29)

[14]Every year King Solomon received over twenty-five tons of gold, [15]in addition to the taxes[g] paid by merchants, the profits from trade, and tribute paid by the Arabian kings and the governors of the Israelite districts.

[16]Solomon made two hundred large shields and had each one overlaid with almost fifteen pounds of gold. [17]He also made three hundred smaller shields, overlaying each one of them with nearly four pounds of gold. He had all these shields placed in the Hall of the Forest of Lebanon.[h]

[18]He also had a large throne made. Part of it was covered with ivory and the rest of it was covered with the finest gold. [19-20]The

---

[e] **10:6** you; *or your deeds.*   [f] **10:8** *Some ancient translations* wives; *Hebrew* men.   [g] **10:15** *Some ancient translations* taxes; *Hebrew* men.   [h] **10:17** HALL OF THE FOREST OF LEBANON: *See 7:2–3.*

If a ton is two thousand pounds, what was the weight in pounds of the queen of Sheba's gift of five tons of gold?

A Royal Visit

The queen of Sheba is quite a character! Hearing of Solomon's fame she comes with lavish gifts and examines everything about Solomon's kingdom. She quizzes Solomon and finds that he is even wiser than she expected. She was known for being noble and wise. Her respect means a lot and helps make Solomon even more famous.

— 1 Kings 10:1–13

throne had six steps leading up to it, with the figure of a lion at each end of every step, a total of twelve lions. At the back of the throne was the figure of a bull's head, and beside each of the two armrests was the figure of a lion. No throne like this had ever existed in any other kingdom.

21 All of Solomon's drinking cups were made of gold, and all the utensils in the Hall of the Forest of Lebanon were of pure gold. No silver was used, since it was not considered valuable in Solomon's day. 22 He had a fleet of ocean-going ships sailing with Hiram's fleet. Every three years his fleet would return, bringing gold, silver, ivory, apes, and monkeys.

23 King Solomon was richer and wiser than any other king, 24 and the whole world wanted to come and listen to the wisdom that God had given him. 25 Everyone who came brought him a gift—articles of silver and gold, robes, weapons, spices, horses, and mules. This continued year after year.

26 Solomon built up a force of fourteen hundred chariots and twelve thousand cavalry horses. Some of them he kept in Jerusalem and the rest he stationed in various other cities. 27 During his reign silver was as common in Jerusalem as stone, and cedar was as plentiful as ordinary sycamore in the foothills of Judah. 28 The king's agents controlled the export of horses from Musri[i] and Cilicia,[j] 29 and the export of chariots from Egypt. They supplied the Hittite and Syrian kings with horses and chariots, selling chariots for 600 pieces of silver each and horses for 150 each.

Solomon Turns Away from God

11 1 Solomon loved many foreign women. Besides the daughter of the king of Egypt he married Hittite women and women from Moab, Ammon, Edom, and Sidon. 2 He married them even though the LORD had commanded the Israelites not to intermarry with these people, because they would cause the Israelites to give their loyalty to other gods. 3 Solomon married seven hundred princesses and also had three hundred concubines. They made him turn away from God, 4 and by the time he was old they had led him into the worship of foreign gods. He was not faithful to the LORD his God, as his father David had been. 5 He worshiped Astarte, the goddess of Sidon, and Molech, the disgusting god of Ammon. 6 He sinned against the LORD and was not true to him as his father David had been. 7 On the mountain east of Jerusalem he built a place to worship Chemosh, the disgusting god of Moab, and a place to worship Molech, the disgusting god of Ammon. 8 He also built places of worship where all his foreign wives could burn incense and offer sacrifices to their own gods.

9-10 Even though the LORD, the God of Israel, had appeared to Solomon twice and had commanded him not to worship foreign

i **10:28** *Probable text* Musri; *Hebrew* Egypt.   j **10:28** MUSRI AND CILICIA: *Two ancient countries in what is now southeast Turkey which were centers of horse breeding in Solomon's time.*
10:26 1 Kings 4:26   **10:27** Deut 17:17   **10:28** Deut 17:16   **11:1** Deut 17:17   **11:2** Ex 34:16; Deut 7:3, 4

Can you find the names of a foreign goddess and two foreign gods that Solomon worshiped (1 Kings 11:1–8)?

gods, Solomon did not obey the LORD but turned away from him. So the LORD was angry with Solomon [11]and said to him, "Because you have deliberately broken your covenant with me and disobeyed my commands, I promise that I will take the kingdom away from you and give it to one of your officials. [12]However, for the sake of your father David I will not do this in your lifetime, but during the reign of your son. [13]And I will not take the whole kingdom away from him; instead, I will leave him one tribe for the sake of my servant David and for the sake of Jerusalem, the city I have made my own."

Solomon's Enemies

[14]So the LORD caused Hadad, of the royal family of Edom, to turn against Solomon. [15-16]Long before this, when David had conquered Edom, Joab the commander of his army had gone there to bury the dead. He and his men remained in Edom six months, and during that time they killed every male in Edom [17]except Hadad and some of his father's Edomite servants, who escaped to Egypt. (At that time Hadad was just a child.) [18]They left Midian and went to Paran, where some other men joined them. Then they traveled to Egypt and went to the king, who gave Hadad some land and a house and provided him with food. [19]Hadad won the friendship of the king, and the king gave his sister-in-law, the sister of Queen Tahpenes, to Hadad in marriage. [20]She bore him a son, Genubath, who was raised by the queen in the palace, where he lived with the king's sons.

[21]When the news reached Hadad in Egypt that David had died and that Joab the commander of the army was dead, Hadad said to the king, "Let me go back to my own country."

[22]"Why?" the king asked. "Have I failed to give you something? Is that why you want to go back home?"

"Just let me go," Hadad answered the king. And he went back to his country.[k]

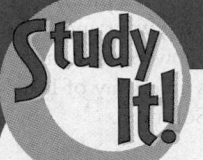

Too Many Gods . . . or Wives?

You knew it would happen. Throughout 1 Kings the author keeps reminding us that God's blessing will stay with Solomon *as long as* he is obedient to God. But he wasn't. According to this passage, he turned away from God and started worshiping foreign gods and goddesses. What happened to the man who prayed, "Make us obedient to him [God], so that we will always live as he wants us to live" (1 Kings 8:58)?

Maybe it had something to do with the fact that Solomon had seven hundred wives! That is surely an exaggeration, but the fact remains that he married many foreign princesses as a way of creating alliances with other people. These princesses wanted to worship the gods and goddesses of their people, and Solomon not only let them, he built altars and shrines for them. God warned the Israelites not to marry foreign people for this very reason, but Solomon ignored that warning.

Solomon broke the Covenant, and the nation began to crumble.

— 1 Kings 11:1–8

As king of Edom, Hadad was an evil, bitter enemy of Israel.[l]

[23]God also caused Rezon son of Eliada to turn against Solomon. Rezon had fled from his master, King Hadadezer of Zobah, [24]and had become the leader of a gang of outlaws. (This happened after David had defeated

[k] **11:22** *One ancient translation* And he went back to his country; *Hebrew does not have these words.*
[l] **11:22** *One ancient translation* As king . . . Israel; *in Hebrew this sentence, with some differences, comes at the end of verse 25.*

Hadadezer and had slaughtered his Syrian allies.) Rezon and his gang went and lived in Damascus, where his followers made him king of Syria. 25He was an enemy of Israel during the lifetime of Solomon.

God's Promise to Jeroboam

26Another man who turned against King Solomon was one of his officials, Jeroboam son of Nebat, from Zeredah in Ephraim. His mother was a widow named Zeruah. 27This is the story of the revolt.

Solomon was filling in the land on the east side of Jerusalem and repairing the city walls. 28Jeroboam was an able young man, and when Solomon noticed how hard he worked, he put him in charge of all the forced labor in the territory of the tribes of Manasseh and Ephraim. 29One day, as Jeroboam was traveling from Jerusalem, the prophet Ahijah from Shiloh met him alone on the road in the open country. 30Ahijah took off the new robe he was wearing, tore it into twelve pieces, 31and said to Jeroboam, "Take ten pieces for yourself, because the LORD, the God of Israel, says to you, 'I am going to take the kingdom away from Solomon, and I will give you ten tribes.

"Take ten pieces for yourself." (11:31)

32Solomon will keep one tribe for the sake of my servant David and for the sake of Jerusalem, the city I have chosen to be my own from the whole land of Israel. 33I am going to do this because Solomon has rejected me and has[m] worshiped foreign gods: Astarte, the god-

dess of Sidon; Chemosh, the god of Moab; and Molech, the god of Ammon. Solomon has[n] disobeyed me; he has done wrong and has not kept my laws and commands as his father David did. 34But I will not take the whole kingdom away from Solomon, and I will keep him in power as long as he lives. This I will do for the sake of my servant David, whom I chose and who obeyed my laws and commands. 35I will take the kingdom away from Solomon's son and will give you ten tribes, 36but I will let Solomon's son keep one tribe, so that I will always have a descendant of my servant David ruling in Jerusalem, the city I have chosen as the place where I am worshiped. 37Jeroboam, I will make you king of Israel, and you will rule over all the territory that you want. 38If you obey me completely, live by my laws, and win my approval by doing what I command, as my servant David did, I will always be with you. I will make you king of Israel and will make sure that your descendants rule after you, just as I have done for David. 39Because of Solomon's sin I will punish the descendants of David, but not for all time.' "

40And so Solomon tried to kill Jeroboam, but he escaped to King Shishak of Egypt and stayed there until Solomon's death.

The Death of Solomon
(2 Chronicles 9:29–31)

41Everything else that Solomon did, his career, and his wisdom, are all recorded in *The History of Solomon.* 42He was king in Jerusalem over all Israel for forty years. 43He died and was buried in David's City, and his son Rehoboam succeeded him as king.

The Northern Tribes Revolt
(2 Chronicles 10:1–19)

12 1Rehoboam went to Shechem, where all the people of northern Israel had gathered to make him king. 2When Jeroboam son of Nebat, who had gone to Egypt to escape from King Solomon, heard this news, he returned from[o]

---

m **11:33** *Some ancient translations* Solomon has . . . and has; *Hebrew* they have . . . and have.   *n* **11:33** *Some ancient translations* Solomon has; *Hebrew* They have.   *o* **12:2** *Some ancient translations (and see 2 Chr 10:2)* returned from; *Hebrew* remained in.

Egypt. ³The people of the northern tribes sent for him, and then they all went together to Rehoboam and said to him, ⁴"Your father Solomon treated us harshly and placed heavy burdens on us. If you make these burdens lighter and make life easier for us, we will be your loyal subjects."

⁵"Come back in three days and I will give you my answer," he replied. So they left.

⁶King Rehoboam consulted the older men who had served as his father Solomon's advisers. "What answer do you advise me to give these people?" he asked.

⁷They replied, "If you want to serve this people well, give a favorable answer to their request, and they will always serve you loyally."

⁸But he ignored the advice of the older men and went instead to the young men who had grown up with him and who were now his advisers. ⁹"What do you advise me to do?" he asked. "What shall I say to the people who are asking me to make their burdens lighter?"

¹⁰They replied, "This is what you should tell them: 'My little finger is thicker than my father's waist!' ¹¹Tell them, 'My father placed heavy burdens on you; I will make them even heavier. He beat you with whips; I'll flog you with bullwhips!' "

¹²Three days later Jeroboam and all the people returned to King Rehoboam, as he had instructed them. ¹³The king ignored the advice of the older men and spoke harshly to the people, ¹⁴as the younger men had advised. He said, "My father placed heavy burdens on you; I will make them even heavier. He beat you with whips; I'll flog you with bullwhips!" ¹⁵It was the will of the LORD to bring about what he had spoken to Jeroboam son of Nebat through the prophet Ahijah from Shiloh. This is why the king did not pay any attention to the people.

¹⁶When the people saw that the king would not listen to them, they shouted, "Down with David and his family! What have they ever done for us? People of Israel,

12:16 2 Sam 20:1

Not So Smart

Rehoboam gets two conflicting pieces of advice. He asks the experienced, older advisers on whom his father depended for their advice. He also asks the young, inexperienced men to tell him what to do. The young men are impatient and arrogant. They seem to want to stay in power and boss everybody around. Like his dad, Solomon, Rehoboam does not choose wisely in this case. He follows the advice of the younger men and tries to increase his own power instead of thinking what is best for the people.

Being older doesn't necessarily mean being wiser. But neither does being younger. When someone gives you advice, consider it carefully. A wise person doesn't think about his or her own needs first. A wise person thinks about what will be best for everyone. What impact will your choices have on others?

— 1 Kings 12:1

let's go home! Let Rehoboam look out for himself!"

So the people of Israel rebelled, ¹⁷leaving Rehoboam as king only of the people who lived in the territory of Judah.

¹⁸Then King Rehoboam sent Adoniram, who was in charge of the forced labor, to go to the Israelites, but they stoned him to death. At this, Rehoboam hurriedly got in his chariot and escaped to Jerusalem. ¹⁹Ever since that time the people of the northern

The split! Israel has one king through the reigns of Saul, David, and Solomon. Now after Solomon's death there will be two kingdoms.

kingdom of Israel have been in rebellion against the dynasty of David.

20 When the people of Israel heard that Jeroboam had returned from Egypt, they invited him to a meeting of the people and made him king of Israel. Only the tribe of Judah remained loyal to David's descendants.

Shemaiah's Prophecy
(2 Chronicles 11:1–4)

21 When Rehoboam arrived in Jerusalem, he called together 180,000 of the best soldiers from the tribes of Judah and Benjamin. He intended to go to war and restore his control over the northern tribes of Israel. 22 But God told the prophet Shemaiah 23 to give this message to Rehoboam and to all the people of the tribes of Judah and Benjamin: 24 "Do not attack your own relatives, the people of Israel. Go home, all of you. What has happened is my will." They all obeyed the LORD's command and went back home.

Jeroboam Turns Away from God

25 King Jeroboam of Israel fortified the town of Shechem in the hill country of Ephraim and lived there for a while. Then he left and fortified the town of Penuel. 26-27 He said to himself, "As things are now, if my people go to Jerusalem and offer sacrifices to the LORD in the Temple there, they will transfer their allegiance to King Rehoboam of Judah and will kill me."

28 After thinking it over, he made two bull-calves of gold and said to his people, "You have been going long enough to Jerusalem to worship. People of Israel, here are your gods who brought you out of Egypt!" 29 He placed one of the gold bull-calves in Bethel and the other in Dan. 30 And so the people sinned, going to worship in Bethel and in Dan.P 31 Jeroboam also built places of worship on hilltops, and he chose priests from families who were not of the tribe of Levi.

Worship at Bethel Is Condemned

32 Jeroboam also instituted a religious festival on the fifteenth day of the eighth month, like the festival in Judah. On the altar in Bethel he offered sacrifices to the gold bull-calves he had made, and he placed there in Bethel the priests serving at the places of worship he had built. 33 And on the fifteenth day of the eighth month, the day that he himself had set, he went to Bethel and offered a sacrifice on the altar in celebration of the festival he had instituted for the people of Israel.

13 1 At the LORD's command a prophet from Judah went to Bethel and arrived there as Jeroboam stood at the altar to offer the sacrifice. 2 Following the LORD's command, the prophet denounced the altar: "O altar, altar, this is what the LORD says: A child, whose name will be Josiah, will be born to the family of David. He will slaughter on you the priests serving at the pagan altars who offer sacrifices on you, and he will burn human bones on you." 3 And the prophet went on to say, "This altar will fall apart, and the ashes on it will be scattered. Then you will know that the LORD has spoken through me."

4 When King Jeroboam heard this, he pointed at him and ordered, "Seize that man!" At once the king's arm became paralyzed so that he couldn't pull it back. 5 The altar suddenly fell apart and the ashes spilled to the ground, as the prophet had predicted in the name of the LORD. 6 King Jeroboam said to the prophet, "Please pray for me to the LORD your God, and ask him to heal my arm!"

The prophet prayed to the LORD, and the king's arm was healed. 7 Then the king said to the prophet, "Come home with me and have something to eat. I will reward you for what you have done."

8 The prophet answered, "Even if you gave me half of your wealth, I would not go with you or eat or drink anything with you. 9 The

p **12:30** *One ancient translation* in Bethel and in Dan; *Hebrew* in Dan.
12:28 Ex 32:4   **12:32, 33** Lev 23:33, 34   **13:2** 2 Kings 23:15, 16

Bethel was the place where Jacob had a vision and built an altar to God (*Genesis 35:1–15*).

LORD has commanded me not to eat or drink a thing, and not to return home the same way I came." 10 So he did not go back the same way he had come, but by another road.

The Old Prophet of Bethel

11 At that time there was an old prophet living in Bethel. His sons[q] came and told him what the prophet from Judah had done in Bethel that day and what he had said to King Jeroboam. 12 "Which way did he go when he left?" the old prophet asked them. They showed him[r] the road 13 and he told them to saddle his donkey for him. They did so, and he rode off 14 down the road after the prophet from Judah and found him sitting under an oak tree. "Are you the prophet from Judah?" he asked.

"I am," the man answered.

15 "Come home and have a meal with me," he said.

16 But the prophet from Judah answered, "I can't go home with you or accept your hospitality. And I won't eat or drink anything with you here, 17 because the LORD has commanded me not to eat or drink a thing, and not to return home the same way I came."

18 Then the old prophet from Bethel said to him, "I, too, am a prophet just like you, and at the LORD's command an angel told me to take you home with me and offer you my hospitality." But the old prophet was lying.

19 So the prophet from Judah went home with the old prophet and had a meal with him. 20 As they were sitting at the table, the word of the LORD came to the old prophet, 21 and he cried out to the prophet from Judah, "The LORD says that you disobeyed him and did not do what he commanded. 22 Instead, you returned and ate a meal in a place he had ordered you not to eat in. Because of this you will be killed, and your body will not be buried in your family grave."

23 After they had finished eating, the old prophet saddled the donkey for the prophet from Judah, 24 who rode off. On the way a lion met him and killed him. His body lay on the road, and the donkey and the lion

stood beside it. 25 Some men passed by and saw the body on the road, with the lion standing near by. They went on into Bethel and reported what they had seen.

26 When the old prophet heard about it, he said, "That is the prophet who disobeyed the LORD's command! And so the LORD sent the lion to attack and kill him, just as the LORD said he would." 27 Then he said to his sons, "Saddle my donkey for me." They did so, 28 and he rode off and found the prophet's body lying on the road, with the donkey and the lion still standing by it. The lion had not eaten the body or attacked the donkey. 29 The old prophet picked up the body, put it on the donkey, and brought it back to Bethel to mourn over it and bury it. 30 He buried it in his own family grave, and he and his sons mourned over it, saying, "Oh my brother, my brother!" 31 After the burial the prophet said to his sons, "When I die, bury me in this grave and lay my body next to his. 32 The words that he spoke at the LORD's command against the altar in Bethel and against all the places of worship in the towns of Samaria will surely come true."

Jeroboam's Fatal Sin

33 King Jeroboam of Israel still did not turn from his evil ways but continued to choose priests from ordinary families to serve at the altars he had built. He ordained as priest anyone who wanted to be one. 34 This sin on his part brought about the ruin and total destruction of his dynasty.

The Death of Jeroboam's Son

14 1 At that time King Jeroboam's son Abijah got sick. 2 Jeroboam said to his wife, "Disguise yourself so that no one will recognize you, and go to Shiloh, where the prophet Ahijah lives, the one who said I would be king of Israel. 3 Take him ten loaves of bread, some cakes, and a jar of honey. Ask him what is going to happen to our son, and he will tell you."

4 So she went to Ahijah's home in Shiloh. Old age had made Ahijah blind. 5 The LORD

---

q **13:11** *Some ancient translations* sons; *Hebrew* son.　　r **13:12** *Some ancient translations* showed him; *Hebrew* saw.

had told him that Jeroboam's wife was coming to ask him about her son, who was sick. And the LORD told Ahijah what to say.

When Jeroboam's wife arrived, she pretended to be someone else. 6But when Ahijah heard her coming in the door, he said, "Come in. I know you are Jeroboam's wife. Why are you pretending to be someone else? I have bad news for you. 7Go and tell Jeroboam that this is what the LORD, the God of Israel, says to him: 'I chose you from among the people and made you the ruler of my people Israel. 8I took the kingdom away from David's descendants and gave it to you. But you have not been like my servant David, who was completely loyal to me, obeyed my commands, and did only what I approve of. 9You have committed far greater sins than those who ruled before you. You have rejected me and have aroused my anger by making idols and metal images to worship. 10Because of this I will bring disaster on your dynasty and will kill all your male descendants, young and old alike. I will get rid of your family; they will be swept away like dung. 11Any members of your family who die in the city will be eaten by dogs, and any who die in the open country will be eaten by vultures. I, the LORD, have spoken.' "

12And Ahijah went on to say to Jeroboam's wife, "Now go back home. As soon as you enter the town, your son will die. 13All the people of Israel will mourn for him and bury him. He will be the only member of Jeroboam's family who will be properly buried, because he is the only one with whom the LORD, the God of Israel, is pleased. 14The LORD is going to place a king over Israel who will put an end to Jeroboam's dynasty.⁵ 15The LORD will punish Israel, and she will shake like a reed shaking in a stream. He will uproot the people of Israel from this good land which he gave to their ancestors, and he will scatter them beyond the Euphrates River, because they have aroused his anger by making idols of the goddess Asherah. 16The LORD will abandon Israel because Jeroboam sinned and led the people of Israel into sin."

17Jeroboam's wife went back to Tirzah. Just as she entered her home, the child died. 18The people of Israel mourned for him and buried him, as the LORD had said through his servant, the prophet Ahijah.

The Death of Jeroboam

19Everything else that King Jeroboam did, the wars he fought and how he ruled, are all recorded in *The History of the Kings of Israel.* 20Jeroboam ruled as king for twenty-two years. He died and was buried, and his son Nadab succeeded him as king.

King Rehoboam of Judah
(2 Chronicles 11:5—12:15)

21Solomon's son Rehoboam was forty-one years old when he became king of Judah, and he ruled seventeen years in Jerusalem, the city which the LORD had chosen from all the territory of Israel as the place where he was to be worshiped. Rehoboam's mother was Naamah from Ammon.

22The people of Judah sinned against the LORD and did more to arouse his anger against them than all their ancestors had done. 23They built places of worship for false gods and put up stone pillars and symbols of Asherah to worship on the hills and under shady trees. 24Worst of all, there were men and women who served as prostitutes at those pagan places of worship. The people of Judah practiced all the shameful things done

They built places of worship for false gods. (14:23)

Live It!

Constantly Fighting

Unlike Solomon, whose reign was marked by peace, the new kings are at war with each other. Is there someone in your family whom you have a hard time getting along with? Constant fighting, whether it's between countries or family members, is destructive.

Did you ever get stuck in the middle of an argument between friends? When friends get angry with each other, it's easy to take sides and have things blow up into a huge disagreement. The next time conflict begins, ask yourself:

- Is this an argument I should get involved in, or would it be better if I let the people involved work it out?
- What could I do or say to help people get along better?

Remember to avoid gossiping or bullying. Encourage your friends to talk to each other. Don't let them use you to deliver hurtful messages. Even when somebody has said or done something hurtful, it is possible to forgive and to be friends again. People need to be willing to talk to each other and say, "I'm sorry."

— 1 Kings 14:21–30

26 He took away all the treasures in the Temple and in the palace, including the gold shields Solomon had made. 27 To replace them, King Rehoboam made bronze shields and entrusted them to the officers responsible for guarding the palace gates. 28 Every time the king went to the Temple, the guards carried the shields and then returned them to the guardroom.

29 Everything else that King Rehoboam did is recorded in *The History of the Kings of Judah*. 30 During all this time Rehoboam and Jeroboam were constantly at war with each other. 31 Rehoboam died and was buried in the royal tombs in David's City and his son Abijah succeeded him as king.

King Abijah of Judah
(2 Chronicles 13:1—14:1)

15 ¹In the eighteenth year of the reign of King Jeroboam of Israel, Abijah became king of Judah, ²and he ruled three years in Jerusalem. His mother was Maacah, the daughter of Absalom. ³He committed the same sins as his father and was not completely loyal to the LORD his God, as his great-grandfather David had been. ⁴But for David's sake the LORD his God gave Abijah a son to rule after him in Jerusalem and to keep Jerusalem secure. ⁵The LORD did this because David had done what pleased him and had never disobeyed any of his commands, except in the case of Uriah the Hittite. ⁶The war which had begun between Rehoboam and Jeroboam continued throughout Abijah's lifetime. ⁷And everything else that Abijah did is recorded in *The History of the Kings of Judah*.

⁸Abijah died and was buried in David's City, and his son Asa succeeded him as king.

King Asa of Judah
(2 Chronicles 14:1–5; 15:16—16:6; 11–14)

⁹In the twentieth year of the reign of King Jeroboam of Israel, Asa became king of

by the people whom the LORD had driven out of the land as the Israelites advanced into the country.

25 In the fifth year of Rehoboam's reign King Shishak of Egypt attacked Jerusalem.

14:25 2 Chr 12:2–8　**14:26** 1 Kings 10:16, 17; 2 Chr 9:15, 16　**15:4** 1 Kings 11:36　**15:5** 2 Sam 11:1–27
15:6 2 Chr 13:3–21

Jeroboam was the first king of Israel, the kingdom in the north. Rehoboam was the first king of Judah, the kingdom in the south. It can be confusing!

Judah, [10]and he ruled forty-one years in Jerusalem. His grandmother was Maacah, the daughter of Absalom. [11]Asa did what pleased the LORD, as his ancestor David had done. [12]He expelled from the country all the male and female prostitutes serving at the pagan places of worship, and he removed all the idols his predecessors had made. [13]He removed his grandmother Maacah from her position as queen mother, because she had made an obscene idol of the fertility goddess Asherah. Asa cut down the idol and burned it in Kidron Valley. [14]Even though Asa did not destroy all the pagan places of worship, he remained faithful to the LORD all his life. [15]He placed in the Temple all the objects his father had dedicated to God, as well as the gold and silver objects that he himself dedicated.

[16]King Asa of Judah and King Baasha of Israel were constantly at war with each other as long as they were in power. [17]Baasha invaded Judah and started to fortify Ramah in order to cut off all traffic in and out of Judah. [18]So King Asa took all the silver and gold that was left in the Temple and the palace, and sent it by some of his officials to Damascus, to King Benhadad of Syria, the son of Tabrimmon and grandson of Hezion, with this message: [19]"Let us be allies, as our fathers were. This silver and gold is a present for you. Now break your alliance with King Baasha of Israel, so that he will have to pull his troops out of my territory."

[20]King Benhadad agreed to Asa's proposal and sent his commanding officers and their armies to attack the cities of Israel. They captured Ijon, Dan, Abel Beth Maacah, the area near Lake Galilee, and the whole territory of Naphtali. [21]When King Baasha heard what had happened, he stopped fortifying Ramah and went to Tirzah.

[22]Then King Asa sent out an order throughout all of Judah requiring everyone, without exception, to help carry away from Ramah the stones and timber that Baasha had been using to fortify it. With this material Asa fortified Mizpah and Geba, a city in the territory of Benjamin.

[23]Everything else that King Asa did, his brave deeds and the towns he fortified, are all recorded in *The History of the Kings of Judah*. But in his old age he was crippled by a foot disease. [24]Asa died and was buried in the royal tombs in David's City, and his son Jehoshaphat succeeded him as king.

King Nadab of Israel

[25]In the second year of the reign of King Asa of Judah, King Jeroboam's son Nadab became king of Israel, and he ruled for two years. [26]Like his father before him, he sinned against the LORD and led Israel into sin.

[27]Baasha son of Ahijah, of the tribe of Issachar, plotted against Nadab and killed him as Nadab and his army were besieging the city of Gibbethon in Philistia. [28]This happened during the third year of the reign of King Asa of Judah. And so Baasha succeeded Nadab as king of Israel. [29]At once he began killing all the members of Jeroboam's family. In accordance with what the LORD had said through his servant, the prophet Ahijah from Shiloh, all of Jeroboam's family were killed; not one survived. [30]This happened because Jeroboam aroused the anger of the LORD, the God of Israel, by the sins that he committed and that he caused Israel to commit.

[31]Everything else that Nadab did is recorded in *The History of the Kings of Israel*. [32]King Asa of Judah and King Baasha of Israel were constantly at war with each other as long as they were in power.

King Baasha of Israel

[33]In the third year of the reign of King Asa of Judah, Baasha son of Ahijah became king of all Israel, and he ruled in Tirzah for twenty-four years. [34]Like King Jeroboam before him, he sinned against the LORD and led Israel into sin.

15:12 2 Chr 15:8–15   **15:29** 1 Kings 14:10

Maacah was the daughter of Absalom. Who was Absalom?

16

¹The LORD spoke to the prophet Jehu son of Hanani and gave him this message for Baasha: ²"You were a nobody, but I made you the leader of my people Israel. And now you have sinned like Jeroboam and have led my people into sin. Their sins have aroused my anger, ³and so I will do away with you and your family, just as I did with Jeroboam. ⁴Any members of your family who die in the city will be eaten by dogs, and any who die in the open country will be eaten by vultures."

⁵Everything else that Baasha did and all his brave deeds are recorded in *The History of the Kings of Israel*. ⁶Baasha died and was buried in Tirzah, and his son Elah succeeded him as king.

⁷That message from the LORD against Baasha and his family was given by the prophet Jehu because of the sins that Baasha committed against the LORD. He aroused the LORD's anger not only because of the evil he did, just as King Jeroboam had done before him, but also because he killed all of Jeroboam's family.

King Elah of Israel

⁸In the twenty-sixth year of the reign of King Asa of Judah, Elah son of Baasha became king of Israel, and he ruled in Tirzah for two years. ⁹Zimri, one of his officers who was in charge of half of the king's chariots, plotted against him. One day in Tirzah, Elah was getting drunk in the home of Arza, who was in charge of the palace. ¹⁰Zimri entered the house, assassinated Elah, and succeeded him as king. This happened in the twenty-seventh year of the reign of King Asa of Judah.

¹¹As soon as Zimri became king he killed off all the members of Baasha's family. Every male relative and friend was put to death. ¹²And so, in accordance with what the LORD had said against Baasha through the prophet Jehu, Zimri killed all the family of Baasha. ¹³Because of their idolatry and because they led Israel into sin, Baasha and his son Elah had aroused the anger of the LORD, the God of Israel. ¹⁴Everything else that Elah did is recorded in *The History of the Kings of Israel*.

King Zimri of Israel

¹⁵In the twenty-seventh year of the reign of King Asa of Judah, Zimri ruled in Tirzah over Israel for seven days. The Israelite troops were besieging the city of Gibbethon in Philistia, ¹⁶and when they heard that Zimri had plotted against the king and assassinated him, then and there they all proclaimed their commander Omri king of Israel. ¹⁷Omri and his troops left Gibbethon and went and besieged Tirzah. ¹⁸When Zimri saw that the city had fallen, he went into the palace's inner fortress, set the palace on fire, and died in the flames. ¹⁹This happened because of his sins against the LORD. Like his predecessor Jeroboam, he displeased the LORD by his own sins and by leading Israel into sin. ²⁰Everything else that Zimri did, including the account of his conspiracy, is recorded in *The History of the Kings of Israel*.

King Omri of Israel

²¹The people of Israel were divided: some of them wanted to make Tibni son of Ginath king, and the others were in favor of Omri. ²²In the end, those in favor of Omri won out; Tibni died and Omri became king. ²³So in the thirty-first year of the reign of King Asa of Judah, Omri became king of Israel, and he ruled for twelve years. The first six years he ruled in Tirzah, ²⁴and then he bought the hill of Samaria for six thousand pieces of silver from a man named Shemer. Omri fortified the hill, built a town there, and named it Samaria, after Shemer, the former owner of the hill.

²⁵Omri sinned against the LORD more than any of his predecessors. ²⁶Like Jeroboam before him, he aroused the anger of the LORD, the God of Israel, by his sins and by leading the people into sin and idolatry. ²⁷Everything else that Omri did and all his accomplishments are recorded in *The History of the Kings of Israel*. ²⁸Omri died and was buried in Samaria, and his son Ahab succeeded him as king.

King Ahab of Israel

²⁹In the thirty-eighth year of the reign of King Asa of Judah, Ahab son of Omri

became king of Israel, and he ruled in Samaria for twenty-two years. ³⁰He sinned against the LORD more than any of his predecessors. ³¹It was not enough for him to sin like King Jeroboam; he went further and married Jezebel, the daughter of King Ethbaal of Sidon, and worshiped Baal. ³²He built a temple to Baal in Samaria, made an altar for him, and put it in the temple. ³³He also put up an image of the goddess Asherah. He did more to arouse the anger of the LORD, the God of Israel, than all the kings of Israel before him. ³⁴During his reign Hiel from Bethel rebuilt Jericho. As the LORD had foretold through Joshua son of Nun, Hiel lost his oldest son Abiram when he laid the foundation of Jericho, and his youngest son Segub when he built the gates.

Elijah and the Drought

17 ¹A prophet named Elijah, from Tishbe in Gilead, said to King Ahab, "In the name of the LORD, the living God of Israel, whom I serve, I tell you that there will be no dew or rain for the next two or three years until I say so."

²Then the LORD said to Elijah, ³"Leave this place and go east and hide yourself near Cherith Brook, east of the Jordan. ⁴The brook will supply you with water to drink, and I have commanded ravens to bring you food there."

I have commanded ravens to bring you food. (17:4)

⁵Elijah obeyed the LORD's command, and went and stayed by Cherith Brook. ⁶He drank water from the brook, and ravens brought him bread and meat every morning and every evening. ⁷After a while the brook dried up because of the lack of rain.

Elijah and the Widow in Zarephath

⁸Then the LORD said to Elijah, ⁹"Now go to the town of Zarephath, near Sidon, and stay there. I have commanded a widow who lives there to feed you." ¹⁰So Elijah went to Zarephath, and as he came to the town gate, he saw a widow gathering firewood. "Please bring me a drink of water," he said to her. ¹¹And as she was going to get it, he called out, "And please bring me some bread, too."

¹²She answered, "By the living LORD your God I swear that I don't have any bread. All I have is a handful of flour in a bowl and a bit of olive oil in a jar. I came here to gather some firewood to take back home and prepare what little I have for my son and me. That will be our last meal, and then we will starve to death."

¹³"Don't worry," Elijah said to her. "Go on and prepare your meal. But first make a small loaf from what you have and bring it to me, and then prepare the rest for you and your son. ¹⁴For this is what the LORD, the God of Israel, says: 'The bowl will not run out of flour or the jar run out of oil before the day that I, the LORD, send rain.'"

"Go on and prepare your meal." (17:13)

¹⁵The widow went and did as Elijah had told her, and all of them had enough food for many days. ¹⁶As the LORD had promised through Elijah, the bowl did not run out of flour nor did the jar run out of oil.

16:34 Josh 6:26   **17:1** Jas 5:17   **17:9** Lk 4:25, 26 did you do this to me? Did you come here to remind God of my sins and so cause my son's death?"

19 "Give the boy to me," Elijah said. He took the boy from her arms, carried him upstairs to the room where he was staying, and laid him on the bed. 20 Then he prayed aloud, "O LORD my God, why have you done such a terrible thing to this widow? She has been kind enough to take care of me, and now you kill her son!" 21 Then Elijah stretched himself out on the boy three times and prayed, "O LORD my God, restore this child to life!" 22 The LORD answered Elijah's prayer; the child started breathing again and he...

23 Elijah took the boy back downstairs to his mother and said to her, "Look, your son is alive!"

24 She answered, "Now I know that you are a man of God and that the LORD really speaks through you!"

Elijah and the Prophets of Baal

18 1 After some time, in the third year of the drought, the LORD said to Elijah, "Go and present yourself to King Ahab, and I will send rain." 2 So Elijah started out.

The famine in Samaria was at its worst, 3 so Ahab called in Obadiah, who was in charge of the palace. (Obadiah was a devout worshiper of the LORD, 4 and when Jezebel was killing the LORD's prophets, Obadiah took a hundred of them, hid them in caves in two groups of fifty, and provided them with food and water.) 5 Ahab said to Obadiah, "Let us go and look[*i*] at every spring and every stream bed in the land to see if we can find enough grass to keep the horses and mules alive. Maybe we won't have to kill any of our animals." 6 They agreed on which part of the land each one would explore, and set off in different directions.

7 As Obadiah was on his way, he suddenly

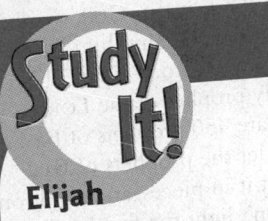

Elijah

This passage marks a shift in 1 Kings. We'll still be hearing the stories of the kings, but now we prop... in to find out about the very impor... ... meet Elijah, a cle worker. Elijah predict... mira- He stays with a widow and her son. God saves all of them from starvation with a bowl of flour that is always full and a jar of oil that never runs dry. Later, when the son dies, Elijah brings him back to life. Do these miracles remind you of anything Jesus did?

Then God sends Elijah as a prophet to the evil King Ahab. To show that the foreign god Baal is powerless, he challenges the prophets of Baal to a contest. They will both set up altars with wood to burn an animal sacrifice. Then they will each pray to their god to light the fire. Of course nothing happens to the altar of Baal. Elijah douses his wood with jars of water for dramatic effect. When he prays, God sends down fire that burns everything, including the stones! Seems like that would get Ahab's attention, but unfortunately it doesn't.

— 1 Kings, chapters 17–18

---

17 Some time later the widow's son got sick; he got worse and worse, and finally he died. 18 She said to Elijah, "Man of God, why

---

i **18:5** *One ancient translation* Let us go and look; *Hebrew* You go and look.
17:21 2 Kings 4:34, 35

---

met Elijah. He recognized him, bowed low before him, and asked, "Is it really you, sir?"

8"Yes, I'm Elijah," he answered. "Go and tell your master the king that I am here."

9Obadiah answered, "What have I done that you want to put me in danger of being killed by King Ahab? 10By the living LORD, your God, I swear that the king has made a search for you in every country in the world. Whenever the ruler of a country reported that you were not in his country, Ahab would require that ruler to swear that you could not be found. 11And now you want me to go and tell him that you are here? 12What if the spirit of the LORD carries you off to some unknown place as I leave? Then, when I tell Ahab that you are here and he can't find you, he will put me to death. Remember that I have been a devout worshiper of the LORD ever since I was a boy. 13Haven't you heard that when Jezebel was killing the prophets of the LORD I hid a hundred of them in caves, in two groups of fifty, and supplied them with food and water? 14So how can you order me to go and tell the king that you are here? He will kill me!"

15Elijah answered, "By the living LORD Almighty, whom I serve, I promise that I will present myself to the king today."

16So Obadiah went to King Ahab and told him, and Ahab set off to meet Elijah. 17When Ahab saw him, he said, "So there you are—the worst troublemaker in Israel!"

18"I'm not the troublemaker," Elijah answered. "You are—you and your father. You are disobeying the LORD's commands and worshiping the idols of Baal. 19Now order all the people of Israel to meet me at Mount Carmel. Bring along the 450 prophets of Baal and the 400 prophets of the goddess Asherah who are supported by Queen Jezebel."

20So Ahab summoned all the Israelites and the prophets of Baal to meet at Mount Carmel. 21Elijah went up to the people and said, "How much longer will it take you to make up your minds? If the LORD is God, worship him; but if Baal is God, worship him!" But the people didn't say a word. 22Then Elijah said, "I am the only prophet of the LORD still left, but there are 450 prophets of Baal. 23Bring two bulls; let the prophets of Baal take one, kill it, cut it in pieces, and put it on the wood—but don't light the fire. I will do the same with the other bull. 24Then let the prophets of Baal pray to their god, and I will pray to the LORD, and the one who answers by sending fire—he is their approval.

The prophets of Baal, since there are so many of you, you take a bull and prepare it first. Pray to your god, but don't set fire to the wood."

26They took the bull that was brought to them, prepared it, and prayed to Baal until noon. They shouted, "Answer us, Baal!" and kept dancing around the altar they had built. But no answer came.

27At noon Elijah started making fun of them: "Pray louder! He is a god! Maybe he is day-dreaming or relieving himself, or perhaps he's gone off on a trip! Or maybe he's sleeping, and you've got to wake him up!" 28So the prophets prayed louder and cut themselves with knives and daggers, according to their ritual, until blood flowed. 29They kept on ranting and raving until the middle of the afternoon; but no answer came, not a sound was heard.

30Then Elijah said to the people, "Come closer to me," and they all gathered around him. He set about repairing the altar of the LORD which had been torn down. 31He took twelve stones, one for each of the twelve tribes named for the sons of Jacob, the man to whom the LORD had given the name Israel. 32With these stones he rebuilt the altar for the worship of the LORD. He dug a trench around it, large enough to hold about four gallons of water. 33Then he placed the wood on the altar, cut the bull in pieces, and laid it on the wood. He said, "Fill four jars with water and pour it on the

18:31 Gen 32:28; 35:10

Elijah used twelve stones to make his altar. For another story about twelve stones that represent the Twelve Tribes, read Joshua, chapter 4.

offering and the wood." They did so, 34and he said, "Do it again"—and they did. "Do it once more," he said—and they did. 35The water ran down around the altar and filled the trench.

36At the hour of the afternoon sacrifice the prophet Elijah approached the altar and prayed, "O LORD, the God of Abraham, Isaac, and Jacob, prove now that you are the God of Israel and that I am your servant and have done all this at your command. 37Answer me, LORD, answer me, so that this people will know that you, the LORD, are God and that you are bringing them back to yourself." u

38The LORD sent fire down, and it burned up the sacrifice, the wood, and the stones, scorched the earth and dried up the water in the trench. 39When the people saw this, they threw themselves on the ground and exclaimed, "The LORD is God; the LORD alone is God!"

The LORD sent fire down. (18:38)

40Elijah ordered, "Seize the prophets of Baal; don't let any of them get away!" The people seized them all, and Elijah led them down to Kishon Brook and killed them.

The End of the Drought

41Then Elijah said to King Ahab, "Now, go and eat. I hear the roar of rain approaching." 42While Ahab went to eat, Elijah climbed to the top of Mount Carmel, where he bowed down to the ground, with his

head between his knees. 43He said to his servant, "Go and look toward the sea."

The servant went and returned, saying, "I didn't see a thing." Seven times in all Elijah told him to go and look. 44The seventh time he returned and said, "I saw a little cloud no bigger than a man's hand, coming up from the sea."

Elijah ordered his servant, "Go to King Ahab and tell him to get in his chariot and go back home before the rain stops him."

"I saw a little cloud." (18:44)

45In a little while the sky was covered with dark clouds, the wind began to blow, and a heavy rain began to fall. Ahab got in his chariot and started back to Jezreel. 46The power of the LORD came on Elijah; he fastened his clothes tight around his waist and ran ahead of Ahab all the way to Jezreel.

Elijah on Mount Sinai

19 1King Ahab told his wife Jezebel everything that Elijah had done and how he had put all the prophets of Baal to death. 2She sent a message to Elijah: "May the gods strike me dead if by this time tomorrow I don't do the same thing to you that you did to the prophets." 3Elijah was afraid and fled for his life; he took his servant and went to Beersheba in Judah.

Leaving the servant there, 4Elijah walked a whole day into the wilderness. He stopped and sat down in the shade of a tree and wished he would die. "It's too much, LORD,"

u **18:37** you are bringing them back to yourself; *or* you yourself made them turn away from you.
18:42-45 Jas 5:18   **19:4** Jon 4:3

Pray It!

A Whisper

Now we get to meet King Ahab's wife, Queen Jezebel. She is just as evil as Ahab, maybe even worse! She threatens to kill Elijah. Elijah goes into hiding in the wilderness in fear and despair. He is overwhelmed with the task before him and the situation he is in. He even prays that he will die. God has a different plan though. Elijah is fed by an angel, witnesses an earthquake, a great wind, and fire. But he doesn't see God in any of these dramatic events. Then in a soft whisper, God speaks to him.

Dear God,
I want to hear your voice.
I want it to be loud and dramatic, something I can't miss!
But that's not the way you usually speak to us.
Help me to be patient and listen for you
in the quiet of my heart.
Help me to make time and space
where I can hear the gentle whisper of your voice. Amen.

— 1 Kings, chapter 19

---

he prayed. "Take away my life; I might as well be dead!"

⁵He lay down under the tree and fell asleep. Suddenly an angel touched him and said, "Wake up and eat." ⁶He looked around and saw a loaf of bread and a jar of water near his head. He ate and drank, and lay down again. ⁷The LORD's angel returned and woke him up a second time, saying, "Get up and eat, or the trip will be too much for you." ⁸Elijah got up, ate and drank, and the food gave him enough strength to walk forty days to Sinai, the holy mountain. ⁹There he went into a cave to spend the night.

Suddenly the LORD spoke to him, "Elijah, what are you doing here?"

¹⁰He answered, "LORD God Almighty, I have always served you—you alone. But the people of Israel have broken their covenant with you, torn down your altars, and killed all your prophets. I am the only one left— and they are trying to kill me!"

¹¹"Go out and stand before me on top of the mountain," the LORD said to him. Then the LORD passed by and sent a furious wind that split the hills and shattered the rocks— but the LORD was not in the wind. The wind stopped blowing, and then there was an earthquake—but the LORD was not in the earthquake. ¹²After the earthquake there was a fire—but the LORD was not in the fire. And after the fire there was the soft whisper of a voice.

¹³When Elijah heard it, he covered his face with his cloak and went out and stood at the entrance of the cave. A voice said to him, "Elijah, what are you doing here?"

¹⁴He answered, " LORD God Almighty, I have always served you—you alone. But the people of Israel have broken their covenant with you, torn down your altars, and killed all your prophets. I am the only one left— and they are trying to kill me."

¹⁵The LORD said, "Return to the wilderness near Damascus, then enter the city and anoint Hazael as king of Syria; ¹⁶anoint Jehu son of Nimshi as king of Israel, and anoint Elisha son of Shaphat from Abel Meholah to succeed you as prophet. ¹⁷Anyone who escapes being put to death by Hazael will be

19:10, 14 Rom 11:3   **19:15** 2 Kings 8:7–13   **19:16** 2 Kings 9:1–6

killed by Jehu, and anyone who escapes Jehu will be killed by Elisha. ¹⁸Yet I will leave seven thousand people alive in Israel—all those who are loyal to me and have not bowed to Baal or kissed his idol."

The Call of Elisha

¹⁹Elijah left and found Elisha plowing with a team of oxen; there were eleven teams ahead of him, and he was plowing with the last one. Elijah took off his cloak and put it on Elisha. ²⁰Elisha then left his oxen, ran after Elijah, and said, "Let me kiss my father and mother good-bye, and then I will go with you."

Elijah answered, "All right, go back. I'm not stopping you!"^v

²¹Then Elisha went to his team of oxen, killed them, and cooked the meat, using the yoke as fuel for the fire. He gave the meat to the people, and they ate it. Then he went and followed Elijah as his helper.

War with Syria

20 ¹King Benhadad of Syria gathered all his troops, and supported by thirty-two other rulers with their horses and chariots, he marched up, laid siege to Samaria, and launched attacks against it. ²He sent messengers into the city to King Ahab of Israel to say, "King Benhadad demands that ³you surrender to him your silver and gold, your women and the strongest of your children."

⁴"Tell my lord, King Benhadad, that I agree; he can have me and everything I own," Ahab answered.

⁵Later the messengers came back to Ahab with another demand from Benhadad: "I sent you word that you were to hand over to me your silver and gold, your women and your children. ⁶Now, however, I will send my officers to search your palace and the homes of your officials, and to take every-

Elisha

Elisha was a wealthy farmer who gives up everything to take over for Elijah. Like the call of the Apostles in the Gospels, the call in this story is one that Elisha answers almost immediately. It is hard to imagine what we might do if a messenger from God came up to us in the middle of a school day and said, "Leave everything and come follow me. God has work for you to do." Okay, maybe there are some things we would be happy to give up, like homework and chores. But it would be hard to leave everything behind, such as your favorite things and the people you love and care about.

But God *does* ask us every day not to be attached to the things of this world. Every day we need to live as God wants and stay focused on God's will for us. God has called you through your Baptism to speak his truth to the people you meet, just like he called Elisha.

— 1 Kings 19:19–21

thing they^w consider valuable. They will be there about this time tomorrow."

⁷King Ahab called in all the leaders of the country and said, "You see that this man wants to ruin us. He sent me a message demanding my wives and children, my silver and gold, and I agreed."

^v **19:20** All right . . . you; *or* Go on, but come back, because what I have just done to you is important.
^w **20:6** *Some ancient translations* they; *Hebrew* you.
19:18 Rom 11:4

When the kings of his Chosen People won't listen, God uses foreign kings like Hazael of Syria *(I Kings 19:15–17)* to get their attention.

[8] The leaders and the people answered, "Don't pay any attention to him; don't give in."

[9] So Ahab replied to Benhadad's messengers, "Tell my lord the king that I agreed to his first demand, but I cannot agree to the second."

The messengers left and then returned with another message [10] from Benhadad: "I will bring enough men to destroy this city of yours and carry off the rubble in their hands. May the gods strike me dead if I don't!"

[11] King Ahab answered, "Tell King Benhadad that a real soldier does his bragging *after* a battle, not before it."

[12] Benhadad received Ahab's answer as he and his allies, the other rulers, were drinking in their tents. He ordered his men to get ready to attack the city, and so they moved into position.

[13] Meanwhile, a prophet went to King Ahab and said, "The LORD says, 'Don't be afraid of that huge army! I will give you victory over it today, and you will know that I am the LORD.' "

[14] "Who will lead the attack?" Ahab asked.

The prophet answered, "The LORD says that the young soldiers under the command of the district governors are to do it."

"Who will command the main force?" the king asked.

"You," the prophet answered.

[15] So the king called out the young soldiers who were under the district commanders, 232 in all. Then he called out the Israelite army, a total of seven thousand men.

[16] The attack began at noon, as Benhadad and his thirty-two allies were getting drunk in their tents. [17] The young soldiers advanced first. Scouts sent out by Benhadad reported to him that a group of soldiers was coming out of Samaria. [18] He ordered, "Take them alive, no matter whether they are coming to fight or to ask for peace."

[19] The young soldiers led the attack, followed by the Israelite army, [20] and each one killed the man he fought. The Syrians fled, with the Israelites in hot pursuit, but Benhadad escaped on horseback, accompanied by some of the cavalry. [21] King Ahab took to the field, captured[x] the horses and chariots, and inflicted a severe defeat on the Syrians.

[22] Then the prophet went to King Ahab and said, "Go back and build up your forces and make careful plans, because the king of Syria will attack again next spring."

The Second Syrian Attack

[23] King Benhadad's officials said to him, "The gods of Israel are mountain gods, and that is why the Israelites defeated us. But we will certainly defeat them if we fight them in the plains. [24] Now, remove the thirty-two rulers from their commands and replace them with field commanders. [25] Then call up an army as large as the one that deserted you, with the same number of horses and chariots. We will fight the Israelites in the plains, and this time we will defeat them."

King Benhadad agreed and followed their advice. [26] The following spring he called up his men and marched with them to the city of Aphek to attack the Israelites. [27] The Israelites were called up and equipped; they marched out and camped in two groups facing the Syrians. The Israelites looked like two small flocks of goats compared to the Syrians, who spread out over the countryside.

[28] A prophet went to King Ahab and said, "This is what the LORD says: 'Because the Syrians say that I am a god of the hills and not of the plains, I will give you victory over their huge army, and you and your people will know that I am the LORD.' "

[29] For seven days the Syrians and the Israelites stayed in their camps, facing each other. On the seventh day they started fighting, and the Israelites killed a hundred thousand Syrians. [30] The survivors fled into the city of Aphek, where the city walls fell on twenty-seven thousand of them.

---

[x] **20:21** *One ancient translation* captured; *Hebrew* destroyed.

Find Syria on Map 3 in the back of this Bible. According to the map, what is another name for Syria?

Benhadad also escaped into the city and took refuge in the back room of a house. ³¹His officials went to him and said, "We have heard that the Israelite kings are merciful. Give us permission to go to the king of Israel with sackcloth around our waists and ropes around our necks, and maybe he will spare your life." ³²So they wrapped sackcloth around their waists and ropes around their necks, went to Ahab and said, "Your servant Benhadad pleads with you for his life."

Ahab answered, "Is he still alive? Good! He's like a brother to me!"

They wrapped . . . ropes around their necks. (20:32)

³³Benhadad's officials were watching for a good sign, and when Ahab said "brother," they took it up at once, and said, "As you say, Benhadad is your brother!"

"Bring him to me," Ahab ordered. When Benhadad arrived, Ahab invited him to get in the chariot with him. ³⁴Benhadad said to him, "I will restore to you the towns my father took from your father, and you may set up a commercial center for yourself in Damascus, just as my father did in Samaria."

Ahab replied, "On these terms, then, I will set you free." He made a treaty with him and let him go.

A Prophet Condemns Ahab

³⁵At the LORD's command a member of a group of prophets ordered a fellow prophet to hit him. But he refused, ³⁶so he said to him, "Because you have disobeyed the LORD's command, a lion will kill you as soon as you leave me." And as soon as he left, a lion came along and killed him.

³⁷Then this same prophet went to another man and said, "Hit me!" This man did so; he hit him a hard blow and hurt him. ³⁸The prophet bandaged his face with a cloth, to disguise himself, and went and stood by the road, waiting for the king of Israel to pass. ³⁹As the king was passing by, the prophet called out to him and said, "Your Majesty, I was fighting in the battle when a soldier brought a captured enemy to me and said, 'Guard this man; if he escapes, you will pay for it with your life or else pay a fine of three thousand pieces of silver.' ⁴⁰But I got busy with other things, and the man escaped."

The king answered, "You have pronounced your own sentence, and you will have to pay the penalty."

⁴¹The prophet tore the cloth from his face, and at once the king recognized him as one of the prophets. ⁴²The prophet then said to the king, "This is the word of the LORD: 'Because you have allowed the man to escape whom I had ordered to be killed, you will pay for it with your life, and your army will be destroyed for letting his army escape.' "

⁴³The king went back home to Samaria, worried and depressed.

Naboth's Vineyard

21 ¹Near King Ahab's palace in Jezreel there was a vineyard owned by a man named Naboth. ²One day Ahab said to Naboth, "Let me have your vineyard; it is close to my palace, and I want to use the land for a vegetable garden. I will give you a better vineyard for it or, if you prefer, I will pay you a fair price."

³"I inherited this vineyard from my ancestors," Naboth replied. "The LORD forbid that I should let you have it!"

⁴Ahab went home, depressed and angry over what Naboth had said to him. He lay down on his bed, facing the wall, and would not eat. ⁵His wife Jezebel went to him and

asked, "Why are you so depressed? Why won't you eat?"

⁶He answered, "Because of what Naboth said to me. I offered to buy his vineyard or, if he preferred, to give him another one for it, but he told me that I couldn't have it!"

⁷"Well, are you the king or aren't you?" Jezebel replied. "Get out of bed, cheer up, and eat. I will get you Naboth's vineyard!"

⁸Then she wrote some letters, signed Ahab's name to them, sealed them with his seal, and sent them to the officials and leading citizens of Jezreel. ⁹The letters said: "Proclaim a day of fasting, call the people together, and give Naboth the place of honor. ¹⁰Get a couple of scoundrels to accuse him to his face of cursing God and the king. Then take him out of the city and stone him to death."

¹¹The officials and leading citizens of Jezreel did what Jezebel had commanded. ¹²They proclaimed a day of fasting, called the people together, and gave Naboth the place of honor. ¹³The two scoundrels publicly accused him of cursing God and the king, and so he was taken outside the city and stoned to death. ¹⁴The message was sent to Jezebel: "Naboth has been put to death."

¹⁵As soon as Jezebel received the message, she said to Ahab, "Naboth is dead. Now go and take possession of the vineyard which he refused to sell to you." ¹⁶At once Ahab went to the vineyard to take possession of it.

¹⁷Then the LORD said to Elijah, the prophet from Tishbe, ¹⁸"Go to King Ahab of Samaria. You will find him in Naboth's vineyard, about to take possession of it. ¹⁹Tell him that I, the LORD, say to him, 'After murdering the man, are you taking over his property as well?' Tell him that this is what I say: 'In the very place that the dogs licked up Naboth's blood they will lick up your blood!'"

²⁰When Ahab saw Elijah, he said, "Have you caught up with me, my enemy?"

"Yes, I have," Elijah answered. "You have devoted yourself completely to doing what is wrong in the LORD's sight. ²¹So the LORD says to you, 'I will bring disaster on you. I will do away with you and get rid of every

No Shame

Naboth is a holy man who is devoted to God and holds sacred the trust God has given him, the land of his ancestors. He is the opposite of the greedy, pouty King Ahab who sulks because he can't get what he wants—Naboth's vineyard. To make Ahab happy, Queen Jezebel sets up Naboth to be stoned to death by falsely accusing him of cursing God. All in a day's work for this evil, greedy couple.

Ahab and his wife Jezebel have already rejected God's guidance and worshiped the idols of foreign gods. Now by having Naboth murdered, they have broken one of the most important Israelite laws about land ownership. They have abused their power at the expense of a lowly person. This is the last straw for God. He sends Elijah to prophesy that they will die shamefully.

— 1 Kings, chapter 21

male in your family, young and old alike. ²²Your family will become like the family of King Jeroboam son of Nebat and like the family of King Baasha son of Ahijah, because you have stirred up my anger by leading Israel into sin.' ²³And concerning Jezebel, the LORD says that dogs will eat her body in the city of Jezreel. ²⁴Any of your relatives who die in the city will be eaten by dogs, and any who die in the open country will be eaten by vultures."

(²⁵There was no one else who had devoted himself so completely to doing wrong in the LORD's sight as Ahab—all at the urging of his wife Jezebel. ²⁶He committed the most shameful sins by worshiping idols, as the Amorites had done, whom the LORD had driven out of the land as the people of Israel advanced.)

27 When Elijah finished speaking, Ahab tore his clothes, took them off, and put on sackcloth. He refused food, slept in the sackcloth, and went about gloomy and depressed.

28 The LORD said to the prophet Elijah, 29 "Have you noticed how Ahab has humbled himself before me? Since he has done this, I will not bring disaster on him during his lifetime; it will be during his son's lifetime that I will bring disaster on Ahab's family."

The Prophet Micaiah Warns Ahab
(2 Chronicles 18:2–27)

22 1 There was peace between Israel and Syria for the next two years, 2 but in the third year King Jehoshaphat of Judah went to see King Ahab of Israel.

3 Ahab asked his officials, "Why is it that we have not done anything to get back Ramoth in Gilead from the king of Syria? It belongs to us!" 4 And Ahab asked Jehoshaphat, "Will you go with me to attack Ramoth?"

"I am ready when you are," Jehoshaphat answered, "and so are my soldiers and my cavalry. 5 But first let's consult the LORD."

6 So Ahab called in the prophets, about four hundred of them, and asked them, "Should I go and attack Ramoth, or not?"

"Attack it," they answered. "The Lord will give you victory."

7 But Jehoshaphat asked, "Isn't there another prophet through whom we can consult the LORD?"

8 Ahab answered, "There is one more, Micaiah son of Imlah. But I hate him because he never prophesies anything good for me; it's always something bad."

"You shouldn't say that!" Jehoshaphat replied.

9 Then Ahab called in a court official and told him to go and get Micaiah at once.

10 The two kings, dressed in their royal robes, were sitting on their thrones at the threshing place just outside the gate of Samaria, and all the prophets were prophesying in front of them. 11 One of them, Zedekiah son of Chenaanah, made iron horns and said to Ahab, "This is what the LORD says: 'With these you will fight the Syrians and totally defeat them.' " 12 All the other prophets said the same thing. "March against Ramoth and you will win," they said. "The LORD will give you victory."

13 Meanwhile, the official who had gone to get Micaiah said to him, "All the other prophets have prophesied success for the king, and you had better do the same."

14 But Micaiah answered, "By the living LORD I promise that I will say what he tells me to!"

15 When he appeared before King Ahab, the king asked him, "Micaiah, should King Jehoshaphat and I go and attack Ramoth, or not?"

"Attack!" Micaiah answered. "Of course you'll win. The LORD will give you victory."

16 But Ahab replied, "When you speak to me in the name of the LORD, tell the truth! How many times do I have to tell you that?"

17 Micaiah answered, "I can see the army of Israel scattered over the hills like sheep without a shepherd. And the LORD said, 'These men have no leader; let them go home in peace.' "

18 Ahab said to Jehoshaphat, "Didn't I tell you that he never prophesies anything good for me? It's always something bad!"

19 Micaiah went on: "Now listen to what the LORD says! I saw the LORD sitting on his throne in heaven, with all his angels standing beside him. 20 The LORD asked, 'Who will deceive Ahab so that he will go and be killed at Ramoth?' Some of the angels said one thing, and others said something else, 21 until

22:17 Num 27:17; Mt 9:36; Mk 6:34   22:19 Job 1:6; Isa 6:1

"**Ahab tore his clothes**" (*I Kings 21:27*). **This is a sign that a person has realized she or he has done something terrible.**

a spirit stepped forward, approached the LORD, and said, 'I will deceive him.' 22'How?' the LORD asked. The spirit replied, 'I will go and make all of Ahab's prophets tell lies.' The LORD said, 'Go and deceive him. You will succeed.' "

23And Micaiah concluded: "This is what has happened. The LORD has made these prophets of yours lie to you. But he himself has decreed that you will meet with disaster!"

24Then the prophet Zedekiah went up to Micaiah, slapped his face, and asked, "Since when did the LORD's spirit leave me and speak to you?"

25"You will find out when you go into some back room to hide," Micaiah replied.

26Then King Ahab ordered one of his officers, "Arrest Micaiah and take him to Amon, the governor of the city, and to Prince Joash. 27Tell them to throw him in prison and to put him on bread and water until I return safely."

28"If you return safely," Micaiah exclaimed, "then the LORD has not spoken through me!" And he added, "Listen, everyone, to what I have said!"

The Death of Ahab
(2 Chronicles 18:28–34)

29Then King Ahab of Israel and King Jehoshaphat of Judah went to attack the city of Ramoth in Gilead. 30Ahab said to Jehoshaphat, "As we go into battle, I will disguise myself, but you wear your royal garments." So the king of Israel went into battle in disguise.

31The king of Syria had ordered his thirty-two chariot commanders to attack no one else except the king of Israel. 32So when they saw King Jehoshaphat, they all thought that he was the king of Israel, and they turned to attack him. But when he cried out, 33they realized that he was not the king of Israel, and they stopped their attack. 34By chance, however, a Syrian soldier shot an arrow which struck King Ahab

between the joints of his armor. "I'm wounded!" he cried out to his chariot driver. "Turn around and pull out of the battle!"

35While the battle raged on, King Ahab remained propped up in his chariot, facing the Syrians. The blood from his wound ran down and covered the bottom of the chariot, and at evening he died. 36Near sunset the order went out through the Israelite ranks: "Each of you go back to your own country and city!"

37So died King Ahab. His body was taken to Samaria and buried. 38His chariot was cleaned up at the pool of Samaria, where dogs licked up his blood and prostitutes washed themselves, as the LORD had said would happen.

39Everything else that King Ahab did, including an account of his palace decorated with ivory and of all the cities he built, is recorded in *The History of the Kings of Israel*. 40At his death his son Ahaziah succeeded him as king.

King Jehoshaphat of Judah
(2 Chronicles 20:31—21:1)

41In the fourth year of the reign of King Ahab of Israel, Jehoshaphat son of Asa became king of Judah 42at the age of thirty-five, and he ruled in Jerusalem for twenty-five years. His mother was Azubah, the daughter of Shilhi. 43Like his father Asa before him, he did what was right in the sight of the LORD; but the places of worship were not destroyed, and the people continued to offer sacrifices and burn incense there. 44Jehoshaphat made peace with the king of Israel.

45Everything else that Jehoshaphat did, all his bravery and his battles, are recorded in *The History of the Kings of Judah*. 46He got rid of all the male and female prostitutes serving at the pagan altars who were still left from the days of his father Asa.

47The land of Edom had no king; it was

Many kings had court prophets like Zedekiah. Rather than speaking for God, they often told the king what he wanted to hear.

ruled by a deputy appointed by the king of Judah.

⁴⁸King Jehoshaphat had ocean-going ships built to sail to the land of Ophir for gold; but they were wrecked at Eziongeber and never sailed. ⁴⁹Then King Ahaziah of Israel offered to let his men sail with Jehoshaphat's men, but Jehoshaphat refused the offer.

⁵⁰Jehoshaphat died and was buried in the royal tombs in David's City, and his son Jehoram succeeded him as king.

King Ahaziah of Israel

⁵¹In the seventeenth year of the reign of King Jehoshaphat of Judah, Ahaziah son of Ahab became king of Israel, and he ruled in Samaria for two years. ⁵²He sinned against the LORD, following the wicked example of his father Ahab, his mother Jezebel, and King Jeroboam, who had led Israel into sin. ⁵³He worshiped and served Baal, and like his father before him, he aroused the anger of the LORD, the God of Israel.

Your Next Step

Congratulations on finishing the First Book of Kings! Use this space to write your thoughts and questions about this book. If you are following the suggested reading plan, go ahead to the Second Book of Kings. It continues with the story of the prophets Elijah and Elisha and the kings of Israel and Judah.

Have you ever watched a character in a movie and you just knew they were going to make a big mistake? The other characters warn them, but they just can't seem to stop themselves. The people of Israel are kind of like that in the Second Book of Kings. This book continues the story of the Israelites' history, but it doesn't end well. The two kingdoms—Judah in the south and Israel in the north—each have their own challenges even though their stories are still connected.

The prophet Elisha and other prophets continue the work begun by Elijah in calling the leaders and the people away from idolatry and injustice. In the end, the warning is ignored, and the people are led farther and farther away from their promise to serve only God. Eventually, all is lost.

Chap. 25

Headlines

- Elijah Rides Fiery Chariot to Heaven (2:1–18)
- Elisha Brings Boy Back to Life (4:8–37)
- Evil Queen Meets Her Fate (9:30–37)
- A Great Prophet Dies (13:14–21)
- Assyrians Conquer Samaria (Israel)! (17:5–23)
- Faithful King Rules Judah (18:1–8)
- Jerusalem and the Temple Destroyed (25:1–17)

FACTOIDS

How does this book fit into the Bible? This book concludes the story of Israel's kings. It is a major turning point in the history of the Israelites. The Temple and city of Jerusalem are destroyed, and the people are led away in exile.

Why was it written? It was written to show that Israel's history was guided by God.

Jesus connection: The story of Jesus feeding the crowds in all four Gospels recalls Elisha's feeding the prophets in 2 Kings 4:42–44.

Important themes

- God answers those who call on his name.
- God continually calls his people to repent and be faithful.
- Those who refuse to repent and turn to God will suffer the consequences and be expelled from God's presence.

2 KINGS

Elijah and King Ahaziah

1 ¹After the death of King Ahab of Israel the country of Moab rebelled against Israel.

²King Ahaziah of Israel fell off the balcony on the roof of his palace in Samaria and was seriously injured. So he sent some messengers to consult Baalzebub, the god of the Philistine city of Ekron, in order to find out whether or not he would recover. ³But an angel of the LORD commanded Elijah, the prophet from Tishbe, to go and meet the messengers of King Ahaziah and ask them, "Why are you going to consult Baalzebub, the god of Ekron? Is it because you think there is no god in Israel? ⁴Tell the king that the LORD says, 'You will not recover from your injuries; you will die!' "

Elijah did as the LORD commanded, ⁵and the messengers returned to the king. "Why have you come back?" he asked.

⁶They answered, "We were met by a man who told us to come back and tell you that the LORD says to you, 'Why are you sending messengers to consult Baalzebub, the god of Ekron? Is it because you think there is no god in Israel? You will not recover from your injuries; you will die!' "

⁷"What did the man look like?" the king asked.

⁸"He was wearing a cloak made of animal skins, tied with*a* a leather belt," they answered.

"It's Elijah!" the king exclaimed.

⁹Then he sent an officer with fifty men to get Elijah. The officer found him sitting on a hill and said to him, "Man of God, the king orders you to come down."

¹⁰"If I am a man of God," Elijah answered, "may fire come down from heaven and kill you and your men!" At once fire came down and killed the officer and his men.

¹¹The king sent another officer with fifty men, who went up*b* and said to Elijah, "Man of God, the king orders you to come down at once!"

¹²"If I am a man of God," Elijah answered, "may fire come down from heaven and kill you and your men!" At once the fire of God came down and killed the officer and his men.

¹³Once more the king sent an officer with fifty men. He went up the hill, fell on his knees in front of Elijah, and pleaded, "Man of God, be merciful to me and my men. Spare our lives! ¹⁴The two other officers and their men were killed by fire from heaven; but please be merciful to me!"

¹⁵The angel of the LORD said to Elijah, "Go down with him, and don't be afraid." So Elijah went with the officer to the king ¹⁶and said to him, "This is what the LORD says: 'Because you sent messengers to consult Baalzebub, the god of Ekron—as if there were no god in Israel to consult—you will not get well; you will die!' "

¹⁷Ahaziah died, as the LORD had said through Elijah. Ahaziah had no sons, so his brother*c* Joram succeeded him as king in the second year of the reign of Jehoram son of Jehoshaphat, king of Judah.

¹⁸Everything else that King Ahaziah did is recorded in *The History of the Kings of Israel.*

Elijah Is Taken Up to Heaven

2 ¹The time came for the LORD to take Elijah up to heaven in a whirlwind. Elijah and Elisha set out from Gilgal, ²and on the way Elijah said to Elisha, "Now stay here; the LORD has ordered me to go to Bethel."

But Elisha answered, "I swear by my loyalty to the living LORD and to you that I will not leave you." So they went on to Bethel.

³A group of prophets who lived there went to Elisha and asked him, "Do you

a **1:8** was wearing . . . with; *or was a hairy man and wore.* *b* **1:11** *One ancient translation* went up; *Hebrew* answered. *c* **1:17** *Some ancient translations* his brother; *Hebrew does not have these words.*
1:8 Mt 3:4; Mk 1:6 **1:10, 12** Lk 9:54

Saying Good-bye

Have you ever had to say good-bye to someone close to you? Maybe a friend moved, or someone you love passed away. Letting go of someone you care about is a very hard thing to do. Elisha doesn't want Elijah to leave him, but Elijah knows that it's his time to go. Something of Elijah remains with Elisha, though—Elijah's cloak. It is a symbol that Elisha now has Elijah's power.

Even when someone leaves us, we keep a part of him or her. It doesn't have to be a piece of clothing or even a picture. Our memories, the lessons we learned from the person, the love we have shared remains with us. When we entrust the person we love to God, we can stay connected. If you've lost someone, pray for him or her. If he or she has died or is just far away, ask God to look after him or her.

— 2 Kings 2:1–15

⁵A group of prophets who lived there went to Elisha and asked him, "Do you know that the LORD is going to take your master away from you today?"

"Yes, I know," Elisha answered. "But let's not talk about it."

⁶Then Elijah said to Elisha, "Now stay here; the LORD has ordered me to go to the Jordan River."

But Elisha answered, "I swear by my loyalty to the living LORD and to you that I will not leave you." So they went on, ⁷and fifty of the prophets followed them to the Jordan. Elijah and Elisha stopped by the river, and the fifty prophets stood a short distance away. ⁸Then Elijah took off his cloak, rolled it up, and struck the water with it; the water divided, and he and Elisha crossed to the other side on dry ground. ⁹There, Elijah said to Elisha, "Tell me what you want me to do for you before I am taken away."

"Let me receive the share of your power that will make me your successor,"ᵈ Elisha answered.

¹⁰"That is a difficult request to grant," Elijah replied. "But you will receive it if you see me as I am being taken away from you; if you don't see me, you won't receive it."

¹¹They kept talking as they walked on; then suddenly a chariot of fire pulled by horses of fire came between them, and Elijah was taken up to heaven by a whirlwind. ¹²Elisha saw it and cried out to Elijah, "My father, my father! Mighty defender of Israel! You are gone!" And he never saw Elijah again.

In grief Elisha tore his cloak in two. ¹³Then he picked up Elijah's cloak that had fallen from him, and went back and stood on the bank of the Jordan. ¹⁴He struck the water with Elijah's cloak and said, "Where is the LORD, the God of Elijah?" Then he struck the water again, and it divided, and he walked over to the other side. ¹⁵The fifty prophets from Jericho saw him and said,

know that the LORD is going to take your master away from you today?"

"Yes, I know," Elisha answered. "But let's not talk about it."

⁴Then Elijah said to Elisha, "Now stay here; the LORD has ordered me to go to Jericho."

But Elisha answered, "I swear by my loyalty to the living LORD and to you that I will not leave you." So they went on to Jericho.

ᵈ **2:9** THE SHARE . . . SUCCESSOR: *Elisha asked for the share that the first-born son inherited by law from his father (see Deut 21:17).*

2:9 Deut 21:17   **2:12** 2 Kings 13:14; Sir 48:9, 12

Can you find a story in 1 Kings in which God also sent down fire from heaven in response to Elijah's prayer?

"My father! . . . You are gone!" (2:12)

"The power of Elijah is on Elisha!" They went to meet him, bowed down before him, 16and said, "There are fifty of us here, all strong men. Let us go and look for your master. Maybe the spirit of the LORD has carried him away and left him on some mountain or in some valley."

"No, you must not go," Elisha answered.

17But they insisted until he gave in and let them go. The fifty of them went and looked high and low for Elijah for three days, but didn't find him. 18Then they returned to Elisha, who had waited at Jericho, and he said to them, "Didn't I tell you not to go?"

Miracles of Elisha

19Some men from Jericho went to Elisha and said, "As you know, sir, this is a fine city, but the water is bad and causes miscarriages."

20"Put some salt in a new bowl and bring it to me," he ordered. They brought it to him, 21and he went to the spring, threw the salt in the water, and said, "This is what the LORD says: 'I make this water pure, and it will not cause any more deaths or miscarriages.' " 22And that water has been pure ever since, just as Elisha said it would be.

23Elisha left Jericho to go to Bethel, and on the way some boys came out of a town and made fun of him. "Get out of here, baldy!" they shouted.

24Elisha turned around, glared at them, and cursed them in the name of the LORD. Then two she-bears came out of the woods and tore forty-two of the boys to pieces.

25Elisha went on to Mount Carmel and later returned to Samaria.

War between Israel and Moab

3 1In the eighteenth year of the reign of King Jehoshaphat of Judah, Joram son of Ahab became king of Israel, and he ruled in Samaria for twelve years. 2He sinned against the LORD, but he was not as bad as his father or his mother Jezebel; he pulled down the image his father had made for the worship of Baal. 3Yet, like King Jeroboam son of Nebat before him, he led Israel into sin and would not stop.

4King Mesha of Moab raised sheep, and every year he gave as tribute to the king of Israel 100,000 lambs and the wool from 100,000 sheep. 5But when King Ahab of Israel died, Mesha rebelled against Israel. 6At once King Joram left Samaria and gathered all his troops. 7He sent word to King Jehoshaphat of Judah: "The king of Moab has rebelled against me; will you join me in war against him?"

"I will," King Jehoshaphat replied. "I am at your disposal, and so are my men and my horses. 8What route shall we take for the attack?"

"We will go the long way through the wilderness of Edom," Joram answered.

9So King Joram and the kings of Judah and Edom set out. After marching seven days, they ran out of water, and there was none left for the men or the pack animals. 10"We're done for!" King Joram exclaimed. "The LORD has put the three of us at the mercy of the king of Moab!"

11King Jehoshaphat asked, "Is there a prophet here through whom we can consult the LORD?"

An officer of King Joram's forces answered, "Elisha son of Shaphat is here. He was Elijah's assistant."

12"He is a true prophet," King Jehoshaphat said. So the three kings went to Elisha.

13"Why should I help you?" Elisha said to the king of Israel. "Go and consult those prophets that your father and mother consulted."

"No!" Joram replied. "It is the LORD who has put us three kings at the mercy of the king of Moab."

14Elisha answered, "By the living LORD,

whom I serve, I swear that I would have nothing to do with you if I didn't respect your ally, King Jehoshaphat of Judah. [15]Now get me a musician."

As the musician played his harp, the power of the LORD came on Elisha, [16]and he said, "This is what the LORD says: 'Dig ditches all over this dry stream bed. [17]Even though you will not see any rain or wind, this stream bed will be filled with water, and you, your livestock, and your pack animals will have plenty to drink.'" [18]And Elisha continued, "But this is an easy thing for the LORD to do; he will also give you victory over the Moabites. [19]You will conquer all their beautiful fortified cities; you will cut down all their fruit trees, stop all their springs, and ruin all their fertile fields by covering them with stones."

"This is what the LORD says." (3:16)

[20]The next morning, at the time of the regular morning sacrifice, water came flowing from the direction of Edom and covered the ground.

[21]When the Moabites heard that the three kings had come to attack them, all the men who could bear arms, from the oldest to the youngest, were called out and stationed at the border. [22]When they got up the following morning, the sun was shining on the water, making it look as red as blood. [23]"It's blood!" they exclaimed. "The three enemy armies must have fought and killed each other! Let's go and loot their camp!"

[24]But when they reached the camp, the Israelites attacked them and drove them back. The Israelites kept up the pursuit,[e] slaughtering the Moabites [25]and destroying their cities. As they passed by a fertile field,

every Israelite would throw a stone on it until finally all the fields were covered; they also stopped up the springs and cut down the fruit trees. At last only the capital city of Kir Heres[f] was left, and the slingers surrounded it and attacked it.

[26]When the king of Moab realized that he was losing the battle, he took seven hundred swordsmen with him and tried to force his way through the enemy lines and escape to the king of Syria,[g] but he failed. [27]So he took his oldest son, who was to succeed him as king, and offered him on the city wall as a sacrifice to the god of Moab. The Israelites were terrified[h] and so they drew back from the city and returned to their own country.

Elisha Helps a Poor Widow

4 [1]The widow of a member of a group of prophets went to Elisha and said, "Sir, my husband has died! As you know, he was a God-fearing man, but now a man he owed money to has come to take away my two sons as slaves in payment for my husband's debt."

[2]"What shall I do for you?" he asked. "Tell me, what do you have at home?"

"Nothing at all, except a small jar of olive oil," she answered.

[3]"Go to your neighbors and borrow as many empty jars as you can," Elisha told her. [4]"Then you and your sons go into the house, close the door, and start pouring oil into the jars. Set each one aside as soon as it is full."

[5]So the woman went into her house with her sons, closed the door, took the small jar of olive oil, and poured oil into the jars as her sons brought them to her. [6]When they had filled all the jars, she asked if there were any more. "That was the last one," one of her sons answered. And the olive oil stopped flowing. [7]She went back to Elisha, the prophet, who said to her, "Sell the olive oil and pay all your debts, and there will be enough money left over for you and your sons to live on."

---

e **3:24** *One ancient translation* kept up the pursuit; *Hebrew unclear.* *f* **3:25** *Probable text* only the capital city of Kir Heres; *Hebrew unclear.* *g* **3:26** *One ancient translation* Syria; *Hebrew* Edom. *h* **3:27** TERRIFIED: *either because of what Chemosh, the god of the Moabites, might do, or because of what the LORD, the God of the Israelites, might do.*

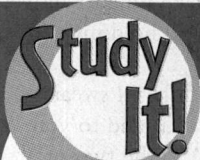

Elisha the Rescuer

It may not sound like a very important miracle, making one small jar of olive oil enough to fill many bottles, but for this poor widow it made all the difference. Her husband had been a prophet. The family had lived simply. Now her sons were to be taken away as slaves to pay off the family's debt. This practice was one of the ways that poor people were robbed of their land.

The woman was about to lose everything. Olive oil was very precious; it was even used as a kind of money. But more importantly it was one of the basic foods for both rich people and poor people. Elisha's miracle saved the woman's land and her sons. It was a sign of God's care for poor and powerless people.

— 2 Kings 4:1–7

Elisha and the Rich Woman from Shunem

⁸One day Elisha went to Shunem, where a rich woman lived. She invited him to a meal, and from then on every time he went to Shunem he would have his meals at her house. ⁹She said to her husband, "I am sure that this man who comes here so often is a holy man. ¹⁰Let's build a small room on the roof, put a bed, a table, a chair, and a lamp in it, and he can stay there whenever he visits us."

¹¹One day Elisha returned to Shunem and went up to his room to rest. ¹²He told his servant Gehazi to go and call the woman. When she came, ¹³he said to Gehazi, "Ask her what I can do for her in return for all the trouble she has had in providing for our needs. Maybe she would like me to go to the king or the army commander and put in a good word for her."

"I have all I need here among my own people," she answered.

¹⁴Elisha asked Gehazi, "What can I do for her then?"

He answered, "Well, she has no son, and her husband is an old man."

¹⁵"Tell her to come here," Elisha ordered. She came and stood in the doorway, ¹⁶and Elisha said to her, "By this time next year you will be holding a son in your arms."

"Oh!" she exclaimed. "Please, sir, don't lie to me. You are a man of God!"

¹⁷But, as Elisha had said, at about that time the following year she gave birth to a son.

¹⁸Some years later, at harvest time, the boy went out one morning to join his father, who was in the field with the harvest workers. ¹⁹Suddenly he cried out to his father, "My head hurts! My head hurts!"

"Carry the boy to his mother," the father said to a servant. ²⁰The servant carried the boy back to his mother, who held him in her lap until noon, at which time he died.

So the woman . . . poured oil into the jars. (4:5)

4:16 Gen 18:4

What horrible thing did the king of Moab do that terrified the Israelites and made them turn back?

2 Kings

21She carried him up to Elisha's room, put him on the bed and left, closing the door behind her. 22Then she called her husband and said to him, "Send a servant here with a donkey. I need to go to the prophet Elisha. I'll be back as soon as I can."

23"Why do you have to go today?" her husband asked. "It's neither a Sabbath nor a New Moon Festival."*i*

"Never mind," she answered. 24Then she had the donkey saddled, and ordered the servant, "Make the donkey go as fast as it can, and don't slow down unless I tell you to." 25So she set out and went to Mount Carmel, where Elisha was.

"Make the donkey go as fast as it can." (4:24)

Elisha saw her coming while she was still some distance away, and he said to his servant Gehazi, "Look, there comes the woman from Shunem! 26Hurry to her and find out if everything is all right with her, her husband, and her son."

She told Gehazi that everything was all right, 27but when she came to Elisha, she bowed down before him and took hold of his feet. Gehazi was about to push her away, but Elisha said, "Leave her alone. Can't you see she's deeply distressed? And the LORD has not told me a thing about it."

28The woman said to him, "Sir, did I ask you for a son? Didn't I tell you not to get my hopes up?"

29Elisha turned to Gehazi and said, "Hurry! Take my walking stick and go. Don't stop to greet anyone you meet, and if anyone greets you, don't take time to answer. Go straight to the house and hold my stick over the boy."

30The woman said to Elisha, "I swear by my loyalty to the living LORD and to you that I will not leave you!" So the two of them started back together. 31Gehazi went on ahead and held Elisha's stick over the child, but there was no sound or any other sign of life. So he went back to meet Elisha and said, "The boy didn't wake up."

32When Elisha arrived, he went alone into the room and saw the boy lying dead on the bed. 33He closed the door and prayed to the LORD. 34Then he lay down on the boy, placing his mouth, eyes, and hands on the boy's mouth, eyes, and hands. As he lay stretched out over the boy, the boy's body started to get warm. 35Elisha got up, walked around the room, and then went back and again stretched himself over the boy. The boy sneezed seven times and then opened his eyes. 36Elisha called Gehazi and told him to call the boy's mother. When she came in, he said to her, "Here's your son." 37She fell at Elisha's feet, with her face touching the ground; then she took her son and left.

Two More Miracles

38Once, when there was a famine throughout the land, Elisha returned to Gilgal. While he was teaching a group of prophets, he told his servant to put a big pot on the fire and make some stew for them. 39One of them went out in the fields to get some herbs. He found a wild vine and picked as many gourds as he could carry. He brought them back and sliced them up into the stew, not knowing what they were. 40The stew was poured out for the men to eat, but as soon as they tasted it they exclaimed to Elisha, "It's poisoned!"—and wouldn't eat it. 41Elisha asked for some meal, threw it into the pot, and said, "Pour out

---

i 4:23 SABBATH . . . NEW MOON FESTIVAL: *Such holy days were thought to be the best time to consult a prophet.*
4:34, 35 1 Kings 17:21

Pray It!

Seek Healing

Naaman, the commander of the mighty Syrian army, had a bad skin disease. He heard from a captured Israelite girl that he could be cured. Naaman went to his own king, who sent him to the king of Israel, who sent him to Elisha, who sent him to the Jordan River. And he was healed! One of the signs of the power and presence of God throughout the Bible is healing. We know that God wants to heal us. God wants to heal our bodies, but more importantly God wants to heal our hearts.

> *Healing God,*
> *Naaman sought healing from the prophet Elisha.*
> *He washed in the Jordan River, and his suffering ended.*
> *I come to you now in need of healing.*
> *Heal my heart in the broken places,*
> *   just as you healed Naaman.*
> *Make me whole again.*
> *Give me a fresh start. Amen.*

— 2 Kings 5:1–14

some more stew for them." And then there was nothing wrong with it.

42 Another time, a man came from Baal Shalishah, bringing Elisha twenty loaves of bread made from the first barley harvested that year, and some freshly-cut heads of grain. Elisha told his servant to feed the group of prophets with this, **43** but he answered, "Do you think this is enough for a hundred men?"

Elisha replied, "Give it to them to eat, because the LORD says that they will eat and still have some left over." **44** So the servant set the food before them, and as the LORD had said, they all ate, and there was still some left over.

Naaman Is Cured

5 ¹ Naaman, the commander of the Syrian army, was highly respected and esteemed by the king of Syria, because through Naaman the LORD had given victory to the Syrian forces. He was a great soldier, but he suf-

fered from a dreaded skin disease. **2** In one of their raids against Israel, the Syrians had carried off a little Israelite girl, who became a servant of Naaman's wife. **3** One day she said to her mistress, "I wish that my master could go to the prophet who lives in Samaria! He would cure him of his disease." **4** When Naaman heard of this, he went to the king and told him what the girl had said. **5** The king said, "Go to the king of Israel and take this letter to him."

So Naaman set out, taking thirty thousand pieces of silver, six thousand pieces of gold, and ten changes of fine clothes. **6** The letter that he took read: "This letter will introduce my officer Naaman. I want you to cure him of his disease."

7 When the king of Israel read the letter, he tore his clothes in dismay and exclaimed, "How can the king of Syria expect me to cure this man? Does he think that I am God,ʲ with the power of life and death? It's plain that he is trying to start a quarrel with me!"

ʲ **5:7** God; *or* a god.
5:1–14 Lk 4:27

8When the prophet Elisha heard what had happened, he sent word to the king: "Why are you so upset? Send the man to me, and I'll show him that there is a prophet in Israel!"

9So Naaman went with his horses and chariot and stopped at the entrance to Elisha's house. 10Elisha sent a servant out to tell him to go and wash himself seven times in the Jordan River, and he would be completely cured of his disease. 11But Naaman left in a rage, saying, "I thought that he would at least come out to me, pray to the LORD his God, wave his hand over the diseased spot,k and cure me! 12Besides, aren't the rivers Abana and Pharpar, back in Damascus, better than any river in Israel? I could have washed in them and been cured!"

13His servants went up to him and said, "Sir, if the prophet had told you to do something difficult, you would have done it. Now why can't you just wash yourself, as he said, and be cured?" 14So Naaman went down to the Jordan, dipped himself in it seven times, as Elisha had instructed, and he was completely cured. His flesh became firm and healthy like that of a child. 15He returned to Elisha with all his men and said, "Now I know that there is no god but the God of Israel; so please, sir, accept a gift from me."

"If the prophet had told you to do something difficult, you would have done it." (5:13)

16Elisha answered, "By the living LORD, whom I serve, I swear that I will not accept a gift."

Naaman insisted that he accept it, but he would not. 17So Naaman said, "If you won't accept my gift, then let me have two mule-loads of earth to take home with me,l

because from now on I will not offer sacrifices or burnt offerings to any god except the LORD. 18So I hope that the LORD will forgive me when I accompany my king to the temple of Rimmon, the god of Syria, and worship him. Surely the LORD will forgive me!"

19"Go in peace," Elisha said. And Naaman left.

He had gone only a short distance, 20when Elisha's servant Gehazi said to himself, "My master has let Naaman get away without paying a thing! He should have accepted what that Syrian offered him. By the living LORD I will run after him and get something from him." 21So he set off after Naaman. When Naaman saw a man running after him, he got down from his chariot to meet him, and asked, "Is something wrong?"

22"No," Gehazi answered. "But my master sent me to tell you that just now two members of the group of prophets in the hill country of Ephraim arrived, and he would like you to give them three thousand pieces of silver and two changes of fine clothes."

23"Please take six thousand pieces of silver," Naaman replied. He insisted on it, tied up the silver in two bags, gave them and two changes of fine clothes to two of his servants, and sent them on ahead of Gehazi. 24When they reached the hill where Elisha lived, Gehazi took the two bags and carried them into the house. Then he sent Naaman's servants back. 25He went back into the house, and Elisha asked him, "Where have you been?"

"Oh, nowhere, sir," he answered.

26But Elisha said, "Wasn't I there in spirit when the man got out of his chariot to meet you? This is no time to accept money and clothes, olive groves and vineyards, sheep and cattle, or servants! 27And now Naaman's disease will come upon you, and you and your descendants will have it forever!"

When Gehazi left, he had the disease—his skin was as white as snow.

---

k **5:11** the diseased spot; *or this place.* l **5:17** EARTH TO TAKE HOME WITH ME: *It was then believed that a god could be worshiped only on his own land.*

The Recovery of the Ax Head

6 ¹One day the group of prophets that Elisha was in charge of complained to him, "The place where we live is too small! ²Give us permission to go to the Jordan and cut down some trees, so that we can build a place to live."

"All right," Elisha answered.

³One of them urged him to go with them; he agreed, ⁴and they set out together. When they arrived at the Jordan, they began to work. ⁵As one of them was cutting down a tree, suddenly his iron ax head fell in the water. "What shall I do, sir?" he exclaimed to Elisha. "It was a borrowed ax!"

⁶"Where did it fall?" Elisha asked.

The man showed him the place, and Elisha cut off a stick, threw it in the water, and made the ax head float. ⁷"Take it out," he ordered, and the man reached down and picked it up.

The Syrian Army Is Defeated

⁸The king of Syria was at war with Israel. He consulted his officers and chose a place to set up his camp. ⁹But Elisha sent word to the king of Israel, warning him not to go near that place, because the Syrians were waiting in ambush there. ¹⁰So the king of Israel warned the people who lived in that place, and they were on guard. This happened several times.

¹¹The Syrian king became greatly upset over this; he called in his officers and asked them, "Which one of you is on the side of the king of Israel?"

¹²One of them answered, "No one is, Your Majesty. The prophet Elisha tells the king of Israel what you say even in the privacy of your own room."

¹³"Find out where he is," the king ordered, "and I will capture him."

When he was told that Elisha was in Dothan, ¹⁴he sent a large force there with horses and chariots. They reached the town at night and surrounded it. ¹⁵Early the next morning Elisha's servant got up, went out of

Mercy Not Revenge

It must have been so tempting for Elisha. The king would have been happy to kill these enemy soldiers who had come to kill Elisha. He would have been justified, right? But Elisha makes a different choice—feed them and send them home! Have you ever had a chance at revenge that you passed up? Did you ever face a situation where someone had been unkind to you, but you responded with kindness to him or her? It's a pretty good feeling. The story goes that after this, the King of Syria stopped raiding the land of Israel. Mercy can be a powerful force. Try it!

— 2 Kings 6:8–23

the house, and saw the Syrian troops with their horses and chariots surrounding the town. He went back to Elisha and exclaimed, "We are doomed, sir! What shall we do?"

¹⁶"Don't be afraid," Elisha answered. "We have more on our side than they have on theirs." ¹⁷Then he prayed, "O LORD, open his eyes and let him see!" The LORD answered his prayer, and Elisha's servant looked up and saw the hillside covered with horses and chariots of fire all around Elisha.

¹⁸When the Syrians attacked, Elisha prayed, "O LORD, strike these men blind!" The LORD answered his prayer and struck them blind. ¹⁹Then Elisha went to them and said, "You are on the wrong road; this is not the town you are looking for. Follow me, and I will lead you to the man you are after." And he led them to Samaria.

²⁰As soon as they had entered the city,

Check Map 3 in the back of this Bible to see how far Naaman traveled. He started in Syria and ended up at the Jordan River near Samaria.

Elisha prayed, "Open their eyes, LORD, and let them see." The LORD answered his prayer; he restored their sight, and they saw that they were inside Samaria.

21 When the king of Israel saw the Syrians, he asked Elisha, "Shall I kill them, sir? Shall I kill them?"

22 "No," he answered. "Not even soldiers you had captured in combat would you put to death. Give them something to eat and drink, and let them return to their king." 23 So the king of Israel provided a great feast for them; and after they had eaten and drunk, he sent them back to the king of Syria. From then on the Syrians stopped raiding the land of Israel.

The Siege of Samaria

24 Some time later King Benhadad of Syria led his entire army against Israel and laid siege to the city of Samaria. 25 As a result of the siege the food shortage in the city was so severe that a donkey's head cost eighty pieces of silver, and half a pound of dove's dung[m] cost five pieces of silver.

26 The king of Israel was walking by on the city wall when a woman cried out, "Help me, Your Majesty!"

27 He replied, "If the LORD won't help you, what help can I provide? Do I have any wheat or wine? 28 What's your trouble?"

She answered, "The other day this woman here suggested that we eat my child, and then eat her child the next day. 29 So we cooked my son and ate him. The next day I told her that we would eat her son, but she had hidden him!"

30 Hearing this, the king tore his clothes in dismay, and the people who were close to the wall could see that he was wearing sackcloth under his clothes. 31 He exclaimed, "May God strike me dead if Elisha is not beheaded before the day is over!" 32 And he sent a messenger to get Elisha.

Meanwhile Elisha was at home with some elders who were visiting him. Before the king's messenger arrived, Elisha said to the elders, "That murderer is sending someone to kill me! Now, when he gets here, shut the door and don't let him come in. The king himself will be right behind him." 33 He had hardly finished saying this, when the king[n] arrived and said, "It's the LORD who has brought this trouble on us! Why should I wait any longer for him to do something?"

7 1 Elisha answered, "Listen to what the LORD says! By this time tomorrow you will be able to buy in Samaria ten pounds of the best wheat or twenty pounds of barley for one piece of silver."

2 The personal attendant of the king said to Elisha, "That can't happen—not even if the LORD himself were to send grain[o] at once!"

"You will see it happen, but you won't get to eat any of the food," Elisha replied.

The Syrian Army Leaves

3 Four men who were suffering from a dreaded skin disease were outside the gates of Samaria, and they said to each other, "Why should we wait here until we die? 4 It's no use going into the city, because we would starve to death in there; but if we stay here, we'll die also. So let's go to the Syrian camp; the worst they can do is kill us, but maybe they will spare our lives." 5 So, as it began to get dark, they went to the Syrian camp, but when they reached it, no one was there. 6 The Lord had made the Syrians hear what sounded like the advance of a large army with horses and chariots, and the Syrians thought that the king of Israel had hired Hittite and Egyptian kings and their armies to attack them. 7 So that evening the Syrians had fled for their lives, abandoning their tents, horses, and donkeys, and leaving the camp just as it was.

8 When the four men reached the edge of the camp, they went into a tent, ate and drank

---

m 6:25 DOVE'S DUNG: *This may be a popular term for a vegetable such as wild onions.*   n 6:33 *Probable text* king: *Hebrew* messenger.   o 7:2 grain; *or* rain.
6:29 Deut 28:57; Lam 4:10

A *siege* is when an army surrounds a city for days or weeks and does not let supplies in. A city's defenses are weakened so that the army can enter easily.

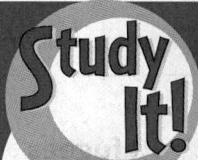

The Last Shall Be First

The Syrians are winning. Their siege is starving out the people of the city of Samaria. Just when all seems to be lost, some lepers discover the Syrian army's camp has been suddenly deserted. In this dramatic story of despair turned to victory, the people at the bottom of society are the first ones to realize the good news. Lepers are outcasts. Because of their contagious skin disease, they have to live outside the city. People turn away from them. Now they are the heroes and get to deliver the good news that the Syrians are gone.

Throughout the Bible we see unlikely heroes, people no one would notice who end up playing key roles in God's plans. God seems to have a special place in his heart for the people who don't have it all together.

— 2 Kings 7:3–9

11 The guards announced the news, and it was reported in the palace. 12 It was still night, but the king got out of bed and said to his officials, "I'll tell you what the Syrians are planning! They know about the famine here, so they have left their camp to go and hide in the countryside. They think that we will leave the city to find food, and then they will take us alive and capture the city."

13 One of his officials said, "The people here in the city are doomed anyway, like those that have already died. So let's send some men with five of the horses that are left, so that we can find out what has happened."p 14 They chose some men, and the king sent them in two chariots with instructions to go and find out what had happened to the Syrian army. 15 The men went as far as the Jordan, and all along the road they saw the clothes and equipment that the Syrians had abandoned as they fled. Then they returned and reported to the king. 16 The people of Samaria rushed out and looted the Syrian camp. And as the LORD had said, ten pounds of the best wheat or twenty pounds of barley were sold for one piece of silver.

17 It so happened that the king of Israel had put the city gate under the command of the officer who was his personal attendant. The officer was trampled to death there by the people and died, as Elisha had predicted when the king went to see him. 18 Elisha had told the king that by that time the following day ten pounds of the best wheat or twenty pounds of barley would be sold in Samaria for one piece of silver, 19 to which the officer had answered, "That can't happen—not even if the LORD himself were to send grainq at once!" And Elisha had replied, "You will see it happen, but you won't get to eat any of the food." 20 And that is just what happened to him—he died, trampled to death by the people at the city gate.

The Woman from Shunem Returns

8 ¹ Now Elisha had told the woman who lived in Shunem, whose son he had brought back to life, that the LORD was

what was there, grabbed the silver, gold, and clothing they found, and went off and hid them; then they returned, entered another tent, and did the same thing. 9 But then they said to each other, "We shouldn't be doing this! We have good news, and we shouldn't keep it to ourselves. If we wait until morning to tell it, we are sure to be punished. Let's go right now and tell the king's officers!" 10 So they left the Syrian camp, went back to Samaria, and called out to the guards at the gates: "We went to the Syrian camp and didn't see or hear anybody; the horses and donkeys have not been untied, and the tents are just as the Syrians left them."

p **7:13** *Verse 13 in Hebrew is unclear.* q **7:19** grain; *or rain.*
8:1 2 Kings 4:8–37

2 Kings

sending a famine on the land, which would last for seven years, and that she should leave with her family and go and live somewhere else. ²She had followed his instructions and had gone with her family to live in Philistia for the seven years.

³At the end of the seven years she returned to Israel and went to the king to ask that her house and her land be restored to her. ⁴She found the king talking with Gehazi, Elisha's servant; the king wanted to know about Elisha's miracles. ⁵While Gehazi was telling the king how Elisha had brought a dead person back to life, the woman made her appeal to the king. Gehazi said to him, "Your Majesty, here is the woman and here is her son whom Elisha brought back to life!" ⁶In answer to the king's question, she confirmed Gehazi's story, and so the king called an official and told him to give back to her everything that was hers, including the value of all the crops that her fields had produced during the seven years she had been away.

Elisha and King Benhadad of Syria

⁷Elisha went to Damascus at a time when King Benhadad of Syria was sick. When the king was told that Elisha was there, ⁸he said to Hazael, one of his officials, "Take a gift to the prophet and ask him to consult the LORD to find out whether or not I am going to get well." ⁹So Hazael loaded forty camels with all kinds of the finest products of Damascus and went to Elisha. When Hazael met him, he said, "Your servant King Benhadad has sent me to ask you whether or not he will recover from his sickness."

¹⁰Elisha answered, "The LORD has revealed to me that he will die; but go to him and tell him that he will recover." ¹¹Then Elisha stared at him with a horrified look on his face until Hazael became ill at ease. Suddenly Elisha burst into tears. ¹²"Why are you crying, sir?" Hazael asked.

"Because I know the horrible things you will do against the people of Israel," Elisha

Live It!

Refugees

Do you know anyone who is a refugee? A refugee is someone who has been forced to leave his or her home and land because of war, famine, natural disaster, or persecution. Elisha showed a special concern for people in need— widows, sick people, poor people. He had warned this same woman that there would be a famine, and he comes to her aid once again so that she can regain her land.

There are thousands of refugees in the world today. As Christians we are called to actively help those in need. Find out about refugees in your area. Where are they from? What needs do they have? Why did they have to leave their homes? What can you do to help them?

— 2 Kings 8:1–6

answered. "You will set their fortresses on fire, slaughter their finest young men, batter their children to death, and rip open their pregnant women."

¹³"How could I ever be that powerful?" Hazael asked. "I'm a nobody!"

"The LORD has shown me that you will be king of Syria," Elisha replied.

¹⁴Hazael went back to Benhadad, who asked him, "What did Elisha say?"

"He told me that you would certainly get well," Hazael answered. ¹⁵But on the following day Hazael took a blanket, soaked it in water, and smothered the king.

And Hazael succeeded Benhadad as king of Syria.

King Jehoram of Judah
(2 Chronicles 21:1–20)

16In the fifth year of the reign of Joram son of Ahab as king of Israel,r Jehoram son of Jehoshaphat became king of Judah 17at the age of thirty-two, and he ruled in Jerusalem for eight years. 18His wife was Ahab's daughter, and like the family of Ahab he followed the evil ways of the kings of Israel. He sinned against the LORD, 19but the LORD was not willing to destroy Judah, because he had promised his servant David that his descendants would always continue to rule.

20During Jehoram's reign Edom revolted against Judah and became an independent kingdom. 21So Jehoram set out with all his chariots to Zair, where the Edomite army surrounded them. During the night he and his chariot commanders managed to break out and escape, and his soldiers scattered to their homes. 22Edom has been independent ofs Judah ever since. During this same period the city of Libnah also revolted.

23Everything else that Jehoram did is recorded in *The History of the Kings of Judah.* 24Jehoram died and was buried in the royal tombs in David's City, and his son Ahaziah succeeded him as king.

King Ahaziah of Judah
(2 Chronicles 22:1–6)

25In the twelfth year of the reign of Joram son of Ahab as king of Israel, Ahaziah son of Jehoram became king of Judah 26at the age of twenty-two, and he ruled in Jerusalem for one year. His mother was Athaliah, the daughter of King Ahab and granddaughter of King Omri of Israel. 27Since Ahaziah was related to King Ahab by marriage, he sinned against the LORD, just as Ahab's family did.

28King Ahaziah joined King Joram of Israel in a war against King Hazael of Syria. The armies clashed at Ramoth in Gilead,

and Joram was wounded in battle. 29He returned to the city of Jezreel to recover from his wounds, and Ahaziah went there to visit him.

Jehu Is Anointed King of Israel

9 1Meanwhile the prophet Elisha called one of the young prophets and said to him, "Get ready and go to Ramoth in Gilead. Take this jar of olive oil with you, 2and when you get there look for Jehu, the son of Jehoshaphat and grandson of Nimshi. Take him to a private room away from his companions, 3pour this olive oil on his head, and say, 'The LORD proclaims that he anoints you king of Israel.' Then leave there as fast as you can."

4So the young prophet went to Ramoth, 5where he found the army officers in a conference. He said, "Sir, I have a message for you."

Jehu asked, "Which one of us are you speaking to?"

"To you, sir," he replied. 6Then the two of them went indoors, and the young prophet poured the olive oil on Jehu's head and said to him, "The LORD, the God of Israel, proclaims: 'I anoint you king of my people Israel. 7You are to kill your master the king, that son of Ahab, so that I may punish Jezebel for murdering my prophets and my other servants. 8All of Ahab's family and descendants are to die; I will get rid of every male in his family, young and old alike. 9I will treat his family as I did the families of King Jeroboam of Israel and of King Baasha of Israel. 10Jezebel will not be buried; her body will be eaten by dogs in the territory of Jezreel.' " After saying this, the young prophet left the room and fled.

11Jehu went back to his fellow officers, who asked him, "Is everything all right? What did that crazy fellow want with you?"

---

r **8:16** *Some ancient translations* Israel; *Hebrew* Israel, Jehoshaphat being king of Judah.   s **8:22** independent of; *or* in revolt against.
8:19 1 Kings 11:36   **8:20** Gen 27:40   **9:6** 1 Kings 19:16   **9:10** 1 Kings 21:23

Edom *(2 Kings 8:20–22)* **was not one of the Twelve Tribes of Israel. The people of Edom were descendants of Esau, Jacob's twin brother.**

"You know what he wanted," Jehu answered.

12 "No we don't!" they replied. "Tell us what he said!"

"He told me that the LORD proclaims: 'I anoint you king of Israel.' "

13 At once Jehu's fellow officers spread their cloaks at the top of the steps for Jehu to stand on, blew trumpets, and shouted, "Jehu is king!"

King Joram of Israel Is Killed

14-15 Then Jehu plotted against King Joram, who was in Jezreel, where he had gone to recover from the wounds which he had received in the battle at Ramoth against King Hazael of Syria. So Jehu said to his fellow officers, "If you are with me, make sure that no one slips out of Ramoth to go and warn the people in Jezreel." 16 Then he got into his chariot and set off for Jezreel. Joram had still not recovered, and King Ahaziah of Judah was there, visiting him.

17 A guard on duty in the watchtower at Jezreel saw Jehu and his men approaching. "I see some men riding up!" he called out.

Joram replied, "Send a rider to find out if they are friends or enemies."

18 The messenger rode out to Jehu and said to him, "The king wants to know if you come as a friend."

"That's none of your business!" Jehu answered. "Fall in behind me."

The guard on the watchtower reported that the messenger had reached the group but was not returning. 19 Another messenger was sent out, who asked Jehu the same question. Again Jehu answered, "That's none of your business! Fall in behind me."

20 Once more the guard reported that the messenger had reached the group but was not returning. And he added, "The leader of the group is driving his chariot like a madman, just like Jehu!"

21 "Get my chariot ready," King Joram ordered. It was done, and he and King Ahaziah rode out, each in his own chariot, to meet Jehu. They met him at the field which had belonged to Naboth. 22 "Are you coming in peace?" Joram asked him.

"How can there be peace," Jehu answered, "when we still have all the witchcraft and idolatry that your mother Jezebel started?"

23 "It's treason, Ahaziah!" Joram cried out, as he turned his chariot around and fled. 24 Jehu drew his bow, and with all his strength shot an arrow that struck Joram in the back and pierced his heart. Joram fell dead in his chariot, 25 and Jehu said to his aide Bidkar, "Get his body and throw it in the field that belonged to Naboth. Remember that when you and I were riding together behind King Joram's father Ahab, the LORD spoke these words against Ahab: 26 'I saw the murder of Naboth and his sons yesterday. And I promise that I will punish you here in this same field.' So take Joram's body," Jehu ordered his aide, "and throw it in the field that belonged to Naboth, so as to fulfill the LORD's promise."

King Ahaziah of Judah Is Killed

27 King Ahaziah saw what happened, so he fled in his chariot toward the town of Beth Haggan, pursued by Jehu. "Kill him too!" Jehu ordered his men, and they wounded him[i] as he drove his chariot on the road up to Gur, near the town of Ibleam. But he managed to keep on going until he reached the city of Megiddo, where he died. 28 His officials took his body back to Jerusalem in a chariot and buried him in the royal tombs in David's City.

29 Ahaziah had become king of Judah in the eleventh year that Joram son of Ahab was king of Israel.

---

[i] 9:27 *Some ancient translations* and they wounded him; *Hebrew does not have these words.*
9:26 1 Kings 21:19

Jezebel insults Jehu by calling him a Zimri. Read the story of Zimri in 1 Kings 16:8–12 to see what he did.

Queen Jezebel Is Killed

30Jehu arrived in Jezreel. Jezebel, having heard what had happened, put on eye shadow, arranged her hair, and stood looking down at the street from a window in the palace. 31As Jehu came through the gate, she called out, "You Zimri!ᵘ You assassin! Why are you here?"

32Jehu looked up and shouted, "Who is on my side?" Two or three palace officials looked down at him from a window, 33and Jehu said to them, "Throw her down!" They threw her down, and her blood spattered on the wall and on the horses. Jehu drove his horses and chariot over her body, 34entered the palace, and had a meal. Only then did he say, "Take that cursed woman and bury her; after all, she is a king's daughter." 35But the men who went out to bury her found nothing except her skull and the bones of her hands and feet. 36When they reported this to Jehu, he said, "This is what the LORD said would happen, when he spoke through his servant Elijah: 'Dogs will eat Jezebel's body in the territory of Jezreel. 37Her remains will be scattered there like dung, so that no one will be able to identify them.' "

The Descendants of Ahab Are Killed

10 ¹There were seventy descendants of King Ahab living in the city of Samaria. Jehu wrote a letter and sent copies to the rulers of the city,ᵛ to the leading citizens, and to the guardians of Ahab's descendants. The letter read: 2"You are in charge of the king's descendants, and you have at your disposal chariots, horses, weapons, and fortified cities. So then, as soon as you receive this letter, 3you are to choose the best qualified of the king's descendants, make him king, and fight to defend him."

4The rulers of Samaria were terrified. "How can we oppose Jehu," they said, "when neither King Joram nor King Ahaziah could?" 5So the officer in charge of the palace and the official in charge of the city, together with the leading citizens and the

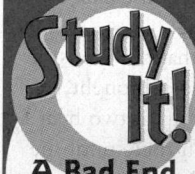

A Bad End

Do you remember the evil Queen Jezebel from the end of 1 Kings? The story of her death is told with drama and graphic violence. The author wanted to make a point—those who did not obey God would be punished. After she falls to her death, she is consumed by dogs—just as Elijah had prophesied. This was a great dishonor for someone who expected to be buried in a royal tomb.

The death of Queen Jezebel, King Joram, and his son King Ahaziah of Judah mark the end of the Omri dynasty. King Omri and his descendants all got the "thumbs down" from the author. They had each sinned against the Lord by worshiping foreign gods and treating the people of their kingdoms with injustice. Their violent deaths are seen as punishment for leading Israel astray.

— 2 Kings 9:30–37

guardians, sent this message to Jehu: "We are your servants, and we are ready to do anything you say. But we will not make anyone king; do whatever you think best."

6Jehu wrote them another letter: "If you are with me and are ready to follow my orders, bring the heads of King Ahab's descendants to me at Jezreel by this time tomorrow."

The seventy descendants of King Ahab were under the care of the leading citizens of Samaria, who were bringing them up. 7When Jehu's letter was received, the leaders of Samaria killed all seventy of Ahab's

ᵘ 9:31 ZIMRI: *An Israelite army officer who assassinated the king of Israel (see 1 Kings 16:8–12).*   ᵛ 10:1 *Some ancient translations* the city; *Hebrew* Jezreel.
9:36 1 Kings 21:23

descendants, put their heads in baskets, and sent them to Jehu at Jezreel.

⁸When Jehu was told that the heads of Ahab's descendants had been brought, he ordered them to be piled up in two heaps at the city gate and to be left there until the following morning. ⁹In the morning he went out to the gate and said to the people who were there, "I was the one who plotted against King Joram and killed him; you are not responsible for that. But who killed all these? ¹⁰This proves that everything that the LORD said about the descendants of Ahab will come true. The LORD has done what he promised through his prophet Elijah." ¹¹Then Jehu put to death all the other relatives of Ahab living in Jezreel, and all his officers, close friends, and priests; not one of them was left alive.

The Relatives of King Ahaziah Are Killed

¹²Jehu left Jezreel to go to Samaria. On the way, at a place called "Shepherds' Camp," ¹³he met some relatives of the late King Ahaziah of Judah and asked them, "Who are you?"

"Ahaziah's relatives," they answered. "We are going to Jezreel to pay our respects to the children of Queen Jezebel and to the rest of the royal family." ¹⁴Jehu ordered his men, "Take them alive!" They seized them, and he put them to death near a pit there. There were forty-two people in all, and not one of them was left alive.

All Remaining Relatives of Ahab Are Killed

¹⁵Jehu started out again, and on his way he was met by Jonadab son of Rechab. Jehu greeted him and said, "You and I think alike. Will you support me?"

"I will," Jonadab answered.

"Give me your hand, then," Jehu replied. They clasped hands, and Jehu helped him up into the chariot, ¹⁶saying, "Come with me and see for yourself how devoted I am to the LORD." And they rode on together to

Samaria. ¹⁷When they arrived there, Jehu killed all of Ahab's relatives, not sparing even one. This is what the LORD had told Elijah would happen.

The Worshipers of Baal Are Killed

¹⁸Jehu called the people of Samaria together and said, "King Ahab served the god Baal a little, but I will serve him much more. ¹⁹Call together all the prophets of Baal, all his worshipers, and all his priests. No one is excused; I am going to offer a great sacrifice to Baal, and whoever is not present will be put to death." (This was a trick on the part of Jehu by which he meant to kill all the worshipers of Baal.) ²⁰Then Jehu ordered, "Proclaim a day of worship in honor of Baal!" The proclamation was made, ²¹and Jehu sent word throughout all the land of Israel. All who worshiped Baal came; not one of them failed to come. They all went into the temple of Baal, filling it from one end to the other. ²²Then Jehu ordered the priest in charge of the sacred robes to bring the robes out and give them to the worshipers. ²³After that, Jehu himself went into the temple with Jonadab son of Rechab and said to the people there, "Make sure that only worshipers of Baal are present and that no worshiper of the LORD has come in." ²⁴Then he and Jonadab went in to offer sacrifices and burnt offerings to Baal. He had stationed eighty men outside the temple and had instructed them: "You are to kill all these people; anyone who lets one of them escape will pay for it with his life!"

²⁵As soon as Jehu had presented the offerings, he said to the guards and officers, "Go in and kill them all; don't let anyone escape!" They went in with drawn swords, killed them all, and dragged the bodies outside. Then they went on into the inner sanctuary of the temple, ²⁶brought out the sacred pillar that was there, and burned it. ²⁷So they destroyed the sacred pillar and the temple, and turned the temple into a latrine—which it still is today.

²⁸That was how Jehu wiped out the worship of Baal in Israel. ²⁹But he imitated

the sin of King Jeroboam, who led Israel into the sin of worshiping the gold bull-calves he set up in Bethel and in Dan. ³⁰The LORD said to Jehu, "You have done to Ahab's descendants everything I wanted you to do. So I promise you that your descendants, down to the fourth generation, will be kings of Israel." ³¹But Jehu did not obey with all his heart the Law of the LORD, the God of Israel; instead, he followed the example of Jeroboam, who led Israel into sin.

The Death of Jehu

³²At that time the LORD began to reduce the size of Israel's territory. King Hazael of Syria conquered all the Israelite territory ³³east of the Jordan, as far south as the town of Aroer on the Arnon River—this included the territories of Gilead and Bashan, where the tribes of Gad, Reuben, and East Manasseh lived.

³⁴Everything else that Jehu did, including his brave deeds, is recorded in *The History of the Kings of Israel.* ³⁵He died and was buried in Samaria, and his son Jehoahaz succeeded him as king. ³⁶Jehu had ruled in Samaria as king of Israel for twenty-eight years.

Queen Athaliah of Judah
(2 Chronicles 22:10—23:15)

11 ¹As soon as King Ahaziah's mother Athaliah learned of her son's murder, she gave orders for all the members of the royal family to be killed. ²Only Ahaziah's son Joash escaped. He was about to be killed with the others, but was rescued by his aunt Jehosheba, who was King Jehoram's daughter and Ahaziah's half sister. She took him and his nurse into a bedroom in the Temple and hid him from Athaliah, so that he was not killed. ³For six years Jehosheba took care of the boy and kept him hidden in the Temple, while Athaliah ruled as queen.

⁴But in the seventh year Jehoiada the priest sent for the officers in charge of the royal

Protectors and Defenders

The child Joash would never have survived if he had not been rescued by his aunt and then guarded by the priest. Most of us don't have to worry about assassination attempts, but we do face different kinds of troubles and need people around us who can protect us. Sometimes this protection comes when others help us make good choices. Young people are sometimes faced with things like cheating, lying, stealing, smoking, drinking, fighting, and other risky behaviors. If you make bad choices about these things, you could get hurt or even killed.

Who are the people in your life who have looked out for you? Who gives you guidance in making good choices to keep you from danger? Do you have friends who give you good advice? Is there an adult in your life you can really count on if you have a question or a problem? Think about who those protectors are in your life. Let them know how important they are to you.

— 2 Kings 11:1–12

bodyguard and of the palace guards, and told them to come to the Temple, where he made them agree under oath to what he planned to do. He showed them King Ahaziah's son Joash ⁵and gave them the following orders: "When you come on duty on the Sabbath, one third of you are to guard the palace; ⁶another third

Queen Athaliah tore her clothes when she saw that Joash had been crowned as king. This was an expression of sorrow or dismay.

are to stand guard at the Sur Gate, and the other third are to stand guard at the gate behind the other guards.[w] 7 The two groups that go off duty on the Sabbath are to stand guard at the Temple to protect the king. 8 You are to guard King Joash with drawn swords and stay with him wherever he goes. Anyone who comes near you is to be killed."

9 The officers obeyed Jehoiada's instructions and brought their men to him—those going off duty on the Sabbath and those going on duty. 10 He gave the officers the spears[x] and shields that had belonged to King David and had been kept in the Temple, 11 and he stationed the men with drawn swords all around the front of the Temple, to protect the king. 12 Then Jehoiada led Joash out, placed the crown on his head, and gave him a copy of the laws governing kingship. Then Joash was anointed and proclaimed king. The people clapped their hands and shouted, "Long live the king!"

13 Queen Athaliah heard the noise being made by the guards and the people, so she hurried to the Temple, where the crowd had gathered. 14 There she saw the new king standing by the column at the entrance of the Temple, as was the custom. He was surrounded by the officers and the trumpeters, and the people were all shouting joyfully and blowing trumpets. Athaliah tore her clothes in distress and shouted, "Treason! Treason!"

Athaliah tore her clothes in distress. (11:14)

15 Jehoiada did not want Athaliah killed in the Temple area, so he ordered the army officers: "Take her out between the rows of guards, and kill anyone who tries to rescue her." 16 They seized her, took her to the palace, and there at the Horse Gate they killed her.

Jehoiada's Reforms
(2 Chronicles 23:16–21)

17 The priest Jehoiada had King Joash and the people make a covenant with the LORD that they would be the LORD's people; he also made a covenant between the king and the people. 18 Then the people went to the temple of Baal and tore it down; they smashed the altars and the idols, and killed Mattan, the priest of Baal, in front of the altars.

Jehoiada put guards on duty at the Temple, 19 and then he, the officers, the royal bodyguard, and the palace guards escorted the king from the Temple to the palace, followed by all the people. Joash entered by the Guard Gate and took his place on the throne. 20 All the people were filled with happiness, and the city was quiet, now that Athaliah had been killed in the palace.

21 Joash became king of Judah at the age of seven.

King Joash of Judah
(2 Chronicles 24:1–16)

12 1 In the seventh year of the reign of King Jehu of Israel, Joash became king of Judah, and he ruled in Jerusalem for forty years. His mother was Zibiah from the city of Beersheba. 2 Throughout his life he did what pleased the LORD, because Jehoiada the priest instructed him. 3 However, the pagan places of worship were not destroyed, and the people continued to offer sacrifices and burn incense there.

---

[w] **11:6** *Hebrew has an additional word, the meaning of which is unclear.*   [x] **11:10** *Some ancient translations (and see 2 Chr 23:9)* spears; *Hebrew* spear.
11:14 2 Kings 23:3

4Joash called the priests and ordered them to save up the money paid in connection with the sacrifices in the Temple, both the dues paid for the regular sacrifices and the money given as freewill gifts. 5Each priest was to be responsible for the money brought by those he served, and the money was to be used to repair the Temple, as needed.

6But by the twenty-third year of Joash's reign the priests still had not made any repairs in the Temple. 7So he called in Jehoiada and the other priests and asked them, "Why aren't you repairing the Temple? From now on you are not to keep the money you receive; you must hand it over, so that the repairs can be made." 8The priests agreed to this and also agreed not to make the repairs in the Temple.

9Then Jehoiada took a box, made a hole in the lid, and placed the box by the altar, on the right side as one enters the Temple. The priests on duty at the entrance put in the box all the money given by the worshipers. 10Whenever there was a large amount of money in the box, the royal secretary and the High Priest would come, melt down the silver, and weigh it.*y* 11After recording the exact amount, they would hand the silver over to the men in charge of the work in the Temple, and these would pay the carpenters, the builders, 12the masons, and the stone cutters, buy the timber and the stones used in the repairs, and pay all other necessary expenses. 13None of the money, however, was used to pay for making silver cups, bowls, trumpets, or tools for tending the lamps, or any other article of silver or of gold. 14It was all used to pay the workers and to buy the materials used in the repairs. 15The men in charge of the work were thoroughly honest, so there was no need to require them to account for the funds. 16The money given for the repayment offerings and for the offerings for sin was not deposited in the box; it belonged to the priests.

17At that time King Hazael of Syria attacked the city of Gath and conquered it; then he decided to attack Jerusalem. 18King Joash of Judah took all the offerings that his predecessors Jehoshaphat, Jehoram, and Ahaziah had dedicated to the LORD, added to them his own offerings and all the gold in the treasuries of the Temple and the palace, and sent them all as a gift to King Hazael, who then led his army away from Jerusalem.

19Everything else that King Joash did is recorded in *The History of the Kings of Judah.*

20-21King Joash's officials plotted against him, and two of them, Jozacar son of Shimeath and Jehozabad son of Shomer, killed him at the house built on the land that was filled in on the east side of Jerusalem, on the road that goes down to Silla. Joash was buried in the royal tombs in David's City, and his son Amaziah succeeded him as king.

King Jehoahaz of Israel

13 1In the twenty-third year of the reign of Joash son of Ahaziah as king of Judah, Jehoahaz son of Jehu became king of Israel, and he ruled in Samaria for seventeen years. 2Like King Jeroboam before him, he sinned against the LORD and led Israel into sin; he never gave up his evil ways. 3So the LORD was angry with Israel, and he allowed King Hazael of Syria and his son Benhadad to defeat Israel time after time. 4Then Jehoahaz prayed to the LORD, and the LORD, seeing how harshly the king of Syria was oppressing the Israelites, answered his prayer. 5The LORD sent Israel a leader, who freed them from the Syrians, and so the Israelites lived in peace, as before. 6But they still did not give up the sins into which King Jeroboam had led Israel, but kept on*z* committing them; and the image of the goddess Asherah remained in Samaria.

7Jehoahaz had no armed forces left except fifty cavalry troops, ten chariots, and ten thousand foot soldiers, because the king of Syria had destroyed the rest, trampling them down like dust.

8Everything else that Jehoahaz did and all his brave deeds are recorded in *The History of the Kings of Israel.* 9He died and was buried

---

y **12:10** melt down the silver, and weigh it; *or* count the money, and tie it up in bags.   *z* **13:6** *Some ancient translations* kept on; *Hebrew* he kept on.
12:4 Ex 30:11–16   **12:15** 2 Kings 22:7   **12:16** Lev 7:7

Pray It!

The Same Old Sins

The Israelites kept committing the same sins. They couldn't seem to break their sinful habits. We can be like that sometimes. When we fall into bad or sinful habits, they can be very hard to break.

> God of Love,
> I know you want me to stay close to you.
> Whenever I sin it's like I'm
>   turning my back on you,
>   taking a step away from you,
>   refusing your gift of love.
> Help me to avoid the things that lead me into sin.
> Help me to seek you when I need forgiveness.
> Help me to remember both your love and your mercy. Amen.

— 2 Kings 13:1–11

in Samaria, and his son Jehoash succeeded him as king.

King Jehoash of Israel

10 In the thirty-seventh year of the reign of King Joash of Judah, Jehoash son of Jehoahaz became king of Israel, and he ruled in Samaria for sixteen years. 11 He too sinned against the LORD and followed the evil example of King Jeroboam, who had led Israel into sin. 12 Everything else that Jehoash did, including his bravery in the war against King Amaziah of Judah, is recorded in *The History of the Kings of Israel*. 13 Jehoash died and was buried in the royal tombs in Samaria, and his son Jeroboam II succeeded him as king.

The Death of Elisha

14 The prophet Elisha was sick with a fatal disease, and as he lay dying, King Jehoash of Israel went to visit him. "My father, my father!" he exclaimed as he wept. "You have been the mighty defender of Israel!"

15 "Get a bow and some arrows," Elisha ordered him. Jehoash got them, 16 and Elisha told him to get ready to shoot. The king did so, and Elisha placed his hands on the king's hands. 17 Then, following the prophet's instructions, the king opened the window that faced toward Syria. "Shoot the arrow!" Elisha ordered. As soon as the king shot the arrow, the prophet exclaimed, "You are the LORD's arrow, with which he will win victory over Syria. You will fight the Syrians in Aphek until you defeat them."

18 Then Elisha told the king to take the other arrows and strike the ground with them. The king struck the ground three times, and then stopped. 19 This made Elisha angry, and he said to the king, "You should have struck five or six times, and then you would have won complete victory over the Syrians; but now you will defeat them only three times."

20 Elisha died and was buried.

Every year bands of Moabites used to invade the land of Israel. 21 One time during a funeral, one of those bands was seen, and the people threw the corpse into Elisha's tomb and ran off.*a* As soon as the body came

---

a **13:21** *One ancient translation* and ran off; *Hebrew* and he ran off.
13:14 2 Kings 2:12

into contact with Elisha's bones, the man came back to life and stood up.

War between Israel and Syria

22King Hazael of Syria oppressed the Israelites during all of Jehoahaz' reign, 23but the LORD was kind and merciful to them. He would not let them be destroyed, but helped them because of his covenant with Abraham, Isaac, and Jacob. He has never forgotten his people.

24At the death of King Hazael of Syria his son Benhadad became king. 25Then King Jehoash of Israel defeated Benhadad three times and recaptured the cities that had been taken by Benhadad during the reign of Jehoahaz, the father of Jehoash.

King Amaziah of Judah
(2 Chronicles 25:1–24)

14 1In the second year of the reign of Jehoash son of Jehoahaz as king of Israel, Amaziah son of Joash became king of Judah 2at the age of twenty-five, and he ruled in Jerusalem for twenty-nine years. His mother was Jehoaddin from Jerusalem. 3He did what was pleasing to the LORD, but he was not like his ancestor King David; instead, he did what his father Joash had done. 4He did not tear down the pagan places of worship, and the people continued to offer sacrifices and burn incense there.

5As soon as Amaziah was firmly in power, he executed the officials who had killed his father, the king. 6However, he did not kill their children but followed what the LORD had commanded in the Law of Moses: "Parents are not to be put to death for crimes committed by their children, and children are not to be put to death for crimes committed by their parents; people are to be put to death only for a crime they themselves have committed."

7Amaziah killed ten thousand Edomite soldiers in Salt Valley; he captured the city of Sela in battle and called it Joktheel, the name it still has.

8Then Amaziah sent messengers to King Jehoash of Israel, challenging him to fight.b 9But King Jehoash sent back the following reply: "Once a thorn bush on the Lebanon Mountains sent a message to a cedar: 'Give your daughter in marriage to my son.' A wild animal passed by and trampled the bush down. 10Now Amaziah, you have defeated the Edomites, and you are filled with pride. Be satisfied with your fame and stay at home. Why stir up trouble that will only bring disaster on you and your people?"

11But Amaziah refused to listen, so King Jehoash marched out with his men and fought against him at Beth Shemesh in Judah. 12Amaziah's army was defeated, and all his soldiers fled to their homes. 13Jehoash took Amaziah prisoner, advanced on Jerusalem, and tore down the city wall from Ephraim Gate to the Corner Gate, a distance of two hundred yards. 14He took all the silver and gold he could find, all the Temple equipment and all the palace treasures, and carried them back to Samaria. He also took hostages with him.

15Everything else that Jehoash did, including his bravery in the war against King Amaziah of Judah, is recorded in *The History of the Kings of Israel*. 16Jehoash died and was buried in the royal tombs in Samaria, and his son Jeroboam II succeeded him as king.

The Death of King Amaziah of Judah
(2 Chronicles 25:25–28)

17King Amaziah of Judah lived fifteen years after the death of King Jehoash of Israel. 18Everything else that Amaziah did is recorded in *The History of the Kings of Judah*.

19There was a plot in Jerusalem to assassinate Amaziah, so he fled to the city of Lachish, but his enemies followed him there

---

b 14:8 challenging him to fight; *or* inviting him to a conference.
14:6 Deut 24:16

2 Kings

and killed him. 20His body was carried back to Jerusalem on a horse and was buried in the royal tombs in David's City. 21The people of Judah then crowned his sixteen-year-old son Uzziah as king. 22Uzziah reconquered and rebuilt Elath after his father's death.

King Jeroboam II of Israel

23In the fifteenth year of the reign of Amaziah son of Joash as king of Judah, Jeroboam son of Jehoash became king of Israel, and he ruled in Samaria for forty-one years. 24He sinned against the LORD, following the wicked example of his predecessor King Jeroboam son of Nebat, who led Israel into sin. 25He reconquered all the territory that had belonged to Israel, from Hamath Pass in the north to the Dead Sea in the south. This was what the LORD, the God of Israel, had promised through his servant the prophet Jonah son of Amittai from Gath Hepher. 26The LORD saw the terrible[c] suffering of the Israelites; there was no one at all to help them. 27But it was not the LORD's purpose to destroy Israel completely and forever, so he rescued them through King Jeroboam II. 28Everything else that Jeroboam II did, his brave battles, and how he restored Damascus and Hamath to Israel,[d] are all recorded in The History of the Kings of Israel. 29Jeroboam died and was buried in the royal tombs, and his son Zechariah succeeded him as king.

King Uzziah of Judah
(2 Chronicles 26:1–23)

15 1In the twenty-seventh year of the reign of King Jeroboam II of Israel, Uzziah son of Amaziah became king of Judah 2at the age of sixteen, and he ruled in Jerusalem for fifty-two years. His mother was Jecoliah from Jerusalem. 3Following the example of his father, he did what was pleasing to the LORD. 4But the pagan places of worship were not destroyed, and the people continued to offer sacrifices and burn incense there. 5The LORD struck Uzziah with a dreaded skin disease that stayed with him the rest of his life. He lived in a separate house, relieved of all duties, while his son Jotham governed the country.

6Everything else that Uzziah did is recorded in The History of the Kings of Judah. 7Uzziah died and was buried in the royal burial ground in David's City, and his son Jotham succeeded him as king.

King Zechariah of Israel

8In the thirty-eighth year of the reign of King Uzziah of Judah, Zechariah son of Jeroboam II became king of Israel, and he ruled in Samaria for six months. 9He, like his predecessors, sinned against the LORD. He followed the wicked example of King Jeroboam son of Nebat, who led Israel into sin. 10Shallum son of Jabesh conspired against King Zechariah, assassinated him at Ibleam,[e] and succeeded him as king. 11Everything else that Zechariah did is recorded in The History of the Kings of Israel. 12So the promise was fulfilled which the LORD had made to King Jehu: "Your descendants down to the fourth generation[f] will be kings of Israel."

King Shallum of Israel

13In the thirty-ninth year of the reign of King Uzziah of Judah, Shallum son of Jabesh became king of Israel, and he ruled in Samaria for one month. 14Menahem son of Gadi went from Tirzah to Samaria, assassinated Shallum, and succeeded him as king. 15Everything else that Shallum did, including an account of his

---

[c] **14:26** Some ancient translations terrible; Hebrew rebellious.   [d] **14:28** One ancient translation to Israel; Hebrew for Judah in Israel.   [e] **15:10** One ancient translation at Ibleam; Hebrew before people.   [f] **15:12** FOURTH GENERATION: Zechariah was Jehu's great-great-grandson.
14:25 Jon 1:1   **15:7** Isa 6:1   **15:12** 2 Kings 10:30

The History of the Kings of Judah and *The History of the Kings of Israel* are books that were lost long ago.

Plots and Schemes

Chapter 15 of 2 Kings mentions seven different kings, four of whom were assassinated! This was not a bright spot in the history of God's people. Their leaders were not good men, and they were not committed to following God.

You don't have to kill someone to plot against him or her. Once there was a group of teens who wanted to get revenge on another student. The group hacked into this student's computer and used it to write nasty posts about teachers on the student's Facebook page. At first the group got away with it. Everyone thought that the student being picked on was guilty. But soon a teacher realized what was really happening. All the people in the group received detentions for their behavior.

Beware of things that are done in secret! Plots and schemes—except for planning surprise birthday parties—are big trouble for everyone involved.

— 2 Kings, chapter 15

conspiracy, is recorded in *The History of the Kings of Israel*. 16 As Menahem was on his way from Tirzah, he completely destroyed the city of Tappuah,g its inhabitants, and the surrounding territory, because the city did not surrender to him. He even ripped open the bellies of all the pregnant women.

King Menahem of Israel

17 In the thirty-ninth year of the reign of King Uzziah of Judah, Menahem son of Gadi became king of Israel, and he ruled in Samaria for ten years. 18 He sinned against the LORD, for until the day of his death he followed the wicked example of King Jeroboam son of Nebat, who led Israel into sin. 19 Tiglath Pileser, the emperor of Assyria, invaded Israel, and Menahem gave him thirty-eight tons of silver to gain his support in strengthening Menahem's power over the country. 20 Menahem got the money from the rich men of Israel by forcing each one to contribute fifty pieces of silver. So Tiglath Pileser went back to his own country.

21 Everything else that Menahem did is recorded in *The History of the Kings of Israel*. 22 He died and was buried, and his son Pekahiah succeeded him as king.

King Pekahiah of Israel

23 In the fiftieth year of the reign of King Uzziah of Judah, Pekahiah son of Menahem became king of Israel, and he ruled in Samaria for two years. 24 He sinned against the LORD, following the wicked example of King Jeroboam son of Nebat, who led Israel into sin. 25 An officer of Pekahiah's forces, Pekah son of Remaliah, plotted with fifty men from Gilead, assassinated Pekahiah in the palace's inner fortressh in Samaria, and succeeded him as king.

26 Everything else that Pekahiah did is recorded in *The History of the Kings of Israel*.

King Pekah of Israel

27 In the fifty-second year of the reign of King Uzziah of Judah, Pekah son of Remaliah became king of Israel, and he ruled in Samaria for twenty years. 28 He sinned against the LORD, following the wicked example of King Jeroboam son of Nebat, who led Israel into sin.

29 It was while Pekah was king that Tiglath Pileser, the emperor of Assyria, captured the cities of Ijon, Abel Beth Maacah, Janoah, Kedesh, and Hazor, and the territories of Gilead, Galilee, and Naphtali, and took the people to Assyria as prisoners.

g 15:16 One ancient translation Tappuah; Hebrew Tiphsah, which is unclear.

h 15:25 Hebrew has two additional words, the meaning of

30In the twentieth year of the reign of Jotham son of Uzziah as king of Judah, Hoshea son of Elah plotted against King Pekah, assassinated him, and succeeded him as king. 31Everything else that Pekah did is recorded in *The History of the Kings of Israel*.

King Jotham of Judah
(2 Chronicles 27:1–9)

32In the second year of the reign of Pekah son of Remaliah as king of Israel, Jotham son of Uzziah became king of Judah 33at the age of twenty-five, and he ruled in Jerusalem for sixteen years. His mother was Jerusha, the daughter of Zadok. 34Following the example of his father Uzziah, Jotham did what was pleasing to the LORD. 35But the pagan places of worship were not destroyed, and the people continued to offer sacrifices and burn incense there. It was Jotham who built the North Gate of the Temple.

36Everything else that Jotham did is recorded in *The History of the Kings of Judah*. 37It was while he was king that the LORD first sent King Rezin of Syria and King Pekah of Israel to attack Judah. 38Jotham died and was buried in the royal tombs in David's City, and his son Ahaz succeeded him as king.

King Ahaz of Judah
(2 Chronicles 28:1–27)

16 1In the seventeenth year of the reign of Pekah son of Remaliah as king of Israel, Ahaz son of Jotham became king of Judah 2at the age of twenty, and he ruled in Jerusalem for sixteen years. He did not follow the good example of his ancestor King David; instead, he did what was not pleasing to the LORD his God 3and followed the example of the kings of Israel. He even sacrificed his own son as a burnt offering to idols, imitating the disgusting practice of the people whom the LORD had driven out of the land as the Israelites advanced. 4At the pagan places of worship, on the hills, and under every shady tree, Ahaz offered sacrifices and burned incense.

5King Rezin of Syria and King Pekah of Israel attacked Jerusalem and besieged it, but could not defeat Ahaz. (6At the same time the king of Edom*i* regained control of the city of Elath and drove out the Judeans who lived there. The Edomites settled in Elath and still live there.) 7Ahaz sent men to Tiglath Pileser, the emperor of Assyria, with this message: "I am your devoted servant. Come and rescue me from the kings of Syria and of Israel, who are attacking me." 8Ahaz took the silver and gold from the Temple and the palace treasury, and sent it as a present to the emperor. 9Tiglath Pileser, in answer to Ahaz' plea, marched out with his army against Damascus, captured it, killed King Rezin, and took the people to Kir as prisoners.

10When King Ahaz went to Damascus to meet Emperor Tiglath Pileser, he saw the altar there and sent back to Uriah the priest an exact model of it, down to the smallest details. 11So Uriah built an altar just like it and finished it before Ahaz returned. 12On his return from Damascus, Ahaz saw that the altar was finished, 13so he burned animal sacrifices and grain offerings on it and poured a wine offering and the blood of a fellowship offering on it. 14The bronze altar dedicated to the LORD was between the new altar and the Temple, so Ahaz moved it to the north side of his new altar. 15Then he ordered Uriah: "Use this large altar of mine for the morning burnt offerings and the evening grain offerings, for the burnt offerings and grain offerings of the king and the people, and for the people's wine offerings. Pour on it the blood of all the animals that are sacrificed. But keep the bronze altar for me to use for divination." 16Uriah did as the king commanded.

17King Ahaz took apart the bronze carts used in the Temple and removed the basins that were on them. He also took the bronze tank from the backs of the twelve bronze bulls and placed it on a stone foundation. 18And in order to please the Assyrian emperor, Ahaz also removed from the Temple the

---

i **16:6** *Probable text* the king of Edom; *Hebrew* King Rezin of Syria.
16:3 Deut 12:31   **16:5** Isa 7:1   **16:14** Ex 27:1, 2; 2 Chr 4:1   **16:17** 1 Kings 7:23–39; 2 Chr 4:2–6

2 Kings

platform for the royal throne and closed up the king's private entrance to the Temple.*j*

19Everything else that King Ahaz did is recorded in *The History of the Kings of Judah.* **20**Ahaz died and was buried in the royal tombs in David's City, and his son Hezekiah succeeded him as king.

King Hoshea of Israel

17 **1**In the twelfth year of the reign of King Ahaz of Judah, Hoshea son of Elah became king of Israel, and he ruled in Samaria for nine years. **2**He sinned against the LORD, but not as much as the kings who had ruled Israel before him. **3**Emperor Shalmaneser of Assyria made war against him; Hoshea surrendered to Shalmaneser and paid him tribute every year. **4**But one year Hoshea sent messengers to So, king of Egypt,*k* asking for his help, and stopped paying the annual tribute to Assyria. When Shalmaneser learned of this, he had Hoshea arrested and put in prison.

The Fall of Samaria

5Then Shalmaneser invaded Israel and besieged Samaria. In the third year of the siege, **6**which was the ninth year of the reign of Hoshea, the Assyrian emperor*l* captured Samaria, took the Israelites to Assyria as prisoners, and settled some of them in the city of Halah, some near the Habor River in the district of Gozan and some in the cities of Media.

7Samaria fell because the Israelites sinned against the LORD their God, who had rescued them from the king of Egypt and had led them out of Egypt. They worshiped other gods, **8**followed the customs of the people whom the LORD had driven out as his people advanced, and adopted customs introduced by the kings of Israel.*m* **9**The Israelites did*n* things that the LORD their

They worshiped other gods. (17:7)

God disapproved of. They built pagan places of worship in all their towns, from the smallest village to the largest city. **10**On all the hills and under every shady tree they put up stone pillars and images of the goddess Asherah, **11**and they burned incense on all the pagan altars, following the practice of the people whom the LORD had driven out of the land. They aroused the LORD's anger with all their wicked deeds **12**and disobeyed the LORD's command not to worship idols.

13The LORD had sent his messengers and prophets to warn Israel and Judah: "Abandon your evil ways and obey my commands, which are contained in the Law I gave to your ancestors and which I handed on to you through my servants the prophets." **14**But they would not obey; they were stubborn like their ancestors, who had not trusted in the LORD their God. **15**They refused to obey his instructions, they did not keep the covenant he had made with their ancestors, and they disregarded his warnings. They worshiped worthless idols and became worthless themselves, and they followed the customs of the surrounding nations, disobeying the LORD's command not to imitate them. **16**They broke all the laws of the LORD their God and made two metal bullcalves to worship; they also made an image of the goddess Asherah, worshiped the stars, and served the god Baal. **17**They sacrificed their sons and daughters as burnt offerings to pagan gods; they consulted mediums and fortunetellers, and they devoted themselves completely to doing what is wrong in the LORD's sight, and so aroused his anger. **18**The LORD was

---

j **16:18** *Verse 18 in Hebrew is unclear.*   *k* **17:4** So, king of Egypt; *or* the king of Egypt at Sais.   *l* **17:6** ASSYRIAN EMPEROR: *Probably Sargon II, the successor of Shalmaneser.*   *m* **17:8** *Probable text* and adopted . . . Israel; *Hebrew unclear.*   *n* **17:9** did; *or* said.
16:20 Isa 14:28   **17:10** 1 Kings 14:23   **17:16** 1 Kings 12:28   **17:17** Deut 18:10

Ahaz was a very bad king. Make a list of all the evil things he did from chapter 16. For a short chapter, it will be a pretty big list!

2 Kings

They disregarded his warnings. (17:15)

angry with the Israelites and banished them from his sight, leaving only the kingdom of Judah.

¹⁹But even the people of Judah did not obey the laws of the LORD their God; they imitated the customs adopted by the people of Israel. ²⁰The LORD rejected all the Israelites, punishing them and handing them over to cruel enemies until at last he had banished them from his sight.

²¹After the LORD had separated Israel from Judah, the Israelites made Jeroboam son of Nebat their king. Jeroboam caused them to abandon the LORD and led them into terrible sins. ²²They followed Jeroboam and continued to practice all the sins he had committed, ²³until at last the LORD banished them from his sight, as he had warned through his servants the prophets that he would do. So the people of Israel were taken into exile to Assyria, where they still live.

The Assyrians Settle in Israel

²⁴The emperor of Assyria took people from the cities of Babylon, Cuth, Ivvah, Hamath, and Sepharvaim, and settled them in the cities of Samaria*ᵒ* in place of the exiled Israelites. They took possession of these cities and lived there. ²⁵When they first settled there, they did not worship the LORD, and so he sent lions, which killed some of them. ²⁶The emperor of Assyria was told that the people he had settled in the cities of Samaria did not know the law of the god of that land, and so the god had sent

Monkey See Monkey Do

People have a funny habit of imitating one another's behavior. The Israelites who settled in Samaria began to imitate the practices of the people who had lived there before them. They worshiped other gods and even built idols to them. People imitate bad behavior for all kinds of reasons—to fit in, so people will be impressed with them, sometimes just out of curiosity.

Maybe you've had friends do this. They start hanging around with a new group of people. They dress differently than they used to, listen to different music, and do things they wouldn't have done before. Maybe you've even done this yourself. Part of it is just the process of finding out who you want to be. It can be a problem, though. If you're always looking for someone else to decide what's right and wrong for you, you can end up like the Israelites. You will be doing things that you know are really wrong. It's okay to want to fit in, but take a close look at your behavior. Does it match up with what you say you believe? Do your actions fit the person you are and want to become?

— 2 Kings 17:7–18

lions, which were killing them. ²⁷So the emperor commanded: "Send back one of the priests we brought as prisoners; have him*ᵖ* go back and live there, in order to teach the

---

ᵒ **17:24** SAMARIA: *The name of the capital city was applied to the territory of the former kingdom of Israel.*
ᵖ **17:27** *Some ancient translations* him; *Hebrew* them.

In Jesus' time Samaria was seen as a place of polluted religion. Read these stories about Samaritans in the New Testament: John 4:1–26 and Luke 10:30–37.

people the law of the god of that land." 28So an Israelite priest who had been deported from Samaria went and lived in Bethel, where he taught the people how to worship the LORD.

29But the people who settled in Samaria continued to make their own idols, and they placed them in the shrines that the Israelites had built. Each different group made idols in the cities they were living in: 30the people of Babylon made idols of the god Succoth Benoth; the people of Cuth, idols of Nergal; the people of Hamath, idols of Ashima; 31the people of Ivvah, idols of Nibhaz and Tartak; and the people of Sepharvaim sacrificed their children as burnt offerings to their gods Adrammelech and Anammelech. 32These people also worshiped the LORD and chose from among their own number all sorts of people to serve as priests at the pagan places of worship and to offer sacrifices for them there. 33So they worshiped the LORD, but they also worshiped their own gods according to the customs of the countries from which they had come.

34They still carry on their old customs to this day. They do not worship the LORD nor do they obey the laws and commands which he gave to the descendants of Jacob, whom he named Israel. 35The LORD had made a covenant with them and had ordered them: "Do not worship other gods; do not bow down to them or serve them or offer sacrifices to them. 36You shall obey me, the LORD, who brought you out of Egypt with great power and strength; you are to bow down to me and offer sacrifices to me. 37You shall always obey the laws and commands that I wrote for you. You shall not obey other gods, 38and you shall not forget the covenant I made with you. 39You shall obey me, the LORD your God, and I will rescue you from your enemies." 40But those people would not listen, and they continued to follow their old customs.

41So those people worshiped the LORD, but they also worshiped their idols; and to this day their descendants continue to do the same.

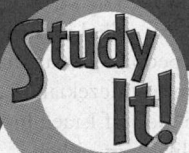

One of the Good Guys

As each king is named in 1 and 2 Kings, the author tells us either that "he sinned against the LORD" or "he did what was pleasing to the LORD." The kings who worshiped only God, resisted the pagan gods, treated people fairly, and destroyed their idols and altars are the good guys. King Hezekiah was one of the good guys. He is even compared with the great King David who was thought of as the most faithful, the most devoted to the Lord, of any king, ever.

This doesn't mean that King Hezekiah's life was without problems. The Assyrians tried to conquer the kingdom of Judah after taking over the northern kingdom of Israel. Because Hezekiah turned to God and relied on the advice of the prophet Isaiah, the Assyrians eventually turned away. But Hezekiah got a good scare.

— 2 Kings 18:1–8

King Hezekiah of Judah
(2 Chronicles 29:1, 2; 31:1)

18 1In the third year of the reign of Hoshea son of Elah as king of Israel, Hezekiah son of Ahaz became king of Judah 2at the age of twenty-five, and he ruled in Jerusalem for twenty-nine years. His mother was Abijah, the daughter of Zechariah. 3Following the example of his ancestor King David, he did what was pleasing to the LORD. 4He destroyed the pagan places of worship, broke the stone pillars, and cut down the images of the goddess Asherah. He

also broke in pieces the bronze snake that Moses had made, which was called Nehushtan. Up to that time the people of Israel had burned incense in its honor. [5] Hezekiah trusted in the LORD, the God of Israel; Judah never had another king like him, either before or after his time. [6] He was faithful to the LORD and never disobeyed him, but carefully kept all the commands that the LORD had given Moses. [7] So the LORD was with him, and he was successful in everything he did. He rebelled against the emperor of Assyria and refused to submit to him. [8] He defeated the Philistines and raided their settlements, from the smallest village to the largest city, including Gaza and its surrounding territory.

[9] In the fourth year of Hezekiah's reign—which was the seventh year of King Hoshea's reign over Israel—Emperor Shalmaneser of Assyria invaded Israel and besieged Samaria. [10] In the third year of the siege Samaria fell; this was the sixth year of Hezekiah's reign and the ninth year of Hoshea's reign. [11] The Assyrian emperor[q] took the Israelites to Assyria as prisoners and settled some of them in the city of Halah, some near the Habor River in the district of Gozan, and some in the cities of Media.

[12] Samaria fell because the Israelites did not obey the LORD their God, but broke the covenant he had made with them and disobeyed all the laws given by Moses, the servant of the LORD. They would not listen and they would not obey.

The Assyrians Threaten Jerusalem
(2 Chronicles 32:1–19; Isaiah 36:1–22)

[13] In the fourteenth year of the reign of King Hezekiah, Sennacherib, the emperor of Assyria, attacked the fortified cities of Judah and conquered them. [14] Hezekiah sent a message to Sennacherib, who was in Lachish: "I have done wrong; please stop your attack, and I will pay whatever you demand." The emperor's answer was that Hezekiah should send him ten tons of silver and one ton of gold. [15] Hezekiah sent him all the silver in the Temple and in the palace treasury; [16] he also

stripped the gold from the temple doors and the gold with which he himself had covered the doorposts, and he sent it all to Sennacherib. [17] The Assyrian emperor sent a large army from Lachish to attack Hezekiah at Jerusalem; it was commanded by his three highest officials. When they arrived at Jerusalem, they occupied the road where the cloth makers work by the ditch that brings water from the upper pool. [18] Then they sent for King Hezekiah, and three of his officials went out to meet them: Eliakim son of Hilkiah, who was in charge of the palace; Shebna, the court secretary; and Joah son of Asaph, who was in charge of the records. [19] One of the Assyrian officials told them that the emperor wanted to know what made King Hezekiah so confident. [20] He demanded, "Do you think that words can take the place of military skill and might? Who do you think will help you rebel against Assyria? [21] You are expecting Egypt to help you, but that would be like using a reed as a walking stick—it would break and jab your hand. That is what the king of Egypt is like when anyone relies on him."

[22] The Assyrian official went on, "Or will you tell me that you are relying on the LORD your God? It was the LORD's shrines and altars that Hezekiah destroyed, when he told the people of Judah and Jerusalem to worship only at the altar in Jerusalem. [23] I will make a bargain with you in the name of the emperor. I will give you two thousand horses if you can find that many men to ride them! [24] You are no match for even the lowest ranking Assyrian official, and yet you

Sennacherib . . . attacked the fortified cities. (18:13)

expect the Egyptians to send you chariots and cavalry! 25Do you think I have attacked your country and destroyed it without the LORD's help? The LORD himself told me to attack it and destroy it."

26Then Eliakim, Shebna, and Joah told the official, "Speak Aramaic to us, sir. We understand it. Don't speak Hebrew; all the people on the wall are listening."

27He replied, "Do you think you and the king are the only ones the emperor sent me to say all these things to? No, I am also talking to the people who are sitting on the wall, who will have to eat their excrement and drink their urine, just as you will."

28Then the official stood up and shouted in Hebrew, "Listen to what the emperor of Assyria is telling you! 29He warns you not to let Hezekiah deceive you. Hezekiah can't save you. 30And don't let him persuade you to rely on the LORD. Don't think that the LORD will save you and that he will stop our Assyrian army from capturing your city. 31Don't listen to Hezekiah. The emperor of Assyria commands you to come out of the city and surrender. You will all be allowed to eat grapes from your own vines and figs from your own trees, and to drink water from your own wells—32until the emperor resettles you in a country much like your own, where there are vineyards to give wine and there is grain for making bread; it is a land of olives, olive oil, and honey. If you do what he commands, you will not die, but live. Don't let Hezekiah fool you into thinking that the LORD will rescue you. 33Did the gods of any other nations save their countries from the emperor of Assyria? 34Where are they now, the gods of Hamath and Arpad? Where are the gods of Sepharvaim, Hena, and Ivvah? Did anyone save Samaria? 35When did any of the gods of all these countries ever save their country from our emperor? Then what makes you think the LORD can save Jerusalem?"

36The people kept quiet, just as King Hezekiah had told them to; they did not say a word. 37Then Eliakim, Shebna, and Joah

The official stood up and shouted in Hebrew. (18:28)

tore their clothes in grief, and went and reported to the king what the Assyrian official had said.

The King Asks Isaiah's Advice
(Isaiah 37:1–7)

19 1As soon as King Hezekiah heard their report, he tore his clothes in grief, put on sackcloth, and went to the Temple of the LORD. 2He sent Eliakim, the official in charge of the palace, Shebna, the court secretary, and the senior priests to the prophet Isaiah son of Amoz. They also were wearing sackcloth. 3This is the message which he told them to give Isaiah: "Today is a day of suffering; we are being punished and are in disgrace. We are like a woman who is ready to give birth, but is too weak to do it. 4The Assyrian emperor has sent his chief official to insult the living God. May the LORD your God hear these insults and punish those who spoke them. So pray to God for those of our people who survive."

5When Isaiah received King Hezekiah's message, 6he sent back this answer: "The LORD tells you not to let the Assyrians frighten you with their claims that he cannot save you. 7The LORD will cause the emperor to hear a rumor that will make him go back to his own country, and the LORD will have him killed there."

Remember how Israel split into two kingdoms? Second Kings 18:9–12 tells how the northern kingdom was taken over by the Assyrians in 721 BC.

Pray It!

Pour Out Your Heart

Have you ever felt hopeless? Like the world was closing in on you? King Hezekiah must have felt like that. The Assyrian Emperor sent a threatening letter meant to frighten Hezekiah and drive him to despair. Instead Hezekiah went to the Temple and poured out his heart to the Lord. Sometimes we need to do that, too.

> *Dear God,*
> *I don't know what to do,*
> *The situation seems hopeless.*
> *I don't want to give up, but I don't see a way out.*
> *I know we cannot solve this by ourselves.*
> *We can only do it with your help.*
> *Be with us, Lord.*
> *Guide us, protect us, and give us courage.*
> *I know we can only get through this with you. Amen.*

— 2 Kings 19:14–19

The Assyrians Send Another Threat
(Isaiah 37:8–20)

⁸The Assyrian official learned that the emperor had left Lachish and was fighting against the nearby city of Libnah; so he went there to consult him. ⁹Word reached the Assyrians that the Egyptian army, led by King Tirhakah of Ethiopia,ʳ was coming to attack them. When the emperor heard this, he sent a letter to King Hezekiah of Judah ¹⁰to tell him, "The god you are trusting in has told you that you will not fall into my hands, but don't let that deceive you. ¹¹You have heard what an Assyrian emperor does to any country he decides to destroy. Do you think that you can escape? ¹²My ancestors destroyed the cities of Gozan, Haran, and Rezeph, and killed the people of Betheden who lived in Telassar, and none of their gods could save them. ¹³Where are the kings of the cities of Hamath, Arpad, Sepharvaim, Hena, and Ivvah?"

¹⁴King Hezekiah took the letter from the messengers and read it. Then he went to the Temple, placed the letter there in the presence of the LORD, ¹⁵and prayed, "O LORD, the God of Israel, seated on your throne above the winged creatures, you alone are God, ruling all the kingdoms of the world. You created the earth and the sky. ¹⁶Now, LORD, look at what is happening to us. Listen to all the things that Sennacherib is saying to insult you, the living God. ¹⁷We all know, LORD, that the emperors of Assyria have destroyed many nations, made their lands desolate, ¹⁸and burned up their gods—which were no gods at all, only images of wood and stone made by human hands. ¹⁹Now, LORD our God, rescue us from the Assyrians, so that all the nations of the world will know that only you, O LORD, are God."

ʳ **19:9** *Hebrew* Cush: *Cush is the ancient name of the extensive territory south of the First Cataract of the Nile River. This region was called Ethiopia in Graeco-Roman times, and included within its borders most of modern Sudan and some of present-day Ethiopia (Abyssinia).*

19:15 Ex 25:22

How does Hezekiah know that he will recover from his illness? What sign does he ask for?

Isaiah's Message to the King
(Isaiah 37:21–38)

20 Then Isaiah sent a message telling King Hezekiah that in answer to the king's prayer 21 the LORD had said, "The city of Jerusalem laughs at you, Sennacherib, and makes fun of you. 22 Whom do you think you have been insulting and ridiculing? You have been disrespectful to me, the holy God of Israel. 23 You sent your messengers to boast to me that with all your chariots you had conquered the highest mountains of Lebanon. You boasted that there you cut down the tallest cedars and the finest cypress trees and that you reached the deepest parts of the forests. 24 You boasted that you dug wells and drank water in foreign lands and that the feet of your soldiers tramped the Nile River dry.

25 "Have you never heard that I planned all this long ago? And now I have carried it out. I gave you the power to turn fortified cities into piles of rubble. 26 The people who lived there were powerless; they were frightened and stunned. They were like grass in a field or weeds growing on a roof when the hot east wind blasts them.ˢ

27 "But I know everything about you, what you do and where you go. I know how you rage against me. 28 I have received the report of that rage and that pride of yours, and now I will put a hook through your nose and a bit in your mouth, and take you back by the same road you came."

29 Then Isaiah said to King Hezekiah, "Here is a sign of what will happen. This year and next you will have only wild grain to eat, but the following year you will be able to plant your grain and harvest it, and plant vines and eat grapes. 30 Those in Judah who survive will flourish like plants that send roots deep into the ground and produce fruit. 31 There will be people in Jerusalem and on Mount Zion who will survive, because the LORD is determined to make this happen.

32 "And this is what the LORD has said about the Assyrian emperor: 'He will not enter this city or shoot a single arrow against it. No soldiers with shields will come near the city, and no siege mounds will be built

around it. 33 He will go back by the same road he came, without entering this city. I, the LORD, have spoken. 34 I will defend this city and protect it, for the sake of my own honor and because of the promise I made to my servant David.' "

35 That night an angel of the LORD went to the Assyrian camp and killed 185,000 soldiers. At dawn the next day there they lay, all dead! 36 Then the Assyrian emperor Sennacherib withdrew and returned to Nineveh. 37 One day, when he was worshiping in the temple of his god Nisroch, two of his sons, Adrammelech and Sharezer, killed him with their swords and then escaped to the land of Ararat. Another of his sons, Esarhaddon, succeeded him as emperor.

King Hezekiah's Illness and Recovery
(Isaiah 38:1–8, 21, 22; 2 Chronicles 32:24–26)

20 1 About this time King Hezekiah became sick and almost died. The prophet Isaiah son of Amoz went to see him and said to him, "The LORD tells you that you are to put everything in order, because you will not recover. Get ready to die."

2 Hezekiah turned his face to the wall and prayed: 3 "Remember, LORD, that I have served you faithfully and loyally and that I have always tried to do what you wanted me to." And he began to cry bitterly.

4 Isaiah left the king, but before he had passed through the central courtyard of the palace the LORD told him 5 to go back to Hezekiah, ruler of the LORD's people, and say to him, "I, the LORD, the God of your ancestor David, have heard your prayer and seen your tears. I will heal you, and in three days you will go to the Temple. 6 I will let you live fifteen years longer. I will rescue you and this city Jerusalem from the emperor of Assyria. I will defend this city, for the sake of my own honor and because of the promise I made to my servant David."

7 Then Isaiah told the king's attendants to put on his boil a paste made of figs, and he would get well.ᵗ 8 King Hezekiah asked, "What is the sign to prove that the LORD

ˢ **19:26** *Probable text* when the hot east wind blasts them; *Hebrew* blasted before they are grown.   ᵗ **20:7** *One ancient translation (and see Isa 38:21)* figs, and he would get well; *Hebrew* figs. They did so, and he got well.

will heal me and that three days later I will be able to go to the Temple?"

9Isaiah replied, "The LORD will give you a sign to prove that he will keep his promise. Now, would you prefer to have the shadow on the stairway go forward ten steps or go back ten steps?"*u*

10Hezekiah answered, "It's easy to have the shadow go forward ten steps!*v* Have it go back ten steps."*v*

11Isaiah prayed to the LORD, and the LORD made the shadow go back ten steps*v* on the stairway*w* set up by King Ahaz.

Messengers from Babylonia
(Isaiah 39:1–8)

12About that same time the king of Babylonia, Merodach Baladan, the son of Baladan, heard that King Hezekiah had been sick, so he sent him a letter and a present. 13Hezekiah welcomed the messengers and showed them his wealth—his silver and gold, his spices and perfumes, and all his military equipment. There was nothing in his storerooms or anywhere in his kingdom that he did not show them. 14Then the prophet Isaiah went to King Hezekiah and asked, "Where did these men come from and what did they say to you?"

Hezekiah answered, "They came from a very distant country, from Babylonia."

15"What did they see in the palace?"

"They saw everything. There is nothing in the storerooms that I didn't show them."

16Isaiah then told the king, "The LORD Almighty says that 17a time is coming when everything in your palace, everything that your ancestors have stored up to this day, will be carried off to Babylonia. Nothing will be left. 18Some of your own direct descendants will be taken away and made eunuchs to serve in the palace of the king of Babylonia."

19King Hezekiah understood this to mean that there would be peace and security during his lifetime, so he replied, "The message you have given me from the LORD is good."

The End of Hezekiah's Reign
(2 Chronicles 32:32, 33)

20Everything else that King Hezekiah did, his brave deeds, and an account of how he built a reservoir and dug a tunnel to bring water into the city, are all recorded in *The History of the Kings of Judah.* 21Hezekiah died, and his son Manasseh succeeded him as king.

King Manasseh of Judah
(2 Chronicles 33:1–20)

21 1Manasseh was twelve years old when he became king of Judah, and he ruled in Jerusalem for fifty-five years. His mother was Hephzibah. 2Following the disgusting practices of the nations whom the LORD had driven out of the land as his people advanced, Manasseh sinned against the LORD. 3He rebuilt the pagan places of worship that his father Hezekiah had destroyed; he built altars for the worship of Baal and made an image of the goddess Asherah, as King Ahab of Israel had done. Manasseh also worshiped the stars. 4He built pagan altars in the Temple, the place that the LORD had said was where he should be worshiped. 5In the two courtyards of the Temple he built altars for the worship of the stars. 6He sacrificed his son as a burnt offering. He practiced divination and magic and consulted*x* fortunetellers and mediums. He sinned greatly against the LORD and stirred up his anger. 7He placed the symbol of the goddess Asherah in the Temple, the place about which the LORD had said to David and his son Solomon: "Here in Jerusalem, in this Temple, is the place that I have chosen out of all the territory of the twelve tribes of Israel as the place where I am to be worshiped. 8And if the people of Israel will obey all my commands and keep the whole Law that my servant Moses gave them, then I will not allow them to be driven out of the land that I gave to their ancestors." 9But the people of Judah did not obey the LORD, and

Pray It!

In the Face of Evil

King Manasseh was powerful, violent, and brutal. He ruled longer than any other Israelite king. He followed the good King Hezekiah and led people astray. How could Hezekiah's son turn out so bad?

Where do we see this kind of behavior in the world today? Think of some of the places, people, or situations that are violent today: war, fighting, abuse, murder. What about the things that lead people astray? Greed, materialism, the media, peer pressure. How do you deal with these things in your own life? Do you try not to think about them? One thing we can do in the face of evil is to pray—for strength to resist it and for the power to change it. Read Psalm 71 for comfort and strength against evil.

— 2 Kings 21:1–10

Manasseh led them to commit even greater sins than those committed by the nations whom the LORD had driven out of the land as his people advanced.

[10] Through his servants the prophets the LORD said, [11] "King Manasseh has done these disgusting things, things far worse than what the Canaanites did; and with his idols he has led the people of Judah into sin. [12] So I, the LORD God of Israel, will bring such a disaster on Jerusalem and Judah that everyone who hears about it will be stunned. [13] I will punish Jerusalem as I did Samaria, as I did King Ahab of Israel and his descendants. I will wipe Jerusalem clean of its people, as clean as a plate that has been wiped and turned upside down. [14] I will abandon the people who survive, and will hand them over to their enemies, who will conquer them and plunder their land. [15] I will do this to my people because they have sinned against me and have stirred up my anger from the time their ancestors came out of Egypt to this day."

[16] Manasseh killed so many innocent people that the streets of Jerusalem were flowing with blood; he did this in addition to leading the people of Judah into idolatry, causing them to sin against the LORD.

[17] Everything else that Manasseh did, including the sins he committed, is recorded in *The History of the Kings of Judah*. [18] Manasseh died and was buried in the palace garden, the garden of Uzza, and his son Amon succeeded him as king.

King Amon of Judah
(2 Chronicles 33:21–25)

[19] Amon was twenty-two years old when he became king of Judah, and he ruled in Jerusalem for two years. His mother was Meshullemeth, the daughter of Haruz from the town of Jotbah. [20] Like his father Manasseh, he sinned against the LORD; [21] he imitated his father's actions, and he worshiped the idols that his father had worshiped. [22] He rejected the LORD, the God of his ancestors, and disobeyed the LORD's commands.

[23] Amon's officials plotted against him and assassinated him in the palace. [24] The people of Judah killed Amon's assassins and made his son Josiah king.

[25] Everything else that Amon did is recorded in *The History of the Kings of Judah*.

Compare King Manasseh with King Josiah in 2 Kings, chapters 22–23. What words would you use to describe each of them?

26 Amon was buried in the tomb in the garden of Uzza, and his son Josiah succeeded him as king.

King Josiah of Judah
(2 Chronicles 34:1, 2)

22 ¹Josiah was eight years old when he became king of Judah, and he ruled in Jerusalem for thirty-one years. His mother was Jedidah, the daughter of Adaiah from the town of Bozkath. ²Josiah did what was pleasing to the LORD; he followed the example of his ancestor King David, strictly obeying all the laws of God.

The Book of the Law Is Discovered
(2 Chronicles 34:8–28)

³In the eighteenth year of his reign, King Josiah sent the court secretary Shaphan, the son of Azaliah and grandson of Meshullam, to the Temple with the order: ⁴"Go to the High Priest Hilkiah and get a report on the amount of money that the priests on duty at the entrance to the Temple have collected from the people. ⁵Tell him to give the money to the men who are in charge of the repairs in the Temple. They are to pay ⁶the carpenters, the builders, and the masons, and buy the timber and the stones used in the repairs. ⁷The men in charge of the work are thoroughly honest, so there is no need to require them to account for the funds."

⁸Shaphan delivered the king's order to Hilkiah, and Hilkiah told him that he had found the book of the Law in the Temple. Hilkiah gave him the book, and Shaphan read it. ⁹Then he went back to the king and reported: "Your servants have taken the money that was in the Temple and have handed it over to the men in charge of the repairs." ¹⁰And then he said, "I have here a book that Hilkiah gave me." And he read it aloud to the king.

¹¹When the king heard the book being read, he tore his clothes in dismay, ¹²and gave

the following order to Hilkiah the priest, to Ahikam son of Shaphan, to Achbor son of Micaiah, to Shaphan, the court secretary, and to Asaiah, the king's attendant: ¹³"Go and consult the LORD for me and for all the people of Judah about the teachings of this book. The LORD is angry with us because our ancestors have not done what this book says must be done."

¹⁴Hilkiah, Ahikam, Achbor, Shaphan, and Asaiah went to consult a woman named Huldah, a prophet who lived in the newer part of Jerusalem. (Her husband Shallum, the

Live It!

An Amazing Woman

We know that King Josiah is going to be a good king because he "did what was pleasing to the LORD" (2 Kings 22:2). But after all those years of evil under King Manasseh, people didn't know how God wanted them to live anymore. Then someone found a book of the Law of Moses. After reading it and realizing how far astray they had gone from the Law, King Josiah was worried and afraid.

So King Josiah looked for guidance. He sent his aides out to find the prophet and holy woman Huldah. Huldah had words of challenge and words of comfort for the king. To whom do you go when you need guidance or advice, when you are worried or afraid? Who are the Huldahs in your life? Who are the people who can help you see right and wrong?

— 2 Kings, chapter 22

22:1 Jer 3:6   22:7 2 Kings 12:15

Before reading 2 Kings, had you ever heard of the prophet Huldah? How many other women can you name from the Bible?

son of Tikvah and grandson of Harhas, was
in charge of the Temple robes.) They
described to her what had happened, ¹⁵and
she told them to go back to the king and
give him ¹⁶the following message from the
LORD: "I am going to punish Jerusalem and
all its people, as written in the book that the
king has read. ¹⁷They have rejected me and
have offered sacrifices to other gods, and so
have stirred up my anger by all they have
done. My anger is aroused against Jerusalem,
and it will not die down. ¹⁸As for the king
himself, this is what I, the LORD God of
Israel, say: You listened to what is written in
the book, ¹⁹and you repented and humbled
yourself before me, tearing your clothes and
weeping, when you heard how I threatened
to punish Jerusalem and its people. I will
make it a terrifying sight, a place whose
name people will use as a curse. But I have
heard your prayer, ²⁰and the punishment
which I am going to bring on Jerusalem will
not come until after your death. I will let
you die in peace."

The men returned to King Josiah with
this message.

Josiah Does Away with Pagan Worship
(2 Chronicles 34:3–7, 29–33)

23 ¹King Josiah summoned all the leaders of Judah and Jerusalem, ²and
together they went to the Temple, accompanied by the priests and the prophets and all
the rest of the people, rich and poor alike.
Before them all the king read aloud the
whole book of the covenant which had been
found in the Temple. ³He stood by the royal
column and made a covenant with the
LORD to obey him, to keep his laws and
commands with all his heart and soul, and to
put into practice the demands attached to
the covenant, as written in the book. And all
the people promised to keep the covenant.

⁴Then Josiah ordered the High Priest
Hilkiah, his assistant priests, and the guards
on duty at the entrance to the Temple to
bring out of the Temple all the objects used
in the worship of Baal, of the goddess Asherah, and of the stars. The king burned all

The king read aloud the whole book of the covenant.
(23:2)

The king burned all these objects outside the city. (23:4)

these objects outside the city near Kidron
Valley and then had the ashes taken to
Bethel. ⁵He removed from office the priests
that the kings of Judah had ordained to offer
sacrifices*ʸ* on the pagan altars in the cities of
Judah and in places near Jerusalem—all the

ʸ **23:5** *Some ancient translations* to offer sacrifices; *Hebrew* and he offered sacrifices
23:4–6 2 Kings 21:3; 2 Chr 33:3

priests who offered sacrifices to Baal, to the sun, the moon, the planets, and the stars. [6]He removed from the Temple the symbol of the goddess Asherah, took it out of the city to Kidron Valley, burned it, pounded its ashes to dust, and scattered it over the public burying ground. [7]He destroyed the living quarters in the Temple occupied by the temple prostitutes.[z] (It was there that women wove robes used in the worship of Asherah.) [8]He brought to Jerusalem the priests who were in the cities of Judah, and throughout the whole country he desecrated the altars where they had offered sacrifices. He also tore down the altars dedicated to the goat demons near the gate built by Joshua, the city governor, which was to the left of the main gate as one enters the city. [9]Those priests were not allowed to serve in the Temple, but they could eat the unleavened bread provided for their fellow priests.

[10]King Josiah also desecrated Topheth, the pagan place of worship in Hinnom Valley, so that no one could sacrifice his son or daughter as a burnt offering to the god Molech. [11]He also removed the horses that the kings of Judah had dedicated to the worship of the sun, and he burned the chariots used in this worship. (These were kept in the temple courtyard, near the gate and not far from the living quarters of Nathan Melech, a high official.) [12]The altars which the kings of Judah had built on the palace roof above King Ahaz' quarters, King Josiah tore down, along with the altars put up by King Manasseh in the two courtyards of the Temple; he smashed the altars to bits[a] and threw them into Kidron Valley. [13]Josiah desecrated the altars that King Solomon had built east of Jerusalem, south of the Mount of Olives,[b] for the worship of disgusting idols—Astarte the goddess of Sidon, Chemosh the god of Moab, and Molech the god of Ammon. [14]King Josiah broke the stone pillars to pieces, cut down the symbols of the goddess

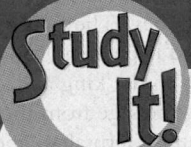

A Faith-Filled King

King Josiah gathered all the people together and had the book of the Law read to them. By doing this he imitated Moses and Joshua:

- "Then [Moses] took the book of the covenant, in which the LORD's commands were written, and read it aloud to the people" (Exodus 24:7).
- "Joshua then read aloud the whole Law . . . Every one of the commandments of Moses was read by Joshua to the whole gathering" (Joshua 8:34–35).

Josiah began a renewal. He tore down all the altars and places of worship that had been built to false gods. The people began to follow God again. They stopped worshiping idols and pagan gods. Josiah helped the people of Israel regain their sense of identity and their faith in God.

— 2 Kings 23:1–14

Asherah, and the ground where they had stood he covered with human bones.

[15]Josiah also tore down the place of worship in Bethel, which had been built by King Jeroboam son of Nebat, who led Israel into sin. Josiah pulled down the altar, broke its stones into pieces,[c] and pounded them to dust; he also burned the image of Asherah. [16]Then Josiah looked around and saw some tombs there on the hill; he had the bones taken out of them and burned on the altar. In this way he desecrated the altar, doing

---

[z] **23:7** TEMPLE PROSTITUTES: *Men and women who practiced prostitution in the worship of fertility gods.*
[a] **23:12** *Probable text* smashed . . . to bits; *Hebrew unclear.*   [b] **23:13** MOUNT OF OLIVES: *Hebrew here refers to it as* "Mount of Destruction" *or* "Mount of Sin."   [c] **23:15** *One ancient translation* broke its stones into pieces; *Hebrew* burned the altar.
23:10 a Jer 7:31; 19:1–6; 32:35; **b** Lev 18:21   **23:12** 2 Kings 21:5; 2 Chr 33:5   **23:13** 1 Kings 11:7
23:15 1 Kings 12:33   **23:16** 1 Kings 13:2

what the prophet had predicted long before during the festival as King Jeroboam was standing by the altar. King Josiah looked around and saw the tomb of the prophet[d] who had made this prediction. 17"Whose tomb is that?" he asked.

The people of Bethel answered, "It is the tomb of the prophet who came from Judah and predicted these things that you have done to this altar."

18"Leave it as it is," Josiah ordered. "His bones are not to be moved."

So his bones were not moved, neither were those of the prophet who had come from Samaria.

19In every city of Israel King Josiah tore down all the pagan places of worship which had been built by the kings of Israel, who thereby aroused the LORD's anger. He did to all those altars what he had done in Bethel. 20He killed all the pagan priests on the altars where they served, and he burned human bones on every altar. Then he returned to Jerusalem.

Josiah Celebrates the Passover
(2 Chronicles 35:1–19)

21King Josiah ordered the people to celebrate the Passover in honor of the LORD their God, as written in the book of the Covenant. 22No Passover like this one had ever been celebrated by any of the kings of Israel or of Judah, since the time when judges ruled the nation. 23Now at last, in the eighteenth year of the reign of Josiah, the Passover was celebrated in Jerusalem.

Other Changes Made by Josiah

24In order to enforce the laws written in the book that the High Priest Hilkiah had found in the Temple, King Josiah removed from Jerusalem and the rest of Judah all the mediums and fortunetellers, and all the household gods, idols, and all other pagan objects of worship. 25There had never been a king like him before, who served the LORD with all his heart, mind, and strength, obeying all the Law of Moses; nor has there been a king like him since.

There had never been a king like him before. (23:25)

26But the LORD's fierce anger had been aroused against Judah by what King Manasseh had done, and even now it did not die down. 27The LORD said, "I will do to Judah what I have done to Israel: I will banish the people of Judah from my sight, and I will reject Jerusalem, the city I chose, and the Temple, the place I said was where I should be worshiped."

The End of Josiah's Reign
(2 Chronicles 35:20—36:1)

28Everything else that King Josiah did is recorded in *The History of the Kings of Judah.* 29While Josiah was king, King Neco of Egypt led an army to the Euphrates River to help the emperor of Assyria. King Josiah tried to stop the Egyptian army at Megiddo and was killed in battle. 30His officials placed his body in a chariot and took it back to Jerusalem, where he was buried in the royal tombs.

The people of Judah chose Josiah's son Joahaz and anointed him king.

---

[d] **23:16** *One ancient translation* during the festival . . . the prophet; *Hebrew does not have these words.*
23:17 1 Kings 13:30–32

Josiah "served the LORD with all his heart, mind, and strength" *(2 Kings 23:25).* Read Deuteronomy 6:5 and Matthew 22:34–38. Notice anything similar?

King Joahaz of Judah
(2 Chronicles 36:2–4)

31Joahaz was twenty-three years old when he became king of Judah, and he ruled in Jerusalem for three months. His mother was Hamutal, the daughter of Jeremiah from the city of Libnah. 32Following the example of his ancestors, he sinned against the LORD. 33His reign ended when King Neco of Egypt took him prisoner in Riblah, in the land of Hamath, and made Judah pay 7,500 pounds of silver and 75 pounds of gold as tribute. 34King Neco made Josiah's son Eliakim king of Judah as successor to Josiah, and changed his name to Jehoiakim. Joahaz was taken to Egypt by King Neco, and there he died.

King Jehoiakim of Judah
(2 Chronicles 36:5–8)

35King Jehoiakim collected a tax from the people in proportion to their wealth, in order to raise the amount needed to pay the tribute demanded by the king of Egypt.

36Jehoiakim was twenty-five years old when he became king of Judah, and he ruled in Jerusalem for eleven years. His mother was Zebidah, the daughter of Pedaiah from the town of Rumah. 37Following the example of his ancestors, Jehoiakim sinned against the LORD.

24 1While Jehoiakim was king, King Nebuchadnezzar of Babylonia invaded Judah, and for three years Jehoiakim was forced to submit to his rule; then he rebelled. 2The LORD sent armed bands of Babylonians, Syrians, Moabites, and Ammonites against Jehoiakim to destroy Judah, as the LORD had said through his servants the prophets that he would do. 3This happened at the LORD's command, in order to banish the people of Judah from his sight because of all the sins that King Manasseh had committed, 4and especially

because of all the innocent people he had killed. The LORD could not forgive Manasseh for that.

5Everything that Jehoiakim did is recorded in *The History of the Kings of Judah*. 6Jehoiakim died, and his son Jehoiachin succeeded him as king.

7The king of Egypt and his army never marched out of Egypt again, because the king of Babylonia now controlled all the territory that had belonged to Egypt, from the Euphrates River to the northern border of Egypt.

King Jehoiachin of Judah
(2 Chronicles 36:9, 10)

8Jehoiachin was eighteen years old when he became king of Judah, and he ruled in Jerusalem for three months. His mother was Nehushta, the daughter of Elnathan from Jerusalem. 9Following the example of his father, Jehoiachin sinned against the LORD.

10It was during his reign that the Babylonian army, commanded by King Nebuchadnezzar's officers, marched against Jerusalem and besieged it. 11During the siege Nebuchadnezzar himself came to Jerusalem, 12and King Jehoiachin, along with his mother, his sons, his officers, and the palace officials, surrendered to the Babylonians. In the eighth year of Nebuchadnezzar's reign he took Jehoiachin prisoner 13and carried off to Babylon all the treasures in the Temple and the palace. As the LORD had foretold, Nebuchadnezzar broke up all the gold utensils which King Solomon had made for use in the Temple. 14Nebuchadnezzar carried away as prisoners the people of Jerusalem, all the royal princes, and all the leading men, ten thousand in all. He also deported all the skilled workers, including the blacksmiths, leaving only the poorest of the people behind in Judah.

15Nebuchadnezzar took Jehoiachin to

23:34 Jer 22:11, 12   **23:36** Jer 22:18, 19; 26:1–6; 35:1–19   **24:1** Jer 25:1–38; Dan 1:1, 2   **24:12** Jer 22:24–30; 24:1–10; 29:1, 2   **24:15** Ezek 17:12

Jehoiachin became king when he was 18 years old. Who was Jehoiachin's father?

The Cost of Sin

**King Manasseh had killed inno-
cent people and had been
unfaithful to God. The author
viewed the destruction and loss of
the southern Kingdom as the cost
of the king's sin. Sin has a cost in
our own lives. When we lie it
destroys our relationships. When
we cheat we lose our own sense
of self-worth. What price have
you paid for sin? What can you do
to repair the damage you've
done? In addition to receiving the
sacrament of Reconciliation, here
are a few things you could do:**

- **If you've lost a friend or friends
  because of gossip or unkindness,
  apologize to the person or people you've hurt. See if you can
  do something good that would
  help repair the relationship.**
- **If you've disobeyed your parents,
  offer to help out around the
  house a little more than usual.**
- **If you've done something to
  hurt your own self-esteem, build
  it back up by working extra hard
  on a tough assignment or challenging yourself to give up a
  bad habit and start a good one.**

— 2 Kings 24:1–4

Babylon as a prisoner, together with
Jehoiachin's mother, his wives, his officials,
and the leading men of Judah. ¹⁶Nebuchad-
nezzar deported all the important men to
Babylonia, seven thousand in all, and one
thousand skilled workers, including the
blacksmiths, all of them able-bodied men fit
for military duty.

¹⁷Nebuchadnezzar made Jehoiachin's

uncle Mattaniah king of Judah and changed
his name to Zedekiah.

King Zedekiah of Judah
(2 Chronicles 36:11, 12; Jeremiah 52:1–3a)

¹⁸Zedekiah was twenty-one years old
when he became king of Judah, and he
ruled in Jerusalem for eleven years. His
mother was Hamutal, the daughter of Jeremiah from the city of Libnah. ¹⁹King
Zedekiah sinned against the LORD, just as
King Jehoiakim had done. ²⁰The LORD
became so angry with the people of
Jerusalem and Judah that he banished them
from his sight.

The Fall of Jerusalem
*(2 Chronicles 36:13–21; Jeremiah
52:3b–11)*

25 ¹Zedekiah rebelled against King
Nebuchadnezzar of Babylonia, and
so Nebuchadnezzar came with all his army
and attacked Jerusalem on the tenth day of
the tenth month of the ninth year of Zedekiah's reign. They set up camp outside the
city, built siege walls around it, ²and kept it
under siege until Zedekiah's eleventh year.
³On the ninth day of the fourth month*ᵉ* of
that same year, when the famine was so bad
that the people had nothing left to eat, ⁴the
city walls were broken through. Although
the Babylonians were surrounding the city,
all the soldiers escaped during the night.
They left by way of the royal garden, went
through the gateway connecting the two
walls, and fled in the direction of the Jordan Valley. ⁵But the Babylonian army pursued King Zedekiah, captured him in the
plains near Jericho, and all his soldiers
deserted him. ⁶Zedekiah was taken to King
Nebuchadnezzar, who was in the city of
Riblah, and there Nebuchadnezzar passed
sentence on him. ⁷While Zedekiah was
looking on, his sons were put to death;
then Nebuchadnezzar had Zedekiah's eyes
put out, placed him in chains, and took
him to Babylon.

ᵉ **25:3** *Probable text (see Jer 52:6)* the fourth month; *Hebrew* the month.
24:17 Jer 37:1; Ezek 17:13   **24:18** Jer 27:1–22; 28:1–17   **24:20** Ezek 17:15   **25:1** Jer 21:1–10; 34:1–5;
Ezek 24:2   **25:4** Ezek 33:21   **25:7** Ezek 12:13

Pray It!

Utter Destruction

You don't know what you have until you lose it. Have you ever heard someone say that? Have you ever felt that way yourself? In this chapter we see the utter destruction of what the Israelites once had. King Zedekiah's sons are killed; the king is taken away, blinded, and put in chains. The Temple is looted and destroyed. All the important officials are taken away as prisoners, then beaten and put to death.

First the northern kingdom was taken over, and now the southern kingdom of Judah is no more. Can you imagine the despair the people must have felt? Maybe you can. Maybe you've experienced a loss that made you feel like your whole world was coming to an end.

> O God,
> I don't know what to do.
> I feel like life will never be the same again.
> There seems to be no reason to hope.
> I want to hide and cry.
> Hold me and comfort me.
> Remind me that you're here with me.
> Help me find something to be hopeful about.
> Bring me back to life. Amen.

— 2 Kings 25:1–21

The Destruction of the Temple
(Jeremiah 52:12–33)

⁸On the seventh day of the fifth month of the nineteenth year of King Nebuchadnezzar of Babylonia, Nebuzaradan, adviser to the king and commander of his army, entered Jerusalem. ⁹He burned down the Temple, the palace, and the houses of all the important people in Jerusalem, ¹⁰and his soldiers tore down the city walls. ¹¹Then Nebuzaradan took away to Babylonia the people who were left in the city, the remaining skilled workers,ᶠ and those who had deserted to the Babylonians. ¹²But he left in Judah some of the poorest people, who owned no property, and put them to work in the vineyards and fields.

¹³The Babylonians broke in pieces the bronze columns and the carts that were in the Temple, together with the large bronze tank, and they took all the bronze to Babylon. ¹⁴They also took away the shovels and the ash containers used in cleaning the altar, the tools used in tending the lamps, the bowls used for catching the blood from the sacrifices, the bowls used for burning incense, and all the other bronze articles used in the Temple service. ¹⁵They took away everything that was made of gold or silver, including the small bowls and the pans used for carrying live coals. ¹⁶The bronze objects that King Solomon had made for the Temple—the two columns, the carts, and the large tank—were too heavy to weigh. ¹⁷The two columns were identical: each one was 27 feet high, with a bronze capital on top, 4½ feet high. All around each capital was a bronze grillwork decorated with pomegranates made of bronze.

ᶠ **25:11** *Probable text (see Jer 52:15)* skilled workers; *Hebrew* crowd.
25:9 1 Kings 9:8 **25:13 a** 1 Kings 7:15–26; 2 Chr 3:15–17; **b** 1 Kings 7:23–26; 2 Chr 4:2–5 **25:14** 1 Kings 7:45; 2 Chr 4:16

The people of Judah were carried away from their land into exile. (25:21)

The People of Judah Are Taken to Babylonia
(Jeremiah 52:24–27)

¹⁸In addition, Nebuzaradan, the commanding officer, took away as prisoners Seraiah the High Priest, Zephaniah the priest next in rank, and the three other important Temple officials. ¹⁹From the city he took the officer who had been in command of the troops, five of the king's personal advisers who were still in the city, the commander's assistant, who was in charge of military records, and sixty other important men. ²⁰Nebuzaradan took them to the king of Babylonia, who was in the city of Riblah ²¹in the territory of Hamath. There the king had them beaten and put to death.

So the people of Judah were carried away from their land into exile.

Gedaliah, Governor of Judah
(Jeremiah 40:7–9; 41:1–3)

²²King Nebuchadnezzar of Babylonia made Gedaliah, the son of Ahikam and grandson of Shaphan, governor of Judah, and placed him in charge of all those who had not been taken away to Babylonia. ²³When the Judean officers and soldiers who had not

surrendered heard about this, they joined Gedaliah at Mizpah. These officers were Ishmael son of Nethaniah, Johanan son of Kareah, Seraiah son of Tanhumeth from the town of Netophah, and Jezaniah from Maacah. ²⁴Gedaliah said to them, "I give you my word that there is no need for you to be afraid of the Babylonian officials. Settle in this land, serve the king of Babylonia, and all will go well with you."

²⁵But in the seventh month of that year, Ishmael, the son of Nethaniah and grandson of Elishama, a member of the royal family, went to Mizpah with ten men, attacked Gedaliah, and killed him. He also killed the Israelites and Babylonians who were there with him. ²⁶Then all the Israelites, rich and poor alike, together with the army officers, left and went to Egypt, because they were afraid of the Babylonians.

Jehoiachin Is Released from Prison
(Jeremiah 52:31–34)

²⁷In the year that Evilmerodach became king of Babylonia, he showed kindness to King Jehoiachin of Judah by releasing him from prison. This happened on the twenty-seventh day of the twelfth month of the

25:22–24 Jer 40:7–9   25:25 Jer 41:1–3   25:26 Jer 43:5–7

The destruction of Jerusalem leads to the Babylonian Exile, when all the leaders of Judah are taken to Babylon as slaves in 587 BC.

thirty-seventh year after Jehoiachin had been taken away as prisoner. 28Evilmerodach treated him kindly and gave him a position of greater honor than he gave the other kings who were exiles with him in Babylo-

nia. 29So Jehoiachin was permitted to change from his prison clothes and to dine at the king's table for the rest of his life. 30Each day, for as long as he lived, he was given a regular allowance for his needs.

Your Next Step

Congratulations on finishing the Second Book of Kings! Use this space to write your thoughts and questions about this book. If you are following the suggested reading plan, move ahead to the Book of Isaiah. The prophet Isaiah and his followers have many things to say about the idolatry and injustice that happened during the time of the kings.

"Wow, that was an interesting Web site, wasn't it? The Mesopotamian people sure had lots of enemies, didn't they?" Doug's dad said. "Let's see what the next site listed on your homework sheet is like." When they opened the next Web site, the same time period was highlighted, but this site gave different information. It talked about how the kings of the Mesopotamian people came to power.

The First Book of Chronicles is similar. It covers the same period of history that the books of Samuel and Kings cover but from a different viewpoint. The writer (called the Chronicler) wants the reader to know the family tree of Israel's leaders. Most importantly, he wants to make sure the Israelites have hope for the future and continue their religious practices.

Chap. 15

Head lines

- Lists, Lists, and More Lists (chapters 1–9)
- Famous Soldiers Help David (11:10–25)
- Victory Declared! (14:8–17)
- Covenant Box Moved to Jerusalem (15:25–29)
- Giants Defeated in Battle (20:4–8)
- Levites Assigned Temple Duties (23:2–5)
- David Declares Temple to Be Built (28:1–8)

FACTOIDS

Who wrote this book? The author (or authors) of First and Second Chronicles was called the Chronicler. He was a scribe who wrote sometime after the people returned to Jerusalem after the Exile.

What time period does it cover? First Chronicles covers the events that took place from Creation until King David's death.

Why was it written? It was written to give hope for the future. It also emphasizes the importance of the priests and the Jerusalem Temple.

What is the literary style? The Chronicler used both stories and genealogies (family histories) to record the history of the Israelites.

Important themes

- Even though the Israelites have experienced many disasters, there is still hope for the future.
- The future of Israel can be secured if the people continue to worship God and keep their religious practices.

1 CHRONICLES

From Adam to Abraham
(Genesis 5:1–32; 10:1–32; 11:10–26)

1 **1**Adam was the father of Seth, Seth was the father of Enosh, Enosh the father of Kenan, **2**Kenan the father of Mahalalel, Mahalalel the father of Jared. **3**Jared was the father of Enoch, who was the father of Methuselah; Methuselah was the father of Lamech, **4**who was the father of Noah. Noah had three sons: Shem, Ham, and Japheth.

5The sons of Japheth—Gomer, Magog, Madai, Javan, Tubal, Meshech, and Tiras—were the ancestors of the peoples who bear their names. **6**The descendants of Gomer were the people of Ashkenaz, Riphath, and Togarmah. **7**The descendants of Javan were the people of Elishah, Spain, Cyprus, and Rhodes.

8The sons of Ham—Cush, Egypt, Libya, and Canaan—were the ancestors of the peoples who bear their names. **9**The descendants of Cush were the people of Seba, Havilah, Sabtah, Raamah, and Sabteca. The descendants of Raamah were the people of Sheba and Dedan. (**10**Cush had a son named Nimrod, who became the world's first great conqueror.) **11**The descendants of Egypt were the people of Lydia, Anam, Lehab, Naphtuh, **12**Pathrus, Casluh, and of Crete (from whom the Philistines were descended). **13**Canaan's sons—Sidon, the oldest, and Heth—were the ancestors of the peoples who bear their names. **14**Canaan was also the ancestor of the Jebusites, the Amorites, Girgashites, **15**Hivites, Arkites, Sinites, **16**Arvadites, Zemarites, and Hamathites.

17Shem's sons—Elam, Asshur, Arpachshad, Lud, Aram, Uz, Hul, Gether, and Meshek—were the ancestors of the peoples who bear their names. **18**Arpachshad was the father of Shelah, who was the father of Eber. **19**Eber had two sons; one was named Peleg,*a* because during his time the people of the world were divided, and the other was named Joktan. **20**The descendants of Joktan were the people of Almodad, Sheleph, Hazarmaveth, Jerah, **21**Hadoram, Uzal, Diklah, **22**Ebal, Abimael, Sheba, **23**Ophir, Havilah, and Jobab.

24The family line from Shem to Abram is as follows: Shem, Arpachshad, Shelah, **25**Eber, Peleg, Reu, **26**Serug, Nahor, Terah, **27**and Abram (also known as Abraham).

The Descendants of Ishmael
(Genesis 25:12–16)

28Abraham had two sons, Isaac and Ishmael. **29**The sons of Ishmael became the heads of twelve tribes: Nebaioth (from the name of Ishmael's oldest son), Kedar, Adbeel, Mibsam, **30**Mishma, Dumah, Massa, Hadad, Tema, **31**Jetur, Naphish, and Kedemah.

32Abraham had a concubine named Keturah, who bore him six sons: Zimran, Jokshan, Medan, Midian, Ishbak, and Shuah. Jokshan had two sons: Sheba and Dedan. **33**Midian had five sons: Ephah, Epher, Hanoch, Abida, and Eldaah.

The Descendants of Esau
(Genesis 36:1–19)

34Abraham's son Isaac had two sons, Esau and Jacob. **35**Esau's sons were Eliphaz, Reuel, Jeush, Jalam, and Korah. **36**Eliphaz became the ancestor of the following tribes: Teman, Omar, Zephi, Gatam, Kenaz, Timna, and Amalek. **37**And Reuel became the ancestor of the tribes of Nahath, Zerah, Shammah, and Mizzah.

The Original Inhabitants of Edom
(Genesis 36:20–30)

38-42 The original inhabitants of Edom were descended from the following sons of Seir:

Lotan, who was the ancestor of the clans of Hori and Homam. (Lotan had a sister named Timna.)

a **1:19** PELEG: *This name sounds like the Hebrew for "divide."*

Shobal, who was the ancestor of the clans of Alvan, Manahath, Ebal, Shephi, and Onam.

Zibeon, who had two sons, Aiah and Anah. Anah was the father of Dishon, and Dishon was the ancestor of the clans of Hamran, Eshban, Ithran, and Cheran.

Ezer, who was the ancestor of the clans of Bilhan, Zaavan, and Jaakan.

Dishan, who was the ancestor of the clans of Uz and Aran.

The Kings of Edom
(Genesis 36:31–43)

43-50 The following kings ruled the land of Edom one after the other, in the time before there were any kings in Israel:

Bela son of Beor from Dinhabah

Jobab son of Zerah from Bozrah

Husham from the region of Teman

Hadad son of Bedad from Avith (he defeated the Midianites in a battle in the country of Moab)

Samlah from Masrekah

Shaul from Rehoboth-on-the-River

Baal Hanan son of Achbor

Hadad from Pau (his wife was Mehetabel, the daughter of Matred and granddaughter of Mezahab)

51The people of Edom were divided into the following tribes: Timna, Alvah, Jetheth, **52**Oholibamah, Elah, Pinon, **53**Kenaz, Teman, Mibzar, **54**Magdiel, and Iram.

The Descendants of Judah

2 **1**Jacob had twelve sons: Reuben, Simeon, Levi, Judah, Issachar, Zebulun, **2**Dan, Joseph, Benjamin, Naphtali, Gad, and Asher.

3Judah had five sons in all. By his wife Bathshua, a Canaanite, he had three sons: Er, Onan, and Shelah. His oldest son, Er, was so evil that the LORD killed him. **4**By his daughter-in-law Tamar, Judah had two more sons, Perez and Zerah.

5Perez had two sons, Hezron and Hamul. **6**His brother Zerah had five sons: Zimri, Ethan, Heman, Calcol, and Darda. **7**Achan[b] son of Carmi, one of Zerah's descendants, brought disaster on the people of Israel by keeping loot that had been devoted to God. **8**Ethan had one son, Azariah.

The Family Tree of King David

9Hezron had three sons: Jerahmeel, Ram, and Caleb.

10The family line from Ram to Jesse is as follows: Ram, Amminadab, Nahshon (a prominent man of the tribe of Judah), **11**Salmon, Boaz, **12**Obed, and Jesse.

13Jesse had seven sons. In order of age they were: Eliab, Abinadab, Shammah, **14**Nethanel, Raddai, **15**Ozem, and David. **16**He also had two daughters, Zeruiah and Abigail.

Jesse's daughter Zeruiah had three sons: Abishai, Joab, and Asahel. **17**His other daughter Abigail married Jether, a descendant of Ishmael, and they had a son named Amasa.

The Descendants of Hezron

18Hezron's son Caleb married Azubah and had a daughter named Jerioth. She had[c] three sons: Jesher, Shobab, and Ardon. **19**After the death of Azubah, Caleb married Ephrath, and they had a son named Hur. **20**Hur's son was Uri, and his grandson was Bezalel.

21When Hezron was sixty years old, he married Machir's daughter, the sister of Gilead. They had a son named Segub, **22**and Segub had a son named Jair. Jair ruled[d] twenty-three cities in the territory of Gilead. **23**But the kingdoms of Geshur and Aram conquered sixty towns there, including the villages of Jair and Kenath, and the towns nearby. All the people who lived there were descendants of Machir, the father of Gilead. **24**After Hezron died, his son Caleb married Ephrath, his father's widow.[e] They had a son named Ashhur, who founded the town of Tekoa.

---

b **2:7** ACHAN: *This is his name in Josh 7:1. The Hebrew text here calls him "Achar," which means "disaster."*
c **2:18** *Some ancient translations* had a daughter . . . She had; *Hebrew unclear.*   *d* **2:22** ruled; *or* owned.
e **2:24** *Some ancient translations* his son . . . widow; *Hebrew unclear.*
2:7 Josh 7:1

The Descendants of Jerahmeel

25 Jerahmeel, the oldest son of Hezron, had five sons: Ram, the oldest, Bunah, Oren, Ozem, and Ahijah. 26-27 Ram had three sons: Maaz, Jamin, and Eker. Jerahmeel had another wife, a woman named Atarah, and they had a son, Onam. 28 Onam had two sons, Shammai and Jada, and Shammai also had two sons, Nadab and Abishur.

29 Abishur married a woman named Abihail, and they had two sons, Ahban and Molid. 30 Abishur's brother Nadab had two sons, Seled and Appaim, but Seled died without having any sons. 31 Appaim was the father of Ishi, Ishi was the father of Sheshan, and Sheshan the father of Ahlai.

32 Jada, the brother of Shammai, had two sons, Jether and Jonathan, but Jether died without having any sons. 33 Jonathan had two sons, Peleth and Zaza. All these were descendants of Jerahmeel.

34 Sheshan had no sons, only daughters. He had an Egyptian servant named Jarha, 35 to whom he gave one of his daughters in marriage. They had a son named Attai. 36 The family line from Attai to Elishama is as follows: Attai, Nathan, Zabad, 37 Ephlal, Obed, 38 Jehu, Azariah, 39 Helez, Eleasah, 40 Sismai, Shallum, 41 Jekamiah, and Elishama.

Other Descendants of Caleb

42 The oldest son of Caleb, Jerahmeel's brother, was named Mesha. Mesha was the father of Ziph, who was the father of Mareshah, who was the father of Hebron.ƒ 43 Hebron had four sons: Korah, Tappuah, Rekem, and Shema. 44 Shema was the father of Raham and the grandfather of Jorkeam. Rekem, Shema's brother, was the father of Shammai, 45 who was the father of Maon, who was the father of Bethzur.

46 Caleb had a concubine named Ephah, and by her he had three more sons: Haran, Moza, and Gazez. Haran also had a son named Gazez.

(47 A man named Jahdai had six sons: Regem, Jotham, Geshan, Pelet, Ephah, and Shaaph.)

48 Caleb had another concubine, Maacah, who bore him two sons, Sheber and Tirhanah. 49 Later she had two more sons: Shaaph, who founded the town of Madmannah; and Shevah, who founded the towns of Machbenah and Gibea.

In addition, Caleb had a daughter named Achsah.

50 The following are also descendants of Caleb.

Hur was the oldest son of Caleb and his wife Ephrath. Hur's son Shobal founded Kiriath Jearim, 51 his second son Salma founded Bethlehem, and his third son Hareph founded Bethgader.

52 Shobal, the founder of Kiriath Jearim, was the ancestor of the people of Haroeh, of half the inhabitants of Menuhoth, 53 and of the following clans that lived in Kiriath Jearim: the Ithrites, Puthites, Shumathites, and Mishraites. (The people of the cities of Zorah and Eshtaol were members of these clans.)

54 Salma, the founder of Bethlehem, was the ancestor of the people of Netophath, of Atroth Beth Joab, and of the Zorites, who were one of the two clans in Manahath.

(55 The following clans of experts in writing and copying documents lived in the town of Jabez: the Tirathites, Shimeathites, and Sucathites. They were Kenites who had intermarried with the Rechabites.)

King David's Children

3 1-3 The following, in order of age, are David's sons who were born while he was in Hebron:

Amnon, whose mother was Ahinoam from Jezreel

Daniel, whose mother was Abigail from Carmel

Absalom, whose mother was Maacah, daughter of King Talmai of Geshur

Adonijah, whose mother was Haggith

Shephatiah, whose mother was Abital

Ithream, whose mother was Eglah

4 All six were born in Hebron during the seven and a half years that David ruled there.

ƒ 2:42 *Probable text* father of Mareshah . . . Hebron; *Hebrew unclear.*
3:4 2 Sam 5:4, 5; 1 Kings 2:11; 1 Chr 29:27

In Jerusalem he ruled as king for thirty-three years, 5and many sons were born to him there.

His wife Bathsheba, daughter of Ammiel, bore him four sons: Shimea, Shobab, Nathan, and Solomon.

6He had nine other sons: Ibhar, Elishua, Elpelet, 7Nogah, Nepheg, Japhia, 8Elishama, Eliada, and Eliphelet. 9In addition to all these sons, David had sons by his concubines. He also had a daughter, Tamar.

The Descendants of King Solomon

10This is the line of King Solomon's descendants from father to son: Solomon, Rehoboam, Abijah, Asa, Jehoshaphat, 11Jehoram, Ahaziah, Joash, 12Amaziah, Uzziah, Jotham, 13Ahaz, Hezekiah, Manasseh, 14Amon, and Josiah. 15Josiah had four sons: Johanan, Jehoiakim, Zedekiah, and Joahaz. 16Jehoiakim had two sons: Jehoiachin and Zedekiah.

The Descendants of King Jehoiachin

17These are the descendants of King Jehoiachin, who was taken prisoner by the Babylonians. Jehoiachin had seven sons: Shealtiel, 18Malchiram, Pedaiah, Shenazzar, Jekamiah, Hoshama, and Nedabiah. 19Pedaiah had two sons, Zerubbabel and Shimei. Zerubbabel was the father of two sons, Meshullam and Hananiah, and one daughter, Shelomith. 20He had five other sons: Hashubah, Ohel, Berechiah, Hasadiah, and Jushab Hesed.

21Hananiah had two sons, Pelatiah and Jeshaiah. Jeshaiah was the father of Rephaiah, who was the father of Arnan, the father of Obadiah, the father of Shecaniah.g 22Shecaniah had one son, Shemaiah, and five grandsons: Hattush, Igal, Bariah, Neariah, and Shaphat. 23Neariah had three sons: Elioenai, Hizkiah, and Azrikam. 24Elioenai had seven sons: Hodaviah, Eliashib, Pelaiah, Akkub, Johanan, Delaiah, and Anani.

The Descendants of Judah

4 1These are some of the descendants of Judah: Perez, Hezron, Carmi, Hur, and Shobal. 2Shobal was the father of Reaiah, who was the father of Jahath, the father of Ahumai and Lahad, the ancestors of the people who lived in Zorah.

3-4Hur was the oldest son of his father Caleb's wife Ephrath, and his descendants founded the city of Bethlehem. Hur had three sons: Etam, Penuel, and Ezer. Etam had three sons:h Jezreel, Ishma, and Idbash, and one daughter, Hazzelelponi. Penuel founded the city of Gedor, and Ezer founded Hushah.

5Ashhur, who founded the town of Tekoa, had two wives, Helah and Naarah. 6He and Naarah had four sons: Ahuzzam, Hepher, Temeni, and Haahashtari. 7Ashhur and Helah had three sons: Zereth, Izhar, and Ethnan.

8Koz was the father of Anub and Zobebah, and the ancestor of the clans descended from Aharhel son of Harum.

9There was a man named Jabez, who was the most respected member of his family. His mother had given him the name Jabez,i because his birth had been very painful. 10But Jabez prayed to the God of Israel, "Bless me, God, and give me much land. Be with me and keep me from anything evil that might cause me pain." And God gave him what he prayed for.

Other Family Lists

11Caleb, the brother of Shuhah, had a son, Mehir. Mehir was the father of Eshton, 12who had three sons: Bethrapha, Paseah, and Tehinnah. Tehinnah was the founder of the city of Nahash. The descendants of these men lived in Recah.

13Kenaz had two sons, Othniel and Seraiah. Othniel also had two sons, Hathath and Meonothai.j 14Meonothai was the father of Ophrah.

Seraiah was the father of Joab, the founder of Handcraft Valley, where all the people were skilled workers.

---

g 3:21 *Verse 21 in Hebrew is unclear.*   h 4:3–4 *Some ancient translations* sons; *Hebrew* fathers.   i 4:9 JABEZ: *This name sounds like the Hebrew for "pain."*   j 4:13 *Some ancient translations* Meonothai; *Hebrew does not have this name.*
3:5 2 Sam 11:3

15Caleb son of Jephunneh had three sons: Iru, Elah, and Naam. And Elah was the father of Kenaz.

16Jehallelel had four sons: Ziph, Ziphah, Tiria, and Asarel.

17-18Ezrah had four sons: Jether, Mered, Epher, and Jalon. Mered married Bithiah, a daughter of the king of Egypt, and they had a daughter, Miriam, and two sons, Shammai and Ishbah. Ishbah founded the town of Eshtemoa. Mered also married a woman from the tribe of Judah, and they had three sons: Jered, who founded the town of Gedor; Heber, founder of the town of Soco; and Jekuthiel, founder of the town of Zanoah.

19Hodiah married the sister of Naham. Their descendants founded the clan of Garm, which lived in the town of Keilah, and the clan of Maacath, which lived in the town of Eshtemoa.*k*

20Shimon had four sons: Amnon, Rinnah, Benhanan, and Tilon.

Ishi had two sons: Zoheth and Benzoheth.

The Descendants of Shelah

21Shelah was one of Judah's sons. His descendants included Er, who founded the town of Lecah; Laadah, founder of the town of Mareshah; the clan of linen weavers, who lived in the town of Beth Ashbea; 22Jokim and the people who lived in the town of Cozeba; and Joash and Saraph, who married Moabite women and then settled in Bethlehem.*l* (These traditions are very old.) 23They were potters in the service of the king and lived in the towns of Netaim and Gederah.

The Descendants of Simeon

24Simeon had five sons: Nemuel, Jamin, Jarib, Zerah, and Shaul. 25Shaul's son was Shallum, his grandson was Mibsam, and his great-grandson was Mishma. 26Then from Mishma the line descended through Hammuel, Zaccur, and Shimei. 27Shimei had sixteen sons and six daughters, but his relatives had fewer children, and the tribe of Simeon did not grow as much as the tribe of Judah did.

28Down to the time of King David the descendants of Simeon lived in the following towns: Beersheba, Moladah, Hazarshual, 29Bilhah, Ezem, Tolad, 30Bethuel, Hormah, Ziklag, 31Beth Marcaboth, Hazarsusim, Bethbiri, and Shaaraim. 32They also lived in five other places: Etam, Ain, Rimmon, Tochen, and Ashan, 33and the surrounding villages, as far southwest as the town of Baalath. These are the records which they kept of their families and of the places where they lived.

34-38The following men were the heads of their clans:

Meshobab, Jamlech, Joshah son of Amaziah, Joel,

Jehu (the son of Joshibiah, the son of Seraiah, the son of Asiel),

Elioenai, Jaakobah, Jeshohaiah, Asaiah, Adiel, Jesimiel, Benaiah,

Ziza (the son of Shiphi, the son of Allon, a descendant of Jedaiah, Shimri, and Shemaiah).

Because their families continued to grow, 39they spread out westward almost to Gerar*m* and pastured their sheep on the eastern side of the valley in which that city is located.

Potters in the service of the king (4:23)

They . . . pastured their sheep. (4:39)

---

k **4:19** *Verse 19 in Hebrew is unclear.* *l* **4:22** *Probable text* settled in Bethlehem; *Hebrew unclear.* *m* **4:39** *Some ancient translations* Gerar; *Hebrew* Gedor.
4:28-33 Josh 19:2-8

40 They found plenty of fertile pasture lands there in a stretch of open country that was quiet and peaceful. The people who had lived there before were Hamites.

41 In the time of King Hezekiah of Judah, the men named above went to Gerar and destroyed the tents and huts of the people who lived there.ⁿ They drove the people out and settled there permanently because there was plenty of pasture for their sheep. 42 Five hundred other members of the tribe of Simeon went east to Edom. They were led by the sons of Ishi: Pelatiah, Neariah, Rephaiah, and Uzziel. 43 There they killed the surviving Amalekites, and they have lived there ever since.

The Descendants of Reuben

5 ¹These are the descendants of Reuben, the oldest of Jacob's sons. (Because he had sex with one of his father's concubines, he lost the rights belonging to the first-born son, and those rights were given to Joseph. 2 It was the tribe of Judah, however, that became the strongest and provided a ruler for all the tribes.) 3 Reuben, the oldest of Jacob's sons, had four sons: Hanoch, Pallu, Hezron, and Carmi.

4-6 These are the descendants of Joel from generation to generation: Shemaiah, Gog, Shimei, Micah, Reaiah, Baal, and Beerah. The Assyrian emperor, Tiglath Pileser, captured Beerah, a leader of the tribe, and deported him.

7 The family records list the following clan leaders in the tribe of Reuben: Jeiel, Zechariah, 8 and Bela, the son of Azaz and grandson of Shema, of the clan of Joel. This clan lived in Aroer and in the territory from there north to Nebo and Baal Meon. 9 They had large herds in the land of Gilead, and so they occupied the land as far east as the desert that stretches all the way to the Euphrates River.

10 In the time of King Saul the tribe of Reuben attacked the Hagrites, killed them in battle, and occupied their land in the eastern part of Gilead.

The Descendants of Gad

11 The tribe of Gad lived to the north of Reuben in the land of Bashan as far east as Salecah. 12 Joel was the founder of the leading clan, and Shapham of the second most important clan. Janai and Shaphat were founders of other clans in Bashan. 13 The other members of the tribe belonged to the following seven clans: Michael, Meshullam, Sheba, Jorai, Jacan, Zia, and Eber. 14 They were descendants of Abihail son of Huri, whose ancestors were traced back as follows: Abihail, Huri, Jaroah, Gilead, Michael, Jeshishai, Jahdo, Buz. 15 Ahi, the son of Abdiel and grandson of Guni, was head of these clans. 16 They lived in the territory of Bashan and Gilead, in the towns there and all over the pasture lands of Sharon. (17 These records were compiled in the days of King Jotham of Judah and King Jeroboam II of Israel.)

The Armies of the Eastern Tribes

18 In the tribes of Reuben, Gad, and East Manasseh there were 44,760 soldiers, well-trained in the use of shields, swords, and bows. 19 They went to war against the Hagrite tribes of Jetur, Naphish, and Nodab. 20 They put their trust in God and prayed to him for help, and God answered their prayers and made them victorious over the Hagrites and their allies. 21 They captured from the enemy 50,000 camels, 250,000 sheep, and 2,000 donkeys, and took 100,000 prisoners of war. 22 They killed many of the enemy, because the war was God's will. And they went on living in that territory until the exile.ᵒ

The People of East Manasseh

23 The people of East Manasseh settled in the territory of Bashan as far north as Baal Hermon, Senir, and Mount Hermon, and their population increased greatly. 24 The

---

ⁿ 4:41 the tents and huts . . . there; or the tents of the people who lived there, and the Meunites also.
ᵒ 5:22 THE EXILE: About 733 B.C. the Assyrians conquered northern Israel and the Israelite territory east of the Jordan River and deported the people (see 2 Kings 15:29).
5:1 Gen 35:22; 49:3, 4   5:2 Gen 49:8–10   5:6 2 Kings 15:29

following were the heads of their clans: Epher, Ishi, Eliel, Azriel, Jeremiah, Hodaviah, and Jahdiel. They were all outstanding soldiers, well-known leaders of their clans.

The Eastern Tribes Are Deported

25 But the people were unfaithful to the God of their ancestors and deserted him to worship the gods of the nations whom God had driven out of the land. 26 So God caused Emperor Pul of Assyria (also known as Tiglath Pileser) to invade their country. He deported the tribes of Reuben, Gad, and East Manasseh and settled them permanently in Halah, Habor, and Hara, and by the Gozan River.

The Family Line of the High Priests

6 1 Levi had three sons: Gershon, Kohath, and Merari. 2 Kohath had four sons: Amram, Izhar, Hebron, and Uzziel.

3 Amram had two sons, Aaron and Moses, and one daughter, Miriam.

Aaron had four sons: Nadab, Abihu, Eleazar, and Ithamar.

4 The descendants of Eleazar from generation to generation are as follows: Phinehas, Abishua, 5 Bukki, Uzzi, 6 Zerahiah, Meraioth, 7 Amariah, Ahitub, 8 Zadok, Ahimaaz, 9 Azariah, Johanan, 10 Azariah (the one who served in the Temple which King Solomon built in Jerusalem), 11 Amariah, Ahitub, 12 Zadok, Shallum, 13 Hilkiah, Azariah, 14 Seraiah, Jehozadak. 15 King Nebuchadnezzar deported Jehozadak along with the other people of Judah and Jerusalem whom the LORD sent into exile.

Other Descendants of Levi

16 Levi had three sons: Gershon, Kohath, and Merari. 17 Each of them also had sons. Gershon was the father of Libni and Shimei; 18 Kohath was the father of Amram, Izhar, Hebron, and Uzziel; 19 and Merari was the father of Mahli and Mushi.

20 These are the descendants of Gershon from generation to generation: Libni, Jahath, Zimmah, 21 Joah, Iddo, Zerah, Jeatherai.

22 These are the descendants of Kohath from generation to generation: Amminadab, Korah, Assir, 23 Elkanah, Ebiasaph, Assir, 24 Tahath, Uriel, Uzziah, Shaul.

25 Elkanah had two sons, Amasai and Ahimoth. 26 These are Ahimoth's descendants from generation to generation: Elkanah, Zophai, Nahath, 27 Eliab, Jeroham, Elkanah.

28 Samuel had two sons: Joel,p the older, and Abijah, the younger.

29 These are the descendants of Merari from generation to generation: Mahli, Libni, Shimei, Uzzah, 30 Shimea, Haggiah, Asaiah.

The Temple Musicians

31 These are the men whom King David put in charge of the music at the place of worship in Jerusalem after the Covenant Box was moved there. 32 They took regular turns of duty at the Tent of the LORD's presence during the time before King Solomon built the Temple. 33 The family lines of those who held this office are as follows:

The clan of Kohath: Heman, the leader of the first choir, was the son of Joel. His family line went back to Jacob as follows: Heman, Joel, Samuel, 34 Elkanah, Jeroham, Eliel, Toah, 35 Zuph, Elkanah, Mahath, Amasai, 36 Elkanah, Joel, Azariah, Zephaniah, 37 Tahath, Assir, Ebiasaph, Korah, 38 Izhar, Kohath, Levi, Jacob.

39 Asaph was leader of the second choir. His family line went back to Levi as follows: Asaph, Berechiah, Shimea, 40 Michael, Baaseiah, Malchijah, 41 Ethni, Zerah, Adaiah, 42 Ethan, Zimmah, Shimei, 43 Jahath, Gershon, Levi.

44 Ethan of the clan of Merari was the leader of the third choir. His family line went back to Levi as follows: Ethan, Kishi, Abdi, Malluch, 45 Hashabiah, Amaziah, Hilkiah, 46 Amzi, Bani, Shemer, 47 Mahli, Mushi, Merari, Levi.

48 The other Levites were assigned all the other duties at the place of worship.

---

p *6:28 Some ancient translations (see also 1 Sam 8:2) Joel; Hebrew does not have this name.*
5:26 a 2 Kings 15:19; b 2 Kings 15:29; c 2 Kings 17:6   **6:16–19** Ex 6:16–19

The Descendants of Aaron

49 Aaron and his descendants presented the offerings of incense and offered the sacrifices that were burnt on the altar. They were responsible for all the worship in the Most Holy Place and for the sacrifices by which God forgives Israel's sins. They did all this in accordance with the instructions given by Moses, God's servant. 50 This is the line of Aaron's descendants: Eleazar, Phinehas, Abishua, 51 Bukki, Uzzi, Zerahiah, 52 Meraioth, Amariah, Ahitub, 53 Zadok, Ahimaaz.

Where the Levites Lived

54 This is the territory assigned to the descendants of Aaron of the clan of Kohath. They received the first share of the land assigned to the Levites. 55 This included Hebron in the territory of Judah and the pasture lands around it. 56 The fields and villages, however, that belonged to the city were assigned to Caleb son of Jephunneh. 57-59 The following towns were assigned to Aaron's descendants: Hebron, a city of refuge,*q* Jattir, and the towns of Libnah, Eshtemoa, Hilen, Debir, Ashan, and Beth Shemesh, with their pasture lands. 60 In the territory of Benjamin they were assigned the following towns with their pasture lands: Geba, Alemeth, and Anathoth. This made a total of thirteen towns for all their families to live in. 61 Ten towns in the territory of West Manasseh were assigned by lot to the rest of the clan of Kohath, family by family. 62 To the clan of Gershon, family by family, were assigned thirteen towns in the territories of Issachar, Asher, Naphtali, and East Manasseh in Bashan. 63 In the same way, twelve towns in the territories of Reuben, Gad, and Zebulun were assigned to the clan of Merari, family by family. 64 In this way the people of Israel assigned towns for the Levites to live in, together with the pasture lands around the towns. (65 The towns in the territories of Judah, Simeon, and Benjamin, mentioned above, were also assigned by drawing lots.) 66 Some of the families of the clan of Kohath were assigned towns and pasture lands in the territory of Ephraim: 67 Shechem, the city of refuge in the hills of Ephraim, Gezer, 68 Jokmeam, Beth Horon, 69 Aijalon, and Gath Rimmon. 70 In the territory of West Manasseh they were assigned the towns of Aner and Bileam with the surrounding pasture lands.

71 The families of the clan of Gershon were assigned the following towns, with the surrounding pasture lands:

In the territory of East Manasseh: Golan in Bashan, and Ashtaroth.

72 In the territory of Issachar: Kedesh, Daberath, 73 Ramoth, and Anem.

74 In the territory of Asher: Mashal, Abdon, 75 Hukok, and Rehob.

76 In the territory of Naphtali: Kedesh in Galilee, Hammon, and Kiriathaim.

77 The remaining families of the clan of Merari were assigned the following towns with the surrounding pasture lands:

In the territory of Zebulun: Rimmono and Tabor.

78 In the territory of Reuben, east of the Jordan River beyond Jericho: Bezer on the plateau, Jahzah, 79 Kedemoth, and Mephaath.

80 In the territory of Gad: Ramoth in Gilead, Mahanaim, 81 Heshbon, and Jazer.

The Descendants of Issachar

7 1 Issachar had four sons: Tola, Puah, Jashub, and Shimron.

2 Tola had six sons: Uzzi, Rephaiah, Jeriel, Jahmai, Ibsam, and Shemuel. They were heads of families of the clan of Tola and were famous soldiers. At the time of King David their descendants numbered 22,600.

3 Uzzi had one son, Izrahiah. Izrahiah and his four sons, Michael, Obadiah, Joel, and Isshiah, were all heads of families. 4 They had so many wives and children that their descendants were able to provide 36,000 men for military duty.

5 The official records of all the families of the tribe of Issachar listed 87,000 men eligible for military duty.

---

q 6:57–59 CITY OF REFUGE: *If anyone accidentally killed someone, he could escape to one of these cities and be safe from revenge (see Josh 20:1–9).*

The Descendants of Benjamin and Dan

6 Benjamin had three sons: Bela, Becher, and Jediael.

7 Bela had five sons: Ezbon, Uzzi, Uzziel, Jerimoth, and Iri. They were heads of families in the clan and were all famous soldiers. Their descendants included 22,034 men eligible for military duty.

8 Becher had nine sons: Zemirah, Joash, Eliezer, Elioenai, Omri, Jeremoth, Abijah, Anathoth, and Alemeth. 9 The official record of their descendants by families listed 20,200 men eligible for military duty.

10 Jediael had one son, Bilhan, and Bilhan had seven sons: Jeush, Benjamin, Ehud, Chenaanah, Zethan, Tarshish, and Ahishahar. 11 They were heads of families in the clan and were all famous soldiers. Their descendants included 17,200 men eligible for military duty. 12 Shuppim and Huppim also belonged to this tribe.

Dan had one son, Hushim.ʳ

The Descendants of Naphtali

13 Naphtali had four sons: Jahziel, Guni, Jezer, and Shallum. (They were descendants of Bilhah.ˢ)

The Descendants of Manasseh

14 By his Aramean concubine, Manasseh had two sons, Asriel and Machir. Machir was the father of Gilead. 15 Machir found a wife for Huppim and one for Shuppim. His sister's name was Maacah. Machir's second son was Zelophehad, and he had only daughters.

16 Maacah, Machir's wife, gave birth to two sons, whom they named Peresh and Sheresh. Peresh had two sons, Ulam and Rakem, 17 and Ulam had a son named Bedan. These are all descendants of Gilead, the son of Machir and grandson of Manasseh.

18 Gilead's sister Hammolecheth had three sons: Ishod, Abiezer, and Mahlah. (19 Shemida had four sons: Ahian, Shechem, Likhi, and Aniam.)

The Descendants of Ephraim

20 These are the descendants of Ephraim from generation to generation: Shuthelah, Bered, Tahath, Eleadah, Tahath, 21 Zabad, Shuthelah. Ephraim had two other sons besides Shuthelah: Ezer and Elead, who were killed when they tried to steal the livestock belonging to the native inhabitants of Gath. 22 Their father Ephraim mourned for them for many days, and his relatives came to comfort him. 23 Then he had intercourse with his wife again, and she became pregnant and had a son. They named him Beriah,ᵗ because of the trouble that had come to their family.

24 Ephraim had a daughter named Sheerah. She built the towns of Upper and Lower Beth Horon, and Uzzen Sheerah.

25 Ephraim also had a son named Rephah, whose descendants were as follows: Resheph, Telah, Tahan, 26 Ladan, Ammihud, Elishama, 27 Nun, Joshua.

28 The territory which they took and settled included Bethel and the towns around it, as far east as Naaran and as far west as Gezer and the towns around it. It also included the cities of Shechem and Ayyah, and the towns around them. 29 The descendants of Manasseh controlled the cities of Beth Shan, Taanach, Megiddo, and Dor, and the towns around them.

All these are the places where the descendants of Joseph son of Jacob lived.

The Descendants of Asher

30 These are the descendants of Asher. He had four sons: Imnah, Ishvah, Ishvi, and Beriah; and one daughter, Serah.

31 Beriah had two sons, Heber and Malchiel. (Malchiel founded the city of Birzaith.)

32 Heber had three sons: Japhlet, Shomer, and Hotham; and one daughter, Shua.

33 Japhlet also had three sons: Pasach, Bimhal, and Ashvath.

34 His brother Shomer had three sons: Rohgah, Jehubbah, and Aram.

ʳ **7:12** *Probable text* Shuppim . . . Hushim *(see Gen 46:23; Num 26:39, 42); Hebrew* And Shuppim and Huppim, sons of Ir; Hushim son of Aher.   ˢ **7:13** BILHAH: *A concubine of Jacob and the mother of his two sons Dan and Naphtali.*   ᵗ **7:23** BERIAH: *This name sounds like the Hebrew for "in trouble."*

35 His brother Hotham[u] had four sons: Zophah, Imna, Shelesh, and Amal.

36 The descendants of Zophah were Suah, Harnepher, Shual, Beri, Imrah, **37** Bezer, Hod, Shamma, Shilshah, Ithran, and Beera.

38 The descendants of Jether were Jephunneh, Pispa, and Ara, **39** and the descendants of Ulla were Arah, Hanniel, and Rizia.

40 All of these were descendants of Asher. They were heads of families, famous fighting men, outstanding leaders. Asher's descendants included 26,000 men eligible for military duty.

The Descendants of Benjamin

8 **1** Benjamin had five sons. In order of age they were Bela, Ashbel, Aharah, **2** Nohah, and Rapha.

3 The descendants of Bela were Addar, Gera, Abihud, **4** Abishua, Naaman, Ahoah, **5** Gera, Shephuphan, and Huram.

6-7 The descendants of Ehud were Naaman, Ahijah, and Gera. They were heads of families that lived in Geba, but which were forced out and went to live in Manahath. Gera, the father of Uzza and Ahihud, led them in this move.

8-9 Shaharaim divorced two wives, Hushim and Baara. Later, when he lived in the country of Moab, he married Hodesh and had seven sons: Jobab, Zibia, Mesha, Malcam, **10** Jeuz, Sachia, and Mirmah. His sons all became heads of families.

11 He also had two sons by Hushim: Abitub and Elpaal.

12 Elpaal had three sons: Eber, Misham, and Shemed. It was Shemed who built the cities of Ono and Lod and the surrounding villages.

The Benjaminites in Gath and Aijalon

13 Beriah and Shema were heads of families that settled in the city of Aijalon and drove out the people who lived in the city of Gath. **14** Beriah's descendants included Ahio, Shashak, Jeremoth, **15** Zebadiah, Arad, Eder, **16** Michael, Ishpah, and Joha.

M...
and Jo... **Jerusalem**
19 Shim... included Zebadia...
Zichri, Zabdi, ...Ishmerai, Izliah,
21 Adaiah, Beraiah, ...
22 Shashak's descended Jakim,
Eber, Eliel, **23** Abdon, Zic... Eliel,
...niah, Elam, Anthothijah, **25** Ip...hpan,
Penuel.
...Hana-
26 Jeroham's descendants included ...
sherai, Shehariah, Athaliah, **27** Jaareshiah, ...
jah, and Zichri.

28 These were the ancestral heads of families and their principal descendants who lived in Jerusalem.

The Benjaminites in Gibeon and Jerusalem

29 Jeiel[v] founded the city of Gibeon and settled there. His wife was named Maacah, **30** and his oldest son, Abdon. His other sons were Zur, Kish, Baal, Ner,[w] Nadab, **31** Gedor, Ahio, Zechariah, **32** and Mikloth, the father of Shimeah. Their descendants lived in Jerusalem near other families of their clan.

The Family of King Saul

33 Ner was the father of Kish, and Kish was the father of King Saul. Saul had four sons: Jonathan, Malchishua, Abinadab, and Eshbaal.[x] **34** Jonathan was the father of Meribbaal,[y] who was the father of Micah.

35 Micah had four sons: Pithon, Melech, Tarea, and Ahaz. **36** Ahaz was the father of Jehoaddah, who was the father of three sons: Alemeth, Azmaveth, and Zimri. Zimri was the father of Moza, **37** Moza the father of Binea, Binea of Raphah, Raphah of Eleasah, and Eleasah of Azel.

38 Azel had six sons: Azrikam, Bocheru, Ishmael, Sheariah, Obadiah, and Hanan. **39** Azel's brother Eshek had three sons: Ulam, Jeush, and Eliphelet.

I Chronicles

u 7:35 *Probable text (see verse 32)* Hotham; *Hebrew* Helem.
w 8:30 *One ancient translation (and see 9:36)* Ner; *Hebrew does not have this name.*
x 8:33 ESHBAAL: *Called Ishbosheth in 2 Sam 2:8 and elsewhere in 2 Samuel.*
v 8:29 *Probable text (and see 9:35)* Jeiel; *Hebrew does not have this name.*
y 8:34 MERIBBAAL: *Called Mephibosheth in 2 Sam 4:4 and elsewhere in 2 Samuel.*

oldiers

Chronicles nd fifty sons

named above

⁴⁰Ulam's of Benjamin.

and archers

and grand

were m **Returned**

The

fro eople of Israel were listed

ng to their families, and this

ion was recorded in *The History of*

gs *of Israel.*

he people of Judah had been deported

o Babylon as punishment for their sins. ²The first to return to their property in the cities included Israelite citizens, priests, Levites, and Temple workers. ³People from the tribes of Judah, Benjamin, Ephraim, and Manasseh went to live in Jerusalem.

⁴⁻⁶There were 690 families of the tribe of Judah who lived in Jerusalem.

The descendants of Judah's son Perez had as their leader Uthai, the son of Ammihud and grandson of Omri. His other ancestors included Imri and Bani.

The descendants of Judah's son Shelah had as their leader Asaiah, who was the head of his family.

The descendants of Judah's son Zerah had Jeuel as their leader.

⁷⁻⁸The following members of the tribe of Benjamin lived in Jerusalem:

Sallu son of Meshullam, who was the son of Hodaviah, the son of Hassenuah

Ibneiah son of Jeroham

Elah, the son of Uzzi and grandson of Michri

Meshullam son of Shephatiah, who was the son of Reuel, the son of Ibnijah

⁹There were 956 families of this tribe living there. All the men named above were heads of families.

The Priests Who Lived in Jerusalem

¹⁰⁻¹²The following priests lived in Jerusalem:

Jedaiah, Jehoiarib, and Jachin

Azariah son of Hilkiah (the chief

official in the Temple), whose ancestors included Meshullam, Zadok, Meraioth, and Ahitub

Adaiah son of Jeroham, whose ancestors included Pashhur and Malchijah

Maasai son of Adiel, whose ancestors included Jahzerah, Meshullam, Meshillemith, and Immer

¹³The priests who were heads of families totaled 1,760. They were experts in all the work carried on in the Temple.

The Levites Who Lived in Jerusalem

¹⁴⁻¹⁶The following Levites lived in Jerusalem:

Shemaiah son of Hasshub, whose ancestors included Azrikam and Hashabiah, of the clan of Merari

Bakbakkar, Heresh, and Galal

Mattaniah son of Mica, whose ancestors included Zichri and Asaph

Obadiah son of Shemaiah, whose ancestors included Galal and Jeduthun

Berechiah, the son of Asa and grandson of Elkanah, who lived in the territory that belonged to the town of Netophah

The Temple Guards Who Lived in Jerusalem

¹⁷The following Temple guards lived in Jerusalem: Shallum, Akkub, Talmon, and Ahiman. Shallum was their leader. ¹⁸Down to that time members of their clans had been stationed at the eastern entrance to the King's Gate. ᶻ Formerly they had stood guard at the gates to the camps of the Levites.

¹⁹Shallum, the son of Kore and grandson of Ebiasaph, together with his fellow members of the clan of Korah, was responsible for guarding the entrance to the Tent of the LORD's presence, just as their ancestors had been when they were in charge of the LORD's camp. ²⁰Phinehas son of Eleazar— may the LORD be with him!—had supervised them at one time.

ᶻ **9:18** KING'S GATE: *The east gate of the Temple, through which the king usually entered.*
9:2, 3 Ezra 2:70; 7:6-9; Neh 7:73

21 Zechariah son of Meshelemiah was also a guard at the entrance to the Tent of the LORD's presence.

22 In all, 212 men were chosen as guards for the entrances and gates. They were registered according to the villages where they lived. It was King David and the prophet Samuel who had put their ancestors in these responsible positions. 23 They and their descendants continued to guard the gates to the Temple. 24 There was a gate facing in each direction, north, south, east, and west, and each had a chief guard. 25 These guards were assisted by their relatives, who lived in the villages and who had to take turns at guard duty for seven days at a time. 26 The four chief guards were Levites and had the final responsibility. They were also responsible for the rooms in the Temple and for the supplies kept there. 27 They lived near the Temple, because it was their duty to guard it and to open the gates every morning.

The Other Levites

28 Other Levites were responsible for the utensils used in worship. They checked them out and checked them back in every time they were used. 29 Others were in charge of the other sacred equipment, and of the flour, wine, olive oil, incense, and spices. 30 But the responsibility for mixing the spices belonged to the priests.

31 A Levite named Mattithiah, oldest son of Shallum, of the clan of Korah, was responsible for preparing the baked offerings.[a] 32 Members of the clan of Kohath were responsible for preparing the sacred bread[b] for the Temple every Sabbath.

33 Some Levite families were responsible for the Temple music. The heads of these families lived in some of the Temple buildings and were free from other duties, because they were on call day and night.

34 The men named above were heads of Levite families, according to their ancestral

lines. They were the leaders who lived Jerusalem.

The Ancestors and Descendants of King Saul
(1 Chronicles 8:29–38)

35 Jeiel founded the city of Gibeon and settled there. His wife was named Maacah. 36 His oldest son was Abdon, and his other sons were Zur, Kish, Baal, Ner, Nadab, 37 Gedor, Ahio, Zechariah, and Mikloth, 38 the father of Shimeah. Their descendants lived in Jerusalem near other families of their clan.

39 Ner was the father of Kish, and Kish was the father of Saul. Saul had four sons: Jonathan, Malchishua, Abinadab, and Eshbaal.[c] 40 Jonathan was the father of Meribbaal,[d] who was the father of Micah. 41 Micah had four sons: Pithon, Melech, Tarea, and Ahaz.[e] 42 Ahaz was the father of Jarah, who was the father of three sons: Alemeth, Azmaveth, and Zimri. Zimri was the father of Moza, 43 Moza the father of Binea, Binea of Rephaiah, Rephaiah of Eleasah, and Eleasah of Azel.

44 Azel had six sons: Azrikam, Bocheru, Ishmael, Sheariah, Obadiah, and Hanan.

The Death of King Saul
(1 Samuel 31:1–13)

10 1 The Philistines fought a battle against the Israelites on Mount Gilboa. Many Israelites were killed there, and the rest of them, including King Saul and his sons, fled. 2 But the Philistines caught up with them and killed three of Saul's sons, Jonathan, Abinadab, and Malchishua. 3 The fighting was heavy around Saul, and he was hit by enemy arrows and badly wounded. 4 He said to the young man carrying his weapons, "Draw your sword and kill me, to keep these godless Philistines from gloating over me." But the young man was too terrified to do it. So Saul took his own sword and threw himself on it. 5 The young man

---

a **9:31** BAKED OFFERINGS: *Thin cakes of flour and olive oil which were baked and then presented as offerings to God (see Lev 2:4–6).* b **9:32** SACRED BREAD: *Twelve loaves of bread which were placed on a table in the Temple each Sabbath as an offering to God (see Lev 24:5–9).* c **9:39** ESHBAAL: *Called Ishbosheth in 2 Sam 2:8 and elsewhere in 2 Samuel.* d **9:40** MERIBBAAL: *Called Mephibosheth in 2 Sam 4:4 and elsewhere in 2 Samuel.* e **9:41** *Some ancient translations* Ahaz (see 1 Chr 8:35); *Hebrew does not have this name.*

"My son Solomon is the one." (29:1)

volunteered to give [7]the following for the work on the Temple: 190 tons of gold, 380 tons of silver, 675 tons of bronze, and 3,750 tons of iron. [8]Those who had precious stones gave them to the Temple treasury, which was administered by Jehiel of the Levite clan of Gershon. [9]The people had given willingly to the LORD, and they were happy that so much had been given. King David also was extremely happy.

David Praises God

[10]There in front of the whole assembly King David praised the LORD. He said, "LORD God of our ancestor Jacob, may you be praised forever and ever! [11]You are great and powerful, glorious, splendid, and majestic. Everything in heaven and earth is yours, and you are king, supreme ruler over all. [12]All riches and wealth come from you; you rule everything by your strength and power; and you are able to make anyone great and strong. [13]Now, our God, we give you thanks, and we praise your glorious name.

[14]"Yet my people and I cannot really give you anything, because everything is a gift from you, and we have only given back what is yours already. [15]You know, O LORD, that we pass through life like exiles and strangers, as our ancestors did. Our days are like a passing shadow, and we cannot escape death. [16]O LORD, our God, we have brought together all this wealth to build a temple to honor your holy name, but it all came from you and all belongs to you. [17]I know that you test everyone's heart and are pleased with people of integrity. In honesty and sincerity I have willingly given all this to you, and I have seen

how your people who are gathered here have been happy to bring offerings to you. [18]LORD God of our ancestors Abraham, Isaac, and Jacob, keep such devotion forever strong in your people's hearts and keep them always faithful to you. [19]Give my son Solomon a wholehearted desire to obey everything that you command and to build the Temple for which I have made these preparations."

[20]Then David commanded the people, "Praise the LORD your God!" And the whole assembly praised the LORD, the God of their ancestors, and they bowed low and gave honor to the LORD and also to the king.

[21]The following day they killed animals as sacrifices, dedicating them to the LORD, and then gave them to the people to eat. In addition, they sacrificed a thousand bulls, a thousand rams, and a thousand lambs, which they burned whole on the altar. They also brought the offerings of wine. [22]So that day they were very happy as they ate and drank in the presence of the LORD.

For a second time they proclaimed Solomon king. In the name of the LORD they anointed him as their ruler and Zadok as priest. [23]So Solomon succeeded his father David on the throne which the LORD had established. He was a successful king, and the whole nation of Israel obeyed him. [24]All the officials and soldiers, and even all of David's other sons, promised to be loyal to Solomon as king. [25]The LORD made the whole nation stand in awe of Solomon, and he made him more glorious than any other king that had ruled Israel.

Summary of David's Reign

[26]David son of Jesse ruled over all Israel [27]for forty years. He ruled in Hebron for seven years and in Jerusalem for thirty-three. [28]He died at a ripe old age, wealthy and respected, and his son Solomon succeeded him as king. [29]The history of King David from beginning to end is recorded in the records of the three prophets, Samuel, Nathan, and Gad. [30]The records tell how he ruled, how powerful he was, and all the things that happened to him, to Israel, and to the surrounding kingdoms.

"That was a great movie, but I want to know what happens to the hero. I can't wait for part two! When do you think it'll come out?" When a movie ends and gives a hint that there is another part of the story, most likely a sequel is in the making. It's a good way for moviemakers to get people to come back again. If you just read First Chronicles, you don't have to wait another year to read the sequel. It is right here.

It was natural for the first book to end when David dies and Solomon takes over as king. Second Chronicles continues the history of the Israelite kings and how the kingdom is divided after Solomon's death. But, unlike Second Kings, Second Chronicles focuses on the history and kings of Judah, paying little attention to the northern kingdom of Israel.

Chap. 9:17–19

Headlines

- Work Starts on Temple Building (2:17—3:14)
- Dedication Marked by Fire from Sky (7:1–6)
- African Queen Visits Solomon (9:1–12)
- King Jehoshaphat Begins Reforms (17:1–9)
- King Hezekiah Rededicates Temple (29:18–36)
- Josiah Promises to Keep Covenant (34:29–33)
- Decree Calls for Jews to Return (36:22–23)

FACTOIDS

How does this book fit into the Bible? This book is a continuation of First Chronicles and records the history of Judah from King Solomon to the end of the Babylonian captivity.

Why was it written? It was written to remind the Israelites that God is always with them, even in exile, and to give them hope for the future.

Who are the young people in this book? Joash was seven, Uzziah was sixteen, Manasseh was twelve, Josiah was eight, and Jehoiachin was eighteen when they were named as kings of Judah.

Important themes
- The kings of Judah are measured by their faithfulness to God.
- Israelites must maintain proper worship in the Temple.
- God's faithful people will see Jerusalem and the Temple rebuilt.

Jehoiada's Policies Are Reversed

As long as Jehoiada was alive, sacrifices were offered regularly at the Temple. 15 After reaching the very old age of a hundred and thirty, he died. 16 They buried him in the royal tombs in David's City in recognition of the service he had done for the people of Israel, for God, and for the Temple.

17 But once Jehoiada was dead, the leaders of Judah persuaded King Joash to listen to them instead. 18 And so the people stopped worshiping in the Temple of the LORD, the God of their ancestors, and began to worship idols and the images of the goddess Asherah. Their guilt for these sins brought the LORD's anger on Judah and Jerusalem. 19 The LORD sent prophets to warn them to return to him, but the people refused to listen. 20 Then the spirit of God took control of Zechariah son of Jehoiada the priest. He stood where the people could see him and called out, "The LORD God asks why you have disobeyed his commands and are bringing disaster on yourselves! You abandoned him, so he has abandoned you!" 21 King Joash joined in a conspiracy against Zechariah, and on the king's orders the people stoned Zechariah in the Temple courtyard. 22 The king forgot about the loyal service that Zechariah's father Jehoiada had given him, and he had Zechariah killed. As Zechariah was dying, he called out, "May the LORD see what you are doing and punish you!"

The End of Joash's Reign

23 When autumn came that year, the Syrian army attacked Judah and Jerusalem, killed all the leaders, and took large amounts of loot back to Damascus. 24 The Syrian army was small, but the LORD let them defeat a much larger Judean army because the people had abandoned him, the LORD God of their ancestors. In this way King Joash was punished. 25 He was severely wounded, and when the enemy withdrew, two of his officials plotted against him and killed him in his bed to avenge the murder of the son[i] of Jehoiada the priest. He was buried in David's City, but not

in the royal tombs. (26 Those who plotted against him were Zabad, the son of an Ammonite woman named Shimeath, and Jehozabad, the son of a Moabite woman named Shimrith.) 27 The *Commentary on the Book of Kings* contains the stories of the sons of Joash, the prophecies spoken against him, and the record of how he rebuilt the Temple. His son Amaziah succeeded him as king.

King Amaziah of Judah
(2 Kings 14:2–6)

25 1 Amaziah became king at the age of twenty-five, and he ruled in Jerusalem for twenty-nine years. His mother was Jehoaddin from Jerusalem. 2 He did what was pleasing to the LORD, but did it reluctantly. 3 As soon as he was firmly in power, he executed the officials who had murdered his father. 4 He did not, however, execute their children, but followed what the LORD had commanded in the Law of Moses: "Parents are not to be put to death for crimes committed by their children, and children are not to be put to death for crimes committed by their parents; people are to be put to death only for crimes they themselves have committed."

War against Edom
(2 Kings 14:7)

5 King Amaziah organized all the men of the tribes of Judah and Benjamin into army units, according to the clans they belonged to, and placed officers in command of units of a thousand and units of a hundred. This included all men twenty years of age or older, 300,000 in all. They were picked troops, ready for battle, skilled in using spears and shields. 6 In addition, he hired 100,000 soldiers from Israel at a cost of about four tons of silver. 7 But a prophet went to the king and said to him, "Don't take these Israelite soldiers with you. The LORD is not with these people from the Northern Kingdom. 8 You may think that they will make you stronger[j] in battle, but it is God who has

---

i 24:25 Some ancient translations son; *Hebrew* sons.   *j 25:8 Some ancient translations* You may . . . stronger; *Hebrew* unclear.

24:20, 21 Mt 23:35; Lk 11:51   **25:4** Deut 24:16

the power to give victory or defeat, and he will let your enemies defeat you."

9 Amaziah asked the prophet, "But what about all that silver I have already paid for them?"

The prophet replied, "The LORD can give you back more than that!" 10 So Amaziah sent the hired troops away and told them to go home. At this they went home, bitterly angry with the people of Judah.

11 Amaziah summoned up his courage and led his army to Salt Valley. There they fought and killed ten thousand Edomite soldiers 12 and captured another ten thousand. They took the prisoners to the top of the cliff at the city of Sela and threw them off, so that they were killed on the rocks below.

13 Meanwhile the Israelite soldiers that Amaziah had not allowed to go into battle with him attacked the Judean cities between Samaria and Beth Horon, killed three thousand men, and captured quantities of loot.

14 When Amaziah returned from defeating the Edomites, he brought their idols back with him, set them up, worshiped them, and burned incense to them. 15 This made the LORD angry, so he sent a prophet to Amaziah. The prophet demanded, "Why have you worshiped foreign gods that could not even save their own people from your power?"

16 "Since when," Amaziah interrupted, "have we made you adviser to the king? Stop talking, or I'll have you killed!"

The prophet stopped, but not before saying, "Now I know that God has decided to destroy you because you have done all this and have ignored my advice."

War against Israel
(2 Kings 14:8–20)

17 King Amaziah of Judah and his advisers plotted against Israel. He then sent a message to King Jehoash of Israel, who was the son of Jehoahaz and grandson of Jehu, challenging him to fight.[k] 18 Jehoash sent this answer to Amaziah: "Once a thorn bush in the Lebanon Mountains sent a message to a cedar: 'Give your daughter in marriage to my son.' A wild animal passed by and trampled the bush down. 19 Now Amaziah, you boast that you have defeated the Edomites, but I advise you to stay at home. Why stir up trouble that will only bring disaster on you and your people?"

20 But Amaziah refused to listen. It was God's will for Amaziah to be defeated, because he had worshiped the Edomite idols. 21 So King Jehoash of Israel went into battle against King Amaziah of Judah. They met at Beth Shemesh in Judah, 22 the Judean army was defeated, and the soldiers fled to their homes. 23 Jehoash captured Amaziah and took him to Jerusalem. There he tore down the city wall from Ephraim Gate to the Corner Gate, a distance of two hundred yards. 24 He took back to Samaria as loot all the gold and silver in the Temple, the Temple equipment guarded by the descendants of Obed Edom, and the palace treasures. He also took hostages with him.

25 King Amaziah of Judah outlived King Jehoash of Israel by fifteen years. 26 All the other things that Amaziah did from the beginning to the end of his reign are recorded in *The History of the Kings of Judah and Israel*. 27 Ever since the time when he rebelled against the LORD, there had been a plot against him in Jerusalem. Finally he fled to the city of Lachish, but his enemies followed him there and killed him. 28 His body was carried to Jerusalem on a horse, and he was buried in the royal tombs in David's City.

King Uzziah of Judah
(2 Kings 14:21, 22; 15:1–7)

26 1 All the people of Judah chose Amaziah's sixteen-year-old son Uzziah to succeed his father as king. (2 It was after the death of Amaziah that Uzziah recaptured Elath and rebuilt the city.)

3 Uzziah became king at the age of sixteen, and he ruled in Jerusalem for fifty-two years. His mother was Jecoliah from Jerusalem. 4 Following the example of his father, he did what was pleasing to the LORD. 5 As long as Zechariah, his religious

_____

k **25:17** challenging him to fight; *or* inviting him to a conference.

When the Galliano family left for vacation, they never imagined what would happen. First, they couldn't get home because their car died. When they got the car fixed, they still couldn't go home because of a hurricane. When they finally got back to their home in Florida, they found out the hurricane had ruined part of their house. It seemed so hopeless.

That is probably how the Israelites felt when they returned to Jerusalem—only a whole lot worse. After being in exile for 50 years, they came home to a city that needed a lot of repair. The Temple needed to be rebuilt so they could worship God again, and the city walls needed to be rebuilt for their protection. It was a big job that took a lot of work and cooperation. The books of Ezra and Nehemiah tell part of the rebuilding story.

Chap. 2

Head**lines**

- Jewish Exiles Free After Fifty Years (Ezra 1:1–10)
- Dispute Over Rebuilding the Temple (Ezra 4:1–5)
- Returned Exiles Celebrate Passover (Ezra 6:19–22)
- Ezra Delivers Gifts from King Cyrus (Ezra 8:24–30)
- Nehemiah Asks to Help Rebuild (Nehemiah 2:1–8)
- Wealthy Leaders Take Advantage of Poor People (Nehemiah 5:1–13)
- Nehemiah Dedicates Rebuilt City Wall (Nehemiah 12:27–40)

FACTOIDS

Who wrote these books? The author is unknown, but these books were probably written by a scribe who used personal accounts, or memoirs, from Ezra and Nehemiah to compose them.

What time period do they cover? These books cover the return of the exiles to Jerusalem from the Babylonian captivity to Nehemiah's rule as governor.

Why were they written? These books were written to give an account of the rebuilding of Jerusalem and the Temple after the Exile.

Jesus connection: In the Gospels, Jesus referred to his Resurrection as the rebuilding of the Temple (John 2:19).

Important themes
- The Israelites return from captivity and rebuild Jerusalem and the Temple.
- Prayer, worship, cooperation, strong leadership, and a renewed commitment to God were necessary for the Israelites to rebuild.

EZRA

Cyrus Commands the Jews to Return

1 ¹In the first year that Cyrus of Persia was emperor,ª the LORD made what he had said through the prophet Jeremiah come true. He prompted Cyrus to issue the following command and send it out in writing to be read aloud everywhere in his empire:

²"This is the command of Cyrus, Emperor of Persia. The LORD, the God of Heaven, has made me ruler over the whole world and has given me the responsibility of building a temple for him in Jerusalem in Judah. ³May God be with all of you who are his people. You are to go to Jerusalem and rebuild the Temple of the LORD, the God of Israel, the God who is worshiped in Jerusalem. ⁴If any of his people in exile need help to return, their neighbors are to give them this help. They are to provide them with silver and gold, supplies and pack animals, as well as offerings to present in the Temple of God in Jerusalem."

⁵Then the heads of the clans of the tribes of Judah and Benjamin, the priests and Levites, and everyone else whose heart God had moved got ready to go and rebuild the LORD's Temple in Jerusalem. ⁶All their neighbors helped them by giving them many things: silver utensils, gold, supplies, pack animals, other valuables, and offerings for the Temple.

⁷Emperor Cyrus gave them back the bowls and cups that King Nebuchadnezzar had taken from the Temple in Jerusalem and had put in the temple of his gods. ⁸He handed them over to Mithredath, chief of the royal treasury, who made an inventory of them for Sheshbazzar, the governor of Judah, ⁹⁻¹⁰as follows:

gold bowls for offerings	30
silver bowls for offerings	1,000
other bowls	29
small gold bowls	30
small silver bowls	410
other utensils	1,000

¹¹In all there were 5,400 gold and silver

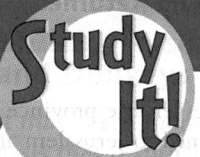

Persian Connection

Persia is an ancient region that is now called Iran. It is in the Middle East, near Iraq, Afghanistan, and Turkey. Three large bodies of water are near it: the Persian Gulf, the Caspian Sea, and the Gulf of Oman. Persia was an important place for the Jewish people who were exiled in Babylon. From Persia came their deliverer, Cyrus the Great.

Cyrus was the emperor in Persia in the sixth century BC. He was called Cyrus the Great because he was a strong warrior, and he also ruled fairly. It is possible that he is the author of the first declaration of human rights. The Jews were finally allowed to return from exile under Cyrus. He also did other good things for the people who lived in his kingdom. The name Cyrus means "like the sun." Even today men are named Cyrus.

Do you know who you are named after and what your name means? If it was someone from the Bible or a saint, find out what he or she did. If not, look up your name in a name book and find out what it means.

— Ezra, chapter 1

ª **1:1** EMPEROR: *King Cyrus of Persia occupied the city of Babylon in 539 B.C. and began to reign as the emperor of Babylonia.*
1:1 Jer 25:11; 29:10   **1:2** Isa 44:28

"O Lord . . . help me with what I am about to do."
(13:4)

glory of Jerusalem. ⁵Now is the time to rescue your chosen people and to help me carry out my plan to destroy the enemies who are threatening us." ⁶Judith went to the bedpost by Holofernes' head and took down his sword. ⁷She came closer, seized Holofernes by the hair of his head, and said, "O Lord, God of Israel, give me strength now." ⁸Then Judith raised the sword and struck him twice in the neck as hard as she could, chopping off his head. ⁹She rolled his body off the bed and took down the mosquito net from the bedposts. Then she came out and gave Holofernes' head to her slave, ¹⁰who put it in the food bag.

Judith and Her Slave Return to Bethulia

Then the two women left together, as they always did when they went to pray. After they had walked through the Assyrian camp, they crossed the valley and went up the mountainside until they came to the gates of Bethulia. ¹¹When they were a short distance away, Judith called out to the guards at the gate, "Open the gate! Open the gate! Our God is still with us. Today he has once again shown his strength in Israel and used his power against our enemies." ¹²When the men heard her voice, they hurried down to the gates and called for the town officials. ¹³Everyone, young and old, ran together to the gate. No one could believe that Judith had come back. They opened the gate for her and her slave and welcomed them. Then, when they had lit a fire to give some light and had gathered around the two women, ¹⁴Judith shouted, "Praise God, give him praise! Praise God,

Peace, Not Violence

What Judith did was very violent. What the Israelites did once they had control of the situation was also very violent. It might make you think that violence is okay with God. But that is not really what the Bible teaches. In the Old Testament, many of the victories attributed to God are violent because the Israelites saw military victories as symbolic victories over the gods of other nations. Gradually they came to realize that there aren't any other gods; Yahweh is the only God, and he is God of all people. Jesus reinforced this by teaching that we must love all people, even our enemies, because God loves all people, too.

It's often tempting to use violence because it seems like a quick solution. But it's never a final solution. It always creates more violence, or at least the desire for more violence, once strength is regained. There can never be "a war to end all wars." It's important to put the violence of the Bible in proper perspective. The real message in the Bible is that God is calling us to be peacemakers.

Isaiah (2:4) and Micah (4:3) both speak of a time when people will "hammer their swords into plows," when "nations will never again go to war." That's the vision we need to work toward. Jesus also warned us, "All who take the sword will die by the sword" (Matthew 26:52).

— Judith 13:1–10

Aaron & Miriam

Breakthrough!: You two come from a pretty famous family.

Aaron [AIR-uhn]: You could say that; our brother, Moses, is really the famous one.

B: But it would be fair to say that the three of you really worked as a team, wouldn't it?

Miriam [MIR-ee-uhm]: Well, yes. The three of us are very close. Aaron was actually Moses' spokesman. Moses has a bit of a speech problem, you see, and so God said that Aaron could be the one to speak to the people. Later, Aaron became the first high priest of the Israelites [IZ-ry-el-yts].

Aaron: And Miriam acted as the leader of the Hebrew [HEE-broo] women in the group that escaped from slavery.

B: And if it weren't for you, Miriam, Moses might never have survived to lead the Hebrew slaves out of Egypt, right?

Miriam: Yes, I helped hide him as a baby. Pharaoh [FAIR-oh] had commanded that all the baby boys be thrown into the river and drowned.

The Egyptians were afraid that soon there would be so many Hebrew slaves that we would rise up and revolt. My mother made a basket that floated, and I followed the basket and made sure that Moses was safe.

B: Is it true that you two were angry with Moses about the woman he married?

Aaron: Yes, that is true. We thought he should have married a Hebrew woman, but instead he chose an outsider. God let us know that we should trust him and Moses, though Miriam was struck with leprosy. I pleaded with Moses and Moses pleaded with God for her to be healed.

B: What advice would you like to give our readers?

Miriam: Well, brothers and sisters don't always get along, but with God's help you can be a great support to each other.

Ruth

Breakthrough!: Your story is kind of a sad one, isn't it, Ruth?

Ruth: Oh, I wouldn't say so. I mean, it started out sad; my husband, my father-in-law, and my brother-in-law had all died. My mother-in-law, Naomi [NAY-oh-mee], my sister-in-law, Orpah [OHR-puh], and I were all widows. In my time widows didn't have any way to support themselves; that's why Naomi decided to go back to her own home. She had come to my country, Moab [MOH-ab], when there was a famine in Bethlehem.

B: Didn't Naomi tell you and Orpah to go back to your own families?

Ruth: She did, but when it came time to say good-bye, I just couldn't leave her. We had become so close. I love her. She taught me about life and about God. She is my family now.

B: People say that you were pretty clever. You and Naomi returned to her hometown, and all of sudden you were married to one of the wealthiest men in town!

Ruth: I guess you could say I'm clever. Naomi gave me good advice, though, and Boaz [BOH-az] was so kind; he really looked out for me. Boaz was my dead husband's relative, and that made it easier to approach him. But he really didn't have to marry me—because I was a foreign woman and all.

B: So would you say you're a "glass half full" kind of person?

Ruth: Well I've always tried to see the good in any situation. It really helped to learn that the God of the Israelites [IZ-ry-el-yts] cared for me, too—a foreign woman. Can you believe that King David, the greatest king of the Israelites, was one of my descendants!

Samuel

Breakthrough!: Tell us, Samuel, did you always know that you'd be a prophet?

Samuel: Well, my mother, Hannah [HAN-uh], seemed to think I'd be special. She prayed and prayed that God would send her a son. When I was finally born, she dedicated me to God.

B: You anointed the first king of Israel [IZ-ry-el]—that's pretty impressive. How did you feel about that?

Samuel: I actually tried to convince the people that they didn't need a king and that having a king would only bring them trouble. They wanted to be like other nations though. The Lord told me that Saul was the one to anoint.

B: And was he a good king?

Samuel: Hmph! Well, yes and no. Sometimes he was great; he defeated the Ammonites [AM-uh-nyts]. But there were times when I had to remind Saul that he was supposed to do things God's way, not just do whatever he felt like.

B: Is it true that the first time God spoke to you, you didn't realize it was God?

Samuel: That's actually a pretty funny story. God was calling me in the middle of the night, and I thought it was my master, Eli [EE-ly]. I kept waking Eli up thinking he needed something. Eli helped me understand that it was really the Lord who was calling me.

B: Didn't you anoint another king after Saul had disobeyed the Lord?

Samuel: I was pretty depressed after Saul was disobedient to God. God sent me out to Bethlehem to anoint a new king. I almost overlooked David; his older brothers were so much bigger and stronger. But David was handsome, heroic, and he really loved the Lord. Through David, God was able to unite the Twelve Tribes of Israel into one nation.

Saul

Breakthrough!: King Saul, you were the first king of Israel [IZ-ry-el]. How were you chosen?

Saul: I was a soldier and a military leader, and one day the prophet Samuel came to me and anointed me to be king. He told me that I had been chosen by God.

B: How did the people respond?

Saul: They seemed pleased to have me for their king, and I tried my best. But somewhere along the line, things started to go bad.

B: What happened?

Saul: I made some decisions that showed my lack of faith in God. Samuel told me that because I disobeyed God, God had turned away from me.

B: So what happened?

Saul: Our enemies, the Philistines [fih-LIHS-teenz], were getting the best of us until David came along and killed Goliath [guh-LY-uhth]. From then on, everything seemed to go his way. When I found out that he had been anointed to be the next king, it bothered me.

B: What did you do?

Saul: I became very jealous of David and how popular he was getting. He had won over my son Jonathan and my daughter Michal [MY-kuhl], who became his wife. I know it was wrong, but I was determined to get rid of David.

B: Did you succeed?

Saul: No, and now it doesn't matter. My sons and I lost our lives in a battle on Mount Gilboa [gil-BOH-uh], fighting against the Philistines. I pray that David forgives me for my insane jealousy and for persecuting him.

B: Any words for our readers?

Saul: Have faith in God and do not disobey him, especially when God chooses you to be a leader.

When the men heard her voice . . . (13:12)

Judith's Plan

14 [1]Then Judith said to them, "My friends, please follow my advice. In the morning, take this head and hang it on the town wall. [2]Appoint a leader for yourselves, and at sunrise have all your able-bodied men take their weapons and march out of the town with him, as if they were going down into the valley to attack the Assyrian outpost. [3]The Assyrian guards will grab their weapons and rush back to camp to wake up their officers. The officers will run to Holofernes' tent but will not find him, and the whole army will be terrified and retreat as you advance against them. [4]Then you and all the other Israelites will be able to follow them and kill them as they retreat. [5]But before you do any of this, send Achior the Ammonite to me. I want to see if he recognizes Holofernes, the man who spoke of Israel with contempt and sent Achior to us, thinking he would be killed along with the rest of us."

who has not held back his mercy from the people of Israel. Tonight he has used me to destroy our enemies." [15]She then took the head out of the food bag and showed it to the people. "Here," she said, "is the head of Holofernes, the general of the Assyrian army, and here is the mosquito net from his bed, where he lay in a drunken stupor. The Lord used a woman to kill him. [16]As the Lord lives, I swear that Holofernes never touched me, although my beauty deceived him and brought him to his ruin. I was not defiled or disgraced; the Lord took care of me through it all."

[17]Everyone in the city was utterly amazed. They bowed down and worshiped God, praying together, "Our God, you are worthy of great praise. Today you have triumphed over the enemies of your people."

[18]Then Uzziah said, "Judith, my dear, the Most High God has blessed you more than any other woman on earth. How worthy of praise is the Lord God who created heaven and earth! He guided you as you cut off the head of our deadliest enemy. [19]Your trust in God will never be forgotten by those who tell of God's power. [20]May God give you everlasting honor for what you have done. May he reward you with blessings, because you remained faithful to him and did not hesitate to risk your own life to relieve the oppression of your people."

All the people replied, "Amen, amen!"

Achior's Conversion

[6]So they called Achior from Uzziah's house. But when he came and saw the head of Holofernes in the hands of one of the men, Achior fainted and fell to the floor. [7]When they had helped him up, Achior bowed at Judith's feet in respect. "May every family in the land of Judah praise you," he said, "and may every nation tremble with terror when they hear your name. [8]Please tell me how you managed to do this."

While all the people were gathered around, Judith told him everything that she had done from the day she left the town until that moment. [9]When she had finished her story, the people cheered so loudly that the whole town echoed with sounds of joy. [10]When Achior heard all that the God of Israel had done, he became a firm believer. He was circumcised and made a member of the Israelite community, as his descendants are to the present day.

13:18 Judg 5:24; Lk 1:28, 42

Panic in Holofernes' Camp

11 The next morning the Israelites hung the head of Holofernes on the wall of the town. All of them took up their weapons and went out in companies to the slopes in front of the town. 12 When the Assyrians saw what was happening, they sent word to their officers, and these reported the matter to their superiors. 13 These men then went to Holofernes' tent and said to Bagoas, "Wake up the general! Those worthless Israelites have dared to come down from the mountain to attack us; they are just asking to be destroyed."

14 Bagoas went in and clapped his hands in front of the sleeping quarters of the tent, thinking that Holofernes was in bed with Judith. 15 When there was no answer, he drew the curtain aside and went in, and there he found the headless body sprawled over a footstool. 16 Bagoas let out a yell. He screamed, tore his clothes, and started groaning and weeping. 17 He went into the tent where Judith had stayed, but of course he did not find her. He rushed out and shouted to the officers, 18 "They have tricked us! One Israelite woman has disgraced Nebuchadnezzar's whole kingdom. Look in there! Holofernes is lying dead on the ground and his head is gone!" 19 When the officers heard this, they tore their clothes in grief; and as the panic spread, wild cries and shouts were heard throughout the camp.

Israel's Victory

15 1 When the soldiers heard what had happened, they were horrified 2 and began to tremble with fear. They all scattered in different directions from the camp, making no effort to stay together as they tried to escape along the paths in the mountains and valleys. 3 The soldiers who had camped in the mountains around Bethulia also began to retreat. Then all the Israelite soldiers came charging down on them.

4 Uzziah sent messengers to the towns of Betomesthaim, Bebai, Choba, and Kola, and throughout the land of Israel to tell everyone what had happened and to urge them to join in pursuing and destroying the enemy.

5 When they received the message, they all attacked the Assyrians and chased them as far as Choba, slaughtering them as they went. Even the people of Jerusalem and others living in the mountains joined the attack when the messengers told them what had happened in the Assyrian camp. The people of the regions of Gilead and Galilee blocked the path of the retreating Assyrians and inflicted heavy losses on them. They pursued them as far as the region around Damascus.

6 The rest of the people in Bethulia went down to the Assyrian camp, plundered it and carried away enough loot to make themselves very rich. 7 When the Israelite soldiers returned from the slaughter, they helped themselves to what was left. There was so much of it that the people of the towns and villages in the hill country also shared in the loot.

Israel Celebrates the Victory

8 The High Priest Joakim and the Council of Israel came from Jerusalem to see for themselves what great things the Lord had done for his people and to meet Judith and congratulate her. 9 When they arrived, they all praised her, "You are Jerusalem's crowning glory, the heroine of Israel, the pride and joy of our people! 10 You have won this great victory for Israel by yourself. God, the Almighty, is pleased with what you have done. May he bless you as long as you live."

All the people responded, "Amen."

11 It took the people thirty days to finish

"You are . . . the heroine of Israel!" (15:9)

looting the camp of the Assyrians. Judith was given Holofernes' tent, all his silver, his bowls, his couches, and all his furniture. She took them and loaded as much as she could on her mule; then she brought her wagons and loaded them too. 12 All the Israelite women came to see her; they sang her praises and danced in her honor. On this joyful occasion Judith and the other women waved ivy-covered branches 13 and wore wreaths of olive leaves on their heads. Judith took her place at the head of the procession to lead the women as they danced. All the men of Israel followed, wearing wreaths of flowers on their heads, carrying their weapons, and singing songs of praise.

Judith's Song of Praise

16 1 Then Judith sang a song of thanksgiving there with all Israel present, and the people joined in this song of praise. 2 She sang,

"Praise my God and sing to him;
    praise the Lord with drums and cymbals;
    play a new song for him.
Praise him and call on him for help.
3 The Lord is a warrior who ends war.
    He rescued me from my pursuers
    and brought me back to his people's
       camp.
4 Down from the mountains of the north
       came the Assyrians,
    with their tens of thousands of soldiers.
Their troops blocked the rivers in the
       valleys;
    their cavalry covered the mountains.
5 They threatened to set fire to our
       country,
    slaughter our young men,
    dash our babies to the ground,
    take our children away as captives,
    and carry off all our young women.
6 But the Lord Almighty tricked them;
    he used a woman to stop them.
7 Their hero was not slain by young soldiers
    or attacked and killed by mighty giants.
It was Judith, the daughter of Merari,
    who brought him down with her
       beauty.

8 She gave victory to the oppressed people
       of Israel,
    when she took off her widow's clothes,
    and put on a linen dress to entice him.
She put on her rich perfumes
    and tied a ribbon around her hair.
9 Her dainty sandal caught his eye;
    her beauty captured his heart.
Then the sword slashed through his neck.
10 The Persians trembled at her daring;
    the Medes were amazed at her bravery.
11 Then our people shouted in victory.
    They had been weak and oppressed,
    but they forced the enemy to retreat in
       panic and fear.
12 We are the descendants of slaves,
    but our enemies turned and ran;
    we killed them like runaway slaves.
    They were destroyed by the army of the
       Lord.

13 "I will sing a new song to my God.
    O Lord, you are strong and glorious!
    You have never been defeated.
14 Let all your creatures serve you.
    You gave the command,
    and all of them came into being;
    you breathed on them,
    and all of them were created.
    No one can oppose your command.
15 The mountains and the seas tremble,
    and rocks melt like wax when you
       come near.
But there is mercy for all who obey you.
16 The Lord is more pleased with those who
       obey him
    than with all the choice meat on the
       altar,
    or with all the most fragrant sacrifices.
17 The nations who rise up against my
       people are doomed.
    The Lord Almighty will punish them
       on Judgment Day.
    He will send fire and worms to devour
       their bodies,
    and they will weep in pain forever."

Judith's Fame

18 When the people arrived in Jerusalem, they purified themselves and worshiped

God. They presented their burnt offerings, freewill offerings, and gifts. ¹⁹Judith dedicated to God all of Holofernes' property, which the people had given to her. And as a special offering in fulfillment of a vow, she presented to the Lord the mosquito net which she had taken from Holofernes' bed. ²⁰For three months the people continued to celebrate in front of the Temple in Jerusalem, and Judith stayed there with them.

²¹When the celebrations had ended, everyone returned home, and Judith went back to Bethulia to live on her own estate. For the rest of her life she was famous throughout the land of Israel. ²²Many men wanted to marry her, but she never remarried after the death of her husband Manasseh. ²³⁻²⁴Her fame continued to spread, and she lived in the house her husband had left her. Before she died, Judith divided her property among her husband's and her own close relatives and set her slave woman free. When she died in Bethulia at the age of 105, she was buried beside her husband, and the people of Israel mourned her death for seven days. ²⁵As long as Judith lived, and for many years after her death, no one dared to threaten the people of Israel.

Have you ever made an enemy? A grudge can lead to hate, opening the door to power struggles, plots, counterplots . . . and before you know it, more people are involved—and are getting hurt.

This is the unfolding drama in the story of Queen Esther. Her cousin Mordecai, a Jew like her, refuses to honor the court official, Haman's ancestors were enemies of the Jews. He uses his influence with the king in an attempt to destroy not only Mordecai but the entire Jewish population of the empire. Esther courageously seeks the king's help and, with Mordecai, manages to save the Jews. This victory gives birth to the Jewish festival Purim, which is still celebrated today.

Chap. C:12–16

Head lines

- Dream Predicts Future Drama (chapters A and F)
- Queen Defies King, Loses Crown (1:10–20)
- Mordecai Saves King's Life (2:21–23)
- Haman Plots to Kill All Jews (3:1–13)
- Esther Is Called to Save Her People (chapter 4)
- Haman's Evil Plan Is Revealed (chapter 7)

FACTOIDS

Who are the central characters? Queen Esther, her cousin Mordecai, King Xerxes, and his top official Haman

Who wrote this book? Written by unknown author(s), this book has both a Hebrew and Greek version. The parts of both versions are identified by numbers, chapters 1–10. The parts that are only in the Greek version are labeled by letters, chapters A–F. The parts labeled by letters are not part of the Protestant Bible.

What is the literary style? This is a short novel, written to explain the origins of the Jewish festival Purim.

Important themes
- Hatred and jealousy lead to destruction.
- Those in positions of power and esteem have a responsibility to help the powerless.
- God saves the innocent through the courageous acts of people he calls.

ESTHER

Mordecai's Strange Dream

A[a] 1-3 Mordecai, a Jew who belonged to the tribe of Benjamin, was taken into exile, along with King Jehoiachin of Judah, when King Nebuchadnezzar of Babylonia captured Jerusalem. Mordecai was the son of Jair, a descendant of Kish and Shimei. He now lived in the Persian city of Susa, where he was an important official in the royal court of Xerxes the great king.

During the second year of Xerxes' reign, on the first day of the month of Nisan, Mordecai had a dream. 4 He dreamed that there was great noise and confusion, loud thunder, and an earthquake, with terrible turmoil on the earth. 5 Then two huge dragons appeared, ready to fight each other. 6 They made a dreadful noise, and all the nations got ready to make war against God's nation of righteous people. 7 For the world it was a day of darkness and gloom, trouble and distress, destruction and ruin. 8 All of God's righteous people were troubled, in great fear of what was about to happen to them. They prepared for death, 9 but they cried out to God for help. In the dream their prayer was answered by a great river which came flowing out of a small spring. 10 The day dawned, the sun rose, and the humble people were made strong and destroyed their arrogant enemies.

11 Mordecai woke up from this dream in which he saw what God planned to do. He thought about it all day and tried to understand what it meant.

Mordecai Saves the King's Life

12 While Mordecai was resting in the courtyard of the palace, where two of the king's eunuchs, Gabatha and Tharra, were on guard, 13 he overheard them plotting together. He listened carefully to what they were saying and learned that they were making plans to kill the king. So Mordecai went to King Xerxes and told him about the plot of the two eunuchs. 14 The king had them questioned, and when they confessed, they were led away and executed.

He overheard them plotting together. (A:13)

15 The king had an account of this written in the official records, and Mordecai also wrote an account of it. 16 Then the king appointed Mordecai to a position at court and gave him many gifts as a reward for what he had done.

17 But Haman son of Hammedatha, a Bougaean who was respected by the king, tried to cause trouble for Mordecai and his people the Jews, because Mordecai had been responsible for the death of the two eunuchs.

Queen Vashti Defies King Xerxes

1 1-2 These things happened in the time of King Xerxes, who ruled 127 provinces, all the way from India to Ethiopia,[b] from his royal throne in Susa, Persia's capital city. 3 In the third year of his reign, the king gave a banquet for all his advisers, the representatives

---

[a] **A** Chapter A:1—17 corresponds to chapters 11:2—12:6 in a number of English translations. [b] **1:1-2** Greek Ethiopia: Ethiopia is the name given in Graeco-Roman times to the extensive territory south of the First Cataract of the Nile River. Cush was the ancient (Hebrew) name of this region which included within its borders most of modern Sudan and some of present-day Ethiopia (Abyssinia).
A:1-3 2 Kings 24:10–16 **1:1, 2** Ezra 4:6

of the other countries, the noblemen from Persia and Media, and the governors of the provinces. [4]For six whole months he made a show of the riches of the imperial court with magnificent and expensive celebrations.

[5]After the feast[c] the king gave a banquet for the people of other nations who were in the city. It lasted a week and was held in the palace courtyard, [6]which was decorated with linen and cotton curtains, held by cords of purple linen attached to silver and gold blocks on marble and stone columns. Couches made of gold and silver had been placed in the courtyard, which was paved with green and white marble and mother-of-pearl. The couches were spread with a fine, thin fabric of many colors, with roses around the edges. [7]There were gold and silver cups, and one of them, decorated with jewels worth more than a thousand tons of silver, had been set out for display. There was plenty of good wine from the king's own supply. [8]There were no limits on the drinks. The king had given orders to the palace servants that they should provide him and his guests with as much as they wanted.

[9]Meanwhile, inside the royal palace Queen Vashti was giving a banquet for the women.

[10]On the seventh day of his banquet the king was feeling happy, so he called in the seven eunuchs who were his personal servants, Haman, Bazan, Tharra, Boraze, Zatholta, Abataza, and Tharaba.[d] [11]He ordered them to bring in the queen, so that he could place the royal crown on her head and show her off to the officials and all his guests, for she was a beautiful woman. [12]But Queen Vashti refused to obey and would not come with the servants. This embarrassed the king and made him furious.

[13]He told his advisers about Vashti's reply and asked them to give a legal opinion about

R-e-s-p-e-c-t!

Queen Vashti is not about to let herself be used as an object of pleasure for her drunk husband and his friends. Women were not permitted to feast at the king's banquet, but they could be commanded to show up as entertainment! Vashti will not stand for such humiliation, so she refuses to go. Her decision costs her a hefty price—her queenship.

Then, King Xerxes has the nerve to send out a decree to all households in his empire that women should respect their husbands, the masters of their homes! Please! Who needs to respect whom?

Respect is an essential ingredient for strong, healthy, and loving relationships. More importantly, as the courageous Queen Vashti shows us, respect between people must begin with *self*-respect.

— Esther 1:10–22

what he should do. [14-15]Three of them, who were closest to the king and held the highest offices, came and told him what the law required and what should be done to Queen Vashti for disobeying the command he had given her through his servants. They were Arkesaeus, Sarsathaeus, and Malesear, officials of Persia and Media.[e]

Esther

---

[c] **1:5** feast; *some manuscripts have* wedding feast.   [d] **1:10** *Greek* Haman . . . Tharaba; *Hebrew* Mehuman, Biztha, Harbona, Bigtha, Abagtha, Zethar, and Carkas.   [e] **1:14–15** *Greek* Three of them . . . Arkesaeus, Sarsathaeus, and Malesear, officials of Persia and Media; *Hebrew* [14] Those he most often turned to for advice were Carshena, Shethar, Admatha, Tarshish, Meres, Marsena, and Memucan—seven officials of Persia and Media who held the highest offices in the kingdom. [15] He said to these men, "I, King Xerxes, sent my servant to Queen Vashti with a command, and she refused to obey it! What does the law say we should do with her?"

Tribe of Benjamin: One of the Twelve Tribes of Israel; Benjamin was one of Jacob's twelve sons.

16 Then the king told his officials and the governors of Media and Persia how the queen had defied him. So Muchaeus[f] said to the king and everyone present: "Queen Vashti has insulted not only you but all of us as well. 17-18 As soon as our wives hear what the queen has done, they will be bold enough to defy their husbands and treat them with disrespect in the same way that Vashti has treated you. 19 If, then, it please Your Majesty, issue a royal proclamation that Vashti may never again appear before the king. Have it written into the laws of Media and Persia. Then give her place as queen to some better woman. There is no other way. 20 When your proclamation is made known all over this empire, then every woman will treat her husband with proper respect, whether he is rich or poor."

21 The king and his officials liked this idea, and the king did as Muchaeus suggested. 22 To each of the royal provinces he sent a message in the language of that province, saying that every husband must be respected in his own home.

Esther Becomes Queen

2 ¹Later the king's anger cooled down. Although he no longer mentioned Vashti, he kept thinking about how he had condemned her. ²So some of the king's advisers suggested, "Why don't you make a search to find some beautiful young women of good character? ³You can appoint officials in every province of the empire and have them bring all these beautiful young virgins to your harem here in Susa. Put them in the care of Hegai, the eunuch who is in charge of your women, and let them be given cosmetics and whatever else they may need. ⁴Then take the young woman you like best and make her queen in Vashti's place."

The king thought this was good advice, so he followed it.

5 There in Susa lived a Jew named Mordecai son of Jair; he was from the tribe of Benjamin and was a descendant of Kish and Shimei. ⁶He was among the captives whom King Nebuchadnezzar of Babylonia had taken into exile from Jerusalem. ⁷Mordecai was the guardian of Esther, the daughter of his uncle Aminadab.[g] She was a beautiful young woman, and after the death of her parents, Mordecai brought her up until she was grown.[h]

8 When the king had issued his new proclamation, many young women were being brought to Susa, and Esther was among them. She too was put in the royal palace in the care of Hegai, who had charge of the harem. ⁹Hegai liked Esther, and she won his favor. He lost no time in beginning her beauty treatment of massage and special diet. He assigned seven young women specially chosen from the royal palace to serve her, and he treated her and her servants well.

10 Now, on the advice of Mordecai, Esther had kept secret the fact that she was Jewish. 11 Every day Mordecai would walk back and forth in front of the courtyard of the harem, watching to see what was going to happen to her.

12 The regular beauty treatment for the young women lasted a year: massages with oil of myrrh for six months and with beauty

The regular beauty treatment . . . lasted a year. (2:12)

---

f **1:16** Greek *Muchaeus;* Hebrew *Memucan.*   *g* **2:7** Greek Esther, the daughter of his uncle Aminadab; Hebrew Esther, whose Hebrew name was Hadassah.   *h* **2:7** until she was grown; *or* and planned to marry her.
2:6 2 Kings 24:10–16; 2 Chr 36:10

Esther

Supporting Immigrants

Catholic Connections

Mordecai and Esther were part of the Jewish Diaspora—the group of Jews who were forced to move to other places when Jerusalem was destroyed by the Babylonians in 587 BC. In their new homes, they learned new languages and customs, but they also held on to their Jewish traditions. When Esther is chosen as the new queen of Persia, her cousin Mordecai advises her not to reveal her Jewish heritage—to avoid trouble. Only later, when the Jews in her empire are about to be destroyed, does she tell her secret in order to save them.

Immigrants in our country today experience similar challenges. For many reasons, they are forced to leave their homes and move to this country. As they try to fit in, they also try to maintain their religious and cultural identities from their homelands. But often they face hostility from others.

The Catholic bishops in the United States encourage Americans to welcome and support immigrants to this land. Whatever their religious background or customs, immigrants are children of God, and we are called to help them feel safe and at home. How can you help do this in your school or community?

— Esther 2:10–11

creams and cosmetics for six more. ¹³After that, each young woman was handed over to the person appointed to conduct her from the harem to the palace, and she was taken to the king. ¹⁴She would go there in the evening, and the next morning she would be taken to another harem and put in the care of Hegai,ⁱ the eunuch in charge. She would not go to the king again unless he asked for her by name.

¹⁵The time came for Esther, the daughter of Aminadabʲ the uncle of Mordecai, to go to the king. She had done everything that Hegai had advised, and she was admired by everyone who saw her. ¹⁶So in Xerxes' seventh year as king, in the twelfth month, the month of Adar,ᵏ she was brought to the king. ¹⁷He fell in love with Esther, who pleased him more than any of the others, and he placed the queen's crown on her head. ¹⁸Then the king gave a week-long banquet for all his

advisers and administrators to celebrate his marriage to Esther. He also granted a reduction of taxes for the whole empire.

Mordecai Saves the King's Life

¹⁹Meanwhile Mordecai had been appointed to a high administrative position. ²⁰As for Esther, she had still not let it be known that she was Jewish. Mordecai had told her not to tell anyone, and she obeyed him in this, just as she had obeyed him when she was a little girl under his care. She continued to worship God and carry out God's commands, without abandoning her Jewish ways.ˡ

²¹When the king promoted Mordecai to a higher position, the two palace eunuchsᵐ who were officers of the king's bodyguard became angry and plotted to assassinate the king. ²²Mordecai learned about it and told Queen Esther, who then told the king the

Esther

ⁱ **2:14** *Greek* Hegai; *Hebrew* Shaashgaz.   ʲ **2:15** *Greek* Aminadab; *Hebrew* Abihail.   ᵏ **2:16** *Greek* twelfth month, the month of Adar; *Hebrew* tenth month, the month of Tebeth.   ˡ **2:20b** *Greek* She continued to worship God and carry out God's commands, without abandoning her Jewish ways: *These words are not in the Hebrew text.*   ᵐ **2:21** *Greek* the two palace eunuchs; *Hebrew* Bigthana and Teresh, two of the palace eunuchs.

details of the plot. 23 The king had the two men questioned, and both men were hanged. To honor Mordecai, the king ordered an account of this to be written down in the royal records, so that his valuable service would be remembered.

Haman Plots to Destroy the Jews

3 ¹Some time later King Xerxes honored a man named Haman son of Hammedatha, a Bougaean,ⁿ by promoting him to the position of prime minister. ²The king ordered all the officials in his service to show their respect for Haman by bowing to him. They all did so, except Mordecai, who refused to bow to Haman. ³The other officials in the royal service asked him why he was disobeying the king's command. ⁴Day after day they urged him to give in, but he would not listen to them. "I am a Jew," he explained, "and I cannot bow to Haman." So they told Haman how Mordecai was defying the king's orders. ⁵Haman was furious when he realized that Mordecai was not going to bow to him, ⁶and so he made plans to kill every Jew in the whole Persian Empire.

⁷In the twelfth year of King Xerxes' reign,ᵒ Haman ordered the lots to be castᵖ to find out the right day and month to destroy the Jews, all in a single day. The fourteenth day of the month of Adar was the date chosen.

⁸So Haman told the king, "There is a certain race of people scattered among the nations all over your empire. They observe customs that are not like those of any other people. Moreover, they do not obey the laws of the empire, so it is not in your best interests to tolerate them. ⁹If it please Your Majesty, issue a decree that they are to be put to death. If you do this, I promise to put 375 tons of silver into the royal treasury."�q

¹⁰The king took off his ring, which was used to stamp official proclamations, and gave it to Hamanʳ to seal the decree that was to be written against the Jews. ¹¹The king

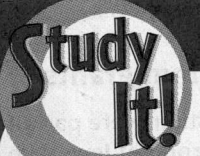

The Final Solution

It is amazing how far the evil of one person can reach. Haman is furious with Mordecai, so Haman convinces the king to sign an order to kill every Jewish person in the empire. Wow! But not too long ago one man, Adolf Hitler, actually tried to kill every Jewish person in Europe. He called it the final solution. He was well on his way to doing it, too, before being defeated.

What is even more amazing is that seemingly good people go along with this evil. "Good" soldiers and people in Esther's time would have carried out the king's orders. Soldiers who were otherwise good people carried out Hitler's orders. This is why it is so important that people don't simply follow orders that they know are wrong. We do what God has revealed as good and true—even if it might put us in danger. That is what Queen Esther will do.

— Esther, chapter 3

told him, "Keep the money, and do whatever you want with that race of people."

¹²So on the thirteenth day of the first month, Haman called the king's secretaries and dictated a proclamation to be translated into every language in the empire and to be sent to all the rulers and governors. It was issued in the name of King Xerxes and sent to all the 127 provinces, which stretched from India to Ethiopia.ˢ ¹³Runners took this

---

ⁿ **3:1** *Greek* a Bougaean; *Hebrew* a descendant of Agag. ᵒ **3:7** *Greek* twelfth year of King Xerxes' reign; *Hebrew* twelfth year of King Xerxes' rule, in the first month, the month of Nisan. ᵖ **3:7** *Greek* lots to be cast; *Hebrew* lots to be cast ("purim," they were called). q **3:9** *Greek* royal treasury; *Hebrew* royal treasury for the administration of the empire. ʳ **3:10** *Greek* Haman; *Hebrew* the enemy of the Jewish people, Haman, son of Hammedatha, the descendant of Agag. ˢ **3:12** *Greek* Ethiopia: *Ethiopia is the name given in Graeco-Roman times to the extensive territory south of the First Cataract of the Nile River. Cush was the ancient (Hebrew) name of this region which included within its borders most of modern Sudan and some of present-day Ethiopia (Abyssinia).*

Esther

proclamation to every province of the empire. It contained the instructions that on a single day in the twelfth month, the month of Adar, all Jews were to be killed and their belongings confiscated. [t u]

Xerxes' Proclamation against the Jews

B [v] [1]This is a copy of the decree:
"King Xerxes the Great sends the following decree to the governors of his 127 provinces, from India to Ethiopia, [w] and to their subordinate officials:

[2]"After I became ruler of many nations and master of the whole world, I resolved that my subjects should always live at peace. I wanted this, not because of pride in my power but because I was always reasonable and governed my subjects with kindness. I determined to renew the peace that everyone longs for and to do what was necessary to create a civilized kingdom, safe for travel from one border to another.

[3]"I asked my advisers how to accomplish this goal, and Haman made a suggestion. He is distinguished among us as a man of great wisdom, and at all times he has demonstrated his concern for the welfare of the kingdom. Because of his unfailing loyalty, he has been raised to the second highest position in the empire. [4]Recently Haman told us about a certain unruly people scattered among all the other peoples of the empire. He explained to us that these people have their own laws, are opposed to every other nation, and constantly ignore royal commands. As a result of their attitude, we are not able to establish the kind of unified government which we earnestly intend for the empire. [5]"These people are hostile to our government and commit terrible crimes which

threaten the security of the empire. They follow strange customs, obey their own laws, and stand alone in their constant opposition to all people. [6]In the light of these facts, we recommend the slaughter of the people referred to by Haman, our prime minister. All of them, including women and children, must be put to death; no one is to be spared. They are our enemies; we will show them no pity. This order is to be carried out this year on the fourteenth day of the twelfth month, the month of Adar. [7]These people, who have caused so much trouble for so long, will all die a violent death in a single day. From then on, our government will be secure and stable."

3 [14]The contents of the proclamation were made public in every province, and everyone was ordered to be prepared for that day.

[15]The decree was also rapidly made public in the capital city of Susa. And while the king and Haman got drunk, [x] the city of Susa was thrown into confusion.

Mordecai Asks for Esther's Help

4 [1]When Mordecai learned of all that had been done, he tore his clothes in anguish. Then he dressed in sackcloth, covered his head with ashes, and ran through the city crying loudly, "An innocent nation is being destroyed!" [y] [2]When he came to the entrance of the palace, he stopped. He did not go in because no one in sackcloth and ashes was allowed inside. [3]Throughout all the provinces, wherever the king's proclamation was made known, there was loud mourning among the Jews. They wept, wailed, and put on sackcloth and ashes. [z]

[4]When Esther's servant women and eunuchs told her what Mordecai was doing, she was deeply disturbed. She sent Mordecai

Esther

[t] **3:13b** *Greek* on a single day . . . confiscated; *Hebrew* on a single day, the thirteenth day of Adar, all Jews—young and old, women and children—were to be killed. They were to be slaughtered without mercy and their belongings were to be taken.   [u] **3:13** *Chapter 3 continues after chapter B.*   [v] **B:1** *Chapter B:1–7 corresponds to chapter 13:1 7 in a number of English translations.*   [w] **B:1** *Greek* Ethiopia: *Ethiopia is the name given in Graeco-Roman times to the extensive territory south of the First Cataract of the Nile River. Cush was the ancient (Hebrew) name of this region which included within its borders most of modern Sudan and some of present-day Ethiopia (Abyssinia).*   [x] **3:15** *Greek* got drunk; *Hebrew* sat down and had a drink.   [y] **4:1** *Greek* "An innocent nation is being destroyed!": *These words are not in the Hebrew text.*   [z] **4:3** *Greek* They wept . . . ashes; *Hebrew* They fasted, wept, wailed, and most of them put on sackcloth and lay in ashes.

Mordecai refused to bow to Haman because that would have been treating Haman like a god.

some clothes to put on instead of the sackcloth, but he would not accept them. [5]Then she called Hathach, one of the palace eunuchs appointed as her servant, and told him to go to Mordecai and get the details of what was happening. [a] [7]Mordecai told him everything that had happened and how Haman had promised to put 375 tons of silver into the royal treasury if all the Jews were killed. [8]He gave Hathach a copy of the proclamation that had been issued in Susa, ordering the destruction of the Jews. Mordecai asked him to take it to Esther so that she might go and plead with the king and beg him to have mercy on her people. "Tell her," he said, "to remember the days when she was just an ordinary person being brought up under my care. Now, since Haman, the king's prime minister, has spoken against us and demands our death, she must pray to the Lord and then speak to the king about us. She must save us from death." [b]

[9]So Hathach did this, [10]and Esther gave him this message to take back to Mordecai: [11]"If anyone, man or woman, goes to the inner courtyard and sees the king without being summoned, that person will be sentenced to death. Everyone in the empire knows that. Only if the king holds out his gold scepter to him can his life be spared. But it has been a month now since the king has sent for me."

[12]When Mordecai received Esther's message, [13]he sent her this warning: "Esther, don't imagine that you are safer than any of the other Jews in the empire. [14]If you keep quiet at a time like this, help will come to the Jews in some other way[c] and they will be saved, but you will die and your father's family will come to an end. Yet, who knows? Maybe it was for a time like this that you were made queen!"

[15]Esther sent Mordecai this reply: [16]"Go and gather all the Jews in Susa together; hold a fast and pray for me. Don't eat or drink anything for three days and nights. My servant women and I will be doing the same. After that, I will go to the king, even though it is against the law. If I must die for doing it, I will die."

[17]Mordecai then left and did everything that Esther had told him to do.

Mordecai's Prayer

C[d] [1]Mordecai prayed to the Lord, calling to mind what the Lord had done in the past: [2]"O Lord, you are the Lord and King of all creation, and everything obeys your commands. If you wish to save Israel, no one can stop you. [3]You made heaven and earth and all the wonderful things on earth. [4]You are the Lord of all, and there is no one who can stand against you. [5]You know all things. You know, Lord, that when I refused to bow to that arrogant Haman, it was not because I was arrogant or trying to impress people. [6-7]I simply did not want to honor any human being more than I honor God. I refuse to bow to anyone but you, my Lord; and this is not because of pride. If it would help to save Israel, I would be willing even to kiss the soles of his feet.

[8-9]"And now, O Lord, God and King, God of Abraham, spare your people; save us from our enemies. They are determined to destroy us; they are looking for a chance. Long ago you chose us to be your people and rescued us from the land of Egypt. Do not abandon us now. [10]We are your chosen people, so listen to my prayer and be gracious to us. Turn our misfortune into joy so that we may live to sing your praises. Save us from death so that we can keep on praising you."

[11]And all the people of Israel prayed loudly and earnestly because they were sure that they were going to die.

---

[a] 4:5 *Some manuscripts add verse 6:* Hathach went to Mordecai in the city square at the entrance to the palace.
[b] 4:8b *Greek* "Tell her," he said . . . "She must save us from death.": *These words are not in the Hebrew text.*
[c] 4:14 *Greek* in some other way; *Hebrew* from heaven.   [d] C:1 *Chapter C:1–30 corresponds to chapters 13:8—14:19 in a number of English translations.*
C:8, 9 Ex 3:6

"Come to our rescue, O Lord. Help me; I am all alone, and I have no one to turn to but you" (*Esther C:25*).

Pray It!

Let Nothing Disturb You

This prayer is from the great saint Teresa of Ávila, who lived from AD 1515 to 1582. She had great courage and lived a life filled with sacrifice. This prayer could also have been said by Esther.

> Let nothing disturb you,
> Nothing dismay you.
> All things pass.
> But God never changes.
>
> Whoever has God lacks nothing.
> If you have only God,
> You have more than enough.

— Esther C:23–25

Esther's Prayer

12 Queen Esther, in deep agony, turned to the Lord. **13** She took off her splendid robes and put on garments of mourning and grief. Instead of her rich perfumes, she put ashes and dung on her head. She did all she could to destroy any dignity in her appearance. She let her tangled and uncombed hair hang down over her body that she had always taken such care to beautify. **14** She prayed to the Lord God of Israel, "My Lord and King, only you are God. I am all alone, and I have no one to turn to but you. Help me! **15** I am about to risk my life. **16** O Lord, as long as I can remember, my family has told me how you chose Israel from all the nations and how in ancient times you singled out our ancestors to be your people forever. You have kept all your promises to them.

17 "But we sinned against you. You handed us over to our enemies because we worshiped their gods. **18** We deserved your punishment, O Lord. **19** But our enemies are no longer satisfied just to see us in slavery. They have made a solemn promise to their idols **20** not only to destroy the people who praise you, but to do away with your Law and to remove forever the glory of your house and altar. **21** They want the whole world to praise worthless idols and stand in awe of mortal kings forever.

22 "Lord, these gods are nothing; do not surrender your power to them or give our enemies the chance to laugh at our downfall. Instead, turn their evil plans against them, and make an example of that man who first planned our destruction.

23 "Remember us, O Lord. Come to us in this time of trouble. Give me courage, King of all gods and Ruler over all earthly powers. **24** Give me the right words to say when I go in to face Xerxes, that savage lion. Change his heart so that he will turn against Haman, our

Esther's prayer (C:12)

Esther

The Courage of a Queen

Like Vashti, who stood up to her husband, the king, Esther must gather all her courage to do the right thing. The royal court had a rule that only those who were summoned by the king could speak with him. If someone dared to approach him without being invited, they were put to death. Esther desperately needs to speak with the king about Haman's plan to destroy Mordecai and all the Jews in the empire. But she knows she could lose her life if she just appears before the king without being invited.

She does it anyway, even though "in her heart she was ter-ror-stricken" (Esther D:5). Esther makes a critical decision to risk her life for the sake of the many Jews who are innocent and do not deserve to be slaughtered. Her courage and her passion to do what is right are truly inspiring!

What are you facing in your life right now that requires courage? What risk do you face if you do the right thing? Who can be there to support and help you?

— Esther 4:9–17; D:1–16

enemy, and destroy him and his gang. 25Come to our rescue, O Lord. Help me; I am all alone, and I have no one to turn to but you.

26"You know everything, Lord. You know that I hate the honor I receive from these Gentiles. I detest the thought of having sex with any of these uncircumcised heathen. 27But you know that I have no choice. I hate the crown I have to wear as queen on offi-cial occasions. I never wear it unless I have

to; it's as disgusting as last month's rag. 28I refuse to eat at Haman's table or honor the king by attending his parties, and I have never drunk any of the wine dedicated to his gods. 29Since I came here, the only thing that has brought me joy is my worship of you, Lord God of Abraham.

30"Almighty God, listen to the prayer of your people. Rescue us from these evildoers, and take away my fear."

Esther Goes to the King

De 1Queen Esther prayed for three days. Then she took off the clothes she had been wearing and put on her splendid robes again. 2-3In all her royal splendor, she prayed again to her God and savior, who sees everything. Walking like a queen, she left her room accompanied by two servant women, one of them escorting her by the arm and 4the other holding up the train of her robe. 5Queen Esther's face was radiantly beautiful. She looked as cheerful as she was lovely, but in her heart she was terror-stricken. 6She passed through all the doors and entered the throne room, where she stood before the king. He was seated on his royal throne, dressed in his glorious robes, which were covered with gold and precious jewels. It was an awe-inspiring sight. 7His face glowed with splendor, but when he saw Esther, he stared at her with fierce anger. She grew weak and turned pale; she almost fainted and

In all her royal splendor (D:2)

---

e **D:1** *Chapter D:1–15 corresponds to chapter 15:1–16 in a number of English translations.*
C:28 Dan 1:8; Jdt 12:2

had to lean her head on her attendant's shoulder.

8 But God changed the king's anger into tender concern. He quickly rose from his throne and took her in his arms until she was able to stand. He calmed her with comforting words. 9 "What is it, Esther?" he said to her. "I am your husband. There's no need to be afraid. 10 Our law applies only to ordinary people; you will not die. 11 Come here to me." 12 He lifted his gold scepter and touched her on the neck with it. Then he kissed her and said, "Tell me what you want."

13 "When I looked at you, my lord, I thought I was seeing an angel of God," the queen answered, "and I was overcome by your awesome majesty. 14 You are so marvelous and your face is so full of kindness."

15 But while she was speaking, she fainted again. 16 The king was concerned about her, and all his attendants tried to revive her.

Esther Invites the King and Haman to a Banquet

5 f 3 "What is it, Esther?" the king asked. "Tell me what you want, and you shall have it—even if it is half of my empire."

4 Esther replied, "Today is a special day for me. If it please my lord, I would like you and Haman to be my guests tonight at a banquet I am preparing for you."

5 The king then ordered Haman to come quickly, so that they could be Esther's guests. So the king and Haman went to Esther's banquet. 6 Over the wine the king again said to her, "Tell me what you want, Queen Esther."

7 Esther replied, 8 "If my lord is kind enough to grant my request, I would like

you and Haman to be my guests tomorrow at another banquet that I will prepare for you. It will be just like this one." g

Haman Plots to Kill Mordecai

9 When Haman left the king he was happy and in a good mood, until he saw Mordecai the Jew in the courtyard of the palace. That made him furious, 10 but he went on home. h Then he invited his friends to his house and asked his wife Zeresh to join them. 11 He boasted to them about how rich he was i and about the honor the king had paid him when he promoted him to high office and made him prime minister. 12 "What is more," Haman said, "Queen Esther gave a banquet for no one but the king and me, and we are invited back tomorrow. 13 But none of this means a thing to me as long as I see that Jew Mordecai sitting in the courtyard of the palace."

14 Then his wife and all his friends suggested, "Why don't you have a gallows put up, seventy-five feet high? Tomorrow morning you can ask the king to have Mordecai hanged on it, and then you can go with the king to the banquet and enjoy yourself." Haman thought it was a good idea, so he had the gallows built.

The King Honors Mordecai

6 1 That night the Lord kept the king from sleeping, so the king ordered his private secretary to bring the official records of the empire and read them to him. 2 He read the account of how Mordecai had uncovered a plot to assassinate the king—the plot made by the two eunuchs who served as palace

---

f **5:1** In Greek, chapter D replaces verses 1 and 2 in Hebrew: 1 On the third day of her fast Esther put on her royal robes and went and stood in the inner courtyard of the palace, facing the throne room. The king was inside, seated on the royal throne, facing the entrance. 2 When the king saw Queen Esther standing outside, she won his favor, and he held out to her the gold scepter. She then came up and touched the tip of it. g **5:8b** Greek It will be just like this one; Hebrew At that time I will tell you what I want. h **5:10** Greek but he went on home; Hebrew but he controlled himself and went on home. i **5:11** Greek how rich he was; Hebrew how rich he was, how many sons he had.
5:3 Mk 6:23

Esther was terrified to face the king without being summoned. How many times did she faint or almost faint while talking to him?

Pray It!

Forgiving Our Enemies

Mordecai and Haman become enemies whose deep hatred leads to a violent death. Haman wants to hang Mordecai on a gallows seventy-five feet high! Our battles are usually much less intense, but they start with something minor, like this: Jen snickered when she saw Sara's new haircut. It was a quiet little snort, almost unnoticeable, but Sara didn't miss it. This was just like Jen to act that way.

How would you handle this if you were Sara? Find a way to hurt Jen back? Shrug it off and tell yourself she's just insecure? Be extra kind to Jen because you would rather have a friend than an enemy?

Our grudges and battles suck up a lot of energy and time, don't they? Jesus told us to forgive (and love!) our enemies (see Matthew 5:43–48), not just because God desires peace among his children, but because we're healthier and happier when we're not carrying all that hate around. Hate weighs a lot!

Do you have any enemies? Any battles stirring? Talk to God about these and ask for help. Forgiveness is one of the hardest things for humans—we need God's strength to let go of hurts and learn to live peacefully with one another. In the end, we will feel better and stronger.

— Esther 5:9–14

Esther

guards.*j* 3 The king asked, "How have we honored and rewarded Mordecai for this?"

His servants answered, "You have done nothing for him."

4 Now just as the king was inquiring about Mordecai's good deed, Haman entered the courtyard. He had come to ask the king to have Mordecai hanged on the gallows that was now ready.

"Who is that in the courtyard?" the king asked.

5 The servants answered, "It is Haman; he is waiting to see you."*k*

"Show him in," said the king.

6 So Haman came in, and the king said to him, "There is someone I wish very much to honor. What should I do for this man?"

Haman thought to himself, "Now who could the king want to honor so much? Me, of course."

7-8 So he answered the king, "Let the royal servants bring a fine linen robe for this man—one that you yourself wear. And let them bring a horse that you yourself ride. 9 Then put that robe on the man you like so much and then have the nobleman lead him, mounted on the horse, through the city square. Have the nobleman announce as they go: 'See how the king rewards a man whom he wishes to honor!'"

10 Then the king said to Haman, "Fine! Do all that for Mordecai the Jew, who holds a high position in the palace;*l* don't leave out a thing."

j **6:2** *Greek* the plot . . . palace guards; *Hebrew* the plot made by Bigthana and Teresh, the two palace eunuchs who had guarded the king's rooms. *k* **6:4–5a** *Greek* Now just as the king . . . he is waiting to see you; *Hebrew* 4 "Are any of my officials in the palace?" the king asked. / Now Haman had just entered the courtyard; he had come to ask the king to have Mordecai hanged on the gallows that was now ready. 5 So the servants answered, "Haman is here, waiting to see you." *l* **6:10b** *Greek* who holds a high position in the palace: *These words are not in the Hebrew text.*

Why did the king first decide to honor Mordecai? What did the king have Haman do for Mordecai that was so humiliating for Haman?

Esther and Joseph

Have you seen the musical *Joseph and the Amazing Technicolor Dreamcoat*? It is based on a wonderful story from Genesis about Joseph, the young son of Jacob. If you are not familiar with the story, read Genesis, chapters 37–50. It is entertaining and teaches an important lesson about forgiveness.

Joseph, like Esther and Mordecai, was a Jew who rose to power in a foreign government and ended up having a great deal of influence. None of these Jews sought out their powerful positions, but by strange circumstances wound up there anyway. Joseph, Esther, and Mordecai were able to use their influence to save their people, the Jews.

Joseph's brothers sold him as a slave, hoping to get rid of him for good, and next thing you know, he has saved their lives during a famine. Vashti stood up to the king, and next thing, she is replaced by a new queen, Esther. Esther does what Vashti could not do—save the Jews. God's plans are interesting and complex! At any moment, something could happen to us that is meant to have greater meaning in time. At any moment, someone could enter our life who will change the way we live.

— Esther 6:1–10

. . . and Haman led him through the city. (6:11)

11So Haman got the robe and the horse, and he put the robe on Mordecai. Mordecai got on the horse, and Haman led him through the city square, announcing to the people as they went: "See how the king rewards a man whom he wishes to honor!"

12Mordecai then went back to the courtyard while Haman hurried home, covering his face in embarrassment. **13**He told his wife and all his friends everything that had happened to him. Then they all said to him, "You are beginning to lose power to Mordecai. He is a Jew, and you cannot overcome him. He will certainly defeat you, for the living God is with him!" *m*

Haman Is Put to Death

14While they were still talking, the palace eunuchs arrived to take Haman to Esther's banquet.

7 **1**And so the king and Haman went to eat with Esther **2**for a second time. Over the wine the king asked her again, "Now, Queen Esther, what do you want? Tell me and you shall have it. I'll even give you half the empire."

3Queen Esther answered, "If it please Your Majesty to grant my humble request, my wish is that I may live and that my people may live. **4**My people and I have been sold into slavery; our possessions have been plundered, and now we are to be destroyed—all of us, including our children, will be slaves—and so far I have kept quiet. It isn't right that our enemy should be a member of the royal court." *n*

Esther

---

m **6:13b** *Greek for the living God is with him!: These words are not in the Hebrew text.* *n* **7:4** *Greek My people . . . the royal court; Hebrew My people and I have been sold for slaughter. If it were nothing more serious than being sold into slavery, I would have kept quiet [and not bother you about it]; but we are about to be destroyed—exterminated!"; Probable text and not . . . it; Hebrew unclear.*

⁵Then King Xerxes asked Esther, "Who dares to do such a thing?"

⁶Esther answered, "Our enemy is this evil man Haman!"

"Our enemy is this evil man Haman!" (7:6)

In terror Haman faced the king and queen. ⁷The king got up from the table and went outside to the palace gardens. Haman could see that he was in a dangerous situation, so he stayed behind to beg Queen Esther for his life. ⁸He had just thrown himself down on Esther's couch to beg for mercy, when the king came back into the room from the gardens. Seeing this, the king cried out, "Are you going to rape my wife° here in my own palace?"

When Haman heard this, he turned away in despair. ⁹Then one of the eunuchs, whose name was Bougathan,ᵖ said, "Haman has even gone so far as to build a gallows at his house so that he can hang Mordecai, who warned Your Majesty about the plot. And it's seventy-five feet high!"

"Hang Haman on it!" the king commanded.

¹⁰So Haman was hanged on the gallows that he had built for Mordecai. Then the king's anger cooled down.

The Jews Are Told to Fight Back

8 ¹That same day King Xerxes gave Queen Esther all the property of Haman, the enemy of the Jews. Esther told the king that Mordecai was related to her, and Mordecai was invited to enter the king's presence. ²The king took off his ring with his seal on it (which he had taken back from Haman) and gave it to Mordecai. Esther put Mordecai in charge of Haman's property.

³Then Esther spoke to the king again, throwing herself at his feet. She begged him to do something to stop the evil plot that Haman�q had made against the Jews. ⁴The king held out the gold scepter to her, so she stood up ⁵and said, "If it please Your Majesty and if you care about me, please issue a proclamation to keep Haman's orders from being carried out—those orders heʳ gave for the destruction of all the Jews in the empire. ⁶How can I endure it if this disaster comes on my people? How can I go on living if my whole nation is destroyed?"

⁷Then the king said to Esther,ˢ "I have hanged Haman for his plot against the Jews, and I have given you his property. If that is not enough, ⁸you may write to the Jews whatever you like; and you may writeᵗ it in my name and stamp it with the royal seal, for a proclamation issued in the king's name and stamped with the royal seal cannot be revoked."

⁹On the twenty-third day of the first month, the month of Nisan,ᵘ the king's secretaries were calledᵛ and letters were written to the Jews and to the governors and administrators of all 127 provinces from India to Ethiopia.ʷ The letters were written to each province in its own language. ¹⁰They were written in the name of the king and stamped with the royal seal and they were delivered by runners.ˣ

° **7:8a** *Greek* my wife; *Hebrew* the queen.　ᵖ **7:8, 9** *Greek* When Haman heard this . . . whose name was Bougathan; *Hebrew* The king had no sooner said this than the eunuchs covered Haman's head. Then one of them, who was named Harbonah.　q **8:3** *Greek* Haman; *Hebrew* Haman, the descendant of Agag.
ʳ **8:5b** *Greek* he; *Hebrew* that the son of Hammedatha the descendant of Agag.　ˢ **8:7** *Greek* to Esther; *Hebrew* to Queen Esther and Mordecai, the Jew.　ᵗ **8:7, 8** *Greek* If that is not enough . . . you may write; *Hebrew* But a proclamation issued in the king's name and stamped with the royal seal cannot be revoked. You may, however, write.　ᵘ **8:9** *Greek* first month, the month of Nisan; *Hebrew* third month, the month of Sivan.　ᵛ **8:9** *Greek* the king's secretaries were called; *Hebrew* Mordecai called the king's secretaries.　ʷ **8:9** *Greek* Ethiopia: *Ethiopia is the name given in Graeco-Roman times to the extensive territory south of the First Cataract of the Nile River. Cush was the ancient (Hebrew) name of this region which included within its borders most of modern Sudan and some of present-day Ethiopia (Abyssinia).*　ˣ **8:10** *Greek* by runners; *Hebrew* by riders mounted on fast horses from the royal stables.
8:8 Dan 6:8

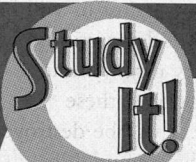

Saving the Jews

Once King Xerxes learns of Haman's evil plot to kill Mordecai and all the Jews in his kingdom, he takes action. First, he punishes Haman by having him hanged. Unfortunately, he cannot undo the order to kill all the Jews, but he does help Mordecai and Esther to send out another order. This order permits the Jews to form armies and defend themselves against their attackers.

On the day of the planned attack, the Jews are prepared—and so they are saved from destruction. It was a great victory for the Jews, who believed that God was once again on their side, protecting the Chosen People who remained faithful to God.

— Esther 8:1–12

---

11 These letters explained that the king would allow the Jews in every city of the empire to live by their own laws and organize for self-defense. They were permitted to treat their opponents and enemies in any way they liked.*y* 12 This decree was to take effect throughout the Persian Empire on the thirteenth day of Adar, the twelfth month.*z a*

The King's Decree in Favor of the Jews

E*b* 1 This is a copy of the decree:

"Greetings from King Xerxes the Great to the governors of the 127 provinces, which extend from India to Ethiopia,*c* and to all those who are loyal to us.

2 "Many people become increasingly arrogant when honors are given to them and favors are done for them. 3 They do not know what to do with so much good fortune, so they not only try to harm our subjects, but they even scheme against those who grant them favors. 4 They are never grateful for what people do for them, and they even think they can escape the judgment of God, who hates evil and sees everything. In their arrogance they listen to the flattery of ignorant, sinful people.

5 "It often happens also that friends who have been entrusted with administrative responsibilities exert pressure on those in authority. They make their leaders their partners in killing people and bring about misfortunes that can never be remedied. 6 These friends, by their lies and deceitful ways, take advantage of the good will of their rulers.

7 "You can see examples of this misuse of power not only in the stories that have been handed down to us from the past, but in the more recent outrageous things which have happened among you.

8 "I intend to make sure that in the future my kingdom will remain untroubled and peaceful for all people. 9 This can be done by changing certain policies and by judging fairly each situation that comes to my attention.

10 "Consider, for example, the case of Haman son of Hammedatha, a Macedonian. He is a foreigner with no Persian blood and

---

y **8:11** *Greek* These letters . . . in any way they liked; *Hebrew* These letters explained that the king would allow the Jews in every city to organize for self-defense. If armed men of any nationality in any province attacked the Jewish men, their children, or their women, the Jews could fight back and destroy the attackers; they could slaughter them to the last man and take their possessions.   *z* **8:12** *Greek* the thirteenth day of Adar, the twelfth month; *Hebrew* the day set for the slaughter of the Jews, the thirteenth of Adar, the twelfth month.   *a* **8:12** *Chapter 8 continues after chapter E.*   *b* **E:1** *Chapter E:1–24 corresponds to chapter 16:1–24 in a number of English translations.*   *c* **E:1** *Greek Ethiopia: Ethiopia is the name given in Graeco-Roman times to the extensive territory south of the First Cataract of the Nile River. Cush was the ancient (Hebrew) name of this region which included within its borders most of modern Sudan and some of present-day Ethiopia (Abyssinia).*

Esther

Why do you think Esther invites the king to *two* banquets before she makes her request?

with no trace of my generosity; but I welcomed him, [11] and he received the benefit of my concern and love for all people. He was, in fact, proclaimed 'Father' of the empire and received more honor than anyone else, except the king.

[12] "But his arrogance knew no limits, and he tried to murder me and take over the empire. [13] In his crafty and deceitful way, he asked that Mordecai be put to death— Mordecai, who once saved my life and who has always supported me. He even asked for the death of Esther, our blameless queen, and in fact, the death of all the Jewish people. [14] His purpose was to leave us helpless and to allow the Macedonians to take over the Persian Empire. [15] Even though this wicked criminal plotted to wipe out the Jews, I find that they are not traitors at all but are governed by very just laws. [16] They worship the living God, the highest and greatest God, who has kept our empire in its excellent condition from the time of our ancestors until our own day.

[17] "Therefore I advise you not to carry out the instructions issued in the letters sent out by Haman. [18] He is the person responsible for all of this, and he has been hanged, along with his entire family, at the gates of Susa. God, who governs all things, has given him the speedy punishment that he deserved.

[19] "I order you to post copies of this decree in every public place. Permit the Jews to live by their own customs, [20] and give them support when they defend themselves against those who attack them on the day set for their destruction, the thirteenth day of Adar, the twelfth month. [21] God, who governs all things, has turned that day of destruction into a day of celebration for his chosen people.

[22] "Include this day among your national holidays and celebrate it as a festival. [23] Now and in the future it will remind us and all our allies of the way God watches over our nation, and those who plot against us will be reminded of God's threat of destruction.

[24] "Every province, every city, without exception, which does not obey these orders will feel my anger. It will be destroyed in battle and burned to the ground. No human being will ever go there again, and even the birds and wild animals will avoid it forever.

8 [d] [13] "Post copies of this decree in plain view in every province, so that all the Jews can be ready to fight their enemies when that day comes."

[14] Messengers on horses rode off at top speed to carry out the orders of the king, and the decree was also made public in Susa.

[15] Mordecai left the palace, wearing royal robes, a turban of fine purple linen, and a gold crown. When the people of Susa saw him, they cheered, [16] and the Jews were happy and joyful. [17] They held a joyful holiday with feasting and happiness in every city and province, wherever the king's proclama-

Post copies of this decree in plain view in every province . . . Messengers on horses rode off at top speed.
(8:13, 14)

[d] **8:13** *Verses 1–12 precede chapter E.*

Read the king's decree in Esther, chapter E. Do you think he is a good king? Why or why not?

tion was posted. In fact, many Gentiles were circumcised and became Jews, because they were now afraid of them.

The Jews Destroy Their Enemies

9 [1]On the thirteenth day of Adar, the day on which the royal proclamation was to take effect, [2]it was the enemies of the Jews who were wiped out.[e] People everywhere were afraid of the Jews, and no one could stand against them. [3]In fact, the provincial governors, the administrators, and the royal scribes showed respect for the Jews, because they were all afraid of Mordecai. [4-5]The royal decree had made his name known throughout the empire.[f]

[6]In Susa, the capital city itself, the Jews killed five hundred people [7-10]and looted their property.[g] Among them were the ten sons of Haman son of Hammedatha, a Bougaean, the enemy of the Jews: Pharsannestain, Delphon, Phasga, Pharadatha, Barea, Sarbacha, Marmasima, Arouphaeus, Arsaeus, and Zabouthaeus.[h]

[11]That same day the number of people killed in Susa was reported to the king. [12]He then said to Esther,[i] "In Susa alone the Jews have killed five hundred people.[j] What must they have done out in the provinces! Tell me[k] what else you want, and you shall have it."

[13]Esther answered, "Let the Jews in Susa do again tomorrow what they were allowed to do today. And have the bodies of Haman's ten sons hung up." [14]The king agreed and permitted the Jews to put the bodies of Haman's ten sons on public display. [15]On the fourteenth day of Adar the Jews of Susa got together again and killed three hundred more people in the city. But they did no looting.

[16]The Jews in the provinces also organized and defended themselves. They rid themselves of their enemies by killing 15,000 people[l] on the thirteenth day of Adar, but they did no looting. [17]On the next day, the fourteenth, there was no more killing, and the Jews made it a joyful holiday of rest and feasting.[m] [18]The Jews of Susa, however, made the fifteenth a holiday, since they had slaughtered their enemies on the thirteenth and fourteenth and did not stop until the fifteenth. [19]This is why Jews who live in small towns observe the fourteenth day of the month of Adar as a holiday, a time of giving gifts of food to one another, while the Jews in the large cities celebrate the holiday in the same way on the fifteenth.[n]

The Festival of Purim

[20]Mordecai had these events written down in a book and sent it to all the Jews, near and far, throughout the Persian Empire, [21]telling them to observe the fourteenth and fifteenth days of Adar as holidays.[o] [22]These were the days on which the Jews had rid themselves of their enemies. The Jews were to observe the whole month as a holiday,[p] for this was a month that had been turned from a time of grief and despair into a time of joy and happiness. They were told to observe these days with feasts and parties, giving gifts of food to friends and to the poor. [23]So the Jews accepted all that Mordecai had written.[q]

[24]Mordecai had recorded how Haman son

[e] 9:2 *Greek* it was the enemies . . . wiped out; *Hebrew* 9:1b the day when the enemies of the Jews were hoping to get them in their power. But instead, the Jews triumphed over them. [2] In the Jewish quarter of every city [or In every Jewish city] in the empire the Jews organized to attack anyone who tried to harm them.   [f] 9:4-5 *Greek* The royal decree . . . empire; *Hebrew* It was well-known throughout the empire that Mordecai was now a powerful man in the palace and was growing more powerful. So the Jews could do what they wanted with their enemies. They attacked them with swords and slaughtered them.   [g] 9:7-10 *Greek* and looted their property: *These words are not in the Hebrew text.*   [h] 9:7-10 *Greek* Haman son of Hammedatha, a Bougaean . . . Zabouthaeus; *Hebrew* Haman son of Hammedatha, the enemy of the Jews: Parshandatha, Dalphon, Aspatha, Poratha, Adalia, Aridatha, Parmashta, Arisai, Aridai, and Vaizatha. However, there was no looting.   [i] 9:12 *Greek* Esther; *Hebrew* Queen Esther.   [j] 9:12 *Greek* five hundred people; *Hebrew* five hundred people, including Haman's sons.   [k] 9:12 *Greek* provinces! Tell me; *Hebrew* provinces! What do you want now? You shall have it. Tell me.   [l] 9:16 *Greek* 15,000 people; *Hebrew* seventy-five thousand people who hated them.
[m] 9:17 *Greek* joyful holiday of rest and feasting; *Hebrew* joyful day of feasting.   [n] 9:19 *Greek* while the Jews in the larger cities celebrate the holiday in the same way on the fifteenth: *These words are not in the Hebrew text.*
[o] 9:21 *Greek* as holidays; *Hebrew* as holidays every year.   [p] 9:22 *Greek* The Jews were to observe the whole month as a holiday: *These words are not in the Hebrew text.*   [q] 9:23 *Greek* So the Jews accepted all that Mordecai had written; *Hebrew* So the Jews followed Mordecai's instructions, and the celebration became an annual custom.
9:1 1 Macc 7:49; 2 Macc 15:36   **9:24-28** Esth 3:7

Esther

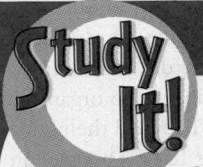

The Festival of Purim

Purim is a Hebrew word that means "lots." The Jewish festival of Purim that celebrates the victory of the Jews was named after the method that decided when the attack would be held. Haman chose lots (similar to picking a date out of a hat) to choose a date. It was on that day, and the next (upon the request of Esther), that the Jews defended themselves against their enemies and were saved. On the days after battle, the Jews celebrated by feasting, giving thanks, and sharing their food with poor people.

Today, the Jewish people celebrate the courage and determination of Esther and Mordecai on the Festival of Purim. On those days they give thanks to God for his faithfulness, and share gifts and meals with one another, especially with poor people.

— **Esther 9:20–31**

of Hammedatha, a Macedonian,ʳ had fought against the Jewish people, how he had made a decree and cast lotsˢ to determine the day

he would destroy them, 25 and how he had gone to the king to request that Mordecai be hanged.ᵗ But Haman suffered the same fate he had planned for the Jews—he and his sons were hanged from the gallows. 26-28 Because of Mordecai's letter,ᵘ because of all they had suffered, and because of all that had happened to them, the Jews accepted Mordecai's suggestion and made it a rule for themselves, their descendants, and anyone that might become a Jew, that these days should be properly observed as a memorial, generation after generation, in every city, province, and country. The Jews were to remember and observe these days of Purim for all time to come and never neglect them. (The holidays are called Purim because "purim" in their language is the word for "lots.")ᵛ

29-30 Then Queen Esther, the daughter of Aminadab,ʷ along with Mordecai the Jew, wrote down what they had done, putting the queen's full authority behind the letter about Purim. 31 They both took responsibility for establishing the festival and made up their minds to observe it at all costs.ˣʸ 32 Esther established the festival forever, and a written record was made of her official decree.

The Greatness of Xerxes and Mordecai

10 ¹King Xerxes imposed taxesᶻ on the people of the coastal regions of his empire as well as on those of the interior. ²His power and virtue, as well as the wealth and splendor of his empire,ᵃ are recorded in the official records of the kings of Persia and Media. ³Mordecaiᵇ was second in rank only to King Xerxes himself. He was a great man in the empire and was honored by his fellow

ʳ **9:24** *Greek* a Macedonian; *Hebrew* the descendant of Agog.   ˢ **9:24** *Greek* cast lots; *Hebrew* cast lots ("purim," they were called).   ᵗ **9:24, 25** *Greek* day he would destroy them . . . that Mordecai would be hanged. But; *Hebrew* for destroying the Jews; he had planned to wipe them out. But Esther went to the king, and the king issued written orders with the result that.   ᵘ **9:26–28** *Greek* Because of Mordecai's letter; *Hebrew* That is why the holidays are called Purim. Because of Mordecai's letter.   ᵛ **9:26–28** *Greek* and never neglect them. (The holidays are called Purim because "purim" in their language is the word for "lots."): *These words are not in the Hebrew text.* ʷ **9:29–30** *Greek* Aminadab; *Hebrew* Abihail.   ˣ **9:31** *Greek* They both . . . at all costs; *Hebrew* ³⁰ The letter was addressed to all the Jews, and copies were sent to all the 127 provinces of the Persian Empire. It wished the Jews peace and security ³¹ and directed them and their descendants to observe the days of Purim at the proper time, just as they had adopted rules for the observance of fasts and times of mourning. This was commanded by both Mordecai and Queen Esther.   ʸ **9:31** at all costs; *Greek unclear.*   ᶻ **10:1** *Greek* taxes; *Hebrew* forced labor. ᵃ **10:2** *Greek* His power and virtue . . . his empire; *Hebrew* All the great and wonderful things he did, as well as the whole story of how he promoted Mordecai to high office.   ᵇ **10:3** *Greek* Mordecai; *Hebrew* Mordecai the Jew.

Jews. He was greatly loved, for he sought the welfare of his people.

Mordecai Remembers His Dream

F[c] [1]Then Mordecai said, "God has caused all these things to happen! [2]And I am reminded of the dream I had about all of this. Every detail of the dream has come true: [3]the small spring that became a river, the dawn that turned into sunlight, and the abundance of water. The river is Esther, whom the king married and made his queen. [4]The two dragons represent Haman and me. [5]The nations are all those who have gathered together to destroy the Jews. [6]My nation is Israel, which cried out to God for help and was saved. The Lord saved his people! He rescued us from all these evils and performed great miracles and wonders that have never happened among other nations. [7]That is because God prepared one destiny for his own people and another for all other nations. [8]Then came the day and the hour when these two destinies were to be decided; the time had come for God to make a decision about the nations. [9]God remembered his chosen people and gave the verdict in their favor. [10]So each year for all time to come God's people will gather together in his presence on the fourteenth and fifteenth of the month of Adar, and celebrate with joy and happiness."

Postscript

During the fourth year of the reign of Ptolemy and Cleopatra, a man named

Dreams

In ancient times, dreams were believed to be messages from God. Here are some other interesting dreams to check out:
- Genesis 28:10–22 (Jacob)
- Genesis 37:1–11; 40:1—41:36 (Joseph)
- 1 Samuel 3:1–10 (Samuel)
- 1 Kings 3:5–15 (Solomon)
- Daniel 7:1–14 (Daniel)
- Matthew 1:18–25; 2:13–15 (Joseph)

Does God speak to us in our dreams? It's possible. We believe God dwells inside us, in our hearts and minds. So when our brains are resting (sleeping), what a great time for God to get through to us!

— Esther F:1–10

Dositheus, who claimed to be a levitical priest, brought the preceding letter about the Purim festival. He was accompanied by his son Ptolemy, and they declared that the letter was genuine and that it had been translated by Lysimachus, son of Ptolemy, a member of a Jerusalem family.

[c] **F:1** *Chapter F:1–10 corresponds to chapters 10:4—11:1 in a number of English translations.*

Esther

Your Next Step

Congratulations on finishing the Book of Esther! Use this space to write your thoughts and questions about this book. If you are following the suggested reading plan, move ahead to the Book of Daniel in the Old Testament. It is another book with stories about Jewish people living in foreign countries.

First they came in and took over our country. Then they threw out all the holy objects from our sacred Temple and brought in statues of their pagan gods. Then they wanted us to perform sacrifices to those pagan gods. *Enough!*

This is how the Jews felt when the Greek (Seleucid) rulers took over Palestine (Israel) 150 years before Jesus was born. The First Book of Maccabees has stories of evil rulers, rebellion, courage, and war as it tells the story of the Jewish resistance to the Greek rulers. It focuses on the family of Mattathias and is named for his sons—the Maccabees. Judas Maccabeus is the most famous Maccabee and the one who led much of the revolt against the Greeks.

Chap. 5:40–44

Headlines

- Judas Leads Victories for Israel (3:1–9)
- The Temple Is Purified (4:36–59)
- Judas Dead, Brother Takes Over (9:1–31)
- Traitors' Plans Fail (11:20–27)
- Jonathan Captured and Assumed Dead (12:39–53)
- Simon's Reign Brings Peace to Judea (14:4–15)
- Murderous Plot to Kill Simon Succeeds (16:11–17)

FACTOIDS

Who wrote this book? An unknown author wrote this book sometime after 100 BC.
Who are the central characters? Judas Maccabeus and his brothers, John, Simon, Eleazar, and Jonathan.
What time period does it cover? This book covers from 175 to 134 BC.
Why was it written? It was written to emphasize the kingly and priestly authority of the Maccabees and to help the Israelites see that God used the Maccabees to bring freedom to Israel.

Important themes
- God is absolutely reliable through all generations.
- God, not bloodlines, chooses who will serve and save his people.

1 MACCABEES

Alexander the Great

1 ¹This history begins when Alexander the Great, son of Philip of Macedonia, marched from Macedonia and attacked Darius, king of Persia and Media. Alexander enlarged the Greek Empire by defeating Darius and seizing his throne. ²He fought many battles, captured fortified cities, and put the kings of the region to death. ³As he advanced to the ends of the earth, he plundered many nations; and when he had conquered the world, he became proud and arrogant. ⁴By building up a strong army, he dominated whole nations and their rulers, and forced everyone to pay him taxes.

⁵⁻⁷When Alexander had been emperor for twelve years, he fell ill and realized that he was about to die. He called together his generals, noblemen who had been brought up with him since his early childhood, and he divided his empire, giving a part to each of them. ⁸After his death, the generals took control, ⁹and each had himself crowned king of his own territory. The descendants of these kings ruled for many generations and brought a great deal of misery on the world.

Antiochus Epiphanes and the Renegade Jews
(2 Maccabees 4:7–17)

¹⁰The wicked ruler Antiochus Epiphanes, son of King Antiochus the Third of Syria, was a descendant of one of Alexander's generals. Antiochus Epiphanes had been a hostage in Rome before he became king of Syria in the year 137.*ᵃ*

¹¹At that time there appeared in the land of Israel a group of traitorous Jews who had no regard for the Law and who had a bad influence on many of our people. They said, "Let's come to terms with the Gentiles, for our refusal to associate with them has brought us nothing but trouble." ¹²This proposal appealed to many people, ¹³and some of them became so enthusiastic about it that they went to the king and received from him permission to follow Gentile customs. ¹⁴They built in Jerusalem a stadium like those in the Greek cities. ¹⁵They had surgery performed to hide their circumcision, abandoned the holy covenant, started associating with*ᵇ* Gentiles, and did all sorts of other evil things.

Antiochus Attacks Egypt

¹⁶When Antiochus had firmly established himself as king, he decided to conquer Egypt and rule that country as well as Syria. ¹⁷He invaded Egypt with a large fleet of ships and a powerful army, including chariots, elephants, and cavalry. ¹⁸When the attack came, King Ptolemy of Egypt turned and fled, and many of his soldiers were killed. ¹⁹Antiochus was able to capture the fortified cities of Egypt and plunder the whole land.

Antiochus Persecutes the Jews

²⁰In the year 143,*ᶜ* after the conquest of Egypt, Antiochus marched with a great army against the land of Israel and the city of Jerusalem. ²¹In his arrogance, he entered the Temple and took away the gold altar, the lampstand with all its equipment, ²²the table for the bread offered to the Lord, the cups and bowls, the gold fire pans, the curtain, and the crowns. He also stripped all the gold from the front of the Temple ²³and carried off the silver and gold and everything else of value, including all the treasures that he could find stored there. ²⁴Then he took it all to his own country. He had also murdered many people and boasted arrogantly about it. ²⁵There was great mourning everywhere in the land of Israel.

ᵃ **1:10** THE YEAR 137: *The dates in this book are counted from the beginning of the Syrian Kingdom in 312 B.C. The year 137 corresponds to 175 B.C.* *ᵇ* **1:15** started associating with; *or* married. *ᶜ* **1:20** THE YEAR 143: *This corresponds to 169 B.C.*
1:10 2 Macc 4:7 **1:15** 1 Cor 7:18

Then he took it all to his own country. (1:24)

26 Rulers and leaders groaned in sorrow.
   Young men and young women grew weak.
   The beauty of our women faded.
27 Every bridegroom sang a funeral song,
   and every bride sat mourning in her room.
28 All our people were clothed with shame,
   and our land trembled for them.

29 Two years later Antiochus sent a large army from Mysia*d* against the towns of Judea. When the soldiers entered Jerusalem, 30 their commander spoke to the people, offering them terms of peace and completely deceiving them. Then he suddenly launched a fierce attack on the city, dealing it a major blow and killing many of the people. 31 He plundered the city, set it on fire, and tore down its buildings and walls. 32 He and his army took the women and children as prisoners and seized the cattle.

33 Then Antiochus and his forces built high walls and strong towers in the area north of the Temple, turning it into a fort. 34 They brought in a group of traitorous Jews and installed them there. 35 They also brought in arms and supplies and stored in the fort all the loot that they had taken in Jerusalem. This fort became a great threat to the city.

36 The fort was a threat to the Temple,
   a constant, evil menace for Israel.
37 Innocent people were murdered around
      the altar;
   the Holy Place was defiled by murderers.
38 The people of Jerusalem fled in fear,
   and the city became a colony of foreigners.
   Jerusalem was foreign to its own people,

who had been forced to abandon the city.
39 Her Temple was as empty as a wilderness;
   her festivals were turned into days of
      mourning,
   her Sabbath joy into shame.
   Her honor became an object of ridicule.
40 Her shame was as great as her former
      glory,
   and her pride was turned into deepest
      mourning.

41-43 Antiochus now issued a decree that all nations in his empire should abandon their own customs and become one people. All the Gentiles and even many of the Israelites submitted to this decree. They adopted the official pagan religion, offered sacrifices to idols, and no longer observed the Sabbath.

44 The king also sent messengers with a decree to Jerusalem and all the towns of Judea, ordering the people to follow customs that were foreign to the country. 45 He ordered them not to offer burnt offerings, grain offerings, or wine offerings in the Temple, and commanded them to treat Sabbaths and festivals as ordinary work days. 46 They were even ordered to defile the Temple and the holy things in it.*e* 47 They were commanded to build pagan altars, temples, and shrines, and to sacrifice pigs and other unclean animals there. 48 They were forbidden to circumcise their sons and were required to make themselves ritually unclean in every way they could, 49 so that they would forget the Law which the Lord had given through Moses and would disobey all its commands. 50 The penalty for disobeying the king's decree was death.

51 The king not only issued the same decree throughout his whole empire, but he also appointed officials to supervise the people and commanded each town in Judea to offer pagan sacrifices. 52 Many of the Jews were ready to forsake the Law and to obey these officials. They defiled the land with their evil, 53 and their conduct forced all true Israelites to hide wherever they could.

54 On the fifteenth day of the month of

---

d **1:29** *Probable text* a large army from Mysia; *Greek* a tax collector with a large army.   *e* **1:46** the holy things in it; *or* the priests.
1:54 Dan 9:27; 11:31; 12:11; 1 Macc 6:7; Mt 24:15; Mk 13:14

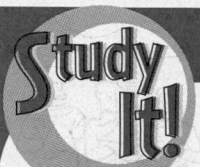

Where Are the Maccabees?

"Wow, I read this great story—actually it was two whole books—in my Bible last night. There were tons of battles and other military stuff. It was so good I stayed up late." Mike was enthusiastic as he talked to his friend, Pat. "Pat, have you read 1 Maccabees yet?"

"Where are the Maccabees?" Pat answered.

"In the Bible, the Maccabees, you know," Mike said.

"I've never heard of them, but I'll look tonight."

The next day they had a big discussion about the Book of Maccabees. Pat couldn't find it in his Bible, and his mom said their Bibles don't include it. Mike couldn't believe it because all the Bibles at his house had it.

They decided to ask around. Pat asked his youth pastor, and Mike asked his youth minister. Both explained to the boys how this happened and why each faith preferred to include or not include these books. Some Protestant Bibles don't have 1 and 2 Maccabees (or Tobit, Judith, Wisdom, Sirach, Baruch, and parts of Esther and Daniel). These Old Testament books were not originally written in Hebrew and have been rejected by some Christians. Other Christians, including Catholics, believe that these books—originally written in Greek—are also inspired books and include them in their Bibles.

Pat and Mike decided that they wouldn't argue over whose Bible was right. There are too many other things they agree on.

Kislev in the year 145,^{f} King Antiochus set up "The Awful Horror" on the altar of the Temple, and pagan altars were built in the towns throughout Judea. 55 Pagan sacrifices were offered in front of houses and in the streets. 56 Any books of the Law which were found were torn up and burned, 57 and anyone who was caught with a copy of the sacred books or who obeyed the Law was put to death by order of the king. 58 Month after month these wicked people used their power against the Israelites caught in the towns.

59 On the twenty-fifth of the month, these same evil people offered sacrifices on the pagan altar erected on top of the altar in the Temple. 60 Mothers who had allowed their babies to be circumcised were put to death in accordance with the king's decree. 61 Their babies were hung around their necks, and their families and those who had circumcised them were put to death. 62 But many people in Israel firmly resisted the king's decree and refused to eat food that was ritually unclean. 63 They preferred to die rather than break the holy covenant and eat unclean food—and many did die. 64 In his anger God made Israel suffer terribly.

The Faithfulness of Mattathias

2 ¹During that time, a priest of the Jehoiarib family named Mattathias, who was the son of John and the grandson of Simeon, moved from Jerusalem and settled in Modein. ²Mattathias had five sons: John (also called Gaddi), ³Simon (also called Thassi), ⁴Judas (also called Maccabeus), ⁵Eleazar (also called Avaran), and Jonathan (also called Apphus).

⁶When Mattathias saw all the sins that were being committed in Judea and Jerusalem, ⁷he said:

"Why was I born to see these terrible
        things,
    the ruin of my people and of the holy
        city?
Must I sit here helpless
    while the city is surrendered to enemies
    and the Temple falls into the hands of
        foreigners?

f **1:54** THE YEAR 145: *This corresponds to 167 B.C.*
1:60 2 Macc 6:10

I Maccabees

8 The Temple is like someone without
   honor.
9 Its splendid furnishings
   have been carried away as loot.
 Our children have been killed in the
   streets,
   and our young men by the sword of
   the enemy.
10 Every nation in the world has occupied
   the city
   and robbed her of her possessions.
11 All her ornaments have been stripped
   away;
   she is now a slave, no longer free.
12 Look at our Temple, profaned by the
   Gentiles,
   emptied of all its splendor.
13 Why should we go on living?"

14 In their grief, Mattathias and his sons
tore their clothes, put on sackcloth, and continued in deep mourning.

15 Then the king's officials, who were forcing the people to turn from God, came to
the town of Modein to force the people
there to offer pagan sacrifices. 16 Many of the
Israelites came to meet them, including Mattathias and his sons. 17 The king's officials said
to Mattathias, "You are a respected leader in
this town, and you have the support of your
sons and relatives. 18 Why not be the first one
here to do what the king has commanded?
All the Gentiles, the people of Judea, and all
the people left in Jerusalem have already
done so. If you do, you and your sons will be
honored with the title of 'Friends of the
King,' and you will be rewarded with silver
and gold and many gifts."

19 Mattathias answered in a loud voice, "I
don't care if every Gentile in this empire has
obeyed the king and yielded to the command to abandon the religion of his ancestors. 20 My children, my relatives, and I will
continue to keep the covenant that God
made with our ancestors. 21 With God's help
we will never abandon his Law or disobey
his commands. 22 We will not obey the king's
decree, and we will not change our way of
worship in the least."

23 Just as he finished speaking, one of the
men from Modein decided to obey the king's

"We will not obey the king's decree." (2:22)

decree and stepped out in front of everyone
to offer a pagan sacrifice on the altar that
stood there. 24 When Mattathias saw him, he
became angry enough to do what had to be
done. Shaking with rage, he ran forward and
killed the man right there on the altar. 25 He
also killed the royal official who was forcing
the people to sacrifice, and then he tore down
the altar. 26 In this way Mattathias showed his
deep devotion for the Law, just as Phinehas
had done when he killed Zimri son of Salu.

The Guerrilla Warfare of Mattathias

27 Then Mattathias went through the town
shouting, "Everyone who is faithful to God's
covenant and obeys his Law, follow me!"
28 With this, he and his sons fled to the
mountains, leaving behind all they owned.

29-30 At that time also many of the
Israelites who were seeking to be right with
God through obedience to the Law went
out to live in the wilderness, taking their
children, their wives, and their livestock with
them, because of the terrible oppression they
were suffering. 31 The report soon reached
the king's officials and the soldiers in the fort
at Jerusalem that some men who had defied
the king's command had gone into hiding in
the wilderness. 32 A large force of soldiers
pursued them, caught up with them, set up
camp opposite them, and prepared to attack
them on the Sabbath. 33 "There is still time,"
they shouted out to the Jews. "Come out
and obey the king's command, and we will
spare your lives."

2:26 Num 25:6–15   2:32 2 Macc 6:11

I Maccabees

34"We will not come out," they answered. "We will not obey the king's command, and we will not profane the Sabbath."

35The soldiers attacked them immediately, 36but the Jews did nothing to resist; they did not even throw stones or block the entrances to the caves where they were hiding. 37They said, "We will all die with a clear conscience. Let heaven and earth bear witness that you are slaughtering us unjustly." 38So the enemy attacked them on the Sabbath and killed the men, their wives, their children, and their livestock. A thousand people died.

39When Mattathias and his friends heard the news about this, they were greatly saddened 40and said to one another, "If all of us do as these other Jews have done and refuse to fight the Gentiles to defend our lives and our religion, we will soon be wiped off the face of the earth." 41On that day they decided that if anyone attacked them on the Sabbath, they would defend themselves, so that they would not all die as other Jews had died in the caves.

42Then Mattathias and his friends were joined by a group of devout and patriotic Jews, the strongest and bravest men in Israel, who had all volunteered to defend the Law. 43In addition, everyone who was fleeing from the persecution joined them and strengthened their forces. 44Now that they had an army, they gave vent to their anger by attacking the renegade Jews. Those who escaped were forced to flee to the Gentiles for safety. 45Mattathias and his friends went everywhere tearing down pagan altars 46and circumcising by force every uncircumcised boy they found within the borders of Israel. 47They were also successful in hunting down the arrogant Gentile officials. 48They rescued the Law of Moses from the Gentiles and their kings and broke the power of the wicked King Antiochus.

The Death of Mattathias

49When the time came for Mattathias to die, he said to his sons, "These are times of violence and distress. Arrogant people are in control and have made us an object of ridicule. 50But you, my sons, must be devoted to the Law and ready to die to defend God's covenant with our ancestors. 51Remember what our ancestors did and how much they accomplished in their day. Follow their example, and you will be rewarded with great glory and undying fame. 52Remember how Abraham put his trust in the Lord when he was tested and how the Lord was pleased with him and accepted him. 53Joseph, in his time of trouble, obeyed God's commands and became ruler over the land of Egypt. 54Phinehas, our ancestor, because of his burning devotion, was given the promise that his descendants would always be priests. 55Joshua was made a judge in Israel because he obeyed the command of Moses. 56Caleb brought back a good report to the community and was given a part of the land as a reward. 57David was made king and was given the promise that his descendants would always be kings because of his steadfast loyalty to God. 58Elijah, because of his great devotion to the Law, was taken up into heaven. 59Hananiah, Azariah, and Mishael were saved from the flames because they had faith. 60Daniel was a man of integrity, and the Lord rescued him from the mouth of the lions. 61Take each of these ancestors of ours as an example, and you will realize that no one who puts his trust in the Lord will ever lack strength. 62Don't be afraid of the threats of a wicked man. Remember that he will die and all his splendor will end with worms feeding on his decaying body. 63Today he may be highly honored, but tomorrow he will disappear; his body will return to the earth and his scheming will come to an end. 64But you, my sons, be strong and courageous in defending the Law, because it is through the Law that you will earn great glory.

65"Your brother Simon is wise, so always listen to him as you would to me. 66Judas Maccabeus has been strong all his life; he will be your commander and will lead you in battle against the enemy. 67Call everyone who obeys God's Law to rally around you; then avenge the wrongs done to your people. 68Pay back the Gentiles for what they have done, and always obey the Law and its commands."

2:52 Gen 15:6; 22:15–18   2:53 Gen 39:1—45:28   2:55, 56 Num 13:1—14:12   2:57 2 Sam 7:16
2:58 2 Kings 2:9–12   2:59 Dan 3:8–30   2:60 Dan 6:1–24; Dan C:31–42

69 Then Mattathias gave them his blessing and died. 70 He was buried in the family tomb at Modein, and all the people of Israel went into deep mourning for him. This happened in the year 146.g

The Early Victories of Judas
(2 Maccabees 8:1–7)

3 1 Judas Maccabeus took the place of his father Mattathias. 2 All his brothers and all the loyal followers of his father gave him their support, and they were happy to carry on Israel's war.

3 Judas brought greater glory to his people.
In his armor, he was like a giant.
He took up his weapons and went to war;
   with his own sword he defended his camp.
4 He was like a ferocious lion roaring as it attacks.
5 Judas hunted down those who broke the Law
   and set fire to all who oppressed his people.
6 In fear of him, lawless men huddled together in terror,
   not knowing which way to turn.
He advanced the cause of freedom by what he did.
7 He made life miserable for many kings,
   but brought joy to the people of Israel.
We will praise him forever for what he did.
8 He went through the towns of Judea
   and destroyed all the godless men.
He relieved Israel of its terrible suffering.h
9 His fame spread to the ends of the earth,
   as he gathered together those who were threatened with death.

10 Then Apollonius assembled a Gentile army, including a large force from Samaria, to attack the people of Israel. 11 When Judas learned of this, he marched out to battle, defeated the army, and killed Apollonius. Many Gentiles lost their lives, and the rest fled. 12 When the spoils of war were collected, Judas took the sword of Apollonius and used it in battle until the day he died.

13 Seron, the general of the Syrian forces, learned that Judas had gathered together an army, consisting of a band of loyal men who were ready to fight under his command. 14 Seron said to himself, "I will make a reputation for myself throughout the empire by defeating Judas and his men, who have no respect for the king's command." 15 Then he began a new campaign against Judas and was joined by a strong force of godless men who were eager to help him take vengeance on Israel. 16 When he approached the pass at Beth Horon, Judas went out to meet him with a small group of men. 17 When Judas' men saw the army coming against them, they asked, "How can our little group of men fight an army as big as that? Besides, we have not eaten all day, and we are tired!"

"It is the Lord's power that determines the outcome."
(3:19)

18 "It is not difficult," Judas answered, "for a small group to overpower a large one. It makes no difference to the Lord whether we are rescued by many people or by just a few. 19 Victory in battle does not depend on who has the largest army; it is the Lord's power that determines the outcome. 20 Our enemies are coming against us with great violence, intending to plunder our possessions and kill our wives and children. 21 But we are fighting for our lives and for our religion. 22 When we attack, the Lord will crush our enemies, so don't be afraid of them."

23 As soon as Judas had finished speaking, he and his men made a sudden attack against Seron and his army and crushed them. 24 They pursued them down the pass at Beth

---

g 2:70 THE YEAR 146: This corresponds to 166 B.C.   h 3:8 relieved Israel of its terrible suffering; or saved Israel from God's anger.

Horon to the plain and killed about 800 men. Those who escaped fled to Philistia. 25After that, Gentiles everywhere began to be afraid of Judas and his brothers. 26His fame reached the ears of King Antiochus, and people in every nation talked about Judas and his victories.

The King Appoints Lysias as Governor

27When Antiochus heard what had happened, he was furious. He ordered all the armies of his empire to assemble in one huge force. 28From his treasury he paid a full year's wages to his soldiers and ordered them to be prepared for any emergency. 29But then he found that the funds in his treasury were exhausted. Income from taxes had decreased because of the disorder and the troubles he had brought on the world by doing away with the laws which had been in force from the earliest times. 30Antiochus had always given presents more lavishly than earlier kings, but now he was worried that he might not be able to continue this, or even to meet expenses—this had happened once or twice before. 31He was very disturbed; but finally he decided to go to Persia, collect the taxes from the provinces there, and bring together a large sum of ready cash.

32He appointed Lysias, an important man who had been granted the title "Relative of the King," as governor to take care of the king's affairs in the whole territory between the Euphrates River and the Egyptian border. 33The king also made Lysias the guardian of his son Antiochus the Fifth until his own return. 34He put Lysias in charge of all the elephants and of half his army, and then gave him detailed instructions about what he wanted done, and in particular, what he wanted done with the inhabitants of Judea and Jerusalem. 35Lysias was ordered to send an army against the Jews, especially the Jews in Jerusalem, to break their power and destroy them, so that no trace of them would remain. 36He was ordered to take their land and give it to foreigners, who would settle the whole area. 37Taking the other half of his army, the king set out from

Antioch, his capital city, in the year 147.*i* He crossed the Euphrates River and marched through Mesopotamia.

The Victories of Judas
(2 Maccabees 8:8–29, 34–36)

38Lysias chose Nicanor, Gorgias, and Ptolemy son of Dorymenes as army commanders; all three were able men who bore the title "Friend of the King." 39He put them in charge of 40,000 infantry and 7,000 cavalry and ordered them to invade the land of Judea and destroy it as the king had commanded. 40These commanders set out with their entire force, and when they came to the plains near Emmaus, they made camp. 41A force from Idumea*j* and Philistia joined them. The merchants of the region heard about the strength of the army, and they came to the camp with chains and a large amount of money, hoping to buy some Jewish slaves.

42Judas and his brothers saw that their situation was getting more and more difficult, with foreign armies camped within their own borders. They also learned that the king had commanded the complete destruction of the people. 43So they determined to rebuild their ruined nation and fight for their country and the Temple. 44Then the whole community came together to prepare for war and to pray for God's mercy.

45Jerusalem was as empty as a wilderness;
   no citizens left or entered the city.
The holy Temple was profaned by
      foreigners,
and Gentiles camped in the city's fort;
so joy departed from the people of Israel,
and the sound of music was heard no
      more.

46Then Judas and his men assembled and marched to Mizpah, opposite Jerusalem, because the people of Israel had previously had a place of worship there. 47In deep mourning, they fasted all that day, put on sackcloth, threw ashes on their heads, and tore their clothes. 48The Gentiles would have consulted their idols in such a situation, but the Israelites unrolled the book of the Law to search for God's guidance. 49They

I Maccabees

brought the priests' robes, the offerings of the first grain, and the tithes, and then they brought in some Nazirites who had completed their vows. 50 The whole community prayed, "Lord, what shall we do with these things? Where shall we take them, 51 now that your holy Temple has been trampled and profaned by Gentiles, and your priests mourn in disgrace? 52 The Gentiles have come to attack and destroy us. You know what they plan to do! 53 If you don't help us, how can we stand up against them?" 54 Then they blew trumpets and shouted loudly.

55 After that, Judas divided his men into groups of ten, fifty, a hundred, and a thousand, placing officers in charge of each group. 56 Then, in obedience to the Law, he sent home everyone who had recently been married, built a house, or planted a vineyard, as well as anyone who was afraid. 57 Finally, the army marched out and took up positions south of Emmaus, 58 where Judas said to them: "Prepare yourselves for battle and be courageous! Be ready early tomorrow morning to fight these Gentiles who have joined forces to attack us and destroy us and our Temple. 59 It is better for us to die fighting than to stand idly by and watch the destruction of our nation and our Temple. 60 But the Lord will do what he pleases."

4 1 Gorgias took 5,000 infantry and 1,000 of his most experienced cavalry and left camp by night, 2 with men from the fort in Jerusalem as his guides. He had planned to make a surprise attack on the Jewish army, 3 but Judas learned of the plan and moved out with his men to attack the king's army at Emmaus 4 while Gorgias and his troops were still away from the camp. 5 When Gorgias and his army reached Judas' camp that night, they found no one there. They thought Judas and his men were trying to escape, so they started looking for them in the mountains.

6 At dawn Judas appeared in the plain with 3,000 men, not all of them as well armed as they would have liked. 7 They saw the huge Gentile army of experienced troops wearing armor and protected by cavalry. 8 But Judas said to his men, "Don't worry about the size of their army, and don't be frightened when they attack. 9 Remember how our ancestors were saved at the Red Sea when the king of Egypt was pursuing them with his army! 10 Now let us ask the Lord to have mercy on us. Let us pray that he will honor his covenant with our ancestors and crush this army when we attack today. 11 Then all the Gentiles will know that Israel has a God who rescues and saves them."

12 When the Gentiles saw Judas and his men preparing for battle, 13 they moved out of their camp to fight. Then Judas and his men sounded their trumpets 14 and attacked. The Gentiles broke ranks and fled to the plain, 15 but all the stragglers were killed. The Israelites pursued the enemy as far as Gezer, the plains of Idumea, and the towns of Azotus and Jamnia. Altogether they killed about 3,000 of the enemy.

16 When Judas and his army came back from the pursuit, 17-18 he said to his men, "Don't be greedy for loot. Gorgias and his army are nearby in the mountains, so there is still heavy fighting ahead of us. We must stand firm and fight. After that, you can safely take all the loot you want." 19 Judas was just finishing his speech when an enemy patrol on a scouting mission looked down from the mountains 20 and saw that their army had been put to flight; they could tell from the smoke that their camp was burning. 21 When they saw all this, they were terrified, and when they also saw that Judas' army was in the plain ready for battle, 22 they all fled to Philistia. 23 Then Judas returned to loot the enemy camp; he took large amounts of gold and silver, blue and purple cloth, and other rich plunder. 24 When the Jews came back to their own camp, they sang a hymn: "The Lord is worthy of praise; his mercy endures forever." 25 That day brought a great victory to the people of Israel.

Victory over Lysias
(2 Maccabees 11:1–12)

26 The Gentile troops that escaped went to Lysias and reported all that had happened. 27 When Lysias heard that his troops had lost the battle, he was shocked and disappointed

that Israel had not been defeated as the king had commanded.

28 In the following year Lysias gathered an army of 60,000 well-trained infantry and 5,000 cavalry, intending to conquer the Jews. 29 They marched into Idumea and camped at Bethzur. Judas came to meet them with 10,000 men. 30 When Judas saw how strong the enemy's army was, he prayed, "We will praise you, Savior of Israel. You broke the attack of the giant by the hand of your servant David and you let Saul's son Jonathan and the young man who carried his weapons defeat the entire Philistine army. 31 Now in the same way let your people Israel defeat our enemy. Put them to shame, in spite of all their confidence in their infantry and cavalry. 32 Make them afraid; let their bold strength melt away; let them tremble at the prospect of defeat. 33 We love and worship you; so let us kill our enemies, that we may then sing your praises."

34 The battle began, and in the hand-to-hand fighting about 5,000 of Lysias' men were killed. 35 When Lysias saw that his army was being defeated and when he saw the reckless courage of Judas and his men, who showed that they were ready to live or die with honor, he returned to Antioch. There he recruited some mercenaries and planned to return to Judea later with a much larger army.

The Purification of the Temple
(2 Maccabees 10:1–8)

36 Judas and his brothers said, "Now that our enemies have been defeated, let's go to Jerusalem to purify the Temple and rededicate it." 37 So the whole army was assembled and went up to Mount Zion. 38 There they found the Temple abandoned, the altar profaned, the gates burned down, the courtyards grown up in a forest of weeds, and the priests' rooms torn down. 39 In their sorrow, they tore their clothes, cried loudly, threw ashes on their heads, 40 and fell face down on the ground. When the signal was given on the trumpets, everyone cried out to the Lord.

41 Then Judas ordered some of his soldiers to attack the men in the fort, while he purified the Temple. 42 He chose some priests who were qualified and who were devoted to the Law. 43 They purified the Temple and took the stones that had been defiled and put them in an unclean place. 44 They discussed what should be done with the altar of burnt offerings, which had been desecrated 45 by the Gentiles, and decided to tear it down, so that it would not stand there as a monument to their shame. So they tore down the altar 46 and put the stones in a suitable place on the Temple hill, where they were to be kept until a prophet should appear and decide what to do with them. 47 Then they took uncut stones, as the Law of Moses required, and built a new altar like the old one. 48 They repaired the Temple, inside and out, and dedicated its courtyards. 49 They made new utensils for worship and brought the lampstand, the altar of incense, and the table for the bread into the Temple. 50 They burned incense on the altar and lit the lamps on the lampstand, and there was light in the Temple! 51 They placed the loaves of bread on the table, hung the curtains, and completed all the work.

52-54 The twenty-fifth day of the ninth month, the month of Kislev, in the year 148 k was the anniversary of the day the Gentiles had desecrated the altar. On that day a sacrifice was offered on the new altar in accordance with the Law of Moses. The new altar was dedicated and hymns were sung to the accompaniment of harps, lutes, and cymbals. 55 All the people bowed down with their faces to the ground and worshiped and praised the Lord for giving them victory.

56 For eight days they celebrated the rededication of the altar. With great joy they brought burnt offerings and offered fellowship offerings and thank offerings. 57 They decorated the front of the Temple with gold crowns and shields, rebuilt the gates and the priests' rooms and put doors on them. 58 Now that the Jews had removed the shame which the Gentiles had brought, they held a great celebration. 59 Then Judas, his brothers,

k 4:52–54 THE YEAR 148: *This corresponds to 164 B.C.*
4:30 1 Sam 17:41–54; 14:1–23   4:47 Ex 20:25; Deut 27:5, 6   4:52–54 1 Macc 1:54

and the entire community of Israel decreed that the rededication of the altar should be celebrated with a festival of joy and gladness at the same time each year, beginning on the twenty-fifth of the month of Kislev and lasting for eight days.

60 Then they built high walls and strong towers around Mount Zion, so that the Gentiles could not come in and trample and defile it again. 61 Judas placed a detachment of soldiers there to guard the Temple. He also fortified the town of Bethzur, so that the people of Israel would have a fortress facing Idumea.

Wars with Neighboring Nations
(2 Maccabees 10:14–33; 12:10–45)

5 1 When the neighboring nations heard that the Jews had built the altar and restored the Temple as it had been before, they were so furious 2 that they made up their minds to destroy all the Jews who were living among them. So they began to murder and kill our people.

3 The Idumeans were blockading the Israelites, so Judas went to war against them at Akrabattene, crushed them, and looted them. 4 He also dealt with the people of Baean, who were a constant threat to the people of Israel, because they would lie in ambush waiting to trap Israelite travelers. 5 He shut the Baeanites up in their forts, took a solemn oath that he would destroy them, and burned their forts with everyone in them. 6 Then he marched against the land of Ammon, where he met a large and powerful army under the command of a man named Timothy. 7 Judas won many battles against them and finally defeated them. 8 He captured Jazer and its surrounding villages and then returned to Judea.

9 The Gentiles in Gilead assembled to attack and destroy the Israelites living in their territory. But the Israelites fled to the fortress of Dathema 10-11 and sent the following letter to Judas and his brothers: "The Gentiles around us are joining forces under Timothy. We have fled to this fortress for protection, and now they are getting ready

to capture it and destroy us. 12 Many of us have already been killed. Come rescue us! 13 All the Jewish men in the region of Tob[l] have been killed, their wives and their children have been taken captive, and their possessions have been carried off. A force of about 1,000 men has been destroyed there."

14 This letter was still being read when other messengers, who had torn their clothes in sorrow, arrived with a report from Galilee. 15 They said, "An army from Ptolemais, Tyre, Sidon, and all of Galilee has come together to destroy us."

16 When Judas and the people heard all this, a great assembly was held to decide what should be done to help these countrymen, who were in such difficulty under enemy attack. 17 Judas said to his brother Simon, "Choose some men and go rescue our fellow Jews in Galilee; our brother Jonathan and I will go to Gilead." 18 Judas left the rest of his army to defend Judea and put the two leaders, Azariah and Joseph son of Zechariah, in charge of the people. 19 He told them: "I am leaving you in command here, but don't go out and fight the Gentiles until we get back." 20 Then 3,000 men joined Simon for the march into Galilee, and 8,000 remained with Judas for the march into Gilead.

21 Simon went into Galilee and fought many battles with the Gentiles. He defeated them 22 and pursued them all the way to the city of Ptolemais, killing about 3,000 of them, and taking the loot. 23 Then he took the Jews who were in Galilee and Arbatta, with their wives, their children, and all they owned, and brought them back to Judea with him. There was great rejoicing.

24 During this time, Judas Maccabeus and his brother Jonathan had crossed the Jordan River and had marched for three days through the desert. 25 They met some friendly Nabateans who told them all that had happened to the Jews in Gilead. 26 They reported that many Jews were imprisoned in the fortified cities of Bozrah, Bosor, Alema, Chaspho, Maked, and Karnaim, 27 while others were imprisoned in the smaller towns of Gilead. They also reported that the enemy

---

l 5:13 in the region of Tob; or who were fighting with Tobias.

was drawn up to make an attack the next day on the Jewish fortresses, hoping to destroy all the Jews in a single day.

28 So Judas and his army suddenly turned and attacked Bozrah by the desert road, captured the town, and killed every man in it. They looted the town and set it on fire. 29 They left there and marched all night to the fortress at Dathema. 30 At dawn Judas and his men saw a vast army attacking the fortress; they were bringing up ladders, siege platforms, and battering rams in an effort to capture it. 31 When Judas heard the noise, the shouts, and the sound of trumpets coming from the city, he realized that the battle had begun, 32 so he said to his men, "Fight today for our fellow Jews!"

Judas and his men saw a vast army attacking the fortress. (5:30)

33 He ordered his men to march in three columns and attack the enemy from the rear. As they moved forward, they blew trumpets and shouted prayers. 34 When the army under Timothy's command saw that it was Judas Maccabeus, the soldiers turned and fled. Judas crushed them and killed about 8,000 men that day.

35 Then Judas turned aside to attack the town of Alema;*m* he captured it and killed all the men in it. He looted the town and set fire to it. 36 From there he went on and captured Chaspho, Maked, Bosor, and the other towns of Gilead.

37 After this, Timothy gathered another army and camped opposite Raphon, on the other side of a river. 38 Judas sent some men to spy on the camp, and they reported back to him that all the Gentiles in the region had joined Timothy and had formed a large army. 39 Timothy had also hired Arab mercenaries to help him, and these were camped on the other side of the river ready to attack Judas. So Judas went out to meet them in battle.

40 As Judas and his army came closer to the water, Timothy said to his officers, "If he keeps on coming and crosses the river, we won't be able to turn back his attack, and he will defeat us. 41 But if he is afraid and stops on the other side of the river, we will cross over to attack and defeat him." 42 When Judas reached the bank of the river, he gave orders to his officers to let no one stop but to push everyone forward into battle. 43 Judas was the first to cross the river against the enemy, and all his men followed him. The Gentiles broke ranks before them, threw away their arms, and fled to the pagan temple at Karnaim. 44 But Judas and his men took the city and burned down the temple with all who were in it. With Karnaim overthrown, the Gentiles could no longer offer any resistance to Judas.

45 Then Judas gathered together all the Jews in Gilead to take them back to Judea with him. It was a large group of all kinds of people, together with their wives and children and all that they owned. 46 They went as far as Ephron, a large, well-fortified town. It was impossible to go around it on either side, and the road passed directly through the town. 47 But the people there would not let them pass and blocked the town gates with stones. 48 Then Judas sent a friendly message to them: "Let us pass through your territory to return home. No one will harm you; we will just pass through." But they still refused to open the gates.

49 So Judas told everyone in the group, except the fighting men, to camp where they were. 50 The fighting men were ordered to take up their positions and attack the town. They fought all day and all night, until they had taken it. 51 Judas had all the men of Ephron put to death, plundered the town, and leveled it. Then he and his army marched through the town over the dead bodies. 52 They crossed the Jordan into the wide plain opposite Beth Shan. 53 Throughout the whole march Judas kept gathering up the stragglers and encouraging the people until they reached the land of Judea. 54 With

m 5:35 ALEMA: The name of the town is not certain.

thanksgiving and rejoicing, they went up to Mount Zion and sacrificed burnt offerings because they had returned safely without a single loss.

55 While Judas and Jonathan were in Gilead and their brother Simon was attacking Ptolemais in Galilee, 56 Joseph and Azariah, the commanders of the army in Judea, heard about their brave deeds and victories. 57 They said to one another, "Let's go to war with the Gentiles around us and win some fame for ourselves." 58 So they and their men attacked Jamnia. 59 Gorgias and his men went out of the town to meet them in battle. 60 They defeated Joseph and Azariah and pursued them as far as the borders of Judea. At least 2,000 Israelite men were killed that day. 61 This great defeat came about because the Jewish commanders wanted to be heroes and refused to obey Judas and his brothers. 62 Besides, they did not belong to the family of the Maccabees, whom God had chosen to bring freedom to the people of Israel.

63 But Judas Maccabeus and his brothers won great respect among all the Israelites and all the Gentiles. When people heard of their fame, 64 large crowds gathered to praise them.

65 Then Judas and his brothers went to war against the Edomites to the south. He attacked Hebron and its surrounding towns, destroyed its fortifications, and burned down the towers around it. 66 Then he marched into the land of the Philistines and passed through Marisa.[n] 67 That day a number of priests were killed in battle because they wanted to be heroes and foolishly went out to fight. 68 Judas turned aside to Azotus in Philistia. He pulled down the altars, burned the images of their gods, plundered their towns, and then returned to Judea.

The Death of Antiochus the Fourth
(2 Maccabees 1:11–17; 9:1–29; 10:9–11)

6 ¹ As King Antiochus the Fourth was passing through Mesopotamia, he heard of a city in Persia, named Elymais, which was famous for its riches in silver and gold. ² The temple was very rich, containing gold

shields, armor, and weapons left there by Alexander, son of King Philip of Macedonia, who was the first to rule the Greek Empire. ³ Antiochus came and tried to take the city and loot it, but he didn't succeed, because the citizens had learned what he was planning to do, ⁴ and they drew up their troops to resist him. In great frustration he withdrew to return to Babylonia.

⁵ In Persia a messenger reached him with the news that the armies he had sent into Judea had been defeated. ⁶ Lysias and his strong army had been forced to flee from the Jews, who were now reinforced by the additional weapons, supplies, and loot they had taken from the defeated armies. ⁷ The Jews had pulled down the thing they called "The Awful Horror" that Antiochus had built on the altar in Jerusalem. They had also surrounded the Temple with high walls, as it had been before, and had taken and fortified the town of Bethzur, one of the king's own towns.

⁸ When the king heard this report, he was so dumbfounded and terribly shaken that he went to bed in a fit of deep depression because things had not turned out as he had hoped. ⁹ He remained ill for a long time, as waves of despair swept over him, until he finally realized that he was going to die. ¹⁰ He called together all those to whom he had given the title "Friends of the King" and said to them, "I cannot sleep, and my heart is broken with grief and worry. ¹¹ At first I asked myself why these great waves of trouble were sweeping over me, since I have been kind and well-liked during my reign.

The king . . . went to bed in a fit of deep depression. (6:8)

---

[n] **5:66** *Some ancient translations* Marisa; *Greek* Samaria.
6:7 1 Macc 1:54

12But then I remembered the wrongs I did in Jerusalem when I took all the silver and gold objects from the Temple and tried without any good reason to destroy the inhabitants of Judea. 13I know this is why all these terrible things have happened to me and I am about to die in deep despair here in this foreign land."

14Then he called Philip, one of his most trusted advisers, and put him in charge of his whole empire. 15He gave him his crown, robe, and official ring, and authorized him to educate his son Antiochus the Fifth and bring him up to be king. 16King Antiochus died there in the year 149.o

17When Lysias learned that the king had died, he made the young Antiochus king in place of his father. He had brought up Antiochus from childhood and now gave him the name Eupator.

The Campaign of Antiochus the Fifth and Lysias
(2 Maccabees 13:1–26; 11:22–26)

18Meanwhile, the enemies in the fort at Jerusalem had been blockading the people of Israel in the area around the Temple, constantly causing them trouble and giving support to the Gentiles. 19So Judas decided to get rid of them and called all the people together to besiege the fort. 20The people assembled and laid siege to the fort in the year 150.p They built siege platforms and battering rams.

21But some of the men under siege escaped, and together with some of the renegade Jews, they went to the king and said, 22"How long are you going to wait before you take revenge for what was done to our countrymen? 23We were willing to serve your father, follow his orders, and obey his decrees. 24But what good did it do us? Now our own countrymen have become our enemies.q In fact, they have killed as many of us as they could find and have stolen our possessions. 25But we are not the only ones they have harmed; they have attacked all their neighbors. 26And now they have laid siege to the fort in Jerusalem and

are planning to take it. They have also fortified the Temple and Bethzur. 27Unless you act immediately, they will do even more, and you will not be able to stop them."

28When the king heard this, he was furious. He brought together all the army commanders, the cavalry officers, and his most trusted advisers. 29He also hired mercenary soldiers from other countries and from the Greek islands. 30His forces numbered 100,000 infantry, 20,000 cavalry, and 32 elephants trained for war. 31The king and his army passed through Idumea and laid siege to Bethzur, where they fought for a long time. They built battering rams and siege platforms, but the defenders fought bravely and came out of the town and burned down the platforms.

32Then Judas withdrew his troops from the fort in Jerusalem and set up his camp at Beth Zechariah, blocking the advance of the king's army. 33Early the next morning, the king rapidly moved his army along the road to Beth Zechariah, where his troops took up battle positions and blew trumpets. 34They got the elephants ready for battle by showing them grape juice and mulberry juice. 35The huge animals were distributed among the infantry units. A thousand men, protected by chain armor and bronze helmets, were stationed with each elephant. Each animal was also accompanied by a special force of 500 cavalry, 36which always remained with the elephant. 37A strong, protected wooden platform was securely fastened by a special harness to the back of each elephant. Threer soldiers rode on each animal, in addition to the elephant driver. 38Lysias placed the rest of the cavalry on the two flanks of the army where they could be protected by the infantry while harassing the enemy. 39The sunlight, reflected off the bronze and gold shields, shone on the mountains and flashed like burning torches. 40Part of the king's army was spread out over the higher ground of the mountain slopes and part over the lower land, but they all moved forward steadily and in good order. 41All the people were terrified when they heard the noise made by the clashing of weapons and the marching of that great and powerful army.

42Judas and his army advanced into battle, and immediately killed 600 of the king's army. **43**When Eleazar Avaran saw that one of the elephants was larger than the others and that it was covered with royal armor, he thought that the king was riding on it. **44**Eleazar sacrificed his life to save his people and to gain eternal fame. **45**He ran boldly toward the elephant, which was in the middle of a battalion of infantry. He rushed forward killing men to the right and left, so that the enemy soldiers fell back before him on both sides. **46**He slipped in under the elephant and stabbed it to death, and it fell on him and killed him. **47**But when the Jews realized how strong the royal army was and how determined it was to fight, they retreated.

48The king and his army advanced to fight the Jews at Jerusalem and laid siege to the whole of Judea and Jerusalem. **49**He made peace with the Jews of Bethzur, who then left the town. There had not been enough food in the town for them to withstand the siege because it was the sabbatical year, when no crops were planted. **50**The king occupied Bethzur and stationed a body of troops there to guard it. **51**Then he surrounded the Temple and besieged it for a long time. He set up siege platforms, battering rams, catapults for throwing fire and stones, and other weapons to throw spears and rocks. **52**The defenders also made war machines to oppose those of the enemy, and so the battle went on for a long time. **53**But there was no food left in the Temple storage bins because it was the sabbatical year, and the people who had fled from the Gentiles and taken refuge in Judea had eaten all the food that had been stored there. **54**The shortage of food had been so severe that many people had scattered to their homes, and only a few men were left in the Temple.

55Meanwhile, Philip, who had been appointed by King Antiochus before his death to educate his son to be king, **56**returned from Persia and Media. He had come back with the royal army and planned to take control of the government. When Lysias heard this news, **57**he made rapid preparations to depart. He said to the young king, to his officers, and to his men, "We are growing weaker each day; we are short of provisions, and this place we are besieging is strong. Besides, there are pressing government affairs which need our attention. **58**So now let's arrange a truce and make a peace treaty with the Jews and their whole nation. **59**We will allow them to follow their own laws and customs as they did before. All this trouble started when we provoked them by abolishing their laws and customs."

60This recommendation was well received by the king and the officers, so Lysias proposed peace terms to the Jews, and they accepted them. **61**When the king and his officers solemnly agreed to abide by these terms, the Jews came out of their fortress. **62**But when the king entered the Temple area on Mount Zion and saw the strong fortifications, he broke his word and ordered the walls surrounding the Temple to be torn down. **63**Then he hurriedly left and returned to Antioch, where he found Philip in control of the city. The king attacked the city and took it by force.

The High Priest Alcimus and the Campaign of Nicanor
(2 Maccabees 14:1–36; 15:1–36)

7 **1**In the year 151,*s* Demetrius son of Seleucus left Rome and with a few men landed at a town on the Mediterranean coast, where he proclaimed himself king. **2**As he was making his way to the royal palace of his ancestors, the soldiers arrested Antiochus the Fifth and Lysias, planning to take them to Demetrius. **3**When Demetrius heard about it, he said, "I don't want to see them." **4**So the soldiers killed them, and Demetrius took the throne.

5Then all the godless traitorous Jews led by Alcimus, who wanted to be High Priest, went to Demetrius. **6**They brought accusations against the other Jews and said, "Judas and his brothers have killed everybody who supported you, and they have driven us out of our country. **7**We advise you to send

---

s 7:1 THE YEAR 151: *This corresponds to 161 B.C.*

someone whom you can trust to go and inspect all the damage done to our property and the king's territory and to punish Judas, his brothers, and all who support them."

⁸King Demetrius chose one of his advisers, a man by the name of Bacchides, who was the governor of Greater Syria. He was an important man in the empire and loyal to the king. ⁹He was sent along with the godless Alcimus, whom the king had appointed High Priest; Alcimus had orders to take revenge on the Jews. ¹⁰They left Antioch and arrived in Judea with a large army. Bacchides tried to trick Judas and his brothers by sending to them messengers with offers of peace. ¹¹But when Judas and his brothers saw what a large army they had brought, they did not believe what the messengers said.

¹²A group of teachers of the Law came to Alcimus and Bacchides, asking for justice. ¹³These devout and patriotic men were the first of the Jews to try to make peace with Alcimus and Bacchides. ¹⁴They trusted Alcimus, who was a priest descended from Aaron, and they thought he would not cause them any harm. ¹⁵Alcimus assured them of his peaceful intentions and solemnly promised that no harm would come to them or their friends. ¹⁶But as soon as they began to trust him, he arrested 60 of them and put them all to death on the same day. As the scripture says,

¹⁷"The blood of your faithful people was
        poured out,
    their bodies were scattered around
        Jerusalem,
    and there was no one left to bury the
        dead."

¹⁸When this happened, all the people were afraid of Alcimus and Bacchides, and they said, "They don't know what truth or justice means. They gave their solemn word and then broke it!" ¹⁹Bacchides left Jerusalem and set up his headquarters at Beth Zaith. He ordered the arrest of some of the faithful Jews and even many of the renegades who had willingly joined him; he had them killed and thrown into a deep pit. ²⁰Bacchides put the country under the control of Alcimus, left troops there to help him, and returned to the king.

²¹Alcimus then began his struggle to establish himself as High Priest. ²²Every troublemaker in the country joined him. They gained control of the land of Judea and caused great difficulties for the Jews. ²³Judas saw that the trouble Alcimus and his men had caused was even worse than the damage done by the Gentiles. ²⁴So he went around the whole country of Judea taking revenge on all the men who had willingly joined Alcimus and preventing them from leaving the towns and going into the country. ²⁵When Alcimus saw that Judas and his men were growing more powerful and when he realized that he would not be able to stand against them, he returned to the king and accused them of great crimes.

²⁶Then the king sent Nicanor, one of his most honored officers, who hated the Jews, with orders to exterminate them. ²⁷Nicanor came to Jerusalem with a big army. He tried to trick Judas and his brothers by sending peace offers. He said, ²⁸"There need not be any quarrel between you and me. I will come to you with a small escort for a friendly private conversation." ²⁹When he came to Judas, they exchanged polite greetings, but Judas' enemies were ready to kidnap him. ³⁰When Judas learned that Nicanor's visit was part of a plot against him, he was afraid and decided not to meet him again. ³¹Nicanor realized that his plan had been discovered, so he left Jerusalem to meet Judas in battle near Capharsalama. ³²About 500 of Nicanor's men were killed, and the rest of the army escaped to the fort in Jerusalem.

³³Some time later Nicanor went to Mount Zion. Some of the priests left the Temple and, along with some of the leaders of the people, went to welcome him with words of peace and to show him the burnt offering that was being sacrificed on behalf of the king. ³⁴But he ridiculed them and made them ceremonially unclean by spitting on them. He spoke proudly ³⁵and angrily threatened them with an oath, "Unless Judas and his army are surrendered to me immediately, I will burn this Temple down as soon as I return after my victory." And he left in a rage.

I Maccabees

36 The priests went into the courtyard and stood facing the altar and the Temple. They started weeping and prayed, 37 "Lord, you chose this Temple to bear your name and to be a place of prayer and intercession for your people. 38 Now, take vengeance on this man and his army; let them die in battle. Remember how they spoke evil of you, and let none of them survive."

39 Nicanor left Jerusalem and set up his headquarters at Beth Horon, where the Syrian army joined him. 40 Meanwhile, Judas set up camp at Adasa with 3,000 men. There Judas prayed, 41 "Lord, the Scriptures tell us that when a king sent messengers to insult you, your angel went out and killed 185,000 of his soldiers. 42 Now, in the same way, crush this army before us today and let everyone know that Nicanor is being punished because he insulted your holy Temple. Punish him as his wickedness deserves."

43 The armies met in battle on the thirteenth day of the month of Adar, and Nicanor's army was defeated. Nicanor himself was the first to be killed in the battle, 44 and when his soldiers saw that he was dead, they threw down their weapons and fled. 45 The Jews pursued them all day long from Adasa to Gezer. As they followed, they kept sounding the call to battle on the trumpets, 46 and from all the surrounding villages of Judea people came out and attacked the fleeing enemy from the sides. This forced them back toward the Jews who were chasing them, and all of the enemy were killed in the fight. Not one of them survived.

47 The Jews took the loot and then cut off Nicanor's head and his right arm, which he had extended so arrogantly. They brought his head and his arm to be put on display outside Jerusalem. 48 There was great rejoicing among the Jews. They set that day aside as a special day of celebration, 49 and decreed that the thirteenth day of Adar should be observed as an annual day of celebration. 50 There was peace in the land of Judea for a little while.

The Treaty with the Romans

8 ¹Judas had heard about the Romans and their reputation as a military power. He knew that they welcomed all those who joined them as allies and that those who came to them could be sure of the friendship of Rome. 2 People had told him about the wars the Romans had fought and their heroic acts among the Gauls, whom they had conquered and forced to pay taxes. 3 He had been told what they had done in Spain when they captured the silver mines and the gold mines there. 4 By careful planning and persistence, they had conquered the whole country, even though it was far from Rome. They had overcome the kings from distant lands who had fought against them; they had defeated them so badly that the survivors had to pay annual taxes. 5 They had fought and conquered Philip and Perseus, kings of Macedonia, and all who had joined them against Rome. 6 They had even defeated Antiochus the Great, king of Syria, who had attacked them with 120 elephants, cavalry, chariots, and a powerful army. 7 They took him alive and forced him and his successors to pay heavy taxes, to give hostages, and to surrender 8 India, Media, Lydia, and some of their best lands. They took these and gave them to King Eumenes. ᶠ

9 When the Greeks made plans to attack and destroy them, 10 the Romans learned of the plans and sent a general to fight against them. The Romans killed many of the Greeks, took their wives and children captive, plundered their possessions, occupied their land, tore down their fortresses, and made them slaves, as they are today. 11 They also destroyed or made slaves of other kingdoms, the islands, and everyone who had ever fought against them. 12 But they maintained their friendship with their allies and those who relied on them for protection. They conquered kings near and far, and everyone who heard of their reputation was afraid of them. 13 They helped some men to become kings, while they deposed others; they had become a world power. 14 In spite of all this, no Roman ever tried to advance

---

ᶠ **8:8** KING EUMENES: *This is King Eumenes II, king of Pergamum from 197—158 B.C.*
7:41 2 Kings 19:35

his own position by wearing a crown or putting on royal robes. 15They created a senate, and each day 320 senators came together to deliberate about the affairs of the people and their well-being. 16Each year they entrusted to one man the responsibility of governing them and controlling their whole territory. Everyone obeyed this one man, and there was no envy or jealousy among them.

17Judas chose Eupolemus, the son of John and grandson of Accos, and Jason son of Eleazar and sent them to Rome to make a treaty of friendship and alliance with the Romans. 18He did this to eliminate Syrian oppression, since the Jews clearly saw that they were being reduced to slavery. 19After a long and difficult journey, Eupolemus and Jason reached Rome and entered the Senate. They addressed the assembly in these terms: 20"Judas Maccabeus, his brothers, and the Jewish people have sent us here to make a mutual defense treaty with you, so that we may be officially recorded as your friends and allies."

21The Romans accepted the proposal, 22and what follows is a copy of the letter which was engraved on bronze tablets and sent to Jerusalem to remain there as a record of the treaty:

23"May things go well forever for the Romans and for the Jewish nation on land and sea! May they never have enemies, and may they never go to war! 24But if war is declared first against Rome or any of her allies anywhere, 25the Jewish nation will come to her aid with wholehearted support, as the situation may require. 26And to those at war with her, the Jews shall not give or supply food, arms, money, or ships, as was agreed in Rome. The Jews must carry out their obligations without receiving anything in return.

27"In the same way, if war is declared first against the Jewish nation, the Romans will come to their aid with hearty support, as the situation may require. 28And to their enemies there shall not be given or supplied food, arms, money, or ships, as was agreed in Rome. The Romans must carry out their obligations without deception.

29"These are the terms of the treaty that the Romans have made with the Jewish people. 30But if, in the future, both parties shall agree to add or remove anything, they shall act on their decision, and whatever they add or remove shall be valid.

31"Furthermore, concerning the wrongs which King Demetrius is doing against the Jews, we have written him as follows, 'Why have you treated our friends and allies, the Jews, so harshly? 32If they complain to us about you one more time, we will support their cause and go to war against you on land and sea.' "

The Death of Judas

9 1When Demetrius heard that Nicanor and his army had been annihilated, he again sent Bacchides and Alcimus to the land of Judea, this time with the Syrian wing of the army. 2They moved along Gilgal Road, laid siege to Mesaloth in Arbela, captured it, and killed many people. 3In the first month of the year 152,ᵘ they set up camp opposite Jerusalem. 4From there they marched to Berea with 20,000 infantry and 2,000 cavalry.

5Judas had camped at Elasa, with 3,000 experienced soldiers. 6But when they saw the enormous size of the enemy army, they were terrified. So many men deserted that only 800 Jewish soldiers were left. 7When Judas saw that his army was dwindling away and that the battle was about to begin, he was worried because there was not enough time to bring his army together. 8He was discouraged, but he said to those who were still with him, "Let's prepare for the attack; maybe we can still defeat them."

9His men tried to talk him out of it. "We are not strong enough," they said. "Let's retreat now and save our lives. Then we can return with reinforcements and fight the enemy. We don't have enough men now."

10Judas replied, "Never let it be said that I ran from a battle. If our time has come, let's die bravely for our fellow Jews and not leave any stain on our honor."

11The Syrian army came out of the camp

ᵘ **9:3** THE YEAR 152: *This corresponds to 160 B.C.*
8:17 2 Macc 4:11   **8:22** 1 Macc 14:18

and took up battle positions against the Jews. The cavalry was divided into two parts. The shock troops were in the front lines, but the archers and those who used slings went ahead of the main formation. 12Bacchides took his position on the right. The infantry advanced, protected on both sides by the cavalry, and the war trumpets were blown. The soldiers of Judas also sounded their trumpets. 13The ground shook from the noise when the two armies met, and they fought from morning until evening.

14When Judas saw that Bacchides and the main force of the Syrian army was on the right, all his bravest men joined him, 15and they crushed the Syrians' right wing. They pursued them as far as the foothills. *v* 16But when the Syrians on the left wing saw that their right wing had been crushed, they turned to attack Judas and his men from the rear. 17The fighting became very fierce, and many on both sides were killed. 18Finally Judas himself was killed. Then all his men fled. 19Jonathan and Simon took their brother's body and buried it in the family tomb at Modein, 20and there at the tomb they wept for him. All Israel mourned for him in great sorrow for many days. They said, 21"It can't be! The mighty hero and savior of Israel has been killed!"

22The other deeds of Judas, his battles, his courageous deeds, and his great accomplishments, were too many to write down.

Jonathan Succeeds Judas

23After the death of Judas, the lawless traitors began to reappear everywhere in Judea, and all the wicked people returned. 24Also at that time there was a severe famine, and the whole country went over to the side of the renegades. 25Bacchides deliberately appointed some renegade Jews as rulers over the country. 26These men hunted down the friends of Judas and brought them all before Bacchides, and he subjected them to torture and humiliation. 27It was a time of great trouble for Israel, worse than anything that had happened to them since the time prophets ceased to appear among them.

28Then all the friends of Judas came together and said to Jonathan, 29"Since your brother Judas died, there has been no one like him to lead us against our enemies, against Bacchides and those of our own nation who oppose us. 30So today we choose you to succeed him as our ruler and commander to carry on our war." 31Jonathan accepted the leadership that day and took the place of his brother Judas.

The Campaigns of Jonathan

32When Bacchides learned of this, he made up his mind to kill Jonathan. 33But when this news reached Jonathan, he fled, with his brother Simon and their men, to the wilderness of Tekoa and set up camp at the pool of Asphar. (34Bacchides learned about this on the Sabbath and crossed the Jordan with his whole army. *w*) 35Jonathan sent his brother John, who was responsible for the soldiers' families, to ask the Nabateans, with whom he was on friendly terms, for permission to store with them the large amount of baggage they had. 36But the Jambrites of Medeba attacked John, took him captive, and carried off all the baggage. 37Some time later Jonathan and his brother Simon learned that the Jambrites were about to celebrate an important wedding and that there would be a bridal procession from the town of Nadabath. The bride was the daughter of one of the great princes of Canaan. 38Jonathan and Simon had wanted revenge for the death of their brother John, so they and their men went up on one of the mountains and hid. 39They kept watch and saw a noisy crowd loaded down with baggage. The bridegroom, his friends, and his relatives were on their way to meet the bride's party. They were heavily armed and were playing musical instruments and drums. 40The Jews attacked from their ambush and killed many of them; the rest escaped into the mountains, while the Jews carried off all their possessions. 41So the wedding was turned into a time of mourning and their joyful music into funeral songs. 42Jonathan and Simon had taken full revenge for the death of their brother, and they returned to the marshes along the Jordan.

v 9:15 Probable text the foothills; Greek Mount Azotus. verse 43.   *w 9:34 Verse 34 is probably misplaced and belongs with*

They kept watch and saw a noisy crowd loaded down with baggage. (9:39)

43Bacchides heard about this and arrived on the Sabbath at the banks of the Jordan with a large army. **44**Jonathan said to his men, "Now we must fight for our lives. We are in a worse situation than we have ever been in before. **45**The enemy is in front of us, the river is behind us, and marshes and thickets are on both sides of us; there is no way out. **46**So pray now for the Lord to save us from our enemies."

47The battle began and Jonathan and his men were just about to kill Bacchides, when he escaped to the rear of the army. **48**So Jonathan and his men jumped into the Jordan and swam to the other side to escape, and the Syrian army did not cross the river to follow them. **49**That day Bacchides lost about 1,000 men.

50After Bacchides returned to Jerusalem, the Syrians built fortifications with high walls and barred gates for a number of towns in Judea: Emmaus, Beth Horon, Bethel, Timnath, Pirathon, Tephon, and the fortress in Jericho. **51**In all of these he placed troops to harass the Jews. **52**He also strengthened the fortifications of the towns of Bethzur and Gezer and of the fort in Jerusalem. He placed army units in them and stored up supplies there. **53**Then he took the sons of the leading men of the country as hostages and imprisoned them in the fort.

54In the second month of the year 153,ˣ the High Priest Alcimus ordered that the wall of the inner court of the Temple be torn down. This would have destroyed what the prophets had accomplished; but just as the work began, **55**he had a stroke, and work was stopped. Paralyzed and unable to open his mouth, he could not speak or even make

a will for his family. **56**He died in great torment. **57**When Bacchides learned that Alcimus was dead, he returned to King Demetrius, and the land of Judea had peace for two years.

58Then all the renegades got together and said, "Look, Jonathan and his men are living in peace and security. If we bring Bacchides here now, he can capture them all in a single night." **59**They went to discuss the matter with Bacchides, **60**and he set out with a large army. He sent secret letters to all his allies in Judea, asking them to seize Jonathan and his men. But they were not able to do so because the plot was discovered. **61**Jonathan and his men captured 50 of the traitorous leaders who had been involved in the plot and put them to death. **62**Then Jonathan, Simon, and their forces withdrew to Bethbasi in the wilderness. They rebuilt the fallen fortifications and strengthened the town's defenses. **63**When Bacchides learned about all this, he got his whole army together and alerted his supporters in Judea. **64**He attacked Bethbasi from all sides and built siege platforms. After the battle had gone on for a long time, **65**Jonathan slipped out into the country with a small body of men and left his brother Simon in charge of the town. **66**Jonathan defeated Odomera and his people, and then attacked and destroyed the Phasirite camp. Once defeated, they joined Jonathan and advanced with him in his attack against Bacchides. **67**At the same time, Simon and his men rushed from the town and burned the siege platforms. **68**In the battle Bacchides was pressed so hard that all his plans came to nothing, and he was defeated. **69**He was so furious with the traitorous Jews who had urged him to come to Judea that he put many of them to death.

Then Bacchides decided to return to his own country, **70**but when Jonathan learned of this, he sent ambassadors to Bacchides to arrange for peace terms and the return of Jewish prisoners. **71**Bacchides agreed to do as Jonathan asked and gave him his solemn promise that he would let him live in peace the rest of his life. **72**Bacchides handed over the prisoners and returned to his own

I Maccabees

country. Never again did he come into Jewish territory. [73]War came to an end in Israel. Jonathan settled in Michmash and began to govern the people and to eliminate the renegade Jews from Israel.

Alexander Epiphanes Makes Jonathan High Priest

10 [1]In the year 160,[y] Alexander Epiphanes,[z] son of Antiochus the Fourth, landed at Ptolemais and captured it. The people welcomed him as their king. [2]When King Demetrius heard of it, he gathered a large army and went out to meet him in battle. [3]At that time Demetrius sent Jonathan a friendly letter full of flattery, [4]in the hope of winning Jonathan over to his side and making peace with the Jews before Alexander made a treaty with them against him. [5]Demetrius thought that Jonathan would certainly remember all the wrongs he had done to him, his brothers, and the entire Jewish nation. [6]And so Demetrius made Jonathan his ally and gave him authority to raise an army and equip it. He also ordered that the hostages held in the fort at Jerusalem should be handed over to Jonathan. [7]So Jonathan went to Jerusalem and read the letter to all the people and to the men in the fort. [8]These men were terrified when they learned that the king had given Jonathan authority to raise an army. [9]They handed the hostages over to him, and he returned them to their parents.

[10]Jonathan set up headquarters in Jerusalem and began to rebuild and restore the city. [11]He ordered the builders to use squared stones for the city walls and for the protecting wall around Mount Zion. This was done. [12]The foreigners deserted the fortresses that Bacchides had built; [13]each man left his post and returned to his own country. [14]But some of the Jews who had abandoned the Law of Moses and its commands were still left in Bethzur, which served as their last place of refuge.

[15]King Alexander learned of the promises Demetrius had made to Jonathan and he also learned about Jonathan himself, about the battles he had fought, his courageous deeds, and the troubles he and his brothers had endured. [16]He was certain that he would never find another man like Jonathan and so decided to make him his friend and ally. [17]He wrote Jonathan a letter:

[18]"King Alexander to his friend Jonathan, greetings.

[19]"I have heard that you are a brave man who has earned the right to be a friend of the king. [20]I have this day appointed you as High Priest of your nation and conferred upon you the title of 'Friend of the King.' You are to be our ally and give us your support."

He also sent him a royal robe and a gold crown. [21]Jonathan put on the robes of the High Priest in the seventh month of the year 160[a] at the Festival of Shelters. He raised an army and stored up a large supply of weapons.

Jonathan Supports Alexander Epiphanes

[22]When Demetrius heard this, he was distressed and said, [23]"How did we manage to let Alexander get ahead of us? He has strengthened his position by making an alliance with the Jews. [24]I also will write them a friendly letter offering high positions and gifts, so that they will support me."

[25]He wrote:

"King Demetrius to the nation of the Jews, greetings. [26]We are delighted to learn that you have kept your obligations under our treaty, remained loyal to us, and have not gone over to the side of our enemies. [27]Now if you continue to remain loyal to us, we will reward you well. [28]We will grant you exemptions from many taxes and allow you other privileges. [29]I hereby grant all the Jewish people release and exemption from payment of regular taxes, salt taxes, and other special taxes. [30]Furthermore, from this day I release you from your obligation to pay me one third of the grain harvest and one half of the fruit harvest. From now on I will not

---

[y] **10:1** THE YEAR 160: *This corresponds to 152 B.C.*   [z] **10:1** ALEXANDER EPIPHANES: *Alexander Epiphanes is more widely known as Alexander Balas.*   [a] **10:21** THE YEAR 160: *This corresponds to 152 B.C.*
10:30 1 Macc 11:34

demand these payments from Judea or from the three districts that have been added to Judea from Samaria and Galilee. ³¹Jerusalem and its surrounding territory is to be recognized as a holy city and to be exempt from the payment of all taxes. ³²I also give up my authority over the fort in Jerusalem and place it under the High Priest, who may station there anyone he wishes to guard it. ³³I freely grant release to all Jews who are prisoners of war anywhere in my kingdom. All of them will be exempt from taxes, even on their cattle.ᵇ ³⁴No taxes shall be collected from any Jew anywhere in my kingdom on Sabbaths, New Moon Festivals, and other holy days. Furthermore, no taxes shall be collected three days before or after the major holy days. ³⁵No one has the right on any of these days to demand payment or to trouble you in any way.

³⁶"Jews may be enlisted in the royal army up to a total of 30,000 men, and they will receive the same pay as other royal troops. ³⁷Some of them may be stationed in the great royal fortresses, and others assigned to responsible positions in the government. They shall have Jews as their leaders and officers, and they shall be allowed to follow their own laws and customs, just as the king has permitted for the people of Judea.

³⁸"The three districts added to Judea from the territory of Samaria will be completely incorporated into Judea and placed under the authority of the High Priest alone. ³⁹I give to the Temple in Jerusalem for its operating expenses the revenues from the city of Ptolemais and the lands belonging to it. ⁴⁰I also promise to make an annual gift of 15,000 silver coins from appropriate accounts within the royal treasury. ⁴¹The total accumulated state subsidy, which we have failed to pay in recent years, shall be paid, and the payments continued from now on for the work of the Temple. ⁴²In addition to this, we will no longer require the 5,000 silver coins annually from the Temple income.

This money belongs to the priests serving in the Temple. ⁴³Whoever owes a debt to the king or any other debt and takes refuge in the Temple in Jerusalem or in any area that belongs to it may not be arrested nor may his property anywhere in my kingdom be confiscated. ⁴⁴The expenses for rebuilding and renovating the Temple shall be provided from the royal treasury. ⁴⁵Likewise, the expenses for rebuilding the walls of Jerusalem and its surrounding fortifications, as well as the walls of designated towns in Judea, shall be provided from the royal treasury."

⁴⁶When Jonathan and the people heard the proposals made by King Demetrius, they refused to believe them or accept them, because they remembered how harshly he had treated them and what terrible troubles he had caused them. ⁴⁷They preferred to give their allegiance to Alexander because he had been the first to open peace negotiations, and they remained his allies as long as he lived.

⁴⁸King Alexander raised a large army and took up battle positions facing Demetrius. ⁴⁹But when the armies of the two kings met in battle, the army of Alexanderᶜ turned and ran. Demetriusᵈ pursued them and won the battle. ⁵⁰Alexanderᵉ fought bitterly until sundown, but Demetrius was killed that day.

⁵¹Then Alexander sent ambassadors to King Ptolemy the Sixth of Egypt with this message:

⁵²"I have returned to my kingdom and taken my seat on the throne of my ancestors. I have taken over the government, and I am now in control of the country. ⁵³I made war on Demetrius, defeated him and his army, and I have taken over his kingdom. ⁵⁴Now I am ready to make an alliance. Give me your daughter in marriage, and I will give both of you such gifts as you deserve."

⁵⁵King Ptolemy replied, "It was a great day when you returned to your country and took the throne of your ancestors. ⁵⁶I agree to your proposals, but first meet me at Ptolemais. We can get acquainted there, and I will give you my daughter in marriage."

ᵇ **10:33** *This sentence in Greek is unclear.*   ᶜ **10:49** Alexander; *some manuscripts have* Demetrius.
ᵈ **10:49** Demetrius; *some manuscripts have* Alexander.   ᵉ **10:50** Alexander; *some manuscripts have* Demetrius.

Ptolemy and his daughter Cleopatra left Egypt. (10:57)

57 So in the year 162[f] Ptolemy and his daughter Cleopatra[g] left Egypt and arrived at Ptolemais. **58** King Alexander met them, and Ptolemy gave him his daughter in marriage. The wedding was celebrated there in Ptolemais with royal splendor.

59 King Alexander wrote asking Jonathan to come to meet him. **60** So Jonathan, in a show of splendor, went to Ptolemais and met the two kings. He presented them with gifts of silver and gold, and he also gave many gifts to the high officials who had accompanied them. Everyone was favorably impressed with him. **61** At the same time some traitorous Jews who wanted to make trouble for Jonathan made accusations against him, but King Alexander paid no attention to them. **62** He gave orders that Jonathan should be given royal robes to wear, **63** and he honored him by letting him sit at his side. Alexander told his officers to take Jonathan into the center of the city and to announce that no one was to bring charges against him for any reason and no one was to cause him any kind of trouble. **64** When his accusers saw the honors given to him, heard the announcement, and saw him clothed in royal robes, they all fled. **65** The king further honored Jonathan by enrolling him in the First Order of the "Friends of the King" and by making him general and governor of his province. **66** Jonathan returned to Jerusalem pleased and successful.

Jonathan's Victory over Apollonius

67 In the year 165[h] Demetrius the Second, the son of Demetrius the First, left Crete and arrived in Syria, the land of his ancestors. **68** When King Alexander heard about this, he was worried and returned to Antioch, the capital of Syria. **69** Demetrius reappointed Apollonius governor of Greater Syria. Apollonius raised a large army, set up camp near Jamnia, and sent the following message to Jonathan the High Priest:

70 "Because of you I am being ridiculed, but why do you, there in your mountains, continue this rebellion when no one supports you? **71** If you really have any confidence in your army, come down here on the plain and fight, where we can test each other's strength. Study the situation, and you will find that I have the support of the forces from the cities. **72** You will learn who I am and who our allies are, and you will discover that you have no chance of standing against us. Your predecessors have already been beaten twice on their own ground; **73** so how do you expect to defeat my cavalry and the kind of army I have here on the plain? Down here there is not so much as a pebble to hide behind and no way to escape."

74 When Jonathan received this message from Apollonius, he became angry. He took 10,000 elite troops from Jerusalem; his brother Simon also brought troops, and their two forces **75** set up camp outside of Joppa. The men of the city refused to let them in because there was a detachment of Apollonius' troops there, but Jonathan attacked, **76** and the men in the city became so frightened that they opened the gates, allowing Jonathan to capture Joppa. **77** When Apollonius heard what had happened, he took 3,000 cavalry and a large army of infantry and pretended to retreat south toward Azotus. However, relying upon the strength of his cavalry, he marched into the plain with his main force, **78-79** positioning 1,000 cavalry where they could attack Jonathan's forces from the rear. Jonathan continued his pursuit

f **10:57** THE YEAR 162: *This corresponds to 150 B.C.*   g **10:57** CLEOPATRA: *This was Cleopatra Thea, also known as Cleopatra the Third, and not to be confused with Cleopatra the Seventh (69—30 B.C.), who was involved in the history of Caesar and Mark Antony.*   h **10:67** THE YEAR 165: *This corresponds to 147 B.C.*

as far as Azotus, where the two armies met in battle. 80Not until then did Jonathan realize that he was caught in an ambush. His army was surrounded, and enemy arrows rained down on them from morning until evening. 81But Jonathan's men stood firm, as he had ordered, and the attacking cavalry grew tired. 82Then, when the cavalry was exhausted, Simon appeared on the scene with his forces and attacked and overwhelmed the enemy infantry, who broke ranks and fled. 83The cavalry, which by now was scattered all over the battlefield, fled to Azotus, where they took refuge in the temple of Dagon, their god. 84But Jonathan set fire to the city and to the temple of Dagon, burning to death all those who had taken refuge there. Then he set fire to the surrounding towns and looted them. 85That day about 8,000 were either killed in the battle or burned to death. 86Jonathan left and set up camp at Ascalon, where the people of the city came out to welcome him with great honors. 87Jonathan and his men returned to Jerusalem with large quantities of loot.

88When King Alexander heard what Jonathan had done, he gave him even greater honors. 89He sent him a gold shoulder buckle, which is given only to those honored with the title "Relative of the King." He also gave him the city of Ekron and its surrounding territory.

The Fall of Alexander Epiphanes

11 1King Ptolemy the Sixth of Egypt assembled an army of soldiers more numerous than the grains of sand along the seashore, and he also gathered a great fleet of ships. He intended to trap Alexander, take his kingdom, and add it to his own, 2so he went to Syria with promises of peace, and the citizens opened their gates to him and welcomed him. King Alexander had ordered them to do this because Ptolemy was his father-in-law. 3But as Ptolemy moved north, he stationed a detachment of troops in each town. 4When he reached Azotus, the people there showed him the burned ruins of the temple of Dagon and all the destruction in the city and the surrounding towns. There were corpses everywhere. The bodies of the men Jonathan had burned to death during the battle were now stacked up along Ptolemy's route. 5The people told him what Jonathan had done, hoping that he would hold him responsible, but Ptolemy said nothing. 6Jonathan, with all the proper ceremony, went to Joppa to meet him. They exchanged greetings and spent the night there. 7Jonathan accompanied him as far as the Eleutherus River before returning to Jerusalem. 8In this way King Ptolemy, in his plot against Alexander, took control of the towns along the coast as far north as Seleucia-by-the-sea.

9From there King Ptolemy sent this message to King Demetrius: "Let's make a treaty. My daughter is now Alexander's wife, but I will take her back and give her to you and let you rule over your father's kingdom. 10I regret that I ever gave her to Alexander, because he has tried to kill me." 11Ptolemy made this accusation against Alexander because he wanted to take over his kingdom. 12So he took his daughter away from Alexander and gave her to Demetrius; he broke off all relations with Alexander, and they became open enemies. 13Then Ptolemy entered Antioch and assumed the crown of Syria; so he wore both the crown of Egypt and the crown of Syria.

14King Alexander was in Cilicia at the time because the people of that region were in a state of rebellion. 15But when he heard what Ptolemy had done, he moved to attack him. Ptolemy met him with a large force and won a decisive victory. 16While Ptolemy reached the peak of his power, Alexander fled to Arabia to find protection, 17but an Arab named Zabdiel cut off his head and sent it to Ptolemy. 18Two days later Ptolemy himself died, and the troops he had left in the fortresses were then killed by the local citizens. 19So in the year 167i Demetrius the Second became king.

Jonathan Wins the Favor of Demetrius the Second

20About that time Jonathan gathered the men of Judea to attack the fort in Jerusalem.

i 11:19 THE YEAR 167: This corresponds to 145 B.C.

They built many siege platforms to use in the attack. 21But some traitorous Jews who hated their own nation went to King Demetrius the Second and told him that Jonathan was laying siege to the fort in Jerusalem. 22When Demetrius heard this, he was furious and immediately moved his headquarters to Ptolemais. He wrote to Jonathan and ordered him to lift the siege and to meet him for a conference in Ptolemais without a moment's delay.

23When Jonathan got the message, he gave orders for the siege to continue, and then chose some Jewish leaders and some priests to go with him. At the risk of his life, 24he went to the king in Ptolemais, taking along robes, silver and gold, and many other gifts. He made a good impression on the king. 25Although some lawless traitors of his own nation had made accusations against Jonathan, 26the king still treated him just as his predecessors had done. He honored him in the presence of all his advisers, 27and confirmed him as High Priest, restoring all his former honors and appointing him to the highest rank among the "Friends of the King."

28Jonathan asked the king to release the territory of Judea and the three regions of Samaria*j* from the payment of taxes, promising that if Demetrius would do that, he would pay him a lump sum of 22,000 pounds of silver. 29The king agreed and wrote a letter to Jonathan to confirm all this:

30"King Demetrius to King Jonathan and to the Jewish nation, greetings.

31"For your information I am sending a copy of the letter I have written to the Honorable Lasthenes about you:

32" 'King Demetrius to the Honorable Lasthenes, greetings. 33I have decided to grant the Jewish nation certain benefits because they are our loyal allies and keep their treaty obligations. 34I confirm their rights to the land of Judea and the three regions of Ephraim, Lydda, and Arimathea, which are hereby annexed to Judea from Samaria with all the lands belonging to them. This will be of benefit to everyone who goes to Jerusalem to offer sacrifice, since payments of the annual tax on pro-

duce and fruit from these lands will no longer be made to the king, but to the Temple. 35And I also grant them relief from the payment of revenues now due me from tithes, tolls, salt taxes, and special taxes. 36None of the provisions mentioned in this letter shall ever be canceled in the future.

37" 'You are required to see that a complete copy of this decree is made and given to Jonathan, to be posted in a prominent place on the Temple hill.' "

Jonathan Helps Demetrius the Second

38When King Demetrius saw that the land was peaceful under his rule and there was no further resistance, he disbanded his whole army and sent everyone home, except the soldiers he had hired from the Greek islands. This made all the soldiers who had served under his predecessors hate him because they had lost their source of income. 39One of Alexander's former supporters, Trypho, saw that all the soldiers were complaining about Demetrius, so he went to Imalkue, the Arab who was responsible for bringing up Alexander's young son Antiochus. 40Trypho stayed there for a long time and kept urging Imalkue to hand the boy over to him, so that he could make him king in place of his father. He also told Imalkue about the decrees of Demetrius and how the soldiers hated him.

41Jonathan sent a message to King Demetrius asking him to remove his troops from the fort in Jerusalem and from the fortresses in Judea, since they kept harassing the Jews. 42Demetrius replied: "I will do what you request, and when the opportunity presents itself, I will bestow upon you and your nation the highest honors. 43But now you can help me by sending soldiers to fight for me, because all of my troops have revolted."

44So Jonathan sent 3,000 trained soldiers to Antioch. The king was delighted when they arrived, 45because a mob of 120,000 had gathered in the city determined to kill him. 46But he escaped to the palace while the mob took control of the streets and began to riot. 47Then the king called on the

---

j 11:28 *Probable text* three regions of Samaria; *Greek* three regions and Samaria.
11:34 1 Macc 10:30

Jewish soldiers for help, and they all rushed to his aid. They went through the whole city and killed at least 100,000 people. [48]They saved the king's life, but they plundered and burned the city. [49]When the people saw that the Jews had complete control of the city, they lost courage and appealed to the king, requesting [50]him to arrange a truce and stop the Jewish attack. [51]The rebels threw down their arms and surrendered. The king and everyone in his kingdom now had great respect for the Jews, who returned to Jerusalem with a great deal of loot. [52]Demetrius was firmly established as king, and the country was at peace under his rule, [53]but he broke all his promises and turned against Jonathan. He did not reward him for his loyal service, but instead continued to harass him.

Jonathan Supports Antiochus the Sixth

[54]Some time later, Trypho returned with the young boy Antiochus and crowned him king. [55]All the soldiers that Demetrius had dismissed then came to the support of the young king. They defeated Demetrius, and he fled. [56]Trypho captured the elephants and took control of Antioch. [57]The young King Antiochus wrote to Jonathan and confirmed him as High Priest and as ruler over the four regions and gave him the title "Friend of the King." [58]He sent him a set of gold tableware and authorized him to drink from gold cups, to wear a royal robe, and to wear the gold shoulder buckle awarded to "Relatives of the King." [59]He also appointed Jonathan's brother Simon as governor of the territory from the Phoenician coast to the Egyptian border. [60]Jonathan then marched with his army through the towns of Greater Syria, and all the Syrian forces joined him as allies. He went to Ascalon, where the people welcomed him with great honors. [61]Then he went to Gaza, but the people there barred their gates against him. So he laid siege to the city and burned and looted the surrounding area. [62]The people of Gaza then asked for peace, and Jonathan arranged a truce. He took the sons of the leaders and

sent them to Jerusalem as hostages. After that he marched on as far as Damascus.

[63]Jonathan learned that the officers of Demetrius had come to Kedesh in Galilee with a large army, intending to keep him from carrying out his plan. [64]So he left his brother Simon in Judea and set out to meet them in battle. [65]Then Simon laid siege to Bethzur and fought against it for a long time. [66]The people asked for peace terms, and Simon agreed. He then took over the town, drove the people out, and stationed a detachment of troops there.

[67]Jonathan and his army set up camp by Lake Galilee. Early the next morning he marched his troops to the plain of Hazor, [68]where the main force of the foreign army was advancing to meet him. Unknown to Jonathan, they had left a detachment of troops in ambush in the mountains, [69]and when the men in ambush came out and attacked, [70]Jonathan's entire army turned and ran. No one was left, except two officers, Mattathias son of Absalom and Judas son of Chalphi. [71]Jonathan was humiliated, so he tore his clothes, threw dust on his head, and prayed. [72]Then he turned back to the battle, crushed the enemy, and put them to flight. [73]When his own fleeing soldiers saw this, they turned back and joined him in pursuit. They chased the enemy all the way back to their camp at Kedesh and then took over the camp. [74]At least 3,000 enemy soldiers were killed that day. Jonathan then returned to Jerusalem.

Alliances with Rome and Sparta

12 [1]When Jonathan saw that things were working out to his advantage, he chose ambassadors and sent them to Rome to confirm and renew friendship with the Romans. [2]He also sent letters with a similar message to Sparta and other places. [3]The ambassadors went to Rome, where they were admitted to the Senate chamber, and reported that the High Priest Jonathan and the Jewish nation had sent them to renew the earlier ties of friendship and alliance with Rome. [4]The Romans provided them with letters to the authorities in each country through which they would pass,

guaranteeing them safe conduct in their return to the land of Judea.

5 Here is a copy of the letter Jonathan wrote to the Spartans:

6 "Jonathan the High Priest, the national council of leaders, the priests, and the rest of the people of Judea, to our brothers in Sparta, greetings. 7 At an earlier time, your King Arius sent a letter to our High Priest Onias, stating that our two nations are related, as the attached copy shows. 8 Onias received your ambassador with full honors and acknowledged receipt of your letter, which declared our alliance and friendship. 9 And now, although we are not in need of such alliances, since we find our source of strength in the holy books we possess, 10 we have written to renew our ties of brotherhood and friendship with you. We do not wish to become total strangers, and it has now been many years since your last communication. 11 Throughout the years we have taken every opportunity, on our festival days and other suitable days, to remember you when we have offered our sacrifices and made our prayers, as it is fitting and proper for brothers to do. 12 We also are pleased that fame has come to you. 13 But we have had one series of troubles after another and have had to fight many wars, because we have been under constant attack by surrounding nations. 14 During this time of war, we did not wish to trouble you or our other allies and friends, 15 since we do have the help of the Lord, who has defeated our enemies and rescued us from them. 16 So we have chosen Numenius son of Antiochus together with Antipater son of Jason and sent them as ambassadors to Rome to renew our ties of friendship and alliance with the Romans. 17 We have also ordered them to go to you with our greetings and deliver this letter about the renewal of our ties of brotherhood. 18 And now we request an answer to this letter.

19 "The following is a copy of the earlier letter:

20 " 'King Arius of Sparta to Onias the High Priest, greetings. 21 We have found a document about the Spartans and the Jews indicating that we are related and that both of our nations are descended from Abraham. 22 Now that we have discovered this, please send us a report about your situation. 23 In reply, we will send you a letter indicating that we are willing to share our possessions, including cattle and property, if you will do the same. We have given orders to our ambassadors to give you a full report about these matters.' "

Campaigns of Jonathan and Simon

24 Jonathan learned that the officers of Demetrius had returned to attack him with an even larger army than before. 25 Jonathan did not want to give them an opportunity to penetrate his own territory, so he left Jerusalem and went to meet them in the region of Hamath. 26 Jonathan sent spies into the enemy camp, who reported to him that the enemy forces were making plans to attack the Jews by night. 27 At sunset Jonathan ordered all his soldiers to be on the alert and to have their weapons ready for a surprise attack any time during the night. He also stationed guards all around the camp. 28 When the enemy soldiers learned that Jonathan and his men were ready for battle, they were panic-stricken and fled, leaving their campfires burning. 29 Jonathan and his men saw the campfires but did not realize what had happened until the next morning. 30 Jonathan then set out after them, but he could not overtake them because they had already crossed the Eleutherus River. 31 Then Jonathan turned aside and

They were panic-stricken and fled, leaving their campfires burning. (12:28)

attacked a tribe of Arabs called Zabadeans. He defeated them and plundered their possessions. 32Then he broke camp and went to Damascus, inspecting the entire area along the way.

33Meanwhile, Simon had also set out on a campaign and had advanced as far as Ascalon and the neighboring fortresses. Then he turned aside to Joppa 34and stationed a detachment of soldiers there because he had heard that the people were planning to hand over the fortress of Joppa to the soldiers of Demetrius.

35When Jonathan returned, he called the council of the leaders together and made plans with them to build fortresses in Judea, 36to increase the height of the walls of Jerusalem, and to build a high wall to separate the fort from the city. This would isolate the fort, making it impossible for the enemy to buy or sell anything. 37The people worked together to strengthen the city's defenses because a part of the east wall along the Kidron Valley had collapsed and the Chaphenatha section was in need of repair. 38Simon also rebuilt the town of Adida in the foothills. He fortified it and constructed barred gates for it.

Trypho Captures Jonathan

39Then Trypho plotted a rebellion against King Antiochus so that he could make himself king of Syria. 40He was afraid, however, that Jonathan would not agree to this and would go to war against him to prevent it. So Trypho got his army ready and went to Beth Shan in the hope of capturing Jonathan and putting him to death. 41But Jonathan also came to Beth Shan with 40,000 well-trained soldiers. 42When Trypho saw how large an army Jonathan had brought with him, he was afraid to take action. 43So he received Jonathan with all honors, presented him to all his advisers, gave him gifts, and ordered his advisers and soldiers to obey Jonathan as they would him. 44He asked Jonathan, "Why have you put these soldiers to so much trouble when we are not at war? 45Why don't you send them home? Choose a few men to stay with you, and then accompany me to Ptolemais. I will hand the

city over to you, as well as the rest of the fortresses, the troops, and all the officials. Then I will turn around and leave. In fact, that's why I am here." 46Jonathan believed him, and following his advice, sent his soldiers back to Judea. 47He took 3,000 men with him, but left 2,000 of them in Galilee, while only 1,000 accompanied him the rest of the way. 48But when Jonathan entered Ptolemais, the people of the city locked the gates, arrested him, and killed everyone who had come with him.

49Trypho sent infantry and cavalry units to Galilee and Jezreel Valley to kill the rest of Jonathan's soldiers. 50The Jewish troops thought that Jonathan had been captured and killed, along with all those who had accompanied him, so they encouraged one another and marched out in battle formation. 51When the approaching enemy forces saw that the Jews were ready to fight for their lives, they turned back. 52Then the Jewish soldiers returned to Judea safely, but terribly afraid. The whole nation was in deep mourning, assuming that Jonathan and all his men had been killed. 53All the surrounding nations now tried to destroy them. They thought that the Jews had no leaders or allies and that the time was ripe to annihilate them and put an end to their history.

Simon Leads the Jews

13 1Simon learned that Trypho had assembled a large army and that he had plans to invade Judea and devastate it. 2He realized that this news had brought panic and fear to the people, so he went to Jerusalem, called the people together, 3and tried to encourage them by saying, "You know how much my father's family, my brothers, and I have done for the sake of the Law of Moses and the Temple. You also know about the wars we have fought and the troubles we have had. 4All my brothers have been killed fighting for our Law, our Temple, and our nation, and I am the only one left. 5But never let it be said that I tried to save my own life in a time of danger; I do not consider myself better than my brothers. 6Not in the least! It is true that in their hatred all the Gentile nations have gathered together to

destroy us, but I will fight to defend my nation, the Temple, and your loved ones."

7 These words immediately revived the morale of the people, 8 and they answered with a loud shout, "You are now our leader in place of your brothers Judas and Jonathan. 9 Fight our wars, and we will do whatever you ask." 10 So Simon gathered together all the soldiers and hurried to complete the walls of Jerusalem and to strengthen all its defenses. 11 He sent Jonathan son of Absalom to Joppa with a large army. This Jonathan drove out the people who were there and occupied the town.

12 Trypho left Ptolemais with a large army to invade Judea, taking Simon's brother Jonathan along with him as a prisoner. 13 Simon set up camp at Adida at the edge of the plain. 14 When Trypho learned that Simon had succeeded his brother Jonathan and that he was ready to meet him in battle, he sent this message to him: 15 "I am holding your brother Jonathan under arrest because while he was in office he did not pay his debts to the royal treasury. 16 However, I will release him if you will pay me 6,000 pounds of silver and send two of his sons as hostages to guarantee that he will not revolt against us when he is released."

17 Although Simon knew that they were deceiving him, he sent for the money and the two sons because he did not want to arouse the hostility of the Jews. 18 He was afraid that they might later say that Jonathan was put to death because Simon would not send the money and the boys. 19 So he did as Trypho had demanded, but Trypho broke his promise and did not release Jonathan.

20 Then Trypho made his move to invade the land and destroy it, circling around by the road to Adora. But Simon and his army moved along facing him wherever he went. 21 The enemy soldiers in the fort in Jerusalem kept sending messengers to Trypho urging him to come to them quickly by way of the desert and to send them supplies. 22 Trypho got all his cavalry ready for the invasion, but that night there was a heavy snowstorm, and he was not able to move up into the hills. So he withdrew and went into Gilead. 23 When he was near

Baskama, he had Jonathan put to death and his body buried there. 24 Then Trypho turned and went back to his own country.

25 Simon had the body of his brother Jonathan brought to Modein, to be buried in the town of their ancestors. 26 Everyone in Israel was in deep sorrow at the loss of Jonathan, and they mourned for him a long time. 27 Over the tomb of his father and his brothers Simon built a high monument that could be seen from a great distance. It was covered front and back with polished stone. 28 He constructed seven pyramids side by side for his father, his mother, and his four brothers. 29 For the pyramids he created a setting of tall columns on which there were carvings. Some of these carvings were of suits of armor and some were of ships. It was a monument to their victories, which travelers from overseas could visit. k 30 The tomb which he built in Modein is still there today.

31 Meanwhile, Trypho assassinated the young king, Antiochus the Sixth, 32 and took over his kingdom in Syria. He brought that country great troubles.

33 Simon rebuilt the fortresses of Judea with high towers, strong walls, and barred gates; then he placed stores of supplies there. 34 He sent ambassadors to King Demetrius the Second to ask for tax relief for the land, since Trypho was doing nothing but robbing them. 35 King Demetrius sent the following letter in reply:

36 "King Demetrius to the High Priest Simon, the friend of kings, to the Jewish nation, and to their leaders, greetings. 37 I have received the gold crown and the gold palm branch which you sent, and I am prepared to make a peace treaty with you and to instruct our tax officials to grant you exemptions. 38 Our previous agreements with you are confirmed, and the fortresses which you have built are to remain yours. 39 I grant you pardon for treaty violations committed up to the present date, and I release you from payment of the special tax still due and any other taxes that have been collected up to this time in Jerusalem. 40 All Jews who are qualified may enroll in the royal service. Let us have peace."

k **13:29** Verses 28–29 in Greek are unclear.

41 So in the year 170[l] the yoke of the Gentile oppressors was removed from the Jews. 42 People began to date their documents and contracts with these words: "In the first year of Simon, the great High Priest, commander and leader of the Jews."

43 At that time Simon laid siege to Gezer and surrounded it with his army. He built a movable siege platform, brought it up to the town wall, attacked one of the towers, and captured it. 44 The men who had been on the siege platform then moved rapidly into the town, and this created great confusion. 45 The men of the town, their wives, and their children tore their clothes in distress and climbed up on the top of the town wall. They pleaded loudly with Simon for a truce. 46 "Have mercy on us," they begged. "Don't punish us as we deserve!"

47 So Simon came to terms with them and ended the fighting. He made the people leave the town; then he purified the houses in which there had been idols. When that was done, he and his men entered the town singing hymns and songs of praise. 48 He eliminated everything that would make the town ritually unclean and settled it with people who would obey every command contained in the Law of Moses. He strengthened the defenses of the town and built himself a palace there.

49 Those in the fort in Jerusalem were now prevented from leaving to buy or sell anything. They were suffering from severe hunger and many of them had died of starvation. 50 Finally they appealed to Simon for a truce. He agreed, removed them from the fort, and purified it. 51 On the twenty-third day of the second month, in the year 171,[m] there was a great celebration in the city because this terrible threat to the security of Israel had come to an end. Simon and his men entered the fort singing hymns of praise and thanksgiving, while carrying palm branches and playing harps, cymbals, and lyres. 52 Simon issued a decree that the day should be joyfully celebrated every year. He strengthened the defenses of the Temple hill on the side facing the fort, and he and his

men made their headquarters there. 53 Simon's son John was now a grown man, so Simon made him commander of the whole army, and John set up headquarters at Gezer.

Simon and his men entered the fort. (13:51)

In Praise of Simon

14 ¹ In the year 172[n] King Demetrius the Second gathered his army and went to Media to seek additional help for his war against Trypho. 2 When King Arsaces the Sixth of Persia and Media heard that Demetrius had entered his territory, he sent one of his commanders with some troops to capture Demetrius alive. 3 They attacked and defeated the army of Demetrius, took him captive, and brought him back to King Arsaces, who threw him in prison.

4 The land of Judea was at peace as long as Simon lived. During his entire reign, he used his position of power and influence to do what was good for his people, and they were always pleased with him as their ruler. 5 He added to his reputation when he captured the port of Joppa and opened up the route to the Greek islands. 6 He not only enlarged the territory of his nation and gained control of the whole country, 7 but he brought back many

---

l **13:41** THE YEAR 170: *This corresponds to 142 B.C.*   m **13:51** THE YEAR 171: *This corresponds to 141 B.C.*
n **14:1** THE YEAR 172: *This corresponds to 140 B.C.*
13:43 2 Macc 10:32–38

prisoners of war and captured Gezer, Bethzur, and the fort in Jerusalem. He purified the fort, and there was no one to oppose him.

8 The Jews farmed their land in peace; the land produced its crops and the trees bore fruit. 9 The young men showed off their splendid military uniforms, while the old men sat around the city squares and talked about the great things that had happened. 10 Simon supplied the cities with food and provided them with weapons of defense. His fame spread everywhere. 11 He brought peace to the country, and Israel's joy knew no bounds. 12 Everyone lived in peace among his own grapevines and fig trees, and no one made them afraid. 13 In those days all the enemy kings had been defeated, and there was no one left in the land to fight the Jews. 14 Simon provided help for all the poor among his people, and guided by the Law of Moses, he eliminated all wicked and lawless men. 15 He provided the Temple with splendid furnishings and added a large number of utensils for use in worship.

16 When the news that Jonathan had died reached Rome and Sparta, it brought great sorrow. 17 But when the Spartans heard that Simon had succeeded his brother as High Priest and that he was in control of the country and its towns, 18 they engraved on bronze tablets a renewal of the treaty of friendship which they had made with his brothers Judas and Jonathan and sent the tablets to him. 19 These were read to the assembly in Jerusalem. 20 What follows is a copy of the letter sent by the Spartans:

"The people of Sparta and their rulers to Simon the High Priest, to the leaders and the priests of the Jews, and to all our Jewish brothers, greetings. 21 The delegation that you sent to our people has told us how respected and renowned you are. Their visit has been a source of joy for us, 22 and a report of their visit has been written down in our public records, as follows: 'Numenius son of Antiochus and Antipater son of Jason, honored representatives of the Jews, appeared before us to renew their treaty of friendship. 23 The assembly of the people was pleased to receive these men with all honors and to place a copy of their report in the public archives, so that the people of Sparta may have it on record. A copy of this document has been made for the High Priest Simon.' "

24 Later, Simon sent Numenius to Rome with the gift of a large gold shield weighing half a ton, to confirm the Jews' alliance with the Romans.

25 When the people of Israel heard about all this, they asked themselves, "How can we express our thanks to Simon and his sons? 26 He, his brothers, and his father's whole family have been towers of strength for our nation. They have fought off our enemies and set the nation free."

So they recorded this on bronze tablets and set them up on columns on Mount Zion. 27 The inscription read as follows:

"On the eighteenth day of the month of Elul in the year 172,[n] that is, in the third year of Simon, the High Priest,[o] 28 at a great assembly of priests, people, officials, and national leaders the following facts were made known to us: 29 Often when wars broke out in the country, Simon son of Mattathias, a priest of the Jehoiarib family, and his brothers risked their lives in protecting our nation, our Temple, and our Law against our enemies. They have brought great glory to our nation. 30 Jonathan united our people and became the High Priest before he died. 31 The enemies of the Jews plotted to invade the land and defile the Temple. 32 Then Simon assumed command and fought for his country. He spent a large amount of his own money to provide weapons and wages for his nation's armed forces. 33 He fortified the towns of Judea, and especially Bethzur on the border, where enemy weapons had previously been stored. He stationed a detachment of soldiers there. 34 He fortified the seaport of Joppa and the city of Gezer on the border of Azotus, which was previously occupied by enemy soldiers. He settled Jews there and provided the towns with everything that the people needed.[p]

---

n **14:27** THE YEAR 172: *This corresponds to 140 B.C.*   o **14:27** *Greek has an additional word, the meaning of which is unclear.*   p **14:34** *that the people needed; or that was needed to keep them in repair.*
14:18 1 Macc 8:22

35 When the people saw Simon's patriotism and how he wanted to bring glory to his nation, they made him their leader and High Priest. They did this because of all that he had accomplished through his loyalty and because he had brought about justice and had tried in every way to bring glory to his nation.

36 "Under his leadership the Gentiles were driven out of the land. Enemy soldiers were forced out of the area north of the Temple, where they had built the fort, from which the soldiers used to go out and defile the holy Temple. 37 Simon settled Jews in the fort, strengthened it for the security of the country and the city of Jerusalem, and increased the height of the city walls. 38 As a result, King Demetrius confirmed him as High Priest, 39 gave him the title of "Friend of the King," and treated him with great honor. 40 Demetrius did this because he had heard that the Romans were calling the Jews their friends, allies, and brothers and that they had received Simon's delegation with full honors.

41 "Therefore, q the Jews and their priests are happy to have Simon and his descendants as their leaders and High Priests, until a true prophet appears. 42 Simon shall govern their country, have charge of the Temple, and shall be their military commander. He shall be in charge of military supplies, fortifications, and public works. 43 The people must obey him in everything. All government contracts shall be drawn up in his name. He shall have the right to wear royal robes with the gold shoulder buckle.

44 "No one, priest or people, shall have the legal right to annul any of these decisions, to alter or change any of Simon's orders, to convene any assembly in the country without his permission, or to wear royal robes with the gold shoulder buckle. 45 Anyone who disobeys or disregards these regulations shall be subject to punishment.

46 "The people gave their unanimous approval to grant Simon the right to act in accordance with these regulations. 47 Simon consented and agreed to be supreme leader: High Priest, commander of the armies, and governor of the Jews and the priests."

48 It was decided that this declaration should be engraved on bronze tablets and set up in a prominent place within the Temple area 49 and that copies should be placed in the Temple treasury, where Simon and his sons would have access to them.

Antiochus the Seventh Asks for Simon's Support

15 1 From the Greek islands Antiochus son of King Demetrius wrote the following letter to Simon the High Priest and governor of the Jews and to the whole nation:

2 "King Antiochus to Simon, the High Priest and governor, and to the Jewish nation, greetings. 3 As you know, the kingdom of my ancestors has been seized by traitors. I have decided to reclaim it and restore its former greatness. I have raised a large army of mercenary troops and have fitted out warships. 4 I plan to invade the land and to attack those who have destroyed many of the towns and ruined the country.

5 "Now therefore, I confirm all exemptions from taxes and payments granted you by former kings. 6 I authorize you to mint your own coins as legal currency in your own country. 7 Jerusalem and the Temple shall be free of taxation. All the weapons that you have manufactured and the defenses you have built and now occupy shall remain yours. 8 In addition, all debts now owed to the royal treasury, or which may in the future fall due, are permanently canceled. 9 As soon as I have regained control of my kingdom, I will confer upon you, your nation, and the Temple such great honors that the glory of your country will be evident to the whole world."

10 In the year 174 r Antiochus invaded the land of his ancestors. Most of the soldiers came over to his side, so that there were very

few left with Trypho. ¹¹Trypho, pursued by
Antiochus, fled to the coastal city of Dor,
¹²realizing that he was in a desperate situa-
tion, now that all his troops had deserted
him. ¹³Then Antiochus laid siege to Dor
with 120,000 well-trained soldiers and 8,000
cavalry. ¹⁴With his ships joining the attack,
he completely surrounded the town and
brought such pressure on it that no one was
able to enter or leave.

Rome Supports the Jews

¹⁵Meanwhile, Numenius and those with
him arrived in Jerusalem from Rome with
the following letter addressed to various
kings and countries:

¹⁶"From Lucius, consul of the Romans,
to King Ptolemy, greetings. ¹⁷A delegation
from our friends and allies the Jews has
come to us to renew the earlier treaty of
friendship and alliance. They were sent by
the High Priest Simon and the Jewish
people, ¹⁸and they have brought as a gift a
gold shield weighing half a ton. ¹⁹So we
have decided to write to various kings and
countries urging them not to harm the
Jews, their towns, or their country in any
way. They must not make war against the
Jews or give support to those who attack
them. ²⁰We have decided to accept the
shield and grant them protection. ²¹There-
fore if any traitors escape from Judea and
seek refuge in your land, hand them over
to Simon the High Priest, so that he may
punish them according to Jewish law."

²²Lucius wrote the same letter to King
Demetrius, to Attalus, Ariarathes, and Arsaces,
²³and to all the following countries: Samp-
sames, Sparta, Delos, Myndos, Sicyon, Caria,
Samos, Pamphylia, Lycia, Halicarnassus,
Rhodes, Phaselis, Cos, Side, Aradus, Gortyna,
Cnidus, Cyprus, and Cyrene. ²⁴A copy of the
letter was also sent to Simon the High Priest.

Antiochus the Seventh Breaks with Simon

²⁵King Antiochus laid siege to Dor for a
second time, keeping it under constant attack.
He built siege platforms, and his blockade kept

Trypho and his men from going in or out.
²⁶Simon sent 2,000 well-trained soldiers to
help Antiochus, as well as silver and gold and a
great deal of equipment. ²⁷But Antiochus
refused to accept them, canceled all the previous agreements that he had made with Simon,
and became his enemy. ²⁸Then Antiochus sent
his trusted official Athenobius to negotiate
with Simon. He told Simon, "You are occupying Joppa, Gezer, and the fort in Jerusalem,
cities that belong to my kingdom. ²⁹You have
devastated those regions and brought great
trouble to the country. You have seized control
of many places in my kingdom. ³⁰Now you
must hand back these cities that you have captured, and you must give me the tax money
that you have taken from places that you occupied outside the territory of Judea. ³¹If you are
unwilling to do this, then you must pay me
30,000 pounds of silver, and 30,000 additional
pounds of silver to compensate me for dam-
ages and for lost taxes. If you refuse to do
either of these, we will go to war against you."

³²When Athenobius came to Jerusalem and
saw the splendor of Simon's court, the gold
and silver tableware in his banquet hall, and
the rest of the display of great wealth, he was
amazed. He delivered the king's message to
Simon, ³³and Simon answered, "We have
never taken land away from other nations or
confiscated anything that belonged to other
people. On the contrary, we have simply taken
back property that we inherited from our
ancestors, land that had been unjustly taken
away from us by our enemies at one time or
another. ³⁴We are now only making use of
this opportunity to recover our ancestral heritage. ³⁵As for Joppa and Gezer, which you
claim, we will give you 6,000 pounds of silver,
in spite of the fact that the people of those
cities have done great harm to our nation."

Athenobius made no reply, ³⁶but he
returned to the king in a rage. When he told
the king what Simon had said, and reported
on the splendor of Simon's court and all that
he had seen, the king became violently angry.

John's Victory over Cendebeus

³⁷In the meantime, Trypho had boarded a
ship and escaped to the town of Orthosia.

15:15 1 Macc 12:16

38King Antiochus appointed Cendebeus as commander of the coastal area, provided him with infantry and cavalry, 39and gave him orders to move against Judea. He also ordered him to rebuild the town of Kedron and fortify its gates, so that he could fight against the Jewish people. The king himself continued to pursue Trypho.

40Cendebeus then came to Jamnia and began to harass the Jews by invading Judea, capturing people, and murdering them. 41He rebuilt Kedron and stationed some cavalry and infantry units there, so that they could make attacks and patrol the roads of Judea, as the king had ordered.

16 1Simon's son John left Gezer and went to report to his father what Cendebeus had done. 2Simon said to John and Judas, his two oldest sons, "All my father's family, my brothers, and I have fought Israel's battles all our lives, and many times we have been successful in saving Israel. 3I am old now, but you, thanks to God, are in the prime of life. You must take my place and that of my brother in fighting for our nation. And may God himself be with you."

4Then John raised an Israelite army of 20,000 trained soldiers and cavalry and marched out against Cendebeus. They spent the night in Modein, 5and then early the next morning they moved into the plain. There a large army of infantry and cavalry moved to meet them, but there was a river between the two armies. 6John and his army took up battle positions facing the enemy, but when John saw that his soldiers were afraid to cross the river, he crossed ahead of them, and his men saw him and followed. 7John divided his army and placed his cavalry in the middle of the infantry, because there was a large number of enemy cavalry. 8The trumpets sounded the attack, and Cendebeus and his army were defeated, and many of them were killed. The rest ran back to their fortress at Kedron. 9Judas was wounded in the battle, but his brother John continued to pursue the enemy as far as Kedron, which Cendebeus had rebuilt. 10The escaping soldiers fled to the towers in the fields at Azotus, and John set fire to the city. On that day, 2,000 enemy soldiers were killed, and John returned safely to Judea.

The Murder of Simon and Two of His Sons

11Simon the High Priest had appointed Ptolemy son of Abubus commander for the Plain of Jericho. Ptolemy was very rich, 12because he was Simon's son-in-law. 13But he became too ambitious and wanted to take over the country. So he devised a plan to assassinate Simon and his sons. 14Simon, together with his sons Mattathias and Judas, was visiting the towns in the area, in order to take care of their needs. They arrived in Jericho in the month of Shebat, the eleventh month, in the year 177.s 15Ptolemy, still plotting to murder Simon and his two sons, received them in a small fortress called Dok, which he had built. He gave a great banquet for them, but he had men hidden within the fortress. 16When Simon and his sons were drunk, Ptolemy and his men came out of hiding and with swords in hand rushed into the banquet hall, where they killed Simon, his two sons, and some of the servants. 17With this horrible act of treachery, Ptolemy returned evil for good.

18Then Ptolemy wrote a report of what he had done and sent it to the king. In the letter he requested that troops be sent to help him and that the country and the cities be turned over to him. 19He wrote a letter to the army officers inviting them to join him and promising them silver, gold, and gifts. Then he sent some of his men to Gezer to kill John, 20and others to take control of Jerusalem and the Temple hill. 21But someone ran to Gezer ahead of Ptolemy's men and reported to John that his father and his brothers had been killed and that Ptolemy was sending his soldiers to kill him. 22John was horrified at this news, but, because he had been warned in advance, he was able to capture and put to death the men who had been sent to kill him.

23Now the rest of what John did from the time he succeeded his father: his wars, his deeds of courage, his rebuilding of walls, and his other accomplishments, 24are all written in the chronicles of his reign as High Priest.

I Maccabees

"What goes around, comes around!" This expresses a simple truth presented in 2 Maccabees. Living a good, just, faithful life—keeping God in front—will bring you great blessings. If not in this life, then your blessings will come in eternal life—heaven. If you are evil and power hungry and thrive on hurting others, you will suffer—either in this life or the next.

The Second Book of Maccabees reveals stories of the best and worst kinds of people. It tells why and how they love God faithfully or reject God completely. As you read this book, you will be inspired, angered, horrified, and challenged by their stories. You will also understand the ups and downs the Jewish people faced during a time of persecution.

Headlines

- Heavenly Warriors Defend Temple (3:1–28)
- Corrupt High Priest Tries to Be Greek (4:7–22)
- Eleazar Remains Faithful, Sets Example for Youth (6:18–31)
- Martyrs Tortured and Die for Faith (chapter 7)
- First Hanukkah Celebrated (10:1–8)
- Judas' Vision Inspires Victory (15:6–37)

FACTOIDS

Who are the central characters? Judas Maccabeus and other faithful Jews who fight to save their faith; Onias, the just and faithful High Priest; corrupt leaders who work to destroy the Jews.

Who wrote this book? An unknown author who was concerned with the meaning of history rather than the facts. Second Maccabees is a summary of a lost five-volume story of the Maccabees written by Jason of Cyrene.

Why was it written? It was written to show how the Jewish faith grew even during difficult years, and to offer the Jews hope in their suffering.

What time period does it cover? From 180 to 160 BC, approximately the same period as 1 Maccabees.

Important themes
- Pray for your enemies. There are many paths to peace—besides war.
- God's faithful may suffer, but justice will eventually be served—if not in this life, then in the resurrection of the dead.
- Pray for those who have died, and know that they pray for you too.

2 MACCABEES

A Letter to the Jews in Egypt

1 ¹"From the Jews of Jerusalem and Judea to those in Egypt, warm greetings.

²"May God be good to you and keep the covenant he made with Abraham, Isaac, and Jacob, his faithful servants. ³May he fill each of you with the desire to worship him and to do his will eagerly with all your heart and soul. ⁴May he enable you to understand his Law and his commands. May he give you peace, ⁵answer your prayers, forgive your sins, and never abandon you in times of trouble. ⁶Here in Judah we are now praying for you.

⁷"In the year 169,ᵃ when Demetrius the Second was king of Syria, we wrote to tell you about the persecution and the hard times that came upon us in the years after Jason revolted against authority in the Holy Land. ⁸Jason and his men set fire to the Temple gates and slaughtered innocent people. Then we prayed to the Lord and he answered our prayers. So we sacrificed animals, gave offerings of grain, lit the lamps in the Temple, and set out the sacred loaves. ⁹This is why we urge you to celebrate in the month of Kislev a festival similar to the Festival of Shelters. Written in the year 188."ᵇ

A LETTER TO ARISTOBULUS

The Death of King Antiochus

¹⁰"From the Jews of Jerusalem and Judea, the Jewish Senate, and Judas, to Aristobulus, a descendant of priests and the teacher of King Ptolemy, and to the Jews in Egypt, greetings and good health.

¹¹"We thank God because he saved us from great danger. We were like men ready to fight against a king, ¹²but God drove the enemy from our holy city. ¹³When King Antiochus arrived in Persia, his army seemed impossible to defeat, but they were cut to pieces in the temple of the goddess Nanea by an act of treachery on the part of her priests. ¹⁴King Antiochus had gone to the temple with some of his most trusted advisers, so that he might marry the goddess and then take away most of the temple treasures as a wedding gift. ¹⁵After the priests had laid out the treasure, he and a few of his men went into the temple to collect it. But the priests closed the doors behind him ¹⁶and stoned him and his men from trap doors hidden in the ceiling. Then they cut up the bodies and threw the heads to the people outside. ¹⁷Praise God for punishing those evil men! Praise him for everything!

Fire Consumes Nehemiah's Sacrifice

¹⁸"On the twenty-fifth day of the month of Kislev we will celebrate the Festival of Rededication just as we celebrate the Festival of Shelters. We thought it important to remind you of this, so that you too may celebrate this festival. In this way you will remember how fire appeared when Nehemiah offered sacrifices after he had rebuilt the Temple and the altar. ¹⁹At the time when our ancestors were being taken to exile in Persia, a few devout priests took some fire from the altar and secretly hid it in the bottom of a dry cistern. They hid the fire so well that no one ever discovered it. ²⁰Years later, when it pleased God, the Persian emperor sent Nehemiah back to Jerusalem, and Nehemiah told the descendants of those priests to find the fire. They reported to us that they had found no fire but only some oily liquid. Nehemiah then told them to scoop some up and bring it to him. ²¹When everything for the sacrifice had been placed on the altar, he told the priests to pour the liquid over both the wood and the sacrifice. ²²After this was done and some time had passed, the sun appeared from behind the clouds, and suddenly everything on the altar burst into flames. Everyone looked on in amazement. ²³Then, while the fire was

---

ᵃ **1:7** THE YEAR 169: *This corresponds to 143 B.C.*   ᵇ **1:9** THE YEAR 188: *This corresponds to 124 B.C.*
1:13–16 1 Macc 6:1–4; 2 Macc 9:1–10

Everyone looked on in amazement. (1:22)

consuming the sacrifice, Jonathan the High Priest led the people in prayer, and Nehemiah and all the people responded.

Nehemiah's Prayer

24"Nehemiah's prayer went something like this: 'Lord God, Creator of all things, you are awesome and strong, yet merciful and just. You alone are king. No one but you is kind; 25no one but you is gracious and just. You are almighty and eternal, forever ready to rescue Israel from trouble. You chose our ancestors to be your own special people. 26Accept this sacrifice which we offer on behalf of all Israel; protect your chosen people and make us holy. 27Free those who are slaves in foreign lands and gather together our scattered people. Have mercy on our people, who are mistreated and despised, so that all other nations will know that you are our God. 28Punish the brutal and arrogant people who have oppressed us, 29and then establish your people in your holy land, as Moses said you would.'

The Persian Emperor Hears about the Fire

30"Then the priests sang hymns. 31After the sacrifices had been consumed, Nehemiah gave orders for the rest of the liquid to be poured over some large stones. 32Immediately a fire blazed up, but it was extinguished by a flame from the fire on the altar.

33"News of what had happened spread everywhere. The Persian emperor heard that a liquid had been found in the place where the priests had hidden the altar fire, just before they were taken into exile. He also heard that Nehemiah and his friends had used this liquid to burn the sacrifice on the altar. 34When the emperor investigated the matter and found out that this was true, he had the area fenced off and made into a shrine. 35It became a substantial source of income for him, and he used the money for gifts to anyone who was in his good favor. 36Nehemiah and his friends called the liquid *nephthar* which means 'purification,' but most people call it 'naphtha.'

Jeremiah Hides the Tent of the Lord's Presence

2 1"We know from the records that Jeremiah the prophet instructed the people who were being taken into exile to hide some of the fire from the altar, as we have just mentioned. 2We also know that he taught them God's Law and warned them not to be deceived by the ornamented gold and silver idols which they would see in the land of their exile. 3And then he urged them never to abandon the Law.

4"These same records also tell us that Jeremiah, acting under divine guidance, commanded the Tent of the Lord's Presence and the Covenant Box to follow him to the mountain where Moses had looked down on the land which God had promised our people. 5When Jeremiah got to the mountain, he found a huge cave and there he hid the Tent of the Lord's Presence, the Covenant Box, and the altar of incense. Then he sealed up the entrance.

6"Some of Jeremiah's friends tried to follow him and mark the way, but they could not find the cave. 7When Jeremiah learned what they had done, he reprimanded them, saying, 'No one must know about this place

Read 2 Maccabees 1:2–5 as if it were a blessing being prayed for you.

Pray It!

Please and Thanks, God!

There are lots of ways to pray, including asking God for help. We call prayers asking God for help prayers of petition. God welcomes our requests. But our prayer can't just be about what we need—that's kind of selfish, right? We need to also recognize how much God loves us and cares for us (which is why we know we can come to God for help). Nehemiah gives us a great example of praying this way (2 Maccabees 1:24–29) and so does this young person.

Dear God,

Sometimes I can't believe how lucky I've been to have so many friends in my life. Thank you for each and every one of them! And thanks for teaching me what it means to be a good (not perfect!) friend.

God, my best friend, Molly, and I are in the middle of a terrible fight. I mean, it's bad. It might be the end for us. I won't go into all the details, and you already know what happened. Anyway, we're really stuck.

God, you know all the ins and outs of friendship—being the best friend anyone could have. So please, help Molly and me! Give us the courage to fix this, forgive each other, and start over fresh.

Thanks! Amen.

Love, Amanda

— 2 Maccabees 1:24–29

until God gathers his people together again and shows them mercy. [8]At that time he will reveal where these things are hidden, and the dazzling light of his presence will be seen in the cloud, as it was in the time of Moses and on the occasion when Solomon prayed that the Temple might be dedicated in holy splendor.'

. . . but they could not find the cave. (2:6)

2:8 Ex 16:10; 24:16; 1 Kings 8:10, 11

How Solomon Celebrated the Festival

[9]"We are also told how the wise King Solomon offered a sacrifice of dedication at the completion of the Temple, [10]and that when he prayed, fire came down from heaven and consumed the sacrifices, just as it had done earlier when Moses prayed. [11]Moses had explained that the sin offering was consumed by fire because it was not eaten. [12]Solomon celebrated the festival for eight days.

Nehemiah's Library

[13]"These same facts are found in the royal records and in the memoirs of Nehemiah, who established a library and collected the writings of David, letters of the kings concerning offerings, and books about the kings and prophets. [14]Judas also collected the books that had been scattered because of the war, and we still have them. [15]If you ever need any of these books, let us know, and we will send them.

An Invitation to Celebrate the Festival

16"Since we are about to celebrate the Festival of Rededication, we are writing to you, advising you to celebrate it as well. 17God has saved all his people and has restored to all of us our holy land, the kingship, the priesthood, and the Temple services, 18just as he promised in his Law. He has rescued us from terrible evils and has purified the Temple, and we are confident that in his mercy he will soon gather us to his holy Temple from every nation under the sun."

Author's Preface

19Jason of Cyrene has recorded in five volumes the story of Judas Maccabeus and his brothers, the purification of the great Temple, and the dedication of its altar. 20He has described the battles with Antiochus Epiphanes and with his son Eupator, 21and he has told of the heavenly visions that appeared to those who fought bravely and enthusiastically to defend Judaism. Our forces were few in number, but they plundered the entire country and routed the heathen forces. 22They recaptured the Temple famous throughout the world, liberated Jerusalem, and restored the laws that were in danger of being abolished. They were able to do all these things because the Lord was merciful and kind to them.

23I will now try to summarize in a single book the five volumes written by Jason. 24The number of details and the bulk of material can be overwhelming for anyone who wants to read an account of the events. 25But I have attempted to simplify it for all readers; those who read for sheer pleasure will find enjoyment and those who want to memorize the facts will not find it difficult. 26Writing such a summary is a difficult task, demanding hard work and sleepless nights. 27It is as difficult as preparing a banquet that people of different tastes will enjoy. But I am happy to undergo this hardship in order to please my readers. 28I will leave the matter of details to the original author and

attempt to give only a summary of the events. 29I am not the builder of a new house who is concerned with every detail of the structure, but simply a painter whose only concern is to make the house look attractive. 30The historian must master his subject, examine every detail, and then explain it carefully, 31but whoever is merely writing a summary should be permitted to give a brief account without going into a detailed discussion. 32So then, without any further comment, I will begin my story. It would be foolish to write such a long introduction that the story itself would have to be cut short.

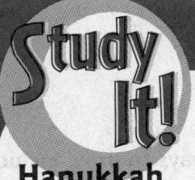

Hanukkah

Second Maccabees actually starts with two letters written to the Jews in Egypt. In this second letter, the Jews in Egypt are being invited to celebrate the festival of Rededication of the Temple in Jerusalem, also known as Hanukkah. Possibly the Jewish community in Jerusalem wanted to keep the Jews in Egypt connected to their roots. The actual event that Hanukkah is based on is covered later in the book.

Hanukkah is celebrated for eight days during December, to remember how the Maccabees rededicated the Temple after it was robbed and damaged by Antiochus IV Epiphanes (see 1 Maccabees 4:52–56 and 2 Maccabees 10:1–8). Each day a candle is lit as the Jews rejoice and give God thanks that their faith has survived through time. Hanukkah is still celebrated by Jewish people today.

— 2 Maccabees 2:16–18

The Argument between Onias and Simon

3 ¹When Onias*ᶜ* was High Priest in Jerusalem, the holy city enjoyed peace and prosperity, and its laws were strictly obeyed, because he was devout and hated evil. ²The kings of Syria and Egypt honored the Temple and presented it with expensive gifts, ³and King Seleucus,*ᵈ* ruler of all Asia, even used to pay the costs of the Temple sacrifices from the revenues he collected.

⁴But a man by the name of Simon, of the tribe of Bilgah,*ᵉ* the chief administrative official of the Temple, lost an argument he had with Onias over the regulations governing the city market. ⁵At this time Apollonius son of Thraseus was the governor of Greater Syria. Simon went to him ⁶and said that there was so much money in the Temple treasury that it could not be counted, and since the money was not needed for sacrifices, it might as well be placed under the king's control.

Heliodorus Is Sent to Jerusalem

⁷When Apollonius met with the king, he told him about the money, and the king ordered Heliodorus, his chief minister, to get it for him. ⁸Heliodorus set out at once on his mission, but he claimed that he was only making a tour of inspection of the cities of Greater Syria. ⁹After he had arrived in Jerusalem and had been warmly received by the High Priest, he explained the real reason for his visit and asked if what he had been told was true. ¹⁰⁻¹¹The High Priest then stated that Simon, that devil of a man, had not been telling the truth. There was indeed some money in the Temple treasury, but part of it was set aside for widows and orphans and part of it belonged to Hyrcanus son of Tobias, a very important man. He also pointed out that the total amount was only 30,000 pounds of silver and 15,000 pounds

of gold. ¹²He added that it was absolutely impossible that anyone should be permitted to take the money of those people who had placed their trust in the sanctity and safety of this world-famous Temple.

Heliodorus Plans to Enter the Temple

¹³But Heliodorus insisted that the money should be taken for the royal treasury, as the king had ordered. ¹⁴So he set a day and went into the Temple to supervise the counting of the money. This caused an uproar throughout the entire city. ¹⁵Priests, wearing their priestly robes, threw themselves face downward before the altar and begged God to keep the money safe, since he had given the laws designed to protect the money that people deposited in the Temple. ¹⁶It was heartbreaking to see the High Priest. His face turned pale, revealing the agony of his soul, ¹⁷and his body was trembling with fear, reflecting the pain in his heart. ¹⁸People ran

It was heartbreaking to see the High Priest. (3:16)

ᶜ **3:1** ONIAS: *This is Onias the Third, son of Simon the Second (see 4:4–6; Sir 50:1–21).* ᵈ **3:3** SELEUCUS: *This is Seleucus the Fourth, known as Philopator, son of Antiochus the Third, 187—175 B.C.* ᵉ **3:4** *Some ancient translations* Bilgah *(see Neh 12:5,18); Greek* Benjamin.

Where else in this book, besides 2 Maccabees 2:23–32, does the author of 2 Maccabees write a personal note to his readers, about his writing?

Pray It!

Praying for Enemies

Jesus taught us that when someone hurts us, we should not hurt them back—which is normally just the thing we want to do. Not only should we not hurt them, but, we are supposed to *love* our enemies (see Matthew 5:38–48)! How many examples can you think of when loving an enemy seems impossible?

The High Priest, Onias, shows us one way to do this. The Greek king's representative, Heliodorus, was going to take all the gold from the Jewish treasury in the Temple. But when Heliodorus arrived at the Temple, he was attacked by angels. As Heliodorus lay on the Temple floor, near death, Onias had the perfect chance to destroy him. But what did he do? Onias prayed for Heliodorus! God heard the prayer of Onias and spared the life of Heliodorus. Heliodorus praised God and left the Temple treasury alone.

Loving, forgiving, or praying for an enemy may be one of the hardest things to face in life, but we can ask God for the courage and strength to do it. And we can be sure that God will bless us for loving instead of hating.

— 2 Maccabees 3:29–40

from their houses to join together in prayer that the Temple might not be defiled. ¹⁹Women, wearing nothing but skirts of sackcloth, crowded the streets. Young girls whose parents had never allowed them to be seen in public ran to the gates or to the walls of the city, or just stared out of their windows. ²⁰But wherever they went, they lifted their hands to God in prayer. ²¹What a pitiful sight it was to see the High Priest in such great agony and frustration and to see everyone in the city confused and lying face down on the ground.

The Lord Protects His Temple

²²While everyone was begging the Lord Almighty to protect the money that had been entrusted to his care, ²³Heliodorus went on with his plan. ²⁴But at the very moment that he and his bodyguards arrived at the treasury, the Lord of all supernatural powers caused such a vision to appear that everyone who had dared to enter with Heliodorus was panic-stricken and weak with fear at this display of the Lord's power. ²⁵In the vision they saw a horse and a rider. The horse had a richly decorated bridle, and its rider, dressed in gold armor, was frightening. Suddenly the horse rushed at Heliodorus, then reared up and struck at him with its hoofs. ²⁶Heliodorus also saw two unusually strong and handsome young men, wearing very fine clothes. They stood on either side of him and beat him unmercifully. ²⁷He immediately fell to the ground unconscious, and his men put him on a stretcher ²⁸and carried him out. Only a moment earlier this man had entered the treasury with a large group of men, including all his bodyguards, but now he was being carried away helpless. So they all*ƒ* openly acknowledged the mighty power of God.

ƒ 3:28 they all; *some manuscripts have* he.

The Temple also functioned like a bank. It had a special room, the treasury, where gold, silver, and other valuables were kept.

Onias Prays for Heliodorus' Recovery

29 Heliodorus lay there unable to speak and without hope of recovery from this demonstration of God's power. 30 But the Jews praised Almighty God because he had miraculously protected his Temple and had brought great happiness where only minutes before there had been fear and confusion. 31 Some of Heliodorus' friends quickly asked Onias the High Priest to pray that the Most High would spare the life of this man who was at the point of death. 32 So the High Priest offered a sacrifice in the hope that God would save Heliodorus, for he did not want the king to think that the Jews had done this to the man he had sent. 33 While Onias was offering the sacrifice, the two young men, wearing the same clothes as before, again appeared to Heliodorus and said, "Be grateful to the High Priest; the Lord has spared your life because of him. 34 Remember that it was the Lord of heaven who punished you. Now go and tell everyone of his great power." When they had said this, they disappeared.

Heliodorus Praises God

35 So Heliodorus offered a sacrifice to the Lord and made many promises, because the Lord had spared his life. Then he said goodbye to Onias and returned with his army to the king. 36 There he told everyone what the Lord, the most powerful of all gods, had done.

37 When the king asked Heliodorus who would be the best man to send on the next mission to Jerusalem, Heliodorus replied, 38 "If you have an enemy or know of someone plotting against your government, send him. He will come back badly beaten, if he comes back at all, for some strange power from God is at work there. 39 The God of heaven watches over the Temple, he strikes down and destroys anyone who comes to harm it." 40 That is the story of how the Temple treasury was protected from Heliodorus.

Simon Accuses Onias

4 ¹But Simon (mentioned earlier as the one who informed Apollonius about the money and brought trouble on the nation) also lied about Onias, claiming that he was responsible for the attack on Heliodorus and for the difficulties that followed. ²He dared to accuse Onias of plotting against the government—Onias who not only had made donations to Jerusalem and had protected the Temple, but who was eager to see that all our laws were obeyed. ³-⁴Apollonius son of Menestheus, the governor of Greater Syria, encouraged Simon in every evil thing he did, and Simon's opposition finally grew so strong that one of his trusted followers committed several murders. Onias realized how dangerous the situation had become, ⁵so he went to the king, not for the purpose of making accusations against his own people, but for the common good of all Jews, both in their private and public lives. ⁶He realized that without the king's cooperation there was no hope for peace, and Simon would keep on with his foolishness.

Jason Introduces Greek Customs

⁷Later, when King Seleucus died and Antiochus (known as Epiphanes) became king, Jason the brother of Onias became High Priest by corrupt means. ⁸He went to see*g* the king and offered him 27,000 pounds of silver with 6,000 more pounds to be paid later. ⁹Jason also offered him an additional 11,250 pounds of silver for the authority to establish a stadium where young men could train and to enroll the people of Jerusalem as citizens of Antioch.*h*

¹⁰The king gave his approval, and just as soon as Jason took over the office of High Priest, he made the people of Jerusalem change to the Greek way of life. ¹¹He began by abolishing the favors that John had secured for the Jews from previous Syrian kings. (John was the father of the Eupolemus who later went to Rome to make an alliance

---

g **4:8** went to see; *or* wrote to.   *h* **4:9** the people . . . Antioch; *or* the men of Jerusalem as supporters of King Antiochus.
4:7 1 Macc 1:10   **4:11** 1 Macc 8:17

2 Maccabees

The Price of Evil

Good and faithful Onias has his office of High Priest snatched away by Jason, who later loses his place to Menelaus. Both Jason and Menelaus are selfish, greedy, controlling men whose evil acts bring God's punishment upon the Jews.

Instead of honoring his faith, Jason forced the Greek way of life on the Jewish population. The Temple, the Law, and Jewish values are tossed out the window in favor of Greek customs and ideals (2 Maccabees 4:10–17). Menelaus steals and cheats and even has Onias killed.

Evil does not go unpunished. Unfortunately, innocent people can suffer the consequences of evil, as well as the wicked people who caused the trouble. From this point on in 2 Maccabees, faithful Jews are caught in battle after battle, and many are tortured and killed by their enemies.

What are some of the differences you see in Onias, Jason, and Menelaus—both as religious leaders and as men? What lessons can you learn from them?

— 2 Maccabees, chapter 4

craze for the Greek way of life and for foreign customs reached such a point [14]that even the priests lost all interest in their sacred duties. They lost interest in the Temple services and neglected the sacrifices. Just as soon as the signal was given, they would rush off to take part in the games that were forbidden by our Law. [15]They did not care about anything their ancestors had valued; they prized only Greek honors. [16]And this turned out to be the source of all their troubles, for the very people whose ways they admired and whose customs they tried to imitate became their enemies and oppressed them. [17]It is a serious thing to disregard God's Law, as you will see from the following events.

Jerusalem under Syrian Influence

[18]Once when the king was present for the athletic games that were held every five[i] years in the city of Tyre, [19]that worthless Jason sent some men there from Jerusalem, who were also enrolled as citizens of Antioch, to take 22,500 pounds of silver to pay for a sacrifice to the god Hercules. But even these men did not think it was fitting to use such a large sum of money for a sacrifice, and [20]so the money originally intended as a sacrifice to Hercules was used for the construction of warships.

[21]When Apollonius son of Menestheus was sent to Egypt to attend the crowning of Philometor as king, Antiochus learned that Philometor was opposed to his policies. Antiochus became concerned about the security of his own kingdom, so he went to Joppa and then on to Jerusalem. [22]There he was welcomed with great splendor by Jason and the people of the city who went out to greet him, shouting and carrying torches. From Jerusalem Antiochus led his army to Phoenicia.

Menelaus Becomes High Priest

[23]Three years later, Jason sent Menelaus (brother of the Simon[j] mentioned earlier) to take some money to the king and to get his decision on several important matters. [24]But

and to establish ties of friendship.) Jason also did away with our Jewish customs and introduced new customs that were contrary to our Law. [12]With great enthusiasm he built a stadium near the Temple hill and led our finest young men to adopt the Greek custom of participating in athletic events. [13]Because of the unrivaled wickedness of Jason, that ungodly and illegitimate High Priest, the when he stood before the king, Menelaus impressed him with his show of authority and offered 22,500 pounds of silver more than Jason had offered for his appointment to the office of High Priest. 25 As a result Menelaus returned to Jerusalem with papers from the king, confirming him as High Priest. But he possessed no other qualifications; he had the temper of a cruel tyrant and could be as fierce as a wild animal. 26 So Jason, who had cheated his own brother out of the office of High Priest, was now forced to flee to the land of Ammon. 27 Menelaus continued to be High Priest, but he never paid any of the money he had promised the king. 28 However, Sostratus, the captain of the fort in Jerusalem, kept demanding the money, since it was his responsibility to collect it. So finally, the two men were summoned to appear before the king concerning the matter. 29 Menelaus left his brother Lysimachus as acting High Priest, while Sostratus left the fort under the command of Crates, the commander of the mercenary troops from Cyprus.

The Murder of Onias

30 Meanwhile, there was a revolt in the Cilician cities of Tarsus and Mallus, because the king had given those cities to Antiochis, his mistress. 31 So the king left Andronicus, one of his high officials, in command, while he hurried off to Cilicia to restore order. 32 Menelaus took advantage of this opportunity and presented Andronicus with some of the gold objects he had removed from the Temple in Jerusalem. He had already sold some of them to the city of Tyre and to other nearby cities. 33 When Onias heard about this, he fled for safety to a temple at Daphne near the city of Antioch and openly accused Menelaus. 34 Then Menelaus secretly persuaded Andronicus to kill Onias. So Andronicus went to Onias and deceived him with a friendly greeting and with promises of safety. Although Onias was suspicious, Andronicus finally lured him away from the safety of the temple and immediately murdered him in cold blood.

Andronicus Is Punished

35 The Jews and Gentiles were very angry because Onias had been murdered. 36 So when the king returned from the territory of Cilicia, the Jews of Antioch went to him and protested against this senseless killing. Many Gentiles felt the same way about the crime. 37 King Antiochus was deeply grieved and was so filled with sorrow that he was moved to tears when he recalled the wisdom and self-control that Onias had shown throughout his life. 38 Antiochus became so angry that he tore off Andronicus' royal robe, stripped him naked, and marched him around the city to the very spot where Onias had been murdered. Then Antiochus had this bloodthirsty murderer put to death. This was how the Lord gave him the punishment he deserved.

Lysimachus Is Killed

39 Meanwhile, with the support of his brother Menelaus, Lysimachus had on numerous occasions robbed the Jerusalem Temple and had taken many of its gold objects. When word of this spread around, crowds began to gather in protest against Lysimachus. 40 Finally, the crowds were becoming dangerous and were beginning to get out of control, so Lysimachus sent 3,000 armed men to attack them. They were led by Auranus, a man as stupid as he was old. 41 When the Jews in the Temple courtyard realized what was happening, they picked up rocks, pieces of wood, or simply handfuls of ashes from the altar and threw them at Lysimachus and his men in the confusion. 42 They killed a few of Lysimachus' men, wounded many of them, and all the rest ran for their lives. Lysimachus himself, that temple robber, was killed near the Temple treasury.

4:34 Dan 9:26

"It is a serious thing to disregard God's Law" (2 Maccabees 4:17).

Menelaus Is Brought to Trial

43Because of this incident Menelaus was brought to trial. 44When the king came to the city of Tyre, the Jewish authorities in Jerusalem sent three men to bring charges against Menelaus. 45When Menelaus saw that he was losing the case, he offered Ptolemy son of Dorymenes a large bribe to persuade the king to decide in his favor. 46Ptolemy then asked the king to go outside the courtroom with him, as though to get some fresh air, and there he persuaded him to change his mind 47and declare Menelaus innocent of the charges against him. So Menelaus was set free, although he had caused the trouble; but the three men, whom even the cruel Scythians would have declared innocent, were sentenced to death. 48The three men had spoken in defense of Jerusalem, its people,k and the sacred objects stolen from the Temple, but they were quickly and unjustly executed. 49Some of the people of Tyre, however, showed their disgust with this crime and their respect for these men by giving them a splendid funeral. 50Menelaus stayed on in his position because of the greed of those in power. He grew more evil every day and became the worst enemy of his own people.

Visions of a Battle

5 1About this time Antiochus the Fourth made a second attack against Egypt. 2For nearly forty days people all over Jerusalem saw visions of cavalry troops in gold armor charging across the sky. The riders were armed with spears and their swords were drawn. 3They were lined up in battle against one another, attacking and counterattacking. Shields were clashing, there was a rain of spears, and arrows flew through the air. All the different kinds of armor and the gold bridles on the horses flashed in the sunlight. 4Everyone in the city prayed that these visions might be a good sign.

Attacking and counterattacking (5:3)

Jason Attacks Jerusalem

5 When a false report began to spread that Antiochus had died, Jason took more than a thousand men and suddenly attacked Jerusalem. They drove back those stationed on the city walls and finally captured the city. Menelaus fled for safety to the fort, near the Temple hill, 6while Jason and his men went on slaughtering their fellow Jews without mercy. Jason did not realize that success against one's own people is the worst kind of failure. He even considered his success a victory over enemies, rather than a defeat of his own people. 7But Jason did not take over the government. Instead he was forced to flee once again to the territory of the Ammonites, and in the end his evil plot brought him nothing but shame and disgrace, 8and he died in misery. Aretas, the ruler of the Arabs, imprisoned him; he was looked upon as a criminal and despised because he had betrayed his own people; everyone was hunting for him, and he had to run from town to town. He fled to Egypt for safety, 9then to Greece, hoping to find refuge among the Spartans, who were related to the Jews. Finally, this man, who had forced so many others to flee from their own country, died as a fugitive in a foreign land. 10Jason had killed many people and left their bodies unburied, but now his own death was unmourned. He was not given a funeral or even buried with his ancestors.

k **4:48** its people; *some manuscripts also have* the surrounding villages.

It was bad enough when Jason, the former High Priest, attacked Jerusalem. Then King Antiochus attacked. How many people did he kill?

Antiochus Attacks Jerusalem
(1 Maccabees 1:20–63)

11 When the news of what had happened in Jerusalem reached Antiochus, he thought the whole country of Judea was in revolt, and he became as furious as a wild animal. So he left Egypt and took Jerusalem by storm, 12 giving his men orders to cut down without mercy everyone they met and to slaughter anyone they found hiding in the houses. 13 They murdered everyone—men and women, boys and girls; even babies were butchered. 14 Three days later Jerusalem had lost 80,000 people: 40,000 killed in the attack and at least that many taken away to be sold as slaves.

15 But Antiochus was still not satisfied. He even dared to enter the holiest Temple in all the world, guided by Menelaus, who had become a traitor both to his religion and to his people. 16 With his filthy and unholy hands, Antiochus swept away the sacred objects of worship and the gifts which other kings had given to increase the glory and honor of the Temple. 17 He was so thrilled with his conquest that he did not realize that the Lord had let his holy Temple be defiled because the sin of the people of Jerusalem had made him angry for a while. 18 If the people of Jerusalem had not been involved in so many sins, Antiochus would have been punished immediately and prevented from taking such a foolish action. He would have suffered the same fate as Heliodorus, who was sent by King Seleucus to inspect the treasury. 19 But the Lord did not choose his people for the sake of his Temple; he established his Temple for the sake of his people. 20 So the Temple shared in the people's suffering but also later shared in their prosperity. The Lord abandoned it when he became angry, but restored it when his anger had cooled down.

Another Attack against Jerusalem

21 Antiochus took 135,000 pounds of silver from the Temple and hurried off to Antioch. Such was his arrogance that he felt he could make ships sail across dry land or troops march across the sea. 22 He appointed governors to cause trouble for the people. In Jerusalem he placed Philip, a man from Phrygia who was more evil than Antiochus himself. 23 At Mount Gerizim he placed Andronicus. In addition to these, there was Menelaus, who mistreated his fellow Jews far worse than the governors did. Antiochus hated the Jews so much 24 that he sent an army of 22,000 mercenary troops from Mysia to Jerusalem under the command of a man named Apollonius, with orders to kill every man in the city and to sell the women and boys as slaves. 25 Apollonius arrived in Jerusalem, pretending to be on a peace mission. Then on a Sabbath, when all the Jews were observing the day of rest, he led his troops, who were fully armed, in a parade outside the city. 26 Suddenly he commanded his men to kill everyone who had come out to see them. They rushed into the city and murdered a great many people.

27 But Judas Maccabeus and about nine others escaped into the barren mountains, where they lived like wild animals. In order not to defile themselves, they ate only plants which they found growing there.

The Jews Are Persecuted Because of Their Faith

6 ¹Not long after that, the king sent an elderly Athenian[l] to force the Jews to abandon their religion and the customs of their ancestors. ²He was also to defile their Temple by dedicating it to the Olympian god Zeus.[m] The temple on Mount Gerizim was to be officially named "Temple of Zeus the God of Hospitality," as the people who lived there had requested.

³The oppression was harsh and almost intolerable. ⁴Gentiles filled the Temple with drinking parties and all sorts of immorality. They even had intercourse with prostitutes there. Forbidden objects were brought into the Temple, ⁵and the altar was covered with detestable sacrifices prohibited by our Law. ⁶It

---

[l] **6:1** elderly Athenian; *or* an elder of Athens, *or* Athenaios the elder, *or* Geron an Athenian; *some manuscripts have* an elderly Antiochean; *or* an elder of Antioch.   [m] **6:2** ZEUS: *The supreme god of the Greeks; Mount Olympus was thought to be his home.*

2 Maccabees

was impossible to observe the Sabbath, to celebrate any of the traditional festivals, or even so much as to admit to being a Jew. [7] Each month when the king's birthday was celebrated, the Jews were compelled by brute force to eat the intestines of sacrificial animals. Then, during the festival in honor of the wine god Dionysus, they were required to wear ivy wreaths on their heads and march in procession. [8] On the advice of Ptolemy,[n] the neighboring Greek cities were also instructed to require Jews to eat the sacrifices; [9] they were told to put to death every Jew who refused to adopt the Greek way of life. It was easy to see that hard times were ahead. [10] For example, two women were arrested for having their babies circumcised. They were paraded around the city with their babies hung from their breasts; then they were thrown down from the city wall. [11] On another occasion, Philip was told that some Jews had gathered in a nearby cave to observe the Sabbath in secret. Philip attacked and burned them all alive. They had such respect for the Sabbath that they would not fight to defend themselves.

The Lord Punishes and Shows Mercy

[12] I beg you not to become discouraged as you read about the terrible things that happened. Consider that this was the Lord's way of punishing his people, not of destroying them. [13] In fact, it is a sign of kindness to punish a person immediately for his sins, rather than to wait a long time. [14] The Lord does not treat us as he does other nations: he waits patiently until they have become deeply involved in sin before he punishes them, [15] but he punishes us before we have sinned too much. [16] So the Lord is always merciful to us, his own people. Although he punishes us with disasters, he never abandons us. [17] I have made these few observations by way of reminder. We will now get on with the story.

Eleazar Dies for His Faith

[18] There was an elderly and highly respected teacher of the Law by the name of

Integrity

Eleazar had the chance to trick the Greeks and save his life. But he wouldn't do it. He was concerned that the young Jews would think he had compromised his faith and believe it was okay for them to do the same.

Doing the right thing, no matter the consequences, is what *integrity* is all about. Some people are tempted to think that lying, cheating, or stealing a little isn't so bad if no one seems to get hurt because of it. But when we do these things, they slowly destroy our character. We become untrustworthy, selfish, and greedy. We lose track of what is right and wrong and care less and less about how our actions affect other people.

Integrity is important for ourselves, for those around us, and ultimately to the world. We must trust that God sees our actions and blesses us for choosing what is right. A person of integrity is strong, good, and courageous. This is truly a prize for any human—more precious than gold.

Who do you know who is like this?

— 2 Maccabees 6:18–31

Eleazar, whose mouth was being forced open to make him eat pork. [19-20] But he preferred an honorable death rather than a life of disgrace. So he spit out the meat and went willingly to the place of torture, showing how people should have courage to refuse unclean food, even if it costs them their lives. [21-22] Those in charge of the sacrifice

---

[n] **6:8** Ptolemy *(see 4:45); some manuscripts have* the people of Ptolemais.
6:10 1 Macc 1:60, 61   **6:11** 1 Macc 2:32–38   **6:18** Lev 11:7, 8; Heb 11:35

had been friends of Eleazar for a long time, and because of this friendship they told him privately to bring meat that was lawful for him to eat. He need only pretend to eat the pork, they said, and in this way he would not be put to death.

23 But Eleazar made a decision worthy of his gray hair and advanced age. All his life he had lived in perfect obedience to God's holy laws, so he replied, "Kill me, here and now. 24 Such deception is not worthy of a man of my years. Many young people would think that I had denied my faith after I was ninety years old. 25 If I pretended to eat this meat, just to live a little while longer, it would bring shame and disgrace on me and lead many young people astray. 26 For the present I might be able to escape what you could do to me, but whether I live or die, I cannot escape Almighty God. 27 If I die bravely now, it will show that I deserved my long life. 28 It will also set a good example of the way young people should be willing and glad to die for our sacred and respected laws."

As soon as he said these things, he went° off to be tortured, 29 and the very people who had treated him kindly a few minutes before, now turned against him, because they thought he had spoken like a madman. 30 When they had beaten him almost to the point of death, he groaned and said, "The Lord possesses all holy knowledge. He knows I could have escaped these terrible sufferings and death, yet he also knows that I gladly suffer these things, because I fear him."

31 So Eleazar died. But his courageous death was remembered as a glorious example, not only by young people, but by the entire nation as well.

A Mother and Her Sons Die for Their Faith

7 1 On another occasion a Jewish mother and her seven sons were arrested. The king was having them beaten to force them

° **6:28** went; *some manuscripts have* was dragged.
7:1–42 Heb 11:35, 36   **7:6** Deut 32:36

His courageous death was remembered as a glorious example. (6:31)

to eat pork. 2 Then one of the young men said, "What do you hope to gain by doing this? We would rather die than abandon the traditions of our ancestors."

3 This made the king so furious that he gave orders for huge pans and kettles to be heated red hot, 4 and it was done immediately. Then he told his men to cut off the tongue of the one who had spoken and to scalp him and chop off his hands and feet, while his mother and six brothers looked on. 5 After the young man had been reduced to a helpless mass of breathing flesh, the king gave orders for him to be carried over and thrown into one of the pans. As a cloud of smoke streamed up from the pan, the brothers and their mother encouraged one another to die bravely, saying, 6 "The Lord God is looking on and understands our suffering. Moses made this clear when he wrote a song condemning those who had abandoned the Lord. He said, 'The Lord will have mercy on those who serve him.' "

7 After the first brother had died in this way, the soldiers started amusing themselves with the second one by tearing the hair and skin from his head. Then they asked him, "Now will you eat this pork, or do you want us to chop off your hands and feet one by one?"

8 He replied in his native language, "I will

Eternal Life

Ca✝holic Connec✝ions

This is one of the most painful and gruesome stories in the Bible! Imagine being that mother, watching the slow torture and death of each of her seven sons, then suffering the same fate herself. Why is this story here?

Not only does this family provide us with another example of courage and integrity in the face of religious persecution, but it also teaches us about the reality of eternal life. This family knew that those who live with justice and love, even if they suffer for it, will be raised from the dead and live with God forever. And those who reject God and live a wicked life will be punished for all eternity. This is one of the first places in the Bible that eternal life is spoken about.

— 2 Maccabees, chapter 7

never eat it!" So the soldiers tortured him, just as they had the first one, 9but with his dying breath he cried out to the king, "You butcher! You may kill us, but the King of the universe will raise us from the dead and give us eternal life, because we have obeyed his laws."

10The soldiers began entertaining themselves with the third brother. When he was ordered to stick out his tongue, he quickly did so. Then he bravely held out his hands 11and courageously said, "God gave these to me. But his laws mean more to me than my hands, and I know God will give them back to me again." 12The king and those with him were amazed at his courage and at his willingness to suffer.

13After he had died, the soldiers tortured the fourth one in the same cruel way, 14but his final words were, "I am glad to die at your hands, because we have the assurance that God will raise us from death. But there will be no resurrection to life for you, Antiochus!"

15When the soldiers took the fifth boy and began torturing him, 16he looked the king squarely in the eye and said, "You have the power to do whatever you want with us, even though you also are mortal. But do not think that God has abandoned our people. 17Just wait. God will use his great power to torture you and your descendants."

18Then the soldiers took the sixth boy, and just before he died he said, "Make no mistake. We are suffering what we deserve, because we have sinned against our God. That's why all these terrible things are happening to us. 19But don't think for a minute that you will avoid being punished for fighting against God."

20The mother was the most amazing one of them all, and she deserves a special place in our memory. Although she saw her seven sons die in a single day, she endured it with great courage because she trusted in the Lord. 21She combined womanly emotion with manly courage and spoke words of encouragement to each of her sons in their native language. 22"I do not know how your life began in my womb," she would say, "I was not the one who gave you life and breath and put together each part of

See Daniel 12:23 for an inspiring description of those who are resurrected from the dead.

Nonviolent Resistance

Eleazar and the woman and her seven sons give us wonderful examples of nonviolent resistance to injustice. These Jews did not cooperate with their persecutors. They did not fight them (matching violence with violence), but neither did they just give in to them. They held on firmly to their beliefs and confronted the evil facing them.

In recent times people like Rosa Parks, Martin Luther King, and Mahatma Gandhi powerfully stood up against injustice in a nonviolent way. They fought against racism and neglect of poor people. And each one suffered for it. But they accepted this because they knew God brings good out of the suffering of the just. Many laws protecting human rights have been established because of their nonviolent resistance to injustice.

— 2 Maccabees, chapters 6–7

your body. ²³It was God who did it, God who created the universe, the human race, and all that exists. He is merciful and he will give you back life and breath again, because you love his laws more than you love yourself."

²⁴Antiochus was sure that the mother was making fun of him, so he did his best to convince her youngest son to abandon the traditions of his ancestors. He promised not only to make the boy rich and famous, but to place him in a position of authority and to give him the title "Friend of the King." ²⁵But the boy paid no attention to him, so Antiochus tried to persuade the boy's mother to talk him into saving his life, ²⁶and after much persuasion she agreed to do so. ²⁷Leaning over her son, she fooled the cruel

tyrant by saying in her native language, "My son, have pity on me. Remember that I carried you in my womb for nine months and nursed you for three years. I have taken care of you and looked after all your needs up to the present day. ²⁸So I urge you, my child, to look at the sky and the earth. Consider everything you see there, and realize that God made it all from nothing, just as he made the human race. ²⁹Don't be afraid of this butcher. Give up your life willingly and prove yourself worthy of your brothers, so that by God's mercy I may receive you back with them at the resurrection."

³⁰Before she could finish speaking, the boy said, "King Antiochus, what are you waiting for? I refuse to obey your orders. I only obey the commands in the Law which Moses gave to our ancestors. ³¹You have thought up all kinds of cruel things to do to our people, but you won't escape the punishment that God has in store for you. ³²⁻³³It is true that our living Lord is angry with us and is making us suffer because of our sins, in order to correct and discipline us. But this will last only a short while, for we are still his servants, and he will forgive us. ³⁴But you are the cruelest and most disgusting thing that ever lived. So don't fool yourself with illusions of greatness while you punish God's people. ³⁵There is no way for you to escape punishment at the hands of the almighty and all-seeing God. ³⁶My brothers suffered briefly because of our faithfulness to God's covenant, but now they have entered eternal

"King Antiochus . . . I refuse to obey your orders."
(7:30)

life.*p* But you will fall under God's judgment and be punished as you deserve for your arrogance. ³⁷I now give up my body and my life for the laws of our ancestors, just as my brothers did. But I also beg God to show mercy to his people quickly and to torture you until you are forced to acknowledge that he alone is God. ³⁸May my brothers and I be the last to suffer the anger of Almighty God, which he has justly brought upon our entire nation."

³⁹These words of ridicule made Antiochus so furious that he had the boy tortured even more cruelly than his brothers. ⁴⁰And so the boy died, with absolute trust in the Lord, never unfaithful for a minute.

⁴¹Last of all, the mother was put to death.

⁴²But I have said enough about the Jews being tortured and being forced to eat the intestines of sacrificial animals.

Judas Maccabeus Revolts
(1 Maccabees 3:1–26)

8 ¹Judas Maccabeus and his friends went secretly from village to village until they had gathered a force of about 6,000 Jewish men who had remained faithful to their religion. ²They begged the Lord to help his people, now trampled under foot by all nations, to take pity on the Temple, now defiled by pagans, ³and to have mercy on Jerusalem, now destroyed and almost leveled to the ground. ⁴They also asked the Lord to show his hatred of evil by taking revenge on those who were murdering his people, mercilessly slaughtering innocent children, and saying evil things against the Lord.

⁵When Judas had finally organized his forces, the Gentiles were unable to stand against him, because the Lord's anger against Israel had now turned to mercy. ⁶⁻⁷Judas would make sudden attacks on towns and villages and burn them. He captured strategic positions and routed many enemy troops, finding that he was most successful at night. People everywhere spoke of his bravery.

God's Mercy Returns

Judas Maccabeus and his friends have been hiding out, praying for God's help, protection, and strength to fight their enemies. Now Judas has gathered a small army of Jews, and they begin winning battles. They believe God's anger has turned to mercy and that they will be unbeatable.

In 2 Maccabees we once again see the pattern of salvation history that is repeated again and again throughout the Bible:

- We are blessed and are faithful to God.
- We fall into sin.
- We suffer because of our sin.
- We beg God for help, and we promise to be more faithful.
- God is merciful and saves us.
- God blesses us again, and we are faithful to God.

— 2 Maccabees 8:1–7

Ptolemy Sends Nicanor to Attack Judas
(1 Maccabees 3:38–41)

⁸When Philip, governor of Jerusalem, realized that Judas was gaining ground little by little and that his victories were becoming more and more frequent, he wrote a letter to Ptolemy, governor of Greater Syria, requesting his help in defending the royal interests. ⁹Ptolemy immediately appointed Nicanor son of Patroclus, who was also in the closest circle of the King's Friends, and sent him with more than 20,000 troops of various nationalities to wipe out the entire Jewish race. Ptolemy also appointed Gorgias, a general of wide military experience, to go with him. ¹⁰King Antiochus owed the Romans

p 7:36 briefly . . . life; *or* briefly, but now they have entered eternal life because of our covenant with God.

150,000 pounds of silver; Nicanor planned to pay off the debt by selling Jewish prisoners of war as slaves.

11 So he at once sent word to the towns along the coast, informing them that he would be selling Jews for less than a pound of silver each. But he did not know of the judgment that Almighty God had in store for him.

Judas Learns of Nicanor's Plans
(1 Maccabees 3:42–54)

12 Judas learned that Nicanor was advancing with his army toward Judea, so he informed his men. 13 Some were cowardly and did not believe in the justice of God, and they ran away as fast as they could. 14 But others sold all their remaining possessions so that the Lord would consider them worthy to be saved from the godless Nicanor, who had sold them as slaves even before the battle had taken place. 15 They prayed that if God was not willing to do this for their sake alone, he might be willing to rescue them because of the covenants he had made with their ancestors, and because he, the great and wonderful God, had called them to be his people. 16 Judas brought together all 6,000 of his men and encouraged them not to be frightened or to flee in panic at the sight of the large number of Gentile troops who were marching against them without cause. Instead they should fight bravely, 17 never forgetting the crimes the Gentiles had committed against the Temple and how they had made Jerusalem suffer terribly and had done away with Jewish traditions. 18 "They rely on their weapons and their daring," Judas said, "but we trust in Almighty God, who is able to destroy not only these troops, but, if necessary, the entire world, with a mere nod of his head."

19 Then Judas went on to remind them of the ways God had helped their ancestors: during the time of Sennacherib 185,000 of the enemy had been destroyed; 20 and once in Babylonia 8,000 Jews came to the aid of 4,000 Macedonians, defeating 120,000 Galatians and taking a great deal of loot, all because of God's help.

Judas Defeats Nicanor
(1 Maccabees 3:55—4:27)

21 Judas' words encouraged his men and made them willing to die for their religion and their country. He then divided his army into four divisions 22 of about 1,500 men each, with himself and his brothers Simon, Joseph, and Jonathan each in charge of a division. 23 After ordering Eleazar to read aloud[q] from the holy book, he gave his men the battle cry: "God will help us," and personally led the attack against Nicanor.

24 Almighty God fought on their side, and they killed more than 9,000 of the enemy. They wounded many others and put the entire enemy army to flight. 25 They seized the money from the people who had come to buy them as slaves. Then they pursued the enemy a long way, until they had to return, 26 because it was almost time for the Sabbath to begin. 27 When they had collected the enemy's weapons and looted the dead, they celebrated the Sabbath, praising the Lord and giving thanks to him, because he had brought them safely to that day and had given them the first sign of his mercy. 28 When the Sabbath was over, they gave some of the loot to the victims of persecution and to the widows and orphans; then they divided the rest among their own families. 29 Afterward they joined together in prayer to the merciful Lord, asking him to look favorably upon his servants.

Judas Defeats Timothy and Bacchides

30 The Jews later fought against the forces of Timothy and Bacchides and killed more than 20,000 of them. They captured some very high fortresses and took a lot of loot, which they divided equally among

---

q 8:23 *Probable text* After . . . aloud; *Greek unclear.*
8:23 1 Macc 3:48

themselves and the widows, orphans, old men, and the victims of persecution. ³¹They carefully collected all the enemy's weapons and stored them in strategic places, but the rest of the loot was taken to Jerusalem. ³²They executed the commanding officer of Timothy's forces, a godless man who had caused the Jews much suffering. ³³While celebrating their victory in the city of their ancestors, they burned alive those men who had set fire to the Temple gates. The dead included Callisthenes, who had hidden in a small house; and so he received the punishment he deserved for his evil deeds.

³⁴In this way, the evil Nicanor, who had brought a thousand merchants to buy the Jews, ³⁵was defeated with the help of the Lord by the very people he despised so much. He threw off his splendid uniform and fled all alone like a runaway slave, until he reached Antioch. He had succeeded only in destroying his entire army. ³⁶This man, who had tried to pay a debt to Rome by selling the people of Jerusalem, showed that the Jews could not be defeated. God was their mighty Defender, because they obeyed the laws he had given them.

The Lord Punishes Antiochus
(1 Maccabees 6:1–7; 2 Maccabees 1:11–17)

9 ¹About this time Antiochus was retreating in disorder from Persia, ²where he had entered the city of Persepolis and had attempted to rob a temple and take control of the city. The people took up arms and attacked Antiochus, forcing his army to retreat in disgrace. ³When he reached Ecbatana, he was told what had happened to the forces of Nicanor and Timothy. ⁴He became furious and decided to make the Jews pay for the defeat he had suffered. So he ordered his chariot driver not to stop until they reached Jerusalem. With great arrogance he said, "I will turn Jerusalem into a graveyard full of Jews."

But he did not know that he was heading straight for God's judgment. ⁵In fact, as soon as he had said these words, the all-seeing Lord, the God of Israel, struck him down with an invisible but fatal blow. He was seized with sharp intestinal pains for which there was no relief— ⁶a fitting punishment for the man who had tortured others in so many terrible ways! ⁷But this in no way caused him to give up his pride. Instead he became more arrogant than ever, and breathing out fiery threats against the Jews, he gave orders to drive even faster. As a result he fell out of his chariot with such a thud that it made every bone in his body ache. ⁸His arrogant pride made him think he had the superhuman strength to make ocean waves obey him and to weigh high mountains on a pair of scales. But suddenly he fell flat on the ground and had to be carried off on a stretcher, a clear sign to everyone of God's power. ⁹Even the eyes of this godless man were crawling with worms and he lived in terrible pain and agony. The stink was so bad that his entire army was sickened, ¹⁰and no one was able to come close enough to carry him around. Yet only a short while before, he thought he could take hold of the stars.

No one was able to come close enough. (9:10)

Antiochus Makes a Promise to God
(1 Maccabees 6:8–17)

¹¹Antiochus was deeply depressed and suffered constant pain because of the punishment that God had brought on him, so he finally came to his senses and gave up his arrogant pride. ¹²Then, when he could no longer endure his own stink, he said, "It is

right that all mortals should be subject to God and not think that they are his equal." [13]The time of the Lord's mercy had come to an end for Antiochus, but this worthless man made the Lord a promise: [14]"I once intended to level Jerusalem to the ground and make that holy city a graveyard full of Jews," he said, "but now I declare it a free city. [15]I had planned to throw out the dead bodies of the Jews and their children for the wild animals and the birds to eat, for I did not consider them worth burying. But now I intend to grant them the same privileges as the citizens of Athens enjoy. [16]I once looted the Temple and took its sacred utensils, but I will fill it with splendid gifts and with better utensils than before, and I will pay the cost of the sacrifices from my own resources. [17]Besides all this, I will become a Jew myself and go wherever people live, telling them of God's power."

Antiochus' Letter to the Jews

[18]Antiochus was in despair and could find no relief from his pain, because God was punishing him as he deserved, so he wrote the following letter to the Jews:

[19]"King Antiochus to the Jews, my most distinguished subjects. Warm greetings and best wishes for your health and prosperity.

[20]"I hope that you and your families are in good health and that all goes well with you. My hope is in God, [21]and I remember with a deep sense of joy the respect and kindness that you have shown me.

"On my way home from Persia I fell violently ill, and so I thought it best to begin making plans for the general welfare of the people. [22]I have not given up hopes of getting well; in fact I am fully confident that I will recover. [23]But I recall that my father used to appoint a successor whenever he went on a military campaign east of the Euphrates. [24]He did this so that if something unexpected happened, or if some bad news came back, then his subjects would not be afraid, for they knew who had been left in command. [25]Also, I know how the rulers along the frontiers of my kingdom are constantly on the lookout for any opportunity that may

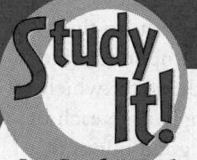

Is God Violent?

The Maccabees believed God punished evil, therefore God caused their military victories. This thinking can lead us to believe that God is in favor of war and will assist in any violence necessary to defeat evil people. But doesn't this sound odd, when we've been taught to believe that God is all-loving, compassionate, merciful, and more? Does God have a split personality?

No. Jesus made it very clear to us: God is love and calls us to love one another, even our enemies.

So why is God painted to be a great warrior in the Old Testament? The Jews were special to God—God's Chosen People. The survival of the Jews, their faith and customs, and the Temple—all were part of God's will for them. War was what they knew, and they drew upon war as the only way they knew to survive. So it made sense to them that God wanted them to fight violence with violence and that God was behind their victories.

But Jesus corrected this way of thinking and told us that *love*, not violence, was the way to live. We need to trust that God is still close to us, protecting us—even in our suffering. War might sometimes be justifiable in self-defense, but violence and war are not the ultimate answers to injustice. Love, forgiveness, and mercy are.

— 2 Maccabees, chapter 9

come along. That is why I have appointed my son Antiochus to succeed me as king. I have frequently entrusted him to your care and recommended him to you when I went on my regular visits to the provinces east of the Euphrates. (He is receiving a copy of the letter which follows.) 26 Now I strongly urge each of you to keep in mind the good things that I have done for you, both individually and as a nation, and to continue in your good will toward me and my son. 27 I am confident that he will treat you with fairness and kindness, just as I have always done."

28 And so, this murderer, who had cursed God, suffered the same terrible agonies he had brought on others, and then died a miserable death in the mountains of a foreign land. 29 One of his close friends, Philip, took his body home; but, because he was afraid of Antiochus' son, he went on to King Ptolemy Philometor of Egypt.

The Rededication of the Temple
(1 Maccabees 4:36–61)

10 1 Judas Maccabeus and his followers, under the leadership of the Lord, recaptured the Temple and the city of Jerusalem. 2 They tore down the altars which foreigners had set up in the marketplace and destroyed the other places of worship that had been built. 3 They purified the Temple and built a new altar. Then, with new fire started by striking flint, they offered sacrifice for the first time in two years, burned incense, lighted the lamps, and set out the sacred loaves. 4 After they had done all this, they lay face down on the ground and prayed that the Lord would never again let such disasters strike them. They begged him to be merciful when he punished them for future sins and not hand them over any more to barbaric, pagan Gentiles. 5 They rededicated the Temple on the twenty-fifth day of the month of Kislev, the same day of the same month on which the Temple had been desecrated by the Gentiles. 6 The happy celebration lasted eight days, like the Festival of Shelters, and the people remembered how only a short time before, they had spent the Festival of Shelters wandering like wild animals in the mountains and living in caves. 7 But now, carrying green palm branches and sticks decorated with ivy, they paraded around, singing grateful praises to him who had brought about the purification of his own Temple. 8 Everyone agreed that the entire Jewish nation should celebrate this festival each year.

Ptolemy Macron Commits Suicide

9 The days of Antiochus Epiphanes had come to an end. 10 Now we will tell about Antiochus Eupator, the son of this godless man, and give a summary of the evil effects of his wars. 11 When he became king he appointed a man by the name of Lysias to be in charge of the affairs of state and to be chief governor of Greater Syria, 12 replacing Ptolemy Macron, who had been the first governor to treat the Jews fairly. Macron had established peaceful relations with them in an attempt to make up for the wrongs they had suffered. 13 As a result the King's Friends went to Eupator and accused Macron of treachery, because he had abandoned the island of Cyprus, which King Philometor of Egypt had placed under his command, and had gone over to Antiochus Epiphanes. In fact, everyone called Macron a traitor. No longer able to maintain the respect that his office demanded, he committed suicide by taking poison.

Judas Maccabeus Defeats the Idumeans
(1 Maccabees 5:1–8)

14 When Gorgias became governor of Idumea, he kept a force of mercenaries and attacked the Jews at every opportunity. 15 Not only this, but the Idumeans themselves controlled certain strategic fortresses and were constantly harassing the Jews. They welcomed those who fled from Jerusalem and did everything they could to keep the country in a perpetual state of war. 16 So Judas Maccabeus and his men, after offering prayers for God's help, rushed out and made a vigorous attack against the Idumean fortresses. 17 They beat back those who were defending the walls and captured the fortresses, killing everyone they found, a total of about 20,000 people.

18About 9,000 of the enemy, however, managed to take refuge in two easily defended forts, with everything they needed to withstand a siege. 19Judas had to go on to some other places in the country, where he was more urgently needed, but he left behind Simon and Joseph, together with Zacchaeus and his men. This force was large enough to continue the siege, 20but some of Simon's men were greedy, and when they were offered 140 pounds of silver, they let some of the enemy escape from the forts. 21When Judas heard what had happened, he called together the leaders of his troops and accused those men of selling their brothers by setting their enemies free to fight against them. 22Then he executed the traitors and immediately captured the two forts. 23Judas was always successful in battle, and in his assault on those two forts he killed more than 20,000 men.

Judas Defeats Timothy

24Timothy, who had been defeated by the Jews once before, had gathered a large number of cavalry from Asia and a tremendous force of mercenary troops and was now advancing to take Judea by armed attack. 25But as the enemy forces were approaching, Judas and his men prayed to God. They put on sackcloth, threw dirt on their heads, 26and lay face downward on the steps of the altar, begging God to help them by fighting against their enemies, as he had promised in his Law.

27When they had finished praying, they took up their weapons, went out a good distance from Jerusalem, and stopped for the night not far from the enemy. 28At daybreak the two armies joined in battle. The Jewish forces depended upon both their bravery and their trust in the Lord for victory, while the enemy relied only on their ability to fight fiercely. 29When the fighting was at its worst, the enemy saw five handsome men riding on horses with gold bridles and leading the Jewish forces. 30These five men surrounded Judas, protecting him with their own armor and showering the enemy with arrows and thunderbolts. The enemy forces then became so confused and bewildered that they broke ranks, and the Jews cut them to pieces, 31slaughtering 20,500 infantry and 600 cavalry.

32Timothy himself escaped to the strongly defended fort of Gezer, where his brother Chaereas was in command. 33Judas and his men besieged the fort for four days with great enthusiasm, 34but those inside trusted to the security of their positions and shouted all sorts of terrible insults against the Jews and their God. 35At dawn on the fifth day, twenty of Judas' men, burning with anger at these insults, bravely climbed the wall and with savage fury chopped down everyone they met. 36At the same time, others climbed the walls on the other side of the fort and set the towers on fire. Many of the enemy were burned to death as the flames spread. A third force broke down the gates and let in the rest of Judas' men to capture the city. 37Timothy had hidden in a cistern, but they killed

---

Pray It!

Prayer for Protection

Read Psalm 140. Judas and the other Jews who were crying out to God for help may have said a prayer similar to this one. Page through the Book of Psalms and see how many other prayers you can find that have a similar theme. Notice that there are two ideas woven through these prayers: asking God for help and protection and praising God for his love and mercy.

Try writing your own prayer to God for protection.

— 2 Maccabees 10:25–26

When the Maccabees won control of the Temple, they immediately cleaned and purified it. Who is responsible for keeping your church clean and beautiful?

Twenty of Judas' men . . . bravely climbed the wall.
(10:35)

him, as well as his brother Chaereas and
Apollophanes.

38 When it was over, the Jews celebrated
by singing hymns and songs of thanksgiving
to the Lord, who had shown them great
kindness and had given them victory.

Judas Maccabeus Defeats Lysias
(1 Maccabees 4:26–35)

11 **1** Not long after Timothy was defeated, Lysias, the King's guardian and
relative, and head of the government, heard
what had happened. He became angry **2** and
led 80,000 infantry and all his cavalry against
the Jews with the intention of turning
Jerusalem into a Greek city. **3** The Temple
would be taxed, as were all Gentile places of
worship, and the office of High Priest would
be up for sale each year. **4** Lysias was so
pleased with his tens of thousands of
infantry, his thousands of cavalry, and his
eighty elephants that he failed to take into

account the power of God. **5** He invaded
Judea and attacked the fort of Bethzur, about
twenty miles south of Jerusalem.

6 When Judas and his men heard that
Lysias was laying siege to their forts, they
and all the people cried and wept, begging
the Lord to send a good angel to save them.
7 Judas was the first to take up his weapons,
and he urged the others to join him in risk-
ing their lives to help the other Jews. So
with great eagerness they all set out together. **8** But they had not gone far from
Jerusalem, when suddenly they noticed they
were being led by a horseman dressed in
white and carrying gold weapons. **9** Immediately all of them together thanked God for
his mercy; he had made them brave enough
to attack not only men, but even the most
savage animals or even walls of iron. **10** So
they marched in battle formation, and with
them went the one whom the Lord in his
mercy had sent to fight on their side. **11** Then
they charged into the enemy like lions,
killing 11,000 infantry and 1,600 cavalry, and
forcing the rest to run for their lives. **12** Most
of those who ran were wounded and had
lost their weapons, and Lysias himself managed to escape only because he ran away like
a coward.

Lysias Makes Peace with the Jews
(1 Maccabees 6:56–61)

13 Lysias was no fool. As he thought about
the defeat he had suffered, he realized it was
because the mighty God had fought for the
Jews, making it impossible for them to be
defeated. So he sent a message to the Jews,
14 trying to persuade them to agree to a just
settlement and promising to do all he could
to make the king friendly toward them.*ʳ*
15 Judas Maccabeus considered what would
be best for the people, and so he agreed to
all the proposals Lysias had made, since the
king had granted every written request that
Judas had presented to Lysias.*ˢ*

ʳ **11:14** to do . . . them; *Greek unclear.*   *ˢ* **11:15** since . . . Lysias; *or* and the king granted every written request
that Judas presented to Lysias.

The Letter of Lysias to the Jews

16Here is a copy of the letter which Lysias wrote to the Jews:

"Lysias to the Jewish people, greetings. **17**Your representatives John and Absalom have delivered to me the official document you sent with them, and they have asked me to agree to what is contained in it. **18**I have informed the king of the matters that needed to be brought to his attention, and he has agreed to do whatever is possible. **19**If you continue to be loyal to the government, I will do everything I can in the future to benefit your nation. **20**I have instructed your representatives and mine to meet with you to discuss the details of these matters. **21**May all go well with you. Dated the twenty-fourth day of the month of Dioscorinthius in the year 148."*t*

The King's Letter to Lysias

22Here is a copy of the King's letter:

"King Antiochus to the honorable Lysias, greetings. **23**Now that my father has gone to be with the gods, I want the subjects of my kingdom to conduct their own affairs without interference. **24**I understand that the Jews do not wish to adopt the Greek way of life, as my father had intended, but prefer their own way of life and have requested that they be allowed to live according to their own customs. **25**Since I desire that they live undisturbed like the other nations in my empire, I hereby decree that their Temple be restored to them and that they be allowed to live according to the customs of their ancestors. **26**Please inform them of this decision and assure them of my friendship, so that they may conduct their own affairs in peace, without anything to worry about."

27Here is a copy of the king's letter to the Jewish people:

"King Antiochus to the Jewish leaders and all the Jews, greetings. **28**I hope that all is going well for you. I am in good health. **29**Menelaus has informed me of

your desire to return home and attend to your own affairs. **30**So then, those of you who return home by the thirtieth of the month of Xanthicus may rest assured that you have nothing to fear. **31**You may continue to observe your food laws and other laws, as you used to do, and no Jew will be punished for any crime done in ignorance. **32**I am sending Menelaus to set your minds at ease. **33**May all go well with you. Dated the fifteenth day of the month of Xanthicus in the year 148."*t*

The Letter of the Romans to the Jews

34The Romans also sent the Jews the following letter:

"Quintus Memmius and Titus Manius, representatives of the Romans, to the Jews, greetings. **35**We are in complete agreement with all that has been granted to you by the honorable Lysias. **36**We are now on our way to Antioch, so please examine carefully those matters that Lysias referred to the king. Then send a reply to us immediately so that we can represent your best interests before him. Do this as soon as you can, **37**without delay, so that we may know what you have decided. **38**May all go well with you. Dated the fifteenth day of the month of Xanthicus in the year 148."

The Jews of Joppa Are Murdered

12 **1**When the peace agreement between the Jews and the Syrians was completed, Lysias returned to the king, and the Jews went back to their farming. **2**But some of the local governors, Timothy and Apollonius son of Gennaeus, as well as Hieronymus and Demophon, would not let them live in peace; and neither would Nicanor, the commander of the mercenaries from Cyprus.

3About this time, the people of Joppa did a cruel thing to the Jews of their city. They pretended to be friendly to the Jews and invited them and their families to go sailing with them on ships they had provided. **4**Since all the people of the town had decided to do this, the Jews suspected nothing and

t **11:21, 33** THE YEAR 148: *This corresponds to 164 B.C.*

accepted the invitation out of a feeling of good will. But when they were out at sea, the people of Joppa drowned all two hundred of them.

The people of Joppa drowned all two hundred of them. (12:4)

5As soon as Judas heard of this inhuman thing that had been done to those Jews, he informed his men. 6After they had prayed to God, the just judge, they attacked the murderers. Under cover of darkness they set fire to the harbor, burning all the ships, and killing everyone they found hiding there. 7The gates of the city were locked, so Judas withdrew; but he was determined to return at some other time and wipe out everyone living there.

8Judas heard that the people of Jamnia had plans to kill the Jews of their city also. 9So he attacked Jamnia at night, setting fire to its harbor and the ships there. The flames could be seen as far as Jerusalem, thirty miles away.

Judas' Victories in the Region of Gilead
(1 Maccabees 5:9–54)

10When Judas and his men were about a mile away from Jamnia on their way to meet Timothy in battle, they were attacked by more than 5,000 Arabs, supported by 500 cavalry. 11It was a hard fight, but with the help of God they defeated these desert tribesmen, who then asked to be on friendly terms with the Jews, promising to give them some livestock and offering to help them in other ways as well. 12Judas thought their friendship might prove useful in many ways,

so he agreed to make peace with them; after that the Arabs returned to their tents.

13Judas also attacked the heavily fortified walled city of Caspin. The people who lived there were a mixed population of Gentiles 14who relied on the strength of their walls and felt confident that they had enough food stored up to last through a siege. So they made fun of Judas and his men, shouting out insults against them and profanities against their God. 15But the Jews prayed to the Almighty Lord of the universe, who had torn down the walls of Jericho in the days of Joshua without using battering rams or siege weapons. Then they made a fierce attack against the wall 16and because it was God's will, they captured the city. The Jews slaughtered so many people that a nearby lake, which was about a quarter of a mile wide, seemed to be overflowing with blood.

Judas Defeats Timothy's Army
(1 Maccabees 5:37–44)

17From the city of Caspin, Judas and his men marched about 95 miles, until they came to the Jewish settlement of Charax, near the city of Tob. 18But they did not find Timothy there, because he had already left the region. He had been able to do nothing there except leave behind a strong garrison in one place. 19Two of Judas' generals, Dositheus and Sosipater, attacked the garrison and killed all 10,000 men stationed there. 20Then Judas divided his army into several divisions, placing Dositheus and Sosipater each in command of a division, and hurried after Timothy, who had a force of 120,000 infantry and 2,500 cavalry. 21When Timothy found out that Judas was coming after him, he sent the women and the children on ahead with the baggage to the city of Karnaim, which was almost impossible to besiege or even to reach, because of the narrow passes that led up to it. 22But at the moment that Judas' first division came into sight, the enemy forces were thrown into panic by a vision sent by God, who sees everything. In terror they began to run wildly about and many of them were wounded by the swords of their own men. 23So Judas and his men pursued them as hard as they

He sent the women and the children on ahead with the baggage. (12:21)

could, killing at least 30,000 of the enemy. [24]Timothy himself was captured by the troops of Dositheus and Sosipater. But he was very shrewd and managed to convince them that many of their relatives were his prisoners and would be put to death if anything happened to him. [25]Finally, after he had promised to send their relatives home safely, they let him go free.

Judas Wins Other Victories
(1 Maccabees 5:45–54)

[26]Next, Judas attacked the city of Karnaim and the temple of the goddess Atargatis there, killing 25,000 people [27]and completely destroying both the city and the temple. Then he attacked the fortified city of Ephron where Lysias and[u] people of all nationalities were living. Strong young men took up their positions in front of the walls and fought bravely, while inside the city were stored large quantities of military supplies and weapons. [28]But the Jews prayed for help to the Lord, who crushes the power of his enemies. So they captured the city and killed about 25,000 people. [29]From there they hurried on to the city of Beth Shan, seventy-five miles north of Jerusalem. [30]The Jews there told Judas how kindly the people of the city had treated them, especially during hard

times. [31]So Judas and his men thanked the people and urged them to show the same good will toward the Jews in the future. Then they left for Jerusalem, where they arrived shortly before the Harvest Festival.

Judas Defeats Gorgias

[32]After Pentecost (as the Harvest Festival is called in Greek) Judas and his men quickly marched out against Gorgias, the governor of Idumea, [33]who met them with 3,000 infantry and 400 cavalry. [34]In the battle that followed, a few Jews were killed. [35]Then a Jew from the city of Tob,[v] a powerful cavalry soldier by the name of Dositheus, grabbed Gorgias by his cloak and started dragging him away by brute force, intending to take the worthless man alive. But suddenly one from the Thracian cavalry rushed at Dositheus and chopped off his arm, allowing Gorgias to escape to the city of Marisa.

[36]By now the Jewish men under the command of Esdrias had been fighting for a long time and were exhausted. So Judas prayed that the Lord would show that he was on their side and in command of their troops. [37]Then, while Judas sang a hymn in his native language as a battle cry, the Jews made a surprise attack against Gorgias and his men and put them to flight.

Prayers for Those Killed in Battle

[38]After the battle Judas led his men to the town of Adullam. It was the day before the Sabbath, so they purified themselves according to Jewish custom and then observed the holy day. [39]By the following day it was urgent that they gather up the bodies of the men who had been killed in battle and bury them in their family tombs. [40]But on each of the dead, hidden under their clothes, they found small images of the gods worshiped in Jamnia, which the Law forbids Jews to wear.

---

[u] **12:27** Lysias and; *some manuscripts do not have these words.*   [v] **12:35** a Jew from the city of Tob; *some manuscripts have* one of Bacenor's men.
12:32 Ex 23:16   **12:40** Deut 7:25

Praying for the Dead

Catholic Connections

The Jewish fighters killed in battle were found wearing small idols of a foreign god. This was a serious sin. Judas Maccabeus made an offering of silver and prayed for the sins of his dead warriors. He believed in the resurrection of the dead and that the dead must be made clean from their sins before they could enjoy God's reward of eternal life in heaven.

This passage supports the Catholic teaching about purgatory. Purgatory is a state where the souls of the dead who died in God's friendship are purified of any remaining sin and of any of the effects of sin which have yet to be healed. Then they will be ready to fully experience the joy of God's immense love in heaven. The Church teaches us to pray for the dead so that God will have mercy on them, forgive their sins, and bring them quickly to heaven.

This is a Catholic prayer (sometimes said with the rosary) that makes this plea to God:

O my Jesus, forgive us our sins, and save us from the fires of hell. Lead all the souls to heaven, especially those in most need of your mercy. Amen.

— 2 Maccabees 12:39–45

Everyone then knew why these men had been killed. [41]So they praised the ways of the Lord, the just judge, who reveals what is hidden, [42]and they begged him that this sin might be completely blotted out. Then, Judas, that great man, urged the people to keep away from sin, because they had seen for themselves what had happened to those men who had sinned. [43]He also took up a collection from all his men, totaling about four pounds of silver, and sent it to Jerusalem to provide for a sin offering. Judas did this noble thing because he believed in the resurrection of the dead. [44]If he had not believed that the dead would be raised, it would have been foolish and useless to pray for them. [45]In his firm and devout conviction that all of God's faithful people would receive a wonderful reward, Judas made provision for a sin offering to set free from their sin those who had died.

Menelaus Is Put to Death

13 [1]In the year 149[w] Judas Maccabeus and his followers found out that Antiochus Eupator was marching against Judea with a large army [2]and that Lysias, the young king's guardian and the head of his government, was with him. They[x] had a force of Greek troops consisting of 110,000 infantry, 5,300 cavalry, 22 elephants, and 300 chariots with sharp blades attached to their wheels.

[3]Menelaus, trying to take advantage of the situation, went over to their side and urged them on, not because he was concerned for the country, but because he hoped to be confirmed as High Priest. [4]But God, the King of kings, made Antiochus furious with Menelaus. Lysias proved to Antiochus that this criminal had been the source of all his troubles, so Antiochus ordered him to be

w **13:1** THE YEAR 149: *This corresponds to 163 B.C.*   x **13:2** They; *Greek unclear.*

Check out what Jesus has to say about violence in Matthew 26:51–52.

taken to the city of Berea and put to death in the way that it was done there. 5In that city there is a tower about 75 feet high. It is filled with ashes, and all around the inside of the tower is a platform sloping down into the ashes. 6People accused of crimes against the gods or of any other serious crime are taken there and thrown down to their death. 7Menelaus was put to death in that way, without even having the privilege of a burial, 8and that was just what he deserved. He had often profaned the sacred ashes of the altar fire in the Temple, and now he met his death in ashes.

A Battle Near the City of Modein

9King Antiochus arrogantly continued his barbaric invasion of Judah, intending to deal with the Jews more harshly than his father had ever done. 10When Judas learned of this, he told the people to pray to the Lord day and night, because they were in danger of losing their Law, their country, and their holy Temple. As never before, they needed his help and protection 11to keep their newly restored country from falling into the hands of godless Gentiles. 12For three days the people did nothing but lie face down on the ground, fasting and crying, begging the merciful Lord for his help. Then Judas spoke words of encouragement to the people, urging them to get ready for action.

13Afterward, Judas met privately with the Jewish leaders and decided to march out with God's help to battle against the king, rather than to wait for Antiochus to invade Judea and besiege Jerusalem. 14Then, leaving the outcome of the battle to the Creator of the world, Judas encouraged his men to fight bravely and to be willing to die for their laws, the Temple, Jerusalem, their country, and their whole way of life. They set up camp near the city of Modein. 15Judas gave his men the battle cry, "Victory comes from God," and that night, with a picked force of his bravest young men, he attacked the area near the king's tent and killed as many as 2,000 men. They also stabbed to death*y* the lead elephant and its keeper. 16Everyone in camp was terrified and in panic when Judas and his men finally left victoriously 17just before dawn. The help and protection of the Lord had made all this possible.

Antiochus the Fifth Makes a Treaty with the Jews
(1 Maccabees 6:48–63)

18This taste of Jewish daring was enough to convince King Antiochus that he had to find some better way of capturing the Jewish positions. 19He attacked the strong Jewish fort of Bethzur, but was repeatedly beaten back and finally defeated. 20Judas sent supplies to the men who were defending the fort, 21but a Jewish soldier by the name of Rhodocus gave some secret information to the enemy. He was found out, however, caught, and put to death. 22The king made a second attempt to come to terms with the people of Bethzur, and when he had reached an agreement with them, he withdrew his forces. Then he went to attack Judas, but again he was defeated. 23Meanwhile, Philip had been left at Antioch in charge of the government, but King Antiochus learned that he had revolted. The king did not know what to do, so he initiated peace talks with the Jews, agreed to their terms, and promised to be just in his treatment of them. To put the treaty into effect, he offered a sacrifice, gave a generous gift to show his respect for the Temple, 24and graciously received Judas Maccabeus. After that, the king appointed Hegemonides to be governor of the territory between the cities of Ptolemais and Gerar, 25and then he himself went on to Ptolemais. The people there were angry because of the treaty he had made with the Jews—so angry, in fact, that they wanted the treaty canceled. 26But Lysias made a public speech, defending the treaty as well as he could. After he had calmed the people down and convinced them that he was right, he returned to Antioch.

In this way King Antiochus' invasion was turned into a retreat.

y 13:15 Probable text stabbed to death; Greek unclear.

Peace Talks

King Antiochus saw that war was getting him nowhere, fast! So he sat down with the Jews and tried to talk out a peaceful solution. This isn't an easy way out. In fact, the challenge to make peace through talking and compromise can sometimes be more challenging than a bloody battle.

How do you deal with the battles in your life? Do you enlist friends to turn on the person who hurt you? Do you turn to violence? Or do you try to talk things out? Will you admit where you're wrong and try to understand the other person's actions and feelings?

Next time you find yourself fighting with someone, try a peace talk. Maybe ask for help from a teacher, parent, counselor, or friend who has strong relationship-building skills. Pray to God for wisdom and courage. And peace.

— 2 Maccabees 13:23–26

Alcimus Speaks against Judas
(1 Maccabees 7:1–21)

14 ¹Three years later, Judas and his men learned that Demetrius son of Seleucus had sailed into the port of Tripolis with a powerful army and a fleet. ²It was reported that he had killed King Antiochus and his guardian Lysias and had taken over the country.

³There was a man by the name of Alcimus, who had formerly been High Priest but who had gladly adopted the Greek way of life during the revolt. Realizing that he could never again be High Priest

and fearful of what the Jews might do to him, ⁴he went to see King Demetrius in the year 151.ᶻ On this occasion he presented the king with a gold crown and a palm branch, together with some olive branches traditionally presented to the Temple, but he said nothing about his plans. ⁵Later, however, he got the chance to put his foolish plans into effect when Demetrius summoned him to a meeting of his advisers and asked him what the Jews were intending to do.

Alcimus said, ⁶"The followers of Judas Maccabeus think of themselves as devout and patriotic; they love war and are constantly inciting the people to rebellion and will never leave the nation in peace. ⁷It is their fault that I no longer hold the glorious position of High Priest, to which I am entitled by birth. And so I have come here, ⁸primarily out of a genuine concern for your interests as king, but also out of consideration for my own people, for the foolish policies of Judas and his followers have brought terrible suffering on our entire nation. ⁹When Your Majesty has examined all the details of these matters, please act in your

He went to see King Demetrius. (14:4)

usual kind and generous manner to relieve the oppression of our nation and its people. 10As long as Judas is alive, it will be impossible for our nation to enjoy peace."

Demetrius Sends Nicanor to Attack Judas

11As soon as Alcimus had finished his speech, the other advisers quickly seized this opportunity to arouse Demetrius' anger against Judas, because they also hated him. 12So King Demetrius immediately appointed Nicanor, who was the commander of his elephant forces, to be governor of Judea, and sent him there 13with orders to kill Judas, scatter his followers, and make Alcimus High Priest of the greatest Temple in all the world. 14All the foreigners in Judea, who had fled from Judas' attacks, now rushed to join forces with Nicanor, because they thought that any defeat or trouble that came to the Jews would be to their own advantage.

15The Jews heard that Nicanor was attacking and that the foreigners in their country were giving him their support. So they threw dirt on themselves and prayed to their God, who had chosen their nation as his possession forever and had never failed to help them in time of need. 16Then Judas, their leader, gave the orders, and they immediately marched out to engage the enemy in battle near the village of Adasa.a 17Judas' brother Simon was fighting Nicanor but was gradually losing the battle because of an unexpected move on the part of the enemy. 18However, when Nicanor heard how bravely and courageously Judas and his men were fighting for their country, he decided not to settle the matter in battle. 19Instead, he sent Posidonius, Theodotus, and Mattathias to make a treaty with the Jews.

20After the terms of the treaty had been worked out in detail, Nicanor informed his troops, and they unanimously agreed. 21Then a day was set on which the leaders would meet

in private. Ceremonial chairs were brought out from each camp and set up. 22Judas had taken the precaution of placing battle-ready troops in strategic places, in case of sudden treachery on the part of the enemy. But the two leaders had a friendly meeting. 23Nicanor stayed on in Jerusalem for some time after that. He did not mistreat the Jews in any way, and even sent away the people who had come over to his side. 24The two men became the best of friends, and Judas was Nicanor's constant companion. 25Nicanor urged him to marry and start a family. So Judas did this and settled down to a peaceful life.

Nicanor Turns against Judas

26When Alcimus noticed how well Nicanor and Judas were getting along, he obtained a copy of the treaty and went to see King Demetrius. He told the king that Nicanor was disloyal to the government, because he had appointed the traitor Judas to be his successor. 27These false accusations infuriated the king, and in his anger he wrote to Nicanor, informing him that he was dissatisfied with the treaty and ordering him to arrest Judas Maccabeus and send him to Antioch at once.

28When this message reached Nicanor, he was hurt and didn't know what to do, because he did not like having to break an agreement with a man who had kept his part of the bargain. 29Yet it was impossible for him to ignore the king's command, so he began looking for a way to trap Judas. 30Judas, however, noticed that Nicanor was becoming hostile and rude toward him, and he knew that this was a bad sign. So he gathered a large number of his followers and went into hiding.

31When Nicanor realized that Judas had outsmarted him, he went to the great and holy Temple at the time when the priests were offering sacrifice and ordered them to surrender Judas to him. 32But the priests declared under oath that they had no idea where Judas was hiding. 33Then Nicanor raised his right

---

a **14:16** *Probable text* Adasa; *Greek* Dessau.
14:15–25 1 Macc 7:27, 28　**14:31** 1 Macc 7:29, 30

The Greek governor, Nicanor, betrayed his best friend, Judas Maccabeus. Nicanor felt forced to do this by the king. Do you agree with Nicanor?

arm in the direction of the Temple and made a solemn threat: "If you do not hand Judas over to me as a prisoner, I will level God's Temple to the ground, demolish this altar, and on this spot build a glorious temple to Dionysus." ³⁴Then he left, and immediately the priests lifted their arms toward heaven and prayed to God, the faithful Defender of our nation: ³⁵"Lord, you are in need of nothing, yet it has pleased you to place your Temple here and to live among us. ³⁶You alone are holy, and your Temple has only recently been purified, so now protect its holiness forever."

Razis Dies for His Country

³⁷One of the leaders in Jerusalem, a man by the name of Razis, was denounced to Nicanor. It was said that he had helped his people in many ways and was so highly respected by them that he was known as "the Father of the Jews." ³⁸During the early days of the revolution he had risked his life for Judaism and had been brought to trial because of his loyalty. ³⁹Wanting to show clearly how much he disliked the Jews, Nicanor sent more than 500 soldiers to arrest Razis, ⁴⁰because he thought his arrest would be a crippling blow to the Jews. ⁴¹The soldiers were about to capture the tower where Razis had gone. They were forcing open the gates to the courtyard, and the order had been given to set the door on fire. Razis realized there was no escape, so he tried to commit suicide with his sword, ⁴²preferring to die with honor rather than suffer humiliation at the hands of evil men.

⁴³Under the pressure of the moment, Razis misjudged the thrust of the sword, and it did not kill him. So, while the soldiers were swarming into the room, he rushed to the wall and jumped off like a brave hero into the crowd below. ⁴⁴The crowd quickly moved back, and he fell in the space they left. ⁴⁵Still alive, and burning with courage, he got up, and with blood gushing from his wounds, he ran through the crowd and finally climbed a steep rock. ⁴⁶Now completely drained of blood, he tore out his intestines with both hands and threw them at the crowd, and as he did so, he prayed for the Lord of life and breath to give them back to him. That was how he died.

Nicanor's Cruel Plan

15 ¹Nicanor learned that Judas and his men were in the region of Samaria, and so he decided to attack them on a Sabbath, when he could do so without any danger to himself. ²The Jews who were forced to accompany his army begged him not to do such a cruel and savage thing, but to respect the day that the all-seeing God had honored and made the most holy of all days. ³Then Nicanor, the lowest creature on earth, asked if there was some sovereign ruler in heaven who had commanded them to honor the Sabbath. ⁴And the Jews replied, "Yes; the living Lord, who rules in heaven, commanded us to honor the Sabbath."

⁵But Nicanor answered, "I am the ruler on earth, and I order you to take up your weapons and to do what the king commands." However, he did not succeed in carrying out his cruel plan.

Judas Prepares His Troops for Battle

⁶In his arrogance Nicanor had boasted that he would set up a monument in honor of his victory over Judas. ⁷But Judas was fully confident that the Lord would help him, ⁸so he urged his men not to be afraid of the enemy. He encouraged them to remember how the Almighty had helped them in times past and to rest assured that he would give them victory this time also. ⁹He renewed their hope by reading to them from the Law and the Prophets and by reminding them of the battles they had already won. ¹⁰When his men were ready for battle, he gave them their orders and at the same time pointed out how the Gentiles could not be trusted, because they never kept their treaties. ¹¹He armed all his men, not by encouraging them to trust in shields and spears, but by inspiring them with

---

"Lord, you are in need of nothing, yet it has pleased you to place your Temple here and to live among us" (2 Maccabees 14:35).

Intercession of the Saints

Catholic Connections

Judas is a powerful leader—he prepares his army through prayer and inspires them to be courageous. Before their battle with Nicanor, Judas has a vision about two highly respected Jews who have already died: Onias, the just and faithful High Priest of the Temple, and Jeremiah, the great prophet. In the vision, Onias says that Jeremiah "loves the Jewish people and offers many prayers for us" (2 Maccabees 15:14).

We believe that the faithful saints who have gone to heaven pray for us, as well. We believe in the Communion of Saints, which means that all believers, living and dead, are connected as one family. The saints in heaven intercede (go to God on our behalf) in prayer for us. The greatest saint of all is Mary, the mother of Jesus. That's why we tell her about our needs; we know her prayers to God for us are very powerful.

— 2 Maccabees 15:11–14

courageous words. He also lifted their morale by telling them about his dream, a kind of vision that they could trust in.

12 He told them that he had seen a vision of Onias, the former High Priest, that great and wonderful man of humble and gentle disposition, who was an outstanding orator and who had been taught from childhood how to live a virtuous life. With outstretched arms Onias was praying for the entire Jewish nation. **13** Judas then saw an impressive white-haired man of great dignity and authority. **14** Onias said: "This is God's prophet Jeremiah, who loves the Jewish people and offers many prayers for us and for Jerusalem, the holy city."

15 Then Jeremiah stretched out his right hand and gave Judas a gold sword, saying as he did so, **16** "This holy sword is a gift from God. Take it and destroy your enemies."

17 The eloquent words that Judas spoke encouraged everyone to be brave, and inspired boys to fight like men. Their city, their religion, and their Temple were in danger. So the Jews made up their minds not to waste any time, but to make a daring attack against the enemy and bravely decide their fate in hand-to-hand combat. **18** They were

not so concerned about their own families and relatives as they were about their sacred Temple. **19** And the people who had to stay in Jerusalem were deeply concerned about how a battle on open ground would turn out.

The Defeat and Death of Nicanor

20 Everyone was waiting to see who would win the battle. The enemy troops were already moving forward, with their cavalry on each

"This holy sword is a gift from God." (15:16)

side of them, and their elephants placed in strategic positions. 21 Judas Maccabeus looked at the huge enemy force, the variety of their weapons, and their fierce elephants. Then he raised his hands toward heaven and prayed to the Lord, who works miracles, because he knew that the Lord gives victory to those who deserve it, not to those who have a strong army. 22 Judas said: "Lord, when Hezekiah was king of Judah, you sent your angel, who killed 185,000 of King Sennacherib's men. 23 Now once again, Lord of heaven, send your good angel to make our enemies shake and tremble with fear. 24 With your great power, destroy these people who have slandered you and have come out to attack your chosen people." So Judas ended his prayer.

25 Nicanor and his army moved forward to the sound of trumpets and battle songs, 26 but Judas and his men went into battle calling on God for help. 27 So by fighting with their hands and praying to God in their hearts, the Jews killed more than 35,000 of the enemy. How grateful they were for the help they had received from God! 28 When the battle was over and they were going home celebrating their victory, they noticed Nicanor in full armor lying dead on the battlefield. 29 Then with loud shouts they praised the Lord in their native language.

30 Judas Maccabeus, who had always fought with all his body and soul for his own people, never losing the patriotism of his youth, ordered his men to cut off Nicanor's head and right arm and to take them to Jerusalem. 31 When they arrived in the city, he called together all the people, stationed the priests before the altar, and sent for the men in the fort. 32 He showed them the head of the evil Nicanor and the arm which that wicked man had arrogantly stretched out against the sacred Temple of the Almighty God. 33 Then he cut out the tongue of that godless man, promising to feed it bit by bit to the birds and to hang up his head opposite the Temple, as evidence of what his foolishness did for him. 34 Everyone there looked up to heaven and praised the Lord, who had revealed his power and had kept his Temple from being defiled. 35 Judas hung Nicanor's head from the wall of the fort, as a clear proof to everyone of the Lord's help. 36 By unanimous vote it was decided that this day would never be forgotten, but would be celebrated each year on the eve of Mordecai's Day, *b* which is the thirteenth day of the twelfth month, called Adar in Aramaic.

Concluding Words

37 That is how things turned out for Nicanor. The city of Jerusalem remained in the possession of the Jewish people from that time on, so I will end my story here. 38 If it is well written and to the point, I am pleased; if it is poorly written and uninteresting, I have still done my best. 39 We know it is unhealthy to drink wine or water alone, whereas wine mixed with water makes a delightfully tasty drink. So also a good story skillfully written gives pleasure to those who read it. With this I conclude.

b **15:36** MORDECAI'S DAY: *The Festival of Purim (see Esth 9:17–22).*
15:22 2 Kings 19:35   **15:25–35** 1 Macc 7:43–50   **15:36** 1 Macc 7:49

Your Next Step — Congratulations on finishing the Second Book of the Maccabees! Use this space to write your thoughts and questions about this book. If you are following the suggested reading plan, move ahead to the Gospel of John in the New Testament. John emphasizes that Jesus is the key to the resurrection.

Like a volcano that violently and surprisingly erupts, heaping steaming lava upon a city that was minding its own business . . . probably that's what it felt like when Job's good and faithful life shattered to pieces. That's often what tragedy and suffering feel like to us, too. We don't see it coming, we didn't do anything to deserve it, and it shakes our peaceful life to its very core.

Why? Why does God let innocent people suffer? That is the big question in the Book of Job. It is one of the greatest mysteries we ponder in our world. As Job's dramatic story unfolds and you enter into the intense discussions about God's justice, you will learn more about God's deep and awesome wisdom.

Chap 1:13–22

Headlines

- Tragedy: Job Loses Everything! (1:13–22)
- Curse the Day I Was Born! (3:1–26)
- Friends Blame Job for His Troubles (11:1–20)
- Job Argues His Case (31:5–40)
- Young Bystander Speaks Out (32:1–22)
- God Speaks, Ends Debate! (38:1–41)
- Job Repents, Receives Blessing (chapter 42)

FACTOIDS

Who are the central characters? Job; his three friends, Bildad, Zophar, and Eliphaz; Elihu, a young bystander; and God.

Who wrote this book? An unknown author or authors wrote this book to address questions about suffering, integrity, and the mysterious ways of God, and to teach us about trust.

What literary style is used? Folktale, with poetic speeches.

Who are the young people in this book? Elihu, a young man who had his own ideas to add to the debate between Job and his friends.

Important themes

- Tragedy and suffering happen to everyone and are not punishments sent by God.
- No matter what emotions we feel or thoughts we have, we can share them openly with God.
- God's ways are far beyond our ability to understand, and trusting in God is the only way to have peace of mind and heart.

JOB

Satan tests Job

1 ¹There was a man named Job, living in the land of Uz,ᵃ who worshiped God and was faithful to him. He was a good man, careful not to do anything evil. ²He had seven sons and three daughters, ³and owned seven thousand sheep, three thousand camels, one thousand head of cattle, and five hundred donkeys. He also had a large number of servants and was the richest man in the East.

⁴Job's sons used to take turns giving a feast, to which all the others would come, and they always invited their three sisters to join them. ⁵The morning after each feast, Job would get up early and offer sacrifices for each of his children in order to purify them. He always did this because he thought that one of them might have sinned by insulting God unintentionally.

⁶When the day came for the heavenly beingsᵇ to appear before the LORD, Satanᶜ was there among them. ⁷The LORD asked him, "What have you been doing?"

Satan answered, "I have been walking here and there, roaming around the earth."

⁸"Did you notice my servant Job?" the LORD asked. "There is no one on earth as faithful and good as he is. He worships me and is careful not to do anything evil."

⁹Satan replied, "Would Job worship you if he got nothing out of it? ¹⁰You have always protected him and his family and everything he owns. You bless everything he does, and you have given him enough cattle to fill the whole country. ¹¹But now suppose you take away everything he has—he will curse you to your face!"

¹²"All right," the LORD said to Satan, "everything he has is in your power, but you must not hurt Job himself." So Satan left.

The Fall from a Good Life

What happens to Job is very sad. In the space of a few minutes, he gets the news that all his animals, servants, and even his children have been stolen or killed. It is also possible for us to experience sudden loss. A terrible accident, sickness, a violent fight, death, divorce, natural disaster—life can change for us in an instant! Our good and solid life falls apart, and chaos and sadness take over.

That's why it's so important to be thankful for all you have been given, and to appreciate all of it—*today*. Say thanks when someone is kind to you. Notice the ways your parents show their love for you, and find ways to show it back. Take some time to just hang out with brothers and sisters—what if they weren't there tomorrow? Cherish the good times you have with your friends.

Most of all, *thank God* for all the blessings in your life: family, friends, talents, health, your home, and everything you enjoy doing. Being thankful when times are good helps us remember that God is also with us during times of tragedy and loss.

— Job, chapter 1

ᵃ **1:1** UZ: *An area whose exact location is unknown.*   ᵇ **1:6** HEAVENLY BEINGS: *Supernatural beings who serve God in heaven.*   ᶜ **1:6** SATAN: *A supernatural being whose name indicates he was regarded as the opponent of human beings.*
1:6 Gen 6:2; Job 38:7; Ps 29:1   **1:9–11** Rev 12:10

Job's Children and Wealth Are Destroyed

13 One day when Job's children were having a feast at the home of their oldest brother, 14 a messenger came running to Job. "We were plowing the fields with the oxen," he said, "and the donkeys were in a nearby pasture. 15 Suddenly the Sabeans[d] attacked and stole them all. They killed every one of your servants except me. I am the only one who escaped to tell you."

16 Before he had finished speaking, another servant came and said, "Lightning struck the sheep and the shepherds and killed them all. I am the only one who escaped to tell you."

17 Before he had finished speaking, another servant came and said, "Three bands of Chaldean[e] raiders attacked us, took away the camels, and killed all your servants except me. I am the only one who escaped to tell you."

18 Before he had finished speaking, another servant came and said, "Your children were having a feast at the home of your oldest son, 19 when a storm swept in from the desert. It blew the house down and killed them all. I am the only one who escaped to tell you."

20 Then Job got up and tore his clothes in grief. He shaved his head and threw himself face downward on the ground. 21 He said, "I was born with nothing, and I will die with nothing. The LORD gave, and now he has taken away. May his name be praised!"

22 In spite of everything that had happened, Job did not sin by blaming God.

Satan Tests Job Again

2 ¹ When the day came for the heavenly beings to appear before the LORD again, Satan was there among them. ² The LORD asked him, "Where have you been?"

Satan answered, "I have been walking here and there, roaming around the earth."

"The LORD gave, and now he has taken away."
(1:21)

3 "Did you notice my servant Job?" the LORD asked. "There is no one on earth as faithful and good as he is. He worships me and is careful not to do anything evil. You persuaded me to let you attack him for no reason at all, but Job is still as faithful as ever."

4 Satan replied, "A person will give up everything in order to stay alive. 5 But now suppose you hurt his body—he will curse you to your face!"

6 So the LORD said to Satan, "All right, he is in your power, but you are not to kill him."

7 Then Satan left the LORD's presence and made sores break out all over Job's body. 8 Job went and sat by the garbage dump and took a piece of broken pottery to scrape his sores. 9 His wife said to him, "You are still as faithful as ever, aren't you? Why don't you curse God and die?"

10 Job answered, "You are talking nonsense! When God sends us something good, we welcome it. How can we complain when he sends us trouble?" Even in all this suffering Job said nothing against God.

---

d **1:15** SABEANS: *A tribe of wandering raiders from the south.*
1:21 Sir 40:1; 11:14

e **1:17** CHALDEANS: *A tribe of wandering raiders from the north.*

"Why don't you curse God and die?" (2:9)

Job's Friends Come

11 Three of Job's friends were Eliphaz, from the city of Teman, Bildad, from the land of Shuah, and Zophar, from the land of Naamah. When they heard how much Job had been suffering, they decided to go and comfort him. **12** While they were still a long way off they saw Job, but did not recognize him. When they did, they began to weep and wail, tearing their clothes in grief and throwing dust into the air and on their heads. **13** Then they sat there on the ground with him for seven days and nights without saying a word, because they saw how much he was suffering.

Job's Complaint to God

3 **1** Finally Job broke the silence and cursed the day on which he had been born.

Job

2-3 O God, put a curse on the day I was born;
put a curse on the night when I was conceived!
4 Turn that day into darkness, God.
Never again remember that day;
never again let light shine on it.

5 Make it a day of gloom and thick darkness;
cover it with clouds, and blot out the sun.
6 Blot that night out of the year,
and never let it be counted again;
7 make it a barren, joyless night.
8 Tell the sorcerers to curse that day,
those who know how to control Leviathan.*ʃ*

Live It!

Being There Is Enough

Jenni was getting ready to attend a wake—her first one—for her best friend's dad. She felt sick to her stomach with nervousness because she didn't know what she would say or do. Have you ever been in a situation like this? A friend is suffering, and you don't know how to respond?

Job's friends rushed to his side as soon as they heard about his tragedies. They stayed with him seven days and nights! And they simply sat with him, quietly. No words were necessary.

Sometimes, this is all our friends need from us. Just to be there for them. Having the right words to say isn't important. Simply let them know you're there if they need you. Then just stay close.

Our presence is the best gift we can offer when someone is suffering.

— Job 2:11–13

ʃ **3:8** LEVIATHAN: *Some take this to be the crocodile, others a legendary monster. Magicians were thought to be able to make him cause eclipses of the sun.*
3:1–19 Jer 20:14–18 **3:3** Sir 23:14

Are any of your friends going through a difficult time? How can you show them you are there for them?

Pray It!

Let Me Feel Peace

Job finally lets his grief out in chapter 3. He doesn't hold back. He tells God exactly what he's feeling. Here is a prayer of a young person pouring her heart out to God. Would you feel okay praying like this?

Dear Lord,
Today it feels like everyone hates me. My parents are mad at me, and I'm grounded.
My friend Keesha is acting weird and pretty much ignoring me. I don't know what
her problem is. I played a horrible game, and my coach and the team really came
down hard on me. Geez, everybody has a bad day sometimes. My teachers don't even
notice I'm there. And worst of all, Jayden, who I thought was interested in me, started
going out with Angelana.
*   I hate my life! I don't even know why I'm here. Nobody cares, anyway.*
*   God, I need to feel some peace. Show me it won't always be like today. I know*
you love me, at least. I need your peace and love to fill me up so I can keep going.
Help me, Lord!

— Job, chapter 3

9 Keep the morning star from shining;
    give that night no hope of dawn.
10 Curse that night for letting me be born,
    for exposing me to trouble and grief.

11 I wish I had died in my mother's womb
    or died the moment I was born.
12 Why did my mother hold me on her
    knees?
    Why did she feed me at her breast?
13 If I had died then, I would be at rest now,
14   sleeping like the kings and rulers
    who rebuilt ancient palaces.
15 Then I would be sleeping like princes
    who filled their houses with gold and
    silver,
16   or sleeping like a stillborn child.
17 In the grave wicked people stop their evil,
    and tired workers find rest at last.
18 Even prisoners enjoy peace,
    free from shouts and harsh commands.
19 Everyone is there, the famous and the
    unknown,
    and slaves at last are free.

20 Why let people go on living in misery?
    Why give light to those in grief

21 They wait for death, but it never
    comes;
    they prefer a grave to any treasure.
22 They are not happy till they are dead and
    buried;
23   God keeps their future hidden
    and hems them in on every side.
24 Instead of eating, I mourn,
    and I can never stop groaning.
25 Everything I fear and dread comes true.
26 I have no peace, no rest,
    and my troubles never end.

The First Dialogue
(4:1—14:22)

4

Eliphaz

1-2 Job, will you be annoyed if I speak?
    I can't keep quiet any longer.
3 You have taught many people
    and given strength to feeble hands.
4 When someone stumbled, weak and tired,
    your words encouraged him to stand.

3:21 Rev 9:6

Job

The (Really, Really) Long Debate

After a week of being quietly present to Job in his grief, his friends try to make some sense out of things. From chapter 4 through chapter 32, Job and his friends get into a huge debate about why Job has suffered so much. Job's friends are certain his tragedies happened because Job or someone in his family sinned against God. They believe God punishes people who are unjust or wicked (this is what the Israelites believed about disaster, disease, and other problems). Job insists he has done nothing wrong to bring on his troubles. He feels like God has abandoned him and treated him unjustly.

What do you think? Are Job's friends correct when they say that God punishes us for our sins? Read on for the answer.

— Job, chapter 4

5 Now it's your turn to be in trouble,
   and you are too stunned to face it.
6 You worshiped God, and your life was
   blameless;
   and so you should have confidence and
   hope.
7 Think back now. Name a single case
   where someone righteous met with
   disaster.
8 I have seen people plow fields of evil
   and plant wickedness like seed;
   now they harvest wickedness and evil.
9 Like a storm, God destroys them in his
   anger.

10 The wicked roar and growl like lions,
   but God silences them and breaks their
   teeth.
11 Like lions with nothing to kill and eat,
   they die, and all their children are
   scattered.

12 Once a message came quietly,
   so quietly I could hardly hear it.
13 Like a nightmare it disturbed my sleep.
14   I trembled and shuddered;
   my whole body shook with fear.
15 A light breeze touched my face,
   and my skin crawled with fright.
16 I could see something standing there;
   I stared, but couldn't tell what it was.
   Then I heard a voice out of the silence:
17 "Can anyone be righteous in the sight of[g]
   God
   or be pure before[h] his Creator?
18 God does not trust his heavenly servants;
   he finds fault even with his angels.
19 Do you think he will trust a creature of
   clay,
   a thing of dust that can be crushed like
   a moth?
20 We may be alive in the morning,
   but die unnoticed before evening
   comes.
21 All that we have is taken away;
   we die, still lacking wisdom."

5 ¹Call out, Job. See if anyone answers.
   Is there any angel to whom you can
   turn?
2 To worry yourself to death with
   resentment
   would be a foolish, senseless thing
   to do.
3 I have seen fools who looked secure,
   but I called down a sudden curse on
   their homes.
4 Their children can never find safety;
   no one stands up to defend them in
   court.
5 Hungry people will eat the fool's crops—
   even the grain growing among
   thorns[i]—
   and thirsty people will envy his wealth.

g **4:17** righteous in the sight of; or more righteous than.   h **4:17** be pure before; or be more pure than.
i **5:5** Probable text even . . . thorns; Hebrew unclear.
4:13 Job 33:15

⁶Evil does not grow in the soil,
    nor does trouble grow out of the
        ground.
⁷No indeed! We bring trouble on
        ourselves,
    as surely as sparks fly up from a fire.ʲ

⁸If I were you, I would turn to God
    and present my case to him.
⁹We cannot understand the great things he
        does,
    and to his miracles there is no end.
¹⁰He sends rain on the land
    and he waters the fields.
¹¹Yes, it is God who raises the humble
    and gives joy to all who mourn.
¹²⁻¹³He upsets the plans of cunning
        people,
    and traps the wise in their own
        schemes,
    so that nothing they do succeeds;
¹⁴   even at noon they grope in darkness.
¹⁵But God saves the poorᵏ from death;
    he saves the needy from oppression.
¹⁶He gives hope to the poor and silences
        the wicked.

¹⁷Happy is the person whom God corrects!
    Do not resent it when he rebukes you.
¹⁸God bandages the wounds he makes;
    his hand hurts you, and his hand heals.
¹⁹Time after time he will save you from
        harm;
²⁰   when famine comes, he will keep you
        alive,
    and in war protect you from death.
²¹God will rescue you from slander;
    he will save you when destruction
        comes.
²²You will laugh at violence and hunger
    and not be afraid of wild animals.
²³The fields you plow will be free of rocks;
    wild animals will never attack you.
²⁴Then you will live at peace in your tent;
    when you look at your sheep, you will
        find them safe.

²⁵You will have as many children
    as there are blades of grass in a pasture.
²⁶Like wheat that ripens till harvest time,
    you will live to a ripe old age.
²⁷Job, we have learned this by long study.
    It is true, so now accept it.

6
Job

¹⁻²If my troubles and griefs were weighed
        on scales,
³   they would weigh more than the sands
        of the sea,
    so my wild words should not surprise
        you.
⁴Almighty God has shot me with arrows,
    and their poison spreads through my
        body.
    God has lined up his terrors against me.

⁵A donkey is content when eating grass,
    and a cow is quiet when eating hay.
⁶But who can eat flat, unsalted food?
    What taste is there in the white of an
        egg?
⁷I have no appetite for food like that,
    and everything I eat makes me sick.ˡ

⁸Why won't God give me what I ask?
    Why won't he answer my prayer?
⁹If only he would go ahead and kill me!
¹⁰If I knew he would, I would leap for joy,
    no matter how great my pain.
    I know that God is holy;
    I have never opposed what he
        commands.
¹¹What strength do I have to keep on
        living?
    Why go on living when I have no hope?
¹²Am I made of stone? Is my body bronze?
¹³I have no strength left to save myself;
    there is nowhere I can turn for help.

¹⁴In troubleᵐ like this I need loyal friends—
    whether I've forsaken God or not.

ʲ **5:7** *sparks fly up from a fire; or birds fly up to the sky.*   ᵏ **5:15** *Probable text* poor; *Hebrew unclear.*
ˡ **6:7** *Probable text* sick; *Hebrew unclear.*   ᵐ **6:14** *Probable text* trouble; *Hebrew unclear.*
5:9 Sir 43:32   **5:13** 1 Cor 3:19   **5:17** Prov 3:11, 12; Heb 12:5, 6   **5:18** Hos 6:1

**Eliphaz encourages Job to talk to God about his problems. Do you need to talk
with God about anything in your life?**

Job

15 But you, my friends, you deceive me like
   streams
      that go dry when no rain comes.
16 The streams are choked with snow and
   ice,
17   but in the heat they disappear,
      and the stream beds lie bare and dry.
18 Caravans get lost looking for water;
      they wander and die in the desert.
19 Caravans from Sheba and Tema search,
20   but their hope dies beside dry streams.
21 You are like[n] those streams to me,[o]
      you see my fate and draw back in fear.
22 Have I asked you to give me a gift
      or to bribe someone on my behalf
23   or to save me from some enemy or
      tyrant?

24 All right, teach me; tell me my faults.
      I will be quiet and listen to you.
25 Honest words are convincing,
      but you are talking nonsense.
26 You think I am talking nothing but wind;
      then why do you answer my words of
      despair?
27 You would even roll dice for orphan
   slaves
      and make yourselves rich off your
      closest friends!

"You think I am talking nothing but wind." (6:26)

28 Look me in the face. I won't lie.
29 You have gone far enough. Stop being
   unjust.
      Don't condemn me. I'm in the right.
30 But you think I am lying—
      you think I can't tell right from wrong.

7 ¹ Human life is like forced army service,
      like a life of hard manual labor,
2   like a slave longing for cool
      shade;
      like a worker waiting to be paid.

Open to Criticism?

Sometimes it feels so good to point out someone's faults to them, doesn't it? But what about when someone points out your faults to you? Do you react in anger? Do you brush it off as ridiculous? Do you automatically believe it and add it to your list of reasons you're no good?

Job is struggling to listen to his friends. It's usually a good idea to listen when people point out our faults. Look at yourself honestly: Is there some truth to what they say? Is that fault showing up in the things you say and do? Sometimes they are wrong, but sometimes they are right—especially if it's a person who knows you well. Instead of resenting someone for criticizing you, think of it as an opportunity to check and see if there is some room for personal growth and improvement.

— Job 6:24–25

---

n **6:21** *Probable text* like; *Hebrew* indeed.   o **6:21** *probable text* to me; *Hebrew unclear*

Pray It!

Honestly, God!

See how honest Job is in talking to God. He's upset with God and lets God know it. Of all the ways there are to pray, God loves it best when we just talk to him. Honestly. We can tell God everything that's on our mind—even what we think of him! God doesn't want us to just say what we think he wants to hear. He already knows our real thoughts, anyway, so why try to hide them?

Sit down and have a conversation with God, or write a letter to God in your journal. Tell God exactly what's going on in your life, how you feel about it, what disappointments you're experiencing, what makes you mad, what your questions and hopes and dreams are, and so on. Tell God everything.

We can be this honest with God. Anytime, anywhere—God welcomes it!

— Job 7:7–21

---

³Month after month I have nothing to live for;

night after night brings me grief.

⁴When I lie down to sleep, the hours drag;

I toss all night and long for dawn.

⁵My body is full of worms;

it is covered with scabs;

pus runs out of my sores.

⁶My days pass by without hope,

pass faster than a weaver's shuttle.ᵖ

⁷Remember, O God, my life is only a breath;

my happiness has already ended.

⁸You see me now, but never again.

If you look for me, I'll be gone.

⁹⁻¹⁰Like a cloud that fades and is gone,

we humans die and never return;

we are forgotten by all who knew us.

¹¹No! I can't be quiet!

I am angry and bitter.

I have to speak.

¹²Why do you keep me under guard?

Do you think I am a sea monster?�q

¹³I lie down and try to rest;

I look for relief from my pain.

¹⁴But you—you terrify me with dreams;

you send me visions and nightmares

¹⁵ until I would rather be strangled

than live in this miserable body.

¹⁶I give up; I am tired of living.

Leave me alone. My life makes no sense.

¹⁷Why are people so important to you?

Why pay attention to what they do?

¹⁸You inspect them every morning

and test them every minute.

¹⁹Won't you look away long enough

for me to swallow my spit?

"I give up; I am tired of living." (7:16)

ᵖ **7:6** WEAVER'S SHUTTLE: *A small device in the loom which carries threads back and forth rapidly in weaving cloth.*

�q **7:12** SEA MONSTER: *A reference to ancient stories in which sea monsters had to be guarded so that they would not escape and do damage.*

7:9, 10 Wis 2:1–4   **7:17** Ps 8:4; 144:3

Pleading Our Case with God

Last night, Mario's parents told him and his sister that they were getting a divorce. Today, his dad moved out of their house. Mario's head is spinning—he didn't see it coming. Was there something he could have done to stop it? Could he stop it, still? Maybe if he didn't complain so much about helping around the house, or if he wasn't so moody. All that could cause a lot of stress, right? So, if he was more pleasant and helpful, his parents might try again? Maybe if he pleased God *and* his parents, God would bring his family back together again.

Don't we think this way sometimes? Job's friend Bildad thought that way. He said if Job didn't sin, then Job's misfortunes must have been his children's fault. All Job has to do is plead with God and things will get better. But of course that isn't what happened at all.

Although improving our behavior is always worthwhile, it doesn't mean we can control outcomes by doing so. Sometimes bad things just happen to us, and we can do nothing to change the situation. The challenge for us is to accept what is happening and pray for the strength to face it. That's a gigantic challenge for our faith! We need to trust that God does indeed want only good for us, and sometimes God's ways are very mysterious.

— Job 8:1–6

20 Are you harmed by my sin, you jailer?
    Why use me for your target practice?
    Am I so great a burden to you?
21 Can't you ever forgive my sin?
    Can't you pardon the wrong I do?
  Soon I will be in my grave,
    and I'll be gone when you look for me.

8

Bildad

1-2 Are you finally through with your windy
    speech?
3 God never twists justice;
    he never fails to do what is right.
4 Your children must have sinned against
    God,
    and so he punished them as they
    deserved.
5 But turn now and plead with Almighty
    God;
6   if you are so honest and pure,
    then God will come and help you
    and restore your household as your
    reward.
7 All the wealth you lost will be nothing
    compared with what God will give you
    then.

8 Look for a moment at ancient wisdom;
    consider the truths our ancestors
    learned.
9 Our life is short, we know nothing at all;
    we pass like shadows across the earth.
10 But let the ancient wise people teach you;
    listen to what they had to say:

11 "Reeds can't grow where there is no
    water;
    they are never found outside a swamp.
12 If the water dries up, they are the first to
    wither,
    while still too small to be cut and used.
13 Godless people are like those reeds;
    their hope is gone, once God is
    forgotten.
14 They trust a thread—a spider's web.
15   If they lean on a web, will it hold them
    up?
    If they grab for a thread, will it help
    them stand?"

Praying for Help

A long tradition of prayer in our Church is intercessory prayer, or prayer of petition. In intercessory prayer, we bring our needs to God and ask for his help and blessing.

Job wonders if it's worth it to ask God for help. He doubts if God is really listening or even if he cares. God truly does care and is always listening to our prayers! But here's the tricky part: we might not get exactly what we ask for. That doesn't mean God doesn't answer our prayers. It just means that God answers our prayers in the ways he knows are best for us.

For instance, Susan's grandmother died of cancer, even though Susan prayed and prayed with all her heart for her grandmother to be healed and to live a long life. Was God busy when Susan was praying? Didn't he get the message? Or did he ignore Susan's prayers?

God did answer Susan's prayers, but not the way she hoped. In time, she realized God showed his love for her in other ways: through the care of friends and family, by showing her how to be kind to someone who is very sick, and by giving her the desire to start hanging out at the nursing home (Susan thought her grandma would really like that).

Trust God—he hears you and is working on your prayer. Keep your eyes and heart open to how your prayer is being answered!

— Job 9:1–16

16 Evil people sprout like weeds in the sun,
    like weeds that spread all through the
       garden.
17 Their roots wrap around the stones
    and hold fast to^r every rock.
18 But then pull them up—
    no one will ever know they were there.
19 Yes, that's all the joy evil people have;
    others now come and take their places.

20 But God will never abandon the faithful
    or ever give help to evil people.
21 He will let you laugh and shout again,
22   but he will bring disgrace on those
      who hate you,
    and the homes of the wicked will
      vanish.

9
Job

1-2 Yes, I've heard all that before.
    But how can a human being win a case
      against God?
3 How can anyone argue with him?
    He can ask a thousand questions
    that no one could ever answer.^s
4 God is so wise and powerful;
    no one can stand up against him.
5 Without warning he moves mountains
    and in anger he destroys them.
6 God sends earthquakes and shakes the
      ground;
    he rocks the pillars that support the earth.

^r **8:17** *Probable text* hold fast to; *Hebrew* see.   ^s **9:3** He can ask . . . answer; *or* Someone could ask him a thousand questions, and he would not answer.
9:2 Job 4:17

"Are you finally through with your windy speech?" (*Job 8:1–2*). Job and his friends sure are honest with one another!

7 He can keep the sun from rising,
  and the stars from shining at night.
8 No one helped God spread out the heavens
  or trample the sea monster's back. *t*
9 God hung the stars in the sky—the Dipper,
  Orion, the Pleiades, and the stars of the south.
10 We cannot understand the great things he does,
  and to his miracles there is no end.

11 God passes by, but I cannot see him.
12 He takes what he wants, and no one can stop him;
  no one dares ask him, "What are you doing?"
13 God's anger is constant. He crushed his enemies
  who helped Rahab, *u* the sea monster, oppose him.
14 So how can I find words to answer God?
15 Though I am innocent, all I can do
  is beg for mercy from God my judge.
16 Yet even then, if he lets me speak,
  I can't believe he would listen to me.
17 He sends storms to batter and bruise me
  without any reason at all.
18 He won't let me catch my breath;
  he has filled my life with bitterness.
19 Should I try force? Try force on God?
  Should I take him to court? Could anyone make him go? *v*
20 I am innocent and faithful, but my words sound guilty,
  and everything I say seems to condemn me.
21-22 I am innocent, but I no longer care.
  I am sick of living. Nothing matters;
  innocent or guilty, God will destroy us.
23 When an innocent person suddenly dies,
  God laughs.
24 God gave the world to the wicked.
  He made all the judges blind.
  And if God didn't do it, who did?

25 My days race by, not one of them good.
26 My life passes like the swiftest boat,
  as fast as an eagle swooping down on a rabbit.
27-28 If I smile and try to forget my pain,
  all my suffering comes back to haunt me;
  I know that God does hold me guilty.
29 Since I am held guilty, why should I bother?
30   No soap can wash away my sins.
31 God throws me into a pit with filth,
  and even my clothes are ashamed of me.
32 If God were human, I could answer him;
  we could go to court to decide our quarrel.
33 But there is no one to step between us—
  no one to judge both God and me.
34 Stop punishing me, God!
  Keep your terrors away!
35 I am not afraid. I am going to talk
  because I know my own heart.

10

1 I am tired of living.
  Listen to my bitter complaint.
2 Don't condemn me, God.
  Tell me! What is the charge against me?
3 Is it right for you to be so cruel?
  To despise what you yourself have made?
  And then to smile on the schemes of wicked people?
4 Do you see things as we do?
5   Is your life as short as ours?
6 Then why do you track down all my sins
  and hunt down every fault I have?
7 You know that I am not guilty,
  that no one can save me from you.

8 Your hands formed and shaped me,
  and now *w* those same hands destroy me.

---

t **9:8** TRAMPLE THE SEA MONSTER'S BACK: *A reference to ancient stories in which a sea monster was killed and then trampled (see also 26:13).*   *u* **9:13** RAHAB: *A legendary sea monster which represented the forces of chaos and evil.*
v **9:19** *Probable text* make him go; *Hebrew* make me go.   *w* **10:8** *Some ancient translations* and now; *Hebrew* together.
9:7, 8 Bar 3:34, 35   **9:9** Job 38:31; Am 5:8   **10:7** Wis 16:15

"We cannot understand the great things he does, / and to his miracles there is no end" (Job 9:10).

9 Remember that you made me from clay; x
    are you going to crush me back to
    dust?
10 You gave my father strength to beget me;
    you made me grow in my mother's
    womb.
11 You formed my body with bones and
    sinews
    and covered the bones with muscles
    and skin.
12 You have given me life and constant love,
    and your care has kept me alive.
13 But now I know that all that time
    you were secretly planning to harm
    me.
14 You were watching to see if I would sin,
    so that you could refuse to forgive me.
15 As soon as I sin, I'm in trouble with you,
    but when I do right, I get no credit.
    I am miserable and covered with shame. y
16 If I have any success at all,
    you hunt me down like a lion;
    to hurt me you even work miracles.
17 You always have some witness against me;
    your anger toward me grows and
    grows;
    you always plan some new attack.

18 Why, God, did you let me be born?
    I should have died before anyone saw
    me.
19 To go from the womb straight to the grave
    would have been as good as never
    existing.
20 Isn't my life almost over? Leave me alone!
    Let me enjoy the time I have left.
21 I am going soon and will never come
    back—
    going to a land that is dark and gloomy,
22 a land of darkness, shadows, and
    confusion,
    where the light itself is darkness.

11
Zophar

1-2 Will no one answer all this nonsense?
    Does talking so much put you in the
    right?

3 Job, do you think we can't answer you?
    That your mocking words will leave us
    speechless?
4 You claim that what you say is true;
    you claim you are pure in the sight of
    God.
5 How I wish God would answer you!
6 He would tell you there are many sides to
    wisdom;
    there are things too deep for human
    knowledge.
    God is punishing you less than you
    deserve.
7 Can you discover the limits and bounds
    of the greatness and power of God?
8 The sky is no limit for God,
    but it lies beyond your reach.
    God knows the world of the dead,
    but you do not know it.
9 God's greatness is broader than the earth,
    wider than the sea.
10 If God arrests you and brings you to trial,
    who is there to stop him?
11 God knows which people are worthless;
    he sees all their evil deeds.
12 Stupid people will start being wise
    when wild donkeys are born tame.

13 Put your heart right, Job. Reach out to
    God.
14 Put away evil and wrong from your home.
15 Then face the world again, firm and
    courageous.
16 Then all your troubles will fade from
    your memory,
    like floods that are past and
    remembered no more.
17 Your life will be brighter than sunshine at
    noon,
    and life's darkest hours will shine like
    the dawn.
18 You will live secure and full of hope;
    God will protect you and give you rest.
19 You won't be afraid of your enemies;
    many people will ask you for help.
20 But the wicked will look around in
    despair
    and find that there is no way to escape.
    Their one hope is that death will come.

x **10:9** *One ancient translation* from clay; *Hebrew* like clay.
my shame.
10:10 Wis 7:1, 2   y **10:15** *Probable text* covered with shame; *Hebrew* see

The Sacrament of Penance and Reconciliation

Catholic Connections

Job's friend Zophar tells him: "Put your heart right, Job. Reach out to God" (Job 11:13).
This is what the sacrament of Penance and Reconciliation is all about for us. We want to put our hearts right and our lives back on track. We know we'll feel better when we admit our sin to God and let him purify us and set us back on the path of goodness. The sacrament lets us reach out to God and ask for forgiveness and healing.

Like the father of the prodigal son (see the parable in Luke 15:11–32), God is waiting for us with open arms, before we even say we're sorry! God will never let us down when we reach out to him. God happily forgives and helps us when we want to change our hearts. Then everything seems lighter and brighter in our lives.

— Job 11:13–18

12

Job

1-2 Yes, you are the voice of the people.
    When you die, wisdom will die with
        you.
3 But I have as much sense as you have;
    I am in no way inferior to you;
    everyone knows all that you have
        said.
4 Even my friends laugh at me now;
    they laugh, although I am righteous
        and blameless;
    but there was a time when God
        answered my prayers.
5 You have no troubles, and yet you make
        fun of me;
    you hit someone who is about to
        fall.
6 But thieves and godless people live in
        peace,
    though their only god is their own
        strength.

7 Even birds and animals have much they
        could teach you;
8   ask the creatures of earth and sea for
        their wisdom.
9 All of them know that the LORD's hand
        made them.

10 It is God who directs the lives of his
        creatures;
    everyone's life is in his power.
11 But just as your tongue enjoys tasting
        food,
    your ears enjoy hearing words.
12-13 Old people have wisdom,
    but God has wisdom and power.
    Old people have insight;
    God has insight and power to act.
14 When God tears down, who can
        rebuild,
    and who can free those God imprisons?
15 Drought comes when God withholds
        rain;
    floods come when he turns water
        loose.

16 God is strong and always victorious;
    both deceived and deceiver are in his
        power.
17 He takes away the wisdom of rulers
    and makes leaders act like fools.
18 He dethrones kings and makes them
        prisoners;
19   he humbles priests and men of
        power.
20 He silences those who are trusted,
    and takes the wisdom of old people
        away.

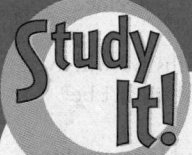

Is God a Director?

Some people believe God controls everything and everybody. They think that he knows exactly what will happen and when, and that he makes it all happen. On the other hand, we are told God gives us free will to make our own choices. So which is it? Is God like a movie director? Does he control us? Or does he give us freedom?

The Bible tells us that we are made in God's image. Which means that God gave us the ability to choose love and goodness. But the flip side of that is we can also choose hate and evil. We are free to choose how to respond to life even if we do not choose everything that happens to us. The mystery is that God sees the whole picture of how our lives are going to unfold, but that doesn't mean he forces it to happen that way.

— Job 12:10

13 ¹⁻²Everything you say, I have heard before.
I understand it all; I know as much as you do.
I'm not your inferior.
³But my dispute is with God, not you;
I want to argue my case with him.
⁴You cover up your ignorance with lies;
you are like doctors who can't heal anyone.
⁵Say nothing, and someone may think you are wise!

⁶Listen while I state my case.
⁷ Why are you lying?
Do you think your lies will benefit God?
⁸Are you trying to defend him?
Are you going to argue his case in court?
⁹If God looks at you closely, will he find anything good?
Do you think you can fool God the way you fool others?
¹⁰Even though your prejudice is hidden, he will reprimand you,
¹¹ and his power will fill you with terror.
¹²Your proverbs are as useless as ashes;
your arguments are as weak as clay.
¹³Be quiet and give me a chance to speak, and let the results be what they will.

²¹He disgraces those in power
and puts an end to the strength of rulers.
²²He sends light to places dark as death.
²³He makes nations strong and great,
but then he defeats and destroys them.
²⁴He makes their leaders foolish
and lets them wander confused and lost;
²⁵ they grope in the dark and stagger like drunkards.

"Be quiet and give me a chance to speak." (13:13)

Job

14 I am z ready to risk my life.

15 I've lost all hope, so what if God kills me?
I am going to state my case to him.

16 It may even be that my boldness will save me,
since no wicked person would dare to face God.

17 Now listen to my words of explanation.

18 I am ready to state my case,
because I know I am in the right.

19 Are you coming to accuse me, God?
If you do, I am ready to be silent and die.

20 Let me ask for two things; agree to them,
and I will not try to hide from you:

21 stop punishing me, and don't crush me with terror.

22 Speak first, O God, and I will answer.
Or let me speak, and you answer me.

23 What are my sins? What wrongs have I done?
What crimes am I charged with?

24 Why do you avoid me?
Why do you treat me like an enemy?

25 Are you trying to frighten me? I'm
nothing but a leaf;
you are attacking a piece of dry straw.

26 You bring bitter charges against me,
even for what I did when I was young.

27 You bind chains on my feet;
you watch every step I take,
and even examine my footprints.

28 As a result, I crumble like rotten wood,
like a moth-eaten coat.

14

1 We are all born weak and helpless.
All lead the same short, troubled life.

2 We grow and wither as quickly as flowers;
we disappear like shadows.

3 Will you even look at me, God,
or put me on trial and judge me?

4 Nothing clean can ever come
from anything as unclean as human beings.

5 The length of our lives is decided beforehand—
the number of months we will live.
You have settled it, and it can't be changed.

6 Look away from us and leave us alone; a
let us enjoy our hard life—if we can. b

7 There is hope for a tree that has been cut down;
it can come back to life and sprout.

There is hope for a tree that has been cut down. (14:7)

8 Even though its roots grow old,
and its stump dies in the ground,

9 with water it will sprout like a young plant.

10 But we die, and that is the end of us;
we die, and where are we then?

11 Like rivers that stop running,
and lakes that go dry,

12 people die, never to rise.
They will never wake up while the sky endures;
they will never stir from their sleep.

13 I wish you would hide me in the world of the dead;
let me be hidden until your anger is over,
and then set a time to remember me.

---

z **13:14** *One ancient translation* I am; *Hebrew* Why am I.
Hebrew manuscripts so that we may rest. b **14:6** let us . . . can; *or until we finish our day of hard work.*
a **14:6** *One Hebrew manuscript* and leave us alone; *most*
13:27 Job 33:11 **14:1, 2** Wis 2:1; Sir 40:1–11; 41:1–4

Think of someone you know who has died. Now imagine him or her living in heaven with God, happier than ever.

Eternal Life

Ca+holic Connec+ions

Atheists are people who do not believe in the existence of God. They would share the belief of Job: when we die, that's the end of us. Or, as others say, we're just food for the worms. Catholics and all Christians believe something very different! Death is hardly the end, but a new beginning—the beginning of an amazingly wonderful life with God for all of eternity. Forever and ever—more happiness and peace than we can even imagine!

How do we know this? Because when Jesus died, it wasn't over. He rose from the dead! Furthermore, Jesus tells us that those who love God will also share in his Resurrection. We will live forever with God and know complete joy.

When someone we love dies, believing in the Resurrection can bring us great comfort. The Resurrection is God's promise that those people who die in Gods grace shall be raised—body and soul—into a new and incredible life. And when we are facing death one day, we will also have this hope to hold onto. Death isn't the end!

— Job 14:10–12

14 If a man dies, can he come back to life?
But I will wait for better times,
    wait till this time of trouble is ended.
15 Then you will call, and I will answer,
    and you will be pleased with me, your
        creature.
16 Then you will watch every step I take,
    but you will not keep track of my sins.
17 You will forgive them and put them
        away;
    you will wipe out all the wrongs I have
        done.

18 There comes a time when mountains fall
    and solid cliffs are moved away.
19 Water will wear down rocks,
    and heavy rain will wash away the soil;
    so you destroy our hope for life.
20 You overpower us and send us away
        forever;
    our faces are twisted in death.
21 Our children win honor, but we never
        know it,
    nor are we told when they are
        disgraced.
22 We feel only the pain of our own bodies
    and the grief of our own minds.

The Second Dialogue
(15:1—21:34)

15
Eliphaz

1-2 Empty words, Job! Empty words!
3 No one who is wise would talk the way
        you do
    or defend himself with such
        meaningless words.
4 If you had your way, no one would fear
        God;
    no one would pray to him.
5 Your wickedness is evident by what you
        say;
    you are trying to hide behind clever
        words.
6 There is no need for me to condemn
        you;
    you are condemned by every word you
        speak.

7 Do you think you were the first person
        born?
    Were you there when God made the
        mountains?

Job

8 Did you overhear the plans God made?
　Does human wisdom belong to you
　　alone?
9 There is nothing you know that we don't
　know.
10 We learned our wisdom from gray-haired
　people—
　those born before your father.

11 God offers you comfort; why still reject
　it?
　We have spoken for him with calm,
　even words.
12 But you are excited and glare at us in
　anger.
13 You are angry with God and denounce
　him.

14 Can any human being be really pure?
　Can anyone be right with God?
15 Why, God does not trust even his
　angels;
　even they are not pure in his sight.
16 And we drink evil as if it were water;
　yes, we are corrupt; we are worthless.

17 Now listen, Job, to what I know.
18 Those who are wise have taught me
　truths
　which they learned from their
　　ancestors,
　and they kept no secrets hidden.
19 Their land was free from foreigners;
　there was no one to lead them away
　　from God.

20 The wicked who oppress others
　will be in torment as long as they live.
21 Voices of terror will scream in their ears,
　and robbers attack when they think
　　they are safe.
22 They have no hope of escaping from
　darkness,
　for somewhere a sword is waiting to
　　kill them,
23 　and vultures*c* are waiting*d* to eat their
　　corpses.
　They know their future is dark;
24 　disaster, like a powerful king,
　is waiting to attack them.

Pray It!

Choosing the Right Path

Eliphaz is trying to prove to Job that our sins cause the hurt and pain we experience. That is often true. What is also true is that sometimes evil or trouble comes our way even when we have tried to make good choices and live moral lives. That's a mystery beyond our understanding. But although we can't control everything that happens to us, we can do our best to bring goodness into our world, by being our best and most faithful selves. Read Psalm 16 and spend some time praying about this.

— Job 15:20–35

25 That is the fate of those
　who shake their fists at God
　and defy the Almighty.
26-27 They are proud and rebellious;
　they stubbornly hold up their shields
　and rush to fight against God.

28 They are the ones who captured cities
　and seized houses whose owners had
　　fled,
　but war will destroy those cities and
　　houses.
29 They will not remain rich for long;
　nothing they own will last.
　Even their shadows*e* will vanish,
30 　and they will not escape from darkness.
　They will be like trees
　whose branches are burned by fire,
　whose blossoms*f* are blown away by the
　　wind.
31 If they are foolish enough to trust in evil,
　then evil will be their reward.

c **15:23** *One ancient translation* vultures; *Hebrew* where is he?　*d* **15:23** *One ancient translation* are waiting; *Hebrew* he wanders.　*e* **15:29** *One ancient translation* shadows; *Hebrew unclear.*　*f* **15:30** *One ancient translation* blossoms; *Hebrew* mouth.
15:14–16 Job 25:4–6

32 Before their time is up they will wither,*g*
     wither like a branch and never be
          green again.
33 They will be like vines that lose their
          unripe grapes;
     like olive trees that drop their blossoms.
34 There will be no descendants for godless
          people,
     and fire will destroy the homes built by
          bribery.
35 These are the ones who plan trouble and
          do evil;
     their hearts are always full of deceit.

16
Job

1-2 I have heard words like that before;
     the comfort you give is only torment.

"The comfort you give is only torment." (16:1)

3 Are you going to keep on talking forever?
     Do you always have to have the last
          word?
4 If you were in my place and I in yours,
     I could say everything you are saying.
   I could shake my head wisely
     and drown you with a flood of words.
5 I could strengthen you with advice
     and keep talking to comfort you.
6 But nothing I say helps,
     and being silent does not calm my pain.

Shut Up and Just Listen!

At the beginning of Job, chapter
16, Job is tired of hearing his
friends giving him advice. It isn't
really what he needs right now.
When friends have troubles, we
often want to help by offering
advice or telling a story of a similar experience we had, so they'll
know we understand what they're
going through. Our intentions are
good, but that's not really the
best way to help.

   When you want to be there
for a friend, just listen. Be quiet!
Let your friend talk it out. Don't
try to fix your friend or their
problem. By letting your friend
talk, you're allowing them to tap
into their own wisdom and find
an answer. *Then*, you can talk: Tell
your friend that you believe in
them and ask how you can help.

— Job 16:1–5

7 You have worn me out, God;
     you have let my family be killed.
8   You have seized me; you are my enemy.
   I am skin and bones,
     and people take that as proof of my
          guilt.*h*

9 In anger God tears me limb from limb;
     he glares at me with hate.
10 People sneer at me;
     they crowd around me and slap my
          face.
11 God has handed me over to evil
          people.

g **15:32** *Some ancient translations* wither; *Hebrew* be filled.   *h* **16:8** *Verses 7-8 in Hebrew are unclear.*

**Fearing God is another way of saying that we are in awe of God's power and
wisdom.**

Job

12 I was living in peace,
    but God took me by the throat
    and battered me and crushed me.
God uses me for target practice
13   and shoots arrows at me from every
      side—
    arrows that pierce and wound me;
    and even then he shows no pity.
14 He wounds me again and again;
    he attacks like a soldier gone mad with
      hate.

15 I mourn and wear clothes made of
      sackcloth,
    and I sit here in the dust defeated.
16 I have cried until my face is red,
    and my eyes are swollen and circled
      with shadows,
17   but I am not guilty of any violence,
    and my prayer to God is sincere.

18 O Earth, don't hide the wrongs done to
      me!
    Don't let my call for justice be silenced!
19 There is someone in heaven
    to stand up for me and take my side.
20 My friends scorn me;
    my eyes pour out tears to God.
21 I want someone to plead with God for
      me,
    as one pleads for a friend.
22 My years are passing now,
    and I walk the road of no return.

17   1 The end of my life is near. I can
        hardly breathe;
    there is nothing left for me but the
      grave.
2 I watch how bitterly everyone mocks me.
3 I am being honest, God. Accept my word.
    There is no one else to support what I
      say.
4 You have closed their minds to reason;
    don't let them triumph over me now.
5 In the old proverb someone betrays his
      friends for money,
    and his children suffer for it. *i*

6 And now people use this proverb against
      me;
    they come and spit in my face.
7 My grief has almost made me blind;
    my arms and legs are as thin as shadows.
8 Those who claim to be honest are shocked,
    and they all condemn me as godless.
9 Those who claim to be respectable
    are more and more convinced they are
      right.
10 But if all of them came and stood before
      me,
    I would not find even one of them
      wise.

Pray It!

The Turning of Friends

alone in my room
no peace joy hope, only tears
bring back just one friend
    —Alisha, 13 years old

Like Alisha—and Job—our hearts break when friends turn away from us. When you are sad, confused, lonely, or anxious, it can help to express your feelings creatively. You could try writing a haiku verse, like Alisha's. Haiku is a Japanese form of poetry with three lines of seventeen syllables—five syllables in the first line, seven in the second, and five in the third line. Pour your thoughts and emotions into the words of the haiku. Make a work of art out of it! Writing and creating can bring healing to your heart.

      — Job 17:1–6

i **17:5** someone . . . suffer for it; *or* someone entertains his friends while his children go hungry.
16:19 Job 19:25

11 My days have passed; my plans have failed;
   my hope is gone.
12 But my friends say night is daylight;
   they say that light is near,
   but I know I remain in darkness.
13 My only hope is the world of the dead,
   where I will lie down to sleep in the
   dark.
14 I will call the grave my father,
   and the worms that eat me
   I will call my mother and my sisters.
15 Where is there any hope for me?
   Who sees any?
16 Hope will not go with me[j]
   when I go down to the world of the
   dead.

18
Bildad

1-2 Job, can't people like you ever be quiet?
   If you stopped to listen, we could talk
   to you.
3 What makes you think we are as stupid as
   cattle?
4 You are only hurting yourself with your
   anger.
   Will the earth be deserted because you
   are angry?
   Will God move mountains to satisfy
   you?

5 The light of the wicked will still be put
   out;
   its flame will never burn again.
6 The lamp in their tents will be darkened.
7 Their steps were firm, but now they
   stumble;
   they fall—victims of their own advice.
8 They walk into a net, and their feet are
   caught;
9   a trap catches their heels and holds them.
10 On the ground a snare is hidden;
   a trap has been set in their path.

11 All around them terror is waiting;
   it follows them at every step.
12 They used to be rich, but now they go
   hungry;
   disaster stands and waits at their side.

The Power of Anger

Anger can be a powerful force in our lives—often a destructive force. When we hold on to our anger, it eats away at us like a disease. We begin concentrating on ways to get revenge, our mood gets darker, we snap at people, and we get ugly lines in our forehead from frowning all the time! At its worst, unhealed anger can result in violence or contribute to serious illness. This is why Job's friend warns Job that he may be hurting himself with his anger. Curiously, our anger hurts us more than it hurts anyone else.

We need to bring our anger to God and ask for healing—for our own good. We experience healing when we choose forgiveness instead of revenge. We are also healed of anger when we focus on the positive things in our lives and see the good in others instead of focusing only on the negative things.

Can anger ever be good? It's never healthy to hold in our feelings, so if we can express anger in a way that is respectful and not violent to others, that's helpful. But then, we need to *let it go* so it doesn't grow deeper in us. Pray for peace in your heart, your words, and your actions!

— Job 18:4

13 A deadly disease spreads over their bodies
   and causes their arms and legs to rot.
14 They are torn from the tents where they
   lived secure,
   and are dragged off to face King Death.

---

j **17:16** *One ancient translation* with me; *Hebrew unclear.*
18:5, 6 Job 21:17

Job

15 Now anyone may live in their tents—*k*
   after sulfur is sprinkled to disinfect them!*l*
16 Their roots and branches are withered
   and dry.
17 Their fame is ended at home and abroad;
   no one remembers them any more.
18 They will be driven out of the land of the
   living,
   driven from light into darkness.
19 They have no descendants, no survivors.
20 From east to west, all who hear of their
   fate
   shudder and tremble with fear.
21 That is the fate of evil people,
   the fate of those who care nothing for
   God.

19
Job

1-2 Why do you keep tormenting me with
   words?
3 Time after time you insult me
   and show no shame for the way you
   abuse me.
4 Even if I have done wrong,
   how does that hurt you?
5 You think you are better than I am,
   and regard my troubles as proof of my
   guilt.
6 Can't you see it is God who has done this?
   He has set a trap to catch me.
7 I protest his violence,
   but no one is listening;
   no one hears my cry for justice.
8 God has blocked the way, and I can't get
   through;
   he has hidden my path in darkness.
9 He has taken away all my wealth
   and destroyed my reputation.
10 He batters me from every side.
  He uproots my hope
   and leaves me to wither and die.
11 God is angry and rages against me;
   he treats me like his worst enemy.
12 He sends his army to attack me;
   they dig trenches and lay siege to my
   tent.

13 God has made my own family forsake
   me;
  I am a stranger to those who knew
   me;
14   my relatives and friends are gone.
15 Those who were guests in my house have
   forgotten me;
  my servant women treat me like a
   stranger and a foreigner.
16 When I call a servant, he doesn't
   answer—
  even when I beg him to help me.
17 My wife can't stand the smell of my
   breath,
  and my own brothers won't come near
   me.
18 Children despise me and laugh when they
   see me.
19 My closest friends look at me with
   disgust;
  those I loved most have turned against
   me.
20 My skin hangs loose on my bones;
  I have barely escaped with my life.*m*
21 You are my friends! Take pity on me!
  The hand of God has struck me down.

"You are my friends! Take pity on me!" (19:21)

22 Why must you persecute me the way
   God does?
  Haven't you tormented me enough?

23 How I wish that someone would
   remember my words
   and record them in a book!

k **18:15** Now anyone may live in their tents; *Hebrew unclear.*   *l* **18:15** TO DISINFECT THEM: *Sulfur was used in the ancient world as a disinfectant and to clean rooms that had contained corpses.*   *m* **19:20** *Verse 20 in Hebrew is unclear.*
19:19 Sir 6:8

29 But now, be afraid of the sword—
  the sword that brings God's wrath on
    sin,
  so that you will know there is one who
    judges. *q*

20
Zophar

1-2 Job, you upset me. Now I'm impatient to
    answer.
3 What you have said is an insult,
  but I know how to reply to you.

4 Surely you know that from ancient times,
  when we humans were first placed on
    earth,
5 no wicked people have been happy for
    long.
6 They may grow great, towering to the sky,
  so great that their heads reach the
    clouds,
7 but they will be blown away like dust.
  Those who used to know them
    will wonder where they have gone.
8 They will vanish like a dream, like a
    vision at night,
  and never be seen again.
9 The wicked will disappear from the place
    where they used to live;
10 and their children will make good what
    they stole from the poor.
11 Their bodies used to be young and
    vigorous,
  but soon they will turn to dust.

12-13 Evil tastes so good to them
  that they keep some in their mouths to
    enjoy its flavor.
14 But in their stomachs the food turns bitter,
  as bitter as any poison could be.
15 The wicked vomit up the wealth they
    stole;
  God takes it back, even out of their
    stomachs.

Live It!

True Blue Friendship

Marcia was truly at a low point in her life. Some of her problems were her own fault, and others weren't. But she was at her lowest low and felt like everyone was tired of her troubles—and her. This is exactly how Job felt about his family and friends.

What kind of a friend are you during the tough times? Do you get frustrated and walk away? Do you start pointing out faults and try to change your friends? Or do you believe in them and stick by them through thick and thin? Can you wait it out with them, until life gets easier?

This is the kind of friend God is to us. Job doesn't get that—yet!

— Job 19:13–22

---

24 Or with a chisel carve my words in
    stone
  and write them so that they would last
    forever. *n*

25 But I know there is someone in heaven
  who will come at last to my defense.
26 Even after my skin is eaten by disease,
  while still in this body *o* I will see
    God. *p*
27 I will see him with my own eyes,
  and he will not be a stranger.

  My courage failed because you said,
28 "How can we torment him?"
  You looked for some excuse to attack
    me.

---

n **19:24** last forever; *or* be on record.   *o* **19:26** while still in this body; *or* although not in this body.
p **19:26** *Verse 26 in Hebrew is unclear.*   *q* **19:29** one who judges; *or* a judgment.
20:8 Wis 5:14

---

17 They will not live to see rivers of olive
oil[r]
or streams that flow with milk and
honey.
18 They will have to give up all they have
worked for;
they will have no chance to enjoy their
wealth,
19 because they oppressed and neglected
the poor
and seized houses someone else had
built.
20 Their greed is never satisfied.
21 When they eat, there is nothing left over,
but now their prosperity comes to an
end.
22 At the height of their success
all the weight of misery will crush them.
23 Let them eat all they want!
God will punish them in fury and
anger.
24 When they try to escape from an iron
sword,
a bronze bow will shoot them down.
25 Arrows stick through their bodies;
the shiny points drip with their blood,
and terror grips their hearts.
26 Everything they have saved is destroyed;
a fire not lit by human hands
burns them and all their family.
27 Heaven reveals their sin,
and the earth gives testimony against
them.
28 All their wealth will be destroyed
in the flood of God's anger.

29 This is the fate of wicked people,
the fate that God assigns to them.

Live It!

Greed

Is it wrong to be wealthy? Sinful, even? The wicked ones Zophar is talking about are not just wealthy and successful—they are *greedy*. Greed is evil because it leads people to neglect poor people and steal what is not theirs (Job 20:19), so they will have even more wealth. Their money, property, and material things are never enough—like a spoiled child, they want more, more, more, and they're not going to share any of it!

Where do you see greed at work in our world? in our nation? Do you experience greed at school, or in your family? Is greed lurking inside you?

Wealth itself is not evil—but those who are wealthy have a responsibility to be generous with those who have less. And wealthy people need to be careful that money and material things don't start to become the center of their lives. That is the slippery slope toward greed! Our deepest happiness comes when God is at the center of our lives. Everyone, rich and poor, needs to trust that God will take care of all their needs (see Luke 12:22–34).

— Job 20:15–28

21
Job

1-2 Listen to what I am saying;
that is all the comfort I ask from you.
3 Give me a chance to speak and then,
when I am through, sneer if you like.

16 What the evil people swallow is like poison;
it kills them like the bite of a deadly
snake.

[r] 20:17 *Probable text* They will . . . oil; *Hebrew unclear.*
20:24 Wis 5:17–23

While reading Job, chapter 20, make a list of all the bad things that Zophar
says will happen to wicked or evil people.

4 My quarrel is not with mortals;
    I have good reason to be impatient.
5 Look at me. Isn't that enough
    to make you stare in shocked silence?
6 When I think of what has happened to
        me,
    I am stunned, and I tremble and shake.

7 Why does God let evil people live,
    let them grow old and prosper?
8 They have children and grandchildren,
    and live to watch them all grow up.
9 God does not bring disaster on their
        homes;
    they never have to live in terror.
10 Yes, all their cattle breed
    and give birth without trouble.
11 Their children run and play like lambs
12   and dance to the music of harps and
        flutes.
13 They live out their lives in peace
    and quietly die without suffering.

14 The wicked tell God to leave them alone;
    they don't want to know his will for
        their lives.
15 They think there is no need to serve God
    nor any advantage in praying to him.
16 They claim they succeed by their own
        strength,
    but their way of thinking I can't accept.

17 Was a wicked person's light ever put out?
    Did one of them ever meet with
        disaster?
    Did God ever punish the wicked in anger
18   and blow them away like straw in the
        wind,
    or like dust carried away in a storm?

19 You claim God punishes a child for the
        sins of his father.
    No! Let God punish the sinners
        themselves;
    let him show that he does it because of
        their sins.
20 Let sinners bear their own punishment;
    let them feel the wrath of Almighty
        God.
21 When our lives are over,
    do we really care whether our children
        are happy?
22 Can anyone teach God,
    who judges even those in high places?

Study It!

Reward and Punishment

The debate seems to be going in endless circles! Job's friends will not give up the idea that Job is being punished for his sins. That was the belief of the Israelites: grief and failure were punishment for unfaithfulness, and happiness and success were rewards for being faithful to God. Job is familiar with that reasoning and doesn't disagree with his friends. And he isn't upset with God because he is suffering. What he's upset about is that he *has* been faithful, and yet he suffers. It doesn't make any sense! This is what he is desperate to have his friends understand.

We know that some people who suffer or struggle with failure are faithful and others are not. And some happy or successful people are faithful, while others are not. Jesus set us straight about how God works: God does not reward and punish in the way the Israelites believed. All people are equally deserving of God's love and generosity. And suffering is a possibility for anyone, not just sinners—Jesus is the best example of this.

So why do innocent people suffer? This is the urgent question in the Book of Job. Keep reading!

— Job, chapter 21

23-24 Some people stay healthy till the day
        they die;
    they die happy and at ease,
    their bodies well-nourished.
25 Others have no happiness at all;
    they live and die with bitter hearts.
26 But all alike die and are buried;
    they all are covered with worms.

27 I know what spiteful thoughts you have.
28 You ask, "Where are the homes of great
     people now,
       those who practiced evil?"

29 Haven't you talked with people who
       travel?
     Don't you know the reports they bring
       back?
30 On the day God is angry and punishes,
     it is the wicked who are always spared.
31 There is no one to accuse the wicked
     or pay them back for all they have
       done.
32 When they are carried to the graveyard,
     to their well-guarded tombs,
33   thousands join the funeral procession,
     and even the earth lies gently on their
       bodies.

34 And you! You try to comfort me with
     nonsense!
     Every answer you give is a lie!

The Third Dialogue
(22:1—27:23)

22

Eliphaz

1-2 Is there anyone, even the wisest,
     who could ever be of use to God?
3 Does your doing right benefit God,
     or does your being good help him at
       all?
4 It is not because you stand in awe of God
     that he reprimands you and brings you
       to trial.
5 No, it's because you have sinned so much;
     it's because of all the evil you do.
6 To make a brother repay you the money
       he owed,
     you took away his clothes and left him
       nothing to wear.
7 You refused water to those who were tired,
     and refused to feed those who were
       hungry.
8 You used your power and your position
     to take over the whole land.

9 You not only refused to help widows,
     but you also robbed and mistreated
       orphans.
10 So now there are pitfalls all around you,
     and suddenly you are full of fear.
11 It has grown so dark that you cannot see,
     and a flood overwhelms you.

12 Doesn't God live in the highest heavens
     and look down on the stars, even
       though they are high?
13 And yet you ask, "What does God know?
     He is hidden by clouds—how can he
       judge us?"
14 You think the thick clouds keep him
     from seeing,
     as he walks on the dome of the sky.

15 Are you determined to walk in the paths
     that evil people have always followed?
16 Even before their time had come,
     they were washed away by a flood.
17 These are the ones who rejected God
     and believed that he could do nothing
       to them.
18 And yet it was God who made them
       prosperous—
     I can't understand the thoughts of the
       wicked.
19 Good people are glad and the innocent
       laugh
     when they see the wicked punished.
20 All that the wicked own is destroyed,
     and fire burns up anything that is left.

21 Now, Job, make peace with God
     and stop treating him like an enemy;
     if you do, then he will bless you.
22 Accept the teaching he gives;
     keep his words in your heart.
23 Yes, you must humbly*s* return to God
     and put an end to all the evil
     that is done in your house.
24 Throw away your gold;
     dump your finest gold in the dry
       stream bed.
25 Let Almighty God be your gold,
     and let him be silver, piled high for you.
26 Then you will always trust in God
     and find that he is the source of your
       joy.

s **22:23** *One ancient translation* humbly; *Hebrew* be built up.
22:2, 3 Job 35:6—8

27 When you pray, he will answer you,
     and you will keep the vows you made.
28 You will succeed in all you do,
     and light will shine on your path.
29 God brings down the proud[t]
     and saves the humble.
30 He will rescue you if you are innocent,[u]
     if what you do is right.[v]

23
Job

1-2 I still rebel and complain against God;
     I cannot keep from groaning.
3 How I wish I knew where to find him,
     and knew how to go where he is.
4 I would state my case before him
     and present all the arguments in my
     favor.
5 I want to know what he would say
     and how he would answer me.
6 Would God use all his strength against me?
     No, he would listen as I spoke.
7 I am honest; I could reason with God;
     he would declare me innocent[w] once
     and for all.

8 I have searched in the East, but God is
     not there;
     I have not found him when I searched
     in the West.
9 God has been at work in the North and
     the South,
     but still I have not seen him.
10 Yet God knows every step I take;
     if he tests me, he will find me pure.
11 I follow faithfully the road he chooses,
     and never wander to either side.
12 I always do what God commands;
     I follow his will, not my own desires.

13 He never changes. No one can oppose him
     or stop him from doing what he wants
     to do.
14 He will fulfill what he has planned for me;
     that plan is just one of the many he has;

Pray It!

Where Is God Found?

Job wants a face-to-face meeting with God, and he has looked everywhere, but he can't find him. Where do you find God? Where do you look?

     Some people believe Church is where God lives, and in our celebration of the sacraments. Others believe God is found in nature. Still others believe we meet God in other people and in the good works we do. Some find God is as close to them as their heartbeat. Which is correct? All of the above! God is in us and around us and everywhere! God is always waiting for us to seek and find him.

— *Job 23:3–9*

"I tremble with fear before him." (23:15)

15   I tremble with fear before him.
16-17 Almighty God has destroyed my
     courage.

---

[t] **22:29** *Probable text* proud; *Hebrew unclear.*   [u] **22:30** *Some ancient translations* innocent; *Hebrew* not innocent.
[v] **22:30** *Verse 30 in Hebrew is unclear.*   [w] **23:7** he would declare me innocent; *or* then my rights would be safe.

"Let Almighty God be your gold. . . . / Then you will always trust in God / and find that he is the source of your joy" (*Job 22:25–26*).

It is God, not the dark, that makes me
    afraid—
  even though the darkness has made me
    blind.

24

¹Why doesn't God set a time for
    judging,
  a day of justice for those who serve
    him?

²People move property lines to get more
    land;
  they steal sheep and put them with
    their own flocks.
³They take donkeys that belong to orphans,
  and keep a widow's ox till she pays her
    debts.
⁴They prevent the poor from getting their
    rights
  and force the needy to run and hide.

⁵So the poor, like wild donkeys,
  search for food in the dry wilderness;
  nowhere else can they find food for
    their children.
⁶They have to harvest fields they don't
    own,ˣ
  and gather grapes in vineyards of the
    wicked.
⁷At night they sleep with nothing to cover
    them,
  nothing to keep them from the cold.
⁸They are drenched by the rain that falls
    on the mountains,
  and they huddle beside the rocks for
    shelter.

⁹Evil people make slaves of fatherless infants
  and take the children of the poor in
    payment for debts.
¹⁰But the poor must go out with no clothes
    to protect them;
  they must go hungry while harvesting
    wheat.
¹¹They press olives for oil, and grapes for
    wine,
  but they themselves are thirsty.

¹²In the cities the wounded and dying cry
    out,
  but God ignores their prayers.
¹³There are those who reject the light;
  they don't understand it or go where it
    leads.
¹⁴At dawn the murderer gets up
  and goes out to kill the poor,
  and at night he steals.
¹⁵The adulterer waits for twilight to come;
  he covers his face so that no one can
    see him.
¹⁶At night thieves break into houses,
  but by day they hide and avoid the light.
¹⁷They fear the light of day,
  but darkness holds no terror for them.

[Zophar]ʸ

¹⁸The wicked are swept away by floods,
  and the land they own is under God's
    curse;
  they no longer go to work in their
    vineyards.
¹⁹As snow vanishes in heat and drought,
  so sinners vanish from the land of the
    living.
²⁰Not even their mothers remember them
    now;
  they are eaten by worms and destroyed
    like fallen trees.
²¹That happens because they mistreated
    widows
  and showed no kindness to childless
    women.
²²God, in his strength, destroys the mighty;
  God acts—and the wicked die.
²³God may let them live secure,
  but keeps an eye on them all the time.
²⁴For a while the wicked prosper,
  but then they wither like weeds,
  like stalks of grain that have been cut
    down.
²⁵Can anyone deny that this is so?
  Can anyone prove that my words are not
    true?

ˣ **24:6** FIELDS THEY DON'T OWN: *Having been cheated out of their own land, the poor are forced to work for others for very small pay.* ʸ **24:18** Zophar *is not named in the text, but this speech is usually assigned to him.*

Job asks why God doesn't "set a time for judging" *(Job 24:1).* **We know that God does! Read Revelation, chapters 20–22, about God's judgment day.**

Pray It!

Whispers of God's Power

Bildad is poetic in his telling of God's power in nature—yet admits we have only hints of God's greatness.

Thank you, God—
for the unconditional love of dogs,
for the amazing way our bodies work,
for the variety of trees and plants and flowers in the world,
for the strength of my dad's arms when he holds me tight,
for the sparkle of fireflies,
for the ability of our hearts to forgive,
for music and sunsets and pizza and electricity!
You are truly an awesome God! Amen.

— **Job 26:5–14**

25

Bildad

1-2 God is powerful; all must stand in awe of him;

he keeps his heavenly kingdom in peace.

3 Can anyone count the angels who serve him?

Is there any place where God's light does not shine?

4 Can anyone be righteous or pure in God's sight?

5 In his eyes even the moon is not bright, or the stars pure.

6 Then what about a human being, that worm, that insect?

What is a human life worth in God's eyes?

26

Job

1-2 What a big help you are to me— poor, weak man that I am!

3 You give such good advice

and share your knowledge with a fool like me!

4 Who do you think will hear all your words?

Who inspired you to speak like this?

[Bildad] *z*

5 The spirits of the dead tremble in the waters under the earth.

6 The world of the dead lies open to God;

no covering shields it from his sight.

7 God stretched out the northern sky and hung the earth in empty space.

8 It is God who fills the clouds with water

and keeps them from bursting with the weight.

9 He hides the full moon behind a cloud.

10 He divided light from darkness

by a circle drawn on the face of the sea.

11 When he threatens the pillars that hold up the sky,

they shake and tremble with fear.

12 It is his strength that conquered the sea; *a*

by his skill he destroyed the monster Rahab. *b*

---

z **26:5** Bildad *is not named in the text, but this speech is usually assigned to him.*　　*a* **26:12** CONQUERED THE SEA: *A reference to an ancient story in which the sea fought against God.*　　*b* **26:12** RAHAB: *See 9:13.*

Job

13 It is his breath that made the sky clear,
and his hand that killed the escaping
monster.^c
14 But these are only hints of his power,
only the whispers that we have heard.
Who can know how truly great God is?

27
Job

1-2 I swear by the living Almighty God,
who refuses me justice and makes my
life bitter—
3   as long as God gives me breath,
4   my lips will never say anything evil,
my tongue will never tell a lie.
5 I will never say that you men are right;
I will insist on my innocence to my
dying day.
6 I will never give up my claim to be right;
my conscience is clear.

7 May all who oppose me and fight against
me
be punished like the wicked and the
unrighteous.
8 What hope is there for the godless
in the hour when God demands their
life?
9 When trouble comes, will God hear their
cries?
10 They should have desired the joy he gives;
they should have constantly prayed to
him.

11 Let me teach you how great is God's
power,
and explain what Almighty God has
planned.
12 But no, after all, you have seen for
yourselves;
so why do you talk such nonsense?

[Zophar]^d

13 This is how Almighty God
punishes wicked, violent people.
14 They may have many sons,
but all will be killed in war;
their children never have enough to eat.

Integrity

This much can be said about Job:
he is a person of *integrity*. Integrity
means that you know the truth,
and you stand by it. You don't give
in to pressure from other people's
opinions. You do the right thing,
no matter what the cost.

Job knows with all his heart
that he is innocent. He will not
budge on that truth, and, further,
he knows God would not want
him to back down from the truth
either.

Some people keep a list of the
things that they know are true.
Whenever they learn a new truth
about life, they add it to that list.
Maybe you want to start such a
list. Then make a commitment to
live by the truths God has revealed
to you. Growing up to be a person
of integrity is a gift you can give to
the world.

— Job 27:1–6

15 Those who survive will die from disease,
and even their widows will not mourn
their death.
16 The wicked may have too much silver to
count
and more clothes than anyone needs;
17 but some good person will wear the
clothes,
and someone honest will get the silver.
18 The wicked build houses like a spider's
web^e
or like the hut of a slave guarding the
fields.
19 One last time^f they will lie down rich,
and when they wake up, they will find
their wealth gone.

^c **26:13** ESCAPING MONSTER: *See 9:8.*   ^d **27:13** Zophar *is not named in the text, but this speech is usually assigned to
him.*   ^e **27:18** *Some ancient translations* spider's web; *Hebrew* moth *or* bird's nest.   ^f **27:19** *Some ancient translations*
One last time; *Hebrew* They will not be gathered.

20 Terror will strike like a sudden flood;
    a wind in the night will blow them
      away;
21   the east wind will sweep them from
      their homes;
22   it will blow down on them without
      pity
    while they try their best to escape.
23 The wind howls at them as they run,
    frightening them with destructive
    power.

In Praise of Wisdom§

28 ¹There are mines where silver is dug;
    There are places where gold is
      refined.
2 We dig iron out of the ground
  And melt copper out of the stones.
3 Miners explore the deepest darkness.
  They search the depths of the earth
  And dig for rocks in the darkness.
4 Far from where anyone lives
  Or human feet ever travel,
  They dig the shafts of mines.
  There they work in loneliness,
  Clinging to ropes in the pits.
5 Food grows out of the earth,
  But underneath the same earth
  All is torn up and crushed.
6 The stones of the earth contain sapphires,
  And its dust contains gold.
7 No hawk sees the roads to the mines,
  And no vulture ever flies over them.
8 No lion or other fierce beast
  Ever travels those lonely roads.

9 Miners dig the hardest rocks,
  Dig mountains away at their base.
10 As they tunnel through the rocks,
  They discover precious stones.
11 They dig to the sources of ʰ rivers
  And bring to light what is hidden.
12 But where can wisdom be found?
  Where can we learn to understand?

13 Wisdom is not to be found among
    mortals;
  No one knows its true value.
14 The depths of the oceans and seas
  Say that wisdom is not found there.
15 It cannot be bought with silver or
    gold.
16 The finest gold and jewels
  Cannot equal its value.
17 It is worth more than gold,
  Than a gold vase or finest glass.
18 The value of wisdom is more
  Than coral or crystal or rubies.
19 The finest topaz and the purest gold
  Cannot compare with the value of
    wisdom.

20 Where, then, is the source of wisdom?
  Where can we learn to understand?
21 No living creature can see it,
  Not even a bird in flight.
22 Even death and destruction
  Admit they have heard only rumors.

23 God alone knows the way,
  Knows the place where wisdom is
      found,
24 Because he sees the ends of the earth,
  Sees everything under the sky.
25 When God gave the wind its power
  And determined the size of the sea;
26 When God decided where the rain would
    fall,
  And the path that the thunderclouds
    travel;
27 It was then he saw wisdom and tested its
    worth—
  He gave it his approval.

28 God said to us humans,
  "To be wise, you must have reverence for
    the Lord.
  To understand, you must turn from
    evil."

§ **28** *The Hebrew text does not indicate who is speaking in this chapter.* ʰ **28:11** *Some ancient translations* dig to the sources of; *Hebrew* bind from trickling.
28:12 Sir 1:6; Bar 3:15 **28:13** Bar 3:29–31 **28:23** Bar 3:35–37 **28:27** Sir 1:9, 19 **28:28** Ps 111:10; Prov 1:7; 9:10

"As long as God gives me breath, / my lips will never say anything evil, / my tongue will never tell a lie" *(Job 27:3–4).*

Pray It!

Keepin' an Eye Out

Job feels that his life crumbled because God stopped watching over him. God abandoned him, he believes, and so began his many troubles. We can certainly understand how someone who experienced Job's losses could feel like this.

This couldn't be further from the truth about how God acts, though. We believe that God is *omnipresent*, meaning, he is watching over everyone all the time, all at once! Don't even try to understand how that can be—it's a great mystery of our faith. Just believe it, and know that problems or not, God never leaves our side for a minute.

— Job 29:2–5

Job's Final Statement of His Case
(29:1—31:40)

29 ¹Job began speaking again.

²If only my life could once again
be as it was when God watched over me.
³God was always with me then
and gave me light as I walked through the darkness.
⁴Those were the days when I was prosperous,
and the friendship of God protected my home.
⁵Almighty God was with me then,
and I was surrounded by all my children.
⁶My cows and goats gave plenty of milk,
and my olive trees grew in the rockiest soil.
⁷Whenever the city elders met
and I took my place among them,
⁸   young men stepped aside as soon as they saw me,
and old men stood up to show me respect.
⁹The leaders of the people would stop talking;

¹⁰   even the most important men kept silent.
¹¹Everyone who saw me or heard of me
had good things to say about what I had done.
¹²When the poor cried out, I helped them;
I gave help to orphans who had nowhere to turn.
¹³People who were in deepest misery praised me,
and I helped widows find security.
¹⁴I have always acted justly and fairly.
¹⁵I was eyes for the blind,
and feet for the lame.
¹⁶I was like a father to the poor
and took the side of strangers in trouble.
¹⁷I destroyed the power of cruel men
and rescued their victims.
¹⁸I always expected to live a long life
and to die at home in comfort.
¹⁹I was like a tree whose roots always have water
and whose branches are wet with dew.
²⁰Everyone was always praising me,
and my strength never failed me.
²¹When I gave advice, people were silent
and listened carefully to what I said;

"I smiled on them when they had lost confidence; / my cheerful face encouraged them" (Job 29:24). **Who needs your encouragement today?**

22   they had nothing to add when I had
         finished.
   My words sank in like drops of rain;
23   everyone welcomed them
      just as farmers welcome rain in spring.
24 I smiled on them when they had lost
         confidence;
   my cheerful face encouraged them.
25 I took charge and made the decisions;
      I led them as a king leads his troops,
      and gave them comfort in their despair.

30 ¹But men younger than I am make
      fun of me now!
   Their fathers have always been so
         worthless
      that I wouldn't let them help my dogs
         guard sheep.
² They were a bunch of worn-out men,
      too weak to do any work for me.
³ They were so poor and hungry
      that they would gnaw dry roots—
      at night, in wild, desolate places.
⁴ They pulled up the plants of the desert
         and ate them,
      even the tasteless roots of the broom
         tree!
⁵ Everyone drove them away with shouts,
      as if they were shouting at thieves.
⁶ They had to live in caves,
      in holes dug in the sides of cliffs.
⁷ Out in the wilds they howled like animals
      and huddled together under the bushes.
⁸ A worthless bunch of nameless nobodies!
   They were driven out of the land.

⁹ Now they come and laugh at me;
   I am nothing but a joke to them.
10 They treat me with disgust;
      they think they are too good for me,
      and even come and spit in my face.
11 Because God has made me weak and
         helpless,
      they turn against me with all their fury.
12 This mob attacks me head-on;
      they send me running; they prepare
         their final assault.
13 They cut off my escape and try to destroy
         me;
      and there is no one to stopⁱ them.

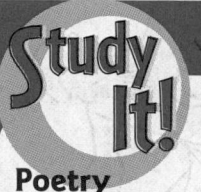

Poetry

The speeches in the Book of Job
are written as poems. These are
not poems that rhyme or have a
certain rhythm (they may have, in
the original Hebrew language), but
they include a feature of poetry
called *parallelism*.

Parallelism can be two lines in
which the same thought is repeated: "Now they come and laugh at
me; / I am nothing but a joke to
them" (Job 30:9).

Or it can be two lines with
opposite thoughts: "Where once I
heard joyful music, / now I hear
only mourning and weeping" (Job
30:31).

Or, the second line can add to
or build upon the thought of the
first line: "Out in the wilds they
howled like animals / and huddled
together under the bushes" (Job
30:7).

In your journal, try writing a
prayer to God using parallel lines
as your pattern.

— Job, chapter 30

14 They pour through the holes in my
         defenses
      and come crashing down on top of me;
15 I am overcome with terror;
      my dignity is gone like a puff of
         wind,
      and my prosperity like a cloud.

16 Now I am about to die;
      there is no relief for my suffering.
17 At night my bones all ache;
      the pain that gnaws me never stops.
18 God seizes me by my collar
      and twists my clothes out of shape.

ⁱ **30:13** *Probable text* stop; *Hebrew* help.

Job

"He throws me down in the mud." (30:19)

19 He throws me down in the mud;
  I am no better than dirt.

20 I call to you, O God, but you never answer;
  and when I pray, you pay no attention.
21 You are treating me cruelly;
  you persecute me with all your power.
22 You let the wind blow me away;
  you toss me about in a raging storm.
23 I know you are taking me off to my death,
  to the fate in store for everyone.
24 Why do you attack a ruined man,
  one who can do nothing but beg for
    pity?[j]
25 Didn't I weep with people in trouble
  and feel sorry for those in need?
26 I hoped for happiness and light,
  but trouble and darkness came instead.
27 I am torn apart by worry and pain;
  I have had day after day of suffering.
28 I go about in gloom, without any sunshine;
  I stand up in public and plead for help.
29 My voice is as sad and lonely
  as the cries of a jackal or an ostrich.
30 My skin has turned dark; I am burning
    with fever.
31 Where once I heard joyful music,
  now I hear only mourning and
    weeping.

31

1 I have made a solemn promise
  never to look with lust at a woman.

2 What does Almighty God do to us?
  How does he repay human deeds?
3 He sends disaster and ruin
  to those who do wrong.

4 God knows everything I do;
  he sees every step I take.

5 I swear I have never acted wickedly
  and never tried to deceive others.
6 Let God weigh me on honest scales,
  and he will see how innocent I am.
7 If I have turned from the right path
  or let myself be attracted to evil,
  if my hands are stained with sin,
8   then let my crops be destroyed,
  or let others eat the food I grow.

9 If I have been attracted to my neighbor's
    wife,
  and waited, hidden, outside her door,
10   then let my wife cook another man's
    food
  and sleep in another man's bed.
11 Such wickedness should be punished by
    death.
12 It would be like a destructive, hellish fire,
  consuming everything I have.

13 When any of my servants complained
    against me,
  I would listen and treat them fairly.
14 If I did not, how could I then face God?
  What could I say when God came to
    judge me?
15 The same God who created me
  created my servants also.

16 I have never refused to help the poor;
  never have I let widows live in despair
17   or let orphans go hungry while I ate.
18 All my life I have taken care of them.[k]

19 When I found someone in need,
  too poor to buy clothes,
20   I would give him clothing made of wool
  that had come from my own flock of
    sheep.
  Then he would praise me with all his
    heart.

21 If I have ever cheated an orphan,
  knowing I could win in court,
22   then may my arms be broken;
  may they be torn from my shoulders.
23 Because I fear God's punishment,
  I could never do such a thing.

[j] **30:24** *Verse 24 in Hebrew is unclear.*   [k] **31:18** *All my life . . . them; Hebrew unclear.*
31:16–18 Tob 4:7–11, 16

Examination of Conscience

Catholic Connections

In his mind, Job was thinking about all his behaviors to see if he had done anything wrong. He thought about his faithfulness to his wife, how he treated the people who work for him, how he cared for poor people, the importance of riches in his life, how he acted toward his enemies, and so on.

We practice this exercise as part of the sacrament of Penance and Reconciliation. Before we confess our sins to the priest, we honestly examine our conscience to determine if and how we are guilty of sin. Many written guides are available to help you think about the different areas of your life. Look for patterns of behavior and attitudes that keep showing up. This helps you prepare what you will confess to God in the sacrament.

Look at Job's list, and see which concerns of his conscience match yours. How would your examination of conscience differ from Job's?

— Job 31:5–40

24 I have never trusted in riches
25   or taken pride in my wealth.
26 I have never worshiped the sun in its
         brightness
     or the moon in all its beauty.
27 I have not been led astray to honor them
     by kissing my hand in reverence to
         them.
28 Such a sin should be punished by death;
     it denies Almighty God.

29 I have never been glad when my enemies
         suffered,
     or pleased when they met with disaster;
30   I never sinned by praying for their death.
31 All those who work for me know
     that I have always welcomed strangers.
32 I invited travelers into my home
     and never let them sleep in the streets.

33 Others try to hide their sins,
     but I have never concealed mine.
34 I have never feared what people would
     say;

I have never kept quiet or stayed indoors
     because I feared their scorn.

35 Will no one listen to what I am saying?
     I swear that every word is true.
     Let Almighty God answer me.

If the charges my opponent brings against
         me
     were written down so that I could see
         them,
36 I would wear them proudly on my shoulder
     and place them on my head like a
         crown.
37 I would tell God everything I have done,
     and hold my head high in his presence.

38 If I have stolen the land I farm
     and taken it from its rightful owners—
39   if I have eaten the food that grew there
     but let the farmers that grew it starve—
40   then instead of wheat and barley,
     may weeds and thistles grow.

The words of Job are ended.

31:24 Sir 31:5–10

"God knows everything I do; / he sees every step I take" (Job 31:4).

Job

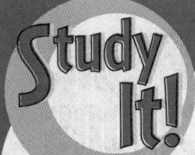

The Gifts of Youth

Elihu hesitates to speak up because he is young, but when he gathers up the courage to speak, he has a lot to say! His thoughts reflect the wisdom of a young soul. God calls young people, as well as mature adults, to share their gifts and their wisdom. Here are some stories of young people in the Bible—stories of how they were called by God, the wisdom they possessed, missions they accomplished with courage, and gifts they shared with others:

- Joseph, son of Jacob (Genesis, chapters 37–50)
- Samuel (1 Samuel, chapter 3)
- David (1 Samuel, chapters 16–18)
- Jeremiah (Jeremiah 1:4–10)
- Mary (Luke 1:26–56)
- Jesus (Luke 2:41–52)
  Check out these stories, and let them inspire you!

— Job, chapters 32–37

The Speeches of Elihu
(32:1—37:24)

32 ¹Because Job was convinced of his own innocence, the three men gave up trying to answer him. ²But a bystander named Elihu could not control his anger any longer, because Job was justifying himself and blaming God. (Elihu was the son of Barakel, a descendant of Buz, and belonged to the clan of Ram.) ³He was also angry with Job's three friends. They could not find any way to answer Job, and this made it appear that God was in the wrong. ⁴Because Elihu was the youngest one there, he had waited until everyone finished speaking. ⁵When he saw that the three men could not answer Job, he was angry ⁶and began to speak.

Elihu

I am young, and you are old,
    so I was afraid to tell you what I think.
⁷I told myself that you ought to speak,
    that you older men should share your wisdom.
⁸But it is the spirit of Almighty God
    that comes to us and gives us wisdom.
⁹It is not growing old that makes us wise
    or helps us to know what is right.
¹⁰So now I want you to listen to me;
    let me tell you what I think.

¹¹I listened patiently while you were speaking
    and waited while you searched for wise phrases.
¹²I paid close attention and heard you fail;
    you have not disproved what Job has said.
¹³How can you claim you have discovered wisdom?
    God must answer Job, for you have failed.
¹⁴Job was speaking to you, not to me,
    but I would never answer the way you did.
¹⁵Words have failed them, Job;
    they have no answer for you.
¹⁶Shall I go on waiting when they are silent?
    They stand there with nothing more to say.
¹⁷No, I will give my own answer now
    and tell you what I think.
¹⁸I can hardly wait to speak.
    I can't hold back the words.
¹⁹If I don't get a chance to speak,
    I will burst like a wineskin full of new wine.
²⁰I can't stand it; I have to speak.
²¹I will not take sides in this debate;
    I am not going to flatter anyone.

Wine was made in goatskins that stretched as the fermenting grape juice produced gases—if the skins didn't stretch enough, they would burst.

22 I don't know how to flatter,
and God would quickly punish me if I
did.

33 1 And now, Job, listen carefully
to all that I have to say.
2 I am ready to say what's on my mind.
3 All my words are sincere,
and I am speaking the truth.
4 God's spirit made me and gave me life.

5 Answer me if you can. Prepare your
arguments.
6 You and I are the same in God's sight,
both of us were formed from clay.
7 So you have no reason to fear me;
I will not overpower you.

8 Now this is what I heard you say:
9 "I am not guilty; I have done nothing
wrong.
I am innocent and free from sin.
10 But God finds excuses for attacking me
and treats me like an enemy.
11 He binds chains on my feet;
he watches every move I make."

12 But I tell you, Job, you are wrong.
God is greater than any human being.
13 Why do you accuse God
of never answering our complaints?
14 Although God speaks again and again,
no one pays attention to what he
says.
15 At night when people are asleep,
God speaks in dreams and visions.
16 He makes them listen to what he says,
and they are frightened at his warnings.
17 God speaks to make them stop their
sinning
and to save them from becoming
proud.
18 He will not let them be destroyed;
he saves them from death itself.
19 God corrects us by sending sickness
and filling our bodies with pain.
20 Those who are sick lose their appetites,
and even the finest food looks revolting.
21 Their bodies waste away to nothing;
you can see all their bones;
22 they are about to go to the world of
the dead.

God's Messengers

Have you heard the story about the woman who slipped off a cliff, was hanging from a tree limb, and cried out to God: "Help, God! Please save me!" Soon, a helicopter flew near her and a ladder was let down so she could climb up to safety. "No, thanks," she told them, "God's going to save me." Next, a fire truck arrived and a crash pad was placed below her so that she could jump without getting injured. "Thanks, but I'm waiting for God—he'll be saving me any minute now!" Finally, she called out again: "God? Are you there? I don't know how much longer I can hang on! Please save me!" God responded to her, "I sent you a helicopter and a fire truck. What more do you want?"

Elihu tells Job he is wrong about God not answering his prayers. God speaks to us and offers us help all the time, but most of the time we miss it! Some of the ways God can speak to us:
- through the guidance of parents and other caring adults
- through the support and example of friends
- when a situation, such as an illness or loss, causes us to look at what is truly important in life
- through the dreams and desires that God plants in our hearts
Ask God to keep your eyes and ears and heart open to his presence in your life.

— Job 33:12–19

23 Perhaps an angel may come to their aid—
     one of God's thousands of angels,
     who remind us of our duty.
24 In mercy the angel will say, "Release them!
     They are not to go down to the world
     of the dead.
     Here is the ransom to set them free."
25 Their bodies will grow young and strong
     again;
26   when they pray, God will answer;
     they will worship God with joy;
     God will set things right for them
     again.
27 Each one will say in public, "I have
     sinned.
     I have not done right, but God spared
     me.
28 He kept me from going to the world of
     the dead,
     and I am still alive."

29 God does all this again and again;
30   each one saves a person's life,
     and gives him the joy of living.

31 Now, Job, listen to what I am saying;
     be quiet and let me speak.
32 But if you have something to say, let me
     hear it;
     I would gladly admit you are in the
     right.
33 But if not, be quiet and listen to me,
     and I will teach you how to be wise.

34

1-2 You men are so wise, so clever;
     listen now to what I am saying.
3 You know good food when you taste it,
     but not wise words when you hear
     them.
4 It is up to us to decide the case.
5 Job claims that he is innocent,
     that God refuses to give him justice.
6 He asks, "How could I lie and say I am
     wrong?
     I am fatally wounded, but I am sinless."

7 Have you ever seen anyone like this man
     Job?
     He never shows respect for God.
8 He likes the company of evil people
     and goes around with sinners.

9 He says that it never does any good
     to try to follow God's will.
10 Listen to me, you men who understand!
     Will Almighty God do what is wrong?
11 He rewards people for what they do
     and treats them as they deserve.
12 Almighty God does not do evil;
     he is never unjust to anyone.
13 Did God get his power from someone else?
     Did someone put him in charge of the
     world?
14 If God took back the breath of life,
15   then everyone living would die
     and turn into dust again.

16 Now listen to me, if you are wise.
17 Are you condemning the righteous God?
     Do you think that *he* hates justice?
18 God condemns kings and rulers
     when they are worthless or wicked.
19 He does not take the side of rulers
     nor favor the rich over the poor,
     for he created everyone.
20 We may suddenly die at night.
     God strikes us down and we perish;
     he kills the mighty with no effort at all.
21 He watches every step we take.
22 There is no darkness dark enough
     to hide a sinner from God.
23 God does not need to set a time*l*
     for us to go and be judged by him.
24 He does not need an investigation
     to remove leaders and replace them
     with others.
25 Because he knows what they do;
     he overthrows them and crushes them
     by night.
26 He punishes sinners where all can see it,
27   because they have stopped following him
     and ignored all his commands.
28 They forced the poor to cry out to God,
     and he heard their calls for help.
29 If God decided to do nothing at all,
     no one could criticize him.
     If he hid his face, we would be helpless.
30 There would be nothing that nations
     could do
     to keep godless oppressors from ruling
     them.

---

l **34:23** *Probable text* a time; *Hebrew* yet.
34:11 Ps 62:12

³¹ Job, have you confessed your sins to God
  and promised not to sin again?
³² Have you asked God to show you your
  faults,
  and have you agreed to stop doing evil?
³³ Since you object to what God does,
  can you expect him to do what you
  want?
  The decision is yours, not mine;
  tell us now what you think.

³⁴ Any sensible person will surely agree;
  and the wise who hear me will say
³⁵   that Job is speaking from ignorance
  and that nothing he says makes sense.
³⁶ Think through everything that Job says;
  you will see that he talks like an evil
  man.
³⁷ To his sins he adds rebellion;
  in front of us all he mocks God.

35 ¹⁻² It is not right, Job, for you to say
      that you are innocent in God's sight,
³ or to ask God, "How does my sin affect
  you?
  What have I gained by not sinning?"
⁴ I am going to answer you and your
  friends too.
⁵ Look at the sky! See how high the clouds
  are!
⁶ If you sin, that does no harm to God.
  If you do wrong many times, does that
  affect him?
⁷ Do you help God by being so righteous?
  There is nothing God needs from you.
⁸ Others suffer from your sins,
  and the good you do helps them.

⁹ When people are oppressed, they groan;
  they cry for someone to save them.
¹⁰ But they don't turn to God, their Creator,
  who gives them hope in their darkest
  hours.
¹¹ They don't turn to God, who makes us
  wise,
  wiser than any animal or bird.

¹² They cry for help, but God doesn't
  answer,
  for they are proud and evil.
¹³ It is useless for them to cry out;
  Almighty God does not see or hear
  them.

Live It!

Making a Difference

Jackson climbed into bed, and before he fell asleep he thought about his day. He was really sorry that he had borrowed Al's homework to finish his own. He didn't mean to copy quite as much as he did. But they both got caught anyway, and both received big fat zeros for the assignment—a zero he didn't need. Al was pretty mad, and Jackson couldn't blame him. He hoped their friendship wasn't ruined.

Then he remembered the lunchroom incident. Maggie dropped her tray right behind him! Everyone cheered and clapped, of course—that's just what you do during a tray dropping. But something made Jackson turn around in his seat and help her pick up the dishes and food that crashed to the ground. He wasn't sure if he saw tears of embarrassment pooling up in her eyes, but he did recognize gratitude in the smile she gave him.

Our actions do make a difference for other people, as Elihu says in Job 35:8. We choose what *kind* of difference.

— Job 35:8

35:6–8 Job 22:2, 3

"If God took back the breath of life, / then everyone living would die / and turn into dust again" (Job 34:14–15). See Genesis 2:7.

Job

14 Job, you say you can't see God;
but wait patiently—your case is before
him.
15 You think that God does not punish,
that he pays little attention to sin.
16 It is useless for you to go on talking;
it is clear you don't know what you are
saying.

36 1-2 Be patient and listen a little
longer
to what I am saying on God's behalf.
3 My knowledge is wide; I will use what I
know
to show that God, my Creator, is just.
4 Nothing I say to you is false;
you see before you a truly wise man.

5 How strong God is! He despises no one;
there is nothing he doesn't understand.
6 He does not let sinners live on,
and he always treats the poor with justice.
7 He protects those who are righteous;
he allows them to rule like kings
and lets them be honored forever.
8 But if people are bound in chains,
suffering for what they have done,
9　God shows them their sins and their
pride.
10 He makes them listen to his warning
to turn away from evil.
11 If they obey God and serve him,
they live out their lives in peace and
prosperity.
12 But if not, they will die in ignorance
and cross the stream into the world of
the dead.

13 Those who are godless keep on being
angry,
and even when punished, they don't
pray for help.
14 They die while they are still young,
worn out by a life of disgrace.
15 But God teaches people through suffering
and uses distress to open their eyes.

16 God brought you out of trouble,
and let you enjoy security;

your table was piled high with food.
17 But now you are being punished as you
deserve.
18 Be careful not to let bribes deceive you,
or riches lead you astray.
19 It will do you no good to cry out for
help;
all your strength can't help you now.
20 Don't wish for night to come,
the time when nations will perish.
21 Be careful not to turn to evil;
your suffering was sent to keep you
from it.
22 Remember how great is God's power;
he is the greatest teacher of all.
23 No one can tell God what to do
or accuse him of doing evil.
24 He has always been praised for what he
does;
you also must praise him.
25 Everyone has seen what he has done;
but we can only watch from a
distance. *m*
26 We cannot fully know his greatness
or count the number of his years.

27 It is God who takes water from the earth
and turns it into drops of rain.
28 He lets the rain pour from the clouds
in showers for all human beings.

Everyone has seen what he has done. (36:25)

---

m **36:25** but we can only watch from a distance; *or* no one understands it all.

Euthanasia

Catholic Connections

"But God teaches people through suffering / and uses distress to open their eyes" (Job 36:15). No one welcomes suffering, no matter whether it is our own or the suffering of someone we love. We pray to God to take suffering away. But we also believe that suffering has a purpose, no matter how bad the pain might be. That is why euthanasia, which is sometimes called mercy killing, is wrong. People who approve of euthanasia feel that it is okay for someone to ask to be killed to end intense suffering. But killing someone before their natural death—even if it is to end the person's suffering—is morally wrong.

What good can come from suffering? Suffering can teach us patience, trust, willingness to let others help us, compassion, humility, faithfulness, and hope, among other lessons. Jesus gave us the best example of facing suffering with courage, forgiveness, and love. Without his violent death, we could not experience his victorious Resurrection, which is the main event of Christianity.

We can't escape suffering—at some point in our lives most of us will experience it. But we can look to God to be near us, to strengthen us, and to teach us important lessons about life, death, and love.

— Job 36:15

29 No one knows how the clouds move
   or how the thunder roars
   through the sky, where God dwells.
30 He sends lightning through all the
      sky,
   but the depths of the sea remain
      dark.
31 This is how he feeds[n] the people
   and provides an abundance of food.
32 He seizes the lightning with his hands
   and commands it to hit the mark.
33 Thunder announces the approaching
      storm,
   and the cattle know it is coming.

37 1 The storm makes my heart beat
         wildly.
2 Listen, all of you, to the voice of God,
   to the thunder that comes from his
      mouth.
3 He sends the lightning across the sky,
   from one end of the earth to the
      other.

4 Then the roar of his voice is heard,
   the majestic sound of thunder,
   and all the while the lightning
      flashes.
5 At God's command amazing things
      happen,
   wonderful things that we can't
      understand.
6 He commands snow to fall on the
      earth,
   and sends torrents of drenching rain.
7 He brings our work to a stop;
   he shows us what he can do.[o]
8 The wild animals go to their dens.
9 The storm winds come from the south,
   and the biting cold from the north.
10 The breath of God freezes the waters,
   and turns them to solid ice.
11 Lightning flashes from the clouds,[p]
12   as they move at God's will.
   They do all that God commands,
      everywhere throughout the world.

[n] **36:31** *Probable text* feeds; *Hebrew* judges.   [o] **37:7** *One ancient translation* us what he can do; *Hebrew* this to those whom he has made.   [p] **37:11** *Verse 11 in Hebrew is unclear.*

Job

13 God sends rain to water the earth;
　　he may send it to punish us,
　　or to show us his favor.

14 Pause a moment, Job, and listen;
　　consider the wonderful things God
　　does.
15 Do you know how God gives the
　　command
　　and makes lightning flash from the
　　clouds?
16 Do you know how clouds float in the sky,
　　the work of God's amazing skill?
17 No, you can only suffer in the heat
　　when the south wind oppresses the
　　land.
18 Can you help God stretch out the sky
　　and make it as hard as polished metal?
19 Teach us what to say to God;
　　our minds are blank; we have nothing
　　to say.
20 I won't ask to speak with God;
　　why should I give him a chance to
　　destroy me?

21 And now the light in the sky is dazzling,
　　too bright for us to look at it;
　　and the sky has been swept clean by
　　the wind.
22 A golden glow is seen in the north,
　　and the glory of God fills us with awe.
23 God's power is so great that we cannot
　　come near him;
　　he is righteous and just in his dealings
　　with us.
24 No wonder, then, that everyone is awed
　　by him,
　　and that he ignores those who claim to
　　be wise.

The LORD Answers Job

38 ¹ Then out of the storm the LORD
　　　spoke to Job.

The LORD

2 Who are you to question my wisdom
　　with your ignorant, empty words?
3 Now stand up straight
　　and answer the questions I ask you.

Pray It!

God's View of Creation

God finally speaks up! In chapters 38–39, God asks Job a series of questions, all concerning the creation of the world. Job has no answers to these questions. Awesome, complex, curious, marvelous, amazing—those words can't even begin to describe the miracle of Creation or its architect and maker, God. Spend some time reading those chapters; try reading them out loud as the beautiful poems they are. Let your reading be a prayer, praising God, our Creator.

— Job, chapters 38–39

---

4 Were you there when I made the world?
　　If you know so much, tell me about it.
5 Who decided how large it would be?
　　Who stretched the measuring line over
　　　it?
　　Do you know all the answers?
6 What holds up the pillars that support the
　　　earth?
　　Who laid the cornerstone of the
　　　world?
7 In the dawn of that day the stars sang
　　together,
　　and the heavenly beings[q] shouted for
　　joy.

8 Who closed the gates to hold back the sea[r]
　　when it burst from the womb of the
　　earth?
9 It was I who covered the sea with clouds
　　and wrapped it in darkness.
10 I marked a boundary for the sea
　　and kept it behind bolted gates.
11 I told it, "So far and no farther!
　　Here your powerful waves must stop."

---

q **38:7** HEAVENLY BEINGS: *See 1:6.*　　r **38:8** TO HOLD BACK THE SEA: *See 26:12.*
38:7 Bar 3:34　　**38:8–11** Jer 5:22

12 Job, have you ever in all your life
    commanded a day to dawn?
13 Have you ordered the dawn to seize the
    earth
    and shake the wicked from their hiding
    places?
14 Daylight makes the hills and valleys stand
    out
    like the folds of a garment,
    clear as the imprint of a seal on clay.
15 The light of day is too bright for the
    wicked
    and restrains them from doing
    violence.

16 Have you been to the springs in the
    depths of the sea?
    Have you walked on the floor of the
    ocean?
17 Has anyone ever shown you the gates
    that guard the dark world of the dead?
18 Have you any idea how big the world is?
    Answer me if you know.

19 Do you know where the light comes from
    or what the source of darkness is?
20 Can you show them how far to go,
    or send them back again?
21 I am sure you can, because you're so old
    and were there when the world was
    made!

22 Have you ever visited the storerooms,
    where I keep the snow and the hail?
23 I keep them ready for times of trouble,
    for days of battle and war.
24 Have you been to the place where the
    sun comes up,
    or the place from which the east wind
    blows?
25 Who dug a channel for the pouring rain
    and cleared the way for the
    thunderstorm?
26 Who makes rain fall where no one lives?
27 Who waters the dry and thirsty land,
    so that grass springs up?

28 Does either the rain or the dew have a
    father?
29 Who is the mother of the ice and the
    frost,
30   which turn the waters to stone
    and freeze the face of the sea?
31 Can you tie the Pleiades together
    or loosen the bonds that hold Orion?
32 Can you guide the stars season by season
    and direct the Big and the Little
    Dipper?
33 Do you know the laws that govern the
    skies,
    and can you make them apply to the
    earth?
34 Can you shout orders to the clouds
    and make them drench you with rain?
35 And if you command the lightning to
    flash,
    will it come to you and say, "At your
    service"?
36 Who tells the ibis⁵ when the Nile will
    flood,
    or who tells the rooster that rain will
    fall?ᵗ
37 Who is wise enough to count the clouds
    and tilt them over to pour out the rain,
38   rain that hardens the dust into lumps?

39 Do you find food for lions to eat,
    and satisfy hungry young lions
40   when they hide in their caves,
    or lie in wait in their dens?
41 Who is it that feeds the ravens
    when they wander about hungry,
    when their young cry to me for food?

39

¹ Do you know when mountain
    goats are born?
    Have you watched wild deer give
    birth?
² Do you know how long they carry their
    young?
    Do you know the time for their birth?

ˢ **38:36** IBIS: *A bird in ancient Egypt that was believed to announce the flooding of the Nile River.*   ᵗ **38:36** *Verse 36 in
Hebrew is unclear.*
38:31 Job 9:9; Am 5:8

**"Have you ever visited the storerooms, / where I keep the snow and the
hail?"** (*Job 38:22*).

Pray It!

Earth Prayer

The beauty of the trees,
the softness of the air,
the fragrance of the grass,
    speaks to me.
The summit of the mountain,
the thunder of the sky,
the rhythm of the sea,
    speaks to me.
The faintness of the stars,
the freshness of the morning,
the dewdrop on the flower,
    speaks to me.
The strength of fire,
the taste of salmon,
the trail of the sun,
and the life that never goes away,
    they speak to me.
And my heart soars.
    —Chief Dan George

    — Job, chapter 39

3 Do you know when they will crouch
   down
    and bring their young into the world?
4 In the wilds their young grow strong;
    they go away and don't come back.

5 Who gave the wild donkeys their
   freedom?
    Who turned them loose and let them
    roam?
6 I gave them the desert to be their home,
    and let them live on the salt plains.
7 They keep far away from the noisy cities,
    and no one can tame them and make
    them work.
8 The mountains are the pastures where
   they feed,
    where they search for anything green
    to eat.

9 Will a wild ox work for you?
   Is he willing to spend the night in your
    stable?
10 Can you hold one with a rope and make
   him plow?
   Or make him pull a harrow in your
    fields?
11 Can you rely on his great strength
    and expect him to do your heavy
    work?
12 Do you expect him to bring in your
   harvest
   and gather the grain from your
    threshing place?

13 How fast the wings of an ostrich beat!
   But no ostrich can fly like a stork. *u*
14 The ostrich leaves her eggs on the ground
    for the heat in the soil to warm them.
15 She is unaware that a foot may crush
    them
    or a wild animal break them.
16 She acts as if the eggs were not hers,
    and is unconcerned that her efforts
    were wasted.
17 It was I who made her foolish
    and did not give her wisdom.
18 But when she begins to run, *v*
    she can laugh at any horse and rider.

19 Was it you, Job, who made horses so
   strong
   and gave them their flowing manes?
20 Did you make them leap like locusts
   and frighten people with their
    snorting?
21 They eagerly paw the ground in the
   valley;
   they rush into battle with all their
    strength.
22 They do not know the meaning of fear,
    and no sword can turn them back.
23 The weapons which their riders carry
    rattle and flash in the sun.
24 Trembling with excitement, the horses
   race ahead;
   when the trumpet blows, they can't
    stand still.

u **39:13** *Verse 13 in Hebrew is unclear.*   *v* **39:18** *Probable text* run; *Hebrew unclear.*

Do ostriches make good mothers? Check out Job 39:13–18.

*The ostrich . . . the horses . . . an eagle . . .
the monster . . . (39:14, 24, 27; 40:15)*

25 At each blast of the trumpet they snort;
    they can smell a battle before they get
        near,
    and they hear the officers shouting
        commands.

26 Does a hawk learn from you how to fly
    when it spreads its wings toward the
        south?
27 Does an eagle wait for your command
    to build its nest high in the mountains?
28 It makes its home on the highest rocks
    and makes the sharp peaks its fortress.
29 From there it watches near and far
    for something to kill and eat.
30 Around dead bodies the eagles gather,
    and the young eagles drink the
        blood.

40 1-2 Job, you challenged Almighty
        God;
    will you give up now, or will you
        answer?

Job

3-4 I spoke foolishly, LORD. What can I
        answer?
    I will not try to say anything else.
5 I have already said more than I should.

6 Then out of the storm the LORD spoke
to Job once again.

The LORD

7 Now stand up straight
    and answer my questions.
8 Are you trying to prove that I am
        unjust—
    to put me in the wrong and yourself in
        the right?
9 Are you as strong as I am?
    Can your voice thunder as loud as
        mine?

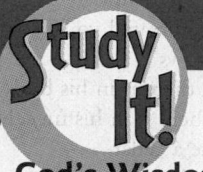

God's Wisdom

So, what is the point of God's speech? Job gets it right away. We cannot even get close to understanding the mind of God. Our brains simply aren't equipped to take in a mystery like that. God is teaching us that, like Creation, human nature is extremely complicated—often beyond our understanding. Why would God allow an innocent person to suffer? Even if God revealed the answer to us, we would not be able to grasp the meaning. God's wisdom is so wide and so deep that it's way beyond the limits of our imagination and control.

Is this supposed to be comforting? We still don't have an answer to the question about why people suffer. Like Job, we each may have times in our lives when all we can do is trust in the wisdom of God's plans—even if we don't like them. For now, we do our best to cope with the mystery of suffering, and to believe that it can teach us, bless us, and deepen our faith and love.

— Job 40:1–5

10 If so, stand up in your honor and pride;
    clothe yourself with majesty and glory.
11 Look at those who are proud;
    pour out your anger and humble them.
12 Yes, look at them and bring them down;
    crush the wicked where they stand.
13 Bury them all in the ground;
    bind them in the world of the dead.
14 Then I will be the first to praise you
    and admit that you won the victory
        yourself.

15 Look at the monster Behemoth;*w*
    I created him and I created you.
  He eats grass like a cow,
16   but what strength there is in his body,
    and what power there is in his muscles!
17 His tail stands up like a cedar,
    and the muscles in his legs are strong.
18 His bones are as strong as bronze,
    and his legs are like iron bars.

19 The most amazing of all my creatures!
    Only his Creator can defeat him.
20 Grass to feed him grows
    on the hills where wild beasts play.*x*
21 He lies down under the thorn bushes,
    and hides among the reeds in the swamp.
22 The thorn bushes and the willows by the
        stream
    give him shelter in their shade.
23 He is not afraid of a rushing river;
    he is calm when the Jordan dashes in
        his face.
24 Who can blind his eyes and capture him?
    Or who can catch his snout in a trap?

41 ¹Can you catch Leviathan*y* with a
        fishhook
    or tie his tongue down with a rope?
2 Can you put a rope through his snout
    or put a hook through his jaws?
3 Will he beg you to let him go?
    Will he plead with you for mercy?
4 Will he make an agreement with you
    and promise to serve you forever?
5 Will you tie him like a pet bird,
    like something to amuse your servant
        women?
6 Will fishermen bargain over him?
    Will merchants cut him up to sell?
7 Can you fill his hide with fishing spears
    or pierce his head with a harpoon?
8 Touch him once and you'll never try it
        again;
    you'll never forget the fight!

9 Anyone who sees Leviathan
    loses courage and falls to the ground.
10 When he is aroused, he is fierce;
    no one would dare to stand before him.

11 Who can attack him and still be safe?
    No one in all the world can do it.*z*
12 Let me tell you about Leviathan's legs
    and describe how great and strong
        he is.
13 No one can tear off his outer coat
    or pierce the armor*a* he wears.
14 Who can make him open his jaws,
    ringed with those terrifying teeth?
15 His back*b* is made of rows of shields,
    fastened together and hard as stone.
16 Each one is joined so tight to the next,
    not even a breath can come between.
17 They all are fastened so firmly together
    that nothing can ever pull them apart.
18 Light flashes when he sneezes,
    and his eyes glow like the rising sun.
19 Flames blaze from his mouth,
    and streams of sparks fly out.
20 Smoke comes pouring out of his nose,
    like smoke from weeds burning under
        a pot.
21 His breath starts fires burning;
    flames leap out of his mouth.
22 His neck is so powerful
    that all who meet him are terrified.
23 There is not a weak spot in his skin;
    it is as hard and unyielding as iron.
24 His stony heart is without fear,
    as unyielding and hard as a millstone.
25 When he rises up, even the strongest*c* are
        frightened;
    they are helpless with fear.
26 There is no sword that can wound
        him;
    no spear or arrow or lance that can
        harm him.
27 For him iron is as flimsy as straw,
    and bronze as soft as rotten wood.
28 There is no arrow that can make him
        run;
    rocks thrown at him are like bits of
        straw.
29 To him a club is a piece of straw,
    and he laughs when men throw
        spears.

---

w **40:15** BEHEMOTH: *Some identify this with the hippopotamus, others with a legendary creature.*   *x* **40:20** *Verse 20 in Hebrew is unclear.*   *y* **41:1** LEVIATHAN: *See 3:8.*   *z* **41:11** *Verse 11 in Hebrew is unclear.*   *a* **41:13** *One ancient translation* armor; *Hebrew* bridle.   *b* **41:15** *Some ancient translations* back; *Hebrew* pride.   *c* **41:25** strongest; *or gods.*
41:1 Ps 74:14; 104:26; Isa 27:1

Job

³⁰ The scales on his belly are like jagged
pieces of pottery;
they tear up the muddy ground like a
threshing sledge. *ᵈ*
³¹ He churns up the sea like boiling water
and makes it bubble like a pot of oil.
³² He leaves a shining path behind him
and turns the sea to white foam.
³³ There is nothing on earth to compare
with him;
he is a creature that has no fear.
³⁴ He looks down on even the proudest
animals;
he is king of all wild beasts.

42

Job

¹ Then Job answered the LORD.

² I know, LORD, that you are all-powerful;
that you can do everything you want.
³ You ask how I dare question your
wisdom
when I am so very ignorant.
I talked about things I did not
understand,
about marvels too great for me to
know.
⁴ You told me to listen while you spoke
and to try to answer your questions.
⁵ In the past I knew only what others had
told me,
but now I have seen you with my own
eyes.
⁶ So I am ashamed of all I have said
and repent in dust and ashes.

Conclusion

⁷ After the LORD had finished speaking to
Job, he said to Eliphaz, "I am angry with you
and your two friends, because you did not
speak the truth about me, the way my servant Job did. ⁸ Now take seven bulls and
seven rams to Job and offer them as a sacrifice for yourselves. Job will pray for you, and

God's Blessing for Job

Shockingly—to us—God admits
that Job was correct. God did
indeed allow suffering to trample
the life of an innocent person.
Job's friends claimed that God
would never do such a thing, and
God angrily informs them that
they spoke untruthfully about him.

The Israelites' view of God's
justice—rewarding the good and
punishing the wicked—is proven to
be too simple. While God does not
cause or *will* Job's suffering, we are
led to understand that God *allows*
it. This is not at all comforting to
us! But, remember, God's plans are
a deep mystery—we cannot grasp
all the ways God works in our lives
and our world. We are asked to do
what seems impossible at times:
trust.

Because Job spoke the truth
about God, God blessed him—
twice as much as before! The
author's claim that Job lived to the
age of 140 is another way of saying
that Job's life was good and long
(twice as many years as the average life span, to match the twice-
as-many blessings), so that he had
plenty of time to enjoy all of God's
blessings poured upon him.

— Job, chapter 42

I will answer his prayer and not disgrace you
the way you deserve. You did not speak the
truth about me as he did."

ᵈ **41:30** THRESHING SLEDGES: *These had sharp pieces of iron or stone fastened beneath them.*
42:3 Job 38:2   **42:4** Job 38:3

Job

The LORD made him prosperous again. (42:10)

⁹Eliphaz, Bildad, and Zophar did what the LORD had told them to do, and the LORD answered Job's prayer.

¹⁰Then, after Job had prayed for his three friends, the LORD made him prosperous again and gave him twice as much as he had had before. ¹¹All Job's brothers and sisters and former friends came to visit him and feasted with him in his house. They expressed their sympathy and comforted him for all the troubles the LORD had brought on him. Each of them gave him some money and a gold ring.

¹²The LORD blessed the last part of Job's life even more than he had blessed the first. Job owned fourteen thousand sheep, six thousand camels, two thousand head of cattle, and one thousand donkeys. ¹³He was the father of seven sons and three daughters. ¹⁴He called the oldest daughter Jemimah, the second Keziah, and the youngest Keren Happuch.ᵉ ¹⁵There were no other women in the whole world as beautiful as Job's daughters. Their father gave them a share of the inheritance along with their brothers.

¹⁶Job lived a hundred and forty years after this, long enough to see his grandchildren and great-grandchildren. ¹⁷And then he died at a very great age.

ᵉ **42:14** *In Hebrew the names of Job's daughters suggest beauty both by their sound and by their meaning.* JEMIMAH *means "dove";* KEZIAH *means "cassia," a variety of cinnamon used as a perfume; and* KEREN HAPPUCH *means a small box used for eye make-up.*
42:10 Job 1:1–3

Your Next Step

Congratulations on finishing the Book of Job! Use this space to write your thoughts and questions about this book. If you are following the suggested reading plan, move ahead to the First Letter of Peter in the New Testament. This letter also discusses suffering, connecting our suffering to the suffering of Christ.

Each Sunday, as the cantor leads the assembly in the responsorial psalm, Debbie sings her heart out. Sometimes, when her youth group plans their special Masses, she leads them in the responsorial psalm. She knows it is good practice, and she likes it a lot. She imagines that one day she will lead the whole church.

Debbie, like many people, loves the Psalms. She especially likes the words and themes of the Psalms. The Psalms are poetic, dramatic, comforting, and inspirational. They sing gratitude for God's blessings, cry for help in times of need, seek wisdom and direction, praise God during worship, and express wonder and awe at the greatness of God. All of these things make the Psalms one of the most beloved books of the Bible.

Psalm 150

Headlines

- The Key to True Happiness! (Psalm 1)
- Fools Say There Is No God (Psalm 14)
- Desperate Cry for Help Is Answered (Psalm 22)
- Hope Found in Time of Despair (Psalm 23)
- Plea for Forgiveness and God's Mercy (Psalm 51)
- Youth Prays for Help (Psalm 102)
- Everyone and Everything Praise God! (Psalms 148–150)

FACTOIDS

Who wrote this book? There are many authors, called psalmists, who contributed to the collection of Psalms.

Why was it written? Psalms was written as a hymnbook and prayer book for God's people. They are still used and sung in Catholic liturgy and devotions, often as a response to another Bible reading.

How is it organized? Psalms is divided into five books: Book 1 (1–41), Book 2 (42–72), Book 3 (73–89), Book 4 (90–106), and Book 5 (107–150).

Jesus connection: Jesus quoted Psalms; some of his last words are from the Psalms (Psalm 22).

Important themes

- There are many kinds of psalms: songs of praise and thanksgiving, songs of lament and petition, songs of wisdom, liturgical or worship psalms, and historical psalms.
- No matter what emotions we are feeling, we can bring them to God in prayer.

PSALMS

BOOK ONE
(Psalms 1–41)

True Happiness

1 ¹Happy are those
who reject the advice of evil people,
who do not follow the example of
sinners
or join those who have no use for God.
²Instead, they find joy in obeying the Law
of the LORD,
and they study it day and night.
³They are like trees that grow beside a
stream,
that bear fruit at the right time,
and whose leaves do not dry up.
They succeed in everything they do.

⁴But evil people are not like this at all;
they are like straw that the wind blows
away.
⁵Sinners will be condemned by God
and kept apart from God's own people.
⁶The righteous are guided and protected
by the LORD,
but the evil are on the way to their
doom.

God's Chosen King

2 ¹Why do the nations plan rebellion?
Why do people make their useless
plots?
²Their kings revolt,
their rulers plot together against the
LORD
and against the king he chose.
³"Let us free ourselves from their rule,"
they say;
"let us throw off their control."

⁴From his throne in heaven the Lord laughs
and mocks their feeble plans.
⁵Then he warns them in anger
and terrifies them with his fury.

Sing a Psalm!

Some people like to play a special song or type of music when they are feeling a certain way. They may put on country music when they are feeling low. They might put on rock when they are feeling happy. Maybe they listen to classical music when they need to calm down. This is like the Psalms. There are songs that celebrate as well as ones that express grief. There are songs that are joyful and others that are sad. Almost every emotion can be found in the Psalms.

The Psalms, written in a poetic style, were put to music. They still are! Both Jewish and Christian musicians continue to write music for the Psalms. They are so popular that in many New Testament Bibles (Bibles that only contain the New Testament books), the Psalms are also included. Psalms are included in many Catholic prayer services and liturgies. In a Catholic Mass, a psalm is sung or read after the first reading.

— Psalm 1

⁶"On Zion,ᵃ my sacred hill," he says,
"I have installed my king."

⁷"I will announce," says the king, "what
the LORD has declared.
He said to me: 'You are my son;
today I have become your father.

ᵃ **2:6** ZION: *The term "Zion" (originally a designation for "David's City," the Jebusite stronghold captured by King David's forces) was later extended in meaning to refer to the hill on which the Temple stood.*
1:3 Jer 17:8   **2:1, 2** Acts 4:25, 26   **2:7** Acts 13:33; Heb 1:5; 5:5

8 Ask, and I will give you all the nations;
   the whole earth will be yours.
9 You will break them with an iron rod;
   you will shatter them in pieces like a
   clay pot.' "

10 Now listen to this warning, you kings;
   learn this lesson, you rulers of the world:
11 Serve the LORD with fear;
   tremble 12 and bow down to him; [b]
   or else his anger will be quickly aroused,
   and you will suddenly die.
   Happy are all who go to him for protection.

Morning Prayer for Help [c]

3 ¹ I have so many enemies, LORD,
      so many who turn against me!
2 They talk about me and say,
   "God will not help him."

3 But you, O LORD, are always my shield
      from danger;
   you give me victory
   and restore my courage.
4 I call to the LORD for help,
   and from his sacred hill [d] he answers me.

5 I lie down and sleep,
   and all night long the LORD protects me.
6 I am not afraid of the thousands of enemies
   who surround me on every side.

7 Come, LORD! Save me, my God!
   You punish all my enemies
   and leave them powerless to harm me.
8 Victory comes from the LORD —
   may he bless his people.

Evening Prayer for Help [e]

4 ¹ Answer me when I pray,
      O God, my defender!
   When I was in trouble, you helped me.
   Be kind to me now and hear my
      prayer.

Pray It!

Sleep Soundly

One way to get a good night's sleep is to do a few things before going to bed. Your parents would probably tell you that before going to bed you should be brushing your teeth and putting your dirty clothes in the laundry. But after the work is done, there is one last thing: prayer. That's right. A good prayer at the end of the day can help you rest well. Psalm 4 can be used as an evening psalm. It probably doesn't describe your average day, but it does remind you that God protects, loves, and blesses you. Those are great thoughts for sweet dreams!
   You might even want to write your own closing prayer to end your day. Say a prayer just before going to bed and see how well you sleep.

— Psalm 4

2 How long will you people insult me?
   How long will you love what is
      worthless
   and go after what is false?

3 Remember that the LORD has chosen the
      righteous for his own,
   and he hears me when I call to him.

4 Tremble with fear and stop sinning;
   think deeply about this,
   when you lie in silence on your beds.

[b] **2:12** *Probable text* tremble . . . him; *some other possible texts* with trembling kiss his feet *and* with trembling kiss the Son *and* tremble and kiss the mighty one; *Hebrew unclear.*   [c] **3** HEBREW TITLE: *A psalm by David, after he ran away from his son Absalom.*   [d] **3:4** SACRED HILL: *See 2:6.*   [e] **4** HEBREW TITLE: *A psalm by David.*
2:9 Rev 2:26, 27; 12:5; 19:15   **3 Title** 2 Sam 15:13—17:22   **4:4** Eph 4:26

What do people in our society think makes someone happy? What does Psalm 1 say that really makes a person happy?

Psalms

5 Offer the right sacrifices to the LORD,
and put your trust in him.

6 There are many who pray:
"Give us more blessings, O LORD.
Look on us with kindness!"

7 But the joy that you have given me
is more than they will ever have
with all their grain and wine.

8 When I lie down, I go to sleep in peace;
you alone, O LORD, keep me perfectly
safe.

A Prayer for Protection*e*

5 1 Listen to my words, O LORD,
and hear my sighs.
2 Listen to my cry for help,
my God and king!

I pray to you, O LORD;
3 you hear my voice in the morning;
at sunrise I offer my prayer*f*
and wait for your answer.

4 You are not a God who is pleased with
wrongdoing;
you allow no evil in your presence.
5 You cannot stand the sight of the proud;
you hate all wicked people.
6 You destroy all liars
and despise violent, deceitful people.

7 But because of your great love
I can come into your house;
I can worship in your holy Temple
and bow down to you in reverence.
8 LORD, I have so many enemies!
Lead me to do your will;
make your way plain for me to follow.

9 What my enemies say can never be
trusted;
they only want to destroy.
Their words are flattering and smooth,
but full of deadly deceit.
10 Condemn and punish them, O God;
may their own plots cause their ruin.

Drive them out of your presence
because of their many sins
and their rebellion against you.

11 But all who find safety in you will
rejoice;
they can always sing for joy.
Protect those who love you;
because of you they are truly happy.
12 You bless those who obey you, LORD;
your love protects them like a shield.

A Prayer for Help in Time of Trouble*g*

6 1 LORD, don't be angry and rebuke me!
Don't punish me in your anger!
2 I am worn out, O LORD; have pity on
me!
Give me strength; I am completely
exhausted
3 and my whole being is deeply troubled.
How long, O LORD, will you wait to help
me?

4 Come and save me, LORD;
in your mercy rescue me from death.
5 In the world of the dead you are not
remembered;
no one can praise you there.

6 I am worn out with grief;
every night my bed is damp from my
weeping;
my pillow is soaked with tears.
7 I can hardly see;
my eyes are so swollen
from the weeping caused by my
enemies.

8 Keep away from me, you evil people!
The LORD hears my weeping;
9 he listens to my cry for help
and will answer my prayer.
10 My enemies will know the bitter shame
of defeat;
in sudden confusion they will be
driven away.

e **5** HEBREW TITLE: *A psalm by David.* *f* **5:3** prayer; *or* sacrifice. *g* **6** HEBREW TITLE: *A psalm by David.*
5:9 Rom 3:13 **6:1** Ps 38:1 **6:8** Mt 7:23; Lk 13:27

What makes you feel safe? What type of protection do you ask God for?

Big Kids Don't Cry?

Maybe you have heard that big kids don't cry. But this can be misleading. It is true that as we age, we learn to control our emotions. But emotions are healthy, and it isn't wrong to show them appropriately. Even tears—for both women and men—have their place. The psalmist isn't afraid to cry. "I am worn out with grief; / every night my bed is damp from my weeping; / my pillow is soaked with tears" (Psalm 6:6).

So, don't worry if every once in a while you feel like crying. It's only human. Life is sad and hard sometimes, and tears can help us express the feelings of frustration and grief. Sometimes people even shed tears when they are feeling great joy. But if you feel like *all* you do is cry (or if you are always angry or sad), talk to an adult you can trust about what you are feeling.

— Psalm 6

A Prayer for Justice[h]

7 ¹O LORD, my God, I come to you for
    protection;
  rescue me and save me from all who
    pursue me,
² or else like a lion they will carry me off
  where no one can save me,
  and there they will tear me to pieces.

³⁻⁴O LORD, my God, if I have wronged
    anyone,
  if I have betrayed a friend

or without cause done violence to my
  enemy[i] —
  if I have done any of these things—
⁵ then let my enemies pursue me and catch
    me,
  let them cut me down and kill me
  and leave me lifeless on the ground!

⁶Rise in your anger, O LORD!
  Stand up against the fury of my enemies;
  rouse yourself and help me!
 Justice is what you demand,
⁷ so bring together all the peoples
    around you,
  and rule over them from above.[j]
⁸You are the judge of all people.
  Judge in my favor, O LORD;
  you know that I am innocent.
⁹You are a righteous God
  and judge our thoughts and desires.
 Stop the wickedness of evildoers
  and reward those who are good.

¹⁰God is my protector;
  he saves those who obey him.
¹¹God is a righteous judge
  and always condemns the wicked.
¹²If they do not change their ways,
  God will sharpen his sword.
 He bends his bow and makes it ready;
¹³ he takes up his deadly weapons
  and aims his burning arrows.

¹⁴See how wicked people think up evil;
  they plan trouble and practice
    deception.
¹⁵But in the traps they set for others,
  they themselves get caught.
¹⁶So they are punished by their own evil
  and are hurt by their own violence.

¹⁷I thank the LORD for his justice;
  I sing praises to the LORD, the Most
    High.

God's Glory and Human Dignity[k]

8 ¹O LORD, our Lord,
    your greatness is seen in all the world!
 Your praise reaches up to the heavens;

---

[h] **7** HEBREW TITLE: *A song which David sang to the LORD because of Cush the Benjaminite.*   [i] **7:3–4** without cause done violence to my enemy; *or* shown mercy to someone who wronged me unjustly.   [j] **7:7** *Probable text* rule over them from above; *Hebrew* return above over them.   [k] **8** HEBREW TITLE: *A psalm by David.*

7:9 Rev 2:23

Psalms

2   it is sung by children and babies.
> You are safe and secure from all your
> enemies;
>> you stop anyone who opposes you.

3 When I look at the sky, which you have
> made,
>> at the moon and the stars, which you
>> set in their places—
4 what are human beings, that you think of
> them;
>> mere mortals, that you care for them?

5 Yet you made them inferior only to
> yourself;[l]
>> you crowned them with glory and
>> honor.
6 You appointed them rulers over
> everything you made;
>> you placed them over all creation:
7   sheep and cattle, and the wild animals
> too;
8   the birds and the fish
> and the creatures in the seas.

9 O LORD, our Lord,
> your greatness is seen in all the world!

Thanksgiving to God for His Justice [m]

9 1 I will praise you, LORD, with all my
> heart;
>> I will tell of all the wonderful things
>> you have done.
2 I will sing with joy because of you.
> I will sing praise to you, Almighty God.

I will praise you, LORD. *(9:1)*

3 My enemies turn back when you appear;
> they fall down and die.
4 You are fair and honest in your
> judgments,
>> and you have judged in my favor.

5 You have condemned the heathen
> and destroyed the wicked;
>> they will be remembered no more.
6 Our enemies are finished forever;
> you have destroyed their cities,
>> and they are completely forgotten.

7 But the LORD is king forever;
> he has set up his throne for judgment.
8 He rules the world with righteousness;
> he judges the nations with justice.

9 The LORD is a refuge for the oppressed,
> a place of safety in times of trouble.
10 Those who know you, LORD, will trust
> you;
>> you do not abandon anyone who
>> comes to you.

11 Sing praise to the LORD, who rules in
> Zion!
>> Tell every nation what he has done!
12 God remembers those who suffer;
> he does not forget their cry,
>> and he punishes those who wrong
>> them.

13 Be merciful to me, O LORD!
> See the sufferings my enemies cause
> me!
>> Rescue me from death, O LORD,
14   that I may stand before the people of
> Jerusalem
>> and tell them all the things for which I
>> praise you.
> I will rejoice because you saved me.

15 The heathen have dug a pit and fallen in;
> they have been caught in their own
> trap.
16 The LORD has revealed himself by his
> righteous judgments,
>> and the wicked are trapped by their
>> own deeds.

---

[l] **8:5** yourself; *or the gods, or the angels.*   [m] **9** HEBREW TITLE: *A psalm by David.*
8:2 Mt 21:16   **8:4** Job 7:17, 18; Ps 144:3; Heb 2:6–8   **8:5** Wis 2:23; Sir 17:1–4   **8:6** 1 Cor 15:27; Eph
1:22; Heb 2:8   **9:13** Wis 16:13

17 Death is the destiny of all the wicked,
of all those who reject God.
18 The needy will not always be neglected;
the hope of the poor will not be
crushed forever.

19 Come, LORD! Do not let anyone defy
you!
Bring the heathen before you
and pronounce judgment on them.
20 Make them afraid, O LORD;
make them know that they are only
mortal beings.

A Prayer for Justice

10 1 Why are you so far away, O LORD?
Why do you hide yourself when
we are in trouble?
2 The wicked are proud and persecute the
poor;
catch them in the traps they have
made.

3 The wicked are proud of their evil
desires;
the greedy curse and reject the LORD.
4 The wicked do not care about the LORD;
in their pride they think that God
doesn't matter.

"They think that God doesn't matter." (10:4)

5 The wicked succeed in everything.
They cannot understand God's
judgments;
they sneer at their enemies.
6 They say to themselves, "We will never
fail;

10:7 Rom 3:14

we will never be in trouble."
7 Their speech is filled with curses, lies, and
threats;
they are quick to speak hateful, evil
words.

8 They hide themselves in the villages,
waiting to murder innocent people.
They spy on their helpless victims;
9   they wait in their hiding place like lions.
They lie in wait for the poor;
they catch them in their traps and drag
them away.

10 The helpless victims lie crushed;
brute strength has defeated them.
11 The wicked say to themselves, "God
doesn't care!
He has closed his eyes and will never
see me!"

12 O LORD, punish those wicked people!
Remember those who are suffering!
13 How can the wicked despise God
and say to themselves, "He will not
punish me"?
14 But you do see; you take notice of trouble
and suffering
and are always ready to help.
The helpless commit themselves to you;
you have always helped the needy.

15 Break the power of wicked and evil people;
punish them for the wrong they have
done
until they do it no more.

16 The LORD is king forever and ever.
Those who worship other gods
will vanish from his land.

17 You will listen, O LORD, to the prayers of
the lowly;
you will give them courage.
18 You will hear the cries of the oppressed
and the orphans;
you will judge in their favor,
so that mortal men may cause terror no
more.

**When does it seem like God is hiding? When does it seem that God takes
"notice of trouble and suffering"** *(Psalm 10:14)?*

Psalms

Confidence in the LORD[n]

11 ¹I trust in the LORD for safety.
How foolish of you to say to me,
"Fly away like a bird to the mountains,[o]
² because the wicked have drawn their
bows and aimed their arrows
to shoot from the shadows at good
people.
³There is nothing a good person can do
when everything falls apart."

⁴The LORD is in his holy temple;
he has his throne in heaven.
He watches people everywhere
and knows what they are doing.
⁵He examines the good and the wicked
alike;
the lawless he hates with all his heart.

⁶He sends down flaming coals[p] and
burning sulfur on the wicked;
he punishes them with scorching
winds.
⁷The LORD is righteous and loves good
deeds;
those who do them will live in his
presence.

Those who do them will live in his presence. (11:7)

A Prayer for Help[q]

12 ¹Help us, LORD!
There is not a good person left;
honest people can no longer be found.
²All of them lie to one another;
they deceive each other with flattery.

³Silence those flattering tongues, O LORD!
Close those boastful mouths that say,
⁴"With our words we get what we want.
We will say what we wish,
and no one can stop us."

⁵"But now I will come," says the LORD,
"because the needy are oppressed
and the persecuted groan in pain.
I will give them the security they long
for."

⁶The promises of the LORD can be trusted;
they are as genuine as silver
refined seven times in the furnace.

⁷⁻⁸The wicked are everywhere,
and everyone praises what is evil.
Keep us always safe, O LORD,
and preserve us from such people.

A Prayer for Help[q]

13 ¹How much longer will you forget
me, LORD? Forever?
How much longer will you hide
yourself from me?
²How long must I endure trouble?
How long will sorrow fill my heart day
and night?
How long will my enemies triumph
over me?

³Look at me, O LORD my God, and
answer me.
Restore my strength; don't let me die.
⁴Don't let my enemies say, "We have
defeated him."
Don't let them gloat over my downfall.

⁵I rely on your constant love;
I will be glad, because you will rescue
me.
⁶I will sing to you, O LORD,
because you have been good to me.

---

[n] **11** HEBREW TITLE: *By David.*   [o] **11:1** *Some ancient translations* like a bird to the mountains; *Hebrew* bird, to your *(plural)* mountain.   [p] **11:6** *One ancient translation* coals; *Hebrew* traps.   [q] **12; 13** HEBREW TITLE: *A psalm by David.*

Who are the needy in your community, and how can you help them?

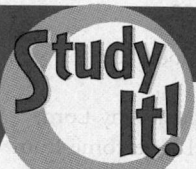

A Psalm for Everything!

Do you know how many psalms there are? If you said 150, you are correct. And do you know how many different types of psalms there are? Thirteen! Psalm 13 is a lament. A lament expresses deep sorrow or grief. There are two types of lament psalms—those of an individual and those of a community. The Israelites experienced many wars and hardships, so they had lots of sorrows and grief.

Other psalm types include thanksgiving by an individual, hymns, songs of Zion, enthronement psalms, royal psalms, wisdom psalms, Torah psalms, entrance psalms, pilgrimage psalms, history psalms, and acrostics. Some people divide the psalms into even more categories. As you read through the psalms, look at the titles—they'll give you a hint as to what type each is. You don't have to know what all these categories mean, though, to appreciate the psalms. When you finish reading all 150, look over them again and decide which type you like best. You may even discover that you have a favorite psalm.

— Psalm 13

Human Wickedness[r]
(Psalm 53)

14 ¹Fools say to themselves,
"There is no God!"
They are all corrupt,
and they have done terrible things;
there is no one who does what is right.

²The LORD looks down from heaven at us humans
to see if there are any who are wise,
any who worship him.
³But they have all gone wrong;
they are all equally bad.
Not one of them does what is right,
not a single one.

⁴"Don't they know?" asks the LORD.
"Are all these evildoers ignorant?
They live by robbing my people,
and they never pray to me."

⁵But then they will be terrified,
for God is with those who obey him.
⁶Evildoers frustrate the plans of the humble,
but the LORD is their protection.

⁷How I pray that victory
will come to Israel from Zion.
How happy the people of Israel will be
when the LORD makes them
prosperous again!

What God Requires[s]

15 ¹LORD, who may enter your Temple?
Who may worship on Zion, your
sacred hill?[t]

²Those who obey God in everything
and always do what is right,
whose words are true and sincere,
³ and who do not slander others.
They do no wrong to their friends
nor spread rumors about their
neighbors.
⁴They despise those whom God rejects,
but honor those who obey the LORD.
They always do what they promise,
no matter how much it may cost.
⁵They make loans without charging
interest
and cannot be bribed to testify against
the innocent.

Whoever does these things will always be
secure.

Psalms

I Don't Need Anyone

"When I grow up, I'm going to depend on myself and not on anyone else," Javier told his mom after school one day. "I won't need parents because I'll have a job. I'll be able to buy my own food and clothes and video games."

His mom sighed, "Javi, it isn't about having all the money and stuff."

"Well, I hate having to ask for stuff all the time. It'll be great when I can get it all myself."

"Javi, your papa and I have good jobs, and we have a house, and you have food and clothes, right?"

"Yes, mama but . . ." he interrupted. She wouldn't let him finish, "Wait a minute, let me finish. We have all that and more, and yet your papa and I still depend on something."

"Yeah, each other, right?" he said.

"That's right, but it isn't the whole story. We also depend on God. Every day we ask God for help."

"Every day?" Javi asked.

"Yes, we depend on God every day. We pray Psalm 16, which says, 'You will show me the path that leads to life; your presence fills me with joy and brings me pleasure forever.' So, even when you're old, and responsible, and buying Papa and me food, remember that! Maybe then you'll understand that you need to depend on God, just like Papa and I do, okay Javi?"

— Psalm 16

A Prayer of Confidence [u]

16 ¹Protect me, O God; I trust in you for safety.
²I say to the LORD, "You are my Lord;
all the good things I have come from you."

³How excellent are the LORD's faithful people!
My greatest pleasure is to be with them.

⁴Those who rush to other gods
bring many troubles on themselves. [v]
I will not take part in their sacrifices;
I will not worship their gods.

⁵You, LORD, are all I have,
and you give me all I need;
my future is in your hands.
⁶How wonderful are your gifts to me;
how good they are!

⁷I praise the LORD, because he guides me,
and in the night my conscience warns me.
⁸I am always aware of the LORD's presence;
he is near, and nothing can shake me.

⁹And so I am thankful and glad,
and I feel completely secure,
¹⁰because you protect me from the power of death.
I have served you faithfully,
and you will not abandon me to the world of the dead.

¹¹You will show me the path that leads to life;
your presence fills me with joy
and brings me pleasure forever.

The Prayer of an Innocent Person [w]

17 ¹Listen, O LORD, to my plea for justice;
pay attention to my cry for help!
Listen to my honest prayer.
²You will judge in my favor,
because you know what is right.

u **16** HEBREW TITLE: *A psalm by David.*
v **16:4** *Probable text* Those . . . themselves; *Hebrew unclear.* *w* **17** HEBREW TITLE: *A prayer by David.*
16:10 Acts 13:35   **16:8–11** Acts 2:25–28

3 You know my heart.
You have come to me at night;
you have examined me completely
and found no evil desire in me.
I speak no evil, 4 as others do;
I have obeyed your command
and have not followed paths of
violence.
5 I have always walked in your way
and have never strayed from it.

6 I pray to you, O God, because you answer
me;
so turn to me and listen to my words.
7 Reveal your wonderful love and save
me;
at your side I am safe from my
enemies.

8 Protect me as you would your very eyes;
hide me in the shadow of your wings
9   from the attacks of the wicked.

Deadly enemies surround me;
10   they have no pity and speak proudly.
11 They are around me now, wherever I
turn,
watching for a chance to pull me
down.
12 They are like lions, waiting for me,
wanting to tear me to pieces.

13 Come, LORD! Oppose my enemies and
defeat them!
Save me from the wicked by your
sword;
14   save me from those who in this life
have all they want.
Punish them with the sufferings you have
stored up for them;
may there be enough for their children
and some left over for their children's
children!

15 But I will see you, because I have done
no wrong;
and when I awake, your presence will
fill me with joy.

David's Song of Victory [x]
(2 Samuel 22:1–51)

18   1 How I love you, LORD!
         You are my defender.

2 The LORD is my protector;
he is my strong fortress.
My God is my protection,
and with him I am safe.
He protects me like a shield;
he defends me and keeps me safe.
3 I call to the LORD,
and he saves me from my enemies.
Praise the LORD!

4 The danger of death was all around me;
the waves of destruction rolled over
me.
5 The danger of death was around me,
and the grave set its trap for me.
6 In my trouble I called to the LORD;
I called to my God for help.
In his temple he heard my voice;
he listened to my cry for help.

7 Then the earth trembled and shook;
the foundations of the mountains
rocked and quivered,
because God was angry.
8 Smoke poured out of his nostrils,
a consuming flame and burning coals
from his mouth.
9 He tore the sky open and came down
with a dark cloud under his feet.
10 He flew swiftly on his winged creature; [y]
he traveled on the wings of the wind.
11 He covered himself with darkness;
thick clouds, full of water, surrounded
him.
12 Hailstones and flashes of fire
came from the lightning before him
and broke through the dark clouds.
13 Then the LORD thundered from the sky;
and the voice of the Most High was
heard. [z]

---

x **18** HEBREW TITLE: *The words that David, the LORD's servant, sang to the LORD on the day the LORD saved him from Saul and all his other enemies.*   *y* **18:10** WINGED CREATURE: *See Word List.*   *z* **18:13** *One ancient translation (and see 2 Sam 22:14) was heard; Hebrew was heard hailstones and flashes of fire.*

"Reveal your wonderful love and save me; / at your side I am safe from my enemies" (Psalm 17:7).

Psalms

¹⁴ He shot his arrows and scattered his
   enemies;
   with flashes of lightning he sent them
   running.
¹⁵ The floor of the ocean was laid bare,
   and the foundations of the earth were
   uncovered,
   when you rebuked your enemies, LORD,
   and roared at them in anger.

¹⁶ The LORD reached down from above and
   took hold of me;
   he pulled me out of the deep waters.
¹⁷ He rescued me from my powerful
   enemies
   and from all those who hate me—
   they were too strong for me.
¹⁸ When I was in trouble, they attacked me,
   but the LORD protected me.
¹⁹ He helped me out of danger;
   he saved me because he was pleased
   with me.

²⁰ The LORD rewards me because I do what
   is right;
   he blesses me because I am innocent.
²¹ I have obeyed the law of the LORD;
   I have not turned away from my God.
²² I have observed all his laws;
   I have not disobeyed his commands.
²³ He knows that I am faultless,
   that I have kept myself from doing
   wrong.
²⁴ And so he rewards me because I do what
   is right,
   because he knows that I am innocent.

²⁵ O LORD, you are faithful to those who
   are faithful to you;
   completely good to those who are
   perfect.
²⁶ You are pure to those who are pure,
   but hostile to those who are wicked.
²⁷ You save those who are humble,
   but you humble those who are
   proud.

²⁸ O LORD, you give me light;
   you dispel my darkness.

²⁹ You give me strength to attack my enemies
   and power to overcome their defenses.

³⁰ This God—how perfect are his deeds!
   How dependable his words!
   He is like a shield
   for all who seek his protection.
³¹ The LORD alone is God;
   God alone is our defense.
³² He is the God who makes me strong,
   who makes my pathway safe.
³³ He makes me sure-footed as a deer;
   he keeps me safe on the mountains.
³⁴ He trains me for battle,
   so that I can use the strongest bow.

³⁵ O LORD, you protect me and save me;
   your care has made me great,
   and your power has kept me safe.
³⁶ You have kept me from being captured,
   and I have never fallen.
³⁷ I pursue my enemies and catch them;
   I do not stop until I destroy them.
³⁸ I strike them down, and they cannot rise;
   they lie defeated before me.
³⁹ You give me strength for the battle
   and victory over my enemies.
⁴⁰ You make my enemies run from me;
   I destroy those who hate me.
⁴¹ They cry for help, but no one saves them;
   they call to the LORD, but he does not
   answer.
⁴² I crush them, so that they become like dust
   which the wind blows away.
   I trample on them like mud in the streets.

⁴³ You saved me from a rebellious people
   and made me ruler over the nations;
   people I did not know have now
   become my subjects.
⁴⁴ Foreigners bow before me;
   when they hear me, they obey.
⁴⁵ They lose their courage
   and come trembling from their
   fortresses.
⁴⁶ The LORD lives! Praise my defender!
   Proclaim the greatness of the God who
   saves me.

18:33 Hab 3:19

**What do you know about King David? Read 2 Samuel 22:1–51 and then read
Psalm 18.**

47 He gives me victory over my enemies;
   he subdues the nations under me
48   and saves me from my foes.

O LORD, you give me victory over my
   enemies
and protect me from violent people.
49 And so I praise you among the nations;
   I sing praises to you.

50 God gives great victories to his king;
   he shows constant love to the one he
      has chosen,
   to David and his descendants forever.

God's Glory in Creation[a]

19 ¹How clearly the sky reveals God's
       glory!
   How plainly it shows what he has
      done!
² Each day announces it to the following
      day;
   each night repeats it to the next.
³ No speech or words are used,
   no sound is heard;
⁴ yet their message[b] goes out to all the world
   and is heard to the ends of the earth.
   God made a home in the sky for the sun;
5   it comes out in the morning like a
      happy bridegroom,
   like an athlete eager to run a race.
⁶ It starts at one end of the sky
   and goes across to the other.
   Nothing can hide from its heat.

The Law of the LORD

⁷ The law of the LORD is perfect;
   it gives new strength.
   The commands of the LORD are
      trustworthy,
   giving wisdom to those who lack it.
⁸ The laws of the LORD are right,
   and those who obey them are happy.
   The commands of the LORD are just
   and give understanding to the mind.
⁹ Reverence for the LORD is good;
   it will continue forever.
   The judgments of the LORD are just;
   they are always fair.

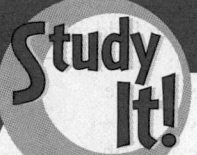

Celebrating Saints

Catholics honor saints in many
ways. Churches are named after
them, statues are built in their
honor, and we often take on a
saint's name when we are confirmed. Most saints also have feast
days, that is, a particular day on
which they are remembered each
year. On a saint's feast day, special
Bible readings can be used at
Masses celebrated in honor of the
saint. Psalm 19 is the responsorial
psalm chosen for saints Andrew,
Simon, Jude, Matthew, Philip, and
James, on each of their feast days.

   What does Psalm 19 have to do
with these saints? These saints
were all Apostles who preached
the gospel message to people who
had not heard it. With this in
mind, read Psalm 19. Do you see
the connection?

   If you are interested in a particular saint, you might want to read
the Scripture readings chosen for
his or her feast day. You can find
the readings in a special book
called the lectionary. Ask a priest,
deacon, or other leader in your
church to help you.

— Psalm 19

10 They are more desirable than the finest
      gold;
   they are sweeter than the purest
      honey.
11 They give knowledge to me, your servant;
   I am rewarded for obeying them.

---

a **19** HEBREW TITLE: *A psalm by David.*   *b* **19:4** *Some ancient translations* message; *Hebrew* line.
18:49 Rom 15:9   **19:4** Rom 10:18

12 None of us can see our own errors;
     deliver me, LORD, from hidden faults!
13 Keep me safe, also, from willful sins;
     don't let them rule over me.
   Then I shall be perfect
     and free from the evil of sin.

14 May my words and my thoughts be
     acceptable to you,
   O LORD, my refuge and my redeemer!

A Prayer for Victory[c]

20 ¹May the LORD answer you when
     you are in trouble!
   May the God of Jacob protect you!
2 May he send you help from his Temple
     and give you aid from Mount
       Zion.
3 May he accept all your offerings
     and be pleased with all your sacrifices.
4 May he give you what you desire
     and make all your plans succeed.
5 Then we will shout for joy over your
     victory
     and celebrate your triumph by praising
       our God.
   May the LORD answer all your requests.

6 Now I know that the LORD gives victory
     to his chosen king;
   he answers him from his holy heaven
     and by his power gives him great
       victories.
7 Some trust in their war chariots
     and others in their horses,
   but we trust in the power of the LORD
     our God.
8 Such people will stumble and fall,
     but we will rise and stand firm.

9 Give victory to the king, O LORD;
     answer[d] us when we call.

Praise for Victory[e]

21 ¹The king is glad, O LORD, because
     you gave him strength;
   he rejoices because you made him
     victorious.

2 You have given him his heart's desire;
     you have answered his request.

3 You came to him with great blessings
     and set a crown of gold on his head.
4 He asked for life, and you gave it,
     a long and lasting life.

5 His glory is great because of your help;
     you have given him fame and majesty.
6 Your blessings are with him forever,
     and your presence fills him with joy.

7 The king trusts in the LORD Almighty;
     and because of the LORD's constant
       love
     he will always be secure.
8 The king will capture all his enemies;
     he will capture everyone who hates him.
9 He will destroy them like a blazing fire
     when he appears.

   The LORD will devour them in his anger,
     and fire will consume them.
10 None of their descendants will survive;
     the king will kill them all.

11 They make their plans, and plot against
       him,
     but they will not succeed.
12 He will shoot his arrows at them
     and make them turn and run.

13 We praise you, LORD, for your great
       strength!
   We will sing and praise your power.

A Cry of Anguish and a Song of Praise[e]

22 ¹My God, my God, why have you
     abandoned me?
   I have cried desperately for help,
     but still it does not come.
2 During the day I call to you, my God,
     but you do not answer;
   I call at night,
     but get no rest.

3 But you are enthroned as the Holy One,
     the one whom Israel praises.
4 Our ancestors put their trust in you;
     they trusted you, and you saved them.

---

[c] **20** HEBREW TITLE: *A psalm by David.*   [d] **20:9** *Some ancient translations* answer; *Hebrew* he will answer.
[e] **21; 22** HEBREW TITLE: *A psalm by David.*
22:1 Mt 27:46; Mk 15:34

5 They called to you and escaped from
      danger;
   they trusted you and were not
      disappointed.

6 But I am no longer a human being; I am
      a worm,
   despised and scorned by everyone!
7 All who see me make fun of me;
   they stick out their tongues and shake
      their heads.
8 "You relied on the LORD," they say.
   "Why doesn't he save you?
   If the LORD likes you,
   why doesn't he help you?"

9 It was you who brought me safely
      through birth,
   and when I was a baby, you kept me
      safe.
10 I have relied on you since the day I was
      born,
   and you have always been my God.
11 Do not stay away from me!
   Trouble is near,
   and there is no one to help.

12 Many enemies surround me like bulls;
   they are all around me,
   like fierce bulls from the land of
      Bashan.
13 They open their mouths like lions,
   roaring and tearing at me.

14 My strength is gone,
   gone like water spilled on the ground.
   All my bones are out of joint;
   my heart is like melted wax.
15 My throatᶠ is as dry as dust,
   and my tongue sticks to the roof of my
      mouth.
   You have left me for dead in the dust.

16 An evil gang is around me;
   like a pack of dogs they close in on
      me;
   they tear atᵍ my hands and feet.

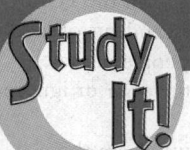

Jesus and the Psalms

"My God, my God, why have you abandoned me?"

These are words from Psalm 22 that Jesus cried out from the cross. It is not surprising that the Psalms were part of Jesus' last prayer. He prayed the Psalms his whole life. When he was baptized, a voice from heaven proclaimed words that sound a lot like Psalm 2, "This is my own dear Son, with whom I am pleased" (Matthew 3:17). Jesus knew a lot of Scripture by heart. His parents and rabbis prayed with him and taught him the Psalms. We can imagine him turning to the Psalms, both in times of joy and sorrow. Maybe you will find some psalms that you want to memorize and pray.

— **Psalm 22**

17 All my bones can be seen.
   My enemies look at me and stare.
18 They gamble for my clothes
   and divide them among themselves.

19 O LORD, don't stay away from me!
   Come quickly to my rescue!
20 Save me from the sword;
   save my life from these dogs.
21 Rescue me from these lions;
   I am helplessʰ before these wild bulls.

22 I will tell my people what you have done;
   I will praise you in their assembly:

ᶠ **22:15** *Probable text* throat; *Hebrew* strength.   ᵍ **22:16** *Some ancient translations* they tear at; *others* they tie; *Hebrew* like a lion.   ʰ **22:21** *Some ancient translations* I am helpless; *Hebrew* you answered me.
22:7 Mt 27:39; Mk 15:29; Lk 23:35   **22:8** Mt 27:43   **22:18** Mt 27:35; Mk 15:24; Lk 23:34; Jn 19:24
22:22 Heb 2:12

Read Psalm 22 and see how it moves from hopelessness to praising God.

23 "Praise him, you servants of the LORD!
   Honor him, you descendants of Jacob!
   Worship him, you people of Israel!
24 He does not neglect the poor or ignore
       their suffering;
   he does not turn away from them,
       but answers when they call for help."

25 In the full assembly I will praise you for
       what you have done;
   in the presence of those who worship
       you
   I will offer the sacrifices I promised.
26 The poor will eat as much as they want;
   those who come to the LORD will
       praise him.
   May they prosper forever!

27 All nations will remember the LORD.
   From every part of the world they will
       turn to him;
   all races will worship him.
28 The LORD is king,
   and he rules the nations.

29 All proud people will bow down to
       him;[i]
   all mortals will bow down before
       him.
30 Future generations will serve him;
   they will speak of the Lord to the
       coming generation.
31 People not yet born will be told:
   "The Lord saved his people."

The LORD Our Shepherd[j]

23 ¹The LORD is my shepherd;
       I have everything I need.
   ²He lets me rest in fields of green
       grass
   and leads me to quiet pools of fresh
       water.
   ³He gives me new strength.
   He guides me in the right paths,
       as he has promised.

4 Even if I go through the deepest darkness,
   I will not be afraid, LORD,
   for you are with me.
   Your shepherd's rod and staff protect me.

Even if I go through the deepest darkness . . . (23:4)

5 You prepare a banquet for me,
   where all my enemies can see me;
   you welcome me as an honored guest
   and fill my cup to the brim.
6 I know that your goodness and love will
       be with me all my life;
   and your house will be my home as
       long as I live.

The Great King[j]

24 ¹The world and all that is in it
           belong to the LORD;
   the earth and all who live on it are his.
   ²He built it on the deep waters beneath
       the earth
   and laid its foundations in the ocean
       depths.

   ³Who has the right to go up the LORD's
       hill?[k]
   Who may enter his holy Temple?
   ⁴Those who are pure in act and in thought,
   who do not worship idols
   or make false promises.

---

[i] **22:29** *Probable text* will bow down to him; *Hebrew* will eat and bow down.   [j] **23; 24** HEBREW TITLE: *A psalm by David.*   [k] **24:3** THE LORD'S HILL: *The hill in Jerusalem on which the Temple was built.*
23:2 Rev 7:17   **24:1** 1 Cor 10:26   **24:4** Mt 5:8

Pray It!

I Trust in You

Psalm 25 is a prayer of trust in God, like this one.

This prayer is for you, God.
You teach me, and I trust in you.
Sometimes I mess up.
   I did when I was little, and still do.
   You loved me through it all.
Because you are awesome,
      you show me what to do, and
      I try to do what is good.
I turn to you for help, and
      you help me not worry.
I trust in you.
You protect me and keep me safe.
I trust in you. Amen.

— Psalm 25

5 The LORD will bless them and save them;
   God will declare them innocent.
6 Such are the people who come to God,
   who come into the presence of the
      God of Jacob.

7 Fling wide the gates,
   open the ancient doors,
   and the great king will come in.
8 Who is this great king?
He is the LORD, strong and mighty,
   the LORD, victorious in battle.

9 Fling wide the gates,
   open the ancient doors,
   and the great king will come in.
10 Who is this great king?
   The LORD Almighty—he is the great
      king!

A Prayer for Guidance and Protection[l]

25 ¹To you, O LORD, I offer my prayer;
      ²in you, my God, I trust.
Save me from the shame of defeat;
   don't let my enemies gloat over me!

3 Defeat does not come to those who trust
   in you,
      but to those who are quick to rebel
      against you.

4 Teach me your ways, O LORD;
   make them known to me.
5 Teach me to live according to your truth,
   for you are my God, who saves me.
   I always trust in you.

6 Remember, O LORD, your kindness and
      constant love
   which you have shown from long ago.
7 Forgive the sins and errors of my youth.
   In your constant love and goodness,
   remember me, LORD!

8 Because the LORD is righteous and good,
   he teaches sinners the path they should
      follow.
9 He leads the humble in the right way
   and teaches them his will.
10 With faithfulness and love he leads
   all who keep his covenant and obey his
      commands.

l 25 HEBREW TITLE: *By David.*

11 Keep your promise, LORD, and forgive my
     sins,
   for they are many.
12 Those who have reverence for the LORD
     will learn from him the path they
     should follow.
13 They will always be prosperous,
     and their children will possess the land.
14 The LORD is the friend of those who
     obey him
     and he affirms his covenant with them.

15 I look to the LORD for help at all times,
     and he rescues me from danger.
16 Turn to me, LORD, and be merciful to
     me,
   because I am lonely and weak.
17 Relieve me of my worries
     and save me from all my troubles.
18 Consider my distress and suffering
     and forgive all my sins.

19 See how many enemies I have;
     see how much they hate me.
20 Protect me and save me;
     keep me from defeat.
     I come to you for safety.
21 May my goodness and honesty preserve
     me,
   because I trust in you.

22 From all their troubles, O God,
     save your people Israel!

The Prayer of a Good Person [l]

26 ¹Declare me innocent, O LORD,
     because I do what is right
   and trust you completely.
   ²Examine me and test me, LORD;
     judge my desires and thoughts.
   ³Your constant love is my guide;
     your faithfulness always leads me. [m]

   ⁴I do not keep company with worthless
     people;
     I have nothing to do with hypocrites.
   ⁵I hate the company of the evil
     and avoid the wicked.

   ⁶LORD, I wash my hands to show that I am
     innocent

     and march in worship around your
     altar.
   ⁷I sing a hymn of thanksgiving
     and tell of all your wonderful deeds.

   ⁸I love the house where you live, O LORD,
     the place where your glory dwells.
   ⁹Do not destroy me with the sinners;
     spare me from the fate of murderers—
10   those who do evil all the time
     and are always ready to take bribes.

11 As for me, I do what is right;
     be merciful to me and save me!

12 I am safe from all dangers;
     in the assembly of his people I praise
     the LORD.

A Prayer of Praise [n]

27 ¹The LORD is my light and my
     salvation;
   I will fear no one.
   The LORD protects me from all danger;
   I will never be afraid.

   ²When evil people attack me and try to
     kill me,
     they stumble and fall.
   ³Even if a whole army surrounds me,
     I will not be afraid;
   even if enemies attack me,
     I will still trust God. [o]

   ⁴I have asked the LORD for one thing;
     one thing only do I want:
   to live in the LORD's house all my
     life,
     to marvel there at his goodness,
     and to ask for his guidance.
   ⁵In times of trouble he will shelter me;
     he will keep me safe in his Temple
     and make me secure on a high rock.
   ⁶So I will triumph over my enemies
     around me.
     With shouts of joy I will offer sacrifices
       in his Temple;
     I will sing, I will praise the LORD.

   ⁷Hear me, LORD, when I call to you!
     Be merciful and answer me!
   ⁸When you said, "Come worship me,"

---

l 26 HEBREW TITLE: *By David.*   m 26:3 your faithfulness always leads me; *or* I live in loyalty to you.
n 27 HEBREW TITLE: *By David.*   o 27:3 still trust God; *or* not lose courage.

I answered, "I will come, LORD."
9 Don't hide yourself from me!

Don't be angry with me;
   don't turn your servant away.
You have been my help;
   don't leave me, don't abandon me,
   O God, my savior.
10 My father and mother may abandon me,
   but the LORD will take care of me.

11 Teach me, LORD, what you want me to do,
   and lead me along a safe path,
   because I have many enemies.
12 Don't abandon me to my enemies,
   who attack me with lies and threats.

13 I know that I will live to see
   the LORD's goodness in this present life.
14 Trust in the LORD.
   Have faith, do not despair.
   Trust in the LORD.

A Prayer for Help *p*

28 ¹O LORD, my defender, I call to you.
      Listen to my cry!
  If you do not answer me,
   I will be among those who go down to
    the world of the dead.
2 Hear me when I cry to you for help,
   when I lift my hands toward your holy
    Temple.
3 Do not condemn me with the wicked,
   with those who do evil—
   those whose words are friendly,
   but who have hatred in their hearts.
4 Punish them for what they have done,
   for the evil they have committed.
   Punish them for all their deeds;
   give them what they deserve!
5 They take no notice of what the LORD
    has done
   or of what he has made;
  so he will punish them
   and destroy them forever.

6 Give praise to the LORD;
   he has heard my cry for help.
7 The LORD protects and defends me;
   I trust in him.
He gives me help and makes me glad;
   I praise him with joyful songs.
8 The LORD protects his people;
   he defends and saves his chosen king.
9 Save your people, LORD,
   and bless those who are yours.
Be their shepherd,
   and take care of them forever.

The Voice of the LORD in the Storm *q*

29 ¹Praise the LORD, you heavenly
      beings;
   praise his glory and power.
2 Praise the LORD's glorious name;
   bow down before the Holy One when
    he appears. *r*

3 The voice of the LORD is heard on the
    seas;
   the glorious God thunders,
   and his voice echoes over the
    ocean.
4 The voice of the LORD is heard
   in all its might and majesty.

5 The voice of the LORD breaks the
    cedars,
   even the cedars of Lebanon.
6 He makes the mountains of Lebanon
    jump like calves
   and makes Mount Hermon leap like a
    young bull.

7 The voice of the LORD makes the
    lightning flash.
8 His voice makes the desert shake;
   he shakes the desert of Kadesh.
9 The LORD's voice shakes the oaks *s*
   and strips the leaves from the trees
   while everyone in his Temple shouts,
   "Glory to God!"

p **28** HEBREW TITLE: *By David.*   *q* **29** HEBREW TITLE: *A psalm by David.*   *r* **29:2** when he appears; *or* in garments of worship; *or* in his beautiful Temple.   *s* **29:9** *Probable text* shakes the oaks; *Hebrew* makes the deer give birth.
28:4 Rev 22:12   **29:1, 2** Ps 96:7–9

How many of the qualities in Psalm 26 do you have?

Turning Sadness to Joy

It was Jill's first swim meet, and she was really nervous. She dove in right after the gun went off and swam as fast as she could. She missed her turn, but when she finished, she looked around and no one else was at the edge. "I won!" she thought, then she realized they had all finished and gotten out of the pool. Embarrassed, she got out of the pool and wanted to disappear.

The next week she almost didn't go to practice, but remembering a verse from a psalm she read, "I will never be defeated" (30:6), encouraged her to go. She went back that week and the next and the next. She practiced her turns each time she went to practice, even if it wasn't a drill.

It was time for her second meet. This time, she didn't finish last and even got out of the pool at the same time as the rest of the heat. By the end of the season, she had won two ribbons. She was so happy, she could barely remember that first meet. The end of Psalm 30 became her motto: "You have changed my sadness into a joyful dance; / you have taken away my sorrow / and surrounded me with joy" (verse 11).

— Psalm 30

10 The LORD rules over the deep waters;
　　he rules as king forever.
11 The LORD gives strength to his people
　　and blesses them with peace.

A Prayer of Thanksgiving[t]

30 1 I praise you, LORD, because you
　　　　have saved me
　　and kept my enemies from gloating
　　　over me.
2 I cried to you for help, O LORD my God,
　　and you healed me;
3 　you kept me from the grave.
I was on my way to the depths below,[u]
　　but you restored my life.

4 Sing praise to the LORD,
　　all his faithful people!
Remember what the Holy One has done,
　　and give him thanks!
5 His anger lasts only a moment,
　　his goodness for a lifetime.
Tears may flow in the night,
　　but joy comes in the morning.

6 I felt secure and said to myself,
　　"I will never be defeated."
7 You were good to me, LORD;
　　you protected me like a mountain
　　　fortress.
But then you hid yourself from me,
　　and I was afraid.

8 I called to you, LORD;
　　I begged for your help:
9 "What will you gain from my death?
　　What profit from my going to the grave?
Are dead people able to praise you?
　　Can they proclaim your unfailing
　　　goodness?
10 Hear me, LORD, and be merciful!
　　Help me, LORD!"

11 You have changed my sadness into a
　　joyful dance;
you have taken away my sorrow
　　and surrounded me with joy.

---

[t] **30** HEBREW TITLE: *A song for the dedication of the Temple; a psalm by David.*   [u] **30:3** THE DEPTHS BELOW: *The world of the dead* (see 6:5).

Who do you turn to when you need protection? Check out the beginning of Psalm 31 to see who the psalmist turns to.

12 So I will not be silent;
    I will sing praise to you.
LORD, you are my God;
    I will give you thanks forever.

A Prayer of Trust in God[v]

31 ¹I come to you, LORD, for protection;
        never let me be defeated.
    You are a righteous God;
        save me, I pray!
²Hear me! Save me now!
Be my refuge to protect me;
    my defense to save me.

³You are my refuge and defense;
    guide me and lead me as you have
        promised.
⁴Keep me safe from the trap that has been
        set for me;
    shelter me from danger.
⁵I place myself in your care.
You will save me, LORD;
    you are a faithful God.

⁶You hate those who worship false gods,
    but I trust in you.
⁷I will be glad and rejoice
    because of your constant love.
You see my suffering;
    you know my trouble.
⁸You have not let my enemies capture
        me;
    you have given me freedom to go
        where I wish.

⁹Be merciful to me, LORD,
    for I am in trouble;
my eyes are tired from so much crying;
    I am completely worn out.
¹⁰I am exhausted by sorrow,
    and weeping has shortened my life.
I am weak from all my troubles;[w]
    even my bones are wasting away.

¹¹All my enemies, and especially my
        neighbors,
    treat me with contempt.
Those who know me are afraid of me;
    when they see me in the street, they
        run away.

¹²Everyone has forgotten me, as though I
        were dead;
    I am like something thrown away.
¹³I hear many enemies whispering;
    terror is all around me.
They are making plans against me,
    plotting to kill me.
¹⁴But my trust is in you, O LORD;
    you are my God.
¹⁵I am always in your care;
    save me from my enemies,
    from those who persecute me.
¹⁶Look on your servant with kindness;
    save me in your constant love.
¹⁷I call to you, LORD;
    don't let me be disgraced.
May the wicked be disgraced;
    may they go silently down to the world
        of the dead.
¹⁸Silence those liars—
    all the proud and arrogant
    who speak with contempt about the
        righteous.

¹⁹How wonderful are the good things
    you keep for those who honor you!
Everyone knows how good you are,
    how securely you protect those who
        trust you.
²⁰You hide them in the safety of your
        presence
    from the plots of others;
in a safe shelter you hide them
    from the insults of their enemies.

²¹Praise the LORD!
How wonderfully he showed his love for
        me
    when I was surrounded and attacked!
²²I was afraid and thought
    that he had driven me out of his
        presence.
But he heard my cry,
    when I called to him for help.

²³Love the LORD, all his faithful people.
The LORD protects the faithful,
    but punishes the proud as they deserve.
²⁴Be strong, be courageous,
    all you that hope in the LORD.

ᵛ 31 HEBREW TITLE: *A psalm by David.*   ʷ 31:10 *Some ancient translations* troubles; *Hebrew* iniquity.
31:5 Lk 23:46

Psalms

Trinity Sunday

On the Sunday after Pentecost, the Catholic Church celebrates Trinity Sunday. As part of the Mass that Sunday, sometimes the responsorial psalm is from Psalm 33: "Blessed the people the Lord has chosen to be his own." All three persons of the Holy Trinity—Father, Son, and Holy Spirit—make God's love known. They are the one, true God, the God who chooses all people to be his own. If we take Psalm 33 to heart, we will respond by praising, worshiping, and thanking God.

— Psalm 33

Confession and Forgiveness *x*

32 ¹Happy are those whose sins are forgiven,
whose wrongs are pardoned.
²Happy is the one whom the LORD does not accuse of doing wrong
and who is free from all deceit.

³When I did not confess my sins,
I was worn out from crying all day long.
⁴Day and night you punished me, LORD;
my strength was completely drained,
as moisture is dried up by the summer heat.

⁵Then I confessed my sins to you;
I did not conceal my wrongdoings.
I decided to confess them to you,
and you forgave all my sins.

⁶So all your loyal people should pray to you in times of need; *y*
when a great flood of trouble comes rushing in,
it will not reach them.
⁷You are my hiding place;
you will save me from trouble.
I sing aloud of your salvation,
because you protect me.

⁸The LORD says, "I will teach you the way you should go;
I will instruct you and advise you.

⁹Don't be stupid like a horse or a mule,
which must be controlled with a bit and bridle
to make it submit."

¹⁰The wicked will have to suffer,
but those who trust in the LORD
are protected by his constant love.
¹¹You that are righteous, be glad and rejoice
because of what the LORD has done.
You that obey him, shout for joy!

A Song of Praise

33 ¹All you that are righteous,
shout for joy for what the LORD has done;
praise him, all you that obey him.
²Give thanks to the LORD with harps,
sing to him with stringed instruments.
³Sing a new song to him,
play the harp with skill, and shout for joy!

⁴The words of the LORD are true,
and all his works are dependable.
⁵The LORD loves what is righteous and just;
his constant love fills the earth.

⁶The LORD created the heavens by his command,
the sun, moon, and stars by his spoken word.

---

x **32** HEBREW TITLE: *A poem by David.*   *y* **32:6** *Some ancient translations* need; *Hebrew* finding only.
32:1, 2 Rom 4:7, 8

7 He gathered all the seas into one place;
  he shut up the ocean depths in
    storerooms.

8 Worship the LORD, all the earth!
  Honor him, all peoples of the world!
9 When he spoke, the world was created;
  at his command everything appeared.

10 The LORD frustrates the purposes of the
     nations;
   he keeps them from carrying out their
     plans.
11 But his plans endure forever;
   his purposes last eternally.
12 Happy is the nation whose God is the
     LORD;
   happy are the people he has chosen for
     his own!

13 The LORD looks down from heaven
   and sees all of us humans.
14 From where he rules, he looks down
   on all who live on earth.
15 He forms all their thoughts
   and knows everything they do.

16 A king does not win because of his
     powerful army;
   a soldier does not triumph because of
     his strength.
17 War horses are useless for victory;
   their great strength cannot save.

18 The LORD watches over those who obey
     him,
   those who trust in his constant love.
19 He saves them from death;
   he keeps them alive in times of famine.

20 We put our hope in the LORD;
   he is our protector and our help.
21 We are glad because of him;
   we trust in his holy name.

22 May your constant love be with us,
     LORD,
   as we put our hope in you.

In Praise of God's Goodness z

34 1 I will always thank the LORD;
         I will never stop praising him.
2 I will praise him for what he has done;
  may all who are oppressed listen and be
    glad!
3 Proclaim with me the LORD's greatness;
  let us praise his name together!

4 I prayed to the LORD, and he answered
    me;
  he freed me from all my fears.
5 The oppressed look to him and are glad;
  they will never be disappointed.
6 The helpless call to him, and he answers;
  he saves them from all their troubles.
7 His angel guards those who honor the
    LORD
  and rescues them from danger.

8 Find out for yourself how good the
    LORD is.
  Happy are those who find safety with
    him.
9 Honor the LORD, all his people;
  those who obey him have all they
    need.
10 Even lions go hungry for lack of food,
   but those who obey the LORD lack
     nothing good.

11 Come, my young friends, and listen to me,
   and I will teach you to honor the
     LORD.
12 Would you like to enjoy life?
   Do you want long life and happiness?
13 Then keep from speaking evil
   and from telling lies.
14 Turn away from evil and do good;
   strive for peace with all your heart.

15 The LORD watches over the righteous
   and listens to their cries;
16 but he opposes those who do evil,
   so that when they die, they are soon
     forgotten.

z **34** HEBREW TITLE: *By David, who left the presence of Abimelech after pretending to be crazy and being sent away by him.*
33:16 Jdt 9:7; 1 Macc 3:19   **34 Title** 1 Sam 21:13–15   **34:8** 1 Pet 2:3   **34:12–16** 1 Pet 3:10–12

Which is greater, the time you spend asking God for things, or the time you spend praising God? According to Psalm 34, which should be greater?

Psalms

Psalms

17 The righteous call to the LORD, and he
   listens;
   he rescues them from all their troubles.
18 The LORD is near to those who are
   discouraged;
   he saves those who have lost all hope.

19 Good people suffer many troubles,
   but the LORD saves them from them
   all;
20 the LORD preserves them completely;
   not one of their bones is broken.
21 Evil will kill the wicked;
   those who hate the righteous will be
   punished.

22 The LORD will save his people;
   those who go to him for protection
   will be spared.

A Prayer for Help[a]

35 1 Oppose those who oppose me,
    LORD,
   and fight those who fight against me!
2 Take your shield and armor
   and come to my rescue.
3 Lift up your spear and war ax
   against those who pursue me.
   Promise that you will save me.

4 May those who try to kill me
   be defeated and disgraced!
   May those who plot against me
   be turned back and confused!
5 May they be like straw blown by the
   wind
   as the angel of the LORD pursues them!
6 May their path be dark and slippery
   while the angel of the LORD strikes
   them down!

7 Without any reason they laid a trap for me
   and dug a deep hole to catch me.
8 But destruction will catch them before
   they know it;
   they will be caught in their own trap
   and fall to their destruction!

9 Then I will be glad because of the LORD;
   I will be happy because he saved me.
10 With all my heart I will say to the LORD,
   "There is no one like you.
   You protect the weak from the strong,
   the poor from the oppressor."

11 Evil people testify against me
   and accuse me of crimes I know
   nothing about.
12 They pay me back evil for good,
   and I sink in despair.
13 But when they were sick, I dressed in
   mourning;
   I deprived myself of food;
   I prayed with my head bowed low,
14   as I would pray for a friend or a
   brother.
   I went around bent over in mourning,
   as one who mourns for his mother.

15 But when I was in trouble, they were all
   glad
   and gathered around to make fun of me;
   strangers beat me
   and kept striking me.
16 Like those who would mock a cripple,[b]
   they glared at me with hate.

17 How much longer, Lord, will you just
   look on?
   Rescue me from their attacks;
   save my life from these lions!
18 Then I will thank you in the assembly of
   your people;
   I will praise you before them all.

19 Don't let my enemies, those liars,
   gloat over my defeat.
   Don't let those who hate me for no
   reason
   smirk with delight over my sorrow.

20 They do not speak in a friendly way;
   instead they invent all kinds of lies
   about peace-loving people.
21 They accuse me, shouting,
   "We saw what you did!"

a 35 HEBREW TITLE: *By David.*   *b* 35:16 *Probable text* Like those . . . cripple; *Hebrew unclear.*
34:20 Jn 19:36   35:19 Ps 69:4; Jn 15:25

Read Psalm 36:6. Isn't it nice to know that animals are under God's care?

22 But you, O LORD, have seen this.
   So don't be silent, Lord;
   don't keep yourself far away!
23 Rouse yourself, O Lord, and defend me;
   rise up, my God, and plead my cause.
24 You are righteous, O LORD, so declare me
      innocent;
   don't let my enemies gloat over me.
25 Don't let them say to themselves,
   "We are rid of him!
   That's just what we wanted!"

26 May those who gloat over my suffering
   be completely defeated and confused;
   may those who claim to be better than I
      am
   be covered with shame and disgrace.

27 May those who want to see me acquitted
   shout for joy and say again and
      again,
   "How great is the LORD!
   He is pleased with the success of his
      servant."
28 Then I will proclaim your righteousness,
   and I will praise you all day long.

Human Wickedness[c]

36

1 Sin speaks to the wicked deep in
      their hearts;
   they reject God and do not have
      reverence for him.
2 Because they think so highly of
      themselves,
   they think that God will not discover
      their sin and condemn it.
3 Their speech is wicked and full of lies;
   they no longer do what is wise and
      good.
4 They make evil plans as they lie in bed;
   nothing they do is good,
   and they never reject anything evil.

The Goodness of God

5 LORD, your constant love reaches the
      heavens;
   your faithfulness extends to the skies.

6 Your righteousness is towering like the
      mountains;
   your justice is like the depths of the sea.
   People and animals are in your care.

7 How precious, O God, is your constant
      love!
   We find[d] protection under the shadow
      of your wings.
8 We feast on the abundant food you
      provide;
   you let us drink from the river of your
      goodness.
9 You are the source of all life,
   and because of your light we see the
      light.

10 Continue to love those who know you
   and to do good to those who are
      righteous.
11 Do not let proud people attack me
   or the wicked make me run away.

12 See where evil people have fallen.
   There they lie, unable to rise.

The Destiny of the Wicked and of the Good[e]

37

1 Don't be worried on account of
      the wicked;
   don't be jealous of those who do
      wrong.
2 They will soon disappear like grass that
      dries up;
   they will die like plants that wither.

3 Trust in the LORD and do good;
   live in the land and be safe.
4 Seek your happiness in the LORD,
   and he will give you your heart's desire.

5 Give yourself to the LORD;
   trust in him, and he will help you;
6 he will make your righteousness shine
   like the noonday sun.

7 Be patient and wait for the LORD to act;
   don't be worried about those who
      prosper
   or those who succeed in their evil
      plans.

---

c **36** HEBREW TITLE: *By David, the LORD's servant.*   d **36:7** *precious, O God, is . . . find; or precious is your
constant love! Gods and people find.*   e **37** HEBREW TITLE: *By David.*
36:1 Rom 3:18

Psalms

Cheaters!

"I can't stand it when they cheat; they mess the curve up and make the rest of us look bad," Noah complained to his friends. When tests came back in history, it was obvious that a group of kids had cheated.

"It almost makes me want to cheat too, just to get the grades," Greg answered.

"Yeah, they're getting a movie day, and we have to study on Friday. No fair," Elliot added.

"It's not worth it," Noah tried to calm them a little. "Besides, haven't you ever heard, 'Cheaters never prosper'? I wish I could tell Mr. Shimkis, but I don't have proof!"

"Yeah, I guess there is a chance they'll get caught," Greg said.

"You know, I read a psalm today that said, 'The LORD loves what is right / and does not abandon his faithful people' (Psalm 37:28). We just have to study and do our best. That's what's important," Elliot said.

"Yeah, and let's get a snack and start studying!" Noah added.

— Psalm 37

8 Don't give in to worry or anger;
   it only leads to trouble.
9 Those who trust in the LORD will possess
      the land,
   but the wicked will be driven out.

10 Soon the wicked will disappear;
   you may look for them, but you won't
      find them;

11 but the humble will possess the land
   and enjoy prosperity and peace.

12 The wicked plot against good people
   and glare at them with hate.
13 But the Lord laughs at wicked people,
   because he knows they will soon be
      destroyed.

14 The wicked draw their swords and bend
      their bows
   to kill the poor and needy,
   to slaughter those who do what is
      right;
15 but they will be killed by their own
      swords,
   and their bows will be smashed.

16 The little that a good person owns
   is worth more than the wealth of all
      the wicked,
17 because the LORD will take away the
      strength of the wicked,
   but protect those who are good.

18 The LORD takes care of those who obey
      him,
   and the land will be theirs forever.
19 They will not suffer when times are bad;
   they will have enough in time of
      famine.
20 But the wicked will die;
   the enemies of the LORD will vanish
      like wild flowers;
   they will disappear like smoke.

21 The wicked borrow and never pay back,
   but good people are generous with
      their gifts.
22 Those who are blessed by the LORD will
      possess the land,
   but those who are cursed by him will
      be driven out.

23 The LORD guides us in the way we
      should go
   and protects those who please him.
24 If they fall, they will not stay down,
   because the LORD will help them up.

25 I am old now; I have lived a long time,
   but I have never seen good people
      abandoned by the LORD
   or their children begging for food.

26 At all times they give freely and lend to
   others,
      and their children are a blessing.

27 Turn away from evil and do good,
      and your descendants will always live in
      the land;
28 for the LORD loves what is right
      and does not abandon his faithful
      people.
   He protects them forever,
      but the descendants of the wicked will
      be driven out.
29 The righteous will possess the land
      and live in it forever.

30 The words of good people are wise,
      and they are always fair.
31 They keep the law of their God in their
      hearts
      and never depart from it.

32 Wicked people watch good people
      and try to kill them;
33 but the LORD will not abandon them to
      their enemy's power
      or let them be condemned when they
      are on trial.

34 Put your hope in the LORD and obey his
      commands;
   he will honor you by giving you the
      land,
   and you will see the wicked driven
      out.

35 I once knew someone wicked who was a
      tyrant;
   he towered over everyone like a cedar
      of Lebanon;f
36 but later Ig passed by, and he wasn't there;
   I looked for him, but couldn't find
      him.

37 Notice good people, observe the
      righteous;
   peaceful people have descendants,
38 but sinners are completely destroyed,
      and their descendants are wiped out.

39 The LORD saves the righteous
      and protects them in times of trouble.
40 He helps them and rescues them;
   he saves them from the wicked,
   because they go to him for protection.

The Prayer of a Sufferer h

38

1 O LORD, don't punish me in your
      anger!
2 You have wounded me with your arrows;
   you have struck me down.

3 Because of your anger, I am in great pain;
   my whole body is diseased because of
   my sins.
4 I am drowning in the flood of my sins;
   they are a burden too heavy to bear.

5 Because I have been foolish,
   my sores stink and rot.
6 I am bent over, I am crushed;
   I mourn all day long.
7 I am burning with fever
   and I am near death.
8 I am worn out and utterly crushed;
   my heart is troubled, and I groan with
   pain.

9 O Lord, you know what I long for;
   you hear all my groans.
10 My heart is pounding, my strength is
   gone,
   and my eyes have lost their brightness.
11 My friends and neighbors will not come
   near me,
   because of my sores;
   even my family keeps away from me.
12 Those who want to kill me lay traps for
   me,
   and those who want to hurt me
      threaten to ruin me;
   they never stop plotting against me.

13 I am like the deaf and cannot hear,
   like the dumb and cannot speak.
14 I am like those who do not answer,
   because they cannot hear.

---

f **37:35** *One ancient translation* like a cedar of Lebanon; *Hebrew unclear.* g **37:36** *Some ancient translations* I; *Hebrew he.* h **38** HEBREW TITLE: *A psalm by David; a lament.*

Think of someone you know who is good. What does he or she do that makes you know that? How does it feel to be with that person?

Psalms

Pray It!

Live Through This

Young people around the world have suffered like the writer of Psalm 38. Here is a poem from a 13-year-old Rwandan-born girl who lost many of her relatives when one tribe of people tried to kill everyone who belonged to a different tribe.

A once peaceful land
With loving neighbors and friends
Torn apart by war.
A saddening event
Too horrible to accept
Yet, it's not the first.
The world shuts them out
A country with such beauty
Now filled with anger
So much bitterness
My heart is soaked with sadness
For I lost so much.
My roots forgotten
The cousins I never met
All ripped apart by hatred.
My blood, family, roots
All lost over ignorance
The Tutsis tortured.
Betrayed by their friends
In their homes, churches and towns
Hiding in horror.
What is our next step?
To regain humanity
Compassion . . . and love?
Is it possible?
Or is it lost forever?
My pride is not lost.

— Psalm 38

(Valerie N. Piraino, Catholic Relief Services)

15 But I trust in you, O LORD;
    and you, O Lord my God, will answer me.
16 Don't let my enemies gloat over my distress;
    don't let them boast about my downfall!
17 I am about to fall
    and am in constant pain.
18 I confess my sins;
    they fill me with anxiety.
19 My enemies are healthy and strong;
    there are many who hate me for no reason.
20 Those who pay back evil for good
    are against me because I try to do right.
21 Do not abandon me, O LORD;
    do not stay away, my God!
22 Help me now, O Lord my savior!

The Confession of a Sufferer[i]

39 1 I said, "I will be careful about what I do
    and will not let my tongue make me sin;
  I will not say anything
    while evil people are near."
2 I kept quiet, not saying a word,
    not even about anything good!
  But my suffering only grew worse,
3   and I was overcome with anxiety.
  The more I thought, the more troubled I became;
    I could not keep from asking:
4 " LORD, how long will I live?
    When will I die?
  Tell me how soon my life will end."

5 How short you have made my life!
  In your sight my lifetime seems nothing.
  Indeed every living being is no more than a puff of wind,

i **39** HEBREW TITLE: *A psalm by David.*

Read Psalm 40:4–11. What does the psalmist suggest that God asks of us?

6   no more than a shadow.
    All we do is for nothing;
        we gather wealth, but don't know who
            will get it.

7 What, then, can I hope for, Lord?
    I put my hope in you.
8 Save me from all my sins,
    and don't let fools make fun of me.
9 I will keep quiet, I will not say a word,
    for you are the one who made me
        suffer like this.
10 Don't punish me any more!
    I am about to die from your blows.
11 You punish our sins by your rebukes,
    and like a moth you destroy what we
        love.
    Indeed we are no more than a puff of
        wind!

12 Hear my prayer, LORD,
    and listen to my cry;
        come to my aid when I weep.
    Like all my ancestors
        I am only your guest for a little while.
13 Leave me alone so that I may have some
        happiness
    before I go away and am no more.

A Song of Praise[i]

40 1 I waited patiently for the LORD's
            help;
        then he listened to me and heard my cry.
2 He pulled me out of a dangerous pit,
    out of the deadly quicksand.
    He set me safely on a rock
        and made me secure.
3 He taught me to sing a new song,
    a song of praise to our God.
    Many who see this will take warning
        and will put their trust in the LORD.

4 Happy are those who trust the LORD,
    who do not turn to idols
        or join those who worship false gods.
5 You have done many things for us,
    O LORD our God;
        there is no one like you!

You have made many wonderful plans
    for us.
I could never speak of them all—
    their number is so great!

6 You do not want sacrifices and offerings;
    you do not ask for animals burned
        whole on the altar
    or for sacrifices to take away sins.
    Instead, you have given me ears to hear
        you,
7   and so I answered, "Here I am;
        your instructions for me are in the
            book of the Law.[j]
8 How I love to do your will, my God!
    I keep your teaching in my heart."

9 In the assembly of all your people, LORD,
    I told the good news that you save us.
    You know that I will never stop
        telling it.

I told the good news. (40:9)

10 I have not kept the news of salvation to
        myself;
    I have always spoken of your
        faithfulness and help.
    In the assembly of all your people I have
        not been silent
    about your loyalty and constant love.

11 LORD, I know you will never stop being
        merciful to me.
    Your love and loyalty will always keep
        me safe.

A Prayer for Help
(Psalm 70)

12 I am surrounded by many troubles—
    too many to count!

---

i **40** HEBREW TITLE: *A psalm by David.*   *j* **40:7** your instructions . . . Law; *or* my devotion to you is recorded in
your book.
40:6–8 Heb 10:5–7

Psalms

You Want Me to Do What?

If you have poor or homeless people in your community, you may think they look dirty or are weird. Maybe they haven't had a shower for a while. It is hard to shower when you don't have a place to live. (Some homeless people try to use public restroom sinks to get clean.) Some homeless people have mental illnesses that make it hard for them to keep a job and own a home. But they are children of God, just like you and your parents and your friends.

Helping needy people is a key part of following God. Psalm 41 reminds us that God blesses those who help the poor (verses 1–3). So the next time you help with a food drive or volunteer to work on a Habitat for Humanity house, notice how good it makes you feel.

— Psalm 41:1–3

My sins have caught up with me,
    and I can no longer see;
they are more than the hairs of my
        head,
    and I have lost my courage.
13 Save me, LORD! Help me now!
14 May those who try to kill me
    be completely defeated and confused.
May those who are happy because of my
        troubles
    be turned back and disgraced.
15 May those who make fun of me
    be dismayed by their defeat.

16 May all who come to you
    be glad and joyful.

May all who are thankful for your
        salvation
    always say, "How great is the LORD!"
17 I am weak and poor, O Lord,
    but you have not forgotten me.
You are my savior and my God—
    hurry to my aid!

A Prayer in Sickness [k]

41 ¹Happy are those who are
        concerned for the poor;
    the LORD will help them when they
        are in trouble.
² The LORD will protect them and preserve
        their lives;
    he will make them happy in the
        land;
    he will not abandon them to the power
        of their enemies.
³ The LORD will help them when they are
        sick
    and will restore them to health.

⁴ I said, "I have sinned against you,
        LORD;
    be merciful to me and heal me."
⁵ My enemies say cruel things about me.
    They want me to die and be forgotten.
⁶ Those who come to see me are not
        sincere;
    they gather bad news about me
    and then go out and tell it everywhere.
⁷ All who hate me whisper to each other
        about me,
    they imagine the worst about [l] me.
⁸ They say, "He is fatally ill;
    he will never leave his bed again."
⁹ Even my best friend, the one I trusted
        most,
    the one who shared my food,
    has turned against me.
¹⁰ Be merciful to me, LORD, and restore my
        health,
    and I will pay my enemies back.
¹¹ They will not triumph over me,
    and I will know that you are pleased
        with me.

---

k **41** HEBREW TITLE: *A psalm by David.*   *l* **41:7** imagine the worst about; *or* make evil plans to harm.
41:9 Mt 26:23; Mk 14:18; Lk 22:21; Jn 13:18

12 You will help me, because I do what is
   right;
   you will keep me in your presence
   forever.

13 Praise the LORD, the God of Israel!
   Praise him now and forever!

       Amen! Amen!

BOOK TWO
(Psalms 42–72)

The Prayer of Someone in Exile [m]

42 ¹ As a deer longs for a stream of cool
       water,
   so I long for you, O God.
2 I thirst for you, the living God.
   When can I go and worship in your
   presence?
3 Day and night I cry,
   and tears are my only food;
   all the time my enemies ask me,
   "Where is your God?"

4 My heart breaks when I remember the
   past,
   when I went with the crowds to the
   house of God
   and led them as they walked along,
   a happy crowd, singing and shouting
   praise to God.
5 Why am I so sad?
   Why am I so troubled?
   I will put my hope in God,
   and once again I will praise him,
   my savior and my God.

6-7 Here in exile my heart is breaking,
   and so I turn my thoughts to him.
   He has sent waves of sorrow over my soul;
   chaos roars at me like a flood,
   like waterfalls thundering down to the
   Jordan
   from Mount Hermon and Mount
   Mizar.

8 May the LORD show his constant love
   during the day,
   so that I may have a song at night,
   a prayer to the God of my life.

9 To God, my defender, I say,
   "Why have you forgotten me?
   Why must I go on suffering
   from the cruelty of my enemies?"
10 I am crushed by their insults,
   as they keep on asking me,
   "Where is your God?"

11 Why am I so sad?
   Why am I so troubled?
   I will put my hope in God,
   and once again I will praise him,
   my savior and my God.

The Prayer of Someone in Exile
(Continuation of Psalm 42)

43 ¹ O God, declare me innocent,
       and defend my cause against the
       ungodly;
   deliver me from lying and evil people!
2 You are my protector;
   why have you abandoned me?
   Why must I go on suffering
   from the cruelty of my enemies?

3 Send your light and your truth;
   may they lead me
   and bring me back to Zion, your sacred
   hill, [n]
   and to your Temple, where you live.
4 Then I will go to your altar, O God;
   you are the source of my happiness.
   I will play my harp and sing praise to you,
   O God, my God.

5 Why am I so sad?
   Why am I so troubled?
   I will put my hope in God,
   and once again I will praise him,
   my savior and my God.

m 42 HEBREW TITLE: *A poem by the clan of Korah.*   n 43:3 SACRED HILL: See 2:6.
41:13 Ps 106:48

Psalms

Masses for the Dead

Have you ever been to a Catholic funeral? Do you remember some of the symbols that were used? You may see a white cloth, called a pall, that represents the baptismal cloth. You may also see holy water, a cross, incense, the Book of the Gospels, a Paschal candle, and of course, the bread and wine. These are all symbols that recall God's saving love.

When people plan funerals, they have some choices for the readings that are read at the funeral. Parts of Psalms 42 and 43 are combined as a choice for the responsorial psalm. They express sadness, abandonment, and also hope. Read them over. Can you see how someone who has lost a loved one could relate to these psalms?

Catholic Connections

— Psalm 43

A Prayer for Protection°

44 ¹With our own ears we have heard it, O God—
our ancestors have told us about it,
about the great things you did in their time,
in the days of long ago:
²how you yourself drove out the heathen
and established your people in their land;
how you punished the other nations
and caused your own to prosper.
³Your people did not conquer the land with their swords;
they did not win it by their own power;
it was by your power and your strength,
by the assurance of your presence,
which showed that you loved them.

⁴You are my king and my God;
you give^p victory to your people,
5   and by your power we defeat our enemies.
⁶I do not trust in my bow
or in my sword to save me;

⁷but you have saved us from our enemies
and defeated those who hate us.
⁸We will always praise you
and give thanks to you forever.

⁹But now you have rejected us and let us be defeated;
you no longer march out with our armies.
¹⁰You made us run from our enemies,
and they took for themselves what was ours.
¹¹You allowed us to be slaughtered like sheep;
you scattered us in foreign countries.
¹²You sold your own people for a small price
as though they had little value.^q

¹³Our neighbors see what you did to us,
and they mock us and laugh at us.
¹⁴You have made us a joke among the nations;
they shake their heads at us in scorn.
¹⁵I am always in disgrace;
I am covered with shame
16   from hearing the sneers and insults
of my enemies and those who hate me,

° **44** HEBREW TITLE: *A poem by the clan of Korah.*   ^p **44:4** *Some ancient translations* and my God; you give; *Hebrew* O God; give.   ^q **44:12** *as . . . value; or* and made no profit from the sale.

Verse 22 of Psalm 44 is quoted in Romans 8:34–39. Read that passage to see an example of how the New Testament writers referred to the Psalms.

¹⁷All this has happened to us,
even though we have not forgotten you
or broken the covenant you made with
us.

¹⁸We have not been disloyal to you;
we have not disobeyed your
commands.

¹⁹Yet you left us helpless among wild
animals;
you abandoned us in deepest darkness.

²⁰If we had stopped worshiping our God
and prayed to a foreign god,

²¹you would surely have discovered it,
because you know our secret thoughts.

²²But it is on your account that we are
being killed all the time,
that we are treated like sheep to be
slaughtered.

²³Wake up, Lord! Why are you asleep?
Rouse yourself! Don't reject us forever!

²⁴Why are you hiding from us?
Don't forget our suffering and trouble!

²⁵We fall crushed to the ground;
we lie defeated in the dust.

²⁶Come to our aid!
Because of your constant love save us!

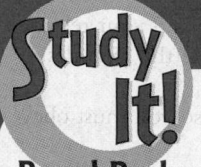

Royal Psalms

Want to be like a king or a queen? Recite Psalm 45! It is called a royal psalm and was probably part of royal weddings. Royal psalms are found throughout the whole Book of Psalms. There may be more than ten royal psalms in it. The king is usually the central figure in a royal psalm. Because in ancient Israel the king was seen as God's representative, by praising the king you are also praising God.

As you read Psalm 45, count the number of times you find words that represent royalty—words such as king, queen, majestic, palace, court, and throne.

— Psalm 45

A Royal Wedding Song^r

45 ¹Beautiful words fill my mind,
as I compose this song for the king.
Like the pen of a good writer
my tongue is ready with a poem.

²You are the most handsome of men;
you are an eloquent speaker.
God has always blessed you.

³Buckle on your sword, mighty king;
you are glorious and majestic.

⁴Ride on in majesty to victory
for the defense of truth and justice!^s
Your strength will win you great
victories!

⁵Your arrows are sharp,
they pierce the hearts of your enemies;
nations fall down at your feet.

⁶The kingdom that God has given you^t
will last forever and ever.
You rule over your people with justice;

⁷   you love what is right and hate what is
evil.
That is why God, your God, has chosen
you
and has poured out more happiness on
you
than on any other king.

⁸The perfume of myrrh and aloes is on
your clothes;
musicians entertain you in palaces
decorated with ivory.

⁹Among the women of your court are
daughters of kings,
and at the right of your throne stands
the queen,
wearing ornaments of finest gold.

---

^r **45** HEBREW TITLE: *A poem by the clan of Korah; a love song.* ^s **45:4** *Probable text* and justice; *Hebrew* and meekness of justice. ^t **45:6** The kingdom that God has given you; *or* Your kingdom, O God; *or* Your divine kingdom.

44:22 Rom 8:36   **45:6, 7** Heb 1:8, 9

10 Bride of the king, listen to what I say—
   forget your people and your relatives.
11 Your beauty will make the king desire
   you;
   he is your master, so you must obey
   him.
12 The people of Tyre will bring you gifts;
   rich people will try to win your favor.

13 The princess is in the palace—how
   beautiful she is!
   Her gown is made of gold thread.
14 In her colorful gown she is led to the king,
   followed by her bridesmaids,
   and they also are brought to him.
15 With joy and gladness they come
   and enter the king's palace.

16 You, my king, will have many sons
   to succeed your ancestors as kings,
   and you will make them rulers over the
   whole earth.
17 My song will keep your fame alive
   forever,
   and everyone will praise you for all
   time to come.

God Is with Us [u]

46 ¹God is our shelter and strength,
      always ready to help in times of
      trouble.
2 So we will not be afraid, even if the earth
   is shaken
   and mountains fall into the ocean
   depths;
3 even if the seas roar and rage,
   and the hills are shaken by the
   violence.

We will not be afraid. (46:2)

4 There is a river that brings joy to the city
   of God,
   to the sacred house of the Most High.
5 God is in that city, and it will never be
   destroyed;
   at early dawn he will come to its aid.
6 Nations are terrified, kingdoms are
   shaken;
   God thunders, and the earth dissolves.

7 The LORD Almighty is with us;
   the God of Jacob is our refuge.

8 Come and see what the LORD has
   done.
   See what amazing things he has done
   on earth.
9 He stops wars all over the world;
   he breaks bows, destroys spears,
   and sets shields on fire.
10 "Stop fighting," he says, "and know that I
   am God,
   supreme among the nations,
   supreme over the world."

11 The LORD Almighty is with us;
   the God of Jacob is our refuge.

Clap your hands for joy. (47:1)

The Supreme Ruler [v]

47 ¹Clap your hands for joy, all peoples!
      Praise God with loud songs!
2 The LORD, the Most High, is to be
   feared;
   he is a great king, ruling over all the
   world.
3 He gave us victory over the peoples;
   he made us rule over the nations.

---

[u] **46** HEBREW TITLE: *A song by the clan of Korah.*   [v] **47** HEBREW TITLE: *A psalm by the clan of Korah.*

Ascension Sunday

"Let's get going. You don't want to miss this Sunday or be late, do you?" Julio's mom was hurrying him more than usual this morning.

"Uh, it's just like any other Sunday, isn't it?" Julio yawned as he answered.

"No, it's Ascension Sunday! It's like Christmas!" she replied.

This conversation is probably not one that kids and their parents have. It is very unlikely that people invite family over, have big meals, and do all the usual holiday activities on Ascension Sunday. But maybe they should. Ascension is one of the ten days listed in the *Catechism of the Catholic Church* as holy days of obligation. It is celebrated either forty days after Easter or on the following Sunday. Why is the Ascension so special for Catholics? Here are a few reasons:

- At the Ascension Jesus left this world to return to his Father and be with him forever.
  - Because of this, we too can spend eternity with God.
    - Through the Holy Spirit, Jesus is now able to be everywhere, with everyone, for all time!

— Psalm 47

Psalms

"Sing praise to God." (47:6)

⁴He chose for us the land where we live,
  the proud possession of his people,
    whom he loves.

⁵God goes up to his throne.
  There are shouts of joy and the blast of
    trumpets,
  as the LORD goes up.

⁶Sing praise to God;
  sing praise to our king!
⁷God is king over all the world;
  praise him with songs!

⁸God sits on his sacred throne;
  he rules over the nations.
⁹The rulers of the nations assemble
  with the people*w* of the God of Abraham.
  More powerful than all armies is he;
    he rules supreme.

Zion, the City of God *x*

48 ¹The LORD is great and is to be
  highly praised
  in the city of our God, on his sacred hill.*y*
²Zion, the mountain of God, is high and
  beautiful;
  the city of the great king brings joy to
    all the world.

---

w **47:9** *Probable text* with the people; *Hebrew* the people.   *x* **48** HEBREW TITLE: *A psalm by the clan of Korah; a song.*   *y* **48:1** SACRED HILL: *See 2:6.*
48:2 Mt 5:35

Read Psalm 46. How does it feel to know that God is there, even when you are the most scared?

3 God has shown that there is safety with
him
inside the fortresses of the city.

4 The kings gathered together
and came to attack Mount Zion.

5 But when they saw it, they were
amazed;
they were afraid and ran away.

6 There they were seized with fear and
anguish,
like a woman about to bear a child,

7 like ships tossing in a furious storm.

8 We have heard what God has done,
and now we have seen it
in the city of our God, the LORD
Almighty;
he will keep the city safe forever.

9 Inside your Temple, O God,
we think of your constant love.

10 You are praised by people everywhere,
and your fame extends over all the
earth.
You rule with justice;

11 let the people of Zion be glad!
You give right judgments;
let there be joy in the cities of Judah!

12 People of God, walk around Zion and
count the towers;

13 take notice of the walls and examine
the fortresses,
so that you may tell the next generation:

14 "This God is our God forever and
ever;
he will lead us for all time to come."

The Foolishness of Trusting in Riches z

49 ¹ Hear this, everyone!
Listen, all people everywhere,

2 great and small alike,
rich and poor together.

3 My thoughts will be clear;
I will speak words of wisdom.

4 I will turn my attention to proverbs
and explain their meaning as I play the
harp.

5 I am not afraid in times of danger
when I am surrounded by enemies,

6 by evil people who trust in their riches
and boast of their great wealth.

7 We can never redeem ourselves;
we cannot pay God the price for our
lives,

8 because the payment for a human life is
too great.
What we could pay would never be
enough

9 to keep us from the grave,
to let us live forever.

10 Anyone can see that even the wise die,
as well as the foolish and stupid.
They all leave their riches to their
descendants.

11 Their graves a are their homes forever;
there they stay for all time,
though they once had lands of their
own.

12 Our greatness cannot keep us from
death;
we will still die like the animals.

13 See what happens to those who trust in
themselves,
the fate of those b who are satisfied with
their wealth—

14 they are doomed to die like sheep,
and Death will be their shepherd.
The righteous will triumph over them,
as their bodies quickly decay
in the world of the dead far from their
homes. c

15 But God will rescue me;
he will save me from the power of
death.

16 Don't be upset when someone becomes
rich,
when his wealth grows even greater;

z 49 HEBREW TITLE: A psalm by the clan of Korah.   a 49:11 Some ancient translations graves; Hebrew inner thoughts.
b 49:13 One ancient translation the fate of those; Hebrew after them.   c 49:14 in . . . homes.; Hebrew unclear.
49:10 Sir 11:19

Zion: The hill in Jerusalem the Temple was built on. So the city of Zion was
Jerusalem.

17 he cannot take it with him when he dies;
his wealth will not go with him to the
grave.

He cannot take it with him when he dies. (49:17)

18 Even if someone is satisfied with this life
and is praised because he is successful,
19 he will join all his ancestors in death,
where the darkness lasts forever.
20 Our greatness cannot keep us from death;
we will still die like the animals.

True Worship *d*

50 ¹The Almighty God, the LORD,
speaks;
he calls to the whole earth from east to
west.
² God shines from Zion,
the city perfect in its beauty.

³ Our God is coming, but not in silence;
a raging fire is in front of him,
a furious storm around him.
⁴ He calls heaven and earth as witnesses
to see him judge his people.
⁵ He says, "Gather my faithful people to me,
those who made a covenant with me
by offering a sacrifice."
⁶ The heavens proclaim that God is
righteous,
that he himself is judge.

⁷ "Listen, my people, and I will speak;
I will testify against you, Israel.
I am God, your God.
⁸ I do not reprimand you because of your
sacrifices
and the burnt offerings you always
bring me.

⁹ And yet I do not need bulls from your
farms
or goats from your flocks;
¹⁰ all the animals in the forest are mine
and the cattle on thousands of hills.
¹¹ All the wild birds are mine
and all living things in the fields.
¹² "If I were hungry, I would not ask you
for food,
for the world and everything in it is
mine.
¹³ Do I eat the flesh of bulls
or drink the blood of goats?
¹⁴ Let the giving of thanks be your sacrifice
to God, *e*
and give the Almighty all that you
promised.
¹⁵ Call to me when trouble comes;
I will save you,
and you will praise me."

¹⁶ But God says to the wicked,
"Why should you recite my
commandments?
Why should you talk about my
covenant?
¹⁷ You refuse to let me correct you;
you reject my commands.
¹⁸ You become the friend of every thief you
see,
and you associate with adulterers.

¹⁹ "You are always ready to speak evil;
you never hesitate to tell lies.

All the animals in the forest are mine. (50:10)

d **50** HEBREW TITLE: *A psalm by Asaph.* *e* **50:14** Let the giving . . . to God; *or* Offer your thanksgiving sacrifice
to God.

Examination of Conscience

Psalm 51 is a prayer for forgiveness and reminds Catholics of the sacrament of Penance and Reconciliation. Before celebrating the sacrament, it is a great idea to have an examination of conscience. And no, that is not like going to the doctor for a physical examination, or like taking a final exam. It is something you can do by yourself or with others.

Most group reconciliation services include an examination of conscience. Sometimes that means a person will read some questions based on the Ten Commandments or the Beatitudes or general Christian values. The questions are only for you to answer in your heart. They help you think about your words, actions, and even your failure to act. If the service includes the opportunity to celebrate the actual sacrament of Penance and Reconciliation, the examination of conscience is followed by an opportunity to go to confession.

It is a good idea to examine your conscience on your own each night, while things are still fresh in your mind. Start by asking yourself these simple questions:

- What did I do today that showed others God's love?
  - Did any of my actions or words keep me from experiencing God's love?

— Psalm 51

20 You are ready to accuse your own
    relatives
    and to find fault with them.
21 You have done all this, and I have said
    nothing,
    so you thought that I am like you.
But now I reprimand you
    and make the matter plain to you.

22 "Listen to this, you that ignore me,
    or I will destroy you,
    and there will be no one to save you.
23 Giving thanks is the sacrifice that honors
    me,
    and I will surely save all who obey me."

A Prayer for Forgiveness[f]

51 ¹Be merciful to me, O God,
    because of your constant love.
Because of your great mercy
    wipe away my sins!

² Wash away all my evil
    and make me clean from my sin!
³ I recognize my faults;
    I am always conscious of my sins.
⁴ I have sinned against you—only against
    you—
    and done what you consider evil.
So you are right in judging me;
    you are justified in condemning me.
⁵ I have been evil from the day I was born;
    from the time I was conceived, I have
    been sinful.

⁶ Sincerity and truth are what you require;
    fill my mind with your wisdom.
⁷ Remove my sin, and I will be clean;
    wash me, and I will be whiter than snow.
⁸ Let me hear the sounds of joy and gladness;
    and though you have crushed me and
    broken me,
    I will be happy once again.

f 51 HEBREW TITLE: *A psalm by David, after the prophet Nathan had spoken to him about his adultery with Bathsheba.*
51 Title 2 Sam 12:1–15   **51:4** Rom 3:4

9 Close your eyes to my sins
and wipe out all my evil.

10 Create a pure heart in me, O God,
and put a new and loyal spirit in me.

"Create a pure heart in me, O God." (51:10)

11 Do not banish me from your presence;
do not take your holy spirit away from
me.

12 Give me again the joy that comes from
your salvation,
and make me willing to obey you.

13 Then I will teach sinners your
commands,
and they will turn back to you.

14 Spare my life, O God, and save me,*g*
and I will gladly proclaim your
righteousness.

15 Help me to speak, Lord,
and I will praise you.

16 You do not want sacrifices,
or I would offer them;
you are not pleased with burnt offerings.

17 My sacrifice is a humble spirit, O God;
you will not reject a humble and
repentant heart.

18 O God, be kind to Zion and help her;
rebuild the walls of Jerusalem.

19 Then you will be pleased with proper
sacrifices
and with our burnt offerings;
and bulls will be sacrificed on your
altar.

God's Judgment and Grace *h*

52 1 Why do you boast, great one, of
your evil?
God's faithfulness is eternal.

2 You make plans to ruin others;
your tongue is like a sharp razor.
You are always inventing lies.

3 You love evil more than good
and falsehood more than truth.

4 You love to hurt people with your words,
you liar!

5 So God will ruin you forever;
he will take hold of you and snatch you
from your home;
he will remove you from the world of
the living.

6 Righteous people will see this and be
afraid;
then they will laugh at you and say,

7 "Look, here is someone who did not
depend on God for safety,
but trusted instead in great wealth
and looked for security in being
wicked."

8 But I am like an olive tree growing in the
house of God;
I trust in his constant love forever and
ever.

---

g **51:14** Spare my life . . . me; *or* O God my savior, keep me from the crime of murder.   *h* **52** HEBREW TITLE: *A
poem by David, after Doeg the Edomite went to Saul and told him that David had gone to the house of Ahimelech.*
52 Title 1 Sam 22:9, 10

**How does Psalm 52 compare those who depend on God and those who do not
depend on God?**

⁹I will always thank you, God, for what
    you have done;
in the presence of your people
    I will proclaim that you are good.

Human Wickedness[i]
(Psalm 14)

53 ¹Fools say to themselves,
    "There is no God."
They are all corrupt,
    and they have done terrible things;
    there is no one who does what is
        right.

²God looks down from heaven at people
    to see if there are any who are wise,
    any who worship him.
³But they have all turned away;
    they are all equally bad.
Not one of them does what is right,
    not a single one.

⁴"Don't they know?" God asks.
    "Are these evildoers ignorant?
They live by robbing my people,
    and they never pray to me."

⁵But then they will become terrified,
    as they have never been before,
    for God will scatter the bones of the
        enemies of his people.
God has rejected them,
    and so Israel will totally defeat them.

⁶How I pray that victory
    will come to Israel from Zion.
How happy the people of Israel will be
    when God makes them prosperous
        again!

A Prayer for Protection from Enemies[j]

54 ¹Save me by your power, O God;
    set me free by your might!
²Hear my prayer, O God;
    listen to my words!

³Proud people are coming to attack me;
    cruel people are trying to kill me—
    those who do not care about God.

⁴But God is my helper.
    The Lord is my defender.
⁵May God use their own evil to punish my
        enemies.
He will destroy them because he is
        faithful.

⁶I will gladly offer you a sacrifice,
    O LORD;
I will give you thanks
    because you are good.
⁷You have rescued me from all my
        troubles,
    and I have seen my enemies defeated.

The Prayer of Someone Betrayed by a Friend[k]

55 ¹Hear my prayer, O God;
    don't turn away from my plea!
²Listen to me and answer me;
    I am worn out by my worries.
³I am terrified by the threats of my
        enemies,
    crushed by the oppression of the
        wicked.
They bring trouble on me;
    they are angry with me and hate me.

⁴I am terrified,
    and the terrors of death crush me.
⁵I am gripped by fear and trembling;
    I am overcome with horror.
⁶I wish I had wings like a dove.
    I would fly away and find rest.
⁷I would fly far away
    and make my home in the desert.
⁸I would hurry and find myself a shelter
    from the raging wind and the storm.
⁹Confuse the speech of my enemies,
    O Lord!

I see violence and riots in the city,

---

[i] **53** HEBREW TITLE: *A poem by David.*   [j] **54** HEBREW TITLE: *A poem by David, after the men from Ziph went to Saul and told him that David was hiding in their territory.*   [k] **55** HEBREW TITLE: *A poem by David.*
53:1–3 Rom 3:10–12   **54 Title** 1 Sam 23:19; 26:1

10 surrounding it day and night,
   filling it with crime and trouble.
11 There is destruction everywhere;
   the streets are full of oppression and
      fraud.

12 If it were an enemy making fun of me,
      I could endure it;
   if it were an opponent boasting over me,
      I could hide myself from him.
13 But it is you, my companion,
      my colleague and close friend.
14 We had intimate talks with each other
      and worshiped together in the Temple.
15 May my enemies die before their time;
      may they go down alive into the world
         of the dead!
   Evil is in their homes and in their hearts.

16 But I call to the LORD God for help,
      and he will save me.
17 Morning, noon, and night
      my complaints and groans go up to
         him,
      and he will hear my voice.
18 He will bring me safely back
      from the battles that I fight
      against so many enemies.
19 God, who has ruled from eternity,
      will hear me and defeat them;
   for they refuse to change,
      and they do not fear him.

20 My former companion attacked his
      friends;
      he broke his promises.
21 His words were smoother than cream,
      but there was hatred in his heart;
   his words were as soothing as oil,
      but they cut like sharp swords.

22 Leave your troubles with the LORD,
      and he will defend you;
      he never lets honest people be
         defeated.

23 But you, O God, will bring those
      murderers and liars to their graves
      before half their life is over.
   As for me, I will trust in you.

Why Did They Do That?

"I have no friends!"
    Have you ever said that?
Maybe you said it when a friend
or friends did or said something
that really hurt you or betrayed
you. Most people have had a time
in their life when it felt like this.
The person who wrote Psalm 55
must have had that same experience. What he wrote in verse 12 is
so true: "If it were an enemy making fun of me, I could endure it."
When strangers or enemies make
fun of us or hurt us, it feels like
less of a betrayal than when our
friends do it.
    This is a great psalm to read
when feeling bad about your own
friends, but it also is a good
reminder of how to live. Think
about a friend you may have hurt
in the past. Maybe you could take
some time to write to him or her,
name what happened, and apologize if you haven't already done
so. If there isn't someone for you
to apologize to, good for you!
And keep Psalm 55 in mind whenever you feel like telling a friend's
secret or gossiping about something she or he did.

— Psalm 55

A Prayer of Trust in God[1]

56 ¹Be merciful to me, O God,
      because I am under attack;
   my enemies persecute me all the
      time.
²All day long my opponents attack me.
   There are so many who fight against
      me.

---

[1] 56 HEBREW TITLE: *A psalm by David, after the Philistines captured him in Gath.*
56 Title 1 Sam 21:13–15

³ When I am afraid, O LORD Almighty,
  I put my trust in you.
⁴ I trust in God and am not afraid;
  I praise him for what he has promised.
  What can a mere human being do to
    me?

⁵ My enemies make trouble for me all day
    long;
  they are always thinking up some way
    to hurt me!
⁶ They gather in hiding places
  and watch everything I do,
    hoping to kill me.
⁷ Punish[m] them, O God, for their evil;
  defeat those people in your anger!

⁸ You know how troubled I am;
  you have kept a record of my tears.
  Aren't they listed in your book?
⁹ The day I call to you,
  my enemies will be turned back.
  I know this: God[n] is on my side—
¹⁰   the LORD, whose promises I praise.
¹¹ In him I trust, and I will not be afraid.
  What can a mere human being do to
    me?

¹² O God, I will offer you what I have
    promised;
  I will give you my offering of
    thanksgiving,
¹³ because you have rescued me from
    death
  and kept me from defeat.
  And so I walk in the presence of God,
  in the light that shines on the living.

A Prayer for Help [o]

57 ¹ Be merciful to me, O God, be
    merciful,
  because I come to you for safety.
  In the shadow of your wings I find
    protection
  until the raging storms are over.

² I call to God, the Most High,
  to God, who supplies my every
    need.

³ He will answer from heaven and save me;
  he will defeat my oppressors.
  God will show me his constant love
    and faithfulness.

⁴ I am surrounded by enemies,
  who are like lions hungry for human
    flesh.
  Their teeth are like spears and arrows;
    their tongues are like sharp swords.

⁵ Show your greatness in the sky, O God,
  and your glory over all the earth.

⁶ My enemies have spread a net to catch
    me;
  I am overcome with distress.
  They dug a pit in my path,
    but fell into it themselves.

⁷ I have complete confidence, O God;
  I will sing and praise you!
⁸ Wake up, my soul!
  Wake up, my harp and lyre!
  I will wake up the sun.
⁹ I will thank you, O Lord, among the
    nations.
  I will praise you among the peoples.
¹⁰ Your constant love reaches the heavens;
  your faithfulness touches the skies.
¹¹ Show your greatness in the sky, O God,
  and your glory over all the earth.

A Prayer for God to Punish
the Wicked [p]

58 ¹ Do you rulers[q] ever give a just
    decision?
  Do you judge everyone fairly?
² No! You think only of the evil you can
    do,
  and commit crimes of violence in the
    land.

³ Evildoers go wrong all their lives;
  they tell lies from the day they are
    born.
⁴ They are full of poison like snakes;
  they stop up their ears like a deaf
    cobra,

[m] **56:7** *Probable text* Punish; *Hebrew* Save.   [n] **56:9** I know this: God; *or* Because I know that God.
[o] **57** HEBREW TITLE: *A psalm by David, after he fled from Saul in the cave.*   [p] **58** HEBREW TITLE: *A psalm by David.*
[q] **58:1** rulers; *or* gods.
57 Title 1 Sam 22:1; 24:3

5 which does not hear the voice of the
   snake charmer,
   or the chant of the clever magician.

6 Break the teeth of these fierce lions,
   O God.
7 May they disappear like water draining
   away;
   may they be crushed like weeds on a
   path.[r]
8 May they be like snails that dissolve into
   slime;
   may they be like a baby born dead that
   never sees the light.
9 Before they know it, they are cut down
   like weeds;
   in his fierce anger God will blow them
   away
   while they are still living.[s]

10 The righteous will be glad when they see
   sinners punished;
   they will wade through the blood of
   the wicked.
11 People will say, "The righteous are indeed
   rewarded;
   there is indeed a God who judges the
   world."

A Prayer for Safety[t]

59 ¹Save me from my enemies, my God;
       protect me from those who attack
       me!
2 Save me from those evil people;
   rescue me from those murderers!

3 Look! They are waiting to kill me;
   cruel people are gathering against
   me.
   It is not because of any sin or wrong I
   have done,
4   nor because of any fault of mine,
   O LORD,
   that they hurry to their places.

5 Rise, LORD God Almighty, and come to
   my aid;
   see for yourself, God of Israel!
   Wake up and punish the heathen;
   show no mercy to evil traitors!

6 They come back in the evening,
   snarling like dogs as they go about the
   city.
7 Listen to their insults and threats.
   Their tongues are like swords in their
   mouths,
   yet they think that no one hears them.

8 But you laugh at them, LORD;
   you mock all the heathen.
9 I have confidence in your strength;
   you are my refuge, O God.
10 My God loves me and will come to me;
   he will let me see my enemies
   defeated.

11 Do not kill them, O God, or my people
   may forget.
   Scatter them by your strength and
   defeat them,
   O Lord, our protector.
12 Sin is on their lips; all their words are
   sinful;
   may they be caught in their pride!
   Because they curse and lie,
13   destroy them in your anger;
   destroy them completely.
   Then everyone will know that God rules
   in Israel,
   that his rule extends over all the earth.

14 My enemies come back in the evening,
   snarling like dogs as they go about the
   city,
15   like dogs roaming about for food
   and growling if they do not find
   enough.

16 But I will sing about your strength;
   every morning I will sing aloud of your
   constant love.

[r] **58:7** *Probable text* may . . . path; *Hebrew unclear.* [s] **58:9** *Verse 9 in Hebrew is unclear.* [t] **59** HEBREW TITLE: *A psalm by David, after Saul sent men to watch his house in order to kill him.*
59 Title 1 Sam 19:11

How would you describe your enemies? How does the psalmist describe the enemies in Psalm 59?

You have been a refuge for me,
a shelter in my time of trouble.
17 I will praise you, my defender.
My refuge is God,
the God who loves me.

A Prayer for Deliverance[u]

60 1 You have rejected us, God, and
defeated us;
you have been angry with us—but
now turn back to us.[v]
2 You have made the land tremble, and you
have cut it open;
now heal its wounds, because it is
falling apart.
3 You have made your people suffer greatly;
we stagger around as though we were
drunk.
4 You have warned those who have
reverence for you,
so that they might escape destruction.
5 Save us by your might; answer our prayer,
so that the people you love may be
rescued.

6 From his sanctuary[w] God has said,
"In triumph I will divide Shechem
and distribute Sukkoth Valley to my
people.
7 Gilead is mine, and Manasseh too;
Ephraim is my helmet
and Judah my royal scepter.
8 But I will use Moab as my washbowl,
and I will throw my sandals on Edom,
as a sign that I own it.
Did the Philistines think they would
shout in triumph over me?"

9 Who, O God, will take me into the
fortified city?
Who will lead me to Edom?
10 Have you really rejected us?
Aren't you going to march out with
our armies?

11 Help us against the enemy;
human help is worthless.
12 With God on our side we will win;
he will defeat our enemies.

A Prayer for Protection[x]

61 1 Hear my cry, O God;
listen to my prayer!
2 In despair and far from home
I call to you!

Take me to a safe refuge,
3 for you are my protector,
my strong defense against my enemies.

"Take me to a safe refuge." (61:2)

4 Let me live in your sanctuary all my life;
let me find safety under your wings.
5 You have heard my promises, O God,
and you have given me what belongs
to those who honor you.

6 Add many years to the king's life;
let him live on and on!
7 May he rule forever in your presence,
O God;
protect him with your constant love
and faithfulness.

8 So I will always sing praises to you,
as I offer you daily what I have
promised.

---

[u] **60** HEBREW TITLE: *A psalm by David, for teaching, when he fought against the Arameans from Naharaim and from Zobah, and Joab turned back and killed 12,000 Edomites in Salt Valley.*   [v] **60:1** angry with us . . . us; *or* angry with us and turned your back on us.   [w] **60:6** From his sanctuary; *or* In his holiness.   [x] **61** HEBREW TITLE: *By David.*
60 Title 2 Sam 8:13; 1 Chr 18:12

Is God on your side even when you lose at something? How is that similar to or different from what is said in Psalm 60:12?

Pray It!

Every Day?

Did you know that if you do something twenty-one days in a row, it becomes a habit? And that some habits are bad for you (like smoking or eating junk food), but that others are good (like brushing your teeth or exercise)? That's right, if you want to create a good habit, make yourself do something *every day* for twenty-one days in a row. Why not start with prayer? The author of Psalm 61 says he promised to sing to God daily. If you read a psalm or say a memorized prayer or pray spontaneously every day for twenty-one days, you will have a good habit of prayer started.

— Psalm 61:8

Confidence in God's Protection ʸ

62 ¹I wait patiently for God to save me;
I depend on him alone.
²He alone protects and saves me;
he is my defender,
and I shall never be defeated.

³How much longer will all of you attack someone
who is no stronger than a broken-down fence?
⁴You only want to bring him down from his place of honor;
you take pleasure in lies.
You speak words of blessing,
but in your heart you curse him.

⁵I depend on God alone;
I put my hope in him.
⁶He alone protects and saves me;
he is my defender,
and I shall never be defeated.

⁷My salvation and honor depend on God;
he is my strong protector;
he is my shelter.

⁸Trust in God at all times, my people.
Tell him all your troubles,
for he is our refuge.

⁹Human beings are all like a puff of breath;
great and small alike are worthless.
Put them on the scales, and they weigh nothing;
they are lighter than a mere breath.
¹⁰Don't put your trust in violence;
don't hope to gain anything by robbery;
even if your riches increase,
don't depend on them.

¹¹More than once I have heard God say
that power belongs to him
¹² and that his love is constant.
You yourself, O Lord, reward everyone
according to their deeds.

Longing for God ᶻ

63 ¹O God, you are my God,
and I long for you.
My whole being desires you;
like a dry, worn-out, and waterless land,
my soul is thirsty for you.
²Let me see you in the sanctuary;
let me see how mighty and glorious
you are.
³Your constant love is better than life itself,
and so I will praise you.
⁴I will give you thanks as long as I live;
I will raise my hands to you in prayer.
⁵My soul will feast and be satisfied,
and I will sing glad songs of praise to
you.

⁶As I lie in bed, I remember you;
all night long I think of you,
⁷ because you have always been my help.
In the shadow of your wings I sing for joy.
⁸I cling to you,
and your hand keeps me safe.

⁹Those who are trying to kill me
will go down into the world of the
dead.

ʸ **62** HEBREW TITLE: *A psalm by David.*   ᶻ **63** HEBREW TITLE: *A psalm by David, when he was in the desert of Judea.*
62:12 Job 34:11; Jer 17:10; Mt 16:27; Rom 2:6; Rev 2:23   **63 Title** 1 Sam 23:14

10 They will be killed in battle,
   and their bodies eaten by wolves.
11 Because God gives him victory,
   the king will rejoice.
Those who make promises in God's name
   will praise him,
but the mouths of liars will be shut.

A Prayer for Protection[a]

64 ¹I am in trouble, God—listen to my
        prayer!
   I am afraid of my enemies—save my
      life!
2 Protect me from the plots of the wicked,
   from mobs of evil people.
3 They sharpen their tongues like swords
   and aim cruel words like arrows.
4 They are quick to spread their shameless
      lies;
   they destroy good people with
      cowardly slander.
5 They encourage each other in their evil
      plots;
   they talk about where they will place
      their traps.
   "No one can see them," they say.
6 They make evil plans and say,
   "We have planned a perfect crime."
The human heart and mind are a mystery.

7 But God shoots his arrows at them,
   and suddenly they are wounded.
8 He will destroy them because of those
      words;[b]
   all who see them will shake their
      heads.
9 They will all be afraid;
   they will think about what God has
      done
   and tell about his deeds.
10 All righteous people will rejoice
   because of what the LORD has done.
They will find safety in him;
   all good people will praise him.

Praise and Thanksgiving[c]

65 ¹O God, it is right for us to praise
        you in Zion
   and keep our promises to you,
2   because you answer prayers.
People everywhere will come to you
3   on account of their sins.
Our faults defeat us,[d]
   but you forgive them.
4 Happy are those whom you choose,
   whom you bring to live in your
      sanctuary.
We shall be satisfied with the good things
      of your house,
   the blessings of your sacred Temple.

5 You answer us by giving us victory,
   and you do wonderful things to save
      us.
People all over the world
   and across the distant seas trust in
      you.
6 You set the mountains in place by your
      strength,
   showing your mighty power.
7 You calm the roar of the seas
   and the noise of the waves;
   you calm the uproar of the peoples.
8 The whole world stands in awe
   of the great things that you have done.
Your deeds bring shouts of joy
   from one end of the earth to the other.

9 You show your care for the land by
      sending rain;
   you make it rich and fertile.
You fill the streams with water;
   you provide the earth with crops.
This is how you do it:
10   you send abundant rain on the plowed
         fields
   and soak them with water;
   you soften the soil with showers
      and cause the young plants to grow.
11 What a rich harvest your goodness
      provides!
   Wherever you go there is plenty.
12 The pastures are filled with flocks;
   the hillsides are full of joy.

---

a **64** HEBREW TITLE: *A psalm by David.*   *b* **64:8** *Probable text* He will destroy them because of those words;
Hebrew They will destroy him, those words are against them.   *c* **65** HEBREW TITLE: *A psalm by David; a song.*
d **65:3** *One ancient translation* us; *Hebrew* me.

Thanksgiving

The word *thanksgiving* usually brings to mind images of pilgrims and turkeys. For Catholics, thanksgiving isn't something that just happens on a Thursday in November. We are called to be thankful daily, or even more often. The name of our central sacrament, the Eucharist, is a Greek word meaning "thanksgiving." This tells us that the Mass is a form of prayerful thanksgiving.

One of the types of prayer found in the Psalms is thanksgiving. The people writing the Psalms knew how important it is to give thanks to God. How do you give thanks to God? Have you said "thank God" (and made it a prayer) when you got a good grade or won an award? At the end of the day, do you make a list of things to be grateful for and give thanks in your evening prayer? Do you keep a prayer journal that lists your prayers and your thanks when they are answered? If you haven't done anything like these suggestions, try one or more of them. You'll be doing what the writer of Psalm 65 did (and check out what Saint Paul says in 1 Thessalonians 5:18).

— Psalm 65

13 The fields are covered with sheep;
   the valleys are full of wheat.
Everything shouts and sings for
   joy.

A Song of Praise and Thanksgiving [e]

66 ¹Praise God with shouts of joy, all
     people!
²Sing to the glory of his name;
   offer him glorious praise!
³Say to God, "How wonderful are the
    things you do!
Your power is so great
that your enemies bow down in fear
   before you.
⁴Everyone on earth worships you;
   they sing praises to you,
   they sing praises to your name."

Sing to the glory of his name! (66:2)

⁵Come and see what God has done,
   his wonderful acts among people.
⁶He changed the sea into dry land;
   our ancestors crossed the river on
    foot.
There we rejoiced because of what he
   did.
⁷He rules forever by his might
   and keeps his eyes on the nations.
Let no rebels rise against him.
⁸Praise our God, all nations;
   let your praise be heard.

e **66** HEBREW TITLE: *A song.*
66:6 a Ex 14:21; b Josh 3:14–17

Psalms

Celebrating Mary, Mother of God

Catholic Connections

In the Catholic Church, January 1, the first day of the calendar year, is dedicated to Mary. During the Mass that day, we pray part of Psalm 67, which talks about the mercy of God. Mary knew God's mercy and blessing firsthand and praised God for it just as this psalm does.

This feast day for Mary is celebrated one week after we celebrate Jesus' birth. Why don't you celebrate your mom, or another woman who is significant to you, one week after your birthday? Celebrate it with a psalm you pick just for her by creating a symbol for her and decorating it with the words from the psalm. Surprise her with breakfast in bed or another special meal. Make one week after your birthday *her* day.

— Psalm 67

9 He has kept us alive
  and has not allowed us to fall.

10 You have put us to the test, God;
  as silver is purified by fire,
  so you have tested us.

11 You let us fall into a trap
  and placed heavy burdens on our backs.

12 You let our enemies trample us;
  we went through fire and flood,
  but now you have brought us to a place
  of safety.ᶠ

13 I will bring burnt offerings to your
  house;
  I will offer you what I promised.

14 I will give you what I said I would
  when I was in trouble.

15 I will offer sheep to be burned on the
  altar;
  I will sacrifice bulls and goats,
  and the smoke will go up to the sky.

16 Come and listen, all who honor God,
  and I will tell you what he has done for
  me.

17 I cried to him for help;
  I praised him with songs.

18 If I had ignored my sins,
  the Lord would not have listened to
  me.

19 But God has indeed heard me;
  he has listened to my prayer.

20 I praise God,
  because he did not reject my prayer
  or keep back his constant love from me.

A Song of Thanksgivingᵍ

67 1 God, be merciful to us and bless us;
  look on us with kindness,

2 so that the whole world may know your
  will;
  so that all nations may know your
  salvation.

3 May the peoples praise you, O God;
  may all the peoples praise you!

4 May the nations be glad and sing for joy,
  because you judge the peoples with
  justice
  and guide every nation on earth.

5 May the peoples praise you, O God;
  may all the peoples praise you!

ᶠ 66:12 *Some ancient translations* safety; *Hebrew* overflowing.   ᵍ 67 HEBREW TITLE: *A psalm; a song.*

"God, be merciful to us and bless us; look on us with kindness" *(Psalm 67:1).*

6 The land has produced its harvest;
    God, our God, has blessed us.
7 God has blessed us;
    may all people everywhere honor him.

A National Song of Triumph[h]

68 ¹God rises up and scatters his
            enemies.
    Those who hate him run away in
        defeat.
² As smoke is blown away, so he drives
        them off;
    as wax melts in front of the fire,
    so do the wicked perish in God's
        presence.
³ But the righteous are glad and rejoice in
        his presence;
    they are happy and shout for joy.

⁴ Sing to God, sing praises to his name;
    prepare a way for him who rides on
        the clouds.[i]
    His name is the LORD —be glad in his
        presence!

⁵ God, who lives in his sacred Temple,
    cares for orphans and protects widows.
⁶ He gives the lonely a home to live in
    and leads prisoners out into happy
        freedom,
    but rebels will have to live in a desolate
        land.

⁷ O God, when you led your people,
    when you marched across the
        desert,
⁸ the earth shook, and the sky poured
        down rain,
    because of the coming of the God of
        Sinai,[j]
    the coming of the God of Israel.
⁹ You caused abundant rain to fall
    and restored your worn-out land;
¹⁰ your people made their home there;
    in your goodness you provided for the
        poor.

¹¹ The Lord gave the command,
    and many women carried the news:

¹² "Kings and their armies are running away!"
    The women at home divided what was
        captured:
¹³   figures of doves covered with silver,
        whose wings glittered with fine gold.
    (Why did some of you stay among the
        sheep pens on the day of battle?)
¹⁴ When Almighty God scattered the kings
        on Mount Zalmon,
    he caused snow to fall there.

¹⁵ What a mighty mountain is Bashan,
    a mountain of many peaks!
¹⁶ Why from your mighty peaks do you
        look with scorn
    on the mountain[k] on which God chose
        to live?
    The LORD will live there forever!

¹⁷ With his many thousands of mighty
        chariots
    the Lord comes from Sinai[l] into the
        holy place.
¹⁸ He goes up to the heights,
    taking many captives with him;
    he receives gifts from rebellious people.
    The LORD God will live there.

¹⁹ Praise the Lord,
    who carries our burdens day after day;
    he is the God who saves us.
²⁰ Our God is a God who saves;
    he is the LORD, our Lord,
    who rescues us from death.

²¹ God will surely break the heads of his
        enemies,
    of those who persist in their sinful ways.
²² The Lord has said, "I will bring your
        enemies back from Bashan;
    I will bring them back from the depths
        of the ocean,
²³ so that you may wade in their blood,
    and your dogs may lap up as much as
        they want."

²⁴ O God, your march of triumph is seen by
        all,
    the procession of God, my king, into
        his sanctuary.

h **68** HEBREW TITLE: *A psalm by David; a song.*   i **68:4** on the clouds; *or* across the desert.   j **68:8** GOD OF SINAI:
As the people of Israel went from Egypt to Canaan, God revealed himself to them at Mount Sinai (see Ex 19:16–25).
k **68:16** MOUNTAIN: See 2:6.   l **68:17** Probable text comes from Sinai; *Hebrew* in them, Sinai.
68:8 Ex 19:18   **68:18** Eph 4:8

Psalms

Praise the Lord, who carries our burdens day after day. (68:19)

25 The singers are in front, the musicians are behind,

in between are the young women beating the tambourines.

26 "Praise God in the meeting of his people; praise the LORD, all you descendants of Jacob!"

27 First comes Benjamin, the smallest tribe, then the leaders of Judah with their group,

followed by the leaders of Zebulun and Naphtali.

28 Show your power, O God, the power you have used on our behalf

29 from your Temple in Jerusalem, where kings bring gifts to you.

30 Rebuke Egypt, that wild animal in the reeds;

rebuke the nations, that herd of bulls with their calves,

until they all bow down and offer you their silver.

Scatter those people who love to make war!^m

31 Ambassadors^n will come from Egypt; the Ethiopians^o will raise their hands in prayer to God.

32 Sing to God, kingdoms of the world, sing praise to the Lord,

33 to him who rides in the sky, the ancient sky.

Listen to him shout with a mighty roar.

34 Proclaim God's power; his majesty is over Israel, his might is in the skies.

35 How awesome is God as he comes from his sanctuary— the God of Israel!

He gives strength and power to his people.

Praise God!

A Cry for Help ^p

69 ¹ Save me, O God!
The water is up to my neck;

² I am sinking in deep mud, and there is no solid ground;

I am out in deep water, and the waves are about to drown me.

³ I am worn out from calling for help, and my throat is aching.

I have strained my eyes, looking for your help.

⁴ Those who hate me for no reason are more numerous than the hairs of my head.

My enemies tell lies against me; they are strong and want to kill me.

They made me give back things I did not steal.

⁵ My sins, O God, are not hidden from you;

you know how foolish I have been.

⁶ Don't let me bring shame on those who trust in you,

Sovereign LORD Almighty!

---

^m **68:30** *Verse 30 in Hebrew is unclear.*   ^n **68:31** *Some ancient translations* Ambassadors; *Hebrew unclear.*
^o **68:31** *Hebrew* Cushites: *Cush is the ancient name of the extensive territory south of the First Cataract of the Nile River. This region was called Ethiopia in Graeco-Roman time, and included within its borders most of modern Sudan and some of present-day Ethiopia (Abyssinia).*   ^p **69** HEBREW TITLE: *By David.*
69:4 Ps 35:19; Jn 15:25

Psalms

Don't let me bring disgrace to those who
  worship you,
    O God of Israel!
7 It is for your sake that I have been
  insulted
  and that I am covered with shame.
8 I am like a stranger to my relatives,
  like a foreigner to my family.

9 My devotion to your Temple burns in me
  like a fire;
  the insults which are hurled at you fall
    on me.
10 I humble myself*q* by fasting,
  and people insult me;
11 I dress myself in clothes of mourning,
  and they laugh at me.
12 They talk about me in the streets,
  and drunkards make up songs about me.

13 But as for me, I will pray to you, LORD;
  answer me, God, at a time you choose.
  Answer me because of your great love,
  because you keep your promise to save.
14 Save me from sinking in the mud;
  keep me safe from my enemies,
  safe from the deep water.
15 Don't let the flood come over me;
  don't let me drown in the depths
  or sink into the grave.

16 Answer me, LORD, in the goodness of
  your constant love;
  in your great compassion turn to me!
17 Don't hide yourself from your servant;
  I am in great trouble—answer me now!
18 Come to me and save me;
  rescue me from my enemies.

19 You know how I am insulted,
  how I am disgraced and dishonored;
  you see all my enemies.
20 Insults have broken my heart,
  and I am in despair.
  I had hoped for sympathy, but there was
    none;
  for comfort, but I found none.

21 When I was hungry, they gave me poison;
  when I was thirsty, they offered me
    vinegar.
22 May their banquets cause their ruin;
  may their sacred feasts cause their
    downfall.
23 Strike them with blindness!
  Make their backs always weak!
24 Pour out your anger on them;
  let your indignation overtake them.
25 May their camps be left deserted;
  may no one be left alive in their tents.
26 They persecute those whom you have
  punished;
  they talk about the sufferings of those
    you have wounded.
27 Keep a record of all their sins;
  don't let them have any part in your
    salvation.
28 May their names be erased from the book
  of the living;
  may they not be included in the list of
    your people.

29 But I am in pain and despair;
  lift me up, O God, and save me!

30 I will praise God with a song;
  I will proclaim his greatness by giving
    him thanks.
31 This will please the LORD more than
  offering him cattle,
  more than sacrificing a full-grown bull.
32 When the oppressed see this, they will be
    glad;
  those who worship God will be
    encouraged.
33 The LORD listens to those in need
  and does not forget his people in
    prison.

34 Praise God, O heaven and earth,
  seas and all creatures in them.
35 He will save Jerusalem
  and rebuild the towns of Judah.

---

q **69:10** *Some ancient translations* humble myself; *Hebrew* cry.
69:9 a Jn 2:17; **b** Rom 15:3   **69:21** Mt 27:48; Mk 15:36; Lk 23:26; Jn 19:28, 29   **69:22, 23** Rom 11:9, 10
69:25 Acts 1:20   **69:28** Ex 32:32; Rev 3:5; 13:8; 17:8

When do you feel like saying, "The water is up to my neck . . ." *(Psalm 69:1)*?
What do you do when you feel that way?

Psalms

His people will live there and possess the
land;

36 the descendants of his servants will
inherit it,
and those who love him will live there.

A Prayer for Help[r]
(Psalm 40:13–17)

70 ¹Save me, O God!
LORD, help me now!

²May those who try to kill me
be defeated and confused.

May those who are happy because of my
troubles
be turned back and disgraced.

³May those who make fun of me
be dismayed by their defeat.

⁴May all who come to you
be glad and joyful.

May all who are thankful for your salvation
always say, "How great is God!"

⁵I am weak and poor;
come to me quickly, O God.

You are my savior and my LORD —
hurry to my aid!

The Prayer of an Elderly Person

71 ¹LORD, I have come to you for
protection;
never let me be defeated!

²Because you are righteous, help me and
rescue me.

Listen to me and save me!

³Be my secure shelter
and a strong fortress[s] to protect me;
you are my refuge and defense.

⁴My God, rescue me from wicked people,
from the power of cruel and evil
people.

⁵Sovereign LORD, I put my hope in you;
I have trusted in you since I was
young.

⁶I have relied on you all my life;
you have protected[t] me since the day I
was born.

I will always praise you.

⁷My life has been an example to many,
because you have been my strong
defender.

⁸All day long I praise you
and proclaim your glory.

⁹Do not reject me now that I am old;
do not abandon me now that I am
feeble.

¹⁰My enemies want to kill me;
they talk and plot against me.

¹¹They say, "God has abandoned him;
let's go after him and catch him;
there is no one to rescue him."

¹²Don't stay so far away, O God;
my God, hurry to my aid!

¹³May those who attack me
be defeated and destroyed.

May those who try to hurt me
be shamed and disgraced.

¹⁴I will always put my hope in you;
I will praise you more and more.

¹⁵I will tell of your goodness;
all day long I will speak of your
salvation,
though it is more than I can
understand.

¹⁶I will go in the strength of the LORD God;
I will proclaim your goodness, yours
alone.

¹⁷You have taught me ever since I was
young,
and I still tell of your wonderful acts.

¹⁸Now that I am old and my hair is gray,
do not abandon me, O God!

Be with me while I proclaim your power
and might
to all generations to come.

¹⁹Your righteousness, God, reaches the skies.
You have done great things;
there is no one like you.

---

[r] **70** HEBREW TITLE: *A psalm by David; a lament.*   [s] **71:3** *One ancient translation* a strong fortress; *Hebrew* to go
always you commanded.   [t] **71:6** *Some ancient translations* protected; *Hebrew unclear.*

Why, do you think, was the psalmist going to play hymns on a harp (see *Psalm
71:22*)**? What instrument would you use?**

Now that I am old . . . (71:18)

20 You have sent troubles and suffering on
    me,
    but you will restore my strength;
    you will keep me from the grave.
21 You will make me greater than ever;
    you will comfort me again.

22 I will indeed praise you with the harp;
    I will praise your faithfulness, my
      God.
  On my harp I will play hymns to you,
    the Holy One of Israel.
23 I will shout for joy as I play for you;
    with my whole being I will sing
    because you have saved me.
24 I will speak of your righteousness all day
    long,
    because those who tried to harm me
    have been defeated and disgraced.

A Prayer for the King[u]

72 ¹Teach the king to judge with your
       righteousness, O God;
  share with him your own justice,
  ²so that he will rule over your people with
    justice
    and govern the oppressed with
      righteousness.
³May the land enjoy prosperity;
    may it experience righteousness.

4 May the king judge the poor fairly;
    may he help the needy
    and defeat their oppressors.
5 May your people worship you as long as
    the sun shines,
    as long as the moon gives light, for ages
    to come.

6 May the king be like rain on the fields,
    like showers falling on the land.
7 May righteousness flourish in his lifetime,
    and may prosperity last as long as the
    moon gives light.

8 His kingdom will reach from sea to sea,
    from the Euphrates to the ends of the
    earth.
9 The peoples of the desert will bow down
    before him;
    his enemies will throw themselves to
    the ground.
10 The kings of Spain and of the islands will
    offer him gifts;
    the kings of Sheba and Seba[v] will bring
    him offerings.
11 All kings will bow down before him;
    all nations will serve him.

12 He rescues the poor who call to him,
    and those who are needy and
    neglected.
13 He has pity on the weak and poor;
    he saves the lives of those in need.
14 He rescues them from oppression and
    violence;
    their lives are precious to him.

15 Long live the king!
    May he be given gold from Sheba;[w]
    may prayers be said for him at all times;
    may God's blessings be on him always!
16 May there be plenty of grain in the land;
    may the hills be covered with crops,
    as fruitful as those of Lebanon.
  May the cities be filled with people,
    like fields full of grass.
17 May the king's name never be forgotten;
    may his fame last as long as the sun.
  May all nations ask God to bless them
    as he has blessed the king.[x]

---

[u] **72** HEBREW TITLE: *By Solomon.*   *[v]* **72:10** SHEBA AND SEBA: *Sheba was toward the south in Arabia and Seba was on the opposite side of the Red Sea.*   *[w]* **72:15** SHEBA: See 72:10.   *[x]* **72:17** as he has blessed the king; *or* and may they wish happiness for the king.
72:8 Zech 9:10; Sir 44:21

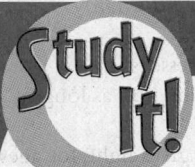

Dividing the Psalms

You may have noticed that before Psalm 73, there is a heading that says "Book Three (Psalms 73–89)." Psalms is divided into five parts, called books. Book 1 contains Psalms 1–41, Book 2 has Psalms 42–72, Book 3 runs from 73–89, Book 4 includes 90–106, and Book 5 contains Psalms 107–150.

Experts really aren't sure how or why the Psalms were divided into these different books. There is evidence that shows smaller collections of the Psalms were made before the whole group was done. Because psalms were written and sung over a long period of time, scholars say it isn't surprising that we know so little about how they were organized. We do know, however, that they are loved by many people and that they express many different emotions and situations.

— **Psalm 73**

18 Praise the LORD, the God of Israel!
   He alone does these wonderful things.
19 Praise his glorious name forever!
   May his glory fill the whole world.

Amen! Amen!

20 This is the end of the prayers of David
   son of Jesse.

BOOK THREE
(Psalms 73–89)

The Justice of God y

73 ¹God is indeed good to Israel,
   to those who have pure hearts.

2 But I had nearly lost confidence;
   my faith was almost gone
3 because I was jealous of the proud
   when I saw that things go well for the
      wicked.

4 They do not suffer pain;
   they are strong and healthy.
5 They do not suffer as other people do;
   they do not have the troubles that
      others have.
6 And so they wear pride like a necklace
   and violence like a robe;
7 their hearts pour out evil, z
   and their minds are busy with wicked
      schemes.
8 They laugh at other people and speak of
      evil things;
   they are proud and make plans to
      oppress others.
9 They speak evil of God in heaven
   and give arrogant orders to everyone
      on earth,
10 so that even God's people turn to them
   and eagerly believe whatever they say. a
11 They say, "God will not know;
   the Most High will not find out."
12 That is what the wicked are like.
   They have plenty and are always
      getting more.

13 Is it for nothing, then, that I have kept
      myself pure
   and have not committed sin?
14 O God, you have made me suffer all day
      long;
   every morning you have punished me.

15 If I had said such things,
   I would not be acting as one of your
      people.
16 I tried to think this problem through,
   but it was too difficult for me
17   until I went into your Temple.
   Then I understood what will happen to
      the wicked.

18 You will put them in slippery places
   and make them fall to destruction!
19 They are instantly destroyed;
   they go down to a horrible end.

y **73** HEBREW TITLE: By Asaph.   z **73:7** Some ancient translations their hearts pour out evil; Hebrew unclear.
a **73:10** Verse 10 in Hebrew is unclear.

Psalms

20 They are like a dream that goes away in
    the morning;
    when you rouse yourself, O Lord, they
    disappear.

21 When my thoughts were bitter
    and my feelings were hurt,
22 I was as stupid as an animal;
    I did not understand you.
23 Yet I always stay close to you,
    and you hold me by the hand.
24 You guide me with your instruction
    and at the end you will receive me
    with honor.
25 What else do I have in heaven but you?
    Since I have you, what else could I
    want on earth?
26 My mind and my body may grow
    weak,
    but God is my strength;
    he is all I ever need.

27 Those who abandon you will certainly
    perish;
    you will destroy those who are
    unfaithful to you.
28 But as for me, how wonderful to be near
    God,
    to find protection with the Sovereign
    LORD
    and to proclaim all that he has done!

A Prayer for National Deliverance[b]

74 ¹Why have you abandoned us like
    this, O God?
    Will you be angry with your own
    people forever?
2 Remember your people, whom you
    chose for yourself long ago,
    whom you brought out of slavery to be
    your own tribe.
    Remember Mount Zion, where once
    you lived.
3 Walk over these total ruins;

our enemies have destroyed everything
    in the Temple.
4 Your enemies have shouted in triumph in
    your Temple;
    they have placed their flags there as
    signs of victory.
5 They looked like woodsmen
    cutting down trees with their axes.[c]
6 They smashed all the wooden panels
    with their axes and sledge hammers.
7 They wrecked your Temple and set it on
    fire;
    they desecrated the place where you
    are worshiped.
8 They wanted to crush us completely;
    they burned down every holy place in
    the land.

9 All our sacred symbols are gone;
    there are no prophets left,
    and no one knows how long this will
    last.
10 How long, O God, will our enemies
    laugh at you?
    Will they insult your name forever?
11 Why have you refused to help us?
    Why do you keep your hands behind
    you?[d]

12 But you have been our king from the
    beginning, O God;
    you have saved us many times.
13 With your mighty strength you divided
    the sea
    and smashed the heads of the sea
    monsters;
14 you crushed the heads of the monster
    Leviathan[e]
    and fed his body to desert animals.[f]
15 You made springs and fountains
    flow;
    you dried up large rivers.
16 You created the day and the night;
    you set the sun and the moon in their
    places;

---

b 74 HEBREW TITLE: *A poem by Asaph.*   c 74:5 *Verse 5 in Hebrew is unclear.*   d 74:11 *Probable text* Why do you
keep your hands behind you; *Hebrew unclear.*   e 74:14 LEVIATHAN: *A legendary monster which was a symbol of the
forces of chaos and evil.*   f 74:14 animals; *or* people.
74:13 Ex 14:21   74:14 Job 41:1; Ps 104:26; Isa 27:1

**"But as for me, how wonderful to be near God, / to find protection with the
Sovereign LORD / and to proclaim all that he has done!"** (Psalm 73:28).

17 you set the limits of the earth;
  you made summer and winter.

18 But remember, O LORD, that your
    enemies laugh at you,
  that they are godless and despise
    you.
19 Don't abandon your helpless people to
    their cruel enemies;
  don't forget your persecuted people!

20 Remember the covenant you made with
    us.
  There is violence in every dark corner
    of the land.
21 Don't let the oppressed be put to shame;
  let those poor and needy people praise
    you.

22 Rouse yourself, God, and defend your
    cause!
  Remember that godless people laugh at
    you all day long.
23 Don't forget the angry shouts of your
    enemies,
  the continuous noise made by your
    foes.

God the Judgeᵍ

75 1 We give thanks to you, O God, we
    give thanks to you!
  We proclaim how great you are
  and tell ofʰ the wonderful things you
    have done.

2 "I have set a time for judgment," says
    God,
  "and I will judge with fairness.
3 Though every living creature tremble
  and the earth itself be shaken,
  I will keep its foundations firm.
4 I tell the wicked not to be arrogant;
5   I tell them to stop their boasting."

6 Judgment does not come from the east or
    from the west,
  from the north or from the south;ⁱ

7 it is God who is the judge,
  condemning some and acquitting
    others.
8 The LORD holds a cup in his hand,
  filled with the strong wine of his anger.
  He pours it out, and all the wicked drink
    it;
  they drink it down to the last drop.

9 But I will never stop speaking of the God
    of Jacob
  or singing praises to him.
10 He will break the power of the wicked,
  but the power of the righteous will be
    increased.

God the Victorʲ

76 1 God is known in Judah;
    his name is honored in Israel.
2 He has his home in Jerusalem;
  he lives on Mount Zion.
3 There he broke the arrows of the enemy,
  their shields and swords, yes, all their
    weapons.

4 How glorious you are, O God!
  How majestic, as you return from the
    mountains
  where you defeated your foes.
5 Their brave soldiers have been stripped of
    all they had
  and now are sleeping the sleep of death;
  all their strength and skill was useless.
6 When you threatened them, O God of
    Jacob,
  the horses and their riders fell dead.

7 But you, LORD, are feared by all.
  No one can stand in your presence
  when you are angry.
8 You made your judgment known from
    heaven;
  the world was afraid and kept silent,
9 when you rose up to pronounce
    judgment,
  to save all the oppressed on earth.

ᵍ 75 HEBREW TITLE: *A psalm by Asaph; a song.*   ʰ 75:1 *Some ancient translations* We proclaim how great you are
and tell of; *Hebrew* Your name is near and they tell of.   ⁱ 75:6 *Probable text* from the north or from the south;
Hebrew from the wilderness of the mountains.   ʲ 76 HEBREW TITLE: *A psalm by Asaph; a song.*

What do you think it means to say that God judges "with fairness"?
(Psalm 75:2).

10 Human anger only results in more praise
   for you;
      those who survive the wars will keep
      your festivals. *k*

11 Give the LORD your God what you
   promised him;
      bring gifts to him, all you nearby
      nations.
      God makes everyone fear him;
12   he humbles proud princes
      and terrifies great kings.

Comfort in Time of Distress*l*

77 ¹I cry aloud to God;
         I cry aloud, and he hears me.
 ²In times of trouble I pray to the Lord;
   all night long I lift my hands in prayer,
   but I cannot find comfort.
 ³When I think of God, I sigh;
   when I meditate, I feel discouraged.

 ⁴He keeps me awake all night;
   I am so worried that I cannot speak.
 ⁵I think of days gone by and remember
   years of long ago.

 ⁶I spend the night in deep   thought;*m*
   I meditate, and this is what I ask myself:
 ⁷"Will the Lord always reject us?
   Will he never again be pleased with us?
 ⁸Has he stopped loving us?
   Does his promise no longer stand?
 ⁹Has God forgotten to be merciful?
   Has anger taken the place of his
   compassion?"
10 Then I said, "What hurts me most is this—
   that God is no longer powerful."*n*

11 I will remember your great deeds, LORD;
   I will recall the wonders you did in the
   past.
12 I will think about all that you have done;
   I will meditate on all your mighty acts.

13 Everything you do, O God, is holy.
   No god is as great as you.
14 You are the God who works miracles;
   you showed your might among the
   nations.

15 By your power you saved your people,
   the descendants of Jacob and of Joseph.
16 When the waters saw you, O God, they
   were afraid,
   and the depths of the sea trembled.
17 The clouds poured down rain;
   thunder crashed from the sky,
   and lightning flashed in all directions.
18 The crash of your thunder rolled out,
   and flashes of lightning lit up the world;
   the earth trembled and shook.
19 You walked through the waves;
   you crossed the deep sea,
   but your footprints could not be seen.
20 You led your people like a shepherd,
   with Moses and Aaron in charge.

God and His People*o*

78 ¹Listen, my people, to my teaching,
         and pay attention to what I say.
 ²I am going to use wise sayings
   and explain mysteries from the past,
 ³   things we have heard and known,
   things that our ancestors told us.
 ⁴We will not keep them from our children;
   we will tell the next generation
   about the LORD's power and his great
   deeds
   and the wonderful things he has done.

 ⁵He gave laws to the people of Israel
   and commandments to the descendants
   of Jacob.
   He instructed our ancestors
   to teach his laws to their children,
 ⁶so that the next generation might learn
   them
   and in turn should tell their children.
 ⁷In this way they also will put their trust in
   God
   and not forget what he has done,
   but always obey his commandments.
 ⁸They will not be like their ancestors,
   a rebellious and disobedient people,
   whose trust in God was never firm
   and who did not remain faithful to
   him.

k **76:10** *One ancient translation* will keep your festivals; *verse 10 in Hebrew is unclear.* *l* **77** HEBREW TITLE: *A psalm by Asaph.* *m* **77:6** *Some ancient translations* deep thought; *Hebrew* song. *n* **77:10** *Verse 10 in Hebrew is unclear.* *o* **78** HEBREW TITLE: *A poem by Asaph.*
78:2 Mt 13:35

Psalms

Pray It!

Manna from Heaven

Psalm 78 is kind of an overview of the important people and events in the Old Testament. You may recognize the names of some of the people and events mentioned. One of the events was when God provided manna, or food, for the Israelites during a time when they were starving in the desert (verses 23–25).

Many of us often exaggerate our hunger by saying something like, "I'm starving." But for many people around the world, even in the United States, these are real words. Millions of people in the world do not have enough to eat. To help the cause of ending world hunger, join in this prayer:

Giver of life, you helped the Israelites when they were hungry. I know you will continue to help the hungry in our time, too. Help me be more aware of the needs of others, and make me eager to join in works of service to help those who are hungry every day. Amen.

— **Psalm 78:23–25**

12 While their ancestors watched, God performed miracles
in the plain of Zoan in the land of Egypt.
13 He divided the sea and took them through it;
he made the waters stand like walls.
14 By day he led them with a cloud
and all night long with the light of a fire.
15 He split rocks open in the desert
and gave them water from the depths.
16 He caused a stream to come out of the rock
and made water flow like a river.

17 But they continued to sin against God,
and in the desert they rebelled against the Most High.
18 They deliberately put God to the test
by demanding the food they wanted.
19 They spoke against God and said,
"Can God supply food in the desert?
20 It is true that he struck the rock,
and water flowed out in a torrent;
but can he also provide us with bread
and give his people meat?"

21 And so the LORD was angry when he heard them;
he attacked his people with fire,
and his anger against them grew,
22 because they had no faith in him
and did not believe that he would save them.
23 But he spoke to the sky above
and commanded its doors to open;
24 he gave them grain from heaven,
by sending down manna for them to eat.
25 So they ate the food of angels,
and God gave them all they wanted.
26 He also caused the east wind to blow,
and by his power he stirred up the south wind;
27 and to his people he sent down birds,
as many as the grains of sand on the shore;
28 they fell in the middle of the camp
all around the tents.
29 So the people ate and were satisfied;
God gave them what they wanted.

9 The Ephraimites, armed with bows and arrows,
ran away on the day of battle.
10 They did not keep their covenant with God;
they refused to obey his law.
11 They forgot what he had done,
the miracles they had seen him perform.

78:12 Ex 7:8—12:32 **78:13** Ex 14:21, 22 **78:14** Ex 13:21, 22 **78:12–16** Wis 16:1—19:22 **78:15, 16** Ex 17:1–7; Num 20:2–13 **78:18–31** Ex 16:2–15; Num 11:4–23, 31–35 **78:24** Wis 16:20–29; Jn 6:31

30 But they had not yet satisfied their craving
   and were still eating,
31 when God became angry with them
   and killed their strongest men,
   the best young men of Israel.

32 In spite of all this the people kept sinning;
   in spite of his miracles they did not
      trust him.
33 So he ended their days like a breath
   and their lives with sudden disaster.
34 Whenever he killed some of them,
   the rest would turn to him;
   they would repent and pray earnestly
      to him.
35 They remembered that God was their
      protector,
   that the Almighty came to their aid.
36 But their words were all lies;
   nothing they said was sincere.
37 They were not loyal to him;
   they were not faithful to their covenant
      with him.

38 But God was merciful to his people.
   He forgave their sin
   and did not destroy them.
Many times he held back his anger
   and restrained his fury.
39 He remembered that they were only
      mortal beings,
   like a wind that blows by and is gone.

40 How often they rebelled against him in
      the desert;
   how many times they made him sad!
41 Again and again they put God to the test
   and brought pain to the Holy God of
      Israel.
42 They forgot his great power
   and the day when he saved them from
      their enemies
43 and performed his mighty acts and
      miracles
   in the plain of Zoan in the land of
      Egypt.

44 He turned the rivers into blood,
   and the Egyptians had no water to
      drink.
45 He sent flies among them, that tormented
      them,
   and frogs that ruined their land.
46 He sent locusts to eat their crops
   and to destroy their fields.
47 He killed their grapevines with hail
   and their fig trees with frost.
48 He killed their cattle with hail
   and their flocks with lightning.ᵖ
49 He caused them great distress
   by pouring out his anger and fierce
      rage,
   which came as messengers of death.
50 He did not restrain his anger
   or spare their lives,
   but killed them with a plague.
51 He killed the first-born sons
   of all the families of Egypt.

52 Then he led his people out like a
      shepherd
   and guided them through the desert.
53 He led them safely, and they were not
      afraid;
   but the sea came rolling over their
      enemies.
54 He brought them to his holy land,
   to the mountains which he himself
      conquered.
55 He drove out the inhabitants as his people
      advanced;
   he divided their land among the tribes
      of Israel
   and gave their homes to his people.

56 But they rebelled against Almighty God
   and put him to the test.
They did not obey his commandments,
57 but were rebellious and disloyal like
      their ancestors,
   unreliable as a crooked arrow.

---

p **78:48** hail . . . lightning; *or* terrible disease . . . deadly plague.
78:37 Acts 8:21   **78:44** Ex 7:17–21   **78:45 a** Ex 8:20–24; **b** Ex 8:1–6   **78:46** Ex 10:12–15   **78:47, 48** Ex
9:22–25   **78:51** Ex 12:29   **78:52** Ex 13:17–22   **78:53** Ex 14:26–28   **78:54** Ex 15:17; Josh 3:14–17
78:55 Josh 11:16–23   **78:56** Judg 2:11–15

Can you find the ten plagues from Exodus in Psalm 78?

58 They angered him with their heathen
places of worship,
and with their idols they made him
furious.
59 God was angry when he saw it,
so he rejected his people completely.
60 He abandoned his tent in Shiloh,*q*
the home where he had lived among
us.
61 He allowed our enemies to capture the
Covenant Box,
the symbol of his power and glory.
62 He was angry with his own people
and let them be killed by their
enemies.
63 Young men were killed in war,
and young women had no one to
marry.
64 Priests died by violence,
and their widows were not allowed to
mourn.

65 At last the Lord woke up as though from
sleep;
he was like a strong man excited by
wine.
66 He drove his enemies back
in lasting and shameful defeat.
67 But he rejected the descendants of Joseph;
he did not select the tribe of Ephraim.
68 Instead he chose the tribe of Judah
and Mount Zion, which he dearly loves.
69 There he built his Temple
like his home in heaven;
he made it firm like the earth itself,
secure for all time.

70 He chose his servant David;
he took him from the pastures,
71 where he looked after his flocks,
and he made him king of Israel,
the shepherd of the people of God.
72 David took care of them with unselfish
devotion
and led them with skill.

A Prayer for the Nation's Deliverance*r*

79 1 O God, the heathen have invaded
your land.
They have desecrated your holy Temple
and left Jerusalem in ruins.
2 They left the bodies of your people for
the vultures,
the bodies of your servants for wild
animals to eat.
3 They shed your people's blood like water;
blood flowed like water all through
Jerusalem,
and no one was left to bury the dead.
4 The surrounding nations insult us;
they laugh at us and mock us.

5 LORD, will you be angry with us forever?
Will your anger continue to burn like
fire?
6 Turn your anger on the nations that do
not worship you,
on the people who do not pray to you.
7 For they have killed your people;
they have ruined your country.

8 Do not punish us for the sins of our
ancestors.
Have mercy on us now;
we have lost all hope.
9 Help us, O God, and save us;
rescue us and forgive our sins
for the sake of your own honor.
10 Why should the nations ask us,
"Where is your God?"
Let us see you punish the nations
for shedding the blood of your
servants.

11 Listen to the groans of the prisoners,
and by your great power free those
who are condemned to die.
12 Lord, pay the other nations back seven
times
for all the insults they have hurled at
you.

q **78:60** SHILOH: *The central place of worship for the people of Israel before the time of King David.*   *r* **79** HEBREW
TITLE: *A psalm by Asaph.*
78:60 Josh 18:1; Jer 7:12–14; 26:6   **78:61** 1 Sam 4:4–22   **78:70, 71** 1 Sam 16:11, 12; 2 Sam 7:8; 1 Chr 17:7
79:1 2 Kings 25:8–10; 2 Chr 36:17–19; Jer 52:12–14

"Bring us back, O God! / Show us your mercy, and we will be saved!"
(Psalm 80:3).

13 Then we, your people, the sheep of your
 flock,
  will thank you forever
  and praise you for all time to come.

A Prayer for the Nation's Restoration

80 1 Listen to us, O Shepherd of Israel;
  hear us, leader of your flock.
 Seated on your throne above the winged
  creatures,
2 reveal yourself to the tribes of Ephraim,
  Benjamin, and Manasseh.
 Show us your strength;
  come and save us!

3 Bring us back, O God!
  Show us your mercy, and we will be
  saved!

4 How much longer, LORD God Almighty,
  will you be angry with your people's
  prayers?
5 You have given us sorrow to eat,
  a large cup of tears to drink.
6 You let the surrounding nations fight over
  our land;
  our enemies insult us.

7 Bring us back, Almighty God!
  Show us your mercy, and we will be
  saved!

8 You brought a grapevine out of Egypt;
  you drove out other nations and
  planted it in their land.
9 You cleared a place for it to grow;
  its roots went deep, and it spread out
  over the whole land.
10 It covered the hills with its shade;
  its branches overshadowed the giant
  cedars.
11 It extended its branches to the
  Mediterranean Sea
  and as far as the Euphrates River.
12 Why did you break down the fences
  around it?
  Now anyone passing by can steal its
  grapes;
13 wild hogs trample it down,
  and wild animals feed on it.

14 Turn to us, Almighty God!
  Look down from heaven at us;
  come and save your people!
15 Come and save this grapevine that you
  planted,
  this young vine you made grow so
  strong!
16 Our enemies have set it on fire and cut it
  down;
  look at them in anger and destroy
  them!
17 Preserve and protect the people you have
  chosen,
  the nation you made so strong.
18 We will never turn away from you again;
  keep us alive, and we will praise you.

19 Bring us back, LORD God Almighty.
  Show us your mercy, and we will be
  saved.

A Song for a Festival

81 1 Shout for joy to God our defender;
  sing praise to the God of Jacob!
2 Start the music and beat the tambourines;
  play pleasant music on the harps and
  the lyres.
3 Blow the trumpet for the festival,
  when the moon is new and when the
  moon is full.
4 This is the law in Israel,
  an order from the God of Jacob.
5 He gave it to the people of Israel
  when he attacked the land of
  Egypt.

 I hear an unknown voice saying,
6 "I took the burdens off your backs;
  I let you put down your loads of
  bricks.
7 When you were in trouble, you called to
  me, and I saved you.
  From my hiding place in the storm, I
  answered you.
  I put you to the test at the springs of
  Meribah.
8 Listen, my people, to my warning;
  Israel, how I wish you would listen to
  me!

---

s **80** HEBREW TITLE: *A psalm by Asaph; a testimony.*   *t* **81** HEBREW TITLE: *By Asaph.*
80:1 Ex 25:22   **81:3** Num 10:10   **81:7** Ex 17:7; Num 20:13

9 You must never worship another god.
10 I am the LORD your God,
   who brought you out of Egypt.
   Open your mouth, and I will feed you.

11 "But my people would not listen to
      me;
   Israel would not obey me.
12 So I let them go their stubborn ways
   and do whatever they wanted.
13 How I wish my people would listen to
      me;
   how I wish they would obey me!
14 I would quickly defeat their enemies
   and conquer all their foes.
15 Those who hate me would bow in fear
      before me;
   their punishment would last forever.
16 But I would feed you with the finest
      wheat
   and satisfy you with wild honey."

God the Supreme Ruler [u]

82 ¹God presides in the heavenly council;
      in the assembly of the gods he
         gives his decision:
2 "You must stop judging unjustly;
   you must no longer be partial to the
      wicked!
3 Defend the rights of the poor and the
      orphans;
   be fair to the needy and the helpless.
4 Rescue them from the power of evil
      people.

5 "How ignorant you are! How stupid!
   You are completely corrupt,
   and justice has disappeared from the
      world.
6 'You are gods,' I said;
   'all of you are children of the Most
      High.'
7 But you will die like mortals;
   your life will end like that of any
      prince."

8 Come, O God, and rule the world;
   all the nations are yours.

A Prayer for the Defeat of Israel's Enemies [v]

83 ¹O God, do not keep silent;
      do not be still, do not be quiet!
2 Look! Your enemies are in revolt,
   and those who hate you are rebelling.
3 They are making secret plans against your
      people;
   they are plotting against those you
      protect.
4 "Come," they say, "let us destroy their
      nation,
   so that Israel will be forgotten forever."

5 They agree on their plan
   and form an alliance against you:
6 the people of Edom and the Ishmaelites;
   the people of Moab and the Hagrites;
7 the people of Gebal, Ammon, and
      Amalek,
   and of Philistia and Tyre.
8 Assyria has also joined them
   as a strong ally of the Ammonites and
      Moabites, the descendants of Lot.

9 Do to them what you did to the
      Midianites,
   and to Sisera and Jabin at the Kishon
      River.
10 You defeated them at Endor,
   and their bodies rotted on the ground.
11 Do to their leaders what you did to Oreb
      and Zeeb;
   defeat all their rulers as you did Zebah
      and Zalmunna,
12 who said, "We will take for our own
   the land that belongs to God."

13 Scatter them like dust, O God,
   like straw blown away by the wind.
14 As fire burns the forest,
   as flames set the hills on fire,
15 chase them away with your storm
   and terrify them with your fierce winds.
16 Cover their faces with shame, O LORD,
   and make them acknowledge your
      power.
17 May they be defeated and terrified
      forever;
   may they die in complete disgrace.

---

u 82 HEBREW TITLE: *A psalm by Asaph.*   v 83 HEBREW TITLE: *A psalm by Asaph; a song.*
81:9 Ex 20:2, 3; Deut 5:6, 7   **82:6** Jn 10:34   **83:9 a** Judg 7:1–23; **b** Judg 4:6–22   **83:11 a** Judg 7:25; **b** Judg 8:12

18 May they know that you alone are the
Lord,
supreme ruler over all the earth.

Longing for God's House _w_

84 1 How I love your Temple, Lord
Almighty!
2 How I want to be there!
I long to be in the Lord's Temple.
With my whole being I sing for joy
to the living God.
3 Even the sparrows have built a nest,
and the swallows have their own home;
they keep their young near your altars,
Lord Almighty, my king and my God.

Even the sparrows have built a nest. (84:3)

4 How happy are those who live in your
Temple,
always singing praise to you.

5 How happy are those whose strength
comes from you,
who are eager to make the pilgrimage
to Mount Zion.
6 As they pass through the dry valley of
Baca,
it becomes a place of springs;
the autumn rain fills it with pools.
7 They grow stronger as they go;
they will see the God of gods on
Zion.

_w_ **84; 85** HEBREW TITLE: _A psalm by the clan of Korah._

8 Hear my prayer, Lord God Almighty.
Listen, O God of Jacob!
9 Bless our king, O God,
the king you have chosen.

10 One day spent in your Temple
is better than a thousand anywhere
else;
I would rather stand at the gate of the
house of my God
than live in the homes of the wicked.
11 The Lord is our protector and glorious
king,
blessing us with kindness and honor.
He does not refuse any good thing
to those who do what is right.
12 Lord Almighty, how happy are those
who trust in you!

A Prayer for the Nation's Welfare _w_

85 1 Lord, you have been merciful to
your land;
you have made Israel prosperous again.
2 You have forgiven your people's sins
and pardoned all their wrongs.
3 You stopped being angry with them
and held back your furious rage.

4 Bring us back, O God our savior,
and stop being displeased with us!
5 Will you be angry with us forever?
Will your anger never cease?
6 Make us strong again,
and we, your people, will praise you.
7 Show us your constant love, O Lord,
and give us your saving help.

8 I am listening to what the Lord God is
saying;
he promises peace to us, his own
people,
if we do not go back to our foolish
ways.
9 Surely he is ready to save those who
honor him,
and his saving presence will remain in
our land.

"One day spent in your Temple / is better than a thousand anywhere else"
(Psalm 84:10).

Let God Help

Doing things alone can be difficult! Imagine trying to play tug of war against a whole team—by yourself. Some people think they can live without God's help. But that is like playing tug-of-war by yourself against a whole team. Psalm 85 reminds us that we especially need God's help. If we really listen to the message of verses 10–11, we will hear how good life is when we work with God: "Love and faithfulness will meet; / righteousness and peace will embrace. / Human loyalty will reach up from the earth, / and God's righteousness will look down from heaven."

Can't you just picture your hand reaching up from the earth and God's hand reaching down toward you? If you're trying to do it without God, life will most likely be harder, and the path will be rougher. If there is an area of your life where you can use some strength, remember Psalm 85 and reach your hand out to God. That area might be like a tug-of-war in your heart. Imagine how well you will play with God pulling with you!

— Psalm 85

10 Love and faithfulness will meet;
    righteousness and peace will embrace.
11 Human loyalty will reach up from the
    earth,
    and God's righteousness will look
    down from heaven.

12 The LORD will make us prosperous,
    and our land will produce rich
    harvests.
13 Righteousness will go before the LORD
    and prepare the path for him.

A Prayer for Help ˣ

86 1 Listen to me, LORD, and answer me,
    for I am helpless and weak.
2 Save me from death, because I am loyal to
    you;
    save me, for I am your servant and I
    trust in you.

3 You are my God, so be merciful to me;
    I pray to you all day long.
4 Make your servant glad, O Lord,
    because my prayers go up to you.
5 You are good to us and forgiving,
    full of constant love for all who pray to
    you.

6 Listen, LORD, to my prayer;
    hear my cries for help.
7 I call to you in times of trouble,
    because you answer my prayers.

8 There is no god like you, O Lord,
    not one has done what you have done.
9 All the nations that you have created
    will come and bow down to you;
    they will praise your greatness.
10 You are mighty and do wonderful things;
    you alone are God.

11 Teach me, LORD, what you want me
    to do,
    and I will obey you faithfully;
    teach me to serve you with complete
    devotion.
12 I will praise you with all my heart,
    O Lord my God;
    I will proclaim your greatness forever.
13 How great is your constant love for me!
    You have saved me from the grave
    itself.

"Teach me, LORD, what you want me to do, / and I will obey you faithfully; / teach me to serve you with complete devotion" *(Psalm 86:11).*

¹⁴Proud people are coming against me,
O God;
a cruel gang is trying to kill me—
people who pay no attention to you.
¹⁵But you, O Lord, are a merciful and
loving God,
always patient, always kind and faithful.
¹⁶Turn to me and have mercy on me;
strengthen me and save me,
because I serve you just as my mother
did.
¹⁷Show me proof of your goodness, LORD;
those who hate me will be ashamed
when they see that you have given me
comfort and help.

In Praise of Jerusalem*y*

87 ¹The LORD built his city on the
sacred hill;*z*
² more than any other place in Israel
he loves the city of Jerusalem.
³Listen, city of God,
to the wonderful things he says about
you:

⁴"I will include Egypt and Babylonia
when I list the nations that obey me;
the people of Philistia, Tyre, and Ethiopia*a*
I will number among the inhabitants of
Jerusalem."

⁵Of Zion it will be said
that all nations belong there
and that the Almighty will make her
strong.
⁶The LORD will write a list of the peoples
and include them all as citizens of
Jerusalem.
⁷They dance and sing,
"In Zion is the source of all our
blessings."

A Cry for Help*b*

88 ¹LORD God, my savior, I cry out all
day,
and at night I come before you.

Pray It!
Lowest of the Low

Feeling really low, bluer than blue, and just rotten? Check out Psalm 88. It is called the most miserable of all the individual laments (a type of psalm expressing sadness). So you can read it when you're really blue and know that even the psalmist felt that way.

Or maybe you want to write your own individual lament. First, start with a cry to God, then list your troubles, and end with a description of how you are feeling right now. Psalms are very poetic and use symbolic words, so be creative in describing your feelings. Just writing out how you feel can sometimes help you feel better.

— Psalm 88

---

²Hear my prayer;
listen to my cry for help!

³So many troubles have fallen on me
that I am close to death.
⁴I am like all others who are about to
die;
all my strength is gone.*c*
⁵I am abandoned among the dead;
I am like the slain lying in their
graves,
those you have forgotten completely,
who are beyond your help.
⁶You have thrown me into the depths of
the tomb,
into the darkest and deepest pit.
⁷Your anger lies heavy on me,
and I am crushed beneath its waves.

---

y **87** HEBREW TITLE: *A psalm by the clan of Korah; a song*   *z* **87:1** SACRED HILL: See 2:6.   *a* **87:4** *Hebrew Cush: Cush is the ancient name of the extensive territory south of the First Cataract of the Nile River. This region was called Ethiopia in Graeco-Roman time, and included within its borders most of modern Sudan and some of present-day Ethiopia (Abyssinia).*   *b* **88** HEBREW TITLE: *A psalm by the clan of Korah; a song. A poem by Heman the Ezrahite.*   *c* **88:4** *all my strength is gone; or there is no help for me.*

Psalms

8 You have caused my friends to abandon
  me;
  you have made me repulsive to them.
I am closed in and cannot escape;
9   my eyes are weak from suffering.
LORD, every day I call to you
  and lift my hands to you in prayer.

10 Do you perform miracles for the dead?
  Do they rise up and praise you?
11 Is your constant love spoken of in the
  grave
  or your faithfulness in the place of
  destruction?
12 Are your miracles seen in that place of
  darkness
  or your goodness in the land of the
  forgotten?

13 LORD, I call to you for help;
  every morning I pray to you.
14 Why do you reject me, LORD?
  Why do you turn away from me?
15 Ever since I was young, I have suffered
  and been near death;
  I am worn out[d] from the burden of
  your punishments.
16 Your furious anger crushes me;
  your terrible attacks destroy me.
17 All day long they surround me like a
  flood;
  they close in on me from every side.
18 You have made even my closest friends
  abandon me,
  and darkness is my only companion.

A Hymn in Time of National Trouble[e]

89 ¹ O LORD, I will always sing of your
  constant love;
  I will proclaim your faithfulness
  forever.
2 I know that your love will last for all
  time,
  that your faithfulness is as permanent as
  the sky.
3 You said, "I have made a covenant with
  the man I chose;
  I have promised my servant David,

4 'A descendant of yours will always be
  king;
  I will preserve your dynasty forever.' "

5 The heavens sing of the wonderful things
  you do;
  the holy ones sing of your faithfulness,
  LORD.
6 No one in heaven is like you, LORD;
  none of the heavenly beings is your
  equal.
7 You are feared in the council of the holy
  ones;
  they all stand in awe of you.

8 LORD God Almighty, none is as mighty as
  you;
  in all things you are faithful, O LORD.
9 You rule over the powerful sea;
  you calm its angry waves.
10 You crushed the monster Rahab[f] and
  killed it;
  with your mighty strength you defeated
  your enemies.
11 Heaven is yours, the earth also;
  you made the world and everything
  in it.
12 You created the north and the south;
  Mount Tabor and Mount Hermon sing
  to you for joy.
13 How powerful you are!
  How great is your strength!
14 Your kingdom is founded on
  righteousness and justice;
  love and faithfulness are shown in all
  you do.

15 How happy are the people who worship
  you with songs,
  who live in the light of your kindness!
16 Because of you they rejoice all day long,
  and they praise you for your goodness.
17 You give us great victories;
  in your love you make us triumphant.
18 You, O LORD, chose our protector;
  you, the Holy God of Israel, gave us
  our king.

---

[d] **88:15** *Probable text* I am worn out; *Hebrew unclear.*   [e] **89** HEBREW TITLE: *A poem by Ethan the Ezrahite.*
[f] **89:10** RAHAB: *A legendary sea monster which represented the forces of chaos and evil.*
89 Title 1 Kings 4:31   **89:4** 2 Sam 7:12–16; 1 Chr 17:11–14; Ps 132:11; Acts 2:30

Catholic Connections

Electing a Pope

"Who will it be?"
"Will he be like the last one?"
"Will it be someone we have heard of?"
"Will it be an Italian?"
"Will it be an African?"

These are some of the many questions that people ask when a pope dies and a new one is soon to be elected. The cardinals elect the pope in a process that includes prayer and conversation. The most important thing in their decision is the Holy Spirit. It is the Holy Spirit that guides the cardinals as they elect their (and our) leader. Masses are held around the world as the new pope is being chosen. The psalm response in these Masses is from Psalm 89, which reminds us that God is faithful in his promises to us.

— Psalm 89

God's Promise to David

19 In a vision long ago you said to your
     faithful servants,
   "I have given help to a famous
     soldier;
   I have given the throne to one I chose
     from the people.
20 I have made my servant David king
     by anointing him with holy oil.
21 My strength will always be with him,
   my power will make him strong.
22 His enemies will never succeed against
     him;
   the wicked will not defeat him.
23 I will crush his foes
     and kill everyone who hates him.
24 I will love him and be loyal to him;
   I will make him always victorious.
25 I will extend his kingdom
     from the Mediterranean to the
     Euphrates River.
26 He will say to me,
   'You are my father and my God;
   you are my protector and savior.'

27 I will make him my first-born son,
     the greatest of all kings.
28 I will always keep my promise to him,
     and my covenant with him will last
     forever.
29 His dynasty will be as permanent as the
     sky;
   a descendant of his will always be king.

30 "But if his descendants disobey my law
     and do not live according to my
     commands,
31 if they disregard my instructions
     and do not keep my commandments,
32 then I will punish them for their sins;
   I will make them suffer for their wrongs.
33 But I will not stop loving David
     or fail to keep my promise to him.
34 I will not break my covenant with him
     or take back even one promise I made
     him.

35 "Once and for all I have promised by my
     holy name:
   I will never lie to David.
36 He will always have descendants,

89:20 a 1 Sam 13:14; Acts 13:22; b 1 Sam 16:12   **89:27** Rev 1:5

Find the questions the psalmist asks God in Psalm 88. How do you think God would answer them?

Psalms

and I will watch over his kingdom as
  long as the sun shines.
37 It will be as permanent as the moon,
  that faithful witness in the sky."

Lament over the Defeat of the King

38 But you are angry with your chosen king;
  you have deserted and rejected him.
39 You have broken your covenant with
    your servant
  and thrown his crown in the dirt.
40 You have torn down the walls of his city
  and left his forts in ruins.
41 All who pass by steal his belongings;
  all his neighbors laugh at him.
42 You have given the victory to his
    enemies;
  you have made them all happy.
43 You have made his weapons useless
  and let him be defeated in battle.
44 You have taken away his royal scepter[g]
  and knocked his throne to the ground.
45 You have made him old before his time
  and covered him with disgrace.

A Prayer for Deliverance

46 LORD, will you hide yourself forever?
  How long will your anger burn like fire?
47 Remember how short my life is;
  remember that you created all of us
    mortal!
48 Who can live and never die?
  How can we humans keep ourselves
    from the grave?
49 Lord, where are the former proofs of your
    love?
  Where are the promises you made to
    David?
50 Don't forget how I, your servant, am
    insulted,
  how I endure all the curses[h] of the
    heathen.

51 Your enemies insult your chosen king,
  O LORD!
  They insult him wherever he goes.

52 Praise the LORD forever!

Amen! Amen!

BOOK FOUR
(Psalms 90–106)

Of God and Human Beings[i]

90
1 O Lord, you have always been our
    home.
2 Before you created the hills
  or brought the world into being,
  you were eternally God,
  and will be God forever.

3 You tell us to return to what we were;
  you change us back to dust.
4 A thousand years to you are like one day;
  they are like yesterday, already gone,
  like a short hour in the night.
5 You carry us away like a flood;
  we last no longer than a dream.
  We are like weeds that sprout in the
    morning,
6   that grow and burst into bloom,
  then dry up and die in the evening.

7 We are destroyed by your anger;
  we are terrified by your fury.
8 You place our sins before you,
  our secret sins where you can see them.

9 Our life is cut short by your anger;
  it fades away like a whisper.
10 Seventy years is all we have—
  eighty years, if we are strong;
  yet all they bring us is trouble and sorrow;
  life is soon over, and we are gone.

11 Who has felt the full power of your
    anger?
  Who knows what fear your fury can
    bring?

---

[g] **89:44** *Probable text* royal scepter; *Hebrew* purity.   [h] **89:50** *Probable text* curses; *Hebrew* crowds.   [i] **90** HEBREW
TITLE: *A prayer by Moses, the man of God.*
90:4 2 Pet 3:8   **90:10** Sir 18:8, 9

How many minutes "old" would you be if a thousand years were like a day?
(See Psalm 90:4.)

12 Teach us how short our life is,
     so that we may become wise.

13 How much longer will your anger last?
     Have pity, O LORD, on your servants!
14 Fill us each morning with your constant
     love,
     so that we may sing and be glad all our
     life.
15 Give us now as much happiness as the
     sadness you gave us
     during all our years of misery.
16 Let us, your servants, see your mighty
     deeds;
     let our descendants see your glorious
     might.
17 Lord our God, may your blessings be with
     us.
     Give us success in all we do!

God Our Protector

91 ¹Whoever goes to the LORD for safety,
          whoever remains under the
               protection of the Almighty,
² can say to him,
     "You are my defender and protector.
     You are my God; in you I trust."
³ He will keep you safe from all hidden
     dangers
     and from all deadly diseases.
⁴ He will cover you with his wings;
     you will be safe in his care;
     his faithfulness will protect and defend
     you.
⁵ You need not fear any dangers at night
     or sudden attacks during the day
⁶   or the plagues that strike in the dark
     or the evils that kill in daylight.

⁷ A thousand may fall dead beside you,
     ten thousand all around you,
     but you will not be harmed.
⁸ You will look and see
     how the wicked are punished.

⁹ You have made the LORD your[j] defender,
     the Most High your protector,
10 and so no disaster will strike you,
     no violence will come near your
     home.

11 God will put his angels in charge of you
     to protect you wherever you go.
12 They will hold you up with their hands
     to keep you from hurting your feet on
     the stones.
13 You will trample down lions and snakes,
     fierce lions and poisonous snakes.

14 God says, "I will save those who love me
     and will protect those who
          acknowledge me as LORD.
15 When they call to me, I will answer them;
     when they are in trouble, I will be with
     them.
     I will rescue them and honor them.
16 I will reward them with long life;
     I will save them."

A Song of Praise[k]

92 ¹How good it is to give thanks to
          you, O LORD,
     to sing in your honor, O Most High
          God,
² to proclaim your constant love every
     morning
     and your faithfulness every night,
³ with the music of stringed instruments
     and with melody on the harp.
⁴ Your mighty deeds, O LORD, make me
     glad;
     because of what you have done, I sing
     for joy.

⁵ How great are your actions, LORD!
     How deep are your thoughts!
⁶ This is something a fool cannot know;
     someone who is stupid cannot
          understand:
⁷ the wicked may grow like weeds,
     those who do wrong may prosper;
     yet they will be totally destroyed,
⁸   because you, LORD, are supreme
          forever.

⁹ We know that your enemies will die,
     and all the wicked will be defeated.
10 You have made me as strong as a wild ox;
     you have blessed me with happiness.
11 I have seen the defeat of my enemies
     and heard the cries of the wicked.

12 The righteous will flourish like palm
    trees;
    they will grow like the cedars of
      Lebanon.
13 They are like trees planted in the house of
    the LORD,
    that flourish in the Temple of our God,
14   that still bear fruit in old age
    and are always green and strong.
15 This shows that the LORD is just,
    that there is no wrong in my protector.

God the King

93 ¹ The LORD is king.
    He is clothed with majesty and
      strength.
The earth is set firmly in place
    and cannot be moved.
2 Your throne, O LORD, has been firm from
    the beginning,
    and you existed before time began.

3 The ocean depths raise their voice,
    O LORD;
    they raise their voice and roar.
4 The LORD rules supreme in heaven,
    greater than the roar of the ocean,
    more powerful than the waves of the
      sea.

5 Your laws are eternal, LORD,
    and your Temple is holy indeed,
    forever and ever.

God the Judge of All

94 ¹ LORD, you are a God who punishes;
    reveal your anger!
2 You are the judge of us all;
    rise and give the proud what they
      deserve!
3 How much longer will the wicked be
    glad?
    How much longer, LORD?
4 How much longer will criminals be
    proud
    and boast about their crimes?

5 They crush your people, LORD;
    they oppress those who belong to you.

6 They kill widows and orphans,
    and murder the strangers who live in
      our land.
7 They say, "The LORD does not see us;
    the God of Israel does not notice."

8 My people, how can you be such stupid
    fools?
    When will you ever learn?
9 God made our ears—can't he hear?
    He made our eyes—can't he see?
10 He scolds the nations—won't he punish
    them?[l]
    He is the teacher of us all—hasn't he
      any knowledge?
11 The LORD knows what we think;
    he knows how senseless our reasoning
      is.

12 LORD, how happy are those you instruct,
    the ones to whom you teach your law!
13 You give them rest from days of trouble
    until a pit is dug to trap the wicked.
14 The LORD will not abandon his people;
    he will not desert those who belong to
      him.
15 Justice will again be found in the courts,
    and all righteous people will support it.

16 Who stood up for me against the wicked?
    Who took my side against the
      evildoers?
17 If the LORD had not helped me,
    I would have gone quickly to the land
      of silence.[m]
18 I said, "I am falling";
    but your constant love, O LORD, held
      me up.
19 Whenever I am anxious and worried,
    you comfort me and make me glad.

20 You have nothing to do with corrupt
    judges,
    who make injustice legal,
21   who plot against good people
    and sentence the innocent to death.
22 But the LORD defends me;
    my God protects me.
23 He will punish them for their wickedness
    and destroy them for their sins;
    the LORD our God will destroy them.

l **94:10** them?; *or our wicked leaders?*   *m* **94:17** LAND OF SILENCE: *The world of the dead (see 6:5).*
94:11 1 Cor 3:20

Catholic Connections

Praise and Adoration

Alleluia means "Praise the Lord." And praise is what Psalm 95 is all about. Praise is a type of prayer. The Church teaches that praise is very important because it unites all our other prayers and carries them to God. When we praise God, we recognize his uniqueness, his power, and his love for us. If we didn't recognize those things, we would not be praying to God about anything else!

So praise is different from thanking God for what was done, or for asking God for something, and is certainly different from lamenting to God. It is about the joy of God's love. Praise can be heard in some great music, in many of the psalms, and is described in Paul's letter to the Ephesians (see Ephesians 5:19). Praise is also found in you—it's that feeling you get when you are happy and love God just because God *is*.

— Psalm 95:1–7

A Song of Praise

95 ¹Come, let us praise the LORD!
Let us sing for joy to God, who
protects us!
²Let us come before him with
thanksgiving
and sing joyful songs of praise.
³For the LORD is a mighty God,
a mighty king over all the gods.
⁴He rules over the whole earth,
from the deepest caves to the highest
hills.
⁵He rules over the sea, which he made;
the land also, which he himself formed.

⁶Come, let us bow down and worship
him;
let us kneel before the LORD, our
Maker!
⁷He is our God;
we are the people he cares for,
the flock for which he provides.

Listen today to what he says:

"Let us . . . worship him." (95:6)

⁸"Don't be stubborn, as your ancestors
were at Meribah,
as they were that day in the desert at
Massah.
⁹There they put me to the test and tried me,
although they had seen what I did for
them.

95:7–11 Heb 3:7–11   95:7, 8 Heb 3:15; 4:7   95:8, 9 Ex 17:1–7; Num 20:2–13

"He is our God; / we are the people he cares for, / the flock for which he provides" *(Psalm 95:7).*

10 For forty years I was disgusted with those
    people.
  I said, 'How disloyal they are!
  They refuse to obey my commands.'
11 I was angry and made a solemn promise:
  'You will never enter the land
  where I would have given you rest.'"

God the Supreme King
(1 Chronicles 16:23–33)

96 ¹Sing a new song to the LORD!
    Sing to the LORD, all the world!
² Sing to the LORD, and praise him!
  Proclaim every day the good news that
    he has saved us.
³ Proclaim his glory to the nations,
  his mighty deeds to all peoples.

⁴ The LORD is great and is to be highly
    praised;
  he is to be honored more than all the
    gods.
⁵ The gods of all other nations are only
    idols,
  but the LORD created the heavens.
⁶ Glory and majesty surround him;
  power and beauty fill his Temple.

⁷ Praise the LORD, all people on earth;
  praise his glory and might.
⁸ Praise the LORD's glorious name;
  bring an offering and come into his
    Temple.
⁹ Bow down before the Holy One when
    he appears;[n]
  tremble before him, all the earth!

10 Say to all the nations, "The LORD is king!
  The earth is set firmly in place and
    cannot be moved;
  he will judge the peoples with justice."
11 Be glad, earth and sky!
  Roar, sea, and every creature in you;
12   be glad, fields, and everything in you!
  The trees in the woods will shout for joy

The trees in the woods will shout for joy. (96:12)

13   when the LORD comes to rule the
    earth.
  He will rule the peoples of the world
    with justice and fairness.

God the Supreme Ruler

97 ¹The LORD is king! Earth, be glad!
    Rejoice, you islands of the seas!
² Clouds and darkness surround him;
  he rules with righteousness and justice.
³ Fire goes in front of him
  and burns up his enemies around him.
⁴ His lightning lights up the world;
  the earth sees it and trembles.
⁵ The hills melt like wax before the
    LORD,
  before the Lord of all the earth.
⁶ The heavens proclaim his righteousness,
  and all the nations see his glory.

⁷ Everyone who worships idols is put to
    shame;
  all the gods bow down[o] before the
    LORD.

[n] **96:9** when he appears; *or* in garments of worship.   [o] **97:7** all the gods bow down; *or* bow down, all gods.
95:11 a Num 14:20–23; Deut 1:34–36; Heb 4:3, 5; **b** Deut 12:9, 10   **96:7–9** Ps 29:1, 2

Psalm 97 describes God as being a little bit like a superhero. If you were to name God as a superhero, what name would you give God?

8 The people of Zion are glad,
　　and the cities of Judah rejoice
　　because of your judgments, O LORD.
9 LORD Almighty, you are ruler of all the
　　earth;
　　you are much greater than all the gods.

10 The LORD loves those who hate evil;[p]
　　he protects the lives of his people;
　　he rescues them from the power of the
　　　wicked.
11 Light shines on the righteous,
　　and gladness on the good.
12 All you that are righteous be glad
　　because of what the LORD has done!
　Remember what the holy God has done,
　　and give thanks to him.

God the Ruler of the World[q]

98 ¹Sing a new song to the LORD;
　　he has done wonderful things!
By his own power and holy strength
　he has won the victory.
2 The LORD announced his victory;
　he made his saving power known to
　　the nations.
3 He kept his promise to the people of
　　Israel
　with loyalty and constant love for
　　them.
All people everywhere have seen the
　victory of our God.

4 Sing for joy to the LORD, all the earth;
　praise him with songs and shouts of joy!
5 Sing praises to the LORD!
　Play music on the harps!
6 Blow trumpets and horns,
　and shout for joy to the LORD, our
　　king.

7 Roar, sea, and every creature in you;
　sing, earth, and all who live on you!
8 Clap your hands, you rivers;
　you hills, sing together with joy before
　　the LORD,
9 　because he comes to rule the earth.
　He will rule the peoples of the world
　　with justice and fairness.

Pray It!

Highest of the High

So did you do the psalm writing as part of the "lowest of the low" (see Psalm 88)? Well, now is a chance to write the "highest of the high." Psalm 98 does that. It shouts out how great God is, and how well God takes care of his people. It ends by inviting everything in the world to clap and sing and praise God.

When you are feeling great, when life is good and it seems like all is well in the world, take time to write a praise psalm of your own. First, decide how you want to address God—for example, as king or with whatever other title you want to use. Then list the great things God has done. Lastly, end by inviting others to rejoice and remember the good things God has done. Remember to use poetic language and to name some specific things God has done for you and for others.

— Psalm 98

God the Supreme King

99 ¹The LORD is king,
　　and the people tremble.
He sits on his throne above the winged
　creatures,
　and the earth shakes.
2 The LORD is mighty in Zion;
　he is supreme over all the nations.
3 Everyone will praise his great and
　　majestic name.
　Holy is he!

p **97:10** *Probable text* The LORD loves those who hate evil; *Hebrew* Hate evil, you who love the LORD.
q **98** HEBREW TITLE: *A psalm.*
99:1 Ex 25:22

Psalms

Priestly Promises

Ca⊕holic Connec⊕ions

"You mean you have to do everything he says?" Ty asked his uncle.

"Well, yes," his uncle replied.

"So, Uncle T, if he asked you to hurt someone, you have to?" Ty was trying to figure out how far his uncle would go. The had just read Psalm 99, and it bothered him that it was about commands. It sounded like the military.

"No, Little Ty, it doesn't mean that. What do you really want to know?" His uncle, also named Ty, knew that Little Ty was up to something.

"I want to know why you are doing it. Why become a priest? Why follow someone's commands?"

"It's about following God. And following what God calls me to do. I know I am supposed to be a priest. It is how I follow God's command."

"Maybe Little Ty will become the second Father Ty *if* his uncle stops calling him Little Ty." The younger Ty smiled up at his uncle, secretly liking to be called Little Ty by him and hoping his uncle would still use that name.

"Sorry, you'll always be my Little Ty. And, if God wants you to be a priest, I'll be there to help you figure it out. And if not, I'll be there to help you figure out what it is you're supposed to do with your life."

— Psalm 99

4 Mighty king,ʳ you love what is right;
   you have established justice in Israel;
   you have brought righteousness and
      fairness.
5 Praise the LORD our God;
   worship before his throne!
   Holy is he!

6 Moses and Aaron were his priests,
   and Samuel was one who prayed to him;
   they called to the LORD, and he
      answered them.
7 He spoke to them from the pillar of cloud;
   they obeyed the laws and commands
      that he gave them.

8 O LORD, our God, you answered your
      people;
   you showed them that you are a God
      who forgives,
   even though you punished them for
      their sins.

9 Praise the LORD our God,
   and worship at his sacred hill!ˢ
The LORD our God is holy.

A Hymn of Praiseᵗ

100 1 Sing to the LORD, all the world!
   2 Worship the LORD with joy;
      come before him with happy songs!

3 Acknowledge that the LORD is God.
   He made us, and we belong to
      him;
   we are his people, we are his flock.

4 Enter the Temple gates with thanksgiving;
   go into its courts with praise.
   Give thanks to him and praise him.

5 The LORD is good;
   his love is eternal
   and his faithfulness lasts forever.

ʳ **99:4** *Probable text* Mighty king; *Hebrew* The might of the king.   ˢ **99:9** SACRED HILL: *See 2:6.*   ᵗ **100** HEBREW
TITLE: *A psalm of thanksgiving.*
99:7 Ex 33:9   **100:5** 1 Chr 16:34; 2 Chr 5:13; 7:3; Ezra 3:11; Ps 106:1; 107:1; 118:1; 136:1; Jer 33:11

A King's Promise[u]

101 ¹My song is about loyalty and
justice,
and I sing it to you, O LORD.
²My conduct will be faultless.
When will you come to me?

I will live a pure life in my house
³ and will never tolerate evil.
I hate the actions of those who turn away
from God;
I will have nothing to do with them.
⁴I will not be dishonest[v]
and will have no dealings with evil.[w]
⁵I will get rid of anyone
who whispers evil things about
someone else;
I will not tolerate anyone
who is proud and arrogant.

"Enter the Temple gates with thanksgiving." (100:4)

⁶I will approve of those who are faithful to
God
and will let them live in my palace.
Those who are completely honest
will be allowed to serve me.
⁷No liar will live in my palace;
no hypocrite will remain in my
presence.
⁸Day after day I will destroy
the wicked in our land;
I will expel all who are evil
from the city of the LORD.

The Prayer of a Troubled Youth[x]

102 ¹Listen to my prayer, O LORD,
and hear my cry for help!
²When I am in trouble,
don't turn away from me!
Listen to me,
and answer me quickly when I call!

³My life is disappearing like smoke;
my body is burning like fire.
⁴I am beaten down like dry grass;
I have lost my desire for food.
⁵I groan aloud;
I am nothing but skin and bones.
⁶I am like a wild bird in the desert,
like an owl in abandoned ruins.
⁷I lie awake;
I am like a lonely bird on a housetop.
⁸All day long my enemies insult me;
those who mock me use my name in
cursing.

⁹⁻¹⁰Because of your anger and fury,
ashes are my food,
and my tears are mixed with my
drink.
You picked me up and threw me away.
¹¹My life is like the evening shadows;
I am like dry grass.

¹²But you, O LORD, are king forever;
all generations will remember you.

---

[u] **101** HEBREW TITLE: *A psalm by David.*   [v] **101:4** not be dishonest; *or* stay away from dishonest people.
[w] **101:4** evil; *or* evil people.   [x] **102** HEBREW TITLE: *A prayer by a weary sufferer who pours out his complaints to the*
LORD.

The psalmist says to "enter the Temple gates with thanksgiving" *(Psalm 100:4).* **When you enter your church, do you do so with thanks and praise?**

Pray It!

Prayer for a Troubled Youth

If you're having a rough day, Psalm 102 is a great place for inspiration in prayer. And if you're really having a hard time, try this prayer, inspired by Psalm 103.

Praise the Lord!
How do I praise the Lord when everything is so horrible?
How can I remember how kind God is when everyone else is being unkind?
My life doesn't feel like it is filled with good things.
Wait, though, maybe I can praise the Lord:
I am young
God has forgiven me before.
God does love me.
Even if my parents don't seem kind right now,
*   they are good people, trying to do their best.*
And, if I really do believe,
*   then God really is here,*
*   even when life is crummy,*
*   when things don't go my way,*
*   and when I'm feeling troubled.*
So, yeah, I will praise the Lord!
Praise the Lord!
With God, I will get through this!
Amen.

— **Psalm 102**

13 You will rise and take pity on Zion;
   the time has come to have mercy on
      her;
   this is the right time.
14 Your servants love her,
   even though she is destroyed;
   they have pity on her,
   even though she is in ruins.
15 The nations will fear the LORD;
   all the kings of the earth will fear his
      power.
16 When the LORD rebuilds Zion,
   he will reveal his greatness.
17 He will hear his forsaken people
   and listen to their prayer.

18 Write down for the coming generation
   what the LORD has done,
   so that people not yet born will praise
      him.
19 The LORD looked down from his holy
      place on high,
   he looked down from heaven to earth.
20 He heard the groans of prisoners
   and set free those who were
      condemned to die.
21 And so his name will be proclaimed in
      Zion,
   and he will be praised in Jerusalem
22   when nations and kingdoms come
      together
   and worship the LORD.

"When I am in trouble, / don't turn away from me! / Listen to me, / and answer me quickly when I call!" *(Psalm 102:2).*

²³The LORD has made me weak while I am
      still young;
   he has shortened my life.
²⁴O God, do not take me away now
      before I grow old.

   O LORD, you live forever;
²⁵   long ago you created the earth,
      and with your own hands you made
         the heavens.
²⁶They will disappear, but you will
      remain;
   they will all wear out like clothes.
   You will discard them like clothes,
      and they will vanish.
²⁷But you are always the same,
      and your life never ends.
²⁸Our children will live in safety,
      and under your protection
      their descendants will be secure.

The Love of God*ʸ*

103
¹Praise the LORD, my soul!
   All my being, praise his holy
      name!
²Praise the LORD, my soul,
   and do not forget how kind he is.
³He forgives all my sins
   and heals all my diseases.
⁴He keeps me from the grave
   and blesses me with love and mercy.
⁵He fills my life*ᶻ* with good things,
   so that I stay young and strong like an
      eagle.
⁶The LORD judges in favor of the
      oppressed
   and gives them their rights.
⁷He revealed his plans to Moses
   and let the people of Israel see his
      mighty deeds.
⁸The LORD is merciful and loving,
   slow to become angry and full of
      constant love.
⁹He does not keep on rebuking;
   he is not angry forever.
¹⁰He does not punish us as we deserve
   or repay us according to our sins and
      wrongs.

¹¹As high as the sky is above the earth,
   so great is his love for those who honor
      him.
¹²As far as the east is from the west,
   so far does he remove our sins from us.
¹³As a father is kind to his children,
   so the LORD is kind to those who
      honor him.
¹⁴He knows what we are made of;
   he remembers that we are dust.

¹⁵As for us, our life is like grass.
   We grow and flourish like a wild flower;
¹⁶   then the wind blows on it, and it is
      gone—
   no one sees it again.

Then the wind blows on it, and it is gone. (103:16)

¹⁷But for those who honor the LORD, his
      love lasts forever,
   and his goodness endures for all
         generations
¹⁸of those who are true to his covenant
   and who faithfully obey his commands.

¹⁹The LORD placed his throne in heaven;
   he is king over all.
²⁰Praise the LORD, you strong and mighty
      angels,
   who obey his commands,
   who listen to what he says.
²¹Praise the LORD, all you heavenly
      powers,
   you servants of his, who do his will!
²²Praise the LORD, all his creatures
   in all the places he rules.
   Praise the LORD, my soul!

ʸ 103 HEBREW TITLE: *By David.*   *ᶻ* 103:5 *Probable text* my life; *Hebrew unclear.*
102:25–27 Heb 1:10–12   103:8 Jas 5:11

In Praise of the Creator

104

¹Praise the LORD, my soul!
  O LORD, my God, how great
    you are!
You are clothed with majesty and glory;
² you cover yourself with light.
You have spread out the heavens like a
    tent
³ and built your home on the waters
    above.ᵃ
You use the clouds as your chariot
  and ride on the wings of the wind.
⁴You use the winds as your messengers
  and flashes of lightning as your
    servants.

⁵You have set the earth firmly on its
    foundations,
  and it will never be moved.
⁶You placed the ocean over it like a robe,
  and the water covered the mountains.
⁷When you rebuked the waters, they fled;
  they rushed away when they heard
    your shout of command.
⁸They flowed over the mountains and into
    the valleys,
  to the place you had made for them.
⁹You set a boundary they can never pass,
  to keep them from covering the earth
    again.

¹⁰You make springs flow in the valleys,
  and rivers run between the hills.
¹¹They provide water for the wild animals;
  there the wild donkeys quench their
    thirst.
¹²In the trees near by,
  the birds make their nests and sing.
¹³From the sky you send rain on the hills,
  and the earth is filled with your
    blessings.
¹⁴You make grass grow for the cattle
  and plants for us to use,
  so that we can grow our crops
¹⁵ and produce wine to make us happy,
  olive oil to make us cheerful,
  and bread to give us strength.

¹⁶The cedars of Lebanon get plenty of
    rain—
  the LORD's own trees, which he planted.
¹⁷There the birds build their nests;
  the storks nest in the fir trees.
¹⁸The wild goats live in the high
    mountains,
  and the rock badgers hide in the cliffs.

¹⁹You created the moon to mark the
    months;
  the sun knows the time to set.
²⁰You made the night, and in the darkness
  all the wild animals come out.
²¹The young lions roar while they hunt,
  looking for the food that God provides.
²²When the sun rises, they go back
  and lie down in their dens.
²³Then people go out to do their work
  and keep working until evening.

²⁴LORD, you have made so many things!
  How wisely you made them all!
  The earth is filled with your creatures.
²⁵There is the ocean, large and wide,
  where countless creatures live,
  large and small alike.
²⁶The ships sail on it, and in it plays
    Leviathan,
  that sea monster which you made.ᵇ

²⁷All of them depend on you
  to give them food when they need it.
²⁸You give it to them, and they eat it;
  you provide food, and they are satisfied.
²⁹When you turn away, they are afraid;
  when you take away your breath, they
    die
  and go back to the dust from which
    they came.
³⁰But when you give them breath,ᶜ they are
    created;
  you give new life to the earth.

³¹May the glory of the LORD last forever!
  May the LORD be happy with what he
    has made!
³²He looks at the earth, and it trembles;
  he touches the mountains, and they
    pour out smoke.

ᵃ **104:3** THE WATERS ABOVE: *A reference to the waters above the celestial dome (Gen 1:6, 7).*   ᵇ **104:26** in it plays
. . . made; *or* Leviathan is there, that sea monster you made to amuse you.   ᶜ **104:30** give them breath; *or* send
out your spirit.
104:4 Heb 1:7   **104:26** Job 41:1; Ps 74:14; Isa 27:1

33 I will sing to the LORD all my life;
  as long as I live I will sing praises to my
  God.
34 May he be pleased with my song,
  for my gladness comes from him.
35 May sinners be destroyed from the earth;
  may the wicked be no more.

Praise the LORD, my soul!
Praise the LORD!

God and His People
(1 Chronicles 16:8–22)

105 ¹Give thanks to the LORD,
    proclaim his greatness;
  tell the nations what he has done.
² Sing praise to the LORD;
  tell the wonderful things he has
    done.
³ Be glad that we belong to him;
  let all who worship him rejoice.
⁴ Go to the LORD for help;
  and worship him continually.
5-6 You descendants of Abraham, his servant;
  you descendants of Jacob, the man he
    chose:
  remember the miracles that God
    performed
  and the judgments that he gave.

⁷ The LORD is our God;
  his commands are for all the world.
⁸ He will keep his covenant forever,
  his promises for a thousand generations.
⁹ He will keep the agreement he made
    with Abraham
  and his promise to Isaac.
¹⁰ The LORD made a covenant with Jacob,
  one that will last forever.
¹¹ "I will give you the land of Canaan," he
    said.
  "It will be your own possession."

¹² God's people were few in number,
  strangers in the land of Canaan.
¹³ They wandered from country to country,
  from one kingdom to another.

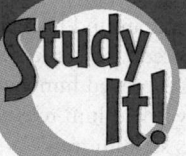

What about the Women?

Where are the women? Why does Psalm 105 just talk about men: Abraham, Jacob, Joseph, Moses, Aaron? What about their wives, their daughters and sisters—why aren't they mentioned? What about the great women of the Bible—why aren't they mentioned? Keep in mind that in the time the Psalms were written, the roles of women were much different than they are now. Women were not typically leaders, were not usually considered strong, and had little say in what went on in society.

That doesn't mean that the time of the Psalms was better or worse than our time; it was just different. When we read the Bible, it helps to know what was going on in society at the time. Today is different for women; they are recognized for their accomplishments, have more of a voice, and are rulers, presidents, and other political leaders throughout the world.

— Psalm 105

¹⁴ But God let no one oppress them;
  to protect them, he warned the kings:
¹⁵ "Don't harm my chosen servants;
  do not touch my prophets."

¹⁶ The LORD sent famine to their country
  and took away all their food.
¹⁷ But he sent a man ahead of them,
  Joseph, who had been sold as a
    slave.

105:9 a Gen 12:7; 17:8; **b** Gen 26:3   **105:10, 11** Gen 28:13   **105:14, 15** Gen 20:3–7

18 His feet were kept in chains,
   and an iron collar was around his neck,
19 until what he had predicted came true.
   The word of the LORD proved him right.
20 Then the king of Egypt had him released;
   the ruler of nations set him free.
21 He put him in charge of his government
   and made him ruler over all the land,
22 with power over the king's officials
   and authority to instruct his advisers.

23 Then Jacob went to Egypt
   and settled in that country.
24 The LORD gave many children to his
   people
   and made them stronger than their
   enemies.
25 He made the Egyptians hate his people
   and treat his servants with deceit.
26 Then he sent his servant Moses,
   and Aaron, whom he had chosen.
27 They did God's mighty acts
   and performed miracles in Egypt.
28 God sent darkness on the country,
   but the Egyptians did not obey[d] his
   command.
29 He turned their rivers into blood
   and killed all their fish.
30 Their country was overrun with frogs;
   even the palace was filled with them.
31 God commanded, and flies and gnats
   swarmed throughout the whole
   country.
32 He sent hail and lightning on their land
   instead of rain;
33 he destroyed their grapevines and fig trees
   and broke down all the trees.
34 He commanded, and the locusts came,
   countless millions of them;
35 they ate all the plants in the land;
   they ate all the crops.

36 He killed the first-born sons
   of all the families of Egypt.

37 Then he led the Israelites out;
   they carried silver and gold,
   and all of them were healthy and
   strong.
38 The Egyptians were afraid of them
   and were glad when they left.
39 God put a cloud over his people
   and a fire at night to give them light.
40 They[e] asked, and he sent quails;
   he gave them food from heaven to
   satisfy them.
41 He opened a rock, and water gushed out,
   flowing through the desert like a river.
42 He remembered his sacred promise
   to Abraham his servant.

43 So he led his chosen people out,
   and they sang and shouted for joy.
44 He gave them the lands of other peoples
   and let them take over their fields,
45 so that his people would obey his laws
   and keep all his commands.

Praise the LORD!

The LORD's Goodness to His People

106
1 Praise the LORD!

Give thanks to the LORD, because he is
   good;
   his love is eternal.
2 Who can tell all the great things he has
   done?
   Who can praise him enough?
3 Happy are those who obey his
   commands,
   who always do what is right.

---

d **105:28** *Some ancient translations* did not obey; *Hebrew* obeyed.   e **105:40** *Some ancient translations* They;
Hebrew he.

105:16 Gen 41:53–57   **105:17** Gen 37:28; 45:5   **105:18, 19** Gen 39:20—40:23   **105:20** Gen 41:14
105:21 Gen 41:39–41   **105:23 a** Gen 46:6; **b** Gen 47:11   **105:24, 25** Ex 1:7–14   **105:26** Ex 3:1—4:17
105:28 Ex 10:21–23   **105:29** Ex 7:17–21   **105:30** Ex 8:1–6   **105:31 a** Ex 8:20–24; **b** Ex 8:16, 17
105:32, 33 Ex 9:22–25   **105:34, 35** Ex 10:12–15   **105:36** Ex 12:29   **105:37, 38** Ex 12:33–36
105:39 Ex 13:21, 22   **105:40** Ex 16:2–15   **105:41** Ex 17:1–7; Num 20:2–13   **105:44** Josh 11:16–23
106:1 1 Chr 16:34; 2 Chr 5:13; 7:3; Ezra 3:11; Ps 100:5; 107:1; 118:1; 136:1; Jer 33:11

**Do you remember the story of the gold bull-calf mentioned in Psalm 106? If
not, you may want to read Exodus 32:1–21.**

4 Remember me, LORD, when you help
      your people;
   include me when you save them.
5 Let me see the prosperity of your people
   and share in the happiness of your
      nation,
   in the glad pride of those who belong
      to you.

6 We have sinned as our ancestors did;
   we have been wicked and evil.
7 Our ancestors in Egypt did not
      understand God's wonderful acts;
   they forgot the many times he showed
      them his love,
   and they rebelled against the Almighty*f*
      at the Red Sea.
8 But he saved them, as he had promised,
   in order to show his great power.
9 He gave a command to the Red Sea,
   and it dried up;
   he led his people across on dry land.
10 He saved them from those who hated
      them;
   he rescued them from their enemies.
11 But the water drowned their enemies;
   not one of them was left.
12 Then his people believed his promises
   and sang praises to him.

13 But they quickly forgot what he had
      done
   and acted without waiting for his
      advice.
14 They were filled with craving in the
      desert
   and put God to the test;
15 so he gave them what they asked for,
   but also sent a terrible disease among
      them.

16 There in the desert they were jealous of
      Moses
   and of Aaron, the LORD's holy servant.
17 Then the earth opened up and swallowed
      Dathan
   and buried Abiram and his family;
18 fire came down on their followers
   and burned up those wicked people.

19 They made a gold bull-calf at Sinai
   and worshiped that idol;
20 they exchanged the glory of God
   for the image of an animal that eats
      grass.
21 They forgot the God who had saved
      them
   by his mighty acts in Egypt.
22 What wonderful things he did there!
   What amazing things at the Red Sea!
23 When God said that he would destroy his
      people,
   his chosen servant, Moses, stood up
      against God
   and kept his anger from destroying
      them.

24 Then they rejected the pleasant land,
   because they did not believe God's
      promise.
25 They stayed in their tents and
      grumbled
   and would not listen to the LORD.
26 So he have them a solomn warning
   that he would make them die in the
      desert
27   and scatter their descendants among
      the heathen,
   letting them die in foreign countries.

28 Then at Peor, God's people joined in the
      worship of Baal
   and ate sacrifices offered to dead
      gods.
29 They stirred up the LORD's anger by their
      actions,
   and a terrible disease broke out among
      them.
30 But Phinehas stood up and punished the
      guilty,
   and the plague was stopped.
31 This has been remembered in his favor
      ever since
   and will be for all time to come.

32 At the springs of Meribah the people
      made the LORD angry,
   and Moses was in trouble on their
      account.

f **106:7** *Probable text* the Almighty; *Hebrew* the sea.

106:7 Ex 14:10–12   **106:9–12** Ex 14:21–31   **106:12** Ex 15:1–21   **106:14, 15** Num 11:4–34
106:16–18 Num 16:1–35   **106:19–23** Ex 32:1–14   **106:24–26** Num 14:1–35   **106:27** Lev 26:33
106:28–31 Num 25:1–13   **106:32, 33** Num 20:2–13

33 They made him so bitter
     that he spoke without stopping to think.

34 They did not kill the heathen,
     as the LORD had commanded them
     to do,
35 but they intermarried with them
     and adopted their pagan ways.
36 God's people worshiped idols,
     and this caused their destruction.
37 They offered their own sons and daughters
     as sacrifices to the idols of Canaan.
38 They killed those innocent children,
     and the land was defiled by those
     murders.
39 They made themselves impure by their
     actions
     and were unfaithful to God.

40 So the LORD was angry with his people;
     he was disgusted with them.
41 He abandoned them to the power of the
     heathen,
     and their enemies ruled over them.
42 They were oppressed by their enemies
     and were in complete subjection to
     them.
43 Many times the LORD rescued his people,
     but they chose to rebel against him
     and sank deeper into sin.
44 Yet the LORD heard them when they
     cried out,
     and he took notice of their distress.
45 For their sake he remembered his covenant,
     and because of his great love he
     relented.
46 He made all their oppressors
     feel sorry for them.

47 Save us, O LORD our God,
     and bring us back from among the
     nations,
     so that we may be thankful
     and praise your holy name.

48 Praise the LORD, the God of Israel;
     praise him now and forever!
     Let everyone say, "Amen!"

          Praise the LORD!

BOOK FIVE
(Psalms 107–150)

In Praise of God's Goodness

107 1 "Give thanks to the LORD,
          because he is good;
     his love is eternal!"
2 Repeat these words in praise to the
     LORD,
     all you whom he has saved.
     He has rescued you from your enemies
3   and has brought you back from foreign
     countries,
     from east and west, from north and
     south.g

4 Some wandered in the trackless desert
     and could not find their way to a city
     to live in.
5 They were hungry and thirsty
     and had given up all hope.
6 Then in their trouble they called to the
     LORD,
     and he saved them from their distress.
7 He led them by a straight road
     to a city where they could live.
8 They must thank the LORD for his
     constant love,
     for the wonderful things he did for
     them.
9 He satisfies those who are thirsty
     and fills the hungry with good things.

10 Some were living in gloom and darkness,
     prisoners suffering in chains,
11 because they had rebelled against the
     commands of Almighty God
     and had rejected his instructions.
12 They were worn out from hard work;
     they would fall down, and no one
     would help.
13 Then in their trouble they called to the
     LORD,
     and he saved them from their distress.
14 He brought them out of their gloom and
     darkness
     and broke their chains in pieces.

g 107:3 *Probable text* south; *Hebrew* the Mediterranean Sea (meaning "west").
106:34–36 Judg 2:1–3; 3:5, 6   **106:37** 2 Kings 17:17   **106:38** Num 35:33   **106:40–46** Judg 2:14–18
106:47, 48 1 Chr 16:35, 36   **107:1** 1 Chr 16:34; 2 Chr 5:13; 7:3; Ezra 3:11; Ps 100:5; 106:1; 118:1; 136:1; Jer
33:11

15 They must thank the LORD for his
constant love,
for the wonderful things he did for
them.
16 He breaks down doors of bronze
and smashes iron bars.

17 Some were fools, suffering because of
their sins
and because of their evil;
18 they couldn't stand the sight of food
and were close to death.
19 Then in their trouble they called to the
LORD,
and he saved them from their distress.
20 He healed them with his command
and saved them from the grave.
21 They must thank the LORD for his
constant love,
for the wonderful things he did for
them.
22 They thank him with sacrifices,
and with songs of joy must tell all that
he has done.

23 Some sailed over the ocean in ships,
earning their living on the seas.
24 They saw what the LORD can do,
his wonderful acts on the seas.
25 He commanded, and a mighty wind
began to blow
and stirred up the waves.
26 The ships were lifted high in the air
and plunged down into the depths.
In such danger the sailors lost their
courage;
27   they stumbled and staggered like
drunks—
all their skill was useless.
28 Then in their trouble they called to the
LORD,
and he saved them from their distress.
29 He calmed the raging storm,
and the waves became quiet.
30 They were glad because of the calm,
and he brought them safe to the port
they wanted.

31 They must thank the LORD for his
constant love,
for the wonderful things he did for
them.
32 They must proclaim his greatness in the
assembly of the people
and praise him before the council of
the leaders.

33 The LORD made rivers dry up completely
and stopped springs from flowing.
34 He made rich soil become a salty
wasteland
because of the wickedness of those
who lived there.
35 He changed deserts into pools of water
and dry land into flowing springs.
36 He let hungry people settle there,
and they built a city to live in.
37 They sowed the fields and planted
grapevines
and reaped an abundant harvest.
38 He blessed his people, and they had many
children;
he kept their herds of cattle from
decreasing.

39 When God's people were defeated and
humiliated
by cruel oppression and suffering,
40 he showed contempt for their oppressors
and made them wander in trackless
deserts.
41 But he rescued the needy from their misery
and made their families increase like
flocks.
42 The righteous see this and are glad,
but all the wicked are put to silence.

He brought them safe to the port. (107:30)

107:34 Sir 39:23

43 May those who are wise think about
　　these things;
　　may they consider the LORD's constant
　　love.

A Prayer for Help against Enemies[h]
(Psalm 57:7-11; 60:5-12)

108

1 I have complete confidence,
　　O God!
　I will sing and praise you!
Wake up, my soul!

2 　Wake up, my harp and lyre!
　　I will wake up the sun.

3 I will thank you, O LORD, among the
　　nations.
　I will praise you among the peoples.

4 Your constant love reaches above the
　　heavens;
　your faithfulness touches the skies.

5 Show your greatness in the sky, O God,
　　and your glory over all the earth.

6 Save us by your might; answer my prayer,
　　so that the people you love may be
　　rescued.

7 From his sanctuary[i] God has said,
　　"In triumph I will divide Shechem
　　and distribute Sukkoth Valley to my
　　people.

8 Gilead is mine, and Manasseh too;
　　Ephraim is my helmet
　　and Judah my royal scepter.

9 But I will use Moab as my washbowl,
　　and I will throw my sandals on Edom,
　　as a sign that I own it.
　I will shout in triumph over the
　　Philistines."

10 Who, O God, will take me into the
　　fortified city?
　Who will lead me to Edom?

11 Have you really rejected us?
　　Aren't you going to march out with
　　our armies?

12 Help us against the enemy;
　　human help is worthless.

13 With God on our side we will win;
　　he will defeat our enemies.

The Complaint of Someone in Trouble[j]

109

1 I praise you, God; don't remain
　　silent!

2 Wicked people and liars have attacked
　　me.
　They tell lies about me,

3 　and they say evil things about me,
　　attacking me for no reason.

4 They oppose me, even though I love
　　them
　and have prayed for them. [k]

5 They pay me back evil for good
　　and hatred for love.

6 Choose some corrupt judge to try my
　　enemy,
　and let one of his own enemies accuse
　　him.

7 May he be tried and found guilty;
　　may even his prayer be considered a
　　crime!

8 May his life soon be ended;
　　may someone else take his job!

9 May his children become orphans,
　　and his wife a widow!

10 May his children be homeless beggars;
　　may they be driven from[l] the ruins
　　they live in!

11 May his creditors take away all his
　　property,
　and may strangers get everything he
　　worked for.

12 May no one ever be kind to him
　　or care for the orphans he leaves
　　behind.

13 May all his descendants die,
　　and may his name be forgotten in the
　　next generation.

---

[h] 108 HEBREW TITLE: *A psalm by David; a song.*　[i] 108:7 From his sanctuary; *or* In his holiness.　[j] 109 HEBREW TITLE: *A psalm by David.*　[k] 109:4 *Probable text* have prayed for them; *Hebrew unclear.*　[l] 109:10 *One ancient translation* be driven from; *Hebrew* seek.
109:8 Acts 1:20

"Wicked people and liars have attacked me. / . . . **They pay me back evil for good / and hatred for love"** (Psalm 109:2-5).

14 May the LORD remember the evil of his
    ancestors
    and never forgive his mother's sins.
15 May the LORD always remember their
    sins,
    but may they themselves be completely
    forgotten!

16 That man never thought of being kind;
    he persecuted and killed
    the poor, the needy, and the helpless.
17 He loved to curse—may he be cursed!
    He hated to give blessings—may no
    one bless him!
18 He cursed as naturally as he dressed
    himself;
    may his own curses soak into his body
    like water
    and into his bones like oil!
19 May they cover him like clothes
    and always be around him like a belt!

20 LORD, punish my enemies in that way—
    those who say such evil things against
    me!
21 But my Sovereign LORD, help me as you
    have promised,
    and rescue me because of the goodness
    of your love.
22 I am poor and needy;
    I am hurt to the depths of my heart.
23 Like an evening shadow I am about to
    vanish;
    I am blown away like an insect.
24 My knees are weak from lack of food;
    I am nothing but skin and bones.
25 When people see me, they laugh at me;
    they shake their heads in scorn.

26 Help me, O LORD my God;
    because of your constant love, save me!
27 Make my enemies know
    that you are the one who saves me.
28 They may curse me, but you will bless
    me.
    May my persecutors be defeated,^m
    and may I, your servant, be glad.
29 May my enemies be covered with disgrace;
    may they wear their shame like a robe.

^m **109:28** *One ancient translation* May my persecutors
be defeated; *Hebrew* They persecuted me and were
defeated.
109:25 Mt 27:39; Mk 15:29

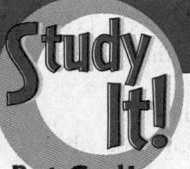

But God!

"Alleluia, alleluia!" The song sounded so joyful, and the people at church were all smiling and singing and seemed to be so happy with God. Not Dena. After Mass, she stayed in the church and looked at Jesus up on the cross. "I am so mad at you!" she said. "I know you did all these great things for humanity, but it doesn't seem like any of it matters for me. I can't believe it!"

"What can't you believe?" Dena almost jumped out of her skin when she heard the voice behind her. It was her second-grade religion teacher, of all people. Dena was embarrassed now.

"Na . . . nothing," she sputtered.

"Well, you sounded pretty mad there," Ms. Jo said.

"I'm not supposed to get mad at God, am I, Ms. Jo?"

"Why not?" Ms. Jo answered.

"Well, you taught us all about God's love, but I'm really mad," Dena said. Dena and Ms. Jo sat on one of the pews.

"Dena, it's okay to get mad at God," Ms. Jo replied. "Don't you remember that we talked about getting close to God? And that one way is by developing a relationship with God? Growing a relationship means being honest, even if we are feeling angry. That doesn't mean we stop loving our friends, or family, or God."

"I think I get it." Dena was thankful for Ms. Jo, just like when she was eight, when Ms. Jo was her teacher. They walked out of church together. Dena was still mad at God, but knew she had someone to talk to about it.

— Psalm 109

Psalms

30 I will give loud thanks to the LORD;
    I will praise him in the assembly of the
      people,
31 because he defends the poor
    and saves them from those who
      condemn them to death.

The LORD and His Chosen King[n]

110   1 The LORD said to my lord,
      "Sit here at my right side
until I put your enemies under your
    feet."
2 From Zion the LORD will extend your
    royal power.
    "Rule over your enemies," he says.
3 On the day you fight your enemies,
    your people will volunteer.
Like the dew of early morning
    your young men will come to you on
      the sacred hills.[o]

4 The LORD made a solemn promise and
    will not take it back:
"You will be a priest forever
    in the priestly order of Melchizedek."[p]

5 The Lord is at your right side;
    when he becomes angry, he will defeat
      kings.
6 He will pass judgment on the nations
    and fill the battlefield with corpses;
    he will defeat kings all over the earth.
7 The king will drink from the stream by
    the road,
    and strengthened, he will stand
      victorious.

In Praise of the LORD

111   1 Praise the LORD!

With all my heart I will thank the
    LORD
in the assembly of his people.
2 How wonderful are the things the LORD
    does!
    All who are delighted with them want
      to understand them.

Pray It!

Acrostic Psalms

An acrostic is a type of poem where the first letter of each line in the poem spells out a word or the entire alphabet. So if you knew Hebrew and saw Psalm 111 written in Hebrew (the language it was first written in), you would see that each line starts with a different letter of the Hebrew alphabet.

Try writing your own acrostic prayer. The first word of each line would start with a different letter of the alphabet. Or for a shorter prayer, write an acrostic based on a word such as *praise*. The first word of the first line would start with *p*. The first word of each of the next five lines would start with one of the following letters, in order: *r, a, i, s, e.* Have fun and be creative!

— Psalm 111

---

3 All he does is full of honor and majesty;
    his righteousness is eternal.

4 The LORD does not let us forget his
    wonderful actions;
    he is kind and merciful.
5 He provides food for those who honor
    him;
    he never forgets his covenant.
6 He has shown his power to his
    people
    by giving them the lands of
      foreigners.

7 In all he does he is faithful and just;
    all his commands are dependable.

---

[n] **110** HEBREW TITLE: *A psalm by David.*   [o] **110:3** *Verse 3 in Hebrew is unclear.*   [p] **110:4** *in the priestly order of* Melchizedek; *or like* Melchizedek; *or in the line of succession to Melchizedek.*
110:1 Mt 22:44; Mk 12:36; Lk 20:42, 43; Acts 2:34, 35; 1 Cor 15:25; Eph 1:20–22; Col 3:1; Heb 1:13; 8:1; 10:12, 13   **110:4** Heb 5:6; 6:20; 7:17, 21

8 They last for all time;
   they were given in truth and
      righteousness.
9 He set his people free
   and made an eternal covenant with
      them.
   Holy and mighty is he!
10 The way to become wise is to honor the
   LORD;*q*
   he gives sound judgment to all who
      obey his commands.
   He is to be praised forever.

The Happiness of a Good Person

112 ¹Praise the LORD!

Happy is the person who honors the LORD,
   who takes pleasure in obeying his
      commands.
2 The good man's children will be powerful
   in the land;
   his descendants will be blessed.
3 His family will be wealthy and rich,
   and he will be prosperous forever.

4 Light shines in the darkness for good
   people,
   for those who are merciful, kind, and
      just.
5 Happy is the person who is generous
   with his loans,
   who runs his business honestly.
6 A good person will never fail;
   he will always be remembered.

7 He is not afraid of receiving bad news;
   his faith is strong, and he trusts in the
      LORD.
8 He is not worried or afraid;
   he is certain to see his enemies defeated.
9 He gives generously to the needy,
   and his kindness never fails;
   he will be powerful and respected.
10 The wicked see this and are angry;
   they glare in hate and disappear;
   their hopes are gone forever.

Words of Wisdom

Is one of your grandparents or an older person you know always giving you little bits of advice? Does it seem like he or she always knows just what to say, better sometImes than your teachers or parents? Listening to these bits of wisdom can help you in your day-to-day life, even if it seems like the same old sayings over and over.

Psalm 112 is one of the wisdom psalms, a group of nearly ten psalms. Becoming wise takes time, and reading about it is one way to help gain wisdom. In the case of Psalm 112, the writer speaks like a wise old person telling the youth the benefits of being a good person. The psalm tells us that the way to become wise is to honor the Lord. If this sounds like the advice you get from older people in your life, then you are receiving true wisdom, indeed!

— Psalm 112

In Praise of the LORD's Goodness

113 ¹Praise the LORD!

You servants of the LORD,
   praise his name!
2 May his name be praised,
   now and forever.
3 From the east to the west
   praise the name of the LORD!

---

q **111:10** The way . . . the LORD; *or* The most important part of wisdom is honoring the LORD.
111:10 Job 28:28; Prov 1:7; 9:10   **112:9** 2 Cor 9:9

Psalms

4 The LORD rules over all nations;
  his glory is above the heavens.

5 There is no one like the LORD our God.
  He lives in the heights above,
6   but he bends down
    to see the heavens and the earth.
7 He raises the poor from the dust;
  he lifts the needy from their misery
8 and makes them companions of princes,
  the princes of his people.
9 He honors the childless wife in her
    home;
  he makes her happy by giving her
    children.

Praise the LORD!

A Passover Song

114 ¹When the people of Israel left
      Egypt,
  when Jacob's descendants left that
    foreign land,
2 Judah became the Lord's holy people,
  Israel became his own possession.

3 The Red Sea looked and ran away;
  the Jordan River stopped flowing.
4 The mountains skipped like goats;
  the hills jumped around like lambs.

5 What happened, Sea, to make you run
    away?
  And you, O Jordan, why did you stop
    flowing?
6 You mountains, why did you skip like
    goats?
  You hills, why did you jump around
    like lambs?

7 Tremble, earth, at the Lord's coming,
  at the presence of the God of Jacob,
8 who changes rocks into pools of water
  and solid cliffs into flowing springs.

The One True God

115 ¹To you alone, O LORD, to you
      alone,
  and not to us, must glory be given
  because of your constant love and
    faithfulness.

2 Why should the nations ask us,
  "Where is your God?"
3 Our God is in heaven;
  he does whatever he wishes.
4 Their gods are made of silver and gold,
  formed by human hands.
5 They have mouths, but cannot speak,
  and eyes, but cannot see.
6 They have ears, but cannot hear,
  and noses, but cannot smell.
7 They have hands, but cannot feel,
  and feet, but cannot walk;
  they cannot make a sound.
8 May all who made them and who trust in
    them
  become* like the idols they have made.

9 Trust in the LORD, you people of Israel.
  He helps you and protects you.
10 Trust in the LORD, you priests of God.
  He helps you and protects you.
11 Trust in the LORD, all you that worship
    him.
  He helps you and protects you.

12 The LORD remembers us and will bless
    us;
  he will bless the people of Israel
  and all the priests of God.
13 He will bless everyone who honors
    him,
  the great and the small alike.

14 May the LORD give you children—
  you and your descendants!
15 May you be blessed by the LORD,
  who made heaven and earth!

16 Heaven belongs to the LORD alone,
  but he gave the earth to us humans.

ʳ 115:8 May all . . . become; or All who made them and who trust in them will become.
114:1 Ex 12:51   **114:3 a** Ex 14:21; **b** Josh 3:16   **114:8** Ex 17:1–7; Num 20:2–13   **115:4–8** Ps 135:15–18;
Bar 6:4–73; Rev 9:20   **115:13** Rev 11:18; 19:5

**Psalm 114 is a Passover psalm. Remember the Passover story? It can be found
in Exodus, chapter 12.**

17 The LORD is not praised by the dead,
  by any who go down to the land of
    silence.[s]
18 But we, the living, will give thanks to him
  now and forever.

  Praise the LORD!

Someone Saved from Death Praises God

116
¹I love the LORD, because he
    hears me;
  he listens to my prayers.
²He listens to me
  every time I call to him.
³The danger of death was all around me;
  the horrors of the grave closed in on
    me;
  I was filled with fear and anxiety.
⁴Then I called to the LORD,
  "I beg you, LORD, save me!"

⁵The LORD is merciful and good;
  our God is compassionate.
⁶The LORD protects the helpless;
  when I was in danger, he saved me.
⁷Be confident, my heart,
  because the LORD has been good to
    me.

⁸The LORD saved me from death;
  he stopped my tears
  and kept me from defeat.
⁹And so I walk in the presence of the
    LORD
  in the world of the living.
¹⁰I kept on believing, even when I said,
  "I am completely crushed,"
¹¹even when I was afraid and said,
  "No one can be trusted."

¹²What can I offer the LORD
  for all his goodness to me?
¹³I will bring a wine offering to the LORD,
  to thank him for saving me.
¹⁴In the assembly of all his people
  I will give him what I have promised.

¹⁵How painful it is to the LORD
  when one of his people dies!

¹⁶I am your servant, LORD;
  I serve you just as my mother did.
  You have saved me from death.
¹⁷I will give you a sacrifice of thanksgiving
  and offer my prayer to you.
¹⁸⁻¹⁹In the assembly of all your people,
  in the sanctuary of your Temple in
    Jerusalem,
  I will give you what I have promised.

  Praise the LORD!

In Praise of the LORD

117
¹Praise the LORD, all nations!
    Praise him, all peoples!
²His love for us is strong,
  and his faithfulness is eternal.

  Praise the LORD!

Prasie the LORD, all nations! (117:1)

A Prayer of Thanks for Victory

118
¹Give thanks to the LORD,
    because he is good,
  and his love is eternal.
²Let the people of Israel say,
  "His love is eternal."
³Let the priests of God say,
  "His love is eternal."

---

s **115:17** LAND OF SILENCE: *The world of the dead (see 6:5).*
116:10 2 Cor 4:13   **117:1** Rom 15:11   **118:1** 1 Chr 16:34; 2 Chr 5:13; 7:3; Ezra 3:11; Ps 100:5; 106:1;
107:1; 136:1; Jer 33:11

Psalms

A Psalm for Confirmation

You will be my witnesses to all the world.
Praise the Lord, all you nations;
glorify him, all you peoples!
You will be my witnesses to all the world.
For steadfast is his kindness toward us,
and the fidelity of the Lord endures forever.

Using the words of Acts 1:8 and Psalm 117:1–2, the cantor leads the responsorial psalm during a Rite of Confirmation. Later, the bishop begins his homily by asking the youth being confirmed this question, "How will you be witnesses to all the world?"

One of the girls raises her hand very slowly. Heart pounding, she answers, "I will . . . Oh, never mind, it's stupid." She turns bright red as the bishop walks toward her. He says, "It's okay. Tell us, how will you be a witness?"

As she sees the bishop up close, she sees the kindness in his eyes. He gives her a small smile that gives her a little courage. She answers: "I will _____."

What did the girl say that answered the bishop's question? How would you answer it?

—Psalm 117

6 The LORD is with me, I will not be afraid;
  what can anyone do to me?
7 It is the LORD who helps me,
  and I will see my enemies defeated.
8 It is better to trust in the LORD
  than to depend on people.
9 It is better to trust in the LORD
  than to depend on human leaders.

10 Many enemies were around me;
  but I destroyed them by the power of the LORD!
11 They were around me on every side;
  but I destroyed them by the power of the LORD!
12 They swarmed around me like bees,
  but they burned out as quickly as a brush fire;
  by the power of the LORD I destroyed them.
13 I was fiercely attacked and was being defeated,
  but the LORD helped me.
14 The LORD makes me powerful and strong;
  he has saved me.

15 Listen to the glad shouts of victory in the tents of God's people:
  "The LORD's mighty power has done it!
16   His power has brought us victory—
  his mighty power in battle!"

17 I will not die; instead, I will live
  and proclaim what the LORD has done.
18 He has punished me severely,
  but he has not let me die.

19 Open to me the gates of the Temple;
  I will go in and give thanks to the LORD!

20 This is the gate of the LORD;
  only the righteous can come in.

21 I praise you, LORD, because you heard me,
  because you have given me victory.

22 The stone which the builders rejected as worthless
  turned out to be the most important of all.

4 Let all who worship him say,
  "His love is eternal."

5 In my distress I called to the LORD;
  he answered me and set me free.

118:6 Heb 13:6 **118:14** Ex 15:2; Isa 12:2 **118:22** Lk 20:17; Acts 4:11; 1 Pet 2:7 **118:22, 23** Mt 21:42; Mk 12:10, 11

23 This was done by the LORD;
   what a wonderful sight it is!
24 This is the day of the LORD's victory;
   let us be happy, let us celebrate!
25 Save us, LORD, save us!
   Give us success, O LORD!

26 May God bless the one who comes in the
   name of the LORD!
   From the Temple of the LORD we bless
   you.
27 The LORD is God; he has been good
   to us.
   With branches in your hands, start the
   festival
   and march around the altar.

28 You are my God, and I give you thanks;
   I will proclaim your greatness.

29 Give thanks to the LORD, because he is
   good,
   and his love is eternal.

The Law of the LORD

119
1 Happy are those whose lives are
   faultless,
   who live according to the law of the
   LORD.
2 Happy are those who follow his
   commands,
   who obey him with all their heart.
3 They never do wrong;
   they walk in the LORD's ways.
4 LORD, you have given us your laws
   and told us to obey them faithfully.
5 How I hope that I shall be faithful
   in keeping your instructions!
6 If I pay attention to all your commands,
   then I will not be put to shame.
7 As I learn your righteous judgments,
   I will praise you with a pure heart.
8 I will obey your laws;
   never abandon me!

Keeping Commandments

If you break rules, you get punished, right? But is that why rules are there? Think about it. Cheating is against the rules, right? Is it against the rules so your teachers can catch you and punish you, or is it against the rules because cheating is lying, and lying leads to more lying, which leads to being unhappy?

It is the same thing with God's commandments. God did not give us commandments so he would have fun catching us breaking them and punishing us for that. God gives us commandments so that we may be happy, holy, and healthy. The benefit of following God's laws is what Psalm 119 is all about. Look at what it says we get by following the commandments:
- more understanding and wisdom
- happiness and joy
- new life and hope
- the ability to answer those who insult you

It may take time and patience to benefit (see verses 81–88, 121–128, and 169–176), but it will be worth it!

— Psalm 119

Obedience to the Law of the LORD

9 How can young people keep their lives
   pure?
   By obeying your commands.

118:25 Mt 21:9; Mk 11:9; Jn 12:13   **118:26** Mt 21:9; 23:39; Mk 11:9; Lk 13:35; 19:38; Jn 12:13

Where have you heard the verse in Psalm 118:22 before? Check the footnotes for places it is quoted in the New Testament.

Psalms

10 With all my heart I try to serve you;
  keep me from disobeying your
  commandments.
11 I keep your law in my heart,
  so that I will not sin against you.
12 I praise you, O LORD;
  teach me your ways.
13 I will repeat aloud
  all the laws you have given.
14 I delight in following your commands
  more than in having great wealth.
15 I study your instructions;
  I examine your teachings.
16 I take pleasure in your laws;
  your commands I will not forget.

Happiness in the Law of the LORD

17 Be good to me, your servant,
  so that I may live and obey your
  teachings.
18 Open my eyes, so that I may see
  the wonderful truths in your law.
19 I am here on earth for just a little while;
  do not hide your commands from
  me.
20 My heart aches with longing;
  I want to know your judgments at all
  times.
21 You reprimand the proud;
  cursed are those who disobey your
  commands.
22 Free me from their insults and scorn,
  because I have kept your laws.
23 The rulers meet and plot against me,
  but I will study your teachings.
24 Your instructions give me pleasure;
  they are my advisers.

Determination to Obey the Law of the LORD

25 I lie defeated in the dust;
  revive me, as you have promised.
26 I confessed all I have done, and you
  answered me;
  teach me your ways.

27 Help me to understand your laws,
  and I will meditate on your wonderful
  teachings.[1]
28 I am overcome by sorrow;
  strengthen me, as you have promised.
29 Keep me from going the wrong way,
  and in your goodness teach me your
  law.
30 I have chosen to be obedient;
  I have paid attention to your
  judgments.
31 I have followed your instructions, LORD;
  don't let me be put to shame.
32 I will eagerly obey your commands,
  because you will give me more
  understanding.

A Prayer for Understanding

33 Teach me, LORD, the meaning of your
  laws,
  and I will obey them at all times.
34 Explain your law to me, and I will obey
  it;
  I will keep it with all my heart.
35 Keep me obedient to your
  commandments,
  because in them I find happiness.
36 Give me the desire to obey your laws
  rather than to get rich.
37 Keep me from paying attention to what is
  worthless;
  be good to me, as you have promised.
38 Keep your promise to me, your servant—
  the promise you make to those who
  obey you.
39 Save me from the insults I fear;
  how wonderful are your judgments!
40 I want to obey your commands;
  give me new life, for you are righteous.

Trusting the Law of the LORD

41 Show me how much you love me, LORD,
  and save me according to your promise.
42 Then I can answer those who insult me
  because I trust in your word.

[1] **119:27** teachings; *or* deeds.

Is Psalm 119 the longest psalm? Can you find a psalm that is longer?

43 Enable me to speak the truth at all times,
    because my hope is in your judgments.
44 I will always obey your law,
    forever and ever.
45 I will live in perfect freedom,
    because I try to obey your teachings.
46 I will announce your commands to kings
    and I will not be ashamed.
47 I find pleasure in obeying your
        commands,
    because I love them.
48 I respect and love your commandments;
    I will meditate on your instructions.

Confidence in the Law of the Lord

49 Remember your promise to me, your
        servant;
    it has given me hope.
50 Even in my suffering I was comforted
    because your promise gave me life.
51 The proud are always scornful of me,
    but I have not departed from your
        law.
52 I remember your judgments of long
        ago,
    and they bring me comfort, O Lord.
53 When I see the wicked breaking your
        law,
    I am filled with anger.
54 During my brief earthly life
    I compose songs about your
        commands.
55 In the night I remember you, Lord,
    and I think about your law.
56 I find my happiness
    in obeying your commands.

Devotion to the Law of the Lord

57 You are all I want, O Lord;
    I promise to obey your laws.
58 I ask you with all my heart
    to have mercy on me, as you have
        promised!
59 I have considered my conduct,
    and I promise to follow your
        instructions.
60 Without delay I hurry
    to obey your commands.
61 The wicked have laid a trap for me,
    but I do not forget your law.

62 In the middle of the night I wake up
    to praise you for your righteous
        judgments.
63 I am a friend of all who serve you,
    of all who obey your laws.
64 Lord, the earth is full of your constant
        love;
    teach me your commandments.

The Value of the Law of the Lord

65 You have kept your promise, Lord,
    and you are good to me, your servant.
66 Give me wisdom and knowledge,
    because I trust in your commands.
67 Before you punished me, I used to go
        wrong,
    but now I obey your word.
68 How good you are—how kind!
    Teach me your commands.
69 The proud have told lies about me,
    but with all my heart I obey your
        instructions.
70 They have no understanding,
    but I find pleasure in your law.
71 My punishment was good for me,
    because it made me learn your
        commands.
72 The law that you gave means more to
        me
    than all the money in the world.

The Justice of the Law of the Lord

73 You created me, and you keep me safe;
    give me understanding, so that I may
        learn your laws.
74 Those who honor you will be glad when
        they see me,
    because I trust in your promise.
75 I know that your judgments are
        righteous, Lord,
    and that you punished me because you
        are faithful.
76 Let your constant love comfort me,
    as you have promised me, your servant.
77 Have mercy on me, and I will live
    because I take pleasure in your law.
78 May the proud be ashamed for falsely
        accusing me;
    as for me, I will meditate on your
        instructions.

⁷⁹ May those who honor you come to me—
    all those who know your commands.
⁸⁰ May I perfectly obey your
    commandments
    and be spared the shame of defeat.

A Prayer for Deliverance

⁸¹ I am worn out, LORD, waiting for you to
    save me;
    I place my trust in your word.
⁸² My eyes are tired from watching for what
    you promised,
    while I ask, "When will you help me?"
⁸³ I am as useless as a discarded wineskin;
    yet I have not forgotten your
    commands.
⁸⁴ How much longer must I wait?
    When will you punish those who
    persecute me?
⁸⁵ The proud, who do not obey your law,
    have dug pits to trap me.
⁸⁶ Your commandments are all trustworthy;
    people persecute me with lies—help
    me!
⁸⁷ They have almost succeeded in killing
    me,
    but I have not neglected your
    commands.
⁸⁸ Because of your constant love be good to
    me,
    so that I may obey your laws.

Faith in the Law of the LORD

⁸⁹ Your word, O LORD, will last forever;
    it is eternal in heaven.
⁹⁰ Your faithfulness endures through all the
    ages;
    you have set the earth in place, and it
    remains.
⁹¹ All things remain to this day because of
    your command,
    because they are all your servants.
⁹² If your law had not been the source of
    my joy,
    I would have died from my sufferings.
⁹³ I will never neglect your instructions,
    because by them you have kept me
    alive.

⁹⁴ I am yours—save me!
    I have tried to obey your commands.
⁹⁵ The wicked are waiting to kill me,
    but I will meditate on your laws.
⁹⁶ I have learned that everything has limits;
    but your commandment is perfect.

Love for the Law of the LORD

⁹⁷ How I love your law!
    I think about it all day long.
⁹⁸ Your commandment is with me all the
    time
    and makes me wiser than my enemies.
⁹⁹ I understand more than all my teachers,
    because I meditate on your
    instructions.
¹⁰⁰ I have greater wisdom than those who are
    old,
    because I obey your commands.
¹⁰¹ I have avoided all evil conduct,
    because I want to obey your word.
¹⁰² I have not neglected your instructions,
    because you yourself are my teacher.
¹⁰³ How sweet is the taste of your
    instructions—
    sweeter even than honey!
¹⁰⁴ I gain wisdom from your laws,
    and so I hate all bad conduct.

Light from the Law of the LORD

¹⁰⁵ Your word is a lamp to guide me
    and a light for my path.
¹⁰⁶ I will keep my solemn promise
    to obey your just instructions.
¹⁰⁷ My sufferings, LORD, are terrible indeed;
    keep me alive, as you have promised.
¹⁰⁸ Accept my prayer of thanks, O LORD,
    and teach me your commands.
¹⁰⁹ I am always ready to risk my life;
    Iᵘ have not forgotten your law.
¹¹⁰ The wicked lay a trap for me,
    but I have not disobeyed your
    commands.
¹¹¹ Your commandments are my eternal
    possession;
    they are the joy of my heart.
¹¹² I have decided to obey your laws
    until the day I die.

ᵘ **119:109** I am always ready to risk my life; I; *or* My life is in constant danger, but I.

Safety in the Law of the LORD

113 I hate those who are not completely loyal
    to you,
  but I love your law.
114 You are my defender and protector;
  I put my hope in your promise.
115 Go away from me, you sinful people.
  I will obey the commands of my God.
116 Give me strength, as you promised, and I
    shall live;
  don't let me be disappointed in my
    hope!
117 Hold me, and I will be safe,
  and I will always pay attention to your
    commands.
118 You reject everyone who disobeys your
    laws;
  their deceitful schemes are useless.
119 You treat all the wicked like rubbish,
  and so I love your instructions.
120 Because of you I am afraid;
  I am filled with fear because of your
    judgments.

Obedience to the Law of the LORD

121 I have done what is right and good;
  don't abandon me to my enemies!
122 Promise that you will help your
    servant;
  don't let the arrogant oppress me!
123 My eyes are tired from watching for your
    saving help,
  for the deliverance you promised.
124 Treat me according to your constant
    love,
  and teach me your commands.
125 I am your servant; give me understanding,
  so that I may know your teachings.
126 LORD, it is time for you to act,
  because people are disobeying your law.
127 I love your commands more than gold,
  more than the finest gold.
128 And so I follow all your instructions;[v]
  I hate all wrong ways.

Desire to Obey the Law of the LORD

129 Your teachings are wonderful;
  I obey them with all my heart.
130 The explanation of your teachings gives
    light
  and brings wisdom to the ignorant.
131 In my desire for your commands
  I pant with open mouth.
132 Turn to me and have mercy on me
  as you do on all those who love you.
133 As you have promised, keep me from
    falling;
  don't let me be overcome by evil.
134 Save me from those who oppress me,
  so that I may obey your commands.
135 Bless me with your presence
  and teach me your laws.
136 My tears pour down like a river,
  because people do not obey your law.

The Justice of the Law of the LORD

137 You are righteous, LORD,
  and your laws are just.
138 The rules that you have given
  are completely fair and right.
139 My anger burns in me like a fire,
  because my enemies disregard your
    commands.
140 How certain your promise is!
  How I love it!
141 I am unimportant and despised,
  but I do not neglect your teachings.
142 Your righteousness will last forever,
  and your law is always true.
143 I am filled with trouble and anxiety,
  but your commandments bring me
    joy.
144 Your instructions are always just;
  give me understanding, and I shall live.

A Prayer for Deliverance

145 With all my heart I call to you;
  answer me, LORD, and I will obey your
    commands!

---

v **119:128** *Some ancient translations* all your instructions; *Hebrew unclear.*

"Your word is a lamp to guide me . . . *(Psalm 119:105).* **How does God's Word, the Bible, guide your life?**

146I call to you;
     save me, and I will keep your laws.
147Before sunrise I call to you for help;
     I place my hope in your promise.
148All night long I lie awake,
     to meditate on your instructions.
149Because your love is constant, hear me,
     O LORD;
     show your mercy, and preserve my life!
150My cruel persecutors are coming
     closer,
     people who never keep your law.
151But you are near to me, LORD,
     and all your commands are permanent.
152Long ago I learned about your
     instructions;
     you made them to last forever.

A Plea for Help

153Look at my suffering, and save me,
     because I have not neglected your law.
154Defend my cause, and set me free;
     save me, as you have promised.
155The wicked will not be saved,
     for they do not obey your laws.
156But your compassion, LORD, is great;
     show your mercy and save me!
157I have many enemies and oppressors,
     but I do not fail to obey your laws.
158When I look at those traitors, I am filled
     with disgust,
     because they do not keep your
     commands.
159See how I love your instructions, LORD.
     Your love never changes, so save me!
160The heart of your law is truth,
     and all your righteous judgments are
     eternal.

Dedication to the Law of the LORD

161Powerful people attack me unjustly,
     but I respect your law.
162How happy I am because of your
     promises—
     as happy as someone who finds rich
     treasure.

163I hate and detest all lies,
     but I love your law.
164Seven times each day I thank you
     for your righteous judgments.
165Those who love your law have perfect
     security,
     and there is nothing that can make
     them fall.
166I wait for you to save me, LORD,
     and I do what you command.
167I obey your teachings;
     I love them with all my heart.
168I obey your commands and your
     instructions;
     you see everything I do.

A Prayer for Help

169Let my cry for help reach you,
     LORD!
     Give me understanding, as you have
     promised.
170Listen to my prayer,
     and save me according to your promise!
171I will always praise you,
     because you teach me your laws.
172I will sing about your law,
     because your commands are just.
173Always be ready to help me,
     because I follow your commands.
174How I long for your saving help,
     O LORD!
     I find happiness in your law.
175Give me life, so that I may praise you;
     may your instructions help me.
176I wander about like a lost sheep;
     so come and look for me, your servant,
     because I have not neglected your laws.

A Prayer for Help

120

1When I was in trouble, I called
     to the LORD,
and he answered me.
2Save me, LORD,
     from liars and deceivers.

3You liars, what will God do to you?
     How will he punish you?

Day and Night

"Is too," Kai said. "Is not," Moe answered. "Is too," Kai repeated. "Is not," Moe said louder.

Sometimes arguments go on like that for a long time. It almost seems as if some people hate peace, like the psalmist says at the end of Psalm 120. Some people argue just for the sake of arguing. Other times they don't stop to see the other person's point of view. Imagine what would happen if everyone, everywhere, instead of arguing, stopped and tried to see what the other person was feeling. A Native American Sioux saying advises that before we judge people, we should walk three miles in their moccasins. That doesn't mean we literally put on their shoes. It just means that we should make every effort to see what they see and experience what they experience. This is one way to start making peace.

So the next time you find yourself in a situation that sounds like the argument between Kai and Moe, take a few minutes to see the other's point of view. Maybe you can be the one who starts the chain of peace.

— Psalm 120:7

7 When I speak of peace,
   they are for war.

The LORD Our Protector

121 ¹I look to the mountains;
   where will my help come from?
²My help will come from the LORD,
   who made heaven and earth.

³He will not let you fall;
   your protector is always awake.

⁴The protector of Israel
   never dozes or sleeps.
⁵The LORD will guard you;
   he is by your side to protect you.
⁶The sun will not hurt you during the day,
   nor the moon during the night.

⁷The LORD will protect you from all danger;
   he will keep you safe.
⁸He will protect you as you come and go
   now and forever.

In Praise of Jerusalem ˣ

122 ¹I was glad when they said to me,
   "Let us go to the LORD's house."
²And now we are here,
   standing inside the gates of Jerusalem!

³Jerusalem is a city restored
   in beautiful order and harmony.

⁴With a soldier's sharp arrows,
   with red-hot coals!

⁵Living among you is as bad as living in Meshech
   or among the people of Kedar. ʷ

⁶I have lived too long
   with people who hate peace!

Let us go to the LORD's house. (122:1)

ʷ **120:5** MESHECH . . . KEDAR: *Two distant regions, whose people were regarded as savages.*   ˣ **122** HEBREW TITLE: *By David.*

Psalms

Pray It!

Peace in Jerusalem

Psalm 122 has a verse about praying for peace in Jerusalem. Even in our time there is much violence in the holy city of Jerusalem. Let's keep praying for peace there and all over the world.

> *On holy ground they walk.*
> *The people of Jerusalem*
>   *going to school*
>   *shopping at the markets*
>   *talking with friends*
>   *running to the bus,*
>   *on holy ground they walk.*
> *God, let that holy ground be peaceful.*
> *Let it be your peaceful city.*
> *The place where pilgrims go*
>   *to be closer to you,*
>   *the place where your people live*
>   *in buildings and out in the open.*
> *Let it be your peaceful city,*
>   *full of love, prayers, laughter, and freedom.*
> *Let it be your peaceful city,*
>   *where all live in unity,*
>   *where all walk on holy ground,*
>   *where all walk in unity.*
> *Amen.*

— Psalm 122

4 This is where the tribes come,
the tribes of Israel,
to give thanks to the LORD
according to his command.
5 Here the kings of Israel
sat to judge their people.

6 Pray for the peace of Jerusalem:
"May those who love you prosper.
7 May there be peace inside your walls
and safety in your palaces."
8 For the sake of my relatives and friends
I say to Jerusalem, "Peace be with
you!"
9 For the sake of the house of the LORD
our God
I pray for your prosperity.

A Prayer for Mercy

123 ¹LORD, I look up to you,
up to heaven, where you
rule.
2 As a servant depends on his master,
as a maid depends on her mistress,
so we will keep looking to you, O LORD
our God,
until you have mercy on us.

3 Be merciful to us, LORD, be
merciful;
we have been treated with so much
contempt.
4 We have been mocked too long by the
rich
and scorned by proud oppressors.

Psalms

God the Protector of His People [x]

124 ¹What if the LORD had not been
on our side?
Answer, O Israel!

² "If the LORD had not been on our side
when our enemies attacked us,
³ then they would have swallowed us alive
in their furious anger against us;
⁴ then the flood would have carried us
away,
the water would have covered us,
⁵ the raging torrent would have drowned
us."

⁶ Let us thank the LORD,
who has not let our enemies destroy us.
⁷ We have escaped like a bird from a
hunter's trap;
the trap is broken, and we are free!
⁸ Our help comes from the LORD,
who made heaven and earth.

The Security of God's People

125 ¹Those who trust in the LORD
are like Mount Zion,
which can never be shaken, never be
moved.
² As the mountains surround Jerusalem,
so the LORD surrounds his people,
now and forever.

³ The wicked will not always rule over the
land of the righteous;
if they did, the righteous themselves
might do evil.
⁴ LORD, do good to those who are good,
to those who obey your commands.
⁵ But when you punish the wicked,
punish also those who abandon your
ways.

Peace be with Israel!

A Prayer for Deliverance

126 ¹When the LORD brought us
back to Jerusalem, [y]
it was like a dream!
² How we laughed, how we sang for joy!
Then the other nations said about us,
"The LORD did great things for them."
³ Indeed he did great things for us;
how happy we were!

⁴ LORD, make us prosperous again, [z]
just as the rain brings water back to dry
riverbeds.
⁵ Let those who wept as they planted their
crops,
gather the harvest with joy!

⁶ Those who wept as they went out
carrying the seed
will come back singing for joy,
as they bring in the harvest.

Gather the harvest with joy. (126:5)

In Praise of God's Goodness [a]

127 ¹If the LORD does not build the
house,
the work of the builders is useless;
if the LORD does not protect the
city,
it does no good for the sentries to
stand guard.

---

[x] **124** HEBREW TITLE: *By David.*   [y] **126:1** brought us back to Jerusalem; *or* made Jerusalem prosperous again.
[z] **126:4** make us prosperous again; *or* take us back to our land.   [a] **127** HEBREW TITLE: *By Solomon.*

How would you answer the question, "What if the LORD had not been on our side?" *(Psalm 124:1).*

Psalms

Holy Families

During the Christmas season, we celebrate the Holy Family: Jesus, Mary, and Joseph. Psalm 128 is the responsorial psalm during Mass that day because it describes a family blessed by God. If we look at the Holy Family, we see an excellent example of a family that followed God. Joseph is an example of doing what God asks even if it results in shame or embarrassment. Remember, Mary, his fiancée, was pregnant, and Joseph wasn't the father.

Mary also risked shame, embarrassment, and more by saying yes to God. In Mary's time, being pregnant without being married meant that Mary would be shunned by nearly everyone. Sometimes it may seem as if following God would be embarrassing, like when your friends want you to do something but you can't because you have to do something with your family. When those times happen, and they will, try to remember the Holy Family.

— Psalm 128

² It is useless to work so hard for a living,
　getting up early and going to bed late.
For the LORD provides for those he
　loves,
　while they are asleep.

³ Children are a gift from the LORD;
　they are a real blessing.

⁴ The sons a man has when he is young
　are like arrows in a soldier's hand.
⁵ Happy is the man who has many such
　arrows.
He will never be defeated
　when he meets his enemies in the
　place of judgment.

The Reward of Obedience to the LORD

128

¹ Happy are those who obey the LORD,
who live by his commands.

² Your work will provide for your needs;
　you will be happy and prosperous.
³ Your wife will be like a fruitful vine in
　your home,
　and your children will be like young
　olive trees around your table.
⁴ A man who obeys the LORD
　will surely be blessed like this.

⁵ May the LORD bless you from Zion!
May you see Jerusalem prosper
　all the days of your life!
⁶ May you live to see your grandchildren!

Peace be with Israel!

A Prayer against Israel's Enemies

129

¹ Israel, tell us how your enemies
have persecuted you
ever since you were young.

² "Ever since I was young,
　my enemies have persecuted me
　cruelly,
　but they have not overcome me.
³ They cut deep wounds in my back
　and made it like a plowed field.
⁴ But the LORD, the righteous one,
　has freed me from slavery."

⁵ May everyone who hates Zion
　be defeated and driven back.
⁶ May they all be like grass growing on the
　housetops,
　which dries up before it can grow;

Why, do you think, the psalmist says, "Children are a gift from the LORD; / they are a real blessing" (Psalm 127:3)?

What Is Prayer?

Catholic Connections

Now that you have read most of the Psalms (there are only twenty left), you have experienced quite a few different types of prayer.

So, what is prayer? Is it a complaint to God or praise? Is it a long list of what God has (or hasn't) done? Is it asking God for something, or is it giving thanks? Prayer is all these things, and it is more, too.

Some people might say that prayer is talking to God. But prayer is not just the words we say to God; it is what is in our minds and hearts. Like a good friendship, it includes learning about and loving the other person. In this case, the other is God. So it means that you realize that you are friends with God. God whispers in your heart, "I love you." That is when the power of prayer hits you. But you must be willing to be open and listen with your heart. The great thing is, when you are aware of God's love for you, the more you can share it with others.

— Psalm 130

Psalms

7   no one gathers it up
       or carries it away in bundles.
8 No one who passes by will say,
       "May the LORD bless you!
       We bless you in the name of the
          LORD."

A Prayer for Help

130
¹From the depths of my despair
       I call to you, LORD.
² Hear my cry, O Lord;
       listen to my call for help!
³ If you kept a record of our sins,
       who could escape being
          condemned?
⁴ But you forgive us,
       so that we should stand in awe of you.

⁵ I wait eagerly for the LORD's help,
       and in his word I trust.
⁶ I wait for the Lord
       more eagerly than sentries wait for the
          dawn—
       than sentries wait for the dawn.

⁷ Israel, trust in the LORD,

because his love is constant
and he is always willing to save.
⁸ He will save his people Israel
from all their sins.

A Prayer of Humble Trust[b]

131
¹LORD, I have given up my pride
       and turned away from my
          arrogance.
I am not concerned with great matters
       or with subjects too difficult for
       me.

. . . more eagerly than sentries wait for the dawn.
(130:6)

[b] **131** HEBREW TITLE: *By David.*
130:8 Mt 1:21; Titus 2:14

2 Instead, I am content and at peace.
As a child lies quietly in its mother's arms,
so my heart is quiet within me.
3 Israel, trust in the LORD
now and forever!

In Praise of the Temple

132 ¹ LORD, do not forget David
and all the hardships he
endured.
2 Remember, LORD, what he promised,
the vow he made to you, the Mighty
God of Jacob:
3 "I will not go home or go to bed;
4   I will not rest or sleep,
5   until I provide a place for the LORD,
a home for the Mighty God of Jacob."

6 In Bethlehem we heard about the
Covenant Box,
and we found it in the fields of Jearim.
7 We said, "Let us go to the LORD's house;
let us worship before his throne."

8 Come to the Temple, LORD, with the
Covenant Box,
the symbol of your power,
and stay here forever.
9 May your priests do always what is right;
may your people shout for joy!

10 You made a promise to your servant
David;
do not reject your chosen king, LORD.
11 You made a solemn promise to David—
a promise you will not take back:
"I will make one of your sons king,
and he will rule after you.
12 If your sons are true to my covenant
and to the commands I give them,
their sons, also, will succeed you for all
time as kings."

13 The LORD has chosen Zion;
he wants to make it his home:
14 "This is where I will live forever;
this is where I want to rule.
15 I will richly provide Zion with all she
needs;
I will satisfy her poor with food.

16 I will bless her priests in all they do,
and her people will sing and shout for
joy.
17 Here I will make one of David's
descendants a great king;
here I will preserve the rule of my
chosen king.
18 I will cover his enemies with shame,
but his kingdom will prosper and
flourish."

In Praise of Living in Peace[b]

133 ¹ How wonderful it is, how
pleasant,
for God's people to live together in
harmony!

*"How wonderful . . . for God's people to live together
in harmony!" (133:1)*

2 It is like the precious anointing oil
running down from Aaron's head and
beard,
down to the collar of his robes.
3 It is like the dew on Mount Hermon,
falling on the hills of Zion.
That is where the LORD has promised his
blessing—
life that never ends.

A Call to Praise God

134 ¹ Come, praise the LORD,
all his servants,
all who serve in his Temple at night.
2 Raise your hands in prayer in the Temple,
and praise the LORD!
3 May the LORD, who made heaven and
earth,
bless you from Zion!

---

b **133** HEBREW TITLE: *By David.*
132:6–10 2 Chr 6:41, 42   **132:11** 2 Sam 7:12–16; 1 Chr 17:11–14; Ps 89:3, 4; Acts 2:30   **132:17** 1 Kings
11:36

A Hymn of Praise

135
¹Praise the LORD!

Praise his name, you servants of the
LORD,
2   who stand in the LORD's house,
in the Temple of our God.
³Praise the LORD, because he is good;
sing praises to his name, because he is
kind.ᶜ
⁴He chose Jacob for himself,
the people of Israel for his own.

⁵I know that our LORD is great,
greater than all the gods.
⁶He does whatever he wishes
in heaven and on earth,
in the seas and in the depths below.
⁷He brings storm clouds from the ends of
the earth;
he makes lightning for the storms,
and he brings out the wind from his
storeroom.

⁸In Egypt he killed all the first-born
of people and animals alike.
⁹There he performed miracles and
wonders
to punish the king and all his officials.
¹⁰He destroyed many nations
and killed powerful kings:
¹¹Sihon, king of the Amorites,
Og, king of Bashan,
and all the kings in Canaan.
¹²He gave their lands to his people;
he gave them to Israel.

¹³LORD, you will always be proclaimed as
God;
all generations will remember you.
¹⁴The LORD will defend his people;
he will take pity on his servants.

¹⁵The gods of the nations are made of silver
and gold;
they are formed by human hands.

¹⁶They have mouths, but cannot speak,
and eyes, but cannot see.
¹⁷They have ears, but cannot hear;
they are not even able to breathe.
¹⁸May all who made them and who trust in
them
becomeᵈ like the idols they have made!

¹⁹Praise the LORD, people of Israel;
praise him, you priests of God!
²⁰Praise the LORD, you Levites;
praise him, all you that worship him!
²¹Praise the LORD in Zion,
in Jerusalem, his home.

Praise the LORD!

A Hymn of Thanksgiving

136
¹Give thanks to the LORD,
because he is good;
his love is eternal.
²Give thanks to the greatest of all gods;
his love is eternal.
³Give thanks to the mightiest of all lords;
his love is eternal.

⁴He alone performs great miracles;
his love is eternal.
⁵By his wisdom he made the heavens;
his love is eternal;
⁶he built the earth on the deep waters;
his love is eternal.
⁷He made the sun and the moon;
his love is eternal;
⁸the sun to rule over the day;
his love is eternal;
⁹the moon and the stars to rule over the
night;
his love is eternal.

¹⁰He killed the first-born sons of the
Egyptians;
his love is eternal.
¹¹He led the people of Israel out of Egypt;
his love is eternal;

ᶜ **135:3** he is kind; or it is pleasant to do so.   ᵈ **135:18** May all . . . become; or All who made them and who
trust in them will become.
135:15–18 Ps 115:4–8; Rev 9:20   **136:1** 1 Chr 16:34; 2 Chr 5:13; 7:3; Ezra 3:11; Ps 100:5; 106:1; 107:1;
118:1; Jer 33:11   **136:5** Gen 1:1   **136:6** Gen 1:2   **136:7–9** Gen 1:16   **136:10** Ex 12:29

**How would your community be different if you were truly living in harmony
as suggested by Psalm 133?**

Psalms

Pray It!

His Love Is Eternal

"His love is eternal," is repeated throughout Psalm 136. Maybe you have read lines in other psalms that are repeated. It is one tool the writers use to emphasize a statement about God. Here is another chance to write your own prayer. Choose a statement you would like to make about God (such as, "God Rocks!"). Then write verses about God that can go in between the statement. It is that simple. Have fun!

— **Psalm 136**

12 with his strong hand, his powerful arm;
     his love is eternal.
13 He divided the Red Sea;
     his love is eternal;
14 he led his people through it;
     his love is eternal;
15 but he drowned the king of Egypt and his army;
     his love is eternal.

16 He led his people through the desert;
     his love is eternal.
17 He killed powerful kings;
     his love is eternal;
18 he killed famous kings;
     his love is eternal;
19 Sihon, king of the Amorites;
     his love is eternal;
20 and Og, king of Bashan;
     his love is eternal.
21 He gave their lands to his people;
     his love is eternal;

22 he gave them to Israel, his servant;
     his love is eternal.
23 He did not forget us when we were defeated;
     his love is eternal;
24 he freed us from our enemies;
     his love is eternal.
25 He gives food to every living creature;
     his love is eternal.

26 Give thanks to the God of heaven;
     his love is eternal.

A Lament of Israelites in Exile

137 1 By the rivers of Babylon we sat down;
     there we wept when we remembered Zion.
2 On the willows near by
     we hung up our harps.
3 Those who captured us told us to sing;
     they told us to entertain them:
     "Sing us a song about Zion."

4 How can we sing a song to the LORD
     in a foreign land?
5 May I never be able to play the harp again
     if I forget you, Jerusalem!
6 May I never be able to sing again
     if I do not remember you,
     if I do not think of you as my greatest joy!

7 Remember, LORD, what the Edomites did
     the day Jerusalem was captured.
     Remember how they kept saying,
     "Tear it down to the ground!"

8 Babylon, you will be destroyed.
     Happy are those who pay you back
     for what you have done to us—
9   who take your babies
     and smash them against a rock.

136:11 Ex 12:51   136:13–15 Ex 14:21–29   136:19 Num 21:21–30   136:20 Num 21:31–35   137:8 Rev 18:6

How many times is the phrase "his love is eternal" repeated in Psalm 136?

Pray It!

Life!

Life—from its very beginning to its natural end—is sacred. It is important to pray for the tiny babies in their mothers' wombs *and* for the aged who are nearing the end of their lives *and* for the person who is on death row. One way to keep life sacred is by praying for all life.

Giver of Life, let us remember that all of life is special. Help us remember the beauty of
  life, newly formed, unborn babies, wrinkled and bald,
  life, old men and women, wrinkled and bald,
  life, sick people, undergoing treatment, wrinkled and bald,
  all of life, the old and young, the sick and the healthy, the prisoner and free.
Help me, Giver of Life, to remember that all of them are special.
Amen.

— Psalm 139

A Prayer of Thanksgiving*e*

138 ¹I thank you, LORD, with all my heart;
  I sing praise to you before the gods.
²I face your holy Temple,
  bow down, and praise your name
because of your constant love and
    faithfulness,
  because you have shown that your
    name and your commands are
    supreme.*f*
³You answered me when I called to you;
  with your strength you strengthened
    me.

⁴All the kings in the world will praise you,
    LORD,
  because they have heard your promises.
⁵They will sing about what you have done
  and about your great glory.
⁶Even though you are so high above,
  you care for the lowly,
  and the proud cannot hide from you.

⁷When I am surrounded by troubles,
  you keep me safe.
  You oppose my angry enemies
  and save me by your power.

⁸You will do everything you have
    promised;
  LORD, your love is eternal.
  Complete the work that you have
    begun.

God's Complete Knowledge and Care*g*

139 ¹LORD, you have examined me
    and you know me.
²You know everything I do;
  from far away you understand all my
    thoughts.
³You see me, whether I am working or
    resting;
  you know all my actions.
⁴Even before I speak,
  you already know what I will say.
⁵You are all around me on every side;
  you protect me with your power.
⁶Your knowledge of me is too deep;
  it is beyond my understanding.

⁷Where could I go to escape from you?
  Where could I get away from your
    presence?

---

e **138** HEBREW TITLE: *By David.* *f* **138:2** *Probable text* your name and your commands are supreme; *Hebrew* your command is greater than all your name. *g* **139** HEBREW TITLE: *A psalm by David.*

3 When I am ready to give up,
   he knows what I should do.
In the path where I walk,
   my enemies have hidden a trap for me.
4 When I look beside me,
   I see that there is no one to help me,
   no one to protect me.
No one cares for me.
5 LORD, I cry to you for help;
   you, LORD, are my protector;
   you are all I want in this life.
6 Listen to my cry for help,
   for I am sunk in despair.
Save me from my enemies;
   they are too strong for me.
7 Set me free from my distress;[p]
   then in the assembly of your people I
   will praise you
   because of your goodness to me.

A Prayer for Help[q]

143 ¹LORD, hear my prayer!
In your righteousness listen to
   my plea;
   answer me in your faithfulness!
2 Don't put me, your servant, on trial;
   no one is innocent in your sight.

3 My enemies have hunted me down
   and completely defeated me.
They have put me in a dark prison,
   and I am like those who died long
   ago.
4 So I am ready to give up;
   I am in deep despair.

5 I remember the days gone by;
   I think about all that you have
   done,
   I bring to mind all your deeds.
6 I lift up my hands to you in prayer;
   like dry ground my soul is thirsty for
   you.

7 Answer me now, LORD!
   I have lost all hope.

Don't hide yourself from me,
   or I will be among those who go
   down to the world of the dead.
8 Remind me each morning of your
   constant love,
   for I put my trust in you.
My prayers go up to you;
   show me the way I should go.

9 I go to you for protection, LORD;
   rescue me from my enemies.
10 You are my God;
   teach me to do your will.
Be good to me, and guide me on a safe
   path.

11 Rescue me, LORD, as you have
   promised;
   in your goodness save me from my
   troubles!
12 Because of your love for me, kill my
   enemies
   and destroy all my oppressors,
   for I am your servant.

A King Thanks God for Victory[r]

144 ¹Praise the LORD, my protector!
He trains me for battle
and prepares me for war.
2 He is my protector and defender,
   my shelter and savior,
   in whom I trust for safety.
He subdues the nations under me.

3 LORD, what are mortals, that you notice
   them;
   mere mortals, that you pay attention
   to us?
4 We are like a puff of wind;
   our days are like a passing shadow.

5 O LORD, tear the sky open and come
   down;
   touch the mountains, and they will
   pour out smoke.

[p] **142:7** distress; *or prison.* [q] **143** HEBREW TITLE: *A psalm by David.* [r] **144** HEBREW TITLE: *By David.*
143:2 Rom 3:20; Gal 2:16 **144:3** Job 7:17, 18; Ps 8:4

Psalm 144 describes good sons and daughters as plants and columns! How do you think your parents would describe you?

Pray It!

Yeah God!

How do you praise God?

As you read Psalms 145–150, notice that the writers were very joyful. Praising God in as many ways as possible, they announce the greatness of God. Music, the stars, princes, kings, all creatures, angels, and all of God's people are invited in the praise.

So, how should we praise God today? Take some time and write your own psalm praising God. Here is an example:

Praise God with text messages and on Facebook!
Praise God with newsflashes and radio announcements!
Praise God with skywriting and billboards!
Praise God with rockets and satellites!
Praise God with electric guitars and synthesizers!

— **Psalm 145**

6 Send flashes of lightning and scatter your
  enemies;
    shoot your arrows and send them
      running.
7 Reach down from above,
    pull me out of the deep water, and
      rescue me;
    save me from the power of foreigners,
8   who never tell the truth
    and lie even under oath.

9 I will sing you a new song, O God;
    I will play the harp and sing to you.
10 You give victory to kings
    and rescue your servant David.
11 Save me from my cruel enemies;
    rescue me from the power of
      foreigners,
    who never tell the truth
    and lie even under oath.

12 May our sons in their youth
    be like plants that grow up strong.
  May our daughters be like stately columns
    which adorn the corners of a palace.
13 May our barns be filled
    with crops of every kind.
  May the sheep in our fields
    bear young by the tens of thousands.

14 May our cattle reproduce plentifully
    without miscarriage or loss.
  May there be no cries of distress in our
    streets.

15 Happy is the nation of whom this is true;
    happy are the people whose God is the
      LORD!

A Hymn of Praise[s]

145

1 I will proclaim your greatness,
    my God and king;
  I will thank you forever and ever.
2 Every day I will thank you;
    I will praise you forever and ever.
3 The LORD is great and is to be highly
    praised;
    his greatness is beyond understanding.
4 What you have done will be praised from
    one generation to the next;
    they will proclaim your mighty acts.
5 They will speak of your glory and
    majesty,
    and I will meditate on your wonderful
      deeds.
6 People will speak of your mighty deeds,
    and I will proclaim your greatness.

s **145** HEBREW TITLE: *A song of praise by David.*

4 The LORD takes pleasure in his
  people;
  he honors the humble with victory.
5 Let God's people rejoice in their
  triumph
  and sing joyfully all night long.
6 Let them shout aloud as they praise
  God,
  with their sharp swords in their hands
7   to defeat the nations
  and to punish the peoples;
8   to bind their kings in chains,
  their leaders in chains of iron;
9   to punish the nations as God has
  commanded.
  This is the victory of God's people.

  Praise the LORD!

149:6 2 Macc 15:27

Praise the LORD!

150 **¹**Praise the LORD!

Praise God in his Temple!
  Praise his strength in heaven!
2 Praise him for the mighty things he has
  done.
  Praise his supreme greatness.
3 Praise him with trumpets.
  Praise him with harps and lyres.
4 Praise him with drums and dancing.
  Praise him with harps and flutes.
5 Praise him with cymbals.
  Praise him with loud cymbals.
6 Praise the LORD, all living creatures!

  Praise the LORD!

"Praise the LORD!" (150:1)

Your Next Step

Congratulations on finishing the Book of Psalms! Use this space to write your thoughts and questions about this book. If you are following the suggested reading plan, move ahead to the Letter to the Philippians in the New Testament. Philippians contains a song from the early Church that is like a psalm.

The Book of Proverbs

"Dear Zelda, I have this problem, and I'm not sure what to do about it. . . ." You've probably read letters that begin this way in a magazine or online. People have always looked for help with life's challenges. The Book of Proverbs gives advice on how to be a good person, how to build relationships, how to deal with tough times, and all kinds of other topics that are as important to you today as they were to young people hundreds of years ago.

Proverbs are short, often clever, and easy-to-memorize statements of wisdom and practical truth. The Book of Proverbs is a collection of advice written by different people over a long period of time. All of these people had one goal in mind: to pass along the wisdom that comes from God so that we can understand life better and live it well.

Chap. 11:1

Head lines

- Purpose and Value of Wisdom (1:1–7)
- A Father's Advice (chapter 4)
- Seek Wisdom, Find Happiness (chapter 8)
- Watch Your Temper and Your Tongue! (10:18–21)
- Pick Your Friends Carefully (24:1–2)
- The Sweet Taste of Gossip (26:20–28)
- Honesty Is the Best Policy (28:1–20)

FACTOIDS

Who wrote this book? King Solomon usually gets the credit, but several people wrote different parts of it over a span of about four hundred years, long before Jesus was born.

Why was it written? To give down-to-earth, practical advice on everyday matters, such as family, society, and relationships.

Who was it written for? Even though the advice applies to everyone, much of this book was written specifically for young people.

How is it organized? The book has two main parts. Chapters 1–9 include speeches about how to be wise and live a good life. Chapters 10–31 are collections of short sayings.

Important themes
- Being a wise person means knowing right from wrong and always doing the right thing, no matter how hard it might be.
- Treat people as you want to be treated.
- God is always with us, no matter what.

PROVERBS

The Value of Proverbs

1 ¹The proverbs of Solomon, son of David and king of Israel.

²Here are proverbs that will help you recognize wisdom and good advice, and understand sayings with deep meaning. ³They can teach you how to live intelligently and how to be honest, just, and fair. ⁴They can make an inexperienced person clever and teach young people how to be resourceful. ⁵These proverbs can even add to the knowledge of the wise and give guidance to the educated, ⁶so that they can understand the hidden meanings of proverbs and the problems that the wise raise.

Advice to the Young

⁷To have knowledge, you must first have reverence for the LORD.*a* Stupid people have no respect for wisdom and refuse to learn.

⁸My child, pay attention to what your father and mother tell you. ⁹Their teaching will improve your character as a handsome turban or a necklace improves your appearance.

¹⁰My child, when sinners tempt you, don't give in. ¹¹Suppose they say, "Come on; let's find someone to kill! Let's attack some innocent people for the fun of it! ¹²They may be alive and well when we find them, but they'll be dead when we're through with them! ¹³We'll find all kinds of riches and fill our houses with loot! ¹⁴Come and join us, and we'll all share what we steal."

¹⁵My child, don't go with people like that. Stay away from them. ¹⁶They can't wait to do something bad. They're always ready to kill. ¹⁷It does no good to spread a net when the

Parental Wisdom

"Go ask your mother!" "Listen to your father!" "See what Grandma says!" "Uncle Harry will show you how to do it!"

You've heard those words many times. The adults you live with play a big role in helping you grow up. They have a responsibility for seeing that you have food to eat, clothes to wear, and a place to live. They also make sure that you go to school, do your homework, and know how to do things for yourself. But maybe their most important job is teaching you what it means to be a good person, a person who makes a positive difference in the world.

The Book of Proverbs starts by telling young people to have reverence for God and to pay attention to their parents. Your parents and other family members have learned a lot in all their years of life. They've had some successes and made mistakes, too. Even though they were teenagers in a very different world, pay close attention to the wisdom they share.

— Proverbs 1:8–9

---

a **1:7** To . . . LORD; *or* The most important part of knowledge is having reverence for the LORD.
1:1 1 Kings 4:32   **1:7** Job 28:28; Ps 111:10; Prov 9:10; Sir 1:14

1:9   *1:11–15*   *1:28*   *1:33*   *2:2*

Pray It!

With Ears and Heart

You listen with your ears, but to really hear and understand someone, you must also listen with your heart. The next time someone needs to talk with you about something important, say this short prayer based on Proverbs 2:1–2.

> *Dear God,*
> *Open my ears that I may hear the words that are spoken.*
> *Open my heart that I might understand their true meaning.*
> *Open my mind that I may always act out of love and respect. Amen.*

— Proverbs 2:1–2

bird you want to catch is watching, [18] but people like that are setting a trap for themselves, a trap in which they will die. [19] Robbery always claims the life of the robber—this is what happens to[b] anyone who lives by violence.

Wisdom Calls

[20] Listen! Wisdom is calling out in the streets and marketplaces, [21] calling loudly at the city gates and wherever people come together:

[22] "Foolish people! How long do you want to be foolish? How long will you enjoy making fun of knowledge? Will you never learn? [23] Listen when I reprimand you; I will give you good advice and share my knowledge with you. [24] I have been calling you, inviting you to come, but you would not listen. You paid no attention to me. [25] You have ignored all my advice and have not been willing to let me correct you. [26] So when you get into trouble, I will laugh at you. I will make fun of you when terror strikes— [27] when it comes on you like a storm, bringing fierce winds of trouble, and you are in pain and misery. [28] Then you will call for wisdom, but

I will not answer. You may look for me everywhere, but you will not find me. [29] You have never had any use for knowledge and have always refused to obey the LORD. [30] You have never wanted my advice or paid any attention when I corrected you. [31] So then, you will get what you deserve, and your own actions will make you sick. [32] Inexperienced people die because they reject wisdom. Stupid people are destroyed by their own lack of concern. [33] But whoever listens to me will have security. He will be safe, with no reason to be afraid."

The Rewards of Wisdom

2 [1] My child, learn what I teach you and never forget what I tell you to do. [2] Listen to what is wise and try to understand it. [3] Yes, beg for knowledge; plead for insight. [4] Look for it as hard as you would for silver or some hidden treasure. [5] If you do, you will know what it means to fear the LORD and you will succeed in learning about God. [6] It is the LORD who gives wisdom; from him come knowledge and understanding. [7] He provides help and protection for those who

[b] **1:19** *One ancient translation* what happens to; *Hebrew* the path of.
1:20, 21 Prov 8:1–3   **2:6** Wis 9:10; Sir 1:1

"It is the LORD who gives wisdom; from him come knowledge and understanding" *(Proverbs 2:6)*.

Proverbs

Wisdom: Guard and Guide

Isabel didn't need to see the hurt in Natalie's eyes to know that what she said was wrong. But the hurt was there. And so were the tears. More than anything, Isabel wanted to eat lunch with Lucy and the other popular girls. As they passed Natalie's table, Lucy made a nasty comment about Natalie's need for special help in reading. When Isabel added her own mean remark, the others giggled. Natalie shot Isabel a glance that said, "Not you, too!" and then her eyes filled with tears. Isabel felt terrible. She was quiet all through lunch at the popular table.

Did you ever do something you knew was wrong, just because someone else did it? God's gift of wisdom does two things: it guards us from evil, and it guides us to make right choices. The gift is yours if you want it. Just ask God.

— Proverbs 2:1–22

say— 13those who have abandoned a righteous life to live in the darkness of sin, 14those who find pleasure in doing wrong and who enjoy senseless evil, 15unreliable people who cannot be trusted.

16You will be able to resist any immoral woman who tries to seduce you with her smooth talk, 17who is faithless to her own husband and forgets her sacred vows. 18If you go to her house, you are traveling the road to death. To go there is to approach the world of the dead. 19No one who visits her ever comes back. He never returns to the road to life. 20So you must follow the example of good people and live a righteous life. 21Righteous people—people of integrity—will live in this land of ours. 22But God will snatch the wicked from the land and pull sinners out of it like plants from the ground.

Advice to the Young

3 1My child, don't forget what I teach you. Always remember what I tell you to do. 2My teaching will give you a long and prosperous life. 3Never let go of loyalty and faithfulness. Tie them around your neck; write them on your heart. 4If you do this, both God and people will be pleased with you.

5Trust in the LORD with all your heart. Never rely on what you think you know. 6Remember the LORD in everything you do, and he will show you the right way. 7Never let yourself think that you are wiser than you are; simply obey the LORD and refuse to do wrong. 8If you do, it will be like good medicine, healing your wounds and easing your pains. 9Honor the LORD by making him an offering from the best of all that your land produces. 10If you do, your barns will be filled with grain, and you will have too much wine to store it all.

11My child, when the LORD corrects you, pay close attention and take it as a warning. 12The LORD corrects those he loves, as parents correct a child of whom they are proud. 13Happy is anyone who becomes wise—

are righteous and honest. 8He protects those who treat others fairly, and guards those who are devoted to him.

9If you listen to me, you will know what is right, just, and fair. You will know what you should do. 10You will become wise, and your knowledge will give you pleasure. 11Your insight and understanding will protect you 12and prevent you from doing the wrong thing. They will keep you away from people who stir up trouble by what they

3:4 Lk 2:52   **3:7** Rom 12:16   **3:11** Job 5:17   **3:11, 12** Heb 12:5, 6   **3:12** Rev 3:19

Read Proverbs 3:27. How would you apply this teaching in your school? your community? your family?

Pray It!

Trust in the Lord

Dear God, sometimes I wonder,
am I doing what you want me to be doing?
Is everything going to turn out okay?
Why do bad things happen?
When the road ahead looks uncertain or fearful
and I don't know where I'm going,
help me see the path you want me to follow.
I believe you will be with me every step of the way,
when everything is going great,
and in times of trouble, danger, and sorrow.
I trust that you will lead me where you want me to go.
And knowing that brings me joy. (Koch, *Garden of a Thousand Gates*, p. 61)

— **Proverbs 3:5–6**

---

who comes to have understanding. ¹⁴There is more profit in it than there is in silver; it is worth more to you than gold. ¹⁵Wisdom is more valuable than jewels; nothing you could want can compare with it. ¹⁶Wisdom offers you long life, as well as wealth and honor. ¹⁷Wisdom can make your life pleasant and lead you safely through it. ¹⁸Those who become wise are happy; wisdom will give you life.

¹⁹The LORD created the earth by his wisdom;
  by his knowledge he set the sky in place.

²⁰His wisdom caused the rivers to flow and the clouds to give rain to the earth.

²¹My child, hold on to your wisdom and insight. Never let them get away from you. ²²They will provide you with life—a pleasant and happy life. ²³You can go safely on your way and never even stumble. ²⁴You will not be afraid when you go to bed, and you will sleep soundly through the night. ²⁵You will not have to worry about sudden disasters, such as come on the wicked like a storm. ²⁶The LORD will keep you safe. He will not let you fall into a trap.

²⁷Whenever you possibly can, do good to those who need it. ²⁸Never tell your neighbors to wait until tomorrow if you can help them now. ²⁹Don't plan anything that will hurt your neighbors; they live beside you, trusting you. ³⁰Don't argue with others for no reason when they have never done you any harm. ³¹Don't be jealous of violent people or decide to act as they do, ³²because the LORD hates people who do evil, but he takes righteous people into his confidence. ³³The LORD puts a curse on the homes of the wicked, but blesses the homes of the righteous. ³⁴He has no use for conceited people, but shows favor to those who are humble.

3:27, 28 Sir 4:3   **3:34** Jas 4:6; 1 Pet 5:5

2:16   3:12   3:20   3:23   3:29

clear, clean, and confident; it cannot be harmed.[d] It loves what is good. It is sharp and unconquerable, 23kind, and a friend of humanity. It is dependable and sure, and has no worries. It has power over everything, and sees everything. It penetrates every spirit that is intelligent and pure, no matter how delicate its substance may be.

24Wisdom moves more easily than motion itself; she is so pure that she penetrates everything. 25She is a breath of God's power—a pure and radiant stream of glory from the Almighty. Nothing that is defiled can ever steal its way into Wisdom. 26She is a reflection of eternal light, a perfect mirror of God's activity and goodness. 27Even though Wisdom acts alone, she can do anything. She makes everything new, although she herself never changes. From generation to generation she enters the souls of holy people, and makes them God's friends and prophets. 28There is nothing that God loves more than people who are at home with Wisdom. 29Wisdom is more beautiful than the sun and all the constellations. She is better than light itself, 30because night always follows day, but evil never overcomes Wisdom.

8 1Her great power reaches into every part of the world, and she sets everything in useful order.

Solomon's Love for Wisdom

2Wisdom has been my love. I courted her when I was young and wanted to make her my bride. I fell in love with her beauty. 3She glorifies her noble origin by living with God, the Lord of all, who loves her. 4She is familiar with God's mysteries and helps determine his course of action.

5Is it good to have riches in this life? Nothing can make you richer than Wisdom, who makes everything function. 6Is knowledge a useful thing to have? Nothing is better than Wisdom, who has given shape to everything that exists. 7Do you love justice? All the virtues are the result of Wisdom's work: justice and courage, self-control and understanding. Life can offer us nothing more valuable than these. 8Do you want to have wide experience? Wisdom knows the lessons of history and can anticipate the future. She knows how to interpret what people say and how to solve problems. She knows the miracles that God will perform, and how the movements of history will develop.

9So I decided to take Wisdom home to live with me, because I knew that she would give me good advice and encourage me in times of trouble and grief. 10I thought to myself, "Because of her I will be honored wherever people come together. The old men will respect me, even though I am young. 11They will find that my opinions show deep insight, and those in power will admire me. 12When I am silent, they will wait for me to speak, and when I speak, they will pay attention. Even when I speak at length, they will listen with concentration. 13Because of Wisdom I will gain immortality; I will live forever in the memory of those who come after me. 14I will hold power over nations and peoples; 15dreaded tyrants will be seized with fear at the mention of my name. I will be famous, as a good king and as a brave soldier. 16When I come home to Wisdom, I will find contentment because there is no conflict or pain in living with her, only happiness and joy."

17And so I thought it over: to be wedded to Wisdom is to live forever, 18to love her is to be perfectly happy, to do her work is to be rich beyond measure, to share her company is to have sound judgment, to converse with her is to be honored. Then I was determined to take Wisdom as my bride. 19I had a pleasant personality even as a child. I had been fortunate enough to receive a good soul, or rather, I was given a sound body to live in because I was already good. 20Still, I realized that I would never receive Wisdom unless God gave her to me—and knowing that only God could give her to me was itself a sign of understanding. So I prayed, begging the Lord with all my heart:

Wisdom

David

Breakthrough!: King David, how long did you rule over Israel [IZ-ry-el]?

David: A total of forty years.

B: Wow, that's a long time. You became king in a rather unusual way. Please describe what happened.

David: Well, I was tending my family's sheep one day, when one of my brothers told me to come to the house. A prophet named Samuel saw me and anointed me with oil! The only problem was that there already was an anointed king, Saul. Plus I had seven older brothers, so I couldn't figure out why I was chosen.

B: What was your relationship with King Saul?

David: At first I was his musician and armorbearer, and then I got to know two of his children well. Saul's son Jonathan became my best friend, and Saul's daughter Michal [MY-kuhl] became my wife. But Saul became very jealous of me and wanted me dead. I was never sure why. That was hard, because I respected Saul. After all, he had also been anointed king.

B: You accomplished a lot in your life. What are you most proud of?

David: I would say making Jerusalem [ji-ROO-suh-luhm] the capital. It gave my people a city to call their own and a resting place for the Covenant Box.

B: Any regrets?

David: Oh, yes. I very much regret my adultery with Bathsheba [bath-SHEE-buh] and the way I arranged for Uriah [yoo-RY-uh] to be killed. I was blinded by my desire for Bathsheba, and that led me to break God's laws.

B: Any words for our readers?

David: Yes. I tried to be a person after God's own heart and God worked through me to make the people of Israel a mighty nation. I recommend that your readers try to please God in everything they do.

c17

Amos

Breakthrough!: Amos, you come from a small town near Bethlehem [BETH-li-hem], correct?

Amos: That's right. I am from Tekoa [tuh-KOH-uh] in Judah, and I was working as a shepherd and tree trimmer when I got my call from God.

B: You were very critical of the kingdom of Israel [IZ-ry-el], and that got a lot of people upset.

Amos: Yes, that's right. I was ordered to leave the shrine at Bethel [BETH-uhl] because the priest Amaziah [am-uh-ZY-uh] didn't like what I was saying.

B: So, then you toned down your message?

Amos: Absolutely not! I would not water down God's message for anyone!

B: And what was God's message?

Amos: Israel and its rulers and its people had gotten fat and lazy. They abused the poor and completely forgot their obligation to serve the less fortunate. They would be destroyed for this.

B: So, you prophesied that Israel was doomed?

Amos: That is exactly what I said. Israel had sinned and turned its back on the poor. They had violated the covenant with God. As a consequence, their kingdom would come to an end.

B: Was there any hope?

Amos: Yes, God would never totally abandon his promises to us. A few people would survive the coming destruction. I knew one day God would restore the kingdom of David.

B: What is your message for our readers?

Amos: To be a follower of God, you must be a person who acts with justice. Then justice will flow like a stream, and righteousness like a river that never goes dry.

Hosea

Breakthrough!: Hosea, I have to get right to the point. You were married to Gomer [GOH-mer], correct?

Hosea [hoh-ZAY-uh]: Yes, that's right.

B: I'm sure you realize that she had quite a reputation around town. She was a . . . well, she was a prostitute who was unfaithful to you.

Hosea: Yes, I know. It made me very sad.

B: So, why did you stay with her when she clearly did not respect you?

Hosea: That is a very important question, and it gets to the heart of my message to my people. Yes, Gomer was unfaithful. Everyone knew it. But God commanded me to marry her. So I loved her and I stayed with her, despite everything.

B: What is the message you spoke of?

Hosea: My marriage was a public symbol of the relationship between God and his people. God committed himself to us. We were his people. However, we were not faithful to God. We turned away from him time and time again.

B: So you are saying that Gomer was like the people of Israel [IZ-ry-el]?

Hosea: That's exactly right. My wife's behavior was very much like Israel's, and yet, God remained faithful through it all. Just as God remained faithful to us, his chosen people, so I remained faithful to Gomer, despite the heartache it caused me.

B: I think I understand now. You are truly an amazing man, Hosea, with a huge heart. Any words for our readers?

Hosea: Yes, they are words I have said before: Return to the Lord. Your sin makes you stumble and fall. Come back to the Lord with all your heart and seek his forgiveness.

Isaiah

Breakthrough!: Hello, Isaiah [eye-ZAY-uh], it looks like you brought some guests.

Isaiah 1: Actually we are all Isaiahs. There are more than one of us.

B: Say that again?

Isaiah 2: The prophecies in the Book of Isaiah were the work of more than one person. The prophecies at the beginning of the book were from the original Isaiah, but then I came along and prophesied in his name.

Isaiah 3: Then I came along and kept it up.

B: So there were just three of you, right?

Isaiah 1: Well, no one really knows for sure. Maybe there were only two. Or maybe there was a whole group that kept prophesying and writing in my name.

B: And what did you do?

Isaiah 2: We were prophets, meaning we spoke God's truth. Our message had to change with the times. The first Isaiah had to tell the people they were being unfaithful to God and would be punished after that. But then Jerusalem [ji-ROO-suh-luhm] was destroyed and the people taken into slavery. So then I had to speak God's words of hope and promise.

B: What challenges did you three face?

Isaiah 3: I think the hardest thing was being faithful to preaching God's message, even when it seemed like no one was listening. It breaks your heart to see your people ignoring God.

B: What period of time do all your prophecies cover?

Isaiah 1: Our prophecies cover a period of time going from about 740 BC to 500 BC or later. You can see that it would be pretty hard for one person to do.

B: Anything else for our Bible readers?

Isaiah 2: Some of our prophecies were about a leader who would be a suffering servant for his people. I bet you can guess who that turned out to be!

Solomon Prays for Wisdom

9 [1]"God of my ancestors, merciful Lord, by your word you created everything. [2]By your Wisdom you made us humans to rule all creation, [3]to govern the world with holiness and righteousness, to administer justice with integrity. [4]Give me the Wisdom that sits beside your throne; give me a place among your children. [5]I am your slave, as was my mother before me. I am only human. I am not strong, and my life will be short. I have little understanding of the Law or of how to apply it. [6]Even if someone is perfect, he will be thought of as nothing without the Wisdom that comes from you. [7]You chose me over everyone else to be the king of your own people, to judge your sons and daughters. [8]You told me to build a temple on your sacred mountain, an altar in Jerusalem, the city you chose as your home. It is a copy of that temple in heaven, which you prepared at the beginning. [9]Wisdom is with you and knows your actions; she was present when you made the world. She knows what pleases you, what is right and in accordance with your commands. [10]Send her from the holy heavens, down from your glorious throne, so that she may work at my side, and I may learn what pleases you. [11]She knows and understands everything, and will guide me intelligently in what I do. Her glory will protect me. [12]Then I will judge your people fairly, and be worthy of my father's throne. My actions will be acceptable.

[13]"Who can ever learn the will of God? [14]Human reason is not adequate for the task, and our philosophies tend to mislead us, [15]because our mortal bodies weigh our souls down. The body is a temporary structure made of earth, a burden to the active mind. [16]All we can do is make guesses about things on earth; we must struggle to learn about things that are close to us. Who, then, can ever hope to understand heavenly things? [17]No one has ever learned your will, unless you first gave him Wisdom, and sent your holy spirit down to him. [18]In this way people on earth have been set on the right path,

have learned what pleases you, and have been kept safe by Wisdom."

Wisdom Protected Adam

10 [1]Wisdom protected the father of the world, the first man that was ever formed, when he alone had been created. She saved him from his own sinful act [2]and gave him the strength to master everything on earth.

Cain Abandoned Wisdom

[3]But there was an unrighteous man who abandoned Wisdom; he destroyed himself by killing his brother in a fit of anger.

Wisdom Protected Noah

[4]Because of that sin, the earth was flooded, but Wisdom saved it again. She guided a righteous man in his flimsy wooden boat.

Wisdom Helped Abraham

[5]Once when the nations were frustrated in their wicked plans, Wisdom recognized a righteous man and kept him innocent in God's sight. She gave him strength to obey God's command in spite of his love for his son.

Wisdom Rescued Lot

[6]Wisdom rescued a righteous man while ungodly people were dying. He escaped the flames that destroyed the Five Cities. [7]You can still see the evidence of their wickedness. The land there is barren and smoking. The plants bear fruit that never ripens, and a pillar of salt stands as a monument to one who did not believe. [8]The people of those cities ignored Wisdom and could not tell right from wrong. Not only that, but the remains of their cities still remind us of the foolish way they lived, so that their failure can never be forgotten. [9]But Wisdom rescued her servants from the danger.

9:1–18 1 Kings 3:6–9; Wis 7:7 **10:1, 2** Gen 1:26–28 **10:3** Gen 4:8–13 **10:4** Gen 7:1—8:22 **10:5** Gen 11:1–9; 12:1–3; 22:1–19 **10:6–9** Gen 19:1–29

3.

13.

4.

6.

18.

10.

Wisdom protects. (Numbers refer to verses of chapter 10)

Wisdom Protected Jacob

10 A righteous man once had to escape from his brother's anger, and Wisdom guided him in the right way. She showed him God's kingdom and allowed him to know about holy things.ᵉ She made him prosperous and successful in his work. **11** When others were greedy for what he had, and wanted to take it away from him, Wisdom stood by him and

ᵉ **10:10** holy things; *or* angels.
10:10–12 Gen 27:43; 28:10–22; 32:24–30

made him rich. [12]She protected him from his enemies who were waiting for a chance to attack him. She gave him victory in a hard fight, so that he might realize that nothing can make a person stronger than serving God.

Wisdom Rescued Joseph

[13]Once a righteous man was sold into slavery, but Wisdom did not abandon him. She kept him safe from sin. She went to prison with him [14]and never left him until she had given him power over an empire and made him the ruler of people who had once oppressed him. She let it be known that a false accusation had been made against him, and she gave him eternal honor.

Wisdom Led the Israelites Out of Egypt

[15]Wisdom once rescued an innocent and holy people from a nation of oppressors. [16]She entered the soul of one of God's servants and[f] stood up to dreaded kings by performing miracles. [17]She rewarded God's people for their hardships. She guided them along a miraculous journey. She gave them shade during the day and brilliant starlight at night. [18]She led them through the deep waters of the Red Sea, [19]but she drowned their enemies and washed their bodies up on the shore. [20]And so the righteous looted the ungodly. They sang hymns to your holy name, O Lord; together they praised you for defending them. [21]Wisdom gave speech to those who could not speak; she even caused babies to speak clearly.

Wisdom Led the Israelites through the Desert

11 [1]Wisdom brought success to the people of Israel through a holy prophet. [2]They traveled across a desert where no one lived and camped in places where no human being had ever been. [3]They stood up to their enemies and fought them off. [4]When your people grew thirsty, they called to you, Lord, and you gave them water flowing out of solid rock. [5]The disasters that punished the Egyptians saved your people when they were in trouble.

The Punishment of the Egyptians

[6-8]Because those enemies decreed that the babies of your people should be killed, you stirred up the sources of their everflowing river and made it foul with blood.

In the desert you let your people go thirsty, to give them a taste of how you had punished their enemies. And then, when they least expected it, you gave them plenty of water. [9]When they were being tested, even though it was a merciful discipline, they learned how wicked people were tortured when you judged them in anger. [10]You tested your people, as parents test their children, to warn them. But you judged their enemies like a stern king and condemned them. [11]They suffered, whether they were near your people or far from them. [12]Their sorrow was doubled; they groaned as they looked back on what had happened. [13]When they learned that their punishment had been of benefit to your people, they realized that it was your work, Lord. [14]The Egyptians had refused to have anything to do with that man who, long before as a baby, had been thrown out and exposed; but as things worked out, they came to be amazed at him. The righteous never suffered a thirst like theirs.

[15]Their wickedness misled them into silly ideas, so that they worshiped snakes and other disgusting animals, creatures without any powers of reason. Because of this, you punished them with millions of such animals, [16]and taught them that punishment for sin takes the same form as the sin itself. [17]Your almighty power, Lord, created the world out of material that had no form at all. You could easily have punished those people by sending an invasion of bears or savage lions. [18]You could have created new and terrible animals, that could breathe fire or roar and send out clouds of smoke, or

f **10:16** and; *or* who.
10:13, 14 Gen 37:12–36; 39:1–23; 41:37–44   **10:15–21** Ex 1:1—15:21   **11:1–5** Ex 15:22—17:16
11:15, 16 Ex 8:1–24; 10:12–15

You could have created new and terrible animals.
(11:18)

shoot out fearful sparks from their eyes.
¹⁹ You could have made animals like these
that would not have to attack those people
to kill them, but could scare them to death
just by looking at them. ²⁰ But this was not
necessary. You could have pursued them with
your justice or struck them dead at the
slightest hint of your power. But you have
chosen to measure, count, and weigh everything you do.

God Is Powerful and Merciful

²¹ You can show your great power any
time you wish, and no one can stand up
against it. ²² In your sight the whole world is
a grain of sand, barely heavy enough to tip a
pair of scales, a drop of dew on the ground
in the morning. ²³ You are powerful enough
to do anything, but you are merciful to
everyone; you overlook our sins and give us
time to repent. ²⁴ You love everything that
exists; you do not despise anything that you
have made. If you had not liked it, you
would not have made it in the first place.
²⁵ How could anything last, if you did not
want it to? How could it endure, if you had
not created it? ²⁶ You have allowed it all to
exist, O Lord, because it is yours, and you
love every living thing.

12 ¹ Your immortal spirit is in every one
of them, ² and so you gently correct
those who sin against you. You remind them
of what they are doing, and warn them about
it, so that they may abandon their evil ways
and put their trust in you, Lord.

The Sins of the Canaanites

³⁻⁴ You hated the people who lived in
your holy land long ago, because they did
horrible things: they practiced magic and
conducted unholy worship; ⁵ they killed children without mercy and ate the flesh and
blood of human beings. They were initiated
into secret rituals.ᵍ ⁶ in which parents murdered their own defenseless children. It was
your will for our ancestors to destroy these
people, ⁷ so that the land which you consider
the most precious of all lands would be a
suitable home for your people. ⁸ But even in
this you showed mercy toward their enemies, since they were only human beings.
You sent hornets ahead of your army, to
destroy the enemy gradually. ⁹ You could
have allowed the righteous to destroy those
ungodly people in battle; you could have
wiped them out immediately with wild animals or with one harsh command. ¹⁰ But
instead, you carried out your sentence gradually, to give them a chance to repent, even
though you knew that they came from evil
stock, that they had been wicked since birth,
and that they would never change their way
of thinking. ¹¹ Their whole nation was
cursed from the start, and though you had
not punished them for their sins, it was not
because you were afraid of anyone.

God Is Sovereign

¹² You created those wicked people, and
no one can speak in their defense or condemn you for destroying them. No one can
question what you have done or challenge
your judgment. ¹³ All things are under your
care, and there is no other god to whom you
must justify your decisions. ¹⁴ No king or
ruler on earth can accuse you of punishing
those people unfairly. ¹⁵ You are righteous,

ᵍ **12:5** They were . . . rituals; *Greek unclear.*
12:3–7 Deut 12:31; 18:9–13　**12:8** Ex 23:28

and you rule everything righteously. You have never used your power to condemn a person who does not deserve to be punished. 16 Your strength is the source of justice. You can show mercy to everyone, because you are the Lord of all. 17 You show your strength when people doubt that your power is perfect, and you punish anyone who knows your power but dares to ignore it. 18 Even though you have absolute power, you are a merciful judge. You could take action against us whenever you like, but instead, you rule us with great patience.

19 By the things you have done you have taught your people that a person who is righteous must also be kind. You have given your people abundant hope by allowing them to repent of their sins. 20 You were very careful and patient in punishing your people's enemies; even when they deserved to die, you gave them every opportunity to give up their sinful ways. 21 But you judged your own people very strictly, even though you had made covenants with their ancestors and had solemnly promised to give them good things.

22 Yes, you punish us, but you punish our enemies ten thousand times more, so that when we judge others, we may remember your goodness, and when we are being judged, we may look for mercy.

The Punishment of the Egyptians

23 And so you tormented those who were foolish enough to live wickedly—you tormented them with the horrible things they worshiped. 24 They had wandered far away from the truth and worshiped the most disgusting and horrible animals. They were deceived as easily as little children. 25 And so you punished them for their stupidity, and your judgment made them look like fools. 26 It was a light punishment, but those who pay no attention to such warnings deserve to feel the full weight of God's judgment. 27 When they were punished with those creatures they considered gods, they became bitterly disillusioned and recognized that the true God was the one they had always refused to acknowledge. That is why they suffered the final punishment.

13:10—14:31 Isa 44:9–20; Jer 10:1–16; Bar 6:8–73

The Foolishness of Nature Worship

13 1 Anyone who does not know God is simply foolish. Such people look at the good things around them and still fail to see the living God. They have studied the things he made, but they have not recognized the one who made them. 2 Instead, they suppose that the gods who rule the world are fire or wind or storm or the circling stars or rushing water or the heavenly bodies. 3 People were so delighted with the beauty of these things that they thought they must be gods, but they should have realized that these things have a master and that he is much greater than all of them, for he is the creator of beauty, and he created them. 4 Since people are amazed at the power of these things, and how they behave, they ought to learn from them that their maker is far more powerful. 5 When we realize how vast and beautiful the creation is, we are learning about the Creator at the same time.

6 But maybe we are too harsh with these people. After all, they may have really wanted to find God, but couldn't. 7 Surrounded by God's works, they keep on looking at them, until they are finally convinced that because the things they see are so beautiful, they must be gods. 8 But still, these people really have no excuse. 9 If they had enough intelligence to speculate about the nature of the universe, why did they never find the Lord of all things?

The Foolishness of Idolatry

10 But the most miserable people of all are those who rest their hopes on lifeless things, who worship things that have been made by human hands—images of animals artistically made from gold and silver, or some useless stone carved by someone years ago. 11 A skilled woodworker may saw down some suitable tree, carefully strip off the bark, and then, with skillful craftsmanship, make from it an object that will serve some useful purpose. 12 He will take the leftover pieces and use them as firewood to cook a meal that he can sit down to and enjoy. 13 But among that scrap wood he may take one piece that isn't

good for anything—maybe it's crooked and full of knots—and carefully carve it in his leisure time, using spare moments to shape it into the crude image of a person, 14or maybe of some worthless animal. He paints it all over with red, covering up every flaw in the work. 15Then he prepares a suitable place in the wall for it and fastens it in place with iron nails. 16He is careful to keep it from falling, because he knows it is only an idol and needs help; it cannot help itself. 17But he is not ashamed to pray to this life-less thing about his marriage, his children, and his possessions. 18It is weak, but he prays to it for health. It is dead, but he prays to it for life. It has no experience, but he prays to it for help. It cannot walk, but he prays to it for a successful journey. 19Its hands have no power, but he asks it to help him—in business, in making money, and in his work.

. . . . It is dead, but he prays to it for life. (13:18)

Wooden Idols Compared with Noah's Wooden Boat

14 1In the same way, a man getting ready to sail on the raging sea will call for help from a piece of wood that is not as strong as the ship he is about to board. 2Someone designed the ship out of a desire for profit, and a craftsman built it with skill. 3But it is your care, O Father, that steers it; you give it a safe path through the waves of the sea. 4People may go to sea even if they have no skill, because you can save them from any danger. 5It is your will that the things you have made by your wisdom should be put to use. And so people can cross the sea in a boat and come safely to land, because they trust their lives to that small piece of wood.

6This was how it was in ancient times, when a proud race of giants was dying away. The hope of the world escaped on such a boat under your guidance and left the world a new generation to carry on the human race. 7A blessing was on Noah's wooden boat that allowed righteousness to survive, 8but a curse is on an idol made by human hands. A curse is also on the one who makes it, because he works on this perishable thing and then calls it a god. 9Ungodly people and these ungodly things they make are equally hated by God, 10who will punish both the things made and the people who made them. 11And so God's judgment will fall on pagan idols, because, even though they are made from something God created, they became horrible things that trap the souls of foolish people.

The Origins of Idolatry

12Sexual immorality began when idols were invented. They have corrupted human life ever since they were first made. 13Idols have not always existed, nor will they exist forever. 14It was human pride that brought them into the world, and that is why a quick end has been planned for them.

15Once there was a father who was over-whelmed with grief at the untimely death of his child, so he made an image of that child who had been suddenly taken from him. He then honored a dead human being as a god, and handed on secret rituals and ceremonies to those who were under his authority. 16As time went on, this ungodly custom became stronger. Finally it became law, and idols were being worshiped at the command of powerful rulers. 17When people lived too far away to honor a ruler in his presence but were eager to pay honor to this absent king, they would imagine what he must look like, and would then make a likeness of him. 18The ambitious artists who made these like-nesses caused this worship to spread, even among people who did not know the king. 19An artist might want to please some ruler, and so he would use his skill to make the likeness better looking than the actual person. 20Then people would be so attracted by the work of art, that the one whom they had earlier honored now became the object of their worship. ²¹So all this became a deadly trap, because people who were grieving, or under royal authority, would take objects of stone or wood, and give them the honor reserved for the One God.

The Results of Idolatry

²²One thing led to another. It was not enough to be wrong about the knowledge of God. They lived in a state of evil warfare, but they were so ignorant that they called it peace. ²³They murdered children in their initiation rituals, celebrated secret mysteries, and held wild ceremonial orgies with unnatural practices. ²⁴They no longer kept their lives or their marriages pure. A man might kill another by an act of treachery or cause him grief by committing adultery with his wife. ²⁵Everything was a complete riot of bloody murder, robbery, deceit, corruption, faithlessness, disorder, falsehood, ²⁶harassment of innocent people, ingratitude, moral decay, sexual perversion, broken marriages, adultery, and immorality. ²⁷The worship of idols, whose names should never be spoken, is the beginning and the end, the cause and the result of every evil. ²⁸People who worship them lose control of themselves in ecstasy, or pass off lies as prophecies, or live wickedly, or break their word without hesitation. ²⁹They tell lies under oath and expect no punishment, because the idols they put their trust in are lifeless. ³⁰But punishment will finally catch up with them, for two reasons: first, they were in error about God when they worshiped idols, and second, they had so little regard for holiness that they made false statements to deceive people. ³¹When unrighteous people commit sin, they will be hunted down, not by the power of whatever thing they swear by, but by the punishment that sinners deserve.

The True God Gives Immortality

15 ¹But you, our God, are kind and true and patient. You rule the universe with mercy. ²Even if we sin, we know your power and are still yours. But because we know that we belong to you, we will not

sin. ³Knowing you is perfect righteousness. Recognizing your power is where immortality begins. ⁴We have not been misled by any evil product of human skill, by any useless object painted by some artist, or by any idol smeared with different colors. ⁵The sight of such things arouses the passions of foolish people and makes them desire a dead, lifeless image. ⁶Anyone who makes such a thing or desires it or worships it is in love with something evil, and gets what he deserves when he places his hopes in it.

The Foolishness of Worshiping Clay Idols

⁷A potter works the soft clay and carefully shapes each object for our use. Some things he makes are put to good use, and some are not, but he makes them all from the same clay, and shapes them in the same manner. The potter himself decides which objects shall be used for what purposes. ⁸He is a human being who was himself formed from earth only a short while earlier, and after a little while, when he must return the soul

You rule the universe with mercy. (15:1)

that was lent to him, he will go back to the same earth. He is a human being, but he wastes his labor shaping a useless god out of the same clay that he uses to make pots. 9His life will be short, and he will soon have to die, but he is not concerned about that. He wants to compete with those who work in gold, silver, and bronze, and make things like they do. He takes great pride in the things he makes, but they are counterfeit. 10His heart is made of ashes. His hope is cheaper than dirt. His life is not worth as much as his clay, 11because he never came to know the God who shaped him, who breathed into him an active soul and a living spirit. 12He thinks of human life as just a game, a market where he can make a profit. He believes that he must make money however he can, even by evil ways. 13This man, who makes idols and fragile pots from the same clay, knows better than anyone else that he is sinning.

This man, who makes idols and fragile pots (15:13)

The Punishment of the Egyptians

14But the most foolish of all people, showing less sense than babies, were the enemies who oppressed your people, O Lord. 15They thought that all their pagan idols were gods, even though idols cannot see with their eyes, cannot breathe through their nose, cannot hear with their ears, cannot feel with their fingers, and cannot walk on their legs. 16Someone whose spirit is only borrowed made them. No one can ever make a god that is equal to a human being. 17Every person will sooner or later die, but anything he makes with his wicked hands is dead from the start. He himself is better than what he worships. He at least is alive, but what he

worships is not, and never has been. 18Such people worship the most disgusting animals, including even the least intelligent ones. 19Even as animals they are not attractive enough to make anyone want them. God himself passed them by when he put his approval and blessing on the rest of creation.

16 1And so it was appropriate that these people were punished by such creatures—tormented by swarms of them.

2But you, O Lord, did not punish your people in this way; instead, you showed them kindness. You sent them quails to eat, a rare, delicious food to satisfy their hunger. 3You did all this so that the idolaters, when they were hungry, would be unable to eat because of the disgusting creatures sent to them. Your people, however, suffered hunger only a short while, and then they ate the finest food. 4It was necessary for the oppressors to suffer relentless need, while your people saw how their enemies were being tormented.

5When terrible, fierce snakes attacked your people and were killing them with their poison, you did not remain angry long enough to destroy your people. 6This trouble lasted for only a little while, as a warning. Then you gave them a healing symbol, the bronze snake, to remind them of what your Law requires. 7If a person looked at that symbol, he was cured of the snakebite—not by what he saw, but by you, the savior of all mankind. 8By doing this, you also convinced our enemies that you are the one who rescues people from every evil. 9Our enemies died from the bites of locusts and flies; no way was found to cure them, because they deserved to be punished by such creatures. 10But even poisonous snakes could not overcome your people, because you had mercy, helped them, and cured them. 11They were bitten so that they would remember your commands, but they were quickly rescued, in order to keep them from forgetting you completely and depriving themselves of your kindness. 12No medicine or ointment cured them. They were restored to health by your word, O Lord, the word which heals all humanity. 13You have power over life and death; you can bring a person to the brink of death and back again. 14A wicked person may kill someone, but cannot bring the dead person back to life or rescue a soul imprisoned in the world of the dead.

Disastrous Storms Hit Egypt

15No one can possibly escape from you. 16Look at those ungodly people: they refused to recognize you as God, so you punished them with your great power. They were overtaken by terrible storms of rain and hail and were completely destroyed by fire. 17The most amazing thing was that the fire burned all the more fiercely in the water, which usually puts fire out. All the forces of nature fight to defend those who are righteous. 18At one point the flames died down, so that they wouldn't destroy the creatures sent to punish the ungodly. Those people had to learn that they were being overtaken by your judgment. 19But at another point, when surrounded by water, the flames burned more fiercely than fire had ever burned before, and so destroyed the crops on the land where those unrighteous people lived.

The Israelites Receive Manna to Eat

20But this disaster did not strike your people. Instead, you gave them the food of angels. From heaven you sent down bread that was ready to eat, and they did not have to prepare it. The food you gave delighted everyone, no matter what his taste. 21All this showed how lovingly you care for your children. That food satisfied the desire of everyone who ate it; it was changed to suit each person's taste. 22It was food that under normal circumstances would vanish away like snow or ice, but now it did not melt even in the fire. This was meant to teach your people that the same fire that was destroying their enemies' crops during the heavy downpour of rain and hail 23held back its power, so that your own righteous people might have food.

24You created the universe; it is at your command. All creation uses its power to punish unrighteous people, but it becomes mild and kind to those who put their trust in you. 25Creation assumed all kinds of forms to show how you provide generously for all who pray to you.h 26This happened so that the people whom you loved, O Lord, might learn that they are not fed by what they can grow. It is your word that maintains those who put their trust in you. 27The food that was not destroyed by the fire melted when the first ray of sunlight warmed it. 28This was to teach us that we must get up before daybreak to give you thanks, and pray as the sun comes up. 29But an ungrateful person's hope will melt away like frost, and drain away like water that is not being used.

Terror Strikes the Egyptians at Night

17 1O Lord, your acts of judgment are marvelous and hard to explain; that is why people who had not been taught about them went astray. 2When lawless people imagined that they had your holy nation in their power, they were themselves imprisoned in a long night of darkness. They lay in their own houses, shut off from your eternal care. 3They thought that their sins had been secret and unnoticed, shielded from view by a dark curtain of forgetfulness, but now they were horribly afraid, confused, and terrified by ghostly forms. 4Not even the dark corners where they lay could protect them from fear. They were surrounded by horrible noises; grim ghosts with gloomy faces appeared before their eyes. 5No fire had power to give them light, and the brilliant stars could do nothing to relieve that deathly darkness. 6There was only a dreadful fire, lit by no human hand, that shone on them, and in their terror they believed that the real world was even worse than the things they imagined. 7The illusions produced by their magic tricks were put to shame, and all the wisdom they had boasted of came to nothing. 8They had claimed they could drive away all the fears and illnesses of sick minds, but now they themselves were sick with silly, groundless fears. 9Even though nothing dangerous had actually happened, they were terrified by hissing snakes and animals advancing on them. 10And so they died, shaking with fear,

h **16:25** pray to you; *or* are in need.
16:20–29 Ex 16:1–36

afraid even to open their eyes, yet unable to keep them shut.

11 Wickedness is cowardly in itself and stands self-condemned.*i* Someone with a guilty conscience will always imagine things to be worse than they really are. 12 Fear is nothing but the failure to use the help that reason gives. 13 When you lack the confidence to rely on reason, you give in to the fears caused by ignorance.

14 All night long those people slept the same restless sleep, even though the night held no power over them, since it came from the powerless depths of the world of the dead. 15 They were chased by hideous forms and lay paralyzed as they surrendered themselves to the sudden, unexpected fear that came over them. 16 People would suddenly collapse and lie locked in the chains of their own fear. 17 Farmers, shepherds, and laborers out in the countryside were captured by the same inevitable fate and bound in the darkness by the same invisible chain. 18-19 They were panic-stricken by the sighing of the wind or by the singing of birds in the trees or by the roar of rushing water or by the rumble of falling rock or by the sound of unseen creatures running about or by the savage roaring of wild animals or by the echoes from the mountains. 20 In the full light of day, the rest of the world went about its business undisturbed. 21 Only those people were covered by this heavy night, a foretaste of the darkness of death that was waiting for them. They were a burden to themselves that was even heavier than the darkness.

Light Shines on the Israelites

18 1 Yet all the while a brilliant light was shining for your holy people. Their enemies heard their voices, but couldn't see them. They envied the good fortune of your people, who were not suffering. 2 Those enemies could at least be thankful that the people they had wronged were not taking vengeance on them now, and so they begged them to leave.*j*

3 Then you guided your people as they traveled through a country they did not know. You guided them with a pillar of fire. It was like a sun that would not harm them on that glorious journey. 4 But their enemies, who were not allowed to see the light, deserved to be prisoners in darkness, because they had made prisoners of your people. And it was through your people that the eternal light of the Law was going to be given to the world.

The Death of the Egyptian First-Born

5 When your enemies were carrying out their resolve to kill the babies of your holy people, there was one child who was abandoned but later rescued. Then you punished your enemies by killing a great number of their own children. You drowned their whole army at one time in the rushing waters. 6 But our ancestors had been told in advance of what would happen that night, so that they would be cheered and encouraged by confident trust in your promises to them. 7 Your people knew that you would rescue the righteous nation and destroy their enemies. 8 With the same act you punished our enemies and did us the glorious honor of calling us to yourself.

9 During all this time devout people from this righteous nation were secretly offering sacrifices, giving their word to each other that they would keep God's law and share each other's blessings and dangers. Already they were chanting those ancient hymns of praise. 10 But their enemies' pitiful cries of grief echoed everywhere, as they mourned for their dead children. 11 Masters suffered the same punishment as their slaves; the king endured the same loss as the common people. 12 There were too many dead bodies to count. There were not enough people left to bury them all. In a single moment their dearest children died; all of them met death in the same way. 13 These people had paid no attention to any warning, but relied instead on their magical powers. But when their first-born sons were killed, then they recognized that Israel was God's son.

---

i **17:11** Wickedness . . . self-condemned; *Greek unclear.*
18:1–4 Ex 13:17–22

j **18:2** begged them to leave; *or* begged their

14 The short night was half over, and all was quiet and peaceful, **15** when suddenly your threats were carried out! An invincible word of judgment sped from your royal throne in heaven, straight down to that doomed land. It came like a soldier in fierce attack, **16** carrying out your firm command with a fearful weapon, standing with feet on the ground and head touching the sky, filling the land with death. **17** At that moment the people who were about to die had terrible nightmares and were seized by sudden fear. **18** All over the land they lay half-dead and let it be known why they were dying. **19** They knew why they were dying, because their horrible dreams had told them.

Aaron's Prayer Saves the Israelites from Death

20 Death also came to the righteous nation, for an epidemic struck many of them while they were in the desert, but your anger did not last long. **21** There was a certain blameless man who quickly took action to defend them. Acting as their priest, Aaron offered prayers and burned the incense used in asking forgiveness of sins. With prayers and incense as his weapons, he withstood your anger and ended the disaster. By doing this he proved that he was your servant. **22** He overcame the bitter difficulty,*k* but not by his own strength or by military force. Instead, he used prayer to stop the punishment, appealing to the promises you solemnly gave to our ancestors. **23** Dead bodies were already lying in piles, but he stepped in to hold your anger back and to keep it from harming those who were left alive. **24** He wore a long robe decorated with symbols of the universe. In honor of our ancestors he wore four rows of engraved stones on his chest, and your own majesty was represented by the ornament on his turban. **25** The Angel of Death was afraid of these things, and gave up. It was only a slight experience of your wrath, but it was enough.

The Suicidal Stupidity of the Egyptians

19 **1** But the godless continued to feel your pitiless anger until the very end. You knew what they would do before they did it. **2** You knew that even though they let your people go and made them leave quickly, they would change their minds and pursue them. **3-4** While the Egyptians were still mourning at the graves of their dead, they forgot why all this had happened, and they foolishly decided that the people they had begged to leave were runaways. So they chased after them. They were led into this as part of the punishment they deserved, so that they would suffer the rest of the torments they were due to receive. **5** They were to meet a strange death, while your people continued on their miraculous journey.

God Guides and Protects His People

6 The whole nature of the universe was changed at your command so that your people would not be harmed. **7** They saw the cloud over their camp and dry land where water had been. There was a grass-covered plain between the stormy waves of the Red Sea, making it easy for them to cross over. **8** All your people, under your protection, saw this miracle and went across. **9** They pranced about like horses let out to pasture; they skipped about like lambs and praised you, Lord, for saving them. **10** They still remembered what life had been like when they were slaves—how the earth bred gnats instead of cattle, how the river produced huge numbers of frogs instead of fish. **11-12** Later, when they desperately wanted better food, quails came up from the sea to satisfy their hunger. The quail was a bird they had never seen before.

The Punishment of the Egyptians

13 But violent thunder gave warning of the punishment that was coming on those

---

k **18:22** *Probable text* bitter difficulty; *Greek* crowd.
18:20–25 Num 16:41–50

sinners. They suffered a well-deserved punishment for their great wickedness. No nation had ever hated strangers so bitterly. 14 Other people had been known to refuse welcome to strangers who came to them, but these people made slaves of those who were their guests and who had shown them kindness. 15 Every nation will be punished if it does not welcome foreigners, 16 but these people, who had earlier welcomed the foreigners with happy celebrations and treated them as equals, later made them suffer cruelly. 17 These people were also struck with blindness, like the men of Sodom who came to the door of that righteous man Lot. They found themselves in total darkness, as each one groped around to find his own door.

God's Miraculous Power

18 On a harp each string keeps its own pitch, but each sound can be combined with others to make different melodies. That is how it was in those days, when the very elements entered into new combinations. Look at what happened! 19 Land animals took to the water, and swimming creatures came up on the land. 20 Fire burned even in water, which could not put it out. 21 And yet the flames could not burn the flesh of the perishable creatures walking in them and did not melt that heavenly food that would ordinarily have melted like frost.

22 Lord, you have made your people great—glorious in all respects. You have never neglected them. You have given them help, always, everywhere.

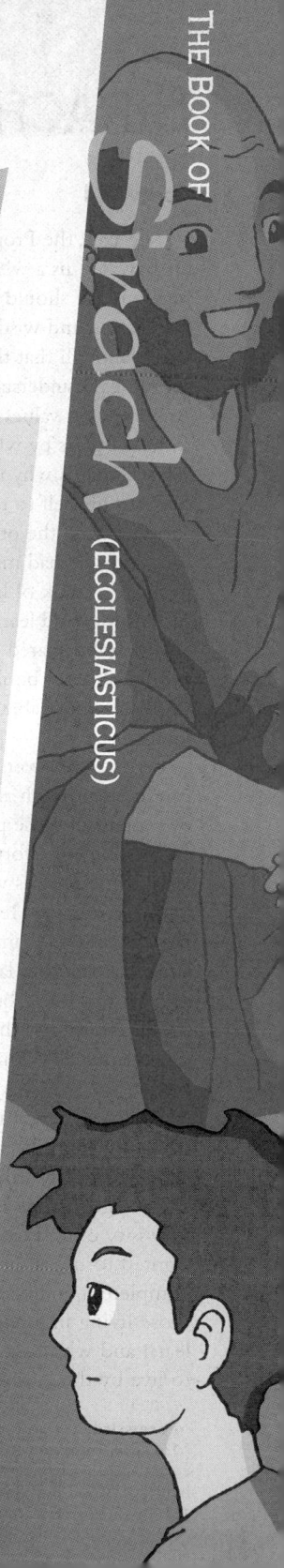

THE BOOK OF*Sirach*

(ECCLESIASTICUS)

Some of the advice in this book might sound out-of-date. Like something your grandfather would say. Actually, somebody's grandfather did say it years before the birth of Jesus. But it is still good advice today!

The author of this book is also named Jesus. Jesus son of Sirach was a wise Jewish teacher who lived in Jerusalem during a time of great change. He saw many Jews forget the ways of their faith and instead accept the Greek customs and beliefs. The author wrote down all kinds of Jewish wisdom. He wrote for the older generation, who were forgetting, and for the younger generation, who had never learned traditional Jewish beliefs. Then his grandson translated it into Greek, so everyone could appreciate the wisdom of the Jewish faith.

Chap. 3

Head_lines_

- Youth: Prepare for Difficult Times (2:1–18)
- Advice on Friendship (6:5–17)
- Honor Your Parents (7:27–28)
- Self-Respect Wins Respect (10:28–29)
- Appearances Can Be Deceiving (11:2–6)
- Only Fools Curse (23:13–15)
- The Works of God Are Beautiful! (43:13–33)

FACTOIDS

Who wrote this book? It was written by Jesus son of Sirach, who lived in the second century BC. It was later translated into Greek by his grandson.
Why was it written? To remind the Jews that traditional Jewish wisdom was better than modern Greek ideas.
What literary style is used? It is a collection of prayers, sayings, hymns, lists, and general advice.
Jesus connection: Jesus' parable about the rich fool (Luke 12:16–21) is very similar to Sirach 11:18–19.
Important themes
- God rewards those who do good and punishes the sinful.
- Small sins can lead to bigger sins.
- We should follow the example of our elders and the great heroes of our faith.

SIRACH

Foreword

The Law, the Prophets, and the later writers have left us a wealth of valuable teachings, and we should praise Israel for the instruction and wisdom they provide. But it is not enough that those who read them should gain understanding for themselves. Anyone who values learning should be able to help others by what he himself says and writes. That is why my grandfather Jesus devoted himself to reading the Law, the Prophets, and the other books of our ancestors. After he had mastered them, he was led to write a book of his own in order to share his wisdom and learning with others, so that anyone who shared his love for learning should have his book available as well, and be all the more able to live according to the Law.

Let me urge you, then, to read this book carefully and with an open mind. And please be patient in those places where, in spite of all my diligent efforts, I may not have translated some phrases very well. What was originally written in Hebrew does not always have exactly the same sense when it is translated into another language.[a] That is true not only of this book, but even of the Law itself, the Prophets, and the other books. The translations differ quite a bit from the original.

I came to Egypt in the thirty-eighth year of King Euergetes' reign and stayed for some time. While I was there, I had the opportunity for a good deal of study and felt the necessity of translating the following book. I wanted to use all my diligence and skill to complete it and make it available for all those living in foreign lands who wish to learn and who have the strength of character to live by the Law of Moses.

In Praise of Wisdom

1 ¹All wisdom comes from the Lord,
   and Wisdom is with him forever.
² Who can count raindrops or the sand
   along the shore?
   Who can count the days of eternity?
³ How high is the sky? How wide is the
   earth?
   How deep is the ocean? How
   profound is Wisdom?
   Can anyone find answers to these
   questions?

Who can count raindrops? (1:2)

⁴ Wisdom was created before anything
   else;
   understanding has always existed.[b]
⁶ Has anyone ever been shown where
   Wisdom originates?
   Does anyone understand her subtle
   cleverness?[c]
⁸ There is only one who is wise,
   and we must stand in awe before his
   throne.
⁹ The Lord himself created Wisdom;
   he saw her and recognized her
   value,
   and so he filled everything he made
   with Wisdom.

---

[a] **Foreword** *The book of Sirach was written in Hebrew, but the writer of this foreword translated it into Greek.*
[b] *1:4 Some manuscripts add verse 5:* The source of Wisdom is the word of God on high; her ways are eternal commands.   [c] *1:6 Some manuscripts add verse 7:* To whom has the knowledge of Wisdom been revealed? Who has understood her great experience?
1:1 Prov 2:6   **1:9** Prov 8:22–31; Sir 24:9

¹⁰He gave some measure of Wisdom to
   everyone,
   but poured her out on those who love
   him.

¹¹If you fear the Lord, honor and pride will
   be yours;
   you will be crowned with happiness
   and joy.

¹²To honor the Lord is a heartfelt delight;
   it will give you a long and happy life,

¹³and at the end of your days all will go
   well for you.
   God will bless you on the day of your
   death.

¹⁴To fear the Lord is the first step to
   Wisdom.
   Wisdom is given to the faithful in their
   mothers' wombs.

¹⁵She has lived with us from ancient times,
   and generations to come will rely on
   her.

¹⁶To fear the Lord is Wisdom at her fullest;
   she satisfies us completely with her gifts

¹⁷and fills our homes and our barns
   with all that our hearts can desire.

¹⁸To fear the Lord is the flower of Wisdom
   that blossoms with peace and good
   health. ᵈ

¹⁹She sends knowledge and understanding
   like the rain,
   and increases the honor of those who
   receive her.

²⁰To fear the Lord is the root of Wisdom;
   her branches are long life. ᵉ

Self-control

²²There is no excuse for unjustified anger;
it can bring about your downfall. ²³Wait and
be patient, and later you will be glad you did.
²⁴Keep quiet until the right time to speak,
and you will gain a reputation for good sense.

Wisdom and Reverence for God

²⁵Wisdom has a treasury of wise sayings,
but sinners have nothing but contempt for
godliness. ²⁶If you want to be wise, keep the
Lord's commands, and he will give you Wisdom in abundance. ²⁷Fearing the Lord is
Wisdom and an education in itself. He is
pleased by loyalty and humility. ²⁸Be faithful
in the practice of your religion; when you
worship the Lord, do it with all your heart.
²⁹Be careful about what you say, and don't
be a hypocrite. ³⁰Don't be arrogant; you may
suffer a fall and be disgraced. The Lord will
reveal your secrets and humble you in front
of everyone in the synagogue, because you
did not come there with reverence for the
Lord, but with a heart full of hypocrisy.

Faithfulness to God

2 ¹My child, if you are going to serve the
   Lord, be prepared for times when you
will be put to the test. ²Be sincere and
determined. Keep calm when trouble comes.
³Stay with the Lord; never abandon him, and
you will be prosperous at the end of your
days. ⁴Accept whatever happens to you.
Even if you suffer humiliation, be patient.
⁵Gold is tested by fire, and human character
is tested in the furnace of humiliation. ⁶Trust
the Lord, and he will help you. Walk straight
in his ways, and put your hope in him.

⁷All you that fear the Lord, wait for him
to show you his mercy. Do not turn away
from him, or you will fall. ⁸All you that fear
the Lord, trust him, and you will certainly be
rewarded. ⁹All you that fear the Lord, look
forward to his blessings of mercy and eternal
happiness.

¹⁰Think back to the ancient generations
and consider this: has the Lord ever disappointed anyone who put his hope in him?
Has the Lord ever abandoned anyone who
held him in constant reverence? Has the
Lord ever ignored anyone who prayed to
him? ¹¹The Lord is kind and merciful; he
forgives our sins and keeps us safe in time of
trouble. ¹²But those who lose their nerve are
doomed—all those sinners who try to have
it both ways! ¹³Doom is sure to come for
those who lose their courage; they have no
faith, and so they will have no protection.
¹⁴Doom is sure to come for those who lose

ᵈ **1:18** *Some manuscripts add:* He saw her and recognized her value *(see 1:9).* ᵉ **1:20** *Some manuscripts add verse*
21: Honoring the Lord takes sin away; where the fear of the Lord is found, it turns away anger.
1:17 Wis 7:11   **1:20** Prov 3:16; 4:10   **2:5** Wis 3:5, 6; 1 Pet 1:7

their hope. What will they do when the Lord comes to judge them?

15 Those who fear the Lord do not disobey his commands; those who love him will live as he wants them to live. 16 Those who fear and love the Lord will try to please him and devote themselves to the Law. 17 Those who fear the Lord are always ready to serve him. They humble themselves before him, and say, 18 "We place our destiny in the hands of the Lord, not in human hands, because his mercy is as great as his majesty."

Duties to Parents

3 1 Children, listen to me; I am your father. Do what I tell you and you will be safe, 2 for the Lord has given fathers authority over their children and given children the obligation to obey their mothers. 3 If you respect your father, you can make up for your sins, 4 and if you honor your mother, you are earning great wealth. 5 If you respect your father, one day your own children will make you happy; the Lord will hear your prayers. 6 If you obey the Lord by honoring your father and making your mother happy, you will live a long life. 7 Obey your parents as if you were their slave. 8 Honor your father

Obey the Lord by . . . making your mother happy.
(3:6)

in everything you do and say, so that you may receive his blessing. 9 When parents give their blessing, they give strength to their children's homes, but when they curse their children, they destroy the very foundations.

10 Never seek honor for yourself at your father's expense; it is not to your credit if he is dishonored. 11 Your own honor comes from the respect that you show to your father. If children do not honor their mothers, it is their own disgrace. 12 My child, take care of your father when he grows old; give him no cause for worry as long as he lives. 13 Be sympathetic even if his mind fails him; don't look down on him just because you are strong and healthy. 14 The Lord will not forget the kindness you show to your father; it will help you make up for your sins. 15 When you are in trouble, the Lord will remember your kindness and will help you; your sins will melt away like frost in warm sunshine. 16 Those who abandon their parents or give them cause for anger may as well be cursing the Lord; they are already under the Lord's curse.

Humility

17 My child, be humble in everything you do, and people will appreciate it more than gifts.[f] 18 The greater you become, the more humble you should be; then the Lord will be pleased with you.[g] 20 The Lord's power is great, and he is honored by those who are humble. 21 Don't try to understand things that are too hard for you, or investigate matters that are beyond your power to know. 22 Concentrate on the Law, which has been given to you. You do not need to know about things which the Lord has not revealed, 23 so don't concern yourself with them. After all, what has been shown to you is beyond human power to understand. 24 Many people have been misled by their own opinions; their wrong ideas have warped their judgment.[h]

[f] 3:17 *Hebrew* people . . . gifts; *Greek* those whom the Lord approves will love you.   [g] 3:18 *Some Greek manuscripts add verse 19:* Many are exalted and esteemed, but God's secrets are revealed to the humble; *Hebrew:* God's mercy is great, and he reveals his secrets to those who are humble.   [h] 3:24 *Some Greek manuscripts add verse 25:* If you have no eyes, you cannot see; don't claim to have knowledge if you don't have it; *Hebrew has, after verse 27:* If you have no eyes, you cannot see; if you have no knowledge, you cannot have Wisdom.
2:15, 16 Wis 6:18; Jn 14:15, 21, 23   **3:8** Ex 20:12   **3:18** Phil 2:3   **3:22** Deut 29:29

The greater you become, the more humble you should be. (3:18)

26Stubbornness will get you into trouble at the end. If you live dangerously, it will kill you. 27A stubborn person will be burdened down with troubles. Sinners go on adding one sin to another. 28There is no cure for the troubles that arrogant people have; wickedness has taken deep root in them. 29Intelligent people will learn from proverbs and parables. They listen well because they want to learn.

Giving to the Poor

30Giving to the poor can make up for sin, just as water can put out a blazing fire. 31Anyone who responds to others with acts of kindness is thinking of the future, because he will find help if he ever falls on hard times.

4 1My child, don't prevent the poor from making a living, or keep them waiting in their need. 2Never give a hungry person any cause for resentment or anger. 3Don't add to the troubles of someone who is already desperate. If he is in need, don't put off giving to him. 4-5Don't refuse to help a beggar who is in distress. Don't turn your back on a poor person or give him any reason to curse you. 6If he becomes so bitter that he does curse you, his Creator will hear his prayer.

7Make yourself popular in the synagogue. Bow your head to men of authority. 8Listen to what the poor have to say, and answer them politely. 9Protect people from those who want to wrong them, and be firm in your judgments. 10Be like a father to orphans, and provide widows with the help their husbands can no longer give them. Then you will be like a child of the Most High, and he will love you more than your own mother does.

Wisdom as a Teacher

11Wisdom takes care of those who look for her; she raises them to greatness. 12Loving her is loving life itself; rising early to look for her is pure joy. 13Anyone who obtains Wisdom will be greatly honored. Wherever he goes, the Lord will bless him. 14Wisdom's servants are the servants of the Holy One, and the Lord loves everyone who loves her. 15Those who obey her will give sound judgments;[i] those who pay attention to her have true security. 16Put your trust in Wisdom, and you will possess her and pass her on to your descendants. 17At first, Wisdom will lead you along difficult paths. She will make you so afraid that you will think you cannot go on. The discipline she demands will be tormenting, and she will put you to the test with her requirements until she trusts you[j] completely. 18Then she will come to you with no delay, reveal her secrets to you, and make you happy. 19But if you go astray, she will abandon you and let you go to your own ruin.

Self-confidence

20Take advantage of opportunities, but guard yourself against evil. Don't underrate yourself. 21Humility deserves honor and respect, but a low opinion of yourself leads to sin. 22Do not let others have their way at your expense; do not bring on your own ruin by giving up your rights. 23Never hesitate to speak out when the occasion[k] calls for it. Don't hide your wisdom.[l] 24Your

Sirach

---

*i 4:15 Hebrew give sound judgments; Greek judge nations.   j 4:17 she trusts you; or you trust her.
k 4:23 Probable text the occasion; Greek safety.   l 4:23 Hebrew Don't hide your wisdom; most Greek manuscripts do not have these words; other Greek manuscripts Don't hide your wisdom for the sake of appearances.*

wisdom and education can be known only by what you say. 25Do not, however, go against the truth, and remember that you do not know everything. 26Don't be ashamed to confess your sins; there's no point in trying to stop a river from flowing. 27Don't allow yourself to be dominated by someone who is stupid or show partiality to influential people. 28Stand up for what is right, even if it costs you your life; the Lord God will be fighting on your side.

29Don't be quick to speak or lazy and negligent in your work. 30Don't act like a lion at home or be suspicious of your servants. 31Don't stick out your hand to get something if you're going to be tightfisted when the time comes to pay it back.

Don't Be Presumptuous

5 1Don't rely on money to make you independent. 2Don't think you have to have everything you want, and then spend your energy trying to get it. 3Don't think that no one can exercise authority over you; if you do, the Lord is certain to punish you. 4Don't think that you can sin and get away with it; the Lord does not mind waiting to punish you. 5Don't be so certain of the Lord's forgiveness that you go on committing one sin after another. 6Don't think that his mercy is so great that he will forgive your sins no matter how many they are. He does show mercy, but he also shows his furious anger with sinners. 7Come back to the Lord quickly. Don't think that you can keep putting it off. His anger can come upon you suddenly, and you will die under his punishment. 8Don't rely on dishonest wealth; it will do you no good on that day of disaster.

Sincerity and Self-control

9-10Be certain about what you believe and consistent in what you say. Don't try to please everyone or agree with everything people say.*m* 11Always be ready to listen, but take your time in answering. 12Answer only

if you know what to say, and if you don't know what to say, keep quiet. 13Speaking can bring you either honor or disgrace; what you say can ruin you.

Answer only if you know what to say, and if you don't . . . keep quiet. (5:12)

14Don't get a reputation for being a gossip, and don't tell tales that will hurt people. Just as robbers will suffer disgrace, so liars will suffer severe condemnation. 15Do nothing destructive,*n* whether it seems insignificant or not,

6 1and do not be an enemy when you should be a friend. A bad reputation brings you the disgrace that lying sinners deserve. 2Do not let your passions carry you away; this can tear your soul to pieces like a bull.*o* 3You will be left like a dead tree without any leaves or fruit. 4Evil desire will destroy you and make you a joke to your enemies.

Friendship

5If you are polite and courteous, you will enjoy the friendship of many people. 6Exchange greetings with many, but take advice from only one person out of a thousand. 7When you make friends, don't be too quick to trust them; make sure that they have proved themselves. 8Some people will be your friends only when it is convenient

---

m 5:9–10 Hebrew everything people say; *Greek adds* That is what double-tongued sinners do.   *n 5:15 Hebrew* Do nothing destructive; *Greek* Do not be ignorant in anything.   *o 6:2 Verse 2 in both Greek and Hebrew is unclear.*
4:31 Acts 20:35   **5:4** Eccl 8:11

for them, but they won't stand by you in trouble. ⁹Others will fall out with you over some argument, and then embarrass you by letting everyone know about it. ¹⁰⁻¹¹Others will sit at your table as long as things are going well; they will stick to you like your shadow and give orders to your servants, but they will not stand by you in trouble. ¹²If your situation takes a turn for the worse, they will turn against you, and you won't be able to find them anywhere.

¹³Stay away from your enemies and be on guard against your friends. ¹⁴A loyal friend is like a safe shelter; find one, and you have found a treasure. ¹⁵Nothing else is as valuable; there is no way of putting a price on it. ¹⁶A loyal friend is like a medicine that keeps you in good health. Only those who fear the Lord can find such a friend. ¹⁷A person who fears the Lord can make real friendships, because he will treat his friends as he does himself.ᵖ

Learn from Wisdom

¹⁸My child, learn to value Wisdom while you are young, and you will still be able to find her when you grow old. ¹⁹Work as hard to find Wisdom as a farmer works to plow and plant his fields; then you can expect a good harvest. You will have to work at it for a while, but you will soon be enjoying what you have earned. ²⁰Undisciplined people find Wisdom's demands too hard and don't have enough determination to meet them. ²¹Her requirements are a burden heavier than they are willing to bear, and they quickly lay them aside. ²²"Discipline" means just that—discipline,�q and not many people are able to discipline themselves.

²³My child, listen to me and take my advice. ²⁴Put Wisdom's chains around your feet and her yoke around your neck. ²⁵Carry her on your shoulder and don't be resentful of her bonds. ²⁶Follow Wisdom, and keep to her ways with all your heart. ²⁷Go looking for her, and she will reveal herself to you. Take hold of her and don't let go. ²⁸Then you will discover the peace of mind she

offers, and she will become your joy. ²⁹⁻³⁰The signs of slavery you wear will become signs of royal majesty. Her chains will be your protection, and you will wear her yoke like a magnificent robe. ³¹You will wear Wisdom like a splendid crown.

³²My child, you can learn if you want to. You can be clever if you are determined to be. ³³If you are willing to listen, you will learn and become wise. ³⁴Go where the old people are; find someone who is wise, and stay with him. ³⁵Be ready to listen when religious people speak, and don't miss anything that shows insight. ³⁶If you find someone with understanding, get up early to call on him; wear out his doorstep with your visits.

³⁷Devote all your time to studying the Lord's commands and thinking about them. He will give you the insight and wisdom you are looking for.

Miscellaneous Advice

7 ¹⁻²If you do no wrong, no wrong will ever come to you. ³Do not plow the ground to plant seeds of injustice; you may reap a bigger harvest than you expect.

⁴Don't ask the Lord for a place of honor or ask the king for an important position. ⁵Don't try to convince the Lord that you are righteous or make a show of your wisdom before the king. ⁶Don't set your heart on being a judge, unless you have the strength of character it takes to put an end to injustice. If you let yourself be influenced by someone in a position of power, your integrity will be damaged. ⁷Don't commit any crime against the general public, and don't disgrace yourself among your townspeople.

⁸Don't commit the same sin twice. The punishment you get the first time ought to be enough.

⁹Don't think that God Most High is going to take into account how very generous you are and so accept any offering you decide to make.

¹⁰Never get tired of praying, and never miss a chance to give to the poor.

ᵖ **6:17** because . . . himself; or because his friends will also fear the Lord.   q **6:22** Hebrew "Discipline" . . . discipline; Greek "Wisdom" . . . wisdom.
6:19 Jas 5:7, 8   **6:37** Josh 1:8; Ps 1:2

¹¹Don't laugh at someone who has been humiliated. It is the Lord who humbles a person, but the Lord also raises him up again.

¹²Don't think up lies to tell about your friends. ¹³Don't tell lies at all. It never does any good.

¹⁴In an official assembly, don't get up and talk a lot of nonsense. And don't repeat yourself when you pray.

¹⁵Don't try to avoid farm work or other hard labor; the Most High has given us these jobs to do.

¹⁶Don't join up with a crowd of sinners; remember that the Lord's punishment is sure to come.

¹⁷Be very humble, because the decay of death awaits us all.ʳ

Relations with Others

¹⁸Don't betray a friend for money. Don't betray a real friend for all the gold in the world.

¹⁹Don't miss your chance to marry a wise and good woman. A gracious wife is worth more than gold.

²⁰Don't mistreat servants who do their work well, or employees who do their best for you.

²¹Show the same love to wise servants that you would show to yourself,ˢ and let them have their freedom.

²²Take good care of any animals you own. If they make money for you, keep them.

²³If you have sons, educate them. Teach them self-discipline while they are young.

²⁴If you have daughters, keep them virtuous, and don't be too indulgent with them.
²⁵When you give your daughter in marriage, you have finished a great task, but give her to a sensible man.

²⁶If you have a good wife, do not divorce her, but do not trust yourself to someone you don't love.

²⁷Honor your father with all your heart, and never forget how your mother suffered when you were born. ²⁸Remember that you

owe your life to them. How can you ever repay them for all they have done for you?

²⁹Fear the Lord with all your heart, and have respect for his priests. ³⁰Love your Creator with all your strength, and give his ministers your support. ³¹Honor the Lord and respect the priests. Supply them with what you have been commanded to give: the first produce, the offering for sin, the shoulder of the sacrificial animal—all the required sacrifices and offerings.

³²Give your help to the poor, and the Lord will give you his perfect blessing. ³³Be generous to every living soul, and be gracious to the memory of the dead. ³⁴Show sympathy to those who have lost a loved one, and mourn with them. ³⁵Do not hesitate to visit the sick. You will be loved for things like these. ³⁶Whatever you do, remember that some day you must die. As long as you keep this in mind, you will never sin.

Teach them self-discipline while they are young. (7:23)

Using Common Sense

8 ¹Do not challenge a person who has influence; you may fall into his power. ²Do not quarrel with someone rich; he may bribe people to turn against you. Gold has destroyed many people and corrupted kings. ³Don't argue with someone who talks too much; you will just be adding fuel to his fire. ⁴Don't make fun of someone who has bad manners; he may insult your ancestors.

ʳ **7:17** *Hebrew* the decay . . . all; *Greek* the punishment of the ungodly is fire and worms.   ˢ **7:21** *Hebrew* Show the same love . . . yourself; *Greek* Show love to a wise servant.
7:21 Ex 21:2; Deut 15:12–15   **7:27, 28** Ex 20:12

5Don't criticize someone if he is already turning away from sin. Remember that we are all guilty. 6Never think less of someone because he is old; some of us are growing old, too. 7Don't be happy over the death of anyone; remember that all of us must die.

8Do not disregard what the wise have said. Study their proverbs; from them you can learn to be cultured and to serve great people. 9Pay attention to what old people say, for they learned from those who came before them. You can learn from them, and they can teach you how to have an answer ready when you need one.

10You should not provide a sinner with more opportunity to sin. You might get hurt yourself; it's as easy as getting burned while adding logs to a fire. 11You should not get up and walk out on someone who is insolent. He might twist your words and use them against you. 12You should not lend anything to someone more powerful than you. If you do, you might as well consider it lost. 13You should not guarantee anyone else's loan to an extent that you cannot afford. You must be prepared to pay any such guarantee. 14You should not bring a lawsuit against a judge. He will win because of his position. 15You should not travel with anyone who is reckless. It will cause you nothing but trouble. He will do any foolish thing he pleases, and you will die with him.

16You should not get into an argument with anyone who has a hot temper or go to some place where the two of you will be alone. Violence means nothing to such a person, and he will attack you when there is no one to help you. 17You should not ask a stupid person for advice. He will not be able to keep secret what you tell him. 18You should not do anything in front of a stranger that should be kept secret. There is no way of knowing what will happen if you do. 19You should not reveal your most private thoughts to anyone. If you do, you may as well throw away any chance of happiness.[t]

Advice about Women

9 1Don't be jealous of the wife you love. You will only be teaching her how to do you harm. 2Do not surrender your dignity to any woman. 3Keep away from other men's wives[u] or they will trap you. 4Don't keep company with female musicians; they will trick you. 5Don't look too intently at a virgin, or you may find yourself forced to pay a bride price. 6Don't give yourself to prostitutes, or you may lose everything you own. 7So don't go looking about in the streets or wandering around in the rundown parts of town. 8When you see a good-looking woman, look the other way; don't let your mind dwell on the beauty of any woman who is not your wife. Many men have been led astray by a woman's beauty. It kindles passion as if it were fire. 9Don't sit down to eat with another man's wife or join her for a drink. You may give in to the temptation of her charms and be destroyed by your passion.

When you see a good-looking woman, look the other way. (9:8)

Friendships with Others

10Never abandon old friends; you will never find a new one who can take their place. Friendship is like wine; it gets better as it grows older. 11Don't be jealous of a sinner's success; you don't know what kind of disaster is in store for him. 12Don't take

[t] **8:19** *Hebrew* If . . . happiness; *Greek* And don't let anyone do you a favor.   [u] **9:3** *Hebrew* other men's wives; *Greek* immoral women.
9:1 Num 5:12–15

Sirach

pleasure in the things that make ungodly people happy; remember that they will be held guilty as long as they live. [13]If you keep away from someone who has the power to put you to death, you will not have to fear for your life; but if you must go near him, be very careful, or he may kill you. Be conscious that you are walking among hidden traps, that you are an easy target.

[14]Get to know the people around you as well as you can, and take advice only from those who are qualified to give it. [15]Engage in conversation with intelligent people, and let the Law of the Most High be the topic of your discussions. [16]Choose righteous people for your dinner companions. Your chief pride should be your fear of the Lord.

Rulers

[17]A skilled worker is admired for the things he makes, and a leader's wisdom is proved by his words. [18]Someone who speaks rashly and recklessly is feared and hated by everyone in town. **10** [1]A wise ruler will educate his people, and his government will be orderly. [2]All the officials and all the citizens will be like their ruler. [3]An uneducated king will ruin his people, but a government will grow strong if its rulers are wise. [4]The Lord sees to the government of the world and brings the right person to power at the right time. [5]The success of that person is in the Lord's hands. The Lord is the source of the honor given to any official.

Pride

[6]Don't be angry with someone for every little thing he does wrong. Don't do anything out of injured pride. [7]Arrogance and injustice are hated by both the Lord and people. [8]Injustice, arrogance, and wealth cause nations to fall from power, and others then rise to take their place. [9]We are only dust and ashes; what have we got to be proud of? Our body decays even while we are alive.[v] [10]A long illness puzzles the

doctor.[w] Even a king may be alive today and dead tomorrow. [11]When a person dies, all he then possesses is worms, flies, and maggots.

[12]Pride has its beginning when a person abandons the Lord, his maker. [13]Pride is like a fountain pouring out sin, and whoever persists in it will be full of wickedness. That is why the Lord brought terrible punishments on some people and completely destroyed them. [14]The Lord has overthrown kings and put humbler people in their place. [15]The Lord has pulled up nations by the roots and established humbler ones in their place. [16]The Lord has overthrown empires and completely devastated their lands. [17]He destroyed some so completely that they are not even remembered any more. [18]The Creator never intended for human beings to be arrogant and violent.

People Who Should Be Honored

[19]Who deserves honor? The human race does, because people fear the Lord. Who does not deserve honor? The human race does not, because people break the Lord's commands. [20]A leader should be honored by those who follow him, and the Lord honors those who fear him.[x]

[22]Rich people, famous people, and poor people all take pride in their fear of the Lord. [23]It is not right to refuse honor to a poor person who is intelligent, and it is not right to give honor to a sinner. [24]People of influence, rulers, and judges will be honored, but none of them is greater than a person who fears the Lord. [25]A slave who is wise will have free citizens serving him; and if they are sensible, they will not resent it.

Humility and Self-respect

[26]When you do your work, don't make a show of your skill, and don't try to put on a show when you are in trouble. [27]It is better to work and have more than you need than to go around boasting but hungry.

[28]My child, keep your self-respect, but

---

v **10:9** Our body . . . alive; *this sentence in both Greek and Hebrew is unclear.*   *w* **10:10** A long . . . doctor; *this sentence in both Greek and Hebrew is unclear.*   *x* **10:20** *Some manuscripts add verse 21:* Success begins with fear of the Lord, but failure begins with stubbornness and arrogance.
10:14 1 Sam 2:8; Lk 1:52

remain modest. Value yourself at your true worth. ²⁹There is no excuse for a person to run himself down. No one respects a person who has no respect for himself. ³⁰Poor people can be honored for their good sense, and rich people can be honored for their wealth. ³¹If someone is honored while he is poor, think how much he will be honored if he becomes rich! If someone is despised while he is rich, think how much more he will be

11 despised if he becomes poor! ¹If a poor person is wise, he has good reason to be proud, and he will be thought of as someone great.

Appearances

²Do not compliment a person on his good looks. On the other hand, do not look down on someone who is unattractive. ³Compared to most flying things, a bee is very small, but the honey it makes is the sweetest of foods. ⁴Don't make fun of someone who has fallen on hard times and is dressed in rags.ʸ The Lord does wonderful things that human beings never notice. ⁵Many are the kings who have ended their careers sitting on the ground, while their crowns were worn by those no one had heard of before. ⁶Many are the rulers who have suffered disgrace. Many are the famous people who have fallen into the power of others.

Be Cautious

⁷Before you start criticizing, get your facts straight and think the matter through. ⁸Don't interrupt while someone is speaking; hear what he has to say before you answer. ⁹Don't get into an argument over something that is none of your business. Don't take part in decisions that are being made by sinners. ¹⁰My child, don't get involved in too many things. If you try to do too much, you will suffer for it. You won't be able to finish your work, and you won't be able to get away from it either. ¹¹For instance, here is someone who never stops working like a slave, but gets further behind all the time.

Don't Judge a Book . . .

Have you ever heard an adult say, "Don't judge a book by its cover"? It means don't be fooled by the outside appearance of a person. Do not think that a good-looking person is brave or considerate or smart or trustworthy just because of good looks. And do not think that a plain-looking person is dull or afraid or uncaring or useless just because of plain looks.

Expensive clothes, jewelry, and shoes do not make a person a good friend. What's more important in a friend—money or trust? What's more important—good looks or a caring heart? What's more important—the color of a person's skin or a person's personality? As Sirach says, the bee is very small and ordinary, but it makes honey, something sweeter than anything a larger animal produces!

Money can make you spoiled and demanding. Popularity can make you selfish and inconsiderate. Don't be fooled! Sometimes the most unpopular students in school would make the nicest, most understanding, and appreciative friends. Good relationships are based on values deeper than money, good looks, or popularity. Remember that when you want to invite someone to a movie or a dance!

— Sirach 11:2–6

¹²On the other hand, someone else may be very poor and not up to his task. He may be slow, and he may need help, but the Lord is

ʸ **11:4** *Hebrew* Don't . . . rags; *Greek* Don't take pride in fine clothes, and don't let compliments go to your head.

pleased with him and pulls him out of his bad situation. ¹³When he is back on his feet again, everyone is astounded.

¹⁴Everything comes from the Lord: success and failure, poverty and wealth, life and death. ¹⁵Wisdom, understanding, knowledge of the Law, love, and the doing of good deeds—all these come from the Lord. ¹⁶Error and darkness have been with sinners from the beginning, and those who enjoy evil will have it with them into their old age. ¹⁷The Lord's gifts to religious people are gifts that endure. If he approves of you, you will always be successful. ¹⁸Someone may grow rich by working hard and denying himself pleasure, but what does he get for it? ¹⁹He says to himself, "Now I can finally sit back and enjoy what I have worked for." But he has no idea how long it will be before he must die and leave his wealth to others.

²⁰Stand by your duty and stick to it; grow old at your work. ²¹Don't be jealous of what sinners achieve; just stick to your own work, and trust the Lord. It is very easy for the Lord to make a poor person suddenly rich. ²²Devout people will receive the Lord's blessing as their reward, and that blessing can be given in a moment. ²³Don't be concerned about what you need, or what success the future holds for you. ²⁴On the other hand, don't think that you have everything you need or that nothing can go wrong for you in the future. ²⁵When things are going well, people don't think about hard times; and when things are going badly, they forget about prosperity. ²⁶The Lord can easily wait until the day of our death to reward or punish us. ²⁷At that time our deeds are open for all to see; all our happiness can be erased in that one moment of misery. ²⁸So then, don't think of anyone's life as happy until it is over, because all the evidence is not in until the person is dead.ᶻ

Be Careful in Choosing Friends

²⁹Be careful about the kind of person you invite into your home, because clever people can fool you in many ways. ³⁰A proud person is a decoy to lure you into danger; like a spy, he will look for your weaknesses.ᵃ ³¹He will make good appear evil and find fault with the noblest actions. ³²A single spark can set a pile of coals ablaze, and a sinner is just waiting for a chance to do violence. ³³Watch out for such people and their evil plans; they will ruin you permanently. ³⁴If you bring a stranger home with you, it will only cause trouble, even between you and your own family.

12 ¹When you do a good deed, make sure you know who is benefiting from it; then what you do will not be wasted.ᵇ ²You will be repaid for any kindness you show to a devout person. If he doesn't repay you, the Most High will. ³No good ever comes to a person who gives comfort to the wicked; it is not a righteous act.ᶜ ⁴Give to religious people, but don't help sinners. ⁵Do good to humble people, but don't give anything to those who are not devout. Don't give them food, or they will use your kindness against you. Every good thing you do for such people will bring you twice as much trouble in return. ⁶The Most High himself hates sinners, and he will punish them. ⁷Give to good people, but do not help sinners.

⁸When things are going well, it is hard to tell who your real friends are, but in hard times you can recognize your enemies; ⁹even your friends will leave you then. But when you are successful, your enemies will act like friends.ᵈ ¹⁰Never trust an enemy; his

But when you are successful, your enemies will act like friends. (12:9)

ᶻ **11:28** *Hebrew* all . . . dead; *Greek* a man will be known by his children.   ᵃ **11:30** *Hebrew* look . . . weaknesses; *Greek* wait for your downfall.   ᵇ **12:1** what you do . . . wasted; *or* you will be thanked for what you do.
ᶜ **12:3** *Hebrew* gives . . . act; *Greek* makes evil a habit or refuses to give to the poor.   ᵈ **12:9** *Hebrew* act like friends; *Greek* be sorry.
11:18, 19 Ps 49:10; Lk 12:16–21   **12:1** Mt 7:6

wickedness is as destructive as rust. ¹¹Watch out, and be on guard against him, even if he acts ever so humble. He is like a metal mirror that rusts away if you don't keep it polished. ¹²Seat an enemy at your right hand, and the next thing you know he'll be trying to get your own place of honor. Put him next to you, and he will overthrow you. Then you will realize the truth of my words, and be stung with regret when you remember them. ¹³Nobody feels sorry for snake charmers or wild animal tamers who get bitten, ¹⁴and nobody will feel sorry for you if you run around with sinners and get involved in their wrongdoing.

¹⁵An enemy will stay with you for a while, but not when trouble comes. ¹⁶He will speak fine words while he plots how to trap you. He will pretend to share your sorrows, but he will kill you if he gets a chance. ¹⁷If trouble comes your way, you will find him waiting, ready to trip you up while he pretends to help you. ¹⁸He will be a different person then, rubbing his hands, nodding his head, and spreading rumors about you.

13

¹If you touch tar, it will stick to you, and if you keep company with arrogant people, you will come to be just like them. ²Don't try to lift something too heavy for you, and don't keep company with people who are richer and more powerful than you. You cannot keep a clay pot next to an iron kettle; the pot will break if it hits the kettle. ³If a rich person wrongs someone, he can afford to add insult to injury; but if a poor person is wronged, he is forced to apologize for himself. ⁴A rich person will use you as long as he can profit from it, but when you need him, he will leave you helpless. ⁵He will live with you as long as you have anything and will gladly drain you dry. ⁶If he needs you, he will trick you with his smiles and cheerful, kindly words. "Do you need anything?" he will ask. ⁷He will feed you until you are embarrassed. Finally, when he has drained you two or three times over, he will laugh at you. If you see him later, he will pretend he doesn't know you, and will pass you by.

⁸Be careful not to be misled; you can be

enjoying yourself and suddenly find yourself humiliated. ⁹If you are invited to the home of someone influential, be reserved in your behavior. Then he will invite you more often. ¹⁰If you push yourself on him, he will put you in your place. On the other hand, if you keep your distance from him, he will forget about you. ¹¹Don't pretend to be his equal or trust everything he says. In spite of all of his long and polite conversation, he is testing you.

¹²If a person does not keep confidences, he is cruel; he will not hesitate to hurt you or have you put in jail. ¹³Keep your secrets to yourself and be very careful, for you are always walking on dangerous ground. *e*

¹⁵Every creature prefers its own kind, and people are no different. ¹⁶Just as animals of the same species flock together, so people keep company with people like themselves. ¹⁷A sinner has no more in common with a devout person than a wolf has with a lamb. ¹⁸Rich people have no more in common with poor people than hyenas have with dogs. ¹⁹The rich hunt down the poor just as lions hunt down wild donkeys in the open country. ²⁰Arrogant people have nothing but scorn for the humble, and the rich think of the poor in the same way. ²¹When a rich person stumbles, his friends will steady him, but if a poor person falls, his friends will have nothing to do with him. ²²When someone rich makes a mistake, there are many people to cover up for him and

He will feed you until you are embarrassed. (13:7)

---

e **13:13** *Some manuscripts add verses 13b–14:* When you hear this in your sleep, wake up! ¹⁴As long as you live, love the Lord and call on him to rescue you.

explain away all the things he never should have said. But let someone poor make a mistake, and he gets nothing but criticism. Even if what he says makes good sense, nobody will listen. ²³When a rich person speaks, everyone is silent, and they praise him to the skies for what he says. But let a poor person speak, and everybody says, "Who is that?" They push him down if he so much as stumbles.

When a rich person speaks, everyone is silent . . .
But let a poor person speak . . . (13:23)

²⁴There is nothing wrong with being rich if you haven't sinned to get that way. But there is nothing sinful about being poor, either. Only the ungodly think so. ²⁵It's what is in your heart that makes the expression on your face happy or sad. ²⁶If you feel cheerful, you will look cheerful, although making up proverbs calls for some intense thought.

14 ¹If a person never says anything carelessly, he is to be congratulated; he doesn't need to feel guilty. ²If a person has a clear conscience and never gives up hope, he is certainly to be congratulated!

Responsible Use of Wealth

³It isn't right for someone who is selfish to be rich. What use is money to a stingy person? ⁴If you deny yourself in order to accumulate wealth, you are only accumulating it for someone else. Others will use your riches to live in luxury. ⁵How can you be generous with others if you are stingy with yourself, if you are not willing to enjoy your own wealth? ⁶No one is worse off than someone who is stingy with himself; it is a sin that brings its own punishment. ⁷When such a person does something good, it is only by accident; his selfishness will sooner or later be evident. ⁸A selfish person is evil; he turns his back on people's needs ⁹and is never satisfied with what he has. Greed*f* will shrivel up a person's soul. ¹⁰Some people are too stingy to put bread on their own table.

¹¹My child, treat yourself as well as you can, and bring worthy offerings to the Lord. ¹²Remember that death is coming for you some day, and you haven't been told when that will be. ¹³Before that day comes, be kind to your friends; be as generous as you can. ¹⁴Don't deny yourself a single day's happiness. If there is something you want to do and it is lawful, go ahead! ¹⁵Some day all that you have worked for will be divided up and given to others. ¹⁶So be generous; but also be willing to receive from others. Enjoy yourself, for you will not find any pleasures in the world of the dead. ¹⁷The human body wears out like a piece of clothing. The ancient law decrees that we must die. ¹⁸Human beings are like leaves on a spreading tree. New growth takes the place of the fallen leaves; while some of us die, others are being born. ¹⁹Everything made by human hands will decay and perish, along with the person who made it.

The Happiness of Having Wisdom

²⁰It is a happy person who is concerned with Wisdom and who uses good sense. ²¹Anyone who studies the ways of Wisdom will also learn her secrets. ²²Go after Wisdom like a hunter looking for game. ²³Look into her windows and listen at her doors. ²⁴Camp

f **14:9** *Probable text* Greed; *Greek* Wicked injustice.
14:20–25 Prov 8:32–35

as close to her house as you can get, 25and you will have a fine place to live. 26-27Build your home there, safe beneath her protecting branches, and shaded from the heat.*g*

15 ¹If you fear the Lord, you will do this. Master his Law, and you will find Wisdom. ²She will come to welcome you, like a mother or a young bride. ³She will give you wisdom and knowledge like food and drink. ⁴Rely on her for support, and you will never know the disgrace of failure. ⁵She will make you more honored than all your neighbors; when you speak in the assembly, she will give you the right words. ⁶You will find happiness and genuine joy; your name will be remembered forever.

⁷But people who are foolish or sinful will never even catch sight of Wisdom. ⁸She will have nothing to do with conceited people; she never enters the mind of liars. ⁹It is not appropriate for a sinner to sing hymns of praise, because his worship is insincere. ¹⁰A hymn should be an expression of wisdom, inspired by the Lord himself.

Free Will

¹¹Don't blame the Lord for your sin; the Lord does not cause what he hates.*h* ¹²Don't claim that he has misled you; he doesn't need the help of sinners to accomplish his purposes. ¹³The Lord hates evil in all its forms, and those who fear the Lord find nothing attractive in evil. ¹⁴When, in the beginning, the Lord created human beings, he left them free to do as they wished. ¹⁵If you want to, you can keep the Lord's commands. You can decide whether you will be loyal to him or not. ¹⁶He has placed fire and water before you; reach out and take whichever you want. ¹⁷You have a choice between life and death; you will get whichever you choose. ¹⁸The Lord's wisdom and power are great and he sees everything. ¹⁹He is aware of everything a person does,

and he takes care of those who fear him. ²⁰He has never commanded anyone to be wicked or given anyone permission to sin.

God's Punishment of Sinners

16 ¹A large family is nothing to be desired if the children are worthless. Godless children are nothing to be proud of. ²No matter how many children you have, don't look on them with pride unless they fear the Lord. ³Don't put much hope in their future or expect them to live a long time. One child who does the Lord's will is better than a thousand who do not.*i* It is better to go to your grave with no children at all than to have children who are godless.

⁴A city's population may grow because of the wisdom of one person, while a whole tribe of lawless people disappears. ⁵I have seen such things many times and have heard of even more striking examples. ⁶The Lord's flaming anger will break out against a small gathering of sinners or a disobedient nation. ⁷He did not forgive those ancient giants who rebelled against him, confident of their own strength. ⁸He detested the arrogance of the people among whom Lot lived, and he did not spare them. ⁹He showed no mercy on that nation which he doomed to destruction for its sins, ¹⁰nor on those 600,000 people on the march through the wilderness who gathered together in stubborn rebellion. ¹¹Even if there had been only one stubborn person, it would have been a miracle if he had escaped punishment. The Lord is merciful, but he can also become angry. He can be overwhelming in his forgiveness or in his anger. ¹²His punishment is as severe as his mercy is great. He judges people by what they have done. ¹³No sinner can escape with what he has stolen. The Lord will reward the patience of devout people. ¹⁴Every righteous person will be rewarded;*j* everyone will get what he deserves.*k*

---

g **14:26–27** *Hebrew* Build . . . heat; *Greek* Let her protect your children. Live safe beneath her branches, shaded from the heat, surrounded by her glory.   *h* **15:11** *Hebrew* the Lord does not cause what he hates; *Greek* do not do what the Lord hates.   *i* **16:3** *Hebrew* who does . . . do not; *Greek* is better than a thousand.
j **16:14** *Hebrew* Every . . . rewarded; *Greek* He makes room for every act of mercy.   *k* **16:14** *Some manuscripts add verses 15–16:* The Lord made the king of Egypt so stubborn that he would not acknowledge the Lord, in order that the world might know the Lord's works. ¹⁶He shows his mercy to all creation; he has divided his light from darkness with a plumb line.
15:11–20 Sir 17:1–12   **16:7** Gen 6:4; Wis 14:6

17Never say, "I will hide from the Lord. Nobody up there is going to give me a thought. How can I be noticed among so many people? The creation is so enormous, what am I worth? 18When the Lord comes, everything will tremble: the earth and the great waters beneath it, the sky and the heavens above it. 19The mountains will shake, and the foundations of the earth will shudder when he looks at them. 20The Lord isn't going to give me a thought. Nobody cares what I do. 21If I sin and am secretly disloyal, nobody will know it.[l] 22If I do what is right, nobody will tell the Lord about it. Who wants to wait for him, anyway? He is too slow in doing what he has said he would." 23Only someone with very little sense, and foolishly misguided, would think things like that.

God's Wisdom in Creation

24My child, listen and pay attention to me; you will gain knowledge if you do. 25I will give you diligent and accurate instruction.

26In the beginning the Lord did his work of creation,[m]
and gave everything a place of its own.
27He arranged everything in an eternal order
and decreed that it should be that way forever.
Not one part of creation ever grows hungry;
no part grows tired or stops its work.
28The parts do not crowd one another,
and they never disobey his word.
29When the Lord had made all this,
he looked at the earth and filled it with good things.
30He covered it with all kinds of creatures

that must die and return to the dust.

17 1Then the Lord formed human beings from the dust
and sent each of them back to it again.
2He gave them only a limited time to live,
but he gave them authority over everything on earth.
3He made them to be like himself,
and gave them his[n] own strength.
4He made all other creatures afraid of them;
he gave them authority over all the animals and birds.[o]
6He gave them their tongues, their eyes, their ears, their minds, and their consciences.
7He filled them with knowledge and understanding
and showed them the difference between good and evil.
8He gave them his own insight
to let them see the majesty of his creation.[p]
10They will praise his holy name
and proclaim the greatness of all he does.
11He made knowledge available to them
and gave them the Law as a source of life.
12He made an eternal covenant with them
and revealed his commands to them.
13They saw the splendor of his majesty
and heard the glory of his voice.
14He warned them against unrighteousness
and taught each person how to treat others.

God Is Judge

15The Lord is always aware of what people do; there is no way to hide from him.[q] 17He gave each nation its own ruler, but Israel is the Lord's own possession.[r] 19The Lord is

---

[l] 16:21 *Hebrew* 20–21The Lord . . . know it; *Greek* 20It is altogether too big for the human mind to handle. No one can understand his ways. 21Most of his works are just as invisible as the storm wind.   [m] 16:26 *Hebrew* In . . . creation; *Greek* In the judgment of the Lord his works are from the beginning.   [n] 17:3 *Probable text* his; *Greek* their.   [o] 17:4 *Some manuscripts add verse 5:* The Lord gave them the five senses, but he also gave them a sixth—intelligence, and a seventh—reason, which enables them to interpret what comes to them through the senses.
[p] 17:8 *Some manuscripts add verse 9:* and he allowed them to take pride forever in his marvelous deeds.
[q] 17:15 *Some manuscripts add verses 16–17a:* From childhood on they tend to be evil; their heart is like stone, and they don't seem to be able to make it more human. 17He divided the nations of the whole earth.
[r] 17:17 *Some manuscripts add verse 18:* Israel is his first-born, whom he disciplines as he brings him up. He gives him the light of his love and never neglects him.
17:1–3 Gen 1:26–28; 2:7   **17:7** Gen 2:17

Sirach

always watching what people do; everything they do is as clear as day to him. 20None of their sins are hidden from him; he is aware of them all.ˢ 22When we give to the poor, the Lord considers it as precious as a valuable ring. Human kindness is as precious to him as life itself. 23Later he will judge the wicked and punish them; they will get what they deserve. 24But the Lord will allow those who repent to return to him. He always gives encouragement to those who are losing hope.

A Call to Repentance

25Come to the Lord, and leave your sin behind. Pray sincerely that he will help you live a better life. 26Return to the Most High and turn away from sin. Have an intense hatred for wickedness. 27Those who are alive can give thanks to the Lord, but can anyone in the world of the dead sing praise to the Most High? 28A person who is alive and well can sing the Lord's praises, but the dead, who no longer exist, have no way to give him thanks. 29How great is the Lord's merciful forgiveness of those who turn to him! 30But this is not the nature of human beings;ᵗ not one of us is immortal. 31Nothing is brighter than the sun, but even the sun's light fails during an eclipse. How much easier it is for human thoughts to be eclipsed by evil! 32The Lord can look out over all the stars in the sky. Human beings? They are dust and ashes.

The Greatness of God

18 1The Lord, who lives forever, created the whole universe, 2and he alone is just.ᵘ 4He has given no one enough power to describe what he has done, and no one can investigate it completely. 5Who can measure his majestic power? Who can tell the whole story of his merciful actions? 6We cannot add to them; we cannot subtract from them. There is no way to comprehend the marvelous things the Lord has done. 7When we come to the end of that story, we

have not even begun; we are simply at a loss for words.

Human Beings Are Nothing

8What are human beings? Of what use are we? The good that we do—the evil that we do—what does it all mean? 9If we live a hundred years, we have lived an unusually long time, 10but compared with all eternity, those years are like a drop of water in the ocean, like a single grain of sand. 11That is why the Lord is so patient with us, why he is so free with his mercy. 12He looks at us and knows that we are doomed to die; that is why he is so willing to forgive us. 13We can show compassion to someone we know, but the Lord shows compassion for all humanity. He corrects us; he disciplines us; he teaches us. Like a shepherd tending sheep, he brings us back to himself. 14He will have compassion on us if we accept his guidance and are eager for him to show us where we are wrong.

Kindness and Charity

15My child, when you help someone, don't reprimand him at the same time. When you make a gift, don't say anything that hurts. 16Your words count for more than what you give. Even dew gives some relief during a spell of hot weather. 17Yes, kind words are more effective than the best of gifts, and if you are really concerned, you will give both. 18It is stupid to be unkind and insulting. No one's eyes are going to sparkle at a gift that you resent giving.

Self-examination

19Know what you are talking about before you speak, and give attention to your health before you get sick. 20Examine your conscience before the Lord judges you; then when that time comes, he will forgive you. 21Humble yourself before you are punished with sickness. When you have sinned, show

ˢ **17:20** *Some manuscripts add verse 21:* But the Lord is gracious and knows his creatures; so he has spared them rather than abandon them.   ᵗ **17:30** But . . . human beings; *or* People cannot have everything.   ᵘ **18:2** *Some manuscripts add verses 2b–3:* and there is no other besides him. ³He guides the world with his hand, and everything obeys him. He is the king of all things, and his power separates what is holy from what is not.
17:25, 26 Jer 3:12   **17:27, 28** Ps 6:5; Isa 38:18; Bar 2:17, 18

. . . a gift you resent giving. (18:18)

repentance. ²²If you make a promise to the Lord, keep it as soon as you can. Don't wait until you are about to die to set things straight. ²³But before you make such a promise, be prepared to keep it. Don't try to test the Lord's patience. ²⁴Think! Do you want him to be angry with you on the day you die? When you face his judgment, do you want him to turn his back on you? ²⁵When you have all you want, think what it is like to be hungry, what it is to be poor. ²⁶Things can change in a single day; the Lord can act very quickly. ²⁷If you are wise, you will be careful in everything you do. When sin is all around you, be especially careful that you do not become guilty. ²⁸Every intelligent person can recognize wisdom and will honor anyone who shows it. ²⁹If you appreciate wisdom when you hear it, you will become wise yourself, and your words will be a source of wisdom for others.

Self-control

³⁰Don't be controlled by your lust; keep your passions in check. ³¹If you allow yourself to satisfy your every desire, you will be a joke to your enemies. ³²Don't indulge in luxurious living; the expense of it will ruin you. ³³Don't make yourself a beggar by borrowing for expensive banquets when you don't have enough money of your own.

19 ¹If you do, you^v will never get rich; if you don't pay attention to small matters, you will gradually ruin yourself. ²Wine and women make sensible men do foolish things. A man who goes to prostitutes gets more and more careless, ³and that carelessness will cost him his life. Worms will feed on his decaying body.

⁴It is silly to trust people too quickly. If you sin, you are hurting yourself. ⁵If wickedness makes you happy, you will be condemned.

Loose Talk

⁶Avoid idle talk, and you will avoid a lot of trouble. ⁷Never repeat what you hear, and you will have no regrets. ⁸Don't tell it to your friends or your enemies unless it would be sinful to keep it to yourself. ⁹Whoever hears you will take note of it, and sooner or later will hate you for it. ¹⁰Have you heard a rumor? Let it die with you. Be brave! It won't make you explode. ¹¹A foolish person trying to keep a secret suffers like a woman in labor. ¹²Any time he hears a secret, it's like an arrow stuck in his leg.

¹³If you hear that a friend has done something wrong, ask him about it. Maybe it isn't true. If it is true, he won't do it again. ¹⁴If you hear that a neighbor has said something he shouldn't, ask him about it. Maybe he didn't say it. If he did, he won't say it again. ¹⁵If you hear something bad about a friend, ask him about it. It might be a lie. Don't believe everything you hear. ¹⁶A person may say something carelessly and not really mean it. Everyone has sinned in this way at one time or another. ¹⁷If you hear something that makes you angry with your neighbor, ask him about it before you threaten him. Leave the matter to the Law of the Most High. ^w

Recognizing Real Wisdom

²⁰Fear the Lord and keep his Law; that is what Wisdom is all about. ^x ²²You may know

---

^v **19:1** *Hebrew* If you do, you; *Greek* A worker who drinks too much.   ^w **19:17** *Some manuscripts add verses 17c–19:* and don't be angry. ¹⁸Fearing the Lord is the first step toward his accepting you; he will love you if you are wise. ¹⁹Learn the Lord's commands. It is a discipline that gives life. Those who do what pleases him enjoy the fruit of the tree of immortality.   ^x **19:20** *Some manuscripts add verses 20b–21:* and what the knowledge of his omnipotence means. ²¹If a servant refuses to obey his master, but later does obey, the master is still angry.

everything there is to know about wickedness, but that does not make you wise. It is not sensible to follow the advice of sinners. 23It is possible to use cleverness for wicked purposes, but some people act like fools because they don't know any better. 24A devout person, even if he is not very intelligent, is better off than the cleverest of sinners. 25It is possible to be marvelously clever and still be dishonest, or to get what you want by being absurdly polite.

26Then there are those wicked people who go about looking very solemn and mournful, but who are only trying to deceive you. 27They will turn their faces away and pretend not to hear you, but they'll take advantage of you when you least expect it. 28If for some reason they are unable to sin now, they'll get around to it at the first opportunity. 29You can know people by their appearance. The first time you look at them, you can tell if they have good sense. 30Their character shows in the way they dress, the way they laugh, and the way they walk.

Knowing When to Talk

20 1A person can be rebuked in the wrong way; it may be wiser to keep quiet than to speak. 2But it is much better to rebuke the person than to keep your

. . . and pretend not to hear you. (19:27)

anger bottled up. 3Admit when you are wrong, and you will avoid embarrassment. 4Using force to get a point across is like a castrated man trying to rape a young woman. 5Some people are thought to be wise because they don't talk much; others are disliked because they talk too much. 6Some people keep quiet because they don't have anything to say; others keep quiet because they know the right time to speak. 7A wise person will not speak until the right moment, but a bragging fool doesn't know when that time is. 8No one can stand a person who talks too long and will not give others a chance to speak.

No one can stand a person who talks too long. (20:8)

Sudden Changes of Fortune

9Bad luck can sometimes lead to success, and a stroke of good luck can sometimes lead to loss.

10Generosity will sometimes do you no good, but at other times it will repay you double.

11Honor can be followed by disgrace, but there are people who have risen from obscurity to places of honor.

12Sometimes what seems like a real bargain can turn out to be a very expensive mistake.

13When a person with good judgment speaks, he wins friends. A stupid person, though, can shower compliments on everybody, and it won't help him a bit. 14If such a person gives you something, it won't do any good; it won't be as valuable as he thinks it is.*y* 15 He isn't generous with anything but criticism, which he will shout for all the world to hear. If he lends you something today, he'll want it back tomorrow. (Don't you hate people like that?) 16 Then that fool will say, "Nobody likes me. Nobody appreciates what I do for them. They'll take what I give them, but then talk about me behind my back." 17 And he's right—he's a constant joke to everyone.

Inappropriate Talk

18 A slip of the tongue is worse than a slip on the pavement; the wicked will go to ruin just as suddenly as a person slips and falls.

19 An impolite person is like one of those off-color stories that ignorant people are always telling.

20 Nobody takes a proverb seriously when some fool quotes it at the wrong time.

21 If a person is too poor to afford sin, he can rest without a guilty conscience.

22 You can lose all your self-respect by being reluctant to speak up in the presence of stupidity.

23 If you promise a friend something because you are too bashful to say no, you're needlessly making an enemy.

24 Lying is an ugly blot on a person's character, but ignorant people do it all the time. 25 A thief is better than a habitual liar, but both are headed for ruin. 26 A liar has no honor. He lives in constant disgrace.

Stewardship of Wisdom

27 Speak wisely, and you will get ahead in the world. Influential people appreciate good sense. 28 They will excuse your errors if they like you, so cultivate the soil and reap the harvest!

29 Gifts and bribes make even the wise blind to the truth, and prevent them from being honest in their criticism.

30 Wisdom that is not expressed is like a treasure that has been hidden—both are useless. 31 But a person who covers up his foolishness is better than one who keeps his wisdom to himself.

Sin

21 1 My child, have you sinned? Don't do it again, and pray for forgiveness for what you have already done. 2 Avoid sin as if it were a snake. If you get too near, it will sink its teeth into your soul like a lion, and destroy you. 3 Every lawless act leaves an incurable wound, like one left by a double-edged sword.

4 If a person is insolent and arrogant, he may lose everything he has.

5 When poor people pray, God hears them and quickly answers their prayers.

6 If you refuse to accept correction, you are committing a sin; and if you fear the Lord, you will make a sincere change in your ways.

7 Someone may be famous as a good speaker, but when he is wrong, a sensible person will detect it.

8 Anyone who borrows money to build a house is just collecting stones for his own tomb.*z*

9 A group of people who have no respect for the Law is like a pile of kindling; they will meet a fiery end. 10 The road that sinners walk is smooth and paved, but it leads to the world of the dead.

Wisdom and Foolishness

11 Whoever wants to keep the Law must learn what the Law means. If you fear the Lord in every sense of the term, you will have wisdom. 12 You have to be intelligent to learn anything; but there is such a thing as just pretending to be intelligent, which only makes people bitter. 13 A wise person's knowledge is like a river that never runs dry, like an everflowing stream of good advice.

14 A fool, on the other hand, has a mind like a jar with a hole in it; anything he learns is soon lost.

15 When an educated person hears something that shows insight, it stimulates his

---

y **20:14** it won't be . . . it is; *or* he only expects to be repaid. *z* **21:8** his own tomb; *some manuscripts have* the winter.
21:5 Sir 35:17–19

*A fool . . . has a mind like a jar with a hole in it.
(21:14)*

mind and leads him on to other ideas. But when someone who is satisfied with ignorance hears it, he won't like it, and will forget it as soon as he can. ¹⁶Listening to a foolish person talk is like traveling with a heavy load on your back, but it is a pleasure to hear what intelligent people have to say. ¹⁷The assembly will be eager to hear from an intelligent person and will take his opinion seriously.

¹⁸To an ignorant person, wisdom is as useless as a house gone to ruin. He has never even thought about the things he is so sure of. ¹⁹To a person without any sense, an education is like handcuffs, ²⁰⁻²¹but to a sensible person, it is like gold bracelets. An intelligent person will smile quietly while a fool roars with laughter. ²²⁻²³A stupid person will peep into someone's house through the door and then march right in, but someone with experience and good manners will have enough respect to wait outside. ²⁴Eavesdropping at doors is bad manners, and anyone with a sense of decency would be ashamed to do it.

²⁵Presumptuous people talk about things that are none of their business,ᵃ but the wise will consider the consequences of what they say. ²⁶Fools say whatever comes to mind; wise people think before they speak.

²⁷When a wicked person curses his enemyᵇ he is cursing himself.

²⁸A gossip ruins his own character, and everyone in the neighborhood hates him.

Laziness and Foolishness

22 ¹⁻²Lazy people are no better than dung; they are repulsive, and no one wants to get near them.

³It is a disgrace to a father to have an undisciplined child, especially if it is a daughter. ⁴A sensible daughter will get a husband, but a shameless daughter brings her father grief. ⁵A girl with no sense of propriety will disgrace both her husband and her father; neither will have any respect for her.

⁶Lecturing your children can sometimes be as out of place as singing to people in mourning, but a whipping is a wise choice of discipline at any time.

⁷Trying to teach a fool is like gluing a broken pot back together, like waking someone out of a deep sleep. ⁸Explaining something to a fool is like explaining it to a sleepy person; when you have finished, he'll say, "What was that again?"ᶜ

¹¹We mourn for the dead because they have no access to light. We ought to mourn for fools, because they have no access to intelligence. In fact, we should go into deeper mourning for fools, because the life they lead is worse than death. The dead are at least at rest. ¹²For seven days we mourn the dead, but a foolish or ungodly person causes a lifetime of grief.

¹³Don't visit stupid people or spend a lot of time talking with them. Avoid them; then they can't contaminate you, and you can live in peace without being troubled or worn down by their foolishness. ¹⁴Such people are a heavier burden to bear than lead; and the only word that fits them is "fools." ¹⁵It is easier to carry a load of sand, salt, and iron than to put up with a stupid person.

¹⁶A wooden beam can be put into a building so firmly that an earthquake cannot

---

ᵃ **21:25** *Probable text* Presumptuous . . . business; *Greek* The lips of strangers speak of these things.   ᵇ **21:27** his enemy; *or* Satan.   ᶜ **22:8** *Some manuscripts add verses 9–10:* Children who are brought up well do not show the humble origin of their parents. ¹⁰Children who are not brought up well, who are arrogant and conceited, are a stain on the noblest family.
22:12 Gen 50:10; Jdt 16:24

shake it loose; a person can be trained to use reason and good sense so well that he keeps his head when a crisis comes. [17]A mind that thinks things through intelligently is like a firm wall, finely decorated. [18]Small stones on top of a wall[d] will not stay put when the wind blows, and a person whose stupid ideas have made him timid will not be able to stand up to frightening situations.

Friendship

[19]If you stick something in your eye, tears will flow; and if you hurt a person deeply, you will discover his true feelings. [20]If you throw rocks at birds, you will scare them away; and if you insult a friend, you will break up the friendship. [21-22]Even if you have a violent argument with a friend, and speak sharply, all is not lost. You can still make up with him. But any friend will leave you if you insult him, if you are arrogant, if you reveal his secrets, or if you turn on him unexpectedly.

[23]Gain the confidence of your neighbor if he is poor; then you can share his happiness if he becomes successful. Stand by him when he is in trouble if you want to share with him when better times come his way.

[24]Fumes and smoke appear before the flames do; insults come before violence.

[25]I will never be afraid to protect a friend, and I will never turn a friend away if he needs me. [26]If I suffer because of him, everyone who learns of it will be on guard against him.

A Prayer for Help against Sin

[27]I wish that a guard could be placed at my mouth, that my lips could be wisely sealed. It would keep me from making mistakes and prevent me from destroying myself with my own tongue!

23 [1]O Lord, my Father and Master of my life, do not leave me at the mercy of my own words; don't let them cause my downfall. [2]I wish I could be whipped for my thoughts, so that Wisdom could discipline my mind. I would not want to be spared when I am wrong; I would not want a single sin to be overlooked! [3]Then I would not keep on sinning, making one mistake after another. I could not fall to my enemies and be humiliated by them.

[4]O Lord, my Father, God of my life, keep me from being arrogant; [5]protect me from evil desires. [6]Keep me from being overcome by greed or lust; do not leave me at the mercy of these shameless passions.

Taking Oaths

[7]My children, listen to what I have to say about proper speech; do as I teach you and you will never get trapped. [8]Sinners are caught by their own arrogant, insulting words.

[9]Don't fall into the habit of taking oaths, and don't use God's holy name too freely. [10]A slave who is constantly beaten will never be free of bruises; someone who is always taking an oath by the Holy Name will never be free of sin. [11]Anyone who takes oaths all the time is sinful to the core, and punishment is never far away from his household. If he fails to fulfill his oath, he is guilty. If he ignores his oath, he is twice as guilty. If his oath was insincere in the first place, he cannot be pardoned and will have a house full of trouble.

Filthy Talk

[12]There is one way of speaking that is like death itself—may no Israelite ever be guilty of it! Devout people do not wallow in such sin, and they will keep away from such behavior. [13]Don't fall into the habit of coarse, profane talk; it is sinful. [14]You might forget yourself while in the company of important people and make a fool of yourself with some foul word that comes to you naturally. Think how your parents would feel! You would curse the day you were born and wish you were dead! [15]If you fall into the habit of using offensive language, you will never break yourself of it as long as you live.

---

[d] **22:18** Small . . . wall; *some manuscripts have* A fence on top of a hill.
23:9 Mt 5:34; Jas 5:12

Sexual Sins

16There are any number of ways to sin and bring down the Lord's anger, but sexual passion is a hot, blazing fire that cannot be put out at will; it can only burn itself out. A man who lives for nothing but sexual enjoyment will keep on until that fire destroys him. **17**To such a man all women are desirable, and he can never get enough as long as he lives.

18The man who is unfaithful to his wife thinks to himself, "No one will ever know. It's dark in here, and no one sees me. I have nothing to worry about. As for the Most High, he won't even notice." **19**This man is only afraid of other people. He doesn't realize that the eyes of the Lord are 10,000 times brighter than the sun, that he sees everything we do, even when we try to hide it. **20**He knew everything before he created the world, as well as after. **21**That sinful man will be caught when he least expects it, and punished publicly.

22The same is true of a woman who is unfaithful to her husband and presents him with a child by another man. **23**In the first place, she has broken the Law of the Most High. In the second place, she has wronged her husband. And in the third place, she has made a whore of herself by committing adultery and bearing the child of a man not her husband. **24-25**The children will suffer for her sin. They will not be able to find a place in society or establish families. She herself will be brought before the assembly **26**and permanently disgraced. There will be a curse on her memory. After she is gone, **27**everyone will realize that nothing is better than fearing the Lord, nothing is sweeter than keeping his commands.

In Praise of Wisdom

24 **1**Listen to Wisdom! She proudly sings her own praises among the Israelites, her own people, **2**in the assembly of the Most High, in the presence of his power.*e*

3"I am the word spoken by the Most High.
   I covered the earth like a mist.
4I made my home in highest heaven,
   my throne on a pillar of cloud.
5Alone I walked around the circle of the sky
   and walked through the ocean beneath the earth.
6I ruled over*f* all the earth and the ocean waves,
   over every nation, over every people.
7I looked everywhere for a place to settle,
   some part of the world to make my home.
8Then my Creator, who created the universe,
   told me where I was to live.
'Make your home in Israel,' he said.
   'The descendants of Jacob will be your people.'
9He created me in eternity, before time began,
   and I will exist for all eternity to come.
10I served him in the Sacred Tent
   and then made my home on Mount Zion.
11He settled me in the Beloved City
   and gave me authority over Jerusalem.
12I put down roots among an honored people
   whom the Lord had chosen as his own.
13I grew tall, like the cedars in Lebanon,
   like the cypresses on Mount Hermon,
14like the palm trees of Engedi,*g*
   like the roses of Jericho,
like beautiful olive trees in the fields,
   like plane trees growing by the water.
15My breath was the spicy smell of cinnamon,
   of sweet perfume and finest myrrh,
of stacte, onycha, and galbanum,
   the fragrant incense in the Sacred Tent.
16Like an oak I spread out my branches,
   magnificent and graceful.
17Like a grapevine I put out lovely shoots;
   my blossoms gave way to rich and glorious fruit.*h*

---

e **24:2** power; *or* angels.   *f* **24:6** ruled over; *some manuscripts have* gained possession of.   *g* **24:14** of Engedi; *some manuscripts have* on the seashore.   *h* **24:17** *Some manuscripts add verse 18:* I am the mother of beautiful love, of fear, knowledge, and holy hope. Since I am eternal, I am given to all my children, who are named by him. **24:4** Ex 33:9, 10

19 Come to me, all you that want me,
  and eat your fill of my fruit.
20 You will remember me as sweeter than
    honey,
  better than honey from the comb.
21 Eat me, and you will hunger for more;
  drink me, and you will thirst for more.
22 Obey me, and you will never have cause
    for embarrassment;
  do as I say, and you will be safe from
    sin."

Wisdom and the Law

23 Wisdom is the Law, the Law which
Moses commanded us to keep, the covenant
of God Most High, the inheritance of the
synagogues of Israel.*i* 25 The Law overflows
with Wisdom like the Pishon River, like the
Tigris at fruit-picking time. 26 The Law
brims over with understanding like the
Euphrates, like the Jordan at harvest time.
27 It sparkles with teachings like the Nile,*j*
like the Gihon at grape-picking time.

28 The first human being ever created
never knew Wisdom completely, and the last
person on earth will be no more successful.
29 The possibilities of Wisdom are vaster
than the ocean; her resources are more profound than the deepest waters beneath the
earth.

30 As for me, I thought of myself as an
irrigation canal bringing water from a river
into a garden. 31 I only intended to water my
orchard and flower beds, but the canal soon
became a river, and the river became a sea.
32 And so I present you with my learning; I
hold it high, so that its light can be seen
everywhere, like that of the rising sun.
33 Like an inspired prophet, I pour out my
teachings, so that future generations can
benefit from them. 34 Please realize that I
have not done all this hard work for myself
alone, but to help anyone who wants to be
wise.

People Who Deserve Praise

25 ¹ There are three things in which I
take special delight—things that are
beautiful to the Lord and people alike:*k*
  brothers who get along with each other,
    neighbors who are friends,
      and a married couple who are happy
        together.
² There are three kinds of people I cannot
stand, whose behavior I find highly offensive:
  poor people who are arrogant,
    rich people who lie,
      and foolish old men who commit
        adultery.
³ Unless you learn what you can while
you are young, you will never be wise when
you reach old age. ⁴ Sound judgment, good
advice, and gray hair go together beautifully.

Three things in which I take special delight . . . (25:1)

i **24:23** *Some manuscripts add verse 24:* Always be strong in the Lord; stay with him, so that he may make you
strong. There is no God but the Lord Almighty, and no savior except him. *j* **24:27** *One ancient translation* It
sparkles . . . Nile; *Greek* It makes teachings shine like light. *k* **25:1** *Some ancient translations* There are . . . alike;
Greek I was made beautiful in three ways and I stood before the Lord and people in beauty.

Sirach

[5] Wisdom, understanding, and sound counsel are appropriate to the aged and the respected. [6] Elderly people wear the crown of long experience, and they can boast of nothing finer than their fear of the Lord.

[7] I will tell you about ten kinds of people that I feel fortunate to know, especially fortunate in the case of the tenth:

someone who takes pride in his children,

someone who lives to see his enemies fall,

[8] a man fortunate enough to have an understanding wife,

a married couple who are well-matched,[l]

a person who never speaks sinfully,

a person who doesn't have to work for someone less competent than himself,

[9] someone fortunate enough to have a real friend,[m]

a person that people are happy to listen to,

[10] and the really great one: someone who is wise.

But the greatest one of all is the person who fears the Lord.

[11] Such a person has no equal, because the fear of the Lord is the most important thing in the world.[n]

Advice about Women

[13] No wound is as serious as wounded love. No troubles are as serious as the troubles that women cause. [14] No sufferings are worse than the sufferings caused by people who hate you. No revenge is worse than revenge taken by an enemy. [15] No poison is deadlier than the poison of a snake, and no anger is deadlier than the anger of a woman.[o]

[16] I would rather live in the same house with a lion or a dragon than with a bad wife. [17] When a wife is in a bad mood, her expression changes until she looks like an angry bear. [18] Her husband has to go and eat with the neighbors, where he can't hold back his bitter sighs.

[19] Compared with the troubles caused by a woman, any other trouble looks small. May such women suffer the fate of sinners!

[20] A quiet man living with a nagging wife is like an old man climbing up a sandy hill.

[21] Never lose your head over a woman's beauty, and don't try to win a woman because she is wealthy.[p] [22] When a man is supported by his wife, there is sure to be anger, arrogance, and humiliation. [23] A bad wife will make her husband gloomy and depressed, and break his heart. Show me a timid man who can never make up his mind, and I will show you a wife who doesn't make her husband happy. [24] Sin began with a woman, and we must all die because of her. [25] Don't let a bad wife have her way, any more than you would allow water to leak from your cistern. [26] If she won't do as you tell her, divorce her.

26

[1] The husband of a good wife is a fortunate man; he will live twice as long because of her. [2] A fine wife is a joy to her husband, and he can live out his years in peace. [3] A good wife is among the precious blessings given to those who fear the Lord. [4] Whether such men are rich or poor, they will be happy and always look cheerful.

[5] There are four things that scare me: vicious rumors spread around town, a gathering mob, false accusations—these are all worse than death. [6] But a woman jealous of another woman causes heartache and grief; her tongue lashes out at everyone.

[7] A bad wife is like a yoke that doesn't fit. Trying to control her is like holding a scorpion. [8] A drunken woman is an infuriating sight; she can't conceal her shameless behavior. [9] You can tell an unfaithful wife by the bold and flirting look in her eyes.

[10] If your daughter is determined to have her own way, keep a close watch on her. If you don't, she'll take advantage of any chance she gets. [11] If she is too self willed, be on guard, and don't be surprised if she disappoints you. [12] She'll spread her legs anywhere for any man who wants her, just as a thirsty traveler will drink whatever water is available.

---

l **25:8** *Hebrew and one ancient translation* a married couple . . . well-matched; *Greek does not have these words.* *m* **25:9** *Some ancient translations* real friend; *Greek* good sense. *n* **25:11** *Some manuscripts add verse 12:* Fearing the Lord is the first step toward loving him, and faith is the first step toward loyalty to him. *o* **25:15** *Some ancient translations* woman; *Greek* enemy. *p* **25:21** *Hebrew* because she is wealthy; *Greek does not have these words.*

You can tell an unfaithful wife by . . . (26:9)

¹³A gracious wife is her husband's delight; her abilities make him a stronger man.*q* ¹⁴A wife who doesn't talk too much is a gift from the Lord. Such restraint is admirable beyond words. ¹⁵A modest wife has endless charm; it is a quality too precious to measure. ¹⁶The beauty of a good wife in her well-kept home is like the noonday sun shining in the Lord's sky. ¹⁷Her beautiful face and attractive figure are*r* as lovely as the light from the sacred lampstand in the Temple, ¹⁸and like its gold shaft set on its silver base are her shapely legs and strong ankles.*s t*

Sad Observations

²⁸There are two things that make me sad, and a third that makes me angry:

a soldier who has become poor,
　　intelligent people who are not
　　　　respected,
　　　and a righteous person who turns to
　　　　evil.

The Lord will punish such a person with death!

²⁹A merchant can hardly avoid doing wrong; every salesman is guilty of sin.

27 ¹Many people have sinned while looking for a profit; if you want to be rich you have to keep blinders on your eyes. ²It is hard to remove a peg that is stuck between two stones of a house, and it is just as hard to remove dishonesty from buying and selling. ³Unless you are determined in your fear of the Lord, your house is going to come down on you.

Speech Reflects True Feelings

⁴Your talk shows your faults; it is like a sieve that separates out the rubbish. ⁵The way you think shows your character just as surely as a kiln shows any flaws in the pottery being fired. ⁶You can tell how well a tree has been cared for by the fruit it bears, and you can tell a person's feelings by the way he expresses himself. ⁷Never praise anyone before you hear him talk; that is the real test.

Honesty

⁸If you try to be honest, you can be, and it will improve your character as handsome clothing improves your appearance. ⁹Birds come to roost with those of their own kind, and the habit of honesty comes to those who try to be honest. ¹⁰Sin waits for those looking for a chance to sin, just as a lion waits for prey.

Foolish Talk

¹¹When devout people talk, what they say always makes sense, but foolish people are always contradicting themselves. ¹²When

q **26:13** her abilities . . . man; *or* she knows how to keep him well-fed.　*r* **26:17** and attractive figure are; *or as* she grows older is.　*s* **26:18** strong ankles; *some manuscripts have* firm breasts *or* determined heart.
t **26:18** *Some manuscripts add verses 19–27:* My child, stay healthy while you are young, and don't give your strength to strangers. ²⁰Search the whole land for a fertile field, and plant it with your own seed, trusting your own good stock. ²¹Then your children will survive and grow up confident of their good family. ²²A prostitute is like spit; a married woman who has affairs brings death to her lovers. ²³A lawless man will get a godless wife, as he deserves, but a man who honors the Lord will have a devout wife. ²⁴A shameless wife enjoys making a disgrace of herself, but a modest wife will act modestly even alone with her husband. ²⁵A self-willed woman is a bitch, but a woman with a sense of decency honors the Lord. ²⁶A wife who honors her husband will seem wise to everyone; but if she dishonors him by her overbearing attitude, everyone will know that she is ungodly. Fortunate is the husband of a good wife, because he will live twice as long. ²⁷A loud-mouthed, talkative woman is like a trumpet sounding the signal for attack, and any man who has such a wife will spend his life at war.
27:6 Mt 7:17; 12:33; Lk 6:44

Sirach

you find yourself with stupid people, look for some excuse to leave, but when you are with serious-minded people, stay as long as you can.

¹³The stories that foolish people tell are offensive, and they make jokes about the worst kinds of sin. ¹⁴When such people curse, it is enough to make your hair stand on end, and when they start arguing among themselves, all you can do is to stop up your ears. ¹⁵It is painful to listen to them insult each other, and such blustering can lead to violence.

All you can do is to stop up your ears. (27:14)

Betraying Secrets

¹⁶If you repeat secrets that have been told to you, you are destroying the confidence others have in you, and you will never have a close friend. ¹⁷Respect your friends, and keep faith with them. If you do betray a friend's confidence, you may as well forget you have a friend. ¹⁸You have killed that friendship just as surely as if you had taken a weapon and killed an enemy. ¹⁹Your friend is gone. You can no more get him back than you can get a bird to come back to your hand once you let it go. ²⁰Don't bother going after him. It's too late. He is gone, like a deer escaped from a trap. ²¹Wounds can be bandaged and insults can be forgiven, but if you betray a confidence, it is hopeless.

Hypocrisy

²²When someone starts winking at you, he has something bad in mind, and nothing can stop him from going through with it. ²³When he's with you, his talk is so nice! He compliments you on every word you say. But behind your back it's a different story; he will take what you have said and turn it against you. ²⁴There is nothing in the world that I hate as much as a person like that— and the Lord hates him too.

²⁵Throw a stone straight up in the air and it will come down on your head. Strike a blow, and you yourself will be wounded. ²⁶People who set traps fall into them themselves. ²⁷People who hurt others will be hurt by their own actions and will have no idea why.

²⁸Arrogant people insult others and make fun of them,^u but someone is waiting like a lion for a chance to take revenge on them. ²⁹Those who are happy to witness the downfall of devout people are going to fall into a trap and die a painful death.

Resentment

³⁰Anger and a hot temper are horrible things, but sinners have both. ¹The Lord is taking note of your sins, and if you take vengeance on someone, the Lord will take vengeance on you. ²But if you forgive someone who has wronged you, your sins will be forgiven when you pray. ³You cannot expect the Lord to pardon you while you are holding a grudge against someone else. ⁴You yourself are a sinner, and if you won't forgive another person, you have no right to pray that the Lord will forgive your sins. ⁵If you cannot get rid of your anger, you have no hope of forgiveness—you are only a human being. ⁶Think about it! Some day you will die, and your body will decay. So give up hate and live by the Lord's commands, ⁷the commands in the covenant of the Most High. Instead of getting upset over your neighbor's faults, overlook them.

Arguments

⁸If you stay out of arguments, you will not sin so much, because a hot temper gets them started. ⁹It is sinful to break up a friendship

---

^u **27:28** insult others . . . them; *or* will be insulted and mocked.
27:16–21 Prov 20:19; 25:9   **28:2** Mt 6:14; Mk 11:25

It is sinful to break up a friendship. (28:9)

by creating hostility among people who get along well together. ¹⁰The more fuel, the hotter the fire. The more stubbornness, the hotter the argument. And the stronger or richer people are, the angrier they can afford to become. ¹¹An argument that blazes out suddenly can lead to violence. ¹²You can blow on a spark to make it glow, or you can spit on it to put it out. Either way, you do it with your mouth.

Vicious Talk

¹³Gossips and liars deserve to be cursed, because they have been the ruin of many people who were minding their own business. ¹⁴Many have had their lives ruined and have been driven from their homes because of people who meddled in their business. Such unwanted interference has resulted in the destruction of strong cities and the homes of respected people. ¹⁵Meddlers have caused faithful wives to be divorced, robbed of everything they had worked for. ¹⁶Anyone who pays attention to slander can never find peace of mind. ¹⁷A whip can raise a welt, but a vicious tongue can break bones. ¹⁸More people have died as a result of loose talk than were ever killed by swords. ¹⁹⁻²⁰Count yourself lucky if you have been spared the experience of having irresponsible talk directed against you—if you have never had that iron yoke around your neck or those heavy chains on your legs. ²¹Slander leads to a miserable death; but in fact, you'd be better off dead.

²²Devout people, however, cannot be overcome by slander; they cannot be burned by its flames. ²³Its victims are those who have abandoned the Lord; once the fire of slander has been lit among them, it cannot be put out. Slander will pounce on them like a lion and tear them to pieces like a leopard.

²⁴Don't you fence in your property? Don't you lock up your money? ²⁵Well, be just as careful with what you say. Weigh every word, and have a lock ready for your mouth. ²⁶Someone may be waiting for you to slip, and if you are not careful, you will stumble over your own words and fall down in front of him.

Loans and Repayment

29 ¹Be kind enough to lend to your neighbor when he needs help. You are keeping the Lord's commands if you help him. ²If he needs something, lend it to him. And when you are in debt, pay it back as soon as you can. ³If you meet your obligations, you will always be able to borrow what you need. ⁴Many people treat a loan as something they found and can keep, causing embarrassment to those who helped them. ⁵Some people will speak politely, bow, and scrape until they get the loan they want, but when the time comes to pay it back, they'll put it off, say that it's inconvenient, and make a lot of worthless excuses. ⁶If the lender insists on being paid, he can count himself lucky to get back half. If he doesn't insist, the borrower has robbed him and made an unnecessary enemy. All the lender will get from him are curses, insults, and disrespect, but never any gratitude.

⁷Many people refuse to lend at all, not because they are stingy, but because*ᵛ* they don't want to be cheated if they can avoid it.

Generosity

⁸Nevertheless, be understanding with those who are poor. Don't keep them waiting for your generosity. ⁹The Lord has commanded us to help the poor; don't refuse them the help they need. ¹⁰It is better to lose your money by helping a relative or a friend than to lose it by letting it rust away

---

v **29:7** not because . . . stingy, but because; *some manuscripts have* therefore, because of this wickedness.
28:13–26 Sir 51:2–6; Jas 3:5–12   **29:1–7** Ex 22:25; Lev 25:35–38

Sirach

Don't keep them waiting for your generosity. (29:8)

under a rock somewhere. 11Use your wealth as the Most High has commanded; this will do you more good than keeping your money for yourself. 12Count among your treasures the fact that you give to the poor. It will save you from all kinds of trouble 13and will be a better defense against your enemies than the strongest shield or stoutest spear.

Guaranteeing Debts

14A good man is willing to guarantee his neighbor's debts. Only someone who has lost all sense of decency would refuse to do so. 15If someone does this favor for you, don't forget it; he has risked his good name for you. 16There are some ungrateful sinners who abandon those who stand behind them, and they cause them loss of property. 17Guaranteeing loans has ruined many prosperous people and caused them unsettling storms of trouble. 18Influential people have lost their homes over it and have had to go wandering in foreign countries. 19A sinner who hopes to make a profit by guaranteeing a loan is going to find himself involved in lawsuits. 20So help your neighbor as much as you can, but protect yourself against the dangers involved.

Home and Hospitality

21The necessities of life are water, food, clothing, and a home where you can have privacy. 22It is better to be poor and live

under your own crude roof than to enjoy lavish banquets in other people's homes. 23Be happy with what you have, even if it isn't very much, and don't listen to anyone who would insult your home and family. *w* 24Going from house to house is a miserable way to live. Anywhere you go, you don't dare speak. 25You welcome the guests and pour the drinks, and nobody thanks you. Instead, people humiliate you by saying things like: 26"Stranger! Come here and set the table! I want to eat what you've got there! Give it here! 27Go away, stranger! I've got an important guest! My brother is coming to visit, and I need the room!"

Going from house to house is a miserable way to live. (29:24)

28Being denied hospitality or having a moneylender hound you—these are hard things for any sensitive person to endure.

Bringing up Children

30

1A father who loves his son will whip him often, so that he can be proud of him later. 2If a son is disciplined, he will be of some use, and his father can boast of him to his friends. 3Anyone who gives good guidance to his son cannot only take pride in him among his friends, but he can make his enemies jealous. 4-5While the father is alive, the sight of his son makes him happy, and when he dies, he has no regrets. He is not really dead, because his son is like him. 6He has left someone to take vengeance on his enemies and to return the favors he owes his friends.

w 29:23 don't listen . . . family; *or* don't listen to insults from your family; *some manuscripts do not have these words;* *one ancient translation has* don't get a reputation for living off other people.

. . . so that he can be proud of him later. (30:1)

7But anyone who spoils his son will have to bandage his wounds.ˣ His heart will stop every time he hears a shout. 8An untamed horse is going to be stubborn, and an undisciplined son is no different. 9If you pamper your child and play with him, he will be a disappointment and a source of grief. 10Laugh with him now, and one day you will have to cry over him, grinding your teeth in regret. 11Don't give him freedom while he is young, and don't overlook what he does wrong. 12Whip him while he is still a child, and make him respect your authority. If you don't, he will be stubborn and disobedient and cause you nothing but sorrow. 13So discipline your son and give him work to do, or else he will be an embarrassment to you.

Health

14It is better to be poor, but strong and healthy, than to be rich, but in poor health. 15A sound, healthy body and a cheerful attitudeʸ are more valuable than gold and jewels. 16Nothing can make you richer or give you greater happiness than those two things. 17It would be better to be dead, asleep forever, than to live in the misery of chronic illness. 18The finest food means nothing if you are too sick to eat it; it might as well be offered to an idol.ᶻ 19But there is no point in offering food to an idol; it can't eat it or smell it. It is just the same with someone whom the Lord has afflicted. 20He looks at his food and sighs, like a castrated man hugging a young woman.

The finest food means nothing if you are too sick to eat it. (30:18)

Cheerfulness and Sadness

21Don't deliberately torture yourself by giving in to depression. 22Happiness makes for a long life and makes it worth living. 23Enjoy yourself and be happy; don't worry all the time. Worry never did anybody any good, and it has destroyed many people. 24It will make you old before your time. Jealousy and anger will shorten your life. 25A cheerful person with a good attitude will have a good appetite and enjoy his food.

Problems Caused by Money

31 1Worrying about money will make you lose weight and lose sleep. 2Worrying about businessᵃ will keep you from sleeping just as surely as a serious illness does.

3Rich people work hard to make a lot of money; then they can sit back and live in luxury. 4Poor people work hard and have nothing to show for it, and when they rest, they are still poor.

5No one who loves money can be judged innocent; his efforts to get rich have led him into sin.ᵇ 6Many people have been ruined

---

ˣ **30:7** *will have . . . wounds; or* is going to be hurt.   ʸ **30:15** *Hebrew* a cheerful attitude; *Greek* a strong body.
ᶻ **30:18** *Hebrew* offered to an idol; *Greek* placed on a grave.   ᵃ **31:2** *Hebrew* Worrying about business; *Greek*
Sleepless worry.   ᵇ **31:5** *Hebrew* have . . . sin; *Greek* will destroy him.
30:21–25 Eccl 11:9, 10

because of money, brought face to face with disaster. ⁷Money is a trap for those who are fascinated by it, a trap that every fool falls into.

Money is a trap for those who are fascinated by it.
(31:7)

⁸A person who gets rich without sinfully chasing after money is fortunate. ⁹Do you know anyone like that? If so, we will congratulate him for performing a miracle that no one else has ever been able to do. ¹⁰If anyone has ever passed this test, he can well be proud. Has anyone ever known that he could get away with cheating someone, and not taken advantage of it? ¹¹If so, he deserves his wealth, and everyone will praise him for his generosity.

Behavior at Dinner Parties

¹²When you sit down at a fancy banquet, don't let your mouth hang open, and don't say, "Look at all that food!" ¹³It is impolite to have a greedy eye; remember that. Nothing in creation is greedier than the eye; that is why it sheds tears so often.ᶜ ¹⁴Don't reach out for everything you see, and don't elbow people out of the way to get at the food. ¹⁵Be considerate of the other people at the table and treat them the way you want to be treated. ¹⁶When you get your food, eat it like a human being. Don't smack and slurp; nobody can stand that. ¹⁷It's good manners to be the first to stop eating; stuffing yourself is offensive. ¹⁸If there are many people pres-

ent, don't try to be the first to be served. ¹⁹A little bit is plenty for anyone with good manners. Besides, you won't be short of breath when you go to bed. ²⁰People who eat too much get stomach aches and cannot sleep. If you don't overeat, you can get a good night's sleep and wake up early the next morning feeling fine. ²¹But if you do get a stomach ache from eating too much, go off and vomitᵈ and you will feel better. ²²My child, if you listen to what I am saying and put it into practice, one of these days you will thank me for it. Be moderateᵉ in everything you do, and you will never get sick.

²³People appreciate a generous host, and he deserves their praise. ²⁴But everybody in town will complain about a host who is stingy with food, and their complaints are justified.

²⁵Don't try to prove your manhood by how much you can drink. Wine has been the ruin of many. ²⁶An arrogant person's character shows through when he is in a drunken argument, in the same way that iron is tested when it is heated red-hot and then dipped in water. ²⁷Wine can put new life into you if you drink it in moderation. What would life be like without it? Wine was created to make us happy. ²⁸If you drink it in moderation and at the right time, it can lift your spirits and make you cheerful, ²⁹but if you drink when you are angry and upset, it leads to headaches, embarrassment, and disgrace.ᶠ ³⁰A drunken fool can lose his temper and hurt himself. His drinking makes him weak and an easy target for angry blows. ³¹Never rebuke a person when you have both been drinking. Don't hurt his feelings while he is having a good time. It's not the time to criticize anyone, or to ask him to pay back a debt.

32 ¹If you are chosen to preside at a banquet, don't put on airs. Just be like everyone else. Look after the guests before you sit down. ²After you have performed your duties, you can sit down and enjoy yourself with the others. They will respect you for doing a good job.

ᶜ **31:13** *Hebrew* so often; *Greek* on every face.   ᵈ **31:21** go off and vomit; *some manuscripts have* get up in the middle of the meal.   ᵉ **31:22** *Hebrew* moderate; *Greek* industrious.   ᶠ **31:29** *Hebrew* when you are . . . disgrace; *Greek* too much, it leads to bitterness, offense, and stumbling.

3If you are older than most of the guests, you may talk; that is your right. But you should know what you are talking about and not interrupt the music. 4If entertainment is being provided, don't keep up a steady conversation; it's the wrong time to show off your wit. 5Music at a banquet where wine is served is like a ruby set in gold. 6Good music and good wine—an emerald set in gold.

7If you are young, don't speak unless you have to, but never more than twice, and only if someone speaks to you first. 8Come to the point and say it all in a few words. Show that you are well-informed, but stay quiet. 9Don't treat important people as if you were their equal and don't make a nuisance of yourself by asking them a lot of questions.*g* 10The reputation of a modest person goes before him, as lightning before thunder.

11Leave the party at the right time and never be the last to go. Don't linger at the door; just go straight home. 12There you can enjoy yourself as you wish, but don't commit the sin of bragging. 13And don't forget to thank your Creator for letting you enjoy so many good things.

Interpreting the Law

14If you fear the Lord, you will accept his correction. He will bless those who get up early in the morning to pray. 15Study his Law, and you will master it, unless you are insincere about it, in which case you will fail. 16If you fear the Lord, you will know what is right, and you will be famous for your fairness. 17Sinners have no use for correction, and will interpret the Law to suit themselves.

18Sensible people will consider every opinion, but arrogant*h* people will let nothing stand in their way. 19Never do anything without thinking it through, and once you have done something, don't look back and wish you had done something else. 20Don't take a course of action that is dangerous, and don't make the same mistake twice.*i* 21Don't

be too sure of yourself, even when the way looks easy. 22Always watch where you are going.*j* 23Whatever you do be careful;*k* this is keeping the Lord's commands.

24Believing in the Law means keeping the Lord's commands.

If you trust the Lord, you cannot lose.

33 1No evil will ever come to a person who fears the Lord; however often danger comes, the Lord will come to the rescue. 2A person who has no use for the Law doesn't have good sense, and anyone who is insincere about it is going to be tossed about like a boat in a storm. 3If you are wise, you will believe in the Law; you will find it as reliable as the sacred lots.

4Prepare what you are going to say and people will listen to you. Use what you have learned before you start talking. 5A foolish person's mind works like a cartwheel, going round and round in circles. 6A sarcastic friend is like a wild horse that neighs no matter who tries to ride him.

People Are Not Alike

7Why are some days holier than others, even though the same sun rises on every day of the year? 8It is because the Lord made them different by setting them apart as religious holidays and festivals. 9He made some days holy and important, and made other days ordinary.

10Every human being was made from the earth, just as Adam was. 11But the Lord, in his wisdom, made them all different and gave them different tasks. 12He blessed some, making them honored and holy, keeping them near him. Others he cursed, humbling them and removing them from their positions. 13Just as clay is in the potter's hands for him to shape as he pleases, so we are in the hands of our Creator for him to do with as he wishes.

14Good is the opposite of evil, life is the opposite of death, and sin is the opposite of devotion to the Lord. 15Think about it: the

g **32:9** *Hebrew* make . . . questions; *Greek* keep talking when someone else is speaking.　*h* **32:18** *Hebrew* arrogant; *Greek* foreign and arrogant.　*i* **32:20** *Hebrew* make . . . twice; *Greek* stumble on stones.
j **32:22** *Hebrew* watch . . . going; *Greek* look out for your children.　*k* **32:23** *Hebrew* be careful; *Greek* have confidence in yourself.
33:3 Ex 28:30; Sir 45:10

Most High has made everything in pairs, each thing the opposite of something else.

16As for me, I have been the last to come on duty, as if going through vineyards to gather whatever the grape-pickers had left behind. But the Lord blessed me, and I did well,[l] like a grape-picker who has filled the wine press. 17But I want you to know that I have not done all this work for myself alone, but for everyone who wants to learn. 18Listen to me, all you great leaders! All you leaders of the assemblies, hear what I have to say!

Be Independent

19Never, as long as you live, give anyone power over you—whether son, wife, brother, or friend. Don't give your property to anyone; you might change your mind and have to ask for it back. 20As long as you have breath in your body, don't let anyone lead your life for you. 21It is better that your children be dependent on you than the other way around. 22Keep control over all that you do; don't let anything stain your reputation. 23Wait until the last moment of your life, when you are breathing your last, and then divide your property among your heirs.

Treatment of Slaves

24A donkey should be given its fodder and its burden, and it should be beaten. A slave should be given food and work, and should be disciplined. 25If you make your slave work, you can set your mind at ease. If you don't keep him busy, he will be looking for freedom. 26You can use a harness and yoke to tame an animal, and a slave can be tortured in the stocks. 27Keep him at work, and don't let him be idle; idleness can only teach him how to make trouble. 28Work is what he needs. If he won't obey you, put him in chains.

29But don't be too severe with anyone, and never be unfair. 30If you have a slave, treat him as you would want to be treated; you bought him with your hard-earned money. 31Treat him as a brother; you need him as you need yourself. If you mistreat him and he runs away, where are you going to look for him?

Dreams Mean Nothing

34 1Foolish people are deceived by vain hopes, and dreams get them all excited. 2A person who pays any attention at all to dreams is like someone who tries to catch shadows or chase the wind. 3What you see in a dream is no more real than the reflection of your face in a mirror. 4What is unreal can no more produce something real than what is dirty can produce something clean. 5Dreams, divination, and omens are all nonsense. You see in them only what you want to see.[m] 6Unless the Most High has sent you the dream, pay no attention to it. 7Dreams have misled many people; they put their faith in them, only to be disappointed. 8The Law is complete without such falsehood. Wisdom, as spoken by the righteous, is also complete without it.

Travel

9A well-traveled[n] person with wide experience knows many things and talks sense. 10You can't know much if you haven't experienced much, but travel can make you more clever. 11In my own travels I have seen many things and learned more than I can put into words. 12I have been in danger of death many times, but I have always been able to escape by relying on past experience.

Fear the Lord

13Those who fear the Lord will live, because they have put their trust in the one who can save them. 14Fear the Lord, and you will have nothing else to fear. If your trust is in him, you will never act like a coward. 15People who fear the Lord are fortunate, because they know where they can look for help. 16The Lord watches over those who love him; he is their strong protection and firm support. He shelters them from the

l 33:16 did well; or overtook the others.　m 34:5 Probable text You see . . . to see; Greek The mind has an imagination like a woman in labor.　n 34:9 A well-traveled; some manuscripts have An educated.
34:1–8 Deut 13:1–5; 18:9–14

heat, shades them from the noonday sun, and keeps them from stumbling and falling. 17 He makes them cheerful and puts a sparkle in their eyes. He blesses them with life and health.

Offering Sacrifices

18 If you offer as a sacrifice an animal that you have obtained dishonestly, it is defective and unacceptable. 19 The Most High gets no pleasure from sacrifices made by ungodly people; no amount of sacrifices can make up for their sins. 20 Anyone who steals an animal from the poor to offer as a sacrifice is like someone who kills a boy before his father's eyes. 21 Food means life itself to poor people, and taking it away from them is murder. 22 It is murder to deprive someone of his living or to cheat an employee of his wages.

. . . taking it away from them is murder. (34:21)

23 When one person builds and somebody else tears down, has anything been accomplished but hard work? 24 When one person blesses and somebody else curses, which one is the Lord going to listen to? 25 If you touch a dead body and then purify yourself by washing, but then go and touch it again, what good did the washing do? 26 If you fast because of your sins, and then go out and commit the same sins over again, what have you gained by going without food? Who do you think is going to listen to your prayers?

35 1 Keeping the Law is worth many offerings; it is a fellowship offering in itself. 2 Returning a kindness is like a grain offering; giving to the poor is like a thanksgiving offering. 3 Keeping away from sin will please the Lord and make atonement for sin. 4 But don't come to the Temple without an offering; 5 the Law requires that you bring one. 6 When someone righteous offers a sacrifice and the fat drips down on the altar, a pleasant smell rises to the Most High. 7 The Lord will accept the offerings made by a righteous person and will not forget them. 8 Praise the Lord by making generous offerings to him; don't be stingy with the first of your crops. 9 Be cheerful with every gift you make, and when you pay your tithes, do it gladly. 10 Give to the Most High as he has given to you, just as generously as you can. 11 The Lord always repays and will do it many times over. 12 But don't try to bribe him or rely on offerings that you have obtained dishonestly. He will not accept them.

God's Justice

The Lord is fair[o] and does not show partiality. 13 He is not prejudiced against the poor; when someone prays who has been wronged, the Lord listens. 14 When orphans and widows pour out their prayers, he does not ignore them. 15 The tears running down a widow's cheek cry out in accusation against the one who has caused her distress.

16 Serve the Lord willingly, and the Lord will accept you; your prayers will reach the skies. 17 The prayer of a humble person goes past the clouds and keeps on going until it reaches the Lord Most High, where it stays until he answers by seeing that justice is done and that the guilty are punished.

18 And the Lord will act quickly. He will show no patience with wicked people. He will take vengeance by crushing the heathen. He will completely wipe out the merciless and the arrogant, and will destroy the authority of the wicked. 19 He will give each of us what our thoughts and actions deserve. Because of the Lord's mercy, his people will

o **35:12** *Hebrew* fair; *Greek* judge.
35:9 2 Cor 9:7

be happy when he has judged their case. ²⁰In times of trouble his mercy is as welcome as rain after a long drought.

A Prayer for Israel

36 ¹O Lord God of the universe, look upon us and have mercy. ²Make every nation stand in fear of you. ³Take action against the foreign nations, and let them witness your power! ⁴You have used us to show them how holy you are; now use them to show us how great you are. ⁵Let them learn, as we have learned, that there is no God, O Lord, but you. ⁶Give new signs, perform new miracles; show us your glorious strength! ⁷⁻⁹Bring on that appointed time when everyone can talk about the great things you do. Pour out your furious, flaming anger, and let none of our enemies survive. Destroy those who have oppressed your people. ¹⁰Crush all those enemy rulers who think they are the only people in the world who matter! ¹¹Gather the tribes of Israel together again, and give them back their land as you gave it to them long ago. ¹²Lord, have mercy on Israel, the people who are known by your name, whom you called your first-born son. ¹³Take pity on Jerusalem, your holy city, where you chose to stay. ¹⁴Fill your Temple*ᵖ* on Mount Zion with your glory and with hymns of praise. ¹⁵Testify for your people, whom you created in the beginning; fulfill the prophecies that have been spoken in your name. ¹⁶Reward those who have put their faith in you, and vindicate your prophets. ¹⁷You have always been gracious to your people;*�q* listen to your servants as we pray. Then everyone on earth will recognize that you are the Lord, the God of the ages.

Choosing a Wife

¹⁸Any kind of food can be eaten, but some foods are better than others. ¹⁹And just as the tongue can distinguish the flavors of different kinds of meat, so a sharp mind can detect lies. ²⁰A person with a warped mind

causes trouble, but an experienced person knows how to pay it back.

²¹A woman has to take any man as a husband, but a man must choose his wife carefully. ²²A woman's beauty makes a man happy; there is no fairer sight for the human eye to see. ²³If the woman is kind and gentle in her speech, her husband is the most fortunate of men. ²⁴When a man marries, he gets the finest thing he will ever have—a wife to help and encourage him.

²⁵If property is not fenced in, thieves will wander in and help themselves. And if a man has no wife, he is a sighing wanderer; ²⁶people have no more trust in a homeless person who sleeps in a different place every night than they have in a wandering thief who goes from town to town.

False Friends

37 ¹Anyone can claim to be your friend, but some people are friends in name only. ²The grief caused when a close friendship turns sour is as bad as death. ³This evil impulse we have! Why was it ever formed? How did it manage to cover the earth with deceit? ⁴Some people will be your friend as long as things are going well, but they will turn against you when trouble comes. ⁵A real*ʳ* friend will help you against your enemies*ˢ* and protect you in the fight. ⁶Never forget such companions in battle;*ᵗ* share the results of your victory with them.

When a close friendship turns sour (37:2)

ᵖ **36:14** *Hebrew* Temple; *Greek* people.   *�q* **36:17** *Hebrew* You have . . . people; *Greek* According to the blessing of Aaron on your people.   *ʳ* **37:5** *Hebrew* real; *Greek* does not have this word.   *ˢ* **37:5** *Hebrew* against your enemies; *Greek* hoping to get a meal.   *ᵗ* **37:6** *Hebrew* in battle; *Greek* in your soul.

Caution in Taking Advice

7 Anyone can give advice, but some people do so only in their own interest. 8 Be careful when somebody offers you advice. Find out first what his interest in the matter is, because you can be sure that he is thinking primarily of himself. Why should he come out on top instead of you?*u* 9 He will assure you that things look good, and then stand back to watch what happens to you.

10 Don't ask advice of anyone who doesn't trust you, and don't give advice to anyone who is jealous of you.

11 Don't ask a woman for advice about a rival of hers,

a coward about war,
a merchant about a bargain,
a buyer about selling,
a stingy person about gratitude,
a cruel person about kindness,
a lazy person about work,
a casual worker about finishing a job,
a lazy slave about a difficult task.

Pay no attention to any advice they may give.

12 Instead, rely on someone who is religious and known to keep the Lord's commands, someone who is sympathetic with you, who will be sorry to see you fail. 13 And trust your own judgment; no one's advice is more reliable. 14 Sometimes your own intuition can tell you more than seven watchmen on a high tower. 15 Above all, pray to the Most High that he will show you the right thing to do.

Wisdom and Confidence

16 Planning and thought lie behind everything that is done. 17-18 The mind concerns itself with four things: these are good and evil, life and death. They all begin in the mind,*v* but the tongue is their absolute ruler.

19 Someone may have the ability to teach, but still not be of much use to himself. 20 He may be clever with words, but end up starving because people hate him. 21 This may happen if he doesn't have good sense, if the Lord has not given him tact. 22 Someone may consider himself wise and let you know that he is certain about what he knows. 23 Anyone who really is wise will be the teacher of his people, and they can be certain that what he teaches is the truth. 24 Everyone will praise such a person and speak of him as fortunate. 25 A person's life has only a limited number of days, but the life of Israel cannot be measured in days at all. 26 The wise will win the confidence of others, and will be remembered forever.

Controlling the Appetite

27 My child, as you go through life, keep your appetite under control, and don't eat anything that you know is bad for you. 28 All food doesn't agree with everyone, and everyone doesn't like the same kinds of food. 29 Don't feel that you just have to have all sorts of fancy food, and don't be a glutton over any food. 30 If you eat too much, you'll get sick; if you do it all the time, you'll always have stomach trouble. 31 Gluttony has been the death of many people. Avoid it and live longer.

Sickness and Medicine

38 1 Give doctors the honor they deserve, for the Lord gave them their work to do.*w* 2 Their skill came from the Most High, and kings reward them for it. 3 Their knowledge gives them a position of importance, and powerful people hold them in high regard.

4 The Lord created medicines from the earth, and a sensible person will not hesitate to use them. 5 Didn't a tree once make bitter water fit to drink, so that the Lord's power*x* might be known? 6 He gave medical knowledge to human beings, so that we would praise him for the miracles he performs. 7-8 The druggist mixes these medicines, and the doctor will use them to cure diseases and

---

u **37:8** *Hebrew* Why . . . you?; *Greek* He may use his influence against you.   *v* **37:17–18** *Hebrew* The mind . . . the mind; *Greek* There are four things that show the changes of the heart: good and evil, life and death.
w **38:1** *Hebrew* gave them their work to do; *Greek* created them.   *x* **38:5** the Lord's power; *or* its healing properties.
38:5 Ex 15:23–25

ease pain. There is no end to the activities of the Lord, who gives health to the people of the world.

⁹My child, when you get sick, don't ignore it. Pray to the Lord, and he will make you well. ¹⁰Confess all your sins and determine that in the future you will live a righteous life. ¹¹Offer incense and a grain offering, as fine as you can afford.ʸ ¹²Then call the doctor—for the Lord created him—and keep him at your side; you need him. ¹³There are times when you have to depend on his skill. ¹⁴The doctor's prayer is that the Lord will make him able to ease his patients' pain and make them well again. ¹⁵As for the person who sins against his Creator, he deserves to be sick.

Mourning for the Dead

¹⁶My child, when someone dies, you should mourn. Weep and wail to show how deeply you feel the loss. Prepare the body in the proper way, and be present at the burial. ¹⁷Weep bitterly and passionately; observe the proper period of mourning for the person. Mourn for a whole day or maybe two, to keep people from talking, but then pull yourself together and reconcile yourself to the loss. ¹⁸Grief can undermine your health and even lead to your own death. ¹⁹Grief lingers on after the death of a loved one, but it is not wise to let it lead you into poverty.

²⁰Don't lose yourself in sorrow; drive it away.ᶻ Remember that we must all die sometime. ²¹There is no way to bring the dead person back. All your sorrow does him no good, and it hurts you. Don't forget that. ²²You will die, just as he did. Today it was his turn; tomorrow it will be yours. ²³When the dead have been laid to rest, let the memory of them fade. Once they are gone, take courage.

Scholarship and Other Occupations

²⁴Scholars must have time to study if they are going to be wise; they must be relieved of other responsibilities. ²⁵How can a farm

All your sorrow does him no good. (38:21)

hand gain knowledge, when his only ambition is to drive the oxen and make them work, when all he knows to talk about is livestock? ²⁶He takes great pains to plow a straight furrow and will work far into the night to feed the animals.

²⁷It is the same with the artist and the craftsman, who work night and day engraving precious stones, carefully working out new designs. They take great pains to produce a lifelike image, and will work far into the night to finish the work.

²⁸It is the same with the blacksmith at his anvil, planning what he will make from a piece of iron. The heat from the fire sears his skin as he sweats away at the forge. The clanging of the hammer deafens himᵃ as he carefully watches the object he is working take shape. He takes great pains to complete his task, and will work far into the night to bring it to perfection.

²⁹It is the same with the potter, sitting at his wheel and turning it with his feet, always concentrating on his work, concerned with how many objects he can produce. ³⁰He works the clay with his feet until he can shape it with his hands; then he takes great pains to glaze it properly, and will work far into the night to clean out the kiln.

³¹All of these people are skilled with their hands, each of them an expert at his own craft. ³²Without such people there could be no cities; no one would live or visit where

ʸ **38:11** *Hebrew* as fine as you can afford; *Greek unclear.* ᶻ **38:20** drive it away; *or put the memory of the person aside.* ᵃ **38:28** *Probable text* deafens him; *Greek* renews his ears.
38:16–23 Sir 22:11, 12

He works the clay with his feet until he can shape it with his hands. (38:30)

these services were not available. ³³These people are not sought out to serve on the public councils, and they never attain positions of great importance. They do not serve as judges, and they do not understand legal matters. They have no education and are not known for their wisdom. You never hear them quoting proverbs. ³⁴But the work they do holds this world together. When they do their work, it is the same as offering prayer.^b

39 ¹But it is different with the person who devotes himself to studying the Law of the Most High. He examines the wisdom of all the ancient writers and concerns himself with the prophecies. ²He memorizes the sayings of famous men and is a skilled interpreter of parables. ³He studies the hidden meaning of proverbs and is able to discuss the obscure points of parables. ⁴Great people call on him for his services, and he is seen in the company of rulers. He travels to foreign lands in his efforts to learn about human good and evil. ⁵It is his practice to get up early and pray aloud to the Lord his Creator, asking the Most High to forgive his sins. ⁶Then, if the great Lord is willing, he will be filled with understanding. He will pour out a stream of wise sayings, and give thanks to the Lord in prayer. ⁷He will have

knowledge to share and good advice to give, as well as insight into the Lord's secrets. ⁸He will demonstrate his learning in what he teaches,^c and his pride will be in the Lord's Law and covenant. ⁹He will be widely praised for his wisdom, and it will never be lost, because people for generations to come will remember him. ¹⁰The Gentiles will talk about his wisdom, and he will be praised aloud in the assembly. ¹¹If he lives to old age, he will die famous, but if he is laid to rest before he is famous, he will be content.^d

A Hymn in Praise of God

¹²Like the moon, I am full—full of more ideas to be discussed. ¹³Listen to me, you devout children of mine, and blossom like a rosebush on a stream bank. ¹⁴Bloom like a sweet-smelling lily, and send your fragrance into the air like incense. Sing the Lord's praises, and thank him for all that he has done. ¹⁵Proclaim his glory in grateful praise! To the music of the harp, sing this song:

¹⁶All that the Lord has done is very good;
　　all that he commands is sooner or later
　　　done.
¹⁷No one should ask why things are as they
　　are;
　　these questions will be answered at the
　　　right time.
He commanded, and the water piled up
　　high,
　　great walls of water arose when he
　　　spoke.
¹⁸Whatever he commands is promptly done;
　　there are no limits to his power to save.
¹⁹He sees all that every human being does;
　　there is no way to hide from his sight.
²⁰He sees the whole of time, from
　　beginning to end,
　　and nothing takes him by surprise.^e
²¹No one should ask why things are as they
　　are;
　　everything in creation has its purpose.
²²His blessings overflow like the Nile,
　　enriching the world in a fertile flood.^f

^b **38:34** When . . . prayer; *or* When they pray, it is about their work.　^c **39:8** his learning . . . teaches; *or the* wisdom of what he has been taught.　^d **39:11** if he is . . . content; *Greek unclear.*　^e **39:20** takes him by surprise; *or* is too marvelous for him.　^f **39:22** *Hebrew* overflow . . . flood; *Greek* cover the dry land like a river and drench it like a flood.

23 He turns fresh water into salt water,
 and he turns his anger on the nations.
24 For the devout, his ways are straight;
 for the wicked, they are laid with traps.
25 From the beginning he has made good
  things for the good
 and terrible things for sinners.
26 The basic needs of life are these:
 water, fire, iron, and salt,
 flour, honey, and milk,
 wine, clothing, and oil.
27 All these things are good for those who
  are devout,
 but they turn into evils for sinners.

28 There are winds that were created to
  bring punishment,
 fierce enough to move mountains.*g*
In times of judgment, they unleash their
  strength
 and calm the anger of their maker.
29-30 Vicious animals, scorpions, and snakes;
 the sword that destroys the wicked;
fire, hail, famine, and disease;
 these have all been created as
  punishments.
31 They are all glad to obey the Lord's
  command
 and are ready to serve him here on
  earth.
When their times of duty come,
 they never disobey.
(32 I was long convinced of this, so after
thinking it over I put*h* it in writing.)
33 Everything made by the Lord is good;
 he meets every need at the proper
  time.
34 No one can claim that some things are
  worse than others,
 for everything is good in its proper
  place.
35 Now then, sing praises with all your heart,
 and praise the name of the Lord!

The Misery of Human Life

40 ¹Every person has been given a great deal of work to do. A heavy burden lies on all of us from the day of our birth until the day we go back to the earth, the mother of us all. ²We are confused and fearful, dreading the day of our death— ³-⁴all of us from the king on his splendid throne wearing royal robes and a crown, to the humblest person dressed in burlap and living in poverty. ⁵All through our lives we meet anger, jealousy, and trouble. Things disturb us; we live with furious conflicts and with the fear of death. Even when we go to bed, we think up new troubles in our sleep. ⁶We get little rest, if any at all. When we sleep, it is as if we were awake, disturbed by our imaginations. If we dream that we are running from an enemy, ⁷just as we are about to be caught,*i* we wake up and are relieved to find there is nothing to be afraid of.

⁸Here is what all creatures, both human and animal, must face (but it is seven times worse for sinners): ⁹death, violence, conflict, murder, disaster, famine, sickness, epidemic. ¹⁰All these things were created because of the wicked; they are the ones who have caused destruction.*j* ¹¹Everything that comes from the earth goes back to the earth, just as all water flows into the sea.

The Results of Evil

¹²Nothing that comes from bribery or injustice will last, but the effects of loyalty will remain forever. ¹³Wealth that has been obtained dishonestly is like a stream that runs full during a thunderstorm, ¹⁴tumbling rocks along as it flows, but then suddenly goes dry.*k* ¹⁵The children of ungodly people will not leave large families; they are like plants trying to take root on rock, ¹⁶like reeds along a river bank, withering*l* before any other plant. ¹⁷Acts of kindness and charity are as lasting as eternity.*m*

The Joys of Human Life

¹⁸Being independently wealthy or working for a living—both can make life pleasant, but it is better to find a treasure.

¹⁹Your name can be preserved if you have

---

g **39:28** *Hebrew* move mountains; *Greek* lash heavily. *h* **39:32** put; *or* left. *i* **40:7** *Probable text* caught; *Greek* rescued. *j* **40:10** *Hebrew* have caused destruction; *Greek* caused the flood. *k* **40:14** *Verses 13–14 are translated from Hebrew; verse 14 in Greek is unclear.* *l* **40:16** *Hebrew* withering; *Greek* pulled up. *m* **40:17** *Hebrew* Acts . . . eternity; *Greek* Kindness is a blessed garden, and charity lasts forever.

children or if you establish a city, but finding Wisdom is a better way.

Owning livestock and orchards will make you famous,[n] but it is better to have a wife you love.[o]

20 Wine and music can make you happy, but a happy marriage[p] is even better.

21 Flutes and harps make fine music, but a pleasant voice is better than either.

22 Gracefulness and beauty please the eye, but not as much as new growth in the spring.

23 You can't go wrong with a good friend or neighbor, but an intelligent wife is[q] better than either.

24 Relatives and helpers are good to have in times of trouble, but it will be an even greater help if you have made a practice of giving to the poor.

25 Gold and silver provide security, but good advice is better.

26 Wealth and strength give confidence, but the fear of the Lord can give you even greater confidence. When you fear the Lord you need nothing more; it is all the support you need. 27 The fear of the Lord is like a rich garden of blessings; you could not want a more glorious shelter.

Begging

28 My child, don't live the life of a beggar; it is better to die than to beg. 29 If you have to depend on someone else for your food, you are not really living your own life. You pollute yourself by accepting food from another. Begging is torture to the soul of any sensitive person.[r] 30 A shameless person can make begging sound sweet, but something inside him burns.

Death

41 1 Death! The very thought of it is bitter to someone who is prosperous, living peacefully with his possessions, free of worries, and still able to enjoy his food.

2 Death! Its sentence is welcome to someone living in poverty, with failing health, very old, burdened with worries, blind, and without hope.[s]

3 Do not be afraid of death's decree. Remember that it came to those before you and will come to those after you. 4 The Lord has decreed it for every living creature. Who are you to object to what the Most High wishes? In the world of the dead no one will care whether you lived ten years, a hundred, or a thousand.

The Fate of the Wicked

5 The children of sinners, brought up in ungodly surroundings, turn out to be hateful people. 6 They will lose whatever they inherit, and their own descendants will live in permanent disgrace. 7 The children will put the blame for their disgrace on their ungodly parents.

8 You are doomed, you irreligious people who have abandoned the Law of the Most High God. 9 When you have children, disaster will strike them and you will be left with nothing but sorrow. There will be great joy whenever you stumble,[t] and even after your death you will be cursed. 10 What comes into being from nothing[u] will return to nothing;[u] so it will be with the godless, doomed to extinction.

11 A person's body amounts to nothing,[v] but a good reputation will last forever. 12 Protect your reputation; it will outlive you and last longer than a thousand treasures of gold. 13 A good life lasts only so long, but a good reputation will last forever.

A Sense of Decency

14 My children, do as I teach you and live at peace. Wisdom that is not expressed is like a treasure that has been hidden—both are useless. 15 A person who covers up his fool-

---

[n] **40:19** *Hebrew* but finding Wisdom . . . famous; *Greek does not have these words.* [o] **40:19** *Hebrew* wife you love; *Greek* blameless wife. [p] **40:20** *Hebrew* a happy marriage; *Greek* the love of Wisdom. [q] **40:23** *Hebrew* an intelligent wife is; *Greek* a wife and a husband are. [r] **40:29** *Hebrew* Begging . . . person; *Greek* An intelligent and understanding person will avoid it. [s] **41:2** *Hebrew* blind, and without hope; *Greek* rebellious and without patience. [t] **41:9** *Hebrew* When you have . . . stumble; *Greek* You are born under a curse. [u] **41:10** *Hebrew* nothing; *Greek* earth. [v] **41:11** *Hebrew* A person's . . . nothing; *Greek* The death of a person's body is mourned.

ishness is better than one who keeps his wisdom to himself.

¹⁶My children, listen and I will teach you the circumstances when it is proper to be ashamed. *w* Sometimes it is entirely out of place.

. . . when it is proper to be ashamed. (41:16)

¹⁷Before your parents, be ashamed of
    immoral behavior.
Before a ruler or an important person, be
    ashamed of a lie.
¹⁸Before a judge, be ashamed of criminal
    behavior.
Before a public assembly, be ashamed of
    breaking the law.
Before a friend or partner, be ashamed of
    dishonesty.
¹⁹Before your neighbors, be ashamed of
    theft.
Be ashamed of breaking a promise, *x*
    of leaning on the dinner table with
      your elbows,
    of stinginess when you are asked for
      something,
²⁰   of not returning a greeting,
    of staring at a prostitute,
²¹   of turning down a relative's request,
    of depriving someone of what is
      rightly his,
    of staring at another man's wife,
²²   of playing around with his slave
      woman (keep away from her bed!)
    of insulting your friends,
    of following up your gifts with
      criticism,
²³   of betraying secrets.
These are times when it is proper for you to be ashamed, and people will respect you for it.

A Sense of Pride

42 ¹On the other hand, it is possible to sin by giving in to other people too much. Here are some things you should not be ashamed of:
²the Law of the Most High and his
    covenant,
    judging even godless people fairly,
³sharing expenses with a business partner
    or a traveling companion,
    sharing an inheritance,
⁴using accurate weights and measures,
⁵making a profit, whether great or small,
    bargaining with a merchant,
    disciplining your children often,
    beating a disloyal slave until the blood
      flows.
⁶It is wise to lock things up if you cannot trust your wife or if too many people are around. ⁷Keep an accurate record of any deposits you make or of anything you give or receive. ⁸Don't hesitate to correct someone who is acting foolishly or an old man who goes around with prostitutes. All of this is worthwhile advice, and if you follow it, everyone will approve of your behavior.

Fathers and Daughters

⁹Although he will not let his daughter know it, a father will lie awake at night worrying about her. If she is young, he worries that she might not get married. If she is already married, he worries about her happiness. ¹⁰If she is a virgin, he worries that she might be seduced and become pregnant while living in his house. If she is married, he worries that she might be unfaithful, or that she might not be able to have children.

¹¹Keep a close watch over your daughter if she is determined to have her own way. If you don't, she may make a fool of you in front of your enemies. You will be a constant joke to everyone in town, a public disgrace. Make sure that her room has no windows or any place where she can look out to the entrance of the house. *y* ¹²Don't let her show

Sirach

---

w **41:16** *Hebrew* My children . . . ashamed; *Greek* Show respect for what I say.   *x* **41:19** *Hebrew* of breaking a promise; *Greek* of yourself before the truth of God.   *y* **42:11** *Hebrew* Make sure . . . house; *Greek* does not have these words.
42:9–11 Sir 7:24, 25; 26:10–12

off her beauty in front of men, or spend her time talking with the women.*z* ¹³Women hurt other women just as moths damage clothing.

¹⁴A man's wickedness is better than a woman's goodness; women bring shame and disgrace.

The Glory of God in Nature

¹⁵Now I will remind you of the works of the Lord
and describe the things I have seen.
The words of the Lord brought his works into being,
and the whole creation obeys his commands.
¹⁶The light of the sun shines down on everything,
and everything is filled with the Lord's glory.
¹⁷Not even to his holy angels has the Lord given power
to describe all his mighty deeds,
even though he has given them power
to stand unharmed in his glorious presence.*a*
¹⁸He sees into the oceans and into the human heart,
and he knows the secrets of both.
The Most High knows everything that can be known
and understands the signs of the ages.
¹⁹He knows all that has ever been and all that ever will be;
he uncovers the deepest of mysteries.
²⁰He takes notice of our every thought
and hears our every word.
²¹The orderly world shows the greatness of his wisdom;
he is the same forever and ever.*b*
Nothing can be added to him, and nothing taken away;
he needs no one to give him advice.
²²All his works are beautiful,
down to the smallest and faintest spark of light.*c*

²³All these things go on forever,
and all of them have their purpose.
²⁴All things are in pairs, each the opposite of the other,
but nothing the Lord made is incomplete.
²⁵Everything completes the goodness of something else.
Could anyone ever see enough of this splendor?

43

¹How beautiful is the bright, clear sky above us!
What a glorious sight it is!
²The sun, when it appears, proclaims as it rises
how marvelous a thing it is, made by the Most High.
³At noon it dries up the land;
no one can stand its blazing heat.
⁴The setting sun sets fire to the hilltops,
like a metal furnace glowing from the heat.*d*
It sends out fiery rays,
blinding the eyes with its brightness.
⁵The Lord, who made it, is great;
it speeds on its way at his command.

⁶There is also the moon, marking the passage of time,*e*
an eternal sign of the changing seasons.
⁷The moon determines the holy days.
Its light grows full and then grows dim.
⁸The "month" is named after the moon,
marvelous to watch as it grows fuller each night,
a signal light for the heavenly armies,
shining out in the dome of the sky.

⁹The shining stars make the night sky lovely,
brilliant ornaments in the Lord's high heavens.
¹⁰They stay in the places assigned to them by the Holy One
and never relax their dutiful watch.

¹¹Look at the rainbow and praise its Creator!
How magnificent, how radiant, its beauty!

z **42:11** *Hebrew* Don't let . . . women; *Greek unclear.* *a* **42:17** *Hebrew* even though . . . presence; *Greek* which the Lord Almighty established so that everything may stand firm in his glory. *b* **42:21** *Hebrew* he is . . . ever; *Greek* he is before eternity and is eternal. *c* **42:22** *Hebrew* down to . . . spark of light; *Greek unclear.*
d **43:4** *Hebrew* The setting . . . heat; *Greek* A man at a furnace works with scorching heat, but the sun burns the hills three times as much. *e* **43:6** *Hebrew* marking . . . time; *Greek unclear.*

¹²Like a bow bent by the hands of the Most
      High,
    it spans the horizon in a circle of glory.

It spans the horizon in a circle of glory. (43:12)

¹³He commands, and snow begins to fall;
    lightning strikes to carry out his
      judgments.
¹⁴The storerooms of the sky are thrown
      open,
    and the clouds roll out like flying birds.
¹⁵With his power he forms great masses of
      clouds
    and shatters the ice into hailstones.
¹⁶⁻¹⁷He speaks, and thunder twists the earth
      in pain;
    the mountains are shaken by his
      strength.ᶠ
    Whenever he wishes, the south wind
      blows,
    whirlwinds come, and windstorms
      from the north.
    He sends the snow fluttering down like
      birds,
    like locusts lighting on the ground.
¹⁸We marvel at its beautiful whiteness,
    and in fascination we watch it fall.
¹⁹He sprinkles frost over the ground like
      salt,
    and it freezes into thorny flowers of
      ice.ᵍ
²⁰He sends the cold north wind blowing
    and the water hardens into ice;
    every lake and pond freezes over,
    putting on a coat of icy armor.

²¹He scorches the wilderness hills with
      drought,
    and the grass turns brown from its heat;
²²but a cloudy mist restores it all to life
    as the weather cools and dew appears.

²³By his wisdom he calmed the great
      oceans
    and placed the islands there.
²⁴Sailors tell about the dangers of the sea,
    and we listen to their tales in
      amazement.
²⁵In the sea are strange and marvelous
      creatures:
    huge monsters and all kinds of living
      things.
²⁶Each of the Lord's messengers succeeds at
      its task.
    Everything is held together by his
      word.

²⁷We could say much more and never
      finish,
    but it all means this: the Lord is
      everything.
²⁸How can we find the power to praise
      him?
    He is greater than all his creation.
²⁹The Lord is awesome in his greatness;
    his power is overwhelming.
³⁰Though you do your best to praise him,
    he is greater than you can ever express.
    Though you honor him tirelessly and
      with all your strength,
    you still cannot praise him enough.
³¹No one has seen him, no one can
      describe him;
    no one can praise him as he deserves.
³²Mysteries greater than these are still
      unknown;
    we know only a fraction of his works.
³³The Lord made the universe
    and then gave wisdom to devout
      people.

The Glory of God in History

44 ¹So let us now give praise to godlyʰ
      men,
    our ancestors of generations past,

ᶠ **43:16–17** *Hebrew* by his strength; *Greek* when he appears.   ᵍ **43:19** *Hebrew* flowers of ice; *Greek* points.
ʰ **44:1** *Hebrew* godly; *Greek* famous.

2 those whom the Lord honored with great
glory,
in whom his greatness has been seen
from the beginning of time.
3 There were some who ruled kingdoms,
and some who were known for their
strength.
Some were wise advisers,
and some spoke prophecies.
4 There were statesmen whose policies
governed the people,
rulers who issued decrees,[i]
scholars who spoke wise words,[j]
and those who used pointed proverbs,[k]
5   poets, and composers of music,
6   rich and powerful men living
peacefully at home.
7 All of these were famous in their own
times,
honored by the people of their day.
8 Some of them left a reputation,
and people still praise them today.
9 There are others who are not
remembered,
as if they had never lived,
who died and were forgotten,
they, and their children after them.
10 But we will praise these godly men,
whose righteous deeds have never been
forgotten.
11 Their reputations will be passed on to
their descendants,
and this will be their inheritance.[l]
12 Their descendants continue to keep the
covenant
and always will, because of what their
ancestors did.
13 Their family line will go on forever,
and their fame will never fade.
14 Their bodies were laid to rest,
but their reputations will live forever.
15 Nations will tell about their wisdom,
and God's people will praise them.

Enoch

16 Enoch pleased the Lord and was taken
up into heaven. He became an inspiration
for repentance for all time to come.

Noah

17 Noah was a perfectly righteous man.
After destruction came, he gave the human
race a new start.[m] Because of him there were
people left on earth when the flood was
over. 18 The Lord made an eternal covenant
with him, promising that life would never
again be destroyed by a flood.

Abraham

19 Abraham was the great ancestor of
many nations; his reputation was faultless.[n]
20 He kept the Law of the Most High and
made a covenant with him, a covenant
marked on his body. When he was put to the
test, he was found faithful. 21 And so the Lord
made him a solemn promise that his descendants would be a blessing to the world; that
their number would be countless, like the
dust of the earth; that they would be honored more than any other people on earth;
and that their land would extend from sea to
sea, from the Euphrates to the ends of the
earth.

Isaac and Jacob

22-23 The Lord renewed that covenant with
Isaac, and then again with Jacob, repeating
the promise that Abraham's descendants
would be a blessing to the whole human
race. The Lord assured Jacob that he would
bless him; he gave him the land that would
be his, dividing it into twelve parts, one for
each of the tribes.

---

[i] *44:4 Probable Hebrew text* rulers who issued decrees; *Greek unclear.* [j] *44:4 Hebrew* scholars . . . words; *Greek
unclear.* [k] *44:4 Hebrew* and those . . . proverbs; *Greek does not have these words.* [l] *44:11 Verse 11 in Greek is
unclear.* [m] *44:17 Hebrew* gave . . . start; *Greek* was taken in exchange for the human race. [n] *44:19 Hebrew* his
reputation was faultless; *Greek* there was no one like him in reputation.
44:16 Gen 5:24; Heb 11:5; Jude 14   **44:17, 18** Gen 6:9—9:17   **44:19–21** Gen 15:1—17:27; 22:1–18
44:22, 23 Gen 17:19; 26:3–5; 27:28; 28:14

Moses

45

¹From Jacob's descendants the Lord raised up a godly man who won the favor of everyone, loved by God and people alike. This man was Moses, whose very memory is a blessing. ²The Lord made him as glorious as the angels and made his enemies fear him. ³There in Egypt at his command the disaster struck.º The Lord made kings hold him in respect. The Lord gave him his commands for his people and showed him the dazzling light of his presence. ⁴The Lord chose Moses out of the whole human race and consecrated him because of his loyalty and humility. ⁵He let him hear his voice and led him into the dark cloud, where, face to face, he gave him the commandments, the Law that gives life and knowledge, so that Moses might teach the covenant regulations to the Israelites.

Aaron

⁶The Lord raised up Aaron, a holy man like his brother Moses, of the tribe of Levi. ⁷He made an eternal covenant with him, giving him the privilege of serving as priest to the Lord's people. He honored him by clothing him with magnificent robes and fine ornaments, ⁸perfect in their splendor. He granted him the symbols of authority: the linen shorts, the shirt, and the robe with the pomegranates around the hem. ⁹Gold bells were also around its hem, so that when he walked, their ringing would be heard in the Temple, and the Lord would remember his people. ¹⁰The Lord gave Aaron the sacred robe with the gold, blue, and purple embroidery; the breastpiece with the Urim and Thummim;ᴾ ¹¹the red yarn, spun by an expert; the precious stones with names engraved on them, mounted in a gold setting by a jeweler, placed on the breastpiece to remind the Lord of the twelve tribes of Israel. ¹²He gave him the turban with the gold ornament engraved with the words "Dedicated to the Lord." It was expertly crafted, a beautiful work of art, and it was a high honor to wear it. ¹³Before Aaron's time such beautiful things were never seen. No one but Aaron and his descendants ever wore them, or ever will. ¹⁴The grain offering is to be presented twice a day and burned completely.

¹⁵Moses ordained Aaron to office by pouring the sacred anointing oil over his head. An eternal covenant was made with him and his descendants, that they would serve the Lord as his priests and bless the people in the Lord's name. ¹⁶The Lord chose Aaron out of the whole human race to offer sacrifices, to burn fragrant incense to remind the Lord of his people, and to take away their sins. ¹⁷He entrusted the commandments to Aaron's keeping and gave him the authority to make legal decisions and to teach Israel the Law.

¹⁸Once, while the people were in the wilderness, an angry group of jealous outsiders conspired against Moses. These were Dathan, Abiram, and Korah with their supporters. ¹⁹The Lord saw what they were doing and became angry, so furious that he performed a miracle and destroyed them in a blazing fire. ²⁰Then he rewarded Aaron again, giving him a special honor: the right to the offerings of the first produce, so that the priests should have enough to eat. ²¹Their food is the sacrifices offered to the Lord; the Lord gave this to Aaron and his descendants. ²²But Aaron, unlike the rest of the people, was to inherit no land, no special portion of his own. The Lord himself would be all he needed.

Phinehas

²³Only Moses and Aaron were more famous for their intense devotion to the Lord than Phinehas son of Eleazar. He brought about forgiveness for Israel's sin by standing firm in brave determination when everyone else was in rebellion. ²⁴And so the Lord made a covenant with him, valid for all time to come, that he should be in charge of

---

º **45:3** *Hebrew* struck; *Greek* stopped. ᴾ **45:10** URIM AND THUMMIM: *Two objects used by the priest to determine God's will; it is not known precisely how they were used.*
45:1–5 Ex 6:28—11:10; 20:1–21 **45:6** Ex 4:14 **45:7–13** Ex 28:1–43 **45:15** Lev 8:1–36
45:18, 19 Num 16:1–35 **45:22** Num 18:20; Deut 12:12 **45:23–26** Num 25:7–13

the sanctuary and of his people, that he and his descendants should hold the office of High Priest forever. 25 Unlike the covenant made with David son of Jesse, from the tribe of Judah, where the kingship passed only from father to son, the priesthood was to pass from Aaron to all his descendants.

26 Now praise the Lord, who is good, who

IN PRAISE OF ANCESTORS (Chapters 44-50)

has crowned you with glory!*q* May he give you wisdom to judge his people fairly, so that their success and your authority*r* may continue for all time to come.

Joshua

46 [1]Joshua*s* son of Nun was a great soldier and the next of the prophets after Moses. He lived up to the meaning of his name as the great deliverer of the Lord's chosen people. He defeated the enemies that attacked them, so that Israel could claim its land. [2]How magnificent it was when he raised his arm and then led the attacks on the cities! [3]No one could stand up to him;*t* he was fighting a holy war for the Lord. [4]Remember how he held back the sun and made one day as long as two? [5]When his enemies were threatening him from every side, he prayed to the mighty Lord Most High, and his prayer was answered with a hailstorm of devastating force. [6]The Lord hurled the hail down on the enemy*u* and destroyed them at the pass at Beth Horon, so that the nations would realize how strong Joshua was, since he was fighting as a devoted follower of the Lord.

Caleb

[7]Joshua was loyal as long as Moses lived, both he and Caleb son of Jephunneh. They stood up to the whole community, made them stop their ungrateful complaining, and kept them from sinning. [8]Out of the 600,000 Israelites who marched through the wilderness, these two were the only ones spared and allowed to enter the rich and fertile land that was to be theirs. [9]The Lord made Caleb strong, and when he was an old man, he was still strong enough to go up into the hill country and capture it for himself and his descendants. [10]Then all of Israel could see how good it is to follow the Lord.

The Judges

[11]Then there were the judges, each of them famous in their own right, who never fell into idolatry and never abandoned the Lord. [12]May their memory be honored! May these whom we honor spring from the grave to new life in their descendants!

Samuel

[13]Samuel was loved by the Lord. As the Lord's prophet he established the kingdom and appointed rulers for the people. [14]He judged the nation in accordance with the Law of the Lord, and the Lord protected Israel. [15]Because Samuel was faithful, he was accepted as a true prophet. People trusted him as a seer because of his words. [16]When his enemies were threatening him from every side, he called upon the mighty Lord and offered him a young lamb as a sacrifice. [17]Then the Lord thundered from heaven with a mighty roar [18]and destroyed all the enemy*v* rulers of Philistia. [19]When Samuel was about to die, he gave assurances before the Lord and the anointed king that he had never taken anyone's property, not even so much as a pair of shoes, and no one contradicted him. [20]Even after he died, he prophesied to King Saul how he would die. Out of the grave he spoke as a prophet, to blot out his people's wickedness.

Nathan

47 [1]After him came Nathan, who was a prophet at the time of David.

David

[2]As the choice fat portion of the fellowship offering is reserved for the Lord, so David was chosen from among the Israelites. [3]He played with lions and bears as if they were lambs or little goats. [4]When he was still

q **45:26** *Hebrew* Now praise . . . glory; *Greek does not have these words.*   *r* **45:26** *Probable Hebrew text* and your authority; *Greek unclear.*   *s* **46:1** JOSHUA: *This name in Hebrew means "the Lord saves."*   *t* **46:3** *Hebrew* no one . . . to him; *Greek* No one before had ever been so brave.   *u* **46:6** *Probable text* The Lord hurled . . . enemy; *Greek unclear.*   *v* **46:18** *Hebrew* enemy; *Greek* rulers of Tyre and.
46:1–6 Josh 1:1—11:23   **46:7–10** Num 14:6–10; 11:21; Josh 14:6–11   **46:11** Judg 1:1—16:31   **46:13–20** 1 Sam 3:19, 20; 7:9–11; 10:1; 12:3; 16:13; 28:18, 19   **47:1** 2 Sam 7:2, 3; 12:1   **47:2–11** 1 Sam 17:34—18:7; 2 Sam 5:7; 8:1; 12:13

a boy, he killed a giant to rescue his people. He put a stone in his sling, took aim, and put an end to Goliath's bragging. ⁵He prayed to the Lord, the Most High, and was given the strength to kill that famous soldier, so that the nations would have respect for the power of his people. ⁶The people honored him for killing his tens of thousands, and when he was crowned king, they praised him for being chosen by the Lord. ⁷He wiped out all his enemies and permanently crushed the Philistines, so that they never again became a threat.

⁸In everything David did, he gave thanks and praise to the Holy Lord, the Most High. He loved his Creator and sang praises to him with all his heart. ⁹He put singers at the altar to provide beautiful music. ¹⁰He set the times of the festivals throughout the year and made them splendid occasions; the Temple rang with the Lord's praises all day long. ¹¹The Lord forgave David's sin and established his power forever. He made a covenant with him that he and his descendants would reign in splendor over Israel.

Solomon

¹²David prepared the way well for his son, a wise man, to rule after him. ¹³There was no war while Solomon was king. God gave him peace on all his borders, so that he could build for the Lord a Temple which would stand forever. ¹⁴How wise you were, Solomon, when you were young! Your knowledge was like the Nile*ʷ* in flood. ¹⁵Your influence reached over all the world; your proverbs and riddles were known everywhere. ¹⁶You were famous everywhere, and people loved you for bringing peace. ¹⁷Nations around the world held you in admiration for your songs, proverbs, parables, and witty sayings. ¹⁸You gathered silver and gold as if it were tin or lead, all in the name of the Lord God of Israel.

¹⁹But your lust for women was your downfall. ²⁰You stained your reputation and that of your descendants. They suffered punishment for that foolishness of yours, which caused them so much grief. ²¹It divided the nation, and a rival kingdom arose in northern Israel. ²²But the Lord will always be merciful and keep all his promises.*ˣ* He will never destroy the descendants of David, whom he chose and who loved him. So for Israel's sake he allowed David's family to survive.

Rehoboam and Jeroboam

²³Solomon followed his ancestors in death and left one of his sons to rule after him. This was Rehoboam, a man of little intelligence and great foolishness,*ʸ* whose policies caused a rebellion.

There was also the unspeakable*ᶻ* Jeroboam, who led northern Israel in sinful ways. ²⁴His people became so sinful that they were exiled from their land. ²⁵They tried all kinds of wickedness until the Lord took vengeance on them.

Elijah

48 ¹Then there arose the fiery prophet Elijah, whose words blazed like a torch. ²He brought a famine on the people, and many of them died because of his persistence. ³Speaking in the name of the Lord, he kept the rain from coming, and on three occasions he called down fire. ⁴Elijah, your miracles were marvelous! No one else can boast of such deeds! ⁵In the name of the Most High, you brought a dead man back to life. ⁶You brought a famous king down to sickness and death. ⁷At Sinai you heard the Lord rebuke you and declare his determination to punish his enemies. ⁸You anointed a king to be the instrument of that punishment, and a prophet to take your place. ⁹You were taken up to heaven in a fiery whirlwind, a chariot drawn by fiery horses. ¹⁰The

ʷ **47:14** *Hebrew* the Nile; *Greek* a river.   *ˣ* **47:22** *Hebrew* keep all his promises; *Greek* will not destroy what he made.   *ʸ* **47:23** *Hebrew* great foolishness; *Greek* the people's fool.   *ᶻ* **47:23** *Hebrew* the unspeakable (one); *Greek* Jeroboam son of Nebat.
47:13–17 1 Kings 4:21–32   **47:18** 1 Kings 10:21, 27   **47:19** 1 Kings 11:1   **47:21** 1 Kings 12:15–20 **47:22** 2 Sam 7:15   **47:23–25** 1 Kings 11:43; 12:10–30; 2 Kings 17:6, 18   **48:1–11** 1 Kings 17:1–24; 18:38; 19:15, 16; 2 Kings 1:10–16; 2:11; Mal 4:5, 6

Sirach

scripture says that you are ready to appear at the designated time,*a* to cool God's anger before it breaks out in fury; that you "will bring parents and children together again," and restore the tribes of Israel. 11Fortunate are those who live to see you come, as well as those who have already died in love, for we too shall live.*b*

Elisha

12When Elijah was hidden by the whirlwind, Elisha was filled with his spirit. As long as he lived, he was not afraid of rulers, and they could not make him do as they wished. 13Nothing was too hard for him. Even when he was dead, his body worked a miracle. 14In life and in death he performed amazing miracles.

15But in spite of all this, the people did not abandon their sinful ways until they were taken from their land as prisoners and scattered all over the world. This left the nation few in number, but those who remained were still ruled by the descendants of David. 16Some of the people did what was pleasing to the Lord, but others committed sin after sin.

Hezekiah

17Hezekiah prepared his city to resist a siege and provided it with a water supply. He had a tunnel built through solid rock with iron tools and had cisterns built to hold the water. 18During his reign Sennacherib attacked the city and sent his chief official from Lachish. He challenged Jerusalem and boasted arrogantly. 19The people lost their courage and shook with fear; they were in pain, like a woman in labor. 20But they prayed to the merciful Lord, the Holy One in heaven, who quickly answered their prayers and sent Isaiah to save them. 21The Lord struck the Assyrian camp; his angel wiped them out. 22Yes, Hezekiah did what

was pleasing to the Lord and firmly followed the example of his ancestor David. This was what was commanded by the great prophet Isaiah, whose visions were trusted. 23He made the sun move backward and lengthened the king's life. 24He comforted the mourners in Jerusalem. His powerful spirit looked into the future, 25and he predicted what was to happen before the end of time, hidden things that had not yet occurred.

Josiah

49

1The memory of Josiah is as sweet as the fragrance of expertly blended incense, sweet as honey to the taste,*c* like music with wine at a banquet. 2He followed the correct policy of reforming the nation and removed the horrors of idolatry. 3He was completely loyal to the Lord and strengthened true religion in those wicked times.

Jeremiah

4All the kings, except David, Hezekiah, and Josiah, were terrible sinners, because they abandoned the Law of the Most High to the very end of the kingdom.*d* 5They surrendered their power and honor to foreigners, 6who set fire to the holy city and left its streets deserted, just as Jeremiah had predicted. 7Jeremiah had been badly treated, even though he was chosen as a prophet before he was born, "to uproot and to pull down, to destroy and to overthrow," but also "to build and to plant."

Ezekiel

8It was Ezekiel who was shown the vision of the divine glory over the chariot and the living creatures. 9He also referred to the prophet Job, who always did the right thing.*e*

---

a **48:10** *Hebrew* you are . . . time; *Greek unclear.*   *b* **48:11** *Verse 11 in Greek is unclear.*   *c* **49:1** *Hebrew* to the taste; *Greek* to everyone.   *d* **49:4** *Hebrew* to the very end of the kingdom; *Greek* and failed.   *e* **49:9** *Probable Hebrew text* He also . . . thing; *Greek unclear.*

48:12 2 Kings 2:9, 13   **48:13** 2 Kings 13:20, 21   **48:15** 2 Kings 18:11, 12   **48:17** 2 Kings 20:20   **48:18** 2 Kings 18:13–17   **48:20, 21** 2 Kings 19:15–20, 35   **48:23** 2 Kings 20:10, 11   **49:1–3** 2 Kings 22:1; 22:11–13; 23:3, 25   **49:6, 7** Jer 1:4–10; 39:8   **49:8, 9** Ezek 1:3–15; 14:14–20

The Twelve Prophets

10 May the bones of the twelve prophets rise to new life, because these men encouraged the people of Israel and saved them with confident hope.

Zerubbabel and Joshua

11 How can we praise Zerubbabel? He was like a signet ring on the Lord's right hand, 12 as was Joshua son of Jehozadak. They rebuilt the Lord's holy Temple, destined for eternal fame.

Nehemiah

13 The memory of Nehemiah is also great. He rebuilt the ruined walls of Jerusalem, installing the gates and bars. He rebuilt our homes.

The Patriarchs

14 No one else like Enoch has ever walked the face of the earth, for he was taken up from the earth. 15 No one else like Joseph has ever been born;f even his bones were honored.g 16 Shem, Seth, and Enoshh were highly honored, but Adam's glory was above that of any other living being.

Simon Son of Onias

50 1 The greatest of his brothers and the pride of his peoplei was the High Priest Simon son of Onias, who repaired the Temple 2 and laid the foundation for the high double wall and the fortifications of the Temple.j 3 The reservoir, as big as the bronze tank, was dugk while he was in office. 4 He made plans to protect his people from attack and fortified the city so that it could withstand a siege.

5 How glorious he was when he came out of the Most Holy Place!l 6 He was like the morning star shining through the clouds, like the full moon, 7 like the sun shining on the Temple of the Most High, like the rainbow gleaming in glory against the clouds, 8 like roses in springtime, like lilies beside a stream, like the cedars of Lebanon in summer, 9 like burning incense, like a cup made of hammered gold and decorated with all kinds of jewels, 10 like an olive tree loaded with fruit, like a cypress tree towering into the clouds.

11 When Simon put on his magnificent robe and went up to the holy altar dressed in perfect splendor, he made the Temple courtyard a majestic sight. 12 When the priests handed him the portions of the sacrifice as he stood beside the altar with his assistants circling him like a wreath, he was like a young cedar of Lebanon surrounded by palm trees. 13 Those were the descendants of Aaron in their splendid garments, standing before the whole assembly of Israel, holding in their hands the offering made to the Lord. 14 When he had finished the service at the altar and had arranged the sacrifice to the Most High, the Almighty, 15 he reached for a cup and poured out sweet-smelling wine at the foot of the altar as an offering to the Most High, the universal King. 16 Then the priests shouted and blew their trumpets of hammered silver. They made a loud noise that the Most High would hear. 17 All the people immediately bowed down with their faces to the ground to worship their Lord, the Almighty, the Most High. 18 Then the choir began to sing his praises, and the beautiful music rang out. 19 The people kept praying to the merciful Lord Most High until the service of worship had come to a close. 20 Then Simon came down from the altar, raised his hands over the whole assembly of Israel, and reverently pronounced the blessing from the Lord, 21 while the people bowed a second time in worship to receive that blessing from the Most High.

---

f 49:15 Greek adds the greatest of his brothers and the pride of his people; Hebrew and one ancient translation place these words in 50:1. g 49:15 even . . . honored; or the Lord watched over his body. h 49:16 Hebrew Shem, Seth, and Enosh; Greek Shem and Seth among people. i 50:1 The greatest . . . people; Hebrew and one ancient translation place the words at this point; Greek places them at 49:15. j 50:2 Verse 2 in Greek is unclear. k 50:2 Hebrew dug; Greek reduced. l 50:5 Hebrew Most Holy Place; Greek Most Holy Place among the people.
49:11 Ezra 3:2; Hag 2:23　49:12 Hag 1:1, 12　49:13 Neh 6:15　50:20 Num 6:24–27

A Benediction

22 Now then, give praise to the God of the universe, who has done great things everywhere, who brings us up[m] from the time we are born, and deals with us mercifully. 23 May he give us happiness and allow us to have peace in Israel forever. 24 May he continue his mercy to us and rescue us in our time of need.

Three Hated Nations

25 There are two nations that I detest, and a third that does not even deserve to be called a nation. 26 These are the Edomites,[n] the inhabitants of the Philistine cities, and the stupid Samaritans.

The Wisdom of Jesus Son of Sirach

27 I, Jesus son of Sirach Eleazar[o] of Jerusalem, put all my wisdom into writing this book to provide instruction and knowledge for others. 28 May God bless everyone who gives attention to these teachings. Whoever takes them to heart will become wise. 29 Whoever lives by them will be strong enough for any occasion, because he will be walking in the light of the Lord.

A Song of Thanksgiving

51

1 I give you thanks, O Lord and King;
  I praise you as my God and Savior.
I give you thanks,
2   for you have helped me and protected me.
You have rescued me from death,
  from dangerous lies and slander.
3 You helped me when no one else would;
  in your great mercy you saved me
  from the many troubles I have known:
  from the glaring hatred of my enemies,
    who wanted to put an end to my life;
4 from suffocation in oppressive smoke
    rising from fires that I did not light;
5 from death itself;
    from vicious slander reported to the king.

6 I was once brought face to face with death;
7   enemies surrounded me everywhere.
I looked for someone to help me,
  but there was no one there.
8 But then, O Lord, I remembered how merciful you are
  and what you had done in times past.
I remembered that you rescue those who rely on you,
  that you save them from their enemies.
9 Then from here on earth I prayed to you
  to rescue me from death.
10 I prayed, "O Lord, you are my father;[p]
  do not abandon me to my troubles
  when I am helpless against arrogant enemies.
11 I will always praise you
  and sing hymns of thanksgiving."
You answered my prayer,
12   and saved me from the threat of destruction.
And so I thank you and praise you.
  O Lord, I praise you!

The Search for Wisdom

13 When I was still young, before I started out on my travels, I boldly prayed for Wisdom. 14 I went to the Temple and asked for her, and I will look for her as long as I live. 15 From my blossoming youth to my ripe old age she has been my delight. I have followed directly in her path ever since I was young. 16 I received Wisdom as soon as I began listening for her, and I have been rewarded with great knowledge. 17 I have always been a learner and am grateful to everyone who has been my teacher. 18 I was determined to live wisely and was devoted to the cause of goodness. I have no regrets. 19 I fought for Wisdom and was strict in my conduct. When I prayed, I sadly confessed how far short of Wisdom I fell. 20 But I was determined to have her, and I found her by keeping myself free from sin. I have grown in Wisdom since first I found her, and I will never be without her. 21 Because I was driven by the desire to find her, I have been richly rewarded. 22 The Lord gave me a gift for words, and I have used it in his praise.

Sirach

---

m 50:22 brings us up; or honors us.   n 50:26 Hebrew Edomites; Greek Samaritans.   o 50:27 Sirach Eleazar; or Sirach son of Eleazar.   p 51:10 Hebrew you are my father; Greek father of my Lord.

23Come to me, all you that need instruction, and learn in my school. 24Why do you admit that you are ignorant and do nothing about it? 25Here is what I say: It costs nothing to be wise. 26Put on the yoke, and be willing to learn. The opportunity is always near. 27See for yourselves! I have really not studied very hard, but I have found great contentment. 28No matter how much it costs you to get Wisdom, it will be well worth it. 29Be joyfully grateful for the Lord's mercy, and never be ashamed to praise him. 30Do your duty at the proper time, and the Lord, at the time he thinks proper, will give you your reward.

THE BOOK OF Isaiah

If you take drugs, you can do permanent damage to your brain. If you miss a lot of school and don't do your homework and study, you may not graduate.

These warnings are real, and yet some people don't take them seriously. As a result, many people suffer needless consequences.

The great prophet Isaiah and some of his followers warned the people of God about the dangers of failing to keep God's Covenant. They warned them about the dangers of worshiping foreign gods and treating the poor unfairly. Isaiah called the people to repent of their sins. But they didn't take him seriously. After the people had been taken as slaves into Babylon, Isaiah's disciples offered the people hope that someday they would return from exile and rebuild Israel. They even foretold of a new earth and heaven where God would rule with peace and justice.

Chap. 5

Headlines

- God, Tired of Sacrifices, Wants Justice! (1:10–20)
- Child to Bring Endless Peace (9:2–7)
- New King Will Defend the Helpless (11:1–9)
- Hope Cries Out in the Wilderness! (40:1–5)
- Servant Chosen to Bring Justice (42:1–9)
- Servant Suffers for Sheep (52:13—53:12)
- Good News for God's People (chapter 61)

FACTOIDS

Who wrote this book? Isaiah is divided into three parts. First Isaiah, chapters 1–39, is a collection of poems written by the great prophet Isaiah before the Babylonian Exile. Second Isaiah, chapters 40–55, and Third Isaiah, chapters 56–66, were written by disciples of Isaiah who wrote during and after the Exile.

What time period does it cover? From 745 to 500 BC.

Why was it written? Isaiah was written to warn the leaders about misusing their power. It also offered hope for those living in exile that God would save them and return them to rebuild Israel.

Jesus connection: Jesus is the Messiah and suffering servant prophesied in First and Second Isaiah.

Important themes

- The sacrifice God asks of us is to be faithful and just.
- God is with those who suffer and trust in God's saving power.
- God will send a leader, a descendant of King David, who will be the perfect ruler and will bring justice and peace to God's people.

ISAIAH

1 ¹This book contains the messages about Judah and Jerusalem which God revealed to Isaiah son of Amoz during the time when Uzziah, Jotham, Ahaz, and Hezekiah were kings of Judah.

God Reprimands His People

²The LORD said, "Earth and sky, listen to what I am saying! The children I brought up have rebelled against me. ³Cattle know who owns them, and donkeys know where their master feeds them. But that is more than my people Israel know. They don't understand at all."

⁴You are doomed, you sinful nation, you corrupt and evil people! Your sins drag you down! You have rejected the LORD, the holy God of Israel, and have turned your backs on him. ⁵Why do you keep on rebelling? Do you want to be punished even more? Israel, your head is already covered with wounds, and your heart and mind are sick. ⁶From head to foot there is not a healthy spot on your body. You are covered with bruises and sores and open wounds. Your wounds have not been cleaned or bandaged. No medicine has been put on them.

⁷Your country has been devastated, and your cities have been burned to the ground. While you look on, foreigners take over your land and bring everything to ruin. ⁸Jerusalem alone is left, a city under siege— as defenseless as a guard's hut in a vineyard or a shed in a cucumber field. ⁹If the LORD Almighty had not let some of the people

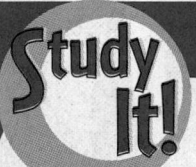

Stories about Jesus?

Does your family or parish put out a nativity scene before Christmas? Besides Jesus, Mary, Joseph, shepherds, and wise men, many nativity scenes include cattle, donkeys, and sheep. What you may not know is that there is a legend that the animals at Jesus' birth knew who he was. This legend was based on the prophecy of Isaiah 1:3. This prophecy says that cattle and donkeys know who their masters are, even if God's people do not recognize their master (God).

That legend is just a legend. There is no record in the Gospels of animals at Jesus' birth. However, it is true that many of the prophecies in Isaiah do point to Christ. Some of the next articles will point out some of those prophecies. As you read Isaiah, you may want to make a list of, or draw a star in the margin next to, the verses that remind you of Jesus.

— Isaiah 1:3

Israel, your head is already covered with wounds. (1:5)

1:1 a 2 Kings 15:1–7; 2 Chr 26:1–23; **b** 2 Kings 15:32–38; 2 Chr 27:1–9; **c** 2 Kings 16:1–20; 2 Chr 28:1–27; **d** 2 Kings 18:1—20:21; 2 Chr 29:1—32:33

survive, Jerusalem would have been totally destroyed, just as Sodom and Gomorrah were.

¹⁰Jerusalem, your rulers and your people are like those of Sodom and Gomorrah. Listen to what the LORD is saying to you. Pay attention to what our God is teaching you. ¹¹He says, "Do you think I want all these sacrifices you keep offering to me? I have had more than enough of the sheep you burn as sacrifices and of the fat of your fine animals. I am tired of the blood of bulls and sheep and goats. ¹²Who asked you to bring me all this when you come to worship me? Who asked you to do all this tramping around in my Temple? ¹³It's useless to bring your offerings. I am disgusted with the smell of the incense you burn. I cannot stand your New Moon Festivals, your Sabbaths, and your religious gatherings; they are all corrupted by your sins. ¹⁴I hate your New Moon Festivals and holy days; they are a burden that I am tired of bearing.

¹⁵"When you lift your hands in prayer, I will not look at you. No matter how much you pray, I will not listen, for your hands are covered with blood. ¹⁶Wash yourselves clean. Stop all this evil that I see you doing. Yes, stop doing evil ¹⁷and learn to do right. See that justice is done—help those who are oppressed, give orphans their rights, and defend widows."

¹⁸The LORD says, "Now, let's settle the

When you lift your hands in prayer . . . (1:15)

matter. You are stained red with sin, but I will wash you as clean as snow.ᵃ Although your stains are deep red, you will be as white as wool.ᵇ ¹⁹If you will only obey me, you will eat the good things the land produces. ²⁰But if you defy me, you are doomed to die. I, the LORD, have spoken."

The Sinful City

²¹The city that once was faithful is behaving like a whore! At one time it was filled with righteous people, but now only murderers remain. ²²Jerusalem, you were once like silver, but now you are worthless; you were like good wine, but now you are only water. ²³Your leaders are rebels and friends of thieves; they are always accepting gifts and bribes. They never defend orphans in court or listen when widows present their case.

²⁴So now, listen to what the LORD Almighty, Israel's powerful God, is saying: "I will take revenge on you, my enemies, and you will cause me no more trouble. ²⁵I will take action against you. I will purify you the way metal is refined, and will remove all your impurity. ²⁶I will give you rulers and advisers like those you had long ago. Then Jerusalem will be called the righteous, faithful city."

²⁷Because the LORD is righteous, he will save Jerusalem and everyone there who repents. ²⁸But he will crush everyone who sins and rebels against him; he will kill everyone who forsakes him.

²⁹You will be sorry that you ever worshiped trees and planted sacred gardens.ᶜ ³⁰You will wither like a dying oak, like a garden that no one waters. ³¹Just as straw is set on fire by a spark, so powerful people will be destroyed by their own evil deeds, and no one will be able to stop the destruction.

ᵃ **1:18** sin, but . . . snow; *or* sin; do you think I will wash you as clean as snow?   ᵇ **1:18** Although your . . . wool; *or* Your stains are deep red; do you think you will be as white as wool?   ᶜ **1:29** SACRED GARDENS: *People believed that dedicating a garden to a fertility god would cause him to bless their crops.*
1:9 Gen 19:24; Rom 9:29   **1:11–14** Am 5:21, 22

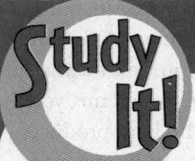

War or Peace

At the beginning of Isaiah, chapter 2, Isaiah makes a prophecy about a time when God's peace will last forever. This vision of everlasting peace is one that many people have worked for over many centuries. There are even Catholic peace organizations, like Pax Christi, that try to prevent and stop wars and violence. Unfortunately, it seems there are still as many wars as there were at the time of Isaiah. The timelines in history books use wars as markers, and many students (maybe even you) study the dates and places of the various wars.

God doesn't want us to be at war. The Creation stories in Genesis tell us that God created us so that we could all live in peace. Isaiah and other books of the Bible promise us that ultimately God's peace will come and last forever. Until that time it is a good idea to practice peace—right where you are. With God's help if you practice peace and if others practice it too, we will eventually get it right.

— Isaiah 2:2–4

Everlasting Peace
(Micah 4:1–3)

2 ¹Here is the message which God gave to Isaiah son of Amoz about Judah and Jerusalem:

²In days to come
the mountain where the Temple stands
will be the highest one of all,
towering above all the hills.
Many nations will come streaming to it,
³ and their people will say,
"Let us go up the hill of the LORD,*d*
to the Temple of Israel's God.
He will teach us what he wants us to do;
we will walk in the paths he has
chosen.
For the LORD's teaching comes from
Jerusalem;
from Zion he speaks to his people."

⁴He will settle disputes among great
nations.
They will hammer their swords into
plows
and their spears into pruning knives.
Nations will never again go to war,
never prepare for battle again.
⁵Now, descendants of Jacob, let us walk in the light which the LORD gives us!

Arrogance Will Be Destroyed

⁶O God, you have forsaken your people, the descendants of Jacob! The land is full of magic practices from the East and from Philistia.*e* The people follow foreign customs. ⁷Their land is full of silver and gold, and there is no end to their treasures. Their land is full of horses, and there is no end to their chariots. ⁸Their land is full of idols, and they worship objects that they have made with their own hands.

⁹Everyone will be humiliated and disgraced. Do not forgive them, LORD! ¹⁰They will hide in caves in the rocky hills or dig holes in the ground to try to escape from the LORD's anger and to hide from his power and glory! ¹¹A day is coming when human pride will be ended and human arrogance destroyed. Then the LORD

d **2:3** HILL OF THE LORD: *Mount Zion, the hill in Jerusalem which formed part of the area on which the Temple was built.* *e* **2:6** *Probable text* The land . . . Philistia; *Hebrew unclear.*
2:4 Joel 3:10; Mic 4:3   **2:10** Rev 6:15; 2 Thess 1:9

"They will hammer their swords into plows / and their spears into pruning knives" *(Isaiah 2:4).*

alone will be exalted. ¹²On that day the LORD Almighty will humble everyone who is powerful, everyone who is proud and conceited. ¹³He will destroy the tall cedars of Lebanon and all the oaks in the land of Bashan. ¹⁴He will level the high mountains and hills, ¹⁵every high tower, and the walls of every fortress. ¹⁶He will sink even the largest and most beautiful ships. ¹⁷⁻¹⁸Human pride will be ended, and human arrogance will be destroyed. Idols will completely disappear, and the LORD alone will be exalted on that day.

¹⁹People will hide in caves in the rocky hills or dig holes in the ground to try to escape from the LORD's anger and to hide from his power and glory, when he comes to shake the earth. ²⁰When that day comes, they will throw away the gold and silver idols they have made, and abandon them to the moles and the bats. ²¹When the LORD comes to shake the earth, people will hide in holes and caves in the rocky hills to try to escape from his anger and to hide from his power and glory.

To escape from the LORD's anger (2:19, 21)

²²Put no more confidence in mortals. What are they worth?

Chaos in Jerusalem

3 ¹Now the Lord, the Almighty LORD, is about to take away from Jerusalem and Judah everything and everyone that the people depend on. He is going to take away their food and their water, ²their heroes and their soldiers, their judges and their prophets, their fortunetellers and their statesmen, ³their military and civilian leaders, their politicians and everyone who uses magic to control events. ⁴The LORD will let the peo-ple be governed by immature boys. ⁵Everyone will take advantage of everyone else. Young people will not respect their elders, and worthless people will not respect their superiors.

⁶A time will come when the members of a clan will choose one of their number and say to him, "You at least have something to wear, so be our leader in this time of trouble."

⁷But he will answer, "Not me! I can't help you. I don't have any food or clothes either. Don't make me your leader!"

⁸Yes, Jerusalem is doomed! Judah is collapsing! Everything they say and do is against the LORD; they openly insult God himself. ⁹Their prejudices will be held against them. They sin as openly as the people of Sodom did. They are doomed, and they have brought it on themselves.

¹⁰The righteous will be happy,*f* and things will go well for them. They will get to enjoy what they have worked for. ¹¹But evil people are doomed; what they have done to others will now be done to them.

¹²Moneylenders oppress my people, and their creditors cheat them.

My people, your leaders are misleading you, so that you do not know which way to turn.

The LORD Judges His People

¹³The LORD is ready to state his case; he is ready to judge his people.*g* ¹⁴The LORD is bringing the elders and leaders of his people to judgment. He makes this accusation: "You have plundered vineyards, and your houses are full of what you have taken from the poor. ¹⁵You have no right to crush my people and take advantage of the poor. I, the Sovereign LORD Almighty, have spoken."

A Warning to the Women of Jerusalem

¹⁶The LORD said, "Look how proud the women of Jerusalem are! They walk along with their noses in the air. They are always flirting. They take dainty little steps, and the bracelets on their ankles jingle. ¹⁷But I will

Isaiah

---

f **3:10** *Probable text* The righteous will be happy; *Hebrew* Say to the righteous.   *g* **3:13** *Some ancient translations* his people; *Hebrew* the peoples.

punish them—I will shave their heads and leave them bald."

18A day is coming when the Lord will take away from the women of Jerusalem everything they are so proud of—the ornaments they wear on their ankles, on their heads, on their necks, 19and on their wrists. He will take away their veils 20and their hats; the magic charms they wear on their arms and at their waists; 21the rings they wear on their fingers and in their noses; 22all their fine robes, gowns, cloaks, and purses; 23their revealing garments, their linen handkerchiefs, and the scarves and long veils they wear on their heads.

24Instead of using perfumes, they will stink; instead of fine belts, they will wear coarse ropes; instead of having beautiful hair, they will be bald; instead of fine clothes, they will be dressed in rags; their beauty will be turned to shame!

With their noses in the air (3:16)
Dressed in rags (3:24)

25The men of the city, yes, even the strongest men, will be killed in war. 26The city gates will mourn and cry, and the city itself will be like a woman sitting on the ground, stripped naked.

4 1When that time comes, seven women will grab hold of one man and say, "We can feed and clothe ourselves, but please let us say you are our husband, so that we won't have to endure the shame of being unmarried."

Jerusalem Will Be Restored

2The time is coming when the LORD will make every plant and tree in the land grow large and beautiful. All the people of Israel who survive will take delight and pride in the crops that the land produces. 3Everyone who is left in Jerusalem, whom God has chosen for survival, will be called holy. 4By his power the Lord will judge and purify the nation and wash away the guilt of Jerusalem and the blood that has been shed there. 5Then over Mount Zion and over all who are gathered there, the LORD will send a cloud in the daytime and smoke and a bright flame at night. God's glory will cover and protect the whole city. 6His glory will shade the city from the heat of the day and make it a place of safety, sheltered from the rain and storm.

The Song of the Vineyard

5 1Listen while I sing you this song,
    a song of my friend and his vineyard:
My friend had a vineyard
    on a very fertile hill.
2He dug the soil and cleared it of stones;
    he planted the finest vines.
He built a tower to guard them,
    dug a pit for treading the grapes.
He waited for the grapes to ripen,
    but every grape was sour.
3So now my friend says, "You people who live in Jerusalem and Judah, judge between my vineyard and me. 4Is there anything I failed to do for it? Then why did it produce sour grapes and not the good grapes I expected?

5"Here is what I am going to do to my vineyard: I will take away the hedge around it, break down the wall that protects it, and let wild animals eat it and trample it down. 6I will let it be overgrown with weeds. I will not trim the vines or hoe the ground; instead, I will let briers and thorns cover it. I will even forbid the clouds to let rain fall on it."

7Israel is the vineyard of the LORD Almighty;
    the people of Judah are the vines he planted.

4:5 Ex 13:21; 24:16   5:1, 2 Mt 21:33; Mk 12:1; Lk 20:9

He expected them to do what was
    good,
  but instead they committed murder.
He expected them to do what was
    right,
  but their victims cried out for justice.

*A very fertile hill . . . he dug the soil . . . cleared it
of stones . . . he planted the finest vines . . . he built
a tower . . . dug a pit . . . he waited for the grapes to
ripen, but every grape was sour. (5:1–2)*

The Evil That People Do

8 You are doomed! You buy more houses
and fields to add to those you already have.
Soon there will be no place for anyone else
to live, and you alone will live in the land. **9** I
have heard the Lord Almighty say, "All these
big, fine houses will be empty ruins. **10** The
grapevines growing on five acres of land will
yield only five gallons of wine. Ten bushels of
seed will produce only one bushel of grain."

11 You are doomed! You get up early in the
morning to start drinking, and you spend
long evenings getting drunk. **12** At your feasts
you have harps and tambourines and flutes—
and wine. But you don't understand what the
Lord is doing, **13** and so you will be carried
away as prisoners. Your leaders will starve to
death, and the common people will die of
thirst. **14** The world of the dead is hungry for
them, and it opens its mouth wide. It gulps
down the nobles of Jerusalem along with the
noisy crowd of common people.

15 Everyone will be disgraced, and all who
are proud will be humbled. **16** But the Lord
Almighty shows his greatness by doing what
is right, and he reveals his holiness by judging his people. **17** In the ruins of the cities
lambs will eat grass and young goats will
find pasture. *h*

18 You are doomed! You are unable to break
free from your sins. **19** You say, "Let the Lord
hurry up and do what he says he will, so that
we can see it. Let Israel's holy God carry out
his plans; let's see what he has in mind."

20 You are doomed! You call evil good and

In the ruins of the cities. (5:17)

---

h **5:17** *Verse 17 in Hebrew is unclear.*
5:11 Wis 2:7–9

**Isaiah, chapter 3, is pretty critical about the way people lived in Isaiah's time.
What would a prophet say about the way people live today?**

Heroes of the wine bottle! (5:22)

Pray It!

Light and Dark

"You are doomed." Isaiah repeats this phrase several times in Isaiah, chapter 5. Because of the Israelites' wickedness, Isaiah says that God is sending soldiers from a distant nation who will come and punish the Israelites. The light that was supposed to be God's Chosen People will be swallowed by darkness.

Light is a symbol for God's presence throughout the Bible. Darkness is very often used as a symbol for the absence of God. Opposites are used in poems and prayers for drama and as ways of contrasting. Write a prayer using the words *light* and *dark,* and any other sets of opposites (such as happy and sad or wise and foolish) that you want to use. In your prayer, talk about what happens when people follow God and what happens when they do not follow God.

— Isaiah, chapter 5

and dry grass shrivel and burn in the fire, your roots will rot and your blossoms will dry up and blow away, because you have rejected what the LORD Almighty, Israel's holy God, has taught us. 25 The LORD is angry with his people and has stretched out his hand to punish them. The mountains will shake, and the bodies of those who die will be left in the streets like rubbish. Yet even then the LORD's anger will not be ended, but his hand will still be stretched out to punish.

26 The LORD gives a signal to call for a distant nation. [i] He whistles for them to come from the ends of the earth. And here they come, swiftly, quickly! 27 None of them grow tired; none of them stumble. They never doze or sleep. Not a belt is loose; not a sandal strap is broken. 28 Their arrows are sharp, and their bows are ready to shoot. Their horses' hoofs are as hard as flint, and their chariot wheels turn like a whirlwind. 29 The soldiers roar like lions that have killed an animal and are carrying it off where no one can take it away from them.

30 When that day comes, they will roar over Israel as loudly as the sea. Look at this country! Darkness and distress! The light is swallowed by darkness.

God Calls Isaiah to Be a Prophet

6 ¹In the year that King Uzziah died, I saw the Lord. He was sitting on his throne, high and exalted, and his robe filled

call good evil. You turn darkness into light and light into darkness. You make what is bitter sweet, and what is sweet you make bitter.

21 You are doomed! You think you are wise, so very clever.

22 You are doomed! Heroes of the wine bottle! Brave and fearless when it comes to mixing drinks! 23 But for just a bribe you let the guilty go free, and you keep the innocent from getting justice. 24 So now, just as straw

---

i **5:26** *Probable text* a distant nation; *Hebrew* distant nations.
6:1 2 Kings 15:7; 2 Chr 26:23

the whole Temple. ²Around him flaming creatures were standing, each of which had six wings. Each creature covered its face with two wings, and its body with two, and used the other two for flying. ³They were calling out to each other:

"Holy, holy, holy!
The LORD Almighty is holy!
His glory fills the world."

⁴The sound of their voices made the foundation of the Temple shake, and the Temple itself became filled with smoke.

⁵I said, "There is no hope for me! I am doomed because every word that passes my lips is sinful, and I live among a people whose every word is sinful. And yet, with my own eyes I have seen the King, the LORD Almighty."

⁶Then one of the creatures flew down to me, carrying a burning coal that he had taken from the altar with a pair of tongs. ⁷He touched my lips with the burning coal and said, "This has touched your lips, and now your guilt is gone, and your sins are forgiven."

⁸Then I heard the Lord say, "Whom shall I send? Who will be our messenger?"

I answered, "I will go! Send me!"

⁹So he told me to go and give the people this message: "No matter how much you listen, you will not understand. No matter how much you look, you will not know what is happening." ¹⁰Then he said to me, "Make the minds of these people dull, their ears deaf, and their eyes blind, so that they cannot see or hear or understand. If they did, they might turn to me and be healed."

¹¹I asked, "How long will it be like this, Lord?"

He answered, "Until the cities are ruined and empty—until the houses are uninhabited—until the land itself is a desolate wasteland. ¹²I will send the people far away and make the whole land desolate. ¹³Even if one person out of ten remains in the land, he too will be destroyed; he will be like the stump of an oak tree that has been cut down."

(The stump represents a new beginning for God's people.)

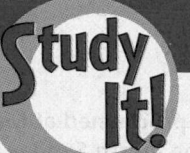

Prophets and Prophecy

The Book of Isaiah includes many visions, judgments, predictions, and promises proclaimed by the prophet Isaiah. We call all of these things prophecy. Prophecy isn't magic or fortunetelling, nor is it guessing or hypothesizing. A *prophet* is a person who speaks for another, in this case God. Isaiah and the other prophets were called by God to deliver God's messages to the Israelites. Chapter 6 tells the story of how Isaiah was called by God to be a prophet.

Many times the prophets warned the people about their behavior. And many times the people ignored the warnings. So sometimes the prophets, such as Isaiah, had to tell the people the same warning over and over. The prophets also spoke God's promises of hope and peace when the people needed to hear that message from God. The prophets did not give their own personal message; they always were giving God's message. And sometimes that got the prophets in trouble because people did not always want to hear God's message!

— Isaiah, chapter 6

A Message for King Ahaz

7 ¹When King Ahaz, the son of Jotham and grandson of Uzziah, ruled Judah, war broke out. Rezin, king of Syria, and Pekah son of Remaliah, king of Israel, attacked Jerusalem, but were unable to capture it.

6:3 Rev 4:8   **6:4** Rev 15:8   **6:9, 10** Mt 13:14, 15; Mk 4:12; Lk 8:10; Jn 12:40; Acts 28:26, 27   **7:1** 2 Kings 16:5; 2 Chr 28:5, 6

Advent

Isaiah 7:10–14 is proclaimed at Mass every three years on the fourth Sunday of Advent, the Sunday just before Christmas. If you are familiar with the Christmas story, you probably know why: "A young woman who is pregnant will have a son and will name him 'Immanuel'" (Isaiah 7:14). These words point toward the birth of Christ. If you read Matthew 1:18–24, which is the Gospel for the fourth Sunday of Advent, you can see how this passage from Isaiah and that Gospel passage go together.

Catholic Connections

— Isaiah 7:10–14

2 When word reached the king of Judah that the armies of Syria were already in the territory of Israel, he and all his people were so terrified that they trembled like trees shaking in the wind.

3 The LORD said to Isaiah, "Take your son Shear Jashub,ʲ and go to meet King Ahaz. You will find him on the road where the cloth makers work, at the end of the ditch that brings water from the upper pool. 4 Tell him to keep alert, to stay calm, and not to be frightened or disturbed. The anger of King Rezin and his Syrians and of King Pekah is no more dangerous than the smoke from two smoldering sticks of wood. 5 Syria, together with Israel and its king, has made a plot. 6 They intend to invade Judah, terrify the people into joining their side, and then put Tabeel's son on the throne.

7 "But I, the LORD, declare that this will never happen. 8 Why? Because Syria is no stronger than Damascus, its capital city, and Damascus is no stronger than King Rezin. As for Israel, within sixty-five years it will be too shattered to survive as a nation. 9 Israel is no stronger than Samaria, its capital city, and Samaria is no stronger than King Pekah.

"If your faith is not enduring, you will not endure."

The Sign of Immanuel

10 The LORD sent another message to Ahaz: 11 "Ask the LORD your God to give you a sign. It can be from deep in the world of the dead or from high up in heaven."

12 Ahaz answered, "I will not ask for a sign. I refuse to put the LORD to the test."

13 To that Isaiah replied, "Listen, now, descendants of King David. It's bad enough for you to wear out the patience of people—do you have to wear out God's patience too? 14 Well then, the Lord himself will give you a sign: a young womanᵏ who is pregnant will have a son and will name him 'Immanuel.'ˡ 15 By the time he is old enough to make his own decisions, people will be drinking milk and eating honey.ᵐ 16 Even before that time comes, the lands of those two kings who terrify you will be deserted.

17 "The LORD is going to bring on you, on your people, and on the whole royal family, days of trouble worse than any that have come since the kingdom of Israel separated from Judah—he is going to bring the king of Assyria.

18 "When that time comes, the LORD will whistle as a signal for the Egyptians to come like flies from the farthest branches of the

---

ʲ 7:3 SHEAR JASHUB: *This name in Hebrew means "A few will come back" (see 10:20–22).* ᵏ 7:14 YOUNG WOMAN: *The Hebrew word here translated "young woman" is not the specific term for "virgin," but refers to any young woman of marriageable age. The use of "virgin" in Mt 1:23 reflects a Greek translation of the Old Testament, made some 500 years after Isaiah.* ˡ 7:14 IMMANUEL: *This name in Hebrew means "God is with us."* ᵐ 7:15 MILK AND HONEY: *These foods were associated with the earlier days of Israel's history.*

7:14 Mt 1:23

Nile, and for the Assyrians to come from their land like bees. 19They will swarm in the rugged valleys and in the caves in the rocks, and they will cover every thorn bush and every pasture.

20"When that time comes, the Lord will hire a barber from across the Euphrates—the emperor of Assyria!—and he will shave off your beards and the hair on your heads and your bodies.

21"When that time comes, even if a farmer has been able to save only one young cow and two goats, 22they will give so much milk that he will have all he needs. Yes, the few survivors left in the land will have milk and honey to eat.

23"When that time comes, the fine vine-yards, each with a thousand vines and each worth a thousand pieces of silver, will be overgrown with thorn bushes and briers. 24People will go hunting there with bows and arrows. Yes, the whole country will be full of briers and thorn bushes. 25All the hills where crops were once planted will be so overgrown with thorns that no one will go there. It will be a place where cattle and sheep graze."

Isaiah's Son as a Sign to the People

8 1The LORD said to me, "Take a large piece of writing material and write on it in large letters:*n* 'Quick Loot, Fast Plunder.' 2Get two reliable men, the priest Uriah and Zechariah son of Jeberechiah, to serve as witnesses."

3Some time later my wife became pregnant. When our son was born, the LORD said to me, "Name him 'Quick-Loot-Fast-Plunder.' 4Before the boy is old enough to say 'Mamma' and 'Daddy,' all the wealth of Damascus and all the loot of Samaria will be carried off by the king of Assyria."

The Emperor of Assyria Is Coming

5The LORD spoke to me again. 6He said, "Because these people have rejected the quiet waters of Shiloah Brook*o* and tremble*p* before King Rezin and King Pekah, 7I, the Lord, will bring the emperor of Assyria and all his forces to attack Judah. They will advance like the flood waters of the Euphrates River, overflowing all its banks. 8They will sweep through Judah in a flood, rising shoulder high and covering every-thing."

God is with us! His outspread wings pro-tect the land.*q*

9Gather together in fear, you nations! Lis-ten, you distant parts of the earth. Get ready to fight, but be afraid! Yes, get ready, but be afraid! 10Make your plans! But they will never succeed. Talk all you want to! But it is all useless, because God is with us.

The LORD Warns the Prophet

11With his great power the LORD warned me not to follow the road which the people were following. He said, 12"Do not join in the schemes of the people and do not be afraid of the things that they fear. 13Remem-ber that I, the LORD Almighty, am holy; I am the one you must fear. 14Because of my awe-some holiness I am like a stone that people stumble over; I am like a trap that will catch the people of the kingdoms of Judah and Israel and the people of Jerusalem. 15Many will stumble; they will fall and be crushed. They will be caught in a trap."

Warning against Consulting the Dead

16You, my disciples, are to guard and pre-serve the messages that God has given me. 17The LORD has hidden himself from his people, but I trust him and place my hope in him.

n **8:1** large letters; *or* letters that everyone can read.   *o* **8:6** SHILOAH BROOK: *A stream which flowed from the large spring on the eastern side of Jerusalem.*   *p* **8:6** *Probable text* tremble; *Hebrew* rejoice.   *q* **8:8** everything." God . . . land; *or* everything. They will spread out over the land. God be with us!"
8:12, 13 1 Pet 3:14, 15   **8:14, 15** 1 Pet 2:8   **8:17** Heb 2:13

Isaiah

The name Immanuel literally means "God is with us."

Bad Feelings

Read Isaiah 8:11–15 and then think about this story:

"We have to cheat; it is the only way to pass. If I don't pass, I won't get into the honors program in high school." Sam tried to convince her friends. "Yeah, I *have* to get into that program or my parents will kill me." Claudia agreed.

"And I have the perfect plan," said Karen. "It's just perfect."

"What is it?" Claudia and Sam said at the same time.

"It's . . ." Karen looked at Kenza. "What about you? Are you in or are you out?"

Kenza looked at her friends. It was tempting. Mr. Gratsi's class was so hard, and the test seemed impossible to prepare for. But the thought of cheating gave her such a bad feeling in her stomach. "I don't know."

"Don't know!" cried Sam. "How can you not know? We have to cheat. Let's listen to Karen's plan."

"I don't think so," Kenza said. She knew this meant her friends may get better grades and into the honors program. But she didn't want to be involved in a scheme. "You guys know this is wrong—please don't go through with it."

As she walked away, she heard the girls whispering, but she wasn't afraid or even worried. She was following her conscience, and that good feeling in her stomach was much better than the bad feeling she had earlier.

— Isaiah 8:11–15

18 Here I am with the children the LORD has given me. The LORD Almighty, whose throne is on Mount Zion, has sent us as living messages to the people of Israel.

19 But people will tell you to ask for messages from fortunetellers and mediums, who chirp and mutter. They will say, "After all, people should ask for messages from the spirits and consult the dead on behalf of the living."

20 You are to answer them, "Listen to what the LORD is teaching you! Don't listen to mediums—what they tell you cannot keep trouble away."[r]

A Time of Trouble

21 The people will wander through the land, discouraged and hungry. In their hunger and their anger they will curse their king and their God. They may look up to the sky 22 or stare at the ground, but they will see nothing but trouble and darkness, terrifying darkness into which they are being 9 driven. 1 There will be no way for them to escape from this time of trouble.

The Future King

The land of the tribes of Zebulun and Naphtali was once disgraced, but the future will bring honor to this region, from the Mediterranean eastward to the land on the other side of the Jordan, and even to Galilee itself, where the foreigners live.

2 The people who walked in darkness
    have seen a great light.
They lived in a land of shadows,
    but now light is shining on them.
3 You have given them great joy,[s] Lord;
    you have made them happy.
They rejoice in what you have done,

r 8:20 *Verse 20 in Hebrew is unclear.* s 9:3 *Probable text* You have given them great joy; *Hebrew* You have increased the nation.
8:18 Heb 2:13   **9:1** Mt 4:15   **9:2** Mt 4:16; Lk 1:79

Isaiah

Read Isaiah 9:2. How do you feel when you finally get a really sunny day after several cloudy and gloomy days?

Pray It!

Names of God

"Wonderful Counselor," "Mighty God," "Eternal Father," "Prince of Peace" (Isaiah 9:6). All of these are names given to God. Here is a prayer that uses them. You can add to it by using other names that you would give to God.

Wonderful
God, you really are wonderful. You do wonderful things and know how to make me feel wonderful. Thank you for being a wonderful friend to me. Amen.

Counselor
Jesus, you are a counselor. You listen when I call and lead me on the right path. Thank you for being there when I need someone to turn to. Amen.

Mighty God
Holy Spirit, you are mighty. You came to Mary and gave courage to the disciples at Pentecost. Thank you for being a mighty force in my life. Amen.

Eternal Father
Lord, you are my Eternal Father. You are there for me; like a loving, kind parent, you hold me close. Thank you for being my Eternal Father. Amen.

Prince of Peace
Jesus, you are the Prince of Peace. You give me a model for peace and show me that peace is the only way. Thank you for giving me your peace. Amen.

— Isaiah 9:6

Now light is shining on them. (9:2)

as people rejoice when they harvest
   grain
or when they divide captured
   wealth.
⁴ For you have broken the yoke that
   burdened them
and the rod that beat their shoulders.
You have defeated the nation
   that oppressed and exploited your
   people,

just as you defeated the army of Midian
   long ago.
⁵ The boots of the invading army
and all their bloodstained clothing
will be destroyed by fire.
⁶ A child is born to us!
A son is given to us!
And he will be our ruler.
He will be called, "Wonderful^t
   Counselor,"
"Mighty God," "Eternal Father,"
"Prince of Peace."
⁷ His royal power will continue to grow;
his kingdom will always be at peace.
He will rule as King David's successor,
basing his power on right and justice,
from now until the end of time.
The Lord Almighty is determined to do
   all this.

Isaiah

^t **9:6** Wonderful; *or* Wise.
9:7 Lk 1:32, 33

The Lord Will Punish Israel

8 The Lord has pronounced judgment on the kingdom of Israel, on the descendants of Jacob. **9** All the people of Israel, everyone who lives in the city of Samaria, will know that he has done this. Now they are proud and arrogant. They say, **10** "The brick buildings have fallen down, but we will replace them with stone buildings. The beams of sycamore wood have been cut down, but we will replace them with the finest cedar."

11 The Lord has stirred up their enemies*u* to attack them. **12** Syria on the east and Philistia on the west have opened their mouths to devour Israel. Yet even so the Lord's anger is not ended; his hand is still stretched out to punish.

13 The people of Israel have not repented; even though the Lord Almighty has punished them, they have not returned to him. **14** In a single day the Lord will punish Israel's leaders and its people; he will cut them off, head and tail. **15** The old and honorable men are the head—and the tail is the prophets whose teachings are lies! **16** Those who lead these people have misled them and totally confused them. **17** And so the Lord will not let any of the young men escape, and he will not show pity on any of the widows and orphans, because all the people are godless and wicked and everything they say is evil. Yet even so the Lord's anger will not be ended, but his hand will still be stretched out to punish.

18 The wickedness of the people burns like a fire that destroys thorn bushes and thistles. It burns like a forest fire that sends up columns of smoke. **19** Because the Lord Almighty is angry, his punishment burns like a fire throughout the land and destroys the people, and it is each of us for ourselves.

Like a forest fire (9:18)

20 Everywhere in the country people snatch and eat any bit of food they can find, but their hunger is never satisfied. They even eat their own children! **21** The people of Manasseh and the people of Ephraim attack each other, and together they attack Judah. Yet even so the Lord's anger is not ended; his hand is still stretched out to punish.

10 **1** You are doomed! You make unjust laws that oppress my people. **2** That is how you keep the poor from having their rights and from getting justice. That is how you take the property that belongs to widows and orphans. **3** What will you do when God punishes you? What will you do when he brings disaster on you from a distant country? Where will you run to find help? Where will you hide your wealth? **4** You will be killed in battle or dragged off as prisoners. Yet even so the Lord's anger will not be ended; his hand will still be stretched out to punish.

The Emperor of Assyria as the Instrument of God

5 The Lord said, "Assyria! I use Assyria like a club to punish those with whom I am angry. **6** I sent Assyria to attack a godless nation, people who have made me angry. I sent them to loot and steal and trample the people like dirt in the streets."

7 But the Assyrian emperor has his own violent plans in mind. He is determined to destroy many nations. **8** He boasts, "Every one of my commanders is a king! **9** I conquered the cities of Calno and Carchemish, the cities of Hamath and Arpad. I conquered Samaria and Damascus. **10** I reached out to punish those kingdoms that worship idols, idols more numerous than those of Jerusalem and Samaria. **11** I have destroyed Samaria and all its idols, and I will do the same to Jerusalem and the images that are worshiped there."

12 But the Lord says, "When I finish what I am doing on Mount Zion and in Jerusalem, I will punish the emperor of Assyria for all his boasting and all his pride."

---

u **9:11** *Probable text* their enemies; *Hebrew* the enemies of Rezin.
10:5–34 Isa 14:24–27; Nah 1:1—3:19; Zeph 2:13–15

13 The emperor of Assyria boasts, "I have done it all myself. I am strong and wise and clever. I wiped out the boundaries between nations and took the supplies they had stored. Like a bull I have trampled the people who live there. 14 The nations of the world were like a bird's nest, and I gathered their wealth as easily as gathering eggs. Not a wing fluttered to scare me off; no beak opened to scream at me!"

15 But the LORD says, "Can an ax claim to be greater than the one who uses it? Is a saw more important than the one who saws with it? A club doesn't lift up a person; a person lifts up a club."

16 The LORD Almighty is going to send disease to punish those who are now well-fed. In their bodies there will be a fire that burns and burns. 17 God, the light of Israel, will become a fire. Israel's holy God will become a flame, which in a single day will burn up everything, even the thorns and thistles. 18 The rich forests and farmlands will be totally destroyed, in the same way that a fatal sickness destroys someone. 19 There will be so few trees left that even a child will be able to count them.

A Few Will Come Back

20 A time is coming when the people of Israel who have survived will not rely any more on the nation that almost destroyed them. They will truly put their trust in the LORD, Israel's holy God. 21 A few of the people of Israel will come back to their mighty God. 22 Even though now there are as many people of Israel as there are grains of sand by the sea, only a few will come back. Destruction is in store for the people, and it is fully deserved. 23 Yes, throughout the whole country the Sovereign LORD Almighty will bring destruction, as he said he would.

The LORD Will Punish Assyria

24 The Sovereign LORD Almighty says to his people who live in Zion, "Do not be afraid of the Assyrians, even though they oppress you as the Egyptians used to do. 25 In only a little while I will finish punishing you, and then I will destroy them. 26 I, the LORD Almighty, will beat them with my whip as I did the people of Midian at Oreb Rock. I will punish Assyria as I punished Egypt. 27 When that time comes, I will free you from the power of Assyria, and their yoke will no longer be a burden on your shoulders." v

The Invader Attacks

28 The enemy army has captured the city of Ai! w They have passed through Migron! They left their supplies at Michmash! 29 They have crossed the pass and are spending the night at Geba! The people in the town of Ramah are terrified, and the people in King Saul's hometown of Gibeah have run away. 30 Shout, people of Gallim! Listen, people of Laishah! Answer, people of Anathoth! 31 The people of Madmenah and Gebim are running for their lives. 32 Today the enemy are in the town of Nob, and there they are shaking their fists at Mount Zion, at the city of Jerusalem.

33 The LORD Almighty will bring them crashing down like branches cut off a tree. The proudest and highest of them will be cut down and humiliated. 34 The LORD will cut them down as trees in the heart of the forest are cut down with an ax, as even the finest trees of Lebanon fall!

The Peaceful Kingdom

11 1 The royal line of David is like a tree that has been cut down; but just as new branches sprout from a stump, so a new king will arise from among David's descendants.

Isaiah

---

v **10:27** *Hebrew has three additional words, the meaning of which is unclear.* w **10:28** *AI: This and the other places mentioned in verses 28–32 were located near Jerusalem, along the way by which an invader would come to attack from the north.*
10:22, 23 Rom 9:27 **11:1** Rev 5:5; 22:16

"Wolves and sheep will live together in peace, / and leopards will lie down with young goats" *(Isaiah 11:6).*

2 The spirit of the LORD will give him
    wisdom
  and the knowledge and skill to rule his
    people.
  He will know the LORD's will and honor
    him,
3   and find pleasure in obeying him.
  He will not judge by appearance or
    hearsay;
4   he will judge the poor fairly
  and defend the rights of the helpless.
  At his command the people will be
    punished,
  and evil persons will die.
5 He will rule his people with justice and
    integrity.

6 Wolves and sheep will live together in
    peace,
  and leopards will lie down with young
    goats.
  Calves and lion cubs will feed^x together,
  and little children will take care of
    them.

And little children will take care of them. (11:6)

7 Cows and bears will eat together,
  and their calves and cubs will lie down
    in peace.
  Lions will eat straw as cattle do.
8 Even a baby will not be harmed
  if it plays near a poisonous snake.
9 On Zion, God's sacred hill,
  there will be nothing harmful or evil.

The land will be as full of knowledge of
    the LORD
  as the seas are full of water.

The Exiled People Will Return

10 A day is coming when the new king
from the royal line of David will be a symbol
to the nations. They will gather in his royal
city and give him honor. 11 When that day
comes, the Lord will once again use his
power and bring back home those of his people who are left in Assyria and Egypt, in the
lands of Pathros, Ethiopia,^y Elam, Babylonia,
and Hamath, and in the coastlands and on the
islands of the sea. 12 The Lord will raise a signal flag to show the nations that he is gathering together again the scattered people of
Israel and Judah and bringing them back from
the four corners of the earth. 13 The kingdom
of Israel will not be jealous of Judah any
more, and Judah will not be the enemy of
Israel. 14 Together they will attack the
Philistines on the west and plunder the people who live to the east. They will conquer
the people of Edom and Moab, and the people of Ammon will obey them. 15 The LORD
will dry up the Gulf of Suez, and he will
bring a hot wind to dry up the Euphrates,
leaving only seven tiny streams, so that anyone
can walk across. 16 There will be a highway
out of Assyria for those of his people Israel
who have survived there, just as there was for
their ancestors when they left Egypt.

Hymn of Thanksgiving

12 ^1 A day is coming when people will
      sing,
  "I praise you, LORD! You were angry with
    me,
  but now you comfort me and are angry
    no longer.

---

x 11:6 *Some ancient translations* will feed; *Hebrew* and well-fed cattle.   y 11:11 *Hebrew* Cush: *Cush is the ancient*
name of the extensive territory south of the First Cataract of the Nile River. This region was called Ethiopia in Graeco-
Roman times, and included within its borders most of modern Sudan and some of present-day Ethiopia (Abyssinia).
11:4 2 Thess 2:8   **11:5** Eph 6:14   **11:6–9** Isa 65:25   **11:9** Hab 2:14   **11:10** Rom 15:12   **11:15** Rev
16:12

Zion: **The name for the mountain that the Temple in Jerusalem was built on.**
Eventually, it became another name for Jerusalem or the whole nation of Israel.

"Tell them how great he is!" (12:4)

2 God is my savior;
  I will trust him and not be afraid.
The LORD gives me power and strength;
  he is my savior.
3 As fresh water brings joy to the thirsty,
  so God's people rejoice when he saves
    them."

4 A day is coming when people will sing,
"Give thanks to the LORD! Call for him
    to help you!
Tell all the nations what he has done!
Tell them how great he is!
5 Sing to the LORD because of the great
    things he has done.
Let the whole world hear the news.
6 Let everyone who lives in Zion shout and
    sing!
Israel's holy God is great,
  and he lives among his people."

God Will Punish Babylon

13 1 This is a message about Babylon, which Isaiah son of Amoz received from God.
2 On the top of a barren hill raise the battle flag! Shout to the soldiers and raise your arm as the signal for them to attack the gates of the proud city. 3 The LORD has called out

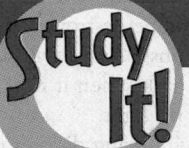

Yesua and Yesayahu

Yesua is the Hebrew word for salvation, and *Yesayahu* is Isaiah in Hebrew. Does this give you a clue about what Isaiah's message is going to be about? It could be said that Isaiah's words are words of salvation. Salvation has to do with how God is saving us. Maybe you don't think you need to be saved, but the truth is, we all need to be saved. Saved from what? We need to be saved from sin and death.

The hymn of thanksgiving in Isaiah, chapter 12, is an example of Isaiah's message of salvation. We hear that God is a savior and of the happiness that comes with that. In the whole Book of Isaiah, the words *salvation, save,* and *savior* are used a total of 78 times.

— Isaiah, chapter 12

his proud and confident soldiers to fight a holy war and punish those he is angry with.

4 Listen to the noise on the mountains— the sound of a great crowd of people, the sound of nations and kingdoms gathering. The LORD of Armies is preparing his troops for battle. 5 They are coming from far-off countries at the ends of the earth. In his anger the LORD is coming to devastate the whole country.

6 Howl in pain! The day of the LORD is near, the day when the Almighty brings destruction. 7 Everyone's hands will hang limp, and everyone's courage will fail. 8 They will all be terrified and overcome with pain, like the pain of a woman in labor. They will look at each other in fear, and their faces will burn with shame. 9 The day of the LORD is coming—that cruel day of his fierce anger

Isaiah

and fury. The earth will be made a wilderness, and every sinner will be destroyed. [10]Every star and every constellation will stop shining, the sun will be dark when it rises, and the moon will give no light.

[11]The LORD says, "I will bring disaster on the earth and punish all wicked people for their sins. I will humble everyone who is proud and punish everyone who is arrogant and cruel. [12]Those who survive will be scarcer than gold. [13]I will make the heavens tremble, and the earth will be shaken out of its place on that day when I, the LORD Almighty, show my anger.

[14]"The foreigners living in Babylon will run away to their homelands, scattering like deer escaping from hunters, like sheep without a shepherd. [15]Anyone who is caught will be stabbed to death. [16]While they look on helplessly, their babies will be battered to death, their houses will be looted, and their wives will be raped."

[17]The LORD says, "I am stirring up the Medes[z] to attack Babylon. They care nothing for silver and are not tempted by gold. [18]With their bows and arrows they will kill the young men. They will show no mercy to babies and take no pity on children. [19]Babylonia is the most beautiful kingdom of all; it is the pride of its people. But I, the LORD, will overthrow Babylon as I did Sodom and Gomorrah! [20]No one will ever live there again. No wandering Arab will ever pitch a tent there, and no shepherd will ever pasture a flock there. [21]It will be a place where desert animals live and where owls build their nests. Ostriches will live there, and wild goats will prance through the ruins. [22]The towers and palaces will echo with the cries of hyenas and jackals. Babylon's time has come! Her days are almost over."

The Return from Exile

14 [1]The LORD will once again be merciful to his people Israel and choose them as his own. He will let them live in their own land again, and foreigners will come and live there with them. [2]Many nations will help the people of Israel return to the land which the LORD gave them, and there the nations will serve Israel as slaves. Those who once captured Israel will now be captured by Israel, and the people of Israel will rule over those who once oppressed them.

The King of Babylon in the World of the Dead

[3]The LORD will give the people of Israel relief from their pain and suffering and from the hard work they were forced to do. [4]When he does this, they are to mock the king of Babylon and say:

"The cruel king has fallen! He will never oppress anyone again! [5]The LORD has ended the power of the evil rulers [6]who angrily oppressed the peoples and never stopped persecuting the nations they had conquered. [7]Now at last the whole world enjoys rest and peace, and everyone sings for joy. [8]The cypress trees and the cedars of Lebanon rejoice over the fallen king, because there is no one to cut them down, now that he is gone!

[9]"The world of the dead is getting ready to welcome the king of Babylon. The ghosts of those who were powerful on earth are stirring about. The ghosts of kings are rising from their thrones. [10]They all call out to him, 'Now you are as weak as we are! You are one of us! [11]You used to be honored with the music of harps, but now here you are in the world of the dead. You lie on a bed of maggots and are covered with a blanket of worms.'"

[12]King of Babylon, bright morning star, you have fallen from heaven! In the past you conquered nations, but now you have been thrown to the ground. [13]You were determined to climb up to heaven and to place your throne above the highest stars. You thought you would sit like a king on that mountain in the north where the gods assemble. [14]You said you would climb to the tops of the clouds and be like the Almighty.

---

[z] **13:17** MEDES: *People of a nation northeast of Babylonia, which became part of the Persian Empire.*
13:10 Ezek 32:7; Mt 24:29; Mk 13:24, 25; Lk 21:25; Rev 6:12, 13; 8:12   **13:19** Gen 19:24   **13:21** Isa 34:14; Zeph 2:14; Rev 18:2   **14:12** Rev 8:10; 9:1   **14:13–15** Mt 11:23; Lk 10:15

15 But instead, you have been brought down to the deepest part of the world of the dead.

16 The dead will stare and gape at you. They will ask, "Is this the man who shook the earth and made kingdoms tremble? 17 Is this the man who destroyed cities and turned the world into a desert? Is this the man who never freed his prisoners or let them go home?"

18 All the kings of the earth lie in their magnificent tombs, 19 but you have no tomb, and your corpse is thrown out to rot. It is covered by the bodies of soldiers killed in battle, thrown with them into a rocky pit, and trampled down. 20 Because you ruined your country and killed your own people, you will not be buried like other kings. None of your evil family will survive. 21 Let the slaughter begin! The sons of this king will die because of their ancestors' sins. None of them will ever rule the earth or cover it with cities.

God Will Destroy Babylon

22 The LORD Almighty says, "I will attack Babylon and bring it to ruin. I will leave nothing—no children, no survivors at all. I, the LORD, have spoken. 23 I will turn Babylon into a marsh, and owls will live there. I will sweep Babylon with a broom that will sweep everything away. I, the LORD Almighty, have spoken."

"I will sweep Babylon." (14:23)

God Will Destroy the Assyrians

24 The LORD Almighty has sworn an oath: "What I have planned will happen. What I have determined to do will be done. 25 I will destroy the Assyrians in my land of Israel and trample them on my mountains. I will free my people from the Assyrian yoke and from the burdens they have had to bear. 26 This is my plan for the world, and my arm is stretched out to punish the nations." 27 The LORD Almighty is determined to do this; he has stretched out his arm to punish, and no one can stop him.

God Will Destroy the Philistines

28 This is a message that was proclaimed in the year that King Ahaz died.

29 People of Philistia, the rod that beat you is broken, but you have no reason to be glad. When one snake dies, a worse one comes in its place. A snake's egg hatches a flying dragon. 30 The LORD will be a shepherd to the poor of his people and will let them live in safety. But he will send a terrible famine on you Philistines, and it will not leave any of you alive.

31 Howl and cry for help, all you Philistine cities! Be terrified, all of you! A cloud of dust is coming from the north—it is an army with no cowards in its ranks.

32 How shall we answer the messengers that come to us from Philistia? We will tell them that the LORD has established Zion and that his suffering people will find safety there.

God Will Destroy Moab

15 1 This is a message about Moab. The cities of Ar and Kir are destroyed in a single night, and silence covers the land of Moab. 2 The people of Dibon[a] climb the hill to weep at the shrine. The people of Moab wail in grief over the cities

---

^a **15:2** *Probable text* people of Dibon; *Hebrew* people and Dibon.
14:24–27 Isa 10:5–34; Nah 1:1—3:19; Zeph 2:13–15 **14:28** 2 Kings 16:20; 2 Chr 28:27 **14:29–31** Jer 47:1–7; Ezek 25:15–17; Joel 3:4–8; Am 1:6–8; Zeph 2:4–7; Zech 9:5–7 **15:1—16:14** Isa 25:10–12; Jer 48:1–47; Ezek 25:8–11; Am 2:1–3; Zeph 2:8–11

Isaiah

Pray It!

Our Enemies Destroyed?

The prophecies in these chapters of Isaiah are about God's punishment of nations that are Israel's enemies: Babylon, Assyria, Moab, and Egypt. Isaiah uses strong and violent imagery to describe how these nations and their people will meet their doom. We have to remember to understand the Old Testament in light of what Jesus teaches. Jesus makes it clear that God loves all people and that we should love our enemies and pray for them. Rather than see them destroyed, followers of Jesus try everything possible to show our enemies the goodness of God and how to live in love and peace. Here's a prayer for people who threaten us.

Mighty God,
Sometimes I feel like Isaiah. I want to see people who do evil and hurt others com-
pletely destroyed. It is hard to understand how people can be so mean and cruel to
other people. But Jesus showed us that you even love mean and evil people. So I pray,
Lord, for people who are our enemies. Help them to know your love. Help us to be an
example of love and forgiveness so that they might come to believe in you, too. With
the help of the Holy Spirit, may we live with understanding, peace, and justice for all
people. Amen.

— Isaiah, chapter 15

of Nebo and Medeba; they have shaved their heads and their beards in grief. ³The people in the streets are dressed in sackcloth; in the city squares and on the rooftops people mourn and cry. ⁴The people of Heshbon and Elealeh cry out, and their cry can be heard as far away as Jahaz. Even the soldiers tremble; their courage is gone. ⁵My heart cries out for Moab! The people have fled to the town of Zoar, and to Eglath Shelishiyah. Some climb the road to Luhith, weeping as they go; some escape to Horonaim, grieving loudly. ⁶Nimrim Brook is dry, the grass beside it has withered, and nothing green is left. ⁷The people go across the Valley of Willows, trying to escape with all their possessions. ⁸Everywhere at Moab's borders the sound of crying is heard. It is heard at the towns of Eglaim and Beerelim. ⁹At the town of Dibon the river is red with blood, and

God has something even worse in store for the people there. Yes, there will be a bloody slaughter of everyone left in Moab.

The people of Moab wail in grief. (15:2)

"Then one of David's descendants will be king, and he will rule the people with faithfulness and love" *(Isaiah 16:5).*

Trying to escape with all their possessions (15:7)

Moab's Hopeless Situation

16 ¹From the city of Sela in the desert the people of Moab send a lamb as a present to the one who rules in Jerusalem. ²They wait on the banks of the Arnon River and move aimlessly back and forth, like birds driven from their nest.

³They say to the people of Judah, "Tell us what to do. Protect us like a tree that casts a cool shadow in the heat of noon, and let us rest in your shade. We are refugees; hide us where no one can find us. ⁴Let us stay in your land. Protect us from those who want to destroy us."

(Oppression and destruction will end, and those who are devastating the country will be gone. ⁵Then one of David's descendants will be king, and he will rule the people with faithfulness and love. He will be quick to do what is right, and he will see that justice is done.)

⁶The people of Judah say, "We have heard how proud the people of Moab are. We know that they are arrogant and conceited, but their boasts are empty."

⁷The people of Moab will weep because of the troubles they suffer. They will all weep when they remember the fine food they used to eat in the city of Kir Heres. They will be driven to despair. ⁸The farms near Heshbon and the vineyards of Sibmah are destroyed—those vineyards whose wine used to make the rulers of the nations drunk. At one time the vines spread as far as the city of Jazer, and eastward into the desert, and westward to the other side of the Dead Sea. ⁹Now I weep for Sibmah's vines as I weep for Jazer. My tears fall for Heshbon and Elealeh, because there is no harvest to make

the people glad. ¹⁰No one is happy now in the fertile fields. No one shouts or sings in the vineyards. No one tramples grapes to make wine; the shouts of joy are ended. *b* ¹¹I groan with sadness for Moab, with grief for Kir Heres. ¹²The people of Moab wear themselves out going to their mountain shrines and to their temples to pray, but it will do them no good.

¹³That is the message the LORD gave earlier about Moab. ¹⁴And now the LORD says, "In exactly three years Moab's great wealth will disappear. Of its many people, only a few will survive, and they will be weak."

God Will Punish Syria and Israel

17 ¹The LORD said, "Damascus will not be a city any longer; it will be only a pile of ruins. ²The cities of Syria will be deserted forever. *c* They will be a pasture for sheep and cattle, and no one will drive them away. ³Israel will be defenseless, and Damascus will lose its independence. Those Syrians who survive will be in disgrace like the people of Israel. I, the LORD Almighty, have spoken."

⁴The LORD said, "A day is coming when Israel's greatness will come to an end, and its wealth will be replaced by poverty. ⁵Israel will be like a field where the grain has been cut and harvested, as desolate as a field in Rephaim Valley when it has been picked bare. ⁶Only a few people will survive, and Israel will be like an olive tree from which all the olives have been picked except two or

Israel will be like an olive tree. (17:6)

Isaiah

---

b **16:10** *One ancient translation* the shouts of joy are ended; *Hebrew* I have ended the shouts of joy.   *c* **17:2** *One ancient translation* The cities . . . forever; *Hebrew* The cities of Aroer are deserted.
17:1–3 Jer 49:23–27; Am 1:3–5; Zech 9:1

three at the very top, or a few that are left on the lower branches. I, the LORD God of Israel, have spoken."

7 When that day comes, people will turn for help to their Creator, the holy God of Israel. 8 They will no longer rely on the altars they made with their own hands, or trust in their own handiwork—symbols of the goddess Asherah and altars for burning incense.

9 When that day comes, well-defended cities will be deserted and left in ruins like the cities that the Hivites and the Amorites*d* abandoned as they fled from the people of Israel.

10 Israel, you have forgotten the God who rescues you and protects you like a mighty rock. Instead, you plant sacred gardens*e* in order to worship a foreign god. 11 But even if they sprouted and blossomed the very morning you planted them, there would still be no harvest. There would be only trouble and incurable pain.

Enemy Nations Are Defeated

12 Powerful nations are in commotion with a sound like the roar of the sea, like the crashing of huge waves. 13 The nations advance like rushing waves, but God reprimands them and they retreat, driven away like dust on a mountainside, like straw in a whirlwind. 14 At evening they cause terror, but by morning they are gone. That is the fate of everyone who plunders our land.

God Will Punish Ethiopia

18 1 Beyond the rivers of Ethiopia*f* there is a land where the sound of wings is heard. 2 From that land ambassadors come down the Nile in boats made of reeds. Go back home, swift messengers! Take a message back to your land divided by rivers, to your strong and powerful nation, to your tall and smooth-skinned people, who are feared all over the world.

Africans in the Bible

Isaiah, chapters 18–19, are prophecies against the people of Ethiopia and Egypt. What continent do these people come from? Africa, of course! Look on a globe or map and see where Egypt and Ethiopia are located in relation to Israel. You will see that to travel on land from Africa to Europe or Asia you have to cross through Israel. That is why the people of Africa were well known to the Israelites. You can see that Isaiah had a great respect for the Ethiopians, calling them a "strong and powerful nation" (18:2).

— Isaiah, chapter 18

3 Listen, everyone who lives on earth! Look for a signal flag to be raised on the mountaintops! Listen for the blowing of the bugle! 4 The LORD said to me, "I will look down from heaven as quietly as the dew forms in the warm nights of harvest time, as serenely as the sun shines in the heat of the day. 5 Before the grapes are gathered, when the blossoms have all fallen and the grapes are ripening, the enemy will destroy the Ethiopians*f* as easily as a knife cuts branches from a vine. 6 The corpses of their soldiers will be left exposed to the birds and the wild animals. In summer the birds will feed on them, and in winter, the animals."

7 A time is coming when the LORD Almighty will receive offerings from this land divided by rivers, this strong and powerful nation, this tall and smooth-skinned people, who are feared all over the world.

d **17:9** *One ancient translation* the Hivites and the Amorites; *Hebrew* woodland and hill country.
e **17:10** SACRED GARDENS: *See 1:29.* *f* **18:1, 5** *Hebrew* Cush(ites): *Cush is the ancient name of the extensive territory south of the First Cataract of the Nile River. This region was called Ethiopia in Graeco-Roman times, and included within its borders most of modern Sudan and some of present-day Ethiopia (Abyssinia).*
18:1–7 Zeph 2:12

They will come to Mount Zion, where the LORD Almighty is worshiped.

God Will Punish Egypt

19 ¹This is a message about Egypt.
The LORD is coming to Egypt, riding swiftly on a cloud. The Egyptian idols tremble before him, and the people of Egypt lose their courage. ²The LORD says, "I will stir up civil war in Egypt and turn brother against brother and neighbor against neighbor. Rival cities will fight each other, and rival kings will struggle for power. ³I am going to frustrate the plans of the Egyptians and destroy their morale. They will ask their idols to help them, and they will go and consult mediums and ask the spirits of the dead for advice. ⁴I will hand the Egyptians over to a tyrant, to a cruel king who will rule them. I, the LORD Almighty, have spoken."

⁵The water will be low in the Nile, and the river will gradually dry up. ⁶The channels of the river will stink as they slowly go dry. Reeds and rushes will wither, ⁷and all the crops planted along the banks of the Nile will dry up and be blown away. ⁸Everyone who earns a living by fishing in the Nile will groan and cry; their hooks and their nets will be useless. ⁹Those who make linen cloth will be in despair; ¹⁰weavers and skilled workers will be broken and depressed.

¹¹The leaders of the city of Zoan are fools! Egypt's wisest people give stupid

Their hooks and their nets will be useless. (19:8)

19:1–25 Jer 46:2–26; Ezek 29:1—32:32

advice! How do they dare to tell the king that they are successors to the ancient scholars and kings? ¹²King of Egypt, where are those clever advisers of yours? Perhaps they can tell you what plans the LORD Almighty has for Egypt. ¹³The leaders of Zoan and Memphis are fools. They were supposed to lead the nation, but they have misled it. ¹⁴The LORD has made them give confusing advice. As a result, Egypt does everything wrong and staggers like a drunk slipping on his own vomit. ¹⁵No one in Egypt, rich or poor, important or unknown, can offer help.

Egypt Will Worship the LORD

¹⁶A time is coming when the people of Egypt will be as timid as women. They will tremble in terror when they see that the LORD Almighty has stretched out his hand to punish them. ¹⁷The people of Egypt will be terrified of Judah every time they are reminded of the fate that the LORD Almighty has prepared for them.

¹⁸When that time comes, the Hebrew language will be spoken in five Egyptian cities. The people there will take their oaths in the name of the LORD Almighty. One of the cities will be called, "City of the Sun."

¹⁹When that time comes, there will be an altar to the LORD in the land of Egypt and a stone pillar dedicated to him at the Egyptian border. ²⁰They will be symbols of the LORD Almighty's presence in Egypt. When the people there are oppressed and call out to the LORD for help, he will send someone to rescue them. ²¹The LORD will reveal himself to the Egyptian people, and then they will acknowledge and worship him, and bring him sacrifices and offerings. They will make solemn promises to him and do what they promise. ²²The LORD will punish the Egyptians, but then he will heal them. They will turn to him, and he will hear their prayers and heal them.

²³When that time comes, there will be a highway between Egypt and Assyria. The

Isaiah

Pray It!

Prayer for the Oppressed

In Isaiah, chapter 19, Isaiah makes an interesting prophecy. First, he says that God will punish the Egyptians with a civil war and the Nile will dry up. But they will eventually recognize the Lord and call out to him. Only when they are oppressed do they finally understand their need for God. Like the Egyptians in this prophecy, there are groups of people who have been suffering for a long time. They have been victims of racism, poverty, or hunger. When this happens we say that these people are oppressed.

Find a current newspaper. Look through it for an article on people who are oppressed. Maybe they are people who are losing their land, are not being paid fairly, or are being treated violently by others because of their race or religion. After reading the article, write a prayer for them, asking God to send them the help they need. Pray that prayer often. As part of your prayer, read Isaiah 19:20: "When the people there are oppressed and call out to the LORD for help, he will send someone to rescue them." You may just be the one God is sending to help them!

— Isaiah 19:20

people of these two countries will travel back and forth between them, and the two nations will worship together. 24 When that time comes, Israel will rank with Egypt and Assyria, and these three nations will be a blessing to all the world. 25 The LORD Almighty will bless them and say, "I will bless you, Egypt, my people; you, Assyria, whom I created; and you, Israel, my chosen people."

The Sign of the Naked Prophet

20 ¹Under the orders of Emperor Sargon of Assyria, the commander-in-chief of the Assyrian army attacked the Philistine city of Ashdod. ²Three years earlier the LORD had told Isaiah son of Amoz to take off his sandals and the sackcloth he was wearing. He obeyed and went around naked and barefoot. ³When Ashdod was captured, the LORD said, "My servant Isaiah has been going around naked and barefoot for three years. This is a sign of what will happen to Egypt and Ethiopia.ʄ ⁴The emperor of Assyria will lead away naked the prisoners he captures from those two countries. Young and old, they will walk barefoot and naked, with their buttocks exposed, bringing shame on Egypt. ⁵Those who have put their trust in Ethiopiaʄ and have boasted about Egypt will be disillusioned, their hopes shattered. ⁶When that time comes, the people who live along the coast of Philistia will say, 'Look at what has happened to the people we relied on to protect us from the emperor of Assyria! How will we ever survive?' "

ʄ 20:3, 5 Hebrew Cush(ites): Cush is the ancient name of the extensive territory south of the First Cataract of the Nile River. This region was called Ethiopia in Graeco-Roman times, and included within its borders most of modern Sudan and some of present-day Ethiopia (Abyssinia).

Isaiah, chapter 20, says that Isaiah went naked and barefoot for three years. He probably wasn't completely naked; he may have just took off his sandals and robe!

A Vision of the Fall of Babylon

21 [1]This is a message about Babylonia. Like a whirlwind sweeping across the desert, disaster will come from a terrifying land. [2]I have seen a vision of cruel events, a vision of betrayal and destruction.

Army of Elam, attack! Army of Media, lay siege to the cities! God will put an end to the suffering which Babylon has caused.

[3]What I saw and heard in the vision has filled me with terror and pain, pain like that of a woman in labor. [4]My head is spinning, and I am trembling with fear. I had been longing for evening to come, but it has brought me nothing but terror.

[5]In the vision a banquet is ready; rugs are spread for the guests to sit on. They are eating and drinking. Suddenly the command rings out: "Officers! Prepare your shields!"

[6]Then the Lord said to me, "Go and post a sentry, and tell him to report what he sees. [7]If he sees riders coming on horseback, two by two, and riders on donkeys and camels, he is to observe them carefully."

[8]The sentry calls out, "Sir, I have been standing guard at my post day and night."

[9]Suddenly, here they come! Riders on horseback, two by two. The sentry gives the news, "Babylon has fallen! All the idols they worshiped lie shattered on the ground."

[10]My people Israel, you have been threshed like wheat, but now I have announced to you the good news that I have heard from the LORD Almighty, the God of Israel.

A Message about Edom

[11]This is a message about Edom.

Someone calls to me from Edom, "Sentry, how soon will the night be over? Tell me how soon it will end."

[12]I answer, "Morning is coming, but night will come again. If you want to ask again, come back and ask."

A Message about Arabia

[13]This is a message about Arabia.

People of Dedan, you whose caravans camp in the barren country of Arabia, [14]give water to the thirsty people who come to you. You people of the land of Tema, give food to the refugees. [15]People are fleeing to escape from swords that are ready to kill them, from bows that are ready to shoot, from all the dangers of war.

[16]Then the Lord said to me, "In exactly one year the greatness of the tribes of Kedar will be at an end. [17]The archers are the bravest warriors of Kedar, but few of them will be left. I, the LORD God of Israel, have spoken."

A Message about Jerusalem

22 [1]This is a message about the Valley of Vision.

What is happening? Why are all the people of the city celebrating on the roofs of the houses? [2]The whole city is in an uproar, filled with noise and excitement.

Your people who died in this war did not die fighting. [3]All your leaders ran away and were captured before they shot a single arrow. [4]Now leave me alone to weep bitterly over all those of my people who have died. Don't try to comfort me. [5]This is a time of panic, defeat, and confusion in the Valley of Vision, and the Sovereign LORD Almighty has sent it on us. The walls of our city have been battered down, and cries for help have echoed among the hills.

[6]The soldiers from the land of Elam came riding on horseback, armed with bows and arrows. Soldiers from the land of Kir had their shields ready. [7]The fertile valleys of Judah were filled with chariots; soldiers on horseback stood in front of Jerusalem's gates. [8]All of Judah's defenses crumbled.

When that happened, you brought weapons out of the arsenal. [9-10]You found the places where the walls of Jerusalem needed repair. You inspected all the houses in Jerusalem and tore some of them down to get stones to repair the city walls. In order to store water, [11]you built a reservoir inside the city to hold the water flowing down from the old pool. But you paid no attention to God, who planned all this long ago and who caused it to happen.

21:9 Rev 14:8; 18:2

Isaiah

Huh?

The prophecy in the first half of Isaiah, chapter 22, may leave you scratching your head. It says that God was upset because the people were celebrating and rejoicing. But why would God be upset at that?

It helps to know some background. Isaiah believed that God was sending foreign armies (from Elam) to attack Jerusalem as punishment for their sins. The people of Jerusalem should have recognized this and asked God for forgiveness—by weeping and mourning, shaving their heads, and wearing sackcloth (Isaiah 22:12). Instead they decided to party because they thought they were going to die anyway. God was trying to get their attention so that they could get on the right path—and they totally missed it!

Has God ever tried to get your attention through good or bad events in your life?

— Isaiah 22:1–14

"That will be the end of everything that was hanging on it." (22:25)

Isaiah *(side tab)*

¹²The Sovereign LORD Almighty was calling you then to weep and mourn, to shave your heads and wear sackcloth. ¹³Instead, you laughed and celebrated. You killed sheep and cattle to eat, and you drank wine. You said, "We might as well eat and drink! Tomorrow we'll be dead."

¹⁴The Sovereign LORD Almighty himself spoke to me and said, "This evil will never be forgiven them as long as they live. I, the Sovereign LORD Almighty, have spoken."

A Warning to Shebna

¹⁵The Sovereign LORD Almighty told me to go to Shebna, the manager of the royal household, and say to him, ¹⁶"Who do you think you are? What right do you have to carve a tomb for yourself out of the rocky hillside? ¹⁷You may be important, but the LORD will pick you up and throw you away. ¹⁸He will pick you up like a ball and throw you into a much larger country. You will die there beside the chariots you were so proud of. You are a disgrace to your master's household. ¹⁹The LORD will remove you from office and bring you down from your high position."

²⁰The LORD said to Shebna, "When that happens, I will send for my servant Eliakim son of Hilkiah. ²¹I will put your official robe and belt on him and give him all the authority you have had. He will be like a father to the people of Jerusalem and Judah. ²²I will give him complete authority under the king, the descendant of David. He will have the keys of office; what he opens, no one will shut, and what he shuts, no one will open. ²³I will fasten him firmly in place like a peg, and he will be a source of honor to his whole family.

²⁴"But all his relatives and dependents will become a burden to him. They will hang on him like pots and bowls hanging from a peg! ²⁵When that happens, the peg that was firmly fastened will pull loose and fall. And that will be the end of everything that was hanging on it." The LORD has spoken.

A Message about Phoenicia

23 ¹This is a message about Tyre.
Howl with grief, you sailors out
on the ocean! Your home port of Tyre has
been destroyed; its houses and its harbor are
in ruins. As your ships return from Cyprus,
you learn the news. ²Wail, you merchants of
Sidon! You sent agents ³across the sea to buy
and sell the grain that grew in Egypt and to
do business with all the nations.

⁴City of Sidon, you are disgraced! The sea
and the great ocean depths disown you and
say, "I never had any children. I never raised
sons or daughters."

⁵Even the Egyptians will be shocked and
dismayed when they learn that Tyre has been
destroyed.

⁶Howl with grief, you people of Phoenicia! Try to escape to Spain! ⁷Can this be the
joyful city of Tyre, founded so long ago? Is
this the city that sent settlers across the sea to
establish colonies? ⁸Who was it that planned
to bring all this on Tyre, that imperial city,
whose merchant princes were the most honored men on earth? ⁹The LORD Almighty
planned it. He planned it in order to put an
end to their pride in what they had done
and to humiliate their honored ones.

¹⁰Go and farm the land, you people in the
colonies in Spain! There is no one to protect
you any more.ᵍ ¹¹The LORD has stretched out
his hand over the sea and overthrown kingdoms. He has commanded that the Phoenician centers of commerce be destroyed.
¹²City of Sidon, your happiness has ended,
and your people are oppressed. Even if they
escape to Cyprus, they will still not be safe.

(¹³It was the Babylonians, not the Assyrians, who let the wild animals overrun Tyre. It
was the Babylonians who put up siege towers, tore down the fortifications of Tyre, and
left the city in ruins.ʰ)

¹⁴Howl with grief, you sailors out on the
ocean! The city you relied on has been
destroyed.

¹⁵A time is coming when Tyre will be forgotten for seventy years, the lifetime of a
king. When those years are over, Tyre will be
like the prostitute in the song:

¹⁶Take your harp, go round the town,
    you poor forgotten whore!
Play and sing your songs again
    to bring men back once more.

¹⁷When the seventy years are over, the
LORD will let Tyre go back to her old trade,
and she will hire herself out to all the kingdoms of the world. ¹⁸The money she earns
by commerce will be dedicated to the
LORD. She will not store it away, but those
who worship the LORD will use her money
to buy the food and the clothing they need.

The LORD Will Punish the Earth

24 ¹The LORD is going to devastate the
earth and leave it desolate. He will
twist the earth's surface and scatter its people. ²Everyone will meet the same fate—the
priests and the people, slaves and masters,
buyers and sellers, lenders and borrowers,
rich and poor. ³The earth will lie shattered
and ruined. The LORD has spoken and it will
be done.

⁴The earth dries up and withers; the
whole world grows weak; both earth and sky
decay. ⁵The people have defiled the earth by
breaking God's laws and by violating the
covenant he made to last forever. ⁶So God
has pronounced a curse on the earth. Its people are paying for what they have done.
Fewer and fewer remain alive. ⁷The
grapevines wither, and wine is becoming
scarce. Everyone who was once happy is now
sad, ⁸and the joyful music of their harps and
drums has ceased. ⁹There is no more happy
singing over wine; no one enjoys its taste any
more. ¹⁰In the city everything is in chaos, and
people lock themselves in their houses for
safety. ¹¹People shout in the streets because
there is no more wine. Happiness is gone
forever; it has been banished from the land.

ᵍ **23:10** *Verse 10 in Hebrew is unclear.*   ʰ **23:13** *Verse 13 in Hebrew is unclear.*
23:1–18 Ezek 26:1—28:19; Joel 3:4–8; Am 1:9, 10; Zech 9:1–4; Mt 11:21, 22; Lk 10:13, 14

Isaiah

**Find Tyre and Sidon on Map 3. Given the location of these cities, what do you
think would be the main ways the people of these places made their living?**

12 The city is in ruins, and its gates have been broken down. 13 This is what will happen in every nation all over the world. It will be like the end of harvest, when the olives have been beaten off every tree and the last grapes picked from the vines.

14 Those who survive will sing for joy. Those in the West will tell how great the LORD is, 15 and those in the East will praise him. The people who live along the sea will praise the LORD, the God of Israel. 16 From the most distant parts of the world we will hear songs in praise of Israel, the righteous nation.

But there is no hope for me! I am wasting away! Traitors continue to betray, and their treachery grows worse and worse. 17 Listen to me, everyone! There are terrors, pits, and traps waiting for you. 18 Anyone who tries to escape from the terror will fall in a pit, and anyone who escapes from the pit will be caught in a trap. Torrents of rain will pour from the sky, and earth's foundations will shake. 19 The earth will crack and shatter and split open. 20 The earth itself will stagger like a drunk, sway like a hut in a storm. The world is weighed down by its sins; it will collapse and never rise again.

21 A time is coming when the LORD will punish the powers above and the rulers of the earth. 22 God will crowd kings together like prisoners in a pit. He will shut them in prison until the time of their punishment comes. 23 The moon will grow dark, and the sun will no longer shine, for the LORD Almighty will be king. He will rule in Jerusalem on Mount Zion, and the leaders of the people will see his glory.

A Hymn of Praise

25 1 LORD, you are my God;
I will honor you and praise your name.
You have done amazing things;
you have faithfully carried out

Kings together like prisoners in a pit (24:22)

the plans you made long ago.
2 You have turned cities into ruins
and destroyed their fortifications.
The palaces which our enemies built
are gone forever.
3 The people of powerful nations will praise you;
you will be feared in the cities of cruel nations.
4 The poor and the helpless have fled to you
and have been safe in times of trouble.
You give them shelter from storms
and shade from the burning heat.
Cruel enemies attack like a winter storm,[i]
5 like drought in a dry land.
But you, LORD, have silenced our enemies;
you silence the shouts of cruel people,
as a cloud cools a hot day.

God Prepares a Banquet

6 Here on Mount Zion the LORD Almighty will prepare a banquet for all the nations of the world—a banquet of the richest food and the finest wine. 7 Here he will suddenly remove the cloud of sorrow that has been hanging over all the nations. 8 The Sovereign LORD will destroy death forever! He will wipe away the tears from everyone's

---

[i] **25:4** *Probable text* winter storm; *Hebrew* storm against a wall.
25:8 a 1 Cor 15:54; **b** Rev 7:17; 21:4

Isaiah

Habitat for Humanity

In 1976 Millard and Linda Fuller started the organization Habitat for Humanity. They had sold all of their possessions to work for poor people—as a response to Christ's message. Their idea was to provide affordable housing for those who could not afford to buy their own homes. They took Isaiah 25:4 seriously: "The poor and helpless have fled to you / . . . You give them shelter from storms / and shade from the burning heat."

In 1984 former U.S. President Jimmy Carter and his wife Rosalyn became personally involved. Their participation gave Habitat for Humanity the publicity it needed to become nationally known. Today, more than 150,000 houses have been built, giving more than 900,000 people a home of their own. Thousands of volunteers, from many different religions, have helped Habitat for Humanity build the homes.

Many churches work with Habitat for Humanity. Find out if your parish has a connection to Habitat for Humanity. Maybe you and your family could volunteer to work on a house. It will give you a very good feeling to know you are helping to shelter the homeless— something God is calling us to do.

— Isaiah 25:4

eyes and take away the disgrace his people have suffered throughout the world. The LORD himself has spoken.

⁹When it happens, everyone will say, "He is our God! We have put our trust in him,

and he has rescued us. He is the LORD! We have put our trust in him, and now we are happy and joyful because he has saved us."

God Will Punish Moab

¹⁰The LORD will protect Mount Zion, but the people of Moab will be trampled down the way straw is trampled in manure. ¹¹They will reach out their hands as if they were trying to swim, but God will humiliate them, and their hands will sink helplessly. ¹²He will destroy the fortresses of Moab with their high walls and bring them tumbling down into the dust.

God Will Give His People Victory

26 ¹A day is coming when the people will sing this song in the land of Judah:

Our city is strong!
God himself defends its walls!
²Open the city gates
and let the faithful nation enter,
the nation whose people do what is
right.
³You, LORD, give perfect peace
to those who keep their purpose firm
and put their trust in you.
⁴Trust in the LORD forever;
he will always protect us.
⁵He has humbled those who were proud;
he destroyed the strong city they lived in,
and sent its walls crashing into the dust.
⁶Those who were oppressed walk over it
now
and trample it under their feet.

⁷LORD, you make the path smooth for
good people;
the road they travel is level.
⁸We follow your will and put our hope in
you;
you are all that we desire.
⁹At night I long for you with all my heart;
when you judge the earth and its people,
they will all learn what justice is.
¹⁰Even though you are kind to the wicked,
they never learn to do what is right.

Isaiah

25:10–12 Isa 15:1—16:14; Jer 48:1–47; Ezek 25:8–11; Am 2:1–3; Zeph 2:8–11

Even here in a land of righteous people
they still do wrong;
they refuse to recognize your greatness.
11 Your enemies do not know that you will
punish them.

LORD, put them to shame and let them
suffer;
let them suffer the punishment you
have prepared.

Show them how much you love your
people.

12 You will give us prosperity, LORD;
everything that we achieve
is the result of what you do.[j]

13 LORD our God, we have been ruled by
others,
but you alone are our LORD.

14 Now they are dead and will not live again;
their ghosts will not rise,
for you have punished them and
destroyed them.

No one remembers them any more.

15 LORD, you have made our nation grow,
enlarging its territory on every side;
and this has brought you honor.

16 You punished your people, LORD,
and in anguish they prayed to you.[k]

17 You, LORD, have made us cry out,
as a woman in labor cries out in pain.

18 We were in pain and agony,
but we gave birth to nothing.

We have won no victory for our land;
we have accomplished nothing.[l]

19 Those of our people who have died will
live again!

Their bodies will come back to life.

All those sleeping in their graves
will wake up and sing for joy.

As the sparkling dew refreshes the earth,
so the LORD will revive those who
have long been dead.

Judgment and Restoration

20 Go into your houses, my people, and
shut the door behind you. Hide yourselves
for a little while until God's anger is over.

21 The LORD is coming from his heavenly
dwelling place to punish the people of the
earth for their sins. The murders that were
secretly committed on the earth will be
revealed, and the ground will no longer hide
those who have been killed.

27 1 On that day the LORD will use his
powerful and deadly sword to pun-
ish Leviathan, that wriggling, twisting dragon, and to kill the monster[m] that lives in the
sea.

2 On that day the LORD will say of his
pleasant vineyard, 3 "I watch over it and
water it continually. I guard it night and day
so that no one will harm it. 4 I am no longer
angry with the vineyard. If there were thorns
and briers to fight against, I would burn
them up completely. 5 But if the enemies of
my people want my protection, let them
make peace with me. Yes, let them make
peace with me."

6 In the days to come the people of Israel,
the descendants of Jacob, will take root like a
tree, and they will blossom and bud. The
earth will be covered with the fruit they
produce.

7 Israel has not been punished by the
LORD as severely as its enemies nor lost as
many people. 8 The LORD punished his people by sending them into exile. He took
them away with a cruel wind from the east.[n]
9 But Israel's sins will be forgiven only when
the stones of pagan altars are ground up like
chalk, and no more incense altars or symbols
of the goddess Asherah are left.

10 The fortified city lies in ruins. It is
deserted like an empty wilderness. It has
become a pasture for cattle, where they can
rest and graze. 11 The branches of the trees

The fortified city lies in ruins. (27:10)

---

j **26:12** *everything that . . . do; or you treat us according to what we do.*   k **26:16** *Verse 16 in Hebrew is unclear.*
l **26:18** *We have won . . . nothing; Hebrew unclear.*   m **27:1** LEVIATHAN . . . MONSTER: *Legendary monsters which
were symbols of the nations oppressing Israel.*   n **27:8** *Verse 8 in Hebrew is unclear.*
26:11 Heb 10:27   **27:1** Job 41:1; Ps 74:14; 104:26

On that Day

There was a lot of bad news in Isaiah's prophecies leading up to Isaiah, chapter 26. Jerusalem, Assyria, Babylon, Philistia, Moab, Syria, Ethiopia, Egypt, Edom, Arabia, Shebna, and Phoenicia all get news of their punishment. It seems like everyone gets bad news. However, throughout those chapters, and especially here in chapters 26–27, Isaiah also has good news. His good news is about a time to come when God's peace and justice will triumph.

Maybe you've been given really bad news sometime in your life. It could be that your parents are splitting up "on that day" or that you have to move to a new city "on that day," or maybe you have to have surgery "on that day." Regardless of the bad news, look for how God is working in a positive way. It could be that you'll meet great new friends in the city you move to, or that by having surgery you'll eventually get better. Sometimes bad news stays bad news, and it is hard to see the good. But most of the time, by looking at all of the angles, we can see that "on that day" God can bring good things out of hard experiences.

— Isaiah, chapter 27

are withered and broken, and women gather them for firewood. Because the people have understood nothing, God their Creator will not pity them or show them any mercy.

12 On that day, from the Euphrates to the Egyptian border, the LORD will gather his people one by one, as threshing separates the wheat from the chaff.

13 When that day comes, a trumpet will be blown to call back from Assyria and Egypt all the Israelites who are in exile there. They will come and worship the LORD in Jerusalem, on his sacred hill. *o*

A Warning to the Northern Kingdom

28 ¹The kingdom of Israel is doomed! Its glory is fading like the crowns of flowers on the heads of its drunken leaders. Their proud heads are well perfumed, but there they lie, dead drunk. ²The Lord has someone strong and powerful ready to attack them, someone who will come like a hailstorm, like a torrent of rain, like a rushing, overpowering flood, and will overwhelm the land. ³The pride of those drunken leaders will be trampled underfoot. ⁴The fading glory of those proud leaders will disappear like the first figs of the season, picked and eaten as soon as they are ripe.

⁵A day is coming when the LORD Almighty will be like a glorious crown of flowers for his people who survive. ⁶He will give a sense of justice to those who serve as judges, and courage to those who defend the city gates from attack.

Isaiah and the Drunken Prophets of Judah

⁷Even the prophets and the priests are so drunk that they stagger. They have drunk so much wine and liquor that they stumble in confusion. The prophets are too drunk to understand the visions that God sends, and the priests are too drunk to decide the cases that are brought to them. ⁸The tables where

o 27:13 SACRED HILL: See 2:3.

Isaiah

So drunk they stagger (28:7)

they sit are all covered with vomit, and not a clean spot is left.

9 They complain about me. They say, "Who does that man think he's teaching? Who needs his message? It's only good for babies that have just stopped nursing! 10 He is trying to teach us letter by letter, line by line, lesson by lesson."

11 If you won't listen to me, then God will use foreigners speaking some strange-sounding language to teach you a lesson. 12 He offered rest and comfort to all of you, but you refused to listen to him. 13 That is why the LORD is going to teach you letter by letter, line by line, lesson by lesson. Then you will stumble with every step you take. You will be wounded, trapped, and taken prisoner.

A Cornerstone for Zion

14 Now you arrogant leaders who rule here in Jerusalem over this people, listen to what the LORD is saying. 15 You boast that you have made a treaty with death and reached an agreement with the world of the dead. You are certain that disaster will spare you when it comes, because you depend on lies and deceit to keep you safe. 16 This, now, is what the Sovereign LORD says: "I am placing in Zion a foundation that is firm and strong. In it I am putting a solid cornerstone

on which are written the words, 'Faith that is firm is also patient.' 17 Justice will be the measuring line for the foundation, and honesty will be its plumb line."

Hailstorms will sweep away all the lies you depend on, and floods will destroy your security. 18 The treaty you have made with death will be abolished, and your agreement with the world of the dead will be canceled. When disaster sweeps down, you will be overcome. 19 It will strike you again and again, morning after morning. You will have to bear it day and night. Each new message from God will bring new terror! 20 You will be like the person in the proverb, who tries to sleep in a bed too short to stretch out on, with a blanket too narrow to wrap himself in. 21 The LORD will fight as he did at Mount Perazim and in the valley of Gibeon, in order to do what he intends to do— strange as his actions may seem. He will complete his work, his mysterious work.

A bed too short, . . . a blanket too narrow (28:20)

22 Don't laugh at the warning I am giving you! If you do, it will be even harder for you to escape. I have heard the LORD Almighty's decision to destroy the whole country.

God's Wisdom

23 Listen to what I am saying; pay attention to what I am telling you. 24 Farmers don't constantly plow their fields and keep getting them ready for planting. 25 Once they have prepared the soil, they plant the seeds of herbs such as dill and cumin. They plant

28:11, 12 1 Cor 14:21   28:15 Wis 1:16; Sir 14:12   28:16 Ps 118:22, 23; Rom 9:33; 10:11; 1 Pet 2:6
28:21 a 2 Sam 5:20; 1 Chr 14:11; b Josh 10:10–12

"All this wisdom comes from the LORD Almighty! The plans God makes are wise, and they always succeed" *(Isaiah 28:29).*

Isaiah

Keeping God Number 1

Isaiah wanted God's people to listen and to keep God Number 1. He tells them in Isaiah 28:22, "Don't laugh at the warning I am giving you!"

How do you keep God Number 1 in your life? Are there times when you get warnings to change your behavior and ignore them? Are there times when you know you're putting God second or even lower on your list? Most people have times like that. We need to be reminded to keep God Number 1 and look for ways we can do that.

Who do you know who does a good job of keeping God Number 1? Take some time to ask that person how he or she does it. Then spend some time in prayer looking for your own ways of keeping God Number 1. By asking others and praying about it, you can create a plan for keeping God first. Once you have a plan, stick to it. It takes practice and discipline to keep God Number 1.

— Isaiah 28:22–29

rows of wheat and barley,*p* and at the edges of their fields they plant other grain. ²⁶They know how to do their work, because God has taught them. ²⁷They never use a heavy club to beat out dill seeds or cumin seeds; instead they use light sticks of the proper size. ²⁸They do not ruin the wheat by threshing it endlessly, and they know how to thresh it by driving a cart over it without bruising the grains. ²⁹All this wisdom comes from the LORD Almighty. The plans God makes are wise, and they always succeed.

The Fate of Jerusalem

29 ¹God's altar, Jerusalem itself, is doomed! The city where David camped is doomed! Let another year or two come and go, with its feasts and festivals, ²and then God will bring disaster on the city that is called "God's altar." There will be weeping and wailing, and the whole city will be like an altar covered with blood. ³God will attack the city, surround it, and besiege it. ⁴Jerusalem will be like a ghost struggling to speak from under the ground, a muffled voice coming from the dust.

⁵Jerusalem, all the foreigners who attack you will be blown away like dust, and their terrifying armies will fly away like straw. Suddenly and unexpectedly ⁶the LORD Almighty will rescue you with violent thunderstorms and earthquakes. He will send windstorms and raging fire; ⁷then all the armies of the nations attacking the city of God's altar, all their weapons and equipment—everything—will vanish like a dream, like something imagined in the night. ⁸All the nations that assemble to attack Jerusalem will be like a starving person who dreams he is eating and wakes up hungry, or like someone dying of thirst who dreams he is drinking and wakes with a dry throat.

Disregarded Warnings

⁹Go ahead and be stupid! Go ahead and be blind! Get drunk without any wine! Stagger without drinking a drop! ¹⁰The LORD has made you drowsy, ready to fall into a deep sleep. The prophets should be the eyes of the people, but God has blindfolded them. ¹¹The meaning of every prophetic vision will be hidden from you; it will be like a sealed scroll. If you take it to someone who knows how to read and ask him to read it to you, he will say he can't because it is sealed. ¹²If you give it to someone who can't read and ask him to read it to you, he will answer that he doesn't know how.

¹³The Lord said, "These people claim to worship me, but their words are meaningless, and their hearts are somewhere else. Their

Isaiah

p **27:25** *Hebrew has an additional word, the meaning of which is unclear.*
29:10 Rom 11:8   **29:13** Mt 15:8, 9; Mk 7:6, 7

Just Putting Your Time In

Catholic Connections

Tina's eyes kept closing, and all she could think of was what she would do when she got out of church. She stood when everyone stood and mumbled the Lord's Prayer, but she wasn't really aware of what she did or said. Afterward her friends were talking about something Father Marco had said. All Tina wanted to do was get to the mall.

While they were shopping, her mom asked what the girls had been talking about after church. When Tina said she didn't know, her mom gave her a hard look. "Tina," she said, "do you listen to anything during church?"

"Mom, don't get on my case. I go. I pray. I stand. I sit. What more do you want?"

"Tina, it isn't about following the rules. It's about putting your heart and soul into it. The prophets made that clear in the Old Testament."

"So, I don't have to sit and stand when you do?"

"Of course it's good to do the gestures, but it's more important to really be part of it. Could you at least try that next week? Maybe what the girls heard was important, and maybe if you really try you'll find something important, too."

"Okay, I'll try," Tina said, "And about these jeans . . ." Tina gave her mom a wink, her signal that she got it.

— Isaiah 29:13–14

religion is nothing but human rules and traditions, which they have simply memorized. ¹⁴So I will startle them with one unexpected blow after another. Those who are wise will turn out to be fools, and all their cleverness will be useless."

Hope for the Future

¹⁵Those who try to hide their plans from the LORD are doomed! They carry out their schemes in secret and think no one will see them or know what they are doing. ¹⁶They turn everything upside down. Which is more important, the potter or the clay? Can something you have made say, "You didn't make me"? Or can it say, "You don't know what you are doing"?

¹⁷As the saying goes, before long the dense forest will become farmland, and the farmland will go back to forest.

¹⁸When that day comes, the deaf will be able to hear a book being read aloud, and the blind, who have been living in darkness, will open their eyes and see. ¹⁹Poor and humble people will once again find the happiness which the LORD, the holy God of Israel, gives. ²⁰It will be the end of those who oppress others and show contempt for God. Every sinner will be destroyed. ²¹God will destroy those who slander others, those who prevent the punishment of criminals, and those who tell lies to keep honest people from getting justice.

²²So now the LORD, the God of Israel, who rescued Abraham from trouble, says, "My people, you will not be disgraced any longer, and your faces will no longer be pale with shame. ²³When you see the children that I will give you, then you will acknowledge that I am the holy God of Israel. You will honor me and stand in awe of me.

Isaiah

29:14 1 Cor 1:19   29:16 Isa 45:9; Sir 33:13; Rom 9:20

24Foolish people will learn to understand, and those who are always grumbling will be glad to be taught."

A Useless Treaty with Egypt

30 1The LORD has spoken: "Those who rule Judah are doomed because they rebel against me. They follow plans that I did not make, and sign treaties against my will, piling one sin on another. 2They go to Egypt for help without asking for my advice. They want Egypt to protect them, so they put their trust in Egypt's king. 3But the king will be powerless to help them, and Egypt's protection will end in disaster. 4Although their ambassadors have already arrived at the Egyptian cities of Zoan and Hanes, 5the people of Judah will regret that they ever trusted that unreliable nation, a nation that fails them when they expect help."

6This is God's message about the animals of the southern desert: "The ambassadors travel through dangerous country, where lions live and where there are poisonous snakes and flying dragons. They load their donkeys and camels with expensive gifts for a nation that cannot give them any help. 7The help that Egypt gives is useless. So I have nicknamed Egypt, 'The Harmless Dragon.' "

The Disobedient People

8God told me to write down in a book what the people are like, so that there would be a permanent record of how evil they are. 9They are always rebelling against God, always lying, always refusing to listen to the LORD's teachings. 10They tell the prophets to keep quiet. They say, "Don't talk to us about what's right. Tell us what we want to hear. Let us keep our illusions. 11Get out of our way and stop blocking our path. We don't want to hear about your holy God of Israel."

12But this is what the holy God of Israel says: "You ignore what I tell you and rely on violence and deceit. 13You are guilty. You are like a high wall with a crack running down

it; suddenly you will collapse. 14You will be shattered like a clay pot, so badly broken that there is no piece big enough to pick up hot coals with or to dip water from a cistern."

15The Sovereign LORD, the Holy One of Israel, says to the people, "Come back and quietly trust in me. Then you will be strong and secure." But you refuse to do it. 16Instead, you plan to escape from your enemies by riding fast horses. And you are right—escape is what you will have to do! You think your horses are fast enough, but those who pursue you will be faster! 17A thousand of you will run away when you see one enemy soldier, and five soldiers will be enough to make you all run away. Nothing will be left of your army except a lonely flagpole on the top of a hill. 18And yet the LORD is waiting to be merciful to you. He is ready to take pity on you because he always does what is right. Happy are those who put their trust in the LORD.

God Will Bless His People

19You people who live in Jerusalem will not weep any more. The LORD is compassionate, and when you cry to him for help, he will answer you. 20The Lord will make you go through hard times, but he himself will be there to teach you, and you will not have to search for him any more. 21If you wander off the road to the right or the left, you will hear his voice behind you saying, "Here is the road. Follow it." 22You will take your idols plated with silver and your idols covered with gold, and will throw them away like filth, shouting, "Out of my sight!" 23Whenever you plant your crops, the Lord will send rain to make them grow and will give you a rich harvest, and your livestock will have plenty of pasture. 24The oxen and donkeys that plow your fields will eat the finest and best fodder. 25On the day when the forts of your enemies are captured and their people are killed, streams of water will flow from every mountain and every hill. 26The moon will be as bright as the sun, and

Isaiah

Isaiah describes what the people are like in Isaiah 30:8–11. Does that description sound like anyone you know?

Pray It!

Just When

The next time your life seems really bad and you think you can't take it anymore, try this prayer.

> Just when I think I can't take it anymore,
> there you are,
> the God who blesses me.
> Just when I have heard so much bad news,
> there you are,
> the God who brings good news.
> Just when I thought I was all wrong,
> there you are,
> the God who makes me want to do what is right.
> Just when I realize that I did wrong,
> there you are,
> the God who forgives.
> Just when I think I can't take it anymore,
> there you are,
> my wonderful God who never leaves me.
> Amen.

— Isaiah 30:19–26

The finest and best fodder (30:24)

the sun will be seven times brighter than usual, like the light of seven days in one. This will all happen when the LORD bandages and heals the wounds he has given his people.

God Will Punish Assyria

27 The LORD's power and glory can be seen in the distance. Fire and smoke show his anger. He speaks, and his words burn like fire. 28 He sends the wind in front of him like a flood that carries everything away. It sweeps nations to destruction and puts an end to their evil plans. 29 But you, God's people, will be happy and sing as you do on the night of a sacred festival. You will be as happy as those who walk to the music of flutes on their way to the Temple of the LORD, the defender of Israel.

30 The LORD will let everyone hear his majestic voice and feel the force of his anger. There will be flames, cloudbursts, hailstones, and torrents of rain. 31 The Assyrians will be terrified when they hear the LORD's voice and feel the force of his punishment. 32 As

"Just as a bird hovers over its nest to protect its young, so I, the LORD Almighty, will protect Jerusalem and defend it" (Isaiah 31:5).

the LORD strikes them again and again, his people will keep time with the music of drums and harps. God himself will fight against the Assyrians. ³³Long ago a place was prepared where a huge fire will burn the emperor of Assyria. It is deep and wide, and piled high with wood. The LORD will breathe out a stream of flame to set it on fire.

God Will Protect Jerusalem

31 ¹Those who go to Egypt for help are doomed! They are relying on Egypt's vast military strength—horses, chariots, and soldiers. But they do not rely on the LORD, the holy God of Israel, or ask him for help. ²He knows what he is doing! He sends disaster. He carries out his threats to punish evil people and those who protect them. ³The Egyptians are not gods—they are only human. Their horses are not supernatural. When the LORD acts, the strong nation will crumble, and the weak nation it helped will fall. Both of them will be destroyed.

⁴The LORD said to me, "No matter how shepherds yell and shout, they can't scare away a lion from an animal that it has killed; in the same way, there is nothing that can keep me, the LORD Almighty, from protecting Mount Zion. ⁵Just as a bird hovers over its nest to protect its young, so I, the LORD Almighty, will protect Jerusalem and defend it."

As a bird hovers over its nest (31:5)

⁶God said, "People of Israel, you have sinned against me and opposed me. But now, come back to me! ⁷A time is coming when all of you will throw away the sinful idols you made out of silver and gold. ⁸Assyria will be destroyed in war, but not by human power. The Assyrians will run from battle, and their young men will be made slaves. ⁹Their emperor will run away in terror, and the officers will be so frightened that they will abandon their battle flags." The LORD has spoken—the LORD who is worshiped in Jerusalem and whose fire burns there for sacrifices.

A King with Integrity

32 ¹Some day there will be a king who rules with integrity, and national leaders who govern with justice. ²Each of them will be like a shelter from the wind and a place to hide from storms. They will be like streams flowing in a desert, like the shadow of a giant rock in a barren land. ³Their eyes and ears will be open to the needs of the people. ⁴They will not be impatient any longer, but they will act with understanding and will say what they mean. ⁵No one will think that a fool is honorable or say that a scoundrel is honest. ⁶A fool speaks foolishly and thinks up evil things to do. What he does and what he says are an insult to the LORD, and he never feeds the hungry or gives thirsty people anything to drink. ⁷A stupid person is evil and does evil things; he plots to ruin the poor with lies and to keep them from getting their rights. ⁸But an honorable person acts honestly and stands firm for what is right.

Judgment and Restoration

⁹You women who live an easy life, free from worries, listen to what I am saying. ¹⁰You may be satisfied now, but this time next year you will be in despair because there will be no grapes for you to gather. ¹¹You have been living an easy life, free from worries; but now, tremble with fear! Strip off your clothes and tie rags around your waist. ¹²Beat your breasts in grief because the fertile fields and the vineyards have been

The Right Thing

"You can survive if you say and do what is right" (Isaiah 33:15).

"If I become student council president, I will make sure we get extra recess time every day. I will make sure the cafeteria serves McDonald's and pizza. So vote for me!" Eric's opponent ended her speech with that promise.

Eric stepped up to the microphone in the gym. He looked around and then down at his speech. His ideas didn't include extra recess and McDonald's. They did include ideas for making his school safe and ways of helping his classmates to be better students. It seemed unlikely that those ideas would get him elected student body president. But he knew his ideas were realistic and that his classmates felt afraid since the recent violence in a school near theirs. So Eric started his speech. It didn't sound as flashy as his opponent's speech, but what he said must have made sense. There was a lot of applause when he finished.

The next day the principal got on the loudspeaker and announced the winners. Eric was sure everyone had voted for the girl running against him, but it was his name being said over the school PA system, not hers. His classmates were interested in being safe and in succeeding, not just in longer breaks and lunchtimes. A lot of the kids congratulated him in the hallway. Even the popular kids said something to him. Eric realized then that saying and doing what is right is always the best plan.

— Isaiah 33:15

destroyed, 13and thorn bushes and briers are growing on my people's land. Weep for all the houses where people were happy and for the city that was full of life. 14Even the palace will be abandoned and the capital city totally deserted. Homes and the forts that guarded them will be in ruins forever. Wild donkeys will roam there, and sheep will find pasture there.

15But once more God will send us his spirit. The wasteland will become fertile, and fields will produce rich crops. 16Everywhere in the land righteousness and justice will be done. 17Because everyone will do what is right, there will be peace and security forever. 18God's people will be free from worries, and their homes peaceful and safe. (19But hail will fall on the forests, and the city will be torn down.) 20How happy everyone will be with plenty of water for the crops and safe pasture everywhere for the donkeys and cattle.

A Prayer for Help

33 1Our enemies are doomed! They have robbed and betrayed, although no one has robbed them or betrayed them. But their time to rob and betray will end, and they themselves will become victims of robbery and treachery.

2LORD, have mercy on us. We have put our hope in you. Protect us day by day and save us in times of trouble. 3When you fight for us, nations run away from the noise of battle. 4Their belongings are pounced upon and taken as loot.

5How great the LORD is! He rules over everything. He will fill Jerusalem with justice and integrity 6and give stability to the nation. He always protects his people and gives them wisdom and knowledge. Their greatest treasure is their reverence for the LORD.

7The brave are calling for help. The ambassadors who tried to bring about peace are crying bitterly. 8The highways are so dangerous that no one travels on them. Treaties are broken and agreements are violated. No one is respected any more. 9The land lies idle and deserted. The forests of Lebanon have withered, the fertile valley of

Sharon is like a desert, and in Bashan and on Mount Carmel the leaves are falling from the trees.

The LORD Warns His Enemies

¹⁰The LORD says to the nations, "Now I will act. I will show how powerful I am. ¹¹You make worthless plans and everything you do is useless. My spirit is like a fire that will destroy you.⁹ ¹²You will crumble like rocks burned to make lime, like thorns burned to ashes. ¹³Let everyone near and far hear what I have done and acknowledge my power."

¹⁴The sinful people of Zion are trembling with fright. They say, "God's judgment is like a fire that burns forever. Can any of us survive a fire like that?" ¹⁵You can survive if you say and do what is right. Don't use your power to cheat the poor and don't accept bribes. Don't join with those who plan to commit murder or to do other evil things. ¹⁶Then you will be safe; you will be as secure as if in a strong fortress. You will have food to eat and water to drink.

The Glorious Future

¹⁷Once again you will see a king ruling in splendor over a land that stretches in all directions. ¹⁸Your old fears of foreign tax collectors and spies will be only a memory. ¹⁹You will no longer see any arrogant foreigners who speak a language that you can't understand. ²⁰Look at Zion, the city where we celebrate our religious festivals. Look at Jerusalem! What a safe place it will be to live in! It will be like a tent that is never moved, whose pegs are never pulled up and whose ropes never break. ²¹The LORD will show us his glory. We will live beside broad rivers and streams, but hostile ships will not sail on them.ʳ ²²⁻²³All the rigging on those ships is

useless; the sails cannot be spread! We will seize all the wealth of enemy armies, and there will be so much that even the lame can get a share. The LORD himself will be our king; he will rule over us and protect us. ²⁴No one who lives in our land will ever again complain of being sick, and all sins will be forgiven.

God Will Punish His Enemies

34 ¹Come, people of all nations! Gather around and listen. Let the whole earth and everyone living on it come here and listen. ²The LORD is angry with all the nations and all their armies. He has condemned them to destruction. ³Their corpses will not be buried, but will lie there rotting and stinking; and the mountains will be red with blood. ⁴The sun, moon, and stars will crumble to dust. The sky will disappear like a scroll being rolled up, and the stars will fall like leaves dropping from a vine or a fig tree.

⁵The LORD has prepared his sword in heaven, and now it will strike Edom, those people whom he has condemned to destruction. ⁶His sword will be covered with their blood and fat, like the blood and fat of lambs and goats that are sacrificed. The LORD will offer this sacrifice in the city of Bozrah; he will make this a great slaughter in the land of Edom. ⁷The people will fall like wild oxen and young bulls, and the earth will be red with blood and covered with fat. ⁸This is the time when the LORD will rescue Zion and take vengeance on her enemies.

⁹The rivers of Edom will turn into tar, and the soil will turn into sulfur. The whole country will burn like tar. ¹⁰It will burn day and night, and smoke will rise from it forever. The land will lie waste age after age, and no one will ever travel through it again. ¹¹Owls and ravens will take over the land. The LORD will make it a barren waste again,

ᵟ **33:11** *One ancient translation* My spirit . . . you; *Hebrew* You are destroying yourselves.　ʳ **33:21** *Verse 21 in Hebrew is unclear.*
34:4 Mt 24:29; Mk 13:25; Lk 21:26; Rev 6:13, 14　**34:5–17** Isa 63:1–6; Jer 49:7–22; Ezek 25:12–14; 35:1–15; Am 1:11, 12; Ob 1–14; Mal 1:2–5　**34:10** Rev 14:11; 19:3

Isaiah

Isaiah describes a glorious future for the Israelites at the end of Isaiah, chapter 33. How would you describe your glorious future?

Owls and ravens will take over the land. (34:11)

as it was before the creation. ¹²There will be no king to rule the country, and the leaders will all be gone.ˢ ¹³Thorns and thistles will grow up in all the palaces and walled towns, and jackals and owls will live in them. ¹⁴Wild animals will roam there, and demons will call to each other. The night monsterᵗ will come there looking for a place to rest. ¹⁵Owls will build their nests, lay eggs, hatch their young, and care for them there. Vultures will gather there, one after another.

¹⁶Search in the LORD's book of living creatures and read what it says. Not one of these creatures will be missing, and not one will be without its mate. The LORD has commanded it to be so; he himself will bring them together. ¹⁷It is the LORD who will divide the land among them and give each of them a share. They will live in the land age after age, and it will belong to them forever.

The Road of Holiness

35 ¹The desert will rejoice,
and flowers will bloom in the wastelands.
²The desert will sing and shout for joy;
it will be as beautiful as the Lebanon Mountains
and as fertile as the fields of Carmel and Sharon.
Everyone will see the LORD's splendor,
see his greatness and power.

³Give strength to hands that are tired
and to knees that tremble with weakness.
⁴Tell everyone who is discouraged,
"Be strong and don't be afraid!
God is coming to your rescue,
coming to punish your enemies."

⁵The blind will be able to see,
and the deaf will hear.
⁶The lame will leap and dance,
and those who cannot speak will shout for joy.
Streams of water will flow through the desert;
⁷ the burning sand will become a lake,
and dry land will be filled with springs.
Where jackals used to live,
marsh grass and reeds will grow.

⁸There will be a highway there,
called "The Road of Holiness."
No sinner will ever travel that road;
no fools will mislead those who follow it.ᵘ
⁹No lions will be there;
no fierce animals will pass that way.
Those whom the LORD has rescued
will travel home by that road.
¹⁰They will reach Jerusalem with gladness,
singing and shouting for joy.
They will be happy forever,
forever free from sorrow and grief.

The Assyrians Threaten Jerusalem
(2 Kings 18:13–27; 2 Chronicles 32:1–19)

36 ¹In the fourteenth year that Hezekiah was king of Judah, Sennacherib, the emperor of Assyria, attacked the fortified cities of Judah and captured them. ²Then he ordered his chief official to go from Lachish to Jerusalem with a large military force to demand that King Hezekiah surrender. The official occupied the road where the cloth makers work, by the ditch that brings water

ˢ **34:12** *Verse 12 in Hebrew begins with a word, the meaning of which is unclear.*   ᵗ **34:14** NIGHT MONSTER: *A female demon, believed to live in desolate places.*   ᵘ **35:8** *Probable text no fools . . . follow it; Hebrew unclear.*
35:3 Heb 12:12   **35:5, 6** Mt 11:5; Lk 7:22

The night monster mentioned in Isaiah 34:14 is called Lilith, a female demon, in other Bible translations.

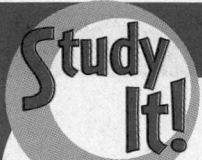

Holiness and Healthiness

Isaiah, chapter 35, talks about the Road of Holiness. This is the path that people follow to get to God. It is a marvelous place, where the blind see, and the lame will leap and dance. Did you ever stop and think, though, that the road to holiness is also the road to healthiness?

Some people may think that being a good follower of Christ is just about praying, going to Mass, and avoiding big sins. But God wants more for us. God is interested in all aspects of our life: our bodies, our souls, our hearts, and our minds. This is why the Church teaches that part of the meaning of the fifth commandment, "You shall not kill," is about taking care of our physical health. If we abuse food, alcohol, tobacco, or drugs, we are causing harm to our bodies. We are, in a sense, killing them. This also includes getting enough sleep and eating healthy foods. Equally important is taking care of our mental health. When we have psychological problems and ignore them, we are also not fully obeying the fifth commandment.

God really does want you to be holy and physically healthy. That is the way we are made to be—wonderfully created by our loving God.

— Isaiah, chapter 35

the records, Joah son of Asaph. ⁴The Assyrian official told them that the emperor wanted to know what made King Hezekiah so confident. ⁵He demanded, "Do you think that words can take the place of military skill and might? Who do you think will help you rebel against Assyria? ⁶You are expecting Egypt to help you, but that would be like using a reed as a walking stick—it would break and would jab your hand. That is what the king of Egypt is like when anyone relies on him."

⁷The Assyrian official went on, "Or will you tell me that you are relying on the LORD your God? It was the LORD's shrines and altars that Hezekiah destroyed when he told the people of Judah and Jerusalem to worship at one altar only. ⁸I will make a bargain with you in the name of the emperor. I will give you two thousand horses if you can find that many riders. ⁹You are no match for even the lowest ranking Assyrian official, and yet you expect the Egyptians to send you chariots and horsemen. ¹⁰Do you think I have attacked your country and destroyed it without the LORD's help? The LORD himself told me to attack it and destroy it."

¹¹Then Eliakim, Shebna, and Joah told the official, "Speak Aramaic to us. We understand it. Don't speak Hebrew; all the people on the wall are listening."

¹²He replied, "Do you think you and the king are the only ones the emperor sent me to say all these things to? No, I am also talking to the people who are sitting on the wall, who will have to eat their excrement and drink their urine, just as you will."

¹³Then the official stood up and shouted in Hebrew, "Listen to what the emperor of Assyria is telling you. ¹⁴He warns you not to let Hezekiah deceive you. Hezekiah can't save you. ¹⁵And don't let him persuade you to rely on the LORD. Don't think that the LORD will save you and that he will stop our Assyrian army from capturing your city. ¹⁶Don't listen to Hezekiah! The emperor of Assyria commands you to come out of the city and surrender. You will all be allowed to eat grapes from your own vines and figs from your own trees, and to drink water

Isaiah

from the upper pool. ³Three Judeans came out to meet him: the official in charge of the palace, Eliakim son of Hilkiah; the court secretary, Shebna; and the official in charge of from your own wells— 17until the emperor resettles you in a country much like your own, where there are vineyards to give wine and there is grain for making bread. 18Don't let Hezekiah fool you into thinking that the LORD will rescue you. Did the gods of any other nations save their countries from the emperor of Assyria? 19Where are they now, the gods of Hamath and Arpad? Where are the gods of Sepharvaim? Did anyone save Samaria? 20When did any of the gods of all these countries ever save their country from our emperor? Then what makes you think the LORD can save Jerusalem?"

21The people kept quiet, just as King Hezekiah had told them to; they did not say a word. 22Then Eliakim, Shebna, and Joah tore their clothes in grief and went and reported to the king what the Assyrian official had said.

The people kept quiet. (36:21)

The King Asks Isaiah's Advice
(2 Kings 19:1–7)

37 1As soon as King Hezekiah heard their report, he tore his clothes in grief, put on sackcloth, and went to the Temple of the LORD. 2He sent Eliakim, the official in charge of the palace, Shebna, the court secretary, and the senior priests to the prophet Isaiah son of AmoMz. They also were wearing sackcloth. 3This is the message which he told them to give to Isaiah: "Today is a day of suffering; we are being punished and are in disgrace. We are like a woman who is ready to give birth, but is too weak to do it. 4The Assyrian emperor has sent his chief official to insult the living God. May the LORD your God hear these insults and punish those who spoke them. So pray to God for those of our people who survive."

Good King Hezekiah

Chapters 36–39 end the first section of the Book of Isaiah. These chapters tell of King Hezekiah of Judah. These chapters are very similar to the story of Hezekiah in 2 Kings or 2 Chronicles. You will see cross-references to those books under the headings.

Hezekiah was ruling at a difficult time. The Assyrians had just taken over the kingdom of Israel, to the north. Now they were coming for the kingdom of Judah.

Hezekiah could have tried fighting the Assyrians on his own, or he could have surrendered. Instead, he prayed to God and asked Isaiah for help. Isaiah told King Hezekiah to stand firm and have faith and God would take care of things. Sure enough, the Assyrian army left, and the Assyrian emperor was later assassinated by his own sons.

— Isaiah, chapter 36

5When Isaiah received King Hezekiah's message, 6he sent back this answer: "The LORD tells you not to let the Assyrians frighten you by their claims that he cannot save you. 7The LORD will cause the emperor to hear a rumor that will make him go back to his own country, and the LORD will have him killed there."

The Assyrians Send Another Threat
(2 Kings 19:8–19)

8The Assyrian official learned that the emperor had left Lachish and was fighting against the nearby city of Libnah; so he went there to consult him. 9Word reached the Assyrians that the Egyptian army, led by

King Tirhakah of Ethiopia,[v] was coming to attack them. When the emperor heard this, he sent a letter to King Hezekiah [10]of Judah to tell him: "The god you are trusting in has told you that you will not fall into my hands, but don't let that deceive you. [11]You have heard what an Assyrian emperor does to any country he decides to destroy. Do you think that you can escape? [12]My ancestors destroyed the cities of Gozan, Haran, and Rezeph, and killed the people of Betheden who lived in Telassar, and none of their gods could save them. [13]Where are the kings of the cities of Hamath, Arpad, Sepharvaim, Hena, and Ivvah?"

[14]King Hezekiah took the letter from the messengers and read it. Then he went to the Temple, placed the letter there in the presence of the LORD, [15]and prayed, [16]"Almighty LORD, God of Israel, seated above the winged creatures, you alone are God, ruling all the kingdoms of the world. You created the earth and the sky. [17]Now, LORD, hear us and look at what is happening to us. Listen to all the things that Sennacherib is saying to insult you, the living God. [18]We all know, LORD, that the emperors of Assyria have destroyed many nations, made their lands desolate, [19]and burned up their gods—which were no gods at all, only images of wood and stone made by human hands. [20]Now, LORD our God, rescue us from the Assyrians, so that all the nations of the world will know that you alone are God."

Isaiah's Message to the King
(2 Kings 19:20–37)

[21]Then Isaiah sent a message telling King Hezekiah that in answer to the king's prayer [22]the LORD had said, "The city of Jerusalem laughs at you, Sennacherib, and makes fun of you. [23]Whom do you think you have been insulting and ridiculing? You have been disrespectful to me, the holy God of Israel. [24]You sent your servants to boast to me that with all your chariots you had conquered the highest mountains of Lebanon. You boasted that there you cut down the tallest cedars and the finest cypress trees, and that you reached the deepest parts of the forests. [25]You boasted that you dug wells and drank water in foreign lands, and that the feet of your soldiers tramped the Nile River dry.

[26]"Have you never heard that I planned all this long ago? And now I have carried it out. I gave you the power to turn fortified cities into piles of rubble. [27]The people who lived there were powerless; they were frightened and stunned. They were like grass in a field or weeds growing on a roof when the hot east wind blasts them.[w]

[28]"But I know everything about you, what you do and where you go. I know how you rage against me. [29]I have received the report of that rage and that pride of yours, and now I will put a hook through your nose and a bit in your mouth and will take you back by the same road you came."

[30]Then Isaiah said to King Hezekiah, "Here is a sign of what will happen. This year and next you will have only wild grain to eat, but the following year you will be able to plant grain and harvest it, and plant vines and eat grapes. [31]Those in Judah who survive will flourish like plants that send roots deep into the ground and produce fruit. [32]There will be people in Jerusalem and on Mount Zion who will survive, because the LORD Almighty is determined to make this happen.

[33]"And this is what the LORD has said about the Assyrian emperor: 'He will not enter this city or shoot a single arrow against it. No soldiers with shields will come near the city, and no siege mounds will be built around it. [34]He will go back by the same road he came, without entering this city. I,

---

[v] **37:9** *Hebrew Cush: Cush is the ancient name of the extensive territory south of the First Cataract of the Nile River. This region was called Ethiopia in Graeco-Roman times, and included within its borders most of modern Sudan and some of present-day Ethiopia (Abyssinia).* [w] **37:27** *Probable text when the hot east wind blasts them; Hebrew blasted before they are grown.*
37:16 Ex 25:22

Isaiah

How did Isaiah know what to say in reply to King Hezekiah's question *(Isaiah 37:6–7)?*

the LORD, have spoken. 35I will defend this city and protect it, for the sake of my own honor and because of the promise I made to my servant David.' "

36An angel of the LORD went to the Assyrian camp and killed 185,000 soldiers. At dawn the next day there they lay, all dead! 37Then the Assyrian emperor Sennacherib withdrew and returned to Nineveh. 38One day when he was worshiping in the temple of his god Nisroch, two of his sons, Adrammelech and Sharezer, killed him with their swords and then escaped to the land of Ararat. Another of his sons, Esarhaddon, succeeded him as emperor.

An angel of the LORD went to the Assyrian camp.
(37:36)

King Hezekiah's Illness and Recovery
(2 Kings 20:1–11; 2 Chronicles 32:24–26)

38 1About this time King Hezekiah became sick and almost died. The prophet Isaiah son of Amoz went to see him and said to him, "The LORD tells you that you are to put everything in order because you will not recover. Get ready to die."

2Hezekiah turned his face to the wall and prayed: 3"Remember, LORD, that I have served you faithfully and loyally, and that I have always tried to do what you wanted me to." And he began to cry bitterly.

4Then the LORD commanded Isaiah 5to go back to Hezekiah and say to him, "I, the LORD, the God of your ancestor David, have heard your prayer and seen your tears; I will

let you live fifteen years longer. 6I will rescue you and this city of Jerusalem from the emperor of Assyria, and I will continue to protect the city."

21Isaiah told the king to put a paste made of figs on his boil, and he would get well. 22Then King Hezekiah asked, "What is the sign to prove that I will be able to go to the Temple?"*x*

7Isaiah replied, "The LORD will give you a sign to prove that he will keep his promise. 8On the stairway built by King Ahaz, the LORD will make the shadow go back ten steps." And the shadow moved back ten steps.*y*

9After Hezekiah recovered from his illness, he wrote this song of praise:

10I thought that in the prime of life
   I was going to the world of the dead,
   Never to live out my life.
11I thought that in this world of the living
   I would never again see the LORD
   Or any living person.
12My life was cut off and ended,
   Like a tent that is taken down,
   Like cloth that is cut from a loom.
   I thought that God was ending my life.*z*
13All night I cried out with pain,
   As if a lion were breaking my bones.
   I thought that God was ending my life.*a*
14My voice was thin and weak,
   And I moaned like a dove.
   My eyes grew tired from looking to
      heaven.
   LORD, rescue me from all this trouble.
15What can I say? The LORD has done this.
   My heart is bitter, and I cannot sleep.*b*

16Lord, I will live for you, for you alone;
   Heal me and let me live.*c*
17My bitterness will turn into peace.
   You save*d* my life from all danger;
   You forgive all my sins.

---

x **38:22** *Verses 21–22 are moved here from the end of the chapter (see 2 Kings 20:6–9).*   *y* **38:8** *stairway . . . ten steps . . . steps; or sundial . . . ten degrees . . . degrees (see 2 Kings 20:9–11).*   *z* **38:12** *I thought . . . my life; Hebrew unclear.*   *a* **38:13** *Verse 13 in Hebrew is unclear.*   *b* **38:15** *One ancient translation suggests* I cannot sleep; *Hebrew unclear.*   *c* **38:16** *Verses 15 and 16 in Hebrew are unclear.*   *d* **38:17** *Some ancient translations* save; *Hebrew* love.
38:18 *Sir 17:27; Bar 2:17*

Second Chance

Imagine being really sick and thinking you are going to die. You would probably pray and ask God for help. Imagine then that someone gives you a cure and you get to live. That is what happened to King Hezekiah. He was near death and was even told he would die; then Isaiah told him that he would live. The prayer in chapter 38 is what King Hezekiah wrote after he recovered. Do you think King Hezekiah lived differently after his life was spared?

If you were near death and then you were given a second chance at life, what would you do with it? Would you live your life any differently? Don't wait until you are in King Hezekiah's place. If you need to make changes in your life, make them now. Write a list of how you want to be, what you want to do. As you create your list, keep in mind all you have read here in Isaiah and throughout the Bible.

— Isaiah, chapter 38

Messengers from Babylonia
(2 Kings 20:12–19)

39 ¹About that same time the king of Babylonia, Merodach Baladan, son of Baladan, heard that King Hezekiah had been sick, so he sent him a letter and a present. ²Hezekiah welcomed the messengers and showed them his wealth—his silver and gold, his spices and perfumes, and all his military equipment. There was nothing in his storerooms or anywhere in his kingdom that he did not show them. ³Then the prophet Isaiah went to King Hezekiah and asked, "Where did these messengers come from and what did they say to you?"

Hezekiah answered, "They came from a very distant country, from Babylonia."

⁴"What did they see in the palace?"

"They saw everything. There is nothing in the storerooms that I didn't show them."

⁵Isaiah then told the king, "The LORD Almighty says that ⁶a time is coming when everything in your palace, everything that your ancestors have stored up to this day, will be carried off to Babylonia. Nothing will be left. ⁷Some of your own direct descendants will be taken away and made eunuchs to serve in the palace of the king of Babylonia."

⁸King Hezekiah understood this to mean that there would be peace and security during his lifetime, so he replied, "The message you have given me from the LORD is good."

Words of Hope

40 ¹"Comfort my people," says our God. "Comfort them!
²Encourage the people of Jerusalem.
Tell them they have suffered long enough and their sins are now forgiven.ᶠ
I have punished them in full for all their sins."

³A voice cries out,
"Prepare in the wilderness a road for the LORD!
Clear the way in the desert for our God!

¹⁸No one in the world of the dead can praise you;
The dead cannot trust in your faithfulness.
¹⁹It is the living who praise you,
As I praise you now.
Parents tell their children how faithful you are.
²⁰LORD, you have healed me.
We will play harps and sing your praise,
Sing praise in your Temple as long as we live.ᵉ

ᵉ **38:20** *Verses 21–22 are placed after verse 6.* ᶠ **40:2** and their sins are now forgiven; *or* they have paid for what they did.
39:7 Dan 1:1–7; 2 Kings 24:10–16; 2 Chr 36:10 **40:3** Sir 48:10; Bar 5:7; Mt 3:3; Mk 1:3; Jn 1:23
40:3–5 Lk 3:4–6

Isaiah

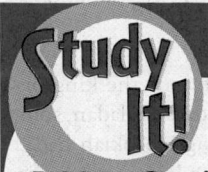

A New Section

Chapters 40–66 of Isaiah take a very different turn from the previous chapters. These chapters are sometimes called the Book of Consolation. Consolation means to comfort someone. It is thought that these chapters were written by a follower of the original Isaiah a hundred years or more after the events of chapter 39. They refer to the captivity in Babylon, which was from 587 to 538 B.C. This was the time when the Babylonians had taken over Judah, the southern kingdom, and destroyed Jerusalem and the Temple.

You will notice that these chapters focus on hope and comfort. After the Babylonians destroyed the Temple, many of the people lost all hope. They thought God had abandoned them. The prophet behind these chapters tells the people that God is still with them, and will restore them to their homes once more.

— Isaiah, chapter 40

Isaiah

4 Fill every valley;
  level every mountain.
The hills will become a plain,
  and the rough country will be made
    smooth.
5 Then the glory of the LORD will be
    revealed,
  and all people will see it.
The LORD himself has promised this."

6 A voice cries out, "Proclaim a message!"
"What message shall I proclaim?" I ask.
"Proclaim that all human beings are like
    grass;
  they last no longer than wild flowers.
7 Grass withers and flowers fade
  when the LORD sends the wind
    blowing over them.
  People are no more enduring than
    grass.
8 Yes, grass withers and flowers fade,
  but the word of our God endures
    forever."

9 Jerusalem, go up on a high mountain
  and proclaim the good news!
Call out with a loud voice, Zion;
  announce the good news!g
Speak out and do not be afraid.
Tell the towns of Judah
  that their God is coming!

"Their God is coming!" (40:9)

10 The Sovereign LORD is coming to rule
    with power,
  bringing with him the people he has
    rescued.h
11 He will take care of his flock like a
    shepherd;
  he will gather the lambs together
  and carry them in his arms;
  he will gently lead their mothers.

g 40:9 Jerusalem, go up . . . news!; or Go up on a high mountain and proclaim the good news to Jerusalem! Call out with a loud voice and announce the good news to Zion! h 40:10 the people he has rescued; or the rewards he has for his people.
40:6–8 Jas 1:10, 11; 1 Pet 1:24, 25   40:10 Isa 62:11; Rev 22:12   40:11 Ezek 34:15; Jn 10:11

Israel's Incomparable God

¹²Can anyone measure the ocean by
    handfuls
  or measure the sky with his hands?
  Can anyone hold the soil of the earth in a
    cup
  or weigh the mountains and hills on
    scales?
¹³Can anyone tell the LORD what to do?
  Who can teach him or give him
    advice?
¹⁴With whom does God consult
  in order to know and understand
  and to learn how things should be
    done?

¹⁵To the LORD the nations are nothing,
  no more than a drop of water;
  the distant islands are as light as dust.
¹⁶All the animals in the forests of Lebanon
  are not enough for a sacrifice to our
    God,
  and its trees are too few to kindle the
    fire.
¹⁷The nations are nothing at all to him.

¹⁸To whom can God be compared?
  How can you describe what he is like?
¹⁹He is not like an idol that workers make,
  that metalworkers cover with gold
  and set in a base of silver.
²⁰Anyone who cannot afford silver or gold*i*
  chooses wood that will not rot.
  He finds a skillful worker
  to make an image that won't fall down.

²¹Do you not know?
  Were you not told long ago?
  Have you not heard how the world
    began?
²²It was made by the one who sits on his
    throne
  above the earth and beyond the sky;
  the people below look as tiny as ants.
  He stretched out the sky like a curtain,
  like a tent in which to live.

²³He brings down powerful rulers
  and reduces them to nothing.
²⁴They are like young plants,
  just set out and barely rooted.
  When the LORD sends a wind,
  they dry up and blow away like straw.

²⁵To whom can the holy God be compared?
  Is there anyone else like him?
²⁶Look up at the sky!
  Who created the stars you see?
  The one who leads them out like an
    army,
  he knows how many there are
  and calls each one by name!
  His power is so great—
  not one of them is ever missing!

²⁷Israel, why then do you complain
  that the LORD doesn't know your
    troubles
  or care if you suffer injustice?
²⁸Don't you know? Haven't you heard?
  The LORD is the everlasting God;
  he created all the world.
  He never grows tired or weary.
  No one understands his thoughts.
²⁹He strengthens those who are weak and
    tired.
³⁰Even those who are young grow weak;
  young people can fall exhausted.
³¹But those who trust in the LORD for help
  will find their strength renewed.
  They will rise on wings like eagles;
  they will run and not get weary;
  they will walk and not grow weak.

God's Assurance to Israel

41 ¹God says,
  "Be silent and listen to me, you
    distant lands!
  Get ready to present your case in court;
  you will have your chance to speak.
  Let us come together to decide who is
    right.

i **40:20** *Verses 19–20a in Hebrew are unclear.*
40:13 Rom 11:34; 1 Cor 2:16   **40:15** Wis 11:22; Sir 10:16, 17   **40:18, 19** Acts 17:29   **40:20** Wis
13:11–19; Bar 6:8–40   **40:26** Bar 3:34, 35

Compare Isaiah, chapter 40, with Isaiah, chapter 6.

Pray It!

FEAR

The dark? spiders? heights? public speaking?

What are you afraid of? A lot of people are afraid of the dark or of spiders or of heights. And being afraid of public speaking is the number one fear. Isaiah knew that the people were afraid and needed courage. He let them know God's message: "Do not be afraid—I am with you! / I am your God—let nothing terrify you!" (Isaiah 41:10). Choose something you are afraid of and include it in this prayer.

I will not be afraid of _____ because I know that you, my God, are with me. I may get scared, but I will remember you and your message in Isaiah: "Do not be afraid!" Amen.

— Isaiah 41:10

2 "Who was it that brought the conqueror
   from the east,*j*
   and makes him triumphant wherever
   he goes?
Who gives him victory over kings and
   nations?
   His sword strikes them down as if they
   were dust.
   His arrows scatter them like straw
   before the wind.
3 He follows in pursuit and marches safely
   on,
   so fast that he hardly touches the
   ground!
4 Who was it that made this happen?
   Who has determined the course of
   history?
I, the LORD, was there at the beginning,
   and I, the LORD, will be there at the
   end.
5 "The people of distant lands have seen
   what I have done;
   they are frightened and tremble with
   fear.
   So they all assemble and come.

6 The skilled workers help and encourage
   each other.
7 The carpenter says to the goldsmith, 'Well
   done!'
   The one who beats the idol smooth
   encourages the one who nails it
   together.
They say, 'The soldering is good'—
   and they fasten the idol in place with
   nails.

8 "But you, Israel my servant,
   you are the people that I have chosen,
   the descendants of Abraham, my friend.
9 I brought you from the ends of the earth;
   I called you from its farthest corners
   and said to you, 'You are my servant.'
   I did not reject you, but chose you.
10 Do not be afraid—I am with you!
   I am your God—let nothing terrify you!
I will make you strong and help you;
   I will protect you and save you.
11 "Those who are angry with you
   will know the shame of defeat.
   Those who fight against you will die

j **41:2** THE CONQUEROR FROM THE EAST: *Cyrus, the emperor of Persia (see 45:1).*
41:8 2 Chr 20:7; Jas 2:23

Isaiah

God is putting the false gods of the nations on trial in chapter 41. Can you find the legal sounding language in verses 1, 21, 22, 28?

12 and will disappear from the earth.
13 I am the LORD your God;
    I strengthen you and tell you,
    'Do not be afraid; I will help you.' "

14 The LORD says,
    "Small and weak as you are, Israel,
    don't be afraid; I will help you.
    I, the holy God of Israel, am the one who
    saves you.
15 I will make you like a threshing board,
    with spikes that are new and sharp.
    You will thresh mountains and destroy
    them;
    hills will crumble into dust.
16 You will toss them in the air;
    the wind will carry them off,
    and they will be scattered by the storm.
    Then you will be happy because I am
    your God;
    you will praise me, the holy God of
    Israel.

17 "When my people in their need look for
    water,
    when their throats are dry with thirst,
    then I, the LORD, will answer their prayer;
    I, the God of Israel, will never abandon
    them.
18 I will make rivers flow among barren hills
    and springs of water run in the valleys.
    I will turn the desert into pools of water
    and the dry land into flowing springs.
19 I will make cedars grow in the desert,
    and acacias and myrtles and olive trees.
    Forests will grow in barren land,
    forests of pine and juniper and cypress.
20 People will see this and know
    that I, the LORD, have done it.
    They will come to understand
    that Israel's holy God has made it
    happen."

I will turn the desert into pools of water. (41:18)

The LORD's Challenge to False Gods

21 The LORD, the king of Israel, has this to
say:
    "You gods of the nations, present your
    case.
    Bring the best arguments you have!
22 Come here and predict what will happen,
    so that we will know it when it takes
    place.
    Explain to the court the events of the
    past,
    and tell us what they mean.
23 Tell us what the future holds—
    then we will know that you are gods!
    Do something good or bring some
    disaster;
    fill us with fear and awe!
24 You and all you do are nothing;
    those who worship you are disgusting!

25 "I have chosen a man who lives in the
    east;*k*
    I will bring him to attack from the
    north.
    He tramples on rulers as if they were
    mud,
    like a potter trampling clay.
26 Which of you predicted that this would
    happen,
    so that we could say that you were
    right?
    None of you said a word about it;
    no one heard you say a thing!
27 I, the LORD, was the first to tell Zion the
    news;
    I sent a messenger to Jerusalem to say,
    'Your people are coming! They are
    coming home!'*l*
28 When I looked among the gods,
    none of them had a thing to say;
    not one could answer the questions I
    asked.
29 All these gods are useless;
    they can do nothing at all—
    these idols are weak and powerless."

k **41:25** A MAN WHO LIVES IN THE EAST: See 41:2.   *l* **41:27** *Verse 27 in Hebrew is unclear.*

"All these gods are useless." (41:29)

The Lord's Servant

42 ¹The Lord says,
"Here is my servant, whom I
strengthen—
the one I have chosen, with whom I
am pleased.
I have filled him with my Spirit,
and he will bring justice to every
nation.
²He will not shout or raise his voice
or make loud speeches in the
streets.
³He will not break off a bent reed
nor put out a flickering lamp.
He will bring lasting justice to all.
⁴He will not lose hope or courage;
he will establish justice on the earth.
Distant lands eagerly wait for his
teaching."

⁵God created the heavens and stretched
them out;
he fashioned the earth and all that lives
there;
he gave life and breath to all its
people.
And now the Lord God says to his
servant,
⁶"I, the Lord, have called you and given
you power
to see that justice is done on earth.

Through you I will make a covenant with
all peoples;
through you I will bring light to the
nations.
⁷You will open the eyes of the blind
and set free those who sit in dark
prisons.

⁸"I alone am the Lord your God.
No other god may share my glory;
I will not let idols share my praise.
⁹The things I predicted have now come
true.
Now I will tell you of new things
even before they begin to happen."

A Song of Praise

¹⁰Sing a new song to the Lord;
sing his praise, all the world!
Praise him, you that sail the sea;
praise him, all creatures of the sea!
Sing, distant lands and all who live there!
¹¹Let the desert and its towns praise God;
let the people of Kedar praise him!
Let those who live in the city of Sela
shout for joy from the tops of the
mountains!
¹²Let those who live in distant lands
give praise and glory to the Lord!
¹³The Lord goes out to fight like a
warrior;
he is ready and eager for battle.
He gives a war cry, a battle shout;
he shows his power against his enemies.

God Promises to Help His People

¹⁴God says,
"For a long time I kept silent;
I did not answer my people.
But now the time to act has come;
I cry out like a woman in labor.
¹⁵I will destroy the hills and mountains
and dry up the grass and trees.
I will turn the river valleys into deserts*m*
and dry up the pools of water.

¹⁶"I will lead my blind people
by roads they have never traveled.

---

m **42:15** *Probable text* deserts; *Hebrew* coastlands.
42:1 Mt 3:17; 17:5; Mk 1:11; Lk 3:22; 9:35   **42:1–4** Mt 12:18–21   **42:5** Acts 17:24, 25   **42:6** Isa 49:6; Lk
2:32; Acts 13:47; 26:23

I will turn their darkness into light
and make rough country smooth
before them.
These are my promises,
and I will keep them without fail.
17 All who trust in idols,
who call images their gods,
will be humiliated and disgraced."

Israel's Failure to Learn

18 The LORD says,
"Listen, you deaf people!
Look closely, you that are blind!
19 Is anyone more blind than my servant,
more deaf than the messenger I send?
20 Israel, you have seen so much,
but what has it meant to you?
You have ears to hear with,
but what have you really heard?"

21 The LORD is a God who is eager to save,
so he exalted his laws and teachings,
and he wanted his people to honor
them.
22 But now his people have been plundered;
they are locked up in dungeons
and hidden away in prisons.
They were robbed and plundered,
with no one to come to their rescue.

23 Will any of you listen to this?
From now on will you listen with care?
24 Who gave Israel up to the looters?
It was the LORD himself, against whom
we sinned!
We would not live as he wanted us to live
or obey the teachings he gave us.
25 So he made us feel the force of his anger
and suffer the violence of war.
Like fire his anger burned throughout
Israel,
but we never knew what was
happening;
we learned nothing at all from it.

God Promises to Rescue His People

43 1 Israel, the LORD who created you
says,
"Do not be afraid—I will save you.
I have called you by name—you are
mine.
2 When you pass through deep waters, I
will be with you;
your troubles will not overwhelm you.
When you pass through fire, you will not
be burned;
the hard trials that come will not hurt
you.

When you pass through deep waters . . . (43:2)

3 For I am the LORD your God,
the holy God of Israel, who saves you.
I will give up Egypt to set you free;
I will give up Ethiopia[n] and Seba.
4 I will give up whole nations to save your
life,
because you are precious to me
and because I love you and give you
honor.
5 Do not be afraid—I am with you!

"From the distant east and the farthest
west
I will bring your people home.
6 I will tell the north to let them go
and the south not to hold them back.
Let my people return from distant lands,
from every part of the world.

---

n **43:3** *Hebrew* Cush: *Cush is the ancient name of the extensive territory south of the First Cataract of the Nile River. This region was called Ethiopia in Graeco-Roman times, and included within its borders most of modern Sudan and some of present-day Ethiopia (Abyssinia).*

Isaiah

I will bring your people home. (43:5)

7 They are my own people,
  and I created them to bring me glory."

Israel Is the LORD's Witness

8 God says,
  "Summon my people to court.
    They have eyes, but they are blind;
    they have ears, but they are deaf!
9 Summon the nations to come to the trial.
    Which of their gods can predict the
      future?
    Which of them foretold what is
      happening now?
  Let these gods bring in their witnesses
    to prove that they are right,
    to testify to the truth of their words.

10 "People of Israel, you are my witnesses;
    I chose you to be my servant,
  so that you would know me and believe
      in me
    and understand that I am the only God.
  Besides me there is no other god;
    there never was and never will be.

11 "I alone am the LORD,
    the only one who can save you.
12 I predicted what would happen,
    and then I came to your aid.
  No foreign god has ever done this;
    you are my witnesses.

13 I am God and always will be.
  No one can escape from my power;
    no one can change what I do."

Escape from Babylon

14 Israel's holy God, the LORD who saves
you, says,
  "To save you, I will send an army against
      Babylon;
    I will break down the city gates,
    and the shouts of her people will turn
      into crying.
15 I am the LORD, your holy God.
    I created you, Israel, and I am your
      king."

16 Long ago the LORD made a road through
      the sea,
    a path through the swirling waters.

The LORD made a road through the sea. (43:16)

17 He led a mighty army to destruction,
    an army of chariots and horses.
  Down they fell, never to rise,
    snuffed out like the flame of a lamp!

18 But the LORD says,
  "Do not cling to events of the past
    or dwell on what happened long ago.
19 Watch for the new thing I am going
      to do.
    It is happening already—you can see it
      now!
  I will make a road through the
      wilderness
    and give you streams of water there.

**In Isaiah, chapter 43, God calls the Israelites to testify that he is the true God.
What evidence could they give from their history to prove this?**

20 Even the wild animals will honor me;
    jackals and ostriches will praise me
when I make rivers flow in the desert
    to give water to my chosen people.
21 They are the people I made for myself,
    and they will sing my praises!"

Israel's Sin

22 The LORD says,
"But you were tired of me, Israel;
    you did not worship me.
23 You did not bring me your burnt
       offerings of sheep;
    you did not honor me with your
       sacrifices.
I did not burden you by demanding
       offerings
    or wear you out by asking for incense.
24 You didn't buy incense for me
    or satisfy me with the fat of your
       animals.
Instead you burdened me with your
       sins;
    you wore me out with the wrongs you
       have committed.
25 And yet, I am the God who forgives your
       sins,
    and I do this because of who I am.
I will not hold your sins against you.

26 "Let us go to court; bring your
       accusation!
    Present your case to prove you are in
       the right!
27 Your earliest ancestor*o* sinned;
    your leaders sinned against me,
28   and your rulers profaned*p* my sanctuary.
So I brought destruction on Israel;
    I let my own people be insulted."

The LORD Is the Only God

44 1 The LORD says,
"Listen now, Israel, my servant,
my chosen people, the descendants of
       Jacob.
2 I am the LORD who created you;
    from the time you were born, I have
       helped you.

For the Thirsty

You know the person. That one in
the lunchroom who sits alone.
The one who eats as fast as possible and then disappears. The one
who is ignored, or worse, made
fun of. Every school has one,
probably more.

    Did you realize that that kid is
thirsty? Even if he or she has something to drink, he or she is thirsty.
Thirsty to know a friendly smile or
a kind word. Thirsty like the dry
ground described in Isaiah 44:3.

    Do you know what this person
is thirsty for? For you. Yes, for you
and your company. It's risky. Your
friends might laugh at you or
ignore you. They may stop eating
with you. But you know it is right.
You know it is what you are called
to do.

    You are called to give water to
the thirsty.

— Isaiah 44:3

Do not be afraid; you are my servant,
    my chosen people whom I love.

3 "I will give water to the thirsty land
    and make streams flow on the dry
       ground.
I will pour out my spirit on your children
    and my blessing on your descendants.
4 They will thrive like well-watered
       grass,
    like willows by streams of running
       water.
5 "One by one, people will say, 'I am the
       LORD's.'
They will come to join the people of
       Israel.

o **43:27** YOUR EARLIEST ANCESTOR: *A reference to Jacob or to Abraham, or possibly to Adam.*   *p* **43:28** *One ancient translation* your rulers profaned; *Hebrew* I profaned the rulers of.

Isaiah

They each will mark the name of the
LORD on their arms
and call themselves one of God's
people."

6 The LORD, who rules and protects Israel,
the LORD Almighty, has this to say:
"I am the first, the last, the only God;
there is no other god but me.
7 Could anyone else have done what I did?
Who could have predicted all that
would happen
from the very beginning to the end of
time?*q*
8 Do not be afraid, my people!
You know that from ancient times until
now
I have predicted all that would happen,
and you are my witnesses.
Is there any other god?
Is there some powerful god I never heard
of?"

Idolatry Is Ridiculed

9 All those who make idols are worthless,
and the gods they prize so highly are useless.
Those who worship these gods are blind and
ignorant—and they will be disgraced. 10 It
does no good to make a metal image to
worship as a god! 11 Everyone who worships
it will be humiliated. The people who make
idols are human beings and nothing more.
Let them come and stand trial—they will be
terrified and will suffer disgrace.
12 The metalworker takes a piece of metal
and works with it over a fire. His strong arm
swings a hammer to pound the metal into
shape. As he works, he gets hungry, thirsty,
and tired.
13 The carpenter measures the wood. He
outlines a figure with chalk, carves it out
with his tools, and makes it in the form of a
man, a handsome human figure, to be placed
in his house. 14 He might cut down cedars to
use, or choose oak or cypress wood from the
forest. Or he might plant a laurel tree and
wait for the rain to make it grow. 15 A person
uses part of a tree for fuel and part of it for
making an idol. With one part he builds a

fire to warm himself and bake bread; with
the other part he makes a god and worships
it. 16 With some of the wood he makes a fire;
he roasts meat, eats it, and is satisfied. He
warms himself and says, "How nice and
warm! What a beautiful fire!" 17 The rest of
the wood he makes into an idol, and then he
bows down and worships it. He prays to it
and says, "You are my god—save me!"
18 Such people are too stupid to know
what they are doing. They close their eyes
and their minds to the truth. 19 The maker of
idols hasn't the wit or the sense to say,
"Some of the wood I burned up. I baked
some bread on the coals, and I roasted meat
and ate it. And the rest of the wood I made
into an idol. Here I am bowing down to a
block of wood!"
20 It makes as much sense*r* as eating ashes.
His foolish ideas have so misled him that he
is beyond help. He won't admit to himself
that the idol he holds in his hand is not a
god at all.

Bowing down to a block of wood (44:19)

The LORD, the Creator and Savior

21 The LORD says,
"Israel, remember this;
remember that you are my servant.
I created you to be my servant,
and I will never forget you.
22 I have swept your sins away like a cloud.
Come back to me; I am the one who
saves you."

---

q **44:7** *Verse 7 in Hebrew is unclear.*   *r* **44:20** *It makes as much sense; or It will do him as much good.*
44:6 Isa 48:12; Rev 1:17; 2:8; 22:13   **44:15** Wis 13:11–19

The idol he holds in his hand is not a god at all.
(44:20)

23 Shout for joy, you heavens!
Shout, deep places of the earth!
Shout for joy, mountains, and every tree
of the forest!
The LORD has shown his greatness
by saving his people Israel.

24 "I am the LORD, your savior;
I am the one who created you.
I am the LORD, the Creator of all things.
I alone stretched out the heavens;
when I made the earth, no one helped
me.

25 I make fools of fortunetellers
and frustrate the predictions of
astrologers.
The words of the wise I refute
and show that their wisdom is
foolishness.

26 But when my servant makes a prediction,
when I send a messenger to reveal my
plans,
I make those plans and predictions
come true.
I tell Jerusalem that people will live there
again,
and the cities of Judah that they will be
rebuilt.
Those cities will rise from the ruins.

27 With a word of command I dry up the
ocean.

28 I say to Cyrus, 'You are the one who will
rule for me;
you will do what I want you to do:
you will order that Jerusalem be
rebuilt
and that the foundations of the Temple
be laid.' "

The LORD Appoints Cyrus

45 ¹ The LORD has chosen Cyrus to be
king.
He has appointed him to conquer
nations;
he sends him to strip kings of their
power;
the LORD will open the gates of cities
for him.
To Cyrus the LORD says,

2 "I myself will prepare your way,
leveling mountains and hills.
I will break down bronze gates
and smash their iron bars.

3 I will give you treasures from dark, secret
places;
then you will know that I am the
LORD
and that the God of Israel has called
you by name.

4 I appoint you to help my servant Israel,
the people that I have chosen.
I have given you great honor,
although you do not know me.

5 "I am the LORD; there is no other god.
I will give you the strength you
need,
although you do not know me.

6 I do this so that everyone
from one end of the world to the other
may know that I am the LORD
and that there is no other god.

7 I create both light and darkness;
I bring both blessing and disaster.
I, the LORD, do all these things.

44:25 1 Cor 1:20   44:28 2 Chr 36:23; Ezra 1:2

8 I will send victory from the sky like rain;
    the earth will open to receive it
    and will blossom with freedom and
        justice.
I, the LORD, will make this happen."

The LORD of Creation and History

9 Does a clay pot dare argue with its maker,
    a pot that is like all the others?
Does the clay ask the potter what he is
        doing?
Does the pot complain that its maker
        has no skill?
10 Do we dare say to our parents,
    "Why did you make me like this?"
11 The LORD, the holy God of Israel,
    the one who shapes the future, says:
"You have no right to question me about
        my children
    or to tell me what I ought to do!
12 I am the one who made the earth
    and created human beings to live there.
By my power I stretched out the heavens;
    I control the sun, the moon, and the
        stars.
13 I myself have stirred Cyrus to action
    to fulfill my purpose and put things
        right.
I will straighten out every road that he
        travels.
He will rebuild my city, Jerusalem,
    and set my captive people free.
No one has hired him or bribed him to
        do this."
The LORD Almighty has spoken.

14 The LORD says to Israel,
"The wealth of Egypt and Ethiopia⁵ will
        be yours,
    and the tall men of Seba will be your
        slaves;
    they will follow you in chains.
They will bow down to you and confess,
    'God is with you—he alone is God.

15 The God of Israel, who saves his people,
    is a God who conceals himself.
16 Those who make idols will all be
        ashamed;
    all of them will be disgraced.
17 But Israel is saved by the LORD,
    and her victory lasts forever;
    her people will never be disgraced.' "

18 The LORD created the heavens—
    he is the one who is God!
He formed and made the earth—
    he made it firm and lasting.
He did not make it a desolate waste,
    but a place for people to live.
It is he who says, "I am the LORD,
    and there is no other god.
19 I have not spoken in secret
    or kept my purpose hidden.
I did not require the people of Israel
    to look for me in a desolate waste.
I am the LORD, and I speak the truth;
    I make known what is right."

The LORD of the World and the Idols of Babylon

20 The LORD says,
"Come together, people of the nations,
    all who survive the fall of the empire;
    present yourselves for the trial!
The people who parade with their idols
        of wood
    and pray to gods that cannot save
        them—
    those people know nothing at all!
21 Come and present your case in court;
    let the defendants consult one
        another.
Who predicted long ago what would
        happen?
Was it not I, the LORD, the God who
    saves his people?
There is no other god.

---

⁵ **45:14** *Hebrew Cush: Cush is the ancient name of the extensive territory south of the First Cataract of the Nile River. This region was called Ethiopia in Graeco-Roman times, and included within its borders most of modern Sudan and some of present-day Ethiopia (Abyssinia).*
45:9 Isa 29:16; Rom 9:20

Isaiah, chapter 45, contains the famous image of God as the potter and us as the clay. What would you like to ask God about how you were created?

22 "Turn to me now and be saved,
   people all over the world!
I am the only God there is.
23 My promise is true,
   and it will not be changed.
I solemnly promise by all that I am:
   Everyone will come and kneel before
     me
   and vow to be loyal to me.
24 "They will say that only through me
   are victory and strength to be found;
but all who hate me will suffer disgrace.
25 I, the LORD, will rescue all the
     descendants of Jacob,
   and they will give me praise.

46

1 "This is the end for Babylon's gods!
   Bel and Nebo once were worshiped,
but now they are loaded on donkeys,
a burden for the backs of tired animals.
2   The idols cannot save themselves;
   they are captured and carried away.
This is the end for Babylon's gods!

The idols cannot save themselves. (46:2)

3 "Listen to me, descendants of Jacob,
   all who are left of my people.
I have cared for you from the time you
     were born.
4 I am your God and will take care of you
   until you are old and your hair is gray.
I made you and will care for you;
   I will give you help and rescue you.
5 "To whom will you compare me?" says
     the LORD.
   "Is there anyone else like me?
6 People open their purses and pour out
     gold;
   they weigh out silver on the scales.

They hire a goldsmith to make a god;
   then they bow down and worship it.
7 They lift it to their shoulders and carry it;
   they put it in place, and there it stands,
   unable to move from where it is.
If any pray to it, it cannot answer
   or save them from disaster.

8 "Remember this, you sinners;
   consider what I have done.
9 Remember what happened long ago;
   acknowledge that I alone am God
   and that there is no one else like me.
10 From the beginning I predicted the
     outcome;
   long ago I foretold what would
     happen.
I said that my plans would never fail,
   that I would do everything I intended
     to do.
11 I am calling a man to come from the
     east;[t]
   he will swoop down like a hawk
   and accomplish what I have planned.
I have spoken, and it will be done.

12 "Listen to me, you stubborn people
   who think that victory is far away.
13 I am bringing the day of victory near—
   it is not far away at all.
My triumph will not be delayed.
   I will save Jerusalem
   and bring honor to Israel there."

Judgment on Babylon

47

1 The LORD says,
   "Babylon, come down from your
     throne,
   and sit in the dust on the ground.
You were once like a virgin, a city
     unconquered,
   but you are soft and delicate no longer!
You are now a slave!
2 Turn the millstone! Grind the flour!
Off with your veil! Strip off your fine
     clothes!
Lift up your skirts to cross the streams![u]
3 People will see you naked;
   they will see you humbled and shamed.

(margin tab) Isaiah

Hocus Pocus

Hocus Pocus! Your room is clean. Hocus Pocus! You get an A on a test. Hocus Pocus! Someone gets well.

Wouldn't it be nice to have a magic spell that works that easily? Some books and movies portray worlds where magic is used to make life easier. But, of course, those books are fictional. There is no easy or magical way out of work or life's problems. The Babylonians thought magic spells would work for them. Isaiah's words remind us that magic is really powerless and that the real power lies with God.

Reading novels for fun is fine, even if they contain magical worlds. It can be fun to read about magic and dragons and other fantastic things. Just remember that it is all fiction. *God,* not magic spells, is the only source of life and real freedom.

— Isaiah 47:11–15

I will take vengeance, and no one will
   stop me."

⁴ The holy God of Israel sets us free—
   his name is the LORD Almighty.

⁵ The LORD says to Babylon,
"Sit in silence and darkness;
   no more will they call you the queen
   of nations!
⁶ I was angry with my people;
   I treated them as no longer mine:
I put them in your power,
   and you showed them no mercy;
   even the aged you treated harshly.

⁷ You thought you would always be a
   queen,
   and did not take these things to heart
   or think how it all would end.

⁸ "Listen to this, you lover of pleasure,
   you that think you are safe and secure.
You claim you are as great as God—
   that there is no one else like you.
You thought that you would never be a
   widow
   or suffer the loss of your children.
⁹ But in a moment, in a single day,
   both of these things will happen.
In spite of all the magic you use,
   you will lose your husband and
   children.

¹⁰ "You felt sure of yourself in your evil;
   you thought that no one could see you.
Your wisdom and knowledge led you
   astray,
   and you said to yourself, 'I am God—
   there is no one else like me.'
¹¹ Disaster will come upon you,
   and none of your magic can stop it.
Ruin will come on you suddenly—
   ruin you never dreamed of!
¹² Keep all your magic spells and charms;
   you have used them since you were
   young.
Perhaps they will be of some help to you;
   perhaps you can frighten your enemies.
¹³ You are powerless in spite of the advice
   you get.
Let your astrologers come forward and
   save you—
   those people who study the stars,
   who map out the zones of the heavens
   and tell you from month to month
   what*ᵛ* is going to happen to you.

¹⁴ "They will be like bits of straw,
   and a fire will burn them up!
They will not even be able to save
   themselves—
   the flames will be too hot for them,
   not a cozy fire to warm themselves by.
¹⁵ That is all the good they will do you—
   those astrologers you've consulted all
   your life.

ᵛ **47:13** *Some ancient translations* what; *Hebrew* from what.
47:8, 9 Rev 18:7, 8

Isaiah

Those people who study the stars (47:13)

They all will leave you and go their own way,
and none will be left to save you."

God Is LORD of the Future

48 ¹Listen to this, people of Israel,
you that are descended from Judah:
You swear by the name of the LORD
and claim to worship the God of Israel—
but you don't mean a word you say.
²And yet you are proud to say
that you are citizens of the holy city
and that you depend on Israel's God,
whose name is the LORD Almighty.

³The LORD says to Israel,
"Long ago I predicted what would take place;
then suddenly I made it happen.
⁴I knew that you would prove to be stubborn,
as rigid as iron and unyielding as bronze.
⁵And so I predicted your future long ago,
announcing events before they took place,
to keep you from claiming
that your idols and images made them happen.

⁶"All I foretold has now taken place;
you have to admit my predictions were right.
Now I will tell you of new things to come,
events that I did not reveal before.
⁷Only now am I making them happen;
nothing like this took place in the past.
If it had, you would claim that you knew all about it.
⁸I knew that you couldn't be trusted,
that you have always been known as a rebel.
That is why you never heard of this at all,
why no word of it ever came to your ears.

⁹"In order that people will praise my name,
I am holding my anger in check;
I am keeping it back and will not destroy you.
¹⁰I have tested you in the fire of suffering,
as silver is refined in a furnace.
But I have found that you are worthless.
¹¹What I do is done for my own sake—
I will not let my name be dishonored
or let anyone else share the glory
that should be mine and mine alone."

Cyrus, the LORD's Chosen Leader

¹²The LORD says,
"Listen to me, Israel, the people I have called!
I am God, the first, the last, the only God!
¹³My hands made the earth's foundations
and spread the heavens out.
When I summon earth and sky,
they come at once and present themselves.

¹⁴"Assemble and listen, all of you!
None of the gods could predict
that the man I have chosen would attack Babylon;
he will do what I want him to do.

48:12 Isa 44:6; Rev 1:17; 22:13

Isaiah

King Cyrus of Persia conquered Babylon in 539 BC. He let the Israelites who were in captivity return to rebuild Jerusalem and the Temple.

15 I am the one who spoke and called him;
  I led him out and gave him success.

16 "Now come close to me and hear what I
    say.
  From the beginning I have spoken
    openly
  and have always made my words come
    true."
(Now the Sovereign LORD has given me his
power and sent me.)

The LORD's Plan for His People

17 The holy God of Israel,
  the LORD who saves you, says:
  "I am the LORD your God,
  the one who wants to teach you for
    your own good
  and direct you in the way you should
    go.

18 "If only you had listened to my
    commands!
  Then blessings would have flowed for you
    like a stream that never goes dry.
  Victory would have come to you
    like the waves that roll on the shore.

19 Your descendants would be as numerous
    as grains of sand,
  and I would have made sure they were
    never destroyed."

20 Go out from Babylon, go free!
  Shout the news gladly; make it known
    everywhere:
    "The LORD has saved his servant
    Israel!"

21 When the LORD led his people through a
    hot, dry desert,
  they did not suffer from thirst.
  He made water come from a rock for
    them;
  he split the rock open, and water
    flowed out.

22 "There is no safety for sinners," says the
  LORD.

Israel, A Light to the Nations

49 ¹Listen to me, distant nations,
    you people who live far away!
  Before I was born, the LORD chose me
    and appointed me to be his servant.

2 He made my words as sharp as a sword.
    With his own hand he protected me.ʷ
  He made me like an arrow,
    sharp and ready for use.

3 He said to me, "Israel, you are my servant;
    because of you, people will praise me."

4 I said, "I have worked, but how hopeless
    it is!
  I have used up my strength, but have
    accomplished nothing."
  Yet I can trust the LORD to defend my
    cause;
  he will reward me for what I do.

5 Before I was born, the LORD appointed
    me;
  he made me his servant to bring back
    his people,
  to bring back the scattered people of
    Israel.

He made water come from a rock. (48:21)

ʷ 49:2 With his own hand . . . me; or He kept me hidden in his hand.
48:20 Rev 18:4   48:22 Isa 57:21   49:1 Jer 1:5   49:2 Heb 4:12; Rev 1:16

"Before I was born, the LORD chose me and appointed me to be his servant"
(Isaiah 49:1).

Isaiah

The LORD gives me honor;
  he is the source of my strength.

⁶The LORD said to me,
"I have a greater task for you, my servant.
  Not only will you restore to greatness
  the people of Israel who have survived,
but I will also make you a light to the
    nations—
  so that all the world may be saved."

⁷Israel's holy God and savior says
  to the one who is deeply despised,
who is hated by the nations
  and is the servant of rulers:
"Kings will see you released
  and will rise to show their respect;
princes also will see it,
  and they will bow low to honor you."

This will happen because the LORD has
  chosen his servant;
the holy God of Israel keeps his promises.

The Restoration of Jerusalem

⁸The LORD says to his people,
"When the time comes to save you, I will
  show you favor
  and answer your cries for help.
I will guard and protect you
  and through you make a covenant with
    all peoples.
I will let you settle once again
  in your land that is now laid waste.
⁹I will say to the prisoners, 'Go free!'
  and to those who are in darkness,
  'Come out to the light!'
They will be like sheep that graze on the
    hills;
¹⁰ they will never be hungry or thirsty.
Sun and desert heat will not hurt
    them,
  for they will be led by one who loves
    them.
He will lead them to springs of water.

¹¹"I will make a highway across the
    mountains
  and prepare a road for my people to
    travel.

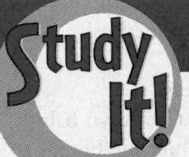

The Suffering Servant

Have you found many things in Isaiah that remind you of Jesus? (See "Stories about Jesus?" on page 1016.) As part of your search, you definitely want to look at the Servant Songs (they can be read in Isaiah 42:1–4; 49:1–6; 50:4–9 and 52:13—53:12). These are verses in which the prophet tells about an unnamed servant of God. Isaiah prophesies that this servant brings about God's justice, but that he will also suffer. His suffering will not be due to his own sins but those of others. We are told that he will suffer for us, even to death.

Remember that Isaiah was writing hundreds of years before the birth of Jesus. So it is remarkable that in these verses about the suffering servant, we see so much that reminds us of Jesus. When Christians read this passage, we see Jesus as that unnamed servant. The writer tells us that the servant Jesus was appointed by God before he was even born. Knowing that Jesus was born, suffered, and died for us helps us know just how much we are loved.

    — Isaiah 49:1–6

¹²My people will come from far away,
  from the north and the west,
  and from Aswanˣ in the south."

¹³Sing, heavens! Shout for joy, earth!
  Let the mountains burst into song!
The LORD will comfort his people;
  he will have pity on his suffering
    people.

14 But the people of Jerusalem said,
"The LORD has abandoned us!
    He has forgotten us."
15 So the LORD answers,
"Can a woman forget her own baby
    and not love the child she bore?
Even if a mother should forget her child,
    I will never forget you.
16 Jerusalem, I can never forget you!
    I have written your name on the palms
        of my hands.
17 "Those who will rebuild you are coming
        soon,
    and those who destroyed you will
        leave.
18 Look around and see what is happening!
    Your people are assembling—they are
        coming home!
As surely as I am the living God,
    you will be proud of your people,
    as proud as a bride is of her jewels.

19 "Your country was ruined and desolate—
    but now it will be too small
    for those who are coming to live there.
And those who left you in ruins
    will be far removed from you.
20 Your people who were born in exile
    will one day say to you,
'This land is too small—
    we need more room to live in!'
21 Then you will say to yourself,
'Who bore all these children for me?
I lost my children and could have no
        more.
I was exiled and driven away—
    who brought these children up?
I was left all alone—
    where did these children come
        from?' "

22 The Sovereign LORD says to his people:
"I will signal to the nations,
    and they will bring your children
        home.
23 Kings will be like fathers to you;
    queens will be like mothers.
They will bow low before you and honor
        you;
    they will humbly show their respect for
        you.

Then you will know that I am the LORD;
    no one who waits for my help will be
        disappointed."
24 Can you take away a soldier's loot?
    Can you rescue the prisoners of a
        tyrant?

25 The LORD replies,
"That is just what is going to happen.
The soldier's prisoners will be taken away,
    and the tyrant's loot will be seized.
I will fight against whoever fights you,
    and I will rescue your children.
26 I will make your oppressors kill each
        other;
    they will be drunk with murder and
        rage.
Then all people will know that I am the
        LORD,
    the one who saves you and sets you free.
They will know that I am Israel's
        powerful God."

50 ¹ The LORD says,
"Do you think I sent my people
        away
    like a man who divorces his wife?
    Where, then, are the papers of divorce?
Do you think I sold you into captivity
    like a man who sells his children as
        slaves?
No, you went away captive because of
        your sins;
    you were sent away because of your
        crimes.

2 "Why did my people fail to respond
    when I went to them to save them?
Why did they not answer when I called?
Am I too weak to save them?
I can dry up the sea with a command
    and turn rivers into a desert,
    so that the fish in them die for lack of
        water.
3 I can make the sky turn dark,
    as if it were in mourning for the dead."

The Obedience of the LORD's Servant

4 The Sovereign LORD has taught me what
    to say,

so that I can strengthen the weary.
Every morning he makes me eager
   to hear what he is going to teach me.
5 The LORD has given me understanding,
   and I have not rebelled
   or turned away from him.
6 I bared my back to those who beat me.
   I did not stop them when they insulted
     me,
   when they pulled out the hairs of my
     beard
   and spit in my face.

7 But their insults cannot hurt me
   because the Sovereign LORD gives me
     help.
   I brace myself to endure them.
   I know that I will not be disgraced,
8   for God is near,
   and he will prove me innocent.
   Does anyone dare bring charges against
     me?
   Let us go to court together!
   Let him bring his accusation!
9 The Sovereign LORD himself defends
     me—
   who, then, can prove me guilty?
   All my accusers will disappear;
   they will vanish like moth-eaten cloth.

10 All of you that honor the LORD
   and obey the words of his servant,
   the path you walk may be dark indeed,
   but trust in the LORD, rely on your
     God.
11 All of you that plot to destroy others
   will be destroyed by your own plots.
   The LORD himself will make this happen;
   you will suffer a miserable fate.

Words of Comfort to Jerusalem

51 1 The LORD says,
   "Listen to me, you that want to be
     saved;
   you that come to me for help.
   Think of the rock from which you came,
   the quarry from which you were cut.

2 Think of your ancestor, Abraham,
   and of Sarah, from whom you are
     descended.
   When I called Abraham, he was childless,
   but I blessed him and gave him children;
   I made his descendants numerous.

3 "I will show compassion to Jerusalem,
   to all who live in her ruins.
   Though her land is a desert, I will make it
     a garden,
   like the garden I planted in Eden.
   Joy and gladness will be there,
   and songs of praise and thanks to me.

4 "Listen to me, my people,
   listen to what I say:
   I give my teaching to the nations;
   my laws will bring them light.
5 I will come quickly and save them;
   the time of my victory is near.
   I myself will rule over the nations.
   Distant lands wait for me to come;
   they wait with hope for me to save
     them.
6 Look up at the heavens; look at the earth!
   The heavens will disappear like smoke;
   the earth will wear out like old
     clothing,
   and all its people will die like flies.
   But the deliverance I bring will last
     forever;
   my victory will be final.

7 "Listen to me, you that know what is
     right,
   who have my teaching fixed in your
     hearts.
   Do not be afraid when people taunt and
     insult you;
8   they will vanish like moth-eaten
     clothing!
   But the deliverance I bring will last
     forever;
   my victory will endure for all time."

9 Wake up, LORD, and help us!
   Use your power and save us;
   use it as you did in ancient times.

50:6 Mt 26:67; Mk 14:65   **50:8, 9** Rom 8:33, 34

Isaiah

Isaiah 50:4–9 is called a suffering servant song. Who does it remind you of?

It was you that cut the sea monster
    Rahab[y] to pieces.
10 It was you also who dried up the sea
    and made a path through the water,
    so that those you were saving could
    cross.
11 Those whom you have rescued
    will reach Jerusalem with gladness,
    singing and shouting for joy.
They will be happy forever,
    forever free from sorrow and grief.

12 The LORD says,
"I am the one who strengthens you.
    Why should you fear mortals,
    who are no more enduring than
    grass?
13 Have you forgotten the LORD who made
    you,
    who stretched out the heavens
    and laid the earth's foundations?
Why should you live in constant fear
    of the fury of those who oppress
    you,
    of those who are ready to destroy
    you?
Their fury can no longer touch you.
14 Those who are prisoners will soon be set
    free;
    they will live a long life
    and have all the food they need.

15 "I am the LORD your God;
    I stir up the sea
    and make its waves roar.
My name is the LORD Almighty!
16 I stretched out[z] the heavens
    and laid the earth's foundations;
I say to Jerusalem, 'You are my people!
I have given you my teaching,
    and I protect you with my hand.' "

The End of Jerusalem's Suffering

17 Jerusalem, wake up!
    Rouse yourself and get up!

You have drunk the cup of punishment
    that the LORD in his anger gave you to
    drink;
    you drank it down, and it made you
    stagger.
18 There is no one to lead you,
    no one among your people
    to take you by the hand.

19 A double disaster has fallen on you:
    your land has been devastated by war,
    and your people have starved.
There is no one to show you sympathy.
20 At the corner of every street
    your people collapse from weakness;
    they are like deer caught in a hunter's
    net.
They have felt the force of God's anger.

21 You suffering people of Jerusalem,
    you that stagger as though you were
    drunk,
22 the LORD your God defends you and says,
"I am taking away the cup
    that I gave you in my anger.
You will no longer have to drink
    the wine that makes you stagger.
23 I will give it to those who oppressed you,
    to those who made you lie down in
    the streets
    and trampled on you as if you were
    dirt."

God Will Rescue Jerusalem

52 1 Jerusalem, be strong and great again!
    Holy city of God, clothe yourself
    with splendor!
The heathen will never enter your gates
    again.
2 Shake yourself free, Jerusalem!
    Rise from the dust and sit on your
    throne!
Undo the chains that bind you,
    captive people of Zion!

3 The Sovereign LORD says to his people,

---

y **51:9** RAHAB: *A legendary sea monster, which represented the forces of chaos and evil, was sometimes a symbol of Egypt.*
z **51:16** *One ancient translation* stretched out; *Hebrew* planted.
51:17 Rev 14:10; 16:19   **52:1** Rev 21:2, 27

Do you remember what happened to Sarah and Abraham *(see Isaiah 51:2)*? **If
not, read Genesis 17:19–22 and 21:1–8.**

"When you became slaves, no money was paid for you; in the same way nothing will be paid to set you free. 4When you went to live in Egypt as foreigners, you did so of your own free will; Assyria, however, took you away by force and paid nothing for you. 5And now in Babylonia the same thing has happened: you are captives, and nothing was paid for you. Those who rule over you boast and brag and constantly show contempt for me. 6In time to come you will acknowledge that I am God and that I have spoken to you."

7 How wonderful it is to see
　　a messenger coming across the
　　　　mountains,
　　bringing good news, the news of
　　　　peace!
He announces victory and says to Zion,
　　"Your God is king!"

A messenger coming across the mountains (52:7)

8 Those who guard the city are
　　　shouting,
　　shouting together for joy.
They can see with their own eyes
　　the return of the LORD to Zion.

9 Break into shouts of joy,
　　you ruins of Jerusalem!
The LORD will rescue his city
　　and comfort his people.
10 The LORD will use his holy
　　　power;
　　he will save his people,
　　and all the world will see it.

Pray It!

Beautiful Feet?

The shoes come off
Revealing skin
Tanned a dark brown
With light stripes from sandal
　　straps
Heels cracked and filled with dust
Toenails hiding more brown dirt
These are the beautiful feet of
　　Jesus
The one who came to us
Born simply
Living humbly
Spreading peace
Preaching freedom
Sharing meals
Healing hearts
Loving friends and enemies
Serving all
Arms wide open
Even on the cross
Dying for all
I am thankful for
Those beautiful feet

— Isaiah 52

11 Be sure to leave Babylonia,
　　all you that carry the Temple
　　　equipment.
Touch no forbidden thing;a
　　keep yourselves holy and leave.
12 This time you will not have to leave in a
　　　hurry;
　　you will not be trying to escape.
The LORD your God will lead you
　　and protect you on every side.

The Suffering Servant

13 The LORD says,
"My servant will succeed in his task;
　　he will be highly honored.b

---

a **52:11** FORBIDDEN THING: *Any object that was considered ritually unclean.*　b **52:13** he will be highly honored; *or* he will be restored to greatness and honor.
52:5 Rom 2:24　**52:7** Nah 1:15; Rom 10:15; Eph 6:15　**52:11** 2 Cor 6:17

Isaiah

14 Many people were shocked when they
    saw him;
  he was so disfigured that he hardly
    looked human.
15 But now many nations will marvel at him,
  and kings will be speechless with
    amazement.
  They will see and understand
  something they had never known."

53

1 The people reply,
  "Who would have believed what we
    now report?
  Who could have seen the LORD's hand
    in this?
2 It was the will of the LORD that his servant
  grow like a plant taking root in dry
    ground.
  He had no dignity or beauty
  to make us take notice of him.
  There was nothing attractive about him,
  nothing that would draw us to him.
3 We despised him and rejected him;
  he endured suffering and pain.
  No one would even look at him—
  we ignored him as if he were nothing.

4 "But he endured the suffering that should
    have been ours,
  the pain that we should have borne.
  All the while we thought that his
    suffering
  was punishment sent by God.
5 But because of our sins he was wounded,
  beaten because of the evil we did.
  We are healed by the punishment he
    suffered,
  made whole by the blows he received.
6 All of us were like sheep that were lost,
  each of us going his own way.
  But the LORD made the punishment fall
    on him,
  the punishment all of us deserved.

7 "He was treated harshly, but endured it
    humbly;
  he never said a word.
  Like a lamb about to be slaughtered,
  like a sheep about to be sheared,
  he never said a word.

8 He was arrested and sentenced and led off
    to die,
  and no one cared about his fate.
  He was put to death for the sins of our
    people.
9 He was placed in a grave with those who
    are evil,
  he was buried with the rich,
  even though he had never committed a
    crime
  or ever told a lie."

10 The LORD says,
  "It was my will that he should suffer;
  his death was a sacrifice to bring
    forgiveness.
  And so he will see his descendants;
  he will live a long life,
  and through him my purpose will
    succeed.
11 After a life of suffering, he will again have
    joy;
  he will know that he did not suffer in
    vain.
  My devoted servant, with whom I am
    pleased,
  will bear the punishment of many
  and for his sake I will forgive them.
12 And so I will give him a place of honor,
  a place among the great and powerful.
  He willingly gave his life
  and shared the fate of evil men.
  He took the place of many sinners
  and prayed that they might be
    forgiven."ᶜ

He never said a word. (53:7)

ᶜ **53:12** prayed that they might be forgiven; *or* suffered the punishment they deserved.
52:15 Rom 15:21   **53:1** Rom 10:16; Jn 12:38   **53:4** Mt 8:17   **53:5** 1 Pet 2:24   **53:6** 1 Pet 2:25
53:7 Rev 5:6   **53:7, 8** Acts 8:32, 33   **53:9** 1 Pet 2:22   **53:12** Mk 15:28; Lk 22:37

The LORD's Love for Israel

54 ¹Jerusalem, you have been like a
childless woman,
but now you can sing and shout for
joy.
Now you will have more children
than a woman whose husband never
left her.
²Make the tent you live in larger;
lengthen its ropes and strengthen the
pegs!
³You will extend your boundaries on all
sides;
your people will get back the land
that the other nations now occupy.
Cities now deserted will be filled with
people.

⁴Do not be afraid—you will not be
disgraced again;
you will not be humiliated.
You will forget your unfaithfulness as a
young wife,
and your desperate loneliness as a
widow.
⁵Your Creator will be like a husband to
you—
the LORD Almighty is his name.
The holy God of Israel will save you—
he is the ruler of all the world.

⁶Israel, you are like a young wife,
deserted by her husband and deeply
distressed.
But the LORD calls you back to him and
says:
⁷"For one brief moment I left you;
with deep love I will take you back.
⁸I turned away angry for only a moment,
but I will show you my love forever."
So says the LORD who saves you.

⁹"In the time of Noah I promised
never again to flood the earth.
Now I promise not to be angry with you
again;
I will not reprimand or punish you.

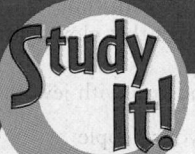

Making Connections

If your history teacher talks about
a TV show you watch, you will
probably listen more carefully to
what he or she is talking about.
The prophecies of Isaiah also mention popular stories of the Israelite
people. Throughout Isaiah there
are references to other parts of the
Old Testament. In chapter 51 the
writer refers to Eden and to Sarah
and Abraham. In chapter 54 Isaiah
mentions the Covenant God made
with Noah after the flood. By using
these stories, the prophet encouraged the people to listen closely
and make connections with their
history.

Is there anyone you know who
helps you make the connections
between the Bible's stories and our
lives today?

— Isaiah 54:9

¹⁰The mountains and hills may crumble,
but my love for you will never end;
I will keep forever my promise of
peace."
So says the LORD who loves you.

The Future Jerusalem

¹¹The LORD says,
"O Jerusalem, you suffering, helpless
city,
with no one to comfort you,
I will rebuild your foundations with
precious stones.

54:1 Gal 4:27   **54:9** Gen 9:8–17   **54:10** Jdt 16:15   **54:11, 12** Rev 21:18–21   **54:11** Tob 13:16, 17

Isaiah

**"We are healed by the punishment he suffered, / made whole by the blows he
received"** *(Isaiah 53:5)*.

12 I will build your towers with rubies,
  your gates with stones that glow like
    fire,
  and the wall around you with jewels.

13 "I myself will teach your people
  and give them prosperity and peace.
14 Justice and right will make you strong.
  You will be safe from oppression and
    terror.
15 Whoever attacks you,
  does it without my consent;
  whoever fights against you will fall.

16 "I create the blacksmith,
  who builds a fire and forges weapons.
  I also create the soldier,
  who uses the weapons to kill.
17 But no weapon will be able to hurt you;
  you will have an answer for all who
    accuse you.
  I will defend my servants
  and give them victory."

The LORD has spoken.

God's Offer of Mercy

55 ¹The LORD says,
  "Come, everyone who is thirsty—
  here is water!
  Come, you that have no money—
  buy grain and eat!
  Come! Buy wine and milk—
  it will cost you nothing!
2 Why spend money on what does not
    satisfy?
  Why spend your wages and still be
    hungry?
  Listen to me and do what I say,
  and you will enjoy the best food of all.

3 "Listen now, my people, and come to me;
  come to me, and you will have life!
  I will make a lasting covenant with you
  and give you the blessings I promised
    to David.
4 I made him a leader and commander of
    nations,

and through him I showed them my
    power.
5 Now you will summon foreign nations;
  at one time they did not know you,
  but now they will come running to
    join you!
  I, the LORD your God, the holy God of
    Israel,
  will make all this happen;
  I will give you honor and glory."

6 Turn to the LORD and pray to him,
  now that he is near.
7 Let the wicked leave their way of life
  and change their way of thinking.
  Let them turn to the LORD, our God;
  he is merciful and quick to forgive.
8 "My thoughts," says the LORD, "are not
    like yours,
  and my ways are different from yours.
9 As high as the heavens are above the
    earth,
  so high are my ways and thoughts
    above yours.

10 "My word is like the snow and the rain
  that come down from the sky to water
    the earth.
  They make the crops grow
  and provide seed for planting and food
    to eat.
11 So also will be the word that I speak—
  it will not fail to do what I plan for it;
  it will do everything I send it to do.

12 "You will leave Babylon with joy;
  you will be led out of the city in peace.
  The mountains and hills will burst into
    singing,
  and the trees will shout for joy.
13 Cypress trees will grow where now there
    are briers;
  myrtle trees will come up in place of
    thorns.
  This will be a sign that will last forever,
  a reminder of what I, the LORD, have
    done."

54:13 Jn 6:45   55:1 Rev 21:6; 22:17   55:2 Sir 24:19–22   55:3 Acts 13:34   55:10 2 Cor 9:10

"My thoughts," says the LORD, "are not like yours. . . . / As high as the heavens are above the earth, / so high are my ways and thoughts above yours" (Isaiah 55:8–9).

God's People Will Include All Nations

56 ¹The LORD says to his people, "Do what is just and right, for soon I will save you. ²I will bless those who always observe the Sabbath and do not misuse it. I will bless those who do nothing evil."

³A foreigner who has joined the LORD's people should not say, "The LORD will not let me worship with his people."

A man who has been castrated should never think that because he cannot have children, he can never be part of God's people. ⁴The LORD says to such a man, "If you honor me by observing the Sabbath and if you do what pleases me and faithfully keep my covenant, ⁵then your name will be remembered in my Temple and among my people longer than if you had sons and daughters. You will never be forgotten."

⁶And the LORD says to those foreigners who become part of his people, who love him and serve him, who observe the Sabbath and faithfully keep his covenant: ⁷"I will bring you to Zion, my sacred hill,ᵈ give you joy in my house of prayer, and accept the sacrifices you offer on my altar. My Temple will be called a house of prayer for the people of all nations."

⁸The Sovereign LORD, who has brought his people Israel home from exile, has promised that he will bring still other people to join them.

Israel's Leaders Are Condemned

⁹The LORD has told the foreign nations to come like wild animals and devour his people. ¹⁰He says, "All the leaders, who are supposed to warn my people, are blind! They know nothing. They are like watch dogs that don't bark—they only lie around and dream. How they love to sleep! ¹¹They are like greedy dogs that never get enough. These leaders have no understanding. They each do as they please and seek their own advantage. ¹²'Let's get some wine,' these drunkards say, 'and drink all we can hold! Tomorrow will be even better than today!'"

All Are Welcome

It really doesn't matter who you are or where you are from. It doesn't matter if you are married or single, if you are rich or poor. It only matters if you love God and keep the Covenant God made with us. God made all of us, equally. God wants all of us— young and old, male and female, foreigner and native—to be included and united.

Read Isaiah 56:1–8. It is pretty clear what God says—all are welcome. If you have been choosing your friends based on where they are from or how they look, think again. Maybe it is time to rethink how you pick your friends and treat outsiders. If you already do a good job of including everyone in your circle of friends, good for you!

— Isaiah 56:1–8

How they love to sleep! (56:10)

Israel's Idolatry Is Condemned

57 ¹Good people die, and no one understands or even cares. But when they die, no calamity can hurt them. ²Those who live good lives find peace and rest in death.

³Come here to be judged, you sinners! You are no better than sorcerers, adulterers, and

ᵈ **56:7** SACRED HILL: *See 2:3.*
56:4, 5 Wis 3:14, 15   **56:7** Mt 21:13; Mk 11:17; Lk 19:46

Isaiah

prostitutes. ⁴Who are you making fun of? Who are you liars jeering at? ⁵You worship the fertility gods by having sex under those sacred trees of yours. You offer your children as sacrifices in the rocky caves near stream beds. ⁶You take smooth stones from there and worship them as gods. You pour out wine as offerings to them and bring them grain offerings. Do you think I am pleased with all this? ⁷You go to the high mountains to offer sacrifices and have sex. ⁸You set up your obscene idols just inside your front doors. You forsake me; you take off your clothes and climb in your large beds with your lovers, whom you pay to sleep with you. And there you satisfy your lust. ⁹You put on your perfumes and ointments and go to worship the god Molech. To find gods to worship, you send messengers far and wide, even to the world of the dead. ¹⁰You wear yourselves out looking for other gods, but you never give up. You think your obscene idols give you strength, and so you never grow weak.

¹¹The LORD says, "Who are these gods that make you afraid, so that you tell me lies and forget me completely? Have you stopped honoring me because I have kept silent for so long? ¹²You think that what you do is right, but I will expose your conduct, and your idols will not be able to help you. ¹³When you cry for help, let those idols of yours save you! A puff of wind will carry them off! But those who trust in me will live in the land and will worship me in my Temple."

God's Promise of Help and Healing

¹⁴The LORD says, "Let my people return to me. Remove every obstacle from their path! Build the road and make it ready!
¹⁵"I am the high and holy God, who lives forever. I live in a high and holy place, but I also live with people who are humble and repentant, so that I can restore their confidence and hope. ¹⁶I gave my people life, and I will not continue to accuse them or be angry with them forever.ᵉ ¹⁷I was angry with them because of their sin and greed, and so I punished them and abandoned them. But they were stubborn and kept on going their own way.

¹⁸"I have seen how they acted, but I will heal them. I will lead them and help them, and I will comfort those who mourn. ¹⁹I offer peace to all, both near and far! I will heal my people. ²⁰But evil people are like the restless sea, whose waves never stop rolling in, bringing filth and muck. ²¹There is no safety for sinners," says the LORD.

True Fasting

58 ¹The LORD says, "Shout as loud as you can! Tell my people Israel about their sins! ²They worship me every day, claiming that they are eager to know my ways and obey my laws. They say they want me to give them just laws and that they take pleasure in worshiping me."

³The people ask, "Why should we fast if the LORD never notices? Why should we go without food if he pays no attention?"

The LORD says to them, "The truth is that at the same time you fast, you pursue your own interests and oppress your workers. ⁴Your fasting makes you violent, and you quarrel and fight. Do you think this kind of fasting will make me listen to your prayers? ⁵When you fast, you make yourselves suffer; you bow your heads low like a blade of grass and spread out sackcloth and ashes to lie on.

The kind of fasting I want is this. (58:6-7)

ᵉ **57:16** I gave my people . . . forever; *or* I will not continue to accuse them or be angry with them forever, for then they would die—the very people to whom I gave life.
57:19 Eph 2:17 **57:21** Isa 48:22

It Takes Two Feet

Polluted oceans, children working in sweat shops, homelessness, corrupt governments, hate crimes, and more. These are common headlines. They are also the opposite of what we as Catholics believe God wants for us. The prophets revealed God's desire that we need to work toward the common good. Working toward the common good means we try to live justly and fairly. As Isaiah prophesied, "Remove the chains of oppression and the yoke of injustice, and let the oppressed go free. Share your food with the hungry and open your homes to the homeless poor. Give clothes to those who have nothing to wear, and do not refuse to help your own relatives" (Isaiah 58:6–7).

In addition to doing direct service (such as collecting food, serving meals at shelters, giving away clothes), we also need to work for change. Working for change includes doing things that help remove the causes of hunger, poverty, and prejudice. These types of work include writing letters to challenge unjust laws or publicly protesting things that are wrong. These are the two feet of service and justice. Just like we need two feet to stay balanced and walk forward, working toward the common good takes two feet, too.

By working toward the common good, your steps of service and justice will combine with the steps of millions of other people to create a better world.

— Isaiah 58:6–7

Is that what you call fasting? Do you think I will be pleased with that?

⁶"The kind of fasting I want is this: Remove the chains of oppression and the yoke of injustice, and let the oppressed go free. ⁷Share your food with the hungry and open your homes to the homeless poor. Give clothes to those who have nothing to wear, and do not refuse to help your own relatives.

⁸"Then my favor will shine on you like the morning sun, and your wounds will be quickly healed. I will always be with you to save you; my presence will protect you on every side. ⁹When you pray, I will answer you. When you call to me, I will respond.

"If you put an end to oppression, to every gesture of contempt, and to every evil word;

¹⁰if you give food to the hungry and satisfy those who are in need, then the darkness around you will turn to the brightness of noon. ¹¹And I will always guide you and satisfy you with good things. I will keep you strong and well. You will be like a garden that has plenty of water, like a spring of water that never goes dry. ¹²Your people will rebuild what has long been in ruins, building again on the old foundations. You will be known as the people who rebuilt the walls, who restored the ruined houses."

The Reward for Keeping the Sabbath

¹³The LORD says, "If you treat the Sabbath as sacred and do not pursue your own

58:7 Mt 25:34

Isaiah

If you want to know the kinds of sinful behaviors people performed in worshiping other gods, read Isaiah 57:3–10.

interests on that day; if you value my holy day and honor it by not traveling, working, or talking idly on that day, 14then you will find the joy that comes from serving me. I will make you honored all over the world, and you will enjoy the land I gave to your ancestor, Jacob. I, the LORD, have spoken."

The Prophet Condemns the People's Sins

59 1Don't think that the LORD is too weak to save you or too deaf to hear your call for help! 2It is because of your sins that he doesn't hear you. It is your sins that separate you from God when you try to worship him. 3You are guilty of lying, violence, and murder.

4You go to court, but you do not have justice on your side. You depend on lies to win your case. You carry out your plans to hurt others. 5-6The evil plots you make are as deadly as the eggs of a poisonous snake. Crush an egg, out comes a snake! But your plots will do you no good—they are as useless as clothing made of cobwebs! 7You are always planning something evil, and you can hardly wait to do it. You never hesitate to murder innocent people. You leave ruin and destruction wherever you go, 8and no one is safe when you are around. Everything you do is unjust. You follow a crooked path, and no one who walks that path will ever be safe.

The People Confess Their Sin

9The people say, "Now we know why God does not save us from those who oppress us. We hope for light to walk by, but there is only darkness, 10and we grope about like blind people. We stumble at noon, as if it were night, as if we were in the dark world of the dead. 11We are frightened and distressed. We long for God to save us from oppression and wrong, but nothing happens. 12"LORD, our crimes against you are many. Our sins accuse us. We are well aware

of them all. 13We have rebelled against you, rejected you, and refused to follow you. We have oppressed others and turned away from you. Our thoughts are false; our words are lies. 14Justice is driven away, and right cannot come near. Truth stumbles in the public square, and honesty finds no place there. 15There is so little honesty that those who stop doing evil find themselves the victims of crime."

The LORD Prepares to Rescue His People

The LORD has seen this, and he is displeased that there is no justice. 16He is astonished to see that there is no one to help the oppressed. So he will use his own power to rescue them and to win the victory. 17He will wear justice like a coat of armor and saving power like a helmet. He will clothe himself with the strong desire to set things right and to punish and avenge the wrongs that people suffer. 18He will punish his enemies according to what they have done, even those who live in distant lands. 19From east to west everyone will fear him and his great power. He will come like a rushing river, like a strong wind.

20The LORD says to his people, "I will come to Jerusalem to defend you and to save all of you that turn from your sins. 21And I make a covenant with you: I have given you my power and my teachings to be yours forever, and from now on you are to obey me and teach your children and your descendants to obey me for all time to come."

The Future Glory of Jerusalem

60 1Arise, Jerusalem, and shine like the sun;
    The glory of the LORD is shining on you!
  2Other nations will be covered by
      darkness,
    But on you the light of the LORD will
      shine;

59:7, 8 Rom 3:15–17   **59:16** Isa 63:5   **59:17** Wis 5:17–23; Eph 6:14, 17; 1 Thess 5:8   **59:20** Rom 11:26

Isaiah

"The LORD has seen this, and he is displeased that there is no justice. He is astonished to see that there is no one to help the oppressed" (Isaiah 59:15–16).

Great caravans of camels will come. (60:6)

The LORD will make his Temple more
    glorious than ever.

Like a strong wind (59:19)

The brightness of his presence will be
    with you.
³ Nations will be drawn to your light,
And kings to the dawning of your new
    day.

⁴ Look around you and see what is
    happening:
Your people are gathering to come home!
Your sons will come from far away;
Your daughters will be carried like
    children.
⁵ You will see this and be filled with joy;
You will tremble with excitement.
The wealth of the nations will be brought
    to you;
From across the sea their riches will
    come.

⁶ Great caravans of camels will come, from
    Midian and Ephah.
They will come from Sheba, bringing
    gold and incense.
People will tell the good news of what
    the LORD has done!
⁷ All the sheep of Kedar and Nebaioth
Will be brought to you as sacrifices
And offered on the altar to please the
    LORD.

⁸ What are these ships that skim along like
    clouds,
Like doves returning home?
⁹ They are ships coming from distant lands,
Bringing God's people home.
They bring with them silver and gold
To honor the name of the LORD,
The holy God of Israel,
Who has made all nations honor his
    people.

What are these ships? (60:8)

¹⁰ The LORD says to Jerusalem,
"Foreigners will rebuild your walls,
And their kings will serve you.
In my anger I punished you,
But now I will show you my favor and
    mercy.
¹¹ Day and night your gates will be open,
So that the kings of the nations
May bring you their wealth.
¹² But nations that do not serve you
Will be completely destroyed.

¹³ "The wood of the pine, the juniper, and
    the cypress,

Isaiah

60:4 Bar 5:5, 6   **60:11** Rev 21.25, 26

The finest wood from the forests of Lebanon (60:13)

The finest wood from the forests of
   Lebanon,
Will be brought to rebuild you, Jerusalem,
To make my Temple beautiful,
To make my city glorious.

14 The descendants of those who oppressed
   you will come
And bow low to show their respect.
All who once despised you will worship
   at your feet.
They will call you 'The City of the
   LORD,'
'Zion, the City of Israel's Holy God.'

Bow low to show their respect (60:14)

15 "You will no longer be forsaken and
   hated,
A city deserted and desolate.
I will make you great and beautiful,
A place of joy forever and ever.

16 Nations and kings will care for you
As a mother nurses her child.
You will know that I, the LORD, have
   saved you,
That the mighty God of Israel sets you
   free.

17 "I will bring you gold instead of bronze,
Silver and bronze instead of iron and wood,
And iron instead of stone.
Your rulers will no longer oppress you;
I will make them rule with justice and
   peace.

18 The sounds of violence will be heard no
   more;
Destruction will not shatter your country
   again.
I will protect and defend you like a wall;
You will praise me because I have saved
   you.

19 "No longer will the sun be your light by
   day
Or the moon be your light by night;
I, the LORD, will be your eternal light;
The light of my glory will shine on you.

20 Your days of grief will come to an end.
I, the LORD, will be your eternal light,
More lasting than the sun and moon.

21 Your people will all do what is right,
And will possess the land forever.

I . . . will be your eternal light. (60:19)

I planted them, I made them,
To reveal my greatness to all.

22 Even your smallest and humblest family
Will become as great as a powerful nation.
When the right time comes,
I will make this happen quickly.
I am the LORD!"

The Good News of Deliverance

61 ¹The Sovereign LORD has filled me
   with his Spirit.
He has chosen me and sent me
To bring good news to the poor,
To heal the broken-hearted,
To announce release to captives
And freedom to those in prison.

60:14 Rev 3:9   **60:19** Rev 21:23; 22:5   **61:1** Mt 11:5; Lk 7:22   **61:1, 2** Lk 4:18, 19

Oh Joy!

The last six chapters of Isaiah are filled with promises of joy. They predict a time when God's love and justice will be brought to all nations. Notice all the nations named in chapter 60 that are sending representatives to honor God. The holy city, Jerusalem, will be rebuilt and become the center of the world's attention. It is a wonderful vision, and we can see some of it repeated in the New Testament, particularly in the Book of Revelation, chapters 21 and 22.

For Christians, the fulfillment of these promises began with Jesus and was confirmed by his death and Resurrection. We live in an in-between time, when Isaiah's promises have begun to be fulfilled but are not yet fully realized. It is an exciting time to be part of. Even though God has triumphed over sin and death, the world is not yet perfect. We are called to be God's messengers, to bring God's good news to the world and help make Isaiah's prophecies more and more real.

— Isaiah, chapter 60

² He has sent me to proclaim
That the time has come
When the LORD will save his people
And defeat their enemies.
He has sent me to comfort all who
    mourn,
³ To give to those who mourn in Zion

61:2 Mt 5:4 61:10 Rev 21:2

Joy and gladness instead of grief,
A song of praise instead of sorrow.
They will be like trees
That the LORD himself has planted.
They will all do what is right,
And God will be praised for what he has
    done.
⁴ They will rebuild cities that have long
    been in ruins.

⁵ My people, foreigners will serve you.
They will take care of your flocks
And farm your land and tend your
    vineyards.
⁶ And you will be known as the priests of
    the LORD,
The servants of our God.
You will enjoy the wealth of the nations
And be proud that it is yours.
⁷ Your shame and disgrace are ended.
You will live in your own land,
And your wealth will be doubled;
Your joy will last forever.

⁸ The LORD says,
"I love justice and I hate oppression and
    crime.
I will faithfully reward my people
And make an eternal covenant with them.
⁹ They will be famous among the nations;
Everyone who sees them will know
That they are a people whom I have
    blessed."

¹⁰ Jerusalem rejoices because of what the
    LORD has done.
She is like a bride dressed for her wedding.
God has clothed her with salvation and
    victory.
¹¹ As surely as seeds sprout and grow,
The Sovereign LORD will save his people,
And all the nations will praise him.

62 ¹ I will speak out to encourage
    Jerusalem;
I will not be silent until she is saved,
And her victory shines like a torch in the
    night.

Isaiah

Jesus quotes this passage from Isaiah *(61:1–2)* **to announce the start of his ministry** *(see Luke 4:18–19).*

Jesus' Mission Is Yours Too

good news
healing
freedom
comfort
gladness
rebuilding
joy
blessing
saving
praising

What a great list! Not only did Isaiah promise all these things, Jesus really did them. If you could choose one of the things on the list to be or do for others, which one would you choose? Once you've chosen it, make a list of ways to live it out. Share your ideas with people you trust. These can be your teachers, catechists, youth minister, parents, or priest. See if they can help you live out your idea.

— Isaiah, chapter 61

Like a torch in the night (62:1)

Because the LORD is pleased with you
And will be like a husband to your land.
5 Like a young man taking a virgin as his
    bride,
He who formed you will marry you.
As a groom is delighted with his bride,
So your God will delight in you.

6 On your walls, Jerusalem, I have placed
    sentries;
They must never be silent day or night.
They must remind the LORD of his
    promises
And never let him forget them.
7 They must give him no rest until he
    restores Jerusalem
And makes it a city the whole world
    praises.

8 The LORD has made a solemn promise,
And by his power he will carry it out:
"Your grain will no longer be food for
    your enemies,
And foreigners will no longer drink your
    wine.
9 But you that planted and harvested the
    grain
Will eat the bread and praise the LORD.
You that tended and gathered the grapes
Will drink the wine in the courts of my
    Temple."

10 People of Jerusalem, go out of the city
And build a road for your returning
    people!
Prepare a highway; clear it of stones!

2 Jerusalem, the nations will see you
    victorious!
All their kings will see your glory.
You will be called by a new name,
A name given by the LORD himself.
3 You will be like a beautiful crown for the
    LORD.
4 No longer will you be called "Forsaken,"
Or your land be called "The Deserted
    Wife."
Your new name will be "God Is Pleased
    with Her."
Your land will be called "Happily
    Married,"

Isaiah

"I will tell of the LORD's unfailing love; / I praise him for all he has done for us" *(Isaiah 63:7).*

Pray It!

Names

In several places Isaiah, chapter 62, talks about old names and new names for places. Jerusalem used to be called Forsaken, but it will be called God Is Pleased with Her or The City That God Loves. These names probably sound really pretty in their original Hebrew language. In the Bible, giving something a new name is a sign that God is at work in a person, a city, or a nation. That is one of the reasons that Catholics have a tradition of taking on a new name at Confirmation.

What is your favorite name for God? What name would you like God to call you? What name would you like for the city or state you live in? Can you write a prayer using all these names?

— Isaiah 62:4,12

Put up a signal so that the nations can know
11 That the LORD is announcing to all the earth:
"Tell the people of Jerusalem
That the LORD is coming to save you,
Bringing with him the people he has rescued."
12 You will be called "God's Holy People,"
"The People the LORD Has Saved."
Jerusalem will be called "The City That God Loves,"
"The City That God Did Not Forsake."

The LORD's Victory over the Nations

63 1 "Who is this coming from the city of Bozrah in Edom? Who is this so splendidly dressed in red, marching along⨍ in power and strength?"

It is the LORD, powerful to save, coming to announce his victory.

2 "Why is his clothing so red, like that of someone who tramples grapes to make wine?"

3 The LORD answers, "I have trampled the nations like grapes, and no one came to help me. I trampled them in my anger, and their blood has stained all my clothing. 4 I decided

that the time to save my people had come; it was time to punish their enemies. 5 I was amazed when I looked and saw that there was no one to help me. But my anger made me strong, and I won the victory myself. 6 In my anger I trampled whole nations and shattered them. I poured out their lifeblood on the ground."

The LORD's Goodness to Israel

7 I will tell of the LORD's unfailing love;
I praise him for all he has done for us.
He has richly blessed the people of Israel because of his mercy and constant love.
8 The LORD said, "They are my people; they will not deceive me." And so he saved them 9 from all their suffering. It was not an angel, but the LORD himself who saved them. In his love and compassion he rescued them. He had always taken care of them in the past, 10 but they rebelled against him and made his holy spirit sad. So the LORD became their enemy and fought against them.

11 But then they⨍ remembered the past, the days of Moses, the servant of the LORD, and they asked, "Where now is the LORD, who saved the leaders of his people from the sea?

Isaiah

⨍ **63:1** *Some ancient translations* marching along; *Hebrew* bowed down.   ⨍ **63:11** *Probable text* they; *Hebrew* he.
62:11 Isa 40:10; Rev 22:12   **63:1–6** Isa 34:5–17; Jer 49:7–22; Ezek 25:12–14; 35:1 15; Am 1.11, 12; Ob 1–14; Mal 1:2–5   **63:3 a** Rev 14:20; 19:15; **b** Rev 19:13   **63:5** Isa 59:16

Where is the LORD, who gave his spirit to Moses? 12-13 Where is the LORD, who by his power did great things through Moses, dividing the waters of the sea and leading his people through the deep water, to win everlasting fame for himself?"

Led by the LORD, they were as sure-footed as wild horses, and never stumbled. 14 As cattle are led into a fertile valley, so the LORD gave his people rest. He led his people and brought honor to his name.

A Prayer for Mercy and Help

15 LORD, look upon us from heaven, where you live in your holiness and glory. Where is your great concern for us? Where is your power? Where are your love and compassion? Do not ignore us. 16 You are our father. Our ancestors Abraham and Jacob do not acknowledge us, but you, LORD, are our father, the one who has always rescued us. 17 Why do you let us stray from your ways? Why do you make us so stubborn that we turn away from you? Come back, for the sake of those who serve you, for the sake of the people who have always been yours.

18 We, your holy people, were driven out by our enemies for a little while; they trampled down your sanctuary.[h] 19 You treat us as though you had never been our ruler, as though we had never been your people.

64 1 Why don't you tear the sky open and come down? The mountains would see you and shake with fear. 2 They would tremble like water boiling over a hot fire. Come and reveal your power to your enemies, and make the nations tremble at your presence! 3 There was a time when you came and did terrifying things that we did not expect; the mountains saw you and shook with fear. 4 No one has ever seen or heard of a God like you, who does such deeds for those who put their hope in him. 5 You welcome those who find joy in doing what is right, those who remember how you want them to live. You were angry with us, but we went on sinning; in spite of your great anger we have continued to do wrong

Build a road for your returning people! (62:10)

since ancient times.[i] 6 All of us have been sinful; even our best actions are filthy through and through. Because of our sins we are like leaves that wither and are blown away by the wind. 7 No one turns to you in prayer; no one goes to you for help. You have hidden yourself from us and have abandoned[j] us because of our sins.

8 But you are our father, LORD. We are like clay, and you are like the potter. You created us, 9 so do not be too angry with us or hold our sins against us forever. We are your people; be merciful to us. 10 Your sacred cities are like a desert; Jerusalem is a deserted ruin, 11 and our Temple, the sacred and beautiful place where our ancestors praised you, has been destroyed by fire. All the places we loved are in ruins. 12 LORD, are you unmoved by all this? Are you going to do nothing and make us suffer more than we can endure?

God's Punishment of the Rebellious

65 1 The LORD said, "I was ready to answer my people's prayers, but they did not pray. I was ready for them to find me, but they did not even try. The nation did not pray to me, even though I was always ready to answer, 'Here I am; I will help you.' 2 I have always been ready to welcome my people, who stubbornly do what is wrong and go their own way. 3 They shamelessly keep on making me angry. They offer pagan sacrifices at sacred gardens[k] and burn incense on pagan altars. 4 At night they go to caves and tombs to consult the spirits of the dead. They eat pork and drink broth made from meat offered in pagan sacrifices. 5 And then they say to others, 'Keep away

---

h **63:18** *Verse 18 in Hebrew is unclear.*   *i* **64:5** *Probable text* in spite of . . . ancient times; *Hebrew unclear.*
j **64:7** *Some ancient translations* abandoned; *Hebrew* melted.   *k* **65:3** SACRED GARDENS: *See 1:29.*
63:12 Ex 14:21   **64:4** 1 Cor 2:9   **65:1** Rom 10:20   **65:2** Rom 10:21

from us; we are too holy for you to touch!' I cannot stand people like that—my anger against them is like a fire that never goes out.

6"I have already decided on their punishment, and their sentence is written down. I will not overlook what they have done, but will repay them 7for their sins and the sins of their ancestors. They have burned incense at pagan hill shrines and spoken evil of me. So I will punish them as their past deeds deserve."

8The LORD says, "No one destroys good grapes; instead, they make wine with them. Neither will I destroy all my people—I will save those who serve me. 9I will bless the Israelites who belong to the tribe of Judah, and their descendants will possess my land of mountains. My chosen people, who serve me, will live there. 10They will worship me and will lead their sheep and cattle to pasture in the Plain of Sharon in the west and in Trouble Valley in the east.

11"But it will be different for you that forsake me, who ignore Zion, my sacred hill,¹ and worship Gad and Meni, the gods of luck and fate. 12It will be your fate to die a violent death, because you did not answer when I called you or listen when I spoke. You chose to disobey me and do evil. 13And so I tell you that those who worship and obey me will have plenty to eat and drink, but you will be hungry and thirsty. They will be happy, but you will be disgraced. 14They will sing for joy, but you will cry with a broken heart. 15My chosen people will use your name as a curse. I, the Sovereign LORD, will put you to death. But I will give a new name to those who obey me. 16Anyone in the land who asks for a blessing will ask to be blessed by the faithful God. Whoever takes an oath will swear by the name of the faithful God. The troubles of the past will be gone and forgotten."

The New Creation

17The LORD says, "I am making a new earth and new heavens. The events of the past will be completely forgotten. 18Be glad and rejoice forever in what I create. The new Jerusalem I make will be full of joy, and her people will be happy. 19I myself will be filled with joy because of Jerusalem and her people. There will be no weeping there, no calling for help. 20Babies will no longer die in infancy, and all people will live out their life span. Those who live to be a hundred will be considered young. To die before that would be a sign that I had punished them. 21-22People will build houses and get to live in them—they will not be used by someone else. They will plant vineyards and enjoy the wine—it will not be drunk by others. Like trees, my people will live long lives. They will fully enjoy the things that they have worked for. 23The work they do will be successful, and their children will not meet with disaster. I will bless them and their descendants for all time to come. 24Even before they finish praying to me, I will answer their prayers. 25Wolves and lambs will eat together; lions will eat straw, as cattle do, and snakes will no longer be dangerous. On Zion, my sacred hill,¹ there will be nothing harmful or evil."

The LORD Judges the Nations

66 ¹The LORD says, "Heaven is my throne, and the earth is my footstool. What kind of house, then, could you build for me, what kind of place for me to live in? 2I myself created the whole universe! I am pleased with those who are humble and repentant, who fear me and obey me.

3"The people do as they please. It's all the same to them whether they kill a bull as a sacrifice or sacrifice a human being; whether they sacrifice a lamb or break a dog's neck;

---

¹ **65:11, 25** SACRED HILL: *See 2:3*.
65:10 Josh 7:24–26   **65:17** Isa 66:22; 2 Pet 3:13; Rev 21:1   **65:19** Rev 21:4   **65:25** Isa 11:6–9
66:1 a Mt 5:34; 23:22; **b** Mt 5:35   **66:1, 2a** Acts 7:49, 50

"No one has ever seen or heard of a God like you, who does such deeds for those who put their hope in him" (Isaiah 64:4).

Pray It!

Help from the Holy Trinity

At the end of Isaiah are some prophecies about a time in the future when God will judge all people. Some people will be condemned for their sins, but those people who loved God and practiced justice will live in the new Jerusalem. This will be a place of joy and will be free from suffering or injustice.

We don't have to wait to die and go to heaven before experiencing the joy God wants us to have. We just have to look around and be open to the joy that God has in store for us right now. The problem is that some people spend so much time thinking about the past, they can't see what God is doing for them right now. Putting your past behind you can be very freeing. If you find yourself spending too much time thinking about something in the past, maybe this prayer idea can help. It is a prayer that involves all three persons of the Holy Trinity.

- First, think of the event or problem you keep remembering and ask God the Father to help you put it behind you.
- Second, if the event was a sin you committed, ask Jesus to forgive you (and remember to celebrate the sacrament of Penance and Reconciliation).
- Third, ask the Holy Spirit for the courage to move into the future.

— Isaiah 65:17–25

whether they present a grain offering or offer pigs' blood; whether they offer incense or pray to an idol. They take pleasure in disgusting ways of worship. 4So I will bring disaster upon them—the very things they are afraid of—because no one answered when I called or listened when I spoke. They chose to disobey me and do evil."

5Listen to what the LORD says, you that fear him and obey him: "Because you are faithful to me, some of your own people hate you and will have nothing to do with you. They mock you and say, 'Let the LORD show his greatness and save you, so that we may see you rejoice.' But they themselves will be disgraced! 6Listen! That loud noise in the city, that sound in the Temple, is the sound of the LORD punishing his enemies!

7"My holy city is like a woman who suddenly gives birth to a child without ever

going into labor. 8Has anyone ever seen or heard of such a thing? Has a nation ever been born in a day? Zion will not have to suffer long, before the nation is born. 9Do not think that I will bring my people to the point of birth and not let them be born." The LORD has spoken.

10Rejoice with Jerusalem; be glad for her, all you that love this city! Rejoice with her now, all you that have mourned for her! 11You will enjoy her prosperity, like a child at its mother's breast.

12The LORD says, "I will bring you lasting prosperity; the wealth of the nations will flow to you like a river that never goes dry. You will be like a child that is nursed by its mother, carried in her arms, and treated with love. 13I will comfort you in Jerusalem, as a mother comforts her child. 14When you see

66:7 Rev 12:5

The last chapter of Isaiah is filled with images of negative punishments and positive promises. How many can you find of each?

this happen, you will be glad; it will make you strong and healthy. Then you will know that I, the LORD, help those who obey me, and I show my anger against my enemies."

15 The LORD will come with fire. He will ride on the wings of a storm to punish those he is angry with. 16 By fire and sword he will punish all the people of the world whom he finds guilty—and many will be put to death.

17 The LORD says, "The end is near for those who purify themselves for pagan worship, who go in procession to sacred gardens,*m* and who eat pork and mice and other disgusting foods. 18 I know*n* their thoughts and their deeds. I am coming*o* to gather the people of all the nations. When they come together, they will see what my power can do 19 and will know that I am the one who punishes them.

"But I will spare some of them and send them to the nations and the distant lands that have not heard of my fame or seen my greatness and power: to Spain, Libya,*p* and Lydia, with its skilled archers, and to Tubal and Greece. Among these nations they will proclaim my greatness. 20 They will bring back all your people from the nations as a gift to me. They will bring them to my sacred hill*q* in Jerusalem on horses, mules, and camels, and in chariots and wagons, just as Israelites bring grain offerings to the Temple in ritually clean containers. 21 I will make some of them priests and Levites.

22 "Just as the new earth and the new heavens will endure by my power, so your descendants and your name will endure. 23 On every New Moon Festival and every Sabbath people of every nation will come to worship me here in Jerusalem," says the LORD. 24 "As they leave, they will see the dead bodies of those who have rebelled against me. The worms that eat them will never die, and the fire that burns them will never be put out. The sight of them will be disgusting to all people."

---

m **66:17** SACRED GARDENS: See 1:29.   *n* **66:18** Some ancient translations I know; Hebrew I.   *o* **66:18** Some ancient translations I am coming; Hebrew He is coming.   *p* **66:19** One ancient translation Libya; Hebrew Pul.
q **66:20** SACRED HILL: See 2:3.
66:22 Isa 65:17; 2 Pet 3:13; Rev 21:1   **66:24** Jdt 16:17; Mk 9:48

Your Next Step

Congratulations on finishing the Book of Isaiah! Use this space to write your thoughts and questions about this book. If you are following the suggested reading plan, move ahead to the Gospel of Matthew in the New Testament. Look for quotes in Matthew that come from Isaiah.

Isaiah

"I just had to tell someone!" Have you ever felt this way? Sometimes we know something that we just can't keep to ourselves, no matter how hard we try.

Jeremiah experienced something similar, except that he knew that what he had to say would get him in trouble. God had chosen him at an early age to be a prophet. He had to proclaim God's words of judgment even though he knew those words would upset people. As a result, Jeremiah was often persecuted because of his message. But he would not back down. Like it or not, he was the one God had chosen to speak the truth—and so he did, no matter what the consequences. And that is the test of a true prophet.

Chap. 38

Headlines

- Youth Chosen As Prophet (1:4–9)
- God's Warning: Keep the Covenant! (11:1–8)
- Jeremiah's Shorts Make a Point (13:1–11)
- Jeremiah Complains to God (20:7–18)
- New Covenant Written on Hearts (31:31–34)
- Prophet Is Rescued from Well (38:1–13)
- God Promises Babylon's Punishment (chapter 51)

FACTOIDS

Who wrote this book? Jeremiah and his disciples, including Baruch.

Why was it written? To tell the story of the prophet Jeremiah and record his messages to God's Chosen People.

What time period does it cover? From 626 to 560 BC.

What literary style is used? This book is part history, part biography, and part prophecy.

Important themes

- God reveals a New Covenant that will be written on the hearts of God's people.
- Sin leads to suffering, but with repentance comes forgiveness and new life.
- Beware of false prophets who tell people what they want to hear.

JEREMIAH

1 ¹This book is the account of what was said by Jeremiah son of Hilkiah, one of the priests of the town of Anathoth in the territory of Benjamin. ²The LORD spoke to Jeremiah in the thirteenth year that Josiah son of Amon was king of Judah, ³and he spoke to him again when Josiah's son Jehoiakim was king. After that, the LORD spoke to him many times, until the eleventh year of the reign of Zedekiah son of Josiah. In the fifth month of that year the people of Jerusalem were taken into exile.

The Call of Jeremiah

⁴The LORD said to me, ⁵"I chose you before I gave you life, and before you were born I selected you to be a prophet to the nations."

⁶I answered, "Sovereign LORD, I don't know how to speak; I am too young."

⁷But the LORD said to me, "Do not say that you are too young, but go to the people I send you to, and tell them everything I command you to say. ⁸Do not be afraid of them, for I will be with you to protect you. I, the LORD, have spoken!"

⁹Then the LORD reached out, touched my lips, and said to me, "Listen, I am giving you the words you must speak. ¹⁰Today I

Who, Me?

"Who, me?"

Do those words sound familiar? We have all used them and heard others use them. You can almost picture someone turning around to see who is calling. Or maybe the person saying "Who, me?" isn't excited about being called. This is sort of what Jeremiah is saying at the beginning of his book. It is the story of his call by God. He isn't too excited about being called by God. He knows that prophets are often not treated very well.

So Jeremiah tries to make excuses for why God shouldn't call him. Jeremiah says that he doesn't know how to speak and that he's too young. However, God is not buying it. God has a plan for young Jeremiah, just as he has a plan for each of us. We can make excuses, but God's plan is already in place before we are even born. Jeremiah is called to be a prophet, to speak God's message to people who don't really want to hear it. God also has a plan for each of us, no excuses accepted!

Ask God to help you understand and follow your call.

— Jeremiah 1:4–10

"I am giving you the words you must speak." (1:9)

1:2 2 Kings 22:3—23:27; 2 Chr 34:8—35:19   **1:3 a** 2 Kings 23:36—24:7; 2 Chr 36:5–8; **b** 2 Kings 24:18—25:21; 2 Chr 36:11–21

give you authority over nations and kingdoms to uproot and to pull down, to destroy and to overthrow, to build and to plant."

Two Visions

11 The LORD asked me, "Jeremiah, what do you see?"

I answered, "A branch of an almond tree."

12 "You are right," the LORD said, "and I am watching[a] to see that my words come true."

13 Then the LORD spoke to me again. "What else do you see?" he asked.

I answered, "I see a pot boiling in the north, and it is about to tip over this way."

14 He said to me, "Destruction will boil over from the north on all who live in this land, 15 because I am calling all the nations in the north to come. Their kings will set up their thrones at the gates of Jerusalem and around its walls and also around the other cities of Judah. 16 I will punish my people because they have sinned; they have abandoned me, have offered sacrifices to other gods, and have made idols and worshiped them. 17 Get ready, Jeremiah; go and tell them everything I command you to say. Do not be afraid of them now, or I will make you even more afraid when you are with them. 18-19 Listen, Jeremiah! Everyone in this land—the kings of Judah, the officials, the priests, and the people—will be against you. But today I am giving you the strength to resist them; you will be like a fortified city, an iron pillar, and a bronze wall. They will not defeat you, for I will be with you to protect you. I, the LORD, have spoken."

God's Care for Israel

2 ¹The LORD told me ²to proclaim this message to everyone in Jerusalem.

"I remember how faithful you were when
　　you were young,
　how you loved me when we were first
　　married;
you followed me through the desert,
　through a land that had not been planted.

³Israel, you belonged to me alone;
　you were my sacred possession.
I sent suffering and disaster
　on everyone who hurt you.
I, the LORD, have spoken."

The Sin of Israel's Ancestors

⁴Listen to the LORD's message, you descendants of Jacob, you tribes of Israel. ⁵The LORD says:

"What accusation did your ancestors
　　bring against me?
　What made them turn away from me?
They worshiped worthless idols
　and became worthless themselves.
⁶They did not care about me,
　even though I rescued them from
　　Egypt
　and led them through the wilderness:
　a land of deserts and sand pits,
　a dry and dangerous land
　where no one lives
　and no one will even travel.
⁷I brought them into a fertile land,
　to enjoy its harvests and its other good
　　things.
But instead they ruined my land;
　they defiled the country I had given
　　them.
⁸The priests did not ask, 'Where is the
　　LORD?'
　My own priests did not know me.
The rulers rebelled against me;
　the prophets spoke in the name of Baal
　and worshiped useless idols.

The LORD's Case against His People

⁹"And so I, the LORD, will state my case
　against my people again.
I will bring charges against their
　descendants.
¹⁰Go west to the island of Cyprus,
　and send someone eastward to the land
　of Kedar.

---

[a] **1:12** WATCHING: *This word in Hebrew sounds like the Hebrew for "almond."*

Baal was the chief god of the Canaanites and appears twice in Jeremiah, chapter 2. Can you find both places?

You will see that nothing like this has
   ever happened before.
11 No other nation has ever changed its
   gods,
   even though they were not real.
But my people have exchanged me,
   the God who has brought them
   honor,
   for gods that can do nothing for
   them.
12 And so I command the sky to shake with
   horror,
   to be amazed and astonished,
13   for my people have committed two
   sins:
they have turned away from me,
   the spring of fresh water,
and they have dug cisterns,
   cracked cisterns that can hold no water
   at all.

The Results of Israel's Unfaithfulness

14 "Israel is not a slave;
   he was not born into slavery.
   Why then do his enemies hunt him
   down?
15 They have roared at him like lions;
   they have made his land a desert,
   and his towns lie in ruins, completely
   abandoned.
16 Yes, the people of Memphis and
   Tahpanhes
have cracked his skull.
17 Israel, you brought this on yourself!
   You deserted me, the LORD your
   God,
   while I was leading you along the
   way.
18 What do you think you will gain by
   going to Egypt
   to drink water from the Nile?
What do you think you will gain by
   going to Assyria
   to drink water from the Euphrates?
19 Your own evil will punish you,
   and your turning from me will
   condemn you.

You will learn how bitter and wrong
   it is
   to abandon me, the LORD your
   God,
   and no longer to remain faithful to me.
I, the Sovereign LORD Almighty, have
   spoken."

Israel Refuses to Worship the LORD

20 The Sovereign LORD says,
"Israel, long ago you rejected my
   authority;
   you refused to obey me and worship
   me.
On every high hill
   and under every green tree
   you worshiped fertility gods.
21 I planted you like a choice vine
   from the very best seed.
But look what you have become!
   You are like a rotten, worthless vine.
22 Even if you washed with the strongest
   soap,
   I would still see the stain of your guilt.
23 How can you say you have not defiled
   yourself,
   that you have never worshiped Baal?
Look how you sinned in the valley;
   see what you have done.
You are like a wild camel in heat,
   running around loose,
24   rushing into the desert.[b]
When she is in heat, who can control
   her?
No male that wants her has to trouble
   himself;
   she is always available in mating season.
25 Israel, don't wear your feet out,
   or let your throat become dry
   from chasing after other gods.
But you say, 'No! I can't turn back.
   I have loved foreign gods
   and will go after them.' "

Israel Deserves to Be Punished

26 The LORD says, "Just as a thief is disgraced when caught, so all you people of
Israel will be disgraced—your kings and

Jeremiah

---

[b] 2:24 *Probable text* rushing into the desert; *Hebrew* a wild donkey used to the desert.

Pray It!

Help! Rescue Me!

"But when you are in trouble, you ask me to come and save you" (Jeremiah 2:27). These words of the Lord can hit home pretty easily. How many times do we pray only when we are in trouble or really need God to help someone we care about? What about when things are going well, when life is good? Take a moment right now and think of five things that happened to you recently that are good things. Think also of five people in your life you would like to pray for. Now, turn to God in prayer, and try this formula:

- Begin with: "Thank you, God, for these blessings . . ."
- Now pray for others in your life: "God, I pray for a blessing upon . . ."
- And if you need God's help, end with: "Dear God, please help me to . . ."

— Jeremiah 2:26–27

officials, your priests and prophets. 27 You will all be disgraced—you that say that a tree is your father and that a rock is your mother. This will happen because you turned away from me instead of turning to me. But when you are in trouble, you ask me to come and save you.

28 "Where are the gods that you made for yourselves? When you are in trouble, let them save you—if they can! Judah, you have as many gods as you have cities. 29 What is your complaint? Why have you rebelled against me? 30 I punished you, but it did no good; you would not let me correct you. Like a raging lion, you have murdered your prophets. 31 People of Israel, listen to what I am saying. Have I been like a desert to you, like a dark and dangerous land? Why, then, do you say that you will do as you please, that you will never come back to me? 32 Does a young woman forget her jewelry, or a bride her wedding dress? But my people have forgotten me for more days than can be counted. 33 You certainly know how to chase after lovers. Even the worst of women can learn from you. 34 Your clothes are stained with the blood of the poor and innocent, not with the blood of burglars.

"But in spite of all this, 35 you say, 'I am innocent; surely the LORD is no longer angry with me.' But I, the LORD, will punish you because you deny that you have sinned.

36 You have cheapened yourself by turning to the gods of other nations. You will be disappointed by Egypt, just as you were by Assyria. 37 You will turn away from Egypt, hanging your head in shame. I, the LORD, have rejected those you trust; you will not gain anything from them."

Unfaithful Israel

3 ¹The LORD says, "If a man divorces his wife, and she leaves him and becomes another man's wife, he cannot take her back again. This would completely defile the land. But, Israel, you have had many lovers, and now you want to return to me! ²Look up at the hilltops. Is there any place where you have not acted like a prostitute? You waited for lovers along the roadside, as an Arab waits for victims in the desert. You have defiled the land with your prostitution. ³That is why the rains were held back, and the spring showers did not come. You even look like a prostitute; you have no shame.

⁴"And now you say to me, 'You are my father, and you have loved me ever since I was a child. ⁵You won't always be angry; you won't be mad at me forever.' Israel, that is what you said, but you did all the evil you could."

Jeremiah

Worshiping stones and trees (3:9)

Israel and Judah Must Repent

⁶When Josiah was king, the LORD said to me, "Have you seen what Israel, that unfaithful woman, has done? She has turned away from me, and on every high hill and under every green tree she has acted like a prostitute. ⁷I thought that after she had done all this, she would surely return to me. But she did not return, and her unfaithful sister Judah saw it all. ⁸Judah also saw that I divorced Israel and sent her away because she had turned from me and had become a prostitute. But Judah, Israel's unfaithful sister, was not afraid. She too became a prostitute ⁹and was not at all ashamed. She defiled the land, and she committed adultery by worshiping stones and trees. ¹⁰And after all this, Judah, Israel's unfaithful sister, only pretended to return to me; she was not sincere. I, the LORD, have spoken."

¹¹Then the LORD told me that, even though Israel had turned away from him, she had proved to be better than unfaithful Judah. ¹²He told me to go and say to Israel, "Unfaithful Israel, come back to me. I am merciful and will not be angry; I will not be angry with you forever. ¹³Only admit that you are guilty and that you have rebelled against the LORD, your God. Confess that under every green tree you have given your love to foreign gods and that you have not obeyed my commands. I, the LORD, have spoken.

3:6 2 Kings 22:1—23:30; 2 Chr 34:1—35:27

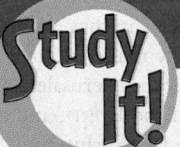

The Roots of Racism

In the beginning of Jeremiah, chapter 3, there is the phrase "as an Arab waits for victims in the desert" (verse 2). The word *Arab* here is used to describe bandits who waited for caravans to pass and then attacked and robbed them. Clearly, the word *Arab* here has negative overtones, and we would describe this as a racist comment because not all Arabs are thieves. Perhaps this is why some other English versions of the Bible use the word *nomad* instead of *Arab.*

Today some of us have the tendency to refer to Arabs as terrorists. We have to be very careful when labeling a group of people, especially an ethnic group. Most likely, few Arabs in the time of Jeremiah were thieves, and certainly very few Arabs today are terrorists. Keep your ears open for times when you hear people lumping everyone from an ethnic group or nation together. It is unfair, and it is wrong.

— Jeremiah 3:2

¹⁴"Unfaithful people, come back; you belong to me. I will take one of you from each town and two from each clan, and I will bring you back to Mount Zion. ¹⁵I will give you rulers who obey me, and they will rule you with wisdom and understanding. ¹⁶Then when you have become numerous in that land, people will no longer talk about

Jeremiah

Israel is the northern kingdom, and Judah is the southern kingdom. Both are mentioned in Jeremiah, chapter 3. See Map 3 to see their boundaries.

my Covenant Box. They will no longer think about it or remember it; they will not even need it, nor will they make another one. 17 When that time comes, Jerusalem will be called 'The Throne of the LORD,' and all nations will gather there to worship me. They will no longer do what their stubborn and evil hearts tell them. 18 Israel will join with Judah, and together they will come from exile in the country in the north and will return to the land that I gave your ancestors as a permanent possession."

The Idolatry of God's People

19 The LORD says,
"Israel, I wanted to accept you as my
    child
    and give you a delightful land,
    the most beautiful land in all the world.
I wanted you to call me father
    and never again turn away from me.
20 But like an unfaithful wife,
    you have not been faithful to me.
I, the LORD, have spoken."

21 A noise is heard on the hilltops:
    it is the people of Israel crying and
        pleading
    because they have lived sinful lives
    and have forgotten the LORD their
        God.
22 Return, all of you who have turned away
        from the LORD;
    he will heal you and make you faithful.

You say, "Yes, we are coming to the LORD because he is our God. 23 We were not helped at all by our pagan worship on the hilltops. Help for Israel comes only from the LORD our God. 24 But the worship of Baal, the god of shame, has made us lose flocks and herds, sons and daughters—everything that our ancestors have worked for since ancient times. 25 We should lie down in shame and let our disgrace cover us. We and our ancestors

have always sinned against the LORD our God; we have never obeyed his commands."

A Call to Repentance

4 ¹The LORD says, "People of Israel, if you want to turn, then turn back to me. If you are faithful to me and remove the idols I hate, ²it will be right for you to swear by my name. Then c all the nations will ask me to bless them, and they will praise me."

Turn back to me. (4:1)

³The LORD says to the people of Judah and Jerusalem, "Plow up your unplowed fields; do not plant your seeds among thorns. ⁴Keep your covenant with me, your LORD, and dedicate yourselves to me, you people of Judah and Jerusalem. If you don't, my anger will burn like fire because of the evil things you have done. It will burn, and there will be no one to put it out."

Judah Is Threatened with Invasion

5 Blow the trumpet throughout the land!
    Shout loud and clear!
Tell the people of Judah and Jerusalem
    to run to the fortified cities.
6 Point the way to Zion!
    Run for safety! Don't delay!
The LORD is bringing disaster
    and great destruction from the north.
7 Like a lion coming from its hiding place,
    a destroyer of nations has set out.

---

c **4:2** it will be right . . . name. Then; *or* and if you swear by my name and are truthful, just, and righteous, then.
4:3 Hos 10:12

Sackcloth is a rough material made from goat's hair. It's uncomfortable to wear. Why would people who are mourning wear sackcloth?

The enemy is coming like clouds. (4:13)

He is coming to destroy Judah.
The cities of Judah will be left in ruins,
    and no one will live in them.
⁸ So put on sackcloth, and weep and wail
    because the fierce anger of the LORD
    has not turned away from Judah.

⁹ The LORD said, "On that day kings and officials will lose their courage; priests will be shocked and prophets will be astonished."

¹⁰ Then I said, "Sovereign LORD, you have completely deceived the people of Jerusalem! You have said there would be peace, but a sword is at their throats."

¹¹ The time is coming when the people of Jerusalem will be told that a scorching wind is blowing in from the desert toward them. It will not be a gentle wind that only blows away the chaff— ¹²the wind that comes at the LORD's command will be much stronger than that! It is the LORD himself who is pronouncing judgment on his people.

Judah Is Surrounded by Enemies

¹³ Look, the enemy is coming like clouds. Their war chariots are like a whirlwind, and their horses are faster than eagles. We are lost! We are doomed!

¹⁴ Jerusalem, wash the evil from your heart, so that you may be saved. How long will you go on thinking sinful thoughts?

¹⁵ Messengers from the city of Dan and from the hills of Ephraim announce the bad news. ¹⁶ They have come to warn the nations and to tell Jerusalem that enemies are coming from a country far away. These enemies will shout against the cities of Judah ¹⁷and will surround Jerusalem like men guarding a field, because her people have rebelled against the LORD. The LORD has spoken.

¹⁸ Judah, you have brought this on yourself by the way you have lived and by the things you have done. Your sin has caused this suffering; it has stabbed you through the heart.

Jeremiah's Sorrow for His People

¹⁹ The pain! I can't bear the pain!
    My heart! My heart is beating wildly!
    I can't keep quiet;
    I hear the trumpets
        and the shouts of battle.
²⁰ One disaster follows another;
        the whole country is left in ruins.
    Suddenly our tents are destroyed;
        their curtains are torn to pieces.
²¹ How long must I see the battle raging
        and hear the blasts of trumpets?
²² The LORD says, "My people are stupid;
        they don't know me.
    They are like foolish children;
        they have no understanding.
    They are experts at doing what is evil,
        but failures at doing what is good."

Jeremiah's Vision of the Coming Destruction

²³ I looked at the earth—it was a barren
        waste;
    at the sky—there was no light.
²⁴ I looked at the mountains—they were
        shaking,
    and the hills were rocking back and
        forth.
²⁵ I saw that there were no people;
        even the birds had flown away.
²⁶ The fertile land had become a desert;
        its cities were in ruins
    because of the LORD's fierce anger.

(²⁷ The LORD has said that the whole earth will become a wasteland, but that he will not completely destroy it.)

Jeremiah

Pray It!

Do You Really Mean It?

In one of his prophecies, Jeremiah says, "Even though you claim to worship the LORD, / you do not mean what you say" (Jeremiah 5:2). Do these words apply to us? If we really worship the Lord, then when we go to Mass or participate in a prayer service, do we really pay attention to what we are saying?

It is so easy to mouth the familiar words of prayers we hear every day. But we can do better than that. If we are truly worshiping the Lord, we have to put our heart and soul into it. And we have to live it. Say each of these prayers slowly and try to put meaning into every word:

- "Lamb of God, you take away the sins of the world, have mercy on us."
- "For yours is the kingdom and the power and the glory, now and forever."
- "Thanks be to God."

— Jeremiah 5:2

28 The earth will mourn;
　　the sky will grow dark.
　The LORD has spoken
　　and will not change his mind.
　He has made his decision
　　and will not turn back.
29 At the noise of the cavalry and archers
　　everyone will run away.
　Some will run to the forest;
　　others will climb up among the
　　　rocks.
　Every town will be left empty,
　　and no one will live in them again.
30 Jerusalem, you are doomed!
　　Why do you dress in scarlet?
　　Why do you put on jewelry and paint
　　　your eyes?
　You are making yourself beautiful for
　　　nothing!
　Your lovers have rejected you
　　and want to kill you.
31 I heard a cry, like a woman in labor,
　　a scream like a woman bearing her first
　　　child.
　It was the cry of Jerusalem gasping for
　　　breath,
　　stretching out her hand and saying,
　"I am doomed!
　　They are coming to kill me!"

The Sin of Jerusalem

5 ¹People of Jerusalem, run through your
　　streets!
　Look around! See for yourselves!
　Search the marketplaces!
　Can you find one person
　　who does what is right
　　and tries to be faithful to God?
　If you can, the LORD will forgive
　　Jerusalem.
² Even though you claim to worship the
　　LORD,
　　you do not mean what you say.
³ Surely the LORD looks for faithfulness.
　He struck you, but you paid no attention;
　　he crushed you, but you refused to
　　　learn.
　You were stubborn and would not turn
　　　from your sins.
⁴ Then I thought, "These are only the poor
　　and ignorant.
　They behave foolishly;
　　they don't know what their God
　　　requires,
　　what the LORD wants them to do.
⁵ I will go to the people in power
　　and talk with them.
　Surely they know what their God
　　　requires,
　　what the LORD wants them to do."

But all of them have rejected the LORD's
authority
and refuse to obey him.
6 That is why lions from the forest will kill
them;
wolves from the desert will tear them
to pieces,
and leopards will prowl through their
towns.
If those people go out, they will be torn
apart
because their sins are numerous
and time after time they have turned
from God.
7 The LORD asked, "Why should I forgive
the sins of my people?
They have abandoned me
and have worshiped gods that are not
real.
I fed my people until they were full,
but they committed adultery
and spent their time with prostitutes.
8 They were like well-fed stallions wild
with desire,
each lusting for his neighbor's wife.
9 Shouldn't I punish them for these
things
and take revenge on a nation such as
this?
10 I will send enemies to cut down my
people's vineyards,
but not to destroy them completely.
I will tell them to strip away the branches,
because those branches are not mine.
11 The people of Israel and Judah
have betrayed me completely.
I, the LORD, have spoken."

The LORD Rejects Israel

12 The LORD's people have denied him
and have said, "He won't really do anything.[d]
We won't have hard times; we won't have
war or famine." 13-14 They have said that the
prophets are nothing but windbags and that
they have no message from the LORD. The

LORD God Almighty said to me, "Jeremiah,
because these people have said such things,
I will make my words like a fire in your
mouth. The people will be like wood, and
the fire will burn them up."

15 People of Israel, the LORD is bringing a
nation from far away to attack you. It is a
strong and ancient nation, a nation whose
language you do not know. 16 Their archers
are mighty soldiers who kill without mercy.
17 They will devour your crops and your
food; they will kill your sons and your
daughters. They will slaughter your flocks
and your herds and destroy your vines and
fig trees. The fortified cities in which you
trust will be destroyed by their army.

18 The LORD says, "Yet even in those days
I will not completely destroy my people.
19 When they ask why I did all these things,
tell them, Jeremiah, that just as they turned
away from me and served foreign gods in
their own land, so they will serve strangers
in a land that is not theirs."

God Warns His People

20 The LORD says, "Tell the descendants
of Jacob, tell the people of Judah: 21 Pay
attention, you foolish and stupid people,
who have eyes, but cannot see, and have
ears, but cannot hear. 22 I am the LORD;
why don't you fear me? Why don't you
tremble before me? I placed the sand as the
boundary of the sea, a permanent boundary
that it cannot cross. The sea may toss, but it
cannot go beyond it; the waves may roar,
but they cannot break through. 23 But you
people! You are stubborn and rebellious;
you have turned aside and left me. 24 You
never thought to honor me, even though I
send the autumn rains and the spring rains
and give you the harvest season each year.
25 Instead, your sins have kept these good
things from you.
26 "Evildoers live among my people; they
lie in wait like those who lay nets to catch

---

d **5:12** He won't . . . anything; *or* We don't want anything to do with him.
5:21 Isa 6:9, 10; Ezek 12:2; Mk 8:18   **5:22** Job 38:8–11

God talks about people "who have eyes, but cannot see, and have ears, but
cannot hear" *(Jeremiah 5:20)*. **What do you think God means?**

birds,*e* but they have set their traps to catch people. 27Just as a hunter fills a cage with birds, they have filled their houses with loot. That is why they are powerful and rich, 28why they are fat and well fed. There is no limit to their evil deeds. They do not give orphans their rights or show justice to the oppressed.

29"But I, the LORD, will punish them for these things; I will take revenge on this nation. 30A terrible and shocking thing has happened in the land: 31prophets speak nothing but lies; priests rule as the prophets command, and my people offer no objections. But what will they do when it all comes to an end?"

Jerusalem Is Surrounded by Enemies

6 1People of Benjamin, run for safety! Escape from Jerusalem! Sound the trumpet in Tekoa and build a signal fire in Beth Haccherem. Disaster and destruction are about to come from the north. 2The city of Zion is beautiful, but it will be destroyed; 3kings will camp there with their armies. They will pitch their tents around the city, and each of them will camp wherever they want. 4They will say, "Prepare to attack Jerusalem! Get ready! We'll attack at noon!" But then they will say, "It's too late, the day is almost over, and the evening shadows are growing long. 5We'll attack by night; we'll destroy the city's fortresses."

6The LORD Almighty has ordered these kings to cut down trees and build mounds in order to besiege Jerusalem. He has said, "I will punish this city because it is full of oppression. 7As a well keeps its water fresh, so Jerusalem keeps its evil fresh. I hear violence and destruction in the city; sickness and wounds are all I see. 8People of Jerusalem, let these troubles be a warning to you, or else I will abandon you; I will turn your city into a desert, a place where no one lives."

Rebellious Israel

9The LORD Almighty said to me, "Israel will be stripped clean like a vineyard from which every grape has been picked. So you must rescue everyone you can while there is still time."

10I answered, "Who would listen to me if I spoke to them and warned them? They are stubborn and refuse to listen to your message; they laugh at what you tell me to say. 11Your anger against them burns in me too, LORD, and I can't hold it in any longer."

Then the LORD said to me, "Pour out my anger on the children in the streets and on the gatherings of the young people. Husbands and wives will be taken away, and even the very old will not be spared. 12Their houses will be given to others, and so will their fields and their wives. I am going to punish the people of this land. 13Everyone, great and small, tries to make money dishonestly; even prophets and priests cheat the people. 14They act as if my people's wounds were only scratches. 'All is well,' they say, when all is not well. 15Were they ashamed because they did these disgusting things? No, they were not at all ashamed; they don't even know how to blush. And so they will fall as others have fallen; when I punish them, that will be the end of them. I, the LORD, have spoken."

Israel Rejects God's Way

16The LORD said to his people, "Stand at the crossroads and look. Ask for the ancient paths and where the best road is. Walk in it, and you will live in peace."

But they said, "No, we will not!" 17Then the LORD appointed sentries to listen for the trumpet's warning. But they said, "We will not listen."

18So the LORD said, "Listen, you nations, and learn what is going to happen to my people. 19Listen, earth! As punishment for all

e 5:26 Probable text they . . . birds; Hebrew unclear.
6:14 Ezek 13:10   **6:12–15** Jer 8:10–12

their schemes I am bringing ruin on these people, because they have rejected my teaching and have not obeyed my words. 20 What do I care about the incense they bring me from Sheba, or the spices from a distant land? I will not accept their offerings or be pleased with their sacrifices. 21 And so I will make these people stumble and fall. Parents and children will die, and so will friends and neighbors."

Invasion from the North

22 The LORD says, "People are coming from a country in the north; a mighty nation far away is preparing for war. 23 They have taken up their bows and swords; they are cruel and merciless. They sound like the roaring sea, as they ride their horses. They are ready for battle against Jerusalem."

24 "We have heard the news," say the people of Jerusalem, "and our hands hang limp; we are seized by anguish and pain like a woman in labor. 25 We don't dare go to the countryside or walk on the roads, because our enemies are armed and terror is all around us."

"We have heard the news, . . . and our hands hang limp." (6:24)

26 The LORD says to his people, "Put on sackcloth and roll in ashes. Mourn with bitter tears as you would for an only child, because the one who comes to destroy you will suddenly attack. 27 Jeremiah, test my

people, as you would test metal, and find out what they are like. 28 They are all stubborn rebels, hard as bronze and iron. They are all corrupt, going around and spreading gossip. 29 The furnace burns fiercely, but the waste metals do not melt and run off. It is useless to go on refining my people, because those who are evil are not taken away. 30 They will be called worthless dross, because I, the LORD, have rejected them."

Jeremiah Preaches in the Temple

7 1-3 The LORD sent me to the gate of the Temple where the people of Judah went in to worship. He told me to stand there and announce what the LORD Almighty, the God of Israel, had to say to them: "Change the way you are living and the things you are doing, and I will let you go on living here. 4 Stop believing those deceitful words, 'We are safe! This is the LORD's Temple, this is the LORD's Temple, this is the LORD's Temple!'

5 "Change the way you are living and stop doing the things you are doing. Be fair in your treatment of one another. 6 Stop taking advantage of aliens, orphans, and widows. Stop killing innocent people in this land. Stop worshiping other gods, for that will destroy you. 7 If you change, I will let you go on living here in the land which I gave your ancestors as a permanent possession.

8 "Look, you put your trust in deceitful words. 9 You steal, murder, commit adultery, tell lies under oath, offer sacrifices to Baal, and worship gods that you had not known before. 10 You do these things I hate, and then you come and stand in my presence, in my own Temple, and say, 'We are safe!' 11 Do you think that my Temple is a hiding place for robbers? I have seen what you are doing. 12 Go to Shiloh,f the first place where I chose to be worshiped, and see what I did to it because of the sins of my people Israel. 13 You have committed all these sins, and even though I spoke to you over and over again, you refused to listen. You would not answer when I called you. 14 And so, what I did to Shiloh I will do to this Temple of

This Is the Lord's Temple

The Lord sends Jeremiah to the Temple to deliver a strong message. The people would come to the Temple and say: "We are safe! This is the LORD's Temple" (Jeremiah 7:4). And yet, they would spend the rest of their time breaking almost every commandment possible. They were taking advantage of widows, orphans, and aliens (immigrants)—the most vulnerable (defenseless) groups in Israelite society. They steal, murder, and worship false gods. Yet they still go to God's Temple pretending to be devout followers of God.

It is this hypocritical attitude that God sends Jeremiah to preach against. The people are making a mockery of the Temple by not living holy lives. Sorry, God says through Jeremiah, but it doesn't work that way. Temples, churches, and mosques are holy places and the people who worship in them are called to live holy lives. You can do this too by living the Gospel message you hear at Sunday Mass all week long.

— Jeremiah 7:1–15

mine, in which you trust. Here in this place that I gave to your ancestors and you, I will do the same thing that I did to Shiloh. [15]I will drive you out of my sight as I drove out your relatives, the people of Israel. I, the LORD, have spoken."

The People's Disobedience

[16]The LORD said, "Jeremiah, do not pray for these people. Do not cry or pray on their behalf; do not plead with me, for I will not listen to you. [17]Don't you see what they are doing in the cities of Judah and in the streets of Jerusalem? [18]The children gather firewood, the men build fires, and the women mix dough to bake cakes for the goddess they call the Queen of Heaven. They also pour out offerings of wine to other gods, in order to hurt me. [19]But am I really the one they are hurting? No, they are hurting themselves and bringing shame on themselves. [20]And so I, the Sovereign LORD, will pour out my fierce anger on this Temple. I will pour it out on people and animals alike, and even on the trees and the crops. My anger will be like a fire that no one can put out.

[21]"My people, some sacrifices you burn completely on the altar, and some you are permitted to eat. But what I, the LORD, say is that you might as well eat them all. [22]I gave your ancestors no commands about burnt offerings or any other kinds of sacrifices when I brought them out of Egypt. [23]But I did command them to obey me, so that I would be their God and they would be my people. And I told them to live the way I had commanded them, so that things would go well for them. [24]But they did not obey or pay any attention. Instead, they did whatever their stubborn and evil hearts told them to do, and they became worse instead of better. [25]From the day that your ancestors came out of Egypt until this very day I have kept on sending to you my servants, the prophets. [26]Yet no one listened or paid any attention. Instead, you became more stubborn and rebellious than your ancestors.

[27]"So, Jeremiah, you will speak all these words to my people, but they will not listen to you; you will call them, but they will not answer. [28]You will tell them that their nation does not obey me, the LORD their God, or learn from their punishment. Faithfulness is dead. No longer is it even talked about.

Sinful Deeds in Hinnom Valley

[29]"Mourn, people of Jerusalem;
    cut off your hair and throw it away.

Sing a funeral song on the hilltops,
　　because I, the LORD, am angry
　　and have rejected my people.

30 "The people of Judah have done an evil
thing. They have placed their idols, which I
hate, in my Temple and have defiled it. 31 In
Hinnom Valley they have built an altar called
Topheth, so that they can sacrifice their sons
and daughters in the fire. I did not command
them to do this—it did not even enter my
mind. 32 And so, the time will come when it
will no longer be called Topheth or Hinnom
Valley, but Slaughter Valley. They will bury
people there because there will be nowhere
else to bury them. 33 The corpses will be
food for the birds and wild animals, and
there will be no one to scare them off.
34 The land will become a desert. In the
cities of Judah and in the streets of Jerusalem
I will put an end to the sounds of joy and
gladness and to the happy sounds of wedding feasts.

8 1 "At that time the bones of the kings
and of the officials of Judah, as well as
the bones of the priests, of the prophets, and
of the other people who lived in Jerusalem,
will be taken out of their graves. 2 Instead of
being gathered and buried, their bones will
be like manure lying on the ground. They
will be spread out before the sun, the moon,
and the stars, which these people have loved
and served, and which they have consulted
and worshiped. 3 And the people of this evil
nation who survive, who live in the places
where I have scattered them, will prefer to
die rather than to go on living. I, the LORD
Almighty, have spoken."

Sin and Punishment

4 The LORD told me to say to his people,
"When someone falls down, doesn't he get
back up? If someone misses the road, doesn't
he turn back? 5 Why then, my people, do
you turn away from me without ever turning back? You cling to your idols and refuse

"You cling to your idols." (8:5)

to return to me. 6 I listened carefully, but you
did not speak the truth. Not one of you has
been sorry for your wickedness; not one of
you has asked, 'What have I done wrong?'
Each of you keep on going your own way,
like a horse rushing into battle. 7 Even storks
know when it is time to return; doves, swallows, and thrushes know when it is time to
migrate. But, my people, you do not know
the laws by which I rule you. 8 How can you
say that you are wise and that you know my
laws? Look, the laws have been changed by
dishonest scribes. 9 Your wise men are put to
shame; they are confused and trapped. They
have rejected my words; what wisdom do
they have now? 10 So I will give their fields
to new owners and their wives to other
men. Everyone, great and small, tries to make
money dishonestly. Even prophets and priests
cheat the people. 11 They act as if my people's wounds were only scratches. 'All is well,'
they say, when all is not well. 12 My people,
were you ashamed because you did these

7:31 a 2 Kings 23:10; Jer 32:35; b Lev 18:21   7:34 Jer 16:9; 25:10; Bar 2:23; Rev 18:23   8:11 Ezek 13:10
8:10–12 Jer 6:12–15

Did you know that child sacrifice *(Jeremiah 7:31)* **was still practiced in Old
Testament times?**

Jeremiah

disgusting things? No, you were not ashamed at all; you don't even know how to blush! And so you will fall as others have fallen; when I punish you, that will be the end of you. I, the LORD, have spoken.

13 "I wanted to gather my people, as a farmer gathers a harvest; but they are like a vine with no grapes, like a fig tree with no figs; even the leaves have withered. Therefore, I have allowed outsiders to take over the land." *g*

Like a vine with no grapes (8:13)

14 "Why are we sitting still?" God's people ask. "Come on, we will run to the fortified cities and die there. The LORD our God has condemned us to die; he has given us poison to drink, because we have sinned against him. 15 We hoped for peace and a time of healing, but it was no use; terror came instead. 16 Our enemies are already in the city of Dan; we hear the snorting of their horses. The whole land trembles when their horses neigh. Our enemies have come to destroy our land and everything in it, our city and all its people."

17 "Watch out!" the LORD says, "I am sending snakes among you, poisonous snakes that cannot be charmed, and they will bite you."

Jeremiah's Sorrow for His People

18 My sorrow cannot be healed; *h*
    I am sick at heart.

I am sick at heart. (8:18)

19 Listen! Throughout the land
    I hear my people crying out,
"Is the LORD no longer in Zion?
    Is Zion's king no longer there?"
The LORD, their king, replies,
"Why have you made me angry by
        worshiping your idols
    and by bowing down to your useless
        foreign gods?"
20 The people cry out,
"The summer is gone, the harvest is over,
    but we have not been saved."

21 My heart has been crushed
    because my people are crushed;
    I mourn; I am completely dismayed.
22 Is there no medicine in Gilead? *i*
    Are there no doctors there?
    Why, then, have my people not been
        healed?

9 1 I wish my head were a well of water,
        and my eyes a fountain of tears,
    so that I could cry day and night
        for my people who have been killed.
2 I wish I had a place to stay in the desert
        where I could get away from my
        people.
    They are all unfaithful,
        a mob of traitors.

g 8:13 Therefore . . . land; Hebrew unclear.   h 8:18 Probable text My sorrow . . . healed; Hebrew unclear.
i 8:22 GILEAD: A region east of the Jordan, famous for plants that were used for medicinal purposes.

Jeremiah expresses his sorrow for his people's suffering, caused because of their sins. What are the sins in our society that cause people to suffer?

³ They are always ready to tell lies;
  dishonesty instead of truth rules the land.

The LORD says,
"My people do one evil thing after
  another
  and do not acknowledge me as their
    God."

⁴ Everyone must be on guard against their
  friends,
  and no one can trust their relatives;
for all relatives are as deceitful as Jacob,
  and everyone slanders their friends.
⁵⁻⁶ They all mislead their friends,
  and no one tells the truth;
they have taught their tongues to lie
  and will not give up their sinning.
They do one violent thing after another,
  and one deceitful act follows another.

The LORD says that his people reject him.
⁷ Because of this the LORD Almighty says,
"I will refine my people like metal
  and put them to the test.
My people have done evil—
  what else can I do with them?
⁸ Their tongues are like deadly arrows;
  they always tell lies.
Everyone speaks friendly words to their
  neighbors,
  but they are really setting a trap for
    them.
⁹ Will I not punish them for these things?
  Will I not take revenge on a nation like
    this?
I, the LORD, have spoken."

¹⁰ I said, "I will mourn for the mountains
  and weep for the pastures,
because they have dried up,
  and no one travels through them.
The sound of livestock is no longer
  heard;
  birds and wild animals have fled and
    gone."

¹¹ The LORD says, "I will make Jerusalem a
  pile of ruins,
  a place where jackals live;
the cities of Judah will become a desert,
  a place where no one lives."

¹² I asked, " LORD, why is the land devastated and dry as a desert, so that no one trav-

The Sharp Tongue

Have you ever seen an arrowhead? In many parts of the United States, particularly near American Indian hunting grounds, arrowheads are fairly common. Chiseled by hand out of small rocks and used as the tips for arrows, they were very sharp and effective. Now, imagine someone's tongue being shaped like an arrowhead. All of us know that our tongues can be deadly weapons because we can use them to ruin someone's reputation or to hurt someone by making fun of him or her. Jeremiah says the tongues of people of his time are like deadly arrows (Jeremiah 9:8). Apparently, things haven't changed all that much in 2,500 years! The next time you are tempted to criticize someone, picture your tongue as an arrow that will be shot at someone else. Think about the harm that arrow can do, and stop before you let it loose!

— Jeremiah 9:8

els through it? Who is wise enough to understand this? To whom have you explained it so that they can tell others?"

¹³ The LORD answered, "This has happened because my people have abandoned the teaching that I gave them. They have not obeyed me or done what I told them. ¹⁴ Instead, they have been stubborn and have worshiped the idols of Baal as their ancestors taught them to do. ¹⁵ So then, listen to what I, the LORD Almighty, the God of Israel, will do: I will give my people bitter plants to eat and poison to drink. ¹⁶ I will scatter them among nations that neither they nor their ancestors have heard about, and I will send

Jeremiah

armies against them until I have completely destroyed them."

The People of Jerusalem Cry Out for Help

17 The LORD Almighty said,
"Think about what is happening!
Call for the mourners to come,
    for the women who sing funeral songs."

18 The people said,
"Tell them to hurry and sing a funeral
        song for us,
    until our eyes fill with tears,
    and our eyelids are wet from crying."

19 Listen to the sound of crying in Zion:
"We are ruined!
    We are completely disgraced!
We must leave our land;
    our homes have been torn down."

20 I said,
"Listen to the LORD, you women,
    and pay attention to his words.
Teach your daughters how to mourn,
    and your friends how to sing a funeral
        song.
21 Death has come in through our windows
        and entered our palaces;
    it has cut down the children in the streets
        and the young men in the
            marketplaces.
22 Dead bodies are scattered everywhere,
        like piles of manure on the fields,
    like grain cut and left behind by the
            reapers,
    grain that no one gathers.
This is what the LORD has told me to say."

23 The LORD says,
"The wise should not boast of their
            wisdom,
    nor the strong of their strength,
    nor the rich of their wealth.
24 If any want to boast,
    they should boast that they know and
            understand me,
    because my love is constant,
    and I do what is just and right.

These are the things that please me.
I, the LORD, have spoken."

25-26 The LORD says, "The time is coming when I will punish the people of Egypt, Judah, Edom, Ammon, Moab, and the desert people, who have their hair cut short.^j All these people are circumcised, but have not kept the covenant it symbolizes. None of these people and none of the people of Israel have kept my covenant."

Idolatry and True Worship

10 1 People of Israel, listen to the message that the LORD has for you. 2 He says,
"Do not follow the ways of other nations;
    do not be disturbed by unusual sights
        in the sky,
    even though other nations are terrified.
3 The religion of these people is worthless.
A tree is cut down in the forest;
    it is carved by the tools of the
        woodworker
4   and decorated with silver and gold.
It is fastened down with nails
    to keep it from falling over.
5 Such idols are like scarecrows in a field of
        melons;
    they cannot speak;
they have to be carried
    because they cannot walk.
Do not be afraid of them:
    they can cause you no harm,
    and they can do you no good."

They cannot speak; they have to be carried. (10:5)

---

j **9:25–26** HAIR CUT SHORT: *The desert people cut their hair short in honor of their god, a pagan practice forbidden to the Israelites (see Lev 19:27).*
9:24 1 Cor 1:31; 2 Cor 10:17

6 LORD, there is no one like you;
   you are mighty,
   and your name is great and powerful.
7 Who would not honor you, the king of
      all nations?
   You deserve to be honored.
   There is no one like you
      among all the wise men of the nations
      or among any of their kings.
8 All of them are stupid and foolish.
   What can they learn from wooden
      idols?[k]
9 Their idols are covered with silver from
      Spain
   and with gold from Uphaz,
      all the work of artists;
   they are dressed in violet and purple cloth
      woven by skilled weavers.
10 But you, LORD, are the true God,
   you are the living God
      and the eternal king.
   When you are angry, the world trembles;
      the nations cannot endure your anger.

(11 You people must tell them that the
gods who did not make the earth and the
sky will be destroyed. They will no longer
exist anywhere on earth.)

A Hymn of Praise to God

12 The LORD made the earth by his power;
   by his wisdom he created the world
      and stretched out the heavens.
13 At his command the waters above the sky[l]
      roar;
   he brings clouds from the ends of the
      earth.
   He makes lightning flash in the rain
      and sends the wind from his storeroom.
14 At the sight of this, people feel stupid and
      senseless;
   those who make idols are disillusioned,
   because the gods they make are false
      and lifeless.

15 They are worthless and should be
      despised;
   they will be destroyed when the LORD
      comes to deal with them.
16 The God of Jacob is not like them;
   he is the one who made everything,
   and he has chosen Israel to be his very
      own people.
   The LORD Almighty is his name.

The Coming Exile

17 People of Jerusalem, you are under
siege! Gather up your belongings. 18 The
LORD is going to throw you out of this land;
he is going to crush you until not one of
you is left. The LORD has spoken.
19 The people of Jerusalem cried out,
   "How badly we are hurt!
   Our wounds will not heal.
   And we thought this was something we
      could endure!
20 Our tents are ruined;
   the ropes that held them have
      broken.
   Our children have all gone away;
   there is no one left to put up our tents
      again;
   there is no one to hang their
      curtains."

21 I answered, "Our leaders are stupid;
   they do not ask the LORD for guidance.
   This is why they have failed,
   and our people have been scattered.
22 Listen! News has come!
   There is a great commotion in a nation
      to the north;
   its army will turn the cities of Judah into
      a desert,
   a place where jackals live."

23 LORD, I know that none of us are in
   charge of our own destiny;
   none of us have control over our own
      life.

---

k 10:8 What can . . . idols?; or What their idols teach is worthless.   l 10:13 WATERS ABOVE THE SKY: See Gen
1:6–8.
10:7 Rev 15:4

Jeremiah

Jeremiah says that Jerusalem is "under siege" (Jeremiah 10:17). **This is often
how an enemy army would defeat a city. Can you describe the process?**

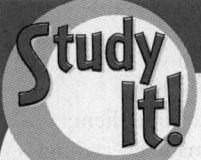

Breaking the Covenant

Why is God so angry with his Chosen People? Why are all these bad things happening? Jeremiah, chapter 11, explains that it is because the Israelites have broken God's Covenant with them. This covenant is the sacred promise or commitment between God and his people. Several covenants are described in the book of Genesis: these include one between God and Noah, one between God and Abraham, and another between God and Jacob.

But the most important covenant was the covenant God made with Moses and the Israelite people at Mount Sinai. You may want to read about that covenant again in Exodus, chapter 24. God's part of the Sinai Covenant was that he would protect the Israelites and give them their own land. Their part of the Sinai Covenant is summarized in the Ten Commandments. Can you see how the Israelites are not keeping their part of the Covenant?

— Jeremiah 11:1–5

24 Correct your people, LORD,
    but do not be too hard on us
    or punish us when you are angry;
    that would be the end of us.
25 Turn your anger on the nations that do
    not worship you
    and on the people who reject you.
They have killed your people;
    they have destroyed us completely
    and left our country in ruins.

Jeremiah and the Covenant

11 ¹The LORD said to me, ²"Listen to the terms of the covenant. Tell the people of Judah and of Jerusalem ³that I, the LORD God of Israel, have placed a curse on everyone who does not obey the terms of this covenant. ⁴It is the covenant I made with their ancestors when I brought them out of Egypt, the land that was like a blazing furnace to them. I told them to obey me and to do everything that I had commanded. I told them that if they obeyed, they would be my people and I would be their God. ⁵Then I would keep the promise I made to their ancestors that I would give them the rich and fertile land which they now have."

I said, "Yes, LORD."

⁶Then the LORD said to me, "Go to the cities of Judah and to the streets of Jerusalem. Proclaim my message there and tell the people to listen to the terms of the covenant and to obey them. ⁷When I brought their ancestors out of Egypt, I solemnly warned them to obey me, and I have kept on warning the people until this day. ⁸But they did not listen or obey. Instead, everyone continued to be as stubborn and evil as ever. I had commanded them to keep the covenant, but they refused. So I brought on them all the punishments described in it."

⁹Then the LORD said to me, "The people of Judah and of Jerusalem are plotting against me. ¹⁰They have gone back to the sins of their ancestors, who refused to do what I said; they have worshiped other gods. Both Israel and Judah have broken the covenant that I made with their ancestors. ¹¹So now I, the LORD, warn them that I am going to bring destruction on them, and they will not escape. And when they cry out to me for help, I will not listen to them. ¹²Then the people of Judah and of Jerusalem will go to the gods to whom they offer sacrifices and will cry out to them for help. But those gods will not be able to save them when this destruction comes. ¹³The people of Judah have as many gods as they have cities, and the inhabitants of Jerusalem have set up as

"When I brought their ancestors out of Egypt, I solemnly warned them to obey me, and I have kept on warning the people until this day" (Jeremiah 11:7).

many altars for sacrifices to that disgusting god Baal as there are streets in the city. ¹⁴Jeremiah, don't pray to me or plead with me on behalf of these people. When they are in trouble and call to me for help, I will not listen to them."

¹⁵The LORD says, "The people I love are doing evil things. What right do they have to be in my Temple? Do they think they can prevent disaster by making promises^m and by offering animal sacrifices? Will they then rejoice? ¹⁶I once called them a leafy olive tree, full of beautiful fruit; but now, with a roar like thunder I will set its leaves on fire and break its branches.

I will set its leaves on fire. (11:16)

¹⁷"I, the LORD Almighty, planted Israel and Judah; but now I threaten them with disaster. They have brought this on themselves because they have done wrong; they have made me angry by offering sacrifices to Baal."

A Plot against Jeremiah's Life

¹⁸The LORD informed me of the plots that my enemies were making against me. ¹⁹I was like a trusting lamb taken out to be killed, and I did not know that it was against me that they were planning evil things. They were saying, "Let's chop down the tree while it is still healthy;^n let's kill him so that no one will remember him any more."

²⁰Then I prayed, "Almighty LORD, you are a just judge; you test people's thoughts

and feelings. I have placed my cause in your hands; so let me watch you take revenge on these people."

²¹The people of Anathoth wanted me killed, and they told me that they would kill me if I kept on proclaiming the LORD's message. ²²So the LORD Almighty said, "I will punish them! Their young men will be killed in war; their children will die of starvation. ²³I have set a time for bringing disaster on the people of Anathoth, and when that time comes, none of them will survive."

Jeremiah Questions the LORD

12 ¹"LORD, if I argued my case with you,
   you would prove to be right.
Yet I must question you about matters of justice.
Why are the wicked so prosperous?
   Why do dishonest people succeed?

---

^m **11:15** *One ancient translation* promises; *Hebrew* many. with its bread.
11:20 Wis 1:6–9

^n **11:19** *Probable text* while it is still healthy; *Hebrew*

2 You plant them, and they take root;
    they grow and bear fruit.
They always speak well of you,
    yet they do not really care about you.
3 But, LORD, you know me;
    you see what I do
    and how I love you.
Drag these evil people away like sheep to
    be butchered;
    guard them until it is time for them to
    be slaughtered.
4 How long will our land be dry,
    and the grass in every field be
    withered?
Animals and birds are dying
    because of the wickedness of our
    people,
    people who say, 'God doesn't see what
    we are doing.' "*o*

5 The LORD said,
"Jeremiah, if you get tired racing against
    people,
    how can you race against horses?
If you can't even stand up in open
    country,
    how will you manage in the jungle by
    the Jordan?
6 Even your relatives, members of your own
    family, have betrayed you;
    they join in the attacks against you.
Do not trust them, even though they
    speak friendly words."

The LORD's Sorrow because of His People

7 The LORD says,
"I have abandoned Israel;
    I have rejected my chosen nation.
I have given the people I love
    into the power of their enemies.
8 My chosen people have turned against
    me;
    like a lion in the forest
    they have roared at me,
    and so I hate them.
9 My chosen people are like a bird
    attacked from all sides by hawks.
Call the wild animals
    to come and join in the feast!

10 Many foreign rulers have destroyed my
    vineyard;
    they have trampled down my fields;
    they have turned my lovely land into a
    desert.
11 They have made it a wasteland;
    it lies desolate before me.
The whole land has become a desert,
    and no one cares.
12 Across all the desert highlands
    people have come to plunder.
I have sent war to destroy the entire land;
    no one can live in peace.
13 My people planted wheat, but gathered
    weeds;
    they have worked hard, but got nothing
    for it.
Because of my fierce anger
    their crops have failed."

The LORD's Promise to Israel's Neighbors

14 The LORD says, "I have something to say about Israel's neighbors who have ruined the land I gave to my people Israel. I will take those wicked people away from their countries like an uprooted plant, and I will rescue Judah from them. 15 But after I have taken them away, I will have mercy on them; I will bring each nation back to its own land and to its own country. 16 If with all their hearts they will accept the religion of my people and will swear, 'As the LORD lives'— as they once taught my people to swear by Baal—then they will also be a part of my people and will prosper. 17 But if any nation will not obey, then I will completely uproot it and destroy it. I, the LORD, have spoken."

The Linen Shorts

13 1 The LORD told me to go and buy myself some linen shorts and to put them on; but he told me not to put them in water. 2 So I bought them and put them on. 3 Then the LORD spoke to me again and said, 4 "Go to the Euphrates River and hide the shorts in a hole in the rocks." 5 So I went and hid them near the Euphrates.

---

o **12:4** *Some ancient translations* what we are doing; *Hebrew* our latter end.

⁶Some time later the LORD told me to go back to the Euphrates and get the shorts. ⁷So I went back, and when I found the place where I had hidden them, I saw that they were ruined and were no longer any good.

⁸Then the LORD spoke to me again. He said, ⁹"This is how I will destroy the pride of Judah and the great pride of Jerusalem. ¹⁰These evil people have refused to obey me. They have been as stubborn and wicked as ever, and have worshiped and served other gods. So then, they will become like these shorts that are no longer any good. ¹¹Just as shorts fit tightly around the waist, so I intended all the people of Israel and Judah to hold tightly to me. I did this so that they would be my people and would bring praise and honor to my name; but they would not obey me."

The Wine Jar

¹²The LORD God said to me, "Jeremiah, tell the people of Israel that every wine jar should be filled with wine. They will answer that they know every wine jar should be filled with wine. ¹³Then tell them that I, the LORD, am going to fill the people in this land with wine until they are drunk: the kings, who are David's descendants, the priests, the prophets, and all the people of Jerusalem. ¹⁴Then I will smash them like jars against one another, old and young alike. No pity, compassion, or mercy will stop me from killing them."

Jeremiah Warns against Pride

¹⁵People of Israel, the LORD has spoken!
    Be humble and listen to him.
¹⁶Honor the LORD, your God,
    before he brings darkness,
    and you stumble on the mountains;
    before he turns into deep darkness
    the light you hoped for.
¹⁷If you will not listen,
    I will cry in secret because of your
        pride;

Clinging to God

A pair of linen shorts isn't exactly your typical biblical image, is it? Some translations use the word *loincloth,* which is the type of underwear men would have worn in Old Testament times. Why would God instruct Jeremiah to use such an image? What's the point?

Think about it. As the passage explains, just as shorts fit tightly around the waist, so God wants the people to cling tightly to him. And after the shorts are hidden in a hole in the rocks, they are ruined by the weather and therefore good for nothing. So the people, through their disobedience, have ruined their relationship with God.

So, there it is: a ruined pair of linen shorts is a prop that Jeremiah can use to get his point across. No doubt it got people's attention! Try to think of anything in your room that could be a symbol of your relationship with God.

— Jeremiah 13:1–11

I will cry bitterly, and my tears will flow
    because the LORD's people have been
    taken away as captives.

¹⁸The LORD said to me, "Tell the king and his mother to come down from their thrones, because their beautiful crowns have fallen from their heads.ᵖ ¹⁹The towns of southern Judah are under siege; no one can

ᵖ **13:18** *Some ancient translations* from their heads; *Hebrew unclear.*

In Jeremiah, chapter 12, can you find examples of how the land itself was affected by people's sin? How have we destroyed or hurt the earth in our time?

get through to them. All the people of Judah have been taken away into exile."

20 Jerusalem, look! Your enemies are coming down from the north! Where are the people entrusted to your care, your people you were so proud of? 21 What will you say when people you thought were your friends conquer you and rule over you?�q You will be in pain like a woman giving birth. 22 If you ask why all this has happened to you—why your clothes have been torn off and you have been raped—it is because your sin is so terrible. 23 Can people change the color of their skin, or a leopard remove its spots? If they could, then you that do nothing but evil could learn to do what is right. 24 The LORD will scatter you like straw that is blown away by the desert wind. 25 He has said that this will be your fate. This is what he has decided to do with you, because you have forgotten him and have trusted in false gods. 26 The LORD himself will strip off your clothes and expose you to shame. 27 He has seen you do the things he hates. He has seen you go after pagan gods on the hills and in the fields, like a man lusting after his neighbor's wife or like a stallion after a mare. People of Jerusalem, you are doomed! When will you ever be pure?

Like straw that is blown away (13:24)

The Terrible Drought

14 1 The LORD said to me concerning the drought,

2 "Judah is in mourning;
     its cities are dying,
   its people lie on the ground in sorrow,
     and Jerusalem cries out for help.
3 The rich people send their servants for
     water;
   they go to the cisterns,
   but find no water;
   they come back with their jars empty.

q **13:21** *Probable text* What . . . over you; *Hebrew unclear.*

They come back with their jars empty. (14:3)

Discouraged and confused,
     they hide their faces.
4 Because there is no rain
     and the ground is dried up,
the farmers are sick at heart;
     they hide their faces.
5 In the field the mother deer
     abandons her newborn fawn
     because there is no grass.
6 The wild donkeys stand on the hilltops
     and pant for breath like jackals;
their eyesight fails them
     because they have no food.
7 My people cry out to me,
     'Even though our sins accuse us,
     help us, LORD, as you have promised.
We have turned away from you many
     times;
     we have sinned against you.
8 You are Israel's only hope;
     you are the one who saves us from
       disaster.
Why are you like a stranger in our land,
     like a traveler who stays for only one
       night?
9 Why are you like someone taken by
     surprise,
     like a soldier powerless to help?
Surely, LORD, you are with us!
     We are your people;
     do not abandon us.' "

Cistern: A type of well that holds rainwater. Cisterns are an important source of water for people in dry lands.

10 The LORD says about these people, "They love to run away from me, and they will not control themselves. So I am not pleased with them. I will remember the wrongs they have done and punish them because of their sins."

11 The LORD said to me, "Do not ask me to help these people. **12** Even if they fast, I will not listen to their cry for help; and even if they offer me burnt offerings and grain offerings, I will not be pleased with them. Instead, I will kill them in war and by starvation and disease."

13 Then I said, "Sovereign LORD, you know that the prophets are telling the people that there will be no war or starvation, because you have promised, they say, that there will be only peace in our land."

14 But the LORD replied, "The prophets are telling lies in my name; I did not send them, nor did I give them any orders or speak one word to them. The visions they talk about have not come from me; their predictions are worthless things that they have imagined. **15** I, the LORD, tell you what I am going to do to those prophets whom I did not send but who speak in my name and say war and starvation will not strike this land—I will kill them in war and by starvation. **16** The people to whom they have said these things will be killed in the same way. Their bodies will be thrown out into the streets of Jerusalem, and there will be no one to bury them. This will happen to all of them—including their wives, their sons, and their daughters. I will make them pay for their wickedness."

17 The LORD commanded me to tell the people about my sorrow and to say:

"May my eyes flow with tears day and
    night,
    may I never stop weeping,
for my people are deeply wounded
    and are badly hurt.
18 When I go out in the fields,
    I see the bodies of men killed in war;
when I go into the towns,
    I see people starving to death.
Prophets and priests carry on their work,
    but they don't know what they are
    doing."ʳ

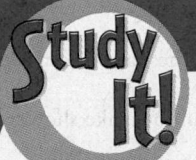

Study It!

False Prophets

One of the reasons Jeremiah was so unpopular is that he preached the truth. He tried to warn the people that bad things would happen to them if they didn't return to the Lord. However, they preferred to listen to other people who called themselves prophets. These prophets told the people what they wanted to hear. But their words did not come from God. So they are called false prophets. As the LORD tells Jeremiah, "The prophets are telling lies in my name" (Jeremiah 14:14).

If the message of a preacher or speaker does not challenge us and only tells us what we want to hear, it is doubtful that these are prophetic words. Check out a more detailed description of false prophets in Jeremiah 23:16–22.

— Jeremiah 14:13–15

The People Plead with the LORD

19 LORD, have you completely rejected Judah?
    Do you hate the people of Zion?
Why have you hurt us so badly
    that we cannot be healed?
We looked for peace, but nothing good
        happened;
    we hoped for healing, but terror came
        instead.
20 We have sinned against you, LORD;
    we confess our own sins
    and the sins of our ancestors.
21 Remember your promises and do not
        despise us;
    do not bring disgrace on Jerusalem,
    the place of your glorious throne.

ʳ **14:18** Prophets . . . doing; *or* Prophets and priests have been dragged away to a land they know nothing about.

Do not break the covenant you made
    with us.
22 None of the idols of the nations can send
    rain;
    the sky by itself cannot make showers
    fall.
We have put our hope in you, O LORD
    our God,
    because you are the one who does
    these things.

Doom for the People of Judah

15 ¹Then the LORD said to me, "Even
if Moses and Samuel were standing
here pleading with me, I would not show
these people any mercy. Make them go
away; make them get out of my sight.
²When they ask you where they should go,
tell them that I have said:
    Some are doomed to die by disease—
        that's where they will go!
    Others are doomed to die in war—
        that's where they will go!
    Some are doomed to die of starvation—
        that's where they will go!
    Others are doomed to be taken away as
        prisoners—
        that's where they will go!
³I, the LORD, have decided that four terrible
things will happen to them: they will be
killed in war; their bodies will be dragged off
by dogs; birds will eat them, and wild animals
will devour what is left over. ⁴I will make all
the people of the world horrified at them
because of what Hezekiah's son Manasseh
did in Jerusalem when he was king of Judah."
⁵The LORD says,
    "Who will pity you, people of Jerusalem,
        and who will grieve over you?
    Who will stop long enough
        to ask how you are?
⁶You people have rejected me;
    you have turned your backs on me.
So I reached out and crushed you
    because I was tired of controlling my
    anger.ˢ
⁷In every town in the land
    I threw you to the wind like straw.

I destroyed you, my people,
    I killed your children
    because you did not stop your evil
    ways.
⁸There are more widows in your land
    than grains of sand by the sea.
I killed your young men in their prime
    and made their mothers suffer.
I suddenly struck them
    with anguish and terror.
⁹The mother who lost her seven children
    has fainted,
    gasping for breath.
Her daylight has turned to darkness;
    she is disgraced and sick at heart.
I will let your enemies kill
    those of you who are still alive.
I, the LORD, have spoken."

Jeremiah Complains to the LORD

¹⁰What an unhappy man I am! Why did
my mother bring me into the world? I have
to quarrel and argue with everyone in the
land. I have not lent any money or borrowed
any; yet everyone curses me. ¹¹LORD, may all
their curses come true if I have not servedᵗ
you well, if I have not pleaded with you on
behalf of my enemies when they were in
trouble and distress. (¹²No one can break
iron, especially the iron from the north that
is mixed with bronze.)

¹³The LORD said to me, "I will send enemies to carry away the wealth and treasures
of my people, in order to punish them for
the sins they have committed throughout
the land. ¹⁴I will make them serve their enemies in a land they know nothing about,
because my anger is like fire, and it will burn
forever."

¹⁵Then I said, " LORD, you understand.
Remember me and help me. Let me have
revenge on those who persecute me. Do not
be so patient with them that they succeed in
killing me. Remember that it is for your sake
that I am insulted. ¹⁶You spoke to me, and I
listened to every word. I belong to you,
LORD God Almighty, and so your words
filled my heart with joy and happiness. ¹⁷I

ˢ 15:6 you because . . . anger; or you; I was tired of feeling sorry for you.   ᵗ 15:11 Probable text LORD, . . .
served; Hebrew unclear.
15:1 a Ex 32:11–14; Num 14:13–19; b 1 Sam 7:5–9   15:2 Rev 13:10   15:4 2 Kings 21:1–16; 2 Chr 33:1–9

Why Me, O Lord?

Check out the conversation between God and Jeremiah in Jeremiah 15:10–21. Jeremiah is unhappy and complains to God. God responds, but Jeremiah has more to say. He has lots of questions for the Lord and doesn't hesitate to ask them. God ends by reassuring Jeremiah that he is not alone. Sometimes that's all we need to know. Think of a time when you sensed God was with you in times of trouble. Are you willing to trust that God is with you even when it seems everyone else is against you?

— Jeremiah 15:10–21

did not spend my time with other people, laughing and having a good time. In obedience to your orders I stayed by myself and was filled with anger. ¹⁸Why do I keep on suffering? Why are my wounds incurable? Why won't they heal? Do you intend to disappoint me like a stream that goes dry in the summer?"

¹⁹To this the LORD replied, "If you return, I will take you back, and you will be my servant again. If instead of talking nonsense you proclaim a worthwhile message, you will be my prophet again. The people will come back to you, and you will not need to go to them. ²⁰I will make you like a solid bronze wall as far as they are concerned. They will fight against you, but they will not defeat you. I will be with you to protect you and keep you safe. ²¹I will rescue you from the power of wicked and violent people. I, the LORD, have spoken."

16:9 Jer 7:34; 25:10; Rev 18:23

The LORD's Will for Jeremiah's Life

16 ¹Again the LORD spoke to me and said, ²"Do not marry or have children in a place like this. ³I will tell you what is going to happen to the children who are born here and to their parents. ⁴They will die of terrible diseases, and no one will mourn for them or bury them. Their bodies will lie like piles of manure on the ground. They will be killed in war or die of starvation, and their bodies will be food for the birds and the wild animals.

⁵"You must not enter a house where there is mourning. Do not grieve for anyone. I will no longer bless my people with peace or show them love and mercy. ⁶The rich and the poor will die in this land, but no one will bury them or mourn for them. Not one of you will gash yourself or shave your head to show your grief. ⁷No one will eat or drink with anyone to offer comfort when a loved one dies. No one will show sympathy, not even for someone who has lost a father or mother.

⁸"Do not enter a house where people are feasting. Do not sit down with them to eat and drink. ⁹Listen to what I, the LORD Almighty, the God of Israel, have to say. I will silence the sounds of joy and gladness and the happy sounds of wedding feasts. The people here will live to see this happen.

¹⁰"When you tell them all this, they will ask you why I have decided to punish them so harshly. They will ask what crime they are guilty of and what sin they have committed against the LORD their God. ¹¹Then tell them that the LORD has said, 'Your ancestors turned away from me and worshiped and served other gods. They abandoned me and did not obey my teachings. ¹²But you have done even worse than your ancestors. All of you are stubborn and evil, and you do not obey me. ¹³So then, I will throw you out of this land into a land that neither you nor your ancestors have ever known. And there

Jeremiah

Moses and Samuel are mentioned at the beginning of Jeremiah, chapter 15. Which of these two men has two books in the Bible named after him?

Single for God

Catholic Connections

God instructs Jeremiah not to marry (Jeremiah 16:2), and so Jeremiah remains single and celibate all his life. He remains single as a sign that the coming destruction is no time to start a family and raise children. Almost all Jewish males married, so staying single would definitely make Jeremiah noticed.

In this way Jeremiah is also like Jesus. Jesus was never married either. Jesus' mission was for all people, and it took all of his energy and time. If he had a wife and children, he could not have been a devoted husband and father and still accomplish his mission.

You are probably aware that in the Catholic Church, priests and women and men in religious communities make vows to remain single for their whole lives. This is also called celibacy. They choose to be single to devote themselves to God's mission and to be a sign that God's love is enough for us.

— Jeremiah 16:1–4

you will serve other gods day and night, and I will show you no mercy.' "

The Return from Exile

14 The LORD says, "The time is coming when people will no longer swear by me as the living God who brought the people of Israel out of the land of Egypt. 15 Instead, they will swear by me as the living God who brought the people of Israel out of a northern land and out of all the other countries where I had scattered them. I will bring them back to their own country, to the land that I gave their ancestors. I, the LORD, have spoken."

The Coming Punishment

16 The LORD says, "I am sending for many fishermen to come and catch these people. Then I will send for many hunters to hunt them down on every mountain and hill and in the caves among the rocks. 17 I see everything they do. Nothing is hidden from me; their sins do not escape my sight. 18 I will make them pay double for their sin and wickedness, because they have defiled my land with idols that are as lifeless as corpses, and have filled it with their false gods."

Jeremiah's Prayer of Confidence in the LORD

19 LORD, you are the one who protects me and gives me strength; you help me in times of trouble. Nations will come to you from the ends of the earth and say, "Our ancestors had nothing but false gods, nothing but useless idols. 20 Can people make their own gods? No, if they did, those would not really be gods."

21 "So then," says the LORD, "once and for all I will make the nations know my power and my might; they will know that I am the LORD."

Jeremiah

Compare Jeremiah 17:6–8 with Psalm 1.

The Sin and Punishment of Judah

17 ¹The LORD says, "People of Judah, your sin is written with an iron pen; it is engraved on your hearts with a diamond point and carved on the corners of your altars. ²Your people worship at the altars and the symbols that have been set up for the goddess Asherah by every green tree and on the hilltops ³and on the mountains in the open country. I will have your enemies take away your wealth and your treasures because of all the sins you have committed*u* throughout your land. ⁴You will have to give up*v* the land I gave you, and I will make you serve your enemies in a land you know nothing about, because my anger is like a fire, and it will burn forever."

Various Sayings

⁵The LORD says,
"I will condemn those
  who turn away from me
and put their trust in human beings,
  in the strength of mortals.
⁶He is like a bush in the desert,
  which grows in the dry wasteland,
  on salty ground where nothing else
    grows.
Nothing good ever happens to him.

⁷"But I will bless the person
  who puts his trust in me.
⁸He is like a tree growing near a stream
  and sending out roots to the water.
It is not afraid when hot weather comes,
  because its leaves stay green;
it has no worries when there is no rain;
  it keeps on bearing fruit.

⁹"Who can understand the human heart?
  There is nothing else so deceitful;
  it is too sick to be healed.
¹⁰I, the LORD, search the minds
  and test the hearts of people.
I treat each of them according to the way
    they live,
  according to what they do."

He is like a bush in the desert. (17:6)

¹¹The person who gets money dishonestly
  is like a bird that hatches eggs it didn't
    lay.
In the prime of life he will lose his riches,
  and in the end he is nothing but a fool.

¹²Our Temple is like a glorious throne,
  standing on a high mountain from the
    beginning.

¹³LORD, you are Israel's hope;
  all who abandon you will be put to
    shame.
They will disappear like names written in
    the dust,*w*
  because they have abandoned you, the
    LORD,
  the spring of fresh water.

Jeremiah Asks the LORD for Help

¹⁴LORD, heal me and I will be completely well; rescue me and I will be perfectly safe. You are the one I praise!

¹⁵The people say to me, "Where are those threats the LORD made against us? Let him carry them out now!"

¹⁶But, LORD, I never urged you to bring

u **17:3** *Probable text* because of all the sins you have committed; *Hebrew* your high places for sins.
v **17:4** *Probable text* You . . . give up; *Hebrew unclear.*   *w* **17:13** disappear . . . dust; *or* go to the world of the dead.
17:8 Ps 1:3   **17:10 a** Rev 2:23; **b** Ps 62:12

Jeremiah

Pray It!

My Place of Safety

Jeremiah says to God, "You are my place of safety when trouble comes" (Jeremiah 17:17).
Where do you go when you are afraid?

Think of a place where you feel safe. Now picture God there with you. Perhaps God is holding you or simply beside you. Stay with this image for a while.

The next time you feel afraid or threatened, try to recapture that image of being in a safe place with God. Let God reassure you and be with you.

— Jeremiah 17:14–18

disaster on them;ˣ I did not wish a time of trouble for them. LORD, you know this; you know what I have said. 17Do not be a terror to me; you are my place of safety when trouble comes. 18Bring disgrace on those who persecute me, but spare me, LORD. Fill them with terror, but do not terrify me. Bring disaster on them and break them to pieces.

On Observing the Sabbath

19The LORD said to me, "Jeremiah, go and announce my message at the People's Gate, through which the kings of Judah enter and leave the city; then go to all the other gates of Jerusalem. 20Tell the kings and all the people of Judah and everyone who lives in Jerusalem and enters these gates, to listen to what I say. 21Tell them that if they love their lives, they must not carry any load on the Sabbath; they must not carry anything in through the gates of Jerusalem 22or carry anything out of their houses on the Sabbath. They must not work on the Sabbath; they

must observe it as a sacred day, as I commanded their ancestors. 23Their ancestors did not listen to me or pay any attention. Instead, they became stubborn; they would not obey me or learn from me.

24"Tell these people that they must obey all my commands. They must not carry any load in through the gates of this city on the Sabbath. They must observe the Sabbath as a sacred day and must not do any work at all. 25Then their kings and princes will enter the gates of Jerusalem and have the same royal power that David had. Together with the people of Judah and of Jerusalem, they will ride in chariots and on horses, and the city of Jerusalem will always be filled with people. 26People will come from the towns of Judah and from the villages around Jerusalem; they will come from the territory of Benjamin, from the foothills, from the mountains, and from southern Judah. They will bring to my Temple burnt offerings and sacrifices, grain offerings and incense, as well as thank offerings. 27But they must obey me and observe the Sabbath as a sacred day. They must not carry any load through the gates of Jerusalem on that day, for if they do, I will set the gates of Jerusalem on fire. Fire will burn down the palaces of Jerusalem, and no one will be able to put it out."

Jeremiah at the Potter's House

18 1The LORD said to me, 2"Go down to the potter's house, where I will give you my message." 3So I went there and saw the potter working at his wheel. 4Whenever a piece of pottery turned out imperfect, he would take the clay and make it into something else.

5Then the LORD said to me, 6"Don't I have the right to do with you people of Israel what the potter did with the clay? You are in my hands just like clay in the potter's hands. 7If at any time I say that I am going to uproot, break down, or destroy any nation or kingdom, 8but then that nation turns from its evil, I will not do what I said I would. 9On the other hand, if I say that I am going to

ˣ 17:16 *Probable text* bring disaster on them; *Hebrew* from being a shepherd after you.
17:21 Neh 13:15–22   **17:22** Ex 20:8–10; Deut 5:12–14

plant or build up any nation or kingdom, [10]but then that nation disobeys me and does evil, I will not do what I said I would. [11]Now then, tell the people of Judah and of Jerusalem that I am making plans against them and getting ready to punish them. Tell them to stop living sinful lives—to change their ways and the things they are doing. [12]They will answer, 'No, why should we? We will all be just as stubborn and evil as we want to be.' "

The People Reject the LORD

[13]The LORD says,
"Ask every nation if such a thing
    has ever happened before.
    The people of Israel have done a
        terrible thing!
[14]Are Lebanon's rocky heights ever without
    snow?
    Do its cool mountain streams ever run
        dry?
[15]Yet my people have forgotten me;
    they burn incense to idols.
They have stumbled in the way they
        should go;
    they no longer follow the old ways;
    they walk on unmarked paths.
[16]They have made this land a thing of
        horror,
    to be despised forever.
All who pass by will be shocked at what
        they see;
    they will shake their heads in
        amazement.
[17]I will scatter my people before their
        enemies,
    like dust blown by the east wind.
I will turn my back on them;
    I will not help them when the disaster
        comes."

A Plot against Jeremiah

[18]Then the people said, "Let's do something about Jeremiah! There will always be priests to instruct us, the wise to give us

counsel, and prophets to proclaim God's message. Let's bring charges against him and stop listening to what he says."

[19]So I prayed, " LORD, hear what I am saying and listen to what my enemies are saying about me. [20]Is evil the payment for good? Yet they have dug a pit for me to fall in. Remember how I came to you and spoke on their behalf, so that you would not deal with them in anger. [21]But now, LORD, let their children starve to death; let them be killed in war. Let the women lose their husbands and children; let the men die of disease and the young men be killed in battle. [22]Send a mob to plunder their homes without warning; make them cry out in terror. They have dug a pit for me to fall in and have set traps to catch me. [23]But, LORD, you know all their plots to kill me. Do not forgive their evil or pardon their sin. Throw them down in defeat and deal with them while you are angry."

"LORD, hear what I am saying." (18:19)

The Broken Jar

19 [1]The LORD told me to go and buy a clay jar. He also told me to take some of the elders of the people and some of the older priests, [2]and to go through

19:2 2 Kings 23:10; Jer 7:30–32; 32:34, 35

Jeremiah

How is what the people say against Jeremiah in 18:18 similar to what people said about Jesus in the Gospels?

Broken Dreams

God tells Jeremiah to break a clay jar in front of the leaders to let the people know that God is upset with their sins. A shattered clay pot or jar is impossible to fully repair. In fact, it really doesn't make sense to even try to put back together all the broken pieces.

This can happen with relationships as well, especially close friendships. Something happens. A secret told in confidence is shared with others. Or one person gets jealous of another. Angry words become weapons, and then it happens: the friendship is broken, and it will be hard to fix. Sometimes, in the process, our heart can be broken as well. Because of misunderstandings and sinful choices we are going to hurt one another at times . Let's remember how hard it is to pick up the pieces of a broken relationship.

— Jeremiah, chapter 19

The LORD told me to break the jar. (19:10)

Judah have known anything about. They have filled this place with the blood of innocent people, 5and they have built altars for Baal in order to burn their children in the fire as sacrifices. I never commanded them to do this; it never even entered my mind. 6So then, the time will come when this place will no longer be called Topheth or Hinnom Valley. Instead, it will be known as Slaughter Valley. 7In this place I will frustrate all the plans of the people of Judah and Jerusalem. I will let their enemies triumph over them and kill them in battle. I will give their corpses to the birds and the wild animals as food. 8I will bring such terrible destruction on this city that everyone who passes by will be shocked and amazed. 9The enemy will surround the city and try to kill its people. The siege will be so terrible that the people inside the city will eat one another and even their own children."

10Then the LORD told me to break the jar in front of those who had gone with me 11and to tell them that the LORD Almighty had said, "I will break this people and this city, and it will be like this broken clay jar that cannot be put together again. People will bury their dead even in Topheth because there will be nowhere else to bury them. 12I promise that I will make this city and its inhabitants like Topheth. 13The houses of Jerusalem, the houses of the kings of Judah,

Potsherd Gate out to Hinnom Valley. There I was to proclaim the message that he would give me. 3The LORD told me to say, "Kings of Judah and people of Jerusalem, listen to what I, the LORD Almighty, the God of Israel, have to say. I am going to bring such a disaster on this place that everyone who hears about it will be stunned. 4I am going to do this because the people have abandoned me and defiled this place by offering sacrifices here to other gods—gods that neither they nor their ancestors nor the kings of

19:5 Lev 18:21

Jeremiah

"I will break this people and this city, and it will be like this broken clay jar that cannot be put together again" *(Jeremiah 19:11).*

and indeed all the houses on whose roofs incense has been burned to the stars and where wine has been poured out as an offering to other gods—they will all be as unclean as Topheth."

14 Then I left Topheth, where the LORD had sent me to proclaim his message. I went and stood in the court of the Temple and told all the people 15 that the LORD Almighty, the God of Israel, had said, "I am going to bring on this city and on every nearby town all the punishment that I said I would, because you are stubborn and will not listen to what I say."

Jeremiah's Conflict with Pashhur the Priest

20 1 When the priest Pashhur son of Immer, who was the chief officer of the Temple, heard me proclaim these things, 2 he had me beaten and placed in chains near the upper Benjamin Gate in the Temple. 3 The next morning, after Pashhur had released me from the chains, I said to him, "The LORD did not name you Pashhur. The name he has given you is 'Terror Everywhere.' 4 The LORD himself has said, 'I am going to make you a terror to yourself and to your friends, and you will see them all killed by the swords of their enemies. I am going to put all the people of Judah under the power of the king of Babylonia; he will take some away as prisoners to his country and put others to death. 5 I will also let their enemies plunder all the wealth of this city and seize all its possessions and property, even the treasures of the kings of Judah, and carry everything off to Babylonia. 6 As for you, Pashhur, you and all your family will also be captured and taken off to Babylonia. There you will die and be buried, along with all your friends to whom you have told so many lies.' "

Jeremiah Complains to the LORD

7 LORD, you have deceived me,
    and I was deceived.
You are stronger than I am,
    and you have overpowered me.
Everyone makes fun of me;
    they laugh at me all day long.

I'm Sick of It!

"Everyone makes fun of me; / they laugh at me all day long" (Jeremiah 20:7).

These words of Jeremiah could easily be our own words, couldn't they? Jeremiah is fed up with his role as a prophet. He is upset and feels that God has tricked him. He is sick and tired of being ridiculed. So Jeremiah complains to God, even cursing the day he was born (Jeremiah 20:14)!

No doubt all of us have been made fun of at one time or another. It can get frustrating, and we want to complain about it. Let God know how you feel. It is dangerous and unwise to keep your feelings bottled up inside of you. If you need to, talk to someone you trust about what is happening. Not so the person can fix it, but so that you can have someone help share your burden. Jeremiah didn't hesitate to share his feelings—maybe that is why he could keep going on.

— Jeremiah 20:7–18

8 Whenever I speak, I have to cry out
    and shout, "Violence! Destruction!"
LORD, I am ridiculed and scorned all the
    time
    because I proclaim your message.
9 But when I say, "I will forget the LORD
    and no longer speak in his name,"
then your message is like a fire
    burning deep within me.
I try my best to hold it in,
    but can no longer keep it back.
10 I hear everybody whispering,
    "Terror is everywhere!
    So let's report him to the authorities!"

Jeremiah

Even my close friends wait for my
downfall.
"Perhaps he can be tricked," they say;
"then we can catch him and get
revenge."
11 But you, LORD, are on my side, strong
and mighty,
and those who persecute me will fail.
They will be disgraced forever,
because they cannot succeed.
Their disgrace will never be forgotten.
12 But, Almighty LORD, you test people
justly;
you know what is in their hearts and
minds.
So let me see you take revenge on my
enemies,
for I have placed my cause in your
hands.
13 Sing to the LORD!
Praise the LORD!
He rescues the oppressed from the power
of evil people.

14 Curse the day I was born!
Forget the day my mother gave me birth!
15 Curse the one who made my father glad
by bringing him the news,
"It's a boy! You have a son!"
16 May he be like those cities
that the LORD destroyed without
mercy.
May he hear cries of pain in the morning
and the battle alarm at noon,
17　for not killing me before I was born.
Then my mother's womb would have
been my grave.
18 Why was I born?
Was it only to have trouble and sorrow,
to end my life in disgrace?

Jerusalem's Defeat Is Predicted

21 ¹King Zedekiah of Judah sent to
me Pashhur son of Malchiah and
the priest Zephaniah son of Maaseiah with
this request: ²"Please speak to the LORD for
us, because King Nebuchadnezzar of Babylonia and his army are besieging the city.
Maybe the LORD will perform one of his

miracles for us and force Nebuchadnezzar
to retreat."

³Then the LORD spoke to me, and I told
those who had been sent to me ⁴to tell
Zedekiah that the LORD, the God of Israel,
had said, "Zedekiah, I am going to defeat
your army that is fighting against the king of
Babylonia and his army. I will pile up your
soldiers' weapons in the center of the city. ⁵I
will fight against you with all my might, my
anger, my wrath, and my fury. ⁶I will kill
everyone living in this city; people and animals alike will die of a terrible disease. ⁷But
as for you, your officials, and the people who
survive the war, the famine, and the disease—I will let all of you be captured by
King Nebuchadnezzar and by your enemies,
who want to kill you. Nebuchadnezzar will
put you to death. He will not spare any of
you or show mercy or pity to any of you. I,
the LORD, have spoken."

⁸Then the LORD told me to say to the
people, "Listen! I, the LORD, am giving you
a choice between the way that leads to life
and the way that leads to death. ⁹Anyone
who stays in the city will be killed in war or
by starvation or disease. But those who go
out and surrender to the Babylonians, who
are now attacking the city, will not be
killed; they will at least escape with their
life. ¹⁰I have made up my mind not to spare
this city, but to destroy it. It will be given
over to the king of Babylonia, and he will
burn it to the ground. I, the LORD, have
spoken."

Judgment on the Royal House of Judah

11-12 The LORD told me to give this message to the royal house of Judah, the
descendants of David: "Listen to what I, the
LORD, am saying. See that justice is done
every day. Protect the person who is being
cheated from the one who is cheating him.
If you don't, the evil you are doing will
make my anger burn like a fire that cannot
be put out. ¹³You, Jerusalem, are sitting ʸ
high above the valleys, like a rock rising

ʸ 21:13 You, Jerusalem, are sitting; *or* You are enthroned.
20:14–18 Job 3:1–19　21:2 2 Kings 25:1–11; 2 Chr 36:17–21

above the plain. But I will fight against you. You say that no one can attack you or break through your defenses. 14But I will punish you for what you have done. I will set your palace on fire, and the fire will burn down everything around it. I, the LORD, have spoken."

Jeremiah's Message to the Royal House of Judah

22 1-2The LORD told me to go to the palace of the king of Judah, the descendant of David, and there tell the king, his officials, and the people of Jerusalem to listen to what the LORD had said: 3"I, the LORD, command you to do what is just and right. Protect the person who is being cheated from the one who is cheating him. Do not mistreat or oppress aliens, orphans, or widows; and do not kill innocent people in this holy place. 4If you really do as I have commanded, then David's descendants will continue to be kings. And they, together with their officials and their people, will continue to pass through the gates of this palace in chariots and on horses. 5But if you do not obey my commands, then I swear to you that this palace will fall into ruins. I, the LORD, have spoken.

6"To me, Judah's royal palace is as beautiful as the land of Gilead and as the Lebanon Mountains; but I will make it a desolate place where no one lives. 7I am sending men to destroy it. They will all bring their axes, cut down its beautiful cedar pillars, and throw them into the fire.

8"Afterward many foreigners will pass by and ask one another why I, the LORD, have done such a thing to this great city. 9Then they will answer that it is because you have abandoned your covenant with me, your God, and have worshiped and served other gods."

Jeremiah's Message concerning Joahaz

10People of Judah, do not weep for King Josiah;
   do not mourn his death.
But weep bitterly for Joahaz, his son;
   they are taking him away, never to return,
   never again to see the land where he was born.

11The LORD says concerning Josiah's son Joahaz, who succeeded his father as king of Judah, "He has gone away from here, never to return. 12He will die in the country where they have taken him, and he will never again see this land."

Jeremiah's Message concerning Jehoiakim

13Doomed is the one who builds his house
   by injustice
   and enlarges it by dishonesty;
who makes his people work for nothing
   and does not pay their wages.
14Doomed is the one who says,
   "I will build myself a mansion
   with spacious rooms upstairs."
So he puts windows in his house,
   panels it with cedar,
   and paints it red.
15Does it make you a better king
   if you build houses of cedar,
   finer than those of others?
Your father enjoyed a full life.
   He was always just and fair,
   and he prospered in everything he did.
16He gave the poor a fair trial,
   and all went well with him.
That is what it means to know the LORD.
17But you can only see your selfish interests;
   you kill the innocent
   and violently oppress your people.
The LORD has spoken.

22:5 Mt 23:28; Lk 13:35   22:11 2 Kings 23:31–34; 2 Chr 36:1–4

Jeremiah

Jeremiah prophesied during the reigns of five kings of Judah: Josiah, Joahaz, Jehoikim, Jehoiachin, and Zedekiah.

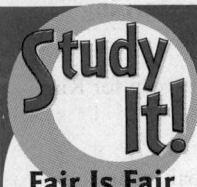

Fair Is Fair

One of the roles of the prophet is to speak out against injustice, and this is what Jeremiah does in Jeremiah 22:13. His words can easily apply to today's world. In the United States, we have something called minimum wage, which assures that a full-time worker will get at least a certain amount per hour. In many parts of the world, no such laws exist, and often people will take any work they can get, no matter how little it pays. Sometimes, at the end of the day, they are not even paid at all, despite being promised a wage. Jeremiah warns against this injustice to workers and says that those who build their houses on this kind of injustice and dishonesty are doomed.

— Jeremiah 22:13–17

18 So then, the LORD says about Josiah's son Jehoiakim, king of Judah,

"No one will mourn his death or say,
  'How terrible, my friend, how terrible!'
No one will weep for him or cry,
  'My lord! My king!'
19 With the funeral honors of a donkey,
  he will be dragged away
  and thrown outside Jerusalem's gates."

Jeremiah's Message about the Fate of Jerusalem

20 People of Jerusalem, go to Lebanon and shout,
  go to the land of Bashan and cry;

call out from the mountains of Moab,
  because all your allies have been
  defeated.
21 The LORD spoke to you when you were
  prosperous,
  but you refused to listen.
That is what you've done all your life;
  you never would obey the LORD.
22 Your leaders will be blown away by the
  wind,
  your allies taken as prisoners of war,
  your city disgraced and put to shame
  because of all the evil you have done.
23 You rest secure among the cedars brought
  from Lebanon;
  but how pitiful you'll be when pains
  strike you,
  pains like those of a woman in labor.

God's Judgment on Jehoiachin

24 The LORD said to King Jehoiachin, son of King Jehoiakim of Judah, "As surely as I am the living God, even if you were the signet ring on my right hand, I would pull you off 25 and give you to people you are afraid of, people who want to kill you. I will give you to King Nebuchadnezzar of Babylonia and his soldiers. 26 I am going to force you and your mother into exile. You will go to a country where neither of you was born, and both of you will die there. 27 You will long to see this country again, but you will never return."

28 I said, "Has King Jehoiachin become like a broken jar that is thrown away and that no one wants? Is that why he and his children have been taken into exile to a land they know nothing about?"
29 O land, land, land!
  Listen to what the LORD has said:
30 "This man is condemned to lose his
  children,
  to be a man who will never succeed.
He will have no descendants
  who will rule in Judah
  as David's successors.
I, the LORD, have spoken."

22:18 2 Kings 23:36—24:6; 2 Chr 36:5–7   22:24 2 Kings 24:8–15; 2 Chr 36:9, 10

King Joahaz ruled only three months before the Egyptian pharaoh took him prisoner and made his brother Jehoiakim king of Judah.

Hope for the Future

23 ¹How terrible will be the LORD's judgment on those rulers who destroy and scatter his people! ²This is what the LORD, the God of Israel, says about the rulers who were supposed to take care of his people: "You have not taken care of my people; you have scattered them and driven them away. Now I am going to punish you for the evil you have done. ³I will gather the rest of my people from the countries where I have scattered them, and I will bring them back to their homeland. They will have many children and increase in number. ⁴I will appoint rulers to take care of them. My people will no longer be afraid or terrified, and I will not punish them again.ᶻ I, the LORD, have spoken."

⁵The LORD says, "The time is coming when I will choose as king a righteous descendant of David. That king will rule wisely and do what is right and just throughout the land. ⁶When he is king, the people of Judah will be safe, and the people of Israel will live in peace. He will be called 'The LORD Our Salvation.'

⁷"The time is coming," says the LORD, "when people will no longer swear by me as the living God who brought the people of Israel out of the land of Egypt. ⁸Instead, they will swear by me as the living God who brought the people of Israel out of a northern land and out of all the other countries where I had scattered them. Then they will live in their own land."

Jeremiah's Message about the Prophets

⁹My heart is crushed,
    and I am trembling.
Because of the LORD,
    because of his holy words,
    I am like a man who is drunk,
        someone who has had too much wine.
¹⁰The land is full of people unfaithful to
        the LORD;
    they live wicked lives and misuse their
        power.

Because of the LORD's curse the land
        mourns
    and the pastures are dry.

¹¹The LORD says,
"The prophets and the priests are godless;
    I have caught them doing evil in the
        Temple itself.
¹²The paths they follow will be slippery
        and dark;
    I will make them stumble and fall.
I am going to bring disaster on them;
    the time of their punishment is
        coming.
I, the LORD, have spoken.
¹³I have seen the sin of Samaria's prophets:
    they have spoken in the name of Baal
    and have led my people astray.
¹⁴But I have seen the prophets in Jerusalem
        do even worse:
    they commit adultery and tell lies;
    they help people to do wrong,
    so that no one stops doing what is evil.
To me they are all as bad
    as the people of Sodom and
        Gomorrah.

¹⁵"So then, this is what I, the LORD Almighty, say about the prophets of Jerusalem:
    I will give them bitter plants to eat
        and poison to drink,
    because they have spread ungodliness
        throughout the land."

¹⁶The LORD Almighty said to the people of Jerusalem, "Do not listen to what the prophets say; they are filling you with false hopes. They tell you what they have imagined and not what I have said. ¹⁷To the people who refuse to listen to what I have said, they keep saying that all will go well with them. And they tell everyone who is stubborn that disaster will never touch them."

¹⁸I said, "None of these prophets has ever known the LORD's secret thoughts. None of them has ever heard or understood his message, or ever listened or paid attention to what he said. ¹⁹His anger is a storm, a furious wind that will rage over the heads of the wicked, ²⁰and it will not end until he has

---

ᶻ **23:4** I will not punish them again; *or* not one of them will be missing.
23:5, 6 Jer 33:14–16   **23:14** Gen 18:20; Ezek 16:49

done everything he intends to do. In days to come his people will understand this clearly."

21 The LORD said, "I did not send these prophets, but even so they went. I did not give them any message, but still they spoke in my name. 22 If they had known my secret thoughts, then they could have proclaimed my message to my people and could have made them give up the evil lives they live and the wicked things they do.

23 "I am a God who is everywhere and not in one place only. 24 No one can hide where I cannot see them. Do you not know that I am everywhere in heaven and on earth? 25 I know what those prophets have said who speak lies in my name and claim that I have given them my messages in their dreams. 26 How much longer will those prophets mislead my people with the lies they have invented? 27 They think that the dreams they tell will make my people forget me, just as their ancestors forgot me and turned to Baal. 28 The prophet who has had a dream should say it is only a dream, but the prophet who has heard my message should proclaim that message faithfully. What good is straw compared with wheat? 29 My message is like a fire and like a hammer that breaks rocks in pieces. 30 I am against those prophets who take each other's words and proclaim them as my message. 31 I am also against those prophets who speak their own words and claim they came from me. 32 Listen to what I, the LORD, say! I am against the prophets who tell their dreams that are full of lies. They tell these dreams and lead my people astray with their lies and their boasting. I did not send them or order them to go, and they are of no help at all to the people. I, the LORD, have spoken."

The LORD's Burden

33 The LORD said to me, "Jeremiah, when one of my people or a prophet or a priest asks you, 'What is the LORD's message?' you are to say, 'You are a burden[a] to the LORD, and he is going to get rid of you.' 34 If any of my people or a prophet or a priest even uses

the words 'the LORD's burden,' I will punish them and their families. 35 Instead, each one of them should ask their friends and their relatives, 'What answer has the LORD given? What has the LORD said?' 36 So they must no longer use the words 'the LORD's burden,' because if any of them do, I will make my message a real burden to them. The people have perverted the words of their God, the living God, the LORD Almighty. 37 Jeremiah, ask the prophets, 'What answer did the LORD give you? What did the LORD say?' 38 And if they disobey my command and use the words 'the LORD's burden,' then tell them that 39 I will certainly pick them up[b] and throw them far away from me, both them and the city that I gave to them and their ancestors. 40 I will bring on them everlasting shame and disgrace that will never be forgotten."

Two Baskets of Figs

24 ¹ The LORD showed me two baskets of figs placed in front of the Temple. (This was after King Nebuchadnezzar of Babylonia had taken away Jehoiakim's son, King Jehoiachin of Judah, as a prisoner from Jerusalem to Babylonia, together with the leaders of Judah, the craftworkers, and the

Two baskets of figs (24:1)

---

a **23:33** *The Hebrew word for* message *and* burden *is the same.*   *b* **23:39** *The Hebrew verb for* pick up *comes from the same root as the Hebrew word for* message *and* burden.
23:24 Wis 1:7; Sir 16:17   **24:1** 2 Kings 24:12–16; 2 Chr 36:10

skilled workers.) ²The first basket contained good figs, those that ripen early; the other one contained bad figs, too bad to eat. ³Then the LORD said to me, "Jeremiah, what do you see?"

I answered, "Figs. The good ones are very good, and the bad ones are very bad, too bad to eat."

⁴So the LORD said to me, ⁵"I, the LORD, the God of Israel, consider that the people who were taken away to Babylonia are like these good figs, and I will treat them with kindness. ⁶I will watch over them and bring them back to this land. I will build them up and not tear them down; I will plant them and not pull them up. ⁷I will give them the desire to know that I am the LORD. Then they will be my people, and I will be their God, because they will return to me with all their heart.

⁸"As for King Zedekiah of Judah, the politicians around him, and the rest of the people of Jerusalem who have stayed in this land or moved to Egypt—I, the LORD, will treat them all like these figs that are too bad to be eaten. ⁹I will bring such a disaster on them that all the nations of the world will be terrified. People will make fun of them, make jokes about them, ridicule them, and use their name as a curse everywhere I scatter them. ¹⁰I will bring war, starvation, and disease on them until there is not one of them left in the land that I gave to them and their ancestors."

One Bad Apple

Jeremiah, chapter 24, uses the symbol of good figs and bad figs. We are probably more familiar with good apples and bad apples. It's easy to spot a bad or rotten apple. It is bruised, mushy, and has brown spots. No one wants to eat it. Perhaps you have heard the expression, "He is one bad apple." We all know what that means. This individual has been judged to be no good. Perhaps he gets into trouble a lot, or maybe he has been arrested a few times. While it is not fair to judge someone by appearances, we do know that people will judge us by how we act.

Imagine yourself as an apple tree. Are you producing good apples or bad apples? That is, do your actions cause good in the world or evil? What do others see when they look at you—good apples or bad apples? Try to name some of both in your life.

— Jeremiah, chapter 24

The Enemy from the North

25 ¹In the fourth year that Jehoiakim son of Josiah was king of Judah, I received a message from the LORD concerning all the people of Judah. (This was the first year that Nebuchadnezzar was king of Babylonia.) ²I said to all the people of Judah and of Jerusalem, ³"For twenty-three years, from the thirteenth year that Josiah son of Amon was king of Judah until this very day, the LORD has spoken to me, and I have

never failed to tell you what he said. But you have paid no attention. ⁴You would not listen or pay attention, even though the LORD has continued to send you his servants the prophets. ⁵They told you to turn from your wicked way of life and from the evil things you are doing, so that you could go on living in the land that the LORD gave you and your ancestors as a permanent possession. ⁶They told you not to worship and serve other gods and not to make the LORD angry

25:1 2 Kings 24:1; 2 Chr 36:5–7; Dan 1:1, 2

Jeremiah

Pay Attention!

Have you ever been daydreaming and suddenly realize that someone is calling your name? That can be pretty embarrassing when it happens in class. Not paying attention can have consequences. Not paying attention while driving can result in an accident and even death. Jeremiah tells the Israelites that they refused to pay attention to the prophets God sent to warn them. Now they have to pay the consequences.

At times all of us have a problem paying attention. Our minds can easily wander. Think about how this can apply to your life. If you aren't paying attention to God, you can easily wander off in a direction different from what God has planned for you. Before long, you find yourself in a situation or problem that makes you wonder, "How did I get into this?" Not paying attention to our soul can also be fatal to our spiritual lives. So Jeremiah's message is pretty clear: pay attention when God is speaking!

— Jeremiah 25:1–7

by worshiping the idols you had made. If you had obeyed the LORD, then he would not have punished you. 7But the LORD himself says that you refused to listen to him. Instead, you made him angry with your idols and have brought his punishment on yourselves.

8"So then, because you would not listen to him, the LORD Almighty says, 9'I am going to send for all the peoples from the north and for my servant, King Nebuchadnezzar of Babylonia. I am going to bring them to fight against Judah and its inhabitants and against all the neighboring nations. I am going to destroy this nation and its neighbors and leave them in ruins forever, a terrible and shocking sight. I, the LORD, have spoken. 10I will silence their shouts of joy and gladness and the happy sounds of wedding feasts. They will have no oil for their lamps, and there will be no more grain. 11This whole land will be left in ruins and will be a shocking sight, and the neighboring nations will serve the king of Babylonia for seventy years. 12After that I will punish Babylonia and its king for their sin. I will destroy that country and leave it in ruins forever. 13I will punish Babylonia with all the disasters that I threatened to bring on the nations when I spoke through Jeremiah—all the disasters recorded in this book. 14I will pay the Babylonians back for what they have done, and many nations and great kings will make slaves of them.' "

God's Judgment on the Nations

15The LORD, the God of Israel, said to me, "Here is a wine cup filled with my anger. Take it to all the nations to whom I send you, and make them drink from it. 16When they drink from it, they will stagger and go out of their minds because of the war I am sending against them."

17So I took the cup from the LORD's hand, gave it to all the nations to whom the LORD had sent me, and made them drink from it. 18Jerusalem and all the towns of Judah, together with its kings and leaders, were made to drink from it, so that they would become a desert, a terrible and shocking sight, and so that people would use their name as a curse—as they still do.

19-26Here is the list of all the others who had to drink from the cup:

25:10 a Jer 7:34; 16:9; b Rev 18:22, 23 **25:11** 2 Chr 36:21; Jer 29:10; Dan 9:2

Locate as many of the lands mentioned in Jeremiah 25:19–26 as you can on Maps 3, 4, and 5 in the back of this Bible.

Jeremiah

the king of Egypt, his officials and leaders;
all the Egyptians and all the foreigners in
    Egypt;
all the kings of the land of Uz;
all the kings of the Philistine cities of
    Ashkelon, Gaza, Ekron, and what
    remains of Ashdod;
all the people of Edom, Moab, and
    Ammon;
all the kings of Tyre and Sidon;
all the kings of the Mediterranean lands;
the cities of Dedan, Tema, and Buz;
all the people who cut their hair short;
all the kings of Arabia;
all the kings of the desert tribes;
all the kings of Zimri, Elam, and Media;
all the kings of the north, far and near,
    one after another.

Every nation on the face of the earth had to drink from it. Last of all, the king of Babylonia will drink from it.

27 Then the LORD said to me, "Tell the people that I, the LORD Almighty, the God of Israel, am commanding them to drink until they are drunk and vomit, until they fall down and cannot get up, because of the war that I am sending against them. **28** And if they refuse to take the cup from your hand and drink from it, then tell them that the LORD Almighty has said that they will still have to drink from it. **29** I will begin my work of destruction in my own city. Do they think they will go unpunished? No, they will be punished, for I am going to send war on all the people on earth. I, the LORD Almighty, have spoken.

30 "You, Jeremiah, must proclaim everything I have said. You must tell these people,
'The LORD will roar from heaven
    and thunder from the heights of
    heaven.
He will roar against his people;
    he will shout like a man treading
    grapes.
Everyone on earth will hear him,
31   and the sound will echo to the ends of
    the earth.
The LORD has a case against the
    nations.

He will bring all people to trial
    and put the wicked to death.
The LORD has spoken.' "

32 The LORD Almighty says that disaster is coming on one nation after another, and a great storm is gathering at the far ends of the earth. **33** On that day the bodies of those whom the LORD has killed will lie scattered from one end of the earth to the other. No one will mourn for them, and they will not be taken away and buried. They will lie on the ground like piles of manure.

34 Cry, you leaders, you shepherds of my people, cry out loud! Mourn and roll in the dust. The time has come for you to be slaughtered,*c* and you will be butchered like rams.*d* **35** There will be no way for you to escape. **36-37** You moan and cry out in distress because the LORD in his anger has destroyed your nation and left your peaceful country in ruins. **38** The LORD has abandoned his people*e* like a lion that leaves its cave. The horrors of war and the LORD's fierce anger have turned the country into a desert.

Jeremiah Is Brought to Trial

26 **1** Soon after Jehoiakim son of Josiah became king of Judah, **2** the LORD said to me, "Stand in the court of the Temple and proclaim all I have commanded you to say to the people who come from the towns of Judah to worship there. Do not leave out anything. **3** Perhaps the people will listen and give up their evil ways. If they do, then I will change my mind about the destruction I plan to bring on them for all their wicked deeds."

4 The LORD told me to say to the people, "I, the LORD, have said that you must obey me by following the teaching that I gave you, **5** and by paying attention to the words of my servants, the prophets, whom I have kept on sending to you. You have never obeyed what they said. **6** If you continue to disobey, then I will do to this Temple what I did to Shiloh,*f* and all the nations of the world will use the name of this city as a curse."

---

c **25:34** *Hebrew has an additional word, the meaning of which is unclear.*   *d* **25:34** *One ancient translation* rams; *Hebrew* vessels.   *e* **25:38** The LORD . . . people; *or* The LORD's people run away.   *f* **26:6** SHILOH: *See 7:12.*
26:1 2 Kings 23:36—24:6; 2 Chr 36:5–7   **26:6** Josh 18:1; Ps 78:60; Jer 7:12–14

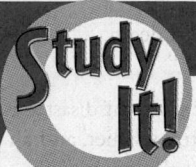

Falsely Accused

Even though they lived six hundred years apart, there are some similarities between the life of Jeremiah and the life of Jesus. In Jeremiah, chapter 26, Jeremiah is brought to trial. Read verses 1–16, and then turn to any of these four Gospel accounts of the arrest and trial of Jesus: Matthew 26:47—27:26, Mark 14:43—15:5, Luke 22:47—23:25, and John 18:3—19:16.

What similarities do you notice between Jeremiah's trial and Jesus' trial? What are some differences?

— Jeremiah, chapter 26

7 The priests, the prophets, and all the people heard me saying these things in the Temple, 8 and as soon as I had finished all that the LORD had commanded me to speak, they grabbed me and shouted, "You ought to be killed for this! 9 Why have you said in the LORD's name that this Temple will become like Shiloh and that this city will be destroyed and no one will live in it?" Then the people crowded around me.

10 When the leaders of Judah heard what had happened, they hurried from the royal palace to the Temple and took their places at the New Gate. 11 Then the priests and the prophets said to the leaders and to the people, "This man deserves to be sentenced to death because he has spoken against our city. You heard him with your own ears."

12 Then I said, "The LORD sent me to proclaim everything that you heard me say against this Temple and against this city. 13 You must change the way you are living and the things you are doing, and must obey the LORD your God. If you do, he will change his mind about the destruction that

he said he would bring on you. 14 As for me, I am in your power! Do with me whatever you think is fair and right. 15 But be sure of this: if you kill me, you and the people of this city will be guilty of killing an innocent man, because it is the LORD who sent me to give you this warning."

16 Then the leaders and the people said to the priests and the prophets, "This man spoke to us in the name of the LORD our God; he should not be put to death."

17 After that, some of the elders stood up and said to the people who had gathered, 18 "When Hezekiah was king of Judah, the prophet Micah of Moresheth told all the people that the LORD Almighty had said,

'Zion will be plowed like a field;
    Jerusalem will become a pile of ruins,
    and the Temple hill will become a
        forest.'

19 King Hezekiah and the people of Judah did not put Micah to death. Instead, Hezekiah honored the LORD and tried to win his favor. And the LORD changed his mind about the disaster that he said he would bring on them. Now we are about to bring a terrible disaster on ourselves."

(20 There was another man, Uriah son of Shemaiah from Kiriath Jearim, who spoke in the name of the LORD against this city and nation just as Jeremiah did. 21 When King Jehoiakim and his soldiers and officials heard what Uriah had said, the king tried to have him killed. But Uriah heard about it; so he fled in terror and escaped to Egypt. 22 King Jehoiakim, however, sent Elnathan son of Achbor and some other men to Egypt to get Uriah. 23 They brought him back to King Jehoiakim, who had him killed and his body thrown into the public burial ground.)

24 But because I had the support of Ahikam son of Shaphan, I was not handed over to the people and killed.

Jeremiah Wears an Ox Yoke

27 1 Soon after Josiah's son Zedekiah became king of Judah, the LORD told me 2 to make myself a yoke out of leather straps and wooden crossbars and to

put it on my neck. ³Then the LORD told me to send a message*g* to the kings of Edom, Moab, Ammon, Tyre, and Sidon through their ambassadors who had come to Jerusalem to see King Zedekiah. ⁴The LORD Almighty, the God of Israel, told me to command them to tell their kings that the LORD had said: ⁵"By my great power and strength I created the world, human beings, and all the animals that live on the earth; and I give it to anyone I choose. ⁶I am the one who has placed all these nations under the power of my servant, King Nebuchadnezzar of Babylonia, and I have made even the wild animals serve him. ⁷All nations will serve him, and they will serve his son and his grandson until the time comes for his own nation to fall. Then his nation will serve powerful nations and great kings.

⁸"But if any nation or kingdom will not submit to his rule, then I will punish that nation by war, starvation, and disease until I have let Nebuchadnezzar destroy it completely. ⁹Do not listen to your prophets or to those who claim they can predict the future, either by dreams or by calling up the spirits of the dead or by magic. They all tell you not to submit to the king of Babylonia. ¹⁰They are deceiving you and will cause you to be taken far away from your country. I will drive you out, and you will be destroyed. ¹¹But if any nation submits to the king of Babylonia and serves him, then I will let it stay on in its own land, to farm it and live there. I, the LORD, have spoken."

¹²I said the same thing to King Zedekiah of Judah, "Submit to the king of Babylonia. Serve him and his people, and you will live. ¹³Why should you and your people die in war or of starvation or disease? That is what the LORD has said will happen to any nation that does not submit to the king of Babylonia. ¹⁴Do not listen to the prophets who tell you not to surrender to him. They are deceiving you. ¹⁵The LORD himself has said

that he did not send them and that they are lying to you in his name. And so he will drive you out, and you will be killed, you and the prophets who are telling you these lies."

¹⁶Then I told the priests and the people that the LORD had said: "Do not listen to the prophets who say that the Temple treasures will soon be brought back from Babylonia. They are lying to you. ¹⁷Don't listen to them! Submit to the king of Babylonia and you will live! Why should this city become a pile of ruins? ¹⁸If they are really prophets and if they have my message, let them ask me, the LORD Almighty, not to allow the treasures that remain in the Temple and in the royal palace to be taken to Babylonia."

(¹⁹⁻²⁰When King Nebuchadnezzar took away to Babylonia the king of Judah, Jehoiachin son of Jehoiakim, and the leading men of Judah and Jerusalem, he left the columns, the bronze tank, the carts, and some of the other Temple treasures.)

²¹"Listen to what I, the LORD Almighty, the God of Israel, say about the treasures that are left in the Temple and in the royal palace in Jerusalem: ²²They will be taken to Babylonia and will remain there until I turn my attention to them. Then I will bring them back and restore them to this place. I, the LORD, have spoken."

Jeremiah and the Prophet Hananiah

28 ¹That same year,*h* in the fifth month of the fourth year that Zedekiah was king, Hananiah son of Azzur, a prophet from the town of Gibeon, spoke to me in the Temple. In the presence of the priests and of the people he told me ²that the LORD Almighty, the God of Israel, had said: "I have broken the power of the king of Babylonia. ³Within two years I will bring back to this place all the Temple treasures that King Nebuchadnezzar took to Babylonia. ⁴I will

g 27:3 *Probable text* a message; *Hebrew* them.   *h 28:1* *One ancient translation* That same year; *Hebrew* That same year at the beginning of his reign.
27:6 Bar 3:16, 17   28:1 2 Kings 24:18–20; 2 Chr 36:11–13

Jeremiah

Yoke: A wood frame put around the neck of an animal, such as an ox. Ropes are attached to the yoke so that the animal can pull a wagon or a plow.

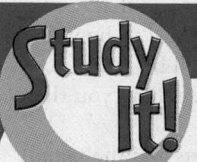

Turning Point

You may notice that Jeremiah's message changes a little in the second half of his book. About this time the Babylonians conquer Jerusalem and take many of the people back to Babylon as captives. The Israelites who survive are hopeless and very upset. They believe that God has abandoned them as a people. So Jeremiah begins to preach a more hopeful message. He prophesies that they will spend years in captivity but that eventually God will have mercy and bring them back to their land. God has not abandoned them!

— Jeremiah 27:21–22

also bring back the king of Judah, Jehoiachin son of Jehoiakim, along with all of the people of Judah who went into exile in Babylonia. Yes, I will break the power of the king of Babylonia. I, the LORD, have spoken."

⁵Then in the presence of the priests and of all the people who were standing in the Temple, I said to Hananiah, ⁶"Wonderful! I hope the LORD will do this! I certainly hope he will make your prophecy come true and will bring back from Babylonia all the Temple treasures and all the people who were taken away as prisoners. ⁷But listen to what I say to you and to the people. ⁸The prophets who spoke long ago, before my time and yours, predicted that war, starvation, and disease would come to many nations and powerful kingdoms. ⁹But a prophet who predicts peace can only be recognized as a prophet whom the LORD has truly sent when that prophet's predictions come true."

¹⁰Then Hananiah took the yoke off my neck, broke it in pieces, ¹¹and said in the presence of all the people, "The LORD has said that this is how he will break the yoke that King Nebuchadnezzar has put on the neck of all the nations; and he will do this within two years." Then I left.

¹²Some time after this the LORD told me ¹³to go and tell Hananiah: "The LORD has said that you may be able to break a wooden yoke, but heⁱ will replace it with an iron yoke. ¹⁴The LORD Almighty, the God of Israel, has said that he will put an iron yoke on all these nations and that they will serve King Nebuchadnezzar of Babylonia. The LORD has said that he will make even the wild animals serve Nebuchadnezzar."

¹⁵Then I told Hananiah this, and added, "Listen, Hananiah! The LORD did not send you, and you are making these people believe a lie. ¹⁶And so the LORD himself says that he is going to get rid of you. Before this year is over you will die because you have told the people to rebel against the LORD."

¹⁷And Hananiah died in the seventh month of that same year.

Jeremiah's Letter to the Jews in Babylonia

29 ¹I wrote a letter to the priests, the prophets, the leaders of the people, and to all the others whom Nebuchadnezzar had taken away as prisoners from Jerusalem to Babylonia. ²I wrote it after King Jehoiachin, his mother, the palace officials, the leaders of Judah and of Jerusalem, the engravers, and the skilled workers had been taken into exile. ³I gave the letter to Elasah son of Shaphan and to Gemariah son of Hilkiah, whom King Zedekiah of Judah was

ⁱ **28:13** *One ancient translation* he; *Hebrew* you.
29:1, 2 2 Kings 24:12–16; 2 Chr 36:10

Hananiah was a false prophet who predicted that Babylonia would only rule for two years. But Babylonia ruled for over fifty years!

Pray It!

Big Plans

Do you spend time wondering where you'll be five or ten years from now? What you'll be doing or who your friends will be? It's all a mystery right now, but one thing is for sure: God knows. Jeremiah, chapter 29, contains a wonderful message from God about our future. The bottom line is God has a plan for us.

For prayer, read through verses 10–13 very slowly. Repeat the words several times. Let them sink in. Imagine God saying them to you.

How do these words make you feel?

Return to this passage whenever you are worried about your future or where your life is headed. Yes, God has big plans for each one of us.

— Jeremiah 29:10–13

sending to King Nebuchadnezzar of Babylonia. It said:

⁴"The LORD Almighty, the God of Israel, says to all those people whom he allowed Nebuchadnezzar to take away as prisoners from Jerusalem to Babylonia: ⁵'Build houses and settle down. Plant gardens and eat what you grow in them. ⁶Marry and have children. Then let your children get married, so that they also may have children. You must increase in numbers and not decrease. ⁷Work for the good of the cities where I have made you go as prisoners. Pray to me on their behalf, because if they are prosperous, you will be prosperous too. ⁸I, the LORD, the God of Israel, warn you not to let yourselves be deceived by the prophets who live among you or by any others who claim they can predict the future. Do not pay any attention to their ʲ dreams. ⁹They are telling you lies in my name. I did not send them. I, the LORD Almighty, have spoken.'

¹⁰"The LORD says, 'When Babylonia's seventy years are over, I will show my concern for you and keep my promise to bring you back home. ¹¹I alone know the plans I have for you, plans to bring you prosperity and not disaster, plans to bring about the future you hope for.ᵏ ¹²Then

you will call to me. You will come and pray to me, and I will answer you. ¹³You will seek me, and you will find me because you will seek me with all your heart. ¹⁴Yes, I say, you will find me, and I will restore you to your land. I will gather you from every country and from every place to which I have scattered you, and I will bring you back to the land from which I had sent you away into exile. I, the LORD, have spoken.'

¹⁵"You say that the LORD has given you prophets in Babylonia. ¹⁶Listen to what the LORD says about the king who rules the kingdom that David ruled and about the people of this city, that is, your relatives who were not taken away as prisoners with you. ¹⁷The LORD Almighty says, 'I am bringing war, starvation, and disease on them, and I will make them like figs that are too rotten to be eaten. ¹⁸I will pursue them with war, starvation, and disease, and all the nations of the world will be horrified at what they see. Everywhere I scatter them, people will be shocked and terrified at what has happened to them. People will make fun of them and use their name as a curse. ¹⁹This will happen to them because they did not obey the message that I kept on sending

ʲ **29:8** *Probable text* their; *Hebrew* your.   ᵏ **29:11** the future you hope for; *or* a future full of hope.
29:10 2 Chr 36:21; Jer 25:11; Dan 9:2   **29:13** Deut 4:29; Wis 6:12, 13

Jeremiah

to them through my servants the prophets. They refused to listen. 20 All of you whom I sent into exile in Babylonia, listen to what I, the LORD, say.'

21 "The LORD Almighty, the God of Israel, has spoken about Ahab son of Kolaiah and Zedekiah son of Maaseiah, who are telling you lies in his name. He has said that he will hand them over to the power of King Nebuchadnezzar of Babylonia, who will put them to death before your eyes. 22 When the people who were taken away as prisoners from Jerusalem to Babylonia want to bring a curse on someone, they will say, 'May the LORD treat you like Zedekiah and Ahab, whom the king of Babylonia roasted alive!' 23 This will be their fate because they are guilty of terrible sins—they have committed adultery and have told lies in the LORD's name. This was against the LORD's will; he knows what they have done, and he is a witness against them.*l* The LORD has spoken."

The Letter of Shemaiah

24-25 The LORD Almighty, the God of Israel, gave me a message for Shemaiah of Nehelam, who had sent a letter in his own name to all the people of Jerusalem and to the priest Zephaniah son of Maaseiah and to all the other priests. In this letter Shemaiah wrote to Zephaniah:

26 "The LORD made you a priest in place of Jehoiada, and you are now the chief officer*m* in the Temple. It is your duty to see that every crazy person who pretends to be a prophet is placed in chains with an iron collar around the neck. 27 Why haven't you done this to Jeremiah of Anathoth, who has been speaking as a prophet to the people? 28 He must be stopped because he told the people in Babylonia that they would be prisoners there a long time and should build houses, settle down, plant gardens, and eat what they grow."

29 Zephaniah read the letter to me, 30 and

then the LORD told me 31-32 to send to all the prisoners in Babylon this message about Shemaiah: "I, the LORD, will punish Shemaiah and all of his descendants. I did not send him, but he spoke to you as if he were a prophet, and he made you believe lies. He will have no descendants among you. He will not live to see the good things that I am going to do for my people, because he told them to rebel against me. I, the LORD, have spoken."

The LORD's Promises to His People

30 1 The LORD, the God of Israel, 2 said to me, "Write down in a book everything that I have told you, 3 because the time is coming when I will restore my people, Israel and Judah. I will bring them back to the land that I gave their ancestors, and they will take possession of it again. I, the LORD, have spoken."

4 The LORD says to the people of Israel and Judah,

5 "I heard a cry of terror,
　　a cry of fear and not of peace.
6 Now stop and think!
　　Can a man give birth to a child?
　Why then do I see every man with his
　　　hands on his stomach
　　like a woman in labor?
　Why is everyone so pale?
7 A terrible day is coming;
　　no other day can compare with it—
　　a time of distress for my people,
　　but they will survive."

8 The LORD Almighty says, "When that day comes, I will break the yoke that is around their neck and remove their chains, and they will no longer be the slaves of foreigners. 9 Instead, they will serve me, the LORD their God, and a descendant of David, whom I will enthrone as king.

10 "My people, do not be afraid;
　　people of Israel, do not be terrified.
　I will rescue you from that faraway land,
　　from the land where you are prisoners.

---

l 29:23 done, and he . . . them; *or* done; he saw them do it.　*m* 29:26 *Some ancient translations* officer; *Hebrew* officers.

30:10, 11 Jer 46:27, 28

It'll Be Okay

What's one of the first things your parent or guardian says when you get hurt or are crying? "It'll be okay." These are reassuring words. We need to hear them from time to time, especially when we're going through rough times. This is the message God is saying to the people in Jeremiah, chapter 30: "It'll be okay." This is the message God wants to say to each of us: "It'll be okay."

Think of the last time someone said those words to you. Now try remembering the last time you said them to someone else. Do you know anyone who needs to hear these words right now?

— Jeremiah 30:8–11

You will come back home and live in
    peace;
    you will be secure, and no one will
      make you afraid.
11 I will come to you and save you.
I will destroy all the nations
    where I have scattered you,
    but I will not destroy you.
I will not let you go unpunished;
    but when I punish you, I will be fair.
I, the LORD, have spoken."

12 The LORD says to his people,
"Your wounds are incurable,
    your injuries cannot be healed.
13 There is no one to take care of you,
    no remedy for your sores,
    no hope of healing for you.
14 All your lovers have forgotten you;
    they no longer care about you.

I have attacked you like an enemy;
    your punishment has been harsh
    because your sins are many
    and your wickedness is great.
15 Complain no more about your injuries;
    there is no cure for you.
I punished you like this
    because your sins are many
    and your wickedness is great.
16 But now, all who devour you will be
    devoured,
    and all your enemies will be taken away
      as prisoners.
All who oppress you will be oppressed,
    and all who plunder you will be
      plundered.
17 I will make you well again;
    I will heal your wounds,
    though your enemies say,
'Zion is an outcast;
    no one cares about her.'
I, the LORD, have spoken."

18 The LORD says,
"I will restore my people to their land
    and have mercy on every family;
Jerusalem will be rebuilt,
    and its palace restored.
19 The people who live there will sing
    praise;
    they will shout for joy.
By my blessing they will increase in
    numbers;
    my blessing will bring them honor.
20 I will restore the nation's ancient power
    and establish it firmly again;
    I will punish all who oppress them.
21-22 Their ruler will come from their own
    nation,
    their prince from their own people.
He will approach me when I invite him,
    for who would dare come uninvited?
They will be my people,
    and I will be their God.
I, the LORD, have spoken."

23-24 The LORD's anger is a storm, a furious wind that will rage over the heads of the wicked. It will not end until he has done all

Jeremiah

that he intends to do. In days to come his people will understand this clearly.

Israel's Return Home

31 [1]The LORD says, "The time is coming when I will be the God of all the tribes of Israel, and they will be my people. [2]In the desert I showed mercy to those people who had escaped death. When the people of Israel longed for rest, [3]I appeared to them[n] from far away. People of Israel, I have always loved you, so I continue to show you my constant love. [4]Once again I will rebuild you. Once again you will take up your tambourines and dance joyfully. [5]Once again you will plant vineyards on the hills of Samaria, and those who plant them will eat what the vineyards produce. [6]Yes, the time is coming when sentries will call out on the hills of Ephraim, 'Let's go up to Zion, to the LORD our God.' "

[7]The LORD says,
"Sing with joy for Israel,
   the greatest of the nations.
Sing your song of praise,
  'The LORD has saved his[o] people;
  he has rescued all who are left.'
[8]I will bring them from the north
   and gather them from the ends of the
     earth.

The young women will dance and be happy, and men, young and old, will rejoice. (31:13)

The blind and the lame will come with
   them,
   pregnant women and those about to
     give birth.
They will come back a great nation.
[9]My people will return weeping,
   praying as I lead them back.
I will guide them to streams of water,
   on a smooth road where they will not
     stumble.
I am like a father to Israel,
   and Ephraim is my oldest son."

[10]The LORD says,
"Nations, listen to me
   and proclaim my words on the far-off
     shores.
I scattered my people, but I will gather
   them
   and guard them as a shepherd guards
     his flock.
[11]I have set Israel's people free
   and have saved them from a mighty
     nation.
[12]They will come and sing for joy on
     Mount Zion
   and be delighted with my gifts—
   gifts of grain and wine and olive oil,
   gifts of sheep and cattle.
They will be like a well-watered garden;
   they will have everything they need.
[13]Then the young women will dance and
     be happy,
   and men, young and old, will rejoice.
I will comfort them and turn their
     mourning into joy,
   their sorrow into gladness.
[14]I will fill the priests with the richest food
   and satisfy all the needs of my people.
I, the LORD, have spoken."

The LORD's Mercy on Israel

[15]The LORD says,
"A sound is heard in Ramah,
   the sound of bitter weeping.

[n] **31:3** *One ancient translation* them; *Hebrew* me.   [o] **31:7** *Some ancient translations* The LORD has saved his; *Hebrew* LORD save your.
31:15 a Gen 35:16–19; **b** Mt 2:18

Rachel and her children are mentioned in Jeremiah 31:15. Read more about Rachel and her children in Genesis 35:16–19.

Rachel is crying for her children;
  they are gone,
  and she refuses to be comforted.
¹⁶ Stop your crying
  and wipe away your tears.
All that you have done for your children
  will not go unrewarded;
  they will return from the enemy's land.
¹⁷ There is hope for your future;
  your children will come back home.
  I, the LORD, have spoken.

¹⁸ "I hear the people of Israel say in grief,
  'LORD, we were like an untamed animal,
  but you taught us to obey.
Bring us back;
  we are ready to return to you,
  the LORD our God.
¹⁹ We turned away from you,
  but soon we wanted to return.
After you had punished us,
  we hung our heads in grief.
We were ashamed and disgraced
  because we sinned when we were
    young.'

²⁰ "Israel, you are my dearest child,
  the one I love best.
Whenever I mention your name,
  I think^p of you with love.
My heart goes out to you;
  I will be merciful.
²¹ Set up signs and mark the road;
  find again the way by which you left.
Come back, people of Israel,
  come home to the towns you left.
²² How long will you hesitate, faithless
    people?
I have created something new and
    different,
  as different as a woman protecting a
    man."^{q}

The Future Prosperity of God's People

²³ The LORD Almighty, the God of Israel,
says, "When I restore the people to their
land, they will once again say in the land of
Judah and in its towns,

Live It!

Wild and Tame

What does it mean to be tame? In the animal kingdom, wild horses and wild dogs run free. They have no master to obey. Tame animals have masters that they follow and who care and provide for them.

In Jeremiah, chapter 31, the people of Israel compare themselves to untamed or wild animals. They did not obey God before they were conquered and led into captivity. Now they tell the Lord, "But you taught us to obey." Aren't we in many ways like that? We enter this world untamed, and our families help to "tame" us by teaching us how to live in peace and harmony. They provide care for us—food, shelter, clothing—and so much more.

Yet it seems there are parts of us that remain untamed. At times, we want to be free and wild. We don't want to have to obey anyone. But we need the people who care for us. We need the love and guidelines they provide to grow and do well in life. We cannot let our "wild" sides get out of control and cut us off from the people we need.

Think about what parts of your life are untamed. Think also about how you can be a more positive member of your family.

— Jeremiah 31:18

'May the LORD bless the sacred hill^r of
  Jerusalem,
  the holy place where he lives.'
²⁴ People will live in Judah and in all its
towns, and there will be farmers, and

---

^{p} **31:20** I mention . . . I think; *or* I threaten to punish, I still think. ^{q} **31:22** as different . . . man; *Hebrew unclear.* ^{r} **31:23** SACRED HILL: *Mount Zion, the hill in Jerusalem which formed part of the Temple and palace area.*

Putting Your Heart in It

You remember that in Exodus, God wrote the original Ten Commandments in stone. Now in Jeremiah, chapter 31, Jeremiah delivers a very important message from God. It is one of the most beautiful prophecies in the whole book. God says he will make a New Covenant, not on stone tablets but on the hearts of the people. In other words, God's New Covenant is with each one of us, and God's law will be within us.

Think of it this way. One of the signs that you are growing up is when you do something just because you know it is the right thing to do. When you are a child, you follow rules so you won't get in trouble. As we mature, we do what is right because the motivation comes from inside of us.

If you avoid doing something wrong because you are afraid of getting caught, that's okay. But if you avoid doing something wrong just because you know it is against God's will, you are following God's law written on your heart!

— Jeremiah 31:31–33

will take care to plant them and to build them up. 29 When that time comes, people will no longer say,

'The parents ate the sour grapes,
But the children got the sour taste.'
30 Instead, those who eat sour grapes will have their own teeth set on edge; and everyone will die because of their own sin."

31 The LORD says, "The time is coming when I will make a new covenant with the people of Israel and with the people of Judah. 32 It will not be like the old covenant that I made with their ancestors when I took them by the hand and led them out of Egypt. Although I was like a husband to them, they did not keep that covenant. 33 The new covenant that I will make with the people of Israel will be this: I will put my law within them and write it on their hearts. I will be their God, and they will be my people. 34 None of them will have to teach a neighbor to know the LORD, because all will know me, from the least to the greatest. I will forgive their sins and I will no longer remember their wrongs. I, the LORD, have spoken."

35 The LORD provides the sun for light by day,
    the moon and the stars to shine at night.
He stirs up the sea and makes it roar;
    his name is the LORD Almighty.
36 He promises that as long as the natural order lasts,
    so long will Israel be a nation.
37 If one day the sky could be measured and the foundations of the earth explored,
    only then would he reject the people of Israel
    because of all they have done.
The LORD has spoken.

38 "The time is coming," says the LORD, "when all of Jerusalem will be rebuilt as my city, from Hananel Tower west to the Corner Gate. 39 And the boundary line will continue from there on the west to the hill of Gareb and then around to Goah. 40 The entire valley, where the dead are buried and garbage is

shepherds with their flocks. 25 I will refresh those who are weary and will satisfy with food everyone who is weak from hunger. 26 So then, people will say, 'I went to sleep and woke up refreshed.'

27 "I, the LORD, say that the time is coming when I will fill the land of Israel and Judah with people and animals. 28 And just as I took care to uproot, to pull down, to overthrow, to destroy, and to demolish them, so I

31:29 Ezek 18:2   31:31 Mt 26:28; Mk 14:24; Lk 22:20; 1 Cor 11:25; 2 Cor 3:6   31:31–34 Heb 8:8–12
31:33 Heb 10:16   31:34 Heb 10:17

Jeremiah

dumped, and all the fields above Kidron Brook as far as the Horse Gate to the east, will be sacred to me. The city will never again be torn down or destroyed."

Jeremiah Buys a Field

32 ¹The LORD spoke to me in the tenth year that Zedekiah was king of Judah, which was also the eighteenth year of King Nebuchadnezzar of Babylonia. ²At that time the army of the king of Babylonia was attacking Jerusalem, and I was locked up in the courtyard of the royal palace. ³King Zedekiah had imprisoned me there and had accused me of announcing that the LORD had said, "I am going to let the king of Babylonia capture this city, ⁴and King Zedekiah will not escape. He will be handed over to the king of Babylonia; he will see him face to face and will speak to him in person. ⁵Zedekiah will be taken to Babylonia, and he will remain there until I deal with him. Even if he fights the Babylonians, he will not be successful. I, the LORD, have spoken."

⁶The LORD told me ⁷that Hanamel, my uncle Shallum's son, would come to me with the request to buy his field at Anathoth in the territory of Benjamin, because I was his nearest relative and had the right to buy it for myself. ⁸Then, just as the LORD had said, Hanamel came to me there in the courtyard and asked me to buy the field. So I knew that the LORD had really spoken to me. ⁹I bought the field from Hanamel and weighed out the money to him; the price came to seventeen pieces of silver. ¹⁰I signed and sealed the deed, had it witnessed, and weighed out the money on scales. ¹¹Then I took both copies of the deed of purchase— the sealed copy containing the contract and its conditions, and the open copy— ¹²and gave them to Baruch, the son of Neriah and grandson of Mahseiah. I gave them to him in the presence of Hanamel and of the witnesses who had signed the deed of purchase and of the people who were sitting in the court-

yard. ¹³Before them all I said to Baruch, ¹⁴"The LORD Almighty, the God of Israel, has ordered you to take these deeds, both the sealed deed of purchase and the open copy, and to place them in a clay jar, so that they may be preserved for years to come. ¹⁵The LORD Almighty, the God of Israel, has said that houses, fields, and vineyards will again be bought in this land."

Jeremiah's Prayer

¹⁶After I had given the deed of purchase to Baruch, I prayed, ¹⁷"Sovereign LORD, you made the earth and the sky by your great power and might; nothing is too difficult for you. ¹⁸You have shown constant love to thousands, but you also punish people for the sins of their parents. You are a great and powerful God; you are the LORD Almighty. ¹⁹You make wise plans and do mighty things; you see everything that people do, and you reward them according to their actions. ²⁰Long ago you performed miracles and wonders in Egypt, and you have continued to perform them to this day, both in Israel and among all the other nations, so that you are now known everywhere. ²¹By means of miracles and wonders that terrified our enemies, you used your power and might to bring your people Israel out of Egypt. ²²You gave them this rich and fertile land, as you had promised their ancestors. ²³But when they came into this land and took possession of it, they did not obey your commands or live according to your teaching; they did nothing that you had ordered them to do. And so you brought all this destruction on them.

²⁴"The Babylonians have built siege mounds around the city to capture it, and they are attacking. War, starvation, and disease will make the city fall into their hands. You can see that all you have said has come true. ²⁵Yet, Sovereign LORD, you are the one who ordered me to buy the field in the presence of witnesses, even though the city is about to be captured by the Babylonians."

32:1 2 Kings 25:1–7

Jeremiah

26 Then the LORD said to me, 27 "I am the LORD, the God of all people. Nothing is too difficult for me. 28 I am going to give this city over to King Nebuchadnezzar of Babylonia and his army; they will capture it 29 and set it on fire. They will burn it down, together with the houses where people have made me angry by burning incense to Baal on the rooftops and by pouring out wine offerings to other gods. 30 From the very beginning of their history the people of Israel and the people of Judah have displeased me and made me angry by what they have done. 31 The people of this city have made me angry and furious from the day it was built. I have decided to destroy it 32 because of all the evil that has been done by the people of Judah and Jerusalem, together with their kings and leaders, their priests and prophets. 33 They turned their backs on me; and though I kept on teaching them, they would not listen and learn. 34 They even placed their disgusting idols in the Temple built for my worship, and they have defiled it. 35 They have built altars to Baal in Hinnom Valley, to sacrifice their sons and daughters to the god Molech. I did not command them to do this, and it did not even enter my mind that they would do such a thing and make the people of Judah sin."

A Promise of Hope

36 The LORD, the God of Israel, said to me, "Jeremiah, the people are saying that war, starvation, and disease will make this city fall into the hands of the king of Babylonia. Now listen to what else I have to say. 37 I am going to gather the people from all the countries where I have scattered them in my anger and fury, and I am going to bring them back to this place and let them live here in safety. 38 Then they will be my people, and I will be their God. 39 I will give them a single purpose in life: to honor me for all time, for their own good and the good of their descendants. 40 I will make an eternal covenant with them. I will never stop doing good things for them, and I will make them fear me with all their heart, so that they will never turn away from me. 41 I will take pleasure in doing good things for them, and I will establish them permanently in this land.

42 "Just as I have brought this disaster on these people, so I am going to give them all the good things that I have promised. 43 The people are saying that this land will be like a desert where neither people nor animals live, and that it will be given over to the Babylonians. But fields will once again be bought in this land. 44 People will buy them, and the deeds will be signed, sealed, and witnessed. This will take place in the territory of Benjamin, in the villages around Jerusalem, in the towns of Judah, and in the towns in the hill country, in the foothills, and in southern Judah. I will restore the people to their land. I, the LORD, have spoken."

Another Promise of Hope

33 1 While I was still in prison in the courtyard, the LORD's message came to me again. 2 The LORD, who made the earth, who formed it and set it in place, spoke to me. He whose name is the LORD said, 3 "Call to me, and I will answer you; I will tell you wonderful and marvelous things that you know nothing about. 4 I, the LORD, the God of Israel, say that the houses of Jerusalem and the royal palace of Judah will be torn down as a result of the siege and the attack. 5 Some will fight against the Babylonians, who will fill the houses[s] with the corpses of those whom I am going to strike down in my anger and fury. I have turned away from this city because of the evil things that its people have done. 6 But I will heal this city and its people and restore them to health. I will show them abundant peace and security. 7 I will make Judah and Israel pros-

---

[s] **33:5** *In verses 4 and 5* as a result . . . houses; *Hebrew unclear.*
32:28 2 Kings 25:1–11; 2 Chr 36:17–21   **32:34** 2 Kings 23:10; Jer 7:30, 31; 19:1–6   **32:35 a** 2 Kings 23:10; Jer 7:31; **b** Lev 18:21

Nebuchadnezzar was the name of four different kings in ancient Mesopotamia. The most famous is the one who captured Jerusalem in 597 BC.

The LORD's message came to me again. (33:1)

perous, and I will rebuild them as they were before. ⁸I will purify them from the sins that they have committed against me, and I will forgive their sins and their rebellion. ⁹Jerusalem will be a source of joy, honor, and pride to me; and every nation in the world will fear and tremble when they hear about the good things that I do for the people of Jerusalem and about the prosperity that I bring to the city."

¹⁰The LORD said, "People are saying that this place is like a desert, that it has no people or animals living in it. And they are right; the towns of Judah and the streets of Jerusalem are empty; no people or animals live there. But in these places you will hear again ¹¹the shouts of gladness and joy and the happy sounds of wedding feasts. You will hear people sing as they bring thank offerings to my Temple; they will say,

'Give thanks to the LORD Almighty,
    because he is good
    and his love is eternal.'

I will make this land as prosperous as it was before. I, the LORD, have spoken."

¹²The LORD Almighty said, "In this land that is like a desert and where no people or animals live, there will once again be pastures where shepherds can take their sheep. ¹³In the towns in the hill country, in the foothills, and in southern Judah, in the territory of Benjamin, in the villages around Jerusalem, and in the towns of Judah, shepherds will once again count their sheep. I, the LORD, have spoken."

¹⁴The LORD said, "The time is coming when I will fulfill the promise that I made to the people of Israel and Judah. ¹⁵At that time I will choose as king a righteous descendant of David. That king will do what is right and just throughout the land. ¹⁶The people of Judah and of Jerusalem will be rescued and will live in safety. The city will be called 'The LORD Our Salvation.' ¹⁷I, the LORD, promise that there will always be a descendant of David to be king of Israel ¹⁸and that there will always be priests from the tribe of Levi to serve me and to offer burnt offerings, grain offerings, and sacrifices."

¹⁹The LORD said to me, ²⁰"I have made a covenant with the day and with the night, so that they always come at their proper times; and that covenant can never be broken. ²¹In the same way I have made a covenant with my servant David that he would always have a descendant to be king, and I have made a covenant with the priests from the tribe of Levi that they would always serve me; and those covenants can never be broken. ²²I will increase the number of descendants of my servant David and the number of priests from the tribe of Levi, so that it will be as impossible to count them as it is to count the stars in the sky or the grains of sand on the seashore."

²³The LORD said to me, ²⁴"Have you noticed how people are saying that I have rejected Israel and Judah, the two families that I chose? And so they look with contempt on my people and no longer consider them a nation. ²⁵But I, the LORD, have a covenant with day and night, and I have made the laws that control earth and sky. ²⁶And just as surely as I have done this, so I will maintain my covenant with Jacob's descendants and with my servant David. I will choose one of David's descendants to rule over the descendants of Abraham, Isaac, and Jacob. I will be merciful to my people and make them prosperous again."

33:11 1 Chr 16:34; 2 Chr 5:13; 7:3; Ezra 3:11; Ps 100:5; 106:1; 107:1; 118:1; 136:1   **33:14–16** Jer 23:5, 6
33:17 2 Sam 7:12–16; 1 Kings 2:4; 1 Chr 17:11–14   **33:18** Num 3:5–10

Jeremiah

Pray It!

Night and Day

In our ever-changing world, there are a few things we can count on. One is the twenty-four hour cycle of each day. We know that night will always give way to day, and vice versa. God uses the trustworthiness of night and day as a symbol of the trustworthiness of his covenant with Israel and Judah. You can count on God's promises!

Let God know how grateful you are for those things in your life that you can count on. Begin with the words in Jeremiah 33:20. Think about other parts of God's Creation that we can count on and thank God for. Check out Psalm 104 and Daniel A:29–59 for songs in the Bible that focus on nature and creation.

— Jeremiah 33:19–26

A Message for Zedekiah

34 ¹The LORD spoke to me when King Nebuchadnezzar of Babylonia and his army, supported by troops from all the nations and races that were subject to him, were attacking Jerusalem and its nearby towns. ²The LORD, the God of Israel, told me to go and say to King Zedekiah of Judah, "I, the LORD, will hand this city over to the king of Babylonia, and he will burn it down. ³You will not escape; you will be captured and handed over to him. You will see him face to face and talk to him in person; then you will go to Babylonia. ⁴Zedekiah, listen to what I say about you. You will not be killed in battle. ⁵You will die in peace, and as people burned incense when they buried your ancestors, who were kings before you, in the same way they will burn incense for you. They will mourn over you and say, 'Our king is dead!' I, the LORD, have spoken."

⁶Then I gave this message to King Zedekiah in Jerusalem ⁷while the army of the king of Babylonia was attacking the city. The army was also attacking Lachish and Azekah, the only other fortified cities left in Judah.

Deceitful Treatment of Slaves

⁸King Zedekiah and the people of Jerusalem had made an agreement to set free ⁹their Hebrew slaves, both male and female, so that no one would have an Israelite as a slave. ¹⁰All the people and their leaders agreed to free their slaves and never to enslave them again. They did set them free, ¹¹but later they changed their minds, took them back, and forced them to become slaves again.

¹²Then the LORD, ¹³the God of Israel, told me to say to the people: "I made a covenant with your ancestors when I rescued them from Egypt and set them free from slavery. I told them that ¹⁴every seven years they were to set free any Hebrew slave who had served them for six years. But your ancestors would not pay any attention to me or listen to what I said. ¹⁵Just a few days ago you changed your minds and did what pleased me. All of you agreed to set all Israelites free, and you made a covenant in my presence, in the Temple where I am worshiped. ¹⁶But then you changed your minds again and dishonored me. All of you took back the slaves whom you had set free as they desired, and you forced them into slavery again. ¹⁷So now, I, the LORD, say that you have disobeyed me; you have not given all Israelites their freedom. Very well, then, I will give you freedom: the freedom to die by war, disease, and starvation. I will make every nation in the world horrified at what I do to you. ¹⁸⁻¹⁹The officials of Judah and of Jerusalem, together with the palace officials, the priests, and all the leaders, made a covenant with me by walking between the

Jeremiah

two halves of a bull that they had cut in two. But they broke the covenant and did not keep its terms. So I will do to these people what they did to the bull. 20I will hand them over to their enemies, who want to kill them, and their corpses will be eaten by birds and wild animals. 21I will also hand over King Zedekiah of Judah and his officials to those who want to kill them. I will hand them over to the Babylonian army, which has stopped its attack against you. 22I will give the order, and they will return to this city. They will attack it, capture it, and burn it down. I will make the towns of Judah like a desert where no one lives. I, the LORD, have spoken."

Jeremiah and the Rechabites

35 1When Jehoiakim son of Josiah was king of Judah, the LORD said to me, 2"Go to the members of the Rechabite clan and talk to them. Then bring them into one of the rooms in the Temple and offer them some wine." 3So I took the entire Rechabite clan—Jaazaniah (the son of another Jeremiah, who was Habazziniah's son) and all his brothers and sons— 4and brought them to the Temple. I took them into the room of the disciples of the prophet Hanan son of Igdaliah. This room was above the room of Maaseiah son of Shallum, an important official in the Temple, and near the rooms of the other officials. 5Then I placed cups and bowls full of wine before the Rechabites, and I said to them, "Have some wine."

6But they answered, "We do not drink wine. Our ancestor Jonadab son of Rechab told us that neither we nor our descendants were ever to drink any wine. 7He also told us not to build houses or farm the land and not to plant vineyards or buy them. He commanded us always to live in tents, so that we might remain in this land where we live like strangers. 8We have obeyed all the instructions that Jonadab gave us. We ourselves never drink wine, and neither do our wives, our sons, or our daughters. 9-10We do not build houses for homes—we live in tents—and we own no vineyards, fields, or grain. We have fully obeyed everything that our ancestor Jonadab commanded us. 11But when King Nebuchadnezzar invaded the country, we decided to come to Jerusalem to get away from the Babylonian and Syrian armies. That is why we are living in Jerusalem."

12-13Then the LORD Almighty, the God of Israel, told me to go and say to the people of Judah and Jerusalem, "I, the LORD, ask you why you refuse to listen to me and to obey my instructions. 14Jonadab's descendants have obeyed his command not to drink wine, and to this very day none of them drink any. But I have kept on speaking to you, and you have not obeyed me. 15I have continued to send you all my servants the prophets, and they have told you to give up your evil ways and to do what is right. They warned you not to worship and serve other gods, so that you could go on living in the land that I gave you and your ancestors. But you would not listen to me or pay any attention to me. 16Jonadab's descendants have obeyed the command that their ancestor gave them, but you people have not obeyed me. 17So now, I, the LORD Almighty, the God of Israel, will bring on you people of Judah and of Jerusalem all the destruction that I promised. I will do this because you would not listen when I spoke to you, and you would not answer when I called you."

18Then I told the Rechabite clan that the LORD Almighty, the God of Israel, had said, "You have obeyed the command that your ancestor Jonadab gave you; you have followed all his instructions, and you have done everything he commanded you. 19So I, the LORD Almighty, the God of Israel, promise that Jonadab son of Rechab will always have a male descendant to serve me."

35:1 2 Kings 23:36—24:6; 2 Chr 36:5–7

Zedekiah was the last king of Judah and was placed on his throne by Nebuchadnezzar in 597 BC.

Baruch wrote it all down on a scroll. Baruch read from the scroll. Then the officials sent Jehudi. (36:4, 10, 14)

Baruch Reads the Scroll in the Temple

36 ¹In the fourth year that Jehoiakim son of Josiah was king of Judah, the LORD said to me, ²"Get a scroll and write on it everything that I have told you about Israel and Judah and all the nations. Write everything that I have told you from the time I first spoke to you, when Josiah was king, up to the present. ³Perhaps when the people of Judah hear about all the destruction that I intend to bring on them, they will turn from their evil ways. Then I will forgive their wickedness and their sins."

⁴So I called Baruch son of Neriah and dictated to him everything that the LORD had said to me. And Baruch wrote it all down on a scroll. ⁵Then I gave Baruch the following instructions: "I am no longer allowed to go into the Temple. ⁶But I want you to go there the next time the people are fasting. You are to read the scroll aloud, so that they will hear everything that the LORD has said to me and that I have dictated to you. Do this where everyone can hear you, including the people of Judah who have come in from their towns. ⁷Perhaps they will pray to the LORD and turn from their evil ways, because the LORD has threatened this people with his terrible anger and fury." ⁸So

Baruch read the LORD's words in the Temple exactly as I had told him to do.

⁹In the ninth month of the fifth year that Jehoiakim was king of Judah, the people fasted to gain the LORD's favor. The fast was kept by all who lived in Jerusalem and by all who came there from the towns of Judah. ¹⁰Then, while all the people were listening, Baruch read from the scroll everything that I had said. He did this in the Temple, from the room of Gemariah son of Shaphan, the court secretary. His room was in the upper court near the entrance of the New Gate of the Temple.

The Scroll Is Read to the Officials

¹¹Micaiah, the son of Gemariah and grandson of Shaphan, heard Baruch read from the scroll what the LORD had said. ¹²Then he went to the royal palace, to the room of the court secretary, where all the officials were in session. Elishama, the court secretary, Delaiah son of Shemaiah, Elnathan son of Achbor, Gemariah son of Shaphan, Zedekiah son of Hananiah, and all the other officials were there. ¹³Micaiah told them everything that he had heard Baruch read to the people. ¹⁴Then the officials sent Jehudi (the son of Nethaniah, grandson of Shelemiah, and great-grandson of Cushi) to tell Baruch to bring the scroll that he had read to the people. Baruch brought them the

36:1 2 Kings 24:1; 2 Chr 36:5–7; Dan 1:1, 2

Baruch was a friend of Jeremiah and served as his secretary, or scribe. He wrote down much of what Jeremiah said.

"We must report this to the king." . . . *As soon as Jehudi finished reading three or four columns, the king cut them off.* . . . *Then I took another scroll. (36:16, 23, 32)*

scroll. 15 "Sit down," they said, "and read the scroll to us." So Baruch did. 16 After he had read it, they turned to one another in alarm and said to Baruch, "We must report this to the king." 17 Then they asked him, "Tell us, now, how did you come to write all this? Did Jeremiah dictate it to you?"

18 Baruch answered, "Jeremiah dictated every word of it to me, and I wrote it down in ink on this scroll."

19 Then they told him, "You and Jeremiah must go and hide. Don't let anyone know where you are."

The King Burns the Scroll

20 The officials put the scroll in the room of Elishama, the court secretary, and went to the king's court, where they reported everything to the king. 21 Then the king sent Jehudi to get the scroll. He took it from the room of Elishama and read it to the king and all the officials who were standing around him. 22 It was winter and the king was sitting in his winter palace in front of the fire. 23 As soon as Jehudi finished reading three or four columns, the king cut them off with a small knife and threw them into the fire. He kept doing this until the entire scroll was burned up. 24 But neither the king nor any of his officials who heard all this was afraid or showed any sign of sorrow. 25 Although Elnathan, Delaiah, and Gemariah begged the king not to burn the scroll, he paid no attention to them. 26 Then he ordered Prince Jerahmeel, together with Seraiah son of Azriel and Shelemiah son of Abdeel, to arrest me and my secretary Baruch. But the LORD had hidden us.

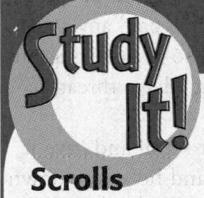

Study It!

Scrolls

It's easy to forget that books did not exist in biblical times. Written words were either carved in stone or written on scrolls. Each book of the Bible would actually have been written on one long scroll. That means one continuous sheet of skin or paper. Each end of the scroll would be attached to a rod so that both ends of the scroll could be rolled up toward the middle. They could be unrolled to locate a particular section or passage. Scrolls eventually gave way to books, which were much more convenient to use. It is also good to remember that all copies of books or scrolls were done by hand until the invention of the printing press fourteen hundred years after Christ!

In Jewish worship, scrolls are still used today.

— Jeremiah, chapter 36

Jeremiah Writes Another Scroll

27 After King Jehoiakim had burned the scroll that I had dictated to Baruch, the LORD told me 28 to take another scroll and write on it everything that had been on the

first one. ²⁹The LORD told me to say to the king, "You have burned the scroll, and you have asked Jeremiah why he wrote that the king of Babylonia would come and destroy this land and kill its people and its animals. ³⁰So now, I, the LORD, say to you, King Jehoiakim, that no descendant of yours will ever rule over David's kingdom. Your corpse will be thrown out where it will be exposed to the sun during the day and to the frost at night. ³¹I will punish you, your descendants, and your officials because of the sins all of you commit. Neither you nor the people of Jerusalem and of Judah have paid any attention to my warnings, and so I will bring on all of you the disaster that I have threatened."

³²Then I took another scroll and gave it to my secretary Baruch, and he wrote down everything that I dictated. He wrote everything that had been on the first scroll and similar messages that I dictated to him.

Zedekiah's Request to Jeremiah

37 ¹King Nebuchadnezzar of Babylonia made Zedekiah son of Josiah king of Judah in the place of Jehoiachin son of Jehoiakim. ²But neither Zedekiah nor his officials nor the people obeyed the message which the LORD had given me.

³King Zedekiah sent Jehucal son of Shelemiah and the priest Zephaniah son of Maaseiah to ask me to pray to the LORD our God on behalf of our nation. ⁴I had not yet been put in prison and was still moving about freely among the people. ⁵The Babylonian army had been besieging Jerusalem, but when they heard that the Egyptian army had crossed the Egyptian border, they retreated.

⁶Then the LORD, the God of Israel, told me ⁷to say to Zedekiah, "The Egyptian army is on its way to help you, but it will return home. ⁸Then the Babylonians will come back, attack the city, capture it, and burn it down. ⁹I, the LORD, warn you not to deceive yourselves into thinking that the Babylonians will not come back, because they will. ¹⁰Even if you defeat the whole Babylonian army, so that only wounded men are left, lying in their tents, they would still get up and burn this city to the ground."

Jeremiah Is Arrested and Imprisoned

¹¹The Babylonian army retreated from Jerusalem because the Egyptian army was approaching. ¹²So I started to leave Jerusalem and go to the territory of Benjamin to take possession of my share of the family property. ¹³But when I reached the Benjamin Gate, the officer in charge of the soldiers on duty there, a man by the name of Irijah, the son of Shelemiah and grandson of Hananiah, stopped me and said, "You are deserting to the Babylonians!"

¹⁴I answered, "That's not so! I'm not deserting." But Irijah would not listen to me. Instead, he arrested me and took me to the officials. ¹⁵They were furious with me and had me beaten and locked up in the house of Jonathan, the court secretary, whose house had been made into a prison. ¹⁶I was put in an underground cell and kept there a long time.

¹⁷Later on King Zedekiah sent for me, and there in the palace he asked me privately, "Is there any message from the LORD?"

"There is," I answered, and added, "You will be handed over to the king of Babylonia." ¹⁸Then I asked, "What crime have I committed against you or your officials or this people, to make you put me in prison? ¹⁹What happened to your prophets who told you that the king of Babylonia would not attack you or the country? ²⁰And now, Your Majesty, I beg you to listen to me and do what I ask. Please do not send me back to the prison in Jonathan's house. If you do, I will surely die there."

²¹So King Zedekiah ordered me to be locked up in the palace courtyard. I stayed there, and each day I was given a loaf of bread from the bakeries until all the bread in the city was gone.

37:1 2 Kings 24:17; 2 Chr 36:10

Pray It!

Down and Out

Sometimes you may feel as if you too are at the bottom of a deep pit, as Jeremiah was when he was thrown into the muddy well. Maybe this prayer will help.

Dear God, right now I feel pretty down and out. It seems that no one cares, and I am just sinking deeper. I believe that you are with me in my troubles. And just as Jeremiah was rescued by someone, I pray that you will send someone to help me. Keep my eyes focused on you and fill me with hope. Let me also have the courage to ask for help when I need it. I can't get through life alone. I look forward to brighter days. Thank you, God. Amen.

— Jeremiah 38:1–13

Jeremiah in a Dry Well

38 ¹Shephatiah son of Mattan, Gedaliah son of Pashhur, Jehucal son of Shelemiah, and Pashhur son of Malchiah heard that I was telling the people that ²the LORD had said, "Whoever stays on in the city will die in war or of starvation or disease. But those who go out and surrender to the Babylonians will not be killed; they will at least escape with their life." ³I was also telling them that the LORD had said, "I am going to give the city to the Babylonian army, and they will capture it."

⁴Then the officials went to the king and said, "This man must be put to death. By talking like this he is making the soldiers in the city lose their courage, and he is doing the same thing to everyone else left in the city. He is not trying to help the people; he only wants to hurt them."

⁵King Zedekiah answered, "Very well, then, do what you want to with him; I can't stop you." ⁶So they took me and let me down by ropes into Prince Malchiah's well, which was in the palace courtyard. There was no water in the well, only mud, and I sank down in it.

⁷However, Ebedmelech the Ethiopian,ᶠ a eunuch who worked in the royal palace, heard that they had put me in the well. At that time the king was holding court at the Benjamin Gate. ⁸So Ebedmelech went there and said to the king, ⁹"Your Majesty, what these men have done is wrong. They have put Jeremiah in the well, where he is sure to die of starvation, since there is no more food in the city." ¹⁰Then the king ordered Ebedmelech to take with him three men and to pull me out of the well before I died. ¹¹So Ebedmelech went with the men to the palace storeroom and got some worn-out clothing which he let down to me by ropes. ¹²He told me to put the rags under my arms, so that the ropes wouldn't hurt me. I did this, ¹³and they pulled me up out of the well. After that I was kept in the courtyard.

Zedekiah Asks Jeremiah's Advice

¹⁴On another occasion King Zedekiah had me brought to him at the third entrance to the Temple, and he said, "I am going to

ᶠ *38:7 Hebrew* Cushite: *Cush is the ancient name of the extensive territory south of the First Cataract of the Nile River. This region was called Ethiopia in Graeco-Roman times, and included within its borders most of modern Sudan and some of present-day Ethiopia (Abyssinia).*

Why do you think Jeremiah's message upset people so much that they wanted to throw him in a well and leave him to die?

Jeremiah

And they pulled me up out of the well. (38:13)

ask you a question, and I want you to tell me the whole truth."

15 I answered, "If I tell you the truth, you will put me to death, and if I give you advice, you won't pay any attention."

16 So King Zedekiah promised me in secret, "I swear by the living God, the God who gave us life, that I will not put you to death or hand you over to the men who want to kill you."

17 Then I told Zedekiah that the LORD Almighty, the God of Israel, had said, "If you surrender to the king of Babylonia's officers, your life will be spared, and this city will not be burned down. Both you and your family will be spared. **18** But if you do not surrender, then this city will be handed over to the Babylonians, who will burn it down, and you will not escape from them."

19 But the king answered, "I am afraid of our own people who have deserted to the Babylonians. I may be handed over to them and tortured."

20 I said, "You will not be handed over to them. I beg you to obey the LORD's message; then all will go well with you, and your life will be spared. **21** But the LORD has shown me in a vision what will happen if

you refuse to surrender. **22** In it I saw all the women left in Judah's royal palace being led out to the king of Babylonia's officers. Listen to what they were saying as they went:

> 'The king's best friends misled him,
> 　they overruled him.
> And now that his feet have sunk in the
> 　mud,
> 　his friends have left him.' "

23 Then I added, "All your women and children will be taken out to the Babylonians, and you yourself will not escape from them. You will be taken prisoner by the king of Babylonia, and this city will be burned to the ground."

24 Zedekiah replied, "Don't let anyone know about this conversation, and your life will not be in danger. **25** If the officials hear that I have talked with you, they will come and ask you what we said. They will promise not to put you to death if you tell them everything. **26** Just tell them you were begging me not to send you back to prison to die there." **27** Then all the officials came and questioned me, and I told them exactly what the king had told me to say. There was nothing else they could do, because no one had overheard the conversation. **28** And I was kept in the palace courtyard until the day Jerusalem was captured.

The Fall of Jerusalem

39 **1** In the tenth month of the ninth year that Zedekiah was king of Judah, King Nebuchadnezzar of Babylonia came with his whole army and attacked Jerusalem. **2** On the ninth day of the fourth month of Zedekiah's eleventh year as king, the city walls were broken through.

(**3** When Jerusalem was captured,*ᵘ* all the high officials of the king of Babylonia came and took their places at the Middle Gate, including Nergal Sharezer, Samgar Nebo, Sarsechim, and another Nergal Sharezer.*ᵛ*)

ᵘ **39:3** When Jerusalem was captured; *these words are moved here from the end of chapter 38.* *ᵛ* **39:3** *The names and titles of these men are unclear.*
38:28 Ezek 33:21

The Babylonians burned down the royal palace and the houses. (39:8)

4When King Zedekiah and all his soldiers saw what was happening, they tried to escape from the city during the night. They left by way of the royal garden, went through the gateway connecting the two walls, and escaped in the direction of the Jordan Valley. 5But the Babylonian army pursued them and captured Zedekiah in the plains near Jericho. Then they took him to King Nebuchadnezzar, who was in the city of Riblah in the territory of Hamath, and there Nebuchadnezzar passed sentence on him. 6At Riblah he put Zedekiah's sons to death while Zedekiah was looking on, and he also had the officials of Judah executed. 7After that, he had Zedekiah's eyes put out and had him placed in chains to be taken to Babylonia. 8Meanwhile, the Babylonians burned down the royal palace and the houses of the people and tore down the walls of Jerusalem. 9Finally Nebuzaradan, the commanding officer, took away as prisoners to Babylonia the people who were left in the city, together with those who had deserted to him. 10He left in the land of Judah some of the poorest people, who owned no property, and he gave them vineyards and fields.

Jeremiah's Release

11But King Nebuchadnezzar commanded Nebuzaradan, the commanding officer, to give the following order: 12"Go and find Jeremiah and take good care of him. Do not harm him, but do for him whatever he wants." 13So Nebuzaradan, together with the high officials Nebushazban and Nergal Sharezer and all the other officers of the king of Babylonia, 14had me brought from the palace courtyard. They put me under the care of Gedaliah, the son of Ahikam and grandson of Shaphan, who was to see that I got home safely. And so I stayed there among the people.

Hope for Ebedmelech

15While I was still imprisoned in the palace courtyard, the LORD told me 16to tell Ebedmelech the Ethiopian*w* that the LORD Almighty, the God of Israel, had said, "Just as I said I would, I am going to bring upon this city destruction and not prosperity. And when this happens, you will be there to see it. 17But I, the LORD, will protect you, and you will not be handed over to the people you are afraid of. 18I will keep you safe, and you will not be put to death. You will escape

w **39:16** *Hebrew* Cushite: *Cush is the ancient name of the extensive territory south of the First Cataract of the Nile River. This region was called Ethiopia in Graeco-Roman times, and included within its borders most of modern Sudan and some of present-day Ethiopia (Abyssinia).*

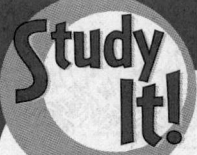

Stories After the Fall

Jeremiah, chapters 39–45, read more like history than prophecy. They tell about what happened to Jeremiah and the land of Judah after the Babylonians left. Jeremiah was not forced to go into captivity in Babylon. So he stayed back in Judah, where he had a number of adventures, including being forced to go to Egypt for a while.

The point of it all seems to be that if people just listened to God's message that Jeremiah delivered, everything would have been much better. They could have lived in peace without making the Babylonians angry with them. There would have been no war or destruction of Jerusalem and the Temple. But they continued to refuse to listen to Jeremiah, leading to more killing and hardships.

— Jeremiah, chapter 40

with your life because you have put your trust in me. I, the LORD, have spoken."

Jeremiah Stays with Gedaliah

40 ¹The LORD spoke to me after Nebuzaradan, the commanding officer, had set me free at Ramah. I had been taken there in chains, along with all the other people from Jerusalem and Judah who were being taken away as prisoners to Babylonia.

²The commanding officer took me aside and said, "The LORD your God threatened this land with destruction, ³and now he has done what he said he would. All this happened because your people sinned against

the LORD and disobeyed him. ⁴Now, I am taking the chains off your wrists and setting you free. If you want to go to Babylonia with me, you may do so, and I will take care of you. But if you don't want to go, you don't have to. You have the whole country to choose from, and you may go wherever you wish."

⁵When I did not answer,ˣ Nebuzaradan said, "Go back to Gedaliah, the son of Ahikam and grandson of Shaphan, whom the king of Babylonia has made governor of the towns of Judah. You may stay with him and live among the people, or you may go anywhere you think you should." Then he gave me a present and some food to take with me, and let me go on my way. ⁶I went to stay with Gedaliah in Mizpah and lived among the people who were left in the land.

Gedaliah, Governor of Judah
(2 Kings 25:22–24)

⁷Some of the Judean officers and soldiers had not surrendered. They heard that the king of Babylonia had made Gedaliah governor of the land and had placed him in charge of all those who had not been taken away to Babylonia—the poorest people in the land. ⁸So Ishmael son of Nethaniah, Johanan son of Kareah, Seraiah son of Tanhumeth, the sons of Ephai from Netophah, and Jezaniah from Maacah went with their men to Gedaliah at Mizpah. ⁹Gedaliah said to them, "I give you my word that there is no need for you to be afraid to surrender to the Babylonians. Settle in this land, serve the king of Babylonia, and all will go well with you. ¹⁰I myself will stay in Mizpah and be your representative when the Babylonians come here. But you can gather and store up wine, fruit, and olive oil, and live in the villages you occupy." ¹¹Meanwhile, all the Israelites who were in Moab, Ammon, Edom, and other countries, heard that the king of Babylonia had allowed some Israelites to stay on in Judah and that he had made Gedaliah their governor. ¹²So they left the places where they had been scattered,

---

ˣ **40:5** When I did not answer; *or* Then, before he left.
40:7–9 2 Kings 25:22–24

Jeremiah

and returned to Judah. They came to Gedaliah at Mizpah, and there they gathered in large amounts of wine and fruit.

Gedaliah Is Murdered
(2 Kings 25:25, 26)

13After this, Johanan and the leaders of the soldiers who had not surrendered came to Gedaliah at Mizpah 14and said to him, "Don't you know that King Baalis of Ammon has sent Ishmael to murder you?" But Gedaliah did not believe it. 15Then Johanan said privately to him, "Let me go and kill Ishmael, and no one will know who did it. Why should he be allowed to murder you? That would cause all the Jews who have gathered around you to be scattered, and it would bring disaster on all the people who are left in Judah."

16But Gedaliah answered, "Don't do it! What you are saying about Ishmael is not true!"

41 1In the seventh month of that year, Ishmael, the son of Nethaniah and grandson of Elishama, a member of the royal family and one of the king's chief officers, went to Mizpah with ten men to see Governor Gedaliah. While they were all eating a meal together, 2Ishmael and the ten men with him pulled out their swords and killed Gedaliah. 3Ishmael also killed all the Israelites who were with Gedaliah at Mizpah and the Babylonian soldiers who happened to be there.

4The next day, before anyone knew about Gedaliah's murder, 5eighty men arrived from Shechem, Shiloh, and Samaria. They had shaved off their beards, torn their clothes, and gashed themselves. They were taking grain and incense to offer in the Temple. 6So Ishmael went out from Mizpah to meet them, weeping as he went. When he came to them, he said, "Please come in to see Gedaliah." 7As soon as they were inside the city, Ishmael and his men killed them and threw their bodies in a well.

8But there were ten men in the group who said to Ishmael, "Please don't kill us! We have wheat, barley, olive oil, and honey hidden in the fields." So he spared them. 9The well into which Ishmael threw the bodies of the men he had killed was the large oneʸ that King Asa had dug when he was being attacked by King Baasha of Israel. Ishmael filled the well with the bodies. 10Then he made prisoners of the king's daughters and all the rest of the people in Mizpah, whom Nebuzaradan the commanding officer had placed under the care of Gedaliah. Ishmael took them prisoner and started off in the direction of the territory of Ammon.

11Johanan and all the army leaders with him heard of the crime that Ishmael had committed. 12So they went after him with their men and overtook him near the large pool at Gibeon. 13When Ishmael's prisoners saw Johanan and the leaders of the forces with him, they were glad, 14and turned and ran to them. 15But Ishmael and eight of his men got away from Johanan and escaped to the land of Ammon.

16Then Johanan and the leaders of the forces with him took charge of the people whom Ishmael had taken away as prisoners from Mizpah after murdering Gedaliah— soldiers, women, children, and eunuchs. 17-18They were afraid of the Babylonians because Ishmael had murdered Gedaliah, whom the king of Babylonia had made governor of the land. So they set out for Egypt, in order to get away from the Babylonians. On the way they stopped at Chimham near Bethlehem.

The People Ask Jeremiah to Pray for Them

42 1Then all the army leaders, including Johanan son of Kareah and Azariahᶻ son of Hoshaiah, came with people

---

ʸ 41:9 *One ancient translation* was the large one; *Hebrew* by means of Gedaliah.   ᶻ 42:1 *One ancient translation* (*see also* 43:2) Azariah; *Hebrew* Jezaniah.
41:1–3 2 Kings 25:25

King Asa (*Jeremiah 41:9*) ruled over Judah from 911 to 870 BC. Check out his story in 1 Kings 15:9–24.

of every class ²and said to me, "Please do what we ask you! Pray to the LORD our God for us. Pray for all of us who have survived. Once there were many of us; but now only a few of us are left, as you can see. ³Pray that the LORD our God will show us the way we should go and what we should do."

⁴I answered, "Very well, then. I will pray to the LORD our God, just as you have asked, and whatever he says, I will tell you. I will not keep back anything from you."

⁵Then they said to me, "May the LORD be a true and faithful witness against us if we do not obey all the commands that the LORD our God gives you for us. ⁶Whether it pleases us or not, we will obey the LORD our God, to whom we are asking you to pray. All will go well with us if we obey him."

The LORD's Answer to Jeremiah's Prayer

⁷Ten days later the LORD spoke to me; ⁸so I called together Johanan, all the army leaders who were with him, and all the other people. ⁹I said to them, "The LORD, the God of Israel, to whom you sent me with your request has said, ¹⁰'If you are willing to go on living in this land, then I will build you up and not tear you down; I will plant you and not pull you up. The destruction I brought on you has caused me great sorrow. ¹¹Stop being afraid of the king of Babylonia. I am with you, and I will rescue you from his power. ¹²Because I am merciful, I will make him have mercy on you and let you go back home. I, the LORD, have spoken.'

¹³⁻¹⁵"But you people who are left in Judah must not disobey the LORD your God and refuse to live in this land. You must not say, 'No, we will go and live in Egypt, where we won't face war any more or hear the call to battle or go hungry.' If you say this, then the LORD Almighty, the God of Israel, says, 'If you are determined to go and live in Egypt, ¹⁶then the war that you fear will

overtake you, and the hunger you dread will follow you, and you will die there in Egypt. ¹⁷All the people who are determined to go and live in Egypt will die either in war or of starvation or disease. Not one of them will survive, not one will escape the disaster that I am going to bring on them.'

¹⁸"The LORD, the God of Israel, says, 'Just as my anger and fury were poured out on the people of Jerusalem, so my fury will be poured out on you if you go to Egypt. You will be a horrifying sight; people will make fun of you and use your name as a curse. You will never see this place again.' "

¹⁹Then I continued, "The LORD has told you people who are left in Judah not to go to Egypt. And so I warn you now ²⁰that you are making a fatal mistake. You asked me to pray to the LORD our God for you, and you promised that you would do everything that he commands. ²¹And now I have told you, but you are disobeying everything that the LORD our God sent me to tell you. ²²So then, remember this: you will die in war or of starvation or disease in the land where you want to go and live."

Jeremiah Is Taken to Egypt

43 ¹I finished telling the people everything that the LORD their God had sent me to tell them. ²Then Azariah son of Hoshaiah and Johanan son of Kareah and all the other arrogant men said to me, "You are lying. The LORD our God did not send you to tell us not to go and live in Egypt. ³Baruch son of Neriah has stirred you up against us, so that the Babylonians will gain power over us and can either kill us or take us away to Babylonia." ⁴So neither Johanan nor any of the army officers nor any of the people would obey the LORD's command to remain in the land of Judah. ⁵Then Johanan and all the army officers took everybody left in Judah away to Egypt, together with all the people who had returned from the nations where they had been scattered: ⁶the men, the

43:5–7 2 Kings 25:26

Jeremiah

They disobeyed the LORD's command and went into Egypt. (43:7)

women, the children, and the king's daughters. They took everyone whom Nebuzaradan the commanding officer had left under the care of Gedaliah, including Baruch and me. ⁷They disobeyed the LORD's command and went into Egypt as far as the city of Tahpanhes.

⁸There the LORD said to me, ⁹"Get some large stones and bury them in the mortar of the pavement*ᵃ* in front of the entrance to the government building here in the city, and let some of the Israelites see you do it. ¹⁰Then tell them that I, the LORD Almighty, the God of Israel, am going to bring my servant King Nebuchadnezzar of Babylonia to this place, and he*ᵇ* will put his throne over these stones that you*ᶜ* buried, and will spread the royal tent over them. ¹¹Nebuchadnezzar will come and defeat Egypt. Those people who are doomed to die of disease will die of disease, those doomed to be taken away as prisoners will be taken away as prisoners, and those doomed to be killed in war will be killed in war. ¹²I will set fire to the temples of Egypt's gods, and the king of Babylonia will either burn their gods or carry them off. As shepherds pick their clothes clean of lice, so the king of Babylonia will pick the land of Egypt clean and then leave victorious. ¹³He will destroy the sacred stone monuments at Heliopolis in Egypt and will burn down the temples of the Egyptian gods."

The LORD's Message to the Israelites in Egypt

44 ¹The LORD spoke to me concerning all the Israelites living in Egypt, in the cities of Migdol, Tahpanhes, and Memphis, and in the southern part of the country. ²The LORD Almighty, the God of Israel, said,

Study It!

Egypt

At the end of his life, Jeremiah was taken off to Egypt, and it is believed that he died there. Egypt plays a very important role in the Bible, and many great figures spent time there.

• Joseph was sold by his brothers into slavery and spent many years in Egypt, eventually becoming governor and being reunited with his family (Genesis, chapters 37–50).

• Moses fled Egypt but was called by God to lead the Israelites out of slavery in Egypt to the Promised Land.

• Jesus was taken to Egypt by Mary and Joseph to protect him from death when Herod ordered that all boys under the age of two be murdered (Matthew 2:13–23).

• Egypt today is famous for its ancient pyramids. Make sure you can find Egypt on a map.

— Jeremiah 43:1–6

"You yourselves have seen the destruction I brought on Jerusalem and all the other cities of Judah. Even now they are still in ruins, and no one lives in them ³because their people had done evil and had made me angry.

ᵃ **43:9** *Probable text* bury them . . . pavement; *Hebrew unclear.*   *ᵇ* **43:10** *Some ancient translations* he; *Hebrew* I.
ᶜ **43:10** *Some ancient translations* you; *Hebrew* I.

Jeremiah

They offered sacrifices to other gods and served gods that neither they nor you nor your ancestors ever worshiped. ⁴I kept sending you my servants the prophets, who told you not to do this terrible thing that I hate. ⁵But you would not listen or pay any attention. You would not give up your evil practice of sacrificing to other gods. ⁶So I poured out my anger and fury on the towns of Judah and on the streets of Jerusalem, and I set them on fire. They were left in ruins and became a horrifying sight, as they are today.

⁷"And so I, the LORD Almighty, the God of Israel, now ask why you are doing such an evil thing to yourselves. Do you want to bring destruction on men and women, children and babies, so that none of your people will be left? ⁸Why do you make me angry by worshiping idols and by sacrificing to other gods here in Egypt, where you have come to live? Are you doing this just to destroy yourselves, so that every nation on earth will make fun of you and use your name as a curse? ⁹Have you forgotten all the wicked things that have been done in the towns of Judah and in the streets of Jerusalem by your ancestors, by the kings of Judah and their wives, and by you and your wives? ¹⁰But to this day you have not humbled yourselves. You have not honored me or lived according to all the laws that I gave you and your ancestors.

¹¹"So then, I, the LORD Almighty, the God of Israel, will turn against you and destroy all Judah. ¹²As for the people of Judah who are left and are determined to go and live in Egypt, I will see to it that all of them are destroyed. All of them, great and small, will die in Egypt, either in war or of starvation. They will be a horrifying sight; people will make fun of them and use their name as a curse. ¹³I will punish those who live in Egypt, just as I punished Jerusalem—with war, starvation, and disease. ¹⁴None of the people of Judah who are left and have come to Egypt to live will escape or survive. Not one of them will return to Judah, where they long to live once again. No one will return except a few refugees."

¹⁵Then all the men who knew that their wives offered sacrifices to other gods, and all the women who were standing there, including the Israelites who lived in southern Egypt—a large crowd in all—said to me, ¹⁶"We refuse to listen to what you have told us in the name of the LORD. ¹⁷We will do everything that we said we would. We will offer sacrifices to our goddess, the Queen of Heaven, and we will pour out wine offerings to her, just as we and our ancestors, our king and our leaders, used to do in the towns of Judah and in the streets of Jerusalem. Then we had plenty of food, we were prosperous, and had no troubles. ¹⁸But ever since we stopped sacrificing to the Queen of Heaven and stopped pouring out wine offerings to her, we have had nothing, and our people have died in war and of starvation."

¹⁹And the women added, "When we baked cakes shaped like the Queen of Heaven, offered sacrifices to her, and poured out wine offerings to her, our husbands approved of what we were doing."

²⁰Then I said to all the men and the women who had answered me in this way, ²¹"As for the sacrifices which you and your ancestors, your kings and your leaders, and the people of the land offered in the towns of Judah and in the streets of Jerusalem—do you think that the LORD did not know about them or that he forgot them? ²²This very day your land lies in ruins and no one lives in it. It has become a horrifying sight, and people use its name as a curse because the LORD could no longer endure your wicked and evil practices. ²³This present disaster has come on you because you offered sacrifices to other gods and sinned against the LORD by not obeying all his commands."

²⁴⁻²⁵I told all the people, especially the women, what the LORD Almighty, the God of Israel, was saying to the people of Judah living in Egypt: "Both you and your wives have made solemn promises to the Queen of Heaven. You promised that you would offer sacrifices to her and pour out wine offerings to her, and you have kept your promises. Very well, then! Keep your promises! Carry out your vows! ²⁶But now listen to the vow that I, the LORD, have made in my mighty name to all you Israelites in Egypt: Never again will I let any of you use my name to

make a vow by saying, 'I swear by the living Sovereign LORD!' 27I will see to it that you will not prosper, but will be destroyed. All of you will die, either in war or of disease, until not one of you is left. 28But a few of you will escape death and return from Egypt to Judah. Then the survivors will know whose words have come true, mine or theirs. 29I, the LORD, will give you proof that I will punish you in this place and that my promise to bring destruction on you will come true. 30I will hand over King Hophra of Egypt to his enemies who want to kill him, just as I handed over King Zedekiah of Judah to King Nebuchadnezzar of Babylonia, who was his enemy and wanted to kill him."

God's Promise to Baruch

45 1In the fourth year that Jehoiakim son of Josiah was king of Judah, Baruch wrote down what I had dictated to him. Then I told him 2that the LORD, the God of Israel, had said, "Baruch, 3you are saying, 'I give up! The LORD has added sorrow to my troubles. I am worn out from groaning, and I can't find any rest!'

4"But I, the LORD, am tearing down what I have built and pulling up what I have planted. I will do this to the entire earth. 5Are you looking for special treatment for yourself? Don't do it. I am bringing disaster on all people, but you will at least escape with your life, wherever you go. I, the LORD, have spoken."

Egypt's Defeat at Carchemish

46 1The LORD spoke to me about the nations, 2beginning with Egypt. This is what he said about the army of King Neco of Egypt, which King Nebuchadnezzar of Babylonia defeated at Carchemish near the Euphrates River in the fourth year that Jehoiakim was king of Judah:

3 "The Egyptian officers shout,
    'Get your shields ready
        and march into battle!
4 Harness your horses and mount them!
    Fall in line and put on your helmets!
        Sharpen your spears!
        Put on your armor!'

5 "But what do I see?" asks the LORD.
    "They are turning back in terror.
    Their soldiers are beaten back;
        overcome with fear, they run as fast as
            they can
        and do not look back.
6 Those who run fast cannot get away;
    the soldiers cannot escape.
    In the north, by the Euphrates,
        they stumble and fall.
7 Who is this that rises like the Nile,
    like a river flooding its banks?
8 It is Egypt, rising like the Nile,
    like a river flooding its banks.
    Egypt said, 'I will rise and cover the world;
        I will destroy cities and the people who
            live there.
9 Command the horses to go
    and the chariots to roll!
    Send out the soldiers:
        men from Ethiopia[d] and Libya,
            carrying shields,
        and skilled archers from Lydia.' "

10 This is the day of the Sovereign LORD
        Almighty:
    today he will take revenge;
    today he will punish his enemies.

Command the horses to go. (46:9)

d **46:9** *Hebrew* Cush: *Cush is the ancient name of the extensive territory south of the First Cataract of the Nile River. This region was called Ethiopia in Graeco-Roman times, and included within its borders most of modern Sudan and some of present-day Ethiopia (Abyssinia).*
44:30 2 Kings 25:1–7   **45:1** 2 Kings 24:1; 2 Chr 36:5–7; Dan 1:1, 2   **46:2–26** Isa 19:1–25; Ezek 29:1—32:32

Jeremiah

The Queen of Heaven referred to in Jeremiah 44:17 is not Jesus' mother, Mary, but a false goddess. That title was later given to Mary by the Church.

His sword will eat them until it is full,
and drink their blood until it is
satisfied.
Today the Almighty sacrifices his victims
in the north, by the Euphrates.
11 People of Egypt, go to Gilead^e
and look for medicine!
All your medicine has proved useless;
nothing can heal you.
12 Nations have heard of your shame;
everyone has heard you cry.
One soldier trips over another,
and both of them fall to the ground.

The Coming of Nebuchadnezzar

13 When King Nebuchadnezzar of Babylonia came to attack Egypt, the LORD spoke to me. He said,

14 "Proclaim it in the towns of Egypt,
in Migdol, Memphis, and Tahpanhes:
'Get ready to defend yourselves;
all you have will be destroyed in
war!
15 Why has your mighty god Apis fallen?
The LORD has struck him down!'
16 Your soldiers have stumbled and fallen;^f
each one says to the other,
'Hurry! Let's go home to our people
and escape the enemy's sword!'
17 "Give the king of Egypt a new name—
'Noisy Braggart Who Missed His
Chance.'
18 I, the LORD Almighty, am king.
I am the living God.
As Mount Tabor towers above the
mountains
and Mount Carmel stands high above
the sea,
so will be the strength of the one who
attacks you.
19 Get ready to be taken prisoner,
you people of Egypt!
Memphis will be made a desert,
a ruin where no one lives.

20 Egypt is like a splendid cow,
attacked by a stinging fly from the
north.
21 Even her hired soldiers
are helpless as calves.
They did not stand and fight;
all of them turned and ran.
The day of their doom had arrived,
the time of their destruction.
22 Egypt runs away, hissing like a snake,
as the enemy's army approaches.
They attack her with axes,
like people cutting down trees
23   and destroying a thick forest.
Their soldiers are too many to count;
they outnumber the locusts.
24 The people of Egypt are put to shame;
they are conquered by the people of
the north.
I, the LORD, have spoken."

25 The LORD Almighty, the God of Israel, says, "I am going to punish Amon, the god of Thebes, together with Egypt and its gods and kings. I am going to take the king of Egypt and all who put their trust in him, 26 and hand them over to those who want to kill them, to King Nebuchadnezzar of Babylonia and his army. But later on, people will live in Egypt again, as they did in times past. I, the LORD, have spoken.

The LORD Will Save His People

27 "My people, do not be afraid,
people of Israel, do not be terrified.
I will rescue you from that faraway land,
from the land where you are prisoners.
You will come back home and live in
peace;
you will be secure, and no one will
make you afraid.
28 I will come to you and save you.
I will destroy all the nations
where I have scattered you,
but I will not destroy you.

---

^e **46:11** GILEAD: *See 8:22.*   ^f **46:16** *Probable text* Your soldiers . . . fallen; *Hebrew unclear.*
46:13 Jer 43:10–13   **46:27, 28** Jer 30:10, 11

Jeremiah (side tab)

Crete and Gaza still exist today. Crete is an island, and Gaza is part of the Holy Land. See if you can locate them on a map.

Fair Punishment

In Jeremiah 46:28, the Lord says, "I will not let you go unpunished; / but when I punish you, I will be fair."

No one likes to get punished, even when the punishment is deserved. Yet it is easier to accept punishment when you know that it is fair. A fair punishment can help you cool down, be honest and admit that you were wrong, and encourage you to make up for any hurt or damage you have caused. God allowed the Israelites to suffer violence and captivity to help them to be honest about their sinful actions. It was a way of getting their attention. So the next time you are punished for something you did wrong, ask God for the grace to accept punishment without trying to blame someone else. Use it as an opportunity to let God help you be a better person.

— Jeremiah 46:28

I will not let you go unpunished;
    but when I punish you, I will be
      fair.
I, the LORD, have spoken."

The LORD's Message about Philistia

47 ¹Before the king of Egypt attacked Gaza, the LORD spoke to me about Philistia. ²He said:

"Look! Waters are rising in the north
    and will rush like a river in flood.
They will cover the land and everything
    on it,
    cities and the people who live there.

People will call out for help;
    everyone on earth will cry bitterly.
³They will hear the hoofbeats of horses,
    the clatter of chariots,
    the rumble of wheels.
Parents will not turn back for their
    children;
    their hands will hang limp at their sides.
⁴The time has come to destroy Philistia,
    to cut off from Tyre and Sidon
    all the help that remains.
I, the LORD, will destroy the Philistines,
    all who came from the shores of Crete.
⁵Great sorrow has come to the people of
    Gaza,
    and Ashkelon's people are silent.
    How long will the rest of Philistia
      mourn?
⁶You cry out, 'Sword of the LORD!
    How long will you go on slashing?
Go back to your scabbard,
    stay there and rest!'
⁷But how can it rest,
    when I have given it work to do?
I have commanded it to attack Ashkelon
    and the people who live on the coast."

The Destruction of Moab

48 ¹This is what the LORD Almighty said about Moab:

"Pity the people of Nebo—
    their town is destroyed!
Kiriathaim is captured,
    its mighty fortress torn down,
    and its people put to shame;
²   the splendor of Moab is gone.
The enemy have captured Heshbon
    and plot to destroy the nation of Moab.
The town of Madmen will be silenced;
    armies will march against it.
³The people of Horonaim cry out,
    'Violence! Destruction!'

⁴"Moab has been destroyed;
    listen to the children crying.
⁵Hear the sound of their sobs
    along the road up to Luhith,
    the cries of distress
    on the way down to Horonaim.

47:1–7 Isa 14:29–31; Ezek 25:15–17; Joel 3:4–8; Am 1:6–8; Zeph 2:4–7; Zech 9:5–7   **48:1–47** Isa 15:1—16:14; 25:10–12; Ezek 25:8–11; Am 2:1–3; Zeph 2:8–11

Jeremiah

⁶'Quick, run for your lives!' they say.
  'Run like a wild desert donkey!'

⁷"Moab, you trusted in your strength and
      your wealth,
  but now even you will be conquered;
  your god Chemosh will go into exile,
      along with his princes and priests.
⁸Not a town will escape the destruction;
  both valley and plain will be ruined.
  I, the LORD, have spoken.
⁹Set up a tombstone for Moab;
  it will soon be destroyed.
  Its towns will be left in ruins,
      and no one will live there again."

(¹⁰Curse those who do not do the LORD's
work with all their heart! Curse those who
do not slash and kill!)

The Cities of Moab Are Destroyed

¹¹The LORD said, "Moab has always lived
secure and has never been taken into exile.
Moab is like wine left to settle undisturbed
and never poured from jar to jar. Its flavor
has never been ruined, and it tastes as good
as ever.

¹²"So now, the time is coming when I will
send people to pour Moab out like wine.
They will empty its wine jars and break
them in pieces. ¹³Then the Moabites will be
disillusioned with their god Chemosh, just as
the Israelites were disillusioned with Bethel, a
god in whom they trusted.

¹⁴"Men of Moab, why do you claim to be
      heroes,
  brave soldiers tested in war?
¹⁵Moab and its cities are destroyed;
  its finest young men have been
      slaughtered.
  I am the king, the LORD Almighty,
      and I have spoken.
¹⁶Moab's doom approaches;
  its ruin is coming soon.

¹⁷"Mourn for that nation, you that live
      nearby,
  all of you that know its fame.
  Say, 'Its powerful rule has been broken;
      its glory and might are no more.'
¹⁸You that live in Dibon,
  come down from your place of
      honor

and sit on the ground in the dust;
  Moab's destroyer is here
      and has left its forts in ruins.
¹⁹You that live in Aroer,
  stand by the road and wait;
      ask those who are running away,
      find out from them what has
          happened.
²⁰'Moab has fallen,' they will answer,
  'weep for it; it is disgraced.
  Announce along the Arnon River
      that Moab is destroyed!'

²¹"Judgment has come on the cities of
the plateau: on Holon, Jahzah, Mephaath,
²²Dibon, Nebo, Beth Diblathaim, ²³Kir-
iathaim, Bethgamul, Bethmeon, ²⁴Kerioth,
and Bozrah. Judgment has come on all the
cities of Moab, far and near. ²⁵Moab's might
has been crushed; its power has been
destroyed. I, the LORD, have spoken."

Moab Will Be Humbled

²⁶The LORD said, "Make Moab drunk,
because it has rebelled against me. Moab will
roll in its own vomit, and people will laugh.
²⁷Moab, remember how you made fun of
the people of Israel? You treated them as
though they had been caught with a gang of
robbers.

²⁸"You people who live in Moab, leave
your towns! Go and live on the cliffs! Be like
the dove that makes its nest in the sides of a
ravine. ²⁹Moab is very proud! I have heard
how proud, arrogant, and conceited the people are, how much they think of themselves.
³⁰I, the LORD, know of their arrogance.
Their boasts amount to nothing, and the
things they do will not last. ³¹And so I will
weep for everyone in Moab and for the people of Kir Heres. ³²I will cry for the people
of Sibmah, even more than for the people of
Jazer. City of Sibmah, you are like a vine
whose branches reach across the Dead Sea
and go as far as Jazer. But now your summer
fruits and your grapes have been destroyed.
³³Happiness and joy have been taken away
from the fertile land of Moab. I have made
the wine stop flowing from the wine presses;
there is no one to make the wine and shout
for joy.
³⁴"The people of Heshbon and Elealeh

cry out,^{g} and their cry can be heard as far as Jahaz; it can be heard by the people in Zoar, and it is heard as far as Horonaim and Eglath Shelishiyah. Even Nimrim Brook has dried up. 35I will stop the people of Moab from making burnt offerings at their places of worship and from offering sacrifices to their gods. I, the LORD, have spoken.

36"So my heart mourns for Moab and for the people of Kir Heres, like someone playing a funeral song on a flute, because everything they owned is gone. 37All of them have shaved their heads and cut off their beards. They have all made gashes on their hands, and everyone is wearing sackcloth. 38On all the housetops of Moab and in all its public squares there is nothing but mourning, because I have broken Moab like a jar that no one wants. 39Moab has been shattered! Cry out! Moab has been disgraced. It is in ruins, and all the surrounding nations make fun of it. I, the LORD, have spoken."

No Escape for Moab

40The LORD has promised that a nation will swoop down on Moab like an eagle with its outspread wings, 41and the towns and fortresses will be captured. On that day Moab's soldiers will be as frightened as a woman in labor. 42Moab will be destroyed and will no longer be a nation, because it rebelled against me. 43Terror, pits, and traps are waiting for the people of Moab. The LORD has spoken. 44Whoever tries to escape the terror will fall into the pits, and whoever climbs out of the pits will be caught in the traps, because the LORD has set the time for Moab's destruction. 45Helpless refugees try to find protection in Heshbon, the city that King Sihon once ruled, but it is in flames.^{h} Fire has burned up the frontiers and the mountain heights of the war-loving people of Moab. 46Pity the people of Moab! The

people who worshiped Chemosh have been destroyed, and their sons and daughters have been taken away as prisoners.

47But in days to come the LORD will make Moab prosperous again. All of this is what the LORD has said will happen to Moab.

The LORD's Judgment on Ammon

49 1This is what the LORD said about Ammon: "Where are the men of Israel? Is there no one to defend their land? Why have they let the people who worship Molech take the territory of the tribe of Gad and settle there? 2But the time is coming when I will make the people of the capital city of Rabbah hear the noise of battle, and it will be left in ruins and its villages burned to the ground. Then Israel will take its land back from those who took it from them. 3People of Heshbon, cry out! Ai is destroyed! Women of Rabbah, go into mourning! Put on sackcloth and mourn. Run about in confusion. Your god Molech will be taken into exile, together with his priests and princes. 4Why do you unfaithful people boast? Your strength is failing. Why do you trust in your power and say that no one would dare attack you? 5I will bring terror on you from every side. You will all run away. Each one will run for his life, and there will be no one to bring your troops together again.

6"But later on I will make Ammon prosperous again. I, the LORD, have spoken."

The LORD's Judgment on Edom

7This is what the LORD Almighty said about Edom: "Have the people of Edom lost their good judgment? Can their advisers no longer tell them what to do? Has all their wisdom disappeared? 8People of Dedan, turn

---

g 48:34 *Probable text* Heshbon . . . cry out; *Hebrew unclear.*   h 48:45 Heshbon, the city . . . flames; *or* the city of Heshbon, but it is in flames and the palace of King Sihon is burning.
49:1–6 Ezek 21:28–32; 25:1–7; Am 1:13–15; Zeph 2:8–11   **49:7–22** Isa 34:5–17; 63:1–6; Ezek 25:12–14; 35:1–15; Am 1:11, 12; Ob 1–14; Mal 1:2–5   **49:7** Bar 3:22, 23

Jeremiah

Locate Moab and the River Arnon on Map 3 in the back of this Bible. What body of water does the Arnon flow into?

Hide! (49:8)

and run! Hide! I am going to destroy Esau's descendants because the time has come for me to punish them. 9When people pick grapes, they leave a few on the vines, and when robbers come at night, they take only what they want. 10But I*ʲ* have stripped Esau's descendants completely and uncovered their hiding places, so that they can no longer hide. All the people of Edom are destroyed. Not one of them is left. 11Leave your orphans with me, and I will take care of them. Your widows can depend on me.

12"If even those who did not deserve to be punished had to drink from the cup of punishment, do you think that you will go unpunished? No, you must drink from the cup! 13I myself have sworn that the city of Bozrah will become a horrifying sight and a desert; people will make fun of it and use its name as a curse. All the nearby villages will be in ruins forever. I, the LORD, have spoken."

14I said, "Edom, I have received a message from the LORD. He has sent a messenger to tell the nations to assemble their armies and to get ready to attack you. 15The LORD is going to make you weak, and no one will respect you. 16Your pride has deceived you. No one fears you as much as you think they do. You live on the rocky cliffs, high on top of the mountain; but even though you live as high up as an eagle, the LORD will bring you down. The LORD has spoken."

17The LORD said, "The destruction that will come on Edom will be so terrible that everyone who passes by will be shocked and terrified. 18The same thing will happen to Edom that happened to Sodom and Gomorrah, when they and the nearby towns were destroyed. No one will ever live there again. I, the LORD, have spoken. 19Like a lion coming out of the thick woods along the Jordan River up to the green pasture land, I will come and make the Edomites run away suddenly from their country. Then the leader I choose will rule the nation. Who can be compared to me? Who would dare challenge me? What ruler could oppose me? 20So listen to the plan that I have made against the people of Edom, and to what I intend to do to the people of the city of Teman. Even their children will be dragged off, and everyone will be horrified. 21When Edom falls, there will be such a noise that the entire earth will shake, and the cries of alarm will be heard as far away as the Gulf of Aqaba. 22The enemy will attack Bozrah like an eagle swooping down with outspread wings. On that day Edom's soldiers will be as frightened as a woman in labor."

The LORD's Judgment on Damascus

23This is what the LORD said about Damascus: "The people in the cities of Hamath and Arpad are worried and troubled because they have heard bad news. Anxiety rolls over them like a sea, and they cannot rest. 24The people of Damascus are weak and have fled in terror. They are in pain and misery like a woman in labor. 25The famous city that used to be happy*ʲ* is completely deserted. 26On that day her young men will be killed in the city streets, and all her soldiers destroyed. 27I will set the walls of Damascus on fire and will burn down King Benhadad's palaces. I, the LORD Almighty, have spoken."

ⁱ **49:10** they leave a few . . . they take only what they want. 10But I; *or* they leave nothing . . . they take everything. 10And so I. *ʲ* **49:25** *Some ancient translations* happy; *Hebrew* my happiness.
49:18 Gen 19:24, 25   **49:19** Wis 12:12   **49:23–27** Isa 17:1–3; Am 1:3–5; Zech 9:1

Read more about Esau's descendants in Genesis, chapter 36. How does this explain why Esau is mentioned in connection with Moab?

Judgment on the Tribe of Kedar and the City of Hazor

28This is what the LORD said about the tribe of Kedar and the districts controlled by Hazor, which were conquered by King Nebuchadnezzar of Babylonia: "Attack the people of Kedar and destroy that tribe of eastern people! 29Seize their tents and their flocks, their tent curtains and everything in their tents. Take their camels and tell the people, 'Terror is all around you!'

30"People of Hazor, I, the LORD, warn you to run far away and hide. King Nebuchadnezzar of Babylonia has plotted against you, and this is what he says, 31'Come on! We'll attack those people that feel safe and secure! Their city has no gates or locks and is completely unprotected.'

32"Take their camels and all their livestock! I will scatter in every direction those people who cut their hair short, and I will bring disaster on them from every side. 33Hazor will be made a desert forever, a place where only jackals live. No one will ever live there again. I, the LORD, have spoken."

The LORD's Judgment on Elam

34Soon after Zedekiah became king of Judah, the LORD Almighty spoke to me about the country of Elam. 35He said, "I will kill all the archers who have made Elam so powerful. 36I will make winds blow against Elam from all directions, and I will scatter her people everywhere, until there is no country where her refugees have not gone. 37I will make the people of Elam afraid of their enemies, who want to kill them. In my great anger I will destroy the people of Elam and send armies against them until I have wiped them out. 38I will destroy their kings and leaders, and set up my throne there. 39But later on I will make the people of Elam prosperous again. I, the LORD, have spoken."

I, the Lord, Have Spoken

You may notice that the phrase, "I, the LORD, have spoken," appears many times in Jeremiah, chapters 49–52. See if you can count how many times that phrase or something close to it appears. Why, do you think, is it repeated so often?

The words, "I have spoken," have an air of authority about them. You can almost hear God saying after each one, "Period." There is no room for excuses or debate. This is the way it will be. End of discussion.

Sometimes we need to know that something that is said is the final word. "I, the LORD, have spoken," is that kind of statement. The word *amen* works the same way. Whenever we say amen, we are saying, "So be it."

— Jeremiah, chapters 49–52

Babylon's Capture

50 1This is the message that the LORD gave me about the city of Babylon and its people:

2"Tell the news to the nations! Proclaim it!
Give the signal and announce the news!
Do not keep it a secret!
Babylon has fallen!
Her god Marduk has been shattered!
Babylon's idols are put to shame;
her disgusting images are crushed!

3"A nation from the north has come to attack Babylonia and will make it a desert. People and animals will run away, and no one will live there."

50:1—51:64 Isa 13:1—14:23; 47:1–15

Jeremiah

Israel's Return

⁴The LORD says, "When that time comes, the people of both Israel and Judah will come weeping, looking for me, their God. ⁵They will ask the way to Zion and then go in that direction. They will make an eternal covenant with me and never break it.

⁶"My people are like sheep whose shepherds have let them get lost in the mountains. They have wandered like sheep from one mountain to another, and they have forgotten where their home is. ⁷They are attacked by all who find them. Their enemies say, 'They sinned against the LORD, and so what we have done is not wrong. Their ancestors trusted in the LORD, and they themselves should have remained faithful to him.'

⁸"People of Israel, run away from Babylonia! Leave the country! Be the first to leave! ⁹I am going to stir up a group of strong nations in the north and make them attack Babylonia. They will line up in battle against the country and conquer it. They are skillful hunters, shooting arrows that never miss the mark. ¹⁰Babylonia will be looted, and those who loot it will take everything they want. I, the LORD, have spoken."

Babylon's Fall

¹¹The LORD says, "People of Babylonia, you plundered my nation. You are happy and glad, going about like a cow threshing grain or like a neighing horse, ¹²but your own great city will be humiliated and disgraced. Babylonia will be the least important nation of all; it will become a dry and waterless desert. ¹³Because of my anger no one will live in Babylon; it will be left in ruins, and all who pass by will be shocked and amazed.

¹⁴"Archers, line up for battle against Babylon and surround it. Shoot all your arrows at Babylon, because it has sinned against me, the LORD. ¹⁵Raise the war cry all around the city! Now Babylon has surrendered. Its walls have been broken through and torn down.ᵏ I am taking my revenge on

the Babylonians. So take your revenge on them, and treat them as they have treated others. ¹⁶Do not let seeds be planted in that country nor let a harvest be gathered. Every foreigner living there will be afraid of the attacking army and will go back home."

Israel's Return

¹⁷The LORD says, "The people of Israel are like sheep, chased and scattered by lions. First, they were attacked by the emperor of Assyria, and then King Nebuchadnezzar of Babylonia gnawed on their bones. ¹⁸Because of this, I, the LORD Almighty, the God of Israel, will punish King Nebuchadnezzar and his country, just as I punished the emperor of Assyria. ¹⁹I will restore the people of Israel to their land. They will eat the food that grows on Mount Carmel and in the region of Bashan, and they will eat all they want of the crops that grow in the territories of Ephraim and Gilead. ²⁰When that time comes, no sin will be found in Israel and no wickedness in Judah, because I will forgive those people whose lives I have spared. I, the LORD, have spoken."

Like sheep . . . scattered by lions (50:17)

God's Judgment on Babylonia

²¹The LORD says, "Attack the people of Merathaim and of Pekod. Kill and destroy them.ˡ Do everything I command you. I, the LORD, have spoken. ²²The noise of battle is heard in the land, and there is great destruction. ²³Babylonia hammered the whole world to pieces, and now that hammer is shattered! All the nations are shocked at what has happened to that country. ²⁴Babylonia, you fought against me, and you have

---

ᵏ **50:15** *Hebrew has an additional word, the meaning of which is unclear.*   ˡ **50:21** *One ancient translation* them; *Hebrew after them.*
50:8 Rev 18:4

been caught in the trap I set for you, even though you did not know it. 25I have opened the place where my weapons are stored, and in my anger I have taken them out, because I, the Sovereign LORD Almighty, have work to do in Babylonia. 26Attack it from every side and break open the places where its grain is stored! Pile up the loot like piles of grain! Destroy the country! Leave nothing at all! 27Kill all their soldiers! Slaughter them! The people of Babylonia are doomed! The time has come for them to be punished!"

(28Refugees escape from Babylonia and come to Jerusalem, and they tell how the LORD our God took revenge for what the Babylonians had done to his Temple.)

29"Tell the archers to attack Babylon. Send out everyone who knows how to use the bow and arrow. Surround the city and don't let anyone escape. Pay it back for all it has done, and treat it as it has treated others, because it acted with pride against me, the Holy One of Israel. 30So its young men will be killed in the city streets, and all its soldiers will be destroyed on that day. I, the LORD, have spoken.

31"Babylonia, you are filled with pride, so I, the Sovereign LORD Almighty, am against you! The time has come for me to punish you. 32Your proud nation will stumble and fall, and no one will help you up. I will set your cities on fire, and everything around will be destroyed."

33The LORD Almighty says, "The people of Israel and of Judah are oppressed. All who captured them are guarding them closely and will not let them go. 34But the one who will rescue them is strong—his name is the LORD Almighty. He himself will take up their cause and will bring peace to the earth, but trouble to the people of Babylonia."

35The LORD says,
"Death to Babylonia!
    Death to its people,
    to its rulers, to its people of wisdom.
36Death to its lying prophets—
    what fools they are!
Death to its soldiers—
    how terrified they are!
37Destroy its horses and chariots!
Death to its hired soldiers—
    how weak they are!
Destroy its treasures;
    plunder and loot.
38Bring a drought on its land
    and dry up its rivers.
Babylonia is a land of terrifying idols
    that have made fools of the people.

39"And so Babylon will be haunted by demons and evil spirits,m and by unclean birds. Never again will people live there, not for all time to come. 40The same thing will happen to Babylon that happened to Sodom and Gomorrah, when I destroyed them and the nearby towns. No one will ever live there again. I, the LORD, have spoken.

41"People are coming from a country in the
    north,
    a mighty nation far away;
    many kings are preparing for war.
42They have taken their bows and swords;
    they are cruel and merciless.
They sound like the roaring sea,
    as they ride their horses.
They are ready for battle against
    Babylonia.
43The king of Babylonia hears the news,
    and his hands hang limp.
He is seized by anguish,
    by pain like a woman in labor.

44"Like a lion coming out of the thick woods along the Jordan up to the green pasture land, I, the LORD, will come and make the Babylonians run away suddenly from their city. Then the leader I choose will rule the nation. Who can be compared to me? Who would dare challenge me? What ruler could oppose me? 45So listen to the plan that I have made against the city of Babylon and to what I intend to do to its people.

---

m **50:39** demons and evil spirits; *or* wildcats and jackals.
50:29 Rev 18:6   **50:39** Rev 18:2   **50:40** Gen 19:24, 25

Jeremiah 50:6 mentions lost sheep, a familiar image in the Bible. Check out Isaiah 53:6 and 1 Peter 2:25.

Even their children will be dragged off, and everyone will be horrified. ⁴⁶When Babylon falls, there will be such a noise that the entire earth will shake, and the cries of alarm will be heard by the other nations."

Further Judgment on Babylonia

51

¹The LORD says, "I am bringing a destructive wind*ⁿ* against Babylonia and its people. ²I will send foreigners to destroy Babylonia like a wind that blows straw away. When that day of destruction comes, they will attack from every side and leave the land bare. ³Don't give its soldiers time to shoot their arrows or to put on their armor. Do not spare the young men! Destroy the whole army! ⁴They will be wounded and die in the streets of their cities. ⁵I, the LORD God Almighty, have not abandoned Israel and Judah, even though they have sinned against me, the Holy One of Israel. ⁶Run away from Babylonia! Run for your lives! Do not be killed because of Babylonia's sin. I am now taking my revenge and punishing it as it deserves. ⁷Babylonia was like a gold cup in my hand, making the whole world drunk. The nations drank its wine and went out of their minds. ⁸Babylonia has suddenly fallen and is destroyed! Mourn over it! Get medicine for its wounds, and maybe it can be healed. ⁹Foreigners living there said, 'We tried to help Babylonia, but it was too late. Let's leave now and go back home. God has punished Babylonia with all his might and has destroyed it completely.' "

Run for your lives! (51:6)

¹⁰The LORD says, "My people shout, 'The LORD has shown that we are in the right. Let's go and tell the people in Jerusalem what the LORD our God has done.' "

¹¹The LORD has stirred up the kings of Media, because he intends to destroy Babylonia. That is how he will take revenge for the destruction of his Temple.

The attacking officers command, "Sharpen your arrows! Get your shields ready! ¹²Give the signal to attack Babylon's walls. Strengthen the guard! Post the sentries! Place troops in ambush!"

Give the signal to attack Babylon's walls. (51:12)

The LORD has done what he said he would do to the people of Babylonia. ¹³That country has many rivers and rich treasures, but its time is up, and its thread of life is cut. ¹⁴The LORD Almighty has sworn by his own life that he will bring many men to attack Babylonia like a swarm of locusts, and they will shout with victory.

A Hymn of Praise to God

¹⁵The LORD made the earth by his power;
　by his wisdom he created the world and stretched out the heavens.
¹⁶At his command the waters above the sky*ᵒ* roar;
　he brings clouds from the ends of the earth.
He makes lightning flash in the rain and sends the wind from his storeroom.

ⁿ **51:1** destructive wind; *or* destroying spirit.　*ᵒ* **51:16** WATERS ABOVE THE SKY: *See Gen 1:6–8.*
51:7 Rev 17:2–4; 18:3　**51:9** Rev 18:5　**51:13** Rev 17:1

"When Babylon falls, there will be such a noise that the entire earth will shake" (Jeremiah 50:46).

17 At the sight of this, people feel stupid and
      senseless;
   those who make idols are disillusioned
   because the gods they make are false
      and lifeless.
18 They are worthless and should be
      despised;
   they will be destroyed when the LORD
      comes to deal with them.
19 The God of Jacob is not like them;
   he is the one who made everything,
   and he has chosen Israel to be his very
      own people.
   The LORD Almighty is his name.

The LORD's Hammer

20 The LORD says,
   "Babylonia, you are my hammer, my
      weapon of war.
   I used you to crush nations and
      kingdoms,
21   to shatter horses and riders,
   to shatter chariots and their drivers,
22   to kill men and women,
   to slay old and young,
   to kill boys and girls,
23   to slaughter shepherds and their flocks,
   to slaughter farmers and their plow
      horses,
   to crush rulers and high officials."

Babylonia's Punishment

24 The LORD says, "You will see me repay
Babylonia and its people for all the evil they
did to Jerusalem. 25 Babylonia, you are like a
mountain that destroys the whole world, but
I, the LORD, am your enemy. I will take hold
of you, level you to the ground, and leave
you in ashes. 26 None of the stones from your
ruins will ever be used again for building.
You will be like a desert forever. I, the
LORD, have spoken.

27 "Give the signal to attack! Blow the
trumpet so that the nations can hear! Prepare
the nations for war against Babylonia! Tell the
kingdoms of Ararat, Minni, and Ashkenaz to
attack. Appoint an officer to lead the attack.
Bring up the horses like a swarm of locusts.
28 Prepare the nations for war against Babylonia. Send for the kings of Media, their leaders

The Hammer

A hammer can be either a positive
image or a negative one. In Jeremiah 51:21, Babylonia is called
God's hammer because it will be
used to crush other nations. In
this case, it is a weapon of war.
But most of the time, a hammer is
a positive image. Hammers are
used to pound nails and to build
things. The international organization Habitat for Humanity,
which builds homes for needy
people around the world, uses the
phrase "Theology of the Hammer." What this means is that a
hammer can be a way of witnessing to God. When a hammer is
used to build shelter for others, it
can be a powerful example of
faith in action. Find out if there is
a chapter of Habitat for Humanity
near you.

— Jeremiah 51:20–23

and officials, and the armies of all the countries they control. 29 The earth trembles and
shakes because the LORD is carrying out his
plan to make Babylonia a desert, where no
one lives. 30 The Babylonian soldiers have
stopped fighting and remain in their forts.
They have lost their courage and have become
helpless. The city gates are broken down, and
the houses are on fire. 31 Messenger after messenger runs to tell the king of Babylonia that
his city has been broken into from every side.
32 The enemy have captured the river crossing
and have set the fortresses on fire. The Babylonian soldiers have panicked. 33 Soon the
enemy will cut them down and trample them
like grain on a threshing place. I, the LORD
Almighty, the God of Israel, have spoken."

34 The king of Babylonia cut Jerusalem up
      and ate it.
   He emptied the city like a jar;
      like a monster he swallowed it.

He took what he wanted
and threw the rest away.
³⁵ Let the people of Zion say,
"May Babylonia be held responsible
for the violence done to us!"
Let the people of Jerusalem say,
"May Babylonia be held responsible
for what we have suffered!"

The LORD Will Help Israel

³⁶ And so the LORD said to the people of
Jerusalem, "I will take up your cause and will
make your enemies pay for what they did to
you. I will dry up the source of Babylonia's
water and make its rivers go dry. ³⁷ That
country will become a pile of ruins where
wild animals live. It will be a horrible sight;
no one will live there, and all who see it will
be terrified. ³⁸ The Babylonians all roar like
lions and growl like lion cubs. ³⁹ Are they
greedy? I will prepare them a feast and make
them drunk and happy. They will go to sleep
and never wake up. ⁴⁰ I will take them to be
slaughtered, like lambs, goats, and rams. I, the
LORD, have spoken."

*That country will become a pile of ruins where
wild animals live. (51:37)*

Babylon's Fate

⁴¹ The LORD says about Babylon: "The
city that the whole world praised has been
captured! What a horrifying sight Babylon
has become to the nations! ⁴² The sea has
rolled over Babylon and covered it with
roaring waves. ⁴³ The towns have become a
horrifying sight and are like a waterless
desert, where no one lives or even travels. ⁴⁴ I
will punish Bel, the god of Babylonia, and
make him give up his stolen goods; the
nations will not worship him any more.

"Babylon's walls have fallen. ⁴⁵ People of
Israel, run away from there! Run for your

life from my fierce anger. ⁴⁶ Do not lose
courage or be afraid because of the rumors
you hear. Every year a different rumor
spreads—rumors of violence in the land and
of one king fighting another. ⁴⁷ And so the
time is coming when I will deal with Babylonia's idols. The whole country will be put
to shame, and all its people will be killed.
⁴⁸ Everything on earth and in the sky will
shout for joy when Babylonia falls to the
people who come from the north to destroy
it. ⁴⁹ Babylonia caused the death of people all
over the world, and now Babylonia will fall
because it caused the death of so many
Israelites. I, the LORD, have spoken."

God's Message to the Israelites in Babylonia

⁵⁰ The LORD says to his people in Babylo-
nia: "You have escaped death! Now go!
Don't wait! Though you are far from home,
think about me, your LORD, and remember
Jerusalem. ⁵¹ You say, 'We've been disgraced
and made ashamed; we feel completely helpless because foreigners have taken over the
holy places in the Temple.' ⁵² So then, I say
that the time is coming when I will deal
with Babylon's idols, and the wounded will
groan throughout the country. ⁵³ Even if
Babylon could climb to the sky and build a
strong fortress there, I would still send people to destroy it. I, the LORD, have spoken."

Further Destruction on Babylon

⁵⁴ The LORD says,
"Listen to the sound of crying in
Babylon,
of mourning for the destruction in the
land.
⁵⁵ I am destroying Babylon
and putting it to silence.
The armies rush in like roaring waves
and attack with noisy shouts.
⁵⁶ They have come to destroy Babylon;
its soldiers are captured,
and their bows are broken.
I am a God who punishes evil,
and I will treat Babylon as it deserves.

57 I will make its rulers drunk—
    men of wisdom, leaders, and soldiers.
They will go to sleep and never wake up.
    I, the king, have spoken;
    I am the LORD Almighty.
58 The walls of mighty Babylon will be
        thrown to the ground,
    and its towering gates burned down.
The work of the nations is all for
        nothing;
    their efforts go up in flames.
I, the LORD Almighty, have spoken."

Jeremiah's Message Is Sent to Babylonia

59 King Zedekiah's personal attendant was
Seraiah, the son of Neriah and grandson of
Mahseiah. In the fourth year that Zedekiah
was king of Judah, Seraiah was going to
Babylonia with him, and I gave him some
instructions. 60 I wrote in a book an account
of all the destruction that would come on
Babylonia, as well as all these other things
about Babylonia. 61 I told Seraiah, "When
you get to Babylon, be sure to read aloud to
the people everything that is written here.
62 Then pray,' LORD, you have said that you
would destroy this place, so that there would
be no living creatures in it, neither people
nor animals, and it would be like a desert
forever.' 63 Seraiah, when you finish reading
this book to the people, then tie it to a rock
and throw it into the Euphrates River 64 and
say, 'This is what will happen to Babylonia—
it will sink and never rise again because of
the destruction that the LORD is going to
bring on it.' "p

The words of Jeremiah end here.

The Fall of Jerusalem
(2 Kings 24:18—25:7)

52 ¹Zedekiah was twenty-one years old
when he became king of Judah, and
he ruled in Jerusalem for eleven years. His

It will sink and never rise again. (51:64)

mother's name was Hamutal, the daughter of
the Jeremiah who lived in the city of Libnah. ²King Zedekiah sinned against the
LORD, just as King Jehoiakim had done.
³The LORD became so angry with the people of Jerusalem and Judah that he banished
them from his sight.

Zedekiah rebelled against King Nebuchadnezzar of Babylonia, ⁴and so Nebuchadnezzar came with all his army and
attacked Jerusalem on the tenth day of the
tenth month of the ninth year of Zedekiah's
reign. They set up camp outside the city,
built siege walls around it, ⁵and kept it under
siege until Zedekiah's eleventh year. ⁶On the
ninth day of the fourth month of that same
year, when the famine was so bad that the
people had nothing left to eat, ⁷the city walls
were broken through. Although the Babylonians were surrounding the city, all the soldiers escaped during the night. They left by
way of the royal garden, went through the
gateway connecting the two walls, and fled

p **51:64** *One ancient translation* on it; *Hebrew* on it and they will become tired out.
51:63, 64 Rev 18:21   **52:4** Ezek 24:2   **52:7** Ezek 33:21

Jeremiah's scroll of prophesies is thrown into the river to sink *(Jeremiah 51:63–64)*. **What is this a sign of?**

The End?

Jeremiah, chapter 52, describes the fall of Jerusalem, the destruction of the Temple, and the people taken in captivity to Babylonia. It seems that all is lost, that it's over. It is the fulfillment of Jeremiah's prophecies and warnings to the people. It proves he was a true prophet. As terrible as this ending seems to be, however, there is hope. We know this begins a completely new and different era for God's Chosen People. It is important to remember that God will never abandon his Chosen People. Stay tuned!

— Jeremiah, chapter 52

in the direction of the Jordan Valley. ⁸But the Babylonian army pursued King Zedekiah, captured him in the plains near Jericho, and all his soldiers deserted him. ⁹Zedekiah was taken to King Nebuchadnezzar, who was in the city of Riblah in the territory of Hamath, and there Nebuchadnezzar passed sentence on him. ¹⁰At Riblah he put Zedekiah's sons to death while Zedekiah was looking on and he also had the officials of Judah executed. ¹¹After that, he had Zedekiah's eyes put out and had him placed in chains and taken to Babylon. Zedekiah remained in prison in Babylon until the day he died.

The Destruction of the Temple
(2 Kings 25:8–17)

¹²On the tenth day of the fifth month of the nineteenth year of King Nebuchadnezzar of Babylonia, Nebuzaradan, adviser to the king and commander of his army, entered Jerusalem. ¹³He burned down the Temple, the palace, and the houses of all the important people in Jerusalem; ¹⁴and his soldiers tore down the city walls. ¹⁵Then Nebuzaradan took away to Babylonia⁹ the people who were left in the city, the remaining skilled workers, and those who had deserted to the Babylonians. ¹⁶But he left in Judah some of the poorest people, who owned no property, and he put them to work in the vineyards and fields.

¹⁷The Babylonians broke in pieces the bronze columns and the carts that were in the Temple, together with the large bronze tank, and they took all the bronze to Babylon. ¹⁸They also took away the shovels and the ash containers used in cleaning the altar, the tools used in tending the lamps, the bowls used for catching the blood from the sacrifices, the bowls used for burning incense, and all the other bronze articles used in the Temple service. ¹⁹They took away everything that was made of gold or silver: the small bowls, the pans used for carrying live coals, the bowls for holding the blood from the sacrifices, the ash containers, the lampstands, the bowls used for incense, and the bowls used for pouring out wine offerings. ²⁰The bronze objects that King Solomon had made for the Temple—the two columns, the carts, the large tank, and the twelve bulls that supported it—were too heavy to weigh. ²¹⁻²²The two columns were identical: each one was 27 feet high and 18 feet around. They were hollow, and the metal was 3 inches thick. On top of each column was a bronze capital 7½ feet high, and all around it was a grillwork decorated with pomegranates, all of which was also made of bronze. ²³On the grillwork of each column there were a hundred pomegranates in all, and ninety-six of these were visible from the ground.

⁹ **52:15** *Probable text* Babylonia; *Hebrew* Babylonia some of the poorest of the people.
52:11 Ezek 12:13   **52:13** 1 Kings 9:8   **52:17–23** 1 Kings 7:15–47

So the people of Judah were carried away. (52:27)

The People of Judah Are Taken to Babylonia
(2 Kings 25:18–21, 27–30)

24 In addition, Nebuzaradan, the commanding officer, took away as prisoners Seraiah the High Priest, Zephaniah the priest next in rank, and the three other important Temple officials. 25 From the city he took the officer who had been in command of the troops, seven of the king's personal advisers who were still in the city, the commander's assistant, who was in charge of military records, and sixty other important men. 26 Nebuzaradan took them to the king of Babylonia, who was in the city of Riblah 27 in the territory of Hamath. There the king had them beaten and put to death.

So the people of Judah were carried away from their land into exile. 28 This is the record of the people that Nebuchadnezzar took away as prisoners: in his seventh year as king he carried away 3,023; 29 in his eighteenth year, 832 from Jerusalem; 30 and in his twenty-third year, 745—taken away by Nebuzaradan. In all, 4,600 people were taken away.

31 In the year that Evilmerodach became king of Babylonia, he showed kindness to King Jehoiachin of Judah by releasing him from prison. This happened on the twenty-fifth day of the twelfth month of the thirty-seventh year after Jehoiachin had been taken away as a prisoner. 32 Evilmerodach treated him kindly and gave him a position of greater honor than he gave the other kings who were exiles with him in Babylonia. 33 So Jehoiachin was permitted to change from his prison clothes and to dine at the king's table for the rest of his life. 34 Each day for as long as he lived, he was given a regular allowance for his needs.

Your Next Step

Congratulations on finishing the Book of Jeremiah! Use this space to write your thoughts and questions about this book. If you are following the suggested reading plan, move ahead to the Letter from James in the New Testament. The Letter from James also emphasizes the importance of being fair and just in the way you treat others.

Jeremiah

When something bad happens in your life, do you turn to a diary, a sketchpad, or a musical instrument? Many people respond to disasters by writing songs or poetry. The words of country music, rock, blues, and other styles of music are often about people's problems. Countless poems have been written in memory of people who have died or about a traumatic event. The people of Israel were extremely upset over the destruction of their beloved city. They were heartbroken because they were taken as captives to Babylonia. They had lost their homes, their freedom, their capital, and their place of worship—the Temple. As a result of their grief, poems were written. The poems of Lamentations give an idea of how much sorrow the Israelites had.

Headlines

- Jerusalem Is Abandoned! (chapter 1)
- People Worn Out with Weeping (2:10–13)
- A Glimmer of Hope (3:19–42)
- Gotta Get Back to the Lord (5:15–21)

FACTOIDS

Who wrote this book? The author of Lamentations is unknown.

What period is covered? The Babylonian Exile between 587 and 538 BC.

Why was it written? Lamentations was written to give the Israelites living in Babylonia a chance to express their grief. They had lost their country, their freedom, and their worship of God in the Temple. It was also written to help them remember the goodness of God.

How is it organized? Lamentations is a collection of five poems, each of which is a separate chapter, or book. Each of the books has twenty-two verses, except the third, which has sixty-six verses.

Important themes

- Grieving our losses and acknowledging our sins are actions that can lead to healing.
- Recalling God's goodness in the past gives us hope for the future.

LAMENTATIONS

The Sorrows of Jerusalem

1 ¹ How lonely lies Jerusalem, once so full
of people!
Once honored by the world, she is
now like a widow;
The noblest of cities has fallen into
slavery.

² All night long she cries; tears run down
her cheeks.
Of all her former friends, not one is left
to comfort her.
Her allies have betrayed her and are all
against her now.

Like a widow . . . all night long she cries. (1:1–2)

³ Judah's people are helpless slaves, forced
away from home.*ᵃ*
They live in other lands, with no place
to call their own—
Surrounded by enemies, with no way
to escape.

⁴ No one comes to the Temple now to
worship on the holy days.
The young women who sang there
suffer, and the priests can only groan.
The city gates stand empty, and Zion is
in agony.

⁵ Her enemies succeeded; they hold her in
their power.
The LORD has made her suffer for all
her many sins;
Her children have been captured and
taken away.

⁶ The splendor of Jerusalem is a thing of
the past.
Her leaders are like deer that are weak
from hunger,
Whose strength is almost gone as they
flee from the hunters.

⁷ A lonely ruin now, Jerusalem recalls her
ancient splendor.
When she fell to the enemy, there was
no one to help her;
Her conquerors laughed at her downfall.

⁸ Her honor is gone; she is naked and held
in contempt.
She groans and hides her face in shame.
Jerusalem made herself filthy with
terrible sin.

⁹ Her uncleanness was easily seen, but she
showed no concern for her fate.
Her downfall was terrible; no one can
comfort her.
Her enemies have won, and she cries to
the LORD for mercy.

¹⁰ The enemies robbed her of all her
treasures.
She saw them enter the Temple itself,
Where the LORD had forbidden
Gentiles to go.

¹¹ Her people groan as they look for
something to eat;
They exchange their treasures for food
to keep themselves alive.
"Look at me, LORD," the city cries; "see
me in my misery."

¹² "Look at me!" she cries to everyone who
passes by.*ᵇ*

ᵃ **1:3** are helpless . . . home; *or* fled from home, from the misery of slavery.   *ᵇ* **1:12** Look . . . by; *or* May this
not happen to you that pass by; *or* Does this mean nothing to you that pass by?
1:1 Bar 4:12

"No one has ever had pain like mine,
Pain that the LORD brought on me in
the time of his anger.

13 "He sent fire from above, a fire that
burned inside me.
He set a trap for me and brought me to
the ground.
Then he abandoned me and left me in
constant pain.

14 "He took note of all my sins and tied
them all together;
He hung them around my neck, and I
grew weak beneath the weight.
The Lord gave me to my foes, and I
was helpless against them.

15 "The Lord laughed at all my strongest
soldiers;
He sent an army to destroy my young
men.
He crushed my people like grapes in a
wine press.

16 "That is why my eyes are overflowing
with tears.
No one can comfort me; no one can
give me courage.
The enemy has conquered me; my
people have nothing left.

17 "I stretch out my hands, but no one will
help me.
The LORD has called enemies against
me from every side;
They treat me like some filthy thing.

18 "But the LORD is just, for I have
disobeyed him.
Listen to me, people everywhere; look
at me in my pain.
My young men and women have been
taken away captive.

19 "I called to my allies, but they refused to
help me.
The priests and the leaders died in the
city streets,
Looking for food to keep themselves
alive.

20 "Look, O LORD, at my agony, at the
anguish of my soul!
My heart is broken in sorrow for my
sins.
There is murder in the streets; even
indoors there is death.

21 "Listen[c] to my groans; there is no one to
comfort me.
My enemies are glad that you brought
disaster on me.
Bring[d] the day you promised; make my
enemies suffer as I do.

22 "Condemn them for all their wickedness;
Punish them as you punished me for
my sins.
I groan in misery, and I am sick at
heart."

The Lord's Punishment of Jerusalem

2 1 The Lord in his anger has covered Zion
with darkness.
Its heavenly splendor he has turned
into ruins.
On the day of his anger he abandoned
even his Temple.

2 The Lord destroyed without mercy every
village in Judah
And tore down the forts that defended
the land.
He brought disgrace on the kingdom
and its rulers.

3 In his fury he shattered the strength of
Israel;
He refused to help us when the enemy
came.
He raged against us like fire, destroying
everything.

4 He aimed his arrows at us like an enemy;
He killed all those who were our joy
and delight.
Here in Jerusalem we felt his burning
anger.

5 Like an enemy, the Lord has destroyed
Israel;
He has left her forts and palaces in ruins.

---

[c] **1:21** *One ancient translation* Listen; *Hebrew* They listened.   [d] **1:21** *One ancient translation* Bring; *Hebrew* You
brought.

Together We Pray

Catholic Connections

"I don't need anybody to help me!" Did you ever say this to your parents when you were little and learning to do something new? Even now, you may not want your parents, teachers, or friends to help with some things. You may want to be as independent as possible. But there are times and places when we need other people's help.

One of those times is prayer. Sometimes, praying alone is just what you need. However, there are times when coming together to pray is important to do. At masses, weddings, Baptisms, and Confirmations, people come together to pray. Funerals bring us together in sadness but in trust of eternal life. Whenever there is a tragedy, people find support in sharing their sadness with one another. The Book of Lamentations has poems that helped the Jewish people do that after the horrible events that led to the destruction of Jerusalem and the Temple.

A modern example of this happening is after the tragedy of September 11. In many churches, temples, and synagogues, people came together to pray in sorrow. These services help us remember what has happened, the people affected, and also our own limitations. Not intended to depress us, praying together after a tragedy helps us to care for ourselves and others.

— Lamentations, chapter 2

He has brought on the people of Judah unending sorrow.

6 He smashed to pieces the Temple where we worshiped him;
He has put an end to holy days and Sabbaths.
King and priest alike have felt the force of his anger.

7 The Lord rejected his altar and deserted his holy Temple;
He allowed the enemy to tear down its walls.
They shouted in victory where once we had worshiped in joy.

8 The LORD was determined that the walls of Zion should fall;
He measured them off to make sure of total destruction.
The towers and walls now lie in ruins together.

9 The gates lie buried in rubble, their bars smashed to pieces.

The king and the noblemen now are in exile.
The Law is no longer taught, and the prophets have no visions from the LORD.

10 Jerusalem's old men sit on the ground in silence,
With dust on their heads and sackcloth on their bodies.
Young women bow their heads to the ground.

11 My eyes are worn out with weeping; my soul is in anguish.
I am exhausted with grief at the destruction of my people.
Children and babies are fainting in the streets of the city.

12 Hungry and thirsty, they cry to their mothers;
They fall in the streets as though they were wounded,
And slowly die in their mothers' arms.

13 O Jerusalem, beloved Jerusalem, what can
        I say?
    How can I comfort you? No one has
        ever suffered like this.
    Your disaster is boundless as the ocean;
        there is no possible hope.

14 Your prophets had nothing to tell you but
        lies;
    Their preaching deceived you by never
        exposing your sin.
    They made you think you did not
        need to repent.

15 People passing by the city look at you in
        scorn.
    They shake their heads and laugh at
        Jerusalem's ruins:
    "Is this that lovely city? Is this the pride
        of the world?"

16 All your enemies mock you and glare at
        you with hate.
    They curl their lips and sneer, "We
        have destroyed it!
    This is the day we have waited for!"

17 The LORD has finally done what he
        threatened to do:
    He has destroyed us without mercy, as
        he warned us long ago.
    He gave our enemies victory, gave
        them joy at our downfall.

18 O Jerusalem, let your very walls cry out
        to the Lord!e
    Let your tears flow like rivers night and
        day;
    Wear yourself out with weeping and
        grief

19 All through the night get up again and
        again to cry out to the Lord;
    Pour out your heart and beg him for
        mercy on your children—
    Children starving to death on every
        street corner!

20 Look, O LORD! Why are you punishing
        us like this?
    Women are eating the bodies of the
        children they loved!
    Priests and prophets are being killed in
        the Temple itself

Get up again . . . . to cry out to the Lord. (2:19)

21 Young and old alike lie dead in the streets,
    Young men and women, killed by
        enemy swords.
    You slaughtered them without mercy
        on the day of your anger.

22 You invited my enemies to hold a
        carnival of terror all around me,
    And no one could escape on that day
        of your anger.
    They murdered my children, whom I
        had raised and loved.

Punishment, Repentance, and Hope

3 1 I am one who knows what it is to be
        punished by God.
2   He drove me deeper and deeper into
        darkness
3   And beat me again and again with
        merciless blows.
4 He has left my flesh open and raw, and
        has broken my bones.
5   He has shut me in a prison of misery
        and anguish.
6   He has forced me to live in the
        stagnant darkness of death.

7 He has bound me in chains; I am a
        prisoner with no hope of escape.
8   I cry aloud for help, but God refuses to
        listen;
9   I stagger as I walk; stone walls block me
        wherever I turn.
10 He waited for me like a bear; he pounced
        on me like a lion.
11 He chased me off the road, tore me to
        pieces, and left me.

e 2:18 *Probable text* O Jerusalem . . . Lord; *Hebrew* Their hearts cried out to the Lord, O wall of Jerusalem.

God refuses to listen. (3:8)

12 He drew his bow and made me the target for his arrows.

13 He shot his arrows deep into my body.

14 People laugh at me all day long; I am a joke to them all.

15 Bitter suffering is all he has given me for food and drink.

16 He rubbed my face in the ground and broke my teeth on rocks.

17 I have forgotten what health and peace and happiness are.

18 I do not have much longer to live; my hope in the LORD is gone.

19 The thought of my pain, my homelessness, is bitter poison.

20 I think of it constantly, and my spirit is depressed.

21 Yet hope returns when I remember this one thing:

22 The LORD's unfailing love and mercy still continue,

23 Fresh as the morning, as sure as the sunrise.

24 The LORD is all I have, and so in him I put my hope.

25 The LORD is good to everyone who trusts in him,

26 So it is best for us to wait in patience— to wait for him to save us—

27 And it is best to learn this patience in our youth.

28 When we suffer, we should sit alone in silent patience;

29 We should bow in submission, for there may still be hope.

30 Though beaten and insulted, we should accept it all.

31 The Lord is merciful and will not reject us forever.

32 He may bring us sorrow, but his love for us is sure and strong.

33 He takes no pleasure in causing us grief or pain.

34 The Lord knows when our spirits are crushed in prison;

35 He knows when we are denied the rights he gave us;

36 When justice is perverted in court, he knows.

37 The will of the Lord alone is always carried out.*ƒ*

38 Good and evil alike take place at his command.

39 Why should we ever complain when we are punished for our sin?*ᵍ*

40 Let us examine our ways and turn back to the LORD.

41 Let us open our hearts to God in heaven and pray,

42 "We have sinned and rebelled, and you, O LORD, have not forgiven us.

43 "You pursued us and killed us; your mercy was hidden by your anger,

44 By a cloud of fury too thick for our prayers to get through.

45 You have made us the garbage dump of the world.

46 "We are insulted and mocked by all our enemies.

47 We have been through disaster and ruin; we live in danger and fear.

48 My eyes flow with rivers of tears at the destruction of my people.

ƒ **3:37** The will . . . out; *or* No one can make anything happen unless the Lord is willing.   ᵍ **3:39** Why should . . . sin?; *or* Why should we complain about being punished for sin, as long as we are still alive?

49 "My tears will pour out in a ceaseless
     stream

50 Until the LORD looks down from
     heaven and sees us.

51 My heart is grieved when I see what
     has happened to the women of the
     city.

52 "I was trapped like a bird by enemies
     who had no cause to hate me.

53 They threw me alive into a pit and
     closed the opening with a stone.

54 Water began to close over me, and I
     thought death was near.

55 "From the bottom of the pit, O LORD,
     I cried out to you,

56 And when I begged you to listen to
     my cry, you heard.

57 You answered me and told me not to
     be afraid.

58 "You came to my rescue, Lord, and saved
     my life.

59 Judge in my favor; you know the
     wrongs done against me.

60 You know how my enemies hate me
     and how they plot against me.

61 "You have heard them insult me,
     O LORD; you know all their plots.

62 All day long they talk about me and
     make their plans.

63 From morning till night they make fun
     of me.

64 "Punish them for what they have done,
     O LORD;

65 Curse them and fill them with despair!

66 Hunt them down and wipe them off
     the earth!"

Jerusalem after Its Fall

4 ¹Our glittering gold has grown dull;
     the stones of the Temple lie scattered
     in the streets.

² Zion's young people were as precious to
     us as gold,
     but now they are treated like common
     clay pots.

3 Even a mother wolf will nurse her cubs,
     but my people are like ostriches, cruel
     to their young.

4 They let their babies die of hunger and
     thirst;
     children are begging for food that no
     one will give them.

5 People who once ate the finest foods die
     starving in the streets;
     those raised in luxury are pawing
     through garbage for food.

6 My people have been punished even
     more than the inhabitants of Sodom,
     which met a sudden downfall at the
     hands of God.

7 Our princes[h] were undefiled and pure as
     snow,
     vigorous and strong, glowing with
     health.

8 Now they lie unknown in the streets,
     their faces blackened in death;
     their skin, dry as wood, has shriveled
     on their bones.

9 Those who died in the war were better
     off than those who died later,
     who starved slowly to death, with no
     food to keep them alive.

10 The disaster that came to my people
     brought horror;
     loving mothers boiled their own
     children for food.

11 The LORD turned loose the full force of
     his fury;
     he lit a fire in Zion that burned it to
     the ground.

12 No one anywhere, not even rulers of
     foreign nations,
     believed that any invader could enter
     Jerusalem's gates.

13 But it happened, because her prophets
     sinned and her priests were guilty
     of causing the death of innocent
     people.

h 4:7 princes; or Nazirites.
4:6 Gen 19:24   4:10 Deut 28:57; Ezek 5:10

14 Her leaders wandered through the streets
  as though blind,
  so stained with blood that no one
  would touch them.

15 "Get away!" people shouted. "You're
  defiled! Don't touch me!"
  So they wandered from nation to
  nation, welcomed by no one.

16 The LORD had no more concern for
  them; he scattered them himself.
  He showed no regard for our priests
  and leaders.

17 For help that never came, we looked until
  we could look no longer.
  We kept waiting for help from a nation
  that had none to give.

18 The enemy was watching for us; we could
  not even walk in the streets.
  Our days were over; the end had come.

19 Swifter than eagles swooping from the
  sky, they chased us down.
  They tracked us down in the hills; they
  took us by surprise in the desert.

20 They captured the source of our life, the
  king the LORD had chosen,
  the one we had trusted to protect us
  from every invader.

21 Laugh on, people of Edom and Uz; be
  glad while you can.
  Your disaster is coming too; you too
  will stagger naked in shame.

22 Zion has paid for her sin; the LORD will
  not keep us in exile any longer.
  But Edom, the LORD will punish you;
  he will expose your guilty acts.

A Prayer for Mercy

5 1 Remember, O LORD, what has
  happened to us.
  Look at us, and see our disgrace.

2 Our property is in the hands of strangers;
  foreigners are living in our homes.

3 Our fathers have been killed by the enemy,
  and now our mothers are widows.

4 We must pay for the water we drink;
  we must buy the wood we need for fuel.

5 Driven hard like donkeys or camels,
  we are tired, but are allowed no rest.

6 To get food enough to stay alive,
  we went begging to Egypt and Assyria.

7 Our ancestors sinned, but now they are
  gone,
  and we are suffering for their sins.

8 Our rulers are no better than slaves,
  and no one can save us from their
  power.

9 Murderers roam through the countryside;
  we risk our lives when we look for food.

10 Hunger has made us burn with fever
  until our skin is as hot as an oven.

11 Our wives have been raped on Mount
  Zion itself;
  in every Judean village our daughters
  have been forced to submit.

12 Our leaders have been taken and hanged;
  our elders are shown no respect.

13 Our young men are forced to grind grain
  like slaves;
  boys go staggering under heavy loads
  of wood.

14 The old people no longer sit at the city
  gate,
  and the young people no longer make
  music.

15 Happiness has gone out of our lives;
  grief has taken the place of our dances.

16 Nothing is left of all we were proud of.
  We sinned, and now we are doomed.

17 We are sick at our very hearts
  and can hardly see through our tears,

18 because Mount Zion lies lonely and
  deserted,
  and wild jackals prowl through its ruins.

19 But you, O LORD, are king forever
  and will rule to the end of time.

20 Why have you abandoned us so long?
  Will you ever remember us again?

21 Bring us back to you, LORD! Bring us back!
  Restore our ancient glory.

22 Or have you rejected us forever?
  Is there no limit to your anger?

Omar, a twelve-year-old boy from Somalia, had been living in refugee camps since he was two. Now he was in a line in an airport in Kenya with what was left of his family, going to a place they had only seen on a map. They were leaving the refugee camp behind, just as they had left their homeland behind years ago. As they boarded the plane, they were full of fear and hope—leaving with only their faith in God, their traditions, and one another. They hoped to return someday.

The Israelites found themselves in a similar situation. Their beloved homeland had been taken over by the Babylonians. Many of the Israelites had been taken into captivity. Now Baruch is telling the Israelites to remember the lessons of the past and pray that God will allow them to return to Jerusalem.

Chap. 1:3–4

Head lines

- Reading Book Results in Tears (1:1–7)
- Wisdom Lives with God's People (3:32—4:4)
- God's Children Go Home (4:27–36)

FACTOIDS

Who wrote this book? The author is unknown, but whoever it was gave credit in the book to Baruch, Jeremiah's secretary.

When was it written? The events took place in the 6th century BC, and the book was written after that. It is estimated that it was written beginning in the second century BC.

Why was it written? It was written to help the Israelite people understand how they could lead a happy and holy life while living in exile.

Important themes
- God's people can find happiness, no matter where they are living, if they are sorry for their sins and try to remain faithful to God's Covenant.
- God's people are able to hold on to their identity in difficult times by remembering and keeping their traditions.

BARUCH

Introduction

1 ¹ This book was written by Baruch son of Neraiah, grandson of Mahseiah, and a descendant of Zedekiah, Hasadiah, and Hilkiah. It was written in Babylon ²on the seventh day of the month*a* in the fifth year after the Babylonians captured Jerusalem and burned it down. ³⁻⁴ Baruch read the book aloud to Jehoiachin son of Jehoiakim, king of Judah, and to all the people who lived in Babylon by the Sud River. Everyone came to hear it read—nobles, children of royal families, elders, in fact, all the people, no matter what their status.

⁵ When the book was read, everyone cried, fasted, and prayed to the Lord. ⁶ Then they all gave as much money as they could, ⁷ and the collection was sent to Jerusalem to Jehoiakim the High Priest, son of Hilkiah and grandson of Shallum, and to the other priests and to all the people who were with him in Jerusalem.

Baruch read the book aloud. (1:3)

⁸ On the tenth day of the month of Sivan, Baruch took the sacred utensils which had been carried away from the Temple and returned them to Judah. These were the silver utensils which Zedekiah son of King Josiah of Judah had ordered made ⁹ after King Nebuchadnezzar of Babylonia had deported Jehoiachin, the rulers, the skilled workers,*b* the nobles, and the common people and had taken them from Jerusalem to Babylon.

A Letter to Jerusalem

¹⁰ The people wrote:

Please use the money we are sending you to buy animals for the burnt offerings and the sin offerings, to buy incense, and to provide the grain offerings. Offer them on the altar of the Lord our God, ¹¹ and pray for King Nebuchadnezzar of Babylonia and his son Belshazzar, that they may live as long as the heavens last. ¹² Then the Lord will strengthen us and be our guide. Nebuchadnezzar and his son Belshazzar will protect us, and we will be loyal to them as long as we live; then they will be pleased with us. ¹³ We ask you also to pray to the Lord God for us, because we have sinned against him, and he is still angry with us. ¹⁴ Please read this book that we are sending you and make your own confession of sin in the Temple on the first day of the Festival of Shelters and on other holy days of assembly.

A Confession of Sin

¹⁵ This is the confession you should make: "The Lord our God is righteous, but we are still covered with shame. All of us— the people of Judah, the people of Jerusalem, ¹⁶ our kings, our rulers, our priests, our prophets, and our ancestors have been put to shame, ¹⁷ because we have sinned against the Lord our God ¹⁸ and have disobeyed him. We did not listen to

---

a **1:2** THE MONTH: *The month is probably the fifth month of the Hebrew calendar (see 2 Kings 25:8; Jer 52:12).*
b **1:9** skilled workers; *Greek* prisoners.
1:1 Jer 36:4   **1:3, 4** 2 Kings 24:8–17

him or live according to his commandments. 19From the day the Lord brought our ancestors out of Egypt until the present day, we have continued to be unfaithful to him, and we have not hesitated to disobey him. 20Long ago, when the Lord led our ancestors out of Egypt, so that he could give us a rich and fertile land, he pronounced curses against us through his servant Moses. And today we are suffering because of those curses. 21We refused to obey the word of the Lord our God which he spoke to us through the prophets. Instead, we all did as we pleased and went on our own evil way. We turned to other gods and did things the Lord hates.

2 1"So the Lord carried out the threat he had made against us and against our judges, our kings, our rulers, and the people of Israel and Judah. 2Nowhere else on earth have such things happened as happened in Jerusalem when the Lord carried out the threats written in the Law of Moses. 3Things were so bad that we even ate the flesh of our own sons and daughters. 4The Lord scattered our people, handing us over to the control of all the nations around us, and they looked on us with reproach and horror. 5We sinned against the Lord our God and refused to obey him. Therefore, our nation was conquered, instead of being victorious.

6"The Lord our God is always righteous, but we and our ancestors are still burdened with our guilt. 7Even though the Lord punished us as he had threatened, 8we still did not turn to him and pray that we would abandon our evil thoughts. 9-10We did not obey him or live by his just commands, so the Lord brought on us all the punishments he had kept ready for us.

The Prayer for Deliverance

11"You, O Lord, are the God of Israel who brought your people out of Egypt with great power and with signs, miracles, and wonders. You showed your mighty strength and gained a glorious reputation, which is still recognized today. 12O Lord our God, we have sinned; we have been unfaithful; we have disobeyed all your commands. 13But do not be angry with us any longer. Here among the nations where you have scattered us, only a few of us are left. 14Listen to our prayer of petition, Lord, and rescue us for the sake of your own honor. Let those who have taken us into exile be pleased with us. 15Then the whole world will know that you are the Lord our God and that you have chosen the nation of Israel to be your own people.

16"O Lord, look down from heaven and see our misery. Listen to our prayer. 17Open your eyes and look upon us. Those in the world of the dead with no breath left in their bodies cannot offer praises to you or proclaim how just you are. 18Only the living, O Lord, can offer you praise and acknowledge your justice, even though they may be suffering greatly, bent and weak, hungry and with failing eyesight.

19"O Lord our God, we pray to you for mercy, but not because of any good things done by our ancestors and our kings. 20You turned your anger and wrath against us, just as you had threatened to do when your servants the prophets spoke your word to us and said, 21'Bend your backs and serve the king of Babylonia, and you can remain in the land that I gave to your ancestors. 22But if you refuse to obey my command to serve him, 23I will bring to an end every sound of joy and celebration in the towns of Judah and in Jerusalem. Even the happy sounds of wedding feasts will no longer be heard. The whole land will be desolate and uninhabited.'

24"But we did not obey your command to serve the king of Babylonia, so you carried out the threat that you had made when you spoke through your servants the prophets, when you said that the bones of our kings and of our ancestors would be taken from their tombs and scattered. 25And now here they lie exposed to the heat of the day and to the frost of the night. They died in torment from famine, war, and disease. 26And because of the sin of the people of

Israel and Judah, you have reduced your own Temple to ruins, even as it is today.

27 "But, Lord, you have been patient with us and have shown us great mercy, 28 as you promised through your servant Moses on the day you commanded him to write your Law in the presence of the Israelites. 29 'If you do not obey me,' you said, 'you will be reduced to a handful among the nations where I will scatter you. 30 I know that you will not obey me, because you are a stubborn people. But when you are taken into exile in another land, you will come to your senses. 31 Then you will realize that I am the Lord your God, and I will give you a desire to know and a mind with which to understand. 32 There in the land of your exile you will praise me and remember me. 33 You will stop being so stubborn and wicked, for you will remember what happened to your ancestors when they sinned against the Lord. 34 Then I will bring you back to the land that I solemnly promised to give to your ancestors, to Abraham, Isaac, and Jacob, and it will be yours again. I will increase your population, and you will never again be reduced to a small number. 35 I will make an everlasting covenant with you; I will be your God and you will be my people. I will never again remove you, the people of Israel, from the land that I gave you.'

3 1 "O Lord Almighty, God of Israel, from the depth of our troubled, weary souls we cry out to you. 2 Hear us, O Lord, and have mercy on us, because we have sinned against you. 3 You reign as king forever, but we die and are gone forever. 4 O Lord Almighty, God of Israel, hear our prayer. We are no better off than the dead. Our ancestors sinned against you, the Lord their God. They refused to obey you, and we are suffering the consequences of their sin. 5 Forget the sinful things that our ancestors did in the past; at a time like this, think only of your power and reputation, 6 for you are the Lord our God, and we will praise you. 7 You have made us fear you, so that we might pray to you. Here in exile we will praise you because we have turned away from the

sins of our ancestors. 8 You have scattered us among the nations, and you have made them despise and curse us. You are punishing us for the sins of our ancestors when they rebelled against you, the Lord our God."

In Praise of Wisdom

9 Listen, Israel, to the commands that promise life; pay attention, and you will become wise. 10 Why is it, Israel, that you find yourself in an enemy land? Why have you grown old in a foreign country? You are ritually unclean, like the dead; 11 you are already counted among the dead. But why? 12 It is because you have left the source of Wisdom! 13 If you had walked in God's ways, you would have lived in peace forever. 14 Learn where understanding, strength, and insight are to be found. Then you will know where to find a long and full life, light to guide you, and peace.

15 No one has ever found where Wisdom lives or has entered her treasure house, 16-17 and those who have tried have vanished: the rulers of the nations, those who hunted wild animals and birds for sport, those who accumulated vast fortunes of silver and gold, which everyone trusts and will do anything to get, 18 and those who worried and schemed to make money, but who left no trace of their work behind. 19 They have all disappeared and gone down to the world of the dead. Others have come along to take their place. 20 A later generation was born and lived in the land, but they too did not discover the way to knowledge. They did not find the path to Wisdom or ever reach her. 21 Their children also failed. 22 Wisdom was not found by the Canaanites. It has not been discovered by the Edomites 23 although they search after knowledge. The way to Wisdom has not been found by the merchants of Merran and Tema or by those who relate fables or by any others who seek understanding.

24 O Israel, how great is the universe in which God dwells! How vast is all that he possesses! 25 There is no end to it; there is no way to measure how wide or how high it is. 26 Here in early times the famous giants were

Where Can You Go?

Consider this type of scavenger hunt—you are told to go to a place where you find the following:
• insight or wisdom
• strength
• understanding
And you are also told to come back with proof that you found those three things.

Where would you look? Who would help you find this place? What would be the proof that you found those three things? If you are having trouble answering this question, don't feel bad. Baruch says, "No one has ever found where Wisdom lives or has entered her treasure house" (3:15). Luckily, Baruch also tells us where to find Wisdom: "Wisdom is the book of God's commandments, the Law that will last forever" (4:1). You can find wisdom, strength, and understanding in this very book you hold! Guess what? You won the scavenger hunt!

— Baruch 3:14–15

born, a mighty race skilled in war. 27But God did not choose them to be his people or show them the way of knowledge. 28They died out because they had neither understanding nor insight.

29No one has ever gone up into heaven to get Wisdom and bring her down out of the clouds. 30No one has sailed across the seas to find Wisdom or bought her with precious gold. 31No one knows how to get to her or how to discover the path that leads to her.

32The only one who knows Wisdom is God, and he knows all things. With his understanding he found her. He established the earth for all time and filled it with all kinds of animals. 33The light trembled and obeyed when he called. He sent it forth, and it appeared. 34He called the stars, and they promptly answered; they took their places and gladly shone to please the one who made them. 35He is our God, and there is none like him. 36He discovered the entire path leading to understanding and gave Wisdom to his servant Israel, whom he loved. 37From that time on, Wisdom appeared on earth and lived among us.

4 1Wisdom is the book of God's commandments, the Law that will last forever. All who hold onto her will live, but those who abandon her will die. 2Turn to Wisdom, people of Israel, and take hold of her. Make your way toward the splendor of her light. 3Do not surrender our glorious privileges to any other people. 4How happy we are, people of Israel; we have the advantage of knowing what is pleasing to God!

Comfort for Jerusalem

5Take courage, my people, you are the ones who keep Israel's name alive. 6You were sold to Gentile nations, but not to be destroyed. Because you made God angry, he handed you over to your enemies. 7When you offered sacrifices to demons instead of to God, you angered the one who made you. 8You forgot the Eternal God, who had nourished you as a child, and so you brought grief to Jerusalem, who had been like a mother to you. 9Jerusalem saw that God was punishing you because he was angry, and she said to all the neighboring cities, "Look at the great misery that God has brought on me. 10I saw my sons and daughters taken into captivity, a captivity brought on them by the Eternal God. 11I brought up my children with great delight, but I cried and mourned when they were taken from me. 12Let no one take pleasure in my suffering now that I am a widow and so many of my children have been taken from me. They turned away from God's Law, and their sins have made me a deserted city. 13They had no respect for his commandments and

Baruch

Consider how the Eternal God has sent my people into exile. (4:14)

would not live by them; they refused to let him guide them in the way of righteousness.

¹⁴"All you neighboring cities, come and consider how the Eternal God has sent my children into exile. ¹⁵He brought against them a nation from far away, a shameless nation that speaks a foreign language and has no respect for the elderly and no pity for children. ¹⁶These people carried off my beloved sons and took away my daughters, and I was left a widow, completely alone.

¹⁷"My children in exile, I can do nothing to help you. ¹⁸Only the one who brought this punishment upon you can rescue you from your enemies. ¹⁹Go your own way, my children; live your own life! I am all alone. ²⁰I have taken off the robes I wore during days of peace, and I have dressed myself like a person in mourning. I will cry out to the Eternal God for help as long as I live.

²¹"Take courage, my children, and cry out to God for help. He will rescue you from oppression, from the power of your enemies. ²²I am confident that the Eternal God will soon set you free. The Holy One, your eternal savior, will make me happy when he shows you mercy. ²³I cried and wailed when you were taken away, but God will bring you back and will make me happy forever. ²⁴Just as the neighboring cities watched as you were taken captive, so they will soon see the Eternal God coming in glorious splendor to rescue you. ²⁵My children, endure God's punishment with patience. Your enemies have persecuted you, but you will soon see them destroyed and at your mercy. ²⁶My children, I spoiled you with love, but you have had to follow rugged paths; you were carried off like sheep caught in an enemy raid.

²⁷"Take courage, my children, and cry out to God for help. He punished you, but he will not forget you. ²⁸Just as you were once determined to turn away from God, now turn back and serve him with ten times more determination. ²⁹The one who brought these calamities upon you will rescue you and bring you everlasting joy."

Jerusalem Is Assured of Help

³⁰Take courage, Jerusalem. God, who gave you your name, will now bring comfort to you. ³¹Misery will come to those who mistreated you and then rejoiced when you fell. ³²Misery will come to those cities that made your children slaves. Misery will be the fate of Babylon, that city which swallowed up your children. ³³Just as that city rejoiced when you fell and took delight in your ruin, so now she will mourn when she herself is deserted. ³⁴I will turn her proud boastings into mourning and take away her large population in which she took pride. ³⁵I, the Eternal God, will send down fire on her, and it will burn for many days. Her ruins will be haunted by demons for a long time to come.

³⁶Look to the east, Jerusalem, and see the joy that God is bringing to you. ³⁷Look, your children are coming home, the children that were taken from you. They have been

I, the Eternal God, will send down fire on her. (4:35)

gathered together from the east and from the west by the command of God, the Holy One. And now they are coming home, rejoicing in the glory of God.

5 ¹Jerusalem, take off the clothes you have worn in your mourning and distress, and put on the eternal splendor of God's glory. ²Put around you the cloak of God's righteousness. Place on your head the crown of the glory of the Eternal God. ³God will show your splendor to every nation on earth. ⁴Forever he will say to you: "Your security comes from your righteousness, and your splendor from your devotion to me."ᶜ

⁵Get up, Jerusalem, stand on the mountaintop; see where God, the Holy One, is bringing your children together from the east and from the west. They are rejoicing that God has remembered them. ⁶Jerusalem, your children were led away by their enemies; they left you on foot, but God is bringing them back to you, carried in royal splendor. ⁷God has commanded that every high mountain and the everlasting hills shall be made low; he has commanded that the valleys shall be filled and the ground leveled, so that the people of Israel may come safely home in the glory of God. ⁸At the command of God, forests of fragrant trees will

spring up to provide shade for the people of Israel. ⁹God will lead Israel home. They will return with great joy, guided by his mercy and righteousness, surrounded by the light of his glorious presence.

The Letter of Jeremiah

6 ¹This is a copy of the letter sent by Jeremiah to the people of Jerusalem just before they were captured by the Babylonian king and taken to Babylon. It contains the message that God had commanded Jeremiah to give them.

The People Face a Long Captivity

²You have sinned against God. That is why you are about to be taken away as prisoners to Babylon by King Nebuchadnezzar. ³You will remain there in exile for many years, as long as seven generations; then God will lead you peacefully home from Babylon.

⁴There in Babylon you will see gods made of wood, silver, and gold—gods which people carry on their shoulders and which fill the heathen with fear. ⁵You must be careful never to imitate those Gentiles. Don't let their gods fill you with fear when you see them being carried in procession and being worshiped. ⁶Instead, say to yourselves, "It is you alone, Lord, that we must worship." ⁷God's angel will be there with you; he will take care of you.

The Helplessness of Idols

⁸Their idols are plated with silver and gold and have tongues that were carved by woodworkers. But they are not real gods, and they cannot speak. ⁹The people make gold crowns and put them on the heads of their gods, as if these idols were girls who love jewelry. ¹⁰Sometimes the priests steal the silver and gold from their gods and spend it on themselves; ¹¹they even give some of it to the temple prostitutes. People take these gods of wood, silver, and gold, and

God will lead Israel home . . . with great joy. (5:9)

ᶜ **5:4** Forever . . . devotion to me; *or* He will give you this name forever: "Peace from Righteousness and Glory from Godliness."
5:1, 2 Isa 52:1; 61:3, 10; Rev 21:2   **6:1** Jer 29:1

put clothes on them, as if they were human. [12] But even though the gods are dressed in purple robes like kings, they still cannot keep themselves from being tarnished or protect themselves from termites. [13] When dust from the temple settles on their faces, someone has to wipe it off for them. [14] Like human judges they hold scepters in their hands, but they have no power to punish anyone who wrongs them. [15] Sometimes they have daggers and axes in their hands, but they cannot protect themselves from being destroyed in war or from being carried off by thieves. [16] All of this proves that they are not gods—do not worship them.

[17] Those gods sitting in their temples are as useless as a broken bowl. Their eyes are filled with the dust that people kick up when they come in. [18] The priests fortify the temples with doors and bars and bolts, so that thieves cannot break in. The gods are locked up as securely as a prisoner about to be executed for a crime against the king. [19] The priests light lamps for the gods, far more than they need for their own use, but the idols can't see even one of them. [20] Their insides are eaten away by termites, just like the wooden beams of the temple, and their clothing is destroyed, but they don't even know it. [21] Their faces are blackened by the smoke in the temple. [22] Bats, swallows, and other birds perch on them, and even cats sit on them. [23] All of this proves that they are not gods—do not worship them.

[24] These idols have been plated with gold to make them beautiful, but they do not shine unless someone polishes them. When they were being poured into molds, they felt nothing. [25] It makes no difference how high a price is paid for them; they are still unable to breathe. [26] See how useless they are! They can't walk on their own feet, but must be carried around. [27] Even those who take care of them are embarrassed when one of their gods falls to the ground and has to be picked up again. When someone stands one of them in a certain place, it cannot move, and if it is leaning over, it can never straighten itself up. Offering gifts to them is like giving gifts to a corpse. [28] Priests sell what is sacrificed to their gods and use the money on themselves. And the wives of the priests preserve the sacrifices with salt for later use, instead of sharing them with the poor and helpless. [29] Even women who are having their monthly period or women who have just given birth are allowed to touch the sacrifices. All of this proves that they are not gods—do not worship them.

[30] How can they ever be called gods, when women are allowed to make offerings to these things made of wood, silver, and gold? [31] The priests even sit in the temples when they are in mourning, with torn clothes and shaved, uncovered heads. [32] The priests roar and shout in the presence of their gods as if they were taking part in a funeral feast. [33] They take the clothing off their gods and give it to their wives and children. [34] It doesn't matter whether a person helps or harms these gods, since they cannot pay him back. They are not able to make anyone a king or to dethrone him, [35] and they cannot make a person wealthy or give him any money. If someone makes a vow to them but does not keep it, they will never make him pay. [36] They can never rescue a person from death, and they never help a weak person against one who is strong. [37] They cannot restore sight to the blind or save anyone in distress. [38] They cannot offer any mercy or give help to widows or orphans. [39] These things made of wood and covered with silver and gold are as powerless as stone taken from the mountains; and the people who worship them will be put to shame. [40] How can anyone think that they are gods or call them gods?

They . . . must be carried around. (6:26)

The Foolishness of Worshiping Idols

The Babylonians bring dishonor on their own gods. 41 When someone cannot speak, they take him to the temple and ask Bel to give him the power of speech, as if Bel could understand anything. 42 But even when the people realize that their gods cannot help, they are stupid enough to go on worshiping them. 43 Not only that, but women wrap cords around themselves and sit alongside the road burning incense and offering themselves as prostitutes. When one of them is taken off for sex, she returns to ridicule the woman next to her who was not beautiful enough to be chosen. 44 Everything about these idols is false. How can anyone think that they are gods or call them gods?

45 Woodworkers and goldsmiths make these gods, so they can never be anything other than what these people want them to be. 46 Even their makers do not live long lives, so how are they able to create gods? 47 These people leave nothing but deceit and disgrace as an inheritance for future generations. 48 When wars and disturbances come, the priests plan where they can go into hiding with their gods. 49 These idols are helpless in the face of wars and disturbances. Why can't people realize that these idols are not gods?

50 These idols are nothing more than wood covered with silver and gold; one day it will be clear that they are really not gods at all. 51 All nations and kings will realize that idols are nothing more than the work of human hands. They do not have the power of a god, 52 and anyone should know that they are not really gods.

53 These gods can never make anyone a king or bring rain. 54 They can't make decisions about their own affairs or give justice to someone who has been wronged; they can do absolutely nothing. They are as useless as crows flying around in the air. 55 When a temple catches on fire, the priests run away to save themselves, while the gods made of wood and covered with silver and gold are left to burn like wooden beams. 56 They can't fight kings or go to war against enemies. How can anyone believe that they are gods?

57 These gods of wood, covered with silver and gold, cannot protect themselves from thieves and robbers 58 who take off the silver and gold and the gods' clothing and walk away with all of it. The gods can do nothing to stop them. 59 Anything from a courageous king to a useful piece of pottery is better than a false god. Even a door is better than a false god; a door at least protects the things in the house. Even a wooden pillar in a palace is better than a false god.

60 God provided the sun, the moon, and the stars to give light, and they obey him. 61 The same is true of lightning and wind. The lightning can be seen far and wide, and the wind blows everywhere. 62 When God commands clouds to spread out over the whole world, they obey. 63 When God sends down fire from heaven to burn up mountains and forests, it does what it is told. Idols cannot do these things—they can't even do a good imitation. 64 Why should they be called gods, when they are not able to help us or harm us in any way? 65 You know that they are not gods—do not worship them.

66 These gods have no power over kings; they cannot pronounce curses on them or grant them blessings. 67 They cannot produce for the nations any signs in the sky; they cannot shine like the sun or the moon. 68 Even wild animals are better off than these idols; animals can at least run from danger to protect themselves. 69 So it is absolutely clear that they are not gods—do not worship them.

70 These gods of theirs, made of wood and covered with silver and gold, are about as helpful as a scarecrow in a cucumber patch; they are no protection at all. 71 They do as much good as a thorn bush in a garden; instead of keeping birds away, they provide a perch for them. These gods are like a dead body thrown out into the darkness. 72 The purple linen[d] robes they wear rot away, so we know that they are not gods. Finally they will be eaten by termites, and then no one anywhere will have any use for them.

73 The righteous person has an advantage over others; he does not own any idols, and they can never make a fool of him.

d **6:72** linen; *Greek* marble.
6:41 Isa 46:1

THE BOOK OF *Ezekiel*

Are you a science fiction or fantasy fan? Do you like movies with imaginary creatures? Then you'll love the Book of Ezekiel! Ezekiel was one of the greatest prophets of Israel. God sends him wild visions to help the Israelites understand that they sinned against God and that God was very angry with them. Among other things, they worshiped idols and neglected poor people. At first they didn't listen, but terrible things happened—the southern kingdom of Judah was taken over, and the Temple was destroyed. The people who survived were taken to Babylonia as war captives. After that, Ezekiel shares God's message of hope—that God promises to rebuild their homeland and to be with them forever.

Chap. 2:8—3:3

Headlines

- Prophet Has Wild Visions (1:4–28)
- Ezekiel Silenced, Tries Acting (3:22—4:17)
- Children Not Punished for Parents' Sins (18:1–31)
- Ezekiel Does Not Mourn Dead Wife (24:15–27)
- Good Shepherd Rescues His Sheep (34:11–31)
- Dry Bones Come to Life! (37:1–14)
- Plans for New Temple Revealed (40:1–5)

FACTOIDS

Who wrote this book? This book was written by the prophet Ezekiel and people called scribes who recorded his words and actions. Ezekiel did all his prophesying in Babylonia, where he was taken captive before the final fall of Jerusalem.

Why was it written? The book has two major sections. Chapters 1–24 occurred before the destruction of Jerusalem (587 BC.) and warned the Israelites about the coming destruction. Chapters 25–48 occurred after Jerusalem was destroyed. In this section Ezekiel began prophesying about the promise of God's salvation through a new covenant.

What is the literary style? Ezekiel is a combination of historical facts, words of warning and hope to the Israelites, and descriptions of Ezekiel's visions.

Important themes
- The Israelites sinned, and they must repent.
- God is glorious, and the name of God is holy.
- God will restore the Temple and create a new covenant with the Israelites.

EZEKIEL

EZEKIEL'S FIRST VISION OF GOD
(1:1—7:27)

God's Throne

1 ¹On the fifth day of the fourth month of the thirtieth year,ᵃ I, Ezekiel the priest, son of Buzi, was living with the Jewish exiles by the Chebar River in Babylonia. The sky opened, and I saw a vision of God. (²It was the fifth year since King Jehoiachin had been taken into exile.) ³There in Babylonia beside the Chebar River, I heard the LORD speak to me, and I felt his power.

⁴I looked up and saw a windstorm coming from the north. Lightning was flashing from a huge cloud, and the sky around it was glowing. Where the lightning was flashing, something shone like bronze. ⁵At the center of the storm I saw what looked like four living creatures in human form, ⁶but each of them had four faces and four wings. ⁷Their legs were straight, and they had hoofs like those of a bull. They shone like polished bronze. ⁸In addition to their four faces and four wings, they each had four human hands, one under each wing. ⁹Two wings of each creature were spread out so that the creatures formed a square, with their wing tips touching. When they moved, they moved as a group without turning their bodies.

¹⁰Each living creature had four different faces: a human face in front, a lion's face at the right, a bull's face at the left, and an eagle's face at the back. ¹¹Two wingsᵇ of each creature were raised so that they touched the tips of the wings of the creatures next to it, and their other two wings were folded against their bodies. ¹²Each creature faced all four directions, and so the group could go wherever they wished, without having to turn.

¹³Amongᶜ the creatures there was something that looked like a blazing torch, constantly moving. The fire would blaze up and shoot out flashes of lightning. ¹⁴The creatures themselves darted back and forth with the speed of lightning.

¹⁵As I was looking at the four creatures I saw four wheels touching the ground, one beside each of them.ᵈ ¹⁶All four wheels were

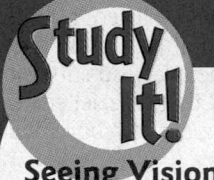

Study It!

Seeing Visions

Creatures with four faces, wheels covered with eyes, a crystal dome, windstorms—those are only a few of the images Ezekiel sees in chapter 1. For the Israelites, these images represented familiar characteristics of God. For example, the throne is placed above the dome (Ezekiel 1:26), symbolizing God's location above the sky. Wheels that could move in any direction (1:17) were a sign that God was with them everywhere they went.

Just as Ezekiel did, a prophet trying to get your attention would use familiar images to tell you about God. For example, a picture of the planet earth might mean that God is everywhere. A goldfish surrounded by water could mean that God's love is all around you.

What other symbols and images could a prophet use to tell you and your friends about God?

— Ezekiel 1:4–28

ᵃ **1:1** THIRTIETH YEAR: *It is not known to what year this refers.* ᵇ **1:11** *Some ancient translations* Two wings; *Hebrew* Their faces, their wings. ᶜ **1:13** *Some ancient translations* Among; *Hebrew* And the likeness of. ᵈ **1:15** *Some ancient translations* them; *Hebrew* their faces.
1:1 Rev 19:11　**1:2** 2 Kings 24:10–16; 2 Chr 36:9, 10　**1:5** Rev 4:6　**1:10** Ezek 10:14; Rev 4:7
1:13 Rev 4:5　**1:15–21** Ezek 10:9–13

alike; each one shone like a precious stone, and each had another wheel intersecting it at right angles, ¹⁷so that the wheels could move in any of the four directions. ¹⁸The rims of the wheels were covered with eyes.ᵉ ¹⁹Whenever the creatures moved, the wheels moved with them, and if the creatures rose up from the earth, so did the wheels. ²⁰The creatures went wherever they wished, and the wheels did exactly what the creatures did, because the creatures controlled them. ²¹So every time the creatures moved or stopped or rose in the air, the wheels did exactly the same.

²²Above the heads of the creatures there was something that looked like a dome made of dazzling crystal. ²³There under the dome stood the creatures, each stretching out two wings toward the ones next to it and covering its body with the other two wings. ²⁴I heard the noise their wings made in flight; it sounded like the roar of the sea, like the noise of a huge army, like the voice of Almighty God. When they stopped flying, they folded their wings, ²⁵but there was still a sound coming from above the dome over their heads.

²⁶Above the dome there was something that looked like a throne made of sapphire, and sitting on the throne was a figure that looked like a human being. ²⁷The figure seemed to be shining like bronze in the middle of a fire. It shone all over with a bright light ²⁸that had in it all the colors of the rainbow. This was the dazzling light which shows the presence of the LORD.

God Calls Ezekiel to Be a Prophet

2 When I saw this, I fell face downward on the ground. Then I heard a voice ¹saying, "Mortal man, stand up. I want to talk to you." ²While the voice was speaking, God's spirit entered me and raised me to my feet, and I heard the voice continue, ³"Mortal

man, I am sending you to the people of Israel. They have rebelled and turned against me and are still rebels, just as their ancestors were. ⁴They are stubborn and do not respect me, so I am sending you to tell them what I, the Sovereign LORD, am saying to them. ⁵Whether those rebels listen to you or not, they will know that a prophet has been among them.

⁶"But you, mortal man, must not be afraid of them or of anything they say. They will defy and despise you; it will be like living among scorpions. Still, don't be afraid of those rebels or of anything they say. ⁷You will tell them whatever I tell you to say, whether they listen or not. Remember what rebels they are.

⁸"Mortal man, listen to what I tell you. Don't be rebellious like them. Open your mouth and eat what I am going to give you." ⁹I saw a hand reaching out toward me, and it was holding a scroll. ¹⁰The hand unrolled the scroll, and I saw that there was writing on both sides—cries of grief were written there, and wails and groans.

I saw a hand reaching out toward me. (2:9)

3 ¹ God said, "Mortal man, eat this scroll; then go and speak to the people of Israel."

²So I opened my mouth, and he gave me

ᵉ **1:18** *Verse 18 in Hebrew is unclear.*
1:18 Rev 4:8   **1:22** Rev 4:6   **1:24** Rev 1:4–15; 19:6   **1:26** Ezek 10:1; Rev 4:2, 3   **1:27** Ezek 8:2
2:9, 10 Rev 5:1

Ezekiel

Only God Is God

When God talks to Ezekiel, God keeps calling him "mortal man." The use of this phrase emphasizes that God is God and Ezekiel is a human being. God demands honor, respect, and obedience from Ezekiel just because God is God.

God requires the same from us. When we refuse to participate in Sunday Mass or show little reverence in church, we dishonor God. When we use bad language or develop a poor attitude at home, we disrespect God. When we waste precious resources or treat others badly, we disobey God.

Ezekiel listened carefully to God and honored, respected, and obeyed him. How will you follow Ezekiel's example?

— Ezekiel, chapters 2–3

the scroll to eat. ³He said, "Mortal man, eat this scroll that I give you; fill your stomach with it." I ate it, and it tasted as sweet as honey.

⁴Then God said, "Mortal man, go to the people of Israel and say to them whatever I tell you to say. ⁵I am not sending you to a nation that speaks a difficult foreign language, but to the Israelites. ⁶If I sent you to great nations that spoke difficult languages you didn't understand, they would listen to you. ⁷But none of the people of Israel will be willing to listen; they will not even listen to me. All of them are stubborn and defiant. ⁸Now I will make you as stubborn and as tough as they are. ⁹I will make you as firm as

3:1–3 Rev 10:9, 10

a rock, as hard as a diamond; don't be afraid of those rebels."

¹⁰God continued, "Mortal man, pay close attention and remember everything I tell you. ¹¹Then go to the people of your nation who are in exile and tell them what I, the Sovereign LORD, am saying to them, whether they pay attention to you or not."

¹²Then God's spirit lifted me up, and I heard behind me the loud roar of a voice that said, "Praise the glory of the LORD in heaven above!" ¹³I heard the wings of the creatures beating together in the air, and the noise of the wheels, as loud as an earthquake. ¹⁴The power of the LORD came on me with great force, and as his spirit carried me off, I felt bitter and angry. ¹⁵So I came to Tel Abib beside the Chebar River, where the exiles were living, and for seven days I stayed there, overcome by what I had seen and heard.

The LORD Appoints Ezekiel as a Lookout
(Ezekiel 33:1–9)

¹⁶After the seven days had passed, the LORD spoke to me. ¹⁷"Mortal man," he said, "I am making you a lookout for the nation of Israel. You will pass on to them the warnings I give you. ¹⁸If I announce that someone evil is going to die but you do not warn him to change his ways so that he can save his life, he will die, still a sinner, but I will hold you responsible for his death. ¹⁹If you do warn an evil man and he doesn't stop sinning, he will die, still a sinner, but your life will be spared.

²⁰"If someone truly good starts doing evil and I put him in a dangerous situation, he will die if you do not warn him. He will die because of his sins—I will not remember the good he did—and I will hold you responsible for his death. ²¹If you do warn a good man not to sin and he listens to you and doesn't sin, he will stay alive, and your life will also be spared."

The scroll that God told Ezekiel to eat was covered with cries of grief. So Ezekiel expected it to taste bitter, but instead it tasted sweet.

Ezekiel Will Be Unable to Talk

22 I felt the powerful presence of the LORD and heard him say to me, "Get up and go out into the valley. I will talk to you there."

23 So I went out into the valley, and there I saw the glory of the LORD, just as I had seen it beside the Chebar River. I fell face downward on the ground, 24 but God's spirit entered me and raised me to my feet. The LORD said to me, "Go home and shut yourself up in the house. 25 You will be tied with ropes, mortal man, and you will not be able to go out in public. 26 I will paralyze your tongue so that you won't be able to warn these rebellious people. 27 Then, when I speak to you again and give you back the power of speech, you will tell them what I, the Sovereign LORD, am saying. Some of them will listen, but some will ignore you, for they are a nation of rebels."

But God's spirit entered me and raised me to my feet. (3:24)

Ezekiel Acts Out the Siege of Jerusalem

4 1 God said, "Mortal man, get a brick, put it in front of you, and scratch lines on it to represent the city of Jerusalem. 2 Then, to represent a siege, put trenches, earthworks, camps, and battering rams all around it. 3 Take an iron pan and set it up like a wall between you and the city. Face the city. It is under siege, and you are the one besieging it. This will be a sign to the nation of Israel.

4-5 "Then lie down on your left side, and I*f*

will place on you the guilt of the nation of Israel. For 390 days you will stay there and suffer because of their guilt. I have sentenced you to one day for each year their punishment will last. 6 When you finish that, turn over on your right side and suffer for the guilt of Judah for forty days—one day for each year of their punishment.

7 "Fix your eyes on the siege of Jerusalem. Shake your fist at the city and prophesy against it. 8 I will tie you up so that you cannot turn from one side to the other until the siege is over.

Shake your fist at the city and prophesy against it. (4:7)

9 "Now take some wheat, barley, beans, peas, millet, and spelt. Mix them all together and make bread. That is what you are to eat during the 390 days you are lying on your left side. 10 You will be allowed eight ounces of bread a day, and it will have to last until the next day. 11 You will also have a limited amount of water to drink, two cups a day. 12 You are to build a fire out of dried human excrement, bake bread on the fire, and eat it where everyone can see you."

13 The LORD said, "This represents the way the Israelites will have to eat food which the Law forbids,*g* when I scatter them to foreign countries."

14 But I replied, "No, Sovereign LORD! I have never defiled myself. From childhood on I have never eaten meat from any animal that died a natural death or was killed by wild animals. I have never eaten any food considered unclean."

15 So God said, "Very well. I will let you use cow dung instead, and you can bake your bread on that."

16 And he added, "Mortal man, I am going to cut off the supply of bread for Jerusalem.

f 4:4–5 *Probable text* I; *Hebrew* you.   *g* 4:13 FOOD WHICH THE LAW FORBIDS: *The Law of Moses prohibited the eating of certain foods as being ritually unclean (see Lev 11).*

Ezekiel

Live It!

Messages from God?

God had Ezekiel use lots of different ways to deliver his message to the Israelites. It's divine instant messaging. First God tells Ezekiel to make a map of the city and then make it look like it's being destroyed. Then Ezekiel is supposed to lie on his side for 430 days to represent the number of years of punishment. God also tells him to make some bread and bake it over a fire made out of . . . well, check out Ezekiel 4:12. And after that Ezekiel shaves his head.

Many people are trying to get God's message to you. Some of them use unusual means, like Ezekiel did. Some use words. Others share God's message just by living a good life. Keep your eyes and ears open. You never know when a message from God is going to pop up in your life.

— Ezekiel 4:1—5:4

The people there will be distressed and anxious as they measure out the food they eat and the water they drink. 17They will run out of bread and water; they will be in despair, and they will waste away because of their sins."

Ezekiel Cuts His Hair

5 1The LORD said, "Mortal man, take a sharp sword and use it to shave off your beard and all your hair. Then weigh the hair on scales and divide it into three parts. 2Burn up a third of it in the city when the siege is over. Take another third and chop it up with your sword as you move around outside the city. Scatter the remaining third to the winds, and I will pursue it with my

sword. 3Keep back a few hairs and wrap them in the hem of your clothes. 4Then take a few of them out again, throw them in the fire, and let them burn up. From them fire will spread to the whole nation of Israel."

5The Sovereign LORD said, "Look at Jerusalem. I put her at the center of the world, with other countries all around her. 6But Jerusalem rebelled against my commands and showed that she was more wicked than the other nations, more disobedient than the countries around her. Jerusalem rejected my commands and refused to keep my laws. 7Now listen, Jerusalem, to what I, the Sovereign LORD, am saying. By not obeying my laws or keeping my commands, you have caused more trouble than the nations around you. You have followed the customs of other nations. 8And so I, the Sovereign LORD, am telling you that I am your enemy. I will pass judgment on you where all the nations can see it. 9Because of all the things you do that I hate, I will punish Jerusalem as I have never done before and will never do again. 10As a result, parents in Jerusalem will eat their children, and children will eat their parents. I will punish you and scatter in every direction any who are left alive.

11"Therefore, as I am the living God—this is the word of the Sovereign LORD— because you defiled my Temple with all the evil, disgusting things you did, I will cut you down without mercy. 12A third of your people will die from sickness and hunger in the city; a third will be cut down by swords outside the city; and I will scatter the last third to the winds and pursue them with a sword.

13"You will feel all the force of my anger and rage until I am satisfied. When all this happens, you will be convinced that I, the LORD, have spoken to you because I am outraged at your unfaithfulness. 14Everyone from the nations around you who passes by will sneer at you and keep their distance.

15"When I am angry and furious with you and punish you, all the nations around you will be terrified. They will look at you with disgust and make fun of you. 16I will cut off your supply of food and let you

Ezekiel's Gift

Ezekiel was not a great poet like some other writers in the Old Testament. He didn't fight bravely in battles. He was not an important leader. But he had an amazing gift for drama. He used this gift to teach others about God.

Do you enjoy acting or playing a musical instrument? Are you good at drawing or painting? Do you like writing stories or poems? Like Ezekiel, you can use these gifts to share God with others. As an artist, a writer, a musician, an actor, or a poet, you reflect God's handiwork and communicate God's message in ways that others cannot.

Look around you. Listen to the sounds of life. Watch people. You will come to know that God is the supreme artist. Keep doing your part to learn about your art and share the gift that God gave you.

— Ezekiel, chapter 5

Sovereign LORD's word—to hear what I, the Sovereign LORD, am telling the mountains, the hills, the gorges, and the valleys: I will send a sword to destroy the places where people worship idols. ⁴The altars will be torn down and the incense altars broken. All the people there will be killed in front of their idols; ⁵I will scatter the corpses of the people of Israel; I will scatter their bones all around the altars. ⁶All the cities of Israel will be destroyed, so that all their altars and their idols will be smashed to pieces, their incense altars will be shattered, and everything they made will disappear. ⁷People will be killed everywhere, and those who survive will acknowledge that I am the LORD.

⁸"I will let some escape the slaughter and be scattered among the nations, ⁹where they will live in exile. There they will remember me and know that I have punished them and disgraced them,ⁱ because their faithless hearts deserted me and they preferred idols to me. And they will be disgusted with themselves because of the evil and degrading things they have done. ¹⁰They will know that I am the LORD and that my warnings were not empty threats."

¹¹The Sovereign LORD said, "Wring your hands! Stamp your feet! Cry in sorrow because of all the evil, disgusting things the Israelites have done. They are going to die in war or of starvation or disease. ¹²Those far away will get sick and die; those nearby will be killed in war; those who survive will starve to death. They will feel all the force of my anger. ¹³Corpses will be scattered among the idols and around

Corpses will be scattered among the idols. (6:13)

starve. You*ʰ* will feel the pains of hunger like sharp arrows sent to destroy you. ¹⁷I will send hunger and wild animals to kill your children, and will send sickness, violence, and war to kill you. I, the LORD, have spoken."

The LORD Condemns Idolatry

6 ¹The LORD spoke to me. ²"Mortal man," he said, "look toward the mountains of Israel and give them my message. ³Tell the mountains of Israel to hear the

---

ʰ **5:16** *Probable text* You; *Hebrew* They.   *ⁱ* **6:9** *Some ancient translations* disgraced them; *Hebrew* I am disgraced.
5:17 Rev 6:8

People who were captured in war were forced to shave their heads. Ezekiel's shaved head was a symbol of what was to come.

Ezekiel

Pray It!

I'm Angry, God

The book of Ezekiel describes God as being angry with the Israelites, and for good reasons. In Ezekiel, chapter 6, he threatens to destroy the mountains and all the places where the people worshiped idols. God sends the message through Ezekiel that they will pay for "all the evil, disgusting things the Israelites have done" (Ezekiel 6:11).

Most people get angry at times. It is not necessarily a sin to feel angry. But anger is such a strong emotion that we must be careful not to be controlled by it. Uncontrolled anger can lead to sinful acts of revenge and violence. The next time you feel angry, say this short prayer asking God to help you control your anger so that you can work out your problems in a mature way.

I'm angry, God,
Help me to understand my feelings.
Help me to see the other person's side of things.
Help me to control my words and my actions.
Help me to look for a solution to the problem
that won't hurt anyone—most of all, me.
Amen.

— Ezekiel, chapter 7

the altars, scattered on every high hill, on the top of every mountain, under every green tree and every large oak, in every place where they burned sacrifices to their idols. Then everyone will know that I am the LORD. 14Yes, I will reach out and destroy their country. I will make it a wasteland from the southern desert to the city of Riblah in the north, not sparing any place where the Israelites live. Then everyone will know that I am the LORD."

The End Is Near for Israel

7 1The LORD spoke to me. 2"Mortal man," he said, "this is what I, the Sovereign LORD, am saying to the land of Israel: This is the end for the whole land!

3"Israel, the end has come. You will feel my anger, because I am judging you for what you have done. I will pay you back for

all your disgusting conduct. 4I will not spare you or show you any mercy. I am going to punish you for the disgusting things you have done, so that you will know that I am the LORD."

5This is what the Sovereign LORD is saying: "One disaster after another is coming on you. 6It's all over. This is the end. You are finished. 7The end is coming for you people who live in the land. The time is near when there will be no more celebrations at the mountain shrines, only confusion.j

8"Very soon now you will feel all the force of my anger. I am judging you for what you have done, and I will pay you back for all your disgusting conduct. 9I will not spare you or show you any mercy. I am going to punish you for the disgusting things you have done, so that you will know that I

j 7:7 *Probable text* celebrations . . . confusion; *Hebrew unclear.*

What are the things that happen in today's world that you think anger God?

am the LORD and that I am the one who punishes you."

10 The day of disaster is coming. Violence is flourishing. Pride is at its height.ᵏ 11 Violence produces more wickedness. Nothing of theirs will remain, nothing of their wealth, their splendor, or their glory.

12 The time is coming. The day is near when buying and selling will have no more meaning, because God's punishment will fall on everyone alike. 13 No merchants will live long enough to get back what they have lost, because God's anger is on everyone. Those who are evil cannot survive.ˡ 14 The trumpet blows, and everyone gets ready. But no one goes off to war, for God's anger will fall on everyone alike.

Punishment for Israel's Sins

15 There is fighting in the streets, and sickness and hunger in the houses. Anyone who is out in the country will die in the fighting, and anyone in the city will be a victim of sickness and hunger. 16 Some will escape to the mountains like doves frightened from the valleys. All of them will moan over their sins.ᵐ 17 Everyone's hands will be weak, and their knees will shake. 18 They will put on sackcloth and they will tremble all over. Their heads will be shaved, and they will all be disgraced. 19 They will throw their gold and silver away in the streets like garbage, because neither silver nor gold can save them when the LORD pours out his fury. They cannot use it to satisfy their desires or fill their stomachs. Gold and silver led them into sin. 20 Once they were proud of their beautiful jewels, but they used them to make disgusting idols. That is why the LORD has made their wealth repulsive to them.

Some will escape to the mountains. (7:16)

21 "I will let foreigners rob them," says the LORD, "and lawbreakers will take all their wealth and defile it. 22 I will not interfere when my treasured Temple is profaned, when robbers break into it and defile it.

They were proud of their beautiful jewels. (7:20)

23 "Everything is in confusionⁿ —the land is full of murders and the cities are full of violence. 24 I will bring the most evil nations here and let them have your homes. Your strongest men will lose their confidence when I let the nations profane the places where you worship. 25 Despair is coming. You will look for peace and never find it. 26 One disaster will follow another, and a steady stream of bad news will pour in. You will beg the prophets to reveal what they foresee. The priests will have nothing to teach the people, and the elders will have no advice to give. 27 The king will mourn, the prince will give up hope, and the people will shake with fear. I will punish you for all you have done, and will judge you in the same way as you have judged others. This will show you that I am the LORD."

ᵏ 7:10 *Probable text* Pride is at its height; *Hebrew unclear.* ˡ 7:13 *Verse 13 in Hebrew is unclear.* ᵐ 7:16 *Verse 16 in Hebrew is unclear.* ⁿ 7:23 *One ancient translation* Everything is in confusion; *Hebrew unclear.*

EZEKIEL'S SECOND VISION OF GOD (8:1—10:22)

Idolatry in Jerusalem

8 ¹On the fifth day of the sixth month of the sixth year of our exile, the leaders of the exiles from Judah were sitting in my house with me. Suddenly the power of the Sovereign LORD came on me. ²I looked up and saw a vision of a fiery human form. From the waist down his body looked like fire, and from the waist up he was shining like polished bronze. ³He reached out what seemed to be a hand and grabbed me by the hair. Then in this vision God's spirit lifted me high in the air and took me to Jerusalem. He took me to the inner entrance of the north gate of the Temple, where there was an idol that was an outrage to God.

⁴There I saw the dazzling light that shows the presence of Israel's God, just as I had seen it when I was by the Chebar River. ⁵God said to me, "Mortal man, look toward the north." I looked, and there near the altar by the entrance of the gateway I saw the idol that was an outrage to God.

⁶God said to me, "Mortal man, do you see what is happening? Look at the disgusting things the people of Israel are doing here, driving me farther and farther away from my holy place. You will see even more disgraceful things than this."

⁷He took me to the entrance of the outer courtyard and showed me a hole in the wall. ⁸He said, "Mortal man, break through the wall here." I broke through it and found a door. ⁹He told me, "Go in and look at the evil, disgusting things they are doing there." ¹⁰So I went in and looked. The walls were covered with drawings of snakes and other unclean animals,ᵒ and of the other things which the Israelites were worshiping. ¹¹Seventy Israelite leaders were there, including Jaazaniah son of Shaphan. Each one was holding an incense burner, and smoke was rising from the incense. ¹²God asked me,

"Mortal man, do you see what the Israelite leaders are doing in secret? They are all worshiping in a room full of images. Their excuse is: 'The LORD doesn't see us! He has abandoned the country.' "

¹³Then the LORD said to me, "You are going to see them do even more disgusting things than that." ¹⁴So he took me to the north gate of the Temple and showed me women weeping over the death of the god Tammuz.ᵖ

¹⁵He asked, "Mortal man, do you see that? You will see even more disgusting things." ¹⁶So he took me to the inner courtyard of the Temple. There near the entrance of the sanctuary, between the altar and the porch, were about twenty-five men. They had turned their backs to the sanctuary and were bowing low toward the east, worshiping the rising sun.

¹⁷The LORD said to me, "Mortal man, do you see that? These people of Judah are not satisfied with merely doing all the disgusting things you have seen here and with spreading violence throughout the country. No, they must come and do them right here in the Temple and make me even more angry. Look how they insult me in the most offensive way possible!�q ¹⁸They will feel all the force of my anger. I will not spare them or show them any mercy. They will shout prayers to me as loud as they can, but I will not listen to them."

Jerusalem Is Punished

9 ¹Then I heard God shout, "Come here, you men who are going to punish the city. Bring your weapons with you." ²At once six men came from the outer north gate of the Temple, each one carrying a weapon. With them was a man dressed in linen clothes, carrying something to write with. They all came and stood by the bronze altar.

³Then the dazzling light of the presence of the God of Israel rose up from the

---

ᵒ **8:10** UNCLEAN ANIMALS: *The Law of Moses prohibited the eating of certain animals as being ritually unclean (see 4:13; Lev 11).* ᵖ **8:14** TAMMUZ: *A god who was thought to die when vegetation died and to come to life the next year. Women would mourn his ritual death.* q **8:17** IN THE MOST OFFENSIVE WAY POSSIBLE: *A reference to a pagan rite of putting a branch to the nose.*

8:2 Ezek 1:27   **8:4** Ezek 1:28

winged creatures[r] where it had been, and moved to the entrance of the Temple. The LORD called to the man dressed in linen, [4]"Go through the whole city of Jerusalem and put a mark on the forehead of everyone who is distressed and troubled because of all the disgusting things being done in the city."

[5]And I heard God say to the other men, "Follow him through the city and kill. Spare no one; have mercy on no one. [6]Kill the old men, young men, young women, mothers, and children. But don't touch anyone who has the mark on his forehead. Start here at my Temple." So they began with the leaders who were standing there at the Temple.

[7]God said to them, "Defile the Temple. Fill its courtyards with corpses. Get to work!" So they began to kill the people in the city.[s]

[8]While the killing was going on, I was there alone. I threw myself face downward on the ground and shouted, "Sovereign LORD, are you so angry with Jerusalem that you are going to kill everyone left in Israel?"

[9]God answered, "The people of Israel and Judah are guilty of terrible sins. They have committed murder all over the land and have filled Jerusalem with crime. They say that I, the LORD, have abandoned their country and that I don't see them. [10]But I will not have pity on them; I will do to them what they have done to others."

[11]Then the man wearing linen clothes returned and reported to the LORD, "I have carried out your orders."

The Glory of the LORD Leaves the Temple

10 [1]I looked at the dome over the heads of the living creatures[t] and above them was something that seemed to be a throne made of sapphire. [2]God said to the man wearing linen clothes, "Go between the wheels under the creatures and fill your

The Mark of Caring

"Go through the whole city of Jerusalem and put a mark on the forehead of everyone who is distressed and troubled because of all the disgusting things being done in the city" (Ezekiel 9:4).

In Ezekiel's vision, the people with a mark on their forehead were the only ones spared when God gave the order to kill the residents of Jerusalem. They were the people who worshiped God as God and treated others fairly. God spared their lives because they cared.

You may not be able to change the attitudes and actions of the people around you, but you can live your life well and care about others. It may be enough to make them think about making some changes. And that's all God asks of you.

— Ezekiel 9:3–6

hands with burning coals. Then scatter the coals over the city."

I watched him go. [3]The creatures were standing to the south of the Temple when he went in, and a cloud filled the inner courtyard. [4]The dazzling light of the LORD's presence rose up from the creatures and moved to the entrance of the Temple. Then the cloud filled the Temple, and the courtyard was blazing with the light. [5]The noise made by the creatures' wings was heard even in the

[r] **9:3** WINGED CREATURES: *See* 1:5–12.   [s] **9:7** work!" So they . . . city.; *or* work! Go on and start killing the people in the city!"   [t] **10:1** LIVING CREATURES: *See* 1:5–12.
9:4 Rev 7:3; 9:4; 14:1   **10:1** Ezek 1:26; Rev 4:2   **10:2** Rev 8:5

"But I will not have pity on them; I will do to them what they have done to others" *(Ezekiel 9:10).*

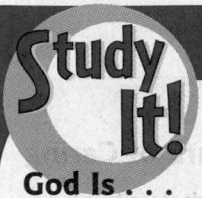

God Is . . .

In Ezekiel's vision, he saw "the dazzling light of the LORD's presence" (Ezekiel 10:4). It is only one of many images that tell us something about God in the Scriptures. Check out these others:

• an eagle (Deuteronomy 32:10–11)
• a shepherd (Psalm 23)
• a mother comforting her child (Isaiah 66:13)
• a baker woman (Luke 13:20–21)
• a vine (John 15:5)

When you think of God, what images come to mind? Be creative.

— Ezekiel 10:4

outer courtyard. It sounded like the voice of Almighty God.

⁶When the LORD commanded the man wearing linen clothes to take some fire from between the wheels that were under the creatures, the man went in and stood by one of the wheels. ⁷One of the creatures reached his hand into the fire that was there among them, picked up some coals, and put them in the hands of the man in linen. The man took the coals and left.

⁸I saw that each creature had what looked like a human hand under each of its wings. ⁹⁻¹⁰I also saw that there were four wheels, all alike, one beside each creature. The wheels shone like precious stones, and each one had another wheel which intersected it at right angles. ¹¹When the creatures moved, they could go in any direction without turning. They all moved together in the direction they wanted to go, without having to turn around. ¹²Their bodies, backs, hands, wings, and wheels were covered with eyes. ¹³I heard a voice calling out, "Whirling wheels."

¹⁴Each creature had four faces. The first was the face of a bull, the second a human face, the third the face of a lion, and the fourth the face of an eagle. ¹⁵(They were the same creatures that I had seen by the Chebar River.) When the creatures rose in the air ¹⁶and moved, the wheels went with them. Whenever they spread their wings to fly, the wheels still went with them. ¹⁷When the creatures stopped, the wheels stopped; and when the creatures flew, the wheels went with them, because the creatures controlled them.

¹⁸Then the dazzling light of the LORD's presence left the entrance of the Temple and moved to a place above the creatures. ¹⁹They spread their wings and flew up from the earth while I was watching, and the wheels went with them. They paused at the east gate of the Temple, and the dazzling light was over them. ²⁰I recognized them as the same creatures which I had seen beneath the God of Israel at the Chebar River.

²¹Each of them had four faces, four wings, and what looked like a human hand under each wing. ²²Their faces looked exactly like the faces[u] I had seen by the Chebar River. Each creature moved straight ahead.

Jerusalem Is Condemned

11 ¹God's spirit lifted me up and took me to the east gate of the Temple. There near the gate I saw twenty-five men, including Jaazaniah son of Azzur and Pelatiah son of Benaiah, two leaders of the nation.

²God said to me, "Mortal man, these men make evil plans and give bad advice in this city. ³They say, 'We will soon be building houses again.[v] The city is like a cooking pot, and we are like the meat in it, but at least it

[u] **10:22** *Probable text* the faces; *Hebrew* the faces and them.   [v] **11:3** We will . . . again; *or* We won't be building houses any time soon.
10:9–13 Ezek 1:15–21   **10:12** Rev 4:8   **10:14** Ezek 1:10; Rev 4:7

Ezekiel, chapter 11, introduces a new name for God, Sovereign LORD.
***Sovereign* means to have supreme authority and power.**

protects us from the fire.' ⁴Now then, denounce them, mortal man."

⁵The spirit of the LORD took control of me, and the LORD told me to give the people this message: "People of Israel, I know what you are saying and what you are planning. ⁶You have murdered so many people here in the city that the streets are full of corpses.

⁷"So this is what I, the Sovereign LORD, am saying to you. This city is a cooking pot all right, but what is the meat? The corpses of those you have killed! You will not be here—I will throw you out of the city! ⁸Are you afraid of swords? I will bring soldiers with swords to attack you. ⁹I will take you out of the city and hand you over to foreigners. I have sentenced you to death, ¹⁰and you will be killed in battle in your own country. Then everyone will know that I am the LORD. ¹¹This city will not protect you the way a pot protects the meat in it. I will punish you wherever you may be in the land of Israel. ¹²You will know that I am the LORD and that while you were keeping the laws of the neighboring nations, you were breaking *my* laws and disobeying *my* commands."

¹³While I was prophesying, Pelatiah dropped dead. I threw myself face downward on the ground and shouted, "No, Sovereign LORD! Are you going to kill everyone left in Israel?"

God's Promise to the Exiles

¹⁴The LORD spoke to me. ¹⁵"Mortal man," he said, "the people who live in Jerusalem are talking about you and those of your nation who are in exile. They say, 'The exiles are too far away to worship the LORD. He has given us possession of the land.'

¹⁶"Now tell your fellow exiles what I am saying. I am the one who sent them to live in far-off nations and scattered them in other countries. Yet, for the time being I will be present with them in the lands where they have gone.

¹⁷"So tell them what I, the Sovereign LORD, am saying. I will gather them out of

> # Pray It!
> ## I Need a New Heart
>
> *I need a new heart, God. Not the one that beats inside of me, but the one that makes me understanding and kind to others.*
>
> *I need a new mind, God. Not the one that gets me through school, but the one that makes me think that I am the center of the universe.*
>
> *Can you help me, God? Can you take away my stubbornness and replace it with faithfulness? I know that you are my God, and I am yours. I just have to keep remembering. Amen.*
>
> **— Ezekiel 11:19–21**

the countries where I scattered them, and will give the land of Israel back to them. ¹⁸When they return, they are to get rid of all the filthy, disgusting idols they find. ¹⁹I will give them a new heart and a new mind. I will take away their stubborn heart of stone and will give them an obedient heart. ²⁰Then they will keep my laws and faithfully obey all my commands. They will be my people, and I will be their God. ²¹But I will punish the people who love to worship filthy, disgusting idols. I will punish them for what they have done." The Sovereign LORD has spoken.

God's Glory Leaves Jerusalem

²²The living creatures began to fly, and the wheels went with them. The dazzling light of the presence of the God of Israel was over them. ²³Then the dazzling light left the city and moved to the mountain east of it. ²⁴In the vision the spirit of God lifted me up and brought me back to the exiles in Babylonia. Then the vision faded, ²⁵and I told the exiles everything that the LORD had shown me.

11:19, 20 Ezek 36:26–28   **11:22, 23** Ezek 43:2–5

Ezekiel

In the vision . . . . (11:24)

The Prophet as a Refugee

12 ¹The LORD spoke to me. ²"Mortal man," he said, "you are living among rebellious people. They have eyes, but they see nothing; they have ears, but they hear nothing, because they are rebellious.

³"Now, mortal man, pack a bundle just as a refugee would and start out before nightfall. Let everyone see you leaving and going to another place. Maybe those rebels will notice you.ʷ ⁴While it is still daylight, pack your bundle for exile, so that they can see you, and then let them watch you leave in the evening as if you were going into exile. ⁵While they are watching, break a hole through the wall of your house and take your pack out through it. ⁶Let them watch you putting your pack on your shoulder and going out into the dark with your eyes covered, so that you can't see where you are going. What you do will be a warning to the Israelites."

⁷I did what the LORD told me to do. That day I packed a bundle as a refugee would, and that evening as it was getting dark I dug a hole in the wall with my hands and went out. While everyone watched, I put the pack on my shoulder and left.

⁸The next morning the LORD spoke to me. ⁹"Mortal man," he said, "now that those Israelite rebels are asking you what you're doing, ¹⁰tell them what I, the Sovereign LORD, am saying to them. This message is for the prince ruling in Jerusalem and for all the people who live there. ¹¹Tell them that what you have done is a sign of what will happen to them—they will be refugees and captives. ¹²The prince who is ruling them will shoulder his pack in the dark and escape through a hole that they dig for him in the wall. He will cover his eyes and not see where he is going. ¹³But I will spread out my net and trap him in it. Then I will take him to the city of Babylon, where he will die without having seen it. ¹⁴I will scatter in every direction all the members of his court and his advisers and bodyguards, and people will search for them to kill them.

¹⁵"When I scatter them among the other nations and in foreign countries, they will know that I am the LORD. ¹⁶I will let a few of them survive the war, the famine, and the diseases, so that there among the nations they will realize how disgusting their actions have been and will acknowledge that I am the LORD."

The Sign of the Trembling Prophet

¹⁷The LORD spoke to me. ¹⁸"Mortal man," he said, "tremble when you eat, and shake with fear when you drink. ¹⁹Tell the whole nation that this is the message of the Sovereign LORD to the people of Jerusalem who are still living in their land: They will tremble when they eat and shake with fear when they drink. Their land will be stripped bare, because everyone who lives there is lawless. ²⁰Cities that are now full of people will be destroyed, and the country will be made a wilderness. Then they will know that I am the LORD."

ʷ **12:3** Maybe those . . . you; *or* Maybe they will then realize that they are rebels.
12:2 Isa 6:9, 10; Jer 5:21; Mk 8:18   **12:13** 2 Kings 25:7; Jer 52:11

A Popular Proverb and an Unpopular Message

21 The LORD spoke to me. 22 "Mortal man," he said, "why do the people of Israel repeat this proverb: 'Time goes by, and predictions come to nothing'? 23 Now tell them what I, the Sovereign LORD, have to say about that. I will put an end to that proverb. It won't be repeated in Israel any more. Tell them instead: The time has come, and the predictions are coming true!

24 "Among the people of Israel there will be no more false visions or misleading prophecies. 25 I, the LORD, will speak to them, and what I say will be done. There will be no more delay. In your own lifetime, you rebels, I will do what I have warned you I would do. I have spoken," says the Sovereign LORD.

26 The LORD said to me, 27 "Mortal man, the Israelites think that your visions and prophecies are about the distant future. 28 So tell them that I, the Sovereign LORD, am saying: There will be no more delay. What I have said will be done. I, the Sovereign LORD, have spoken!"

Prophecy against False Male Prophets

13 1 The LORD spoke to me. 2 "Mortal man," he said, "denounce the prophets of Israel who make up their own prophecies. Tell them to listen to the word of the LORD."

3 This is what the Sovereign LORD says: "These foolish prophets are doomed! They provide their own inspiration and invent their own visions. 4 People of Israel, your prophets are as useless as foxes living among the ruins of a city. 5 They don't guard the places where the walls have crumbled, nor do they rebuild the walls, and so Israel cannot be defended when war comes on the day of the LORD. 6 Their visions are false, and their predictions are lies. They claim that they are speaking my message, but I have not sent them. Yet they expect their words to come true! 7 I tell them:

The Future is N.O.W.

A cable television show about people living their dreams used the title "N.O.W." The letters stand for "No Opportunity Wasted." That message has a lot to do with God's plan for our lives as well.

The Israelites didn't worry too much about Ezekiel's visions. They thought that his warnings about God's punishment would happen sometime in the future. Their attitude was, "It'll never happen to me." But God had other plans. "There will be no more delay. What I have said will be done" (Ezekiel 12:28).

Every day you learn something new about being the person God wants you to be. What have you learned about yourself and God today or this week? Don't wait to put what you learn into practice. The time is N.O.W.

— Ezekiel 12:26–28

Those visions you see are false, and the predictions you make are lies. You say that they are my words, but I haven't spoken to you!"

8 So the Sovereign LORD says to them, "Your words are false, and your visions are lies. I am against you. 9 I am about to punish you prophets who have false visions and make misleading predictions. You will not be there when my people gather to make decisions; your names will not be included in the list of the citizens of Israel; you will never return to your land. Then you will know that I am the Sovereign LORD.

10 "The prophets mislead my people by

Ezekiel

God has Ezekiel act out two more signs of coming troubles in Ezekiel, chapter 12, to warn the Israelites. What did Ezekiel do?

saying that all is well. All is certainly not well! My people have put up a wall of loose stones, and then the prophets have come and covered it with whitewash. 11 Tell the prophets that their wall is going to fall down. I will send a pouring rain. Hailstones will fall on it, and a strong wind will blow against it. 12 The wall will collapse, and everyone will ask you what good the whitewash did."

13 Now this is what the Sovereign LORD says: "In my anger I will send a strong wind, pouring rain, and hailstones to destroy the wall. 14 I intend to break down the wall they whitewashed, to shatter it, and to leave the foundation stones bare. It will collapse and kill you all. Then everyone will know that I am the LORD.

I will send a strong wind, pouring rain, and hailstones to destroy the wall. (13:13)

15 "The wall and those who covered it with whitewash will feel the force of my anger. Then I will tell you that the wall is gone and so are those who whitewashed it— 16 those prophets who assured Jerusalem that all was well, when all was not well!" The Sovereign LORD has spoken.

Prophecy against False Female Prophets

17 The LORD said, "Now, mortal man, look at the women among your people who make up predictions. Denounce them 18 and tell them what the Sovereign LORD is saying to them:

"You women are doomed! You sew magic wristbands for everyone and make magic scarves for everyone to wear on their heads, so that they can have power over other people's lives. You want to possess the power of life and death over my people and to use it for your own benefit. 19 You dishonor me in front of my people in order to get a few handfuls of barley and a few pieces of bread. You kill people who don't deserve to die, and you keep people alive who don't deserve to live. So you tell lies to my people, and they believe you."

20 Now this is what the Sovereign LORD says: "I hate the wristbands that you use in your attempt to control life and death. I will rip them off your arms and set free the people that you were controlling.ˣ 21 I will rip off your scarves and let my people escape from your power once and for all. Then you will know that I am the LORD.

22 "By your lies you discourage good people, whom I do not wish to hurt. You prevent evil people from giving up evil and saving their lives. 23 So now your false visions and misleading predictions are over. I am rescuing my people from your power, so that you will know that I am the LORD."

God Condemns Idolatry

14 1 Some of the leaders of the Israelites came to consult me about the LORD's will. 2 Then the LORD spoke to me. 3 "Mortal man," he said, "these men have given their hearts to idols and are letting idols lead them into sin. Do they think I will give them an answer?

4 "Now speak to them and tell them what I, the Sovereign LORD, am saying to them: Each of you Israelites who have given your heart to idols and let them lead you into sin and who then come to consult a prophet, will get an answer from me—the answer that your many idols deserve! 5 All those idols have turned the Israelites away from me, but

---

ˣ **13:20** *In verse 20 in Hebrew a word occurs twice, the meaning of which is unclear.*

by my answer I hope to win back their loyalty.

6 "Now then, tell the Israelites what I, the
Sovereign LORD, am saying: Turn back and
leave your disgusting idols.

7 "Whenever one of you Israelites or one
of you foreigners who live in the Israelite
community turn away from me and worship
idols, and then go to consult a prophet, I, the
LORD, will give you your answer! 8 I will
oppose you. I will make an example of you.
I will remove you from the community of
my people, so that all of you will know that
I am the LORD.

9 "If any prophets are deceived into giving
a false answer, it is because I, the LORD, have
deceived them. I will remove them from the
people of Israel. 10 Both prophets and anyone
who consults them will get the same punishment. 11 I will do this to keep the Israelites
from deserting me and defiling themselves
by their sins. They are to be my people, and I
will be their God." The Sovereign LORD has
spoken.

Noah, Danel, and Job

12 The LORD spoke to me. 13 "Mortal
man," he said, "if a country sins and is
unfaithful to me, I will reach out and destroy
its supply of food. I will send a famine and
kill people and animals alike. 14 Even if those
three men, Noah, Danel,ʸ and Job, were living there, their goodness would save only
their own lives." The Sovereign LORD has
spoken.

15 "Or I might send wild animals to kill
the people, making the land so dangerous
that no one could travel through it, 16 and
even if those three men lived there—as surely as I, the Sovereign LORD, am the living
God—they would not be able to save even
their own children. They would save only
their own lives, and the land would become
a wilderness.

17 "Or I might bring war on that country
and send destructive weapons to wipe out
people and animals alike, 18 and even if those
three men lived there—as surely as I, the
Sovereign LORD, am the living God—they

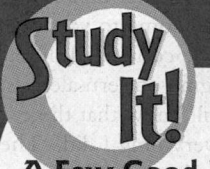

A Few Good Men

Who were Noah, Danel (or Daniel),
and Job, and why do their names
keep coming up? They are good
and holy men from other books of
the Bible. Ezekiel brings them into
his conversation with God to check
if a few good people can save the
lives of everyone in a town, even if
the others have sinned.

- Noah and his family were spared
  from the Flood because he was
  the only good person in the area
  (see Genesis, chapters 6–9).
- Danel was a king famous for his
  wisdom and goodness. (There is
  also the prophet Daniel, but his
  story is later than Ezekiel's.)
- Job was a holy man who was
  always close to God but endured
  many trials (see the Book of Job).
  God's message to Ezekiel was
  simple and direct: each person is
  responsible for his or her own sinfulness. No one can help you stay
  close to God but *you*.

— Ezekiel 14:12–23

Ezekiel

would not be able to save even their children, but only their own lives.

19 "If I send an epidemic on that country
and in my anger take many lives, killing people and animals, 20 even if Noah, Danel, and
Job lived there—as surely as I, the Sovereign
LORD, am the living God—they would not
be able to save even their own children. Their
goodness would save only their own lives."

21 This is what the Sovereign LORD is saying: "I will send my four worst punishments
on Jerusalem—war, famine, wild animals, and
disease—to destroy people and animals alike.

ʸ **14:14** Danel; *or* Daniel *(see 28:3), an ancient hero, known for his righteous life.*
14:21 Rev 6:8

22If some survive and save their children, look at them when they come to you. See how evil they are, and be convinced that the punishment I am bringing on Jerusalem is justified; 23then you will know that there was good reason for everything I did." The Sovereign LORD has spoken.

A Parable about a Vine

15 1The LORD spoke to me. 2"Mortal man," he said, "how does a vine compare with a tree? What good is a branch of a grapevine compared with the trees of the forest? 3Can you use it to make anything? Can you even make a peg out of it to hang things on? 4It is only good for building a fire. And when the ends are burned up and the middle is charred, can you make anything out of it? 5It was useless even before it was burned. Now that the fire has burned it and charred it, it is even more useless."

Can you make anything out of it? (15:4)

6Now this is what the Sovereign LORD is saying: "Just as a vine is taken from the forest and burned, so I will take the people who live in Jerusalem 7and will punish them. They have escaped one fire, but now fire will burn them up. When I punish them, you will know that I am the LORD. 8They have been unfaithful to me, and so I will make the country a wilderness." The Sovereign LORD has spoken.

Jerusalem the Unfaithful

16 1The LORD spoke to me again. 2"Mortal man," he said, "point out to Jerusalem what disgusting things she has done. 3Tell Jerusalem what the Sovereign LORD is saying to her:

"You were born in the land of Canaan. Your father was an Amorite, and your mother was a Hittite.z 4When you were born, no one cut your umbilical cord or washed youd or rubbed you with salt or wrapped you in cloths. 5No one took enough pity on you to do any of these things for you. When you were born, no one loved you. You were thrown out in an open field.

6"Then I passed by and saw you squirming in your own blood. You were covered with blood, but I wouldn't let you die. 7I made you grow like a healthy plant. You grew strong and tall and became a young woman.b Your breasts were well-formed, and your hair had grown, but you were naked.

8"As I passed by again, I saw that the time had come for you to fall in love. I covered your naked body with my coat and promised to love you. Yes, I made a marriage covenant with you, and you became mine." This is what the Sovereign LORD says.

9"Then I took water and washed the blood off you. I rubbed olive oil on your skin. 10I dressed you in embroidered gowns and gave you shoes of the best leather, a linen headband, and a silk cloak. 11I put jewels on you—bracelets and necklaces. 12I gave you a nose ring and earrings and a beautiful crown to wear. 13You had ornaments of gold and silver, and you always wore clothes of embroidered linen and silk. You ate bread made from the best flour, and had honey and olive oil to eat. Your beauty was dazzling, and you became a queen. 14You became famous in every nation for your perfect beauty, because I was the one who made you so lovely." This is what the Sovereign LORD says.

15"But you took advantage of your beauty and fame to sleep with everyone who came along.c 16You used some of your clothes to decorate your places of worship, and just like a prostitute,d you gave yourself to everyone. 17You took the silver and gold jewelry that I had given you, used it to make male images, and committed adultery with them. 18You

---

z **16:3** AMORITE . . . HITTITE: *The Israelites regarded these people as immoral and idolatrous.* a **16:4** *Hebrew has an additional word, the meaning of which is unclear.* b **16:7** *Probable text* young woman; *Hebrew unclear.* c **16:15** *Hebrew has two additional words, the meaning of which is unclear.* d **16:16** *Hebrew has four additional words, the meaning of which is unclear.*

took the embroidered clothes I gave you and put them on the images, and you offered to the images the olive oil and incense I had given you. 19I gave you food—the best flour, olive oil, and honey—but you offered it as a sacrifice to win the favor of idols." This is what the Sovereign LORD says.

20"Then you took the sons and the daughters you had borne me and offered them as sacrifices to idols. Wasn't it bad enough to be unfaithful to me, 21without taking my children and sacrificing them to idols? 22During your disgusting life as a prostitute you never once remembered your childhood—when you were naked, squirming in your own blood."

Jerusalem's Life as a Prostitute

23The Sovereign LORD said, "You are doomed! Doomed! You did all that evil, and then 24by the side of every road you built places to worship idols and practice prostitution. 25You dragged your beauty through the mud. You offered yourself to everyone who came by, and you were more of a prostitute every day. 26You let your lustful neighbors, the Egyptians, go to bed with you, and you used your prostitution to make me angry.

27"Now I have raised my hand to punish you and to take away your share of my blessing. I have handed you over to the Philistines, who hate you and are disgusted with your immoral actions.

28"Because you were not satisfied by the others, you went running after the Assyrians. You were their prostitute, but they didn't satisfy you either. 29You were also a prostitute for the Babylonians, that nation of merchants, but they didn't satisfy you either."

30Thise is what the Sovereign LORD is saying: "You have done all this like a shameless prostitute. 31On every street you built places to worship idols and practice prostitution. But you are not out for money like a common prostitute. 32You are like a woman who commits adultery with strangers instead of loving her husband. 33A prostitute is paid, but you gave presents to all your lovers and bribed them to come from everywhere to sleep with you. 34You are a special kind of prostitute. No one forced you to become one. You didn't get paid; you paid them! Yes, you are different."

God's Judgment on Jerusalem

35Now then, Jerusalem, you whore! Hear what the LORD is saying.

36This is what the Sovereign LORD says: "You stripped off your clothes, and like a prostitute, you gave yourself to your lovers and to all your disgusting idols, and you killed your children as sacrifices to idols. 37Because of this I will bring all your former lovers together—the ones you liked and the ones you hated. I will bring them around you in a circle, and then I will strip off your clothes and let them see you naked. 38I will condemn you for adultery and murder, and in my anger and fury I will punish you with death. 39I will put you in their power, and they will tear down the places where you engage in prostitution and worship idols. They will take away your clothes and jewels and leave you completely naked.

40"They will stir up a crowd to stone you, and they will cut you to pieces with their swords. 41They will burn your houses down and let crowds of women see your punishment. I will make you stop being a prostitute and make you stop giving gifts to your lovers. 42Then my anger will be over, and I will be calm. I will not be angry or jealous any more. 43You have forgotten how I treated you when you were young, and you have made me angry by all the things you did. That is why I have made you pay for them all. Why did you add sexual immorality to all the other disgusting things you did?" The Sovereign LORD has spoken.

e **16:30** *Verse 30 in Hebrew begins with three words, the meaning of which is unclear.*

Just like the Israelites, we sometimes worship idols. Our idols are money, possessions, power, and physical comforts.

Ezekiel

Like Mother, Like Daughter

44 The LORD said, "People will use this proverb about you, Jerusalem: 'Like mother, like daughter.' **45** You really are your mother's daughter. She detested her husband and her children. You are like your sisters, who hated their husbands and their children. You and your sister cities had a Hittite mother and an Amorite*f* father.

46 "Your older sister, with her villages, is Samaria, in the north. Your younger sister, with her villages, is Sodom, in the south. **47** Were you satisfied to follow in their footsteps and copy their disgusting actions? No, in only a little while you were acting worse than they were in everything you did.

48 "As surely as I am the living God," the Sovereign LORD says, "your sister Sodom and her villages never did the evil that you and your villages have done. **49** She and her daughters were proud because they had plenty to eat and lived in peace and quiet, but they did not take care of the poor and the underprivileged. **50** They were proud and stubborn and did the things that I hate, so I destroyed them, as you well know.

51 "Samaria did not sin half as much as you have. You have acted more disgustingly than she ever did. Your corruption makes your sisters look innocent by comparison. **52** And now you will have to endure your disgrace. Your sins are so much worse than those of your sisters that they look innocent beside you. Now blush and bear your shame, because you make your sisters look pure."

Sodom and Samaria Will Be Restored

53 The LORD said to Jerusalem, "I will make them prosperous again—Sodom and her villages and Samaria and her villages. Yes, I will make you prosperous too. **54** You will be ashamed of yourself, and your disgrace will show your sisters how well-off they are. **55** They will become prosperous again, and you and your villages will also be restored.

56 Didn't you joke about Sodom in those days when you were proud **57** and before the evil you did had been exposed? Now you are just like her—a joke to the Edomites, the Philistines, and your other neighbors who hate you. **58** You must suffer for the obscene, disgusting things you have done." The LORD has spoken.

f **16:45** HITTITE . . . AMORITE: *See 16:3.*

Live It!

Feeling Guilty

Sam was a nice guy. He was funny, smart, and kind. He liked to be in the middle of whatever was going on. He also spent his days in a wheelchair, and his words were hard to understand.

One day Isabel made a rude comment to Sam and made fun of the way he talked. Sam pretended not to hear, but he looked hurt. She thought it was funny, but her best friend got mad and told her that there was nothing funny about it. Isabel felt *really* guilty. She avoided Sam for a while, but it was hard because they were in some of the same classes. She never made fun of Sam again. In fact, she and Sam became good friends. But Isabel never really forgot that day, and never really forgave herself for it.

Sometimes you feel guilty for bad things you've done, even after you've made things right again. But God forgives you and keeps on loving you. And if God can do it, shouldn't you?

— Ezekiel 16:63

The city of Sodom is often connected to sexual sin. But in Ezekiel God says that Sodom's sin was neglecting poor people (*Ezekiel 16:49*).

A Covenant That Lasts Forever

59 The Sovereign LORD says, "I will treat you the way you deserve, because you ignored your promises and broke the covenant. 60 But I will honor the covenant I made with you when you were young, and I will make a covenant with you that will last forever. 61 You will remember how you have acted, and be ashamed of it when you get your older sister and your younger sister back. I will let them be like daughters to you, even though this was not part of my covenant with you. 62 I will renew my covenant with you, and you will know that I am the LORD. 63 I will forgive all the wrongs you have done, but you will remember them and be too ashamed to open your mouth." The Sovereign LORD has spoken.

The Parable of the Eagles and the Vine

17 1 The LORD spoke to me. 2 "Mortal man," he said, "tell the Israelites a parable 3 to let them know what I, the Sovereign LORD, am saying to them: There was a giant eagle with beautiful feathers and huge wings, spread wide. He flew to the Lebanon Mountains and broke off the top of a cedar tree, 4 which he carried to a land of commerce and placed in a city of merchants. 5 Then he took a young plant from the land of Israel and planted it in a fertile field,g where there was always water to make it grow. 6 The plant sprouted and became a low, wide-spreading grapevine. The branches grew upward toward the eagle, and the roots grew deep. The vine was covered with branches and leaves.

7 "There was another giant eagle with huge wings and thick plumage. And now the vine sent its roots toward him and turned its leaves toward him, in the hope that he would give it more water than there was in the garden where it was growing.h 8 But the vine had already been planted in a fertile, well-watered field so that it could grow leaves and bear grapes and be a magnificent vine.

9 "So I, the Sovereign LORD, ask: Will this

He . . . broke off the top of a cedar tree. (17:3)

vine live and grow? Won't the first eagle pull it up by its roots, pull off the grapes, and break off the branches and let them wither? It will not take much strength or a mighty nation to pull it up. 10 Yes, it is planted, but will it live and grow? Won't it wither when the east wind strikes it? Won't it wither there where it is growing?"

It is planted, but will it live and grow? (17:10)

The Parable Is Explained

11 The LORD said to me, 12 "Ask these rebels if they know what the parable means. Tell them that the king of Babylonia came to Jerusalem and took the king and his officials back with him to Babylonia. 13 He took one of the king's family, made a treaty with him, and made him swear to be loyal. He took important men as hostages 14 to keep the nation from rising again and to make sure that the treaty would be kept. 15 But the king of Judah rebelled and sent agents to Egypt to get horses and a large army. Will he succeed? Can he get away with that? He cannot break the treaty and go unpunished!

16 "As surely as I am the living God," says the Sovereign LORD, "this king will die in Babylonia because he broke his oath and the

---

g **17:5** *Hebrew has an additional word, the meaning of which is unclear.*   h **17:7** *And now the vine . . . growing; or And now the vine turned away from the garden where it was growing and sent its roots toward him and turned its leaves toward him, in the hope that he would give it water.*
17:12–15 2 Kings 24:15–20; 2 Chr 36:10–13

treaty he had made with the king of Babylonia, who put him on the throne. [17] Even the powerful army of the king of Egypt will not be able to help him fight when the Babylonians build earthworks and dig trenches in order to kill many people. [18] He broke his oath and the treaty he had made. He did all these things, and now he will not escape."

[19] The Sovereign LORD says, "As surely as I am the living God, I will punish him for breaking the treaty which he swore in my name to keep. [20] I will spread out a hunter's net and catch him in it. I will take him to Babylonia and punish him there, because he was unfaithful to me. [21] His best soldiers will be killed in battle, and the survivors will be scattered in every direction. Then you will know that I, the LORD, have spoken."

I will spread out a hunter's net and catch him in it.
(17:20)

God's Promise of Hope

[22] This is what the Sovereign LORD says:
"I will take the top of a tall cedar
    and break off a tender sprout;
I will plant it on on a high mountain,
[23]   on Israel's highest mountain.
It will grow branches and bear seed
    and become a magnificent cedar.
Birds of every kind will live there
    and find shelter in its shade.
[24] All the trees in the land will know
    that I am the LORD.
I cut down the tall trees
    and make small trees grow tall.

You Promised!

Shelby promised her mom that she would clean her room. She went to Laticia's house instead. David promised his teacher that he would finish his assignment. That night he played video games for two hours and never touched it. Grace's dad promised that they would do something together on Saturday. He called her Friday and said he was going to a golf tournament.

Have you ever broken a promise you made to someone? Has anyone ever broken a promise he or she made to you? When you break a promise for no good reason, it's a serious matter. At the end of Ezekiel, chapter 17, God says that King Zedekiah will be punished for breaking his treaties, that is, promises he made to another king. Breaking a promise is a sin against the seventh commandment—just like lying.

Think carefully before you make a promise to someone, and keep the promises you make. You will become known as a person people can trust.

— Ezekiel 17:16–20

I wither up the green trees
    and make the dry trees become green.
I, the LORD, have spoken. I will do what I have said I would do."

Individual Responsibility

18 [1] The LORD spoke to me [2] and said, "What is this proverb people keep repeating in the land of Israel?

Birds of every kind will live there. (17:23)

'The parents ate the sour grapes,
But the children got the sour taste.'

³"As surely as I am the living God," says the Sovereign LORD, "you will not repeat this proverb in Israel any more. ⁴The life of every person belongs to me, the life of the parent as well as that of the child. The person who sins is the one who will die.

⁵"Suppose there is a truly good man, righteous and honest. ⁶He doesn't worship the idols of the Israelites or eat the sacrifices offered at forbidden shrines. He doesn't seduce another man's wife or have intercourse with a woman during her period. ⁷He doesn't cheat or rob anyone. He returns what a borrower gives him as security; he feeds the hungry and gives clothing to the naked. ⁸He doesn't lend money for profit. He refuses to do evil and gives an honest decision in any dispute. ⁹Such a man obeys my commands and carefully keeps my laws. He is righteous, and he will live," says the Sovereign LORD.

¹⁰"Then suppose this man has a son who robs and kills, who does any^i of these things ¹¹that the father never did. He eats sacrifices offered at forbidden shrines and seduces other men's wives. ¹²He cheats the poor, he robs, he keeps what a borrower gives him as security. He goes to pagan shrines, worships disgusting idols, ¹³and lends money for prof-

Be All You Can Be

Alex's family is pretty messed up. His dad left when Alex was a baby. His mom drinks way too much. His older brother is always in trouble with the police. He doesn't really know where his sister is. Thank God for school breakfasts and lunches. Otherwise Alex wouldn't get much to eat.

Alex has a lot of adults watching over him, though. His teachers and his coaches know what's going on. They do their best to guide Alex and to get him the help he needs. He loves his family, and he knows they love him. He also knows that the things they do are wrong. God makes it clear in Ezekiel, chapter 18, that children are not doomed to suffer because their parents do wrong things.

If your family is struggling, talk to someone at school or at church. They will find ways to help you. Rely on the support of people you trust. Above all, know that you are your own person, and you are responsible for yourself. Nothing can stop you from becoming all that you can be. And that's what God wants for you.

— Ezekiel, chapter 18

it. Will he live? No, he will not. He has done all these disgusting things, and so he will die. He will be to blame for his own death.

¹⁴"Now suppose this second man has a son. He sees all the sins his father practiced,

---

^i 18:10 *Some ancient translations* who does any; *Hebrew unclear.*
18:9 Lev 18:5

Ezekiel

but does not follow his example. ¹⁵He doesn't worship the idols of the Israelites or eat the sacrifices offered at forbidden shrines. He doesn't seduce another man's wife ¹⁶or oppress anyone or rob anyone. He returns what a borrower gives him as security. He feeds the hungry and gives clothing to the naked. ¹⁷He refuses to do evil*j* and doesn't lend money for profit. He keeps my laws and obeys my commands. He will not die because of his father's sins, but he will certainly live. ¹⁸His father, on the other hand, cheated and robbed*k* and always did evil to everyone. And so he died because of the sins he himself had committed.

¹⁹"But you ask, 'Why shouldn't the son suffer because of his father's sins?' The answer is that the son did what was right and good. He kept my laws and followed them carefully, and so he will certainly live. ²⁰It is the one who sins who will die. A son is not to suffer because of his father's sins, nor a father because of the sins of his son. Good people will be rewarded for doing good, and evil people will suffer for the evil they do.

²¹"If someone evil stops sinning and keeps my laws, if he does what is right and good, he will not die; he will certainly live. ²²All his sins will be forgiven, and he will live, because he did what is right. ²³Do you think I enjoy seeing evil people die?" asks the Sovereign LORD. "No, I would rather see them repent and live.

²⁴"But if a righteous person stops doing good and starts doing all the evil, disgusting things that evil people do, will he go on living? No! None of the good he did will be remembered. He will die because of his unfaithfulness and his sins.

²⁵"But you say, 'What the Lord does isn't right.' Listen to me, you Israelites. Do you think my way of doing things isn't right? It is your way that isn't right. ²⁶When a righteous person stops doing good and starts doing evil and then dies, he dies because of the evil he has done. ²⁷When someone evil stops sinning

and does what is right and good, he saves his life. ²⁸He realizes what he is doing and stops sinning, so he will certainly not die, but go on living. ²⁹And you Israelites say, 'What the Lord does isn't right.' You think my way isn't right, do you? It is your way that isn't right.

He realizes what he is doing and stops sinning. (18:28)

³⁰"Now I, the Sovereign LORD, am telling you Israelites that I will judge each of you by what you have done. Turn away from all the evil you are doing, and don't let your sin destroy you. ³¹Give up all the evil you have been doing, and get yourselves new minds and hearts. Why do you Israelites want to die? ³²I do not want anyone to die," says the Sovereign LORD. "Turn away from your sins and live."

A Song of Sorrow

19 ¹The LORD told me to sing this song of sorrow for two princes of Israel:

²What a lioness your mother was!
    She raised her cubs among the fierce male lions.
³She raised a cub and taught him to hunt;
    he learned to eat people.
⁴The nations heard about him
    and trapped him in a pit.
    With hooks they dragged him off to Egypt.
⁵She waited until she saw all hope was gone.
    Then she raised another of her cubs,
    and he grew into a fierce lion.

---

j **18:17** *Some ancient translations (see also verse 8)* to do evil; *Hebrew* from the poor.   *k* **18:18** *Some ancient translations* robbed; *Hebrew unclear.*
18:20 Deut 24:16   **18:32** Wis 1:13

6 When he was full-grown,
  he prowled with the other lions.
He too learned to hunt and eat people.
7 He wrecked forts,^l he ruined towns.
  The people of the land were terrified
    every time he roared.
8 The nations gathered to fight him;
  people came from everywhere.
They spread their hunting nets
  and caught him in their trap.
9 They put him in a cage
  and took him to the king of Babylonia.
They kept him under guard,
  so that his roar would never be heard
    again
  on the hills of Israel.

10 Your mother was like a grapevine^m
  planted near a stream.
Because there was plenty of water,
  the vine was covered with leaves and
    fruit.
11 Its branches were strong
  and grew to be royal scepters.
The vine grew tall enough to reach the
    clouds;
  everyone saw how leafy and tall it was.
12 But angry hands pulled it up by the roots
  and threw it to the ground.
The east wind dried up its fruit.
Its branches were broken off;
  they dried up and were burned.
13 Now it is planted in the desert,
  in a dry and waterless land.
14 The stem of the vine caught fire;
  fire burned up its branches and fruit.
The branches will never again be strong,
  will never be royal scepters.
This is a song of sorrow; it has been sung
again and again.

The Lord's Will and Human Defiance

20 ¹It was the tenth day of the fifth
month of the seventh year of our
exile. Some of the leaders of the Israelite community came to consult me about the Lord's
will, and they sat down in front of me. ²Then
the Lord spoke to me. ³"Mortal man," he

said, "speak to these leaders and tell them that
the Sovereign Lord is saying: You have come
to ask my will, have you? As surely as I am the
living God, I will not let you ask me anything.
I, the Sovereign Lord, have spoken.

⁴"Are you ready to pass sentence on them,
mortal man? Then do so. Remind them of the
disgusting things their ancestors did. ⁵Tell
them what I am saying. When I chose Israel,
I made them a promise. I revealed myself to
them in Egypt and told them: I am the Lord
your God. ⁶It was then that I promised to take
them out of Egypt and lead them to a land I
had chosen for them, a rich and fertile land,
the finest land of all. ⁷I told them to throw
away the disgusting idols they loved and not
to make themselves unclean with the false
gods of Egypt, because I am the Lord their
God. ⁸But they defied me and refused to listen. They did not throw away their disgusting
idols or give up the Egyptian gods. I was ready
to let them feel the full force of my anger
there in Egypt. ⁹But I did not, since that
would have brought dishonor to my name, for
in the presence of the people among whom
they were living I had announced to Israel
that I was going to lead them out of Egypt.

¹⁰"And so I led them out of Egypt into
the desert. ¹¹I gave them my commands and
taught them my laws, which bring life to
anyone who obeys them. ¹²I made the keeping of the Sabbath a sign of the agreement
between us, to remind them that I, the
Lord, make them holy. ¹³But even in the

I gave them my commands. (20:11)

---

l **19:7** *One ancient translation* wrecked forts; *Hebrew unclear.*   *m* **19:10** *Hebrew has an additional word, the meaning of which is unclear.*
20:5, 6 Ex 6:2–8   **20:11, 13** Lev 18:5   **20:12** Ex 31:13–17

Ezekiel

desert they defied me. They broke my laws and rejected my commands, which bring life to anyone who obeys them. They completely profaned the Sabbath. I was ready to let them feel the force of my anger there in the desert and to destroy them. ¹⁴But I did not, since that would have brought dishonor to my name among the nations which had seen me lead Israel out of Egypt. ¹⁵So I made a vow in the desert that I would not take them to the land I had given them, a rich and fertile land, the finest land of all. ¹⁶I made the vow because they had rejected my commands, broken my laws, and profaned the Sabbath—they preferred to worship their idols.

¹⁷"But then I took pity on them. I decided not to kill them there in the desert. ¹⁸Instead, I warned the young people among them: Do not keep the laws your ancestors made; do not follow their customs or defile yourselves with their idols. ¹⁹I am the LORD your God. Obey my laws and my commands. ²⁰Make the Sabbath a holy day, so that it will be a sign of the covenant we made, and will remind you that I am the LORD your God.

²¹"But that generation also defied me. They broke my laws and did not keep my commands, which bring life to anyone who obeys them. They profaned the Sabbath. I was ready to let them feel the force of my anger there in the desert and to kill them all. ²²But I did not, since that would have brought dishonor to my name among the nations which had seen me bring Israel out of Egypt. ²³So I made another vow in the desert. I vowed that I would scatter them all over the world. ²⁴I did this because they had rejected my commands, broken my laws, profaned the Sabbath, and worshiped the same idols their ancestors had served.

²⁵"Then I gave them laws that are not good and commands that do not bring life. ²⁶I let them defile themselves with their own offerings, and I let them sacrifice their first-born sons. This was to punish them and show them that I am the LORD.

²⁷"Now then, mortal man, tell the Israelites what I, the Sovereign LORD, am saying to them. This is another way their ancestors insulted me by their unfaithfulness. ²⁸I brought them to the land I had promised to give them. When they saw the high hills and green trees, they offered sacrifices at all of them. They made me angry by the sacrifices they burned and by the wine they brought as offerings. ²⁹I asked them: What are these high places where you go? So they have been called 'High Places'ⁿ ever since. ³⁰Now tell the Israelites what I am saying: Why must you commit the same sins your ancestors did and go running after their idols? ³¹Even today you offer the same gifts and defile yourselves with the same idols by sacrificing your children to them in the fire. And then you Israelites still come to ask what my will is! As surely as I, the Sovereign LORD, am the living God, I will not let you ask me anything. ³²You have made up your minds that you want to be like the other nations, like the people who live in other countries and worship trees and rocks. But that will never be.

God Punishes and Forgives

³³"As surely as I, the Sovereign LORD, am the living God, I warn you that in my anger I will rule over you with a strong hand, with all my power. ³⁴I will show you my power and my anger when I gather you together and bring you back from all the countries where you have been scattered. ³⁵I will bring you into the 'Desert of the Nations,' and there I will condemn you to your face. ³⁶I will now condemn you just as I condemned your ancestors in the Sinai Desert," says the Sovereign LORD.

³⁷"I will take firm control of you and make you obey my covenant. ³⁸I will take away from among you those who are rebellious and sinful. I will take them out of the lands where they are living now, but I will not let them return to the land of Israel. Then you will know that I am the LORD."

³⁹The Sovereign LORD says, "And now, all you Israelites, suit yourselves! Go on and

---

ⁿ **20:29** HIGH PLACES: *Pagan places of worship which the Hebrews were forbidden to use. The Hebrew word translated "High Places" sounds like the Hebrew for "where you go."*
20:15 Num 14:26–35   **20:23** Lev 26:33

The Dreaded Ms. G

Ms. G was the hardest teacher at school. She gave a lot of homework. She assigned projects that kept people at the library for hours. If you didn't do your very best, she kept after you until she was satisfied. If you messed up, you heard about it.

Ms. G also cared about every person in her class. She made you feel as if you were the most important person in the room. She believed in you and loved you. At the end of the year, people had a hard time saying goodbye to Ms. G. They knew that they had learned a great deal. They had done their very best, and all their hard work paid off.

God is like that, too. So much of Ezekiel's prophecies is about God demanding the very best from the Israelites and warning them when they mess up. God's "classroom" is a tough place to be sometimes. But like Ms. G, God believes in you and loves you. And all your hard work will pay off.

— Ezekiel 20:33–44

serve your idols! But I warn you that after this you will have to obey me and stop dishonoring my holy name by offering gifts to your idols. 40 There in the land, on my holy mountain,ᵒ the high mountain of Israel, all you people of Israel will worship me. I will be pleased with you and will expect you to bring me your sacrifices, your best offerings, and your holy gifts. 41 After I bring you out

of the countries where you have been scattered and gather you together, I will accept the sacrifices that you burn, and the nations will see that I am holy. 42 When I bring you back to Israel, the land that I promised I would give to your ancestors, then you will know that I am the LORD. 43 Then you will remember all the disgraceful things you did and how you defiled yourselves. You will be disgusted with yourselves because of all the evil things you did. 44 When I act to protect my honor, you Israelites will know that I am the LORD, because I do not deal with you as your wicked, evil actions deserve." The Sovereign LORD has spoken.

Fire in the South

45 The LORD spoke to me. 46 "Mortal man," he said, "look toward the south. Speak against the south and prophesy against the forest of the south. 47 Tell the southern forest to hear what the Sovereign LORD is saying: Look! I am starting a fire, and it will burn up every tree in you, whether green or dry. Nothing will be able to put it out. It will spread from south to north, and everyone will feel the heat of the flames. 48 They will all see that I, the LORD, set it on fire and that no one can put it out."

49 But I protested, "Sovereign LORD, don't make me do it! Everyone is already complaining that I always speak in riddles."

The LORD's Sword

21 ¹The LORD spoke to me. ²"Mortal man," he said, "denounce Jerusalem. Denounce the places where people worship. Warn the land of Israel ³that I, the LORD, am saying: I am your enemy. I will draw my sword and kill all of you, good and evil alike. ⁴I will use my sword against everyone from south to north. ⁵Everyone will know that I, the LORD, have drawn my sword and that I will not put it away.

⁶"Mortal man, groan as if your heart is

ᵒ 20:40 HOLY MOUNTAIN: Mount Zion, the hill in Jerusalem which formed part of the Temple and palace area.

Ezekiel

"I warned the young people among them: Do not keep the laws your ancestors made; do not . . . defile yourselves with their idols" (Ezekiel 20:18).

Ezekiel

breaking with despair. Groan in sorrow where everyone can watch you. 7 When they ask you why you are groaning, tell them it is because of the news that is coming. When it comes, their hearts will be filled with fear, their hands will hang limp, their courage will fail, and their knees will tremble. The time has come; it is here." The Sovereign LORD has spoken.

8 The LORD said to me, 9 "Mortal man, prophesy. Tell the people what I, the Lord, am saying:

A sword, a sword is sharpened and
    polished.
10 It is sharpened to kill,
    polished to flash like lightning.
There can be no rejoicing,
    for my people have disregarded every
    warning and punishment.p
11 The sword is being polished,
    to make it ready for use.
It is sharpened and polished,
    to be put in the hands of a killer.
12 Howl in grief, mortal man;
    this sword is meant for my people
    and for all the leaders of Israel.
They are going to be killed
    with all the rest of my people.
Beat your breast in despair!
13 I am testing my people,
    and if they refuse to repent,
    all these things will happen to them.q

14 "Now, mortal man, prophesy. Clap your hands, and the sword will strike again and again. It is a sword that kills, a sword that terrifiesr and slaughters. 15 It makes my people lose courage and stumble. I am threatening their city with a swords that flashes like lightning and is ready to kill. 16 Cut to the right and the left, you sharp sword! Cut wherever you turn.t 17 I also will clap my hands, and my anger will be over. I, the LORD, have spoken."

The Sword of the King of Babylonia

18 The LORD spoke to me. 19 "Mortal man," he said, "mark out two roads by which the king of Babylonia can come with his sword. Both of them are to start in the same country. Put up a signpost where the roads fork.u 20 One will show the king the way to the Ammonite city of Rabbah, and the other the way to Judah, to the fortified city, Jerusalem. 21 The king of Babylonia stands by the signpost at the fork of the road. To discover which way to go, he shakes the arrows;v he consults his idols; he examines the liver of a sacrificed animal. 22 Now! His right hand holds the arrow marked 'Jerusalem'! It tells him to go and set up battering rams, to shout the battle cry, to place battering rams against the gates, to throw up earthworks, and to dig trenches. 23 The people of Jerusalem won't believe this because of the treaties they have made. But this prediction is to remind them of their sins and to warn them that they will be captured. 24 This then is what I, the Sovereign LORD, am saying: Your sins are exposed. Everyone knows how guilty you are. You show your sins in your every action. You stand condemned, and I will hand you over to your enemies.

25 "You wicked, unholy ruler of Israel, your day, the day of your final punishment, is coming. 26 I, the Sovereign LORD, have spoken. Take off your crown and your turban. Nothing will be the same again. Raise the poor to power! Bring down those who are ruling! 27 Ruin, ruin! Yes, I will make the city a ruin. But this will not happen until the one comes whom I have chosen to punish the city. To him I will give it.

---

p **21:10** *Probable text* There . . . punishment; *Hebrew unclear.*   q **21:13** *Verse 13 in Hebrew is unclear.*
r **21:14** *Some ancient translations* terrifies; *Hebrew unclear.*   s **21:15** *Probable text* threatening . . . sword; *Hebrew unclear.*   t **21:16** *Verse 16 in Hebrew is unclear.*   u **21:19** *Probable text* Put . . . fork; *Hebrew unclear.*
v **21:21** SHAKES THE ARROWS: *When faced with a decision, people in ancient times would sometimes take a handful of arrows, throw them down, and study the pattern in which they fell, in order to learn what to do.*

In Ezekiel, chapter 21, God has Ezekiel perform several more symbolic actions. Can you find two or three things he must do?

Pray It!

Then and Now

Ezekiel lists the sins of the people of Jerusalem that hurt their relationship with God. Read the list below, which is based on Ezekiel's list. Which of these are we guilty of today?

- killing and hurting human beings
- placing material goods above God
- disregarding laws
- showing no respect for parents
- cheating
- not caring for poor people
- showing no reverence for churches and other holy places
- failing to attend Sunday Mass
- lying
- needing to have everything we want right now
- having sex outside of marriage
- stealing

We need to ask God to help us see where we have sinned. Say a prayer that God will help all people to recognize their sins and ask God's forgiveness for them.

— Ezekiel 22:1–12

A Sword and the Ammonites

28 "Mortal man, prophesy. Announce what I, the Sovereign LORD, am saying to the Ammonites, who are insulting Israel. Say to them:

'A sword is ready to destroy;

It is polished to kill, to flash like lightning. 29 The visions that you see are false, and the predictions you make are lies. You are wicked and evil, and your day is coming, the day of your final punishment. The sword is going to fall on your necks.

30 " 'Put up the sword! I will judge you in the place where you were created, in the land where you were born. 31 You will feel my anger when I turn it loose on you like a blazing fire. And I will hand you over to brutal men, experts at destruction. 32 You will be destroyed by fire. Your blood will be shed in your own country, and no one will remember you any more.' " The LORD has spoken.

The Crimes of Jerusalem

22 1 The LORD spoke to me. 2 "Mortal man," he said, "are you ready to judge the city that is full of murderers? Make clear to her all the disgusting things she has done. 3 Tell the city what I, the Sovereign LORD, am saying: Because you have murdered so many of your own people and have defiled yourself by worshiping idols, your time is coming. 4 You are guilty of those murders and are defiled by the idols you made, and so your day is coming, your time is up! That is why I have let the nations make fun of you and all the countries sneer at you. 5 Countries nearby and countries far away sneer at you because of your lawlessness. 6 All Israel's leaders trust in their own strength and commit murder. 7 None of you in the city honor your parents. You cheat foreigners and take advantage of widows and orphans. 8 You have no respect for the holy places, and you don't keep the Sabbath. 9 Some of your

21:28–32 Jer 49:1–6; Ezek 25:1–7; Am 1:3–15; Zeph 2:8–11　　**22:7 a** Ex 20:12; Deut 5:16; **b** Ex 22:21, 22; Deut 24:17　　**22:8** Lev 19:30; 26:2

people tell lies about others in order to have them put to death. Some of them eat sacrifices offered to idols. Some are always satisfying their lusts. 10Some of them sleep with their father's wife. Some force women to have intercourse with them during their period. 11Some commit adultery, and others seduce their daughters-in-law or their half sisters. 12Some of your people murder for pay. Some charge interest on the loans they make to other Israelites and get rich by taking advantage of them. They have forgotten me." The Sovereign LORD has spoken.

13"I will bring my fist down on your robberies and murders. 14Do you think you will have any courage left or have strength enough to lift your hand when I am finished with you? I, the LORD, have spoken, and I keep my word. 15I will scatter your people to every country and nation and will put an end to your evil actions. 16And so the other nations will dishonor you, but you will know that I am the LORD."

God's Refining Furnace

17The LORD said to me, 18"Mortal man, the Israelites are of no use to me. They are like waste metal—copper, tin, iron, and lead—left over after silver has been refined in a furnace. 19So now I, the Sovereign LORD, am telling them that they are just as useless as that. I will bring them all together in Jerusalem 20in the same way that the ore of silver, copper, iron, lead, and tin is put in a refining furnace. My anger and rage will melt them the way fire melts ore. 21Yes, I will gather them in Jerusalem, build a fire under them, and melt them with my anger. 22They will be melted in Jerusalem the way silver is melted in a furnace, and then they will know that they are feeling the anger of the LORD."

The Sins of Israel's Leaders

23The LORD spoke to me again. 24"Mortal man," he said, "tell the Israelites that their land is unholy, and so I am punishing it in my anger. 25The leaders*w* are like lions roaring over the animals they have killed. They kill the people, take all the money and property they can get, and by their murders leave many widows. 26The priests break my law and have no respect for what is holy. They make no distinction between what is holy and what is not. They do not teach the difference between clean and unclean things, and they ignore the Sabbath. As a result the people of Israel do not respect me. 27The government officials are like wolves tearing apart the animals they have killed. They commit murder in order to get rich. 28The prophets have hidden these sins like workers covering a wall with whitewash. They see false visions and make false predictions. They claim to speak the word of the Sovereign LORD, but I, the LORD, have not spoken to them. 29The wealthy cheat and rob. They mistreat the poor and take advantage of foreigners. 30I looked for someone who could build a wall, who could stand in the places where the walls have crumbled and defend the land when my anger is about to destroy it, but I could find no one. 31So I will turn my anger loose on them, and like a fire I will destroy them for what they have done." The Sovereign LORD has spoken.

The Sinful Sisters

23 1The LORD spoke to me. 2"Mortal man," he said, "there were once two sisters. 3When they were young, living in Egypt, they lost their virginity and became prostitutes. 4The older one was named Oholah*x* (she represents Samaria), and the younger one was named Oholibah*y* (she represents Jerusalem). I married both of them, and they bore me children. 5Although she was mine, Oholah continued to be a prostitute and was full of lust for her lovers from Assyria. 6They were soldiers in uniforms of purple, noblemen and high-ranking officers; all of them were handsome young cavalry officers. 7She was the whore for all the Assyrian officers, and her lust led her to defile her-

w **22:25** *One ancient translation* The leaders; *Hebrew* A conspiracy of her prophets.   *x* **23:4** OHOLAH: *This name in Hebrew means "her sanctuary."*   *y* **23:4** OHOLIBAH: *This name in Hebrew means "my sanctuary is in her."*
22:10, 11 Lev 18:7–20   **22:12** Ex 23:8; Deut 16:19; Ex 22:25; Lev 25:36, 37; Deut 23:19   **22:26** Lev 10:10

self by worshiping Assyrian idols. [8]She continued what she had begun as a prostitute in Egypt, where she lost her virginity. From the time she was a young woman, men slept with her and treated her like a prostitute. [9]So I handed her over to her Assyrian lovers whom she wanted so much. [10]They stripped her naked, seized her sons and daughters, and then killed her with a sword. Women everywhere gossiped about her fate.

[11]"Even though her sister Oholibah saw this, she was wilder and more of a prostitute than Oholah had ever been. [12]She too was full of lust for the Assyrian noblemen and officers—soldiers in bright uniforms—and for the cavalry officers, all of those handsome young men. [13]I saw that she was completely immoral, that the second sister was as bad as the first.

[14-15]"She sank deeper and deeper in her immorality. She was attracted by the images of high Babylonian officials carved into the wall and painted bright red, with sashes around their waists and fancy turbans on their heads. [16]As soon as she saw them, she was filled with lust and sent messengers to them in Babylonia. [17]The Babylonians came to have sex with her. They used her and defiled her so much that finally she became disgusted with them. [18]She exposed herself publicly and let everyone know she was a whore. I was as disgusted with her as I had been with her sister. [19]She became more of a prostitute than ever, acting the way she did as a young woman, when she was a prostitute in Egypt. [20]She was filled with lust for oversexed men who had all the lustfulness of donkeys or stallions." ([21]Oholibah, you wanted to repeat the immorality you were guilty of as a young woman in Egypt, where men played with your breasts and you lost your virginity.)

God's Judgment on the Younger Sister

[22]"Now then, Oholibah, this is what I, the Sovereign LORD, am saying to you. You are tired of those lovers, but I will make them angry with you and bring them to surround you. [23]I will bring all the Babylonians and Chaldeans, men from Pekod, Shoa, and Koa, and all the Assyrians. I will gather all those handsome young noblemen and officers, all those important officials and high-ranking cavalry officers. [24]They will attack you from the north,[z] bringing a large army with chariots and supply wagons. Protected by shields and helmets, they will surround you. I will hand you over to them, and they will judge you by their own laws. [25]Because I am angry with you, I will let them deal with you in their anger. They will cut off your nose and your ears and kill your children. Yes, they will take your sons and daughters from you and burn them alive. [26]They will tear off your clothes and take your jewels. [27]I will put a stop to your lust and to the obscenities you have committed ever since you were in Egypt. You won't look at any more idols or think about Egypt any more."

[28]This is what the Sovereign LORD says: "I will hand you over to people you hate and are disgusted with. [29]And because they hate you, they will take away everything you have worked for and leave you stripped naked, exposed like a prostitute. Your lust and your prostitution [30]have brought this on you. You were a prostitute for the nations and defiled yourself with their idols. [31]You followed in your sister's footsteps, and so I will give you the same cup of punishment to drink."

[32]The Sovereign LORD says,

"You will drink from your sister's cup;
    it is large and deep.
Everyone will scorn and mock you;
    the cup is full.
[33]It will make you miserable and drunk,
    that cup of fear and ruin,
    your sister Samaria's cup.
[34]You will drink and drain it dry,
    and with its broken pieces
    tear your breast.
I, the Sovereign LORD, have spoken."

[35]Now this is what the Sovereign LORD is

[z] **23:24** *One ancient translation* north; *Hebrew unclear.*

Read Ezekiel 22:23–31. Say a prayer that the leaders of the world will listen to God and do what is right.

Ezekiel

saying: "Because you forgot me and turned your back on me, you will suffer for your lust and your prostitution."

God's Judgment on Both Sisters

36 The LORD said to me, "Mortal man, are you ready to judge Oholah and Oholibah? Accuse them of the disgusting things they have done. 37 They have committed adultery and murder—adultery with idols and murder of the children they bore me. They sacrificed my children to their idols. 38 And that is not all they did. They profaned my Temple and broke the Sabbath, which I had established. 39 The very day that they killed my children as sacrifices to idols, they came to my Temple and profaned it!

40 "Again and again they sent messengers to invite men to come from a great distance, and the men came. The two sisters would bathe and put on eye shadow and jewelry. 41 They would sit on a beautiful couch, and in front of them they would have a table covered with good things, including the incense and the olive oil that I had given them. 42 The sound of a carefree crowd could be heard, a group of men brought in from the desert. They put bracelets on the women's arms and beautiful crowns on their heads. 43 And I said to myself that they were using as a prostitute a woman worn out by adultery.a 44 They went back to these prostitutes again and again. They went back to Oholah and Oholibah, those immoral women. 45 Righteous men will condemn them on the charge of adultery and murder, because they practice adultery and their hands are stained with blood."

46 This is what the Sovereign LORD says: "Bring a mob to terrorize them and rob them. 47 Let the mob stone them and attack them with swords, kill their children, and burn down their houses. 48 Throughout the land I will put a stop to immorality, as a warning to every woman not to commit

adultery as they did. 49 And you two sisters—I will punish you for your immorality and your sin of worshiping idols. Then you will know that I am the Sovereign LORD."

The Corroded Cooking Pot

24 1 On the tenth day of the tenth month of the ninth year of our exile, the LORD spoke to me. 2 "Mortal man," he said, "write down today's date, because this is the day that the king of Babylonia is beginning the siege of Jerusalem. 3 Tell my rebellious people this parable that I, the Sovereign LORD, have for them:

Set the pot on the fire
and fill it up with water.
4 Put in the best pieces of meat—

Set the pot on the fire. (24:3)

the shoulders and the legs—
fill it with choice bony pieces too.
5 Use the meat of the finest sheep;
pile the woodb under the pot.
Let the water boil;
boil the bones and the meat."

6 This is what the Sovereign LORD is saying: "The city of murderers is doomed! It is like a corroded pot that is never cleaned. Piece after piece of meat is taken out, and not one is left. 7 There was murder in the city, but the blood was not spilled on the ground where the dust could hide it; it was

---

a 23:43 *Verses 42–43 in Hebrew are unclear.* b 24:5 *Probable text* wood; *Hebrew* bones.
24:2 2 Kings 25:1; Jer 52:4

According to Ezekiel 24:1, the destruction of Jerusalem began on January 15, 588 BC.

Pray It!

Losing Someone Special

Ezekiel's wife died, and God commanded Ezekiel not to show any signs of sorrow or grief. That must have been very hard for Ezekiel. Have you ever lost someone close to you? Losing someone special is one of the hardest things you will go through in life. But death is only one way people leave us. If your parents are divorced, you might feel that you've lost the family you once had. If you and a good friend have a huge fight, you may never be close again. If you move away, you leave part of your heart behind with your old friends and everyone else you were close to.

If you're feeling sad because someone you loved is no longer with you, try this simple prayer: close your eyes and get a picture of the person in your mind. Then say these words over and over, until you feel peaceful: "I will be with you always" (Matthew 28:20). Imagine the person you love is holding God's hand and smiling at you.

— Ezekiel 24:15–27

---

spilled on a bare rock. ⁸I have left the blood there, where it cannot be hidden, where it demands angry revenge."

⁹This is what the Sovereign LORD is saying: "The city of murderers is doomed! I myself will pile up the firewood. ¹⁰Bring more wood! Fan the flames! Cook the meat! Boil away the broth!ᶜ Burn up the bones! ¹¹Now set the empty bronze pot on the coals and let it get red-hot. Then the pot will be ritually pure again after the corrosion is burned off, ¹²although all that corrosion will not disappear in the flames.ᵈ ¹³Jerusalem, your immoral actions have defiled you. Although I tried to purify you, you remained defiled. You will not be pure again until you have felt the full force of my anger. ¹⁴I, the LORD, have spoken. The time has come for me to act. I will not ignore your sins or show pity or be merciful. You will be punished for what you have done." The Sovereign LORD has spoken.

The Death of the Prophet's Wife

¹⁵The LORD spoke to me. ¹⁶"Mortal man," he said, "with one blow I am going to take away the person you love most. You are not to complain or cry or shed any tears. ¹⁷Don't let your sobbing be heard. Do not go bareheaded or barefoot as a sign of mourning. Don't cover your face or eat the food that mourners eat."

¹⁸Early in the day I was talking with the people. That evening my wife died, and the next day I did as I had been told. ¹⁹The people asked me, "Why are you acting like this?"

²⁰So I said to them, "The LORD spoke to me and told me ²¹to give you Israelites this message: You are proud of the strength of the Temple. You like to look at it and to visit it, but the LORD is going to profane it. And the younger members of your families who are left in Jerusalem will be killed in war. ²²Then you will do what I have done. You will not cover your faces or eat the food that mourners eat. ²³You will not go bareheaded or barefoot or mourn or cry. You will waste away because of your sins, and you will groan to one another. ²⁴Then I will be a sign to you; you will do everything I have done. The LORD says that when this happens, you will know that he is the Sovereign LORD."

²⁵The LORD said, "Now, mortal man, I

ᶜ **24:10** *Some ancient translations* Boil away the broth!; *Hebrew unclear.*   ᵈ **24:12** *Verse 12 in Hebrew begins with two words, the meaning of which is unclear.*

Ezekiel

will take away from them the strong Temple that was their pride and joy, which they liked to look at and to visit. And I will take away their sons and daughters. 26 On the day that I do this, some who escape the destruction will come and tell you about it. 27 That same day you will get back the power of speech which you had lost, and you will talk with them. In this way you will be a sign to the people, and they will know that I am the LORD."

Prophecy against Ammon

25 ¹ The LORD spoke to me. 2 "Mortal man," he said, "denounce the country of Ammon. 3 Tell them to listen to what I, the Sovereign LORD, am saying: You were delighted to see my Temple profaned, to see the land of Israel devastated, to see the people of Judah go into exile. 4 Because you were glad, I will let the tribes from the eastern desert conquer you. They will set up their camps in your country and settle there. They will eat the fruit and drink the milk that should have been yours. 5 I will turn the city of Rabbah into a place to keep camels, and the whole country of Ammon will become a place to keep sheep, so that you will know I am the LORD.

6 "This is what the Sovereign LORD is saying: You clapped your hands and jumped for joy. You despised the land of Israel. 7 Because you did, I will hand you over to other nations who will rob you and plunder you. I will destroy you so completely that you will not be a nation any more or have a country of your own. Then you will know that I am the LORD."

Prophecy against Moab

8 The Sovereign LORD said, "Because Moab^e has said that Judah is like all the other nations, 9 I will let the cities that defend the border of Moab be attacked, including even the finest cities—Beth Jeshimoth, Baal Meon, and Kiriathaim. 10 I will let the tribes

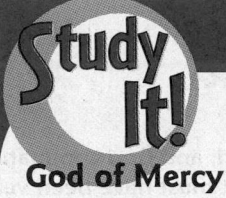

God of Mercy

Ammon. Moab. Edom. Philistia. Tyre. Sidon. Egypt. If you're like most people, you only recognize the last name in that list. These are the names of the countries that surrounded Israel and Judah, the land of God's Chosen People. In Ezekiel, chapters 26–32, Ezekiel sends the message that God will punish the nations that were enemies of the Israelites. For example, the Ammonites rejoiced when the Temple fell, and that angered God. The Edomites turned on the Israelites, and God punished them. The Philistines treated the people of Judah horribly.

The first twenty-four chapters show God's anger at the sins of the Israelites. But even though they had sinned against God, God was still willing to protect them and punish those who hurt them. The God of the Israelites—and our God—is a God of justice and mercy.

— Ezekiel, chapter 25

of the eastern desert conquer Moab, together with Ammon, so that Moab^f will no longer be a nation. 11 I will punish Moab, and they will know that I am the LORD."

Prophecy against Edom

12 The Sovereign LORD said, "The people of Edom took cruel revenge on Judah, and that revenge has brought lasting guilt on Edom. 13 Now I announce that I will punish

^e **25:8** *Some ancient translations* Moab; *Hebrew* Moab and Seir.   ^f **25:10** *Probable text* Moab; *Hebrew* Ammon.
25:1–7 Jer 49:1–6; Ezek 21:28–32; Am 1:13–15; Zeph 2:8–11   **25:8–11** Isa 15:1—16:14; 25:10–12; Jer 48:1–47; Am 2:1–3; Zeph 2:8–11   **25:12–14** Isa 34:5–17; 63:1–6; Jer 49:7–22; Ezek 35:1–15; Am 1:11, 12; Ob 1–14; Mal 1:2–5

Edom and kill every person and animal there. I will make it a wasteland, from the city of Teman to the city of Dedan, and the people will be killed in battle. 14My people Israel will take revenge on Edom for me, and they will make Edom feel my furious anger. Edom will know what it means to be the object of my revenge." The Sovereign LORD has spoken.

Prophecy against Philistia

15The Sovereign LORD said, "The Philistines have taken cruel revenge on their agelong enemies and destroyed them in their hate. 16And so I am announcing that I will attack the Philistines and wipe them out. I will destroy everyone left living there on the Philistine Plain. 17I will punish them severely and take full revenge on them. They will feel my anger. Then they will know that I am the LORD."

Prophecy against Tyre

26 1On the first day of the . . . month*g* of the eleventh year of our exile, the LORD spoke to me. 2"Mortal man," he said, "this is what the people in the city of Tyre are cheering about. They shout, 'Jerusalem is shattered! Her commercial power is gone! She won't be our rival any more!'

3"Now then, this is what I, the Sovereign LORD, am saying: I am your enemy, city of Tyre. I will bring many nations to attack you, and they will come like the waves of the sea. 4They will destroy your city walls and tear down your towers. Then I will sweep away all the dust and leave only a bare rock. 5Fishermen will dry their nets on it, there where it stands in the sea. I, the Sovereign LORD, have spoken. The nations will plunder Tyre, 6and with their swords they will kill those who live in her towns on the

mainland. Then Tyre will know that I am the LORD."

7The Sovereign LORD says, "I am going to bring the greatest king of all—King Nebuchadnezzar of Babylonia—to attack Tyre. He will come from the north with a huge army, with horses and chariots and with cavalry. 8Those who live in the towns on the mainland will be killed in the fighting. The enemy will dig trenches, build earthworks, and make a solid wall of shields against you. 9They will pound in your walls with battering rams and tear down your towers with iron bars. 10The clouds of dust raised by their horses will cover you. The noise of their horses pulling wagons and chariots will shake your walls as they pass through the gates of the ruined city. 11Their cavalry will storm through your streets, killing your people with their swords. Your mighty pillars will be thrown to the ground. 12Your enemies will help themselves to your wealth and merchandise. They will pull down your walls and shatter your luxurious houses. They will take the stones and wood and all the rubble, and dump them into the sea. 13I will put an end to all your songs, and I will silence the music of your harps. 14I will leave only a bare rock where fishermen can dry their nets. The city will never be rebuilt. I, the Sovereign LORD, have spoken."

15The Sovereign LORD has this to say to the city of Tyre: "When you are being conquered, the people who live along the coast will be terrified at the screams of those who are slaughtered. 16All the kings of the seafaring nations will come down from their thrones. They will take off their robes and their embroidered clothes and sit trembling on the ground. They will be so terrified at your fate that they will not be able to stop trembling. 17They will sing this funeral song for you:

Ezekiel

---

g **26:1** month; *the Hebrew text does not specify the month.*
25:15–17 Isa 14:29–31; Jer 47:1–7; Joel 3:4–8; Am 1:6–8; Zeph 2:4–7; Zech 9:5–7   **26:1—28:19** Isa 23:1–18;
Joel 3:4–8; Am 1:9, 10; Zech 9:1–4; Mt 11:21, 22; Lk 10:13, 14   **26:13** Rev 18:22   **26:16–18** Rev 18:9, 10

Ezekiel, chapters 25–32, link the two parts of the Book of Ezekiel: God's judgment in the first half and God's promise in the second half.

Ezekiel

That city which stands at the edge of the sea (27:3)

The famous city is destroyed!
Her ships have been swept[h] from the seas.
The people of this city ruled the seas
And terrified all who lived on the coast.
18 Now, on the day it has fallen,
The islands are trembling,
And their people are shocked at such
destruction."

19 The Sovereign LORD says: "I will make
you as desolate as ruined cities where no one
lives. I will cover you with the water of the
ocean depths. 20 I will send you down to the
world of the dead to join the people who
lived in ancient times. I will make you stay
in that underground world among eternal
ruins, keeping company with the dead. As a
result you will never again be inhabited and
take your place[i] in the land of the living. 21 I
will make you a terrifying example, and that
will be the end of you. People may look for
you, but you will never be found." The Sovereign LORD has spoken.

A Funeral Song for Tyre

27 1 The LORD said to me, 2 "Mortal
man, sing a funeral song for Tyre,
3 that city which stands at the edge of the sea

and does business with the people living on
every seacoast. Tell her what the Sovereign
LORD is saying:
"Tyre, you boasted of your perfect beauty.
4 Your home is the sea.
Your builders made you like a beautiful
ship;
5 They used fir trees from Mount Hermon
for timber
And a cedar from Lebanon for your mast.
6 They took oak trees from Bashan to make
oars;
They made your deck out of pine from
Cyprus
And inlaid it with ivory.
7 Your sails were made of linen,
Embroidered linen from Egypt,
Easily recognized from afar.
Your awnings were made of finest cloth,
Of purple from the island of Cyprus.
8 Your oarsmen were from the cities of
Sidon and Arvad.
Your own skillful men were the sailors.
9 The ship's carpenters
Were well-trained men from Byblos.
Sailors from every seagoing ship
Did business in your shops.
10 "Soldiers from Persia, Lydia, and Libya

h 26:17 *Some ancient translations* swept; *Hebrew* inhabited.
Hebrew unclear.
26:21 Rev 18:21

i 26:20 *One ancient translation* and take your place;

**Check out all the different types of merchandise that were traded in Ezekiel's
time** *(Ezekiel 27:12–24).* **How many different things are mentioned?**

served in your army. They hung their shields and their helmets in your barracks. They are the men who won glory for you. ¹¹Soldiers from Arvad guarded your walls, and troops from Gamad guarded your towers. They hung their shields on your walls. They are the ones who made you beautiful.

¹²"You did business in Spain and took silver, iron, tin, and lead in payment for your abundant goods. ¹³You did business in Greece, Tubal, and Meshech and traded your goods for slaves and for articles of bronze. ¹⁴You sold your goods for workhorses, warhorses, and mules from Beth Togarmah. ¹⁵The people of Rhodes*ʲ* traded with you; people of many coastal lands gave you ivory and ebony in exchange for your goods. ¹⁶The people of Syria bought your merchandise and your many products. They gave emeralds, purple cloth, embroidery, fine linen, coral, and rubies in payment for your wares. ¹⁷Judah and Israel paid for your goods with wheat,*ᵏ* honey, olive oil, and spices. ¹⁸⁻¹⁹The people of Damascus bought your merchandise and your products, paying for them with wine from Helbon and wool from Sahar.*ˡ* They traded wrought iron and spices for your goods. ²⁰The people of Dedan traded saddle blankets for your goods. ²¹The Arabians and the rulers of the land of Kedar paid for your merchandise with lambs, sheep, and goats. ²²For your goods the merchants of Sheba and Raamah traded jewels, gold, and the finest spices. ²³The cities of Haran, Canneh, and Eden, the merchants of Sheba, the cities of Asshur and Chilmad— they all traded with you. ²⁴They sold you luxurious clothing, purple cloth, and embroidery, brightly colored carpets, and well-made cords and ropes. ²⁵Your merchandise was carried in fleets of the largest cargo ships.

"You were like a ship at sea
Loaded with heavy cargo.
²⁶When your oarsmen brought you out to
      sea,
   An east wind wrecked you far from land.
²⁷All your wealth of merchandise,

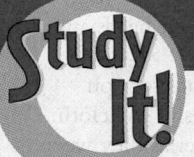

Eden, the Sequel

The people of Tyre had everything. They were rich. The city was perfectly located on the Mediterranean Sea to be the center of trade. Ezekiel 27:12–24 lists some of the products that were traded with other countries in the region.

Even though they had little to do with the fall of Jerusalem, the people of Tyre were destroyed by God. Why? Because of their greed and pride. In Ezekiel 26:2, Ezekiel tells us that the people of Tyre were glad to see Jerusalem fall because it meant they would make more money.

In the Garden of Eden, Adam and Eve had all that they could ever want or need, but they were not satisfied. So they ate the fruit of the forbidden tree. God punished them for it, just like he punished the people of Tyre.

Where do you see greed happening in our world? Do you think people or companies suffer bad things when they get too greedy?

— Ezekiel, chapter 27

All the sailors in your crew,
Your ship's carpenters and your
      merchants,
Every soldier on board the ship—
All, all were lost at sea
When your ship was wrecked.
²⁸The shouts of the drowning sailors
Echoed on the shore.

²⁹"Every ship is now deserted,
And every sailor has gone ashore.

ʲ **27:15** *One ancient translation* Rhodes; *Hebrew* Dedan.   *ᵏ* **27:17** *Hebrew has two additional words, the meaning of which is unclear.*   *ˡ* **27:18–19** *Hebrew has three additional words, the meaning of which is unclear.*
27:25–36 Rev 18:11–19

30 They all mourn bitterly for you,
  Throwing dust on their heads and rolling
    in ashes.
31 They shave their heads for you
  And dress themselves in sackcloth.
  Their hearts are bitter as they weep.
32 They chant a funeral song for you:
  'Who can be compared to Tyre,
  To Tyre now silent in the sea?
33 When your merchandise went overseas,
  You filled the needs of every nation.
  Kings were made rich
  By the wealth of your goods.
34 Now you are wrecked in the sea;
  You have sunk to the ocean depths.
  Your goods and all who worked for you
  Have vanished with you in the sea.'

35 "Everyone who lives along the coast is shocked at your fate. Even their kings are terrified, and fear is written on their faces. 36 You are gone, gone forever, and merchants all over the world are terrified, afraid that they will share your fate."

Prophecy against the King of Tyre

28 1 The LORD spoke to me. 2 "Mortal man," he said, "tell the ruler of Tyre what I, the Sovereign LORD, am saying to him: Puffed up with pride, you claim to be a god. You say that like a god you sit on a throne, surrounded by the seas. You may pretend to be a god, but, no, you are mortal, not divine. 3 You think you are wiser than Danel,[m] that no secret can be kept from you. 4 Your wisdom and skill made you rich with treasures of gold and silver. 5 You made clever business deals and kept on making profits. How proud you are of your wealth!

6 "Now then, this is what I, the Sovereign LORD, am saying: Because you think you are as wise as a god, 7 I will bring ruthless enemies to attack you. They will destroy all the beautiful things you have acquired by skill and wisdom. 8 They will kill you and send you to a watery grave. 9 When they come to kill you, will you still claim that you are a god? When you face your murderers, you will be mortal and not at all divine. 10 You will die like a dog at the hand of godless foreigners. I, the Sovereign LORD, have given the command."

The Fall of the King of Tyre

11 The LORD spoke to me again. 12 "Mortal man," he said, "grieve for the fate that is waiting for the king of Tyre. Tell him what I, the Sovereign LORD, am saying: You were once an example of perfection. How wise and handsome you were! 13 You lived in Eden, the garden of God, and wore gems of every kind: rubies and diamonds; topaz, beryl, carnelian, and jasper; sapphires, emeralds, and garnets. You had ornaments of gold. They were made for you[n] on the day you were created. 14 I put a terrifying angel there to guard you.[o] You lived on my holy mountain and walked among sparkling gems. 15 Your conduct was perfect from the day you were created until you began to do evil. 16 You were busy buying and selling, and this led you to violence and sin. So I forced you to leave my holy mountain, and the angel who guarded you drove you away from the sparkling gems. 17 You were proud of being handsome, and your fame made you act like a fool. Because of this I hurled you to the ground and left you as a warning to other kings. 18 You did such evil in buying and selling that your places of worship were corrupted. So I set fire to the city and burned it to the ground. All who look at you now see you reduced to ashes. 19 You are gone, gone forever, and all the nations that had come to know you are terrified, afraid that they will share your fate."

Prophecy against Sidon

20 The LORD said to me, 21 "Mortal man, denounce the city of Sidon. 22 Tell the people there what I, the Sovereign LORD, say about them: I am your enemy, Sidon; people will praise me because of what I do to you. They will know that I am the LORD, when I show how holy I am by punishing those who live in you. 23 I will send diseases on

---

m **28:3** Danel; or Daniel (see 14:14).   n **28:13** Probable text They were made for you; Hebrew unclear.
o **28:14** One ancient translation I put . . . you; Hebrew unclear.
28:20–26 Joel 3:4–8; Zech 9:1, 2; Mt 11:21, 22; Lk 10:13, 14

you and make blood flow in your streets. You will be attacked from every side, and your people will be killed. Then you will know that I am the LORD."

Israel Will Be Blessed

24 The LORD said, "None of the surrounding nations that treated Israel with scorn will ever again be like thorns and briers to hurt Israel. And they will know that I am the Sovereign LORD."

25 The Sovereign LORD said, "I will bring back the people of Israel from the nations where I scattered them, and all the nations will know that I am holy. The people of Israel will live in their own land, the land that I gave to my servant Jacob. 26 They will live there in safety. They will build houses and plant vineyards. I will punish all their neighbors who treated them with scorn, and Israel will be secure. Then they will know that I am the LORD their God."

Prophecy against Egypt

29 1 On the twelfth day of the tenth month of the tenth year of our exile, the LORD spoke to me. 2 "Mortal man," he said, "denounce the king of Egypt. Tell him how he and all the land of Egypt will be punished. 3 Say that this is what the Sovereign LORD is telling the king of Egypt: I am your enemy, you monster crocodile, lying in the river. You say that the Nile is yours and that you made it.*p* 4 I am going to put a hook through your jaw and make the fish in your river stick fast to you. Then I will pull you up out of the Nile, with all the fish sticking to you. 5 I will throw you and all those fish into the desert. Your body will fall on the ground and be left unburied. I will give it to the birds and animals for food.

I will pull you up out of the Nile. (29:4)

6 Then all the people of Egypt will know that I am the LORD."

The LORD says, "The Israelites relied on you Egyptians for support, but you were no better than a weak stick. 7 When they leaned on you, you broke, pierced their armpits, and made them wrench their backs.*q* 8 Now then, I, the Sovereign LORD, am telling you that I will have troops attack you with swords, and they will kill your people and your animals. 9 Egypt will become an empty wasteland. Then you will know that I am the LORD.

"Because you said that the Nile is yours and you made it, 10 I am your enemy and the enemy of your Nile. I will make all of Egypt an empty wasteland, from the city of Migdol in the north to the city of Aswan in the south, all the way to the Ethiopian*r* border. 11 No human being or animal will walk through it. For forty years nothing will live there. 12 I will make Egypt the most desolate country in the world. For forty years the cities of Egypt will lie in ruins, ruins worse than those of any other city. I will make the Egyptians refugees. They will flee to every country and live among other peoples."

13 The Sovereign LORD says, "After forty years I will bring the Egyptians back from the nations where I have scattered them, 14 and I will let them live in southern Egypt, their original home. There they will be a weak kingdom, 15 the weakest kingdom of all, and they will never again rule other nations. I will make them so unimportant that they will not

---

p 29:3 Some ancient translations *you made it;* Hebrew *you made yourself.*   *q 29:7* One ancient translation *wrench their backs;* Hebrew *make their backs stand.*   *r 29:10* Hebrew *Cushite (Cush): Cush is the ancient name of the extensive territory south of the First Cataract of the Nile River. This region was called Ethiopia in Graeco-Roman times, and included within its borders most of modern Sudan and some of present-day Ethiopia (Abyssinia).*
29:1—32:32 Isa 19:1–25; Jer 46:2–26   **29:6** Isa 36:6

Pride: **Loving yourself or success more than God or others. It is one of the capital sins because it leads to other sins.**

Pray It!

A Prayer for Peace

It seems most of these prophecies against the other nations had to do with war and violence. In Ezekiel, chapter 29, Ezekiel prophesies that there will be war between Egypt and Babylonia. Is there ever an end to war?

God, it seems that war is everywhere. The older I get, the more I hear about it and the more it bothers me. People kill people every day. It happens around the world and right where I live. It seemed like that happened a lot in Ezekiel's time, too. People's lives are shattered because someone they love is hurt or killed, their home is destroyed, or they are wounded beyond repair. I don't know what to do, God, except to pray.

Help me do what I can to change things, God. Please heal the world—one heart at a time. And please start with mine. Amen.

— Ezekiel, chapter 29

be able to bend any other nation to their will. ¹⁶Israel will never again depend on them for help. Egypt's fate will remind Israel how wrong it was to rely on them. Then Israel will know that I am the Sovereign LORD."

King Nebuchadnezzar Will Conquer Egypt

¹⁷On the first day of the first month of the twenty-seventh year of our exile, the LORD spoke to me. ¹⁸"Mortal man," he said, "King Nebuchadnezzar of Babylonia launched an attack on Tyre. He made his soldiers carry such heavy loads that their heads were rubbed bald and their shoulders were worn raw, but neither the king nor his army got anything for all their trouble. ¹⁹So now this is what I, the Sovereign LORD, am saying: I am giving the land of Egypt to King Nebuchadnezzar. He will loot and plunder it and carry off all the wealth of Egypt as his army's pay. ²⁰I am giving him Egypt in payment for his services, because his army was working for me. I, the Sovereign LORD, have spoken.

²¹"When that happens, I will make the people of Israel strong and let you, Ezekiel, speak out where everyone can hear you, so that they will know that I am the LORD."

The LORD Will Punish Egypt

30 ¹The LORD spoke to me again. ²"Mortal man," he said, "prophesy and announce what I, the Sovereign LORD, am saying. You are to shout these words:
   A day of terror is coming!
³The day is near, the day when the LORD
      will act,
   A day of clouds and trouble for the
      nations.
⁴There will be war in Egypt
   And great distress in Ethiopia.ʳ
   Many in Egypt will be killed;
   The country will be plundered
   And left in ruins.
⁵"That war will also kill the soldiers hired from Ethiopia,ʳ Libya, Lydia, Arabia, Kub, and even from among my own people."

⁶The LORD says, "From Migdol in the north to Aswan in the south, all Egypt's defenders will be killed in battle. Egypt's proud army will be destroyed. I, the Sovereign LORD, have spoken. ⁷The land will be the most desolate in the world, and its cities

ʳ 30:4, 5 *Hebrew* Cushite (Cush): *Cush is the ancient name of the extensive territory south of the First Cataract of the Nile River. This region was called Ethiopia in Graeco-Roman times, and included within its borders most of modern Sudan and some of present-day Ethiopia (Abyssinia).*

As king of Babylonia, Nebuchadnezzar conquered Israel. Read more about him (and his dreams) in the Book of Daniel.

will be left totally in ruins. 8When I set fire to Egypt and all her defenders are killed, then they will know that I am the LORD.

9"When that day comes and Egypt is destroyed, I will send messengers in ships to arouse the unsuspecting people of Ethiopia,ʳ and they will be terrified. That day is coming!"

10The Sovereign LORD says, "I will use King Nebuchadnezzar of Babylonia to put an end to Egypt's wealth. 11He and his ruthless army will come to devastate the land. They will attack Egypt with swords, and the land will be full of corpses. 12I will dry up the Nile and put Egypt under the power of evil people. Foreigners will devastate the whole country. I, the LORD, have spoken."

13The Sovereign LORD says, "I will destroy the idols and the false gods in Memphis. There will be no one to rule Egypt, and I will terrify all the people. 14I will make southern Egypt desolate and set fire to the city of Zoan in the north. I will punish the capital city of Thebes. 15I will let the city of Pelusium, Egypt's great fortress, feel my fury. I will destroy the wealth of Thebes. 16I will set fire to Egypt, and Pelusium will be in agony. The walls of Thebes will be broken down, and the city will be flooded.ˢ 17The young men of the cities of Heliopolis and Bubastis will die in the war, and the other people will be taken prisoner. 18Darkness will fall on Tahpanhes when I break the power of Egypt and put an end to the strength they were so proud of. A cloud will cover Egypt, and the people of all her cities will be taken prisoner. 19When I punish Egypt in this way, they will know that I am the LORD."

The Broken Power of the King of Egypt

20On the seventh day of the first month of the eleventh year of our exile, the LORD spoke to me. 21"Mortal man," he said, "I have broken the arm of the king of Egypt. No one has bandaged it or put it in a sling so that it could heal and be strong enough to hold a sword again. 22Now then, this is what

I, the Sovereign LORD, say: I am the enemy of the king of Egypt. I am going to break both his arms—the good one and the one already broken—and the sword will fall from his hand. 23I am going to scatter the Egyptians throughout the world. 24Then I will make the arms of the king of Babylonia strong and put my sword in his hands. But I will break the arms of the king of Egypt, and he will groan and die in front of his enemy. 25Yes, I will weaken him and strengthen the king of Babylonia. When I give him my sword and he points it toward Egypt, everyone will know that I am the LORD. 26I will scatter the Egyptians throughout the world. Then they will know that I am the LORD."

Egypt Is Compared to a Cedar Tree

31 1On the first day of the third month of the eleventh year of our exile, the LORD spoke to me. 2"Mortal man," he said, "say to the king of Egypt and all his people:
How powerful you are!
What can I compare you to?
3 You are likeᵗ a cedar in Lebanon,
With beautiful, shady branches,
A tree so tall it reaches the clouds.ᵘ
4 There was water to make it grow,
And underground rivers to feed it.
They watered the place where the tree
was growing
And sent streams to all the trees of the
forest.
5 Because it was well-watered,
It grew taller than other trees.
Its branches grew thick and long.
6 Every kind of bird built nests in its
branches;
The wild animals bore their young in its
shelter;
The nations of the world rested in its
shade.
7 How beautiful the tree was—
So tall, with such long branches.
Its roots reached down to the deep-
flowing streams.

ʳ **30:9** *Hebrew* Cushite (Cush): *Cush is the ancient name of the extensive territory south of the First Cataract of the Nile River. This region was called Ethiopia in Graeco-Roman times, and included within its borders most of modern Sudan and some of present-day Ethiopia (Abyssinia).* ˢ **30:16** *One ancient translation* flooded; *Hebrew unclear.* ᵗ **31:3** *Probable text* You are like; *Hebrew* Assyria is. ᵘ **31:3** *One ancient translation* clouds; *Hebrew* thick branches.

Catholic Connections

Life's Downs and Ups

You've probably heard the saying, "What goes up must come down." That might apply to balls and flying objects, but when it comes to real life, the opposite is true: what goes down often comes up.

In the first part of the Book of Ezekiel, the Israelites are about as down as they can get. They are almost spiritually dead. But God doesn't give up on them. In the second part that is coming up, God promises to lead them home and be with them forever. The Israelites awake from their spiritual death and are making things right with God.

Catholics believe in the *Paschal mystery,* meaning that God saved us through the life, death, and Resurrection of Jesus. Throughout your life, you have dyings and risings, just like the Israelites and Jesus. It's your way of participating in the Paschal mystery of Jesus.

Know that when things are down, it is not the end of our story. God promised new life for those who have faith, and Jesus' Resurrection is the sign and fulfillment of that promise.

— Ezekiel, chapter 31

8 No cedar in God's garden could compare with it.
No fir tree ever had such branches,
And no plane tree such limbs.
No tree in God's own garden was so beautiful.
9 I made it beautiful, with spreading branches.
It was the envy of every tree in Eden, the garden of God.

10 "Now then, I, the Sovereign LORD, will tell you what is going to happen to that tree that grew until it reached the clouds.*u* As it grew taller it grew proud; 11 so I have rejected it and will let a foreign ruler have it. He will give that tree what it deserves for its wickedness. 12 Ruthless foreigners will cut it down and leave it. Its branches and broken limbs will fall on every mountain and valley in the country. All the nations that have been living in its shade will go away. 13 The birds will come and perch on the fallen tree, and the wild animals will walk over its branches.

14 And so from now on, no tree, no matter how well-watered it is, will grow that tall again or push its top through the clouds*u* and reach such a height. All of them are doomed to die like mortals, doomed to join those who go down to the world of the dead."

15 This is what the Sovereign LORD says: "On the day when the tree goes to the world of the dead, I will make the underground waters cover it as a sign of mourning. I will hold back the rivers and not let the many streams flow out. Because the tree has died, I will bring darkness over the Lebanon Mountains and make all the trees of the forest wither. 16 When I send it down to the world of the dead, the noise of its downfall will shake the nations. All the trees of Eden and all the choice, well-watered trees of Lebanon who have gone to the world below will be pleased at its downfall. 17 They will go with it to the world of the dead to join those that have already fallen. And all who live under its shadow will be scattered among the nations.*v*

u **31:10, 14** *One ancient translation* clouds; *Hebrew* thick branches.   *v* **31:17** *Probable text* And all . . . nations; *Hebrew unclear.*
31:8 Gen 2:9

No tree . . . will grow that tall again. (31:14)

18"The tree is the king of Egypt and all his people. Not even the trees in Eden were so tall and impressive. But now, like the trees of Eden, it will go down to the world of the dead and join the ungodly and those killed in battle. I have spoken," says the Sovereign LORD.

The King of Egypt Is Compared to a Crocodile

32 1On the first day of the twelfth month of the twelfth year of our exile, the LORD spoke to me. 2"Mortal man," he said, "give a solemn warning to the king of Egypt. Give him this message from me: You act like a lion among the nations, but you are more like a crocodile splashing through a river. You muddy the water with your feet and pollute the rivers. 3When many nations gather, I will catch you in my net and let them drag the net ashore. 4I will throw you out on the ground and bring all the birds and animals of the world to feed on you. 5I will cover mountains and valleys with your rotting corpse. 6I will pour out your blood until it spreads over the mountains and fills the streams. 7When I destroy you, I will cover the sky and blot out the stars. The sun will hide behind the clouds, and the moon will give no light. 8I will put out all the lights of heaven and plunge your world into darkness. I, the Sovereign LORD, have spoken.

9"Many nations will be troubled when I spread the news of your destruction through countries you never heard of. 10What I do to you will shock many nations. When I swing my sword, kings will shudder with fright. On the day you fall, all of them will tremble in fear for their own lives."

11The Sovereign LORD says to the king of Egypt, "You will face the sword of the king of Babylonia. 12I will let soldiers from cruel nations draw their swords and kill all your people. All your people and everything else that you are proud of will be destroyed. 13I will slaughter your cattle at every water hole. There will be no people or cattle to muddy the water any more. 14I will let your waters settle and become clear and let your rivers run calm. I, the Sovereign LORD, have spoken. 15When I make Egypt a desolate wasteland and destroy all who live there, they will know that I am the LORD. 16This solemn warning will become a funeral song. The women of the nations will sing it to mourn for Egypt and all its people. I, the Sovereign LORD, have spoken."

The World of the Dead

17On the fifteenth day of the first month*w* of the twelfth year of our exile, the LORD spoke to me. 18"Mortal man," he said, "mourn for all the many people of Egypt. Send them down with the other powerful nations to the world of the dead. 19Say to them:

w **32:17** *One ancient translation* of the first month; *Hebrew does not have these words.*
32:7 Isa 13:10; Mt 24:29; Mk 13:24, 25; Lk 21:25; Rev 6:12, 13; 8:12

Cedar trees were strong, straight, and bug resistant. They were used for ships and large buildings.

Ezekiel

Hey, Beautiful!

Are you good-looking? Do you have a nice body? A lot of people your age are concerned with how they look on the outside. Looking your best is important, but it's not the most important part of who you are. Magazines, television shows, movies, and newspapers are full of things that advertisers say will make you look good. They want you to think that you need their product to be attractive. They want you to forget that you are already beautiful. After all, God made you. It doesn't matter what you look like, what clothes you wear, or what shape your body is in—you are beautiful!

The ancient Egyptians worked hard at looking beautiful. But if you read Ezekiel 32:19, good looks certainly don't matter to God. No one is guaranteed a place in heaven because he or she looks good. What is much more important to God is how you live your life. How beautiful is your life?

— Ezekiel 32:17–19

"Do you think you are more beautiful
        than anyone else?
You will go down to the world of the
        dead
    and lie there among the ungodly.
20 "The people of Egypt will fall with
those who are killed in battle. A sword is
ready to kill them all. x 21 The greatest heroes

and those who fought on the Egyptian side
welcome the Egyptians to the world of the
dead. They shout: 'The ungodly who were
killed in battle have come down here, and
here they lie!'

22 "Assyria is there, with the graves of her
soldiers all around. They were all killed in
battle, 23 and their graves are in the deepest
parts of the world of the dead. All her soldiers fell in battle, and their graves surround
her tomb. Yet once they terrified the land of
the living.

24 "Elam is there, with the graves of her
soldiers all around. They were all killed in
battle, and they went down, uncircumcised,
to the world of the dead. In life they spread
terror, but now they lie dead and disgraced.
25 Elam lies down among those killed in battle, and the graves of her soldiers are all
around her. They are all uncircumcised, all
killed in battle. In life they spread terror, but
now they lie dead and disgraced, sharing the
fate of those killed in battle.

26 "Meshech and Tubal are there, with the
graves of their soldiers all around. They are
all uncircumcised, all killed in battle. Yet
once they terrified the living. 27 They were
not given honorable burial like the heroes of
ancient times, y who went fully armed to the
world of the dead, their swords placed under
their heads and their shields z over their bodies. These heroes were once powerful
enough to terrify the living.

28 "That is how the Egyptians will lie
crushed among the uncircumcised who were
killed in battle.

29 "Edom is there with her kings and
rulers. They were powerful soldiers, but now
they lie in the world of the dead with the
uncircumcised who were killed in battle.

30 "All the princes of the north are there,
and so are the Sidonians. Their power once
spread terror, but now they go down in disgrace with those killed in battle and are laid
to rest, uncircumcised. They share the dis-

---

x **32:20** *Probable text* A sword . . . all; *Hebrew unclear.*   y **32:27** *Some ancient translations* of ancient times; *Hebrew*
of the uncircumcised.   z **32:27** *Probable text* shields; *Hebrew* iniquities.

**Lookouts were usually used for military purposes. But God makes Ezekiel a
spiritual lookout.**

grace of those who go down to the world of the dead.

31 "The sight of all these who were killed in battle will be a comfort to the king of Egypt and his army," says the Sovereign LORD.

32 "I caused the king of Egypt to terrorize the living, but he and all his army will be killed and laid to rest with all the uncircumcised who die in battle." The Sovereign LORD has spoken.

God Appoints Ezekiel as a Lookout
(Ezekiel 3:16–21)

33 **1** The LORD spoke to me. **2** "Mortal man," he said, "tell your people what happens when I bring war to a land. The people of that country choose one of their number to be a lookout. **3** When he sees the enemy approaching, he sounds the alarm to warn everyone. **4** If someone hears it but pays no attention and the enemy comes and kills him, then he is to blame for his own death. **5** His death is his own fault, because he paid no attention to the warning. If he had paid attention, he could have escaped. **6** If, however, the lookout sees the enemy coming and does not sound the alarm, the enemy will come and kill those sinners, but I will hold the lookout responsible for their death.

7 "Now, mortal man, I am making you a lookout for the nation of Israel. You must pass on to them the warnings I give you. **8** If I announce that an evil person is going to die but you do not warn him to change his ways so that he can save his life, then he will die, still a sinner, and I will hold you responsible for his death. **9** If you do warn an evil person and he doesn't stop sinning, he will die, still a sinner, but your life will be spared."

Individual Responsibility

10 The LORD spoke to me. "Mortal man," he said, "repeat to the Israelites what they are saying: 'We are burdened with our sins and the wrongs we have done. We are wasting away. How can we live?' **11** Tell them that as surely as I, the Sovereign LORD, am the living God, I do not enjoy seeing sinners die. I

Wrong Secrets

Jonas knew that Max was heading for trouble. He knew that Max got beer from some older guys in exchange for keeping a lookout. He knew that Max was a shoplifter, too, and proud of it. Max knew that he could count on Jonas not to tell adults about these things. "Friends keep secrets." Max told him one day. "You *are* my friend, right?"

God tells Ezekiel, "If I announce that an evil person is going to die but you do not warn him to change his ways so that he can save his life, then he will die" (Ezekiel 33:8). We have a responsibility to challenge other people when they are doing something that is clearly against God's will. Sooner or later their sinful behavior will lead to their being deeply hurt and also maybe hurting others.

Though keeping secrets is an important part of being a friend, sometimes our friends ask us to keep the wrong secrets. If you know that a friend is doing something wrong or is in danger—and they will not listen to you —tell an adult you trust. Your friend may be angry with you, but it's better to lose the friendship than to watch your friend end up deeply hurt or in worse trouble.

— Ezekiel 33:7–9

would rather see them stop sinning and live. Israel, stop the evil you are doing. Why do you want to die?

12 "Now, mortal man, tell the Israelites that when someone good sins, the good he has done will not save him. If an evil person stops doing evil, he won't be punished, and if a good man starts sinning, his life will not be spared. ¹³I may promise life to someone good, but if he starts thinking that his past goodness is enough and begins to sin, I will not remember any of the good he did. He will die because of his sins. ¹⁴I may warn someone evil that he is going to die, but if he stops sinning and does what is right and good— ¹⁵for example, if he returns the security he took for a loan or gives back what he stole—if he stops sinning and follows the laws that give life, he will not die, but live. ¹⁶I will forgive the sins he has committed, and he will live because he has done what is right and good.

¹⁷"And your people say that what I do isn't right! No, it's their way that isn't right. ¹⁸When someone righteous stops doing good and starts doing evil, he will die for it. ¹⁹When someone evil quits sinning and does what is right and good, he has saved his life. ²⁰But Israel, you say that what I do isn't right. I am going to judge you by what you do."

The News of Jerusalem's Fall

²¹On the fifth day of the tenth month of the twelfth year of our exile, someone who had escaped from Jerusalem came and told me that the city had fallen. ²²The evening before he came, I had felt the powerful presence of the LORD. When the man arrived the next morning, the LORD gave me back the power of speech.

The Sins of the People

²³The LORD spoke to me. ²⁴"Mortal man," he said, "the people who are living in the ruined cities of the land of Israel are saying: 'Abraham was only one man, and he was given the whole land. There are many of us, so now the land is ours.'

²⁵"Tell them what I, the Sovereign LORD, am saying: You eat meat with the blood still in it. You worship idols. You commit murder. What makes you think that the land belongs to you? ²⁶You rely on your swords. Your actions are disgusting. Everyone commits

adultery. What makes you think that the land is yours?

²⁷"Tell them that I, the Sovereign LORD, warn them that as surely as I am the living God, the people who live in the ruined cities will be killed. Those living in the country will be eaten by wild animals. Those hiding in the mountains and in caves will die of disease. ²⁸I will make the country a desolate wasteland, and the power they were so proud of will come to an end. The mountains of Israel will be so wild that no one will be able to travel through them. ²⁹When I punish the people for their sins and make the country a wasteland, then they will know that I am the LORD."

The Results of the Prophet's Message

³⁰The LORD said, "Mortal man, your people are talking about you when they meet by the city walls or in the doorways of their houses. They say to one another, 'Let's go and hear what word has come from the LORD now.' ³¹So my people crowd in to hear what you have to say, but they don't do what you tell them to do. Loving words are on their lips, but they continue their greedy ways. ³²To them you are nothing more than an entertainer singing love songs or playing a harp. They listen to all your words and don't obey a single one of them. ³³But when all your words come true—and they will come true—then they will know that a prophet has been among them."

They listen to all your words and don't obey a single one of them. (33:32)

Catholic Connections

Do You Know Any Good Shepherds?

You've probably never seen a real, live shepherd. Not many of us have. Shepherds check that the sheep have enough good grass to eat and clear water to drink. They make sure the sheep don't wander off and get lost. They protect them from wild animals and take care of them when they are sick or hurt. It was popular in Bible times to compare leaders to shepherds. Ezekiel talks about the leaders of his time being like poor shepherds, failing to care for their people.

You may have never seen a shepherd, but if you think about it, lots of people in your life are like shepherds to you. They care for you, guide you, provide shelter, and protect you. These people follow God's example when they do these things for you.

Jesus is often called the Good Shepherd because he cares for us like a shepherd cares for sheep. Check out John 10:1–18 for more about how Jesus is the Good Shepherd. In the Catholic Church, bishops are also called shepherds. The bishop's crosier, or staff, is to remind us of the staff used by shepherds.

— Ezekiel, chapter 34

The Shepherds of Israel

34 ¹The LORD spoke to me. ²"Mortal man," he said, "denounce the rulers of Israel. Prophesy to them, and tell them what I, the Sovereign LORD, say to them: You are doomed, you shepherds of Israel! You take care of yourselves, but never tend the sheep. ³You drink the milk, wear clothes made from the wool, and kill and eat the finest sheep. But you never tend the sheep. ⁴You have not taken care of the weak ones, healed the ones that are sick, bandaged the ones that are hurt, brought back the ones that wandered off, or looked for the ones that were lost. Instead, you treated them cruelly. ⁵Because the sheep had no shepherd, they were scattered, and wild animals killed and ate them. ⁶So my sheep wandered over the high hills and the mountains. They

were scattered over the face of the earth, and no one looked for them or tried to find them.

⁷"Now, you shepherds, listen to what I, the LORD, am telling you. ⁸As surely as I am the living God, you had better listen to me. My sheep have been attacked by wild animals that killed and ate them because there was no shepherd. My shepherds did not try to find the sheep. They were taking care of themselves and not the sheep. ⁹So listen to me, you shepherds. ¹⁰I, the Sovereign LORD, declare that I am your enemy. I will take my sheep away from you and never again let you be their shepherds; never again will I let you take care only of yourselves. I will rescue my sheep from you and not let you eat them.

34:5 Num 27:17; 1 Kings 22:17; Mt 9:36; Mk 6:34

"Loving words are on their lips, but they continue their greedy ways" (Ezekiel 33:31).

Ezekiel

The Good Shepherd

11 "I, the Sovereign LORD, tell you that I myself will look for my sheep and take care of them 12 in the same way as shepherds take care of their sheep that were scattered and are brought together again. I will bring them back from all the places where they were scattered on that dark, disastrous day. 13 I will take them out of foreign countries, gather them together, and bring them back to their own land. I will lead them back to the mountains and the streams of Israel and will feed them in pleasant pastures. 14 I will let them graze in safety in the mountain meadows and the valleys and in all the green pastures of the land of Israel. 15 I myself will be the shepherd of my sheep, and I will find them a place to rest. I, the Sovereign LORD, have spoken.

I myself will be the shepherd of my sheep. (34:15)

16 "I will look for those that are lost, bring back those that wander off, bandage those that are hurt, and heal those that are sick; but those that are fat and strong I will destroy, because I am a shepherd who does what is right.

17 "Now then, my flock, I, the Sovereign LORD, tell you that I will judge each of you and separate the good from the bad, the sheep from the goats. 18 Some of you are not satisfied with eating the best grass; you even trample down what you don't eat! You drink the clear water and muddy what you don't drink! 19 My other sheep have to eat the grass you trample down and drink the water you muddy.

20 "So now, I, the Sovereign LORD, tell you that I will judge between you strong sheep and the weak sheep. 21 You pushed the sick ones aside and butted them away from the flock. 22 But I will rescue my sheep and not let them be mistreated any more. I will judge each of my sheep and separate the good from the bad. 23 I will give them a king like my servant David to be their one shepherd, and he will take care of them. 24 I, the LORD, will be their God, and a king like my servant David will be their ruler. I have spoken. 25 I will make a covenant with them that guarantees their security. I will get rid of all the dangerous animals in the land, so that my sheep can live safely in the fields and sleep in the forests.

26 "I will bless them and let them live around my sacred hill.^a There I will bless them with showers of rain when they need it. 27 The trees will bear fruit, the fields will produce crops, and everyone will live in safety on his own land. When I break my people's chains and set them free from those who made them slaves, then they will know that I am the LORD. 28 The heathen nations will not plunder them any more, and the wild animals will not kill and eat them. They will live in safety, and no one will terrify them. 29 I will give them fertile fields and put an end to hunger in the land. The other nations will not sneer at them any more. 30 Everyone will know that I protect Israel and that they are my people. I, the Sovereign LORD, have spoken.

31 "You, my sheep, the flock that I feed, are my people, and I am your God," says the Sovereign LORD.

God's Punishment of Edom

35 1 The LORD spoke to me. 2 "Mortal man," he said, "denounce the country of Edom. 3 Tell the people what I, the Sovereign LORD, am saying:

---

^a **34:26** SACRED HILL: *See 20:40.*
34:23 Rev 7:17   **34:24** Ezek 37:24   **35:1–15** Isa 34:5–17; 63:1–6; Jer 49:7–22; Ezek 25:12–14; Am 1:11, 12; Ob 1–14; Mal 1:2–5

"I am your enemy, mountains of Edom!
I will make you a desolate wasteland.
⁴I will leave your cities in ruins
And your land desolate;
Then you will know that I am the LORD.

⁵"You were Israel's constant enemy and let her people be slaughtered in the time of her disaster, the time of final punishment for her sins. ⁶So then—as surely as I, the Sovereign LORD, am the living God—death is your fate, and you cannot escape it. You are guilty of *ᵇ* murder, and murder will follow you. ⁷I will make the hill country of Edom a wasteland and kill everyone who travels through it. ⁸I will cover the mountains with corpses, and the bodies of those who are killed in battle will cover the hills and valleys. ⁹I will make you desolate forever, and no one will live in your cities again. Then you will know that I am the LORD.

¹⁰"You said that the two nations, Judah and Israel, together with their lands, belonged to you and that you would possess them, even though I, the LORD, was their God. ¹¹So then, as surely as I, the Sovereign LORD, am the living God, I will pay you back for your anger, your jealousy, and your hate toward my people. They will know that I am punishing you for what you did to them. ¹²Then you will know that I, the LORD, heard you say with contempt that the mountains of Israel were desolate and that they were yours to devour. ¹³I have heard the wild, boastful way you have talked against me."

¹⁴The Sovereign LORD says, "I will make you so desolate that the whole world will rejoice at your downfall, ¹⁵just as you rejoiced at the devastation of Israel, my own possession. The mountains of Seir, yes, all the land of Edom, will be desolate. Then everyone will know that I am the LORD."

God's Blessing on Israel

36 ¹The LORD said, "Mortal man, speak to the mountains of Israel and tell them to listen to the message which I, ²the Sovereign LORD, have for them: Israel's ene-

Study It!

Punishment and Promises

In the first part of the Book of Ezekiel, God wants the Israelites to know he is a just God who will punish them for their sins. In the second part, God wants them to know that he is a loving God who forgives them. God also lets them know that he will hear their prayers again and bring them back to the land of their birth. It is God's way of restoring his holy name.

Read about all the wonderful promises God makes to the Israelites in Ezekiel, chapter 36. But of all these promises, perhaps the most important is. . . . Well, check out verses 26–27 for the answer.

— Ezekiel, chapter 36

mies gloated and said, 'Now those ancient hills are ours!'

³"Prophesy, then, and announce what I, the Sovereign LORD, am saying. When the neighboring nations captured and plundered the mountains of Israel, everyone made fun of Israel. ⁴So now listen to what I, the Sovereign LORD, say to you mountains and hills, to you brooks and valleys, to you places that were left in ruins, and to you deserted cities which were plundered and mocked by all the surrounding nations.

⁵"I, the Sovereign LORD, have spoken out in the heat of my anger against the surrounding nations, and especially against Edom. With glee and contempt they captured my land and took possession of its pastures.

⁶"So prophesy to the land of Israel; tell the mountains, hills, brooks, and valleys what I, the Sovereign LORD, am saying in jealous anger because of the way the nations have insulted and humiliated them. ⁷I, the

*ᵇ **35:6** One ancient translation* are guilty of; *Hebrew* hate.

Sovereign LORD, solemnly promise that the surrounding nations will be humiliated. 8But on the mountains of Israel the trees will again grow leaves and bear fruit for you, my people Israel. You are going to come home soon. 9I am on your side, and I will make sure that your land is plowed again and crops are planted on it. 10I will make your population grow. You will live in the cities and rebuild everything that was left in ruins. 11I will make people and cattle increase in number. There will be more of you than ever before, and you will have many children. I will let you live there as you used to live, and I will make you more prosperous than ever. Then you will know that I am the LORD. 12I will bring you, my people Israel, back to live again in the land. It will be your own land, and it will never again let your children starve.

13"I, the Sovereign LORD, say: It is true that people say that the land eats people and that it robs the nation of its children. 14But from now on it will no longer eat people and rob you of your children. I, the Sovereign LORD, have spoken. 15The land will no longer have to listen to the nations making fun of it or see the peoples sneer at it. The land will no longer rob the nation of its children. I, the Sovereign LORD, have spoken."

Israel's New Life

16The LORD spoke to me. 17"Mortal man," he said, "when the Israelites were living in their land, they defiled it by the way they lived and acted. I regarded their behavior as being as ritually unclean as a woman is during her monthly period.c 18I let them feel the force of my anger because of the murders they had committed in the land and because of the idols by which they had defiled it. 19I condemned them for the way they lived and acted, and I scattered them through foreign countries. 20Wherever they went, they brought disgrace on my holy name, because people would say, 'These are the people of the LORD, but they had to leave his land.' 21That made me concerned for my holy name, since the Israelites

brought disgrace on it everywhere they went.

22"Now then, give the Israelites the message that I, the Sovereign LORD, have for them: What I am going to do is not for the sake of you Israelites, but for the sake of my holy name, which you have disgraced in every country where you have gone. 23When I demonstrate to the nations the holiness of my great name—the name you disgraced among them—then they will know that I am the LORD. I, the Sovereign LORD, have spoken. I will use you to show the nations that I am holy. 24I will take you from every nation and country and bring you back to your own land. 25I will sprinkle clean water on you and make you clean from all your idols and everything else that has defiled you. 26I will give you a new heart and a new mind. I will take away your stubborn heart of stone and give you an obedient heart. 27I will put my spirit in you and will see to it that you follow my laws and keep all the commands I have given you. 28Then you will live in the land I gave your ancestors. You will be my people, and I will be your God. 29I will save you from everything that defiles you. I will command the grain to be plentiful, so that you will not have any more famines. 30I will increase the yield of your fruit trees and your fields, so that there will be no more famines to disgrace you among the nations. 31You will remember your evil conduct and the wrongs that you committed, and you will be disgusted with yourselves because of your sins and your iniquities. 32Israel, I want you to know that I am not doing all this for your sake. I want you to feel the shame and disgrace of what you are doing. I, the Sovereign LORD, have spoken."

33The Sovereign LORD says, "When I make you clean from all your sins, I will let you live in your cities again and let you rebuild the ruins. 34Everyone who used to walk by your fields saw how overgrown and wild they were, but I will let you farm them again. 35Everyone will talk about how this land, which was once a wilderness, has become like the Garden of Eden, and how

---

c **36:17** RITUALLY UNCLEAN . . . PERIOD: *This is based on the view of ritual uncleanness described in the Law of Moses (see Lev 15:19).*
36:26–28 Ezek 11:19, 20

Ezekiel

Pray It!

Praying with New Life

The beginning of Ezekiel's dream sounds like a scene from a horror movie. The ground is covered with dry bones. He has a conversation with God. All of a sudden he hears rattling. He can't quite believe what he's seeing! The bones are forming into bodies! They're being covered with muscles and skin! Then Ezekiel commands the wind (which represents the Holy Spirit) to blow in the name of God. The bodies start to move. They're alive! But it isn't frightening; it is exciting and hopeful.

Our prayer life can sometimes be like dry bones, that is, it doesn't seem to have much energy or meaning. Have you ever experienced any of the following three situations?

- You said prayers without thinking about their meaning.
- You've gone to Mass but didn't participate.
- You talked to God but didn't listen.

If you said yes to any of these, you've experienced a "dry bones" prayer life. Remember what turned a stack of lifeless bones into live bodies: the Word of God and the Holy Spirit. When you feel like your prayer life needs new life, listen to God's Word and pray to the Holy Spirit to breathe into your heart.

— Ezekiel, chapter 37

the cities which were torn down, looted, and left in ruins, are now inhabited and fortified. 36 Then the neighboring nations that have survived will know that I, the LORD, rebuild ruined cities and replant waste fields. I, the LORD, have promised that I would do this—and I will."

37 The Sovereign LORD says, "I will once again let the Israelites ask me for help, and I will let them increase in numbers like a flock of sheep. 38 The cities that are now in ruins will then be as full of people as Jerusalem was once full of the sheep which were offered as sacrifices at a festival. Then they will know that I am the LORD."

The Valley of Dry Bones

37 ¹I felt the powerful presence of the LORD, and his spirit took me and set me down in a valley where the ground was covered with bones. ²He led me all around the valley, and I could see that there were very many bones and that they were very dry. ³He said to me, "Mortal man, can these bones come back to life?"

I replied, "Sovereign LORD, only you can answer that!"

⁴He said, "Prophesy to the bones. Tell these dry bones to listen to the word of the LORD. ⁵Tell them that I, the Sovereign LORD, am saying to them: I am going to put breath into you and bring you back to life. ⁶I will give you sinews and muscles, and cover you with skin. I will put breath into you and

I could see that there were very many bones. (37:2)

"I will take away your stubborn heart of stone and give you an obedient heart" (Ezekiel 36:26).

Ezekiel

bring you back to life. Then you will know that I am the LORD."

7 So I prophesied as I had been told. While I was speaking, I heard a rattling noise, and the bones began to join together. 8 While I watched, the bones were covered with sinews and muscles, and then with skin. But there was no breath in the bodies.

9 God said to me, "Mortal man, prophesy to the wind.d Tell the wind that the Sovereign LORD commands it to come from every direction, to breathe into these dead bodies, and to bring them back to life."

10 So I prophesied as I had been told. Breath entered the bodies, and they came to life and stood up. There were enough of them to form an army.

11 God said to me, "Mortal man, the people of Israel are like these bones. They say that they are dried up, without any hope and with no future. 12 So prophesy to my people Israel and tell them that I, the Sovereign LORD, am going to open their graves. I am going to take them out and bring them back to the land of Israel. 13 When I open the graves where my people are buried and bring them out, they will know that I am the LORD. 14 I will put my breath in them, bring them back to life, and let them live in their own land. Then they will know that I am the LORD. I have promised that I would do this—and I will. I, the LORD, have spoken."

Judah and Israel in One Kingdom

15 The LORD spoke to me again. 16 "Mortal man," he said, "take a wooden stick and write on it the words, 'The kingdom of Judah.' Then take another stick and write on it the words, 'The kingdom of Israel.' 17 Then hold the two sticks end to end in your hand so that they look like one stick. 18 When your people ask you to tell them what this means, 19 tell them that I, the Sovereign LORD, am going to take the stick representing Israel and put it with the one that repre-

sents Judah. Out of the two I will make one stick and hold it in my hand.

20 "Hold in your hand the two sticks and let the people see them. 21 Then tell them that I, the Sovereign LORD, am going to take all my people out of the nations where they have gone, gather them together, and bring them back to their own land. 22 I will unite them into one nation in the land, on the mountains of Israel. They will have one king to rule over them, and they will no longer be divided into two nations or split into two kingdoms. 23 They will not defile themselves with disgusting idols any more or corrupt themselves with sin. I will free them from all the ways in which they sin and betray me. I will purify them; they will be my people, and I will be their God. 24 A king like my servant David will be their king. They will all be united under one ruler and will obey my laws faithfully. 25 They will live on the land I gave to my servant Jacob, the land where their ancestors lived. They will live there forever, and so will their children and all their descendants. A king like my servant David will rule them forever. 26 I will make a covenant with them that guarantees their security forever. I will establish them and increase their population, and will see to it that my Temple stands forever in their land. 27 I will live there with them; I will be their God, and they will be my people. 28 When I place my Temple there to be among them forever, then the nations will know that I, the LORD, have chosen Israel to be my own people."

Gog as the Instrument of God

38 1 The LORD spoke to me. 2 "Mortal man," he said, "denounce Gog, chief ruler of the nations of Meshech and Tubal in the land of Magog. Denounce him 3 and tell him that I, the Sovereign LORD, am his enemy. 4 I will turn him around, put hooks in his jaws, and drag him and all his troops

---

d **37:9** wind; or spirit. The same Hebrew word may mean wind, or spirit, or breath.
37:10 Rev 11:11   **37:24** Ezek 34:24   **37:27** 2 Cor 6:16; Rev 21:3   **38:2** Rev 20:8

In English, the words *wind, breath,* and *spirit* each have a different meaning. In Hebrew one word, *ruah,* is used to mean all three things.

away. His army, with its horses and uniformed riders, is enormous, and every soldier carries a shield and is armed with a sword. 5 Troops from Persia, Ethiopia,*e* and Libya are with him, and all have shields and helmets. 6 All the fighting men of the lands of Gomer and Beth Togarmah in the north are with him, and so are men from many other nations. 7 Tell him to get ready and have all his troops ready at his command. 8 After many years I will order him to invade a country where the people were brought back together from many nations and have lived without fear of war. He will invade the mountains of Israel, which were desolate and deserted so long, but where all the people now live in safety. 9 He and his army and the many nations with him will attack like a storm and cover the land like a cloud."

10 This is what the Sovereign LORD says to Gog: "When that time comes, you will start thinking up an evil plan. 11 You will decide to invade a helpless country where the people live in peace and security in unwalled towns that have no defenses. 12 You will plunder and loot the people who live in cities that were once in ruins. They have been gathered from the nations, and now they have livestock and property and live at the crossroads of the world. 13 The people of Sheba and Dedan and the merchants from the towns of Spain will ask you, 'Have you assembled your army and attacked in order to loot and plunder? Do you intend to get silver and gold, livestock and property, and march off with all those spoils?' "

14 So the Sovereign LORD sent me to tell Gog what he was saying to him: "Now while my people Israel live in security, you will set out*f* 15 to come from your place in the far north, leading a large, powerful army of soldiers from many nations, all of them on horseback. 16 You will attack my people Israel like a storm moving across the land. When the time comes, I will send you to invade my land in order to show the nations who I am, to show my holiness by what I do through you. 17 You are the one I was talking

about long ago, when I announced through my servants, the prophets of Israel, that in days to come I would bring someone to attack Israel." The Sovereign LORD has spoken.

God's Punishment of Gog

18 The Sovereign LORD says, "On the day when Gog invades Israel, I will become furious. 19 I declare in the heat of my anger that on that day there will be a severe earthquake in the land of Israel. 20 Every fish and bird, every animal large and small, and every human being on the face of the earth will tremble for fear of me. Mountains will fall, cliffs will crumble, and every wall will collapse. 21 I will terrify Gog with all sorts of calamities.*g* I, the Sovereign LORD, have spoken. His men will turn their swords against one another. 22 I will punish him with disease and bloodshed. Torrents of rain and hail, together with fire and sulfur, will pour down on him and his army and on the many nations that are on his side. 23 In this way I will show all the nations that I am great and that I am holy. They will know then that I am the LORD."

The Defeat of Gog

39 1 The Sovereign LORD said, "Mortal man, denounce Gog, the chief ruler of the nations of Meshech and Tubal, and tell him that I am his enemy. 2 I will turn him in a new direction and lead him out of the far north until he comes to the mountains of Israel. 3 Then I will knock his bow out of his left hand and his arrows out of his right hand. 4 Gog and his army and his allies will fall dead on the mountains of Israel, and I will let their bodies be food for all the birds and wild animals. 5 They will fall dead in the open field. I, the Sovereign LORD, have spoken. 6 I will start a fire in the land of Magog and along all the seacoasts where people live undisturbed, and everyone will know that I am the LORD. 7 I will make sure that my

---

e 38:5 Hebrew Cush: Cush is the ancient name of the extensive territory south of the First Cataract of the Nile River. This region was called Ethiopia in Graeco-Roman times, and included within its borders most of modern Sudan and some of present-day Ethiopia (Abyssinia).   f 38:14 One ancient translation set out; Hebrew know.   g 38:21 One ancient translation terrify . . . calamities; Hebrew unclear.

people Israel know my holy name, and I will not let my name be disgraced any more. Then the nations will know that I, the LORD, am the holy God of Israel."

⁸The Sovereign LORD said, "The day I spoke about is certain to come. ⁹The people who live in the cities of Israel will go out and collect the abandoned weapons for firewood. They will build fires with the shields, bows, arrows, spears, and clubs, and have enough to last for seven years. ¹⁰They will not have to gather firewood in the fields or cut down trees in the forest, because they will have the abandoned weapons to burn. They will loot and plunder those who looted and plundered them." The Sovereign LORD has spoken.

The Burial of Gog

¹¹The LORD said, "When all this happens, I will give Gog a burial ground there in Israel, in Travelers' Valley, east of the Dead Sea.ʰ Gog and all his army will be buried there, and the valley will be called 'The Valley of Gog's Army.' ¹²It will take the Israelites seven months to bury all the corpses and make the land clean again. ¹³Everyone in the land will help bury them, and they will be honored for this on the day of my victory. I, the Sovereign LORD, have spoken. ¹⁴After the seven months are over, men will be chosen to travel through the land in order to find and bury those bodiesⁱ remaining on the ground, so that they can make the land clean. ¹⁵As they go up and down the country, every time they find a human bone, they will put a marker beside it so that the gravediggers can come and bury it in the Valley of Gog's Army. ¹⁶(There will be a town nearby named after the army.) And so the land will be made clean again."

¹⁷The Sovereign LORD said to me, "Mortal man, call all the birds and animals to come from all around to eat the sacrifice I am preparing for them. It will be a huge feast on the mountains of Israel, where they can eat meat and drink blood. ¹⁸They are to

eat the bodies of soldiers and drink the blood of the rulers of the earth, all of whom will be killed like rams or lambs or goats or fat bulls. ¹⁹When I kill these people like sacrifices, the birds and animals are to eat all the fat they can hold and to drink blood until they are drunk. ²⁰At my table they will eat all they can hold of horses and their riders and of soldiers and fighting men. I, the Sovereign LORD, have spoken."

The Restoration of Israel

²¹The LORD said, "I will let the nations see my glory and show them how I use my power to carry out my just decisions. ²²The Israelites will know from then on that I am the LORD their God. ²³And the nations will know that the Israelites went into exile because of the sins which they committed against me. I turned away from them and let their enemies defeat them and kill them in battle. ²⁴I gave them what they deserved for their uncleanness and their wickedness, and I turned away from them."

²⁵The Sovereign LORD said, "But now I will be merciful to Jacob's descendants, the people of Israel, and make them prosperous again. I will protect my holy name. ²⁶When they are once more living in safety in their own land, with no one to threaten them, they will be able to forget how they were disgraced for having betrayed me. ²⁷In order to show to the many nations that I am holy, I will bring my people back from all the countries where their enemies live. ²⁸Then my people will know that I am the LORD their God. They will know this, because I sent them into captivity and now gather them and bring them back into their own land, not leaving even one of them behind. ²⁹I will pour out my spirit on the people of Israel and never again turn away from them. I, the Sovereign LORD, have spoken."

ʰ **39:11** *Hebrew has four additional words, the meaning of which is unclear.*   ⁱ **39:14** *Some ancient translations* those bodies; *Hebrew* the travelers.
39:17–20 Rev 19:17, 18

A VISION OF THE FUTURE TEMPLE (40:1—48:35)

Ezekiel Is Taken to Jerusalem

40 ¹It was the tenth day of the new year, which was the twenty-fifth year after we had been taken into exile and the fourteenth year after Jerusalem was captured. On that day I felt the powerful presence of the LORD, and he carried me away. ²In a vision God took me to the land of Israel and put me on a high mountain. I saw in front of me*ʲ* a group of buildings that looked like a city. ³He took me closer, and I saw a man who shone like bronze. He was holding a linen tape measure and a measuring rod and was standing by a gateway.

He was holding a linen tape measure. (40:3)

⁴He said to me, "Watch, mortal man. Listen carefully and pay close attention to everything I show you, because this is why you were brought here. You are to tell the people of Israel everything you see."

The East Gate

⁵What I saw was the Temple, and there was a wall around it. The man took his mea-suring rod, which was 10 feet long, and measured the wall. It was 10 feet high and 10 feet thick. ⁶Then he went to the gateway that faced east. He went up the steps, and at the top he measured the entrance; it was 10 feet deep.*ᵏ* ⁷Beyond it there was a passageway, which had three guardrooms on each side. Each of the rooms was square, 10 feet on each side, and the walls between them were 8 feet thick. Beyond the guardrooms there was a passageway 10 feet long that led to an entrance room which faced the Temple. ⁸⁻⁹He measured this room and found it was 14 feet deep. It formed that end of the gateway which was nearest the Temple, and at its far end the walls were 4 feet thick. (¹⁰These guardrooms on each side of the passageway were all the same size, and the walls between them were all of the same thickness.)

¹¹Next, the man measured the width of the passageway in the gateway. It was 22 feet altogether, and the space between the open gates was 16 feet. ¹²In front of each of the guardrooms there was a low wall 20 inches high and 20 inches thick. (The rooms were 10 feet square.) ¹³Then he measured the distance from the back wall*ˡ* of one room to the back wall*ˡ* of the room across the passageway from it, and it was 42 feet. ¹⁴The room at the far end led out to a courtyard. He measured that room and found it was 34 feet wide.*ᵐ* ¹⁵The total length of the gateway from the outside wall of the gate to the far side of the last room was 84 feet. ¹⁶There were small openings in the outside walls of all the rooms and also in the inner walls between the rooms. There were palm trees carved on the inner walls that faced the passageway.

The Outer Courtyard

¹⁷The man took me through the gateway into the courtyard. There were thirty rooms built against the outer wall, and in front of

---

ʲ **40:2** *One ancient translation* in front of me; *Hebrew* in the south.   *ᵏ* **40:6** *One ancient translation* deep; *Hebrew* deep, one entrance 10 feet deep.   *ˡ* **40:13** *Probable text* back wall; *Hebrew* roof.   *ᵐ* **40:14** *Verse 14 in Hebrew is unclear.*

40:2 Rev 21:10   **40:3** Rev 11:1; 21:15   **40:5—42:20** 1 Kings 6:1–38; 2 Chr 3:1–9 them there was an area paved with stones, [18]which extended around the courtyard. This outer courtyard was at a lower level than the inner courtyard.

[19]There was a gateway at a higher level that led to the inner courtyard. The man measured the distance between the two gateways, and it was 168 feet.[n]

The North Gate

[20]Then the man measured the gateway on the north side that led into the outer courtyard. [21]The three guardrooms on each side of the passageway, the walls between them, and the entrance room all had the same measurements as those in the east gateway. The total length of the gateway was 84 feet and the width 42 feet. [22]The entrance room, the windows, and the carved palm trees were like those in the east gate. Here seven steps led up to the gate, and the entrance room was at the end facing the courtyard. [23]Across the courtyard from this north gateway was another gateway leading to the inner courtyard, just as there was on the east side. The man measured the distance between these two gateways, and it was 168 feet.

The South Gate

[24]Next, the man took me to the south side, and there we saw another gateway. He measured its inner walls and its entrance room, and they were the same as the others. [25]There were windows in the rooms of this gateway just as in the others. The total length of the gateway was 84 feet and the width 42 feet. [26]Seven steps led up to it, and its entrance room was also at the end facing the courtyard. There were palm trees carved on the inner walls that faced the passageway. [27]Here, too, there was a gateway leading to the inner courtyard. The man measured the distance to this second gateway, and it was 168 feet.

The Inner Courtyard: The South Gate

[28]The man took me through the south gateway into the inner courtyard. He measured the gateway, and it was the same size as the gateways in the outer wall. [29-30]Its guardrooms, its entrance room, and its inner walls were the same size as those in the other gateways. There were also windows in the rooms of this gateway. The total length was 84 feet and the width 42 feet. [31]Its entrance room faced the other courtyard, and palm trees were carved on the walls along the passageway. Eight steps led up to this gate.

The Inner Courtyard: The East Gate

[32]The man took me through the east gateway into the inner courtyard. He measured the gateway, and it was the same size as the others. [33]Its guardrooms, its entrance room, and its inner walls measured the same as those in the other gateways. There were windows all around, and in the entrance room also. The total length was 84 feet and the width 42 feet. [34]The entrance room faced the outer courtyard. Palm trees were carved on the walls along the passageway. Eight steps led up to this gate.

The Inner Courtyard: The North Gate

[35]Then the man took me to the north gateway. He measured it, and it was the same size as the others. [36]Like them, it also had guardrooms, decorated inner walls, an entrance room, and windows all around. Its total length was 84 feet and its width 42 feet. [37]The entrance room[o] faced the outer courtyard. Palm trees were carved on the walls along the passageway. Eight steps led up to this gate.

Buildings Near the North Gate

[38]In the outer courtyard there was an annex attached to the inner gateway on the

---

[n] **40:19** Hebrew has two additional words, the meaning of which is unclear.   [o] **40:37** Some ancient translations entrance room; Hebrew inner wall.

Check out 1 Corinthians 3:16–17 for Saint Paul's description of the Church as the Temple of the Holy Spirit.

north side. It opened into the entrance room that faced the courtyard, and there they washed the carcasses of the animals to be burned whole as sacrifices. 39 In this entrance room there were four tables, two on each side of the room. It was on these tables that they killed the animals to be offered as sacrifices, either to be burned whole or to be sacrifices for sin or as repayment offerings. 40 Outside the room there were four similar tables, two on either side of the entrance of the north gate. 41 Altogether there were eight tables on which the animals to be sacrificed were killed: four inside the room and four out in the courtyard. 42 The four tables in the annex, used to prepare the offerings to be burned whole, were of cut stone. They were 20 inches high, and their tops were 30 inches square. All the equipment used in killing the sacrificial animals was kept on these tables. 43 Ledges 3 inches wide ran around the edge of the tables. All the meat to be offered in sacrifice was placed on the tables.*p*

44 Then he brought me into the inner court. There were two rooms opening on the inner court, one facing south beside the north gateway and the other facing north beside the south gateway.*q* 45 The man told me that the room which faced south was for the priests who served in the Temple, 46 and the room which faced north was for the priests who served at the altar. All the priests are descended from Zadok; they are the only members of the tribe of Levi who are permitted to go into the LORD's presence to serve him.

The Inner Courtyard and the Temple Building

47 The man measured the inner courtyard, and it was 168 feet square. The Temple was on the west side, and in front of it was an altar. 48 Then he took me into the entrance room of the Temple. He measured the entranceway: it was 9 feet deep and 24 feet wide,*r* with walls 5 feet thick on either side. 49 Steps led up to the entrance room, which was 34 feet

wide and 20 feet deep.*s* There were two columns, one on each side of the entrance.

41 ¹ Next, the man took me into the central room, the Holy Place. He measured the passageway into it: it was 10 feet deep*t* ² and 18 feet wide, with walls 8 feet thick on either side. He measured the room itself: it was 68 feet long and 34 feet wide.

³ Then he went to the innermost room. He measured the passageway into it: it was 3 feet deep and 10 feet wide, with walls on either side 12 feet thick.*u* ⁴ He measured the room itself, and it was 34 feet square. This room was beyond the central room. Then he said to me, "This is the Most Holy Place."

The Rooms Built against the Temple Walls

⁵ The man measured the thickness of the inner wall of the Temple building, and it was 10 feet. Against this wall, all around the Temple, was a series of small rooms 7 feet wide. ⁶ These rooms were in three stories, with thirty rooms on each floor. The Temple's outer wall on each floor was thinner than on the floor below, so that the rooms could rest on the wall without being anchored into it. ⁷ And so the Temple walls, when seen from the outside, seemed to have the same thickness all the way to the top. Against the Temple's outer wall, on the outside of the rooms, two wide stairways were built, so that it was possible to go from the lower story to the middle and the upper stories.*v* ⁸⁻¹¹ The outside wall of these rooms was 8 feet thick; there was one door into the rooms on the north side of the Temple, and one into those on the south side. I saw that there was a terrace 8 feet wide around the Temple; it was 10 feet above the ground and it was level with the foundation of the rooms by the Temple walls. Between the terrace and the buildings used by the priests there was an open space 34 feet across, along the sides of the Temple.

---

p **40:43** *Verse 43 in Hebrew is unclear.*   *q* **40:44** *One ancient translation* Then . . . south gateway; *verse 44 in Hebrew is unclear.*   *r* **40:48** *One ancient translation* and 24 feet wide; *Hebrew does not have these words.*   *s* **40:49** *One ancient translation* 20 feet deep; *Hebrew* 18 feet deep.   *t* **41:1** *Hebrew has two additional words, the meaning of which is unclear.*   *u* **41:3** *One ancient translation* with walls on either side 12 feet thick; *Hebrew and* 12 feet thick.
v **41:7** *Verse 7 in Hebrew is unclear.*

Ezekiel

God, the Builder

Ca[+]holic Connec[+]ions

Ezekiel's last vision is of a rebuilt Temple in Jerusalem. Chapters 40–42 of Ezekiel are full of measurements, descriptions of areas, and floor plans. Lots of details are included, right down to the palm trees carved on the walls.

The Temple of Jerusalem in Ezekiel's vision was a magnificent place. It was a place where God dwelled again in glory. Ezekiel's vision did come true in the sense that the Temple was rebuilt when King Cyrus allowed the Jews who were in captivity in Babylon to return to Jerusalem.

In the New Testament, Saint Paul calls the Church the Temple of the Holy Spirit. That means that the Holy Spirit lives in all members of the church in a special way. Because of this Catholics do not believe there is only one place where God can be worshiped. Jesus Christ is present with us through the power of the Holy Spirit wherever we gather in God's name.

— Ezekiel 41:15–21

The Building on the West

¹²At the far end of the open space on the west side of the Temple there was a building 150 feet long and 116 feet wide; its walls were 9 feet thick all around.

The Total Measurements of the Temple Building

¹³The man measured the outside of the Temple, and it was 168 feet long. And from the back of the Temple, across the open space to the far side of the building to the west, the distance was also 168 feet. ¹⁴The distance across the front of the Temple, including the open space on either side, was also 168 feet. ¹⁵He measured the length of the building to the west, including its galleries on both sides, and it was also 168 feet.

Details of the Temple Building

The entrance room of the Temple, the Holy Place, and the Most Holy Place ¹⁶were all paneled with wood from the floor to the windows. These windows could be covered. ʷ ¹⁷The inside walls of the Temple, up as high as above the doors, were completely covered with carvings ˣ ¹⁸of palm trees and winged creatures. Palm trees alternated with creatures, one following the other, all the way around the room. Each creature had two faces: ¹⁹a human face that was turned toward the palm tree on one side, and a lion's face that was turned toward the tree on the other side. It was like this all around the wall, ²⁰from the floor to above the doors. ²¹The doorposts of the Holy Place were square.

The Wooden Altar

In front of the entrance of the Most Holy Place there was something that looked like ²²a wooden altar. It was 5 feet high and 4 feet wide. Its corner posts, its base, ʸ and its sides were all made of wood. The man said to me, "This is the table which stands in the presence of the LORD."

ʷ **41:16** *Verse 16 in Hebrew is unclear.*   ˣ **41:17** *Verse 17 in Hebrew is unclear.*   ʸ **41:22** *Some ancient translations* base; *Hebrew* length.

The Doors

23There was a door at the end of the passageway to the Holy Place and one also at the end of the passageway to the Most Holy Place. **24**They were double doors that swung open in the middle. **25**There were palm trees and winged creatures carved on the doors of the Holy Place, just as there were on the walls. And there was a wooden covering over the outside of the doorway of the entrance room. **26**At the sides of this room there were windows, and the walls were decorated with palm trees.ᶻ

Two Buildings Near the Temple

42 **1**Then the man took me into the outer courtyard and led me to a building on the north side of the Temple, not far from the building at the west end of the Temple. **2**This building was 168 feet long and 84 feet wide. **3**On one side it faced the space 34 feet wide which was alongside the Temple, and on the other side it faced the pavement of the outer courtyard. It was built on three levels, each one set further back than the one below it. **4**Along the north side of this building was a passageway 16 feet wide and 168 feet long,ᵃ with entrances on that side. **5**The rooms at the upper level of the building were narrower than those at the middle and lower levels because they were set further back. **6**The rooms at all three levels were on terraces and were not supported by columns like the other buildings in the courtyard. **7-8**At the lower level the outer wall of the building was solid for 84 feet, half its length; and there were rooms in the remaining 84 feet. At the top level there were rooms in the entire length of the building. **9-10**Below these rooms at the east end of the building, where the wall of the courtyard began,ᵇ there was an entrance into the outer courtyard.

At the southᶜ side of the Temple there was an identical building not far from the building at the west end of the Temple. **11**In front of the rooms there was a passageway just like the one on the north side. It had the same measurements, the same design, and the same kind of entrances. **12**There was a door under the rooms on the south side of the building, at the east end where the wall began.

13The man said to me, "Both these buildings are holy. In them the priests who enter the LORD's presence eat the holiest offerings. Because the rooms are holy, the priests will place the holiest offerings there: the offerings of grain and the sacrifices offered for sin or as repayment offerings. **14**When priests have been in the Temple and want to go to the outer courtyard, they must leave in these rooms the holy clothing they wore while serving the LORD. They must put on other clothes before going out to the area where the people gather."

The Measurements of the Temple Area

15When the man had finished measuring inside the Temple area, he took me out through the east gate and then measured the outside of the area. **16**He took the measuring rod and measured the east side, and it was 840 feet. **17-19**Then he measured the north side, the south side, and the west side; each side had the same length, 840 feet,ᵈ **20**so that the wall enclosed a square 840 feet on each side. The wall served to separate what was holy from what was not.

The LORD Returns to the Temple

43 **1**The man took me to the gate that faces east, **2**and there I saw coming from the east the dazzling light of the presence of the God of Israel. God's voice

---

ᶻ **41:26** *Hebrew has three additional words, the meaning of which is unclear.*   ᵃ **41:4** *Some ancient translations* 168 feet long; *Hebrew* a way of 20 inches.   ᵇ **41:9–10** *One ancient translation* where the wall of the courtyard began; *Hebrew* in the breadth of the wall of the courtyard.   ᶜ **41:9–10** *One ancient translation* south; *Hebrew* east. ᵈ **41:17–19** *Verses 16–19 in Hebrew are unclear.* **43:2** Ezek 10:3, 4, 18, 19; 11:22, 23; Rev 1:15

Each wall of the Temple area was 840 feet long. That would make each wall how many football fields long? That is a big area!

Ezekiel

sounded like the roar of the sea, and the earth shone with the dazzling light. ³ This vision was like the one I had seen when God came to destroy Jerusalem, and the one I saw by the Chebar River. Then I threw myself face downward on the ground. ⁴ The dazzling light passed through the east gate and went into the Temple.

The dazzling light passed through the east gate. (43:4)

⁵ The LORD's spirit lifted me up and took me into the inner courtyard, where I saw that the Temple was filled with the glory of the LORD. ⁶ The man stood beside me there, and I heard the LORD speak to me out of the Temple: ⁷ "Mortal man, here is my throne. I will live here among the people of Israel and rule them forever. Neither the people of Israel nor their kings will ever again disgrace my holy name by worshiping other gods or by burying the corpses of ᵉ their dead kings. ⁸ The kings built the doorsills and doorposts of their palace right against the doorsills and doorposts of my Temple, so that there was only a wall between us. They disgraced my holy name by all the disgusting things they did, and so in my anger I destroyed them. ⁹ Now they must stop worshiping other gods and remove the corpses of ᶠ their kings. If they do, I will live among them forever."

¹⁰ And the LORD continued, "Mortal man, tell the people of Israel about the Temple, and let them study its plan. Make them ashamed of their sinful actions. ¹¹ Then if they are ashamed of what they have done, explain the plan of the Temple to them: its design, its entrances and exits, its shape, the arrangement of everything, and all its rules and regulations. Write all this down for them so that they can see how everything is arranged and can carry out all the rules. ¹² This is the law of the Temple: All the area surrounding it on the top of the mountain is sacred and holy."

The Altar

¹³ These are the measurements of the altar, using the same unit of measure as in measuring the Temple. All around the base of the altar there was a gutter 20 inches deep and 20 inches wide, with a rim at the outside edge 10 inches high. ¹⁴ The lowest section of the altar, from the top of the base, was 4 feet high. The next section was set back from the edge 20 inches all around, and was 7 feet high. The section after that was also set back from the edge 20 inches all around. ¹⁵ This top section, on which the sacrifices were burned, was also 7 feet high. The projections on the four corners were higher than the rest of the top. ¹⁶ The top of the altar was a square, 20 feet on each side. ¹⁷ The middle section was also a square, 24 feet on each side, with a rim at the outside edge 10 inches high. (The gutter was 20 inches wide.) The steps going up the altar were on the east side.

The Consecration of the Altar

¹⁸ The Sovereign LORD said to me, "Mortal man, listen to what I tell you. When the altar is built, you are to dedicate it by burn-

---

ᵉ **43:7** *by burying the corpses of; or by putting up monuments to.* ᶠ **43:9** *remove the corpses of; or remove the monuments to.*
43:13–17 Ex 27:1, 2; 2 Chr 4:1 **43:18–27** Ex 29:35–37; 1 Macc 4:52–56

The east gate of the Temple was to stay closed, a sign that God would never leave the Israelites again *(Ezekiel 44:1–2).*

ing sacrifices on it and by sprinkling on it the blood of the animals that were sacrificed. 19 Those priests belonging to the tribe of Levi who are descended from Zadok are the only ones who are to come into my presence to serve me. I, the Sovereign LORD, command this. You will give them a young bull to offer as a sacrifice for sin. 20 You are to take some of its blood and put it on the projections on the top corners of the altar, on the corners of the middle section of the altar, and all around its edges. In this way you will purify the altar and consecrate it. 21 You are to take the bull that is offered as a sacrifice for sin and burn it at the specified place outside the Temple area. 22 The next day you are to take a male goat without any defects and offer it as a sacrifice for sin. Purify the altar with its blood the same way you did with the bull. 23 When you have finished doing that, take a young bull and a young ram, both of them without any defects, 24 and bring them to me. The priests will sprinkle salt on them and burn them as an offering to me. 25 Each day for seven days you are to offer a goat, a bull, and a ram as sacrifices for sin. All of them must be without any defects. 26 For seven days the priests are to consecrate the altar and make it ready for use. 27 When the week is over, the priests are to begin offering on the altar the burnt offerings and the fellowship offerings of the people. Then I will be pleased with all of you. I, the Sovereign LORD, have spoken."

The Use of the East Gate

44 1 The man led me to the outer gate at the east side of the Temple area. The gate was closed, 2 and the LORD said to me, "This gate will stay closed and will never be opened. No human being is allowed to use it, because I, the LORD God of Israel, have entered through it. It is to remain closed. 3 The ruling prince, however, may go there to eat a holy meal in my presence. He is to enter and leave the gateway through the entrance room at the inner end."

Rules for Admission to the Temple

4 Then the man took me through the north gate to the front of the Temple. As I looked, I saw that the Temple of the LORD was filled with the dazzling light of his presence. I threw myself face downward on the ground, 5 and the LORD said to me, "Mortal man, pay attention to everything you see and hear. I am going to tell you the rules and regulations for the Temple. Note carefully which persons are allowed to go in and out of the Temple, and which persons are not allowed.

6 "Tell those rebellious people of Israel that I, the Sovereign LORD, will no longer tolerate the disgusting things that they have been doing. 7 They have profaned my Temple by letting uncircumcised foreigners, people who do not obey me, enter the Temple when the fat and the blood of the sacrifices are being offered to me. So my people have broken my covenant by all the disgusting things they have done. 8 They have not taken charge of the sacred rituals in my Temple, but instead have put foreigners in charge.

9 "I, the Sovereign LORD, declare that no uncircumcised foreigner, no one who disobeys me, will enter my Temple, not even a foreigner who lives among the people of Israel."

The Levites Are Excluded from the Priesthood

10 The LORD said to me, "I am punishing those Levites who, together with the rest of the people of Israel, deserted me and worshiped idols. 11 They may serve me in the Temple by taking charge of the gates and by performing the work of the Temple. They may kill the animals which the people offer for burnt offerings and for sacrifices, and they are to be on duty to serve the people. 12 But because they conducted the worship of idols for the people of Israel and in this way led the people into sin, I, the Sovereign LORD, solemnly swear that they must be punished. 13 They are not to serve me as priests or to go near anything that is holy to me or to enter the Most Holy Place. This is the punishment for the disgusting things they have done. 14 I

am assigning to them the menial work that is to be done in the Temple."

The Priests

15 The Sovereign LORD said, "Those priests belonging to the tribe of Levi who are descended from Zadok, however, continued to serve me faithfully in the Temple when the rest of the people of Israel turned away from me. So now they are the ones who are to serve me and come into my presence to offer me the fat and the blood of the sacrifices. 16 They alone will enter my Temple, serve at my altar, and conduct the Temple worship. 17 When they enter the gateway to the inner courtyard of the Temple, they are to put on linen clothing. They must not wear anything made of wool when they are on duty in the inner courtyard or in the Temple. 18 So that they won't perspire, they are to wear linen turbans and linen trousers, but no belt. 19 Before they go to the outer courtyard where the people are, they must first take off the clothes they wore on duty in the Temple and leave them in the holy rooms. They are to put on other clothing in order to keep their sacred clothing from harming the people.g

20 "Priests must neither shave their heads nor let their hair grow long. They are to keep it a proper length. 21 Priests must not drink any wine before going into the inner courtyard. 22 No priest may marry a divorced woman; he is to marry only an Israelite virgin or the widow of another priest.

23 "The priests are to teach my people the difference between what is holy and what is not, and between what is ritually clean and what is not. 24 When a legal dispute arises, the priests are to decide the case according to my laws. They are to keep the religious festivals according to my rules and regulations, and they are to keep the Sabbaths holy.

25 "A priest is not to become ritually unclean by touching a corpse, unless it is one of his parents, one of his children or a brother or an unmarried sister. 26 After he has become clean again, he must wait seven days 27 and then go into the inner courtyard of the Temple and offer a sacrifice for his purification, so that he can serve in the Temple again. I, the Sovereign LORD, have spoken.

28 "The priests have the priesthood as their share of what I have given Israel to be handed down from one generation to another. They are not to hold property in Israel; I am all they need. 29 The grain offerings, the sin offerings, and the repayment offerings will be the priests' food, and they are to receive everything in Israel that is set apart for me. 30 The priests are to have the best of all the first harvest and of everything else that is offered to me. Each time the people bake bread, they are to give the priests the first loaf as an offering, and my blessing will rest on their homes. 31 The priests must not eat any bird or animal that dies a natural death or is killed by another animal."

The LORD's Portion of the Country

45 1 When the land is divided to give each tribe a share, one part is to be dedicated to the LORD. It is to be 10 miles long by 8 milesh wide. The entire area will be holy. 2 In this area there is to be a square plot of land for the Temple, 840 feet on each side, entirely surrounded by an open space 84 feet wide. 3 Half of this area, a section 10 miles by 4 miles, is to be measured off; it will contain the Temple, the holiest place of all. 4 It will be a holy part of the country, set aside for the priests who serve the LORD in his Temple. It will contain their houses and the section of land for the Temple. 5 The other half of the area is to be set aside as the possession of the Levites, who do the work in the Temple. There will be towns there for them to live in.i

6 Next to the holy area, another section,

g **44:19** HARMING THE PEOPLE: *It was believed that ordinary people would be harmed by touching something holy.* h **45:1** *One ancient translation* 8 miles; *Hebrew* 4 miles. i **45:5** *One ancient translation* towns there for them to live in; *Hebrew* twenty rooms.
44:17, 18 Ex 28:39–43; Lev 16:4 **44:19** Lev 16:23 **44:20** Lev 21:5 **44:21** Lev 10:9 **44:22** Lev 21:7, 13, 14 **44:23** Lev 10:10 **44:25** Lev 21:1–4 **44:28** Num 18:20 **44:29, 30** Num 18:8–19 **44:31** Lev 22:8

10 miles long and 2 miles wide, is to be set aside for a city where any of the people of Israel may live.

Land for the Prince

⁷Land is also to be set aside for the ruling prince. From the west boundary of the holy area it will extend west to the Mediterranean Sea; and from the east boundary it will extend to the eastern border of the country, so that its length will be the same as the length of one of the areas allotted to the tribes of Israel. ⁸This area will be the share the ruling prince will have in the land of Israel, so that he will no longer oppress the people, but will let the rest of the country belong to the tribes of Israel.

Rules for the Prince

⁹The Sovereign LORD said, "You have sinned too long, you rulers of Israel! Stop your violence and oppression. Do what is right and just. You must never again drive my people off their land. I, the Sovereign LORD, am telling you this.

¹⁰"Everyone must use honest weights and measures:

¹¹"The *ephah* for dry measure is to be equal to the *bath* for liquid measure. The standard is the *homer.ʲ* The resulting measures are as follows:

1 *homer* = 10 *ephahs* = 10 *baths*

¹²"Your weights are to be as follows:

20 *gerahs* = 1 *shekelᵏ*

60 *shekels* = 1 *mina*

¹³⁻¹⁵"This is the basis on which you are to make your offerings:

Wheat: 1/60th of your harvest

Barley: 1/60th of your harvest

Olive oil: 1/100th of the yield of your trees

(Measure it by the *bath:* 10 *baths* = 1 *homer* = 1 *kor.*)

Sheep: 1 sheep out of every 200 from the meadows of Israel

"You are to bring grain offerings, animals to be burned whole, and animals for fellowship offerings, so that your sins will be forgiven. I, the Sovereign LORD, command it.

¹⁶"All the people of the land must takeˡ these offerings to the ruling prince of Israel. ¹⁷It will be his duty to provide the animals to be burned whole, the grain offerings, and the wine offerings for the whole nation of Israel at the New Moon Festivals, the Sabbaths, and the other festivals. He is to provide the sin offerings, the grain offerings, the offerings to be burned whole, and the fellowship offerings, to take away the sins of the people of Israel."

The Festivals
(Exodus 12:1–20; Leviticus 23:33–43)

¹⁸The Sovereign LORD said, "On the first day of the first month you are to sacrifice a bull without any defects and purify the Temple. ¹⁹The priest will take some of the blood of this sin offering and put it on the doorposts of the Temple, on the four corners of the altar, and on the posts of the gateways to the inner courtyard. ²⁰On the seventh day of the month you are to do the same thing on behalf of anyone who sins unintentionally or through ignorance. In this way you will keep the Temple holy.

²¹"On the fourteenth day of the first month you will begin the celebration of the Passover Festival. For seven days everyone will eat bread made without yeast. ²²On the first day of the festival the ruling prince must offer a bull as a sacrifice for his sins and for those of all the people. ²³On each of the seven days of the festival he is to sacrifice to the LORD seven bulls and seven rams

Ezekiel

ʲ **45:11** HOMER: *A unit of dry or liquid measure, about 5 bushels or 175 quarts; so an ephah or a bath would be about 1/2 bushel or 17:5 quarts.* ᵏ **45:12** SHEKEL: *In Ezekiel's time this unit of weight was about 0:4 ounce or 11:4 grams.* ˡ **45:16** *Probable text* must take; *Hebrew unclear.*
45:10 Lev 19:36   **45:21** Ex 12:1–20; Num 28:16–25

Chapter 23 in the Book of Leviticus also describes many Jewish feasts and festivals.

Holy Days

Catholic Connections

The Jews honored God through special festivals in the Temple. Some of these feasts are described in Ezekiel 45:18–25, including the offering for each event. As Catholics, we also honor God through special feasts of the Church called *holy days of obligation*. We are required to go to Mass on these days just as we do on Sunday. Some holy days, like Easter, always fall on a Sunday. The bishop in your diocese may decide to move a holy day to a Sunday or sometimes excuse people from attending Mass on a particular holy day. Generally, we observe six holy days of obligation during the Church year.

- December 25: Christmas
- January 1: Solemnity of the Blessed Virgin Mary, the Mother of God
- Sixth Thursday after Easter: Ascension of the Lord
- August 15: Assumption of the Blessed Virgin Mary
  - November 1: All Saints' Day
    - December 8: Immaculate Conception of the Blessed Virgin Mary

— Ezekiel 45:18–26

without any defects and burn them whole. He is also to sacrifice a male goat each day as a sin offering. 24For each bull and each ram that is sacrificed, there is to be an offering of half a bushel of grain and three quarts of olive oil.

25"For the Festival of Shelters, which begins on the fifteenth day of the seventh month, the prince will offer on each of the seven days the same sacrifice for sin, the same offerings to be burned whole, and the same offerings of grain and olive oil."

The Prince and the Festivals

46 1The Sovereign LORD says, "The east gateway to the inner courtyard must be kept closed during the six working days, but it is to be opened on the Sabbath and at the New Moon Festival. 2The ruling prince will go from the outer courtyard into the entrance room of the gateway and stand beside the posts of the gate while the priests burn his sacrifices whole and offer his fellowship offerings. There at the gate he must worship and then go back out. The gate must not be shut until evening. 3Each Sabbath and each New Moon Festival all the people are also to bow down and worship the LORD in front of the gate. 4On the Sabbath the prince is to bring to the LORD, as sacrifices to be burned whole, six lambs and one ram, all without any defects. 5With each ram he is to bring an offering of half a bushel of grain, and with each lamb he is to bring whatever he wants to give. For each half-bushel of grain offering he is to bring three quarts of olive oil. 6At the New Moon Festival he will offer a young bull, six lambs, and a ram, all without any defects. 7With each bull and each ram the offering is to be half a bushel of grain, and with each lamb the offering is to

45:25 Lev 23:33–36; Num 29:12–38

Notice that Ezekiel refers to the ruler as a prince. Perhaps he wants to emphasize that God alone is king.

be whatever the prince wants to give. Three quarts of olive oil are to be offered with each half-bushel of grain. ⁸The prince must leave the entrance room of the gateway and go out by the same way he went in.

⁹"When the people come to worship the LORD at any festival, those who enter by the north gate are to leave by the south gate after they have worshiped, and those who enter by the south gate are to leave by the north gate. No one may go out by the same way he entered, but must leave by the opposite gate. ¹⁰The prince is to come in when the people come, and leave when they leave. ¹¹On the feast days and at the festivals the grain offering will be half a bushel with each bull or ram, and whatever the worshiper wants to give with each lamb. Three quarts of olive oil are to be offered with each half-bushel of grain.

¹²"When the ruling prince wants to make a voluntary offering to the LORD, either an offering to be burned whole or a fellowship offering, the east gate to the inner courtyard will be opened for him. He is to make the offering in the same way he does on the Sabbath, and the gate is to be closed after he goes back out."

The Daily Offering

¹³The LORD says, "Every morning a one-year-old lamb without any defects is to be burned whole as an offering to the LORD. This offering must be made every day. ¹⁴Also an offering of five pounds of flour is to be made every morning, along with one quart of olive oil for mixing with the flour. The rules for this offering to the LORD are to be in force forever. ¹⁵The lamb, the flour, and the olive oil are to be offered to the LORD every morning forever."

The Prince and the Land

¹⁶The Sovereign LORD commands: "If the ruling prince gives any of the land he owns to one of his sons as a present, it will belong to that son as a part of his family property. ¹⁷But if the ruling prince gives any of his land to anyone who is in his service, it will become the prince's property again when the Year of Restoration[m] comes. It belongs to him, and only he and his sons can own it permanently. ¹⁸The ruling prince must not take any of the people's property away from them. Any land he gives to his sons must be from the land that is assigned to him, so that he will not oppress any of my people by taking their land."

The Temple Kitchens

¹⁹Then the man took me to the entrance of the rooms facing north near the gate on the south side of the inner courtyard. These are holy rooms for the priests. He pointed out a place on the west side of the rooms ²⁰and said, "This is the place where the priests are to boil the meat offered as sacrifices for sin or as repayment offerings, and to bake the offerings of flour, so that nothing holy is carried to the outer courtyard, where it might harm the people."[n]

²¹⁻²²Then he led me to the outer courtyard and showed me that in each of its four corners there was a smaller[o] courtyard, 68 feet long and 48 feet wide. ²³Each one had a stone wall around it, with fireplaces built against the wall. ²⁴The man told me, "These are the kitchens where the Temple servants are to boil the sacrifices the people offer."

The Stream Flowing from the Temple

47 ¹The man led me back to the entrance of the Temple. Water was coming out from under the entrance and flowing east, the direction the Temple faced. It was flowing down from under the south part of the Temple past the south side of the altar. ²The man then took me out of the Temple area by way of the north gate and led me around to the gate that faces east. A

---

m **46:17** YEAR OF RESTORATION: *Every fifty years, all Israelites were required to give freedom to any Israelites who had become slaves because of debts; they were also to give back to the original owner, or his heirs, any ancestral land that had been sold for debt (see Lev 25:8–55).* *n* **46:20** HARM THE PEOPLE: *See 44:19.* *o* **46:21–22** *One ancient translation* smaller; *Hebrew* enclosed.
46:17 Lev 25:10   **47:1** Zech 14:8; Jn 7:38; Rev 22:1

Pray It!

The Water of Life

The Dead Sea in Israel is so filled with dissolved minerals that nothing can live in it. But in Ezekiel's vision, the stream that flowed from the Temple put so much fresh water into the Dead Sea that fish would be able to live in it again. Compare this with the waters of Baptism. When you were baptized, the priest poured holy water over your head. Like the stream in Ezekiel's vision, the waters of Baptism are God's living water for you. They wash away original sin and support you as you grow in faith.

    The next time you wash your hands or take a shower, close your eyes and think about God's living water flowing all around you. Imagine that it is washing away the dead parts of your life so that you can start fresh. Think about one thing you will do that day to reflect a new attitude or a new start. Pray that the Holy Spirit will give you the courage to do what you know you need to do.

— Ezekiel 47:1–12

small stream of water was flowing out at the south side of the gate. ³With his measuring rod the man measured 560 yards downstream to the east and told me to wade through the stream there. The water came only to my ankles. ⁴Then he measured another 560 yards, and the water came up to my knees. Another 560 yards farther down, the water was up to my waist. ⁵He measured 560 yards more, and there the stream was so deep I could not wade through it. It was too deep to cross except by swimming. ⁶He said to me, "Mortal man, note all this carefully."

Then the man took me back to the riverbank, ⁷and when I got there, I saw that there were very many trees on each bank. ⁸He said

to me, "This water flows through the land to the east and down into the Jordan Valley and to the Dead Sea. When it flows into the Dead Sea, it replaces the salt water of that sea with fresh water. ⁹Wherever the stream flows, there will be all kinds of animals and fish. The stream will make the water of the Dead Sea fresh, and wherever it flows, it will bring life. ¹⁰From the Springs of Engedi all the way to the Springs of Eneglaim, there will be fishermen on the shore of the sea, and they will spread out their nets there to dry. There will be as many different kinds of fish there as there are in the Mediterranean Sea. ¹¹But the water in the marshes and ponds along the shore will not be made

The man . . . told me to wade through the stream there. (47:3)

fresh. They will remain there as a source of salt. 12On each bank of the stream all kinds of trees will grow to provide food. Their leaves will never wither, and they will never stop bearing fruit. They will have fresh fruit every month, because they are watered by the stream that flows from the Temple. The trees will provide food, and their leaves will be used for healing people."

The Boundaries of the Land

13 The Sovereign LORD said, "These are the boundaries of the land that is to be divided among the twelve tribes, with the tribe of Joseph receiving two sections.p 14I solemnly promised your ancestors that I would give them possession of this land; now divide it equally among you.

15 "The northern boundary runs eastward from the Mediterranean Sea to the city of Hethlon, to Hamath Pass, to the city of Zedad,q 16to the cities of Berothah and Sibraim (they are located between the territory of the kingdom of Damascus and that of the kingdom of Hamath), and to the city of Ticon (located by the border of the district of Hauran). 17So the northern boundary runs from the Mediterranean eastward to Enon City, with the border regions of Damascus and Hamath to the north of it.

18 "The eastern boundary runs south from a point between the territory of Damascus and that of Hauran, with the Jordan River forming the boundary between the land of Israel on the west and Gilead on the east, as far as Tamarr on the Dead Sea.

19 "The southern boundary runs southwest from Tamar to the oasis of Kadesh Meribah and then northwest along the Egyptian border to the Mediterranean Sea.

20 "The western boundary is formed by the Mediterranean and runs north to a point west of Hamath Pass.

21 "Divide this land among your tribes; 22it is to be your permanent possession. The foreigners who are living among you and who have had children born here are also to receive their share of the land when you divide it. They are to be treated like full Israelite citizens and are to draw lots for shares of the land along with the tribes of Israel. 23All foreign residents will receive their share with the people of the tribe among whom they are living. I, the Sovereign LORD, have spoken."

The Division of the Land among the Tribes

48 1-7The northern boundary of the land runs eastward from the Mediterranean Sea to the city of Hethlon, to Hamath Pass, to Enon City, to the boundary between the kingdoms of Damascus and Hamath. Each tribe is to receive one section of land extending from the eastern boundary west to the Mediterranean Sea,s in the following order from north to south:

Dan
Asher
Naphtali
Manasseh
Ephraim
Reuben
Judah

The Special Section in the Center of the Land

8 The next section of the land is to be set apart for special use. It is to be 10 miles wide from north to south, and the same length from east to west as the sections given to the tribes. The Temple will be located within this section.

9 In the center of this section, a special area 10 miles by 8 milest is to be dedicated to the

p 47:13 TWO SECTIONS: The tribes of Manasseh and Ephraim, the sons of Joseph, were each given one section.
q 47:15 One ancient translation Hamath Pass, to the city of Zedad; Hebrew Zedad Pass to the city of Hamath.
r 47:18 Some ancient translations Tamar; Hebrew unclear.   s 48:1–7 One ancient translation extending . . . Sea; Hebrew having an eastern boundary and a western boundary.   t 48:9 Probable text (see 45:1) 8 miles; Hebrew 4 miles.
47:12 Rev 22:2

Ezekiel

LORD. ¹⁰The priests are to have a portion of this holy area. From east to west their portion is to measure 10 miles, and from north to south, 4 miles. The Temple of the LORD is to be located in the middle of this area. ¹¹This holy area is to be for the priests who are descendants of Zadok. They served me faithfully and did not join the rest of the Israelites in doing wrong, as the other members of the tribe of Levi did. ¹²So they are to have a special area next to the area belonging to the Levites, and it will be the holiest of all. ¹³The Levites also are to have a special area, south of that of the priests. It too is to be 10 miles from east to west, by 4 miles from north to south. ¹⁴The area dedicated to the LORD is the best part of all the land, and none of it may be sold or exchanged or transferred to anyone else. It is holy and belongs to the LORD.

¹⁵The part of the special area that is left, 10 miles by 2 miles, is not holy, but is for the general use of the people. They may live there and use the land. The city is to be in the center of it, ¹⁶and it will be a square, 2,520 yards on each side. ¹⁷All around the city on each side there will be an open space 140 yards across. ¹⁸The land that is left after the city has been built in the area immediately to the south of the holy area—4 miles by 2 miles on the east and 4 miles by 2 miles on the west—is to be used as farmland by the people who live in the city. ¹⁹Anyone who lives in the city, no matter which tribe he comes from, may farm that land.

²⁰And so the total area in the center of the section which was set apart will be a square measuring 10 miles on each side, and it will include the area occupied by the city.

²¹⁻²²To the east and to the west of this area which contains the Temple, the priests' land, the Levites' land, and the city, the remaining land belongs to the ruling prince. It reaches east to the eastern boundary and west to the Mediterranean Sea, and is bounded on the north by the section belonging to Judah and on the south by the one belonging to Benjamin.

A Place Called God

Have you ever felt like God is ignoring you? When you pray, do you wonder if there's really a God out there who is listening? The Israelites probably felt that way, too. In the first half of the Book of Ezekiel, God was so angry with the Israelites that they might have thought that God was ready to give up on them.

In the second part of the book, things change. Jerusalem and the Temple have been destroyed. Many of the people are in exile in Babylon. God shows them that he is forgiving and merciful. He promises to lead them back to their homeland and make it a place where they can live well and worship God only. Ezekiel's visions are a promise that even the Temple will be rebuilt.

God even changes the name of the city of Jerusalem: "The name of the city from now on will be 'The-LORD-Is-Here!'" (Ezekiel 48:35). It will be a rough journey, and it will take a long time to get back, but the Israelites are headed home.

— Ezekiel 48:35

Land for the Other Tribes

²³⁻²⁷South of this special section, each of the remaining tribes is to receive one section of land running from the eastern boundary west to the Mediterranean Sea, in the following order from north to south:

Zadok (Ezekiel 48:11) **was a priest who supported King David and King Solomon. His descendants served as the high priests of the Temple.**

Benjamin
Simeon
Issachar
Zebulun
Gad

28On the south side of the portion given to the tribe of Gad, the boundary runs southwest from Tamar to the oasis of Kadesh, and then northwest along the Egyptian border to the Mediterranean Sea.

29The Sovereign LORD said, "That is the way the land is to be divided into sections for the tribes of Israel to possess."

48:30–34 Rev 21:12, 13

The Gates of Jerusalem

30-34There are twelve entrances to the city of Jerusalem. Each of the four walls measures 2,520 yards and has three gates in it, each named for one of the tribes. The gates in the north wall are named for Reuben, Judah, and Levi; those in the east wall, for Joseph, Benjamin, and Dan; those in the south wall, for Simeon, Issachar, and Zebulun; and those in the west wall are named for Gad, Asher, and Naphtali. 35The total length of the wall on all four sides of the city is 10,080 yards. The name of the city from now on will be "The-LORD-Is-Here!"

Ezekiel

Your Next Step

Congratulations on finishing the Book of Ezekiel! Use this space to write your thoughts and questions about this book. If you are following the suggested reading plan, go ahead to the Book of Jonah. Jonah is a story of another prophet, who was even less eager than Ezekiel to speak for God.

Why are we so fascinated by superheroes? Is it because they are "super," with special gifts that allow them to do great things? Or is it because they are "heroes," willing to put themselves in danger to help other people or even save the planet?

Daniel is a superhero in both senses. In 164 BC, the Jewish people were being treated horribly by an evil king. In their suffering they needed to hear the stories of a Jewish hero from an earlier time. Daniel was that hero. He had a special gift, the ability to interpret dreams, which allowed him to do great things. But he and his friends also put themselves in danger several times in order to remain faithful to God. In the end they always came out ahead—which is the way superhero stories usually end! Daniel's courage gave God's people hope that, in the end, they would be rewarded for their faithfulness.

Chap. 3

Headlines

- A King's Disturbing Dream (2:24–45)
- Three Friends Survive Fiery Furnace! (3:19–23; A:23–27)
- Daniel Reads Handwriting on the Wall (5:5–30)
- Daniel Is Thrown to the Lions (6:11–28)
- Susanna Falsely Accused! (chapter B)
- Daniel Slays a Dragon (C:23–32)

FACTOIDS

Who wrote this book? The author is unknown.

Why was it written? These heroic stories and prophetic writings were written to comfort the Jewish people during a time of persecution by Antiochus IV Epiphanes, around 164 BC.

What time period does it cover? A time in the sixth century B.C. during the Babylonian Exile.

Jesus connection: Jesus often calls himself the Son of Man, a term that appears in Daniel (7:13).

Important themes

- It is important to do what is right in the eyes of God.
- God is in control of all events.
- Despite persecution and oppression, God will be victorious, and the Kingdom of God will eventually be realized.

DANIEL

THE STORY OF DANIEL AND HIS FRIENDS (1:1—6:28)

The Young Men at Nebuchadnezzar's Court

1 ¹In the third year that Jehoiakim was king of Judah, King Nebuchadnezzar of Babylonia attacked Jerusalem and surrounded the city. ²The Lord let him capture King Jehoiakim and seize some of the Temple treasures. He took some prisoners back with him to the temple of his gods in Babylon, and put the captured treasures in the temple storerooms.

³The king ordered Ashpenaz, his chief official, to select from among the Israelite exiles some young men of the royal family and of the noble families. ⁴They had to be handsome, intelligent, well-trained, quick to learn, and free from physical defects, so that they would be qualified to serve in the royal court. Ashpenaz was to teach them to read and write the Babylonian language. ⁵The king also gave orders that every day they were to be given the same food and wine as the members of the royal court. After three years of this training they were to appear before the king. ⁶Among those chosen were Daniel, Hananiah, Mishael, and Azariah, all of whom were from the tribe of Judah. ⁷The chief official gave them new names: Belteshazzar, Shadrach, Meshach, and Abednego.

⁸Daniel made up his mind not to let himself become ritually unclean by eating the food and drinking the wine of the royal court, so he asked Ashpenaz to help him, ⁹and God made Ashpenaz sympathetic to Daniel. ¹⁰Ashpenaz, however, was afraid of the king, so he said to Daniel, "The king has decided what you are to eat and drink, and if you don't look as fit as the other young men, he may kill me."

¹¹So Daniel went to the guard whom Ashpenaz had placed in charge of him and his three friends. ¹²"Test us for ten days," he

Live It!

Eat Your Vegetables!

To avoid eating food that the Law of Moses forbids (such as pork), Daniel and his three friends make a deal with Ashpenaz, the king's chief official. They are granted the right to eat only vegetables and drink water for the next ten days, and they ask to be compared with the other young men of the court who are on a regular diet. When the time is up, Daniel and his friends are actually healthier and stronger than the others are!

The point of this story isn't that a vegetarian diet is better for you, although there might be some truth to that. The point is that our lives are better off when we follow God's commandments. We might think that cheating on a test doesn't hurt us, but it does. We might think that taking time to rest and go to church on Sunday isn't a big deal, but it is.

God doesn't give us commandments to make life difficult. He gives us laws to live by so we can live healthy, happy, and holy lives and be with him forever in heaven. So eat your vegetables and make God's laws the rule of your life.

— Daniel 1:11–16

said. "Give us vegetables to eat and water to drink. ¹³Then compare us with the young men who are eating the food of the royal

1:1 2 Kings 24:1; 2 Chr 36:5–7 **1:2–4** 2 Kings 20:17, 18; 24:10–16; 2 Chr 36:10; Isa 39:7, 8

court, and base your decision on how we look."

14He agreed to let them try it for ten days. 15When the time was up, they looked healthier and stronger than all those who had been eating the royal food. 16So from then on the guard let them continue to eat vegetables instead of what the king provided.

17God gave the four young men knowledge and skill in literature and philosophy. In addition, he gave Daniel skill in interpreting visions and dreams.

18At the end of the three years set by the king, Ashpenaz took all the young men to Nebuchadnezzar. 19The king talked with them all, and Daniel, Hananiah, Mishael, and Azariah impressed him more than any of the others. So they became members of the king's court. 20No matter what question the king asked or what problem he raised, these four knew ten times more than any fortuneteller or magician in his whole kingdom. 21Daniel remained at the royal court until Cyrus, the emperor of Persia, conquered Babylonia.

Nebuchadnezzar's Dream

2 1In the second year that Nebuchadnezzar was king, he had a dream. It worried him so much that he couldn't sleep, 2so he sent for his fortunetellers, magicians, sorcerers, and wizards to come and explain the dream to him. When they came and stood before the king, 3he said to them, "I'm worried about a dream I've had. I want to know what it means."

4They answered the king in Aramaic,*a* "May Your Majesty live forever! Tell us your dream, and we will explain it to you."

5The king said to them, "I have made up my mind that you must tell me the dream and then tell me what it means. If you can't, I'll have you torn limb from limb and make your houses a pile of ruins. 6But if you can tell me both the dream and its meaning, I will reward you with gifts and great honor.

Now then, tell me what the dream was and what it means."

7They answered the king again, "If Your Majesty will only tell us what the dream was, we will explain it."

8At that, the king exclaimed, "Just as I thought! You are trying to gain time, because you see that I have made up my mind 9to give all of you the same punishment if you don't tell me the dream. You have agreed among yourselves to go on telling me lies because you hope that in time things will change. Tell me what the dream was, and then I will know that you can also tell me what it means."

10The advisers replied, "There is no one on the face of the earth who can tell Your Majesty what you want to know. No king, not even the greatest and most powerful, has ever made such a demand of his fortunetellers, magicians, and wizards. 11What Your Majesty is asking for is so difficult that no one can do it for you except the gods, and they do not live among human beings."

12At that, the king flew into a rage and ordered the execution of all the royal advisers in Babylon. 13So the order was issued for all of them to be killed, including Daniel and his friends.

God Shows Daniel What the Dream Means

14Then Daniel went to Arioch, commander of the king's bodyguard, who had been ordered to carry out the execution. Choosing his words carefully, 15he asked Arioch why the king had issued such a harsh order. So Arioch told Daniel what had happened.

16Daniel went at once and obtained royal permission for more time, so that he could tell the king what the dream meant. 17Then Daniel went home and told his friends Hananiah, Mishael, and Azariah what had happened. 18He told them to pray to the God of heaven for mercy and to ask him to

---

a 2:4 From here to the end of chapter 7, the language used is Aramaic, not Hebrew. The language of the addition from the ancient Greek translation—The Prayer of Azariah and the Song of the Three Young Men (A.1–68)—between 3.23 and 3.24 is Greek.

King Jehoiakim ruled over Judah from 609 to 598 BC. Read more about him in 2 Kings 24:1–6.

Daniel

Pray It!

Daniel's Prayer

Daniel's prayer of praise to God is a beautiful one. Why not adapt it and make it your own? Here's a suggestion.

God, you are wise and powerful! I praise you forever and ever. You control the time and the seasons; you make and unmake presidents and rulers; it is you who give wisdom and understanding. You reveal things that are deep and secret; you know what is hidden in darkness, and you are surrounded by light. I praise you and honor you, God of my parents and grandparents. Please give me wisdom and strength, and let my whole life be a song of praise to you. Amen.

— Daniel 2:20–23

explain the mystery to them so that they would not be killed along with the other advisers in Babylon. 19 Then that same night the mystery was revealed to Daniel in a vision, and he praised the God of heaven:

20 "God is wise and powerful!
    Praise him forever and ever.
21 He controls the times and the seasons;
    he makes and unmakes kings;
    it is he who gives wisdom and
      understanding.
22 He reveals things that are deep and secret;
    he knows what is hidden in darkness,
    and he himself is surrounded by light.
23 I praise you and honor you, God of my
      ancestors.
  You have given me wisdom and strength;
    you have answered my prayer
    and shown us what to tell the king."

Daniel Tells the King the Dream and Explains It

24 So Daniel went to Arioch, whom the king had commanded to execute the royal advisers. He said to him, "Don't put them to death. Take me to the king, and I will tell him what his dream means."

25 At once Arioch took Daniel into King Nebuchadnezzar's presence and told the king, "I have found one of the Jewish exiles who can tell Your Majesty the meaning of your dream."

26 The king said to Daniel (who was also called Belteshazzar), "Can you tell me what I dreamed and what it means?"

27 Daniel replied, "Your Majesty, there is no wizard, magician, fortuneteller, or astrologer who can tell you that. 28 But there is a God in heaven, who reveals mysteries. He has informed Your Majesty what will happen in the future. Now I will tell you the dream, the vision you had while you were asleep.

29 "While Your Majesty was sleeping, you dreamed about the future; and God, who reveals mysteries, showed you what is going to happen. 30 Now, this mystery was revealed to me, not because I am wiser than anyone else, but so that Your Majesty may learn the meaning of your dream and understand the thoughts that have come to you.

31 "Your Majesty, in your vision you saw standing before you a giant statue, bright and shining, and terrifying to look at. 32 Its head was made of the finest gold; its chest and arms were made of silver; its waist and hips of bronze, 33 its legs of iron, and its feet partly of iron and partly of clay. 34 While you were looking at it, a great stone broke loose from a cliff without anyone touching it, struck the iron and clay feet of the statue, and shattered them. 35 At once the iron, clay, bronze, silver, and gold crumbled and became like the dust on a threshing place in summer. The wind carried it all away, leaving not a trace. But the stone grew to be a mountain that covered the whole earth.

36 "This was the dream. Now I will tell Your Majesty what it means. 37 Your Majesty, you are the greatest of all kings. The God of heaven has made you emperor

and given you power, might, and honor. ³⁸He has made you ruler of all the inhabited earth and ruler over all the animals and birds. You are the head of gold. ³⁹After you there will be another empire, not as great as yours, and after that a third, an empire of bronze, which will rule the whole earth. ⁴⁰And then there will be a fourth empire,

HIGHLIGHTS FROM NEBUCHADNEZZAR'S DREAM INTERPRETED BY DANIEL
(Numbers refer to chapter and verse in Daniel)

as strong as iron, which shatters and breaks everything. And just as iron shatters everything, it will shatter and crush all the earlier empires. 41 You also saw that the feet and the toes were partly clay and partly iron. This means that it will be a divided empire. It will have something of the strength of iron, because there was iron mixed with the clay. 42 The toes—partly iron and partly clay—mean that part of the empire will be strong and part of it weak. 43 You also saw that the iron was mixed with the clay. This means that the rulers of that empire will try to unite their families by intermarriage, but they will not be able to, any more than iron can mix with clay. 44 At the time of those rulers the God of heaven will establish a kingdom that will never end. It will never be conquered, but will completely destroy all those empires and then last forever. 45 You saw how a stone broke loose from a cliff without anyone touching it and how it struck the statue made of iron, bronze, clay, silver, and gold. The great God is telling Your Majesty what will happen in the future. I have told you exactly what you dreamed, and have given you its true meaning."

The King Rewards Daniel

46 Then King Nebuchadnezzar bowed to the ground and gave orders for sacrifices and offerings to be made to Daniel. 47 The king said, "Your God is the greatest of all gods, the Lord over kings, and the one who reveals mysteries. I know this because you have been able to explain this mystery." 48 Then he gave Daniel a high position, presented him with many splendid gifts, put him in charge of the province of Babylon, and made him the head of all the royal advisers. 49 At Daniel's request the king put Shadrach, Meshach, and Abednego in charge of the affairs of the province of Babylon; Daniel, however, remained at the royal court.

Nebuchadnezzar Commands Everyone to Worship a Gold Statue

3 1 King Nebuchadnezzar had a gold statue made, ninety feet high and nine feet wide, and he had it set up in the plain of Dura in the province of Babylon. 2 Then the king gave orders for all his officials to come together—the princes, governors, lieutenant governors, commissioners, treasurers, judges, magistrates, and all the other officials of the provinces. They were to attend the dedication of the statue which King Nebuchadnezzar had set up. 3 When all these officials gathered for the dedication and stood in front of the statue, 4 a herald announced in a loud voice, "People of all nations, races, and languages! 5 You will hear the sound of the trumpets, followed by the playing of oboes, lyres, zithers, and harps; and then all the other instruments will join in. As soon as the music starts, you are to bow down and worship the gold statue that King Nebuchadnezzar has set up. 6 Anyone who does not bow down and worship will immediately be thrown into a blazing furnace." 7 And so, as soon as they heard the sound of the instruments, the people of all the nations, races, and languages bowed down and worshiped the gold statue which King Nebuchadnezzar had set up.

Daniel's Three Friends Are Accused of Disobedience

8 It was then that some Babylonians took the opportunity to denounce the Jews. 9 They said to King Nebuchadnezzar, "May Your Majesty live forever! 10 Your Majesty has issued an order that as soon as the music starts, everyone is to bow down and worship the gold statue, 11 and that anyone who does not bow down and worship it is to be thrown into a blazing furnace. 12 There are some Jews whom you put in charge of the province of Babylon—Shadrach, Meshach, and Abednego—who are disobeying Your Majesty's orders. They do not worship your god or bow down to the statue you set up."

Daniel

Like Daniel, Joseph had the ability to interpret dreams (see Genesis, chapter 41). Both men are given important positions because of their God-given gift.

Daniel

We Believe . . . No Matter What

Daniel's three friends—Shadrach, Meshach, and Abednego—are about to be thrown into a fiery furnace for refusing to worship a gold statue. They tell the king that if God decides to rescue them from the furnace, then they will be saved. But even if he doesn't, it doesn't matter. They will not bow down to the gold statue. No way. Their faith in God is without conditions. They believe, whether they survive or not. Their strong faith makes the king very angry, and he has the furnace heated seven times hotter than usual.

This is a story told to encourage the faith of the Jewish people who were being persecuted several centuries later by the Greeks. After Jesus, the early Christian martyrs were also inspired by the story. It helped them to endure and to know that God would not let them down in the end.

What happens to us when the pressure is on? Do we make excuses about our faith? Do we try to make deals with God? Pray for strong and courageous faith, like that of the three young men in this story.

— Daniel, chapter 3

[13] At that, the king flew into a rage and ordered the three men to be brought before him. [14] He said to them, "Shadrach, Meshach, and Abednego, is it true that you refuse to worship my god and to bow down to the gold statue I have set up? [15] Now then, as soon as you hear the sound of the trumpets, oboes, lyres, zithers, harps, and all the other instruments, bow down and worship the statue. If you do not, you will immediately be thrown into a blazing furnace. Do you think there is any god who can save you?"

[16] Shadrach, Meshach, and Abednego answered, "Your Majesty, we will not try to defend ourselves. [17] If the God whom we serve is able to save us from the blazing furnace and from your power, then he will.[b] [18] But even if he doesn't, Your Majesty may be sure that we will not worship your god, and we will not bow down to the gold statue that you have set up."

Daniel's Three Friends Are Sentenced to Death

[19] Then Nebuchadnezzar lost his temper, and his face turned red with anger at Shadrach, Meshach, and Abednego. So he ordered the furnace to be heated seven times hotter than usual. [20] And he commanded the strongest men in his army to tie the three men up and throw them into the blazing furnace. [21] So they tied them up, fully dressed—shirts, robes, caps, and all—and threw them into the blazing furnace. [22] Now because the king had given strict orders for the furnace to be made extremely hot, the flames burned up the guards who took the men to the furnace. [23] Then Shadrach, Meshach, and Abednego, still tied up, fell into the heart of the blazing fire.

[b] **3:17** If the God . . . will; or If it is true that we refuse to worship your god or bow down to the gold statue you set up, the God whom we serve is able to save us from the blazing furnace and from your power—and he will.
3:23 Dan A:1

Not all Bibles include the chapters labeled A, B, and C, which were probably added after the original book was written.

The Prayer of Azariah

A¹ The three young men, Hananiah, Mishael, and Azariah,ᶜ started walking around in the flames, singing hymns to God, and praising him as Lord. ²Then Azariah stood still and there in the fire he prayed aloud: ³"O Lord, the God of our ancestors, we praise and adore you; may your name be honored forever. ⁴You have treated us as we deserve. In everything you have done to us you are always honest, and when you bring us to judgment, you are always fair. ⁵You did what was right when you brought disaster upon Jerusalem, the holy city of our ancestors. We deserved that judgment because of our sins. ⁶We disobeyed you, we turned our backs on you, and we are guilty of every sin. ⁷We did not do the things that you commanded us to do. If we had obeyed your laws, we would have prospered, ⁸but now we deserve the judgment and punishment that you have brought upon us. ⁹You have handed us over to lawless, hateful, and defiant enemies—to the most wicked king in the world. ¹⁰And now all of us who worship you are humiliated; we are too ashamed to open our mouths.

¹¹"Yet for the sake of your own honor, do not break your covenant with us and abandon us forever. ¹²Do not withhold your mercy from us. Keep your promises to Abraham, whom you loved, to Isaac, your servant, and to Jacob, the father of your holy people Israel. ¹³You promised to give them as many descendants as the stars in the sky or as the grains of sand along the seashore. ¹⁴But now, Lord, we are fewer in number than any other nation; wherever we are, we live in disgrace because of our sins. ¹⁵We are left without a king, without any prophets or leaders. There is no longer a Temple where we can go to offer you burnt offerings, sacrifices, gifts, or incense, no place where we can make offerings to you and find your mercy. ¹⁶But we come to you with repentant hearts and humble spirits, begging you to accept us just as if we had come with burnt offerings of rams and bulls and thousands of fat lambs.

¹⁷Accept our repentance as our sacrifice to you today, so that we may obey you with all our hearts. No one who trusts you will ever be disappointed. ¹⁸⁻¹⁹Now with all our hearts we promise to obey you, worship you, and come to you in prayer. Treat us with kindness and mercy, and let us never be put to shame. ²⁰O Lord, rescue us with one of your miracles; bring honor to your name.

²¹"Bring disgrace and shame on all who harm us. Take away their might and power and crush their strength. ²²Let them know that you alone are Lord and God and that you rule in majesty over the whole world."

²³The king's servants who had thrown the three men into the furnace kept the fire hot by feeding it with oil, tar, flax, and brushwood. ²⁴The flames blazed up to a height of seventy-five feet ²⁵and even spread out and burned up the Babylonians standing near the furnace. ²⁶But an angel of the Lord came down into the fire where the three men were. He pushed aside the flames ²⁷so that it felt as if a cool breeze were blowing, and the fire did not touch the men at all or hurt them in any way.

The Song of the Three Young Men

²⁸There in the furnace the three young men again started singing together in praise of God:

²⁹"We praise you, O Lord, the God of our ancestors.

The three young men again started singing. (A:28)

Daniel

30 May your glorious, holy name
    be held in honor and reverence forever.
31 May hymns be sung to your glory forever
    and may your holy presence be praised
        in that temple,
32 where you sit on your heavenly throne
        above the winged creatures
    and look down to the world of the
        dead.
    May you be praised and honored
        forever.
33 May you be praised as you sit on your
        royal throne.
    May hymns be sung to your glory
        forever.
34 May you be praised in the dome of the
        heavens.
    May hymns be sung to your glory
        forever.

35 "Praise the Lord, all creation;
    sing his praise and honor him forever.
36 Praise the Lord, skies above;
    sing his praise and honor him forever.
37 Praise the Lord, all angels of the Lord;
    sing his praise and honor him forever.
38 Praise the Lord, all waters above the sky;
    sing his praise and honor him forever.
39 Praise the Lord, all heavenly powers;
    sing his praise and honor him forever.
40 Praise the Lord, sun and moon;
    sing his praise and honor him forever.
41 Praise the Lord, stars of heaven;
    sing his praise and honor him forever.
42 Praise the Lord, rain and dew;
    sing his praise and honor him forever.
43 Praise the Lord, all winds;
    sing his praise and honor him forever.
44 Praise the Lord, fire and heat;
    sing his praise and honor him forever.
45 Praise the Lord, bitter cold and scorching
        heat;
    sing his praise and honor him forever.
46 Praise the Lord, dews and snows;
    sing his praise and honor him forever.
47 Praise the Lord, nights and days;
    sing his praise and honor him forever.
48 Praise the Lord, daylight and darkness;
    sing his praise and honor him forever.
49 Praise the Lord, ice and cold;
    sing his praise and honor him forever.
50 Praise the Lord, frost and snow;
    sing his praise and honor him forever.

Pray It!

Group Prayer

The long prayer of praise sung by the three men in the furnace seems very repetitive, but try to picture these three young men singing their hearts out and perhaps each taking the first half of each verse, and all three joining in on the refrain, "Sing his praise and honor him forever."

Why not try this in a group—perhaps a class or youth group? Everyone can say together verses 29–34. Then a different person says the first part of each verse, and everyone says the second part together. Better yet, why not get into a rhythm or even set it to music?

Conclude by having everyone say the last three verses together.

— Daniel A:29–68

51 Praise the Lord, lightning and storm
        clouds;
    sing his praise and honor him forever.
52 "Let the earth praise the Lord;
    sing his praise and honor him forever.
53 Praise the Lord, mountains and hills;
    sing his praise and honor him forever.
54 Praise the Lord, everything that grows;
    sing his praise and honor him forever.
55 Praise the Lord, lakes and rivers;
    sing his praise and honor him forever.
56 Praise the Lord, springs of water;
    sing his praise and honor him forever.
57 Praise the Lord, whales and sea creatures;
    sing his praise and honor him forever.
58 Praise the Lord, all birds;
    sing his praise and honor him forever.
59 Praise the Lord, all cattle and wild
        animals;
    sing his praise and honor him forever.

Jeremiah

Breakthrough!: Jeremiah [jehr-eh-MY-uh], you are one of the most famous prophets of Israel [IZ-ry-el]! God must have chosen you for your great wisdom.

Jeremiah: Actually, I feel like it was just the opposite. I was barely more than a boy when God first called me.

B: Really? Why did you answer God's call?

Jeremiah: Not for the fame; I did it because it was what God wanted of me—to speak for him.

B: What was your life like?

Jeremiah: At first it was easy. Josiah was king when I first started to prophesy. I liked his reforms, and King Josiah [joh-SY-uh] respected me. But after Josiah died, King Jehoiakim [ji-HOI-uh-kim] and King Zedekiah [zed-uh-KY-uh], who followed him, were evil and corrupt men. They were interested in power and money and not in taking care of their people.

B: So things got worse?

Jeremiah: It was then that I had some bad experiences because I spoke out against those kings and their practices. At different times I had to hide from the kings, was in prison, and was beaten. I even was thrown into a well and left to die. But the very worst thing was seeing the great city of Jerusalem [ji-ROO-suh-luhm] totally destroyed by the Babylonians [ba-buh-LOH-nee-uhns].

B: How did you handle all those bad things?

Jeremiah: (laughing) I was really upset with God, and let him know it. You can see how honest I was with God by reading Jeremiah 20:7–18.

B: What else would you like our readers to know?

Jeremiah: I know the message from God that I gave was very harsh at times. But remember God's message of hope that I also preached. God wants the best for his people!

Ezekiel

Breakthrough!: Ezekiel [eh-ZEE-kee-uhl]! We've been looking forward to interviewing you. Tell us about your call from God.

Ezekiel: I was called by God when I was thirty. I was a priest, and God also called me to be a prophet. God had a special name for me, "Mortal man." Oh, yeah, I had to eat a scroll, too. It tasted sweet.

B: How did you feel when you started to have visions of God?

Ezekiel: It was a little scary at first; God's power is so awesome that it tends to be a little overpowering. Some people thought my visions were a little too wild, but I needed to get the message to the people any way I could. I shaved my head once to get the point across.

B: You certainly did some wild things. Did anyone call you crazy? Didn't you once cook your food on . . . ?

Ezekiel: Yes, I cooked my food on dried cow's dung. It was meant to show the people the extreme conditions they would have to face once the kingdom was conquered. I had a good imagination and liked acting, so God used those gifts to make his points.

B: What message did you deliver for God?

Ezekiel: God wanted people to renew their hearts and spirits. I taught that each person is responsible for his or her own sins. I also had hopes that the kingdom of Judah might renew itself and follow God faithfully once again.

B: What was your biggest challenge?

Ezekiel: Getting people to understand and take what I was saying seriously.

B: Anything else you want the Bible readers to know?

Ezekiel: Read the book—you'll get all the wild details.

Ezra & Nehemiah

Breakthrough!: Could you tell us which one of you is which?

Ezra: My name is Ezra [EHZ-ruh].

Nehemiah: And I am Nehemiah [nee-eh-MY-uh].

B: Why are you two put together all the time?

(Both together): Because our stories are very similar. And, originally, our stories were told in one book.

B: Tell us a little about yourselves.

Ezra: I'll go first. I was a priest and scribe, a Jewish religious official who was born in captivity in Babylon [BAB-uh-luhn].

Nehemiah: And I was an administrator; I actually worked in the emperor's household.

B: So, what was the important part of your story?

Ezra: Well, after years in Babylon, a Persian king conquered Babylon and let us go home and rebuild Jerusalem [ji-ROO-suh-luhm] and the Temple. It was an amazing time.

B: Was it all smooth sailing?

Nehemiah: Ezra had to deal with people who opposed the rebuilding. He also had a big problem with the way Israelite [IZ-ry-el-yt] men were marrying foreign women.

Ezra: And Nehemiah first had to convince the emperor to let him go to Jerusalem. Then he really had to deal with rebuilding the city walls. He had a lot of people helping, which took lots of coordination. He had to be sure that all the people had food and a place to live.

B: And what were your joys?

Ezra: I was so happy when God answered our prayers so we could return home. I was also honored to see the gifts the Persian king gave us to help our rebuilding.

Nehemiah: It was a great day when the wall was finished. We had quite a party, dancing and singing so loudly it could be heard from miles away.

Judith

Breakthrough!: Hello, Judith. Can you tell us a little about yourself?

Judith: Yes, and thank you for this opportunity. My story was told to inspire people to be courageous and trust in God. I was very religious and observed all our religious laws.

B: What was your biggest challenge?

Judith: It is really gory.

B: That's okay.

Judith: Well, I beheaded General Holofernes [hohl-uh-FER-neez].

B: What!

Judith: I needed to do something that would help the Israelites [IZ-ry-el-yts] win a hopeless battle. I made myself very attractive, and Holofernes invited me and my servant into his tent, probably hoping to have sex. Then, when he got very drunk, I chopped off his head with his sword. It created such panic in King Nebuchadnezzar's [neb-uh-kuhd-NEZ-uhr's] army that the Israelites had an easy victory.

B: Why do you think people like your story?

Judith: Because it shows the power of people usually thought of as weak. In my society women were thought of as powerless, but my faith in God made me strong.

B: Did you celebrate the victory?

Judith: We sure did. It lasted for three months! I was given rewards (that I offered to God) and I celebrated with the other women. We put olive branches on our heads and danced. The men wore flower wreaths and sang songs of praise as they carried their weapons. I also sang a special song; you can find it in Judith 16:1–17.

B: What else would you like to tell the Bible readers?

Judith: Read the book—it is all in there. And remember how much power you have when you trust in God!

Esther

Breakthrough!: Queen Esther, you certainly look splendid!

Esther: Yes, the king always wants me to look my best for interviews.

B: How is it that you, a Jewish woman, became a queen in Persia?

Esther: Well, the Queen Vashti [VASH-tee] displeased King Xerxes [ZUHRK-seez], and so the king divorced her. The king's advisers looked for a beautiful, young woman to become the next queen, and, amazingly, the king picked me. I never told him about my Jewish faith until later.

B: You were an orphan, too?

Esther: Yes, my relative Mordecai [MOHR-deh-ky] raised me.

B: Didn't Mordecai uncover a plot against your people?

Esther: Actually, Mordecai uncovered a plan to assassinate the king. The king rewarded Mordecai by giving him a high government position. This made another official called Haman [HAY-muhn] jealous. Haman decided to get revenge by telling the king lies about my people. Haman tricked the king into sending out a letter ordering that all Jews be hunted down and killed.

B: How horrible! What happened?

Esther: Mordecai wanted me to go to the king immediately and plead for our people's lives. But no one, not even the queen, could go before the king without being called. I was afraid I would be killed, too. I was not that brave a person. But I found my courage and told the king that I was a Jew and that he had been lied to about my people. The king was so angry he ordered Haman to be hanged. The king let Mordecai send a letter out in the king's name allowing the Jews to defend themselves. Then the king sent out another letter telling the truth about our people.

B: So, do the Jewish people today still remember what you did?

Esther: Yes, they do, in a feast called Purim [PUR-em].

The Maccabees

Breakthrough!: Hi, guys, could you give us your names?

Maccabees: We are Judas, John, Simon, Eleazar [el-ee-AY-zuhr], and Jonathan—known as the Maccabees [MAK-uh-beez]. We lived before Christ was born—about 175 years before. This was when Alexander the Great was dying. We are named after our most famous brother, Judas, who was called Judas Maccabeus [mak-uh-BEE-uhs], meaning "Judas, the Hammer."

B: Why is Judas most famous?

Maccabees: Our father was Mattathias [mat-uh-THY-uhs], and he started a revolt against the Greeks, who were persecuting us. When our father died, Judas was the one who successfully led the revolt and pushed the Greeks out of Jerusalem [ji-ROO-suh-luhm]. He was a brilliant warrior.

B: Was Judas the only leader?

Maccabees: When Judas died, Jonathan took over as leader; he became a High Priest. Unfortunately, he was captured and killed. After him it was Simon who led. He, too, was murdered.

B: Wow, you certainly were a family of leaders willing to give your lives for God's cause. What else are you guys proud of?

Maccabees: Besides the revolt, we also purified the Temple. The Greeks had it filled with statues and images of Greek gods and goddesses, which we threw out.

B: Was that occasion called Hanukkah [HAH-nuh-kah]?

Maccabees: We didn't call it that, but later on the Jewish people named it the feast of Hanukkah, the feast of lights. Jewish people celebrate Hanukkah around the same time Christians celebrate Christmas.

B: What do the Bible readers need to know about your story?

Maccabees: Our story is told in two slightly different versions, 1 Maccabees and 2 Maccabees. We hope you read them.

Job

Breakthrough!: So, Job [JOHB], tell us a little about yourself.

Job: I had a really hard time for a while. I lost everything, really everything! It was horrible. I was a good man; I followed God and tried not to do anything evil.

B: So what happened?

Job: I lost most of my servants, all of my sheep and camels, and every one of my ten children. Then I got a really bad skin disease. My wife thought I should just curse God and die.

B: Did you?

Job: No, I told her this: "When God sends us something good, we welcome it. How can we complain when he sends us trouble?" (Job 2:10). I never said anything against God, until my friends showed up.

B: Tell us about your friends.

Job: My friends are Eliphaz [EL-i-faz], Bildad [BIL-dad], and Zophar [ZOH-far]. For seven days they just sat with me in silence. Then we started arguing about why this happened to me.

B: What was your discussion about?

Job: Divine justice, whether my suffering was due to some sin I had committed, that sort of thing. I finally did complain to God. But eventually my friends gave up on me.

B: So, what about God? Didn't you have an encounter with God?

Job: Yes, God did come and help me out. God challenged me about wonderful and awesome things that no human being can explain. He made me realize that some things are beyond human understanding. But God did tell my friends that they weren't right about the cause of my suffering.

B: What happened after that?

Job: God restored my health and all my wealth. And, I had more children and lived to see my grandchildren and great-grand-children!

Lady Wisdom

Breakthrough!: Lady Wisdom. That is an interesting name.

LW: Lady Wisdom is a name that some ancient Israelites [IZ-ry-el-yts] used to describe the wisdom of God. They felt that pursuing wisdom was so important, it was like having a relationship with another person. I'm actually described as a person in Proverbs 1:20–33 and 8:22–31, Sirach [SER-ak] 24:1–31, Wisdom 9:9–11, and Job 28:1–28.

B: Tell us some of your major achievements.

LW: First off, I am sort of the inspiration for the Books of Wisdom: Proverbs, Job [JOHB], Ecclesiastes [eh-klee-zee-AS-teez], Sirach, the Song of Songs, and the Wisdom of Solomon. I also taught people lots of things.

B: Like what things?

LW: Like the need for order in human affairs. There is an order in God's creation that must be respected. I also help them understand that almost all actions have consequences. When you do something,

it affects other people and things, for better or worse. For example, if you want to get really good at something, you have to practice at it, not just wish for it. That's part of God's order.

B: What was hard to teach people?

LW: Suffering has meaning, living a good life is possible, and humans have the responsibility of caring for God's creation. Some people have a hard time learning these things.

B: Anything else you want to tell the Bible readers?

LW: Yes, I'd like them to know that I do have my limits. Wisdom alone can't tell them everything about God because some things are just beyond our limits. But following the advice in the Books of Wisdom is a good way to live a full and rich life.

60 "Praise the Lord, all people on earth;
    sing his praise and honor him forever.
61 Praise the Lord, people of Israel;
    sing his praise and honor him forever.
62 Praise the Lord, priests of the Lord;
    sing his praise and honor him forever.
63 Praise the Lord, servants of the Lord;
    sing his praise and honor him forever.
64 Praise the Lord, all faithful people;
    sing his praise and honor him forever.
65 Praise the Lord, all who are humble and
    holy;
    sing his praise and honor him forever.
66 Praise the Lord, Hananiah, Azariah, and
    Mishael;
    sing his praise and honor him forever.
    He rescued us from the world of the dead
    and saved us from the power of death.
    He brought us out from the burning
    furnace
    and saved us from the fire.
67 Give thanks to the Lord, for he is good
    and his mercy lasts forever.
68 Praise the Lord, all who worship him;
    sing praise to the God of gods and give
    him thanks,
    for his mercy lasts forever."

3 24 Suddenly Nebuchadnezzar leaped to his feet in amazement. He asked his officials, "Didn't we tie up three men and throw them into the blazing furnace?"

They answered, "Yes, we did, Your Majesty."

25 "Then why do I see four men walking around in the fire?" he asked. "They are not tied up, and they show no sign of being hurt—and the fourth one looks like an angel." *d*

The Three Men Are Released and Promoted

26 So Nebuchadnezzar went up to the door of the blazing furnace and called out, "Shadrach! Meshach! Abednego! Servants of the Supreme God! Come out!" And they

d **3:25** angel; *or* a son of the gods; *or* a son of God.

came out at once. 27 All the princes, governors, lieutenant governors, and other officials of the king gathered to look at the three men, who had not been harmed by the fire. Their hair was not singed, their clothes were not burned, and there was no smell of smoke on them.

28 The king said, "Praise the God of Shadrach, Meshach, and Abednego! He sent his angel and rescued these men who serve and trust him. They disobeyed my orders and risked their lives rather than bow down and worship any god except their own.

29 "And now I command that if anyone of any nation, race, or language speaks disrespectfully of the God of Shadrach, Meshach, and Abednego, he is to be torn limb from limb, and his house is to be made a pile of ruins. There is no other god who can rescue like this."

30 And the king promoted Shadrach, Meshach, and Abednego to higher positions in the province of Babylon.

The fourth one looks like an angel. (3:25)

Nebuchadnezzar's Second Dream

4 1 King Nebuchadnezzar sent the following message to the people of all nations, races, and languages in the world:

"Greetings! 2 Listen to my account of the wonders and miracles which the Supreme God has shown me.

3 "How great are the wonders God shows
us!

How powerful are the miracles he
performs!

God is king forever; he will rule for all
time.

4 "I was living comfortably in my palace,
enjoying great prosperity. 5 But I had a
frightening dream and saw terrifying visions
while I was asleep. 6 I ordered all the royal
advisers in Babylon to be brought to me so
that they could tell me what the dream
meant. 7 Then all the fortunetellers, magicians, wizards, and astrologers were brought
in, and I told them my dream, but they
could not explain it to me. 8 Then Daniel
came in. (He is also called Belteshazzar, after
the name of my god.) The spirit of the holy
gods^e is in him, so I told him what I had
dreamed. I said to him: 9 Belteshazzar, chief
of the fortunetellers, I know that the spirit of
the holy gods^e is in you and that you understand all mysteries. This is^f my dream. Tell me
what it means.

10 "While I was asleep, I had a vision of a
huge tree in the middle of the earth. 11 It
grew bigger and bigger until it reached the
sky and could be seen by everyone in the
world. 12 Its leaves were beautiful, and it was
loaded down with fruit—enough for the
whole world to eat. Wild animals rested in its
shade, birds built nests in its branches, and
every kind of living being ate its fruit.

13 "While I was thinking about the vision,
I saw coming down from heaven an angel,
alert and watchful. 14 He proclaimed in a
loud voice, 'Cut the tree down and chop off
its branches; strip off its leaves and scatter its
fruit. Drive the animals from under it and
the birds out of its branches. 15 But leave the
stump in the ground with a band of iron and
bronze around it. Leave it there in the field
with the grass.

" 'Now let the dew fall on this man, and
let him live with the animals and the plants.
16 For seven years he will not have a human

mind, but the mind of an animal. 17 This is
the decision of the alert and watchful angels.
So then, let all people everywhere know that
the Supreme God has power over human
kingdoms and that he can give them to anyone he chooses—even to those who are least
important.'

18 "This is the dream I had," said King
Nebuchadnezzar. "Now, Belteshazzar, tell me
what it means. None of my royal advisers
could tell me, but you can, because the spirit
of the holy gods^g is in you."

Daniel Explains the Dream

19 At this, Daniel, who is also called Belteshazzar, was so alarmed that he could not say
anything. The king said to him, "Belteshazzar, don't let the dream and its message alarm
you."

Belteshazzar replied, "Your Majesty, I wish
that the dream and its explanation applied to
your enemies and not to you. 20 The tree, so
tall that it reached the sky, could be seen by
everyone in the world. 21 Its leaves were beautiful, and it had enough fruit on it to feed the

So tall that it reached the sky (4:20)

whole world. Wild animals rested under it,
and birds made their nests in its branches.

22 "Your Majesty, you are the tree, tall and
strong. You have grown so great that you

---

^e **4:8, 9** gods; *or God.* ^f **4:9** *Probable text* This is; *Aramaic* Visions of. ^g **4:18** gods; *or God.*

**"And now, I, Nebuchadnezzar, praise, honor, and glorify the King of Heaven.
Everything he does is right and just"** *(Daniel 4:37).*

reach the sky, and your power extends over the whole world. 23 While Your Majesty was watching, an angel came down from heaven and said, 'Cut the tree down and destroy it, but leave the stump in the ground. Wrap a band of iron and bronze around it, and leave it there in the field with the grass. Let the

Leave the stump in the ground. (4:23)

dew fall on this man, and let him live there with the animals for seven years.'

24 "This, then, is what it means, Your Majesty, and this is what the Supreme God has declared will happen to you. 25 You will be driven away from human society and will live with wild animals. For seven years you will eat grass like an ox and sleep in the open air, where the dew will fall on you. Then you will admit that the Supreme God controls all human kingdoms and that he can give them to anyone he chooses. 26 The angel ordered the stump to be left in the ground. This means that you will become king again when you acknowledge that God rules all the world. 27 So then, Your Majesty, follow my advice. Stop sinning, do what is right, and be merciful to the poor.*h* Then you will continue to be prosperous."

28 All this did happen to King Nebuchadnezzar. 29 Only twelve months later, while he was walking around on the roof of his royal palace in Babylon, 30 he said, "Look how great Babylon is! I built it as my capital city to display my power and might, my glory and majesty."

31 Before the words were out of his mouth, a voice spoke from heaven, "King Nebuchadnezzar, listen to what I say! Your royal power is now taken away from you. 32 You will be driven away from human society, live with wild animals, and eat grass like an ox for seven years. Then you will acknowledge that the Supreme God has

Down to Earth

There's a saying that states, The bigger they are, the harder they fall. This certainly seems to be the case with King Nebuchadnezzar. Just as Daniel tells him when he interprets the king's dream, the proud king does indeed spend seven years living as an animal in the wild and eating grass. The word *humility* comes from a word that originally meant "dirt" or "earth." So it seems fitting that the king is suddenly very close to the earth. It is hoped that we don't need to eat grass to be humble, but we do need to remind ourselves—and one another—that we are human beings and need to keep our egos in check.

   Think of someone you know who has accomplished much but is still humble. What are some signs of his or her humility?

— Daniel 4:19–33

power over human kingdoms and that he can give them to anyone he chooses."

33 The words came true immediately. Nebuchadnezzar was driven out of human society and ate grass like an ox. The dew fell on his body, and his hair grew as long as eagle feathers and his nails as long as bird claws.

Nebuchadnezzar Praises God

34 "When the seven years had passed," said the king, "I looked up at the sky, and my sanity returned. I praised the Supreme God and gave honor and glory to the one who lives forever.

---

h **4:27** Stop sinning . . . to the poor; *or* Make up for your sins by doing what is right and by being merciful to the poor.
4:27 Tob 12:9; Sir 3:30   **4:34** Sir 18:1

"He will rule forever,
  and his kingdom will last for all time.
35 He looks on the people of the earth as
    nothing;
  angels in heaven and people on earth
    are under his control.
No one can oppose his will
  or question what he does.

36 "When my sanity returned, my honor, my majesty, and the glory of my kingdom were given back to me. My officials and my noblemen welcomed me, and I was given back my royal power with even greater honor than before.

37 "And now, I, Nebuchadnezzar, praise, honor, and glorify the King of Heaven. Everything he does is right and just, and he can humble anyone who acts proudly."

Belshazzar's Banquet

5 ¹One night King Belshazzar invited a thousand noblemen to a great banquet, and they drank wine together. ²While they were drinking, Belshazzar gave orders to bring in the gold and silver cups and bowls which his father[i] Nebuchadnezzar had carried off from the Temple in Jerusalem. The king sent for them so that he, his noblemen, his wives, and his concubines could drink out of them. ³At once the gold cups and bowls were brought in, and they all drank wine out of them ⁴and praised gods made of gold, silver, bronze, iron, wood, and stone.

⁵Suddenly a human hand appeared and began writing on the plaster wall of the palace, where the light from the lamps was shining most brightly. And the king saw the hand as it was writing. ⁶He turned pale and

Suddenly a human hand appeared. (5:5)

was so frightened that his knees began to shake. ⁷He shouted for someone to bring in the magicians, wizards, and astrologers. When they came in, the king said to them, "Anyone who can read this writing and tell me what it means will be dressed in robes of royal purple, wear a gold chain of honor around his neck, and be the third in power in the kingdom." ⁸The royal advisers came forward, but none of them could read the writing or tell the king what it meant. ⁹In his distress King Belshazzar grew even paler, and his noblemen had no idea what to do.

¹⁰The queen mother heard the noise made by the king and his noblemen and entered the banquet hall. She said, "May Your Majesty live forever! Please do not be so disturbed and look so pale. ¹¹There is a man in your kingdom who has the spirit of the holy gods[j] in him. When your father was king, this man showed good sense, knowledge, and wisdom like the wisdom of the gods. And King Nebuchadnezzar, your father,[k] made him chief of the fortunetellers, magicians, wizards, and astrologers. ¹²He has unusual ability and is wise and skillful in interpreting dreams, solving riddles, and explaining mysteries; so send for this man Daniel, whom the king named Belteshazzar, and he will tell you what all this means."

Daniel Explains the Writing

¹³Daniel was brought at once into the king's presence, and the king said to him, "Are you Daniel, that Jewish exile whom my father the king brought here from Judah? ¹⁴I have heard that the spirit of the holy gods[l] is in you and that you are skillful and have knowledge and wisdom. ¹⁵The advisers and magicians were brought in to read this writing and tell me what it means, but they could not discover the meaning. ¹⁶Now I have heard that you can find hidden meanings and explain mysteries. If you can read this writing and tell me what it means, you will be dressed in robes of royal purple, wear a gold chain of honor around your neck, and be the third in power in the kingdom."

---

[i] **5:2** *There were several kings of Babylonia between Nebuchadnezzar and Belshazzar. Father may mean predecessor, or the name* Nebuchadnezzar *may be used for Nabonidus.*   [j] **5:11** gods; *or* God.   [k] **5:11** your father (see 5:2).
[l] **5:14** gods; *or* God.

The Writing's on the Wall

Have you ever heard the expression, The writing's on the wall? This is where it comes from: the fifth chapter of the Book of Daniel. It generally means that the end is near. That is certainly true for King Belshazzar. He is told by Daniel that his days are numbered. In fact, Belshazzar is killed that night.

Think about a time when someone might have said this to you. He or she might have been predicting a break-up in a relationship, or perhaps that some goal you had been working toward was about to come true. When someone tells you that the writing is on the wall, he or she is generally telling you that you are about to face the consequences of your actions.

If God were to send you a message written on a wall, what three words do you think would appear? What would they mean?

— Daniel, chapter 5

17 Daniel replied, "Keep your gifts for yourself or give them to someone else. I will read for Your Majesty what has been written and tell you what it means.

18 "The Supreme God made your father Nebuchadnezzar a great king and gave him dignity and majesty. 19 He was so great that people of all nations, races, and languages were afraid of him and trembled. If he wanted to kill someone, he did; if he wanted to keep someone alive, he did. He honored or disgraced anyone he wanted to. 20 But because he became proud, stubborn, and cruel, he was removed from his royal throne and lost his place of honor. 21 He was driven away from human society, and his mind became like that of an animal. He lived with wild donkeys, ate grass like an ox, and slept in the open air with nothing to protect him from the dew. Finally he admitted that the Supreme God controls all human kingdoms and can give them to anyone he chooses.

22 "But you, his son, have not humbled yourself, even though you knew all this. 23 You acted against the Lord of heaven and brought in the cups and bowls taken from his Temple. You, your noblemen, your wives, and your concubines drank wine out of them and praised gods made of gold, silver, bronze, iron, wood, and stone—gods that cannot see or hear and that do not know anything. But you did not honor the God who determines whether you live or die and who controls everything you do. 24 That is why God has sent the hand to write these words.

25 "This is what was written: 'Number, number, weight, divisions.' 26 And this is what it means: *number,* God has numbered the days of your kingdom and brought it to an end; 27 *weight,* you have been weighed on the scales and found to be too light; 28 *divisions,* your kingdom is divided up and given to the Medes and Persians." *m*

29 Immediately Belshazzar ordered his servants to dress Daniel in a robe of royal purple and to hang a gold chain of honor around his neck. And he made him the third in power in the kingdom. 30 That same night Belshazzar, the king of Babylonia, was killed; 31 and Darius the Mede, who was then sixty-two years old, seized the royal power.

Daniel in the Pit of Lions

6 1 Darius decided to appoint a hundred and twenty governors to hold office throughout his empire. 2 In addition, he chose Daniel and two others to supervise the

m **5:28** PERSIANS: *In Aramaic the word for "Persians" sounds like the word for "division."*

The gold and silver cups the king is using *(Daniel 5:2)* **were the sacred bowls and cups taken from the Temple in Jerusalem.**

Daniel

Pray It!

Thrown to the Lions

The incident of Daniel in the lions' pit, or den, is one of the most famous of the Old Testament. Because Daniel was so good at his job, he was promoted. That made his coworkers jealous, and they figured out a way to bring him down. Jealousy and envy can make people do some pretty awful things to others. If you ever feel you are the victim of jealous people, be like Daniel and keep trusting God to protect you.

Heavenly Father,
I didn't mean to make people jealous
    or act snobby or proud.
Yet they seem to dislike me anyway.
Dear God, help them to see
    that my joy in life comes from you.
Anything good or precious that I have
    is the result of your blessing and love.
They can have that, too,
    if they only trust in you. Amen.

— Daniel, chapter 6

governors and to look after the king's interests. ³Daniel soon showed that he could do better work than the other supervisors or the governors. Because he was so outstanding, the king considered putting him in charge of the whole empire. ⁴Then the other supervisors and the governors tried to find something wrong with the way Daniel administered the empire, but they couldn't, because Daniel was reliable and did not do anything wrong or dishonest. ⁵They said to each other, "We are not going to find anything of which to accuse Daniel unless it is something in connection with his religion."

⁶So they went to see the king and said, "King Darius, may Your Majesty live forever! ⁷All of us who administer your empire—the supervisors, the governors, the lieutenant governors, and the other officials—have agreed that Your Majesty should issue an order and enforce it strictly. Give orders that for thirty days no one be permitted to request anything from any god or from any human being except from Your Majesty. Anyone who violates this order is to be thrown into a pit filled with lions. ⁸So let Your Majesty issue this order and sign it, and it will be in force, a law of the Medes and Persians, which cannot be changed." ⁹And so King Darius signed the order. ¹⁰When Daniel learned that the order had been signed, he went home. In an upstairs room of his house there were windows that faced toward Jerusalem. There, just as he had always done, he knelt down at the open windows and prayed to God three times a day.

¹¹When Daniel's enemies observed him praying to God, ¹²all of them went together to the king to accuse Daniel. They said, "Your Majesty, you signed an order that for the next thirty days anyone who requested anything from any god or from any human being except you, would be thrown into a pit filled with lions."

Notice that Daniel faces Jerusalem to pray. Muslims today always face the holy city of Mecca when they pray.

He knelt down at the open windows. (6:10)

The king replied, "Yes, that is a strict order, a law of the Medes and Persians, which cannot be changed."

13 Then they said to the king, "Daniel, one of the exiles from Judah, does not respect Your Majesty or obey the order you issued. He prays regularly three times a day."

14 When the king heard this, he was upset and did his best to find some way to rescue Daniel. He kept trying until sunset. 15 Then Daniel's enemies came back to the king and said to him, "Your Majesty knows that according to the laws of the Medes and Persians no order which the king issues can be changed."

16 So the king gave orders for Daniel to be taken and thrown into the pit filled with lions. He said to Daniel, "May your God, whom you serve so loyally, rescue you." 17 A stone was put over the mouth of the pit, and the king placed his own royal seal and the seal of his noblemen on the stone, so that no one could rescue Daniel. 18 Then the king returned to the palace and spent a sleepless night, without food or any form of entertainment.

19 At dawn the king got up and hurried to the pit. 20 When he got there, he called out anxiously, "Daniel, servant of the living God! Was the God you serve so loyally able to save you from the lions?"

21 Daniel answered, "May Your Majesty live forever! 22 God sent his angel to shut the mouths of the lions so that they would not hurt me. He did this because he knew that I was innocent and because I have not wronged you, Your Majesty."

23 The king was overjoyed and gave orders for Daniel to be pulled up out of the pit. So they pulled him up and saw that he had not been hurt at all, for he trusted God. 24 Then the king gave orders to arrest all those who had accused Daniel, and he had them thrown, together with their wives and children, into the pit filled with lions. Before they even reached the bottom of the pit, the lions pounced on them and broke all their bones.

25 Then King Darius wrote to the people of all nations, races, and languages on earth:

"Greetings! 26 I command that throughout my empire everyone should fear and respect Daniel's God.

"He is a living God,
  and he will rule forever.
His kingdom will never be destroyed,
  and his power will never come to an
    end.
27 He saves and rescues;
  he performs wonders and miracles
    in heaven and on earth.
He saved Daniel from being killed by the
    lions."

28 Daniel prospered during the reign of Darius and the reign of Cyrus the Persian.

DANIEL DESCRIBES HIS VISIONS (7:1—12:13)

Daniel's Vision of the Four Beasts

7 1 In the first year that Belshazzar was king of Babylonia, I had a dream and saw a vision in the night. I wrote the dream down, and this is the record 2 of what I saw that night:

He knew that I was innocent. (6:22)

6:16 Dan C:31–42 **6:22** Tob 4:17; 12:14, 15

Daniel

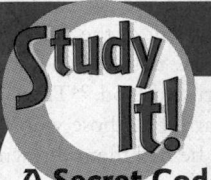

A Secret Code

The second part of the Book of Daniel is very different from the first. The type of writing in the second part of the book is called apocalyptic writing. *Apocalypse* is a Greek word meaning "to uncover" or "to reveal." Apocalyptic writing often has symbolic images that are revealed in visions. These images can be confusing to the reader. These symbolic images were like codes meant to reveal God's plans or purposes. Apocalyptic writing sometimes happened during times of persecution, and the code would be understood by the people being persecuted, but not by the persecutors. The last book of the Bible, the Book of Revelation, is almost all apocalyptic writing.

Scholars have identified many of the historical people represented by Daniel's visions. One of them is Alexander the Great (Daniel 11:3–4). The purpose of these visions is to assure the people that God would triumph over all earthly kingdoms and powers.

— Daniel, chapter 7

Winds were blowing from all directions and lashing the surface of the ocean. ³Four huge beasts came up out of the ocean, each one different from the others. ⁴The first one looked like a lion, but had wings like an eagle. While I was watching, the wings were torn off. The beast was lifted up and made to stand up straight. And then a human mind was given to it.

⁵The second beast looked like a bear standing on its hind legs. It was holding three ribs between its teeth, and a voice said to it, "Go on, eat as much meat as you can!"

⁶While I was watching, another beast appeared. It looked like a leopard, but on its back there were four wings, like the wings of a bird, and it had four heads. It had a look of authority about it.

⁷As I was watching, a fourth beast appeared. It was powerful, horrible, terrifying. With its huge iron teeth it crushed its victims, and then it trampled on them. Unlike the other beasts, it had ten horns. ⁸While I was staring at the horns, I saw a little horn coming up among the others. It tore out three of the horns that were already there. This horn had human eyes and a mouth that was boasting proudly.

The Vision of the One Who Has Been Living Forever

⁹While I was looking, thrones were put in place. One who had been living forever sat down on one of the thrones. His clothes were white as snow, and his hair was like pure wool. His throne, mounted on fiery wheels, was blazing with fire, ¹⁰and a stream of fire was pouring out from it. There were many thousands of people there to serve him, and millions of people stood before him. The court began its session, and the books were opened.

¹¹While I was looking, I could still hear the little horn bragging and boasting. As I watched, the fourth beast was killed, and its body was thrown into the flames and destroyed. ¹²The other beasts had their power taken away, but they were permitted to go on living for a limited time.

¹³During this vision in the night, I saw what looked like a human being. He was approaching me, surrounded by clouds, and he went to the one who had been living forever and was presented to him. ¹⁴He was given authority, honor, and royal power, so that the people of all nations, races, and languages would serve him. His authority would last forever, and his kingdom would never end.

7:3 Rev 13:1; 17:8   **7:4–6** Rev 13:2   **7:7** Rev 12:3; 13:1   **7:8** Rev 13:5, 6   **7:9 a** Rev 20:4; **b** Rev 1:14
7:10 a Rev 5:11; **b** Rev 20:12   **7:13** Mt 24:30; 26:64; Mk 13:26; 14:62; Lk 21:27; Rev 1:7, 13; 14:14
7:14 Rev 11:15

The Visions Are Explained

15 The visions I saw alarmed me, and I was deeply disturbed.[n] **16** I went up to one of those standing there and asked him to explain it all. So he told me the meaning. **17** He said, "These four huge beasts are four empires which will arise on earth. **18** And the people of the Supreme God will receive royal power and keep it forever and ever."

19 Then I wanted to know more about the fourth beast, which was not like any of the others—the terrifying beast which crushed its victims with its bronze claws and iron teeth and then trampled on them. **20** And I wanted to know about the ten horns on its head and the horn that had come up afterward and had made three of the horns fall. It had eyes and a mouth and was boasting proudly. It was more terrifying than any of the others.

21 While I was looking, that horn made war on God's people and conquered them. **22** Then the one who had been living forever came and pronounced judgment in favor of[o] the people of the Supreme God. The time had arrived for God's people to receive royal power.

23 This is the explanation I was given: "The fourth beast is a fourth empire that will be on the earth and will be different from all other empires. It will crush the whole earth and trample it down. **24** The ten horns are ten kings who will rule that empire. Then another king will appear; he will be very different from the earlier ones and will overthrow three kings. **25** He will speak against the Supreme God and oppress God's people. He will try to change their religious laws and festivals, and God's people will be under his power for three and a half years. **26** Then the heavenly court will sit in judgment, take away his power, and destroy him completely. **27** The power and greatness of all the kingdoms on earth will be given to the people of the Supreme God. Their royal power will never end, and all rulers on earth will serve and obey them."

28 This is the end of the account. I was so frightened that I turned pale, and I kept everything to myself.

Daniel's Vision of a Ram and a Goat

8 **1** In the third year that Belshazzar was king, I saw a second vision.[p] **2** In the vision I suddenly found myself in the walled city of Susa in the province of Elam. I was standing by the Ulai River, **3** and there beside the river I saw a ram that had two long horns, one of which was longer and newer than the other. **4** I watched the ram butting with his horns to the west, the north, and the south. No animal could stop him or escape his power. He did as he pleased and grew arrogant.

5 While I was wondering what this meant, a goat came rushing out of the west, moving so fast that his feet didn't touch the ground. He had one prominent horn between his eyes. **6** He came toward the ram, which I had seen standing beside the river, and rushed at him with all his force. **7** I watched him attack the ram. He was so angry that he smashed into him and broke the two horns. The ram had no strength to resist. He was thrown to the ground and trampled on, and there was no one who could save him.

8 The goat grew more and more arrogant, but at the height of his power his horn was broken. In its place four prominent horns came up, each pointing in a different direction. **9** Out of one of these four horns grew a little horn, whose power extended toward the south and the east and toward the Promised Land. **10** It grew strong enough to attack the army of heaven, the stars themselves, and it threw some of them to the ground and trampled on them. **11** It even

Daniel

---

[n] **7:15** *Aramaic has two additional words, the meaning of which is unclear.*   [o] **7:22** pronounced judgment in favor of; *or* gave the right to judge to.   [p] **8:1** *Beginning at 8:1, the rest of this book is in Hebrew (see 2:4).*
7:18 Rev 22:5   **7:21** Rev 13:7   **7:22** Rev 20:4   **7:24** Rev 17:12   **7:25** Rev 12:14; 13:5, 6   **7:27 a** Rev 20:4; **b** Rev 22:5   **8:10** Rev 12:4

Other translations of the Bible use the term "son of man" to describe the person in Daniel 7:13–14. This is a title used for Jesus in the New Testament.

Daniel

defied the Prince of the heavenly army, stopped the daily sacrifices offered to him, and ruined the Temple. 12People sinned there instead of offering the proper daily sacrifices,*q* and true religion was thrown to the ground. The horn was successful in everything it did.

13Then I heard one angel ask another, "How long will these things that were seen in the vision continue? How long will an awful sin replace the daily sacrifices? How long will the army of heaven and the Temple be trampled on?"

14I heard the other angel answer, "It will continue for 2,300 evenings and mornings, during which sacrifices will not be offered. Then the Temple will be restored."

The Angel Gabriel Explains the Vision

15I was trying to understand what the vision meant, when suddenly someone was standing in front of me. 16I heard a voice call out over the Ulai River, "Gabriel, explain to him the meaning of what he saw." 17Gabriel came and stood beside me, and I was so terrified that I fell to the ground.

He said to me, "Mortal man, understand the meaning. The vision has to do with the end of the world." 18While he was talking, I fell to the ground unconscious. But he took hold of me, raised me to my feet, 19and said, "I am showing you what the result of God's anger will be. The vision refers to the time of the end.

20"The ram you saw that had two horns represents the kingdoms of Media and Persia. 21The goat represents the kingdom of Greece, and the prominent horn between his eyes is the first king. 22The four horns that came up when the first horn was broken represent the four kingdoms into which that nation will be divided and which will not be as strong as the first kingdom.

23"When the end of those kingdoms is

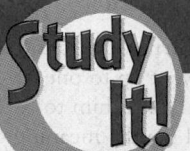

The Archangel Gabriel

Most of us know Gabriel as the angel who appeared to Mary to announce to her that she would become the mother of Jesus (see Luke 1:26). But it is here in the Book of Daniel that Gabriel appears for the first time in the Bible as a messenger from God. Gabriel, along with Raphael and Michael, are three archangels, or chief angels. In chapter 8 of Daniel, Gabriel explains to Daniel what his vision means.

Angels are spiritual beings and do not have physical bodies as we do. So why, do you think, are angels usually pictured with wings? It has to do with the role they play in God's plan.

— Daniel 8:15–26

---

near and they have become so wicked that they must be punished, there will be a stubborn, vicious, and deceitful king. 24He will grow strong—but not by his own power. He will cause terrible destruction and be successful in everything he does. He will bring destruction on powerful men and on God's own people. 25Because he is cunning, he will succeed in his deceitful ways. He will be proud of himself and destroy many people without warning. He will even defy the greatest King of all, but he will be destroyed without the use of any human power. 26This vision about the evening and morning sacrifices which has been explained to you will

---

q **8:12** People . . . sacrifices; *Hebrew unclear.*
8:16 Lk 1:19, 26

Goats in the Bible are sometimes symbolic of evil or disobedient people.

come true. But keep it secret now, because it will be a long time before it does come true."

27I was depressed and ill for several days. Then I got up and went back to the work that the king had assigned to me, but I was puzzled by the vision and could not understand it.

Daniel Prays for His People

9 1Darius the Mede, who was the son of Xerxes, ruled over the kingdom of Babylonia. 2In the first year of his reign I was studying the sacred books and thinking about the seventy years that Jerusalem would be in ruins, according to what the LORD had told the prophet Jeremiah. 3And I prayed earnestly to the Lord God, pleading with him, fasting, wearing sackcloth, and sitting in ashes. 4I prayed to the LORD my God and confessed the sins of my people.

I said, "Lord God, you are great, and we honor you. You are faithful to your covenant and show constant love to those who love you and do what you command.

5"We have sinned, we have been evil, we have done wrong. We have rejected what you commanded us to do and have turned away from what you showed us was right. 6We have not listened to your servants the prophets, who spoke in your name to our kings, our rulers, our ancestors, and our whole nation. 7You, Lord, always do what is right, but we have always brought disgrace on ourselves. This is true of all of us who live in Judea and in Jerusalem and of all the Israelites whom you scattered in countries near and far because they were unfaithful to you. 8Our kings, our rulers, and our ancestors have acted shamefully and sinned against you, Lord. 9You are merciful and forgiving, although we have rebelled against you. 10We did not listen to you, O LORD our God, when you told us to live according to the laws which you gave us through your servants the prophets. 11All Israel broke your laws and refused to listen to what you said. We sinned against you, and so you brought on us the curses that are written in the Law of Moses, your servant. 12You did what you said you would do to us and our rulers. You punished Jerusalem more severely than any other city on earth, 13giving us all the punishment described in the Law of Moses. But even now, O LORD our God, we have not tried to please you by turning from our sins or by following your truth. 14You, O LORD our God, were prepared to punish us, and you did, because you always do what is right, and we did not listen to you.

15"O Lord our God, you showed your power by bringing your people out of Egypt, and your power is still remembered. We have sinned; we have done wrong. 16You have defended us in the past, so do not be angry with Jerusalem any longer. It is your city, your sacred hill.r All the people in the neighboring countries look down on Jerusalem and on your people because of our sins and the evil our ancestors did. 17O God, hear my prayer and pleading. Restore your Temple, which has been destroyed; restore it so that everyone will know that you are God. 18Listen to us, O God; look at us and see the trouble we are in and the suffering of the city that bears your name. We are praying to you because you are merciful, not because we have done right. 19Lord, hear us. Lord, forgive us. Lord, listen to us, and act! In order that everyone will know that you are God, do not delay! This city and these people are yours."

"God, do not delay!" (9:19)

r **9:16** SACRED HILL: *Mount Zion (see Zion in Word List).*
9:2 Jer 25:11; 29:10   **9:7** Bar 1:15–17   **9:11** Bar 1:19–23   **9:15** Bar 2:11–13   **9:17** Bar 2:14   **9:18** Bar 2:19

Gabriel Explains the Prophecy

20I went on praying, confessing my sins and the sins of my people Israel and pleading with the LORD my God to restore his holy Temple. **21**While I was praying, Gabriel, whom I had seen in the earlier vision, came flying down to where I was. It was the time for the evening sacrifice to be offered. **22**He explained, "Daniel, I have come here to help you understand the prophecy. **23**When you began to plead with God, he answered you. He loves you, and so I have come to tell you the answer. Now pay attention while I explain the vision.

24"Seven times seventy years is the length of time God has set for freeing your people and your holy city from sin and evil. Sin will be forgiven and eternal justice established, so that the vision and the prophecy will come true, and the holy Temple*s* will be rededicated. **25**Note this and understand it: From the time the command is given to rebuild Jerusalem until God's chosen leader comes, seven times seven years will pass. Jerusalem will be rebuilt with streets and strong defenses, and will stand for seven times sixty-two years, but this will be a time of troubles. **26**And at the end of that time God's chosen leader will be killed unjustly.*t* The city and the Temple will be destroyed by the invading army of a powerful ruler. The end will come like a flood, bringing the war and destruction which God has prepared. **27**That ruler will have a firm agreement with many people for seven years, and when half this time is past, he will put an end to sacrifices and offerings. The Awful Horror*u* will be placed on the highest point of the Temple and will remain there until the one who put it there meets the end which God has prepared for him."

Daniel's Vision by the Tigris River

10 **1**In the third year that Cyrus was emperor of Persia, a message was revealed to Daniel, who is also called Belteshazzar. The message was true but extremely hard to understand.*v* It was explained to him in a vision.

2At that time I was mourning for three weeks. **3**I did not eat any rich food or any meat, drink any wine, or comb my hair until the three weeks were past.

4On the twenty-fourth day of the first month of the year I was standing on the bank of the mighty Tigris River. **5**I looked up and saw someone who was wearing linen clothes and a belt of fine gold. **6**His body shone like a jewel. His face was as bright as a flash of lightning, and his eyes blazed like fire. His arms and legs shone like polished bronze, and his voice sounded like the roar of a great crowd.

7I was the only one who saw the vision. Those who were with me did not see anything, but they were terrified and ran and hid. **8**I was left there alone, watching this amazing vision. I had no strength left, and my face was so changed that no one could have recognized me. **9**When I heard his voice, I fell to the ground unconscious and lay there face downward. **10**Then a hand took hold of me and raised me to my hands and knees; I was still trembling.

11The angel said to me, "Daniel, God loves you. Stand up and listen carefully to what I am going to say. I have been sent to you." When he had said this, I stood up, still trembling.

12Then he said, "Daniel, don't be afraid. God has heard your prayers ever since the first day you decided to humble yourself in order to gain understanding. I have come in answer to your prayer. **13**The angel prince of the kingdom of Persia opposed me for twenty-one days. Then Michael, one of the chief angels, came to help me, because I had been left there alone in Persia. **14**I have come to make you understand what will happen to your people in the future. This is a vision about the future."

15When he said this, I stared at the ground, speechless. **16**Then the angel, who looked like a human being, reached out and

---

s **9:24** *Temple; or* altar.   *t* **9:26** *One ancient translation* unjustly; *Hebrew unclear.*   *u* **9:27** THE AWFUL HORROR: *A pagan image set up in the Jerusalem Temple by foreign conquerors (see 1 Macc 1:54–61).*   *v* **10:1** but extremely hard to understand; *or* and it was about a great war.
9:21 Lk 1:19, 26   **9:27** Dan 11:31; 12:11; 1 Macc 1:44–50, 54; Mt 24:15; Mk 13:14   **10:5, 6** Rev 1:13–15; 2:18; 19:12   **10:13, 21** Rev 12:7

Michael, the Guardian

Ca+holic Connec+ions

Michael is the second of the archangels to be introduced in the Book of Daniel. The name Michael means "who is like God?" in Hebrew. Michael is referred to as Israel's guardian angel in Daniel 10:20–21. He is also famous for leading the good angels in the heavenly battle against the forces of evil in Revelation 12:7. As the guardian angel of Israel, he is responsible for protecting and helping the people of Israel. That is why he is often pictured dressed in armor with a sword.

There are also angels assigned to protect and defend every human being. These angels are also called guardian angels. You can find the story of Raphael, an archangel who helped a man named Tobias, in the Book of Tobit. The feast of the archangels Michael, Gabriel, and Raphael is celebrated on September 29. The feast of the guardian angels is on October 2.

— Daniel 10:12—11:2

Daniel

touched my lips. I said to him, "Sir, this vision makes me so weak that I can't stop trembling. ¹⁷I am like a slave standing before his master. How can I talk to you? I have no strength or breath left in me."

¹⁸Once more he took hold of me, and I felt stronger. ¹⁹He said, "God loves you, so don't let anything worry you or frighten you."

When he had said this, I felt even stronger and said, "Sir, tell me what you have to say. You have made me feel better."

²⁰⁻²¹He said, "Do you know why I came to you? It is to reveal to you what is written in the book of Truth. Now I have to go back and fight the guardian angel of Persia. After that the guardian angel of Greece will appear. There is no one to help me except Michael, **11** ¹Israel's guardian angel.ʷ ¹He isˣ responsible for helping and defending me. ²And what I am now going to tell you is true."

The Kingdoms of Egypt and Syria

The angel said, "Three more kings will rule over Persia, followed by a fourth, who will be richer than all the others. At the height of his power and wealth he will challenge the kingdom of Greece.

³"Then a heroic king will appear. He will rule over a huge empire and do whatever he wants. ⁴But at the height of his power his empire will break up and be divided into four parts. Kings not descended from him will rule in his place, but they will not have the power that he had.

⁵"The king of Egypt will be strong. One of his generals, however, will be even stronger and rule a greater kingdom. ⁶After a number of years the king of Egypt will make an alliance with the king of Syria and give him his daughter in marriage. But the alliance will not last, and she, her husband, her child,ʸ and the servants who went with her will all be killed. ⁷Soon afterward one of her relatives will become king. He will

ʷ **10:20–21** *Probable text* guardian angel; *Hebrew* guardian angel. And I, in the first year of Darius the Mede.
ˣ **11:20–21** *One ancient translation* He is; *Hebrew* I am.   ʸ **11:6** *Some ancient translations* her child; *Hebrew* her father.

The number 7 (see Daniel 9:24) **appears often in the Bible and signifies perfection or the right amount of time.**

attack the army of the king of Syria, enter their fortress, and defeat them. 8 He will carry back to Egypt the images of their gods and the articles of gold and silver dedicated to those gods. After several years of peace 9 the king of Syria will invade Egypt, but he will be forced to retreat.

10 "The sons of the king of Syria will prepare for war and gather a large army. One of them will sweep on like a flood and attack an enemy fortress. 11 In his anger the king of Egypt will go to war against the king of Syria and capture his huge army. 12 He will be proud of his victory and of the many soldiers he has killed, but he will not continue to be victorious.

13 "The king of Syria will go back and gather a larger army than he had before. When the proper time comes, he will return with a large, well-equipped army. 14 Then many people will rebel against the king of Egypt. And some violent people from your nation, Daniel, will rebel because of a vision they have seen, but they will be defeated. 15 So the king of Syria will lay siege to a fortified city and capture it. The soldiers of Egypt will not continue to fight; even the best of them will not have enough strength. 16 The Syrian invader will do with them as he pleases, without opposition. He will stand in the Promised Land and have it completely in his power.

17 "The king of Syria will plan an expedition, using his whole army. Then, in order to destroy his enemy's kingdom, he will make an alliance with him and offer him his daughter^z in marriage; but his plan will not succeed. 18 After that he will attack the nations by the sea and conquer many of them. But a foreign leader will defeat him and put an end to his arrogance; indeed he will turn the arrogance of Syria's king back on him.^a 19 The king will return to the fortresses of his own land, but he will be defeated, and that will be the end of him.

20 "He will be followed by another king, who will send an officer to oppress the people with taxes in order to increase the wealth of his kingdom. In a short time that king will be killed, but not publicly and not in battle."

The Evil King of Syria

21 The angel went on to explain: "The next king of Syria will be an evil man who has no right to be king, but he will come unexpectedly and seize power by trickery. 22 Anyone who opposes him, even God's High Priest, will be swept away and wiped out. 23 By making treaties, he will deceive other nations, and he will grow stronger and stronger, even though he rules only a small nation. 24 He will invade a wealthy province without warning and will do things that none of his ancestors ever did. Then he will divide among his followers the goods and property he has captured in war. He will make plans to attack fortresses, but his time will soon run out.

25 "He will boldly raise a large army to attack the king of Egypt, who will prepare to fight back with a huge and powerful army. But the king of Egypt will be deceived and will not be successful. 26 His closest advisers will ruin him. Many of his soldiers will be killed, and his army will be wiped out. 27 Then the two kings will sit down to eat at the same table, but their motives will be evil, and they will lie to each other. They will not get what they want, because the time for it has not yet come. 28 The king of Syria will return home with all the loot he has captured, determined to destroy the religion of God's people. He will do as he pleases and then return to his own land.

29 "Later on he will invade Egypt again, but this time things will turn out differently. 30 The Romans will come in ships and oppose him, and he will be frightened.

"Then he will turn back in a rage and try to destroy the religion of God's people. He

Four nations that still exist today are mentioned in Daniel, chapter 11. Can you identify them and find them on a map?

will follow the advice of those who have abandoned that religion. ³¹Some of his soldiers will make the Temple ritually unclean. They will stop the daily sacrifices and set up The Awful Horror.^b ³²By deceit the king will win the support of those who have already abandoned their religion, but those who follow God will fight back. ³³Wise leaders of the people will share their wisdom with many others. But for a while some of them will be killed in battle or be burned to death, and some will be robbed and made prisoners. ³⁴While the killing is going on, God's people will receive a little help, even though many who join them will do so for selfish reasons. ³⁵Some of those wise leaders will be killed, but as a result of this the people will be purified. This will continue until the end comes, the time that God has set.

³⁶"The king of Syria will do as he pleases. He will boast that he is greater than any god, superior even to the Supreme God. He will be able to do this until the time when God punishes him. God will do exactly what he has planned. ³⁷The king will ignore the god his ancestors served, and also the god that women love. In fact, he will ignore every god, because he will think he is greater than any of them. ³⁸Instead, he will honor the god who protects fortresses. He will offer gold, silver, jewels, and other rich gifts to a god his ancestors never worshiped. ³⁹To defend his fortresses, he will use people who worship a foreign god. He will give great honor to those who accept him as ruler, put them into high offices, and give them land as a reward.

⁴⁰"When the king of Syria's final hour has almost come, the king of Egypt will attack him, and the king of Syria will fight back with all his power, using chariots, horses, and many ships. He will invade many countries, like the waters of a flood. ⁴¹He will even invade the Promised Land and kill tens of thousands, but the countries of Edom, Moab, and what is left of Ammon will

escape. ⁴²When he invades all those countries, even Egypt will not be spared. ⁴³He will take away Egypt's hidden treasures of gold and silver and its other prized possessions. He will conquer Libya and Ethiopia.^c ⁴⁴Then news that comes from the east and the north will frighten him, and he will fight furiously, killing many people. ⁴⁵He will even set up his huge royal tents between the sea and the mountain on which the Temple stands. But he will die, with no one there to help him."

The Time of the End

12 ¹The angel wearing linen clothes said, "At that time the great angel Michael, who guards your people, will appear. Then there will be a time of troubles, the worst since nations first came into existence. When that time comes, all the people of your nation whose names are written in God's book will be saved. ²Many of those who have already died will live again: some will enjoy eternal life, and some will suffer eternal disgrace. ³The wise leaders will shine with all the brightness of the sky. And those who have taught many people to do what is right will shine like the stars forever."

⁴He said to me, "And now, Daniel, close the book and put a seal on it until the end of the world. Meanwhile, many people will

Daniel, close the book. (12:4)

^b **11:31** THE AWFUL HORROR: *See 9:27.* ^c **11:43** *Hebrew* Cush: *Cush is the ancient name of the extensive territory south of the First Cataract of the Nile River. This region was called Ethiopia in Graeco-Roman times, and included within its borders most of modern Sudan and some of present-day Ethiopia (Abyssinia).*

11:31 Dan 9:27; 12:11; Mt 24:15; Mk 13:14 **11:36 a** 2 Thess 2:3, 4; **b** Rev 13:5, 6 **12:1 a** Rev 12:7; **b** Mt 24:21; Mk 13:19; Rev 7:14; 12:7 **12:2** Isa 26:19; 2 Macc 7:9–11, 14; Mt 25:46; Jn 5:29 **12:4** Rev 22:10

waste their efforts trying to understand what is happening."

5 Then I saw two men standing by a river, one on each bank. 6 One of them asked the angel who was standing further upstream, "How long will it be until these amazing events come to an end?"

7 The angel raised both hands toward the sky and made a solemn promise in the name of the Eternal God. I heard him say, "It will be three and a half years. When the persecution of God's people ends, all these things will have happened."

8 I heard what he said, but I did not understand it. So I asked, "But, sir, how will it all end?"

9 He answered, "You must go now, Daniel, because these words are to be kept secret and hidden until the end comes. 10 Many people will be purified. Those who are wicked will not understand but will go on being wicked; only those who are wise will understand.

11 "From the time the daily sacrifices are stopped, that is, from the time of The Awful Horror,*d* 1,290 days will pass. 12 Happy are those who remain faithful until 1,335 days are over!

13 "And you, Daniel, be faithful to the end. Then you will die, but you will rise to receive your reward at the end of time."

Susanna's Beauty Attracts Two Judges

B 1 In Babylon there lived a man named Joakim, 2 who was married to Susanna, daughter of Hilkiah. Susanna was a beautiful woman and deeply religious. 3 Her parents were devout Jews who had brought up their daughter to live according to the Law of Moses. 4 Her husband Joakim was very wealthy. Lovely gardens surrounded his house, and the other Jews often gathered there for meetings, because they all thought so highly of him. 5-6 Everyone who had a legal case to present would also go to Joakim's house, where two judges held court. These two leaders of the Jewish com-

Live It!

Lust and Self-Control

Do you know what the word *lust* means? A very good example of it is in Daniel, chapter B, the story of Susanna. Lust refers to a strong desire or craving. For example, you can lust after a candy bar, which means you really want a candy bar. Lust usually refers to sexual desire, though. In the story of Susanna, two judges lust after Susanna. They see her only as a sexual object, and they try to force her into having sex. When she refuses, the judges try to condemn her. Daniel saves the day and the life of innocent Susanna.

Lust can lead us to treat others not as human beings but as objects. Pornography is all about lust. What it does is to make sexual objects out of human beings and bring out the worst in us. We need to avoid pornography because it only increases our lust while decreasing our respect for others. Human bodies are wonderful, but not when they are used simply to bring out the worst in us. That is what pornography is about.

Think about why giving in to lust is such a dangerous thing to do.

— Daniel, chapter B

munity had recently been appointed to office. They were the ones about whom the Lord said, "There is wickedness in Babylon; judges are failing to give guidance to the people."

7 Every day at noon, when all the people left for lunch, Susanna used to take a walk in

the gardens. 8The two judges were so attracted to her that they would wait around and watch for her. 9They became so obsessed with their desire for her that they lost interest both in prayer and in their responsibility as judges. 10They each wanted Susanna, but neither told the other how he felt, 11for each was ashamed to admit his lust. 12So day after day they watched eagerly to catch sight of her.

13One day at noon they said to each other, "It's time for lunch; let's go home." 14So they both left and went their separate ways, but soon each one came back for a look at Susanna, and by accident they met each other. At first each tried to explain what he was doing there, but finally they both confessed their desire for Susanna. They decided to watch for a time when they might find her alone. 15-17So they kept waiting for the right opportunity.

Each one came back for a look at Susanna. (B:14)

The Judges Try to Seduce Susanna

One day Susanna went into the garden as usual with her two servant women. No one else was there, except the two judges, who had hidden themselves and were watching

B:22 Lev 20:10; Deut 22:22

Susanna. It was very hot and she decided to take a bath. So she said to her servants, "Bring me some bath oil and some perfume, and lock the gates, so that I won't be disturbed." 18The servants locked the main gates and went out by the side door to get what Susanna had asked for. They did not notice the two men.

19As soon as the servants had left, the two judges jumped out from their hiding place, ran to Susanna, 20and said to her, "The gates are locked and no one will see us. We are burning to have sex with you, so give us what we want. 21If you don't, we will go to court and swear that we saw you send your servants away, so that you could be alone with a young man."

22"There is no way out," Susanna moaned. "If I give in to you, I could be put to death for adultery. If I refuse, you will still have me trapped. 23But I would rather be your innocent victim than sin against the Lord." 24So she started screaming as loud as she could, and the two judges began shouting accusations, 25while one of them ran and unlocked the gates.

26As soon as the servants in the house heard all the noise, they ran into the gardens through the side door to find out what had happened to Susanna. 27The judges told their story, and the servants were shocked and ashamed. Such a thing had never before been said about Susanna.

The Judges Testify against Susanna

28The next day, when the people assembled at Joakim's house, the two judges arrived, fully determined to carry out their wicked plan to have Susanna put to death. 29In front of all the people they said, "Send for Joakim's wife Susanna, the daughter of Hilkiah." When she was called, 30she came in with her parents, her children, and all her other relatives. 31Susanna was so graceful and beautiful 32that the two wicked men ordered her veil to be removed, so that they might enjoy looking at her. ³³Her family and everyone else were in tears.

³⁴Then the two judges stood up in front of the people, placed their hands on Susanna's head, and began making their accusations against her. ³⁵She was crying, but she looked up to heaven because she trusted the Lord. ³⁶The two men gave the following testimony: "We were walking in the gardens when this woman came in with her two servant women. She locked the main gates and asked the servants to leave. ³⁷Then a young man who had been hiding in the gardens came to her, and they lay down together. ³⁸We were in a corner of the gardens, and when we saw what was happening, we ran over ³⁹and caught them in the act. We tried to hold on to the man, but he was too strong for us. He ran and opened the gates and got away, ⁴⁰but we were able to hold the woman. We asked her who the man was, but she refused to tell us. We swear that our testimony is true." ⁴¹Because the two men were not only leaders in the community but also judges, the people believed their story and condemned Susanna to death.

Daniel Rescues Susanna

⁴²Then Susanna cried out in a loud voice, "Eternal God, nothing can be kept secret from you; you know everything before it happens. ⁴³Here I am about to die, but you know that I am innocent, that these men are lying. Why must I die?"

⁴⁴The Lord heard her prayer ⁴⁵and led a young man named Daniel to speak out, just as Susanna was being taken away to her death. ⁴⁶He shouted, "I refuse to be a party to her death!"

⁴⁷Everyone turned around to look at him and asked, "What are you talking about?"

⁴⁸Daniel stood up before them and said, "People of Israel, how foolish can you be? Are you going to condemn an Israelite woman to death on this kind of evidence? You haven't even tried to find out the truth. ⁴⁹Reopen the case. The testimony these men gave was a lie."

⁵⁰So all the people hurried back to where the trial had taken place, and the officials said to Daniel, "God has given you wisdom beyond your years, so come and join us and explain to us what you mean."

⁵¹Daniel said to them, "Separate the two judges, and let me question them one at a time." ⁵²Then Daniel called the first judge and said, "You wicked old man, now you will have to answer for all the sins you have committed. ⁵³You have been giving unjust sentences. You have condemned the innocent and released the guilty, even though the Lord has said, 'Do not put an innocent person to death.' ⁵⁴Now if you really did see this couple making love, tell me, what tree were they under?"

"Under a small gum tree," he answered.

⁵⁵Daniel said, "All right! That lie will cost you your life. God's angel has already been given orders to chop*ᵉ* you in two."

⁵⁶Then the first judge was led away and the second one was brought before Daniel. "You are more like a Canaanite than a Jew," Daniel said to him. "This woman's beauty has warped your judgment, and lust has corrupted your thinking. ⁵⁷You are used to having your way with the women of Israel because they have been afraid of you, but here is a Jewish woman, and she would not give in. ⁵⁸Now, tell me what tree you saw them under."

"Under a large oak tree," he answered.

⁵⁹Daniel said, "All right! That lie will cost you your life; God's angel is waiting with his sword in his hand, ready to cut*ᶠ* you in two. Then we shall be rid of you both."

⁶⁰Then all the people shouted and praised God, who saves those who put their trust in him. ⁶¹They turned against the two judges because Daniel had proved that they had lied

---

ᵉ **B:55** CHOP: *This word in Greek sounds like the Greek for "a small gum tree."*   *ᶠ* **B:59** CUT: *This word in Greek sounds like the Greek for "a large oak tree."*
B:53 Ex 23:7

---

under oath. 62The Law of Moses states that people who give false testimony shall receive the same punishment that the accused person would have received. And so the two judges were put to death, and the life of an innocent woman was saved. 63Susanna's parents, her husband, and all her relatives praised God because she had been proved innocent of the charges. 64From that day on, Daniel was held in high regard.

Daniel and the Priests of Bel

C ¹After the death of King Astyages, Cyrus of Persia took over his kingdom. ²Daniel was one of King Cyrus' closest companions, and the king thought more highly of Daniel than of any other of his advisers.

³The Babylonians had an idol named Bel. Each day the people had to provide Bel with an offering of twelve bushels of fine flour, forty sheep, and fifty gallons of wine. ⁴King Cyrus believed that Bel was a god, and each day he used to go and worship it. But Daniel worshiped his own God.

⁵One day the king asked Daniel, "Why don't you worship Bel?"

Daniel answered, "I do not worship idols made with human hands. I worship only the living God, who created heaven and earth and is the Lord of all human beings."

⁶"And don't you believe that our god Bel is really alive?" asked the king. "Haven't you seen how much he eats and drinks every day?"

⁷Daniel laughed and said, "Don't be fooled, Your Majesty. This god you call Bel is nothing more than clay covered with bronze; it has never eaten or drunk anything."

⁸⁻¹⁰At this the king became angry and called in all seventy of the priests of Bel. He said to them, "I warn you that you will be put to death, unless you can show me that it is Bel who is eating these offerings. If you prove to me that it is Bel, then I will have Daniel put to death for claiming that Bel is not a god."

Daniel agreed to this proposal.

¹¹Then they all went with the king into Bel's temple, where the priests said to the king, "Your Majesty, we will go out and let you place the food on the table and prepare the wine. When you leave, you may lock the door behind you and seal it with the royal seal. ¹²In the morning when you return, if you find that Bel has not eaten everything, you can put us to death. But if he has, Daniel will die for making false accusations against us."

¹³But the priests were not worried, because they had made a secret entrance underneath a table in the temple, so that they could go in every night and eat the offerings.

¹⁴When the priests had left, the king set out the food for Bel. Then Daniel ordered his servants to bring some ashes and scatter them all over the floor of the temple. No one except the king saw them do this. After that they all went out, locked the door, sealed it with the royal seal, and left.

The king set out the food for Bel. (C:14)

¹⁵That night, as usual, the priests with their wives and children came into the temple by the secret entrance and ate all the food and drank all the wine.

¹⁶Early the next morning, the king and Daniel went to the temple. ¹⁷The king asked, "Have the seals been broken, Daniel?"

"No, Your Majesty, they have not been broken," he replied.

¹⁸As soon as the door was opened, the king saw the empty table and shouted, "You are great, O Bel! You really are a god."

¹⁹But Daniel began to laugh and said to the king, "Before you enter the temple, look at the floor and tell me whose footprints you see there."

²⁰"I see the footprints of men, women, and children," said the king, ²¹and he became so angry that he had the priests and their families arrested and brought to him. They showed him the secret doors through which they had come in each night to eat the food placed on the table. ²²So the king had the priests put to death, and he gave Bel to Daniel, who destroyed the idol and tore down its temple.

He gave Bel to Daniel, who destroyed the idol.
(C:22)

Daniel Kills the Dragon

²³There was also a huge dragon which the Babylonians worshiped. ²⁴One day the king said to Daniel, "You can't tell me that this god is not alive. So worship him!"

²⁵"I worship the Lord," replied Daniel. "He is the only living God. ²⁶And if Your Majesty will give me permission, I will kill this dragon of yours without using a sword or a club."

"You have my permission," answered the king.

²⁷So Daniel took some tar, some fat, and some hair and boiled them all together. He made cakes out of the mixture and fed them to the dragon. When the dragon ate them, it swelled up and burst open. "That's the kind of thing you Babylonians worship," said Daniel.

²⁸When the people of Babylon heard what had happened, they staged an angry demonstration against the king. "The king has become a Jew," they shouted. "First he destroyed Bel and slaughtered the priests, and now he has killed our dragon." ²⁹They went to the king and demanded that Daniel be handed over to them. "If you refuse," they warned the king, "we will put you and your family to death."

³⁰When the king saw that they meant what they said, he was forced to hand Daniel over to them. ³¹They threw him into a pit of lions, where they left him for six days. ³²There were seven lions in the pit, and normally they were fed two human bodies and two sheep each day. But they were given nothing to eat during these six days, in order to make sure that Daniel would be eaten.

Daniel Is Rescued from the Pit of Lions

³³At that time the prophet Habakkuk was in the land of Judah. He had cooked a stew and crumbled bread into it. He was carrying a bowl of it to the workers who were out in the fields harvesting grain, ³⁴when an angel of the Lord spoke to him, "Take the food you are carrying and give it to Daniel, who is in Babylon in a pit of lions."

³⁵Habakkuk answered, "Sir, I have never been to Babylon, and I don't know where the pit of lions is."

³⁶So the angel grabbed the prophet by the hair and took him to Babylon with the speed of the wind.^g He set him down near the pit of lions. ³⁷Habakkuk called out, "Daniel! Daniel! God has sent you some food. Here, take it."

³⁸When Daniel heard Habakkuk, he prayed, "God, you did remember me; you never abandon those who love you." ³⁹Then he got up and ate the meal, and God's angel immediately took Habakkuk home.

⁴⁰Seven days after Daniel had been thrown to the lions, the king went to the pit to mourn for him. When he got there and looked in, there sat Daniel. ⁴¹The king

g **C:36** with the speed of the wind; *or* by the power of his spirit.
C:31, 32 Dan 6:16–24 **C:36** Ezek 8:3

Daniel

The king shouted, "O Lord, the God of Daniel, how great you are." (C:41)

shouted, "O Lord, the God of Daniel, how great you are. You alone are God." ⁴²So he pulled Daniel out of the pit and had those who had tried to kill Daniel thrown into it. And the lions ate them immediately, while the king watched.

Your Next Step

Congratulations on finishing the Book of Daniel! Use this space to write your thoughts and questions about this book. If you are following the suggested reading plan, go back to the Book of Job in the Old Testament. This book is a reflection on why God allows people to suffer.

Why would God tell a prophet to marry and have children with a prostitute who would be unfaithful to him? To make a point—to show the people of Israel how they were unfaithful to God.

God told Hosea to marry a prostitute named Gomer. Hosea did what he was told and had three children with her. Their names communicated God's message to his people. Jezreel is named for a place of great bloodshed and tells of God's punishment to come. The second child was named "Unloved," which tells that God no longer shows mercy to Israel. The third, "Not-My-People" tells that God's people were unfaithful. But no matter how often God's people were unfaithful, God is always faithful. Like Hosea's love for Gomer, God's love for us is unfailing.

Chap. 11:3

Head lines

- Prophet Marries Prostitute (1:2–8)
- God's Great Love for His People (2:19–23)
- God Desires Love Not Sacrifice (6:1–6)
- Israelites Sow the Wind, Reap a Storm! (8:1–10)
- God Extends Loving Arms! (11:1–4)

FACTOIDS

Who wrote this book? Hosea, who preached to the northern kingdom of Israel before the Israelites were conquered by the Assyrians.

What period does it cover? Around 786–722 BC.

Why was it written? Hosea used his marriage to the unfaithful prostitute Gomer to illustrate the unfaithfulness of the Israelites and God's faithful and persistent love for them.

Jesus connection: Just as Hosea forgave Gomer every time she left him and was unfaithful, Jesus forgives all of our sins. The reference to Jesus in Matthew 2:15, "I called my Son out of Egypt," is taken from Hosea 11:1.

Important themes

- Those who rely on wealth and power are likely to forget all about God.
- Like a loving parent, God loves us, is waiting for us, and is ready to take us back—even when we are "not worthy."
- Poor choices will have poor results, and evil actions will have evil consequences.

HOSEA

1 ¹This is the message which the LORD gave Hosea son of Beeri during the time that Uzziah, Jotham, Ahaz, and Hezekiah were kings of Judah, and Jeroboam son of Jehoash was king of Israel.

Hosea's Wife and Children

²When the LORD first spoke to Israel through Hosea, he said to Hosea, "Go and get married; your wife will be unfaithful, and your children will be just like her.ᵃ In the same way my people have left me and become unfaithful."

³So Hosea married a woman named Gomer, the daughter of Diblaim. After the birth of their first child, a son, ⁴the LORD said to Hosea, "Name him 'Jezreel,' because it will not be long before I punish the king of Israel for the murders that his ancestor Jehu committed at Jezreel.ᵇ I am going to put an end to Jehu's dynasty.ᶜ ⁵And in Jezreel Valley I will at that time destroy Israel's military power."

⁶Gomer had a second child—this time it was a daughter. The LORD said to Hosea, "Name her 'Unloved,' because I will no longer show love to the people of Israel or forgive them. ⁷But to the people of Judah I will show love. I, the LORD their God, will save them, but I will not do it by war—with swords or bows and arrows or with horses and horsemen."

⁸After Gomer had weaned her daughter, she became pregnant again and had another son. ⁹The LORD said to Hosea, "Name him 'Not-My-People,' because the people of Israel are not my people, and I am not their God."

Israel Is to Be Restored

¹⁰The people of Israel will become like the sand of the sea, more than can be counted or measured. Now God says to them, "You are not my people," but the day is coming when he will say to them, "You are the children of the living God!" ¹¹The people of Judah and the people of Israel will be reunited. They will choose for themselves a single leader, and once again they will grow and prosper in their land. Yes, the day of **2** Jezreelᵈ will be a great day! ¹So call your fellow Israelites "God's People" and "Loved-by-the-Lord."

Unfaithful Gomer—Unfaithful Israel

²My children, plead with your mother— though she is no longer a wife to me, and I am no longer her husband. Plead with her to stop her adultery and prostitution. ³If she does not, I will strip her as naked as she was on the day she was born. I will make her like a dry and barren land, and she will die of thirst. ⁴⁻⁵I will not show mercy to her children; they are the children of a shameless prostitute.ᵉ She herself said, "I will go to my lovers—they give me food and water, wool and linen, olive oil and wine."

⁶So I am going to fence her in with thorn bushes and build a wall to block her way. ⁷She will run after her lovers but will not catch them. She will look for them but will not find them. Then she will say, "I am going back to my first husband—I was better off then than I am now."

⁸She would never acknowledge that I am the one who gave her the grain, the wine, the olive oil, and all the silver and gold that she used in the worship of Baal. ⁹So at harvest time I will take back my gifts of grain and wine, and will take away the wool and the linen I gave her for clothing. ¹⁰I will strip her naked in front of her lovers, and no one will be able to save her from my power.

ᵃ **1.2** get married; your wife . . . her; *or* marry a prostitute, and have children by her who will be just as bad as she is. ᵇ **1.4** JEZREEL: *At this city Jehu assassinated the king of Israel and all the rest of the royal family, and became the first king of a new dynasty (see 2 Kings 9–10).* ᶜ **1.4** Jehu's dynasty; *or* the kingdom of Israel. ᵈ **1.11** JEZREEL: *This name in Hebrew means "God sows" and suggests growth and prosperity.* ᵉ **2.4–5** the children of a shameless prostitute; *or as shameless as their mother, a* prostitute.
1:1 a 2 Kings 15:1–7; 2 Chr 26:1–23; **b** 2 Kings 15:32–38; 2 Chr 27:1–8; **c** 2 Kings 16:1–20; 2 Chr 28:1–27; **d** 2 Kings 18:1—20:21; 2 Chr 29:1—32:33; **e** 2 Kings 14:23–29 **1:4** 2 Kings 10:11 **1:10** Rom 9:26

11 I will put an end to all her festivities—her annual and monthly festivals and her Sabbath celebrations—all her religious meetings. 12 I will destroy her grapevines and her fig trees, which she said her lovers gave her for serving them. I will turn her vineyards and orchards into a wilderness; wild animals will destroy them. 13 I will punish her for the times that she forgot me, when she burned incense to Baal and put on her jewelry to go chasing after her lovers. The LORD has spoken.

The LORD's Love for His People

14 So I am going to take her into the desert again; there I will win her back with words of love. 15 I will give back to her the vineyards she had and make Trouble Valley a door of hope. She will respond to me there as she did when she was young, when she came from Egypt. 16 Then once again she will call me her husband—she will no longer call me her Baal./ 17 I will never let her speak the name of Baal again.

18 At that time I will make a covenant with all the wild animals and birds, so that they will not harm my people. I will also remove all weapons of war from the land, all swords and bows, and will let my people live in peace and safety.

Let my people live in peace. (2:18)

19 Israel, I will make you my wife;
 I will be true and faithful;
 I will show you constant love and
   mercy
 and make you mine forever.
20 I will keep my promise and make you
   mine,
 and you will acknowledge me as
   LORD.
21-22 At that time I will answer the prayers of
   my people Israel.g
 I will make rain fall on the earth,
 and the earth will produce grain and
   grapes and olives.
23 I will establish my people in the land and
   make them prosper.
 I will show love to those who were called
   "Unloved,"
 and to those who were called "Not-
   My-People"
 I will say, "You are my people,"
 and they will answer, "You are our God."

Hosea and the Unfaithful Woman

3 1 The LORD said to me, "Go againh and show your love for a woman who is committing adultery with a lover. You must love her just as I still love the people of Israel, even though they turn to other gods and like to take offerings of raisins to idols."i

2 So I paid fifteen pieces of silver and seven bushels of barley to buy her. 3 I told her that for a long time she would have to wait for me without being a prostitute or committing adultery; and during this time I would wait for her. 4 In just this way the people of Israel will have to live for a long time without kings or leaders, without sacrifices or sacred stone pillars, without idols or images to use for divination. 5 But the time will come when the people of Israel will once again turn to the LORD their God and to a descendant of David their king. Then they will fear the LORD and will receive his good gifts.

/ 2.16 BAAL: *This title of the Canaanite god means "Lord"; another meaning of the word is "husband."*
g 2.21–22 ISRAEL: *The Hebrew text here refers to Israel as Jezreel (see 1.4, 11).* h 3.1 The LORD . . . again; or The LORD spoke to me again. He said, "Go . . . " i 3.1 OFFERINGS OF RAISINS TO IDOLS: *Dried grapes were used in the worship of fertility gods, who were believed to give abundant harvests to their worshipers.*
2:15 Josh 7:24–26 2:23 Rom 9:25; 1 Pet 2:10

The Lord's Accusation against Israel

4 ¹The Lord has an accusation to bring against the people who live in this land. Listen, Israel, to what he says: "There is no faithfulness or love in the land, and the people do not acknowledge me as God. ²They make promises and break them; they lie, murder, steal, and commit adultery. Crimes increase, and there is one murder after another. ³And so the land will dry up, and everything that lives on it will die. All the animals and birds, and even the fish, will die."

The Lord Accuses the Priests

⁴The Lord says, "Let no one accuse the people or reprimand them—my complaint is against you priests.ʲ ⁵Night and day you blunder on, and the prophets do no better than you. I am going to destroy Israel, your mother. ⁶My people are doomed because they do not acknowledge me. You priests have refused to acknowledge me and have rejected my teaching, and so I reject you and will not acknowledge your sons as my priests.

⁷"The more of you priests there are, the more you sin against me, and so I will turn your honor into disgrace. ⁸You grow rich from the sins of my people, and so you want them to sin more and more. ⁹You will suffer the same punishment as the people! I will punish you and make you pay for the evil you do. ¹⁰You will eat your share of the sacrifices, but still be hungry. You will worship the fertility gods, but still have no children, because you have turned away from me to follow other gods."

The Lord Condemns Pagan Worship

¹¹The Lord says, "Wine, both old and new, is robbing my people of their senses! ¹²They ask for revelations from a piece of wood! A stick tells them what they want to

They ask for revelations from a piece of wood! (4:12)

know! They have left me. Like a woman who becomes a prostitute, they have given themselves to other gods. ¹³At sacred places on the mountaintops they offer sacrifices, and on the hills they burn incense under tall, spreading trees, because the shade is so pleasant!

"As a result, your daughters serve as prostitutes, and your daughters-in-law commit adultery. ¹⁴Yet I will not punish them for this, because you yourselves go off with temple prostitutes,ᵏ and together with them you offer pagan sacrifices. As the proverb says, 'A people without sense will be ruined.'

¹⁵"Even though you people of Israel are unfaithful to me, may Judah not be guilty of the same thing. Don't worship at Gilgal or Bethaven,ˡ or make promises there in the name of the living Lord. ¹⁶The people of Israel are as stubborn as mules. How can I feed them like lambs in a meadow? ¹⁷The people of Israel are under the spell of idols. Let them go their own way. ¹⁸After drinking much wine, they delight in their prostitution, preferring disgrace to honor. ¹⁹They will be carried away as by the wind, and they will be ashamed of their pagan sacrifices.ᵐ,ⁿ

5 ¹"Listen to this, you priests! Pay attention, people of Israel! Listen, you that belong to the royal family! You are supposed

---

ʲ **4.4** *Probable text* my complaint is against you priests; *Hebrew* your people are like those with a complaint against the priests.   ᵏ **4.14** TEMPLE PROSTITUTES: *These women were found in Canaanite temples, where fertility gods were worshiped. It was believed that intercourse with these prostitutes assured fertile fields and herds.*   ˡ **4.15** BETHAVEN: *This name means "house of evil" or "house of idolatry" and in this passage refers to the city of Bethel, a name which means "house of God." See also 10.8.*   ᵐ **4.19** sacrifices; *some ancient translations* altars.   ⁿ **4.19** *Verses 17–19 in Hebrew are unclear.*

to judge with justice—so judgment will fall on you! You have become a trap at Mizpah, a net spread on Mount Tabor, [2]a deep pit at Acacia City,[o] and I will punish all of you. [3]I know what Israel is like—she cannot hide from me. She has been unfaithful, and her people are unfit to worship me."

Hosea Warns against Idolatry

[4]The evil that the people have done keeps them from returning to their God. Idolatry has a powerful hold on them, and they do not acknowledge the LORD. [5]The arrogance of the people of Israel cries out against them. Their sins make them stumble and fall, and the people of Judah fall with them. [6]They take their sheep and cattle to offer as sacrifices to the LORD, but it does them no good. They cannot find him, for he has left them. [7]They have been unfaithful to the LORD; their children do not belong to him. So now they and their lands will soon be destroyed.

War between Judah and Israel

[8]Blow the war trumpets in Gibeah! Sound the alarm in Ramah! Raise the war cry at Bethaven![p] Into battle, men of Benjamin! [9]The day of punishment is coming, and Israel will be ruined. People of Israel, this will surely happen!

[10]The LORD says, "I am angry because the leaders of Judah have invaded Israel and stolen land from her. So I will pour out punishment on them like a flood. [11]Israel is suffering oppression; she has lost land that was rightfully hers, because she insisted on going for help to those who had none to give.[q] [12]I will bring destruction on Israel and ruin on the people of Judah.

[13]"When Israel saw how sick she was and when Judah saw her own wounds, then Israel went to Assyria to ask the great emperor for help, but he could not cure them or heal their wounds. [14]I will attack the people of Israel and Judah like a lion. I myself will tear them to pieces and then leave them. When I drag them off, no one will be able to save them.

[15]"I will abandon my people until they have suffered enough for their sins and come looking for me. Perhaps in their suffering they will try to find me."

The People's Insincere Repentance

6 [1]The people say, "Let's return to the LORD! He has hurt us, but he will be sure to heal us; he has wounded us, but he will bandage our wounds, won't he? [2]In two or three days he will revive us, and we will live in his presence. [3]Let us try to know the LORD. He will come to us as surely as the day dawns, as surely as the spring rains fall upon the earth."

[4]But the LORD says, "Israel and Judah, what am I going to do with you? Your love for me disappears as quickly as morning mist; it is like dew, that vanishes early in the day. [5]That is why I have sent my prophets to you with my message of judgment and destruction. What I want from you is plain and clear: [6]I want your constant love, not your animal sacrifices. I would rather have my people know me than burn offerings to me.

[7]"But as soon as they entered the land at Adam,[r] they broke the covenant I had made with them. [8]Gilead is a city full of evil people and murderers. [9]The priests are like a gang of robbers who wait in ambush for someone. Even on the road to the holy place at Shechem they commit murder. And they do all this evil deliberately! [10]I have seen a horrible thing in Israel: my people have defiled themselves by worshiping idols.

[11]"And as for you, people of Judah, I have set a time to punish you also for what you are doing.

7 [1]"Whenever I want to heal my people Israel and make them prosperous again, all I can see is their wickedness and the evil

---

[o] **5.2** *Probable text* a deep pit at Acacia City; *Hebrew unclear.*   [p] **5.8** BETHAVEN: *This name means "house of evil" or "house of idolatry" and in this passage refers to the city of Bethel, a name which means "house of God." See also 10.8.*
[q] **5.11** *Probable text* those who had none to give; *Hebrew* command.   [r] **6.7** *Probable text* But . . . at Adam; *Hebrew* But like Adam.
6:6 Mt 9:13; 12:7

they do. They cheat one another; they break into houses and steal; they rob people in the streets. [2] It never enters their heads that I will remember all this evil; but their sins surround them, and I cannot avoid seeing them."

Conspiracy in the Palace

[3] The LORD says, "People deceive the king and his officers by their evil plots. [4] They are all treacherous and disloyal. Their hatred smolders like the fire in an oven, which is not stirred by the baker until the dough is ready to bake. [5] On the day of the king's celebration they made the king and his officials drunk and foolish with wine. [6] Yes, they burned[s] like an oven with their plotting. All night their anger smoldered, and in the morning it burst into flames.

[7] "In the heat of their anger they murdered their rulers. Their kings have been assassinated one after another, but no one prays to me for help."

Israel and the Nations

[8] The LORD says, "The people of Israel are like a half-baked loaf of bread. They rely on the nations around them [9] and do not realize that this reliance on foreigners has robbed them of their strength. Their days are numbered, but they don't even know it. [10] The arrogance of the people of Israel cries out against them. In spite of everything that has happened, they have not returned to me, the LORD their God. [11] Israel flits around like a silly pigeon; first her people call on Egypt for help, and then they run to Assyria! [12] But I will spread out a net and catch them like birds as they go by. I will punish them for the evil they have done.[t]

[13] "They are doomed! They have left me and rebelled against me. They will be destroyed. I wanted to save them, but their worship of me was false. [14] They have not prayed to me sincerely, but instead they throw themselves down and wail as the heathen do. When they pray for grain and wine, they gash themselves like pagans. What rebels

they are! [15] Even though I was the one who brought them up and made them strong, they plotted against me. [16] They keep on turning away from me to a god that is powerless.[u] They are as unreliable as a crooked bow. Because their leaders talk arrogantly, they will die a violent death, and the Egyptians will laugh."

The LORD Condemns Israel for Idol Worship

8 [1] The LORD says, "Sound the alarm! Enemies are swooping down on my land like eagles! My people have broken the covenant I made with them and have rebelled against my teaching. [2] Even though they call me their God and claim that they are my people and that they know me, [3] they have rejected what is good. Because of this their enemies will pursue them.

[4] "My people chose kings, but they did it on their own. They appointed leaders, but without my approval. They took their silver and gold and made idols—for their own destruction. [5] I hate the gold bull worshiped by the people of the city of Samaria. I am furious with them. How long will it be before they give up their idolatry? [6] An Israelite craftsman made the idol, and it is not a god at all! The gold bull worshiped in Samaria will be smashed to pieces! [7] When they sow the wind, they will reap a storm! A field of grain that doesn't ripen can never produce any bread. But even if it did, foreigners would eat it up. [8] Israel has become like any other nation and is as useless as a broken pot. [9] Stubborn as wild donkeys, the people of Israel go their own way. They have gone off to seek help from Assyria and have paid other nations to protect them. [10] But now I am going to gather them together and punish them. Soon they will writhe in pain when the emperor of Assyria oppresses them.

[11] "The more altars the people of Israel build for removing sin, the more places they have for sinning! [12] I write down countless teachings for the people, but they reject them as strange and foreign. [13] They offer

[s] **7.6** *One ancient translation* burned; *Hebrew* drew near. report to their congregation. [u] **7.16** *Probable text* a god that is powerless; *Hebrew unclear.* [t] **7.12** *Probable text* the evil they have done; *Hebrew* the

Hosea

sacrifices to me and eat the meat of the sacrifices.*v* But I, the LORD, am not pleased with them, and now I will remember their sin and punish them for it; I will send them back to Egypt!

14 "The people of Israel have built palaces, but they have forgotten their own Maker. The people of Judah have built fortified cities. But I will send fire that will burn down their palaces and their cities."

Hosea Announces Punishment for Israel

9 ¹People of Israel, stop celebrating your festivals like pagans. You have turned away from your God and have been unfaithful to him. All over the land you have sold yourselves like prostitutes to the god Baal and have loved the grain you thought he paid you with! ²But soon you will not have enough grain and olive oil, and there will be no wine. ³The people of Israel will not remain in the LORD's land, but will have to go back to Egypt and will have to eat forbidden food*w* in Assyria. ⁴In those foreign lands they will not be able to make wine offerings to the LORD or bring their sacrifices to him. Their food will defile everyone who eats it, like food eaten at funerals. It will be used only to satisfy their hunger; none of it will be taken as an offering to the LORD's Temple. ⁵And when the time comes for the appointed festivals in honor of the LORD, what will they do then? ⁶When the disaster comes and the people are scattered, the Egyptians will gather them up—gather them for burial there at Memphis! Their treasures of silver and the places where their homes once stood will be overgrown with weeds and thorn bushes.

⁷The time for punishment has come, the time when people will get what they deserve. When that happens, Israel will know it! "This prophet," you say, "is a fool. This inspired man is insane." You people hate me so much because your sin is so great. ⁸God has sent me as a prophet to warn his people

Israel. Yet wherever I go, you try to trap me like a bird. Even in God's Temple the people are the prophet's enemies. ⁹They are hopelessly evil in what they do, just as they were at Gibeah.*x* God will remember their sin and punish them for it.

Israel's Sin and Its Consequences

¹⁰The LORD says, "When I first found Israel, it was like finding grapes growing in the desert. When I first saw your ancestors, it was like seeing the first ripe figs of the season. But when they came to Mount Peor, they began to worship Baal and soon became as disgusting as the gods they loved. ¹¹Israel's greatness will fly away like a bird, and there will be no more children born to them, no more women pregnant, no more children conceived. ¹²But even if they did bring up children, I would take them away and not leave one alive. When I abandon these people, terrible things will happen to them."

¹³LORD, I can see their children being hunted down*y* and killed. ¹⁴What shall I ask you to do to these people? Make their women barren! Make them unable to nurse their babies!

The LORD's Judgment on Israel

¹⁵The LORD says, "All their evildoing began in Gilgal. It was there that I began to hate them. And because of the evil they have done, I will drive them out of my land. I will not love them any more; all their leaders have rebelled against me. ¹⁶The people of Israel are like a plant whose roots have dried up and which bears no fruit. They will have no children, but even if they did, I would kill the children so dear to them."

The Prophet Speaks about Israel

¹⁷The God I serve will reject his people, because they have not listened to him. They will become wanderers among the nations.

---

v **8.13** They offer . . . the sacrifices; *Hebrew unclear.*   *w* **9.3** FORBIDDEN FOOD: *The Law of Moses prohibited the eating of certain foods as being ritually unclean (see Lev 11).*   *x* **9.9** GIBEAH: *At this city some Israelites of the tribe of Benjamin raped a Levite's concubine; this caused a civil war that almost wiped out the Benjaminites (see Judg 19—21).*
y **3** *Probable text* being hunted down; *Hebrew unclear.*

Lk 21:22   **9:9** Judg 19:1–30   **9:10** Num 25:1–5

10

¹The people of Israel were like a grapevine that was full of grapes. The more prosperous they were, the more altars they built. The more productive their land was, the more beautiful they made the sacred stone pillars they worship. ²The people whose hearts are deceitful must now suffer for their sins. God will break down their altars and destroy their sacred pillars.

³These people will soon be saying, "We have no king because we did not fear the LORD. But what could a king do for us anyway?" ⁴They utter empty words and make false promises and useless treaties. Justice has become injustice, growing like poisonous weeds in a plowed field.

⁵The people who live in the city of Samaria will be afraid and will mourn the loss of the gold bull ᶻ at Bethaven. ᵃ They and the priests who serve the idol will weep over it. They will wail when it is stripped of its golden splendor. ⁶The idol will be carried off to Assyria as tribute to the great emperor. The people of Israel will be disgraced and put to shame because of the advice they followed. ⁷Their king will be carried off, like a chip of wood on water. ⁸The hilltop shrines of Aven, ᵃ where the people of Israel worship idols, will be destroyed. Thorns and weeds will grow up over their altars. The people will call out to the mountains, "Hide us!" and to the hills, "Cover us!"

Thorns and weeds will grow up over their altars. (10:8)

The LORD Pronounces Judgment on Israel

⁹The LORD says, "The people of Israel have not stopped sinning against me since the time of their sin at Gibeah. ᵇ So at Gibeah war will catch up with them. ¹⁰I will attack ᶜ this sinful people and punish them. Nations will join together against them, and they will be punished for their many sins.

¹¹"Israel was once like a well-trained young cow, ready and willing to thresh grain. But I decided to put a yoke ᵈ on her beautiful neck and to harness her for harder work. I made Judah pull the plow and Israel pull the harrow. ¹²I said, 'Plow new ground for yourselves, plant righteousness, and reap the blessings that your devotion to me will produce. It is time for you to turn to me, your LORD, and I will come and pour out blessings upon you.' ¹³But instead you planted evil and reaped its harvest. You have eaten the fruit produced by your lies.

"Because you trusted in your chariots ᵉ and in the large number of your soldiers, ¹⁴war will come to your people, and all your fortresses will be destroyed. It will be like the day when King Shalman destroyed the city of Betharbel in battle, and mothers and their children were crushed to death. ¹⁵That is what will happen to you, people of Bethel, because of the terrible evil that you have done. As soon as the battle begins, the king of Israel will die."

God's Love for His Rebellious People

11

¹The LORD says,
"When Israel was a child, I loved him
and called him out of Egypt as my son.ᶠ

ᶻ **10.5** *Some ancient translations* bull; *Hebrew* cows.   ᵃ **10.5, 8** BETHAVEN: *This name means "house of evil" or "house of idolatry" and in this passage refers to the city of Bethel, a name which means "house of God." In verse 8, Bethaven is called Aven. See also 4.15 and 5.8.*   ᵇ **10.9** GIBEAH: *See 9.9.*   ᶜ **10.10** *One ancient translation* I will attack; *Hebrew* In my desire.   ᵈ **10.11** *Probable text* put a yoke; *Hebrew* spare.   ᵉ **10.13** *One ancient translation* chariots; *Hebrew* way.   ᶠ **11.1** him, and called him . . . son; *or* him; from the time he left Egypt I have called him my son.
10:8 Lk 23:30; Rev 6:16   **10:9** Judg 19:1–30   **10:12** Jer 4:3   **11:1** Ex 4:22; Mt 2:15

Hosea

2 But the more I *g* called to him,
the more he turned away from me. *h*
My people sacrificed to Baal;
they burned incense to idols.
3 Yet I was the one who taught Israel to
walk.
I took my people up in my arms, *i*
but they did not acknowledge that I
took care of them.
4 I drew them to me with affection and love.
I picked them up and held them to my
cheek;
I bent down to them and fed them. *j*

5 "They refuse to return to me, and so
they must return to Egypt, and Assyria will
rule them. 6 War will sweep through their
cities and break down the city gates. It will
destroy my people because they do what
they themselves think best. 7 They insist on
turning away from me. They will cry out
because of the yoke that is on them, but no
one will lift it from them. *k*

"They insist on turning away from me." (11:7)

8 "How can I give you up, Israel?
How can I abandon you?
Could I ever destroy you as I did Admah,
or treat you as I did Zeboiim?
My heart will not let me do it!
My love for you is too strong.
9 I will not punish you in my anger;
I will not destroy Israel again.
For I am God and not a mere human
being.
I, the Holy One, am with you.
I will not come to you in anger.

10 "My people will follow me when I roar
like a lion at their enemies. They will hurry

Parents Sacrifice
for Their Children

A section in Hosea, chapter 11,
describes God as a loving parent:
*Yet I was the one who taught
Israel to walk.*
I took my people up in my arms,
*but they did not acknowledge
that I took care of them.*
*I drew them to me with affection
and love.*
*I picked them up and held
them to my cheek;*
*I bent down to them and fed
them. (Verses 3–4)*
We often forget about the sacrifices our parents make for us.
They did everything for us when
we were tiny and completely
dependent on them. Sometimes,
they have to let us suffer painful
consequences in order to learn
important lessons. Sometimes in
the difficult process of growing
up, we rebel against our parents,
we insult them, or we even turn
away from them. Despite this,
most parents continue to love
their children.

God also lets us suffer the consequences of our actions. God
knows we have to learn the hard
way sometimes. But God is always
there, like a loving parent, waiting
for us to come back. A good thing
to think about every day—not just
on Mother's Day or Father's Day.

— Hosea 11:1–4

g **11.2** *One ancient translation* I; *Hebrew* they.   *h* **11.2** *One ancient translation* me; *Hebrew* them.   *i* **11.3** *One
ancient translation* I . . . my arms; *Hebrew* He . . . his arms.   *j* **11.4** *Verse 4 in Hebrew is unclear.*   *k* **11.7** *Verse 7 in
Hebrew is unclear.*
11:8 Deut 29:23

to me from the west. ¹¹They will come from Egypt, as swiftly as birds, and from Assyria, like doves. I will bring them to their homes again. I, the LORD, have spoken."

Israel and Judah Are Condemned

¹²The LORD says, "The people of Israel have surrounded me with lies and deceit, and the people of Judah are still rebelling against me, the faithful and holy God.

12 ¹Everything that the people of Israel do from morning to night is useless and destructive. Treachery and acts of violence increase among them. They make treaties with Assyria and do business with Egypt."

²The LORD has an accusation to bring against the people of Judah; he is also going to punish Israel for the way her people act. He will pay them back for what they have done. ³Their ancestor Jacob struggled with his twin brother Esau while the two of them were still in their mother's womb; when Jacob grew up, he fought against God— ⁴he fought against an angel and won. He wept and asked for a blessing. And at Bethel God came to our ancestor Jacob and spoke with him.ˡ ⁵This was the LORD God Almighty—the LORD is the name by which he is to be worshiped. ⁶So now, descendants of Jacob, trust in your God and return to him. Be loyal and just, and wait patiently for your God to act.

Further Words of Judgment

⁷The LORD says, "The people of Israel are as dishonest as the Canaanites; they love to cheat their customers with false scales. ⁸'We are rich,' they say. 'We've made a fortune. And no one can accuse us of getting rich dishonestly.' ⁹But I, the LORD your God who led you out of Egypt, I will make you live in tents again, as you did when I came to you in the desert. ¹⁰"I spoke to the prophets and gave them many visions, and through the prophets I gave my people warnings. ¹¹Yet idols are worshiped in Gilead, and those who worship them will die. Bulls are sacrificed in Gilgal,

and the altars there will become piles of stone in the open fields."

The altars there will become piles of stone. (12:11)

¹²Our ancestor Jacob had to flee to Mesopotamia, where, in order to get a wife, he worked for another man and took care of his sheep. ¹³The LORD sent a prophet to rescue the people of Israel from slavery in Egypt and to take care of them. ¹⁴The people of Israel have made the LORD bitterly angry; they deserve death for their crimes. Their Lord will punish them for the disgrace they have brought on him.

Final Judgment on Israel

13 ¹In the past, when the tribe of Ephraim spoke, the other tribes of Israel were afraid; they looked up to Ephraim. But the people sinned by worshiping Baal, and for this they will die. ²They still keep on sinning by making metal images to worship—idols of silver, designed by human minds, made by human hands. And then they say, "Offer sacrifices to them!" How can anyone kiss those idols—idols in the shape of bulls!ᵐ ³And so these people will disappear like morning mist, like the dew that vanishes early in the day. They will be like chaff which the wind blows from the threshing place, like smoke from a chimney.

How can anyone kiss those idols? (13:2)

ˡ **12.4** *Some ancient translations* him; *Hebrew* us.   ᵐ **13.2** *Probable text* And then they . . . bulls!; *Hebrew unclear.*
12:3 Gen 25:26   **12:3, 4** Gen 32:24–26   **12:4** Gen 28:10–22   **12:9** Lev 23:42, 43   **12:12** Gen 29:1–20
12:13 Ex 12:50, 51

Hosea

⁴The LORD says, "I am the LORD your God, who led you out of Egypt. You have no God but me. I alone am your savior. ⁵I took care of you in a dry, desert land. ⁶But when you entered the good land, you became full and satisfied, and then you grew proud and forgot me. ⁷So I will attack you like a lion. Like a leopard I will lie in wait along your path. ⁸I will attack you like a bear that has lost her cubs, and I will tear you open. Like a lion I will devour you on the spot, and will tear you to pieces like a wild animal.

⁹"I will destroy you, people of Israel! Then who can help you?[n] ¹⁰You asked for a king and for leaders, but how can they save the nation?[o] ¹¹In my anger I have given you kings, and in my fury I have taken them away.

¹²"Israel's sin and guilt are on record, and the records are safely stored away. ¹³Israel has a chance to live, but is too foolish to take it— like a child about to be born, who refuses to come out of the womb. ¹⁴I will not save this people from the world of the dead or rescue them from the power of death. Bring on[p] your plagues, death! Bring on[p] your destruction, world of the dead! I will no longer have pity for this people. ¹⁵Even though Israel flourishes like weeds,[q] I will send a hot east wind from the desert, and it will dry up their springs and wells. It will take away everything of value. ¹⁶Samaria must be punished for rebelling against me. Her people will die in war; babies will be dashed to the ground, and pregnant women will be ripped open."

Hosea's Plea to Israel

14 ¹Return to the LORD your God, people of Israel. Your sin has made you stumble and fall. ²Return to the LORD, and let this prayer be your offering to him: "Forgive all our sins and accept our prayer, and we will praise you as we have promised. ³Assyria can never save us, and war horses cannot protect us. We will never again say to our idols that they are our God. O LORD, you show mercy to those who have no one else to turn to."

Like a leopard I will lie in wait. (13:7)

The LORD Promises New Life for Israel

⁴The LORD says,
"I will bring my people back to me.
I will love them with all my heart;
    no longer am I angry with them.
⁵I will be to the people of Israel
    like rain in a dry land.
They will blossom like flowers;
    they will be firmly rooted
    like the trees of Lebanon.
⁶They will be alive with new growth,
    and beautiful like olive trees.
They will be fragrant
    like the cedars of Lebanon.
⁷Once again they will live under my
    protection.
They will grow crops of grain
    and be fruitful like a vineyard.
They will be as famous as the wine of
    Lebanon.
⁸The people of Israel[r] will have nothing
    more to do with idols;
I will answer their prayers and take care
    of them.
Like an evergreen tree I will shelter them;
    I am the source of all their blessings."

Conclusion

⁹May those who are wise understand what is written here, and may they take it to heart. The LORD's ways are right, and righteous people live by following them, but sinners stumble and fall because they ignore them.

---

[n] **13.9** *One ancient translation* who can help you?; *Hebrew* in me is your help.   [o] **13.10** *Verse 10 in Hebrew is unclear.*   [p] **13.14** *Some ancient translations* Bring on; *Hebrew* I will be.   [q] **13.15** *Probable text* like weeds; *Hebrew* among brothers.   [r] **14.8** *One ancient translation* The people of Israel; *Hebrew* Israel, I.
13.5, 6 Deut 8:11–17   **13.10** 1 Sam 8:5, 6   **13.11** a 1 Sam 10:17–24; b 1 Sam 15:26   **13.14** 1 Cor 15:55

A plague of locusts came and destroyed the land! Locusts swarmed and hopped everywhere! They were destroying everything in their path.

Joel uses the locusts as an opportunity to get people to pay more attention to God. He talks about the "Day of the Lord," which means the end of time, and describes it in two ways—as bad news and good news. The bad news is "The day of the LORD is coming soon. It will be a dark and gloomy day" (2:1–2). The good news is "Be glad . . . rejoice at what the LORD your God has done for you. . . . [God] will give you back what you lost . . . you will have plenty to eat, and be satisfied" (2:23, 25, 26). The bad news is that we sin—that has to stop. But the good news is that God loves us and cares for us—that is a great comfort.

Chap. 1:4

Headlines

- The Day of the Lord Is Near! (1:15—2:1)
- Spirit Poured Out on Women and Men! (2:28–29)
- Stream of Blessings Flow from Temple (3:16–18)

FACTOIDS

Who wrote this book? The prophet Joel, and perhaps other scribes (writers). It was probably written some time after the Babylonian Exile.

Why was it written? To help people cope with the locusts and to understand that despite plagues and natural disasters, there is still hope because God is with them.

Who are the young people in this book? Young people see visions in Joel 2:28–29. This is read each year during Mass on Pentecost Sunday.

Important themes

- God is always with us, in suffering and in celebration.
- Eventually, the wrongs we commit will catch up with us, and we will have to answer to God for our sins.
- All of our blessings come from God. When the time for suffering ends, there will be great joy.

JOEL

1 ¹This is the LORD's message to Joel son of Pethuel.

The People Mourn the Destruction of the Crops

²Pay attention, you older people;
  everyone in Judah, listen.
Has anything like this ever happened
  in your time or the time of your
    ancestors?
³Tell your children about it;
  they will tell their children,
  who in turn will tell the next
    generation.

⁴Swarm after swarm of locusts settled on
    the crops;
  what one swarm left, the next swarm
    devoured.
⁵Wake up and weep, you drunkards;
  cry, you wine-drinkers;
  the grapes for making new wine have
    been destroyed.

⁶An army of locusts has attacked our land;
  they are powerful and too many to
    count;
  their teeth are as sharp as those of a
    lion.
⁷They have destroyed our grapevines
  and chewed up our fig trees.
They have stripped off the bark,
  till the branches are white.

⁸Cry, you people, like a young woman
    who mourns the death
  of the man she was going to marry.
⁹There is no grain or wine to offer in the
    Temple;
  the priests mourn because they have no
    offerings for the LORD.
¹⁰The fields are bare;
  the ground mourns
    because the grain is destroyed,
    the grapes are dried up,
    and the olive trees are withered.

The ground mourns. (1:10)

¹¹Grieve, you farmers;
  cry, you that take care of the vineyards,
    because the wheat, the barley,
    yes all the crops are destroyed.
¹²The grapevines and fig trees have
    withered;
  all the fruit trees have wilted and
    died.
The joy of the people is gone.
¹³Put on sackcloth and weep,
  you priests who serve at the altar!
Go into the Temple and mourn all
    night!
There is no grain or wine to offer your
    God.
¹⁴Give orders for a fast;
  call an assembly!
Gather the leaders
  and all the people of Judah
  into the Temple of the LORD your God
  and cry out to him!
¹⁵The day of the LORD is near,
  the day when the Almighty brings
    destruction.
What terror that day will bring!

¹⁶We look on helpless as our crops are
    destroyed.
There is no joy in the Temple of our
    God.
¹⁷The seeds die in the dry earth.
There is no grain to be stored,
  and so the empty granaries are in ruins.
¹⁸The cattle are bellowing in distress
  because there is no pasture for them;
  the flocks of sheep also suffer.

1:6 Rev 9:8   1:15 Isa 13:6

¹⁹ I cry out to you, LORD,
　　because the pastures and trees are dried
　　　up,
　　as though a fire had burned them.
²⁰ Even the wild animals cry out to you
　　because the streams have become dry.

The Locusts as a Warning of the Day of the LORD

2 ¹ Blow the trumpet; sound the alarm
　　on Zion, God's sacred hill.*ᵃ*
　　Tremble, people of Judah!
　　The day of the LORD is coming soon.
² It will be a dark and gloomy day,
　　a black and cloudy day.
　　The great army of locusts advances
　　like darkness spreading over the
　　　mountains.
　　There has never been anything like it,
　　and there never will be again.

³ Like fire they eat up the plants.
　　In front of them the land is like the
　　　Garden of Eden,
　　but behind them it is a barren desert.
　　Nothing escapes them.
⁴ They look like horses;
　　they run like war-horses.
⁵ As they leap on the tops of the mountains,
　　they rattle like chariots;
　　they crackle like dry grass on fire.
　　They are lined up like a great army ready
　　　for battle.
⁶ As they approach, everyone is terrified;
　　every face turns pale.
⁷ They attack like warriors;
　　they climb the walls like soldiers.
　　They all keep marching straight ahead
　　and do not change direction
⁸ 　or get in each other's way.
　　They swarm through defenses,
　　and nothing can stop them.
⁹ They rush against the city;
　　they run over the walls;
　　they climb up the houses
　　and go in through the windows like
　　　thieves.
¹⁰ The earth shakes as they advance;
　　the sky trembles.

The sun and the moon grow dark,
　　and the stars no longer shine.
¹¹ The LORD thunders commands to his
　　　army.
　　The troops that obey him
　　are many and mighty.
　　How terrible is the day of the LORD!
　　Who will survive it?

A Call to Repentance

¹² "But even now," says the LORD,
　　"repent sincerely and return to me
　　with fasting and weeping and
　　　mourning.
¹³ Let your broken heart show your sorrow;
　　tearing your clothes is not enough."
　　Come back to the LORD your God.
　　He is kind and full of mercy;
　　he is patient and keeps his promise;
　　he is always ready to forgive and not
　　　punish.

Let your broken heart show your sorrow. (2:13)

¹⁴ Perhaps the LORD your God will change
　　　his mind
　　and bless you with abundant crops.
　　Then you can offer him grain and wine.

¹⁵ Blow the trumpet on Mount Zion;
　　give orders for a fast and call an
　　　assembly!
¹⁶ Gather the people together;
　　prepare them for a sacred meeting;
　　bring the old people;
　　gather the children
　　and the babies too.
　　Even newly married couples
　　must leave their homes and come.

ᵃ **2:1** SACRED HILL: *Mount Zion (see Zion in Word List).*
2:4, 5 Rev 9:7–9　**2:10** Rev 8:12　**2:11** Rev 6:17

Joel

Ash Wednesday and Lent

Catholic Connections

Have you heard of prayer, fasting, and alms-giving—the traditional spiritual practices of Lent?

- By spending more time at prayer, we refocus on God. We remember our sinfulness and God's love.
- By fasting, or eating less, we remind ourselves that we depend on God for what we need to live. Fasting also helps make us aware of the needs of people who are poor.
- By almsgiving—donating money, food, or clothing to poor and needy people—we put into practice what Jesus taught. Our material things are meant to be shared.

In the Old Testament reading on Ash Wednesday, we listen to Joel 2:12–18. The prophet reminds us to return to the Lord with all our heart, with fasting and weeping. In the Gospel for Ash Wednesday, Jesus tells us how to be during Lent—humble and quiet. Don't brag about how much money we give to poor people. Don't try to impress people with our perfect prayers. Don't complain about how hungry we are while fasting. Then, by the time Easter comes around, we really will have something to celebrate!

— Joel 2:12–18

17 The priests, serving the LORD
  between the altar and the entrance of
   the Temple,
must weep and pray:
  "Have pity on your people, LORD.
  Do not let other nations despise us and
   mock us
  by saying, 'Where is your God?'"

God Restores Fertility to the Land

18 Then the LORD showed concern for his
  land;
  he had mercy on his people.
19 He answered them:
  "Now I am going to give you
  grain and wine and olive oil,
  and you will be satisfied.
  Other nations will no longer despise
   you.

20 I will remove the locust army that came
   from the north
  and will drive some of them into the
   desert.
Their front ranks will be driven into the
   Dead Sea,
  their rear ranks into the Mediterranean.
  Their dead bodies will stink.
I will destroy them because of all they
  have done to you.

21 "Fields, don't be afraid,
  but be joyful and glad
  because of all the LORD has done for
   you.
22 Animals, don't be afraid.
  The pastures are green;
  the trees bear their fruit,
  and there are plenty of figs and grapes.

23 "Be glad, people of Zion,
  rejoice at what the LORD your God has
   done for you.

He has given you the right amount of
autumn rain;[b]
he has poured down the winter rain for
you
and the spring rain as before.
24 The threshing places will be full of grain;
the pits beside the presses will overflow
with wine and olive oil.
25 I will give you back what you lost
in the years when swarms of locusts ate
your crops.
It was I who sent this army against
you.
26 Now you will have plenty to eat, and be
satisfied.
You will praise the LORD your God,
who has done wonderful things for
you.
My people will never be despised
again.
27 Then, Israel, you will know that I am
among you
and that I, the LORD, am your God
and there is no other.
My people will never be despised
again.

The Day of the LORD

28 "Afterward I will pour out my Spirit on
everyone:
your sons and daughters will proclaim
my message;
your old people will have dreams,
and your young people will see visions.
29 At that time I will pour out my Spirit
even on servants, both men and
women.

30 "I will give warnings of that day
in the sky and on the earth;
there will be bloodshed, fire, and clouds
of smoke.
31 The sun will be darkened,
and the moon will turn red as blood
before the great and terrible day of the
LORD comes.

32 But all who ask the LORD for help will be
saved.
As the LORD has said,
'Some in Jerusalem will escape;
those whom I choose will survive.' "

God Will Judge the Nations

3 1 The LORD says,
"At that time I will restore
the prosperity of Judah and Jerusalem.
2 I will gather all the nations
and bring them to the Valley of
Judgment.
There I will judge them
for all they have done to my people.
They have scattered the Israelites in
foreign countries
and divided Israel, my land.
3 They threw dice to decide
who would get the captives.
They sold boys and girls into slavery
to pay for prostitutes and wine.

4 "What are you trying to do to me, Tyre,
Sidon, and all of Philistia? Are you trying to
pay me back for something? If you are, I will
quickly pay you back! 5 You have taken my
silver and gold and carried my rich treasures
into your temples. 6 You have taken the people of Judah and Jerusalem far from their
own country and sold them to the Greeks.
7 Now I am going to bring them out of the
places to which you have sold them. I will
do to you what you have done to them. 8 I
will let your sons and daughters be sold to
the people of Judah; they will sell them to
the far-off Sabeans. I, the LORD, have spoken.

9 "Make this announcement among the
nations:
'Prepare for war;
call your warriors;
gather all your soldiers and march!
10 Hammer the points of your plows into
swords
and your pruning knives into spears.
Even the weak must fight.

---

b **2:23** right amount of autumn rain; *or* autumn rain because he is just.
2:31 Mt 24:29; Mk 13:24, 25; Lk 21:25; Rev 6:12, 13   **2:28–32** Acts 2:17–21   **2:32** Rom 10:13   **3:4–8** Isa
23:1–18; Ezek 26:1—28:26; Am 1:9, 10; Zech 9:1–4; Mt 11:21, 22; Lk 10:13, 14   **3:4–8** Isa 14:29–31; Jer
47:1–7; Ezek 25:15–17; Am 1:6–8; Zeph 2:4–7; Zech 9:5–7   **3:10** Isa 2:4; Mic 4:3

11 Hurry[c] and come,
     all you surrounding nations,
     and gather in the valley.' "

Send down, O LORD, your army to attack
     them!

12 "The nations must get ready
     and come to the Valley of Judgment.
   There I, the LORD, will sit to judge
     all the surrounding nations.
13 They are very wicked;
   cut them down like grain
     at harvest time;
   crush them as grapes are crushed
     in a full wine press
     until the wine runs over."

14 Thousands and thousands
     are in the Valley of Judgment.
   It is there that the day of the LORD
     will soon come.
15 The sun and the moon grow dark,
     and the stars no longer shine.

God Will Bless His People

16 The LORD roars from Mount Zion;
     his voice thunders from Jerusalem;
     earth and sky tremble.

But he will defend his people.
17 "Then, Israel, you will know that I am
     the LORD your God.
   I live on Zion, my sacred hill.
   Jerusalem will be a sacred city;
     foreigners will never conquer it
     again.
18 At that time the mountains will be
     covered with vineyards,
   and cattle will be found on every
     hill;
   there will be plenty of water for all of
     Judah.
   A stream will flow from the Temple of the
     LORD,
     and it will water Acacia Valley.

19 "Egypt will become a desert,
     and Edom a ruined waste,
   because they attacked the land of Judah
     and killed its innocent people.
20-21 I will avenge[d] those who were
     killed;
   I will not spare the guilty.
   But Judah and Jerusalem will be inhabited
     forever,
   and I, the LORD, will live on Mount
     Zion."

---

c 3:11 *Probable text* Hurry; *Hebrew* Help.   d 3:20–21 *Some ancient translations* avenge; *Hebrew* declare innocent.
3:13 a Rev 14:14–16; **b** Rev 14:19, 20; 19:15   **3:16** Am 1:2

Isn't it crystal clear? Don't lie, steal, kill, take advantage of poor people, or worship anything other than God. If we live by God's teachings, life is better—for everyone. God gave the Israelites and us laws to live by because he loves us deeply and wants us to know real joy in our day-to-day living. It's so simple. But humanity doesn't seem to be able to pull it off. And people suffer as a result.

That is why Amos is so mad! He is exploding with rage at the people in the northern kingdom of Israel and their neighbors. They disobey God's teachings and take advantage of poor people and worship foreign gods. This time, Amos says, they have gone too far, and God will punish them, Israel most of all because God had done so much for them.

Chap. 2:6–8

Headlines

- Honest People Sold into Slavery! (2:6—3:2)
- Wealthy Women Condemned (4:1–3)
- God Wants Justice, Not Festivals (5:21–27)
- Amos Refuses to Be Silent (7:10–17)
- Merchants Use Crooked Scales! (8:4–6)
- God's Future Plans (9:11–15)

FACTOIDS

Who wrote this book? Amos (or scribes recording his words), the earliest prophet whose words were recorded as a separate book of the Bible.

Why was it written? Amos, a shepherd and farmer, was called by God to prophesy in the northern kingdom of Israel. Amos especially challenged corrupt and greedy people taking advantage of poor people.

What period does it cover? 786–746 BC.

Important themes

- God will punish the sinful, especially those who mistreat poor people.
- Religious acts mean nothing if people will not change their wicked lifestyle.
- God will save those who are faithful, even if there is only a few of them.

THE BOOK OF *Amos*

AMOS

1 ¹These are the words of Amos, a shepherd from the town of Tekoa. Two years before the earthquake, when Uzziah was king of Judah and Jeroboam son of Jehoash was king of Israel, God revealed to Amos all these things about Israel.

²Amos said,

"The LORD roars from Mount Zion;
   his voice thunders from Jerusalem.
The pastures dry up,
   and the grass on Mount Carmel turns
     brown."

God's Judgment on Israel's Neighbors

Syria

³The LORD says, "The people of Damascus have sinned again and again, and for this I will certainly punish them. They treated the people of Gilead with savage cruelty. ⁴So I will send fire upon the palace built by King Hazael and I will burn down the fortresses of King Benhadad. ⁵I will smash the city gates of Damascus and remove the inhabitants of Aven Valley and the ruler of Betheden. The people of Syria will be taken away as prisoners to the land of Kir."

Philistia

⁶The LORD says, "The people of Gaza have sinned again and again, and for this I will certainly punish them. They carried off a whole nation and sold them as slaves to the people of Edom. ⁷So I will send fire upon the city walls of Gaza and burn down its fortresses. ⁸I will remove the rulers of the cities of Ashdod and Ashkelon. I will punish the city of Ekron, and all the Philistines who are left will die."

Tyre

⁹The LORD says, "The people of Tyre have sinned again and again, and for this I will certainly punish them. They carried off a whole nation into exile in the land of Edom, and did not keep the treaty of friendship they had made. ¹⁰So I will send fire upon the city walls of Tyre and burn down its fortresses."

"I will send fire." (1:4—2:5)

1:1 a 2 Kings 15:1–7; 2 Chr 26:1–23; **b** 2 Kings 14:23–29 **1:2** Joel 3:16 **1:3–5** Isa 17:1–3; Jer 49:23–27; Zech 9:1 **1:6–8** Isa 14:29–31; Jer 47:1–7; Ezek 25:15–17; Joel 3:4–8; Zeph 2:4–7; Zech 9:5–7 **1:9, 10** Isa 23:1–18; Ezek 26:1—28:19; Joel 3:4–8; Zech 9:1–4; Mt 11:21, 22; Lk 10:13, 14

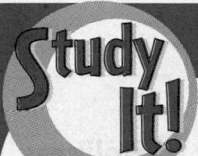

The Sins of the Cities

What's got God in such a rage, according to Amos? What exactly are the sins of Israel and its neighboring cities? Amos accuses them of:

- treating people with savage cruelty
- selling people as slaves
- not keeping the promises they had made
- showing no mercy, only extreme anger
- ripping open pregnant women
- dishonoring the king
- despising God's teachings and ignoring his Commandments
- being led astray by false gods
- abusing honest people who had debt, especially poor people
- trampling weak, helpless, and poor people
- sexual immorality

If God were addressing your city today, could the people of your city be charged with any of these sins?

— Amos 1:1—2:8

Edom

11 The LORD says, "The people of Edom have sinned again and again, and for this I will certainly punish them. They hunted down their relatives,*a* the Israelites, and showed them no mercy. Their anger had no limits, and they never let it die. 12 So I will send fire upon the city of Teman and burn down the fortresses of Bozrah."

Ammon

13 The LORD says, "The people of Ammon have sinned again and again, and for this I will certainly punish them. In their wars for more territory they even ripped open pregnant women in Gilead. 14 So I will send fire upon the city walls of Rabbah and burn down its fortresses. Then there will be shouts on the day of battle, and the fighting will rage like a storm. 15 Their king and his officers will go into exile."

Moab

2 1 The LORD says, "The people of Moab have sinned again and again, and for this I will certainly punish them. They dishonored the bones of the king of Edom by burning them to ashes. 2 I will send fire upon the land of Moab and burn down the fortresses of Kerioth. The people of Moab will die in the noise of battle while soldiers are shouting and trumpets are sounding. 3 I will kill the ruler of Moab and all the leaders of the land."

Judah

4 The LORD says, "The people of Judah have sinned again and again, and for this I will certainly punish them. They have despised my teachings and have not kept my commands. They have been led astray by the same false gods that their ancestors served. 5 So I will send fire upon Judah and burn down the fortresses of Jerusalem."

God's Judgment on Israel

6 The LORD says, "The people of Israel have sinned again and again, and for this I

---

a **1:11** THEIR RELATIVES: *The Israelites were descended from Jacob, who was the brother of Esau, the ancestor of the Edomites.*
1:11, 12 Isa 34:5–17; 63:1–6; Jer 49:7–22; Ezek 25:12–14; 35:1–15; Ob 1–14; Mal 1:2–5 **1:13–15** Jer 49:1–6; Ezek 21:28–32; 25:1–7; Zeph 2:8–11 **2:1–3** Isa 15:1—16:14; 25:10–12; Jer 48:1–47; Ezek 25:8–11; Zeph 2:8–11

Amos

Find the eight kingdoms or cities named in Amos, chapters 1–2, on Map 3 in the back of this Bible.

will certainly punish them. They sell into slavery honest people who cannot pay their debts, the poor who cannot repay even the price of a pair of sandals. [7] They trample[b] down the weak and helpless and push the poor out of the way. A man and his father have intercourse with the same slave woman, and so profane my holy name. [8] At every place of worship people sleep on clothing that they have taken from the poor as security for debts. In the temple of their God they drink wine which they have taken from those who owe them money.

[9] "And yet, my people, it was for your sake that I totally destroyed the Amorites, who were as tall as cedar trees and as strong as oaks. [10] I brought you out of Egypt, led you through the desert for forty years, and gave you the land of the Amorites to be your own. [11] I chose some of your sons to be prophets and some of your young men to be nazirites.[c] Isn't this true, people of Israel? I, the LORD, have spoken. [12] But you made the nazirites drink wine, and ordered the prophets not to speak my message. [13] And now I will crush you to the ground, and you will groan like a cart loaded with grain. [14] Not even fast runners will escape; strong men will lose their strength, and soldiers will not be able to save their own lives. [15] Archers will not stand their ground, fast runners will not get away, and men on horses will not escape with their lives. [16] On that day even the bravest soldiers will drop their weapons and run." The LORD has spoken.

3 [1] People of Israel, listen to this message which the LORD has spoken about you, the entire nation that he brought out of Egypt: [2] "Of all the nations on earth, you are the only one I have known and cared for. That is what makes your sins so terrible, and that is why I must punish you for them."

Test of Holiness

Craig owns a very successful chain of fast-food restaurants that are sweeping the country. In his own town, he and his family are known for their support and generosity in the community and their church.

Not many people know this, but Craig's heart stretches to poor people. There's a guy in town, Samuel, who is homeless and suffers from a variety of problems. He rides a bike everywhere, sleeps outside, depends on the kindness of strangers, and generally causes no trouble. Craig has instructed his employees at his restaurant to take care of Samuel. Samuel comes in twice a day to eat at Craig's restaurant. The workers treat him as respectfully as any other customer, and Samuel always eats for free.

Amos tells us that the real test of holiness is not only what happens in church on Sundays, but how we act outside of church—at work, school, in politics, and community activities. Are we looking out for the needs of poor and powerless people and acting to help them? If not, then our religious practices are empty.

— Amos 2:6–8

The Prophet's Task

[3] Do two people start traveling together without arranging to meet?

---

[b] **2:7** trample; *Hebrew unclear.* [c] **2:11** NAZIRITES: *Israelites who showed their devotion to God by taking vows not to drink wine or beer or cut their hair or touch corpses (see Num 6:1–8).*
2:9 Deut 3:8–11   **2:11** Num 6:1–8

Read Amos 3:10. What kinds of crimes do people commit today to try to gain great wealth?

⁴Does a lion roar in the forest unless he has found a victim?

Does a young lion growl in his den unless he has caught something?

⁵Does a bird get caught in a trap if the trap has not been baited?

Does a trap spring unless something sets it off?

⁶Does the war trumpet sound in a city without making the people afraid?

Does disaster strike a city unless the LORD sends it?

⁷The Sovereign LORD never does anything without revealing his plan to his servants, the prophets.

⁸When a lion roars, who can keep from being afraid?

When the Sovereign LORD speaks, who can keep from proclaiming his message?

The Doom of Samaria

⁹Announce to those who live in the palaces of Egypt and Ashdod: "Gather together in the hills around Samaria and see the great disorder and the crimes being committed there."

¹⁰The LORD says, "These people fill their mansions with things taken by crime and violence. They don't even know how to be honest. ¹¹And so an enemy will surround their land, destroy their defenses, and plunder their mansions."

¹²The LORD says, "As a shepherd recovers only two legs or an ear of a sheep that a lion has eaten, so only a few will survive of Samaria's people, who now recline on luxurious couches.ᵈ ¹³Listen now, and warn the descendants of Jacob," says the Sovereign LORD Almighty. ¹⁴"On the day when I punish the people of Israel for their sins, I will destroy the altars of Bethel. The corners of every altar will be broken off and will fall to the ground. ¹⁵I will destroy winter houses and summer houses. The houses decorated with ivory will fall in ruins; every large house will be destroyed."

4 ¹Listen to this, you women of Samaria, who grow fat like the well-fed cows of Bashan, who mistreat the weak, oppress the

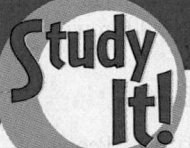

Why Is God So Hard on Israel?

Blair is sitting in a jail cell, in shock. She can't believe she got caught stealing. Worse, she can't believe the person who turned her in was her mom! What's the big deal? So she borrowed twenty bucks from the cash register at her mom's store. So what? How horrible can a mother be, to have her own child arrested!

The police officer asked Blair's mom why she turned her daughter in. Blair's mom said: "More than anyone else, she knows better. I've given her everything she could want, and I've taught her right from wrong. She's been warned— this is not the first time I've caught her stealing. I hope it will be her last. She needs to learn that there are consequences when you do something wrong."

This is why God is so angry at Israel. They are his Chosen People. They have been given everything, including the Law of Moses. More than any nation, they should know better than to neglect poor people and allow injustice to grow. Because they know better, God is going to let them experience the full consequences of their sins!

— Amos 3:1–2

poor, and demand that your husbands keep you supplied with liquor! ²As the Sovereign LORD is holy, he has promised, "The days will come when they will drag you away with hooks; every one of you will be like a

ᵈ **3:12** luxurious couches; *Hebrew unclear.*
3:14 2 Kings 23:15

Amos

fish on a hook. ³You will be dragged to the nearest break in the wall and thrown out."ᵉ

Israel's Failure to Learn

⁴The Sovereign LORD says, "People of Israel, go to the holy place in Bethel and sin, if you must! Go to Gilgal and sin with all your might! Go ahead and bring animals to be sacrificed morning after morning, and bring your tithes every third day. ⁵Go on and offer your bread in thanksgiving to God, and brag about the extra offerings you bring! This is the kind of thing you love to do.

⁶"I was the one who brought famine to all your cities, yet you did not come back to me. ⁷I kept it from raining when your crops needed it most. I sent rain on one city, but not on another. Rain fell on one field, but another field dried up. ⁸Weak with thirst, the people of several cities went to a city where they hoped to find water, but there was not enough to drink. Still you did not come back to me.

⁹"I sent a scorching wind to dry up your crops. The locusts ate up all your gardens and vineyards, your fig trees and olive trees. Still you did not come back to me.

Still you did not come back to me. (4:9)

¹⁰"I sent a plague on you like the one I sent on Egypt. I killed your young men in battle and took your horses away. I filled your nostrils with the stink of dead bodies in your camps. Still you did not come back to me.

¹¹"I destroyed some of you as I destroyed Sodom and Gomorrah. Those of you who survived were like a burning stick saved from a fire. Still you did not come back to me," says the LORD. ¹²"So then, people of Israel, I

am going to punish you. And because I am going to do this, get ready to face my judgment!"

¹³ God is the one who made the mountains
  and created the winds.
He makes his thoughts known to people;
  he changes day into night.
He walks on the heights of the earth.
This is his name: the LORD God
  Almighty!

A Call to Repentance

5 ¹Listen, people of Israel, to this funeral song which I sing over you:

²Virgin Israel has fallen,
  Never to rise again!
She lies abandoned on the ground,
  And no one helps her up.

³The Sovereign LORD says, "A city in Israel sends out a thousand soldiers, but only a hundred return; another city sends out a hundred, but only ten come back."

⁴The LORD says to the people of Israel, "Come to me, and you will live. ⁵Do not go to Beersheba to worship. Do not try to find me at Bethel—Bethel will come to nothing. Do not go to Gilgal—her people are doomed to exile."

⁶Go to the LORD, and you will live. If you do not go, he will sweep down like fire on the people of Israel. The fire will burn up the people of Bethel, and no one will be able to put it out. ⁷You are doomed, you that twist justice and cheat people out of their rights!

⁸The LORD made the stars,
  the Pleiades and Orion.
He turns darkness into daylight
  and day into night.
He calls for the waters of the sea
  and pours them out on the earth.
His name is the LORD.
⁹He brings destruction on the mighty and
  their strongholds.

¹⁰You people hate anyone who challenges injustice and speaks the whole truth in

---

ᵉ 4:3 *Hebrew has an additional word, the meaning of which is unclear.*
4:6 Wis 12:2, 10 4:11 Gen 19:24 5:8 Job 9:9; 38:31

The Working Poor

Olivia's parents work four jobs between them. Still, it seems like they hardly have what they need. Frustrated, she asked: "Why do you work so much? Where is all the money you make?" Her parents helped her understand: They are hard workers, but without college degrees, they cannot get jobs that pay much more than the minimum wage. Plus, none of their employers provide health insurance, which costs as much as her mom earns. One whole job, just for health insurance! Olivia's parents got angrier as they spoke. It wasn't fair! Business owners who offer only part-time jobs and the lowest possible wages are doing so to save money—but they ignore the needs of the people who work for them. The workers who are struggling to make ends meet just keep struggling and working harder—and never get ahead.

The employers might be acting within the law, but that doesn't mean they are acting justly. Amos pointed this same accusation at Israel: "You are doomed, you that twist justice and cheat people out of their rights!" (Amos 5:7).

How can you be more just and fair with others?

— Amos 5:7–15

plant. [12] I know how terrible your sins are and how many crimes you have committed. You persecute good people, take bribes, and prevent the poor from getting justice in the courts. [13] And so, keeping quiet in such evil times is the smart thing to do!

[14] Make it your aim to do what is right, not what is evil, so that you may live. Then the LORD God Almighty really will be with you, as you claim he is. [15] Hate what is evil, love what is right, and see that justice prevails in the courts. Perhaps the LORD will be merciful to the people of this nation who are still left alive.

[16] And so the Sovereign LORD Almighty says, "There will be wailing and cries of sorrow in the city streets. Even farmers will be called to mourn the dead along with those who are paid to mourn. [17] There will be wailing in all the vineyards. All this will take place because I am coming to punish you." The LORD has spoken.

There will be wailing and cries of sorrow. (5:16)

[18] How terrible it will be for you who long for the day of the LORD! What good will that day do you? For you it will be a day of darkness and not of light. [19] It will be like someone who runs from a lion and meets a bear! Or like someone who comes home and puts his hand on the wall—only to be bitten by a snake! [20] The day of the LORD will bring darkness and not light; it will be a day of gloom, without any brightness.

court. [11] You have oppressed the poor and robbed them of their grain. And so you will not live in the fine stone houses you build or drink wine from the beautiful vineyards you

Like someone who runs from a lion (5:19)

²¹ The LORD says, "I hate your religious festivals; I cannot stand them! ²² When you bring me burnt offerings and grain offerings, I will not accept them; I will not accept the animals you have fattened to bring me as offerings. ²³ Stop your noisy songs; I do not want to listen to your harps. ²⁴ Instead, let justice flow like a stream, and righteousness like a river that never goes dry.

²⁵ "People of Israel, I did not demand sacrifices and offerings during those forty years that I led you through the desert. ²⁶ But now, because you have worshiped images of Sakkuth, your king god, and of Kaiwan, your star god, you will have to carry those images ²⁷ when I take you into exile in a land beyond Damascus," says the LORD, whose name is Almighty God.

The Destruction of Israel

6 ¹ How terrible it will be for you that have such an easy life in Zion and for you that feel safe in Samaria—you great leaders of this great nation Israel, you to whom the people go for help! ² Go and look at the city of Calneh. Then go on to the great city of Hamath and on down to the Philistine city of Gath. Were they any better than the kingdoms of Judah and Israel? Was their territory larger than yours? ³ You refuse to admit that a day of disaster is coming, but what you do only brings that day closer. ⁴ How terrible

it will be for you that stretch out on your luxurious couches, feasting on veal and lamb! ⁵ You like to compose songs, as David did, and play them on harps. ⁶ You drink wine by the bowlful and use the finest perfumes, but you do not mourn over the ruin of Israel. ⁷ So you will be the first to go into exile. Your feasts and banquets will come to an end.

⁸ The Sovereign LORD Almighty has given this solemn warning: "I hate the pride of the people of Israel; I despise their luxurious mansions. I will give their capital city and everything in it to the enemy."

"I hate the pride of the people of Israel." (6:8)

⁹ If there are ten men left in a family, they will die. ¹⁰ The dead man's relative, the one in charge of the funeral, will take the body out of the house. The relative will call to whoever is still left in the house, "Is anyone else there with you?"

The person will answer, "No!"

Then the relative will say, "Be quiet! We

5:21, 22 Isa 1:11–14　　**5:25–27** Acts 7:42, 43

How important are money and material things to you? What do you do to help poor people?

Woe to the Wealthy!

Amos is clearly addressing the wealthy people of Israel, not all Israelites. Are we to understand that living a wealthy lifestyle is sinful? Yes, says Amos, if you think only of your own comfort and luxuries. Yes, if your wealth was earned at the expense of poor people, or dishonestly in any way. Yes, if you are not learning about the needs of poor people and how you can help them. But, Amos says, if justice and mercy for poor and weak people are a high priority and you share your wealth generously, then being wealthy is not sinful.

Jesus echoed Amos's warning: "It is much harder for a rich person to enter the Kingdom of God than for a camel to go through the eye of a needle" (Matthew 19:24).

— Amos 6:4–7

must be careful not even to mention the LORD's name."*f*

11When the LORD gives the command, houses large and small will be smashed to pieces. 12Do horses gallop on rocks? Does anyone plow the sea with oxen? Yet you have turned justice into poison, and right into wrong.

13You brag about capturing the town of Lodebar.*g* You boast, "We were strong enough to take Karnaim."*h*

14The LORD God Almighty himself says, "People of Israel, I am going to send a foreign army to occupy your country. It will oppress you from Hamath Pass in the north to the Brook of the Arabah in the south."

A Vision of Locusts

7 1I had a vision from the Sovereign LORD. In it I saw him create a swarm of locusts just after the king's share of the hay had been cut and the grass was starting to grow again. 2In my vision I saw the locusts eat up every green thing in the land, and then I said, "Sovereign LORD, forgive your people! How can they survive? They are so small and weak!"

3The LORD changed his mind and said, "What you saw will not take place."

A Vision of Fire

4I had another vision from the Sovereign LORD. In it I saw him preparing to punish his people with fire. The fire burned up the great ocean under the earth and started to burn up the land. 5Then I said, "Stop, O Sovereign LORD! How can your people survive? They are so small and weak!"

"Stop, O Sovereign LORD!" (7:5)

6The LORD changed his mind again and said, "This will not take place either."

A Vision of a Plumb Line

7I had another vision from the LORD. In it I saw him standing beside a wall that had been built with the use of a plumb line, and there was a plumb line in his hand. 8He asked me, "Amos, what do you see?"

"A plumb line," I answered.

Then he said, "I am using it to show that my people are like a wall that is out of line. I will not change my mind again about punishing them. 9The places where Isaac's descendants worship will be destroyed. The

f **6:10** *Verse 10 in Hebrew is unclear.*   *g* **6:13** LODEBAR: *This name sounds like the Hebrew for "nothing."*
h **6:13** KARNAIM: *The name of this small town means "horns," a symbol of strength.*

Pray It!

Called to Be a Prophet

Lord, are you calling me? Like Amos, I get so angry when I see someone acting dishonestly. I want to yell when I am aware of unfairness. In my city, there are homeless people living downtown, and almost everyone pretends they are invisible. God, I know you must be upset about these things. Do you want me to say something? Amen.

— *Amos, chapter 7*

holy places of Israel will be left in ruins. I will bring the dynasty of King Jeroboam to an end."

Amos and Amaziah

¹⁰Amaziah, the priest of Bethel, then sent a report to King Jeroboam of Israel: "Amos is plotting against you among the people. His speeches will destroy the country. ¹¹This is what he says: 'Jeroboam will die in battle, and the people of Israel will be taken away from their land into exile.' "

¹²Amaziah then said to Amos, "That's enough, prophet! Go on back to Judah and do your preaching there. Let *them* pay you for it. ¹³Don't prophesy here at Bethel any more. This is the king's place of worship, the national temple."

¹⁴Amos answered, "I am not the kind of prophet who prophesies for pay. I am a herdsman, and I take care of fig trees. ¹⁵But the LORD took me from my work as a shepherd and ordered me to come and prophesy to his people Israel. ¹⁶So now listen to what the LORD says. You tell me to stop prophesying, to stop raving against the people of Israel. ¹⁷And so, Amaziah, the LORD says to you, 'Your wife will become a prostitute in the city, and your children will be killed in

war. Your land will be divided up and given to others, and you yourself will die in a heathen country. And the people of Israel will certainly be taken away from their own land into exile.' "

A Vision of a Basket of Fruit

8 ¹I had another vision from the Sovereign LORD. In it I saw a basket of fruit. ²The LORD asked, "Amos, what do you see?"

"A basket of fruit," I answered.

The LORD said to me, "The end*ⁱ* has come for my people Israel. I will not change my mind again about punishing them. ³On that day the songs in the palace will become cries of mourning. There will be dead bodies everywhere. They will be cast out in silence."*ʲ*

Amos, what do you see? "A basket of fruit" (8:2)

Israel's Doom

⁴Listen to this, you that trample on the needy and try to destroy the poor of the country. ⁵You say to yourselves, "We can hardly wait for the holy days to be over so that we can sell our grain. When will the Sabbath end, so that we can start selling again? Then we can overcharge, use false measures, and fix the scales to cheat our customers. ⁶We can sell worthless wheat at a high price. We'll find someone poor who can't pay his debts, not even the price of a pair of sandals, and we'll buy him as a slave."

⁷The LORD, the God of Israel, has sworn, "I will never forget their evil deeds. ⁸And so the earth will quake, and everyone in the land will be in distress. The whole country

ⁱ 8:2 END: *The Hebrew words for "end" and "fruit" sound alike.* *ʲ 8:3* out in silence; *or* out. Silence!

Archbishop Oscar Romero

The 1980s were difficult years for Central American countries. The wealthy families who controlled the military were trying to keep the poor people in their place. Poor families were desperately trying to lift themselves out of poverty. Many religious and human rights workers tried helping the people who lived in poverty, especially through education. And many of them died for their efforts, killed by death squads who worked for the wealthy people in power.

Archbishop Oscar Romero of El Salvador was a good friend of the wealthy citizens of his country. But then he became aware of the severe injustices the poor people in his country suffered. He had a deep change of heart, and became the champion for people living in poverty. He challenged the wealthy leaders to share their wealth and respect the human rights of all people.

Bishop Romero was killed in 1983 while saying Mass. He was one of thousands of martyrs who nonviolently fought against injustice to poor people. Today, faithful followers of Christ are still martyred, or killed, for trying to improve the lives of poor people. Pray for missionaries and others who are tirelessly working on behalf of poor people.

— Amos 8:4–6

will be shaken; it will rise and fall like the Nile River. [9]The time is coming when I will make the sun go down at noon and the earth grow dark in daytime. I, the Sovereign LORD, have spoken. [10]I will turn your festivals into funerals and change your glad songs into cries of grief. I will make you shave your heads and wear sackcloth, and you will be like parents mourning for their only child. That day will be bitter to the end.

[11]"The time is coming when I will send famine on the land. People will be hungry, but not for bread; they will be thirsty, but not for water. They will hunger and thirst for a message from the LORD. I, the Sovereign LORD, have spoken. [12]People will wander from the Dead Sea to the Mediterranean and then on around from the north to the east. They will look everywhere for a message from the LORD, but they will not find it. [13]On that day even healthy young men and women will collapse from thirst. [14]Those who swear by the idols of Samaria, who say, 'By the god of Dan' or 'By the god of Beersheba'—those people will fall and not rise again."

The LORD's Judgments

9 [1]I saw the Lord standing by the altar. He gave the command: "Strike the tops of the Temple columns so hard that the foundation will shake. Break them off and let them fall on the heads of the people. I will kill the rest of the people in war. No one will get away; not one will escape. [2]Even if they dig their way down to the world of the dead, I will catch them. Even if they climb up to heaven, I will bring them down. [3]If they hide on the top of Mount Carmel, I will search for them and catch them. If they hide from me at the bottom of the sea, I will command the sea monster[k] to bite them. [4]If they are taken away into captivity by their enemies, I will order them to be put to

k **9:3** SEA MONSTER: *It was believed that the sea was inhabited by a great monster. This creature, like all others, was regarded as under God's control.*

Amos

"People will be hungry, but not for bread; they will be thirsty, but not for water. They will hunger and thirst for a message from the LORD" *(Amos 8:11)*.

Catholic Social Teaching

Catholic Connections

The Catholic Church has been as vocal as Amos about social justice and human dignity. Our concern is rooted in the teachings of the Bible, such as those found in Amos. But the Catholic Church also has a rich collection of documents that explains what is called Catholic social teaching. Some of the key themes of Catholic social teaching are as follows:

- All people have a unique dignity from God that must be respected.
- We must care for the common good of our world community, not just our own individual concerns.
- We must have a concern for poor people.
- We must protect the rights of workers.
- We must care for God's Creation.
- We must promote peace and rid ourselves of weapons of mass destruction.
- We must work so that the world's wealth is distributed fairly among all people.

Amos tells the Israelites of the doom that awaits them for their selfish and unjust ways—and how God will one day restore Israel. Catholic social teaching tells us how to live more justly, share more generously, and act with mercy—so that we will not fall into the same kind of sinful behavior as the Israelites.

— Amos, chapters 8–9

death. I am determined to destroy them, not to help them."

5 The Sovereign LORD Almighty touches
　　the earth,
　　and it quakes;
　　all who live there mourn.
The whole world rises and falls like the
　　Nile River.
6 The LORD builds his home in the heavens,
　　and over the earth he puts the dome of
　　the sky.
He calls for the waters of the sea
　　and pours them out on the earth.
His name is the LORD!

7 The LORD says, "People of Israel, I think as much of the people of Ethiopia[l] as I do of you. I brought the Philistines from Crete and the Syrians from Kir, just as I brought you from Egypt. 8 I, the Sovereign LORD, am watching this sinful kingdom of Israel, and I will destroy it from the face of the earth. But I will not destroy all the descendants of Jacob.

9 "I will give the command and shake the people of Israel like grain in a sieve. I will shake them among the nations to remove all who are worthless. 10 The sinners among my people will be killed in war—all those who say, 'God will not let any harm come near us.' "

---

[l] **9:7** *Hebrew* Cush: *Cush is the ancient name of the extensive territory south of the First Cataract of the Nile River. This region was called Ethiopia in Graeco-Roman times, and included within its borders most of modern Sudan and some of present-day Ethiopia (Abyssinia).*

Read Amos's vision of a better world in 9:13–15. How can you tell that he lived in a rural area?

The Future Restoration of Israel

11 The LORD says, "A day is coming when I will restore the kingdom of David, which is like a house fallen into ruins. I will repair its walls and restore it. I will rebuild it and make it as it was long ago. 12 And so the people of Israel will conquer what is left of the land of Edom and all the nations that were once mine," says the LORD, who will cause this to happen.

13 "The days are coming," says the LORD,
"when grain will grow faster than it
can be harvested,
and grapes will grow faster than the
wine can be made.

The mountains will drip with sweet
wine,
and the hills will flow with it.
14 I will bring my people back to their
land.
They will rebuild their ruined cities
and live there;
they will plant vineyards and drink the
wine;
they will plant gardens and eat what
they grow.
15 I will plant my people on the land I gave
them,
and they will not be pulled up
again."
The LORD your God has spoken.

9:11, 12 Acts 15:16–18

Your Next Step

Congratulations on finishing the Book of Amos! Use this space to write your thoughts and questions about this book. If you are following the suggested reading plan, go ahead to the Book of Micah in the Old Testament. Micah is another prophet who spoke out against worshiping foreign gods and treating people unfairly.

Amos

"Just you wait! You're gonna get it!" You may have heard these words at one time or another, maybe from a brother or sister who was threatening to tell on you. The message is clear—you did something wrong, and you are going to be punished.

Obadiah's message to the Edomites is similar. The Israelites and the Edomites are related through Jacob and his twin brother, Esau. Even though they are related, the Edomites did nothing to help the people of Judah when they were captured by the Babylonians. In fact, the Edomites actually gloated over the ruin of Jerusalem. Obadiah's warning to the Edomites in verse 15 could easily apply to us, too. He says: "What you have done will be done to you. You will get back what you have given."

Headlines

- God to Edom: You Are Warned! (verses 1–9)
- Edom Gets Rich; Judah Suffers (verses 10–14)
- Final Victory Belongs to Judah (verses 15–21)

FACTOIDS

Who wrote this book? Obadiah is the shortest book in the Old Testament. It is thought to have been written by the prophet Obadiah.

Why was it written? Obadiah warns the people of Edom that they will be punished for their abuse of Judah.

What period does it cover? The fifth century, sometime after the Babylonian Exile.

How does it fit into the Bible? Obadiah is one of the minor prophets who wrote after the Babylonian Exile.

Important themes

- What you have done to others will come back to you.
- Even though God's people suffer now, someday they will be reunited and return to the land God promised.

OBADIAH

¹This is the prophecy of Obadiah—what the Sovereign LORD said about the nation of Edom.

The LORD Will Punish Edom

The LORD has sent his messenger to the
nations,
and we have heard his message:
"Get ready! Let us go to war against
Edom!"
²The LORD says to Edom,
"I will make you weak;
everyone will despise you.
³Your pride has deceived you.
Your capital is a fortress of solid rock;
your home is high in the mountains,
and so you say to yourself,
'Who can ever pull me down?'
⁴Even though you make your home
as high as an eagle's nest,
so that it seems to be among the stars,
yet I will pull you down.

Yet I will pull you down. (4)

⁵"When thieves come at night,
they take only what they want.
When people gather grapes,
they always leave a few.
But your enemies have wiped you out
completely.
⁶Descendants of Esau, your treasures have
been looted.
⁷Your allies have deceived you;
they have driven you from your country.

People who were at peace with you have
now conquered you.
Those friends who ate with you have
laid a trap for you;
they say of you, 'Where is all that
cleverness he had?'

⁸"On the day I punish Edom,
I will destroy their clever men
and wipe out all their wisdom.
⁹The fighting men of Teman will be
terrified,
and every soldier in Edom will be
killed.

Reasons for Edom's Punishment

¹⁰"Because you robbed and killed
your relatives,ᵃ the descendants of
Jacob,
you will be destroyed and dishonored
forever.
¹¹You stood aside on that day
when enemies broke down their gates.
You were as bad as those strangers
who carried off Jerusalem's wealth
and divided it among themselves.
¹²You should not have gloated
over the misfortune of your relatives in
Judah.
You should not have been glad
on the day of their ruin.
You should not have laughed at them
in their distress.

You should not have gloated. (12)

ᵃ **10** YOUR RELATIVES: *The Israelites were descended from Jacob, who was the brother of Esau, the ancestor of the Edomites.*
1–14 Isa 34:5–17; 63:1–6; Jer 49:7–22; Ezek 25:12–14; 35:1–15; Am 1:11, 12; Mal 1:2–5

13 You should not have entered the city of
     my people
  to gloat over their suffering
  and to seize their riches
  on the day of their disaster.
14 You should not have stood at the
     crossroads
  to catch those trying to escape.
  You should not have handed them over to
     the enemy
  on the day of their distress.

God Will Judge the Nations

15 "The day is near when I, the LORD,
     will judge all nations.
  Edom, what you have done
  will be done to you.
     You will get back what you have given.
16 My people have drunk a bitter cup of
     punishment
  on my sacred hill.*b*
  But all the surrounding nations will drink
  a still more bitter cup of punishment;
  they will drink it all and vanish away.

The Victory of Israel

17 "But on Mount Zion some will escape,
  and it will be a sacred place.

b **16** SACRED HILL: *Mount Zion (see Zion in Word List).*

The people of Jacob will possess
  the land that is theirs by right.
18 The people of Jacob and of Joseph will be
     like fire;
  they will destroy the people of
     Esau
  as fire burns stubble.
  No descendant of Esau will survive.
  I, the LORD, have spoken.

19 "People from southern Judah will occupy
     Edom;
  those from the western foothills will
     capture Philistia.
  Israelites will possess the territory of
     Ephraim and Samaria;
  the people of Benjamin will take
     Gilead.
20 The army of exiles from northern
     Israel
  will return and conquer Phoenicia as
     far north as Zarephath.
  The exiles from Jerusalem who are in
     Sardis
  will capture the towns of southern
     Judah.
21 The victorious men of Jerusalem
  will attack Edom and rule over it.
  And the LORD himself will be king."

Obadiah

Where is Edom? Locate it on Map 3 in the back of this Bible.

Jonah had an attitude problem. God had a job for him—to go to Nineveh and tell the people to change their ways. Jonah didn't want to go, so he ran away. But God wouldn't let Jonah get away; Jonah ended up in the belly of a large fish. When he finally went to Nineveh, he never expected that the people would listen to him. But amazingly they did! Instead of being happy, Jonah was angry. He didn't want to share God's love with Ninevites. He didn't think they deserved it.

The story of Jonah is full of lessons about respecting others, listening to God, understanding God's love, and believing that God knows best—even when we don't understand God's plans.

Chap. 2

Headlines

- God Calls, Jonah Runs (1:1–16)
- Jonah Becomes Fish Food! (1:17–2:10)
- Jonah Gets a Second Chance (3:1–10)
- God Spares Nineveh, Jonah Throws a Fit! (4:1–10)

FACTOIDS

Who wrote this book? The author is unknown, but the story focuses on the activities of an imaginary prophet named Jonah.

Why was it written? The Israelites believed that God loved only them and that God would destroy their enemies. This book was written to teach them that God cares for everyone, including their enemies.

How does it fit into the Bible? The Book of Jonah is one of eighteen prophetic books and the only one that is a parable, that is, a story that teaches a lesson.

Jesus connection: Just as Jonah spent three days and three nights in the belly of a large fish before being spit up on the shore, Jesus spent three days in the tomb before his Resurrection.

Important themes

- God loves everyone, even those we consider our enemies.
- God forgives those who are sorry for their sins and gives them a second chance.

JONAH

Jonah Disobeys the LORD

1 ¹One day the LORD spoke to Jonah son of Amittai. ²He said, "Go to Nineveh, that great city, and speak out against it; I am aware of how wicked its people are." ³Jonah, however, set out in the opposite direction in order to get away from the LORD. He went to Joppa, where he found a ship about to go to Spain. He paid his fare and went aboard with the crew to sail to Spain, where he would be away from the LORD.

⁴But the LORD sent a strong wind on the sea, and the storm was so violent that the ship was in danger of breaking up. ⁵The sailors were terrified and cried out for help, each one to his own god. Then, in order to lessen the danger,ᵃ they threw the cargoᵇ overboard. Meanwhile, Jonah had gone below and was lying in the ship's hold, sound asleep.

⁶The captain found him there and said to him, "What are you doing asleep? Get up and pray to your god for help. Maybe he will feel sorry for us and spare our lives."

⁷The sailors said to each other, "Let's draw lots and find out who is to blame for getting us into this danger." They did so, and Jonah's name was drawn. ⁸So they said to him, "Now, then, tell us! Who is to blame for this? What are you doing here? What country do you come from? What is your nationality?"

⁹"I am a Hebrew," Jonah answered. "I worship the LORD, the God of heaven, who made land and sea." ¹⁰Jonah went on to tell them that he was running away from the LORD.

The sailors were terrified, and said to him, "That was an awful thing to do!"ᶜ ¹¹The storm was getting worse all the time, so the sailors asked him, "What should we do to you to stop the storm?"

¹²Jonah answered, "Throw me into the sea, and it will calm down. I know it is my fault that you are caught in this violent storm."

You Disobey, You Pay

Martin pretended he didn't hear his dad as he rode away on his bike. He was supposed to clean out the garage. Martin knew he would be in trouble, but he and Jon had plans. When Martin arrived at Jon's house, his dad was waiting for him. Martin's dad didn't say much, except to tell Martin that he was grounded.

God told Jonah to go to Nineveh, but Jonah boarded a ship instead. God sent a powerful storm, and when the sailors realized that it was Jonah's fault, they threw him overboard and a large fish swallowed him.

Martin and Jonah both realized that wrong actions have unpleasant consequences. Being grounded is no fun. Neither is spending three days in the belly of a fish, only to be vomited up on the shore! It's a hard lesson to learn, but if you disobey, you will pay.

— Jonah, chapter 1

¹³Instead, the sailors tried to get the ship to shore, rowing with all their might. But the storm was becoming worse and worse, and they got nowhere. ¹⁴So they cried out to the LORD, "O LORD, we pray, don't punish us with death for taking this man's life! You, O LORD, are responsible for all this; it is your doing." ¹⁵Then they picked Jonah up and threw him into the sea, and it calmed down

ᵃ **1:5** lessen the danger; *or* lighten the ship.   ᵇ **1:5** cargo; *or* equipment.   ᶜ **1:10** and said . . . to do!; *or* and asked him, "Why did you have to run away like that?"
1:1 2 Kings 14:25

Pray It!

Jonah's Prayer, Your Prayer

While he was in the belly of the fish, Jonah had a lot of time to think and pray. He realized that he was running away from God because he didn't want to do what God was asking. In his prayer he did three things:

- He told God about his fears.
- He proclaimed his love for God by praising God.
- He promised to do what he had promised to do.

Jonah's prayer can become your prayer as often as you like. It will change every time, depending on what is going on in your life. Just go to a quiet place and do the same three things that Jonah did.

God answered Jonah's prayer by ordering the fish to spit him out. Don't forget to listen and watch for God's response to you.

— Jonah, chapter 2

at once. 16This made the sailors so afraid of the LORD that they offered a sacrifice and promised to serve him.

17At the LORD's command a large fish swallowed Jonah, and he was inside the fish for three days and three nights.

Jonah's Prayer

2 1From deep inside the fish Jonah prayed to the LORD his God:

2"In my distress, O LORD, I called to you,
and you answered me.
From deep in the world of the dead
I cried for help, and you heard me.
3 You threw me down into the depths,
to the very bottom of the sea,
where the waters were all around me,
and all your mighty waves rolled over
me.
4 I thought I had been banished from your
presence
and would never see your holy Temple
again.

5 The water came over me and choked me;
the sea covered me completely,
and seaweed wrapped around my
head.
6 I went down to the very roots of the
mountains,
into the land whose gates lock shut
forever.*d*
But you, O LORD my God,
brought me back from the depths
alive.
7 When I felt my life slipping away,
then, O LORD, I prayed to you,
and in your holy Temple you heard me.
8 Those who worship worthless idols
have abandoned their loyalty to you.
9 But I will sing praises to you;
I will offer you a sacrifice
and do what I have promised.
Salvation comes from the LORD!"

10Then the LORD ordered the fish to spit Jonah up on the beach, and it did.

d **2:6** THE LAND WHOSE GATES LOCK SHUT FOREVER: *A reference to the world of the dead (see 2:2).*
1:17 Mt 12:40

Jonah

As a child, you probably heard that Jonah was swallowed by a whale. The Bible just says "a large fish."

Prayer is communicating with God in a relationship of love. What signs do you see of Jonah's love for God in his prayer?

HIGHLIGHTS FROM THE LIFE OF JONAH (1, 2, 3, 4)

Jonah Obeys the LORD

3 ¹Once again the LORD spoke to Jonah. ²He said, "Go to Nineveh, that great city, and proclaim to the people the message I have given you." ³So Jonah obeyed the LORD and went to Nineveh, a city so large that it took three days to walk through it. ⁴Jonah started through the city, and after walking a whole day, he proclaimed, "In forty days Nineveh will be destroyed!"

⁵The people of Nineveh believed God's message. So they decided that everyone should fast, and all the people, from the greatest to the least, put on sackcloth to show that they had repented.

⁶When the king of Nineveh heard about it, he got up from his throne, took off his robe, put on sackcloth, and sat down in ashes. ⁷He sent out a proclamation to the people of Nineveh: "This is an order from the king and his officials: No one is to eat anything; all persons, cattle, and sheep are forbidden to eat or drink. ⁸All persons and animals must wear sackcloth. Everyone must pray earnestly to God and must give up their wicked behavior and their evil actions. ⁹Perhaps God will change his mind; perhaps he will stop being angry, and we will not die!"

¹⁰God saw what they did; he saw that they had given up their wicked behavior. So he changed his mind and did not punish them as he had said he would.

One World Under God

Jonah had a strong wish that God would punish the people of Nineveh, whom he considered enemies—mostly because they were not Jews. When he finally agreed to go to the Ninevites with God's message, he was shocked that they listened. He was also angry because it meant that they would not be punished. At the end of the story, God tells Jonah that he has no right to be angry; everyone is entitled to God's love.

The story of Jonah was written to teach the Israelites—and us—a lesson about God: no group of people is any more deserving of God's love than another group. This is true of countries, and it is also true of the groups you belong to. God never chooses sides. He does not care who is popular, athletic, or rich. God's love is big enough for everyone.

— Jonah, chapters 3–4

Jonah's Anger and God's Mercy

4 ¹Jonah was very unhappy about this and became angry. ²So he prayed, "LORD, didn't I say before I left home that this is just what you would do? That's why I did my best to run away to Spain! I knew that you are a loving and merciful God, always patient, always kind, and always ready to change your mind and not punish. ³Now then, LORD, let me die. I am better off dead than alive."

⁴The LORD answered, "What right do you have to be angry?"

⁵Jonah went out east of the city and sat down. He made a shelter for himself and sat in its shade, waiting to see what would happen to Nineveh. ⁶Then the LORD God made a plant grow up over Jonah to give him some shade, so that he would be more comfortable. Jonah was extremely pleased with the plant. ⁷But at dawn the next day, at God's command, a worm attacked the plant, and it died. ⁸After the sun had risen, God sent a hot east wind, and Jonah was about to faint from the heat of the sun beating down on his head. So he wished he were dead.ᵉ "I am better off dead than alive," he said.

⁹But God said to him, "What right do you have to be angry about the plant?"

ᵉ **4:8** wished he were dead; *or prayed that he would die.*
3:4, 5 Mt 12:41; Lk 11:32   **4:2** Ex 34:6   **4:3** 1 Kings 19:4

Jonah replied, "I have every right to be angry—angry enough to die!"

10 The LORD said to him, "This plant grew up in one night and disappeared the next; you didn't do anything for it and you didn't make it grow—yet you feel sorry for it! **11** How much more, then, should I have pity on Nineveh, that great city. After all, it has more than 120,000 innocent children in it, as well as many animals!"

Your Next Step

Congratulations on finishing the Book of Jonah! Use this space to write your thoughts and questions about this book. If you are following the suggested reading plan, go back to the Book of Ezra. Ezra tells the story of how the people returned to rebuild the city of Jerusalem and the Temple after their captivity in Babylon.

Jonah

You've probably heard people say: "I've got good news and bad news. Which do you want to hear first?" The Book of Micah is very much like that. The book starts with the bad news. Because the Israelites worship false gods and mistreat one another, their two kingdoms are heading for ruin.

But wait, there is good news. Micah says that after the destruction, God will restore their country. There will also be a new ruler, one who is strong and who will bring peace and justice. And this new ruler will come from a humble place, a small country village called Bethlehem. Any guesses who that might be?

Chap. 2:1–2

Headlines

- Micah Tells of Abuses (2:8–10; 3:1–3)
- Weapons Will Be Farming Tools! (4:1–5)
- Peaceful Ruler Coming from Bethlehem (5:1–5)
- Do You Know What God Requires? (6:6–8)

FACTOIDS

Who wrote this book? Micah (or scribes recording his words), who left his country village and went to the big city of Jerusalem to prophecy when God called.

Why was it written? It was written to record the words of the prophet Micah. He warned God's people that war and violence would be the result of not following God and not treating other people fairly.

Jesus connection: Jesus is the great ruler, born in Bethlehem, who Micah says will bring peace to God's people (5:2–5).

Important themes

- If God's people truly believe in God, then they will care for all people and treat them justly, especially poor people.
- God will not abandon his people; he will send a ruler who will bring a time of peace.

MICAH

1 ¹ During the time that Jotham, Ahaz, and Hezekiah were kings of Judah, the LORD gave this message to Micah, who was from the town of Moresheth. The LORD revealed to Micah all these things about Samaria and Jerusalem.

A Lament for Samaria and Jerusalem

²Hear this, all you nations;
  listen to this, all who live on earth!
The Sovereign LORD will testify against
    you.
  Listen! He speaks from his heavenly
    temple.
³The LORD is coming from his holy place;
  he will come down and walk on the
    tops of the mountains.
⁴Then the mountains will melt under him
  like wax in a fire;
they will pour down into the valleys
  like water pouring down a hill.

⁵All this will happen because the people of Israel have sinned and rebelled against God. Who is to blame for Israel's rebellion? Samaria, the capital city itself! Who is guilty of idolatry in Judah? Jerusalem itself! ⁶So the LORD says, "I will make Samaria a pile of ruins in the open country, a place for planting grapevines. I will pour the rubble of the city down into the valley, and will lay bare the city's foundations. ⁷All its precious idols will be smashed to pieces, everything given to its temple prostitutes will be destroyed by fire, and all its images will become a desolate heap. Samaria acquired these things for its fertility rites, and now her enemies will carry them off for temple prostitutes elsewhere."

⁸Then Micah said, "Because of this I will mourn and lament. To show my sorrow, I will walk around barefoot and naked. I will howl like a jackal and wail like an ostrich.

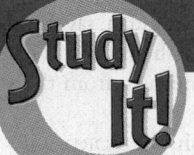

Israel and Judah, Samaria and Jerusalem

About 150 years before Micah was born, the Israelite nation split into two separate kingdoms. This happened after the death of King Solomon. The kingdom in the north was called Israel, and the kingdom in the south was called Judah. Samaria was the capital of Israel. Micah first predicts Samaria's destruction (Micah 1:6). Then Micah condemns the sins of Judah and predicts the destruction of Judah's capital, Jerusalem (3:12). Micah realizes that both kingdoms have been unfaithful to God. They will come to a bad end because of this.

— Micah, chapter 1

⁹Samaria's wounds cannot be healed, and Judah is about to suffer in the same way; destruction has reached the gates of Jerusalem itself, where my people live."

The Enemy Approaches Jerusalem

¹⁰Don't tell our enemies in Gath about our defeat; don't let them see you weeping. People of Beth Leaphrah,ᵃ show your despair by rolling in the dust! ¹¹You people of Shaphir, go into exile, naked and ashamed. Those who live in Zaanan do not dare to come out of their city. When you hear the people of Bethezel mourn, you will know that there is no refuge there. ¹²The

---

ᵃ **1:10** BETH LEAPHRAH: *The prophet speaks of outlying towns (verses 10–14) which an enemy army approaching Jerusalem would attack.*
1:1 a 2 Kings 15:32–38; 2 Chr 27:1–7; **b** 2 Kings 16:1–20; 2 Chr 28:1–27; **c** 2 Kings 18:1—20:21; 2 Chr 29:1—32:33

people of Maroth anxiously wait for relief, because the LORD has brought disaster close to Jerusalem. 13 You that live in Lachish, hitch the horses to the chariots. You imitated the sins of Israel and so caused Jerusalem to sin. 14 And now, people of Judah, say good-bye to the town of Moresheth Gath. The kings of Israel will get no help from the town of Achzib.

15 People of Mareshah, the LORD will hand you over to an enemy, who is going to capture your town. The leaders of Israel will go and hide in the cave at Adullam. 16 People of Judah, cut off your hair in mourning for the children you love. Make yourselves as bald as vultures, because your children will be taken away from you into exile.

The Fate of Those Who Oppress the Poor

2 ¹How terrible it will be for those who lie awake and plan evil! When morning comes, as soon as they have the chance, they do the evil they planned. ²When they want fields, they seize them; when they want houses, they take them. No one's family or property is safe.

³And so the LORD says, "I am planning to bring disaster on you, and you will not be able to escape it. You are going to find yourselves in trouble, and then you will not walk so proudly any more. ⁴When that time comes, people will use the story about you as an example of disaster, and they will sing this song of despair about your experience:

We are completely ruined!
The LORD has taken our land away
And given it to those who took us
captive."ᵇ

⁵So then, when the time comes for the land to be given back to the LORD's people, there will be no share for any of you.

⁶The people preach at me and say, "Don't preach at us. Don't preach about all that. God is not going to disgrace us. ⁷Do you think the people of Israel are under a curse?ᶜ Has the LORD lost his patience? Would he really do such things? Doesn't heᵈ speak kindly to those who do right?"

"Don't preach at us." (2:6)

⁸The LORD replies, "You attack my peopleᵉ like enemies. Men return from battle, thinking they are safe at home, but there you are, waiting to steal the coats off their backs. ⁹You drive the women of my people out of the homes they love, and you have robbed their children of my blessings forever. ¹⁰Get up and go; there is no safety here any more. Your sins have doomed this place to destruction.

¹¹"These people want the kind of prophet who goes around full of lies and deceit and says, 'I prophesy that wine and liquor will flow for you.'

¹²"But I will gather you together, all you people of Israel that are left. I will bring you together like sheep returning to the fold. Like a pasture full of sheep, your land will once again be filled with many people."

¹³God will open the way for them and lead them out of exile. They will break out of the city gates and go free. Their king, the LORD himself, will lead them out.

ᵇ 2:4 *Probable text* those who took us captive; *Hebrew* rebels.   ᶜ 2:7 *Probable text* under a curse; *Hebrew unclear.*
ᵈ 2:7 *One ancient translation* Doesn't he; *Hebrew* Don't I.   ᵉ 2:8 *Probable text* You attack my people; *Hebrew* Recently my people have attacked.

Micah may have been a farmer. How many farm images can you find in his book?

Peer Pressure

Peer pressure means doing something only because other people tell you to do it. Micah knew about peer pressure. The people kept telling him: "Don't preach at us. Don't preach about all that" (Micah 2:6). But he didn't give in to peer pressure. He preached the message God gave him.

Some of Joe's friends are stealing from a local store. They keep telling Joe that it is exciting and will make him brave. Joe wants to keep his friends, but he knows that stealing is a sin. What do you think Micah would tell Joe? What are some of the peer pressures that you face?

— **Micah 2:6–11**

Micah Denounces Israel's Leaders

3 ¹Listen, you rulers of Israel! You are supposed to be concerned about justice, ²yet you hate what is good and you love what is evil. You skin my people alive and tear the flesh off their bones. ³You eat my people up. You strip off their skin, break their bones, and chop them up like meat for the pot. ⁴The time is coming when you will cry out to the LORD, but he will not answer you. He will not listen to your prayers, for you have done evil.

⁵My people are deceived by prophets who promise peace to those who pay them, but threaten war for those who don't. To these prophets the LORD says, ⁶"Prophets, your day is almost over; the sun is going down on you. Because you mislead my people, you will have no more prophetic visions, and you will not be able to predict anything." ⁷Those who predict the future will be disgraced by their failure. They will all be humiliated because God does not answer them.

⁸But as for me, the LORD fills me with his spirit and power, and gives me a sense of justice and the courage to tell the people of Israel what their sins are. ⁹Listen to me, you rulers of Israel, you that hate justice and turn right into wrong. ¹⁰You are building God's city, Jerusalem, on a foundation of murder and injustice. ¹¹The city's rulers govern for bribes, the priests interpret the Law for pay, the prophets give their revelations for money—and they all claim that the LORD is with them. "No harm will come to us," they say. "The LORD is with us."

The prophets give their revelations for money. (3:11)

¹²And so, because of you, Zion will be plowed like a field, Jerusalem will become a pile of ruins, and the Temple hill will become a forest.

The LORD's Universal Reign of Peace
(Isaiah 2:2–4)

4 ¹In days to come
    the mountain where the Temple stands
      will be the highest one of all,
      towering above all the hills.
Many nations will come streaming
      to it,
²   and their people will say,
"Let us go up the hill of the LORD,ᶠ
      to the Temple of Israel's God.

ᶠ **4:2** HILL OF THE LORD: *Mount Zion (see Zion in Word List).*
3:12 Jer 26:18

Micah

Pray It!

Micah says that a time will come when God will bring peace to the whole world. You can pray this prayer for peace, written by Marisa Garfinkel, a high school student. *Adonai Shalom* means "Lord of peace."

Adonai Shalom
Lord, let there be peace in my heart,
so that it may be open to feel love,
kindness, and goodness.

Adonai Shalom
Lord, let there be peace in my life,
so that I can listen to and learn from others
who seem so different from me.

Adonai Shalom
Lord, may I have the opportunity to create
a peaceful environment with lifestyles
that include all my neighbors.

Adonai Shalom
Lord, please grant me peace,
that I may find contentment in your world,
so that "nations will never again go to war, / never prepare for battle again"
(Isaiah 2:4).

— Micah 4:1–4

He will teach us what he wants us to do;
   we will walk in the paths he has
      chosen.
For the LORD's teaching comes from
      Jerusalem;
   from Zion he speaks to his people."

3 He will settle disputes among the nations,
   among the great powers near and far.
They will hammer their swords into plows
   and their spears into pruning knives.
Nations will never again go to war,
   never prepare for battle again.
4 Everyone will live in peace
   among their own vineyards and fig trees,
   and no one will make them afraid.
The LORD Almighty has promised this.

5 Each nation worships and obeys its own god, but we will worship and obey the LORD our God forever and ever.

Israel Will Return from Exile

6 "The time is coming," says the LORD, "when I will gather together the people I punished, those who have suffered in exile. 7 They are crippled and far from home, but I will make a new beginning with those who are left, and they will become a great nation. I will rule over them on Mount Zion from that time on and forever."

8 And you, Jerusalem, where God, like a shepherd from his lookout tower, watches over his people, will once again be the capi-

4:3 Isa 2:4; Joel 3:10   4:4 Zech 3:10

Micah

Jesus' Birthplace

Catholic Connections

Micah predicts that a new ruler will come from Bethlehem, the smallest of towns. That new ruler is Jesus. He was born to poor parents in a little town (see Luke 2:1–7). You might think the Savior of the world should have been born in an important town. But Jesus lived a simple life to show it doesn't matter how wealthy your family is. You do not need to be rich or important to please God—in some ways being rich or famous can make it harder to follow God. What God truly desires is a humble heart—so we recognize that everything we have is a gift from God.

— Micah 5:2–5

tal of the kingdom that was yours. ⁹Why do you cry out so loudly? Why are you suffering like a woman in labor? Is it because you have no king, and your counselors are dead? ¹⁰Twist and groan,ᵍ people of Jerusalem, like a woman giving birth, for now you will have to leave the city and live in the open country. You will have to go to Babylon, but there the LORD will save you from your enemies. ¹¹Many nations have gathered to attack you. They say, "Jerusalem must be destroyed! We will see this city in ruins!" ¹²But these nations do not know what is in the LORD's mind. They do not realize that they have been gathered together to be punished in the same way that grain is brought in to be threshed.

¹³The LORD says, "People of Jerusalem, go and punish your enemies! I will make you as strong as a bull with iron horns and bronze hoofs. You will crush many nations, and the wealth they got by violence you will present to me, the Lord of the whole world."

5 ¹People of Jerusalem, gather your forces!ʰ We are besieged! They are attacking the leader of Israel!

God Promises a Ruler from Bethlehem

²The LORD says, "Bethlehem Ephrathah, you are one of the smallest towns in Judah, but out of you I will bring a ruler for Israel, whose family line goes back to ancient times."

³So the LORD will abandon his people to their enemies until the woman who is to give birth has her son. Then those Israelites who are in exile will be reunited with their own people. ⁴When he comes, he will rule his people with the strength that comes from the LORD and with the majesty of the LORD God himself. His people will live in safety because people all over the earth will acknowledge his greatness, ⁵and he will bring peace.

Deliverance and Punishment

When the Assyrians invade our country and break through our defenses, we will send our strongest leaders to fight them. ⁶By force of arms they will conquer Assyria, the land of Nimrod, and theyⁱ will save us from the Assyrians when they invade our territory.

ᵍ **4:10** *Probable text* groan; *Hebrew* bring forth. ʰ **5:1** *Probable text* People . . . forces!; *Hebrew unclear.*
ⁱ **5:6** *Probable text* they; *Hebrew* he.
5:2 Mt 2:6; Jn 7:42 **5:6** Gen 10:8–11

Micah

[7] The people of Israel who survive will be like refreshing dew sent by the LORD for many nations, like showers on growing plants. They will depend on God, not people. [8] Those who are left among the nations will be like a lion hunting for food in a forest or a pasture: it gets in among the sheep, pounces on them, and tears them to pieces—and there is no hope of rescue. [9] Israel will conquer her enemies and destroy them all.

[10] The LORD says, "At that time I will take away your horses and destroy your chariots. [11] I will destroy the cities in your land and tear down all your defenses. [12] I will destroy the magic charms you use and leave you without any fortunetellers. [13] I will destroy your idols and sacred stone pillars; no longer will you worship the things that you yourselves have made. [14] I will pull down the images of the goddess Asherah in your land and destroy your cities. [15] And in my great anger I will take revenge on all nations that have not obeyed me."

The LORD's Case against Israel

6 [1] Listen to the LORD's case against Israel. Arise, O LORD, and present your case; let the mountains and the hills hear what you say.

[2] You mountains, you everlasting foundations of the earth, listen to the LORD's case! The LORD has a case against his people. He is going to bring an accusation against Israel.

[3] The LORD says, "My people, what have I done to you? How have I been a burden to you? Answer me. [4] I brought you out of Egypt; I rescued you from slavery; I sent Moses, Aaron, and Miriam to lead you. [5] My people, remember what King Balak of Moab planned to do to you and how Balaam son of Beor answered him. Remember the things that happened on the way from the camp at Acacia to Gilgal. Remember these things and you will realize what I did in order to save you."

What the LORD Requires

[6] What shall I bring to the LORD, the God of heaven, when I come to worship him? Shall I bring the best calves to burn as offerings to him? [7] Will the LORD be pleased if I bring him thousands of sheep or endless streams of olive oil? Shall I offer him my first-born child to pay for my sins? [8] No, the LORD has told us what is good. What he requires of us is this: to do what is just, to show constant love, and to live in humble fellowship with our God.

[9] It is wise to fear the LORD. He calls to the city, "Listen, you people who assemble in the city![j] [10] In the houses of evil people are treasures which they got dishonestly. They use false measures, a thing that I hate.[k] [11] How can I forgive those who use false scales and weights? [12] Your rich people exploit the poor, and all of you are liars. [13] So I have already begun[l] your ruin and destruction because of your sins. [14] You will eat, but not be satisfied—in fact you will still be hungry. You will carry things off, but

How can I forgive those who use false scales and weights? (6:11)

---

[j] **6:9** *Probable text* who assemble in the city; *Hebrew* and who appointed it. Yet.   [k] **6:10** *Verse 10 in Hebrew is unclear.*   [l] **6:13** *Some ancient translations* begun; *Hebrew* made sick.
6:4 a Ex 12:50, 51; b Ex 4:10–16; c Ex 15:20   **6:5** a Num 22:2—24:25; b Josh 3:1—4:19

Worship: **To adore God in prayer, particularly as part of a public religious ritual such as the Mass.**

Pray It!

Empty Worship

The Temple at Jerusalem had regular religious rituals to worship God. During the rituals there were animal sacrifices (Micah 6:6). The rituals were attended by all the powerful people of the city. Yet these same people cheated poor people (6:10–12). It upset Micah that these wealthy people pretended to be so religious! Their rituals meant nothing to God if they did not treat others fairly (6:7–8).

Catholics worship God at Mass and other prayer services. But just as in Micah's time, it isn't enough just to attend worship services. We must follow God the rest of the week. To help you remember this, before going to Mass each week, say this prayer:

Dear God, I know I am not perfect. Show me where I need to change. Let Jesus's body and blood in the Eucharist strengthen me to do what is right in the week ahead. Do not let my prayers become empty promises. Amen.

— Micah 6:6–16

you will not be able to save them; anything you do save I will destroy in war. ¹⁵You will sow grain, but not harvest the crop. You will press oil from olives, but never get to use it. You will make wine, but never drink it. ¹⁶This will happen because you have followed the evil practices of King Omri and of his son, King Ahab. You have continued their policies, and so I will bring you to ruin, and everyone will despise you. People*ᵐ* everywhere will treat you with contempt."*ⁿ*

Israel's Moral Corruption

7 ¹It's hopeless! I am like a hungry person who finds no fruit left on the trees and no grapes on the vines. All the grapes and all the tasty figs have been picked. ²There is not an honest person left in the land, no one loyal to God. Everyone is waiting for a chance to commit murder. Everyone hunts down their own people. ³They are all experts at doing evil. Officials and judges ask for bribes. The influential people tell them what they want, and so they scheme togeth-

er.*º* ⁴Even the best and most honest of them are as worthless as weeds.

The day has come when God will punish the people, as he warned them through their watchmen, the prophets. Now they are in confusion. ⁵Don't believe your neighbor or trust your friend. Be careful what you say even to your husband or wife. ⁶In these times sons treat their fathers like fools, daughters oppose their mothers, and young women quarrel with their mothers-in-law; your enemies are the members of your own family.

⁷But I will watch for the LORD; I will wait confidently for God, who will save me. My God will hear me.

The LORD Brings Salvation

⁸Our enemies have no reason to gloat over us. We have fallen, but we will rise again. We are in darkness now, but the LORD will give us light. ⁹We have sinned against the LORD, so now we must endure his anger for a while. But in the end he will defend us and right the wrongs that have been done to us.

Micah

ᵐ **6:16** *One ancient translation* People; *Hebrew* My people.   *ⁿ* **6:16** People . . . contempt; *or* As my people you will everywhere be treated with contempt.   *º* **7:3** and so they scheme together; *Hebrew unclear.*
6:16 a 1 Kings 16:23–28; **b** 1 Kings 16:29–34; 21:25, 26   **7:6** Mt 10:35, 36; Lk 12:53

Your people will return to you from everywhere. (7:12)

He will bring us out to the light; we will live to see him save us. ¹⁰Then our enemies will see this and be disgraced—the same enemies who taunted us by asking, "Where is the LORD your God?" We will see them defeated, trampled*ᵖ* down like mud in the streets.

¹¹People of Jerusalem, the time to rebuild the city walls is coming. At that time your territory will be enlarged. ¹²Your people will return to you from everywhere—from Assyria in the east, from Egypt in the south, from the region of the Euphrates River, from distant seas and far-off mountains. ¹³But the earth will become a desert because of the wickedness of those who live on it.

The LORD's Compassion on Israel

¹⁴Be a shepherd to your people, LORD, the people you have chosen. Although they live apart in the wilderness, there is fertile land around them. Let them go and feed in the rich pastures of Bashan and Gilead, as they did long ago.

¹⁵Work miracles for us,*�q* LORD, as you did in the days when you brought us out of Egypt. ¹⁶The nations will see this and be frustrated in spite of all their strength. In dismay they will close their mouths and cover their ears. ¹⁷They will crawl in the dust like snakes; they will come from their fortresses, trembling and afraid. They will turn in fear to the LORD our God.

¹⁸There is no other god like you, O LORD; you forgive the sins of your people who have survived. You do not stay angry forever, but you take pleasure in showing us your constant love. ¹⁹You will be merciful to us once again. You will trample our sins underfoot and send them to the bottom of the sea! ²⁰You will show your faithfulness and constant love to your people, the descendants of Abraham and of Jacob, as you promised our ancestors long ago.

ᵖ **7:10** We will see . . . trampled; *or* We will gloat over them as they lie trampled.   *�q* **7:15** *Probable text* Work miracles for us; *Hebrew* I will work miracles for him.

Micah

Your Next Step

Congratulations on finishing the Book of Micah! Use this space to write your thoughts and questions about this book. If you are following the suggested reading plan, go back to the Book of Jeremiah in the Old Testament. Jeremiah was a prophet who saw the destruction of Jerusalem and the holy Temple.

Think about the last time that you were really angry
with someone. What made you so angry? How did you deal with
your anger? Did you keep it inside? Or did you express your
anger? Maybe you talked about it—or "vented"—with a friend.

In this short book, Nahum describes God's anger at the Assyrians. God vows to destroy Nineveh, the glittering capital of the
Assyrians, as cruelly as the Assyrians dealt with the Israelites.
And that is Nahum's point. God takes care of his Chosen People
and punishes the guilty. Nineveh will meet the same fate that it
inflicted on others. This may sound like pure revenge, but for the
people of Nahum's time, this is simply justice carried out by God.

THE BOOK OF *Nahum*

Chap. 2:4–5

Head lines

- Storm Warning: God's Judgment Coming (chapter 1)
- Nineveh Falls! (2:1—3:19)

FACTOIDS

Who wrote this book? The prophet Nahum.

Why was it written? It was written to the Israelites who had experienced cruel
treatment at the hands of the Assyrians. Nahum's prophecies assure God's people that God will avenge them. The book describes the fall of the evil city of
Nineveh and celebrates God's victory.

What period does it cover? 663–612 BC.

How does it fit into the Bible? Nahum wrote after the Assyrians had destroyed
the northern kingdom of Israel and invaded the southern kingdom of Judah
(but before the Babylonian Exile).

Important theme
- God will not allow evil people to go unpunished.
- God protects and comforts those who turn to the Lord in times of trouble.

NAHUM

1 ¹This is a message about Nineveh, the account of a vision seen by Nahum, who was from Elkosh.

The LORD's Anger against Nineveh

²The LORD God tolerates no rivals;
he punishes those who oppose him.
In his anger he pays them back.
³The LORD does not easily become angry,
but he is powerful
and never lets the guilty go unpunished.

Where the LORD walks, storms arise;
the clouds are the dust raised by his feet!
⁴He commands the sea, and it dries up!
He makes the rivers go dry.
The fields of Bashan wither,
Mount Carmel turns brown,
and the flowers of Lebanon fade.
⁵Mountains quake in the presence of the
LORD;
hills melt before him.
The earth shakes when the LORD appears;
the world and all its people tremble.
⁶When he is angry, who can survive?
Who can survive his terrible fury?
He pours out his flaming anger;
rocks crumble to dust before him.

⁷The LORD is good;
he protects his people in times of trouble;
he takes care of those who turn to him.
⁸Like a great rushing flood he completely
destroys his enemies;ᵃ
he sends to their death those who
oppose him.
⁹What are you plotting against the LORD?
He will destroy you.
No one opposes him more than once.
¹⁰Like tangled thorns and dry straw
you drunkards will be burned up!

¹¹From you, Nineveh, there came someone full of wicked schemes, who plotted against the LORD. ¹²This is what the LORD

ᵃ **1:8** *Some ancient translations* his enemies; *Hebrew* its place.
1:1—3:19 Isa 10:5–34; 14:24–27; Zeph 2:13–15

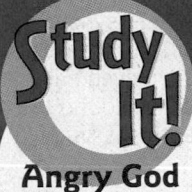

Angry God

"He pours out his flaming anger;
    rocks crumble to dust before
    him.

The LORD is good;
    he protects his people in times
    of trouble;
    he takes care of those who turn
    to him." (Nahum 1:6–7)

These two verses follow one another in the Book of Nahum, and seem to describe two different images of God. One is an image of an angry, punishing God. The other is an image of a loving, caring God. The Israelite people had no trouble with these different images of God. They had experienced many wars and conflicts. Throughout this violent time they felt God's support. They had an image of God as a strong warrior, defeating their enemies as long as they remained faithful to their Covenant with God. But they also knew God's love, care, and mercy, and so they also had gentle and tender images of God.

God sent Jesus to fully reveal God's message of love and forgiveness for all people. Because of what Jesus taught us, it has become harder to imagine God as a warrior, taking one people's side against another people's. Thanks to Jesus, we now see forgiveness— more than victory in battle—as a sign of God's presence.

— Nahum 1:6–7

says to his people Israel: "Even though the Assyrians are strong and numerous, they will be destroyed and disappear. My people, I made you suffer, but I will not do it again. [13] I will now end Assyria's power over you and break the chains that bind you."

[14] This is what the LORD has decreed about the Assyrians: "They will have no descendants to carry on their name. I will destroy the idols that are in the temples of their gods. I am preparing a grave for the Assyrians—they don't deserve to live!"

[15] Look, a messenger is coming over the mountains with good news! He is on his way to announce the victory! People of Judah, celebrate your festivals and give God what you solemnly promised him. The wicked will never invade your land again. They have been totally destroyed!

The Fall of Nineveh

2 [1] Nineveh, you are under attack!
The power that will shatter you has come.
Prepare the defenses!
Guard the road!
Prepare for battle!
([2] The LORD is about to restore the glory of Israel, as it was before her enemies plundered her.)
[3] The enemy soldiers carry red shields and wear uniforms of red.
They are preparing to attack!

Look, a messenger is coming! (1:15)

Their chariots flash like fire!
Their horses[b] prance!

[4] Chariots dash wildly through the streets, rushing back and forth in the city squares.
They flash like torches and dart about like lightning.
[5] The officers are summoned; they stumble as they press forward.

The attackers rush to the wall and set up the shield for the battering ram.
[6] The gates by the river burst open; the palace is filled with terror.
[7] The queen is taken captive; her servants moan like doves and beat their breasts in sorrow.
[8] Like water from a broken dam the people rush from Nineveh![c]

The fall of Nineveh (2)

Nahum

[b] *2:3 Some ancient translations* horses; *Hebrew* cypresses.   [c] *2:8 Probable text* Like water . . . Nineveh; *Hebrew unclear.*
1:15 Isa 52:7

"Stop! Stop!" the cry rings out—
  but no one turns back.

9 Plunder the silver!
  Plunder the gold!
  The city is full of treasure!

10 Nineveh is destroyed, deserted, desolate!
  Hearts melt with fear;
  knees tremble, strength is gone;
  faces grow pale.

11 Where now is the city
  that was like a den of lions,
  the place where young lions were fed,
  where the lion and the lioness would go
  and their cubs would be safe?
12 The lion killed his prey
  and tore it to pieces for his mate and
    her cubs;
  he filled his den with torn flesh.

13 "I am your enemy!" says the LORD
Almighty. "I will burn up your chariots. Your
soldiers will be killed in war, and I will take
away everything that you took from others.
The demands of your envoys will no longer
be heard."

Nineveh's Suffering

3 1 Doomed is the lying, murderous city,
    full of wealth to be looted and
      plundered!
2 Listen! The crack of the whip,
  the rattle of wheels,
  the gallop of horses,
  the jolting of chariots!
3 Cavalry troops charge,
  swords flash, spears gleam!
  Corpses are piled high,
    dead bodies without number—
    men stumble over them!
4 Nineveh the whore is being punished.
  Attractive and full of deadly charms,
    she enchanted nations and enslaved[d]
    them.

5 The LORD Almighty says,
  "I will punish you, Nineveh!
  I will strip you naked
  and let the nations see you,

see you in all your shame.
6 I will treat you with contempt
  and cover you with filth.
  People will stare at you in horror.
7 All who see you will shrink back.
  They will say, 'Nineveh lies in ruins!
  Who has any sympathy for her?
  Who will want to comfort her?' "

8 Nineveh, are you any better than Thebes,
the capital of Egypt? She too had a river to
protect her like a wall—the Nile was her
defense. 9 She ruled Ethiopia[e] and Egypt,
there was no limit to her power; Libya was
her ally. 10 Yet the people of Thebes were
carried off into exile. At every street corner
their children were beaten to death. Their
leading men were carried off in chains and
divided among their captors.

11 Nineveh, you too will fall into a drunken
stupor! You too will try to escape from your
enemies. 12 All your fortresses will be like fig
trees with ripe figs: shake the trees, and the
fruit falls right into your mouth! 13 Your soldiers are helpless, and your country stands
defenseless before your enemies. Fire will
destroy the bars across your gates. 14 Draw
water to prepare for a siege, and strengthen
your fortresses! Trample the clay to make
bricks, and get the brick molds ready! 15 No
matter what you do, you will still be burned
to death or killed in battle. You will be wiped
out like crops eaten up by locusts.

You multiplied like locusts! 16 You produced more merchants than there are stars in
the sky! But now they are gone, like locusts
that spread their wings and fly away. 17 Your
officials are like a swarm of locusts that stay
in the walls on a cold day. But when the sun
comes out, they fly away, and no one knows
where they have gone!

18 Emperor of Assyria, your governors are
dead, and your noblemen are asleep forever!
Your people are scattered on the mountains,
and there is no one to bring them home
again. 19 There is no remedy for your
injuries, and your wounds cannot be healed.
All those who hear the news of your
destruction clap their hands for joy. Did anyone escape your endless cruelty?

---

d **3:4** enslaved; or seduced. e **3:9** Hebrew Cush: Cush is the ancient name of the extensive territory south of the First
Cataract of the Nile River. This region was called Ethiopia in Graeco-Roman times, and included within its borders most of
modern Sudan and some of present-day Ethiopia (Abyssinia).

"O God! All this waiting! What's up with that? What are you waiting for? Why do you let them get away with that, God? If I were in charge of the world, I would do things differently and make things right!"

Habakkuk was right in God's face, telling God what he thought, and offering his own suggestions. Do you ever do that? Sometimes, when we complain to God, we feel guilty. But Habakkuk shows us that it is okay to yell at God. God can take it. God doesn't hold it against us when we get frustrated. Part of growing in faith is learning how to cope with our frustrations. Habakkuk struggled to understand how a loving God could allow evil and suffering. In the end, he placed his trust in God's saving power.

Chap. 1:2

Headlines

- Habakkuk Complains, Debates with God! (1:2–11)
- Habakkuk Rejoices in God's Saving Power (3:1–19)

FACTOIDS

Who wrote this book? Habakkuk, a prophet in the southern kingdom of Judah.

Why was it written? Habakkuk expresses frustration at God's silence when bad things were happening to God's people. He also expresses the importance of having faith in God's eventual justice.

What literary style is used? The reflections in this book are similar to those in the wisdom literature. The dialog sections between Habakkuk and God resemble the Book of Job.

Jesus connection: Habakkuk's cry, "How long, O Lord?" is similar to Jesus' cry to God in the garden at Gethsemane when he asks God to remove the cup of suffering from him. (See Matthew 26:39.)

Important themes

- It is okay for God's people to ask the hard questions, such as, "Why do bad things happen to good people?"
- We may never understand the ways of God while on this earth. Things happen in God's time, not in our own time.

HABAKKUK

1 ¹This is the message that the LORD revealed to the prophet Habakkuk.

Habakkuk Complains of Injustice

²O LORD, how long must I call for help before you listen, before you save us from violence? ³Why do you make me see such trouble? How can you stand to look on such wrongdoing? Destruction and violence are all around me, and there is fighting and quarreling everywhere. ⁴The law is weak and useless, and justice is never done. Evil people get the better of the righteous, and so justice is perverted.

The LORD's Reply

⁵Then the LORD said to his people, "Keep watching the nations around you, and you will be astonished at what you see. I am going to do something that you will not believe when you hear about it. ⁶I am bringing the Babylonians to power, those fierce, restless people. They are marching out across the world to conquer other lands. ⁷They spread fear and terror, and in their pride they are a law to themselves.

⁸"Their horses are faster than leopards,

fiercer than hungry wolves. Their cavalry troops come riding from distant lands; their horses paw the ground. They come swooping down like eagles attacking their prey. ⁹"Their armies advance in violent conquest, and everyone is terrified as they approach.*ᵃ* Their captives are as numerous as grains of sand. ¹⁰They treat kings with contempt and laugh at high officials. No fortress can stop them—they pile up earth against it and capture it. ¹¹Then they sweep on like the wind and are gone, these men whose power is their god."

Habakkuk Complains to the LORD Again

¹²LORD, from the very beginning you are God. You are my God, holy and eternal. LORD, my God and protector, you have chosen the Babylonians and made them strong so that they can punish us. ¹³But how can you stand these treacherous, evil men? Your eyes are too holy to look at evil, and you cannot stand the sight of people doing wrong. So why are you silent while they destroy people who are more righteous than they are?

¹⁴How can you treat people like fish or

"LORD . . . how can you stand these treacherous, evil men?" (1:12–13)

ᵃ **1:9** *Probable text* and everyone . . . approach; *Hebrew unclear.*
1:5 Acts 13:41   **1:6** 2 Kings 24:2

like a swarm of insects that have no ruler to direct them? 15The Babylonians catch people with hooks, as though they were fish. They drag them off in nets and shout for joy over their catch! 16They even worship their nets and offer sacrifices to them, because their nets provide them with the best of everything.

17Are they going to use their swords forever and keep on destroying nations without mercy?

The Lord's Answer to Habakkuk

2 1I will climb my watchtower and wait to see what the Lord will tell me to say and what answer he[b] will give to my complaint.

2The Lord gave me this answer: "Write down clearly on tablets what I reveal to you, so that it can be read at a glance. 3Put it in writing, because it is not yet time for it to come true. But the time is coming quickly, and what I show you will come true. It may seem slow in coming, but wait for it; it will certainly take place, and it will not be delayed. 4And this is the message: 'Those who are evil will not survive,[c] but those who are righteous will live because they are faithful to God.' "

Doom on the Unrighteous

5Wealth is deceitful. Greedy people are proud and restless—like death itself they are never satisfied. That is why they conquer nation after nation for themselves. 6The conquered people will taunt their conquerors and show their scorn for them. They will say, "You take what isn't yours, but you are doomed! How long will you go on getting rich by forcing your debtors to pay up?"

7But before you know it, you that have conquered others will be in debt yourselves and be forced to pay interest. Enemies will come and make you tremble. They will plunder you! 8You have plundered the people of many nations, but now those who have survived will plunder you because of the murders you have committed and because of your violence against the people of the world and its cities.[d]

9You are doomed! You have made your family rich with what you took by violence, and have tried to make your own home safe from harm and danger! 10But your schemes have brought shame on your family; by destroying many nations you have only brought ruin on yourself. 11Even the stones of the walls cry out against you, and the rafters echo the cry.

12You are doomed! You founded a city on crime and built it up by murder. 13The nations you conquered wore themselves out in useless labor, and all they have built goes up in flames. The Lord Almighty has done this. 14But the earth will be as full of the knowledge of the Lord's glory as the seas are full of water.

15You are doomed! In your fury you humiliated and disgraced your neighbors; you made them stagger as though they were drunk. 16You in turn will be covered with shame instead of honor. You yourself will drink and stagger. The Lord will make you drink your own cup of punishment, and your honor will be turned to disgrace. 17You have cut down the forests of Lebanon; now you will be cut down. You killed its animals; now animals will terrify you. This will happen because of the murders you have committed and because of your violence against the people of the world and its cities.[d]

18What's the use of an idol? It is only something that a human being has made, and it tells you nothing but lies. What good does it do for its maker to trust it—a god that can't even talk! 19You are doomed! You say to a piece of wood, "Wake up!" or to a block of stone, "Get up!" Can an idol reveal anything to you? It may be covered with silver and gold, but there is no life in it.

20The Lord is in his holy Temple; let everyone on earth be silent in his presence.

Habakkuk

---

b 2:1 *One ancient translation* he; *Hebrew* I.   c 2:4 *Probable text* will not survive; *Hebrew unclear.*   d 2:8, 17 the people . . . cities; *or* the land, the city, and those who live in it.
2:3 Heb 10:37   2:4 Rom 1:17; Gal 3:11; Heb 10:38   2:13 Sir 14:19   2:14 Isa 11:9

Pray It!

After Winter, Comes the Spring

Read Habakkuk 3:17–19. How can the prophet say that even if all the crops fail and the animals die, he will still be joyful and glad? The answer is simple: Faith. He is confident that God cares for him and sooner or later things will get better. Can you think of examples like that? When good times follow hard times? How about:

- After months of painful exercise, I can run faster.
- After nine months of preparation and many hours of pain, a new baby is born.
- After years of playing boring scales and studying music theory, I become a musician.
- After thunder, lightning, and pounding rain, the clouds lighten, and a rainbow forms.
- After the suffering death of Good Friday, the glorious life of Easter Sunday comes.

So Habakkuk's prayer doesn't seem so strange after all. It doesn't mean that praying with the confidence of Habakkuk will be easy. But we need to keep trying to have that kind of faith.

— Habakkuk 3:17–18

A Prayer of Habakkuk

3 ¹This is a prayer of the prophet Habakkuk:ᵉ

²O LORD, I have heard of what you have done,
　and I am filled with awe.
Now do again in our times
　the great deeds you used to do.
Be merciful, even when you are angry.

³God is coming again from Edom;
　the holy God is coming from the hills of Paran.
His splendor covers the heavens,
　and the earth is full of his praise.
⁴He comes with the brightness of lightning;
　light flashes from his hand,
　there where his power is hidden.
⁵He sends disease before him
　and commands death to follow him.
⁶When he stops, the earth shakes;
　at his glance the nations tremble.

The eternal mountains are shattered;
　the everlasting hills sink down,
　the hills where he walked in ancient times.

⁷I saw the people of Cushan afraid
　and the people of Midian tremble.
⁸Was it the rivers that made you angry, LORD?
　Was it the sea that made you furious?
You rode upon the clouds;
　the storm cloud was your chariot,
　as you brought victory to your people.
⁹You got ready to use your bow,
　ready to shoot your arrows.ᶠ
Your lightning split open the earth.
¹⁰When the mountains saw you, they trembled;
　water poured down from the skies.
The waters under the earth roared,
　and their waves rose high.

ᵉ **3:1** Hebrew has an additional phrase, the meaning of which is unclear. ᶠ **3:9** Probable text ready to shoot your arrows; Hebrew unclear.

Habakkuk

11 At the flash of your speeding arrows
 and the gleam of your shining spear,
 the sun and the moon stood still.
12 You marched across the earth in
 anger;
 in fury you trampled the nations.
13 You went out to save your people,
 to save your chosen king.
 You struck down the leader of the wicked
 and completely destroyed his
 followers.g
14 Your arrows pierced the commander of
 his army
 when it came like a storm to scatter
 us,
 gloating like those who secretly oppress
 the poor.h
15 You trampled the sea with your
 horses,
 and the mighty waters foamed.

16 I hear all this, and I tremble;
 my lips quiver with fear.
 My body goes limp,
 and my feet stumblei beneath me.

I will quietly wait for the time to
 come
 when God will punish those who
 attack us.

17 Even though the fig trees have no
 fruit
 and no grapes grow on the vines,
 even though the olive crop fails
 and the fields produce no grain,
 even though the sheep all die
 and the cattle stalls are empty,
18 I will still be joyful and glad,
 because the LORD God is my
 savior.
19 The Sovereign LORD gives me strength.
 He makes me sure-footed as a
 deer
 and keeps me safe on the mountains.

g **3:13** *Probable text* completely . . . followers; *Hebrew unclear.*   h **3:14** *Verse 14 in Hebrew is unclear.*
i **3:16** *Probable text* my feet stumble; *Hebrew* I am excited, because.
3:19 2 Sam 22:34; Ps 18:33

Habakkuk

Gloom, doom, and happiness. This really could be the title of this book because there is some of all three. It is a book about sin and the need to repent—to turn back to the Lord. Zephaniah warns his people that gloom and doom lie ahead because they have forgotten who they are. They are worshiping pagan gods such as Baal and Milcom. It is time to shape up and face the consequences—because there are some to face. Whenever we stray from what is good and right, we need to be ready to accept the consequences of our sin.

Yet even though most of this book seems pretty negative, it concludes on a joyful and promising note: "Sing and shout for joy, people of Israel!" (Zephaniah 3:14). There is a happy ending, after all!

Chap. 2:8–15

Head lines

- You Will Hear Wailing! (chapter 1)
- Sing and Shout for Joy! (3:14–20)

FACTOIDS

Who wrote this book? The prophet Zephaniah, who preached to the southern kingdom of Judah around 630 BC, and probably a later editor.

Why was it written? Zephaniah urged the people of Judah to turn from sin and idolatry and to repent.

How does it fit into the Bible? Zephaniah is one of the prophets who wrote during the reign of Josiah (640–609 BC), about the same time as Jeremiah.

Important theme

- God's punishment for sinful actions is meant to teach us, not destroy us. We should never despair, but place our trust in God's loving care.

ZEPHANIAH

1

¹This is the message that the LORD gave to Zephaniah during the time that Josiah son of Amon was king of Judah. (Zephaniah was descended from King Hezekiah through Amariah, Gedaliah, and Cushi.)

The Day of the LORD's Judgment

²The LORD said, "I am going to destroy everything on earth, ³all human beings and animals, birds and fish. I will bring about the downfall of[a] the wicked. I will destroy everyone, and no survivors will be left. I, the LORD, have spoken.

⁴"I will punish the people of Jerusalem and of all Judah. I will destroy the last trace of the worship of Baal there, and no one will even remember the pagan priests who serve him. ⁵I will destroy anyone who goes up on the roof and worships the sun, the moon, and the stars. I will also destroy those who worship me and swear loyalty to me, but then take oaths in the name of the god Milcom. ⁶I will destroy those who have turned back and no longer follow me, those who do not come to me or ask me to guide them."

⁷The day is near when the LORD will sit in judgment; so be silent in his presence. The LORD is preparing to sacrifice his people and has invited enemies to plunder Judah. ⁸"On that day of slaughter," says the LORD, "I will punish the officials, the king's sons, and all who practice foreign customs. ⁹I will punish all who worship like pagans and who steal and kill in order to fill their master's house[b] with loot.

¹⁰"On that day," says the LORD, "you will hear the sound of crying at the Fish Gate in Jerusalem. You will hear wailing in the newer part of the city and a great crashing sound in the hills. ¹¹Wail and cry when you hear this, you that live in the lower part of the city, because all the merchants will be dead!

¹²"At that time I will take a lamp and search Jerusalem. I will punish the people who are self-satisfied and confident, who say to themselves, 'The LORD never does anything, one way or the other.' ¹³Their wealth will be looted and their houses destroyed. They will never live in the houses they are building or drink wine from the vineyards they are planting."

The LORD never does anything, one way or the other. (1:12)

¹⁴The great day of the LORD is near—very near and coming fast! That day will be bitter, for even[c] the bravest soldiers will cry out in despair! ¹⁵It will be a day of fury, a day of trouble and distress, a day of ruin and destruction, a day of darkness and gloom, a black and cloudy day, ¹⁶a day filled with the sound of war trumpets and the battle cry of soldiers attacking fortified cities and high towers.

¹⁷The LORD says, "I will bring such disasters on the human race that everyone will grope about like someone blind. They have sinned against me, and now their blood will be poured out like water, and their dead bodies will lie rotting on the ground."

---

[a] **1:3** *Probable text* I will bring about the downfall of; *Hebrew* the stumbling blocks. [b] **1:9** their master's house; *or* the temple of their god. [c] **1:14** That day . . . even; *or* Listen! That terrible day is coming when even.
1:1 2 Kings 22:1—23:30; 2 Chr 34:1—35:27

18 On the day when the LORD shows his fury, not even all their silver and gold will save them. The whole earth will be destroyed by the fire of his anger. He will put an end—a sudden end—to everyone who lives on earth.

A Plea for Repentance

2 ¹Shameless nation, come to your senses ²before you are driven away like chaff blown by the wind, before the burning anger of the LORD comes upon you, before the day when he shows his fury. ³Turn to the LORD, all you humble people of the land, who obey his commands. Do what is right, and humble yourselves before the LORD. Perhaps you will escape punishment on the day when the LORD shows his anger.

The Doom of the Nations around Judah

⁴No one will be left in the city of Gaza. Ashkelon will be deserted. The people of Ashdod will be driven out in half a day,ᵈ and the people of Ekron will be driven from their city. ⁵You Philistines are doomed, you people who live along the coast. The LORD has passed sentence on you. He will destroy you, and not one of you will be left. ⁶Your land by the sea will become open fields with shepherd's huts and sheep pens. ⁷The people of Judah who survive will occupy your land. They will pasture their flocks there and sleep in the houses of Ashkelon. The LORD their God will be with them and make them prosper again.

⁸The LORD Almighty says, "I have heard the people of Moab and Ammon insulting and taunting my people, and boasting that they would seize their land. ⁹As surely as I am the living LORD, the God of Israel, I swear that Moab and Ammon are going to be destroyed like Sodom and Gomorrah.

They will become a place of salt pits and everlasting ruin, overgrown with weeds. Those of my people who survive will plunder them and take their land."

¹⁰That is how the people of Moab and Ammon will be punished for their pride and arrogance and for insulting the people of the LORD Almighty. ¹¹The LORD will terrify them. He will reduce the gods of the earth to nothing, and then every nation will worship him, each in its own land.

¹²The LORD will also put the people of Ethiopiaᵉ to death.

¹³The LORD will use his power to destroy Assyria. He will make the city of Nineveh a deserted ruin, a waterless desert. ¹⁴It will be a place where flocks, herds, and animals of every kind will lie down. Owls will live among its ruins and hoot from the windows. Crowsᶠ will caw on the doorsteps. The cedar wood of her buildings will be stripped away. ¹⁵That is what will happen to the city that is so proud of its own power and thinks it is safe. Its people think that their city is the greatest in the world. What a desolate place it will become, a place where wild animals will rest! Everyone who passes by will shrink back in horror.

Owls will live among its ruins. (2:14)

Jerusalem's Sin and Redemption

3 ¹Jerusalem is doomed, that corrupt, rebellious city that oppresses its own people. ²It has not listened to the LORD or accepted his discipline. It has not put its trust in the LORD or asked for his help. ³Its officials are like roaring lions; its judges are

---

ᵈ **2:4** *in half a day; or by a surprise attack at noontime.*   ᵉ **2:12** *Hebrew* Cush: *Cush is the ancient name of the extensive territory south of the First Cataract of the Nile River. This region was called Ethiopia in Graeco-Roman times, and included within its borders most of modern Sudan and some of present-day Ethiopia (Abyssinia).*   ᶠ **2:14** *Some ancient translations* Crows; *Hebrew* Desolation.

2:4–7 Isa 14:29–31; Jer 47:1–7; Ezek 25:15–17; Joel 3:4–8; Am 1:6–8; Zech 9:5–7   **2:8–11 a** Isa 15:1—16:14; 25:10–12; Jer 48:1–47; Ezek 25:8–11; Am 1:13–15; **b** Jer 49:1–6; Ezek 21:28–32; 25:1–7; Am 1:13–15   **2:9** Gen 19:24   **2:12** Isa 18:1–7   **2:13–15** Isa 10:5–34; 14:24–27; Nah 1:1—3:19

Pray It!

A Festival of Delight!

Delight is a word some people don't put together with God. Yet that word appears many times in the Bible, especially in the Old Testament. Pray these beautiful lines from Zephaniah, chapter 3.

> The LORD will take delight in you,
>   and in his love he will give you new life.
> He will sing and be joyful over you,
>   as joyful as people at a festival. (Verses 17–18)

Now read them a second time, slowly and prayerfully. Imagine God smiling at the thought of you, at the sound of your name. Ask God to help you take delight in others as well. And don't forget to sing, for God sings a song of joy for you!

— Zephaniah 3:17–18

like hungry wolves, too greedy to leave a bone until morning. [4] The prophets are irresponsible and treacherous; the priests defile what is sacred, and twist the law of God to their own advantage. [5] But the LORD is still in the city; he does what is right and never what is wrong. Every morning without fail, he brings justice to his people. And yet the unrighteous people there keep on doing wrong and are not ashamed.

[6] The LORD says, "I have wiped out whole nations; I have destroyed their cities and left their walls and towers in ruins. The cities are deserted; the streets are empty—no one is left. [7] I thought that then my people would have reverence for me and accept my discipline, that they would never forget[g] the lesson I taught them. But soon they were behaving as badly as ever.

[8] "Just wait," the LORD says. "Wait for the day when I rise to accuse the nations. I have made up my mind to gather nations and kingdoms in order to let them feel the force of my anger. The whole earth will be destroyed by the fire of my fury.

[9] "Then I will change the people of the nations, and they will pray to me alone and not to other gods. They will all obey me. [10] Even from distant Ethiopia[h] my scattered people will bring offerings to me. [11] At that time you, my people, will no longer need to be ashamed that you rebelled against me. I will remove everyone who is proud and arrogant, and you will never again rebel against me on my sacred hill.[i] [12] I will leave there a humble and lowly people, who will come to me for help. [13] The people of Israel who survive will do no wrong to anyone, tell no lies, nor try to deceive. They will be prosperous and secure, afraid of no one."

A Song of Joy

[14] Sing and shout for joy, people of Israel!
    Rejoice with all your heart, Jerusalem!
[15] The LORD has stopped your punishment;
    he has removed all your enemies.
The LORD, the king of Israel, is with you;
    there is no reason now to be afraid.
[16] The time is coming when they will say to
    Jerusalem,
"Do not be afraid, city of Zion!

---

[g] **3:7** *Some ancient translations* they would never forget; *Hebrew* their dwelling would not be cut off.
[h] **3:10** *Hebrew* Cush: *Cush is the ancient name of the extensive territory south of the First Cataract of the Nile River. This region was called Ethiopia in Graeco-Roman times, and included within its borders most of modern Sudan and some of present-day Ethiopia (Abyssinia).* [i] **3:11** SACRED HILL: *Mount Zion (see Zion in Word List).*
3:13 Rev 14:5

Zephaniah

Do not let your hands hang limp!
17 The LORD your God is with you;
　　his power gives you victory.
　The LORD will take delight in you,
　　and in his love he will give you new life.*j*
　He will sing and be joyful over you,
18　　as joyful as people at a festival."
The LORD says,
　"I have ended the threat of doom
　　and taken away your disgrace.*k*
19 The time is coming!

I will punish your oppressors;
　I will rescue all the lame
　and bring the exiles home.
I will turn their shame to honor,
　and all the world will praise them.
20 The time is coming!
I will bring your scattered people home;
　I will make you famous throughout the
　　world
　and make you prosperous once again."
The LORD has spoken.

j **3:17** *Some ancient translations* give you new life; *Hebrew* be silent.　　*k* **3:18** *Verse 18 in Hebrew is unclear.*

Imagine that your town or neighborhood was hit by a tornado or hurricane. Almost every house and building were destroyed, including the church. What should be rebuilt first? Well, people's homes, of course. Everyone needs a safe place to live. Besides, no one has money to rebuild the church, right?

The prophet Haggai would tell us that it is just as important to rebuild God's house as our own. It's a matter of priorities. Why is the church—or in Haggai's time, the Temple—so important? Having a community place to worship God says that God is very important to a community's life. It's not so important that the new church or temple is the biggest or the best, but rather that God is at the center of our lives together.

Head lines

- Command Issued to Rebuild Temple (chapter 1)
- Future Temple Filled with God's Glory (2:1–9)

FACTOIDS

Who wrote this book? This collection of brief prophetic messages is attributed to the prophet Haggai.

Why was it written? Haggai urged those who have returned to Judah after the Babylonian Exile to rebuild the Temple.

How does it fit into the Bible? Haggai is the first prophet to write after the return from Exile, around 520 BC.

Important theme
- Rebuilding God's Temple will bring blessings and peace to the people.

HAGGAI

The LORD's Command to Rebuild the Temple

1 ¹During the second year that Darius was emperor of Persia, on the first day of the sixth month, the LORD spoke through the prophet Haggai. The message was for the governor of Judah, Zerubbabel son of Shealtiel, and for the High Priest, Joshua son of Jehozadak.

²The LORD Almighty said to Haggai, "These people say that this is not the right time to rebuild the Temple." ³The LORD then gave this message to the people through the prophet Haggai: ⁴"My people, why should you be living in well-built houses while my Temple lies in ruins? ⁵Don't you see what is happening to you? ⁶You have planted much grain, but have harvested very little. You have food to eat, but not enough to make you full. You have wine to drink, but not enough to get drunk on! You have clothing, but not enough to keep you warm. And workers cannot earn enough to live on. ⁷Can't you see why this has happened?

⁸Now go up into the hills, get lumber, and rebuild the Temple; then I will be pleased and will be worshiped as I should be.

⁹"You hoped for large harvests, but they turned out to be small. And when you brought the harvest home, I blew it away.ᵃ Why did I do that? Because my Temple lies in ruins while every one of you is busy working on your own house. ¹⁰That is why there is no rain and nothing can grow. ¹¹I have brought drought on the land—on its hills, grainfields, vineyards, and olive orchards—on every crop the ground produces, on people and animals, on everything you try to grow."

The People Obey the LORD's Command

¹²Then Zerubbabel and Joshua and all the people who had returned from the exileᵇ in Babylonia, did what the LORD their God told them to do. They were afraid and obeyed the prophet Haggai, the LORD's

Why should you be living in well-built houses while my Temple lies in ruins? (1:4)

ᵃ **1:9** I blew it away; *or* I spoiled it.　ᵇ **1:12** who had returned from the exile; *or* who had not gone into exile.
1:1 Ezra 4:24—5:2; 6:14

Pray It!

Working Together

Have you ever been part of a service project where you helped build something? You may have heard of Habitat for Humanity. This organization brings volunteers together to build homes for people who cannot afford to buy a house. The family that will be buying the house (at a very reasonable price) must help build the house, together with lots of volunteers. Habitat is well known and respected because it brings a lot of people together to do a very good thing. This is what happened at the time of Haggai, when the people worked together to rebuild the Temple in Jerusalem.

Is there some local project that you and your friends or classmates can get involved in? See if there is a Habitat for Humanity chapter in your area. And don't forget that Jesus was a carpenter. Try to picture Jesus working right alongside you.

— Haggai 1:12—2:5

---

messenger. [13]Then Haggai gave the LORD's message to the people: "I will be with you—that is my promise." [14]The LORD inspired everyone to work on the Temple: Zerubbabel, the governor of Judah; Joshua, the High Priest, and all the people who had returned from the exile.[b] They began working on the Temple of the LORD Almighty, their God, [15]on the twenty-fourth day of the sixth month of the second year that Darius was emperor.

The Splendor of the New Temple

2 [1]On the twenty-first day of the seventh month of that same year, the LORD spoke again through the prophet Haggai. [2]He told Haggai to speak to Zerubbabel, the governor of Judah, to Joshua, the High Priest, and to the people, and to say to them, [3]"Is there anyone among you who can still remember how splendid the Temple used to be? How does it look to you now? It must seem like nothing at all. [4]But now don't be discouraged, any of you. Do the work, for I am with you. [5]When you came out of

Egypt, I promised that I would always be with you. I am still with you, so do not be afraid.

[6]"Before long I will shake heaven and earth, land and sea. [7]I will overthrow all the nations, and their treasures will be brought here, and the Temple will be filled with wealth. [8]All the silver and gold of the world is mine. [9]The new Temple will be more splendid than the old one, and there I will give my people prosperity and peace." The LORD Almighty has spoken.

The Prophet Consults the Priests

[10]On the twenty-fourth day of the ninth month of the second year that Darius was emperor, the LORD Almighty spoke again to the prophet Haggai. [11]He said, "Ask the priests for a ruling on this question: [12]Suppose someone takes a piece of consecrated meat from a sacrifice and carries it in a fold of his robe. If he then lets his robe touch any bread, cooked food, wine, olive oil, or any kind of food at all, will it make that food consecrated also?"

[b] **1:14** who had returned from the exile; *or* who had not gone into exile.
2:3 Ezra 3:12   **2:5** Ex 29:45, 46   **2:6** Heb 12:26

When the question was asked, the priests answered, "No."

13 Then Haggai asked, "Suppose someone is defiled because he has touched a dead body. If he then touches any of these foods, will that make them defiled too?"

The priests answered, "Yes."

14 Then Haggai said, "The LORD says that the same thing applies to the people of this nation and to everything they produce; and so everything they offer on the altar is defiled."

The LORD Promises His Blessing

15 The LORD says, "Can't you see what has happened to you? Before you started to rebuild the Temple, **16** you would go to a pile of grain expecting to find twenty bushels, but there would be only ten. You would go to draw fifty gallons of wine from a vat, but find only twenty. **17** I sent scorching winds and hail to ruin everything you tried to

2:13 Num 19:11–22

grow, but still you did not repent. **18** Today is the twenty-fourth day of the ninth month, the day that the foundation of the Temple has been completed. See what is going to happen from now on. **19** Although there is no grain left, and the grapevines, fig trees, pomegranates, and olive trees have not yet produced, yet from now on I will bless you."

The LORD's Promise to Zerubbabel

20 On that same day, the twenty-fourth of the month, the LORD gave Haggai a second message **21** for Zerubbabel, the governor of Judah: "I am about to shake heaven and earth **22** and overthrow kingdoms and end their power. I will overturn chariots and their drivers; the horses will die, and their riders will kill one another. **23** On that day I will take you, Zerubbabel my servant, and I will appoint you to rule in my name. You are the one I have chosen." The LORD Almighty has spoken.

Cheer up! Things will get better.

This is the main message of the Book of Zechariah. But you have to read through lots of strange visions to see it. The book has two parts, probably written by two different prophets, just as the Book of Isaiah was. The first part calls the people to rebuild the Temple. Through a series of visions, it also promises a future when God will make everything right. Then the second part tells of a future great battle between good and evil in which God will triumph.

The combined message is meant to give hope to God's people, promising them better days ahead. It's a lot like when we try to comfort people who are going through hard times or suffering from an illness. We try to encourage them and offer them hope that things will eventually get better. That is the main message of this next-to-the-last book of the Old Testament.

THE BOOK OF *Zechariah*

Chap. 4:1–14

Headlines

- Vision Foretells Rebuilding of Temple! (1:7–17)
- Vision of a New Jerusalem (2:6–13)
- Woman in a Basket! (5:5–11)
- Future King Rides Donkey (9:9–17)
- God Saves Jerusalem! (12:1–9)

FACTOIDS

Who wrote this book? The prophet Zechariah is thought to have written chapters 1–8 around 520 to 518 BC. But an unknown prophet, (or prophets), is thought to have written chapters 9–14 much later, sometime after 333 BC.

How does it fit into the Bible? Zechariah is one of the prophets who wrote during the same time as Haggai (520 BC).

Jesus connection: Zachariah's prophecies are quoted in the New Testament as proof that Jesus is the promised Messiah. (See Matthew 26:31 and Zechariah 13:7.)

Important theme

- The Temple, Jerusalem, and God's Covenant with the people will be restored.
- The final victory over evil belongs to God.

ZECHARIAH

The LORD Calls His People to Return to Him

1 ¹In the eighth month of the second year that Darius was emperor of Persia, the LORD gave this message to the prophet Zechariah, the son of Berechiah and grandson of Iddo. ²The LORD Almighty told Zechariah to say to the people, "I, the LORD, was very angry with your ancestors, ³but now I say to you, 'Return to me, and I will return to you. ⁴Do not be like your ancestors. Long ago the prophets gave them my message, telling them not to live evil, sinful lives any longer. But they would not listen to me or obey me. ⁵Your ancestors and those prophets are no longer alive. ⁶Through my servants the prophets I gave your ancestors commands and warnings, but they disregarded them and suffered the consequences. Then they repented and acknowledged that I, the LORD Almighty, had punished them as they deserved and as I had determined to do.'"

The Prophet's Vision of the Horses

⁷In the second year that Darius was emperor, on the twenty-fourth day of the eleventh month (the month of Shebat), the LORD gave me a message in a vision at night. ⁸I saw someone riding a red horse. He had stopped among some myrtle trees in a valley, and behind him were other horses—red, dappled, and white. ⁹I asked him, "Sir, what do these horses mean?"

He answered, "I will show you what they mean. ¹⁰The LORD sent them to go and inspect the earth."

¹¹They reported to the angel: "We have been all over the world and have found that the whole world lies helpless and subdued."

¹²Then the angel said, "Almighty LORD, you have been angry with Jerusalem and the cities of Judah for seventy years now. How much longer will it be before you show them mercy?"

¹³The LORD answered the angel with comforting words, ¹⁴and the angel told me to proclaim what the LORD Almighty had said: "I have a deep love and concern for Jerusalem, my holy city, ¹⁵and I am very angry with the nations that enjoy quiet and peace. For while I was holding back my anger against my people, those nations made the sufferings of my people worse. ¹⁶So I have come back to Jerusalem to show mercy to the city. My Temple will be restored, and the city will be rebuilt."

¹⁷The angel also told me to proclaim: "The LORD Almighty says that his cities will be prosperous again and that he will once again help Jerusalem and claim the city as his own."

The Vision of the Horns

¹⁸In another vision I saw four ox horns. ¹⁹I asked the angel that had been speaking to me, "What do these horns mean?"

He answered, "They stand for the world powers that have scattered the people of Judah, Israel, and Jerusalem."

²⁰Then the LORD showed me four workers with hammers. ²¹I asked, "What have they come to do?"

He answered, "They have come to terrify and overthrow the nations that completely crushed the land of Judah and scattered its people."

The Vision of the Measuring Line

2 ¹In another vision I saw a man with a measuring line in his hand. ²"Where are you going?" I asked.

"To measure Jerusalem," he answered, "to see how long and how wide it is."

³Then I saw the angel who had been speaking to me step forward, and another angel came to meet him. ⁴The first one said to the other, "Run and tell that young man with the measuring line that there are going

to be so many people and so much livestock in Jerusalem that it will be too big to have walls. ⁵The LORD has promised that he himself will be a wall of fire around the city to protect it and that he will live there in all his glory."

The Exiles Are Called to Come Home

⁶⁻⁷The LORD said to his people, "I scattered you in all directions. But now, you exiles, escape from Babylonia and return to Jerusalem. ⁸Anyone who strikes you strikes what is most precious to me."

So the LORD Almighty*ᵃ* sent me with this message for the nations that had plundered his people: ⁹"The LORD himself will fight against you, and you will be plundered by the people who were once your servants."

When this happens, everyone will know that the LORD Almighty sent me.

¹⁰The LORD said, "Sing for joy, people of Jerusalem! I am coming to live among you!"

¹¹At that time many nations will come to the LORD and become his people. He will live among you, and you will know that he has sent me to you. ¹²Once again Judah will be the special possession of the LORD in his sacred land, and Jerusalem will be the city he loves most of all.

¹³Be silent, everyone, in the presence of the LORD, for he is coming from his holy dwelling place.

The Prophet's Vision of the High Priest

3 ¹In another vision the LORD showed me the High Priest Joshua standing before the angel of the LORD. And there beside Joshua stood Satan,*ᵇ* ready to bring an accusation against him. ²The angel of the LORD*ᶜ* said to Satan, "May the LORD condemn you, Satan! May the LORD, who loves Jerusalem, condemn you. This man is like a stick snatched from the fire."

³Joshua was standing there, wearing filthy clothes. ⁴The angel said to his heavenly

attendants, "Take away the filthy clothes this man is wearing." Then he said to Joshua, "I have taken away your sin and will give you new clothes to wear."

⁵He commanded the attendants to put*ᵈ* a clean turban on Joshua's head. They did so, and then they put the new clothes on him while the angel of the LORD stood there.

⁶Then the angel told Joshua that ⁷the LORD Almighty had said: "If you obey my laws and perform the duties I have assigned you, then you will continue to be in charge of my Temple and its courts, and I will hear your prayers, just as I hear the prayers of the angels who are in my presence. ⁸Listen then, Joshua, you who are the High Priest; and listen, you fellow priests of his, you that are the sign of a good future: I will reveal my servant, who is called The Branch! ⁹I am placing in front of Joshua a single stone with seven facets. I will engrave an inscription on it, and in a single day I will take away the sin of this land. ¹⁰When that day comes, each of you will invite your neighbor to come and enjoy peace and security, surrounded by your vineyards and fig trees."

A single stone with seven facets (3:9)

The Vision of the Lampstand

4 ¹The angel who had been speaking to me came again and roused me as if I had been sleeping. ²"What do you see?" he asked.

ᵃ 2:8 *Hebrew has two additional words, the meaning of which is unclear.*   *ᵇ 3:1* SATAN: *A supernatural being whose name indicates he was regarded as the opponent of human beings.*   *ᶜ 3:2* *One ancient translation* The angel of the LORD; *Hebrew* The LORD.   *ᵈ 3:5* *Some ancient translations* He commanded the attendants to put; *Hebrew* I said, "Let them put.

3:1 a Ezra 5:2; b Rev 12:10   **3:2** Jude 9   **3:8** Jer 23:5; 33:15; Zech 6:12   **3:10** Mic 4:4

"A lampstand made of gold," I answered. "At the top is a bowl for the oil. On the lampstand are seven lamps, each one with places for seven wicks. ³There are two olive trees beside the lampstand, one on each side of it." ⁴Then I asked the angel, "What do these things stand for, sir?"

⁵"Don't you know?" he asked me.

"No, I don't, sir," I replied.

¹⁰ᵇThe angel said to me, "The seven lamps are the seven eyes of the LORD, which see all over the earth."ᵉ

¹¹Then I asked him, "What do the two olive trees on either side of the lampstand mean? ¹²And what is the meaning of the two olive branches beside the two gold pipes from which the olive oil pours?"

¹³He asked me, "Don't you know?"

"No, I don't, sir," I answered.

¹⁴Then he said, "These are the two men whom God has chosen and anointed to serve him, the Lord of the whole earth."

God's Promise to Zerubbabel

⁶The angel told me to give Zerubbabel this message from the LORD: "You will succeed, not by military might or by your own strength, but by my spirit. ⁷Obstacles as great as mountains will disappear before you. You will rebuild the Temple, and as you put the last stone in place, the people will shout, 'Beautiful, beautiful!'"

⁸Another message came to me from the LORD. ⁹He said, "Zerubbabel has laid the foundation of the Temple, and he will finish the building. When this happens, my people will know that it is I who sent you to them. ¹⁰ᵃThey are disappointed because so little progress is being made. But they will see Zerubbabel continuing to build the Temple, and they will be glad."

The Vision of the Flying Scroll

5 ¹I looked again, and this time I saw a scroll flying through the air. ²The angel asked me what I saw. I answered, "A scroll flying through the air; it is thirty feet long and fifteen feet wide."

³Then he said to me, "On it is written the curse that is to go out over the whole land. On one side of the scroll it says that every thief will be removed from the land; and on the other side it says that everyone who tells lies under oath will also be taken away. ⁴The LORD Almighty says that he will send this curse out, and it will enter the house of every thief and the house of everyone who tells lies under oath. It will remain in their houses and leave them in ruins."

The Vision of the Woman in the Basket

⁵The angel appeared again and said, "Look! Something else is coming!"

⁶"What is it?" I asked.

He replied, "It is a basket, and it stands for the sinᶠ of the whole land."

⁷The basket had a lid made of lead. As I watched, the lid was raised, and there in the basket sat a woman!

There in the basket sat a woman! (5:7)

⁸The angel said, "This represents wickedness." Then he pushed her down into the basket and put the lid back down. ⁹I looked up and saw two women flying toward me with

---

ᵉ **4:10b** *Verses 10b–14 are moved here from the end of the chapter in order to retain the natural sequence of the narrative.*
ᶠ **5:6** *Some ancient translations* sin; *Hebrew* eye.
4:3 Rev 11:4   **4:6** Ezra 5:2   **4:10** Rev 5:6   **4:11** Rev 11:4

Pray It!
Horses, Flying Scrolls, and Women in Baskets!

Spend some time reading through the eight visions that Zechariah has. Everything from colored horses, to lamps, to a woman in a basket! Notice how many of them are ordinary objects. This is a reminder that almost anything can remind you of God. Look around the room you are in right now. There's probably a light or a window. You are probably sitting on a chair. Are there any pictures on the wall? Focus on one thing and make up a prayer based on how that thing reminds you of God. Here's an example, using the floor:

Dear God, you are the floor of my life. You provide me with support even though I don't realize it. You keep me level. Thank you!

How about an electrical outlet?
Dear God, like an outlet, you are a source of energy. Remind me often to plug myself in to your energy. Let the current of your grace flow through me and keep me going. Amen.

What else can you use around you for prayer?

— Zechariah, chapter 5

powerful wings like those of a stork. They picked up the basket and flew off with it.

¹⁰I asked the angel, "Where are they taking it?"

¹¹He answered, "To Babylonia, where they will build a temple for it. When the temple is finished, the basket will be placed there to be worshiped."

The Vision of the Four Chariots

6 ¹I had another vision. This time I saw four chariots coming out from between two bronze mountains. ²The first chariot was pulled by red horses, the second by black horses, ³the third by white horses, and the fourth by dappled horses. ⁴Then I asked the angel, "Sir, what do these chariots mean?"

⁵He answered, "These are the four winds; they have just come from the presence of the Lord of all the earth."

⁶The chariot pulled by the black horses was going north to Babylonia, the white horses were going to the west, and the dappled horses were going to the country in the south. ⁷As the dappled horses came out, they were impatient to go and inspect the earth. The angel said, "Go and inspect the earth!"—and they did. ⁸Then the angel cried out to me, "The horses that went north to Babylonia have quieted the LORD's anger."

The Command to Crown Joshua

⁹The LORD gave me this message. ¹⁰He said, "Take the gifts given by the exiles Heldai, Tobijah, and Jedaiah, and go at once to the home of Josiah son of Zephaniah. All of them have returned from exile in Babylonia. ¹¹Make a crown out of the silver and gold they have given, and put it on the head of the High Priest, Joshua son of Jehozadak. ¹²Tell him that the LORD Almighty says, 'The man who is called The Branch will flourish where he is and rebuild the LORD's Temple. ¹³He is the one who will build it and receive the honor due a king, and he will rule his people. A priest will stand by his throne, and they will work together in peace and harmony.' ¹⁴The crown will be a

memorial in the LORD's Temple in honor of Heldai,ᵍ Tobijah, Jedaiah, and Josiah."ʰ

¹⁵Men who live far away will come and help to rebuild the Temple of the LORD. And when it is rebuilt, you will know that the LORD Almighty sent me to you. This will all happen if you fully obey the commands of the LORD your God.

The LORD Condemns Insincere Fasting

7 ¹In the fourth year that Darius was emperor, on the fourth day of the ninth month (the month of Kislev), the LORD gave me a message.

²The people of Bethel had sent Sharezer and Regemmelech and their men to the Temple of the LORD Almighty to pray for the LORD's blessing ³and to ask the priests and the prophets this question: "Should we continue to mourn because of the destruction of the Temple, by fasting in the fifth month as we have done for so many years now?"

⁴This is the message of the LORD that came to me. ⁵He said, "Tell the people of the land and the priests that when they fasted and mourned in the fifth and seventh months during these seventy years, it was not in honor of me. ⁶And when they ate and drank, it was for their own satisfaction."

⁷This is what the LORD said through the earlier prophets at the time when Jerusalem was prosperous and filled with people and when there were many people living not only in the towns around the city but also in the southern region and in the western foothills.

Disobedience, the Cause of Exile

⁸The LORD gave this message to Zechariah: ⁹"Long ago I gave these commands to my people: 'You must see that justice is done, and must show kindness and mercy to one another. ¹⁰Do not oppress widows, orphans, foreigners who live among you, or anyone else in need. And do not plan ways of harming one another.'

¹¹"But my people stubbornly refused to listen. They closed their minds ¹²and made their hearts as hard as rock. Because they would not listen to the teaching which I sent through the prophets who lived long ago, I became very angry. ¹³Because they did not listen when I spoke, I did not answer when they prayed. ¹⁴Like a storm I swept them away to live in foreign countries. This good land was left a desolate place, with no one living in it."

The LORD Promises to Restore Jerusalem

8 ¹The LORD Almighty gave this message to Zechariah: ²"I have longed to help Jerusalem because of my deep love for her people, a love which has made me angry with her enemies. ³I will return to Jerusalem, my holy city, and live there. It will be known as the faithful city, and the hill of the LORD Almightyⁱ will be called the sacred hill. ⁴Once again old men and women, so old that they use canes when they walk, will be sitting in the city squares. ⁵And the streets will again be full of boys and girls playing.

⁶"This may seem impossible to those of the nation who are now left, but it's not impossible for me. ⁷I will rescue my people from the lands where they have been taken, ⁸and will bring them back from east and west to live in Jerusalem. They will be my people, and I will be their God, ruling over them faithfully and justly.

⁹"Have courage! You are now hearing the same words the prophets spoke at the time the foundation was being laid for rebuilding my Temple. ¹⁰Before that time no one could afford to hire either men or animals, and no one was safe from enemies. I turned people against one another. ¹¹But now I am treating the survivors of this nation differently. ¹²They will plant their crops in peace. Their vines will bear grapes, the earth will produce crops, and there will be plenty of rain. I will give all these blessings to the people of my nation who survive. ¹³People of Judah and Israel! In the past foreigners have cursed one another by saying, 'May the same disasters

ᵍ **6:14** *One ancient translation* Heldai; *Hebrew* Helem.   ʰ **6:14** *One ancient translation* Josiah; *Hebrew* Hen.
ⁱ **8:3** HILL OF THE LORD ALMIGHTY: *Mount Zion (see Zion in Word List).*

fall on you that fell on Judah and Israel!' But I will save you, and then those foreigners will say to one another, 'May you receive the same blessings that came to Judah and Israel!' So have courage and don't be afraid."

May you receive the same blessings that came to Judah and Israel! (8:13)

14 The LORD Almighty says, "When your ancestors made me angry, I planned disaster for them and did not change my mind, but carried out my plans. 15 But now I am planning to bless the people of Jerusalem and Judah. So don't be afraid. 16 These are the things you should do: Speak the truth to one another. In the courts give real justice—the kind that brings peace. 17 Do not plan ways of harming one another. Do not give false testimony under oath. I hate lying, injustice, and violence."

18 The LORD Almighty gave this message to Zechariah: 19 "The fasts held in the fourth, fifth, seventh, and tenth months will become festivals of joy and gladness for the people of Judah. You must love truth and peace."

20 The LORD Almighty says, "The time is coming when people from many[j] cities will come to Jerusalem. 21 Those from one city will say to those from another, 'We are going to worship the LORD Almighty and pray for his blessing. Come with us!' 22 Many[j] peoples and powerful nations will come to Jerusalem to worship the LORD Almighty and to pray for his blessing. 23 In those days ten foreigners will come to one Jew and say, 'We want to share in your destiny, because we have heard that God is with you.' "

Judgment on Neighboring Nations

9 1 This is the LORD's message:
He has decreed punishment for the land of Hadrach and for the city of Damascus. Not only the tribes of Israel but also the capital of Syria belong to the LORD. 2 Hamath, which borders on Hadrach, also belongs to him, and so do the cities of Tyre and Sidon, with all their skill. 3 Tyre has built fortifications for herself and has piled up so much silver and gold that it is as common as dirt! 4 But the Lord will take away everything she has. He will throw her wealth into the sea, and the city will be burned to the ground.

5 The city of Ashkelon will see this and be afraid. The city of Gaza will see it and suffer great pain. So will Ekron, and her hopes will be shattered. Gaza will lose her king, and Ashkelon will be left deserted. 6 People of mixed race will live in Ashdod. The LORD says, "I will humble all these proud Philistines. 7 They will no longer eat meat with blood in it, or other forbidden food. All the survivors will become part of my people and be like a clan in the tribe of Judah. Ekron will become part of my people, as the Jebusites[k] did. 8 I will guard my land and keep armies from passing through it. I will not allow tyrants to oppress my people any more. I have seen how my people have suffered."

The Future King

9 Rejoice, rejoice, people of Zion!
Shout for joy, you people of Jerusalem!
Look, your king is coming to you!

Look, your king is coming to you! (9:9)

---

[j] 8:20, 22 many; *or* great.   [k] 9:7 JEBUSITES: *The original inhabitants of Jerusalem, who became David's subjects after he captured the city.*
8:16 Eph 4:25   9:1 Isa 17:1–3; Jer 49:23–27; Am 1:3–5   9:1–4 Isa 23:1–18; Ezek 26:1—28:26; Joel 3:4–8; Am 1:9, 10; Mt 11:21, 22; Lk 10:13, 14   9:5–7 Isa 14:29–31; Jer 47:1–7; Ezek 25:15–17; Joel 3:4–8; Am 1:6–8; Zeph 2:4–7   9:9 Mt 21:5; Jn 12:15

He comes triumphant and victorious,
    but humble and riding on a donkey—
    on a colt, the foal of a donkey.
10 The LORD says,
    "I will remove the war chariots from Israel
    and take the horses from Jerusalem;
    the bows used in battle will be destroyed.
Your king will make peace among the
    nations;
    he will rule from sea to sea,
    from the Euphrates River to the ends
    of the earth."

The Restoration of God's People

11 The LORD says,
    "Because of my covenant with you
    that was sealed by the blood of
    sacrifices,
I will set your people free—
    free from the waterless pit of exile.
12 Return, you exiles who now have hope;
    return to your place of safety.
Now I tell you that I will repay you twice
    over
    with blessing for all you have suffered.
13 I will use Judah like a soldier's bow
    and Israel like the arrows.
I will use the men of Zion like a sword,
    to fight the men of Greece."

14 The LORD will appear above his people;
    he will shoot his arrows like lightning.
The Sovereign LORD will sound the
    trumpet;
    he will march in the storms from the
    south.
15 The LORD Almighty will protect his
    people,
    and they will destroy their enemies.
They will shout in battle like drunk men
    and will shed the blood of their
    enemies;
    it will flow like the blood of a sacrifice
    poured on the altar from a bowl.[l]

16 When that day comes, the LORD will save
    his people,
    as a shepherd saves his flock from
    danger.

They will shine in his land
    like the jewels of a crown.
17 How good and beautiful the land will be!
    The young people will grow strong on
    its grain and wine.

The LORD Promises Deliverance

10 ¹Ask the LORD for rain in the spring of the year. It is the LORD who sends rain clouds and showers, making the fields green for everyone. ²People consult idols and fortunetellers, but the answers they get are lies and nonsense. Some interpret dreams, but only mislead you; the comfort they give is useless. So the people wander about like lost sheep. They are in trouble because they have no leader.

³ The LORD says, "I am angry with those foreigners who rule my people, and I am going to punish them. The people of Judah are mine, and I, the LORD Almighty, will take care of them. They will be my powerful warhorses. ⁴From among them will come rulers, leaders, and commanders to govern my people.[m] ⁵The people of Judah will be victorious like soldiers who trample their enemies in the mud of the streets. They will fight because the LORD is with them, and they will defeat even the enemy cavalry.

6 "I will make the people of Judah strong;
    I will rescue the people of Israel.
I will have compassion on them
    and bring them all back home.
They will be as though I had never
    rejected them.
    I am the LORD their God; I will answer
    their prayers.
7 The people of Israel will be strong like
    soldiers,
    happy like those who have been
    drinking wine.
Their descendants will remember this
    victory
    and be glad because of what the LORD
    has done.

8 "I will call my people
    and gather them together.

---

l **9:15** *Verse 15 in Hebrew is unclear.*   *m* **10:4** *From among . . . people; or* All oppressors—rulers, leaders, and commanders—will depart together from Judah.
9:10 Ps 72:8   **9:11** Ex 24:8   **10:2** Mt 9:36; Mk 6:34

I will rescue them
　　and make them as numerous as they
　　　　used to be.
9 Though I have scattered them among the
　　nations,
　　yet in far-off places they will remember
　　me.
They and their children will survive
　　and return home together.
10 From Egypt and Assyria I will bring them
　　home
　　and settle them in their own country.
I will settle them in Gilead and Lebanon
　　also;
　　the whole land will be filled with
　　people.
11 When they pass through their sea of
　　trouble,
　　I, the LORD, will strike the waves,
　　and the depths of the Nile will go
　　dry.
Proud Assyria will be humbled,
　　and mighty Egypt will lose her power.
12 I will make my people strong;
　　they will worship and obey me."
The LORD has spoken.

The Fall of the Tyrants

11 ¹Open your doors, Lebanon,
　　　so that fire can burn down your
　　　　cedar trees!ⁿ
2 Weep and wail, cypress trees—
　　the cedars have fallen;
　　those glorious trees have been
　　destroyed!
Weep and wail, oaks of Bashan—
　　the dense forest has been cut down!
3 The rulers cry out in grief;
　　their glory is gone!
Listen to the roaring of the lions;
　　their forest home along the Jordan is
　　destroyed!

The Two Shepherds

4 The LORD my God said to me, "Act the
part of the shepherdᵒ of a flock of sheep that
are going to be butchered. 5 Their owners
kill them and go unpunished. They sell the
meat and say, 'Praise the LORD! We are rich!'
Even their own shepherds have no pity on
them."

(6 The LORD said, "I will no longer pity
anyone on earth. I myself will put all the
people in the power of their rulers. These
rulers will devastate the earth, and I will not
save it from their power.")

7 Those who bought and sold the sheep
hired me, and I became the shepherd of the
sheep that were going to be butchered. I
took two sticks: one I called "Favor" and the
other "Unity." And I took care of the flock.
8 I lost patience with three other shepherds,
who hated me, and I got rid of them all in a
single month. 9 Then I said to the flock, "I
will not be your shepherd any longer. Let
those die who are to die. Let those be
destroyed who are to be destroyed. Those
who are left will destroy one another."
10 Then I took the stick called "Favor" and
broke it, to cancel the covenant which the
LORD had made with all the nations. 11 So
the covenant was canceled on that day. Those
who bought and sold the sheep were watching me, and they knew that the LORD was
speaking through what I did. 12 I said to
them, "If you are willing, give me my wages.
But if not, keep them." So they paid me
thirty pieces of silver as my wages.

13 The LORD said to me, "Put them in the
Temple treasury."ᵖ So I took the thirty
pieces of silver—the magnificent sum they
thought I was worth—and put them in the
Temple treasury. 14 Then I broke the second
stick, the one called "Unity," and the unity of
Judah and Israel was shattered.

15 Then the LORD said to me, "Once again
act the part of a shepherd, this time a worthless one. 16 I have put a shepherd in charge of
my flock, but he does not help the sheep
that are threatened by destruction; nor does
he look for the lost, or heal those that are
hurt, or feed the healthy. Instead, he eats the
meat of the fattest sheep and tears off their
hoofs. 17 That worthless shepherd is doomed!

ⁿ **11:1** CEDAR TREES: *Trees are used here as symbols of powerful nations or their kings.* ᵒ **11:4** SHEPHERD: *Shepherd is used here as a symbol of a king or leader, and sheep as symbols of his people or followers.* ᵖ **11:13** *Some ancient translations* Put them in the Temple treasury; *Hebrew* Give them to the potter.
10:9, 10 Bar 2:20–32　　**11:12, 13** Mt 27:9, 10　　**11:12** Mt 26:15

He has abandoned his flock. (11:17)

He has abandoned his flock. War will totally destroy his power. His arm will wither, and his right eye will go blind."

The Future Deliverance of Jerusalem

12 [1] This is a message about Israel from the LORD, the LORD who spread out the skies, created the earth, and gave life to man. He says, [2] "I will make Jerusalem like a cup of wine; the nations around her will drink and stagger like drunks. And when they besiege Jerusalem, the cities of the rest of Judah will also be besieged. [3] But when that time comes, I will make Jerusalem like a heavy stone—any nation that tries to lift it will be hurt. All the nations of the world will join forces to attack her. [4] At that time I will terrify all their horses and make all their riders go crazy. I will watch over the people of Judah, but I will make the horses of their enemies blind. [5] Then the clans of Judah will say to themselves, 'The LORD God Almighty gives strength to his people who live in Jerusalem.'

[6] "At that time I will make the clans of Judah like a fire in a forest or in a field of ripe grain—they will destroy all the surrounding nations. The people of Jerusalem will remain safe in the city.

[7] "I, the LORD, will give victory to the armies of Judah first, so that the honor which the descendants of David and the people of Jerusalem will receive will be no greater than that of the rest of Judah. [8] At that time the LORD will protect those who live in Jerusalem, and even the weakest among them will become as strong as David was. The descendants of David will lead them like the angel of the LORD, like God

himself. [9] At that time I will destroy every nation that tries to attack Jerusalem.

[10] "I will fill the descendants of David and the other people of Jerusalem with the spirit of mercy and the spirit of prayer. They will look at the one whom they stabbed to death, and they will mourn for him like those who mourn for an only child. They will mourn bitterly, like those who have lost their first-born son. [11] At that time the mourning in Jerusalem will be as great as the mourning for Hadad Rimmon[q] in the plain of Megiddo. [12-14] Each family in the land will mourn by itself: the family descended from David, the family descended from Nathan, the family descended from Levi, the family descended from Shimei, and all the other families. Each family will mourn by itself, and the men of each family will mourn separately from the women.

13 [1] "When that time comes," says the LORD Almighty, "a fountain will be opened to purify the descendants of David and the people of Jerusalem from their sin and idolatry. [2] At that time I will remove the names of the idols from the land, and no one will remember them any more. I will get rid of anyone who claims to be a prophet and will take away the desire to worship idols. [3] Then if anyone still insists on prophesying, his own father and mother will tell him that he must be put to death, because he claimed to speak the LORD's word, but spoke lies instead. When he prophesies, his own father and mother will stab him to death. [4] When that time comes, no prophet will be proud of his visions or act like a prophet or wear a prophet's coarse garment in order to deceive people. [5] Instead, he will say, 'I am not a prophet. I am a farmer—I have farmed the land all my life.' [6] Then if someone asks him, 'What are those wounds on your chest?' he will answer, 'I got them at a friend's house.' "

The Command to Kill God's Shepherd

[7] The LORD Almighty says, "Wake up, sword, and attack the shepherd[r] who works for me! Kill him, and the sheep will be scat-

---

q **12:11** HADAD RIMMON: *Probably a name for Baal, the god of vegetation in Canaan and Syria. When the vegetation died each year, the worshipers thought that the god had died, and they mourned his death.*　*r* **13:7** SHEPHERD: *See 11:4.*
12:10 Jn 19:37; Rev 1:7　**12:10–14** Mt 24:20; Rev 1:7　**13:7** Mt 26:31; Mk 14:27

tered. I will attack my people 8and throughout the land two-thirds of the people will die. 9And I will test the third that survives and will purify them as silver is purified by fire. I will test them as gold is tested. Then they will pray to me, and I will answer them. I will tell them that they are my people, and they will confess that I am their God."

Jerusalem and the Nations

14 1The day when the LORD will sit in judgment is near. Then Jerusalem will be looted, and the loot will be divided up before your eyes. 2The LORD will bring all the nations together to make war on Jerusalem. The city will be taken, the houses looted, and the women raped. Half of the people will go into exile, but the rest of them will not be taken away from the city. 3Then the LORD will go out and fight against those nations, as he has fought in times past. 4At that time he will stand on the Mount of Olives, to the east of Jerusalem. Then the Mount of Olives will be split in two from east to west by a large valley. Half of the mountain will move northward, and half of it southward. 5You will escape through this valley that divides the mountain in two.ˢ You will flee as your ancestors did when the earthquake struck in the time of King Uzziah of Judah. The LORD my God will come, bringing all the angels with him.

6When that time comes, there will no longer be cold or frost,ᵗ 7nor any darkness. There will always be daylight, even at nighttime. When this will happen is known only to the LORD.

8When that day comes, fresh water will flow from Jerusalem, half of it to the Dead Sea and the other half to the Mediterranean. It will flow all year long, in the dry season as well as the wet. 9Then the LORD will be king over all the earth; everyone will worship him as God and know him by the same name.

10The whole region, from Geba in the north to Rimmon in the south, will be made level. Jerusalem will tower above the land around it; the city will reach from the Benjamin Gate to the Corner Gate, where there had been an earlier gate, and from the Tower of Hananel to the royal wine presses. 11The people will live there in safety, no longer threatened by destruction.

12The LORD will bring a terrible disease on all the nations that make war on Jerusalem. Their flesh will rot away while they are still alive; their eyes and their tongues will rot away.

13At that time the LORD will make them so confused and afraid that everyone will seize the man next to him and attack him. 14The men of Judah will fight to defend Jerusalem. They will take as loot the wealth of all the nations—gold, silver, and clothing in great abundance.

15A terrible disease will also fall on the horses, the mules, the camels, and the donkeys—on all the animals in the camps of the enemy.

16Then all of the survivors from the nations that have attacked Jerusalem will go there each year to worship the LORD Almighty as king and to celebrate the Festival of Shelters. 17If any nation refuses to go and worship the LORD Almighty as king, then rain will not fall on their land. 18If the Egyptians refuse to celebrate the Festival of Shelters, then they will be struck by the same disease that the LORD will send on every nation that refuses to go. 19This will be the punishment that will fall on Egypt and on all the other nations if they do not celebrate the Festival of Shelters.

20At that time even the harness bells of the horses will be inscribed with the words "Dedicated to the LORD." The cooking pots in the Temple will be as sacred as the bowls before the altar. 21Every cooking pot in Jerusalem and in all Judah will be set apart for use in the worship of the LORD Almighty. The people who offer sacrifices will use them for boiling the meat of the sacrifices. When that time comes, there will no longer be any merchant in the Temple of the LORD Almighty.

ˢ 14:5 *Probable text* You will escape . . . in two; *Hebrew unclear.*   ᵗ 14:6 *Probable text* cold or frost; *Hebrew unclear.*
14:8 Ezek 47:1; Jn 7:38; Rev 22:1   14:11 Rev 22:3   14:16 Lev 23:39–43

THE BOOK OF

Malachi

We expect that when promises are made to us, they will be kept. A broken promise leads to mistrust and hurt.

Malachi calls for faithfulness to promises made to God. This book addresses two areas where men of power broke their promises and were unfaithful—priesthood and marriage. Malachi challenged Israel's priests, who were being dishonest and corrupt, to be faithful in providing good leadership and honoring God. The prophet also challenged husbands, who were divorcing and leaving their Jewish wives for foreign (non-Jewish) wives, to remain faithful to their Jewish wives. Malachi's final prophecy serves as a bridge between the promises God made in the Old Testament and Jesus' fulfillment of those promises in the New Testament.

Chap. 3:1–3

Head lines

- God Sends Warning to Priests! (2:1–9)
- God Hates Broken Promises (2:10–16)
- Messenger Coming to Prepare the People (3:1–5)

FACTOIDS

Who wrote this book? We do not know for sure. Because Malachi means "my messenger," we are not sure if it is the name of an actual prophet. It may be a title describing the book.

Who is this book addressed to? Men of power—priests who were not faithful to the Law and husbands who were not faithful to their wives.

Jesus connection: The messenger who prepares the way for the Lord's coming (Malachi 3:1) is fulfilled in the person of John the Baptist, who prepares the way for Jesus.

Important themes
- God's people are called to keep their promises and to be faithful to God. God will reward those who are just and faithful—all wrongs will be made right.
- The Day of the Lord is coming, and it will be terrible for those who have abused power.

MALACHI

1 ¹This is the message that the LORD gave Malachi to tell the people of Israel.

The LORD's Love for Israel

²The LORD says to his people, "I have always loved you."

But they reply, "How have you shown your love for us?"

The LORD answers, "Esau and Jacob were brothers, but I have loved Jacob and his descendants, ³and have hated Esau and his descendants. I have devastated Esau's hill country and abandoned the land to jackals."

⁴If Esau's descendants, the Edomites, say, "Our towns have been destroyed, but we will rebuild them," then the LORD will reply, "Let them rebuild—I will tear them down again. People will call them 'The evil country' and 'The nation with whom the LORD is angry forever.' "

⁵The people of Israel are going to see this with their own eyes, and they will say, "The LORD is mighty even outside the land of Israel!"

The LORD Reprimands the Priests

⁶The LORD Almighty says to the priests, "Children honor their parents, and servants honor their masters. I am your father—why don't you honor me? I am your master—why don't you respect me? You despise me, and yet you ask, 'How have we despised you?' ⁷This is how—by offering worthless food on my altar. Then you ask, 'How have we failed to respect you?' I will tell you—by showing contempt for my altar. ⁸When you bring a blind or sick or lame animal to sacrifice to me, do you think there's nothing wrong with that? Try giving an animal like that to the governor! Would he be pleased with you or grant you any favors?"

⁹Now, you priests, try asking God to be good to us. He will not answer your prayer, and it will be your fault. ¹⁰The LORD Almighty says, "I wish one of you would close the Temple doors so as to prevent you from lighting useless fires on my altar. I am not pleased with you; I will not accept the offerings you bring me. ¹¹People from one end of the world to the other honor me. Everywhere they burn incense to me and offer acceptable sacrifices. All of them honor me! ¹²But you dishonor me when you say that my altar is worthless and when you offer on it food that you despise. ¹³You say, 'How tired we are of all this!' and you turn up your nose at me. As your offering to me you bring a stolen animal or one that is lame or sick. Do you think I will accept that from you? ¹⁴A curse on the cheater who sacrifices a worthless animal to me, when he has in his flock a good animal that he promised to give me! For I am a great king, and people of all nations fear me."

One that is lame or sick (1:13)

2 ¹The LORD Almighty says to the priests, "This command is for you: ²You must honor me by what you do. If you will not listen to what I say, then I will bring a curse on you. I will put a curse on the things you receive for your support. In fact, I have already put a curse on them, because you do not take my command seriously. ³I will punish your children and rub your faces in the dung of the animals you sacrifice—and you

1:2, 3 Rom 9:13   1:2–5 Isa 34:5–17; 63:1–6; Jer 49:7–22; Ezek 25:12–14; 35:1–15; Am 1:11, 12; Ob 1–14
1:8 Deut 15:21

will be taken out to the dung heap. ⁴Then you will know that I have given you this command, so that my covenant with the priests, the descendants of Levi, will not be broken.

⁵"In my covenant I promised them life and well-being, and this is what I gave them, so that they might respect me. In those days they did respect and fear me. ⁶They taught what was right, not what was wrong. They lived in harmony with me; they not only did what was right themselves, but they also helped many others to stop doing evil. ⁷It is the duty of priests to teach the true knowledge of God. People should go to them to learn my will, because they are the messengers of the LORD Almighty.

⁸"But now you priests have turned away from the right path. Your teaching has led many to do wrong. You have broken the covenant I made with you. ⁹So I, in turn, will make the people of Israel despise you because you do not obey my will, and when you teach my people, you do not treat everyone alike."

The People's Unfaithfulness to God

¹⁰Don't we all have the same father? Didn't the same God create us all? Then why do we break our promises to one another, and why do we despise the covenant that God made with our ancestors? ¹¹The people of Judah have broken their promise to God and done a horrible thing in Jerusalem and all over the country. They have defiled the Temple which the LORD loves. Men have married women who worship foreign gods. ¹²May the LORD remove from the community of Israel those who did this, and never again let them participate in the offerings our nation brings to the LORD Almighty.ᵃ

¹³This is another thing you do. You drown the LORD's altar with tears, weeping and wailing because he no longer accepts the offerings you bring him. ¹⁴You ask why he no longer accepts them. It is because he knows you have broken your promise to the wife you married when you were young. She was your partner, and you have broken your promise to her, although you promised before God that you would be faithful to her. ¹⁵Didn't God make you one body and spirit with her?ᵇ What was his purpose in this? It was that you should have children who are truly God's people. So make sure that none of you breaks his promise to his wife. ¹⁶"I hate divorce," says the LORD God of Israel. "I hate it when one of you does such a cruel thing to his wife. Make sure that you do not break your promise to be faithful to your wife."

The Day of Judgment Is Near

¹⁷You have tired the LORD out with your talk. But you ask, "How have we tired him?" By saying, "The LORD Almighty thinks all evildoers are good; in fact he likes them." Or by asking, "Where is the God who is supposed to be just?"

3 ¹The LORD Almighty answers, "I will send my messenger to prepare the way for me. Then the Lord you are looking for will suddenly come to his Temple. The messenger you long to see will come and proclaim my covenant."

²But who will be able to endure the day when he comes? Who will be able to survive when he appears? He will be like strong soap, like a fire that refines metal. ³He will come to judge like one who refines and purifies silver. As a metalworker refines silver and gold, so the LORD's messenger will purify the priests, so that they will bring to the LORD the right kind of offerings. ⁴Then the offerings which the people of Judah and Jerusalem bring to the LORD will be pleasing to him, as they used to be in the past.

⁵The LORD Almighty says, "I will appear among you to judge, and I will testify at once against those who practice magic, against adulterers, against those who give false testimony, those who cheat employees out of their wages, and those who take

---

ᵃ **2:12** *One ancient translation* May . . . Almighty; *Hebrew unclear.*   ᵇ **2:15** *Probable text* Didn't God . . . her; *Hebrew unclear.*
2:4 Num 3:11–13   **2:5** Num 25:12   **3:1** Mt 11:10; Mk 1:2; Lk 1:76; 7:27   **3:2** Joel 2:11; Rev 6:17

advantage of widows, orphans, and foreigners—against all who do not respect me.

The Payment of Tithes

6 "I am the LORD, and I do not change. And so you, the descendants of Jacob, are not yet completely lost. 7 You, like your ancestors

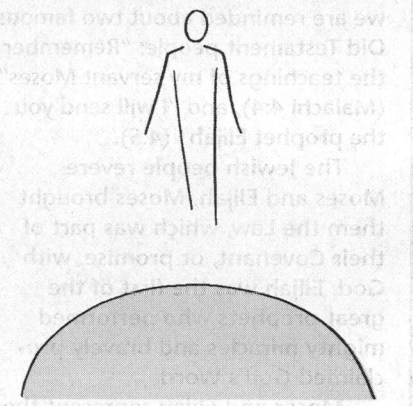

I am the LORD, and I do not change. (3:6)

before you, have turned away from my laws and have not kept them. Turn back to me, and I will turn to you. But you ask, 'What must we do to turn back to you?' 8 I ask you, is it right for a person to cheat God? Of course not, yet you are cheating me. 'How?' you ask. In the matter of tithes and offerings. 9 A curse is on all of you because the whole nation is cheating me. 10 Bring the full amount of your tithes to the Temple, so that there will be plenty of food there. Put me to the test and you will see that I will open the windows of heaven and pour out on you in abundance all kinds of good things. 11 I will not let insects destroy your crops, and your grapevines will be loaded with grapes. 12 Then the people of all nations will call you happy, because your land will be a good place to live.

God's Promise of Mercy

13 "You have said terrible things about me," says the LORD. "But you ask, 'What have we said about you?' 14 You have said, 'It's useless to serve God. What's the use of doing

what he says or of trying to show the LORD Almighty that we are sorry for what we have done? 15 As we see it, proud people are the ones who are happy. Evil people not only prosper, but they test God's patience with their evil deeds and get away with it.'"

16 Then the people who feared the LORD spoke to one another, and the LORD listened and heard what they said. In his presence, there was written down in a book a record of those who feared the LORD and respected him. 17 "They will be my people," says the LORD Almighty. "On the day when I act, they will be my very own. I will be merciful to them as parents are merciful to the children who serve them. 18 Once again my people will see the difference between what happens to the righteous and to the wicked, to the person who serves me and the one who does not."

The Day of the LORD Is Coming

4 ¹ The LORD Almighty says, "The day is coming when all proud and evil people will burn like straw. On that day they will burn up, and there will be nothing left of them. 2 But for you who obey me, my saving power will rise on you like the sun and bring healing like the sun's rays. You will be as free and happy as calves let out of a stall.

My saving power will rise on you like the sun. (4:2)

3:6 Sir 48:10   **3:10** Lev 27:30; Num 18:21–24; Deut 12:6; 14:22–29; Neh 13:12

Malachi

³On the day when I act, you will overcome the wicked, and they will be like dust under your feet.

⁴"Remember the teachings of my servant Moses, the laws and commands which I gave him at Mount Sinai for all the people of Israel to obey.

⁵"But before the great and terrible day of the LORD comes, I will send you the prophet Elijah. ⁶He will bring fathers and children together again; otherwise I would have to come and destroy your country."

4:5 Mt 11:14; 17:10–13; Mk 9:11–13; Lk 1:17; Jn 1:21

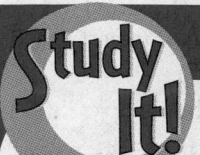

Moses, Elijah, and Jesus

At the end of the Book of Malachi, we are reminded about two famous Old Testament people: "Remember the teachings of my servant Moses" (Malachi 4:4), and "I will send you the prophet Elijah" (4:5).

The Jewish people revere Moses and Elijah. Moses brought them the Law, which was part of their Covenant, or promise, with God. Elijah was the first of the great prophets who performed mighty miracles and bravely proclaimed God's Word.

Moses and Elijah represent the Law and the prophets to the Jewish people. No wonder these two men appeared at Jesus' Transfiguration, when Jesus' glory as the Son of God was revealed (Matthew 17:1–9, Mark 9:2–13, Luke 9:28–36). No wonder the three Apostles who saw the sight were amazed. This was one of the most dazzling signs that Jesus was indeed the Messiah, the one they had been waiting for.

Why do you think the last chapter of the last book of the Old Testament has this connection with the life of Jesus to be revealed in the New Testament?

— Malachi, chapter 4

NEW TESTAMENT

The Bible is divided into two major sections, the Old Testament and the New Testament. The New Testament contains twenty-seven books. These books contain several kinds of writings. You will find Gospels, religious history, letters to individuals, letters to communities, homilies, and visions. All these books are in some way about God's biggest breakthrough in history: the coming of Jesus Christ. The New Testament stories tell how Jesus' mission starts with God's Chosen People, who today we call the Jews. They also tell how Jesus' first disciples quickly expanded the mission to include non-Jews, who were called Gentiles.

Testament is another word for *covenant,* and a covenant is a holy promise made between God and human beings. The Old Testament is about the original Covenant that God made with his Chosen People. The New Testament writings show how the promises of the Covenant in the Old Testament were fulfilled by Jesus Christ. Through Jesus, God extended the Covenant to the whole human race. We call this the New Covenant, the promise that every person—Jew or Gentile—can have eternal life with God. This New Testament tells how this was made possible by Jesus' life, death, and Resurrection.

Breakthrough! The Bible for Young Catholics divides the New Testament into two sections. The table of contents shows the books that are in each section. Here's some information on each section:

The Gospels and the Acts of the Apostles. *Gospel* literally means "good news." We call Matthew, Mark, Luke, and John Gospels because they tell the Good News of Jesus Christ. These four books each have their unique picture of Jesus Christ. It is believed that Mark was written first. The writers of Matthew and Luke probably used Mark as a starting point in creating their Gospels. That is why these three Gospels have some very similar stories.

The Gospel of John is quite different from the other three. There are fewer miracles and fewer parables, and John more clearly presents Jesus as God's Son. Having four Gospels gives us a more complete understanding of Jesus than having just one.

The Acts of the Apostles picks up where the Gospels leave off. It was written by the same person who wrote the Gospel of Luke. Acts tells the exciting story of the first Christians. By traveling and preaching, they spread the Good News of Jesus Christ throughout the known world.

The Letters and Revelation. Back at the time of Jesus, there was no telephone, television, radio, or Internet. So when the early leaders of the Church wanted to communicate, they did so by writing letters. These letters were written to groups and to individuals. They helped the first Christians—and they help us—understand what it means to be a follower of Jesus.

The majority of the letters were written by Saint Paul or by people writing in his name. It was not uncommon at that time to honor a great person by writing letters or books in his or her name. So some letters that say they were written by Saint Paul or Saint Peter may have been written by other early Christians.

The Revelation to John is not a letter but a collection of prophecies and visions. It is about the struggle between the good and evil forces of creation. Revelation promises that even though believers will suffer and be persecuted, God will make everything right in the end.

To fully understand God's plan for the human race, we need both the Old and the New Testament. The New Testament reveals the great love God has for us by sending his Son into the world. Through the Gospels and letters, God shows us that we can be saved from fear, anxiety, sin, and even death by putting our faith in Jesus Christ. Then, as disciples empowered by the Holy Spirit, we can bring God's love to other people.

If the Gospel of Matthew were a popular movie, it might be titled *God Saves*. Then the Old Testament books of the Bible might be called *God Saves: The Beginning*. In the Old Testament, we hear the story of a God who loves his people and wants to save them from sin and the effects of sin. In the Gospel of Matthew—really in all the books of the New Testament—we hear how God's plans are fulfilled in the life, death, and Resurrection of Jesus Christ.

The Gospel of Matthew shows how Jesus takes the ancient teachings and makes them new. He challenges his followers, including us today, to love as completely as he does. And keep watching! Matthew gives a preview of *God Saves: The Conclusion*, when Jesus will conquer evil and death once and for all at his Second Coming.

Chap. 28:1–3

Headlines

- Future King Born In a Stable! (1:1—2:23)
- Jesus' Extreme Message: *Love Your Enemies* (5:43–48)
- Dead Girl Brought Back to Life! (9:23–26)
- Jesus Responds to Criticisms (12:1–42)
- Jesus Seen Talking to Dead Prophets (17:1–13)
- Women Claim to See Resurrected Jesus! (28:1–9)
- Jesus' Followers Sent to the Whole World (28:16–20)

FACTOIDS

Who wrote this book? An old tradition says it was the Apostle Matthew but no one knows for sure. We do know that the author was a Jew who had become a Christian.

When was it written? Probably between AD 75 and 90, or about fifty years after Jesus' Resurrection.

Whom was it written for? It was originally written for Jews who had become followers of Christ. These Jewish Christians were becoming outcasts in the Jewish community.

Why was it written? Matthew was written to reassure the early Jewish Christians that Jesus was the Messiah promised in the Hebrew Scriptures.

Important themes

- Jesus proclaims the Kingdom of heaven.
- Jesus is in conflict with religious leaders who are not open to his message.
- Jesus has miraculous power over sickness, storms, evil, and even death.

MATTHEW

The Ancestors of Jesus Christ
(Luke 3:23–38)

1 **1**This is the list of the ancestors of Jesus Christ, a descendant of David, who was a descendant of Abraham.

2-6a From Abraham to King David, the following ancestors are listed: Abraham, Isaac, Jacob, Judah and his brothers; then Perez and Zerah (their mother was Tamar), Hezron, Ram, Amminadab, Nahshon, Salmon, Boaz (his mother was Rahab), Obed (his mother was Ruth), Jesse, and King David.

6b-11 From David to the time when the people of Israel were taken into exile in Babylon, the following ancestors are listed: David, Solomon (his mother was the woman who had been Uriah's wife), Rehoboam, Abijah, Asa, Jehoshaphat, Jehoram, Uzziah, Jotham, Ahaz, Hezekiah, Manasseh, Amon, Josiah, and Jehoiachin and his brothers.

12-16 From the time after the exile in Babylon to the birth of Jesus, the following ancestors are listed: Jehoiachin, Shealtiel, Zerubbabel, Abiud, Eliakim, Azor, Zadok, Achim, Eliud, Eleazar, Matthan, Jacob, and Joseph, who married Mary, the mother of Jesus, who was called the Messiah.

17So then, there were fourteen generations from Abraham to David, and fourteen from David to the exile in Babylon, and fourteen from then to the birth of the Messiah.

The Birth of Jesus Christ
(Luke 2:1–7)

18This was how the birth of Jesus Christ took place. His mother Mary was engaged to Joseph, but before they were married, she found out that she was going to have a baby by the Holy Spirit. **19**Joseph was a man who always did what was right, but he did not want to disgrace Mary publicly; so he made plans to break the engagement privately. **20**While he was thinking about this, an angel

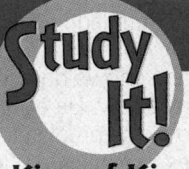

King of Kings

The Gospel of Matthew begins with a genealogy, or listing of Jesus' ancestors. The genealogy shows that God is doing what he promised to do. Look at some of the names in the list. Many of them are names that you will recognize from the Old Testament. God promised Abraham that he would be the father of a great nation (Genesis 12:2). God promised David that the Messiah, the one who would save the people, would be a descendant of David's (2 Samuel 7:12–16).

— Matthew 1:1–17

of the Lord appeared to him in a dream and said, "Joseph, descendant of David, do not be afraid to take Mary to be your wife. For it is by the Holy Spirit that she has conceived. **21**She will have a son, and you will name him Jesus—because he will save his people from their sins."

22Now all this happened in order to make come true what the Lord had said through the prophet, **23**"A virgin will become pregnant and have a son, and he will be called Immanuel" (which means, "God is with us").

24So when Joseph woke up, he married Mary, as the angel of the Lord had told him to. **25**But he had no sexual relations with her before she gave birth to her son. And Joseph named him Jesus.

1:11 2 Kings 24:14, 15; 2 Chr 36:10; Jer 27:20 **1:18** Lk 1:27 **1:21** Sir 46:1; Lk 1:31 **1:23** Isa 7:14 (LXX)
1:25 Lk 2:21

The Liturgical Year

Catholic Connections

After the genealogy Matthew continues with the stories about Jesus' birth and the visit of the wise men, or magi. The Catholic Church celebrates these events during the Christmas season. These are special seasons during the Church year.

The Church has its own calendar called the liturgical calendar. It moves through seasons just like any other calendar does. The seasons are connected to the important moments in Jesus' life. Advent is the season before Christmas. During Advent we remember and celebrate the events leading up to and surrounding the birth of Jesus. The liturgical year reminds us that God's saving action continues today and will be fulfilled when Jesus returns at the end of time.

— Matthew 1:18—2:12

Matthew

Visitors from the East

2 ¹Jesus was born in the town of Bethlehem in Judea, during the time when Herod was king. Soon afterward, some men who studied the stars came from the East to Jerusalem ²and asked, "Where is the baby born to be the king of the Jews? We saw his star when it came up in the east, and we have come to worship him."

³When King Herod heard about this, he was very upset, and so was everyone else in Jerusalem. ⁴He called together all the chief priests and the teachers of the Law and asked them, "Where will the Messiah be born?"

⁵"In the town of Bethlehem in Judea," they answered. "For this is what the prophet wrote:

⁶ 'Bethlehem in the land of Judah,
    you are by no means the least of the
        leading cities of Judah;
for from you will come a leader
    who will guide my people Israel.' "

⁷So Herod called the visitors from the East to a secret meeting and found out from them the exact time the star had appeared. ⁸Then he sent them to Bethlehem with these instructions: "Go and make a careful search for the child; and when you find him, let me know, so that I too may go and worship him."

⁹⁻¹⁰And so they left, and on their way they saw the same star they had seen in the East. When they saw it, how happy they were, what joy was theirs! It went ahead of them until it stopped over the place where the child was. ¹¹They went into the house, and when they saw the child with his mother

The star . . . went ahead of them (2:9–10)

2:6 Mic 5:2

Do you think Joseph was scared? How would you feel if an angel asked you to do something for God?

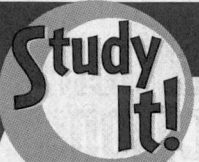

Remember Moses?

Jesus was hidden as a baby so that he would not be killed. The same thing happened to Moses (see Exodus 1:22—2:10). The story of Moses was important to the people for whom Matthew's Gospel was written. They were Jews. They would have recognized this comparison to Moses, one of their greatest leaders. Matthew's Gospel includes other similarities between Jesus and Moses. For example, by fleeing to Egypt and returning to Israel, Jesus takes the same journey that Moses and his people, the Israelites, took.

— Matthew 2:13–18

Mary, they knelt down and worshiped him. They brought out their gifts of gold, frankincense, and myrrh, and presented them to him.

¹²Then they returned to their country by another road, since God had warned them in a dream not to go back to Herod.

The Escape to Egypt

¹³After they had left, an angel of the Lord appeared in a dream to Joseph and said, "Herod will be looking for the child in order to kill him. So get up, take the child and his mother and escape to Egypt, and stay there until I tell you to leave."

¹⁴Joseph got up, took the child and his mother, and left during the night for Egypt, ¹⁵where he stayed until Herod died. This was done to make come true what the Lord had said through the prophet, "I called my Son out of Egypt."

The Killing of the Children

¹⁶When Herod realized that the visitors from the East had tricked him, he was furious. He gave orders to kill all the boys in Bethlehem and its neighborhood who were two years old and younger—this was done in accordance with what he had learned from the visitors about the time when the star had appeared.

¹⁷In this way what the prophet Jeremiah had said came true:
¹⁸"A sound is heard in Ramah,
    the sound of bitter weeping.
Rachel is crying for her children;
    she refuses to be comforted,
    for they are dead."

The Return from Egypt

¹⁹After Herod died, an angel of the Lord appeared in a dream to Joseph in Egypt ²⁰and said, "Get up, take the child and his mother, and go back to the land of Israel, because those who tried to kill the child are dead." ²¹So Joseph got up, took the child and his mother, and went back to Israel.

²²But when Joseph heard that Archelaus had succeeded his father Herod as king of Judea, he was afraid to go there. He was given more instructions in a dream, so he went to the province of Galilee ²³and made his home in a town named Nazareth. And so what the prophets had said came true: "He will be called a Nazarene."

The Preaching of John the Baptist
(Mark 1:1–8; Luke 3:1–18; John 1:19–28)

3 ¹At that time John the Baptist came to the desert of Judea and started preaching. ²"Turn away from your sins," he said, "because the Kingdom of heaven is near!"

2:15 Hos 11:1   2:18 Jer 31:15   2:23 Mk 1:24; Lk 2:39; Jn 1:45   3:2 Mt 4:17; Mk 1:15

The visitors from the East represent all of us who are not descended from the Jewish people. They show that God's salvation is for everyone.

Pray It!

Announcing God's Kingdom!

John the Baptist went ahead of Jesus. He let everybody know that something special was about to happen. The way his clothes are described would have reminded people of the prophet Elijah (2 Kings 1:8). People of Jesus' time believed that Elijah would return from heaven to announce the coming of the Day of the Lord. The author compares John to Elijah to let people know that Jesus is the one they have been waiting for.

> Saving God,
> Help me to be like John
>   by my words and actions.
> Help me to announce Jesus' coming.
> Help me to make a path for Jesus in my heart. Amen.

— Matthew 3:1–12

³John was the man the prophet Isaiah was talking about when he said,

"Someone is shouting in the desert,
'Prepare a road for the Lord;
make a straight path for him to travel!' "

⁴John's clothes were made of camel's hair; he wore a leather belt around his waist, and his food was locusts and wild honey. ⁵People came to him from Jerusalem, from the whole province of Judea, and from all over the country near the Jordan River. ⁶They confessed their sins, and he baptized them in the Jordan.

⁷When John saw many Pharisees and Sadducees coming to him to be baptized, he said to them, "You snakes—who told you that you could escape from the punishment God is about to send? ⁸Do those things that will show that you have turned from your sins. ⁹And don't think you can escape punishment by saying that Abraham is your ancestor. I tell you that God can take these rocks and make descendants for Abraham! ¹⁰The ax is ready to cut down the trees at the roots; every tree that does not bear good fruit will be cut down and thrown in the fire. ¹¹I baptize you with water to show that you have repented, but the one who will come after me will baptize you with the Holy Spirit and fire. He is much greater than I am; and I am not good enough even to carry his sandals. ¹²He has his winnowing shovel with him to thresh out all the grain. He will gather his wheat into his barn, but he will burn the chaff in a fire that never goes out."

The Baptism of Jesus
(Mark 1:9–11; Luke 3:21, 22)

¹³At that time Jesus arrived from Galilee and came to John at the Jordan to be baptized by him. ¹⁴But John tried to make him change his mind. "I ought to be baptized by you," John said, "and yet you have come to me!"

¹⁵But Jesus answered him, "Let it be so for now. For in this way we shall do all that God requires." So John agreed.

¹⁶As soon as Jesus was baptized, he came up out of the water. Then heaven was opened to him, and he saw the Spirit of God coming down like a dove and lighting on him. ¹⁷Then a voice said from heaven, "This is my own dear Son, with whom I am pleased."

3:3 Isa 40:3 (LXX) 3:4 2 Kings 1:8 3:7 Mt 12:34; 23:33 3:9 Jn 8:33 3:10 Mt 7:19 3:12 Wis 5:14, 23 3:17 Gen 22:2; Ps 2:7; Isa 42:1; Mt 12:18; 17:5; Mk 1:11; Lk 9:35

Pray It!

Facing the Devil

Jesus is hungry, tired, and probably lonely after fasting for forty days and nights in the desert. The Devil chooses this time to come and tempt him. It is often when we are feeling our worst that temptation is the strongest. When things are going badly at school or at home, when we feel lonely or lost, it is easy to listen to the voice of doubt. It is easy to think that God has abandoned us. Where does Jesus find strength? Jesus relies on God.

Dear God,
I don't feel very good right now.
Like Jesus in the desert, I'm tired.
I feel weak.
Be my strength and my courage.
Help me to rely on you
when I'm tempted to do things that I know I shouldn't.
I know that you will get me through.
Amen.

— Matthew 4:1–11

The Temptation of Jesus
(Mark 1:12, 13; Luke 4:1–13)

4 ¹Then the Spirit led Jesus into the desert to be tempted by the Devil. ²After spending forty days and nights without food, Jesus was hungry. ³Then the Devil came to him and said, "If you are God's Son, order these stones to turn into bread."

⁴But Jesus answered, "The scripture says, 'Human beings cannot live on bread alone, but need every word that God speaks.' "

⁵Then the Devil took Jesus to Jerusalem, the Holy City, set him on the highest point of the Temple, ⁶and said to him, "If you are God's Son, throw yourself down, for the scripture says,

'God will give orders to his angels about
      you;
    they will hold you up with their hands,
    so that not even your feet will be hurt
      on the stones.' "

⁷Jesus answered, "But the scripture also says, 'Do not put the Lord your God to the test.' "

⁸Then the Devil took Jesus to a very high mountain and showed him all the kingdoms of the world in all their greatness. ⁹"All this I will give you," the Devil said, "if you kneel down and worship me."

¹⁰Then Jesus answered, "Go away, Satan! The scripture says, 'Worship the Lord your God and serve only him!' "

"Order these stones to turn into bread!" (4:3)

4:1 Heb 2:18; 4:15   4:4 Deut 8:3   4:6 Ps 91:11, 12   4:7 Deut 6:16   4:10 Deut 6:13

11 Then the Devil left Jesus; and angels came and helped him.

Jesus Begins His Work in Galilee
(Mark 1:14, 15; Luke 4:14, 15)

12 When Jesus heard that John had been put in prison, he went away to Galilee. 13 He did not stay in Nazareth, but went to live in Capernaum, a town by Lake Galilee, in the territory of Zebulun and Naphtali. 14 This was done to make come true what the prophet Isaiah had said,

15 "Land of Zebulun and land of Naphtali,
    on the road to the sea, on the other
      side of the Jordan,
    Galilee, land of the Gentiles!
16 The people who live in darkness
    will see a great light.
On those who live in the dark land of death
    the light will shine."

17 From that time Jesus began to preach his message: "Turn away from your sins, because the Kingdom of heaven is near!"

Jesus Calls Four Fishermen
(Mark 1:16–20; Luke 5:1–11)

18 As Jesus walked along the shore of Lake Galilee, he saw two brothers who were fishermen, Simon (called Peter) and his brother Andrew, catching fish in the lake with a net. 19 Jesus said to them, "Come with me, and I will teach you to catch people." 20 At once they left their nets and went with him.

21 He went on and saw two other brothers, James and John, the sons of Zebedee. They were in their boat with their father Zebedee, getting their nets ready. Jesus called them, 22 and at once they left the boat and their father, and went with him.

Jesus Teaches, Preaches, and Heals
(Luke 6:17–19)

23 Jesus went all over Galilee, teaching in the synagogues, preaching the Good News

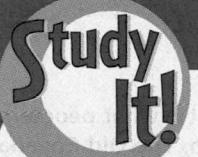

Jesus' Most Famous Sermon

Many well-known teachings of Jesus are collected in chapters 5–7 of the Gospel of Matthew, including the Beatitudes, the Golden Rule, and the Lord's Prayer. This section of Matthew's Gospel is called the Sermon on the Mount. Some of these teachings echo ideas that were already present in Jesus' time. Some of them are radical. Jesus says all these things, and then in the chapters to come, we see him live out all these teachings. He trusts in God. When he is treated cruelly, he responds with forgiveness and mercy. Read Matthew, chapters 5–7, carefully. It is a sneak preview of what lies ahead.

about the Kingdom, and healing people who had all kinds of disease and sickness. 24 The news about him spread through the whole country of Syria, so that people brought to him all those who were sick, suffering from all kinds of diseases and disorders: people with demons, and epileptics, and paralyzed people—and Jesus healed them all. 25 Large crowds followed him from Galilee and the Ten Towns, from Jerusalem, Judea, and the land on the other side of the Jordan.

The Sermon on the Mount

5 1 Jesus saw the crowds and went up a hill, where he sat down. His disciples gathered around him, 2 and he began to teach them:

4:12 Mt 14:3; Mk 6:17; Lk 3:19,20   4:13 Jn 2:12   4:15,16 Isa 9:1,2   4:17 Mt 3:2   4:23 Mt 9:35; Mk 1:39

Jesus spent forty days in the desert. Moses and the Israelites spent forty years. What's the connection? (See the article "Remember Moses?" in chapter 2.)

Matthew

A New Law

The Old Covenant is what people of Jesus' time were used to. The Old Covenant was a promise. God promised that the Israelites would be his special people, and the people promised that they would worship him alone. As a sign of their commitment, they followed the special law that God gave to Moses. This Old Law was symbolized by the Ten Commandments.

But the Israelites failed to be faithful to God over and over again. So Jesus brought a New Covenant. The New Covenant had a New Law that did not do away with the Old Law (Matthew 5:17–20) but fulfilled and completed it. The New Law focuses not just on our actions but also on what is in our hearts. In chapter 5 watch for the phrase "You have heard that it was said." Each time this phrase appears, Jesus gives a teaching from the Law of Moses and focuses on its true meaning.

The first section of the Sermon on the Mount is called the Beatitudes. The Beatitudes summarize what God's New Law is all about. They focus on the attitudes in our hearts rather than on specific actions. They are the key to human happiness. In the Beatitudes we see the wisdom of the Old Law brought to a new level.

— Matthew 5:1–12

True Happiness
(Luke 6:20–23)

3 "Happy are those who know they are
   spiritually poor;
   the Kingdom of heaven belongs to
   them!
4 "Happy are those who mourn;
   God will comfort them!
5 "Happy are those who are humble;
   they will receive what God has
   promised!
6 "Happy are those whose greatest desire is
   to do what God requires;
   God will satisfy them fully!
7 "Happy are those who are merciful to
   others;

   God will be merciful to them!
8 "Happy are the pure in heart;
   they will see God!
9 "Happy are those who work for peace;
   God will call them his children!
10 "Happy are those who are persecuted
   because they do what God requires;
   the Kingdom of heaven belongs to
   them!

11 "Happy are you when people insult you and persecute you and tell all kinds of evil lies against you because you are my followers. 12 Be happy and glad, for a great reward is kept for you in heaven. This is how the prophets who lived before you were persecuted.

5:4 Isa 61:2 5:5 Ps 37:11 5:6 Isa 55:1,2; Sir 24:21 5:8 Ps 24:3,4 5:10 1 Pet 3:14 5:11 1 Pet 4:14
5:12 2 Chr 36:16; Sir 2:8; Acts 7:52

Salt and Light
(Mark 9:50; Luke 14:34, 35)

13 "You are like salt for the whole human race. But if salt loses its saltiness, there is no way to make it salty again. It has become worthless, so it is thrown out and people trample on it.

14 "You are like light for the whole world. A city built on a hill cannot be hid. 15 No one lights a lamp and puts it under a bowl; instead it is put on the lampstand, where it gives light for everyone in the house. 16 In the same way your light must shine before people, so that they will see the good things you do and praise your Father in heaven.

Teaching about the Law

17 "Do not think that I have come to do away with the Law of Moses and the teachings of the prophets. I have not come to do away with them, but to make their teachings come true. 18 Remember that as long as heaven and earth last, not the least point nor the smallest detail of the Law will be done away with—not until the end of all things.*a* 19 So then, whoever disobeys even the least important of the commandments and teaches others to do the same, will be least in the Kingdom of heaven. On the other hand, whoever obeys the Law and teaches others to do the same, will be great in the Kingdom of heaven. 20 I tell you, then, that you will be able to enter the Kingdom of heaven only if you are more faithful than the teachers of the Law and the Pharisees in doing what God requires.

Teaching about Anger

21 "You have heard that people were told in the past, 'Do not commit murder; anyone who does will be brought to trial.' 22 But now I tell you: if you are angry*b* with your brother you will be brought to trial, if you call your brother 'You good-for-nothing!' you will be brought before the Council, and if you call your brother a worthless fool you will be in

---

> ## *Pray It!*
>
> ### Shine Bright!
>
> In this passage we are told "your light must shine before people" (Matthew 5:16). Light a candle in a dark room. Now shield the flame with your hand. Notice how dark the room gets. Now hold the light up over your head. See how it lights up the whole room? God wants us to do the same thing with our lives. God asks us to live so that the good we do shines on others and lights up the whole world.
>
> **— Matthew 5:13–16**

---

danger of going to the fire of hell. 23 So if you are about to offer your gift to God at the altar and there you remember that your brother has something against you, 24 leave your gift there in front of the altar, go at once and make peace with your brother, and then come back and offer your gift to God.

25 "If someone brings a lawsuit against you and takes you to court, settle the dispute while there is time, before you get to court. Once you are there, you will be turned over to the judge, who will hand you over to the police, and you will be put in jail. 26 There you will stay, I tell you, until you pay the last penny of your fine.

Teaching about Adultery

27 "You have heard that it was said, 'Do not commit adultery.' 28 But now I tell you: anyone who looks at a woman and wants to possess her is guilty of committing adultery with her in his heart. 29 So if your right eye causes you to sin, take it out and throw it away! It is

---

a **5:18** *the end of all things; or all its teachings come true.*   *b* **5:22** *if you are angry; some manuscripts have if without cause you are angry.*
5:13 Mk 9:50; Lk 14:34,35   **5:14** Jn 8:12; 9:5   **5:15** Mk 4:21; Lk 8:16; 11:33   **5:16** 1 Pet 2:12   **5:18** Lk 16:17   **5:21** Ex 20:13; Deut 5:17   **5:27** Ex 20:14; Deut 5:18   **5:29** Mt 18:9; Mk 9:47

much better for you to lose a part of your body than to have your whole body thrown into hell. 30If your right hand causes you to sin, cut it off and throw it away! It is much better for you to lose one of your limbs than to have your whole body go off to hell.

Teaching about Divorce
(Matthew 19:9; Mark 10:11, 12; Luke 16:18)

31"It was also said, 'Anyone who divorces his wife must give her a written notice of divorce.' 32But now I tell you: if a man divorces his wife for any cause other than her unfaithfulness, then he is guilty of making her commit adultery if she marries again; and the man who marries her commits adultery also.

Teaching about Vows

33"You have also heard that people were told in the past, 'Do not break your promise, but do what you have vowed to the Lord to do.' 34But now I tell you: do not use any oath when you make a promise. Do not swear by heaven, for it is God's throne; 35nor by earth, for it is the resting place for his feet; nor by Jerusalem, for it is the city of the great King. 36Do not even swear by your head, because you cannot make a single hair white or black. 37Just say 'Yes' or 'No'—anything else you say comes from the Evil One.

Teaching about Revenge
(Luke 6:29, 30)

38"You have heard that it was said, 'An eye for an eye, and a tooth for a tooth.' 39But now I tell you: do not take revenge on someone who wrongs you. If anyone slaps you on the right cheek, let him slap your left cheek too. 40And if someone takes you to court to sue you for your shirt, let him have your coat as well. 41And if one of the occupation troops forces you to carry his pack one mile, carry it two miles. 42When someone asks you for something, give it to him; when someone wants to borrow something, lend it to him.

Love for Enemies
(Luke 6:27, 28, 32–36)

43"You have heard that it was said, 'Love your friends, hate your enemies.' 44But now I tell you: love your enemies and pray for those who persecute you, 45so that you may become the children of your Father in heaven. For he makes his sun to shine on bad and good people alike, and gives rain to those who do good and to those who do evil. 46Why should God reward you if you love only the people who love you? Even the tax collectors do that! 47And if you speak only to your friends, have you done anything out of the ordinary? Even the pagans do that! 48You must be perfect—just as your Father in heaven is perfect.

Teaching about Charity

6 1"Make certain you do not perform your religious duties in public so that people will see what you do. If you do these things publicly, you will not have any reward from your Father in heaven.

2"So when you give something to a needy person, do not make a big show of it, as the hypocrites do in the houses of worship and on the streets. They do it so that

Do not make a big show of it. (6:2)

5:30 Mt 18:8; Mk 9:43 **5:31** Deut 24:1-4; Mt 19:7; Mk 10:4 **5:32** Mt 19:9; Mk 10:11,12; Lk 16:18; 1 Cor 7:10,11 **5:33 a** Lev 19:12; **b** Num 30:2; Deut 23:21 **5:34 a** Jas 5:12; **b** Isa 66:1; Mt 23:22 **5:35 a** Isa 66:1; **b** Ps 48:2 **5:38** Ex 21:24; Lev 24:20; Deut 19:21 **5:43** Sir 12:4-7 **5:45** Sir 4:10 **5:48** Lev 19:2; Deut 18:13 **6:1** Mt 23:5

people will praise them. I assure you, they have already been paid in full. ³But when you help a needy person, do it in such a way that even your closest friend will not know about it. ⁴Then it will be a private matter. And your Father, who sees what you do in private, will reward you.

Teaching about Prayer
(Luke 11:2–4)

⁵"When you pray, do not be like the hypocrites! They love to stand up and pray in the houses of worship and on the street corners, so that everyone will see them. I assure you, they have already been paid in full. ⁶But when you pray, go to your room, close the door, and pray to your Father, who is unseen. And your Father, who sees what you do in private, will reward you.

⁷"When you pray, do not use a lot of meaningless words, as the pagans do, who think that their gods will hear them because their prayers are long. ⁸Do not be like them. Your Father already knows what you need before you ask him. ⁹This, then, is how you should pray:

'Our Father in heaven:
May your holy name be honored;
¹⁰ may your Kingdom come;
may your will be done on earth as it is in heaven.
¹¹ Give us today the food we need.ᶜ
¹² Forgive us the wrongs we have done, as we forgive the wrongs that others have done to us.
¹³ Do not bring us to hard testing, but keep us safe from the Evil One.'ᵈ

¹⁴"If you forgive others the wrongs they have done to you, your Father in heaven will also forgive you. ¹⁵But if you do not forgive others, then your Father will not forgive the wrongs you have done.

No Show-Offs

Hypocrites are people whose beliefs and actions don't match. They say one thing and do the opposite. They may do the right thing, but it is just for show and doesn't really mean anything because their hearts aren't in it. In this section Jesus criticizes this kind of behavior. He tells his followers that when they do something good, they should keep it a secret. When you pray don't show off. When you help someone else, don't brag about it. Then you know that you are doing the right thing for the right reason.

— Matthew 6:5–7

Teaching about Fasting

¹⁶"And when you fast, do not put on a sad face as the hypocrites do. They neglect their appearance so that everyone will see that they are fasting. I assure you, they have already been paid in full. ¹⁷When you go without food, wash your face and comb your hair, ¹⁸so that others cannot know that you are fasting—only your Father, who is unseen, will know. And your Father, who sees what you do in private, will reward you.

Riches in Heaven
(Luke 12:33, 34)

¹⁹"Do not store up riches for yourselves here on earth, where moths and rust destroy,

---

ᶜ **6:11** *we need; or for today, or for tomorrow.*   ᵈ **6:13** *Some manuscripts add* For yours is the kingdom, and the power, and the glory forever. Amen.
6:5 Lk 18:10-14   **6:7** Sir 7:14   **6:14,15** Mk 11:25,26   **6:14** Sir 28:1-5   **6:17** Jdt 10:3   **6:19** Jas 5:2,3

During Jesus' time a Roman soldier could force a bystander to carry his pack for a mile *(Matthew 5:41).* **Such packs weighed about seventy pounds!**

Pray It!

Remember God's Goodness

Do you worry a lot? Many people do. In chapter 6 Matthew reminds us that God takes care of us. The next time you find yourself worrying about the future, use this meditation to regain your perspective.

A flower in the field starts as a seed. The sun warms the seed. The soil feeds the tiny plant through its delicate but growing root system. The rain falls, the plant grows, and finally the bud becomes a bright beautiful blossom. God made this whole process. It takes place without any work or worry on the part of the flower. God has a plan for you too. You are so much more valuable to God than a tiny flower, so much more complex. Imagine the process that has brought you to where you are today—from a tiny creature growing inside your mother to the person you are now. And God's not through with you! God has a plan to make something bright and beautiful happen with you too!

— **Matthew 6:25–34**

The Light of the Body
(Luke 11:34–36)

22 "The eyes are like a lamp for the body. If your eyes are sound, your whole body will be full of light; 23 but if your eyes are no good, your body will be in darkness. So if the light in you is darkness, how terribly dark it will be!

God and Possessions
(Luke 16:13; 12:22–31)

24 "You cannot be a slave of two masters; you will hate one and love the other; you will be loyal to one and despise the other. You cannot serve both God and money.

25 "This is why I tell you: do not be worried about the food and drink you need in order to stay alive, or about clothes for your body. After all, isn't life worth more than food? And isn't the body worth more than clothes? 26 Look at the birds: they do not plant seeds, gather a harvest and put it in barns; yet your Father in heaven takes care of them! Aren't you worth much more than birds? 27 Can any of you live a bit longer*e* by worrying about it?

Aren't you worth much more than birds? (6:26)

28 "And why worry about clothes? Look how the wild flowers grow: they do not work or make clothes for themselves. 29 But I tell you that not even King Solomon with all his wealth had clothes as beautiful as one of these flowers. 30 It is God who clothes the

and robbers break in and steal. 20 Instead, store up riches for yourselves in heaven, where moths and rust cannot destroy, and robbers cannot break in and steal. 21 For your heart will always be where your riches are.

e **6:27** live a bit longer; *or* grow a bit taller.
6:20 Sir 29:11   **6:29** 1 Kings 10:4-7; 2 Chr 9:3-6

Jesus wants more than words! You can't just *say* you believe. You've got to act like you do too!

wild grass—grass that is here today and gone tomorrow, burned up in the oven. Won't he be all the more sure to clothe you? What little faith you have!

31"So do not start worrying: 'Where will my food come from? or my drink? or my clothes?' 32(These are the things the pagans are always concerned about.) Your Father in heaven knows that you need all these things. 33Instead, be concerned above everything else with the Kingdom of God and with what he requires of you, and he will provide you with all these other things. 34So do not worry about tomorrow; it will have enough worries of its own. There is no need to add to the troubles each day brings.

Judging Others
(Luke 6:37, 38, 41, 42)

7 1"Do not judge others, so that God will not judge you, 2for God will judge you in the same way you judge others, and he will apply to you the same rules you apply to others. 3Why, then, do you look at the speck in your brother's eye and pay no attention to the log in your own eye? 4How dare you say to your brother, 'Please, let me take that speck out of your eye,' when you have a log in your own eye? 5You hypocrite! First take the log out of your own eye, and then you will be able to see clearly to take the speck out of your brother's eye.

6"Do not give what is holy to dogs—they will only turn and attack you. Do not throw your pearls in front of pigs—they will only trample them underfoot.

Ask, Seek, Knock
(Luke 11:9–13)

7"Ask, and you will receive; seek, and you will find; knock, and the door will be opened to you. 8For everyone who asks will receive, and anyone who seeks will find, and the door will be opened to those who knock. 9Would any of you who are fathers give your son a stone when he asks for bread? 10Or would you give him a snake when he asks for a fish? 11As bad as you are,

you know how to give good things to your children. How much more, then, will your Father in heaven give good things to those who ask him!

12"Do for others what you want them to do for you: this is the meaning of the Law of Moses and of the teachings of the prophets.

The Narrow Gate
(Luke 13:24)

13"Go in through the narrow gate, because the gate to hell is wide and the road that leads to it is easy, and there are many who travel it. 14But the gate to life is narrow and the way that leads to it is hard, and there are few people who find it.

A Tree and Its Fruit
(Luke 6:43, 44)

15"Be on your guard against false prophets; they come to you looking like sheep on the outside, but on the inside they are really like wild wolves. 16You will know them by what they do. Thorn bushes do not bear grapes, and briers do not bear figs. 17A healthy tree bears good fruit, but a poor tree bears bad fruit. 18A healthy tree cannot bear bad fruit, and a poor tree cannot bear good fruit. 19And any tree that does not bear good fruit is cut down and thrown in the fire. 20So then, you will know the false prophets by what they do.

I Never Knew You
(Luke 13:25–27)

21"Not everyone who calls me 'Lord, Lord' will enter the Kingdom of heaven, but only those who do what my Father in heaven wants them to do. 22When the Judgment Day comes, many will say to me, 'Lord, Lord! In your name we spoke God's message, by your name we drove out many demons and performed many miracles!' 23Then I will say to them, 'I never knew you. Get away from me, you wicked people!'

7:2 Mk 4:24   **7:12** Tob 4:15; Lk 6:31   **7:13, 14** Sir 15:17   **7:16** Sir 27:6   **7:19** Mt 3:10; Lk 3:9   **7:20** Mt 12:33   **7:23** Ps 6:8

Pray It!

Good as Gold

Even though they might have different ways of saying it, Buddhists, Hindus, Taoists, Jews, Muslims, and Christians all share the central teaching of this section of Matthew, "Do for others what you want them to do for you" (Matthew 7:12). We call this teaching the Golden Rule. The message of the Golden Rule seems to be a part of most cultures and religions. Imagine if everyone in the world lived by this teaching! How would the world be different? How about your own life? In what ways do you live out this teaching?

Loving God,
You showed us how to love one another.
It is easy to say, but sometimes it is hard to do.
When I am angry or tired or annoyed,
*   it is easy to forget the needs of another person.*
It is easy to forget that I should treat them the way I want to be treated.
Please help me to remember each person's humanity.
Help me to remember that each person I meet is your son or daughter.
Help the leaders of this world, Lord.
Whenever they have a decision to make that affects others,
*   help them remember the Golden Rule. Amen.*

— Matthew 7:12

The Two House Builders
(Luke 6:47–49)

24 "So then, anyone who hears these words of mine and obeys them is like a wise man who built his house on rock. 25 The rain poured down, the rivers flooded over, and the wind blew hard against that house. But it did not fall, because it was built on rock.

26 "But anyone who hears these words of mine and does not obey them is like a foolish man who built his house on sand. 27 The rain poured down, the rivers flooded over, the wind blew hard against that house, and it fell. And what a terrible fall that was!"

The Authority of Jesus

28 When Jesus finished saying these things, the crowd was amazed at the way he taught. 29 He wasn't like the teachers of the Law; instead, he taught with authority.

Jesus Heals a Man
(Mark 1:40–45; Luke 5:12–16)

8 1 When Jesus came down from the hill, large crowds followed him. 2 Then a man suffering from a dreaded skin disease came to him, knelt down before him, and said, "Sir, if you want to, you can make me clean."f

3 Jesus reached out and touched him. "I do want to," he answered. "Be clean!" At once the man was healed of his disease. 4 Then Jesus said to him, "Listen! Don't tell anyone, but go straight to the priest and let him examine you; then in order to prove to everyone that you are cured, offer the sacrifice that Moses ordered."

Jesus Heals a Roman Officer's Servant
(Luke 7:1–10)

5 When Jesus entered Capernaum, a Roman officer met him and begged for help:

f 8:2 MAKE ME CLEAN: *This disease was considered to make a person ritually unclean.*
7:28,29 Mk 1:22; Lk 4:32   8:4 Lev 14:1-32

6 "Sir, my servant is sick in bed at home, unable to move and suffering terribly."

7 "I will go and make him well," Jesus said.

8 "Oh no, sir," answered the officer. "I do not deserve to have you come into my house. Just give the order, and my servant will get well. 9 I, too, am a man under the authority of superior officers, and I have soldiers under me. I order this one, 'Go!' and he goes; and I order that one, 'Come!' and he comes; and I order my slave, 'Do this!' and he does it."

10 When Jesus heard this, he was surprised and said to the people following him, "I tell you, I have never found anyone in Israel with faith like this. 11 I assure you that many will come from the east and the west and sit down with Abraham, Isaac, and Jacob at the feast in the Kingdom of heaven. 12 But those who should be in the Kingdom will be thrown out into the darkness, where they will cry and gnash their teeth." 13 Then Jesus said to the officer, "Go home, and what you believe will be done for you."

And the officer's servant was healed that very moment.

Jesus Heals Many People
(Mark 1:29–34; Luke 4:38–41)

14 Jesus went to Peter's home, and there he saw Peter's mother-in-law sick in bed with a fever. 15 He touched her hand; the fever left her, and she got up and began to wait on him.

16 When evening came, people brought to Jesus many who had demons in them. Jesus drove out the evil spirits with a word and healed all who were sick. 17 He did this to make come true what the prophet Isaiah had said, "He himself took our sickness and carried away our diseases."

The Would-Be Followers of Jesus
(Luke 9:57–62)

18 When Jesus noticed the crowd around him, he ordered his disciples to go to the

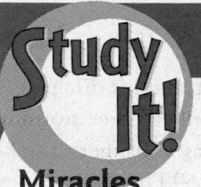

Study It!

Miracles

The miracles in Matthew's Gospel are one more sign that the Kingdom of heaven is not some far off place but right here, right now! The miracles show the power of God clearly present and acting in the world. For example, Jesus comes across a man with a skin disease (Matthew 8:1–3). Because of the laws of the time, the man had to live outside the town, away from his friends and family. By the Jewish Law, people with skin diseases and other illnesses were considered unclean. The law was meant to keep the disease from spreading.

When Jesus healed the man with a skin disease, he not only made the man healthy again but changed his whole life! Now he could go back to his family and friends. Miracles like this are an example of Jesus' healing power. The other miracle stories in chapter 8 show that Jesus also has power over nature and power over evil.

— Matthew, chapter 8

other side of the lake. 19 A teacher of the Law came to him. "Teacher," he said, "I am ready to go with you wherever you go."

20 Jesus answered him, "Foxes have holes, and birds have nests, but the Son of Man has no place to lie down and rest."

21 Another man, who was a disciple, said, "Sir, first let me go back and bury my father."

22 "Follow me," Jesus answered, "and let the dead bury their own dead."

8:9 Bar 3:33-35   **8:11** Lk 13:29   **8:12** Mt 22:13; 25:30; Lk 13:28   **8:17** Isa 53:4   **8:21** Tob 4:3, 4

Love your enemies. Jesus says this (Matthew 5:44), **then he does it in chapter 8! Whom did Jesus heal who was considered an enemy of the Jews?**

Jesus Calms a Storm
(Mark 4:35–41; Luke 8:22–25)

23 Jesus got into a boat, and his disciples went with him. 24 Suddenly a fierce storm hit the lake, and the boat was in danger of sinking. But Jesus was asleep. 25 The disciples went to him and woke him up. "Save us, Lord!" they said. "We are about to die!"

26 "Why are you so frightened?" Jesus answered. "What little faith you have!" Then he got up and ordered the winds and the waves to stop, and there was a great calm.

27 Everyone was amazed. "What kind of man is this?" they said. "Even the winds and the waves obey him!"

Jesus Heals Two Men with Demons
(Mark 5:1–20; Luke 8:26–39)

28 When Jesus came to the territory of Gadara on the other side of the lake, he was met by two men who came out of the burial caves there. These men had demons in them and were so fierce that no one dared travel on that road. 29 At once they screamed, "What do you want with us, you Son of God? Have you come to punish us before the right time?"

30 Not far away there was a large herd of pigs feeding. 31 So the demons begged Jesus, "If you are going to drive us out, send us into that herd of pigs."

32 "Go," Jesus told them; so they left and went off into the pigs. The whole herd rushed down the side of the cliff into the lake and was drowned.

33 The men who had been taking care of the pigs ran away and went into the town, where they told the whole story and what had happened to the men with the demons. 34 So everyone from the town went out to meet Jesus; and when they saw him, they begged him to leave their territory.

Jesus Heals a Paralyzed Man
(Mark 2:1–12; Luke 5:17–26)

9 1 Jesus got into the boat and went back across the lake to his own town,g 2 where some people brought to him a paralyzed man, lying on a bed. When Jesus saw how much faith they had, he said to the paralyzed man, "Courage, my son! Your sins are forgiven."

3 Then some teachers of the Law said to themselves, "This man is speaking blasphemy!"

4 Jesus perceived what they were thinking, and so he said, "Why are you thinking such evil things? 5 Is it easier to say, 'Your sins are forgiven,' or to say, 'Get up and walk'? 6 I will prove to you, then, that the Son of Man has authority on earth to forgive sins." So he said to the paralyzed man, "Get up, pick up your bed, and go home!"

7 The man got up and went home. 8 When the people saw it, they were afraid, and praised God for giving such authority to people.

Jesus Calls Matthew
(Mark 2:13–17; Luke 5:27–32)

9 Jesus left that place, and as he walked along, he saw a tax collector, named Matthew, sitting in his office. He said to him, "Follow me."

Matthew got up and followed him.

10 While Jesus was having a meal in Matthew's house,h many tax collectors and other outcasts came and joined Jesus and his disciples at the table. 11 Some Pharisees saw this and asked his disciples, "Why does your teacher eat with such people?"

12 Jesus heard them and answered, "People who are well do not need a doctor, but only those who are sick. 13 Go and find out what is meant by the scripture that says: 'It is kindness that I want, not animal sacrifices.' I have not come to call respectable people, but outcasts."

g **9:1** HIS OWN TOWN: *Capernaum (see 4:13).*   h **9:10** in Matthew's house; *or* in his *(that is,* Jesus') house.
9:10,11 Lk 15:1,2   **9:13** a Mt 12:7; b Hos 6:6

Blasphemy **is insulting God or being disrespectful toward God** *(Matthew 9:3)*. **People thought it was blasphemous to claim to forgive sins.**

Live It!

Friends to the Rescue

The man who couldn't walk had to be carried by his friends to Jesus. They took a risk. It could not have been easy to take the man from his house and carry him on a stretcher to where Jesus was. Jesus might have turned them away. Then all their hard work, the risk they took, would have been for nothing. But "when Jesus saw how much faith they had" (Matthew 9:2), he responded by forgiving the man's sins. Sometimes people can be so paralyzed by sin or fear that it is hard for them to ask for what they need from God. They need another person to help them overcome that paralysis.

Think of your friends. Do any of them need help approaching God? Are you being called to "carry" someone to Jesus for healing? How can you help? It can be as easy as telling someone that you will pray for him or her. You can tell them about your own belief in God—that God will always forgive anyone who asks. When someone needs healing, they need to hear about God's love and mercy. You could even share this story with them.

— Matthew 9:1–8

The Question about Fasting
(Mark 2:18–22; Luke 5:33–39)

14 Then the followers of John the Baptist came to Jesus, asking, "Why is it that we and the Pharisees fast often, but your disciples don't fast at all?"

15 Jesus answered, "Do you expect the guests at a wedding party to be sad as long as the bridegroom is with them? Of course not! But the day will come when the bride-groom will be taken away from them, and then they will fast.

16 "No one patches up an old coat with a piece of new cloth, for the new patch will shrink and make an even bigger hole in the coat. 17 Nor does anyone pour new wine into used wineskins, for the skins will burst, the wine will pour out, and the skins will be ruined. Instead, new wine is poured into fresh wineskins, and both will keep in good condition."

The Official's Daughter and the Woman Who Touched Jesus' Cloak
(Mark 5:21–43; Luke 8:40–56)

18 While Jesus was saying this, a Jewish official came to him, knelt down before him, and said, "My daughter has just died; but come and place your hands on her, and she will live."

19 So Jesus got up and followed him, and his disciples went along with him.

20 A woman who had suffered from severe bleeding for twelve years came up behind Jesus and touched the edge of his cloak. 21 She said to herself, "If only I touch his cloak, I will get well."

"If only I touch his cloak . . . " (9:21)

22 Jesus turned around and saw her, and said, "Courage, my daughter! Your faith has made you well." At that very moment the woman became well.

23 Then Jesus went into the official's house. When he saw the musicians for the funeral and the people all stirred up, 24 he said, "Get out, everybody! The little girl is not dead—she is only sleeping!" Then they all started making fun of him. 25 But as soon as the people had been put out, Jesus went

into the girl's room and took hold of her hand, and she got up. 26The news about this spread all over that part of the country.

Jesus Heals Two Blind Men

27Jesus left that place, and as he walked along, two blind men started following him. "Have mercy on us, Son of David!" they shouted.

28When Jesus had gone indoors, the two blind men came to him, and he asked them, "Do you believe that I can heal you?"

"Yes, sir!" they answered.

29Then Jesus touched their eyes and said, "Let it happen, then, just as you believe!"— 30and their sight was restored. Jesus spoke sternly to them, "Don't tell this to anyone!"

31But they left and spread the news about Jesus all over that part of the country.

Jesus Heals a Man Who Could Not Speak

32As the men were leaving, some people brought to Jesus a man who could not talk because he had a demon. 33But as soon as the demon was driven out, the man started talking, and everyone was amazed. "We have never seen anything like this in Israel!" they exclaimed.

34But the Pharisees said, "It is the chief of the demons who gives Jesus the power to drive out demons."

Jesus Has Pity for the People

35Jesus went around visiting all the towns and villages. He taught in the synagogues, preached the Good News about the Kingdom, and healed people with every kind of disease and sickness. 36As he saw the crowds, his heart was filled with pity for them, because they were worried and helpless, like sheep without a shepherd. 37So he said to his disciples, "The harvest is large, but there are few workers to gather it in. 38Pray to the owner of the harvest that he will send out workers to gather in his harvest."

The Twelve Apostles
(Mark 3:13–19; Luke 6:12–16)

10 1Jesus called his twelve disciples together and gave them authority to drive out evil spirits and to heal every disease and every sickness. 2These are the names of the twelve apostles: first, Simon (called Peter) and his brother Andrew; James and his brother John, the sons of Zebedee; 3Philip and Bartholomew; Thomas and Matthew, the tax collector; James son of Alphaeus, and Thaddaeus; 4Simon the Patriot, and Judas Iscariot, who betrayed Jesus.

The Mission of the Twelve
(Mark 6:7–13; Luke 9:1–6)

5These twelve men were sent out by Jesus with the following instructions: "Do not go to any Gentile territory or any Samaritan towns. 6Instead, you are to go to the lost sheep of the people of Israel. 7Go and preach, 'The Kingdom of heaven is near!' 8Heal the sick, bring the dead back to life, heal those who suffer from dreaded skin diseases, and drive out demons. You have received without paying, so give without being paid. 9Do not carry any gold, silver, or copper money in your pockets; 10do not carry a beggar's bag for the trip or an extra shirt or shoes or a walking stick. Workers should be given what they need.

11"When you come to a town or village, go in and look for someone who is willing to welcome you, and stay with him until you leave that place. 12When you go into a house, say, 'Peace be with you.' 13If the people in that house welcome you, let your greeting of peace remain; but if they do not welcome you, then take back your greeting. 14And if some home or town will not welcome you or listen to you, then leave that place and shake the dust off your feet. 15I assure you that on the Judgment Day God will show more mercy to the people of Sodom and Gomorrah than to the people of that town!

9:34 Mt 10:25; 12:24; Mk 3:22; Lk 11:15   **9:35** Mt 4:23; Mk 1:39; Lk 4:44   **9:36** Num 27:17; 1 Kings 22:17; 2 Chr 18:16; Ezek 34:5; Mk 6:34   **9:37,38** Lk 10:2   **10:10** 1 Cor 9:14; 1 Tim 5:18   **10:14** Acts 13:51 **10:15 a** Mt 11:24; **b** Gen 19:24-28   **10:7-15** Lk 10:4-12

The Twelve

Catholic Connections

Twelve is an important number. There were twelve tribes of Israel. The number of Apostles was meant to remind people that Jesus came to save the whole Jewish nation and to be a sign of the connection between the Old Covenant and the New Covenant.

If you look over the list of people at the beginning of Matthew, chapter 10, you might wonder what Jesus was thinking. These were not powerful or important people. One was a tax collector, shunned by others. Simon the Patriot may have been committed to the violent overthrow of the Roman occupation. Judas would betray Jesus. But Jesus knew what he was doing. Eleven of these men, changed by watching and listening to Jesus, would do mighty things. They would endure persecution, torture, and death as the first leaders of the Church, just as Jesus predicts in verses 16–25. All future popes and bishops receive their authority from the authority and mission Christ gave to the original Apostles.

You don't have to be rich or powerful to make a difference. Simple and humble people do great things because greed and pride do not get in the way of God working through them.

— Matthew 10:1–4

Matthew

Coming Persecutions
(Mark 13:9–13; Luke 21:12–17)

16"Listen! I am sending you out just like sheep to a pack of wolves. You must be as cautious as snakes and as gentle as doves. 17Watch out, for there will be those who will arrest you and take you to court, and they will whip you in the synagogues. 18For my sake you will be brought to trial before rulers and kings, to tell the Good News to them and to the Gentiles. 19When they bring you to trial, do not worry about what you are going to say or how you will say it; when the time comes, you will be given what you will say. 20For the words you will speak will not be yours; they will come from the Spirit of your Father speaking through you.

21"People will hand over their own brothers to be put to death, and fathers will do the same to their children; children will turn against their parents and have them put to death. 22Everyone will hate you because of me. But whoever holds out to the end will be saved. 23When they persecute you in one town, run away to another one. I assure you that you will not finish your work in all the towns of Israel before the Son of Man comes.

24"No pupil is greater than his teacher; no slave is greater than his master. 25So a pupil should be satisfied to become like his teacher, and a slave like his master. If the head of the family is called Beelzebul, the members of the family will be called even worse names!

10:16 Lk 10:3   **10:17-20** Mk 13:9-11; Lk 12:11,12; 21:12-15   **10:21** Mk 13:12; Lk 21:16   **10:22 a** Mt 24:9; Mk 13:13; Lk 21:17; **b** Mt 24:13; Mk 13:13   **10:24 a** Lk 6:40; **b** Jn 13:16; 15:20   **10:25** Mt 9:34; 12:24; Mk 3:22; Lk 11:15

Apostle comes from a Greek word meaning "one who is sent."

Hard Times

Have you ever done the right thing and then gotten in trouble for it? Maybe you told the truth about something, and then someone got mad at you. Maybe you stood up for one friend but lost another friend in the process. This part of chapter 10 is challenging and confusing! Up to this point Jesus has spoken words of love and comfort. Now he is telling his followers that he will cause fighting between family members (Matthew 10:35–36).

Actually this is meant to encourage his followers. He's warning them—especially those who are going out as missionaries—that this is not going to be easy! Even your own family may turn against you. You're doing the right thing, but it's going to be hard!

— Matthew 10:34–39

Whom to Fear
(Luke 12:2–7)

26 "So do not be afraid of people. Whatever is now covered up will be uncovered, and every secret will be made known. 27 What I am telling you in the dark you must repeat in broad daylight, and what you have heard in private you must announce from the housetops. 28 Do not be afraid of those who kill the body but cannot kill the soul; rather be afraid of God, who can destroy both body and soul in hell. 29 For only a penny you can buy two sparrows, yet not one sparrow falls to the

ground without your Father's consent. 30 As for you, even the hairs of your head have all been counted. 31 So do not be afraid; you are worth much more than many sparrows!

Confessing and Rejecting Christ
(Luke 12:8, 9)

32 "Those who declare publicly that they belong to me, I will do the same for them before my Father in heaven. 33 But those who reject me publicly, I will reject before my Father in heaven.

Not Peace, but a Sword
(Luke 12:51–53; 14:26, 27)

34 "Do not think that I have come to bring peace to the world. No, I did not come to bring peace, but a sword. 35 I came to set sons against their fathers, daughters against their mothers, daughters-in-law against their mothers-in-law; 36 your worst enemies will be the members of your own family.

37 "Those who love their father or mother more than me are not fit to be my disciples; those who love their son or daughter more than me are not fit to be my disciples. 38 Those who do not take up their cross and follow in my steps are not fit to be my disciples. 39 Those who try to gain their own life will lose it; but those who lose their life for my sake will gain it.

Rewards
(Mark 9:41)

40 "Whoever welcomes you welcomes me; and whoever welcomes me welcomes the one who sent me. 41 Whoever welcomes God's messenger because he is God's messenger, will share in his reward. And whoever welcomes a good man because he is good, will share in his reward. 42 You can be sure that whoever gives even a drink of cold water to one of the least of these my follow-

10:26 Mk 4:22; Lk 8:17   10:33 2 Tim 2:12   10:35,36 Mic 7:6   10:38 Mt 16:24; Mk 8:34; Lk 9:23
10:39 Mt 16:25; Mk 8:35; Lk 9:24; 17:33; Jn 12:25   10:40 a Lk 10:16; Jn 13:20; b Mk 9:37; Lk 9:48

"So do not be afraid; you are worth much more than many sparrows!"
(Matthew 10:31).

Matthew

ers because he is my follower, will certainly receive a reward."

The Messengers from John the Baptist
(Luke 7:18–35)

11 ¹When Jesus finished giving these instructions to his twelve disciples, he left that place and went off to teach and preach in the towns near there.

²When John the Baptist heard in prison about the things that Christ was doing, he sent some of his disciples to him. ³"Tell us," they asked Jesus, "are you the one John said was going to come, or should we expect someone else?"

⁴Jesus answered, "Go back and tell John what you are hearing and seeing: ⁵the blind can see, the lame can walk, those who suffer from dreaded skin diseases are made clean,ⁱ the deaf hear, the dead are brought back to life, and the Good News is preached to the poor. ⁶How happy are those who have no doubts about me!"

⁷While John's disciples were leaving, Jesus spoke about him to the crowds: "When you went out to John in the desert, what did you expect to see? A blade of grass bending in the wind? ⁸What did you go out to see? A man dressed up in fancy clothes? People who dress like that live in palaces! ⁹Tell me, what did you go out to see? A prophet? Yes indeed, but you saw much more than a prophet. ¹⁰For John is the one of whom the scripture says: 'God said, I will send my messenger ahead of you to open the way for you.' ¹¹I assure you that John the Baptist is greater than anyone who has ever lived. But the one who is least in the Kingdom of heaven is greater than John. ¹²From the time John preached his message until this very day the Kingdom of heaven has suffered violent attacks,ʲ and violent men try to seize it. ¹³Until the time of John all the prophets and the Law of Moses spoke about the Kingdom; ¹⁴and if you are willing to believe their message, John is Elijah, whose coming was predicted. ¹⁵Listen, then, if you have ears!

¹⁶"Now, to what can I compare the people

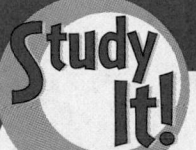

The Blind Can See

When John's disciples come to ask Jesus, "Are you the one John said was going to come?" (Matthew 11:3), they are really asking Jesus if he is the Messiah. Jesus answers them with the words of the prophet Isaiah, "The blind can see, the lame can walk" (Matthew 11:5). The people of Jesus' time knew that this prophecy from Isaiah described signs of the coming of the Messiah. So without actually saying so, Jesus is telling John's followers that he is indeed the Messiah.

— Matthew 11:1–6

of this day? They are like children sitting in the marketplace. One group shouts to the other, ¹⁷'We played wedding music for you, but you wouldn't dance! We sang funeral songs, but you wouldn't cry!' ¹⁸When John came, he fasted and drank no wine, and everyone said, 'He has a demon in him!' ¹⁹When the Son of Man came, he ate and drank, and everyone said, 'Look at this man! He is a glutton and wine drinker, a friend of tax collectors and other outcasts!' God's wisdom, however, is shown to be true by its results."

The Unbelieving Towns
(Luke 10:13–15)

²⁰The people in the towns where Jesus had performed most of his miracles did not turn from their sins, so he reproached those towns. ²¹"How terrible it will be for you, Chorazin! How terrible for you too, Bethsaida! If the miracles which were performed in you had been performed in Tyre and

ⁱ **11:5** MADE CLEAN: *See 8:2.* ʲ **11:12** has suffered violent attacks; *or* has been coming violently.
11:5 a Isa 35:5,6; b Isa 61:1   **11:10** Mal 3:1   **11:12,13** Lk 16:16   **11:14** Mal 4:5; Mt 17:10-13; Mk 9:11-13   **11:21** Isa 23:1-18; Ezek 26:1—28:26; Joel 3:4-8; Am 1:9,10; Zech 9:2-4

Matthew

Pray It!

Come to Me

At the end of this section, we hear these very comforting words from Jesus, "Come to me, all of you who are tired from carrying heavy loads, and I will give you rest" (Matthew 11:28). Jesus wasn't just talking about being physically tired but being spiritually tired. We can be spiritually tired from the burden of worrying about someone we love or the burden of the guilt of sin. So when you are feeling worn out by life, read these words of Jesus and say this prayer to yourself.

> *Jesus, help me to remember to come to you*
> *when I am feeling overwhelmed.*
> *You promise to take my heavy burdens,*
> *and replace them with things that are much easier to carry.*
> *When I am tired and sad, remind me to come to you,*
> *the One who loves me, and let me rest in you. Amen.*

— Matthew 11:25–30

Sidon, the people there would have long ago put on sackcloth and sprinkled ashes on themselves, to show that they had turned from their sins! 22I assure you that on the Judgment Day God will show more mercy to the people of Tyre and Sidon than to you! 23And as for you, Capernaum! Did you want to lift yourself up to heaven? You will be thrown down to hell! If the miracles which were performed in you had been performed in Sodom, it would still be in existence today! 24You can be sure that on the Judgment Day God will show more mercy to Sodom than to you!"

Come to Me and Rest
(Luke 10:21, 22)

25At that time Jesus said, "Father, Lord of heaven and earth! I thank you because you have shown to the unlearned what you have hidden from the wise and learned. 26Yes, Father, this was how you were pleased to have it happen.

27"My Father has given me all things. No one knows the Son except the Father, and no one knows the Father except the Son

and those to whom the Son chooses to reveal him.

28"Come to me, all of you who are tired from carrying heavy loads, and I will give you rest. 29Take my yoke and put it on you, and learn from me, because I am gentle and humble in spirit; and you will find rest. 30For the yoke I will give you is easy, and the load I will put on you is light."

Come to me, all of you who are tired. (11:28)

The Question about the Sabbath
(Mark 2:23–28; Luke 6:1–5)

12 1Not long afterward Jesus was walking through some wheat fields on a Sabbath. His disciples were hungry, so they began to pick heads of wheat and eat the grain. 2When the Pharisees saw this, they said to Jesus, "Look, it is against our Law for your disciples to do this on the Sabbath!"

11:23 a Isa 14:13-15; **b** Gen 19:24-28   **11:24** Mt 10:15; Lk 10:12   **11:27 a** Jn 3:35; **b** Jn 1:18; 10:15
11:28-30 Sir 6:24-30; 24:19; 51:23-26   **11:29** Jer 6:16   **12:1** Deut 23:25

[3]Jesus answered, "Have you never read what David did that time when he and his men were hungry? [4]He went into the house of God, and he and his men ate the bread offered to God, even though it was against the Law for them to eat it—only the priests were allowed to eat that bread. [5]Or have you not read in the Law of Moses that every Sabbath the priests in the Temple actually break the Sabbath law, yet they are not guilty? [6]I tell you that there is something here greater than the Temple. [7]The scripture says, 'It is kindness that I want, not animal sacrifices.' If you really knew what this means, you would not condemn people who are not guilty; [8]for the Son of Man is Lord of the Sabbath."

The Man with a Paralyzed Hand
(Mark 3:1–6; Luke 6:6–11)

[9]Jesus left that place and went to a synagogue, [10]where there was a man who had a paralyzed hand. Some people were there who wanted to accuse Jesus of doing wrong, so they asked him, "Is it against our Law to heal on the Sabbath?"

[11]Jesus answered, "What if one of you has a sheep and it falls into a deep hole on the Sabbath? Will you not take hold of it and lift it out? [12]And a human being is worth much more than a sheep! So then, our Law does allow us to help someone on the Sabbath."

[13]Then he said to the man with the paralyzed hand, "Stretch out your hand."

He stretched it out, and it became well again, just like the other one. [14]Then the Pharisees left and made plans to kill Jesus.

God's Chosen Servant

[15]When Jesus heard about the plot against him, he went away from that place; and large crowds followed him. He healed all the sick [16]and gave them orders not to tell others about him. [17]He did this so as to make come true what God had said through the prophet Isaiah:

[18]"Here is my servant, whom I have chosen, the one I love, and with whom I am pleased.

I will send my Spirit upon him,

The Letter of the Law

The Pharisees criticize Jesus first for allowing his disciples to pick grain on the Sabbath and then for healing a man on the Sabbath. Some religious leaders in Jesus' time saw these actions as violations of the Jewish Law. Jesus responds by reminding the Pharisees that mercy is more important than following their narrow understanding of the Law. We can be like that sometimes too, can't we? How might we respond more mercifully to the following people?

- The young mother who struggles to get to church with her baby and then gets dirty looks from the people around her because the baby makes noise
- The homeless man that we make fun of because he smells
- The people of a different religion whom we label weird because they express their faith in God differently than we do
- Any people we judge because we think we're better than them

Jesus teaches to not let anything get in the way of reaching out to another person.

— Matthew 12:1–8

Matthew

12:3,4 1 Sam 21:1-6   **12:4** Lev 24:9   **12:5** Num 28:9,10   **12:7 a** Mt 9:13; **b** Hos 6:6   **12:11** Lk 14:5
12:18-21 Isa 42:1-4 (LXX)

"Come to me, all of you who are tired from carrying heavy loads, and I will give you rest" *(Matthew 11:28)*.

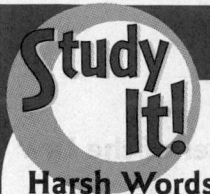

Harsh Words

In this section the conflict between Jesus and the religious leaders is steadily increasing. They accuse him of using the power of Beelzebul (another name for Satan) to drive out demons (Matthew 12:24). Jesus calls them snakes (12:34)! This isn't just name-calling though. The religious leaders challenge Jesus' authority and question his understanding of the Jewish Law. Jesus challenges them about whether their hearts are in the right place. Jesus says: "How can you say good things when you are evil? For the mouth speaks what the heart is full of" (12:34).

Jesus' harshest criticism is for people who say one thing and do another or for people who do the right actions but with evil things in their hearts. Jesus will continue to be in conflict with these people for the rest of his ministry, and this conflict will eventually lead to his death. We must all pray for God's help to see when our words, our actions, and our hearts are not acting as one.

— Matthew 12:22–37

and he will announce my judgment to
the nations.
19 He will not argue or shout,
or make loud speeches in the streets.
20 He will not break off a bent reed,
nor put out a flickering lamp.

He will persist until he causes justice to
triumph,
21 and on him all peoples will put their
hope."

Jesus and Beelzebul
(Mark 3:20–30; Luke 11:14–23)

22 Then some people brought to Jesus a man who was blind and could not talk because he had a demon. Jesus healed the man, so that he was able to talk and see. 23 The crowds were all amazed at what Jesus had done. "Could he be the Son of David?" they asked.

24 When the Pharisees heard this, they replied, "He drives out demons only because their ruler Beelzebul gives him power to do so."

25 Jesus knew what they were thinking, and so he said to them, "Any country that divides itself into groups which fight each other will not last very long. And any town or family that divides itself into groups which fight each other will fall apart. 26 So if one group is fighting another in Satan's kingdom, this means that it is already divided into groups and will soon fall apart! 27 You say that I drive out demons because Beelzebul gives me the power to do so. Well, then, who gives your followers the power to drive them out? What your own followers do proves that you are wrong! 28 No, it is not Beelzebul, but God's Spirit, who gives me the power to drive out demons, which proves that the Kingdom of God has already come upon you.

29 "No one can break into a strong man's house and take away his belongings unless he first ties up the strong man; then he can plunder his house.

30 "Anyone who is not for me is really against me; anyone who does not help me gather is really scattering. 31 For this reason I tell you: people can be forgiven any sin and any evil thing they say;*k* but whoever says evil things against the Holy Spirit will not

---

k **12:31** evil thing they say; *or* evil thing they say against God.
12:24 Mt 9:34; 10:25   **12:29** Tob 8:3   **12:30** Mk 9:40

Jesus talks about the miracle of Jonah (Matthew 12:39). **The book of the prophet Jonah is very short. Have you read it?**

be forgiven. [32]Anyone who says something against the Son of Man can be forgiven; but whoever says something against the Holy Spirit will not be forgiven—now or ever.

A Tree and Its Fruit
(Luke 6:43–45)

[33]"To have good fruit you must have a healthy tree; if you have a poor tree, you will have bad fruit. A tree is known by the kind of fruit it bears. [34]You snakes—how can you say good things when you are evil? For the mouth speaks what the heart is full of. [35]A good person brings good things out of a treasure of good things; a bad person brings bad things out of a treasure of bad things.

[36]"You can be sure that on the Judgment Day you will have to give account of every useless word you have ever spoken. [37]Your words will be used to judge you—to declare you either innocent or guilty."

The Demand for a Miracle
(Mark 8:11, 12; Luke 11:29–32)

[38]Then some teachers of the Law and some Pharisees spoke up. "Teacher," they said, "we want to see you perform a miracle."

[39]"How evil and godless are the people of this day!" Jesus exclaimed. "You ask me for a miracle? No! The only miracle you will be given is the miracle of the prophet Jonah. [40]In the same way that Jonah spent three days and nights in the big fish, so will the Son of Man spend three days and nights in the depths of the earth. [41]On the Judgment Day the people of Nineveh will stand up and accuse you, because they turned from their sins when they heard Jonah preach; and I tell you that there is something here greater than Jonah! [42]On the Judgment Day the Queen of Sheba will stand up and accuse you, because she traveled all the way from her country to listen to King Solomon's wise teaching; and I assure you that there is something here greater than Solomon!

The Return of the Evil Spirit
(Luke 11:24–26)

[43]"When an evil spirit goes out of a person, it travels over dry country looking for a place to rest. If it can't find one, [44]it says to itself, 'I will go back to my house.' So it goes back and finds the house empty, clean, and all fixed up. [45]Then it goes out and brings along seven other spirits even worse than itself, and they come and live there. So when it is all over, that person is in worse shape than at the beginning. This is what will happen to the evil people of this day."

Jesus' Mother and Brothers
(Mark 3:31–35; Luke 8:19–21)

[46]Jesus was still talking to the people when his mother and brothers arrived. They stood outside, asking to speak with him. [47]So one of the people there said to him, "Look, your mother and brothers are standing outside, and they want to speak with you."[l]

[48]Jesus answered, "Who is my mother? Who are my brothers?" [49]Then he pointed to his disciples and said, "Look! Here are my mother and my brothers! [50]Whoever does what my Father in heaven wants is my brother, my sister, and my mother."

The Parable of the Sower
(Mark 4:1–9; Luke 8:4–8)

13 [1]That same day Jesus left the house and went to the lakeside, where he sat down to teach. [2]The crowd that gathered around him was so large that he got into a boat and sat in it, while the crowd stood on the shore. [3]He used parables to tell them many things.

"Once there was a man who went out to sow grain. [4]As he scattered the seed in the field, some of it fell along the path, and the birds came and ate it up. [5]Some of it fell on rocky ground, where there was little soil. The seeds soon sprouted, because the soil wasn't deep. [6]But when the sun came up, it burned

---

[l] **12:47** *Some manuscripts do not have verse 47.*
12:32 Lk 12:10   **12:33** Sir 27:6; Mt 7:20; Lk 6:44   **12:34 a** Mt 3:7; 23:33; Lk 3:7; **b** Mt 15:18; Lk 6:45
12:38 Mt 16:1; Mk 8:11; Lk 11:16   **12:39** Mt 16:4; Mk 8:12   **12:40** Jon 1:17   **12:41** Jon 3:5
12:42 1 Kings 10:1-10; 2 Chr 9:1-12   **13:2** Lk 5:1-3

Pray It!

Are You Good Soil?

The parable of the sower that begins Matthew, chapter 13, is about receiving the Word of God and letting it take root in our lives. Even if we hear the good news of God's love, there is so much that can distract us from living the way God wants us to. When we experience disappointment or when we focus on material things, these "rocks and weeds" of the world can choke out the Word of God in us. Spend some quiet time reflecting on or even journaling about the following questions:

- Do you feel like you understand the Word of God? What can you do to learn more?
- What are the worries and distractions that pull you away from living the life God wants for you? Is there anything you can do to get rid of these things?
- What do you need so that you can be "good soil"? Do you need to visit with a mentor or to set aside time for Bible study or to share your faith with other people? Maybe you need a ride to church or to be less busy with activities? How can you make those things happen?

— Matthew 13:1–23

the plants bore grain: some had one hundred grains, others sixty, and others thirty."

9 And Jesus concluded, "Listen, then, if you have ears!"

The Purpose of the Parables
(Mark 4:10–12; Luke 8:9, 10)

10 Then the disciples came to Jesus and asked him, "Why do you use parables when you talk to the people?"

11 Jesus answered, "The knowledge about the secrets of the Kingdom of heaven has been given to you, but not to them. 12 For the person who has something will be given more, so that he will have more than enough; but the person who has nothing will have taken away from him even the little he has. 13 The reason I use parables in talking to them is that they look, but do not see, and they listen, but do not hear or understand. 14 So the prophecy of Isaiah applies to them:

'This people will listen and listen, but not
    understand;
  they will look and look, but not see,
15 because their minds are dull,
    and they have stopped up their ears
    and have closed their eyes.
Otherwise, their eyes would see,
    their ears would hear,
    their minds would understand,
and they would turn to me, says God,
    and I would heal them.'

16 "As for you, how fortunate you are! Your eyes see and your ears hear. 17 I assure you that many prophets and many of God's people wanted very much to see what you see, but they could not, and to hear what you hear, but they did not.

Jesus Explains the Parable of the Sower
(Mark 4:13–20; Luke 8:11–15)

18 "Listen, then, and learn what the parable of the sower means. 19 Those who hear the message about the Kingdom but do not understand it are like the seeds that fell along the path. The Evil One comes and snatches

the young plants; and because the roots had not grown deep enough, the plants soon dried up. 7 Some of the seed fell among thorn bushes, which grew up and choked the plants. 8 But some seeds fell in good soil, and

13:12 Mt 25:29; Mk 4:25; Lk 8:18; 19:26   **13:14,15** Isa 6:9,10 (LXX)   **13:16,17** Lk 10:23,24

away what was sown in them. 20 The seeds that fell on rocky ground stand for those who receive the message gladly as soon as they hear it. 21 But it does not sink deep into them, and they don't last long. So when trouble or persecution comes because of the message, they give up at once. 22 The seeds that fell among thorn bushes stand for those who hear the message; but the worries about this life and the love for riches choke the message, and they don't bear fruit. 23 And the seeds sown in the good soil stand for those who hear the message and understand it: they bear fruit, some as much as one hundred, others sixty, and others thirty."

The Parable of the Weeds

24 Jesus told them another parable: "The Kingdom of heaven is like this. A man sowed good seed in his field. 25 One night, when everyone was asleep, an enemy came and sowed weeds among the wheat and went away. 26 When the plants grew and the heads of grain began to form, then the weeds showed up. 27 The man's servants came to him and said, 'Sir, it was good seed you sowed in your field; where did the weeds come from?' 28 'It was some enemy who did this,' he answered. 'Do you want us to go and pull up the weeds?' they asked him. 29 'No,' he answered, 'because as you gather the weeds you might pull up some of the wheat along with them. 30 Let the wheat and the weeds both grow together until harvest. Then I will tell the harvest workers to pull up the weeds first, tie them in bundles and burn them, and then to gather in the wheat and put it in my barn.' "

The Parable of the Mustard Seed
(Mark 4:30–32; Luke 13:18, 19)

31 Jesus told them another parable: "The Kingdom of heaven is like this. A man takes a mustard seed and sows it in his field. 32 It is the smallest of all seeds, but when it grows

up, it is the biggest of all plants. It becomes a tree, so that birds come and make their nests in its branches."

Pray It!

The God Box

On a retreat, the leaders brought a box filled with all sorts of strange things: marbles, rubber bands, a stick of gum, a toy car, a Super Ball, a red crayon, a smiley face sticker. They called it the God Box. Throughout the retreat, people could pick an item from the box and explain to the rest of the retreatants how God is like that object: "God is like this eraser, erasing all your mistakes." "God is like this glue stick, holding things together." "God is like this pair of glasses, helping us see things clearly."

In this chapter Jesus uses parables to explain the Kingdom of heaven (God). Parables are stories that use objects and activities from people's everyday lives. You can create modern parables by making your own God Box. Decorate the outside of a shoebox and fill it with small, simple objects—a coin, a pebble, a birthday candle. Keep it on your dresser or beside your bed. When you wake up in the morning or before you go to sleep at night, take an object out and think about how it is like God. You might even want to write down your ideas and keep a list inside the box!

— Matthew, chapter 13

Matthew

Parables are stories that use objects and experiences that people are familiar with to explain important ideas about God.

The Parable of the Yeast
(Luke 13:20, 21)

33Jesus told them still another parable:
"The Kingdom of heaven is like this. A
woman takes some yeast and mixes it with a
bushel of flour until the whole batch of
dough rises."

Jesus' Use of Parables
(Mark 4:33, 34)

34Jesus used parables to tell all these things
to the crowds; he would not say a thing to
them without using a parable. 35He did this
to make come true what the prophet had
said,

"I will use parables when I speak to them;
I will tell them things unknown since
the creation of the world."

Jesus Explains the Parable
of the Weeds

36When Jesus had left the crowd and gone
indoors, his disciples came to him and said,
"Tell us what the parable about the weeds in
the field means."
37Jesus answered, "The man who sowed
the good seed is the Son of Man; 38the field
is the world; the good seed is the people
who belong to the Kingdom; the weeds are
the people who belong to the Evil One;
39and the enemy who sowed the weeds is
the Devil. The harvest is the end of the age,
and the harvest workers are angels. 40Just as
the weeds are gathered up and burned in the
fire, so the same thing will happen at the end
of the age: 41the Son of Man will send out
his angels to gather up out of his Kingdom
all those who cause people to sin and all
others who do evil things, 42and they will
throw them into the fiery furnace, where
they will cry and gnash their teeth. 43Then
God's people will shine like the sun in their
Father's Kingdom. Listen, then, if you have
ears!

The Parable of the Hidden Treasure

44"The Kingdom of heaven is like this. A
man happens to find a treasure hidden in a
field. He covers it up again, and is so happy
that he goes and sells everything he has, and
then goes back and buys that field.

The Parable of the Pearl

45"Also, the Kingdom of heaven is like
this. A man is looking for fine pearls, 46and
when he finds one that is unusually fine, he
goes and sells everything he has, and buys
that pearl.

The Parable of the Net

47"Also, the Kingdom of heaven is like
this. Some fishermen throw their net out in
the lake and catch all kinds of fish. 48When
the net is full, they pull it to shore and sit
down to divide the fish: the good ones go
into the buckets, the worthless ones are
thrown away. 49It will be like this at the end
of the age: the angels will go out and gather
up the evil people from among the good
50and will throw them into the fiery furnace,
where they will cry and gnash their teeth.

New Truths and Old

51"Do you understand these things?" Jesus
asked them.
"Yes," they answered.
52So he replied, "This means, then, that
every teacher of the Law who becomes a
disciple in the Kingdom of heaven is like a
homeowner who takes new and old things
out of his storage room."

Jesus Is Rejected at Nazareth
(Mark 6:1–6; Luke 4:16–30)

53When Jesus finished telling these parables, he left that place 54and went back to his
hometown. He taught in the synagogue, and

13:35 Ps 78:2

those who heard him were amazed. "Where did he get such wisdom?" they asked. "And what about his miracles? 55 Isn't he the carpenter's son? Isn't Mary his mother, and aren't James, Joseph, Simon, and Judas his brothers? 56 Aren't all his sisters living here? Where did he get all this?" 57 And so they rejected him.

Jesus said to them, "A prophet is respected everywhere except in his hometown and by his own family." 58 Because they did not have faith, he did not perform many miracles there.

The Death of John the Baptist
(Mark 6:14–29; Luke 9:7–9)

14 ¹At that time Herod, the ruler of Galilee, heard about Jesus. 2 "He is really John the Baptist, who has come back to life," he told his officials. "That is why he has this power to perform miracles."

³ For Herod had earlier ordered John's arrest, and he had him tied up and put in prison. He had done this because of Herodias, his brother Philip's wife. 4 For some time John the Baptist had told Herod, "It isn't right for you to be married to Herodias!" 5 Herod wanted to kill him, but he was afraid of the Jewish people, because they considered John to be a prophet.

⁶ On Herod's birthday the daughter of Herodias danced in front of the whole group. Herod was so pleased 7 that he promised her, "I swear that I will give you anything you ask for!"

⁸ At her mother's suggestion she asked him, "Give me here and now the head of John the Baptist on a plate!"

⁹ The king was sad, but because of the promise he had made in front of all his guests he gave orders that her wish be granted. 10 So he had John beheaded in prison. 11 The head was brought in on a plate and given to the girl, who took it to her mother. 12 John's disciples came, carried away his body, and buried it; then they went and told Jesus.

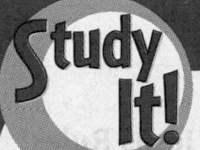

Study It!

Foreshadowing

The story of John the Baptist's death in the middle of Matthew's Gospel, gives us a preview of what will happen at the end of the Gospel. Consider the many parallels between the way John dies and what lies ahead for Jesus himself: John is arrested and treated as a criminal even though he has done nothing wrong (Matthew 14:3), just as Jesus will be. Herod gives in to pressure from others demanding John's death, just as Pilate will give in to the pressure from people who want Jesus sentenced to death. The word *foreshadow* is sometimes used to describe prophecies or events in the Bible that remind us of future events that occur in the life of Jesus.

— Matthew 14:1–12

Jesus Feeds Five Thousand
(Mark 6:30–44; Luke 9:10–17; John 6:1–14)

¹³ When Jesus heard the news about John, he left there in a boat and went to a lonely place by himself. The people heard about it, and so they left their towns and followed him by land. 14 Jesus got out of the boat, and when he saw the large crowd, his heart was filled with pity for them, and he healed their sick.

¹⁵ That evening his disciples came to him and said, "It is already very late, and this is a lonely place. Send the people away and let them go to the villages to buy food for themselves."

¹⁶ "They don't have to leave," answered Jesus. "You yourselves give them something to eat!"

¹⁷ "All we have here are five loaves and two fish," they replied.

13:57 Jn 4:44   **14:3,4** Lk 3:19,20   **14:4** Lev 18:16; 20:21

Jesus Rules!

In the middle of the night, the wind was rising, and the waves tossed the boat. Jesus, who rules over fear, who rules over wind and waves, and who rules over chaos walks across the lake. When Peter decides to follow Jesus, his faith isn't quite strong enough. This story tells us these important lessons:

- **Jesus shares in the power of God.**
- **Jesus may challenge us, but he will also rescue us.**
- **Jesus rules!**

The next time you experience a storm in your life—like an argument with your parents or a disagreement with your friends—remember that Jesus is there with you!

— Matthew 14:22–33

18"Then bring them here to me," Jesus said. 19He ordered the people to sit down on the grass; then he took the five loaves and the two fish, looked up to heaven, and gave thanks to God. He broke the loaves and gave them to the disciples, and the disciples gave them to the people. 20Everyone ate and had enough. Then the disciples took up twelve baskets full of what was left over. 21The number of men who ate was about five thousand, not counting the women and children.

Jesus Walks on the Water
(Mark 6:45–52; John 6:15–21)

22Then Jesus made the disciples get into the boat and go on ahead to the other side of the lake, while he sent the people away. 23After sending the people away, he went up a hill by himself to pray. When evening came, Jesus was there alone; 24and by this time the boat was far out in the lake, tossed about by the waves, because the wind was blowing against it.

25Between three and six o'clock in the morning Jesus came to the disciples, walking on the water. 26When they saw him walking on the water, they were terrified. "It's a ghost!" they said, and screamed with fear. 27Jesus spoke to them at once. "Courage!" he said. "It is I. Don't be afraid!"

28Then Peter spoke up. "Lord, if it is really you, order me to come out on the water to you."

29"Come!" answered Jesus. So Peter got out of the boat and started walking on the water to Jesus. 30But when he noticed the strong wind, he was afraid and started to sink down in the water. "Save me, Lord!" he cried.

31At once Jesus reached out and grabbed hold of him and said, "What little faith you have! Why did you doubt?"

32They both got into the boat, and the wind died down. 33Then the disciples in the boat worshiped Jesus. "Truly you are the Son of God!" they exclaimed.

Jesus Heals the Sick in Gennesaret
(Mark 6:53–56)

34They crossed the lake and came to land at Gennesaret, 35where the people recognized Jesus. So they sent for the sick people in all the surrounding country and brought them to Jesus. 36They begged him to let the sick at least touch the edge of his cloak; and all who touched it were made well.

The Teaching of the Ancestors
(Mark 7:1–13)

15 1Then some Pharisees and teachers of the Law came from Jerusalem to Jesus and asked him, 2"Why is it that your disciples disobey the teaching handed down by our ancestors? They don't wash their hands in the proper way before they eat!"

3Jesus answered, "And why do you disobey God's command and follow your own teaching? 4For God said, 'Respect your father and your mother,' and 'If you curse your father or your mother, you are to be put to death.' 5But you teach that if people have something they could use to help their father or mother, but say, 'This belongs to God,' 6they do not need to honor their father.*m* In this way you disregard God's command, in order to follow your own teaching. 7You hypocrites! How right Isaiah was when he prophesied about you!

8 'These people, says God, honor me with
      their words,
    but their heart is really far away from
      me.
9 It is no use for them to worship me,
    because they teach human rules as
      though they were my laws!' "

The Things That Make a Person Unclean
(Mark 7:14–23)

10Then Jesus called the crowd to him and said to them, "Listen and understand! 11It is not what goes into your mouth that makes you ritually unclean; rather, what comes out of it makes you unclean."

12Then the disciples came to him and said, "Do you know that the Pharisees had their feelings hurt by what you said?"

They are blind leaders of the blind. (15:14)

13"Every plant which my Father in heaven did not plant will be pulled up," answered Jesus. 14"Don't worry about them! They are blind leaders of the blind; and when one blind man leads another, both fall into a ditch."

15Peter spoke up, "Explain this saying to us."

16Jesus said to them, "You are still no more intelligent than the others. 17Don't you understand? Anything that goes into your mouth goes into your stomach and then on out of your body. 18But the things that come out of the mouth come from the heart, and these are the things that make you ritually unclean. 19For from your heart come the evil ideas which lead you to kill, commit adultery, and do other immoral things; to rob, lie, and slander others. 20These are the things that make you unclean. But to eat without washing your hands as they say you should—this doesn't make you unclean."

A Woman's Faith
(Mark 7:24–30)

21Jesus left that place and went off to the territory near the cities of Tyre and Sidon. 22A Canaanite woman who lived in that region came to him. "Son of David!" she cried out. "Have mercy on me, sir! My daughter has a demon and is in a terrible condition."

23But Jesus did not say a word to her. His disciples came to him and begged him, "Send her away! She is following us and making all this noise!"

24Then Jesus replied, "I have been sent only to the lost sheep of the people of Israel."

25At this the woman came and fell at his feet. "Help me, sir!" she said.

26Jesus answered, "It isn't right to take the children's food and throw it to the dogs."

27"That's true, sir," she answered, "but even the dogs eat the leftovers that fall from their masters' table."

28So Jesus answered her, "You are a woman of great faith! What you want will

m **15:6** their father; *some manuscripts have* their father or mother.
15:4 a Ex 20:12; Deut 5:16; **b** Ex 21:17; Lev 20:9   **15:8,9** Isa 29:13 (LXX)   **15:14** Lk 6:39   **15:18** Mt 12:34

Water represents chaos. When Jesus walks on the water, it is a sign that he is divine because he rules over the chaos. Read Psalm 65:7.

Matthew

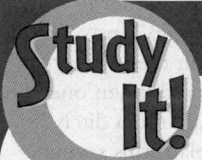

Feeding the Crowds

At the end of chapter 15, we have a second story about Jesus feeding a large crowd (the first story was in chapter 14). These miracle stories link Jesus with the past and the future. The way the story is told would remind the audience of two important people from the Old Testament: Elisha, and Moses. Elisha fed the people with almost nothing (2 Kings 4:42–44), and so does Jesus. Everyone eats, and there is food left.

We can find a similar story in Exodus, chapter 16. After crossing the Red Sea, God feeds the Israelites with manna—which is like bread—in the wilderness. In Matthew, chapter 14, Jesus crosses Lake Galilee and feeds the people with bread in a deserted place. These stories also foreshadow (see earlier article) the story of the Last Supper and hint at the heavenly banquet at the end of time.

— Matthew 15:32–39

be done for you." And at that very moment her daughter was healed.

Jesus Heals Many People

29 Jesus left there and went along by Lake Galilee. He climbed a hill and sat down. 30 Large crowds came to him, bringing with them the lame, the blind, the crippled, the dumb, and many other sick people, whom they placed at Jesus' feet; and he healed them. 31 The people were amazed as they saw the dumb speaking, the crippled made whole, the lame walking, and the blind seeing; and they praised the God of Israel.

Jesus Feeds Four Thousand
(Mark 8:1–10)

32 Jesus called his disciples to him and said, "I feel sorry for these people, because they have been with me for three days and now have nothing to eat. I don't want to send them away without feeding them, for they might faint on their way home."

33 The disciples asked him, "Where will we find enough food in this desert to feed this crowd?"

34 "How much bread do you have?" Jesus asked.

"Seven loaves," they answered, "and a few small fish."

35 So Jesus ordered the crowd to sit down on the ground. 36 Then he took the seven loaves and the fish, gave thanks to God, broke them, and gave them to the disciples; and the disciples gave them to the people. 37 They all ate and had enough. Then the disciples took up seven baskets full of pieces left over. 38 The number of men who ate was four thousand, not counting the women and children.

39 Then Jesus sent the people away, got into a boat, and went to the territory of Magadan.

The Demand for a Miracle
(Mark 8:11–13; Luke 12:54–56)

16 1 Some Pharisees and Sadducees who came to Jesus wanted to trap him, so they asked him to perform a miracle for them, to show that God approved of him. 2 But Jesus answered, "When the sun is setting, you say, 'We are going to have fine weather, because the sky is red.' 3 And early in the morning you say, 'It is going to rain,

16:1 Mt 12:38; Lk 11:16

Peter the Rock

Catholic Connections

Once again we read how the religious leaders do not believe in Jesus. In contrast, Peter says confidently, "You are the Messiah, the Son of the living God" (Matthew 16:16). Jesus affirms Peter's faith by telling Peter that he will have a special role in history. Peter's leadership will be the foundation of the Church. He will become the first pope.

This Scripture passage explains why Peter and all the popes that followed him are the spiritual leaders and highest authority of the Church. Jesus gave Peter a special role as leader of the Apostles. That special role did not end with Peter but is passed on to every pope who followed Peter since the start of the Church.

— Matthew 16:13–20

Matthew

because the sky is red and dark.' You can predict the weather by looking at the sky, but you cannot interpret the signs concerning these times!ⁿ [n] 4How evil and godless are the people of this day! You ask me for a miracle? No! The only miracle you will be given is the miracle of Jonah."

So he left them and went away.

The Yeast of the Pharisees and Sadducees
(Mark 8:14–21)

5When the disciples crossed over to the other side of the lake, they forgot to take any bread. 6Jesus said to them, "Take care; be on your guard against the yeast of the Pharisees and Sadducees."

7They started discussing among themselves, "He says this because we didn't bring any bread."

8Jesus knew what they were saying, so he asked them, "Why are you discussing among yourselves about not having any bread? What little faith you have! 9Don't you understand yet? Don't you remember when I broke the five loaves for the five thousand men? How many baskets did you fill? 10And what about the seven loaves for the four thousand men? How many baskets did you fill? 11How is it

that you don't understand that I was not talking to you about bread? Guard yourselves from the yeast of the Pharisees and Sadducees!"

12Then the disciples understood that he was not warning them to guard themselves from the yeast used in bread but from the teaching of the Pharisees and Sadducees.

Peter's Declaration about Jesus
(Mark 8:27–30; Luke 9:18–21)

13Jesus went to the territory near the town of Caesarea Philippi, where he asked his disciples, "Who do people say the Son of Man is?"

14"Some say John the Baptist," they answered. "Others say Elijah, while others say Jeremiah or some other prophet."

15"What about you?" he asked them. "Who do you say I am?"

16Simon Peter answered, "You are the Messiah, the Son of the living God."

17"Good for you, Simon son of John!" answered Jesus. "For this truth did not come to you from any human being, but it was given to you directly by my Father in heaven. 18And so I tell you, Peter: you are a rock, and on this rock foundation I will build my church, and not even death will ever be able to overcome it. 19I will give you the keys of

ⁿ **16:3** *Some manuscripts do not have the words of Jesus in verses 2-3.*
16:4 Mt 12:39; Lk 11:29 **16:6** Lk 12:1 **16:9** Mt 14:17-21 **16:10** Mt 15:34-38 **16:14** Mt 14:1,2; Mk 6:14,15; Lk 9:7,8 **16:16** Jn 6:68,69 **16:19** Mt 18:18; Jn 20:23

Matthew

Pray It!

A Glimpse of Glory

"Jesus . . . led them up a high mountain where they were alone. As they looked on, a change came over Jesus: his face was shining like the sun, and his clothes were dazzling white" (Matthew 17:1–2).

> Lord Jesus,
> I need you to lead me up the mountain
>   because it is so easy for me to get discouraged.
> Let me see your shining presence
>   because it is so easy for me to get distracted.
> Help me focus on what your love requires of me
>   because it is so easy to want to keep things easy.
> Lead me back down the mountain to everyday life
>   with you by my side
>   and help me do what God asks me to do in the world. Amen.

— Matthew 17:1–13

the Kingdom of heaven; what you prohibit on earth will be prohibited in heaven, and what you permit on earth will be permitted in heaven."

20 Then Jesus ordered his disciples not to tell anyone that he was the Messiah.

Jesus Speaks about His Suffering and Death
(Mark 8:31—9:1; Luke 9:22–27)

21 From that time on Jesus began to say plainly to his disciples, "I must go to Jerusalem and suffer much from the elders, the chief priests, and the teachers of the Law. I will be put to death, but three days later I will be raised to life."

22 Peter took him aside and began to rebuke him. "God forbid it, Lord!" he said. "That must never happen to you!"

23 Jesus turned around and said to Peter, "Get away from me, Satan! You are an obstacle in my way, because these thoughts of yours don't come from God, but from human nature."

24 Then Jesus said to his disciples, "If any of you want to come with me, you must forget yourself, carry your cross, and follow me. 25 For if you want to save your own life, you will lose it; but if you lose your life for my sake, you will find it. 26 Will you gain anything if you win the whole world but lose your life? Of course not! There is nothing you can give to regain your life. 27 For the Son of Man is about to come in the glory of his Father with his angels, and then he will reward each one according to his deeds. 28 I assure you that there are some here who will not die until they have seen the Son of Man come as King."

The Transfiguration
(Mark 9:2–13; Luke 9:28–36)

17 ¹Six days later Jesus took with him Peter and the brothers James and John and led them up a high mountain where they were alone. ²As they looked on, a change came over Jesus: his face was shining like the sun, and his clothes were dazzling white. ³Then the three disciples saw Moses and Elijah talking with Jesus. ⁴So

16:24 Mt 10:38; Lk 14:27   **16:25** Mt 10:39; Lk 17:33; Jn 12:25   **16:27 a** Mt 25:31; **b** Ps 62:12; Rom 2:6

Peter spoke up and said to Jesus, "Lord, how good it is that we are here! If you wish, I will make three tents here, one for you, one for Moses, and one for Elijah."

5 While he was talking, a shining cloud came over them, and a voice from the cloud said, "This is my own dear Son, with whom I am pleased—listen to him!"

6 When the disciples heard the voice, they were so terrified that they threw themselves face downward on the ground. **7** Jesus came to them and touched them. "Get up," he said. "Don't be afraid!" **8** So they looked up and saw no one there but Jesus.

9 As they came down the mountain, Jesus ordered them, "Don't tell anyone about this vision you have seen until the Son of Man has been raised from death."

10 Then the disciples asked Jesus, "Why do the teachers of the Law say that Elijah has to come first?"

11 "Elijah is indeed coming first," answered Jesus, "and he will get everything ready. **12** But I tell you that Elijah has already come and people did not recognize him, but treated him just as they pleased. In the same way they will also mistreat the Son of Man."

13 Then the disciples understood that he was talking to them about John the Baptist.

Jesus Heals a Boy with a Demon
(Mark 9:14–29; Luke 9:37–43a)

14 When they returned to the crowd, a man came to Jesus, knelt before him, **15** and said, "Sir, have mercy on my son! He is an epileptic and has such terrible attacks that he often falls in the fire or into water. **16** I brought him to your disciples, but they could not heal him."

17 Jesus answered, "How unbelieving and wrong you people are! How long must I stay with you? How long do I have to put up with you? Bring the boy here to me!"

18 Jesus gave a command to the demon, and it went out of the boy, and at that very moment he was healed.

19 Then the disciples came to Jesus in private and asked him, "Why couldn't we drive the demon out?"

20 "It was because you do not have enough faith," answered Jesus. "I assure you that if you have faith as big as a mustard seed, you can say to this hill, 'Go from here to there!' and it will go. You could do anything!" *o*

Jesus Speaks Again about His Death
(Mark 9:30–32; Luke 9:43b–45)

22 When the disciples all came together in Galilee, Jesus said to them, "The Son of Man is about to be handed over to those **23** who will kill him; but three days later he will be raised to life."

The disciples became very sad.

Payment of the Temple Tax

24 When Jesus and his disciples came to Capernaum, the collectors of the Temple tax came to Peter and asked, "Does your teacher pay the Temple tax?"

25 "Of course," Peter answered.

When Peter went into the house, Jesus spoke up first, "Simon, what is your opinion? Who pays duties or taxes to the kings of this world? The citizens of the country or the foreigners?"

26 "The foreigners," answered Peter.

"Well, then," replied Jesus, "that means that the citizens don't have to pay. **27** But we don't want to offend these people. So go to the lake and drop in a line. Pull up the first fish you hook, and in its mouth you will find a coin worth enough for my Temple tax and yours. Take it and pay them our taxes."

o **17:20** *Some manuscripts add verse 21:* But only prayer and fasting can drive this kind out; nothing else can *(see Mk 9:29).*

17:5 a Gen 22:2; Ps 2:7; Isa 42:1; Mt 3:17; 12:18; Mk 1:11; Lk 3:22; **b** Deut 18:15   **17:1-5** 2 Pet 1:17,18   **17:10** Mal 4:5   **17:11** Sir 48:10   **17:12** Mt 11:14   **17:20** Mt 21:21; Mk 11:23; 1 Cor 13:2   **17:24** Ex 30:13; 38:26

What do Moses and Elijah have in common? Unscramble the letters "sperothp" to find a word that completes this sentence: "They are both _____."

Who Is the Greatest?
(Mark 9:33–37; Luke 9:46–48)

18 ¹At that time the disciples came to Jesus, asking, "Who is the greatest in the Kingdom of heaven?"

²So Jesus called a child to come and stand in front of them, ³and said, "I assure you that unless you change and become like children, you will never enter the Kingdom of heaven. ⁴The greatest in the Kingdom of heaven is the one who humbles himself and becomes like this child. ⁵And whoever welcomes in my name one such child as this, welcomes me.

"Unless you change and become like children . . ."
(18:3)

Temptations to Sin
(Mark 9:42–48; Luke 17:1, 2)

⁶"If anyone should cause one of these little ones to lose his faith in me, it would be better for that person to have a large millstone tied around his neck and be drowned in the deep sea. ⁷How terrible for the world that there are things that make people lose their faith! Such things will always happen—but how terrible for the one who causes them!

⁸"If your hand or your foot makes you lose your faith, cut it off and throw it away! It is better for you to enter life without a hand or a foot than to keep both hands and both feet and be thrown into the eternal fire. ⁹And if your eye makes you lose your faith, take it

When You Are Lost

Isn't it great to know that we have a God who will search for us? The parable of the lost sheep (Matthew 18:10–14) reminds us that God seeks us out even when we have wandered off. When we sin, Jesus the good shepherd comes to find us. We just have to open our hearts and let him in.

This story has a second message: Christians have a responsibility to other people. We should live our lives so that we do not lead others astray. And when a friend, family member, or even a stranger has lost his or her way, it is our responsibility to go and bring them back to God if we can.

— Matthew 18:10–14

out and throw it away! It is better for you to enter life with only one eye than to keep both eyes and be thrown into the fire of hell.

The Parable of the Lost Sheep
(Luke 15:3–7)

¹⁰"See that you don't despise any of these little ones. Their angels in heaven, I tell you, are always in the presence of my Father in heaven.ᵖ

¹²"What do you think a man does who has one hundred sheep and one of them gets lost? He will leave the other ninety-nine grazing on the hillside and go and look for the lost sheep. ¹³When he finds it, I tell you, he feels far happier over this one sheep than over the ninety-nine that did not get lost. ¹⁴In just the

ᵖ **18:10** *Some manuscripts add verse 11: For the Son of Man came to save the lost (see Lk 19:10).*
18:1 Lk 22:24   **18:3** Mk 10:15; Lk 18:17   **18:8** Mt 5:30   **18:9** Mt 5:29   **18:10** Tob 12:15   **18:11** Lk 19:10

Matthew 18:15–17 gives great advice for solving a problem. Would it work for you?

He will go . . . and look for the lost sheep. (18:12)

same way your*q* Father in heaven does not want any of these little ones to be lost.

When Someone Sins

15 "If your brother sins against you,*r* go to him and show him his fault. But do it privately, just between yourselves. If he listens to you, you have won your brother back. 16 But if he will not listen to you, take one or two other persons with you, so that 'every accusation may be upheld by the testimony of two or more witnesses,' as the scripture says. 17 And if he will not listen to them, then tell the whole thing to the church. Finally, if he will not listen to the church, treat him as though he were a pagan or a tax collector.

Prohibiting and Permitting

18 "And so I tell all of you: what you prohibit on earth will be prohibited in heaven, and what you permit on earth will be permitted in heaven.

19 "And I tell you more: whenever two of you on earth agree about anything you pray for, it will be done for you by my Father in heaven. 20 For where two or three come together in my name, I am there with them."

The Parable of the Unforgiving Servant

21 Then Peter came to Jesus and asked, "Lord, if my brother keeps on sinning

Forgive, Forgive, Then Forgive Again!

In response to Peter's question, "How many times do I have to forgive?" (Matthew 18:21), Jesus tells the parable of the unforgiving servant. This story is a way of saying "You're asking the wrong question Peter!" It's not about how many times you have to forgive someone. It's about being a person of forgiveness, having an attitude of mercy. Is it hard to forgive other people? How can you become a more forgiving person? Remember God's love and mercy for you. Then the next time someone needs your forgiveness, it might not be so hard to forgive that person.

— Matthew 18:21–35

against me, how many times do I have to forgive him? Seven times?"

22 "No, not seven times," answered Jesus, "but seventy times seven,*s* 23 because the Kingdom of heaven is like this. Once there was a king who decided to check on his servants' accounts. 24 He had just begun to do so when one of them was brought in who owed him millions of dollars. 25 The servant did not have enough to pay his debt, so the king ordered him to be sold as a slave, with his wife and his children and all that he had, in order to pay the debt. 26 The servant fell on his knees before the king. 'Be patient with me,' he begged, 'and I will pay you everything!' 27 The king felt sorry for him, so he forgave him the debt and let him go.

28 "Then the man went out and met one of his fellow servants who owed him a few dollars. He grabbed him and started choking

---

q **18:14** your; *some manuscripts have* my.   *r* **18:15** *Some manuscripts do not have* against you.   *s* **18:22** seventy times seven; *or* seventy-seven times.
18:15 Lk 17:3   **18:16** Deut 19:15   **18:18** Mt 16:19; Jn 20:23   **18:21,22** Lk 17:3,4   **18:22** Gen 4:24

Truly Free

As you read this chapter, you might find that the way Jesus describes the Kingdom of heaven can seem confusing! Do not marry for the sake of the Kingdom . . . be like a child . . . sell everything you have and follow me . . . the last shall be first. In our culture these ideas can seem crazy! We like power and prestige; a little child does not have these. We like to own things; giving away our money seems so strange! We like being in first place over almost anything else; choosing to be last is just weird.

Jesus' ideas can seem to make no sense at all—unless you are willing to put your full trust in Jesus, unless you are willing to listen to our saints. Their lives show us that if we can let go of our attachments to things, power, money, and position, then we will be truly free, and we will experience the Kingdom of heaven right now!

— Matthew, chapter 19

him. 'Pay back what you owe me!' he said. ²⁹His fellow servant fell down and begged him, 'Be patient with me, and I will pay you back!' ³⁰But he refused; instead, he had him thrown into jail until he should pay the debt. ³¹When the other servants saw what had happened, they were very upset and went to the king and told him everything. ³²So he called the servant in. 'You worthless slave!' he said. 'I forgave you the whole amount you owed me, just because you asked me to. ³³You should have had mercy on your fellow servant, just as I had mercy on you.' ³⁴The king was very angry, and he

sent the servant to jail to be punished until he should pay back the whole amount."

³⁵And Jesus concluded, "That is how my Father in heaven will treat every one of you unless you forgive your brother from your heart."

Jesus Teaches about Divorce
(Mark 10:1–12)

19 ¹When Jesus finished saying these things, he left Galilee and went to the territory of Judea on the other side of the Jordan River. ²Large crowds followed him, and he healed them there.

³Some Pharisees came to him and tried to trap him by asking, "Does our Law allow a man to divorce his wife for whatever reason he wishes?"

⁴Jesus answered, "Haven't you read the scripture that says that in the beginning the Creator made people male and female? ⁵And God said, 'For this reason a man will leave his father and mother and unite with his wife, and the two will become one.' ⁶So they are no longer two, but one. No human being must separate, then, what God has joined together."

⁷The Pharisees asked him, "Why, then, did Moses give the law for a man to hand his wife a divorce notice and send her away?"

⁸Jesus answered, "Moses gave you permission to divorce your wives because you are so hard to teach. But it was not like that at the time of creation. ⁹I tell you, then, that any man who divorces his wife for any cause other than her unfaithfulness, commits adultery if he marries some other woman."

¹⁰His disciples said to him, "If this is how it is between a man and his wife, it is better not to marry."

¹¹Jesus answered, "This teaching does not apply to everyone, but only to those to whom God has given it. ¹²For there are different reasons why men cannot marry: some, because they were born that way; others, because men made them that way; and others do not marry for the sake of the Kingdom of heaven. Let him who can accept this teaching do so."

19:4 Gen 1:27; 5:2   **19:5** Gen 2:24   **19:7** Deut 24:1-4; Mt 5:31   **19:9** Mt 5:32; 1 Cor 7:10,11

Jesus Blesses Little Children
(Mark 10:13–16; Luke 18:15–17)

13Some people brought children to Jesus for him to place his hands on them and to pray for them, but the disciples scolded the people. 14Jesus said, "Let the children come to me and do not stop them, because the Kingdom of heaven belongs to such as these."

15He placed his hands on them and then went away.

The Rich Young Man
(Mark 10:17–31; Luke 18:18–30)

16Once a man came to Jesus. "Teacher," he asked, "what good thing must I do to receive eternal life?"

17"Why do you ask me concerning what is good?" answered Jesus. "There is only One who is good. Keep the commandments if you want to enter life."

18"What commandments?" he asked.

Jesus answered, "Do not commit murder; do not commit adultery; do not steal; do not accuse anyone falsely; 19respect your father and your mother; and love your neighbor as you love yourself."

20"I have obeyed all these commandments," the young man replied. "What else do I need to do?"

21Jesus said to him, "If you want to be perfect, go and sell all you have and give the money to the poor, and you will have riches in heaven; then come and follow me."

22When the young man heard this, he went away sad, because he was very rich.

23Jesus then said to his disciples, "I assure you: it will be very hard for rich people to enter the Kingdom of heaven. 24I repeat: it is much harder for a rich person to enter the Kingdom of God than for a camel to go through the eye of a needle."

25When the disciples heard this, they were completely amazed. "Who, then, can be saved?" they asked.

26Jesus looked straight at them and answered, "This is impossible for human beings, but for God everything is possible."

27Then Peter spoke up. "Look," he said, "we have left everything and followed you. What will we have?"

28Jesus said to them, "You can be sure that when the Son of Man sits on his glorious throne in the New Age, then you twelve followers of mine will also sit on thrones, to rule the twelve tribes of Israel. 29And everyone who has left houses or brothers or sisters or father or mother or children or fields for my sake, will receive a hundred times more and will be given eternal life. 30But many who now are first will be last, and many who now are last will be first.

The Workers in the Vineyard

20 1"The Kingdom of heaven is like this. Once there was a man who went out early in the morning to hire some men to work in his vineyard. 2He agreed to pay them the regular wage, a silver coin a day, and sent them to work in his vineyard. 3He went out again to the marketplace at nine o'clock and saw some men standing there doing nothing, 4so he told them, 'You also go and work in the vineyard, and I will pay you a fair wage.' 5So they went. Then at twelve o'clock and again at three o'clock he did the same thing. 6It was nearly five o'clock when he went to the marketplace and saw some other men still standing there. 'Why are you wasting the whole day here doing nothing?' he asked them. 7'No one hired us,' they answered. 'Well, then, you go and work in the vineyard,' he told them.

8"When evening came, the owner told his foreman, 'Call the workers and pay them their wages, starting with those who were hired last and ending with those who were hired first.' 9The men who had begun to work at five o'clock were paid a silver coin

19:18 a Ex 20:13; Deut 5:17; b Ex 20:14; Deut 5:18; c Ex 20:15; Deut 5:19; d Ex 20:16; Deut 5:20
19:19 a Ex 20:12; Deut 5:16; b Lev 19:18 **19:28** a Mt 25:31; b Lk 22:30 **19:30** Mt 20:16; Lk 13:30
20:8 Lev 19:13; Deut 24:15

Matthew

In Jesus' time women had almost no rights. Can you find where Jesus tells husbands to fulfill their responsibilities to their wives?

each. 10So when the men who were the first to be hired came to be paid, they thought they would get more; but they too were given a silver coin each. 11They took their money and started grumbling against the employer. 12'These men who were hired last worked only one hour,' they said, 'while we put up with a whole day's work in the hot sun—yet you paid them the same as you paid us!' 13'Listen, friend,' the owner answered one of them, 'I have not cheated you. After all, you agreed to do a day's work for one silver coin. 14Now take your pay and go home. I want to give this man who was hired last as much as I gave you. 15Don't I have the right to do as I wish with my own money? Or are you jealous because I am generous?' "

16And Jesus concluded, "So those who are last will be first, and those who are first will be last."

Jesus Speaks a Third Time about His Death
(Mark 10:32–34; Luke 18:31–34)

17As Jesus was going up to Jerusalem, he took the twelve disciples aside and spoke to them privately, as they walked along. 18"Listen," he told them, "we are going up to Jerusalem, where the Son of Man will be handed over to the chief priests and the teachers of the Law. They will condemn him to death 19and then hand him over to the Gentiles, who will make fun of him, whip him, and crucify him; but three days later he will be raised to life."

A Mother's Request
(Mark 10:35–45)

20Then the wife of Zebedee came to Jesus with her two sons, bowed before him, and asked him for a favor.

21"What do you want?" Jesus asked her. She answered, "Promise me that these two sons of mine will sit at your right and your left when you are King."

22"You don't know what you are asking for," Jesus answered the sons. "Can you drink the cup of suffering that I am about to drink?"

"We can," they answered.

23"You will indeed drink from my cup," Jesus told them, "but I do not have the right to choose who will sit at my right and my left. These places belong to those for whom my Father has prepared them."

24When the other ten disciples heard about this, they became angry with the two brothers. 25So Jesus called them all together and said, "You know that the rulers of the heathen have power over them, and the leaders have complete authority. 26This, however, is not the way it shall be among you. If one of you wants to be great, you must be the servant of the rest; 27and if one of you wants to be first, you must be the slave of the others— 28like the Son of Man, who did not come to be served, but to serve and to give his life to redeem many people."

Jesus Heals Two Blind Men
(Mark 10:46–52; Luke 18:35–43)

29As Jesus and his disciples were leaving Jericho, a large crowd was following. 30Two blind men who were sitting by the road heard that Jesus was passing by, so they began to shout, "Son of David! Have mercy on us, sir!"

31The crowd scolded them and told them to be quiet. But they shouted even more loudly, "Son of David! Have mercy on us, sir!"

32Jesus stopped and called them. "What do you want me to do for you?" he asked them.

33"Sir," they answered, "we want you to give us our sight!"

34Jesus had pity on them and touched their eyes; at once they were able to see, and they followed him.

20:16 Mt 19:30; Mk 10:31; Lk 13:30　**20:25,26** Lk 22:25,26　**20:26,27** Mt 23:11; Mk 9:35; Lk 22:26

The roads of Jesus' time were dirty from travelers and animal waste. This explains why people would cover it up with palm branches!

Pray It!   **Defending Poor People**

Jesus has been telling his disciples that he needs to go to Jerusalem. Jerusalem is the political and religious center of Jesus' people. People from all over travel to Jerusalem to offer their sacrifices to God at the Temple. Jesus knew he had to share God's message in that great city.

By now Jesus is so famous that people greet him like a triumphant king. So what is the very first thing that Jesus does? He turns over the tables of the people who sell animals and change money in the Temple. He is angry with them because they are making money unfairly off poor people, and they are doing so in a holy place. Jesus spends so much of his ministry caring for those who have been overlooked or mistreated. Sick and poor people come first for Jesus.

Lord, you showed great care for people that others overlooked.
Help me to always be aware of those in need.
Give me the courage to speak out for the people to whom no one else listens.
Amen

— Matthew 21:1–17

Matthew

The Triumphant Entry into Jerusalem
(Mark 11:1–11; Luke 19:28–40;
John 12:12–19)

21 ¹As Jesus and his disciples approached Jerusalem, they came to Bethphage at the Mount of Olives. There Jesus sent two of the disciples on ahead ²with these instructions: "Go to the village there ahead of you, and at once you will find a donkey tied up with her colt beside her. Untie them and bring them to me. ³And if anyone says anything, tell him, 'The Master¹ needs them'; and then he will let them go at once."

⁴This happened in order to make come true what the prophet had said:
⁵"Tell the city of Zion,
   Look, your king is coming to you!
He is humble and rides on a donkey
   and on a colt, the foal of a donkey."

⁶So the disciples went and did what Jesus had told them to do: ⁷they brought the donkey and the colt, threw their cloaks over them, and Jesus got on. ⁸A large crowd of people spread their cloaks on the road while others cut branches from the trees and spread them on the road. ⁹The crowds walking in

"God bless him who comes in the name of the Lord!" (21:9)

front of Jesus and those walking behind began to shout, "Praise to David's Son! God bless him who comes in the name of the Lord! Praise be to God!"

¹ **21:3** The Master; *or* Their owner.
21:5 Zech 9:9   **21:9** Ps 118:25,26

10When Jesus entered Jerusalem, the whole city was thrown into an uproar. "Who is he?" the people asked.

11"This is the prophet Jesus, from Nazareth in Galilee," the crowds answered.

Jesus Goes to the Temple
(Mark 11:15–19; Luke 19:45–48; John 2:13–22)

12Jesus went into the Temple and drove out all those who were buying and selling there. He overturned the tables of the moneychangers and the stools of those who sold pigeons, 13and said to them, "It is written in the Scriptures that God said, 'My Temple will be called a house of prayer.' But you are making it a hideout for thieves!"

14The blind and the crippled came to him in the Temple, and he healed them. 15The chief priests and the teachers of the Law became angry when they saw the wonderful things he was doing and the children shouting in the Temple, "Praise to David's Son!" 16So they asked Jesus, "Do you hear what they are saying?"

"Indeed I do," answered Jesus. "Haven't you ever read this scripture? 'You have trained children and babies to offer perfect praise.' "

17Jesus left them and went out of the city to Bethany, where he spent the night.

Jesus Curses the Fig Tree
(Mark 11:12–14, 20–24)

18On his way back to the city early next morning, Jesus was hungry. 19He saw a fig tree by the side of the road and went to it, but found nothing on it except leaves. So he said to the tree, "You will never again bear fruit!" At once the fig tree dried up.

20The disciples saw this and were astounded. "How did the fig tree dry up so quickly?" they asked.

21Jesus answered, "I assure you that if you believe and do not doubt, you will be able to do what I have done to this fig tree. And not only this, but you will even be able to say to this hill, 'Get up and throw yourself in the sea,' and it will. 22If you believe, you will receive whatever you ask for in prayer."

The Question about Jesus' Authority
(Mark 11:27–33; Luke 20:1–8)

23Jesus came back to the Temple; and as he taught, the chief priests and the elders came to him and asked, "What right do you have to do these things? Who gave you such right?"

24Jesus answered them, "I will ask you just one question, and if you give me an answer, I will tell you what right I have to do these things. 25Where did John's right to baptize come from: was it from God or from human beings?"

They started to argue among themselves, "What shall we say? If we answer, 'From God,' he will say to us, 'Why, then, did you not believe John?' 26But if we say, 'From human beings,' we are afraid of what the people might do, because they are all convinced that John was a prophet." 27So they answered Jesus, "We don't know."

And he said to them, "Neither will I tell you, then, by what right I do these things.

The Parable of the Two Sons

28"Now, what do you think? There was once a man who had two sons. He went to the older one and said, 'Son, go and work in the vineyard today.' 29'I don't want to,' he answered, but later he changed his mind and went. 30Then the father went to the other son and said the same thing. 'Yes, sir,' he answered, but he did not go. 31Which one of the two did what his father wanted?"

"The older one," they answered.

So Jesus said to them, "I tell you: the tax collectors and the prostitutes are going into the Kingdom of God ahead of you. 32For John the Baptist came to you showing you the right path to take, and you would not believe him; but the tax collectors and the prostitutes believed him. Even when you saw this, you did not later change your minds and believe him.

21:13 Isa 56:7; Jer 7:11 **21:16** Ps 8:2 (LXX) **21:21** Mt 17:20; 1 Cor 13:2 **21:32** Lk 3:12; 7:29,30

The Parable of the Tenants in the Vineyard
(Mark 12:1–12; Luke 20:9–19)

33 "Listen to another parable," Jesus said. "There was once a landowner who planted a vineyard, put a fence around it, dug a hole for the wine press, and built a watchtower. Then he rented the vineyard to tenants and left home on a trip. 34 When the time came to gather the grapes, he sent his slaves to the tenants to receive his share of the harvest. 35 The tenants grabbed his slaves, beat one, killed another, and stoned another. 36 Again the man sent other slaves, more than the first time, and the tenants treated them the same way. 37 Last of all he sent his son to them. 'Surely they will respect my son,' he said. 38 But when the tenants saw the son, they said to themselves, 'This is the owner's son. Come on, let's kill him, and we will get his property!' 39 So they grabbed him, threw him out of the vineyard, and killed him.

40 "Now, when the owner of the vineyard comes, what will he do to those tenants?" Jesus asked.

41 "He will certainly kill those evil men," they answered, "and rent the vineyard out to other tenants, who will give him his share of the harvest at the right time."

42 Jesus said to them, "Haven't you ever read what the Scriptures say?

'The stone which the builders rejected as worthless
turned out to be the most important of all.
This was done by the Lord;
what a wonderful sight it is!'

43 "And so I tell you," added Jesus, "the Kingdom of God will be taken away from you and given to a people who will produce the proper fruits."*u*

45 The chief priests and the Pharisees heard Jesus' parables and knew that he was talking about them, 46 so they tried to arrest him. But they were afraid of the crowds, who considered Jesus to be a prophet.

The Parable of the Wedding Feast
(Luke 14:15–24)

22 1 Jesus again used parables in talking to the people. 2 "The Kingdom of heaven is like this. Once there was a king who prepared a wedding feast for his son. 3 He sent his servants to tell the invited guests to come to the feast, but they did not want to come. 4 So he sent other servants with this message for the guests: 'My feast is ready now; my steers and prize calves have been butchered, and everything is ready. Come to the wedding feast!' 5 But the invited guests paid no attention and went about their business: one went to his farm, another to his store, 6 while others grabbed the servants, beat them, and killed them. 7 The king was very angry; so he sent his soldiers, who killed those murderers and burned down their city. 8 Then he called his servants and said to them, 'My wedding feast is ready, but the people I invited did not deserve it. 9 Now go to the main streets and invite to the feast as many people as you find.' 10 So the servants went out into the streets and gathered all the people they could find, good and bad alike; and the wedding hall was filled with people.

11 "The king went in to look at the guests and saw a man who was not wearing wedding clothes. 12 'Friend, how did you get in here without wedding clothes?' the king asked him. But the man said nothing. 13 Then the king told the servants, 'Tie him up hand and foot, and throw him outside in the dark. There he will cry and gnash his teeth.' "

14 And Jesus concluded, "Many are invited, but few are chosen."

u 21:43 *Some manuscripts add verse 44:* Whoever falls on this stone will be cut to pieces; and if the stone falls on someone, it will crush him to dust *(see Lk 20:18).*
21:33 Isa 5:1,2   21:42 Ps 118:22,23   22:13 Mt 8:12; 25:30; Lk 13:28

Are you more like the older son or the younger son in the parable of the two sons?

Matthew

The Question about Paying Taxes
(Mark 12:13–17; Luke 20:20–26)

15 The Pharisees went off and made a plan to trap Jesus with questions. 16 Then they sent to him some of their disciples and some members of Herod's party. "Teacher," they said, "we know that you tell the truth. You teach the truth about God's will for people, without worrying about what others think, because you pay no attention to anyone's status. 17 Tell us, then, what do you think? Is it against our Law to pay taxes to the Roman Emperor, or not?"

18 Jesus, however, was aware of their evil plan, and so he said, "You hypocrites! Why are you trying to trap me? 19 Show me the coin for paying the tax!"

They brought him the coin, 20 and he asked them, "Whose face and name are these?"

21 "The Emperor's," they answered.

So Jesus said to them, "Well, then, pay to the Emperor what belongs to the Emperor, and pay to God what belongs to God."

22 When they heard this, they were amazed; and they left him and went away.

The Question about Rising from Death
(Mark 12:18–27; Luke 20:27–40)

23 That same day some Sadducees came to Jesus and claimed that people will not rise from death. 24 "Teacher," they said, "Moses said that if a man who has no children dies, his brother must marry the widow so that they can have children who will be considered the dead man's children. 25 Now, there were seven brothers who used to live here. The oldest got married and died without having children, so he left his widow to his brother. 26 The same thing happened to the second brother, to the third, and finally to all seven. 27 Last of all, the woman died. 28 Now, on the day when the dead rise to life, whose wife will she be? All of them had married her."

29 Jesus answered them, "How wrong you are! It is because you don't know the Scrip-

Loving God Full Blast

"Love God with everything you've got!"

In Matthew 22:34–40 the religious leaders try to trap Jesus again with a question that they thought had no right answer. For these religious leaders, all the commandments or laws were equally important. But Jesus avoids the trap by talking about love instead of laws.

How would your life be different if you loved God full blast? With the volume turned all the way up? The second part of Jesus' answer is connected to the first part of his answer. If we truly love God, then we show it by loving the people around us—friends *and* enemies!

— Matthew 22:34–40

tures or God's power. 30 For when the dead rise to life, they will be like the angels in heaven and will not marry. 31 Now, as for the dead rising to life: haven't you ever read what God has told you? He said, 32 'I am the God of Abraham, the God of Isaac, and the God of Jacob.' He is the God of the living, not of the dead."

33 When the crowds heard this, they were amazed at his teaching.

The Great Commandment
(Mark 12:28–34; Luke 10:25–28)

34 When the Pharisees heard that Jesus had silenced the Sadducees, they came together, 35 and one of them, a teacher of the Law, tried

22:23 Acts 23:8 22:24 Deut 25:5 22:30 Wis 5:5 22:32 Ex 3:6

"Love the Lord your God with all your heart, with all your soul, and with all your mind" *(Matthew 22:37).*

to trap him with a question. 36 "Teacher," he asked, "which is the greatest commandment in the Law?"

37 Jesus answered, " 'Love the Lord your God with all your heart, with all your soul, and with all your mind.' 38 This is the greatest and the most important commandment. 39 The second most important commandment is like it: 'Love your neighbor as you love yourself.' 40 The whole Law of Moses and the teachings of the prophets depend on these two commandments."

The Question about the Messiah
(Mark 12:35–37; Luke 20:41–44)

41 When some Pharisees gathered together, Jesus asked them, 42 "What do you think about the Messiah? Whose descendant is he?"

"He is David's descendant," they answered.

43 "Why, then," Jesus asked, "did the Spirit inspire David to call him 'Lord'? David said,

44 'The Lord said to my Lord:

Sit here at my right side

until I put your enemies under your feet.'

45 If, then, David called him 'Lord,' how can the Messiah be David's descendant?"

46 No one was able to give Jesus any answer, and from that day on no one dared to ask him any more questions.

Jesus Warns against the Teachers of the Law and the Pharisees
(Mark 12:38, 39; Luke 11:43, 46; 20:45, 46)

23 1 Then Jesus spoke to the crowds and to his disciples. 2 "The teachers of the Law and the Pharisees are the authorized interpreters of Moses' Law. 3 So you must obey and follow everything they tell you to do; do not, however, imitate their actions, because they don't practice what they preach. 4 They tie onto people's backs loads that are heavy and hard to carry, yet they aren't willing even to lift a finger to help them carry those loads. 5 They do everything

They aren't willing even to lift a finger to help them. (23:4)

so that people will see them. Look at the straps with scripture verses on them which they wear on their foreheads and arms, and notice how large they are! Notice also how long are the tassels on their cloaks! v 6 They love the best places at feasts and the reserved seats in the synagogues; 7 they love to be greeted with respect in the marketplaces and to have people call them 'Teacher.' 8 You must not be called 'Teacher,' because you are all equal and have only one Teacher. 9 And you must not call anyone here on earth 'Father,' because you have only the one Father in heaven. 10 Nor should you be called 'Leader,' because your one and only leader is the Messiah. 11 The greatest one among you must be your servant. 12 Whoever makes himself great will be humbled, and whoever humbles himself will be made great.

Jesus Condemns Their Hypocrisy
(Mark 12:40; Luke 11:39–42, 44, 52; 20:47)

13 "How terrible for you, teachers of the Law and Pharisees! You hypocrites! You lock the door to the Kingdom of heaven in people's faces, but you yourselves don't go in, nor do you allow in those who are trying to enter! w

---

v **23:5** TASSELS ON THEIR CLOAKS: *These tassels were worn as a sign of devotion to God (see Num 15:37–41).*
w **23:13** *Some manuscripts add verse 14:* How terrible for you, teachers of the Law and Pharisees! You hypocrites! You take advantage of widows and rob them of their homes, and then make a show of saying long prayers! Because of this your punishment will be all the worse! *(see Mk 12:40).*
22:37 Deut 6:5 **22:39** Lev 19:18 **22:35-40** Lk 10:25-28 **22:44** Ps 110:1 **23:5 a** Mt 6:1; **b** Deut 6:8; **c** Num 15:38 **23:11** Mt 20:26,27; Mk 9:35; 10:43,44; Lk 22:26 **23:12** Lk 14:11; 18:14

How terrible for you, teachers of the Law! (23:15)

15 "How terrible for you, teachers of the Law and Pharisees! You hypocrites! You sail the seas and cross whole countries to win one convert; and when you succeed, you make him twice as deserving of going to hell as you yourselves are!

16 "How terrible for you, blind guides! You teach, 'If someone swears by the Temple, he isn't bound by his vow; but if he swears by the gold in the Temple, he is bound.' 17 Blind fools! Which is more important, the gold or the Temple which makes the gold holy? 18 You also teach, 'If someone swears by the altar, he isn't bound by his vow; but if he swears by the gift on the altar, he is bound.' 19 How blind you are! Which is the more important, the gift or the altar which makes the gift holy? 20 So then, when a person swears by the altar, he is swearing by it and by all the gifts on it; 21 and when he swears by the Temple, he is swearing by it and by God, who lives there; 22 and when someone swears by heaven, he is swearing by God's throne and by him who sits on it.

23 "How terrible for you, teachers of the Law and Pharisees! You hypocrites! You give to God one tenth even of the seasoning herbs, such as mint, dill, and cumin, but you neglect to obey the really important teachings of the Law, such as justice and mercy and honesty. These you should practice, without neglecting the others. 24 Blind guides! You strain a fly out of your drink, but swallow a camel!

25 "How terrible for you, teachers of the Law and Pharisees! You hypocrites! You clean the outside of your cup and plate, while the inside is full of what you have gotten by violence and selfishness. 26 Blind Pharisee! Clean what is inside the cup first, and then the outside will be clean too!

27 "How terrible for you, teachers of the Law and Pharisees! You hypocrites! You are like whitewashed tombs, which look fine on the outside but are full of bones and decaying corpses on the inside. 28 In the same way, on the outside you appear good to everybody, but inside you are full of hypocrisy and sins.

Jesus Predicts Their Punishment
(Luke 11:47–51)

29 "How terrible for you, teachers of the Law and Pharisees! You hypocrites! You make fine tombs for the prophets and decorate the monuments of those who lived good lives; 30 and you claim that if you had lived during the time of your ancestors, you would not have done what they did and killed the prophets. 31 So you actually admit that you are the descendants of those who murdered the prophets! 32 Go on, then, and finish up what your ancestors started! 33 You snakes and children of snakes! How do you expect to escape from being condemned to hell? 34 And so I tell you that I will send you prophets and wise men and teachers; you will kill some of them, crucify others, and whip others in the synagogues and chase them from town to town. 35 As a result, the punishment for the murder of all innocent people will fall on you, from the murder of innocent Abel to the murder of Zechariah son of Berechiah, whom you murdered between the Temple and the altar. 36 I tell you indeed: the punishment for all these murders will fall on the people of this day!

Jesus' Love for Jerusalem
(Luke 13:34, 35)

37 "Jerusalem, Jerusalem! You kill the prophets and stone the messengers God has sent you! How many times I wanted to put

23:22 Isa 66:1; Mt 5:34 23:23 Lev 27:30 23:27 Acts 23:3 23:33 Mt 3:7; 12:34; Lk 3:7 23:35 a Gen 4:8; b 2 Chr 24:20,21

Pray It!

Let Me Love You

At the end of Matthew, chapter 23, Jesus mourns for the people of Jerusalem. His anger at the religious leaders is turned to sorrow and compassion. "How many times I wanted to put my arms around all your people . . . but you would not let me!" (Matthew 23:37). Jesus wants to give his love to everyone, but our hearts must be open to receiving Jesus.

Jesus, help me to be open to the amazing love you have for me.
I don't want to turn my back on you.
I will follow you; I will accept your love.
I will follow you; I will listen to your words.
I will follow you; I will live as you command. Amen.

— Matthew 23:37–39

my arms around all your people, just as a hen gathers her chicks under her wings, but you would not let me! ³⁸And so your Temple will be abandoned and empty. ³⁹From now on, I tell you, you will never see me again until you say, 'God bless him who comes in the name of the Lord.' "

Jesus Speaks of the Destruction of the Temple
(Mark 13:1, 2; Luke 21:5, 6)

24 ¹Jesus left and was going away from the Temple when his disciples came to him to call his attention to its buildings. ²"Yes," he said, "you may well look at all these. I tell you this: not a single stone here will be left in its place; every one of them will be thrown down."

Troubles and Persecutions
(Mark 13:3–13; Luke 21:7–19)

³As Jesus sat on the Mount of Olives, the disciples came to him in private. "Tell us when all this will be," they asked, "and what

will happen to show that it is the time for your coming and the end of the age."

⁴Jesus answered, "Watch out, and do not let anyone fool you. ⁵Many men, claiming to speak for me, will come and say, 'I am the Messiah!' and they will fool many people. ⁶You are going to hear the noise of battles close by and the news of battles far away; but do not be troubled. Such things must happen, but they do not mean that the end has come. ⁷Countries will fight each other; kingdoms will attack one another. There will be famines and earthquakes everywhere. ⁸All these things are like the first pains of childbirth.

⁹"Then you will be arrested and handed over to be punished and be put to death. Everyone will hate you because of me. ¹⁰Many will give up their faith at that time; they will betray one another and hate one another. ¹¹Then many false prophets will appear and fool many people. ¹²Such will be the spread of evil that many people's love will grow cold. ¹³But whoever holds out to the end will be saved. ¹⁴And this Good News about the Kingdom will be preached

23:38 Jer 22:5   23:39 Ps 118:26   24:9 Mt 10:22   24:13 Mt 10:22

A *hypocrite* is someone whose actions do not match his or her words. Jesus condemned all hypocrisy.

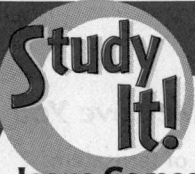

Jesus Comes Again

Jesus promised that he would come back again; he even describes his coming "on the clouds of heaven with power and great glory" (Matthew 24:30). The Church has a special name for the Second Coming of Christ: the Parousia. *Parousia* is a Greek word that means "arrival." The early Christians thought that Jesus would be coming back in their life-time. They looked forward to it with excitement.

Some people are afraid of the Parousia. Sometimes when we don't know what to expect, we can get nervous, even scared. The Catholic Church teaches that Christ will return at the end of time and judge all the nations. His Kingdom will be fully established, and his victory over evil will be complete. Like the early Christians, we should look forward with joy to Jesus' coming again!

— Matthew, chapter 24

through all the world for a witness to all people; and then the end will come.

The Awful Horror
(Mark 13:14–23; Luke 21:20–24)

15 "You will see 'The Awful Horror' of which the prophet Daniel spoke. It will be standing in the holy place." (Note to the reader: understand what this means!)

16 "Then those who are in Judea must run away to the hills. 17 Someone who is on the roof of a house must not take the time to go down and get any belongings from the house. 18 Someone who is in the field must not go back to get a cloak. 19 How terrible it will be in those days for women who are pregnant and for mothers with little babies! 20 Pray to God that you will not have to run away during the winter or on a Sabbath! 21 For the trouble at that time will be far more terrible than any there has ever been, from the beginning of the world to this very day. Nor will there ever be anything like it again. 22 But God has already reduced the number of days; had he not done so, nobody would survive. For the sake of his chosen people, however, God will reduce the days.

23 "Then, if anyone says to you, 'Look, here is the Messiah!' or 'There he is!'—do not believe it. 24 For false Messiahs and false prophets will appear; they will perform great miracles and wonders in order to deceive even God's chosen people, if possible. 25 Listen! I have told you this ahead of time.

26 "Or, if people should tell you, 'Look, he is out in the desert!'—don't go there; or if they say, 'Look, he is hiding here!'—don't believe it. 27 For the Son of Man will come like the lightning which flashes across the whole sky from the east to the west.

28 "Wherever there is a dead body, the vultures will gather.

The Coming of the Son of Man
(Mark 13:24–27; Luke 21:25–28)

29 "Soon after the trouble of those days, the sun will grow dark, the moon will no longer shine, the stars will fall from heaven, and the powers in space will be driven from their courses. 30 Then the sign of the Son of Man will appear in the sky; and all the peoples of earth will weep as they see the Son of Man coming on the clouds of heaven

24:15 Dan 9:27; 11:31; 12:11; 1 Macc 1:54; 6:7   24:17,18 Lk 17:31   24:21 Dan 12:1; Rev 7:14
24:26,27 Lk 17:23,24   24:28 Lk 17:37   24:29 a Isa 13:10; Joel 2:10,31; 3:15; Rev 6:12; b Isa 13:10; Ezek 32:7; Joel 2:10; 3:15; c Isa 34:4; Rev 6:13   24:30 Dan 7:13; Zech 12:10-14; Rev 1:7

What is the "Awful Horror" mentioned in Matthew 24:15? A war? a plague? a pagan image? a terrible beast? Find out by reading Daniel 9:27.

with power and great glory. ³¹The great trumpet will sound, and he will send out his angels to the four corners of the earth, and they will gather his chosen people from one end of the world to the other.

The Lesson of the Fig Tree
(Mark 13:28–31; Luke 21:29–33)

³²"Let the fig tree teach you a lesson. When its branches become green and tender and it starts putting out leaves, you know that summer is near. ³³In the same way, when you see all these things, you will know that the time is near, ready to begin.ˣ ³⁴Remember that all these things will happen before the people now living have all died. ³⁵Heaven and earth will pass away, but my words will never pass away.

No One Knows the Day and Hour
(Mark 13:32–37; Luke 17:26–30, 34–36)

³⁶"No one knows, however, when that day and hour will come—neither the angels in heaven nor the Son;ʸ the Father alone knows. ³⁷The coming of the Son of Man will be like what happened in the time of Noah. ³⁸In the days before the flood people ate and drank, men and women married, up to the very day Noah went into the boat; ³⁹yet they did not realize what was happening until the flood came and swept them all away. That is how it will be when the Son of Man comes. ⁴⁰At that time two men will be working in a field: one will be taken away, the other will be left behind. ⁴¹Two women will be at a mill grinding meal: one will be taken away, the other will be left behind. ⁴²Watch out, then, because you do not know what day your Lord will come. ⁴³If the owner of a house knew the time when the thief would come, you can be sure that he would stay awake and not let the thief break into his house. ⁴⁴So then, you also must always be ready, because the Son of Man will come at an hour when you are not expecting him.

The Faithful or the Unfaithful Servant
(Luke 12:41–48)

⁴⁵"Who, then, is a faithful and wise servant? It is the one that his master has placed in charge of the other servants to give them their food at the proper time. ⁴⁶How happy that servant is if his master finds him doing this when he comes home! ⁴⁷Indeed, I tell you, the master will put that servant in charge of all his property. ⁴⁸But if he is a bad servant, he will tell himself that his master will not come back for a long time, ⁴⁹and he will begin to beat his fellow servants and to eat and drink with drunkards. ⁵⁰Then that servant's master will come back one day when the servant does not expect him and at a time he does not know. ⁵¹The master will cut him in piecesᶻ and make him share the fate of the hypocrites. There he will cry and gnash his teeth.

The Parable of the Ten Young Women

25 ¹"At that time the Kingdom of heaven will be like this. Once there were ten young women who took their oil lamps and went out to meet the bridegroom. ²Five of them were foolish, and the other five were wise. ³The foolish ones took their lamps but did not take any extra oil with them, ⁴while the wise ones took containers full of oil for their lamps. ⁵The bridegroom was late in coming, so they began to nod and fall asleep.

⁶"It was already midnight when the cry rang out, 'Here is the bridegroom! Come and meet him!' ⁷The ten young women woke up and trimmed their lamps. ⁸Then the foolish ones said to the wise ones, 'Let us have some of your oil, because our lamps are going out.' ⁹'No, indeed,' the wise ones answered, 'there is not enough for you and for us. Go to the store and buy some for yourselves.' ¹⁰So the foolish ones went off to buy some oil; and while they were gone, the bridegroom arrived. The five who were ready went in with him to the wedding feast, and the door was closed.

ˣ **24:33** the time is near, ready to begin; *or* he is near, ready to come.   ʸ **24:36** *Some manuscripts do not have* nor the Son.   ᶻ **24:51** cut him in pieces; *or* throw him out.
24:37 Gen 6:5-8   **24:39** Gen 7:6-24   **24:43,44** Lk 12:39,40   **25:1** Lk 12:35

Pray It!

Find Us Ready, Lord

When you return Lord, I want to be ready.
Help me clean out the dusty corners of my life
   and keep my heart ready for your return.
Through prayer I will grow closer to you.
By loving others I will prepare myself for your coming.
By knowing that you might come at any moment,
I will remain ready for your return
   because I wish to live always in your love. Amen.

— *Matthew 25:1–13*

11 "Later the others arrived. 'Sir, sir! Let us in!' they cried out. 12 'Certainly not! I don't know you,' the bridegroom answered."

13 And Jesus concluded, "Watch out, then, because you do not know the day or the hour.

The Parable of the Three Servants
(Luke 19:11–27)

14 "At that time the Kingdom of heaven will be like this. Once there was a man who was about to leave home on a trip; he called his servants and put them in charge of his property. 15 He gave to each one according to his ability: to one he gave five thousand gold coins, to another he gave two thousand, and to another he gave one thousand. Then he left on his trip. 16 The servant who had received five thousand coins went at once and invested his money and earned another five thousand. 17 In the same way the servant who had received two thousand coins earned another two thousand. 18 But the servant who had received one thousand coins went off, dug a hole in the ground, and hid his master's money.

19 "After a long time the master of those servants came back and settled accounts with them. 20 The servant who had received five thousand coins came in and handed over the other five thousand. 'You gave me five thou-

sand coins, sir,' he said. 'Look! Here are another five thousand that I have earned.' 21 'Well done, you good and faithful servant!' said his master. 'You have been faithful in managing small amounts, so I will put you in charge of large amounts. Come on in and share my happiness!' 22 Then the servant who had been given two thousand coins came in and said, 'You gave me two thousand coins, sir. Look! Here are another two thousand that I have earned.' 23 'Well done, you good and faithful servant!' said his master. 'You have been faithful in managing small amounts, so I will put you in charge of large amounts. Come on in and share my happiness!' 24 Then the servant who had received one thousand coins came in and said, 'Sir, I know you are a hard man; you reap harvests where you did not plant, and you gather crops where you did not scatter seed. 25 I was afraid, so I went off and hid your money in the ground. Look! Here is what belongs to you.' 26 'You bad and lazy servant!' his master said. 'You knew, did you, that I reap harvests where I did not plant, and gather crops where I did not scatter seed? 27 Well, then, you should have deposited my money in the bank, and I would have received it all back with interest when I returned. 28 Now, take the money away from him and give it to the one who has ten thousand coins. 29 For to every person who has something, even more

25:11,12 Lk 13:25   **25:14–30** Lk 19:11–27   **25:29** Mt 13:12; Mk 4:25; Lk 8:18

will be given, and he will have more than enough; but the person who has nothing, even the little that he has will be taken away from him. ³⁰As for this useless servant— throw him outside in the darkness; there he will cry and gnash his teeth.'

The Final Judgment

³¹"When the Son of Man comes as King and all the angels with him, he will sit on his royal throne, ³²and the people of all the nations will be gathered before him. Then he will divide them into two groups, just as a shepherd separates the sheep from the goats. ³³He will put the righteous people at his right and the others at his left. ³⁴Then the King will say to the people on his right, 'Come, you that are blessed by my Father! Come and possess the kingdom which has been prepared for you ever since the creation of the world. ³⁵I was hungry and you fed me, thirsty and you gave me a drink; I was a stranger and you received me in your homes, ³⁶naked and you clothed me; I was sick and you took care of me, in prison and you visited me.' ³⁷The righteous will then answer him, 'When, Lord, did we ever see you hungry and feed you, or thirsty and give you a drink? ³⁸When did we ever see you a stranger and welcome you in our homes, or naked and clothe you? ³⁹When did we ever see you sick or in prison, and visit you?' ⁴⁰The King will reply, 'I tell you, whenever you did this for one of the least important of these followers of mine, you did it for me!'

⁴¹"Then he will say to those on his left, 'Away from me, you that are under God's curse! Away to the eternal fire which has been prepared for the Devil and his angels! ⁴²I was hungry but you would not feed me, thirsty but you would not give me a drink; ⁴³I was a stranger but you would not welcome me in your homes, naked but you would not clothe me; I was sick and in prison but you would not take care of me.' ⁴⁴Then they will answer him, 'When, Lord, did we ever see you hun-

Seeing Christ, Being Christ

Jesus tells his followers that if they show an act of kindness to anyone, it is as if they did it to him (Matthew 25:40). As Christians we are called to see Christ in others and to be Christ for others. You can volunteer at a nursing home or a food pantry. Or encourage your church or school to do a food drive or collect blankets and winter coats. One youth group has a "Change the World" jar. The young people collect all the loose change in people's pockets each week at youth group and then a few times a year donate it to a group that helps poor people. It helps remind them of the people in need. You could have your own "Change the World" jar. Encourage your family, maybe even your whole parish or school, to start this tradition.

— Matthew 25:31–46

gry or thirsty or a stranger or naked or sick or in prison, and we would not help you?' ⁴⁵The King will reply, 'I tell you, whenever you refused to help one of these least important ones, you refused to help me.' ⁴⁶These, then, will be sent off to eternal punishment, but the righteous will go to eternal life."

The Plot against Jesus
(Mark 14:1, 2; Luke 22:1, 2; John 11:45–53)

26 ¹When Jesus had finished teaching all these things, he said to his disci-

Who are the least important *(Matthew 25:40)* **in the world today? Who is in need of food, clothing, visits? What can you do about it?**

Matthew

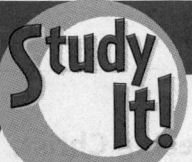

What She Has Done

In a dramatic story at the beginning of Matthew, chapter 26, the unnamed woman anoints Jesus' head in the same way that the kings of the Old Testament were anointed. Anointing on the head was a sign that this person was God's choice. The woman may have suspected that Jesus was in danger of being killed, and this kind of anointing was also a way of preparing a body for burial. She wanted to recognize that Jesus was chosen by God. Jesus in turn recognizes the woman's compassion for him and praises her extravagance in using this very expensive oil. She put her resources at the service of someone in need. It is this act of compassion that will be remembered.

— Matthew 26:6–13

dreaded skin disease. 7 While Jesus was eating, a woman came to him with an alabaster jar filled with an expensive perfume, which she poured on his head. 8 The disciples saw this and became angry. "Why all this waste?" they asked. 9 "This perfume could have been sold for a large amount and the money given to the poor!"

10 Jesus knew what they were saying, and so he said to them, "Why are you bothering this woman? It is a fine and beautiful thing that she has done for me. 11 You will always have poor people with you, but you will not always have me. 12 What she did was to pour this perfume on my body to get me ready for burial. 13 Now, I assure you that wherever this gospel is preached all over the world, what she has done will be told in memory of her."

Judas Agrees to Betray Jesus
(Mark 14:10, 11; Luke 22:3–6)

14 Then one of the twelve disciples—the one named Judas Iscariot—went to the chief priests 15 and asked, "What will you give me if I betray Jesus to you?" They counted out thirty silver coins and gave them to him. 16 From then on Judas was looking for a good chance to hand Jesus over to them.

ples, 2 "In two days, as you know, it will be the Passover Festival, and the Son of Man will be handed over to be crucified."

3 Then the chief priests and the elders met together in the palace of Caiaphas, the High Priest, 4 and made plans to arrest Jesus secretly and put him to death. 5 "We must not do it during the festival," they said, "or the people will riot."

Jesus Is Anointed at Bethany
(Mark 14:3–9; John 12:1–8)

6 Jesus was in Bethany at the house of Simon, a man who had suffered from a

Thirty silver coins (26:15)

26:2 Ex 12:1-27 **26:7** Lk 7:37,38 **26:11** Deut 15:11 **26:15** Zech 11:12

" 'Take and eat it,' he said; 'this is my body' " *(Matthew 26:26).*

Jesus Eats the Passover Meal with His Disciples
(Mark 14:12–21; Luke 22:7–13, 21–23; John 13:21–30)

17 On the first day of the Festival of Unleavened Bread the disciples came to Jesus and asked him, "Where do you want us to get the Passover meal ready for you?"

18 "Go to a certain man in the city," he said to them, "and tell him: 'The Teacher says, My hour has come; my disciples and I will celebrate the Passover at your house.' "

19 The disciples did as Jesus had told them and prepared the Passover meal.

20 When it was evening, Jesus and the twelve disciples sat down to eat. **21** During the meal Jesus said, "I tell you, one of you will betray me."

22 The disciples were very upset and began to ask him, one after the other, "Surely, Lord, you don't mean me?"

23 Jesus answered, "One who dips his bread in the dish with me will betray me. **24** The Son of Man will die as the Scriptures say he will, but how terrible for that man who will betray the Son of Man! It would have been better for that man if he had never been born!"

25 Judas, the traitor, spoke up. "Surely, Teacher, you don't mean me?" he asked.

Jesus answered, "So you say."

The Lord's Supper
(Mark 14:22–26; Luke 22:14–20; 1 Corinthians 11:23–25)

26 While they were eating, Jesus took a piece of bread, gave a prayer of thanks, broke it, and gave it to his disciples. "Take and eat it," he said; "this is my body."

27 Then he took a cup, gave thanks to God, and gave it to them. "Drink it, all of you," he said; **28** "this is my blood, which seals God's covenant, my blood poured out for many for the forgiveness of sins. **29** I tell you, I will never again drink this wine until the day I drink the new wine with you in my Father's Kingdom."

30 Then they sang a hymn and went out to the Mount of Olives.

Jesus Predicts Peter's Denial
(Mark 14:27–31; Luke 22:31–34; John 13:36–38)

31 Then Jesus said to them, "This very night all of you will run away and leave me, for the scripture says, 'God will kill the shepherd, and the sheep of the flock will be scattered.' **32** But after I am raised to life, I will go to Galilee ahead of you."

33 Peter spoke up and said to Jesus, "I will never leave you, even though all the rest do!"

34 Jesus said to Peter, "I tell you that before the rooster crows tonight, you will say three times that you do not know me."

35 Peter answered, "I will never say that, even if I have to die with you!"

And all the other disciples said the same thing.

Jesus Prays in Gethsemane
(Mark 14:32–42; Luke 22:39–46)

36 Then Jesus went with his disciples to a place called Gethsemane, and he said to them, "Sit here while I go over there and pray." **37** He took with him Peter and the two sons of Zebedee. Grief and anguish came over him, **38** and he said to them, "The sorrow in my heart is so great that it almost crushes me. Stay here and keep watch with me."

39 He went a little farther on, threw himself face downward on the ground, and prayed, "My Father, if it is possible, take this cup of suffering from me! Yet not what I want, but what you want."

"Take this cup of suffering from me!" (26:39)

26:23 Ps 41:9   **26:28** a Ex 24:8; b Jer 31:31–34   **26:31** Zech 13:7   **26:32** Mt 28:16

Matthew

Matthew

Obstacles to Prayer

Ca**h**olic Connec**i**ons

Jesus asks his closest friends to "stay here and keep watch with me" (Matthew 26:38). But after a full meal, they fall asleep. The disciples love Jesus. But their human limits keep them from praying as they want to.

Prayer can be a very difficult thing at times. You can be distracted by the radio or television. Maybe noisy people in your house make it difficult to find some quiet. Maybe you are so busy with your friends, family, and school activities that it's hard to find time for prayer.

If you find prayer difficult, don't be discouraged. Even the greatest saints found it very difficult to pray at times. These obstacles can be overcome. Turn off the television and radio. Wake up early or find a quiet room. Pray in the car on your way to or from your activities. Make prayer a priority and keep your relationship with Jesus alive!

— Matthew 26:36–46

40 Then he returned to the three disciples and found them asleep; and he said to Peter, "How is it that you three were not able to keep watch with me for even one hour? 41 Keep watch and pray that you will not fall into temptation. The spirit is willing, but the flesh is weak."

42 Once more Jesus went away and prayed, "My Father, if this cup of suffering cannot be taken away unless I drink it, your will be done." 43 He returned once more and found the disciples asleep; they could not keep their eyes open.

44 Again Jesus left them, went away, and prayed the third time, saying the same words. 45 Then he returned to the disciples and said, "Are you still sleeping and resting? Look! The hour has come for the Son of Man to be handed over to the power of sinners. 46 Get up, let us go. Look, here is the man who is betraying me!"

The Arrest of Jesus
(Mark 14:43–50; Luke 22:47–53; John 18:3–12)

47 Jesus was still speaking when Judas, one of the twelve disciples, arrived. With him was a large crowd armed with swords and clubs and sent by the chief priests and the elders. 48 The traitor had given the crowd a signal: "The man I kiss is the one you want. Arrest him!"

49 Judas went straight to Jesus and said, "Peace be with you, Teacher," and kissed him. 50 Jesus answered, "Be quick about it, friend!"[a]

Then they came up, arrested Jesus, and held him tight. 51 One of those who were with Jesus drew his sword and struck at the High Priest's slave, cutting off his ear. 52 "Put

They could not keep their eyes open. (26:43)

[a] **26:50** Be quick about it, friend!; *or* Why are you here, friend?

your sword back in its place," Jesus said to him. "All who take the sword will die by the sword. 53 Don't you know that I could call on my Father for help, and at once he would send me more than twelve armies of angels? 54 But in that case, how could the Scriptures come true which say that this is what must happen?"

55 Then Jesus spoke to the crowd, "Did you have to come with swords and clubs to capture me, as though I were an outlaw? Every day I sat down and taught in the Temple, and you did not arrest me. 56 But all this has happened in order to make come true what the prophets wrote in the Scriptures."

Then all the disciples left him and ran away.

Jesus before the Council
(Mark 14:53–65; Luke 22:54, 55, 63–71; John 18:13, 14, 19–24)

57 Those who had arrested Jesus took him to the house of Caiaphas, the High Priest, where the teachers of the Law and the elders had gathered together. 58 Peter followed from a distance, as far as the courtyard of the High Priest's house. He went into the courtyard and sat down with the guards to see how it would all come out. 59 The chief priests and the whole Council tried to find some false evidence against Jesus to put him to death; 60 but they could not find any, even though many people came forward and told lies about him. Finally two men stepped up 61 and said, "This man said, 'I am able to tear down God's Temple and three days later build it back up.' "

62 The High Priest stood up and said to Jesus, "Have you no answer to give to this accusation against you?" 63 But Jesus kept quiet. Again the High Priest spoke to him, "In the name of the living God I now put you under oath: tell us if you are the Messiah, the Son of God."

64 Jesus answered him, "So you say. But I tell all of you: from this time on you will see the Son of Man sitting at the right side of the Almighty and coming on the clouds of heaven!"

65 At this the High Priest tore his clothes and said, "Blasphemy! We don't need any more witnesses! You have just heard his blasphemy! 66 What do you think?"

They answered, "He is guilty and must die."

67 Then they spat in his face and beat him; and those who slapped him 68 said, "Prophesy for us, Messiah! Guess who hit you!"

Peter Denies Jesus
(Mark 14:66–72; Luke 22:56–62; John 18:15–18, 25–27)

69 Peter was sitting outside in the courtyard when one of the High Priest's servant women came to him and said, "You, too, were with Jesus of Galilee."

70 But he denied it in front of them all. "I don't know what you are talking about," he answered, 71 and went on out to the entrance of the courtyard. Another servant woman saw him and said to the men there, "He was with Jesus of Nazareth."

72 Again Peter denied it and answered, "I swear that I don't know that man!"

73 After a little while the men standing there came to Peter. "Of course you are one of them," they said. "After all, the way you speak gives you away!"

74 Then Peter said, "I swear that I am telling the truth! May God punish me if I am not! I do not know that man!"

Just then a rooster crowed, 75 and Peter remembered what Jesus had told him: "Before the rooster crows, you will say three times that you do not know me." He went out and wept bitterly.

Jesus Is Taken to Pilate
(Mark 15:1; Luke 23:1, 2; John 18:28–32)

27 1 Early in the morning all the chief priests and the elders made their plans against Jesus to put him to death. 2 They put him in chains, led him off, and

---

26:55 Lk 19:47; 21:37   **26:61** Jn 2:19   **26:64** Dan 7:13   **26:65,66** Lev 24:16   **26:67** Isa 50:6

Why did Peter deny Jesus? He was afraid he might be arrested and killed too.

Good Friday

Catholic Connections

During Holy Week, which begins on Palm Sunday, we remember Jesus' suffering and death on Good Friday. For the Good Friday liturgy, the Church is kept simple, sometimes statues are covered or removed. The Gospel reading is taken from John, chapters 18 and 19, which is another version of what Matthew's Gospel describes here.

The Good Friday liturgy is serious and can even feel sad because we are focusing on Jesus' death. During the liturgy we show special reverence for the cross in appreciation of Christ's sacrifice. This is called the veneration of the cross. This liturgy reminds us of Jesus' sacrifice, but even on Good Friday we are people of hope because we know how the story ends. We leave the Good Friday liturgy knowing that Easter is coming soon!

— Matthew 26:57—27:56

handed him over to Pilate, the Roman governor.

The Death of Judas
(Acts 1:18, 19)

3 When Judas, the traitor, learned that Jesus had been condemned, he repented and took back the thirty silver coins to the chief priests and the elders. 4 "I have sinned by betraying an innocent man to death!" he said.

"What do we care about that?" they answered. "That is your business!"

5 Judas threw the coins down in the Temple and left; then he went off and hanged himself.

6 The chief priests picked up the coins and said, "This is blood money, and it is against our Law to put it in the Temple treasury." 7 After reaching an agreement about it, they used the money to buy Potter's Field, as a cemetery for foreigners. 8 That is why that field is called "Field of Blood" to this very day.

9 Then what the prophet Jeremiah had said came true: "They took the thirty silver

coins, the amount the people of Israel had agreed to pay for him, 10 and used the money to buy the potter's field, as the Lord had commanded me."

Pilate Questions Jesus
(Mark 15:2–5; Luke 23:3–5; John 18:33–38)

11 Jesus stood before the Roman governor, who questioned him. "Are you the king of the Jews?" he asked.

"So you say," answered Jesus. 12 But he said nothing in response to the accusations of the chief priests and elders.

13 So Pilate said to him, "Don't you hear all these things they accuse you of?"

14 But Jesus refused to answer a single word, with the result that the Governor was greatly surprised.

Jesus Is Sentenced to Death
(Mark 15:6–15; Luke 23:13–25; John 18:39—19:16)

15 At every Passover Festival the Roman governor was in the habit of setting free any

27:3-8 Acts 1:18,19   27:9,10 Zech 11:12,13

Matthew 27:25 is also known as the blood curse. It has been wrongly used to justify hatred against the Jewish people.

one prisoner the crowd asked for. 16At that time there was a well-known prisoner named Jesus Barabbas. 17So when the crowd gathered, Pilate asked them, "Which one do you want me to set free for you? Jesus Barabbas or Jesus called the Messiah?" 18He knew very well that the Jewish authorities had handed Jesus over to him because they were jealous.

19While Pilate was sitting in the judgment hall, his wife sent him a message: "Have nothing to do with that innocent man, because in a dream last night I suffered much on account of him."

20The chief priests and the elders persuaded the crowd to ask Pilate to set Barabbas free and have Jesus put to death. 21But Pilate asked the crowd, "Which one of these two do you want me to set free for you?"

"Barabbas!" they answered.

22"What, then, shall I do with Jesus called the Messiah?" Pilate asked them.

"Crucify him!" they all answered.

23But Pilate asked, "What crime has he committed?"

Then they started shouting at the top of their voices: "Crucify him!"

24When Pilate saw that it was no use to go on, but that a riot might break out, he took some water, washed his hands in front of the crowd, and said, "I am not responsible for the death of this man! This is your doing!"

25The whole crowd answered, "Let the responsibility for his death fall on us and on our children!"

26Then Pilate set Barabbas free for them; and after he had Jesus whipped, he handed him over to be crucified.

The Soldiers Make Fun of Jesus
(Mark 15:16–20; John 19:2, 3)

27Then Pilate's soldiers took Jesus into the governor's palace, and the whole company gathered around him. 28They stripped off his clothes and put a scarlet robe on him. 29Then they made a crown out of thorny branches and placed it on his head, and put a stick in his right hand; then they knelt before him and made fun of him. "Long live the King of the Jews!" they said. 30They spat on him, and took the stick and hit him over the head. 31When they had finished making fun of him, they took the robe off and put his own clothes back on him. Then they led him out to crucify him.

Jesus Is Crucified
(Mark 15:21–32; Luke 23:26–43; John 19:17–27)

32As they were going out, they met a man from Cyrene named Simon, and the soldiers forced him to carry Jesus' cross. 33They came to a place called Golgotha, which means, "The Place of the Skull." 34There they offered Jesus wine mixed with a bitter substance; but after tasting it, he would not drink it.

35They crucified him and then divided his clothes among them by throwing dice. 36After that they sat there and watched him. 37Above his head they put the written notice of the accusation against him: "This is Jesus, the King of the Jews." 38Then they crucified two bandits with Jesus, one on his right and the other on his left.

39People passing by shook their heads and hurled insults at Jesus: 40"You were going to tear down the Temple and build it back up in three days! Save yourself if you are God's Son! Come on down from the cross!"

41In the same way the chief priests and the teachers of the Law and the elders made fun of him: 42"He saved others, but he cannot save himself! Isn't he the king of Israel? If he will come down off the cross now, we will believe in him! 43He trusts in God and claims to be God's Son. Well, then, let us see if God wants to save him now!"

44Even the bandits who had been crucified with him insulted him in the same way.

The Death of Jesus
(Mark 15:33–41; Luke 23:44–49; John 19:28–30)

45At noon the whole country was covered with darkness, which lasted for three hours. 46At about three o'clock Jesus cried out with

27:24 Deut 21:6-9   **27:34** Ps 69:21   **27:35** Ps 22:18   **27:39** Ps 22:7; 109:25; Sir 12:17,18; 13:7
27:40 Mt 26:61; Jn 2:19   **27:43** Ps 22:8; Wis 2:18-20   **27:46** Ps 22:1

Pray It!

Thank You, Lord

Lord Jesus, when I see you on the cross, it makes me wonder.
Why did you have to suffer? Was this the only way?
I am so amazed that you, the Son of God, were willing to become human, even if
that meant enduring the worst treatment that human beings have to offer—
mockery, torture, death.
Thank you.
Thank you for following your Father's will.
Thank you for standing in the face of hatred and showing such amazing love. Amen.

— **Matthew 27:32–50**

a loud shout, *"Eli, Eli, lema sabachthani?"* which means, "My God, my God, why did you abandon me?"

47 Some of the people standing there heard him and said, "He is calling for Elijah!" 48 One of them ran up at once, took a sponge, soaked it in cheap wine, put it on the end of a stick, and tried to make him drink it.

49 But the others said, "Wait, let us see if Elijah is coming to save him!"

50 Jesus again gave a loud cry and breathed his last.

51 Then the curtain hanging in the Temple was torn in two from top to bottom. The earth shook, the rocks split apart, 52 the graves broke open, and many of God's people who had died were raised to life. 53 They left the graves, and after Jesus rose from death, they went into the Holy City, where many people saw them.

54 When the army officer and the soldiers with him who were watching Jesus saw the earthquake and everything else that happened, they were terrified and said, "He really was the Son of God!"

55 There were many women there, looking on from a distance, who had followed Jesus from Galilee and helped him. 56 Among them were Mary Magdalene, Mary the mother of James and Joseph, and the wife of Zebedee.

The Burial of Jesus
(Mark 15:42–47; Luke 23:50–56; John 19:38–42)

57 When it was evening, a rich man from Arimathea arrived; his name was Joseph, and he also was a disciple of Jesus. 58 He went into the presence of Pilate and asked for the body of Jesus. Pilate gave orders for the body to be given to Joseph. 59 So Joseph took it, wrapped it in a new linen sheet, 60 and placed it in his own tomb, which he had just recently dug out of solid rock. Then he rolled a large stone across the entrance to the tomb and went away. 61 Mary Magdalene and the other Mary were sitting there, facing the tomb.

The Guard at the Tomb

62 The next day, which was a Sabbath, the chief priests and the Pharisees met with Pilate 63 and said, "Sir, we remember that while that liar was still alive he said, 'I will be raised to life three days later.' 64 Give orders, then, for his tomb to be carefully guarded until the third day, so that his disciples will not be able to go and steal the body, and then tell the people that he was raised from death. This last lie would be even worse than the first one."

65 "Take a guard," Pilate told them; "go and make the tomb as secure as you can."

27:48 Ps 69:21 27:51 Ex 26:31-33 27:55,56 Lk 8:2,3 27:63 Mt 16:21; 17:23; 20:19; Mk 8:31; 9:31; 10:33,34; Lk 9:22; 18:31-33

Holy Trinity

Ca☩holic Connec☩ions

The Gospel of Matthew ends with two stories of the resurrected Jesus. In the first story he appears to the women leaving the tomb (Matthew 28:9–10). In the second story he appears to the eleven disciples who were also the Apostles. He gives them this command, "Go, then, to all peoples everywhere and make them my disciples: baptize them in the name of the Father, the Son, and the Holy Spirit" (28:19). You probably recognize these words; we say them when we make the sign of the cross.

God the Father, God the Son, and God the Holy Spirit are one God even though they are revealed as three persons. This is why we also call God the Holy Trinity. This belief is a mystery that we do not fully understand. But it does tell us that God is not solitary. The Father, Son, and Holy Spirit are in relationship with one another and form a loving communion. We, too, are not meant to be alone but to live in community. We are all invited to be a part of God's family, as is the whole world!

— Matthew 28:16–20

Matthew

⁶⁶So they left and made the tomb secure by putting a seal on the stone and leaving the guard on watch.

The Resurrection
(Mark 16:1–10; Luke 24:1–12; John 20:1–10)

28 ¹After the Sabbath, as Sunday morning was dawning, Mary Magdalene and the other Mary went to look at the tomb. ²Suddenly there was a violent earthquake; an angel of the Lord came down from heaven, rolled the stone away, and sat on it. ³His appearance was like lightning, and his clothes were white as snow. ⁴The guards were so afraid that they trembled and became like dead men.

⁵The angel spoke to the women. "You must not be afraid," he said. "I know you are looking for Jesus, who was crucified. ⁶He is not here; he has been raised, just as he said. Come here and see the place where he was lying. ⁷Go quickly now, and tell his disciples, 'He has been raised from death, and now he is going to Galilee ahead of you; there you will see him!' Remember what I have told you."

⁸So they left the tomb in a hurry, afraid and yet filled with joy, and ran to tell his disciples.

⁹Suddenly Jesus met them and said, "Peace be with you." They came up to him, took hold of his feet, and worshiped him. ¹⁰"Do not be afraid," Jesus said to them. "Go and tell my brothers to go to Galilee, and there they will see me."

The Report of the Guard

¹¹While the women went on their way, some of the soldiers guarding the tomb went back to the city and told the chief priests everything that had happened. ¹²The chief priests met with the elders and made their plan; they gave a large sum of money to the soldiers ¹³and said, "You are to say that his disciples came during the night and stole his body while you were asleep. ¹⁴And if the Governor should hear of this, we will

"He is not here; he has been raised, just as he said" *(Matthew 28:6).*

convince him that you are innocent, and you will have nothing to worry about."

15 The guards took the money and did what they were told to do. And so that is the report spread around by the Jews to this very day.

Jesus Appears to His Disciples
(Mark 16:14–18; Luke 24:36–49; John 20:19–23; Acts 1:6–8)

16 The eleven disciples went to the hill in Galilee where Jesus had told them to go.

28:16 Mt 26:32; Mk 14:28   **28:19** Acts 1:8

17 When they saw him, they worshiped him, even though some of them doubted. **18** Jesus drew near and said to them, "I have been given all authority in heaven and on earth. **19** Go, then, to all peoples everywhere and make them my disciples: baptize them in the name of the Father, the Son, and the Holy Spirit, **20** and teach them to obey everything I have commanded you. And I will be with you always, to the end of the age."

Your Next Step   **Congratulations on finishing the Gospel of Matthew! Use this space to write your thoughts and questions about this book. If you are following the suggested reading plan, go back to the Book of Psalms in the Old Testament. The Psalms were an important part of Jesus and his followers' prayer life.**

The Gospel According to Mark

Are you a person who likes to get right to the facts? Then you will definitely enjoy the Gospel according to Mark. It was the first Gospel to be written and is also the shortest of the four Gospels. The Gospel according to Mark was probably intended for new believers in Rome, which was far away from where Jesus walked, taught, and performed miracles.

Mark does not tell about Jesus' teachings as much as the other Gospels do. Instead it focuses on what it really means to be a disciple and how to live what Jesus taught. At the heart of Mark's Gospel is Jesus' suffering. The message to Mark's readers was that someday they would see the Risen Jesus because of how they lived and accepted their suffering like Jesus accepted his suffering.

Chap. 15:22–32

Headlines

- Names of Jesus' Apostles Revealed (3:13–19)
- Apostles Struggle to Understand Stories (chapter 4)
- Jesus Asks, "Who Do You Say I Am?" (8:27–30)
- Jesus Predicts Suffering and Death (8:31–38; 9:30–32; 10:32–34)
- Trouble Predicted for Jesus' Disciples (13:3–13)
- Jesus Crucified on Friday! (chapter 15)
- Women Frightened by Empty Tomb (16:1–8)

FACTOIDS

Who wrote this book? An old tradition says the author was a follower of Peter called John Mark, but no one really knows for sure.

When was it written? Probably between AD 60 and 70, about thirty-five years after Jesus' Resurrection.

Who was it written for? Mark was originally written for Christians in Rome who were being persecuted.

How does it fit into the Bible? The Gospels of Matthew, Mark, and Luke are called the *synoptic* Gospels. The authors of Matthew and Luke probably used Mark as the starting point for writing their Gospels.

Important themes
- Jesus suffers and so will his followers.
- Jesus tries to keep his identity secret, but the word still gets out.
- Disciples of Jesus recognize him as their Savior, follow his teachings, and tell other people about Jesus.

MARK

The Preaching of John the Baptist
(Matthew 3:1–12; Luke 3:1–18; John 1:19–28)

1 ¹This is the Good News about Jesus Christ, the Son of God.*ᵃ* ²It began as the prophet Isaiah had written:

"God said, 'I will send my messenger
  ahead of you
to open the way for you.'

³Someone is shouting in the desert,
  'Get the road ready for the Lord;
  make a straight path for him to
    travel!' "

⁴So John appeared in the desert, baptizing and preaching.*ᵇ* "Turn away from your sins and be baptized," he told the people, "and God will forgive your sins." ⁵Many people from the province of Judea and the city of Jerusalem went out to hear John. They confessed their sins, and he baptized them in the Jordan River.

⁶John wore clothes made of camel's hair, with a leather belt around his waist, and his food was locusts and wild honey. ⁷He announced to the people, "The man who will come after me is much greater than I am. I am not good enough even to bend down and untie his sandals. ⁸I baptize you with water, but he will baptize you with the Holy Spirit."

The Baptism and Temptation of Jesus
(Matthew 3:13—4:11; Luke 3:21, 22; 4:1–13)

⁹Not long afterward Jesus came from Nazareth in the province of Galilee, and was baptized by John in the Jordan. ¹⁰As soon as Jesus came up out of the water, he saw heaven opening and the Spirit coming down on him like a dove. ¹¹And a voice came from heaven, "You are my own dear Son. I am pleased with you."

¹²At once the Spirit made him go into the desert, ¹³where he stayed forty days, being tempted by Satan. Wild animals were there also, but angels came and helped him.

Jesus Calls Four Fishermen
(Matthew 4:12–22; Luke 4:14, 15; 5:1–11)

¹⁴After John had been put in prison, Jesus went to Galilee and preached the Good News from God. ¹⁵"The right time has come," he said, "and the Kingdom of God is near! Turn away from your sins and believe the Good News!"

¹⁶As Jesus walked along the shore of Lake Galilee, he saw two fishermen, Simon and his brother Andrew, catching fish with a net. ¹⁷Jesus said to them, "Come with me, and I will teach you to catch people." ¹⁸At once they left their nets and went with him.

At once they left their nets. (1:18)

ᵃ **1:1** *Some manuscripts do not have* the Son of God.   *ᵇ* **1:4** John appeared in the desert, baptizing and preaching; *some manuscripts have* John the Baptist appeared in the desert, preaching.
1:2 Mal 3:1   **1:3** Isa 40:3 (LXX)   **1:6** 2 Kings 1:8   **1:11** Gen 22:2; Ps 2:7; Isa 42:1; Mt 3:17; 12:18; Mk 9:7; Lk 3:22   **1:15** Mt 3:2

Lent

Catholic Connections

Before Jesus began his work of teaching and healing, he went to the desert for forty days to pray and fast (Mark 1:12–13). It was his way of preparing for the road ahead of him, the road that would lead him to his passion, death, and Resurrection.

In memory of Jesus' time in the desert, the Church observes Lent. Lent is a special season of the Church year that is the preparation for the mysteries of Easter. It begins on Ash Wednesday, and lasts forty days, until Easter (the forty days do not include the Sundays during Lent). During that time we focus on our sinfulness and try to change our ways to better follow Christ.

Many people do things to help them focus on God during Lent. They might fast from food, spend extra time in prayer, contribute to causes that help poor people, and reach out to people who are in need of extra help and prayers. How does your family celebrate Lent?

— Mark 1:12–13

19 He went a little farther on and saw two other brothers, James and John, the sons of Zebedee. They were in their boat getting their nets ready. 20 As soon as Jesus saw them, he called them; they left their father Zebedee in the boat with the hired men and went with Jesus.

A Man with an Evil Spirit
(Luke 4:31–37)

21 Jesus and his disciples came to the town of Capernaum, and on the next Sabbath Jesus went to the synagogue and began to teach. 22 The people who heard him were amazed at the way he taught, for he wasn't like the teachers of the Law; instead, he taught with authority. 23 Just then a man with an evil spirit came into the synagogue and screamed, 24 "What do you want with us, Jesus of Nazareth? Are you here to destroy us? I know who you are—you are God's holy messenger!" 25 Jesus ordered the spirit, "Be quiet, and come out of the man!"

26 The evil spirit shook the man hard, gave a loud scream, and came out of him. 27 The people were all so amazed that they started saying to one another, "What is this? Is it some kind of new teaching? This man has authority to give orders to the evil spirits, and they obey him!" 28 And so the news about Jesus spread quickly everywhere in the province of Galilee.

Jesus Heals Many People
(Matthew 8:14–17; Luke 4:38–41)

29 Jesus and his disciples, including James and John, left the synagogue and went straight to the home of Simon and Andrew. 30 Simon's mother-in-law was sick in bed with a fever, and as soon as Jesus arrived, he was told about her. 31 He went to her, took her by the hand, and helped her up. The fever left her, and she began to wait on them. 32 After the sun had set and evening had come, people brought to Jesus all the sick and those who had demons. 33 All the people of the town gathered in front of the house.

1:22 Mt 7:28, 29

Mark

How many other events in the Bible can you think of that lasted forty days or forty years?

Took her by the hand, and . . . the fever left her. (1:31)

34 Jesus healed many who were sick with all kinds of diseases and drove out many demons. He would not let the demons say anything, because they knew who he was.

Jesus Preaches in Galilee
(Luke 4:42–44)

35 Very early the next morning, long before daylight, Jesus got up and left the house. He went out of town to a lonely place, where he prayed. 36 But Simon and his companions went out searching for him, 37 and when they found him, they said, "Everyone is looking for you."

38 But Jesus answered, "We must go on to the other villages around here. I have to preach in them also, because that is why I came."

39 So he traveled all over Galilee, preaching in the synagogues and driving out demons.

Jesus Heals a Man
(Matthew 8:1–4; Luke 5:12–16)

40 A man suffering from a dreaded skin disease came to Jesus, knelt down, and begged him for help. "If you want to," he said, "you can make me clean."c

41 Jesus was filled with pity,d and reached out and touched him. "I do want to," he answered. "Be clean!" 42 At once the disease left the man, and he was clean. 43 Then Jesus spoke sternly to him and sent him away at once, 44 after saying to him, "Listen, don't tell anyone about this. But go straight to the priest and let him examine you; then in order to prove to everyone that you are cured, offer the sacrifice that Moses ordered."

45 But the man went away and began to spread the news everywhere. Indeed, he talked so much that Jesus could not go into a town publicly. Instead, he stayed out in lonely places, and people came to him from everywhere.

Jesus Heals a Paralyzed Man
(Matthew 9:1–8; Luke 5:17–26)

2 1 A few days later Jesus went back to Capernaum, and the news spread that he was at home. 2 So many people came together that there was no room left, not even out in front of the door. Jesus was preaching the message to them 3 when four men arrived, carrying a paralyzed man to Jesus. 4 Because of the crowd, however, they could not get the man to him. So they made a hole in the roof right above the place where Jesus was. When they had made an opening, they let the man down, lying on his mat. 5 Seeing how much faith they had, Jesus said to the paralyzed man, "My son, your sins are forgiven."

6 Some teachers of the Law who were sitting there thought to themselves, 7 "How does he dare talk like this? This is blasphemy! God is the only one who can forgive sins!"

8 At once Jesus knew what they were thinking, so he said to them, "Why do you think such things? 9 Is it easier to say to this paralyzed man, 'Your sins are forgiven,' or to say, 'Get up, pick up your mat, and walk'? 10 I will prove to you, then, that the Son of Man has authority on earth to forgive sins." So he said to the paralyzed man, 11 "I tell you, get up, pick up your mat, and go home!"

12 While they all watched, the man got up, picked up his mat, and hurried away. They were all completely amazed and praised

c **1:40** MAKE ME CLEAN: *This disease was considered to make a person ritually unclean.*   d **1:41** pity; *some manuscripts have* anger.
1:39 Mt 4:23; 9:35   **1:44** Lev 14:1-32

Read Mark 2:13–17. Who are the outcasts in your life? How have you reached out to them? If you haven't, what keeps you from doing it?

God, saying, "We have never seen anything like this!"

Jesus Calls Levi
(Matthew 9:9–13; Luke 5:27–32)

¹³Jesus went back again to the shore of Lake Galilee. A crowd came to him, and he started teaching them. ¹⁴As he walked along, he saw a tax collector, Levi son of Alphaeus, sitting in his office. Jesus said to him, "Follow me." Levi got up and followed him.

¹⁵Later on Jesus was having a meal in Levi's house.ᵉ A large number of tax collectors and other outcasts was following Jesus, and many of them joined him and his disciples at the table. ¹⁶Some teachers of the Law, who were Pharisees, saw that Jesus was eating with these outcasts and tax collectors, so they asked his disciples, "Why does he eat with such people?"

¹⁷Jesus heard them and answered, "People who are well do not need a doctor, but only those who are sick. I have not come to call respectable people, but outcasts."

The Question about Fasting
(Matthew 9:14–17; Luke 5:33–39)

¹⁸On one occasion the followers of John the Baptist and the Pharisees were fasting. Some people came to Jesus and asked him, "Why is it that the disciples of John the Baptist and the disciples of the Pharisees fast, but yours do not?"

¹⁹Jesus answered, "Do you expect the guests at a wedding party to go without food? Of course not! As long as the bridegroom is with them, they will not do that. ²⁰But the day will come when the bridegroom will be taken away from them, and then they will fast.

²¹"No one uses a piece of new cloth to patch up an old coat, because the new patch will shrink and tear off some of the old cloth, making an even bigger hole. ²²Nor does anyone pour new wine into used wineskins, because the wine will burst the skins, and both the wine and the skins will be ruined. Instead, new wine must be poured into fresh wineskins."

Forgiveness

Did you ever ask someone to keep a secret, only to find out that the entire school knows about it? Did you ever get your feelings hurt? Has anyone ever told a lie that got you in trouble? Have you ever done these things to someone else?

When people hurt you, you may be angry and upset. That's a normal human reaction. But eventually you have to get to a point where you can forgive them. Otherwise the negative feelings might begin to affect other relationships. That's why Jesus first forgave the paralyzed man's sins (Mark 2:5). Jesus wanted to show that healing someone from sin is even more important than physical healing.

When you forgive someone, you free yourself to move on to other important concerns. When you are forgiven for your sins—by God and the people you have hurt—you are free to move on and learn from your mistake.

- God forgives you for all your sins if you are truly sorry. Shouldn't you do the same for others?
- Who do you need to forgive?
- From whom do you need forgiveness?

— Mark 2:1–12

The Question about the Sabbath
(Matthew 12:1–8; Luke 6:1–5)

²³Jesus was walking through some wheat fields on a Sabbath. As his disciples walked along with him, they began to pick the heads of wheat. ²⁴So the Pharisees said to

Mark

ᵉ **2:15** in Levi's house; *or* in his *(that is, Jesus')* house.
2:23 Deut 23:25

Jesus, "Look, it is against our Law for your disciples to do that on the Sabbath!"

25 Jesus answered, "Have you never read what David did that time when he needed something to eat? He and his men were hungry, 26 so he went into the house of God and ate the bread offered to God. This happened when Abiathar was the High Priest. According to our Law only the priests may eat this bread—but David ate it and even gave it to his men."

27 And Jesus concluded, "The Sabbath was made for the good of human beings; they were not made for the Sabbath. 28 So the Son of Man is Lord even of the Sabbath."

The Man with a Paralyzed Hand
(Matthew 12:9–14; Luke 6:6–11)

3 1 Then Jesus went back to the synagogue, where there was a man who had a paralyzed hand. 2 Some people were there who wanted to accuse Jesus of doing wrong; so they watched him closely to see whether he would cure the man on the Sabbath. 3 Jesus said to the man, "Come up here to the front." 4 Then he asked the people, "What does our Law allow us to do on the Sabbath? To help or to harm? To save someone's life or to destroy it?"

But they did not say a thing. 5 Jesus was angry as he looked around at them, but at the same time he felt sorry for them, because they were so stubborn and wrong. Then he said to the man, "Stretch out your hand." He stretched it out, and it became well again. 6 So the Pharisees left the synagogue and met at once with some members of Herod's party, and they made plans to kill Jesus.

A Crowd by the Lake

7 Jesus and his disciples went away to Lake Galilee, and a large crowd followed him. They had come from Galilee, from Judea, 8 from Jerusalem, from the territory of Idumea, from the territory on the east side of the Jordan, and from the region around the cities of Tyre and Sidon. All these people came to Jesus because they had heard of the things he was doing. 9 The crowd was so large that Jesus told his disciples to get a boat ready for him, so that the people would not crush him. 10 He had healed many people, and all the sick kept pushing their way to him in order to touch him. 11 And whenever the people who had evil spirits in them saw him, they would fall down before him and scream, "You are the Son of God!"

The crowd was so large . . . (3:9)

2:26 Lev 24:9   **2:25,26** 1 Sam 21:1-6   **3:9,10** Mk 4:1; Lk 5:1-3

Pray It!

Called and Sent

Jesus chose twelve men to be his closest followers. He called them Apostles, which is from a word that means "one who is sent out." Many other men and women followed Jesus, but the Twelve (as they are often called) were singled out by name. They are listed in Mark 3:16–19.

The number 12 had special meaning to Jesus, who was a devout Jew. It represented the twelve sons of Jacob and the Twelve Tribes of Israel.

The Apostles were twelve people with different personalities and different jobs. Some were young, some were old. Some were married, some single. Though they weren't all perfect, the thing they had in common was that they were willing to follow Jesus. After Jesus' Resurrection the Apostles who remained continued Jesus' mission in building the Church.

> Jesus,
> Help me to hear your call.
> I want to follow you, wherever you lead me.
> I don't need to start a church.
> I just need to let the Church guide me and strengthen me
>   so that I can share your love with others.
> Thank you, Jesus, for calling me to be part of your family.
> Amen.

— Mark 3:13–19

Mark

---

12 Jesus sternly ordered the evil spirits not to tell anyone who he was.

Jesus Chooses the Twelve Apostles
(Matthew 10:1–4; Luke 6:12–16)

13 Then Jesus went up a hill and called to himself the men he wanted. They came to him, 14 and he chose twelve, whom he named apostles. "I have chosen you to be with me," he told them. "I will also send you out to preach, 15 and you will have authority to drive out demons."

16 These are the twelve he chose: Simon (Jesus gave him the name Peter); 17 James and his brother John, the sons of Zebedee (Jesus gave them the name Boanerges, which means "Men of Thunder"); 18 Andrew, Philip, Bartholomew, Matthew, Thomas, James son

of Alphaeus, Thaddaeus, Simon the Patriot, 19 and Judas Iscariot, who betrayed Jesus.

Jesus and Beelzebul
(Matthew 12:22–32; Luke 11:14–23; 12:10)

20 Then Jesus went home. Again such a large crowd gathered that Jesus and his disciples had no time to eat. 21 When his family heard about it, they set out to take charge of him, because people were saying, "He's gone mad!"

22 Some teachers of the Law who had come from Jerusalem were saying, "He has Beelzebul in him! It is the chief of the demons who gives him the power to drive them out."

23 So Jesus called them to him and spoke to them in parables: "How can Satan drive out Satan? 24 If a country divides itself into groups which fight each other, that country

3:22 Mt 9:34; 10:25

The Apostle Judas killed himself after he betrayed Jesus. Do you know who replaced him? Check out Acts 1:15–26.

The Church Is the Family of God

Ca holic Connec ions

In the little story about Jesus' mother and brothers (Mark 3:31–35), it almost seems as if Jesus is putting down his family. But that wasn't his intention. Jesus was trying to make a bigger point. His point is that the family of God is bigger than blood relatives or relationships. The family of God is anyone who believes in Jesus and does what God asks.

Starting with teachings such as this, Jesus put into motion everything that was needed to start the Catholic Church. The Church was in God's plan from the very beginning, from the moment of Creation. God calls everyone together in Jesus and the Holy Spirit and invites everyone to become his children. Jesus started the Church to be God's family on earth—which is why the Church is sometimes called the family of God.

— Mark 3:31–35

will fall apart. 25 If a family divides itself into groups which fight each other, that family will fall apart. 26 So if Satan's kingdom divides into groups, it cannot last, but will fall apart and come to an end.

27 "No one can break into a strong man's house and take away his belongings unless he first ties up the strong man; then he can plunder his house.

28 "I assure you that people can be forgiven all their sins and all the evil things they may say.ʄ 29 But whoever says evil things against the Holy Spirit will never be forgiven, because he has committed an eternal sin." (30 Jesus said this because some people were saying, "He has an evil spirit in him.")

Jesus' Mother and Brothers
(Matthew 12:46–50; Luke 8:19–21)

31 Then Jesus' mother and brothers arrived. They stood outside the house and sent in a message, asking for him. 32 A crowd was sitting around Jesus, and they said to him, "Look, your mother and your brothers and sisters are outside, and they want you."

33 Jesus answered, "Who is my mother? Who are my brothers?" 34 He looked at the people sitting around him and said, "Look! Here are my mother and my brothers! 35 Whoever does what God wants is my brother, my sister, my mother."

The Parable of the Sower
(Matthew 13:1–9; Luke 8:4–8)

4 1 Again Jesus began to teach beside Lake Galilee. The crowd that gathered around him was so large that he got into a boat and sat in it. The boat was out in the water, and the crowd stood on the shore at the water's edge. 2 He used parables to teach them many things, saying to them:

3 "Listen! Once there was a man who went out to sow grain. 4 As he scattered the seed in the field, some of it fell along the path, and the birds came and ate it up. 5 Some of it fell on rocky ground, where there was little soil. The seeds soon sprouted,

ʄ 3:28 evil things they may say; or evil things they may say against God.
3:29 Lk 12:10   4:1 Lk 5:1-3

" 'Whoever does what God wants is my brother, my sister, my mother' "
(Mark 3:35).

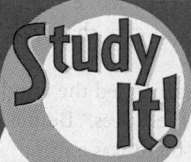

Stories That Teach

When you were a child, you probably heard stories like *The Little Engine That Could, Runaway Bunny,* and *Rainbow Fish.* These are interesting stories that teach a lesson about life.

Jesus also used stories to teach people how to live the way God wants them to. These stories with a spiritual message are called parables. To make his point, Jesus told parables about people, places, and things that were familiar to his audience. But his stories often ended in ways that surprised people and made them think about what God was like.

How many different parables can you find in Mark, chapter 4?

— Mark, chapter 4

because the soil wasn't deep. 6Then, when the sun came up, it burned the young plants; and because the roots had not grown deep enough, the plants soon dried up. 7Some of the seed fell among thorn bushes, which grew up and choked the plants, and they didn't bear grain. 8But some seeds fell in good soil, and the plants sprouted, grew, and bore grain: some had thirty grains, others sixty, and others one hundred."

9And Jesus concluded, "Listen, then, if you have ears!"

The Purpose of the Parables
(Matthew 13:10–17; Luke 8:9, 10)

10When Jesus was alone, some of those who had heard him came to him with the twelve disciples and asked him to explain the parables. 11"You have been given the secret of the Kingdom of God," Jesus answered. "But the others, who are on the outside, hear all things by means of parables, 12so that,

'They may look and look,
    yet not see;
they may listen and listen,
    yet not understand.
For if they did, they would turn to God,
    and he would forgive them.' "

Jesus Explains the Parable of the Sower
(Matthew 13:18–23; Luke 8:11–15)

13Then Jesus asked them, "Don't you understand this parable? How, then, will you ever understand any parable? 14The sower sows God's message. 15Some people are like the seeds that fall along the path; as soon as they hear the message, Satan comes and takes it away. 16Other people are like the seeds that fall on rocky ground. As soon as they hear the message, they receive it gladly. 17But it does not sink deep into them, and they don't last long. So when trouble or persecution comes because of the message, they give up at once. 18Other people are like the seeds sown among the thorn bushes. These are the ones who hear the message, 19but the worries about this life, the love for riches, and all other kinds of desires crowd in and choke the message, and they don't bear fruit. 20But other people are like seeds sown in good soil. They hear the message, accept it, and bear fruit: some thirty, some sixty, and some one hundred."

A Lamp under a Bowl
(Luke 8:16–18)

21Jesus continued, "Does anyone ever bring in a lamp and put it under a bowl or under the bed? Isn't it put on the lampstand? 22Whatever is hidden away will be brought out into the open, and whatever is covered up will be uncovered. 23Listen, then, if you have ears!"

24He also said to them, "Pay attention to what you hear! The same rules you use to judge others will be used by God to judge

Mark

4:12 Isa 6:9,10 (LXX)   4:21 Mt 5:15; Lk 11:33   4:22 Mt 10:26; Lk 12:2   4:24 Mt 7:2; Lk 6:38

you—but with even greater severity. 25 Those who have something will be given more, and those who have nothing will have taken away from them even the little they have."

The Parable of the Growing Seed

26 Jesus went on to say, "The Kingdom of God is like this. A man scatters seed in his field. 27 He sleeps at night, is up and about during the day, and all the while the seeds are sprouting and growing. Yet he does not know how it happens. 28 The soil itself makes the plants grow and bear fruit; first the tender stalk appears, then the head, and finally the head full of grain. 29 When the grain is ripe, the man starts cutting it with his sickle, because harvest time has come.

The Parable of the Mustard Seed
(Matthew 13:31, 32, 34; Luke 13:18, 19)

30 "What shall we say the Kingdom of God is like?" asked Jesus. "What parable shall we use to explain it? 31 It is like this. A man takes a mustard seed, the smallest seed in the world, and plants it in the ground. 32 After a while it grows up and becomes the biggest of all plants. It puts out such large branches that the birds come and make their nests in its shade."

33 Jesus preached his message to the people, using many other parables like these; he told them as much as they could understand. 34 He would not speak to them without using parables, but when he was alone with his disciples, he would explain everything to them.

Jesus Calms a Storm
(Matthew 8:23–27; Luke 8:22–25)

35 On the evening of that same day Jesus said to his disciples, "Let us go across to the other side of the lake." 36 So they left the crowd; the disciples got into the boat in which Jesus was already sitting, and they took him with them. Other boats were there too. 37 Suddenly a strong wind blew up, and the waves began to spill over into the boat, so that it was about to fill with water. 38 Jesus was in the back of the boat, sleeping with his head on a pillow. The disciples woke him up and said, "Teacher, don't you care that we are about to die?"

39 Jesus stood up and commanded the wind, "Be quiet!" and he said to the waves, "Be still!" The wind died down, and there was a great calm. 40 Then Jesus said to his disciples, "Why are you frightened? Do you still have no faith?"

Waves began to spill over into the boat (4:37) . . . and there was a great calm. (4:39)

41 But they were terribly afraid and began to say to one another, "Who is this man? Even the wind and the waves obey him!"

Jesus Heals a Man with Evil Spirits
(Matthew 8:28–34; Luke 8:26–39)

5 1 Jesus and his disciples arrived on the other side of Lake Galilee, in the territory of Gerasa. 2 As soon as Jesus got out of the boat, he was met by a man who came out of the burial caves there. This man had an evil spirit in him 3 and lived among the tombs. Nobody could keep him tied with chains any more; 4 many times his feet and his hands had been tied, but every time he broke the chains and smashed the irons on his feet. He was too strong for anyone to control him. 5 Day and night he wandered among the tombs and through the hills, screaming and cutting himself with stones.

6 He was some distance away when he saw Jesus; so he ran, fell on his knees before him, 7 and screamed in a loud voice, "Jesus, Son of the Most High God! What do you want with me? For God's sake, I beg you, don't

4:25 Mt 13:12; 25:29; Lk 19:26 **4:29** Joel 3:13

Pray It!

God Is Good!

I know I ask for a lot, God.
Just like the people who saw Jesus at Galilee,
*   I'm usually asking you for help.*
But this prayer is going to be different.
I don't want anything.
I don't need help with a problem.
And I know you're right here with me.
Right now, I just want to say thank you.
Thanks for all you do for me.
Thanks for making me who I am.
Thanks for the people who love me.
Thanks for this wonderful world.
Thanks for being right here with me.
Just one small request: Please give me the courage
*   to tell my friends how great you are. Amen.*

— Mark 5:18–20

Mark

punish me!" (⁸He said this because Jesus was saying, "Evil spirit, come out of this man!")

⁹So Jesus asked him, "What is your name?"

The man answered, "My name is 'Mob'—there are so many of us!" ¹⁰And he kept begging Jesus not to send the evil spirits out of that region.

¹¹There was a large herd of pigs near by, feeding on a hillside. ¹²So the spirits begged Jesus, "Send us to the pigs, and let us go into them." ¹³He let them go, and the evil spirits went out of the man and entered the pigs. The whole herd—about two thousand pigs in all—rushed down the side of the cliff into the lake and was drowned.

¹⁴The men who had been taking care of the pigs ran away and spread the news in the town and among the farms. People went out to see what had happened, ¹⁵and when they came to Jesus, they saw the man who used to have the mob of demons in him. He was sitting there, clothed and in his right mind; and they were all afraid. ¹⁶Those who had seen it told the people what had happened to the man with the demons, and about the pigs.

¹⁷So they asked Jesus to leave their territory.

¹⁸As Jesus was getting into the boat, the man who had had the demons begged him, "Let me go with you!"

¹⁹But Jesus would not let him. Instead, he told him, "Go back home to your family and tell them how much the Lord has done for you and how kind he has been to you."

²⁰So the man left and went all through the Ten Towns, telling what Jesus had done for him. And all who heard it were amazed.

Jairus' Daughter and the Woman Who Touched Jesus' Cloak
(Matthew 9:18–26; Luke 8:40–56)

²¹Jesus went back across to the other side of the lake. There at the lakeside a large crowd gathered around him. ²²Jairus, an official of the local synagogue, arrived, and when he saw Jesus, he threw himself down

Read Mark 4:35–41. What rough and stormy times in your life do you need Jesus' help with?

at his feet 23and begged him earnestly, "My little daughter is very sick. Please come and place your hands on her, so that she will get well and live!"

24Then Jesus started off with him. So many people were going along with Jesus that they were crowding him from every side.

25There was a woman who had suffered terribly from severe bleeding for twelve years, 26even though she had been treated by many doctors. She had spent all her money, but instead of getting better she got worse all the time. 27She had heard about Jesus, so she came in the crowd behind him, 28saying to herself, "If I just touch his clothes, I will get well."

29She touched his cloak, and her bleeding stopped at once; and she had the feeling inside herself that she was healed of her trouble. 30At once Jesus knew that power had gone out of him, so he turned around in the crowd and asked, "Who touched my clothes?"

31His disciples answered, "You see how the people are crowding you; why do you ask who touched you?"

32But Jesus kept looking around to see who had done it. 33The woman realized what had happened to her, so she came, trembling with fear, knelt at his feet, and told him the whole truth. 34Jesus said to her, "My daughter, your faith has made you well. Go in peace, and be healed of your trouble."

35While Jesus was saying this, some messengers came from Jairus' house and told him, "Your daughter has died. Why bother the Teacher any longer?"

36Jesus paid no attention tog what they said, but told him, "Don't be afraid, only believe." 37Then he did not let anyone else go on with him except Peter and James and his brother John. 38They arrived at Jairus' house, where Jesus saw the confusion and heard all the loud crying and wailing. 39He went in and said to them, "Why all this confusion? Why are you crying? The child is not dead—she is only sleeping!"

40They started making fun of him, so he put them all out, took the child's father and mother and his three disciples, and went into the room where the child was lying. 41He took her by the hand and said to her, *"Talitha, koum,"* which means, "Little girl, I tell you to get up!"

42She got up at once and started walking around. (She was twelve years old.) When this happened, they were completely amazed. 43But Jesus gave them strict orders not to tell anyone, and he said, "Give her something to eat."

Jesus Is Rejected at Nazareth
(Matthew 13:53–58; Luke 4:16–30)

6 1Jesus left that place and went back to his hometown, followed by his disciples. 2On the Sabbath he began to teach in the synagogue. Many people were there; and when they heard him, they were all amazed. "Where did he get all this?" they asked. "What wisdom is this that has been given him? How does he perform miracles? 3Isn't he the carpenter, the son of Mary, and the brother of James, Joseph, Judas, and Simon? Aren't his sisters living here?" And so they rejected him.

4Jesus said to them, "Prophets are respected everywhere except in their own hometown and by their relatives and their family."

5He was not able to perform any miracles there, except that he placed his hands on a few sick people and healed them. 6He was greatly surprised, because the people did not have faith.

Jesus Sends Out the Twelve Disciples
(Matthew 10:5–15; Luke 9:1–6)

Then Jesus went to the villages around there, teaching the people. 7He called the twelve disciples together and sent them out two by two. He gave them authority over the evil spirits 8and ordered them, "Don't take anything with you on the trip except a walking stick—no bread, no beggar's bag, no

---

g **5:36** paid no attention to; *or* overheard.
5:26 Tob 2:10   **6:4** Jn 4:44

What? No Cell Phone?

Can you imagine going away for a while with nothing but the clothes and shoes you have on? No money, no extra clothes, no cell phone, nothing! That's what Jesus tells the disciples to do when he sends them off to preach (Mark 6:7–9). He tells them to rely on the goodness of the people they meet.

Most of us have too many things. Our lives are cluttered with possessions we think we can't live without. We get so caught up in the things we think we need for day-to-day living that we forget the most important thing: God.

Next time you're packing up for school or to go to a friend's house, remind yourself to pack the knowledge that God is with you, God cares for you, and God wants you to spread the Good News to others. And to do that, you don't need anything but the love in your heart.

— Mark 6:6–13

money in your pockets. ⁹Wear sandals, but don't carry an extra shirt." ¹⁰He also told them, "Wherever you are welcomed, stay in the same house until you leave that place. ¹¹If you come to a town where people do not welcome you or will not listen to you, leave it and shake the dust off your feet. That will be a warning to them!"

¹²So they went out and preached that people should turn away from their sins. ¹³They drove out many demons, and rubbed olive oil on many sick people and healed them.

The Death of John the Baptist
(Matthew 14:1–12; Luke 9:7–9)

¹⁴Now King Herod[h] heard about all this, because Jesus' reputation had spread everywhere. Some people were saying, "John the Baptist has come back to life! That is why he has this power to perform miracles."

¹⁵Others, however, said, "He is Elijah."

Others said, "He is a prophet, like one of the prophets of long ago."

¹⁶When Herod heard it, he said, "He is John the Baptist! I had his head cut off, but he has come back to life!" ¹⁷Herod himself had ordered John's arrest, and he had him tied up and put in prison. Herod did this because of Herodias, whom he had married, even though she was the wife of his brother Philip. ¹⁸John the Baptist kept telling Herod, "It isn't right for you to marry your brother's wife!"

¹⁹So Herodias held a grudge against John and wanted to kill him, but she could not because of Herod. ²⁰Herod was afraid of John because he knew that John was a good and holy man, and so he kept him safe. He liked to listen to him, even though he became greatly disturbed every time he heard him.

²¹Finally Herodias got her chance. It was on Herod's birthday, when he gave a feast for all the top government officials, the military chiefs, and the leading citizens of Galilee. ²²The daughter of Herodias[i] came in and danced, and pleased Herod and his guests. So the king said to the girl, "What would you like to have? I will give you anything you want." ²³With many vows he said to her, "I swear that I will give you anything you ask for, even as much as half my kingdom!"

²⁴So the girl went out and asked her mother, "What shall I ask for?"

"The head of John the Baptist," she answered.

²⁵The girl hurried back at once to the king and demanded, "I want you to give me here and now the head of John the Baptist on a plate!"

Mark

---

[h] **6:14** KING HEROD: *Herod Antipas, ruler of Galilee.*   [i] **6:22** The daughter of Herodias; *some manuscripts have* His daughter Herodias.
6:11 Acts 13:51   **6:8–11** Lk 10:4–11   **6:13** Jas 5:14   **6:14,15** Mt 16:14; Mk 8:28; Lk 9:19   **6:17,18** Lk 3:19,20

Feeding the Hungry

Millions of people in this world—and in this country—don't get enough to eat. Most of us can't understand what such hunger feels like. We can barely make it from lunch to dinner without a snack. But many people get nothing to eat for days.

Jesus took a few loaves of bread and a couple of fish and fed thousands of people who came to see him. You can't perform miracles like that, but you can make a difference in lots of ways:

- Give up a few treats each week and give the money you save to poor people.
- Donate food when your school runs a food drive.
- Collect food from your neighbors and friends and donate it.
- Pray for people who are starving.

Jesus is a special friend of poor people, and as members of the Body of Christ, we need to befriend them too. You probably don't know what it's like to go hungry, but you can be a special friend to those who do.

— Mark 6:30–44

26 This made the king very sad, but he could not refuse her because of the vows he had made in front of all his guests. 27 So he sent off a guard at once with orders to bring John's head. The guard left, went to the prison, and cut John's head off; 28 then he brought it on a plate and gave it to the girl, who gave it to her mother. 29 When John's disciples heard about this, they came and got his body, and buried it.

Jesus Feeds Five Thousand
(Matthew 14:13–21; Luke 9:10–17; John 6:1–14)

30 The apostles returned and met with Jesus, and told him all they had done and taught. 31 There were so many people coming and going that Jesus and his disciples didn't even have time to eat. So he said to them, "Let us go off by ourselves to some place where we will be alone and you can rest a while." 32 So they started out in a boat by themselves to a lonely place.

33 Many people, however, saw them leave and knew at once who they were; so they went from all the towns and ran ahead by land and arrived at the place ahead of Jesus and his disciples. 34 When Jesus got out of the boat, he saw this large crowd, and his heart was filled with pity for them, because they were like sheep without a shepherd. So he began to teach them many things. 35 When it was getting late, his disciples came to him and said, "It is already very late, and this is a lonely place. 36 Send the people away, and let them go to the nearby farms and villages in order to buy themselves something to eat."

37 "You yourselves give them something to eat," Jesus answered.

They asked, "Do you want us to go and spend two hundred silver coins[j] on bread in order to feed them?"

38 So Jesus asked them, "How much bread do you have? Go and see."

When they found out, they told him, "Five loaves and also two fish."

39 Jesus then told his disciples to make all the people divide into groups and sit down on the green grass. 40 So the people sat down in rows, in groups of a hundred and groups of fifty. 41 Then Jesus took the five loaves and the two fish, looked up to heaven, and gave thanks to God. He broke the loaves and gave them to his disciples to distribute to the people. He also divided the two fish among them all. 42 Everyone ate and had enough. 43 Then the disciples took up twelve baskets full of what was left of the bread and the fish. 44 The number of men who were fed was five thousand.

j **6:37** SILVER COINS: *A silver coin was the daily wage of a rural worker (see Mt 20:2).*
6:34 Num 27:17; 1 Kings 22:17; 2 Chr 18:16; Ezek 34:5; Mt 9:36

Mark

"It's a ghost!" (6:49)

Jesus Walks on the Water
(Matthew 14:22–33; John 6:15–21)

⁴⁵At once Jesus made his disciples get into the boat and go ahead of him to Bethsaida, on the other side of the lake, while he sent the crowd away. ⁴⁶After saying good-bye to the people, he went away to a hill to pray. ⁴⁷When evening came, the boat was in the middle of the lake, while Jesus was alone on land. ⁴⁸He saw that his disciples were straining at the oars, because they were rowing against the wind; so sometime between three and six o'clock in the morning, he came to them, walking on the water. He was going to pass them by,ᵏ ⁴⁹but they saw him walking on the water. "It's a ghost!" they thought, and screamed. ⁵⁰They were all terrified when they saw him.

Jesus spoke to them at once, "Courage!" he said. "It is I. Don't be afraid!" ⁵¹Then he got into the boat with them, and the wind died down. The disciples were completely amazed, ⁵²because they had not understood the real meaning of the feeding of the five thousand; their minds could not grasp it.

Jesus Heals the Sick in Gennesaret
(Matthew 14:34–36)

⁵³They crossed the lake and came to land at Gennesaret, where they tied up the boat. ⁵⁴As they left the boat, people recognized Jesus at once. ⁵⁵So they ran throughout the whole region; and wherever they heard he was, they brought to him the sick lying on their mats. ⁵⁶And everywhere Jesus went, to villages, towns, or farms, people would take their sick to the marketplaces and beg him to let the sick at least touch the edge of his cloak. And all who touched it were made well.

The Teaching of the Ancestors
(Matthew 15:1–9)

7 ¹Some Pharisees and teachers of the Law who had come from Jerusalem gathered around Jesus. ²They noticed that some of his disciples were eating their food with hands that were ritually unclean—that is, they had not washed them in the way the Pharisees said people should.

(³For the Pharisees, as well as the rest of the Jews, follow the teaching they received from their ancestors: they do not eat unless they wash their hands in the proper way; ⁴nor do they eat anything that comes from the market unless they wash it first.ˡ And they follow many other rules which they have received, such as the proper way to wash cups, pots, copper bowls, and beds.ᵐ)

⁵So the Pharisees and the teachers of the Law asked Jesus, "Why is it that your disciples do not follow the teaching handed down by our ancestors, but instead eat with ritually unclean hands?"

⁶Jesus answered them, "How right Isaiah was when he prophesied about you! You are hypocrites, just as he wrote:

'These people, says God, honor me with
     their words,
   but their heart is really far away from
     me.
⁷It is no use for them to worship me,
   because they teach human rules
   as though they were my laws!'

⁸"You put aside God's command and obey human teachings."

⁹And Jesus continued, "You have a clever way of rejecting God's law in order to

---

ᵏ **6:48** pass them by; *or* join them.   ˡ **7:4** anything that comes from the market unless they wash it first; *or* anything after they come from the market unless they wash themselves first.   ᵐ **7:4** *Some manuscripts do not have* and beds.
7:6,7 Isa 29:13 (LXX)

Jesus probably fed more than five thousand people with the loaves and fishes. Read Mark 6:44 carefully and see if you can explain why.

Mark

uphold your own teaching. 10For Moses commanded, 'Respect your father and your mother,' and, 'If you curse your father or your mother, you are to be put to death.' 11But you teach that if people have something they could use to help their father or mother, but say, 'This is Corban' (which means, it belongs to God), 12they are excused from helping their father or mother. 13In this way the teaching you pass on to others cancels out the word of God. And there are many other things like this that you do."

The Things That Make a Person Unclean
(Matthew 15:10–20)

14Then Jesus called the crowd to him once more and said to them, "Listen to me, all of you, and understand. 15There is nothing that goes into you from the outside which can make you ritually unclean. Rather, it is what comes out of you that makes you unclean."[n]

17When he left the crowd and went into the house, his disciples asked him to explain this saying. 18"You are no more intelligent than the others," Jesus said to them. "Don't you understand? Nothing that goes into you from the outside can really make you unclean, 19because it does not go into your heart but into your stomach and then goes on out of the body." (In saying this, Jesus declared that all foods are fit to be eaten.)

20And he went on to say, "It is what comes out of you that makes you unclean. 21For from the inside, from your heart, come the evil ideas which lead you to do immoral things, to rob, kill, 22commit adultery, be greedy, and do all sorts of evil things; deceit, indecency, jealousy, slander, pride, and folly— 23all these evil things come from inside you and make you unclean."

A Woman's Faith
(Matthew 15:21–28)

24Then Jesus left and went away to the territory near the city of Tyre. He went into a house and did not want anyone to know he was there, but he could not stay hidden. 25A woman, whose daughter had an evil spirit in her, heard about Jesus and came to him at once and fell at his feet. 26The woman was a Gentile, born in the region of Phoenicia in Syria. She begged Jesus to drive the demon out of her daughter. 27But Jesus answered, "Let us first feed the children. It isn't right to take the children's food and throw it to the dogs."

28"Sir," she answered, "even the dogs under the table eat the children's leftovers!"

29So Jesus said to her, "Because of that answer, go back home, where you will find that the demon has gone out of your daughter!"

30She went home and found her child lying on the bed; the demon had indeed gone out of her.

Jesus Heals a Deaf-Mute

31Jesus then left the neighborhood of Tyre and went on through Sidon to Lake Galilee, going by way of the territory of the Ten Towns. 32Some people brought him a man who was deaf and could hardly speak, and they begged Jesus to place his hands on him. 33So Jesus took him off alone, away from the crowd, put his fingers in the man's ears, spat, and touched the man's tongue. 34Then Jesus looked up to heaven, gave a deep groan, and said to the man, *"Ephphatha,"* which means, "Open up!"

35At once the man was able to hear, his speech impediment was removed, and he began to talk without any trouble. 36Then Jesus ordered the people not to speak of it to anyone; but the more he ordered them not to, the more they told it. 37And all who

---

[n] *7:15 Some manuscripts add verse 16: Listen, then, if you have ears! (see 4:23).*
7:10 a Ex 20:12; Deut 5:16; b Ex 21:17; Lev 20:9

Jews followed strict laws for preparing and eating food (see Mark 7:3–4). Check out Leviticus, chapter 11, for more laws about food.

Watch Those "Isms"!

The woman's daughter was sick. She had heard about Jesus and decided to take a chance, even though he was a Jew and she was not. In Jesus' culture Jews were expected to stay away from non-Jews, but out of mercy and love he healed the girl (Mark 7:24–30).

Some people refuse to associate with those who aren't like them. They may believe that people who are different are inferior. These people are *prejudiced,* that is, they "pre-judge" others.

Some common prejudices include *racism* (judging on the basis of skin color or home country), *sexism* (stereotyping or treating someone unfairly because of gender), and *ageism* (discriminating against people because of their age). These attitudes are contrary to Jesus' law of love. They are sinful. What prejudices or "isms" exist in your community? How can you help eliminate them?

— Mark 7:24–30

heard were completely amazed. "How well he does everything!" they exclaimed. "He even causes the deaf to hear and the dumb to speak!"

Jesus Feeds Four Thousand People
(Matthew 15:32–39)

8 ¹Not long afterward another large crowd came together. When the people had nothing left to eat, Jesus called the disciples to him and said, ²"I feel sorry for these people, because they have been with me for three days and now have nothing to eat. ³If I send them home without feeding them, they will faint as they go, because some of them have come a long way."

⁴His disciples asked him, "Where in this desert can anyone find enough food to feed all these people?"

⁵"How much bread do you have?" Jesus asked.

"Seven loaves," they answered.

⁶He ordered the crowd to sit down on the ground. Then he took the seven loaves, gave thanks to God, broke them, and gave them to his disciples to distribute to the crowd; and the disciples did so. ⁷They also had a few small fish. Jesus gave thanks for these and told the disciples to distribute them too. ⁸⁻⁹Everybody ate and had enough—there were about four thousand people. Then the disciples took up seven baskets full of pieces left over. Jesus sent the people away ¹⁰and at once got into a boat with his disciples and went to the district of Dalmanutha.

The Pharisees Ask for a Miracle
(Matthew 16:1–4)

¹¹Some Pharisees came to Jesus and started to argue with him. They wanted to trap him, so they asked him to perform a miracle to show that God approved of him. ¹²But Jesus gave a deep groan and said, "Why do the people of this day ask for a miracle? No, I tell you! No such proof will be given to these people!"

¹³He left them, got back into the boat, and started across to the other side of the lake.

The Yeast of the Pharisees and of Herod
(Matthew 16:5–12)

¹⁴The disciples had forgotten to bring enough bread and had only one loaf with them in the boat. ¹⁵"Take care," Jesus warned them, "and be on your guard against the yeast of the Pharisees and the yeast of Herod."

¹⁶They started discussing among themselves: "He says this because we don't have any bread."

¹⁷Jesus knew what they were saying, so he asked them, "Why are you discussing about

Mark

8:11 Mt 12:38; Lk 11:16   8:12 Mt 12:39; Lk 11:29   8:15 Lk 12:1

What's Your Answer?

You've probably noticed that you're changing. Your body is growing, you think deeper thoughts, and your emotions are more complicated. You are on an exciting road to becoming an adult.

Your understanding of God is also changing. When you were a child, your thoughts about God were simple. Now that you're older, you have deeper faith, but you may also have more questions. You may even have doubts.

Your understanding of God must grow with you. Jesus will keep asking the question, "Who do you say I am?" just as he asked his first disciples in the middle of this chapter (Mark 8:29). Keep thinking about your answer and pray for the Holy Spirit to guide your thoughts. Peter must have been thinking for some time about who Jesus was. If you do the same, you can answer Jesus as confidently as he did: "You are the Messiah" (8:29).

— Mark 8:27–30

21 "And you still don't understand?" he asked them.

Jesus Heals a Blind Man at Bethsaida

22 They came to Bethsaida, where some people brought a blind man to Jesus and begged him to touch him. 23 Jesus took the blind man by the hand and led him out of the village. After spitting on the man's eyes, Jesus placed his hands on him and asked him, "Can you see anything?"

24 The man looked up and said, "Yes, I can see people, but they look like trees walking around."

25 Jesus again placed his hands on the man's eyes. This time the man looked intently, his eyesight returned, and he saw everything clearly. 26 Jesus then sent him home with the order, "Don't go back into the village."

Peter's Declaration about Jesus
(Matthew 16:13–20; Luke 9:18–21)

27 Then Jesus and his disciples went away to the villages near Caesarea Philippi. On the way he asked them, "Tell me, who do people say I am?"

28 "Some say that you are John the Baptist," they answered; "others say that you are Elijah, while others say that you are one of the prophets."

29 "What about you?" he asked them. "Who do you say I am?"

Peter answered, "You are the Messiah."

30 Then Jesus ordered them, "Do not tell anyone about me."

Jesus Speaks about His Suffering and Death
(Matthew 16:21–28; Luke 9:22–27)

31 Then Jesus began to teach his disciples: "The Son of Man must suffer much and be rejected by the elders, the chief priests, and the teachers of the Law. He will be put to death, but three days later he will rise to life." 32 He made this very clear to them. So Peter took him aside and began to rebuke him. 33 But Jesus turned around, looked at his disciples, and rebuked Peter. "Get away from

not having any bread? Don't you know or understand yet? Are your minds so dull? 18 You have eyes—can't you see? You have ears—can't you hear? Don't you remember 19 when I broke the five loaves for the five thousand people? How many baskets full of leftover pieces did you take up?"

"Twelve," they answered.

20 "And when I broke the seven loaves for the four thousand people," asked Jesus, "how many baskets full of leftover pieces did you take up?"

"Seven," they answered.

8:18 Jer 5:21; Ezek 12:2; Mk 4:12   **8:28** Mk 6:14,15; Lk 9:7,8   **8:29** Jn 6:68,69

Dazzled by Glory

Catholic Connections

The scene described at the beginning of Mark, chapter 9, is known as the Transfiguration. It was a moment when Jesus was literally changed so that his glory as the divine Son of God was revealed. The dazzling sight overwhelmed Peter, James, and John, who were with Jesus on the mountaintop that day. It was a sneak peek for the three Apostles of the time when Jesus would be resurrected.

In the Transfiguration the Holy Trinity was present. The Father was the voice, Jesus the Son was there, and the Holy Spirit was represented by the cloud. The Church has many prayers that praise the Holy Trinity. Following is the most common of these prayers. It is usually called the Glory Be. Memorize it and say it the next time you are dazzled by God's brilliance!

> *Glory be to the Father, and to the Son, and to the Holy Spirit:*
> *As it was in the beginning, is now,*
> *and will be forever. Amen.*

— Mark 9:2–8

Mark

me, Satan," he said. "Your thoughts don't come from God but from human nature!"

34 Then Jesus called the crowd and his disciples to him. "If any of you want to come with me," he told them, "you must forget yourself, carry your cross, and follow me. **35** For if you want to save your own life, you will lose it; but if you lose your life for me and for the gospel, you will save it. **36** Do you gain anything if you win the whole world but lose your life? Of course not! **37** There is nothing you can give to regain your life. **38** If you are ashamed of me

. . . . you must forget yourself, carry your cross, and follow me. (8:34)

and of my teaching in this godless and wicked day, then the Son of Man will be ashamed of you when he comes in the glory of his Father with the holy angels."

9 **1** And he went on to say, "I tell you, there are some here who will not die until they have seen the Kingdom of God come with power."

The Transfiguration
(Matthew 17:1–13; Luke 9:28–36)

2 Six days later Jesus took with him Peter, James, and John, and led them up a high mountain, where they were alone. As they looked on, a change came over Jesus, **3** and his clothes became shining white—whiter than anyone in the world could wash them. **4** Then the three disciples saw Elijah and Moses talking with Jesus. **5** Peter spoke up and said to Jesus, "Teacher, how good it is that we are here! We will make three tents,

8:34 Mt 10:38; Lk 14:27   **8:35** Mt 10:39; Lk 17:33; Jn 12:25   **9:2-7** 2 Pet 1:17,18

one for you, one for Moses, and one for Elijah." [6]He and the others were so frightened that he did not know what to say.

[7]Then a cloud appeared and covered them with its shadow, and a voice came from the cloud, "This is my own dear Son—listen to him!" [8]They took a quick look around but did not see anyone else; only Jesus was with them.

[9]As they came down the mountain, Jesus ordered them, "Don't tell anyone what you have seen, until the Son of Man has risen from death."

[10]They obeyed his order, but among themselves they started discussing the matter, "What does this 'rising from death' mean?" [11]And they asked Jesus, "Why do the teachers of the Law say that Elijah has to come first?"

[12]His answer was, "Elijah is indeed coming first in order to get everything ready. Yet why do the Scriptures say that the Son of Man will suffer much and be rejected? [13]I tell you, however, that Elijah has already come and that people treated him just as they pleased, as the Scriptures say about him."

Jesus Heals a Boy with an Evil Spirit
(Matthew 17:14–21; Luke 9:37–43a)

[14]When they joined the rest of the disciples, they saw a large crowd around them and some teachers of the Law arguing with them. [15]When the people saw Jesus, they were greatly surprised, and ran to him and greeted him. [16]Jesus asked his disciples, "What are you arguing with them about?"

[17]A man in the crowd answered, "Teacher, I brought my son to you, because he has an evil spirit in him and cannot talk. [18]Whenever the spirit attacks him, it throws him to the ground, and he foams at the mouth, grits his teeth, and becomes stiff all over. I asked your disciples to drive the spirit out, but they could not."

[19]Jesus said to them, "How unbelieving you people are! How long must I stay with you? How long do I have to put up with

you? Bring the boy to me!" [20]They brought him to Jesus.

As soon as the spirit saw Jesus, it threw the boy into a fit, so that he fell on the ground and rolled around, foaming at the mouth. [21]"How long has he been like this?" Jesus asked the father.

"Ever since he was a child," he replied. [22]"Many times the evil spirit has tried to kill him by throwing him in the fire and into water. Have pity on us and help us, if you possibly can!"

[23]"Yes," said Jesus, "if you yourself can! Everything is possible for the person who has faith."

[24]The father at once cried out, "I do have faith, but not enough. Help me have more!"

[25]Jesus noticed that the crowd was closing in on them, so he gave a command to the evil spirit. "Deaf and dumb spirit," he said, "I order you to come out of the boy and never go into him again!"

[26]The spirit screamed, threw the boy into a bad fit, and came out. The boy looked like a corpse, and everyone said, "He is dead!" [27]But Jesus took the boy by the hand and helped him rise, and he stood up.

[28]After Jesus had gone indoors, his disciples asked him privately, "Why couldn't we drive the spirit out?"

[29]"Only prayer can drive this kind out," answered Jesus; "nothing else can."

Jesus Speaks Again about His Death
(Matthew 17:22, 23; Luke 9:43b–45)

[30]Jesus and his disciples left that place and went on through Galilee. Jesus did not want anyone to know where he was, [31]because he was teaching his disciples: "The Son of Man will be handed over to those who will kill him. Three days later, however, he will rise to life."

[32]But they did not understand what this teaching meant, and they were afraid to ask him.

9:7 Mt 3:17; Mk 1:11; Lk 3:22   **9:11** Mal 4:5; Mt 11:14   **9:12** Sir 48:10

Who Is the Greatest?
(Matthew 18:1–5; Luke 9:46–48)

33They came to Capernaum, and after going indoors Jesus asked his disciples, "What were you arguing about on the road?" **34**But they would not answer him, because on the road they had been arguing among themselves about who was the greatest. **35**Jesus sat down, called the twelve disciples, and said to them, "Whoever wants to be first must place himself last of all and be the servant of all." **36**Then he took a child and had him stand in front of them. He put his arms around him and said to them, **37**"Whoever welcomes in my name one of these children, welcomes me; and whoever welcomes me, welcomes not only me but also the one who sent me."

Whoever Is Not against Us Is for Us
(Luke 9:49, 50)

38John said to him, "Teacher, we saw a man who was driving out demons in your name, and we told him to stop, because he doesn't belong to our group." **39**"Do not try to stop him," Jesus told them, "because no one who performs a miracle in my name will be able soon afterward to say evil things about me. **40**For whoever is not against us is for us. **41**I assure you that anyone who gives you a drink of water because you belong to me will certainly receive a reward.

Temptations to Sin
(Matthew 18:6–9; Luke 17:1, 2)

42"If anyone should cause one of these little ones to lose faith in me, it would be better for that person to have a large millstone tied around the neck and be thrown into the sea. **43**So if your hand makes you lose your faith, cut it off! It is better for you to enter life without a hand than to keep both hands

and go off to hell, to the fire that never goes out.º **45**And if your foot makes you lose your faith, cut it off! It is better for you to enter life without a foot than to keep both feet and be thrown into hell.ᵖ **47**And if your eye makes you lose your faith, take it out! It is better for you to enter the Kingdom of God with only one eye than to keep both eyes and be thrown into hell. **48**There 'the worms that eat them never die, and the fire that burns them is never put out.'

49"Everyone will be purified by fire as a sacrifice is purified by salt.

50"Salt is good; but if it loses its saltiness, how can you make it salty again?

"Have the salt of friendship among yourselves, and live in peace with one another."

Jesus Teaches about Divorce
(Matthew 19:1–12; Luke 16:18)

10 **1**Then Jesus left that place, went to the province of Judea, and crossed the Jordan River. Crowds came flocking to him again, and he taught them, as he always did.

2Some Pharisees came to him and tried to trap him. "Tell us," they asked, "does our Law allow a man to divorce his wife?"

3Jesus answered with a question, "What law did Moses give you?"

4Their answer was, "Moses gave permission for a man to write a divorce notice and send his wife away."

5Jesus said to them, "Moses wrote this law for you because you are so hard to teach. **6**But in the beginning, at the time of creation, 'God made them male and female,' as the scripture says. **7**'And for this reason a man will leave his father and mother and unite with his wife,�q **8**and the two will become one.' So they are no longer two, but one. **9**No human being must separate, then, what God has joined together."

10When they went back into the house, the disciples asked Jesus about this matter. **11**He said to them, "A man who divorces his

---

º **9:43** *Some manuscripts add verse 44:* There 'the worms that eat them never die, and the fire that burns them is never put out' *(see verse 48).*   ᵖ **9:45** *Some manuscripts add verse 46:* There 'the worms that eat them never die, and the fire that burns them is never put out' *(see verse 48).*   q **10:7** *Some manuscripts do not have* and unite with his wife.
9:34 Lk 22:24   **9:35** Mt 20:26,27; 23:11; Mk 10:43,44; Lk 22:26   **9:37** Mt 10:40; Lk 10:16; Jn 13:20
9:40 Mt 12:30; Lk 11:23   **9:41** Mt 10:42   **9:43** Mt 5:30   **9:47** Mt 5:29   **9:48** Isa 66:24   **9:50** Mt 5:13;
Lk 14:34,35   **10:4** Deut 24:1-4; Mt 5:31   **10:6** Gen 1:27; 5:2   **10:7,8** Gen 2:24   **10:11,12** Mt 5:32; 1 Cor
7:10,11

The Challenge

It's no wonder the guy was upset. He went to see Jesus, thinking that he was well on his way to heaven. After all, he followed the rules. But Jesus told him that it wasn't enough. He told the man to sell everything, give the money to poor people, and then follow him (Mark 10:17–23).

Jesus made it clear that just following rules is not enough. Just because someone goes to church doesn't mean an automatic ticket to heaven. We have to live the life we hear about in church. That means being honest, being a peacemaker, helping poor people, loving our enemies, praying, and doing all the other things Jesus taught.

The man in the story walked away. We don't know what he did after that. Maybe he did what Jesus told him to do and came back. What would you do?

— Mark 10:17–31

wife and marries another woman commits adultery against his wife. ¹²In the same way, a woman who divorces her husband and marries another man commits adultery."

Jesus Blesses Little Children
(Matthew 19:13–15; Luke 18:15–17)

¹³Some people brought children to Jesus for him to place his hands on them, but the disciples scolded the people. ¹⁴When Jesus noticed this, he was angry and said to his disciples, "Let the children come to me, and do not stop them, because the Kingdom of God belongs to such as these. ¹⁵I assure you that

whoever does not receive the Kingdom of God like a child will never enter it." ¹⁶Then he took the children in his arms, placed his hands on each of them, and blessed them.

The Rich Man
(Matthew 19:16–30; Luke 18:18–30)

¹⁷As Jesus was starting on his way again, a man ran up, knelt before him, and asked him, "Good Teacher, what must I do to receive eternal life?"

¹⁸"Why do you call me good?" Jesus asked him. "No one is good except God alone. ¹⁹You know the commandments: 'Do not commit murder; do not commit adultery; do not steal; do not accuse anyone falsely; do not cheat; respect your father and your mother.' "

²⁰"Teacher," the man said, "ever since I was young, I have obeyed all these commandments."

²¹Jesus looked straight at him with love and said, "You need only one thing. Go and sell all you have and give the money to the poor, and you will have riches in heaven; then come and follow me." ²²When the man heard this, gloom spread over his face, and he went away sad, because he was very rich.

²³Jesus looked around at his disciples and said to them, "How hard it will be for rich people to enter the Kingdom of God!"

²⁴The disciples were shocked at these words, but Jesus went on to say, "My children, how hard it is to enter the Kingdom of God! ²⁵It is much harder for a rich person to enter the Kingdom of God than for a camel to go through the eye of a needle."

²⁶At this the disciples were completely amazed and asked one another, "Who, then, can be saved?"

²⁷Jesus looked straight at them and answered, "This is impossible for human beings but not for God; everything is possible for God."

²⁸Then Peter spoke up, "Look, we have left everything and followed you."

²⁹"Yes," Jesus said to them, "and I tell you that those who leave home or brothers or sisters or mother or father or children or fields for me and for the gospel, ³⁰will

10:15 Mt 18:3   10:19 **a** Ex 20:13; Deut 5:17; **b** Ex 20:14; Deut 5:18; **c** Ex 20:15; Deut 5:19; **d** Ex 20:16; Deut 5:20; **e** Ex 20:12; Deut 5:16

receive much more in this present age. They will receive a hundred times more houses, brothers, sisters, mothers, children, and fields—and persecutions as well; and in the age to come they will receive eternal life. 31But many who are now first will be last, and many who are now last will be first."

Jesus Speaks a Third Time about His Death
(Matthew 20:17–19; Luke 18:31–34)

32Jesus and his disciples were now on the road going up to Jerusalem. Jesus was going ahead of the disciples, who were filled with alarm; the people who followed behind were afraid. Once again Jesus took the twelve disciples aside and spoke of the things that were going to happen to him. 33"Listen," he told them, "we are going up to Jerusalem where the Son of Man will be handed over to the chief priests and the teachers of the Law. They will condemn him to death and then hand him over to the Gentiles, 34who will make fun of him, spit on him, whip him, and kill him; but three days later he will rise to life."

The Request of James and John
(Matthew 20:20–28)

35Then James and John, the sons of Zebedee, came to Jesus. "Teacher," they said, "there is something we want you to do for us." 36"What is it?" Jesus asked them. 37They answered, "When you sit on your throne in your glorious Kingdom, we want you to let us sit with you, one at your right and one at your left." 38Jesus said to them, "You don't know what you are asking for. Can you drink the cup of suffering that I must drink? Can you be baptized in the way I must be baptized?" 39"We can," they answered.
Jesus said to them, "You will indeed drink the cup I must drink and be baptized in the way I must be baptized. 40But I do not have the right to choose who will sit at my right and my

Me First!

James and John were brothers with big plans—they wanted to be leaders and sit beside Jesus. Jesus gave them a quick lesson in leadership. He said that being a leader is not about being first or most important. "If one of you wants to be great, you must be the servant of the rest" (Mark 10:43).

Are you a leader? People in student government or officers of clubs are leaders. So are people who tutor children, work with young groups of scouts, or help coach sports teams. You are also a leader if you have younger brothers and sisters or babysit children.

Leadership is not about having power over someone. It's not about telling people what to do and what not to do. It's about making hard choices and giving people what they need to be all that God created them to be. It means putting yourself last, not first.

Jesus was the ultimate leader. When you lead someone else, follow his example and be a servant first.

— Mark 10:35–45

left. It is God who will give these places to those for whom he has prepared them."

41When the other ten disciples heard about it, they became angry with James and John. 42So Jesus called them all together to him and said, "You know that those who are considered rulers of the heathen have power

10:31 Mt 20:16; Lk 13:30   **10:38** Lk 12:50   **10:42,43** Lk 22:25,26

Chapter 10 of Mark mentions a province and two cities. Name them and find them on the map "Ministry of Jesus" in the back of this Bible.

over them, and the leaders have complete authority. 43 This, however, is not the way it is among you. If one of you wants to be great, you must be the servant of the rest; 44 and if one of you wants to be first, you must be the slave of all. 45 For even the Son of Man did not come to be served; he came to serve and to give his life to redeem many people."

Jesus Heals Blind Bartimaeus
(Matthew 20:29–34; Luke 18:35–43)

46 They came to Jericho, and as Jesus was leaving with his disciples and a large crowd, a blind beggar named Bartimaeus son of Timaeus was sitting by the road. 47 When he heard that it was Jesus of Nazareth, he began to shout, "Jesus! Son of David! Have mercy on me!"

48 Many of the people scolded him and told him to be quiet. But he shouted even more loudly, "Son of David, have mercy on me!"

49 Jesus stopped and said, "Call him."

So they called the blind man. "Cheer up!" they said. "Get up, he is calling you."

50 So he threw off his cloak, jumped up, and came to Jesus.

51 "What do you want me to do for you?" Jesus asked him.

"Teacher," the blind man answered, "I want to see again."

52 "Go," Jesus told him, "your faith has made you well."

At once he was able to see and followed Jesus on the road.

The Triumphant Entry into Jerusalem
(Matthew 21:1–11; Luke 19:28–40; John 12:12–19)

11 1 As they approached Jerusalem, near the towns of Bethphage and Bethany, they came to the Mount of Olives. Jesus sent two of his disciples on ahead 2 with these instructions: "Go to the village there ahead of you. As soon as you get there, you will find a colt tied up that has never been ridden. Untie it and bring it here. 3 And if someone asks you why you are doing that, say that the Master[r] needs it and will send it back at once."

4 So they went and found a colt out in the street, tied to the door of a house. As they were untying it, 5 some of the bystanders asked them, "What are you doing, untying that colt?"

6 They answered just as Jesus had told them, and the crowd let them go. 7 They brought the colt to Jesus, threw their cloaks over the animal, and Jesus got on. 8 Many people spread their cloaks on the road, while others cut branches in the field and spread them on the road. 9 The people who were in front and those who followed behind began to shout, "Praise God! God bless him who comes in the name of the Lord! 10 God bless the coming kingdom of King David, our father! Praise be to God!"

11 Jesus entered Jerusalem, went into the Temple, and looked around at everything. But since it was already late in the day, he went out to Bethany with the twelve disciples.

Jesus Curses the Fig Tree
(Matthew 21:18, 19)

12 The next day, as they were coming back from Bethany, Jesus was hungry. 13 He saw in the distance a fig tree covered with leaves, so he went to see if he could find any figs on it. But when he came to it, he found only leaves, because it was not the right time for figs. 14 Jesus said to the fig tree, "No one shall ever eat figs from you again!"

And his disciples heard him.

Jesus Goes to the Temple
(Matthew 21:12–17; Luke 19:45–48; John 2:13–22)

15 When they arrived in Jerusalem, Jesus went to the Temple and began to drive out all

---

r **11:3** the Master; *or* its owner.
10:43,44 Mt 23:11; Mk 9:35; Lk 22:26   **11:9** Ps 118:25,26

The event described in Mark 11:1–11 is observed in the Church as Palm Sunday, the first day of Holy Week.

Pray It!

Forgive Me, God

Jesus was upset because the religious leaders of his time were more concerned with making money than with true worship of God (Mark 11:15–19). When we find ourselves putting more value on material things than on our relationship with God, we must seek God's forgiveness.

For being greedy, forgive me, God.
For putting possessions over people, forgive me, God.
For worshiping material things instead of you, forgive me, God.
For being jealous of what others have, forgive me, God.
For not being satisfied with what I have, forgive me, God.
For not being grateful to you for all you have given me, forgive me, God.
Amen.

— Mark 11:15–19

those who were buying and selling. He overturned the tables of the moneychangers and the stools of those who sold pigeons, [16]and he would not let anyone carry anything through the Temple courtyards. [17]He then taught the people: "It is written in the Scriptures that God said, 'My Temple will be called a house of prayer for the people of all nations.' But you have turned it into a hideout for thieves!"

[18]The chief priests and the teachers of the Law heard of this, so they began looking for some way to kill Jesus. They were afraid of him, because the whole crowd was amazed at his teaching.

[19]When evening came, Jesus and his disciples left the city.

The Lesson from the Fig Tree
(Matthew 21:20–22)

[20]Early next morning, as they walked along the road, they saw the fig tree. It was dead all the way down to its roots. [21]Peter remembered what had happened and said to Jesus, "Look, Teacher, the fig tree you cursed has died!"

[22]Jesus answered them, "Have faith in God. [23]I assure you that whoever tells this

hill to get up and throw itself in the sea and does not doubt in his heart, but believes that what he says will happen, it will be done for him. [24]For this reason I tell you: When you pray and ask for something, believe that you have received it, and you will be given whatever you ask for. [25]And when you stand and pray, forgive anything you may have against anyone, so that your Father in heaven will forgive the wrongs you have done."[s]

The Question about Jesus' Authority
(Matthew 21:23–27; Luke 20:1–8)

[27]They arrived once again in Jerusalem. As Jesus was walking in the Temple, the chief priests, the teachers of the Law, and the elders came to him [28]and asked him, "What right do you have to do these things? Who gave you such right?"

[29]Jesus answered them, "I will ask you just one question, and if you give me an answer, I will tell you what right I have to do these things. [30]Tell me, where did John's right to baptize come from: was it from God or from human beings?"

[31]They started to argue among themselves: "What shall we say? If we answer,

---

[s] **11:25** *Some manuscripts add verse 26:* If you do not forgive others, your Father in heaven will not forgive the wrongs you have done (*see Mt 6:15*).
11:17 a Isa 56:7; **b** Jer 7:11   **11:23** Mt 17:20; 1 Cor 13:2   **11:25,26** Mt 6:14,15

'From God,' he will say, 'Why, then, did you not believe John?' ³²But if we say, 'From human beings . . . ' " (They were afraid of the people, because everyone was convinced that John had been a prophet.) ³³So their answer to Jesus was, "We don't know."

Jesus said to them, "Neither will I tell you, then, by what right I do these things."

The Parable of the Tenants in the Vineyard
(Matthew 21:33–46; Luke 20:9–19)

12 ¹ Then Jesus spoke to them in parables: "Once there was a man who planted a vineyard, put a fence around it, dug a hole for the wine press, and built a watchtower. Then he rented the vineyard to tenants and left home on a trip. ²When the time came to gather the grapes, he sent a slave to the tenants to receive from them his share of the harvest. ³The tenants grabbed the slave, beat him, and sent him back without a thing. ⁴Then the owner sent another slave; the tenants beat him over the head and treated him shamefully. ⁵The owner sent another slave, and they killed him; and they treated many others the same way, beating some and killing others. ⁶The only one left to send was the man's own dear son. Last of all, then, he sent his son to the tenants. 'I am sure they will respect my son,' he said. ⁷But those tenants said to one another, 'This is the owner's son. Come on, let's kill him, and his property will be ours!' ⁸So they grabbed the son and killed him and threw his body out of the vineyard.

⁹"What, then, will the owner of the vineyard do?" asked Jesus. "He will come and kill those tenants and turn the vineyard over to others. ¹⁰Surely you have read this scripture?

'The stone which the builders rejected as worthless
turned out to be the most important of all.
¹¹ This was done by the Lord;
what a wonderful sight it is!' "

¹²The Jewish leaders tried to arrest Jesus, because they knew that he had told this parable against them. But they were afraid of the crowd, so they left him and went away.

The Question about Paying Taxes
(Matthew 22:15–22; Luke 20:20–26)

¹³Some Pharisees and some members of Herod's party were sent to Jesus to trap him with questions. ¹⁴They came to him and said, "Teacher, we know that you tell the truth, without worrying about what people think. You pay no attention to anyone's status, but teach the truth about God's will for people. Tell us, is it against our Law to pay taxes to the Roman Emperor? Should we pay them or not?"

¹⁵But Jesus saw through their trick and answered, "Why are you trying to trap me? Bring a silver coin, and let me see it."

¹⁶They brought him one, and he asked, "Whose face and name are these?"

"The Emperor's," they answered.

¹⁷So Jesus said, "Well, then, pay to the Emperor what belongs to the Emperor, and pay to God what belongs to God."

And they were amazed at Jesus.

The Question about Rising from Death
(Matthew 22:23–33; Luke 20:27–40)

¹⁸Then some Sadducees, who say that people will not rise from death, came to Jesus and said, ¹⁹"Teacher, Moses wrote this law for us: 'If a man dies and leaves a wife but no children, that man's brother must marry the widow so that they can have children who will be considered the dead man's children.' ²⁰Once there were seven brothers; the oldest got married and died without having children. ²¹Then the second one married the woman, and he also died without having children. The same thing happened to the third brother, ²²and then to the rest: all seven brothers married the woman and died without having children. Last of all, the woman died. ²³Now, when all the dead rise to life on the day of resurrection, whose wife will she be? All seven of them had married her."

²⁴Jesus answered them, "How wrong you are! And do you know why? It is because you don't know the Scriptures or God's power. ²⁵For when the dead rise to life, they will be like the angels in heaven and will not

12:1 Isa 5:1,2 **12:10,11** Ps 118:22,23 **12:18** Acts 23:8 **12:19** Deut 25:5

Laws of Love

Catholic Connections

Take a close look at the story in the middle of this chapter with its key question, "Which commandment is the most important of all?" (Mark 12:28). When the man asks the question, everyone looks at Jesus, waiting to see what he will say. To some, it seemed like a trick. After all, how can anyone say one law of God is better than another law? But Jesus is a quick thinker. He quoted the Old Testament, which sums up the first three commandments in one statement: love God (Deuteronomy 6:5). The other seven commandments were also summed up in a second Old Testament statement: love your neighbor as yourself (Leviticus 19:18). These, he says, are the two greatest commandments.

All the moral teachings of the Catholic Church are rooted in these two commandments. If a person does not love God and other people, religion is just meaningless prayers and empty practices.

Write those laws of love in your mind and in your heart. Let them guide everything that you think, do, and say.

— Mark 12:28–34

Mark

marry. 26 Now, as for the dead being raised: haven't you ever read in the Book of Moses the passage about the burning bush? There it is written that God said to Moses, 'I am the God of Abraham, the God of Isaac, and the God of Jacob.' 27 He is the God of the living, not of the dead. You are completely wrong!"

The Great Commandment
(Matthew 22:34–40; Luke 10:25–28)

28 A teacher of the Law was there who heard the discussion. He saw that Jesus had given the Sadducees a good answer, so he came to him with a question: "Which commandment is the most important of all?"

29 Jesus replied, "The most important one is this: 'Listen, Israel! The Lord our God is the only Lord.ᵗ 30 Love the Lord your God with all your heart, with all your soul, with all your mind, and with all your strength.' 31 The second most important commandment is this: 'Love your neighbor as you love yourself.' There is no other commandment more important than these two."

32 The teacher of the Law said to Jesus, "Well done, Teacher! It is true, as you say, that only the Lord is God and that there is no other god but he. 33 And you must love God with all your heart and with all your mind and with all your strength; and you must love your neighbor as you love yourself. It is more important to obey these two commandments than to offer on the altar animals and other sacrifices to God."

34 Jesus noticed how wise his answer was, and so he told him, "You are not far from the Kingdom of God."

After this nobody dared to ask Jesus any more questions.

ᵗ **12:29** The Lord our God is the only Lord; or The Lord is our God, the Lord alone.
12:26 Ex 3:6 **12:29,30** Deut 6:4,5 **12:31** Lev 19:18 **12:32** Deut 4:35 **12:33** Hos 6:6 **12:28–34** Lk 10:25–28

Jesus said, "Love your neighbor *as you love yourself*" (Mark 12:31). **How are you doing at loving yourself?**

The Question about the Messiah
(Matthew 22:41–46; Luke 20:41–44)

35 As Jesus was teaching in the Temple, he asked the question, "How can the teachers of the Law say that the Messiah will be the descendant of David? 36 The Holy Spirit inspired David to say:

'The Lord said to my Lord:
  Sit here at my right side
  until I put your enemies under your
    feet.'

37 David himself called him 'Lord'; so how can the Messiah be David's descendant?"

Jesus Warns against the Teachers of the Law
(Matthew 23:1–36; Luke 20:45–47)

A large crowd was listening to Jesus gladly. 38 As he taught them, he said, "Watch out for the teachers of the Law, who like to walk around in their long robes and be greeted with respect in the marketplace, 39 who choose the reserved seats in the synagogues and the best places at feasts. 40 They take advantage of widows and rob them of their homes, and then make a show of saying long prayers. Their punishment will be all the worse!"

The Widow's Offering
(Luke 21:1–4)

41 As Jesus sat near the Temple treasury, he watched the people as they dropped in their money. Many rich people dropped in a lot of money; 42 then a poor widow came along and dropped in two little copper coins, worth about a penny. 43 He called his disciples together and said to them, "I tell you that this poor widow put more in the offering box than all the others. 44 For the others put in what they had to spare of their riches; but she, poor as she is, put in all she had—she gave all she had to live on."

A poor widow came along. (12:42)

Jesus Speaks of the Destruction of the Temple
(Matthew 24:1, 2; Luke 21:5, 6)

13 1 As Jesus was leaving the Temple, one of his disciples said, "Look, Teacher! What wonderful stones and buildings!"

2 Jesus answered, "You see these great buildings? Not a single stone here will be left in its place; every one of them will be thrown down."

Troubles and Persecutions
(Matthew 24:3–14; Luke 21:7–19)

3 Jesus was sitting on the Mount of Olives, across from the Temple, when Peter, James, John, and Andrew came to him in private. 4 "Tell us when this will be," they said, "and tell us what will happen to show that the time has come for all these things to take place."

5 Jesus said to them, "Watch out, and don't let anyone fool you. 6 Many men, claiming to speak for me, will come and say, 'I am he!' and they will fool many people. 7 And don't be troubled when you hear the noise of battles close by and news of battles far away. Such things must happen, but they do not mean that the end has come. 8 Countries will fight each other; kingdoms will attack one another. There will be earthquakes everywhere, and there will be famines.

Can you list all the terrible things Jesus talks about in Mark, chapter 13? Of all these things, which do you think is the worst?

The End Is Near

Someday the world is going to end. The term commonly used for the end of the world is *apocalypse.* No one knows the time. It may be today, or it may be five billion years away. But it will end. And even if the world doesn't end soon, each of us only has a limited amount of time on earth.

In Mark, chapter 13, Jesus talks about the end of time. It may seem strange to think about the end of life before you even get to high school. But Jesus says that everyone should be prepared because we have no idea when it will happen. Above all, he says, we must remain faithful to God. When the end finally comes—whether it's the end of the world or the end of a life—only those who are watchful and faithful will be united with God for all eternity.

Do you know anyone who died at a young age? If today were the last day of your life on earth, what would you do? Are you ready to meet God face-to-face?

— Mark, chapter 13

These things are like the first pains of childbirth.

9"You yourselves must watch out. You will be arrested and taken to court. You will be beaten in the synagogues; you will stand before rulers and kings for my sake to tell them the Good News. 10But before the end comes, the gospel must be preached to all peoples. 11And when you are arrested and taken to court, do not worry ahead of time about what you are going to say; when the time comes, say whatever is then given to you. For the words you speak will not be yours; they will come from the Holy Spirit. 12Men will hand over their own brothers to be put to death, and fathers will do the same to their children. Children will turn against their parents and have them put to death. 13Everyone will hate you because of me. But whoever holds out to the end will be saved.

The Awful Horror
(Matthew 24:15–28; Luke 21:20–24)

14"You will see 'The Awful Horror' standing in the place where he should not be." (Note to the reader: understand what this means!) "Then those who are in Judea must run away to the hills. 15Someone who is on the roof of a house must not lose time by going down into the house to get anything to take along. 16Someone who is in the field must not go back to the house for a cloak. 17How terrible it will be in those days for women who are pregnant and for mothers with little babies! 18Pray to God that these things will not happen in the winter! 19For the trouble of those days will be far worse than any the world has ever known from the very beginning when God created the world until the present time. Nor will there ever be anything like it again. 20But the Lord has reduced the number of those days; if he had not, nobody would survive. For the sake of his chosen people, however, he has reduced those days.

21"Then, if anyone says to you, 'Look, here is the Messiah!' or, 'Look, there he is!'—do not believe it. 22For false Messiahs and false prophets will appear. They will perform miracles and wonders in order to deceive even God's chosen people, if possible. 23Be on your guard! I have told you everything ahead of time.

The Coming of the Son of Man
(Matthew 24:29–31; Luke 21:25–28)

24"In the days after that time of trouble the sun will grow dark, the moon will no longer shine, 25the stars will fall from heaven,

Mark

13:9-11 Mt 10:17-20; Lk 12:11,12   **13:13** Mt 10:22   **13:14** Dan 9:27; 11:31; 12:11; 1 Macc 1:54; 6:7
13:15,16 Lk 17:31   **13:19** Dan 12:1; Rev 7:14   **13:24 a** Isa 13:10; Joel 2:10,31; 3:15; Rev 6:12; **b** Isa 13:10;
Ezek 32:7   **13:25 a** Isa 34:4; Rev 6:13; **b** Joel 2:10

and the powers in space will be driven from their courses. 26 Then the Son of Man will appear, coming in the clouds with great power and glory. 27 He will send the angels out to the four corners of the earth to gather God's chosen people from one end of the world to the other.

The Lesson of the Fig Tree
(Matthew 24:32–35; Luke 21:29–33)

28 "Let the fig tree teach you a lesson. When its branches become green and tender and it starts putting out leaves, you know that summer is near. 29 In the same way, when you see these things happening, you will know that the time is near, ready to begin.ᵘ 30 Remember that all these things will happen before the people now living have all died. 31 Heaven and earth will pass away, but my words will never pass away.

No One Knows the Day or Hour
(Matthew 24:36–44)

32 "No one knows, however, when that day or hour will come—neither the angels in heaven, nor the Son; only the Father knows. 33 Be on watch, be alert, for you do not know when the time will come. 34 It will be like a man who goes away from home on a trip and leaves his servants in charge, after giving to each one his own work to do and after telling the doorkeeper to keep watch. 35 Watch, then, because you do not know when the master of the house is coming—it might be in the evening or at midnight or before dawn or at sunrise. 36 If he comes suddenly, he must not find you asleep. 37 What I say to you, then, I say to all: Watch!"

The Plot against Jesus
(Matthew 26:1–5; Luke 22:1, 2; John 11:45–53)

14 1 It was now two days before the Festival of Passover and Unleavened Bread. The chief priests and the teachers of the Law were looking for a way to arrest

Jesus secretly and put him to death. 2 "We must not do it during the festival," they said, "or the people might riot."

Jesus Is Anointed at Bethany
(Matthew 26:6–13; John 12:1–8)

3 Jesus was in Bethany at the house of Simon, a man who had suffered from a dreaded skin disease. While Jesus was eating, a woman came in with an alabaster jar full of a very expensive perfume made of pure nard. She broke the jar and poured the perfume on Jesus' head. 4 Some of the people there became angry and said to one another, "What was the use of wasting the perfume? 5 It could have been sold for more than three hundred silver coinsᵛ and the money given to the poor!" And they criticized her harshly.

6 But Jesus said, "Leave her alone! Why are you bothering her? She has done a fine and beautiful thing for me. 7 You will always have poor people with you, and any time you want to, you can help them. But you will not always have me. 8 She did what she could; she poured perfume on my body to prepare it ahead of time for burial. 9 Now, I assure you that wherever the gospel is preached all over the world, what she has done will be told in memory of her."

Judas Agrees to Betray Jesus
(Matthew 26:14–16; Luke 22:3–6)

10 Then Judas Iscariot, one of the twelve disciples, went off to the chief priests in order to betray Jesus to them. 11 They were pleased to hear what he had to say, and promised to give him money. So Judas started looking for a good chance to hand Jesus over to them.

Jesus Eats the Passover Meal with His Disciples
(Matthew 26:17–25; Luke 22:7–14, 21–23; John 13:21–30)

12 On the first day of the Festival of Unleavened Bread, the day the lambs for the Passover meal were killed, Jesus' disciples

---

ᵘ **13:29** the time is near, ready to begin; *or* he is near, ready to come. ᵛ **14:5** SILVER COINS: *See 6:37.*
13:26 Dan 7:13; Rev 1:7 **13:32** Mt 24:36 **13:34** Lk 12:36-38 **14:1** Ex 12:1-27 **14:3** Lk 7:37,38
14:7 Deut 15:11

The Real Deal

"This is my body. . . . This is my blood"
(Mark 14:22–24).

Ca holic Connec ions

    Jesus spoke those words at the last
Passover meal he had with his Apostles before he died. He didn't say "this
bread is *like* my body" or "this wine *represents* my blood." The bread and the
wine that you see at Mass is really Jesus Christ, whose body and blood
comes to us in that form. We refer to this as the Real Presence.

    During the Eucharistic prayer, the priest recites the same words Jesus
used at the Last Supper. At that point—which is known as the consecra-
tion—the bread and wine are changed into the body and blood of Christ.

    Later, when you say amen to the person who offers you the host and the
cup, you are saying, "Yes, I believe it's really Jesus." Really.

— Mark 14:22–25

asked him, "Where do you want us to go and get the Passover meal ready for you?"

¹³Then Jesus sent two of them with these instructions: "Go into the city, and a man carrying a jar of water will meet you. Follow him ¹⁴to the house he enters, and say to the owner of the house: 'The Teacher says, Where is the room where my disciples and I will eat the Passover meal?' ¹⁵Then he will show you a large upstairs room, fixed up and furnished, where you will get everything ready for us."

¹⁶The disciples left, went to the city, and found everything just as Jesus had told them; and they prepared the Passover meal.

¹⁷When it was evening, Jesus came with the twelve disciples. ¹⁸While they were at the table eating, Jesus said, "I tell you that one of you will betray me—one who is eating with me."

¹⁹The disciples were upset and began to ask him, one after the other, "Surely you don't mean me, do you?"

²⁰Jesus answered, "It will be one of you twelve, one who dips his bread in the dish

with me. ²¹The Son of Man will die as the Scriptures say he will; but how terrible for that man who will betray the Son of Man! It would have been better for that man if he had never been born!"

The Lord's Supper
*(Matthew 26:26–30; Luke 22:14–20;
I Corinthians 11:23–25)*

²²While they were eating, Jesus took a piece of bread, gave a prayer of thanks, broke

"This is my body." (14:22)

14:18 Ps 41:9

For a description of the event in Jewish history that the feast of Passover
recalls, see Exodus 12:1–28.

it, and gave it to his disciples. "Take it," he said, "this is my body."

23 Then he took a cup, gave thanks to God, and handed it to them; and they all drank from it. 24 Jesus said, "This is my blood which is poured out for many, my blood which seals God's covenant. 25 I tell you, I will never again drink this wine until the day I drink the new wine in the Kingdom of God."

26 Then they sang a hymn and went out to the Mount of Olives.

Jesus Predicts Peter's Denial
(Matthew 26:31–35; Luke 22:31–34; John 13:36–38)

27 Jesus said to them, "All of you will run away and leave me, for the scripture says, 'God will kill the shepherd, and the sheep will all be scattered.' 28 But after I am raised to life, I will go to Galilee ahead of you."

29 Peter answered, "I will never leave you, even though all the rest do!"

30 Jesus said to Peter, "I tell you that before the rooster crows two times tonight, you will say three times that you do not know me."

31 Peter answered even more strongly, "I will never say that, even if I have to die with you!"

And all the other disciples said the same thing.

Jesus Prays in Gethsemane
(Matthew 26:36–46; Luke 22:39–46)

32 They came to a place called Gethsemane, and Jesus said to his disciples, "Sit here while I pray." 33 He took Peter, James, and John with him. Distress and anguish came over him, 34 and he said to them, "The sorrow in my heart is so great that it almost crushes me. Stay here and keep watch."

35 He went a little farther on, threw himself on the ground, and prayed that, if possible, he might not have to go through that time of suffering. 36 "Father," he prayed, "my

Father! All things are possible for you. Take this cup of suffering away from me. Yet not what I want, but what you want."

37 Then he returned and found the three disciples asleep. He said to Peter, "Simon, are you asleep? Weren't you able to stay awake for even one hour?" 38 And he said to them, "Keep watch, and pray that you will not fall into temptation. The spirit is willing, but the flesh is weak."

39 He went away once more and prayed,

Pray It!

I Messed Up Again, Jesus

I try so hard, Jesus. I try to do everything you said I should do. I love you. I believe in you. I try to be good to others. But sometimes I really make a mess of things. I feel terrible about it. It's like I've got a hole in my soul. I just want things to be right between us again.

Then I remember the Apostles. They messed up too. When you needed them most in the garden at Gethsemane, Peter, James, and John fell asleep (Mark 14:33–41). When the soldiers came to arrest you, the Apostles ran away (Mark 14:50). On top of that, Peter denied that he even knew you (14:66–72). You forgave them all, though.

I know you'll do the same for me, Jesus. I know I keep messing up, but I also keep trying. That is what the Apostles did, and that is what I'll do too. Amen.

— Mark 14:32–72

14:24 a Ex 24:8; b Jer 31:31-34 14:27 Zech 13:7 14:28 Mt 28:16

saying the same words. 40 Then he came back to the disciples and found them asleep; they could not keep their eyes open. And they did not know what to say to him.

41 When he came back the third time, he said to them, "Are you still sleeping and resting? Enough! The hour has come! Look, the Son of Man is now being handed over to the power of sinners. 42 Get up, let us go. Look, here is the man who is betraying me!"

The Arrest of Jesus
(Matthew 26:47–56; Luke 22:47–53; John 18:3–12)

43 Jesus was still speaking when Judas, one of the twelve disciples, arrived. With him was a crowd armed with swords and clubs and sent by the chief priests, the teachers of the Law, and the elders. 44 The traitor had given the crowd a signal: "The man I kiss is the one you want. Arrest him and take him away under guard."

So they arrested Jesus and held him tight. (14:46)

45 As soon as Judas arrived, he went up to Jesus and said, "Teacher!" and kissed him. 46 So they arrested Jesus and held him tight. 47 But one of those standing there drew his sword and struck at the High Priest's slave, cutting off his ear. 48 Then Jesus spoke up and said to them, "Did you have to come with swords and clubs to capture me, as though I were an outlaw? 49 Day after day I was with you teaching in the Temple, and you did not arrest me. But the Scriptures must come true."

50 Then all the disciples left him and ran away.

51 A certain young man, dressed only in a linen cloth, was following Jesus. They tried to arrest him, 52 but he ran away naked, leaving the cloth behind.

Jesus before the Council
(Matthew 26:57–68; Luke 22:54, 55, 63–71; John 18:13, 14, 19–24)

53 Then Jesus was taken to the High Priest's house, where all the chief priests, the elders, and the teachers of the Law were gathering. 54 Peter followed from a distance and went into the courtyard of the High Priest's house. There he sat down with the guards, keeping himself warm by the fire. 55 The chief priests and the whole Council tried to find some evidence against Jesus in order to put him to death, but they could not find any. 56 Many witnesses told lies against Jesus, but their stories did not agree.

57 Then some men stood up and told this lie against Jesus: 58 "We heard him say, 'I will tear down this Temple which men have made, and after three days I will build one that is not made by men.' " 59 Not even they, however, could make their stories agree.

60 The High Priest stood up in front of them all and questioned Jesus, "Have you no answer to the accusation they bring against you?"

61 But Jesus kept quiet and would not say a word. Again the High Priest questioned him, "Are you the Messiah, the Son of the Blessed God?"

62 "I am," answered Jesus, "and you will all see the Son of Man seated at the right side of the Almighty and coming with the clouds of heaven!"

63 The High Priest tore his robes and said, "We don't need any more witnesses! 64 You heard his blasphemy. What is your decision?"

They all voted against him: he was guilty and should be put to death.

65 Some of them began to spit on Jesus, and they blindfolded him and hit him. "Guess who hit you!" they said. And the guards took him and slapped him.

Peter Denies Jesus
(Matthew 26:69–75; Luke 22:56–62;
John 18:15–18, 25–27)

⁶⁶Peter was still down in the courtyard when one of the High Priest's servant women came by. ⁶⁷When she saw Peter warming himself, she looked straight at him and said, "You, too, were with Jesus of Nazareth."

⁶⁸But he denied it. "I don't know . . . I don't understand what you are talking about," he answered, and went out into the passageway. Just then a rooster crowed.ʷ

⁶⁹The servant woman saw him there and began to repeat to the bystanders, "He is one of them!" ⁷⁰But Peter denied it again.

A little while later the bystanders accused Peter again, "You can't deny that you are one of them, because you, too, are from Galilee."

⁷¹Then Peter said, "I swear that I am telling the truth! May God punish me if I am not! I do not know the man you are talking about!"

⁷²Just then a rooster crowed a second time, and Peter remembered how Jesus had said to him, "Before the rooster crows two times, you will say three times that you do not know me." And he broke down and cried.

He broke down and cried. (14:72)

Jesus before Pilate
(Matthew 27:1, 2, 11–14; Luke 23:1–5;
John 18:28–38)

15 ¹Early in the morning the chief priests met hurriedly with the elders, the teachers of the Law, and the whole Council, and made their plans. They put Jesus in chains, led him away, and handed him over to Pilate. ²Pilate questioned him, "Are you the king of the Jews?"

Jesus answered, "So you say."

³The chief priests were accusing Jesus of many things, ⁴so Pilate questioned him again, "Aren't you going to answer? Listen to all their accusations!"

⁵Again Jesus refused to say a word, and Pilate was amazed.

Jesus Is Sentenced to Death
(Matthew 27:15–26; Luke 23:13–25;
John 18:39—19:16)

⁶At every Passover Festival Pilate was in the habit of setting free any one prisoner the people asked for. ⁷At that time a man named Barabbas was in prison with the rebels who had committed murder in the riot. ⁸When the crowd gathered and began to ask Pilate for the usual favor, ⁹he asked them, "Do you want me to set free for you the king of the Jews?" ¹⁰He knew very well that the chief priests had handed Jesus over to him because they were jealous.

¹¹But the chief priests stirred up the crowd to ask, instead, that Pilate set Barabbas free for them. ¹²Pilate spoke again to the crowd, "What, then, do you want me to do with the one you call the king of the Jews?"

¹³They shouted back, "Crucify him!"

¹⁴"But what crime has he committed?" Pilate asked.

They shouted all the louder, "Crucify him!"

¹⁵Pilate wanted to please the crowd, so he set Barabbas free for them. Then he had Jesus whipped and handed him over to be crucified.

The Soldiers Make Fun of Jesus
(Matthew 27:27–31; John 19:2, 3)

¹⁶The soldiers took Jesus inside to the courtyard of the governor's palace and called together the rest of the company. ¹⁷They put a purple robe on Jesus, made a crown out of thorny branches, and put it on his head.

ʷ **14:68** *Some manuscripts do not have* Just then a rooster crowed.

18 Then they began to salute him: "Long live the King of the Jews!" 19 They beat him over the head with a stick, spat on him, fell on their knees, and bowed down to him. 20 When they had finished making fun of him, they took off the purple robe and put his own clothes back on him. Then they led him out to crucify him.

Jesus Is Crucified
(Matthew 27:32–44; Luke 23:26–43; John 19:17–27)

21 On the way they met a man named Simon, who was coming into the city from the country, and the soldiers forced him to carry Jesus' cross. (Simon was from Cyrene and was the father of Alexander and Rufus.) 22 They took Jesus to a place called Golgotha, which means "The Place of the Skull." 23 There they tried to give him wine mixed with a drug called myrrh, but Jesus would not drink it. 24 Then they crucified him and divided his clothes among themselves,

throwing dice to see who would get which piece of clothing. 25 It was nine o'clock in the morning when they crucified him.

Throwing dice (15:24)

26 The notice of the accusation against him said: "The King of the Jews." 27 They also crucified two bandits with Jesus, one on his right and the other on his left.ˣ

29 People passing by shook their heads and hurled insults at Jesus: "Aha! You were going to tear down the Temple and build it back up in three days! 30 Now come down from the cross and save yourself!"

31 In the same way the chief priests and the teachers of the Law made fun of Jesus, saying to one another, "He saved others, but he cannot save himself! 32 Let us see the Messiah, the king of Israel, come down from the cross now, and we will believe in him!"

"Come down from the cross!" (15:30)

And the two who were crucified with Jesus insulted him also.

The Death of Jesus
(Matthew 27:45–56; Luke 23:44–49; John 19:28–30)

33 At noon the whole country was covered with darkness, which lasted for three hours. 34 At three o'clock Jesus cried out with a loud shout, *"Eloi, Eloi, lema sabachthani?"* which means, "My God, my God, why did you abandon me?"

35 Some of the people there heard him and

ˣ **15:27** *Some manuscripts add verse 28:* In this way the scripture came true which says, "He shared the fate of criminals" *(see Lk 22:37).*
15:21 Rom 16:13   **15:24** Ps 22:18   **15:28** Isa 53:12   **15:29 a** Ps 22:7; 109:25; **b** Mk 14:58; Jn 2:19
15:34 Ps 22:1

The words of Jesus in Mark 15:34 are in Aramaic, an ancient language related to Hebrew. Compare the English translation with the opening of Psalm 22.

said, "Listen, he is calling for Elijah!" 36 One of them ran up with a sponge, soaked it in cheap wine, and put it on the end of a stick. Then he held it up to Jesus' lips and said, "Wait! Let us see if Elijah is coming to bring him down from the cross!"

37 With a loud cry Jesus died.

38 The curtain hanging in the Temple was torn in two, from top to bottom. 39 The army officer who was standing there in front of the cross saw how Jesus had died.ʸ "This man was really the Son of God!" he said.

40 Some women were there, looking on from a distance. Among them were Mary Magdalene, Mary the mother of the younger James and of Joseph, and Salome. 41 They had followed Jesus while he was in Galilee and had helped him. Many other women who had come to Jerusalem with him were there also.

The Burial of Jesus
(Matthew 27:57–61; Luke 23:50–56; John 19:38–42)

42-43 It was toward evening when Joseph of Arimathea arrived. He was a respected member of the Council, who was waiting for the coming of the Kingdom of God. It was Preparation day (that is, the day before the Sabbath), so Joseph went boldly into the presence of Pilate and asked him for the body of Jesus. 44 Pilate was surprised to hear that Jesus was already dead. He called the army officer and asked him if Jesus had been dead a long time. 45 After hearing the officer's report, Pilate told Joseph he could have the body. 46 Joseph bought a linen sheet, took the body down, wrapped it in the sheet, and placed it in a tomb which had been dug out of solid rock. Then he rolled a large stone across the entrance to the tomb. 47 Mary Magdalene and Mary the mother of Joseph were watching and saw where the body of Jesus was placed.

An Act of Courage

Joseph of Arimathea was a secret follower of Jesus. He was a leader in the city and was afraid that if he made his beliefs known, he would lose friends and business associates. Still, he was curious about this man who preached a message of hope and freedom. After Jesus died, Joseph took a chance. He found the courage to go to Pilate and asked for Jesus' body so he could bury him. His loyalty to Jesus was no longer a secret.

Sometimes it's hard to talk about God, no matter how deep your faith is. For example, you might be afraid to say a prayer before lunch because you think your friends will make fun of you. You would like to talk more in religion class, but you don't because you're afraid that people will think you're too religious. If you ask for help, the Holy Spirit will give you the right words at the right time in the right place. And like Joseph, your faith won't be a secret anymore.

— Mark 15:42–47

The Resurrection
(Matthew 28:1–8; Luke 24:1–12; John 20:1–10)

16 1 After the Sabbath was over, Mary Magdalene, Mary the mother of James, and Salome bought spices to go and anoint the body of Jesus. 2 Very early on

---

ʸ **15:39** had died; *some manuscripts have* had cried out and died.
15:36 Ps 69:21   **15:38** Ex 26:31-33   **15:40,41** Lk 8:2,3

The *stations of the cross* is a Catholic devotion on fourteen scenes from Christ's passion and death.

A Model Friend

Mary Magdalene was a close friend of Jesus. She was part of a group of women disciples who followed Jesus and stayed with him during the horrible events of his passion and death. She was the one who discovered the empty tomb and told the Apostles that Jesus had risen.

Mary was a true friend. She supported Jesus when others questioned him. She stuck with him through the roughest time of his life, even though his other friends deserted him. She told the world how wonderful he was. She announced his great moment of glory. But most of all, she was just there for him, walking with him as he made his way through life. She is a model of a great friend.

- Who are your true friends? What makes them true?
- Who would consider you to be a true friend? What do you do to earn that title?

— Mark 16:1–11

Sunday morning, at sunrise, they went to the tomb. ³⁻⁴On the way they said to one another, "Who will roll away the stone for us from the entrance to the tomb?" (It was a very large stone.) Then they looked up and saw that the stone had already been rolled back. ⁵So they entered the tomb, where they saw a young man sitting at the right, wearing a white robe—and they were alarmed.

⁶"Don't be alarmed," he said. "I know you are looking for Jesus of Nazareth, who was crucified. He is not here—he has been raised! Look, here is the place where he was placed. ⁷Now go and give this message to his disciples, including Peter: 'He is going to Galilee ahead of you; there you will see him, just as he told you.' "

⁸So they went out and ran from the tomb, distressed and terrified. They said nothing to anyone, because they were afraid.

So they went out and ran. (16:8)

AN OLD ENDING TO THE GOSPELᶻ

Jesus Appears to Mary Magdalene
(Matthew 28:9, 10; John 20:11–18)

[⁹After Jesus rose from death early on Sunday, he appeared first to Mary Magdalene, from whom he had driven out seven demons. ¹⁰She went and told his companions. They were mourning and crying; ¹¹and when they heard her say that Jesus was alive and that she had seen him, they did not believe her.

Jesus Appears to Two Followers
(Luke 24:13–35)

¹²After this, Jesus appeared in a different manner to two of them while they were on their way to the country. ¹³They returned and told the others, but these would not believe it.

Jesus Appears to the Eleven
(Matthew 28:16–20; Luke 24:36–49; John 20:19–23; Acts 1:6–8)

¹⁴Last of all, Jesus appeared to the eleven disciples as they were eating. He scolded them, because they did not have faith and

---

ᶻ **16:8** *Some manuscripts and ancient translations do not have this ending to the Gospel (verses 9–20).*
16:7 Mt 26:32; Mk 14:28

Mark

because they were too stubborn to believe those who had seen him alive. ¹⁵He said to them, "Go throughout the whole world and preach the gospel to all people. ¹⁶Whoever believes and is baptized will be saved; whoever does not believe will be condemned. ¹⁷Believers will be given the power to perform miracles: they will drive out demons in my name; they will speak in strange tongues; ¹⁸if they pick up snakes or drink any poison, they will not be harmed; they will place their hands on sick people, and these will get well."

The disciples went and preached everywhere. (16:20)

Jesus Is Taken Up to Heaven
(Luke 24:50–53; Acts 1:9–11)

¹⁹After the Lord Jesus had talked with them, he was taken up to heaven and sat at the right side of God. ²⁰The disciples went and preached everywhere, and the Lord worked with them and proved that their preaching was true by the miracles that were performed.]

ANOTHER OLD ENDING *ᵃ*

[⁹The women went to Peter and his friends and gave them a brief account of all they had been told. ¹⁰After this, Jesus himself sent out through his disciples from the east to the west the sacred and everliving message of eternal salvation.]

ᵃ **16:20** *Some manuscripts and ancient translations have this shorter ending to the Gospel in addition to the longer ending (verses 9–20).*
16:15 Acts 1:8   **16:19** Acts 1:9–11

Your Next Step

Congratulations on finishing the Gospel of Mark! Use this space to write your thoughts and questions about this book. If you are following the suggested reading plan, go back to the Book of Genesis in the Old Testament. This is the first book of the Bible, filled with interesting stories about our ancestors in the faith.

"Come on in!"

These are words we are often greeted with as we enter some-one's home. They are very welcoming words. In many ways, these words also capture the message of Luke's Gospel. It makes sure to let us know that Jesus welcomes all, not just a certain group of people. Just as the words *come on in* are often said with a smile, Luke also emphasizes the joy that comes with entering into life with Jesus. The Gospel begins and ends with stories of joy and good news. It's almost as if Luke pictures Jesus as stand-ing at the front door with both hands open and saying to us with a welcoming smile: "Come on in—there's room for everyone!"

Chap. 1:26–38

Headlines

- Angel Predicts Miracle Pregnancy (1:26–38)
- Child Jesus Lost for Three Days (2:41–52)
- Jesus Brings Young Man Back to Life (7:11–17)
- Stories Challenge Accepted Beliefs (10:25–37; 15:11–32)
- Rich Challenged to Care for Poor (16:19–31; 18:18–30)
- Jesus Shocks Crowd, Befriends Tax Collector (19:1–10)
- Travelers Surprised by the Risen Jesus (24:13–35)

FACTOIDS

Who wrote this book? Many think the author was a Gentile (non-Jewish) Chris-tian named Luke, who may have traveled with Saint Paul.

When was it written? Probably around AD 80 to 90, about fifty years after the Resurrection of Christ.

Who was it written for? The Gospel is addressed to Theophilus, which means "friend of God" in Greek. So it is for anyone who wishes to be a friend of God.

Why was it written? Luke wanted to share the Good News of Jesus with other Gentile Christians of the early Church.

Important themes
- The action of the Holy Spirit is present and working in our lives.
- Jesus came for everyone: Jew and Gentile, women and men, the poor people and the rich people.
- There is great joy in following Jesus.

Of note: Luke also wrote a sequel to this book called the Acts of the Apostles, which you will find after John's Gospel.

LUKE

Introduction

1 ¹Dear Theophilus:

Many people have done their best to write a report of the things that have taken place among us. ²They wrote what we have been told by those who saw these things from the beginning and who proclaimed the message. ³And so, Your Excellency, because I have carefully studied all these matters from their beginning, I thought it would be good to write an orderly account for you. ⁴I do this so that you will know the full truth about everything which you have been taught.

The Birth of John the Baptist Is Announced

⁵During the time when Herod was king of Judea,ᵃ there was a priest named Zechariah, who belonged to the priestly order of Abijah. His wife's name was Elizabeth; she also belonged to a priestly family. ⁶They both lived good lives in God's sight and obeyed fully all the Lord's laws and commands. ⁷They had no children because Elizabeth could not have any, and she and Zechariah were both very old.

⁸One day Zechariah was doing his work as a priest in the Temple, taking his turn in the daily service. ⁹According to the custom followed by the priests, he was chosen by lot to burn incense on the altar. So he went into the Temple of the Lord, ¹⁰while the crowd of people outside prayed during the hour when the incense was burned. ¹¹An angel of the Lord appeared to him, standing at the right side of the altar where the incense was burned. ¹²When Zechariah saw him, he was alarmed and felt afraid. ¹³But the angel said to him, "Don't be afraid, Zechariah! God has heard your prayer, and your wife Elizabeth will bear you a son. You are to name him John. ¹⁴How glad and happy you will be,

and how happy many others will be when he is born! ¹⁵John will be great in the Lord's sight. He must not drink any wine or strong drink. From his very birth he will be filled with the Holy Spirit, ¹⁶and he will bring back many of the people of Israel to the Lord their God. ¹⁷He will go ahead of the Lord, strong and mighty like the prophet Elijah. He will bring fathers and children together again; he will turn disobedient people back to the way of thinking of the righteous; he will get the Lord's people ready for him."

¹⁸Zechariah said to the angel, "How shall I know if this is so? I am an old man, and my wife is old also."

¹⁹"I am Gabriel," the angel answered. "I stand in the presence of God, who sent me to speak to you and tell you this good news. ²⁰But you have not believed my message, which will come true at the right time. Because you have not believed, you will be unable to speak; you will remain silent until the day my promise to you comes true."

²¹In the meantime the people were waiting for Zechariah and wondering why he was spending such a long time in the Temple. ²²When he came out, he could not speak to them, and so they knew that he had seen a vision in the Temple. Unable to say a word, he made signs to them with his hands.

²³When his period of service in the Temple was over, Zechariah went back home. ²⁴Some time later his wife Elizabeth became pregnant and did not leave the house for five months. ²⁵"Now at last the Lord has helped me," she said. "He has taken away my public disgrace!"

The Birth of Jesus Is Announced

²⁶In the sixth month of Elizabeth's pregnancy God sent the angel Gabriel to a town in Galilee named Nazareth. ²⁷He had a message for a young woman promised in mar-

---

ᵃ **1:5** JUDEA: *The term here refers to the whole land of Palestine.*

1:5 1 Chr 24:10   **1:15** Num 6:3   **1:17** Mal 4:5, 6; Sir 48:10, 11   **1:19** Dan 8:16; 9:21; Tob 12:15
1:27 Mt 1:18

"Born of the Virgin Mary"

Catholic Connections

The story of Jesus' conception is one of the greatest and holiest mysteries of the Catholic Church. Catholics believe that Jesus was conceived in the womb of Mary by the power of the Holy Spirit. This means that, unlike normal human births, no human father was involved. Because Jesus was conceived by God and a human parent, we know that Jesus Christ is both fully God and fully human. Mary's virginity is an important sign of that.

When Mary agreed to become the mother of Jesus, she accepted that she would become the mother of the Son of God. The man she was to marry was Joseph, who served as the foster father to Jesus. The moment Mary agreed to become the mother of Jesus, she was helping to set in motion the most important event in human history: the coming of Jesus, the Savior of the World.

— Luke 1:26–38

riage to a man named Joseph, who was a descendant of King David. Her name was Mary. ²⁸The angel came to her and said, "Peace be with you! The Lord is with you and has greatly blessed you!"

²⁹Mary was deeply troubled by the angel's message, and she wondered what his words meant. ³⁰The angel said to her, "Don't be afraid, Mary; God has been gracious to you. ³¹You will become pregnant and give birth to a son, and you will name him Jesus. ³²He will be great and will be called the Son of the Most High God. The Lord God will make him a king, as his ancestor David was, ³³and he will be the king of the descendants of Jacob forever; his kingdom will never end!"

³⁴Mary said to the angel, "I am a virgin. How, then, can this be?"

³⁵The angel answered, "The Holy Spirit will come on you, and God's power will rest upon you. For this reason the holy child will be called the Son of God. ³⁶Remember your relative Elizabeth. It is said that she cannot have children, but she herself is now six

months pregnant, even though she is very old. ³⁷For there is nothing that God cannot do."

³⁸"I am the Lord's servant," said Mary; "may it happen to me as you have said." And the angel left her.

Mary Visits Elizabeth

³⁹Soon afterward Mary got ready and hurried off to a town in the hill country of Judea. ⁴⁰She went into Zechariah's house and greeted Elizabeth. ⁴¹When Elizabeth heard Mary's greeting, the baby moved within her. Elizabeth was filled with the Holy Spirit ⁴²and said in a loud voice, "You are the most blessed of all women, and blessed is the child you will bear! ⁴³Why should this great thing happen to me, that my Lord's mother comes to visit me? ⁴⁴For as soon as I heard your greeting, the baby within me jumped with gladness. ⁴⁵How happy you are to believe that the Lord's message to you will come true!"

1:31 Mt 1:21   **1:32, 33** 2 Sam 7:12, 13, 16; Isa 9:7   **1:37** Gen 18:14   **1:42** Jdt 13:18

" 'Don't be afraid, Mary; God has been gracious to you' " *(Luke 1:30).*

Pray It!

Hail Mary!

Elizabeth's greeting to her relative Mary probably sounds familiar to you (Luke 1:42). This greeting forms part of one of the most well-known Catholic prayers, the Hail Mary. The words in this Bible are slightly different from the prayer. See if you can find the part that matches Elizabeth's greeting.

Hail Mary, full of grace,
The Lord is with you!
Blessed are you among women,
and blessed is the fruit of your
*   womb, Jesus.*
Holy Mary, Mother of God,
pray for us sinners,
now and at the hour of our death.
Amen.

By saying yes to God's plan, Mary has become the mother of all of the living. Through the Hail Mary, we can pray with Mary and ask her to pray for us. The Hail Mary also serves as the main prayer of the Rosary.

— Luke 1:41–42

Mary's Song of Praise

46 Mary said,
"My heart praises the Lord;
47   my soul is glad because of God my
        Savior,
48   for he has remembered me, his lowly
        servant!
From now on all people will call me
        happy,

49   because of the great things the Mighty
        God has done for me.
His name is holy;
50   from one generation to another
        he shows mercy to those who honor
        him.
51 He has stretched out his mighty arm
        and scattered the proud with all their
        plans.
52 He has brought down mighty kings from
        their thrones,
        and lifted up the lowly.
53 He has filled the hungry with good things,
        and sent the rich away with empty
        hands.
54 He has kept the promise he made to our
        ancestors,
        and has come to the help of his servant
        Israel.
55 He has remembered to show mercy to
        Abraham
        and to all his descendants forever!"
56 Mary stayed about three months with Elizabeth and then went back home.

The Birth of John the Baptist

57 The time came for Elizabeth to have her baby, and she gave birth to a son. 58 Her neighbors and relatives heard how wonderfully good the Lord had been to her, and they all rejoiced with her.

59 When the baby was a week old, they came to circumcise him, and they were going to name him Zechariah, after his father. 60 But his mother said, "No! His name is to be John."

61 They said to her, "But you don't have any relative with that name!" 62 Then they made signs to his father, asking him what name he would like the boy to have.

63 Zechariah asked for a writing pad and wrote, "His name is John." How surprised they all were! 64 At that moment Zechariah was able to speak again, and he started praising God. 65 The neighbors were all filled with fear, and the news about these things spread

1:48 1 Sam 1:11   1:52 Job 5:11; 12:19; Sir 10:14   1:55 Gen 17:7   1:46–55 1 Sam 2:1–10   1:59 Lev 12:3

Mary's song of praise in Luke 1:46–55 is called the *Magnificat* and has become an important prayer in the Catholic Church.

Christmas

Santa Claus. Jingle bells. Presents under the Christmas tree. These are all part of the Christmas tradition today, but none of them would exist without the event that the authors of both Luke and Matthew write about at the beginning of their Gospels: the birth of Jesus. Each December 25, just as the days are beginning to get longer, Roman Catholics and most other Christians celebrate the birth of Jesus, the light of the world.

The Christmas story in the Bible is a beautiful and familiar one. As we are busy preparing for this joyful celebration, we need to remember, as the saying goes, that Jesus is the reason for the season. How does your family celebrate the birth of Jesus?

— Luke 2:1–21

through all the hill country of Judea. 66 Everyone who heard of it thought about it and asked, "What is this child going to be?" For it was plain that the Lord's power was upon him.

Zechariah's Prophecy

67 John's father Zechariah was filled with the Holy Spirit, and he spoke God's message:
68 "Let us praise the Lord, the God of Israel!
He has come to the help of his people
and has set them free.
69 He has provided for us a mighty Savior,
a descendant of his servant David.
70 He promised through his holy prophets
long ago
71 that he would save us from our enemies,
from the power of all those who hate us.
72 He said he would show mercy to our
ancestors
and remember his sacred covenant.
73-74 With a solemn oath to our ancestor
Abraham
he promised to rescue us from our
enemies
and allow us to serve him without fear,
75 so that we might be holy and righteous
before him
all the days of our life.

76 "You, my child, will be called a prophet
of the Most High God.
You will go ahead of the Lord
to prepare his road for him,
77 to tell his people that they will be
saved
by having their sins forgiven.
78 Our God is merciful and tender.
He will cause the bright dawn of
salvation to rise on us
79 and to shine from heaven on all those
who live in the dark shadow of
death,
to guide our steps into the path of
peace."

80 The child grew and developed in body and spirit. He lived in the desert until the day when he appeared publicly to the people of Israel.

The Birth of Jesus
(Matthew 1:18–25)

2 1 At that time Emperor Augustus ordered a census to be taken throughout the Roman Empire. 2 When this first census took place, Quirinius was the governor of Syria. 3 Everyone, then, went to register himself, each to his own hometown.

1:76 Mal 3:1   1:79 Isa 9:2

⁴Joseph went from the town of Nazareth in Galilee to the town of Bethlehem in Judea, the birthplace of King David. Joseph went there because he was a descendant of David. ⁵He went to register with Mary, who was promised in marriage to him. She was pregnant, ⁶and while they were in Bethlehem, the time came for her to have her baby. ⁷She gave birth to her first son, wrapped him in cloths and laid him in a manger—there was no room for them to stay in the inn.

The Shepherds and the Angels

⁸There were some shepherds in that part of the country who were spending the night in the fields, taking care of their flocks. ⁹An angel of the Lord appeared to them, and the glory of the Lord shone over them. They were terribly afraid, ¹⁰but the angel said to them, "Don't be afraid! I am here with good news for you, which will bring great joy to all the people. ¹¹This very day in David's town your Savior was born—Christ the Lord! ¹²And this is what will prove it to you: you will find a baby wrapped in cloths and lying in a manger."

¹³Suddenly a great army of heaven's angels appeared with the angel, singing praises to God:

"Glory to God in the highest heaven!" (2:14)

¹⁴"Glory to God in the highest heaven,
and peace on earth to those with
whom he is pleased!"

¹⁵When the angels went away from them back into heaven, the shepherds said to one another, "Let's go to Bethlehem and see this thing that has happened, which the Lord has told us."

¹⁶So they hurried off and found Mary and Joseph and saw the baby lying in the manger. ¹⁷When the shepherds saw him, they told them what the angel had said about the child. ¹⁸All who heard it were amazed at what the shepherds said. ¹⁹Mary remembered all these things and thought deeply about them. ²⁰The shepherds went back, singing praises to God for all they had heard and seen; it had been just as the angel had told them.

Mary remembered all these things. (2:19)

Jesus Is Named

²¹A week later, when the time came for the baby to be circumcised, he was named Jesus, the name which the angel had given him before he had been conceived.

Jesus Is Presented in the Temple

²²The time came for Joseph and Mary to perform the ceremony of purification, as the Law of Moses commanded. So they took the child to Jerusalem to present him to the Lord, ²³as it is written in the law of the Lord: "Every first-born male is to be dedicated to the Lord." ²⁴They also went to offer a sacrifice of a pair of doves or two young pigeons, as required by the law of the Lord.

2:9 Tob 5:4   **2:21** a Lev 12:3; b Lk 1:31   **2:23** Ex 13:2, 12   **2:22–24** Lev 12:6–8

25 At that time there was a man named Simeon living in Jerusalem. He was a good, God-fearing man and was waiting for Israel to be saved. The Holy Spirit was with him 26 and had assured him that he would not die before he had seen the Lord's promised Messiah. 27 Led by the Spirit, Simeon went into the Temple. When the parents brought the child Jesus into the Temple to do for him what the Law required, 28 Simeon took the child in his arms and gave thanks to God:

29 "Now, Lord, you have kept your promise, and you may let your servant go in peace.

30 With my own eyes I have seen your salvation,

31 which you have prepared in the presence of all peoples:

32 A light to reveal your will to the Gentiles and bring glory to your people Israel."

33 The child's father and mother were amazed at the things Simeon said about him. 34 Simeon blessed them and said to Mary, his mother, "This child is chosen by God for the destruction and the salvation of many in Israel. He will be a sign from God which many people will speak against 35 and so reveal their secret thoughts. And sorrow, like a sharp sword, will break your own heart."

36-37 There was a very old prophet, a widow named Anna, daughter of Phanuel of the tribe of Asher. She had been married for only seven years and was now eighty-four years old. [b] She never left the Temple; day and night she worshiped God, fasting and praying. 38 That very same hour she arrived and gave thanks to God and spoke about the child to all who were waiting for God to set Jerusalem free.

The Return to Nazareth

39 When Joseph and Mary had finished doing all that was required by the Law of the Lord, they returned to their hometown of Nazareth in Galilee. 40 The child grew and

"Where Were You?"

Have you ever heard those words? Probably many times, especially if someone was very concerned about you. Jesus faced the same question from his parents when he was twelve years old. They thought he was lost and were very worried about him. On the third day of their frantic search, they found him in the Temple. Jesus seemed surprised at their concern.

Like the boy Jesus, you are at an age where you are growing more independent. You will be on your own more, which will be an adjustment for both you and your parents. Try to imagine yourself as the parents of a missing child. Next time you are gone longer than you thought or something comes up, let the adults in your life know where you are. Their concern for your safety is a sign of their love for you, and by staying in touch you show your love for them.

— Luke 2:41–51

became strong; he was full of wisdom, and God's blessings were upon him.

The Boy Jesus in the Temple

41 Every year the parents of Jesus went to Jerusalem for the Passover Festival. 42 When Jesus was twelve years old, they went to the festival as usual. 43 When the festival was

---

[b] **2:36–37** was now eighty-four years old; *or* had been a widow eighty-four years.
2:32 Isa 42:6; 49:6; 52:10   **2:36, 37** Jdt 8:4, 5   **2:39** Mt 2:23   **2:41** Ex 12:1–27; Deut 16:1–8

Augustus was the first emperor of the Roman Empire. Check out the time line in the front of this Bible to find out when the Romans conquered the Holy Land.

over, they started back home, but the boy Jesus stayed in Jerusalem. His parents did not know this; 44they thought that he was with the group, so they traveled a whole day and then started looking for him among their relatives and friends. 45They did not find him, so they went back to Jerusalem looking for him. 46On the third day they found him in the Temple, sitting with the Jewish teachers, listening to them and asking questions. 47All who heard him were amazed at his intelligent answers. 48His parents were astonished when they saw him, and his mother said to him, "Son, why have you done this to us? Your father and I have been terribly worried trying to find you."

. . . sitting with the Jewish teachers (2:46)

49He answered them, "Why did you have to look for me? Didn't you know that I had to be in my Father's house?" 50But they did not understand his answer.

51So Jesus went back with them to Nazareth, where he was obedient to them. His mother treasured all these things in her heart. 52Jesus grew both in body and in wisdom, gaining favor with God and people.

The Preaching of John the Baptist
(Matthew 3:1–12; Mark 1:1–8; John 1:19–28)

3 1It was the fifteenth year of the rule of Emperor Tiberius; Pontius Pilate was governor of Judea, Herod was ruler of Galilee, and his brother Philip was ruler of the territory of Iturea and Trachonitis; Lysanias was ruler of Abilene, 2and Annas and Caiaphas were High Priests. At that time the word of God came to John son of Zechariah in the desert. 3So John went throughout the whole territory of the Jordan River, preaching, "Turn away from your sins and be baptized, and God will forgive your sins." 4As it is written in the book of the prophet Isaiah:

"Someone is shouting in the desert:
  'Get the road ready for the Lord;
    make a straight path for him to travel!'
5Every valley must be filled up,
  every hill and mountain leveled off.
The winding roads must be made straight,
  and the rough paths made smooth.
6The whole human race will see God's salvation!'"

7Crowds of people came out to John to be baptized by him. "You snakes!" he said to them. "Who told you that you could escape from the punishment God is about to send? 8Do those things that will show that you have turned from your sins. And don't start saying among yourselves that Abraham is your ancestor. I tell you that God can take these rocks and make descendants for Abraham! 9The ax is ready to cut down the trees at the roots; every tree that does not bear good fruit will be cut down and thrown in the fire."

10The people asked him, "What are we to do, then?"

11He answered, "Whoever has two shirts must give one to the man who has none, and whoever has food must share it."

12Some tax collectors came to be baptized, and they asked him, "Teacher, what are we to do?"

13"Don't collect more than is legal," he told them.

14Some soldiers also asked him, "What about us? What are we to do?"

He said to them, "Don't take money from anyone by force or accuse anyone falsely. Be content with your pay."

2:52 1 Sam 2:26; Prov 3:4   **3:4–6** Isa 40:3–5 (LXX)   **3:7** Mt 12:34; 23:33   **3:8** Jn 8:33   **3:9** Mt 7:19
3:12 Lk 7:29

In Luke, chapter 3, we meet Pontius Pilate, Herod, Annas, and Caiaphas. They will play important roles in the arrest and death of Jesus.

Advent

Catholic Connections

"Get the road ready for the Lord." These words of John the Baptist serve as the theme for the season of Advent, which means "coming." John is at the Jordan River, urging people to prepare for the coming of the Messiah. Advent, which begins on the fourth Sunday before Christmas, is a time for us to get a road ready for Jesus in our own lives. The tradition of the Advent wreath with its four candles is a symbol of Advent. Each Sunday another candle is lit as a sign that Jesus is the light that comes into the world. The wreath grows brighter as we get closer to Christmas, and it reminds us to focus on what we need to do to let God enter more fully into our hearts.

— Luke 3:1–18

15 People's hopes began to rise, and they began to wonder whether John perhaps might be the Messiah. 16 So John said to all of them, "I baptize you with water, but someone is coming who is much greater than I am. I am not good enough even to untie his sandals. He will baptize you with the Holy Spirit and fire. 17 He has his winnowing shovel with him, to thresh out all the grain and gather the wheat into his barn; but he will burn the chaff in a fire that never goes out."

18 In many different ways John preached the Good News to the people and urged them to change their ways. 19 But John reprimanded Governor Herod, because he had married Herodias, his brother's wife, and had done many other evil things. 20 Then Herod did an even worse thing by putting John in prison.

The Baptism of Jesus
(Matthew 3:13–17; Mark 1:9–11)

21 After all the people had been baptized, Jesus also was baptized. While he was praying, heaven was opened, 22 and the Holy Spirit came down upon him in bodily form like a dove. And a voice came from heaven,

"You are my own dear Son. I am pleased with you."

The Ancestors of Jesus
(Matthew 1:1–17)

23 When Jesus began his work, he was about thirty years old. He was the son, so people thought, of Joseph, who was the son of Heli, 24 the son of Matthat, the son of Levi, the son of Melchi, the son of Jannai, the son of Joseph, 25 the son of Mattathias, the son of Amos, the son of Nahum, the son of Esli, the son of Naggai, 26 the son of Maath, the son of Mattathias, the son of Semein, the son of Josech, the son of Joda, 27 the son of Joanan, the son of Rhesa, the son of Zerubbabel, the son of Shealtiel, the son of Neri, 28 the son of Melchi, the son of Addi, the son of Cosam, the son of Elmadam, the son of Er, 29 the son of Joshua, the son of Eliezer, the son of Jorim, the son of Matthat, the son of Levi, 30 the son of Simeon, the son of Judah, the son of Joseph, the son of Jonam, the son of Eliakim, 31 the son of Melea, the son of Menna, the son of Mattatha, the son of Nathan, the son of David, 32 the son of Jesse, the son of Obed, the son of Boaz, the son of Salmon, the son of Nahshon, 33 the son of Amminadab, the

Luke

All in the Family

Do you know the names of your great-grandparents? How about *their* great-grandparents? In chapter 3, Luke traces Jesus' ancestors all the way back to Adam, the first human! Family is a very important part of who we are, and we need to take pride in our family and ethnic heritage. Next time you see your grandparents, ask them about their parents and grandparents. Find out what they were like. Each one of us, like Jesus, is part of a long line of people who came before us. And all of us are part of the human family.

— Luke 3:23–38

son of Admin, the son of Arni, the son of Hezron, the son of Perez, the son of Judah, ³⁴the son of Jacob, the son of Isaac, the son of Abraham, the son of Terah, the son of Nahor, ³⁵the son of Serug, the son of Reu, the son of Peleg, the son of Eber, the son of Shelah, ³⁶the son of Cainan, the son of Arphaxad, the son of Shem, the son of Noah, the son of Lamech, ³⁷the son of Methuselah, the son of Enoch, the son of Jared, the son of Mahalaleel, the son of Kenan, ³⁸the son of Enosh, the son of Seth, the son of Adam, the son of God.

The Temptation of Jesus
(Matthew 4:1–11; Mark 1:12, 13)

4 ¹Jesus returned from the Jordan full of the Holy Spirit and was led by the Spirit into the desert, ²where he was tempted by the Devil for forty days. In all that time he ate nothing, so that he was hungry when it was over.

³The Devil said to him, "If you are God's Son, order this stone to turn into bread."

⁴But Jesus answered, "The scripture says, 'Human beings cannot live on bread alone.'"

⁵Then the Devil took him up and showed him in a second all the kingdoms of the world. ⁶"I will give you all this power and all this wealth," the Devil told him. "It has all been handed over to me, and I can give it to anyone I choose. ⁷All this will be yours, then, if you worship me."

⁸Jesus answered, "The scripture says, 'Worship the Lord your God and serve only him!'"

⁹Then the Devil took him to Jerusalem and set him on the highest point of the Temple, and said to him, "If you are God's Son, throw yourself down from here. ¹⁰For the scripture says, 'God will order his angels to take good care of you.' ¹¹It also says, 'They will hold you up with their hands so that not even your feet will be hurt on the stones.'"

¹²But Jesus answered, "The scripture says, 'Do not put the Lord your God to the test.'"

¹³When the Devil finished tempting Jesus in every way, he left him for a while.

Jesus Begins His Work in Galilee
(Matthew 4:12–17; Mark 1:14, 15)

¹⁴Then Jesus returned to Galilee, and the power of the Holy Spirit was with him. The news about him spread throughout all that territory. ¹⁵He taught in the synagogues and was praised by everyone.

Jesus Is Rejected at Nazareth
(Matthew 13:53–58; Mark 6:1–6)

¹⁶Then Jesus went to Nazareth, where he had been brought up, and on the Sabbath he went as usual to the synagogue. He stood up to read the Scriptures ¹⁷and was handed the book of the prophet Isaiah. He unrolled the scroll and found the place where it is written,

¹⁸"The Spirit of the Lord is upon me, because he has chosen me to bring good news to the poor.

4:4 Deut 8:3   4:8 Deut 6:13   4:10, 11 Ps 91:11, 12   4:12 Deut 6:16   4:18, 19 Isa 61:1, 2 (LXX)

He has sent me to proclaim liberty to the
    captives
  and recovery of sight to the blind,
  to set free the oppressed
19   and announce that the time has come
    when the Lord will save his people."

20 Jesus rolled up the scroll, gave it back to
the attendant, and sat down. All the people
in the synagogue had their eyes fixed on
him, 21 as he said to them, "This passage of
scripture has come true today, as you heard it
being read."

22 They were all well impressed with him
and marveled at the eloquent words that he
spoke. They said, "Isn't he the son of Joseph?"

23 He said to them, "I am sure that you
will quote this proverb to me, 'Doctor, heal
yourself.' You will also tell me to do here in
my hometown the same things you heard
were done in Capernaum. 24 I tell you this,"
Jesus added, "prophets are never welcomed
in their hometown. 25 Listen to me: it is true
that there were many widows in Israel during the time of Elijah, when there was no
rain for three and a half years and a severe
famine spread throughout the whole land.
26 Yet Elijah was not sent to anyone in Israel,
but only to a widow living in Zarephath in
the territory of Sidon. 27 And there were
many people suffering from a dreaded skin
disease who lived in Israel during the time
of the prophet Elisha; yet not one of them
was healed, but only Naaman the Syrian."

28 When the people in the synagogue
heard this, they were filled with anger.
29 They rose up, dragged Jesus out of town,
and took him to the top of the hill on which
their town was built. They meant to throw
him over the cliff, 30 but he walked through
the middle of the crowd and went his way.

A Man with an Evil Spirit
(Mark 1:21–28)

31 Then Jesus went to Capernaum, a town
in Galilee, where he taught the people on
the Sabbath. 32 They were all amazed at the
way he taught, because he spoke with
authority. 33 In the synagogue was a man
who had the spirit of an evil demon in him;
he screamed out in a loud voice, 34 "Ah!
What do you want with us, Jesus of
Nazareth? Are you here to destroy us? I
know who you are: you are God's holy
messenger!"

35 Jesus ordered the spirit, "Be quiet and
come out of the man!" The demon threw
the man down in front of them and went
out of him without doing him any harm.

36 The people were all amazed and said to
one another, "What kind of words are these?
With authority and power this man gives
orders to the evil spirits, and they come
out!" 37 And the report about Jesus spread
everywhere in that region.

Jesus Heals Many People
(Matthew 8:14–17; Mark 1:29–34)

38 Jesus left the synagogue and went to
Simon's home. Simon's mother-in-law was
sick with a high fever, and they spoke to
Jesus about her. 39 He went and stood at her
bedside and ordered the fever to leave her.
The fever left her, and she got up at once
and began to wait on them.

40 After sunset all who had friends who
were sick with various diseases brought them
to Jesus; he placed his hands on every one of
them and healed them all. 41 Demons also
went out from many people, screaming,
"You are the Son of God!"

Jesus gave the demons an order and would
not let them speak, because they knew he
was the Messiah.

Jesus Preaches in the Synagogues
(Mark 1:35–39)

42 At daybreak Jesus left the town and
went off to a lonely place. The people started
looking for him, and when they found him,
they tried to keep him from leaving. 43 But
he said to them, "I must preach the Good

Luke

4:24 Jn 4:44   4:25 1 Kings 17:1   4:26 1 Kings 17:8–16   4:27 2 Kings 5:1–14   4:32 Mt 7:28, 29

Jesus refers to Naaman the Syrian (Luke 4:27). **Check out his story in 2 Kings
5:1–14.**

Pray It!

Turn Down the Noise

Twice Luke mentions that Jesus would go away to a lonely place (Luke 4:42, 5:16).
Jesus was almost always surrounded by people, so it makes sense that sometimes
he just needed to get away to a quiet spot where he could rest and pray. That's
important for us too. We all need to have somewhere to go where we can be alone
and spend some time in God's presence. Where is your quiet place to rest and play?

   Where do you go to be alone with your thoughts? The next time you are
there, try this prayer.

> *Dear God, here I am alone with you.*
> *Life gets so crazy sometimes.*
> *It's good just to hang out with you.*
> *It helps me to know that even Jesus needed to get away once in awhile.*
> *Help me as I sort through what's going on in my life,*
>   *especially with my family and friends.*
> *Thank you for being here with me.*
> *Amen.*

— Luke 4:42–43

News about the Kingdom of God in other
towns also, because that is what God sent me
to do."

   44So he preached in the synagogues
throughout the country.

Jesus Calls the First Disciples
(Matthew 4:18–22; Mark 1:16–20)

5 1One day Jesus was standing on the
shore of Lake Gennesaret while the
people pushed their way up to him to listen
to the word of God. 2He saw two boats
pulled up on the beach; the fishermen had
left them and were washing the nets. 3Jesus
got into one of the boats—it belonged to
Simon—and asked him to push off a little
from the shore. Jesus sat in the boat and
taught the crowd.

   4When he finished speaking, he said to
Simon, "Push the boat out further to the

deep water, and you and your partners let
down your nets for a catch."

   5"Master," Simon answered, "we worked
hard all night long and caught nothing. But if
you say so, I will let down the nets." 6They
let them down and caught such a large number of fish that the nets were about to break.
7So they motioned to their partners in the
other boat to come and help them. They

They . . . caught such a large number of fish. (5:6)

5:1–3 Mt 13:1, 2; Mk 3:9, 10; 4:1   5:5 Jn 21:3   5:6 Jn 21:6

Jesus calls his first four disciples in Luke, chapter 5. Can you list their names
and the jobs they had?

came and filled both boats so full of fish that the boats were about to sink. 8 When Simon Peter saw what had happened, he fell on his knees before Jesus and said, "Go away from me, Lord! I am a sinful man!"

9 He and the others with him were all amazed at the large number of fish they had caught. 10 The same was true of Simon's partners, James and John, the sons of Zebedee. Jesus said to Simon, "Don't be afraid; from now on you will be catching people."

11 They pulled the boats up on the beach, left everything, and followed Jesus.

Jesus Heals a Man
(Matthew 8:1–4; Mark 1:40–45)

12 Once Jesus was in a town where there was a man who was suffering from a dreaded skin disease. When he saw Jesus, he threw himself down and begged him, "Sir, if you want to, you can make me clean!"*c*

13 Jesus reached out and touched him. "I do want to," he answered. "Be clean!" At once the disease left the man. 14 Jesus ordered him, "Don't tell anyone, but go straight to the priest and let him examine you; then to prove to everyone that you are cured, offer the sacrifice as Moses ordered."

15 But the news about Jesus spread all the more widely, and crowds of people came to hear him and be healed from their diseases. 16 But he would go away to lonely places, where he prayed.

Jesus Heals a Paralyzed Man
(Matthew 9:1–8; Mark 2:1–12)

17 One day when Jesus was teaching, some Pharisees and teachers of the Law were sitting there who had come from every town in Galilee and Judea and from Jerusalem. The power of the Lord was present for Jesus to heal the sick. 18 Some men came carrying a paralyzed man on a bed, and they tried to carry him into the house and put him in front of Jesus. 19 Because of the crowd, however, they could find no way to take him in. So they carried him up on the roof, made an opening in the tiles, and

let him down on his bed into the middle of the group in front of Jesus. 20 When Jesus saw how much faith they had, he said to the man, "Your sins are forgiven, my friend."

21 The teachers of the Law and the Pharisees began to say to themselves, "Who is this man who speaks such blasphemy! God is the only one who can forgive sins!"

They . . . let him down on his bed into the middle of the group. (5:19)

22 Jesus knew their thoughts and said to them, "Why do you think such things? 23 Is it easier to say, 'Your sins are forgiven you,' or to say, 'Get up and walk'? 24 I will prove to you, then, that the Son of Man has authority on earth to forgive sins." So he said to the paralyzed man, "I tell you, get up, pick up your bed, and go home!"

25 At once the man got up in front of them all, took the bed he had been lying on, and went home, praising God. 26 They were all completely amazed! Full of fear, they praised God, saying, "What marvelous things we have seen today!"

Jesus Calls Levi
(Matthew 9:9–13; Mark 2:13–17)

27 After this, Jesus went out and saw a tax collector named Levi, sitting in his office. Jesus said to him, "Follow me." 28 Levi got up, left everything, and followed him.

29 Then Levi had a big feast in his house

---

c **5:12** MAKE ME CLEAN: *This disease was considered to make a person ritually unclean.*
5:14 Lev 14:1–32

for Jesus, and among the guests was a large number of tax collectors and other people. 30Some Pharisees and some teachers of the Law who belonged to their group complained to Jesus' disciples. "Why do you eat and drink with tax collectors and other outcasts?" they asked.

31Jesus answered them, "People who are well do not need a doctor, but only those who are sick. 32I have not come to call respectable people to repent, but outcasts."

The Question about Fasting
(Matthew 9:14–17; Mark 2:18–22)

33Some people said to Jesus, "The disciples of John fast frequently and offer prayers, and the disciples of the Pharisees do the same; but your disciples eat and drink."

34Jesus answered, "Do you think you can make the guests at a wedding party go without food as long as the bridegroom is with them? Of course not! 35But the day will come when the bridegroom will be taken away from them, and then they will fast."

36Jesus also told them this parable: "You don't tear a piece off a new coat to patch up an old coat. If you do, you will have torn the new coat, and the piece of new cloth will not match the old. 37Nor do you pour new wine into used wineskins, because the new wine will burst the skins, the wine will pour out, and the skins will be ruined. 38Instead, new wine must be poured into fresh wineskins! 39And you don't want new wine after drinking old wine. 'The old is better,' you say."

The Question about the Sabbath
(Matthew 12:1–8; Mark 2:23–28)

6 1Jesus was walking through some wheat fields on a Sabbath. His disciples began to pick the heads of wheat, rub them in their hands, and eat the grain. 2Some Pharisees asked, "Why are you doing what our Law says you cannot do on the Sabbath?"

3Jesus answered them, "Haven't you read what David did when he and his men were hungry? 4He went into the house of God,

Old and New

So what's up with the parable of the patches and the wineskins? When is the last time you had a piece of clothing patched? And what in the world is a wineskin? These are images we have a hard time understanding because they are probably not part of our lives. What Jesus is really talking about here is the difference between the old and the new. For example, if your family or school has an old computer, and you try to install a brand new program, it probably won't work. The old computer simply can't handle the new software.

Jesus is making a point about the new message he is trying to share with his followers. People were sometimes more concerned with following rules rather than getting closer to God. It's not so much about all the rules, as it is about acting out of love and compassion. That is the good NEWs! That's the new program to install within our hearts and souls.

— Luke 5:36–39

took the bread offered to God, ate it, and gave it also to his men. Yet it is against our Law for anyone except the priests to eat that bread."

5And Jesus concluded, "The Son of Man is Lord of the Sabbath."

The Man with a Paralyzed Hand
(Matthew 12:9–14; Mark 3:1–6)

6On another Sabbath Jesus went into a synagogue and taught. A man was there whose right hand was paralyzed. 7Some teachers of the Law and some Pharisees wanted a reason to accuse Jesus of doing wrong, so they watched him closely to see if he would heal on the Sabbath. 8But Jesus knew their thoughts and said to the man, "Stand up and come here to the front." The man got up and stood there. 9Then Jesus said to them, "I ask you: What does our Law allow us to do on the Sabbath? To help or to harm? To save someone's life or destroy it?" 10He looked around at them all; then he said*d* to the man, "Stretch out your hand." He did so, and his hand became well again.

11They were filled with rage and began to discuss among themselves what they could do to Jesus.

Jesus Chooses the Twelve Apostles
(Matthew 10:1–4; Mark 3:13–19)

12At that time Jesus went up a hill to pray and spent the whole night there praying to God. 13When day came, he called his disciples to him and chose twelve of them, whom he named apostles: 14Simon (whom he named Peter) and his brother Andrew; James and John, Philip and Bartholomew, 15Matthew and Thomas, James son of Alphaeus, and Simon (who was called the Patriot), 16Judas son of James, and Judas Iscariot, who became the traitor.

Jesus Teaches and Heals
(Matthew 4:23–25)

17When Jesus had come down from the hill with the apostles, he stood on a level place with a large number of his disciples. A large crowd of people was there from all over Judea and from Jerusalem and from the coast cities of Tyre and Sidon; 18they had come to hear him and to be healed of their diseases. Those who were troubled by evil spirits also came and were healed. 19All the people tried to touch him, for power was going out from him and healing them all.

Happiness and Sorrow
(Matthew 5:1–12)

20Jesus looked at his disciples and said,
"Happy are you poor;
    the Kingdom of God is yours!
21"Happy are you who are hungry now;
    you will be filled!

"Happy are you who weep now;
    you will laugh!
22"Happy are you when people hate you, reject you, insult you, and say that you are evil, all because of the Son of Man! 23Be glad when that happens and dance for joy, because a great reward is kept for you in heaven. For their ancestors did the very same things to the prophets.
24"But how terrible for you who are rich now;
    you have had your easy life!
25"How terrible for you who are full now;
    you will go hungry!

"How terrible for you who laugh now;
    you will mourn and weep!
26"How terrible when all people speak well of you; their ancestors said the very same things about the false prophets.

Love for Enemies
(Matthew 5:38–48; 7:12a)

27"But I tell you who hear me: Love your enemies, do good to those who hate you, 28bless those who curse you, and pray for those who mistreat you. 29If anyone hits you on one cheek, let him hit the other one too; if someone takes your coat, let him have your shirt as well. 30Give to everyone who asks you for something, and when someone takes what is yours, do not ask for it back. 31Do for others just what you want them to do for you.

32"If you love only the people who love you, why should you receive a blessing? Even sinners love those who love them! 33And if you do good only to those who do

---

d **6:10** said; *some manuscripts have* said angrily.
6:22 1 Pet 4:14   **6:23** 2 Chr 36:16; Acts 7:52   **6:31** Tob 4:15; Mt 7:12

Luke

The Beatitudes is the name given to the teachings of Jesus in Luke 6:20–26. See how they compare with the version in Matthew 5:1–12.

Going the Extra Mile

How do we treat people who are mean to us? How do we react to people who we can't stand? Jesus has a pretty clear answer. We are to pray for those who mistreat us and actually bless those people who curse us (to bless someone is to ask God to bring good things to that person)! Jesus goes on to say that it's easy to be nice and kind to the people we like. Anyone can do that. The real challenge—the Christian challenge—is to love the people we don't like and to do good things to and for them.

Who do you have trouble liking? Pray right now that God will bless that person. Think of a specific way that you could follow this tough teaching of Jesus by doing something nice or kind for that person.

— Luke 6:27–36

Judging Others
(Matthew 7:1–5)

37 "Do not judge others, and God will not judge you; do not condemn others, and God will not condemn you; forgive others, and God will forgive you. 38 Give to others, and God will give to you. Indeed, you will receive a full measure, a generous helping, poured into your hands—all that you can hold. The measure you use for others is the one that God will use for you."

39 And Jesus told them this parable: "One blind man cannot lead another one; if he does, both will fall into a ditch. 40 No pupils are greater than their teacher; but all pupils, when they have completed their training, will be like their teacher.

41 "Why do you look at the speck in your brother's eye, but pay no attention to the log in your own eye? 42 How can you say to your brother, 'Please, brother, let me take that speck out of your eye,' yet cannot even see the log in your own eye? You hypocrite! First take the log out of your own eye, and then you will be able to see clearly to take the speck out of your brother's eye.

A Tree and Its Fruit
(Matthew 7:16–20; 12:33–35)

43 "A healthy tree does not bear bad fruit, nor does a poor tree bear good fruit. 44 Every tree is known by the fruit it bears; you do not pick figs from thorn bushes or gather grapes from bramble bushes. 45 A good person brings good out of the treasure of good things in his heart; a bad person brings bad out of his treasure of bad things. For the mouth speaks what the heart is full of.

The Two House Builders
(Matthew 7:24–27)

46 "Why do you call me, 'Lord, Lord,' and yet don't do what I tell you? 47 Anyone who comes to me and listens to my words and

good to you, why should you receive a blessing? Even sinners do that! 34 And if you lend only to those from whom you hope to get it back, why should you receive a blessing? Even sinners lend to sinners, to get back the same amount! 35 No! Love your enemies and do good to them; lend and expect nothing back. You will then have a great reward, and you will be children of the Most High God. For he is good to the ungrateful and the wicked. 36 Be merciful just as your Father is merciful.

6:35 Sir 4:10, 11   **6:39** Mt 15:14   **6:40** Mt 10:24, 25; Jn 13:16; 15:20   **6:44** Mt 12:33   **6:45** Mt 12:34

" 'Do not judge others, and God will not judge you; . . . forgive others, and God will forgive you' " *(Luke 6:37)*.

Measure for Measure

Have you ever seen those old-fashioned balances? They are used for weighing and seeing if two things are more-or-less equal. Keep that image in mind as you think about judging another person or about doing a good deed for someone. Jesus tells us that what we do will come back to us (Luke 6:38). If we constantly judge others, the same will happen to us. If we give generously to others, the same will happen to us. Let's try to keep that balance in mind.

— Luke 6:37–42

obeys them—I will show you what he is like. [48]He is like a man who, in building his house, dug deep and laid the foundation on rock. The river flooded over and hit that house but could not shake it, because it was well built. [49]But anyone who hears my words and does not obey them is like a man who built his house without laying a foundation; when the flood hit that house it fell at once—and what a terrible crash that was!"

Jesus Heals a Roman Officer's Servant
(Matthew 8:5–13)

7 [1]When Jesus had finished saying all these things to the people, he went to Capernaum. [2]A Roman officer there had a servant who was very dear to him; the man was sick and about to die. [3]When the officer heard about Jesus, he sent some Jewish elders to ask him to come and heal his servant. [4]They came to Jesus and begged him earnestly, "This man really deserves your help. [5]He loves our people and he himself built a synagogue for us."

[6]So Jesus went with them. He was not far from the house when the officer sent friends to tell him, "Sir, don't trouble yourself. I do not deserve to have you come into my house, [7]neither do I consider myself worthy to come to you in person. Just give the order, and my servant will get well. [8]I, too, am a man placed under the authority of superior officers, and I have soldiers under me. I order this one, 'Go!' and he goes; I order that one, 'Come!' and he comes; and I order my slave, 'Do this!' and he does it."

[9]Jesus was surprised when he heard this; he turned around and said to the crowd following him, "I tell you, I have never found faith like this, not even in Israel!"

[10]The messengers went back to the officer's house and found his servant well.

Jesus Raises a Widow's Son

[11]Soon afterward[e] Jesus went to a town named Nain, accompanied by his disciples and a large crowd. [12]Just as he arrived at the gate of the town, a funeral procession was coming out. The dead man was the only son of a woman who was a widow, and a large crowd from the town was with her. [13]When the Lord saw her, his heart was filled with pity for her, and he said to her, "Don't cry." [14]Then he walked over and touched the coffin, and the men carrying it stopped. Jesus said, "Young man! Get up, I tell you!" [15]The dead man sat up and began to talk, and Jesus gave him back to his mother.

[16]They all were filled with fear and praised God. "A great prophet has appeared among us!" they said; "God has come to save his people!"

[17]This news about Jesus went out through all the country and the surrounding territory.

The Messengers from John the Baptist
(Matthew 11:2–19)

[18]When John's disciples told him about all these things, he called two of them [19]and sent them to the Lord to ask him, "Are you

Luke

---

[e] **7:11** Soon afterward; *some manuscripts have* The next day.

the one John said was going to come, or should we expect someone else?"

20 When they came to Jesus, they said, "John the Baptist sent us to ask if you are the one he said was going to come, or should we expect someone else?"

21 At that very time Jesus healed many people from their sicknesses, diseases, and evil spirits, and gave sight to many blind people. 22 He answered John's messengers, "Go back and tell John what you have seen and heard: the blind can see, the lame can walk, those who suffer from dreaded skin diseases are made clean,ƒ the deaf can hear, the dead are raised to life, and the Good News is preached to the poor. 23 How happy are those who have no doubts about me!"

24 After John's messengers had left, Jesus began to speak about him to the crowds: "When you went out to John in the desert, what did you expect to see? A blade of grass bending in the wind? 25 What did you go out to see? A man dressed up in fancy clothes? People who dress like that and live in luxury are found in palaces! 26 Tell me, what did you go out to see? A prophet? Yes indeed, but you saw much more than a prophet. 27 For John is the one of whom the scripture says: 'God said, I will send my messenger ahead of you to open the way for you.' 28 I tell you," Jesus added, "John is greater than anyone who has ever lived. But the one who is least in the Kingdom of God is greater than John."

29 All the people heard him; they and especially the tax collectors were the ones who had obeyed God's righteous demands and had been baptized by John. 30 But the Pharisees and the teachers of the Law rejected God's purpose for themselves and refused to be baptized by John.

31 Jesus continued, "Now to what can I compare the people of this day? What are they like? 32 They are like children sitting in the marketplace. One group shouts to the other, 'We played wedding music for you, but you wouldn't dance! We sang funeral songs, but you wouldn't cry!' 33 John the Baptist came, and he fasted and drank no wine, and you said, 'He has a demon in him!'

It's Always Something

Sometimes you just can't win.

In a certain neighborhood, a small, old building had been empty for a long time, and people complained because it was an eyesore. Then one day the place came alive with construction, and before long, a little grocery opened. It was doing very well, but there wasn't a parking lot, so soon a lot more cars were parking on the streets. People in the neighborhood started complaining because now they couldn't always park right in front of their homes or apartments. They finally complained to the neighborhood council, who put up signs along the streets restricting parking. As the weather got colder, customers of the store started going to other places where parking was easier. Eventually the once-successful grocery went out of business. Once again, the building was empty, and soon the neighbors started complaining about the empty building.

This is the very thing Jesus is talking about in this passage as he compares people's reactions with those of John's followers and his own. Sometimes you just can't win! Think about what you have complained about recently. Can you think of something positive to say as well?

— Luke 7:31-35

34 The Son of Man came, and he ate and drank, and you said, 'Look at this man! He is a glutton and wine drinker, a friend of tax

---

ƒ 7:22 MADE CLEAN: See 5:12.

7:22 a Isa 35:5,6; **b** Isa 61:1   **7:27** Mal 3:1   **7:29, 30** Mt 21:32; Lk 3:12

collectors and other outcasts!' 35 God's wisdom, however, is shown to be true by all who accept it."

Jesus at the Home of Simon the Pharisee

36 A Pharisee invited Jesus to have dinner with him, and Jesus went to his house and sat down to eat. 37 In that town was a woman who lived a sinful life. She heard that Jesus was eating in the Pharisee's house, so she brought an alabaster jar full of perfume 38 and stood behind Jesus, by his feet, crying and wetting his feet with her tears. Then she dried his feet with her hair, kissed them, and poured the perfume on them. 39 When the Pharisee saw this, he said to himself, "If this man really were a prophet, he would know who this woman is who is touching him; he would know what kind of sinful life she lives!"

40 Jesus spoke up and said to him, "Simon, I have something to tell you."

"Yes, Teacher," he said, "tell me."

41 "There were two men who owed money to a moneylender," Jesus began. "One owed him five hundred silver coins, and the other owed him fifty. 42 Neither of them could pay him back, so he canceled the debts of both. Which one, then, will love him more?"

43 "I suppose," answered Simon, "that it would be the one who was forgiven more."

"You are right," said Jesus. 44 Then he turned to the woman and said to Simon, "Do you see this woman? I came into your home, and you gave me no water for my feet, but she has washed my feet with her tears and dried them with her hair. 45 You did not welcome me with a kiss, but she has not stopped kissing my feet since I came. 46 You provided no olive oil for my head, but she has covered my feet with perfume. 47 I tell you, then, the great love she has shown proves that her many sins have been forgiven. But whoever has been forgiven little shows only a little love."

48 Then Jesus said to the woman, "Your sins are forgiven."

49 The others sitting at the table began to say to themselves, "Who is this, who even forgives sins?"

50 But Jesus said to the woman, "Your faith has saved you; go in peace."

Women Who Accompanied Jesus

8 1 Some time later Jesus traveled through towns and villages, preaching the Good News about the Kingdom of God. The twelve disciples went with him, 2 and so did some women who had been healed of evil spirits and diseases: Mary (who was called Magdalene), from whom seven demons had been driven out; 3 Joanna, whose husband Chuza was an officer in Herod's court; and Susanna, and many other women who used their own resources to help Jesus and his disciples.

The Parable of the Sower
(Matthew 13:1–9; Mark 4:1–9)

4 People kept coming to Jesus from one town after another; and when a great crowd gathered, Jesus told this parable:

5 "Once there was a man who went out to sow grain. As he scattered the seed in the field, some of it fell along the path, where it was stepped on, and the birds ate it up. 6 Some of it fell on rocky ground, and when the plants sprouted, they dried up because the soil had no moisture. 7 Some of the seed fell among thorn bushes, which grew up with the plants and choked them. 8 And some seeds fell in good soil; the plants grew and bore grain, one hundred grains each."

And Jesus concluded, "Listen, then, if you have ears!"

Luke

A *glutton* (Luke 7:34) **is someone who eats or drinks way too much. Gluttony is one of the seven deadly sins.**

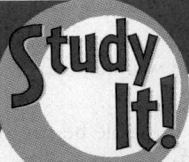

Jesus: A Friend and Teacher to All

Mary. Joanna. Susanna. Luke provides us with the names of three of the women who followed Jesus along with the twelve disciples. Women are also an important part of the Easter story, as they are the ones who first get the news about Jesus' Resurrection. Luke tells us that many other women used their resources to help Jesus and his disciples.

The status of women in Jesus' time was very different from the status of women today in our culture. Women in Jesus' culture had very few rights and were basically considered the property of their husbands. A woman did not speak to men in public, and a man would not speak to a woman who was not his wife. But Jesus broke through these cultural limitations and reached out to women, who played an important role in his life and mission.

— Luke 8:1–3

The Purpose of the Parables
(Matthew 13:10–17; Mark 4:10–12)

9His disciples asked Jesus what this parable meant, 10and he answered, "The knowledge of the secrets of the Kingdom of God has been given to you, but to the rest it comes by means of parables, so that they may look but not see, and listen but not understand.

Jesus Explains the Parable of the Sower
(Matthew 13:18–23; Mark 4:13–20)

11"This is what the parable means: the seed is the word of God. 12The seeds that fell along the path stand for those who hear; but the Devil comes and takes the message away from their hearts in order to keep them from believing and being saved. 13The seeds that fell on rocky ground stand for those who hear the message and receive it gladly. But it does not sink deep into them; they believe only for a while but when the time of testing comes, they fall away. 14The seeds that fell among thorn bushes stand for those who hear; but the worries and riches and pleasures of this life crowd in and choke them, and their fruit never ripens. 15The seeds that fell in good soil stand for those who hear the message and retain it in a good and obedient heart, and they persist until they bear fruit.

A Lamp under a Bowl
(Mark 4:21–25)

16"No one lights a lamp and covers it with a bowl or puts it under a bed. Instead, it is put on the lampstand, so that people will see the light as they come in.

17"Whatever is hidden away will be brought out into the open, and whatever is covered up will be found and brought to light.

18"Be careful, then, how you listen; because those who have something will be given more, but whoever has nothing will have taken away from them even the little they think they have."

Jesus' Mother and Brothers
(Matthew 12:46–50; Mark 3:31–35)

19Jesus' mother and brothers came to him, but were unable to join him because of the crowd. 20Someone said to Jesus, "Your mother and brothers are standing outside and want to see you."

8:10 Isa 6:9 (LXX)   **8:16** Mt 5:15; Lk 11:33   **8:17** Mt 10:26; Lk 12:2   **8:18** Mt 25:29; Lk 19:26

Jesus casts the demons into a herd of pigs *(Luke 8:32–33)*. **In the Old Law, pigs re unclean animals, so Jews did not eat pork.**

21 Jesus said to them all, "My mother and brothers are those who hear the word of God and obey it."

Jesus Calms a Storm
(Matthew 8:23–27; Mark 4:35–41)

22 One day Jesus got into a boat with his disciples and said to them, "Let us go across to the other side of the lake." So they started out. 23 As they were sailing, Jesus fell asleep. Suddenly a strong wind blew down on the lake, and the boat began to fill with water, so that they were all in great danger. 24 The disciples went to Jesus and woke him up, saying, "Master, Master! We are about to die!"

Jesus got up and gave an order to the wind and to the stormy water; they quieted down, and there was a great calm. 25 Then he said to the disciples, "Where is your faith?"

But they were amazed and afraid, and said to one another, "Who is this man? He gives orders to the winds and waves, and they obey him!"

Jesus Heals a Man with Demons
(Matthew 8:28–34; Mark 5:1–20)

26 Jesus and his disciples sailed on over to the territory of Gerasa,*g* which is across the lake from Galilee. 27 As Jesus stepped ashore, he was met by a man from the town who had demons in him. For a long time this man had gone without clothes and would not stay at home, but spent his time in the burial caves. 28 When he saw Jesus, he gave a loud cry, threw himself down at his feet, and shouted, "Jesus, Son of the Most High God! What do you want with me? I beg you, don't punish me!" 29 He said this because Jesus had ordered the evil spirit to go out of him. Many times it had seized him, and even though he was kept a prisoner, his hands and feet tied with chains, he would break the chains and be driven by the demon out into the desert.

30 Jesus asked him, "What is your name?"

"My name is 'Mob,' " he answered—because many demons had gone into him.

31 The demons begged Jesus not to send them into the abyss.*h*

32 There was a large herd of pigs near by, feeding on a hillside. So the demons begged Jesus to let them go into the pigs, and he let them. 33 They went out of the man and into the pigs. The whole herd rushed down the side of the cliff into the lake and was drowned.

34 The men who had been taking care of the pigs saw what happened, so they ran off and spread the news in the town and among the farms. 35 People went out to see what had happened, and when they came to Jesus, they found the man from whom the demons had gone out sitting at the feet of Jesus, clothed and in his right mind; and they were all afraid. 36 Those who had seen it told the people how the man had been cured. 37 Then all the people from that territory asked Jesus to go away, because they were terribly afraid. So Jesus got into the boat and left. 38 The man from whom the demons had gone out begged Jesus, "Let me go with you."

But Jesus sent him away, saying, 39 "Go back home and tell what God has done for you."

The man went through the town, telling what Jesus had done for him.

Jairus' Daughter and the Woman Who Touched Jesus' Cloak
(Matthew 9:18–26; Mark 5:21–43)

40 When Jesus returned to the other side of the lake, the people welcomed him, because they had all been waiting for him. 41 Then a man named Jairus arrived; he was an official in the local synagogue. He threw himself down at Jesus' feet and begged him to go to his home, 42 because his only daughter, who was twelve years old, was dying.

As Jesus went along, the people were crowding him from every side. 43 Among them was a woman who had suffered from severe bleeding for twelve years; she had spent all she had on doctors,*i* but no one had been able to cure her. 44 She came up in the crowd behind Jesus and touched the

g **8:26** Gerasa; *some manuscripts have* Gadara *(see Mt 8:28); others have* Gergesa.   *h* **8:31** ABYSS: *It was thought that the demons were to be imprisoned in the depths of the earth until their final punishment.*   *i* **8:43** *Some manuscripts do not have* she had spent all she had on doctors.

edge of his cloak, and her bleeding stopped at once. 45 Jesus asked, "Who touched me?"

Everyone denied it, and Peter said, "Master, the people are all around you and crowding in on you."

46 But Jesus said, "Someone touched me, for I knew it when power went out of me." 47 The woman saw that she had been found out, so she came trembling and threw herself at Jesus' feet. There in front of everybody, she told him why she had touched him and how she had been healed at once. 48 Jesus said to her, "My daughter, your faith has made you well. Go in peace."

49 While Jesus was saying this, a messenger came from the official's house. "Your daughter has died," he told Jairus; "don't bother the Teacher any longer."

50 But Jesus heard it and said to Jairus, "Don't be afraid; only believe, and she will be well."

51 When he arrived at the house, he would not let anyone go in with him except Peter, John, and James, and the child's father and mother. 52 Everyone there was crying and mourning for the child. Jesus said, "Don't cry; the child is not dead—she is only sleeping!" 53 They all made fun of him, because they knew that she was dead. 54 But Jesus took her by the hand and called out, "Get up, child!" 55 Her life returned, and she got up at once, and Jesus ordered them to give her something to eat. 56 Her parents were astounded, but Jesus commanded them not to tell anyone what had happened.

Jesus Sends Out the Twelve Disciples
(Matthew 10:5–15; Mark 6:7–13)

9 ¹Jesus called the twelve disciples together and gave them power and authority to drive out all demons and to cure diseases. 2 Then he sent them out to preach the Kingdom of God and to heal the sick, 3 after saying to them, "Take nothing with you for the trip: no walking stick, no beggar's bag, no food, no money, not even an extra shirt. 4 Wherever you are welcomed, stay in the same house until you leave that town; 5 wherever people don't welcome you, leave

that town and shake the dust off your feet as a warning to them."

6 The disciples left and traveled through all the villages, preaching the Good News and healing people everywhere.

Herod's Confusion
(Matthew 14:1–12; Mark 6:14–29)

7 When Herod, the ruler of Galilee, heard about all the things that were happening, he was very confused, because some people were saying that John the Baptist had come back to life. 8 Others were saying that Elijah had appeared, and still others that one of the prophets of long ago had come back to life. 9 Herod said, "I had John's head cut off; but who is this man I hear these things about?" And he kept trying to see Jesus.

Jesus Feeds Five Thousand
(Matthew 14:13–21; Mark 6:30–44; John 6:1–14)

10 The apostles came back and told Jesus everything they had done. He took them with him, and they went off by themselves to a town named Bethsaida. 11 When the crowds heard about it, they followed him. He welcomed them, spoke to them about the Kingdom of God, and healed those who needed it.

12 When the sun was beginning to set, the twelve disciples came to him and said, "Send the people away so that they can go to the villages and farms around here and find food and lodging, because this is a lonely place."

13 But Jesus said to them, "You yourselves give them something to eat."

They answered, "All we have are five loaves and two fish. Do you want us to go and buy food for this whole crowd?" 14 (There were about five thousand men there.)

Jesus said to his disciples, "Make the people sit down in groups of about fifty each."

15 After the disciples had done so, 16 Jesus took the five loaves and two fish, looked up to heaven, thanked God for them, broke them, and gave them to the disciples to distribute to the people. 17 They all ate and had

enough, and the disciples took up twelve baskets of what was left over.

Peter's Declaration about Jesus
(Matthew 16:13–19; Mark 8:27–29)

18 One day when Jesus was praying alone, the disciples came to him. "Who do the crowds say I am?" he asked them.

19 "Some say that you are John the Baptist," they answered. "Others say that you are Elijah, while others say that one of the prophets of long ago has come back to life."

20 "What about you?" he asked them. "Who do you say I am?"

Peter answered, "You are God's Messiah."

They all ate and had enough. (9:17)

Jesus Speaks about His Suffering and Death
(Matthew 16:20–28; Mark 8:30—9:1)

21 Then Jesus gave them strict orders not to tell this to anyone. 22 He also told them, "The Son of Man must suffer much and be rejected by the elders, the chief priests, and the teachers of the Law. He will be put to death, but three days later he will be raised to life."

23 And he said to them all, "If you want to come with me, you must forget yourself, take up your cross every day, and follow me. 24 For if you want to save your own life, you will lose it, but if you lose your life for my sake,

you will save it. 25 Will you gain anything if you win the whole world but are yourself lost or defeated? Of course not! 26 If you are ashamed of me and of my teaching, then the Son of Man will be ashamed of you when he comes in his glory and in the glory of the Father and of the holy angels. 27 I assure you that there are some here who will not die until they have seen the Kingdom of God."

Shame on You!

Have you ever been in a situation where you felt embarrassed to be a Catholic? Have you ever felt ashamed about being Christian? Maybe someone was making fun of religion and how stupid it is, and you pretended to agree with them. Or perhaps they made fun of you when you said that you couldn't do something with them because you were going to Church. Whatever was happening, you were in a position where you didn't want to stand out or to stand up for what you believe. Reread Luke 9:26 to hear Jesus' response.

 None of us would want Jesus to be ashamed of us. If you need help, remember that one of the gifts of the Holy Spirit is courage. The next time you find yourself embarrassed about being a Catholic, pray to the Holy Spirit— it can make a world of difference!

     — **Luke 9:23–27**

Luke

9:19 Mt 14:1, 2; Mk 6:14, 15; Lk 9:7, 8 **9:20** Jn 6:68, 69 **9:23** Mt 10:38; Lk 14:27 **9:24** Mt 10:39; Lk 17:33; Jn 12:25

Learn more about the prophet Elijah in the biography of Elijah and Elisha on page c21.

The Transfiguration
(Matthew 17:1–8; Mark 9:2–8)

28 About a week after he had said these things, Jesus took Peter, John, and James with him and went up a hill to pray. 29 While he was praying, his face changed its appearance, and his clothes became dazzling white. 30 Suddenly two men were there talking with him. They were Moses and Elijah, 31 who appeared in heavenly glory and talked with Jesus about the way in which he would soon fulfill God's purpose by dying in Jerusalem. 32 Peter and his companions were sound asleep, but they woke up and saw Jesus' glory and the two men who were standing with him. 33 As the men were leaving Jesus, Peter said to him, "Master, how good it is that we are here! We will make three tents, one for you, one for Moses, and one for Elijah." (He did not really know what he was saying.) 34 While he was still speaking, a cloud appeared and covered them with its shadow; and the disciples were afraid as the cloud came over them. 35 A voice said from the cloud, "This is my Son, whom I have chosen—listen to him!" 36 When the voice stopped, there was Jesus all alone. The disciples kept quiet about all this and told no one at that time anything they had seen.

Jesus Heals a Boy with an Evil Spirit
(Matthew 17:14–18; Mark 9:14–27)

37 The next day Jesus and the three disciples went down from the hill, and a large crowd met Jesus. 38 A man shouted from the crowd, "Teacher! I beg you, look at my son—my only son! 39 A spirit attacks him with a sudden shout and throws him into a fit, so that he foams at the mouth; it keeps on hurting him and will hardly let him go! 40 I begged your disciples to drive it out, but they couldn't."
41 Jesus answered, "How unbelieving and wrong you people are! How long must I stay with you? How long do I have to put up with you?" Then he said to the man, "Bring your son here."
42 As the boy was coming, the demon knocked him to the ground and threw him into a fit. Jesus gave a command to the evil spirit, healed the boy, and gave him back to his father. 43 All the people were amazed at the mighty power of God.

Jesus Speaks Again about His Death
(Matthew 17:22, 23; Mark 9:30–32)

The people were still marveling at everything Jesus was doing, when he said to his disciples, 44 "Don't forget what I am about to tell you! The Son of Man is going to be handed over to the power of human beings." 45 But the disciples did not know what this meant. It had been hidden from them so that they could not understand it, and they were afraid to ask him about the matter.

Who Is the Greatest?
(Matthew 18:1–5; Mark 9:33–37)

46 An argument broke out among the disciples as to which one of them was the greatest. 47 Jesus knew what they were thinking, so he took a child, stood him by his side, 48 and said to them, "Whoever welcomes this child in my name, welcomes me; and whoever welcomes me, also welcomes the one who sent me. For the one who is least among you all is the greatest."

Whoever Is Not against You Is for You
(Mark 9:38–40)

49 John spoke up, "Master, we saw a man driving out demons in your name, and we told him to stop, because he doesn't belong to our group."
50 "Do not try to stop him," Jesus said to him and to the other disciples, "because whoever is not against you is for you."

9:35 Isa 42:1; Mt 3:17; 12:18; Mk 1:11; Lk 3:22 **9:28–35** 2 Pet 1:17, 18 **9:46** Lk 22:24 **9:48** Mt 10:40; Lk 10:16; Jn 13:20

Transfiguration: **The event where Jesus was revealed in his full glory as the Son of God.**

A Samaritan Village Refuses to Receive Jesus

51 As the time drew near when Jesus would be taken up to heaven, he made up his mind and set out on his way to Jerusalem. 52 He sent messengers ahead of him, who went into a village in Samaria to get everything ready for him. 53 But the people there would not receive him, because it was clear that he was on his way to Jerusalem. 54 When the disciples James and John saw this, they said, "Lord, do you want us to call fire down from heaven to destroy them?"[j]

55 Jesus turned and rebuked them.[k] 56 Then Jesus and his disciples went on to another village.

The Would-Be Followers of Jesus
(Matthew 8:19–22)

57 As they went on their way, a man said to Jesus, "I will follow you wherever you go."

58 Jesus said to him, "Foxes have holes, and birds have nests, but the Son of Man has no place to lie down and rest."

59 He said to another man, "Follow me."

But that man said, "Sir, first let me go back and bury my father."

60 Jesus answered, "Let the dead bury their own dead. You go and proclaim the Kingdom of God."

61 Someone else said, "I will follow you, sir; but first let me go and say good-bye to my family."

62 Jesus said to him, "Anyone who starts to plow and then keeps looking back is of no use for the Kingdom of God."

Jesus Sends Out the Seventy-Two

10 1 After this the Lord chose another seventy-two[l] men and sent them out two by two, to go ahead of him to every town and place where he himself was about to go. 2 He said to them, "There is a large harvest, but few workers to gather it in. Pray to the owner of the harvest that he will send out workers to gather in his harvest. 3 Go! I am sending you like lambs among wolves. 4 Don't take a purse or a beggar's bag or shoes; don't stop to greet anyone on the road. 5 Whenever you go into a house, first say, 'Peace be with this house.' 6 If someone who is peace-loving lives there, let your greeting of peace remain

Two by Two

When you're traveling with a friend and busy talking and visiting, doesn't time seem to go so much faster? Jesus knew this, and when he sent his disciples out on a mission, he made sure they went in pairs (Luke 10:1). He knew that the miles go so much faster when they are shared. He also knew that two people traveling together could support one another through the hard times that would certainly happen. We need each other. That's the way God made us and the way Jesus sends us forth to serve.

When a friend is going through hard times or when a family member is sick and needs extra care, those are times when we are called to be good companions. Sometimes, in a hospital room or at a funeral home, the best thing we can do is just to be there. We don't have to say a lot. We can be a quiet companion. Who are persons you count on as companions on the road of life? How can you be a companion to someone in your life right now?

— Luke 10:1–12

Luke

---

j **9:54** *Some manuscripts add* as Elijah did.   k **9:55** *Some manuscripts add* and said, "You don't know what kind of a Spirit you belong to; for the Son of Man did not come to destroy human lives, but to save them."
l **10:1** seventy-two; *some manuscripts have* seventy.
9:54 2 Kings 1:9–16   **9:61** 1 Kings 19:20   **10:2** Mt 9:37, 38   **10:3** Mt 10:16

on that person; if not, take back your greeting of peace. [7]Stay in that same house, eating and drinking whatever they offer you, for workers should be given their pay. Don't move around from one house to another. [8]Whenever you go into a town and are made welcome, eat what is set before you, [9]heal the sick in that town, and say to the people there, 'The Kingdom of God has come near you.' [10]But whenever you go into a town and are not welcomed, go out in the streets and say, [11]'Even the dust from your town that sticks to our feet we wipe off against you. But remember that the Kingdom of God has come near you!' [12]I assure you that on the Judgment Day God will show more mercy to Sodom than to that town!

The Unbelieving Towns
(Matthew 11:20–24)

[13]"How terrible it will be for you, Chorazin! How terrible for you too, Bethsaida! If the miracles which were performed in you had been performed in Tyre and Sidon, the people there would have long ago sat down, put on sackcloth, and sprinkled ashes on themselves, to show that they had turned from their sins! [14]God will show more mercy on the Judgment Day to Tyre and Sidon than to you. [15]And as for you, Capernaum! Did you want to lift yourself up to heaven? You will be thrown down to hell!"

[16]Jesus said to his disciples, "Whoever listens to you listens to me; whoever rejects you rejects me; and whoever rejects me rejects the one who sent me."

The Return of the Seventy-Two

[17]The seventy-two[m] men came back in great joy. "Lord," they said, "even the demons obeyed us when we gave them a command in your name!"

[18]Jesus answered them, "I saw Satan fall like lightning from heaven. [19]Listen! I have

given you authority, so that you can walk on snakes and scorpions and overcome all the power of the Enemy, and nothing will hurt you. [20]But don't be glad because the evil spirits obey you; rather be glad because your names are written in heaven."

Jesus Rejoices
(Matthew 11:25–27; 13:16, 17)

[21]At that time Jesus was filled with joy by the Holy Spirit[n] and said, "Father, Lord of heaven and earth! I thank you because you have shown to the unlearned what you have hidden from the wise and learned. Yes, Father, this was how you were pleased to have it happen.

[22]"My Father has given me all things. No one knows who the Son is except the Father, and no one knows who the Father is except the Son and those to whom the Son chooses to reveal him."

[23]Then Jesus turned to the disciples and said to them privately, "How fortunate you are to see the things you see! [24]I tell you that many prophets and kings wanted to see what you see, but they could not, and to hear what you hear, but they did not."

The Parable of the Good Samaritan

[25]A teacher of the Law came up and tried to trap Jesus. "Teacher," he asked, "what must I do to receive eternal life?"

[26]Jesus answered him, "What do the Scriptures say? How do you interpret them?"

[27]The man answered, " 'Love the Lord your God with all your heart, with all your soul, with all your strength, and with all your mind'; and 'Love your neighbor as you love yourself.' "

[28]"You are right," Jesus replied; "do this and you will live."

[29]But the teacher of the Law wanted to justify himself, so he asked Jesus, "Who is my neighbor?"

---

[m] **10:17** seventy-two; *some manuscripts have* seventy *(see verse 1).*   [n] **10:21** by the Holy Spirit; *some manuscripts have* by the Spirit; *others have* in his spirit.
10:7 1 Cor 9:14; 1 Tim 5:18   **10:10,11** Acts 13:51   **10:4–11** Mt 10:7–14; Mk 6:8–11; Lk 9:3–5
10:12 a Gen 19:24–28; Mt 11:24; **b** Mt 10:15   **10:13** Isa 23:1–18; Ezek 26:1—28:26; Joel 3:4–8; Am 1:9, 10; Zech 9:2–4   **10:15** Isa 14:13–15   **10:16** Mt 10:40; Mk 9:37; Lk 9:48; Jn 13:20   **10:19** Ps 91:13
10:22 a Jn 3:35; **b** Jn 10:15   **10:25–28** Mt 22:35–40; Mk 12:28–34   **10:27 a** Deut 6:5; **b** Lev 19:18
10:28 Lev 18:5

Walk Right By

Have you ever walked into the lunchroom and seen someone eating alone? What is your first reaction? Do you think, "Thank God that's not me?" Do you think about joining him or her or maybe inviting him or her to join you at your table? Does it matter whether you know the person or not? Should it matter? Let's not be too quick to judge the priest and the Levite in the Good Samaritan story. They had reasons for not stopping. They may have been afraid of being attacked by bandits themselves. Or if they had contact with blood, it would have made them ritually unclean for a week according to the Old Testament Law.

We probably have reasons for walking right by someone we would rather not deal with. But Jesus reminds us that if those reasons mean neglecting a person in need, they probably aren't good reasons. We need to remember that someday we could be the one sitting alone. Let's think about that the next time we see someone sitting alone.

— Luke 10:25–37

he walked on by on the other side. 32In the same way a Levite also came there, went over and looked at the man, and then walked on by on the other side. 33But a Samaritan who was traveling that way came upon the man, and when he saw him, his heart was filled with pity. 34He went over to him, poured oil and wine on his wounds and bandaged them; then he put the man on his own animal and took him to an inn, where he took care of him. 35The next day he took out two silver coins and gave them to the innkeeper. 'Take care of him,' he told the innkeeper, 'and when I come back this way, I will pay you whatever else you spend on him.' "

His heart was filled with pity. (10:33)

36And Jesus concluded, "In your opinion, which one of these three acted like a neighbor toward the man attacked by the robbers?"

37The teacher of the Law answered, "The one who was kind to him."

Jesus replied, "You go, then, and do the same."

Jesus Visits Martha and Mary

38As Jesus and his disciples went on their way, he came to a village where a woman named Martha welcomed him in her home. 39She had a sister named Mary, who sat down at the feet of the Lord and listened to his teaching. 40Martha was upset over all the

30Jesus answered, "There was once a man who was going down from Jerusalem to Jericho when robbers attacked him, stripped him, and beat him up, leaving him half dead. 31It so happened that a priest was going down that road; but when he saw the man,

10:33, 34 2 Chr 28:15   10:38, 39 Jn 11:1

Many Jews were prejudiced against Samaritans. How does this make the Good Samaritan's actions even more generous?

The Our Father: Another Version

Catholic Connections

As you read through the beginning of Luke, chapter 11, you'll notice a second version of the prayer we often call the Our Father. The version of the prayer in Matthew 6:9–13 is probably more familiar to you. Study the two versions closely. What similarities and differences do you notice? What does this tell us about the Gospel writers?

Because it came directly from Jesus, the Our Father is probably the most important prayer that we have. That is why Christians pray it so often when we gather. If you look carefully, you'll notice that the first part of the prayer praises God and asks that God's Kingdom will come. The second part of the prayer is a series of petitions, or requests, for the things that we need. We can follow that pattern in our own prayer to God.

Here's an idea. Try putting the Our Father in your own words. For example, you might start your prayer by saying, "My Father, Lord of heaven and earth, I praise your holy name." This may help you look at this old prayer in a new way.

— *Luke 11:1–4*

Luke

work she had to do, so she came and said, "Lord, don't you care that my sister has left me to do all the work by myself? Tell her to come and help me!"

⁴¹ The Lord answered her, "Martha, Martha! You are worried and troubled over so many things, ⁴²but just one is needed. Mary has chosen the right thing, and it will not be taken away from her."

Jesus' Teaching on Prayer
(Matthew 6:9–13; 7:7–11)

11 ¹One day Jesus was praying in a certain place. When he had finished, one of his disciples said to him, "Lord, teach us to pray, just as John taught his disciples."

²Jesus said to them, "When you pray, say this:

'Father:
  May your holy name be honored;
  may your Kingdom come.

3   Give us day by day the food we need.ᵒ
4   Forgive us our sins,
       for we forgive everyone who does us
         wrong.
   And do not bring us to hard testing.' "

⁵And Jesus said to his disciples, "Suppose one of you should go to a friend's house at midnight and say, 'Friend, let me borrow three loaves of bread. ⁶A friend of mine who is on a trip has just come to my house, and I don't have any food for him!' ⁷And suppose your friend should answer from inside, 'Don't bother me! The door is already locked, and my children and I are in bed. I can't get up and give you anything.' ⁸Well, what then? I tell you that even if he will not get up and give you the bread because you are his friend, yet he will get up and give you everything you need because you are not ashamed to keep on asking. ⁹And so I say to you: Ask, and you will receive; seek, and you will find; knock, and the door will be opened to you.

ᵒ **11:3** the food we need; *or* food for the next day.

" 'Ask, and you will receive; seek, and you will find; knock, and the door will be opened to you' " *(Luke 11:9)*.

Prayers of Petition

Catholic Connections

"Please help me with this test, God." "Lord, help my sister get better." These are examples of one of the simplest forms of prayer. They are called petitions, meaning that we ask, or petition, God for something. During the Mass we hear the petitions of the whole community after the homily. The petitions at Mass are called the Prayer of the Faithful. The most common response is, "Lord, hear our prayer."

Most of us pray petitions a lot. This isn't wrong; in fact Jesus tells us that we should ask for God's help, and we should expect a response (Luke 11:9–13). Do not hesitate to share with God the needs you have in your heart. Even though it's hard sometimes, it's good to say your prayers out loud. It does two things: it helps to raise awareness of the needs of others, plus it gives others courage to share their own prayers. When you give voice to the needs in your heart and on your mind, others can pray with you. That is the power of community prayer.

— Luke 11:9–13

¹⁰For those who ask will receive, and those who seek will find, and the door will be opened to anyone who knocks. ¹¹Would any of you who are fathers give your son a snake when he asks for fish? ¹²Or would you give him a scorpion when he asks for an egg? ¹³As bad as you are, you know how to give good things to your children. How much more, then, will the Father in heaven give the Holy Spirit to those who ask him!"

Jesus and Beelzebul
(Matthew 12:22–30; Mark 3:20–27)

¹⁴Jesus was driving out a demon that could not talk; and when the demon went out, the man began to talk. The crowds were amazed, ¹⁵but some of the people said, "It is Beelzebul, the chief of the demons, who gives him the power to drive them out."

¹⁶Others wanted to trap Jesus, so they asked him to perform a miracle to show that God approved of him. ¹⁷But Jesus knew what they were thinking, so he said to them, "Any country that divides itself into groups which fight each other will not last very long; a family divided against itself falls apart. ¹⁸So if Satan's kingdom has groups fighting each other, how can it last? You say that I drive out demons because Beelzebul gives me the power to do so. ¹⁹If this is how I drive them out, how do your followers drive them out? Your own followers prove that you are wrong! ²⁰No, it is rather by means of God's power that I drive out demons, and this proves that the Kingdom of God has already come to you.

²¹"When a strong man, with all his weapons ready, guards his own house, all his belongings are safe. ²²But when a stronger man attacks him and defeats him, he carries away all the weapons the owner was depending on and divides up what he stole.

²³"Anyone who is not for me is really against me; anyone who does not help me gather is really scattering.

The Return of the Evil Spirit
(Matthew 12:43–45)

²⁴"When an evil spirit goes out of a person, it travels over dry country looking for a

Luke

11:15 Mt 9:34; 10:25   **11:16** Mt 12:38; 16:1; Mk 8:11   **11:23** Mk 9:40

place to rest. If it can't find one, it says to itself, 'I will go back to my house.' 25So it goes back and finds the house clean and all fixed up. 26Then it goes out and brings seven other spirits even worse than itself, and they come and live there. So when it is all over, that person is in worse shape than at the beginning."

True Happiness

27When Jesus had said this, a woman spoke up from the crowd and said to him, "How happy is the woman who bore you and nursed you!"

28But Jesus answered, "Rather, how happy are those who hear the word of God and obey it!"

The Demand for a Miracle
(Matthew 12:38–42)

29As the people crowded around Jesus, he went on to say, "How evil are the people of this day! They ask for a miracle, but none will be given them except the miracle of Jonah. 30In the same way that the prophet Jonah was a sign for the people of Nineveh, so the Son of Man will be a sign for the people of this day. 31On the Judgment Day the Queen of Sheba will stand up and accuse the people of today, because she traveled all the way from her country to listen to King Solomon's wise teaching; and there is something here, I tell you, greater than Solomon. 32On the Judgment Day the people of Nineveh will stand up and accuse you, because they turned from their sins when they heard Jonah preach; and I assure you that there is something here greater than Jonah!

The Light of the Body
(Matthew 5:15; 6:22, 23)

33"No one lights a lamp and then hides it or puts it under a bowl;*p* instead, it is put on the lampstand, so that people may see the light as they come in. 34Your eyes are like a lamp for the body. When your eyes are sound,

The Eyes Have it!

"Look me in the eyes!" Why is this so important? Jesus says in Luke 11:34 that our eyes are like a lamp for our bodies. An old saying expresses a similar thought: "The eyes are the mirror of the soul." It is very difficult for young children to lie while looking someone in the eye. As we get older, we learn to disguise our emotions better. Imagine what it would be like to gaze into the eyes of Jesus. What would you see in those eyes?

— Luke 11:33–36

your whole body is full of light; but when your eyes are no good, your whole body will be in darkness. 35Make certain, then, that the light in you is not darkness. 36If your whole body is full of light, with no part of it in darkness, it will be bright all over, as when a lamp shines on you with its brightness."

Jesus Accuses the Pharisees and the Teachers of the Law
(Matthew 23:1–36; Mark 12:38–40)

37When Jesus finished speaking, a Pharisee invited him to eat with him; so he went in and sat down to eat. 38The Pharisee was surprised when he noticed that Jesus had not washed before eating. 39So the Lord said to him, "Now then, you Pharisees clean the outside of your cup and plate, but inside you are full of violence and evil. 40Fools! Did not God, who made the outside, also make the inside? 41But give what is in your cups and plates to the poor, and everything will be ritually clean for you.

42"How terrible for you Pharisees! You give to God one tenth of the seasoning

p **11:33** *Some manuscripts do not have* or puts it under a bowl.
11:29 Mt 16:4; Mk 8:12　**11:30** Jon 3:4　**11:31** 1 Kings 10:1–10; 2 Chr 9:1–12　**11:32** Jon 3:5　**11:33** Mt 5:15; Mk 4:21; Lk 8:16　**11:42** Lev 27:30

herbs, such as mint and rue and all the other herbs, but you neglect justice and love for God. These you should practice, without neglecting the others.

43 "How terrible for you Pharisees! You love the reserved seats in the synagogues and to be greeted with respect in the marketplaces. 44 How terrible for you! You are like unmarked graves which people walk on without knowing it."

45 One of the teachers of the Law said to him, "Teacher, when you say this, you insult us too!"

46 Jesus answered, "How terrible also for you teachers of the Law! You put onto people's backs loads which are hard to carry, but you yourselves will not stretch out a finger to help them carry those loads. 47 How terrible for you! You make fine tombs for the prophets—the very prophets your ancestors murdered. 48 You yourselves admit, then, that you approve of what your ancestors did; they murdered the prophets, and you build their tombs. 49 For this reason the Wisdom of God said, 'I will send them prophets and messengers; they will kill some of them and persecute others.' 50 So the people of this time will be punished for the murder of all the prophets killed since the creation of the world, 51 from the murder of Abel to the murder of Zechariah, who was killed between the altar and the Holy Place. Yes, I tell you, the people of this time will be punished for them all!

52 "How terrible for you teachers of the Law! You have kept the key that opens the door to the house of knowledge; you yourselves will not go in, and you stop those who are trying to go in!"

53 When Jesus left that place, the teachers of the Law and the Pharisees began to criticize him bitterly and ask him questions about many things, 54 trying to lay traps for him and catch him saying something wrong.

A Warning against Hypocrisy
(Matthew 10:26, 27)

12 1 As thousands of people crowded together, so that they were stepping on each other, Jesus said first to his disciples, "Be on guard against the yeast of the Pharisees—I mean their hypocrisy. 2 Whatever is covered up will be uncovered, and every secret will be made known. 3 So then, whatever you have said in the dark will be heard in broad daylight, and whatever you have whispered in private in a closed room will be shouted from the housetops.

Whom to Fear
(Matthew 10:28–31)

4 "I tell you, my friends, do not be afraid of those who kill the body but cannot afterward do anything worse. 5 I will show you whom to fear: fear God, who, after killing, has the authority to throw into hell. Believe me, he is the one you must fear!

6 "Aren't five sparrows sold for two pennies? Yet not one sparrow is forgotten by God. 7 Even the hairs of your head have all been counted. So do not be afraid; you are worth much more than many sparrows!

Confessing and Rejecting Christ
(Matthew 10:32, 33; 12:32; 10:19, 20)

8 "I assure you that those who declare publicly that they belong to me, the Son of Man will do the same for them before the angels of God. 9 But those who reject me publicly, the Son of Man will also reject them before the angels of God.

10 "Whoever says a word against the Son of Man can be forgiven; but whoever says evil things against the Holy Spirit will not be forgiven.

11 "When they bring you to be tried in the synagogues or before governors or rulers, do not be worried about how you

11:51 a Gen 4:8; b 2 Chr 24:20, 21   12:1 Mt 16:6; Mk 8:15   12:2 Mk 4:22; Lk 8:17   12:10 Mt 12:32; Mk 3:29   12:11, 12 Mt 10:19, 20; Mk 13:11; Lk 21:14, 15

The Queen of Sheba appears in 1 Kings, chapter 10. Find out who she visits and why.

What Does It Mean to Be Rich?

Perhaps you have heard the saying, "You can't take it with you." The parable of the rich fool is about that very idea (Luke 12:13–21). Some rich people are very generous with their money and end up doing a lot of good in the world. But others, like the rich fool in the story, simply hoard what they have and look for ways to get richer.

What does it mean to be rich in God's sight? It certainly doesn't have anything to do with money. There's a young man who invites his friends to his birthday party every year. Instead of bringing gifts for him, he asks his friends to bring specific gifts for a needy school that he knows. What a wonderful way to show that the needs of others should come before our own desires. Now that is a rich young man!

— Luke 12:13–21

will defend yourself or what you will say. [12]For the Holy Spirit will teach you at that time what you should say."

The Parable of the Rich Fool

[13]A man in the crowd said to Jesus, "Teacher, tell my brother to divide with me the property our father left us."

[14]Jesus answered him, "Friend, who gave me the right to judge or to divide the property between you two?" [15]And he went on

12:19 Sir 11:19

to say to them all, "Watch out and guard yourselves from every kind of greed; because your true life is not made up of the things you own, no matter how rich you may be."

[16]Then Jesus told them this parable: "There was once a rich man who had land which bore good crops. [17]He began to think to himself, 'I don't have a place to keep all my crops. What can I do? [18]This is what I will do,' he told himself; 'I will tear down my barns and build bigger ones, where I will store the grain and all my other goods. [19]Then I will say to myself, Lucky man! You have all the good things you need for many years. Take life easy, eat, drink, and enjoy yourself!' [20]But God said to him, 'You fool! This very night you will have to give up your life; then who will get all these things you have kept for yourself?' "

[21]And Jesus concluded, "This is how it is with those who pile up riches for themselves but are not rich in God's sight."

Trust in God
(Matthew 6:25–34)

[22]Then Jesus said to the disciples, "And so I tell you not to worry about the food you need to stay alive or about the clothes you need for your body. [23]Life is much more important than food, and the body much more important than clothes. [24]Look at the crows: they don't plant seeds or gather a harvest; they don't have storage rooms or barns; God feeds them! You are worth so much more than birds! [25]Can any of you live a bit

So I tell you not to worry. (12:22)

The words in Luke 12:33–34 serve as a good description of Saint Francis of Assisi, who lived from AD 1182 to 1226. What do you know about Saint Francis?

longerq by worrying about it? 26If you can't manage even such a small thing, why worry about the other things? 27Look how the wild flowers grow: they don't work or make clothes for themselves. But I tell you that not even King Solomon with all his wealth had clothes as beautiful as one of these flowers. 28It is God who clothes the wild grass—grass that is here today and gone tomorrow, burned up in the oven. Won't he be all the more sure to clothe you? What little faith you have!

29"So don't be all upset, always concerned about what you will eat and drink. 30(For the pagans of this world are always concerned about all these things.) Your Father knows that you need these things. 31Instead, be concerned with his Kingdom, and he will provide you with these things.

Riches in Heaven
(Matthew 6:19–21)

32"Do not be afraid, little flock, for your Father is pleased to give you the Kingdom. 33Sell all your belongings and give the money to the poor. Provide for yourselves purses that don't wear out, and save your riches in heaven, where they will never decrease, because no thief can get to them, and no moth can destroy them. 34For your heart will always be where your riches are.

Watchful Servants

35"Be ready for whatever comes, dressed for action and with your lamps lit, 36like servants who are waiting for their master to come back from a wedding feast. When he comes and knocks, they will open the door for him at once. 37How happy are those servants whose master finds them awake and ready when he returns! I tell you, he will take off his coat, have them sit down, and will wait on them. 38How happy they are if he finds them ready, even if he should come at midnight or even later! 39And you can be sure that if the owner of a house knew the time when the thief would come, he would not let the thief break into his house. 40And you, too, must be

ready, because the Son of Man will come at an hour when you are not expecting him."

The Faithful or the Unfaithful Servant
(Matthew 24:45–51)

41Peter said, "Lord, does this parable apply to us, or do you mean it for everyone?"

42The Lord answered, "Who, then, is the faithful and wise servant? He is the one that his master will put in charge, to run the household and give the other servants their share of the food at the proper time. 43How happy that servant is if his master finds him doing this when he comes home! 44Indeed, I tell you, the master will put that servant in charge of all his property. 45But if that servant says to himself that his master is taking a long time to come back and if he begins to beat the other servants, both the men and the women, and eats and drinks and gets drunk, 46then the master will come back one day when the servant does not expect him and at a time he does not know. The master will cut him in piecesr and make him share the fate of the disobedient.

47"The servant who knows what his master wants him to do, but does not get himself ready and do it, will be punished with a heavy whipping. 48But the servant who does not know what his master wants, and yet does something for which he deserves a whipping, will be punished with a light whipping. Much is required from the person to whom much is given; much more is required from the person to whom much more is given.

Jesus the Cause of Division
(Matthew 10:34–36)

49"I came to set the earth on fire, and how I wish it were already kindled! 50I have a baptism to receive, and how distressed I am until it is over! 51Do you suppose that I came to bring peace to the world? No, not peace, but division. 52From now on a family of five will be divided, three against two and two against three. 53Fathers will be against

Luke

q **12:25** live a bit longer; *or* grow a bit taller.   r **12:46** cut him in pieces; *or* throw him out.
12:27 1 Kings 10:4–7; 2 Chr 9:3–6   **12:35** Mt 25:1–13   **12:36** Mk 13:34–36   **12:39,40** Mt 24:43, 44
12:50 Mk 10:38   **12:53** Mic 7:6

Family Feud

Jesus has some rather startling words in Luke 12:49–53. We are used to words like *peace* and *harmony* as signs of Christ's presence in our lives. But Jesus is telling his followers that some tough times are ahead. By following him, they will get people upset, even within their own families. This happened in the time of Jesus, and it certainly happens today.

When we take our Christianity seriously, our values may be challenging to other family members. We may need to confront a family member who is being abusive to someone or who is lying or who is involved with something illegal. We do this to encourage them to change their lives so that they can know God's love. This can cause a lot of stress and even division in a family. Jesus also uses the image of fire (Luke 12:49) to show that he wants his followers to be on fire with his message. As we all know, fire can bring both warmth and destruction.

— Luke 12:49–53

their sons, and sons against their fathers; mothers will be against their daughters, and daughters against their mothers; mothers-in-law will be against their daughters-in-law, and daughters-in-law against their mothers-in-law."

Understanding the Time
(Matthew 16:2, 3)

54Jesus said also to the people, "When you see a cloud coming up in the west, at once you say that it is going to rain—and it does. 55And when you feel the south wind blow-ing, you say that it is going to get hot—and it does. 56Hypocrites! You can look at the earth and the sky and predict the weather; why, then, don't you know the meaning of this present time?

Settle with Your Opponent
(Matthew 5:25, 26)

57"Why do you not judge for yourselves the right thing to do? 58If someone brings a lawsuit against you and takes you to court, do your best to settle the dispute before you get to court. If you don't, you will be dragged before the judge, who will hand you over to the police, and you will be put in jail. 59There you will stay, I tell you, until you pay the last penny of your fine."

Turn from Your Sins or Die

13 1At that time some people were there who told Jesus about the Galileans whom Pilate had killed while they were offering sacrifices to God. 2Jesus answered them, "Because those Galileans were killed in that way, do you think it proves that they were worse sinners than all other Galileans? 3No indeed! And I tell you that if you do not turn from your sins, you will all die as they did. 4What about those eighteen people in Siloam who were killed when the tower fell on them? Do you suppose this proves that they were worse than all the other people living in Jerusalem? 5No indeed! And I tell you that if you do not turn from your sins, you will all die as they did."

The Parable of the Unfruitful Fig Tree

6Then Jesus told them this parable: "There was once a man who had a fig tree growing in his vineyard. He went looking for figs on it but found none. 7So he said to his gardener, 'Look, for three years I have been coming here looking for figs on this fig tree, and I haven't found any. Cut it down! Why should it go on using up the soil?' 8But the gardener answered, 'Leave it alone, sir, just one more year; I will dig around it and put in

One More Chance

"Just give me one more chance. I promise I'll do better." No doubt each of us has spoken these words at some time. If the fig tree in the parable (Luke 13:6–9) could talk, this is probably what it would be saying. The gardener seems to sense this and asks the owner to give the fruitless tree one more year. We are not told how the story ends, but we hope that the gardener gets the okay to give the fig tree some more attention. That extra year of care and concern could make all the difference.

Try to think of someone to whom you could give one more chance. Maybe you had a fight with a good friend. Maybe you need to try a little harder to see a parent's point of view. Or maybe there's a teacher who made you upset. Whoever it is, ask God for the patience to make the relationship better again.

— Luke 13:6–9

some fertilizer. ⁹Then if the tree bears figs next year, so much the better; if not, then you can have it cut down.' "

Jesus Heals a Crippled Woman on the Sabbath

¹⁰One Sabbath Jesus was teaching in a synagogue. ¹¹A woman there had an evil spirit that had kept her sick for eighteen years; she was bent over and could not straighten up at all. ¹²When Jesus saw her, he called out to her, "Woman, you are free from your sickness!" ¹³He placed his hands on her, and at once she straightened herself up and praised God.

¹⁴The official of the synagogue was angry that Jesus had healed on the Sabbath, so he spoke up and said to the people, "There are six days in which we should work; so come during those days and be healed, but not on the Sabbath!"

¹⁵The Lord answered him, "You hypocrites! Any one of you would untie your ox or your donkey from the stall and take it out to give it water on the Sabbath. ¹⁶Now here is this descendant of Abraham whom Satan has kept in bonds for eighteen years; should she not be released on the Sabbath?" ¹⁷His answer made his enemies ashamed of themselves, while the people rejoiced over all the wonderful things that he did.

The Parable of the Mustard Seed
(Matthew 13:31, 32; Mark 4:30–32)

¹⁸Jesus asked, "What is the Kingdom of God like? What shall I compare it with? ¹⁹It is like this. A man takes a mustard seed and plants it in his field. The plant grows and becomes a tree, and the birds make their nests in its branches."

The Parable of the Yeast
(Matthew 13:33)

²⁰Again Jesus asked, "What shall I compare the Kingdom of God with? ²¹It is like this. A woman takes some yeast and mixes it with a bushel of flour until the whole batch of dough rises."

The Narrow Door
(Matthew 7:13, 14, 21–23)

²²Jesus went through towns and villages, teaching the people and making his way

Luke

13:14 Ex 20:9, 10; Deut 5:13, 14

toward Jerusalem. 23Someone asked him, "Sir, will just a few people be saved?"

Jesus answered them, 24"Do your best to go in through the narrow door; because many people will surely try to go in but will not be able. 25The master of the house will get up and close the door; then when you stand outside and begin to knock on the door and say, 'Open the door for us, sir!' he will answer you, 'I don't know where you come from!' 26Then you will answer, 'We ate and drank with you; you taught in our town!' 27But he will say again, 'I don't know where you come from. Get away from me, all you wicked people!' 28How you will cry and gnash your teeth when you see Abraham, Isaac, and Jacob, and all the prophets in the Kingdom of God, while you are thrown out! 29People will come from the east and the west, from the north and the south, and sit down at the feast in the Kingdom of God. 30Then those who are now last will be first, and those who are now first will be last."

Jesus' Love for Jerusalem
(Matthew 23:37–39)

31At that same time some Pharisees came to Jesus and said to him, "You must get out of here and go somewhere else, because Herod wants to kill you."

32Jesus answered them, "Go and tell that fox: 'I am driving out demons and performing cures today and tomorrow, and on the third day I shall finish my work.' 33Yet I must be on my way today, tomorrow, and the next day; it is not right for a prophet to be killed anywhere except in Jerusalem.

34"Jerusalem, Jerusalem! You kill the prophets, you stone the messengers God has sent you! How many times I wanted to put my arms around all your people, just as a hen gathers her chicks under her wings, but you would not let me! 35And so your Temple will be abandoned. I assure you that you will not

see me until the time comes when you say, 'God bless him who comes in the name of the Lord.' "

Jesus Heals a Sick Man

14 1One Sabbath Jesus went to eat a meal at the home of one of the leading Pharisees; and people were watching Jesus closely. 2A man whose legs and arms were swollen came to Jesus, 3and Jesus spoke up and asked the teachers of the Law and the Pharisees, "Does our Law allow healing on the Sabbath or not?"

4But they would not say a thing. Jesus took the man, healed him, and sent him away. 5Then he said to them, "If any one of you had a child or an ox that happened to fall in a well on a Sabbath, would you not pull it out at once on the Sabbath itself?"

6But they were not able to answer him about this.

Humility and Hospitality

7Jesus noticed how some of the guests were choosing the best places, so he told this parable to all of them: 8"When someone invites you to a wedding feast, do not sit down in the best place. It could happen that someone more important than you has been invited, 9and your host, who invited both of you, would have to come and say to you, 'Let him have this place.' Then you would be embarrassed and have to sit in the lowest place. 10Instead, when you are invited, go and sit in the lowest place, so that your host will come to you and say, 'Come on up, my friend, to a better place.' This will bring you honor in the presence of all the other guests. 11For those who make themselves great will be humbled, and those who humble themselves will be made great."

12Then Jesus said to his host, "When you give a lunch or a dinner, do not invite your friends or your brothers or your relatives or

13:27 Ps 6:8   **13:28** Mt 22:13; 25:30   **13:28, 29** Mt 8:11, 12   **13:30** Mt 19:30; 20:16; Mk 10:31
13:35 Ps 118:26   **14:5** Mt 12:11   **14:8–10** Prov 25:6, 7   **14:11** Mt 23:12; Lk 18:14

Remember that the Sabbath begins Friday at sunset and ends on Saturday at sunset. For the Jews, this is a time of rest and worship.

Pray It!

Humility and Hospitality

Humility and *hospitality:* These two *h* words are key descriptions of being a true follower of Christ. Humility simply means knowing that we are completely dependent on God and that every one of us is created in God's image. Hospitality is about making people, especially strangers, feel at home and welcome. Take some time to slowly read Luke 14:7–14 and reflect on how important these two virtues are.

Dear God,
Help me to remember I need the two h's, humility and hospitality.
Whenever I think that I can handle life all by myself,
    remind me that I always need you.
Remind me to look for opportunities to make others feel welcome,
    at school, at home, and at church.
Through humility and hospitality, draw me closer to you each day.
Amen.

— Luke 14:7–14

your rich neighbors—for they will invite you back, and in this way you will be paid for what you did. [13] When you give a feast, invite the poor, the crippled, the lame, and the blind; [14] and you will be blessed, because they are not able to pay you back. God will repay you on the day the good people rise from death."

The Parable of the Great Feast
(Matthew 22:1–10)

[15] When one of the guests sitting at the table heard this, he said to Jesus, "How happy are those who will sit down at the feast in the Kingdom of God!"

[16] Jesus said to him, "There was once a man who was giving a great feast to which he invited many people. [17] When it was time for the feast, he sent his servant to tell his guests, 'Come, everything is ready!' [18] But they all began, one after another, to make excuses. The first one told the servant, 'I have bought a field and must go and look at it; please accept my apologies.' [19] Another one said, 'I have bought five pairs of oxen and am

on my way to try them out; please accept my apologies.' [20] Another one said, 'I have just gotten married, and for that reason I cannot come.' [21] The servant went back and told all this to his master. The master was furious and said to his servant, 'Hurry out to the streets and alleys of the town, and bring back the poor, the crippled, the blind, and the lame.' [22] Soon the servant said, 'Your order has been carried out, sir, but there is room for more.' [23] So the master said to the servant, 'Go out to the country roads and lanes and make people come in, so that my house will be full. [24] I tell you all that none of those who were invited will taste my dinner!' "

The Cost of Being a Disciple
(Matthew 10:37, 38)

[25] Once when large crowds of people were going along with Jesus, he turned and said to them, [26] "Those who come to me cannot be my disciples unless they love me more than they love father and mother, wife and children, brothers and sisters, and themselves as

14:26 Mt 10:37

well. 27 Those who do not carry their own cross and come after me cannot be my disciples. 28 If one of you is planning to build a tower, you sit down first and figure out what it will cost, to see if you have enough money to finish the job. 29 If you don't, you will not be able to finish the tower after laying the foundation; and all who see what happened will make fun of you. 30 'You began to build but can't finish the job!' they will say. 31 If a king goes out with ten thousand men to fight another king who comes against him with twenty thousand men, he will sit down first and decide if he is strong enough to face that other king. 32 If he isn't, he will send messengers to meet the other king to ask for terms of peace while he is still a long way off. 33 In the same way," concluded Jesus, "none of you can be my disciple unless you give up everything you have.

Worthless Salt
(Matthew 5:13; Mark 9:50)

34 "Salt is good, but if it loses its saltiness, there is no way to make it salty again. 35 It is no good for the soil or for the manure pile; it is thrown away. Listen, then, if you have ears!"

The Lost Sheep
(Matthew 18:12–14)

15 1 One day when many tax collectors and other outcasts came to listen to Jesus, 2 the Pharisees and the teachers of the Law started grumbling, "This man welcomes outcasts and even eats with them!" 3 So Jesus told them this parable:

4 "Suppose one of you has a hundred sheep and loses one of them—what do you do? You leave the other ninety-nine sheep in the pasture and go looking for the one that got lost until you find it. 5 When you find it, you are so happy that you put it on your shoulders 6 and carry it back home. Then you call your friends and neighbors together and say to them, 'I am so happy I found my lost sheep. Let us celebrate!' 7 In the same way, I tell you, there will be more joy in heaven over one

sinner who repents than over ninety-nine respectable people who do not need to repent.

The Lost Coin

8 "Or suppose a woman who has ten silver coins loses one of them—what does she do? She lights a lamp, sweeps her house, and looks carefully everywhere until she finds it. 9 When she finds it, she calls her friends and neighbors together, and says to them, 'I am so happy I found the coin I lost. Let us celebrate!' 10 In the same way, I tell you, the angels of God rejoice over one sinner who repents."

The Lost Son

11 Jesus went on to say, "There was once a man who had two sons. 12 The younger one said to him, 'Father, give me my share of the property now.' So the man divided his property between his two sons. 13 After a few days the younger son sold his part of the property and left home with the money. He went to a country far away, where he wasted his money in reckless living. 14 He spent everything he had. Then a severe famine spread over that country, and he was left without a thing. 15 So he went to work for one of the citizens of that country, who sent him out to his farm to take care of the pigs. 16 He wished he could fill himself with the bean pods the pigs ate, but no one gave him anything to eat. 17 At last he came to his senses and said, 'All my father's hired workers have more than they can eat, and here I am about to starve! 18 I will get up and go to my father

"Here I am about to starve!" (15:17)

Oh, Brother!

If you are the oldest in the family, you might be able to identify with the older brother in the famous parable of the lost son, sometimes called the parable of the prodigal son. Can you blame the older brother for being upset? His spoiled younger brother trashes his life and comes crawling back home. And what happens? Dad throws him a huge party. Thanks a lot, Dad!

The older son most likely feels hurt and angry. What he doesn't realize is that he is as special as his younger brother, and his father loves both brothers with all his heart. But because he has been the good son for so long, he feels ignored and left out when his lost brother returns home.

The father in this parable stands for God, who always welcomes us back, no matter what. How do you think this story ends? What does the older brother do next? What would you do?

— Luke 15:11–32

said. 'Bring the best robe and put it on him. Put a ring on his finger and shoes on his feet. 23 Then go and get the prize calf and kill it, and let us celebrate with a feast! 24 For this son of mine was dead, but now he is alive; he was lost, but now he has been found.' And so the feasting began.

25 "In the meantime the older son was out in the field. On his way back, when he came close to the house, he heard the music and dancing. 26 So he called one of the servants and asked him, 'What's going on?' 27 'Your

"Now he is alive." (15:24)

brother has come back home,' the servant answered, 'and your father has killed the prize calf, because he got him back safe and sound.' 28 The older brother was so angry that he would not go into the house; so his father came out and begged him to come in. 29 But he spoke back to his father, 'Look, all these years I have worked for you like a slave, and I have never disobeyed your orders. What have you given me? Not even a goat for me to have a feast with my friends! 30 But this son of yours wasted all your property on prostitutes, and when he comes back home, you kill the prize calf for him!' 31 'My son,' the

and say, "Father, I have sinned against God and against you. 19 I am no longer fit to be called your son; treat me as one of your hired workers." ' 20 So he got up and started back to his father.

"He was still a long way from home when his father saw him; his heart was filled with pity, and he ran, threw his arms around his son, and kissed him. 21 'Father,' the son said, 'I have sinned against God and against you. I am no longer fit to be called your son.' 22 But the father called to his servants. 'Hurry!' he

Luke

father answered, 'you are always here with me, and everything I have is yours. 32But we had to celebrate and be happy, because your brother was dead, but now he is alive; he was lost, but now he has been found.'"

The Shrewd Manager

16 1Jesus said to his disciples, "There was once a rich man who had a servant who managed his property. The rich man was told that the manager was wasting his master's money, 2so he called him in and said, 'What is this I hear about you? Turn in a complete account of your handling of my property, because you cannot be my manager any longer.' 3The servant said to himself, 'My master is going to dismiss me from my job. What shall I do? I am not strong enough to dig ditches, and I am ashamed to beg. 4Now I know what I will do! Then when my job is gone, I shall have friends who will welcome me in their homes.' 5So he called in all the people who were in debt to his master. He asked the first one, 'How much do you owe my master?' 6'One hundred barrels of olive oil,' he answered. 'Here is your account,' the manager told him; 'sit down and write fifty.' 7Then he asked another one, 'And you—how much do you owe?' 'A thousand bushels of wheat,' he answered. 'Here is your account,' the manager told him; 'write eight hundred.' 8As a result the master of this dishonest manager praised him for doing such a shrewd thing; because the people of this world are much more shrewd in handling their affairs than the people who belong to the light."

9And Jesus went on to say, "And so I tell you: make friends for yourselves with worldly wealth, so that when it gives out, you will be welcomed in the eternal home. 10Whoever is faithful in small matters will be faithful in large ones; whoever is dishonest in small matters will be dishonest in large ones. 11If, then, you have not been faithful in handling worldly wealth, how can you be trusted with true wealth? 12And if you have not

Dollars and Sense

Jesus tells his disciples, "You cannot serve both God and money" (Luke 16:13). Why not? The key is in the meaning of the word *serve*. We know that we are called to serve God because God is so much greater than we are and because God has given us so many blessings. It makes sense to serve God. Money, however, is not God. Not even close. But the way some people live, you would think that money is their master. Make God number one in your life, and the other things, including money, will fall into place.

— Luke 16:9–13

been faithful with what belongs to someone else, who will give you what belongs to you?

13"No servant can be the slave of two masters; such a slave will hate one and love the other or will be loyal to one and despise the other. You cannot serve both God and money."

Some Sayings of Jesus
(Matthew 11:12, 13; 5:31, 32; Mark 10:11, 12)

14When the Pharisees heard all this, they made fun of Jesus, because they loved money. 15Jesus said to them, "You are the ones who make yourselves look right in other people's sight, but God knows your hearts. For the things that are considered of great value by people are worth nothing in God's sight.

16"The Law of Moses and the writings of the prophets were in effect up to the time of

16:9 Tob 4:9–11   **16:13** Mt 6:24   **16:16** Mt 11:12, 13

Shrewd: **To be clever and smart in dealing with people, so that you come out ahead.**

Pray It!

It's Too Late!

You almost feel sorry for the rich man in the parable of the rich man and Lazarus. Almost. Then you think of poor Lazarus, covered with sores, hoping for just a crumb of food. All he got was the dogs who came to lick his sores. Here's a prayer to help us see the Lazaruses in our own lives.

Dear God, it is so easy to ignore people we would rather not have to deal with. Give me the grace to notice the forgotten and the ignored, especially the elderly, the homeless, or the people others call crazy. If I can do anything to brighten their day, let me have the courage to do it. Help me to see the unseen. Amen.

Take a moment to pray about the forgotten and ignored people in your neighborhood or town. Ask God to open your eyes and heart to people in need. Who might be a Lazarus in your life?

— Luke 16:19–31

John the Baptist; since then the Good News about the Kingdom of God is being told, and everyone forces their way in. ¹⁷But it is easier for heaven and earth to disappear than for the smallest detail of the Law to be done away with.

¹⁸"Any man who divorces his wife and marries another woman commits adultery; and the man who marries a divorced woman commits adultery.

The Rich Man and Lazarus

¹⁹"There was once a rich man who dressed in the most expensive clothes and lived in great luxury every day. ²⁰There was also a poor man named Lazarus, covered with sores, who used to be brought to the rich man's door, ²¹hoping to eat the bits of food that fell from the rich man's table. Even the dogs would come and lick his sores. ²²The poor man died and was carried by the angels to sit beside Abraham at the feast in heaven. The rich man died and was buried, ²³and in Hades,ˢ where he was in great pain, he looked up and saw Abraham, far away, with Lazarus at his side. ²⁴So he called out,

'Father Abraham! Take pity on me, and send Lazarus to dip his finger in some water and cool off my tongue, because I am in great pain in this fire!' ²⁵But Abraham said, 'Remember, my son, that in your lifetime you were given all the good things, while Lazarus got all the bad things. But now he is enjoying himself here, while you are in pain. ²⁶Besides all that, there is a deep pit lying between us, so that those who want to cross over from here to you cannot do so, nor can anyone cross over to us from where you are.' ²⁷The rich man said, 'Then I beg you, father Abraham, send Lazarus to my father's house, ²⁸where I have five brothers. Let him go and warn them so that they, at least, will not come to this place of pain.' ²⁹Abraham said, 'Your brothers have Moses and the prophets to warn them; your brothers should listen to what they say.' ³⁰The rich man answered, 'That is not enough, father Abraham! But if someone were to rise from death and go to them, then they would turn from their sins.' ³¹But Abraham said, 'If they will not listen to Moses and the prophets, they will not be convinced even if someone were to rise from death.' "

ˢ **16:23** HADES: *The world of the dead.*
16:17 Mt 5:18   **16:18** Mt 5:32; 1 Cor 7:10, 11

Sin
(Matthew 18:6, 7, 21, 22; Mark 9:42)

17 ¹Jesus said to his disciples, "Things that make people fall into sin are bound to happen, but how terrible for the one who makes them happen! ²It would be better for him if a large millstone were tied around his neck and he were thrown into the sea than for him to cause one of these little ones to sin. ³So watch what you do!

"If your brother sins, rebuke him, and if he repents, forgive him. ⁴If he sins against you seven times in one day, and each time he comes to you saying, 'I repent,' you must forgive him."

Faith

⁵The apostles said to the Lord, "Make our faith greater."

⁶The Lord answered, "If you had faith as big as a mustard seed, you could say to this mulberry tree, 'Pull yourself up by the roots and plant yourself in the sea!' and it would obey you.

A Servant's Duty

⁷"Suppose one of you has a servant who is plowing or looking after the sheep. When he comes in from the field, do you tell him to hurry along and eat his meal? ⁸Of course not! Instead, you say to him, 'Get my supper ready, then put on your apron and wait on me while I eat and drink; after that you may have your meal.' ⁹The servant does not deserve thanks for obeying orders, does he? ¹⁰It is the same with you; when you have done all you have been told to do, say, 'We are ordinary servants; we have only done our duty.' "

Jesus Heals Ten Men

¹¹As Jesus made his way to Jerusalem, he went along the border between Samaria and Galilee. ¹²He was going into a village when he was met by ten men suffering from a dreaded skin disease. They stood at a distance ¹³and shouted, "Jesus! Master! Have pity on us!"

Thanks a Lot

Two of the loveliest words in the English language are *thank you*. So simple, but so easy to forget to say. Think about all the nice things that various people do for you each day. How often do you thank them? Sometimes a grown-up will remind you by asking, "Now, what do you say?"

We shouldn't have to be reminded to express our gratitude. It feels so good to be thanked. How do you think Jesus felt when one of the ten people who were healed came back to thank him (Luke 17:15)? What happened to the other nine? Maybe they were just so excited they forgot. Let's try to make thanking someone the first thing we do rather than an afterthought.

— Luke 17:11–19

¹⁴Jesus saw them and said to them, "Go and let the priests examine you."

On the way they were made clean.ᶠ ¹⁵When one of them saw that he was healed, he came back, praising God in a loud voice. ¹⁶He threw himself to the ground at Jesus' feet and thanked him. The man was a Samaritan. ¹⁷Jesus spoke up, "There were ten who were healed; where are the other nine? ¹⁸Why is this foreigner the only one who came back to give thanks to God?" ¹⁹And Jesus said to him, "Get up and go; your faith has made you well."

The Coming of the Kingdom
(Matthew 24:23–28, 37–41)

²⁰Some Pharisees asked Jesus when the Kingdom of God would come. His answer

---

ᶠ **17:14** MADE CLEAN: *See 5:12.*
17:3 Mt 18:15   **17:14** Lev 14:1–32

Luke

"Where are the other nine?" (17:17)

was, "The Kingdom of God does not come in such a way as to be seen. ²¹No one will say, 'Look, here it is!' or, 'There it is!'; because the Kingdom of God is within you."ᵘ

²²Then he said to the disciples, "The time will come when you will wish you could see one of the days of the Son of Man, but you will not see it. ²³There will be those who will say to you, 'Look, over there!' or, 'Look, over here!' But don't go out looking for it. ²⁴As the lightning flashes across the sky and lights it up from one side to the other, so will the Son of Man be in his day. ²⁵But first he must suffer much and be rejected by the people of this day. ²⁶As it was in the time of Noah so shall it be in the days of the Son of Man. ²⁷Everybody kept on eating and drinking, and men and women married, up to the very day Noah went into the boat and the flood came and killed them all. ²⁸It will be as

it was in the time of Lot. Everybody kept on eating and drinking, buying and selling, planting and building. ²⁹On the day Lot left Sodom, fire and sulfur rained down from heaven and killed them all. ³⁰That is how it will be on the day the Son of Man is revealed.

³¹"On that day someone who is on the roof of a house must not go down into the house to get any belongings; in the same way anyone who is out in the field must not go back to the house. ³²Remember Lot's wife! ³³Those who try to save their own life will lose it; those who lose their life will save it. ³⁴On that night, I tell you, there will be two people sleeping in the same bed: one will be taken away, the other will be left behind. ³⁵Two women will be grinding meal together: one will be taken away, the other will be left behind."ᵛ

³⁷The disciples asked him, "Where, Lord?" Jesus answered, "Wherever there is a dead body, the vultures will gather."

The Parable of the Widow and the Judge

18 ¹Then Jesus told his disciples a parable to teach them that they should always pray and never become discouraged. ²"In a certain town there was a judge who neither feared God nor respected people. ³And there was a widow in that same town who kept coming to him and pleading for her rights, saying, 'Help me against my opponent!' ⁴For a long time the judge refused to act, but at last he said to himself, 'Even though I don't fear God or respect people, ⁵yet because of all the trouble this widow is giving me, I will see to it that she gets her rights. If I don't, she will keep on coming and finally wear me out!' "

⁶And the Lord continued, "Listen to what that corrupt judge said. ⁷Now, will God not

---

ᵘ **17:21** within you; *or* among you, *or* will suddenly appear among you.   ᵛ **17:35** *Some manuscripts add verse 36:* Two men will be working in a field: one will be taken away, the other will be left behind *(see Mt 24:40).*
17:26 Gen 6:5–8   **17:27** Gen 7:6–24   **17:28, 29** Gen 18:20—19:25   **17:31** Mt 24:17, 18; Mk 13:15, 16
17:32 Gen 19:26   **17:33** Mt 10:39; 16:25; Mk 8:35; Lk 9:24; Jn 12:25   **18:7** Sir 35:19

A *millstone* is a very heavy stone used in a mill to grind wheat. This type of stone was very common in the time of Jesus.

judge in favor of his own people who cry to him day and night for help? Will he be slow to help them? [8]I tell you, he will judge in their favor and do it quickly. But will the Son of Man find faith on earth when he comes?"

The Parable of the Pharisee and the Tax Collector

[9]Jesus also told this parable to people who were sure of their own goodness and despised everybody else. [10]"Once there were two men who went up to the Temple to pray: one was a Pharisee, the other a tax collector. [11]The Pharisee stood apart by himself and prayed,[w] 'I thank you, God, that I am not greedy, dishonest, or an adulterer, like everybody else. I thank you that I am not like that tax collector over there. [12]I fast two days a week, and I give you one tenth of all my income.' [13]But the tax collector stood at a distance and would not even raise his face to heaven, but beat on his breast and said, 'God, have pity on me, a sinner!' [14]I tell you," said Jesus, "the tax collector, and not the Pharisee, was in the right with God when he went home. For those who make themselves great will be humbled, and those who humble themselves will be made great."

Jesus Blesses Little Children
(Matthew 19:13–15; Mark 10:13–16)

[15]Some people brought their babies to Jesus for him to place his hands on them. The disciples saw them and scolded them for doing so, [16]but Jesus called the children to him and said, "Let the children come to me and do not stop them, because the Kingdom of God belongs to such as these. [17]Remember this! Whoever does not receive the Kingdom of God like a child will never enter it."

Pray It!
Holier Than Thou

Look closely at the two prayers in the parable of the Pharisee and the tax collector. Say each prayer slowly. Describe the attitude revealed in each one. Why does Jesus tell us that the second prayer is better? Why was the tax collector "in the right with God" (Luke 18:14) when he went home? Next time you pray, admit your sinfulness and ask for God's mercy. It's that simple.

— Luke 18:9–14

The Rich Man
(Matthew 19:16–30; Mark 10:17–31)

[18]A Jewish leader asked Jesus, "Good Teacher, what must I do to receive eternal life?"

[19]"Why do you call me good?" Jesus asked him. "No one is good except God alone. [20]You know the commandments: 'Do not commit adultery; do not commit murder; do not steal; do not accuse anyone falsely; respect your father and your mother.'"

[21]The man replied, "Ever since I was young, I have obeyed all these commandments."

[22]When Jesus heard this, he said to him, "There is still one more thing you need to do. Sell all you have and give the money to the poor, and you will have riches in heaven; then come and follow me." [23]But when the man heard this, he became very sad, because he was very rich.

[24]Jesus saw that he was sad and said, "How

---

w **18:11** stood apart by himself and prayed; *some manuscripts have* stood up and prayed to himself.
18:14 Mt 23:12; Lk 14:11   **18:20 a** Ex 20:14; Deut 5:18; **b** Ex 20:13; Deut 5:17; **c** Ex 20:15; Deut 5:19; **d** Ex 20:16; Deut 5:20; **e** Ex 20:12; Deut 5:16

In the time of Jesus, tax collectors were hated because they worked for the Romans and often charged much more than they needed to.

Luke

hard it is for rich people to enter the Kingdom of God! 25It is much harder for a rich person to enter the Kingdom of God than for a camel to go through the eye of a needle."

26The people who heard him asked, "Who, then, can be saved?"

27Jesus answered, "What is humanly impossible is possible for God."

28Then Peter said, "Look! We have left our homes to follow you."

29"Yes," Jesus said to them, "and I assure you that anyone who leaves home or wife or brothers or parents or children for the sake of the Kingdom of God 30will receive much more in this present age and eternal life in the age to come."

Jesus Speaks a Third Time about His Death
(Matthew 20:17–19; Mark 10:32–34)

31Jesus took the twelve disciples aside and said to them, "Listen! We are going to Jerusalem where everything the prophets wrote about the Son of Man will come true. 32He will be handed over to the Gentiles, who will make fun of him, insult him, and spit on him. 33They will whip him and kill him, but three days later he will rise to life."

34But the disciples did not understand any of these things; the meaning of the words was hidden from them, and they did not know what Jesus was talking about.

Jesus Heals a Blind Beggar
(Matthew 20:29–34; Mark 10:46–52)

35As Jesus was coming near Jericho, there was a blind man sitting by the road, begging. 36When he heard the crowd passing by, he asked, "What is this?"

37"Jesus of Nazareth is passing by," they told him.

38He cried out, "Jesus! Son of David! Have mercy on me!"

39The people in front scolded him and told him to be quiet. But he shouted even more loudly, "Son of David! Have mercy on me!"

40So Jesus stopped and ordered the blind man to be brought to him. When he came

near, Jesus asked him, 41"What do you want me to do for you?"

"Sir," he answered, "I want to see again."

42Jesus said to him, "Then see! Your faith has made you well."

43At once he was able to see, and he followed Jesus, giving thanks to God. When the crowd saw it, they all praised God.

Jesus and Zacchaeus

19 1Jesus went on into Jericho and was passing through. 2There was a chief tax collector there named Zacchaeus, who was rich. 3He was trying to see who Jesus was, but he was a little man and could not see Jesus because of the crowd. 4So he ran ahead of the crowd and climbed a sycamore tree to see Jesus, who was going to pass that way. 5When Jesus came to that place, he looked up and said to Zacchaeus, "Hurry down, Zacchaeus, because I must stay in your house today."

He was a little man. (19:3)

6Zacchaeus hurried down and welcomed him with great joy. 7All the people who saw it started grumbling, "This man has gone as a guest to the home of a sinner!"

8Zacchaeus stood up and said to the Lord, "Listen, sir! I will give half my belongings to the poor, and if I have cheated anyone, I will pay back four times as much."

9Jesus said to him, "Salvation has come to

The Long and Short of It

Poor Zacchaeus. He was not only a tax collector but he was also short. The day Jesus came to town, Zacchaeus, like everyone else, wanted to see him. But he came late, and no one was going to make room for him. That didn't stop Zacchaeus. He was determined to see this man whom everyone was talking about. He climbed a tree, and when Jesus saw him, he invited himself over to Zacchaeus's house for dinner.

That encounter changed Zacchaeus's life. One of the morals of the story? Don't let your size or status stop you from following Jesus. Here's another moral. Don't let what others think stop you from being Jesus' friend. Think of little Zacchaeus. Jesus saw inside to his big heart. That's what counts!

— Luke 19:1–10

this house today, for this man, also, is a descendant of Abraham. 10The Son of Man came to seek and to save the lost."

The Parable of the Gold Coins
(Matthew 25:14–30)

11While the people were listening to this, Jesus continued and told them a parable. He was now almost at Jerusalem, and they supposed that the Kingdom of God was just about to appear. 12So he said, "There was once a man of high rank who was going to a country far away to be made king, after which he planned to come back home. 13Before he left, he called his ten servants and gave them each a gold coin and told

them, 'See what you can earn with this while I am gone.' 14Now, his own people hated him, and so they sent messengers after him to say, 'We don't want this man to be our king.'

15"The man was made king and came back. At once he ordered his servants to appear before him, in order to find out how much they had earned. 16The first one came and said, 'Sir, I have earned ten gold coins with the one you gave me.' 17'Well done,' he said; 'you are a good servant! Since you were faithful in small matters, I will put you in charge of ten cities.' 18The second servant came and said, 'Sir, I have earned five gold coins with the one you gave me.' 19To this one he said, 'You will be in charge of five cities.' 20Another servant came and said, 'Sir, here is your gold coin; I kept it hidden in a handkerchief. 21I was afraid of you, because you are a hard man. You take what is not yours and reap what you did not plant.' 22He said to him, 'You bad servant! I will use your own words to condemn you! You know that I am a hard man, taking what is not mine and reaping what I have not planted. 23Well, then, why didn't you put my money in the bank? Then I would have received it back with interest when I returned.' 24Then he said to those who were standing there, 'Take the gold coin away from him and give it to the servant who has ten coins.' 25But they said to him, 'Sir, he already has ten coins!' 26'I tell you,' he replied, 'that to those who have something, even more will be given; but those who have nothing, even the little that they have will be taken away from them. 27Now, as for those enemies of mine who did not want me to be their king, bring them here and kill them in my presence!' "

The Triumphant Approach to Jerusalem
(Matthew 21:1–11; Mark 11:1–11; John 12:12–19)

28After Jesus said this, he went on in front of them toward Jerusalem. 29As he came near Bethphage and Bethany at the Mount of Olives, he sent two disciples ahead 30with these instructions: "Go to the village there ahead of you; as you go in, you will find a colt tied up that has never been ridden. Untie it and bring it here. 31 If someone asks you why you are untying it, tell him that the Master[x] needs it."

32 They went on their way and found everything just as Jesus had told them. 33 As they were untying the colt, its owners said to them, "Why are you untying it?"

34 "The Master needs it," they answered, 35 and they took the colt to Jesus. Then they threw their cloaks over the animal and helped Jesus get on. 36 As he rode on, people spread their cloaks on the road.

37 When he came near Jerusalem, at the place where the road went down the Mount of Olives, the large crowd of his disciples began to thank God and praise him in loud voices for all the great things that they had seen: 38 "God bless the king who comes in the name of the Lord! Peace in heaven and glory to God!"

39 Then some of the Pharisees in the crowd spoke to Jesus. "Teacher," they said, "command your disciples to be quiet!"

40 Jesus answered, "I tell you that if they keep quiet, the stones themselves will start shouting."

Jesus Weeps over Jerusalem

41 He came closer to the city, and when he saw it, he wept over it, 42 saying, "If you only knew today what is needed for peace! But now you cannot see it! 43 The time will come when your enemies will surround you with barricades, blockade you, and close in on you from every side. 44 They will completely destroy you and the people within your walls; not a single stone will they leave in its place, because you did not recognize the time when God came to save you!"

Jesus Goes to the Temple
(Matthew 21:12–17; Mark 11:15–19; John 2:13–22)

45 Then Jesus went into the Temple and began to drive out the merchants, 46 saying to them, "It is written in the Scriptures that God said, 'My Temple will be a house of prayer.' But you have turned it into a hideout for thieves!"

47 Every day Jesus taught in the Temple. The chief priests, the teachers of the Law, and the leaders of the people wanted to kill him, 48 but they could not find a way to do it, because all the people kept listening to him, not wanting to miss a single word.

The Question about Jesus' Authority
(Matthew 21:23–27; Mark 11:27–33)

20 ¹One day when Jesus was in the Temple teaching the people and preaching the Good News, the chief priests and the teachers of the Law, together with the elders, came ²and said to him, "Tell us, what right do you have to do these things? Who gave you such right?"

3 Jesus answered them, "Now let me ask you a question. Tell me, 4 did John's right to baptize come from God or from human beings?"

5 They started to argue among themselves, "What shall we say? If we say, 'From God,' he will say, 'Why, then, did you not believe John?' 6 But if we say, 'From human beings,' this whole crowd here will stone us, because they are convinced that John was a prophet." 7 So they answered, "We don't know where it came from."

8 And Jesus said to them, "Neither will I tell you, then, by what right I do these things."

---

x **19:31** the Master; *or* its owner.
19:38 Ps 118:26   **19:46** Isa 56:7; Jer 7:11   **19:47** Lk 21:37

Did you know that Jesus wept (Luke 19:41)? **His heart was so big that when he saw people headed for destruction, he couldn't help but be overcome with grief.**

Luke

Gotcha!

Twice in Luke, chapter 20, the enemies of Jesus try to trap him with a question, but both times Jesus traps them with his response. They are trying to get Jesus to say something that can be used against him. And they do it in public places where lots of people are gathered so that everyone will hear what he says. It's clear that they are more interested in finding fault with Jesus than in listening to what he has to say.

Jesus is clearly very wise and clever. And the people only grow to admire Jesus even more than before because of how well he handles his questioners. He beats them at their own game.

Sometimes we use words in unkind ways. Examine your heart when you ask a question that may make another person feel mad or sad. Do you really want to know the answer, or are you trying to make yourself look good by making the other person look bad?

— Luke 20:1–8,19–26

The Parable of the Tenants in the Vineyard
(Matthew 21:33–46; Mark 12:1–12)

9 Then Jesus told the people this parable: "There was once a man who planted a vineyard, rented it out to tenants, and then left home for a long time. 10 When the time came to gather the grapes, he sent a slave to the tenants to receive from them his share of the harvest. But the tenants beat the slave and sent him back without a thing. 11 So he sent another slave; but the tenants beat him also, treated him shamefully, and sent him back without a thing. 12 Then he sent a third slave; the tenants wounded him, too, and threw him out. 13 Then the owner of the vineyard said, 'What shall I do? I will send my own dear son; surely they will respect him!' 14 But when the tenants saw him, they said to one another, 'This is the owner's son. Let's kill him, and his property will be ours!' 15 So they threw him out of the vineyard and killed him.

"What, then, will the owner of the vineyard do to the tenants?" Jesus asked. 16 "He will come and kill those men, and turn the vineyard over to other tenants."

When the people heard this, they said, "Surely not!"

17 Jesus looked at them and asked, "What, then, does this scripture mean?

'The stone which the builders rejected as worthless
    turned out to be the most important of all.'

18 Everyone who falls on that stone will be cut to pieces; and if that stone falls on someone, that person will be crushed to dust."

The Question about Paying Taxes
(Matthew 22:15–22; Mark 12:13–17)

19 The teachers of the Law and the chief priests tried to arrest Jesus on the spot, because they knew that he had told this parable against them; but they were afraid of the people. 20 So they looked for an opportunity. They bribed some men to pretend they were sincere, and they sent them to trap Jesus with questions, so that they could hand him over to the authority and power of the Roman Governor. 21 These spies said to Jesus, "Teacher, we know that what you say and teach is right. We know that you pay no attention to anyone's status, but teach the truth about God's will for people. 22 Tell us, is

20:9 Isa 5:1   20:17 Ps 118:22

The Hebrew word *Messiah* translates into *Christos* in Greek, which becomes *Christ* in English. All three mean "the anointed one."

Pray It!

Common Cents

In this passage Jesus handles a coin and uses it to make a point. We can use a coin to make a prayer. Take a look at any U. S. coin. Two four-word phrases appear on each. One is, "The United States of America." Can you find the other? That's right. It's "In God We Trust." Check out paper money too.

Interesting that such a religious phrase appears on every piece of U.S. money. So why not let our money—pennies, nickels, dimes, quarters, and dollar bills—be a source for prayer?

Dear God, perhaps the last place I expect to see your name is on a coin or a dollar bill. Yet there you are. Thanks for the reminder that even money calls me to an awareness of your presence in my life and my need to trust in you. Increase my trust in you and decrease my trust in money. And help me be generous with the money I have and spend it wisely. Amen.

— Luke 20:19–26

---

it against our Law for us to pay taxes to the Roman Emperor, or not?"

23 But Jesus saw through their trick and said to them, 24 "Show me a silver coin. Whose face and name are these on it?"

"The Emperor's," they answered.

25 So Jesus said, "Well, then, pay to the Emperor what belongs to the Emperor, and pay to God what belongs to God."

26 There before the people they could not catch him in a thing, so they kept quiet, amazed at his answer.

The Question about Rising from Death
(Matthew 22:23–33; Mark 12:18–27)

27 Then some Sadducees, who say that people will not rise from death, came to Jesus and said, 28 "Teacher, Moses wrote this law for us: 'If a man dies and leaves a wife but no children, that man's brother must marry the widow so that they can have children who will be considered the dead man's children.' 29 Once there were seven brothers; the oldest got married and died without having children. 30 Then the second one married the woman, 31 and then the third.

The same thing happened to all seven—they died without having children. 32 Last of all, the woman died. 33 Now, on the day when the dead rise to life, whose wife will she be? All seven of them had married her."

34 Jesus answered them, "The men and women of this age marry, 35 but the men and women who are worthy to rise from death and live in the age to come will not then marry. 36 They will be like angels and cannot die. They are the children of God, because they have risen from death. 37 And Moses clearly proves that the dead are raised to life. In the passage about the burning bush he speaks of the Lord as 'the God of Abraham, the God of Isaac, and the God of Jacob.' 38 He is the God of the living, not of the dead, for to him all are alive."

39 Some of the teachers of the Law spoke up, "A good answer, Teacher!" 40 For they did not dare ask him any more questions.

The Question about the Messiah
(Matthew 22:41–46; Mark 12:35–37)

41 Jesus asked them, "How can it be said that the Messiah will be the descendant of

Luke

David? ⁴²For David himself says in the book of Psalms,

'The Lord said to my Lord:
    Sit here at my right side
⁴³ until I put your enemies as a footstool
      under your feet.'

⁴⁴David called him 'Lord'; how, then, can the Messiah be David's descendant?"

Jesus Warns against the Teachers of the Law
(Matthew 23:1–36; Mark 12:38–40)

⁴⁵As all the people listened to him, Jesus said to his disciples, ⁴⁶"Be on your guard against the teachers of the Law, who like to walk around in their long robes and love to be greeted with respect in the marketplace; who choose the reserved seats in the synagogues and the best places at feasts; ⁴⁷who take advantage of widows and rob them of their homes, and then make a show of saying long prayers! Their punishment will be all the worse!"

The Widow's Offering
(Mark 12:41–44)

21 ¹Jesus looked around and saw rich people dropping their gifts in the Temple treasury, ²and he also saw a very poor widow dropping in two little copper coins. ³He said, "I tell you that this poor widow put in more than all the others. ⁴For the others offered their gifts from what they had to spare of their riches; but she, poor as she is, gave all she had to live on."

Jesus Speaks of the Destruction of the Temple
(Matthew 24:1, 2; Mark 13:1, 2)

⁵Some of the disciples were talking about the Temple, how beautiful it looked with its fine stones and the gifts offered to God. Jesus said, ⁶"All this you see—the time will come when not a single stone here will be left in its place; every one will be thrown down."

You Better Watch Out

Jesus says something very important in this passage. He basically tells his followers that many people will come claiming to speak for him, but Jesus says, "Be careful who you follow."

How do we sort out all the people who claim to speak for Jesus? There are preachers and ministers on television and radio, and all of them claim to be speaking for Jesus. It's easy to be deceived. There are many stories, for instance, where people tell their followers that on a certain date, the world is going to end. Followers make plans and prepare themselves. The date comes and goes, and the world goes on.

The best course to take is to learn all you can about what the Catholic Church teaches. The Catholic Church goes all the way back to Jesus and the Apostles. The Holy Spirit guides the Church into the fullness of truth.

Have you ever been fooled by someone's words or message? Think through what happened and what you will do if it happens again. Ask God to help you stay on the right path and not be misled.

— Luke 21:7–19

Troubles and Persecutions
(Matthew 24:3–14; Mark 13:3–13)

⁷"Teacher," they asked, "when will this be? And what will happen in order to show that the time has come for it to take place?"

⁸Jesus said, "Watch out; don't be fooled. Many men, claiming to speak for me, will come and say, 'I am he!' and, 'The time has

come!' But don't follow them. [9]Don't be afraid when you hear of wars and revolutions; such things must happen first, but they do not mean that the end is near."

[10]He went on to say, "Countries will fight each other; kingdoms will attack one another. [11]There will be terrible earthquakes, famines, and plagues everywhere; there will be strange and terrifying things coming from the sky. [12]Before all these things take place, however, you will be arrested and persecuted; you will be handed over to be tried in synagogues and be put in prison; you will be brought before kings and rulers for my sake. [13]This will be your chance to tell the Good News. [14]Make up your minds ahead of time not to worry about how you will defend yourselves, [15]because I will give you such words and wisdom that none of your enemies will be able to refute or contradict what you say. [16]You will be handed over by your parents, your brothers, your relatives, and your friends; and some of you will be put to death. [17]Everyone will hate you because of me. [18]But not a single hair from your heads will be lost. [19]Stand firm, and you will save yourselves.

Jesus Speaks of the Destruction of Jerusalem
(Matthew 24:15–21; Mark 13:14–19)

[20]"When you see Jerusalem surrounded by armies, then you will know that it will soon be destroyed. [21]Then those who are in Judea must run away to the hills; those who are in the city must leave, and those who are out in the country must not go into the city. [22]For those will be 'The Days of Punishment,' to make come true all that the Scriptures say. [23]How terrible it will be in those days for women who are pregnant and for mothers with little babies! Terrible distress will come upon this land, and God's punishment will fall on this people. [24]Some will be killed by the sword, and others will be taken

as prisoners to all countries; and the heathen will trample over Jerusalem until their time is up.

The Coming of the Son of Man
(Matthew 24:29–31; Mark 13:24–27)

[25]"There will be strange things happening to the sun, the moon, and the stars. On earth whole countries will be in despair, afraid of the roar of the sea and the raging tides. [26]People will faint from fear as they wait for what is coming over the whole earth, for the powers in space will be driven from their courses. [27]Then the Son of Man will appear, coming in a cloud with great power and glory. [28]When these things begin to happen, stand up and raise your heads, because your salvation is near."

The Lesson of the Fig Tree
(Matthew 24:32–35; Mark 13:28–31)

[29]Then Jesus told them this parable: "Think of the fig tree and all the other trees. [30]When you see their leaves beginning to appear, you know that summer is near. [31]In the same way, when you see these things happening, you will know that the Kingdom of God is about to come.

[32]"Remember that all these things will take place before the people now living have all died. [33]Heaven and earth will pass away, but my words will never pass away.

The Need to Watch

[34]"Be careful not to let yourselves become occupied with too much feasting and drinking and with the worries of this life, or that Day may suddenly catch you [35]like a trap. For it will come upon all people everywhere on earth. [36]Be on watch and pray always that you will have the strength to go safely through all those things that will happen and to stand before the Son of Man."

21:14, 15 Lk 12:11, 12 **21:22** Hos 9:7 **21:25** Isa 13:10; Ezek 32:7; Joel 2:31; Rev 6:12, 13 **21:27** Dan 7:13; Rev 1:7

Fig trees are very common in the Holy Land. Have you ever seen or tasted a fig?

37 Jesus spent those days teaching in the Temple, and when evening came, he would go out and spend the night on the Mount of Olives. 38 Early each morning all the people went to the Temple to listen to him.

The Plot against Jesus
(Matthew 26:1–5; Mark 14:1, 2; John 11:45–53)

22 1 The time was near for the Festival of Unleavened Bread, which is called the Passover. 2 The chief priests and the teachers of the Law were afraid of the people, and so they were trying to find a way of putting Jesus to death secretly.

Judas Agrees to Betray Jesus
(Matthew 26:14–16; Mark 14:10, 11)

3 Then Satan entered into Judas, called Iscariot, who was one of the twelve disciples. 4 So Judas went off and spoke with the chief priests and the officers of the Temple guard about how he could betray Jesus to them. 5 They were pleased and offered to pay him money. 6 Judas agreed to it and started looking for a good chance to hand Jesus over to them without the people knowing about it.

Jesus Prepares to Eat the Passover Meal
(Matthew 26:17–25; Mark 14:12–21; John 13:21–30)

7 The day came during the Festival of Unleavened Bread when the lambs for the Passover meal were to be killed. 8 Jesus sent Peter and John with these instructions: "Go and get the Passover meal ready for us to eat."

9 "Where do you want us to get it ready?" they asked him.

10 He answered, "As you go into the city, a man carrying a jar of water will meet you. Follow him into the house that he enters,

11 and say to the owner of the house: 'The Teacher says to you, Where is the room where my disciples and I will eat the Passover meal?' 12 He will show you a large furnished room upstairs, where you will get everything ready."

13 They went off and found everything just as Jesus had told them, and they prepared the Passover meal.

The Lord's Supper
(Matthew 26:26–30; Mark 14:22–26; 1 Corinthians 11:23–25)

14 When the hour came, Jesus took his place at the table with the apostles. 15 He said to them, "I have wanted so much to eat this Passover meal with you before I suffer! 16 For I tell you, I will never eat it until it is given its full meaning in the Kingdom of God."

17 Then Jesus took a cup, gave thanks to God, and said, "Take this and share it among yourselves. 18 I tell you that from now on I will not drink this wine until the Kingdom of God comes."

19 Then he took a piece of bread, gave thanks to God, broke it, and gave it to them, saying, "This is my body, which is given for you. Do this in memory of me." 20 In the same way, he gave them the cup after the supper, saying, "This cup is God's new covenant sealed with my blood, which is poured out for you.γ

21 "But, look! The one who betrays me is here at the table with me! 22 The Son of Man will die as God has decided, but how terrible for that man who betrays him!"

23 Then they began to ask among themselves which one of them it could be who was going to do this.

The Argument about Greatness

24 An argument broke out among the disciples as to which one of them should be

γ **22:20** Some manuscripts do not have the words of Jesus after This is my body in verse 19, and all of verse 20.
21:37 Lk 19:47   **22:1** Ex 12:1–27   **22:20** Jer 31:31–34   **22:21** Ps 41:9   **22:24** Mt 18:1; Mk 9:34; Lk 9:46

The Festival of Unleavened Bread is also known as Passover, and it is celebrated each spring by the Jewish people. See Exodus, chapter 12.

Pray It!

Who's Number One?

Try to imagine how Jesus felt at his last meal with his closest followers, when they began to argue about which of them should be thought of as the greatest (Luke 22:24). You can almost hear Jesus saying to himself, "Haven't they been listening to anything I've said?" Following Jesus is about putting others before yourself. It is about serving others and not being served.

Wanting to be number one is definitely *not* what being a Christian is about. Aim to live out the words of Jesus, "I am among you as one who serves." Think of ways that you can be of service to others. Here is a prayer to help you keep your priorities straight.

Dear Jesus, you came to tell us that being number one is not *what it's all about. Help me to keep you as number one in my life and keep the needs of others close behind. Let me wake up each day and think of how I can serve others, especially at home or in school. Help me to keep my priorities straight, which means they are directed toward you. Amen.*

— Luke 22:24–27

---

thought of as the greatest. 25 Jesus said to them, "The kings of the pagans have power over their people, and the rulers claim the title 'Friends of the People.' 26 But this is not the way it is with you; rather, the greatest one among you must be like the youngest, and the leader must be like the servant. 27 Who is greater, the one who sits down to eat or the one who serves? The one who sits down, of course. But I am among you as one who serves.

28 "You have stayed with me all through my trials; 29 and just as my Father has given me the right to rule, so I will give you the same right. 30 You will eat and drink at my table in my Kingdom, and you will sit on thrones to rule over the twelve tribes of Israel.

Jesus Predicts Peter's Denial
(Matthew 26:31–35; Mark 14:27–31; John 13:36–38)

31 "Simon, Simon! Listen! Satan has received permission to test all of you, to sep-arate the good from the bad, as a farmer sep-arates the wheat from the chaff. 32 But I have prayed for you, Simon, that your faith will not fail. And when you turn back to me, you must strengthen your brothers."

33 Peter answered, "Lord, I am ready to go to prison with you and to die with you!"

34 "I tell you, Peter," Jesus said, "the rooster will not crow tonight until you have said three times that you do not know me."

Purse, Bag, and Sword

35 Then Jesus asked his disciples, "When I sent you out that time without purse, bag, or shoes, did you lack anything?"

"Not a thing," they answered.

36 "But now," Jesus said, "whoever has a purse or a bag must take it; and whoever does not have a sword must sell his coat and buy one. 37 For I tell you that the scripture which says, 'He shared the fate of criminals,' must come true about me, because what was written about me is coming true."

Luke

22:26 Mt 23:11; Mk 9:35   22:25, 26 Mt 20:25–27; Mk 10:42–44   22:27 Jn 13:12–15   22:30 Mt 19:28
22:35 Mt 10:9, 10; Mk 6:8, 9; Lk 9:3; 10:4   22:37 Isa 53:12

"Simon, Simon! Listen!" (22:31)

38 The disciples said, "Look! Here are two swords, Lord!"

"That is enough!"*z* he replied.

Jesus Prays on the Mount of Olives
(Matthew 26:36–46; Mark 14:32–42)

39 Jesus left the city and went, as he usually did, to the Mount of Olives; and the disciples went with him. **40** When he arrived at the place, he said to them, "Pray that you will not fall into temptation."

41 Then he went off from them about the distance of a stone's throw and knelt down and prayed. **42** "Father," he said, "if you will, take this cup of suffering away from me. Not my will, however, but your will be done." **43** An angel from heaven appeared to him and strengthened him. **44** In great anguish he prayed even more fervently; his sweat was like drops of blood falling to the ground.*a*

45 Rising from his prayer, he went back to the disciples and found them asleep, worn out by their grief. **46** He said to them, "Why are you sleeping? Get up and pray that you will not fall into temptation."

The Arrest of Jesus
(Matthew 26:47–56; Mark 14:43–50; John 18:3–11)

47 Jesus was still speaking when a crowd arrived, led by Judas, one of the twelve disciples. He came up to Jesus to kiss him. **48** But

Jesus said, "Judas, is it with a kiss that you betray the Son of Man?"

49 When the disciples who were with Jesus saw what was going to happen, they asked, "Shall we use our swords, Lord?" **50** And one of them struck the High Priest's slave and cut off his right ear.

51 But Jesus said, "Enough of this!" He touched the man's ear and healed him.

52 Then Jesus said to the chief priests and the officers of the Temple guard and the elders who had come there to get him, "Did you have to come with swords and clubs, as though I were an outlaw? **53** I was with you in the Temple every day, and you did not try to arrest me. But this is your hour to act, when the power of darkness rules."

Peter Denies Jesus
(Matthew 26:57, 58, 69–75; Mark 14:53, 54, 66–72; John 18:12–18, 25–27)

54 They arrested Jesus and took him away into the house of the High Priest; and Peter followed at a distance. **55** A fire had been lit in the center of the courtyard, and Peter joined those who were sitting around it. **56** When one of the servant women saw him sitting there at the fire, she looked straight at him and said, "This man too was with Jesus!"

57 But Peter denied it, "Woman, I don't even know him!"

"Woman, I don't even know him!" (22:57)

58 After a little while a man noticed Peter and said, "You are one of them, too!"

But Peter answered, "Man, I am not!"

59 And about an hour later another man insisted strongly, "There isn't any doubt that

---

z **22:38** *That is enough; or* Enough of this.   *a* **22:44** *Some manuscripts do not have verses 43–44.*
22:53 Lk 19:47; 21:37

It Wasn't Me!

How could Peter do it? Right when Jesus needed him most, three times he denied even knowing him. And Jesus had even warned Peter that he would do it!

We have all been in a situation where we denied doing anything wrong, even though we were guilty. We may have lied about it and maybe even blamed others. Peter was wrong, and once he realized it, he "wept bitterly" (Luke 22:62). Think of the last time you felt regret for not admitting to the truth about something you did. Did you try to blame someone else? Try not to let that happen. It takes courage to face up to the truth, especially when it comes to standing up for a friend. Resist the temptation to deny the truth. You won't regret it.

— Luke 22:54–62

this man was with Jesus, because he also is a Galilean!"

⁶⁰But Peter answered, "Man, I don't know what you are talking about!"

At once, while he was still speaking, a rooster crowed. ⁶¹The Lord turned around and looked straight at Peter, and Peter remembered that the Lord had said to him, "Before the rooster crows tonight, you will say three times that you do not know me." ⁶²Peter went out and wept bitterly.

Jesus Is Mocked and Beaten
(Matthew 26:67, 68; Mark 14:65)

⁶³The men who were guarding Jesus made fun of him and beat him. ⁶⁴They blindfolded him and asked him, "Who hit you? Guess!" ⁶⁵And they said many other insulting things to him.

Jesus before the Council
(Matthew 26:59–66; Mark 14:55–64; John 18:19–24)

⁶⁶When day came, the elders, the chief priests, and the teachers of the Law met together, and Jesus was brought before the Council. ⁶⁷"Tell us," they said, "are you the Messiah?"

He answered, "If I tell you, you will not believe me; ⁶⁸and if I ask you a question, you will not answer. ⁶⁹But from now on the Son of Man will be seated at the right side of Almighty God."

⁷⁰They all said, "Are you, then, the Son of God?"

He answered them, "You say that I am."

⁷¹And they said, "We don't need any witnesses! We ourselves have heard what he said!"

Jesus before Pilate
(Matthew 27:1, 2, 11–14; Mark 15:1–5; John 18:28–38)

23 ¹The whole group rose up and took Jesus before Pilate, ²where they began to accuse him: "We caught this man misleading our people, telling them not to pay taxes to the Emperor and claiming that he himself is the Messiah, a king."

³Pilate asked him, "Are you the king of the Jews?"

"So you say," answered Jesus.

⁴Then Pilate said to the chief priests and the crowds, "I find no reason to condemn this man."

⁵But they insisted even more strongly, "With his teaching he is starting a riot among the people all through Judea. He began in Galilee and now has come here."

Galilean: Someone who lives in Galilee, which is in the north of Judea. Galileans had a distinct accent. Both Jesus and Peter were Galileans.

Jesus before Herod

6 When Pilate heard this, he asked, "Is this man a Galilean?" 7 When he learned that Jesus was from the region ruled by Herod, he sent him to Herod, who was also in Jerusalem at that time. 8 Herod was very pleased when he saw Jesus, because he had heard about him and had been wanting to see him for a long time. He was hoping to see Jesus perform some miracle. 9 So Herod asked Jesus many questions, but Jesus made no answer. 10 The chief priests and the teachers of the Law stepped forward and made strong accusations against Jesus. 11 Herod and his soldiers made fun of Jesus and treated him with contempt; then they put a fine robe on him and sent him back to Pilate. 12 On that very day Herod and Pilate became friends; before this they had been enemies.

Jesus Is Sentenced to Death
(Matthew 27:15–26; Mark 15:6–15; John 18:39—19:16)

13 Pilate called together the chief priests, the leaders, and the people, 14 and said to them, "You brought this man to me and said that he was misleading the people. Now, I have examined him here in your presence, and I have not found him guilty of any of the crimes you accuse him of. 15 Nor did Herod find him guilty, for he sent him back to us. There is nothing this man has done to deserve death. 16 So I will have him whipped and let him go."[b]

18 The whole crowd cried out, "Kill him! Set Barabbas free for us!" (19 Barabbas had been put in prison for a riot that had taken place in the city, and for murder.)

20 Pilate wanted to set Jesus free, so he appealed to the crowd again. 21 But they shouted back, "Crucify him! Crucify him!"

22 Pilate said to them the third time, "But what crime has he committed? I cannot find anything he has done to deserve death! I will have him whipped and set him free."

23 But they kept on shouting at the top of their voices that Jesus should be crucified, and finally their shouting succeeded. 24 So Pilate passed the sentence on Jesus that they were asking for. 25 He set free the man they wanted, the one who had been put in prison for riot and murder, and he handed Jesus over for them to do as they wished.

Jesus Is Crucified
(Matthew 27:32–44; Mark 15:21–32; John 19:17–27)

26 The soldiers led Jesus away, and as they were going, they met a man from Cyrene named Simon who was coming into the city from the country. They seized him, put the cross on him, and made him carry it behind Jesus.

They . . . put the cross on him, and made him carry it. (23:26)

27 A large crowd of people followed him; among them were some women who were weeping and wailing for him. 28 Jesus turned to them and said, "Women of Jerusalem! Don't cry for me, but for yourselves and your children. 29 For the days are coming when people will say, 'How lucky are the women who never had children, who never bore babies, who never nursed them!' 30 That will be the time when people will say to the

---

[b] **23:16** *Some manuscripts add verse 17:* At every Passover Festival Pilate had to set free one prisoner for them (*see Mk 15:6*).
23:30 Hos 10:8; Rev 6:16

Can you find three wondrous things that happened at Jesus' death? They involved the sun, the Temple, and a Roman officer.

Pray It!

Jesus, Remember Me!

Two criminals were crucified alongside Jesus. One of them insulted Jesus. The other, often referred to as the good thief, respected Jesus and knew he was innocent. He asked to be remembered by Jesus, and Jesus assured him that he would share Paradise with him.

Take a moment to pray for all those accused of crimes, especially the innocent and those given the death penalty.

God, help me always to remember that you love every one of us, no matter what we have done. Your Son was given the death penalty, even though he was innocent. I pray for everyone who has been falsely accused and convicted. I pray also for all those who have been sentenced to death. No matter what they have done, they are still your children. Your love knows no bounds. Remind me of that when my heart is too small and judgmental. Amen.

— Luke 23:39–43

mountains, 'Fall on us!' and to the hills, 'Hide us!' ³¹For if such things as these are done when the wood is green, what will happen when it is dry?"

³²Two other men, both of them criminals, were also led out to be put to death with Jesus. ³³When they came to the place called "The Skull," they crucified Jesus there, and the two criminals, one on his right and the other on his left. ³⁴Jesus said, "Forgive them, Father! They don't know what they are doing."ᶜ

They divided his clothes among themselves by throwing dice. ³⁵The people stood there watching while the Jewish leaders made fun of him: "He saved others; let him save himself if he is the Messiah whom God has chosen!"

³⁶The soldiers also made fun of him: they came up to him and offered him cheap wine, ³⁷and said, "Save yourself if you are the king of the Jews!"

³⁸Above him were written these words: "This is the King of the Jews."

³⁹One of the criminals hanging there hurled insults at him: "Aren't you the Messiah? Save yourself and us!"

⁴⁰The other one, however, rebuked him, saying, "Don't you fear God? You received the same sentence he did. ⁴¹Ours, however, is only right, because we are getting what we deserve for what we did; but he has done no wrong." ⁴²And he said to Jesus, "Remember me, Jesus, when you come as King!"

⁴³Jesus said to him, "I promise you that today you will be in Paradise with me."

The Death of Jesus
(Matthew 27:45–56; Mark 15:33–41; John 19:28–30)

⁴⁴⁻⁴⁵It was about twelve o'clock when the sun stopped shining and darkness covered the whole country until three o'clock; and the curtain hanging in the Temple was torn in two. ⁴⁶Jesus cried out in a loud voice, "Father! In your hands I place my spirit!" He said this and died.

⁴⁷The army officer saw what had happened, and he praised God, saying, "Certainly he was a good man!"

⁴⁸When the people who had gathered there to watch the spectacle saw what happened, they all went back home, beating their breasts in sorrow. ⁴⁹All those who

Luke

ᶜ **23:34** *Some manuscripts do not have* Jesus said, "Forgive them, Father! They don't know what they are doing."
23:34 Ps 22:18   **23:35** Ps 22:7   **23:36** Ps 69:21   **23:45** Ex 26:31–33   **23:46** Ps 31:5   **23:49** Lk 8:2, 3

"Father! In your hands I place my spirit!" (23:46)

knew Jesus personally, including the women who had followed him from Galilee, stood at a distance to watch.

The Burial of Jesus
(Matthew 27:57–61; Mark 15:42–47; John 19:38–42)

50-51 There was a man named Joseph from Arimathea, a town in Judea. He was a good and honorable man, who was waiting for the coming of the Kingdom of God. Although he was a member of the Council, he had not agreed with their decision and action. **52** He went into the presence of Pilate and asked for the body of Jesus. **53** Then he took the body down, wrapped it in a linen sheet, and placed it in a tomb which had been dug out of solid rock and which had never been used. **54** It was Friday, and the Sabbath was about to begin.

55 The women who had followed Jesus from Galilee went with Joseph and saw the tomb and how Jesus' body was placed in it. **56** Then they went back home and prepared the spices and perfumes for the body.

On the Sabbath they rested, as the Law commanded.

The Resurrection
(Matthew 28:1–10; Mark 16:1–8; John 20:1–10)

24 **1** Very early on Sunday morning the women went to the tomb, carrying the spices they had prepared. **2** They found

the stone rolled away from the entrance to the tomb, **3** so they went in; but they did not find the body of the Lord Jesus. **4** They stood there puzzled about this, when suddenly two men in bright shining clothes stood by them. **5** Full of fear, the women bowed down to the ground, as the men said to them, "Why are you looking among the dead for one who is alive? **6** He is not here; he has been raised. Remember what he said to you while he was in Galilee: **7** 'The Son of Man must be handed over to sinners, be crucified, and three days later rise to life.' "

"He is not here; he has been raised." (24:6)

8 Then the women remembered his words, **9** returned from the tomb, and told all these things to the eleven disciples and all the rest. **10** The women were Mary Magdalene, Joanna, and Mary the mother of James; they and the other women with them told these things to the apostles. **11** But the apostles thought that what the women said was nonsense, and they did not believe them. **12** But Peter got up and ran to the tomb; he bent down and saw the grave cloths but nothing else. Then he went back home amazed at what had happened. *d*

The Walk to Emmaus
(Mark 16:12, 13)

13 On that same day two of Jesus' followers were going to a village named Emmaus, about seven miles from Jerusalem, **14** and they

d **24:12** *Some manuscripts do not have verse 12.*
23:56 Ex 20:10; Deut 5:14   **24:6, 7** Mt 16:21; 17:22, 23; 20:18, 19; Mk 8:31; 9:31; 10:33, 34; Lk 9:22; 18:31–33

Luke

Celebrate Easter

Catholic Connections

Even though the word *Easter* never appears in the Bible, it is the word used in English to describe the most important Christian feast. Easter is the day on which Christians celebrate Jesus' Resurrection from the dead in a special way. It is one of the holiest days of the Church year, and the Easter season lasts fifty days until Pentecost. It truly is a time to celebrate the great joy and wonder of the Resurrection. The Sunday readings focus on the appearances of Jesus that are recorded in the four Gospels and the stories of the start of the Church, from the Acts of the Apostles. The Easter season gives each of us hope and joy because death has been overcome. Throughout the Easter season we sing, "Alleluia!"

— Luke 24:1–12

were talking to each other about all the things that had happened. 15As they talked and discussed, Jesus himself drew near and walked along with them; 16they saw him, but somehow did not recognize him. 17Jesus said to them, "What are you talking about to each other, as you walk along?"

They stood still, with sad faces. 18One of them, named Cleopas, asked him, "Are you the only visitor in Jerusalem who doesn't know the things that have been happening there these last few days?"

19"What things?" he asked.

"The things that happened to Jesus of Nazareth," they answered. "This man was a prophet and was considered by God and by all the people to be powerful in everything he said and did. 20Our chief priests and rulers handed him over to be sentenced to death, and he was crucified. 21And we had hoped that he would be the one who was going to set Israel free! Besides all that, this is now the third day since it happened. 22Some of the women of our group surprised us; they went at dawn to the tomb, 23but could not find his body. They came back saying they had seen a vision of angels who told them that he is alive. 24Some of our group

went to the tomb and found it exactly as the women had said, but they did not see him."

25Then Jesus said to them, "How foolish you are, how slow you are to believe everything the prophets said! 26Was it not necessary for the Messiah to suffer these things and then to enter his glory?" 27And Jesus explained to them what was said about himself in all the Scriptures, beginning with the books of Moses and the writings of all the prophets.

28As they came near the village to which they were going, Jesus acted as if he were going farther; 29but they held him back, saying, "Stay with us; the day is almost over and it is getting dark." So he went in to stay with them. 30He sat down to eat with them, took the bread, and said the blessing; then he broke the bread and gave it to them. 31Then their eyes were opened and they recognized him, but he disappeared from their sight. 32They said to each other, "Wasn't it like a fire burning in us when he talked to us on the road and explained the Scriptures to us?"

33They got up at once and went back to Jerusalem, where they found the eleven disciples gathered together with the others 34and saying, "The Lord is risen indeed! He has appeared to Simon!"

Luke

Mary Magdalene and Joanna are mentioned earlier in this Gospel. Try to find the passage (hint: it's near the parable of the sower).

Pray It!

Walking with Jesus

Doesn't it seem odd that Jesus' followers would not have recognized him after his Resurrection? But Cleopas and his companion were so upset by what had happened to Jesus in Jerusalem, that he was probably the last person they expected to join them on the road. Jesus always seems to be either teaching or healing. In this wonderful Emmaus story, he does both. He helps these two people understand what has happened and then shares a meal with them. Once he breaks the bread—a familiar gesture to Jesus' followers—they know who he is. They can't wait to tell the others the Good News!

You, too, might not always recognize that Jesus is walking with you, but he is there. It is easy to get too distracted by our busy lives or by our worries to notice him. The next time you are feeling alone or upset, find a quiet place and pray. Think about the disciples on the road to Emmaus and remember that Jesus walks with you too. Ask Jesus to let you see his presence. And be sure to remember that when the priest blesses the bread and wine, Jesus is there!

— Luke 24:13–35

35 The two then explained to them what had happened on the road, and how they had recognized the Lord when he broke the bread.

Jesus Appears to His Disciples
(Matthew 28:16–20; Mark 16:14–18; John 20:19–23; Acts 1:6–8)

36 While the two were telling them this, suddenly the Lord himself stood among them and said to them, "Peace be with you."*e*

37 They were terrified, thinking that they were seeing a ghost. 38 But he said to them, "Why are you alarmed? Why are these doubts coming up in your minds? 39 Look at my hands and my feet, and see that it is I myself. Feel me, and you will know, for a ghost doesn't have flesh and bones, as you can see I have."

40 He said this and showed them his hands and his feet.*f* 41 They still could not believe, they were so full of joy and wonder; so he asked them, "Do you have anything here to eat?" 42 They gave him a piece of cooked fish, 43 which he took and ate in their presence.

44 Then he said to them, "These are the very things I told you about while I was still with you: everything written about me in the Law of Moses, the writings of the prophets, and the Psalms had to come true."

45 Then he opened their minds to understand the Scriptures, 46 and said to them, "This is what is written: the Messiah must suffer and must rise from death three days later, 47 and in his name the message about repentance and the forgiveness of sins must be preached to all nations, beginning in Jerusalem. 48 You are witnesses of these

e 24:36 Some manuscripts do not have and said to them, "Peace be with you." f 24:40 Some manuscripts do not have verse 40.

" 'Everything written about me in the Law of Moses, the writings of the prophets, and the Psalms had to come true' " *(Luke 24:44).*

things. ⁴⁹And I myself will send upon you
what my Father has promised. But you
must wait in the city until the power from
above comes down upon you."

Jesus Is Taken Up
to Heaven
(Mark 16:19, 20; Acts 1:9–11)

⁵⁰Then he led them out of the city as far
as Bethany, where he raised his hands and
blessed them. ⁵¹As he was blessing them, he
departed from them and was taken up into
heaven.^g ⁵²They worshiped him and went
back into Jerusalem, filled with great joy,
⁵³and spent all their time in the Temple giv-
ing thanks to God.

As he was blessing them . . . (24:51)

^g **24:51** *Some manuscripts do not have* and was taken up into heaven.
24:49 Acts 1:4   **24:50, 51** Acts 1:9–11   **24:51** Sir 50:20

Your Next Step

Congratulations on finishing the Gospel of Luke!
Use this space to write your thoughts and questions about this book. If you are following the suggested reading plan, move ahead to the Acts of the
Apostles. This is the second part of Luke's two-part
series and tells the exciting story of the Apostles
and the early Church.

Luke

Have you ever heard the same family story told by different people? Maybe your grandmother tells it one way, and your dad another, and your serious aunt a very different way. Each of these stories is about the same event and is true, but the story is told from different viewpoints. That is the way it is with John's Gospel. The Gospels of Matthew, Mark, and Luke tell Jesus' story in similar ways, but John is like your aunt.

Because of this the Gospel according to John is less action oriented and more teaching oriented. Jesus performs far fewer miracles than he does in the other three Gospels. From the very beginning, John focuses on how Jesus is really the Messiah and the Son of God.

Chap. 11

Head lines

- Wedding Saved! Water Turns to Wine (2:1–12)
- Samaritan Woman's Secrets Revealed (4:4–19)
- A Few Loaves Feed Thousands (6:1–15)
- Dead Man Raised Four Days Later! (11:1–44)
- Jesus Washes Feet, Peter Shocked (chapter 13)
- Jesus Offers Prayer for Friends (chapter 17)
- Mary Magdalene Is First Witness (20:1–18)

FACTOIDS

Who wrote this book? Probably someone who knew John because the Gospel is named after the Apostle John, son of Zebedee.

When was it written? Around AD 90 to 100, about sixty years after Jesus' Resurrection.

Who was it written for? It was originally written for a community of both Jewish and Gentile (non-Jewish) Christians. John shows that Jesus is the Messiah the Jewish people expected and the Savior of all people.

Why was it written? It was written to show that Jesus is the Messiah and the Son of God and that eternal life comes only through faith in him.

What is the literary style? The book is a Gospel, which is a religious explanation of Jesus' life. It uses a lot of symbolic language.

Important themes
- Jesus is the Messiah and the divine Son of God.
- Contrasts between light and darkness, life and death, and truth and lies are made in many places.
- The role of the Holy Spirit is emphasized.

Pray It!

In the Beginning

God of all time,
As I learn about you in John's Gospel,
Help me keep my mind on the Word
    so that I stay focused on you.
Help me hear the Word
    so that I understand it with my heart.
Help me understand the Word
    so that I both know and Live It!
And help me live the Word
    so that I do more than just think about it.
When I know, and understand, and live,
    and do your Word
I will live in your love forever.
Amen.

— John 1:1–14

The Word of Life

1 ¹In the beginning the Word already existed; the Word was with God, and the Word was God. ²From the very beginning the Word was with God. ³Through him God made all things; not one thing in all creation was made without him. ⁴The Word was the source of life,ᵃ and this life brought light to people. ⁵The light shines in the darkness, and the darkness has never put it out.

⁶God sent his messenger, a man named John, ⁷who came to tell people about the light, so that all should hear the message and believe. ⁸He himself was not the light; he came to tell about the light. ⁹This was the real light—the light that comes into the world and shines on all people.

¹⁰The Word was in the world, and though God made the world through him, yet the world did not recognize him. ¹¹He came to his own country, but his own people did not receive him. ¹²Some, however, did receive him and believed in him; so he gave them the right to become God's children. ¹³They did not become God's children by natural means, that is, by being born as the children of a human father; God himself was their Father.

¹⁴The Word became a human being and, full of grace and truth, lived among us. We saw his glory, the glory which he received as the Father's only Son.

¹⁵John spoke about him. He cried out, "This is the one I was talking about when I said, 'He comes after me, but he is greater than I am, because he existed before I was born.' "

¹⁶Out of the fullness of his grace he has blessed us all, giving us one blessing after another. ¹⁷God gave the Law through Moses, but grace and truth came through Jesus Christ. ¹⁸No one has ever seen God.

ᵃ **1:4** The Word was the source of life; *or* What was made had life in union with the Word.
1:6 Mt 3:1; Mk 1:4; Lk 3:1, 2

The only Son, who is the same as God and is at the Father's side, he has made him known.

John the Baptist's Message
(Matthew 3:1–12; Mark 1:1–8; Luke 3:1–18)

19 The Jewish authorities in Jerusalem sent some priests and Levites to John to ask him, "Who are you?"

20 John did not refuse to answer, but spoke out openly and clearly, saying: "I am not the Messiah."

21 "Who are you, then?" they asked. "Are you Elijah?"

"No, I am not," John answered.

"Are you the Prophet?"[b] they asked.

"No," he replied.

22 "Then tell us who you are," they said. "We have to take an answer back to those who sent us. What do you say about yourself?"

23 John answered by quoting the prophet Isaiah:

"I am 'the voice of someone shouting in
  the desert:
  Make a straight path for the Lord to
  travel!' "

24 The messengers, who had been sent by the Pharisees, 25 then[c] asked John, "If you are not the Messiah nor Elijah nor the Prophet, why do you baptize?"

26 John answered, "I baptize with water, but among you stands the one you do not know. 27 He is coming after me, but I am not good enough even to untie his sandals."

28 All this happened in Bethany on the east side of the Jordan River, where John was baptizing.

The Lamb of God

29 The next day John saw Jesus coming to him, and said, "There is the Lamb of God, who takes away the sin of the world! 30 This is the one I was talking about when I said, 'A man is coming after me, but he is greater than I am, because he existed before I was born.' 31 I did not know who he would be, but I came baptizing with water in order to make him known to the people of Israel."

32 And John gave this testimony: "I saw the Spirit come down like a dove from heaven and stay on him. 33 I still did not know that he was the one, but God, who sent me to baptize with water, had said to me, 'You will see the Spirit come down and stay on a man; he is the one who baptizes with the Holy Spirit.' 34 I have seen it," said John, "and I tell you that he is the Son of God."

I saw the Spirit come down like a dove. (1:32)

The First Disciples of Jesus

35 The next day John was standing there again with two of his disciples, 36 when he saw Jesus walking by. "There is the Lamb of God!" he said.

37 The two disciples heard him say this and

---

[b] **1:21** THE PROPHET: *The one who was expected to appear and announce the coming of the Messiah.*   [c] **1:25** The messengers, who had been sent by the Pharisees, then; *or* Those who had been sent were Pharisees; they. **1:21** a Mal 4:5; b Deut 18:15, 18; Sir 48:10, 11   **1:23** Isa 40:3 (LXX)

went with Jesus. 38Jesus turned, saw them following him, and asked, "What are you looking for?"

They answered, "Where do you live, Rabbi?" (This word means "Teacher.")

39"Come and see," he answered. (It was then about four o'clock in the afternoon.) So they went with him and saw where he lived, and spent the rest of that day with him.

40One of them was Andrew, Simon Peter's brother. 41At once he found his brother Simon and told him, "We have found the Messiah." (This word means "Christ.") 42Then he took Simon to Jesus.

Jesus looked at him and said, "Your name is Simon son of John, but you will be called Cephas." (This is the same as Peter and means "a rock.")

Jesus Calls Philip and Nathanael

43The next day Jesus decided to go to Galilee. He found Philip and said to him, "Come with me!" (44Philip was from Bethsaida, the town where Andrew and Peter lived.) 45Philip found Nathanael and told him, "We have found the one whom Moses wrote about in the book of the Law and whom the prophets also wrote about. He is Jesus son of Joseph, from Nazareth."

46"Can anything good come from Nazareth?" Nathanael asked.

"Come and see," answered Philip.

47When Jesus saw Nathanael coming to him, he said about him, "Here is a real Israelite; there is nothing false in him!"

48Nathanael asked him, "How do you know me?"

Jesus answered, "I saw you when you were under the fig tree before Philip called you."

49"Teacher," answered Nathanael, "you are the Son of God! You are the King of Israel!"

50Jesus said, "Do you believe just because I told you I saw you when you were under the fig tree? You will see much greater things than this!" 51And he said to them, "I am telling you the truth: you will see heaven open and God's angels going up and coming down on the Son of Man."

What's Your Name?

When Jesus changes Simon's name to Cephas (John 1:42), he's showing the important role Peter would play in the Church. Often people are named for a reason—for example, in honor of a relative or a saint or another significant person. Have your ever found out why you were given the name you have? Do you know what your name means?

Here's an interesting exercise for your imagination. If you were to choose your own secret name, what would it be and why? What does this name say about you and what's important to you? You could even make a symbol of this secret name and keep it on your dresser. It would serve as a reminder of the values you want to live.

— John 1:42

The Wedding in Cana

2 1Two days later there was a wedding in the town of Cana in Galilee. Jesus' mother was there, 2and Jesus and his disciples had also been invited to the wedding. 3When the wine had given out, Jesus' mother said to him, "They are out of wine."

4"You must not tell me what to do," Jesus replied. "My time has not yet come."

5Jesus' mother then told the servants, "Do whatever he tells you."

6The Jews have rules about ritual washing, and for this purpose six stone water jars were there, each one large enough to hold between twenty and thirty gallons. 7Jesus said to the servants, "Fill these jars with water." They filled them to the brim, 8and then he told them, "Now draw some water out and take it

Mary as the First Disciple

Catholic Connections

At the beginning of chapter 2, notice that Jesus was like us—he liked parties! The wedding party was going along great. The bride and groom were happy, and the guests were having a lot of fun. Then Jesus' mother, Mary, noticed that the wine was running out. She believed Jesus could do something about it, and he did!

Mary's belief in Jesus at the wedding feast, her yes to the angel (see Luke 1:26–38), and her place at the foot of the cross (see John 19:25) all show her special place in God's plan. She is so special that she is sometimes called the first disciple. A disciple is a believer. John shows that she was one of the very first people to believe in Jesus' power.

— John 2:1–12

to the man in charge of the feast." They took him the water, ⁹which now had turned into wine, and he tasted it. He did not know where this wine had come from (but, of course, the servants who had drawn out the water knew); so he called the bridegroom ¹⁰and said to him, "Everyone else serves the best wine first, and after the guests have drunk a lot, he serves the ordinary wine. But you have kept the best wine until now!"

¹¹Jesus performed this first miracle in Cana in Galilee; there he revealed his glory, and his disciples believed in him.

"Fill these jars with water." (2:7)

¹²After this, Jesus and his mother, brothers, and disciples went to Capernaum and stayed there a few days.

Jesus Goes to the Temple
(Matthew 21:12, 13; Mark 11:15–17; Luke 19:45, 46)

¹³It was almost time for the Passover Festival, so Jesus went to Jerusalem. ¹⁴There in the Temple he found people selling cattle, sheep, and pigeons, and also the money-changers sitting at their tables. ¹⁵So he made a whip from cords and drove all the animals out of the Temple, both the sheep and the cattle; he overturned the tables of the moneychangers and scattered their coins; ¹⁶and he ordered those who sold the pigeons, "Take them out of here! Stop making my Father's house a marketplace!" ¹⁷His disciples remembered that the scripture says, "My devotion to your house, O God, burns in me like a fire."

¹⁸The Jewish authorities came back at him with a question, "What miracle can you perform to show us that you have the right to do this?"

¹⁹Jesus answered, "Tear down this Temple, and in three days I will build it again."

²⁰"Are you going to build it again in

2:12 Mt 4:13   **2:13** Ex 12:1–27   **2:17** Ps 69:9   **2:19** Mt 26:61; 27:40; Mk 14:58; 15:29

Baptism, Born Again!

Have you seen pictures or heard stories about your own Baptism? Most Catholics are baptized as infants and don't remember their Baptism. If you are like many people, you don't remember the water that was poured over your head. You don't remember the holy oil, or chrism, representing the gift of the Holy Spirit that you were crossed with. Maybe your parents kept the candle that was lit for you as a symbol of Christ's light. You might still have your baptismal clothes, which are usually white as a symbol of having our sins washed away. Baptism is the way Christians enter the Church. It is a spiritual rebirth that makes us part of God's family, and it is open to all.

The story of Jesus and Nicodemus is really about Baptism. Nicodemus gets the wrong idea, thinking that Jesus is talking about physical birth. Jesus' answer to Nicodemus tells us how important Baptism is. "'I am telling you the truth,' replied Jesus, 'that no one can enter the Kingdom of God without being born of water and the Spirit'" (John 3:5).

— John 3:1–8

Ca holic Connec ions

---

three days?" they asked him. "It has taken forty-six years to build this Temple!"

²¹But the temple Jesus was speaking about was his body. ²²So when he was raised from death, his disciples remembered that he had said this, and they believed the scripture and what Jesus had said.

Jesus' Knowledge of Human Nature

²³While Jesus was in Jerusalem during the Passover Festival, many believed in him as they saw the miracles he performed. ²⁴But Jesus did not trust himself to them, because he knew them all. ²⁵There was no need for anyone to tell him about them, because he himself knew what was in their hearts.

Jesus and Nicodemus

3 ¹There was a Jewish leader named Nicodemus, who belonged to the party of the Pharisees. ²One night he went to Jesus and said to him, "Rabbi, we know that you are a teacher sent by God. No one could perform the miracles you are doing unless God were with him."

³Jesus answered, "I am telling you the truth: no one can see the Kingdom of God without being born again."[d]

⁴"How can a grown man be born again?" Nicodemus asked. "He certainly cannot enter his mother's womb and be born a second time!"

⁵"I am telling you the truth," replied Jesus, "that no one can enter the Kingdom of God without being born of water and the Spirit. ⁶A person is born physically of human parents, but is born spiritually of the Spirit. ⁷Do not be surprised because I tell you that you must all be born again.[d] ⁸The wind blows wherever it wishes; you hear the sound it makes, but you do not know where it comes

[d] **3:3,7** again; *or* from above.

John

---

from or where it is going. It is like that with everyone who is born of the Spirit."

9"How can this be?" asked Nicodemus.

10Jesus answered, "You are a great teacher in Israel, and you don't know this? 11I am telling you the truth: we speak of what we know and report what we have seen, yet none of you is willing to accept our message. 12You do not believe me when I tell you about the things of this world; how will you ever believe me, then, when I tell you about the things of heaven? 13And no one has ever gone up to heaven except the Son of Man, who came down from heaven."*ᵉ*

14As Moses lifted up the bronze snake on a pole in the desert, in the same way the Son of Man must be lifted up, 15so that everyone who believes in him may have eternal life. 16For God loved the world so much that he gave his only Son, so that everyone who believes in him may not die but have eternal life. 17For God did not send his Son into the world to be its judge, but to be its savior.

18Those who believe in the Son are not judged; but those who do not believe have already been judged, because they have not believed in God's only Son. 19This is how the judgment works: the light has come into the world, but people love the darkness rather than the light, because their deeds are evil. 20Those who do evil things hate the light and will not come to the light, because they do not want their evil deeds to be shown up. 21But those who do what is true come to the light in order that the light may show that what they did was in obedience to God.

Jesus and John

22After this, Jesus and his disciples went to the province of Judea, where he spent some time with them and baptized. 23John also was baptizing in Aenon, not far from Salim, because there was plenty of water in that place. People were going to him, and he was

John 3:16

John 3:16 is an important line in the Bible. It is God's plan for saving the human race summed up in a simple statement. The whole Gospel is about God's love but this is the first time it is named. Because it is so important, many people memorize it. Some people even hold up signs at ball games that say "John 3:16" so others will read it.

Some people try to memorize as much of the Bible as they can. Memorizing Bible verses can be fun. Choose one that you would really like to learn. It is a good idea to ask someone (like a teacher, catechist, parent, or priest) to help you understand it first. Once you memorize it, keep it in your heart and live it!

— John 3:16

baptizing them. (24This was before John had been put in prison.)

25Some of John's disciples began arguing with a Jewᶠ about the matter of ritual washing. 26So they went to John and told him, "Teacher, you remember the man who was with you on the east side of the Jordan, the one you spoke about? Well, he is baptizing now, and everyone is going to him!"

27John answered, "No one can have anything unless God gives it. 28You yourselves are my witnesses that I said, 'I am not the Messiah, but I have been sent ahead of him.' 29The bridegroom is the one to whom the bride belongs; but the bridegroom's friend,

ᵉ 3:13 *The quotation may continue through verse 21.*   *ᶠ* 3:25 a Jew; *some manuscripts have* some Jews.
3:12 Wis 9:16, 17   **3:13** Bar 3:29   **3:14** Num 21:9; Wis 16:5–7   **3:24** Mt 14:3; Mk 6:17; Lk 3:19, 20
3:28 Jn 1:20

The story about the bronze snake *(John 3:14)* **can be found in Numbers 21:4–9.**

who stands by and listens, is glad when he hears the bridegroom's voice. This is how my own happiness is made complete. 30He must become more important while I become less important."

He Who Comes from Heaven

31He who comes from above is greater than all. He who is from the earth belongs to the earth and speaks about earthly matters, but he who comes from heaven is above all. 32He tells what he has seen and heard, yet no one accepts his message. 33But whoever accepts his message confirms by this that God is truthful. 34The one whom God has sent speaks God's words, because God gives him the fullness of his Spirit. 35The Father loves his Son and has put everything in his power. 36Whoever believes in the Son has eternal life; whoever disobeys the Son will not have life, but will remain under God's punishment.

Jesus and the Samaritan Woman

4 ¹The Pharisees heard that Jesus was winning and baptizing more disciples than John. (²Actually, Jesus himself did not baptize anyone; only his disciples did.) ³So when Jesus heard what was being said, he left Judea and went back to Galilee; ⁴on his way there he had to go through Samaria.

⁵In Samaria he came to a town named Sychar, which was not far from the field that Jacob had given to his son Joseph. ⁶Jacob's well was there, and Jesus, tired out by the trip, sat down by the well. It was about noon.

⁷A Samaritan woman came to draw some water, and Jesus said to her, "Give me a drink of water." (⁸His disciples had gone into town to buy food.)

⁹The woman answered, "You are a Jew, and I am a Samaritan—so how can you ask me for a drink?" (Jews will not use the same cups and bowls that Samaritans use.)ᵍ

10Jesus answered, "If you only knew what God gives and who it is that is asking you for a drink, you would ask him, and he would give you life-giving water."

"Give me a drink of water." (4:7)

11"Sir," the woman said, "you don't have a bucket, and the well is deep. Where would you get that life-giving water? ¹²It was our ancestor Jacob who gave us this well; he and his children and his flocks all drank from it. You don't claim to be greater than Jacob, do you?"

13Jesus answered, "Those who drink this water will get thirsty again, ¹⁴but those who drink the water that I will give them will never be thirsty again. The water that I will give them will become in them a spring which will provide them with life-giving water and give them eternal life."

15"Sir," the woman said, "give me that water! Then I will never be thirsty again, nor will I have to come here to draw water."

16"Go and call your husband," Jesus told her, "and come back."

17"I don't have a husband," she answered.

Jesus replied, "You are right when you say you don't have a husband. ¹⁸You have been married to five men, and the man you live with now is not really your husband. You have told me the truth."

19"I see you are a prophet, sir," the woman said. ²⁰"My Samaritan ancestors worshiped God on this mountain, but you Jews say that Jerusalem is the place where we should worship God."

21Jesus said to her, "Believe me, woman, the time will come when people will not worship the Father either on this mountain or in Jerusalem. ²²You Samaritans do not really know whom you worship; but we

---

ᵍ **4:9** Jews will not use the same cups and bowls that Samaritans use; *or* Jews will have nothing to do with Samaritans.

3:35 Mt 11:27; Lk 10:22 **4:5** Gen 33:19; Josh 24:32 **4:9** Ezra 4:1–5; Neh 4:1, 2

Jews know whom we worship, because it is from the Jews that salvation comes. 23But the time is coming and is already here, when by the power of God's Spirit people will worship the Father as he really is, offering him the true worship that he wants. 24God is Spirit, and only by the power of his Spirit can people worship him as he really is."

25The woman said to him, "I know that the Messiah will come, and when he comes, he will tell us everything."

26Jesus answered, "I am he, I who am talking with you."

27At that moment Jesus' disciples returned, and they were greatly surprised to find him talking with a woman. But none of them said to her, "What do you want?" or asked him, "Why are you talking with her?"

28Then the woman left her water jar, went back to the town, and said to the people there, 29"Come and see the man who told me everything I have ever done. Could he be the Messiah?" 30So they left the town and went to Jesus.

31In the meantime the disciples were begging Jesus, "Teacher, have something to eat!"

32But he answered, "I have food to eat that you know nothing about."

33So the disciples started asking among themselves, "Could somebody have brought him food?"

34"My food," Jesus said to them, "is to obey the will of the one who sent me and to finish the work he gave me to do. 35You have a saying, 'Four more months and then the harvest.' But I tell you, take a good look at the fields; the crops are now ripe and ready to be harvested! 36The one who reaps the harvest is being paid and gathers the crops for eternal life; so the one who plants and the one who reaps will be glad together. 37For the saying is true, 'Someone plants, someone else reaps.' 38I have sent you to reap a harvest in a field where you did not work; others worked there, and you profit from their work."

39Many of the Samaritans in that town believed in Jesus because the woman had said, "He told me everything I have ever done." 40So when the Samaritans came to him, they begged him to stay with them, and Jesus stayed there two days.

Who Are You Talking To?

"You shouldn't hang out with her at lunch. She is so weird."

"Let's walk this way so we don't have to go near them."

"Why is Tim talking to the new kid? He wears that weird hat and talks so funny."

Maybe you've heard, or even said, things like this. It is common for people to avoid those who are different. What is uncommon is taking a step toward getting to know those who are different. What is great about taking that step is discovering that people who are different from you have a lot to offer. When people of other cultures first came to this country as immigrants, their food and art were considered strange. Now we think of pizza, tacos, and egg rolls as regular food!

Jesus is a great example of someone who is not afraid to reach out to someone who is different from him. Not many Jewish men would talk to a woman in public, especially a Samaritan woman. Men and women were often separated, and Samaritans were disliked by the Jews. But Jesus stepped over those lines and sat with the woman at the well. The next time you come across someone who is different from you, remember how Jesus treated the woman at the well.

— John 4:1–42

41Many more believed because of his message, 42and they told the woman, "We believe now, not because of what you said, but because we ourselves have heard him, and we know that he really is the Savior of the world."

Pray It!

Help Me Believe

The father in this story believed in Jesus' power. At first he wanted Jesus to come to his house to heal his son. Jesus did not have to go to the house. He healed the boy because the father believed. Try this prayer when believing is hard for you.

> *Dear God,*
> *You healed the official's son because he believed in you.*
> *Help me to have that much faith.*
> *Help me believe in you even when it is hard.*
> *Show me how you work in my life.*
> *Teach me to give you my cares,*
> *   like the official in the story.*
> *Lead me to where you want me to be.*
> *Amen.*

— John 4:46–54

Jesus Heals an Official's Son

43After spending two days there, Jesus left and went to Galilee. **44**For he himself had said, "Prophets are not respected in their own country." **45**When he arrived in Galilee, the people there welcomed him, because they had gone to the Passover Festival in Jerusalem and had seen everything that he had done during the festival.

46Then Jesus went back to Cana in Galilee, where he had turned the water into wine. A government official was there whose son was sick in Capernaum. **47**When he heard that Jesus had come from Judea to Galilee, he went to him and asked him to go to Capernaum and heal his son, who was about to die. **48**Jesus said to him, "None of you will ever believe unless you see miracles and wonders."

49"Sir," replied the official, "come with me before my child dies."

50Jesus said to him, "Go; your son will live!"

The man believed Jesus' words and went. **51**On his way home his servants met him with the news, "Your boy is going to live!"

52He asked them what time it was when his son got better, and they answered, "It was one o'clock yesterday afternoon when the fever left him." **53**Then the father remembered that it was at that very hour when Jesus had told him, "Your son will live." So he and all his family believed.

54This was the second miracle that Jesus performed after coming from Judea to Galilee.

The Healing at the Pool

5 **1**After this, Jesus went to Jerusalem for a religious festival. **2**Near the Sheep Gate in Jerusalem there is a pool*h* with five porches; in Hebrew it is called Bethzatha.*i* **3**A

h **5:2** Near the Sheep Gate . . . a pool; *or* Near the Sheep Pool . . . a place.   *i* **5:2** Bethzatha; *some manuscripts* have Bethesda.
4:44 Mt 13:57; Mk 6:4; Lk 4:24   **4:45** Jn 2:23   **4:46** Jn 2:1–11

John

What do you know about water? How much of the human body is made of water? How long can you live without drinking?

Pray It!

Working Together

If at times you feel that your homework or chores are too much, try this prayer:

Jesus, you worked hard healing and caring for others. You were able to do all of this because of the love of your Father. Help me to work and care for others with out complaining. Help me be thankful for the ability to work, for my arms and legs—some kids can't use theirs. Help me be thankful for my brain—some kids don't learn well. Help me be thankful for homework—some kids don't have a chance to go to school. Help me be thankful for chores—some kids don't have a kitchen to do dishes in or a rug to vacuum. And most of all, help me remember to be thankful for those who care about me: family, teachers, and, of course, you. Thank you, Jesus, for the example you show me. Amen.

— John 5:1–18

large crowd of sick people were lying on the porches—the blind, the lame, and the paralyzed.[j] 5A man was there who had been sick for thirty-eight years. 6Jesus saw him lying there, and he knew that the man had been sick for such a long time; so he asked him, "Do you want to get well?"

7The sick man answered, "Sir, I don't have anyone here to put me in the pool when the water is stirred up; while I am trying to get in, somebody else gets there first."

8Jesus said to him, "Get up, pick up your mat, and walk." 9Immediately the man got well; he picked up his mat and started walking.

The day this happened was a Sabbath, 10so the Jewish authorities told the man who had been healed, "This is a Sabbath, and it is against our Law for you to carry your mat."

11He answered, "The man who made me well told me to pick up my mat and walk."

12They asked him, "Who is the man who told you to do this?"

13But the man who had been healed did not know who Jesus was, for there was a crowd in that place, and Jesus had slipped away.

14Afterward, Jesus found him in the Temple and said, "Listen, you are well now; so stop sinning or something worse may happen to you."

15Then the man left and told the Jewish authorities that it was Jesus who had healed him. 16So they began to persecute Jesus, because he had done this healing on a Sabbath. 17Jesus answered them, "My Father is always working, and I too must work."

18This saying made the Jewish authorities all the more determined to kill him; not only had he broken the Sabbath law, but he had said that God was his own Father and in this way had made himself equal with God.

The Authority of the Son

19So Jesus answered them, "I tell you the truth: the Son can do nothing on his own; he does only what he sees his Father doing.

j 5:3 *Some manuscripts add verses 3b–4:* They were waiting for the water to move, 4because every now and then an angel of the Lord went down into the pool and stirred up the water. The first sick person to go into the pool after the water was stirred up was healed from whatever disease he had.
5:10 Neh 13:19; Jer 17:21   **5:18** Wis 2:16

If you were the sick man, how would you feel after Jesus healed you? How would you feel when the authorities questioned you (John 5:1–14)?

What the Father does, the Son also does.
20For the Father loves the Son and shows
him all that he himself is doing. He will
show him even greater things to do than
this, and you will all be amazed. 21Just as the
Father raises the dead and gives them life, in
the same way the Son gives life to those he
wants to. 22Nor does the Father himself
judge anyone. He has given his Son the full
right to judge, 23so that all will honor the
Son in the same way as they honor the
Father. Whoever does not honor the Son
does not honor the Father who sent him.

24"I am telling you the truth: those who
hear my words and believe in him who sent
me have eternal life. They will not be
judged, but have already passed from death
to life. 25I am telling you the truth: the time
is coming—the time has already come—
when the dead will hear the voice of the
Son of God, and those who hear it will
come to life. 26Just as the Father is himself
the source of life, in the same way he has
made his Son to be the source of life. 27And
he has given the Son the right to judge,
because he is the Son of Man. 28Do not be
surprised at this; the time is coming when all
the dead will hear his voice 29and come out
of their graves: those who have done good
will rise and live, and those who have done
evil will rise and be condemned.

Witnesses to Jesus

30"I can do nothing on my own authority; I judge only as God tells me, so my judgment is right, because I am not trying to do
what I want, but only what he who sent me
wants.

31"If I testify on my own behalf, what I
say is not to be accepted as real proof. 32But
there is someone else who testifies on my
behalf, and I know that what he says about
me is true. 33John is the one to whom you
sent your messengers, and he spoke on
behalf of the truth. 34It is not that I must
have a human witness; I say this only in
order that you may be saved. 35John was like
a lamp, burning and shining, and you were
willing for a while to enjoy his light. 36But I

have a witness on my behalf which is even
greater than the witness that John gave: what
I do, that is, the deeds my Father gave me to
do, these speak on my behalf and show that
the Father has sent me. 37And the Father,
who sent me, also testifies on my behalf. You
have never heard his voice or seen his face,
38and you do not keep his message in your
hearts, for you do not believe in the one
whom he sent. 39You study the Scriptures,
because you think that in them you will find
eternal life. And these very Scriptures speak
about me! 40Yet you are not willing to come
to me in order to have life.

41"I am not looking for human praise.
42But I know what kind of people you are,
and I know that you have no love for God in
your hearts. 43I have come with my Father's
authority, but you have not received me;
when, however, someone comes with his
own authority, you will receive him. 44You
like to receive praise from one another, but
you do not try to win praise from the one
who alone is God; how, then, can you believe
me? 45Do not think, however, that I am the
one who will accuse you to my Father.
Moses, in whom you have put your hope, is
the very one who will accuse you. 46If you
had really believed Moses, you would have
believed me, because he wrote about me.
47But since you do not believe what he
wrote, how can you believe what I say?"

Jesus Feeds Five Thousand
(Matthew 14:13–21; Mark 6:30–44;
Luke 9:10–17)

6 1After this, Jesus went across Lake
Galilee (or, Lake Tiberias, as it is also
called). 2A large crowd followed him,
because they had seen his miracles of healing
the sick. 3Jesus went up a hill and sat down
with his disciples. 4The time for the Passover
Festival was near. 5Jesus looked around and
saw that a large crowd was coming to him,
so he asked Philip, "Where can we buy
enough food to feed all these people?" (6He
said this to test Philip; actually he already
knew what he would do.)

7Philip answered, "For everyone to have

The Eucharist Is Central!

Catholic Connections

Jesus loved a good meal! He went to weddings and ate, he ate with sinners, and he made sure people didn't go hungry. The story of how a few loaves and fishes fed thousands is in all four Gospels. The Bible references that follow the heading "Jesus Feeds Five Thousand" tell you where this story is in the other Gospels.

In John's Gospel, the story is different from the others. After the miracle, Jesus gives more teaching about the Eucharist (Holy Communion). *Eucharist* means "thanksgiving" in Greek. The Eucharist is central to the Catholic faith. Jesus says, "Those who eat my flesh and drink my blood have eternal life, and I will raise them to life on the last day" (John 6:54). Through the Eucharist we build our relationships with Jesus and with the other members of the Church. As you receive Holy Communion, remind yourself of how it unites you with Christians around the world.

— John, chapter 6

John

even a little, it would take more than two hundred silver coins*k* to buy enough bread."

8 Another one of his disciples, Andrew, who was Simon Peter's brother, said, 9 "There is a boy here who has five loaves of barley bread and two fish. But they will certainly not be enough for all these people."

10 "Make the people sit down," Jesus told them. (There was a lot of grass there.) So all the people sat down; there were about five thousand men. 11 Jesus took the bread, gave thanks to God, and distributed it to the people who were sitting there. He did the same with the fish, and they all had as much as they wanted. 12 When they were all full, he said to his disciples, "Gather the pieces left over; let us not waste a bit." 13 So they gathered them all and filled twelve baskets with the pieces left over from the five barley loaves which the people had eaten.

14 Seeing this miracle that Jesus had performed, the people there said, "Surely this is the Prophet*l* who was to come into the world!" 15 Jesus knew that they were about to come and seize him in order to make him king by force; so he went off again to the hills by himself.

Jesus Walks on the Water
(Matthew 14:22–33; Mark 6:45–52)

16 When evening came, Jesus' disciples went down to the lake, 17 got into a boat, and went back across the lake toward Capernaum. Night came on, and Jesus still had not come to them. 18 By then a strong wind was blowing and stirring up the water. 19 The disciples had rowed about three or four miles when they saw Jesus walking on the water, coming near the boat, and they were terrified. 20 "Don't be afraid," Jesus told them, "it is I!" 21 Then they willingly took him into the boat, and immediately the boat reached land at the place they were heading for.

The People Seek Jesus

22 Next day the crowd which had stayed on the other side of the lake realized that there had been only one boat there. They knew that Jesus had not gone in it with his

k 6:7 SILVER COINS: *A silver coin was the daily wage of a rural worker (see Mt 20:2).* *l* 6:14 THE PROPHET: *See 1:21.*

disciples, but that they had left without him. 23 Other boats, which were from Tiberias, came to shore near the place where the crowd had eaten the bread after the Lord had given thanks. 24 When the crowd saw that Jesus was not there, nor his disciples, they got into those boats and went to Capernaum, looking for him.

Jesus the Bread of Life

25 When the people found Jesus on the other side of the lake, they said to him, "Teacher, when did you get here?"

26 Jesus answered, "I am telling you the truth: you are looking for me because you ate the bread and had all you wanted, not because you understood my miracles. 27 Do not work for food that spoils; instead, work for the food that lasts for eternal life. This is the food which the Son of Man will give you, because God, the Father, has put his mark of approval on him."

28 So they asked him, "What can we do in order to do what God wants us to do?"

29 Jesus answered, "What God wants you to do is to believe in the one he sent."

30 They replied, "What miracle will you perform so that we may see it and believe you? What will you do? 31 Our ancestors ate manna in the desert, just as the scripture says, 'He gave them bread from heaven to eat.'"

32 "I am telling you the truth," Jesus said. "What Moses gave you was not*m* the bread from heaven; it is my Father who gives you the real bread from heaven. 33 For the bread that God gives is he who comes down from heaven and gives life to the world."

34 "Sir," they asked him, "give us this bread always."

35 "I am the bread of life," Jesus told them. "Those who come to me will never be hungry; those who believe in me will never be thirsty. 36 Now, I told you that you have seen me but will not believe. 37 Everyone whom my Father gives me will come to me. I will never turn away anyone who comes to me, 38 because I have come down from heaven to do not my own will but the will of him who sent me. 39 And it is the will of him who sent me that I should not lose any of all those he has given me, but that I should raise them all to life on the last day. 40 For what my Father wants is that all who see the Son and believe in him should have eternal life. And I will raise them to life on the last day."

41 The people started grumbling about him, because he said, "I am the bread that came down from heaven." 42 So they said, "This man is Jesus son of Joseph, isn't he? We know his father and mother. How, then, does he now say he came down from heaven?"

43 Jesus answered, "Stop grumbling among yourselves. 44 People cannot come to me unless the Father who sent me draws them to me; and I will raise them to life on the last day. 45 The prophets wrote, 'Everyone will be taught by God.' Anyone who hears the Father and learns from him comes to me. 46 This does not mean that anyone has seen the Father; he who is from God is the only one who has seen the Father. 47 I am telling you the truth: he who believes has eternal life. 48 I am the bread of life. 49 Your ancestors ate manna in the desert, but they died. 50 But the bread that comes down from heaven is of such a kind that whoever eats it will not die. 51 I am the living bread that came down from heaven. If you eat this bread, you will live forever. The bread that I will give you is my flesh, which I give so that the world may live."

52 This started an angry argument among them. "How can this man give us his flesh to eat?" they asked.

53 Jesus said to them, "I am telling you the truth: if you do not eat the flesh of the Son of Man and drink his blood, you will not have life in yourselves. 54 Those who eat my flesh and drink my blood have eternal life, and I will raise them to life on the last day. 55 For my flesh is the real food; my blood is

m **6:32** What Moses gave you was not; *or* It was not Moses who gave you.
6:27 Sir 24:19–22   **6:31** Ex 16:4, 15; Ps 78:24; Wis 16:20, 21   **6:45** Isa 54:13

John

Why would the people want to make Jesus the king (*John 6:15*)? **Why didn't Jesus want to become a king?**

the real drink. 56 Those who eat my flesh and drink my blood live in me, and I live in them. 57 The living Father sent me, and because of him I live also. In the same way whoever eats me will live because of me. 58 This, then, is the bread that came down from heaven; it is not like the bread that your ancestors ate, but then later died. Those who eat this bread will live forever."

59 Jesus said this as he taught in the synagogue in Capernaum.

The Words of Eternal Life

60 Many of his followers heard this and said, "This teaching is too hard. Who can listen to it?"

61 Without being told, Jesus knew that they were grumbling about this, so he said to them, "Does this make you want to give up? 62 Suppose, then, that you should see the Son of Man go back up to the place where he was before? 63 What gives life is God's Spirit; human power is of no use at all. The words I have spoken to you bring God's life-giving Spirit. 64 Yet some of you do not believe." (Jesus knew from the very beginning who were the ones that would not believe and which one would betray him.) 65 And he added, "This is the very reason I told you that no people can come to me unless the Father makes it possible for them to do so."

66 Because of this, many of Jesus' followers turned back and would not go with him any more. 67 So he asked the twelve disciples, "And you—would you also like to leave?"

68 Simon Peter answered him, "Lord, to whom would we go? You have the words that give eternal life. 69 And now we believe and know that you are the Holy One who has come from God."

70 Jesus replied, "I chose the twelve of you, didn't I? Yet one of you is a devil!" 71 He was talking about Judas, the son of Simon Iscariot. For Judas, even though he was one of the twelve disciples, was going to betray him.

Which Way to Go?

Have you ever thought about not following Jesus? Many of his early followers had a hard time accepting some of the things he said and some left Jesus (John 6:66). His disciples found out it was sometimes hard following Jesus. They also knew that there was no better person to follow. Sometimes we are like the people in this story, and it might seem easier to walk away from what Jesus asks us to do. It might even seem like more fun.

The next time it seems easier not following the things Jesus teaches, ask yourself or someone you trust if it really is. The disciples knew it was better to stick with Jesus. If you give it enough thought, you will realize that doing what Jesus asks is better—not easier, but better.

— John 6:60–71

Jesus and His Brothers

7 1 After this, Jesus traveled in Galilee; he did not want to travel in Judea, because the Jewish authorities there were wanting to kill him. 2 The time for the Festival of Shelters was near, 3 so Jesus' brothers said to him, "Leave this place and go to Judea, so that your followers will see the things that you are doing. 4 People don't hide what they are doing if they want to be well known. Since you are doing these things, let the whole world know about you!" (5 Not even his brothers believed in him.)

6:63 Wis 9:13–18 6:68, 69 Mt 16:16; Mk 8:29; Lk 9:20 7:2 Lev 23:34; Deut 16:13

List all the different things people said about Jesus in chapter 7. Why couldn't they agree on what to think about him?

Pray It!

Loving Either Way

"Stop judging by external standards, and judge by true standards" (John 7:24).

God, you love me whether I am skinny or large, tall or short.
Help me love others who are different from me.
You love me whether I am happy or mad.
Help me love others who are mean or angry.
You love me whether I get straight A's or fail a test.
Help me love others when they seem silly or don't make sense.
You love me whether I win or lose.
Help me love others who compete against me.
You love me no matter what.
Help me to not judge others and to love others the way you do.
Amen.

— John 7:24

---

6 Jesus said to them, "The right time for me has not yet come. Any time is right for you. 7 The world cannot hate you, but it hates me, because I keep telling it that its ways are bad. 8 You go on to the festival. I am not going[n] to this festival, because the right time has not come for me." 9 He said this and then stayed on in Galilee.

Jesus at the Festival of Shelters

10 After his brothers had gone to the festival, Jesus also went; however, he did not go openly, but secretly. 11 The Jewish authorities were looking for him at the festival. "Where is he?" they asked.

12 There was much whispering about him in the crowd. "He is a good man," some people said. "No," others said, "he fools the people." 13 But no one talked about him openly, because they were afraid of the Jewish authorities.

14 The festival was nearly half over when Jesus went to the Temple and began teaching. 15 The Jewish authorities were greatly surprised and said, "How does this man know so much when he has never been to school?"

16 Jesus answered, "What I teach is not my own teaching, but it comes from God, who sent me. 17 Whoever is willing to do what God wants will know whether what I teach comes from God or whether I speak on my own authority. 18 Those who speak on their own authority are trying to gain glory for themselves. But he who wants glory for the one who sent him is honest, and there is nothing false in him. 19 Moses gave you the Law, didn't he? But not one of you obeys the Law. Why are you trying to kill me?"

20 "You have a demon in you!" the crowd answered. "Who is trying to kill you?"

21 Jesus answered, "I performed one miracle, and you were all surprised. 22 Moses ordered you to circumcise your sons (although it was not Moses but your ancestors who started it), and so you circumcise a boy on the Sabbath. 23 If a boy is circumcised on the Sabbath so that Moses' Law is not broken, why are you angry with me because I made a man completely well on the Sabbath? 24 Stop judging by external standards, and judge by true standards."

John

---

n **7:8** I am not going; *some manuscripts have* I am not yet going.
7:22 a Lev 12:3; **b** Gen 17:10   **7:23** Jn 5:9

Is He the Messiah?

25 Some of the people of Jerusalem said, "Isn't this the man the authorities are trying to kill? 26 Look! He is talking in public, and they say nothing against him! Can it be that they really know that he is the Messiah? 27 But when the Messiah comes, no one will know where he is from. And we all know where this man comes from."

28 As Jesus taught in the Temple, he said in a loud voice, "Do you really know me and know where I am from? I have not come on my own authority. He who sent me, however, is truthful. You do not know him, 29 but I know him, because I come from him and he sent me."

30 Then they tried to seize him, but no one laid a hand on him, because his hour had not yet come. 31 But many in the crowd believed in him and said, "When the Messiah comes, will he perform more miracles than this man has?"

Guards Are Sent to Arrest Jesus

32 The Pharisees heard the crowd whispering these things about Jesus, so they and the chief priests sent some guards to arrest him. 33 Jesus said, "I shall be with you a little while longer, and then I shall go away to him who sent me. 34 You will look for me, but you will not find me, because you cannot go where I will be."

35 The Jewish authorities said among themselves, "Where is he about to go so that we shall not find him? Will he go to the Greek cities where our people live, and teach the Greeks? 36 He says that we will look for him but will not find him, and that we cannot go where he will be. What does he mean?"

Streams of Life-Giving Water

37 On the last and most important day of the festival Jesus stood up and said in a loud voice, "Whoever is thirsty should come to me, and 38 whoever believes in me should

Filling Up

There is a saying, "You are what you eat." Of course it doesn't mean you'll turn into a giant carrot if you eat a lot of vegetables. It means that eating a balanced diet usually results in looking and being healthy. And eating a lot of junk food may result in being overweight and out of shape.

How we feed our minds and souls is a little like that as well. Filling up on violent and sexual images in movies or video games, or on any other negative or destructive ideas in the media, can have a bad influence on our thinking and acting.

Instead of a diet of negative images like these, Jesus said we should come to him for life-giving water (John 7:37). Drinking from Jesus comes in many forms. During Communion we drink from the cup, taking in Jesus in a very special way. Another way to drink is through the Word of God. By studying, praying with, and living God's Word, you are feeding your mind and soul in a healthy way.

How can you be what you drink? What games, movies, or Internet sites do you avoid or need to avoid? How is the Eucharist and reading the Bible a regular part of your life?

— John 7:37–39

drink. As the scripture says, 'Streams of life-giving water will pour out from his side.' º 39 Jesus said this about the Spirit, which those

---

º **7:38** *Jesus' words in verses 37–38 may be translated:* "Whoever is thirsty should come to me and drink. 38 As the scripture says, 'Streams of life-giving water will pour out from within anyone who believes in me.' "
7:37 Lev 23:36　**7:38** Ezek 47:1; Zech 14:8

John

who believed in him were going to receive. At that time the Spirit had not yet been given, because Jesus had not been raised to glory.

Division among the People

40Some of the people in the crowd heard him say this and said, "This man is really the Prophet!"*p*

41Others said, "He is the Messiah!"

But others said, "The Messiah will not come from Galilee! **42**The scripture says that the Messiah will be a descendant of King David and will be born in Bethlehem, the town where David lived." **43**So there was a division in the crowd because of Jesus. **44**Some wanted to seize him, but no one laid a hand on him.

The Unbelief of the Jewish Authorities

45When the guards went back, the chief priests and Pharisees asked them, "Why did you not bring him?"

46The guards answered, "Nobody has ever talked the way this man does!"

47"Did he fool you, too?" the Pharisees asked them. **48**"Have you ever known one of the authorities or one Pharisee to believe in him? **49**This crowd does not know the Law of Moses, so they are under God's curse!"

50One of the Pharisees there was Nicodemus, the man who had gone to see Jesus before. He said to the others, **51**"According to our Law we cannot condemn people before hearing them and finding out what they have done."

52"Well," they answered, "are you also from Galilee? Study the Scriptures and you will learn that no prophet ever comes*q* from Galilee."

The Woman Caught in Adultery

8 **1**[Then everyone went home, but Jesus went to the Mount of Olives. **2**Early the next morning he went back to the Temple. All the people gathered around him, and he sat down and began to teach them. **3**The teachers of the Law and the Pharisees brought in a woman who had been caught committing adultery, and they made her stand before them all. **4**"Teacher," they said to Jesus, "this woman was caught in the very act of committing adultery. **5**In our Law Moses commanded that such a woman must be stoned to death. Now, what do you say?" **6**They said this to trap Jesus, so that they could accuse him. But he bent over and wrote on the ground with his finger. **7**As they stood there asking him questions, he straightened up and said to them, "Whichever one of you has committed no sin may throw the first stone at her." **8**Then he bent over again and wrote on the ground. **9**When they heard this, they all left, one by one, the older ones first. Jesus was left alone, with the woman still standing there. **10**He straightened up and said to her, "Where are they? Is there no one left to condemn you?"

11"No one, sir," she answered.

"Well, then," Jesus said, "I do not condemn you either. Go, but do not sin again."]*r*

Jesus the Light of the World

12Jesus spoke to the Pharisees again. "I am the light of the world," he said. "Whoever follows me will have the light of life and will never walk in darkness."

13The Pharisees said to him, "Now you are testifying on your own behalf; what you say proves nothing."

14"No," Jesus answered, "even though I do testify on my own behalf, what I say is true, because I know where I came from and

p **7:40** THE PROPHET: *See 1:21.* *q* **7:52** no prophet ever comes; *one manuscript has* the Prophet will not come. *r* **8:11** *Many manuscripts and early translations do not have this passage (8:1–11); others have it after Jn 21:24; others have it after Lk 21:38; one manuscript has it after Jn 7:36.*
7:42 2 Sam 7:12; Mic 5:2 **7:50** Jn 3:1, 2 **8:5** Lev 20:10; Deut 22:22–24 **8:7** Dan B:34 **8:12** Wis 7:26; Mt 5:14; Jn 9:5 **8:13** Jn 5:31

"I am the light of the world. . . . Whoever follows me will have the light of life and will never walk in darkness" *(John 8:12).*

John

John

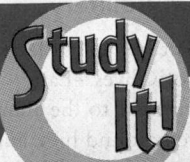

The "I Am" Sayings

In John 8:12 Jesus says, "I am the light of the world." This is one of the "I am" sayings that are found only in the Gospel of John. In these sayings Jesus compares himself to bread (6:35), light (8:12), a gate (10:7), a shepherd (10:11), and a vine (15:5): objects which were common to the people of his time. He also tells us he is "the resurrection and the life" (11:25) and "the way, the truth, and the life" (14:6).

When we read the "I am" sayings, we get a picture of Jesus as one who fills us, lights our way, protects us, provides life, brings us to God, and nurtures us. In these descriptions we come to know and understand that Jesus is the true God.

— John 8:12

where I am going. You do not know where I came from or where I am going. 15 You make judgments in a purely human way; I pass judgment on no one. 16 But if I were to do so, my judgment would be true, because I am not alone in this; the Father who sent me is with me. 17 It is written in your Law that when two witnesses agree, what they say is true. 18 I testify on my own behalf, and the Father who sent me also testifies on my behalf."

19 "Where is your father?" they asked him.

"You know neither me nor my Father," Jesus answered. "If you knew me, you would know my Father also."

20 Jesus said all this as he taught in the Temple, in the room where the offering boxes were placed. And no one arrested him, because his hour had not come.

You Cannot Go Where I Am Going

21 Again Jesus said to them, "I will go away; you will look for me, but you will die in your sins. You cannot go where I am going."

22 So the Jewish authorities said, "He says that we cannot go where he is going. Does this mean that he will kill himself?"

23 Jesus answered, "You belong to this world here below, but I come from above. You are from this world, but I am not from this world. 24 That is why I told you that you will die in your sins. And you will die in your sins if you do not believe that 'I Am Who I Am'."

25 "Who are you?" they asked him.

Jesus answered, "What I have told you from the very beginning.[s] 26 I have much to say about you, much to condemn you for. The one who sent me, however, is truthful, and I tell the world only what I have heard from him."

27 They did not understand that Jesus was talking to them about the Father. 28 So he said to them, "When you lift up the Son of Man, you will know that 'I Am Who I Am'; then you will know that I do nothing on my own authority, but I say only what the Father has instructed me to say. 29 And he who sent me is with me; he has not left me alone, because I always do what pleases him."

30 Many who heard Jesus say these things believed in him.

The Truth Will Set You Free

31 So Jesus said to those who believed in him, "If you obey my teaching, you are really my disciples; 32 you will know the truth, and the truth will set you free."

[s] **8:25** What I have told you from the very beginning; *or* Why should I speak to you at all?
8:17 Deut 19:15

Chapter 8 talks about Jesus' relationship with God the Father. How many times in chapter 8 is Father—with a capital F—mentioned?

33 "We are the descendants of Abraham," they answered, "and we have never been anybody's slaves. What do you mean, then, by saying, 'You will be free'?"

34 Jesus said to them, "I am telling you the truth: everyone who sins is a slave of sin. 35 A slave does not belong to a family permanently, but a son belongs there forever. 36 If the Son sets you free, then you will be really free. 37 I know you are Abraham's descendants. Yet you are trying to kill me, because you will not accept my teaching. 38 I talk about what my Father has shown me, but you do what your father has told you."

39 They answered him, "Our father is Abraham."

"If you really were Abraham's children," Jesus replied, "you would do[t] the same things that he did. 40 All I have ever done is to tell you the truth I heard from God, yet you are trying to kill me. Abraham did nothing like this! 41 You are doing what your father did."

"God himself is the only Father we have," they answered, "and we are his true children."

42 Jesus said to them, "If God really were your Father, you would love me, because I came from God and now I am here. I did not come on my own authority, but he sent me. 43 Why do you not understand what I say? It is because you cannot bear to listen to my message. 44 You are the children of your father, the Devil, and you want to follow your father's desires. From the very beginning he was a murderer and has never been on the side of truth, because there is no truth in him. When he tells a lie, he is only doing what is natural to him, because he is a liar and the father of all lies. 45 But I tell the truth, and that is why you do not believe me. 46 Which one of you can prove that I am guilty of sin? If I tell the truth, then why do you not believe me? 47 He who comes from God listens to God's words. You, however, are not from God, and that is why you will not listen."

Jesus and Abraham

48 They asked Jesus, "Were we not right in saying that you are a Samaritan and have a demon in you?"

49 "I have no demon," Jesus answered. "I honor my Father, but you dishonor me. 50 I am not seeking honor for myself. But there is one who is seeking it and who judges in my favor. 51 I am telling you the truth: whoever obeys my teaching will never die."

52 They said to him, "Now we know for sure that you have a demon! Abraham died, and the prophets died, yet you say that whoever obeys your teaching will never die. 53 Our father Abraham died; you do not claim to be greater than Abraham, do you? And the prophets also died. Who do you think you are?"

54 Jesus answered, "If I were to honor myself, that honor would be worth nothing. The one who honors me is my Father—the very one you say is your God. 55 You have never known him, but I know him. If I were to say that I do not know him, I would be a liar like you. But I do know him, and I obey his word. 56 Your father Abraham rejoiced that he was to see the time of my coming; he saw it and was glad."

57 They said to him, "You are not even fifty years old—and you have seen Abraham?"[u]

58 "I am telling you the truth," Jesus replied. "Before Abraham was born, 'I Am'."

59 Then they picked up stones to throw at him, but Jesus hid himself and left the Temple.

Jesus Heals a Man Born Blind

9 1 As Jesus was walking along, he saw a man who had been born blind. 2 His disciples asked him, "Teacher, whose sin caused him to be born blind? Was it his own or his parents' sin?"

3 Jesus answered, "His blindness has nothing to do with his sins or his parents' sins. He is blind so that God's power might be seen at work in him. 4 As long as it is day, we must do the work of him who sent me;

John

---

t **8:39** If you really were . . . you would do; *some manuscripts have* If you are . . . do.   *u* **8:57** you have seen Abraham?; *some manuscripts have* has Abraham seen you?
8:33 Mt 3:9; Lk 3:8   **8:44** Wis 1:13; 2:24

night is coming when no one can work. [5] While I am in the world, I am the light for the world."

[6] After he said this, Jesus spat on the ground and made some mud with the spittle; he rubbed the mud on the man's eyes [7] and told him, "Go and wash your face in the Pool of Siloam." (This name means "Sent.") So the man went, washed his face, and came back seeing.

[8] His neighbors, then, and the people who had seen him begging before this, asked, "Isn't this the man who used to sit and beg?"

[9] Some said, "He is the one," but others said, "No he isn't; he just looks like him."

So the man himself said, "I am the man."

[10] "How is it that you can now see?" they asked him.

[11] He answered, "The man called Jesus made some mud, rubbed it on my eyes, and told me to go to Siloam and wash my face. So I went, and as soon as I washed, I could see."

[12] "Where is he?" they asked.

"I don't know," he answered.

The Pharisees Investigate the Healing

[13] Then they took to the Pharisees the man who had been blind. [14] The day that Jesus made the mud and cured him of his blindness was a Sabbath. [15] The Pharisees, then, asked the man again how he had received his sight. He told them, "He put some mud on my eyes; I washed my face, and now I can see."

[16] Some of the Pharisees said, "The man who did this cannot be from God, for he does not obey the Sabbath law."

Others, however, said, "How could a man who is a sinner perform such miracles as these?" And there was a division among them.

[17] So the Pharisees asked the man once more, "You say he cured you of your blindness—well, what do you say about him?"

"He is a prophet," the man answered.

[18] The Jewish authorities, however, were not willing to believe that he had been blind and could now see, until they called his par-

Differently Abled

Keith gets around school using a walker. Kids in the hallway sometimes follow him and imitate his limp. He knows they do it and ignores them because he also knows that he is the best speller in school. Even though he can't join the track team or play football, he always wins the spelling bee.

Jesus didn't care if someone was blind or lame or dirty or different from others. He loved everyone equally. Some people ignored these people; Jesus loved them and helped them. Jesus knew that all people have value and something to share with others.

Today people with disabilities sometimes consider themselves "differently abled." Do you know someone who has a disability that makes them stronger in another area? Take the opportunity to get to know someone who is different or has a disability.

— John 9:1–7

ents [19] and asked them, "Is this your son? You say that he was born blind; how is it, then, that he can now see?"

[20] His parents answered, "We know that he is our son, and we know that he was born blind. [21] But we do not know how it is that he is now able to see, nor do we know who cured him of his blindness. Ask him; he is old enough, and he can answer for himself!" [22] His parents said this because they were afraid of the Jewish authorities, who had already agreed that anyone who said he believed that Jesus was the Messiah would be expelled from the synagogue. [23] That is why his parents said, "He is old enough; ask him!"

John

24 A second time they called back the man who had been born blind, and said to him, "Promise before God that you will tell the truth! We know that this man who cured you is a sinner."

25 "I do not know if he is a sinner or not," the man replied. "One thing I do know: I was blind, and now I see."

26 "What did he do to you?" they asked. "How did he cure you of your blindness?"

27 "I have already told you," he answered, "and you would not listen. Why do you want to hear it again? Maybe you, too, would like to be his disciples?"

28 They insulted him and said, "You are that fellow's disciple; but we are Moses' disciples. 29 We know that God spoke to Moses; as for that fellow, however, we do not even know where he comes from!"

30 The man answered, "What a strange thing that is! You do not know where he comes from, but he cured me of my blindness! 31 We know that God does not listen to sinners; he does listen to people who respect him and do what he wants them to do. 32 Since the beginning of the world nobody has ever heard of anyone giving sight to a person born blind. 33 Unless this man came from God, he would not be able to do a thing."

34 They answered, "You were born and brought up in sin—and you are trying to teach us?" And they expelled him from the synagogue.

Spiritual Blindness

35 When Jesus heard what had happened, he found the man and asked him, "Do you believe in the Son of Man?"

36 The man answered, "Tell me who he is, sir, so that I can believe in him!"

37 Jesus said to him, "You have already seen him, and he is the one who is talking with you now."

38 "I believe, Lord!" the man said, and knelt down before Jesus.

39 Jesus said, "I came to this world to judge, so that the blind should see and those who see should become blind."

40 Some Pharisees who were there with him heard him say this and asked him, "Surely you don't mean that we are blind, too?"

41 Jesus answered, "If you were blind, then you would not be guilty; but since you claim that you can see, this means that you are still guilty."

The Parable of the Shepherd

10 1 Jesus said, "I am telling you the truth: the man who does not enter the sheep pen by the gate, but climbs in some other way, is a thief and a robber. 2 The man who goes in through the gate is the shepherd of the sheep. 3 The gatekeeper opens the gate for him; the sheep hear his voice as he calls his own sheep by name, and he leads them out. 4 When he has brought them out, he goes ahead of them, and the sheep follow him, because they know his voice. 5 They will not follow someone else; instead, they will run away from such a person, because they do not know his voice."

6 Jesus told them this parable, but they did not understand what he meant.

Jesus the Good Shepherd

7 So Jesus said again, "I am telling you the truth: I am the gate for the sheep. 8 All others who came before me are thieves and robbers, but the sheep did not listen to them. 9 I am the gate. Those who come in by me will be saved; they will come in and go out and find pasture. 10 The thief comes only in order to steal, kill, and destroy. I have come in order that you might have life—life in all its fullness.

11 "I am the good shepherd, who is willing to die for the sheep. 12 When the hired man, who is not a shepherd and does not own the sheep, sees a wolf coming, he leaves the sheep and runs away; so the wolf snatches the sheep

John

10:11 Sir 18:13

Unscramble these letters to form two words that are the materials Jesus used to heal the man born blind: tpislet, udm.

Jesus the Firefighter?

Who protects you? Your parents? Your teachers? The police and fire departments? Who else? Would these people do anything to keep you safe? If Jesus were speaking today, maybe he would say, "I am the good firefighter."

In Jesus' time and place, shepherds were common. They were protectors of their flocks. The flock Jesus was talking about in John 10:14–18 is not a flock of sheep. It is a group of people—his people. Jesus is saying that he will do anything to protect his people and to bring them together. He loves everyone so much, he tells them he will even die for them. He tells his followers that he will do all of this because God, his Father, wants him to free everyone, to be the Savior of all.

— John 10:7–21

and scatters them. 13The hired man runs away because he is only a hired man and does not care about the sheep. 14-15I am the good shepherd. As the Father knows me and I know the Father, in the same way I know my sheep and they know me. And I am willing to die for them. 16There are other sheep which belong to me that are not in this sheep pen. I must bring them, too; they will listen to my voice, and they will become*v* one flock with one shepherd.

17"The Father loves me because I am willing to give up my life, in order that I may receive it back again. 18No one takes my life away from me. I give it up of my own free will. I have the right to give it up, and I have the right to take it back. This is what my Father has commanded me to do."

19Again there was a division among the people because of these words. 20Many of them were saying, "He has a demon! He is crazy! Why do you listen to him?"

21But others were saying, "A man with a demon could not talk like this! How could a demon give sight to blind people?"

Jesus Is Rejected

22It was winter, and the Festival of the Dedication of the Temple was being celebrated in Jerusalem. 23Jesus was walking in Solomon's Porch in the Temple, 24when the people gathered around him and asked, "How long are you going to keep us in suspense? Tell us the plain truth: are you the Messiah?"

25Jesus answered, "I have already told you, but you would not believe me. The deeds I do by my Father's authority speak on my behalf; 26but you will not believe, for you are not my sheep. 27My sheep listen to my voice; I know them, and they follow me. 28I give them eternal life, and they shall never die. No one can snatch them away from me. 29What my Father has given me is greater*w* than everything, and no one can snatch them away from the Father's care. 30The Father and I are one."

31Then the people again picked up stones to throw at him. 32Jesus said to them, "I have done many good deeds in your presence which the Father gave me to do; for which one of these do you want to stone me?"

33They answered, "We do not want to stone you because of any good deeds, but because of your blasphemy! You are only a man, but you are trying to make yourself God!"

v **10:16** they will become; *some manuscripts have* there will be. *w* **10:29** What my Father has given me is greater; *some manuscripts have* My Father, who gave them to me, is greater.
10:15 Mt 11:27; Lk 10:22 **10:22** 1 Macc 4:36, 52–59; 2 Macc 1:18; 10:5 **10:29** Wis 3:1 **10:33** Lev 24:16

34Jesus answered, "It is written in your own Law that God said, 'You are gods.' 35We know that what the scripture says is true forever; and God called those people gods, the people to whom his message was given. 36As for me, the Father chose me and sent me into the world. How, then, can you say that I blaspheme because I said that I am the Son of God? 37Do not believe me, then, if I am not doing the things my Father wants me to do. 38But if I do them, even though you do not believe me, you should at least believe my deeds, in order that you may know once and for all that the Father is in me and that I am in the Father."

39Once more they tried to seize Jesus, but he slipped out of their hands.

40Jesus then went back again across the Jordan River to the place where John had been baptizing, and he stayed there. 41Many people came to him. "John performed no miracles," they said, "but everything he said about this man was true." 42And many people there believed in him.

The Death of Lazarus

11 1 A man named Lazarus, who lived in Bethany, became sick. Bethany was the town where Mary and her sister Martha lived. (2This Mary was the one who poured the perfume on the Lord's feet and wiped them with her hair; it was her brother Lazarus who was sick.) 3The sisters sent Jesus a message: "Lord, your dear friend is sick."

4When Jesus heard it, he said, "The final result of this sickness will not be the death of Lazarus; this has happened in order to bring glory to God, and it will be the means by which the Son of God will receive glory."

5Jesus loved Martha and her sister and Lazarus. 6Yet when he received the news that Lazarus was sick, he stayed where he was for two more days. 7Then he said to the disciples, "Let us go back to Judea."

8"Teacher," the disciples answered, "just a short time ago the people there wanted to stone you; and are you planning to go back?"

9Jesus said, "A day has twelve hours, doesn't it? So those who walk in broad day-

light do not stumble, for they see the light of this world. 10But if they walk during the night they stumble, because they have no light." 11Jesus said this and then added, "Our friend Lazarus has fallen asleep, but I will go and wake him up."

12The disciples answered, "If he is asleep, Lord, he will get well."

13Jesus meant that Lazarus had died, but they thought he meant natural sleep. 14So Jesus told them plainly, "Lazarus is dead, 15but for your sake I am glad that I was not with him, so that you will believe. Let us go to him."

16Thomas (called the Twin) said to his fellow disciples, "Let us all go along with the Teacher, so that we may die with him!"

Jesus the Resurrection and the Life

17When Jesus arrived, he found that Lazarus had been buried four days before. 18Bethany was less than two miles from Jerusalem, 19and many Judeans had come to see Martha and Mary to comfort them about their brother's death.

20When Martha heard that Jesus was coming, she went out to meet him, but Mary stayed in the house. 21Martha said to Jesus, "If you had been here, Lord, my brother would not have died! 22But I know that even now God will give you whatever you ask him for."

23"Your brother will rise to life," Jesus told her.

24"I know," she replied, "that he will rise to life on the last day."

25Jesus said to her, "I am the resurrection and the life. Those who believe in me will live, even though they die; 26and those who live and believe in me will never die. Do you believe this?"

27"Yes, Lord!" she answered. "I do believe that you are the Messiah, the Son of God, who was to come into the world."

Jesus Weeps

28After Martha said this, she went back and called her sister Mary privately. "The Teacher is here," she told her, "and is asking for you." 29When Mary heard this, she got

John

10:34 Ps 82:6   **10:40** Jn 1:28   **11:1** Lk 10:38, 39   **11:2** Jn 12:3   **11:24** 2 Macc 7:22, 23; 12:44

Pray It!

Jesus Felt Just Like I Do!

Life can be frustrating. If your team loses, if you get a bad grade, if your home life is bad, or if your little sister bugs you too much, it can make you want to cry. Go ahead, Jesus cried when his friend died (John 11:35). Jesus also got upset, had fun with his friends, went to weddings and feasts, and did a lot of other things normal people do. It is great to know that Jesus is really human and that he is really God. So the next time you are feeling some big emotion, remember that Jesus probably felt the same way once too. It can help to take some time and write a prayer to share your emotions with God. Here's a formula you can use.

Jesus, today I feel _____ (write the emotion) because of _____ (write what made you feel that way). Did you feel that way too? I thank you for being human; it's nice to know that you felt _____ (the emotion) sometimes. Help me be more like you in other ways too. Amen.

— John 11:28–37

up and hurried out to meet him. (³⁰Jesus had not yet arrived in the village, but was still in the place where Martha had met him.) ³¹The people who were in the house with Mary comforting her followed her when they saw her get up and hurry out. They thought that she was going to the grave to weep there.

³²Mary arrived where Jesus was, and as soon as she saw him, she fell at his feet. "Lord," she said, "if you had been here, my brother would not have died!"

³³Jesus saw her weeping, and he saw how the people with her were weeping also; his heart was touched, and he was deeply moved. ³⁴"Where have you buried him?" he asked them.

"Come and see, Lord," they answered.

³⁵Jesus wept. ³⁶"See how much he loved him!" the people said.

³⁷But some of them said, "He gave sight to the blind man, didn't he? Could he not have kept Lazarus from dying?"

Lazarus Is Brought to Life

³⁸Deeply moved once more, Jesus went to the tomb, which was a cave with a stone

placed at the entrance. ³⁹"Take the stone away!" Jesus ordered.

Martha, the dead man's sister, answered, "There will be a bad smell, Lord. He has been buried four days!"

⁴⁰Jesus said to her, "Didn't I tell you that you would see God's glory if you believed?" ⁴¹They took the stone away. Jesus looked up and said, "I thank you, Father, that you listen to me. ⁴²I know that you always listen to me, but I say this for the sake of the people here, so that they will believe that you sent me." ⁴³After he had said this, he called out in a loud voice, "Lazarus, come out!" ⁴⁴He came out, his hands and feet wrapped in grave cloths, and with a cloth around his face. "Untie him," Jesus told them, "and let him go."

The Plot against Jesus
(Matthew 26:1–5; Mark 14:1, 2; Luke 22:1, 2)

⁴⁵Many of the people who had come to visit Mary saw what Jesus did, and they believed in him. ⁴⁶But some of them returned to the Pharisees and told them what Jesus had done. ⁴⁷So the Pharisees and

the chief priests met with the Council and said, "What shall we do? Look at all the miracles this man is performing! 48If we let him go on in this way, everyone will believe in him, and the Roman authorities will take action and destroy our Temple and our nation!"

"Lazarus, come out!" (11:43)

49One of them, named Caiaphas, who was High Priest that year, said, "What fools you are! 50Don't you realize that it is better for you to have one man die for the people, instead of having the whole nation destroyed?" 51Actually, he did not say this of his own accord; rather, as he was High Priest that year, he was prophesying that Jesus was going to die for the Jewish people, 52and not only for them, but also to bring together into one body all the scattered people of God.

53From that day on the Jewish authorities made plans to kill Jesus. 54So Jesus did not travel openly in Judea, but left and went to a place near the desert, to a town named Ephraim, where he stayed with the disciples.

55The time for the Passover Festival was near, and many people went up from the country to Jerusalem to perform the ritual of purification before the festival. 56They were looking for Jesus, and as they gathered in the Temple, they asked one another, "What do you think? Surely he will not come to the festival, will he?" 57The chief priests and the Pharisees had given orders that if anyone knew where Jesus was, he must report it, so that they could arrest him.

Jesus Is Anointed at Bethany
(Matthew 26:6–13; Mark 14:3–9)

12 1Six days before the Passover, Jesus went to Bethany, the home of Lazarus, the man he had raised from death. 2They prepared a dinner for him there, which Martha helped serve; Lazarus was one of those who were sitting at the table with Jesus. 3Then Mary took a whole pint of a very expensive perfume made of pure nard, poured it on Jesus' feet, and wiped them with her hair. The sweet smell of the perfume filled the whole house. 4One of Jesus' disciples, Judas Iscariot—the one who was going to betray him—said, 5"Why wasn't this perfume sold for three hundred silver coins*x* and the money given to the poor?" 6He said this, not because he cared about the poor, but because he was a thief. He carried the money bag and would help himself from it.

7But Jesus said, "Leave her alone! Let her keep what she has for the day of my burial. 8You will always have poor people with you, but you will not always have me."

The Plot against Lazarus

9A large number of people heard that Jesus was in Bethany, so they went there, not only because of Jesus but also to see Lazarus, whom Jesus had raised from death. 10So the chief priests made plans to kill Lazarus too, 11because on his account many Jews were rejecting them and believing in Jesus.

The Triumphant Entry into Jerusalem
(Matthew 21:1–11; Mark 11:1–11; Luke 19:28–40)

12The next day the large crowd that had come to the Passover Festival heard that Jesus was coming to Jerusalem. 13So they took branches of palm trees and went out to meet

x **12:5** SILVER COINS: *See 6:7.*
12:3 Lk 7:37, 38   **12:8** Deut 15:11   **12:13** Ps 118:25, 26; 1 Macc 13:51

Jesus was very close friends with Martha, Mary, and Lazarus. Read Luke 10:38–42 for another story about Martha and Mary.

him, shouting, "Praise God! God bless him who comes in the name of the Lord! God bless the King of Israel!"

¹⁴Jesus found a donkey and rode on it, just as the scripture says,

¹⁵"Do not be afraid, city of Zion!
   Here comes your king,
      riding on a young donkey."

¹⁶His disciples did not understand this at the time; but when Jesus had been raised to glory, they remembered that the scripture said this about him and that they had done this for him.

¹⁷The people who had been with Jesus when he called Lazarus out of the grave and raised him from death had reported what had happened. ¹⁸That was why the crowd met him—because they heard that he had performed this miracle. ¹⁹The Pharisees then said to one another, "You see, we are not succeeding at all! Look, the whole world is following him!"

Some Greeks Seek Jesus

²⁰Some Greeks were among those who had gone to Jerusalem to worship during the festival. ²¹They went to Philip (he was from Bethsaida in Galilee) and said, "Sir, we want to see Jesus."

²²Philip went and told Andrew, and the two of them went and told Jesus. ²³Jesus answered them, "The hour has now come for the Son of Man to receive great glory. ²⁴I am telling you the truth: a grain of wheat remains no more than a single grain unless it is dropped into the ground and dies. If it does die, then it produces many grains. ²⁵Those who love their own life will lose it; those who hate their own life in this world will keep it for life eternal. ²⁶Whoever wants to serve me must follow me, so that my servant will be with me where I am. And my Father will honor anyone who serves me.

Live It!

Being Good Seeds

Most kindergarten classes grow beans. The teacher gives each child a paper cup with some earth, then a bean seed. The children cover the seed with soil and they water the seed. Maybe you remember doing this. If so, you probably also remember the wait (which seemed like forever) and the joy when the little sprout first came up from the earth.

Jesus talks about growing things from seeds in John 12:22–26. He talks about how a grain of wheat must fall to the ground in order for plants to grow. In this passage he is talking about himself and how his death will be like a seed that will help others live.

What type of seeds are you planting in your life? If you study and try hard in school, you're planting seeds that may grow into a college education. If you eat a good diet and exercise regularly, you are planting seeds for a healthy body and mind. If you learn about God and follow Jesus, you're planting seeds that will grow into a holy life.

The next time you are making a decision about what to do, ask yourself what type of seed it is that you're planting. If it is a good seed, it'll grow into something good.

— John 12:22–26

12:15 Zech 9:9   12:25 Mt 10:39; 16:25; Mk 8:35; Lk 9:24; 17:33

Which Sunday of the Church year are we given palm branches in honor of Jesus' triumphant entry into Jerusalem?

John

Jesus Speaks about His Death

27"Now my heart is troubled—and what shall I say? Shall I say, 'Father, do not let this hour come upon me'? But that is why I came—so that I might go through this hour of suffering. 28 Father, bring glory to your name!"

Then a voice spoke from heaven, "I have brought glory to it, and I will do so again."

29 The crowd standing there heard the voice, and some of them said it was thunder, while others said, "An angel spoke to him!"

30 But Jesus said to them, "It was not for my sake that this voice spoke, but for yours. 31 Now is the time for this world to be judged; now the ruler of this world will be overthrown. 32 When I am lifted up from the earth, I will draw everyone to me." (33 In saying this he indicated the kind of death he was going to suffer.)

34 The crowd answered, "Our Law tells us that the Messiah will live forever. How, then, can you say that the Son of Man must be lifted up? Who is this Son of Man?"

35 Jesus answered, "The light will be among you a little longer. Continue on your way while you have the light, so that the darkness will not come upon you; for the one who walks in the dark does not know where he is going. 36 Believe in the light, then, while you have it, so that you will be the people of the light."

The Unbelief of the People

After Jesus said this, he went off and hid himself from them. 37 Even though he had performed all these miracles in their presence, they did not believe in him, 38 so that what the prophet Isaiah had said might come true:

"Lord, who believed the message we told?
To whom did the Lord reveal his
   power?"

39 And so they were not able to believe, because Isaiah also said,

40 "God has blinded their eyes
   and closed their minds,

so that their eyes would not see,
   and their minds would not understand,
   and they would not turn to me, says
      God,
   for me to heal them."

41 Isaiah said this because he saw Jesus' glory and spoke about him.

42 Even then, many Jewish authorities believed in Jesus; but because of the Pharisees they did not talk about it openly, so as not to be expelled from the synagogue. 43 They loved human approval rather than the approval of God.

Judgment by Jesus' Words

44 Jesus said in a loud voice, "Whoever believes in me believes not only in me but also in him who sent me. 45 Whoever sees me sees also him who sent me. 46 I have come into the world as light, so that everyone who believes in me should not remain in the darkness. 47 If people hear my message and do not obey it, I will not judge them. I came, not to judge the world, but to save it. 48 Those who reject me and do not accept my message have one who will judge them. The words I have spoken will be their judge on the last day! 49 This is true, because I have not spoken on my own authority, but the Father who sent me has commanded me what I must say and speak. 50 And I know that his command brings eternal life. What I say, then, is what the Father has told me to say."

Jesus Washes His Disciples' Feet

13 1 It was now the day before the Passover Festival. Jesus knew that the hour had come for him to leave this world and go to the Father. He had always loved those in the world who were his own, and he loved them to the very end.

2 Jesus and his disciples were at supper. The Devil had already put into the heart of Judas, the son of Simon Iscariot, the thought of betraying Jesus.y 3 Jesus knew that the Father had given him complete power; he knew

y 13:2 The Devil . . . betraying Jesus; or The Devil had already decided that Judas, the son of Simon Iscariot, would betray Jesus.
12:34 Ps 110:4; Isa 9:7; Ezek 37:25; Dan 7:14   12:38 Isa 53:1 (LXX)   12:40 Isa 6:10 (LXX)

The Triduum, Three Special Days

Catholic Connections

Holy Thursday, Good Friday, and Holy Saturday are three very special days in the Catholic calendar. These three days before Easter Sunday are one celebration called the Triduum. On Holy Thursday, John 13:1–15 is the Gospel read in Church. A foot-washing ritual is part of Thursday's services. On Good Friday, chapters 18–19 of John are read, a dramatic reminder of Jesus' Passion and death. The cross is given special treatment; some people kiss it, and others show love and respect for it in other ways.

On Holy Saturday the Triduum's highlight is the Easter Vigil. The Easter Vigil is the greatest celebration of the year. It is a beautiful liturgy in which we celebrate Christ's Resurrection. The liturgy uses fire and water. It is also the time when the catechumens—those older teens and adults who have been preparing to become Catholic—are baptized, confirmed and receive Holy Communion for the first time.

— John 13:1–17

that he had come from God and was going to God. 4So he rose from the table, took off his outer garment, and tied a towel around his waist. 5Then he poured some water into a washbasin and began to wash the disciples' feet and dry them with the towel around his waist. 6He came to Simon Peter, who said to him, "Are you going to wash my feet, Lord?"

7Jesus answered him, "You do not understand now what I am doing, but you will understand later."

8Peter declared, "Never at any time will you wash my feet!"

"If I do not wash your feet," Jesus answered, "you will no longer be my disciple."

9Simon Peter answered, "Lord, do not wash only my feet, then! Wash my hands and head, too!"

10Jesus said, "Those who have taken a bath are completely clean and do not have to wash themselves, except for their feet. z All of you are clean—all except one." (11Jesus already knew who was going to betray him; that is why he said, "All of you, except one, are clean.")

12After Jesus had washed their feet, he put his outer garment back on and returned to his place at the table. "Do you understand what I have just done to you?" he asked. 13"You call me Teacher and Lord, and it is right that you do so, because that is what I am. 14I, your Lord and Teacher, have just washed your feet. You, then, should wash one another's feet. 15I have set an example for you, so that you will do just what I have done for you. 16I am telling you the truth: no slaves are greater than their master, and no messengers are greater than the one who sent them. 17Now that you know this truth, how happy you will be if you put it into practice!

18"I am not talking about all of you; I know those I have chosen. But the scripture must come true that says, 'The man who shared my food turned against me.' 19I tell you this now before it happens, so that when it does happen, you will believe that 'I Am Who I Am.' 20I am telling you the truth: whoever receives anyone I send receives me also; and whoever receives me receives him who sent me."

z **13:10** *Some manuscripts do not have* except for their feet.
13:12–15 Lk 22:27   **13:16** Mt 10:24; Lk 6:40; Jn 15:20   **13:18** Ps 41:9   **13:20** Mt 10:40; Mk 9:37; Lk 9:48; 10:16

Jesus Predicts His Betrayal

(Matthew 26:20–25; Mark 14:17–21; Luke 22:21–23)

²¹After Jesus had said this, he was deeply troubled and declared openly, "I am telling you the truth: one of you is going to betray me."

The disciples looked at one another. (13:22)

²²The disciples looked at one another, completely puzzled about whom he meant. ²³One of the disciples, the one whom Jesus loved, was sitting next to Jesus. ²⁴Simon Peter motioned to him and said, "Ask him whom he is talking about."

²⁵So that disciple moved closer to Jesus' side and asked, "Who is it, Lord?"

²⁶Jesus answered, "I will dip some bread in the sauce and give it to him; he is the man." So he took a piece of bread, dipped it, and gave it to Judas, the son of Simon Iscariot. ²⁷As soon as Judas took the bread, Satan entered into him. Jesus said to him, "Hurry and do what you must!" ²⁸None of the others at the table understood why Jesus said this to him. ²⁹Since Judas was in charge of the money bag, some of the disciples thought that Jesus had told him to go and buy what they needed for the festival, or to give something to the poor.

³⁰Judas accepted the bread and went out at once. It was night.

The New Commandment

³¹After Judas had left, Jesus said, "Now the Son of Man's glory is revealed; now God's glory is revealed through him. ³²And if God's glory is revealed through him, then God will reveal the glory of the Son of Man in himself, and he will do so at once. ³³My children, I shall not be with you very much

13:33 Jn 7:34

Waiting for Heaven

Kali had to wait for everything. She couldn't get her ears pierced until she turned 13 (even though all the other girls in the sixth grade already had their ears done). She couldn't go to the same movies her older brother went to. She couldn't even stay up to see the 10 o'clock shows. To Kali it seemed like she couldn't do anything, and she was always waiting.

Peter didn't want to wait either. When Jesus talked about leaving his disciples, Peter wanted to know where he was going (John 13:36). Jesus said, "You cannot follow me now where I am going." Peter had to learn to wait, and he made a few mistakes before he was able to follow Jesus. In this passage Jesus tells us that we all have a place in heaven. Jesus himself will lead us there. Our time on earth is a preparation—the more we get to know Jesus now, the better prepared we will be for heaven later.

So don't waste your time! Prepare for heaven by getting to know Jesus. The Church gives us lots of ways to know Jesus better. Receiving Holy Eucharist, receiving the sacrament of Penance and Reconciliation, going to religious education classes, and attending youth retreats are all ways you can get to know Jesus better. Are you putting your best energy into these things or just going through the motions?

— John 13:36—14:7

longer. You will look for me; but I tell you now what I told the Jewish authorities, 'You cannot go where I am going.' 34And now I give you a new commandment: love one another. As I have loved you, so you must love one another. 35If you have love for one another, then everyone will know that you are my disciples."

Jesus Predicts Peter's Denial
(Matthew 26:31–35; Mark 14:27–31; Luke 22:31–34)

36"Where are you going, Lord?" Simon Peter asked him.

"You cannot follow me now where I am going," answered Jesus; "but later you will follow me."

37"Lord, why can't I follow you now?" asked Peter. "I am ready to die for you!"

38Jesus answered, "Are you really ready to die for me? I am telling you the truth: before the rooster crows you will say three times that you do not know me.

Jesus the Way to the Father

14 1"Do not be worried and upset," Jesus told them. "Believe*a* in God and believe also in me. 2There are many rooms in my Father's house, and I am going to prepare a place for you. I would not tell you this if it were not so.*b* 3And after I go and prepare a place for you, I will come back and take you to myself, so that you will be where I am. 4You know the way that leads to the place where I am going."

5Thomas said to him, "Lord, we do not know where you are going; so how can we know the way to get there?"

6Jesus answered him, "I am the way, the truth, and the life; no one goes to the Father except by me. 7Now that you have known me," he said to them, "you will know*c* my Father also, and from now on you do know him and you have seen him."

8Philip said to him, "Lord, show us the Father; that is all we need."

9Jesus answered, "For a long time I have been with you all; yet you do not know me, Philip? Whoever has seen me has seen the Father. Why, then, do you say, 'Show us the Father'? 10Do you not believe, Philip, that I am in the Father and the Father is in me? The words that I have spoken to you," Jesus said to his disciples, "do not come from me. The Father, who remains in me, does his own work. 11Believe me when I say that I am in the Father and the Father is in me. If not, believe because of the things I do. 12I am telling you the truth: those who believe in me will do what I do—yes, they will do even greater things, because I am going to the Father. 13And I will do whatever you ask for in my name, so that the Father's glory will be shown through the Son. 14If you ask me*d* for anything in my name, I will do it.

The Promise of the Holy Spirit

15"If you love me, you will obey my commandments. 16I will ask the Father, and he will give you another Helper, who will stay with you forever. 17He is the Spirit, who reveals the truth about God. The world cannot receive him, because it cannot see him or know him. But you know him, because he remains with you and is*e* in you.

18"When I go, you will not be left all alone; I will come back to you. 19In a little while the world will see me no more, but you will see me; and because I live, you also will live. 20When that day comes, you will know that I am in my Father and that you are in me, just as I am in you.

21"Those who accept my commandments and obey them are the ones who love me.

---

a **14:1** Believe; *or* You believe.   *b* **14:2** There are . . . were not so; *or* There are many rooms in my Father's house; if it were not so, would I tell you that I am going to prepare a place for you?   *c* **14:7** Now that you have known me . . . you will know; *some manuscripts have* If you had known me . . . you would know.   *d* **14:14** *Some manuscripts do not have* me.   *e* **14:17** is; *some manuscripts have* will be.
13:34 Jn 15:12, 17; 1 Jn 3:23; 2 Jn 5   **14:6** Bar 3:13, 14   **14:15** Wis 6:18   **14:21** Wis 6:12, 18; Sir 4:14

In other Bible translations, the Holy Spirit is called the *advocate*, which is another word for helper.

Led by the Holy Spirit

Catholic Connections

Imagine your best friend or teacher telling you he or she was going away and that you wouldn't see him or her again. Would you be scared, sad, confused? The disciples probably felt all those emotions when they were told by Jesus that he was going back to God, his Father. To give them courage, he also told them about the Holy Spirit.

The Holy Spirit, who Jesus calls the Helper, would come to them and help them. It would be the Holy Spirit's job to help teach and lead the Apostles. But the Holy Spirit's help didn't end there. The Holy Spirit continues to help and guide the Church throughout all time. Wherever God sends Jesus, the Holy Spirit is also sent. The three persons of the Holy Trinity—Father, Son, and Holy Spirit—have different roles but share the same saving work. After reading John 14:15–26, read John 20:19–23 and Acts 2:1–12 to see how Jesus' promise was fulfilled.

— John 14:15–26

My Father will love those who love me; I too will love them and reveal myself to them."

²²Judas (not Judas Iscariot) said, "Lord, how can it be that you will reveal yourself to us and not to the world?"

²³Jesus answered him, "Those who love me will obey my teaching. My Father will love them, and my Father and I will come to them and live with them. ²⁴Those who do not love me do not obey my teaching. And the teaching you have heard is not mine, but comes from the Father, who sent me.

²⁵"I have told you this while I am still with you. ²⁶The Helper, the Holy Spirit, whom the Father will send in my name, will teach you everything and make you remember all that I have told you.

²⁷"Peace is what I leave with you; it is my own peace that I give you. I do not give it as the world does. Do not be worried and upset; do not be afraid. ²⁸You heard me say to you, 'I am leaving, but I will come back to you.' If you loved me, you would be glad that I am going to the Father; for he is greater than I. ²⁹I have told you this now before it all happens, so that when it does happen, you will believe. ³⁰I cannot talk with you much longer, because the ruler of this world is coming. He has no power over me,

³¹but the world must know that I love the Father; that is why I do everything as he commands me.

"Come, let us go from this place.

Jesus the Real Vine

15 ¹"I am the real vine, and my Father is the gardener. ²He breaks off every branch in me that does not bear fruit, and he prunes every branch that does bear fruit, so that it will be clean and bear more fruit. ³You have been made clean already by the teaching I have given you. ⁴Remain united to me, and I will remain united to you. A branch cannot bear fruit by itself; it can do so only if it remains in the vine. In the same way you cannot bear fruit unless you remain in me.

⁵"I am the vine, and you are the branches. Those who remain in me, and I in them, will bear much fruit; for you can do nothing without me. ⁶Those who do not remain in me are thrown out like a branch and dry up; such branches are gathered up and thrown into the fire, where they are burned. ⁷If you remain in me and my words remain in you, then you will ask for anything you wish, and you shall have it. ⁸My Father's glory is shown by your bearing much fruit; and in this way

John

you become my disciples. ⁹I love you just as the Father loves me; remain in my love. ¹⁰If you obey my commands, you will remain in my love, just as I have obeyed my Father's commands and remain in his love.

¹¹"I have told you this so that my joy may be in you and that your joy may be complete. ¹²My commandment is this: love one another, just as I love you. ¹³The greatest love you can have for your friends is to give your life for them. ¹⁴And you are my friends if you do what I command you. ¹⁵I do not call you servants any longer, because servants do not know what their master is doing. Instead, I call you friends, because I have told you everything I heard from my Father. ¹⁶You did not choose me; I chose you and appointed you to go and bear much fruit, the kind of fruit that endures. And so the Father will give you whatever you ask of him in my name. ¹⁷This, then, is what I command you: love one another.

The World's Hatred

¹⁸"If the world hates you, just remember that it has hated me first. ¹⁹If you belonged to the world, then the world would love you as its own. But I chose you from this world, and you do not belong to it; that is why the world hates you. ²⁰Remember what I told you: 'Slaves are not greater than their master.' If people persecuted me, they will persecute you too; if they obeyed my teaching, they will obey yours too. ²¹But they will do all this to you because you are mine; for they do not know the one who sent me. ²²They would not have been guilty of sin if I had not come and spoken to them; as it is, they no longer have any excuse for their sin. ²³Whoever hates me hates my Father also. ²⁴They would not have been guilty of sin if I had not done among them the things that no one else ever did; as it is, they have seen what I did, and they hate both me and my Father. ²⁵This, however, was bound to happen so that what is written in their Law may come true: 'They hated me for no reason at all.'

²⁶"The Helper will come—the Spirit, who reveals the truth about God and who comes

Live It!

Love One Another

"I love ice cream and pizza and my dog and the color yellow and you and my best friend and God," Miko said to her mom.

"Really Miko, do you love me the same as ice cream?" her mom asked.

"Of course not! I love you much more than ice cream," she laughed back.

"Good," her mom said, "I hope you remember too what Jesus said about loving others."

"Yes," Miko said, "Jesus wants us to love one another, but does that mean I have to love the munchkin?"

"Yes, Miko, your brother [the munchkin] is included in 'love one another.' And it also means loving your classmates and even your history teacher, Mr. Wilson."

Miko sighed, "I'll try."

Two times in John 15:11–17, Jesus says to us, "Love one another." He not only tells us to love one another, but he also tells us how much he loves us. He calls us friends. He tells us that he loves us so much he would die for us. He loves us more than ice cream and pizza and the color yellow. He wants us to love one another that much too.

— John 15:1–17

from the Father. I will send him to you from the Father, and he will speak about me. ²⁷And you, too, will speak about me, because you have been with me from the very beginning.

16 ¹"I have told you this, so that you will not give up your faith. ²You will be expelled from the synagogues, and the

15:12 Jn 13:34; 15:17; 1 Jn 3:23; 2 Jn 5   **15:20** Mt 10:24; Lk 6:40; Jn 13:16   **15:25** Ps 35:19; 69:4

time will come when those who kill you will think that by doing this they are serving God. ³People will do these things to you because they have not known either the Father or me. ⁴But I have told you this, so that when the time comes for them to do these things, you will remember what I told you.

The Work of the Holy Spirit

"I did not tell you these things at the beginning, for I was with you. ⁵But now I am going to him who sent me, yet none of you asks me where I am going. ⁶And now that I have told you, your hearts are full of sadness. ⁷But I am telling you the truth: it is better for you that I go away, because if I do not go, the Helper will not come to you. But if I do go away, then I will send him to you. ⁸And when he comes, he will prove to the people of the world that they are wrong about sin and about what is right and about God's judgment. ⁹They are wrong about sin, because they do not believe in me; ¹⁰they are wrong about what is right, because I am going to the Father and you will not see me any more; ¹¹and they are wrong about judgment, because the ruler of this world has already been judged.

¹²"I have much more to tell you, but now it would be too much for you to bear. ¹³When, however, the Spirit comes, who reveals the truth about God, he will lead you into all the truth. He will not speak on his own authority, but he will speak of what he hears and will tell you of things to come. ¹⁴He will give me glory, because he will take what I say and tell it to you. ¹⁵All that my Father has is mine; that is why I said that the Spirit will take what I give him and tell it to you.

Sadness and Gladness

¹⁶"In a little while you will not see me any more, and then a little while later you will see me."

¹⁷Some of his disciples asked among themselves, "What does this mean? He tells us that in a little while we will not see him, and then a little while later we will see him; and he also says, 'It is because I am going to the Father.' ¹⁸What does this 'a little while' mean? We don't know what he is talking about!"

¹⁹Jesus knew that they wanted to question him, so he said to them, "I said, 'In a little while you will not see me, and then a little while later you will see me.' Is this what you are asking about among yourselves? ²⁰I am telling you the truth: you will cry and weep, but the world will be glad; you will be sad, but your sadness will turn into gladness. ²¹When a woman is about to give birth, she is sad because her hour of suffering has come; but when the baby is born, she forgets her suffering, because she is happy that a baby has been born into the world. ²²That is how it is with you: now you are sad, but I will see you again, and your hearts will be filled with gladness, the kind of gladness that no one can take away from you.

²³"When that day comes, you will not ask me for anything. I am telling you the truth: the Father will give you whatever you ask of him in my name.ᶠ ²⁴Until now you have not asked for anything in my name; ask and you will receive, so that your happiness may be complete.

Victory over the World

²⁵"I have used figures of speech to tell you these things. But the time will come when I will not use figures of speech, but will speak to you plainly about the Father. ²⁶When that day comes, you will ask him in my name; and I do not say that I will ask him on your behalf, ²⁷for the Father himself loves you. He loves you because you love me and have believed that I came from God. ²⁸I did come from the Father, and I came into

---

ᶠ **16:23** the Father will give you whatever you ask of him in my name; *some manuscripts have* if you ask the Father for anything, he will give it to you in my name.
16:13 Wis 9:11

The disciples were confused by Jesus' words (John 16:17). **Who can you go to for help in understanding the Bible?**

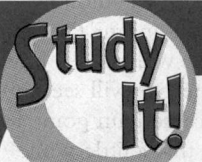

It's Just Too Much!

Tsunamis, hatred, earthquakes, famine, homelessness, war. The list could go on and on. There is so much suffering and sin in the world. Since Adam and Eve's original sin, there always has been. The good news is that Jesus guarantees us victory over suffering and death. Jesus guarantees peace. Jesus says, "The world will make you suffer. But be brave! I have defeated the world!" (John 16:33). So although we will suffer or see others suffer, God's Word assures us that if we are united with Jesus, peace is ours. This also means that we have to do our part to create peace. As you go through your day-to-day activities, remember the promises of Jesus, and let Jesus work through you to make his promises come true for others.

— John 16:25–33

the world; and now I am leaving the world and going to the Father."

29 Then his disciples said to him, "Now you are speaking plainly, without using figures of speech. 30 We know now that you know everything; you do not need to have someone ask you questions. This makes us believe that you came from God."

31 Jesus answered them, "Do you believe now? 32 The time is coming, and is already here, when all of you will be scattered, each of you to your own home, and I will be left all alone. But I am not really alone, because the Father is with me. 33 I have told you this

17:3 Wis 15:3

so that you will have peace by being united to me. The world will make you suffer. But be brave! I have defeated the world!"

Jesus Prays for His Disciples

17 1 After Jesus finished saying this, he looked up to heaven and said, "Father, the hour has come. Give glory to your Son, so that the Son may give glory to you. 2 For you gave him authority over all people, so that he might give eternal life to all those you gave him. 3 And eternal life means to know you, the only true God, and to know Jesus Christ, whom you sent. 4 I have shown your glory on earth; I have finished the work you gave me to do. 5 Father! Give me glory in your presence now, the same glory I had with you before the world was made.

"Father, the hour has come." (17:1)

6 "I have made you known to those you gave me out of the world. They belonged to you, and you gave them to me. They have obeyed your word, 7 and now they know that everything you gave me comes from you. 8 I gave them the message that you gave me, and they received it; they know that it is true that I came from you, and they believe that you sent me.

Pray It!

From Me to We

Here is a short poem prayer called a diamond. It has five lines.

Me

Cool Smart

Playing Learning Praying

Together Christians

We

The first line of a diamond poem starts with one word. The second line uses two words to describe the thing in the first line. The fifth line has the name of something new. The fourth line has two words that describe it. The third line ties both things together. It has three words ending in *ing* that describe both things. A diamond poem is often used to show how opposites are related.

Try writing your own diamond poem prayer that asks God for unity. Maybe the first word is *one* and the last word is *many*. After you write it, pray it often. By praying for unity, we are doing what Jesus did in John 17:21. He was praying that all people of all time would be one—one with one another and one with God.

— John 17:20–23

9"I pray for them. I do not pray for the world but for those you gave me, for they belong to you. 10All I have is yours, and all you have is mine; and my glory is shown through them. 11And now I am coming to you; I am no longer in the world, but they are in the world. Holy Father! Keep them safe by the power of your name, the name you gave me,*g* so that they may be one just as you and I are one. 12While I was with them, I kept them safe by the power of your name, the name you gave me.*h* I protected them, and not one of them was lost, except the man who was bound to be lost—so that the scripture might come true. 13And now I am coming to you, and I say these things in the world so that they might have my joy in their hearts in all its fullness. 14I gave them your message, and the world hated them, because they do not belong to the world, just as I do not belong to the world. 15I do not ask you to take them out of the world, but I do ask you to keep them safe from the Evil One. 16Just as I do not belong to the world, they do not belong to the world. 17Dedicate them to yourself by means of the truth; your word is truth. 18I sent them into the world, just as you sent me into the world. 19And for their sake I dedicate myself to you, in order that they, too, may be truly dedicated to you.

20"I pray not only for them, but also for those who believe in me because of their message. 21I pray that they may all be one. Father! May they be in us, just as you are in me and I am in you. May they be one, so that the world will believe that you sent me. 22I gave them the same glory you gave me, so that they may be one, just as you and I are one: 23I in them and you in me, so that they may be completely one, in order that the world may know that you sent me and that you love them as you love me.

g **17:11** Keep them safe by the power of your name, the name you gave me; *some manuscripts have* By the power of your name keep safe those you have given me.   *h* **17:12** I kept them safe by the power of your name, the name you gave me; *some manuscripts have* By the power of your name I kept safe those you have given me.
17:12 Ps 41:9; Jn 13:18

24"Father! You have given them to me, and I want them to be with me where I am, so that they may see my glory, the glory you gave me; for you loved me before the world was made. 25Righteous Father! The world does not know you, but I know you, and these know that you sent me. 26I made you known to them, and I will continue to do so, in order that the love you have for me may be in them, and so that I also may be in them."

The Arrest of Jesus
(Matthew 26:47–56; Mark 14:43–50; Luke 22:47–53)

18 ¹After Jesus had said this prayer, he left with his disciples and went across Kidron Brook. There was a garden in that place, and Jesus and his disciples went in. ²Judas, the traitor, knew where it was, because many times Jesus had met there with his disciples. ³So Judas went to the garden, taking with him a group of Roman soldiers, and some Temple guards sent by the chief priests and the Pharisees; they were armed and carried lanterns and torches. ⁴Jesus knew everything that was going to happen to him, so he stepped forward and asked them, "Who is it you are looking for?"

⁵"Jesus of Nazareth," they answered.

"I am he," he said.

Judas, the traitor, was standing there with them. ⁶When Jesus said to them, "I am he," they moved back and fell to the ground. ⁷Again Jesus asked them, "Who is it you are looking for?"

"Jesus of Nazareth," they said.

⁸"I have already told you that I am he," Jesus said. "If, then, you are looking for me, let these others go." (⁹He said this so that what he had said might come true: "Father, I have not lost even one of those you gave me.")

¹⁰Simon Peter, who had a sword, drew it and struck the High Priest's slave, cutting off his right ear. The name of the slave was Malchus. ¹¹Jesus said to Peter, "Put your sword back in its place! Do you think that I will not drink the cup of suffering which my Father has given me?"

18:11 Mt 26:39; Mk 14:36; Lk 22:42

John

Nonviolence

Jesus said, "Put your sword back in its place!" (John 18:11) to Peter when Peter cut off the ear of the High Priest's slave. Jesus was willing to accept his suffering and did not want Peter and the others to resort to violence. Jesus reminds us that suffering is indeed difficult but better than retaliation.

Modern examples of the power of nonviolence similarly inspire us. Martin Luther King Jr. practiced nonviolence during the civil rights movement. It was a time when many white Americans were verbally and physically violent against black Americans. But Martin Luther King Jr. insisted that African Americans not respond with violence themselves. Their courage and willingness to love their persecutors brought about a peaceful revolution in this country.

Probably the best-known advocate of nonviolence was a small, quiet man from India, Mahatma Gandhi. His life was dedicated to nonviolence. He once said: "The badge of the violent is his weapon, spear, sword or rifle. God is the shield of the nonviolent."

If you are in a situation where it seems easier to lash out, hit, or verbally hurt someone, try to remember these examples of nonviolence. Jesus wants us to respond to other people's violence with love. It is one of the signs that we are truly his followers.

— John 18:1–11

Jesus before Annas

12Then the Roman soldiers with their commanding officer and the Jewish guards arrested Jesus, tied him up, **13**and took him first to Annas. He was the father-in-law of Caiaphas, who was High Priest that year. **14**It was Caiaphas who had advised the Jewish authorities that it was better that one man should die for all the people.

Peter Denies Jesus
(Matthew 26:69, 70; Mark 14:66–68; Luke 22:55–57)

15Simon Peter and another disciple followed Jesus. That other disciple was well known to the High Priest, so he went with Jesus into the courtyard of the High Priest's house, **16**while Peter stayed outside by the gate. Then the other disciple went back out, spoke to the girl at the gate, and brought Peter inside. **17**The girl at the gate said to Peter, "Aren't you also one of the disciples of that man?"

"No, I am not," answered Peter.

18It was cold, so the servants and guards had built a charcoal fire and were standing around it, warming themselves. So Peter went over and stood with them, warming himself.

The High Priest Questions Jesus
(Matthew 26:59–66; Mark 14:55–64; Luke 22:66–71)

19The High Priest questioned Jesus about his disciples and about his teaching. **20**Jesus answered, "I have always spoken publicly to everyone; all my teaching was done in the synagogues and in the Temple, where all the people come together. I have never said anything in secret. **21**Why, then, do you question me? Question the people who heard me. Ask them what I told them—they know what I said."

22When Jesus said this, one of the guards there slapped him and said, "How dare you talk like that to the High Priest!"

23Jesus answered him, "If I have said anything wrong, tell everyone here what it was. But if I am right in what I have said, why do you hit me?"

24Then Annas sent him, still tied up, to Caiaphas the High Priest.

Peter Denies Jesus Again
(Matthew 26:71–75; Mark 14:69–72; Luke 22:58–62)

25Peter was still standing there keeping himself warm. So the others said to him, "Aren't you also one of the disciples of that man?"

But Peter denied it. "No, I am not," he said.

26One of the High Priest's slaves, a relative of the man whose ear Peter had cut off, spoke up. "Didn't I see you with him in the garden?" he asked.

27Again Peter said "No"—and at once a rooster crowed.

Jesus before Pilate
(Matthew 27:1, 2, 11–14; Mark 15:1–5; Luke 23:1–5)

28Early in the morning Jesus was taken from Caiaphas' house to the governor's palace. The Jewish authorities did not go inside the palace, for they wanted to keep themselves ritually clean, in order to be able to eat the Passover meal. **29**So Pilate went outside to them and asked, "What do you accuse this man of?"

30Their answer was, "We would not have brought him to you if he had not committed a crime."

31Pilate said to them, "Then you yourselves take him and try him according to your own law."

They replied, "We are not allowed to put anyone to death." (**32**This happened in order to make come true what Jesus had said when he indicated the kind of death he would die.)

18:14 Jn 11:49, 50   **18:32** Jn 3:14; 12:32

John

33Pilate went back into the palace and called Jesus. "Are you the king of the Jews?" he asked him.

34Jesus answered, "Does this question come from you or have others told you about me?"

35Pilate replied, "Do you think I am a Jew? It was your own people and the chief priests who handed you over to me. What have you done?"

36Jesus said, "My kingdom does not belong to this world; if my kingdom belonged to this world, my followers would fight to keep me from being handed over to the Jewish authorities. No, my kingdom does not belong here!"

37So Pilate asked him, "Are you a king, then?"

Jesus answered, "You say that I am a king. I was born and came into the world for this one purpose, to speak about the truth. Whoever belongs to the truth listens to me."

38"And what is truth?" Pilate asked.

"And what is truth?" (18:38)

Jesus Is Sentenced to Death
(Matthew 27:15–31; Mark 15:6–20; Luke 23:13–25)

Then Pilate went back outside to the people and said to them, "I cannot find any reason to condemn him. 39But according to the custom you have, I always set free a prisoner for you during the Passover. Do you want me to set free for you the king of the Jews?"

"No, not him! We want Barabbas!" (18:40)

40They answered him with a shout, "No, not him! We want Barabbas!" (Barabbas was a bandit.)

19 1Then Pilate took Jesus and had him whipped. 2The soldiers made a crown out of thorny branches and put it on his head; then they put a purple robe on him 3and came to him and said, "Long live the King of the Jews!" And they went up and slapped him.

4Pilate went back out once more and said to the crowd, "Look, I will bring him out here to you to let you see that I cannot find any reason to condemn him." 5So Jesus came out, wearing the crown of thorns and the purple robe. Pilate said to them, "Look! Here is the man!"

6When the chief priests and the Temple guards saw him, they shouted, "Crucify him! Crucify him!"

Pilate said to them, "You take him, then, and crucify him. I find no reason to condemn him."

7The crowd answered back, "We have a law that says he ought to die, because he claimed to be the Son of God."

8When Pilate heard this, he was even more afraid. 9He went back into the palace and asked Jesus, "Where do you come from?"

But Jesus did not answer. 10Pilate said to him, "You will not speak to me? Remember, I have the authority to set you free and also to have you crucified."

11Jesus answered, "You have authority over me only because it was given to you by

19:11 Wis 6:3

God. So the man who handed me over to you is guilty of a worse sin."

12When Pilate heard this, he tried to find a way to set Jesus free. But the crowd shouted back, "If you set him free, that means that you are not the Emperor's friend! Anyone who claims to be a king is a rebel against the Emperor!"

13When Pilate heard these words, he took Jesus outside and sat down on the judge's seat in the place called "The Stone Pavement." (In Hebrew the name is "Gabbatha.") 14It was then almost noon of the day before the Passover. Pilate said to the people, "Here is your king!"

15They shouted back, "Kill him! Kill him! Crucify him!"

Pilate asked them, "Do you want me to crucify your king?"

The chief priests answered, "The only king we have is the Emperor!"

16Then Pilate handed Jesus over to them to be crucified.

Jesus Is Crucified
(Matthew 27:32–44; Mark 15:21–32; Luke 23:26–43)

So they took charge of Jesus. 17He went out, carrying his cross, and came to "The Place of the Skull," as it is called. (In Hebrew it is called "Golgotha.") 18There they crucified him; and they also crucified two other men, one on each side, with Jesus between them. 19Pilate wrote a notice and

He went out, carrying his cross. (19:17)

had it put on the cross. "Jesus of Nazareth, the King of the Jews," is what he wrote. 20Many people read it, because the place where Jesus was crucified was not far from the city. The notice was written in Hebrew, Latin, and Greek. 21The chief priests said to Pilate, "Do not write 'The King of the Jews,' but rather, 'This man said, I am the King of the Jews.'"

22Pilate answered, "What I have written stays written."

23After the soldiers had crucified Jesus, they took his clothes and divided them into four parts, one part for each soldier. They also took the robe, which was made of one piece of woven cloth without any seams in it. 24The soldiers said to one another, "Let's not tear it; let's throw dice to see who will get it." This happened in order to make the scripture come true:

"They divided my clothes among
     themselves
   and gambled for my robe."
And this is what the soldiers did.

25Standing close to Jesus' cross were his mother, his mother's sister, Mary the wife of Clopas, and Mary Magdalene. 26Jesus saw his mother and the disciple he loved standing there; so he said to his mother, "He is your son."

27Then he said to the disciple, "She is your mother." From that time the disciple took her to live in his home.

The Death of Jesus
(Matthew 27:45–56; Mark 15:33–41; Luke 23:44–49)

28Jesus knew that by now everything had been completed; and in order to make the scripture come true, he said, "I am thirsty."

29A bowl was there, full of cheap wine; so a sponge was soaked in the wine, put on a stalk of hyssop, and lifted up to his lips. 30Jesus drank the wine and said, "It is finished!"

Then he bowed his head and gave up his spirit.

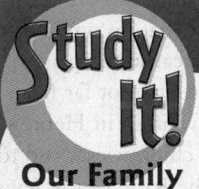

Our Family

"Who is that little old lady? Is she your grandma?" Lisa asked Leslie.

Leslie answered, "No, my mom just helps her out. First her husband died, and then her kids, so now she is all alone."

That night while Leslie was helping her mom with dinner, she asked, "Mom, why do you help Mrs. Collins? Are you hoping you get her stuff when she dies or something?"

"No, Leslie, I help Mrs. Collins because that is what we do for others. Remember the story of Jesus' death on the cross?"

"Mom, what does that have to do with Mrs. Collins?" asked Leslie.

"Leslie, look it up, John 19:26–27," her mother replied.

Leslie went to her Bible and brought it into the kitchen. After reading it she said, "So, Jesus told the disciple to take care of his mother, not you."

"But that's the point, Leslie," her mom replied. "The things Jesus told his followers then are true for us today. Because we are part of the community, we need to take care of one another."

"Hmm. Mom, don't worry, I'll take care of you when you're old like Mrs. Collins," Leslie said.

"Thanks honey, and remember that the Gospel teaches that Mary is also our Mother and cares for us," her mother answered, giving Leslie a big hug.

— John 19:25–27

Jesus' Side Is Pierced

31 Then the Jewish authorities asked Pilate to allow them to break the legs of the men who had been crucified, and to take the bodies down from the crosses. They requested this because it was Friday, and they did not want the bodies to stay on the crosses on the Sabbath, since the coming Sabbath was especially holy. 32 So the soldiers went and broke the legs of the first man and then of the other man who had been crucified with Jesus. 33 But when they came to Jesus, they saw that he was already dead, so they did not break his legs. 34 One of the soldiers, however, plunged his spear into Jesus' side, and at once blood and water poured out. (35 The one who saw this happen has spoken of it, so that you also may believe.[i] What he said is true, and he knows that he speaks the truth.) 36 This was done to make the scripture come true: "Not one of his bones will be broken." 37 And there is another scripture that says, "People will look at him whom they pierced."

The Burial of Jesus
(Matthew 27:57–61; Mark 15:42–47; Luke 23:50–56)

38 After this, Joseph, who was from the town of Arimathea, asked Pilate if he could take Jesus' body. (Joseph was a follower of Jesus, but in secret, because he was afraid of the Jewish authorities.) Pilate told him he could have the body, so Joseph went and took it away. 39 Nicodemus, who at first had gone to see Jesus at night, went with Joseph, taking with him about one hundred pounds of spices, a mixture of myrrh and aloes. 40 The two men took Jesus' body and wrapped it in linen cloths with the spices according to the Jewish custom of preparing a body for burial. 41 There was a garden in the place where Jesus had been put to death, and in it there was a new tomb where no one had ever been buried. 42 Since it was the day before the Sabbath and because the tomb was close by, they placed Jesus' body there.

---

i **19:35** believe; *some manuscripts have* continue to believe.
19:36 Ex 12:46; Num 9:12; Ps 34:20   **19:37** Zech 12:10; Rev 1:7   **19:39** Jn 3:1, 2

The two men took Jesus' body. (19:40)

The Empty Tomb
*(Matthew 28:1–8; Mark 16:1–8;
Luke 24:1–12)*

20 ¹Early on Sunday morning, while it was still dark, Mary Magdalene went to the tomb and saw that the stone had been taken away from the entrance. ²She went running to Simon Peter and the other disciple, whom Jesus loved, and told them, "They have taken the Lord from the tomb, and we don't know where they have put him!"

³Then Peter and the other disciple went to the tomb. ⁴The two of them were running, but the other disciple ran faster than Peter and reached the tomb first. ⁵He bent over and saw the linen cloths, but he did not go in. ⁶Behind him came Simon Peter, and he went straight into the tomb. He saw the linen cloths lying there ⁷and the cloth which had been around Jesus' head. It was not lying with the linen cloths but was rolled up by itself. ⁸Then the other disciple, who had reached the tomb first, also went in; he saw and believed. (⁹They still did not understand the scripture which said that he must rise from death.) ¹⁰Then the disciples went back home.

Jesus Appears to Mary Magdalene
(Matthew 28:9, 10; Mark 16:9–11)

¹¹Mary stood crying outside the tomb. While she was still crying, she bent over and looked in the tomb ¹²and saw two angels there dressed in white, sitting where the body of Jesus had been, one at the head and the other at the feet. ¹³"Woman, why are you crying?" they asked her.

She answered, "They have taken my Lord away, and I do not know where they have put him!"

¹⁴Then she turned around and saw Jesus standing there; but she did not know that it was Jesus. ¹⁵"Woman, why are you crying?" Jesus asked her. "Who is it that you are looking for?"

She thought he was the gardener, so she said to him, "If you took him away, sir, tell me where you have put him, and I will go and get him."

¹⁶Jesus said to her, "Mary!"

She turned toward him and said in Hebrew, "Rabboni!" (This means "Teacher.")

¹⁷"Do not hold on to me," Jesus told her, "because I have not yet gone back up to the Father. But go to my brothers and tell them that I am returning to him who is my Father and their Father, my God and their God."

¹⁸So Mary Magdalene went and told the disciples that she had seen the Lord and related to them what he had told her.

Jesus Appears to His Disciples
*(Matthew 28:16–20; Mark 16:14–18;
Luke 24:36–49)*

¹⁹It was late that Sunday evening, and the disciples were gathered together behind locked doors, because they were afraid of the Jewish authorities. Then Jesus came and stood among them. "Peace be with you," he said. ²⁰After saying this, he showed them his hands and his side. The disciples were filled with joy at seeing the Lord. ²¹Jesus said to them again, "Peace be with you. As the Father sent me, so I send you." ²²Then he breathed on them and said, "Receive the Holy Spirit. ²³If you forgive people's sins, they are forgiven; if you do not forgive them, they are not forgiven."

20:23 Mt 16:19; 18:18

John

Pray It!

Peace

Jesus said, "Peace be with you," two times to his disciples in John 20:19–21. He wants us to be at peace and to share our peace with others. Here is one way to remember how to practice peace:

Practice peace every day.
Enjoy others, especially those who are different.
Always think before you speak and act.
Create peace at home and school.
Echo Jesus' words.

Notice how each line above begins with one of the letters of the word *peace*. What other ways of practicing peace can you think of? Write your own peace reminder:

P
E
A
C
E

— John 20:19–21

Jesus and Thomas

24 One of the twelve disciples, Thomas (called the Twin), was not with them when Jesus came. 25 So the other disciples told him, "We have seen the Lord!"

Thomas said to them, "Unless I see the scars of the nails in his hands and put my finger on those scars and my hand in his side, I will not believe."

26 A week later the disciples were together again indoors, and Thomas was with them. The doors were locked, but Jesus came and stood among them and said, "Peace be with you." 27 Then he said to Thomas, "Put your finger here, and look at my hands; then reach out your hand and put it in my side. Stop your doubting, and believe!"

28 Thomas answered him, "My Lord and my God!"

29 Jesus said to him, "Do you believe because you see me? How happy are those who believe without seeing me!"

The Purpose of This Book

30 In his disciples' presence Jesus performed many other miracles which are not

Jesus came and stood among them. (20:26)

Penance and Reconciliation

One of the powers that Jesus gave to the Apostles after his Resurrection can be found in John 20:21–23. He tells them that they can forgive the sins of others. This is one of the Bible passages that the sacrament of Penance and Reconciliation is based on. The sacrament of Penance and Reconciliation (sometimes called Confession) allows us to experience God's forgiveness for our sins.

During the sacrament we tell or confess our sins to a priest. The priest is Christ's representative. Confessing our sins to a real person who represents Christ helps us understand that sin has real consequences and that God's forgiveness is also very real. The priest shows God's compassion and understanding to the person who is confessing his or her sins.

Ideally Catholics should go to Penance and Reconciliation at least once a year. If you have committed a very serious (mortal) sin, you should go as soon as you can and not receive the Eucharist until you do so. If it has been a while since your last confession, maybe it is time to go. The priest will help you through it, and you can ask a teacher, or a parent for help. Don't miss this chance to feel the amazing forgiveness of God!

— John 20:19–23

"Look at my hands. . . . Stop your doubting, and believe!" (20:27)

written down in this book. ³¹But these have been written in order that you may believe[i] that Jesus is the Messiah, the Son of God, and that through your faith in him you may have life.

Jesus Appears to Seven Disciples

21 ¹After this, Jesus appeared once more to his disciples at Lake Tiberias. This is how it happened. ²Simon Peter, Thomas (called the Twin), Nathanael (the one from Cana in Galilee), the sons of Zebedee, and two other disciples of Jesus were all together. ³Simon Peter said to the others, "I am going fishing."

"We will come with you," they told him. So they went out in a boat, but all that night they did not catch a thing. ⁴As the sun was rising, Jesus stood at the water's edge, but the disciples did not know that it was Jesus. ⁵Then he asked them, "Young men, haven't you caught anything?"

"Not a thing," they answered.

⁶He said to them, "Throw your net out on the right side of the boat, and you will catch some." So they threw the net out and

John

---

[i] **20:31** believe; *some manuscripts have* continue to believe.
21:3 Lk 5:5   **21:6** Lk 5:6

Apostolic Succession

In John, chapter 21, the resurrected Jesus tells Peter three times to feed his sheep. Jesus' sheep are all the people of the world, but especially the Church. The Bible establishes Peter as the first pope and the other Apostles as the first bishops (see also John 13:20, 17:20, 20:21). Through the centuries their special leadership roles have been passed to new popes and bishops in a process called apostolic succession.

Apostolic succession is a big phrase. It is also an important one. When Jesus gave the Apostles the Holy Spirit, he began the chain (succession) of bishops and popes. Today, that chain is continued with our current pope and bishops. The Pope's special role can be traced back to the charge that Jesus gave to Peter in John 21:15–19. The Catholic Church has been, and still is, led by the Holy Spirit through the special teaching authority of the Pope and bishops. At Mass we pray for the Pope, bishop, and the other Church leaders. This helps them lead and strengthen the chain.

Ca**t**holic Connec**t**ions

— John 21:15–19

John

could not pull it back in, because they had caught so many fish.

⁷The disciple whom Jesus loved said to Peter, "It is the Lord!" When Peter heard that it was the Lord, he wrapped his outer garment around him (for he had taken his clothes off) and jumped into the water. ⁸The other disciples came to shore in the boat, pulling the net full of fish. They were not very far from land, about a hundred yards away. ⁹When they stepped ashore, they saw a charcoal fire there with fish on it and some bread. ¹⁰Then Jesus said to them, "Bring some of the fish you have just caught."

¹¹Simon Peter went aboard and dragged the net ashore full of big fish, a hundred and fifty-three in all; even though there were so many, still the net did not tear. ¹²Jesus said to them, "Come and eat." None of the disciples dared ask him, "Who are you?" because they knew it was the Lord. ¹³So Jesus went over, took the bread, and gave it to them; he did the same with the fish.

¹⁴This, then, was the third time Jesus appeared to the disciples after he was raised from death.

Simon Peter . . . dragged the net ashore. (21:11)

Jesus and Peter

¹⁵After they had eaten, Jesus said to Simon Peter, "Simon son of John, do you love me more than these others do?"

"Yes, Lord," he answered, "you know that I love you."

Jesus said to him, "Take care of my lambs." ¹⁶A second time Jesus said to him, "Simon son of John, do you love me?"

"Yes, Lord," he answered, "you know that I love you."

Jesus said to him, "Take care of my sheep." 17A third time Jesus said, "Simon son of John, do you love me?"

Peter became sad because Jesus asked him the third time, "Do you love me?" and so he said to him, "Lord, you know everything; you know that I love you!"

Jesus said to him, "Take care of my sheep. 18I am telling you the truth: when you were young, you used to get ready and go anywhere you wanted to; but when you are old, you will stretch out your hands and someone else will tie you up and take you where you don't want to go." 19(In saying this, Jesus was indicating the way in which Peter would die and bring glory to God.) Then Jesus said to him, "Follow me!"

Jesus and the Other Disciple

20Peter turned around and saw behind him that other disciple, whom Jesus loved— the one who had leaned close to Jesus at the meal and had asked, "Lord, who is going to betray you?" 21When Peter saw him, he asked Jesus, "Lord, what about this man?"

22Jesus answered him, "If I want him to live until I come, what is that to you? Follow me!"

23So a report spread among the followers of Jesus that this disciple would not die. But Jesus did not say he would not die; he said, "If I want him to live until I come, what is that to you?"

24He is the disciple who spoke of these things, the one who also wrote them down; and we know that what he said is true.

Conclusion

25Now, there are many other things that Jesus did. If they were all written down one by one, I suppose that the whole world could not hold the books that would be written.

21:20 Jn 13:25

Your Next Step

Congratulations on finishing the Gospel of John! Use this space to write your thoughts and questions about this book. If you are following the suggested reading plan, move ahead to the First Letter of John. This letter continues to emphasize that God is love!

John

Imagine taking a trip around the world—wouldn't that be a fantastic adventure! In the Acts of the Apostles (Acts) the first followers of Jesus, the Apostles, are on a great journey. But this is no vacation! Instead, they have a huge mission to accomplish: teaching everyone about Jesus and forming new Christian churches.

Acts picks up where the Gospels leave off. The Apostles are on their own, spreading the Good News about Jesus Christ. But they are not really alone, for Jesus has sent them the Holy Spirit to guide them. As they travel about teaching and preaching and healing, they are welcomed by some people and rejected by others. In the midst of it all, a new religion is born: Christianity.

Chap. 7:54–60

Headlines

- Fire! The Spirit's Dramatic Arrival (2:1–13)
- Christians Share Everything (2:43–47)
- Persecutor Becomes Missionary! (9:1–25)
- Jews and Gentiles Form First Church (11:19–26)
- Council Debates Gentile Question (chapter 15)
- Paul Causes Riot in Ephesus! (19:21–41)
- Plot to Assassinate Paul Discovered (23:12–35)

FACTOIDS

Who are the central characters? Peter, Paul, the Apostles, Jewish leaders, Roman leaders, and early Christians.

Who wrote this book? The same person who wrote the Gospel of Luke.

Who was it written for? Just like Luke, Acts is addressed to Theophilus, which means "friend of God" in Greek.

Why was it written? The author wanted to describe how Jesus' mission was carried on by the Apostles after Jesus returned to heaven.

What is the literary style? The style is salvation history. It shows how God's plan for salvation is carried out through special people and events.

Important themes

- Have courage! The Holy Spirit will equip us for the interesting and sometimes perilous journey of living as Christians.
- God wants *all* people on earth to be saved, not only the Jews.
- Living as a Christian means knowing the Gospel, praying together, sharing the Eucharist, and caring for the poor.

ACTS

1

1 Dear Theophilus:

In my first book I wrote about all the things that Jesus did and taught from the time he began his work **2** until the day he was taken up to heaven. Before he was taken up, he gave instructions by the power of the Holy Spirit to the men he had chosen as his apostles. **3** For forty days after his death he appeared to them many times in ways that proved beyond doubt that he was alive. They saw him, and he talked with them about the Kingdom of God. **4** And when they came together, *a* he gave them this order: "Do not leave Jerusalem, but wait for the gift I told you about, the gift my Father promised. **5** John baptized with water, but in a few days you will be baptized with the Holy Spirit."

Jesus Is Taken Up to Heaven

6 When the apostles met together with Jesus, they asked him, "Lord, will you at this time give the Kingdom back to Israel?"

7 Jesus said to them, "The times and occasions are set by my Father's own authority, and it is not for you to know when they will be. **8** But when the Holy Spirit comes upon you, you will be filled with power, and you will be witnesses for me in Jerusalem, in all of Judea and Samaria, and to the ends of the earth." **9** After saying this, he was taken up to heaven as they watched him, and a cloud hid him from their sight.

10 They still had their eyes fixed on the sky as he went away, when two men dressed in white suddenly stood beside them **11** and said, "Galileans, why are you standing there

---

a **1:4** when they came together; *or* while he was staying with them, *or* while he was eating with them.
1:1 Lk 1:1–4   **1:4** Lk 24:49   **1:5** Mt 3:11; Mk 1:8; Lk 3:16; Jn 1:33   **1:8** Mt 28:19; Mk 16:15; Lk 24:47, 48
1:9 Mk 16:19; Lk 24:50, 51

Pray It!

Now What?

The Apostles and other disciples of Jesus had given up everything to follow him: homes, families, and jobs. He touched their hearts, and they changed their lives for him. And now in this first chapter of the Acts of the Apostles, Jesus tells them he is leaving. These first followers might have felt hopeless, abandoned, or lost, but Jesus comforts them, telling them to wait (Acts 1:4). He assures them God has promised a gift for them, the Holy Spirit. The Holy Spirit will fill them with power and give them everything they will need to carry on when he is gone.

> Lord, I don't always know what's next in my life,
> and sometimes the unknown is scary.
> But, I will wait for your gifts.
> Holy Spirit, help me understand what I need to do
> and when I need to do it.
> Give me whatever I need to accomplish it.
> Amen.

— Acts 1:1–11

looking up at the sky? This Jesus, who was taken from you into heaven, will come back in the same way that you saw him go to heaven."

Judas' Successor

12 Then the apostles went back to Jerusalem from the Mount of Olives, which is about half a mile away from the city. 13 They entered the city and went up to the room where they were staying: Peter, John, James and Andrew, Philip and Thomas, Bartholomew and Matthew, James son of Alphaeus, Simon the Patriot, and Judas son of James. 14 They gathered frequently to pray as a group, together with the women and with Mary the mother of Jesus and with his brothers.

15 A few days later there was a meeting of the believers, about a hundred and twenty in all, and Peter stood up to speak. 16 "My friends," he said, "the scripture had to come true in which the Holy Spirit, speaking through David, made a prediction about Judas, who was the guide for those who arrested Jesus. 17 Judas was a member of our group, for he had been chosen to have a part in our work."

(18 With the money that Judas got for his evil act he bought a field, where he fell to his death; he burst open and all his insides spilled out. 19 All the people living in Jerusalem heard about it, and so in their own language they call that field Akeldama, which means "Field of Blood.")

20 "For it is written in the book of Psalms,
'May his house become empty;
    may no one live in it.'
It is also written,
'May someone else take his place of
    service.'
21-22 "So then, someone must join us as a witness to the resurrection of the Lord Jesus. He must be one of the men who were in our group during the whole time that the Lord Jesus traveled about with us, beginning from the time John preached his message of baptism[b] until the day Jesus was taken up from us to heaven."

23 So they proposed two men: Joseph, who was called Barsabbas (also known as Justus), and Matthias. 24 Then they prayed, "Lord, you know the thoughts of everyone, so show us which of these two you have chosen 25 to serve as an apostle in the place of Judas, who left to go to the place where he belongs." 26 Then they drew lots to choose between the two men, and the one chosen was Matthias, who was added to the group of eleven apostles.

The Coming of the Holy Spirit

2 1 When the day of Pentecost came, all the believers were gathered together in one place. 2 Suddenly there was a noise from the sky which sounded like a strong wind blowing, and it filled the whole house where they were sitting. 3 Then they saw what looked like tongues of fire which spread out and touched each person there. 4 They were all filled with the Holy Spirit and began to talk in other languages, as the Spirit enabled them to speak.

5 There were Jews living in Jerusalem, religious people who had come from every country in the world. 6 When they heard this noise, a large crowd gathered. They were all excited, because all of them heard the believers talking in their own languages. 7 In amazement and wonder they exclaimed, "These people who are talking like this are Galileans! 8 How is it, then, that all of us hear them speaking in our own native languages? 9 We are from Parthia, Media, and Elam; from Mesopotamia, Judea, and Cappadocia; from Pontus and Asia, 10 from Phrygia and Pamphylia, from Egypt and the regions of Libya near Cyrene. Some of us are from Rome, 11 both Jews and Gentiles converted to

b 1:21–22 John preached his message of baptism; *or* John baptized him.
1:13 Mt 10:2–4; Mk 3:16–19; Lk 6:14–16 1:18, 19 Mt 27:3–8 1:20 a Ps 69:25; b Ps 109:8 1:22 a Mt 3:16; Mk 1:9; Lk 3:21; b Mk 16:19; Lk 24:51 2:1 Lev 23:15–21; Deut 16:9–11

In the first chapter of Acts, three numbers are mentioned. Can you find them? Do they sound familiar?

Acts

Confirmation

When the Apostles felt the power of the Holy Spirit inside them, they were changed. Suddenly, they could speak and be understood by people who spoke different languages (Acts 2:4–6)! This miracle proved to the Apostles that God was equipping them with the tools they needed for their mission.

When we are confirmed, God changes us too. Confirmation is a sacrament of initiation, one of the Seven Sacraments of the Catholic Church. Through Confirmation the gifts of the Holy Spirit—wisdom, understanding, right judgment, courage, knowledge, reverence, wonder and awe in God's presence—grow stronger within us. Just like the Apostles, we become better equipped to live our faith and share it with others.

— Acts 2:1–13

Catholic Connections

Judaism, and some of us are from Crete and Arabia—yet all of us hear them speaking in our own languages about the great things that God has done!" ¹²Amazed and confused, they kept asking each other, "What does this mean?"

¹³But others made fun of the believers, saying, "These people are drunk!"

"Fellow Jews, . . . listen to me!" (2:14)

Peter's Message

¹⁴Then Peter stood up with the other eleven apostles and in a loud voice began to speak to the crowd: "Fellow Jews and all of you who live in Jerusalem, listen to me and let me tell you what this means. ¹⁵These people are not drunk, as you suppose; it is only nine o'clock in the morning. ¹⁶Instead, this is what the prophet Joel spoke about:

¹⁷'This is what I will do in the last days,
    God says:
    I will pour out my Spirit on everyone.
    Your sons and daughters will proclaim my
        message;
    your young men will see visions,
    and your old men will have dreams.
¹⁸Yes, even on my servants, both men and
        women,
    I will pour out my Spirit in those days,
    and they will proclaim my message.
¹⁹I will perform miracles in the sky above
        and wonders on the earth below.
    There will be blood, fire, and thick
        smoke;
²⁰   the sun will be darkened,
    and the moon will turn red as blood,
    before the great and glorious Day of
        the Lord comes.
²¹And then, whoever calls out to the Lord
    for help will be saved.'

2:17–21 Joel 2:28–32 (LXX)

Acts

22"Listen to these words, fellow Israelites! Jesus of Nazareth was a man whose divine authority was clearly proven to you by all the miracles and wonders which God performed through him. You yourselves know this, for it happened here among you. 23In accordance with his own plan God had already decided that Jesus would be handed over to you; and you killed him by letting sinful men crucify him. 24But God raised him from death, setting him free from its power, because it was impossible that death should hold him prisoner. 25For David said about him,

'I saw the Lord before me at all times;
  he is near me, and I will not be
    troubled.
26And so I am filled with gladness,
  and my words are full of joy.
And I, mortal though I am,
  will rest assured in hope,
27because you will not abandon me in the
    world of the dead;
  you will not allow your faithful servant
    to rot in the grave.
28You have shown me the paths that lead to
    life,
  and your presence will fill me with joy.'

29"My friends, I must speak to you plainly about our famous ancestor King David. He died and was buried, and his grave is here with us to this very day. 30He was a prophet, and he knew what God had promised him: God had made a vow that he would make one of David's descendants a king, just as David was. 31David saw what God was going to do in the future, and so he spoke about the resurrection of the Messiah when he said,

'He was not abandoned in the world of
    the dead;
  his body did not rot in the grave.'

32God has raised this very Jesus from death, and we are all witnesses to this fact. 33He has been raised to the right side of God, his Father, and has received from him the Holy Spirit, as he had promised. What you now see and hear is his gift that he has poured out on us. 34For it was not David who went up into heaven; rather he said,

'The Lord said to my Lord:
  Sit here at my right side

35until I put your enemies as a footstool
    under your feet.'

36"All the people of Israel, then, are to know for sure that this Jesus, whom you crucified, is the one that God has made Lord and Messiah!"

37When the people heard this, they were deeply troubled and said to Peter and the other apostles, "What shall we do, brothers?"

38Peter said to them, "Each one of you must turn away from your sins and be baptized in the name of Jesus Christ, so that your sins will be forgiven; and you will receive God's gift, the Holy Spirit. 39For God's promise was made to you and your children, and to all who are far away—all whom the Lord our God calls to himself."

40Peter made his appeal to them and with many other words he urged them, saying, "Save yourselves from the punishment coming on this wicked people!" 41Many of them believed his message and were baptized, and about three thousand people were added to the group that day. 42They spent their time in learning from the apostles, taking part in the fellowship, and sharing in the fellowship meals and the prayers.

Life among the Believers

43Many miracles and wonders were being done through the apostles, and everyone was filled with awe. 44All the believers continued together in close fellowship and shared their belongings with one another. 45They would sell their property and possessions, and distribute the money among all, according to what each one needed. 46Day after day they met as a group in the Temple, and they had their meals together in their homes, eating with glad and humble hearts, 47praising God, and enjoying the good will of all the people. And every day the Lord added to their group those who were being saved.

A Lame Beggar Is Healed

3 1One day Peter and John went to the Temple at three o'clock in the afternoon, the hour for prayer. 2There at the

2:23 Mt 27:35; Mk 15:24; Lk 23:33; Jn 19:18 **2:24** Mt 28:5, 6; Mk 16:6; Lk 24:5 **2:25–28** Ps 16:8–11 (LXX) **2:30** Ps 132:11; 2 Sam 7:12, 13 **2:34, 35** Ps 110:1 **2:44** Acts 4:32–35

Acts

Beautiful Gate, as it was called, was a man who had been lame all his life. Every day he was carried to the gate to beg for money from the people who were going into the Temple. ³When he saw Peter and John going in, he begged them to give him something. ⁴They looked straight at him, and Peter said, "Look at us!" ⁵So he looked at them, expecting to get something from them. ⁶But Peter said to him, "I have no money at all, but I give you what I have: in the name of Jesus Christ of Nazareth I order you to get up and walk!" ⁷Then he took him by his right hand and helped him up. At once the man's feet and ankles became strong; ⁸he jumped up, stood on his feet, and started walking around. Then he went into the Temple with them, walking and jumping and praising God. ⁹The people there saw him walking and praising God, ¹⁰and when they recognized him as the beggar who had sat at the Beautiful Gate, they were all surprised and amazed at what had happened to him.

"I . . . give you what I have." (3:6)

Peter's Message in the Temple

¹¹As the man held on to Peter and John in Solomon's Porch, as it was called, the people were amazed and ran to them. ¹²When Peter saw the people, he said to them, "Fellow Israelites, why are you surprised at this, and why do you stare at us? Do you think that it was by means of our own power or godliness that we made this man walk? ¹³The God of Abraham, Isaac, and Jacob, the God of our ancestors, has given divine glory to his Servant Jesus. But you handed him over to the authorities, and you rejected him in Pilate's presence, even after Pilate had decided to set him free. ¹⁴He was holy and good, but you rejected him, and instead you asked Pilate to do you the favor of turning loose a murderer. ¹⁵You killed the one who leads to life, but God raised him from death—and we are witnesses to this. ¹⁶It was the power of his name that gave strength to this lame man. What you see and know was done by faith in his name; it was faith in Jesus that has made him well, as you can all see.

¹⁷"And now, my friends, I know that what you and your leaders did to Jesus was due to your ignorance. ¹⁸God announced long ago through all the prophets that his Messiah had to suffer; and he made it come true in this way. ¹⁹Repent, then, and turn to God, so that he will forgive your sins. If you do, ²⁰times of spiritual strength will come from the Lord, and he will send Jesus, who is the Messiah he has already chosen for you. ²¹He must remain in heaven until the time comes for all things to be made new, as God announced through his holy prophets of long ago. ²²For Moses said, 'The Lord your God will send you a prophet, just as he sent me,ᶜ and he will be one of your own people. You are to obey everything that he tells you to do. ²³Anyone who does not obey that prophet shall be separated from God's people and destroyed.' ²⁴And all the prophets who had a message, including Samuel and those who came after him, also announced what has been happening these days. ²⁵The promises of God through his prophets are for you, and you share in the covenant which God made with your ancestors. As he said to Abraham, 'Through your descendants I will bless all the people on earth.' ²⁶And so God chose his Servant and sent him to you first,

ᶜ **3:22** just as he sent me; *or* like me.
3:13 Ex 3:15   **3:14** Mt 27:15–23; Mk 15:6–14; Lk 23:13–23; Jn 19:12–15   **3:22** Deut 18:15, 18 (LXX)
3:23 Deut 18:19   **3:25** Gen 22:18

"It was faith in Jesus that has made him well, as you can all see" *(Acts 3:16).*

Acts

to bless you by making every one of you turn away from your wicked ways."

Peter and John before the Council

4 ¹Peter and John were still speaking to the people when some priests,[d] the officer in charge of the Temple guards, and some Sadducees arrived. ²They were annoyed because the two apostles were teaching the people that Jesus had risen from death, which proved that the dead will rise to life. ³So they arrested them and put them in jail until the next day, since it was already late. ⁴But many who heard the message believed; and the number grew to about five thousand.

⁵The next day the Jewish leaders, the elders, and the teachers of the Law gathered in Jerusalem. ⁶They met with the High Priest Annas and with Caiaphas, John, Alexander, and the others who belonged to the High Priest's family. ⁷They made the apostles stand before them and asked them, "How did you do this? What power do you have or whose name did you use?"

⁸Peter, full of the Holy Spirit, answered them, "Leaders of the people and elders: ⁹if we are being questioned today about the good deed done to the lame man and how he was healed, ¹⁰then you should all know, and all the people of Israel should know, that this man stands here before you completely well through the power of the name of Jesus Christ of Nazareth—whom you crucified and whom God raised from death. ¹¹Jesus is the one of whom the scripture says,

'The stone that you the builders despised turned out to be the most important of all.'

¹²Salvation is to be found through him alone; in all the world there is no one else whom God has given who can save us."

¹³The members of the Council were amazed to see how bold Peter and John were and to learn that they were ordinary men of no education. They realized then that they had been companions of Jesus. ¹⁴But there was nothing that they could say, because they saw the man who had been healed standing there with Peter and John. ¹⁵So they told them to leave the Council room, and then they started discussing among themselves. ¹⁶"What shall we do with these men?" they asked. "Everyone in Jerusalem knows that this extraordinary miracle has been performed by them, and we cannot deny it. ¹⁷But to keep this matter from spreading any further among the people, let us warn these men never again to speak to anyone in the name of Jesus."

¹⁸So they called them back in and told them that under no condition were they to speak or to teach in the name of Jesus. ¹⁹But Peter and John answered them, "You yourselves judge which is right in God's sight— to obey you or to obey God. ²⁰For we cannot stop speaking of what we ourselves have seen and heard." ²¹So the Council warned them even more strongly and then set them free. They saw that it was impossible to punish them, because the people were all praising God for what had happened. ²²The man on whom this miracle of healing had been performed was over forty years old.

The Believers Pray for Boldness

²³As soon as Peter and John were set free, they returned to their group and told them what the chief priests and the elders had said. ²⁴When the believers heard it, they all joined together in prayer to God: "Master and Creator of heaven, earth, and sea, and all that is in them! ²⁵By means of the Holy Spirit you spoke through our ancestor David, your servant, when he said,

'Why were the Gentiles furious; why did people make their useless plots? ²⁶The kings of the earth prepared themselves, and the rulers met together against the Lord and his Messiah.'

[d] **4:1** priests; *some manuscripts have* chief priests.
4:11 Ps 118:22 **4:24** Ex 20:11; Neh 9:6; Ps 146:6 **4:25, 26** Ps 2:1, 2 (LXX)

The Apostles and believers prayed for boldness (Acts 4:29). **What might it look like if you were bold in your faith?**

27 For indeed Herod and Pontius Pilate met together in this city with the Gentiles and the people of Israel against Jesus, your holy Servant, whom you made Messiah. 28 They gathered to do everything that you by your power and will had already decided would happen. 29 And now, Lord, take notice of the threats they have made, and allow us, your servants, to speak your message with all boldness. 30 Reach out your hand to heal, and grant that wonders and miracles may be performed through the name of your holy Servant Jesus."

31 When they finished praying, the place where they were meeting was shaken. They were all filled with the Holy Spirit and began to proclaim God's message with boldness.

The Believers Share Their Possessions

32 The group of believers was one in mind and heart. None of them said that any of their belongings were their own, but they all shared with one another everything they had. 33 With great power the apostles gave witness to the resurrection of the Lord Jesus, and God poured rich blessings on them all. 34 There was no one in the group who was in need. Those who owned fields or houses would sell them, bring the money received from the sale, 35 and turn it over to the apostles; and the money was distributed according to the needs of the people.

36 And so it was that Joseph, a Levite born in Cyprus, whom the apostles called Barnabas (which means "One who Encourages"), 37 sold a field he owned, brought the money, and turned it over to the apostles.

Ananias and Sapphira

5 1 But there was a man named Ananias, who with his wife Sapphira sold some property that belonged to them. 2 But with his wife's agreement he kept part of the money for himself and turned the rest over to the apostles. 3 Peter said to him, "Ananias, why did you let Satan take control of you and make you lie to the Holy Spirit by keeping part of the money you received for

Live It!

Looking Out for One Another

The early Christian communities were determined that no one would be poor; rather, everyone would have as much as they needed. If a family had more money or possessions than they needed, they gave the extra to the Apostles, who then used it to help those who had less than they needed.

Who are the poor people in your community? How good is your church or your family at noticing who is poor and taking care of them? Find out what groups in your community help poor people, and explore how you and your family might get involved.

— Acts 4:34–35

the property? 4 Before you sold the property, it belonged to you; and after you sold it, the money was yours. Why, then, did you decide to do such a thing? You have not lied to people—you have lied to God!" 5 As soon as Ananias heard this, he fell down dead; and all who heard about it were terrified. 6 The young men came in, wrapped up his body, carried him out, and buried him.

7 About three hours later his wife, not knowing what had happened, came in. 8 Peter asked her, "Tell me, was this the full amount you and your husband received for your property?"

"Yes," she answered, "the full amount."

9 So Peter said to her, "Why did you and your husband decide to put the Lord's Spirit to the test? The men who buried your husband are at the door right now, and they will carry you out too!" 10 At once she fell down

Acts

4:27 a Lk 23:7–11; b Mt 27:1, 2; Mk 15:1; Lk 23:1; Jn 18:28, 29   4:32 Acts 2:44, 45   5:5 Dan B:55

Stewardship

Stewardship means sharing generously of our time, our talents, and our money—especially with those in need. God knows what's in our hearts and what we possess. And God knows if we are being generous or selfish; we can fool everyone else, but we can never fool God.

So don't hold back, like Ananias and Sapphira did in the beginning of Acts, chapter 5. Instead, be very generous in sharing your time, talent, and money with others. You may not feel like you have much to offer, but you do. An hour of your time or a couple of dollars of your allowance can make a difference. Then be open to experiencing the abundant blessings God has in store for you for being a good steward!

— Acts 5:1–11

at his feet and died. The young men came in and saw that she was dead, so they carried her out and buried her beside her husband. ¹¹The whole church and all the others who heard of this were terrified.

Miracles and Wonders

¹²Many miracles and wonders were being performed among the people by the apostles. All the believers met together in Solomon's Porch. ¹³Nobody outside the group dared join them, even though the people spoke highly of them. ¹⁴But more and more people were added to the group— a crowd of men and women who believed in the Lord. ¹⁵As a result of what the apostles were doing, sick people were carried out into the streets and placed on beds and mats so that at least Peter's shadow might fall on

some of them as he passed by. ¹⁶And crowds of people came in from the towns around Jerusalem, bringing those who were sick or who had evil spirits in them; and they were all healed.

. . . at least Peter's shadow might fall on some of them. (5:15)

The Apostles Are Persecuted

¹⁷Then the High Priest and all his companions, members of the local party of the Sadducees, became extremely jealous of the apostles; so they decided to take action. ¹⁸They arrested the apostles and put them in the public jail. ¹⁹But that night an angel of the Lord opened the prison gates, led the apostles out, and said to them, ²⁰"Go and stand in the Temple, and tell the people all about this new life." ²¹The apostles obeyed, and at dawn they entered the Temple and started teaching.

The High Priest and his companions called together all the Jewish elders for a full meeting of the Council; then they sent orders to the prison to have the apostles brought before them. ²²But when the officials arrived, they did not find the apostles in prison, so they returned to the Council and reported, ²³"When we arrived at the jail, we found it locked up tight and all the guards on watch at the gates; but when we opened the gates, we found no one inside!" ²⁴When the chief priests and the officer in charge of the Temple guards heard this, they wondered what had happened to the apostles. ²⁵Then a man came in and said to them, "Listen! The

Mary of Nazareth

Breakthrough!: Mary, it is an honor to meet you! How old were you when you became the mother of Jesus?

Mary: I was just a teenager—but that was normal for those times.

B: When did you know Jesus was God's son?

Mary: The angel Gabriel [GAY-bree-uhl] told me first, but I'm not sure I really grasped it. My cousin, Elizabeth, knew it immediately when I visited her. But truly, it took all my life for me to fully understand what it meant to be the mother of God's son . . . well, really, the mother of God!

B: What was it like being Jesus' mom?

Mary: He was a good, hard-working boy. Strong-willed, too! But pure joy. Later, when he was a man, I was amazed by his love, and I was crushed when some people returned his love with hate.

B: That must have been hard. What is your favorite memory of Jesus?

Mary: I shared many meals with him, his disciples, and his close friends, Mary, Martha, and Lazarus [LAZ-uh-ruhs]. I loved seeing him laugh and just relax. And when he brought Lazarus back to life . . . what an amazing day! Of course, Jesus himself was raised later. I don't have words to describe that!

B: You were with him at his death.

Mary: After he died, we brought him down from the cross, and I just held him and kissed him for the longest time. I can still taste his blood on my lips.

B: What would you like your life to teach others?

Mary: From all appearances, I was a poor and insignificant girl, a simple servant of God. But God saw deeper—he saw my faithful, strong, gentle spirit. I would like others to think about those qualities in their lives.

B: What do you think is the most important thing you ever said?

Mary: Saying "yes" to God!

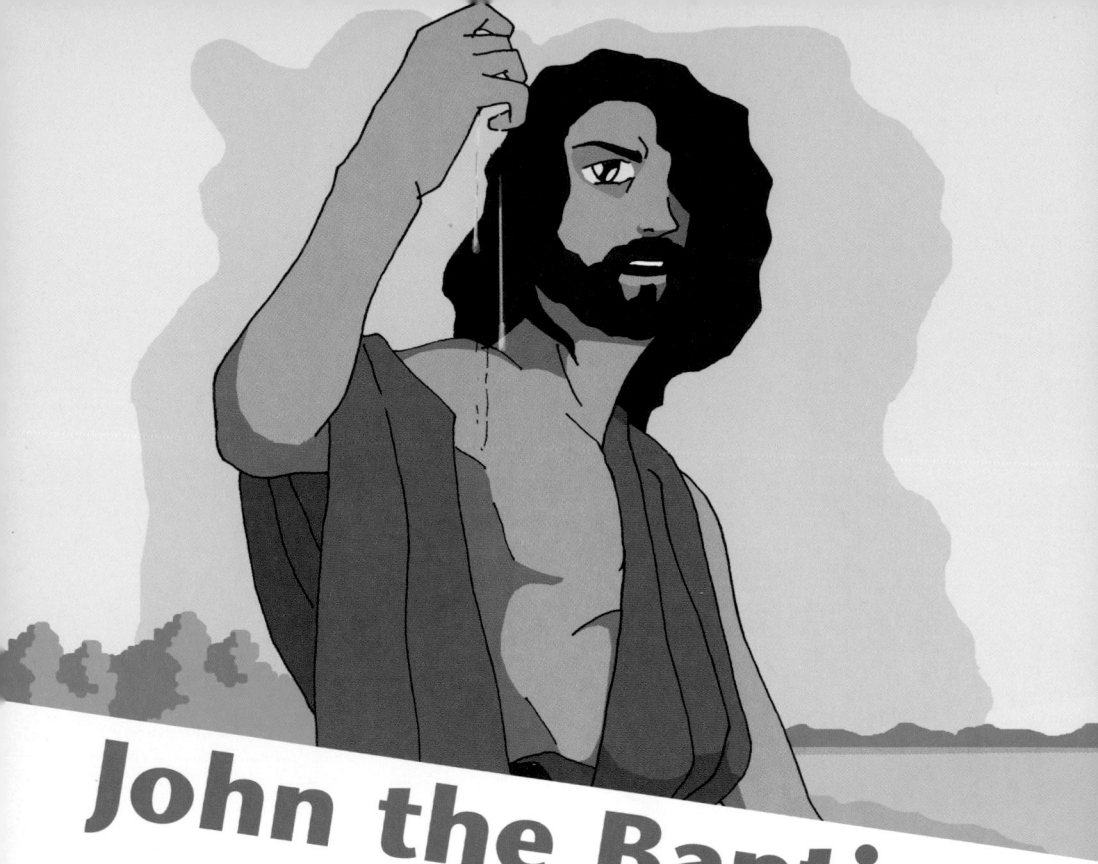

John the Baptist

Breakthrough!: How do you know Jesus?

John: I'm his cousin. When we were grown up, I baptized him and got him started in his ministry.

B: What was it like to baptize Jesus?

John: We both felt very humble about it. When he came out of the water, I saw the Spirit of God rest over Jesus—like a dove, sort of. All of us felt God's presence very powerfully at that moment. I think it was then that Jesus knew it was time to begin his ministry.

B: Tell us a little about your extreme lifestyle.

John: You must be referring to my diet and fashion tastes. It's true; I ate grasshoppers and wild honey, and I wore a camel-hair coat—kind of scratchy, but warm. I lived with a group of believers in the desert. I chose to live very simply so I could keep focused on my mission.

B: What was your mission?

John: I was a baptizer and preacher. I challenged people to change their sinful ways and turn their lives back to God. People said I was a prophet. They also said I was a lot like Jesus, but I knew I wasn't the Messiah; I just pointed people to Jesus, the true Messiah.

B: Your honesty about people's sins got you into trouble, didn't it?

John: Yes, Herod [HAIR-uhd] and his illegitimate wife, Herodias [hi-ROH-dee-uhs], didn't like it when I accused them of adultery. They eventually had me put in prison and killed.

B: Any words you want to leave us with?

John: "Get the road ready for the Lord; make a straight path for him to travel!" (Mark 1:3). It means, prepare a place in your life for God to live. Clean up your act, people!

Peter

Breakthrough!: Sir, what is your connection to Jesus?

Peter: I was one of his twelve apostles; my brother Andrew and I were the first ones Jesus called to follow him.

B: What did you have to give up to do that?

Peter: Give up? Oh, I gained much more than I gave up. I had a good career as a fisherman, which I took a break from. And my family—I wasn't with them as much. But Jesus filled my life with adventures, miracles, challenges . . . and more love than you can imagine. He taught me things I never dreamed I could understand, do, or say.

B: Like what?

Peter: After Jesus left us, everyone looked to me as their leader. I did my best to carry on Jesus' mission and do the work he did, like healing and preaching. Me—a simple fisherman!

B: People say you were an unlikely candidate for taking over. Did you goof up a lot?

Peter: Hmmm . . . yes, I had my moments! But each time I messed up, I got back up and tried again. I think Jesus appreciated my stick-to-it attitude.

B: What was your greatest failure?

Peter: That's easy. After Jesus was arrested, we were terrified that the Romans would come after us, too. So three times I denied to people that Jesus was my friend. It still makes me feel sick to my stomach to recall this.

B: Did Jesus forgive you for that?

Peter: Yes. And he gave me three opportunities to make it up, to tell him just how much I loved him. That's when Jesus asked me to lead his mission.

B: What words would you like our readers to remember you by?

Peter: I'd rather they remember my favorite saying of Jesus: "Don't be afraid."

Mary Magdalene

Breakthrough!: You're the famous prostitute from the Gospels, right?

Mary: NO! That's a common mistake, a terrible rumor that spread. But it's simply not true. There is a prostitute written about, but it is not me. Nor am I the woman caught in adultery. Geesh, my name gets attached to every sinful woman in the Gospels! And I didn't do anything but be a faithful friend to Jesus!

B: Okay, okay, I'm sorry I hit that nerve! Thanks for setting us all straight. So, tell us more about your friendship with Jesus.

Mary: I was sick—in the head, in the heart—some people say I had demons in me, which is true in a sense. Jesus healed me, and I was so moved by this experience that I became one of his followers. I was with Jesus right up to his death—I stood at the foot of his cross, holding up his mother, Mary. Then, on the morning I went to his tomb with the oils and spices, I discovered his body was gone. Then—sorry, it still moves me to tears—he was alive again and he spoke to me outside the tomb! There is no way to describe how awesome that morning was! I was the first person to announce his Resurrection to his apostles, who were hiding out in fear. My fear didn't stop me from trying to give Jesus a proper burial. I would have died for him.

B: What would you like us to remember about you?

Mary: That I was with Jesus through it all. I heard all his stories, saw the miracles, experienced his healing. I was there on all the good days, and on the bad ones, especially the very worst day, when he was tortured and killed. I would do anything for Jesus. I am saved because of him.

Paul

Breakthrough!: Paul, you are one of the most surprising figures in Christianity.

Paul: I started out as a Pharisee [FAIR-ah-see], a devout Jew who lived by the letter of the Law. This new religion, called the Way, was growing rapidly, and some of us felt it had to be stopped before things got out of control. So, I became a defender of the Jewish faith—and ended up persecuting a lot of Christians. I thought I was pleasing God, but I was terribly, terribly misguided.

B: What changed you?

Paul: Jesus appeared to me. To make a long story short, there were flashes from the sky and the voice of Christ saying: "Saul, Saul! Why do you persecute me?" I became a changed man, and learned everything I could about Jesus.

B: Wait, I thought your name was Paul. Why did Christ call you Saul?

Paul: There's an easy explanation. My Jewish name is Saul. But the Roman version of my name is Paul. I became better known as Paul since I spent most of my time preaching in the Roman Empire.

B: You certainly got a lot done after Christ appeared to you.

Paul: I was unstoppable! From the moment of my baptism, I could do nothing but preach the Good News!

B: You must love traveling. You sure got around!

Paul: Honestly, I got terribly seasick! But I had no choice. There were so many people to reach—Jews, Gentiles, the rich, the poor, the educated, the pure of heart. I needed many more years.

B: Under your leadership, the Church expanded from Jerusalem [ji-ROO-suh-luhm] to Rome, the capital of the empire.

Paul: It wasn't just me; there were lots of other Christian missionaries spreading the Good News. It was because of the power of the Holy Spirit. I was just an instrument.

Barnabas

Breakthrough!: How did you first get connected with the apostles?

Barnabas [BAHR-nuh-buhs]: In the early days of the Way (what Christianity was called early on), all the believers took care of one another; we shared our resources to make sure everyone had what they needed. I sold a field I owned and brought the money to the apostles so they could help the poor among us. Later I introduced the apostles to Paul. He originally was a persecutor of the Christians, you see, and they wanted nothing to do with him. Paul needed me to assure the apostles that God had truly changed Paul's heart.

B: So you believed in Paul when no one else would?

Barnabas: I guess so. Next thing I knew, I was traveling with him and sharing the workload with him.

B: The workload?

Barnabas: Preaching and healing, setting up those first Christian communities, appointing leaders, ironing out conflicts, and so on.

B: But you and Paul had a disagreement and split up, right?

Barnabas: My cousin, John Mark, had to drop out of our first mission before it was over, and Paul really held that against him. I guess he didn't trust John Mark or think he was reliable. Anyway, I felt strongly that we should give John Mark another chance. In the end Paul went one way, John Mark and I went the other.

B: That's too bad.

Barnabas: Eventually we worked it out and got back on the road together. In the end, Jesus and his mission are a lot more important than our petty arguments.

B: Your name means "one who encourages." Seems like it fits you!

Barnabas: I hope so.

Timothy

Breakthrough!: Timothy, how is it that Paul came to choose you as a companion and coworker in his mission work?

Timothy: I was a convert of Paul's, when I was young. I think he could see that my faith was sincere and that I loved the Scriptures. I guess he saw other gifts in me as well, and felt I had what it takes to be a missionary.

B: Do you give Paul credit for your faith?

Timothy: Partly. My faith was planted in me and nurtured by my mother, Eunice [YOO-nis], and my grandmother, Lois. Both women were devout Jews and raised me to love my Jewish faith. When I met Paul and learned about Jesus, God moved my heart to believe in him as the Messiah. I am complete now.

B: Was Paul a good traveling companion?

Timothy: Well, he snores . . . but, yes! I never stopped learning from him and never ceased to be inspired by his courage and determination.

B: Did you travel the entire time with Paul?

Timothy: No, I also spent time in Ephesus [EF-uh-suhs] as a leader in the Church there. Paul kept in touch with me by letters, encouraging and supporting me in my pastoral work there.

B: Paul called on you to visit him when he was in prison. Why you?

Timothy: Paul looked on me like a son. We had been through a lot together, and we truly loved each other, like father and son. It was natural that he would call me to be by his side during difficult times.

B: And now you are converting and teaching young people, like Paul did for you?

Timothy: That's what the mission is all about—to keep passing the faith from generation to generation.

Priscilla & Aquila

Breakthrough!: You are friends of Paul's, are you not?

Aquila [AH-kwil-uh]: Yes, Paul lived and worked with my wife and me in Corinth [KAWR-ihnth]. All three of us were tent makers. Paul taught us a lot about Jesus.

B: Priscilla [prih-SIHL-uh], was Paul a good houseguest?

Priscilla: Paul was utterly faithful, and driven to preach the Gospel. It was a privilege to have him in our home. We learned so much from him. Other than his snoring, he was a polite and proper guest!

B: You traveled with Paul a bit, right?

Aquila: It was such an exciting time. We sailed with him to Ephesus [EF-uh-suhs]. We were partners with Paul in starting the Christian community there.

B: So, you've moved around quite a bit yourselves, it seems.

Aquila: It wasn't easy being a follower of Jesus in those days. Before meeting Paul, Priscilla and I lived in Rome. But the emperor wanted the Jews out, so we came to Corinth where we received our call from God.

B: Your call?

Priscilla: Yes, God called us to spread the message of Jesus and become Church leaders. We started a small home church. The believers met in our home to hear the Scriptures and share the holy meal.

B: And you were also teachers.

Aquila: We did whatever we needed to make sure the Gospel was properly taught. For example, there was Apollos [uh-PUHL-ohs], a powerful preacher.

Priscilla: Apollos's heart was in the right place. But Apollos didn't know about being baptized in Jesus' name. We had to sit him down and make sure he understood the whole story.

B: Do you two know that you are one of the few husband and wife missionary teams in the Bible?

Priscilla: Aquila and I were blessed to be able to share our marriage and our ministry together.

Aquila: Yes, and there are lots of married couples working together in the Church all through history. It is all part of God's plan!

men you put in prison are in the Temple teaching the people!" 26So the officer went off with his men and brought the apostles back. They did not use force, however, because they were afraid that the people might stone them.

27They brought the apostles in, made them stand before the Council, and the High Priest questioned them. 28"We gave you strict orders not to teach in the name of this man," he said; "but see what you have done! You have spread your teaching all over Jerusalem, and you want to make us responsible for his death!"

29Peter and the other apostles answered, "We must obey God, not men. 30The God of our ancestors raised Jesus from death, after you had killed him by nailing him to a cross. 31God raised him to his right side as Leader and Savior, to give the people of Israel the opportunity to repent and have their sins forgiven. 32We are witnesses to these things—we and the Holy Spirit, who is God's gift to those who obey him."

33When the members of the Council heard this, they were so furious that they wanted to have the apostles put to death. 34But one of them, a Pharisee named Gamaliel, who was a teacher of the Law and was highly respected by all the people, stood up in the Council. He ordered the apostles to be taken out for a while, 35and then he said to the Council, "Fellow Israelites, be careful what you do to these men. 36You remember that Theudas appeared some time ago, claiming to be somebody great, and about four hundred men joined him. But he was killed, all his followers were scattered, and his movement died out. 37After that, Judas the Galilean appeared during the time of the census; he drew a crowd after him, but he also was killed, and all his followers were scattered. 38And so in this case, I tell you, do not take any action against these men. Leave them alone! If what they have planned and done is of human origin, it will disappear, 39but if it comes from God, you cannot pos-

sibly defeat them. You could find yourselves fighting against God!"

The Council followed Gamaliel's advice. 40They called the apostles in, had them whipped, and ordered them never again to speak in the name of Jesus; and then they set them free. 41As the apostles left the Council, they were happy, because God had considered them worthy to suffer disgrace for the sake of Jesus. 42And every day in the Temple and in people's homes they continued to teach and preach the Good News about Jesus the Messiah.

The Seven Helpers

6 1Some time later, as the number of disciples kept growing, there was a quarrel between the Greek-speaking Jews and the native Jews. The Greek-speaking Jews claimed that their widows were being neglected in the daily distribution of funds. 2So the twelve apostles called the whole group of believers together and said, "It is not right for us to neglect the preaching of God's word in order to handle finances. 3So then, friends, choose seven men among you who are known to be full of the Holy Spirit and wisdom, and we will put them in charge of this matter. 4We ourselves, then, will give our full time to prayer and the work of preaching."

5The whole group was pleased with the apostles' proposal, so they chose Stephen, a man full of faith and the Holy Spirit, and Philip, Prochorus, Nicanor, Timon, Parmenas, and Nicolaus, a Gentile from Antioch who had earlier been converted to Judaism. 6The group presented them to the apostles, who prayed and placed their hands on them.

7And so the word of God continued to spread. The number of disciples in Jerusalem grew larger and larger, and a great number of priests accepted the faith.

5:28 Mt 27:25   **5:39** 2 Macc 7:19

The *Sanhedrin* was the great Council of the Jewish leaders, led by the High Priest. They ruled over religious matters.

Deacons, Ministers of Service

Catholic Connections

The job of making sure widows, orphans, and poor people had everything they needed was becoming a huge job! The Apostles needed to concentrate on preaching and healing, so they found helpers who could help keep track of who needed what and pass out donations fairly. Because the Greek word for service to others is *diakonia*, the people doing this work became known as deacons.

Like in the early Church, today we have deacons, who are ordained to serve the community and assist priests in their ministry. Permanent deacons usually do not have a job in the Church but have regular jobs in the community. If your parish has a permanent deacon, talk to him sometime about his special works of service.

— Acts 6:1–7

The Arrest of Stephen

8Stephen, a man richly blessed by God and full of power, performed great miracles and wonders among the people. 9But he was opposed by some men who were members of the synagogue of the Freedmen*e* (as it was called), which had Jews from Cyrene and Alexandria. They and other Jews from the provinces of Cilicia and Asia started arguing with Stephen. 10But the Spirit gave Stephen such wisdom that when he spoke, they could not refute him. 11So they bribed some men to say, "We heard him speaking against Moses and against God!" 12In this way they stirred up the people, the elders, and the teachers of the Law. They seized Stephen and took him before the Council. 13Then they brought in some men to tell lies about him. "This man," they said, "is always talking against our sacred Temple and the Law of Moses. 14We heard him say that this Jesus of Nazareth will tear down the Temple and change all the customs which have come down to us from Moses!" 15All those sitting in the Council fixed their eyes on Stephen and saw that his face looked like the face of an angel.

Stephen's Speech

7 1The High Priest asked Stephen, "Is this true?"

2Stephen answered, "Brothers and fathers, listen to me! Before our ancestor Abraham had gone to live in Haran, the God of glory appeared to him in Mesopotamia 3and said to him, 'Leave your family and country and go to the land that I will show you.' 4And so he left his country and went to live in Haran. After Abraham's father died, God made him move to this land where you now live. 5God did not then give Abraham any part of it as his own, not even a square foot of ground, but God promised to give it to him, and that it would belong to him and to his descendants. At the time God made this promise, Abraham had no children. 6This is what God said to him: 'Your descendants will live in a foreign country, where they will be slaves and will be badly treated for four hundred years.

e 6:9 FREEDMEN: *These were Jews who had been slaves, but had bought or been given their freedom.*
7:2, 3 Gen 12:1   7:4 a Gen 11:31; b Gen 12:4   7:5 Gen 12:7; 13:15; 15:18; 17:8   7:6, 7 Gen 15:13, 14

Who handles the money at your church? Do you know what the money pays for? To learn more ask your pastor, youth minister, or parents.

Acts

7But I will pass judgment on the people that they will serve, and afterward your descendants will come out of that country and will worship me in this place.' 8Then God gave to Abraham the ceremony of circumcision as a sign of the covenant. So Abraham circumcised Isaac a week after he was born; Isaac circumcised his son Jacob, and Jacob circumcised his twelve sons, the famous ancestors of our race.

9"Jacob's sons became jealous of their brother Joseph and sold him to be a slave in Egypt. But God was with him 10and brought him safely through all his troubles. When Joseph appeared before the king of Egypt, God gave him a pleasing manner and wisdom, and the king made Joseph governor over the country and the royal household. 11Then there was a famine all over Egypt and Canaan, which caused much suffering. Our ancestors could not find any food, 12and when Jacob heard that there was grain in Egypt, he sent his sons, our ancestors, on their first visit there. 13On the second visit Joseph made himself known to his brothers, and the king of Egypt came to know about Joseph's family. 14So Joseph sent a message to his father Jacob, telling him and the whole family, seventy-five people in all, to come to Egypt. 15Then Jacob went to Egypt, where he and his sons died. 16Their bodies were taken to Shechem, where they were buried in the grave which Abraham had bought from the clan of Hamor for a sum of money.

17"When the time drew near for God to keep the promise he had made to Abraham, the number of our people in Egypt had grown much larger. 18At last a king who did not know about Joseph began to rule in Egypt. 19He tricked our ancestors and was cruel to them, forcing them to put their babies out of their homes, so that they would die. 20It was at this time that Moses was born, a very beautiful child. He was cared for at home for three months, 21and when he was put out of his home, the king's daughter adopted him and brought him up

as her own son. 22He was taught all the wisdom of the Egyptians and became a great man in words and deeds.

23"When Moses was forty years old, he decided to find out how his fellow Israelites were being treated. 24He saw one of them being mistreated by an Egyptian, so he went to his help and took revenge on the Egyptian by killing him. (25He thought that his own people would understand that God was going to use him to set them free, but they did not understand.) 26The next day he saw two Israelites fighting, and he tried to make peace between them. 'Listen, men,' he said, 'you are fellow Israelites; why are you fighting like this?' 27But the one who was mistreating the other pushed Moses aside. 'Who made you ruler and judge over us?' he asked. 28'Do you want to kill me, just as you killed that Egyptian yesterday?' 29When Moses heard this, he fled from Egypt and went to live in the land of Midian. There he had two sons.

30"After forty years had passed, an angel appeared to Moses in the flames of a burning bush in the desert near Mount Sinai. 31Moses was amazed by what he saw, and went near the bush to get a better look. But he heard the Lord's voice: 32'I am the God of your ancestors, the God of Abraham, Isaac, and Jacob.' Moses trembled with fear and dared not look. 33The Lord said to him, 'Take your sandals off, for the place where you are standing is holy ground. 34I have seen the cruel suffering of my people in Egypt. I have heard their groans, and I have come down to set them free. Come now; I will send you to Egypt.'

35"Moses is the one who was rejected by the people of Israel. 'Who made you ruler and judge over us?' they asked. He is the one whom God sent to rule the people and set them free with the help of the angel who appeared to him in the burning bush. 36He led the people out of Egypt, performing miracles and wonders in Egypt and at the Red Sea and for forty years in the desert.

Acts

7:7 Ex 3:12   7:8 a Gen 17:10–14; b Gen 21:2–4; c Gen 25:26; d Gen 29:31—35:18   7:9 a Gen 37:11; b Gen 37:28; c Gen 39:2, 21   7:10 Gen 41:39–41   7:11 a Gen 42:1, 2   7:13 a Gen 45:1; b Gen 45:16   7:14 a Gen 45:9, 10, 17, 18; b Gen 46:27 (LXX)   7:15 a Gen 46:1–7; b Gen 49:33   7:16 Gen 23:3–16; 33:19; 50:7–13; Josh 24:32   7:17, 18 Ex 1:7, 8   7:19 a Ex 1:10, 11; b Ex 1:22   7:20 Ex 2:2   7:21 Ex 2:3–10   7:23–29 Ex 2:11–15   7:29 Ex 18:3, 4   7:30–34 Ex 3:1–10   7:35 Ex 2:14   7:36 a Ex 7:3; b Ex 14:21; c Num 14:33

Martyrdom, the Ultimate Sacrifice

Catholic Connections

From the beginning of the Church, many Christians have been persecuted for their faith. The enemies of the faith have tried to force these Christians to speak against God or stop their good works, but the Christians refuse to do so. So they are tortured and often killed. The Christians who are killed because of their faith are called *martyrs*.

Acts, chapter 7, tells the story of Stephen, the first martyr of the Christian Church. Right before Stephen died, he said something that sounded very similar to what Jesus said before his death: "Receive my spirit" and "Do not remember this sin against them" (see Luke 23:34,46).

Bishop Oscar Romero from El Salvador is a modern martyr. After noticing the great injustices against poor people of his country, he started speaking out and became a friend and helper of poor people. This was a threat to the military leaders, who were rich and powerful and wanted to keep the poor people in their place. Even though Bishop Romero received death threats, he did not back down from calling for justice in the name of Jesus Christ. So on March 24, 1983, he was shot to death by his enemies while celebrating the Eucharist.

— Acts, chapter 7

---

37 Moses is the one who said to the people of Israel, 'God will send you a prophet, just as he sent me,* and he will be one of your own people.' 38 He is the one who was with the people of Israel assembled in the desert; he was there with our ancestors and with the angel who spoke to him on Mount Sinai, and he received God's living messages to pass on to us.

39 "But our ancestors refused to obey him; they pushed him aside and wished that they could go back to Egypt. 40 So they said to Aaron, 'Make us some gods who will lead us. We do not know what has happened to that man Moses, who brought us out of Egypt.' 41 It was then that they made an idol in the shape of a bull, offered sacrifice to it, and had a feast in honor of what they themselves had made. 42 So God turned away from them and gave them over to worship the stars of heaven, as it is written in the book of the prophets:

'People of Israel! It was not to me
    that you slaughtered and sacrificed
      animals
    for forty years in the desert.
43 It was the tent of the god Molech that
    you carried,
and the image of Rephan, your star
    god;
they were idols that you had made to
    worship.
And so I will send you into exile beyond
    Babylon.'

44 "Our ancestors had the Tent of God's presence with them in the desert. It had been made as God had told Moses to make it, according to the pattern that Moses had been shown. 45 Later on, our ancestors who received the tent from their fathers carried it with them when they went with Joshua and took over the land from the nations that God drove out as they advanced. And it stayed there until the time of David.

---

f 7:37 just as he sent me; *or* like me.
7:37 Deut 18:15, 18   **7:38** Ex 19:1—20:17; Deut 5:1–33   **7:40** Ex 32:1   **7:41** Ex 32:2–6   **7:42, 43** Am 5:25–27 (LXX)   **7:44** Ex 25:9, 40   **7:45** Josh 3:14–17

Acts

⁴⁶He won God's favor and asked God to allow him to provide a dwelling place for the God of Jacob.ᵍ ⁴⁷But it was Solomon who built him a house.

⁴⁸"But the Most High God does not live in houses built by human hands; as the prophet says,

⁴⁹'Heaven is my throne, says the Lord,
and the earth is my footstool.
What kind of house would you build for me?
Where is the place for me to live in?
⁵⁰Did not I myself make all these things?'

⁵¹"How stubborn you are!" Stephen went on to say. "How heathen your hearts, how deaf you are to God's message! You are just like your ancestors: you too have always resisted the Holy Spirit! ⁵²Was there any prophet that your ancestors did not persecute? They killed God's messengers, who long ago announced the coming of his righteous Servant. And now you have betrayed and murdered him. ⁵³You are the ones who received God's law, that was handed down by angels—yet you have not obeyed it!"

The Stoning of Stephen

⁵⁴As the members of the Council listened to Stephen, they became furious and ground their teeth at him in anger. ⁵⁵But Stephen, full of the Holy Spirit, looked up to heaven and saw God's glory and Jesus standing at the right side of God. ⁵⁶"Look!" he said. "I see heaven opened and the Son of Man standing at the right side of God!"

⁵⁷With a loud cry the Council members covered their ears with their hands. Then they all rushed at him at once, ⁵⁸threw him out of the city, and stoned him. The witnesses left their cloaks in the care of a young man named Saul. ⁵⁹They kept on stoning Stephen as he called out to the Lord, "Lord Jesus, receive my spirit!" ⁶⁰He knelt down and cried out in a loud voice, "Lord! Do not remember this sin against them!" He said this and died.

8 ¹And Saul approved of his murder.

Saul Persecutes the Church

That very day the church in Jerusalem began to suffer cruel persecution. All the believers, except the apostles, were scattered throughout the provinces of Judea and Samaria. ²Some devout men buried Stephen, mourning for him with loud cries.

Saul approved of his murder. (8:1)

³But Saul tried to destroy the church; going from house to house, he dragged out the believers, both men and women, and threw them into jail.

The Gospel Is Preached in Samaria

⁴The believers who were scattered went everywhere, preaching the message. ⁵Philip went to the principal cityʰ in Samaria and preached the Messiah to the people there. ⁶The crowds paid close attention to what Philip said, as they listened to him and saw the miracles that he performed. ⁷Evil spirits came out from many people with a loud cry, and many paralyzed and lame people were healed. ⁸So there was great joy in that city.

ᵍ **7:46** the God of Jacob; *some manuscripts have* the people of Israel. ʰ **8:5** the principal city; *some manuscripts have* a city.
7:46 2 Sam 7:1–16; 1 Chr 17:1–14   **7:47** 1 Kings 6:1–38; 2 Chr 3:1–17   **7:49, 50** Isa 66:1, 2   **7:51** Isa 63:10   **8:3** Acts 22:4, 5; 26:9–11

Acts

Could you forgive your worst enemies as Stephen forgave his? What is the hardest thing you have ever had to forgive someone for?

Pray It!

You Can't Buy Miracles

Have you ever seen a great magician, or learned magic tricks yourself? Magic involves the work of our minds and hands. Simon the magician saw how people received the Holy Spirit when Peter and John laid their hands on them. It looked like magic to him. And he thought if he paid the Apostles, they would show him that trick (Acts 8:19). Peter set him straight, though: These are not magical powers! And they cannot be bought! True healing that comes from God is the work of the heart and the Holy Spirit. God's power works through us if our hearts are pure or "right in God's sight" (8:21). That means we need to trust and be faithful to God.

Dear Lord, sometimes when I pray, I think I might be looking for miracles that act like magic. I need to trust the mysterious ways your power is at work. I have asked for my grandmother's cancer to disappear and for the ankle I sprained yesterday to be better by the playoffs, tomorrow! I know miracles are possible, but they may not look the way I expect or hope. As I grow up, help me to understand more deeply what it means to trust you and what healing truly means. Amen.

— Acts 8:9–25

9 A man named Simon lived there, who for some time had astounded the Samaritans with his magic. He claimed that he was someone great, 10 and everyone in the city, from all classes of society, paid close attention to him. "He is that power of God known as 'The Great Power,' " they said. 11 They paid this attention to him because for such a long time he had astonished them with his magic. 12 But when they believed Philip's message about the good news of the Kingdom of God and about Jesus Christ, they were baptized, both men and women. 13 Simon himself also believed; and after being baptized, he stayed close to Philip and was astounded when he saw the great wonders and miracles that were being performed.

14 The apostles in Jerusalem heard that the people of Samaria had received the word of God, so they sent Peter and John to them. 15 When they arrived, they prayed for the believers that they might receive the Holy Spirit. 16 For the Holy Spirit had not yet come down on any of them; they had only been baptized in the name of the Lord Jesus. 17 Then Peter and John placed their hands on them, and they received the Holy Spirit.

18 Simon saw that the Spirit had been given to the believers when the apostles placed their hands on them. So he offered money to Peter and John, 19 and said, "Give this power to me too, so that anyone I place my hands on will receive the Holy Spirit."

20 But Peter answered him, "May you and your money go to hell, for thinking that you can buy God's gift with money! 21 You have no part or share in our work, because your heart is not right in God's sight. 22 Repent, then, of this evil plan of yours, and pray to the Lord that he will forgive you for thinking such a thing as this. 23 For I see that you are full of bitter envy and are a prisoner of sin."

24 Simon said to Peter and John, "Please pray to the Lord for me, so that none of these things you spoke of will happen to me."

What did the Ethiopian official feel and do after he was baptized (Acts 8:39–40)?

25 After they had given their testimony and proclaimed the Lord's message, Peter and John went back to Jerusalem. On their way they preached the Good News in many villages of Samaria.

Philip and the Ethiopian Official

26 An angel of the Lord said to Philip, "Get ready and go south[i] to the road that goes from Jerusalem to Gaza." (This road is not used nowadays.)[j] 27-28 So Philip got ready and went. Now an Ethiopian eunuch, who was an important official in charge of the treasury of the queen of Ethiopia, was on his way home. He had been to Jerusalem to worship God and was going back home in his carriage. As he rode along, he was reading from the book of the prophet Isaiah. 29 The Holy Spirit said to Philip, "Go over to that carriage and stay close to it." 30 Philip ran over and heard him reading from the book of the prophet Isaiah. He asked him, "Do you understand what you are reading?"

31 The official replied, "How can I understand unless someone explains it to me?" And he invited Philip to climb up and sit in the carriage with him. 32 The passage of scripture which he was reading was this:

"He was like a sheep that is taken to be
      slaughtered,
    like a lamb that makes no sound when
      its wool is cut off.
    He did not say a word.
33 He was humiliated, and justice was denied
      him.
    No one will be able to tell about his
      descendants,
    because his life on earth has come to
      an end."

34 The official asked Philip, "Tell me, of whom is the prophet saying this? Of himself or of someone else?" 35 Then Philip began to speak; starting from this passage of scripture, he told him the Good News about Jesus. 36 As they traveled down the road, they came to a place where there was some water, and

the official said, "Here is some water. What is to keep me from being baptized?"[k]

38 The official ordered the carriage to stop, and both Philip and the official went down into the water, and Philip baptized him. 39 When they came up out of the water, the Spirit of the Lord took Philip away. The official did not see him again, but continued on his way, full of joy. 40 Philip found himself in Azotus; he went on to Caesarea, and on the way he preached the Good News in every town.

The Conversion of Saul
(*Acts 22:6-16; 26:12-18*)

9 1 In the meantime Saul kept up his violent threats of murder against the followers of the Lord. He went to the High Priest 2 and asked for letters of introduction to the synagogues in Damascus, so that if he should find there any followers of the Way of the Lord, he would be able to arrest them, both men and women, and bring them back to Jerusalem.

3 As Saul was coming near the city of Damascus, suddenly a light from the sky flashed around him. 4 He fell to the ground and heard a voice saying to him, "Saul, Saul! Why do you persecute me?"

5 "Who are you, Lord?" he asked.

"I am Jesus, whom you persecute," the

"Who are you, Lord?" (9:5)

---

i **8:26** *south; or* at midday. j **8:26** This road is not used nowadays; *or* This is the desert road. k **8:36** *Some manuscripts add verse 37:* Philip said to him, "You may be baptized if you believe with all your heart." "I do," he answered; "I believe that Jesus Christ is the Son of God."
8:32, 33 Isa 53:7, 8 (LXX)

Capital Punishment

Catholic Connections

The Catholic Church teaches that we should not use capital punishment (also known as the death penalty) to punish criminals as long as they can be kept from hurting someone again.

Why? The Church always works to protect and respect life. The lives of all people—living and unborn, healthy and sick, poor and rich, innocent and guilty—must be respected. Even if we commit a terrible sin, God still loves us. Even the worst criminal is able to change his heart and life. So out of respect for God's gift of life, we should not kill someone just to show that killing is wrong.

Also, the death penalty can be so easily misused. Look at Saint Paul: he led a persecution that led to the unjust execution of many Christians. If the Christians had not been forgiving, they might have tried to put Paul to death for this. But then Paul could not have traveled the world to preach the Gospel and bring people to God after his conversion. If God could change Paul's heart, then our worst criminals can become instruments of God as well. Paul is one of our best arguments against the death penalty.

— Acts, chapter 9

voice said. 6"But get up and go into the city, where you will be told what you must do."

7 The men who were traveling with Saul had stopped, not saying a word; they heard the voice but could not see anyone. 8 Saul got up from the ground and opened his eyes, but could not see a thing. So they took him by the hand and led him into Damascus. 9 For three days he was not able to see, and during that time he did not eat or drink anything.

10 There was a believer in Damascus named Ananias. He had a vision, in which the Lord said to him, "Ananias!"

"Here I am, Lord," he answered.

11 The Lord said to him, "Get ready and go to Straight Street, and at the house of Judas ask for a man from Tarsus named Saul. He is praying, 12 and in a vision he has seen a man named Ananias come in and place his hands on him so that he might see again."

13 Ananias answered, "Lord, many people have told me about this man and about all the terrible things he has done to your people in Jerusalem. 14 And he has come to Damascus with authority from the chief priests to arrest all who worship you."

15 The Lord said to him, "Go, because I have chosen him to serve me, to make my name known to Gentiles and kings and to the people of Israel. 16 And I myself will show him all that he must suffer for my sake."

17 So Ananias went, entered the house where Saul was, and placed his hands on him. "Brother Saul," he said, "the Lord has sent me—Jesus himself, who appeared to you on the road as you were coming here. He sent me so that you might see again and be filled with the Holy Spirit." 18 At once something like fish scales fell from Saul's eyes, and he was able to see again. He stood up and was baptized; 19 and after he had eaten, his strength came back.

9:18 Tob 11:13–15

Saul Preaches in Damascus

Saul stayed for a few days with the believers in Damascus. 20He went straight to the synagogues and began to preach that Jesus was the Son of God.

21All who heard him were amazed and asked, "Isn't he the one who in Jerusalem was killing those who worship that man Jesus? And didn't he come here for the very purpose of arresting those people and taking them back to the chief priests?"

22But Saul's preaching became even more powerful, and his proofs that Jesus was the Messiah were so convincing that the Jews who lived in Damascus could not answer him.

23After many days had gone by, the Jews met together and made plans to kill Saul, 24but he was told of their plan. Day and night they watched the city gates in order to kill him. 25But one night Saul's followers took him and let him down through an opening in the wall, lowering him in a basket.

Saul in Jerusalem

26Saul went to Jerusalem and tried to join the disciples. But they would not believe that he was a disciple, and they were all afraid of him. 27Then Barnabas came to his help and took him to the apostles. He explained to them how Saul had seen the Lord on the road and that the Lord had spoken to him. He also told them how boldly Saul had preached in the name of Jesus in Damascus. 28And so Saul stayed with them and went all over Jerusalem, preaching boldly in the name of the Lord. 29He also talked and disputed with the Greek-speaking Jews, but they tried to kill him. 30When the believers found out about this, they took Saul to Caesarea and sent him away to Tarsus.

31And so it was that the church throughout Judea, Galilee, and Samaria had a time of peace. Through the help of the Holy Spirit it was strengthened and grew in numbers, as it lived in reverence for the Lord.

9:23–25 2 Cor 11:32, 33

Peter in Lydda and Joppa

32Peter traveled everywhere, and on one occasion he went to visit God's people who lived in Lydda. 33There he met a man named Aeneas, who was paralyzed and had not been able to get out of bed for eight years. 34"Aeneas," Peter said to him, "Jesus Christ makes you well. Get up and make your bed." At once Aeneas got up. 35All the people living in Lydda and Sharon saw him, and they turned to the Lord.

36In Joppa there was a woman named Tabitha, who was a believer. (Her name in Greek is Dorcas, meaning "a deer.") She spent all her time doing good and helping the poor. 37At that time she got sick and died. Her body was washed and laid in a room upstairs. 38Joppa was not very far from Lydda, and when the believers in Joppa heard that Peter was in Lydda, they sent two men to him with the message, "Please hurry and come to us." 39So Peter got ready and went with them. When he arrived, he was taken to the room upstairs, where all the widows crowded around him, crying and showing him all the shirts and coats that Dorcas had made while she was alive. 40Peter put them all out of the room, and knelt down and prayed; then he turned to the body and said, "Tabitha, get up!" She opened her eyes, and when she saw Peter, she sat up. 41Peter reached over and helped her get up. Then he called all the believers, including the widows, and presented her alive to them. 42The news about this spread all over Joppa, and many people believed in the Lord. 43Peter stayed on in Joppa for many days with a tanner of leather named Simon.

Peter and Cornelius

10 1There was a man in Caesarea named Cornelius, who was a captain in the Roman army regiment called "The Italian Regiment." 2He was a religious man; he and his whole family worshiped God. He

Acts

The early Christians called themselves the Way (*Acts 9:2*). **Why, do you think, did they call themselves by that name?**

also did much to help the Jewish poor people
and was constantly praying to God. ³It was
about three o'clock one afternoon when he
had a vision, in which he clearly saw an angel
of God come in and say to him, "Cornelius!"

⁴He stared at the angel in fear and said,
"What is it, sir?"

The angel answered, "God is pleased with
your prayers and works of charity, and is
ready to answer you. ⁵And now send some
men to Joppa for a certain man whose full
name is Simon Peter. ⁶He is a guest in the
home of a tanner of leather named Simon,
who lives by the sea." ⁷Then the angel went
away, and Cornelius called two of his house
servants and a soldier, a religious man who
was one of his personal attendants. ⁸He told
them what had happened and sent them off
to Joppa.

⁹The next day, as they were on their way
and coming near Joppa, Peter went up on the
roof of the house about noon in order to
pray. ¹⁰He became hungry and wanted something to eat; while the food was being prepared, he had a vision. ¹¹He saw heaven
opened and something coming down that
looked like a large sheet being lowered by its
four corners to the earth. ¹²In it were all
kinds of animals, reptiles, and wild birds. ¹³A
voice said to him, "Get up, Peter; kill and
eat!"

¹⁴But Peter said, "Certainly not, Lord! I
have never eaten anything ritually unclean
or defiled."

¹⁵The voice spoke to him again, "Do not
consider anything unclean that God has
declared clean." ¹⁶This happened three
times, and then the thing was taken back up
into heaven.

¹⁷While Peter was wondering about the
meaning of this vision, the men sent by Cornelius had learned where Simon's house was,
and they were now standing in front of the
gate. ¹⁸They called out and asked, "Is there a
guest here by the name of Simon Peter?"

¹⁹Peter was still trying to understand what
the vision meant, when the Spirit said, "Lis-

Dreams by God

What's the weirdest dream you've
ever had? God sometimes speaks
to our hearts through dreams and
the symbols they contain. Peter's
dream was about God's desire to
bring Gentiles (non-Jewish people)
into the new Christian community. Jesus was a Jew and preached
mostly to Jewish people. So his
first followers were Jews. Many of
them believed that if you wanted
to become a Christian, you first
had to become a Jew and follow
all the laws of the Jewish religion.

Peter's dream is about Jewish
food, or dietary, laws. According
to these laws, some animals are
unclean, and Jews may not eat
them. But Gentiles did not have
these kinds of food laws, so they
ate those animals. Jewish Christians considered Gentile Christians unclean because of this. In
Peter's dream, God was telling
Peter that people can follow
Christ without following all the
Jewish laws about food! Through
his dream Peter was being guided
to bring Gentiles into the new
Church, without them having to
first become Jews.

God can still speak to people
through dreams. Can you remember any of your dreams? Do you
think God is trying to tell you
something through the dream?

— Acts 10:9—11:10

Gentile is a word used to describe someone who is not Jewish.

ten! Three*¹* men are here looking for you.
²⁰So get ready and go down, and do not
hesitate to go with them, for I have sent
them." ²¹So Peter went down and said to the
men, "I am the man you are looking for.
Why have you come?"

²²"Captain Cornelius sent us," they
answered. "He is a good man who worships
God and is highly respected by all the Jewish
people. An angel of God told him to invite
you to his house, so that he could hear what
you have to say." ²³Peter invited the men in
and had them spend the night there.

The next day he got ready and went with
them; and some of the believers from Joppa
went along with him. ²⁴The following day
he arrived in Caesarea, where Cornelius was
waiting for him, together with relatives and
close friends that he had invited. ²⁵As Peter
was about to go in, Cornelius met him, fell
at his feet, and bowed down before him.
²⁶But Peter made him rise. "Stand up," he
said, "I myself am only a man." ²⁷Peter kept
on talking to Cornelius as he went into the
house, where he found many people gathered. ²⁸He said to them, "You yourselves
know very well that a Jew is not allowed by
his religion to visit or associate with Gentiles. But God has shown me that I must not
consider any person ritually unclean or
defiled. ²⁹And so when you sent for me, I
came without any objection. I ask you, then,
why did you send for me?"

³⁰Cornelius said, "It was about this time
three days ago that I was praying*ᵐ* in my
house at three o'clock in the afternoon. Suddenly a man dressed in shining clothes stood
in front of me ³¹and said: 'Cornelius! God
has heard your prayer and has taken notice
of your works of charity. ³²Send someone to
Joppa for a man whose full name is Simon
Peter. He is a guest in the home of Simon
the tanner of leather, who lives by the sea.'
³³And so I sent for you at once, and you
have been good enough to come. Now we
are all here in the presence of God, waiting
to hear anything that the Lord has instructed
you to say."

Peter's Speech

³⁴Peter began to speak: "I now realize that
it is true that God treats everyone on the
same basis. ³⁵Those who fear him and do
what is right are acceptable to him, no matter
what race they belong to. ³⁶You know the
message he sent to the people of Israel, proclaiming the Good News of peace through
Jesus Christ, who is Lord of all. ³⁷You know
of the great event that took place throughout
the land of Israel, beginning in Galilee after
John preached his message of baptism. ³⁸You
know about Jesus of Nazareth and how God
poured out on him the Holy Spirit and
power. He went everywhere, doing good and
healing all who were under the power of the
Devil, for God was with him. ³⁹We are witnesses of everything that he did in the land of
Israel and in Jerusalem. Then they put him to
death by nailing him to a cross. ⁴⁰But God
raised him from death three days later and
caused him to appear, ⁴¹not to everyone, but
only to the witnesses that God had already
chosen, that is, to us who ate and drank with
him after he rose from death. ⁴²And he commanded us to preach the gospel to the people
and to testify that he is the one whom God
has appointed judge of the living and the
dead. ⁴³All the prophets spoke about him, saying that all who believe in him will have their
sins forgiven through the power of his name."

The Gentiles Receive the Holy Spirit

⁴⁴While Peter was still speaking, the Holy
Spirit came down on all those who were listening to his message. ⁴⁵The Jewish believers
who had come from Joppa with Peter were
amazed that God had poured out his gift of
the Holy Spirit on the Gentiles also. ⁴⁶For
they heard them speaking in strange tongues
and praising God's greatness. Peter spoke up:
⁴⁷"These people have received the Holy
Spirit, just as we also did. Can anyone, then,
stop them from being baptized with water?"
⁴⁸So he ordered them to be baptized in the
name of Jesus Christ. Then they asked him
to stay with them for a few days.

ˡ **10:19** Three; *some manuscripts have* Some; *one manuscript has* Two.   *ᵐ* **10:30** praying; *some manuscripts have*
fasting and praying.
10:34 Deut 10:17

Peter's Report to the Church at Jerusalem

11 ¹The apostles and the other believers throughout Judea heard that the Gentiles also had received the word of God. ²When Peter went to Jerusalem, those who were in favor of circumcising Gentiles criticized him, saying, ³"You were a guest in the home of uncircumcised Gentiles, and you even ate with them!" ⁴So Peter gave them a complete account of what had happened from the very beginning:

⁵"While I was praying in the city of Joppa, I had a vision. I saw something coming down that looked like a large sheet being lowered by its four corners from heaven, and it stopped next to me. ⁶I looked closely inside and saw domesticated and wild animals, reptiles, and wild birds. ⁷Then I heard a voice saying to me, 'Get up, Peter; kill and eat!' ⁸But I said, 'Certainly not, Lord! No ritually unclean or defiled food has ever entered my mouth.' ⁹The voice spoke again from heaven, 'Do not consider anything unclean that God has declared clean.' ¹⁰This happened three times, and finally the whole thing was drawn back up into heaven. ¹¹At that very moment three men who had been sent to me from Caesarea arrived at the house where I was[n] staying. ¹²The Spirit told me to go with them without hesitation. These six fellow believers from Joppa accompanied me to Caesarea, and we all went into the house of Cornelius. ¹³He told us how he had seen an angel standing in his house, who said to him, 'Send someone to Joppa for a man whose full name is Simon Peter. ¹⁴He will speak words to you by which you and all your family will be saved.' ¹⁵And when I began to speak, the Holy Spirit came down on them just as on us at the beginning. ¹⁶Then I remembered what the Lord had said: 'John baptized with water, but you will be baptized with the Holy Spirit.' ¹⁷It is clear that God gave those Gentiles the same gift that he gave us when we believed in the Lord Jesus Christ; who was I, then, to try to stop God!"

¹⁸When they heard this, they stopped their criticism and praised God, saying, "Then God has given to the Gentiles also the opportunity to repent and live!"

The Church at Antioch

¹⁹Some of the believers who were scattered by the persecution which took place when Stephen was killed went as far as Phoenicia, Cyprus, and Antioch, telling the message to Jews only. ²⁰But other believers, who were from Cyprus and Cyrene, went to Antioch and proclaimed the message to Gentiles[o] also, telling them the Good News about the Lord Jesus. ²¹The Lord's power

The More, the Merrier!

God doesn't want us to leave people out just because they are different from us. Variety can make things much more interesting to be a part of. And we can learn more from people who are different from us than from people who are just the same. This is why, as the Church began to form in places such as Antioch, both Jews and Gentiles were included. The variety of histories and gifts made the Church stronger and richer.

Who are the people at your school who get left out because they don't fit in with the popular groups? Try to be the person who looks past their differences and includes them instead of pushing them out. To welcome without judging is a wonderful virtue to possess!

— Acts 11:19–26

---

[n] **11:11** I was; *some manuscripts have* we were.   [o] **11:20** Gentiles; *some manuscripts have* Greek-speaking Jews *or* Greek-speaking people.
11:16 Acts 1:5   **11:19** Acts 8:1–4

Pray It!

The Power of Prayer

After Peter was arrested, everyone in the Church was praying like mad for him! Then, miraculously, Peter escaped from prison.

Do you believe in the power of prayer? Many Catholic parishes have prayer chains. These are groups who make it their business to pray for people. The person on the top of the chain is made aware of a problem, sickness, or other need, then that need gets passed from person to person until everyone in the prayer chain gets the word. Think of something or someone you would want prayers for, then imagine fifty or one hundred or even many hundreds of people praying for your intention. God gets flooded with our prayers!

That's one great thing about being part of a Christian community. We care about what's happening in one another's lives, and when someone is in trouble, we all can pray together for God's help.

Here's an important thing to remember about prayer, however. God always hears and responds to our prayers, but not always in the way we expect or want! Sometimes God's ways are mysterious, but we need to trust in God's constant and deep loving care for us.

— Acts 12:1–19

---

was with them, and a great number of people believed and turned to the Lord.

²²The news about this reached the church in Jerusalem, so they sent Barnabas to Antioch. ²³When he arrived and saw how God had blessed the people, he was glad and urged them all to be faithful and true to the Lord with all their hearts. ²⁴Barnabas was a good man, full of the Holy Spirit and faith, and many people were brought to the Lord.

²⁵Then Barnabas went to Tarsus to look for Saul. ²⁶When he found him, he took him to Antioch, and for a whole year the two met with the people of the church and taught a large group. It was at Antioch that the believers were first called Christians.

²⁷About that time some prophets went from Jerusalem to Antioch. ²⁸One of them, named Agabus, stood up and by the power of the Spirit predicted that a severe famine

was about to come over all the earth. (It came when Claudius was emperor.) ²⁹The disciples decided that they each would send as much as they could to help their fellow believers who lived in Judea. ³⁰They did this, then, and sent the money to the church elders by Barnabas and Saul.

More Persecution

12 ¹About this time King Herod[p] began to persecute some members of the church. ²He had James, the brother of John, put to death by the sword. ³When he saw that this pleased the Jews, he went ahead and had Peter arrested. (This happened during the time of the Festival of Unleavened Bread.) ⁴After his arrest Peter was put in jail, where he was handed over to be guarded by four groups of four soldiers each. Herod

Acts

---

p **12:1** KING HEROD: *Herod Agrippa I, ruler of all Palestine.*
11:28 Acts 21:10   **12:4** Ex 12:1–27

Antioch is where the believers were first called Christians. Can you find Antioch on Map 7 on page c46?

planned to put him on trial in public after Passover. [5] So Peter was kept in jail, but the people of the church were praying earnestly to God for him.

Peter Is Set Free from Prison

[6] The night before Herod was going to bring him out to the people, Peter was sleeping between two guards. He was tied with two chains, and there were guards on duty at the prison gate. [7] Suddenly an angel of the Lord stood there, and a light shone in the cell. The angel shook Peter by the shoulder, woke him up, and said, "Hurry! Get up!" At once the chains fell off Peter's hands. [8] Then the angel said, "Tighten your belt and put on your sandals." Peter did so, and the angel said, "Put your cloak around you and come with me." [9] Peter followed him out of the prison, not knowing, however, if what the angel was doing was real; he thought he was seeing a vision. [10] They passed by the first guard station and then the second, and came at last to the iron gate that opens into the city. The gate opened for them by itself, and they went out. They walked down a street, and suddenly the angel left Peter.

[11] Then Peter realized what had happened to him, and said, "Now I know that it is really true! The Lord sent his angel to rescue me from Herod's power and from everything the Jewish people expected to happen."

[12] Aware of his situation, he went to the home of Mary, the mother of John Mark, where many people had gathered and were praying. [13] Peter knocked at the outside door, and a servant named Rhoda came to answer it. [14] She recognized Peter's voice and was so happy that she ran back in without opening the door, and announced that Peter was standing outside. [15] "You are crazy!" they told her. But she insisted that it was true. So they answered, "It is his angel."

[16] Meanwhile Peter kept on knocking. At last they opened the door, and when they saw him, they were amazed. [17] He motioned with his hand for them to be quiet, and he explained to them how the Lord had brought him out of prison. "Tell this to James and the rest of the believers," he said; then he left and went somewhere else.

[18] When morning came, there was a tremendous confusion among the guards— what had happened to Peter? [19] Herod gave orders to search for him, but they could not find him. So he had the guards questioned and ordered them put to death.

After this, Herod left Judea and spent some time in Caesarea.

The Death of Herod

[20] Herod was very angry with the people of Tyre and Sidon, so they went in a group to see him. First they convinced Blastus, the man in charge of the palace, that he should help them. Then they went to Herod and asked him for peace, because their country got its food supplies from the king's country. [21] On a chosen day Herod put on his royal robes, sat on his throne, and made a speech to the people. [22] "It isn't a man speaking, but a god!" they shouted. [23] At once the angel of the Lord struck Herod down, because he did not give honor to God. He was eaten by worms and died.

[24] Meanwhile the word of God continued to spread and grow.

[25] Barnabas and Saul finished their mission and returned from[q] Jerusalem, taking John Mark with them.

Barnabas and Saul Are Chosen and Sent

13 [1] In the church at Antioch there were some prophets and teachers: Barnabas, Simeon (called the Black), Lucius (from Cyrene), Manaen (who had been brought up with Governor Herod[r]), and Saul. [2] While they were serving the Lord and

---

[q] **12:25** from; *some manuscripts have* to. [r] **13:1** HEROD: *Herod Antipas, ruler of Galilee (see Lk 3:1).*
12:20–23 2 Macc 9:5–28

What needs of others are you aware of that you could pray for? Who else can you ask to pray for those needs?

fasting, the Holy Spirit said to them, "Set apart for me Barnabas and Saul, to do the work to which I have called them."

³They fasted and prayed, placed their hands on them, and sent them off.

In Cyprus

⁴Having been sent by the Holy Spirit, Barnabas and Saul went to Seleucia and sailed from there to the island of Cyprus. ⁵When they arrived at Salamis, they preached the word of God in the synagogues. They had John Mark with them to help in the work.

⁶They went all the way across the island to Paphos, where they met a certain magician named Bar-Jesus, a Jew who claimed to be a prophet. ⁷He was a friend of the governor of the island, Sergius Paulus, who was an intelligent man. The governor called Barnabas and Saul before him because he wanted to hear the word of God. ⁸But they were opposed by the magician Elymas (that is his name in Greek), who tried to turn the governor away from the faith. ⁹Then Saul—also known as Paul—was filled with the Holy Spirit; he looked straight at the magician ¹⁰and said, "You son of the Devil! You are the enemy of everything that is good. You are full of all kinds of evil tricks, and you always keep trying to turn the Lord's truths into lies! ¹¹The Lord's hand will come down on you now; you will be blind and will not see the light of day for a time."

At once Elymas felt a dark mist cover his eyes, and he walked around trying to find someone to lead him by the hand. ¹²When the governor saw what had happened, he believed; for he was greatly amazed at the teaching about the Lord.

In Antioch in Pisidia

¹³Paul and his companions sailed from Paphos and came to Perga, a city in Pamphylia, where John Mark left them and went back to Jerusalem. ¹⁴They went on from Perga and arrived in Antioch in Pisidia, and on the Sabbath they went into the synagogue and sat down. ¹⁵After the reading from the Law of Moses and from the

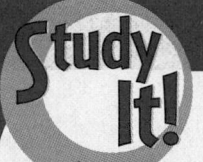

Study It!

Paul's Journeys

In Acts, chapters 13–21, we read about three missionary journeys Paul made over a period of ten years to spread the Gospel message and establish Christian communities, or churches. The first journey (chapters 13–15) begins as a mission to bring Jews to Christ, but soon Paul was converting Gentiles as well. In Acts, the author changes from using Paul's Hebrew name, Saul, to using his Roman name, Paul, symbolizing the importance of his mission. This type of name change happens several other times in the Bible; for example, Abram and Sarai become Abraham and Sarah (Genesis, chapter 17), and Jacob becomes Israel (Genesis, chapter 32).

Paul's second journey (chapters 15–18) takes him into the rest of the Roman Empire, where he begins churches in Thessalonica, Philippi, and Corinth. His letters to these communities (written later) became books in the New Testament: Thessalonians, Philippians, and 1 and 2 Corinthians. Paul also visits the communities he founded on previous journeys.

The third missionary journey (chapters 18–21) is spent primarily in Ephesus and brings Paul back to Jerusalem where he is arrested at the Temple for his preaching about Jesus. Because of his Roman citizenship, he is sent to Rome for a trial and lives the rest of his life there. Check out Map 7 and Map 8 to trace the journeys of Paul.

— Acts, chapters 13–21

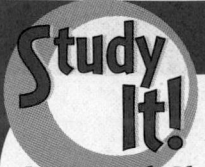

Jews and Christ

A Jew himself, Paul is trying to convert (change the hearts) of other Jews who did not believe in Jesus. In telling the story of Israel's salvation in the middle of Acts, chapter 13, he is connecting Jewish history to the story of Jesus. This is because he wants the Jews to understand that Jesus is the Messiah that the Jewish prophets spoke of. He is not preaching about some new religion that has nothing to do with Judaism. Rather, Jesus and Christianity have everything to do with Judaism. Paul is trying to bring Jews to the Christian faith by helping them understand that Jesus is the Savior they were waiting for!

— Acts 13:13–43

writings of the prophets, the officials of the synagogue sent them a message: "Friends, we want you to speak to the people if you have a message of encouragement for them." 16 Paul stood up, motioned with his hand, and began to speak:

"Fellow Israelites and all Gentiles here who worship God: hear me! 17 The God of the people of Israel chose our ancestors and made the people a great nation during the time they lived as foreigners in Egypt. God brought them out of Egypt by his great power, 18 and for forty years he endured[s] them in the desert. 19 He destroyed seven nations in the land of Canaan and made his people the owners of the land. 20 All of this took about 450 years.

"After this[t] he gave them judges until the time of the prophet Samuel. 21 And when they asked for a king, God gave them Saul son of Kish from the tribe of Benjamin, to be their king for forty years. 22 After removing him, God made David their king. This is what God said about him: 'I have found that David son of Jesse is the kind of man I like, a man who will do all I want him to do.' 23 It was Jesus, a descendant of David, whom God made the Savior of the people of Israel, as he had promised. 24 Before Jesus began his work, John preached to all the people of Israel that they should turn from their sins and be baptized. 25 And as John was about to finish his mission, he said to the people, 'Who do you think I am? I am not the one you are waiting for. But listen! He is coming after me, and I am not good enough to take his sandals off his feet.'

26 "My fellow Israelites, descendants of Abraham, and all Gentiles here who worship God: it is to us that this message of salvation has been sent! 27 For the people who live in Jerusalem and their leaders did not know that he is the Savior, nor did they understand the words of the prophets that are read every Sabbath. Yet they made the prophets' words come true by condemning Jesus. 28 And even though they could find no reason to pass the death sentence on him, they asked Pilate to have him put to death. 29 And after they had done everything that the Scriptures say about him, they took him down from the cross and placed him in a tomb. 30 But God raised him from death, 31 and for many days he appeared to those who had traveled with him from Galilee to Jerusalem. They are now witnesses for him to the people of Israel. 32-33 And we are here to bring the Good News to you: what God promised our ancestors he would do, he has now done for us, who are their descendants, by raising Jesus to life. As it is written in the second Psalm,

'You are my Son;
today I have become your Father.'

s 13:18 he endured; *some manuscripts have* he took care of.   t 13:20 All of this took about 450 years. After this; *or* Some 450 years later.

13:17 a Ex 1:7; b Ex 12:51   13:18 Num 14:34; Deut 1:31   13:19 a Deut 7:1; b Josh 14:1   13:20 a Judg 2:16; b 1 Sam 3:20   13:21 a 1 Sam 8:5; b 1 Sam 10:21   13:22 a 1 Sam 13:14; b 1 Sam 16:12; Ps 89:20   13:24 Mk 1:4; Lk 3:3   13:25 a Jn 1:20; b Mt 3:11; Mk 1:7; Lk 3:16; Jn 1:27   13:28 Mt 27:22, 23; Mk 15:13, 14; Lk 23:21–23; Jn 19:15   13:29 Mt 27:57–61; Mk 15:42–47; Lk 23:50–56; Jn 19:38–42   13:31 Acts 1:3   13:33 Ps 2:7

34 And this is what God said about raising him from death, never to rot away in the grave:

'I will give you the sacred and sure blessings
  that I promised to David.'

35 As indeed he says in another passage,

'You will not allow your faithful servant
  to rot in the grave.'

36 For David served God's purposes in his own time, and then he died, was buried with his ancestors, and his body rotted in the grave. 37 But this did not happen to the one whom God raised from death. 38-39 All of you, my fellow Israelites, are to know for sure that it is through Jesus that the message about forgiveness of sins is preached to you; you are to know that everyone who believes in him is set free from all the sins from which the Law of Moses could not set you free. 40 Take care, then, so that what the prophets said may not happen to you: *u*

41 'Look, you scoffers! Be astonished and die!

For what I am doing today
  is something that you will not believe,
  even when someone explains it to
    you!' "

42 As Paul and Barnabas were leaving the synagogue, the people invited them to come back the next Sabbath and tell them more about these things. 43 After the people had left the meeting, Paul and Barnabas were followed by many Jews and by many Gentiles who had been converted to Judaism. The apostles spoke to them and encouraged them to keep on living in the grace of God.

44 The next Sabbath nearly everyone in the town came to hear the word of the Lord. 45 When the Jews saw the crowds, they were filled with jealousy; they disputed what Paul was saying and insulted him. 46 But Paul and Barnabas spoke out even more boldly: "It was necessary that the word of God should be spoken first to you. But since you reject it and do not consider yourselves worthy of eternal life, we will leave you and go to the Gentiles. 47 For this is the commandment that the Lord has given us:

'I have made you a light for the Gentiles,
  so that all the world may be saved.' "

48 When the Gentiles heard this, they were glad and praised the Lord's message; and those who had been chosen for eternal life became believers.

49 The word of the Lord spread everywhere in that region. 50 But the Jews stirred up the leading men of the city and the Gentile women of high social standing who worshiped God. They started a persecution against Paul and Barnabas and threw them out of their region. 51 The apostles shook the dust off their feet in protest against them and went on to Iconium. 52 The believers in Antioch were full of joy and the Holy Spirit.

In Iconium

14 ¹The same thing happened in Iconium: Paul and Barnabas went to the synagogue and spoke in such a way that a great number of Jews and Gentiles became believers. 2 But the Jews who would not believe stirred up the Gentiles and turned them against the believers. 3 The apostles stayed there for a long time, speaking boldly about the Lord, who proved that their message about his grace was true by giving them the power to perform miracles and wonders. 4 The people of the city were divided: some were for the Jews, others for the apostles.

5 Then some Gentiles and Jews, together with their leaders, decided to mistreat the apostles and stone them. 6 When the apostles learned about it, they fled to the cities of Lystra and Derbe in Lycaonia and to the surrounding territory. 7 There they preached the Good News.

u **13.40** *Some manuscripts do not have* to you.
13.34 Isa 55:3 (LXX)   **13.35** Ps 16:10   **13.41** Hab 1:5 (LXX)   **13.47** Isa 42:6; 49:6   **13.51** Mt 10:14; Mk 6:11; Lk 9:5; 10:11

In Lystra and Derbe

[8]In Lystra there was a crippled man who had been lame from birth and had never been able to walk. [9]He sat there and listened to Paul's words. Paul saw that he believed and could be healed, so he looked straight at him [10]and said in a loud voice, "Stand up straight on your feet!" The man jumped up and started walking around. [11]When the crowds saw what Paul had done, they started shouting in their own Lycaonian language, "The gods have become like men and have come down to us!" [12]They gave Barnabas the name Zeus, and Paul the name Hermes, because he was the chief speaker. [13]The priest of the god Zeus, whose temple stood just outside the town, brought bulls and flowers to the gate, for he and the crowds wanted to offer sacrifice to the apostles.

[14]When Barnabas and Paul heard what they were about to do, they tore their clothes and ran into the middle of the crowd, shouting, [15]"Why are you doing this? We ourselves are only human beings like you! We are here to announce the Good News, to turn you away from these worthless things to the living God, who made heaven, earth, sea, and all that is in them. [16]In the past he allowed all people to go their own way. [17]But he has always given evidence of his existence by the good things he does: he gives you rain from heaven and crops at the right times; he gives you food and fills your hearts with happiness." [18]Even with these words the apostles could hardly keep the crowd from offering a sacrifice to them.

[19]Some Jews came from Antioch in Pisidia and from Iconium; they won the crowds over to their side, stoned Paul and dragged him out of the town, thinking that he was dead. [20]But when the believers gathered around him, he got up and went back into the town. The next day he and Barnabas went to Derbe.

Risking Their Necks

In Acts, chapter 14, we learn that Paul and Barnabas were run out of two towns—Iconium and Lystra—and Paul was almost killed. They were just being faithful to the work God sent them to do. The truth is, sometimes being faithful is risky. For example, when we forgive our enemies, we risk having our friends turn on us. When we give our money to poor people instead of spending it on trendy clothes, we risk being judged by what we wear. When we participate in a service project in our free time, we risk being unpopular because we're doing something out of the ordinary.

Don't be afraid of rejection! Jesus warned us we would be persecuted for being faithful. Even though Paul and Barnabas were run out of town, they were successful in helping some people believe in Jesus. Hang in there and believe that what you gain for living faithfully is far greater than anything you have to lose.

— Acts 14:1–20

The Return to Antioch in Syria

[21]Paul and Barnabas preached the Good News in Derbe and won many disciples. Then they went back to Lystra, to Iconium, and on to Antioch in Pisidia. [22]They strengthened the believers and encouraged them to remain true to the faith. "We must pass through many troubles to enter the Kingdom

14:15 Ex 20:11; Ps 146:6

Elders (Acts 14:23) **were people appointed by the Apostles to have general responsibility for the work of the Church.**

of God," they taught. 23In each church they appointed elders, and with prayers and fasting they commended them to the Lord, in whom they had put their trust.

24After going through the territory of Pisidia, they came to Pamphylia. 25There they preached the message in Perga and then went to Attalia, 26and from there they sailed back to Antioch, the place where they had been commended to the care of God's grace for the work they had now completed.

27When they arrived in Antioch, they gathered the people of the church together and told them about all that God had done with them and how he had opened the way for the Gentiles to believe. 28And they stayed a long time there with the believers.

The Meeting at Jerusalem

15 1Some men came from Judea to Antioch and started teaching the believers, "You cannot be saved unless you are circumcised as the Law of Moses requires." 2Paul and Barnabas got into a fierce argument with them about this, so it was decided that Paul and Barnabas and some of the others in Antioch should go to Jerusalem and see the apostles and elders about this matter.

3They were sent on their way by the church; and as they went through Phoenicia and Samaria, they reported how the Gentiles had turned to God; this news brought great joy to all the believers. 4When they arrived in Jerusalem, they were welcomed by the church, the apostles, and the elders, to whom they told all that God had done through them. 5But some of the believers who belonged to the party of the Pharisees stood up and said, "The Gentiles must be circumcised and told to obey the Law of Moses."

6The apostles and the elders met together to consider this question. 7After a long debate Peter stood up and said, "My friends, you know that a long time ago God chose me from among you to preach the Good News to the Gentiles, so that they could hear and believe. 8And God, who knows the thoughts of everyone, showed his approval of

the Gentiles by giving the Holy Spirit to them, just as he had to us. 9He made no difference between us and them; he forgave their sins because they believed. 10So then, why do you now want to put God to the test by laying a load on the backs of the believers which neither our ancestors nor we ourselves were able to carry? 11No! We believe and are saved by the grace of the Lord Jesus, just as they are."

12The whole group was silent as they heard Barnabas and Paul report all the miracles and wonders that God had performed through them among the Gentiles. 13When they had finished speaking, James spoke up: "Listen to me, my friends! 14Simon has just explained how God first showed his care for the Gentiles by taking from among them a people to belong to him. 15The words of the prophets agree completely with this. As the scripture says,

16'After this I will return, says the Lord,
   and restore the kingdom of David.
 I will rebuild its ruins
   and make it strong again.
17And so all the rest of the human race will
   come to me,
 all the Gentiles whom I have called to
   be my own.
18So says the Lord, who made this known
   long ago.'

19"It is my opinion," James went on, "that we should not trouble the Gentiles who are turning to God. 20Instead, we should write a letter telling them not to eat any food that is ritually unclean because it has been offered to idols; to keep themselves from sexual immorality; and not to eat any animal that has been strangled, or any blood. 21For the Law of Moses has been read for a very long time in the synagogues every Sabbath, and his words are preached in every town."

The Letter to the Gentile Believers

22Then the apostles and the elders, together with the whole church, decided to choose some men from the group and send them to Antioch with Paul and Barnabas. They chose two men who were highly

Acts

respected by the believers, Judas, called Barsabbas, and Silas, 23 and they sent the following letter by them:

"We, the apostles and the elders, your brothers, send greetings to all our brothers of Gentile birth who live in Antioch, Syria, and Cilicia. 24 We have heard that some who went from our group have troubled and upset you by what they said; they had not, however, received any instruction from us. 25 And so we have met together and have all agreed to choose some messengers and send them to you. They will go with our dear friends Barnabas and Paul, 26 who have risked their lives in the service of our Lord Jesus Christ. 27 We send you, then, Judas and Silas, who will tell you in person the same things we are writing. 28 The Holy Spirit and we have agreed not to put any other burden on you besides these necessary rules: 29 eat no food that has been offered to idols; eat no blood; eat no animal that has been strangled; and keep yourselves from sexual immorality. You will do well if you take care not to do these things. With our best wishes."

30 The messengers were sent off and went to Antioch, where they gathered the whole group of believers and gave them the letter. 31 When the people read it, they were filled with joy by the message of encouragement. 32 Judas and Silas, who were themselves prophets, spoke a long time with them, giving them courage and strength. 33 After spending some time there, they were sent off in peace by the believers and went back to those who had sent them.[v]

35 Paul and Barnabas spent some time in Antioch, and together with many others they taught and preached the word of the Lord.

Paul and Barnabas Separate

36 Some time later Paul said to Barnabas, "Let us go back and visit the believers in every town where we preached the word of the Lord, and let us find out how they are getting along." 37 Barnabas wanted to take John Mark with them, 38 but Paul did not think it was right to take him, because he had not stayed with them to the end of their mission, but had turned back and left them in Pamphylia. 39 There was a sharp argument, and they separated: Barnabas took Mark and sailed off for Cyprus, 40 while Paul chose Silas and left, commended by the believers to the care of the Lord's grace. 41 He went through Syria and Cilicia, strengthening the churches.

Timothy Goes with Paul and Silas

16 1 Paul traveled on to Derbe and Lystra, where a Christian named Timothy lived. His mother, who was also a Christian, was Jewish, but his father was a Greek. 2 All the believers in Lystra and Iconium spoke well of Timothy. 3 Paul wanted to take Timothy along with him, so he circumcised him. He did so because all the Jews who lived in those places knew that Timothy's father was Greek. 4 As they went through the towns, they delivered to the believers the rules decided upon by the apostles and elders in Jerusalem, and they told them to obey those rules. 5 So the churches were made stronger in the faith and grew in numbers every day.

In Troas: Paul's Vision

6 They traveled through the region of Phrygia and Galatia because the Holy Spirit did not let them preach the message in the province of Asia. 7 When they reached the border of Mysia, they tried to go into the province of Bithynia, but the Spirit of Jesus did not allow them. 8 So they traveled right on through[w] Mysia and went to Troas. 9 That night Paul had a vision in which he saw a Macedonian standing and begging him, "Come over to Macedonia and help us!" 10 As soon as Paul had this vision, we got ready to leave for Macedonia, because we decided that God had called us to preach the Good News to the people there.

---

v **15:33** *Some manuscripts add verse 34:* But Silas decided to stay there.   *w* **16:8** traveled right on through; *or* passed by.
15:38 Acts 13:13

In Philippi: the Conversion of Lydia

11 We left by ship from Troas and sailed straight across to Samothrace, and the next day to Neapolis. 12 From there we went inland to Philippi, a city of the first district of Macedonia;ˣ it is also a Roman colony. We spent several days there. 13 On the Sabbath we went out of the city to the riverside, where we thought there would be a place where Jews gathered for prayer. We sat down and talked to the women who gathered there. 14 One of those who heard us was Lydia from Thyatira, who was a dealer in purple cloth. She was a woman who worshiped God, and the Lord opened her mind to pay attention to what Paul was saying. 15 After she and the people of her house had been baptized, she invited us, "Come and stay in my house if you have decided that I am a true believer in the Lord." And she persuaded us to go.

In Prison at Philippi

16 One day as we were going to the place of prayer, we were met by a young servant woman who had an evil spirit that enabled her to predict the future. She earned a lot of money for her owners by telling fortunes. 17 She followed Paul and us, shouting, "These men are servants of the Most High God! They announce to you how you can be saved!" 18 She did this for many days, until Paul became so upset that he turned around and said to the spirit, "In the name of Jesus Christ I order you to come out of her!" The spirit went out of her that very moment. 19 When her owners realized that their chance of making money was gone, they seized Paul and Silas and dragged them to the authorities in the public square. 20 They brought them before the Roman officials and said, "These men are Jews, and they are causing trouble in our city. 21 They are teaching customs that are against our law; we are Roman citizens, and we cannot accept these customs or practice them." 22 And the crowd joined in the attack against Paul and Silas.

Then the officials tore the clothes off Paul and Silas and ordered them to be whipped. 23 After a severe beating, they were thrown into jail, and the jailer was ordered to lock them up tight. 24 Upon receiving this order, the jailer threw them into the inner cell and fastened their feet between heavy blocks of wood.

25 About midnight Paul and Silas were praying and singing hymns to God, and the other prisoners were listening to them. 26 Suddenly there was a violent earthquake, which shook the prison to its foundations. At once all the doors opened, and the chains fell off all the prisoners. 27 The jailer woke up, and when he saw the prison doors open, he thought that the prisoners had escaped; so he pulled out his sword and was about to kill himself. 28 But Paul shouted at the top of his voice, "Don't harm yourself! We are all here!"

"Sirs, what must I do to be saved?" (16:30)

29 The jailer called for a light, rushed in, and fell trembling at the feet of Paul and Silas. 30 Then he led them out and asked, "Sirs, what must I do to be saved?"

31 They answered, "Believe in the Lord Jesus, and you will be saved—you and your family." 32 Then they preached the word of

---

ˣ **16:12** a city of the first district of Macedonia; *some manuscripts have* a leading city of the district of Macedonia, *or* a leading city of that district in Macedonia.

Lydia was probably a woman of some wealth. Purple dye was expensive, and she was a dealer in purple cloth *(Acts 16:14).*

Pray It!

Praise God—I'm Miserable!

What would you do if you were put in a prison cell—and you were innocent? Cry? Shout? Curse? Not Paul and Silas! They were praying and singing hymns— loud enough so that all the other prisoners could hear them! The next time you find yourself in trouble or treated unfairly, turn your heart and voice to God:

God, you are amazing!
Over and over you've shown your deep love for me.
I can make it through terrible times because I know you're right here,
*   like always—no matter what happens.*
You are as close to me as my heartbeat.
Help me stay strong and hopeful.
Thank you for your blessings in my life!
Amen.

— Acts 16:25

the Lord to him and to all the others in the house. 33At that very hour of the night the jailer took them and washed their wounds; and he and all his family were baptized at once. 34Then he took Paul and Silas up into his house and gave them some food to eat. He and his family were filled with joy, because they now believed in God.

35The next morning the Roman authorities sent police officers with the order, "Let those men go."

36So the jailer told Paul, "The officials have sent an order for you and Silas to be released. You may leave, then, and go in peace."

37But Paul said to the police officers, "We were not found guilty of any crime, yet they whipped us in public—and we are Roman citizens! Then they threw us in prison. And now they want to send us away secretly? Not at all! The Roman officials themselves must come here and let us out."

38The police officers reported these words to the Roman officials; and when they heard that Paul and Silas were Roman citizens, they were afraid. 39So they went and apologized to them; then they led them out of the prison and asked them to leave the city. 40Paul and Silas left the prison and went to Lydia's house. There they met the believers, spoke words of encouragement to them, and left.

In Thessalonica

17 1Paul and Silas traveled on through Amphipolis and Apollonia and came to Thessalonica, where there was a synagogue. 2According to his usual habit Paul went to the synagogue. There during three Sabbaths he held discussions with the people, quoting 3and explaining the Scriptures, and proving from them that the Messiah had to suffer and rise from death. "This Jesus whom I announce to you," Paul said, "is the Messiah." 4Some of them were convinced and joined Paul and Silas; so did many of the leading women and a large group of Greeks who worshiped God.

5But some Jews were jealous and gathered worthless loafers from the streets and formed a mob. They set the whole city in an uproar and attacked the home of a man named Jason,

How many different cities did Paul and Silas visit in Acts, chapters 17–18? Match them to the route of Paul's second journey on Map 7 on page c46.

in an attempt to find Paul and Silas and bring them out to the people. ⁶But when they did not find them, they dragged Jason and some other believers before the city authorities and shouted, "These men have caused trouble everywhere! Now they have come to our city, ⁷and Jason has kept them in his house. They are all breaking the laws of the Emperor, saying that there is another king, whose name is Jesus." ⁸With these words they threw the crowd and the city authorities in an uproar. ⁹The authorities made Jason and the others pay the required amount of money to be released, and then let them go.

In Berea

¹⁰As soon as night came, the believers sent Paul and Silas to Berea. When they arrived, they went to the synagogue. ¹¹The people there were more open-minded than the people in Thessalonica. They listened to the message with great eagerness, and every day they studied the Scriptures to see if what Paul said was really true. ¹²Many of them believed; and many Greek women of high social standing and many Greek men also believed. ¹³But when the Jews in Thessalonica heard that Paul had preached the word of God in Berea also, they came there and started exciting and stirring up the mobs. ¹⁴At once the believers sent Paul away to the coast; but both Silas and Timothy stayed in Berea. ¹⁵The men who were taking Paul went with him as far as Athens and then returned to Berea with instructions from Paul that Silas and Timothy should join him as soon as possible.

In Athens

¹⁶While Paul was waiting in Athens for Silas and Timothy, he was greatly upset when he noticed how full of idols the city was. ¹⁷So he held discussions in the synagogue with the Jews and with the Gentiles who worshiped God, and also in the public square every day with the people who happened to come by. ¹⁸Certain Epicurean and Stoic teachers also debated with him. Some of

Passing on the Faith

Paul truly had a gift for preaching and teaching! Acts, chapters 17–18, continue the stories of his second missionary journey. Through his speeches and discussions, he spread the news far and wide about Jesus. And many people came to believe in and follow Jesus because of Paul and Silas.

Who taught you about Jesus? Who are the people in your life who continue to show you what living a Christian life means? Take a few minutes to thank God for these people. Better yet, think about sending them a note or small gift that expresses your gratitude.

— Acts, chapters 17–18

them asked, "What is this ignorant show-off trying to say?"

Others answered, "He seems to be talking about foreign gods." They said this because Paul was preaching about Jesus and the resurrection.ʸ ¹⁹So they took Paul, brought him before the city council, the Areopagus, and said, "We would like to know what this new teaching is that you are talking about. ²⁰Some of the things we hear you say sound strange to us, and we would like to know what they mean." (²¹For all the citizens of Athens and the foreigners who lived there liked to spend all their time telling and hearing the latest new thing.)

²²Paul stood up in front of the city council and said, "I see that in every way you Athenians are very religious. ²³For as I walked through your city and looked at the places where you worship, I found an altar on which is written, 'To an Unknown God.'

ʸ **17:18** JESUS AND THE RESURRECTION: *In Greek, the feminine noun "resurrection" could be understood to be the name of a goddess.*
17:23 Wis 13:1

Welcome the Stranger

In Corinth Paul met Priscilla and Aquila, a married couple who invited him to stay with them. No four-star hotels for Paul! Rather, he stayed in homes of people who welcomed him. Some houses were probably fancier or cleaner or had better food than others. But it didn't matter to Paul. Living with other believers filled him up with the energy he needed to continue his ministry.

Hospitality is a wonderful gift! When you have friends or relatives over to your house, what do you do to make them feel welcome and comfortable? What kinds of preparations are made for their visit? Has your family ever welcomed someone to live with you for several weeks or longer?

"Welcome the stranger" is one of the works of mercy. Dorothy Day is a famous American Catholic who spent her adult life serving poor people in New York. She declared that every Christian home should contain a Christ room (that is, an extra room) or a couch where a homeless person could stay. Talk with your family about ways you can help people who need safe shelter and friendship.

— Acts 18:1–3

Catholic Connections

That which you worship, then, even though you do not know it, is what I now proclaim to you. 24 God, who made the world and everything in it, is Lord of heaven and earth and does not live in temples made by human hands. 25 Nor does he need anything that we can supply by working for him, since it is he himself who gives life and breath and everything else to everyone. 26 From one human being he created all races of people and made them live throughout the whole earth. He himself fixed beforehand the exact times and the limits of the places where they would live. 27 He did this so that they would look for him, and perhaps find him as they felt around for him. Yet God is actually not far from any one of us; 28 as someone has said,

'In him we live and move and exist.'

It is as some of your poets have said,

'We too are his children.'

29 Since we are God's children, we should not suppose that his nature is anything like an image of gold or silver or stone, shaped by human art and skill. 30 God has overlooked the times when people did not know him, but now he commands all of them everywhere to turn away from their evil ways. 31 For he has fixed a day in which he will judge the whole world with justice by means of a man he has chosen. He has given proof of this to everyone by raising that man from death!"

32 When they heard Paul speak about a raising from death, some of them made fun of him, but others said, "We want to hear you speak about this again." 33 And so Paul left the meeting. 34 Some men joined him and believed, among whom was Dionysius, a member of the council; there was also a woman named Damaris, and some other people.

In Corinth

18 1 After this, Paul left Athens and went on to Corinth. 2 There he met a Jew named Aquila, born in Pontus, who

17:24, 25 1 Kings 8:27; Isa 42:5; Acts 7:48   **17:25** 2 Macc 14:35   **17:26** 2 Macc 7:23
17:27 Wis 13:6–9

had recently come from Italy with his wife Priscilla, for Emperor Claudius had ordered all the Jews to leave Rome. Paul went to see them, ³and stayed and worked with them, because he earned his living by making tents, just as they did. ⁴He held discussions in the synagogue every Sabbath, trying to convince both Jews and Greeks.

⁵When Silas and Timothy arrived from Macedonia, Paul gave his whole time to preaching the message, testifying to the Jews that Jesus is the Messiah. ⁶When they opposed him and said evil things about him, he protested by shaking the dust from his clothes and saying to them, "If you are lost, you yourselves must take the blame for it! I am not responsible. From now on I will go to the Gentiles." ⁷So he left them and went to live in the house of a Gentile named Titius Justus, who worshiped God; his house was next to the synagogue. ⁸Crispus, who was the leader of the synagogue, believed in the Lord, together with all his family; and many other people in Corinth heard the message, believed, and were baptized.

⁹One night Paul had a vision in which the Lord said to him, "Do not be afraid, but keep on speaking and do not give up, ¹⁰for I am with you. No one will be able to harm you, for many in this city are my people." ¹¹So Paul stayed there for a year and a half, teaching the people the word of God.

¹²When Gallio was made the Roman governor of Achaia, Jews there got together, seized Paul, and took him into court. ¹³"This man," they said, "is trying to persuade people to worship God in a way that is against the law!"

¹⁴Paul was about to speak when Gallio said to the Jews, "If this were a matter of some evil crime or wrong that has been committed, it would be reasonable for me to be patient with you Jews. ¹⁵But since it is an argument about words and names and your own law, you yourselves must settle it. I will not be the judge of such things!" ¹⁶And he drove them out of the court. ¹⁷They all grabbed Sosthenes, the leader of the synagogue, and beat him in front of the court. But that did not bother Gallio a bit.

The Return to Antioch

¹⁸Paul stayed on with the believers in Corinth for many days, then left them and sailed off with Priscilla and Aquila for Syria. Before sailing from Cenchreae he had his head shaved because of a vow he had taken.ᶻ ¹⁹They arrived in Ephesus, where Paul left Priscilla and Aquila. He went into the synagogue and held discussions with the Jews. ²⁰The people asked him to stay longer, but he would not consent. ²¹Instead, he told them as he left, "If it is the will of God, I will come back to you." And so he sailed from Ephesus.

²²When he arrived at Caesarea, he went to Jerusalem and greeted the church, and then went to Antioch. ²³After spending some time there, he left and went through the region of Galatia and Phrygia, strengthening all the believers.

Apollos in Ephesus and Corinth

²⁴At that time a Jew named Apollos, who had been born in Alexandria, came to Ephesus. He was an eloquent speaker and had a thorough knowledge of the Scriptures. ²⁵He had been instructed in the Way of the Lord, and with great enthusiasm he proclaimed and taught correctly the facts about Jesus. However, he knew only the baptism of John. ²⁶He began to speak boldly in the synagogue. When Priscilla and Aquila heard him, they took him home with them and explained to him more correctly the Way of God. ²⁷Apollos then decided to go to Achaia, so the believers in Ephesus helped him by writing to the believers in Achaia, urging them to welcome him. When he arrived, he was a great help to those who through God's

Acts

ᶻ **18:18** A VOW HE HAD TAKEN: *This refers to the Jewish custom of shaving the head as a sign that a vow has been kept.*
18:18 Num 6:18

"Do not be afraid, but keep speaking and do not give up, for I am with you" *(Acts 18:9–10).*

grace had become believers. 28For with his strong arguments he defeated the Jews in public debates by proving from the Scriptures that Jesus is the Messiah.

Paul in Ephesus

19 1While Apollos was in Corinth, Paul traveled through the interior of the province and arrived in Ephesus. There he found some disciples 2and asked them, "Did you receive the Holy Spirit when you became believers?"

"We have not even heard that there is a Holy Spirit," they answered.

3"Well, then, what kind of baptism did you receive?" Paul asked.

"The baptism of John," they answered.

4Paul said, "The baptism of John was for those who turned from their sins; and he told the people of Israel to believe in the one who was coming after him—that is, in Jesus."

5When they heard this, they were baptized in the name of the Lord Jesus. 6Paul placed his hands on them, and the Holy Spirit came upon them; they spoke in strange tongues and also proclaimed God's message. 7They were about twelve men in all.

8Paul went into the synagogue and for three months spoke boldly with the people, holding discussions with them and trying to convince them about the Kingdom of God. 9But some of them were stubborn and would not believe, and before the whole group they said evil things about the Way of the Lord. So Paul left them and took the believers with him, and every day[a] he held discussions in the lecture hall of Tyrannus. 10This went on for two years, so that all the people who lived in the province of Asia, both Jews and Gentiles, heard the word of the Lord.

The Sons of Sceva

11God was performing unusual miracles through Paul. 12Even handkerchiefs and

Demons and Idols and Riots!

Paul's adventure continues! Chapter 19 describes the beginning of his third missionary journey. In his second journey, Paul was thrown out of cities, beaten, and almost stoned to death. Imagine the courage it took for him to start a new journey of evangelizing and healing. Despite the many dangers he faced, Paul stuck with it. Because he was filled with the Holy Spirit, he possessed the courage needed to wake up each day and preach the Good News to all he met.

We don't have to be faced with a dangerous situation to need courage. It can take courage to be kind to a difficult person whom everyone else makes fun of. It can take courage to accept a tough situation that's beyond our control, like a family death or divorce. What do you need courage for in your life? Ask God to give you plenty of it, then keep moving forward!

— Acts 19:1–10

aprons he had used were taken to the sick, and their diseases were driven away, and the evil spirits would go out of them. 13Some Jews who traveled around and drove out evil spirits also tried to use the name of the Lord Jesus to do this. They said to the evil spirits, "I command you in the name of Jesus,

---

[a] **19:9** *Some manuscripts add* from 11:00 a.m. until 4:00 p.m.
19:4 Mt 3:11; Mk 1:4, 7, 8; Lk 3:4, 16; Jn 1:26, 27

Which of the Ten Commandments are the silversmiths breaking in Acts, chapter 19?

whom Paul preaches." 14 Seven brothers, who were the sons of a Jewish High Priest named Sceva, were doing this.

15 But the evil spirit said to them, "I know Jesus, and I know about Paul; but you—who are you?"

16 The man who had the evil spirit in him attacked them with such violence that he overpowered them all. They ran away from his house, wounded and with their clothes torn off. 17 All the Jews and Gentiles who lived in Ephesus heard about this; they were all filled with fear, and the name of the Lord Jesus was given greater honor. 18 Many of the believers came, publicly admitting and revealing what they had done. 19 Many of those who had practiced magic brought their books together and burned them in public. They added up the price of the books, and the total came to fifty thousand silver coins.*b* 20 In this powerful way the word of the Lord*c* kept spreading and growing stronger.

The Riot in Ephesus

21 After these things had happened, Paul made up his mind*d* to travel through Macedonia and Achaia and go on to Jerusalem. "After I go there," he said, "I must also see Rome." 22 So he sent Timothy and Erastus, two of his helpers, to Macedonia, while he spent more time in the province of Asia.

23 It was at this time that there was serious trouble in Ephesus because of the Way of the Lord. 24 A certain silversmith named Demetrius made silver models of the temple of the goddess Artemis, and his business brought a great deal of profit to the workers. 25 So he called them all together with others whose work was like theirs and said to them, "Men, you know that our prosperity comes from this work. 26 Now, you can see and hear for yourselves what this fellow Paul is doing. He says that hand-made gods are not gods at all, and he has succeeded in convincing many people, both here in Ephesus and in nearly the whole province of Asia. 27 There is the danger, then, that this business of ours will get a bad name. Not only that, but there

is also the danger that the temple of the great goddess Artemis will come to mean nothing and that her greatness will be destroyed—the goddess worshiped by everyone in Asia and in all the world!"

28 As the crowd heard these words, they became furious and started shouting, "Great is Artemis of Ephesus!" 29 The uproar spread throughout the whole city. The mob grabbed Gaius and Aristarchus, two Macedonians who were traveling with Paul, and rushed with them to the theater. 30 Paul himself wanted to go before the crowd, but the believers would not let him. 31 Some of the provincial authorities, who were his friends, also sent him a message begging him not to show himself in the theater. 32 Meanwhile the whole meeting was in an uproar: some people were shouting one thing, others were shouting something else, because most of them did not even know why they had come together. 33 Some of the people concluded that Alexander was responsible, since the Jews made him go up to the front. Then Alexander motioned with his hand for the people to be silent, and he tried to make a speech of defense. 34 But when they recognized that he was a Jew, they all shouted together the same thing for two hours: "Great is Artemis of Ephesus!"

35 At last the city clerk was able to calm the crowd. "Fellow Ephesians!" he said. "Everyone knows that the city of Ephesus is the keeper of the temple of the great Artemis and of the sacred stone that fell down from heaven. 36 Nobody can deny these things. So then, you must calm down and not do anything reckless. 37 You have brought these men here even though they have not robbed temples or said evil things about our goddess. 38 If Demetrius and his workers have an accusation against anyone, we have the authorities and the regular days for court; charges can be made there. 39 But if there is something more that you want, it will have to be settled in a legal meeting of citizens. 40 For after what has happened today, there is the danger that we will be accused of a riot. There is no excuse for all

---

b **19:19** SILVER COINS: *A silver coin was the daily wage of a rural worker (see Mt 20:2).*   *c* **19:19** In this . . . Lord; *or* And so, by the power of the Lord, the message.   *d* **19:21** Paul made up his mind; *or* Paul, led by the Spirit, decided.

this uproar, and we would not be able to give a good reason for it." 41After saying this, he dismissed the meeting.

To Macedonia and Achaia

20 ¹After the uproar died down, Paul called together the believers and with words of encouragement said good-bye to them. Then he left and went on to Macedonia. ²He went through those regions and encouraged the people with many messages. Then he came to Achaia, ³where he stayed three months. He was getting ready to go to Syria when he discovered that there were Jews plotting against him; so he decided to go back through Macedonia. ⁴Sopater son of Pyrrhus, from Berea, went with him; so did Aristarchus and Secundus, from Thessalonica; Gaius, from Derbe; Tychicus and Trophimus, from the province of Asia; and Timothy. ⁵They went ahead and waited for us in Troas. ⁶We sailed from Philippi after the Festival of Unleavened Bread, and five days later we joined them in Troas, where we spent a week.

Paul's Last Visit to Troas

⁷On Saturdayᵉ evening we gathered together for the fellowship meal. Paul spoke to the people and kept on speaking until midnight, since he was going to leave the next day. ⁸Many lamps were burning in the upstairs room where we were meeting. ⁹A young man named Eutychus was sitting in the window, and as Paul kept on talking, Eutychus got sleepier and sleepier, until he finally went sound asleep and fell from the third story to the ground. When they picked him up, he was dead. ¹⁰But Paul went down and threw himself on him and hugged him. "Don't worry," he said, "he is still alive!" ¹¹Then he went back upstairs, broke bread, and ate. After talking with them for a long time, even until sunrise, Paul left. ¹²They took the young man home alive and were greatly comforted.

ᵉ 20:7 Saturday; or Sunday.

You Snooze, You Lose!

Do you ever get bored at Mass? Paul was leading a gathering for a small Christian community at someone's home. It was similar to the Catholic Mass—sharing the Word of God and the Eucharist— but more informal. His preaching must have been either boring or too long, because poor Eutychus fell asleep and fell out of the window (Acts 20:9)! The three-story fall killed him, but Paul quickly brought him back to life. Then Paul returned to the group to bless and share the bread and wine. How's that for an interruption in the middle of Mass?

Most people have times when they get bored or tired at Mass. One way to stay alert is by making a mental list before Mass starts of people or situations that need prayers. Then say a prayer to God for each of those after you receive Communion.

— Acts 20:7–12

From Troas to Miletus

¹³We went on ahead to the ship and sailed off to Assos, where we were going to take Paul aboard. He had told us to do this, because he was going there by land. ¹⁴When he met us in Assos, we took him aboard and went on to Mitylene. ¹⁵We sailed from there and arrived off Chios the next day. A day later we came to Samos, and the following day we reached Miletus. ¹⁶Paul had decided to sail on by Ephesus, so as not to lose any time in the province of Asia. He was in a hurry to arrive in Jerusalem by the day of Pentecost, if at all possible.

Paul's Farewell Speech to the Elders of Ephesus

17 From Miletus Paul sent a message to Ephesus, asking the elders of the church to meet him. **18** When they arrived, he said to them, "You know how I spent the whole time I was with you, from the first day I arrived in the province of Asia. **19** With all humility and many tears I did my work as the Lord's servant during the hard times that came to me because of the plots of some Jews. **20** You know that I did not hold back anything that would be of help to you as I preached and taught in public and in your homes. **21** To Jews and Gentiles alike I gave solemn warning that they should turn from their sins to God and believe in our Lord Jesus. **22** And now, in obedience to the Holy Spirit I am going to Jerusalem, not knowing what will happen to me there. **23** I only know that in every city the Holy Spirit has warned me that prison and troubles wait for me. **24** But I reckon my own life to be worth nothing to me; I only want to complete my mission and finish the work that the Lord Jesus gave me to do, which is to declare the Good News about the grace of God.

25 "I have gone about among all of you, preaching the Kingdom of God. And now I know that none of you will ever see me again. **26** So I solemnly declare to you this very day: if any of you should be lost, I am not responsible. **27** For I have not held back from announcing to you the whole purpose of God. **28** So keep watch over yourselves and over all the flock which the Holy Spirit has placed in your care. Be shepherds of the church of God,*f* which he made his own through the blood of his Son.*g* **29** I know that after I leave, fierce wolves will come among you, and they will not spare the flock. **30** The time will come when some men from your own group will tell lies to lead the believers away after them. **31** Watch, then, and remem-

ber that with many tears, day and night, I taught every one of you for three years.

32 "And now I commend you to the care of God and to the message of his grace, which is able to build you up and give you the blessings God has for all his people. **33** I have not wanted anyone's silver or gold or clothing. **34** You yourselves know that I have worked with these hands of mine to provide everything that my companions and I have needed. **35** I have shown you in all things that by working hard in this way we must help the weak, remembering the words that the Lord Jesus himself said, 'There is more happiness in giving than in receiving.' "

36 When Paul finished, he knelt down with them and prayed. **37** They were all crying as they hugged him and kissed him good-bye. **38** They were especially sad because he had said that they would never see him again. And so they went with him to the ship.

Paul Goes to Jerusalem

21 **1** We said good-bye to them and left. After sailing straight across, we came to Cos; the next day we reached Rhodes, and from there we went on to Patara. **2** There we found a ship that was going to Phoenicia, so we went aboard and sailed away. **3** We came to where we could see Cyprus, and then sailed south of it on to Syria. We went ashore at Tyre, where the ship was going to unload its cargo. **4** There we found some believers and stayed with them a week. By the power of the Spirit they told Paul not to go to Jerusalem. **5** But when our time with them was over, we left and went on our way. All of them, together with their wives and children, went with us out of the city to the beach, where we all knelt and prayed. **6** Then we said good-bye to one another, and we went on board the ship while they went back home.

---

f **20:28** God; *some manuscripts have* the Lord.   *g* **20:28** through the blood of his Son; *or* through the sacrificial death of his Son; *or* through his own blood.
20:24 2 Tim 4:7

The people of Ephesus were very sad to see Paul leave. What is the saddest good-bye you have had?

Blessing Paul

Catholic Connections

The people at Tyre worried about Paul as he set sail for Jerusalem, even though he was fearless. So they did the best thing a Christian community can do: they got down on their knees and prayed together for his safety and courage (Acts 21:5). When someone leaves on a long journey or begins a new stage of life, it's good to pray a blessing over her or him. A blessing is a special prayer, asking God's special care and grace for someone. Important moments in life are the perfect time to call upon God to help and protect the person.

All cultures have blessing prayers. Here is one from the Apache Native American tradition. It would have been a perfect blessing for Paul.

May the sun bring you new energy by day.
May the moon softly restore you by night.
May the rain wash away your worries
*   and the breeze blow new strength into your being,*
*   and all of the days of your life may you walk*
*   gently through the world and know its beauty.*

— Acts 21:3–6

7 We continued our voyage, sailing from Tyre to Ptolemais, where we greeted the believers and stayed with them for a day. 8 On the following day we left and arrived in Caesarea. There we stayed at the house of Philip the evangelist, one of the seven men who had been chosen as helpers in Jerusalem. 9 He had four unmarried daughters who proclaimed God's message. 10 We had been there for several days when a prophet named Agabus arrived from Judea. 11 He came to us, took Paul's belt, tied up his own feet and hands with it, and said, "This is what the Holy Spirit says: The owner of this belt will be tied up in this way by the Jews in Jerusalem, and they will hand him over to the Gentiles."

12 When we heard this, we and the others there begged Paul not to go to Jerusalem.

13 But he answered, "What are you doing, crying like this and breaking my heart? I am ready not only to be tied up in Jerusalem but even to die there for the sake of the Lord Jesus."

14 We could not convince him, so we gave up and said, "May the Lord's will be done."

15 After spending some time there, we got our things ready and left for Jerusalem. 16 Some of the disciples from Caesarea also went with us and took us to the house of the man we were going to stay with h — Mnason, from Cyprus, who had been a believer since the early days.

Paul Visits James

17 When we arrived in Jerusalem, the believers welcomed us warmly. 18 The next

h 21:16 and took us to the house of the man we were going to stay with; *or* bringing with them the man at whose house we were going to stay.
21:8 Acts 6:5; 8:5   21:10 Acts 11:28

"May the Lord's will be done" *(Acts 21:14).*

day Paul went with us to see James; and all the church elders were present. 19 Paul greeted them and gave a complete report of everything that God had done among the Gentiles through his work. 20 After hearing him, they all praised God. Then they said, "Brother Paul, you can see how many thousands of Jews have become believers, and how devoted they all are to the Law. 21 They have been told that you have been teaching all the Jews who live in Gentile countries to abandon the Law of Moses, telling them not to circumcise their children or follow the Jewish customs. 22 They are sure to hear that you have arrived. What should be done, then? 23 This is what we want you to do. There are four men here who have taken a vow. 24 Go along with them and join them in the ceremony of purification and pay their expenses; then they will be able to shave their heads.*i* In this way everyone will know that there is no truth in any of the things that they have been told about you, but that you yourself live in accordance with the Law of Moses. 25 But as for the Gentiles who have become believers, we have sent them a letter telling them we decided that they must not eat any food that has been offered to idols, or any blood, or any animal that has been strangled, and that they must keep themselves from sexual immorality."

26 So Paul took the men and the next day performed the ceremony of purification with them. Then he went into the Temple and gave notice of how many days it would be until the end of the period of purification, when a sacrifice would be offered for each one of them.

Paul Is Arrested in the Temple

27 But just when the seven days were about to come to an end, some Jews from the province of Asia saw Paul in the Temple. They stirred up the whole crowd and grabbed Paul. 28 "People of Israel!" they shouted. "Help! This is the man who goes everywhere teaching everyone against the people of Israel, the Law of Moses, and this Temple. And now he has even brought some Gentiles into the Temple and defiled this holy place!" (29 They said this because they had seen Trophimus from Ephesus with Paul in the city, and they thought that Paul had taken him into the Temple.)

30 Confusion spread through the whole city, and the people all ran together, grabbed Paul, and dragged him out of the Temple. At once the Temple doors were closed. 31 The mob was trying to kill Paul, when a report was sent up to the commander of the Roman troops that all of Jerusalem was rioting. 32 At once the commander took some officers and soldiers and rushed down to the crowd. When the people saw him with the soldiers, they stopped beating Paul. 33 The commander went over to Paul, arrested him, and ordered him to be bound with two chains. Then he asked, "Who is this man, and what has he done?" 34 Some in the crowd shouted one thing, others something else. There was such confusion that the commander could not find out exactly what had happened, so he ordered his men to take Paul up into the fort. 35 They got as far as the steps with him, and then the soldiers had to carry him because the mob was so wild. 36 They were all coming after him and screaming, "Kill him!"

Paul Defends Himself

37 As the soldiers were about to take Paul into the fort, he spoke to the commander: "May I say something to you?"

"You speak Greek, do you?" the commander asked. 38 "Then you are not that Egyptian fellow who some time ago started a revolution and led four thousand armed terrorists out into the desert?"

39 Paul answered, "I am a Jew, born in Tarsus in Cilicia, a citizen of an important city. Please let me speak to the people."

40 The commander gave him permission, so Paul stood on the steps and motioned with his hand for the people to be silent.

i **21:24** SHAVE THEIR HEADS: *See 18:18.*
21:23, 24 Num 6:13–21   **21:25** Acts 15:29   **21:29** Acts 20:4

Acts

When they were quiet, Paul spoke to them in Hebrew:

22

¹"My fellow Jews, listen to me as I make my defense before you!" ²When they heard him speaking to them in Hebrew, they became even quieter; and Paul went on:

³"I am a Jew, born in Tarsus in Cilicia, but brought up here in Jerusalem as a student of Gamaliel. I received strict instruction in the Law of our ancestors and was just as dedicated to God as are all of you who are here today. ⁴I persecuted to the death the people who followed this Way. I arrested men and women and threw them into prison. ⁵The High Priest and the whole Council can prove that I am telling the truth. I received from them letters written to fellow Jews in Damascus, so I went there to arrest these people and bring them back in chains to Jerusalem to be punished.

Paul Tells of His Conversion
(Acts 9:1–19; 26:12–18)

⁶"As I was traveling and coming near Damascus, about midday a bright light from the sky flashed suddenly around me. ⁷I fell to the ground and heard a voice saying to me, 'Saul, Saul! Why do you persecute me?' ⁸'Who are you, Lord?' I asked. 'I am Jesus of Nazareth, whom you persecute,' he said to me. ⁹The men with me saw the light, but did not hear the voice of the one who was speaking to me. ¹⁰I asked, 'What shall I do, Lord?' and the Lord said to me, 'Get up and go into Damascus, and there you will be told everything that God has determined for you to do.' ¹¹I was blind because of the bright light, and so my companions took me by the hand and led me into Damascus.

¹²"In that city was a man named Ananias, a religious man who obeyed our Law and was highly respected by all the Jews living there. ¹³He came to me, stood by me, and said, 'Brother Saul, see again!' At that very moment I saw again and looked at him. ¹⁴He said, 'The God of our ancestors has chosen you to know his will, to see his righteous Servant, and to hear him speaking

Turning to God

Conversion simply means turning away from sin and toward God. It means rejecting what is wrong and choosing what is right. At the beginning of Acts, chapter 22, Paul is telling his conversion story to the Jews in Jerusalem, and it's a very dramatic story!

What would you tell people if they asked for your conversion story? Don't panic if you don't have a story like Paul's. Sometimes conversion is connected to a dramatic event in our life. More often, it is about all the little ways we change as we move away from sin and get closer to God. Can you think of one instance when you changed your course—away from sin, toward God? This is part of your conversion story!

— Acts 22:1–21

with his own voice. ¹⁵For you will be a witness for him to tell everyone what you have seen and heard. ¹⁶And now, why wait any longer? Get up and be baptized and have your sins washed away by praying to him.'

Paul's Call to Preach to the Gentiles

¹⁷"I went back to Jerusalem, and while I was praying in the Temple, I had a vision, ¹⁸in which I saw the Lord, as he said to me, 'Hurry and leave Jerusalem quickly, because the people here will not accept your witness about me.' ¹⁹'Lord,' I answered, 'they know very well that I went to the synagogues and arrested and beat those who believe in you. ²⁰And when your witness Stephen was put to death, I myself was there, approving of his murder and taking care of the cloaks of his

22:3 Acts 5:34–39   **22:4, 5** Acts 8:3; 26:9–11   **22:20** Acts 7:58

murderers.' 21 'Go,' the Lord said to me, 'for I will send you far away to the Gentiles.' "

22 The people listened to Paul until he said this; but then they started shouting at the top of their voices, "Away with him! Kill him! He's not fit to live!" 23 They were screaming, waving their clothes, and throwing dust up in the air. 24 The Roman commander ordered his men to take Paul into the fort, and he told them to whip him in order to find out why the Jews were screaming like this against him. 25 But when they had tied him up to be whipped, Paul said to the officer standing there, "Is it lawful for you to whip a Roman citizen who hasn't even been tried for any crime?"

26 When the officer heard this, he went to the commander and asked him, "What are you doing? That man is a Roman citizen!"

27 So the commander went to Paul and asked him, "Tell me, are you a Roman citizen?"

"Yes," answered Paul.

28 The commander said, "I became one by paying a large amount of money."

"But I am one by birth," Paul answered.

29 At once the men who were going to question Paul drew back from him; and the commander was frightened when he realized that Paul was a Roman citizen and that he had put him in chains.

Paul before the Council

30 The commander wanted to find out for sure what the Jews were accusing Paul of; so the next day he had Paul's chains taken off and ordered the chief priests and the whole Council to meet. Then he took Paul and made him stand before them.

23 1 Paul looked straight at the Council and said, "My fellow Israelites! My conscience is perfectly clear about the way in which I have lived before God to this very day." 2 The High Priest Ananias ordered those who were standing close to Paul to strike him on the mouth. 3 Paul said to him,

"God will certainly strike you—you white-washed wall! You sit there to judge me according to the Law, yet you break the Law by ordering them to strike me!"

4 The men close to Paul said to him, "You are insulting God's High Priest!"

5 Paul answered, "My fellow Israelites, I did not know that he was the High Priest. The scripture says, 'You must not speak evil of the ruler of your people.' "

6 When Paul saw that some of the group were Sadducees and the others were Pharisees, he called out in the Council, "Fellow Israelites! I am a Pharisee, the son of Pharisees. I am on trial here because of the hope I have that the dead will rise to life!"

7 As soon as he said this, the Pharisees and Sadducees started to quarrel, and the group was divided. (8 For the Sadducees say that people will not rise from death and that there are no angels or spirits; but the Pharisees believe in all three.) 9 The shouting became louder, and some of the teachers of the Law who belonged to the party of the Pharisees stood up and protested strongly: "We cannot find a thing wrong with this man! Perhaps a spirit or an angel really did speak to him!"

10 The argument became so violent that the commander was afraid that Paul would be torn to pieces. So he ordered his soldiers to go down into the group, get Paul away from them, and take him into the fort.

11 That night the Lord stood by Paul and said, "Don't be afraid! You have given your witness for me here in Jerusalem, and you must also do the same in Rome."

The Plot against Paul's Life

12 The next morning some Jews met together and made a plan. They took a vow that they would not eat or drink anything until they had killed Paul. 13 There were more than forty who planned this together. 14 Then they went to the chief priests and elders and said, "We have taken a solemn

23:3 Mt 23:27, 28   23:5 Ex 22:28   23:6 Acts 26:5; Phil 3:5   23:8 Mt 22:23; Mk 12:18; Lk 20:27

What dangers did Paul face in telling his story (Acts 22:1–25)**? What dangers do you face when you tell how God has worked in your life?**

Pray It!

God Works Through Us

While Paul is being held for questioning, his nephew enters the scene, warning the Roman commander of the plot to kill Paul. Lucky for Paul, and thanks to his nephew, the officers and the commander acted swiftly to make sure their prisoner was kept safe.

Paul's nephew, the officers, the commander, and the army of soldiers were acting as instruments of God, keeping Paul safe from danger. This is how God tends to care for us—through people.

God, at the end of each day, help me remember all the people I was with, and how they showed me a little bit of your love and care. A smile, a helping hand, some advice offered sincerely, kind words, fun . . . I don't always think of these as you peeking into my life, but it is! So, God, thank you for all the people who will show me your love today! And help me think of ways I can show your love to all I meet too. Amen.

— Acts 23:12–35

vow together not to eat a thing until we have killed Paul. 15 Now then, you and the Council send word to the Roman commander to bring Paul down to you, pretending that you want to get more accurate information about him. But we will be ready to kill him before he ever gets here."

16 But the son of Paul's sister heard about the plot; so he went to the fort and told Paul. 17 Then Paul called one of the officers and said to him, "Take this young man to the commander; he has something to tell him." 18 The officer took him, led him to the commander, and said, "The prisoner Paul called me and asked me to bring this young man to you, because he has something to say to you."

19 The commander took him by the hand, led him off by himself, and asked him, "What do you have to tell me?"

20 He said, "The Jewish authorities have agreed to ask you tomorrow to take Paul down to the Council, pretending that the Council wants to get more accurate information about him. 21 But don't listen to them, because there are more than forty men who will be hiding and waiting for him. They

have taken a vow not to eat or drink until they have killed him. They are now ready to do it and are waiting for your decision."

22 The commander said, "Don't tell anyone that you have reported this to me." And he sent the young man away.

Paul Is Sent to Governor Felix

23 Then the commander called two of his officers and said, "Get two hundred soldiers ready to go to Caesarea, together with seventy horsemen and two hundred spearmen, and be ready to leave by nine o'clock tonight. 24 Provide some horses for Paul to ride and get him safely through to Governor Felix." 25 Then the commander wrote a letter that went like this:

26 "Claudius Lysias to His Excellency, Governor Felix: Greetings. 27 The Jews seized this man and were about to kill him. I learned that he is a Roman citizen, so I went with my soldiers and rescued him. 28 I wanted to know what they were accusing him of, so I took him down to their Council. 29 I found out that he had

The Nazarenes (Acts 24:5) was another name for Christians because they were followers of Jesus who was from Nazareth.

not done a thing for which he deserved to die or be put in prison; the accusation against him had to do with questions about their own law. 30 And when I was informed that there was a plot against him, at once I decided to send him to you. I have told his accusers to make their charges against him before you."

31 The soldiers carried out their orders. They got Paul and took him that night as far as Antipatris. 32 The next day the foot soldiers returned to the fort and left the horsemen to go on with him. 33 They took him to Caesarea, delivered the letter to the governor, and turned Paul over to him. 34 The governor read the letter and asked Paul what province he was from. When he found out that he was from Cilicia, 35 he said, "I will hear you when your accusers arrive." Then he gave orders for Paul to be kept under guard in the governor's headquarters.

The Case against Paul

24 1 Five days later the High Priest Ananias went to Caesarea with some elders and a lawyer named Tertullus. They appeared before Governor Felix and made their charges against Paul. 2 Then Paul was called in, and Tertullus began to make his accusation, as follows:

"Your Excellency! Your wise leadership has brought us a long period of peace, and many necessary reforms are being made for the good of our country. 3 We welcome this everywhere and at all times, and we are deeply grateful to you. 4 I do not want to take up too much of your time, however, so I beg you to be kind and listen to our brief account. 5 We found this man to be a dangerous nuisance; he starts riots among Jews all over the world and is a leader of the party of the Nazarenes. 6 He also tried to defile the Temple, and we arrested him.*j* 8 If you question this man, you yourself will be able to learn from him all the things that we are accusing him of." 9 The Jews joined in the accusation and said that all this was true.

Paul's Defense before Felix

10 The governor then motioned to Paul to speak, and Paul said,

"I know that you have been a judge over this nation for many years, and so I am happy to defend myself before you. 11 As you can find out for yourself, it was no more than twelve days ago that I went to Jerusalem to worship. 12 The Jews did not find me arguing with anyone in the Temple, nor did they find me stirring up the people, either in the synagogues or anywhere else in the city. 13 Nor can they give you proof of the accusations they now bring against me. 14 I do admit this to you: I worship the God of our ancestors by following that Way which they say is false. But I also believe in everything written in the Law of Moses and the books of the prophets. 15 I have the same hope in God that these themselves have, namely, that all people, both the good and the bad, will rise from death. 16 And so I do my best always to have a clear conscience before God and people.

17 "After being away from Jerusalem for several years, I went there to take some money to my own people and to offer sacrifices. 18 It was while I was doing this that they found me in the Temple after I had completed the ceremony of purification. There was no crowd with me and no disorder. 19 But some Jews from the province of Asia were there; they themselves ought to come before you and make their accusations if they have anything against me. 20 Or let these who are here tell what crime they found me guilty of when I stood before the Council— 21 except for the one thing I called out when I stood before them: 'I am being tried by you today for believing that the dead will rise to life.'"

22 Then Felix, who was well informed about the Way, brought the hearing to a close. "When the commander Lysias arrives," he told them, "I will decide your case." 23 He ordered the officer in charge of Paul to keep him under guard, but to give him some

Acts

---

j **24:6** *Some manuscripts add verses 6b–8a:* We planned to judge him according to our own law, 7 but the commander Lysias came, and with great violence took him from us. 8 Then Lysias gave orders that his accusers should come before you.
24:17, 18 Acts 21:17–28   **24:21** Acts 23:6

freedom and allow his friends to provide for his needs.

Paul before Felix and Drusilla

24 After some days Felix came with his wife Drusilla, who was Jewish. He sent for Paul and listened to him as he talked about faith in Christ Jesus. 25 But as Paul went on discussing about goodness, self-control, and the coming Day of Judgment, Felix was afraid and said, "You may leave now. I will call you again when I get the chance." 26 At the same time he was hoping that Paul would give him some money; and for this reason he would call for him often and talk with him.

27 After two years had passed, Porcius Festus succeeded Felix as governor. Felix wanted to gain favor with the Jews so he left Paul in prison.

Paul Appeals to the Emperor

25 1 Three days after Festus arrived in the province, he went from Caesarea to Jerusalem, 2 where the chief priests and the Jewish leaders brought their charges against Paul. They begged Festus 3 to do them the favor of having Paul come to Jerusalem, for they had made a plot to kill him on the way. 4 Festus answered, "Paul is being kept a prisoner in Caesarea, and I myself will be going back there soon. 5 Let your leaders go to Caesarea with me and accuse the man if he has done anything wrong."

6 Festus spent another eight or ten days with them and then went to Caesarea. On the next day he sat down in the judgment court and ordered Paul to be brought in. 7 When Paul arrived, the Jews who had come from Jerusalem stood around him and started making many serious charges against him, which they were not able to prove. 8 But Paul defended himself: "I have done nothing wrong against the Law of the Jews or against the Temple or against the Roman Emperor."

9 But Festus wanted to gain favor with the Jews, so he asked Paul, "Would you be willing to go to Jerusalem and be tried on these charges before me there?"

10 Paul said, "I am standing before the Emperor's own judgment court, where I

Longest Wait in a Holding Cell

The governor, Felix, doesn't seem to want to deal with Paul's case. He listens respectfully to Paul, and even brings his Jewish wife to listen. Felix knew about the Way (Acts 24:22), which was another name for the early Church. He might even have been secretly interested in this new religion.

Felix tells Paul that he will hold him in custody while deciding his case and orders the officer to give Paul some liberty and to let his friends take care of him. But then Felix simply ignores Paul and leaves him sitting in prison for two years hoping Paul would bribe his way out of jail (24:26). Finally, Felix retired and let Paul be the next governor's problem.

What do you think Felix was afraid of?

— Acts 24:22–27

should be tried. I have done no wrong to the Jews, as you yourself well know. 11 If I have broken the law and done something for which I deserve the death penalty, I do not ask to escape it. But if there is no truth in the charges they bring against me, no one can hand me over to them. I appeal to the Emperor."

12 Then Festus, after conferring with his advisers, answered, "You have appealed to the Emperor, so to the Emperor you will go."

Paul before Agrippa and Bernice

13 Some time later King Agrippa and Bernice came to Caesarea to pay a visit of welcome to Festus. 14 After they had been there several days, Festus explained Paul's situation to

the king: "There is a man here who was left a prisoner by Felix; 15and when I went to Jerusalem, the Jewish chief priests and elders brought charges against him and asked me to condemn him. 16But I told them that we Romans are not in the habit of handing over any who are accused of a crime before they have met their accusers face to face and have had the chance of defending themselves against the accusation. 17When they came here, then, I lost no time, but on the very next day I sat in the judgment court and ordered the man to be brought in. 18His opponents stood up, but they did not accuse him of any of the evil crimes that I thought they would. 19All they had were some arguments with him about their own religion and about a man named Jesus, who has died; but Paul claims that he is alive. 20I was undecided about how I could get information on these matters, so I asked Paul if he would be willing to go to Jerusalem and be tried there on these charges. 21But Paul appealed; he asked to be kept under guard and to let the Emperor decide his case. So I gave orders for him to be kept under guard until I could send him to the Emperor."

22Agrippa said to Festus, "I would like to hear this man myself."

"You will hear him tomorrow," Festus answered.

23The next day Agrippa and Bernice came with great pomp and ceremony and entered the audience hall with the military chiefs and the leading men of the city. Festus gave the order, and Paul was brought in. 24Festus said, "King Agrippa and all who are here with us: You see this man against whom all the Jewish people, both here and in Jerusalem, have brought complaints to me. They scream that he should not live any longer. 25But I could not find that he had done anything for which he deserved the death sentence. And since he himself made an appeal to the Emperor, I have decided to send him. 26But I have nothing definite about him to write to the Emperor. So I have brought him here before you—and especially before you, King Agrippa!—so

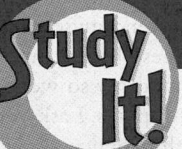

Paul Put to the Test

Paul's situation is similar to what Jesus went through at the beginning of his trial. The chief priests and other Jewish leaders accuse Paul of many offenses, none of which are true. Festus, the new Roman governor, doesn't see the problem and would rather not be bothered with this case. Yet he is worried about keeping the peace with the Jews. So when Paul suggests taking the case to the Emperor, Festus eagerly accepts this solution. Festus also drags the local Jewish king into the picture. He asks King Agrippa to listen to Paul to see what crime Paul has committed. But Agrippa also agrees that Paul is not guilty of any crime against the Jewish faith.

But because Paul has asked for his case to go before the Roman Emperor, they have no choice but to send him to Rome to be tried (Acts 26:32). The rest of Acts tells of Paul's travel to Rome and his time there.

— Acts, chapters 25–26

that, after investigating his case, I may have something to write. 27For it seems unreasonable to me to send a prisoner without clearly indicating the charges against him."

Paul Defends Himself before Agrippa

26 1Agrippa said to Paul, "You have permission to speak on your own behalf." Paul stretched out his hand and defended himself as follows:

This King Agrippa was actually King Agrippa II. His father, King Agrippa I, was also called King Herod (see Acts 12:1–5).

2"King Agrippa! I consider myself fortunate that today I am to defend myself before you from all the things these Jews accuse me of, 3particularly since you know so well all the Jewish customs and disputes. I ask you, then, to listen to me with patience.

4"All the Jews know how I have lived ever since I was young. They know how I have spent my whole life, at first in my own country and then in Jerusalem. 5They have always known, if they are willing to testify, that from the very first I have lived as a member of the strictest party of our religion, the Pharisees. 6And now I stand here to be tried because of the hope I have in the promise that God made to our ancestors— 7the very thing that the twelve tribes of our people hope to receive, as they worship God day and night. And it is because of this hope, Your Majesty, that I am being accused by these Jews! 8Why do you who are here find it impossible to believe that God raises the dead?

9"I myself thought that I should do everything I could against the cause of Jesus of Nazareth. 10That is what I did in Jerusalem. I received authority from the chief priests and put many of God's people in prison; and when they were sentenced to death, I also voted against them. 11Many times I had them punished in the synagogues and tried to make them deny their faith. I was so furious with them that I even went to foreign cities to persecute them.

Paul Tells of His Conversion
(Acts 9:1–19; 22:6–16)

12"It was for this purpose that I went to Damascus with authority and orders from the chief priests. 13It was on the road at midday, Your Majesty, that I saw a light much brighter than the sun, coming from the sky and shining around me and the men traveling with me. 14All of us fell to the ground, and I heard a voice say to me in Hebrew,

'Saul, Saul! Why are you persecuting me? You are hurting yourself by hitting back, like an ox kicking against its owner's stick.' 15'Who are you, Lord?' I asked. And the Lord answered, 'I am Jesus, whom you persecute. 16But get up and stand on your feet. I have appeared to you to appoint you as my servant. You are to tell others what you have seen of me[k] today and what I will show you in the future. 17I will rescue you from the people of Israel and from the Gentiles to whom I will send you. 18You are to open their eyes and turn them from the darkness to the light and from the power of Satan to God, so that through their faith in me they will have their sins forgiven and receive their place among God's chosen people.'

Paul Tells of His Work

19"And so, King Agrippa, I did not disobey the vision I had from heaven. 20First in Damascus and in Jerusalem and then in the whole country of Israel and among the Gentiles, I preached that they must repent of their sins and turn to God and do the things that would show they had repented. 21It was for this reason that these Jews seized me while I was in the Temple, and they tried to kill me. 22But to this very day I have been helped by God, and so I stand here giving my witness to all, to small and great alike. What I say is the very same thing which the prophets and Moses said was going to happen: 23that the Messiah must suffer and be the first one to rise from death, to announce the light of salvation to the Jews and to the Gentiles."

24As Paul defended himself in this way, Festus shouted at him, "You are mad, Paul! Your great learning is driving you mad!"

25Paul answered, "I am not mad, Your Excellency! I am speaking the sober truth. 26King Agrippa! I can speak to you with all boldness, because you know about these things. I am sure that you have taken notice

---

[k] **26:16** *Some manuscripts do not have* of me.

26:5 Acts 23:6; Phil 3:5　**26:8** 2 Macc 7:9　**26:9–11** Acts 8:3; 22:4, 5　**26:20** Acts 9:20, 28, 29
26:23 a 1 Cor 15:20; b Isa 42:6; 49:6

Unscramble this two-word phrase to see what Paul was doing before his conversion: eeiutpgnsrc sseuj. Find the answer in Acts 26:14.

of every one of them, for this thing has not happened hidden away in a corner. 27King Agrippa, do you believe the prophets? I know that you do!"

28Agrippa said to Paul, "In this short time do you think you will make me a Christian?"

29"Whether a short time or a long time," Paul answered, "my prayer to God is that you and all the rest of you who are listening to me today might become what I am—except, of course, for these chains!"

30Then the king, the governor, Bernice, and all the others got up, 31and after leaving they said to each other, "This man has not done anything for which he should die or be put in prison." 32And Agrippa said to Festus, "This man could have been released if he had not appealed to the Emperor."

Paul Sails for Rome

27 1When it was decided that we should sail to Italy, they handed Paul and some other prisoners over to Julius, an officer in the Roman army regiment called "The Emperor's Regiment." 2We went aboard a ship from Adramyttium, which was ready to leave for the seaports of the province of Asia, and we sailed away. Aristarchus, a Macedonian from Thessalonica, was with us. 3The next day we arrived at Sidon. Julius was kind to Paul and allowed him to go and see his friends, to be given what he needed. 4We went on from there, and because the winds were blowing against us, we sailed on the sheltered side of the island of Cyprus. 5We crossed over the sea off Cilicia and Pamphylia and came to Myra in Lycia. 6There the officer found a ship from Alexandria that was going to sail for Italy, so he put us aboard.

7We sailed slowly for several days and with great difficulty finally arrived off the town of Cnidus. The wind would not let us go any farther in that direction, so we sailed down the sheltered side of the island of Crete, passing by Cape Salmone. 8We kept close to the coast and with great difficulty came to a place called Safe Harbors, not far from the town of Lasea.

9We spent a long time there, until it became dangerous to continue the voyage, for by now the Day of Atonement[l] was already past. So Paul gave them this advice: 10"Men, I see that our voyage from here on will be dangerous; there will be great damage to the cargo and to the ship, and loss of life as well." 11But the army officer was convinced by what the captain and the owner of the ship said, and not by what Paul said. 12The harbor was not a good one to spend the winter in; so almost everyone was in favor of putting out to sea and trying to reach Phoenix, if possible, in order to spend the winter there. Phoenix is a harbor in Crete that faces southwest and northwest.[m]

The Storm at Sea

13A soft wind from the south began to blow, and the men thought that they could carry out their plan, so they pulled up the anchor and sailed as close as possible along the coast of Crete. 14But soon a very strong wind—the one called "Northeaster"—blew down from the island. 15It hit the ship, and since it was impossible to keep the ship headed into the wind, we gave up trying and let it be carried along by the wind. 16We got some shelter when we passed to the south of the little island of Cauda. There, with some difficulty we managed to make the ship's boat secure. 17They pulled it aboard and then fastened some ropes tight around the ship. They were afraid that they might run into the sandbanks off the coast of Libya, so they lowered the sail and let the ship be carried by the wind. 18The violent storm continued, so on the next day they began to throw some of the ship's cargo overboard, 19and on the following day they threw part of the ship's equipment overboard. 20For many days we could not see the sun or the stars, and the wind kept on blowing very hard. We finally gave up all hope of being saved.

21After everyone had gone a long time without food, Paul stood before them and said, "You should have listened to me and not have sailed from Crete; then we would have avoided all this damage and loss. 22But

l 27:9 DAY OF ATONEMENT: *This was celebrated toward the end of September or beginning of October, at which time bad weather made sailing dangerous.* m 27:12 southwest and northwest; *or* northeast and southeast.

Pray It!

Holding On for Dear Life

Although this story is made up, it is based on the stories of real people: There were a hundred of us in a boat that should hold only forty people. Then the sea turned into an awful storm, and we were unable to keep everyone safe. When our boat found the shore, weeks later, we had lost twenty-two people. Would we have taken this journey if we had known of the danger? Yes! So terrible is the hatred and violence in Haiti, we could no longer survive there. I believe God heard my cries at sea. It is not easy, but God will help me build a new life here.

Does your life ever seem like you're in the midst of a great storm—things are out of control, you're being tossed about, and it feels like you might never reach safety? That's the perfect time to call out for God!

God, help! This is too big, too scary. I know you are near, but I need to feel your presence—comforting me, protecting me, guiding me to a safe place again. Please calm these waves of trouble, and keep me calm too. And when the storm is over, help me become wiser and stronger and less fearful when the waters of life get choppy again. Thanks, God, for rescuing me—again and again! Amen.

— Acts 27:13–44

now I beg you, take courage! Not one of you will lose your life; only the ship will be lost. 23For last night an angel of the God to whom I belong and whom I worship came to me 24and said, 'Don't be afraid, Paul! You must stand before the Emperor. And God in his goodness to you has spared the lives of all those who are sailing with you.' 25So take courage, men! For I trust in God that it will be just as I was told. 26But we will be driven ashore on some island."

27It was the fourteenth night, and we were being driven in the Mediterranean by the storm. About midnight the sailors suspected that we were getting close to land. 28So they dropped a line with a weight tied to it and found that the water was one hundred and twenty feet deep; a little later they did the same and found that it was ninety feet deep. 29They were afraid that the ship would go on the rocks, so they lowered four anchors from the back of the ship and prayed for daylight. 30Then the sailors tried to escape from the ship; they lowered the boat into the water and pretended that they

were going to put out some anchors from the front of the ship. 31But Paul said to the army officer and soldiers, "If the sailors don't stay on board, you have no hope of being saved." 32So the soldiers cut the ropes that held the boat and let it go.

33Just before dawn, Paul begged them all to eat some food: "You have been waiting for fourteen days now, and all this time you have not eaten a thing. 34I beg you, then, eat some food; you need it in order to survive. Not even a hair of your heads will be lost." 35After saying this, Paul took some bread, gave thanks to God before them all, broke it, and began to eat. 36They took courage, and every one of them also ate some food. 37There was a total of 276[n] of us on board. 38After everyone had eaten enough, they lightened the ship by throwing all the wheat into the sea.

The Shipwreck

39When day came, the sailors did not recognize the coast, but they noticed a bay with

[n] **27:37** *276; some manuscripts have 275; others have* about 76.

a beach and decided that, if possible, they would run the ship aground there. ⁴⁰So they cut off the anchors and let them sink in the sea, and at the same time they untied the ropes that held the steering oars. Then they raised the sail at the front of the ship so that the wind would blow the ship forward, and we headed for shore. ⁴¹But the ship hit a sandbank and went aground; the front part of the ship got stuck and could not move, while the back part was being broken to pieces by the violence of the waves.

The ship hit a sandbank. (27:41)

⁴²The soldiers made a plan to kill all the prisoners, in order to keep them from swimming ashore and escaping. ⁴³But the army officer wanted to save Paul, so he stopped them from doing this. Instead, he ordered everyone who could swim to jump overboard first and swim ashore; ⁴⁴the rest were to follow, holding on to the planks or to some broken pieces of the ship. And this was how we all got safely ashore.

In Malta

28 ¹When we were safely ashore, we learned that the island was called Malta. ²The natives there were very friendly to us. It had started to rain and was cold, so they built a fire and made us all welcome. ³Paul gathered up a bundle of sticks and was putting them on the fire when a snake came out on account of the heat and fastened itself to his hand. ⁴The natives saw the snake hanging on Paul's hand and said to one another, "This man must be a murderer, but

Fate will not let him live, even though he escaped from the sea." ⁵But Paul shook the snake off into the fire without being harmed at all. ⁶They were waiting for him to swell up or suddenly fall down dead. But after waiting for a long time and not seeing anything unusual happening to him, they changed their minds and said, "He is a god!"

⁷Not far from that place were some fields that belonged to Publius, the chief of the island. He welcomed us kindly and for three days we were his guests. ⁸Publius' father was in bed, sick with fever and dysentery. Paul went into his room, prayed, placed his hands on him, and healed him. ⁹When this happened, all the other sick people on the island came and were healed. ¹⁰They gave us many gifts, and when we sailed, they put on board what we needed for the voyage.

From Malta to Rome

¹¹After three months we sailed away on a ship from Alexandria, called "The Twin Gods," which had spent the winter in the island. ¹²We arrived in the city of Syracuse and stayed there for three days. ¹³From there we sailed on and arrived in the city of Rhegium. The next day a wind began to blow from the south, and in two days we came to the town of Puteoli. ¹⁴We found some believers there who asked us to stay with them a week. And so we came to Rome. ¹⁵The believers in Rome heard about us and came as far as the towns of Market of Appius and Three Inns to meet us. When Paul saw them, he thanked God and was greatly encouraged.

In Rome

¹⁶When we arrived in Rome, Paul was allowed to live by himself with a soldier guarding him.

¹⁷After three days Paul called the local Jewish leaders to a meeting. When they had gathered, he said to them, "My fellow Israelites, even though I did nothing against

Acts

our people or the customs that we received from our ancestors, I was made a prisoner in Jerusalem and handed over to the Romans. 18After questioning me, the Romans wanted to release me, because they found that I had done nothing for which I deserved to die. 19But when the Jews opposed this, I was forced to appeal to the Emperor, even though I had no accusation to make against my own people. 20That is why I asked to see you and talk with you. As a matter of fact, I am bound in chains like this for the sake of him for whom the people of Israel hope."

21They said to him, "We have not received any letters from Judea about you, nor have any of our people come from there with any news or anything bad to say about you. 22But we would like to hear your ideas, because we know that everywhere people speak against this party to which you belong."

23So they set a date with Paul, and a large number of them came that day to the place where Paul was staying. From morning till night he explained to them his message about the Kingdom of God, and he tried to convince them about Jesus by quoting from the Law of Moses and the writings of the prophets. 24Some of them were convinced by his words, but others would not believe. 25So they left, disagreeing among themselves, after Paul had said this one thing: "How well the Holy Spirit spoke through the prophet Isaiah to your ancestors! 26For he said,

'Go and say to this people:
You will listen and listen, but not
    understand;
    you will look and look, but not see,
27because this people's minds are dull,
    and they have stopped up their ears
    and closed their eyes.
Otherwise, their eyes would see,
    their ears would hear,
    their minds would understand,
and they would turn to me, says God,
    and I would heal them.' "

28And Paul concluded: "You are to know,

28:19 Acts 25:11   **28:26, 27** Isa 6:9, 10 (LXX)

Live It!

Paul's Last Years

The Book of Acts ends with Paul living alone in Rome as he awaits his trial. For two years we know he lives like this, all the while receiving visitors and preaching about the Kingdom of God "with all boldness and freedom" (Acts 28:31). During that time he also continued writing letters to the Christian communities he helped establish, some of which are included as books in the New Testament. We are not told when or how Paul dies, but ancient tradition claims he was martyred in Rome shortly after that two-year period, around AD 64.

When Paul gathers the Jews to explain his arrest, he quotes the prophet Isaiah (Acts 28:26–27). Paul is pointing out what a tremendous loss their lack of belief is for them. The Jews have waited and waited and waited for the Messiah, yet when he came they could not accept that Jesus was the Messiah.

Through the Holy Spirit, Jesus is present to us. How will we know when we see or hear Jesus? Whenever we experience kindness, comfort, forgiveness, patience, peace, prayerfulness, joy, justice, courage, selflessness, and love—we are meeting Jesus in and through other people.

— Acts 28:17–31

then, that God's message of salvation has been sent to the Gentiles. They will listen!"ᵒ

30 For two years Paul lived in a place he rented for himself, and there he welcomed all who came to see him. **31** He preached about the Kingdom of God and taught about the Lord Jesus Christ, speaking with all boldness and freedom.

ᵒ **28:28** *Some manuscripts add verse 29:* After Paul said this, the Jews left, arguing violently among themselves.

Your Next Step

Congratulations on finishing the Acts of the Apostles! Use this space to write your thoughts and questions about this book. If you are following the suggested reading plan, go back to the Book of Judges in the Old Testament. Like the Apostles, the judges were also leaders who had some pretty exciting adventures.

Acts

Have you ever been confused by the directions for playing a new video game? Or have you ever had trouble really understanding a chapter in one of your textbooks?

Reading Paul's Letter to the Romans is kind of like that for some people. It's full of messages about being a Christian, but it can be very difficult to understand. Despite this difficulty most people say that it is Saint Paul's most important writing. In the letter he explains how God has a plan to save all people from sin and death. So it may not be easy to read, but it is worth the effort. You will find that Paul's central message is clear enough: We must believe that God sent Jesus to save everyone—and if we believe this, our lives will change.

Chap. 4:1–6;5:14

Headlines

- The Key to Being Right with God (1:16–17)
- Faith Is Answer to Sinner's Plight (3:9–31)
- At War with Yourself! (7:14–25)
- God Works with Those Who Love (8:28–30)
- Need Help? Love God! (10:5–21)
- Paul Reveals Rules for Holy Living (12:1—14:23)

FACTOIDS

Who wrote this book? Saint Paul, in preparation for making a visit to Rome. He wanted to explain his teachings to the Christians who lived there.

When was it written? Around AD 56 to 58, about twenty-five years after Jesus' Resurrection. It was one of Paul's last letters.

Who was it written for? It was written for people who had recently become Christians in Rome.

How does it fit into the Bible? It is one of thirteen letters Paul or his followers wrote to new Christians. It is Paul's longest letter.

Important themes

- Everyone has sinned against God, but instead of punishing us, God sent Jesus to save us.
- The Jewish people have a special place in God's plan. But God's plan also includes salvation for non-Jewish people.
- If we believe in Jesus, we are called to live a life of love and service to others.

ROMANS

1 ¹From Paul, a servant of Christ Jesus and an apostle chosen and called by God to preach his Good News.

²The Good News was promised long ago by God through his prophets, as written in the Holy Scriptures. ³It is about his Son, our Lord Jesus Christ: as to his humanity, he was born a descendant of David; ⁴as to his divine holiness, he was shown with great power to be the Son of God by being raised from death. ⁵Through him God gave me the privilege of being an apostle for the sake of Christ, in order to lead people of all nations to believe and obey. ⁶This also includes you who are in Rome, whom God has called to belong to Jesus Christ.

⁷And so I write to all of you in Rome whom God loves and has called to be his own people:

May God our Father and the Lord Jesus Christ give you grace and peace.

Prayer of Thanksgiving

⁸First, I thank my God through Jesus Christ for all of you, because the whole world is hearing about your faith. ⁹God is my witness that what I say is true—the God whom I serve with all my heart by preaching the Good News about his Son. God knows that I remember you ¹⁰every time I pray. I ask that God in his good will may at last make it possible for me to visit you now. ¹¹For I want very much to see you, in order to share a spiritual blessing with you to make you strong. ¹²What I mean is that both you and I will be helped at the same time, you by my faith and I by yours.

¹³You must remember, my friends, that many times I have planned to visit you, but something has always kept me from doing so. I want to win converts among you also, as I have among other Gentiles. ¹⁴For I have an obligation to all peoples, to the civilized and to the savage, to the educated and to the

ignorant. ¹⁵So then, I am eager to preach the Good News to you also who live in Rome.

The Power of the Gospel

¹⁶I have complete confidence in the gospel; it is God's power to save all who believe, first the Jews and also the Gentiles. ¹⁷For the gospel reveals how God puts people right with himself: it is through faith from beginning to end. As the scripture says, "The person who is put right with God through faith shall live."ᵃ

Human Guilt

¹⁸God's anger is revealed from heaven against all the sin and evil of the people whose evil ways prevent the truth from being known. ¹⁹God punishes them, because what can be known about God is plain to them, for God himself made it plain. ²⁰Ever since God created the world, his invisible qualities, both his eternal power and his divine nature, have been clearly seen; they are perceived in the things that God has made. So those people have no excuse at all! ²¹They know God, but they do not give him the honor that belongs to him, nor do they thank him. Instead, their thoughts have become complete nonsense, and their empty minds are filled with darkness. ²²They say

Their thoughts have become complete nonsense.
(1:21)

ᵃ **1:17** put right with God through faith shall live; *or* put right with God shall live through faith.
1:13 Acts 19:21 **1:16** Mk 8:38 **1:17** Hab 2:4 **1:20** Wis 13:1–9; Sir 17:8 **1:21** Eph 4:17, 18

they are wise, but they are fools; ²³instead of worshiping the immortal God, they worship images made to look like mortals or birds or animals or reptiles.

²⁴And so God has given those people over to do the filthy things their hearts desire, and they do shameful things with each other. ²⁵They exchange the truth about God for a lie; they worship and serve what God has created instead of the Creator himself, who is to be praised forever! Amen.

²⁶Because they do this, God has given them over to shameful passions. Even the women pervert the natural use of their sex by unnatural acts. ²⁷In the same way the men give up natural sexual relations with women and burn with passion for each other. Men do shameful things with each other, and as a result they bring upon themselves the punishment they deserve for their wrongdoing.

²⁸Because those people refuse to keep in mind the true knowledge about God, he has given them over to corrupted minds, so that they do the things that they should not do. ²⁹They are filled with all kinds of wickedness, evil, greed, and vice; they are full of jealousy, murder, fighting, deceit, and malice. They gossip ³⁰and speak evil of one another; they are hateful to God, insolent,ᵇ proud, and boastful; they think of more ways to do evil; they disobey their parents; ³¹they have no conscience; they do not keep their promises, and they show no kindness or pity for others. ³²They know that God's law says that people who live in this way deserve death. Yet, not only do they continue to do these very things, but they even approve of others who do them.

God's Judgment

2 ¹Do you, my friend, pass judgment on others? You have no excuse at all, whoever you are. For when you judge others and then do the same things which they do, you condemn yourself. ²We know that God is right when he judges the people who do

Guilty as Charged!

Do you know people who commit the sins Paul describes in Romans 1:28–32? They gossip, fight a lot, and lie. They are greedy and don't care about other people. They say hateful things about their parents and teachers, put down others, and do not keep their promises. They do not respect their own bodies or anyone else's.

Why do they do these things? One simple reason: they don't know God as they should. They refuse to believe that God loves them, has a plan for them, and wants them to be happy forever. If they knew God, they would try to make things right with God by following Jesus.

Remember that through the Bible God speaks to us today too. As you start to read the Letter to the Romans, think about what God might be saying to you. Could Paul have been writing about people at your school? Could he have been writing about you? Are you right with God?

— Romans 1:28–32

such things as these. ³But you, my friend, do those very things for which you pass judgment on others! Do you think you will escape God's judgment? ⁴Or perhaps you despise his great kindness, tolerance, and patience. Surely you know that God is kind, because he is trying to lead you to repent. ⁵But you have a hard and stubborn heart,

ᵇ **1:30** are hateful to God, insolent; *or* hate God, and are insolent.
1:23 Deut 4:16–18; Wis 11:15; 12:24; 13:10–19   **2:1** Mt 7:1; Lk 6:37   **2:4** Wis 11:23

How many times does Paul mention the Law (with a capital L) in Romans, chapter 2? Why is it so important to the Jews?

and so you are making your own punishment even greater on the Day when God's anger and righteous judgments will be revealed. 6For God will reward each of us according to what we have done. 7Some people keep on doing good, and seek glory, honor, and immortal life; to them God will give eternal life. 8Other people are selfish and reject what is right, in order to follow what is wrong; on them God will pour out his anger and fury. 9There will be suffering and pain for all those who do what is evil, for the Jews first and also for the Gentiles. 10But God will give glory, honor, and peace to all who do what is good, to the Jews first and also to the Gentiles. 11For God judges everyone by the same standard.

12The Gentiles do not have the Law of Moses; they sin and are lost apart from the Law. The Jews have the Law; they sin and are judged by the Law. 13For it is not by hearing the Law that people are put right with God, but by doing what the Law commands. 14The Gentiles do not have the Law; but whenever they do by instinct what the Law commands, they are their own law, even though they do not have the Law. 15Their conduct shows that what the Law commands is written in their hearts. Their consciences also show that this is true, since their thoughts sometimes accuse them and sometimes defend them. 16And so, according to the Good News I preach, this is how it will be on that Day when God through Jesus Christ will judge the secret thoughts of all.

The Jews and the Law

17What about you? You call yourself a Jew; you depend on the Law and boast about God; 18you know what God wants you to do, and you have learned from the Law to choose what is right; 19you are sure that you are a guide for the blind, a light for those who are in darkness, 20an instructor for the foolish, and a teacher for the ignorant. You are certain that in the Law you have the full content of knowledge and truth. 21You teach others—why don't you teach yourself? You preach, "Do not steal"—but do you

Know It. Live It.

Carlos can name the Ten Commandments in order. Hannah can recite most parts of the Mass from memory. Loren aced his last religion test, as he usually does. But the three friends declared yesterday "Make Fun of Fat Kids Day." All day they poked fun at people who were overweight and played cruel jokes on them.

Knowing what is right and doing what is right are two different things. Paul makes this point to his Jewish brothers and sisters in the middle of chapter 2 of Romans. Like them, all your life you have been learning the difference between right and wrong. You know the difference. Now it's time to live the difference. Don't put your faith in a notebook and leave it in your locker. Carry it with you in the halls, on the playground, the field, the school bus, the gym, and everyplace else you go. Through your actions give people a good impression about what Christians are like.

— Romans 2:17–29

yourself steal? 22You say, "Do not commit adultery"—but do you commit adultery? You detest idols—but do you rob temples? 23You boast about having God's law—but do you bring shame on God by breaking his law? 24The scripture says, "Because of you Jews, the Gentiles speak evil of God."

25If you obey the Law, your circumcision is of value; but if you disobey the Law, you might as well never have been circumcised. 26If the Gentile, who is not circumcised, obeys the commands of the Law, will not

Romans

God regard him as though he were circumcised? 27 And so you Jews will be condemned by the Gentiles because you break the Law, even though you have it written down and are circumcised; but they obey the Law, even though they are not physically circumcised. 28 After all, who is a real Jew, truly circumcised? It is not the man who is a Jew on the outside, whose circumcision is a physical thing. 29 Rather, the real Jew is the person who is a Jew on the inside, that is, whose heart has been circumcised, and this is the work of God's Spirit, not of the written Law. Such a person receives praise from God, not from human beings.

3 1 Do the Jews then have any advantage over the Gentiles? Or is there any value in being circumcised? 2 Much, indeed, in every way! In the first place, God trusted his message to the Jews. 3 But what if some of them were not faithful? Does this mean that God will not be faithful? 4 Certainly not! God must be true, even though all human beings are liars. As the scripture says,

"You must be shown to be right when
    you speak;
  you must win your case when you are
    being tried."

5 But what if our doing wrong serves to show up more clearly God's doing right? Can we say that God does wrong when he punishes us? (This would be the natural question to ask.) 6 By no means! If God is not just, how can he judge the world?

7 But what if my untruth serves God's glory by making his truth stand out more clearly? Why should I still be condemned as a sinner? 8 Why not say, then, "Let us do evil so that good may come"? Some people, indeed, have insulted me by accusing me of saying this very thing! They will be condemned, as they should be.

No One Is Righteous

9 Well then, are we Jews in any better condition than the Gentiles? Not at all! c I have already shown that Jews and Gentiles alike are all under the power of sin. 10 As the Scriptures say:

"There is no one who is righteous,
11   no one who is wise
  or who worships God.
12 All have turned away from God;
  they have all gone wrong;
  no one does what is right, not even one.
13 Their words are full of deadly deceit;
  wicked lies roll off their tongues,
  and dangerous threats, like snake's
    poison, from their lips;
14   their speech is filled with bitter curses.
15 They are quick to hurt and kill;
16   they leave ruin and destruction
    wherever they go.
17 They have not known the path of peace,
18   nor have they learned reverence for
    God."

19 Now we know that everything in the Law applies to those who live under the Law, in order to stop all human excuses and bring the whole world under God's judgment. 20 For no one is put right in God's sight by doing what the Law requires; what the Law does is to make us know that we have sinned.

How We Are Put Right with God

21 But now God's way of putting people right with himself has been revealed. It has nothing to do with law, even though the Law of Moses and the prophets gave their witness to it. 22 God puts people right through their faith in Jesus Christ. God does this to all who believe in Christ, because there is no difference at all: 23 everyone has sinned and is far away from God's saving presence. 24 But by the free gift of God's grace all are put right with him through Christ Jesus, who sets them free. 25-26 God offered him, so that by his blood d he should become the means by which people's sins are forgiven through their faith in him. God did this in order to demonstrate that he is righteous. In the past he was patient and overlooked people's sins;

---

c **3:9** any better condition than the Gentiles? Not at all!; or any worse condition than the Gentiles? Not altogether. d **3:25–26** by his blood; or by his sacrificial death.
2:29 Deut 30:6 **3:4** Ps 51:4 (LXX) **3:10–12** Ps 14:1–3 (LXX); Ps 53:1–3 (LXX) **3:13 a** Ps 5:9 (LXX); **b** Ps 140:3 **3:14** Ps 10:7 (LXX) **3:15–17** Isa 59:7, 8 **3:18** Ps 36:1 **3:20** Ps 143:2; Gal 2:16 **3:22** Gal 2:16

Sin Happens

Catholic Connections

Sin. It's a strong word. It's more than a little mistake. Sin is disobeying God on purpose. You can sin by thinking, saying, or doing something that offends God. When you choose to do wrong instead of doing good, you sin. You are not following the example of Jesus. You hurt your relationship with God, with other people, and with yourself.

Every night before you go to sleep, think about what thoughts, words, and actions hurt your relationships. Say a prayer admitting you were wrong and ask God for forgiveness. This is called an *examination of conscience*.

Along with this daily routine, the sacrament of Penance and Reconciliation gives Catholics a chance to confess their sins. In the sacrament the priest grants you absolution—God's complete forgiveness for your sins.

— Romans 3:9–20

but in the present time he deals with their sins, in order to demonstrate his righteousness. In this way God shows that he himself is righteous and that he puts right everyone who believes in Jesus.

27 What, then, can we boast about? Nothing! And what is the reason for this? Is it that we obey the Law? No, but that we believe. 28 For we conclude that a person is put right with God only through faith, and not by doing what the Law commands. 29 Or is God the God of the Jews only? Is he not the God of the Gentiles also? Of course he is. 30 God is one, and he will put the Jews right with himself on the basis of their faith, and will put the Gentiles right through their faith. 31 Does this mean that by this faith we do away with the Law? No, not at all; instead, we uphold the Law.

The Example of Abraham

4 1 What shall we say, then, of Abraham, the father of our race? What was his experience? 2 If he was put right with God by the things he did, he would have something to boast about—but not in God's sight. 3 The scripture says, "Abraham believed God, and because of his faith God accepted him as righteous." 4 A person who works is paid wages, but they are not regarded as a gift; they are something that has been earned. 5 But those who depend on faith, not on deeds, and who believe in the God who declares the guilty to be innocent, it is this faith that God takes into account in order to put them right with himself. 6 This is what David meant when he spoke of the happiness of the person whom God accepts as righteous, apart from anything that person does:

7 "Happy are those whose wrongs are forgiven,
    whose sins are pardoned!
8 Happy is the person whose sins the Lord will not keep account of!"

9 Does this happiness that David spoke of belong only to those who are circumcised? No indeed! It belongs also to those who are not circumcised. For we have quoted the

Romans

3:30 Deut 6:4; Gal 3:20   4:3 Gen 15:6; Gal 3:6   4:7, 8 Ps 32:1, 2

An *Act of Contrition* is a prayer telling God that you are sorry for your sins.

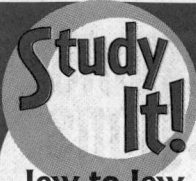

Jew to Jew

Saint Paul was a Jewish Christian. He wrote to both Jews and non-Jews. To get his point across, he used words and names of people that his Jewish readers would understand. In chapter 4 he makes a point about faith by writing about Abraham and Sarah, who had a son even though they were old (see Genesis, chapter 18). He quotes a psalm about forgiveness (see Psalm 32:1–2), because many Jews knew the Psalms by heart. He writes about circumcision, a ritual that was performed on all Jewish males when they were eight days old (see Genesis 17:9–14) to distinguish Jews from non-Jews.

Then Paul says something shocking. He tells them the important thing isn't whether you are circumcised or not but whether you have true faith. Faith in God and faith in Christ. Then he tells them that in God's eyes there is no difference between a circumcised Jew and an uncircumcised non-Jew if they both have faith.

What modern men and women would you name as people who show true faith? What saints, historical figures, and even people you know personally come to mind?

— Romans, chapter 4

scripture, "Abraham believed God, and because of his faith God accepted him as righteous." 10When did this take place? Was it before or after Abraham was circumcised? It was before, not after. 11He was circumcised later, and his circumcision was a sign to show that because of his faith God had accepted him as righteous before he had been circumcised. And so Abraham is the spiritual father of all who believe in God and are accepted as righteous by him, even though they are not circumcised. 12He is also the father of those who are circumcised, that is, of those who, in addition to being circumcised, also live the same life of faith that our father Abraham lived before he was circumcised.

God's Promise Is Received through Faith

13When God promised Abraham and his descendants that the world would belong to him, he did so, not because Abraham obeyed the Law, but because he believed and was accepted as righteous by God. 14For if what God promises is to be given to those who obey the Law, then faith means nothing and God's promise is worthless. 15The Law brings down God's anger; but where there is no law, there is no disobeying of the law.

16And so the promise was based on faith, in order that the promise should be guaranteed as God's free gift to all of Abraham's descendants—not just to those who obey the Law, but also to those who believe as Abraham did. For Abraham is the spiritual father of us all; 17as the scripture says, "I have made you father of many nations." So the promise is good in the sight of God, in whom Abraham believed—the God who brings the dead to life and whose command brings into being what did not exist. 18Abraham believed and hoped, even when there was no reason for hoping, and so became "the father of many nations." Just as the scripture says, "Your descendants will be as

4:11 Gen 17:10   4:13 Gen 17:4–6; 22:17, 18; Gal 3:29   4:14 Gal 3:18   4:16 Gal 3:7   4:17 Gen 17:5
4:18 Gen 15:5

Jews are the spiritual relatives of Christians. We share a special relationship and can learn much from each other.

Romans

Pray It!

A Simple Prayer

After reading the section on being right with God (Romans 5:1–11), try praying this prayer. Does it express the relationship you want with God?

More than anything, God, I want to be right with you.
I know that Jesus died for me, just because you love me.
Now it's my turn to show my love.
I want to live the life you want for me.
I want to be the person you made me to be.
I want to feel all the love you have for me.
I want the world to be a better place because I'm in it.
Help me be right with you, God.
Amen.

— Romans 5:1–11

many as the stars." [19]He was then almost one hundred years old; but his faith did not weaken when he thought of his body, which was already practically dead, or of the fact that Sarah could not have children. [20]His faith did not leave him, and he did not doubt God's promise; his faith filled him with power, and he gave praise to God. [21]He was absolutely sure that God would be able to do what he had promised. [22]That is why Abraham, through faith, "was accepted as righteous by God." [23]The words "he was accepted as righteous" were not written for him alone. [24]They were written also for us who are to be accepted as righteous, who believe in him who raised Jesus our Lord from death. [25]Because of our sins he was given over to die, and he was raised to life in order to put us right with God.

Right with God

5 [1]Now that we have been put right with God through faith, we have[e] peace with God through our Lord Jesus Christ. [2]He has brought us by faith into this experience of God's grace, in which we now live. And so we boast[f] of the hope we have of sharing God's glory! [3]We also boast[g] of our troubles, because we know that trouble produces endurance, [4]endurance brings God's approval, and his approval creates hope. [5]This hope does not disappoint us, for God has poured out his love into our hearts by means of the Holy Spirit, who is God's gift to us.

[6]For when we were still helpless, Christ died for the wicked at the time that God chose. [7]It is a difficult thing for someone to die for a righteous person. It may even be that someone might dare to die for a good person. [8]But God has shown us how much he loves us—it was while we were still sinners that Christ died for us! [9]By his blood[h] we are now put right with God; how much more, then, will we be saved by him from God's anger! [10]We were God's enemies, but he made us his friends through the death of his Son. Now that we are God's friends, how much more will we be saved by Christ's life! [11]But that is not all; we rejoice because of what God has done through our Lord Jesus Christ, who has now made us God's friends.

e **5:1** we have; *some manuscripts have* let us have.   *f* **5:2** we boast; *or* let us boast.   *g* **5:3** We also boast; *or* Let us also boast.   *h* **5:9** By his blood; *or* By his sacrificial death.
4:19 Gen 17:17   **4:25** Isa 53:4, 5

Adam and Christ

12 Sin came into the world through one man, and his sin brought death with it. As a result, death has spread to the whole human race because everyone has sinned. **13** There was sin in the world before the Law was given; but where there is no law, no account is kept of sins. **14** But from the time of Adam to the time of Moses, death ruled over all human beings, even over those who did not sin in the same way that Adam did when he disobeyed God's command.

Adam was a figure of the one who was to come. **15** But the two are not the same, because God's free gift is not like Adam's sin. It is true that many people died because of the sin of that one man. But God's grace is much greater, and so is his free gift to so many people through the grace of the one man, Jesus Christ. **16** And there is a difference between God's gift and the sin of one man. After the one sin, came the judgment of "Guilty"; but after so many sins, comes the undeserved gift of "Not guilty!" **17** It is true that through the sin of one man death began to rule because of that one man. But how much greater is the result of what was done by the one man, Jesus Christ! All who receive God's abundant grace and are freely put right with him will rule in life through Christ.

18 So then, as the one sin condemned all people, in the same way the one righteous act sets all people free and gives them life. **19** And just as all people were made sinners as the result of the disobedience of one man, in the same way they will all be put right with God as the result of the obedience of the one man.

20 Law was introduced in order to increase wrongdoing; but where sin increased, God's grace increased much more. **21** So then, just as sin ruled by means of death, so also God's grace rules by means of righteousness, leading us to eternal life through Jesus Christ our Lord.

Dead to Sin but Alive in Union with Christ

6 **1** What shall we say, then? Should we continue to live in sin so that God's grace will increase? **2** Certainly not! We have died to sin—how then can we go on living in it? **3** For surely you know that when we were baptized into union with Christ Jesus, we were baptized into union with his death. **4** By our baptism, then, we were buried with him and shared his death, in order that, just as Christ was raised from death by the glorious power of the Father, so also we might live a new life.

5 For since we have become one with him in dying as he did, in the same way we shall be one with him by being raised to life as he was. **6** And we know that our old being has been put to death with Christ on his cross, in order that the power of the sinful self might be destroyed, so that we should no longer be the slaves of sin. **7** For when we die, we are set free from the power of sin. **8** Since we have died with Christ, we believe that we will also live with him. **9** For we know that Christ has been raised from death and will never die again—death will no longer rule over him. **10** And so, because he died, sin has no power over him; and now he lives his life in fellowship with God. **11** In the same way you are to think of yourselves as dead, so far as sin is concerned, but living in fellowship with God through Christ Jesus.

So that we should no longer be slaves of sin. (6:6)

12 Sin must no longer rule in your mortal bodies, so that you obey the desires of your natural self. **13** Nor must you surrender any part of yourselves to sin to be used for wicked purposes. Instead, give yourselves to God, as those who have been brought from death to life, and surrender your whole being to him to be used for righteous pur-

Romans

Yes, YOU!

"Are you holy?" Megan looked around. "Yes, you, Megan. Are you holy?" She didn't know what to say. The new leader had a habit of asking questions that really made people think—and sometimes squirm a little. Megan thought quickly. She was a good person. She always did her best. When she did something wrong, she was sorry for it. She was kind. Finally, she answered quietly, "I guess so."

The word *holy* comes from the same word as *whole.* The original word meant unbroken, healthy, or complete. Someone who is holy has a solid relationship with God.

Everything God created is holy—including you! Sometimes, though, holiness is hard to recognize. The whole point of chapter 6 is that Christians must always choose holiness. And that means choosing to say no to sin.

Are you holy? Yes, YOU!

— Romans, chapter 6

poses. ¹⁴Sin must not be your master; for you do not live under law but under God's grace.

Slaves of Righteousness

¹⁵What, then? Shall we sin, because we are not under law but under God's grace? By no means! ¹⁶Surely you know that when you surrender yourselves as slaves to obey someone, you are in fact the slaves of the master you obey—either of sin, which results in death, or of obedience, which results in being put right with God. ¹⁷But thanks be to God! For though at one time you were slaves to sin, you have obeyed with all your heart the truths found in the teaching you received. ¹⁸You were set free from sin and became the slaves of righteousness. ¹⁹(I use everyday language because of the weakness of your natural selves.) At one time you surrendered yourselves entirely as slaves to impurity and wickedness for wicked purposes. In the same way you must now surrender yourselves entirely as slaves of righteousness for holy purposes.

²⁰When you were the slaves of sin, you were free from righteousness. ²¹What did you gain from doing the things that you are now ashamed of? The result of those things is death! ²²But now you have been set free from sin and are the slaves of God. Your gain is a life fully dedicated to him, and the result is eternal life. ²³For sin pays its wage—death; but God's free gift is eternal life in union with Christ Jesus our Lord.

An Illustration from Marriage

7 ¹Certainly you will understand what I am about to say, my friends, because all of you know about law. The law rules over people only as long as they live. ²A married woman, for example, is bound by the law to her husband as long as he lives; but if he dies, then she is free from the law that bound her to him. ³So then, if she lives with another man while her husband is alive, she will be called an adulteress; but if her husband dies, she is legally a free woman and does not commit adultery if she marries another man. ⁴That is how it is with you, my friends. As far as the Law is concerned, you also have died because you are part of the body of Christ; and now you belong to him who was raised from death in order that we might be useful in the service of God. ⁵For when we lived according to our human nature, the sinful desires stirred up by the Law were at work in our bodies, and all we did ended in death. ⁶Now, however, we are free from the Law, because we died to that which once

Romans

held us prisoners. No longer do we serve in the old way of a written law, but in the new way of the Spirit.

Law and Sin

7 Shall we say, then, that the Law itself is sinful? Of course not! But it was the Law that made me know what sin is. If the Law had not said, "Do not desire what belongs to someone else," I would not have known such a desire. 8 But by means of that commandment sin found its chance to stir up all kinds of selfish desires in me. Apart from law, sin is a dead thing. 9 I myself was once alive apart from law; but when the commandment came, sin sprang to life, 10 and I died. And the commandment which was meant to bring life, in my case brought death. 11 Sin found its chance, and by means of the commandment it deceived me and killed me.

12 So then, the Law itself is holy, and the commandment is holy, right, and good. 13 But does this mean that what is good caused my death? By no means! It was sin that did it; by using what is good, sin brought death to me, in order that its true nature as sin might be revealed. And so, by means of the commandment sin is shown to be even more terribly sinful.

The Conflict in Us

14 We know that the Law is spiritual; but I am a mortal, sold as a slave to sin. 15 I do not understand what I do; for I don't do what I would like to do, but instead I do what I hate. 16 Since what I do is what I don't want to do, this shows that I agree that the Law is right. 17 So I am not really the one who does this thing; rather it is the sin that lives in me. 18 I know that good does not live in me— that is, in my human nature. For even though the desire to do good is in me, I am not able to do it. 19 I don't do the good I want to do; instead, I do the evil that I do

not want to do. 20 If I do what I don't want to do, this means that I am no longer the one who does it; instead, it is the sin that lives in me.

21 So I find that this law is at work: when I want to do what is good, what is evil is the only choice I have. 22 My inner being delights in the law of God. 23 But I see a different law at work in my body—a law that fights against the law which my mind approves of. It makes me a prisoner to the law of sin which is at work in my body. 24 What an unhappy man I am! Who will rescue me from this body that is taking me to death? 25 Thanks be to God, who does this through our Lord Jesus Christ!

This, then, is my condition: on my own I can serve God's law only with my mind, while my human nature serves the law of sin.

Life in the Spirit

8 1 There is no condemnation now for those who live in union with Christ Jesus. 2 For the law of the Spirit, which brings us life in union with Christ Jesus, has set me[i] free from the law of sin and death. 3 What the Law could not do, because human nature was weak, God did. He condemned sin in human nature by sending his own Son, who came with a nature like our sinful nature, to do away with sin. 4 God did this so that the righteous demands of the Law might be fully satisfied in us who live according to the Spirit, and not according to human nature. 5 Those who live as their human nature tells them to, have their minds controlled by what human nature wants. Those who live as the Spirit tells them to, have their minds controlled by what the Spirit wants. 6 To be controlled by human nature results in death; to be controlled by the Spirit results in life and peace. 7 And so people become enemies of God when they are controlled by their human nature; for they do not obey God's law, and in fact they

i **8:2** me; *some manuscripts have* you; *others have* us.
7:7 Ex 20:17; Deut 5:21   **7:11** Gen 3:13   **7:15** Gal 5:17

"To be controlled by human nature results in death; to be controlled by the Spirit results in life and peace" *(Romans 8:6)*.

cannot obey it. ⁸Those who obey their human nature cannot please God.

⁹But you do not live as your human nature tells you to; instead, you live as the Spirit tells you to—if, in fact, God's Spirit lives in you. Whoever does not have the Spirit of Christ does not belong to him. ¹⁰But if Christ lives in you, the Spirit is life for youʲ because you have been put right with God, even though your bodies are going to die because of sin. ¹¹If the Spirit of God, who raised Jesus from death, lives in you, then he who raised Christ from death will also give life to your mortal bodies by the presence of his Spirit in you.

¹²So then, my friends, we have an obligation, but it is not to live as our human nature wants us to. ¹³For if you live according to your human nature, you are going to die; but if by the Spirit you put to death your sinful actions, you will live. ¹⁴Those who are led by God's Spirit are God's children. ¹⁵For the Spirit that God has given you does not make you slaves and cause you to be afraid; instead, the Spirit makes you God's children, and by the Spirit's power we cry out to God, "Father! my Father!" ¹⁶God's Spirit joins himself to our spirits to declare that we are God's children. ¹⁷Since we are his children, we will possess the blessings he keeps for his people, and we will also possess with Christ what God has kept for him; for if we share Christ's suffering, we will also share his glory.

The Future Glory

¹⁸I consider that what we suffer at this present time cannot be compared at all with the glory that is going to be revealed to us. ¹⁹All of creation waits with eager longing for God to reveal his children. ²⁰For creation was condemned to lose its purpose, not of its own will, but because God willed it to be so. Yet there was the hope ²¹that creation itself would one day be set free from its slavery to decay and would share the glorious freedom of the children of God. ²²For we know that

God's Big Job

God created the universe and everything in it. And God promised to take care of everything he created. It's a huge job. Human beings often work against God when it comes to taking care of the planet earth. We pollute the air and water with our cars and factories. We waste natural resources like forests and oil so that we can make life super easy. The earth "groans with pain" because of what people have done to it (see Romans 8:22).

The Native American Iroquois Nations hold to the Great Law, which requires that chiefs think about how their decisions will affect people seven generations later. That means they have to think of how the decision might affect their great-great-great-great-great grandchildren. It's a way of saying that some decisions can affect people and the earth for a long time. The earth would not be groaning as much if everyone followed the Great Law of the Iroquois.

— Romans 8:18–25

up to the present time all of creation groans with pain, like the pain of childbirth. ²³But it is not just creation alone which groans; we who have the Spirit as the first of God's gifts also groan within ourselves as we wait for God to make us his children andᵏ set our whole being free. ²⁴For it was by hope that we were saved; but if we see what we hope for, then it is not really hope. For who of us

ʲ **8:10** the Spirit is life for you; *or* your spirit is alive. and.   ᵏ **8:23** *Some manuscripts do not have* make us his children

8:11 1 Cor 3:16   **8:15–17** Gal 4:5–7   **8:15** Mk 14:36; Gal 4:6   **8:18** Wis 3:5, 6   **8:20** Gen 3:17–19
8:23 2 Cor 5:2–4

Romans

hopes for something we see? 25But if we hope for what we do not see, we wait for it with patience.

26In the same way the Spirit also comes to help us, weak as we are. For we do not know how we ought to pray; the Spirit himself pleads with God for us in groans that words cannot express. 27And God, who sees into our hearts, knows what the thought of the Spirit is; because the Spirit pleads with God on behalf of his people and in accordance with his will.

28We know that in all things God works for good with those who love him,[l] those whom he has called according to his purpose. 29Those whom God had already chosen he also set apart to become like his Son, so that the Son would be the first among many believers. 30And so those whom God set apart, he called; and those he called, he put right with himself, and he shared his glory with them.

God's Love in Christ Jesus

31In view of all this, what can we say? If God is for us, who can be against us? 32Certainly not God, who did not even keep back his own Son, but offered him for us all! He gave us his Son—will he not also freely give us all things? 33Who will accuse God's chosen people? God himself declares them not guilty! 34Who, then, will condemn them? Not Christ Jesus, who died, or rather, who was raised to life and is at the right side of God, pleading with him for us! 35Who, then, can separate us from the love of Christ? Can trouble do it, or hardship or persecution or hunger or poverty or danger or death? 36As the scripture says,

> "For your sake we are in danger of death at all times;
> we are treated like sheep that are going to be slaughtered."

37No, in all these things we have complete victory through him who loved us! 38For I am certain that nothing can separate us from his love: neither death nor life, neither angels nor other heavenly rulers or powers, neither the present nor the future, 39neither the world above nor the world below—there is nothing in all creation that will ever be able to separate us from the love of God which is ours through Christ Jesus our Lord.

God and His People

9 1I am speaking the truth; I belong to Christ and I do not lie. My conscience, ruled by the Holy Spirit, also assures me that I am not lying 2when I say how great is my sorrow, how endless the pain in my heart 3for my people, my own flesh and blood! For their sake I could wish that I myself were under God's curse and separated from Christ. 4They are God's people; he made them his children and revealed his glory to them; he made his covenants[m] with them and gave them the Law; they have the true worship; they have received God's promises; 5they are descended from the famous Hebrew ancestors; and Christ, as a human being, belongs to their race. May God, who rules over all, be praised forever![n] Amen.

6I am not saying that the promise of God has failed; for not all the people of Israel are the people of God. 7Nor are all of Abraham's descendants the children of God. God said to Abraham, "It is through Isaac that you will have the descendants I promised you." 8This means that the children born in the usual way[o] are not the children of God; instead, the children born as a result of God's promise are regarded as the true descendants. 9For God's promise was made in these words: "At the right time[p] I will come back, and Sarah will have a son."

10And this is not all. For Rebecca's two sons had the same father, our ancestor Isaac. 11-12But in order that the choice of one son might be completely the result of God's own purpose, God said to her, "The older will

---

[l] **8:28** in all things God works for good with those who love him; *some manuscripts have* all things work for good for those who love God. [m] **9:4** covenants; *some manuscripts have* covenant. [n] **9:5** May God, who rules over all, be praised forever!; *or* And may he, who is God ruling over all, be praised forever! [o] **9:8** CHILDREN BORN IN THE USUAL WAY: *This refers to the descendants Abraham had through Ishmael, his son by Hagar (see Gal 4:22–23).* [p] **9:9** At the right time; *or* At this time next year.
8:36 Ps 44:22   **9:4** Ex 4:22   **9:7** Gen 21:12   **9:9** Gen 18:10   **9:12** Gen 25:23

Pray It!

A Lump on God's Wheel

In Romans 9:20–21 Paul compares us to a clay pot made by God. Did you ever watch a potter at a wheel? She starts with a cold, wet lump of clay. As the wheel spins, she delicately shapes the clay into a form using her fingers and hands. Sometimes the wheel spins fast, sometimes slowly. The form might be a pot, a cup, a bowl, or anything else the potter wants it to be.

Find a quiet place and sit for a few minutes. Imagine yourself as a lump of clay on God's wheel. Feel yourself spinning around as God's hand forms you into what God wants you to be. Are you spinning fast or slowly? What does it feel like to be shaped by God? What is God shaping you into? Don't resist or try to fight it. God is the potter; you are the clay.

— Romans 9:20–21

serve the younger." He said this before they were born, before they had done anything either good or bad; so God's choice was based on his call, and not on anything they had done. 13 As the scripture says, "I loved Jacob, but I hated Esau."

14 Shall we say, then, that God is unjust? Not at all. 15 For he said to Moses, "I will have mercy on anyone I wish; I will take pity on anyone I wish." 16 So then, everything depends, not on what we humans want or do, but only on God's mercy. 17 For the scripture says to the king of Egypt, "I made you king in order to use you to show my power and to spread my fame over the whole world." 18 So then, God has mercy on anyone he wishes, and he makes stubborn anyone he wishes.

God's Anger and Mercy

19 But one of you will say to me, "If this is so, how can God find fault with anyone? Who can resist God's will?" 20 But who are you, my friend, to talk back to God? A clay pot does not ask the man who made it, "Why did you make me like this?" 21 After all, the man who makes the pots has the right to use the clay as he wishes, and to make two pots from the same lump of clay, one for special occasions and the other for ordinary use.

22 And the same is true of what God has done. He wanted to show his anger and to make his power known. But he was very patient in enduring those who were the objects of his anger, who were doomed to destruction. 23 And he also wanted to reveal his abundant glory, which was poured out on us who are the objects of his mercy, those of us whom he has prepared to receive his glory. 24 For we are the people he called, not only from among the Jews but also from among the Gentiles. 25 This is what he says in the book of Hosea:

"The people who were not mine
  I will call 'My People.'
The nation that I did not love
  I will call 'My Beloved.'
26 And in the very place where they were
  told, 'You are not my people,'
  there they will be called the children of
  the living God."

9:13 Mal 1:2, 3   9:15 Ex 33:19   9:17 Ex 9:16 (LXX)   9:20 Isa 29:16; 45:9; Wis 12:12   9:21 Wis 15:7; Sir 33:13   9:22 Wis 12:20, 21   9:25 Hos 2:23   9:26 Hos 1:10

Check out Isaiah 64:8–12 and Jeremiah 18:1–12 for more images of potter God.

Romans

27 And Isaiah exclaims about Israel: "Even if the people of Israel are as many as the grains of sand by the sea, yet only a few of them will be saved; 28 for the Lord will quickly settle his full account with the world." 29 It is as Isaiah had said before, "If the Lord Almighty had not left us some descendants, we would have become like Sodom, we would have been like Gomorrah."

Israel and the Gospel

30 So we say that the Gentiles, who were not trying to put themselves right with God, were put right with him through faith; 31 while God's people, who were seeking a law that would put them right with God, did not find it. 32 And why not? Because they did not depend on faith but on what they did. And so they stumbled over the "stumbling stone" 33 that the scripture speaks of:

"Look, I place in Zion a stone
that will make people stumble,
a rock that will make them fall.
But whoever believes in him will not be
disappointed."

10 1 My friends, how I wish with all my heart that my own people might be saved! How I pray to God for them! 2 I can assure you that they are deeply devoted to God; but their devotion is not based on true knowledge. 3 They have not known the way in which God puts people right with himself, and instead, they have tried to set up their own way; and so they did not submit themselves to God's way of putting people right. 4 For Christ has brought the Law to an end, so that everyone who believes is put right with God.

Salvation Is for All

5 Moses wrote this about being put right with God by obeying the Law: "Whoever obeys the commands of the Law will live." 6 But what the scripture says about being put right with God through faith is this: "You are not to ask yourself, Who will go up into heaven?" (that is, to bring Christ down). 7 "Nor are you to ask, Who will go down

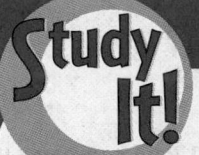

Don't Get Too Comfortable!

Paul comes down hard on his people, the Jews. He tells them that even though they are God's special people, they need to follow Jesus. Paul may seem a little harsh with his criticism. As Catholics, we respect other people's faith and honor their beliefs. We know that many of us worship the same God—the God who created us all. But Paul loved his people so much he wanted them to know the fullness of God's love.

Part of the problem was that some Jews were too comfortable or too stubborn. They did things out of habit rather than out of belief. They followed the rules, but didn't take care of people—especially people who were not like them. They thought they were always right and refused to listen to other people's ideas. Paul could have been talking to some of us!

Don't get too comfortable or too stubborn. Think about why you do what you do as a Catholic. Be open to new ideas. Let go of your prejudices. Above all, be *thought-full* and *faith-full*.

— Romans 9:30—10:4

9:27, 28 Isa 10:22, 23 (LXX) **9:29** Isa 1:9 (LXX) **9:33** Isa 28:16 (LXX) **10:5** Lev 18:5 **10:6–8** Deut 30:12–14

God's Mighty Messengers

Catholic Connections

Paul says that the only way people can hear God's Good News is if someone is spreading it. You spread the Good News about Jesus by your words and actions. This is the job of everyone who is baptized. Many Catholics take this job to heart in a special way: they become involved in Church ministries. They read at Mass, sing in the choir, or teach religious education. Some work with young people or the elderly. Others run soup kitchens. Still others help out with the daily tasks of running a parish.

Some men hear a special call from God to be ordained as a priest or a deacon. Still others respond to God's call to join other women or men as a religious sister or brother. They serve the needs of the Church along with those who are married and single. Every young person should listen carefully and be open to whether God is calling him or her in this way.

The Church needs you—now and when you are an adult. As you think about the future, listen carefully to how God is calling you to be a mighty messenger.

— Romans 10:14–17

into the world below?" (that is, to bring Christ up from death). 8 What it says is this: "God's message is near you, on your lips and in your heart"—that is, the message of faith that we preach. 9 If you confess that Jesus is Lord and believe that God raised him from death, you will be saved. 10 For it is by our faith that we are put right with God; it is by our confession that we are saved. 11 The scripture says, "Whoever believes in him will not be disappointed." 12 This includes everyone, because there is no difference between Jews and Gentiles; God is the same Lord of all and richly blesses all who call to him. 13 As the scripture says, "Everyone who calls out to the Lord for help will be saved."

14 But how can they call to him for help if they have not believed? And how can they believe if they have not heard the message? And how can they hear if the message is not proclaimed? 15 And how can the message be proclaimed if the messengers are not sent out? As the scripture says, "How wonderful is the coming of messengers who bring

good news!" 16 But not all have accepted the Good News. Isaiah himself said, "Lord, who believed our message?" 17 So then, faith comes from hearing the message, and the message comes through preaching Christ.

18 But I ask: Is it true that they did not hear the message? Of course they did—for as the scripture says:

"The sound of their voice went out to all
    the world;
  their words reached the ends of the
    earth."

19 Again I ask: Did the people of Israel not understand? Moses himself is the first one to answer:

"I will use a so-called nation
    to make my people jealous;
  and by means of a nation of fools
    I will make my people angry."

20 And Isaiah is even bolder when he says,

"I was found by those who were not
    looking for me;
  I appeared to those who were not
    asking for me."

Romans

10:11 Isa 28:16 (LXX)   10:13 Joel 2:32   10:15 Isa 52:7   10:16 Isa 53:1 (LXX)   10:18 Ps 19:4 (LXX)
10:19 Deut 32:21   10:20 Isa 65:1 (LXX)

21 But concerning Israel he says, "All day long I held out my hands to welcome a disobedient and rebellious people."

God's Mercy on Israel

11 1 I ask, then: Did God reject his own people? Certainly not! I myself am an Israelite, a descendant of Abraham, a member of the tribe of Benjamin. 2 God has not rejected his people, whom he chose from the beginning. You know what the scripture says in the passage where Elijah pleads with God against Israel: 3 "Lord, they have killed your prophets and torn down your altars; I am the only one left, and they are trying to kill me." 4 What answer did God give him? "I have kept for myself seven thousand men who have not worshiped the false god Baal." 5 It is the same way now: there is a small number left of those whom God has chosen because of his grace. 6 His choice is based on his grace, not on what they have done. For if God's choice were based on what people do, then his grace would not be real grace.

7 What then? The people of Israel did not find what they were looking for. It was only the small group that God chose who found it; the rest grew deaf to God's call. 8 As the scripture says, "God made their minds and hearts dull; to this very day they cannot see or hear." 9 And David says,

"May they be caught and trapped at their feasts;
　　may they fall, may they be punished!
10 May their eyes be blinded so that they cannot see;
　　and make them bend under their troubles at all times."

11 I ask, then: When the Jews stumbled, did they fall to their ruin? By no means! Because they sinned, salvation has come to the Gentiles, to make the Jews jealous of them. 12 The sin of the Jews brought rich blessings to the world, and their spiritual poverty brought rich blessings to the Gentiles. Then, how much greater the blessings will be when the complete number of Jews is included!

The Salvation of the Gentiles

13 I am speaking now to you Gentiles: As long as I am an apostle to the Gentiles, I will take pride in my work. 14 Perhaps I can make the people of my own race jealous, and so be able to save some of them. 15 For when they were rejected, all other people were changed from God's enemies into his friends. What will it be, then, when they are accepted? It will be life for the dead!

16 If the first piece of bread is given to God, then the whole loaf is his also; and if the roots of a tree are offered to God, the branches are his also. 17 Some of the branches of the cultivated olive tree have been broken off, and a branch of a wild olive tree has been joined to it. You Gentiles are like that wild olive tree, and now you share the strong spiritual life of the Jews. 18 So then, you must not despise those who were broken off like branches. How can you be proud? You are just a branch; you don't support the roots—the roots support you.

19 But you will say, "Yes, but the branches were broken off to make room for me." 20 That is true. They were broken off because they did not believe, while you remain in place because you do believe. But do not be proud of it; instead, be afraid. 21 God did not spare the Jews, who are like natural branches; do you think he will spare you? 22 Here we see how kind and how severe God is. He is severe toward those who have fallen, but kind to you—if you continue in his kindness. But if you do not, you too will be broken off. 23 And if the Jews abandon their unbelief, they will be put back in the place where they were; for God is able to do that. 24 You Gentiles are like the branch of a wild olive tree that is broken off and then, contrary to nature, is joined to a cultivated olive tree. The Jews are like this cultivated tree; and it will be much easier for God to join these broken-off branches to their own tree again.

God's Mercy on All

25 There is a secret truth, my friends, which I want you to know, for it will keep

you from thinking how wise you are. It is that the stubbornness of the people of Israel is not permanent, but will last only until the complete number of Gentiles comes to God. 26And this is how all Israel will be saved. As the scripture says,

"The Savior will come from Zion
    and remove all wickedness from the
        descendants of Jacob.
27 I will make this covenant with them
    when I take away their sins."

28Because they reject the Good News, the Jews are God's enemies for the sake of you Gentiles. But because of God's choice, they are his friends because of their ancestors. 29For God does not change his mind about whom he chooses and blesses. 30As for you Gentiles, you disobeyed God in the past; but now you have received God's mercy because the Jews were disobedient. 31In the same way, because of the mercy that you have received, the Jews now disobey God, in order that they also may now*q* receive God's mercy. 32For God has made all people prisoners of disobedience, so that he might show mercy to them all.

Praise to God

33How great are God's riches! How deep are his wisdom and knowledge! Who can explain his decisions? Who can understand his ways? 34As the scripture says,

"Who knows the mind of the Lord?
    Who is able to give him advice?
35 Who has ever given him anything,
    so that he had to pay it back?"

36For all things were created by him, and all things exist through him and for him. To God be the glory forever! Amen.

Life in God's Service

12 1So then, my friends, because of God's great mercy to us I appeal to you: Offer yourselves as a living sacrifice to

---

Pray It!

Start Your Day Right

"To God be the glory forever! Amen" (Romans 11:36).

The last line of chapter 11 is a powerful statement of faith in an awesome God. Write the verse on a card and put it where you will see it every morning. At the start of each day, read the statement out loud. Think about it during the day. Let everything you do, every decision you make, every word you say reflect God's power in your life.

— Romans 11:36

God, dedicated to his service and pleasing to him. This is the true worship that you should offer. 2Do not conform yourselves to the standards of this world, but let God transform you inwardly by a complete change of your mind. Then you will be able to know the will of God—what is good and is pleasing to him and is perfect.

3And because of God's gracious gift to me I say to every one of you: Do not think of yourself more highly than you should. Instead, be modest in your thinking, and judge yourself according to the amount of faith that God has given you. 4We have many parts in the one body, and all these parts have different functions. 5In the same way, though we are many, we are one body in union with Christ, and we are all joined to each other as different parts of one body. 6So we are to use our different gifts in accordance with the grace that God has

Romans

---

q **11:31** *Some manuscripts do not have* now.
11:26 Isa 59:20, 21 (LXX)   **11:27** Isa 27:9 (LXX)   **11:33** Isa 55:8; Wis 17:1   **11:34** Isa 40:13 (LXX)
11:35 Job 41:11   **11:36** 1 Cor 8:6   **12:4, 5** 1 Cor 12:12   **12:6–8** 1 Cor 12:4–11

Mercy **is having loving kindness for a person who does something wrong, just as God has mercy on us.**

given us. If our gift is to speak God's message, we should do it according to the faith that we have; [7]if it is to serve, we should serve; if it is to teach, we should teach; [8]if it is to encourage others, we should do so. Whoever shares with others should do it generously; whoever has authority should work hard; whoever shows kindness to others should do it cheerfully.

[9]Love must be completely sincere. Hate what is evil, hold on to what is good. [10]Love one another warmly as Christians, and be eager to show respect for one another. [11]Work hard and do not be lazy. Serve the Lord with a heart full of devotion. [12]Let your hope keep you joyful, be patient in your troubles, and pray at all times. [13]Share your belongings with your needy fellow Christians, and open your homes to strangers.

[14]Ask God to bless those who persecute you—yes, ask him to bless, not to curse. [15]Be happy with those who are happy, weep with those who weep. [16]Have the same concern for everyone. Do not be proud, but accept humble duties.[r] Do not think of yourselves as wise.

[17]If someone has done you wrong, do not repay him with a wrong. Try to do what everyone considers to be good. [18]Do everything possible on your part to live in peace with everybody. [19]Never take revenge, my friends, but instead let God's anger do it. For the scripture says, "I will take revenge, I will pay back, says the Lord." [20]Instead, as the scripture says: "If your enemies are hungry, feed them; if they are thirsty, give them a drink; for by doing this you will make them burn with shame." [21]Do not let evil defeat you; instead, conquer evil with good.

Duties toward State Authorities

13 [1]Everyone must obey state authorities, because no authority exists without God's permission, and the existing authorities have been put there by God. [2]Whoever opposes the existing authority opposes what God has ordered; and anyone

Whose Rules?

- **What do your favorite television shows tell you about what it means to be successful?**
- **What do your favorite magazines tell you about what it means to be a man or a woman?**
- **What do your favorite video games tell you about how to handle conflict?**

You learn a lot from the world around you. The world tells you that you need a certain body shape or you won't be attractive to others. It tells you that violence is the best way to resolve differences. It tells you that you need a lot of money and material things to be happy and successful.

Sometimes certain messages in our world try to teach us things that are not what God wants for us. In chapter 12 Paul gives us a list of rules for living the life that God intended. Notice how different that list is from some of the things you see or hear every day. Make a list of these rules from Paul. Keep it near your bed. Before you go to sleep, look it over and think about your day. Whose rules did you follow that day? the world's? or God's?

— Romans, chapter 12

---

[r] **12:16** accept humble duties; *or* make friends with humble people.
12:14 Mt 5:44; Lk 6:28   **12:15** Sir 7:34   **12:16** Prov 3:7   **12:19** Deut 32:35   **12:20** Prov 25:21, 22 (LXX)
13:1 Wis 6:3

"If you love others, you will never do them wrong" *(Romans 13:10).*

Romans

who does so will bring judgment on himself. [3] For rulers are not to be feared by those who do good, but by those who do evil. Would you like to be unafraid of those in authority? Then do what is good, and they will praise you, [4] because they are God's servants working for your own good. But if you do evil, then be afraid of them, because their power to punish is real. They are God's servants and carry out God's punishment on those who do evil. [5] For this reason you must obey the authorities—not just because of God's punishment, but also as a matter of conscience.

[6] That is also why you pay taxes, because the authorities are working for God when they fulfill their duties. [7] Pay, then, what you owe them; pay them your personal and property taxes, and show respect and honor for them all.

Duties toward One Another

[8] Be under obligation to no one—the only obligation you have is to love one another. Whoever does this has obeyed the Law. [9] The commandments, "Do not commit adultery; do not commit murder; do not steal; do not desire what belongs to someone else"—all these, and any others besides, are summed up in the one command, "Love your neighbor as you love yourself." [10] If you love others, you will never do them wrong; to love, then, is to obey the whole Law.

[11] You must do this, because you know that the time has come for you to wake up from your sleep. For the moment when we will be saved is closer now than it was when we first believed. [12] The night is nearly over, day is almost here. Let us stop doing the things that belong to the dark, and let us take up weapons for fighting in the light. [13] Let us conduct ourselves properly, as people who live in the light of day—no orgies or drunkenness, no immorality or indecency, no fighting or jealousy. [14] But take up the weapons of the Lord Jesus Christ, and stop paying attention to your sinful nature and satisfying its desires.

And the Greatest Is Love

Jesus' most important message while he was on earth can be summed up in one word: *love.* Paul shared that message with new believers often, as he does in 13:8–10. He says that if you look through the eyes of love, you could never hurt another person. Loving others the way Jesus taught us to makes a person complete.

Check out some of these other teachings about love in the Bible. Try to memorize some of the verses so that they remain in your mind and your heart.

- **Leviticus 19:18**
- **Matthew 5:43–48**
- **Mark 12:28–31**
- **John 13:34–35**
- **Romans 13:8–10**

— 1 Corinthians 13:4–13

Do Not Judge Others

14 [1] Welcome those who are weak in faith, but do not argue with them about their personal opinions. [2] Some people's faith allows them to eat anything, but the person who is weak in the faith eats only vegetables. [3] The person who will eat anything is not to despise the one who doesn't; while the one who eats only vegetables is not to pass judgment on the one who will eat anything; for God has accepted that person. [4] Who are you to judge the servants of someone else? It is their own Master who

13:6, 7 Mt 22:21; Mk 12:17; Lk 20:25   **13:9 a** Ex 20:14; Deut 5:18; **b** Ex 20:13; Deut 5:17; **c** Ex 20:15; Deut 5:19; **d** Ex 20:17; Deut 5:21; **e** Lev 19:18   **14:1–6** Col 2:16

A World of Difference

Amelia rides the school bus with students who were born in other countries. Most of them are just learning English. A few wear clothing from their native countries. Some of her classmates poke fun at them. Some just ignore them. No one talks to them. Amelia is not sure what to do.

One day an elderly neighbor asked Amelia about school. Amelia told her about her multicultural bus ride. Mrs. Kowalski shared her own story. Her parents came from Poland. When she went to school, her classmates made fun of her accent, her clothing, and everything else about her. She told Amelia how much it hurt and how she didn't want to go to school. It got better, but she never forgot what it felt like to be made fun of, just because she was different. She knew in her heart she was the same on the inside as everyone else.

After that Amelia made a promise to herself to talk to at least one person from another country each day. She learned it was important not to judge people because of what they eat or the clothes they wear or how they talk.

— Romans 14:1–12

will decide whether they succeed or fail. And they will succeed, because the Lord is able to make them succeed.

5 Some people think that a certain day is more important than other days, while others think that all days are the same. We each should firmly make up our own minds.

6 Those who think highly of a certain day do so in honor of the Lord; those who will eat anything do so in honor of the Lord, because they give thanks to God for the food. Those who refuse to eat certain things do so in honor of the Lord, and they give thanks to God. 7 We do not live for ourselves only, and we do not die for ourselves only. 8 If we live, it is for the Lord that we live, and if we die, it is for the Lord that we die. So whether we live or die, we belong to the Lord. 9 For Christ died and rose to life in order to be the Lord of the living and of the dead. 10 You then, who eat only vegetables—why do you pass judgment on others? And you who eat anything—why do you despise other believers? All of us will stand before God to be judged by him. 11 For the scripture says,

"As surely as I am the living God, says the Lord,
    everyone will kneel before me,
    and everyone will confess that I am God."

12 Every one of us, then, will have to give an account to God.

Do Not Make Others Fall

13 So then, let us stop judging one another. Instead, you should decide never to do anything that would make others stumble or fall into sin. 14 My union with the Lord Jesus makes me certain that no food is of itself ritually unclean; but if you believe that some food is unclean, then it becomes unclean for you. 15 If you hurt others because of something you eat, then you are no longer acting from love. Do not let the food that you eat ruin the person for whom Christ died! 16 Do not let what you regard as good get a bad name. 17 For God's Kingdom is not a matter of eating and drinking, but of the righteousness, peace, and joy which the Holy Spirit gives. 18 And when you serve Christ in this way, you please God and are approved by others.

19 So then, we must always aim[s] at those things that bring peace and that help strengthen one another. 20 Do not, because of food, destroy what God has done. All foods

s 14:19 we must always aim; *some manuscripts have* we always aim.
14:10 2 Cor 5:10   14:11 Isa 45:23 (LXX)

Romans

may be eaten, but it is wrong to eat anything that will cause someone else to fall into sin. 21 The right thing to do is to keep from eating meat, drinking wine, or doing anything else that will make other believers fall. 22 Keep what you believe about this matter, then, between yourself and God. Happy are those who do not feel guilty when they do something they judge is right! 23 But if they have doubts about what they eat, God condemns them when they eat it, because their action is not based on faith. And anything that is not based on faith is sin.

Please Others, Not Yourselves

15 1 We who are strong in the faith ought to help the weak to carry their burdens. We should not please ourselves. 2 Instead, we should all please other believers for their own good, in order to build them up in the faith. 3 For Christ did not please himself. Instead, as the scripture says, "The insults which are hurled at you have fallen on me." 4 Everything written in the Scriptures was written to teach us, in

Help the weak. (15:1)

order that we might have hope through the patience and encouragement which the Scriptures give us. 5 And may God, the source of patience and encouragement, enable you to have the same point of view among yourselves by following the example of Christ Jesus, 6 so that all of you together may praise with one voice the God and Father of our Lord Jesus Christ.

The Gospel to the Gentiles

7 Accept one another, then, for the glory of God, as Christ has accepted you. 8 For I tell you that Christ's life of service was on behalf of the Jews, to show that God is faithful, to make his promises to their ancestors come true, 9 and to enable even the Gentiles to praise God for his mercy. As the scripture says,

"And so I will praise you among the
        Gentiles;
    I will sing praises to you."
10 Again it says,
    "Rejoice, Gentiles, with God's people!"
11 And again,
    "Praise the Lord, all Gentiles;
        praise him, all peoples!"
12 And again, Isaiah says,
    "A descendant of Jesse will appear;
        he will come to rule the Gentiles,
        and they will put their hope in him."

13 May God, the source of hope, fill you with all joy and peace by means of your faith in him, so that your hope will continue to grow by the power of the Holy Spirit.

Paul's Reason for Writing So Boldly

14 My friends: I myself feel sure that you are full of goodness, that you have all knowledge, and that you are able to teach one another. 15 But in this letter I have been quite bold about certain subjects of which I have reminded you. I have been bold because of the privilege God has given me 16 of being a

Romans

15:3 Ps 69:9   **15:4** 1 Macc 12:9; 2 Macc 15:9   **15:9** 2 Sam 22:50; Ps 18:49   **15:10** Deut 32:43   **15:11** Ps 117:1   **15:12** Isa 11:10 (LXX)

The three *theological virtues* are faith, hope, and love. They are gifts to us from God. Can you find all three in chapter 15?

Hopeful People

"I'm hoping for a new bike."

"I hope she cancels that test."

"I hope we win this game."

Many of our hopes are really wishes and wants. We *wish* for something that will make life easier or more fun. We *want* something good to happen. When we truly *hope* for something, we expect it. We don't just want it or wish for it, we *expect* it, and we wait for it to happen.

The Church calls hope a *theological virtue.* We hope for God's blessings and grace, that is, we expect these things from God. We hope that when we die, we will be with God, meaning that we are confident that God will make good on his promise if we lead a good life. A hopeful person trusts God, has faith in Jesus, and relies on the Holy Spirit.

— Romans 15:13

Catholic Connections

---

servant of Christ Jesus to work for the Gentiles. I serve like a priest in preaching the Good News from God, in order that the Gentiles may be an offering acceptable to God, dedicated to him by the Holy Spirit. 17In union with Christ Jesus, then, I can be proud of my service for God. 18I will be bold and speak only about what Christ has done through me to lead the Gentiles to obey God. He has done this by means of words and deeds, 19by the power of miracles and wonders, and by the power of the Spirit of God. And so, in traveling all the way from Jerusalem to Illyricum, I have proclaimed fully the Good News about Christ. 20My ambition has always been to proclaim the Good News in places where Christ has not been heard of, so as not to build on a foundation laid by someone else. 21As the scripture says,

"Those who were not told about him
    will see,
and those who have not heard will
    understand."

Paul's Plan to Visit Rome

22And so I have been prevented many times from coming to you. 23But now that I have finished my work in these regions and since I have been wanting for so many years to come to see you, 24I hope to do so now. I would like to see you on my way to Spain, and be helped by you to go there, after I have enjoyed visiting you for a while. 25Right now, however, I am going to Jerusalem in the service of God's people there. 26For the churches in Macedonia and Achaia have freely decided to give an offering to help the poor among God's people in Jerusalem. 27That decision was their own; but, as a matter of fact, they have an obligation to help them. Since the Jews shared their spiritual blessings with the Gentiles, the Gentiles ought to use their material blessings to help the Jews. 28When I have finished this task and have turned over to them all the money that has been raised for them, I shall leave for Spain and visit you on my way there. 29When I come to you, I know that I shall

Romans

15:21 Isa 52:15 (LXX)   **15:22** Rom 1:13   **15:25, 26** 1 Cor 16:1–4   **15:27** 1 Cor 9:11

come with a full measure of the blessing of Christ.

³⁰I urge you, friends, by our Lord Jesus Christ and by the love that the Spirit gives: join me in praying fervently to God for me. ³¹Pray that I may be kept safe from the unbelievers in Judea and that my service in Jerusalem may be acceptable to God's people there. ³²And so I will come to you full of joy, if it is God's will, and enjoy a refreshing visit with you. ³³May God, our source of peace, be with all of you. Amen.

Personal Greetings

16 ¹I recommend to you our sister Phoebe, who serves the church at Cenchreae. ²Receive her in the Lord's name, as God's people should, and give her any help she may need from you; for she herself has been a good friend to many people and also to me.

³I send greetings to Priscilla and Aquila, my fellow workers in the service of Christ Jesus; ⁴they risked their lives for me. I am grateful to them—not only I, but all the Gentile churches as well. ⁵Greetings also to the church that meets in their house.

Greetings to my dear friend Epaenetus, who was the first in the province of Asia to believe in Christ. ⁶Greetings to Mary, who has worked so hard for you. ⁷Greetings also to Andronicus and Junia,ᵗ fellow Jews who were in prison with me; they are well known among the apostles, and they became Christians before I did.

⁸My greetings to Ampliatus, my dear friend in the fellowship of the Lord. ⁹Greetings also to Urbanus, our fellow worker in Christ's service, and to Stachys, my dear friend. ¹⁰Greetings to Apelles, whose loyalty to Christ has been proved. Greetings to those who belong to the family of Aristobulus. ¹¹Greetings to Herodion, a fellow Jew, and to the Christians in the family of Narcissus.

¹²My greetings to Tryphaena and Tryphosa, who work in the Lord's service, and to my dear friend Persis, who has done

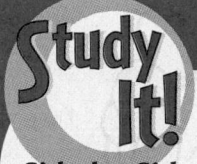

Side by Side

In the final chapter of Paul's letter to the Romans, he mentions several people by name, both women and men. The first person he refers to is Phoebe. She was a friend of his, and she served the growing Church. Paul thanks her for her help and support.

Next Paul names Priscilla and Aquila, a married couple who sometimes traveled with Paul and supported his ministry. They opened their house for Christians to gather for the Eucharist.

Even though women were not allowed to be leaders in the government at that time, they played an important role in the early Church. Even though traveling was dangerous, married couples went on missionary journeys. Working side by side, single women, single men, and married couples spread the Good News of Jesus Christ.

— Romans 16:1–16

so much work for the Lord. ¹³I send greetings to Rufus, that outstanding worker in the Lord's service, and to his mother, who has always treated me like a son. ¹⁴My greetings to Asyncritus, Phlegon, Hermes, Patrobas, Hermas, and all the other Christians with them. ¹⁵Greetings to Philologus and Julia, to Nereus and his sister, to Olympas and to all of God's people who are with them.

¹⁶Greet one another with the kiss of peace. All the churches of Christ send you their greetings.

ᵗ **16:7** Junia; *or* Junias; *some manuscripts have* Julia.
16:3 Acts 18:2   **16:13** Mk 15:21

Romans

Greet one another with the kiss of peace. (16:16)

Final Instructions

17 I urge you, my friends: watch out for those who cause divisions and upset people's faith and go against the teaching which you have received. Keep away from them! **18** For those who do such things are not serving Christ our Lord, but their own appetites. By their fine words and flattering speech they deceive innocent people. **19** Everyone has heard of your loyalty to the gospel, and for this reason I am happy about you. I want you to be wise about what is good, but innocent in what is evil. **20** And God, our source of peace, will soon crush Satan under your feet.

The grace of our Lord Jesus be with you.*u*

21 Timothy, my fellow worker, sends you his greetings; and so do Lucius, Jason, and Sosipater, fellow Jews.

22 I, Tertius, the writer of this letter, send you Christian greetings.

23 My host Gaius, in whose house the church meets, sends you his greetings; Erastus, the city treasurer, and our brother Quartus send you their greetings.*v*

Concluding Prayer of Praise

25 Let us give glory to God! He is able to make you stand firm in your faith, according to the Good News I preach about Jesus Christ and according to the revelation of the secret truth which was hidden for long ages in the past. **26** Now, however, that truth has been brought out into the open through the writings of the prophets; and by the command of the eternal God it is made known to all nations, so that all may believe and obey.

27 To the only God, who alone is all-wise, be glory through Jesus Christ forever! Amen.*w*

---

u **16:20** *Some manuscripts omit this sentence.*   *v* **16:23** *Some manuscripts add verse 24:* The grace of our Lord Jesus Christ be with you all. Amen; *others add this after verse 27.*   *w* **16:27** *Some manuscripts have verses 25–27 here and after 14:23; others have them only after 14:23; one has them after 15:33.*
16:21 Acts 16:1   **16:23** **a** Acts 19:29; 1 Cor 1:14; **b** 2 Tim 4:20

Your Next Step

Congratulations on finishing the Letter to the Romans! Use this space to write your thoughts and questions about this book. If you are following the suggested reading plan, go back to the Book of Proverbs in the Old Testament. Like the Letter to the Romans, it has lots of wise advice for how to live your life.

Do you ever get tired of your parents correcting you? Even though it might get annoying, you probably know deep down that they do it because they care about you. Your parents want you to learn important lessons while you are young—lessons that will serve you well as a teenager and an adult.

The Christian church in the city of Corinth was very young. Paul started the church there. He felt it was his responsibility to correct the people when they were acting badly. He wanted to keep teaching them the important truths about being a Christian. He was acting like a parent—out of love—by correcting his spiritual children.

Chap. 3:5–9

Headlines

- Divisions Threaten New Church (1:10–13)
- Avoid Immoral People! (5:9–13)
- Use Your Body for God's Glory (6:12–20)
- Dangers of Idolatry (10:1–10)
- Paul Says, "Respect the Lord's Supper" (11:17–34)
- Body Parts and the Body of Christ (12:12–31)
- The Primacy of Love (chapter 13)
- Resurrection: Truth or Fiction? (15:12–58)

FACTOIDS

Who are the central characters? Paul, Apollos, and the Christians in Corinth.
Who wrote this book? Saint Paul.
When was it written? A few years after Paul had started the church in Corinth.
Why was it written? Paul wrote to correct mistakes in the new church. He wanted to reinforce some important teachings about the Christian faith.
Jesus connection. In this letter Paul speaks a lot about Jesus' Resurrection. He makes it clear that Christ's Resurrection is the guarantee that we also will be resurrected into new life (15:12–28).

Important themes
- God's wisdom seems like foolishness to some people.
- Christians are not free to do anything they want. We must live moral lives, especially regarding our bodies.
- We are each a part of one body, the Church. The Spirit gives different gifts to each person, all for serving God and the Church.

THE FIRST LETTER TO THE Corinthians

1 CORINTHIANS

1 ¹From Paul, who was called by the will of God to be an apostle of Christ Jesus, and from our brother Sosthenes—

²To the church of God which is in Corinth, to all who are called to be God's holy people, who belong to him in union with Christ Jesus, together with all people everywhere who worship our Lord Jesus Christ, their Lord and ours:

³May God our Father and the Lord Jesus Christ give you grace and peace.

Blessings in Christ

⁴I always give thanks to my God for you because of the grace he has given you through Christ Jesus. ⁵For in union with Christ you have become rich in all things, including all speech and all knowledge. ⁶The message about Christ has become so firmly established in you ⁷that you have not failed to receive a single blessing, as you wait for our Lord Jesus Christ to be revealed. ⁸He will also keep you firm to the end, so that you will be faultless on the Day of our Lord Jesus Christ. ⁹God is to be trusted, the God who called you to have fellowship with his Son Jesus Christ, our Lord.

Divisions in the Church

¹⁰By the authority of our Lord Jesus Christ I appeal to all of you, my friends, to agree in what you say, so that there will be no divisions among you. Be completely united, with only one thought and one purpose. ¹¹For some people from Chloe's family have told me quite plainly, my friends, that there are quarrels among you. ¹²Let me put it this way: each one of you says something different. One says, "I follow Paul"; another, "I follow Apollos"; another, "I follow Peter"; and another, "I follow Christ." ¹³Christ has been divided*a* into groups! Was it Paul who been divided*a* into groups! Was it Paul who

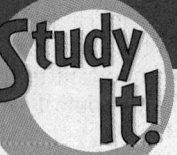

The Scoop on Corinth

Corinth was a seaport city in Greece with a mixture of cultures and religions, as well as very rich and very poor people. Corinth was well-known for its thriving businesses, sports events, variety of people, and—unfortunately—its lack of morality. The church that Paul began there was made up mostly of non-Jewish Christians but also some Jewish Christians. He lived with them about eighteen months, then left the church in the hands of Apollos while he continued his mission in other places. When Paul began hearing reports of divisions, problems with morality, and lack of attention to poor people, he wrote this letter to the Corinthian church to teach and correct its members.

— 1 Corinthians 1:4–9

died on the cross for you? Were you baptized as Paul's disciples?

¹⁴I thank God that I did not baptize any of you except Crispus and Gaius. ¹⁵No one can say, then, that you were baptized as my disciples. (¹⁶Oh yes, I also baptized Stephanas and his family; but I can't remember whether I baptized anyone else.) ¹⁷Christ did not send me to baptize. He sent me to tell the Good News, and to tell it without using the language of human wisdom, in order to make sure that Christ's death on the cross is not robbed of its power.

a Christ has been divided; *some manuscripts have* Christ cannot be divided.

Acts 18:1   **1:12** Acts 18:24   **1:14 a** Acts 18:8; **b** Acts 19:29; Rom 16:23   **1:16** 1 Cor 16:15

Exclusive Groups

It's said that variety is good. It makes life interesting. Right? So why, then, are we so quick to label people? He's popular. She's a jock. He's smart. She's religious. And on and on. Exclusive groups are here to stay, it seems. Paul tells the Corinthians that divisions—or excluding others—are useless, and worse, they are destructive. Have you ever experienced division in your family, class, team, or even in your group of friends? Loyalties change, people are let in or left out, and emotions rage . . . it can get ugly. And what is accomplished?

Being united, as Paul teaches (1 Corinthians 1:10), means keeping your focus on what is truly important. It's important that nobody gets hurt. It's important to treat other people with kindness. It's important to be respected and appreciated—in spite of differences. It's that simple. Judging, labeling, leaving people out, putting people down . . . that's just the opposite of what's important.

Think about the exclusive groups in your school or neighborhood—both those you're part of and those you're not part of. What causes the divisions? How do you treat people inside and outside of the groups? Are you willing to help build bridges between groups?

— 1 Corinthians 1:10–13

Christ the Power and the Wisdom of God

18 For the message about Christ's death on the cross is nonsense to those who are being lost; but for us who are being saved it is God's power. 19 The scripture says,

"I will destroy the wisdom of the wise
    and set aside the understanding of the
       scholars."

20 So then, where does that leave the wise? or the scholars? or the skillful debaters of this world? God has shown that this world's wisdom is foolishness!

21 For God in his wisdom made it impossible for people to know him by means of their own wisdom. Instead, by means of the so-called "foolish" message we preach, God decided to save those who believe. 22 Jews want miracles for proof, and Greeks look for wisdom. 23 As for us, we proclaim the crucified Christ, a message that is offensive to the Jews and nonsense to the Gentiles; 24 but for those whom God has called, both Jews and Gentiles, this message is Christ, who is the power of God and the wisdom of God. 25 For what seems to be God's foolishness is wiser than human wisdom, and what seems to be God's weakness is stronger than human strength.

26 Now remember what you were, my friends, when God called you. From the human point of view few of you were wise or powerful or of high social standing. 27 God purposely chose what the world considers nonsense in order to shame the wise, and he chose what the world considers weak in order to shame the powerful. 28 He chose what the world looks down on and despises and thinks is nothing, in order to destroy what the world thinks is important. 29 This means that no one can boast in God's presence. 30 But God has brought you into union with Christ Jesus, and God has made Christ to be our wisdom. By him we are put right with God; we become God's holy people and are set free. 31 So then, as the scripture says, "Whoever wants to boast must boast of what the Lord has done."

1 Corinthians

1:19 Isa 29:14 (LXX)   **1:20 a** Job 12:17; **b** Isa 44:25   **1:21** Wis 13:1–9   **1:31** Jer 9:24

"God has shown that this world's wisdom is foolishness!" (1 Corinthians 1:20). What do you think that means?

The Message about the Crucified Christ

2 ¹When I came to you, my friends, to preach God's secret truth,[b] I did not use big words and great learning. ²For while I was with you, I made up my mind to forget everything except Jesus Christ and especially his death on the cross. ³So when I came to you, I was weak and trembled all over with fear, ⁴and my teaching and message were not delivered with skillful words of human wisdom, but with convincing proof of the power of God's Spirit. ⁵Your faith, then, does not rest on human wisdom but on God's power.

God's Wisdom

⁶Yet I do proclaim a message of wisdom to those who are spiritually mature. But it is not the wisdom that belongs to this world or to the powers that rule this world—powers that are losing their power. ⁷The wisdom I proclaim is God's secret wisdom, which is hidden from human beings, but which he had already chosen for our glory even before the world was made. ⁸None of the rulers of this world knew this wisdom. If they had known it, they would not have crucified the Lord of glory. ⁹However, as the scripture says,

"What no one ever saw or heard,
what no one ever thought could happen,
is the very thing God prepared for those who love him."

¹⁰But[c] it was to us that God made known his secret by means of his Spirit. The Spirit searches everything, even the hidden depths of God's purposes. ¹¹It is only our own spirit within us that knows all about us; in the same way, only God's Spirit knows all about God. ¹²We have not received this world's spirit; instead, we have received the Spirit sent by God, so that we may know all that God has given us.

¹³So then, we do not speak in words taught by human wisdom, but in words taught by the Spirit, as we explain spiritual truths to those who have the Spirit.[d] ¹⁴Whoever does not have the Spirit cannot receive the gifts that come from God's Spirit. Such a person really does not understand them, and they seem to be nonsense, because their value can be judged only on a spiritual basis. ¹⁵Whoever has the Spirit, however, is able to judge the value of everything, but no one is able to judge him. ¹⁶As the scripture says,

"Who knows the mind of the Lord?
Who is able to give him advice?"

We, however, have the mind of Christ.

Servants of God

3 ¹As a matter of fact, my friends, I could not talk to you as I talk to people who have the Spirit; I had to talk to you as though you belonged to this world, as children in the Christian faith. ²I had to feed you milk, not solid food, because you were not ready for it. And even now you are not ready for it, ³because you still live as the people of this world live. When there is jealousy among you and you quarrel with one another, doesn't this prove that you belong to this world, living by its standards? ⁴When one of you says, "I follow Paul," and another, "I follow Apollos"—aren't you acting like worldly people?

⁵After all, who is Apollos? And who is Paul? We are simply God's servants, by whom you were led to believe. Each one of us does the work which the Lord gave him to do: ⁶I planted the seed, Apollos watered the plant, but it was God who made the plant grow. ⁷The one who plants and the one who waters really do not matter. It is God who matters, because he makes the plant grow. ⁸There is no difference between

---

[b] **2:1** God's secret truth; *some manuscripts have* the testimony about God.   [c] **2:10** But; *some manuscripts have* For.
[d] **2:13** to those who have the Spirit; *or* with words given by the Spirit.
2:3 Acts 18:9   **2:8** Bar 3:14–17   **2:9** Isa 64:4; Sir 1:9, 10   **2:16** Isa 40:13 (LXX)   **3:2** Heb 5:12, 13
3:4 1 Cor 1:12   **3:6 a** Acts 18:4–11; **b** Acts 18:24–28

The *Day of Christ* (*1 Corinthians 3:13*) **refers to the Final Judgment, which Jesus describes in Matthew, chapter 25.**

It was God who made the plant grow. (3:6)

the one who plants and the one who waters; God will reward each one according to the work each has done. ⁹For we are partners working together for God, and you are God's field.

You are also God's building. ¹⁰Using the gift that God gave me, I did the work of an expert builder and laid the foundation, and someone else is building on it. But each of you must be careful how you build. ¹¹For God has already placed Jesus Christ as the one and only foundation, and no other foundation can be laid. ¹²Some will use gold or silver or precious stones in building on the foundation; others will use wood or grass or straw. ¹³And the quality of each person's work will be seen when the Day of Christ exposes it. For on that Day fire will reveal everyone's work; the fire will test it and show its real quality. ¹⁴If what was built on the foundation survives the fire, the builder will receive a reward. ¹⁵But if your work is burnt up, then you will lose it; but you yourself will be saved, as if you had escaped through the fire.

¹⁶Surely you know that you are God's temple and that God's Spirit lives in you! ¹⁷God will destroy anyone who destroys God's temple. For God's temple is holy, and you yourselves are his temple.

¹⁸You should not fool yourself. If any of you think that you are wise by this world's standards, you should become a fool, in

Live It!

U-Build It

If you were a building, what would you look like? a skyscraper made of glass and steel? a log cabin? a concrete warehouse? a stone castle? Is it a welcoming place? Could it survive a hurricane or an earthquake?

In chapter 3 Saint Paul uses this image to have us pay attention to how we are building our character and our life. Then it's up to us to design and build the rest. For example, take a look at your personality—are you kind or mean to others? Are your friendships strong or stormy? Do you treat your family members with patience or is there a lot of yelling that you're part of? What about your interests—is your life all about video games or shopping, or do you take time to help out others? What about your values— do you value honesty, or are you okay with doing something wrong as long as you can get away with it? All of your personality qualities, values, interests, and relationships are indicators of what your building will look like. Lastly, ask yourself: Is Jesus at the heart of it all? Is the Spirit living within you?

— 1 Corinthians 3:9–15

order to be really wise. ¹⁹For what this world considers to be wisdom is nonsense in God's sight. As the scripture says, "God traps the wise in their cleverness"; ²⁰and another scripture says, "The Lord knows that the thoughts of the wise are worthless." ²¹No one, then, should boast about what human beings can do. Actually everything belongs

I Corinthians

to you: ²²Paul, Apollos, and Peter; this world, life and death, the present and the future—all these are yours, ²³and you belong to Christ, and Christ belongs to God.

Apostles of Christ

4 ¹You should think of us as Christ's servants, who have been put in charge of God's secret truths. ²The one thing required of such servants is that they be faithful to their master. ³Now, I am not at all concerned about being judged by you or by any human standard; I don't even pass judgment on myself. ⁴My conscience is clear, but that does not prove that I am really innocent. The Lord is the one who passes judgment on me. ⁵So you should not pass judgment on anyone before the right time comes. Final judgment must wait until the Lord comes; he will bring to light the dark secrets and expose the hidden purposes of people's minds. And then all will receive from God the praise they deserve.

⁶For your sake, my friends, I have applied all this to Apollos and me, using the two of us as an example, so that you may learn what the saying means, "Observe the proper rules." None of you should be proud of one person and despise another. ⁷Who made you superior to others? Didn't God give you everything you have? Well, then, how can you boast, as if what you have were not a gift?

⁸Do you already have everything you need? Are you already rich? Have you become kings, even though we are not? Well, I wish you really were kings, so that we could be kings together with you. ⁹For it seems to me that God has given the very last place to us apostles, like people condemned to die in public as a spectacle for the whole world of angels and of human beings. ¹⁰For Christ's sake we are fools; but you are wise in union with Christ! We are weak, but you are strong! We are despised, but you are honored! ¹¹To this very moment we go hungry and thirsty; we are clothed in rags; we are beaten; we wander from place to place; ¹²we wear ourselves out with hard work. When we are cursed, we bless; when we are perse-

cuted, we endure; ¹³when we are insulted, we answer back with kind words. We are no more than this world's garbage; we are the scum of the earth to this very moment!

¹⁴I write this to you, not because I want to make you feel ashamed, but to instruct you as my own dear children. ¹⁵For even if you have ten thousand guardians in your Christian life, you have only one father. For in your life in union with Christ Jesus I have become your father by bringing the Good News to you. ¹⁶I beg you, then, to follow my example. ¹⁷For this purpose I am sending to you Timothy, who is my own dear and faithful son in the Christian life. He will remind you of the principles which I follow in the new life in union with Christ Jesus and which I teach in all the churches everywhere.

¹⁸Some of you have become proud because you have thought that I would not be coming to visit you. ¹⁹If the Lord is willing, however, I will come to you soon, and

---

Pray It!

Prayer for Humility

Dear God,
Help me understand what it means to be humble. There are some things I can do really well, and some parts of me that are easy to like. I want to remember that you have given all that to me. Whenever I am complimented by others or I am feeling good about myself, let me stop and whisper a thanks to you. If I start feeling like I'm better than others, stop me in my tracks and remind me where my gifts come from. And, on those days when I don't believe there is anything good about me, show me the best parts of myself that you've helped build inside me. Amen.

— 1 Corinthians 4:7

4:4 Wis 17:11   **4:12** Acts 18:3   **4:16** 1 Cor 11:1; Phil 3:17

then I will find out for myself the power which these proud people have, and not just what they say. 20For the Kingdom of God is not a matter of words but of power. 21Which do you prefer? Shall I come to you with a whip, or in a spirit of love and gentleness?

Immorality in the Church

5 1Now, it is actually being said that there is sexual immorality among you so terrible that not even the heathen would be guilty of it. I am told that a man is sleeping with his stepmother! 2How, then, can you be proud? On the contrary, you should be filled with sadness, and the man who has done such a thing should be expelled from your fellowship. 3-4And even though I am far away from you in body, still I am there with you in spirit; and as though I were there with you, I have in the name of our Lord Jesus already passed judgment on the man who has done this terrible thing. As you meet together, and I meet with you in my spirit, by the power of our Lord Jesus present with us, 5you are to hand this man over to Satan for his body to be destroyed, so that his spirit may be saved in the Day of the Lord.

6It is not right for you to be proud! You know the saying, "A little bit of yeast makes the whole batch of dough rise." 7You must remove the old yeast of sin so that you will be entirely pure. Then you will be like a new batch of dough without any yeast, as indeed I know you actually are. For our Passover Festival is ready, now that Christ, our Passover lamb, has been sacrificed. 8Let us celebrate our Passover, then, not with bread having the old yeast of sin and wickedness, but with the bread that has no yeast, the bread of purity and truth.

9In the letter that I wrote you I told you not to associate with immoral people. 10Now I did not mean pagans who are immoral or greedy or are thieves, or who worship idols. To avoid them you would have to get out of the world completely.

Help from Your Friends

From the time we are babies, people have been teaching us right from wrong: our parents, grandparents, teachers, coaches, and priests to name a few. We also learn about morality from the Bible and from our Church teachings. It gets exhausting!

Our friends and peers can teach us about living morally too. Sometimes they teach us good things, and sometimes not so good. We make our own choices, but we can be influenced to act one way or another. Paul has this to say, straight and simply: Stay away from immoral people! Their bad morals can rub off on us. Don't be judgmental or rude toward them, but don't hang out with them either. Paul's talking about peer pressure at its worst!

Pray that God will help you resist the bad influences that are all around us. Pray, too, to be surrounded by people who are trying to live good, moral lives—to be influenced by peer pressure at its best!

— 1 Corinthians 5:9–11

11What I meant was that you should not associate with a person who calls himself a believer but is immoral or greedy or worships idols or is a slanderer or a drunkard or a thief. Don't even sit down to eat with such a person.

12-13After all, it is none of my business to judge outsiders. God will judge them. But

5:1 Deut 22:30   5:6 Gal 5:9   5:7 Ex 12:5   5:8 Ex 13:7; Deut 16:3

I Corinthians

Occasionally, Saint Paul used sarcasm to make his point (1 Corinthians 4:8–14). **He must have been pretty frustrated!**

should you not judge the members of your own fellowship? As the scripture says, "Remove the evil person from your group."

Lawsuits against Fellow Christians

6 ¹If any of you have a dispute with another Christian, how dare you go before heathen judges instead of letting God's people settle the matter? ²Don't you know that God's people will judge the world? Well, then, if you are to judge the world, aren't you capable of judging small matters? ³Do you not know that we shall judge the angels? How much more, then, the things of this life! ⁴If such matters come up, are you going to take them to be settled by people who have no standing in the church? ⁵Shame on you! Surely there is at least one wise person in your fellowship who can settle a dispute between fellow Christians. ⁶Instead, one Christian goes to court against another and lets unbelievers judge the case!

⁷The very fact that you have legal disputes among yourselves shows that you have failed completely. Would it not be better for you to be wronged? Would it not be better for you to be robbed? ⁸Instead, you yourselves wrong one another and rob one another, even other believers! ⁹Surely you know that the wicked will not possess God's Kingdom. Do not fool yourselves; people who are immoral or who worship idols or are adulterers or homosexual perverts ¹⁰or who steal or are greedy or are drunkards or who slander others or are thieves—none of these will possess God's Kingdom. ¹¹Some of you were like that. But you have been purified from sin; you have been dedicated to God; you have been put right with God by the Lord Jesus Christ and by the Spirit of our God.

Use Your Bodies for God's Glory

¹²Someone will say, "I am allowed to do anything." Yes; but not everything is good for you. I could say that I am allowed to do anything, but I am not going to let anything make me its slave. ¹³Someone else will say, "Food is for the stomach, and the stomach is for food." Yes; but God will put an end to both. The body is not to be used for sexual immorality, but to serve the Lord; and the Lord provides for the body. ¹⁴God raised the Lord from death, and he will also raise us by his power.

¹⁵You know that your bodies are parts of the body of Christ. Shall I take a part of Christ's body and make it part of the body of a prostitute? Impossible! ¹⁶Or perhaps you don't know that the man who joins his body to a prostitute becomes physically one with her? The scripture says quite plainly, "The two will become one body." ¹⁷But he who joins himself to the Lord becomes spiritually one with him.

¹⁸Avoid immorality. Any other sin a man commits does not affect his body; but the man who is guilty of sexual immorality sins against his own body. ¹⁹Don't you know that your body is the temple of the Holy Spirit, who lives in you and who was given to you by God? You do not belong to yourselves but to God; ²⁰he bought you for a price. So use your bodies for God's glory.

Questions about Marriage

7 ¹Now, to deal with the matters you wrote about.

A man does well not to marry.ᵉ ²But because there is so much immorality, every man should have his own wife, and every woman should have her own husband. ³A man should fulfill his duty as a husband, and a woman should fulfill her duty as a wife, and each should satisfy the other's needs. ⁴A wife is not the master of her own body, but her husband is; in the same way a husband is not the master of his own body, but his wife is. ⁵Do not deny yourselves to each other, unless you first agree to do so for a while in order to spend your time in prayer; but then resume

ᵉ **7:1** A man does well not to marry; or You say that a man does well not to marry.
5:13 Deut 13:5; 17:7 (LXX)   **6:12** 1 Cor 10:23   **6:16** Gen 2:24   **6:19** 1 Cor 3:16; 2 Cor 6:16

"The body is not to be used for sexual immorality, but to serve the Lord" (I Corinthians 6:13).

Vocations

Catholic Connections

Do you think you'll get married someday? Most people do believe that when they're young, but not everyone is meant to be married. God might want you to be single. These are two examples of vocations that Paul speaks about in 1 Corinthians, chapter 7. Both of these—marriage and single life—offer special gifts, as well as many opportunities to serve God and other people.

Marriage offers the gifts of lifelong companionship, children, and daily lessons in becoming a less self-centered person. At the end of a long life, the greatest gift of marriage is sharing your days and memories with your best friend. Single life offers freedom to do and be many things, to go anywhere, and to be available for whatever might pop up. If you let God steer your life, it's amazing how many people and adventures fill it up!

You might also receive God's call to become a religious sister or brother, or a priest. These are also wonderful vocations and bring you deeply into prayer and doing the work Jesus showed us how to do: helping poor people, comforting sick people, providing the sacraments, teaching, and confronting injustice, for example.

— 1 Corinthians, chapter 7

normal marital relations. In this way you will be kept from giving in to Satan's temptation because of your lack of self-control.

6 I tell you this not as an order, but simply as a permission. **7** Actually I would prefer that all of you were as I am; but each one has a special gift from God, one person this gift, another one that gift.

8 Now, to the unmarried and to the widows I say that it would be better for you to continue to live alone as I do. **9** But if you cannot restrain your desires, go ahead and marry—it is better to marry than to burn with passion.

10 For married people I have a command which is not my own but the Lord's: a wife must not leave her husband; **11** but if she does, she must remain single or else be reconciled to her husband; and a husband must not divorce his wife.

12 To the others I say (I, myself, not the Lord): if a Christian man has a wife who is an unbeliever and she agrees to go on living with him, he must not divorce her. **13** And if a Christian woman is married to a man who is an unbeliever and he agrees to go on living with her, she must not divorce him. **14** For the unbelieving husband is made acceptable to God by being united to his wife, and the unbelieving wife is made acceptable to God by being united to her Christian husband. If this were not so, their children would be like pagan children; but as it is, they are acceptable to God. **15** However, if the one who is not a believer wishes to leave the Christian partner, let it be so. In such cases the Christian partner, whether husband or wife, is free to act. God has called you to live in peace. **16** How can you be sure, Christian wife, that you will not save *f* your husband? Or how can you be sure, Christian husband, that you will not save *f* your wife?

f **7:16** How can you be sure . . . that you will not save; *or* How do you know . . . that you will save.
7:10, 11 Mt 5:32; 19:9; Mk 10:11, 12; Lk 16:18

Live As God Called You

17 Each of you should go on living according to the Lord's gift to you, and as you were when God called you. This is the rule I teach in all the churches. 18 If a circumcised man has accepted God's call, he should not try to remove the marks of circumcision; if an uncircumcised man has accepted God's call, he should not get circumcised. 19 For whether or not a man is circumcised means nothing; what matters is to obey God's commandments. 20 Each of you should remain as you were when you accepted God's call. 21 Were you a slave when God called you? Well, never mind; but if you have a chance to become free, use it.g 22 For a slave who has been called by the Lord is the Lord's free person; in the same way a free person who has been called by Christ is his slave. 23 God bought you for a price; so do not become slaves of people. 24 My friends, each of you should remain in fellowship with God in the same condition that you were when you were called.

Questions about the Unmarried and the Widows

25 Now, concerning what you wrote about unmarried people: I do not have a command from the Lord, but I give my opinion as one who by the Lord's mercy is worthy of trust. 26 Considering the present distress, I think it is better for a man to stay as he is. 27 Do you have a wife? Then don't try to get rid of her. Are you unmarried? Then don't look for a wife. 28 But if you do marry, you haven't committed a sin; and if an unmarried woman marries, she hasn't committed a sin. But I would rather spare you the everyday troubles that married people will have.

29 What I mean, my friends, is this: there is not much time left, and from now on married people should live as though they were not married; 30 those who weep, as though they were not sad; those who laugh, as though they were not happy; those who buy, as though they did not own what they bought; 31 those who deal in material goods, as though they were not fully occupied with them. For this world, as it is now, will not last much longer.

32 I would like you to be free from worry. An unmarried man concerns himself with the Lord's work, because he is trying to please the Lord. 33 But a married man concerns himself with worldly matters, because he wants to please his wife; 34 and so he is pulled in two directions. An unmarried woman or a virgin concerns herself with the Lord's work, because she wants to be dedicated both in body and spirit; but a married woman concerns herself with worldly matters, because she wants to please her husband.

35 I am saying this because I want to help you. I am not trying to put restrictions on you. Instead, I want you to do what is right and proper, and to give yourselves completely to the Lord's service without any reservation.

36 In the case of an engaged couple who have decided not to marry: if the man feels that he is not acting properly toward the young woman and if his passions are too strong and he feels that they ought to marry, then they should get married, as he wants to.h There is no sin in this. 37 But if a man, without being forced to do so, has firmly made up his mind not to marry,i and if he has his will under complete control and has already decided in his own mind what to do—then he does well not to marry the young woman.j 38 So the man who marriesk does well, but the one who doesn't marryl does even better.

39 A married woman is not free as long as her husband lives; but if her husband dies, then she is free to be married to any man she wishes, but only if he is a Christian. 40 She will be happier, however, if she stays as she is. That is my opinion, and I think that I too have God's Spirit.

---

g 7:21 but if you have a chance to become free, use it; or but even if you have a chance to become free, choose rather to make the best of your condition as a slave.   h 7:36 an engaged couple . . . as he wants to; or a man and his unmarried daughter: if he feels that he is not acting properly toward her, and if she is at the right age to marry, then he should do as he wishes and let her get married.   i 7:37 not to marry; or not to let his daughter get married.   j 7:37 marry the young woman; or let her get married.   k 7:38 marries; or lets his daughter get married.   l 7:38 doesn't marry; or doesn't let her get married.

7:18 1 Macc 1:15

The Question about Food Offered to Idols

8 ¹Now, concerning what you wrote about food offered to idols.

It is true, of course, that "all of us have knowledge," as they say. Such knowledge, however, puffs a person up with pride; but love builds up. ²Those who think they know something really don't know as they ought to know. ³But the person who loves God is known by him.

⁴So then, about eating the food offered to idols: we know that an idol stands for something that does not really exist; we know that there is only the one God. ⁵Even if there are so-called "gods," whether in heaven or on earth, and even though there are many of these "gods" and "lords," ⁶yet there is for us only one God, the Father, who is the Creator of all things and for whom we live; and there is only one Lord, Jesus Christ, through whom all things were created and through whom we live.

⁷But not everyone knows this truth. Some people have been so used to idols that to this day when they eat such food they still think of it as food that belongs to an idol; their conscience is weak, and they feel they are defiled by the food. ⁸Food, however, will not improve our relation with God; we shall not lose anything if we do not eat, nor shall we gain anything if we do eat.

⁹Be careful, however, not to let your freedom of action make those who are weak in the faith fall into sin. ¹⁰Suppose a person whose conscience is weak in this matter sees you, who have so-called "knowledge," eating in the temple of an idol; will not this encourage him to eat food offered to idols? ¹¹And so this weak person, your brother for whom Christ died, will perish because of your "knowledge"! ¹²And in this way you will be sinning against Christ by sinning against other Christians and wounding their weak conscience. ¹³So then, if food makes a believer sin, I will never eat meat again, so as not to make a believer fall into sin.

Rights and Duties of an Apostle

9 ¹Am I not a free man? Am I not an apostle? Haven't I seen Jesus our Lord? And aren't you the result of my work for the Lord? ²Even if others do not accept me as an apostle, surely you do! Because of your life in union with the Lord you yourselves are proof of the fact that I am an apostle.

³When people criticize me, this is how I defend myself: ⁴Don't I have the right to be given food and drink for my work? ⁵Don't I have the right to follow the example of the other apostles and the Lord's brothers and Peter, by taking a Christian wife with me on my trips? ⁶Or are Barnabas and I the only ones who have to work for our living? ⁷What soldiers ever have to pay their own expenses in the army? What farmers do not eat the grapes from their own vineyard? What shepherds do not use the milk from their own sheep?

⁸I don't have to limit myself to these everyday examples, because the Law says the same thing. ⁹We read in the Law of Moses, "Do not muzzle an ox when you are using it to thresh grain." Now, is God concerned about oxen? ¹⁰Didn't he really mean us when he said that? Of course that was written for us. Anyone who plows and anyone who reaps should do their work in the hope of getting a share of the crop. ¹¹We have sown spiritual seed among you. Is it too much if we reap material benefits from you? ¹²If others have the right to expect this from you, don't we have an even greater right?

But we haven't made use of this right. Instead, we have endured everything in order not to put any obstacle in the way of the Good News about Christ. ¹³Surely you know that the men who work in the Temple get their food from the Temple and that those who offer the sacrifices on the altar get a share of the sacrifices. ¹⁴In the same way,

9:9 Deut 25:4; 1 Tim 5:18   **9:11** Rom 15:27   **9:13** Deut 18:1   **9:14** Mt 10:10; Lk 10:7

In Corinth much of the meat sold in markets was from animals slaughtered in pagan temples as sacrifices to a god or a goddess.

Focus on the Finish Line

On your mark! Get set! Go!

Corinth was well-known for its sports events, so when Paul spoke of running, he caught people's attention. But the race he talks about is our life here on earth; the finish line is our eternal life with God. Eternal life is the treasured prize that we can look forward to after a well-run race, that is, a faithful life.

To reach the prize, we need to stay focused on God—in the same way a good athlete stays focused on his or her game. When we stay focused, God gives us strength and endurance in our race, and we will win our prize.

— 1 Corinthians 9:23–27

the Lord has ordered that those who preach the gospel should get their living from it.

15But I haven't made use of any of these rights, nor am I writing this now in order to claim such rights for myself. I would rather die first! Nobody is going to turn my rightful boast into empty words! 16I have no right to boast just because I preach the gospel. After all, I am under orders to do so. And how terrible it would be for me if I did not preach the gospel! 17If I did my work as a matter of free choice, then I could expect to be paid; but I do it as a matter of duty, because God has entrusted me with this task. 18What pay do I get, then? It is the privilege of preaching the Good News without charging for it, without claiming my rights in my work for the gospel.

19I am a free man, nobody's slave; but I

make myself everybody's slave in order to win as many people as possible. 20While working with the Jews, I live like a Jew in order to win them; and even though I myself am not subject to the Law of Moses, I live as though I were when working with those who are, in order to win them. 21In the same way, when working with Gentiles, I live like a Gentile, outside the Jewish Law, in order to win Gentiles. This does not mean that I don't obey God's law; I am really under Christ's law. 22Among the weak in faith I become weak like one of them, in order to win them. So I become all things to all people, that I may save some of them by whatever means are possible.

23All this I do for the gospel's sake, in order to share in its blessings. 24Surely you know that many runners take part in a race, but only one of them wins the prize. Run, then, in such a way as to win the prize. 25Every athlete in training submits to strict discipline, in order to be crowned with a wreath that will not last; but we do it for one that will last forever. 26That is why I run straight for the finish line; that is why I am like a boxer who does not waste his punches. 27I harden my body with blows and bring it under complete control, to keep myself from being disqualified after having called others to the contest.

Only one of them wins the prize. (9:24)

Warnings against Idols

10 1I want you to remember, my friends, what happened to our ancestors who followed Moses. They were all

9:25 Wis 4:2; 5:16   **10:1** a Ex 13:21, 22; b Ex 14:22–29

(side tab) **I Corinthians**

Read I Corinthians 10:16–17. Do you see how the Body of Christ names three things? (1) Jesus himself, (2) the consecrated bread, and (3) the people of God.

under the protection of the cloud, and all passed safely through the Red Sea. ²In the cloud and in the sea they were all baptized as followers of Moses. ³All ate the same spiritual bread ⁴and drank the same spiritual drink. They drank from the spiritual rock that went with them; and that rock was Christ himself. ⁵But even then God was not pleased with most of them, and so their dead bodies were scattered over the desert.

⁶Now, all of this is an example for us, to warn us not to desire evil things, as they did, ⁷nor to worship idols, as some of them did. As the scripture says, "The people sat down to a feast which turned into an orgy of drinking and sex." ⁸We must not be guilty of sexual immorality, as some of them were— and in one day twenty-three thousand of them fell dead. ⁹We must not put the Lord^m to the test, as some of them did—and they were killed by snakes. ¹⁰We must not complain, as some of them did—and they were destroyed by the Angel of Death.

¹¹All these things happened to them as examples for others, and they were written down as a warning for us. For we live at a time when the end is about to come.

¹²If you think you are standing firm you had better be careful that you do not fall. ¹³Every test that you have experienced is the kind that normally comes to people. But God keeps his promise, and he will not allow you to be tested beyond your power to remain firm; at the time you are put to the test, he will give you the strength to endure it, and so provide you with a way out.

¹⁴So then, my dear friends, keep away from the worship of idols. ¹⁵I speak to you as sensible people; judge for yourselves what I say. ¹⁶The cup we use in the Lord's Supper and for which we give thanks to God: when we drink from it, we are sharing in the blood of Christ. And the bread we break: when we eat it, we are sharing in the body of Christ. ¹⁷Because there is the one loaf of bread, all of us, though many, are one body, for we all share the same loaf.

¹⁸Consider the people of Israel; those who

American Idols

Money. Popularity. Sports. Fashion. Sex. Food. Success. Comfort. Beauty. These are examples of things that we can idolize. One or more of these can become more important to us than anything else, even God.

In the first commandment, we're told God and only God should come first in our life. "I am the LORD your God. . . . Do not bow down to any idol or worship it" (Exodus 20:2–5). And Paul stresses it again. He goes so far as to call idolatry evil (1 Corinthians 10:6).

Do you have idols in your life? Think about how you spend your money or your time. Is God or the Church anywhere in your priorities? Do you often or always brush these aside for something you consider more fun or interesting? If so, some idols might have snuck into your life.

God has made the most amazing promise to us: he will be with us always, through thick and thin—no matter what. But if we've got a bunch of idols crowding our life—there's not much room left to experience God's promised love. It might even seem like life is falling apart sometimes. But if we put God first, our problems seem lighter, and we just feel more peaceful.

— 1 Corinthians 10:1–13

---

^m **10:9** the Lord; *some manuscripts have* Christ.

10:3 Ex 16:35   **10:4** Ex 17:6; Num 20:11   **10:5** Num 14:29, 30   **10:6** Num 11:4   **10:7** Ex 32:6
10:8 Num 25:1–18   **10:9** Num 21:5, 6   **10:10** Num 16:41–49   **10:13** Jdt 8:25–27; Sir 15:11–20
10:16 Mt 26:26–28; Mk 14:22–24; Lk 22:19, 20   **10:18** Lev 7:6

We all share the same loaf. (10:17)

eat what is offered in sacrifice share in the altar's service to God. ¹⁹Do I imply, then, that an idol or the food offered to it really amounts to anything? ²⁰No! What I am saying is that what is sacrificed on pagan altars is offered to demons, not to God. And I do not want you to be partners with demons. ²¹You cannot drink from the Lord's cup and also from the cup of demons; you cannot eat at the Lord's table and also at the table of demons. ²²Or do we want to make the Lord jealous? Do we think that we are stronger than he?

²³"We are allowed to do anything," so they say. That is true, but not everything is good. "We are allowed to do anything"—but not everything is helpful. ²⁴None of you should be looking out for your own interests, but for the interests of others.

²⁵You are free to eat anything sold in the meat market, without asking any questions because of your conscience. ²⁶For, as the scripture says, "The earth and everything in it belong to the Lord."

²⁷If an unbeliever invites you to a meal and you decide to go, eat what is set before you, without asking any questions because of your conscience. ²⁸But if someone tells you, "This food was offered to idols," then do not eat that food, for the sake of the one who told you and for conscience' sake— ²⁹that is, not your own conscience, but the other person's conscience.

"Well, then," someone asks, "why should my freedom to act be limited by another person's conscience? ³⁰If I thank God for my food, why should anyone criticize me about food for which I give thanks?"

³¹Well, whatever you do, whether you eat or drink, do it all for God's glory. ³²Live in such a way as to cause no trouble either to Jews or Gentiles or to the church of God. ³³Just do as I do; I try to please everyone in all that I do, not thinking of my own good, but of the good of all, so that they might be saved.

11 ¹Imitate me, then, just as I imitate Christ.

Covering the Head in Worship

²I praise you because you always remember me and follow the teachings that I have handed on to you. ³But I want you to understand that Christ is supreme over every man, the husband is supreme over his wife, and God is supreme over Christ. ⁴So a man who prays or proclaims God's message in public worship with his head covered disgraces Christ. ⁵And any woman who prays or proclaims God's message in public worship with nothing on her head disgraces her husband; there is no difference between her and a woman whose head has been shaved. ⁶If the woman does not cover her head, she might as well cut her hair. And since it is a shameful thing for a woman to shave her head or cut her hair, she should cover her head. ⁷A man has no need to cover his head, because he reflects the image and glory of God. But woman reflects the glory of man; ⁸for man was not created from woman, but woman from man. ⁹Nor was man created for woman's sake, but woman was created for man's sake. ¹⁰On account of the angels, then, a woman should have a covering over her head to show that she is under her husband's authority. ¹¹In our life in the Lord, however, woman is not independent of man, nor is man independent of woman. ¹²For as woman was made from man, in the same way man is born of woman; and it is God who brings everything into existence.

¹³Judge for yourselves whether it is proper for a woman to pray to God in public worship with nothing on her head. ¹⁴Why, nature itself teaches you that long hair on a

The Eucharistic Meal

Catholic Connections

Do you ever find yourself during Communion time looking around to see who's walking up the aisle, worrying about tomorrow's big test, remembering the fight you had earlier that morning with your dad, observing the cute three-year-old in front of you, or thinking about the soccer game coming up? A million distractions, right there in church or in our heads!

Saint Paul teaches us that receiving the body and blood of Christ is precious—so take it seriously (1 Corinthians 11:29)! Next time you're at Mass and it's time to receive the Eucharist, really concentrate on what you're doing. Listen to the words, take communion, be quiet and focus on the presence of Jesus within you. For in the same way that bread and wine is changed into Jesus' body and blood, when we eat and drink the Eucharist, we are changed. Jesus becomes part of us, so we become more like Jesus. Pray to feel the power of that change happening inside you. Pray that the love of Jesus will be noticeable in the things you say and do. Pray for peace—in you and around you.

— 1 Corinthians 11:23–33

man is a disgrace, 15but on a woman it is a thing of beauty. Her long hair has been given her to serve as a covering. 16But if anyone wants to argue about it, all I have to say is that neither we nor the churches of God have any other custom in worship.

The Lord's Supper
(Matthew 26:26–29; Mark 14:22–25; Luke 22:14–20)

17In the following instructions, however, I do not praise you, because your meetings for worship actually do more harm than good. 18In the first place, I have been told that there are opposing groups in your meetings; and this I believe is partly true. (19No doubt there must be divisions among you so that the ones who are in the right may be clearly seen.) 20When you meet together as a group, it is not the Lord's Supper that you eat. 21For as you eat, you each go ahead with your own meal, so that some are hungry while others get drunk. 22Don't you have your own homes in which to eat and drink? Or would you rather despise the church of God and put to shame the people who are in need? What do you expect me to say to you about this? Shall I praise you? Of course I don't!

23For I received from the Lord the teaching that I passed on to you: that the Lord Jesus, on the night he was betrayed, took a piece of bread, 24gave thanks to God, broke it, and said, "This is my body, which is for you. Do this in memory of me." 25In the same way, after the supper he took the cup and said, "This cup is God's new covenant, sealed with my blood. Whenever you drink it, do so in memory of me."

26This means that every time you eat this bread and drink from this cup you proclaim the Lord's death until he comes. 27It follows that if one of you eats the Lord's bread or drinks from his cup in a way that dishonors

11:25 a Ex 24:8; Jer 31:31–34; b Ex 24:6–8

I Corinthians

"Every time you eat this bread and drink from this cup you proclaim the Lord's death until he comes" *(I Corinthians 11:26).* **Where have you heard this before?**

Pray It!

Come, Holy Spirit!

The beginning of 1 Corinthians, chapter 12, talks about the gifts of the Holy Spirit, gifts that we receive more fully during the sacrament of Confirmation. The bishop prays this blessing over the Confirmation candidates before they are anointed with oil:

> All powerful God, Father of our Lord Jesus Christ,
> by water and the Holy Spirit
> you freed your sons and daughters from sin
> And gave them new life.
> Send your Holy Spirit upon them
> to be their helper and guide.
> Give them the spirit of wisdom and understanding,
> the spirit of right judgment and courage,
> the spirit of knowledge and reverence.
> Fill them with the spirit of wonder and awe in your presence.
> We ask this through Christ our Lord.

(*Rite of Confirmation*, 42)

— 1 Corinthians 12:1–11

him, you are guilty of sin against the Lord's body and blood. ²⁸So then, you should each examine yourself first, and then eat the bread and drink from the cup. ²⁹For if you do not recognize the meaning of the Lord's body when you eat the bread and drink from the cup, you bring judgment on yourself as you eat and drink. ³⁰That is why many of you are sick and weak, and several have died. ³¹If we would examine ourselves first, we would not come under God's judgment. ³²But we are judged and punished by the Lord, so that we shall not be condemned together with the world.

³³So then, my friends, when you gather together to eat the Lord's Supper, wait for one another. ³⁴And if any of you are hungry, you should eat at home, so that you will not come under God's judgment as you meet together. As for the other matters, I will settle them when I come.

Gifts from the Holy Spirit

12 ¹Now, concerning what you wrote about the gifts from the Holy Spirit. I want you to know the truth about them, my friends. ²You know that while you were still heathen, you were led astray in many ways to the worship of lifeless idols. ³I want you to know that no one who is led by God's Spirit can say "A curse on Jesus!" and no one can confess "Jesus is Lord," without being guided by the Holy Spirit.

⁴There are different kinds of spiritual gifts, but the same Spirit gives them. ⁵There are different ways of serving, but the same Lord is served. ⁶There are different abilities to perform service, but the same God gives ability to all for their particular service. ⁷The Spirit's presence is shown in some way in each person for the good of all. ⁸The Spirit gives one person a message full of wisdom, while to another person the same Spirit

12:4–11 Rom 12:6–8

"Set your hearts, then, on the more important gifts" (*I Corinthians 12:31*).

gives a message full of knowledge. 9One and the same Spirit gives faith to one person, while to another person he gives the power to heal. 10The Spirit gives one person the power to work miracles; to another, the gift of speaking God's message; and to yet another, the ability to tell the difference between gifts that come from the Spirit and those that do not. To one person he gives the ability to speak in strange tongues, and to another he gives the ability to explain what is said. 11But it is one and the same Spirit who does all this; as he wishes, he gives a different gift to each person.

One Body with Many Parts

12Christ is like a single body, which has many parts; it is still one body, even though it is made up of different parts. 13In the same way, all of us, whether Jews or Gentiles, whether slaves or free, have been baptized into the one body by the same Spirit, and we have all been given the one Spirit to drink.

14For the body itself is not made up of only one part, but of many parts. 15If the foot were to say, "Because I am not a hand, I don't belong to the body," that would not keep it from being a part of the body. 16And if the ear were to say, "Because I am not an eye, I don't belong to the body," that would not keep it from being a part of the body. 17If the whole body were just an eye, how could it hear? And if it were only an ear, how could it smell? 18As it is, however, God put every different part in the body just as he wanted it to be. 19There would not be a body if it were all only one part! 20As it is, there are many parts but one body.

21So then, the eye cannot say to the hand, "I don't need you!" Nor can the head say to the feet, "Well, I don't need you!" 22On the contrary, we cannot do without the parts of the body that seem to be weaker; 23and those parts that we think aren't worth very much are the ones which we treat with greater care; while the parts of the body which don't look very nice are treated with special modesty, 24which the more beautiful parts do not

need. God himself has put the body together in such a way as to give greater honor to those parts that need it. 25And so there is no division in the body, but all its different parts have the same concern for one another. 26If one part of the body suffers, all the other parts suffer with it; if one part is praised, all the other parts share its happiness.

27All of you are Christ's body, and each one is a part of it. 28In the church God has put all in place: in the first place apostles, in the second place prophets, and in the third place teachers; then those who perform miracles, followed by those who are given the power to heal or to help others or to direct them or to speak in strange tongues. 29They are not all apostles or prophets or teachers. Not everyone has the power to work miracles 30or to heal diseases or to speak in strange tongues or to explain what is said. 31Set your hearts, then, on the more important gifts.

Best of all, however, is the following way.

Love

13 1I may be able to speak the languages of human beings and even of angels, but if I have no love, my speech is no more than a noisy gong or a clanging bell. 2I may have the gift of inspired preaching; I may have all knowledge and understand all secrets; I may have all the faith needed to move mountains—but if I have no love, I am nothing. 3I may give away everything I have, and even give up my body to be burned[n] but if I have no love, this does me no good.

4Love is patient and kind; it is not jealous or conceited or proud; 5love is not ill-mannered or selfish or irritable; love does not keep a record of wrongs; 6love is not happy with evil, but is happy with the truth. 7Love never gives up; and its faith, hope, and patience never fail.

8Love is eternal. There are inspired messages, but they are temporary; there are gifts of speaking in strange tongues, but they will cease; there is knowledge, but it will pass. 9For our gifts of knowledge and of inspired messages are only partial; 10but when what is

---

n **13:3** to be burned; *some manuscripts have* in order to boast.
12:12 Rom 12:4, 5   **12:28** Eph 4:11   **13:2** Mt 17:20; 21:21; Mk 11:23

True Love

Think of five things you said or did today. Five concrete examples. Now, reread 1 Corinthians 13:4–7. How do your words and actions measure up? Do they show that you are patient? kind? unselfish?

It's one thing to say, "I love God" or "I love my parents" or "I love my best friend." It's another thing to really live in a loving way.

Write out the words of these verses, and hang them up where you'll see them every day. This is a good way to keep checking if you are being faithful to the kind of love God is asking us to offer to ourselves and others.

— 1 Corinthians 13:4–7

perfect comes, then what is partial will disappear.

11 When I was a child, my speech, feelings, and thinking were all those of a child; now that I am an adult, I have no more use for childish ways. 12 What we see now is like a dim image in a mirror; then we shall see face to face. What I know now is only partial;

What we see now is like a dim image in a mirror. (13:12)

Then we shall see face to face. (13:12)

then it will be complete—as complete as God's knowledge of me.

13 Meanwhile these three remain: faith, hope, and love; and the greatest of these is love.

More about Gifts from the Spirit

14 1 It is love, then, that you should strive for. Set your hearts on spiritual gifts, especially the gift of proclaiming God's message. 2 Those who speak in strange tongues do not speak to others but to God, because no one understands them. They are speaking secret truths by the power of the Spirit. 3 But those who proclaim God's message speak to people and give them help, encouragement, and comfort. 4 Those who speak in strange tongues help only themselves, but those who proclaim God's message help the whole church.

5 I would like for all of you to speak in strange tongues; but I would rather that you had the gift of proclaiming God's message. For the person who proclaims God's message is of greater value than the one who speaks in strange tongues—unless there is someone present who can explain what is said, so that the whole church may be helped. 6 So when I come to you, my friends, what use will I be to you if I speak in strange tongues? Not a bit, unless I bring you some revelation from God or some knowledge or some inspired message or some teaching.

7 Take such lifeless musical instruments as the flute or the harp—how will anyone

Pray It!

Strange Tongues?

What does it mean to speak in strange tongues? It's a way of praying. Some people possess this gift of the Spirit described in 1 Corinthians, chapter 14. When they pray out loud, it sometimes sounds like strange, foreign-sounding words. This is said to be the Holy Spirit speaking through them, even though they have no idea what it means. They are praying with their spirit, not their mind. Paul explains that while some people have the gift of speaking in tongues, others might have the gift of understanding what they are saying.

If you ever hear someone speaking in tongues, it can be shocking or disturbing at first. But trust that it is prayer and is another mysterious way that God can work in us.

Paul is making a more important point, however. What comes out of your mouth? Everything we say is important. Our words can offer "help, encouragement, and comfort" (1 Corinthians 14:3). Or our words can be hurtful and destructive or useless. Screaming and cursing is harmful. Laughter and singing can bring joy.

Think about that the next time you're about to open your mouth to God in prayer!

— 1 Corinthians 14:1–6

know the tune that is being played unless the notes are sounded distinctly? [8]And if the one who plays the bugle does not sound a clear call, who will prepare for battle? [9]In the same way, how will anyone understand what you are talking about if your message given in strange tongues is not clear? Your words will vanish in the air! [10]There are many different languages in the world, yet none of them is without meaning. [11]But if I do not know the language being spoken, those who use it will be foreigners to me and I will be a foreigner to them. [12]Since you are eager to have the gifts of the Spirit, you must try above everything else to make greater use of those which help to build up the church.

[13]The person who speaks in strange tongues, then, must pray for the gift to explain what is said. [14]For if I pray in this way, my spirit prays indeed, but my mind has

no part in it. [15]What should I do, then? I will pray with my spirit, but I will pray also with my mind; I will sing with my spirit, but I will sing also with my mind. [16]When you give thanks to God in spirit only, how can ordinary people taking part in the meeting say "Amen" to your prayer of thanksgiving? They have no way of knowing what you are saying. [17]Even if your prayer of thanks to God is quite good, other people are not helped at all.

[18]I thank God that I speak in strange tongues much more than any of you. [19]But in church worship I would rather speak five words that can be understood, in order to teach others, than speak thousands of words in strange tongues.

[20]Do not be like children in your thinking, my friends; be children so far as evil is concerned, but be grown up in your thinking. [21]In the Scriptures it is written,

14:21 Isa 28:11, 12

1 Corinthians

Speaking in strange tongues (1 Corinthians 14:2) **sometimes happens in charismatic prayer groups that are part of some Catholic parishes.**

"By means of people speaking strange
    languages
  I will speak to my people, says the Lord.
I will speak through lips of foreigners,
    but even then my people will not listen
    to me."

22 So then, the gift of speaking in strange tongues is proof for unbelievers, not for believers, while the gift of proclaiming God's message is proof for believers, not for unbelievers.

23 If, then, the whole church meets together and everyone starts speaking in strange tongues—and if some ordinary people or unbelievers come in, won't they say that you are all crazy? 24 But if everyone is proclaiming God's message when some unbelievers or ordinary people come in, they will be convinced of their sin by what they hear. They will be judged by all they hear, 25 their secret thoughts will be brought into the open, and they will bow down and worship God, confessing, "Truly God is here among you!"

Order in the Church

26 This is what I mean, my friends. When you meet for worship, one person has a hymn, another a teaching, another a revelation from God, another a message in strange tongues, and still another the explanation of what is said. Everything must be of help to the church. 27 If someone is going to speak in strange tongues, two or three at the most should speak, one after the other, and someone else must explain what is being said. 28 But if no one is there who can explain, then the one who speaks in strange tongues must be quiet and speak only to himself and to God. 29 Two or three who are given God's message should speak, while the others are to judge what they say. 30 But if someone sitting in the meeting receives a message from God, the one who is speaking should stop. 31 All of you may proclaim God's message, one by one, so that everyone will learn and

be encouraged. 32 The gift of proclaiming God's message should be under the speaker's control, 33 because God does not want us to be in disorder but in harmony and peace.

As in all the churches of God's people, 34 the women should keep quiet in the meetings. They are not allowed to speak; as the Jewish Law says, they must not be in charge. 35 If they want to find out about something, they should ask their husbands at home. It is a disgraceful thing for a woman to speak in a church meeting.

36 Or could it be that the word of God came from you? Or are you the only ones to whom it came? 37 If anyone supposes he is God's messenger or has a spiritual gift, he must realize that what I am writing to you is the Lord's command. 38 But if he does not pay attention to this, pay no attention to him.

39 So then, my friends, set your heart on proclaiming God's message, but do not forbid the speaking in strange tongues. 40 Everything must be done in a proper and orderly way.

The Resurrection of Christ

15 1 And now I want to remind you, my friends, of the Good News which I preached to you, which you received, and on which your faith stands firm. 2 That is the gospel, the message that I preached to you. You are saved by the gospel if you hold firmly to it—unless it was for nothing that you believed.

3 I passed on to you what I received, which is of the greatest importance: that Christ died for our sins, as written in the Scriptures; 4 that he was buried and that he was raised to life three days later, as written in the Scriptures; 5 that he appeared to Peter and then to all twelve apostles. 6 Then he appeared to more than five hundred of his followers at once, most of whom are still alive, although some have died. 7 Then he appeared to James, and afterward to all the apostles.

8 Last of all he appeared also to me—even

15:3 Isa 53:5–12   **15:4** Ps 16:8–10; Mt 12:40; Acts 2:24–32   **15:5 a** Lk 24:34; **b** Mt 28:16, 17; Mk 16:14; Lk 24:36; Jn 20:19   **15:8** Acts 9:3–6

Read I Corinthians 15:19. Would you be a Christian if you didn't believe in the Resurrection?

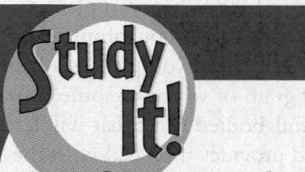

An African Creed

In 1 Corinthians 15:3–5, Paul proclaims one of the earliest creeds of
the Church. A creed is a statement
of beliefs about our faith, especially about the death and Resurrection of Jesus. Here is the beginning
of another creed from the Masai
tribe of the African tradition:

*We believe in the one High God,
who out of love created the beautiful
world and everything good in it. He
created man and wanted man to be
happy in the world. God loves the
world and every nation and tribe on
the earth. We have known this High
God in the darkness, and now we
know him in the light. God promised
in the book of his word, the Bible,
that he would save the world and all
the nations and tribes.*

*We believe that God made good
his promise by sending his Son, Jesus
Christ, a man in the flesh, a Jew by
tribe, born poor in a little village,
who left his home and was always on
safari doing good, curing people by
the power of God, teaching about
God and man, showing that the
meaning of religion is love. He was
rejected by his people, tortured and
nailed hands and feet to a cross, and
died.*

— 1 Corinthians 15:3–5

grace that he gave me was not without effect.
On the contrary, I have worked harder than
any of the other apostles, although it was not
really my own doing, but God's grace working with me. ¹¹So then, whether it came from
me or from them, this is what we all preach,
and this is what you believe.

Our Resurrection

¹²Now, since our message is that Christ has
been raised from death, how can some of you
say that the dead will not be raised to life? ¹³If
that is true, it means that Christ was not
raised; ¹⁴and if Christ has not been raised from
death, then we have nothing to preach and
you have nothing to believe. ¹⁵More than that,
we are shown to be lying about God, because
we said that he raised Christ from death—but
if it is true that the dead are not raised to life,
then he did not raise Christ. ¹⁶For if the dead
are not raised, neither has Christ been raised.
¹⁷And if Christ has not been raised, then your
faith is a delusion and you are still lost in your
sins. ¹⁸It would also mean that the believers in
Christ who have died are lost. ¹⁹If our hope in
Christ is good for this life only and no more,ᵖ
then we deserve more pity than anyone else in
all the world.

²⁰But the truth is that Christ has been
raised from death, as the guarantee that those
who sleep in death will also be raised. ²¹For

Those who sleep in death will also be raised.
(15:20)

though I am like someone whose birth was
abnormal.ᵒ ⁹For I am the least of all the apostles—I do not even deserve to be called an
apostle, because I persecuted God's church.
¹⁰But by God's grace I am what I am, and the

ᵒ **15:8** whose birth was abnormal; *or* who was born at the wrong time.   ᵖ **15:19** If our hope in Christ is good
for this life only and no more; *or* If all we have in this life is our hope in Christ.
15:9 Acts 8:3

1 Corinthians

just as death came by means of a man, in the same way the rising from death comes by means of a man. 22For just as all people die because of their union with Adam, in the same way all will be raised to life because of their union with Christ. 23But each one will be raised in proper order: Christ, first of all; then, at the time of his coming, those who belong to him. 24Then the end will come; Christ will overcome all spiritual rulers, authorities, and powers, and will hand over the Kingdom to God the Father. 25For Christ must rule until God defeats all enemies and puts them under his feet. 26The last enemy to be defeated will be death. 27For the scripture says, "God put *all* things under his feet." It is clear, of course, that the words "all things" do not include God himself, who puts all things under Christ. 28But when all things have been placed under Christ's rule, then he himself, the Son, will place himself under God, who placed all things under him; and God will rule completely over all.

29Now, what about those people who are baptized for the dead? What do they hope to accomplish? If it is true, as some claim, that the dead are not raised to life, why are those people being baptized for the dead? 30And as for us—why would we run the risk of danger every hour? 31My friends, I face death every day! The pride I have in you, in our life in union with Christ Jesus our Lord, makes me declare this. 32If I have, as it were, fought "wild beasts" here in Ephesus simply from human motives, what have I gained? But if the dead are not raised to life, then, as the saying goes, "Let us eat and drink, for tomorrow we will die."

33Do not be fooled. "Bad companions ruin good character." 34Come back to your right senses and stop your sinful ways. I declare to your shame that some of you do not know God.

The Resurrection Body

35Someone will ask, "How can the dead be raised to life? What kind of body will they have?" 36You fool! When you plant a seed in the ground, it does not sprout to life unless it dies. 37And what you plant is a bare seed, perhaps a grain of wheat or some other grain, not the full-bodied plant that will later grow up. 38God provides that seed with the body he wishes; he gives each seed its own proper body.

39And the flesh of living beings is not all the same kind of flesh; human beings have one kind of flesh, animals another, birds another, and fish another.

40And there are heavenly bodies and earthly bodies; the beauty that belongs to heavenly bodies is different from the beauty that belongs to earthly bodies. 41The sun has its own beauty, the moon another beauty, and the stars a different beauty; and even among stars there are different kinds of beauty.

42This is how it will be when the dead are raised to life. When the body is buried, it is mortal; when raised, it will be immortal. 43When buried, it is ugly and weak; when raised, it will be beautiful and strong. 44When buried, it is a physical body; when raised, it will be a spiritual body. There is, of course, a physical body, so there has to be a spiritual body. 45For the scripture says, "The first man, Adam, was created a living being"; but the last Adam is the life-giving Spirit. 46It is not the spiritual that comes first, but the physical, and then the spiritual. 47The first Adam, made of earth, came from the earth; the second Adam came from heaven. 48Those who belong to the earth are like the one who was made of earth; those who are of heaven are like the one who came from heaven. 49Just as we wear the likeness of the man made of earth, so we will wear*q* the likeness of the Man from heaven.

50What I mean, friends, is that what is made of flesh and blood cannot share in God's Kingdom, and what is mortal cannot possess immortality.

51-52Listen to this secret truth: we shall not all die, but when the last trumpet sounds, we shall all be changed in an instant, as quickly as the blinking of an eye. For when the

---

q **15:49** we will wear; *some manuscripts have* let us wear.
15:25 Ps 110:1   **15:27** Ps 8:6   **15:29** 2 Macc 12:44   **15:32** Isa 22:13   **15:45** Gen 2:7
15:51, 52 1 Thess 4:15–17

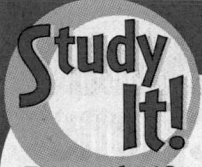

Study It!

Eternal Life

When someone we love dies, it's the saddest moment of our lives. It feels as though we have lost that person forever—and a big, horrible, painful hole is left inside us. But wait—there's great news! Because of Jesus' Resurrection, we believe death is not the end. Our loved ones will be raised up from the dead and given new, resurrected bodies! And we will be together again one day.

If Jesus had died, and that was that—then you wouldn't be reading this right now because it would all be meaningless. But death wasn't the end! Jesus rose from the dead, and that event is at the heart of all our religious beliefs.

Death isn't the end for us, either. We, too, will rise and be with God forever and ever—we call this eternal life. What do you think that will be like? Paul says we will not look the same, just as a seed planted in the soil looks completely different after it dies and rises up out of the ground as a plant or flower (1 Corinthians 15:35–37). Our new bodies will be "spiritual bodies," and they will be "beautiful and strong" (15:44,43).

This is truly the best news of all the Good News!

— 1 Corinthians, chapter 15

trumpet sounds, the dead will be raised, never to die again, and we shall all be changed. 53 For what is mortal must be changed into what is immortal; what will die must be changed into what cannot die. 54 So when this takes place, and the mortal has been changed into the immortal, then the scripture will come true: "Death is destroyed; victory is complete!"

55 "Where, Death, is your victory?

Where, Death, is your power to hurt?" 56 Death gets its power to hurt from sin, and sin gets its power from the Law. 57 But thanks be to God who gives us the victory through our Lord Jesus Christ!

58 So then, my dear friends, stand firm and steady. Keep busy always in your work for the Lord, since you know that nothing you do in the Lord's service is ever useless.

The Offering for Needy Believers

16 1 Now, concerning what you wrote about the money to be raised to help God's people in Judea. You must do what I told the churches in Galatia to do. 2 Every Sunday each of you must put aside some money, in proportion to what you have earned, and save it up, so that there will be no need to collect money when I come. 3 After I come, I shall give letters of introduction to those you have approved, and send them to take your gift to Jerusalem. 4 If it seems worthwhile for me to go, then they can go along with me.

Paul's Plans

5 I shall come to you after I have gone through Macedonia—for I have to go through Macedonia. 6 I shall probably spend some time with you, perhaps the whole winter, and then you can help me to continue my trip, wherever it is I shall go next. 7 I want to see you more than just briefly in passing; I hope to spend quite a long time with you, if the Lord allows.

I Corinthians

15:54 Isa 25:8   15:55 Hos 13:14 (LXX)   16:1 Rom 15:25, 26   16:5 Acts 19:21

"Where, Death, is your victory? Where, Death, is your power to hurt?"
(1 Corinthians 15:55).

Tithing

Saint Paul instructs the Corinthians to put aside an amount of money "in proportion to what you have earned" (1 Corinthians 16:2) for poor people. Our church calls this the practice of tithing (also described in Deuteronomy 26:12). A tithe means 10 percent and is the amount of crops required in Deuteronomy to set aside for poor and needy people.

If you were to practice tithing, it would look like this: If you earn $20 for a job, you save 10 percent ($2) to give to poor people. If you bring home a paycheck of $2,000, then $200 of it goes to charity—before it gets spent on other things!

Today, the Church doesn't require people to give 10 percent, but we are all challenged to give as generously as we can. Some people might be able to give more than 10 percent, and for others 5 percent is a big commitment. Tithing is something to start now. Do you get an allowance? Figure out how much 10 percent of it is, and before you spend a penny of your allowance, put that amount aside and give it to someone or some group that helps poor people.

Ca†holic Connec†ions

— 1 Corinthians 16:1–2

---

8 I will stay here in Ephesus until the day of Pentecost. 9 There is a real opportunity here for great and worthwhile work, even though there are many opponents.

10 If Timothy comes your way, be sure to make him feel welcome among you, because he is working for the Lord, just as I am. 11 No one should look down on him, but you must help him continue his trip in peace, so that he will come back to me; for I am expecting him back with the believers.

12 Now, about brother Apollos. I have often encouraged him to visit you with the other believers, but he is not completely convinced[r] that he should go at this time. When he gets the chance, however, he will go.

Final Words

13 Be alert, stand firm in the faith, be brave, be strong. 14 Do all your work in love.

15 You know about Stephanas and his family; they are the first Christian converts in Achaia and have given themselves to the service of God's people. I beg you, my friends, 16 to follow the leadership of such people as these, and of anyone else who works and serves with them.

17 I am happy about the coming of Stephanas, Fortunatus, and Achaicus; they have made up for your absence 18 and have cheered me up, just as they cheered you up. Such men as these deserve notice.

19 The churches in the province of Asia send you their greetings; Aquila and Priscilla and the church that meets in their house

---

r 16:12 he is not completely convinced; *or* it is not at all God's will.
16:8 Lev 23:15–21; Deut 16:9–11　**16:8, 9** Acts 19:8–10　**16:10** 1 Cor 4:17　**16:15** 1 Cor 1:16
16:19 Acts 18:2

I Corinthians

Do the names of Paul's coworkers sound familiar: Timothy, Apollos, Aquila, and Priscilla? We met them in the Acts of the Apostles.

send warm Christian greetings. 20All the believers here send greetings.

Greet one another with the kiss of peace.

21With my own hand I write this: *Greetings from Paul.*

22Whoever does not love the Lord—a curse on him!

Maran atha—Our Lord, come!

23The grace of the Lord Jesus be with you.

24My love be with you all in Christ Jesus.

Your Next Step

Congratulations on finishing the First Letter to the Corinthians! Use this space to write your thoughts and questions about this book. If you are following the suggested reading plan, move back to the Second Book of Samuel in the Old Testament. This book tells the story of King David.

Nobody likes to be criticized unfairly, especially by people you thought were your friends. When Paul wrote his first letter to the people of Corinth, they had a good relationship. But then some outsiders came to the city and criticized Paul. They said he was a bad person, he was a poor speaker, and he was untrustworthy.

Paul didn't like this conflict. He wrote this second letter to the Christians in Corinth to defend himself and help them get back on the right track. He also wanted to encourage them to be generous to the needs of the poor.

Chap. 8:1–9

Head lines

- Paul Does Everything Out of Love! (1:12—2:4)
- Treasure Contained in Clay Pots (4:1–15)
- Faith, Not Sight, Guides Believers (5:6–7)
- Corinthians Told to Be Generous (8:1–15)
- Paul Describes His Amazing Life (11:16–33)

FACTOIDS

Who wrote this book? It was written by Saint Paul, who started Christian communities in several cities, including Corinth.

When was it written? Around AD 57, about a year after Paul wrote his first letter to the Corinthians.

Why was it written? Paul wanted to defend himself and his ministry against the people who criticized him. He wanted to improve his relationship with the Christian people of Corinth.

Jesus connection. Jesus was without sin. When we unite ourselves to Christ by believing in him, his goodness is reflected in us. This changes us from God's enemies into his friends! (5:16–21)

Important themes

- Paul shows us how to stay faithful to Jesus even when we are personally attacked or put down.
- We are weak and imperfect so that everyone knows that treasure of faith we have comes from God.
- We must be generous in sharing what we have with those in need.

2 CORINTHIANS

1 ¹ From Paul, an apostle of Christ Jesus by God's will, and from our brother Timothy—

To the church of God in Corinth, and to all God's people throughout Achaia:

²May God our Father and the Lord Jesus Christ give you grace and peace.

Paul Gives Thanks to God

³Let us give thanks to the God and Father of our Lord Jesus Christ, the merciful Father, the God from whom all help comes! ⁴He helps us in all our troubles, so that we are able to help others who have all kinds of troubles, using the same help that we ourselves have received from God. ⁵Just as we have a share in Christ's many sufferings, so also through Christ we share in God's great help. ⁶If we suffer, it is for your help and salvation; if we are helped, then you too are helped and given the strength to endure with patience the same sufferings that we also endure. ⁷So our hope in you is never shaken; we know that just as you share in our sufferings, you also share in the help we receive.

Help others who have all kinds of troubles. (1.4)

⁸We want to remind you, friends, of the trouble we had in the province of Asia. The burdens laid upon us were so great and so heavy that we gave up all hope of staying alive. ⁹We felt that the death sentence had been passed on us. But this happened so that we should rely, not on ourselves, but only on God, who raises the dead. ¹⁰From such terrible dangers of death*ᵃ* he saved us, and will save us; and we have placed our hope in him that he will save us again, ¹¹as you help us by means of your prayers for us. So it will be that the many prayers for us will be answered, and God will bless us; and many will raise their voices to him in thanksgiving for us.

The Change in Paul's Plans

¹²We are proud that our conscience assures us that our lives in this world, and especially our relations with you, have been ruled by God-given frankness*ᵇ* and sincerity, by the power of God's grace and not by human wisdom. ¹³⁻¹⁴We write to you only what you can read and understand. But even though you now understand us only in part, I hope that you will come to understand us completely, so that in the Day of our Lord Jesus you can be as proud of us as we shall be of you.

¹⁵I was so sure of all this that I made plans at first to visit you, in order that you might be blessed twice. ¹⁶For I planned to visit you on my way to Macedonia and again on my way back, in order to get help from you for my trip to Judea. ¹⁷In planning this, did I appear fickle? When I make my plans, do I make them from selfish motives, ready to say "Yes, yes" and "No, no" at the same time? ¹⁸As surely as God speaks the truth, my promise to you was not a "Yes" and a "No." ¹⁹For Jesus Christ, the Son of God, who was preached among you by Silas, Timothy, and myself, is not one who is "Yes" and "No." On the contrary, he is God's "Yes"; ²⁰for it is he who is the "Yes" to all of God's promises. This is why through Jesus Christ our "Amen" is said to the glory of God. ²¹It is

---

ᵃ **1:10** terrible dangers of death; *some manuscripts have* terrible death.   *ᵇ* **1:12** frankness; *some manuscripts have* holiness.

1:1 Acts 18:1   **1:8** 1 Cor 15:32   **1:16** Acts 19:21   **1:19** Acts 18:5

God himself who makes us, together with you, sure of our life in union with Christ; it is God himself who has set us apart, 22who has placed his mark of ownership upon us, and who has given us the Holy Spirit in our hearts as the guarantee of all that he has in store for us.

23I call God as my witness—he knows my heart! It was in order to spare you that I decided not to go to Corinth. 24We are not trying to dictate to you what you must believe; we know that you stand firm in the faith. Instead, we are working with you for your own happiness.

2 1So I made up my mind not to come to you again to make you sad. 2For if I were to make you sad, who would be left to cheer me up? Only the very persons I had made sad. 3That is why I wrote that letter to you—I did not want to come to you and be made sad by the very people who should make me glad. For I am convinced that when I am happy, then all of you are happy too. 4I wrote you with a greatly troubled and distressed heart and with many tears; my purpose was not to make you sad, but to make you realize how much I love you all.

Forgiveness for the Offender

5Now, if anyone has made somebody sad, he has not done it to me but to all of you—in part, at least. (I say this because I do not want to be too hard on him.) 6It is enough that this person has been punished in this way by most of you. 7Now, however, you should forgive him and encourage him, in order to keep him from becoming so sad as to give up completely. 8And so I beg you to let him know that you really do love him. 9I wrote you that letter because I wanted to find out how well you had stood the test and whether you are always ready to obey my instructions. 10When you forgive people for what they have done, I forgive them too. For when I forgive—if, indeed, I need to forgive anything—I do it in Christ's presence because of you, 11in order to keep Satan from getting the upper hand over us; for we know what his plans are.

Paul's Anxiety in Troas

12When I arrived in Troas to preach the Good News about Christ, I found that the Lord had opened the way for the work there. 13But I was deeply worried, because I could not find our brother Titus. So I said good-bye to the people there and went on to Macedonia.

Victory through Christ

14But thanks be to God! For in union with Christ we are always led by God as prisoners in Christ's victory procession. God uses us to make the knowledge about Christ spread everywhere like a sweet fragrance. 15For we are like a sweet-smelling incense offered by Christ to God, which spreads among those who are being saved and those who are being lost. 16For those who are being lost, it is a deadly stench that kills; but for those who are being saved, it is a fragrance that brings life. Who, then, is capable for such a task? 17We are not like so many others, who handle God's message as if it were cheap merchandise; but because God has sent us, we speak with sincerity in his presence, as servants of Christ.

Servants of the New Covenant

3 1Does this sound as if we were again boasting about ourselves? Could it be that, like some other people, we need letters of recommendation to you or from you? 2You yourselves are the letter we have, written on our hearts for everyone to know and read. 3It is clear that Christ himself wrote this letter and sent it by us. It is written, not with ink but with the Spirit of the living God, and not on stone tablets but on human hearts.

4We say this because we have confidence in God through Christ. 5There is nothing in us that allows us to claim that we are capable of doing this work. The capacity we have comes from God; 6it is he who made us capable of serving the new covenant, which consists not of a written law but of the Spir-

2:12, 13 Acts 20:1   3:3 a Ex 24:12; b Jer 31:33; Ezek 11:19; 36:26   3:6 Jer 31:31

it. The written law brings death, but the Spirit gives life.

7 The Law was carved in letters on stone tablets, and God's glory appeared when it was given. Even though the brightness on Moses' face was fading, it was so strong that the people of Israel could not keep their eyes fixed on him. If the Law, which brings death when it is in force, came with such glory, 8 how much greater is the glory that belongs to the activity of the Spirit! 9 The system which brings condemnation was glorious; how much more glorious is the activity which brings salvation! 10 We may say that because of the far brighter glory now the glory that was so bright in the past is gone. 11 For if there was glory in that which lasted for a while, how much more glory is there in that which lasts forever!

12 Because we have this hope, we are very bold. 13 We are not like Moses, who had to put a veil over his face so that the people of Israel would not see the brightness fade and disappear. 14 Their minds, indeed, were closed; and to this very day their minds are covered with the same veil as they read the books of the old covenant. The veil is removed only when a person is joined to Christ. 15 Even today, whenever they read the Law of Moses, the veil still covers their minds. 16 But it can be removed, as the scripture says about Moses: "His veil was removed when he turned to the Lord."*c* 17 Now, "the Lord" in this passage is the Spirit; and where the Spirit of the Lord is present, there is freedom. 18 All of us, then, reflect the glory of the Lord with uncovered faces; and that same glory, coming from the Lord, who is the Spirit, transforms us into his likeness in an ever greater degree of glory.

Spiritual Treasure in Clay Pots

4 1 God in his mercy has given us this work to do, and so we do not become discouraged. 2 We put aside all secret and shameful deeds; we do not act with deceit, nor do we falsify the word of God. In the full light of truth we live in God's sight and try to commend ourselves to everyone's

good conscience. 3 For if the gospel we preach is hidden, it is hidden only from those who are being lost. 4 They do not believe, because their minds have been kept in the dark by the evil god of this world. He keeps them from seeing the light shining on them, the light that comes from the Good News about the glory of Christ, who is the exact likeness of God. 5 For it is not ourselves that we preach; we preach Jesus Christ as Lord, and ourselves as your servants for Jesus' sake. 6 The God who said, "Out of darkness the light shall shine!" is the same God who made his light shine in our hearts, to bring us the knowledge of God's glory shining in the face of Christ.

7 Yet we who have this spiritual treasure are like common clay pots, in order to show that the supreme power belongs to God, not to us. 8 We are often troubled, but not crushed; sometimes in doubt, but never in despair; 9 there are many enemies, but we are never without a friend; and though badly hurt at times, we are not destroyed. 10 At all times we carry in our mortal bodies the death of Jesus, so that his life also may be seen in our bodies. 11 Throughout our lives we are always in danger of death for Jesus' sake, in order that his life may be seen in this mortal body of ours. 12 This means that death is at work in us, but life is at work in you.

13 The scripture says, "I spoke because I believed." In the same spirit of faith we also speak because we believe. 14 We know that God, who raised the Lord Jesus to life, will also raise us up with Jesus and take us, together with you, into his presence. 15 All this is for your sake; and as God's grace reaches more and more people, they will offer to the glory of God more prayers of thanksgiving.

Living by Faith

16 For this reason we never become discouraged. Even though our physical being is gradually decaying, yet our spiritual being is renewed day after day. 17 And this small and temporary trouble we suffer will bring us a tremendous and eternal glory, much greater

c **3:16** *Verse 16 may be translated:* But the veil is removed whenever someone turns to the Lord.
3:7 Ex 34:29   **3:13** Ex 34:33   **3:16** Ex 34:34   **4:6** Gen 1:3   **4:13** Ps 116:10 (LXX)

Pray It!

Are You a Clay Pot?

"Yet we who have this spiritual treasure are like common clay pots" (2 Corinthians 4:7). Saint Paul knew the Jewish Scriptures. He knew that the prophet Isaiah describes us as clay in the hands of God, the potter (Isaiah 64:8).

Almighty God, our potter,
I am the work of your hands.
Even though I am like an ordinary clay pot,
*   you trust me to carry the wonderful treasure of Jesus, your Son.*
Help me keep my body, mind, and soul healthy and strong
*   so that I am worthy of this great honor.*
And keep me humble, always pointing others to Jesus
*   and not to myself.*
Because I am just an ordinary clay pot
*   made beautiful by you living within me.*
Amen.

— 2 Corinthians 4:5–7

than the trouble. ¹⁸For we fix our attention, not on things that are seen, but on things that are unseen. What can be seen lasts only for a time, but what cannot be seen lasts forever.

5 ¹For we know that when this tent we live in—our body here on earth—is torn down, God will have a house in heaven for us to live in, a home he himself has made, which will last forever. ²And now we sigh, so great is our desire that our home which comes from heaven should be put on over us; ³by being clothed with it we shall not be without a body. ⁴While we live in this earthly tent, we groan with a feeling of oppression; it is not that we want to get rid of our earthly body, but that we want to have the heavenly one put on over us, so that what is mortal will be transformed by life. ⁵God is the one who has prepared us for this change, and he gave us his Spirit as the guarantee of all that he has in store for us.

⁶So we are always full of courage. We know that as long as we are at home in the body we are away from the Lord's home.

⁷For our life is a matter of faith, not of sight. ⁸We are full of courage and would much prefer to leave our home in the body and be at home with the Lord. ⁹More than anything else, however, we want to please him, whether in our home here or there. ¹⁰For all of us must appear before Christ, to be judged by him. We will each receive what we deserve, according to everything we have done, good or bad, in our bodily life.

Friendship with God through Christ

¹¹We know what it means to fear the Lord, and so we try to persuade others. God knows us completely, and I hope that in your hearts you know me as well. ¹²We are not trying again to recommend ourselves to you; rather, we are trying to give you a good reason to be proud of us, so that you will be able to answer those who boast about people's appearance and not about their character. ¹³Are we really insane? It is for God's sake. Or are we sane? Then it is for your

5:1 Wis 9:15   **5:10** Rom 14:10

sake. 14We are ruled by the love of Christ, now that we recognize that one man died for everyone, which means that they all share in his death. 15He died for all, so that those who live should no longer live for themselves, but only for him who died and was raised to life for their sake.

16No longer, then, do we judge anyone by human standards. Even if at one time we judged Christ according to human standards, we no longer do so. 17Anyone who is joined to Christ is a new being; the old is gone, the new has come. 18All this is done by God, who through Christ changed us from enemies into his friends and gave us the task of making others his friends also. 19Our message is that God was making all human beings his friends through Christ.*d* God did not keep an account of their sins, and he has given us the message which tells how he makes them his friends.

20Here we are, then, speaking for Christ, as though God himself were making his appeal through us. We plead on Christ's behalf: let God change you from enemies into his friends! 21Christ was without sin, but for our sake God made him share our sin in order that in union with him we might share the righteousness of God.

6 1In our work together with God, then, we beg you who have received God's grace not to let it be wasted. 2Hear what God says:

"When the time came for me to show
    you favor,
I heard you;
when the day arrived for me to save you,
    I helped you."

Listen! This is the hour to receive God's favor; today is the day to be saved!

3We do not want anyone to find fault with our work, so we try not to put obstacles in anyone's way. 4Instead, in everything we do we show that we are God's servants by patiently enduring troubles, hardships, and difficulties. 5We have been beaten, jailed, and mobbed; we have been overworked and have gone without sleep or food. 6By our purity,

knowledge, patience, and kindness we have shown ourselves to be God's servants—by the Holy Spirit, by our true love, 7by our message of truth, and by the power of God. We have righteousness as our weapon, both to attack and to defend ourselves. 8We are honored and disgraced; we are insulted and praised. We are treated as liars, yet we speak the truth; 9as unknown, yet we are known by all; as though we were dead, but, as you see, we live on. Although punished, we are not killed; 10although saddened, we are always glad; we seem poor, but we make many people rich; we seem to have nothing, yet we really possess everything.

11Dear friends in Corinth! We have spoken frankly to you; we have opened our hearts wide. 12It is not we who have closed our hearts to you; it is you who have closed your hearts to us. 13I speak now as though you were my children: show us the same feelings that we have for you. Open your hearts wide!

Warning against Pagan Influences

14Do not try to work together as equals with unbelievers, for it cannot be done. How can right and wrong be partners? How can light and darkness live together? 15How can Christ and the Devil agree? What does a believer have in common with an unbeliever? 16How can God's temple come to terms with pagan idols? For we are the temple of the living God! As God himself has said,

"I will make my home with my people
    and live among them;
I will be their God,
    and they shall be my people."
17And so the Lord says,
"You must leave them
    and separate yourselves from them.
Have nothing to do with what is unclean,
    and I will accept you.
18I will be your father,
    and you shall be my sons and
       daughters,
    says the Lord Almighty."

d **5:19** God was making all human beings his friends through Christ; *or* God was in Christ making all human beings his friends.
6:2 Isa 49:8   **6:5** Acts 16:23   **6:16 a** 1 Cor 3:16; 6:19; **b** Lev 26:12; Ezek 37:27   **6:17** Isa 52:11
6:18 2 Sam 7:14; 1 Chr 17.13; Isa 43:6; Jer 31:9

7 ¹All these promises are made to us, my dear friends. So then, let us purify ourselves from everything that makes body or soul unclean, and let us be completely holy by living in awe of God.

Paul's Joy

²Make room for us in your hearts. We have wronged no one; we have ruined no one, nor tried to take advantage of anyone. ³I do not say this to condemn you; for, as I have said before, you are so dear to us that we are always together, whether we live or die. ⁴I am so sure of you; I take such pride in you! In all our troubles I am still full of courage; I am running over with joy.

⁵Even after we arrived in Macedonia, we did not have any rest. There were troubles everywhere, quarrels with others, fears in our hearts. ⁶But God, who encourages the downhearted, encouraged us with the coming of Titus. ⁷It was not only his coming that cheered us, but also his report of how you encouraged him. He told us how much you want to see me, how sorry you are, how ready you are to defend me; and so I am even happier now.

⁸For even if that letter of mine made you sad, I am not sorry I wrote it. I could have been sorry when I saw that it made you sad for a while. ⁹But now I am happy—not because I made you sad, but because your sadness made you change your ways. That sadness was used by God, and so we caused you no harm. ¹⁰For the sadness that is used by God brings a change of heart that leads to salvation—and there is no regret in that! But sadness that is merely human causes death. ¹¹See what God did with this sadness of yours: how earnest it has made you, how eager to prove your innocence! Such indignation, such alarm, such feelings, such devotion, such readiness to punish wrongdoing! You have shown yourselves to be without fault in the whole matter.

¹²So, even though I wrote that letter, it was not because of the one who did wrong or the one who was wronged. Instead, I wrote it to make plain to you, in God's sight,

how deep your devotion to us really is. ¹³That is why we were encouraged.

Not only were we encouraged; how happy Titus made us with his happiness over the way in which all of you helped to cheer him up! ¹⁴I did boast of you to him, and you have not disappointed me. We have always spoken the truth to you, and in the same way the boast we made to Titus has proved true. ¹⁵And so his love for you grows stronger, as he remembers how all of you were ready to obey his instructions, how you welcomed him with fear and trembling. ¹⁶How happy I am that I can depend on you completely!

Christian Giving

8 ¹Our friends, we want you to know what God's grace has accomplished in the churches in Macedonia. ²They have been severely tested by the troubles they went through; but their joy was so great that they were extremely generous in their giving, even though they are very poor. ³I can assure you that they gave as much as they could, and even more than they could. Of their own free will ⁴they begged us and pleaded for the privilege of having a part in helping God's people in Judea. ⁵It was more than we could have hoped for! First they gave themselves to the Lord; and then, by God's will they gave themselves to us as well. ⁶So we urged Titus, who began this work, to continue it and help you complete this special service of love. ⁷You are so rich in all you have: in faith, speech, and knowledge, in your eagerness to help and in your love for us.ᵉ And so we want you to be generous also in this service of love.

⁸I am not laying down any rules. But by showing how eager others are to help, I am trying to find out how real your own love is. ⁹You know the grace of our Lord Jesus Christ; rich as he was, he made himself poor for your sake, in order to make you rich by means of his poverty.

¹⁰My opinion is that it is better for you to finish now what you began last year. You were the first, not only to act, but also to be

---

ᵉ **8:7** *your love for us; some manuscripts have* our love for you.
7:5 2 Cor 2:13   **8:1–4** Rom 15:26

willing to act. ¹¹On with it, then, and finish the job! Be as eager to finish it as you were to plan it, and do it with what you now have. ¹²If you are eager to give, God will accept your gift on the basis of what you have to give, not on what you don't have.

¹³⁻¹⁴I am not trying to relieve others by putting a burden on you; but since you have plenty at this time, it is only fair that you should help those who are in need. Then, when you are in need and they have plenty, they will help you. In this way both are treated equally. ¹⁵As the scripture says, "The one who gathered much did not have too much, and the one who gathered little did not have too little."

Titus and His Companions

¹⁶How we thank God for making Titus as eager as we are to help you! ¹⁷Not only did he welcome our request; he was so eager to help that of his own free will he decided to go to you. ¹⁸With him we are sending the brother who is highly respected in all the churches for his work in preaching the gospel. ¹⁹And besides that, he has been chosen and appointed by the churches to travel with us as we carry out this service of love for the sake of the Lord's glory and in order to show that we want to help.

²⁰We are being careful not to stir up any complaints about the way we handle this generous gift. ²¹Our purpose is to do what is right, not only in the sight of the Lord, but also in the sight of others.

²²So we are sending our brother with them; we have tested him many times and found him always very eager to help. And now that he has so much confidence in you, he is all the more eager to help. ²³As for Titus, he is my partner and works with me to help you; as for the other brothers who are going with him, they represent the churches and bring glory to Christ. ²⁴Show your love to them, so that all the churches will be sure of it and know that we are right in boasting about you.

Help for Needy Believers

9 ¹There is really no need for me to write you about the help being sent to God's people in Judea. ²I know that you are willing to help, and I have boasted of you to the people in Macedonia. "The believers in Achaia," I said, "have been ready to help since last year." Your eagerness has stirred up most of them. ³Now I am sending these believers, so that our boasting about you in this matter may not turn out to be empty words. But, just as I said, you will be ready with your help. ⁴However, if the people from Macedonia should come with me and find out that you are not ready, how ashamed we would be—not to speak of your shame—for feeling so sure of you! ⁵So I thought it was necessary to urge these believers to go to you ahead of me and get ready in advance the gift you promised to make. Then it will be ready when I arrive, and it will show that you give because you want to, not because you have to.

⁶Remember that the person who plants few seeds will have a small crop; the one who plants many seeds will have a large crop. ⁷You should each give, then, as you have decided, not with regret or out of a sense of duty; for God loves the one who gives gladly. ⁸And God is able to give you more than you need, so that you will always have all you need for yourselves and more than enough for every good cause. ⁹As the scripture says,

"He gives generously to the needy; his kindness lasts forever."

¹⁰And God, who supplies seed for the sower and bread to eat, will also supply you with all the seed you need and will make it grow and produce a rich harvest from your generosity. ¹¹He will always make you rich enough to be generous at all times, so that many will thank God for your gifts which they receive from us. ¹²For this service you perform not only meets the needs of God's people, but also produces an outpouring of gratitude to God. ¹³And because of the proof which this service of yours brings, many will give glory to God for your loyalty to the gospel of Christ, which you profess, and for your generosity in sharing with them

8:15 Ex 16:18   **8:21** Prov 3:4 (LXX)   **9:7** Sir 20:10–15   **9:9** Ps 112:9   **9:10** Isa 55:10

and everyone else. ¹⁴And so with deep affection they will pray for you because of the extraordinary grace God has shown you. ¹⁵Let us thank God for his priceless gift!

Paul Defends His Ministry

10 ¹I, Paul, make a personal appeal to you—I who am said to be meek and mild when I am with you, but harsh with you when I am away. By the gentleness and kindness of Christ ²I beg you not to force me to be harsh when I come; for I am sure I can deal harshly with those who say that we act from worldly motives. ³It is true that we live in the world, but we do not fight from worldly motives. ⁴The weapons we use in our fight are not the world's weapons but God's powerful weapons, which we use to destroy strongholds. We destroy false arguments; ⁵we pull down every proud obstacle that is raised against the knowledge of God; we take every thought captive and make it obey Christ. ⁶And after you have proved your complete loyalty, we will be ready to punish any act of disloyalty.

⁷You are looking at the outward appearance of things. Are there some there who reckon themselves to belong to Christ? Well, let them think again about themselves, because we belong to Christ just as much as they do. ⁸For I am not ashamed, even if I have boasted somewhat too much about the authority that the Lord has given us—authority to build you up, not to tear you down. ⁹I do not want it to appear that I am trying to frighten you with my letters. ¹⁰Someone will say, "Paul's letters are severe and strong, but when he is with us in person, he is weak, and his words are nothing!" ¹¹Such a person must understand that there is no difference between what we write in our letters when we are away and what we will do when we are there with you.

¹²Of course we would not dare classify ourselves or compare ourselves with those who rate themselves so highly. How stupid they are! They make up their own standards to measure themselves by, and they judge themselves by their own standards! ¹³As for

Preach the Good News in other countries beyond you. (10:16)

us, however, our boasting will not go beyond certain limits; it will stay within the limits of the work which God has set for us, and this includes our work among you. ¹⁴And since you are within those limits, we were not going beyond them when we came to you, bringing the Good News about Christ. ¹⁵So we do not boast about the work that others have done beyond the limits God set for us. Instead, we hope that your faith may grow and that we may be able to do a much greater work among you, always within the limits that God has set. ¹⁶Then we can preach the Good News in other countries beyond you and shall not have to boast about work already done in someone else's field.

¹⁷But as the scripture says, "Whoever wants to boast must boast about what the Lord has done." ¹⁸For it is when the Lord thinks well of us that we are really approved, and not when we think well of ourselves.

Paul and the False Apostles

11 ¹I wish you would tolerate me, even when I am a bit foolish. Please do! ²I am jealous for you, just as God is; you are like a pure virgin whom I have promised in marriage to one man only, Christ himself. ³I am afraid that your minds will be corrupted and that you will abandon your full and pure devotion to Christ—in the same way that Eve was deceived by the snake's clever lies. ⁴For you gladly tolerate anyone who comes to you and preaches a different Jesus, not the one we preached; and you accept a spirit and

10:17 Jer 9:24   **11:3** Gen 3:1–5, 13

a gospel completely different from the Spirit and the gospel you received from us!

⁵I do not think that I am the least bit inferior to those very special so-called "apostles" of yours! ⁶Perhaps I am an amateur in speaking, but certainly not in knowledge; we have made this clear to you at all times and in all conditions.

⁷I did not charge you a thing when I preached the Good News of God to you; I humbled myself in order to make you important. Was that wrong of me? ⁸While I was working among you, I was paid by other churches. I was robbing them, so to speak, in order to help you. ⁹And during the time I was with you I did not bother you for help when I needed money; the believers who came from Macedonia brought me everything I needed. As in the past, so in the future: I will never be a burden to you! ¹⁰By Christ's truth in me, I promise that this boast of mine will not be silenced anywhere in all of Achaia. ¹¹Do I say this because I don't love you? God knows I love you!

¹²I will go on doing what I am doing now, in order to keep those other "apostles" from having any reason for boasting and saying that they work in the same way that we do. ¹³Those men are not true apostles—they are false apostles, who lie about their work and disguise themselves to look like real apostles of Christ. ¹⁴Well, no wonder! Even Satan can disguise himself to look like an angel of light! ¹⁵So it is no great thing if his servants disguise themselves to look like servants of righteousness. In the end they will get exactly what their actions deserve.

Paul's Sufferings as an Apostle

¹⁶I repeat: no one should think that I am a fool. But if you do, at least accept me as a fool, just so I will have a little to boast of. ¹⁷Of course what I am saying now is not what the Lord would have me say; in this matter of boasting I am really talking like a fool. ¹⁸But since there are so many who boast for merely human reasons, I will do the same. ¹⁹You yourselves are so wise, and so you gladly tolerate fools! ²⁰You tolerate anyone who

Satan can disguise himself. (11:14)

orders you around or takes advantage of you or traps you or looks down on you or slaps you in the face. ²¹I am ashamed to admit that we were too timid to do those things!

But if anyone dares to boast about something—I am talking like a fool—I will be just as daring. ²²Are they Hebrews? So am I. Are they Israelites? So am I. Are they Abraham's descendants? So am I. ²³Are they Christ's servants? I sound like a madman—but I am a better servant than they are! I have worked much harder, I have been in prison more times, I have been whipped much more, and I have been near death more often. ²⁴Five times I was given the thirty-nine lashes by the Jews; ²⁵three times I was whipped by the Romans; and once I was stoned. I have been in three shipwrecks, and once I spent twenty-four hours in the water. ²⁶In my many travels I have been in danger from floods and from robbers, in danger from my own people and from Gentiles; there have been dangers in the cities, dangers in the wilds, dangers on the high seas, and dangers from false friends. ²⁷There has been work and toil; often I have gone without sleep; I have been hungry and thirsty; I have often been without enough food, shelter, or clothing. ²⁸And not to

11:9 Phil 4:15–18 **11:23** Acts 16:23 **11:24** Deut 25:3 **11:25 a** Acts 16:22; **b** Acts 14:19 **11:26 a** Acts 9:23; **b** Acts 14:5

mention other things, every day I am under the pressure of my concern for all the churches. 29 When someone is weak, then I feel weak too; when someone is led into sin, I am filled with distress.

30 If I must boast, I will boast about things that show how weak I am. 31 The God and Father of the Lord Jesus—blessed be his name forever!—knows that I am not lying. 32 When I was in Damascus, the governor under King Aretas placed guards at the city gates to arrest me. 33 But I was let down in a basket through an opening in the wall and escaped from him.

Paul's Visions and Revelations

12 1 I have to boast, even though it doesn't do any good. But I will now talk about visions and revelations given me by the Lord. 2 I know a certain Christian man who fourteen years ago was snatched up to the highest heaven (I do not know whether this actually happened or whether he had a vision—only God knows). 3-4 I repeat, I know that this man was snatched to Paradise (again, I do not know whether this actually happened or whether it was a vision—only God knows), and there he heard things which cannot be put into words, things that human lips may not speak. 5 So I will boast about this man—but I will not boast about myself, except the things that show how weak I am. 6 If I wanted to boast, I would not be a fool, because I would be telling the truth. But I will not boast, because I do not want any of you to have a higher opinion of me than you have as a result of what you have seen me do and heard me say.

7 But to keep me from being puffed up with pride because of the many wonderful things I saw, I was given a painful physical ailment, which acts as Satan's messenger to beat me and keep me from being proud. 8 Three times I prayed to the Lord about this and asked him to take it away. 9 But his answer was: "My grace is all you need, for my power is greatest when you are weak." I am most happy, then, to be proud of my weaknesses, in order to feel the protection of

Christ's power over me. 10 I am content with weaknesses, insults, hardships, persecutions, and difficulties for Christ's sake. For when I am weak, then I am strong.

Paul's Concern for the Corinthians

11 I am acting like a fool—but you have made me do it. You are the ones who ought to show your approval of me. For even if I am nothing, I am in no way inferior to those very special "apostles" of yours. 12 The many miracles and wonders that prove that I am an apostle were performed among you with much patience. 13 How were you treated any worse than the other churches, except that I did not bother you for financial help? Please forgive me for being so unfair!

14 This is now the third time that I am ready to come to visit you—and I will not make any demands on you. It is you I want, not your money. After all, children should not have to provide for their parents, but parents should provide for their children. 15 I will be glad to spend all I have, and myself as well, in order to help you. Will you love me less because I love you so much?

16 You will agree, then, that I was not a burden to you. But someone will say that I was tricky, and trapped you with lies. 17 How? Did I take advantage of you through any of the messengers I sent? 18 I begged Titus to go, and I sent the other believer with him. Would you say that Titus took advantage of you? Do not he and I act from the very same motives and behave in the same way?

19 Perhaps you think that all along we have been trying to defend ourselves before you. No! We speak as Christ would have us speak in the presence of God, and everything we do, dear friends, is done to help you. 20 I am afraid that when I get there I will find you different from what I would like you to be and you will find me different from what you would like me to be. I am afraid that I will find quarreling and jealousy, hot tempers and selfishness, insults and gossip, pride and disorder. 21 I am afraid that the next time I come my God will humiliate me in your

presence, and I shall weep over many who sinned in the past and have not repented of the immoral things they have done—their lust and their sexual sins.

Final Warnings and Greetings

13 ¹This is now the third time that I am coming to visit you. "Any accusation must be upheld by the evidence of two or more witnesses"—as the scripture says. ²I want to tell those of you who have sinned in the past, and all the others; I said it before during my second visit to you, but I will say it again now that I am away: the next time I come nobody will escape punishment. ³You will have all the proof you want that Christ speaks through me. When he deals with you, he is not weak; instead, he shows his power among you. ⁴For even though it was in weakness that he was put to death on the cross, it is by God's power that he lives. In union with him we also are weak; but in our relations with you we shall share God's power in his life.

⁵Put yourselves to the test and judge yourselves, to find out whether you are living in faith. Surely you know that Christ Jesus is in you?—unless you have completely failed. ⁶I trust you will know that we are not failures. ⁷We pray to God that you will do no wrong—not in order to show that we are a success, but so that you may do what is right, even though we may seem to be failures. ⁸For we cannot do a thing against the truth, but only for it. ⁹We are glad when we are weak but you are strong. And so we also pray that you will become perfect. ¹⁰That is why I write this while I am away from you; it is so that when I arrive I will not have to deal harshly with you in using the authority that the Lord has given me—authority to build you up, not to tear you down.

¹¹And now, my friends, good-bye! Strive for perfection; listen to my appeals; agree with one another; live in peace. And the God of love and peace will be with you.

¹²Greet one another with the kiss of peace.

All of God's people send you their greetings.

¹³The grace of the Lord Jesus Christ, the love of God, and the fellowship of the Holy Spirit be with you all.

13:1 Deut 17:6; 19:15

Galatians

Do you sometimes know what your mom, dad, or teacher is feeling just by their voice? The people of Galatia knew what Paul was feeling just by reading the first few paragraphs of this letter: *angry!*

The Galatians were a group of people Paul had visited. When he visited them, he helped them learn about Jesus and probably set up churches in their homes. After Paul left, some of those he taught started to change the way they acted and who they believed. When Paul heard about their behavior, he wrote this letter. He wrote it to remind them of the importance of faith and to get them back on track.

Chap. 2:11–14

Headlines

- An Angry Message (1:6–10)
- Paul Defends His Role as Apostle (1:11—2:14)
- Galatians Warned That Only Faith Saves (3:1–14)
- Galatians Told to Live Like Christians! (5:16–26)

FACTOIDS

Who wrote this book? Saint Paul, after his missionary trip to Galatia.

When was it written? Around AD 54 to 55, about twenty years after Jesus' Resurrection.

Who was it written for? Paul wrote this letter to the Gentile (non-Jewish) Christians in Galatia who were being influenced by missionaries who were preaching something different from what Paul had taught.

Why was it written? Paul wrote to remind the Galatians that they must live by faith in Christ and that non-Jewish Christians were not required to follow Jewish ceremonial laws.

Jesus connection. Paul reminds the Galatians of Jesus' commandment to love one another (5:1–15).

Important themes

- Salvation comes from faith, not just from following rules.
- All God's children are equal and have the same rights and responsibilities.
- Living as faithful Christians means loving and caring for one another.

GALATIANS

1 ¹From Paul, whose call to be an apostle did not come from human beings or by human means, but from Jesus Christ and God the Father, who raised him from death. ²All the believers who are here join me in sending greetings to the churches of Galatia:

³May God our Father and the Lord Jesus Christ give you grace and peace.

⁴In order to set us free from this present evil age, Christ gave himself for our sins, in obedience to the will of our God and Father. ⁵To God be the glory forever and ever! Amen.

The One Gospel

⁶I am surprised at you! In no time at all you are deserting the one who called you by the grace of Christ,ᵃ and are accepting another gospel. ⁷Actually, there is no "other gospel," but I say this because there are some people who are upsetting you and trying to change the gospel of Christ. ⁸But even if we or an angel from heaven should preach to you a gospel that is different from the one we preached to you, may he be condemned to hell! ⁹We have said it before, and now I say it again: if anyone preaches to you a gospel that is different from the one you accepted, may he be condemned to hell!

¹⁰Does this sound as if I am trying to win human approval? No indeed! What I want is God's approval! Am I trying to be popular with people? If I were still trying to do so, I would not be a servant of Christ.

How Paul Became an Apostle

¹¹Let me tell you, my friends, that the gospel I preach is not of human origin. ¹²I did not receive it from any human being, nor did anyone teach it to me. It was Jesus Christ himself who revealed it to me.

¹³You have been told how I used to live when I was devoted to the Jewish religion, how I persecuted without mercy the church of God and did my best to destroy it. ¹⁴I was ahead of most other Jews of my age in my practice of the Jewish religion, and was much more devoted to the traditions of our ancestors.

¹⁵But God in his grace chose me even before I was born, and called me to serve him. And when he decided ¹⁶to reveal his Son to me, so that I might preach the Good News about him to the Gentiles, I did not go to anyone for advice, ¹⁷nor did I go to Jerusalem to see those who were apostles before me. Instead, I went at once to Arabia, and then I returned to Damascus. ¹⁸It was three years later that I went to Jerusalem to obtain information from Peter, and I stayed with him for two weeks. ¹⁹I did not see any other apostle except James,ᵇ the Lord's brother.

²⁰What I write is true. God knows that I am not lying!

²¹Afterward I went to places in Syria and Cilicia. ²²At that time the members of the churches in Judea did not know me personally. ²³They knew only what others were saying: "The man who used to persecute us is now preaching the faith that he once tried to destroy!" ²⁴And so they praised God because of me.

Paul and the Other Apostles

2 ¹Fourteen years later I went back to Jerusalem with Barnabas, taking Titus along with me. ²I went because God revealed to me that I should go. In a private meeting with the leaders I explained the gospel message that I preach to the Gentiles. I did not want my work in the past or in the present to be a failure. ³My companion Titus, even though he is Greek, was not forced to be circumcised, ⁴although some

---

ᵃ **1:6** by the grace of Christ; *some manuscripts have* by his grace.   ᵇ **1:19** any other apostle except James; *or any other apostle; the only other person I saw was James.*

1:13 Acts 8:3; 22:4, 5; 26:9–11   **1:14** Acts 22:3   **1:15, 16** Acts 9:3–6; 22:6–10; 26:13–18   **1:18** Acts 9:26–30   **2:1** Acts 11:30; 15:2

Galatians

Salvation by Faith

Do you know someone who does things to look like they have a good and honest life but when you talk to them, it seems like something is missing? They may be missing an important part of a relationship with God: faith. In Galatians Saint Paul insists that having faith in Jesus Christ as our Savior is what saves us from sin and death. The Old Law that emphasized doing the right things is not enough. Because of original sin we can never live perfectly. Our own actions alone will never restore our true relationship with God.

The Catholic Church teaches that actions are important but faith is necessary for salvation. Salvation means our relationship with God is restored to what God intended from the beginning. This means that you can do all sorts of things to look like you have a good life, but it is faith that is the first step toward salvation.

— Galatians 2:15—3:5

wanted it done. Pretending to be believers, these men slipped into our group as spies, in order to find out about the freedom we have through our union with Christ Jesus. They wanted to make slaves of us, ⁵but in order to keep the truth of the gospel safe for you, we did not give in to them for a minute.

⁶But those who seemed to be the leaders— I say this because it makes no difference to me what they were; God does not judge by outward appearances—those leaders, I say, made no new suggestions to me. ⁷On the contrary, they saw that God had given me the task of preaching the gospel to the Gentiles, just as he had given Peter the task of preaching the gospel to the Jews. ⁸For by God's power I was made an apostle to the Gentiles, just as Peter was made an apostle to the Jews. ⁹James, Peter, and John, who seemed to be the leaders, recognized that God had given me this special task; so they shook hands with Barnabas and me, as a sign that we were all partners. We agreed that Barnabas and I would work

among the Gentiles and they among the Jews. ¹⁰All they asked was that we should remember the needy in their group, which is the very thing I have*ᶜ* been eager to do.

Paul Rebukes Peter at Antioch

¹¹But when Peter came to Antioch, I opposed him in public, because he was clearly wrong. ¹²Before some men who had been sent by James arrived there, Peter had been eating with the Gentile believers. But after these men arrived, he drew back and would not eat with the Gentiles, because he was afraid of those who were in favor of circumcising them. ¹³The other Jewish believers also started acting like cowards along with Peter; and even Barnabas was swept along by their cowardly action. ¹⁴When I saw that they were not walking a straight path in line with the truth of the gospel, I said to Peter in front of them all, "You are a Jew, yet you have been living like a Gentile, not like a

ᶜ **2:10** have; *or* had.
2:6 Deut 10:17

Saint Paul sure could get upset when people were falling away from the truth. Read Galatians 3:1–4 to find out just how mad he was.

Jew. How, then, can you try to force Gentiles to live like Jews?"

Jews and Gentiles Are Saved by Faith

15 Indeed, we are Jews by birth and not "Gentile sinners," as they are called. 16 Yet we know that a person is put right with God only through faith in Jesus Christ, never by doing what the Law requires. We, too, have believed in Christ Jesus in order to be put right with God through our faith in Christ, and not by doing what the Law requires. For no one is put right with God by doing what the Law requires. 17 If, then, as we try to be put right with God by our union with Christ, we are found to be sinners, as much as the Gentiles are—does this mean that Christ is serving the cause of sin? By no means! 18 If I start to rebuild the system of Law that I tore down, then I show myself to be someone who breaks the Law. 19 So far as the Law is concerned, however, I am dead—killed by the Law itself—in order that I might live for God. I have been put to death with Christ on his cross, 20 so that it is no longer I who live, but it is Christ who lives in me. This life that I live now, I live by faith in the Son of God, who loved me and gave his life for me. 21 I refuse to reject the grace of God. But if a person is put right with God through the Law, it means that Christ died for nothing!

Law or Faith

3 1 You foolish Galatians! Who put a spell on you? Before your very eyes you had a clear description of the death of Jesus Christ on the cross! 2 Tell me this one thing: did you receive God's Spirit by doing what the Law requires or by hearing the gospel and believing it? 3 How can you be so foolish! You began by God's Spirit; do you now want to finish by your own power? 4 Did all your experience mean nothing at all? Surely it meant something! 5 Does God give you the Spirit and work miracles among you because you do what the Law requires or because you hear the gospel and believe it?

6 Consider the experience of Abraham; as the scripture says, "He believed God, and because of his faith God accepted him as righteous." 7 You should realize, then, that the real descendants of Abraham are the people who have faith. 8 The scripture predicted that God would put the Gentiles right with himself through faith. And so the scripture announced the Good News to Abraham: "Through you God will bless all people." 9 Abraham believed and was blessed; so all who believe are blessed as he was.

10 Those who depend on obeying the Law live under a curse. For the scripture says, "Whoever does not always obey everything that is written in the book of the Law is under God's curse!" 11 Now, it is clear that no one is put right with God by means of the Law, because the scripture says, "Only the person who is put right with God through faith shall live."d 12 But the Law has nothing to do with faith. Instead, as the scripture says, "Whoever *does* everything the Law requires will live."

13 But by becoming a curse for us Christ has redeemed us from the curse that the Law brings; for the scripture says, "Anyone who is hanged on a tree is under God's curse." 14 Christ did this in order that the blessing which God promised to Abraham might be given to the Gentiles by means of Christ Jesus, so that through faith we might receive the Spirit promised by God.

The Law and the Promise

15 My friends, I am going to use an everyday example: when two people agree on a matter and sign an agreement, no one can break it or add anything to it. 16 Now, God made his promises to Abraham and to his descendant. The scripture does not use the plural "descendants," meaning many people, but the singular "descendant," meaning one person only, namely, Christ. 17 What I mean is that God made a covenant with Abraham and promised to keep it. The Law, which was given four hundred and thirty years later, cannot break that covenant and cancel God's promise. 18 For if God's gift depends on the

d **3:11** put right with God through faith shall live; *or* put right with God shall live through faith.
2:16 a Ps 143:2; Rom 3:20; **b** Rom 3:22   **3:6** Gen 15:6; Rom 4:3   **3:7** Rom 4:16   **3:8** Gen 12:3
3:10 Deut 27:26 (LXX)   **3:11** Hab 2:4   **3:12** Lev 18:5   **3:13** Deut 21:23   **3:17** Ex 12:40   **3:18** Rom 4:14

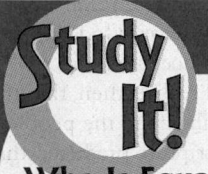

Who Is Equal?

Sometimes in the Old Testament, some people are treated better than others. Men had more freedom and privileges than women. People who were wealthy enough to own slaves thought God favored them over poor people. Jewish people believed that God favored them over all other peoples.

Jesus' message of equality and his new commandment to love one another changed that thinking. His message that all people are equally loved by God was scary to the Jews who had been living with the Old Law. Paul had to remind the Galatians that his teaching about faith, and not the Old Law his opponents were trying to bring back, was the truth revealed by Jesus. Paul reminded the Galatians that equality was one of the cornerstones of Jesus' message. Paul's list included gender (man and woman), religion (Jews and Gentiles), and status (free or slave). What categories would Paul write about if he looked at our society?

— Galatians 3:26–29

Law, then it no longer depends on his promise. However, it was because of his promise that God gave that gift to Abraham.

19 What, then, was the purpose of the Law? It was added in order to show what wrongdoing is, and it was meant to last until the coming of Abraham's descendant, to whom the promise was made. The Law was handed down by angels, with a man acting as a go-between. 20 But a go-between is not needed when only one person is involved; and God is one.[e]

---

e **3:20** and God is one; or and God acts alone.
3:29 Rom 4:13

The Purpose of the Law

21 Does this mean that the Law is against God's promises? No, not at all! For if human beings had received a law that could bring life, then everyone could be put right with God by obeying it. 22 But the scripture says that the whole world is under the power of sin; and so the gift which is promised on the basis of faith in Jesus Christ is given to those who believe.

23 But before the time for faith came, the Law kept us all locked up as prisoners until this coming faith should be revealed. 24 And so the Law was in charge of us until Christ came, in order that we might then be put right with God through faith. 25 Now that the time for faith is here, the Law is no longer in charge of us.

26 It is through faith that all of you are God's children in union with Christ Jesus. 27 You were baptized into union with Christ, and now you are clothed, so to speak, with the life of Christ himself. 28 So there is no difference between Jews and Gentiles, between slaves and free people, between men and women; you are all one in union with Christ Jesus. 29 If you belong to Christ, then

You are all one in union with Christ Jesus. (3:28)

you are the descendants of Abraham and will receive what God has promised.

4 ¹But now to continue—the son who will receive his father's property is treated just like a slave while he is young, even though he really owns everything. ²While he is young, there are men who take care of him and manage his affairs until the time set by his father. ³In the same way, we too were slaves of the ruling spirits of the universe before we reached spiritual maturity. ⁴But when the right time finally came, God sent his own Son. He came as the son of a human mother and lived under the Jewish Law, ⁵to redeem those who were under the Law, so that we might become God's children.

⁶To show that you are *f* his children, God sent the Spirit of his Son into our hearts, the Spirit who cries out, "Father, my Father." ⁷So then, you are no longer a slave but a child. And since you are his child, God will give you all that he has for his children.

You are not longer a slave. (4:7)

Paul's Concern for the Galatians

⁸In the past you did not know God, and so you were slaves of beings who are not gods. ⁹But now that you know God—or, I should say, now that God knows you—how is it that you want to turn back to those weak and pitiful ruling spirits? Why do you want to become their slaves all over again? ¹⁰You pay special attention to certain days,

Shape Up!

Paul might sound a little conceited in Galatians 4:12. But he's not bragging. It was common in his time to use this method to tell people how to behave. So he tells the Galatians to act better. He reminds them about how happily they first received his message (4:13–15). He reminds them that he cares about them deeply, in fact, so much that he calls them his children (4:19).

If you have friends that need to act better, what is a way for you to be a good example to them, without bragging?

— Galatians 4:8–21

months, seasons, and years. ¹¹I am worried about you! Can it be that all my work for you has been for nothing?

¹²I beg you, my friends, be like me. After all, I am like you. You have not done me any wrong. ¹³You remember why I preached the gospel to you the first time; it was because I was sick. ¹⁴But even though my physical condition was a great trial to you, you did not despise or reject me. Instead, you received me as you would an angel from heaven; you received me as you would Christ Jesus. ¹⁵You were so happy! What has happened? I myself can say that you would have taken out your own eyes, if you could, and given them to me. ¹⁶Have I now become your enemy by telling you the truth?

¹⁷Those other people show a deep interest in you, but their intentions are not good. All they want is to separate you from me, so that

f **4:6** To show that you are; *or* Because you are.
4:5–7 Rom 8:15–17

you will have the same interest in them as they have in you. 18 Now, it is good to have such a deep interest if the purpose is good— this is true always, and not merely when I am with you. 19 My dear children! Once again, just like a mother in childbirth, I feel the same kind of pain for you until Christ's nature is formed in you. 20 How I wish I were with you now, so that I could take a different attitude toward you. I am so worried about you!

The Example of Hagar and Sarah

21 Let me ask those of you who want to be subject to the Law: do you not hear what the Law says? 22 It says that Abraham had two sons, one by a slave woman, the other by a free woman. 23 His son by the slave woman was born in the usual way, but his son by the free woman was born as a result of God's promise. 24 These things can be understood as a figure: the two women represent two covenants. The one whose children are born in slavery is Hagar, and she represents the covenant made at Mount Sinai. 25 Hagar, who stands for Mount Sinai in Arabia, is*g* a figure of the present city of Jerusalem, in slavery with all its people. 26 But the heavenly Jerusalem is free, and she is our mother. 27 For the scripture says,

"Be happy, you childless woman!
　　Shout and cry with joy, you who never
　　　　felt the pains of childbirth!
For the woman who was deserted will
　　have more children
　　than the woman whose husband never
　　　　left her."

28 Now, you, my friends, are God's children as a result of his promise, just as Isaac was. 29 At that time the son who was born in the usual way persecuted the one who was born because of God's Spirit; and it is the same now. 30 But what does the scripture say? It says, "Send the slave woman and her son away; for the son of the slave woman will

not have a part of the father's property along with the son of the free woman." 31 So then, my friends, we are not the children of a slave woman but of a free woman.

Preserve Your Freedom

5 1 Freedom is what we have—Christ has set us free! Stand, then, as free people, and do not allow yourselves to become slaves again.

2 Listen! I, Paul, tell you that if you allow yourselves to be circumcised, it means that Christ is of no use to you at all. 3 Once more I warn any man who allows himself to be circumcised that he is obliged to obey the whole Law. 4 Those of you who try to be put right with God by obeying the Law have cut yourselves off from Christ. You are outside God's grace. 5 As for us, our hope is that God will put us right with him; and this is what we wait for by the power of God's Spirit working through our faith. 6 For when we are in union with Christ Jesus, neither circumcision nor the lack of it makes any difference at all; what matters is faith that works through love.

7 You were doing so well! Who made you stop obeying the truth? How did he persuade you? 8 It was not done by God, who calls you. 9 "It takes only a little yeast to make the whole batch of dough rise," as they say. 10 But I still feel confident about you. Our life in union with the Lord makes me confident that you will not take a different view and that whoever is upsetting you will be punished by God.

11 But as for me, my friends, if I continue to preach that circumcision is necessary, why am I still being persecuted? If that were true, then my preaching about the cross of Christ would cause no trouble. 12 I wish that the people who are upsetting you would go all the way; let them go on and castrate themselves!

13 As for you, my friends, you were called

---

g **4:25** Hagar . . . is; *some manuscripts have* Sinai is a mountain in Arabia, and it is.
4:22 *a* Gen 16:15; *b* Gen 21:2　**4:27** Isa 54:1　**4:29** Gen 21:9　**4:30** Gen 21:10　**5:9** 1 Cor 5:6

The things listed in Galatians 5:22–23 are called the *fruits of the Holy Spirit*: love, joy, peace, patience, kindness, goodness, faithfulness, humility, and self-control.

Who Do You Follow?

"C'mon, just do it. One little puff won't kill you." It seemed like every guy in Jack's class had tried smoking. Even Jack's best friend, Carlo, was now urging him to try it. Jack just walked home, ignoring Carlo and the other guys. He heard them laughing as he walked away and felt hurt.

Jack was surprised when Carlo called him that night. During the conversation he asked Carlo who had convinced him to try smoking. When Carlo didn't answer, Jack said: "It doesn't matter who it is, what matters is that we shouldn't be doing it. I don't want to lose my new curfew over a stupid cigarette." Carlo didn't answer for a little bit then said: "Whatever, Jack. I'll talk to you tomorrow, and maybe we can hang out after school, and avoid the other guys together. It's probably better that I follow you."

Saint Paul is concerned that someone has turned the Galatians away from the truth (Galatians 5:7). He hopes his good example and urging can bring them back. How can you help the people you know stay on the right path?

— Galatians 5:7–10

to be free. But do not let this freedom become an excuse for letting your physical desires control you. Instead, let love make you serve one another. 14For the whole Law is summed up in one commandment: "Love your neighbor as you love yourself." 15But if you act like wild animals, hurting and harming each other, then watch out, or you will completely destroy one another.

The Spirit and Human Nature

16What I say is this: let the Spirit direct your lives, and you will not satisfy the desires of the human nature. 17For what our human nature wants is opposed to what the Spirit wants, and what the Spirit wants is opposed to what our human nature wants. These two are enemies, and this means that you cannot do what you want to do. 18If the Spirit leads you, then you are not subject to the Law.

19What human nature does is quite plain. It shows itself in immoral, filthy, and indecent actions; 20in worship of idols and witchcraft. People become enemies and they fight; they become jealous, angry, and ambitious. They separate into parties and groups; 21they are envious, get drunk, have orgies, and do other things like these. I warn you now as I have before: those who do these things will not possess the Kingdom of God.

22But the Spirit produces love, joy, peace, patience, kindness, goodness, faithfulness, 23humility, and self-control. There is no law against such things as these. 24And those who belong to Christ Jesus have put to death their human nature with all its passions and desires. 25The Spirit has given us life; he must also control our lives. 26We must not be proud or irritate one another or be jealous of one another.

Bear One Another's Burdens

6 1My friends, if someone is caught in any kind of wrongdoing, those of you who are spiritual should set him right; but you must do it in a gentle way. And keep an eye on yourselves, so that you will not be tempted, too. 2Help carry one another's burdens, and in this way you will obey^h the law

Help carry one another's burdens. (6:2)

^h 6:2 you will obey; *some manuscripts have* obey.
5:14 Lev 19:18   5:17 Rom 7:15–23

Pray It!

The Real Me

Some people act like they are more than they really are. Maybe you have tried to be something you aren't. The next time you need help in being yourself, say this prayer.

Dear God,
I want to be me.
But my parents tell me to be one thing,
my friends tell me to be my own person,
and television, music, and movies make me think
I should be something else.
It's all very confusing.
Then I remember you.
Who do you want me to be?
You have given me direction in your word.
Help me to hear your call.
Help me be the person you created me to be.
The real me.
Amen.

— **Galatians 6:3–4**

of Christ. ³If you think you are something when you really are nothing, you are only deceiving yourself. ⁴You should each judge your own conduct. If it is good, then you can be proud of what you yourself have done, without having to compare it with what someone else has done. ⁵For each of you have to carry your own load.

⁶If you are being taught the Christian message, you should share all the good things you have with your teacher.

⁷Do not deceive yourselves; no one makes a fool of God. You will reap exactly what you plant. ⁸If you plant in the field of your natural desires, from it you will gather the harvest of death; if you plant in the field of the Spirit, from the Spirit you will gather the harvest of eternal life. ⁹So let us not become tired of doing good; for if we do not give up, the time will come when we will reap the harvest. ¹⁰So then, as often as we have the chance, we should do good to

everyone, and especially to those who belong to our family in the faith.

Final Warning and Greeting

¹¹See what big letters I make as I write to you now with my own hand! ¹²The people who are trying to force you to be circumcised are the ones who want to show off and boast about external matters. They do it, however, only so that they may not be persecuted for the cross of Christ. ¹³Even those who practice circumcision do not obey the Law; they want you to be circumcised so that they can boast that you submitted to this physical ceremony. ¹⁴As for me, however, I will boast only about the cross of our Lord Jesus Christ; for by means of his cross the world is dead to me, and I am dead to the world. ¹⁵It does not matter at all whether or not one is circumcised; what does matter is being a new creature. ¹⁶As for those who follow this

rule in their lives, may peace and mercy be with them—with them and with all of God's people!

17 To conclude: let no one give me any more trouble, because the scars I have on my body show that I am the slave of Jesus.

18 May the grace of our Lord Jesus Christ be with you all, my friends. Amen.

Your Next Step

Congratulations on finishing the Letter to the Galatians! Use this space to write your thoughts and questions about this book. If you are following the suggested reading plan, go back to the Book of Esther in the Old Testament. It is a fascinating story about people who put their faith in God and who God saved from destruction.

Ephesians

Have you ever disagreed with someone on what was important to believe as a Christian? Saint Paul's Letter to the Ephesians was about overcoming disagreements between the Christians who were circumcised (Jewish Christians) and those who were not circumcised (the Gentile Christians). Think of the conflicts in our time between Jews and Arabs and between Christians, Jews, and Muslims. This lesson of unity is still important for us to learn today.

This letter also uses images of war to speak about peace. Chapter 6 mentions the armor of God, the breastplate of righteousness, the shield of faith, the helmet of salvation, and the sword of the Spirit. The way to find peace is to begin with the struggles and conflicts inside of us. Once we are peaceful people ourselves, then we can start to bring peace to others.

Chap. 5:21–33

Head lines

- Prayer for God's People (1:15–23)
- Unite in Christ! (2:11–22; 4:1–6)
- A Beautiful Prayer (3:14–21)
- Rules for Living as God's Children (5:1–10; 6:1–4)
- Prepare for Spiritual Battle! (6:10–20)

FACTOIDS

Who wrote this book? Probably a follower of Paul who wanted to summarize or introduce Paul's teachings about church.

When was it written? After Paul died, sometime between AD 70 and 95.

Who was it written for? Most likely this letter was not written directly for the people in the city of Ephesus, even though it's called the Letter to the Ephesians. It was a general letter, written for Christian communities in several different places.

Important themes

- There is a need for unity and peace, especially among Jews and Gentiles (non-Jews).
- Jesus' followers require inner strength to resist evil and do God's work.

EPHESIANS

1

1From Paul, who by God's will is an apostle of Christ Jesus—

To God's people in Ephesus,*a* who are faithful in their life in union with Christ Jesus:

2May God our Father and the Lord Jesus Christ give you grace and peace.

Spiritual Blessings in Christ

3Let us give thanks to the God and Father of our Lord Jesus Christ! For in our union with Christ he has blessed us by giving us every spiritual blessing in the heavenly world. **4**Even before the world was made, God had already chosen us to be his through our union with Christ, so that we would be holy and without fault before him.

Because of his love **5**God*b* had already decided that through Jesus Christ he would make us his children—this was his pleasure and purpose. **6**Let us praise God for his glorious grace, for the free gift he gave us in his dear Son! **7**For by the blood of Christ*c* we are set free, that is, our sins are forgiven. How great is the grace of God, **8**which he gave to us in such large measure!

In all his wisdom and insight **9**God did what he had purposed, and made known to us the secret plan he had already decided to complete by means of Christ. **10**This plan, which God will complete when the time is right, is to bring all creation together, everything in heaven and on earth, with Christ as head.

11All things are done according to God's plan and decision; and God chose us to be his own people in union with Christ because of his own purpose, based on what he had decided from the very beginning. **12**Let us, then, who were the first to hope in Christ, praise God's glory!

13And you also became God's people when you heard the true message, the Good News that brought you salvation. You believed in Christ, and God put his stamp of

Let us . . . praise God's glory. (1:12)

ownership on you by giving you the Holy Spirit he had promised. **14**The Spirit is the guarantee that we shall receive what God has promised his people, and this assures us that God will give complete freedom to those who are his. Let us praise his glory!

Paul's Prayer

15For this reason, ever since I heard of your faith in the Lord Jesus and your love for all of God's people, **16**I have not stopped giving thanks to God for you. I remember you in my prayers **17**and ask the God of our Lord Jesus Christ, the glorious Father, to give you the Spirit, who will make you wise and reveal God to you, so that you will know him. **18**I ask that your minds may be opened to see his light, so that you will know what is the hope to which he has called you, how rich are the wonderful blessings he promises his people, **19**and how very great is his power at work in us who believe. This power working in us is the same as the mighty strength **20**which he

---

a **1:1** *Some manuscripts do not have* in Ephesus.   *b* **1:5** before him. Because of his love God; *or* before him, and to live in love. God.   *c* **1:7** by the blood of Christ; *or* by the sacrificial death of Christ.

1:1 Acts 18:19–21; 19:1   **1:7** Col 1:14   **1:20** Ps 110:1

used when he raised Christ from death and seated him at his right side in the heavenly world. 21Christ rules there above all heavenly rulers, authorities, powers, and lords; he has a title superior to all titles of authority in this world and in the next. 22God put all things under Christ's feet and gave him to the church as supreme Lord over all things. 23The church is Christ's body, the completion of him who himself completes all things everywhere. *d*

From Death to Life

2 1In the past you were spiritually dead because of your disobedience and sins. 2At that time you followed the world's evil way; you obeyed the ruler of the spiritual powers in space, the spirit who now controls the people who disobey God. 3Actually all of us were like them and lived according to our natural desires, doing whatever suited the wishes of our own bodies and minds. In our natural condition we, like everyone else, were destined to suffer God's anger.

4But God's mercy is so abundant, and his love for us is so great, 5that while we were spiritually dead in our disobedience he brought us to life with Christ. It is by God's grace that you have been saved. 6In our union with Christ Jesus he raised us up with him to rule with him in the heavenly world. 7He did this to demonstrate for all time to come the extraordinary greatness of his grace in the love he showed us in Christ Jesus. 8-9For it is by God's grace that you have been saved through faith. It is not the result of your own efforts, but God's gift, so that no one can boast about it. 10God has made us what we are, and in our union with Christ Jesus he has created us for a life of good deeds, which he has already prepared for us to do.

One in Christ

11You Gentiles by birth—called "the uncircumcised" by the Jews, who call them-

selves the circumcised (which refers to what men do to their bodies)—remember what you were in the past. 12At that time you were apart from Christ. You were foreigners and did not belong to God's chosen people. You had no part in the covenants, which were based on God's promises to his people, and you lived in this world without hope and without God. 13But now, in union with Christ Jesus you, who used to be far away, have been brought near by the blood of Christ. *e* 14For Christ himself has brought us peace by making Jews and Gentiles one people. With his own body he broke down the wall that separated them and kept them enemies. 15He abolished the Jewish Law with its commandments and rules, in order to create out of the two races one new people in union with himself, in this way making peace. 16By his death on the cross Christ destroyed their enmity; by means of the cross he united both races into one body and brought them back to God. 17So Christ came and preached the Good News of peace to all—to you Gentiles, who were far away from God, and to the Jews, who were near to him. 18It is through Christ that all of us, Jews and Gentiles, are able to come in the one Spirit into the presence of the Father.

19So then, you Gentiles are not foreigners or strangers any longer; you are now citizens together with God's people and members of the family of God. 20You, too, are built upon the foundation laid by the apostles and prophets, *f* the cornerstone being Christ Jesus himself. 21He is the one who holds the whole building together and makes it grow into a sacred temple dedicated to the Lord. 22In union with him you too are being built together with all the others into a place where God lives through his Spirit.

Paul's Work for the Gentiles

3 1For this reason I, Paul, the prisoner of Christ Jesus for the sake of you Gentiles, pray to God. 2Surely you have heard

---

d **1:23** who himself completes all things everywhere; *or* who is himself completely filled with God's fullness. *e* **2:13** by the blood of Christ; *or* by the sacrificial death of Christ. *f* **2:20** the foundation laid by the apostles and prophets; *or* the foundation, that is, the apostles and prophets.
1:22 Ps 8:6   **1:22, 23** Col 1:18   **2:1–5** Col 2:13   **2:15** Col 2:14   **2:16** Col 1:20   **2:17** Isa 57:19

Pray It!

This Is a Prayer for Us!

The writer of the Letter to the Ephesians is praying an awesome prayer for us in chapter 3. It's not just for people long ago but for anyone who reads it throughout all time. Here's a simple version of the Ephesians' prayer you can say yourself.

I kneel before you, the Creator of heaven and earth.
I ask to receive the power of the Holy Spirit to strengthen my inner self.
I pray that your Son, Jesus Christ, lives in my heart.
I pray that my life is built on love.
I pray that I can know how huge your love is for me and for all the world.
Finally, I pray that your power will work in me to do more than I can ever
*   imagine or think to ask for.*
Glory to God forever!
Amen.

— **Ephesians 3:14–21**

that God in his grace has given me this work to do for your good. ³God revealed his secret plan and made it known to me. (I have written briefly about this, ⁴and if you will read what I have written, you can learn about my understanding of the secret of Christ.) ⁵In past times human beings were not told this secret, but God has revealed it now by the Spirit to his holy apostles and prophets. ⁶The secret is that by means of the gospel the Gentiles have a part with the Jews in God's blessings; they are members of the same body and share in the promise that God made through Christ Jesus.

⁷I was made a servant of the gospel by God's special gift, which he gave me through the working of his power. ⁸I am less than the least of all God's people; yet God gave me this privilege of taking to the Gentiles the Good News about the infinite riches of Christ, ⁹and of making all people see how God's secret plan is to be put into effect. God, who is the Creator of all things, kept his secret hidden through all the past ages, ¹⁰in order that at the present time, by means of the church, the angelic rulers and powers in the heavenly world might learn of his wis-

dom in all its different forms. ¹¹God did this according to his eternal purpose, which he achieved through Christ Jesus our Lord. ¹²In union with Christ and through our faith in him we have the boldness to go into God's presence with all confidence. ¹³I beg you, then, not to be discouraged because I am suffering for you; it is all for your benefit.

The Love of Christ

¹⁴For this reason I fall on my knees before the Father, ¹⁵from whom every family in heaven and on earth receives its true name. ¹⁶I ask God from the wealth of his glory to give you power through his Spirit to be strong in your inner selves, ¹⁷and I pray that Christ will make his home in your hearts through faith. I pray that you may have your roots and foundation in love, ¹⁸so that you, together with all God's people, may have the power to understand how broad and long, how high and deep, is Christ's love. ¹⁹Yes, may you come to know his love—although it can never be fully known—and so be completely filled with the very nature of God.

3:4–6 Col 1:26, 27   3:18 Sir 1:3

20 To him who by means of his power working in us is able to do so much more than we can ever ask for, or even think of: **21** to God be the glory in the church and in Christ Jesus for all time, forever and ever! Amen.

The Unity of the Body

4 **1** I urge you, then—I who am a prisoner because I serve the Lord: live a life that measures up to the standard God set when he called you. **2** Be always humble, gentle, and patient. Show your love by being tolerant with one another. **3** Do your best to preserve the unity which the Spirit gives by means of the peace that binds you together. **4** There is one body and one Spirit, just as there is one hope to which God has called you. **5** There is one Lord, one faith, one baptism; **6** there is one God and Father of all people, who is Lord of all, works through all, and is in all.

7 Each one of us has received a special gift in proportion to what Christ has given. **8** As the scripture says,

"When he went up to the very heights,
    he took many captives with him;
    he gave gifts to people."

9 Now, what does "he went up" mean? It means that first he came down to the lowest depths of the earth.*g* **10** So the one who came down is the same one who went up, above and beyond the heavens, to fill the whole universe with his presence. **11** It was he who "gave gifts to people"; he appointed some to be apostles, others to be prophets, others to be evangelists, others to be pastors and teachers. **12** He did this to prepare all God's people for the work of Christian service, in order to build up the body of Christ. **13** And so we shall all come together to that oneness in our faith and in our knowledge of the Son of God; we shall become mature people, reaching to the very height of Christ's full stature. **14** Then we shall no longer be children, carried by the waves and blown about by every shifting wind of the teaching of deceitful people, who lead others into error by the tricks they invent. **15** Instead, by speak-

ing the truth in a spirit of love, we must grow up in every way to Christ, who is the head. **16** Under his control all the different parts of the body fit together, and the whole body is held together by every joint with which it is provided. So when each separate part works as it should, the whole body grows and builds itself up through love.

The New Life in Christ

17 In the Lord's name, then, I warn you: do not continue to live like the heathen, whose thoughts are worthless **18** and whose minds are in the dark. They have no part in the life that God gives, for they are completely ignorant and stubborn. **19** They have lost all feeling of shame; they give themselves over to vice and do all sorts of indecent things without restraint.

20 That was not what you learned about Christ! **21** You certainly heard about him, and as his followers you were taught the truth that is in Jesus. **22** So get rid of your old self, which made you live as you used to—the old self that was being destroyed by its deceitful desires. **23** Your hearts and minds must be made completely new, **24** and you must put on the new self, which is created in God's likeness and reveals itself in the true life that is upright and holy.

25 No more lying, then! Each of you must tell the truth to the other believer, because we are all members together in the body of Christ. **26** If you become angry, do not let your anger lead you into sin, and do not stay angry all day. **27** Don't give the Devil a chance. **28** If you used to rob, you must stop robbing and

Do not let your anger lead you into sin. (4:26)

g **4:9** the lowest depths of the earth; *or* the lower depths, the earth itself.
4:2 Col 3:12, 13   **4:8** Ps 68:18   **4:16** Col 2:19   **4:22** Col 3:9   **4:24** a Col 3:10; b Gen 1:26; Wis 9:3
4:25 Zech 8:16   **4:26** Ps 4:4 (LXX)

start working, in order to earn an honest living for yourself and to be able to help the poor. 29Do not use harmful words, but only helpful words, the kind that build up and provide what is needed, so that what you say will do good to those who hear you. 30And do not make God's Holy Spirit sad; for the Spirit is God's mark of ownership on you, a guarantee that the Day will come when God will set you free. 31Get rid of all bitterness, passion, and anger. No more shouting or insults, no more hateful feelings of any sort. 32Instead, be kind and tender-hearted to one another, and forgive one another, as God has forgiven you through Christ.

Living in the Light

5 1Since you are God's dear children, you must try to be like him. 2Your life must be controlled by love, just as Christ loved us and gave his life for us as a sweet-smelling offering and sacrifice that pleases God.

3Since you are God's people, it is not right that any matters of sexual immorality or indecency or greed should even be mentioned among you. 4Nor is it fitting for you to use language which is obscene, profane, or vulgar. Rather you should give thanks to God. 5You may be sure that no one who is immoral, indecent, or greedy (for greed is a form of idolatry) will ever receive a share in the Kingdom of Christ and of God.

6Do not let anyone deceive you with foolish words; it is because of these very things that God's anger will come upon those who do not obey him. 7So have nothing at all to do with such people. 8You yourselves used to be in the darkness, but since you have become the Lord's people, you are in the light. So you must live like people who belong to the light, 9for it is the light*h* that brings a rich harvest of every kind of goodness, righteousness, and truth. 10Try to learn what pleases the Lord. 11Have nothing to do with the worthless things that people do, things that belong to the darkness. Instead, bring them out to the light. (12It is

really too shameful even to talk about the things they do in secret.) 13And when all things are brought out to the light, then their true nature is clearly revealed; 14for anything that is clearly revealed becomes light.*i* That is why it is said,

"Wake up, sleeper,
    and rise from death,
and Christ will shine on you."

15So be careful how you live. Don't live like ignorant people, but like wise people. 16Make good use of every opportunity you have, because these are evil days. 17Don't be fools, then, but try to find out what the Lord wants you to do.

18Do not get drunk with wine, which will only ruin you; instead, be filled with the Spirit. 19Speak to one another with the words of psalms, hymns, and sacred songs; sing hymns and psalms to the Lord with praise in your hearts. 20In the name of our Lord Jesus Christ, always give thanks for everything to God the Father.

Wives and Husbands

21Submit yourselves to one another because of your reverence for Christ.

22Wives, submit yourselves to your husbands as to the Lord. 23For a husband has authority over his wife just as Christ has authority over the church; and Christ is himself the Savior of the church, his body. 24And so wives must submit themselves completely to their husbands just as the church submits itself to Christ.

25Husbands, love your wives just as Christ loved the church and gave his life for it. 26He did this to dedicate the church to God by his word, after making it clean by washing it in water, 27in order to present the church to himself in all its beauty—pure and faultless, without spot or wrinkle or any other imperfection. 28Men ought to love their wives just as they love their own bodies. A man who loves his wife loves himself. (29None of us ever hate our own bodies. Instead, we feed them, and take care of them, just as Christ

Ephesians (side tab)

---

h **5:9** the light; *some manuscripts have* the Spirit.   *i* **5:14** anything that is clearly revealed becomes light; *or it is* light that clearly reveals everything.
4:32 Col 3:13   **5:2** Ex 29:18; Ps 40:6   **5:16** Col 4:5   **5:19, 20** Col 3:16, 17   **5:22** Col 3:18; 1 Pet 3:1
5:25 Col 3:19; 1 Pet 3:7

does the church; 30for we are members of his body.) 31As the scripture says, "For this reason a man will leave his father and mother and unite with his wife, and the two will become one." 32There is a deep secret truth revealed in this scripture, which I understand as applying to Christ and the church. 33But it also applies to you: every husband must love his wife as himself, and every wife must respect her husband.

Children and Parents

6 ¹Children, it is your Christian duty to *j* obey your parents, for this is the right thing to do. ²"Respect your father and mother" is the first commandment that has a promise added: ³"so that all may go well with you, and you may live a long time in the land."

⁴Parents, do not treat your children in such a way as to make them angry. Instead, raise them with Christian discipline and instruction.

Slaves and Masters

⁵Slaves, obey your human masters with fear and trembling; and do it with a sincere heart, as though you were serving Christ. ⁶Do this not only when they are watching you, because you want to gain their approval; but with all your heart do what God wants, as slaves of Christ. ⁷Do your work as slaves cheerfully, as though you served the Lord, and not merely human beings. ⁸Remember that the Lord will reward each of us, whether slave or free, for the good work we do.

⁹Masters, behave in the same way toward your slaves and stop using threats. Remember that you and your slaves belong to the same Master in heaven, who judges everyone by the same standard.

The Whole Armor of God

¹⁰Finally, build up your strength in union with the Lord and by means of his mighty power. ¹¹Put on all the armor that God gives you, so that you will be able to stand up against the Devil's evil tricks. ¹²For we are not fighting against human beings but against the wicked spiritual forces in the heavenly world, the rulers, authorities, and cosmic powers of this dark age. ¹³So put on God's armor now! Then when the evil day comes, you will be able to resist the enemy's attacks; and after fighting to the end, you will still hold your ground.

¹⁴So stand ready, with truth as a belt tight around your waist, with righteousness as your breastplate, ¹⁵and as your shoes the readiness to announce the Good News of peace. ¹⁶At all times carry faith as a shield; for with it you will be able to put out all the burning arrows shot by the Evil One. ¹⁷And accept salvation as a helmet, and the word of God as the sword which the Spirit gives you. ¹⁸Do all this in prayer, asking for God's help. Pray on every occasion, as the Spirit leads. For this reason keep alert and never give up; pray always for all God's people. ¹⁹And pray also for me, that God will give me a message when I am ready to speak, so that I may speak boldly and make known the gospel's secret. ²⁰For the sake of this gospel I am an ambassador, though now I am in prison. Pray that I may be bold in speaking about the gospel as I should.

Final Greetings

²¹Tychicus, our dear brother and faithful servant in the Lord's work, will give you all the news about me, so that you may know how I am getting along. ²²That is why I am sending him to you—to tell you how all of us are getting along and to encourage you.

²³May God the Father and the Lord Jesus Christ give to all Christians peace and love with faith. ²⁴May God's grace be with all those who love our Lord Jesus Christ with undying love.

---

j **6:1** *Some manuscripts do not have* it is your Christian duty to.
5:31 Gen 2:24   **6:1** Col 3:20   **6:2, 3** Ex 20:12; Deut 5:16   **6:4** Col 3:21   **6:5–8** Col 3:22–25   **6:9 a** Col 4:1; **b** Deut 10:17; Col 3:25   **6:11** Wis 5:17   **6:14–17** Wis 5:18–23   **6:14 a** Isa 11:5; **b** Isa 59:17   **6:15** Isa 52:7   **6:17** Isa 59:17   **6:21** Acts 20:4; 2 Tim 4:12   **6:21, 22** Col 4:7, 8

Have you heard the song "Joy to the World"? *Joy* seems to be one of those words that we don't hear or see a lot, except in church. Yet for Paul, who is writing from prison, the word *joy* is very important. It captures the attitude that he wants the new Christians in Philippi to live out. It is more than just having a positive attitude; it is about recognizing the many gifts that we have been given by God through Jesus. The best gift is, of course, Jesus himself. Paul feels very close to the Christians in Philippi, and this short letter contains some of his most beautiful messages.

Chap. 3: 1–14

Headlines

- Paul Sends Joyful Prayer from Prison (1:3–11)
- Well-Known Song about Jesus (2:5–11)
- The Prize Worth Running For (3:12–14)

FACTOIDS

Who wrote this book? Paul, probably while he was in prison.

When was it written? About AD 55 to 63.

Why was it written? Paul wanted to express his thanks to the Christians in Philippi and to teach and encourage the people in their faith.

Jesus connection. A famous and beautiful hymn about Jesus talks about him as true God and true man (2:6–11).

Important themes

- The letter speaks often about joy and rejoicing. Can you count the number of times these words appear in this book?
- Those who continue to try to follow Christ, no matter how many times they fail, will be rewarded.

PHILIPPIANS

1 ¹From Paul and Timothy, servants of Christ Jesus—

To all God's people in Philippi who are in union with Christ Jesus, including the church leaders and helpers:

²May God our Father and the Lord Jesus Christ give you grace and peace.

Paul's Prayer for His Readers

³I thank my God for you every time I think of you; ⁴and every time I pray for you all, I pray with joy ⁵because of the way in which you have helped me in the work of the gospel from the very first day until now. ⁶And so I am sure that God, who began this good work in you, will carry it on until it is finished on the Day of Christ Jesus. ⁷You are always in my heart! And so it is only right for me to feel as I do about you. For you have all shared with me in this privilege that God has given me, both now that I am in prison and also while I was free to defend the gospel and establish it firmly. ⁸God is my witness that I tell the truth when I say that my deep feeling for you all comes from the heart of Christ Jesus himself.

⁹I pray that your love will keep on growing more and more, together with true knowledge and perfect judgment, ¹⁰so that you will be able to choose what is best. Then you will be free from all impurity and blame on the Day of Christ. ¹¹Your lives will be filled with the truly good qualities which only Jesus Christ can produce, for the glory and praise of God.

To Live Is Christ

¹²I want you to know, my friends, that the things that have happened to me have really helped the progress of the gospel. ¹³As a result, the whole palace guard and all the others here know that I am in prison because I am a servant of Christ. ¹⁴And my

Heart to Heart

In Paul's greetings to the Philippians, he says, "You are always in my heart!" (1:7). What a beautiful way to express the friendship and closeness we feel to another person or a group of friends. It is clear that Paul feels a strong bond of friendship with the members of the church in Philippi. What are some ways that you express in words your close friendship with others? Why not write a letter to someone you feel close to and let him or her know how much his or her friendship means to you? Or use the words from this passage to make a birthday card or a get-well card for someone you know.

— Philippians 1:3–11

being in prison has given most of the believers more confidence in the Lord, so that they grow bolder all the time to preach the message*a* fearlessly.

¹⁵Of course some of them preach Christ because they are jealous and quarrelsome, but others from genuine good will. ¹⁶These do so from love, because they know that God has given me the work of defending the gospel. ¹⁷The others do not proclaim Christ sincerely, but from a spirit of selfish ambition; they think that they will make more trouble for me while I am in prison.

¹⁸It does not matter! I am happy about it—just so Christ is preached in every way possible, whether from wrong or right motives. And I will continue to be happy, ¹⁹because I know that by means of your

---

a **1:14** the message; *some manuscripts have* God's message.
1:1 Acts 16:12 **1:13** Acts 28:30

True God and True Man

Catholic Connections

You may notice that the words of Philippians 2:6–11 are set apart. It is believed that they were part of an early Christian song. This beautiful hymn provides an excellent description of who Jesus Christ is for us. In Jesus, the human and divine are perfectly united. This mystery is called the Incarnation. As the *Catechism of the Catholic Church* teaches: "[Jesus] is truly the Son of God who, without ceasing to be God and Lord, became a man and our brother" (number 469). This is a core belief for all Christians. Read over these verses slowly and prayerfully. Jesus Christ is Lord!

— Philippians 2:5–11

prayers and the help which comes from the Spirit of Jesus Christ I shall be set free. ²⁰My deep desire and hope is that I shall never fail in my duty, but that at all times, and especially right now, I shall be full of courage, so that with my whole being I shall bring honor to Christ, whether I live or die. ²¹For what is life? To me, it is Christ. Death, then, will bring more. ²²But if by continuing to live I can do more worthwhile work, then I am not sure which I should choose. ²³I am pulled in two directions. I want very much to leave this life and be with Christ, which is a far better thing; ²⁴but for your sake it is much more important that I remain alive. ²⁵I am sure of this, and so I know that I will stay. I will stay on with you all, to add to your progress and joy in the faith, ²⁶so that when I am with you again, you will have even more reason to be proud of me in your life in union with Christ Jesus.

²⁷Now, the important thing is that your way of life should be as the gospel of Christ requires, so that, whether or not I am able to go and see you, I will hear that you are standing firm with one common purpose and that with only one desire you are fighting together for the faith of the gospel.

²⁸Don't be afraid of your enemies; always be courageous, and this will prove to them that they will lose and that you will win, because it is God who gives you the victory. ²⁹For you have been given the privilege of serving Christ, not only by believing in him, but also by suffering for him. ³⁰Now you can take part with me in the battle. It is the same battle you saw me fighting in the past, and as you hear, the one I am fighting still.

Christ's Humility and Greatness

2 ¹Your life in Christ makes you strong, and his love comforts you. You have fellowship with the Spirit,[b] and you have kindness and compassion for one another. ²I urge you, then, to make me completely happy by having the same thoughts, sharing the same love, and being one in soul and mind. ³Don't do anything from selfish ambition or from a cheap desire to boast, but be humble toward one another, always considering others better than yourselves. ⁴And look out for one another's interests, not just for your own. ⁵The attitude you should have is the one that Christ Jesus had:

---

[b] **2:1** You have fellowship with the Spirit; *or* The Spirit has brought you into fellowship with one another.
1:30 Acts 16:19–40

Philippians

⁶He always had the nature of God,
 but he did not think that by force he
  should try to remain*c* equal with God.
⁷Instead of this, of his own free will he
  gave up all he had,
 and took the nature of a servant.
He became like a human being
 and appeared in human likeness.
⁸He was humble and walked the path of
  obedience all the way to death—
  his death on the cross.
⁹For this reason God raised him to the
  highest place above
 and gave him the name that is greater
  than any other name.
¹⁰And so, in honor of the name of Jesus
  all beings in heaven, on earth, and in
   the world below*d*
  will fall on their knees,
¹¹and all will openly proclaim that Jesus
  Christ is Lord,
 to the glory of God the Father.

Shining as Lights in the World

¹²So then, dear friends, as you always
obeyed me when I was with you, it is even
more important that you obey me now
while I am away from you. Keep on working
with fear and trembling to complete your
salvation, ¹³because God is always at work in
you to make you willing and able to obey
his own purpose.

¹⁴Do everything without complaining or
arguing, ¹⁵so that you may be innocent and
pure as God's perfect children, who live in a
world of corrupt and sinful people. You must
shine among them like stars lighting up the
sky, ¹⁶as you offer them the message of life. If
you do so, I shall have reason to be proud of
you on the Day of Christ, because it will
show that all my effort and work have not
been wasted.

¹⁷Perhaps my life's blood is to be poured
out like an offering on the sacrifice that your

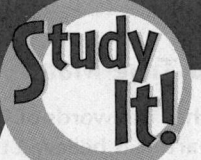

Stop Whining!

Paul tells the Christians of Philippi
to do everything without complaining or arguing (Philippians 2:14).
Does this advice sound familiar? No
doubt you have heard the words,
"Do what you're told and stop
complaining!" Have you ever
noticed how quickly an attitude of
grumbling and complaining can
spread? Soon everyone is whining
about something. So why not
decide to just be upbeat? Today
when you hear someone complaining about something, try to think
of something positive to say. You
can help spread the Good News!

— Philippians 2:12–18

faith offers to God. If that is so, I am glad
and share my joy with you all. ¹⁸In the same
way, you too must be glad and share your joy
with me.

Timothy and Epaphroditus

¹⁹If it is the Lord's will, I hope that I will
be able to send Timothy to you soon, so that
I may be encouraged by news about you.
²⁰He is the only one who shares my feelings
and who really cares about you. ²¹Everyone
else is concerned only with their own affairs,
not with the cause of Jesus Christ. ²²And you
yourselves know how he has proved his
worth, how he and I, like a son and his
father, have worked together for the sake of
the gospel. ²³So I hope to send him to you as

c 2:6 remain; *or* become.   *d* 2:10 WORLD BELOW: *It was thought that the dead continued to exist in a dark world*
under the ground.
2:10, 11 Isa 45:23 (LXX)   2:15 Deut 32:5

Timothy (Philippians 2:19) **is an early Church leader and a companion whom Paul
relied on. Two letters in the New Testament are addressed to Timothy.**

soon as I know how things are going to turn out for me. 24And I trust in the Lord that I myself will be able to come to you soon.

25I have thought it necessary to send to you our brother Epaphroditus, who has worked and fought by my side and who has served as your messenger in helping me. 26He is anxious to see you all and is very upset because you had heard that he was sick. 27Indeed he was sick and almost died. But God had pity on him, and not only on him but on me, too, and spared me an even greater sorrow. 28I am all the more eager, then, to send him to you, so that you will be glad again when you see him, and my own sorrow will disappear. 29Receive him, then, with joy, as a believer in the Lord. Show respect to all such people as he, 30because he risked his life and nearly died for the sake of the work of Christ, in order to give me the help that you yourselves could not give.

Receive him . . . as a believer. (2:29)

The True Righteousness

3 1In conclusion, my friends, be joyful in your union with the Lord. I don't mind repeating what I have written before, and you will be safer if I do so. 2Watch out for those who do evil things, those dogs, those who insist on cutting the body. 3It is we, not they, who have received the true circumcision, for we worship God by means of his Spirit and rejoice in our life in union with Christ Jesus. We do not put any trust in external ceremonies. 4I could, of course, put my trust in such things. If any of you think you can trust in external ceremonies, I have

even more reason to feel that way. 5I was circumcised when I was a week old. I am an Israelite by birth, of the tribe of Benjamin, a pure-blooded Hebrew. As far as keeping the Jewish Law is concerned, I was a Pharisee, 6and I was so zealous that I persecuted the church. As far as a person can be righteous by obeying the commands of the Law, I was without fault. 7But all those things that I might count as profit I now reckon as loss for Christ's sake. 8Not only those things; I reckon everything as complete loss for the sake of what is so much more valuable, the knowledge of Christ Jesus my Lord. For his sake I have thrown everything away; I consider it all as mere garbage, so that I may gain Christ 9and be completely united with him. I no longer have a righteousness of my own, the kind that is gained by obeying the Law. I now have the righteousness that is given through faith in Christ, the righteousness that comes from God and is based on faith. 10All I want is to know Christ and to experience the power of his resurrection, to share in his sufferings and become like him in his death, 11in the hope that I myself will be raised from death to life.

Running toward the Goal

12I do not claim that I have already succeeded or have already become perfect. I keep striving to win the prize for which Christ Jesus has already won me to himself. 13Of course, my friends, I really do not[e] think that I have already won it; the one thing I do, however, is to forget what is behind me and do my best to reach what is ahead. 14So I run straight toward the goal in order to win the prize, which is God's call through Christ Jesus to the life above.

15All of us who are spiritually mature should have this same attitude. But if some of you have a different attitude, God will make this clear to you. 16However that may be, let us go forward according to the same rules we have followed until now.

17Keep on imitating me, my friends. Pay attention to those who follow the right example that we have set for you. 18I have

e **3:13** not; *some manuscripts have* not yet.
3:5 a Rom 11:1; b Acts 23:6; 26:5   **3:6** Acts 8:3; 22:4; 26:9–11   **3:17** 1 Cor 4:16; 11:1

Philippians

I run straight toward the goal. (3:14)

told you this many times before, and now I repeat it with tears: there are many whose lives make them enemies of Christ's death on the cross. ¹⁹They are going to end up in hell, because their god is their bodily desires. They are proud of what they should be ashamed of, and they think only of things that belong to this world. ²⁰We, however, are citizens of heaven, and we eagerly wait for our Savior, the Lord Jesus Christ, to come from heaven. ²¹He will change our weak mortal bodies and make them like his own glorious body, using that power by which he is able to bring all things under his rule.

Their god is their bodily desires. (3:19)

Instructions

4 ¹So then, my friends, how dear you are to me and how I miss you! How happy you make me, and how proud I am of

Keep at it!

The summer Olympics are held every four years. Athletes from all over the world come together to compete in a variety of events. The winners receive gold, silver, and bronze medals. That is often what we see on television or in photos, but we know that behind those medals are years of practice, often for long hours seven days a week. Paul uses the image of a runner trying to win first prize to help us understand that following God's call takes work and dedication. The prize is not a medal, but rather full life in Jesus—in this life and in heaven.

Star athletes may complain about practice, but they know they have to put in their time to be successful. They make a practice schedule to motivate them. Why not make a practice schedule for your spiritual life? When and how long will you spend reading the Bible? When will you spend time learning about your faith? When will you get together to pray with others?

— Philippians 3:12–14

you!—this, dear friends, is how you should stand firm in your life in the Lord.

²Euodia and Syntyche, please, I beg you, try to agree as sisters in the Lord. ³And you too, my faithful partner, I want you to help these women; for they have worked hard with me to spread the gospel, together with Clement and all my other fellow workers, whose names are in God's book of the living.

⁴May you always be joyful in your union with the Lord. I say it again: rejoice!

⁵Show a gentle attitude toward everyone. The Lord is coming soon. ⁶Don't worry

Philippians

about anything, but in all your prayers ask God for what you need, always asking him with a thankful heart. 7And God's peace, which is far beyond human understanding, will keep your hearts and minds safe in union with Christ Jesus.

8In conclusion, my friends, fill your minds with those things that are good and that deserve praise: things that are true, noble, right, pure, lovely, and honorable. 9Put into practice what you learned and received from me, both from my words and from my actions. And the God who gives us peace will be with you.

Thanks for the Gift

10In my life in union with the Lord it is a great joy to me that after so long a time you once more had the chance of showing that you care for me. I don't mean that you had stopped caring for me—you just had no chance to show it. 11And I am not saying this because I feel neglected, for I have learned to be satisfied with what I have. 12I know what it is to be in need and what it is to have more than enough. I have learned this secret, so that anywhere, at any time, I am content, whether I am full or hungry, whether I have too much or too little. 13I have the strength to face all conditions by the power that Christ gives me.

14But it was very good of you to help me in my troubles. 15You Philippians know very well that when I left Macedonia in the early days of preaching the Good News, you were the only church to help me; you were the only ones who shared my profits and losses. 16More than once when I needed help in Thessalonica, you sent it to me. 17It is not that I just want to receive gifts; rather, I want to see profit added to your account. 18Here, then, is my receipt for everything you have given me—and it has been more than enough! I have all I need now that Epaphroditus has brought me all your gifts. They are like a sweet-smelling offering to God, a sacrifice which is acceptable and pleasing to him. 19And with all his abundant wealth through Christ Jesus, my God will supply all your needs. 20To our God and Father be the glory forever and ever! Amen.

Final Greetings

21Greetings to each one of God's people who belong to Christ Jesus. The believers here with me send you their greetings. 22All God's people here send greetings, especially those who belong to the Emperor's palace.

23May the grace of the Lord Jesus Christ be with you all.

4:16 Acts 17:1   **4:15, 16** 2 Cor 11:9   **4:18** Ex 29:18

Philippians

Your Next Step   **Congratulations on finishing the Letter to the Philippians! Use this space to write your thoughts and questions about this book. If you are following the suggested reading plan, go back to the Book of Amos in the Old Testament. This prophet had a real dedication to following God by practicing justice.**

THE LETTER TO THE

Colossians

Did you ever ask anyone for good advice? Even though the Letter to the Colossians was written more than two thousand years ago, it still has good advice for us today. It begins with a rich description of who Christ is. The second chapter warns us about false teachers and incorrect ideas. The third chapter describes how we need to live our lives, and the last chapter closes with final greetings to particular people by name. Those who follow this advice will become happier people, better Christians, and better friends.

Chap. 1:15–18

Head<u>lines</u>

- God Makes Peace Through Son's Death (1:15–20)
- The Secret to a Full Life Revealed! (2:6–10)
- How-To Guide: Living Life in Christ (3:5—4:1)

FACTOIDS

Who wrote this book? Paul or one of Paul's followers using the name of Paul. The author is familiar with Paul's teachings and uses Paul's themes.

When was it written? If Paul wrote it, around AD 61. If one of Paul's followers wrote it, probably after AD 61.

Why was it written? It seems that a group of people were teaching some unusual ideas and practices. This letter reminds the Christian community at Colossae that Jesus needs to be central to their faith.

Jesus connection. Jesus is described as supreme—as the head of the body, the head of the Church. If we know who Christ is, then we know how we must live.

Important themes

- Do not try to be popular by following the latest fads.
- Do not listen to just anyone for advice.
- Know what a Christian needs to do and follow that way of life.

COLOSSIANS

1 ¹From Paul, who by God's will is an apostle of Christ Jesus, and from our brother Timothy—

²To God's people in Colossae, who are our faithful friends in union with Christ:

May God our Father give you grace and peace.

Prayer of Thanksgiving

³We always give thanks to God, the Father of our Lord Jesus Christ, when we pray for you. ⁴For we have heard of your faith in Christ Jesus and of your love for all God's people. ⁵When the true message, the Good News, first came to you, you heard about the hope it offers. So your faith and love are based on what you hope for, which is kept safe for you in heaven. ⁶The gospel keeps bringing blessings and is spreading throughout the world, just as it has among you ever since the day you first heard about the grace of God and came to know it as it really is. ⁷You learned of God's grace from Epaphras, our dear fellow servant, who is Christ's faithful worker on our*ᵃ* behalf. ⁸He has told us of the love that the Spirit has given you.

⁹For this reason we have always prayed for you, ever since we heard about you. We ask God to fill you with the knowledge of his will, with all the wisdom and understanding that his Spirit gives. ¹⁰Then you will be able to live as the Lord wants and will always do what pleases him. Your lives will produce all kinds of good deeds, and you will grow in your knowledge of God. ¹¹⁻¹²May you be made strong with all the strength which comes from his glorious power, so that you may be able to endure everything with patience. And with joy give thanks to*ᵇ* the Father, who has made you fit to have your share of what God has reserved for his people in the kingdom of light. ¹³He rescued us from the power of darkness and brought us safe into the kingdom of his dear Son, ¹⁴by whom we are set free, that is, our sins are forgiven.

The Person and Work of Christ

¹⁵Christ is the visible likeness of the invisible God. He is the first-born Son, superior to all created things. ¹⁶For through him God created everything in heaven and on earth, the seen and the unseen things, including spiritual powers, lords, rulers, and authorities. God created the whole universe through him and for him. ¹⁷Christ existed before all things, and in union with him all things have their proper place. ¹⁸He is the head of his body, the church; he is the source of the body's life. He is the first-born Son, who was raised from death, in order that he alone might have the first place in all things. ¹⁹For it was by God's own decision that the Son has in himself the full nature of God. ²⁰Through the Son, then, God decided to bring the whole universe back to himself. God made peace through his Son's blood*ᶜ* on the cross and so brought back to himself all things, both on earth and in heaven.

²¹At one time you were far away from God and were his enemies because of the evil things you did and thought. ²²But now, by means of the physical death of his Son, God has made you his friends, in order to bring you, holy, pure, and faultless, into his presence. ²³You must, of course, continue faithful on a firm and sure foundation, and must not allow yourselves to be shaken from the hope you gained when you heard the gospel. It is of this gospel that I, Paul, became a servant—this gospel which has been preached to everybody in the world.

ᵃ **1:7** our; *some manuscripts have* your.   *ᵇ* **1:11–12** with patience. And with joy give thanks to; *or* with patience and joy. And give thanks to.   *ᶜ* **1:20** his Son's blood; *or* his Son's sacrificial death.
1:7 Col 4:12; Philem 23   **1:14** Eph 1:7   **1:15** Wis 7:26   **1:18** Eph 1:22, 23   **1:20** Eph 2:16

Paul's Work as a Servant of the Church

24 And now I am happy about my sufferings for you, for by means of my physical sufferings I am helping to complete what still remains of Christ's sufferings on behalf of his body, the church. 25 And I have been made a servant of the church by God, who gave me this task to perform for your good. It is the task of fully proclaiming his message, 26 which is the secret he hid through all past ages from all human beings but has now revealed to his people. 27 God's plan is to make known his secret to his people, this rich and glorious secret which he has for all peoples. And the secret is that Christ is in you, which means that you will share in the glory of God. 28 So we preach Christ to everyone. With all possible wisdom we warn and teach them in order to bring each one into God's presence as a mature individual in union with Christ. 29 To get this done I toil and struggle, using the mighty strength which Christ supplies and which is at work in me.

2 1 Let me tell you how hard I have worked for you and for the people in Laodicea and for all others who do not know me personally. 2 I do this in order that they may be filled with courage and may be drawn together in love, and so have the full wealth of assurance which true understanding brings. In this way they will know God's secret, which is Christ himself. *d* 3 He is the key that opens all the hidden treasures of God's wisdom and knowledge.

4 I tell you, then, do not let anyone deceive you with false arguments, no matter how good they seem to be. 5 For even though I am absent in body, yet I am with you in spirit, and I am glad as I see the resolute firmness with which you stand together in your faith in Christ.

Fullness of Life in Christ

6 Since you have accepted Christ Jesus as Lord, live in union with him. 7 Keep your roots deep in him, build your lives on him, and become stronger in your faith, as you were taught. And be filled with thanksgiving.

8 See to it, then, that no one enslaves you by means of the worthless deceit of human wisdom, which comes from the teachings handed down by human beings and from the ruling spirits of the universe, and not from Christ. 9 For the full content of divine nature lives in Christ, in his humanity, 10 and you have been given full life in union with him. He is supreme over every spiritual ruler and authority.

11 In union with Christ you were circumcised, not with the circumcision that is made by human beings, but with the circumcision made by Christ, which consists of being freed from the power of this sinful self. 12 For when you were baptized, you were buried with Christ, and in baptism you were also raised with Christ through your faith in the active power of God, who raised him from death. 13 You were at one time spiritually dead because of your sins and because you were Gentiles without the Law. But God has now brought you to life with Christ. God forgave us all our sins; 14 he canceled the unfavorable record of our debts with its binding rules and did away with it completely by nailing it to the cross. 15 And on that cross Christ freed himself from the power of the spiritual rulers and authorities; *e* he made a public spectacle of them by leading them as captives in his victory procession.

16 So let no one make rules about what you eat or drink or about holy days or the New Moon Festival or the Sabbath. 17 All such things are only a shadow of things in the future; the reality is Christ. 18 Do not allow yourselves to be condemned by anyone who claims to be superior because of special visions and who insists on false humility and the worship of angels. For no reason at all, such people are all puffed up by their human way of thinking 19 and have stopped holding on to Christ, who is the head of the body. Under Christ's control the whole body is nourished and held together

---

d **2:2** God's secret, which is Christ himself; *some manuscripts have* God's secret; *others have* the secret of God the Father of Christ; *others have* the secret of the God and Father, and of Christ. *e* **2:15** Christ freed himself from the power of the spiritual rulers and authorities; *or* Christ stripped the spiritual rulers and authorities of their power.
2:12 Rom 6:4 **2:13** Eph 2:1–5 **2:14** Eph 2:15 **2:16** Rom 14:1–6 **2:19** Eph 4:16

by its joints and ligaments, and it grows as God wants it to grow.

Dying and Living with Christ

²⁰You have died with Christ and are set free from the ruling spirits of the universe. Why, then, do you live as though you belonged to this world? Why do you obey such rules as ²¹"Don't handle this," "Don't taste that," "Don't touch the other"? ²²All these refer to things which become useless once they are used; they are only human rules and teachings. ²³Of course such rules appear to be based on wisdom in their forced worship of angels, and false humility, and severe treatment of the body; but they have no real value in controlling physical passions.

3 ¹You have been raised to life with Christ, so set your hearts on the things that are in heaven, where Christ sits on his throne at the right side of God. ²Keep your minds fixed on things there, not on things here on earth. ³For you have died, and your life is hidden with Christ in God. ⁴Your real life is Christ and when he appears, then you too will appear with him and share his glory!

The Old Life and the New

⁵You must put to death, then, the earthly desires at work in you, such as sexual immorality, indecency, lust, evil passions, and greed (for greed is a form of idolatry). ⁶Because of such things God's anger will come upon those who do not obey him.ᶠ ⁷At one time you yourselves used to live according to such desires, when your life was dominated by them.

⁸But now you must get rid of all these things: anger, passion, and hateful feelings. No insults or obscene talk must ever come from your lips. ⁹Do not lie to one another, for you have put off the old self with its habits ¹⁰and have put on the new self. This is the new being which God, its Creator, is constantly renewing in his own image, in order to bring you to a full knowledge of himself. ¹¹As a result, there is no longer any

Fashion Advice and More

The Letter to the Colossians has some interesting fashion advice. It says we need to clothe ourselves with compassion, kindness, humility, gentleness, and patience (3:12). What should we take off? Colossians says we need to get rid of sexual immorality, lust, greed (3:5), anger, hateful feelings, insults, obscene language (3:8) and anything else that Jesus wouldn't be part of.

In the world we live in, there are lots of false messages about what's important in life. Colossians challenges many of these false messages. It says we should be tolerant with one another, forgive one another, and love one another. What kind of friend do you want to be? Someone with cool clothes, but bad attitudes? Or someone with less stuff, but who is caring and concerned about your friends and their feelings?

What kind of person do you want to be when you are all grown? Now is the time to start thinking about that. Now is the time to start developing good habits. The advice in chapter 3 is still good for all of us to follow.

— Colossians 3:1–17

distinction between Gentiles and Jews, circumcised and uncircumcised, barbarians, savages, slaves, and free, but Christ is all, Christ is in all.

¹²You are the people of God; he loved you and chose you for his own. So then, you

---

ᶠ **3:6** *Some manuscripts do not have* upon those who do not obey him.
3:1 Ps 110:1   **3:9** Eph 4:22   **3:10 a** Eph 4:24; **b** Gen 1:26   **3:12, 13** Eph 4:2

Colossians

must clothe yourselves with compassion, kindness, humility, gentleness, and patience. [13]Be tolerant with one another and forgive one another whenever any of you has a complaint against someone else. You must forgive one another just as the Lord has forgiven you. [14]And to all these qualities add love, which binds all things together in perfect unity. [15]The peace that Christ gives is to guide you in the decisions you make; for it is to this peace that God has called you together in the one body. And be thankful. [16]Christ's message in all its richness must live in your hearts. Teach and instruct one another with all wisdom. Sing psalms, hymns, and sacred songs; sing to God with thanksgiving in your hearts. [17]Everything you do or say, then, should be done in the name of the Lord Jesus, as you give thanks through him to God the Father.

Personal Relations in the New Life

[18]Wives, submit yourselves to your husbands, for that is what you should do as Christians.

[19]Husbands, love your wives and do not be harsh with them.

[20]Children, it is your Christian duty to obey your parents always, for that is what pleases God.

[21]Parents, do not irritate your children, or they will become discouraged.

[22]Slaves, obey your human masters in all things, not only when they are watching you because you want to gain their approval; but do it with a sincere heart because of your reverence for the Lord. [23]Whatever you do, work at it with all your heart, as though you were working for the Lord and not for people. [24]Remember that the Lord will give you as a reward what he has kept for his people. For Christ is the real Master you serve. [25]And all wrongdoers will be repaid for the wrong things they do, because God judges everyone by the same standard.

4 [1]Masters, be fair and just in the way you treat your slaves. Remember that you too have a Master in heaven.

Instructions

[2]Be persistent in prayer, and keep alert as you pray, giving thanks to God. [3]At the same time pray also for us, so that God will give us a good opportunity to preach his message about the secret of Christ. For that is why I am now in prison. [4]Pray, then, that I may speak, as I should, in such a way as to make it clear.

[5]Be wise in the way you act toward those who are not believers, making good use of every opportunity you have. [6]Your speech should always be pleasant and interesting, and you should know how to give the right answer to everyone.

Final Greetings

[7]Our dear friend Tychicus, who is a faithful worker and fellow servant in the Lord's work, will give you all the news about me. [8]That is why I am sending him to you, in order to cheer you up by telling you how all of us are getting along. [9]With him goes Onesimus, that dear and faithful friend, who belongs to your group. They will tell you everything that is happening here.

[10]Aristarchus, who is in prison with me, sends you greetings, and so does Mark, the cousin of Barnabas. (You have already received instructions to welcome Mark if he comes your way.) [11]Joshua, also called Justus, sends greetings too. These three are the only Jewish believers who work with me for the Kingdom of God, and they have been a great help to me.

[12]Greetings from Epaphras, another member of your group and a servant of Christ Jesus. He always prays fervently for you, asking God to make you stand firm, as mature and fully convinced Christians, in complete obedience to God's will. [13]I can personally testify to his hard work for you and for the

3:13 Eph 4:32   **3:16, 17** Eph 5:19, 20   **3:18** Eph 5:22; 1 Pet 3:1   **3:19** Eph 5:25; 1 Pet 3:7   **3:20** Eph 6:1
3:21 Eph 6:4   **3:22–25** Eph 6:5–8   **3:25** Deut 10:17; Eph 6:9   **4:1** Eph 6:9   **4:5** Eph 5:16   **4:6** Wis
8:12   **4:7** Acts 20:4; 2 Tim 4:12   **4:7, 8** Eph 6:21, 22   **4:9** Philem 10–12   **4:10 a** Acts 19:29; 27:2; Philem
24; **b** Acts 12:12, 25; 13:13; 15:37–39   **4:12** Col 1:7; Philem 23

people in Laodicea and Hierapolis. [14]Luke, our dear doctor, and Demas send you their greetings.

[15]Give our best wishes to the believers in Laodicea and to Nympha and the church that meets in her house.[g] [16]After you read this letter, make sure that it is read also in the church at Laodicea. At the same time, you are to read the letter that the believers in Laodicea will send you. [17]And tell Archippus, "Be sure to finish the task you were given in the Lord's service."

[18]With my own hand I write this: *Greetings from Paul.* Do not forget my chains!

May God's grace be with you.

[g] **4:15** Nympha . . . her house; *some manuscripts have* Nymphas . . . his house.
4:14 a 2 Tim 4:11; Philem 24; **b** 2 Tim 4:10; Philem 24   **4:17** Philem 2

One of life's most difficult experiences is when someone who is close to you dies. We pray that our loved one is at peace with God. We might wonder if we will be united with our loved one again in heaven. It was partly due to concerns like these that Paul wrote to the Thessalonians.

Like many early Christians, the Thessalonians thought that Jesus would come back while they were still alive. They were concerned about their friends who had already died and wondered if they would rise up again when the Lord returned. In this letter Paul wanted to reassure them and tell them not to worry.

Christ's final coming is sometimes called the Second Coming of Christ or the Day of the Lord or the Parousia. When that great day arrives, all the dead who had faith in Christ will be united with Christ and one another.

Chap. 2:9

Head lines

- Missionary Life Is Not Easy (2:8–12)
- Paul Encouraged by Community's Love (3:6–13)
- Death Is Not the End! (4:13–18)
- Followers Told to Stay Awake (5:1–11)

FACTOIDS

Who wrote this book? Paul. He spent time preaching at Thessalonica and started a new Christian community there.

When was it written? This is the oldest book in the New Testament. Most likely it was written around AD 50 to 51. That's only twenty years or so after the death and Resurrection of Jesus. First Thessalonians is even older than the Gospels!

Who was it written for? It was written to the church in Thessalonica, people who were mostly non-Jewish Christians.

Important themes
- Jesus died and rose; so God will raise up all people who have "fallen asleep" (died).
- We do not know when the world will end, but there is no need to be afraid.

1 THESSALONIANS

1 ¹From Paul, Silas, and Timothy—
To the people of the church in Thessalonica, who belong to God the Father and the Lord Jesus Christ:

May grace and peace be yours.

The Life and Faith of the Thessalonians

²We always thank God for you all and always mention you in our prayers. ³For we remember before our God and Father how you put your faith into practice, how your love made you work so hard, and how your hope in our Lord Jesus Christ is firm. ⁴Our friends, we know that God loves you and has chosen you to be his own. ⁵For we brought the Good News to you, not with words only, but also with power and the Holy Spirit, and with complete conviction of its truth. You know how we lived when we were with you; it was for your own good. ⁶You imitated us and the Lord; and even though you suffered much, you received the message with the joy that comes from the Holy Spirit. ⁷So you became an example to all believers in Macedonia and Achaia. ⁸For not only did the message about the Lord go out from you throughout Macedonia and Achaia, but the news about your faith in God has gone everywhere. There is nothing, then, that we need to say. ⁹All those people speak about how you received us when we visited you, and how you turned away from idols to God, to serve the true and living God ¹⁰and to wait for his Son to come from heaven— his Son Jesus, whom he raised from death and who rescues us from God's anger that is coming.

Paul's Work in Thessalonica

2 ¹Our friends, you yourselves know that our visit to you was not a failure. ²You know how we had already been mistreated and insulted in Philippi before we came to you in Thessalonica. And even though there was much opposition, our God gave us courage to tell you the Good News that comes from him. ³Our appeal to you is not based on error or impure motives, nor do we try to trick anyone. ⁴Instead, we always speak as God wants us to, because he has judged us worthy to be entrusted with the Good News. We do not try to please people, but to please God, who tests our motives. ⁵You know very well that we did not come to you with flattering talk, nor did we use words to cover up greed—God is our witness! ⁶We did not try to get praise from anyone, either from you or from others, ⁷even though as apostles of Christ we could have made demands on you. But we were gentle when we were with you, like a mother*a* taking care of her children. ⁸Because of our love for you we were ready to share with you not only the Good News from God but even our own lives. You were so dear to us! ⁹Surely you remember, our friends, how we worked and toiled! We worked day and night so that we would not be any trouble to you as we preached to you the Good News from God.

¹⁰You are our witnesses, and so is God, that our conduct toward you who believe was pure, right, and without fault. ¹¹You know that we treated each one of you just as parents treat their own children. ¹²We encouraged you, we comforted you, and we kept urging you to live the kind of life that pleases God, who calls you to share in his own Kingdom and glory.

¹³And there is another reason why we always give thanks to God. When we brought you God's message, you heard it and accepted it, not as a message from human beings but as God's message, which indeed it is. For God is at work in you who believe. ¹⁴Our friends, the same things happened to

---

a **2:7** we were gentle when we were with you, like a mother; *some manuscripts have* we were like children when we were with you; we were like a mother.
1:1 Acts 17:1   **1:6** Acts 17:5–9   **2:2** a Acts 16:19–24; b Acts 17:1–9

Paul's a Working Man

Saint Paul reminds the Thessalonians that he worked very hard when he was with them. He probably worked hard so that he wouldn't have to beg for his food. But he probably also did it as an example for others to follow. The hard work that Paul and his companions did on their journeys accomplished something huge—it helped establish the Church throughout the Roman Empire.

Work is important. When you do work, it contributes to your community. Maybe you are thinking about what kind of job you might be able to find as a teenager. Maybe you already work—perhaps you have a paper route or you babysit. Some jobs may seem pointless. But almost all honest jobs serve a purpose and help to make the community a better place. So be responsible like Paul, and do your best whenever and wherever you work.

— 1 Thessalonians 2:9–12

you that happened to the churches of God in Judea, to the people there who belong to Christ Jesus. You suffered the same persecutions from your own people that they suffered from the Jews, 15who killed the Lord Jesus and the prophets, and persecuted us. How displeasing they are to God! How hostile they are to everyone! 16They even tried to stop us from preaching to the Gentiles the message that would bring them salvation. In this way they have brought to completion all the sins they have always committed. And now God's anger has at last come down on them!

Paul's Desire to Visit Them Again

17As for us, friends, when we were separated from you for a little while—not in our thoughts, of course, but only in body—how we missed you and how hard we tried to see you again! 18We wanted to return to you. I myself tried to go back more than once, but Satan would not let us. 19After all, it is you—you, no less than others!—who are our hope, our joy, and our reason for boasting of our victory in the presence of our Lord Jesus when he comes. 20Indeed, you are our pride and our joy!

3 1Finally, we could not bear it any longer. So we decided to stay on alone in Athens 2while we sent Timothy, our brother who works with us for God in preaching the Good News about Christ. We sent him to strengthen you and help your faith, 3so that none of you should turn back because of these persecutions. You yourselves know that such persecutions are part of God's will for us. 4For while we were still with you, we told you ahead of time that we were going to be persecuted; and as you well know, that is exactly what happened. 5That is why I had to send Timothy. I could not bear it any longer, so I sent him to find out about your faith. Surely it could not be that the Devil had tempted you and all our work had been for nothing!

6Now Timothy has come back, and he has brought us the welcome news about your faith and love. He has told us that you always think well of us and that you want to see us just as much as we want to see you. 7So, in all our trouble and suffering we have been encouraged about you, friends. It was your faith that encouraged us, 8because now we really live if you stand firm in your life in union with the Lord. 9Now we can give thanks to our God for you. We thank him for the joy we have in his presence because of you. 10Day and night we ask him with all our heart to let us see you personally and supply what is needed in your faith.

11May our God and Father himself and our Lord Jesus prepare the way for us to come to you! 12May the Lord make your love for one another and for all people grow

2:14 Acts 17:5   2:15 Acts 9:23, 29; 13:45, 50; 14:2, 5, 19; 17:5, 13; 18:12   3:1 Acts 17:15   3:6 Acts 18:5

more and more and become as great as our love for you. [13] In this way he will strengthen you, and you will be perfect and holy in the presence of our God and Father when our Lord Jesus comes with all who belong to him. [b]

A Life That Pleases God

4 [1] Finally, our friends, you learned from us how you should live in order to please God. This is, of course, the way you have been living. And now we beg and urge you in the name of the Lord Jesus to do even more. [2] For you know the instructions we gave you by the authority of the Lord Jesus. [3] God wants you to be holy and completely free from sexual immorality. [4] Each of you should know how to live with your wife [c] in a holy and honorable way, [5] not with a lustful desire, like the heathen who do not know God. [6] In this matter, then, none of you should do wrong to other Christians or take advantage of them. We have told you this before, and we strongly warned you that the Lord will punish those who do that. [7] God did not call us to live in immorality, but in holiness. [8] So then, whoever rejects this teaching is not rejecting a human being, but God, who gives you his Holy Spirit.

[9] There is no need to write you about love for each other. You yourselves have been taught by God how you should love one another. [10] And you have, in fact, behaved like this toward all the believers in all of Macedonia. So we beg you, our friends, to do even more. [11] Make it your aim to live a quiet life, to mind your own business, and to earn your own living, just as we told you before. [12] In this way you will win the respect of those who are not believers, and you will not have to depend on anyone for what you need.

The Lord's Coming

[13] Our friends, we want you to know the truth about those who have died, so that you will not be sad, as are those who have no hope. [14] We believe that Jesus died and rose again, and so we believe that God will take back with Jesus those who have died believing in him.

[15] What we are teaching you now is the Lord's teaching: we who are alive on the day the Lord comes will not go ahead of those who have died. [16] There will be the shout of command, the archangel's voice, the sound of God's trumpet, and the Lord himself will come down from heaven. Those who have died believing in Christ will rise to life first; [17] then we who are living at that time will be gathered up along with them in the clouds to meet the Lord in the air. And so we will always be with the Lord. [18] So then, encourage one another with these words.

Be Ready for the Lord's Coming

5 [1] There is no need to write you, friends, about the times and occasions when these things will happen. [2] For you yourselves know very well that the Day of the Lord will come as a thief comes at night. [3] When people say, "Everything is quiet and safe," then suddenly destruction will hit them! It will come as suddenly as the pains that come upon a woman in labor, and people will not escape. [4] But you, friends, are not in the darkness, and the Day should not take you by surprise like a thief. [5] All of you are people who belong to the light, who belong to the day. We do not belong to the night or to the darkness. [6] So then, we should not be sleeping like the others; we should be awake and sober. [7] It is at night when people sleep; it is at night when they get drunk. [8] But we belong to the day, and we should be sober. We must wear faith and love as a breastplate, and our hope of salvation as a helmet. [9] God did not choose us to suffer his anger, but to possess salvation through our Lord Jesus Christ, [10] who died for us in order that we might live together with him, whether we are alive or dead when he comes. [11] And so encourage one another and help one another, just as you are now doing.

1 Thessalonians

---

[b] **3:13** all who belong to him; *or* all his angels.   [c] **4:4** live with your wife; *or* control your body.
4:15–17 1 Cor 15:51, 52   **4:15** Sir 48:11   **5:2** Mt 24:43; Lk 12:39; 2 Pet 3:10   **5:8** Isa 59:17; Eph 6:13–17

Final Instructions and Greetings

12 We beg you, our friends, to pay proper respect to those who work among you, who guide and instruct you in the Christian life. 13 Treat them with the greatest respect and love because of the work they do. Be at peace among yourselves.

14 We urge you, our friends, to warn the idle, encourage the timid, help the weak, be patient with everyone. 15 See that no one pays back wrong for wrong, but at all times make it your aim to do good to one another and to all people.

16 Be joyful always, 17 pray at all times, 18 be thankful in all circumstances. This is what God wants from you in your life in union with Christ Jesus.

19 Do not restrain the Holy Spirit; 20 do not despise inspired messages. 21 Put all things to the test: keep what is good 22 and avoid every kind of evil.

23 May the God who gives us peace make you holy in every way and keep your whole being—spirit, soul, and body—free from every fault at the coming of our Lord Jesus Christ. 24 He who calls you will do it, because he is faithful.

25 Pray also for us, friends.

26 Greet all the believers with the kiss of peace.

27 I urge you by the authority of the Lord to read this letter to all the believers.

28 The grace of our Lord Jesus Christ be with you.

Do you ever think about the end of the world? The Thessalonians did. In his first letter to the Thessalonians, Paul reassures the people who are concerned about the Second Coming of Christ.

This second letter was written much later. But the concerns of the people in Thessalonica are the same—only worse. They are much more worried about when Jesus will return, and some people have even stopped working. They just want to sit around and wait for the end of the world. This letter assures them and tells them to keep working, to keep living their lives normally. No one can predict when Jesus will return. The lesson from this letter is still good advice today. Don't worry. Keep living your life. Have confidence in God.

Chap. 1:6–7

Headlines

- The Final Judgment (chapter 1)
- People Warned about Laziness (3:6–15)

FACTOIDS

When was this book written? If Paul wrote it, around AD 51. If Paul's followers wrote it, which is most likely, sometime between AD 70 and 90.

Who was it written for? Although it was addressed to the church in Thessalonica, it might also have been written for other churches that were having similar troubles.

Why was it written? Paul wanted to reassure the Thessalonians who were confused about the Second Coming of Christ.

Jesus connection. Jesus Christ will come once more at the end of time to bring God's judgment on every person.

Important themes

- Those who do evil and persecute innocent people will receive their just punishment.
- Do not be troubled by news about the end of the world.

2 THESSALONIANS

1 ¹From Paul, Silas, and Timothy—
To the people of the church in Thessalonica, who belong to God our Father and the Lord Jesus Christ:
²May God our Father and the Lord Jesus Christ give you grace and peace.

The Judgment at Christ's Coming

³Our friends, we must thank God at all times for you. It is right for us to do so, because your faith is growing so much and the love each of you has for the others is becoming greater. ⁴That is why we ourselves boast about you in the churches of God. We boast about the way you continue to endure and believe through all the persecutions and sufferings you are experiencing.

⁵All of this proves that God's judgment is just and as a result you will become worthy of his Kingdom, for which you are suffering. ⁶God will do what is right: he will bring suffering on those who make you suffer, ⁷and he will give relief to you who suffer and to us as well. He will do this when the Lord Jesus appears from heaven with his mighty angels, ⁸with a flaming fire, to punish those who reject God and who do not obey the Good News about our Lord Jesus. ⁹They will suffer the punishment of eternal destruction, separated from the presence of the Lord and from his glorious might, ¹⁰when he comes on that Day to receive glory from all his people and honor from all who believe. You too will be among them, because you have believed the message that we told you. ¹¹That is why we always pray for you. We ask our God to make you worthy of the life he has called you to live. May he fulfill by his power all your desire for goodness and complete your work of faith. ¹²In this way the name of our Lord Jesus will receive glory from you, and you from him, by the grace of our God and of the Lord*a* Jesus Christ.

The Wicked One

2 ¹Concerning the coming of our Lord Jesus Christ and our being gathered together to be with him: I beg you, my friends, ²not to be so easily confused in your thinking or upset by the claim that the Day of the Lord has come. Perhaps it is thought that we said this while prophesying or preaching, or that we wrote it in a letter. ³Do not let anyone deceive you in any way. For the Day will not come until the final Rebellion takes place and the Wicked One appears, who is destined to hell. ⁴He will oppose every so-called god or object of worship and will put himself above them all. He will even go in and sit down in God's Temple and claim to be God.

⁵Don't you remember? I told you all this while I was with you. ⁶Yet there is something that keeps this from happening now, and you know what it is. At the proper time, then, the Wicked One will appear. ⁷The Mysterious Wickedness is already at work, but what is going to happen will not happen until the one who holds it back is taken out of the way. ⁸Then the Wicked One will be revealed, but when the Lord Jesus comes, he will kill him with the breath from his mouth and destroy him with his dazzling presence. ⁹The Wicked One will come with the power of Satan and perform all kinds of false miracles and wonders, ¹⁰and use every kind of wicked deceit on those who will perish. They will perish because they did not welcome and love the truth so as to be saved. ¹¹And so God sends the power of error to work in them so that they believe what is false. ¹²The result is that all who have not believed the truth, but have taken pleasure in sin, will be condemned.

You Are Chosen for Salvation

¹³We must thank God at all times for you, friends, you whom the Lord loves. For God

a **1:12** our God and of the Lord; *or* our God and Lord.
1:1 Acts 17:1 **1:9** Isa 2:10 **2:1** 1 Thess 4:15–17 **2:4** Dan 11:36; Ezek 28:2 **2:8** Isa 11:4 **2:9** Mt 24:24

God Has Chosen You!

There's something very comforting about this idea: God chose me to do something important with my life. God has chosen me. I have a calling.

Our calling in life is our vocation. A vocation is not just a career. A vocation means listening for who God is calling you to be; a career is a call to some particular kind of work. A vocation is connected to your state in life, as a single or married person, or as a priest or a religious sister or brother. Often, the greatest fulfillment comes when your vocation helps to determine your career.

Some adults try to figure out which career will bring them the most money. Then to be successful in their career, they may ignore their vocation to their family, their friends, and their Church. And they end up being very unhappy. Other adults listen for the vocations God is calling them to. When they find it, they make sure that their careers support their vocations. And often, they are very happy. When people keep their commitment to their vocations, they are usually successful in their careers too.

When you think about future jobs and careers, ask God to help you see the vocation he is calling you to. That should help guide all your career choices.

— 2 Thessalonians 2:13–17

you to this through the Good News we preached to you; he called you to possess your share of the glory of our Lord Jesus Christ. 15 So then, our friends, stand firm and hold on to those truths which we taught you, both in our preaching and in our letter.

16 May our Lord Jesus Christ himself and God our Father, who loved us and in his grace gave us unfailing courage and a firm hope, 17 encourage you and strengthen you to always do and say what is good.

Pray for Us

3 1 Finally, our friends, pray for us that the Lord's message may continue to spread rapidly and be received with honor, just as it was among you. 2 Pray also that God will rescue us from wicked and evil people; for not everyone believes the message.

3 But the Lord is faithful, and he will strengthen you and keep you safe from the Evil One. 4 And the Lord gives us confidence in you, and we are sure that you are doing and will continue to do what we tell you.

5 May the Lord lead you into a greater understanding of God's love and the endurance that is given by Christ.

The Obligation to Work

6 Our friends, we command you in the name of our Lord Jesus Christ to keep away from all believers who are living a lazy life and who do not follow the instructions that we gave them. 7 You yourselves know very well that you should do just what we did. We were not lazy when we were with you. 8 We did not accept anyone's support without paying for it. Instead, we worked and toiled; we kept working day and night so as not to be an expense to any of you. 9 We did this, not because we do not have the right to demand our support; we did it to be an example for you to follow. 10 While we were with you, we used to tell you, "Whoever refuses to work is not allowed to eat."

11 We say this because we hear that there are some people among you who live lazy lives and who do nothing except meddle in

chose you as the first[b] to be saved by the Spirit's power to make you his holy people and by your faith in the truth. 14 God called

Do not treat them as enemies. (3:15)

other people's business. 12In the name of the Lord Jesus Christ we command these people and warn them to lead orderly lives and work to earn their own living.

13But you, friends, must not become tired of doing good. 14It may be that some there will not obey the message we send you in this letter. If so, take note of them and have nothing to do with them, so that they will be ashamed. 15But do not treat them as enemies; instead, warn them as believers.

Final Words

16May the Lord himself, who is our source of peace, give you peace at all times and in every way. The Lord be with you all.

17With my own hand I write this: *Greetings from Paul.* This is the way I sign every letter; this is how I write.

18May the grace of our Lord Jesus Christ be with you all.

Being young has its advantages and its disadvantages. Most of us are familiar with being told that we're too young for things, or to wait until we're older, or that because of our age we shouldn't try to do or say certain things. Timothy probably felt this way too. This letter encourages Timothy, a young leader in the early Church, and reminds him that he is not too young. This message can be a reminder for anyone who feels too young to serve as a leader. "Do not let anyone look down on you because you are young" (1 Timothy 4:12) are good words to live by. And following Timothy's example is a good practice to live by.

THE FIRST LETTER TO Timothy

Chap. 2:1–8

Headlines

- Beware of False Teachers (1:3–10)
- Church Roles Defined (3:1–13)
- How to Live a Godly Life (4:6–15)

FACTOIDS

Who wrote this book? The author used Paul's name, but the book was probably written by followers of Paul.

When was it written? If Paul wrote it, around AD 65. If Paul's followers wrote it, between AD 90 and 100.

Why was it written? The author wanted to counteract some people who were teaching false beliefs and pulling new Christians away from the truth.

Who are the young people in this book? Timothy is a young church leader.

Important themes

- Prayer and worship are important in helping others come to know Jesus.
- Church leadership requires preparation, sincerity, good character, and spiritual training.
- Leaders in the Church, whether young or old, serve as examples for all believers.

1 TIMOTHY

1 ¹From Paul, an apostle of Christ Jesus by order of God our Savior and Christ Jesus our hope—

²To Timothy, my true son in the faith:

May God the Father and Christ Jesus our Lord give you grace, mercy, and peace.

Warnings against False Teaching

³I want you to stay in Ephesus, just as I urged you when I was on my way to Macedonia. Some people there are teaching false doctrines, and you must order them to stop. ⁴Tell them to give up those legends and those long lists of ancestors, which only produce arguments; they do not serve God's plan, which is known by faith. ⁵The purpose of this order is to arouse the love that comes from a pure heart, a clear conscience, and a genuine faith. ⁶Some people have turned away from these and have lost their way in foolish discussions. ⁷They want to be teachers of God's law, but they do not understand their own words or the matters about which they speak with so much confidence.

⁸We know that the Law is good if it is used as it should be used. ⁹It must be remembered, of course, that laws are made, not for good people, but for lawbreakers and criminals, for the godless and sinful, for those who are not religious or spiritual, for those who kill their fathers or mothers, for murderers, ¹⁰for the immoral, for sexual perverts, for kidnappers, for those who lie and give false testimony or who do anything else contrary to sound doctrine. ¹¹That teaching is found in the gospel that was entrusted to me to announce, the Good News from the glorious and blessed God.

Gratitude for God's Mercy

¹²I give thanks to Christ Jesus our Lord, who has given me strength for my work. I thank him for considering me worthy and appointing me to serve him, ¹³even though in the past I spoke evil of him and persecuted and insulted him. But God was merciful to me because I did not yet have faith and so did not know what I was doing. ¹⁴And our Lord poured out his abundant grace on me and gave me the faith and love which are ours in union with Christ Jesus. ¹⁵This is a true saying, to be completely accepted and believed: Christ Jesus came into the world to save sinners. I am the worst of them. ¹⁶but God was merciful to me in order that Christ Jesus might show his full patience in dealing with me, the worst of sinners, as an example for all those who would later believe in him and receive eternal life. ¹⁷To the eternal King, immortal and invisible, the only God—to him be honor and glory forever and ever! Amen.

¹⁸Timothy, my child, I entrust to you this command, which is in accordance with the words of prophecy spoken in the past about

Christ Jesus came into the world to save sinners. (1:15)

Pray It!

It's PPRT-Y Easy to Pray!

Ricardo tried to lead prayer at the junior high gathering and was tongue-tied. The youth minister whispered in his ear, "Pert, Ricardo, remember pert?" Ricardo took a deep breathe and led the prayer. It was easy, once he remembered *PPRT* (which sounds like *pert*).

 PPRT are the initials of directions for prayer given in 1 Timothy 2:1. The first *P* is "prayers," which simply means taking time out to pray. The second *P* is "petitions." Petitions are your own needs that you pray for. The *R* is for "requests." Requests are other people's needs that you pray for. The *T* is for "thanksgiving." Thanksgiving is taking time to thank God for the things you are grateful for.

 Praying out loud in front of a group can be hard, especially if you haven't had time to practice. So just remember it is pert-y easy to pray if you remember *PPRT*. Give it a try right now.

Prayers: Take a few minutes to pray.
Petitions: Pray for your own personal needs.
Requests: Pray for needs of other people, especially the things people asked you to pray for.
Thanksgiving: Thank God for the things, people, and events you are grateful for.

            — 1 Timothy 2:1

you. Use those words as weapons in order to fight well, [19] and keep your faith and a clear conscience. Some people have not listened to their conscience and have made a ruin of their faith. [20] Among them are Hymenaeus and Alexander, whom I have punished by handing them over to the power of Satan; this will teach them to stop their blasphemy.

Church Worship

2 [1] First of all, then, I urge that petitions, prayers, requests, and thanksgivings be offered to God for all people; [2] for kings and all others who are in authority, that we may live a quiet and peaceful life with all reverence toward God and with proper conduct. [3] This is good and it pleases God our Savior,

[4] who wants everyone to be saved and to come to know the truth. [5] For there is one God, and there is one who brings God and human beings together, the man Christ Jesus, [6] who gave himself to redeem the whole human race. That was the proof at the right time that God wants everyone to be saved, [7] and that is why I was sent as an apostle and teacher of the Gentiles, to proclaim the message of faith and truth. I am not lying; I am telling the truth!

[8] In every church service I want the men to pray, men who are dedicated to God and can lift up their hands in prayer without anger or argument. [9] I also want the women to be modest and sensible about their clothes and to dress properly; not with fancy hair styles or with gold ornaments or pearls or

2:7 2 Tim 1:11 **2:9** 1 Pet 3:3

I Timothy

Doctrines are the official teachings of the Church based on what God revealed through Jesus Christ under the guidance of the Holy Spirit.

Leading the Way

Catholic Connections

In some other Bibles the Church leaders mentioned in 1 Timothy, chapter 3, are called bishops. The Church helpers mentioned in chapter 3 are called deacons. First Timothy was written when the churches that Paul and other missionaries started were getting bigger. They needed strong spiritual leaders to stay on track. This letter provided spiritual advice to those early bishops and deacons for leading their churches.

Over time the Holy Spirit shaped the roles of bishop, priest, and deacon into the ministries we have today. The leaders of the early Church helped maintain true teaching and guided the Church's service, and so do our bishops, priests, and deacons today. DREs, music ministers, youth ministers, and pastoral ministers serve as leaders in many parishes too. Are you called to serve the Church in a leadership role?

— 1 Timothy 3:1–13

expensive dresses, 10but with good deeds, as is proper for women who claim to be religious. 11Women should learn in silence and all humility. 12I do not allow them to teach or to have authority over men; they must keep quiet. 13For Adam was created first, and then Eve. 14And it was not Adam who was deceived; it was the woman who was deceived and broke God's law. 15But a woman will be saved through having children,*a* if she perseveres*b* in faith and love and holiness, with modesty.

Leaders in the Church

3 1This is a true saying: If a man is eager to be a church leader, he desires an excellent work. 2A church leader must be without fault; he must have only one wife,*c* be sober, self-controlled, and orderly; he must welcome strangers in his home; he must be able to teach; 3he must not be a drunkard or a violent man, but gentle and peaceful; he

must not love money; 4he must be able to manage his own family well and make his children obey him with all respect. 5For if a man does not know how to manage his own family, how can he take care of the church of God? 6He must be mature in the faith, so that he will not swell up with pride and be condemned, as the Devil was. 7He should be a man who is respected by the people outside the church, so that he will not be disgraced and fall into the Devil's trap.

Helpers in the Church

8Church helpers must also have a good character and be sincere; they must not drink too much wine or be greedy for money; 9they should hold to the revealed truth of the faith with a clear conscience. 10They should be tested first, and then, if they pass the test, they are to serve. 11Their wives*d* also must be of good character and must not gossip; they must be sober and honest in everything. 12A

a **2:15** will be saved through having children; *or* will be kept safe through childbirth.   *b* **2:15** if she perseveres; *or* if they persevere.   *c* **3:2** have only one wife; *or* be married only once.   *d* **3:11** Their wives; *or* Women helpers.
2:13 a Gen 2:7; b Gen 2:21, 22   **2:14** Gen 3:1–6   **3:2–7** Titus 1:6–9

At the time this letter was written, Church leaders could still be married. The requirement of priests and bishops staying unmarried developed later.

church helper must have only one wife,[e] and be able to manage his children and family well. [13]Those helpers who do their work well win for themselves a good standing and are able to speak boldly about their faith in Christ Jesus.

The Great Secret

[14]As I write this letter to you, I hope to come and see you soon. [15]But if I delay, this letter will let you know how we should conduct ourselves in God's household, which is the church of the living God, the pillar and support of the truth. [16]No one can deny how great is the secret of our religion:

He appeared in human form,
　　was shown to be right by the Spirit,[f]
　　and was seen by angels.
He was preached among the nations,
　　was believed in throughout the world,
　　and was taken up to heaven.

False Teachers

4 [1]The Spirit says clearly that some people will abandon the faith in later times; they will obey lying spirits and follow the teachings of demons. [2]Such teachings are spread by deceitful liars, whose consciences are dead, as if burnt with a hot iron. [3]Such people teach that it is wrong to marry and to eat certain foods. But God created those foods to be eaten, after a prayer of thanks, by those who are believers and have come to know the truth. [4]Everything that God has created is good; nothing is to be rejected, but everything is to be received with a prayer of thanks, [5]because the word of God and the prayer make it acceptable to God.

A Good Servant of Christ Jesus

[6]If you give these instructions to the believers, you will be a good servant of Christ Jesus, as you feed yourself spiritually on the words of faith and of the true teaching which you have followed. [7]But keep away from those godless legends, which are

not worth telling. Keep yourself in training for a godly life. [8]Physical exercise has some value, but spiritual exercise is valuable in every way, because it promises life both for the present and for the future. [9]This is a true saying, to be completely accepted and believed. [10]We struggle[g] and work hard, because we have placed our hope in the living God, who is the Savior of all and especially of those who believe.

[11]Give them these instructions and these teachings. [12]Do not let anyone look down on you because you are young, but be an example for the believers in your speech, your conduct, your love, faith, and purity. [13]Until I come, give your time and effort to the public reading of the Scriptures and to preaching and teaching. [14]Do not neglect the spiritual gift that is in you, which was given to you when the prophets spoke and the elders laid their hands on you. [15]Practice these things and devote yourself to them, in order that your progress may be seen by all. [16]Watch yourself and watch your teaching. Keep on doing these things, because if you do, you will save both yourself and those who hear you.

Responsibilities toward Believers

5 [1]Do not rebuke an older man, but appeal to him as if he were your father. Treat the younger men as your brothers, [2]the older women as mothers, and the younger women as sisters, with all purity.

[3]Show respect for widows who really are all alone. [4]But if a widow has children or grandchildren, they should learn first to carry out their religious duties toward their own family and in this way repay their parents and grandparents, because that is what pleases God. [5]A widow who is all alone, with no one to take care of her, has placed her hope in God and continues to pray and ask him for his help night and day. [6]But a widow who gives herself to pleasure has already died, even though she lives. [7]Give them these instructions, so that no one will find fault with them. [8]But if any do not take

---

[e] **3:12** have only one wife; *or* be married only once.　[f] **3:16** was shown to be right by the Spirit; *or* and, in spiritual form, was shown to be right.　[g] **4:10** struggle; *some manuscripts have* are reviled.
5:5 Jdt 8:4–6

I Timothy

Never Too Young

While growing up, Jeff was constantly reminded that his older brother, Brett, was a good role model. Brett won athletic awards, was class president at the middle school, and all his teachers remembered how great he was. Brett was now in high school and was beginning to do things that his parents weren't too happy about. Jeff was worried that Brett was starting to do bad stuff, and one day told him so. Brett replied, "You're only 12, what do you know?" which of course made Jeff feel hurt.

Imagine Jeff's surprise at the dinner table that night when his parents said to Brett, "You know, you should follow the example of your little brother, he is respectful to us and is well-behaved at school. You could learn from him." Jeff almost fell off his chair.

Because Timothy was a young leader in the Church, other people may not have given him the respect he deserved (1 Timothy 4:12). The author of this letter reminds Timothy—and us—that anyone of any age can be an example by their speech and conduct. Even though you are young, you can be an inspiration for others, even people much older than you!

— 1 Timothy 4:11–16

care of their relatives, especially the members of their own family, they have denied the faith and are worse than an unbeliever.

9 Do not add any widow to the list of widows unless she is over sixty years of age.

In addition, she must have been married only once[h] 10 and have a reputation for good deeds: a woman who brought up her children well, received strangers in her home, performed humble duties for other Christians, helped people in trouble, and devoted herself to doing good.

11 But do not include younger widows in the list; because when their desires make them want to marry, they turn away from Christ, 12 and so become guilty of breaking their earlier promise to him. 13 They also learn to waste their time in going around from house to house; but even worse, they learn to be gossips and busybodies, talking of things they should not. 14 So I would prefer that the younger widows get married, have children, and take care of their homes, so as to give our enemies no chance of speaking evil of us. 15 For some widows have already turned away to follow Satan. 16 But if any Christian woman has widows in her family, she must take care of them and not put the burden on the church, so that it may take care of the widows who are all alone.

17 The elders who do good work as leaders should be considered worthy of receiving double pay, especially those who work hard at preaching and teaching. 18 For the scripture says, "Do not muzzle an ox when you are using it to thresh grain" and "Workers should be given their pay." 19 Do not listen to an accusation against an elder unless it is brought by two or more witnesses. 20 Rebuke publicly all those who commit sins, so that the rest may be afraid.

21 In the presence of God and of Christ Jesus and of the holy angels I solemnly call upon you to obey these instructions without showing any prejudice or favor to anyone in anything you do. 22 Be in no hurry to lay hands on people to dedicate them to the Lord's service. Take no part in the sins of others; keep yourself pure.

23 Do not drink water only, but take a little wine to help your digestion, since you are sick so often.

24 The sins of some people are plain to see, and their sins go ahead of them to judgment; but the sins of others are seen only

h 5:9 married only once; or faithful to her husband.
5:18 a Deut 25:4; b Mt 10:10; Lk 10:7   5:19 Deut 17:6; 19:15

later. 25In the same way good deeds are plainly seen, and even those that are not so plain cannot be hidden.

6 1Those who are slaves must consider their masters worthy of all respect, so that no one will speak evil of the name of God and of our teaching. 2Slaves belonging to Christian masters must not despise them, for they are believers too. Instead, they are to serve them even better, because those who benefit from their work are believers whom they love.

False Teaching and True Riches

You must teach and preach these things. 3Whoever teaches a different doctrine and does not agree with the true words of our Lord Jesus Christ and with the teaching of our religion 4is swollen with pride and knows nothing. He has an unhealthy desire to argue and quarrel about words, and this brings on jealousy, disputes, insults, evil suspicions, 5and constant arguments from people whose minds do not function and who no longer have the truth. They think that religion is a way to become rich.

6Well, religion does make us very rich, if we are satisfied with what we have. 7What did we bring into the world? Nothing! What can we take out of the world? Nothing! 8So then, if we have food and clothes, that should be enough for us. 9But those who want to get rich fall into temptation and are caught in the trap of many foolish and harmful desires, which pull them down

to ruin and destruction. 10For the love of money is a source of all kinds of evil. Some have been so eager to have it that they have wandered away from the faith and have broken their hearts with many sorrows.

What did we bring into the world? Nothing! What can we take out of the world? Nothing! (6:7)

Strive

You can strive for the same character qualities Timothy was told to work toward in 1 Timothy 6:11. For each of the qualities, write a phrase that starts with the same letter as the word. The phrase should explain how you will work toward attaining these qualities. For example, the first word, *righteousness,* begins with *R.* So your phrase might be "Resist cheating." Give it a try:

Righteousness:
R_____

Godliness:
G_____

Faith:
F_____

Love:
L_____

Endurance:
E_____

Gentleness:
G_____

    Once you write your phrases, copy them onto nice paper, decorate the sheet, and put it somewhere to remind yourself of the qualities you are striving for.

— 1 Timothy 6:11–14

1 Timothy

Righteousness is the quality of doing what is right, fair, and just.

Personal Instructions

11But you, man of God, avoid all these things. Strive for righteousness, godliness, faith, love, endurance, and gentleness. **12**Run your best in the race of faith, and win eternal life for yourself; for it was to this life that God called you when you firmly professed your faith before many witnesses. **13**Before God, who gives life to all things, and before Christ Jesus, who firmly professed his faith before Pontius Pilate, I command you **14**to obey your orders and keep them faithfully until the Day when our Lord Jesus Christ will appear. **15**His appearing will be brought about at the right time by God, the blessed and only Ruler, the King of kings and the Lord of lords. **16**He alone is immortal; he lives in the light that no one can approach. No one has ever seen him; no one can ever see him. To him be honor and eternal power! Amen.

17Command those who are rich in the things of this life not to be proud, but to place their hope, not in such an uncertain thing as riches, but in God, who generously gives us everything for our enjoyment. **18**Command them to do good, to be rich in good works, to be generous and ready to share with others. **19**In this way they will store up for themselves a treasure which will be a solid foundation for the future. And then they will be able to win the life which is true life.

20Timothy, keep safe what has been entrusted to your care. Avoid the profane talk and foolish arguments of what some people wrongly call "Knowledge." **21**For some have claimed to possess it, and as a result they have lost the way of faith.

God's grace be with you all.

6:13 Jn 18:33–38

Your Next Step

Congratulations on finishing the First Letter of Timothy! Use this space to write your thoughts and questions about this book. Now move ahead to the Second Letter of Timothy to read even more advice to this young Church leader.

Did you ever get into trouble for something you didn't do? Then you know how this writer feels. Imagine someone who was put in jail—simply for being a Christian!

This letter expresses the sadness of a Church leader who has suffered for the faith. Yet the author still has faith, still has persistence, and still wants to encourage others (especially Timothy) to be strong. It is clear that the author knows Timothy's family well and that he loves and cares about Timothy very much. This letter ends with the author recalling details about many personal friends. Imagine how lonely it would feel to sit in jail without any friends. . . . It seems to make this letter even more special.

Chap. 4:9–13

Head lines

- Encouraging Words from an Apostle (1:8–14)
- The Power of the Word of God! (3:14–17)
- God's Prize Waits for Us (4:7–8)

FACTOIDS

Who wrote this book? Possibly Paul, but more likely one of Paul's followers.
When was it written? If Paul wrote it, possibly as early as AD 65, but more likely around AD 90 to 100.
Who was it written for? It was written for Church leaders in the name of Timothy, a young leader in the early Church.
Why Was It Written? The author wanted to encourage and give advice to Church leaders.
Important themes
- Do not be ashamed of your faith.
- It helps to remember that Jesus suffered, died, and rose again.
- Be persistent in your faith and remember what you have been taught.
- Keep teaching others about the Gospel story.

2 TIMOTHY

1 ¹From Paul, an apostle of Christ Jesus by God's will, sent to proclaim the promised life which we have in union with Christ Jesus—

²To Timothy, my dear son:

May God the Father and Christ Jesus our Lord give you grace, mercy, and peace.

Thanksgiving and Encouragement

³I give thanks to God, whom I serve with a clear conscience, as my ancestors did. I thank him as I remember you always in my prayers night and day. ⁴I remember your tears, and I want to see you very much, so that I may be filled with joy. ⁵I remember the sincere faith you have, the kind of faith that your grandmother Lois and your mother Eunice also had. I am sure that you have it also. ⁶For this reason I remind you to keep alive the gift that God gave you when I laid my hands on you. ⁷For the Spirit that God has given us does not make us timid; instead, his Spirit fills us with power, love, and self-control.

⁸Do not be ashamed, then, of witnessing for our Lord; neither be ashamed of me, a prisoner for Christ's sake. Instead, take your part in suffering for the Good News, as God gives you the strength for it. ⁹He saved us and called us to be his own people, not because of what we have done, but because of his own purpose and grace. He gave us this grace by means of Christ Jesus before the beginning of time, ¹⁰but now it has been revealed to us through the coming of our Savior, Christ Jesus. He has ended the power of death and through the gospel has revealed immortal life.

¹¹God has appointed me as an apostle and teacher to proclaim the Good News, ¹²and it is for this reason that I suffer these things. But I am still full of confidence, because I know whom I have trusted, and I am sure that he is able to keep safe until that Day what he has entrusted to me.*ᵃ* ¹³Hold firmly to the true words that I taught you, as the example for you to follow, and remain in the faith and love that are ours in union with Christ Jesus. ¹⁴Through the power of the Holy Spirit, who lives in us, keep the good things that have been entrusted to you.

¹⁵You know that everyone in the province of Asia, including Phygelus and Hermogenes, has deserted me. ¹⁶May the Lord show mercy to the family of Onesiphorus, because he cheered me up many times. He was not ashamed that I am in prison, ¹⁷but as soon as he arrived in Rome, he started looking for me until he found me. ¹⁸May the Lord grant him his mercy on that Day! And you know very well how much he did for me in Ephesus.

A Loyal Soldier of Christ Jesus

2 ¹As for you, my son, be strong through the grace that is ours in union with Christ Jesus. ²Take the teachings that you heard me proclaim in the presence of many witnesses, and entrust them to reliable people, who will be able to teach others also.

³Take your part in suffering, as a loyal soldier of Christ Jesus. ⁴A soldier on active duty wants to please his commanding officer and so does not get mixed up in the affairs of civilian life. ⁵An athlete who runs in a race cannot win the prize unless he obeys the rules. ⁶The farmer who has done the hard work should have the first share of the harvest. ⁷Think about what I am saying, because the Lord will enable you to understand it all.

⁸Remember Jesus Christ, who was raised from death, who was a descendant of David, as is taught in the Good News I preach. ⁹Because I preach the Good News, I suffer and I am even chained like a criminal. But the word of God is not in chains, ¹⁰and so I endure everything for the sake of God's chosen people, in order that they too may obtain the salvation that comes through Christ Jesus and brings eternal glory. ¹¹This is a true saying:

ᵃ **1:12** what he has entrusted to me; *or* what I have entrusted to him.
1:2 Acts 16:1   **1:5** Acts 16:1   **1:11** 1 Tim 2:7

Pray It!

The Passions of Youth

Joan and Jacob had been seeing each other for two months. It was Joan's first relationship with a guy, and she felt deeply in love. One day at school Jacob said, "Joan, it's been great, but I think we should just be friends. I'm not ready to date just one person." Joan felt deeply hurt, and without thinking she burst out, "That's not fair. We love each other. You can't decide that by yourself." They got into a big argument. All of a sudden they looked around, and it felt like the whole school was staring at them.

As a young person, it is natural that you will feel deep emotions. You will love more, be angrier about injustices, and feel hurt more easily. This is what it means to be passionate, and it is a good thing. So what does 2 Timothy mean when it says, "Avoid the passions of youth" (2:22)? The author is talking about not letting your deep emotions take control of you. Don't let your love or your anger or your hurt lead you to say or do something that you will later regret. When you are feeling strong emotions, take a break. Share your feelings with God in prayer. Talk with someone a little older who can help you sort out what you are feeling and what to say or do.

— 2 Timothy 2:22–26

"If we have died with him,
  we shall also live with him.
12 If we continue to endure,
  we shall also rule with him.
If we deny him,
  he also will deny us.
13 If we are not faithful,
  he remains faithful,
  because he cannot be false to himself."

An Approved Worker

14 Remind your people of this, and give them a solemn warning in God's presence not to fight over words. It does no good, but only ruins the people who listen. 15 Do your best to win full approval in God's sight, as a worker who is not ashamed of his work, one who correctly teaches the message of God's truth. 16 Keep away from profane and foolish discussions, which only drive people farther away from God. 17 Such teaching is like an open sore that eats away the flesh. Two men who have taught such things are Hymenaeus and Philetus. 18 They have left the way of truth and are upsetting the faith of some believers by saying that our resurrection has already taken place. 19 But the solid foundation that God has laid cannot be shaken; and on it are written these words: "The Lord knows those who are his" and "Those who say that they belong to the Lord must turn away from wrongdoing."

20 In a large house there are dishes and bowls of all kinds: some are made of silver and gold, others of wood and clay; some are for special occasions, others for ordinary use. 21 Those who make themselves clean from all those evil things, will be used for special purposes, because they are dedicated and useful to their Master, ready to be used for every good deed. 22 Avoid the passions of youth, and strive for righteousness, faith, love, and peace, together with those who

2:12 Mt 10:33; Lk 12:9   **2:19** Num 16:5

The saying in 2 Timothy 2:11–13 may have been part of an early Christian hymn. Can you create a song using these words?

God's Revealed Truth

Catholic Connections

Are there certain Bible stories you know really well? Maybe you know them because you've heard them all your life. They are probably the stories your grandparents, parents, catechists, and priests told you as you grew up. This is like Timothy, who from an early age learned Scripture (2 Timothy 3:14–15). The advantage you have is that this edition of the Bible is created just for young people. It is important to have parents and teachers teaching you about the Bible, and this Bible will also help you understand the meaning of the Bible stories.

The truth is that by reading and praying with the Bible, you are getting to know God. God is revealed in the Bible, and the more stories about God and the people of God you become familiar with, the easier it is to know God. God also reveals himself and his truths in sacred Tradition. Sacred Tradition includes the truths revealed by Jesus Christ that were taught and passed on by the Apostles, the popes, and the bishops. Sacred Tradition and the Bible are the ways God's revelation for all people is handed on.

— 2 Timothy 3:14–17

with a pure heart call out to the Lord for help. 23 But keep away from foolish and ignorant arguments; you know that they end up in quarrels. 24 As the Lord's servant, you must not quarrel. You must be kind toward all, a good and patient teacher, 25 who is gentle as you correct your opponents, for it may be that God will give them the opportunity to repent and come to know the truth. 26 And then they will come to their senses and escape from the trap of the Devil, who had caught them and made them obey his will.

The Last Days

3 1 Remember that there will be difficult times in the last days. 2 People will be selfish, greedy, boastful, and conceited; they will be insulting, disobedient to their parents, ungrateful, and irreligious; 3 they will be unkind, merciless, slanderers, violent, and fierce; they will hate the good; 4 they will be treacherous, reckless, and swollen with pride; they will love pleasure rather than God; 5 they will hold to the outward form of our religion, but reject its real power. Keep away from such people. 6 Some of them go into people's houses and gain control over weak women who are burdened by the guilt of their sins and driven by all kinds of desires, 7 women who are always trying to learn but who can never come to know the truth. 8 As Jannes and Jambres were opposed to Moses, so also these people are opposed to the truth—people whose minds do not function and who are failures in the faith. 9 But they will not get very far, because everyone will see how stupid they are. That is just what happened to Jannes and Jambres.

3:8 Ex 7:11

Holy Scriptures, or *Scripture* (2 Timothy 3:15–16), **is another name for the Bible. Timothy read the Hebrew Scriptures, or the Old Testament.**

Long, Full Life

This letter was probably written in the name of Paul, recalling the time when Paul was in prison. In prison Paul was sad. He missed Timothy and his other friends and begged them to visit him. He was worried about how everyone was holding up, but he had faith in the people of God. He sensed that he might not live much longer, and he said about his life, "I have done my best in the race, I have run the full distance, and I have kept the faith" (2 Timothy 4:7). The writer knew that Paul was ready to accept his death, and was grateful that he had had such a full life.

Is there someone you know who has lived a long, full life? Perhaps an aging relative or a neighbor? Take a moment to be thankful for that person. Pray for that person's needs. Then decide to spend time with that person and enjoy him or her. Maybe you can get some good advice for your life, as Timothy did.

— 2 Timothy 4:6–8

Last Instructions

[10]But you have followed my teaching, my conduct, and my purpose in life; you have observed my faith, my patience, my love, my endurance, [11]my persecutions, and my sufferings. You know all that happened to me in Antioch, Iconium, and Lystra, the terrible persecutions I endured! But the Lord rescued me from them all. [12]Everyone who wants to live a godly life in union with

Christ Jesus will be persecuted; [13]and evil persons and impostors will keep on going from bad to worse, deceiving others and being deceived themselves. [14]But as for you, continue in the truths that you were taught and firmly believe. You know who your teachers were, [15]and you remember that ever since you were a child, you have known the Holy Scriptures, which are able to give you the wisdom that leads to salvation through faith in Christ Jesus. [16]All Scripture is inspired by God and is useful[b] for teaching the truth, rebuking error, correcting faults, and giving instruction for right living, [17]so that the person who serves God may be fully qualified and equipped to do every kind of good deed.

4 [1]In the presence of God and of Christ Jesus, who will judge the living and the dead, and because he is coming to rule as King, I solemnly urge you [2]to preach the message, to insist upon proclaiming it (whether the time is right or not), to convince, reproach, and encourage, as you teach with all patience. [3]The time will come when people will not listen to sound doctrine, but will follow their own desires and will collect for themselves more and more teachers who will tell them what they are itching to hear. [4]They will turn away from listening to the truth and give their attention to legends. [5]But you must keep control of yourself in all circumstances; endure suffering, do the work of a preacher of the Good News, and perform your whole duty as a servant of God.

[6]As for me, the hour has come for me to be sacrificed; the time is here for me to leave this life. [7]I have done my best in the race, I have run the full distance, and I have kept the faith.[c] [8]And now there is waiting for me the victory prize of being put right with God, which the Lord, the righteous Judge, will give me on that Day—and not only to me, but to all those who wait with love for him to appear.

---

[b] **3:16** All Scripture is inspired by God and is useful; *or* Every scripture inspired by God is also useful.
[c] **4:7** kept the faith; *or* been true to my promise.
3:11 **a** Acts 13:14–52; **b** Acts 14:1–7; **c** Acts 14:8–20

The victory prize . . . (4:8)

Personal Words

9Do your best to come to me soon.
10Demas fell in love with this present world
and has deserted me, going off to Thessalonica. Crescens went to Galatia, and Titus to
Dalmatia. 11Only Luke is with me. Get Mark
and bring him with you, because he can
help me in the work. 12I sent Tychicus to
Ephesus. 13When you come, bring my coat
that I left in Troas with Carpus; bring the
books too, and especially the ones made of
parchment.

14Alexander the metalworker did me great

harm; the Lord will reward him according to
what he has done. 15Be on your guard
against him yourself, because he was violently opposed to our message.

16No one stood by me the first time I
defended myself; all deserted me. May God
not count it against them! 17But the Lord
stayed with me and gave me strength, so that
I was able to proclaim the full message for all
the Gentiles to hear; and I was rescued from
being sentenced to death. 18And the Lord
will rescue me from all evil and take me
safely into his heavenly Kingdom. To him be
the glory forever and ever! Amen.

Final Greetings

19I send greetings to Priscilla and Aquila
and to the family of Onesiphorus. 20Erastus
stayed in Corinth, and I left Trophimus in
Miletus, because he was sick. 21Do your best
to come before winter.

Eubulus, Pudens, Linus, and Claudia send
their greetings, and so do all the other
Christians.

22The Lord be with your spirit.
God's grace be with you all.

4:10 a Col 4:14; Philem 24; b 2 Cor 8:23; Gal 2:3; Titus 1:4   4:11 a Col 4:14; Philem 24; b Acts 12:12, 25;
13:13; 15:37–39; Col 4:10; Philem 24   4:12 Acts 20:4; Eph 6:21, 22; Col 4:7, 8   4:13 Acts 20:6
4:14 a 1 Tim 1:20; b Ps 62:12; Rom 2:6   4:19 a Acts 18:2; b 2 Tim 1:16, 17   4:20 a Acts 19:22; Rom
16:23; b Acts 20:4; 21:29

Your Next Step

Congratulations on finishing the Second Letter of
Timothy! Use this space to write your thoughts and
questions about this book. If you are following the
suggested reading plan, move back to the First Letter to the Corinthians. This letter is about some of
the issues an early Christian church faced.

Did you ever want to give advice to a bishop or leader of the Church? This short letter does exactly that.

It was written to a Church leader and is filled with advice: Advice for elders and leaders (called presbyters and bishops in some Bible translations) and for rebellious people. Advice for men and women, both young and old. Advice for Church leaders on what to do and what not to do. There is even advice for slaves.

After reading it, you might think about your answer to this question, "If I were a Church leader, what advice would I want to follow?"

Chap. 1:5–9

Headlines

- What Makes a Worthy Bishop? (1:5–9)
- Tips for Teaching the Christian Life (2:1–8)
- Be Good in Every Way! (3:1–11)

FACTOIDS

Who wrote this book? Possibly Paul, but more likely one of Paul's followers.

When was it written? If Paul wrote it, as early as AD 65, but more likely between AD 90 and 100.

Who was it written for? This letter was written to Titus, a trusted leader in the early Church.

Why was it written? It was written to encourage Titus in his role as pastor and to give him advice.

Important themes

- Pastors are given advice for teaching people how to live as Christians.
- People need encouragement to keep good habits.

TITUS

1

¹From Paul, a servant of God and an apostle of Jesus Christ.

I was chosen and sent to help the faith of God's chosen people and to lead them to the truth taught by our religion, ²which is based on the hope for eternal life. God, who does not lie, promised us this life before the beginning of time, ³and at the right time he revealed it in his message. This was entrusted to me, and I proclaim it by order of God our Savior.

⁴I write to Titus, my true son in the faith that we have in common.

May God the Father and Christ Jesus our Savior give you grace and peace.

Titus' Work in Crete

⁵I left you in Crete, so that you could put in order the things that still needed doing and appoint church elders in every town. Remember my instructions: ⁶an elder must be without fault; he must have only one wife,*a* and his children must be believers and not have the reputation of being wild or disobedient. ⁷For since a church leader is in charge of God's work, he should be without fault. He must not be arrogant or quick-tempered, or a drunkard or violent or greedy for money. ⁸He must be hospitable and love what is good. He must be self-controlled, upright, holy, and disciplined. ⁹He must hold firmly to the message which can be trusted and which agrees with the doctrine. In this way he will be able to encourage others with the true teaching and also to show the error of those who are opposed to it.

¹⁰For there are many, especially the converts from Judaism, who rebel and deceive others with their nonsense. ¹¹It is necessary to stop their talk, because they are upsetting whole families by teaching what they should not, and all for the shameful purpose of making money. ¹²⁻¹³It was a Cretan himself, one of their own prophets, who spoke the truth when he said, "Cretans are always liars, wicked beasts, and lazy gluttons." For this reason you must rebuke

them sharply, so that they may have a healthy faith ¹⁴and no longer hold on to Jewish legends and to human commandments which come from people who have rejected the truth. ¹⁵Everything is pure to those who are themselves pure; but nothing is pure to those who are defiled and unbelieving, for their minds and consciences have been defiled. ¹⁶They claim that they know God, but their actions deny it. They are hateful and disobedient, not fit to do anything good.

Sound Doctrine

2

¹But you must teach what agrees with sound doctrine. ²Instruct the older men to be sober, sensible, and self-controlled; to be sound in their faith, love, and endurance. ³In the same way instruct the older women to behave as women should who live a holy life. They must not be slanderers or slaves to wine. They must teach what is good, ⁴in order to train the younger women to love their husbands and children, ⁵to be self-controlled and pure, and to be good housewives who submit themselves to their husbands, so that no one will speak evil of the message that comes from God.

⁶In the same way urge the young men to be self-controlled. ⁷In all things you yourself must be an example of good behavior. Be sincere and serious in your teaching. ⁸Use sound words that cannot be criticized, so that your enemies may be put to shame by not having anything bad to say about us.

⁹Slaves are to submit themselves to their masters and please them in all things. They must not talk back to them ¹⁰or steal from them. Instead, they must show that they are always good and faithful, so as to bring credit to the teaching about God our Savior in all they do.

¹¹For God has revealed his grace for the salvation of all people. ¹²That grace instructs us to give up ungodly living and worldly passions,

---

a **1:6** have only one wife; *or* be married only once.
1:4 2 Cor 8:23; Gal 2:3; 2 Tim 4:10   **1:6–9** 1 Tim 3:2–7

and to live self-controlled, upright, and godly lives in this world, [13]as we wait for the blessed Day we hope for, when the glory of our great God and Savior Jesus Christ[b] will appear. [14]He gave himself for us, to rescue us from all wickedness and to make us a pure people who belong to him alone and are eager to do good.

[15]Teach these things and use your full authority as you encourage and rebuke your hearers. Let none of them look down on you.

Christian Conduct

3 [1]Remind your people to submit to rulers and authorities, to obey them, and to be ready to do good in every way. [2]Tell them not to speak evil of anyone, but to be peaceful and friendly, and always to show a gentle attitude toward everyone. [3]For we ourselves were once foolish, disobedient, and wrong. We were slaves to passions and pleasures of all kinds. We spent our lives in malice and envy; others hated us and we hated them. [4]But when the kindness and love of God our Savior was revealed, [5]he saved us. It was not because of any good deeds that we ourselves had done, but because of his own mercy that he saved us, through the Holy Spirit, who gives us new birth and new life by washing us. [6]God poured out the Holy Spirit abundantly on us through Jesus Christ our Savior, [7]so that by his grace we might be put right with God and come into possession of the eternal life we hope for. [8]This is a true saying.

I want you to give special emphasis to these matters, so that those who believe in God may be concerned with giving their time to doing good deeds, which are good and useful for everyone. [9]But avoid stupid arguments, long lists of ancestors, quarrels, and fights about the Law. They are useless and worthless. [10]Give at least two warnings to those who cause divisions, and then have nothing more to do with them. [11]You know that such people are corrupt, and their sins prove that they are wrong.

Final Instructions

[12]When I send Artemas or Tychicus to you,

Making Big Things from Small Beginnings

The Letter to Titus is very short and was written to a Church leader who did not become very famous. And yet a passage from this letter (2:11–14) is used every year at Christmas midnight Mass. Four little verses that are read at Mass begin with, "Beloved: The grace of God has appeared, saving all and training us to reject godless ways and worldly desires" (*The Lectionary*, p. 106).

The Christmas story itself has other examples of God making big things from small beginnings. Mary is just a young girl—a teenager—and she becomes the mother of God. Bethlehem is a tiny town, not very well known for anything, and it becomes the birthplace of our Messiah.

God is very good at making surprising things happen. So don't ever doubt the importance of whatever you do for God. Even if you think it's small, God can make very big things come from it.

— Titus 2:11–14

do your best to come to me in Nicopolis, because I have decided to spend the winter there. [13]Do your best to help Zenas the lawyer and Apollos to get started on their travels, and see to it that they have everything they need. [14]Our people must learn to spend their time doing good, in order to provide for real needs; they should not live useless lives.

[15]All who are with me send you greetings. Give our greetings to our friends in the faith.

God's grace be with you all.

[b] 2:13 our great God and Savior Jesus Christ; *or* the great God and our Savior Jesus Christ.
2:14 **a** Ps 130:8; **b** Ex 19:5; Deut 4:20; 7:6; 14:2; 1 Pet 2:9   **3:12** Acts 20:4; Eph 6:21, 22; Col 4:7, 8; 2 Tim 4:12   **3:13** Acts 18:24; 1 Cor 16:12

Have you ever seen a movie or a TV show about slavery? Have you ever thought about what it's like to be a slave? Masters don't usually treat their slaves very well. In fact, the treatment is often horrible.

While he was in prison, Paul wrote this letter to a slave owner named Philemon. Onesimus was Philemon's slave. He ran away and somehow ended up in prison with Paul, and became a Christian. Paul is trying to convince Philemon to accept Onesimus back as his brother in Christ. Not only does Paul want Onesimus to escape all punishment, he also wants Philemon to give Onesimus freedom.

Picture one of those slave masters in a movie or TV show you have seen. Can you imagine such a person changing his ways and accepting one of his runaway slaves as a brother? That's exactly what Paul is asking.

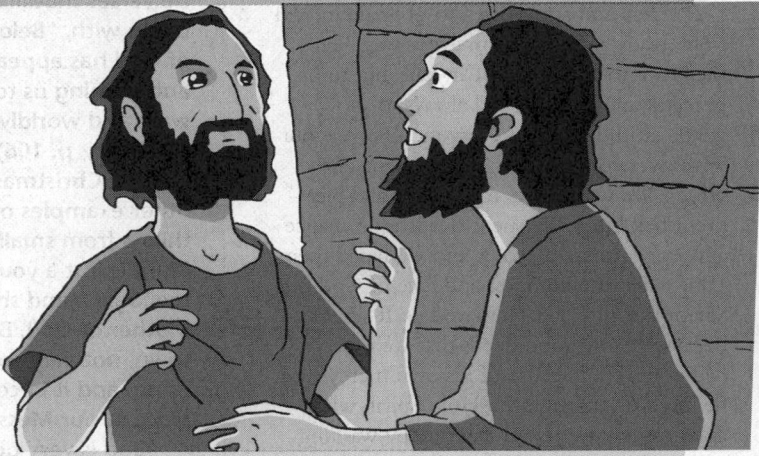

Head lines

- Paul Begs, "Accept Slave as Brother" (verses 17–22)
- Paul gives thanks for Philemon's love and faith (verses 4–7)

FACTOIDS

Who wrote this book? Paul, writing from prison.

When was it written? Around AD 61 to 63.

Who was it written for? It was written to Philemon, one of Paul's friends, who once owned Onesimus as a slave.

Why was it written? The author wanted to convince Philemon to welcome back his former slave Onesimus and accept him as a fellow Christian.

Important theme
- Paul encourages Philemon to accept Onesimus back to his home, no longer just a slave, but now a brother in Christ.

PHILEMON

¹From Paul, a prisoner for the sake of Christ Jesus, and from our brother Timothy—

To our friend and fellow worker Philemon, ²and the church that meets in your house, and our sister Apphia, and our fellow soldier Archippus:

³May God our Father and the Lord Jesus Christ give you grace and peace.

Philemon's Love and Faith

⁴Brother Philemon, every time I pray, I mention you and give thanks to my God. ⁵For I hear of your love for all of God's people and the faith you have in the Lord Jesus. ⁶My prayer is that our fellowship with you as believers will bring about a deeper understanding of every blessing which we have in our life in union with Christ. ⁷Your love, dear brother, has brought me great joy and much encouragement! You have cheered the hearts of all of God's people.

A Request for Onesimus

⁸For this reason I could be bold enough, as your brother in Christ, to order you to do what should be done. ⁹But because I love you, I make a request instead. I do this even though I am Paul, the ambassador of Christ Jesus, and at present also a prisoner for his sake.ᵃ ¹⁰So I make a request to you on behalf of Onesimus, who is my own son in Christ; for while in prison I have become his spiritual father. ¹¹At one time he was of no use to you, but now he is usefulᵇ both to you and to me.

ᵃ **9** the ambassador of Christ Jesus, and at present also a prisoner for his sake; *or* an old man, and at present a prisoner for the sake of Christ Jesus. ᵇ **11** *The Greek name Onesimus means "useful."*
2 Col 4:17 **10** Col 4:9

Pray It!

Slaves Today

Paul probably didn't believe in slavery. In another part of the Bible, he says this: "So there is no difference between Jews and Gentiles, between slaves and free people, between men and women; you are all one in union with Christ Jesus" (Galatians 3:28). In those days, each of these three relationships had one person who was above the other person in some way. Paul is essentially saying, "Not anymore."

In this letter Paul is asking Philemon to welcome Onesimus as a brother in Christ. Paul wants Onesimus to be a free man, not a slave anymore. Even in today's modern world, there are still slaves. People are forced to work in factories or sweatshops. Women and children are kidnapped and forced to work as prostitutes. In some places people are kidnapped and forced to be soldiers.

Think about being chained in a factory and forced to sew clothing or stitch soccer balls. Or worse, forced to sell your body for sex or to kill other people. Think about that cruel existence, day after day, year after year. Say a prayer that some day soon, every country and company in the world will recognize the rights of freedom for all people. Pray that slavery will truly be "not anymore."

Welcome him back. (17)

¹²I am sending him back to you now, and with him goes my heart. ¹³I would like to keep him here with me, while I am in prison for the gospel's sake, so that he could help me in your place. ¹⁴However, I do not want to force you to help me; rather, I would like for you to do it of your own free will. So I will not do anything unless you agree.

¹⁵It may be that Onesimus was away from you for a short time so that you might have him back for all time. ¹⁶And now he is not just a slave, but much more than a slave: he is a dear brother in Christ. How much he means to me! And how much more he will mean to you, both as a slave and as a brother in the Lord!

¹⁷So, if you think of me as your partner, welcome him back just as you would welcome me. ¹⁸If he has done you any wrong or owes you anything, charge it to my account. ¹⁹Here, I will write this with my own hand: *I, Paul, will pay you back* (I should not have to remind you, of course, that you owe your very self to me.) ²⁰So, my brother, please do me this favor for the Lord's sake; as a brother in Christ, cheer me up!

²¹I am sure, as I write this, that you will do what I ask—in fact I know that you will do even more. ²²At the same time, get a room ready for me, because I hope that God will answer the prayers of all of you and give me back to you.

Final Greetings

²³Epaphras, who is in prison with me for the sake of Christ Jesus, sends you his greetings, ²⁴and so do my co-workers Mark, Aristarchus, Demas, and Luke.

²⁵May the grace of the Lord Jesus Christ be with you all.

23 Col 1:7; 4:12   **24 a** Acts 12:12, 25; 13:13; 15:37–39; Col 4:10; **b** Acts 19:29; 27:2; Col 4:10; **c** Col 4:14; 2 Tim 4:10; **d** Col 4:14; 2 Tim 4:11

Have you ever gone to Mass and the priest said something during the homily that really gave you a good idea of who Jesus is? The Letter to the Hebrews is sort of like that but in writing. It is filled with messages of encouragement and great descriptions of Jesus. The writer lets us know just how wonderful Jesus is and tells us that Jesus is more important than the angels. The letter makes a strong case that Jesus is the divine Son of God and that only he could take away the sins of the world.

The writer also encourages Christians (both then and now) to hold fast to the faith that has been given them and to continue moving toward Christ. We can endure whatever comes our way if we keep our faith in Jesus Christ.

Head lines

- Who Is Greater Than the Angels? (1:4–14)
- God's Son Saves People from Sin! (2:9–10)
- God's Promise Is an Anchor (6:13–17)
- Jesus Is the Perfect High Priest (9:6–15)
- Jewish Heroes Kept the Faith (11:1–35)

FACTOIDS

Who wrote this book? Unknown, but sometimes attributed to Paul.
When was it written? Around AD 80 to 90.
Who was it written for? It was written to a group of Greek-speaking Christians, some of whom were possibly Jewish Christians who were in danger of losing their faith.
Why was it written? It was written to tell the Christians to hold on to their faith and to move toward Christ.
What is its literary style? Although called a letter, it is really more like a sermon filled with explanations and metaphors.
Jesus connection. This letter contains many references to Jesus that are found in the Old Testament. The author does this to prove that Jesus fulfills the Jewish Law and is the sacrifice that ends all sacrifices (Hebrews 10:5–7).

Important themes
- God saves us through Jesus' sacrifice.
- Hold fast to faith and move toward Christ.

HEBREWS

God's Word through His Son

1 ¹In the past God spoke to our ancestors many times and in many ways through the prophets, ²but in these last days he has spoken to us through his Son. He is the one through whom God created the universe, the one whom God has chosen to possess all things at the end. ³He reflects the brightness of God's glory and is the exact likeness of God's own being, sustaining the universe with his powerful word. After achieving forgiveness for the sins of all human beings, he sat down in heaven at the right side of God, the Supreme Power.

The Greatness of God's Son

⁴The Son was made greater than the angels, just as the name that God gave him is greater than theirs. ⁵For God never said to any of his angels,

"You are my Son;
today I have become your Father."

Nor did God say about any angel,

"I will be his Father,
and he will be my Son."

⁶But when God was about to send his first-born Son into the world, he said,

"All of God's angels must worship him."

⁷But about the angels God said,

"God makes his angels winds,
and his servants flames of fire."

⁸About the Son, however, God said:

"Your kingdom, O God, will last*a* forever and ever!
You rule over your*b* people with justice.
⁹You love what is right and hate what is wrong.
That is why God, your God, has chosen you
and has given you the joy of an honor far greater
than he gave to your companions."

¹⁰He also said,

"You, Lord, in the beginning created the earth,
and with your own hands you made the heavens.
¹¹They will disappear, but you will remain;
they will all wear out like clothes.
¹²You will fold them up like a coat,
and they will be changed like clothes.
But you are always the same,
and your life never ends."

¹³God never said to any of his angels:

"Sit here at my right side
until I put your enemies
as a footstool under your feet."

¹⁴What are the angels, then? They are spirits who serve God and are sent by him to help those who are to receive salvation.

The Great Salvation

2 ¹That is why we must hold on all the more firmly to the truths we have heard, so that we will not be carried away. ²The message given to our ancestors by the angels was shown to be true, and those who did not follow it or obey it received the punishment they deserved. ³How, then, shall we escape if we pay no attention to such a great salvation? The Lord himself first announced this salvation, and those who heard him proved to us that it is true. ⁴At the same time God added his witness to theirs by performing all kinds of miracles and wonders and by distributing the gifts of the Holy Spirit according to his will.

The One Who Leads Us to Salvation

⁵God has not placed the angels as rulers over the new world to come—the world of

---

a **1:8** Your kingdom, O God, will last; *or* God is your kingdom.   *b* **1:8** your; *some manuscripts have* his.
1:2 Wis 7:22   **1:3** Wis 7:25, 26; 8:1   **1:5 a** Ps 2:7; **b** 2 Sam 7:14; 1 Chr 17:13   **1:6** Deut 32:43 (LXX)
1:7 Ps 104:4 (LXX)   **1:8, 9** Ps 45:6, 7   **1:10–12** Ps 102:25–27 (LXX)   **1:13** Ps 110:1   **1:14** Tob 12:14, 15

Angels

Catholic Connections

Do you believe in angels? Whether you do or not, they are real. In chapters 1 and 2 of Hebrews, the author refers to angels several times. At one point he defines what angels are, "They are spirits who serve God and are sent by him to help those who are to receive salvation" (1:14). The Catholic Church teaches that angels belong to the unseen part of Creation. They cannot be seen, heard, touched, or smelled. They are spiritual beings without physical bodies, and they are immortal; that is, they will live forever. When angels interact with human beings, it is often to deliver messages from God.

But as great and wonderful as angels are, the Letter to the Hebrews makes it clear that Christ Jesus is greater than the angels. Angels are beings created by God, but Jesus is God's Son (1:5) who has existed with God forever (1:2). Jesus, not the angels, will rule the new world to come forever (1:8; 2:5). Angels are wonderful, and it is comforting to know they exist. But Jesus is still greater, and our salvation comes from him.

— Hebrews 1:4—2:8

Hebrews

which we speak. ⁶Instead, as it is said somewhere in the Scriptures:

"What are human beings, O God, that
    you should think of them;
mere human beings, that you should
    care for them?
⁷You made them for a little while lower
    than the angels;
you crowned them with glory and
    honor,ᶜ
⁸ and made them rulers over all things."
It says that God made them "rulers over all things"; this clearly includes everything. We do not, however, see human beings ruling over all things now. ⁹But we do see Jesus, who for a little while was made lower than the angels, so that through God's grace he should die for everyone. We see him now crowned with glory and honor because of the death he suffered. ¹⁰It was only right that God, who creates and preserves all things,

should make Jesus perfect through suffering, in order to bring many children to share his glory. For Jesus is the one who leads them to salvation.

¹¹He purifies people from their sins, and both he and those who are made pure all have the same Father. That is why Jesus is not ashamed to call them his family. ¹²He says to God,

"I will tell my people what you have
    done;
I will praise you in their meeting."
¹³He also says, "I will put my trust in God." And he also says, "Here I am with the children that God has given me."

¹⁴Since the children, as he calls them, are people of flesh and blood, Jesus himself became like them and shared their human nature. He did this so that through his death he might destroy the Devil, who has the power over death, ¹⁵and in this way set free

ᶜ **2:7** *Many manuscripts add:* You made them rulers over everything you made (see Ps 8:6).
2:6–8 Ps 8:4–6   **2:12** Ps 22:22   **2:13 a** Isa 8:17 (LXX); **b** Isa 8:18

"In the past God spoke to our ancestors . . . through the prophets, but in these last days he has spoken to us through his Son" *(Hebrews 1:1–2).*

Hebrews

those who were slaves all their lives because of their fear of death. 16For it is clear that it is not the angels that he helps. Instead, he helps the descendants of Abraham. 17This means that he had to become like his people in every way, in order to be their faithful and merciful High Priest in his service to God, so that the people's sins would be forgiven. 18And now he can help those who are tempted, because he himself was tempted and suffered.

Jesus Is Greater than Moses

3 1My Christian friends, who also have been called by God! Think of Jesus, whom God sent to be the High Priest of the faith we profess. 2He was faithful to God, who chose him to do this work, just as Moses was faithful in his work in God's house. 3A man who builds a house receives more honor than the house itself. In the same way Jesus is worthy of much greater honor than Moses. 4Every house, of course, is built by some-one—and God is the one who has built all things. 5Moses was faithful in God's house as a servant, and he spoke of the things that God would say in the future. 6But Christ is faithful as the Son in charge of God's house. We are his house if we keep up our courage and our confidence in what we hope for.

A Rest for God's People

7So then, as the Holy Spirit says,
"If you hear God's voice today,
8   do not be stubborn, as your ancestors
        were when they rebelled against God,
    as they were that day in the desert
        when they put him to the test.
9There they put me to the test and tried
    me, says God,
    although they had seen what I did for
        forty years.
10And so I was angry with those people
    and said,

'They are always disloyal
    and refuse to obey my commands.'
11I was angry and made a solemn promise:
    'They will never enter the land where I
        would have given them rest!' "

12My friends, be careful that none of you have a heart so evil and unbelieving that you will turn away from the living God. 13Instead, in order that none of you be deceived by sin and become stubborn, you must help one another every day, as long as the word "Today" in the scripture applies to us. 14For we are all partners with Christ if we hold firmly to the end the confidence we had at the beginning.

15This is what the scripture says:
"If you hear God's voice today,
    do not be stubborn, as your ancestors
        were
    when they rebelled against God."

16Who were the people who heard God's voice and rebelled against him? All those who were led out of Egypt by Moses. 17With whom was God angry for forty years? With the people who sinned, who fell down dead in the desert. 18When God made his solemn promise, "They will never enter the land where I would have given them rest"—of whom was he speaking? Of those who rebelled. 19We see, then, that they were not able to enter the land, because they did not believe.

4 1Now, God has offered us the promise that we may receive that rest he spoke about. Let us take care, then, that none of you will be found to have failed to receive that promised rest. 2For we have heard the Good News, just as they did. They heard the message, but it did them no good, because when they heard it, they did not accept it with faith. 3We who believe, then, do receive that rest which God promised. It is just as he said,

"I was angry and made a solemn promise:
    'They will never enter the land where I
        would have given them rest!' "

2:16 Isa 41:8, 9   **3:2** Num 12:7   **3:7–11** Ps 95:7–11 (LXX)   **3:15** Ps 95:7, 8 (LXX)   **3:16–18** Num 14:1–35   **4:3** Ps 95:11

Hebrews 3:7–11 is based on Psalm 95:7–11. Find that psalm and compare it with this passage in Hebrews.

He said this even though his work had been finished from the time he created the world. [4]For somewhere in the Scriptures this is said about the seventh day: "God rested on the seventh day from all his work." [5]This same matter is spoken of again: "They will never enter that land where I would have given them rest." [6]Those who first heard the Good News did not receive that rest, because they did not believe. There are, then, others who are allowed to receive it. [7]This is shown by the fact that God sets another day, which is called "Today." Many years later he spoke of it through David in the scripture already quoted:

"If you hear God's voice today,
    do not be stubborn."

[8]If Joshua had given the people the rest that God had promised, God would not have spoken later about another day. [9]As it is, however, there still remains for God's people a rest like God's resting on the seventh day. [10]For those who receive that rest which God promised will rest from their own work, just as God rested from his. [11]Let us, then, do our best to receive that rest, so that no one of us will fail as they did because of their lack of faith.

[12]The word of God is alive and active, sharper than any double-edged sword. It cuts all the way through, to where soul and spirit meet, to where joints and marrow come together. It judges the desires and thoughts of the heart. [13]There is nothing that can be hid from God; everything in all creation is exposed and lies open before his eyes. And it is to him that we must all give an account of ourselves.

Jesus the Great High Priest

[14]Let us, then, hold firmly to the faith we profess. For we have a great High Priest who has gone into the very presence of God—Jesus, the Son of God. [15]Our High Priest is not one who cannot feel sympathy for our weaknesses. On the contrary, we have a High Priest who was tempted in every way that we are, but did not sin. [16]Let us have confidence, then, and approach God's throne,

Power of God's Word

The Bible has many gory parts, and Hebrews 4:12–13 is just one example. The image of the Word of God slicing through someone is not supposed to be realistic, though. Rather, it is meant to show the power of God's Word. The Word of God is so powerful that nothing in our lives can be hidden from it. Even if you are trying to hide something from others, the Word of God will make it clear whether your life is about doing good or doing bad.

We cannot hide from God's love and concern for us; and we cannot hide our actions, thoughts, and desires from God. This should help us remember to keep God number one in our lives. List the top 10 things that influence the way you live your life. If God isn't on the top of your list, what can you do to put God there?

— Hebrews 4:12–13

where there is grace. There we will receive mercy and find grace to help us just when we need it.

5 [1]Every high priest is chosen from his fellow-men and appointed to serve God on their behalf, to offer sacrifices and offerings for sins. [2]Since he himself is weak in many ways, he is able to be gentle with those who are ignorant and make mistakes. [3]And because he is himself weak, he must offer sacrifices not only for the sins of the people but also for his own sins. [4]No one chooses for himself the honor of being a high priest. It is only by God's call that a man is made a high priest—just as Aaron was.

4:4 Gen 2:2   **4:5** Ps 95:11   **4:7** Ps 95:7, 8 (LXX)   **4:8** Deut 31:7; Josh 22:4   **4:10** Gen 2:2   **4:13** Wis 1:6   **5:3** Lev 9:7   **5:4** Ex 28:1

Hebrews

5 In the same way, Christ did not take upon himself the honor of being a high priest. Instead, God said to him,

"You are my Son;
today I have become your Father."

6 He also said in another place,

"You will be a priest forever,
in the priestly order of Melchizedek."[d]

7 In his life on earth Jesus made his prayers and requests with loud cries and tears to God, who could save him from death. Because he was humble and devoted, God heard him. 8 But even though he was God's Son, he learned through his sufferings to be obedient. 9 When he was made perfect, he became the source of eternal salvation for all those who obey him, 10 and God declared him to be high priest, in the priestly order of Melchizedek.[d]

Warning against Abandoning the Faith

11 There is much we have to say about this matter, but it is hard to explain to you, because you are so slow to understand. 12 There has been enough time for you to be teachers—yet you still need someone to teach you the first lessons of God's message. Instead of eating solid food, you still have to drink milk. 13 Anyone who has to drink milk is still a child, without any experience in the matter of right and wrong. 14 Solid food, on the other hand, is for adults, who through practice are able to distinguish between good and evil.

6 1 Let us go forward, then, to mature teaching and leave behind us the first lessons of the Christian message. We should not lay again the foundation of turning away from useless works and believing in God; 2 of the teaching about baptisms[e] and the laying on of hands; of the resurrection of the dead and the eternal judgment. 3 Let us go forward! And this is what we will do, if God allows.

4 For how can those who abandon their faith be brought back to repent again? They were once in God's light; they tasted heaven's

God's Sure Promise

"I promise to call you tonight," Josefina said to her friend Beth. Beth had had a really bad day and wanted to talk to Josefina about it. When Josefina called her that night, Beth felt better and was able to turn her day around. By keeping her promise, Josefina showed Beth that Beth could trust her.

Chapter 6 in Hebrews tells us that God keeps his promises. This gives us hope and can be a comfort. It gives us an anchor. Anchors keep boats in place through bad weather, and that is what God does for us. The next time you need some hope, read Hebrews 6:9–19 and remind yourself of how God keeps promises.

— Hebrews 6:9–19

gift and received their share of the Holy Spirit; 5 they knew from experience that God's word is good, and they had felt the powers of the coming age. 6 And then they abandoned their faith! It is impossible to bring them back to repent again, because they are again crucifying the Son of God and exposing him to public shame.

7 God blesses the soil which drinks in the rain that often falls on it and which grows plants that are useful to those for whom it is cultivated. 8 But if it grows thorns and weeds, it is worth nothing; it is in danger of being cursed by God and will be destroyed by fire.

9 But even if we speak like this, dear friends, we feel sure about you. We know that you have the better blessings that belong

---

[d] **5:6, 10** in the priestly order of Melchizedek; *or* like Melchizedek; *or* in the line of succession to Melchizedek.
[e] **6:2** baptisms; *or* purification ceremonies.
5:5 Ps 2:7 **5:6** Ps 110:4 **5:7** Mt 26:36–46; Mk 14:32–42; Lk 22:39–46 **5:12, 13** 1 Cor 3:2 **6:8** Gen 3:17, 18

to your salvation. 10God is not unfair. He will not forget the work you did or the love you showed for him in the help you gave and are still giving to other Christians. 11Our great desire is that each of you keep up your eagerness to the end, so that the things you hope for will come true. 12We do not want you to become lazy, but to be like those who believe and are patient, and so receive what God has promised.

God's Sure Promise

13When God made his promise to Abraham, he made a vow to do what he had promised. Since there was no one greater than himself, he used his own name when he made his vow. 14He said, "I promise you that I will bless you and give you many descendants." 15Abraham was patient, and so he received what God had promised. 16When we make a vow, we use the name of someone greater than ourselves, and the vow settles all arguments. 17To those who were to receive what he promised, God wanted to make it very clear that he would never change his purpose; so he added his vow to the promise. 18There are these two things, then, that cannot change and about which God cannot lie. So we who have found safety with him are greatly encouraged to hold firmly to the hope placed before us. 19We have this hope as an anchor for our lives. It is safe and sure, and goes through the curtain of the heavenly temple into the inner sanctuary. 20On our behalf Jesus has gone in there before us and has become a high priest forever, in the priestly order of Melchizedek.ƒ

The Priest Melchizedek

7 1This Melchizedek was king of Salem and a priest of the Most High God. As Abraham was coming back from the battle in which he defeated the four kings,

Melchizedek met him and blessed him, 2and Abraham gave him one tenth of all he had taken. (The first meaning of Melchizedek's name is "King of Righteousness"; and because he was king of Salem, his name also means "King of Peace.") 3There is no record of Melchizedek's father or mother or of any of his ancestors; no record of his birth or of his death. He is like the Son of God; he remains a priest forever.

4You see, then, how great he was. Abraham, our famous ancestor, gave him one tenth of all he got in the battle. 5And those descendants of Levi who are priests are commanded by the Law to collect one tenth from the people of Israel, that is, from their own people, even though they are also descendants of Abraham. 6Melchizedek was not descended from Levi, but he collected one tenth from Abraham and blessed him, the man who received God's promises. 7There is no doubt that the one who blesses is greater than the one who is blessed. 8In the case of the priests the tenth is collected by men who die; but as for Melchizedek the tenth was collected by one who lives, as the scripture says. 9And, so to speak, when Abraham paid the tenth, Levi (whose descendants collect the tenth) also paid it. 10For Levi had not yet been born, but was, so to speak, in the body of his ancestor Abraham when Melchizedek met him.

11It was on the basis of the levitical priesthood that the Law was given to the people of Israel. Now, if the work of the levitical priests had been perfect, there would have been no need for a different kind of priest to appear, one who is in the priestly order of Melchizedek,ƒ not of Aaron. 12For when the priesthood is changed, there also has to be a change in the law. 13And our Lord, of whom these things are said, belonged to a different tribe, and no member of his tribe ever served as a priest. 14It is well known that he was born a member of the tribe of Judah;

Hebrews

ƒ **6:20; 7:11** in the priestly order of Melchizedek (see 5:6).
6:14 Gen 22:16, 17   **6:19** Lev 16:2   **6:20** Ps 110:4   **7:1, 2** Gen 14:17–20   **7:5** Num 18:21

Hebrews

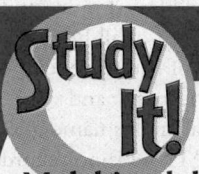

Melchizedek

"Melcheesy who?" Joellen said to Father Raul after Mass.

"Melchizedek, Mel-kiss-a-deck." Joellen had never heard the Eucharistic prayer that Father Raul prayed at Mass. "So, who is Melchizedek, anyway?" Father Raul explained that Melchizedek was a priest and king who, according to the Book of Genesis, offered a sacrifice of bread and wine to God (14:17–20). Because Melchizedek did this, he became Abraham's priest. Father Raul finished his story of Melchizedek by telling Joellen that some early Christians saw similarities between Jesus and Melchizedek. They both offered bread and wine to God.

Melchizedek was an early (but not complete) example of Jesus' priesthood, which is explained in the Letter to the Hebrews.

— Hebrews, chapter 7

and Moses did not mention this tribe when he spoke of priests.

Another Priest, like Melchizedek

15 The matter becomes even plainer; a different priest has appeared, who is like Melchizedek. 16 He was made a priest, not by human rules and regulations, but through the power of a life which has no end. 17 For the scripture says, "You will be a priest forever, in the priestly order of Melchizedek."*f*

18 The old rule, then, is set aside, because it was weak and useless. 19 For the Law of Moses could not make anything perfect. And now a better hope has been provided through which we come near to God.

20 In addition, there is also God's vow. There was no such vow when the others were made priests. 21 But Jesus became a priest by means of a vow when God said to him,

"The Lord has made a solemn promise
    and will not take it back:
'You will be a priest forever.' "

22 This difference, then, also makes Jesus the guarantee of a better covenant.

23 There is another difference: there were many of those other priests, because they died and could not continue their work. 24 But Jesus lives on forever, and his work as priest does not pass on to someone else. 25 And so he is able, now and always, to save those who come to God through him, because he lives forever to plead with God for them.

26 Jesus, then, is the High Priest that meets our needs. He is holy; he has no fault or sin in him; he has been set apart from sinners and raised above the heavens. 27 He is not like other high priests; he does not need to offer sacrifices every day for his own sins first and then for the sins of the people. He offered one sacrifice, once and for all, when he offered himself. 28 The Law of Moses appoints men who are imperfect to be high priests; but God's promise made with the vow, which came later than the Law, appoints the Son, who has been made perfect forever.

Jesus Our High Priest

8 ¹ The whole point of what we are saying is that we have such a High Priest, who sits at the right of the throne of the Divine Majesty in heaven. ² He serves as high priest in the Most Holy Place, that is, in the

f **7:17** in the priestly order of Melchizedek *(see 5:6)*.
7:17 Ps 110:4   **7:21** Ps 110:4   **7:27** Lev 9:7   **8:1** Ps 110:1

The *high priest* of the Jewish people was the only one who could enter the most sacred part of the Temple and offer sacrifice to God.

real tent which was put up by the Lord, not by human hands.

³Every high priest is appointed to present offerings and animal sacrifices to God, and so our High Priest must also have something to offer. ⁴If he were on earth, he would not be a priest at all, since there are priests who offer the gifts required by the Jewish Law. ⁵The work they do as priests is really only a copy and a shadow of what is in heaven. It is the same as it was with Moses. When he was about to build the Sacred Tent, God told him, "Be sure to make everything according to the pattern you were shown on the mountain." ⁶But now, Jesus has been given priestly work which is superior to theirs, just as the covenant which he arranged between God and his people is a better one, because it is based on promises of better things.

⁷If there had been nothing wrong with the first covenant, there would have been no need for a second one. ⁸But God finds fault with his people when he says,

"The days are coming, says the Lord,
    when I will draw up a new covenant
        with the people of Israel and with
        the people of Judah.
⁹It will not be like the covenant that I
        made with their ancestors
    on the day I took them by the hand
        and led them out of Egypt.
They were not faithful to the covenant I
        made with them,
    and so I paid no attention to them.
¹⁰Now, this is the covenant that I will make
        with the people of Israel
    in the days to come, says the Lord:
I will put my laws in their minds
    and write them on their hearts.
I will be their God,
    and they will be my people.
¹¹None of them will have to teach their
        friends
    or tell their neighbors,
    'Know the Lord.'
For they will all know me,
    from the least to the greatest.
¹²I will forgive their sins

and will no longer remember their
        wrongs."
¹³By speaking of a new covenant, God has made the first one old; and anything that becomes old and worn out will soon disappear.

Earthly and Heavenly Worship

9 ¹The first covenant had rules for worship and a place made for worship as well. ²A tent was put up, the outer one, which was called the Holy Place. In it were the lampstand and the table with the bread offered to God. ³Behind the second curtain was the tent called the Most Holy Place. ⁴In it were the gold altar for the burning of incense and the Covenant Box all covered with gold and containing the gold jar with the manna in it, Aaron's stick that had sprouted leaves, and the two stone tablets with the commandments written on them. ⁵Above the Box were the winged creatures representing God's presence, with their wings spread over the place where sins were forgiven. But now is not the time to explain everything in detail.

⁶This is how those things have been arranged. The priests go into the outer tent every day to perform their duties, ⁷but only the high priest goes into the inner tent, and he does so only once a year. He takes with him blood which he offers to God on behalf of himself and for the sins which the people have committed without knowing they were sinning. ⁸The Holy Spirit clearly teaches from all these arrangements that the way into the Most Holy Place has not yet been opened as long as the outer tent still stands. ⁹This is a symbol which points to the present time. It means that the offerings and animal sacrifices presented to God cannot make the worshiper's heart perfect, ¹⁰since they have to do only with food, drink, and various purification ceremonies. These are all outward rules, which apply only until the time when God will establish the new order.

¹¹But Christ has already come as the High Priest of the good things that are already

8:5 Ex 25:40 **8:8–12** Jer 31:31–34 (LXX)   **9:2 a** Ex 26:1–30; **b** Ex 25:31–40; **c** Ex 25:23–30   **9:3** Ex 26:31–33   **9:4 a** Ex 30:1–6; **b** Ex 25:10–16; **c** Ex 16:33; **d** Num 17:8–10; **e** Ex 25:16; Deut 10:3–5   **9:5** Ex 25:18–22   **9:6** Num 18:2–6   **9:7** Lev 16:2–34

here.g The tent in which he serves is greater and more perfect; it is not a tent made by human hands, that is, it is not a part of this created world. 12 When Christ went through the tent and entered once and for all into the Most Holy Place, he did not take the blood of goats and bulls to offer as a sacrifice; rather, he took his own blood and obtained eternal salvation for us. 13 The blood of goats and bulls and the ashes of a burnt calf are sprinkled on the people who are ritually unclean, and this purifies them by taking away their ritual impurity. 14 Since this is true, how much more is accomplished by the blood of Christ! Through the eternal Spirit he offered himself as a perfect sacrifice to God. His blood will purify our consciences from useless rituals, so that we may serve the living God.

15 For this reason Christ is the one who arranges a new covenant, so that those who have been called by God may receive the eternal blessings that God has promised. This can be done because there has been a death which sets people free from the wrongs they did while the first covenant was in effect.

16 In the case of a will it is necessary to prove that the person who made it has died, 17 for a will means nothing while the person who made it is alive; it goes into effect only after his death. 18 That is why even the first covenant h went into effect only with the use of blood. 19 First, Moses proclaimed to the people all the commandments as set forth in the Law. Then he took the blood of bulls and goats, mixed it with water, and sprinkled it on the book of the Law and all the people, using a sprig of hyssop and some red wool. 20 He said, "This is the blood which seals the covenant that God has commanded you to obey." 21 In the same way Moses also sprinkled the blood on the Sacred Tent and over all the things used in worship. 22 Indeed, according to the Law almost everything is purified by blood, and sins are forgiven only if blood is poured out.

Christ's Sacrifice Takes Away Sins

23 Those things, which are copies of the heavenly originals, had to be purified in that way. But the heavenly things themselves require much better sacrifices. 24 For Christ did not go into a Holy Place made by human hands, which was a copy of the real one. He went into heaven itself, where he now appears on our behalf in the presence of God. 25 The Jewish high priest goes into the Most Holy Place every year with the blood of an animal. But Christ did not go in to offer himself many times, 26 for then he would have had to suffer many times ever since the creation of the world. Instead, now when all ages of time are nearing the end, he has appeared once and for all, to remove sin through the sacrifice of himself. 27 Everyone must die once, and after that be judged by God. 28 In the same manner Christ also was offered in sacrifice once to take away the sins of many. He will appear a second time, not to deal with sin, but to save those who are waiting for him.

10 1 The Jewish Law is not a full and faithful model of the real things; it is only a faint outline of the good things to come. The same sacrifices are offered forever, year after year. How can the Law, then, by means of these sacrifices make perfect the people who come to God? 2 If the people worshiping God had really been purified from their sins, they would not feel guilty of sin any more, and all sacrifices would stop. 3 As it is, however, the sacrifices serve year after year to remind people of their sins. 4 For the blood of bulls and goats can never take away sins.

5 For this reason, when Christ was about to come into the world, he said to God:

"You do not want sacrifices and offerings,
  but you have prepared a body for me.
6 You are not pleased with animals burned
    whole on the altar
  or with sacrifices to take away sins.
7 Then I said, 'Here I am,
    to do your will, O God,

---

g **9:11** already here; *some manuscripts have* coming.   h **9:18** COVENANT: *In Greek the same word means "will" and "covenant."*
9:13 a Lev 16:15, 16; **b** Num 19:9, 17–19   **9:19, 20** Ex 24:6–8   **9:21** Lev 8:15   **9:22** Lev 17:11   **9:28** Isa 53:12   **10:5–7** Ps 40:6–8 (LXX)

just as it is written of me in the book of the Law.' "

8 First he said, "You neither want nor are you pleased with sacrifices and offerings or with animals burned on the altar and the sacrifices to take away sins." He said this even though all these sacrifices are offered according to the Law. 9 Then he said, "Here I am, O God, to do your will." So God does away with all the old sacrifices and puts the sacrifice of Christ in their place. 10 Because Jesus Christ did what God wanted him to do, we are all purified from sin by the offering that he made of his own body once and for all.

11 Every Jewish priest performs his services every day and offers the same sacrifices many times; but these sacrifices can never take away sins. 12 Christ, however, offered one sacrifice for sins, an offering that is effective forever, and then he sat down at the right side of God. 13 There he now waits until God puts his enemies as a footstool under his feet. 14 With one sacrifice, then, he has made perfect forever those who are purified from sin.

15 And the Holy Spirit also gives us his witness. First he says,

16 "This is the covenant that I will make
　　with them
　　in the days to come, says the Lord:
I will put my laws in their hearts
　　and write them on their minds."

17 And then he says, "I will not remember their sins and evil deeds any longer." 18 So when these have been forgiven, an offering to take away sins is no longer needed.

Let Us Come Near to God

19 We have, then, my friends, complete freedom to go into the Most Holy Place by means of the death of Jesus. 20 He opened for us a new way, a living way, through the curtain—that is, through his own body. 21 We have a great priest in charge of the house of God. 22 So let us come near to God with a sincere heart and a sure faith, with hearts that have been purified from a guilty conscience and with bodies washed with clean water. 23 Let us hold on firmly to the hope we profess, because we can trust God to keep his promise. 24 Let us be concerned for one another, to help one another to show love and to do good. 25 Let us not give up the habit of meeting together, as some are doing. Instead, let us encourage one another all the more, since you see that the Day of the Lord is coming nearer.

Let us not give up the habit of meeting together.
(10:25)

26 For there is no longer any sacrifice that will take away sins if we purposely go on sinning after the truth has been made known to us. 27 Instead, all that is left is to wait in fear for the coming Judgment and the fierce fire which will destroy those who oppose God! 28 Anyone who disobeys the Law of Moses is put to death without any mercy when judged guilty from the evidence of two or more witnesses. 29 What, then, of those who despise the Son of God? who treat as a cheap thing the blood of God's covenant which purified them from sin? who insult the Spirit of grace? Just think how much worse is the punishment they will deserve! 30 For we know who said, "I will take revenge, I will repay"; and who also said, "The Lord will judge his people." 31 It is a terrifying thing to fall into the hands of the living God!

10:11 Ex 29:38　**10:12, 13** Ps 110:1　**10:16** Jer 31:33　**10:17** Jer 31:34　**10:22** Lev 8:30; Ezek 36:25　**10:27** Isa 26:11 (LXX)　**10:28** Deut 17:6; 19:15　**10:29** Ex 24:8　**10:30** a Deut 32:35; b Deut 32:36

Hebrews

Pray It!

Find Me, God

Staying on God's path can be hard. But going off that path, or turning away from it, gets us lost. In Hebrews 10:39 we are told that "we have faith and are saved." The next time you are feeling lost, try this prayer:

Find me God, I am feeling lost.
Help me get back on your path.
Find me God, I'm ready to turn back.
Help me stay with you.
Find me God, I'm slowing down.
Help me know my faith.
Find me God, I want to be with you.
Help me remember that you never leave.
Amen.

— Hebrews 10:39

32 Remember how it was with you in the past. In those days, after God's light had shone on you, you suffered many things, yet were not defeated by the struggle. 33 You were at times publicly insulted and mistreated, and at other times you were ready to join those who were being treated in this way. 34 You shared the sufferings of prisoners, and when all your belongings were seized, you endured your loss gladly, because you knew that you still possessed something much better, which would last forever. 35 Do not lose your courage, then, because it brings with it a great reward. 36 You need to be patient, in order to do the will of God and receive what he promises. 37 For, as the scripture says,
"Just a little while longer,
    and he who is coming will come;
    he will not delay.
38 My righteous people, however, will
        believe and live;
    but if any of them turns back,
    I will not be pleased with them."

39 We are not people who turn back and are lost. Instead, we have faith and are saved.

Faith

11 ¹To have faith is to be sure of the things we hope for, to be certain of the things we cannot see. ²It was by their faith that people of ancient times won God's approval.

³It is by faith that we understand that the universe was created by God's word, so that what can be seen was made out of what cannot be seen.

⁴It was faith that made Abel offer to God a better sacrifice than Cain's. Through his faith he won God's approval as a righteous man, because God himself approved of his gifts. By means of his faith Abel still speaks, even though he is dead.

⁵It was faith that kept Enoch from dying. Instead, he was taken up to God, and nobody could find him, because God had

10:37, 38 Hab 2:3, 4 (LXX)   **11:2** Sir 44:10—50:21; 1 Macc 2:51–64   **11:3** Gen 1:1; Ps 33:6, 9; Jn 1:3
11:4 Gen 4:3–10   **11:5** Gen 5:21–24 (LXX); Sir 44:16

Hebrews, chapter 11, gives many examples of people from the Old Testament who had faith in God. How many people are named in chapter 11?

To be certain of the things we cannot see (11:1)

It Was Faith

Faith sure has helped a lot of people in the Bible. Chapter 11 of Hebrews gives many examples of how faith helped people live a godly life. It tells us of these men and women, how they lived, how they obeyed God, and what happened as a result.

Write your own version of Hebrews, chapter 11. Start a paragraph like this: "It was faith that helped me . . ." In the paragraph list the ways faith has helped you live the way God wants you to live. Write another paragraph of the ways faith can help you in the future. Keep the paragraphs in a place where you look often. If you have a locker, put them there, or put them on your bedside table, in a notebook, or anywhere you'll see them daily. Add to your paragraphs as new faith-filled events happen in your life.

— Hebrews, chapter 11

taken him up. The scripture says that before Enoch was taken up, he had pleased God. ⁶No one can please God without faith, for whoever comes to God must have faith that God exists and rewards those who seek him.

⁷It was faith that made Noah hear God's warnings about things in the future that he could not see. He obeyed God and built a boat in which he and his family were saved. As a result, the world was condemned, and Noah received from God the righteousness that comes by faith.

⁸It was faith that made Abraham obey when God called him to go out to a country which God had promised to give him. He left his own country without knowing where he was going. ⁹By faith he lived as a foreigner in the country that God had promised him. He lived in tents, as did Isaac and Jacob, who received the same promise from God. ¹⁰For Abraham was waiting for the city which God has designed and built, the city with permanent foundations.

¹¹It was faith that made Abraham able to become a father, even though he was too old and Sarah herself could not have children. He*ⁱ* trusted God to keep his promise. ¹²Though Abraham was practically dead, from this one man came as many descendants as there are stars in the sky, as many as the numberless grains of sand on the seashore.

¹³It was in faith that all these persons died. They did not receive the things God had promised, but from a long way off they saw them and welcomed them, and admitted openly that they were foreigners and refugees on earth. ¹⁴Those who say such things make it clear that they are looking for a country of their own. ¹⁵They did not keep thinking about the country they had left; if they had, they would have had the chance to return. ¹⁶Instead, it was a better country they longed for, the heavenly country. And so God is not ashamed for them to call him their God, because he has prepared a city for them.

ⁱ **11:11** It was faith . . . children. He; *some manuscripts have* It was faith that made Sarah herself able to conceive, even though she was too old to have children. She.
11:7 Gen 6:13–22   **11:8** Gen 12:1–5   **11:9** Gen 35:27   **11:11** Gen 18:11–14; 21:2   **11:12** Gen 15:5; 22:17; 32:12   **11:13** Gen 23:4; 1 Chr 29:15; Ps 39:12

17It was faith that made Abraham offer his son Isaac as a sacrifice when God put Abraham to the test. Abraham was the one to whom God had made the promise, yet he was ready to offer his only son as a sacrifice. 18God had said to him, "It is through Isaac that you will have the descendants I promised." 19Abraham reckoned that God was able to raise Isaac from death—and, so to speak, Abraham did receive Isaac back from death.

20It was faith that made Isaac promise blessings for the future to Jacob and Esau.

21It was faith that made Jacob bless each of the sons of Joseph just before he died. He leaned on the top of his walking stick and worshiped God.

22It was faith that made Joseph, when he was about to die, speak of the departure of the Israelites from Egypt, and leave instructions about what should be done with his body.

23It was faith that made the parents of Moses hide him for three months after he was born. They saw that he was a beautiful child, and they were not afraid to disobey the king's order.

24It was faith that made Moses, when he had grown up, refuse to be called the son of the king's daughter. 25He preferred to suffer with God's people rather than to enjoy sin for a little while. 26He reckoned that to suffer scorn for the Messiah was worth far more than all the treasures of Egypt, for he kept his eyes on the future reward.

27It was faith that made Moses leave Egypt without being afraid of the king's anger. As though he saw the invisible God, he refused to turn back. 28It was faith that made him establish the Passover and order the blood to be sprinkled on the doors, so that the Angel of Death would not kill the first-born sons of the Israelites.

29It was faith that made the Israelites able to cross the Red Sea as if on dry land; when the Egyptians tried to do it, the water swallowed them up.

30It was faith that made the walls of Jericho fall down after the Israelites had marched around them for seven days. 31It was faith that kept the prostitute Rahab from being killed with those who disobeyed God, for she gave the Israelite spies a friendly welcome.

32Should I go on? There isn't enough time for me to speak of Gideon, Barak, Samson, Jephthah, David, Samuel, and the prophets. 33Through faith they fought whole countries and won. They did what was right and received what God had promised. They shut the mouths of lions, 34put out fierce fires, escaped being killed by the sword. They were weak, but became strong; they were mighty in battle and defeated the armies of foreigners. 35Through faith women received their dead relatives raised back to life.

Others, refusing to accept freedom, died under torture in order to be raised to a better life. 36Some were mocked and whipped, and others were put in chains and taken off to prison. 37They were stoned, they were sawed in two, they were killed by the sword. They went around clothed in skins of sheep or goats—poor, persecuted, and mistreated. 38The world was not good enough for them! They wandered like refugees in the deserts and hills, living in caves and holes in the ground.

39What a record all of these have won by their faith! Yet they did not receive what God had promised, 40because God had decided on an even better plan for us. His purpose was that only in company with us would they be made perfect.

God Our Father

12 1As for us, we have this large crowd of witnesses around us. So then, let us rid ourselves of everything that gets in the way, and of the sin which holds on to us so tightly, and let us run with determination the race that lies before us. 2Let us keep our eyes fixed on Jesus, on whom our faith depends from beginning to end. He did not

11:17 Gen 22:1–14 **11:18** Gen 21:12 **11:20** Gen 27:27–29, 39, 40 **11:21 a** Gen 48:1–20; **b** Gen 47:31 (LXX) **11:22** Gen 50:24, 25; Ex 13:19 **11:23 a** Ex 2:2; **b** Ex 1:22 **11:24** Ex 2:10–12 **11:28** Ex 12:21–30 **11:29** Ex 14:21–31 **11:30** Josh 6:12–21 **11:31 a** Josh 6:22–25; **b** Josh 2:1–21 **11:32 a** Judg 6:11—8:32; **b** Judg 4:6—5:31; **c** Judg 13:2—16:31; **d** Judg 11:1—12:7; **e** 1 Sam 16:1—1 Kings 2:11; **11:33** Dan 6:1–27 **11:34** Dan 3:1–30 **11:35** 1 Kings 17:17–24; 2 Kings 4:25–37; 2 Macc 6:18—7:42 **11:36** 1 Kings 22:26, 27; 2 Chr 18:25, 26; Jer 20:2; 37:15; 38:6 **11:37** 2 Chr 24:21

give up because of the cross! On the contrary, because of the joy that was waiting for him, he thought nothing of the disgrace of dying on the cross, and he is now seated at the right side of God's throne.

3 Think of what he went through; how he put up with so much hatred from sinners! So do not let yourselves become discouraged and give up. 4 For in your struggle against sin you have not yet had to resist to the point of being killed. 5 Have you forgotten the encouraging words which God speaks to you as his children?

"My child, pay attention when the Lord
     corrects you,
   and do not be discouraged when he
     rebukes you.
6 Because the Lord corrects everyone he
     loves,
   and punishes everyone he accepts as a
     child."

7 Endure what you suffer as being a father's punishment; your suffering shows that God is treating you as his children. Was there ever a child who was not punished by his father? 8 If you are not punished, as all his children are, it means you are not real children, but bastards. 9 In the case of our human fathers, they punished us and we respected them. How much more, then, should we submit to our spiritual Father and live! 10 Our human fathers punished us for a short time, as it seemed right to them; but God does it for our own good, so that we may share his holiness. 11 When we are punished, it seems to us at the time something to make us sad, not glad. Later, however, those who have been disciplined by such punishment reap the peaceful reward of a righteous life.

Instructions and Warnings

12 Lift up your tired hands, then, and strengthen your trembling knees! 13 Keep walking on straight paths, so that the lame foot may not be disabled, but instead be healed.

14 Try to be at peace with everyone, and try to live a holy life, because no one will see the Lord without it. 15 Guard against turning back from the grace of God. Let no one become like a bitter plant that grows up and causes many troubles with its poison. 16 Let no one become immoral or unspiritual like Esau, who for a single meal sold his rights as the older son. 17 Afterward, you know, he wanted to receive his father's blessing; but he was turned back, because he could not find any way to change what he had done, even though in tears he looked for it.*j*

18 You have not come, as the people of Israel came, to what you can feel, to Mount Sinai with its blazing fire, the darkness and the gloom, the storm, 19 the blast of a trumpet, and the sound of a voice. When the people heard the voice, they begged not to hear another word, 20 because they could not bear the order which said, "If even an animal touches the mountain, it must be stoned to death." 21 The sight was so terrifying that Moses said, "I am trembling and afraid!"

22 Instead, you have come to Mount Zion and to the city of the living God, the heavenly Jerusalem, with its thousands of angels. 23 You have come to the joyful gathering of God's first-born, whose names are written in heaven. You have come to God, who is the judge of all people, and to the spirits of good people made perfect. 24 You have come to Jesus, who arranged the new covenant, and to the sprinkled blood that promises much better things than does the blood of Abel.

25 Be careful, then, and do not refuse to hear him who speaks. Those who refused to hear the one who gave the divine message on earth did not escape. How much less shall we escape, then, if we turn away from the one who speaks from heaven! 26 His voice

---

j **12:17** he looked for it; *or* he tried to get the blessing.
12:5, 6 Job 5:17; Prov 3:11, 12 (LXX)   **12:12** Isa 35:3 (LXX)   **12:13** Prov 4:26 (LXX)   **12:15** Deut 29:18 (LXX)   **12:16** Gen 25:29–34   **12:17** Gen 27:30–40   **12:18, 19** Ex 19:16–22; 20:18–21; Deut 4:11, 12; 5:22–27   **12:20** Ex 19:12, 13   **12:21** Deut 9:19   **12:24** Gen 4:10   **12:25** Ex 20:22   **12:26** Hag 2:6 (LXX)

"Let us keep our eyes fixed on Jesus, on whom our faith depends from beginning to end" *(Hebrews 12:2).*

Hebrews

shook the earth at that time, but now he has promised, "I will once more shake not only the earth but heaven as well." 27 The words "once more" plainly show that the created things will be shaken and removed, so that the things that cannot be shaken will remain.

28 Let us be thankful, then, because we receive a kingdom that cannot be shaken. Let us be grateful and worship God in a way that will please him, with reverence and awe; 29 because our God is indeed a destroying fire.

How to Please God

13 1 Keep on loving one another as Christians. 2 Remember to welcome strangers in your homes. There were some who did that and welcomed angels without knowing it. 3 Remember those who are in prison, as though you were in prison with them. Remember those who are suffering, as though you were suffering as they are.

4 Marriage is to be honored by all, and husbands and wives must be faithful to each other. God will judge those who are immoral and those who commit adultery.

5 Keep your lives free from the love of money, and be satisfied with what you have. For God has said, "I will never leave you; I will never abandon you." 6 Let us be bold, then, and say,

"The Lord is my helper,
I will not be afraid.
What can anyone do to me?"

Keep your lives free from the love of money. (13:5)

Love of Money

Some Native American tribes have a special ceremony called the *otuhan*. In an *otuhan* a person gives away some or all of his or her belongings to mark a special occasion. It is a way of acknowledging the importance of other people in your life. It is also a recognition that a happy life does not come from owning things.

Hebrews reminds us to "Keep your lives free from the love of money" (13:5). Loving stuff is like loving money. The Church calls loving stuff materialism and teaches that materialism is a spiritual danger. If loving stuff stops you from loving people, it is time for a change. People are always more important. You might want to look at all you have and decide if you really need it. If you give some of your extra things away, you may find yourself with more time for people.

— Hebrews 13:5–6

7 Remember your former leaders, who spoke God's message to you. Think back on how they lived and died, and imitate their faith. 8 Jesus Christ is the same yesterday, today, and forever. 9 Do not let all kinds of strange teachings lead you from the right way. It is good to receive inner strength from God's grace, and not by obeying rules about foods; those who obey these rules have not been helped by them.

10 The priests who serve in the Jewish

12:29 Deut 4:24 **13:2** Gen 18:1–8; 19:1–3; Tob 5:4, 5 **13:4** Wis 3:13 **13:5** Deut 31:6, 8; Josh 1:5
13:6 Ps 118:6 (LXX)

"Jesus Christ is the same yesterday, today, and forever" *(Hebrews 13:8).*

place of worship have no right to eat any of the sacrifice on our altar. ¹¹The Jewish high priest brings the blood of the animals into the Most Holy Place to offer it as a sacrifice for sins; but the bodies of the animals are burned outside the camp. ¹²For this reason Jesus also died outside the city, in order to purify the people from sin with his own blood. ¹³Let us, then, go to him outside the camp and share his shame. ¹⁴For there is no permanent city for us here on earth; we are looking for the city which is to come. ¹⁵Let us, then, always offer praise to God as our sacrifice through Jesus, which is the offering presented by lips that confess him as Lord. ¹⁶Do not forget to do good and to help one another, because these are the sacrifices that please God.

For this reason Jesus also died outside the city. (13:12)

¹⁷Obey your leaders and follow their orders. They watch over your souls without resting, since they must give to God an account of their service. If you obey them, they will do their work gladly; if not, they will do it with sadness, and that would be of no help to you.

¹⁸Keep on praying for us. We are sure we have a clear conscience, because we want to do the right thing at all times. ¹⁹And I beg you even more earnestly to pray that God will send me back to you soon.

Closing Prayer

²⁰⁻²¹God has raised from death our Lord Jesus, who is the Great Shepherd of the sheep as the result of his blood,ᵏ by which the eternal covenant is sealed. May the God of peace provide you with every good thing you need in order to do his will, and may he, through Jesus Christ, do in us what pleases him. And to Christ be the glory forever and ever! Amen.

Final Words

²²I beg you, my friends, to listen patiently to this message of encouragement; for this letter I have written you is not very long. ²³I want you to know that our brother Timothy has been let out of prison. If he comes soon enough, I will have him with me when I see you.

²⁴Give our greetings to all your leaders and to all God's people. The believers from Italy send you their greetings.

²⁵May God's grace be with you all.

ᵏ **13:20–21** his blood; *or* his sacrificial death.
13:11 Lev 16:27

Your Next Step

Congratulations on finishing the Letter to the Hebrews! Use this space to write your thoughts and questions about this book. If you are following the suggested reading plan, move back to the Letter to the Romans. Romans is one of the most difficult letters to understand, but it tells us even more about the importance of faith.

Ahhhh . . . freedom! When is the last time you felt this? When you finished a big project or had no homework on a weekend? When you were getting along great with all your friends?

James describes freedom as the way we will feel when we practice living God's Law of love. For example we are most free when we avoid anger, don't judge people, do good deeds for others, be patient, and take care of the poor. God's Law isn't meant to be hard on us. Rather, if we were all following it, our lives would be better and easier. People would treat each other with deeper kindness, respect, and care.

Living in God's love brings true freedom, and James offers lots of practical advice for living that way.

Chap. 2:14–17

Headlines

- Pray Confidently for What You Need! (1:2–7)
- Faith Is Useless Without Action (1:19–27; 2:14–26)
- The Power of the Tongue (3:1–12)
- Boasting Is Bad (4:1–10)
- Prayer Produces Wonders! (5:13–20)

FACTOIDS

Who wrote this book? Possibly James, a relative of Jesus and the first leader of the Christian community in Jerusalem.

When was it written? If James wrote it, around AD 57 to 62. If a later admirer of James wrote it, between AD 70 and 150.

Who was it written for? It was written for Christians living in either Palestine, Syria, or Rome.

What is the literary style? It is a letter to Christians, but it is almost like a Christian advice column.

Important themes

- God is generous and gracious to us, even during difficult times.
- Beware of judging others by their appearance, especially the rich and the poor.
- Our actions and words should reflect our faith.
- Be patient with one another and pray for all in need.

JAMES

1

¹From James, a servant of God and of the Lord Jesus Christ:

Greetings to all God's people scattered over the whole world.

Faith and Wisdom

²My friends, consider yourselves fortunate when all kinds of trials come your way, ³for you know that when your faith succeeds in facing such trials, the result is the ability to endure. ⁴Make sure that your endurance carries you all the way without failing, so that you may be perfect and complete, lacking nothing. ⁵But if any of you lack wisdom, you should pray to God, who will give it to you; because God gives generously and graciously to all. ⁶But when you pray, you must believe and not doubt at all. Whoever doubts is like a wave in the sea that is driven and blown about by the wind. ⁷⁻⁸If you are like that, unable to make up your mind and undecided in all you do, you must not think that you will receive anything from the Lord.

Poverty and Riches

⁹Those Christians who are poor must be glad when God lifts them up, ¹⁰and the rich Christians must be glad when God brings them down. For the rich will pass away like the flower of a wild plant. ¹¹The sun rises with its blazing heat and burns the plant; its flower falls off, and its beauty is destroyed. In the same way the rich will be destroyed while they go about their business.

Testing and Tempting

¹²Happy are those who remain faithful under trials, because when they succeed in passing such a test, they will receive as their reward the life which God has promised to those who love him. ¹³If we are tempted by such trials, we must not say, "This temptation comes from God." For God cannot be tempted by evil, and he himself tempts no one. ¹⁴But we are tempted when we are drawn away and trapped by our own evil desires. ¹⁵Then our evil desires conceive and give birth to sin; and sin, when it is full-grown, gives birth to death.

¹⁶Do not be deceived, my dear friends! ¹⁷Every good gift and every perfect present comes from heaven; it comes down from God, the Creator of the heavenly lights, who does not change or cause darkness by turning. ¹⁸By his own will he brought us into being through the word of truth, so that we should have first place among all his creatures.

Hearing and Doing

¹⁹Remember this, my dear friends! Everyone must be quick to listen, but slow to speak and slow to become angry. ²⁰Human anger does not achieve God's righteous purpose. ²¹So get rid of every filthy habit and all wicked conduct. Submit to God and accept the word that he plants in your hearts, which is able to save you.

²²Do not deceive yourselves by just listening to his word; instead, put it into practice. ²³If you listen to the word, but do not put it into practice you are like people who look in a mirror and see themselves as they are. ²⁴They take a good look at themselves and then go away and at once forget what they look like. ²⁵But if you look closely into the perfect law that sets people free, and keep on paying attention to it and do not simply listen and then forget it, but put it into practice—you will be blessed by God in what you do.

²⁶Do any of you think you are religious? If you do not control your tongue, your religion is worthless and you deceive yourself. ²⁷What God the Father considers to be pure and

Empty Faith?

Mom: Well, that was a nice homily today. Not too long—but lots of pearls of wisdom. I need all the help I can get to become more patient!

Daughter: That last song was cool. I love it when they play drums at church!

Dad: What is this jerk doing? Hey buddy, move it! Where did you get your license? Out of a cereal box?

Daughter: Geez, Dad.

Mom: Honey, did you hear anything at church today? Did anything at all sink in?

Dad: Can't you just be happy that I went to church? Get off my back!

The author of James reminds Christians that listening to God's Word and saying we have faith isn't worth much if we don't show it in our words and actions. What are some ways you see people slipping up on practicing what we claim to believe?

— James 1:19–25

clothes comes to your meeting, and a poor man in ragged clothes also comes. ³If you show more respect to the well-dressed man and say to him, "Have this best seat here," but say to the poor man, "Stand over there, or sit here on the floor by my feet," ⁴then you are guilty of creating distinctions among yourselves and of making judgments based on evil motives.

⁵Listen, my dear friends! God chose the poor people of this world to be rich in faith and to possess the kingdom which he promised to those who love him. ⁶But you dishonor the poor! Who are the ones who oppress you and drag you before the judges? The rich! ⁷They are the ones who speak evil of that good name which has been given to you.

⁸You will be doing the right thing if you obey the law of the Kingdom, which is found in the scripture, "Love your neighbor as you love yourself." ⁹But if you treat people according to their outward appearance, you are guilty of sin, and the Law condemns you as a lawbreaker. ¹⁰Whoever breaks one commandment is guilty of breaking them all. ¹¹For the same one who said, "Do not commit adultery," also said, "Do not commit murder." Even if you do not commit adultery, you have become a lawbreaker if you commit murder. ¹²Speak and act as people who will be judged by the law that sets us free. ¹³For God will not show mercy when he judges the person who has not been merciful; but mercy triumphs over judgment.

genuine religion is this: to take care of orphans and widows in their suffering and to keep oneself from being corrupted by the world.

Warning against Prejudice

2 ¹My friends, as believers in our Lord Jesus Christ, the Lord of glory, you must never treat people in different ways according to their outward appearance. ²Suppose a rich man wearing a gold ring and fine

Faith and Actions

¹⁴My friends, what good is it for one of you to say that you have faith if your actions do not prove it? Can that faith save you? ¹⁵Suppose there are brothers or sisters who need clothes and don't have enough to eat. ¹⁶What good is there in your saying to them, "God bless you! Keep warm and eat well!"—if you don't give them the necessities of life? ¹⁷So it is with faith: if it is alone and includes no actions, then it is dead.

2:8 Lev 19:18   2:11 a Ex 20:14; Deut 5:18; b Ex 20:13; Deut 5:17

"If you do not control your tongue, your religion is worthless and you deceive yourself" *(James 1:26).*

Guilty!
(of Being a Christian)

Someone once posed this question: If you were on trial for being a Christian, would there be enough proof to find you guilty?

The Letter from James suggests that one proof would be your attitude and behavior toward people who are poor, unpopular, unattractive, or just hard to be around. In his earthly life, Jesus spent much of his time with poor people and the people considered the losers of society. He taught us that the least among us are especially blessed—they are precious to God. By his preaching and example, Jesus was teaching us to love and care for poor and outcast people too.

Quickly think of ten things you did and said the past few days. Which things showed patience, fairness, compassion, forgiveness, or generosity? Which things showed acceptance and care for people who are unpopular or less fortunate?

— James 2:1–7

altar. 22 Can't you see? His faith and his actions worked together; his faith was made perfect through his actions. 23 And the scripture came true that said, "Abraham believed God, and because of his faith God accepted him as righteous." And so Abraham was called God's friend. 24 You see, then, that it is by our actions that we are put right with God, and not by our faith alone.

25 It was the same with the prostitute Rahab. She was put right with God through her actions, by welcoming the Israelite spies and helping them to escape by a different road.

26 So then, as the body without the spirit is dead, also faith without actions is dead.

The Tongue

3 1 My friends, not many of you should become teachers. As you know, we teachers will be judged with greater strictness than others. 2 All of us often make mistakes. But if a person never makes a mistake in what he says, he is perfect and is also able to control his whole being. 3 We put a bit into the mouth of a horse to make it obey us, and we are able to make it go where we want. 4 Or think of a ship: big as it is and driven by such strong winds, it can be steered by a very small rudder, and it goes wherever the pilot wants it to go. 5 So it is with the tongue: small as it is, it can boast about great things.

Just think how large a forest can be set on fire by a tiny flame! 6 And the tongue is like a fire. It is a world of wrong, occupying its place in our bodies and spreading evil through our whole being. It sets on fire the entire course of our existence with the fire that comes to it from hell itself. 7 We humans are able to tame and have tamed all other creatures—wild animals and birds, reptiles and fish. 8 But no one has ever been able to tame the tongue. It is evil and uncontrollable, full of deadly poison. 9 We use it to give thanks to our Lord and Father and also to curse other people, who are created in the likeness of God. 10 Words of thanksgiving and cursing pour out from the same mouth.

18 But someone will say, "One person has faith, another has actions." My answer is, "Show me how anyone can have faith without actions. I will show you my faith by my actions." 19 Do you believe that there is only one God? Good! The demons also believe—and tremble with fear. 20 You fool! Do you want to be shown that faith without actions is useless?[a] 21 How was our ancestor Abraham put right with God? It was through his actions, when he offered his son Isaac on the

a **2:20** useless; *some manuscripts have* dead.
2:21 Gen 22:1–14; Sir 44:19–21; 1 Macc 2:52   **2:23 a** Gen 15:6; **b** 2 Chr 20:7; Isa 41:8   **2:25** Josh 2:1–21
3:2 Sir 5:9–15; 14:1; 28:13–26   **3:6** Sir 5:13; 28:22   **3:9** Gen 1:26

You Can Prevent Forest Fires!

Shauna just saw something she couldn't believe. She saw William and Denise holding hands in the drama room after school. But Denise was going out with Travis. Shauna had to tell someone, and soon all their friends knew about it. Travis even tried to start a fight with William. Only later did Shauna hear that Denise and William were only practicing their parts for the school play.

James compares our mean or untrue gossip to a spark that starts a huge forest fire. The words that come out of our mouths can be encouraging and kind, or they can be deadly. God is the best one to help us control our tongues. Ask God to help you stop and think before you speak— so you don't set some person's or some group's reputation on fire!

— James 3:5–12

My friends, this should not happen! ¹¹No spring of water pours out sweet water and bitter water from the same opening. ¹²A fig tree, my friends, cannot bear olives; a grapevine cannot bear figs, nor can a salty spring produce sweet water.

The Wisdom from Above

¹³Are there any of you who are wise and understanding? You are to prove it by your good life, by your good deeds performed with humility and wisdom. ¹⁴But if in your heart you are jealous, bitter, and selfish, don't sin against the truth by boasting of your wis-

dom. ¹⁵Such wisdom does not come down from heaven; it belongs to the world, it is unspiritual and demonic. ¹⁶Where there is jealousy and selfishness, there is also disorder and every kind of evil. ¹⁷But the wisdom from above is pure first of all; it is also peaceful, gentle, and friendly; it is full of compassion and produces a harvest of good deeds; it is free from prejudice and hypocrisy. ¹⁸And goodness is the harvest that is produced from the seeds the peacemakers plant in peace.

Friendship with the World

4 ¹Where do all the fights and quarrels among you come from? They come from your desires for pleasure, which are constantly fighting within you. ²You want things, but you cannot have them, so you are ready to kill; you strongly desire things, but you cannot get them, so you quarrel and fight. You do not have what you want because you do not ask God for it. ³And when you ask, you do not receive it, because your motives are bad; you ask for things to use for your own pleasures. ⁴Unfaithful people! Don't you know that to be the world's friend means to be God's enemy? If you want to be the world's friend, you make yourself God's enemy. ⁵Don't think that there is no truth in the scripture that says, "The spirit that God placed in us is filled with fierce desires."ᵇ ⁶But the grace that God gives is even stronger. As the scripture says, "God resists the proud, but gives grace to the humble."

⁷So then, submit yourselves to God. Resist the Devil, and he will run away from you. ⁸Come near to God, and he will come near to you. Wash your hands, you sinners! Purify your hearts, you hypocrites! ⁹Be sorrowful, cry, and weep; change your laughter into crying, your joy into gloom! ¹⁰Humble yourselves before the Lord, and he will lift you up.

Warning against Judging One Another

¹¹Do not criticize one another, my friends. If you criticize or judge another

ᵇ **4:5** The spirit . . . fierce desires; *or* God yearns jealously over the spirit that he placed in us.
3:13 Sir 19:20–30   **4:6** Prov 3:34 (LXX)

Pray It!

Is *Nice* in Me?

Dear Lord,

Yesterday I was really going at it! Judging people, I mean. I had a clever put-down for quite a few of my classmates—mostly the ones who are "good." Kids who always follow the rules, never get in trouble, are A students . . . the kind of kids you must really love, God!

All that judging felt good at the time because everyone was laughing at the stuff I said. Later, though, I felt kind of sick—a big pit in my stomach. Is that what guilt feels like?

What I'm trying to say, God, is I'm sorry. You know, I can be really snotty. I'm actually getting tired of it, though. And I think other people are getting tired of me. I can't really blame them.

There's this guy in my school, Anthony. He's just nice—plain and simple. I don't think I've ever heard him say a mean thing about anyone. And everybody really likes him. He's popular just because he's nice to everyone. How simple is that? Lord, do you think I can become like that? Can you help me?

— James 4:11–12

James

Christian, you criticize and judge the Law. If you judge the Law, then you are no longer one who obeys the Law, but one who judges it. 12 God is the only lawgiver and judge. He alone can save and destroy. Who do you think you are, to judge someone else?

Warning against Boasting

13 Now listen to me, you that say, "Today or tomorrow we will travel to a certain city, where we will stay a year and go into business and make a lot of money." 14 You don't even know what your life tomorrow will be! You are like a puff of smoke, which appears for a moment and then disappears. 15 What you should say is this: "If the Lord is willing, we will live and do this or that." 16 But now you are proud, and you boast; all such boasting is wrong.

17 So then, if we do not do the good we know we should do, we are guilty of sin.

Warning to the Rich

5 1 And now, you rich people, listen to me! Weep and wail over the miseries that are coming upon you! 2 Your riches have rotted away, and your clothes have been eaten by moths. 3 Your gold and silver are covered with rust, and this rust will be a witness against you and will eat up your flesh like fire. You have piled up riches in these last days. 4 You have not paid any wages to those who work in your fields. Listen to their complaints! The cries of those who gather in your crops have reached the ears of God, the Lord Almighty. 5 Your life here on earth has been full of luxury and pleasure. You have made yourselves fat for the day of slaughter. 6 You have condemned and

4:13, 14 Prov 27:1　4:13 Wis 2:4; 5:9–13　5:2, 3 Mt 6:19　5:3 Sir 29:10–12　5:4 Deut 24:14, 15
5:6 Wis 2:10–20

"Do not criticize one another, my friends" (James 4:11).

James

Prayers of the Faithful

Catholic Connections

Who do you know who needs God's help? One of the best things we can do for one another is pray.

Each week after we pray the Nicene Creed at Mass, usually we pray for our world, our Church, the dead and the sick, and other needs in our community. These prayers are called the Prayer of the Faithful. They are a type of prayer called a petition. After each prayer of petition is read, we say together, "Lord, hear our prayer," or some similar response.

Depending on the size of your church, there might be 100 people joining in those prayers or 600 people or a thousand—all praying to God for the same thing. When we pray alone, we know God hears us. But hundreds of prayers together—imagine how that must get God's attention! Remember, James tells us that our prayers are very powerful (James 5:16).

— James 5:13–18

murdered innocent people, and they do not resist you.[c]

Patience and Prayer

7 Be patient, then, my friends, until the Lord comes. See how patient farmers are as they wait for their land to produce precious crops. They wait patiently for the autumn and spring rains. 8 You also must be patient. Keep your hopes high, for the day of the Lord's coming is near.

9 Do not complain against one another, my friends, so that God will not judge you. The Judge is near, ready to appear. 10 My friends, remember the prophets who spoke in the name of the Lord. Take them as examples of patient endurance under suffering. 11 We call them happy because they endured. You have heard of Job's patience, and you know how the Lord provided for him in the end. For the Lord is full of mercy and compassion.

12 Above all, my friends, do not use an oath when you make a promise. Do not swear by heaven or by earth or by anything else. Say only "Yes" when you mean yes, and "No" when you mean no, and then you will not come under God's judgment.

13 Are any among you in trouble? They should pray. Are any among you happy?

This prayer made in faith will heal the sick. (5:15)

[c] **5:6** people, and they do not resist you; *or* people. Will God not resist you?
5:11 a Job 1:21, 22; 2:10; **b** Ps 103:8   **5:12** Mt 5:34–37

"The prayer of a good person has a powerful effect" *(James 5:16).* **Who needs your prayers today?**

They should sing praises. [14]Are any among you sick? They should send for the church elders, who will pray for them and rub olive oil on them in the name of the Lord. [15]This prayer made in faith will heal the sick; the Lord will restore them to health, and the sins they have committed will be forgiven. [16]So then, confess your sins to one another and pray for one another, so that you will be healed. The prayer of a good person has a powerful effect. [17]Elijah was the same kind of person as we are. He prayed earnestly that there would be no rain, and no rain fell on the land for three and a half years. [18]Once again he prayed, and the sky poured out its rain and the earth produced its crops.

[19]My friends, if any of you wander away from the truth and another one brings you back again, [20]remember this: whoever turns a sinner back from the wrong way will save that sinner's soul[d] from death and bring about the forgiveness of many sins.

[d] **5:20** that sinner's soul; or his own soul.
5:14 Mk 6:13   **5:16** Sir 4:26   **5:17** 1 Kings 17:1; 18:1; Sir 48:2, 3   **5:18** 1 Kings 18:42–45   **5:20** Prov 10:12; Tob 12:9; 1 Pet 4:8

Your Next Step

Congratulations on finishing the Letter of James! Use this space to write your thoughts and questions about this book. If you are following the suggested reading plan, move back to the Letter to the Galatians. Galatians also talks about faith and salvation and a particular issue that almost divided the early Church.

James

Have you ever been picked on or teased? We have all been hurt at some point. It's part of life. It's part of being a human being. The First Letter of Peter was addressed to early Christians who had changed their way of living. For many this new life was very difficult. They were being picked on for being followers of Christ, but it was much more serious than that. They were often mistreated and even persecuted. Suffering for their faith was a way of life.

These Christians lived a long way from Jerusalem and Rome, so you can understand why they needed encouragement. This letter reminded these new Christians of their Baptism and their call to live a good and holy life. It pointed out that their suffering is to be expected because Christ also suffered. In the end, they will be rewarded for their faith. In the meantime, they, like us, need to stay alert and cheer one another on.

Chap. 4:12–16

Headlines

- Rich Blessings Await Us (1:3–5)
- God Will Bless Your Suffering (2:18–25; 3:8–17; 4:12–19)
- Watch Out for the Devil! (5:8–11)

FACTOIDS

Who wrote this book? Possibly Peter, but most likely one of his followers.
When was it written? If it was written by Peter, around AD 60 to 63; if by a follower, AD 70 to 90.
Who was it written for? It was written to Christians living in Asia Minor who were being ridiculed for the way they lived.
Why was it written? The author wanted to encourage the Christian community and help the people make sense of their suffering.
Important themes
- Suffering for following Christ is to be expected.
- Despite suffering, it is important to keep faith in Jesus.
- Older Christians should be good examples. Younger Christians should be open to what their elders have to teach them.

1 PETER

1 ¹From Peter, apostle of Jesus Christ—
To God's chosen people who live as refugees scattered throughout the provinces of Pontus, Galatia, Cappadocia, Asia, and Bithynia. ²You were chosen according to the purpose of God the Father and were made a holy people by his Spirit, to obey Jesus Christ and be purified by his blood.

May grace and peace be yours in full measure.

A Living Hope

³Let us give thanks to the God and Father of our Lord Jesus Christ! Because of his great mercy he gave us new life by raising Jesus Christ from death. This fills us with a living hope, ⁴and so we look forward to possessing the rich blessings that God keeps for his people. He keeps them for you in heaven, where they cannot decay or spoil or fade away. ⁵They are for you, who through faith are kept safe by God's power for the salvation which is ready to be revealed at the end of time.

⁶Be glad about this, even though it may now be necessary for you to be sad for a while because of the many kinds of trials you suffer. ⁷Their purpose is to prove that your faith is genuine. Even gold, which can be destroyed, is tested by fire; and so your faith, which is much more precious than gold, must also be tested, so that it may endure. Then you will receive praise and glory and honor on the Day when Jesus Christ is revealed. ⁸You love him, although you have not seen him, and you believe in him, although you do not now see him. So you rejoice with a great and glorious joy which words cannot express, ⁹because you are receiving the salvation of your souls, which is the purpose of your faith in him.

¹⁰It was concerning this salvation that the prophets made careful search and investigation, and they prophesied about this gift which God would give you. ¹¹They tried to find out when the time would be and how

---

Prayer of Blessing

Catholic Connections

"God bless you!" This is a common expression in English, and a beautiful one. It is a simple form of prayer. A blessing prayer is one that calls on God's power to care for a person, place, thing, or undertaking. A blessing prayer often includes praise for God and for his gifts. First Peter 1:3–9 has several elements of a blessing prayer, beginning with giving thanks and praise to God.

Think of times when a blessing prayer could be used: before a trip, on a birthday or anniversary, before a retreat. There are many ways to pray a blessing, including having all those doing the blessing raise their hands over the person or group to be blessed. The blessing might also involve placing a hand on the person's shoulder or head. No matter how we do it or what words we say, what it comes down to is that we are sharing a simple but deep prayer: "God bless you!"

— 1 Peter 1:3–9

it would come.*a* This was the time to which Christ's Spirit in them was pointing, in predicting the sufferings that Christ would have to endure and the glory that would follow. 12God revealed to these prophets that their work was not for their own benefit, but for yours, as they spoke about those things which you have now heard from the messengers who announced the Good News by the power of the Holy Spirit sent from heaven. These are things which even the angels would like to understand.

A Call to Holy Living

13So then, have your minds ready for action. Keep alert and set your hope completely on the blessing which will be given you when Jesus Christ is revealed. 14Be obedient to God, and do not allow your lives to be shaped by those desires you had when you were still ignorant. 15Instead, be holy in all that you do, just as God who called you is holy. 16The scripture says, "Be holy because I am holy."

17You call him Father, when you pray to God, who judges all people by the same standard, according to what each one has done; so then, spend the rest of your lives here on earth in reverence for him. 18For you know what was paid to set you free from the worthless manner of life handed down by your ancestors. It was not something that can be destroyed, such as silver or gold; 19it was the costly sacrifice of Christ, who was like a lamb without defect or flaw. 20He had been chosen by God before the creation of the world and was revealed in these last days for your sake. 21Through him you believe in God, who raised him from death and gave him glory; and so your faith and hope are fixed on God.

22Now that by your obedience to the truth you have purified yourselves and have come to have a sincere love for other believers, love one another earnestly with all your heart.*b* 23For through the living and eternal word of God you have been born again as the children of a parent who is immortal, not mortal. 24As the scripture says,

"All human beings are like grass,
     and all their glory is like wild flowers.
The grass withers, and the flowers fall,
25   but the word of the Lord remains
       forever."

This word is the Good News that was proclaimed to you.

The Living Stone and the Holy Nation

2 1Rid yourselves, then, of all evil; no more lying or hypocrisy or jealousy or insulting language. 2Be like newborn babies, always thirsty for the pure spiritual milk, so that by drinking it you may grow up and be saved. 3As the scripture says, "You have found out for yourselves how kind the Lord is."

4Come to the Lord, the living stone rejected by people as worthless but chosen by God as valuable. 5Come as living stones, and let yourselves be used in building the spiritual temple, where you will serve as holy priests to offer spiritual and acceptable sacrifices to God through Jesus Christ. 6For the scripture says,

"I chose a valuable stone,
     which I am placing as the cornerstone
     in Zion;
and whoever believes in him will never
     be disappointed."

7This stone is of great value for you that believe; but for those who do not believe:

"The stone which the builders rejected as
     worthless
turned out to be the most important of
     all."

8And another scripture says,

---

a **1:11** when the time would be and how it would come; *or* who the person would be and when he would come.   *b* **1:22** with all your heart; *some manuscripts have* with a pure heart.
1:16 Lev 11:44, 45; 19:2   **1:24, 25** Isa 40:6–8 (LXX)   **2:3** Ps 34:8   **2:6** Isa 28:16 (LXX)   **2:7** Ps 118:22   **2:8** Isa 8:14, 15

The *heathen* (1 Peter 2:12) are those people who do not worship God as revealed in the Bible.

"This is the stone that will make people
    stumble,
    the rock that will make them fall."
They stumbled because they did not believe
in the word; such was God's will for them.

⁹But you are the chosen race, the King's
priests, the holy nation, God's own people,
chosen to proclaim the wonderful acts of
God, who called you out of darkness into his
own marvelous light. ¹⁰At one time you
were not God's people, but now you are his
people; at one time you did not know God's
mercy, but now you have received his mercy.

Slaves of God

¹¹I appeal to you, my friends, as strangers
and refugees in this world! Do not give in to
bodily passions, which are always at war
against the soul. ¹²Your conduct among the
heathen should be so good that when they
accuse you of being evildoers, they will have
to recognize your good deeds and so praise
God on the Day of his coming.

¹³For the sake of the Lord submit yourselves to every human authority: to the
Emperor, who is the supreme authority,
¹⁴and to the governors, who have been
appointed by him to punish the evildoers
and to praise those who do good. ¹⁵For God
wants you to silence the ignorant talk of
foolish people by the good things you do.
¹⁶Live as free people; do not, however, use
your freedom to cover up any evil, but live
as God's slaves. ¹⁷Respect everyone, love
other believers, honor God, and respect the
Emperor.

The Example of Christ's Suffering

¹⁸You servants must submit yourselves to
your masters and show them complete
respect, not only to those who are kind and
considerate, but also to those who are harsh.
¹⁹God will bless you for this, if you endure
the pain of undeserved suffering because you
are conscious of his will. ²⁰For what credit is
there if you endure the beatings you deserve
for having done wrong? But if you endure

suffering even when you have done right,
God will bless you for it. ²¹It was to this that
God called you, for Christ himself suffered
for you and left you an example, so that you
would follow in his steps. ²²He committed
no sin, and no one ever heard a lie come
from his lips. ²³When he was insulted, he did
not answer back with an insult; when he suffered, he did not threaten, but placed his
hopes in God, the righteous Judge. ²⁴Christ
himself carried our sins in his body to the
cross, so that we might die to sin and live for
righteousness. It is by his wounds that you
have been healed. ²⁵You were like sheep that
had lost their way, but now you have been
brought back to follow the Shepherd and
Keeper of your souls.

Wives and Husbands

3 ¹In the same way you wives must submit yourselves to your husbands, so that
if any of them do not believe God's word,
your conduct will win them over to believe.
It will not be necessary for you to say a
word, ²because they will see how pure and
reverent your conduct is. ³You should not
use outward aids to make yourselves beautiful, such as the way you fix your hair, or the
jewelry you put on, or the dresses you wear.
⁴Instead, your beauty should consist of your
true inner self, the ageless beauty of a gentle
and quiet spirit, which is of the greatest
value in God's sight. ⁵For the devout women
of the past who placed their hope in God
used to make themselves beautiful by sub-
mitting themselves to their husbands. ⁶Sarah
was like that; she obeyed Abraham and called
him her master. You are now her daughters if
you do good and are not afraid of anything.

⁷In the same way you husbands must live
with your wives with the proper understanding that they are more delicate than
you. Treat them with respect, because they
also will receive, together with you, God's
gift of life. Do this so that nothing will interfere with your prayers.

2:9 a Ex 19:5, 6; Isa 43:20 (LXX); b Ex 19:5; Deut 4:20; 7:6; 14:2; Titus 2:14; c Isa 43:21; d Isa 9:2   2:10 Hos
2:23   2:22 Isa 53:9   2:23 Isa 53:7   2:24, 25 Isa 53:5, 6 (LXX)   3:1 Eph 5:22; Col 3:18   3:3 1 Tim 2:9
3:6 Gen 18:12   3:7 Eph 5:25; Col 3:19

Suffering for Doing Right

8 To conclude: you must all have the same attitude and the same feelings; love one another, and be kind and humble with one another. 9 Do not pay back evil with evil or cursing with cursing; instead, pay back with a blessing, because a blessing is what God promised to give you when he called you. 10 As the scripture says,

"If you want to enjoy life
and wish to see good times,
you must keep from speaking evil
and stop telling lies.
11 You must turn away from evil and do good;
you must strive for peace with all your heart.
12 For the Lord watches over the righteous
and listens to their prayers;
but he opposes those who do evil."

13 Who will harm you if you are eager to do what is good? 14 But even if you should suffer for doing what is right, how happy you are! Do not be afraid of anyone, and do not worry. 15 But have reverence for Christ in your hearts, and honor him as Lord. Be ready at all times to answer anyone who asks you to explain the hope you have in you, 16 but do it with gentleness and respect. Keep your conscience clear, so that when you are insulted, those who speak evil of your good conduct as followers of Christ will become ashamed of what they say. 17 For it is better to suffer for doing good, if this should be God's will, than for doing evil. 18 For Christ died*c* for sins once and for all, a good man on behalf of sinners, in order to lead you to God. He was put to death physically, but made alive spiritually, 19 and in his spiritual existence he went and preached to the imprisoned spirits. 20 These were the spirits of those who had not obeyed God when he waited patiently during the days that Noah was building his boat. The few people in the boat—eight in all—were saved by the water, 21 which was a symbol pointing to baptism, which now saves you. It is not the washing off of bodily dirt, but the promise made to God from a good conscience. It saves you

You Are Beautiful

What makes a woman beautiful? If you asked advertisers, you would get a variety of answers: the right makeup, the perfect hairstyle, or just the right piece of jewelry, not to mention wearing the latest fashion.

These were pretty much the same things that people in the Roman Empire valued at the time 1 Peter was written (1 Peter 3:3). But the author of this letter suggests that if you asked God the same question, there is little doubt how God would respond: true beauty lies within a person. First Peter 3:4 is a lovely way of describing what real beauty is. And that is true for men as well as women.

Have you ever seen a picture of Mother Teresa? There is more beauty in her wrinkled face than in a hundred fashion models, because we know what lies within her. Nothing is wrong with taking reasonable measures to make ourselves look our best. But when people obsess over makeup and clothes, they are forgetting that what we look like does not define who we are.

How would you define beauty by the world's standards? How would you define beauty by God's standards? Which will you choose to follow?

— 1 Peter 3:3–4

through the resurrection of Jesus Christ, 22 who has gone to heaven and is at the right side of God, ruling over all angels and heavenly authorities and powers.

c 3:18 died; *many manuscripts have* suffered.
3:10–12 Ps 34:12–16 (LXX)   3:14 Mt 5:10   3:14, 15 Isa 8:12, 13   3:20 Gen 6:1—7:24

Changed Lives

4 ¹Since Christ suffered physically, you too must strengthen yourselves with the same way of thinking that he had; because whoever suffers physically is no longer involved with sin. ²From now on, then, you must live the rest of your earthly lives controlled by God's will and not by human desires. ³You have spent enough time in the past doing what the heathen like to do. Your lives were spent in indecency, lust, drunkenness, orgies, drinking parties, and the disgusting worship of idols. ⁴And now the heathen are surprised when you do not join them in the same wild and reckless living, and so they insult you. ⁵But they will have to give an account of themselves to God, who is ready to judge the living and the dead. ⁶That is why the Good News was preached also to the dead, to those who had been judged in their physical existence as everyone is judged; it was preached to them so that in their spiritual existence they may live as God lives.

Good Managers of God's Gifts

⁷The end of all things is near. You must be self-controlled and alert, to be able to pray. ⁸Above everything, love one another earnestly, because love covers over many sins. ⁹Open your homes to each other without complaining. ¹⁰Each one, as a good manager of God's different gifts, must use for the good of others the special gift he has received from God. ¹¹Those who preach must preach God's messages; those who serve must serve with the strength that God gives them, so that in all things praise may be given to God through Jesus Christ, to whom belong glory and power forever and ever. Amen.

Suffering as a Christian

¹²My dear friends, do not be surprised at the painful test you are suffering, as though

4:8 Prov 10:12; Tob 12:9

Watch Out!

When someone tells you to watch out, they are usually giving you a warning. That is exactly what the author is doing in this letter; he tells these Christians to be alert (1 Peter 4:7, 5:8). Why? Because they are being challenged and persecuted because of their faith in Jesus Christ.

It is so easy to get sucked into doing the wrong thing, if we don't stay alert. During a time of national crisis, a government will often raise the alert level. It is a reminder to keep our eyes and ears open and to be aware of what is going on around us. In a way, that is what this letter is telling us: if we are a follower of Christ, our alert level needs to be raised. Because we live in a world that does not yet recognize Jesus as the Lord of all creation, we will get tempted to do things that are not good for us and go against our beliefs.

Think of ways we can help one another to be alert. Church involvement will help you to stay on the right track. Check and see how you can be involved at your Church. If you don't find a way that works for you, talk to your youth minister or parish priest about how you would like to be involved.

— 1 Peter 4:7, 5:8

I Peter

something unusual were happening to you. ¹³Rather be glad that you are sharing Christ's sufferings, so that you may be full of

"If you suffer because you are a Christian, don't be ashamed of it, but thank God that you bear Christ's name" (1 Peter 4:16).

joy when his glory is revealed. [14]Happy are you if you are insulted because you are Christ's followers; this means that the glorious Spirit, the Spirit of God, is resting on you. [15]If you suffer, it must not be because you are a murderer or a thief or a criminal or a meddler in other people's affairs. [16]However, if you suffer because you are a Christian, don't be ashamed of it, but thank God that you bear Christ's name.

[17]The time has come for judgment to begin, and God's own people are the first to be judged. If it starts with us, how will it end with those who do not believe the Good News from God? [18]As the scripture says,

"It is difficult for good people to be
    saved;
what, then, will become of godless
    sinners?"

[19]So then, those who suffer because it is God's will for them, should by their good actions trust themselves completely to their Creator, who always keeps his promise.

The Flock of God

5 [1]I, who am an elder myself, appeal to the church elders among you. I am a witness of Christ's sufferings, and I will share in the glory that will be revealed. I appeal to you [2]to be shepherds of the flock that God gave you and to take care of it willingly, as God wants you to, and not unwillingly. Do your work, not for mere pay, but from a real desire to serve. [3]Do not try to rule over those who have been put in your care, but be examples to the flock. [4]And when the Chief Shepherd appears, you will receive the glorious crown which will never lose its brightness.

[5]In the same way you younger people must submit yourselves to your elders. And all of you must put on the apron of humility, to serve one another; for the scripture says, "God resists the proud, but shows favor to

The kiss of Christian love (5:14)

the humble." [6]Humble yourselves, then, under God's mighty hand, so that he will lift you up in his own good time. [7]Leave all your worries with him, because he cares for you.

[8]Be alert, be on watch! Your enemy, the Devil, roams around like a roaring lion, looking for someone to devour. [9]Be firm in your faith and resist him, because you know that other believers in all the world are going through the same kind of sufferings. [10]But after you have suffered for a little while, the God of all grace, who calls you to share his eternal glory in union with Christ, will himself perfect you and give you firmness, strength, and a sure foundation. [11]To him be the power forever! Amen.

Final Greetings

[12]I write you this brief letter with the help of Silas, whom I regard as a faithful Christian. I want to encourage you and give

---

4:18 Prov 11:31 (LXX) **5:2** Jn 21:15–17 **5:5** Prov 3:34 (LXX) **5:6** Mt 23:12; Lk 14:11; 18:14 **5:7** Sir 2:1–18

Some of the early Christians used *Babylon* as a code word for Rome. They saw the Romans persecuting Christians like the Babylonians persecuted the Jewish people.

my testimony that this is the true grace of
God. Stand firm in it.

13 Your sister church in Babylon,*d* also
chosen by God, sends you greetings, and so

does my son Mark. 14 Greet one another
with the kiss of Christian love.

May peace be with all of you who belong
to Christ.

d **5:13** BABYLON: *As in the book of Revelation, this probably refers to Rome.*
5:12 Acts 15:22, 40   **5:13** Acts 12:12, 25; 13:13; 15:37–39; Col 4:10; Philem 24

Your Next Step

Congratulations on finishing the First Letter of Peter! Use this space to write your thoughts and questions about this book. If you are following the suggested reading plan, go back to the Book of Ezekiel in the Old Testament. Like Peter, Ezekiel encourages his people to live their lives as God wants them to.

When it seems that many things we see and listen to today try to lead us in the wrong direction, this letter gives us hope. Jesus has given us everything we need to live right. It's all a matter of faith, goodness, knowledge, self-control, endurance, godliness, mutual affection, and love.

What about God's promises? When will Jesus return? What will happen?

These are good questions, but we cannot know the answers. To God, one day is like a thousand years, and a thousand years are like one day. We have to be patient and wait. And while we are waiting, let's keep living right.

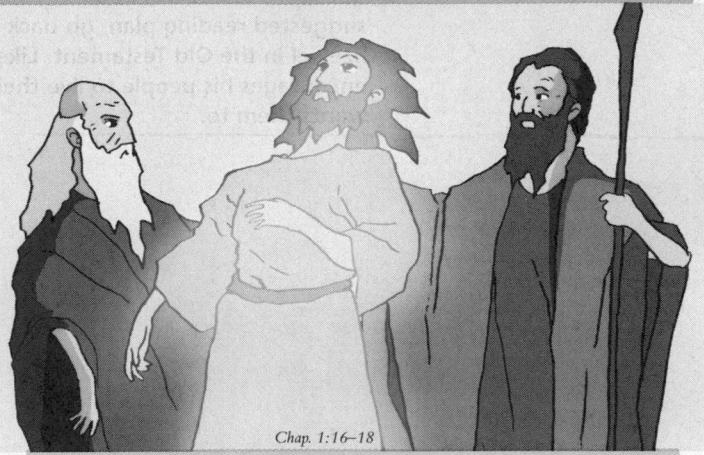

Chap. 1:16–18

Head lines

- Eyewitness to Christ's Glory (1:16–18)
- False Prophets Will Be Punished (chapter 2)
- New Heavens and New Earth Promised (3:10–13)

FACTOIDS

Who wrote this book? An unknown person, writing in Peter's name.

When was it written? Around AD 130, about one hundred years after Jesus' death and Resurrection.

Who was it written for? It was written for a community of early Christians, both Jewish and Gentile (non-Jewish), beginning to question their beliefs.

Why was it written? The author wanted to convince early Christians to ignore false teachings and to hold on to their true faith.

Jesus connection. The author mentions the Transfiguration of Jesus, an event that happened on a mountain while Peter, James, and John were present (Matthew 17:1–8, Mark 9:2–13, and Luke 9:28–36).

Important themes

- Ignore the teachings of false prophets.
- Remain faithful to true Christian teachings.
- Wait patiently and have faith that when the time is right God will make all things new.

2 PETER

1

¹From Simon Peter, a servant and apostle of Jesus Christ—

To those who through the righteousness of our God and Savior Jesus Christ have been given a faith as precious as ours:

²May grace and peace be yours in full measure through your knowledge of God and of Jesus our Lord.

God's Call and Choice

³God's divine power has given us everything we need to live a truly religious life through our knowledge of the one who called us to share in his own*ᵃ* glory and goodness. ⁴In this way he has given us the very great and precious gifts he promised, so that by means of these gifts you may escape from the destructive lust that is in the world, and may come to share the divine nature. ⁵For this very reason do your best to add goodness to your faith; to your goodness add knowledge; ⁶to your knowledge add self-control; to your self-control add endurance; to your endurance add godliness; ⁷to your godliness add Christian affection; and to your Christian affection add love. ⁸These are the qualities you need, and if you have them in abundance, they will make you active and effective in your knowledge of our Lord Jesus Christ. ⁹But if you do not have them, you are so shortsighted that you cannot see and have forgotten that you have been purified from your past sins.

¹⁰So then, my friends, try even harder to make God's call and his choice of you a permanent experience; if you do so, you will never abandon your faith.*ᵇ* ¹¹In this way you will be given the full right to enter the eternal Kingdom of our Lord and Savior Jesus Christ.

¹²And so I will always remind you of these matters, even though you already know them and are firmly grounded in the truth you have received. ¹³I think it only

To make God's call . . . a permanent experience (1:10)

right for me to stir up your memory of these matters as long as I am still alive. ¹⁴I know that I shall soon put off this mortal body, as our Lord Jesus Christ plainly told me. ¹⁵I will do my best, then, to provide a way for you to remember these matters at all times after my death.

Eyewitnesses of Christ's Glory

¹⁶We have not depended on made-up stories in making known to you the mighty coming of our Lord Jesus Christ. With our own eyes we saw his greatness. ¹⁷We were there when he was given honor and glory by God the Father, when the voice came to him from the Supreme Glory, saying, "This is my own dear Son, with whom I am pleased!" ¹⁸We ourselves heard this voice coming from heaven, when we were with him on the holy mountain.

¹⁹So we are even more confident of the message proclaimed by the prophets. You will do well to pay attention to it, because it is like a lamp shining in a dark place until the Day dawns and the light of the morning

---

ᵃ **1:3** to share in his own; *some manuscripts have* through his. *ᵇ* **1:10** abandon your faith; *or* fall into sin.
1:17, 18 Mt 17:1–5; Mk 9:2–7; Lk 9:28–35

star shines in your hearts. 20Above all else, however, remember that none of us can explain by ourselves a prophecy in the Scriptures. 21For no prophetic message ever came just from the human will, but people were under the control of the Holy Spirit as they spoke the message that came from God.

False Teachers

2 1False prophets appeared in the past among the people, and in the same way false teachers will appear among you. They will bring in destructive, untrue doctrines, and will deny the Master who redeemed them, and so they will bring upon themselves sudden destruction. 2Even so, many will follow their immoral ways; and because of what they do, others will speak evil of the Way of truth. 3In their greed these false teachers will make a profit out of telling you made-up stories. For a long time now their Judge has been ready, and their Destroyer has been wide awake!

4God did not spare the angels who sinned, but threw them into hell, where they are kept chained in darkness,c waiting for the Day of Judgment. 5God did not spare the ancient world, but brought the flood on the world of godless people; the only ones he saved were Noah, who preached righteousness, and seven other people. 6God condemned the cities of Sodom and Gomorrah, destroying them with fire, and made them an example of what will happen to the godless. 7He rescued Lot, a good man, who was distressed by the immoral conduct of lawless people. 8That good man lived among them, and day after day he suffered agony as he saw and heard their evil actions. 9And so the Lord knows how to rescue godly people from their trials and how to keep the wicked under punishment for the Day of Judgment, 10especially those who follow their filthy bodily lusts and despise God's authority.

These false teachers are bold and arrogant, and show no respect for the glorious beings above; instead, they insult them. 11Even the angels, who are so much stronger and mightier than these false teachers, do not accuse them with insults in the presence of the Lord. 12But these people act by instinct, like wild animals born to be captured and killed; they attack with insults anything they do not understand. They will be destroyed like wild animals, 13and they will be paid with suffering for the suffering they have caused. Pleasure for them is to do anything in broad daylight that will satisfy their bodily appetites; they are a shame and a disgrace as they join you in your meals, all the while enjoying their deceitful ways! 14They want to look for nothing but the chance to commit adultery; their appetite for sin is never satisfied. They lead weak people into a trap. Their hearts are trained to be greedy. They are under God's curse! 15They have left the straight path and have lost their way; they have followed the path taken by Balaam son of Beor, who loved the money he would get for doing wrong 16and was rebuked for his sin. His donkey spoke with a human voice and stopped the prophet's insane action.

17These people are like dried-up springs, like clouds blown along by a storm; God has reserved a place for them in the deepest darkness. 18They make proud and stupid statements, and use immoral bodily lusts to trap those who are just beginning to escape from among people who live in error. 19They promise them freedom while they themselves are slaves of destructive habits— for we are slaves of anything that has conquered us. 20If people have escaped from the corrupting forces of the world through their knowledge of our Lord and Savior Jesus Christ, and then are again caught and conquered by them, such people are in worse condition at the end than they were at the beginning. 21It would have been much better for them never to have known the way of righteousness than to know it and then turn away from the sacred command that was given them. 22What happened to them shows that the proverbs are true: "A dog goes back to what it has vomited" and "A pig that has been washed goes back to roll in the mud."

c 2:4 chained in darkness; *some manuscripts have* in dark pits.
2:5 Gen 6:1—7:24; Wis 10:4   2:6 Gen 19:24   2:7 Gen 19:1—16; Wis 10:6—8   2:15, 16 Num 22:4—35
2:22 Prov 26:11

The Promise of the Lord's Coming

3 ¹My dear friends, this is now the second letter I have written you. In both letters I have tried to arouse pure thoughts in your minds by reminding you of these things. ²I want you to remember the words that were spoken long ago by the holy prophets, and the command from the Lord and Savior which was given you by your apostles. ³First of all, you must understand that in the last days some people will appear whose lives are controlled by their own lusts. They will make fun of you ⁴and will ask, "He promised to come, didn't he? Where is he? Our ancestors have already died, but everything is still the same as it was since the creation of the world!" ⁵They purposely ignore the fact that long ago God gave a command, and the heavens and earth were created. The earth was formed out of water and by water, ⁶and it was also by water, the water of the flood, that the old world was destroyed. ⁷But the heavens and the earth that now exist are being preserved by the same command of God, in order to be destroyed by fire. They are being kept for the day when godless people will be judged and destroyed.

⁸But do not forget one thing, my dear friends! There is no difference in the Lord's sight between one day and a thousand years; to him the two are the same. ⁹The Lord is not slow to do what he has promised, as some think. Instead, he is patient with you, because he does not want anyone to be destroyed, but wants all to turn away from their sins.

¹⁰But the Day of the Lord will come like a thief. On that Day the heavens will disappear with a shrill noise, the heavenly bodies will burn up and be destroyed, and the earth with everything in it will vanish.ᵈ ¹¹Since all these things will be destroyed in this way, what kind of people should you be? Your lives should be holy and dedicated to God, ¹²as you wait for the Day of God and do your best to make it come soon— the Day when the heavens will burn up and be destroyed, and the heavenly bodies will

be melted by the heat. ¹³But we wait for what God has promised: new heavens and a new earth, where righteousness will be at home.

¹⁴And so, my friends, as you wait for that Day, do your best to be pure and faultless in

What Kind of Person?

The end of 2 Peter talks about the Second Coming of Christ. The letter is saying that even though Christ has not yet returned, he will at some point. "There is no difference in the Lord's sight between one day and a thousand years" (3:8). Knowing that Christ will return when we least expect, we need to consider our response to the question, "What kind of people should you be?" (3:11). Why would the letter writer ask this question? Because the writer knows that every individual life has purpose and meaning in God's plan. Not just the lives of famous people, but the lives of all people.

"Your lives should be holy and dedicated to God" (3:11), not just some of the time but all of the time. What you do each day matters. What you do each day affects your family, your neighborhood, the people in your school, and all of your friends.

What kind of person must you be to have a positive effect on all of those people? What kind of person would have a negative effect? The choice is yours. The results are important. God knows this. So do you.

— 2 Peter 3:1–13

2 Peter

ᵈ **3:10** vanish; *some manuscripts have* be found; *others have* be burned up; *one has* be found destroyed.
3:3 Jude 18   **3:5** Gen 1:6–9   **3:6** Gen 7:11   **3:8** Ps 90:4   **3:10** Mt 24:43; Lk 12:39; 1 Thess 5:2; Rev 16:15   **3:13** Isa 65:17; 66:22; Rev 21:1

God's sight and to be at peace with him.
15Look on our Lord's patience as the opportunity he is giving you to be saved, just as our dear friend Paul wrote to you, using the wisdom that God gave him. 16This is what he says in all his letters when he writes on the subject. There are some difficult things in his letters which ignorant and unstable people explain falsely, as they do with other passages of the Scriptures. So they bring on their own destruction.

17But you, my friends, already know this. Be on your guard, then, so that you will not be led away by the errors of lawless people and fall from your safe position. 18But continue to grow in the grace and knowledge of our Lord and Savior Jesus Christ. To him be the glory, now and forever! Amen.

Has anyone ever asked your advice about something important? Maybe it was a younger brother or sister, or maybe it was a friend. They looked up to you because you were older or because they respected you.

The author of these three letters was considered a respected adviser, or elder, of a Christian community that the Gospel of John had been written for.

In the First Letter of John, the author calls the members of the community little children not because they were actually young people but because the writer cared about them as a spiritual father. In the Second Letter of John, this leader warns the community not to follow those spreading false teachings—to totally avoid them. In the Third Letter of John, the author praises those who show love and care for others and warns against those who cause division in the community.

2 John

Head lines

- Live in God's Light (1 John 2:7–17)
- Love One Another (1 John 3:11–18)
- Perfect Love Drives Out Fear (1 John 4:16–18)
- Deceivers Teach Christ Wasn't Human (2 John, verses 4–11)
- Church Leader Applauded (3 John, verses 5–8)

FACTOIDS

Who wrote these books? A member of the community that produced the Gospel of John, called the elder.

When were they written? Around AD 100.

Who were they written for? They were written for Christians suffering from a split in their community.

Why were they written? The authors wanted to encourage believers to live the right way and to love one another. They also wanted to warn against people teaching falsely about Jesus Christ.

What is the literary style? First John is a teaching homily, and Second John and Third John are both letters.

Important themes

- We are called to walk in the light that is God, in both our words and actions, and to avoid the darkness of sin.
- When we love others, we are showing our love for God.
- Jesus was a real human being even though he was also God's Son.

1 JOHN

The Word of Life

1 ¹We write to you about the Word of life, which has existed from the very beginning. We have heard it, and we have seen it with our eyes; yes, we have seen it, and our hands have touched it. ²When this life became visible, we saw it; so we speak of it and tell you about the eternal life which was with the Father and was made known to us. ³What we have seen and heard we announce to you also, so that you will join with us in the fellowship that we have with the Father and with his Son Jesus Christ. ⁴We write this in order that our[a] joy may be complete.

God Is Light

⁵Now the message that we have heard from his Son and announce is this: God is light, and there is no darkness at all in him. ⁶If, then, we say that we have fellowship with him, yet at the same time live in the darkness, we are lying both in our words and in our actions. ⁷But if we live in the light—just as he is in the light—then we have fellowship with one another, and the blood of Jesus, his Son, purifies us from every sin.

⁸If we say that we have no sin, we deceive ourselves, and there is no truth in us. ⁹But if we confess our sins to God, he will keep his promise and do what is right: he will forgive us our sins and purify us from all our wrongdoing. ¹⁰If we say that we have not sinned, we make a liar out of God, and his word is not in us.

Christ Our Helper

2 ¹I am writing this to you, my children, so that you will not sin; but if anyone does sin, we have someone who pleads with the Father on our behalf—Jesus Christ, the righteous one. ²And Christ himself is the means by which our sins are forgiven, and not our sins only, but also the sins of everyone.

³If we obey God's commands, then we are sure that we know him. ⁴If we say that we know him, but do not obey his commands, we are liars and there is no truth in us. ⁵But if we obey his word, we are the ones whose love for God has really been made perfect. This is how we can be sure that we are in

Live It!

Live in the Light

It was a dark night. There was a thick blanket of clouds that covered the stars. Kim was camping with her family. She was already in her sleeping bag when she remembered that she had left her backpack on the picnic table. If she got up now and tried to find it in the dark, she knew she'd probably trip and fall. She might even get lost in the woods if she strayed off the path. As she lay in the inky blackness, she saw a pinprick of light through the window of her tent, then another. The sky was beginning to clear. Soon the full moon shone round and bright, and everything outside the tent was clearly outlined in silvery white light. Kim knew she could go safely now and find her backpack.

This letter urges the early Christians—and us—to "live in the light" to follow God (1 John 1:7). In the same way that Kim needed the starlight to find her backpack, we need the light of Christ. Jesus Christ will lead us to true happiness and eternal life!

— 1 John 1:5–7

---

[a] **1:4** our; *some manuscripts have* your.
1:1 Jn 1:1 **1:2** Jn 1:14

union with God: 6if we say that we remain in union with God, we should live just as Jesus Christ did.

The New Command

7My dear friends, this command I am writing you is not new; it is the old command, the one you have had from the very beginning. The old command is the message you have already heard. 8However, the command I now write you is new, because its truth is seen in Christ and also in you. For the darkness is passing away, and the real light is already shining.

9If we say that we are in the light, yet hate others, we are in the darkness to this very hour. 10If we love others, we live in the light, and so there is nothing in us that will cause someone else[b] to sin. 11But if we hate others, we are in the darkness; we walk in it and do not know where we are going, because the darkness has made us blind.

If we love others . . . if we hate others. (2:10, 11)

12I write to you, my children, because your sins are forgiven for the sake of Christ. 13I write to you, fathers, because you know him who has existed from the beginning. I write to you, young people, because you have defeated the Evil One.

14I write to you, my children, because you know the Father. I write to you, fathers, because you know him who has existed

from the beginning. I write to you, young people, because you are strong; the word of God lives in you, and you have defeated the Evil One.

15Do not love the world or anything that belongs to the world. If you love the world, you do not love the Father. 16Everything that belongs to the world—what the sinful self desires, what people see and want, and everything in this world that people are so proud of—none of this comes from the Father; it all comes from the world. 17The world and everything in it that people desire is passing away; but those who do the will of God live forever.

The Enemy of Christ

18My children, the end is near! You were told that the Enemy of Christ would come; and now many enemies of Christ have already appeared, and so we know that the end is near. 19These people really did not belong to our fellowship, and that is why they left us; if they had belonged to our fellowship, they would have stayed with us. But they left so that it might be clear that none of them really belonged to us.

20But you have had the Holy Spirit poured out on you by Christ, and so all of you know the truth. 21I write you, then, not because you do not know the truth; instead, it is because you do know it, and you also know that no lie ever comes from the truth.

22Who, then, is the liar? It is those who say that Jesus is not the Messiah. Such people are the Enemy of Christ—they reject both the Father and the Son. 23For those who reject the Son reject also the Father; those who accept the Son have the Father also.

24Be sure, then, to keep in your hearts the message you heard from the beginning. If you keep that message, then you will always live in union with the Son and the Father.

b **2:10** someone else; *or* us.
2:7 Jn 13:34

I John

The author of 1 John uses very personal language. In chapter 2 how many different names does he use for the people he is writing to?

Pray It!

Bigger, Better, Faster

What is the opposite of God? What are the things that pull us away from love? The author warns us away from "anything that belongs to the world" (1 John 2:15). How will you know what these things are? They would be anything that causes you to be selfish, lustful, boastful, or greedy. As Christians we must be especially careful not to be tempted by advertisers who want us to buy the latest gadget or the fastest car. These things will not last. They are "passing away" (2:17).

Holy Spirit,
Help me not to love the things of this world.
Give me the wisdom to know that having the latest and greatest
*   does not bring true happiness.*
Give me the courage to say no to people who promise me good times
*   but only lead me away from you.*
Give me the strength to resist the things that promise instant happiness
*   but in reality bring unhappiness and even death.*
Help me to know the difference between the things
*   that are of God and the things that are only passing away. Amen.*

— 1 John 2:15–17

25 And this is what Christ himself promised to give us—eternal life.

26 I am writing this to you about those who are trying to deceive you. 27 But as for you, Christ has poured out his Spirit on you. As long as his Spirit remains in you, you do not need anyone to teach you. For his Spirit teaches you about everything, and what he teaches is true, not false. Obey the Spirit's teaching, then, and remain in union with Christ.

28 Yes, my children, remain in union with him, so that when he appears we may be full of courage and need not hide in shame from him on the Day he comes. 29 You know that Christ is righteous; you should know, then, that everyone who does what is right is God's child.

Children of God

3 ¹See how much the Father has loved us! His love is so great that we are called God's children—and so, in fact, we are. This is why the world does not know us: it has not known God. ²My dear friends, we are now God's children, but it is not yet clear what we shall become. But we know that when Christ appears, we shall be like him, because we shall see him as he really is. ³Everyone who has this hope in Christ keeps himself pure, just as Christ is pure.

⁴Whoever sins is guilty of breaking God's law, because sin is a breaking of the law. ⁵You know that Christ appeared in order to take away sins,ᶜ and that there is no sin in him. ⁶So everyone who lives in union with Christ does not continue to sin; but whoever

ᶜ **3:5** sins; *some manuscripts have* our sins.
3:1 Jn 1:12   **3:5** Jn 1:29

The author of this letter was connected to the author of the Gospel of John. Look for similarities between I John 3:11–18 and John 15:17–18.

continues to sin has never seen him or known him.

7 Let no one deceive you, my children! Whoever does what is right is righteous, just as Christ is righteous. 8 Whoever continues to sin belongs to the Devil, because the Devil has sinned from the very beginning. The Son of God appeared for this very reason, to destroy what the Devil had done.

9 Those who are children of God do not continue to sin, for God's very nature is in them; and because God is their Father, they cannot continue to sin. 10 Here is the clear difference between God's children and the Devil's children: those who do not do what is right or do not love others are not God's children.

Love One Another

11 The message you heard from the very beginning is this: we must love one another. 12 We must not be like Cain; he belonged to the Evil One and murdered his own brother Abel. Why did Cain murder him? Because the things he himself did were wrong, and the things his brother did were right.

13 So do not be surprised, my friends, if the people of the world hate you. 14 We know that we have left death and come over into life; we know it because we love others. Those who do not love are still under the power of death. 15 Those who hate others are murderers, and you know that murderers do not have eternal life in them. 16 This is how we know what love is: Christ gave his life for us. We too, then, ought to give our lives for others! 17 If we are rich and see others in need, yet close our hearts against them, how can we claim that we love God? 18 My children, our love should not be just words and talk; it must be true love, which shows itself in action.

Courage before God

19 This, then, is how we will know that we belong to the truth; this is how we will be confident in God's presence. 20 If our conscience condemns us, we know that God is

A Closed Heart

It is not wealth alone, but a closed heart, that is contrary to the will of God (1 John 3:17). God's care for poor people is spoken of again and again in the Bible. The Old Law in the Old Testament specifically required that those who have more must share with those who are going without (Deuteronomy 24:10–22).

But the Old Law was not enough. If people's hearts were closed, they found ways around caring for poor people. So Jesus told stories to warn us against having a closed, hard heart. The story of the rich man and Lazarus (Luke 16:19–31), the warning against the teachers of the Law (Mark 12:38–40), and the story of the final judgment (Matthew 25:31–46) are examples of these stories.

What other stories told by Jesus can you think of or find that challenged people to open their hearts to people in need?

— 1 John 3:17–18

greater than our conscience and that he knows everything. 21 And so, my dear friends, if our conscience does not condemn us, we have courage in God's presence. 22 We receive from him whatever we ask, because we obey his commands and do what pleases him. 23 What he commands is that we believe in his Son Jesus Christ and love one another, just as Christ commanded us. 24 Those who obey God's commands live in union with God and God lives in union with them. And because of the Spirit that God has given us we know that God lives in union with us.

I John

Pray It!

God Is Love

Here is a meditation prayer you can try. Read 1 John 4:7–21. Then quiet yourself and imagine you are surrounded by the people you love. Put everyone in the picture: family, friends, other people who have shown love to you, and people whom you have cared about. Now remember what the passage says, "No one has ever seen God, but If we love one another, God lives in union with us, and his love is made perfect in us" (4:12). Imagine all those people's love for you, knowing that through them you are experiencing God's love. Then thank God for all of the love you have been blessed with.

As a follow-up to this meditation, you might want to make a collage with pictures of all the people you imagined. Keep it where you see it regularly to keep in mind God's love for you. Let it serve as a reminder to you to share that love with others.

— 1 John 4:7–21

The True Spirit and the False Spirit

4 ¹My dear friends, do not believe all who claim to have the Spirit, but test them to find out if the spirit they have comes from God. For many false prophets have gone out everywhere. ²This is how you will be able to know whether it is God's Spirit: anyone who acknowledges that Jesus Christ came as a human being has the Spirit who comes from God. ³But anyone who denies this about Jesus does not have the Spirit from God. The spirit that he has is from the Enemy of Christ; you heard that it would come, and now it is here in the world already.

⁴But you belong to God, my children, and have defeated the false prophets, because the Spirit who is in you is more powerful than the spirit in those who belong to the world. ⁵Those false prophets speak about matters of the world, and the world listens to them because they belong to the world. ⁶But we belong to God. Whoever knows God listens to us; whoever does not belong to God does not listen to us. This, then, is how we can tell the difference between the Spirit of truth and the spirit of error.

God Is Love

⁷Dear friends, let us love one another, because love comes from God. Whoever loves is a child of God and knows God. ⁸Whoever does not love does not know God, for God is love. ⁹And God showed his love for us by sending his only Son into the world, so that we might have life through him. ¹⁰This is what love is: it is not that we have loved God, but that he loved us and sent his Son to be the means by which our sins are forgiven.

¹¹Dear friends, if this is how God loved us, then we should love one another. ¹²No one has ever seen God, but if we love one another, God lives in union with us, and his love is made perfect in us.

¹³We are sure that we live in union with God and that he lives in union with us, because he has given us his Spirit. ¹⁴And we have seen and tell others that the Father sent his Son to be the Savior of the world. ¹⁵If we declare that Jesus is the Son of God, we live in union with God and God lives in union with us. ¹⁶And we ourselves know and believe the love which God has for us.

God is love, and those who live in love live in union with God and God lives in

1 John

union with them. [17]Love is made perfect in us in order that we may have courage on the Judgment Day; and we will have it because our life in this world is the same as Christ's. [18]There is no fear in love; perfect love drives out all fear. So then, love has not been made perfect in anyone who is afraid, because fear has to do with punishment.

Perfect love drives out all fear. (4:18)

[19]We love because God first loved us. [20]If we say we love God, but hate others, we are liars. For we cannot love God, whom we have not seen, if we do not love others, whom we have seen. [21]The command that Christ has given us is this: whoever loves God must love others also.

Our Victory over the World

5 [1]Whoever believes that Jesus is the Messiah is a child of God; and whoever loves a father loves his child also. [2]This is

Whoever believes that Jesus is the Messiah is a child of God. (5:1)

5:3 Jn 14:15   5:12 Jn 3:36

how we know that we love God's children: it is by loving God and obeying his commands. [3]For our love for God means that we obey his commands. And his commands are not too hard for us, [4]because every child of God is able to defeat the world. And we win the victory over the world by means of our faith. [5]Who can defeat the world? Only the person who believes that Jesus is the Son of God.

The Witness about Jesus Christ

[6]Jesus Christ is the one who came with the water of his baptism and the blood of his death. He came not only with the water, but with both the water and the blood. And the Spirit himself testifies that this is true, because the Spirit is truth. [7]There are three witnesses: [8]the Spirit, the water, and the blood; and all three give the same testimony. [9]We believe human testimony; but God's testimony is much stronger, and he has given this testimony about his Son. [10]So those who believe in the Son of God have this testimony in their own heart; but those who do not believe God, have made a liar of him, because they have not believed what God has said about his Son. [11]The testimony is this: God has given us eternal life, and this life has its source in his Son. [12]Whoever has the Son has this life; whoever does not have the Son of God does not have life.

Eternal Life

[13]I am writing this to you so that you may know that you have eternal life—you that believe in the Son of God. [14]We have courage in God's presence, because we are sure that he hears us if we ask him for anything that is according to his will. [15]He hears us whenever we ask him; and since we know this is true, we know also that he gives us what we ask from him.

[16]If you see a believer commit a sin that

1 John

does not lead to death, you should pray to God, who will give that person life. This applies to those whose sins do not lead to death. But there is sin which leads to death, and I do not say that you should pray to God about that. 17 All wrongdoing is sin, but there is sin which does not lead to death.

18 We know that no children of God keep on sinning, for the Son of God keeps them safe, and the Evil One cannot harm them.

19 We know that we belong to God even though the whole world is under the rule of the Evil One.

20 We know that the Son of God has come and has given us understanding, so that we know the true God. We live in union with the true God—in union with his Son Jesus Christ. This is the true God, and this is eternal life.

21 My children, keep yourselves safe from false gods!

Your Next Step

Congratulations on finishing the First Letter of John! Use this space to write your thoughts and questions about this book. If you are following the suggested reading plan, move ahead to the Revelation to John. This book is filled with symbolic figures and stories that teach that God's love will triumph over all evil!

The Evil One is another name for Satan or the Devil.

¹From the Elder—

To the dear Lady and to her children, a whom I truly love. And I am not the only one, but all who know the truth love you, 2 because the truth remains in us and will be with us forever.

³May God the Father and Jesus Christ, the Father's Son, give us grace, mercy, and peace; may they be ours in truth and love.

Truth and Love

⁴How happy I was to find that some of your children live in the truth, just as the Father commanded us. ⁵And so I ask you, dear Lady: let us all love one another. This is no new command I am writing you; it is the command which we have had from the beginning. ⁶This love I speak of means that we must live in obedience to God's com-mands. The command, as you have all heard from the beginning, is that you must all live in love.

⁷Many deceivers have gone out over the world, people who do not acknowledge that Jesus Christ came as a human being. Such a person is a deceiver and the Enemy of Christ. ⁸Be on your guard, then, so that you will not lose what we ᵇ have worked for, but will receive your reward in full.

⁹Anyone who does not stay with the teaching of Christ, but goes beyond it, does not have God. Whoever does stay with the teaching has both the Father and the Son. ¹⁰So then, if some come to you who do not bring this teaching, do not welcome them in your homes; do not even say, "Peace be with you." ¹¹For anyone who wishes them peace becomes their partner in the evil things they do.

ᵃ **1** LADY AND . . . HER CHILDREN: *This probably refers to a church and its members (also in verses 4, 5).*   ᵇ **8** we; *some manuscripts have* you.
5 Jn 13:34; 15:12, 17

He Came as a Human Being

Catholic Connections

It seems strange that a Church leader would warn someone *not* to welcome another person. The Second Letter of John reveals a serious conflict within this early Church. The belief that Jesus was a real human being was under attack (verse 7).

This elder writing the letter was worried that believers might be misled. He was very clear that those who taught that Jesus wasn't a human being were deceivers and enemies of Christ (verse 7).

Christians believe that Jesus Christ was both fully God and fully human; or as we sometimes say, "true God and true man." This teaching is called the mystery of the Incarnation. How wonderful to know that Jesus was flesh and blood, just like us! He was hungry, he was tired, he was happy, he was sad, just like us. He was like us in every way except that he never sinned—he never disobeyed God, his Father. Because the Son of God was willing to become a true human being, we know how much we are loved!

— 2 John

Final Words

12I have so much to tell you, but I would rather not do it with paper and ink; instead, I hope to visit you and talk with you personally, so that we shall be completely happy.

13The children of your dear Sister*c* send you their greetings.

c **13** CHILDREN OF YOUR DEAR SISTER: *This probably refers to the members of the church to which the writer belonged.*

¹From the Elder—

To my dear Gaius, whom I truly love.

²My dear friend, I pray that everything may go well with you and that you may be in good health—as I know you are well in spirit. ³I was so happy when some Christians arrived and told me how faithful you are to the truth—just as you always live in the truth. ⁴Nothing makes me happier than to hear that my children live in the truth.

Gaius Is Praised

⁵My dear friend, you are so faithful in the work you do for other Christians, even when they are strangers. ⁶They have spoken to the church here about your love. Please help them to continue their trip in a way that will please God. ⁷For they set out on their trip in the service of Christ without accepting any help from unbelievers. ⁸We Christians, then, must help these people, so that we may share in their work for the truth.

Diotrephes and Demetrius

⁹I wrote a short letter to the church; but Diotrephes, who likes to be their leader, will not pay any attention to what I say. ¹⁰When I come, then, I will bring up everything he has done: the terrible things he says about us and the lies he tells! But that is not enough for him; he will not receive the Christians when they come, and even stops those who want to receive them and tries to drive them out of the church!

¹¹My dear friend, do not imitate what is bad, but imitate what is good. Whoever does good belongs to God; whoever does what is bad has not seen God.

¹²Everyone speaks well of Demetrius; truth itself speaks well of him. And we add our testimony, and you know that what we say is true.

Final Greetings

¹³I have so much to tell you, but I do not want to do it with pen and ink. ¹⁴I hope to see you soon, and then we will talk personally.

¹⁵Peace be with you.

All your friends send greetings. Greet all our friends personally.

What a Guy!

Gaius, the man whom the Third Letter of John is addressed to, was a friend, maybe even a student, of the Elder. Gaius had welcomed missionaries in the past and is now being asked to do so again. He has been a faithful Christian and helped the mission of the Church. Are you like Gaius? Do others recognize you for your faithfulness and love? Even as a young person, you can support the mission of the Church. Get involved in projects sponsored by your parish, school, or community that help other people. Then you will build a reputation as a generous and welcoming person too.

— 3 John

---

1 Acts 19:29; Rom 16:23; 1 Cor 1:14

If you're lucky, you have never met one of the people that the Letter of Jude talks about—people who lie and twist things to look important and cause division. They only seem happy when other people are unhappy. They pretend to like you, but then cause trouble. They are nice to your face, but they complain behind your back. They create problems wherever they go.

These people can be very smooth talkers. They might make you doubt the things you have always known to be true. When you meet one—and you will—don't be fooled. Do as Jude says and "keep yourselves in the love of God" (verse 21).

Verse 7

Head lines

- Harsh Criticism for False Teachers (verses 5–16)
- How to Respond to Manipulators (verses 20–22)

FACTOIDS

Who wrote this book? Unknown.
When was it written? Possibly around AD 90.
Who was it written for? It is unknown who the audience was.
Why was it written? The author wanted to warn people about false teachers and to encourage people to remain faithful.
Important themes
- False teachers are criticized.
- Believers are reminded to stay faithful and pray in the Holy Spirit.

JUDE

¹From Jude, servant of Jesus Christ, and brother of James—

To those who have been called by God, who live in the love of God the Father and the protection of Jesus Christ:

²May mercy, peace, and love be yours in full measure.

False Teachers

³My dear friends, I was doing my best to write to you about the salvation we share in common, when I felt the need of writing at once to encourage you to fight on for the faith which once and for all God has given to his people. ⁴For some godless people have slipped in unnoticed among us, persons who distort the message about the grace of our God in order to excuse their immoral ways, and who reject Jesus Christ, our only Master and Lord. Long ago the Scriptures predicted the condemnation they have received.

⁵For even though you know all this, I want to remind you of how the Lord*a* once rescued the people of Israel from Egypt, but afterward destroyed those who did not believe. ⁶Remember the angels who did not stay within the limits of their proper authority, but abandoned their own dwelling place: they are bound with eternal chains in the darkness below, where God is keeping them for that great Day on which they will be condemned. ⁷Remember Sodom and Gomorrah, and the nearby towns, whose people acted as those angels did and indulged in sexual immorality and perversion: they suffer the punishment of eternal fire as a plain warning to all.

⁸In the same way also, these people have visions which make them sin against their own bodies; they despise God's authority and insult the glorious beings above. ⁹Not even the chief angel Michael did this. In his quarrel with the Devil, when they argued about who would have the body of Moses, Michael did not dare condemn the Devil with insulting words, but said, "The Lord rebuke you!" ¹⁰But these people attack with insults anything they do not understand; and those things that they know by instinct, like wild animals, are the very things that destroy them. ¹¹How terrible for them! They have followed the way that Cain took. For the sake of money they have given themselves over to the error that Balaam committed. They have rebelled as Korah rebelled, and like him they are destroyed. ¹²With their shameless carousing they are like dirty spots in your fellowship meals. They take care only of themselves. They are like clouds carried along by the wind, but bringing no rain. They are like trees that bear no fruit, even in autumn, trees that have been pulled up by the roots and are completely dead. ¹³They are like wild waves of the sea, with their shameful deeds showing up like foam. They are like wandering stars, for whom God has reserved a place forever in the deepest darkness.

¹⁴It was Enoch, the seventh*b* direct descendant from Adam, who long ago prophesied this about them: "The Lord will come with many thousands of his holy angels ¹⁵to bring judgment on all, to condemn them all for the godless deeds they have performed and for all the terrible words that godless sinners have spoken against him!"

¹⁶These people are always grumbling and blaming others; they follow their own evil desires; they brag about themselves and flatter others in order to get their own way.

Warnings and Instructions

¹⁷But remember, my friends, what you were told in the past by the apostles of our Lord Jesus Christ. ¹⁸They said to you,

---

a **5** the Lord; *some manuscripts have* Jesus, *which in Greek is the same as* Joshua.   *b* **14** SEVENTH: *This numbering includes both the first and the last in the series of seven names from Adam to Enoch.*

1 Mt 13:55; Mk 6:3   **5 a** Ex 12:51; **b** Num 14:29, 30   **7** Gen 19:1–24   **9 a** Dan 10:13, 21; 12:1; Rev 12:7; **b** Deut 34:6; **c** Zech 3:2   **11 a** Gen 4:3–8; **b** Num 22:1–35; **c** Num 16:1–35   **14** Gen 5:18, 21–24   **18** 2 Pet 3:3

Pray It!

End with Prayer

The Letter of Jude is full of criticism about some troublesome people. These people are distorting the Christian message and practicing immoral behavior (verse 4). They are even making trouble at the fellowship meals, or the celebration of the Eucharist (verse 12). The author even calls them dirty spots, autumn trees without fruit, wild waves, and wandering stars (verses 12–13). Yet despite all of this negativity, the letter has a lovely, prayerful ending (verses 20–25).

This can serve as a reminder to us during hard times. When you are feeling attacked, when things aren't going your way, when you start feeling negative about life, stop and pray. In your prayer, remember God's love for you. Ask God's help with the things that are bothering you. Pray for the people who seem to be against you. When you stop and pray, you might be surprised by how quickly things can change.

— Jude

"When the last days come, people will appear who will make fun of you, people who follow their own godless desires." ¹⁹These are the people who cause divisions, who are controlled by their natural desires, who do not have the Spirit. ²⁰But you, my friends, keep on building yourselves up on your most sacred faith. Pray in the power of the Holy Spirit, ²¹and keep yourselves in the love of God, as you wait for our Lord Jesus Christ in his mercy to give you eternal life.

²²Show mercy toward those who have doubts; ²³save others by snatching them out of the fire; and to others show mercy mixed with fear, but hate their very clothes, stained by their sinful lusts.

Prayer of Praise

²⁴To him who is able to keep you from falling and to bring you faultless and joyful before his glorious presence— ²⁵to the only God our Savior, through Jesus Christ our Lord, be glory, majesty, might, and authority, from all ages past, and now, and forever and ever! Amen.

Life can seem like it's falling apart at times, even when you're trying to live right. This is what the early Christians felt as they were being persecuted and killed by the Romans who were threatened by their faith. They needed a big dose of hope!

Revelation is filled with weird symbols, coded language, and images that seem like science fiction. But the meaning of it all is that no matter how scary and difficult life gets, there is a happy, hopeful ending. God's love for us is greater than any suffering or evil we experience. If we trust God and try to be faithful in following Jesus, we will one day know the pure joy of being with God forever.

Chap. 12:7–9

THE Revelation TO JOHN

Headlines

- Jesus Appears to John! (1:9–20)
- All Heaven Worships the Lamb (chapters 4–5)
- 144,000 Faithful People Saved (7:1–8)
- War Breaks Out in Heaven (12:7–9)
- The Fall of an Evil Empire (18:1–3)
- Judgment Day Arrives for All (20:11–15)
- No More Sadness: God Lives with Us (21:1–4)

FACTOIDS

Who wrote this book? John, a prophet and disciple of the Apostle John.
When was it written? Probably around AD 92 to 96.
Who was it written for? It was written for Christians of the early Church who were being persecuted and killed by the Roman Empire because of their faith.
Why was it written? To offer hope to the persecuted Christians by reminding them that God ultimately wins over evil, so we must have courage during difficult times and trust in God.
What is the literary style? This book is written in apocalyptic language containing visions, symbols, animals, numbers, coded language, natural disasters, and horrors. It is not meant to be taken literally.

Important themes
- Don't be lukewarm about your faith!
- Jesus is the beginning and end of the entire universe and all history.
- God is victorious over evil; in all things, trust God and have hope!
- A new earth and heaven is waiting for us!

REVELATION

1 ¹This book is the record of the events that Jesus Christ revealed. God gave him this revelation in order to show to his servants what must happen very soon. Christ made these things known to his servant John by sending his angel to him, ²and John has told all that he has seen. This is his report concerning the message from God and the truth revealed by Jesus Christ. ³Happy is the one who reads this book, and happy are those who listen to the words of this prophetic message and obey what is written in this book! For the time is near when all these things will happen.

Greetings to the Seven Churches

⁴From John to the seven churches in the province of Asia:

Grace and peace be yours from God, who is, who was, and who is to come, and from the seven spirits in front of his throne, ⁵and from Jesus Christ, the faithful witness, the first to be raised from death and who is also the ruler of the kings of the world.

He loves us, and by his sacrificial death he has freed us from our sins ⁶and made us a kingdom of priests to serve his God and Father. To Jesus Christ be the glory and power forever and ever! Amen.

⁷Look, he is coming on the clouds! Everyone will see him, including those who pierced him. All peoples on earth will mourn over him. So shall it be!

⁸"I am the first and the last," says the Lord God Almighty, who is, who was, and who is to come.

A Vision of Christ

⁹I am John, your brother, and as a follower of Jesus I am your partner in patiently enduring the suffering that comes to those who belong to his Kingdom. I was put on the island of Patmos because I had proclaimed God's word and the truth that Jesus revealed. ¹⁰On the Lord's day the Spirit took control of me, and I heard a loud voice, that sounded like a trumpet, speaking behind me. ¹¹It said, "Write down what you see, and send the book to the churches in these seven cities: Ephesus, Smyrna, Pergamum, Thyatira, Sardis, Philadelphia, and Laodicea."

¹²I turned around to see who was talking to me, and I saw seven gold lampstands, ¹³and among them there was what looked like a human being, wearing a robe that reached to his feet, and a gold band around his chest. ¹⁴His hair was white as wool, or as snow, and his eyes blazed like fire; ¹⁵his feet shone like brass that has been refined and polished, and his voice sounded like a roaring waterfall. ¹⁶He held seven stars in his right hand, and a sharp two-edged sword came out of his mouth. His face was as bright as the midday sun. ¹⁷When I saw him, I fell down at his feet like a dead man. He placed his right hand on me and said, "Don't be afraid! I am the first and the last. ¹⁸I am the living one! I was dead, but now I am alive forever and ever. I have authority over death and the world of the dead. ¹⁹Write, then, the things you see, both the things that are now and the things that will happen afterward. ²⁰Here is the secret meaning of the seven stars that you see in my right hand, and of the seven gold lampstands: the seven stars are the angels of the seven churches, and the seven lampstands are the seven churches.

The Message to Ephesus

2 ¹"To the angel of the church in Ephesus write:

"This is the message from the one who holds the seven stars in his right hand and who walks among the seven gold lamp-

---

1:4 a Ex 3:14; b Rev 4:5   **1:5** a Isa 55:4; b Ps 89:27   **1:6** Ex 19:6; Rev 5:10   **1:7** a Dan 7:13; Mt 24:30; Mk 13:26; Lk 21:27; 1 Thess 4:17; b Zech 12:10; Jn 19:34, 37; c Zech 12:10; Mt 24:30   **1:8** a Rev 22:13; b Ex 3:14   **1:13** a Dan 7:13; b Dan 10:5   **1:14** Dan 7:9   **1:14, 15** Dan 10:6   **1:15** Ezek 1:24; 43:2   **1:17** Isa 44:6; 48:12; Rev 2:8; 22:13

Pray It!

Hair as White as Snow?

Have you ever imagined Jesus with white hair? Not only that, but in John's vision of Jesus, he had a gold band around his chest, eyes blazing, feet shining like polished brass, his face as bright as the sun (Revelation 1:13–16). Jesus' voice sounded like a trumpet and then a rushing waterfall. The Jesus who appeared in John's vision seems nothing like the Jesus we imagine! Jesus lived in the Middle East, and like other men from that region, he probably had dark skin and hair. But remember, after Jesus' Resurrection, when he appeared to his friends, they didn't recognize him. His glorified body looked completely different than when he was alive.

Close your eyes and picture yourself in a quiet, peaceful place. Imagine that Jesus comes along and sits next to you. What does he look like to you? What do you think he would like to say to you in a meeting like that? What would you share about your life with him? (Meeting Jesus in your imagination is one way to pray, and it can be very comforting and peaceful. You can pray like this anytime, anywhere!)

— Revelation 1:10–16

stands. ²I know what you have done; I know how hard you have worked and how patient you have been. I know that you cannot tolerate evil people and that you have tested those who say they are apostles but are not, and have found out that they are liars. ³You are patient, you have suffered for my sake, and you have not given up. ⁴But this is what I have against you: you do not love me now as you did at first. ⁵Think how far you have fallen! Turn from your sins and do what you did at first. If you don't turn from your sins, I will come to you and take your lampstand from its place. ⁶But this is what you have in your favor: you hate what the Nicolaitans do, as much as I do.

⁷"If you have ears, then, listen to what the Spirit says to the churches!

"To those who win the victory I will give the right to eat the fruit of the tree of life that grows in the Garden of God.

The Message to Smyrna

⁸"To the angel of the church in Smyrna write:

"This is the message from the one who is the first and the last, who died and lived again. ⁹I know your troubles; I know that you are poor—but really you are rich! I know the evil things said against you by those who claim to be Jews but are not; they are a group that belongs to Satan! ¹⁰Don't be afraid of anything you are about to suffer. Listen! The Devil will put you to the test by having some of you thrown into prison, and your troubles will last ten days. Be faithful to me, even if it means death, and I will give you life as your prize of victory.

¹¹"If you have ears, then, listen to what the Spirit says to the churches!

"Those who win the victory will not be hurt by the second death.

2:7 a Gen 2:9; Rev 22:2; b Ezek 28:13; 31:8 (LXX)   2:8 Isa 44:6; 48:12; Rev 1:17; 22:13   2:11 Rev 20:14; 21.8

Revelation

"'I am the first and the last,' says the Lord God Almighty" (Revelation 1:8).

The Message to Pergamum

12 "To the angel of the church in Pergamum write:

"This is the message from the one who has the sharp two-edged sword. 13 I know where you live, there where Satan has his throne. You are true to me, and you did not abandon your faith in me even during the time when Antipas, my faithful witness, was killed there where Satan lives. 14 But there are a few things I have against you: there are some among you who follow the teaching of Balaam, who taught Balak how to lead the people of Israel into sin by persuading them to eat food that had been offered to idols and to practice sexual immorality. 15 In the same way you have people among you who follow the teaching of the Nicolaitans. 16 Now turn from your sins! If you don't, I will come to you soon and fight against those people with the sword that comes out of my mouth.

17 "If you have ears, then, listen to what the Spirit says to the churches!

"To those who win the victory I will give some of the hidden manna. I will also give each of them a white stone on which is written a new name that no one knows except the one who receives it.

The Message to Thyatira

18 "To the angel of the church in Thyatira write:

"This is the message from the Son of God, whose eyes blaze like fire, whose feet shine like polished brass. 19 I know what you do. I know your love, your faithfulness, your service, and your patience. I know that you are doing more now than you did at first. 20 But this is what I have against you: you tolerate that woman Jezebel, who calls herself a messenger of God. By her teaching she misleads my servants into practicing sexual immorality and eating food that has been offered to idols. 21 I have given her time to

Report Cards for Seven Churches

Your heart is racing as you wait for your name to be called. Finally, your teacher calls you up to receive your first-quarter report card. You open it and eagerly read her comments about you: "Your son shows much patience with his fellow students. He is such a friendly and helpful boy, a real pleasure to have in class. But his constant talking is a problem. Because of it, he doesn't hear directions, and he distracts others who are trying to listen. This behavior must change."

In John's vision, Jesus has written a letter to each of the seven churches of Asia Minor. The letters sound a bit like report cards. He offers praise and encouragement to the communities, but he also points out their weaknesses and tells them strongly that they must change and become more faithful.

Remember, these were new churches, still trying to figure out all the ins and outs of living as Christians. They needed guidance and sometimes correction to keep on the right path. If Jesus were writing a letter to your church, what positive things would he have to say? What would he tell you needs to change?

— Revelation, chapters 2–3

2:14 **a** Num 22:5, 7; 31:16; Deut 23:4; **b** Num 25:1–3   2:17 **a** Ex 16:14, 15; 16:33, 34; Jn 6:48–50; **b** Isa 62:2; 65:15   2:20 1 Kings 16:31; 2 Kings 9:22, 30

What does Jesus promise to the seven churches if they are faithful?

repent of her sins, but she does not want to turn from her immorality. 22 And so I will throw her on a bed where she and those who committed adultery with her will suffer terribly. I will do this now unless they repent of the wicked things they did with her. 23 I will also kill her followers, and then all the churches will know that I am the one who knows everyone's thoughts and wishes. I will repay each of you according to what you have done.

24 "But the rest of you in Thyatira have not followed this evil teaching; you have not learned what the others call 'the deep secrets of Satan.' I say to you that I will not put any other burden on you. 25 But until I come, you must hold firmly to what you have. 26-28 To those who win the victory, who continue to the end to do what I want, I will give the same authority that I received from my Father: I will give them authority over the nations, to rule them with an iron rod and to break them to pieces like clay pots. I will also give them the morning star.

29 "If you have ears, then, listen to what the Spirit says to the churches!

The Message to Sardis

3 ¹ "To the angel of the church in Sardis write:

"This is the message from the one who has the seven spirits of God and the seven stars. I know what you are doing; I know that you have the reputation of being alive, even though you are dead! ² So wake up, and strengthen what you still have before it dies completely. For I find that what you have done is not yet perfect in the sight of my God. ³ Remember, then, what you were taught and what you heard; obey it and turn from your sins. If you do not wake up, I will come upon you like a thief, and you will not even know the time when I will come. ⁴ But a few of you there in Sardis have kept your clothes clean. You will walk with me, clothed in white, because you are worthy to do so. ⁵ Those who win the victory will be clothed

like this in white, and I will not remove their names from the book of the living. In the presence of my Father and of his angels I will declare openly that they belong to me.

⁶ "If you have ears, then, listen to what the Spirit says to the churches!

The Message to Philadelphia

⁷ "To the angel of the church in Philadelphia write:

"This is the message from the one who is holy and true. He has the key that belonged to David, and when he opens a door, no one can close it, and when he closes it, no one can open it. ⁸ I know what you do; I know that you have a little power; you have followed my teaching and have been faithful to me. I have opened a door in front of you, which no one can close. ⁹ Listen! As for that group that belongs to Satan, those liars who claim that they are Jews but are not, I will make them come and bow down at your feet. They will all know that I love you. ¹⁰ Because you have kept my command to endure, I will also keep you safe from the time of trouble which is coming upon the world to test all the people on earth. ¹¹ I am coming soon. Keep safe what you have, so that no one will rob you of your victory prize. ¹² I will make those who are victorious pillars in the temple of my God, and they will never leave it. I will write on them the name of my God and the name of the city of my God, the new Jerusalem, which will come down out of heaven from my God. I will also write on them my new name.

¹³ "If you have ears, then, listen to what the Spirit says to the churches!

The Message to Laodicea

¹⁴ "To the angel of the church in Laodicea write:

"This is the message from the Amen, the faithful and true witness, who is the origin*a* of all that God has created. ¹⁵ I know what you have done; I know that you are neither

---

a **3:14** origin; *or* ruler.
2:23 **a** Ps 7:9; Jer 17:10; **b** Ps 62:12   **2:26, 27** Ps 2:8, 9 (LXX)   **3:3** Mt 24:43, 44; Lk 12:39, 40; Rev 16:15
3:5 **a** Ex 32:32, 33; Ps 69:28; Rev 20:12; **b** Mt 10:32; Lk 12:8   **3:7** Isa 22:22; Job 12:14   **3:9** **a** Isa 49:23;
60:14; **b** Isa 43:4   **3:12** **a** Rev 21:2; **b** Isa 62:2; 65:15   **3:14** Prov 8:22

cold nor hot. How I wish you were either one or the other! ¹⁶But because you are lukewarm, neither hot nor cold, I am going to spit you out of my mouth! ¹⁷You say, 'I am rich and well off; I have all I need.' But you do not know how miserable and pitiful you are! You are poor, naked, and blind. ¹⁸I advise you, then, to buy gold from me, pure gold, in order to be rich. Buy also white clothing to dress yourself and cover up your shameful nakedness. Buy also some ointment to put on your eyes, so that you may see. ¹⁹I rebuke and punish all whom I love. Be in earnest, then, and turn from your sins. ²⁰Listen! I stand at the door and knock; if any hear my voice and open the door, I will come into their house and eat with them, and they will eat with me. ²¹To those who win the victory I will give the right to sit beside me on my throne, just as I have been victorious and now sit by my Father on his throne.

I stand at the door and knock. (3:20)

²²"If you have ears, then, listen to what the Spirit says to the churches!"

Worship in Heaven

4 ¹At this point I had another vision and saw an open door in heaven.

And the voice that sounded like a trumpet, which I had heard speaking to me before, said, "Come up here, and I will show

Lukewarm Faith

Jesus is upset with the church in Laodicea because it's boring! "I know that you are neither cold nor hot. How I wish you were either one or the other!" (Revelation 3:15). If these Christians were hot, they'd be on fire with their faith, and of course this is what he wants from all of us. But why would Jesus rather see us cold in our faith than lukewarm? If our faith was cold, we would be greatly in need of saving. Jesus said in the Gospels that he came to save lost, sinful, poor, and suffering people, and those who don't believe. Having a cold faith gives him a lot to work with!

But lukewarm faith is a problem. People with faith that is lukewarm aren't necessarily sinners, but their faith is dull, half-hearted. They just don't care. They might not be bad people, but they don't see any reason to become any better either. And Jesus is saying it's harder to move the hearts of those people.

What's the temperature of your faith?

— Revelation 3:14–15

you what must happen after this." ²At once the Spirit took control of me. There in heaven was a throne with someone sitting on it. ³His face gleamed like such precious stones as jasper and carnelian, and all around the throne there was a rainbow the color of an emerald. ⁴In a circle around the throne were twenty-four other thrones, on which were seated twenty-four elders dressed in white and wearing crowns of gold. ⁵From the

3:19 Prov 3:12; Heb 12:6   **4:2, 3** Ezek 1:26–28; 10:1   **4:5 a** Ex 19:16; Tob 12:15; Rev 8:5; 11:19; 16:18; **b** Ezek 1:13; **c** Rev 1:4; Zech 4:2

Revelation

throne came flashes of lightning, rumblings, and peals of thunder. In front of the throne seven lighted torches were burning, which are the seven spirits of God. [6]Also in front of the throne there was what looked like a sea of glass, clear as crystal.

Surrounding the throne on each of its sides, were four living creatures covered with eyes in front and behind. [7]The first one looked like a lion; the second looked like a bull; the third had a face like a human face; and the fourth looked like an eagle in flight. [8]Each one of the four living creatures had six wings, and they were covered with eyes, inside and out. Day and night they never stop singing:

"Holy, holy, holy, is the Lord God Almighty, who was, who is, and who is to come."

[9]The four living creatures sing songs of glory and honor and thanks to the one who sits on the throne, who lives forever and ever. When they do so, [10]the twenty-four elders fall down before the one who sits on the throne, and worship him who lives forever and ever. They throw their crowns down in front of the throne and say,

[11]"Our Lord and God! You are worthy to receive glory, honor, and power. For you created all things, and by your will they were given existence and life."

The Scroll and the Lamb

5 [1]I saw a scroll in the right hand of the one who sits on the throne; it was covered with writing on both sides and was sealed with seven seals. [2]And I saw a mighty angel, who announced in a loud voice, "Who is worthy to break the seals and open the scroll?" [3]But there was no one in heaven or on earth or in the world below[b] who could open the scroll and look inside it. [4]I cried bitterly because no one could be found who was worthy to open the scroll or look inside it. [5]Then one of the elders said

Unlocking the Code

The language in Revelation was coded so that while the faithful followers of Jesus could understand John's message, their persecutors could not. Here is the meaning of some of the symbols in Revelation:

- *Throne in heaven:* God is seated on a throne, meaning that he holds authority over all of history.
- *Twenty-four thrones around God with twenty-four elders seated:* Twelve, like seven, is symbolic of fullness or perfection; double that, and it is even more perfect. The first twelve thrones are the twelve tribes of Israel and the second twelve thrones are the twelve Apostles. Together they symbolize the fullness of the faith—the Old Covenant and the New Covenant.
- *Four living creatures:* Four means universal (as in the four directions). God rules the entire universe, and all creation praises him. The lion, bull, human being, and eagle represent what is noblest, strongest, wisest, and swiftest in creation.

This first part of John's vision reminds us that God is at the center of everything: all history, the universe, and our faith. That's a good reason for the creatures to be singing God's praise!

— Revelation, chapter 4

[b] **5:3** WORLD BELOW: *The world of the dead (see 1:18).*
4:6 Ezek 1:22   **4:6, 7** Ezek 1:5–10; 10:14   **4:8 a** Ezek 1:18; 10:12; **b** Isa 6:2, 3   **5:1** Ezek 2:9, 10; Isa 29:11
5:5 a Gen 49:9; **b** Isa 11:1, 10

What prayer do we sing at Mass that is similar to the song in Revelation 4:8?

to me, "Don't cry. Look! The Lion from Judah's tribe, the great descendant of David, has won the victory, and he can break the seven seals and open the scroll."

6 Then I saw a Lamb standing in the center of the throne, surrounded by the four living creatures and the elders. The Lamb appeared to have been killed. It had seven horns and seven eyes, which are the seven spirits of God that have been sent through the whole earth. 7 The Lamb went and took the scroll from the right hand of the one who sits on the throne. 8 As he did so, the four living creatures and the twenty-four elders fell down before the Lamb. Each had a harp and gold bowls filled with incense, which are the prayers of God's people.

9 They sang a new song:

"You are worthy to take the scroll
and to break open its seals.
For you were killed, and by your
sacrificial death you bought for God
people from every tribe, language,
nation, and race.
10 You have made them a kingdom of
priests to serve our God,
and they shall rule on earth."

11 Again I looked, and I heard angels, thousands and millions of them! They stood around the throne, the four living creatures, and the elders, 12 and sang in a loud voice:

"The Lamb who was killed is worthy
to receive power, wealth, wisdom, and
strength,
honor, glory, and praise!"

13 And I heard every creature in heaven, on earth, in the world below, and in the sea—all living beings in the universe—and they were singing:

"To him who sits on the throne and to
the Lamb,
be praise and honor, glory and might,
forever and ever!"

14 The four living creatures answered, "Amen!" And the elders fell down and worshiped.

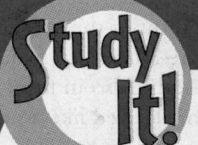

The Lamb of God

As the vision continues, it is helpful to understand the meaning of these symbols in Revelation:

- *Sealed scroll:* Contains messages to sinners, as well as God's plan for the world.
- *Lamb:* Jesus, who had been killed and is now resurrected from the dead. He is in the form of a lamb because he is the Lamb of God. We call Jesus the Lamb of God because he was sacrificed for our sake like the Passover lambs (see Exodus, chapter 12).

His seven horns symbolize perfect power, and his seven eyes symbolize his perfect knowledge. Only he can read the scroll because he alone can reveal and carry out God's divine plan.

Read on to see what messages the scroll contains.

— Revelation, chapter 5

The Seals

6 ¹Then I saw the Lamb break open the first of the seven seals, and I heard one of the four living creatures say in a voice that sounded like thunder, "Come!" ²I looked, and there was a white horse. Its rider held a bow, and he was given a crown. He rode out as a conqueror to conquer.

³Then the Lamb broke open the second seal; and I heard the second living creature say, "Come!" ⁴Another horse came out, a red one. Its rider was given the power to bring

5:6 a Isa 53:7; **b** Zech 4:10   **5:8** Ps 141:2   **5:9** Ps 33:3; 98:1; Isa 42:10   **5:10** Ex 19:6; Rev 1:6   **5:11** Dan 7:10   **6:2** Zech 1:8; 6:3, 6   **6:4** Zech 1:8; 6:2

Chapter 5 of Revelation contains one of many songs of praise to God in the Book of Revelation. How many others can you find in this book?

war on the earth, so that people should kill each other. He was given a large sword.

⁵Then the Lamb broke open the third seal; and I heard the third living creature say, "Come!" I looked, and there was a black horse. Its rider held a pair of scales in his hand. ⁶I heard what sounded like a voice coming from among the four living creatures, which said, "A quart of wheat for a day's wages, and three quarts of barley for a day's wages. But do not damage the olive trees and the vineyards!"

⁷Then the Lamb broke open the fourth seal; and I heard the fourth living creature say, "Come!" ⁸I looked, and there was a pale-colored horse. Its rider was named Death, and Hades[c] followed close behind. They were given authority over one fourth of the earth, to kill by means of war, famine, disease, and wild animals.

⁹Then the Lamb broke open the fifth seal. I saw underneath the altar the souls of those who had been killed because they had proclaimed God's word and had been faithful in their witnessing. ¹⁰They shouted in a loud voice, "Almighty Lord, holy and true! How long will it be until you judge the people on earth and punish them for killing us?" ¹¹Each of them was given a white robe, and they were told to rest a little while longer, until the complete number of other servants and believers were killed, as they had been.

¹²And I saw the Lamb break open the sixth seal. There was a violent earthquake, and the sun became black like coarse black cloth, and the moon turned completely red like blood. ¹³The stars fell down to the earth, like unripe figs falling from the tree when a strong wind shakes it. ¹⁴The sky disappeared like a scroll being rolled up, and every mountain and island was moved from its place. ¹⁵Then the kings of the earth, the rulers and the military chiefs, the rich and the powerful, and all other people, slave and free, hid themselves in caves and under rocks on the mountains. ¹⁶They called out to the mountains and to the rocks, "Fall on us and hide us from the eyes of the one who sits on

Forces of Human Nature Unleashed

Just because we're human, we're bound to have problems! In this vision, seals hold the scroll shut. As the Lamb breaks open the first four seals, horses and riders come out. The riders of the four horses represent power, war, famine, and death—the difficulties and disasters generally brought on by human sin. They are sometimes called the four horsemen of the apocalypse.

Beneath the fifth seal are the martyrs—people who have died for being true to their faith. White is symbolic of joy and victory, and in receiving white robes, they are comforted with knowing their faith will win out over death.

Breaking the sixth seal brings on a violent earthquake, turns the sun black and the moon blood red, and all the stars fall out of the sky. These events symbolize that when God judges us at the end of time, all creation will be affected

What are some of the terrible things going on around the world today—both those caused by natural forces and those brought on by humans? What are people most afraid of? How do you think God might judge our world in these times?

— Revelation, chapter 6

the throne and from the anger of the Lamb! ¹⁷The terrible day of their anger is here, and who can stand up against it?"

Revelation

ᶜ **6:8** HADES: *The world of the dead (see 1:18).*
6:5 Zech 6:2, 6　**6:8** Ezek 14:21　**6:12 a** Rev 11:13; 16:18; **b** Isa 13:10; Joel 2:10, 31; 3:15; Mt 24:29; Mk 13:24, 25; Lk 21:25　**6:13, 14** Isa 34:4　**6:14** Rev 16:20　**6:15** Isa 2:19, 21　**6:16** Hos 10:8; Lk 23:30 **6:17** Joel 2:11; Mal 3:2

Pray It!

Comfort for Those Who Suffer

There are many symbolic numbers in Revelation. What does the number 144,000 mean? One thousand is symbolic of a large number of people, more than can be counted. From each of the twelve tribes of Israel, there are twelve (perfection) thousand (too many to count) people. So twelve tribes multiplied by twelve thousand in each tribe equals 144,000 people.

Revelation isn't saying that exactly 144,000 people are saved. It really means that an enormous number have been faithful to God throughout history—even enduring persecution and death. They had already suffered enough, and now God was going to comfort and refresh them and take away all their pain.

Dear God, too many people are suffering in our world today—from disease, hunger, war, hurricanes, earthquakes, hatred, addictions, violence, and other terrible things. Some live far from me, and some are right here in my town and in my school. You depend on us to help bring your comfort to one another, so help me to listen to those who are afraid, or give a hug to those who are sad, or provide assistance to those who have lost homes and belongings. Let me show them there is hope and that they are loved by you. Amen.

— Revelation, chapter 7

The 144,000 People of Israel

7 ¹After this I saw four angels standing at the four corners of the earth, holding back the four winds so that no wind should blow on the earth or the sea or against any tree. ²And I saw another angel coming up from the east with the seal of the living God. He called out in a loud voice to the four angels to whom God had given the power to damage the earth and the sea. ³The angel said, "Do not harm the earth, the sea, or the trees, until we mark the servants of our God with a seal on their foreheads." ⁴And I was told that the number of those who were marked with God's seal on their foreheads was 144,000. They were from the twelve tribes of Israel, ⁵⁻⁸twelve thousand from each tribe: Judah, Reuben, Gad, Asher, Naphtali, Manasseh, Simeon, Levi, Issachar, Zebulun, Joseph, and Benjamin.

The Enormous Crowd

⁹After this I looked, and there was an enormous crowd—no one could count all the people! They were from every race, tribe, nation, and language, and they stood in front of the throne and of the Lamb, dressed in white robes and holding palm branches in their hands. ¹⁰They called out in a loud voice: "Salvation comes from our God, who sits on the throne, and from the Lamb!" ¹¹All the angels stood around the throne, the elders, and the four living creatures. Then they threw themselves face downward in front of the throne and worshiped God, ¹²saying, "Amen! Praise, glory, wisdom, thanksgiving, honor, power, and might belong to our God forever and ever! Amen!"

¹³One of the elders asked me, "Who are these people dressed in white robes, and where do they come from?"

¹⁴"I don't know, sir. You do," I answered.

He said to me, "These are the people who

7:1 Jer 49:36; Dan 7:2; Zech 6:5 **7:3** Ezek 9:4, 6 **7:14** Dan 12:1; Mt 24:21; Mk 13:19

have come safely through the terrible persecution. They have washed their robes and made them white with the blood of the Lamb. [15] That is why they stand before God's throne and serve him day and night in his temple. He who sits on the throne will protect them with his presence. [16] Never again will they hunger or thirst; neither sun nor any scorching heat will burn them, [17] because the Lamb, who is in the center of the throne, will be their shepherd, and he will guide them to springs of life-giving water. And God will wipe away every tear from their eyes."

The Seventh Seal

8 [1] When the Lamb broke open the seventh seal, there was silence in heaven for about half an hour. [2] Then I saw the seven angels who stand before God, and they were given seven trumpets.

[3] Another angel, who had a gold incense container, came and stood at the altar. He was given a lot of incense to add to the prayers of all God's people and to offer it on the gold altar that stands before the throne. [4] The smoke of the burning incense went up with the prayers of God's people from the hands of the angel standing before God. [5] Then the angel took the incense container, filled it with fire from the altar, and threw it on the earth. There were rumblings and peals of thunder, flashes of lightning, and an earthquake.

The Trumpets

[6] Then the seven angels with the seven trumpets prepared to blow them.

[7] The first angel blew his trumpet. Hail and fire, mixed with blood, came pouring down on the earth. A third of the earth was burned up, a third of the trees, and every blade of green grass.

[8] Then the second angel blew his trumpet.

Many Problems, One Solution

When the seventh seal is broken, there is great silence—like a calm before a storm. Then terrible things start happening, and it seems the entire world is going to be destroyed. Six trumpets blow, each announcing natural disasters, plagues, violent deaths, and more horror than we can imagine!

But wait! The message of this vision is not that the world is coming to an end. This vision, like all of Revelation, is about *hope.* For all those people who lived faithful lives and were marked by God's seal are kept safe from the destruction (Revelation 9:4). God protects them from harm.

This is a hopeful message for us, as well. We no doubt will face suffering or evil in our lives. But if we remain faithful to God, we will not be destroyed by it. Even if it brings physical pain or death here on earth, in eternity we will know nothing but joy and peace.

What does living a faithful life mean to you? Think of five qualities or behaviors that might describe a faithful person. How do you fit the description? How can you be more faithful to God's call?

— Revelation, chapters 8–9

Something that looked like a huge mountain on fire was thrown into the sea. A third of the sea was turned into blood, [9] a third of the

7:16 Isa 49:10   7:17 **a** Ps 23:1; Ezek 34:23; **b** Ps 23:2; Isa 49:10; **c** Isa 25:8   8:3 **a** Am 9:1; **b** Ex 30:1, 3   8:5 **a** Lev 16:12; Ezek 10:2; **b** Ex 19:16; Rev 11:19; 16:18   8:6, 7 Wis 11:5—12:2   8:7 Ex 9:23–25; Ezek 38:22

Revelation

living creatures in the sea died, and a third of the ships were destroyed.

10Then the third angel blew his trumpet. A large star, burning like a torch, dropped from the sky and fell on a third of the rivers and on the springs of water. 11(The name of the star is "Bitterness.") A third of the water turned bitter, and many people died from drinking the water, because it had turned bitter.

12Then the fourth angel blew his trumpet. A third of the sun was struck, and a third of the moon, and a third of the stars, so that their light lost a third of its brightness; there was no light during a third of the day and a third of the night also.

13Then I looked, and I heard an eagle that was flying high in the air say in a loud voice, "O horror! horror! How horrible it will be for all who live on earth when the sound comes from the trumpets that the other three angels must blow!"

9 1Then the fifth angel blew his trumpet. I saw a star which had fallen down to the earth, and it was given the key to the abyss.*d* 2The star opened the abyss, and smoke poured out of it, like the smoke from a large furnace; the sunlight and the air were darkened by the smoke from the abyss. 3Locusts came down out of the smoke upon the earth, and they were given the same kind of power that scorpions have. 4They were told not to harm the grass or the trees or any other plant; they could harm only the people who did not have the mark of God's seal on their foreheads. 5The locusts were not allowed to kill these people, but only to torture them for five months. The pain caused by the torture is like the pain caused by a scorpion's sting. 6During those five months they will seek death, but will not find it; they will want to die, but death will flee from them.

7The locusts looked like horses ready for battle; on their heads they had what seemed to be crowns of gold, and their faces were like human faces. 8Their hair was like women's hair, their teeth were like lions' teeth. 9Their chests were covered with what looked like iron breastplates, and the sound made by their wings was like the noise of many horse-drawn chariots rushing into battle. 10They have tails and stings like those of a scorpion, and it is with their tails that they have the power to hurt people for five months. 11They have a king ruling over them, who is the angel in charge of the abyss. His name in Hebrew is Abaddon; in Greek the name is Apollyon (meaning "The Destroyer").

12The first horror is over; after this there are still two more horrors to come.

13Then the sixth angel blew his trumpet. I heard a voice coming from the four corners of the gold altar standing before God. 14The voice said to the sixth angel, "Release the four angels who are bound at the great Euphrates River!" 15The four angels were released; for this very hour of this very day of this very month and year they had been kept ready to kill a third of all the human race. 16I was told the number of the mounted troops: it was two hundred million. 17And in my vision I saw the horses and their riders: they had breastplates red as fire, blue as sapphire, and yellow as sulfur. The horses' heads were like lions' heads, and from their mouths came out fire, smoke, and sulfur. 18A third of the human race was killed by those three plagues: the fire, the smoke, and the sulfur coming out of the horses' mouths. 19For the power of the horses is in their mouths and also in their tails. Their tails are like snakes with heads, and they use them to hurt people.

20The rest of the human race, all those who had not been killed by these plagues, did not turn away from what they themselves had made. They did not stop worship-

---

d **9:1** ABYSS: *The place in the depths of the earth where the demons were imprisoned until their final punishment.*
8:10 Isa 14:12   **8:11** Jer 9:15   **8:12** Isa 13:10; Ezek 32:7; Joel 2:10, 31; 3:15   **9:2** Gen 19:28   **9:3** Ex 10:12–15; Wis 16:9   **9:4** Ezek 9:4   **9:6** Job 3:21; Jer 8:3   **9:7** Joel 2:4   **9:8** Joel 1:6   **9:9** Joel 2:5   **9:13** Ex 30:1–3   **9:17** Wis 11:17, 18   **9:20** Ps 115:4–7; 135:15–17; Dan 5:23

The angel burns incense in heaven to help the prayers of people on earth (*Revelation 8:3*). **When and where have you seen incense used with prayers?**

ing demons, nor the idols of gold, silver, bronze, stone, and wood, which cannot see, hear, or walk. 21Nor did they repent of their murders, their magic, their sexual immorality, or their stealing.

The Angel and the Little Scroll

10 1Then I saw another mighty angel coming down out of heaven. He was wrapped in a cloud and had a rainbow around his head; his face was like the sun, and his legs were like columns of fire. 2He had a small scroll open in his hand. He put his right foot on the sea and his left foot on the land, 3and called out in a loud voice that sounded like the roar of lions. After he had called out, the seven thunders answered with a roar. 4As soon as they spoke, I was about to write. But I heard a voice speak from heaven, "Keep secret what the seven thunders have said; do not write it down!"

5Then the angel that I saw standing on the sea and on the land raised his right hand to heaven 6and took a vow in the name of God, who lives forever and ever, who created heaven, earth, and the sea, and everything in them. The angel said, "There will be no more delay! 7But when the seventh angel blows his trumpet, then God will accomplish his secret plan, as he announced to his servants, the prophets."

8Then the voice that I had heard speaking from heaven spoke to me again, saying, "Go and take the open scroll which is in the hand of the angel standing on the sea and on the land."

9I went to the angel and asked him to give me the little scroll. He said to me, "Take it and eat it; it will turn sour in your stomach, but in your mouth it will be sweet as honey."

10I took the little scroll from his hand and ate it, and it tasted sweet as honey in my mouth. But after I swallowed it, it turned sour in my stomach. 11Then I was told, "Once again you must proclaim God's message about many nations, races, languages, and kings."

The Two Witnesses

11 1I was then given a stick that looked like a measuring-rod, and was told, "Go and measure the temple of God and the altar, and count those who are worshiping in the temple. 2But do not measure the outer courts, because they have been given to the heathen, who will trample on the Holy City for forty-two months. 3I will send my two witnesses dressed in sackcloth, and they will proclaim God's message during those 1,260 days."

4The two witnesses are the two olive trees and the two lamps that stand before the Lord of the earth. 5If anyone tries to harm them, fire comes out of their mouths and destroys their enemies; and in this way whoever tries to harm them will be killed. 6They have authority to shut up the sky so that there will be no rain during the time they proclaim God's message. They have authority also over the springs of water, to turn them into blood; they have authority also to strike the earth with every kind of plague as often as they wish.

7When they finish proclaiming their message, the beast that comes up out of the abyss will fight against them. He will defeat them and kill them, 8and their bodies will lie in the street of the great city, where their Lord was crucified. The symbolic name of that city is Sodom, or Egypt. 9People from all nations, tribes, languages, and races will look at their bodies for three and a half days and will not allow them to be buried. 10The people of the earth will be happy because of the death of these two. They will celebrate and send presents to each other, because those two prophets brought much suffering upon the whole human race. 11After three and a half days a life-giving breath came from God and entered them, and they stood up; and all who saw them were terrified. 12Then the two prophets heard a loud voice say to them from heaven, "Come up here!" As their enemies watched, they went up into heaven in a cloud. 13At that very moment there was a violent earthquake; a tenth of the

10:5–7 Ex 20:11; Deut 32:40; Dan 12:7; Am 3:7   **10:8–10** Ezek 2:8—3:3   **11:1** Ezek 40:3; Zech 2:1, 2   **11:2** Lk 21:24   **11:4** Zech 4:3, 11–14   **11:6 a** 1 Kings 17:1; **b** Ex 7:17–19; **c** 1 Sam 4:8   **11:7 a** Dan 7:7; Rev 13:5–7; 17:8; **b** Dan 7:21   **11:8** Isa 1:9, 10   **11:11** Ezek 37:10   **11:12** 2 Kings 2:11   **11:13** Rev 6:12; 16:18

The Paschal Mystery

Ca holic Connec ions

How have you experienced suffering in your life? Sickness, depression, death of a loved one, anger, poverty—or something else? Maybe you have suffered for standing up for what is right and moral?

At the heart of the Christian faith is the reality that suffering and death are not the end of life for those with faith in Jesus. God will resurrect us and raise us to a new life, free from the chains of sin and pain and death. Jesus own suffering, death, and Resurrection is called the Paschal Mystery. Those of us who have been baptized already have some share in this mystery. The Paschal Mystery promises that if we remain faithful to Jesus, after we die we shall also be raised to new life.

We can get a taste of the Paschal Mystery here on earth when we go through a time of pain and suffering with faith. Many people find they come through those times with greater faith or as better people.

Sometimes, though, our suffering can last a lifetime. Know that God never abandons you. And at the end of your life, death will not be the end! Like the prophets, we will have new life with Christ—a heaven so wonderful, we can't even imagine it!

— Revelation 11:11–12

city was destroyed, and seven thousand people were killed. The rest of the people were terrified and praised the greatness of the God of heaven.

14 The second horror is over, but the third horror will come soon!

The Seventh Trumpet

15 Then the seventh angel blew his trumpet, and there were loud voices in heaven, saying, "The power to rule over the world belongs now to our Lord and his Messiah, and he will rule forever and ever!" **16** Then the twenty-four elders who sit on their thrones in front of God threw themselves face downward and worshiped God, **17** saying:

"Lord God Almighty, the one who is and who was!
We thank you that you have taken your great power
and have begun to rule!

18 The heathen were filled with rage,
because the time for your anger has come,
the time for the dead to be judged.
The time has come to reward your servants, the prophets,
and all your people, all who have reverence for you,
great and small alike.
The time has come to destroy those who destroy the earth!"

19 God's temple in heaven was opened, and the Covenant Box was seen there. Then there were flashes of lightning, rumblings and peals of thunder, an earthquake, and heavy hail.

The Woman and the Dragon

12 **1** Then a great and mysterious sight appeared in the sky. There was a woman, whose dress was the sun and who had the moon under her feet and a crown of

11:15 Ex 15:18; Dan 2:44; 7:14, 27　**11:18 a** Ps 2:5; 110:5; **b** Ps 115:13　**11:19** 2 Macc 2:4–8; **a** Rev 8:5; 16:18; **b** Rev 16:21

twelve stars on her head. ²She was soon to give birth, and the pains and suffering of childbirth made her cry out.

³Another mysterious sight appeared in the sky. There was a huge red dragon with seven heads and ten horns and a crown on each of his heads. ⁴With his tail he dragged a third of the stars out of the sky and threw them down to the earth. He stood in front of the woman, in order to eat her child as soon as it was born. ⁵Then she gave birth to a son, who will rule over all nations with an iron rod. But the child was snatched away and taken to God and his throne. ⁶The woman fled to the desert, to a place God had prepared for her, where she will be taken care of for 1,260 days.

⁷Then war broke out in heaven. Michael and his angels fought against the dragon, who fought back with his angels; ⁸but the dragon was defeated, and he and his angels were not allowed to stay in heaven any longer. ⁹The huge dragon was thrown out—that ancient serpent, named the Devil, or Satan, that deceived the whole world. He was thrown down to earth, and all his angels with him.

¹⁰Then I heard a loud voice in heaven saying, "Now God's salvation has come! Now God has shown his power as King! Now his Messiah has shown his authority! For the one who stood before our God and accused believers day and night has been thrown out of heaven. ¹¹They won the victory over him by the blood of the Lamb and by the truth which they proclaimed; and they were willing to give up their lives and die. ¹²And so be glad, you heavens, and all you that live there! But how terrible for the earth and the sea! For the Devil has come down to you, and he is filled with rage, because he knows that he has only a little time left."

¹³When the dragon realized that he had been thrown down to the earth, he began to pursue the woman who had given birth to the boy. ¹⁴She was given the two wings of a large eagle in order to fly to her place in the

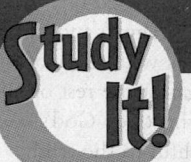

Evil Wages War

This vision symbolizes the battle between Jesus and Satan. The woman is Israel, and the child she gives birth to is Jesus. The pains and sufferings of childbirth are all the problems the Israelites suffered through before God sent them Jesus as their Savior.

The huge red dragon is a symbol of Satan or the terrible forces of evil, ready to devour the child when he is born. But the child is protected and taken to heaven. Satan follows into heaven and war breaks out. Satan and his angels lose the war and are thrown out of heaven, where they once again try to find and destroy the woman. Now, the woman symbolizes the new Christian churches and Jesus' mother, Mary, who brings Christ to the world. She escapes on the wings of a great eagle, which represents the power and swiftness of divine help. But the dragon goes off to continue torturing God's people.

In what ways do you think people are tortured by evil?

— Revelation, chapter 12

desert, where she will be taken care of for three and a half years, safe from the dragon's attack. ¹⁵And then from his mouth the dragon poured out a flood of water after the woman, so that it would carry her away. ¹⁶But the earth helped the woman; it

12:3 Dan 7:7   **12:4** Dan 8:10   **12:5 a** Isa 66:7; **b** Ps 2:9   **12:7** Dan 10:13, 21; 12:1; Jude 9   **12:9 a** Gen 3:1; **b** Lk 10:18   **12:10** Job 1:9–11; Zech 3:1   **12:14** Dan 7:25; 12:7

Michael (Revelation 12:7) **is an archangel, one of God's chief angels. His name was the war cry in the battle against Satan and his followers.**

opened its mouth and swallowed the water that had come from the dragon's mouth. [17]The dragon was furious with the woman and went off to fight against the rest of her descendants, all those who obey God's commandments and are faithful to the truth revealed by Jesus. [18]And the dragon stood[e] on the seashore.

The Two Beasts

13 [1]Then I saw a beast coming up out of the sea. It had ten horns and seven heads; on each of its horns there was a crown, and on each of its heads there was a name that was insulting to God. [2]The beast looked like a leopard, with feet like a bear's feet and a mouth like a lion's mouth. The dragon gave the beast his own power, his throne, and his vast authority. [3]One of the heads of the beast seemed to have been fatally wounded, but the wound had healed. The whole earth was amazed and followed the beast. [4]Everyone worshiped the dragon because he had given his authority to the beast. They worshiped the beast also, saying, "Who is like the beast? Who can fight against it?"

[5]The beast was allowed to make proud claims which were insulting to God, and it was permitted to have authority for forty-two months. [6]It began to curse God, his name, the place where he lives, and all those who live in heaven. [7]It was allowed to fight against God's people and to defeat them, and it was given authority over every tribe, nation, language, and race. [8]All people living on earth will worship it, except those whose names were written before the creation of the world in the book of the living which belongs to the Lamb that was killed.

[9]"Listen, then, if you have ears! [10]Whoever is meant to be captured will surely be captured; whoever is meant to be killed by the sword will surely be killed by the sword.

Evil Today

In Revelation, chapter 13, the vision of the two beasts continues the story about how evil tries to destroy God's people. The power of evil in our world is very real, and it can be terrifying. Just open a newspaper, and stories of murder, war, rape, and other horrible crimes fill the pages.

Evil must be resisted. Like the beasts, it grows in power when good people do not stand against it. It may seem too powerful, too big to do anything about. It happens when a group of good young people gradually get involved deeper and deeper in drinking, drugs, and sexual activity. It starts small, just one drink or some sexual touching. If no one steps in to say this is wrong, the sinful behavior just gets worse and worse.

The way to fight off evil is to keep turning to God. First, pay attention to your sinfulness and do not allow it to get the best of you. Pray for God's strength. Second, speak out when you see sinful behavior happening—even if it isn't the popular thing to do. You may get persecuted. Just remember Revelation. For even though the evil beasts seem powerful, God's love is a million times more powerful.

— Revelation, chapter 13

---

[e] **12:18** And the dragon stood; *some manuscripts have* And I stood, *connecting this verse with what follows.*
13:1 a Dan 7:3; b Rev 17:3, 7–12   **13:2** Dan 7:4–6   **13:5, 6** Dan 7:8, 25; 11:36   **13:7** Dan 7:21   **13:8** Ps 69:28   **13:10** Jer 15:2; 43:11

"This calls for endurance and faith on the part of God's people"
(Revelation 13:10).

Revelation

This calls for endurance and faith on the part of God's people."

11 Then I saw another beast, which came up out of the earth. It had two horns like a lamb's horns, and it spoke like a dragon. 12 It used the vast authority of the first beast in its presence. It forced the earth and all who live on it to worship the first beast, whose wound had healed. 13 This second beast performed great miracles; it made fire come down out of heaven to earth in the sight of everyone. 14 And it deceived all the people living on earth by means of the miracles which it was allowed to perform in the presence of the first beast. The beast told them to build an image in honor of the beast that had been wounded by the sword and yet lived. 15 The second beast was allowed to breathe life into the image of the first beast, so that the image could talk and put to death all those who would not worship it. 16 The beast forced all the people, small and great, rich and poor, slave and free, to have a mark placed on their right hands or on their foreheads. 17 No one could buy or sell without this mark, that is, the beast's name or the number that stands for the name.

18 This calls for wisdom. Whoever is intelligent can figure out the meaning of the number of the beast, because the number stands for the name of someone. Its number is 666.

The Lamb and His People

14 ¹Then I looked, and there was the Lamb standing on Mount Zion; with him were 144,000 people who have his name and his Father's name written on their foreheads. 2 And I heard a voice from heaven that sounded like a roaring waterfall, like a loud peal of thunder. It sounded like the music made by musicians playing their harps. 3 The 144,000 people stood before the throne, the four living creatures, and the elders; they were singing a new song, which only they could learn. Of the whole human race they are the only ones who have been redeemed. 4 They are the men who have kept themselves pure by not having sexual relations with women; they are virgins. They fol-

low the Lamb wherever he goes. They have been redeemed from the rest of the human race and are the first ones to be offered to God and to the Lamb. 5 They have never been known to tell lies; they are faultless.

The Three Angels

6 Then I saw another angel flying high in the air, with an eternal message of Good News to announce to the peoples of the earth, to every race, tribe, language, and nation. 7 He said in a loud voice, "Honor God and praise his greatness! For the time has come for him to judge all people. Worship him who made heaven, earth, sea, and the springs of water!"

8 A second angel followed the first one, saying, "She has fallen! Great Babylon has fallen! She made all peoples drink her wine—the strong wine of her immoral lust!"

9 A third angel followed the first two, saying in a loud voice, "Those who worship the beast and its image and receive the mark on their forehead or on their hand 10 will themselves drink God's wine, the wine of his fury, which he has poured at full strength into the cup of his anger! All who do this will be tormented in fire and sulfur before the holy angels and the Lamb. 11 The smoke of the fire that torments them goes up forever and ever. There is no relief day or night for those who worship the beast and its image, for anyone who has the mark of its name."

12 This calls for endurance on the part of God's people, those who obey God's commandments and are faithful to Jesus.

13 Then I heard a voice from heaven saying, "Write this: Happy are those who from now on die in the service of the Lord!"

"Yes indeed!" answers the Spirit. "They will enjoy rest from their hard work, because the results of their service go with them."

The Harvest of the Earth

14 Then I looked, and there was a white cloud, and sitting on the cloud was what looked like a human being, with a crown of gold on his head and a sharp sickle in his

14:1 Ezek 9:4; Rev 7:3   14:5 Zeph 3:13   14:8 Isa 21:9; Jer 51:8; Rev 18:2   14:10 a Isa 51:17; b Gen 19:24; Ezek 38:22   14:11 Isa 34:10   14:14 Dan 7:13

Pray It!

End of the Day Checkup

It's hard to think about our whole life being judged at the end of time as described in Revelation 14:7! What about just taking one day at a time? How would God judge you at the end of today—for this day only?

Try this self-examination when you go to bed tonight: Think back upon your day, and recall five very specific things you're thankful for. Maybe your coach encouraged you, or you got a new babysitting job. Now, thank God for these five things, events, or people.

Second, think of five things you said or did that you believe were pleasing to God. Ask God to continue to show you how to live faithfully, and to give you the stamina to keep it up every day.

Third, ask yourself—honestly: Were there any times during the day when your actions or words would have disappointed God? Talk to God about those and express your sorrow for those words or actions. Remember how deeply God loves you and wants to help you be forgiving, patient, kind, and caring. If you take care of one day at a time, God's judgment at the end of time doesn't look so scary!

— Revelation 14:6–13

hand. ¹⁵Then another angel came out from the temple and cried out in a loud voice to the one who was sitting on the cloud, "Use your sickle and reap the harvest, because the time has come; the earth is ripe for the harvest!" ¹⁶Then the one who sat on the cloud swung his sickle on the earth, and the earth's harvest was reaped.

¹⁷Then I saw another angel come out of the temple in heaven, and he also had a sharp sickle.

¹⁸Then another angel, who is in charge of the fire, came from the altar. He shouted in a loud voice to the angel who had the sharp sickle, "Use your sickle, and cut the grapes from the vineyard of the earth, because the grapes are ripe!" ¹⁹So the angel swung his sickle on the earth, cut the grapes from the vine, and threw them into the wine press of God's furious anger. ²⁰The grapes were squeezed out in the wine press outside the city, and blood came out of the wine press in a flood two hundred miles long and about five feet deep.

The Angels with the Last Plagues

15 ¹Then I saw in the sky another mysterious sight, great and amazing. There were seven angels with seven plagues, which are the last ones, because they are the final expression of God's anger.

²Then I saw what looked like a sea of glass mixed with fire. I also saw those who had won the victory over the beast and its image and over the one whose name is represented by a number. They were standing by the sea of glass, holding harps that God had given them ³and singing the song of Moses, the servant of God, and the song of the Lamb:

"Lord God Almighty,
    how great and wonderful are your
      deeds!
King of the nations,*f*
    how right and true are your ways!
⁴Who will not stand in awe of you, Lord?
    Who will refuse to declare your
      greatness?
    You alone are holy.

f **15:3** nations; *some manuscripts have* ages.
14:15 Joel 3:13   **14:20** Isa 63:3; Lam 1:15; Rev 19:15   **15:3** Ex 15:1   **15:4 a** Jer 10:7; **b** Ps 86:9

All the nations will come
    and worship you,
        because your just actions are seen by
            all."

⁵After this I saw the temple in heaven open, with the Sacred Tent in it. ⁶The seven angels who had the seven plagues came out of the temple, dressed in clean shining linen and with gold bands tied around their chests. ⁷Then one of the four living creatures gave the seven angels seven gold bowls full of the anger of God, who lives forever and ever. ⁸The temple was filled with smoke from the glory and power of God, and no one could go into the temple until the seven plagues brought by the seven angels had come to an end.

The Bowls of God's Anger

16 ¹Then I heard a loud voice speaking from the temple to the seven angels: "Go and pour out the seven bowls of God's anger on the earth!"

²The first angel went and poured out his bowl on the earth. Terrible and painful sores appeared on those who had the mark of the beast and on those who had worshiped its image.

³Then the second angel poured out his bowl on the sea. The water became like the blood of a dead person, and every living creature in the sea died.

⁴Then the third angel poured out his bowl on the rivers and the springs of water, and they turned into blood. ⁵I heard the angel in charge of the waters say, "The judgments you have made are just, O Holy One, you who are and who were! ⁶They poured out the blood of God's people and of the prophets, and so you have given them blood to drink. They are getting what they deserve!" ⁷Then I heard a voice from the altar saying, "Lord God Almighty! True and just indeed are your judgments!"

⁸Then the fourth angel poured out his

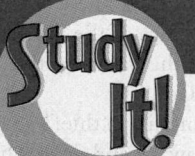

More Disaster Strikes!

The seven bowls described are like the seven seals and seven trumpets. These symbols in Revelation each release a disaster or plague upon the sinful people. Check out the plagues in Exodus, chapters 7 to 12. Each plague came as a warning to the Egyptians to stop tormenting the Israelites and free them from slavery. Again, here in Revelation, disasters and plagues are sent as warnings for people to change their hearts and turn away from evil.

— *Revelation, chapter 16*

bowl on the sun, and it was allowed to burn people with its fiery heat. ⁹They were burned by the fierce heat, and they cursed the name of God, who has authority over these plagues. But they would not turn from their sins and praise his greatness.

¹⁰Then the fifth angel poured out his bowl on the throne of the beast. Darkness fell over the beast's kingdom, and people bit their tongues because of their pain, ¹¹and they cursed the God of heaven for their pains and sores. But they did not turn from their evil ways.

¹²Then the sixth angel poured out his bowl on the great Euphrates River. The river dried up, to provide a way for the kings who come from the east. ¹³Then I saw three unclean spirits that looked like frogs. They were coming out of the mouth of the dragon, the mouth of the beast, and the mouth of the false prophet. ¹⁴They are the spirits of

15:5 Ex 38:21   15:8 Ex 40:34; 1 Kings 8:10, 11; 2 Chr 5:13, 14; Isa 6:4   16:2 Ex 9:10   16:4 Ex 7:17–21; Ps 78:44   16:10 Ex 10:21   16:12 Isa 11:15

Revelation

"Lord God Almighty, / how great and wonderful are your deeds! / King of the nations, / how right and true are your ways!" *(Revelation 15:3)*

demons that perform miracles. These three spirits go out to all the kings of the world, to bring them together for the battle on the great Day of Almighty God.

15 "Listen! I am coming like a thief! Happy is he who stays awake and guards his clothes, so that he will not walk around naked and be ashamed in public!"

16 Then the spirits brought the kings together in the place that in Hebrew is called Armageddon.

17 Then the seventh angel poured out his bowl in the air. A loud voice came from the throne in the temple, saying, "It is done!" 18 There were flashes of lightning, rumblings and peals of thunder, and a terrible earthquake. There has never been such an earthquake since the creation of human beings; this was the worst earthquake of all! 19 The great city was split into three parts, and the cities of all countries were destroyed. God remembered great Babylon and made her drink the wine from his cup—the wine of his furious anger. 20 All the islands disappeared, all the mountains vanished. 21 Huge hailstones, each weighing as much as a hundred pounds, fell from the sky on people, who cursed God on account of the plague of hail, because it was such a terrible plague.

The Famous Prostitute

17 1 Then one of the seven angels who had the seven bowls came to me and said, "Come, and I will show you how the famous prostitute is to be punished, that great city that is built near many rivers. 2 The kings of the earth practiced sexual immorality with her, and the people of the world became drunk from drinking the wine of her immorality."

3 The Spirit took control of me, and the angel carried me to a desert. There I saw a woman sitting on a red beast that had names insulting to God written all over it; the beast

Sins of Nations

The prostitute in Revelation, chapter 17, probably stood for the Roman Empire at the time of John. When John had his visions, the Roman Empire was filled with immoral behavior, greed, and abuse of power. How many nations or empires since then have fallen victim to the same evils? How easy it can be for powerful nations and their leaders to get sucked into the vacuum of sin!

How do you think our country and its leaders measure up in the area of morality? If you could meet with the president, which sins of our nation would you choose to discuss? What concrete suggestions would you make for getting us back on track as a nation that values moral living? If you could deliver a speech to our nation's citizens, what important points would you make?

— Revelation, chapter 17

had seven heads and ten horns. 4 The woman was dressed in purple and scarlet, and covered with gold ornaments, precious stones, and pearls. In her hand she held a gold cup full of obscene and filthy things, the result of her immorality. 5 On her forehead was written a name that has a secret meaning: "Great Babylon, the mother of all prostitutes and perverts in the world." 6 And I saw that the woman was drunk with the blood of God's

16:15 Mt 24:43, 44; Lk 12:39, 40; Rev 3:3 **16:16** 2 Kings 23:29; Zech 12:11 **16:18** Rev 8:5; 11:13, 19 **16:19** Isa 51:17 **16:20** Rev 6:14 **16:21** Ex 9:23; Rev 11:19 **17:1** Jer 51:13 **17:2** Isa 23:17; Jer 51:7 **17:3** Rev 13:1 **17:4** Jer 51:7

Revelation

The author of Revelation connects Rome to the Old Testament by telling the troubles caused by another evil empire, Babylon (see 2 Kings 25:1–21).

people and the blood of those who were killed because they had been loyal to Jesus.

When I saw her, I was completely amazed. 7"Why are you amazed?" the angel asked me. "I will tell you the secret meaning of the woman and of the beast that carries her, the beast with seven heads and ten horns. 8That beast was once alive, but lives no longer; it is about to come up from the abyss and will go off to be destroyed. The people living on earth whose names have not been written before the creation of the world in the book of the living, will all be amazed as they look at the beast. It was once alive; now it no longer lives, but it will reappear.

9"This calls for wisdom and understanding. The seven heads are seven hills, on which the woman sits. They are also seven kings: 10five of them have fallen, one still rules, and the other one has not yet come; when he comes, he must rule only a little while. 11And the beast that was once alive, but lives no longer, is itself an eighth king who is one of the seven and is going off to be destroyed.

12"The ten horns you saw are ten kings who have not yet begun to rule, but who will be given authority to rule as kings for one hour with the beast. 13These ten all have the same purpose, and they give their power and authority to the beast. 14They will fight against the Lamb; but the Lamb, together with his called, chosen, and faithful followers, will defeat them, because he is Lord of lords and King of kings."

15The angel also said to me, "The waters you saw, on which the prostitute sits, are nations, peoples, races, and languages. 16The ten horns you saw and the beast will hate the prostitute; they will take away everything she has and leave her naked; they will eat her flesh and destroy her with fire. 17For God has placed in their hearts the will to carry out his purpose by acting together and giving to the beast their power to rule until God's words come true.

18"The woman you saw is the great city that rules over the kings of the earth."

The Fall of Babylon

18 1After this I saw another angel coming down out of heaven. He had great authority, and his splendor brightened the whole earth. 2He cried out in a loud voice: "She has fallen! Great Babylon has fallen! She is now haunted by demons and unclean spirits; all kinds of filthy and hateful birds live in her. 3For all the nations have drunk her wine—the strong wine of her immoral lust. The kings of the earth practiced sexual immorality with her, and the merchants of the world grew rich from her unrestrained lust."

4Then I heard another voice from heaven, saying,

"Come out, my people! Come out from
   her!
You must not take part in her sins;
   you must not share in her punishment!
5For her sins are piled up as high as
   heaven,
   and God remembers her wicked ways.
6Treat her exactly as she has treated you;
   pay her back double for all she has
   done.
Fill her cup with a drink twice as strong
   as the drink she prepared for you.
7Give her as much suffering and grief
   as the glory and luxury she gave
   herself.
For she keeps telling herself:
'Here I sit, a queen!
   I am no widow,
   I will never know grief!'
8Because of this, in one day she will be
   struck with plagues—
   disease, grief, and famine.
And she will be burned with fire,
   because the Lord God, who judges her,
   is mighty."

9The kings of the earth who took part in her immorality and lust will cry and weep over the city when they see the smoke from the flames that consume her. 10They stand a long way off, because they are afraid of sharing in her suffering. They say, "How terrible! How awful! This great and mighty city

---

17:8 a Dan 7:7; Rev 11:7; **b** Ps 69:28   **17:12** Dan 7:24   **18:2 a** Isa 21:9; Jer 51:8; Rev 14:8; **b** Isa 13:21; Jer 50:39   **18:3** Isa 23:17; Jer 51:7   **18:4** Isa 48:20; Jer 50:8; 51:6, 45   **18:5** Gen 18:20, 21; Jer 51:9   **18:6** Ps 137:8; Jer 50:29   **18:7, 8** Isa 47:7–9   **18:9, 10** Ezek 26:16, 17

This great and mighty city Babylon! (18:10)

Babylon! In just one hour you have been punished!"

11 The merchants of the earth also cry and mourn for her, because no one buys their goods any longer; 12 no one buys their gold, silver, precious stones, and pearls; their goods of linen, purple cloth, silk, and scarlet cloth; all kinds of rare woods and all kinds of objects made of ivory and of expensive wood, of bronze, iron, and marble; 13 and cinnamon, spice, incense, myrrh, and frankincense; wine and oil, flour and wheat, cattle and sheep, horses and carriages, slaves, and even human lives. 14 The merchants say to her, "All the good things you longed to own have disappeared, and all your wealth and glamor are gone, and you will never find them again!" 15 The merchants, who became rich from doing business in that city, will stand a long way off, because they are afraid of sharing in her suffering. They will cry and mourn, 16 and say, "How terrible! How awful for the great city! She used to dress herself in linen, purple, and scarlet, and cover herself with gold ornaments, precious stones, and pearls! 17 And in one hour she has lost all this wealth!"

All the ships' captains and passengers, the sailors and all others who earn their living on the sea, stood a long way off, 18 and cried out as they saw the smoke from the flames that consumed her: "There never has been another city like this great city!" 19 They threw dust on their heads, they cried and mourned, saying, "How terrible! How awful for the great city! She is the city where all who have ships sailing the seas became rich on her wealth! And in one hour she has lost everything!"

20 Be glad, heaven, because of her destruction! Be glad, God's people and the apostles and prophets! For God has condemned her for what she did to you!

21 Then a mighty angel picked up a stone the size of a large millstone and threw it into the sea, saying, "This is how the great city Babylon will be violently thrown down and will never be seen again. 22 The music of harps and of human voices, of players of the flute and the trumpet, will never be heard in you again! No workman in any trade will ever be found in you again; and the sound of the millstone will be heard no more! 23 Never again will the light of a lamp be seen in you; no more will the voices of brides and grooms be heard in you. Your merchants were the most powerful in all the

18:11 Ezek 27:31, 36   **18:12, 13** Ezek 27:12, 13, 22   **18:15** Ezek 27:31, 36   **18:17** Isa 23:14; Ezek 27:26–30   **18:18** Ezek 27:32   **18:19** Ezek 27:30–34   **18:20** Deut 32:43; Jer 51:48   **18:21 a** Jer 51:63, 64; **b** Ezek 26:21   **18:22** Ezek 26:13; Isa 24:8   **18:22, 23** Jer 7:34; 25:10

world, and with your magic you deceived all the peoples of the world!"

²⁴Babylon was punished because the blood of prophets and of God's people was found in the city; yes, the blood of all those who have been killed on earth.

19

¹After this I heard what sounded like the roar of a large crowd of people in heaven, saying, "Praise God! Salvation, glory, and power belong to our God! ²True and just are his judgments! He has condemned the prostitute who was corrupting the earth with her immorality. God has punished her because she killed his servants." ³Again they shouted, "Praise God! The smoke from the flames that consume the great city goes up forever and ever!" ⁴The twenty-four elders and the four living creatures fell down and worshiped God, who was seated on the throne. They said, "Amen! Praise God!"

The Wedding Feast of the Lamb

⁵Then there came from the throne the sound of a voice, saying, "Praise our God, all his servants and all people, both great and small, who have reverence for him!" ⁶Then I heard what sounded like a crowd, like the sound of a roaring waterfall, like loud peals of thunder. I heard them say, "Praise God! For the Lord, our Almighty God, is King! ⁷Let us rejoice and be glad; let us praise his greatness! For the time has come for the wedding of the Lamb, and his bride has prepared herself for it. ⁸She has been given clean shining linen to wear." (The linen is the good deeds of God's people.)

⁹Then the angel said to me, "Write this: Happy are those who have been invited to the wedding feast of the Lamb." And the angel added, "These are the true words of God."

¹⁰I fell down at his feet to worship him,

but he said to me, "Don't do it! I am a servant together with you and with other believers, all those who hold to the truth that Jesus revealed. Worship God!"

For the truth that Jesus revealed is what inspires the prophets.

The Rider on the White Horse

¹¹Then I saw heaven open, and there was a white horse. Its rider is called Faithful and True; it is with justice that he judges and fights his battles. ¹²His eyes were like a flame of fire, and he wore many crowns on his head. He had a name written on him, but no one except himself knows what it is. ¹³The robe he wore was covered with blood. His name is "The Word of God." ¹⁴The armies of heaven followed him, riding on white horses and dressed in clean white linen. ¹⁵Out of his mouth came a sharp sword, with which he will defeat the nations. He will rule over them with a rod of iron, and he will trample out the wine in the wine press of the furious anger of the Almighty God. ¹⁶On his robe and on his thigh was written the name: "King of kings and Lord of lords."

¹⁷Then I saw an angel standing on the sun. He shouted in a loud voice to all the birds flying in midair: "Come and gather together for God's great feast! ¹⁸Come and eat the flesh of kings, generals, and soldiers, the flesh of horses and their riders, the flesh of all people, slave and free, great and small!"

¹⁹Then I saw the beast and the kings of the earth and their armies gathered to fight against the one who was riding the horse and against his army. ²⁰The beast was taken prisoner, together with the false prophet who had performed miracles in his presence. (It was by those miracles that he had deceived those who had the mark of the beast and those who had worshiped the

18:24 Jer 51:49 **19:2** Deut 32:43; 2 Kings 9:7 **19:3** Isa 34:10 **19:5** Ps 115:13 **19:6 a** Ezek 1:24; **b** Ps 93:1; 97:1; 99:1 **19:9** Mt 22:2, 3 **19:11 a** Ezek 1:1; **b** Ps 96:13; Isa 11:4 **19:12** Dan 10:6 **19:13** Wis 18:14–18 **19:15 a** Ps 2:9; **b** Isa 63:3; Joel 3:13; Rev 14:20 **19:17, 18** Ezek 39:17–20 **19:20** Rev 13:1–18

Revelation

Chapter 19 of Revelation includes a wedding feast. See Matthew 22:1–14 and John 2:1–11 for other stories about wedding feasts.

Pray It!

Delivery from Evil!

Just when everything seems to have been swallowed up by evil and destruction, Revelation takes a dramatic turn. Riding into the scene on a white (symbolizing victory and joy) horse is Jesus, called "Faithful and True" (19:11) and "the Word of God" (19:13). The beast is thrown into the lake of fire and all his kings and armies are killed by Jesus and the heavenly armies (the martyrs and all who have been faithful to God). Justice has come at last! Jesus is victorious over evil!

Every time we pray the Our Father, we pray, "Lead us not into temptation, but deliver us from evil." Jesus gave us that prayer (see Matthew 6:13). He knows that we may come face to face with evil, though we often don't even recognize it. Jesus knows we need God's protection from evil and help with resisting temptations to sin.

Try to pray the Our Father each day and remember who leads the charge against evil—Jesus Christ.

— Revelation 19:11–21

image of the beast.) The beast and the false prophet were both thrown alive into the lake of fire that burns with sulfur. 21 Their armies were killed by the sword that comes out of the mouth of the one who was riding the horse; and all the birds ate all they could of their flesh.

The Thousand Years

20 1 Then I saw an angel coming down from heaven, holding in his hand the key of the abyss and a heavy chain. 2 He seized the dragon, that ancient serpent—that is, the Devil, or Satan—and chained him up for a thousand years. 3 The angel threw him into the abyss, locked it, and sealed it, so that he could not deceive the nations any more until the thousand years were over. After that he must be set loose for a little while.

4 Then I saw thrones, and those who sat on them were given the power to judge. I also saw the souls of those who had been executed because they had proclaimed the truth that Jesus revealed and the word of God. They had not worshiped the beast or its image, nor had they received the mark of the beast on their foreheads or their hands. They came to life and ruled as kings with Christ for a thousand years. 5 (The rest of the dead did not come to life until the thousand years were over.) This is the first raising of the dead. 6 Happy and greatly blessed are those who are included in this first raising of the dead. The second death has no power over them; they shall be priests of God and of Christ, and they will rule with him for a thousand years.

The Defeat of Satan

7 After the thousand years are over, Satan will be set loose from his prison, 8 and he will go out to deceive the nations scattered over the whole world, that is, Gog and Magog. Satan will bring them all together

20:2 Gen 3:1   **20:4** Dan 7:9, 22   **20:8 a** Ezek 7:2; **b** Ezek 38:2, 9, 15

Gog and Magog represent pagan nations—those that have no religion and are interested only in what brings them pleasure (see Ezekiel, chapters 38–39).

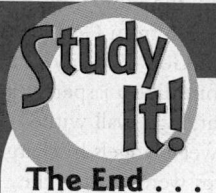

The End . . .

In this vision the dragon (Satan) is chained up or imprisoned for a thousand years. The number 1,000 symbolizes *many*—too many to count. The dragon is not dead, yet, but he doesn't have much power because he's chained. After many years he will be set loose on the earth and cause destruction again. There will be another war between him and God's people, and this time the dragon will be thrown into hell for good. Christ will be victorious over evil for all time! Then all the dead will meet God and be "judged according to what they had done" (Revelation 20:13) with their lives.

— Revelation, chapter 20

for battle, as many as the grains of sand on the seashore. 9They spread out over the earth and surrounded the camp of God's people and the city that he loves. But fire came down from heaven and destroyed them. 10Then the Devil, who deceived them, was thrown into the lake of fire and sulfur, where the beast and the false prophet had already been thrown; and they will be tormented day and night forever and ever.

The Final Judgment

11Then I saw a great white throne and the one who sits on it. Earth and heaven fled from his presence and were seen no more. 12And I saw the dead, great and small alike, standing before the throne. Books were opened, and then another book was opened, the book of the living. The dead were judged according to what they had done, as recorded in the books. 13Then the sea gave up its dead. Death and the world of the dead also gave up the dead they held. And all were judged according to what they had done. 14Then death and the world of the dead were thrown into the lake of fire. (This lake of fire is the second death.) 15Those who did not have their name written in the book of the living were thrown into the lake of fire.

The New Heaven and the New Earth

21 ¹Then I saw a new heaven and a new earth. The first heaven and the first earth disappeared, and the sea vanished. ²And I saw the Holy City, the new Jerusalem, coming down out of heaven from God, prepared and ready, like a bride dressed to meet her husband. ³I heard a loud voice speaking from the throne: "Now God's home is with people! He will live with them, and they shall be his people. God himself will be with them, and he will be their God. ⁴He will wipe away all tears from their eyes. There will be no more death, no more grief or crying or pain. The old things have disappeared."

⁵Then the one who sits on the throne said, "And now I make all things new!" He also said to me, "Write this, because these words are true and can be trusted." ⁶And he said, "It is done! I am the first and the last, the beginning and the end. To anyone who is thirsty I will give the right to drink from the spring of the water of life without paying for it. ⁷Those who win the victory will receive this from me: I will be their God, and they will be my children. ⁸But cowards, traitors, perverts, murderers, the immoral, those who practice magic, those who worship idols, and all liars—the place for them is the lake burning with fire and sulfur, which is the second death."

The New Jerusalem

⁹One of the seven angels who had the seven bowls full of the seven last plagues

20:11, 12 Dan 7:9, 10 **21:1** Isa 65:17; 66:22; 2 Pet 3:13 **21:2 a** Isa 52:1; **b** Rev 3:12; **c** Isa 61:10 **21:3** Ezek 37:27; Lev 26:11, 12 **21:4 a** Isa 25:8; **b** Isa 35:10; 65:19 **21:6** Isa 55:1 **21:7** 2 Sam 7:14; Ps 89:26, 27

Revelation

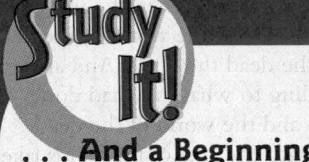

. . . And a Beginning

Genesis begins with creation, and Revelation ends with a new creation! All of earth and heaven are full of God's goodness that we were always meant to enjoy. In this holy city—the new Jerusalem which is a symbol of heaven—there will be nothing that causes us sadness or pain. We will experience only joy and love. The beauty of this city could take your breath away, because the glory of God shines on it and there is no night. Fresh delicious fruit grows all year, and a sparkling river—the river of life—flows from God's throne, for all to drink whenever they wish.

But this hasn't happened yet! John's visions are meant to bring hope to the early Christians when they are being persecuted. This new creation he dreams of will come to us when all evil and suffering are ended. Until that day comes, there will still be people who try to do good with their lives, as well as those who are wrapped up in sinful living. So we must do our part: try to be faithful; remember that God is stronger than pain and evil; and hold on to the hope that one day we will live in God's holy city forever!

— Revelation, chapter 21

came to me and said, "Come, and I will show you the Bride, the wife of the Lamb." [10] The Spirit took control of me, and the angel carried me to the top of a very high mountain.

He showed me Jerusalem, the Holy City, coming down out of heaven from God [11] and shining with the glory of God. The city shone like a precious stone, like a jasper, clear as crystal. [12] It had a great, high wall with twelve gates and with twelve angels in charge of the gates. On the gates were written the names of the twelve tribes of the people of Israel. [13] There were three gates on each side: three on the east, three on the south, three on the north, and three on the west. [14] The city's wall was built on twelve foundation stones, on which were written the names of the twelve apostles of the Lamb. [15] The angel who spoke to me had a gold measuring stick to measure the city, its gates, and its wall. [16] The city was perfectly square, as wide as it was long. The angel measured the city with his measuring stick: it was fifteen hundred miles long and was as wide and as high as it was long. [17] The angel also measured the wall, and it was 216 feet high,[g] according to the standard unit of measure which he was using.[h] [18] The wall was made of jasper, and the city itself was made of pure gold, as clear as glass. [19] The foundation stones of the city wall were adorned with all kinds of precious stones. The first foundation stone was jasper, the second sapphire, the third agate, the fourth emerald, [20] the fifth onyx, the sixth carnelian, the seventh yellow quartz, the eighth beryl, the ninth topaz, the tenth chalcedony, the eleventh turquoise, the twelfth amethyst. [21] The twelve gates were twelve pearls; each gate was made from a single pearl. The street of the city was of pure gold, transparent as glass.

[22] I did not see a temple in the city, because its temple is the Lord God Almighty and the Lamb. [23] The city has no need of the sun or the moon to shine on it, because the glory of God shines on it, and the Lamb is its lamp. [24] The peoples of the world will walk by its light, and the kings of the earth will bring their wealth into it. [25] The gates of the city will stand open all day; they will never be closed, because there will be no night there. [26] The greatness and the wealth

Revelation

---

[g] **21:17** high; *or* thick.   [h] **21:17** *In verses 16 and 17 the Greek text speaks of "12,000 furlongs" and "144 cubits" which may have symbolic significance.*
21:10 Ezek 40:2   **21:12, 13** Ezek 48:30–35   **21:15** Ezek 40:3   **21:18–21** Isa 54:11, 12
21:18 Tob 13:16, 17   **21:23** Isa 60:19, 20   **21:24** Isa 60:3   **21:25, 26** Isa 60:11

Heaven and Hell

Catholic Connections

Some of our images of heaven and hell come from chapters 20 and 21 of Revelation. Hell is described as "the lake of fire and sulfur" where "they will be tormented day and night forever and ever" (20:10). Heaven is like the Holy City described in chapter 21—everything is perfect and amazing. Heaven and hell are not physical places like the images John presents or in the way we usually think of places. But they are very real. And throughout our lives, the choices we make lead us to where we will spend eternity—with or without God, in pure joy or utter despair.

Being with God in heaven will be perfect and amazing! Heaven means perfect unity and joy with God, for eternity. We get glimpses of this on earth. Think of a really fun vacation you've taken or the thrilling moment of victory you share with teammates after a tough game. Those feelings are just a tiny fraction of the joy you'll feel *forever and ever* in heaven!

We experience hell-like moments as well: the death of a family member or getting caught in a serious lie. The sick, horrifying feeling in the pit of your stomach is nothing compared with the misery that hell brings. In life, the person who rejects God moves deeper into sin and unhappiness. At death the separation from God is complete and the suffering is unbearable.

— Revelation, chapters 20–21

of the nations will be brought into the city. [27]But nothing that is impure will enter the city, nor anyone who does shameful things or tells lies. Only those whose names are written in the Lamb's book of the living will enter the city.

22 [1]The angel also showed me the river of the water of life, sparkling like crystal, and coming from the throne of God and of the Lamb [2]and flowing down the middle of the city's street. On each side of the river was the tree of life, which bears fruit twelve times a year, once each month; and its leaves are for the healing of the nations. [3]Nothing that is under God's curse will be found in the city.

The throne of God and of the Lamb will be in the city, and his servants will worship him. [4]They will see his face, and his name will be written on their foreheads. [5]There shall be no more night, and they will not need lamps or sunlight, because the Lord God will be their light, and they will rule as kings forever and ever.

The Coming of Jesus

[6]Then the angel said to me, "These words are true and can be trusted. And the Lord God, who gives his Spirit to the prophets, has sent his angel to show his servants what must happen very soon."

21:27 Isa 52:1; Ezek 44:9   **22:1** Ezek 47:1; Zech 14:8   **22:2** Gen 2:9   **22:3** Zech 14:11 (cp. Gen 3:17)
22:5 a Isa 60:19; **b** Dan 7:18

Revelation

"There will be no more death, no more grief or crying or pain"
(*Revelation 21:4*).

Have Hope!

Poor Antonia. She has three tests this week plus a major project due—and the rest of her project teammates aren't pulling their weight, so she's getting stuck with all the work! She got a detention for chewing gum in class, her volleyball team lost in the last seconds of finals because she missed a play, her parents are constantly fighting, her grandpa's cancer seems to be getting worse, and she caught her best friend saying nasty things about her behind her back. On top of that, she's got a big zit on her nose! She feels like she's getting crushed under the pressure of it all.

Isn't that how life is sometimes? Some days feel like everything is falling apart around us, and it will all come crashing down on us and squish us like a bug!

Hang in there, and keep reading the Book of Revelation! John's message for us is the same one the early Christians needed to hear: Have hope! God is keeping us afloat in our sea of troubles. All the pain, embarrassment, unfairness, anxiety—it will not get the best of us!

— Revelation, chapter 22

7 "Listen!" says Jesus. "I am coming soon! Happy are those who obey the prophetic words in this book!"

8 I, John, have heard and seen all these things. And when I finished hearing and seeing them, I fell down at the feet of the angel who had shown me these things, and I was about to worship him. 9 But he said to me, "Don't do it! I am a servant together with you and with your brothers the prophets and of all those who obey the words in this book. Worship God!" 10 And he said to me, "Do not keep the prophetic words of this book a secret, because the time is near when all this will happen. 11 Whoever is evil must go on doing evil, and whoever is filthy must go on being filthy; whoever is good must go on doing good, and whoever is holy must go on being holy."

12 "Listen!" says Jesus. "I am coming soon! I will bring my rewards with me, to give to each one according to what he has done. 13 I am the first and the last, the beginning and the end."

14 Happy are those who wash their robes clean and so have the right to eat the fruit from the tree of life and to go through the gates into the city. 15 But outside the city are the perverts and those who practice magic, the immoral and the murderers, those who worship idols and those who are liars both in words and deeds.

16 "I, Jesus, have sent my angel to announce these things to you in the churches. I am descended from the family of David; I am the bright morning star."

17 The Spirit and the Bride say, "Come!"

Everyone who hears this must also say, "Come!"

Come, whoever is thirsty; accept the water of life as a gift, whoever wants it.

Conclusion

18 I, John, solemnly warn everyone who hears the prophetic words of this book: if any add anything to them, God will add to their punishment the plagues described in this book. 19 And if any take anything away

Revelation

22:11 Dan 12:10 **22:12 a** Isa 40:10; 62:11; **b** Ps 28:4; Isa 40:10; Jer 17:10 **22:13 a** Rev 1:8; **b** Isa 44:6; 48:12; Rev 1:17; 2:8 **22:14** Gen 2:9; 3:22 **22:16** Isa 11:1, 10 **22:17** Isa 55:1 **22:18, 19** Deut 4:2; 12:32

The phrase "So be it" *(Revelation 22:20)* **is a translation of the word** *amen.* **Whenever we pray, "Amen," we are saying, "So be it!"**

from the prophetic words of this book, God will take away from them their share of the fruit of the tree of life and of the Holy City, which are described in this book.

20 He who gives his testimony to all this says, "Yes indeed! I am coming soon!"

So be it. Come, Lord Jesus!

21 May the grace of the Lord Jesus be with everyone. *i*

i **22:21** everyone; *some manuscripts have* God's people; *others have* all of God's people.

Your Next Step

Congratulations on finishing the Book of Revelation! Use this space to write your thoughts and questions about this book. If you have been reading through the books in order, you have come to the end of this Bible reading plan. But your journey is not over! Here are a some suggestions for continuing your Bible journey:

- Read some of the books that this reading plan skipped.
- Go back and reread some of the books or sections you found especially interesting or confusing. Ask a leader in your church for some help in understanding them.

Let reading and studying the Bible become a lifelong practice!

ABOUT THIS
TRANSLATION

In September 1966 the American Bible Society published *The New Testament in Today's English Version*, the first publication of a new Bible translation intended for people everywhere for whom English is either their mother tongue or an acquired language. Shortly thereafter the United Bible Societies (UBS) requested the American Bible Society (ABS) to undertake on its behalf a translation of the Old Testament following the same principles. Accordingly the American Bible Society appointed a group of translators to prepare the translation. In 1971 this group added a British consultant recommended by the British and Foreign Bible Society. The translation of the Old Testament, which was completed in 1976, was joined to the fourth edition New Testament, thus completing the first edition of the translation that came to be known as the *Good News Bible*.

Two Ways to Present the Deuterocanonical Books

The translation of the books of the Deuterocanon and others classed as Apocrypha was completed in 1978, and the first edition of the *Good News Bible* with Deuterocanonicals and Apocrypha was published in 1979, with the Imprimatur of the Most Reverend John F. Whealon, Archbishop of Hartford, Connecticut. The 1979 publication was an interconfessional edition in which these books were grouped in a separate section between the Old and the New Testaments.

In this present edition, the deuterocanonical books are arranged in the order most familiar to Roman Catholics. The books of Tobit, Judith, and 1 and 2 Maccabees follow the historical books Ezra and Nehemiah. The Book of Esther and its six additions follow Judith in this grouping. Most of these books were written or have their settings in the last several centuries BC.

The Book of Baruch and the Letter of Jeremiah are positioned after Lamentations, as part of the Jeremiah grouping. The books of the Wisdom of Solomon and Sirach, being wisdom books, are located among the other Old Testament Wisdom books, immediately following Song of Songs. The three additions to the Book of Daniel, which are presented as separate books in the interconfessional edition of the Good News Bible, are presented here in the way most familiar to Roman Catholics. Susanna and Bel and the Dragon are traditionally treated as chapters 13 and 14 of Daniel. The third addition has its location between verses 23 and 24 of chapter 3 in the Hebrew text because this is the position it holds in the Septuagint. Known as the Prayer of Azariah and the Song of the Three Young Men, this addition to Daniel provides the text of the prayer offered by Azariah and of the song he and his companions sang while in the midst of the flames in the fiery furnace. The result is an Old Testament with forty-six books, several of which contain significant additions. These books formed part of the Septuagint, the Greek translation of the Old Testament that was in circulation at the time of Christ.

Prior to Jerome's great Latin translation, which came to be known as the *Vulgata* (the common language), there were numerous Latin translations in circulation, all of which had been done from the Greek Septuagint. The great significance of Jerome's work, at least for the Old Testament (AD 389–405), is that he broke from that tradition and based his translation on the received consonantal Hebrew text. His knowledge of Hebrew was excellent, and he had recourse to Jewish text scholars wherever he had questions. For the sections of Esther and Daniel not in the Hebrew canon, Jerome worked from the ancient Greek text. For Tobit and Judith, his base texts were (no longer extant) Aramaic editions of these books. Already before taking on the Old Testament books, Jerome had prepared a revised edition of the Gospels (revising the Old Latin text in light of the best Greek manuscripts available to him). The rest of the Vulgate New Testament text is also attributed to Jerome. The influence of the Vulgate in western Christendom remained unsurpassed from his time until the era of the Reformation and the proliferation of vernacular Bible translations, well over one thousand years later.

The Text Used for This Translation

The basic Hebrew (and Aramaic) text for the Old Testament is the Masoretic text, made available through printed editions published by the UBS, and since 1977 under the title of *Biblia Hebraica Stuttgartensia*. In some instances the words of the printed consonantal text have been divided differently or have been read with a different set of vowels; at times a variant reading in the margin of the Hebrew text *(qere)* has been followed instead of the reading in the text *(kethiv);* and in other instances a variant reading supported by one or more Hebrew manuscripts has been adopted. Where no Hebrew source yields a satisfactory meaning in the context, the translation has either followed one or more of the ancient versions (for example, Greek, Syriac, Latin) or has adopted a reconstructed text (technically referred to as a conjectural emendation) based on scholarly consensus; such departures from the Hebrew are indicated in footnotes.

The basic text for the deuterocanonical books is the Greek text printed in the Septuagint (third edition, 1949), edited by Alfred Rahlfs. For some of these books, the more recently published Goettingen edition of the Septuagint was also consulted.

The basic text for the translation of the New Testament is the *Greek New Testament* published by the UBS (third edition, 1975), but in a few instances the translation is based on a variant reading supported by one or more Greek manuscripts.

The Translation Process

Drafts of the translation in its early stages were sent for comments and suggestions to a Review Panel comprising prominent theologians and biblical scholars appointed by the American Bible Society Board of Managers in its capacity as trustee for the translation. In addition, drafts were sent to major English-speaking Bible Societies throughout the world. Final approval of the translation on behalf of the United Bible Societies was given by the American Bible Society's Board of Managers upon recommendation of its Translations Committee.

The primary concern of the translators was to provide a faithful translation of the meaning of the Hebrew, Aramaic, and Greek texts. Their first task was to understand correctly the meaning of the original. At times the original meaning cannot be precisely known, not only because the meaning of some words and phrases cannot be determined with a great degree of assurance, but also because the underlying cultural and historical context is sometimes beyond recovery. All aids available were used in this task, including the ancient versions (for example, the Septuagint Greek text of the Old Testament, the Vulgate of Jerome, and Old Latin texts as available) and the modern translations in English and other languages.

After ascertaining as accurately as possible the meaning of the original, the translators' next task was to express that meaning in a manner and form easily understood by the readers. Because this translation is intended for all who use English as a means of communication, the translators have tried to avoid words and forms not in current or widespread use; but no artificial limit has been set to the range of the vocabulary employed. Every effort has been made to use language that is natural, clear, simple, and unambiguous. Consequently there has been no attempt to reproduce in English the parts of speech, sentence structure, word order, and grammatical devices of the original languages. Faithfulness in translation also includes a faithful representation of the cultural and historical features of the original. Certain features, however, such as the hours of the day and the measures of weight, capacity, distance, and area, are given their modern equivalents, because the information in those terms conveys more meaning to the reader than the biblical form of those terms.

In cases where a person or place is called by two or more different names in the original, this translation has normally used only the more familiar name in all places: for example, King Jehoiachin of Judah (Jeremiah 52:31), also called Jeconiah (Jeremiah 24:1) and Coniah (Jeremiah 37:1). Where a proper name is spelled two or more different ways in the original text, this translation has used only one spelling: for example, Nebuchadnezzar, also spelled Nebuchadrezzar (Jeremiah 29:3 and 29:21); and Priscilla, also spelled Prisca (Acts 18:26 and Romans 16:3).

Following an ancient tradition, begun by the first translation of the Hebrew Scriptures into Greek (the Septuagint) and followed by the vast majority of English translations, the distinctive Hebrew name for God (usually transliterated *Yahweh,* and earlier *Jehovah)* is in this translation represented by "LORD." When *Adonai,* normally translated "Lord," is followed by *Yahweh,* the combination is rendered by the phrase "Sovereign LORD."

The Revision of the Good News Bible

Since the initial appearance of the *Good News Bible* in *Today's English Version* in 1976, some minor editorial changes and corrections of printing errors have been introduced into the text in connection with various printings. The New Testament was already in its fourth edition at the time the full Bible appeared, but for the Old Testament and the Deuterocanonicals/Apocrypha of the *Good News Bible,* there was no revised edition until 1992. The preparation and publication of the second edition of the full *Good News Bible* in two formats, with and without the Deuterocanonicals and Apocrypha, is the result of a broad international process of careful review and evaluation of the Good News translation by many scholars and experts over a period of several years. This Catholic edition is consequently the beneficiary of all those corrections and revisions.

In December 1986, acting in response to a mounting perception of a need for text revisions, the ABS Board of Managers approved the undertaking of a revision of the Good News translation. The revision was restricted to two main areas of concern that had been raised and discussed over the years since the first appearance of the translation: (1) passages in which the English style had been unnecessarily exclusive and inattentive to gender concerns, and (2) passages in which the translation had been seen as problematic from either a stylistic or an exegetical viewpoint.

The process followed in preparing this revised edition was one of first inviting and collecting proposals for needed revisions from all English-language Bible Societies and English-speaking UBS translations consultants around the world, as well as numerous scholarly consultants in the United States and representatives of various American churches. The proposals received were then assembled for review and evaluation by the same broad array of experts whose specializations included translation, linguistics, English usage, literary and poetic style, biblical studies, and theology. In a series of four stages, consensus was sought on which proposals were necessary and valid, and at each of these review stages, the number of proposals under consideration was reduced until widespread agreement was reached. On the recommendation of the program committee of the ABS Board of Trustees (formerly Board of Managers) and its Translations subcommittee, the ABS Board acted to approve the revisions for the Good News Second Edition.

In the decade and a half since the initial publication of the Good News Bible, many Bible readers had become sensitive to the negative effects of exclusive language; that is, to the ways in which the built-in linguistic biases of the ancient languages and the English language toward the masculine gender has led some Bible readers to feel excluded from being addressed by the scriptural word. This concern has led to the revision of most major English translations during the 1980s, and, increasingly, readers of the Good News translation wrote to request that the Bible Society take this concern into consideration in preparing any revision. In practical terms what this means is that, where references in particular passages are to both men and women, the revision aims at language that is not exclusively masculine-oriented. At the same time, however, great care was taken not to distort the historical reality of the ancient patriarchal culture of Bible times.

Helps for the Reader

To make the text easier to understand, various kinds of readers' helps are supplied. The text itself has been divided into sections, and headings are provided to indicate the contents of the section. Where there are parallel accounts elsewhere in the Bible, as happens frequently in the Gospels, a reference to such a passage appears within parentheses below the heading. There are, in addition, several kinds of notes that appear at the bottom of the page.

(1) *Cultural or historical notes.* These provide information required to enable the modern reader to understand the meaning of the text in terms of its original setting (for example, the explanation of *Rahab* in Psalm 89:10; and the explanation of *Day of Atonement* in Acts 27:9).

(2) *Textual notes.* In the Old Testament, these indicate primarily those passages where the Hebrew word or words may be unclear in meaning, or where one or more of the ancient translations (for example, the Septuagint, Vulgate, or Syriac) appears to preserve the original wording better than the received Hebrew text. In Exodus 8:23, for example, all the above ancient translations have a word meaning "distinction" (cf. Vulgate, *divisionem*) rather than "redemption," which the Hebrew word *pedut* means. The ancient translations point to a Hebrew word *pelut* (division), which is only one letter different from *pedut* (redemption). Where one or more of the ancient versions were followed, the note indicates this by *One ancient translation* (for example, Genesis 1:26) or *Some ancient translations* (for example, Genesis 4:8); where a conjectural emendation was adopted, the note reads *Probable text* (for example, Genesis 10:14). Where the Greek is the primary text, such as in the New Testament or in the Old Testament books based on the Septuagint (also known as the deuterocanonicals), textual notes indicate some of the places where significant differences exist among the ancient manuscripts. These differences may consist of

additions to the text (for example, Matthew 21:43), deletions (for example, Matthew 24:36), or substitutions (for example, Mark 1:41).

(3) *Alternative renderings.* In many places the precise meaning of the original text is in dispute, and there are two or more different ways in which the text may be understood. In some of the more important of such instances, an alternative rendering is given (e.g. Genesis 2:9; Matthew 6:11).

(4) *References to other passages.* In addition, many editions of the Good News Bible include references (by book, chapter, and verse) to other places in the Bible where identical or similar matters or ideas are dealt with.

The line drawings that accompany the text were specially prepared for this translation.

The numbering of chapters and verses in this translation follows the traditional system of major English translations of the Bible. In some instances, however, where the order of thought or events in two or more verses is more clearly represented by a rearrangement of the material, two or more verse numbers are joined (for example, Exodus 2:15–16; Acts 1:21–22). In Old Testament books where additions from the Septuagint have been integrated with the Hebrew text, various strategies of versification have been employed. For these, it will be helpful for the reader to consult the book's introductions and footnotes for guidance.

A Bible that Brings Good News

No one knows better than the translators how difficult their task has been. But they have performed it gladly, conscious always of the presence of the Holy Spirit and of the tremendous debt they owe to the dedication and scholarship of those who have preceded them. The Bible is not simply great literature to be admired and revered; it is Good News for all people everywhere—a message both to be understood and to be applied in daily life. It is with prayer and thankfulness that the translator and staff of the United Bible Societies and American Bible Society offer this translation to the Lord; it is with humility that we pray God will make it fruitful. And to Christ be the glory forever and ever!

ACKNOWLEDGMENTS

The lyrics of "Open My Eyes" on page 442 are from *Spirit and Song* (Portland, OR: OCP Publications, 1999), number 196. Copyright © 1999 by OCP Publications. Song copyright © 1988 by Jesse Manibusan. Published by spiritandsong.com®, 5536 NE Hassalo, Portland, OR 97213. All rights reserved. Used with permission.

The prayer on page 782 is from *Best of Chief Dan George*, by Chief Dan George and Helmut Hirnschall (Blaine, WA: Hancock House Publishers, 1989), page 83. Copyright © 1974, 1989 by Chief Dan George and Helmut Hirnschall. Used with permission.

The prayer on page 814 is by Valerie Piraino, in "Rwanda: Ten Years after Genocide," by Catholic Relief Services, 2005. Used with permission.

The prayer on page 903 is adapted from *Garden of a Thousand Gates: Pathways to Prayer*, by Carl Koch (Winona, MN: Saint Mary's Press, 1998), page 61. Copyright © 1998 by Saint Mary's Press. All rights reserved.

The "Joy" article on page 917 is adapted from *Teaching Guide for Dealing with Tough Times*, by Marilyn Kielbasa (Winona, MN: Saint Mary's Press, 1999), pages 30–31. Copyright © 1999 by Saint Mary's Press. All rights reserved.

The prayer by Marisa T. Garfinkel on page 1354 is from *You Give Me the Sun: Biblical Prayers by Teenagers*, edited by Carl Koch (Winona, MN: Saint Mary's Press, 2000), page 70. Copyright © 2000 by Saint Mary's Press. All rights reserved.

The prayer on page 1692 is from the English translation of *Rite of Confirmation*, (Second Edition) © 1975, International Commission on English in the Liturgy Corporation (ICEL), number 42, in *The Rites of the Catholic Church*, volume one, prepared by the ICEL, a Joint Commission of Catholic Bishops' Conferences (Collegeville, MN: The Liturgical Press, 1990). Copyright © 1990 by the Order of St. Benedict, Collegeville, MN. Used with permission of the ICEL.

The creed on page 1697 is from *Christianity Rediscovered: An Epistle from the Masai*, by Vincent J. Donovan (Notre Dame, IN: Fides/Claretian, 1978), page 200. Copyright © 1978 by Fides/Claretian. Used with permission.

The quotation on page 1733 is from the English translation of the *Catechism of the Catholic Church* for use in the United States of America, second edition, number 469. Copyright © 1994 by the United States Catholic Conference, Inc.—Libreria Editrice Vaticana (LEV). English translation of the *Catechism of the Catholic Church: Modifications from the Editio Typica* copyright © 1997 by the United States Catholic Conference, Inc.—LEV.

The Scripture quotation on page 1769 is taken from the *Lectionary for Mass*, volume one, by the United States Conference of Catholic Bishops (New York: Catholic Book Publishing Company, 1998), page 106. Copyright © 1998, 1997, 1970 by the Confraternity of Christian Doctrine.

The prayers, devotions, beliefs, and practices contained herein have been verified against authoritative sources.

To view copyright terms and conditions for Internet materials cited here, log on to the home pages for the referenced Web sites.

During this book's preparation, all citations, facts, figures, names, addresses, telephone numbers, Internet URLs, and other pieces of information cited within were verified for accuracy. The authors and Saint Mary's Press staff have made every attempt to reference current and valid sources, but we cannot guarantee the content of any source, and we are not responsible for any changes that may have occurred since our verification. If you find an error in, or have a question or concern about, any of the information or sources listed within, please contact Saint Mary's Press.

Illustration Credits

Line drawings by Annie Vallotton.

Cover and inside illustrations by Alex Christ and Erik Lervold of Pernsteiner Creative Group, Inc.

The time line was created by Maps.com.

STUDY AND PRAYER HELPS

INDEX OF
BIBLE STORIES

Events, Prayers, Miracles, Parables, and Jesus' Teachings

Old Testament Events

These events are listed in the order in which they first appear in the Bible.

Creation, *Genesis, chapters 1–2*
original sin and its punishment,
  Genesis, chapter 3
Cain and Abel, *Genesis 4:1–16*
Noah and the Great Flood,
  Genesis, chapters 6–9
God's covenant with Abraham,
  Genesis 17:1—18:15
God's command to sacrifice Isaac,
  Genesis 22:1–19
Isaac's blessing of Jacob, *Genesis 27:1–29*
Jacob's dream, *Genesis 28:10–22*
Joseph and his brothers,
  Genesis, chapters 37–46
birth and youth of Moses,
  Exodus 2:1–10
Moses at the burning bush,
  Exodus 3:1–12
plagues on Egypt, *Exodus, chapters 7–12*
Passover and the Exodus,
  Exodus, chapters 12–14
Ten Commandments, *Exodus 20:1–17*
destruction of Jericho,
  Joshua 5:13—6:27
Gideon and the fleece, *Judges 6:36–40*
Samson, *Judges, chapters 13–16*
Samuel's birth and calling,
  1 Samuel, chapters 1–3
David and Goliath, *1 Samuel, chapter 17*
David and Bathsheba,
  2 Samuel, chapter 11
Solomon's wisdom, *1 Kings, chapter 3*
Elijah's triumph over the priests of Baal,
  1 Kings 18:21–40

miracles of Elisha, *2 Kings 4:1—6:23*
return from Exile, *Ezra, chapter 1*
battles of Judas Maccabeus,
  1 Maccabees, chapters 3–5
Ezekiel and the valley of dry bones,
  Ezekiel 37:1–14
Daniel, *Daniel, chapters 1–6*
Jonah and the Ninevites,
  Jonah, chapters 1–3

New Testament Events

These events are listed in the order in which they first appear in the Bible.

birth of Jesus, *Matthew 1:18—2:12;*
  Luke, chapters 1–2
baptism of Jesus, *Matthew 3:13–17;*
  Mark 1:9–11; Luke 3:21–22
temptation of Jesus, *Matthew 4:1–11;*
  Mark 1:12–13; Luke 4:1–13
Peter's declaration about Jesus,
  Matthew 16:13–20; Mark 8:27–30;
  Luke 9:18–20
Transfiguration of Jesus,
  Matthew 17:1–13; Mark 9:2–13;
  Luke 9:28–36
Jesus' triumphal entry into Jerusalem,
  Matthew 21:1–11; Mark 11:1–11;
  Luke 19:28–40; John 12:12–19
Jesus in the Temple, *Matthew 21:12–17;*
  Mark 11:15–19; Luke 19:45–48;
  John 2:13–17
Judas's betrayal of Jesus,
  Matthew 26:14–16, 47–56;
  Mark 14:10–11, 43–52;
  Luke 22:1–53; John 13:21–30;
  18:1–5

Last Supper, *Matthew 26:17–30;*
  Mark 14:12–26; Luke 22:7–38;
  1 Corinthians 11:23–26
Jesus at Gethsemane, *Matthew 26:36–56;*
  Mark 14:32–52; Luke 22:39–53
Peter's denial of Christ,
  Matthew 26:69–75; Mark 14:66–72;
  Luke 22:54–62; John 18:15–18, 25–27
Crucifixion, *Matthew 27:32–56;*
  Mark 15:21–41; Luke 23:26–49;
  John 19:16–30
Resurrection and appearances,
  Matthew, chapter 28; Mark, chapter 16;
  Luke, chapter 24; John, chapters 20–21;
  Acts 1:1–11
Jesus washing his disciples' feet,
  John 13:1–17
Holy Spirit at Pentecost, *Acts 2:1–41*
stoning of Stephen, *Acts, chapters 6–7*
conversion of Saul, *Acts 9:1–30*
Peter's escape from prison, *Acts 12:1–19*
Paul and Silas's escape from prison,
  Acts 16:16–40
Paul's journey to Rome for his trial,
  Acts, chapters 27–28

Prayers

These prayers are listed in the order in which they first appear in the Bible.

The LORD bless you and take care of
  you, *Numbers 6:24–27*
Hannah's prayer, *1 Samuel 2:1–10*
Speak, LORD, for your servant is listen-
  ing, *1 Samuel 3:9–10*
Blessed be the Lord, *1 Kings 8:56–61*
Tobit's thanksgiving, *Tobit, chapter 13*
Judith's hymn of praise, *Judith 16:1–17*
The LORD is my shepherd, *Psalm 23*
Be merciful to me, O God, *Psalm 51*
LORD, you have examined me and you
  know me, *Psalm 139*

Holy, holy, holy (Hosanna), *Isaiah 6:3;*
  Matthew 21:9; Mark 11:9–10;
  Luke 19:38; John 12:13; Revelation 4:8
Lord's Prayer, *Matthew 6:9–15;*
  Luke 11:2–4
Lord, I am not worthy, *Matthew 8:8*
Jesus' prayer for deliverance,
  Matthew 26:39; Mark 14:36;
  Luke 22:42
Mary's song of praise, *Luke 1:46–55*
Zechariah's prophecy, *Luke 1:68–79*
Glory to God in the highest, *Luke 2:14*
Simeon's prayer, *Luke 2:29–32*
God, have pity on me, a sinner!,
  Luke 18:13
Lamb of God, *John 1:29*
Jesus' prayer for his disciples,
  John, chapter 17
Paul's prayer for the Ephesians,
  Ephesians 3:14–21
Amen, *1 Peter 5:11; Jude, verse 25;*
  Revelation 1:6–7; 22:20–21

Miracles of Jesus

These miracle stories are listed in the order in which they first appear in the Bible.

Healing Individuals
skin disease, *Matthew 8:1–4;*
  Mark 1:40–45; Luke 5:12–16
centurion's servant, *Matthew 8:5–13;*
  Luke 7:1–10
many at Peter's house,
  Matthew 8:14–17; Mark 1:29–34;
  Luke 4:38–41
Gadarene (Gerasene) demoniacs,
  Matthew 8:28–34; Mark 5:1–20;
  Luke 8:26–39
paralytic, *Matthew 9:1–8; Mark 2:1–12;*
  Luke 5:17–26
woman with bleeding,
  Matthew 9:20–22; Mark 5:25–34;
  Luke 8:43–48

two blind men, *Matthew 9:27–31*

mute man, *Matthew 9:32–34*

man with a paralyzed hand,
*Matthew 12:9–13; Mark 3:1–5;
Luke 6:6–11*

blind, mute, and possessed man,
Matthew 12:22

Canaanite woman's daughter,
Matthew 15:21–28; Mark 7:24–30

boy with a demon, *Matthew 17:14–21;
Mark 9:14–29; Luke 9:37–43*

blind man (Bartimaeus),
*Matthew 20:29–34; Mark 10:46–52;
Luke 18:35–43*

man with an unclean spirit,
Mark 1:21–28; Luke 4:31–37

deaf man, *Mark 7:31–37*

blind man at Bethsaida, *Mark 8:22–26*

crippled woman, *Luke 13:11–13*

sick man, *Luke 14:1–4*

ten men with skin diseases,
Luke 17:11–19

High Priest's slave, *Luke 22:50–51*

official's son, *John 4:46–54*

man at the pool of Bethzatha,
John 5:1–9

Controlling Nature

stilling the storm, *Matthew 8:23–27;
Mark 4:35–41; Luke 8:22–25*

feeding five thousand,
*Matthew 14:13–21; Mark 6:30–44;
Luke 9:10–17; John 6:1–14*

walking on water, *Matthew 14:22–33;
Mark 6:45–52; John 6:16–21*

feeding four thousand,
Matthew 15:32–39; Mark 8:1–10

fish with a coin, *Matthew 17:24–27*

fig tree withers, *Matthew 21:18–22;
Mark 11:12–14,20–25*

huge catch of fish, *Luke 5:1–11;
John 21:1–11*

turning water into wine, *John 2:1–11*

Raising the Dead

Jairus's daughter,
*Matthew 9:18–19,23–26;
Mark 5:21–24,35–43;
Luke 8:40–42,49–56*

widow's son at Nain, *Luke 7:11–17*

Lazarus, *John 11:1–44*

Parables of Jesus

These parables are listed in alphabetical order.

canceled debts, *Luke 7:41–43*

cost of discipleship, *Luke 14:25–33*

dishonest manager, *Luke 16:1–8*

faithful or unfaithful slave,
Matthew 24:45–51; Luke 12:42–48

fig tree, *Matthew 24:32–35;
Mark 13:28–31; Luke 21:29–33*

good Samaritan, *Luke 10:30–37*

great feast, *Luke 14:16–24*

growing seed, *Mark 4:26–29*

hidden treasure and pearl,
Matthew 13:44–46

honor at a banquet, *Luke 14:7–14*

light of the world, *Matthew 5:14–16*

lost coin, *Luke 15:8–10*

lost sheep, *Matthew 18:12–14;
Luke 15:3–7*

lost son, *Luke 15:11–32*

mustard seed, *Matthew 13:31–32;
Mark 4:30–32; Luke 13:18–19*

net, *Matthew 13:47–50*

new wine in old wineskins,
*Matthew 9:16–17; Mark 2:21–22;
Luke 5:36–39*

persistent friend, *Luke 11:5–8*

persistent widow, *Luke 18:2–8*

Pharisee and the tax collector,
Luke 18:10–14

rich fool, *Luke 12:16–21*

rich man and Lazarus, *Luke 16:19–31*

salt, *Matthew 5:13; Mark 9:50;
Luke 14:34–35*

sheep and the goats, *Matthew 25:31–46*

sower, *Matthew 13:3–8,18–23;*
  Mark 4:3–9,14–20;
  Luke 8:5–8,11–15
talents, *Matthew 25:14–30*
ten coins, *Luke 19:11–27*
ten young women, *Matthew 25:1–13*
two sons, *Matthew 21:28–31*
unforgiving servant, *Matthew 18:23–35*
unfruitful fig tree, *Luke 13:6–9*
watchful slaves, *Luke 12:35–40*
wedding banquet, *Matthew 22:1–14*
weeds among the wheat,
  Matthew 13:24–30,36–43
wicked tenants, *Matthew 21:33–44;*
  Mark 12:1–12; Luke 20:9–18
wise and foolish builders,
  Matthew 7:24–27; Luke 6:47 49
workers in the vineyard,
  Matthew 20:1–16
worthless slaves, *Luke 17:7–10*
yeast, *Matthew 13:33; Luke 13:20–21*

Teachings of Jesus

These teachings are listed in alphabetical order.

Beatitudes, *Matthew 5:1–12;*
  Luke 6:20–26
born from above, *John 3:1–21*
bread of life, *John 6:25–59*
children, *Mark 10:13–16*
discipleship, *Luke 14:25–33*
do not worry, *Matthew 6:19–21,25–34;*
  Luke 12:22–34
Golden Rule, *Matthew 7:12; Luke 6:31*
good shepherd, *John 10:1–18*
greatest commandment,
  Matthew 22:34–40; Mark 12:28–34;
  Luke 10:25–28
living water, *John 4:1–26*
Lord's Prayer, *Matthew 6:9–13;*
  Luke 11:2–4
mission of the twelve Apostles,
  Matthew 10:1–15

paying taxes, *Matthew 22:15–22;*
  Mark 12:13–17; Luke 20:20–26
rich young man, *Matthew 19:16–30;*
  Mark 10:17–31; Luke 18:18–30
Sermon on the Mount,
  Matthew, chapters 5–7
Sermon on the Plain, *Luke 6:17–49*
vine and branches, *John 15:1–17*
"the way, the truth, and the life,"
  John 14:1–14
"where two or three come together,"
  Matthew 18:20

INDEX OF
ARTICLES

Pray It!, Study It!, Live It!, and Catholic Connections

This subject index is not an index to the Bible itself (sometimes called a concordance). Rather, it is an index to the subjects covered in the various articles in *Breakthrough!*

I

GLOSSARY

This word list identifies many objects or cultural features whose meaning may not be known to all readers.

Abib. The first month of the Hebrew calendar, corresponding to the period from about mid-March to about mid-April. This month is also called Nisan.

Abyss. The place in the depths of the earth where the demons were imprisoned until their final punishment.

Acacia. A flowering tree, a type of mimosa, with hard and durable wood.

Adar. The twelfth month of the Hebrew calendar, corresponding to the period from about mid-February to about mid-March.

Agate. A semiprecious stone of various colors, but usually white and brown.

Alabaster. A soft stone of usually light, creamy color; vases and jars were made from it.

Aloes. A sweet-smelling substance, derived from a plant. It was used medicinally and as a perfume.

Amen. A Hebrew word that means "it is so" or "may it be so." It can also be translated "certainly," "truly," or "surely." In Revelation 3:14 it is used as a title for Christ.

Amethyst. A semiprecious stone, usually purple or violet in color.

Anoint. To pour or rub olive oil on someone in order to honor him or appoint him to some special work. The Israelite kings were anointed as a sign of their taking office, and so the king could be called "the anointed one." In a figurative sense, "The Anointed One" is the title of the one whom God chose and appointed as Savior and Lord.

Apostle. Principally one of the group of twelve men whom Jesus chose to be his special followers and helpers. It is also used in the New Testament to refer to Paul. The word means "one who is sent."

Areopagus. A hill in Athens where the city council used to meet. For this reason the council itself was called Areopagus, even after it no longer met on the hill.

Artemis. The Greek name of an ancient goddess of fertility, worshiped especially in Asia Minor.

Asherah. A goddess of fertility worshiped by the Canaanites; her male counterpart was Baal. After the Hebrews invaded Canaan, many of them began worshiping these two gods.

Astarte. A goddess of fertility and war who was widely worshiped in the ancient Near East.

Atonement, Day of. The most important of Israel's holy days, when the High Priest would offer a sacrifice for the sins of the people of Israel (Leviticus, chapter 16). It was held on the tenth day of the seventh month of the Hebrew calendar (around October 1). The Jewish name for this day is Yom Kippur.

Baal. The god of fertility worshiped by the Canaanites; his female counterpart was Asherah. After the Hebrews invaded Canaan, many of them began worshiping these two gods.

Baal-of-the-Covenant. A name by which the god Baal was known by the people of Shechem.

Babylon. The name of a city and an empire that existed in the ancient Middle East. The Babylonians destroyed Jerusalem and Solomon's Temple in 587 BC. Some early Christians used the name Babylon as a code word for the Roman Empire. They saw the Romans persecuting Christians like the Babylonians persecuted the Israelites.

Balsam. A tree from which sweet-smelling resin was obtained; the resin was used for perfume and medicine.

Barley. A cultivated grain similar to wheat, grown as a food crop.

Beelzebul. A New Testament name given to the Devil as the chief of the evil spirits.

Beryl. A semiprecious stone, usually green or bluish green in color.

Blasphemy. Insulting God or being disrespectful toward God. People thought Jesus was committing blasphemy by claiming to forgive sins.

Breastplate. Part of a soldier's armor, made of leather or metal; it covered the chest and sometimes the back as a protection against arrows and the blows of a sword.

Bul. The eighth month of the Hebrew calendar, corresponding to the period from about mid-October to about mid-November.

Burnt offering. A type of sacrifice in which all the parts of the animal were completely burned on the altar; in other sacrifices only certain parts of the animal were burned.

Calamus. A sweet-smelling reed-like plant.

Capital. The top part of a column supporting a roof.

Carnelian. A semiprecious stone, usually red in color.

Cassia. A spice made from the bark of a tree; it closely resembles cinnamon.

Chalcedony. A semiprecious stone, usually milky or gray in color.

Christ. Originally a title, the Greek equivalent of the Hebrew word *Messiah*. It means "the anointed one." Jesus was called the Christ because he was the one whom God chose and sent as Savior and Lord.

Circumcise. To cut off the foreskin of the penis. As a sign of God's covenant with his people, Israelite boys were circumcised eight days after they were born (Genesis 17:9–14).

Cistern. A type of well that holds rainwater. Cisterns are an important source of water for people in dry lands.

City of refuge. When the people of Israel moved into the land of Canaan, they were told to name certain towns as cities of refuge. If anyone accidentally killed someone, he could escape to one of these cities and be safe from revenge (see Numbers 35:9–34; Deuteronomy 4:41–43, 19:1–13; Joshua 20:1–9).

Concubine. A servant woman who, although not a wife, had sexual relations with her master. She had important legal rights, and her master was referred to as her husband.

Coral. A brightly colored stony substance found in the sea; it was used as jewelry.

Council. The supreme religious court of the Jews, composed of seventy leaders of the Jewish people and presided over by the High Priest.

Covenant. An agreement, either between persons or between God and a person or a people. God made a covenant with Noah (Genesis 9:8–17) and with Abraham (Genesis 17:1–8), but in the Old Testament, the term usually refers to the covenant made between God and the people of Israel at the time of Moses (Exodus 24:4–8).

Covenant Box. The wooden chest covered with gold in which were kept the two stone tablets on which were written the Ten Commandments. It has traditionally been called the Ark of the Covenant.

Cumin. A small plant whose seeds are ground up and used for seasoning foods.

Cush. The term *Cush* in the Old Testament Hebrew text normally designates the territory extending south from the First Cataract of the Nile River at Aswan. It was known in Graeco-Roman times as Ethiopia (Greek, *Aithiopia*), and later as Nubia. In Genesis, chapter 10, the Table of Nations, verses 8–12 are included under the genealogy of Egyptian Cush, yet all the peoples named are in Mesopotamia. Apparently the Hebrew designation for the Babylonian Kassites was "Cush" as well, thus resulting in the mixing of the two regions. Genesis 2:13 may be another reference to Babylonian Cush.

Cymbals. A pair of thin pieces of metal held in the hands and struck together rhythmically in music.

David's City. In the Old Testament, the reference is generally to that part of the city of Jerusalem that was captured from the Jebusites by King David. In the New Testament, the reference is to the town of Bethlehem, David's boyhood home, where Jesus was born.

Dedication, Festival of. The Jewish festival, lasting eight days, that celebrated the restoration and rededication in 165 BC of the Temple altar by the Jewish patriot Judas Maccabeus. The festival began on the twenty-fifth day of the month Kislev (around December 10). The Jewish name for this festival is Hanukkah.

Defile. To make ritually unclean or impure. Certain foods and practices were prohibited by the Law of Moses because they were thought to make a person ritually or ceremonially unclean. Such a person could not take part in the public worship until he had performed certain rituals that would remove the defilement.

Demon. An evil spirit with the power to harm people; it was regarded as a messenger and servant of the Devil.

Dill. A small garden plant whose stems, leaves, and seeds are used for seasoning food.

Dipper: Big Dipper and Little Dipper. Two groups of stars that in the Northern Hemisphere are visible in the northern sky. The star at the end of the "handle" of the Little Dipper is Polaris, the North Star.

Disciple. A person who follows and learns from someone else. In the New Testament, the word is used of the followers of John the Baptist and especially of the followers of Jesus, particularly the twelve Apostles.

Divination. The attempt to discover a message from God or the gods by examining such things as marked stones or the liver of a sacrificed animal.

Dragon. A legendary beast, thought to be like a huge lizard. It is also called a serpent and appears as a figure of the Devil (Revelation 12:3—13:4; 20:2,3).

Elders. In the Old Testament, this is a name given to certain respected leaders of a tribe, nation, or city. In the New Testament, three different groups are called elders: (1) in the Gospels the elders were influential Jewish religious leaders, some of whom were members of the supreme Council; (2) in Acts, chapters 11–21 and the Letters, the elders are Christian Church officers who had a general responsibility for the work of the Church; (3) in Revelation the twenty-four elders are part of God's court in heaven, perhaps as representatives of God's people.

Elul. The sixth month of the Hebrew calendar, corresponding to the period from about mid-August to about mid-September.

Ephod. The Hebrew term traditionally transliterated as "ephod" is of uncertain meaning in a number of contexts. Generally it refers to some type of priestly garment that was worn over the shoulder by the High Priest and with which the Urim and Thummim were associated. In certain contexts, however, the Hebrew term refers to an object of worship, and in some other passages, it evidently refers to an object used to foretell future events.

Epicureans. Those who followed the teaching of Epicurus (died 270 BC), a Greek philosopher who taught that happiness is the highest good in life.

Epileptic. A person who suffers from a nervous disease causing convulsions and fainting.

Ethanim. The seventh month of the Hebrew calendar, corresponding to the period from about mid-September to about mid-October; it was later called Tishri.

Ethiopia. *See* Cush.

Eunuch. A man who has been made physically incapable of having normal sexual relations. Eunuchs were often important officials in the courts of ancient kings, and the term may have come to be used of such officials in general, regardless of their sexual condition.

Exile, the. About 721 BC the Assyrians conquered northern Israel and the Israelite territory east of the Jordan River and deported the people (see 2 Kings 15:29; 1 Chronicles 5:22). In 587 BC the Babylonians conquered the southern kingdom of Judah, destroyed Jerusalem and the Temple, and deported the people to Babylon (see 2 Kings, chapter 25; 2 Chronicles 36:5–21). This is called the Exile.

Exodus. A term that means "departure." The main event in the book with this name is the departure of the Israelites from Egypt.

Fast. To go without food for a while as a religious duty.

Feldspar. A colorful, rather hard rock, often glassy in appearance.

Fellowship offerings. A type of sacrifice offered to ensure a right relationship with God. Only a portion of the animal was burned on the altar; the rest was eaten by the worshipers or the priests.

Flax. A small cultivated plant; the fibers of its stem are spun into thread used in making linen cloth.

Frankincense. A valuable incense, made from the sap of a certain tree. This incense was probably imported from Arabia.

Fruits of the Holy Spirit. The effects in a person's life that come from the work of the Holy Spirit. See Galatians 5:22–23, where the fruits are listed as love, joy, peace, patience, kindness, goodness, faithfulness, humility, and self-control.

Garnet. A semiprecious stone, usually red in color.

Gazelle. A kind of antelope, known for its beauty and gracefulness.

Genesis. A word that means "source" or "beginning." It means that the Book of Genesis is about the beginning of things: the world, human beings, sin, the Covenant with God.

Gentile. A person who is not a Jew.

Hades. The Greek name used in the New Testament to refer to the world of the dead.

Harrow. A farm implement used to break up the ground and level it after plowing.

Harvest Festival. The Israelite festival celebrating the wheat harvest, held in the latter part of May or early June, fifty days after Passover. The Jewish name for this festival is Shavuoth (the Feast of Weeks). It has also been called Pentecost.

Heathens. People who do not worship God as revealed in the Bible.

Hermes. The name of a Greek god who served as messenger of the gods.

Herod's party. A political party in New Testament times composed of Jews who favored being ruled by one of the descendants of Herod the Great rather than by the Roman governor.

High Priest. The priest who occupied the highest office in the Jewish priestly system and was president of the supreme Council of the Jews. Once a year (on the Day of Atonement) he would enter the Most Holy Place in the Temple and offer sacrifice for himself and for the sins of the people of Israel.

Hyssop. A small, bushy plant used in religious ceremonies to sprinkle liquids.

Idolatry. Worshiping false gods, people, or material things in a way that is fitting for God alone.

Incense. Material that is burned to produce a pleasant smell. The Israelites used it in their worship.

Jackal. A small wild animal resembling a fox.

Jasper. A semiprecious stone of various colors. The jasper mentioned in the Bible was probably green, or else clear.

Javelin. A short, light spear used by soldiers in ancient times.

Justice. Being right and fair in relationships with other people. For the prophets it especially meant the quality of caring for the poor and outcast.

Kislev. The ninth month of the Hebrew calendar, corresponding to the period from about mid-November to about mid-December.

Law. The name the Jews applied to the first five books of the Old Testament, also called the Torah or the Pentateuch. Sometimes, however, the name is applied in a more general way to the entire Old Testament.

Leviathan. A legendary animal associated with water, in some passages identified by some scholars as the crocodile. In a figurative sense, it may represent the chaos that existed before God created the world (Job 3:8; Psalm 74:14; Isaiah 27:1).

Levite. (1) A member of the tribe of Levi; (2) a man who assisted the priest in the performance of religious duties.

Levitical priest. A Hebrew priest descended from the tribe of Levi. All priests were supposed to be members of the tribe of Levi, but in later times not all members of the tribe of Levi were priests.

Living creatures. Also referred to as "winged creatures" and traditionally called "cherubim," they were symbols of God's majesty and associated with his presence. For a description of such creatures, see Exodus 25:18–20; Ezekiel 1:5–13, chapter 10; Revelation 4:6–9.

LORD. Where the Hebrew text has Yahweh, sometimes transliterated as Jehovah, this translation employs LORD with capital letters, following a usage that is widespread in English versions. See, for example, Genesis 2:4 and Exodus 3:14. This corresponds either to the occurrence of the name itself or to a pronoun standing for the name.

Lyre. A kind of harp.

Mandrake. A small plant; it was believed that eating its root or fruit would make a woman more easily able to have children.

Manna. A food eaten by the Israelites during their travels in the wilderness. It was white and flaky and looked like small seeds (Exodus 16:14–21; Numbers 11:7–9).

Medium. A person who believes that he or she can communicate with the dead.

Mercy. Having forgiveness and loving-kindness for a person who does something wrong.

Messiah. A Hebrew title (meaning "the anointed one") given to the promised Savior, whose coming was foretold by the Hebrew prophets; the corresponding Greek term "the Christ" has the same meaning.

Michael. An archangel, one of God's chief angels. His name was the war cry of the good angels in the battle against Satan and his followers.

Mildew. A fungus that appears on various objects, especially in damp weather.

Millet. A cultivated grain grown as a food crop.

Molech. One of the gods of the ancient people of Canaan.

Most Holy Place. The innermost room of the Tent of the LORD's presence or the Temple. The Covenant Box was kept there. Only the High Priest could enter the Most Holy Place, and he did so only once a year, on the Day of Atonement.

Mustard. A large plant that grows from a very small seed. The seeds were ground into powder and used as spice on food.

Myrrh. A sweet-smelling resin that was highly prized. It served as a medicine (Mark 15:23) and was used by the Jews in preparing bodies for burial (John 19:39).

Myrtle. A kind of evergreen shrub or tree.

Nard. An expensive perfume made from a plant.

Nazarene. Someone from the town of Nazareth. The name was used as a title for Jesus and also as a name for the early Christians (Acts 24:5).

Nazirite. A person who took a special vow of self-dedication. Such a person was not to drink beer or wine, cut his hair, or touch a dead body (Numbers 6:1–21). The vow could be taken for a certain period of time, but some persons were dedicated to God as Nazirites from their birth.

New Moon Festival. A religious observance held by the Israelites on the day of each new moon.

New Year Festival. The Jewish name for this festival is Rosh Hashanah.

Nisan. The first month of the Hebrew calendar, corresponding to the period from about mid–March to about mid–April. The month is also called Abib.

Onyx. A semiprecious stone of various colors.

Orion. A group of prominent stars visible during winter evenings.

Outcasts. In the Gospels this name, which in many translations appears as "sinners," refers to those Jews who had been excluded from synagogue worship because they violated rules about foods that should not be eaten and about associating with people who were not Jews. Such outcasts were despised by many of their fellow Jews, and Jesus was criticized for associating with them (Mark 2:15–17; Luke 7:34; 15:1–2).

Parable. A story that uses objects and experiences that people are familiar with to teach spiritual truth. It was often used by Jesus.

Paradise. A name for heaven (Luke 23:43; 2 Corinthians 12:3).

Passover. The Israelite festival, which begins on the evening after the fourteenth day of the month Nisan (around April 1), that celebrated the deliverance of the ancient Hebrews from their captivity in Egypt. The Angel of Death killed the firstborn in the Egyptian homes but passed over the Hebrew homes (Exodus 12:23–27). The Jewish name for this festival is Pesach.

Pentecost, Day of. The Greek name for the Israelite festival of wheat harvest (see Harvest Festival). The name Pentecost (meaning "fiftieth") comes from the fact that the feast was held fifty days after Passover.

Pervert. One who commits unnatural sexual acts.

Pharisees. A Jewish religious party during the time of Jesus. They were strict in obeying the Law of Moses and other regulations that had been added to it through the centuries.

Pistachio nut. A small, greenish nut.

Plagues. Disastrous evils or afflictions that cause much destruction and sometimes death.

Pleiades. A small group of stars visible during winter evenings.

Pomegranate. A reddish fruit about the size of a large apple; it has a hard rind and is full of tasty seeds.

Preparation, Day of. The sixth day of the week (Friday), on which the Jews made the required preparation to observe the Sabbath (Saturday).

Pride. Loving yourself or loving success more than God or others. It is one of the capital sins because it leads to other sins.

Prophet. A person who proclaims a message from God. The term usually refers to certain men and women in the Old Testament, but the New Testament speaks of prophets in the early Church. John the Baptist is also called a prophet.

Purim. The Jewish religious holiday held on the fourteenth day of the month Adar (around March 1), celebrating the deliverance of the Jews from Haman by Esther and Mordecai. The story is told in the Book of Esther.

Quartz. A semiprecious stone of various colors, but usually clear.

Rabbi. A Hebrew word that means "my teacher."

Rahab. (1) A legendary sea monster that represented the forces of chaos and evil (Psalm 89:10) and was sometimes used as a symbol of Egypt

(Isaiah, chapter 51); (2) a Canaanite woman who helped the Israelite spies escape from Jericho (Joshua, chapter 2; Hebrews 11:31).

Red Sea. Evidently referred originally to (1) a series of lakes and marshes between the head of the Gulf of Suez and the Mediterranean, the region generally regarded as the site of the events described in Exodus, chapter 13, and was also used to designate (2) the Gulf of Suez, and (3) the Gulf of Aqaba.

Rephan. The name of an ancient god that was worshiped as the ruler of the planet Saturn.

Resin. A fragrant, gummy substance produced from the sap of certain trees and shrubs.

Restoration, Year of. The year, coming every fifty years, when the ancient Israelites returned to the original owner any property they were holding, freed their Israelite slaves, and did not cultivate their fields.

Sabbath. The seventh day of the Jewish week (from sundown on Friday to sundown on Saturday), a holy day on which no work was permitted.

Sackcloth. A coarse cloth made of goats' hair, which was worn as a sign of mourning or distress.

Sadducees. A small Jewish religious party in New Testament times, composed largely of priests. They based their beliefs primarily on the first five books of the Old Testament and differed in several matters of belief and practice from the larger party of the Pharisees.

Samaritan. A name used to refer to a native of Samaria, the region between Judea and Galilee. Because of differences in politics, race, customs, and religion (including especially the central place of worship), there was much bad feeling between the Jews and the Samaritans.

Sanctuary. A building dedicated to the worship of God. Sometimes the word refers to the central place of worship and not to the whole building.

Sapphire. A very valuable stone, usually blue in color.

Scepter. A short rod held by kings to symbolize their authority.

Scorpion. A small creature that has eight legs and a long tail with a poisonous sting. It can inflict a very painful, and sometimes fatal, wound.

Scribe. A person whose business it was to write documents for others or to copy written material. Some scribes were employed by ancient kings to prepare official documents, and some of them became important officials.

Scriptures. In the New Testament, the word refers to the collected body of Hebrew sacred writings known to Christians as the Old Testament. Various names are used: the Law (or the Law of Moses) and the prophets (Matthew 5:17; 7:12; Luke 2:22; 24:44; Acts 13:15; 28:23), the Holy Scriptures (Romans 1:2; 2 Timothy 3:15), the old covenant (2 Corinthians 3:14). For Christians, the Scriptures is another name for the Bible, containing both the Old and New Testaments.

Serpent. A name given to the dragon that appears in the New Testament as a figure of the Devil (Revelation 12:3–17; 20:2,3).

Seventh year. The year, coming every seventh year, when the ancient Israelites did not cultivate their fields and when debts were cancelled.

Study and Prayer Helps

Shebat. The eleventh month of the Hebrew calendar, corresponding to the period from about mid-January to about mid-February.

Shelters, Festival of. A joyous festival celebrated by the Israelites in the fall after the completion of the harvest. To help them remember the years when their ancestors wandered through the wilderness, the Israelites constructed rough shelters to live in during the festival. The Jewish name for this festival is Sukkoth. It has been traditionally called the Feast of Tabernacles or the Feast of Booths.

Shiloh. The central place of worship for the people of Israel before the time of King David. It was here that the Covenant Box was kept in the time of the priest Eli (1 Samuel 1:3). The city was most likely destroyed by the Philistines.

Sickle. A tool consisting of a curved metal blade and a wooden handle, used for cutting wheat and other crops.

Sinai. As the people of Israel went from Egypt to Canaan, God revealed himself to Moses and the people at Mount Sinai, a mountain located somewhere on the Sinai Peninsula but whose exact location is uncertain. It was on this mountain that God gave the Law to Moses (Exodus 19:16–25; 31:18).

Sivan. The third month of the Hebrew calendar, corresponding to the period from about mid-May to about mid-June.

Snuffer. The Hebrew word translated "snuffer" apparently identifies an implement used to trim the oil lamps used in the Tent of the LORD's presence or the Temple.

Sorcerer. A person who works magic for evil purposes.

Stoics. Those who followed the teachings of the Greek philosopher Zeno (died 265 BC), who taught that happiness is to be found in being free from pleasure and pain.

Sulfur. In the Bible this refers to a sulfur compound that burns with great heat and produces an unpleasant smell.

Synagogue. A place where Jews met every Sabbath day for their public worship. It probably also served as a center for Jewish social life and a school for Jewish children.

Tambourine. A small drum with pieces of metal in the rim, held in the hand and shaken. In biblical times it was generally used by women.

Tassel. A group of threads or cords fastened together at one end and loose at the other. The Israelites were commanded to wear these on their clothes (Numbers 15:37–41).

Teachers of the Law. Men who in New Testament times taught and interpreted the teachings of the Old Testament, especially the first five books.

Tebeth. The tenth month of the Hebrew calendar, corresponding to the period from about mid-December to about mid-January.

Tenant. A man who grows crops on land owned by someone else, and turns over a part of the harvest to the owner to pay for the use of his land.

Tent of the LORD's presence. The large tent described in detail in Exodus, chapter 26, where the Israelites worshiped God until Solomon built the Temple. It has traditionally been called the Tabernacle or Tent of meeting.

Threshing, threshing floor, and threshing sledge. Threshing is the process by which farmers separate the edible grain from the husks of crops like wheat and rye. First the stalks are placed on a hard surface called a threshing floor. The farmer then beats the stalks or uses animals to trample them in order to separate the grain from the husks. Sometimes farmers would ride a sledge pulled by oxen over the stalks to speed up the process. These sledges often had bits of iron or stone fastened beneath them. The farmer then used a winnowing shovel to complete the process of separating and gathering the grain (see Winnowing shovel). See also 1 Chronicles 21:18–30; Isaiah 41:15.

Tithe. A tenth part of a person's produce or income, given for religious purposes. See Numbers 18:25–32; Deuteronomy 14:22–29.

Topaz. A semiprecious stone, usually yellow in color.

Turban. A head covering worn by men, made by cloth wrapped around the head.

Turquoise. A semiprecious stone, blue or bluish green in color.

Twelve tribes. The twelve family groups of the nation of Israel, each named for a son of Jacob.

Unleavened Bread, Festival of. The Israelite festival, lasting seven days after Passover; it also celebrated the deliverance of the ancient Hebrews from Egypt. The name came from the practice of not using leaven (yeast) in making bread during that week (Exodus 12:14–20). It was held from the fifteenth to the twenty-second day of the month Nisan (around the first week of April).

Urim and Thummim. Two small objects used by Israelite priests to determine God's will; it is not known precisely how they were used (Numbers 27:21).

Virtue. A habit that leads you to do good things and make choices that are morally right.

Vow. A strong declaration or promise, usually made while calling upon God to punish the speaker if the statement should prove to be not true or if the promise were not kept.

Winged creatures. Also referred to as "living creatures" and traditionally called "cherubim," they were symbols of God's majesty and associated with his presence. For a description of such creatures, see Exodus 25:18–20; Ezekiel 1:5–13, chapter 10; Revelation 4:6–9.

Winnowing shovel. A tool like a shovel or a large fork, used to separate the wheat from the chaff. See Matthew 3:12.

Worship. To adore God in prayer, particularly as part of a public religious ritual.

Wreath. Flowers or leaves arranged in a circle, to be placed on a person's head. In ancient times a wreath of leaves was the prize given to winners in athletic contests.

Year of Restoration. Every fifty years, all Israelites were required to give freedom to any Israelites who had become slaves because of debts; they were also to give back to the original owner, or his heirs, any ancestral land that had been sold for debt (Leviticus 25:8 55; Ezekiel 46:17).

Yeast. A substance, also called leaven, that is added to dough made from the flour of wheat or barley to make it rise before being baked into bread.

Yoke. A heavy bar of wood fitted over the necks of two oxen to make it possible for them to pull a plow or a cart. The word is used figuratively to describe the moral lessons that a teacher passes on to his pupils.

Zeus. The name of the supreme god of the Greeks.

Zion. Originally a name for "David's City," the Jebusite stronghold captured by King David's forces. The term *Zion* was later extended in meaning to refer to the hill on which the Temple stood.

Ziv. The second month of the Hebrew calendar, corresponding to the period from about mid-April to about mid-May.

CATHOLIC PRAYERS

Act of Contrition

My God,
I am sorry for my sins with all my
heart.
In choosing to do wrong and failing to
do good,
I have sinned against you
whom I should love above all things.
I firmly intend, with your help,
to do penance, to sin no more,
and to avoid whatever leads me to sin.
Our savior Jesus Christ suffered and
died for us.
In his name, my God, have mercy.

Act of Faith

My God, I firmly believe you are one
    God in three Divine Persons, Father,
    Son, and Holy Spirit.
I believe in Jesus Christ, your son, who
    became man and died for our sins,
    and who will come to judge the liv
    ing and the dead.
I believe these and all the truths which
    the Holy Catholic Church teaches,
    because you have revealed them, who
    can neither deceive nor be deceived.
    Amen.

Act of Love

My God, I love you above all things,
with my whole heart and soul, because
you are all-good and worthy of all my
love. I love my neighbor as myself for
love of you. I forgive all who have
injured me, and I ask pardon of all
whom I have injured. Amen.

Act of Hope

O my God, trusting in your infinite
goodness and promises, I hope to obtain
pardon of my sins, the help of your
grace, and life everlasting, through the
merits of Jesus Christ, my Lord and
redeemer. Amen.

Apostles' Creed

I believe in God, the Father Almighty,
creator of heaven and earth. I believe in
Jesus Christ, his only son, our Lord. He
was conceived by the power of the
Holy Spirit, and born of the Virgin
Mary. He suffered under Pontius Pilate,
was crucified, died, and was buried. He
descended to the dead. On the third day
he rose again. He ascended into heaven
and is seated at the right hand of the
Father. He will come again to judge the
living and the dead.
   I believe in the Holy Spirit, the holy
catholic Church, the communion of
saints, the forgiveness of sins, the resurrection of the body, and the life everlasting. Amen.

Confiteor (I Confess)

I confess to almighty God, and to you,
my brothers and sisters, that I have
sinned through my own fault in my
thoughts and in my words, in what I
have done and what I have failed to do;
and I ask blessed Mary, ever-virgin, all
the Angels and Saints, and you, my
brothers and sisters, to pray for me to
the Lord our God. May almighty God
have mercy on us, forgive us our sins,
and bring us to everlasting life.

Glory Be

Glory be to the Father, and to the Son, and to the Holy Spirit, as it was in the beginning, is now, and will be forever. Amen.

Grace before Meals

Bless us, O Lord, and these your gifts, which we are about to receive
from your bounty,
through Christ our Lord. Amen.

Grace after Meals

We give you thanks, almighty God, for these and all your gifts
which we have received
through Christ our Lord. Amen.

Hail Mary

Hail Mary, full of grace,
the Lord is with you;
blessed are you among women,
and blessed is the fruit of your womb,
	Jesus.
Holy Mary, Mother of God,
pray for us sinners
now and at the hour of our death.
Amen.

The Lord's Prayer (also called the Our Father)

Our Father who art in heaven,
hallowed be thy name.
Thy kingdom come.
Thy will be done on earth, as it is in
	heaven.
Give us this day our daily bread,
and forgive us our trespasses,
	as we forgive those who trespass
		against us,
and lead us not into temptation,
but deliver us from evil. Amen.

Morning Prayer

Almighty God, I thank you for your past blessings. Today I offer myself— whatever I do, say, or think—to your loving care. Continue to bless me, Lord. I make this morning offering in union with the divine intentions of Jesus Christ, who offers himself daily in the holy sacrifice of the Mass, and in union with Mary, his Virgin Mother and our Mother, who was always the faithful handmaid of the Lord. Amen.

Prayer of Saint Francis

Lord, make me an instrument of your peace:
	where there is hatred, let me sow
		love;
	where there is injury, pardon;
	where there is doubt, faith;
	where there is despair, hope;
	where there is darkness, light;
	where there is sadness, joy.
Divine Master,
grant that I may not so much seek
	to be consoled as to console,
	to be understood as to understand,
	to be loved as to love.
For it is in giving that we receive,
	it is in pardoning that we are
		pardoned,
	it is in dying that we are born to
		eternal life.

Prayer to the Holy Spirit

Come, Holy Spirit, fill the hearts of your faithful. Enkindle in them the fire of your love. Send forth your Spirit, and they will be created. And you will renew the face of the earth.
Let us pray:
Lord, by the light of the Holy Spirit, you have taught the hearts of the faithful. In the same Spirit, help us to relish what is right and always rejoice in your consolation. We ask this through Christ our Lord. Amen.

The Rosary

The Rosary is perhaps the most popular devotion to Mary, the Mother of God. The central part of the Rosary consists of the recitation of five sets of ten Hail Marys (each set is called a decade). This diagram shows you which prayers to use with which parts of the Rosary.

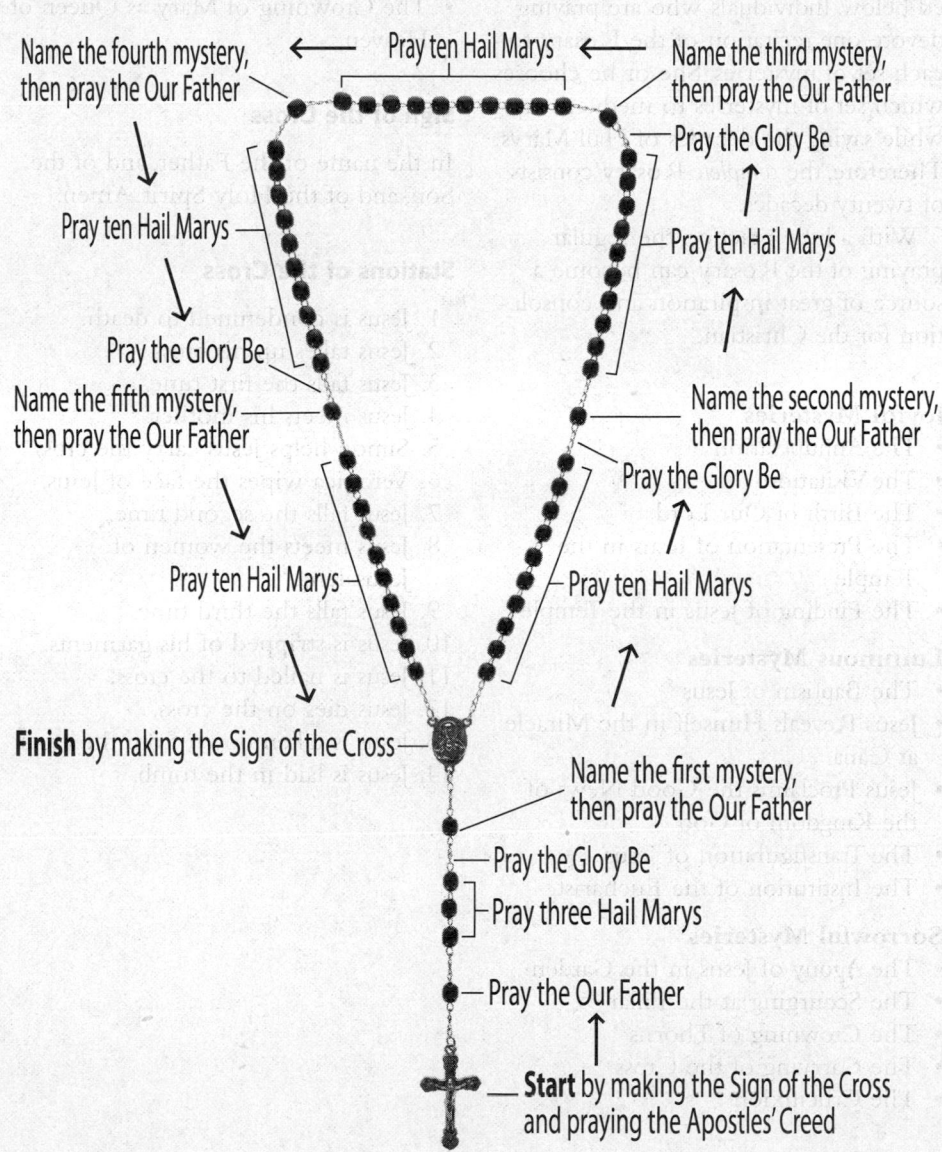

Name the fourth mystery, then pray the Our Father

Pray ten Hail Marys ← Pray ten Hail Marys ← Name the third mystery, then pray the Our Father

Pray the Glory Be

Pray ten Hail Marys

Pray the Glory Be

Name the fifth mystery, then pray the Our Father

Pray ten Hail Marys

Name the second mystery, then pray the Our Father

Pray the Glory Be

Pray ten Hail Marys

Finish by making the Sign of the Cross

Name the first mystery, then pray the Our Father

Pray the Glory Be

Pray three Hail Marys

Pray the Our Father

Start by making the Sign of the Cross and praying the Apostles' Creed

The saying of a five-decade Rosary is connected with meditation on what are called the mysteries of the life of Jesus. These mysteries too are collected into series of five—five joyful, five luminous, five sorrowful, and five glorious mysteries. The mysteries of the Rosary are listed below. Individuals who are praying devote one recitation of the Rosary to each set of mysteries. She or he chooses which set of mysteries to meditate on while saying the decades of Hail Marys. Therefore, the *complete* Rosary consists of twenty decades.

With a little practice, the regular praying of the Rosary can become a source of great inspiration and consolation for the Christian.

Joyful Mysteries

- The Annunciation
- The Visitation
- The Birth of Our Lord
- The Presentation of Jesus in the Temple
- The Finding of Jesus in the Temple

Luminous Mysteries

- The Baptism of Jesus
- Jesus Reveals Himself in the Miracle at Cana
- Jesus Proclaims the Good News of the Kingdom of God
- The Transfiguration of Jesus
- The Institution of the Eucharist

Sorrowful Mysteries

- The Agony of Jesus in the Garden
- The Scourging at the Pillar
- The Crowning of Thorns
- The Carrying of the Cross
- The Crucifixion

Glorious Mysteries

- The Resurrection of Jesus
- The Ascension of Jesus into Heaven
- The Descent of the Holy Spirit on the Apostles (Pentecost)
- The Assumption of Mary into Heaven
- The Crowning of Mary as Queen of Heaven

Sign of the Cross

In the name of the Father, and of the Son, and of the Holy Spirit. Amen.

Stations of the Cross

1. Jesus is condemned to death.
2. Jesus takes up his cross.
3. Jesus falls the first time.
4. Jesus meets his mother.
5. Simon helps Jesus carry the cross.
6. Veronica wipes the face of Jesus.
7. Jesus falls the second time.
8. Jesus meets the women of Jerusalem.
9. Jesus falls the third time.
10. Jesus is stripped of his garments.
11. Jesus is nailed to the cross.
12. Jesus dies on the cross.
13. Jesus is taken down from the cross.
14. Jesus is laid in the tomb.

CATHOLIC TEACHINGS

Two Great Commandments (see Matthew 22:37–40, Mark 12:29–31, Luke 10:27)

- You shall love the Lord your God with all your heart, with all your soul, with all your mind, and with all your strength.
- You shall love your neighbor as yourself.

Ten Commandments (see Exodus 20:1–17)

1. I am the Lord your God: you shall not have strange gods before me.
2. You shall not take the name of the Lord, your God, in vain.
3. Remember to keep holy the Lord's Day.
4. Honor your father and mother.
5. You shall not kill.
6. You shall not commit adultery.
7. You shall not steal.
8. You shall not bear false witness against your neighbor.
9. You shall not covet your neighbor's wife.
10. You shall not covet your neighbor's goods.

Beatitudes (see Matthew 5:3–10)

- Blessed are the poor in spirit; the kingdom of heaven is theirs.
- Blessed are they who mourn; they will be comforted.
- Blessed are the meek; they will inherit the earth.
- Blessed are they who hunger and thirst for righteousness; they will be satisfied.
- Blessed are the merciful; they will be shown mercy.
- Blessed are the clean of heart; they will see God.
- Blessed are the peacemakers; they will be called children of God.
- Blessed are they who are persecuted for the sake of righteousness; the kingdom of heaven is theirs.

Corporal Works of Mercy (see Matthew 25:35–36)

- Feed the hungry.
- Give drink to the thirsty.
- Shelter the homeless.
- Clothe the naked.
- Care for the sick.
- Help the imprisoned.
- Bury the dead.

Spiritual Works of Mercy

- Share knowledge.
- Give advice to those who need it.
- Comfort those who suffer.
- Be patient with others.
- Forgive those who hurt you.
- Give correction to those who need it.
- Pray for the living and the dead.

Theological Virtues (see 1 Corinthians 13:13)

- Faith
- Hope
- Love

Study and Prayer Helps

Cardinal Virtues

- Prudence
- Justice
- Fortitude
- Temperance

Seven Gifts of the Holy Spirit (see Isaiah 11:2–3)

- Wisdom. A wise person recognizes where the Holy Spirit is at work in the world.
- Understanding. Understanding helps us recognize how God wants us to live.
- Right judgment. This gift helps us make choices that will lead us closer to God rather than away from God. The gift of right judgment, sometimes called counsel, helps us figure out what God wants.
- Courage. The gift of courage, also called fortitude, is the special help we need when faced with challenges or struggles.
- Knowledge. This gift helps us understand the meaning of what God has revealed, particularly the Good News of Jesus Christ.
- Reverence. This gift, sometimes called piety, gives us a deep sense of respect for God and the Church. A reverent person honors God and approaches him with humility, trust, and love.
- Wonder and awe. The gift of wonder and awe makes us aware of God's greatness and power.

Fruits of the Holy Spirit (see Galatians 5:22–23)

- Charity
- Joy
- Peace
- Patience
- Goodness
- Kindness
- Long-suffering
- Humility
- Faithfulness
- Modesty
- Continence
- Chastity

Four Marks of the Catholic Church

- One
- Holy
- Catholic
- Apostolic

Liturgical Year

- Advent
- Christmas
- Ordinary Time
- Lent
- Easter Triduum
- Easter
- Pentecost
- Ordinary Time

Seven Sacraments

- Baptism
- Confirmation
- The Eucharist
- Penance and Reconciliation
- Anointing of the Sick
- Matrimony
- Holy Orders

Precepts of the Church

- Attend Mass on Sundays and holy days of obligation and rest from unnecessary labor on these days.
- Confess your sins in the Sacrament of Penance and Reconciliation at least once a year.

- Receive the Eucharist at least during the Easter season.
- Observe the days of fasting and abstinence established by the Church.
- Help to provide for the material needs of the Church according to your ability.

Holy Days of Obligation

- Christmas (December 25)
- Solemnity of the Blessed Virgin Mary, the Mother of God (January 1)
- Ascension of the Lord (the Sunday that follows forty days after Easter)
- Assumption of the Blessed Virgin Mary (August 15)
- All Saints' Day (November 1)
- Immaculate Conception of the Blessed Virgin Mary (December 8)

BIBLE PASSAGES
FOR SPECIAL OCCASIONS

God speaks to us through the words of the Bible. Here are some suggestions for passages to read and reflect on at important moments in your life. Approach these passages in confidence that God wants you to feel his love and presence.

When you need a good friend or want to be a good friend:
- ☐ 1 Samuel, chapter 20
- ☐ Sirach 6:5–17
- ☐ John 15:12–17
- ☐ Colossians 3:12–17

When you are feeling hopeless:
- ☐ Psalm 42
- ☐ Matthew 11:28–30
- ☐ Romans 8:18–39
- ☐ 1 Peter 1:3–9

When you are feeling happy:
- ☐ Psalm 40
- ☐ Psalm 150
- ☐ Sirach 25:1–11
- ☐ Philippians 4:4–9

When you are acting as a leader:
- ☐ 1 Kings 3:4–14
- ☐ Mark 10:35–45
- ☐ 1 Timothy 4:4–12

When preparing for a big game or competition:
- ☐ 1 Corinthians 9:23–27
- ☐ 2 Timothy 2:5

When someone you love has died:
- ☐ Psalm 90
- ☐ John 3:16–17
- ☐ 1 Corinthians 15:50–57
- ☐ 1 Thessalonians 4:13–18

When you are facing temptation:
- ☐ Genesis 3:1–21
- ☐ Matthew 4:1–11
- ☐ 1 Timothy 6:6–10
- ☐ James 1:12–18

At the beginning of the school year:
- ☐ Proverbs, chapter 1
- ☐ Proverbs 10:1,4,13–14,23
- ☐ 1 Corinthians 2:6–8

When you want to be a better follower of Jesus:
- ☐ Mark 8:34–38
- ☐ Luke 6:20–49

When you want to be a better follower of Jesus: (continued)
- ☐ Ephesians 5:1–20
- ☐ James 1:19–27

When you are feeling angry or want revenge:
- ☐ Proverbs 25:21–22
- ☐ Matthew 5:21–24,38–42
- ☐ Romans 12:17–21
- ☐ Ephesians 4:25–32

When you want to know that God loves you:
- ☐ Exodus 34:5–6
- ☐ Psalm 36:5–12
- ☐ Psalm 59:16–17
- ☐ Psalm 139
- ☐ John 15:1–17
- ☐ Romans 5:6–8

When you or someone you know is sick:
- ☐ Psalm 23
- ☐ Luke 7:21–23
- ☐ James 5:14–15
- ☐ 1 Peter 3:3–17

When you are having problems controlling your tongue:
- ☐ Proverbs 10:18–21
- ☐ Sirach 28:12–26
- ☐ Matthew 12:33–37
- ☐ James 3:1–12

During times of violence or war:
- ☐ Proverbs 3:31–33
- ☐ Micah 4:1–4
- ☐ Luke 12:4–7
- ☐ John 14:27–31

When you are overcome by sexual feelings:
- ☐ Genesis 1:26–31
- ☐ Matthew 19:3–9
- ☐ 1 Corinthians 6:12–20
- ☐ Ephesians 5:1–5

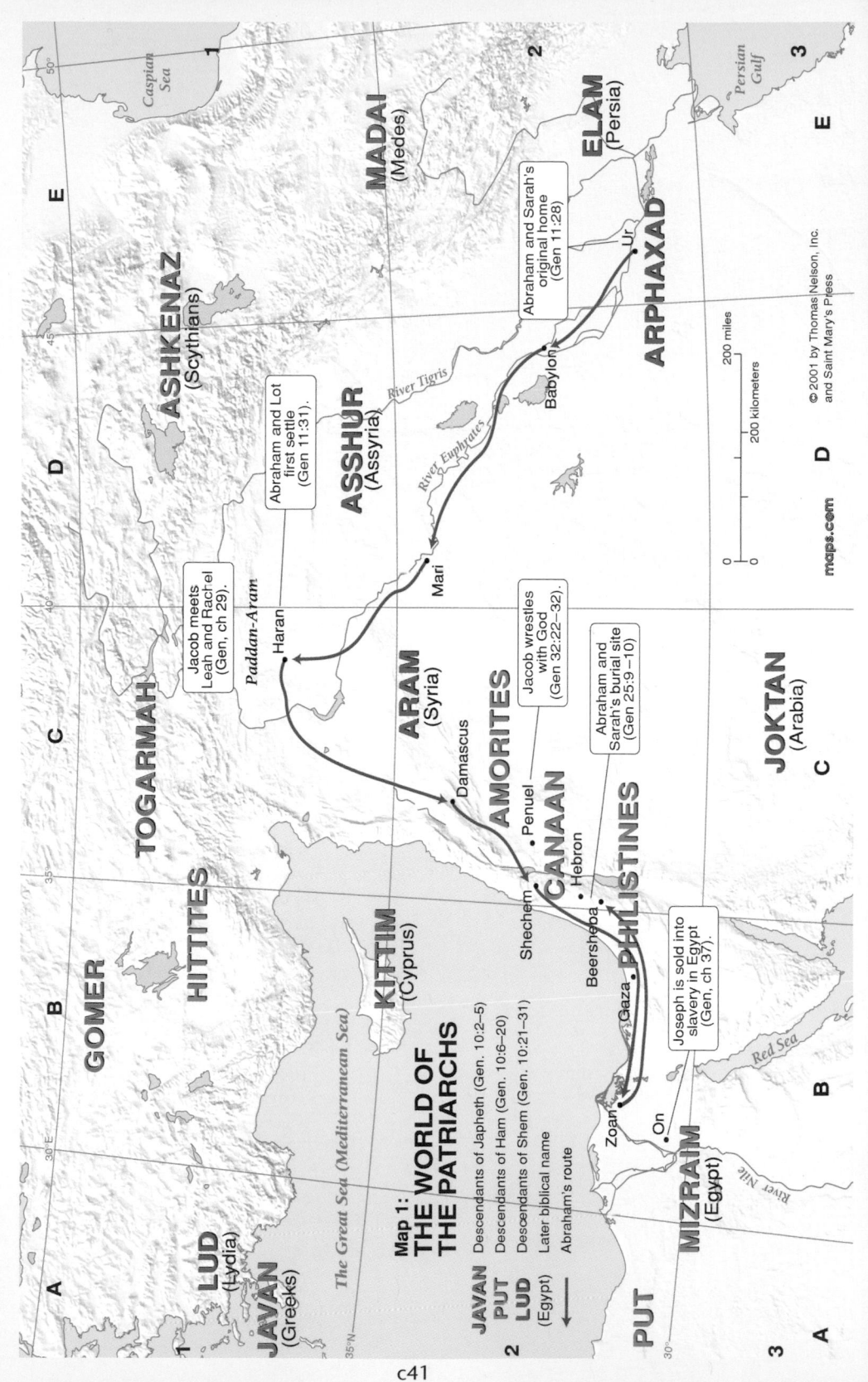

Map 1:
**THE WORLD OF
THE PATRIARCHS**

Descendants of Japheth (Gen. 10:2–5)
Descendants of Ham (Gen. 10:6–20)
Descendants of Shem (Gen. 10:21–31)
Later biblical name
Abraham's route

JAVAN
PUT
LUD
(Egypt)

The Great Sea (Mediterranean Sea)

LUD
(Lydia)

JAVAN
(Greeks)

GOMER

TOGARMAH

HITTITES

KITTIM
(Cyprus)

ASHKENAZ
(Scythians)

MADAI
(Medes)

ELAM
(Persia)

ARPHAXAD

ASSHUR
(Assyria)

River Tigris

River Euphrates

Babylon

Ur

Caspian Sea

Persian Gulf

Abraham and Sarah's
original home
(Gen 11:28)

Abraham and Lot
first settle
(Gen 11:31).

Jacob meets
Leah and Rachel
(Gen, ch 29).

Paddan-Aram

Haran

Mari

ARAM
(Syria)

AMORITES

Damascus

Penuel

CANAAN

Shechem

Hebron

Beersheba

Gaza

PHILISTINES

Jacob wrestles
with God
(Gen 32:22–32).

Abraham and
Sarah's burial site
(Gen 25:9–10)

Joseph is sold into
slavery in Egypt
(Gen, ch 37).

On

Zoan

MIZRAIM
(Egypt)

PUT

River Nile

Red Sea

JOKTAN
(Arabia)

© 2001 by Thomas Nelson, Inc.
and Saint Mary's Press

maps.com

0   200 miles
0   200 kilometers

c41

Map 2:
THE EXODUS FROM EGYPT

Route of the Exodus
Alternate routes of Red Sea crossing
Unsuccessful invasion of Canaan (Num. 14:39–45)
Trade routes
? Exact location questionable

0   75 miles
0   75 kilometers

Moses' death (Deut, ch 34)
Desert wandering (Deut, ch 2)
God gives the Ten Commandments (Ex, ch 20).
Miracles of manna and quail (Ex, ch 16)

Ammon
Moab
Edom
Midian
MT. NEBO
River Arnon
River Jabbok
Dead Sea (Salt Sea)
Punon
Zoar
Arad
Hebron
Beersheba
Gaza
Wilderness of Zin
Kadesh Barnea
Arabah
Ezion Geber
Gulf of Aqaba
MT. SINAI / HOREB
Wilderness of Paran
Route from Egypt to Arabia
Way of the Philistines
Way of Shur
Red Sea
Marah?
Elim?
The Great Sea (Mediterranean Sea)
Baal Zephon
Avaris
Qantir
Pithom
Succoth
Land of Goshen
Memphis
River Nile

© 2001 by Thomas Nelson, Inc, and Saint Mary's Press

maps.com

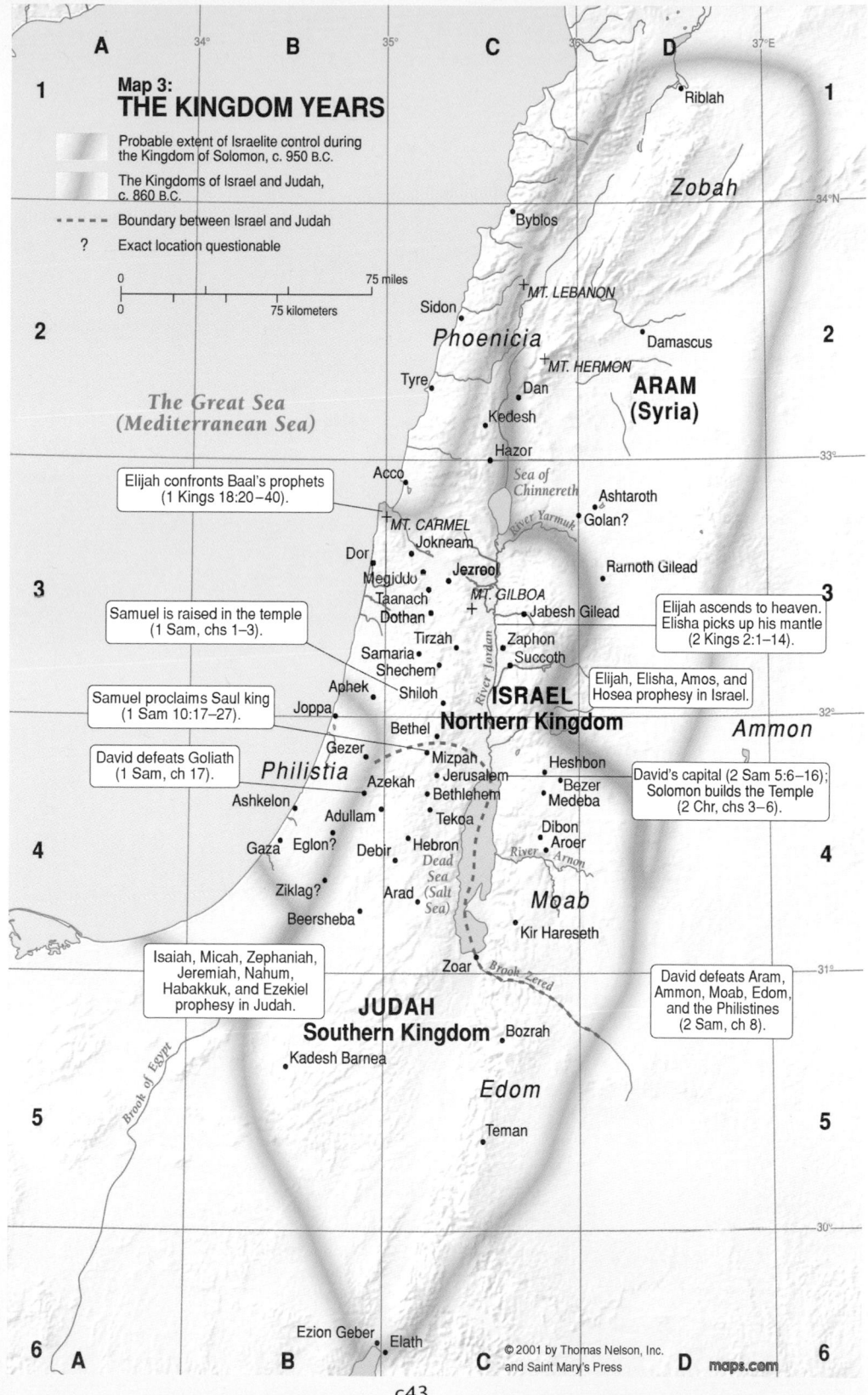

Map 3:
THE KINGDOM YEARS

Probable extent of Israelite control during
the Kingdom of Solomon, c. 950 B.C.

The Kingdoms of Israel and Judah,
c. 860 B.C.

---- Boundary between Israel and Judah

? Exact location questionable

0   75 miles
0   75 kilometers

A   B   C   D

34°   35°   36°   37°E

Riblah

Zobah

34°N

Byblos

+*MT. LEBANON*

Sidon

Phoenicia

Damascus

Tyre

Dan

+*MT. HERMON*

**ARAM
(Syria)**

Kedesh

*The Great Sea
(Mediterranean Sea)*

Hazor

33°

Acco

*Sea of
Chinnereth*

Ashtaroth

Golan?

Elijah confronts Baal's prophets
(1 Kings 18:20–40).

+*MT. CARMEL*

Jokneam

River Yarmuk

Ramoth Gilead

Dor

Megiddo

Jezreel

Taanach

MT. GILBOA

Jabesh Gilead

Elijah ascends to heaven.
Elisha picks up his mantle
(2 Kings 2:1–14).

Dothan

Samuel is raised in the temple
(1 Sam, chs 1–3).

Tirzah

Zaphon

Succoth

Samaria

Shechem

River Jordan

Aphek

Shiloh

ISRAEL
Northern Kingdom

Elijah, Elisha, Amos, and
Hosea prophesy in Israel.

Samuel proclaims Saul king
(1 Sam 10:17–27).

Joppa

Bethel

Ammon

32°

Gezer

Mizpah

Heshbon

David defeats Goliath
(1 Sam, ch 17).

Philistia

Azekah

Jerusalem

Bezer

Medeba

David's capital (2 Sam 5:6–16);
Solomon builds the Temple
(2 Chr, chs 3–6).

Ashkelon

Bethlehem

Adullam

Tekoa

Dibon

Gaza

Eglon?

Debir

Hebron

Aroer

River Arnon

Ziklag?

*Dead
Sea
(Salt
Sea)*

Arad

Moab

Beersheba

Kir Hareseth

Isaiah, Micah, Zephaniah,
Jeremiah, Nahum,
Habakkuk, and Ezekiel
prophesy in Judah.

Zoar

Brook Zered

31°

David defeats Aram,
Ammon, Moab, Edom,
and the Philistines
(2 Sam, ch 8).

JUDAH
Southern Kingdom

Bozrah

Kadesh Barnea

Brook of Egypt

Edom

Teman

30°

Ezion Geber

Elath

Map 4:
THE ASSYRIAN EMPIRE
(C. 700 B.C.)

→ Exiles from Israel into Assyrian captivity (721 B.C.)

©2000 by Thomas Nelson, Inc.

Map 5:
THE BABYLONIAN EMPIRE
(C. 600 B.C.)

▪▪▪▪ Exiles from Judah into Babylonian captivity (605, 597, 587 B.C.)
── Return of exiles under Shesbazzar and Zerubbabel (538 B.C.)
┅┅ Return of exiles under Ezra and Nehemiah (445 B.C.)

©2000 by Thomas Nelson, Inc.

Map 6:
THE MINISTRY OF JESUS

(1,742) Elevation, in feet

? Exact location questionable

0 — 30 miles

0 — 30 kilometers

34°30'E   A   35°00'   B   35°30'   C   36°00'   D

33°30'N

Sidon

Damascus

Zarephath

MT. LEBANON (11,000)

MT. HERMON (9,200)

Iturea

Tyre

Phoenicia

Panias (Caesarea Philippi)

1

Trachonitis

33°00'

Galilee

Ptolemais

Chorazin   Bethsaida?

Feeds five thousand (Lk 9:10–17)

Capernaum

Heals centurion's servant (Mt 8:5–13) and a paralytic (Mt 9:2–8), and raises Jairus's daughter (Mt 9:18–26)

Magdala   Sea of Galilee   Gergesa

MT. CARMEL (1,742)   Cana

Tiberias

River Kishon

Calms the storm (Mk 4:35–41); walks on water (Mt 14:22–33)

River Yarmuk

2

Performs wedding feast miracle (Jn 2:1–11)

Nazareth

MT. TABOR (1,843)   Gadara?

Nain

Grows up in Nazareth (Lk 2:39–40)

Esdraelon

River Jezreel

Transfiguration? (Mt 17:1–13)

Caesarea

Raises widow's son (Lk 7:11–17)

Scythopolis

MT. GILBOA (1,696)

Decapolis

32°30'

The Great Sea (Mediterranean Sea)

Samaria

Talks to Samaritan woman (Jn 4:1–42)

Samaria

Gerasa

3

Sychar

MT. GERIZIM (2,890)

River Jordan   River Jabbok

Antipatris

Joppa

Perea

Arimathea

Ephraim

Gadara?

32°00'

Lydda

Philadelphia

Crucifixion and Resurrection

Heals Bartimaeus (Mk 10:46–52); calls Zacchaeus (Lk 19:1–10)

Appears to two disciples after Resurrection (Lk 24:13–35)

Emmaus

Jericho

Kirjath Jearim

Jerusalem   Bethabara

Jesus' baptism? (Mk 1:9–11)

Beth Haccerem

Bethany   Qumran

4

Azotus

Bethlehem

Raises Lazarus (Jn 11:1–44)

Medeba

Ashkelon

Herodium

Jesus' birth (Lk 2:1–7)

Judea

Machaerus

Hebron

Dead Sea (Salt Sea) (-1,300)

River Arnon

31°30'

Gaza

Idumea

Masada

5

Beersheba

© 2001 by Thomas Nelson, Inc. and Saint Mary's Press

maps.com

A   B   C   D

c45

Map 7:
PAUL'S FIRST AND SECOND JOURNEYS
(ACTS 13–14; 15:39—18:22)

→ First missionary journey, with Barnabas and Mark (c. A.D. 46–48)

→ Second missionary journey, with Silas (c. A.D. 49–52)

© 2001 by Thomas Nelson, Inc.

maps.com

Labels: Illyricum, Italy, Adriatic Sea, Sicily, Macedonia, Thrace, Amphipolis, Philippi, Thessalonica, Neapolis, Berea, Apollonia, Troas, Achaia, Athens, Corinth, Ephesus, Phrygia, Antioch, Iconium, Lystra, Derbe, Pisidia, Tarsus, Attalia, Pamphylia, Antioch, Lycia, Cilicia, Seleucia, Perga, Cyprus, Syria, Patmos, Salamis, Crete, Paphos, The Great Sea (Mediterranean Sea), Caesarea, Jerusalem, Palestine, Black Sea, Pontus, Bithynia, Galatia, Cappadocia

Map 8:
PAUL'S THIRD AND FOURTH JOURNEYS
(ACTS 18:23—21:16; 27—28:16)

→ Third missionary journey (c. A.D. 53–57)

→ Fourth missionary journey (c. A.D. 59–62)

© 2001 by Thomas Nelson, Inc.

maps.com

Labels: Illyricum, Italy, Rome, Three Inns, Appii Forum, Puteoli, Adriatic Sea, Rhegium, Sicily, Syracuse, Malta, Macedonia, Thrace, Amphipolis, Philippi, Thessalonica, Berea, Apollonia, Troas, Assos, Achaia, Mitylene, Chios, Colossae, Phrygia, Antioch, Corinth, Athens, Ephesus, Pisidia, Iconium, Samos, Miletus, Lystra, Derbe, Cos, Cnidus, Lycia, Pamphylia, Tarsus, Rhodes, Myra, Cilicia, Antioch, Patara, Cyprus, Syria, Crete, Fair Havens, The Great Sea (Mediterranean Sea), Tyre, Sidon, Ptolemais, Caesarea, Antipatris, Jerusalem, Palestine, Black Sea, Pontus, Bithynia, Galatia, Cappadocia

c46

Alphabetical List of Bible Books and Abbreviations

Book	Abbreviation	Page	Book	Abbreviation	Page
Acts	Acts	1600	1 Kings	1 Kings	427
Amos	Am	1327	2 Kings	2 Kings	468
Baruch	Bar	1202	Lamentations	Lam	1194
1 Chronicles	1 Chr	511	Leviticus	Lev	150
2 Chronicles	2 Chr	543	Luke	Lk	1493
Colossians	Col	1738	1 Maccabees	1 Macc	672
1 Corinthians	1 Cor	1677	2 Maccabees	2 Macc	706
2 Corinthians	2 Cor	1702	Malachi	Mal	1388
Daniel	Dan	1280	Mark	Mk	1455
Deuteronomy	Deut	223	Matthew	Mt	1395
Ecclesiastes	Eccl	939	Micah	Mic	1350
Ephesians	Eph	1724	Nahum	Nah	1359
Esther	Esth	653	Nehemiah	Neh	597
Exodus	Ex	90	Numbers	Num	181
Ezekiel	Ezek	1211	Obadiah	Ob	1340
Ezra	Ezra	582	1 Peter	1 Pet	1798
Galatians	Gal	1714	2 Peter	2 Pet	1806
Genesis	Gen	19	Philemon	Philem	1770
Habakkuk	Hab	1363	Philippians	Phil	1731
Haggai	Hag	1373	Proverbs	Prov	899
Hebrews	Heb	1773	Psalms	Ps	787
Hosea	Hos	1310	Revelation	Rev	1825
Isaiah	Isa	1033	Romans	Rom	1652
James	Jas	1790	Ruth	Ruth	335
Jeremiah	Jer	1114	1 Samuel	1 Sam	342
Job	Job	739	2 Samuel	2 Sam	388
Joel	Joel	1321	Sirach	Sir	981
1 John	1 Jn	1811	Song of Songs	Song	951
2 John	2 Jn	1819	1 Thessalonians	1 Thess	1744
3 John	3 Jn	1821	2 Thessalonians	2 Thess	1749
John	Jn	1554	1 Timothy	1 Tim	1753
Jonah	Jon	1343	2 Timothy	2 Tim	1761
Joshua	Josh	264	Titus	Titus	1767
Jude	Jude	1822	Tobit	Tob	618
Judges	Judg	299	Wisdom	Wis	961
Judith	Jdt	635	Zechariah	Zech	1377
			Zephaniah	Zeph	1368

All scripture is inspired by God and is useful for teaching, for reproof, for correction, and for training in righteousness, so that everyone who belongs to God may be proficent, equipped for every good work.

(2 Tim 3:16-17)